THE OXFORD DICTIONARY *of* **ART**

For Joshua, Joseph, and William

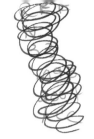

THE OXFORD
DICTIONARY
of

ART

THIRD EDITION

EDITED BY

IAN CHILVERS

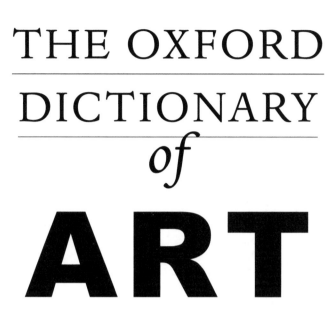

OXFORD
UNIVERSITY PRESS

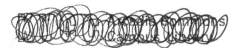

OXFORD
UNIVERSITY PRESS

Great Clarendon Street, Oxford OX2 6DP

Oxford University Press is a department of the University of Oxford.
It furthers the University's objective of excellence in research, scholarship,
and education by publishing worldwide in

Oxford New York

Auckland Bangkok Buenos Aires Cape Town Chennai
Dar es Salaam Delhi Hong Kong Istanbul Karachi Kolkata
Kuala Lumpur Madrid Melbourne Mexico City Mumbai Nairobi
São Paulo Shanghai Taipei Tokyo Toronto

Oxford is a registered trade mark of Oxford University Press
in the UK and in certain other countries

Published in the United States
by Oxford University Press Inc., New York

© Oxford University Press 1988, 1997, 2004

Database right Oxford University Press (maker)

First edition published 1988

Second edition published 1997

Third edition published 2004

British Library Cataloguing in Publication Data
Data available

Library of Congress Cataloging in Publication Data
Data available

ISBN 0–19–860476–9

1 3 5 7 9 10 8 6 4 2
Typeset by Kolam Information Services Pvt. Ltd, Pondicherry, India
Printed in Great Britain by Biddles Ltd

PREFACE

THE first edition of this book, published in 1988, was based on the *Oxford Companion to Art*, edited by Harold Osborne. In the course of successive revisions, however, I have altered the text so much that it now bears little resemblance to its original starting point. Consequently, Harold Osborne's name, which appeared on the title page of the first and second editions, has been omitted in this third version. However, while the book's contents have changed greatly over the years, its aims remain essentially the same: as Dr Dennis Farr wrote in his foreword to the first edition, the *Oxford Dictionary of Art* 'is meant for the layman who needs reliable information in an easily accessible form; it is also designed to be a handy reference book for students and teachers'.

The territory covered by the book is difficult to define exactly, as its boundaries are somewhat elastic. Primarily it deals with Western and Western-inspired painting, sculpture, printmaking, and drawing from ancient times to the present day, but in its treatment of the modern period it also touches on various other fields of activity that are now usually grouped with the more traditional visual arts—Conceptual art, Video art, and so on. Architecture, design, photography, and the applied arts are outside the book's scope, although they are often mentioned in passing, and there are entries on various individuals who were active mainly in these fields but who also worked as painters, sculptors, printmakers, or draughtsmen; the architects Bramante and Brunelleschi are examples. Oriental art, too, is excluded, although there is an entry on Ukiyo-e, as the influence of Japanese prints is mentioned so frequently in the discussion of late 19th-century French painting.

Roughly three-quarters of the book's 3,000 entries are biographical; in addition to artists (who account for about 2,000 of the entries), they deal with patrons, collectors, dealers, administrators, and writers. The non-biographical material is devoted largely to such topics as styles, movements, materials, and techniques. There are also entries on famous museums and galleries, on various other institutions, including academies and schools, and on individual works of art from the ancient and medieval worlds (where the biographical approach that characterizes the rest of the book is less viable). In particular, there are numerous entries on the celebrated antique sculptures (such as the *Apollo Belvedere*, the *Belvedere Torso*, and the *Laocoön*) that were so influential on European art from the Renaissance onwards, as well as a few on ancient statues whose fame is more recent (such as the *Venus de Milo*).

While detailed coverage begins with Classical Greece, a handful of entries have been included on earlier topics that are likely to be of interest to the general reader, for example Altamira (the 'Sistine Chapel of Cave Art') and the '*Venus of Willendorf*'. At the other end of the time scale, an arbitrary cut-off point has been adopted in that no artist born after 1965 has an entry of his or her own. Artists born later than this are occasionally mentioned within other entries, for example that on the Turner Prize, but no attempt is made to provide detailed coverage of the contemporary art scene, in which reputations are so often ephemeral.

The length of an entry can usually be taken as an indication of the significance of the subject, but with many qualifications, some topics and some lives being much more easily summarized than others. Those artists who travelled a great deal, or had fingers in many pies, or who for one reason or another led especially interesting lives are likely to have longer entries than equally accomplished artists who stayed at home and devoted themselves to one speciality.

The order of entries is strictly alphabetical up to the first comma or other punctuation mark, ignoring any spaces in the wording. With certain artists there are problems in deciding which part of the name should determine the alphabetical position, for it is impossible to be entirely logical and consistent in this matter without offending against well-established conventions. Thus, one says 'van Dyck' or 'van Gogh', rather than 'Dyck' or 'Gogh', but they are almost invariably indexed under D and G (as they are here) rather than V. The following general rules may be taken as guidelines to alphabetical positioning, but in cases of doubt the reader is advised to try alternative headings before deciding that a particular artist is not included. Prefixes such as 'de', 'van', and 'von' are generally ignored, but an exception is 'La' or 'Le' (thus La Tour, Georges de). There are certain names where usage goes against this principle; thus Willem de Kooning and Peter De Wint are found under D. Early Italian artists whose names include 'da', 'del', or 'di' are usually found under their first name (Leonardo da Vinci, rather than Vinci, Leonardo da), but again usage sometimes dictates otherwise; thus Andrea del Verrocchio is found under Verrocchio, not Andrea. Names beginning with Mc or St are ordered as though they were spelled Mac and Saint respectively.

Artists' names are given in the form most commonly used in English, so various elements of them have sometimes been dropped, and nicknames or pseudonyms are used as the heading where these are better known than the artist's real name; the names of galleries are also sometimes given in slightly shortened form. Both Tate Britain and Tate Modern are usually cited as 'Tate, London'. In most instances it will be obvious from the context which of the two galleries is meant (a Turner will be in Tate Britain, a Matisse in Tate Modern). With modern British works, however, the situation is different; such works are displayed in both institutions, and they are liable to be transferred between them, so it is not usually possible to specify one location or the other as the permanent home—hence the use of the umbrella title. When a gallery is mentioned more than once within the same entry, the town in which it is located is generally omitted after the first mention. Locations are not given for prints unless they are known to be exceptionally rare.

Cross-references from one article to another are indicated by an asterisk (*) within the main part of the text or by the use of SMALL CAPITALS when the formula 'see so-and-so' is employed. Names of all people who have their own entries are automatically asterisked on their first mention in another entry, and this is also the policy with groups and movements, but cross-references are used more selectively for art media, technical terms, etc., and given only when further elucidation under that heading might be helpful.

For this third edition of the book, almost every entry has been amended in some way and many have been expanded or substantially rewritten. There are also more than 200 new entries, and as a result of the changes the overall wordage of the book has increased by about a quarter. Also new to this edition are two features that I hope will prove useful to readers. First, there is a classified list of entries, making it easy to see which collectors, say, or 18th-century French artists, or printmaking terms, are included. Secondly, in biographical entries the places and exact dates of the subject's birth (or baptism) and death (or burial) are given whenever possible.

Finding such information—and ensuring it is accurate—is at times no easy matter. Often this reflects the haphazard survival of documentary material from early periods, but even with modern artists there can be problems: for example, Milton Avery and Tamara de Lempicka seem to have deliberately provided false information about their origins. Moreover, authoritative sources sometimes disagree even over points that might appear to be matters of easily accessible record. For example, the first three books in which I checked the basic biographical information on Gwen John gave three different dates of death: the Macmillan (Grove) *Dictionary of Art* has 3 September 1939, the Tate Gallery's catalogue of modern British paintings, drawings, and sculpture has 13 September, and the *Dictionary of National Biography* has 18 September. All the specialist literature I consulted to settle the point agreed with the *DNB*, but even the most scholarly monographs can sometimes err surprisingly in this regard. The first line of the standard modern work on Lord Leighton (by Leonée and Richard Ormond, 1975) reads, 'Frederic Leighton was born at Scarborough on the Yorkshire coast on 31 December 1830'; however, almost all other sources say he was born on 3 December, and the Leighton House Museum assures me that this is the correct date.

Whenever I have been unable to resolve such discrepancies myself, I have tried to secure expert help. The literature on Natalia Goncharova, for example, is about equally divided in giving two slightly different dates of birth for her (17 days apart). I was baffled by this until Dr Anthony Parton, author of a forthcoming monograph on the artist, explained that there are two conflicting documentary sources concerning the date, between which it is difficult to choose: a copy of a birth certificate in Goncharova's student dossier at the Moscow School of Art; and a sworn statement she made in 1936 when she was applying for French citizenship (in her entry I have given both dates). Similarly, Sandra de Laszlo, who is compiling a catalogue raisonné of the work of Philip de László (her husband's grandfather), kindly provided me with ample evidence to show which birth date is correct among the three different ones I've seen cited for him. In spite of such help, and weeks of checking, there are still numerous dates that I've had to accept as a matter of probability or trust, rather than conviction.

A more general difficulty with dates comes from the fact that various parts of the Western world have at certain periods used calendar conventions that have differed from the norm. The calendar that we use now, the Gregorian calendar, was introduced in 1582 when Pope Gregory XIII decreed that ten days (5–14 October) would be omitted that year and that centennial years would in future be leap years only if the initial two numbers were divisible by four (so 1600 was a leap year but 1700 was not). These measures were taken to correct the Julian calendar (authorized by Julius Caesar in 46 BC), which had been slowly getting out of step with the seasons. Gregory's reformed calendar was quickly adopted in most Catholic countries, but more slowly elsewhere—not until 1752 in Britain, for example, and not until 1918 in Russia (following the Revolution).

At the same time that it adopted the Gregorian system, England fell into line with Scotland and most of the rest of Europe by dating the new year from 1 January, rather than as previously from 25 March. In addition to these national differences there were local peculiarities: for example, most places used AD 1 as the starting point for counting the years, but some counted from 1 BC, notably Pisa, which was therefore one year ahead of its neighbour Florence; and Venice observed 1 March as the beginning of the year, maintaining this idiosyncracy until it fell to Napoleon in 1797 (these points merely scratch the surface of a complex subject; it is treated in depth in the *Oxford Companion to the Year*). Thus up to the mid-18th century (later in Russia and some other countries) the same event could be assigned a different date in different places, a situation neatly summed up by Robert Ritter in the *Oxford Guide to Style*: 'the execution of Charles I was officially dated 30 January 1648 in England, but 30 January 1649 in Scotland. In Florence . . . the same day was 9 February 1648, in France and Pisa 9 February 1649.'

The upshot of all this is that, from a British point of view, any exact date between 1582 and 1752 is potentially ambiguous, and ideally one needs to know what set of rules has governed it. In this book Continental dates in the period 1582–1752 can generally be assumed to be given according to the Gregorian system, and British (and American) dates of the period according to the Julian system, but with the year in all cases deemed to begin on 1 January, not 25 March. However, when dates are taken from a great variety of sources, as they are in a book such as this, it is not always possible to be sure which system has been used; complete consistency is therefore in practice unattainable and it is likely that an occasional 'error in translation' has crept in.

For dates after 1752, only Russia is really affected as far as this book is concerned. Whenever possible I have given appropriate dates in both Old Style (Julian) and New Style (Gregorian) forms, as in the following example: Aivazovsky, Ivan (b Theodosia [now Feodosiya, Ukraine], 17 [29] July 1817; d Theodosia, 19 Apr. [2 May] 1900). This means that the date of Aivazovsky's birth was 17 July in Russia (which still used the Julian calendar), but 29 July in western Europe. At this time the Gregorian calendar was twelve days ahead of the Julian, but by the time of Aivazovsky's death it was thirteen days ahead, as 1900 was a leap year in the Julian system but not in the Gregorian. When only a single date is given in pre-Revolutionary Russian contexts I have been unable to discover whether it is Old Style or New Style; however, the likelihood is that it is New Style, as the sources I have used are predominantly Western rather than Russian.

When dates are qualified with a question mark, this is placed directly in front of the part of the date that is in doubt. Thus with Antonio Pollaiuolo's date of death, ?4 Feb. 1498, the month and year are certain and there is evidence for the day but it is not conclusive; with Michael Dahl's date of birth, 29 Sept. ?1659, the day and month are known but there is some doubt about the year; and with Pieter Bruegel's date of death, ?(5 Sept.) 1569, the year is recorded reliably, but the evidence for the day and month is questionable. Places of birth and death generally do not present as many pitfalls as dates, but nevertheless require careful checking. Many places have changed their names over the years and this can be a source of confusion, as can the existence of more than one place with the same (or very similar) name. A few sources, for example, give Alexandra Exter's place of birth as what is now Białystok in Poland, but most accounts say she was born at a small place called Bielostok (the spelling varies), near Kiev, several hundred miles away; and Robert Motherwell evidently died in Provincetown, Massachusetts, not – as some sources have it – in Princeton (or Princetown, which I suspect exists only as the result of a typing error). For current spellings of place names I have usually followed the *Times Atlas of the World* and the *Times Index-Gazetteer of the World*, but standard English names of famous foreign cities are used rather than the local version (Florence rather than Firenze, Munich rather than München, and so on).

Dr Johnson defined a lexicographer as 'a writer of dictionaries, a harmless drudge'. I can vouch for the drudgery, but there is also much satisfaction involved in compiling a book such as this, and I would like to thank the various people who have helped to make the task often such an enjoyable one. My chief indebtedness is to Dr Dennis Farr, formerly director of the Courtauld Institute Galleries, London. As consultant editor for the first edition of the book, he read all the text and—with learning, tact, and wit—made numerous corrections and a great many suggestions for improvements to both content and style. Subsequently I have had the benefit of his advice and specialist knowledge on several occasions.

At the Oxford University Press, I am grateful to everyone who has worked on successive editions of the book (and on its concise offspring)—for their enthusiasm and encouragement no less than for their skills: Rowena Anketell, Judith Colleran, Pam Coote, Kathie Gill, Joanna Harris, Pat Lawrence, Hilary McGlynn, Betty Palmer, Angus Phillips, Edwin and Jackie Pritchard, Thomas Webster, and Nicholas Wilson. Staff at several overseas branches of the OUP have also been helpful in providing up-to-date information about artists in their countries.

In a more general sense, I would like to say what a comfort it is to anyone involved in the field of reference books to be able to draw on the resources and tradition of the OUP. I have been able to use the various members of the family of Oxford English Dictionaries to help with definitions, and I have taken much information from the *Dictionary of National Biography* and the various *Oxford Companions* outside the field of art. Margaret Drabble's edition of the *Oxford Companion to English Literature*, for example, contains many excellent entries (by Helen Langdon) on artists and their relationship to literature, and I have also made frequent use of the *Oxford Companions* to *Children's Literature*, *French Literature*, and *German Literature*, and of the *Oxford Classical Dictionary* and the *Oxford Dictionary of the Christian Church*. The *Oxford Companions to Film, Music*, and the *Theatre* have likewise proved helpful when their fields overlapped with mine, and, less obviously, I have also benefited from the *Oxford Companion to Ships and the Sea* (in relation to Clarkson Stanfield) and from the

Oxford Companion to Chess (for some information concerning a Lucas van Leyden painting and for the delightful anecdote in the Duchamp entry).

On a more personal note, I owe a great deal to various members of my family, particularly my sister Doreen Chilvers, who has helped me in ways too numerous to mention; my niece Kendra Hall, for expert advice on government publications; my nephew Gavin Chilvers, for checking some facts and figures; and my cousin Harry Allsop, for help with computer problems and other technical matters. I am also especially grateful to four friends who generously gave up time to help me in the tedious business of checking dates, by consulting sources to which I did not have access: Célestine Dars, John Glaves-Smith, Dr Claudia Stumpf, and Iain Zaczek. Many other friends and former colleagues have given me advice, information, or encouragement, among them Jonathan Alden, Dr Tim Ayers, Rachel Bean, Alison Bolus, Ashley Brown, Caroline Bugler, Rachel Bulbulian, Caroline Christian, Sue Churchill, Emma Clifton, Alison Cole, Erica Davies, Nic Dean, Celia de la Hey, Lorraine Dickey, Lavinia Down, Dr Tom Faulkner, Roz Fishel, Vanessa Fletcher, John Gaisford, Amy Glossop, Bina Goldman, Suzie Green, Clive Gregory, Julia Hanson, Juliet Hardwicke, Flavia Howard, James Hughes, Dr Michael Jacobs, Jessica Johnson, Celia Jones, Heather Jones, Caroline Juler, Frances Kelly, Blaise Keogh, Vanessa Lacey, Frank Landamore, Dr Adrian Lewis, Robin Loerch, Cathy Lowne, Calista Lucy, Lorrie Mack, Margaret Mauger, Latha Menon, Albert Moore, Sir Felix Moore, Anna Morter, Jenny Mulherin, Lucie Nason, Ruth Nason, Nigel O'Gorman, George Otigbah, Alice Peebles, David Pinder, Richard Platt, Maggie Ramsay, Clare Randall, Benedict Read, John Roberts, Guy Robson, Carolyn Rogers, Penelope Byrde Ruddock, Antonia Spowers, Pauline Stride, Jack Tresidder, Nicholas Turner, Dr Malcolm Warner, Christine Webb, Jude Welton, Dr Peter Willis, and Liz Workman. Staff at various libraries, museums, and other institutions have been unfailingly helpful in answering my queries, and I must make special mentions of the Hyman Kreitman Research Centre at Tate Britain and the Anthony Petullo Collection of Self-Taught and Outsider Art, Milwaukee, both of which, at the eleventh hour, provided information that I had despaired of finding. I am also particularly grateful to Valerie Levitt, whose wonderful Newcastle Bookshop (now at Haltwhistle, Northumberland) has supplied me with many publications that I could not otherwise have obtained. Finally, for inspiration from afar, thanks to Deborah Lambert and Victoria Kirkham.

IAN CHILVERS
Jesmond, Newcastle upon Tyne

October 2003

CONTENTS

CLASSIFIED LIST OF ENTRIES

ALL the entries in the book are listed here under various thematic headings. The arrangement is as follows:

> Ancient and medieval
> Artists' biographies
> Other biographies
> Museums and galleries
> Academies, schools, and other institutions
> Exhibitions and prizes
> Styles, groups, and movements
> Materials, tools, and techniques
> Miscellaneous terms

The artists' biographies, which make up the bulk of the book, are arranged by country (and with the major national schools subdivided by century). Western European countries are listed first, in alphabetical order (Austria and Switzerland are grouped with Germany, and Portugal with Spain), followed by central and eastern Europe, Russia, and Scandinavia; then come the Americas, Australasia, and other non-European countries. In line with the practice of the National Gallery in London and the Witt Library at the Courtauld Institute of Art, artists from the Low Countries are called Netherlandish up to about 1600; they are then distinguished as either Dutch or Flemish; and after about 1830 'Flemish' becomes 'Belgian'.

Those artists whose careers do not fit neatly into one country or one century sometimes pose problems as to which list is most appropriate for them. In such instances I have not tried to apply rules but have simply made an intuitive decision for each individual. Thus Annibale Carracci (1560–1609) spent most of his life and career in the 16th century, but I have put him (with the other members of his family) in the 17th-century Italian list because he is regarded as one of the founders of Baroque painting and figures in histories of 17th-century art much more than he does in histories of 16th-century art. Similarly, although Michael Rysbrack and Peter Scheemakers were Flemish by birth, they appear in the 18th-century British list, as they are invariably considered part of the history of British rather than Flemish art.

I have resisted the temptation to include such 'problematic' artists in more than one list or to make cross-references from one list to another, as this would over-complicate what is intended to be a quick guide for the reader rather than an elaborate and precise tool. However, individuals who were notable as both artists and writers (for example Giorgio Vasari) are listed twice—in each of the appropriate sections of the lists. I have also sometimes drawn attention to artists or topics that do not have entries of their own but which are discussed under another heading. In these instances I have used the following convention: Ghe, Nikolai (*Wanderers). This means that Nikolai Ghe does not have an entry of his own, but that information about him will be found under the heading Wanderers.

Egg, Augustus
Etty, William
Farquharson, Joseph
Fielding, Copley
Fildes, Sir Luke
Foster, Myles Birket
Frith, William Powell
Gibson, John
Grant, Sir Francis
Greenaway, Kate
Grimshaw, Atkinson
Haydon, Benjamin Robert
Hayter, Sir George
Herkomer, Sir Hubert von
Herring, John Frederick
Hughes, Arthur
Hunt, William Henry
Hunt, William Holman
Inchbold, J. W.
Keene, Charles
Landseer, Sir Edwin
Lawrence, Sir Thomas
Leader, Benjamin Williams
Lear, Edward
Leech, John
Legros, Alphonse
Leighton, Frederic
Leslie, C. R.
Lewis, J. F.
Linnell, John
Maclise, Daniel
McTaggart, William
Marshall, Benjamin
Martin, John
May, Phil
Millais, Sir John Everett
Moore, Albert
Morris, William
Mulready, William
Muybridge, Eadweard
Orchardson, Sir William Quiller
Nasmyth, Patrick
Palmer, Samuel
Paton, Sir Joseph Noel
Pettie, John
Phillip, John
Phillips, Thomas
Poynter, Sir Edward
Prout, Samuel
Redgrave, Richard
Richmond, George
Roberts, David

Rossetti, Dante Gabriel
Scott, William Bell
Shee, Sir Martin Arthur
Solomon, Simeon
Stanfield, Clarkson
Stevens, Alfred
Stone, Frank and Marcus
Stothard, Thomas
Tenniel, Sir John
Theed, William
Thornycroft, Sir Hamo
Tuke, Henry Scott
Turner, J. M. W.
Turner, William ('Turner of Oxford')
Varley, John
Walker, Fred
Wallis, Henry
Ward, James
Waterhouse, J. W.
Watts, G. F.
Westall, Richard
Westmacott, Sir Richard
Wilkie, Sir David
Woolner, Thomas
Yeames, William Frederick

20th century
Andrews, Michael
Anrep, Boris
Ardizzone, Edward
Armitage, Kenneth
Auerbach, Frank
Ayrton, Michael
Bacon, Francis
Bawden, Edward
Bayes, Gilbert and Walter
Beerbohm, Sir Max
'Beggarstaff, J. & W.'
Bell, Graham
Bell, Vanessa
Bellany, John
Bevan, Robert
Blake, Sir Peter
Bomberg, David
Bone, Sir Muirhead
Boshier, Derek
Brangwyn, Sir Frank
Bratby, John
Brockhurst, Gerald Leslie
Burra, Edward
Butler, Reg
Caro, Sir Anthony

Classified List of Entries

Scarfe, Gerald
Scott, Kathleen and Sir Peter
Scott, William
Shannon, Charles
Sickert, Walter Richard
Smith, Sir Matthew
Spencelayh, Charles
Spencer, Sir Stanley
Steer, Philip Wilson
Stone, Reynolds
Sutherland, Graham
Tonks, Henry
Topolski, Feliks
Tucker, William
Turnbull, William
Uglow, Euan
Underwood, Leon
Vaughan, Keith
Wadsworth, Edward
Walker, Dame Ethel
Wallis, Alfred
Weight, Carel
Wheeler, Sir Charles
Whistler, Rex
Whiteread, Rachel
Wilson, Scottie
Wood, Christopher
Yeats, Jack Butler

FRANCE

15th century
Boucicaut Master
Fouquet, Jean
Froment, Nicolas
Master of Moulins
Master of St Giles
Quarton, Enguerrand

16th century
Bontemps, Pierre
Bourdichon, Jean
Caron, Antoine
Clouet, Jean and François
Colombe, Michel
Corneille de Lyon
Cousin, Jean
Dubois, Ambroise
Dubreuil, Toussaint
Dumonstier family

Duvet, Jean
Giusti, Giovanni (Jean Juste)
Goujon, Jean
Perréal, Jean
Pilon, Germain
Quesnel family
Richier, Ligier
Sambin, Hugues

17th century
Anguier, François and Michel
Baugin, Lubin
Bellange, Jacques
Bigot, Trophime
Blanchard, Jacques
Bosse, Abraham
Boullogne family
Bourdon, Sébastien
Callot, Jacques
Champaigne, Philippe de
Claude
Courtois, Jacques and
   Guillaume
Coysevox, Antoine
Deruet, Claude
Dufresnoy, Charles-Alphonse
Dughet, Gaspard
Edelinck, Gerard
Errard, Charles
François, Guy
Fréminet, Martin
Girardon, François
Jouvenet, Jean
La Fosse, Charles
La Hyre, Laurent de
La Tour, Georges de
Le Brun, Charles
Legros, Pierre
Le Nain brothers
Le Sueur, Eustache
Mellan, Claude
Mignard, Pierre
Millet, Francisque
'Monsù Desiderio'
Nanteuil, Robert
Patel, Pierre
Pérelle, Gabriel
Perrier, François
Poussin, Nicolas
Puget, Pierre
Sarrazin, Jacques

Chodowiecki, Daniel Nikolaus
Dietrich, Christian Wilhelm Ernst
Feuchtmayer, Joseph Anton
Graff, Anton
Günther, Ignaz
Hackert, Jakob Philipp
Kändler, Johann Joachim
Mengs, Anton Raphael
Permoser, Balthasar
Tischbein family
Zick family
Zimmermann, Johann Baptist

19th century
  Blechen, Karl
  Cornelius, Peter
  Feuerbach, Anselm
  Friedrich, Caspar David
  Hildebrand, Adolf von
  Kaulbach, Wilhelm von
  Kersting, Georg Friedrich
  Klinger, Max
  Leibl, Wilhelm
  Lenbach, Franz von
  Lessing, Karl Friedrich
  Marées, Hans von
  Menzel, Adolph
  Overbeck, Friedrich
  Pforr, Frans
  Piloty, Karl von
  Rauch, Christian Daniel
  Rethel, Alfred
  Richter, Ludwig
  Rottmann, Carl
  Runge, Philipp Otto
  Schadow, Johann Gottfried
  Schinkel, Karl Friedrich
  Schnorr von Carolsfeld, Julius
  Senefelder, Aloys
  Spitzweg, Karl
  Stuck, Frans von
  Thoma, Hans
  Uhde, Fritz von
  Winterhalter, Franz Xaver

20th century
  Barlach, Ernst
  Baselitz, Georg
  Baumeister, Willi
  Beckmann, Max
  Beuys, Joseph
  Corinth, Lovis

Dix, Otto
Ernst, Max
Freundlich, Otto
Gropius, Walter
Grosz, George
Heartfield, John
Heckel, Eric
Hofer, Carl
Kiefer, Anselm
Kirchner, Ernst Ludwig
Klee, Paul
Kollwitz, Käthe
Lehmbruck, Wilhelm
Liebermann, Max
Macke, August
Marc, Franz
Modersohn-Becker, Paula
Nolde, Emil
Pechstein, Max
Rohlfs, Christian
Schlemmer, Oscar
Schmidt-Rottluff, Karl
Schwitters, Kurt
Slevogt, Max
Vostell, Wolf
Wols

AUSTRIA

Donner, Georg Raphael
Führich, Joseph
Gerstl, Richard
Gran, Daniel
Huber, Wolfgang
Hundertwasser, Fritz
Klimt, Gustav
Koch, Joseph Anton
Kokoschka, Oskar
Kubin, Alfred
Makart, Hans
Maulbertsch, Franz Anton
Messerschmidt, Franz Xaver
Pacher, Michael
Rottmayr, Johann Michael
Schiele, Egon
Schwarzkogler, Rudolf
Schwind, Moritz von
Seisenegger, Jakob
Stifter, Adalbert
Troger, Paul
Waldmüller, Ferdinand Georg
Wotruba, Fritz

Classified List of Entries

Classified List of Entries

Peruzzi, Baldassare
Piero di Cosimo
Polidoro da Caravaggio
Pontormo
Pordenone
Primaticcio, Francesco
Procaccini, Giulio Cesare
Raimondi, Marcantonio
Raphael
Riccio, Il
Roncalli, Cristoforo
Rosso Fiorentino
Salviati, Francesco
Sansovino, Andrea
Sansovino, Jacopo
Sarto, Andrea del
Savoldo, Giovanni Girolamo
Schiavone, Andrea
Sebastiano del Piombo
Sodoma, Il
Solari family
Solario, Antonio
Tempesta, Antonio
Tibaldi, Pellegrino
Tintoretto, Jacopo
Titian
Torrigiano, Pietro
Udine, Giovanni da
Ugo da Carpi
Vasari, Giorgio
Veronese, Paolo
Vittoria, Alessandro
Zuccaro, Taddeo and Federico

17th century
Albani, Francesco
Algardi, Alessandro
Allori, Cristofano
Baschenis, Evaristo
Bella, Stefano della
Bernini, Gianlorenzo
Cagnacci, Guido
Cantarini, Simone
Caracciolo, Giovanni Battista
Caravaggio, Michelangelo Merisi da
Carracci family
Castiglione, Giovanni Benedetto
Cavallino, Bernardo
Cerquozzi, Michelangelo
Cesari, Giuseppe
Cignani, Carlo
Cigoli, Il

Cortona, Pietro da
Crespi, Daniele
Crespi, Giovanni Battista
Dolci, Carlo
Domenichino
Falcone, Aniello
Feti, Domenico
Furini, Francesco
Gaulli, Giovanni Battista
Gentileschi, Orazio and Artemisia
Giordano, Luca
Grimaldi, Giovanni Francesco
Guercino
Lanfranco, Giovanni
Maderno, Stefano
Maffei, Francesco
Manfredi, Bartolommeo
Maratta, Carlo
Mazzoni, Sebastiano
Mochi, Francesco
Mola, Pier Francesco
Pozzo, Andrea
Preti, Mattia
Recco, Giuseppe
Reni, Guido
Romanelli, Francesco
Rosa, Salvator
Ruoppolo, Giovanni Battista
Sacchi, Andrea
Saraceni, Carlo
Sassoferrato
Scarsellino, Lo
Schedoni, Bartolommeo
Stanzione, Massimo
Strozzi, Bernardo
Tacca, Pietro
Tassi, Agostino
Testa, Pietro

18th century
Amigoni, Jacopo
Appiani, Andrea
Bartolozzi, Francesco
Batoni, Pompeo
Bellotto, Bernardo
Bibiena family
Canaletto
Canova, Antonio
Carlevaris, Luca
Carriera, Rosalba
Castiglione, Giuseppe
Cignaroli, Giambettino

Classified List of Entries

Bruegel, Pieter
Bueckelaer, Joachim
Calvaert, Denys
Cock family
Coecke van Aelst, Pieter
Coninxloo, Gillis van
Cornelisz. van Oostsanen, Jacob
Crabeth, Dirck and Wouter
Dubroeucq, Jacques
Engelbrechtsz., Cornelis
Floris, Cornelis and Frans
Gossaert, Jan
Grimmer, Jacob and Abel
Heemskerck, Maerten van
Hemessen, Jan Sanders van
Joest, Jan
Joos van Cleve
Juan de Flandes
Key, Willem
Lombard, Lambert
Lucas van Leyden
Mander, Karel van
Marinus van Reymerswaele
Massys, Quentin
Master of Alkmaar
Master of Frankfurt
Master of the Brunswick Monogram
Mone, Jean
Mor, Anthonis
Mostaert, Jan
Orley, Bernard van
Patinir, Joachim
Pourbus family
Provost Jan
Scorel, Jan van
Spranger, Bartholomeus
Straet, Jan van der
Swart van Groningen, Jan
Valckenborch family
Veen, Otto van
Vellert, Dirk
Verhaecht, Tobias
Vermeyen, Jan Cornelisz.
Vos, Maerten de
Vredeman de Vries, Hans
Vries, Adriaen de
Ysenbrandt, Adriaen

Dutch

17th century
Aelst, Willem van

Arentsz., Arent
Asselyn, Jan
Ast, Balthasar van der
Avercamp, Hendrick
Baburen, Dirck van
Backer, Jacob
Baen, Jan de
Bakhuizen, Ludolf
Bassen, Bartholomeus van
Beerstraten, Jan
Berchem, Nicolaes
Berckheyde, Gerrit
Beyeren, Abraham van
Bloemaert, Abraham
Bol, Ferdinand
Both, Jan
Boursse, Esias
Bramer, Leonaert
Bray, Jan de
Breenbergh, Bartholomeus
Buytewech, Willem
Campen, Jacob van
Camphuysen, Govert
Cappelle, Jan van de
Claesz., Pieter
Codde, Pieter
Coorte, Adriaen
Cornelis van Haarlem
Cuyp family
Dou, Gerrit
Droochsloot, Joost Cornelisz.
Drost, Willem
Duck, Jacob
Dujardin, Karel
Dusart, Cornelis
Duyster, Willem
Eeckhout, Gerbrand van den
Everdingen, Allart and Caesar van
Fabritius, Carel
Flinck, Govert
Gelder, Aert de
Gheyn, Jacob de
Goltzius, Hendrick
Goyen, Jan van
Hackaert, Jan
Hals, Frans
Hanneman, Adriaen
Heda, Willem Claesz.
Heem, Jan Davidsz. de
Helst, Bartholomeus van der
Heyden, Jan van der
Hobbema, Meindert

Classified List of Entries

ARTISTS' BIOGRAPHIES: AMERICAS, AUSTRALASIA, AND OTHER NON-EUROPEAN

Classified List of Entries

Bellows, George Wesley
Benton, Thomas Hart
Berman, Eugene
Biederman, Charles
Bolotowsky, Ilya
Borglum, Gutzon
Bourgeois, Louise
Burchfield, Charles
Cadmus, Paul
Calder, Alexander
Chamberlain, John
Christo
Close, Chuck
Cornell, Joseph
Curry, John Steuart
Davies, Arthur Bowen
Davis, Stuart
De Andrea, John
de Kooning, Willem
De Maria, Walter
Demuth, Charles
Dickinson, Edwin
Dickinson, Preston
Diebenkorn, Richard
Diller, Burgoyne
Dine, Jim
Dove, Arthur
Evergood, Philip
Feininger, Lyonel
Flavin, Dan
Francis, Sam
Frankenthaler, Helen
Gibson, Charles Dana
Glackens, William
Gorky, Arshile
Gottlieb, Adolph
Gropper, William
Guston, Philip
Hanson, Duane
Hare, David
Hartley, Marsden
Hassam, Childe
Held, Al
Henri, Robert
Hesse, Eva
Hofmann, Hans
Hopper, Edward
Indiana, Robert
Johns, Jasper
Judd, Donald
Kane, John
Kaprow, Allan

Kauffer, E. McKnight
Kelly, Ellsworth
Kent, Rockwell
Kienholz, Edward
Kitaj, Ron B.
Kline, Franz
Kosuth, Joseph
Kuhn, Walt
Lachaise, Gaston
Lawson, Ernest
LeWitt, Sol
Lichtenstein, Roy
Lindner, Richard
Louis, Morris
Luks, George
Macdonald-Wright, Stanton
MacMonnies, Frederick
Man Ray
Manship, Paul
Marin, John
Marsh, Reginald
Morris, Robert
Moses, Grandma
Motherwell, Robert
Nadelman, Elie
Nevelson, Louise
Newman, Barnett
Noguchi, Isamu
Noland, Kenneth
O'Keeffe, Georgia
Oldenburg, Claes
Olitski, Jules
Parrish, Maxfield
Pearlstein, Philip
Pollock, Jackson
Prendergast, Maurice
Ramos, Mel
Rauschenberg, Robert
Reinhardt, Ad
Rivers, Larry
Rockwell, Norman
Rothko, Mark
Russell, Morgan
Sage, Kay
Samaras, Lucas
Schnabel, Julian
Segal, George
Seligmann, Kurt
Serra, Richard
Shahn, Ben
Sheeler, Charles
Shinn, Everett

Sloan, John
Smith, David
Smith, Tony
Smithson, Robert
Soyer, Moses and Raphael
Stella, Frank
Stella, Joseph
Still, Clyfford
Taft, Lorado
Tanguy, Yves
Tchelitchew, Pavel
Tobey, Mark
Tomlin, Bradley Walker
Tooker, George
Twombly, Cy
Warhol, Andy
Weber, Max
Wesselmann, Tom
Wood, Grant
Wyeth, Andrew
Zorach, William

CANADA

Baillargé family
Borduas, Paul
Bush, Jack Hamilton
Carmichael, Franklin (*Group of Seven)
Carr, Emily
Colville, Alex
Cullen, Maurice
Hamel, Théophile
Harris, Lawren Stewart
Jackson, A. Y.
Johnston, Frank (*Group of Seven)
Kane, Paul
Krieghoff, Cornelius
Leduc, Ozias
Levasseur family
Lismer, Arthur (*Group of Seven)
MacDonald, J. E. H. (*Group of Seven)
Macdonald, Jock
Milne, David
Morrice, James Wilson
Plamondon, Antoine
Riopelle, Jean-Paul
Ronald, William
Town, Harold
Thomson, Tom
Varley, Frederick (*Group of Seven)
Watson, Homer

MEXICO

Atl, Dr
Juarez family
Kahlo, Frida
O'Gorman, Juan
Orozco, José Clemente
Posada, José Guadalupe
Rivera, Diego
Siqueiros, David Alfaro
Tamayo, Rufino
Tolsà, Manuel

SOUTH AMERICA AND CARIBBEAN

Batlle Planas, Juan (Argentina)
Botero, Fernando (Colombia)
Cavalcanti, Emiliano di (Brazil)
Clark, Lygia (Brazil)
Cruz-Diez, Carlos (Venezuela)
Figari, Pedro (Uruguay)
Holguín, Melchor Pérez (Bolivia)
Hyppolite, Hector (Haiti)
Lam, Wifredo (Cuba)
Le Parc, Julio (Argentina)
Lisboa, António Francisco (Brazil)
Matta (Chile)
Mérida, Carlos (Guatemala)
Pettoruti, Emilio (Argentina)
Portinari, Cândido (Brazil)
Segall, Lasar (Brazil)
Torres-García, Joaquín (Uruguay)
Xul Zolar (Argentina)

AUSTRALIA

Boyd, Arthur
Bunny, Rupert
Dobell, Sir William
Drysdale, Sir Russell
Heysen, Sir Hans
Lindsay family
McCubbin, Frederick
Meldrum, Max
Nolan, Sir Sidney
Olsen, John
Preston, Margaret
Roberts, Tom
Smith, Grace Cossington
Streeton, Sir Arthur
Whiteley, Brett
Williams, Fred

Classified List of Entries

NEW ZEALAND

Angus, Rita
Goldie, C. F.
Gully, John
Heaphy, Charles
Hodgkins, Frances
Low, Sir David
McCahon, Colin
Woollaston, Sir Mountford Tosswill

OTHER COUNTRIES

Agam, Yaacov (Israel)
Arikha, Avigdor (Israel)
Foujita, Tsuguharu (Japan)
Nagare, Masayuki (Japan)
Stern, Irma (South Africa)
Tretchikoff, Vladimir (South Africa)
Xu Beihong (China)
Yoshihara, Jiro (Japan)

OTHER BIOGRAPHIES

WRITERS/ADMINISTRATORS

15th and 16th centuries
Alberti, Leon Battista
Cellini, Benvenuto
Cennini, Cennino
Condivi, Ascanio
Holanda, Francisco de
Lomazzo, Giovanni Paolo
Mander, Karel van
Ridolfi, Carlo
Vasari, Giorgio

17th century
Baglione, Giovanni
Baldinucci, Filippo
Bellori, Giovanni Pietro
Carducho, Vicente
Dufresnoy, Charles-Alphonse
Félibien, André
Fréart, Roland
Hoogstraten, Samuel van
Huygens, Constantijn
Malvasia, Carlo
Passeri, Giovanni Battista
Piles, Roger de
Sandrart, Joachim von

18th century
Addison, Joseph
Algarotti, Francesco
Burke, Edmund
Cunningham, Allan
Diderot, Denis
Dionysius of Fourna
Edwards, Edward
Gilpin, William
Goethe, Johann Wolfgang von
Home, Henry
Houbraken, Arnold
Hutcheson, Francis
Kant, Immanuel
Lairesse, Gérard de
Lanzi, Luigi
Lessing, Gotthold Ephraim
Palomino, Antonio
Price, Sir Uvedale
Reynolds, Sir Joshua
Richardson, Jonathan
Smith, J. T.
Vertue, George
Walpole, Horace
Winckelmann, Johann
   Joachim

19th century
Bartsch, Adam von
Baudelaire, Charles
Bernard, Émile
Burckhardt, Jacob
Champfleury
Crowe and Cavalcaselle
Denon, Dominique-Vivant
Dunlap, William
Duranty, Edmond
Eastlake, Sir Charles Lock
Farington, Joseph
Fromentin, Eugène
Goncourt, Edmond and Jules de
Hazlitt, William
Hildebrand, Adolf von
Jameson, Anna
Leslie, C. R.
Morelli, Giovanni
Nagler, Georg Kaspar
Northcote, James
Pater, Walter
Quatremère de Quincy, Antoine
Redgrave, Samuel
Riegl, Alois

Ruskin, John
Sérusier, Paul
Taine, Hippolyte
Thoré, Théophile
Tolstoy, Leo
Waagen, Gustav
Zola, Émile

20th century
Alloway, Lawrence
Antal, Frederick
Apollinaire, Guillaume
Barr, Alfred H.
Bell, Clive
Benesch, Otto
Bénézit, Emmanuel
Berenson, Bernard
Biederman, Charles
Blunt, Anthony
Bode, Wilhelm von
Bredius, Abraham
Breton, André
Chastel, André
Clark, Kenneth
Croce, Benedetto
Denis, Maurice
Focillon, Henri
Friedlaender, Walter
Friedländer, Max J.
Fry, Roger
Golding, John
Gombrich, Sir Ernst
Gowing, Sir Lawrence
Grabar, Igor
Greenberg, Clement
Hofstede de Groot, Cornelis
Hughes, Robert
Hulten, Pontus
Longhi, Roberto
MacColl, D. S.
Mâle, Émile
Malraux, André
Marinetti, Filippo Tommaso
Newton, Eric
Ozenfant, Amédée
Panofsky, Erwin
Penrose, Sir Roland
Pevsner, Sir Nikolaus
Pope-Hennessy, Sir John
Read, Sir Herbert
Rewald, John
Rosenberg, Harold

Rothenstein, Sir John
Santayana, George
Seuphor, Michel
Soffici, Ardengo
Stokes, Adrian
Thieme-Becker
Valentiner, Wilhelm
Venturi, Adolfo and Lionello
Veth, Jan
Voss, Hermann
Warburg, Aby
Waterhouse, Sir Ellis
Wilde, Johannes
Wilenski, R. H.
Wittkower, Rudolf
Wölfflin, Heinrich
Worringer, Wilhelm

PATRONS/COLLECTORS

Albani, Cardinal Alessandro
Aldobrandini family
Arundel, Thomas Howard, 2nd Earl of
Barberini family
Barnes, Albert C.
Beaumont, Sir George
Beckford, William
Borghese family
Bourgeois, Sir Peter
Bowes, John
Burgundy, House of
Burrell, Sir William
Caillebotte, Gustave
Caylus, Comte de
Chigi, Agostino
Cooper, Douglas
Courtauld, Samuel
Crozat, Pierre
Diaghilev, Sergei
Dreier, Katherine S.
Este family
Farnese family
Fréart, Paul
Frick, Henry Clay
Gardner, Isabella Stewart
Getty, J. Paul
Giustiniani family
Gonzaga family
Guggenheim, Solomon R.
Gulbenkian, Calouste
Habsburg family
Hope, Thomas

Classified List of Entries

Huntington, Henry E.
Jabach, Everard
Knight, William Payne
Kress, Samuel H.
Lane, Sir Hugh
Ludwig, Peter
Lugt, Frits
Mahon, Sir Denis
Malatesta, Sigismondo
Mariette, Pierre-Jean
Medici family
Mellon, Andrew W. and Paul
Monro, Dr Thomas
Montefeltro family
Morgan, J. Pierpont
Pamphili family
Phillipps, Sir Thomas
Phillips, Duncan
Rothschild family
Rovere family
Royal Collection
Saatchi, Charles
Sforza family
Slade, Sir Felix
Stein, Gertrude
Tate, Sir Henry
Thyssen-Bornemisza family
Tretyakov, Pavel
Uhde, Wilhelm
Wedgwood, Josiah
Whitney, Gertrude Vanderbilt
Wicar, Jean-Baptiste

The popes featured in these
   entries are:
Sixtus IV (Rovere), 1471–84
Julius II (Rovere), 1503–13
Leo X (Medici), 1513–21
Clement VII (Medici), 1523–34
Paul III (Farnese), 1534–49
Clement VIII (Aldobrandini),
   1592–1605
Paul V (Borghese), 1605–21
Urban VIII (Barberini), 1623–44
Innocent X (Pamphili), 1644–55
Alexander VII (Chigi), 1655–67

DEALERS

Agnew's
Castelli, Leo

Christie's
Colnaghi's
Durand-Ruel, Paul
Duveen, Joseph
Gambart, Ernest
Goupil
Grosvenor Gallery
Guggenheim, Peggy
Janis, Sidney
Kahnweiler, Henri-Daniel
Knoedler's
Matisse, Pierre
Parsons, Betty
Sotheby's
Stieglitz, Alfred
Sturm Gallery
Vollard, Ambroise
Wildenstein

NON-BIOGRAPHICAL ENTRIES

MUSEUMS AND GALLERIES

Accademia, Venice
Albertina, Vienna
Alte Pinakothek, Munich (*pinacotheca)
Ambrosiana, Milan
Ashmolean Museum, Oxford
Bargello, Florence
Borghese Gallery, Rome
Brera, Milan
British Museum, London
Dulwich Picture Gallery, London
   (*Bourgeois, Sir Peter)
Escorial
Fitzwilliam Museum, Cambridge
Gemäldegalerie, Berlin and
   Dresden
Hermitage, St Petersburg
Kunsthistorisches Museum, Vienna
Louvre, Paris
Mauritshuis, The Hague
Metropolitan Museum, New York
Musée d'Orsay, Paris
Museum of Modern Art, New York
National Gallery, London
National Portrait Gallery,
   London
Pitti, Florence

Pompidou Centre, Paris
Prado, Madrid
Rijksmuseum, Amsterdam
Uffizi, Florence
Vatican Museums, Rome
Victoria and Albert Museum,
　London
Wallace Collection, London

In addition, museums and other collections
　named after their founders are discussed in
　the following entries:

Barnes, Albert C.
Bowes, John
Burrell, Sir William
Courtauld, Samuel
Frick, Henry Clay
Gardner, Isabella Stewart
Getty, J. Paul
Guggenheim, Solomon R.
Gulbenkian, Calouste
Huntington, Henry E.
Ludwig, Peter
Morgan, J. Pierpont
Phillips, Duncan
Saatchi, Charles
Tate, Sir Henry
Thyssen-Bornemisza family
Tretyakov, Pavel
Whitney, Gertrude Vanderbilt

ACADEMIES, SCHOOLS, AND OTHER INSTITUTIONS

Arts Council
Art Students League
Bauhaus
Beaux-Arts, École des
Black Mountain College
Courtauld Institute of Art
Dilettanti, Society of
Glasgow School of Art
Institute of Contemporary Arts
National Academy of Design
National Art Collections Fund
Pennsylvania Academy of the Fine Arts
Royal Academy
Royal College of Art
St Martin's Lane Academy
St Martin's School of Art

Smithsonian Institution
Société Anonyme
Society of Artists
Society of Independent Artists

EXHIBITIONS AND PRIZES

Armory Show
Biennale
Documenta
Donkey's Tail
Entartete Kunst (*degenerate art)
Forum Exhibition
Great Exhibition
Prix de Rome
Salon
Salon d'Automne
Salon de la Rose + Croix
Salon des Indépendants
Salon des Refusés
Sensation (*Young British Artists)
Situation
Sonderbund
Target
Turner Prize

STYLES, GROUPS, MOVEMENTS

ABC art
Abramtsevo Colony
Abstract Expressionism
Abstract Impressionism
Abstraction-Création
Aestheticism
Allied Artists' Association
American Abstract Artists
American Scene Painting
Ancients
Antipodeans
Antwerp Mannerism
Art Autre
Art Brut
Art Deco
Arte Povera
Art Informel
Art Nouveau
Arts and Crafts movement
Ashcan School
Auto-Destructive art
Automatistes, Les
Avignon, School of

Classified List of Entries

Barbizon School
Baroque
Biedermeier
Blaue Reiter
Blaue Vier
Bloomsbury Group
Blue Rose
Body art
Bohemian School
Brücke, Die
Camden Town Group
Canadian Group of Painters
Caravaggisti
Cercle et Carré
Churrigueresque
Clique, The
Cloissonism
Cobra
Colour Field Painting
Conceptual art
Concrete art
Constructivism
Corrente
Cubism
Cumberland Market Group
Dada
Danube School
Divisionism
École de Paris
Eight, The
Elementarism
Euston Road School
Expressionism
Fantastic Realism
Fauvism
Feminist art
Field Painting
Fluxus
Fontainebleau, School of
Fronte Nuovo delle Arti
Funk art
Futurism
Giottesques
Glasgow School
Gothic Revival
Graffiti art
Groupe de Recherche d'Art Visuel
Group of Seven
Gutai Group
Hague School
Hard-Edge Painting
Harlem Renaissance

Heidelberg School
Hispano-Flemish style
Hudson River School
Impressionism
Independent Group
International Gothic
Intimisme
Jeune Peinture Belge
Junk art
Kinetic art
Kitchen Sink School
Knave of Diamonds
Kukryniksky
Land art
Light art
Little Masters
London Group
Luminism
Macchiaioli
Magical Realism
Mannerism
Metaphysical Painting
Minimal art
Nabis
Nazarenes
Neoclassicism
Neo-Dada
Neo-Expressionism
Neo-Geo
Neo-Impressionism
Neo-Plasticism
Neo-Romanticism
Neue Künstlervereinigung
Neue Sachlichkeit
New British Sculpture
New English Art Club
New Figuration
New Generation
New Image Painting
Newlyn School
New Realism
New Sculpture
New York Realists
New York School
Non-Objective art
Norwich School
Novecento Italiano
November Group
Novembergruppe
Omega Workshops
Op art
Orientalism

Classified List of Entries

gouache
graphite
grisaille
ground
gum
hatching
impasto
imprimatura
ink
intonaco
kit-cat
linseed oil
marouflage
mastic
maulstick
medium
megilp
metalpoint
millboard (*cardboard)
oil paint
palette
palette knife
panel
pantograph
paper
papyrus
parchment
pastel
pen
pencil
pigment
plumbago
pointillism
poppy oil
pouncing
priming
resin
sandarac
sanguine
scumble
secco
sepia
siccative
sinopia
size
stereochromy
stretcher
stump
stylus
support
tempera
tube

turpentine
underdrawing
underpainting
varnish
vehicle
walnut oil
wash
watercolour
water-glass painting

printmaking
aquatint
Baxter prints
burin
burr
chiaroscuro woodcut
chromolithography
crayon manner
Currier & Ives prints
drypoint
Dutch mordant
engraving
etching
flock print
glass print
line engraving
linocut
lithography
livre d'artiste
manière criblée
metal cut
mezzotint
monotype
oleograph
pastel manner (*crayon manner)
print
relief etching
retroussage
rocker
roulette
scorper
scraper
screenprinting
soft-ground etching
state
stencil
stipple engraving
stopping-out varnish
tint tool
woodcut
wood engraving
xylography

Classified List of Entries

boss
bozzetto
Brussels tapestries
bust
cabinet painting
cadavre exquis
calvary
cameo
capital
capriccio
caricature
carnations
cartoon
caryatid
cassone
chiaroscuro
chinoiserie
choir stalls
ciborium
Circle
classicism
continuous representation
contrapposto
conversation piece
craquelure
decorative arts
degenerate art
desco da parto
devotional painting
diaper
diorama
diptych
disegno
donor
drapery painter
drollery
eclectic
Eidophusikon
emblem
ex-voto
fancy picture
Federal Art Project
fête champêtre
Fiammingo
figurative art
fine arts
formalism
gargoyle
genre
Gesamtkunstwerk
gisant
Gobelins

Golden Section
Grand Manner
Grand Tour
graphic art
grotesque
Haggadah
happening
herm
history painting
hue
Hypnerotomachia Poliphili
icon
iconography
iconostasis
ideal
ideal landscape
illusionism
Kelmscott Press
Kunstkammer
liberal arts
limner
local colour
lunette
lyrical abstraction
Maestà
mandorla
maquette
Master of . . .
masterpiece
medal
Megillah
miniature
misericord
mobile
modello
morbidezza
mural
naive art
naturalism
obelisk
object
objet trouvé
Official War Art
Old Master
pala
panorama
paragone
pastiche
patina
peep-show box
peintre-graveur
pendant

ABBREVIATIONS

AG	Art Gallery
Alte Pin.	Alte Pinakothek
ARA	Associate of the Royal Academy
Bib. Nat.	Bibliothèque Nationale
BL	British Library
BM	British Museum
Coll.	Collection(s)
DNB	*Dictionary of National Biography*
Gal.	Gallery, Galerie, Galleria
Gal. Naz.	Galleria Nazionale
Inst.	Institute
KH Mus.	Kunsthistorisches Museum
Lib.	Library
Met. Mus.	Metropolitan Museum
MFA	Museum of Fine Arts
MoMA	Museum of Modern Art
Mus.	Museum(s), Musée(s), Museo
Mus. B.-A.	Musée des Beaux-Arts, Museo de Bellas Artes
Mus. Naz.	Museo Nazionale
Nat. Mus.	National Museum
Neue Pin.	Neue Pinakothek
NG	National Gallery, Nationalgalerie, Nasjonalgalleriet
NPG	National Portrait Gallery
NT	National Trust
OED	*Oxford English Dictionary*
PRA	President of the Royal Academy
priv. coll.	private collection
RA	Royal Academy, Royal Academician
Univ.	University
V&A	Victoria and Albert Museum

Aa, Dirck van der (*b* The Hague, 1731; *d* The Hague, 23 Feb. 1809). The best-known member of a family of Dutch painters from The Hague. He specialized in *grisaille decorative paintings for patrician houses in the city, carrying on the tradition of Jacob de *Wit. His style was strongly influenced by French *Rococo art; indeed his work has sometimes passed under the name of *Fragonard, as with a pair of panels of Cupids in the Victoria and Albert Museum, London. There was another van der Aa family of artists active in the 18th century in Leiden; most of the members were illustrators or engravers.

AAA. See ALLIED ARTISTS' ASSOCIATION and AMERICAN ABSTRACT ARTISTS.

Aachen, Hans von (*b* Cologne, 1552; *d* Prague, 4 Mar. 1615). German painter; his name derives from his father's birthplace, rather than his own. He had an international career, working principally in Italy (*c.*1574–87) and Prague, where he was appointed court painter by the Emperor Rudolf II (see HABSBURG) in 1592. In 1596 he settled permanently in the city (although he made several visits to Germany), and after Rudolf's death in 1612 he worked for his successor, the Emperor Matthias. His paintings, featuring elegant, elongated figures, are—like those of his colleague Bartholomeus *Spranger—leading examples of the sophisticated *Mannerist art then in vogue at the courts of northern Europe, and he was particularly good with playfully erotic nudes (*The Triumph of Truth*, 1598, Alte Pin., Munich). Engravings after his work gave his style wide influence and he ranks as one of the most important German artists of his time.

Aalto, Alvar (*b* Kuortane, 3 Feb. 1898; *d* Helsinki, 11 May 1976). Finnish architect, designer, sculptor, and painter. One of the outstanding architects of the 20th century, he was also an important furniture designer and a talented abstract sculptor and painter. Appropriately for an artist from a land of forests, he made extensive use of timber in his work, and in 1933 he patented a method of bending plywood for furniture. In the 1930s he engaged in what have been described as artistic laboratory experiments, using laminated wood to make abstract reliefs and free-standing sculptures, characterized by irregularly curved forms. These sculptural experiments served the dual purpose of solving technical problems concerning the pliancy of wood and of developing spatial ideas for his architectural work. In the 1950s he took up sculpture on a large scale, working in bronze, marble, and mixed media. His outstanding work in this field is his memorial (1960) for the Battle of Suomussalmi, a leaning bronze pillar on a stone pedestal set up in the arctic wastes of the battlefield. Aalto was noteworthy also for helping to introduce modern art to the Finnish public, particularly the works of his friends *Calder and *Léger.

Aaltonen, Wäinö (*b* Marttila, nr. Turku, 8 Mar. 1894; *d* Helsinki, 30 May 1966). Finnish sculptor, whose work was regarded as an embodiment of his country's national spirit, particularly of the patriotic ardour that flourished in the years following the declaration of independence from Russia (1917). He made his name as a sculptor of war memorials, and his most characteristic works are tributes to national heroes, such as the monument to the runner Paavo Nurmi (1925, the best-known cast is outside the athletics stadium in Helsinki) and the bust of the composer Sibelius (1928, various casts exist). Aaltonen worked in bronze, stone, and other materials, including glass (he also painted and made collages). His style was heroic and essentially naturalistic, although sometimes touched with *Cubist stylizations.

Abakanowicz, Magdalena (*b* Felenty, nr. Warsaw, 20 June 1930). Polish abstract sculptor, the pioneer and leading exponent of sculpture made from woven fabrics. Initially she worked in conventional media in painting and sculpture, but from 1960 she concentrated on textiles, using hessian and rope (in some works she has also incorporated wood). Sometimes she obtained her raw materials by visiting Poland's Baltic ports and collecting old ropes, which she then unravelled and dyed. At first she made reliefs, but she soon moved on to large three-dimensional works. In 1962 she first exhibited in the West (at the International Tapestry Biennial in Lausanne) and thereafter her work appeared often outside Poland in both solo and group shows, winning her an international reputation and numerous awards.

Abate (or Abbate), **Niccolò dell'** (*b* Modena, *c.*1510; *d* ?Fontainebleau, 1571). Italian *Mannerist painter, active for much of his career in France. He spent his early career in and around Modena, mainly as a decorator of secular buildings (little of this work survives intact). From 1547 to 1552 he lived in Bologna, his work of this period including decorations in the Palazzo Poggi (now part of the university). The subjects include landscapes and musical parties, with elegantly dressed, elongated figures influenced particularly by *Parmigianino. In 1552 Niccolò moved to France, where he remained for the rest of his life. For much of this time he worked at *Fontainebleau, initially under *Primaticcio. Most of his work in the palace itself has been lost, and he is now remembered more for his landscapes with figures from mythological stories (*Landscape with the Death of Eurydice*, NG, London). In these he was a precursor of *Claude and *Poussin in the long-lived tradition of French classical landscape. Niccolò also painted portraits in both Italy and France.

Abbey, Edwin Austin (*b* Philadelphia, 1 Apr. 1852; *d* London, 1 Aug. 1911). American painter, etcher, and book illustrator, highly successful in England (where he settled in 1878) as well as in his native country. He specialized in historical scenes and had several large and prestigious commissions, most notably a set of murals (completed 1902) in Boston Public Library representing the quest for the Holy Grail (his friend *Sargent also painted murals in the library) and the official painting commemorating Edward VII's coronation in 1902 (Buckingham Palace, London). Such paintings now seem rather overblown and ponderous, and his reputation rests mainly on his lively book illustrations. He was particularly prolific for *Harper's Weekly*, his association with the magazine lasting from 1870 until his death. Although he always remained an American citizen, Abbey was devoted to cricket and had a private ground at his house at Fairford in Gloucestershire.

Abbott, Lemuel Francis (*b* Leicestershire, *c.*1760; *d* London, 5 Dec. 1802). English portrait painter. All his pictures are of male sitters; his clientele included many naval officers and he is best known for his portrayals of Lord Nelson, of whom he did several portraits with slight variations (1797–8). In 1798 he was declared insane, and some of his unfinished works were completed by other hands.

ABC art. An alternative term for *Minimal art.

Abildgaard, Nicolai Abraham (*b* Copenhagen, 11 Sept. 1743; *d* Frederiksdal, nr. Copenhagen, 4 June 1809). Danish *Neoclassical painter, mainly of historical, literary, and mythological subjects. He studied at the Copenhagen Academy and then from 1772 to 1777 in Rome, where his friendship with *Fuseli helped to introduce *Romantic elements to his style. On his return to Denmark his work became more classical, as is best seen in his cycles of paintings illustrating the Roman writers Terence and Apuleius (1802–4 and 1808–9 respectively, Statens Mus., Copenhagen). He became one of the leading figures in Danish art and had great influence as director of the Copenhagen Academy (1789–91 and 1801–9), where his pupils included *Runge and *Thorvaldsen. Abildgaard occasionally worked as an architect, sculptor, and designer, and he also wrote on art. His most ambitious work, a huge decorative scheme (1778–91) at Christiansborg Palace, Copenhagen, was largely destroyed by fire in 1794.

Abramtsevo Colony. A name applied to a circle of Russian artists associated with the country estate of the patron Savva Mamontov (1841–1918) at Abramtsevo, about 60 km (40 miles) north of Moscow. Mamontov, who earned a fortune from railway building, bought the estate in 1870, and from then until about the end of the century he often played host to distinguished artists, some of whom stayed for several months at a time during the summer, enjoying the attractive surroundings as well as the stimulating company. One of them, Victor *Vasnetsov, said of Mamontov: 'There was in him a sort of electric current that ignited other people's energies. God gave him a special talent for stimulating the creativity of others.' Among the other visitors were *Repin, *Serov, and *Vrubel. Serov's celebrated *Girl with Peaches* (1887, Tretyakov Gal., Moscow), a portrait of Mamontov's 12-year-old daughter Vera, was painted at Abramtsevo. The estate is now a national museum.

abstract art. Art that does not depict recognizable scenes or objects, but instead is made up of forms and colours that exist for their own expressive sake. Much decorative art can thus be described as abstract, but in normal usage the term refers to modern painting and sculpture that abandon the traditional European conception of art as the imitation of nature. Abstract art in this sense was born and achieved its distinctive identity in the decade 1910–20 and is now regarded as the most characteristic form of 20th-century art. It has developed into many different movements and 'isms', but two or three basic tendencies are recognizable. In *Cubism and Abstract Art* (1936), Alfred H. *Barr, 'at the risk of grave oversimplification', divided abstraction into two main currents: the first (represented by *Malevich) he described as 'intellectual, structural, architectonic, geometrical, rectilinear and classical in its austerity and dependence upon logic and calculation'; the second (exemplified by *Kandinsky) he described as 'intuitional and emotional rather than intellectual; organic or *biomorphic rather than geometrical in its forms; curvilinear rather than rectilinear, decorative rather than structural, and romantic rather than classical in its exaltation of the mystical, the spontaneous and the irrational'. Looking at the subject in a slightly different way (and from a later viewpoint than Barr's), it is possible to see three main strands in abstract art: (i) the reduction of natural appearances to radically simplified forms, exemplified in the sculpture of *Brancusi (one meaning of the verb 'abstract' is to summarize or concentrate); (ii) the construction of works of art from non-representational basic forms (often simple geometric shapes), as in Ben *Nicholson's reliefs; (iii) spontaneous, 'free' expression, as in the *Action Painting of Jackson *Pollock. Many exponents of such art dislike the word 'abstract' (*Arp, for example, hated it, insisting on the word *'Concrete'), but the alternatives they prefer, although perhaps more precise, are usually cumbersome, notably non-figurative, non-representational, and *Non-Objective.

The basic aesthetic premiss of abstract art—that formal qualities can be thought of as existing independently of subject matter—existed long before the 20th century. Ultimately the idea can be traced back to Plato, who in his dialogue *Philebus* (*c.*350 BC) puts the following words into Socrates' mouth: 'I do not mean by beauty of form such beauty as that of animals and pictures . . . but understand me to mean straight lines and circles, and the plane or solid figures which are formed out of them by turning-lathes and rulers and measures of angles; for these I affirm to be not only relatively beautiful, like other things, but eternally and absolutely beautiful.' More explicitly, in his Tenth *Discourse* (1780) to the students of the *Royal Academy, Sir Joshua *Reynolds advised that 'we are sure from experience that the beauty of form alone, without the assistance of any other quality, makes of itself a great work, and justly claims our esteem and admiration'; and in discussing the *Belvedere Torso* he referred to 'the perfection of this science of abstract form'. Several notable critics followed this line in the 19th century. In 1846, for example, Charles *Baudelaire wrote that 'painting is interesting only in virtue of line and colour'; in 1890—in a much-quoted remark—Maurice *Denis said: 'Remember that a picture—before being a war horse or a nude woman or an anecdote—is essentially a flat surface covered with colours assembled in a certain order'; and in 1896 George *Santayana, after noting that colour may produce unpleasant as well as pleasant effects, 'almost like a musical discord', proposed that 'a more general development of this sensibility would make possible a new abstract art, an art that should deal with colours as music does with sound' (the analogy with music was often pursued; *Whistler, for example, sometimes gave his paintings pseudo-musical titles, as later did Kandinsky, *Kupka, and other artists, including the Lithuanian composer-painter M. K. Čiurlionis (1875–1911). Many of the leading painters of the 1890s—notably the *Symbolists—stressed the expressive properties of colour, line, and shape rather than their representative function, and this process was taken further by the major avant-garde movements of the first decade of the 20th century—especially *Cubism, *Expressionism, and *Fauvism.

By 1910, then, the time was ripe for abstract art, and it developed more or less simultaneously in various countries. Kandinsky is often cited as the first person to paint an abstract picture, but no artist can in fact be singled out for the distinction. (A work by Kandinsky known as 'First Abstract Watercolour' (Pompidou Centre, Paris) is signed and dated 1910, but some scholars believe that it is later and was inscribed by Kandinsky several years after its execution. This kind of problem arises not only with Kandinsky: several early abstract artists were keen to stress the primacy of their ideas and were not above backdating works.) Among the other artists who produced abstract paintings at about the same early date as Kandinsky were the American Arthur *Dove and the Swiss Augusto Giacometti, cousin of Alberto *Giacometti.

The individual pioneers were soon followed by abstract groups and movements—among the first were *Orphism and *Synchromism in France. There was a particularly rich crop in Russia, with *Constructivism, *Rayonism, and *Suprematism all launched by 1915. With some artists, abstraction represented merely a brief phase in their careers (among them the British artists Vanessa *Bell, Duncan *Grant, and Wyndham *Lewis), but with others it was a vocation or even a mission. The almost religious fervour with which some of the Russian artists pursued their ideals was matched by the members of the De *Stijl group in Holland, founded in 1917. To such artists, abstraction was not simply a matter of style, but a question of finding a visual idiom capable of expressing their most deeply felt ideas. *Mondrian, for example, believed that his art of clarity and balance would lead to a society in which life would be governed by a universal visual harmony.

In the period between the two world wars, the severely geometrical style of De Stijl and the technologically orientated Constructivism were the most influential currents in abstraction (they came together in the *Bauhaus). Paris was the main centre of abstract art at this time, partly because it attracted so many refugee artists from Germany and Russia, where abstract art was banned in the 1930s under Hitler and Stalin. There was also a strong abstract element in *Surrealism, which was born in Paris. The first exhibition devoted solely to abstract art was held there by the *Cercle et Carré group in 1930, and its successor, the *Abstraction-Création association, founded in 1931, brought together a large number of abstract artists of various types and provided a focus for their activities. However, in general figurative art was dominant in the interwar period and abstract art won little public acceptance. It was very much a minority taste in Britain and the USA, for example, in spite of such outstanding individual contributions as the sculptures of *Hepworth and *Calder and the efforts of groups such as *Unit One (founded in 1933) and *American Abstract Artists (founded in 1936).

The second heroic period of abstract art came after the Second World War, when the enormous success of *Abstract Expressionism in the USA and its European equivalent *Art Informel made abstraction for a time virtually the dominant

orthodoxy in Western art. Abstract art no longer seemed to need philosophical justification of the kind given by Kandinsky and Mondrian (although several of the Abstract Expressionists were equally high-minded in approach); however, abstraction was sometimes invested with a moral dimension as an embodiment of Western freedom of thought, as opposed to the totalitarianism that had banned avant-garde art in Nazi Germany and Soviet Russia (see DEGENERATE ART and SOCIALIST REALISM). In this respect it is significant that many of the Abstract Expressionists were influenced by European Surrealists who had fled to New York during the Second World War to escape the fear of such repression. Thus, in the USA particularly, support for abstract art could be regarded almost as a form of patriotism. Abstract Expressionism represented a great watershed in art and many later developments were either evolutions from it or reactions against it. These included a revival of figuration, in the form particularly of *Pop art, but also new styles of abstraction, including *Post-Painterly Abstraction, *Op art, and *Minimal art, all of which flourished in the 1960s.

Abstract Expressionism. The dominant movement in American painting in the late 1940s and 1950s, characterized by a desire to convey powerful emotions through the sensuous qualities of paint, often on canvases of huge size. It was the first major development in American art to achieve international status and influence, and it is often reckoned the most significant art movement anywhere since the Second World War. The energy and excitement it brought to the American art scene helped New York to replace Paris as the world capital of contemporary art, and to many Americans the heyday of the movement has already acquired a kind of legendary status as a golden age.

The phrase 'Abstract Expressionism' had originally been used in 1919 to describe certain paintings by *Kandinsky, but in the context of modern American painting it was first used by the *New Yorker* art critic Robert Coates (1897–1973) in 1945; by the end of the decade it had become part of the standard critical vocabulary. The painters embraced by the term worked mainly in New York and there were various ties of friendship and loose groupings among them, but they shared a similarity of outlook rather than of style—an outlook characterized by a spirit of revolt against tradition and a desire for spontaneous freedom of expression. The stylistic roots of Abstract Expressionism are complex, but despite its name it owed more to *Surrealism—with its stress on *automatism and intuition—than to *Expressionism. A direct source of inspiration came from the European Surrealists who took refuge in the USA during the Second World War, most notably *Matta, who promoted what the American art historian Meyer Schapiro (1904–96) called the 'idea of the canvas as a field of prodigious excitement, unleashed energies'. The war also brought Peggy *Guggenheim back to America, and during its brief lifetime (1942–7) her Art of This Century gallery was the main showcase for Abstract Expressionism during its formative period.

The most famous Abstract Expressionist is Jackson *Pollock, whose explosive *Action Painting best sums up the movement, but the work of other leading exponents was sometimes neither abstract (the leering Women of *de Kooning) nor expressionist (the serene visions of *Rothko). Even allowing for these wide differences, however, there are certain qualities that are basic to most Abstract Expressionist painting: the preference for working on a huge scale; the emphasis placed on surface qualities, so that the flatness of the canvas is stressed; the adoption of an *all-over type of treatment, in which the whole area of the picture is regarded as equally important; the glorification of the act of painting itself; the conviction that abstract painting could convey significant meaning and should not be viewed in *formalist terms alone; and a belief in the absolute individuality of the artist (for which reason most of the Abstract Expressionists disliked being labelled with an 'ism', preferring *New York School as a group designation).

Alongside de Kooning, Pollock, and Rothko, the painters who are considered central to Abstract Expressionism include *Gorky, *Gottlieb, *Guston, *Kline, *Motherwell, *Newman, and *Still. Most of them struggled for recognition early in their careers, but during the 1950s the movement became an enormous critical and financial success. It had passed its peak by 1960, but several of the major figures continued productively after this and a younger generation of painters carried on the Abstract Expressionist torch. Sculptors as well as painters were influenced by the movement, the leading figures including Ibram Lassaw (1913–), Seymour Lipton (1903–86), and Theodore Roszak (1907–81). By 1960, also, reaction against the emotionalism of Abstract Expressionism was under way, in the shape principally of *Pop art and *Post-Painterly Abstraction. Indeed, much of the subsequent history of American art can be written in terms of developments from or responses to the movement, and Robert *Hughes considers that its success has 'encouraged a phony grandiloquence, a confusion of pretentious size with scale, that has plagued American painting ever since'.

Abstract Impressionism. A term coined by Elaine *de Kooning to describe paintings that resemble certain late Impressionist pictures (notably those of *Monet) in their brushwork but have no representative content: 'Retaining the quiet uniform pattern of strokes that spread over the canvas without climax or emphasis, these followers keep the Impressionist manner of looking at a scene but leave out the scene.' In 1958 Lawrence *Alloway used the term as the title of an exhibition he organized in London; the artists represented included Sam *Francis, Patrick *Heron, and Nicolas de *Staël. The term has also been applied to various French abstract painters of the same period, for example *Manessier.

Abstraction-Création. An association of abstract painters and sculptors formed in Paris in February 1931, a successor to the short-lived *Cercle et Carré. It was open to artists of all nationalities and its organization was loose, so that at one time its numbers rose to as many as 400 (among the members were *Arp, *Kandinsky, and *Mondrian, as well as several artists who were never permanently resident in Paris, notably Barbara *Hepworth and Ben *Nicholson). The association was extremely catholic in its outlook and embraced many kinds of non-figurative art, although the emphasis was increasingly on geometrical abstraction. It operated by arranging group exhibitions and by publishing an illustrated annual called Abstraction-Création: art non-figuratif, which appeared from 1932 to 1936; after this its activities declined.

académie. A French term for a private art school, several of which flourished in Paris in the late 19th and early 20th centuries. The term 'atelier libre' has also been used to refer to such establishments. Entry to the official École des *Beaux-Arts was difficult (almost impossible for foreigners, who from 1884 had to take a vicious examination in French) and teaching there was conservative, so private art schools, with their more liberal regimes, were often frequented by progressive young artists. Four of them are particularly well known.

The **Académie Carrière** was opened in 1890 by Eugène Carrière (1849–1906), a painter of portraits, religious pictures, and—his special-ity—scenes of motherhood. His style was misty, monochromatic, and vaguely *Symbolist. *Rodin was a great admirer of his work. There was no regular teaching at the school, though Carrière visited it once a week. It was here that *Matisse met *Derain, thus helping to form the nucleus of the future *Fauves. The **Académie Julian** was founded in 1873 by Rodolphe Julian (1839–1907), whose work as a painter is now forgotten. The school had no entrance require-ments, was open from 8 a.m. to nightfall, and was soon the most popular establishment of its type. Julian opened several branches throughout Paris, one of them for women artists, and by the 1880s the student population was about 600. Although the Académie Julian became famous for the unruly behaviour of its students, it was regarded as a stepping stone to the École des Beaux-Arts (Julian had shown astuteness in en-gaging teachers from the École as visiting pro-fessors). Among the French artists who studied there were *Bonnard, *Denis, Matisse, and *Vuillard. The list of distinguished foreign stu-dents is very long. The **Académie Ranson** was founded in 1908 by Paul Ranson (1864–1909), who had studied at the Académie Julian. After Ranson's early death, his wife took over as dir-ector, and his friends Denis and *Sérusier were among the teachers. Among later teachers the most important was Roger *Bissière, whose style of expressive abstraction influenced many young painters in the 1930s; his pupils included *Manessier. The **Académie Suisse** was founded in about 1850 by a former artists' model called Suisse 'in an old and sordid building where a well-known dentist pulled teeth at one franc apiece . . . artists could for a small fee work from the living model without any examinations or tuition' (John *Rewald, *The History of Impres-sionism*). *Courbet, *Manet, and several of the *Impressionists drew at the Académie Suisse, and it was there in 1861 that Camille *Pissarro first noticed the 'strange Provençal' Paul *Cézanne, whose life drawings were ridiculed by his fellow students.

Académie Montparnasse. See LHOTE.

Académie Royale de Peinture et de Sculpture, Paris. See ACADEMY.

academy. An association of artists, scholars, etc. that aims to maintain professional standards and to promote the affairs of its members. The original Academy was an olive grove outside Athens where Plato and his successors taught philosophy, and his school of philosophy was therefore known as 'The Academy'. In the Italian *Renaissance the word began to be applied to almost any philosophical or literary circle and was sometimes employed of groups of artists who discussed theoretical as well as practical problems. Lorenzo de' *Medici's sculpture garden, supervised in the 1480s by *Bertoldo di Giovanni, is sometimes described as a kind of proto-academy, for example, but the first formal art academy was not set up until 1563, when the Accademia del Disegno was founded in Florence. It was the brainchild of Giorgio *Vasari, whose aim was to emancipate artists from control by the guilds, and to confirm the rise in social stand-ing they had achieved during the previous hun-dred years. *Michelangelo, who more than anyone else embodied this change of status, was made one of the two honorary heads; the other was Duke Cosimo I de' Medici.

The next important step was taken in Rome, where the Accademia di S. Luca was founded in 1593, with Federico *Zuccaro as its first presi-dent. More stress was laid on practical instruc-tion than at Florence, but the Academy was unsuccessful in its war against the guilds until it received support from Pope Urban VIII (Maffeo *Barberini, reigned 1623–44), who rec-ognized it as 'an authority superior to the crafts guilds'. Thereafter it grew in wealth and pres-tige. There were few other permanent acad-emies in Italy before the 18th century, but the word was frequently used of private institutions where artists met to draw from life. The most famous example of this kind was organized by the *Carracci in Bologna in the 1580s.

Several institutions of the Carracci type were set up in northern Europe (the 'academy' founded in Haarlem in about 1600 by *Cornelis van Haarlem, Hendrick *Goltzius, and Karel van *Mander was probably some kind of life drawing class). However, the first official art academy outside Italy was not established until 1648. In that year a group of French painters, moved by the same reasons of prestige as had earlier inspired the Italians, successfully peti-tioned Louis XIV to found the Académie Royale de Peinture et de Sculpture. Here too the guilds put up powerful opposition, and the Académie's supremacy was not assured until Louis' chief minister, Jean-Baptiste Colbert (1619–83), was elected vice-protector in 1661 and saw that he could use it as an instrument of state—for im-posing official standards and principles of taste that would help to create a national artistic identity and a style appropriate for glorifying the king. *Le Brun was appointed director of the Académie in 1663 and he and Colbert ensured that it assumed a virtual monopoly of teaching and of the exhibiting of works of art. Implicit in the Academy's theories and teaching was the assumption that everything to do with art can be brought within the scope of rational understanding and reduced to logical precepts that can be studied and taught.

After the middle of the 17th century, art academies were founded in Germany, Spain, and other countries and by the end of the 18th century well over 100 were flourishing throughout Europe. Among these was the *Royal Academy in London, founded in 1768. Everywhere the academies became champions of *Neoclassicism in opposition to the *Baroque and *Rococo styles. There was some antagonism towards these bodies from the start, and at the end of the 18th century French revolutionary sentiment was especially bitter about the exclusive privileges enjoyed by members of the Académie; many artists, with J.-L. *David in the lead, demanded its dissolution. This step was taken in 1793, but the École des *Beaux-Arts, which took over its teaching role, embodied much the same principles.

The principal threat to academies came not from political developments, however, but from the *Romantic notion of the artist as a genius who produces his masterpieces by the light of inspiration that cannot be taught or subjected to rule. Virtually all the most creative artists of the later 19th century stood outside the academies and sought alternative channels for exhibiting their works, although *Manet, for example, always craved traditional success at the *Salon. Academies still retained prestige in conservative circles, but they were condemned out of hand by the adventurous, and in 1898, in his book *Modern Painting*, the novelist and critic George Moore (1852–1933) wrote: 'that nearly all artists dislike and despise the Royal Academy is a matter of common knowledge.' In the face of competition from rival teaching institutions and artists' groups (such as the *Slade School and the *New English Art Club in England and the *Sezessionen in Germany and Austria) academies tended to become more liberal, but by the middle of the 20th century they were increasingly marginalized. Although the word 'academic' can be used neutrally, it now usually carries a pejorative meaning, and is associated with mediocrity and lack of originality.

academy board. A type of cardboard sheet used as a *support for painting, especially in oils. It is made of sheets of paper sized and pressed together, treated with a *ground, and sometimes embossed with an imitation canvas grain. Academy board was introduced in about 1850 and because of its relative cheapness was popular in art schools and with amateur painters, although it was also used by professional artists for sketches and studies. It has now largely been superseded by *canvas board.

academy figure. A careful painting or drawing (usually about half life-size) from the nude human figure made as an exercise, typically in an art school or academy. The figure is usually depicted in a heroic pose, and there is a tradition of suitable postures that goes back to the *Carracci. Two early 19th-century French examples are in the National Gallery, London.

Accademia (Gallerie dell'Accademia), Venice. The major picture gallery of Venice. It takes its name from the city's Academy of Fine Arts, founded in 1756, but it did not open as a picture gallery until 1809, as part of the administrative reforms carried out by Napoleon when Italy was under his rule. It is housed in a complex of Gothic and Renaissance buildings on the Grand Canal—the church, monastery, and Scuola of S. Maria della Carità. The architect Giovanni Antonio Selva supervised the conversion. Part of the complex is still used for the teaching activities of the Academy (which was administratively separated from the gallery in 1878), but most of it is devoted to exhibition space. Selva kept much of the character of the old buildings, and *Titian's huge *Presentation of the Virgin* (1534–8) remains on the wall for which it was produced, in what was then the Scuola's committee room. The Accademia contains the most comprehensive collection of Venetian painting in the world (although a few major names, such as *Canaletto, are modestly represented); there are few works from other schools.

Acconci, Vito. See BODY ART.

Achilles Painter. Greek vase painter, active in Athens in the mid-5th century BC, named after a *red-figure amphora decorated with a figure of Achilles (Vatican Mus.). He was a contemporary of *Phidias and his paintings have some of the nobility associated with the great sculptor's work. His compositions are simple (usually limited to one or two figures) and his figures are serene and graceful.

Ackermann, Rudolph. See ROWLANDSON.

acroterion (plural: acroteria). An ornamental block on the apex and at the lower angles of a pediment on a classical building (particularly a Greek or Roman temple), bearing a statue or a carved finial.

acrylic. A modern synthetic paint, made with a resin derived from acrylic acid, that combines some of the properties of oils and watercolour. It was the first new painting medium in centuries and has become a serious rival to oil paint. Acrylics are a refined version of paints developed for industrial use and can be applied to almost any surface with a variety of tools (brush, *air-brush, knife, sponge, and so on) to create effects ranging from thin washes to rich impasto and with a matt or gloss finish. Most acrylic paints are water based, although some are oil compatible, using turpentine as a thinner. Thinly applied paint dries in a matter of minutes, thickly applied paint in hours—much quicker than oils. Acrylic paint first became available to artists in the 1940s in the USA and certain American painters discovered that it offered them advantages over oils. Colour Stain painters (see COLOUR FIELD PAINTING) such as Helen *Frankenthaler and Morris *Louis, for example, found that they could thin the paint so that it flowed over the canvas yet still retained its full brilliance of colour. David *Hockney took up acrylic during his first visit to Los Angeles in 1963; he had earlier tried and rejected the medium, but American-manufactured acrylic was at this time far superior to that available in Britain, and he felt that the flat, bold colours helped him to capture the strong Californian light. Hockney used acrylic almost exclusively for his paintings until 1972, when he returned to oils because he now regarded their slow-drying properties as an advantage: 'you can work for days and keep altering it as well; you can scrape it off if you don't like it. Once acrylic is down you can't get it off.' In spite of these differences in properties, the finished appearance of an acrylic painting is sometimes more or less indistinguishable from an oil, and some artists have combined the two techniques in the same painting. In addition to being versatile, acrylics are less susceptible to heat and damp than traditional media, but in the 1990s some doubts began to be expressed about their permanence.

Action Painting. A type of dynamic, impulsive painting in which the artist applies paint with energetic *gestural movements—sometimes by dribbling or splashing—and with no preconceived idea of what the picture will look like. Sometimes the term is employed loosely as a synonym for *Abstract Expressionism, but such usage is misleading, as Action Painting represents only one aspect of that movement. The term was coined by the critic Harold *Rosenberg in an article entitled 'The American Action Painters' in Art News in December 1952. Rosenberg regarded Action Painting as a means of giving free expression to the artist's instinctive creative forces and he regarded the act of painting itself as more significant than the finished work. Although the term soon became established, many critics were unconvinced by Rosenberg's idea of the canvas being 'not a picture but an event': Mary McCarthy, for example, wrote that 'you cannot hang an event on a wall, only a picture'. Rosenberg's article did not mention individual painters and was unillustrated, but the artist who is associated above all with Action Painting is Jackson *Pollock, who vividly described how he felt when working on a canvas laid on the floor: 'I feel nearer, more a part of the painting, since this way I can walk around it, work from the four sides and literally be *in* the painting . . . When I am *in* my painting, I am not aware of what I'm doing. It is only after a sort of "get acquainted" period that I see what I have been about. I have no fears about making changes, destroying the image, etc., because the painting has a life of its own. I try to let it come through.'

There have been numerous accounts of how Pollock came to develop his drip technique, including an unlikely story that the idea came to him when he accidentally kicked over a can of paint. A theory that has been much discussed is that he was influenced by sand paintings of the Navajo Indians of New Mexico, who in certain rituals spill coloured earth onto the ground to form elaborate patterns. Whatever his sources, Pollock used Action Painting to create what are generally regarded as some of the greatest abstract pictures ever created. In the work of lesser artists, however, the technique could easily degenerate into messy self-indulgence, and it generated a good deal of outrage and mockery, especially after the British painter William Green (1934–2001) took to riding a bicycle over the canvas, a feat imitated by the comedian Tony Hancock in the film *The Rebel* (1961). These burlesque aspects of Action Painting were anticipated by the great Japanese artist Katsushika Hokusai (see UKIYO-E), who in his early years used to create huge pictures in front of festival crowds, using a broom and a bucket of ink, and on one occasion dipped the feet of a chicken in paint and let it run over his paper.

Ada Group. Term applied to a group of stylistically related *Carolingian manuscripts from the Middle Rhine region; they take their name from the Ada Gospels (Stadtbibliothek, Trier), which has a dedication to Ada, 'the servant of God', who is said to have been a sister of Charlemagne. The manuscripts are sumptuously illuminated, with much use of gold and heavy colours, combining *Early Christian and *Byzantine models in style and *iconography. A few ivory book covers closely related in style to the manuscripts have also been included within the group, notably those for the Lorsch Gospels (c.820); the front is in the Vatican, the back in the Victoria and Albert Museum, London (the manuscript itself is divided between the Vatican and the library at Alba Iulia, Romania).

Adam, François-Gaspard (b Nancy, 23 May 1710; d Paris, 18 Aug. 1761); **Lambert-Sigisbert** (b Nancy, 10 Oct. 1700; d Paris, 12 May 1759); and **Nicolas-Sébastien** (b Nancy, 22 Mar. 1705; d Paris, 27 Mar. 1778). French sculptors, brothers. All three spent several years in Rome after training with their father **Jacob-Sigisbert** (b Nancy, 28 Oct. 1670; d Nancy, 6 May 1747), and on their return adapted the Roman *Baroque style to French *Rococo taste. Lambert-Sigisbert was the most distinguished member of the family. His masterpiece is the Neptune Fountain (1735–40) at Versailles, a work showing the influence of *Bernini in its exuberant movement. Nicolas-Sébastien often collaborated with Lambert-Sigisbert, notably on the Neptune Fountain; his most important independent work is the monument of Queen Catharina Opalinska (1749) in the church of Notre-Dame-de-Bon-Secours in Nancy. François-Gaspard was the least accomplished of the brothers; his best works are probably his garden statues for Frederick the Great of Prussia at Sanssouci, Potsdam. Better known than any of the three brothers is their nephew *Clodion.

Adam, Henri-Georges (b Paris, 14 Jan. 1904; d La Clarté, Brittany, 27 Aug. 1967). French sculptor, graphic artist, and tapestry designer. He worked in various fields but became best known for sculpture, which he took up in 1938. His early sculptures were figurative and conceived in large expressive planes somewhat in the manner of *Brancusi; later he produced geometrical abstracts, influenced by *Arp, which he sometimes decorated with engraved patterns. Among his best-known works is the *Beacon of the Dead* monument at Auschwitz (1957–8). He designed tapestries for *Aubusson, as well as ones for the United Nations and the French Embassy in Washington.

Adami, Valerio (b Bologna, 17 Mar. 1935). Italian painter and graphic artist, his country's leading exponent of *Pop art and one of the few non-American or non-British artists to achieve international success in the field. Characteristically his pictures resemble frames from comic strips, with firm outlines and clear colours. His subject matter has been taken largely from advertising, but he has also used literary, philosophical, and political themes.

Addison, Joseph (b Milston, nr. Amesbury, Wiltshire, 1 May 1672; d London, 17 June 1719). English writer and statesman. Addison was a Whig MP from 1708 until his death, a classical scholar, a poet, a playwright, and one of the leading journalists of his age. His journalism appeared mainly in the *Tatler* and its successor the *Spectator*, both of which had a large middle-class readership, and he said, 'I shall be ambitious to have it said of me, that I have brought philosophy out of closets and libraries, schools and colleges, to dwell in clubs and assemblies, at tea-tables and coffee-houses.' In terms of aesthetics, his most important writings are a series of essays 'On the Pleasures of the Imagination' published in the *Spectator* in 1712. They show a pragmatic outlook and a belief that the arts should 'deduce their laws and rules from the general sense and taste of mankind, and not from the principles of those arts themselves'. In these writings he helped lay the basis for the notion of 'sensibility' and for that of an 'inner sense' of beauty later taken up by *Hutcheson and the philosopher David Hume (1711–76). As a member of the *Kit-Cat Club, Addison was painted by *Kneller.

Adler, Jankel (b Tuszyn, nr. Łódź, 26 July 1895; d Aldbourne, Wiltshire, 25 Apr. 1949). Polish painter, active mainly in Germany (until 1933, when he left because of the rise of Nazism), France, and Britain (where he settled in 1940). He was primarily a figure painter, best known for his portrayals of Jewish life in Poland (as a youth he had considered becoming a rabbi). His style in his mature work was eclectic and expressionistic, influenced by *Klee and *Picasso. In turn his cosmopolitanism was a stimulus against wartime isolation for several young British artists, notably Robert *Colquhoun and

Robert MacBryde (in the mid-1940s Adler shared a house with them in London).

Aelst, Pieter Coecke van. See COECKE VAN AELST.

Aelst, Pieter van. See BRUSSELS TAPESTRIES.

Aelst, Willem van (*b* Delft, *c*.1625; *d* ?Amsterdam, *c*.1683). Dutch painter of lavish flower pieces and still-lifes. He was a pupil in Delft of his uncle **Evert van Aelst** (1602–57), by whom no works are known. From 1645 to 1649 Willem worked in France (1645–9) and from 1649 to 1656 in Florence, where he was court painter to Ferdinando II de' *Medici, Grand Duke of Tuscany. In 1657, following a brief stay in Delft, he settled in Amsterdam, where his pupils included Rachel *Ruysch.

aerial perspective. Term describing the means of producing a feeling of distance in a painting by imitating the effect of atmosphere whereby objects look paler and bluer the further away they are from the viewer. Dust and large moisture particles in the atmosphere cause some scattering of light as it passes through them, the amount of scattering depending on the wavelength (hence colour) of the light. Short wavelength (blue) light is scattered most and long wavelength (red) is scattered least. This is the reason why the sky is blue and why distant dark objects appear to lie behind a veil of blue.

The term 'aerial perspective' ('prospettiva aerea') was invented by *Leonardo, but the device was used much earlier by Roman painters, for example at Pompeii. In the work of Italian painters of Leonardo's time, backgrounds sometimes look artificially blue, and in general aerial perspective has been more subtly exploited in northern Europe, where the atmosphere tends to be hazier. No one used it more beautifully than *Turner, in some of whose late works it is virtually the subject of the painting.

Aertgen van Leyden. See LUCAS VAN LEYDEN.

Aertsen, Pieter (*b* Amsterdam, *c*.1508; *bur.* Amsterdam, 3 June 1575). Netherlandish painter, active mainly in Antwerp. A pioneer of still-life and *genre painting, he is best known for scenes that at first glance look like pure examples of these types, but which in fact incorporate a religious scene (*Butcher's Stall with the Flight into Egypt*, 1551, Univ. of Uppsala). Aertsen had two painter sons, **Pieter the Younger** (1540–1603) and **Aert** (1550–1612), and he also taught his nephew Joachim *Bueckelaer.

Aestheticism. A term applied to exaggerated expression of the doctrine that art is self-sufficient and need serve no ulterior purpose, whether moral, social, political, or religious. Both the doctrine and its exaggeration are succinctly expressed in the phrase 'art for art's sake', which in England became the slogan of the 'Aesthetic Movement' in the late 19th century. The phrase was used first in French ('l'art pour l'art'), the earliest known occurrence being in 1818, in lectures at the Sorbonne, Paris, by the philosopher Victor Cousin (1792–1867); they were published in 1836 as *Du vrai, du beau, et du bien*. In English, one of the first to use the phrase, in 1868, was Walter *Pater, who ranks among the key figures of the Aesthetic Movement. Among the others were *Whistler and Oscar Wilde, both of them notorious dandies, and the movement was often satirized for its tendency towards preciousness and affectation, most notably in Gilbert and Sullivan's *Patience* (see GROSVENOR GALLERY). Nevertheless, the movement helped to focus attention on the formal qualities of works of art, and so contributed to the critical outlook of writers such as *Berenson and *Fry.

aesthetics. The branch of philosophy dealing with questions of beauty and taste. The term, which derives from a Greek word meaning 'to perceive', was coined by the German philosopher Alexander Gottlieb Baumgarten (1714–62), the author of a two-volume Latin treatise called *Aesthetica* (1750–8). It is usually used in connection with the arts, but it can also embrace beauty in nature.

Afro (Afro Basaldella) (*b* Udine, 4 Mar. 1912; *d* Zurich, 24 July 1976). Italian painter and stage designer. His early work, which included landscapes, portraits, and still-lifes, was influenced by *Cubism, but after the Second World War he developed a loose improvisatory abstract style influenced by *Abstract Expressionism and he came to be regarded as one of the leading Italian artists working in this *Art Informel idiom. He was awarded the city of Venice painting prize at the 1956 Venice *Biennale and had several public commissions, notably a mural entitled *The Garden of Hope* for the restaurant of the Unesco building in Paris (1958). He was the brother of the sculptors **Dino Basaldella** (1909–77) and **Mirko Basaldella** (1910–69); like Afro, Mirko preferred to be known simply by his first name.

Agam, Yaacov (Jacob Gipstein) (*b* Rishon-le-Zion, Palestine [now Rishon Le Ziyyon,

Israel], 11 May 1928). Israeli sculptor and experimental artist, active mainly in Paris, where he settled in 1951. In 1955 he participated, with *Bury, *Calder, *Tinguely, and other artists, in the exhibition 'Le Mouvement' at the Denise René Gallery, the exhibition that put *Kinetic art on the map, and from this time he established a reputation as one of the most inventive figures working with the kinds of abstract art that lay stress on movement and spectator participation. Agam often uses light and sound effects in conjunction with his sculptures, and sometimes the components of his works can be rearranged by the spectator. He has had several major public commissions in France, among them the design of a square in the Défense quarter of Paris (1973).

Agasse, Jacques-Laurent (b Geneva, 24 Mar. 1767; d London, 27 Dec. 1849). Swiss-born animal painter who settled permanently in England in 1800 and became one of the principal successors to *Stubbs. He studied veterinary science in Paris as well as painting (with J.-L. *David) and his work is distinguished by anatomical accuracy as well as grace of line. Although Agasse was initially successful in England (George IV was among his patrons), he died poor and virtually forgotten (his decline was perhaps connected with his difficult temperament). The Musée d'Art et d'Histoire in Geneva has the best collection of his work.

Agnew's (Thomas Agnew & Sons Ltd.), London. One of Britain's most distinguished firms of art dealers. It was founded by **Thomas Agnew** (1794–1871), who in 1817 became a partner in the firm of Victor Zanetti, a Manchester frame maker, art dealer, and print publisher. Agnew became sole proprietor of the business in 1835, and in 1850 he made two of his sons partners, giving the firm its present name. The sons were **Sir William Agnew** (1825–1910) and **Thomas Agnew** (1827–83). In 1860 the firm opened a branch in London, operating first in Waterloo Place and from 1876 in Old Bond Street, where it still has its premises. Sir William Agnew was the leading British art dealer of his time. He helped to create a buoyant market in contemporary British art (partly through his success as a publisher of engravings) and he also dealt in Old Masters. The firm continues to be particularly associated with Old Masters and also with English watercolours.

Agoracritus. Greek sculptor from Paros, active in the second half of the 5th century BC, a pupil of *Phidias. His most celebrated work was a colossal marble statue of Nemesis at Rhamnus, near Marathon, fragments of which survive, including part of the head (BM, London). Several ancient writers, including *Pausanias, attributed the statue to Phidias himself, and it is said that he sometimes made works that he generously allowed his pupil to sign.

Agostino di Duccio (b Florence, c.1418; d ?Perugia, c.1481). Florentine sculptor and architect. He was an artist of distinction and originality—the only 15th-century sculptor born in Florence who owed little to *Donatello or *Ghiberti. His fresh and lively style was linear and graceful, with attractive swirling draperies. Agostino led a peripatetic life, working in various places in north Italy. He is first recorded as a sculptor in 1442, in Modena, and nothing is known of his training or career before this. In 1446 he fled from Florence to Venice after being accused of stealing silver from a church, and from 1449 to 1456 he worked in Rimini on his masterpiece—the sculptural decoration of the Tempio Malatestiano (see MALATESTA). His other major surviving work is the series of reliefs, partly in terracotta, on the façade of the oratory of S. Bernadino at Perugia, on which he worked 1457–61, as architect as well as sculptor. Agostino also executed several delightful reliefs of the Virgin and Child. In 1464 he began a large marble sculpture for Florence Cathedral but abandoned the work; the block was later used by *Michelangelo for his David. He is last documented in 1481, working as architect on the Porta S. Pietro, an ornamental gate in Perugia's town wall.

Aikman, William. See MEDINA.

airbrush. An instrument for spraying paint or varnish by means of compressed air. It looks rather like an outsize fountain pen and is held in a similar fashion, the pressure of the forefinger on a lever regulating the air supply. Various types of nozzle can be fitted and the instrument can be controlled so as to give large areas of flat colour, delicate gradations, or a fine mist. The paint is typically held in a small container attached to the airbrush, and the air compressor is connected by a flexible tube. Originally the compressors were cumbersome, noisy, and expensive, but modern versions are quiet and portable; small cans of compressed air can also be used, but these are not suitable for prolonged use. The airbrush was invented by Charles Burdick, an American watercolour painter, who patented it in England in 1893 and in the same year set up a manufacturing firm called the Fountain Brush Company. In 1900 he founded the Aerograph Company, and the tradename Aerograph was for many years used as a general term for airbrushes (like Biro for ballpoints); *Man Ray called paintings he did with an airbrush 'aerographs'. In the early 20th century airbrushes were used mainly for photographic retouching, and their principal use is now in commercial art. Artists who have made distinctive use of them in this field include the British designer Abram Games (1914–96), who created many memorable posters for the War Office during the Second World War, and the Peruvian-born Alberto Vargas (1895–1982), whose pictures of pin-up girls appeared in almost every issue of *Playboy* magazine from 1960 to 1978. Airbrushes are also often used by painters such as *Hard-Edge abstractionists and *Superrealists who require a very smooth, impersonal finish.

Aivazovsky, Ivan (*b* Theodosia [now Feodosiya, Ukraine], 17 [29] July 1817; *d* Theodosia, 19 Apr. [2 May] 1900). Russian painter. He spent most of his life in the Crimean seaport of Theodosia and the bulk of his huge output (he is said to have painted more than 6,000 pictures) was devoted to marine subjects. They are often treated in a highly charged *Romantic style, notably in his storm scenes and mysterious moonlit views; his repertoire also included naval battles, ports, rocky shores, icebergs, paddle steamers, and indeed virtually every conceivable kind of subject concerned with the sea or waterways. His work was highly popular at home and abroad (he organized dozens of one-man exhibitions), and he was honoured by several foreign academies (he travelled extensively in western Europe and also visited the USA). The best collection of his paintings is in the museum named after him in Feodosia.

Aken, Joseph van (*b* ?Antwerp, *c*.1699; *d* London, 4 July 1749). Flemish-born painter who settled in London around 1720, and in the 1730s and 1740s became the leading specialist *drapery painter of his day, working for numerous portraitists, notably *Hudson and *Ramsay, who were his executors. He also painted some *genre scenes and *conversation pieces. His younger brother **Alexander** (*d* 1757) was his assistant and also made *mezzotints. **Arnold van Aken** (*d* 1736), a painter and engraver, is presumed to have been another brother. Almost nothing is known of him. The family name was also spelled 'Haecken'.

alabaster. A term applied to two types of soft, translucent stone that are similar in appearance but different in composition. The first, known variously as calcite alabaster, Egyptian alabaster, or onyx marble, is a form of calcium carbonate. It was much used by the ancient Egyptians, particularly for small items, including vases and boxes, but also for larger objects such as sarcophagi. Subsequently it has been used in various types of carving (generally small scale), sometimes to exploit beautiful colours streaking the stone (caused by the presence of iron or other minerals). The second type, sometimes distinguished as gypsum alabaster or true alabaster, is a form of gypsum (calcium sulphate). It was extensively used in sculpture in the later Middle Ages. In addition to being easily cut and polished, it has the advantage that it can be painted and gilded without any priming. Its most notable use was in small altarpieces, which from about 1350 to 1550 were made in great numbers in England, many of them for export—they were sent mainly to France but also as far afield as Iceland and Russia. The best collection of such altarpieces is in the Victoria and Albert Museum, London, and other fine examples are in the Castle Museum at Nottingham, a town that was famed for its 'alabaster-men' (the industry was mainly based in the Midlands, the chief quarries being in Derbyshire and Staffordshire). The production of religious images was ended by the Reformation, but alabaster continued to be used for tomb sculpture until the 18th century. Some modern sculptors, for example Henry *Moore, have used it for small-scale works.

Albani, Cardinal Alessandro (*b* Urbino, 15 Oct. 1692; *d* Rome, 11 Dec. 1779). Italian churchman, collector, and art patron, a dominant figure in the art world of Rome for half a century. He came from a distinguished family that included several cardinals and also Pope Clement XI (his uncle), but he led a worldly life and was notorious for his lucrative dealings in the art market, not hesitating to have *antique sculptures heavily restored if it made them sell better. His own superb collection (much of which is now in the Glyptothek at Munich) was housed in a sumptuous villa he had built in Rome (now the villa Torlonia); the decoration included *Mengs's famous ceiling painting *Parnassus* (1761), one of the key works of *Neoclassicism. *Winckelmann was Albani's friend and protégé.

Albani (or **Albano**), **Francesco** (*b* Bologna, 17 Mar. 1578; *d* Bologna, 4 Oct. 1660). Bolognese painter. After a period in the studio of Denys *Calvaert and subsequently in the *Carracci academy, he moved to Rome in about 1601 and for the next fifteen years worked mainly on fresco decorations, initially as an assistant to Annibale Carracci and Guido *Reni (of whom he later became obsessively jealous), then winning important commissions of his own. By 1617 he had returned to Bologna, where he became one of the leading painters of the day and a notable teacher, his pupils including *Cignani, *Mola, and *Sacchi. His later works were mainly altarpieces for local churches and small pictures (sometimes on copper) of allegorical or mythological subjects with prominent landscape backgrounds—very much in the *ideal landscape tradition of Annibale Carracci and *Domenichino. These charmingly light-hearted works were highly popular with collectors in the 18th century.

Albers, Josef (*b* Bottrop, 19 Mar. 1888; *d* New Haven, 25 Mar. 1976). German-born painter, designer, writer, and teacher, who became an American citizen in 1939. He studied (1920–3) and taught (1923–33) at the *Bauhaus, where his activities embraced stained glass, typography, and furniture design. When the Bauhaus closed in 1933 he emigrated to the USA. He was one of the first of the Bauhaus teachers to move there and one of the most energetic in propagating its ideas. From 1933 to 1949 he taught at *Black Mountain College, and from 1950 to 1959 he was head of the department of design at Yale University (the art gallery there has an outstanding collection of his work); he lectured at many other places and won numerous academic awards. From 1949 until his death he worked on a long series of paintings called *Homage to the Square* and it is for these uncompromisingly abstract pictures that he is best known; they consist of three or four squares of carefully planned size set inside one another, painted in flat, usually fairly subdued colours. He favoured the square so much because he believed that of all geometrically regular shapes it best distanced a work of art from nature, emphasizing its man-made quality. The hues in which they were painted often demonstrated the tendency of colours placed in proximity to expand or contract, advance or recede, in relation to each other. Albers's research in this area appeared in *Interaction of Color* (1963), the most important of his numerous publications. His rational approach and disciplined technique were influential on geometrical abstract painters such as *Op artists. Albers's

wife **Anni Albers** (1899–1994), whom he met when she was a student at the Bauhaus, was a weaver; her rectilinear designs have something of the severe economy of her husband's paintings.

Albert, Prince. See ROYAL COLLECTION.

Alberti, Leon Battista (*b* Genoa, 14 Feb. 1404; *d* Rome, Apr. 1472). Italian architect, sculptor, painter, and writer, the most important art theorist of the *Renaissance. The illegitimate son of an exiled Florentine banker, he was educated in Padua and at Bologna University, and was an outstanding Latinist (at the age of 20 he wrote a Latin comedy that was acclaimed as a rediscovered Roman work). For most of his career he was based in Rome (he held a secretarial post in the papal court from 1432 to 1464), but he travelled extensively and had close contacts with the most advanced Florentine artists of the day, particularly *Brunelleschi. His first artistic treatise was written in Latin as *De pictura* in 1435 and translated into Italian the following year (as *Della pittura*) with a dedication to Brunelleschi (*Donatello, *Ghiberti, Luca della *Robbia, and *Masaccio are mentioned alongside him). Alberti wrote on a wide variety of other topics, complementing *De pictura* with a lengthy treatise on architecture (*De re aedificatoria*) and a much shorter one on sculpture (*De statua*). *De re aedificatoria* was probably written in the late 1440s and was presumably finished by 1452, when it was presented to Pope Nicholas V; it became the first printed book on architecture in 1485. *De statua* is generally dated to the 1460s. In these works Alberti turned away from the medieval outlook in which art was considered a symbolic expression of theological truths. Instead he emphasized the rational basis of the arts, and the necessity for the artist to have a thorough grounding in such 'sciences' as history, poetry, and mathematics (*De pictura* contains the first written exposition of the principles of perspective).

At about the time he was writing *De re aedificatoria* Alberti began to work as an architectural designer, his first certain work in this field (*c*.1450) being the exterior remodelling of the church of S. Francesco in Rimini (now known as the Tempio Malatestiano; see MALATESTA). His other buildings include the churches of S. Andrea and S. Sebastiano in Mantua, and in Florence the façades of S. Maria Novella and the Palazzo Rucellai—all of them ranking among the outstanding architectural works of the early Renaissance. Alberti also practised as a painter and sculptor, but little trace survives of his work in these fields. No paintings by him are extant, but two bronze self-portrait plaques are attributed to him (Louvre, Paris, and NG, Washington); judging by his apparent age, these are usually assigned to the mid-1430s, so they may well antedate (and perhaps influenced) *Pisanello's first portrait medals.

Albertina (Graphische Sammlung Albertina), Vienna. One of the world's most celebrated collections of Old Master drawings and prints. It is named after Archduke Albert of Sachsen-Teschen (1738–1822), son of Augustus III, Elector of Saxony and King of Poland, and son-in-law of the Empress Maria-Theresa (see HABSBURG). Albert led a cosmopolitan life and he formed his remarkable collection mainly whilst he was governor of Hungary (1765–80) and then the Netherlands (1780–92). In 1793 he settled in Vienna and soon afterwards took up residence in the palace on the Augustinerstrasse in which his collection is still housed. The collection was enlarged by his successors and taken over by the state in 1918. It is particularly rich in drawings by the great Italian and German masters of the 16th century (among them a superlative group by *Dürer that can be traced back directly to the artist's widow), by Dutch and Flemish artists of the 17th century, and by French artists of the 18th century. A changing selection of its treasures is on view to the public.

Albertinelli, Mariotto (b Florence, 13 Oct. 1474; d Florence, 5 Nov. 1515). Florentine painter, trained by Cosimo *Rosselli, in whose studio he met Fra *Bartolommeo. The two worked in partnership in the 1490s and again in 1509–13. Evidently the arrangement ended because Albertinelli temporarily abandoned painting to become an innkeeper, saying (according to *Vasari) that he was fed up with criticism and wanted a 'less difficult and more cheerful craft'. Vasari also comments that he was 'a restless man, a follower of Venus, and a good liver'. His paintings are elegant but rather insipid.

Albright, Ivan Le Lorraine (b North Harvey, Ill., 20 Feb. 1897; d Woodstock, Vt., 18 Nov. 1983). American painter, the son of **Adam Emery Albright** (1862–1957), a painter who had studied under *Eakins. During the First World War Albright served in France as a medical draughtsman and worked with a meticulous detail and clinical precision that anticipated the paintings of his later career, which show a morbid obsession with death and corruption: sagging, almost putrescent flesh (which he described as 'corrugated

mush'), decrepit, decaying objects, and lurid lighting are typical of his work. Often it evokes a feeling of melancholy for a beauty that is past. He came from a wealthy family and his financial independence allowed him to work slowly, producing a small number of elaborate, highly finished paintings. For most of his life he lived in or near Chicago, and the city's Art Institute has the best collection of his works. It includes the painting Albright did for the Hollywood film (1943) of Oscar Wilde's *The Picture of Dorian Gray*, showing the loathsomely corrupted title figure; Albright's identical twin brother **Malvin Marr Albright** (1897–1983) did the portrait of the young and beautiful Dorian for this film. Malvin died three months before Ivan.

Alcamenes. Greek sculptor of the second half of the 5th century BC, a contemporary of *Phidias and according to some ancient sources his pupil. Alcamenes had a high reputation (*Pliny calls him 'an artist of the first rank'), and after the end of Phidias' career in Athens, he was probably the leading sculptor in the city, but the evidence concerning him is meagre and in places confusing. According to the normally reliable *Pausanias, he made the sculptures of the west pediment of the celebrated temple of Zeus at Olympia (completed by 457 BC), but in another passage Pausanias suggests that he was active as late as 403 BC, and it seems scarcely credible that he could be prominent enough to be engaged on a commission of the highest importance in the 450s and yet still be working more than half a century later (it has been suggested that there were an elder and a younger sculptor of the same name, or alternatively that Alcamenes carved only the *acroterion surmounting the pediment rather than the great pediment figures themselves, the surviving parts of which are in the Archaeological Museum at Olympia). Several other works associated with Alcamenes are known from copies, and a badly mutilated marble statue in the Acropolis Museum in Athens is perhaps an original by him representing Procne and Itys.

Alciati, Andrea. See EMBLEM.

Aldegrever, Heinrich (b Paderborn, 1502; d Soest, Westphalia, c.1555). German printmaker and painter. He worked mainly in Soest and was one of the leading artists in Westphalia in his day. His numerous prints, which include religious subjects, portraits, and ornamental designs, show the all-pervading influence of *Dürer (he even signed his work with an AG monogram shaped much like Dürer's AD). These prints are mainly line engravings, but Aldegrever also made a few etchings. Little is known of his activity as a painter.

Aldine Press. See HYPNEROTOMACHIA POLIPHILI.

Aldobrandini. Italian family of lawyers and ecclesiastics that came to prominence with the election of **Ippolito Aldobrandini** (1536–1605) as Pope Clement VIII in 1592. He commissioned a great deal of art, notably for the decoration of St Peter's, but most of it was of undistinguished quality. His favourite artist was Giuseppe *Cesari. Ippolito's nephew Cardinal **Pietro Aldobrandini** (1572–1621) was a patron and collector of more discriminating and advanced taste. He is particularly remembered for commissioning Annibale *Carracci in about 1604 to paint a series of six pictures—each showing a biblical scene in a landscape setting—to decorate a chapel in the family palace in Rome. These paintings stand at the head of the whole tradition of *ideal landscape. They were largely executed by assistants from Annibale's designs, but the celebrated *Flight into Egypt* is from his own hand and is regarded as one of his greatest works. The six paintings were more or less semicircular in shape to fit into wall areas framed by arches and they are known collectively as the 'Aldobrandini *lunettes'. The chapel has been destroyed, but the paintings all survive in the Galleria Doria Pamphili, Rome. Pietro's cousin Cardinal **Cinzio Aldobrandini** (originally Cinzio Passeri) (1551–1610) was an avid collector of art and antiquities. Most notably he owned a famous ancient Roman fresco now known after him as the *Aldobrandini Wedding* (Vatican Mus). The Aldobrandini male line became extinct in 1638 and the family palace and art collection passed through marriage to the *Pamphili family.

Alechinsky, Pierre (*b* Brussels, 19 Oct. 1927). Belgian painter, printmaker, draughtsman, and film-maker, active mainly in France. In 1947 he became a member of *Jeune Peinture Belge and in 1949 joined the *Cobra group. He left Cobra in 1951 and settled in Paris, where he studied under S. W. *Hayter. In 1955 he visited the Far East and produced a prize-winning film, *Calligraphie japonaise*. Subsequently he has travelled widely in Europe, the USA, and Mexico. His paintings are in a style of vigorous, even violent, expressive abstraction. They retain residual figurative motifs and their sense of turbulent fantasy shows a strong debt to his countryman

*Ensor. Alechinsky is regarded as one of the leading Belgian artists of the 20th century and has an international reputation.

Aleijadinho, O. See LISBOA.

Aleš, Mikuláš. See MÁNES.

Alexander VII, Pope. See CHIGI.

Alexander Mosaic. A floor *mosaic (*c*.100 BC, Archaeological Mus., Naples), discovered in the House of the Faun in Pompeii, depicting Alexander the Great defeating Darius III, the king of Persia, at the Battle of Issus (333 BC). It is impressive in size (more than 5 m (16 ft) wide), spectacular and dynamic in composition, and one of the finest mosaics to survive (albeit substantially damaged) from the ancient world. *Pliny praises a painting of the subject by Philoxenos of Eretria, and the mosaic is probably modelled on this lost original, dating from about two centuries earlier. Curiously, Darius rather than Alexander is the dominant figure in the composition.

Alexander Sarcophagus. A marble *sarcophagus (*c*.310 BC, Archaeological Mus., Istanbul), shaped like a chest with a lid in the form of a temple roof, found in the royal cemetery at Sidon in the Lebanon. It is very richly carved, with high-*relief panels on each of the four sides depicting battle and hunting scenes, including Alexander the Great at the Battle of Issus (the same subject shown in the *Alexander Mosaic*); Sidon was conquered by Alexander in 332 BC and the sarcophagus must have been made for Abdalonymos, whom he installed as ruler. The sculpture, of Greek workmanship, is of good quality, but it is remarkable mainly because it preserves much of its original colouring (see POLYCHROME).

Algardi, Alessandro (*b* Bologna, 31 July 1598; *d* Rome, 10 June 1654). Italian sculptor. He had his initial training in the *Carracci academy in Bologna, and in 1625 he settled in Rome, where he became, apart from *Bernini, the leading sculptor of the day. During the pontificate of Innocent X (Giambattista *Pamphili), 1644–55, Bernini was out of favour and Algardi replaced him at the papal court. His three most prestigious commissions were the tomb of Leo XI (1634–44) and the huge relief of *Pope Leo Driving Attila from Rome* (1646–53), both in St Peter's, Rome, and the free-standing group of *The Decapitation of St Paul* (1641–7) in S. Paolo, Bologna. He was a prolific sculptor of portrait *busts, and these are his works that are now generally most admired—indeed he ranks as one of the greatest portrait sculptors of all time. His style was more sober and classical than Bernini's (although portraits have occasionally been disputed between them), reflecting his Bolognese upbringing, his work as a restorer of *antique statuary, and his friendship with artists such as *Domenichino, *Duquesnoy, *Poussin, and *Sacchi. In his early career Algardi worked mainly in stucco and terracotta (Bologna lacked local stone), but he became a highly sensitive carver in marble. He was also an accomplished draughtsman (he made designs for engravers) and in addition worked as an architect, although his activity in this field is unclear. He ran a busy studio and copies and casts of his work continued to be made long after his death.

Algarotti, Francesco (b Venice, 11 Dec. 1712; d Pisa, 3 May 1764). The foremost Italian art critic of his day, also a collector and patron. He travelled widely and his friendship with some of the leading men of Europe—notably the French philosopher Voltaire and Frederick the Great of Prussia—played a part in spreading the culture of his native Venice. His writings proclaimed a watered-down version of the *Neoclassicism that was then gaining ground in Europe (though not yet in Venice). For some years he influenced the practice of his friends Giambattista *Tiepolo ('restraining his wilder fantasies' as he claimed) and *Canaletto (encouraging his architectural *capricci), as well as *Piazzetta and other Venetian painters. His many publications include *Saggio sopra la pittura* (1762), translated into English as *An Essay on Painting* (1764).

Alkamenes. See ALCAMENES.

Alken. Family of British sporting artists of Danish origin. The family tradition was begun by **Samuel Alken Sen.** (1750–1815), who engraved hunting and sporting landscapes in the manner of *Stubbs. Four of his sons became artists, including **Samuel Jun.** (1784–c.1825) and most notably **Henry** (1785–1851), who was one of the most prolific sporting painters and illustrators of his time. His sprightly style was already archaic in his day, but he excelled at representing the life and movement of the hunting field and produced a huge output of coloured prints (some of them created under the pseudonym 'Ben Tally-Ho'), which continue to be popular with collectors. He had four sons, among them **Samuel Henry Gordon Alken** (1810–94), generally known as Henry Alken Jun., with whose work his own is often confused.

Allais, Alphonse. See MINIMAL ART.

Allan, David (b Alloa, 13 Feb. 1744; d Edinburgh, 6 Aug. 1796). Scottish portrait and *genre painter. From about 1767 to 1777 he lived in Rome, where he studied with Gavin *Hamilton and won a prize for *history painting at the Accademia di S. Luca. In 1777 he moved to London, then in 1780 settled in Edinburgh as a painter of portraits and *conversation pieces. When abroad he had made studies of French and Italian peasants and he painted scenes of Scottish life in a similar vein, which earned him the misleading title of 'the Scottish *Hogarth'. Such works influenced *Wilkie. See also SILHOUETTE.

Allan, Sir William (b Edinburgh, 1782; d Edinburgh, 23 Feb. 1850). Scottish historical painter. From 1805 to 1814 he travelled extensively in Russia, and this gave him a taste for exotic subject matter involving Circassians, Cossacks, Tartars, and Turks (he collected arms and armour and other artefacts to use as props and sometimes wore Circassian costume himself). These pictures did not sell well, but in the 1820s he successfully took up Scottish subjects, including scenes from the novels of Sir Walter Scott, who was Allan's enthusiastic supporter. With his friend *Wilkie, Allan did much to establish the vogue for historical *genre painting in Scotland. He also painted portraits.

alla prima. Method of painting, primarily in oils, in which the finished surface is achieved in a single application of paint rather than through the traditional method of building up successive layers. *Alla prima* is Italian for 'at first'; synonymous terms are 'direct painting', 'wet on wet', and the French *au premier coup* (at first stroke). Direct painting was practised from the 17th century (for example by *Hals), but it was not until the middle of the 19th century that it became the chief method in oil painting. Its growing popularity was connected with the availability of commercial paints of a buttery consistency, as well as with *Romantic ideas about spontaneity of expression.

Allegri, Antonio and **Lorenzo.** See CORREGGIO.

Allied Artists' Association (AAA). A society of British artists formed in London in 1908 by the critic Frank Rutter (1876–1937) and artists in *Sickert's circle for the purpose of organizing annual exhibitions of progressive painters in the jury-free manner of the French *Salon des

Indépendants. It held annual exhibitions at the Albert Hall from 1908 (more than 3,000 works were shown at the first show) and then smaller shows at the Grafton Galleries between 1916 and 1920. *Brancusi (1913), *Kandinsky (1909), and *Zadkine (1913) received the first British showing of their works at these exhibitions. The *Camden Town Group, founded in 1911, was made up largely of members of the Allied Artists' Association.

Allori, Alessandro (b Florence, 31 May 1535; d Florence, 22 Sept. 1607). Florentine painter, the pupil and adopted son of *Bronzino. From 1554 to 1560 he was in Rome, where he added the influence of *Michelangelo's *Last Judgement* to that of his master's courtly *Mannerism. His varied output included altarpieces, portraits, and tapestry designs. *The Pearl Fishers* (1570–1, Studiolo of Francesco I, Palazzo Vecchio, Florence) is generally considered his masterpiece; playful and full of artifice, it combines nude figures obviously drawn from Michelangelo with Bronzino's sveltness and enamelled colouring. He was one of the last notable Italian exponents of Mannerism, painting in a style that was becoming outmoded by the time of his death. His son **Cristofano** (b Florence, 17 Oct. 1577; d Florence, 1 Apr. 1621) was one of the leading Florentine painters of his period, and his style was more naturalistic and *Baroque than that of his father. He produced various types of work, but he is remembered primarily for one picture, *Judith with the Head of Holofernes* (c.1615, Pitti, Florence, and other versions), which in the 18th and 19th centuries was one of the most famous paintings in Italy. Allori led a notoriously dissipated life (interspersed with bouts of pious asceticism) and here his *femme fatale* mistress is portrayed as Judith and he has depicted his own features in Holofernes' severed head. The Ashmolean Museum in Oxford possesses portraits by both Alessandro and Cristofano Allori.

all-over painting. A type of painting in which the whole surface of the canvas is treated in a relatively uniform manner and traditional ideas of composition—of the picture having a top, bottom, or centre—are abandoned. The term was first used in the 1950s with reference to the 'drip' paintings of Jackson *Pollock, and it has since been applied to other pictures in which the overall treatment of the canvas is relatively uniform, whether relying on texture or on 'scribbled' material, as with Cy *Twombly, or on colour, as with the *Colour Field Painters.

Alloway, Lawrence (b London, 17 Sept. 1926; d New York, 2 Jan., 1990). British critic and curator, active for much of his career in the USA. In the 1950s he worked at the *Institute of Contemporary Arts, London (he was deputy director, 1957–9), and he was one of the leading figures in the *Independent Group, the cradle of British *Pop art (Alloway himself coined this term). He was also a strong supporter of American *Abstract Expressionism, and in 1961 he emigrated to the USA, settling in New York, where he became a curator at the *Guggenheim Museum and art critic for the *Nation*. His books include *American Pop Art* (1974) and *Topics in American Art since 1945* (1975). He was married to the British-born painter Sylvia Sleigh (1916–) (see FEMINIST ART), who settled with him in the USA.

Allston, Washington (b on the family plantation, Georgetown County, SC, 5 Nov. 1779; d Cambridge, Mass., 9 July 1843). American painter and writer, considered the most important artistic personality of the first generation of *Romanticism in the USA. Samuel Taylor Coleridge, whose portrait Allston painted (NPG, London, 1814), considered him 'a man of . . . high and rare genius . . . whether I contemplate him in the character of a Poet, a Painter, or a Philosophic Analyst'. Allston spent most of his working life in or near Boston apart from two lengthy visits to Europe: during the first, 1801–8, he studied under Benjamin *West in London and visited Paris and Rome; the second stay in Europe was from 1811 to 1818. Up to c.1818 his Romanticism was expressed in the grandiose and dramatic (*The Rising of a Thunderstorm at Sea*, 1804, MFA, Boston). In his later period he was a forerunner of the subjective and visionary trend in American landscape painting, which relied more on mood and reverie than on observation or drama, as in his famous *Moonlight Landscape* (1819, MFA, Boston). Through his example this type of landscape painting became indigenous to the USA. Allston's writing included poetry, a Gothic novel entitled *Monaldi* (1841), and the posthumously published *Lectures on Art* (1850), the first art treatise by an American.

Alma-Tadema, Sir Lawrence (b Dronrijp, Friesland, 8 Jan. 1836; d Wiesbaden, 25 June 1912). Dutch-born painter who settled in London in 1870 and became a British citizen in 1873. He trained at the Antwerp Academy under *Wappers and de *Keyser, then became an assistant to *Leys. In spite of this background in the Low Countries, he has come to be regarded as one of the quintessential Victorian artists. He specialized in historical *genre scenes, beginning with medieval subjects, but then—following a visit to Pompeii in 1863—turning to the ancient world. His paintings evoke a Hollywood vision of ancient Greece and Rome (and sometimes Egypt), with their sensuous depiction of beautiful women, exotic costumes, and marbled settings—*Punch* called him a 'marvellous artist'. Such works were enormously successful and Alma-Tadema had a sumptuous lifestyle in his house in St John's Wood (previously owned by *Tissot), which he remodelled as a Roman villa. He was knighted in 1899 and received the Order of Merit in 1905. His success encouraged several imitators, including his wife **Laura** (1852–1909), his daughter (by a previous wife) **Anna** (1865–1943), and painters such as John William Godward (1861–1922) and Edwin Long (1829–91). However, Alma-Tadema's work went completely out of favour after his death, and his reputation did not greatly revive until the 1970s. Now he once again pleases a large public; visitor surveys at the Getty Museum, Los Angeles, have revealed that his *Spring* (1894) is the most popular work in the collection.

Alsloot, Denis van (*b* Brussels, *c.*1570; *d* Brussels, 1625/6). Flemish painter. Most of his surviving pictures are forest landscapes in the manner of *Coninxloo; some of them have figures painted by Hendrik de *Clerck. His best-known works, however, are a series, painted for the Infanta Isabella (see RUBENS), of the annual Ommeganck (procession) in Brussels in 1615 (examples are in the Prado, Madrid, and the Victoria and Albert Museum, London). They are undistinguished artistically but of great documentary interest.

Altamira. The site of the first prehistoric rock paintings to be discovered, about 30 km (20 miles) west of Santander, near the village of Santillana del Mar, in northern Spain. The entrance to the cave that contains the paintings was found by a hunter in 1868. Excavations were started in 1879 by a local landowner, Don Marcelino de Sautuola, and the now famous roof paintings were spotted by his infant daughter. The antiquity and authenticity of the paintings were at first denied by most prehistorians, but the doubts were dispelled after the discoveries in 1901 of cave art near Les Eyzies in France by Henri Breuil (1877–1961), the scholar who did more than anyone else to establish the scientific study of cave art. The Altamira cave extends for about 300 m (330 yds) into a limestone massif,

but the paintings are in a gallery, often no more than 2 m (6 ft) high, about 30 m (33 yds) from the entrance. Best-preserved among them are those on the roof—polychrome figures of animals, mainly bison, drawn almost life-size with the contours accentuated here and there by engraving. The paintings are naturalistic in style, displaying a remarkable grasp of essential form and an eye for characteristic attitude and movement. They have gained Altamira the nickname of the 'Sistine Chapel of Cave Art'. The cave also contains rock engravings of animal heads. The polychrome paintings are dated to about *c.*12,000 BC and are regarded, with those at *Lascaux, France, as the outstanding paintings known from the prehistoric era.

altarpiece. A picture, sculpture, screen, decorated wall, or combination of any of these, standing on or behind an altar in a Christian church. Altarpieces vary enormously in size and conception, from tiny portable pictures to huge structures embracing the arts of architecture, sculpture, and painting. In theory, a useful distinction can be made between two broad types: the reredos, which rises from ground level behind the altar; and the retable, which stands either on the back of the altar itself or on a pedestal behind it. In practice, however, the words are not usually used with any precision; 'retable' is often used more or less as a synonym for altarpiece and in particular is commonly applied to the type of enormous structure—sometimes filling the entire east wall of a church—that became popular in Spain and Portugal and their American colonies in the *Baroque period.

Altdorfer, Albrecht (*b c.*1480; *d* Regensburg, 12 Feb. 1538). German painter, printmaker, draughtsman, and architect, active in Regensburg, where he became a citizen in 1505. Nothing is recorded of his training, but his early work was influenced by *Cranach and he was also familiar with *Dürer's woodcuts and engravings. Mingled with these German elements was a knowledge of the art of *Mantegna, perhaps through the mediation of Michael *Pacher. Yet in spite of these varied influences Altdorfer's style always remained personal. Most of his paintings are religious works, but he was one of the first artists to show an interest in landscape as an independent genre. In works such as *Christ Taking Leave of his Mother* (?1520, NG, London) he achieved a wonderful unity of mood between action and landscape, and two pure landscape paintings (without any figures) by him are known (NG, London, and Alte Pin., Munich) (see also DANUBE SCHOOL). His patrons included the Emperor Maximilian I (see HABSBURG) and also Louis X, Duke of Bavaria, for whom he painted the celebrated *Battle of Issus* (1529, Alte Pin., Munich), which formed part of a large series of famous battle pieces from classical antiquity. With its dazzling light effects, teeming figures, and brilliant colours, it is one of the finest examples of Altdorfer's rich imaginative powers. In addition to his paintings, he produced engravings, etchings, and woodcuts, and he was an outstanding draughtsman. From 1526 until his death he also worked as town architect of Regensburg. No architectural work by him survives, but his interest in architecture and his skill in handling intricate problems of perspective are demonstrated in several of his paintings, including *Susannah and the Elders* (1526, Alte Pin., Munich).

Alte Pinakothek, Munich. See PINACOTHECA.

Altichiero (active 1370s and 1380s). Italian painter. He probably came from Zevio near Verona and is sometimes considered to be the founder of the Veronese School, although the only surviving example of his work in that city is a fresco in S. Anastasia. Most of his surviving work is in Padua, where he had a hand in fresco cycles in the basilica of St Anthony (1372–9) and in the oratory of St George (1377–84), in the latter of which he collaborated with an artist called Avanzo, who is otherwise unknown and whose contribution to the work is uncertain. A document of 1393 implies that Altichiero had died by then. The solidity and solemnity of his figures clearly reveal his debt to *Giotto's frescos in the Arena Chapel of Padua. But his pageant-like scenes with their elaborate architectural views express the taste of the late 14th century for *Gothic intricacy, while his naturalism in the study of plants and animals formed the point of departure for a new style that is reflected in *Pisanello.

Alvarez Cubero, José (*b* Priego de Córdoba, 23 Apr. 1768; *d* Madrid, 26 Nov. 1827). The leading Spanish sculptor of the *Neoclassical period. He spent much of his career in Rome (1805–25), where he was a friend and disciple of Canova, and he is sometimes called 'the Spanish Canova'. His work included classical subjects and portraits, but his best-known piece is the marble *Defence of Saragossa* (1823) on the façade of the *Prado, Madrid, celebrating Spanish heroism during the Peninsular War.

amateur. An artist who works for pleasure rather than for a livelihood. In Western art, the idea of amateur status began to have meaning only with the *Renaissance, for before this time the visual arts were considered mere crafts and therefore were socially unacceptable (see LIBERAL ARTS). By the 17th century Renaissance ideals had spread to England, where Sir Nathaniel *Bacon and Prince *Rupert were notable amateur artists of the time. With the popularization of *watercolour in the 18th and 19th centuries, amateur painters proliferated all over Europe. At the same time, sketching and watercolour became accepted 'accomplishments' for young ladies; Queen Victoria (see ROYAL COLLECTION) practised both painting and etching. Local drawing and painting societies increased steadily in numbers in the 19th and early 20th centuries, and amateurs were well represented at exhibitions of associations such as the *London Group. They even invaded the once jealously guarded exhibitions of the *Royal Academy, and one of the most famous of all amateur artists, Sir Winston Churchill (1874–1965), author of *Painting as a Pastime* (1948), was appointed an Honorary Academician Extraordinary. The success of numerous *naive painters, together with the dubious economic status of the many professional artists who are not in regular employment, has further tended to obscure any sharp distinction between professional and amateur.

The word 'amateur', transplanted from France, is first recorded in English in 1784, as a term for a person who had a taste for any subject, not necessarily as an executant (French sale catalogues of the 18th century were often of the collections of 'un grand amateur'). In 1786 the word was used in the more specialized sense of a person who cultivates a pursuit purely as a pastime. Before the word came into use, the term 'virtuoso' (see VIRTU) was sometimes used in similar senses, as was the term 'dilettante' after the founding of the Society of *Dilettanti in 1732. Both 'amateur' and 'dilettante' are now apt to suggest a lack of serious aim or study; the words are sometimes used more or less synonymously, although 'dilettante' stresses 'enjoyment rather than effort, a frittering rather than a concentration of one's energies' (*Webster's New Dictionary of Synonyms*, 1968) and in addition implies a degree of social distinction.

In China, contrary to the position in the West, art has always been accorded a noble position, and the amateur has enjoyed a higher status than the professional. (The difference in status might be seen as analogous to the distinction between

'Gentlemen' and 'Players' that applied in English cricket until 1963.) The Emperor Hui Tsung (1082–1135) was perhaps the most distinguished of all such amateurs.

amber. A fossil *resin derived from various trees, found in many parts of the world but mainly on the southern shores of the Baltic; it has been used in art to make jewellery, decorative items, and small-scale sculpture, and also perhaps as an ingredient of some *varnishes. Amber is usually yellow, but many other colours are found and it varies greatly in opacity. It has been used since prehistoric times, notably in amulets because it was believed to have magical properties (it becomes charged with static electricity when rubbed on the hair). Although it is easy to carve, it can be brittle and skill is needed to prevent fracturing. The golden age of amber carving was the 16th and 17th centuries, and the most famous of all works in the medium was a room lined with amber commissioned by Frederick I of Prussia in 1701. It was originally installed in Schloss Charlottenberg, Berlin, but following Frederick's death in 1714 it was presented to Peter the Great of Russia in 1717 and reconstructed in the Great Palace (or Catherine Palace) at Tsarskoye Selo (now Pushkin), near St Petersburg. The room was looted by the Germans in the Second World War and has never been recovered, but a replica was unveiled in 2003 to commemorate the 300th anniversary of the founding of St Petersburg; a team of craftsmen took more than 20 years to produce it.

Amber has also been used to make a dark, slow-drying varnish, but it is doubtful if it has been used much, if at all, in painting (when medieval writers refer to it in recipes they may be confusing it with other resins).

Amberger, Christoph (d Augsburg, 1561/2). German painter (mainly of portraits) and designer. He spent most of his life in Augsburg, which had many cultural and economic ties with Italy (he met *Titian when he visited the city in 1548), and his style emulates the grandeur and richness of the Venetian School, paying as much attention to dress and jewellery as to characterization (*Charles V, c.*1532, Gemäldegalerie, Berlin). His rare figure compositions (*Virgin and Child between Sts Ulrich and Afra*, 1554, Augsburg Cathedral) are less distinguished. Amberger also designed coins, façade paintings, and statuary.

Ambrosiana (Pinacoteca Ambrosiana), Milan. Picture gallery established in 1618 by Cardinal Federico Borromeo (see CRESPI, GIOVANNI BATTISTA) as a sister institution to the Ambrosian Library (Biblioteca Ambrosiana), which he founded in 1609 in honour of St Ambrose, patron saint of the city. In his book *De pictura sacra* (1624) Borromeo explains that the gallery was intended as a public resource in line with the Council of Trent's call for the faithful to be educated through images as well as words. It has a small but choice collection of Italian and Flemish paintings (Borromeo's friend Jan *Brueghel is well represented) and an important collection of drawings, including works by *Leonardo and *Raphael. In Borromeo's time the Ambrosiana also included an art academy (formally founded in 1620, but active from about 1613); however, it stopped functioning soon after his death in 1631.

American Abstract Artists (AAA). An association of American abstract painters and sculptors formed in New York in 1936 with the aim of promoting their work and fostering public understanding of it. The association held annual exhibitions (the first in 1937) and disseminated the principles of abstract art by lectures, publications, etc. The first president was Balcomb Greene (1904–90) and among the early members were Josef *Albers, Willem *de Kooning, Jackson *Pollock, and David *Smith. In 1940 members picketed the *Museum of Modern Art, demanding that it should show American art, but by the mid-1940s abstract art had achieved recognition and the activities of the association dwindled. In the 1950s, however, it revived and had more than 200 members.

American Academy of the Fine Arts. See NATIONAL ACADEMY OF DESIGN.

American Scene Painting. A broad term applied to the work of various painters who in the 1920s and 1930s depicted aspects of American life and landscape in a naturalistic, descriptive style. The term does not signify an organized movement, but rather an aspect of a general tendency for American artists to move away from abstraction and the avant-garde in the period between the two world wars. Part of this tendency was a patriotic repudiation of European, specifically French, influence; in 1933, Edward *Hopper declared that 'we are not French and never can be and any attempt to do so is to deny our inheritance and to try to impose upon ourselves a character that can be nothing but a veneer upon the surface'. Apart from Hopper, the best-known exponent of American Scene Painting is Charles *Burchfield;

in an essay on Burchfield published in 1928, Hopper wrote that he captured 'all the sweltering, tawdry life of the American small town, and . . . the sad desolation of our suburban landscapes'. The term also embraces the *Regionalists, who were more self-conscious in their nationalism.

Amigoni, Jacopo (*b* ?Venice, *c*.1685; *d* Madrid, 22 Aug. 1752). Italian *Rococo decorative painter and portraitist. His early life is obscure, but he was probably born and trained in Venice. From about 1715 he had an international career, working in Bavaria, England, France, and finally Spain. His English sojourn lasted from 1729 to 1739 (with a break for a visit to Paris in 1736); his finest surviving work from this period is a series of four paintings on the story of Jupiter and Io at Moor Park (now Moor Park Golf Club) in Hertfordshire. He was the last of the Venetian decorators to come to England in the wake of *Pellegrini and the *Ricci, for the demand for large-scale decorative painting was fairly short-lived. Amigoni, however, earned a good living with his portraits and is said to have persuaded *Canaletto to try his fortune in England.

Amman, Jost (*bapt*. Zurich, 13 June 1539; *d* Nuremberg, 17 Mar. 1591). Swiss printmaker and draughtsman, active mainly in Nuremberg, Germany, where he is documented from 1561. He was perhaps the most prolific book illustrator of his day and one of his pupils boasted that he produced more drawings in four years than could be carted away in a hay-wagon (in spite of this huge productivity, he was constantly in financial trouble). His woodcuts and engravings are more important as documents of contemporary life than for their artistic value and in particular there is a wealth of material on 16th-century crafts in his *Eygentliche Beschreibung aller Stände auff Erden* (Frankfurt, 1568; an expanded Latin edition was published in the same year, with 132 woodcuts in place of the 114 in the German original). The title translates as 'Exact Description of All Ranks on Earth' and the book is popularly known as the *Ständebuch* (Book of Trades).

Ammanati, Bartolommeo (*b* Settignano, 18 June 1511; *d* Florence, 22 Apr. 1592). Florentine *Mannerist architect and sculptor. His best-known works in Florence are the Ponte S. Trinità (1567–70, destroyed during the Second World War, but rebuilt) and his additions to the *Pitti Palace (1558–70), including the rusticated court-yard. In sculpture he was strongly influenced by *Michelangelo and by the suaver style of *Sansovino (on whose Library in Venice he worked); his chief work in this field is the rather ponderous fountain (1560–75) in the Piazza della Signoria, Florence, with its marble *Neptune* and bronze *Nymphs*. Ammanati beat several sculptors, including *Cellini and *Giambologna, in a competition for this commission, but the work was not well received. In old age, influenced by Counter-Reformation piety, he wrote a recantation of his secular works (denouncing nude figures as lustful) and he is said to have destroyed some. He was married to Laura Battiferri, a poet who was the subject of a memorable portrait by *Bronzino.

amoretto. See PUTTO.

Analytical Cubism. See CUBISM.

anamorphosis. A picture (or a part of one) executed in such a way that the image appears distorted or unintelligible until it is seen from an unusual angle or by means of a special lens or mirror, when it appears in lifelike aspect. Anamorphosis is first mentioned in the notes of *Leonardo da Vinci, and perhaps the most famous example of its use is in *Holbein's *The Ambassadors* (1533, NG, London), which features a distorted skull, probably a symbol of the brevity of life. Generally, however, the purpose of anamorphosis was to mystify or amuse, and it rarely occurs in major works such as this.

Ancher, Michael (*b* Rutsker, 9 June 1849; *d* Skagen, 19 Sept. 1927) and **Anna** (née Brøndum) (*b* Skagen, 18 Aug. 1859; *d* Skagen, 15 Apr. 1935). Danish painters, husband and wife (they married in 1880), the central figures of the artists' colony that flourished at Skagen in Jutland in the late 19th and early 20th centuries, particularly the 1870s and 1880s (Anna's family ran a hotel that was much frequented by artists; she was the only member of the colony who was a native of Skagen). Many leading Scandinavian painters (as well as writers and musicians) were associated with the colony during its heyday, most notably P. S. *Krøyer. The Anchers' work included domestic interiors and scenes of the life of local fishermen. Their daughter **Helga Ancher** (1881–1964) was also a painter. The family home at Skagen opened as a museum in 1967.

Ancients. Group of English *Romantic artists inspired by William *Blake and active for about a decade in the late 1820s and early 1830s. Their name (evidently first used in May 1827, shortly before Blake's death) expressed their admiration for the more spiritual art of the past in preference to that of their own day. At most there were about nine members, of whom the best known was Samuel *Palmer. Others included Edward *Calvert and George *Richmond, with John *Linnell on the fringes; the remainder were very minor figures. The Ancients sometimes worked at Shoreham in Kent, where Palmer had a house from 1826 to 1835, and they also held meetings in London (at Blake's house in the early days). Usually they worked on a small scale, concentrating on biblical and pastoral subjects in an idyllic or visionary vein. The Ancients attracted little attention at the time and were virtually forgotten for almost a century until they were rediscovered in the 1920s, at the same time as the revival of interest in Blake.

Anderson, Laurie. See PERFORMANCE ART.

Andre, Carl (b Quincy, Mass., 16 Sept. 1935). American sculptor, a leading exponent of *Minimal art. Typically he produces his works by placing identical ready-made commercial units such as bricks, cement blocks, metal plates, etc. (occasionally 'natural products' like logs or bales of hay) in simple geometrical arrangements without adhesives or joints; the works are dismantled when not on exhibition. His most characteristic products abjure height and are arranged as horizontal configurations on the ground ('more like roads than buildings', in his own words); some of them are even intended to be walked over. In Britain Andre is best known for the sensational publicity accompanying the 'Tate bricks' incident in 1976. His *Equivalent VIII* (1966) (consisting of 120 bricks arranged two deep in a rectangle) was vandalized and there was an outcry about the alleged waste of public money on its purchase by the Tate Gallery. In 1985 Andre again made headlines when he was charged with murdering his wife (who died after falling from a window); he was acquitted at his trial.

Andrea da Firenze (Andrea Bonaiuti) (d ?Florence, ?1378). Florentine painter, first documented in 1346. He is remembered mainly for his frescos (1366–8) in the chapter house (now known as the Spanish Chapel) of S. Maria Novella, Florence. This is a church of the Dominican Order, and the frescos—which form the most impressive Florentine cycle of the time—are concerned with the power of the Church in general and the importance of the Dominicans in particular. The best-known scene in the scheme, covering an entire wall of the chapel, is *The Triumph of the Church*, which features a pack of dogs protecting the sheep of the Christian flock (*domini canes*—'dogs of the Lord'—a pun on Dominicans), and also a view of Florence Cathedral showing it imaginatively completed, with a dome similar to the one eventually begun by *Brunelleschi in 1420 (Andrea was among the artists who had been consulted over the construction of the building). Andrea's dignified style is similar to that of *Orcagna.

Andrea del Castagno. See CASTAGNO.

Andrea del Sarto. See SARTO.

Andrea del Verrocchio. See VERROCCHIO.

Andrea di Bartolo. See BARTOLO DI FREDI.

Andrews, Michael (b Norwich, 30 Oct. 1928; d London, 19 July 1995). British painter. He studied at the *Slade School under *Coldstream, 1949–53. A slow, fastidious worker, he concentrated on ambitious figure compositions, subtly handled and often with an underlying emotional tension. He shunned publicity and was little known to the public until an *Arts Council exhibition of his work in 1980, after which he achieved a considerable reputation, although some critics found his work rather plodding. In the mid-1980s he had a change of direction with a series of huge, brilliantly coloured landscapes featuring Ayers Rock in Australia. See also SCHOOL OF LONDON.

Andriessen, Jurriaen (b Amsterdam, 12 June 1742; d Amsterdam, 31 July 1819). Dutch painter, draughtsman, and designer. He specialized in painted wallpapers for private houses, work in which he was assisted by his brother **Anthonie Andriessen** (1747–1813). For much of his career he also ran Amsterdam's Tekenacademie (Drawing Academy), where his many pupils included *Troostwijck and his son **Christiaan Andriessen** (1775–1846). From 1805 to 1808 Christiaan kept a journal, from which about 700 drawings survive, providing a fascinating record of the daily life of the time. They were formerly wrongly attributed to his father.

Angelico, Fra (Guido di Piero (or Pietro)) (b nr. Vicchio, c.1395; d Rome, 18 Feb. 1455). Florentine painter, a Dominican friar. His nickname means 'the angelic brother', and in popular tradition he has been seen as 'not an artist properly so-called but an inspired saint' (*Ruskin); however, he was in fact a highly professional painter, who was in touch with the most advanced developments in contemporary Florentine art, and in later life he travelled extensively for prestigious commissions. He is first recorded as a painter in 1417 and by 1423 he had become a member of the Dominican Order at S. Domenico, Fiesole, near Florence, where he took the name Fra Giovanni. He probably began his career as a manuscript *illuminator, and his early paintings are strongly influenced by *International Gothic. But even in the most lavishly decorative of these works—the *Annunciation* (c.1432) in the Diocesan Museum in Cortona—*Masaccio's influence is evident in the insistent perspective of the architecture.

For most of his career Angelico was based in Fiesole (he became prior there in 1450), but his most famous works were painted at S. Marco in Florence (now an Angelico museum), a Sylvestrine monastery that was taken over by his Order in 1436. He and his assistants painted about 50 frescos there (c.1438–45)—works that are at once the expression of and a guide to the spiritual life of the community. Many of the frescos are in the friars' cells and were intended as aids to devotion; with their immaculate colouring, their economy in drawing and composition, and their freedom from the accidents of time and place, they attain a sense of blissful serenity. In the last decade of his life Angelico also worked in Orvieto and Perugia, and most importantly in Rome, where he frescoed the private chapel of Pope Nicholas V in the Vatican with scenes from the lives of Sts Stephen and Lawrence (1447–50). These differ considerably from the S. Marco frescos, with new emphasis on the story and on circumstantial detail, bringing Angelico more clearly into the mainstream of 15th-century Italian fresco painting.

Angelico died in Rome and was buried in the church of S. Maria sopra Minerva, where his tombstone still exists. He painted numerous altarpieces as well as frescos, several outstanding examples being in the S. Marco museum, including a *Madonna and Saints* (c.1438–40) commissioned by Piero de' *Medici for the high altar of S. Marco, Florence. His work influenced numerous Italian painters, notably Benozzo *Gozzoli (who was probably his pupil), *Domenico Veneziano, and *Piero della Francesca. *Vasari, who referred to Fra Giovanni as 'a simple and most holy man', popularized the use of the name Angelico for him, but he says it is the name by which he was always known, and it was certainly used as early as 1469. He has long been called 'Beato Angelico' (the Blessed Angelico), but his beatification was not made official by the Vatican until 1984.

Angerstein, John Julius. See NATIONAL GALLERY.

Angry Penguins. An Australian avant-garde quarterly journal (1940–6) devoted to art and literature, published first in Adelaide and then from 1943 in Melbourne; the title comes from a line in a poem by its founder, the writer Max Harris (1921–96). It encouraged and provided a focus for a group of young painters who worked in an *Expressionist vein and attempted to create an authentic Australian art free from European influences; among them were Arthur *Boyd, Sidney *Nolan, John Perceval (b 1923), and Albert Tucker (1914–99). They were opposed by a group of *Social Realist painters, among them Noel Counihan (1913–86), and the debate between the two factions in the pages of *Angry Penguins* helped to make Melbourne a lively artistic centre in the early 1940s. In 1944 the journal was the victim of a celebrated hoax when it devoted an issue to the poems of the non-existent 'Ern Malley', whose works were concocted from arbitrarily selected quotations put together by two fairly traditional poets who thought the journal was pretentious and wanted to test the critical judgement of the editors. It never really recovered from the bad publicity this caused.

Anguier, François (b Eu, c.1604; d Paris, 9 Aug. 1669) and **Michel** (b Eu, c.1613; d Paris, 11 July 1686). French sculptors, brothers, who stood somewhat apart from the mainstream, which in the middle of the 17th century was dominated by the classical style of *Sarrazin. They are said to have gone to Rome in about 1641 and joined the studio of *Algardi. On their return to France (François by 1649, Michel in 1651), the brothers collaborated on the tomb of Henry de Montmorency in the chapel of the Lycée at Moulins (1649–52), which reveals the new Roman influence they introduced into France. Later the two brothers worked mainly apart, Michel having the more interesting career. His work includes the decoration of the interior of the church of the Val-de-Grâce, Paris (1662–7), and the *Nativity* group in St Roch, Paris (1665).

Anguissola, Sofonisba (b Cremona, c.1535; bur. Palermo, 16 Nov. 1625). Italian painter, mainly of portraits, the first woman artist to win international renown. She came from an aristocratic family and her father encouraged all his children (six daughters, of whom Sofonisba was the eldest, and a son) to develop their talents in art, literature, and music. Her sisters all became painters too, but none of them made much of a mark (three died young). Sofonisba studied with Bernardino Campi (1522–91), one of the leading painters of the time in Cremona. His patrons included the governor of Milan (a Spanish possession at this time), through whom Sofonisba was invited to Spain to work at the court of Philip II (see HABSBURG) in 1559. She remained there for more than a decade, serving as a lady-in-waiting to the queen as well as working as a painter, before marrying a Sicilian nobleman and settling with him in Sicily (another Spanish possession). After his death she moved to the mainland and married a Genoese aristocrat, but she returned to spend her final years in Sicily. In 1624, when she was about 90, she was visited in Palermo by van *Dyck, who drew a portrait of her (BM, London) and described her as 'still possessed of a good memory, clear senses and a friendly manner'. Her self-portraits (of which about a dozen survive) and portraits of her family are considered her finest works; they are somewhat stiff, but can have great charm. She also painted religious pictures.

Angus, Rita (b Hastings, 12 Mar. 1908; d Wellington, 26 Jan. 1970). New Zealand painter, mainly of portraits and landscapes. Alongside Colin *McCahon and Toss *Woollaston she is considered one of the leading figures in New Zealand art of her time. Working in both oils and watercolours, she painted in a forthright, brightly coloured style that won her a reputation as a pioneer of modernism in her country. She also painted under her married name, Rita Cook.

animaliers. See BARYE.

Anker, Albert (b Ins, Berne canton, 1 Apr. 1831; d Ins, 16 July 1910). Swiss painter. He specialized in rather sentimental scenes of peasant village life that were once very popular. His chief claim to fame is that he was one of Adolf Hitler's favourite artists.

Annigoni, Pietro (b Milan, 7 June 1910; d Florence, 28 Oct. 1988). Italian painter (and occasional sculptor), the only artist of his time to become internationally famous as a society and state portraitist. The turning point in his career was a commission from the Worshipful Company of Fishmongers to paint a portrait of Queen Elizabeth II (1954–5, Fishmongers' Hall, London); it was reproduced endlessly, notably on the postage stamps and banknotes of various countries, and the jacket blurb of Annigoni's autobiography (An Artist's Life, 1977) claims that it made him 'the most famous artist in the

world—not excluding even *Picasso'. Subsequently he painted many other celebrity sitters, including several other members of the British royal family, Presidents Kennedy and Johnson, and Pope John XXIII. In style and technique he based himself on the masters of the Italian *Renaissance, placing great stress on draughtsmanship and often working in *tempera. Characteristically his work was smoothly finished, melodramatic in lighting, and often rather melancholy in mood. Annigoni also painted religious works (including frescos in Italian churches) and ambitious allegorical scenes, and he regarded these as more important than his portraits. Critics often dismissed his work as portentously inflated and tasteless, but he was admired by many traditionalists (*Munnings called him 'the greatest painter of the age') and he sometimes attracted remarkable public attention; more than 200,000 people went to see his second portrait of the Queen (NPG, London) during the fortnight when it was first exhibited in 1970, although this rather severe, schoolmarmish image had a mixed reception, proving much less popular than the glamorous 1954–5 painting.

Anquetin, Louis (b Étrépagny, Eure, 26 Jan. 1861; d Paris, 19 Aug. 1932). French painter, designer, and writer. Early in his career he moved in circles that included some of the outstanding avant-garde painters of the day, including *Bernard, van *Gogh, and *Toulouse-Lautrec (all four had been pupils of *Cormon). With Bernard, he was one of the pioneers of *Cloisonnism, but after about 1890 his work was much more traditional, and he became interested in research into the techniques of the Old Masters, notably *Rubens, on whom he wrote a book (1924). He was a prolific draughtsman and made tapestry cartoons for the Beauvais and Gobelins factories.

Anrep, Boris (b St Petersburg, 28 Sept. 1883; d London, 7 June 1969). Russian-born mosaicist and painter, active mainly in England. He organized the Russian section of Roger *Fry's second *Post-Impressionist exhibition in 1912 and after the First World War, in which he served in the Russian army, he settled in London, although he lived for a time in Paris after his wife left him for Fry in 1926. Anrep was deeply interested in Byzantine art and came to specialize in mosaic pavements, the best-known examples being in Tate Britain, representing William Blake's Proverbs (1923), and the National Gallery—four floors on and around the main staircase, executed between 1926 and 1952. The subjects are *The Awakening of the Muses*, *The Modern Virtues*, *The Labours of Life*, and *The Pleasures of Life*; portraits of many well-known contemporaries are incorporated in them, for example the philosopher Bertrand Russell representing 'Lucidity' and the film actress Greta Garbo as Melpomene, the Muse of Tragedy. They were paid for by Samuel *Courtauld and other benefactors.

Anshutz, Thomas. See HENRI.

Antal, Frederick (*b* Budapest, 21 Dec. 1887; *d* London, 4 Apr. 1954). Hungarian-born art historian who settled in England in 1933 and became a British citizen in 1946. He was deeply interested in historical methodology, and is regarded as the leading exponent of the Marxist interpretation of art history. His views are most fully expressed in *Florentine Painting and its Social Background* (1948), in which he argues that developments in style and subject matter were directly influenced by social and political changes. The book was widely admired, but it was also attacked as being over-rigid in the way it linked artistic phenomena with social and economic causes. Antal's other books include the posthumously published *Hogarth and his Place in European Art* (1962), in which he applied his methods more subtly and flexibly, revealing his fascination with *Hogarth as an expression of English middle-class morality and culture. A collection of his articles, *Classicism and Romanticism, with Other Studies in Art History* (1966), includes 'Remarks on the Method of Art History', which is a statement of his own credo. Antal never held a regular teaching post in England (he occasionally lectured at the *Courtauld Institute), but he was an influential figure. Ernst *Gombrich described him as 'by far the most learned and sophisticated' of the Marxist art historians of his time; 'He was very doctrinaire in his political views, but he had a good eye.'

Antelami, Benedetto (active late 12th century). Italian *Romanesque sculptor, the most notable figure in the history of Italian sculpture before Nicola *Pisano. His name first appears on a *relief of the *Descent from the Cross* (1178) in Parma Cathedral. The major works associated with him are the three carved portals of the adjacent Baptistery, one of which is signed and dated 1196; it has been suggested that he may have overseen the whole structure as architect as well as sculptor. On stylistic grounds he or his workshop have been credited with other work in north Italy. His sculptures have a gravity and

dramatic expressiveness hitherto unknown in the region.

Antenor. Athenian sculptor active in the late 6th century BC. In antiquity he was famous for his bronze group of the *Tyrannicides* (*c*.510 BC, now lost), which stood in the agora (market place) in Athens until it was carried off as booty by the Persian king Xerxes after he sacked the city in 480 BC. The group was restored by Alexander the Great or one of his successors; meanwhile a replacement by *Critius and Nesiotes had been set up, and in *Pausanias' day the two groups still stood together. An impressively solid marble *kore from the Acropolis at Athens (now Acropolis Mus.) may belong to a base signed by Antenor; and by comparison of style some archaeologists attribute to him or his workshop the pedimental sculpture of the late *Archaic temple of Apollo at Delphi.

Anthonisz., Cornelis (*b* Amsterdam, *c*.1505; *d* Amsterdam, 1553). Netherlandish printmaker, painter, and cartographer. He was active mainly in Amsterdam, where he was the leading printmaker of his time. In 1544 he published a large bird's-eye view of the city in woodcut and he also worked as a cartographer in the service of the Emperor Charles V (see HABSBURG). In addition he painted portraits, most notably *The Civic Guard* (1533, Historical Mus., Amsterdam), an early example of a type of group portrait for which Frans *Hals later became renowned.

Antico (Pier Jacopo Alari Bonacolsi) (*b* ?Mantua, *c*.1460; *d* Gazzuolo, July 1528). Italian sculptor, goldsmith, and medallist. His nickname derived from his classically inspired bronze statuettes, many of which were versions of famous antique statues such as the *Apollo Belvedere* (he also restored ancient sculpture). He visited Rome in the 1490s, but worked mainly in and around Mantua, particularly for members of the *Gonzaga family and Isabella d'*Este.

Antinous. A representation in sculpture of the beautiful youth of this name who was a favourite of the Emperor Hadrian. After Antinous was drowned while accompanying Hadrian up the Nile in AD 130 his name became surrounded by romantic legend, and the grief-stricken emperor commemorated him in lavish fashion. He founded a city called Antinoöpolis in Egypt, erected temples in his memory, and had him honoured in festivals. Antinous was frequently represented in sculpture, sometimes as Apollo or Dionysus, and several examples survive;

typically he is shown with curly hair and a sad-sweet expression, although the identification is not always certain, and the title 'Antinous' has sometimes been given loosely to similar figures of beautiful and graceful youths. Particularly famous were the Belvedere Antinous (Vatican Mus.), which was regarded as one of the standards of male beauty (for *Bernini's views on it, see ANTIQUE), and a relief excavated at Hadrian's Villa at Tivoli in 1735. It was one of the greatest treasures of Cardinal *Albani and was regarded by his librarian *Winckelmann as one of the peaks of ancient art; it is still in Albani's villa in Rome, now renamed the Villa Torlonia.

Antipodeans (or **Antipodean Group**). The name adopted by a group of Australian painters (Arthur *Boyd was the best known) who held an exhibition in Melbourne in 1959; the catalogue contained a manifesto of their aims and ideas, attacking abstraction and championing figurative art.

antique, the. The physical remains of the Greek and Roman world, or more particularly the remains of antique sculpture, which have been for later artists an inspiration, a challenge, and a canon of perfection. Such remains have never been totally forgotten or disregarded. Stone from ruined Roman buildings was often reused, and memories of classical ornament or drapery forms recur throughout the Middle Ages; occasionally a true classical dignity was attained, as in the Visitation group (c.1250) on the central portal of the west façade at Reims Cathedral. However, it was not until the Italian *Renaissance that the recovery and revival of the classical past became a deliberate ideal. *Ghiberti's writings, for example, testify to his admiration for antique statues and *cameos, and much of *Donatello's sculpture would be unthinkable without a close study of the antique (most obviously, the *Marcus Aurelius is the work against which he measured himself in his Gattamelata). Lorenzo de' *Medici and Pope Julius II (Giuliano della *Rovere) were among the pioneer collectors of ancient art, and *Vasari attributed the attainment of perfection by the generation of *Leonardo, *Michelangelo, and *Raphael in no small measure to the discovery of such famous marbles as the *Apollo Belvedere and the *Laocoön, although it was mainly the next generation, particularly visitors from northern Europe (*Heemskerck for example), who systematically drew after the antique. Towards the middle of the 16th century the role of the antique in the curriculum of artists became

firmly established. In De' veri precetti della pittura (1587), the painter and writer Giovanni Battista Armenini (c.1525–1609) already gives a list of 'canonic' antiques, including the famous *Belvedere Torso, and such works were carried by means of engravings, casts, and copies into every artist's studio.

The philosophical justification for this dependence on antique models was given in *Bellori's famous oration, Idea (1664), where he claimed that ancient statuary embodied a revelation of an absolute beauty that had been discovered once and for all (see IDEAL). To the followers of the academic doctrine, each of the great antiques, to which now were added the *Farnese Hercules, the *Borghese Warrior, the *Medici Venus, and the *Barberini Faun, represented a type of physique that could serve as a permanent standard for the artist. Nor was antique influence confined to those artists whose work was most obviously classical (such as *Poussin). *Bernini, for example, when he addressed the *Academy in Paris in 1666, said: 'In my early youth I drew a great deal from classical figures, and when I was in difficulties with my first statue I turned to the *Antinous as to the oracle.' Reverence for the antique was given a new lease of life when the *Neoclassical movement reacted against the frivolities of the *Rococo style. In opposition to earlier ideas, *Winckelmann preached the belief that classical artists had deliberately avoided representing extreme passions, and he regarded the antique less as a source of expressive formulas than as a model of noble restraint. The authority of the antique declined with the onset of *Romanticism, with its stress on self-expression, but its influence has still continued. Making drawings from casts of antique sculpture remained a part of most official art training into the 20th century, and *Picasso, for example, often used classical art as a source of inspiration; in particular, his 'Neoclassical' paintings of the 1920s owed much to visits to the Archaeological Museum in Naples.

Antolínez, José (bapt. Madrid, 7 Nov. 1635; d Madrid, 30 May 1675). Spanish painter, active in Madrid. Like *Murillo in Seville, he had a penchant for paintings of the Immaculate Conception (an example, c.1670, is in the Ashmolean Museum, Oxford), and his colourful, sweet style has much in common with Murillo's. His temperament was anything but sweet, however, for he was renowned for his arrogance and vanity; according to *Palomino, he died of a fever after overexerting himself and suffering wounds in a fencing bout. Apart from religious works, his output included a few portraits and *genre scenes, notably the *Picture Dealer* (*c*.1670, Alte Pin., Munich), an intriguing glimpse into the studio of a poor artist.

Antonello da Messina (*b* Messina, *c*.1430; *d* Messina, 14/25 Feb. 1479). Italian painter, mainly active at Messina in Sicily, the most famous artist to come from the island. He was one of the major pioneers of *oil painting in Italy. According to *Vasari, he learnt the technique from Jan van *Eyck, but there is no evidence that he ever visited northern Europe and he was in any case still probably a boy when Jan died in 1441. It is more likely that he acquired his knowledge of northern techniques in Naples, then artistically dominated by the Netherlands; an early 16th-century source indicates that he studied there under Niccolò Colantonio (?*c*.1420–?*c*.1460), probably the leading Neapolitan painter of his time. He made at least two extensive visits to the Italian mainland, and in 1475–6 he was in Venice, where he painted a large altarpiece for the church of S. Cassiano, of which only three fragments remain (KH Mus., Vienna). Vasari says that Antonello brought the 'secret' of oil painting to Venice, and while this is an exaggeration, his altarpiece and other works he painted there did have 'a far-reaching influence . . . during the decade or two succeeding his visit' (Johannes *Wilde, *Venetian Art from Bellini to Titian*, 1974). He showed how oils could be used to create previously unknown atmospheric and colouristic effects, and Giovanni *Bellini, most notably, was greatly impressed by the lucidity and spaciousness of his work.

Antonello's bust portraits—in three-quarter view, of Netherlandish type—also enjoyed a notable vogue in Venice: their expressions were more lively than in the portraits by *Memlinc then being imported and, like Antonello's religious works, they show a remarkable ability to combine northern particularity of detail with the Italian tradition of grandeur and clarity of form. Examples of Antonello's portraits are in the National Gallery, London (this one is often considered a self-portrait), and the Louvre, Paris.

An Túr Gloine. See PURSER.

Antwerp Mannerism. A term coined by Max J. *Friedländer in 1915 to describe a style characteristic of various painters working in Antwerp from about 1500 to about 1530. The style has little to do with Italian *Mannerism, although

Italianate buildings often feature in Antwerp paintings of the time. Rather, as James Snyder writes (*Northern Renaissance Art*, 1985), the style 'marks the final stage of many latent features of earlier Flemish painting . . . Details of costume are elaborated and ornamental effects are exaggerated . . . The result is indeed mannered if one thinks of it as a style gone to seed and losing contact with naturalism . . . The actors, which they are, resemble ceramic figurines with elegant curlicues breaking the drapery contours; their heads are reduced to cute caricatures of wrinkled old men, foppish pages, and demure maidens . . . They tiptoe and prance agilely along their carpeted stages before theatrical backdrops of lofty architectural ruins through which we catch glimpses of distant Disneyland towers and romantic landscapes.' As this description suggests, the term is sometimes used mildly pejoratively, but pictures in the style (almost always on religious subjects) can be lively and charmingly artificial as well as merely overwrought. Most of the artists associated with Antwerp Mannerism are anonymous, but the identified practitioners include Jan de Beer (*c*.1475–1519/28) and (in his early work) Jan *Gossaert. The stylistic features described above, although most highly developed in Antwerp (a major centre for the international art trade), were not confined to the city; indeed they were broadly characteristic of Netherlandish art as a whole at this time.

Anuszkiewicz, Richard. See OP ART.

Apelles. Greek painter active in the 4th century BC, born at Colophon in Asia Minor. None of his work survives, but in antiquity he was reckoned the greatest of Greek painters, excelling all others in grace and also described as a master of composition and of *chiaroscuro. He was court painter to Philip II of Macedon and his son Alexander the Great, and one of the many anecdotes concerning him tells how Alexander gave him his mistress Pancaspe after the artist had fallen in love with her while painting her in the nude. The names of about 30 of his works are recorded by ancient sources. Among his subjects were portraits of Alexander the Great (particularly famous was one for the temple of Artemis at Ephesus), *Calumny*, and *Aphrodite Anadyomene* (Venus Rising from the Sea), made for the temple of Asclepius at Cos, brought to Rome by Augustus, and set up in the temple of Caesar. Descriptions of his work by classical authors were well known during the *Renaissance and inspired several major artists to emulate them.

*Botticelli made a painting and *Mantegna a drawing of *Calumny* (Uffizi, Florence, and BM, London, respectively), and *Titian painted an *Aphrodite Anadyomene* (NG, Edinburgh). A small but majestic painting of *Zeus Enthroned* in the House of the Vettii at Pompeii may well be a reminiscence of Apelles' picture of Alexander holding a thunderbolt.

Aphrodite of Cnidus. Statue by *Praxiteles, made for the city of Cnidus in Asia Minor. It is now lost, but it was his most famous work in antiquity (*Pliny thought it was the finest statue in the world), and was the ancestress of the modern female nude—the first life-size statue showing the goddess completely naked. Several Roman copies survive (for example in the Vatican): they show Aphrodite (Venus) in a gently twisted pose, with the right hand casually masking the pudenda and the left hand dropping her robe over an urn. The statue was placed in an open shrine so it could be seen from all four sides, each view being equally admired. According to some ancient sources, Praxiteles' mistress, the celebrated courtesan Phryne, was his model for the statue. See also DEMETER OF CNIDUS.

Apollinaire, Guillaume (*b* Rome, 26 Aug. 1880; *d* Paris, 9 Nov. 1918). French poet and art critic. The illegitimate son of a high-class Polish-Russian courtesan, he was originally called Wilhelm Apollinaris de Kostrowitzky, but he adopted his pseudonym in 1902, about two years after he settled in Paris; his father was probably an Italian nobleman, although Apollinaire liked to hint he was the offspring of a high-ranking clergyman. In addition to being a major poet, he was 'the most influential art critic writing in France during the decade before the outbreak of war in 1914 . . . a cardinal figure in creating the artistic climate of Paris early in this century—a climate in which anything and everything was thought possible' (John *Golding, *Visions of the Modern*, 1994). He earned his living mainly with journalism and was one of the prototypes of the modern critic, his writing containing much that is superficial and gossipy. His importance stems not so much from the quality of his writing as from his brilliance as a propagandist on behalf of those artists he most admired. In particular he championed *Picasso (his first substantial articles, in 1905, were on him) and later the *Cubists in general (including the *Orphists, whose name he coined). Among the other artists whose reputations he either established or consolidated were *Chagall, de

*Chirico, *Derain, *Matisse, and Henri *Rousseau. He was also influential on *Dada (his friend Marcel *Duchamp's interest in visual punning was partly inspired by Apollinaire's love of jest and linguistic acrobatics) and on *Surrealism (he coined the term in 1917 and his suggestion that artists should explore 'interior universes' stimulated André *Breton, who dedicated the first Surrealist manifesto to his memory). In an entirely different artistic context, he became briefly notorious in 1911 when the *Mona Lisa* was stolen from the Louvre and he spent several days in police custody on false suspicion of being involved in the crime. Apollinaire was wounded in the head serving in the French army in 1916; weakened by this, he died of influenza two years later.

Apollo Belvedere. Marble statue (Vatican Mus.) of the Greek god Apollo, discovered towards the end of the 15th century and long regarded as one of the supreme masterpieces of world art and the absolute standard for male beauty (it is named after the Belvedere Court in the Vatican, in which it was once displayed). The statue is a copy from the Roman period of a *Classical or *Hellenistic Greek bronze, and *Leochares has been proposed as the sculptor of the lost original. It was often copied or adapted, for example by *Bernini in his *Apollo and Daphne* and by *Reynolds, who painted his *Commodore Keppel* in the posture of the statue but in 18th-century dress. *Winckelmann's rapturous description of the *Apollo Belvedere* enshrined it as one of the models of *Neoclassicism, but from the later 19th century its reputation declined and it now seems cold and academic to many critics. Whereas to Winckelmann it appeared 'the highest ideal of art among all the works of antiquity', to Kenneth *Clark it seemed that 'in no other famous work of art are idea and execution more distressingly divorced'.

Apollodorus. Athenian painter of the late 5th century BC. None of his works survive, but ancient writers rated him as one of the leading painters of his period. He was nicknamed *Sciagraphus* (Shadow Painter) because he was the first to model his figures in light and shade, a notable step forward in pictorial illusion that was carried further by *Zeuxis.

Apollonio di Giovanni. See CASSONE.

Apollonius. See BELVEDERE TORSO.

Apoxyomenus. See LYSIPPUS.

Appel, Karel (*b* Amsterdam, 25 Apr. 1921). Dutch abstract painter, sculptor, printmaker, ceramicist, designer, and writer, regarded as the most powerful of the post-war generation of Dutch artists. In 1948 he was a founder of the *Cobra group. He moved to Paris in 1950 and by the end of the decade he had gained an international reputation, having travelled widely and won several prestigious prizes. His most characteristic paintings are in an extremely uninhibited and agitated *Expressionist vein, with strident colours and violent brushwork applied with very thick *impasto. The images usually look purely abstract at first glance, but they often retain suggestions of human masks or of animal or fantasy figures, sometimes fraught with terror as well as a childlike naivety: Herbert *Read wrote that in looking at his pictures one has the impression 'of a spiritual tornado that has left these images of its passage'. Such works were influential on *Neo-Expressionism. Appel has also made sculpture, prints, and ceramics, and he has done a wide range of design work, including the scenery for a ballet, *Can We Dance a Landscape*, for which he also wrote the plot; it was performed at the Paris Opéra in 1987.

Appiani, Andrea (*b* Milan, 31 May 1754; *d* Milan, 8 Nov. 1817). Italian painter. He was the leading Italian painter of the *Neoclassical period, but more on account of the lack of native competition than because of the quality of his work, which is graceful and impeccably finished but often rather bland. Most of his career was spent in Milan; his work there includes the fresco decoration of the church of S. Maria presso S. Celso (1792–8). This is sometimes described as his masterpiece, but his portraits have generally appealed more to modern taste than his decorative work.

applied art. Term describing the design or decoration of functional objects so as to make them aesthetically pleasing. It is used in distinction to *fine art, although there is often no clear dividing line between the two areas.

Apt, Ulrich the Elder (*d* Augsburg, 1532). German painter. He worked in Augsburg, painting altarpieces, portraits, and in 1516 a series of wall paintings (destroyed) in the town hall in collaboration with his pupil Jörg *Breu. Apt had three painter sons, about whom little is known: Jacob, Michael, and Ulrich the Younger.

aquarelle. The French word for *watercolour; it is sometimes used in English to distinguish 'true' watercolour painting—in transparent washes—from *gouache, which is opaque.

aquatint. A printmaking method related to *etching but producing finely granulated tonal areas rather than lines; the term applies also to a print made by this method. There are several variants of the technique, but in essence the process is as follows. A metal plate is sprinkled with acid-resistant resin, which is fused to the plate by heating. When the plate is immersed in an acid bath the acid bites between the tiny particles of resin, creating correspondingly tiny cavities in the metal to hold the ink; the evenly granulated surface produced in this way will eventually print as a speckled grey tone, the coarseness or fineness of the texture depending on the size and density of the grains of resin. The design is created by drawing on the plate with acid-resistant varnish, and variety of tone is obtained in stages by a process called 'stopping out'—that is, progressively varnishing over areas that have been sufficiently bitten and then re-immersing the plate in the acid (the longer the acid bites, the darker the tone). This method of working means that the artist has to create the image in negative, since the areas that are covered with varnish from the beginning (the initial design) will print white.

A version of aquatint was first used in the Netherlands in the mid-17th century (at about the same time as *mezzotint was invented), but it initially made almost no impact. The technique then lay dormant until a satisfactory system was evolved by the French artist Jean-Baptiste Le Prince (1733–81), whose first plates date from 1768. From France the technique soon spread to England, a country especially partial to tonal methods of printmaking, and it was much used there in the late 18th and early 19th centuries for reproducing the luminosity and transparency of watercolours (the combination of 'aqua' and 'tint' in the name suggests its qualities). Colour could be added by hand or by using separate plates with different coloured inks.

The principal English pioneer of aquatint was Paul *Sandby, who published his first examples in 1775 and is said to have coined the term. He was resourceful in technique, inventing a new process for preparing the metal plate—the spirit-ground method. In this, resin dissolved in alcohol is poured over the plate, the evaporation of the spirit leaving the resin to crystallize so as to produce a regularly granulated ground. He combined this process with a technique known as sugar aquatint (or sugar-lift aquatint or lift-ground etching), which allows the artist to make the design positively rather than negatively and therefore to work with greater spontaneity. The design is made directly on the plate with a fluid (typically black ink or watercolour) in which sugar has been dissolved, applied either by pen or by brush. The plate is then varnished and immersed in lukewarm water. While under water the sugar swells, lifts off the plate, and dislodges the varnish, leaving the bare copper beneath, the result being a copper plate covered with varnish except where the drawing was made with sugar solution. An aquatint ground is next laid over the whole surface and the plate bitten in acid. By this means the drawing alone is etched in an aquatint texture, for the rest of the plate, being protected by the varnish, remains unbitten. Finally both ground and varnish are cleaned off and the plate is printed, showing the design as a dark tone on a white background. *Gainsborough learnt the technique from Sandby.

Aquatint has often been combined with etching, notably by *Goya, most of whose prints use the two techniques together in varying proportions. With his great exception, aquatint was used mainly as a reproductive technique until late in the 19th century, when *Cassatt, *Degas, and Camille *Pissarro made a number of highly original prints in which aquatint was combined with etching and other *intaglio methods. In the 20th century the technique became much more popular with creative printmakers as part of the general revival of interest in the print as an independent art form—a revival in which S. W. *Hayter played a central role. *Masson, *Picasso, and *Rouault are among the major modern artists who have used it.

Ara Pacis Augustae (Altar of Augustan Peace). A monumental marble altar (13–9 BC) set up by the first Roman emperor, Augustus, on the Campus Martius in Rome to commemorate his return from a long sojourn in Spain and Gaul and to celebrate the peace and prosperity the empire enjoyed under his rule; it is described by Donald Strong (*Roman Art*, 1976) as 'a masterpiece of political and social propaganda'. The altar proper (which survives only in part) is on a podium, enclosed by screen walls and approached by a stairway. The lavish sculptural decoration of the complex ranks among the finest products of Roman art, and the reliefs representing the ceremonial procession at the dedication of the altar are the first in Western art that can strictly be called documentary, that is, showing identifiable individuals in a contemporary event. Other panels contain allegorical figures, such as Italia flanked by the personifications of the ocean and inland waters, and scenes from Roman mythology and legend. This combination of realistic representation with symbolism and allegory set a tradition that had a long history in Western commemorative sculpture. Several of the sculptured slabs came to light in the 16th century, others in 1859 and 1903. In 1937–8 the site was thoroughly excavated and the monument was reconstructed in a pavilion slightly to the north of its original situation, where the Palazzo Fiano now stands. The sculptural decoration is substantially complete, although fragments are dispersed in various European museums.

Archaic art. Term applied to Greek art in the period before the *Classical period, from about 650 BC until about 480 BC (the date of the Persian sack of Athens). The Archaic period is marked by the development of the life-size stone statue (the *kouros and *kore) and by the change from *black-figure vase painting to *red-figure.

Archaic smile. Conventional smiling expression, often seen in Greek statues of the *Archaic period, especially during the second quarter of the 6th century BC. A smile was suggested by drawing the mouth upwards in a clear, flat curve. Various theories have been offered to explain the convention, which has been described by John Boardman as an expression of 'strained cheerfulness'. According to one view it may have originated in the technical difficulty of fitting the curved mouth into the blocklike form that early sculptors of *kouroi gave to the head: certainly as the century progressed the increasing use of chisels led to a disappearance of the blocklike character and the Archaic smile gave place to a straighter, graver, and more serious or almost sulky expression of the mouth. Other writers have suggested that the smile was intended to express a state of health and well-being. A similar shift from a patterned smile to a more naturalistic gravity may be seen in some *Gothic sculpture, for example in figures carved early and late in the 13th century at Bamberg Cathedral.

Archipenko, Alexander (*b* Kiev, 30 May 1887; *d* New York, 25 Feb. 1964). Russian-born sculptor who became an American citizen in 1928. In 1908 he moved from Moscow to Paris, where he was introduced to *Cubism by *Léger and became one of the outstanding sculptors of the movement. In works such as the bronze *Walking Woman* (1912, Denver Art Mus.), he analysed the human figure into geometrical forms and opened parts of it up with concavities and a central hole to create a contrast of solid and void, issuing in a new idiom in modern sculpture. At about the same time he began making sculptures that were assembled from pieces of commonplace materials, paralleling the work of *Picasso. Archipenko quickly built up a reputation in France and elsewhere (especially Germany), and although his career was interrupted by the First World War, he vigorously relaunched it afterwards, and by the time of his first one-man show in the USA (given by the *Société Anonyme in 1921) he was the best known and most influential of all Cubist sculptors. In 1921–3 he lived in Berlin, then settled in the USA. He taught in various places, but principally in New York, where he ran his own school of sculpture from 1939 until his death. The work he produced in America did not compare in quality or historical importance with that of his European period, but he continued to be imaginative and technically resourceful. In 1924, for example, he invented the *Archipentura* (a kind of *Kinetic painting), and after the Second World War he experimented with 'light' sculptures, making structures of plastic lit from within. His work was influential in both Europe and America, notably in the revival of *polychromy, in the use of new materials, and in pointing the way from a sculpture of solid form towards one of space and light.

Arch of Constantine, Arch of Septimius Severus, and **Arch of Titus.** See TRIUMPHAL ARCH.

Arcimboldo, Giuseppe (*b* ?Milan, *c*.1527; *d* Milan, 11 July 1593). Milanese painter, famous for his allegorical or symbolical compositions in which he arranged objects such as fruits and vegetables into the form of the human face. He began his career as a designer of stained-glass windows for Milan Cathedral, but from 1562 to 1587 he worked successively for the Emperors Ferdinand I, Maximilian II, and Rudolf II (see HABSBURG), first in Vienna and then in Prague. A typical work is *Rudolf II as Vertumnus* (*c*.1590, Skokloster Castle, near Stockholm), showing the emperor as the Roman god of orchards, his head composed of fruit, flowers, and so on. Arcimboldo returned to Milan in 1587. His paintings, though much imitated, were generally regarded merely as curiosities until the *Surrealists revived interest in 'visual punning'.

Ardizzone, Edward (*b* Haiphong, French Indo-China [now Hai Phong, Vietnam], 16 Oct. 1900; *d* Rodmersham, Kent, 8 Nov. 1979). British illustrator, painter, printmaker, and writer, best known as an illustrator of children's literature. His output in this field was huge and he won several distinctions, including in 1956 the first Kate *Greenaway Medal (awarded annually by the Library Association for the best work in the illustration of a children's book). Ardizzone also wrote such books himself, beginning with *Little Tim and the Brave Sea Captain* (1936). In *The Oxford Companion to Children's Literature* (1984), he is described as 'the most eminent British children's illustrator between 1945 and 1970, with a reputation as high in America as in his own country. His characteristic style, which makes great use of cross-hatching, appears casual, but was worked out over many years, and only became fully developed after the Second World War. It is particularly suited to nostalgic scenes of Edwardian city life, with fogbound streets and the cosy interiors of sitting-rooms.' His son **Philip Ardizzone** (1931–78) was a painter and etcher.

Arentsz., Arent (*b* Amsterdam, *c*.1585; *bur.* Amsterdam, 18 Aug. 1631). Dutch painter of winter and summer activities on the seashore and canals of Holland. He is often known as Cabel, after the name of the house in which he was born. His paintings are sometimes difficult to distinguish from Hendrick *Avercamp's, although 'his colours are darker and more vivid than Hendrick's delicate hues' and his figures are 'somewhat larger and cruder' (Seymour Slive, *Dutch Painting: 1600–1800*, 1995).

Arikha, Avigdor (*b* Rădăuţi, 28 Apr. 1929). Romanian-born Israeli painter, draughtsman, printmaker, designer, and writer on art who has worked mainly in France. Initially he made his name as a book illustrator, then from 1957 to 1965 he was primarily an abstract painter, working in an *Art Informel vein. Between 1965 and 1973 he abandoned painting for drawing and etching, his work of this period including a series of portraits of the writer Samuel Beckett, who was a close friend. When he resumed painting in 1973, he concentrated on working from the life, his subjects including landscapes, interiors, still-lifes, and portraits, among which are a few commissioned portraits (*Queen Elizabeth, the Queen Mother*, 1983, NPG, Edinburgh). Such works have won him a reputation as one of the leading figurative painters of his day. Arikha has also written on art and organized exhibitions at the Houston Museum of Fine Arts on the work of *Poussin (1982) and *Ingres (1986).

Arman (Armand Fernandez) (*b* Nice, 17 Nov. 1928). French-born artist who became an American citizen in 1972. In 1957, with his friend Yves *Klein, he decided to be known by his first name only, and the form 'Arman' was adopted in 1958 as a result of a printer's error on the cover of a catalogue. He moved to New York in 1963. Arman is best known for his assemblages of junk material, ranging from modest collections of household debris (*Accumulation of Sliced Teapots*, 1964, Walker Art Center, Minneapolis) to towers of crushed automobiles encased in concrete.

armature. A framework or skeleton (typically of wood or stiff wire) round which a figure of soft material such as clay or wax can be modelled. The term is also applied to the iron framework of *stained-glass windows.

Armenini, Giovanni Battista. See ANTIQUE.

Armitage, Kenneth (*b* Leeds, 18 July 1916; *d* London, 22 Jan. 2002). British sculptor. In 1952 he had his first one-man show in London and in the same year his work was exhibited in the Venice *Biennale; thereafter he rapidly developed an international reputation. His pre-war work consisted mainly of carvings (most of which he later destroyed), but soon after the war he began to work in bronze, which remained a favourite material for what he described as 'the fluid, unifying and sensual quality it can give'. Bronze was also much more suitable than carving for the spindly-legged, slab-bodied shapes that were characteristic of his figures at this time; he depicted them singly or in groups, in everyday attitudes, with a sense of affection and often humour: 'I find most satisfying work which derives from careful study and preparation but which is fashioned in an attitude of pleasure and playfulness.' *People in the Wind* (1951, Tate, London, and other casts) is a well-known example from this phase of his career and one of the first works in which he achieved a distinctively individual style. From the mid-1950s his figures became more impersonal in character and often larger in scale, and from the late 1960s he became more experimental in technique, combining sculpture and drawing in figures of wood, plaster, and paper. In the 1970s he returned to bronze and began to explore non-human subject matter. He also worked in fibreglass.

Armory Show. An art exhibition (officially entitled the International Exhibition of Modern Art) held in New York, 17 February–15 March 1913, at the Armory of the National Guard's Sixty-Ninth Regiment, Lexington Avenue, Manhattan. It was a daring presentation of new and still controversial art on a mammoth scale (about 1,300 works by about 300 artists) and is regarded as the most important exhibition ever held in the country and one of the milestones in 20th-century American culture. The initiative for it came from a group of artists, several of them from the circle of Robert *Henri, who in 1911 formed an organization called the Association of American Painters and Sculptors to find exhibition space for young artists. The breadth of vision with which the show was conceived was primarily due to the Association's president, Arthur B. *Davies, whose enthusiasm for presenting a comprehensive picture of current European movements largely overshadowed the original idea of an exhibition of American art. In effect, the Armory Show was two exhibitions in one. The American portion presented a cross-section of contemporary art from the USA, heavily weighted in favour of younger and more radical artists. The foreign section, which was the core of the exhibition and became the main centre of controversy, traced the evolution of modern art, showing work by *Goya, *Delacroix, *Courbet, and the *Impressionists and *Post-Impressionists, as well as leading contemporary artists including *Kandinsky, *Matisse, and *Picasso. French artists were best represented, and there was comparatively little German art.

From New York a reduced version of the exhibition went to Chicago (Art Institute) and Boston (Copley Hall). More than a quarter of a million visitors paid to see it, and its impact was enormous on a public that generally knew little of Post-Impressionism, let alone *Fauvism, *Cubism, or abstract art (the Metropolitan Museum, New York, bought a *Cézanne at the Show and this was the first picture by the artist to enter an American public collection). Though there was a good deal of ridicule and indignation (directed particularly at Marcel *Duchamp's *Nude Descending a Staircase*), there were also many favourable reviews and the show stirred up public interest in art and created a climate more favourable to experimentation. It had a profound effect on many American artists, for example Stuart *Davis, who regarded it as the turning point of his career, and several important patrons and collectors made their first tentative purchases of modern art at the show, among them Katherine *Dreier. It has therefore become a commonplace to speak of the Armory Show as the real beginning of an interest in modern art in the USA.

Armstrong, Elizabeth. See NEWLYN SCHOOL.

Arnold, Ann and **Graham.** See BLAKE, SIR PETER.

Arnolfo di Cambio (b Colle di Val d'Elsa, nr. Siena, c.1240/5; d Florence, 1302/10). Italian sculptor and architect. He is first mentioned in 1265 as Nicola *Pisano's assistant on the pulpit for Siena Cathedral. In 1277 he is documented in Rome, where he seems to have spent most of the 1280s and 1290s, before settling in Florence in his final years. In Rome he worked in the service of Charles I of Naples and Sicily (Charles of Anjou); his portrait of Charles (c.1280, Capitoline Mus., Rome) was one of the earliest portrait statues since the ancient world. The famous bronze statue of St Peter (c.1290) in St Peter's, Rome, has also been attributed to him. His most important surviving sculpture, however, is the tomb of Cardinal de Braye (d 1282), in S. Domenico at Orvieto, which set the type of wall tomb for more than a century. As an architect, Arnolfo had a great reputation in his day and began the building of Florence Cathedral. No other buildings are documented as being by him, but several other important Florentine buildings, including S. Croce and the Palazzo Vecchio, have been attributed to him, notably by *Vasari. If they really are to be credited to Arnolfo, he must rank as one of the greatest architects of the Middle Ages, as well as a distinguished sculptor.

Arp, Jean (or **Hans**) (b Strasbourg, 16 Sept. 1886; d Basle, 7 June 1966). French sculptor, painter, and poet who was prominently involved with several major avant-garde groups and movements in the first half of the 20th century. At the time of his birth his home city in Alsace was under German rule and he spoke French and German with equal ease (he wrote poetry in both languages). In 1912 he met Robert and Sonia *Delaunay in Paris and *Kandinsky in Munich, where he participated in the second *Blaue Reiter exhibition. In 1915 he moved to Zurich, where he was one of the founders of the *Dada movement and met his future wife Sophie *Taeuber (they married in 1922), with whom he collaborated in experiments with cut-out paper compositions and *collages. During the war years in Zurich he also made his first abstract polychrome relief carvings in wood

(*Dada Relief*, 1916, Kunsthaus, Basle). In 1919–20 he lived in Cologne, where he continued his Dada activities in collaboration with his friend Max *Ernst. From 1920 Arp worked mainly in Paris and in 1928 he settled at nearby Meudon. At this time he was involved in the *Surrealist movement, his work including experiments with chance arrangements. He joined *Cercle et Carré in 1930 and he was a founder member of *Abstraction-Création in 1931. Also in 1931 he took up sculpture in the round (previously he had made only reliefs) and began to produce what are now his most familiar and distinctive works—sensuous abstract pieces (usually in bronze or marble) that convey a suggestion of organic forms without reproducing actual plant or animal shapes (*Growth*, 1938, Guggenheim Mus., New York). In 1941 Arp fled to Grasse on the French Riviera, then in 1942 to Switzerland. After the war he returned to Meudon. In his post-war work he did not seriously add to his earlier achievements, but he won many honours and prestigious public commissions; in 1954, for example, he was awarded the International Sculpture Prize at the Venice *Biennale, and in 1958 he made a relief for the Unesco building in Paris.

Arpino, Cavaliere d'. See CESARI.

Arras tapestries. Tapestries produced in the 14th and 15th centuries at Arras in northern France. They are first mentioned in 1313 and their pre-eminent reputation during the later Middle Ages is attested by the fact that the name of the town passed into several European languages as a generic term for tapestry hangings (Polonius is hiding 'behind the arras' when he is killed by Hamlet). However, production was in decline by the mid-15th century (Tournai had become the leading centre of the art) and the industry was brought to an end when Louis XI of France captured Arras in 1477 (at this time it was part of Burgundy) and expelled the citizens. Subsequent attempts to re-establish it bore little fruit. A number of surviving tapestries have been ascribed to Arras looms, but the only one that is documented is that in Tournai Cathedral depicting the lives of Sts Piat and Eleutherius; it formerly bore the signature of Pierrot Feré of Arras and the date 1402.

arriccio (or **arricciato**). In *fresco painting, a layer of fairly coarse plaster applied to the wall before the *intonaco (the smoother top layer of plaster that forms the painting surface).

Ars moriendi (The Art of Dying). A late medieval compilation of texts (prayers, maxims, exhortations, and so on), intended as a guide for the comforting and counselling of the dying; it was issued as a *block book *c.*1460–5 and subsequently in various editions, including an English translation by Caxton (1491), made from an abridged French version. The block book has eleven full-page illustrations showing a dying man being alternately comforted by angels and tempted by demons to vices such as avarice and despair; on the final page, virtue triumphs in the hour of death. A very similar set of engraved illustrations by the *Master E. S. appeared at about the same time (probably slightly earlier) and both sets no doubt derive in part from prototypes in illuminated manuscripts. The illustrations were a popular source for painters; the deathbed scene in *Bosch's *Tabletop of the Seven Deadly Sins and the Four Last Things* (*c.*1480–90, Prado, Madrid), for example, derives from a similar image in the block book.

Art Autre. A term coined by the French critic Michel Tapié (1909–87) in his book *Un art autre* (1952) to describe a type of art that he regarded as appropriate to the turbulent mood in France in the post-war period—an art than worked through 'paroxysm, magic, total ecstasy'. The term is a vague one and is sometimes used synonymously with *Art Informel (also coined by Tapié). However, Art Autre can be seen as a broader term, for it embraces figurative art (for example that of *Dubuffet) as well as abstract art. In using the phrase 'art autre' (other art) Tapié claimed that post-war art showed a complete break with the past. In addition to Dubuffet, he cited *Mathieu, *Matta, and *Wols as leading representatives of Art Autre.

Art Brut (French: 'Raw Art'). Term coined by Jean *Dubuffet for art produced by people outside the established art world—solitaries, the maladjusted, patients in psychiatric hospitals, prisoners, and fringe-dwellers of all kinds. In English, the term 'Outsider art' (the title of a book by Roger Cardinal, 1972) is sometimes used to cover this type of work. Dubuffet claimed that such art—'springing from pure invention and in no way based, as cultural art constantly is, on chameleon- or parrot-like processes'—is evidence of a power of originality that all people possess but which in most has been stifled by educational training and social constraints. He began to make a collection of Art Brut in 1945, and in 1972 he presented it, by then numbering more than 5,000 items, to the city of Lausanne, where it was opened to the public at the Château de Beaulieu in 1976. Although nearly half the collection was produced by patients, usually schizophrenics, in psychiatric hospitals, Dubuffet repudiated the concept of psychiatric art, claiming that 'there is no art of the insane any more than there is an art of dyspeptics or an art of people with knee complaints'. He also distinguished Art Brut from *naive art on the more dubious ground that naive painters remain within the cultural mainstream, hoping for public recognition, whereas Art Brut artists create their works for their own use as a kind of private theatre.

Art Deco. The most fashionable style of design and interior decoration in the 1920s and 1930s in Europe and the USA, characterized by sleek geometrical or stylized forms and bright, sometimes garish colours. The style takes its name from the Exposition Internationale des Arts Décoratifs et Industriels Modernes, held in Paris in 1925. The emphasis of the exhibition was on individuality and fine craftsmanship (at the opposite extreme from the contemporary doctrines of the *Bauhaus), and Art Deco was originally a luxury style, with costly materials such as ivory, jade, and lacquer much in evidence. However, when the exhibition 'Machine Art'—another great showcase of the style—was held at the Museum of Modern Art, New York, in 1934, the emphasis was on the general style and impression of an interior rather than upon the individual craft object. Perhaps partly because of the effects of the Depression, materials that could be easily mass produced (such as plastics) were adapted to the style. Art Deco may have owed something to several of the major art movements of the early 20th century—the geometry of *Cubism (it has been described as 'Cubism tamed'), the bold colours of *Fauvism, and the machine forms of *Constructivism and *Futurism. Similarly, although the term is not often applied to painting or sculpture, the Art Deco style is clearly reflected in the streamlined forms of certain artists of the period, for example the painter Tamara de *Lempicka and the sculptor Paul *Manship. There was a revival of interest in Art Deco during the 1960s (it was then that the name was coined) and its bold, bright forms have a kinship with *Pop art.

Arte Povera (or **Art Povera**). Term (Italian: 'poor' or 'impoverished art') coined by the Italian art critic Germano Celant (1940–) to describe a type of work, related to *Conceptual and *Minimal art, in which the materials used—

such as soil, twigs, and newspaper—are deliberately chosen for their 'worthlessness'. The term has been used in a bewilderingly diffuse way. It has been applied to *happenings, *installations, and *Land art, for example, and to the work of many non-Italian artists, including Carl *Andre, Joseph *Beuys, Walter *De Maria, Richard *Long, and Robert *Morris. Celant organized several exhibitions on the theme, and in 1969 edited a book entitled *Arte Povera* (it was translated into English the same year as *Art Povera: Conceptual, Actual or Impossible Art?*). He hoped that the use of meagre materials and the avoidance of the traditional idea of art as a collectable 'product' would undermine the art world's commercialism. However, dealers have shown that even this kind of art can be commercially exploited.

art for art's sake. See AESTHETICISM.

Arthois, Jacques d' (*bapt.* Brussels, 12 Oct. 1613; *d* Brussels, ?May 1686). Flemish landscape painter, active in Brussels. He specialized in wooded landscapes, with figures that were often added by other artists, notably *Teniers the Younger. Few dated works exist, the development of his style is not easily followed, and the work of his brother **Nicolas** (1617–?) and his son **Jean-Baptiste** (1638–?) is sometimes indistinguishable from his. D'Arthois was the outstanding landscape painter of his time in Brussels and earned a good living from his work, but he led an extravagant life (he was briefly imprisoned for debt in 1658) and died in poverty. Paintings from his busy studio were often used to decorate churches; examples are in Brussels Cathedral.

Art Informel. Term coined by the French critic Michel Tapié to describe a type of spontaneous abstract painting popular among European artists in the 1940s and 1950s, roughly equivalent to *Abstract Expressionism in the USA. Tapié popularized the term in his book *Un art autre* (1952), and these two terms—*Art Autre and Art Informel—are sometimes used more or less synonymously. They are rarely used with any precision, but some critics regard Art Informel as a narrower term, representing only one aspect of the broader trend of Art Autre (which includes figurative as well as abstract work). In English the term 'Informalism' is sometimes used as an equivalent to Art Informel, but the word 'informel' (which Tapié himself devised) might be translated as 'without form' rather than 'informal'. See also TACHISME.

art mobilier (French: 'portable art'). A term used in the study of prehistoric and primitive art for small movable works of art such as figurines, engraved stones, and bone carvings. According to *The Thames and Hudson Dictionary of Art Terms* (1984), the term is also applied in the sense of 'furnishing art' to 'small portable art objects used for decorative purposes, e.g. *Renaissance bronze statuettes'.

Art Nouveau. Decorative style flourishing in most of western Europe and in the USA from about 1890 to the First World War. As the name suggests, it was a deliberate attempt to create a new style in reaction against the imitation of historical forms that had been such a prominent feature of 19th-century architecture and design. Its most characteristic theme was the use of sinuous asymmetrical lines based on plant forms; flower, leaf, and tendril motifs are common features, as are female figures with abundant flowing hair. At their most typical these motifs are found in the decorative and applied arts, such as interior design, metalwork, glassware, and jewellery, but Art Nouveau also had a major vogue in illustration and poster design and its influence can be seen to varying degrees in much of the painting and sculpture of the period—in a fairly pure form in the work of Alfred *Gilbert and Jan *Toorop, for example, and in certain aspects of such diverse artists as Munch (his penchant for undulating lines) and Matisse (the flat arabesque forms of the trees in some of the landscapes of his *Fauve period).

The style takes its name from a shop called La Maison de l'Art Nouveau opened in Paris in 1895 by the German-born art dealer Siegfried Bing (1838–1905), a leading propagandist for modern design. Paris was one of its most important centres, but its origins were diverse (Celtic and Japanese art have been cited as influences) and its roots were less on the Continent than in England, where the *Arts and Crafts movement had established a tradition of vitality in the applied arts. In France, indeed, Art Nouveau is sometimes known by the name 'Modern Style', reflecting these English origins. In Germany the style was called Jugendstil (from the Munich journal *Die Jugend*, founded in 1896); in Austria, Sezessionstil (after the Vienna *Sezession); in Spain, Modernista; and in Italy, Stile Liberty (after the London store that played so large a part in disseminating its designs). The style was truly international, its archetypal exponents ranging from *Mucha, a Czech whose most characteristic work was done in Paris, to

*Tiffany in New York, and to the Spanish architect Antoni Gaudí (1852–1926) in Barcelona, the centre of a distinctive regional version of the style characterized by exaggerated bulbous forms. This cosmopolitanism was encouraged by the great international exhibitions that flourished during this period, and the style perhaps reached its apogee at the Paris Exposition Universelle of 1900. It nowhere survived the outbreak of the First World War to any extent, but with its stress on the expressive qualities of form, line, and colour, it played a significant part in shaping modern aesthetic attitudes.

arts, classification of. See APPLIED ART, DECORATIVE ARTS, FINE ARTS, LIBERAL ARTS.

Arts and Crafts movement. A social and aesthetic movement of the late 19th and early 20th centuries that championed good design and craftsmanship at a time of increasing mechanization and mass production. The movement, which was concerned mainly with architecture and the decorative arts, originated in Britain and chiefly flourished there, but it also had a significant impact in several Continental countries and in the USA. It was a very broad, loosely structured movement, embracing numerous strands of thought and practice; for the most serious-minded adherents, it involved fundamental issues about human society, but for others it was little more than a decorative fad. There was no particular style associated with the movement (influences came from many different sources), but there was an emphasis on 'honesty'—on producing products that showed clearly what they were made of and how they worked. This advocacy of simplicity and integrity often involved emphasizing plain materials and surfaces, an approach that has had a lasting influence on modern design.

The movement's name derives from the Arts and Crafts Exhibition Society, founded in 1888, but its origins go back to the 1850s, particularly to the ideas of John *Ruskin, who was the most eloquent and influential of the writers who deplored the aesthetic as well as the social effects of industrialization. He hated the type of highly decorated, machine-made products that dominated the *Great Exhibition (1851) and believed that the beauty of medieval art sprang from pride in individual craftsmanship. His ideas greatly influenced William *Morris, who wrote that art was 'man's expression of his joy in labour' and believed that good design could help create a better society. Through the decorative arts firm he established in 1861, Morris set about the re-creation of hand industry in a machine age, producing textiles, printed books, wallpaper, furniture, and so forth. Aesthetically his work was a triumph, and his firm was a commercial success, but his ideal of producing art for the masses failed for the simple reason that only rich people could afford his products. Nevertheless, his ideas had great influence on craftsmen, teachers, and propagandists, and in the 1880s various organizations were founded to promote Arts and Crafts ideas, including the Art Workers' Guild (1884), which aimed to increase understanding and collaboration between different branches of the visual arts. Walter *Crane was one of the leading figures of the Guild. The movement had passed its peak in Britain by the time of the First World War, but its ideas continued to be influential, for example on Eric *Gill. Outside Britain, the movement had a particularly strong impact in Austria, notably on the *Wiener Werkstätte.

Arts Council. An organization established in 1945 and incorporated by Royal Charter in 1946 'to preserve and improve standards of performance in the various arts'. It was a successor to the Council for the Encouragement of Music and the Arts (CEMA), a wartime organization that had operated from 1940 to 1945. Originally it was called the Arts Council of Great Britain, with separate committees for Scotland and Wales, but in 1994 the Scottish and Welsh Arts Councils became autonomous bodies and the main organization was renamed the Arts Council of England. There is also an Arts Council of Northern Ireland (likewise a successor to CEMA), and the Republic of Ireland has its own Arts Council, founded in 1951. In the visual arts, the main activity of the Arts Council consists of the organization of exhibitions, many of which are accompanied by scholarly catalogues. It has two galleries in London for such exhibitions: the Hayward Gallery, part of the South Bank arts complex alongside the Thames—a large, rather grim concrete building opened in 1968; and the much smaller and prettier Serpentine Gallery in Kensington Gardens, which was originally an Edwardian tea-house and was opened as a gallery in 1970. Many exhibitions travel to other venues in Britain. The Arts Council inherited from CEMA the policy of purchasing works by living artists and it has built up a large collection of 20th-century British art. In 2003 the sculpture it owns was moved to the Yorkshire Sculpture Park, near Wakefield. The rest of the collection does not have a permanent home, but works are often loaned to public institutions. The Arts Council also makes grants directly to artists and galleries. It is one of the most important sources of art patronage in Britain, but it is frequently attacked for alleged shortcomings, including too much bureaucracy and too little vision.

Art Students League of New York. An art school established in 1875 when that of the *National Academy of Design temporarily closed. Unlike the Academy School (which reopened in 1877), the Art Students League had no entrance requirements and no set course. Its more progressive methods soon attracted many students—by the turn of the century the enrolment stood at nearly 1,000 and it was established as the most important art school in the country. The teachers have included *Benton, *Chase, *Eakins, *Henri, *Saint-Gaudens, and *Sloan; and the students have included many of the most illustrious figures in 20th-century American art.

Arundel, Thomas Howard, 2nd Earl of (*b* Finchingfield, Essex, 7 July 1585; *d* Padua, 4 Oct. 1646). English diplomat, collector, and patron. Apart from Charles I, he was the greatest English collector of his time. His knowledge of art was based partly on extensive travels in Europe, his most important journey being made with Inigo *Jones in 1613–14. His agents sought out antiquities from all over Europe and even the Levant. He also patronized living artists, notably *Rubens and van *Dyck (both of whom painted him), and he brought *Hollar to England in 1636. Among the Old Masters, he was particularly interested in *Holbein, whose *Christina, Duchess of Milan* (1538, NG, London) he owned. Arundel became bankrupt in 1639, leading to the break-up of his collections; they are now widely dispersed, but much of his classical sculpture is in the *Ashmolean Museum, Oxford.

Asam, Cosmas Damian (*bapt.* Benediktbeuren, 28 Sept. 1686; *d* Munich, 10 May 1739) and **Egid Quirin** (*bapt.* Tegernsee, 1 Sept. 1692; *d* Mannheim, 29 Apr. 1750). German architects and decorators, brothers. They had their first training from their father, the painter **Hans Georg Asam** (1649–1711). After his death, Cosmas Damian spent three years studying in Rome (1711–14); it is generally assumed that Egid Quirin accompanied him, although there is no documentary evidence for this. Cosmas Damian was a fresco painter; Egid Quirin also painted, but he was primarily a sculptor and *stuccoist. Both brothers also worked as architects. They

did much of their work as a team, specializing in the interior decoration of churches—uniting architecture, painting, and sculpture in a sumptuous display and developing the dramatic effects of light and illusionism pioneered by Italian *Baroque artists such as *Bernini and *Pozzo. The best known of their churches is that of St John Nepomuk, Munich (1733–46). The brothers themselves paid for the building (which was attached to Egid Quirin's house), and it is often referred to simply as the 'Asamkirche'. It is a fairly small building but creates an overpowering feeling of religious fervour. Apart from their native Bavaria, they worked in other parts of Germany and also in Austria, Switzerland, Bohemia, and Silesia.

Ashcan School. A term (first used in print in 1934) applied to a loose group of American painters active in New York from about 1908 until the First World War, in reference to the everyday urban subject matter they favoured. The painters embraced by the term were inspired largely by Robert *Henri (one of whose dictums was that 'Art cannot be separated from life'), and the four central figures—*Glackens, *Luks, *Shinn, and *Sloan—had been members of The *Eight, a short-lived group founded by Henri in 1908. (The two terms are often confused, but 'The Eight' has a precise meaning, whereas 'Ashcan School' is a broader and vaguer notion; there is overlap between them, but some of the members of The Eight did not paint Ashcan-type subjects.) Before settling in New York, the four central Ashcan artists had all been artist-reporters on the *Philadelphia Press* and so had been used to making rapid sketches of scenes of everyday life. In style and technique, however, they are now seen to have differed less from contemporary academic painting than they themselves believed. Although they often painted slum life and outcasts, they were interested more in the picturesque aspects of these subjects than in the social issues they raised. *Bellows and *Hopper are among the other artists associated with the group.

Ashmolean Museum, Oxford. The most important of the museums belonging to the University of Oxford. It is named after the antiquary Elias Ashmole (1617–92), who in 1675 offered his collection to the university as a gesture of 'filial respect'. The collection had been largely formed by John Tradescant the Elder (*c.*1570–1638) and his son John the Younger (1608–62), gardeners and travellers. They assembled a remarkable 'closet of rarities' (a collection of curiosities rather than works of art), which John the Younger gave to his friend Ashmole in 1659. Ashmole stipulated that a building should be erected to house the collection, and this was constructed in 1679–83, probably to the design of Thomas Wood, a local mason and sculptor (although it has sometimes been groundlessly attributed to Christopher Wren). When it opened in 1683 it was the first public museum in Britain.

Throughout most of the 18th century the museum was neglected, but it began to receive more attention in the early 19th century, as did other collections of objects that had come into the university's possession in various ways—often through the bequests of former students like Ashmole. It was decided to create a new and much larger museum to house them, and this—an impressive Neoclassical building, designed by C. R. Cockerell—opened in 1845; at this time it was known as the University Galleries. The new museum soon attracted additional bequests, including a collection of 40 Italian paintings (among them *Uccello's celebrated *Hunt in the Forest*) presented in 1850 by William Fox-Strangways (1795–1865), later 4th Earl of Ilchester; he had spent several years in Italy during his career as a diplomat and the pictures he bought there were mainly of the 14th and 15th centuries—a period of Italian art which at this time was much less fashionable than the later years of the Renaissance. An extension to the building was opened in 1894, and the institution was renamed the Ashmolean Museum in 1899. In 1908 it was formally titled the Ashmolean Museum of Art and Archaeology; the original building is now known as the 'Old Ashmolean Building' and houses the Museum of the History of Science.

Little of the Tradescant–Ashmole collection remains in the Ashmolean, having been distributed to other institutions (the famous stuffed dodo that was an inspiration to Lewis Carroll in *Alice in Wonderland* is now in the University Museum, opened in 1860, which is devoted to natural history). The Ashmolean has four departments—Western Art, Eastern Art, Antiquities, and Coins—and has great riches in all of them. Among the antiquities are marbles from the collection formed by Lord *Arundel in the 17th century, and the Old Master drawings include a superlative representation of *Michelangelo and *Raphael from the collection of Sir Thomas *Lawrence.

Aspertini, Amico (*b* Bologna, *c*.1475; *d* Bologna, ?19 Nov. 1552). Italian *Mannerist painter, sculptor, and draughtsman, the best-known member of a family of artists. *Vasari describes him as 'a capricious man with a strange personality' and his unconventionality comes out in his paintings, which are often bizarre in expression: *The Holy Family with Saints* (St Nicolas-aux-Champs, Paris) is described by S. J. Freedberg (*Painting in Italy: 1500–1600*, 1971) as 'suggesting to the spectator the image of what he would expect from a demented Michelangelo'. Aspertini spent several years in Rome and two sketchbooks of Roman remains by him (BM, London) are important sources about contemporary knowledge of the *antique.

Asselyn (or **Asselijn**), **Jan** (*b* Dieppe, *c*.1615; *bur.* Amsterdam, 3 Oct. 1652). Dutch painter of French descent, active mainly in Amsterdam. He spent several years in Italy in the late 1630s and early 1640s and came to specialize in real and imaginary scenes of the Roman Campagna, his glowing light effects owing much to *Claude. His most famous painting, however, is not a landscape, but *The Threatened Swan* (*c*.1650, Rijksmuseum, Amsterdam), an unusual work—showing a bird defending its nest against a dog—that is said to be an allegory of Dutch nationalism (inscriptions added by an unknown hand identify one of the swan's eggs as 'Holland' and the dog as 'the enemy of the state'). Because of a crippled hand Asselyn was nicknamed Crabbetje (little crab). His friend *Rembrandt made an etched portrait of him (*c*.1647) in which he hid the deformed hand through the position of the arm.

assemblage. Term coined by Jean *Dubuffet in 1953 to describe a type of work made from fragments of natural or preformed materials, such as household debris. Some critics maintain that the term should apply only to three-dimensional found material and not to *collage, but it is not usually employed with precision and has been used to embrace *photomontage at one extreme and room *environments at the other. It gained wide currency with an exhibition called 'The Art of Assemblage' held at the Museum of Modern Art, New York, in 1961. The exhibits included *ready-mades by Marcel *Duchamp, boxed constructions by Joseph *Cornell, 'sacking' pictures by *Burri, compressed automobile bodies by *César, tableaux by *Kienholz, collages by a wide range of artists, sculptures by *Nevelson and *Tinguely, and much else besides.

Ast, Balthasar van der (*b* Middelburg, *c*.1594; *bur.* Delft, 19 Dec. 1657). Dutch still-life painter, the brother-in-law of Ambrosius *Bosschaert the Elder, with whom he trained in Middelburg. He worked in Utrecht (where he influenced the early work of Jan Davidsz. de *Heem) before settling in Delft in 1632. His touch was less exquisite than Bosschaert's, but his range was wider, his paintings often including fruit and shells as well as flowers. Because of some similarity in brushwork, it has been suggested that Van der Ast may have been the teacher of *Vermeer.

atelier. French term for an artist's workshop or studio. The term 'ateliers libres' was sometimes applied to the private *académies that became centres for avant-garde art in 19th-century Paris.

Atl, Dr (Gerardo Murillo) (*b* Guadalajara, 3 Oct. 1875; *d* Mexico City, 14 Aug. 1964). Mexican painter and art administrator. He was an ardent nationalist and a key figure in the 20th-century renaissance of his country's art. He travelled and studied in Europe, 1897–1903, obtained a doctoral degree in philosophy and law at Rome in 1898, and adopted the name Atl—an Aztec word for 'water'—in 1902. After his return to Mexico he became a teacher at the Academy of San Carlos in Mexico City, where his pupils included *Orozco, *Rivera, and *Siqueiros. In the 1920s he held a government post in which he promoted the mural decoration of public buildings that was Mexico's greatest contribution to 20th-century art. He painted murals himself, but his talent in this field was modest, and as an artist he is better known for his landscapes, particularly those featuring volcanoes, a subject in which he was passionately interested. He often worked in 'Atl-colour' (a kind of wax crayon). Late in life—already a semi-legendary figure—he became a recluse.

Atlan, Jean-Michel (*b* Constantine, Algeria, 23 Jan. 1913; *d* Paris, 12 Feb. 1960). French painter, lithographer, and poet of Jewish-Berber stock. He settled in Paris in 1930, took a degree in philosophy at the Sorbonne, and was self-taught as an artist. His early work was violently expressionistic and semi-figurative, but after the Second World War he developed an abstract style featuring rhythmical forms in deep, rich colours, often enhanced by thick black outlines. Initially he was successful in this idiom, but from 1948 he went through a period of neglect and poverty. His fortunes were re-established with a one-man show at the Galerie Bing, Paris, in 1956, and thereafter his work was widely exhibited in France and elsewhere.

atlas (plural: atlantes). A sculpted male figure functioning as a column or other supporting feature in architecture, particularly popular in the *Baroque period. In Greek mythology, Atlas was the giant who held up the sky, and atlantes are often depicted so as to suggest the strain of carrying a huge weight on the shoulders. The female equivalent—the *caryatid—is, in contrast, usually shown standing serenely upright.

atmospheric perspective. An alternative term for *aerial perspective.

attributes. Objects conventionally associated with a person (real or imaginary) by means of which he or she can be identified when portrayed in art. Saints are often shown with the instruments of their martyrdom or torture— Catherine with her wheel and Lawrence with his gridiron, for instance. Other examples are Jove's thunderbolts, the club of Hercules, the scales of Justice, or the anchor of Hope. While some of these were used widely and in many contexts, other attributes were more variable, and in certain periods the invention of esoteric or enigmatic attributes was rife.

attribution. A term in art history and criticism for the assignment to an artist of a work of uncertain authorship. Attributions are sometimes made on the evidence of documents. A painting of unknown authorship may, for example, be found to accord with a description in an inventory where the artist is named, and depending on how closely particularized the description is, it may be a likely assumption that the two are one and the same. More usually, however, attribution depends on stylistic evidence, and is based on the notion that an artist, consciously or unconsciously, expresses his individuality through his work to such an extent that, to the expert eye, not even his closest contemporary or most talented imitator will be indistinguishable from him. Given a work that is authenticated beyond reasonable doubt by external evidence such as signatures, contracts, or contemporary accounts, we can therefore proceed to group around it works of a similar character and attribute them to the same master.

In the 19th century an attempt was made to put attribution on a scientific footing by closely studying small points of detail such as the way a painter represents fingernails, but although this kind of system (advocated particularly by Giovanni *Morelli) has its uses, it is now felt that we recognize the work of individual artists more by the general effect than by details, and that the details rather than the general effect are what an imitator will be able to reproduce most closely. Attribution, then, is necessarily a highly subjective business, which explains why experts so often disagree and not infrequently change their minds (Bernard *Berenson, the most famous of all connoisseurs, often changed his attributions in the course of his long career). The uncertainty of attribution can have important financial as well as scholarly consequences, even now that the days are gone when the certificate of authenticity of a man such as Berenson could add several noughts to the price of a painting. Moreover, disputes over the authenticity of prominent (which usually means expensive) works of art are one of the few ways in which art becomes a public issue. George de *La Tour's *Fortune-Teller* (which some people consider to be a fake) has been the subject of television documentaries on both sides of the Atlantic, and in 1982 its publicity-conscious owner (the Metropolitan Museum of Art in New York) billed it as 'the world's most controversial painting'.

Various terms are used in connection with attribution, rarely with any precision. 'Ascription' is sometimes used as a synonym for attribution, but some writers prefer to use it to imply a greater degree of doubt (it is often found in the expression 'tentatively ascribed to') or to indicate an old but not firmly accepted attribution. When a work is described as 'autograph' it is thought to be entirely the work of the artist named. The terms 'studio (or workshop) of', 'school of', and 'circle of' all imply that the work was done in more or less close contact with the artist named, but 'follower of' and 'imitator of' may be much later in date; 'manner of' implies only a general stylistic relationship. Auction rooms and dealers have for about 200 years used a system to catalogue works whereby the use of an artist's full name indicates that the work in question is 'in our opinion a work by the artist', the use of his surname and initials indicates that the work is from the artist's period and 'may be in whole or part the work of the artist', and the use of his surname alone may imply no more than that the work is in the style of the artist. Thus a painting catalogued simply 'Rubens' may be no more than a modern pastiche. In saleroom and other contexts, the term 'after' indicates a copy of a known work of the artist in question.

Aubusson tapestries. Tapestries produced at Aubusson in central France. Production of

tapestries began there in the 16th century and its greatest period was the second half of the 18th century, when large quantities of hangings and furniture coverings were woven with pastoral and *chinoiserie designs by *Oudry, *Boucher, and *Huet. During the 19th century skilful reproductions of earlier pieces were made, and in the 20th century it was in the forefront of modern tapestry design, notably through the work of Jean *Lurçat.

Audran, Claude III (*b* Lyons, 25 Aug. 1658; *d* Paris, 28 May 1734). The best-known member of a family of French painters and decorators. He was one of the leading decorative painters of the time, his output including such things as painted panelling and harpsichord cases, but most of his work has been destroyed or obscured by later additions. A great number of drawings survive, however (mainly in the Nationalmuseum, Stockholm), and these show him to have been a significant figure in the creation of the *Rococo style. In 1704 he was appointed curator at the Luxembourg Palace, Paris, where *Rubens's Marie de Médicis cycle was then housed, and he introduced his assistant *Watteau to this masterpiece by an artist who was to have an enormous influence on his work.

Audubon, John James (*b* Les Cayes, 26 Apr. 1785; *d* New York, 27 Jan. 1851). American painter-naturalist. Born in the French colony of Saint-Domingue (now Haiti), the illegitimate son of a chambermaid and a French sea captain, he was brought up in France and received instruction in drawing from J.-L. *David. He moved to the USA in 1803 to avoid conscription in Napoleon's army and lived as a naturalist, hunter, and taxidermist, also earning some money as a portraitist and drawing master. His combined interests in art and ornithology grew into a plan to make a complete pictorial record of all the bird species of North America. Unable to find a publisher in America, Audubon spent three years in England (1826–9) and found an engraver and publisher in the London firm of Robert Havell and Son. His *The Birds of America, from Original Drawings, with 435 Plates Showing 1,065 Figures* appeared in four volumes of hand-tinted aquatints (1827–38) and now ranks among the most famous and prized books of the world. It was followed by *The Viviparous Quadrupeds of America* (1845–8), which was completed by his son **John Woodhouse Audubon** (1812–62) after the master's sight failed in 1846. His other son, **Victor Gifford Audubon** (1809–60), also assisted his father. Many of Audubon's original drawings are in the New-York Historical Society. See also BE-WICK.

Auerbach, Frank (*b* Berlin, 29 Apr. 1931). German-born painter who moved to England in 1939 as a refugee from Nazism and became a British citizen in 1947. He studied under David *Bomberg, whom he found an inspiring teacher. His work (characteristically nudes and town-scapes) is in the *Expressionist vein of Bom-berg's late paintings and is remarkable for its use of extreme *impasto, so thick that the paint at times seems modelled rather than brushed. He has a reputation as one of the leading British painters of his time, although some critics find his pictures muddy and over-worked.

Augustus III, King of Poland. See GEMÄLDE-GALERIE.

Ault, George. See PRECISIONISM.

Auto-Destructive art. A term applied to works deliberately intended to self-destruct. Works of art that are inherently short-lived are found in various ages and cultures—witness the butter sculptures of Tibet, the sand paintings of some North American Indian tribes, and the snowman made by the young *Michelangelo for Piero de' *Medici. However, the idea of using self-destruction as the point of a work did not emerge until the late 1950s. The most com-mitted exponent of the genre has been the German-born Gustav Metzger (1926–), who originated the term and wrote several mani-festos on the subject, the first in 1959, when he was living in England. From 1960 he gave public demonstrations in which he 'painted' with acid, spraying it on nylon cloth, creating rapidly changing patterns until the nylon was destroyed. Such displays have been interpreted as expres-sions of fatalism at the impermanence of all things and as protests against consumerism. Metzger himself maintained that he was protest-ing against arms expenditure. He also believed that Auto-Destructive art could provide an ac-ceptable channel for human aggression. Among those who are said to have been influenced by his ideas is the rock musician Pete Townshend, whose stage act with his group the Who used to include smashing guitars. Apart from Metzger, the artist most associated with Auto-Destructive art is Jean *Tinguely, whose approach was very different, stressing fancifulness and humour.

automatism. Method of producing paintings or drawings (or writing or other work) in which the artist suppresses conscious control over the movements of the hand, allowing the uncon-scious mind to take over; more broadly, the term can be applied to working procedures that embrace chance, improvisation, and free association. Automatism is mainly a modern phenomenon, but it has various precedents, most notably the 'blot drawings' of Alexander *Cozens, who stimulated his imagination by using accidental blots on the paper to suggest landscape forms. Cozens remarks that *Leo-nardo da Vinci had proposed a similar method and quotes him as saying: 'If you look upon an old wall covered with dirt, or the odd appear-ance of some streaked stones, you may discover several things like landscapes, battles, clouds, uncommon attitudes, humorous faces, draper-ies, &c. Out of this confused mass of objects, the mind will be furnished with abundance of designs and subjects perfectly new.' Slightly before Leonardo, Leon Battista *Alberti (in his treatise *De statua, c.*1460) gives an imaginative account of the origins of sculpture, describing ancient peoples observing 'in tree trunks, clumps of earth, or other objects of this sort, certain outlines which through some slight changes could be made to resemble a natural shape'. Alberti's version of events may be not far from the truth, for scholars of prehistoric art have found examples of such spontaneous dis-covery of representational images in chance nat-ural formations of cave walls.

In its fully developed form, however, automa-tism did not appear until the 20th century. The *Dadaists made some use of the idea, but they were more interested in chance effects than in automatism as such, and it was the *Surrealists who first made automatism an important part of their creative outlook; whereas the Dadaists used the idea dispassionately, to the Surrealists exploration of the unconscious through such methods was deeply personal. They devised various means to facilitate automatism (see DE-CALCOMANIA and FROTTAGE, for example) and some of them regarded the use of dream im-agery (as in the work of *Dalí) as a kind of psychological—as opposed to mechanical—au-tomatism. The Surrealist interest in automatism had a strong influence on the *Abstract Expres-sionists, some of whom took their ideas further. With Surrealists, once an image had been formed by automatic or chance means, it was often exploited deliberately with fully conscious purpose, but with *Action Painters such as Jack-son *Pollock, automatism in principal perme-ated the whole creative process.

Other types of automatism are those in which the artist works under the influence of drugs or by alleged occult means. The offbeat British painter Austin Spare (1886–1956) claimed to be able to conjure up horrific survivals of man's pre-human ancestry from deep within his mind, but more usually the artist is said to work under the inspiration of a beneficent spirit guide (a notion not necessarily to be taken lightly, as no less an artist than William *Blake claimed to have direct inspiration from his dead brother). Unlike Blake, most psychic artists of this kind have no particular artistic gifts or inclinations in their 'normal' life.

Automatistes, Les. A radical group of seven Canadian abstract painters active in Montreal from 1946 to 1951. The oldest of them, mainly responsible for the formation of the group, was Paul-Émile *Borduas, and the other outstanding member was Jean-Paul *Riopelle. Members of the group were influenced by the *Surrealists, from whom they took over their techniques of *automatism. Their first exhibition, in 1946, was the first exhibition by a group of abstract painters to be held in Canada. In 1948 they caused outrage by publishing *Refus global* (Total Refusal), an anarchistic manifesto attacking various aspects of Canadian life and culture, including the Church.

avant-garde. A term originally used to describe the foremost part of an army advancing into battle (also called the vanguard) and now applied to any group, particularly of artists, that considers itself innovative and ahead of the majority; as an adjective, the word is applied to work characteristic of such groups. In its original sense the term is first recorded in English in the late 15th century (in Malory's *Morte d'Arthur*). During the 19th century, it was associated particularly with radical political thought, but from the early 20th century it was used more neutrally to denote cultural innovators of any persuasion; the earliest quotation in the *Oxford English Dictionary* to illustrate this sense ('the pioneers or innovators in any art in a particular period') dates from 1910.

Avanzo. See ALTICHIERO.

Aved, Jacques (*b* Douai, 12 Jan. 1702; *d* Paris, 4 Mar. 1766). French portrait painter. He was brought up in Amsterdam and earned the nickname Camelot (pedlar) because in his youth he is said to have drawn portraits at travelling fairs in the Netherlands. In 1721 he moved to Paris, where he became one of the leading portraitists of the day, especially favoured by middle-class sitters, whom he often showed in the activities of everyday life. The naturalism and directness of his style shows a move away from the florid manner of *Largillière and reflects both his Dutch background and his friendship with *Chardin. His best-known portrait is perhaps *Mme Crozat* (1741, Mus. Fabre, Montpellier), which was attributed to Chardin in the 19th century. A portrait of Aved by Chardin (1734) is in the Louvre. His success made him wealthy enough to form a distinguished art collection.

Avercamp, Hendrick (*bapt.* Amsterdam, 25 Jan. 1585; *bur.* Kampen, 15 May 1634). Dutch painter and draughtsman, active in Kampen, the most famous exponent of the winter landscape, which he established as a distinct category in Dutch art. He was deaf and dumb and known as de Stomme van Kampen (the mute of Kampen). His paintings are colourful and lively, with carefully observed skaters, tobogganers, golfers, and pedestrians. Such works enjoyed great popularity and Avercamp also sold his drawings, many of which are tinted with watercolour, as finished pictures (an outstanding collection is at Windsor Castle). His nephew and pupil **Barent Avercamp** (1612–79) carried on his style in an accomplished manner.

Avery, Milton (*b* Altmar, NY, 7 Mar. 1885; *d* New York, 3 Jan. 1965). American painter, active mainly in New York. (His date of birth is usually given as 1893, but there is good evidence to indicate that he was born in 1885; it was possibly to improve his chances in courting his wife, who was appreciably younger than him, that he deducted eight years from his age.) Avery was an independent figure, described by Robert *Hughes as 'a mild, unassuming man who disliked publicity and at best made a bare living from his work'. At a time when most of his leading contemporaries were working in fairly sober, naturalistic styles (see AMERICAN SCENE PAINTING), he followed the example of *Matisse in using flat areas of colour within flowing outlines. He was the main and practically only channel through which this subtle colouristic tradition was sustained in America until a new interest was taken in it during the 1940s by younger artists such as *Rothko (his close friend) and *Gottlieb. Rothko in particular acknowledged the debt that he and other abstract painters owed to the 'sheer loveliness' of Avery's work, in which he had 'invented sonorities never seen nor heard before'. Although Avery himself never abandoned representation (his favourite subjects included landscapes and beach scenes), some of his later works are so broadly conceived and ethereally painted that they can at first glance be mistaken for abstracts (*Spring Orchard*, 1959, Nat. Mus. of American Art, Washington).

Avignon, School of. Tradition of painting associated with the city of Avignon in southern France, originating during the period when the papal court was transferred there because of anarchic conditions in Rome (1309–77). The presence of this great source of patronage drew many artists to the city, including illustrious Italian masters, among them Simone *Martini and possibly *Giotto. The centre of artistic activities was the Palace of the Popes, begun in the 1330s, which has several frescos dating from around 1350. After the departure of the popes, Avignon became the centre of a school of painting that amalgamated Italian with Netherlandish influences, notably in the work of Enguerrand *Quarton and Nicolas *Froment. The famous *Pietà* from Villeneuve-lès-Avignon (*c*.1460, Louvre, Paris), is now generally attributed to Quarton, but many works that were at one time attributed to the School of Avignon have since been reassigned and it is no longer a clearly defined stylistic entity.

Aycock, Alice. See LAND ART.

Ayres, Gillian. See SITUATION.

Ayrton, Michael (*b* London, 20 Feb. 1921; *d* London, 17 Nov. 1975). British painter, sculptor, theatre designer, book illustrator, writer on art, and broadcaster. His career was often marred by ill health, but he travelled widely and had a long and varied list of works to his credit. He was an erudite, inventive, and highly individual artist, much of whose work revolved around his obsession with the myth of Daedalus and Icarus, which he treated as analogous to his own artistic endeavours. The most extreme expression of his obsession is the enormous maze of brick and stone (1968) he built for an American millionaire at Arkville in New York State, imitating the labyrinth Daedalus built for King Minos of Crete at Knossos. He wrote several books, including *The Testament of Daedalus* (1962), and illustrated many others. From 1944 to 1946 he was art critic of the *Spectator* (succeeding John *Piper), in which position he was a leading spokesman for *Neo-Romanticism, and at about the same time he became a regular radio broadcaster on art (he also appeared often in the BBC's *Round Britain Quiz*).

B

Baburen, Dirck van (*b* Wijk bij Duurstede, nr. Utrecht, ?*c*.1595; *d* Utrecht, 21 Feb. 1624). Dutch figure painter, mainly of religious scenes. He is first documented in 1611, in Utrecht, where he was a pupil of *Moreelse. Soon afterwards he moved to Italy, where he stayed until about 1620, mainly in Rome. During this time his style became strongly influenced by *Caravaggio, and his patrons included Cardinal Scipione *Borghese and Marchese Vincenzo *Giustiniani, both of whom were important collectors of Caravaggio's work. His most prestigious commission in Rome was an altarpiece of the *Entombment* (?1617) for the church of S. Pietro in Montorio (*in situ*); more than a dozen copies of the painting are known, dating from the 17th century to the 19th century, showing the high regard it long enjoyed; in his *Cicerone* (1855), Jacob *Burckhardt compared it favourably with Caravaggio's famous painting of the subject (1602–4, Pinacoteca, Vatican), on which it is clearly based. Baburen returned to the Netherlands in about 1620 and although he died only a few years after this, he played a leading role, with *Honthorst and *Terbrugghen, in establishing Utrecht as a stronghold of the Caravaggesque style (see UTRECHT CARAVAGGISTI). His best-known work is *The Procuress* (1622, MFA, Boston). This picture is seen in the background of two paintings by *Vermeer, whose mother-in-law evidently owned it.

Baciccio, Il. See GAULLI.

Backer, Jacob (*b* Harlingen, *c*.1608; *d* Amsterdam, 27 Aug. 1651). Dutch portrait and history painter, active mainly in Amsterdam, where he had a prosperous career. The tradition (stemming from *Houbraken) that he was a pupil of *Rembrandt is now doubted, but his work was certainly strongly influenced by him; indeed, attributions have sometimes been disputed between them (see BOL). His best-known painting is the beautiful *Portrait of a Boy in Grey* (1634, Mauritshuis, The Hague). His nephew **Adriaen Backer** (1630/2–84) also had a successful career as a portraitist in Amsterdam.

Baço, Jaime (also called **Master Jacomart**) (*b* Valencia, *c*.1411; *d* Valencia, 16 July 1461). Spanish painter. He was the leading artist of his day in Valencia, working at the court of Alfonso V of Aragon and his son and successor John II. Documents show that he was held in high regard by his royal masters and he twice accompanied Alfonso on military campaigns in Italy. However, little or nothing survives from his own hand. The main work associated with him is a *polyptych of St Lawrence and St Peter in the church at Catí near Valencia, commissioned in 1460, but it is believed to have been executed largely by assistants or collaborators. He had a frequent collaborator called Juan Rexach (active 1431–84) and also seems to have worked with a painter called Pere Rexach (active 1452–72), who was presumably related to Juan.

Bacon, Francis (*b* Dublin, 28 Oct. 1909; *d* Madrid, 28 Apr. 1992). British painter, born in Ireland of English parents, a collateral descendant of the Elizabethan statesman and writer of the same name. His father, a racehorse trainer, was a puritanical figure and sent his son away from home when he was 16 after he was discovered trying on some of his mother's underwear. He spent about two months in Berlin and then about eighteen months in Paris (where he was powerfully impressed by an exhibition of *Picasso's work in 1928) before settling in London in 1929. Initially he made a living there designing furniture and rugs, and he had no formal training as a painter. In the 1930s he began exhibiting in London commercial galleries, but he destroyed much of his early work and dropped out of sight until 1945, when his *Three Studies for Figures at the Base of a Crucifixion* (Tate, London), painted in the previous year, was exhibited at the Lefevre Gallery, London, and made him overnight the most controversial painter in the country. John Russell (*Francis Bacon*, 1971) writes that visitors to the exhibition were shocked by 'images so unrelievedly awful that the mind shut snap at the sight of them. Their anatomy was half-human, half-animal, and they were confined in a low-ceilinged, windowless and oddly proportioned space. They could bite, probe, and suck, and they had very long eel-like necks, but their functioning in other respects was mysterious. Ears and mouths they had, but two at least were sightless. One was unpleasantly bandaged.'

Bacon's imagery later became more naturalistic, but at the same time the emotional impact of his work was increased by a change in technique, as he moved away from fairly impersonal brushwork to develop a highly distinctive handling of paint, by means of which he smudged and twisted faces and bodies into ill-defined jumbled protuberances suggestive of formless, sluglike creatures from some nightmare fantasy: 'I would like my pictures to look as if a human being had passed between them, like a snail, leaving a trail of the human presence and memory trace of past events as the snail leaves its slime.' Characteristically his paintings show single figures in isolation or despair, set in a bleak, sometimes cagelike space, and at times accompanied by hunks of raw meat: 'we are all meat, we are potential carcasses.' Often his work was based on his own everyday world (he did numerous self-portraits), but he also used imagery from photographs and film-stills as a starting point. In particular he based a series of paintings (begun in 1951) on *Velázquez's celebrated portrait of Pope Innocent X, but in place of the implacable expression of the original, he sometimes gave the pope a screaming face derived from a still from Sergei Eisenstein's film *The Battleship Potemkin*.

Bacon's work was so novel and unsettling that for many years 'Critics and public vacillated uneasily between the opinions that he was a flashy sensationalist and that he was the most significant painter whom Britain had produced for several generations' (John *Rothenstein, *Francis Bacon*, 1967). In 1962, however, a retrospective exhibition of 90 of his paintings was held at the Tate Gallery, London, subsequently touring to several venues on the Continent, and this event firmly established him as a major figure. Thereafter his international reputation grew rapidly, and in the catalogue of a second major retrospective exhibition at the Tate, in 1985, the director of the Gallery, Alan Bowness, wrote that Bacon was 'surely the greatest living painter; no artist in our century has presented the human predicament with such insight and feeling'. Many critics at the time concurred in this judgement, although others found his despairing vision—his view of life as a 'game with-

out reason'—hard to take. Alongside his reputation as a painter he built up a sulphurous personal legend on account of his promiscuous homosexuality, hard drinking, and heavy gambling. In spite of the huge amount of attention he has attracted, his work has had comparatively little stylistic effect on his contemporaries, for it is so personal that it has been difficult for other artists to absorb it without producing a mere pastiche. However, his obituary in *The Times* commented that 'His influence on younger artists during the 1950s and 1960s was very considerable—not stylistically, for he had few imitators—but through his attitude to his work and the sense he gave of the ultimate seriousness of art.'

Bacon, John (*b* London, 24 Nov. 1740; *d* London, 7 Aug. 1799). English sculptor. His style was essentially *Neoclassical, but he had none of the intellectual interest in the *antique that characterized contemporaries such as *Banks and *Flaxman (unlike them, Bacon never visited Italy). He began his career as a modeller in a porcelain factory and this experience left a permanent mark on him, as his work, even in marble, tends to be soft in feeling, often with much pretty detail. His large output consisted mainly of church monuments, but also included numerous statues and portrait busts. In addition he worked as chief designer to the *Coade artificial stone company from 1771. His career was helped by the favouritism of George III, of whom he produced a portrait in 1774 (Windsor Castle and other versions), and one of his most conspicuous works is *George III and the River Thames* (1780–6) in the courtyard of Somerset House, London (this is unusual in being in bronze at a time when English sculptors favoured marble almost exclusively for monumental work). The king helped him to gain the commission for his largest work, the monument to William Pitt, Earl of Chatham (1779–83), in Westminster Abbey. His finest work is the much smaller and more intimate monument to Thomas Guy (1779) in Guy's Hospital, showing the founder of the hospital succouring a sick man. Bacon ran a large workshop, whose efficiency was aided by an improved *pointing machine he devised. The practice was carried on by his son **John the Younger** (1777–1859).

Bacon, Sir Nathaniel (*b* 1585; *d* ?Culford, Suffolk, 1 July 1627). The first English amateur painter of note. He was a high-born country gentleman, nephew of the Lord Chancellor Francis Bacon. Fewer than a dozen paintings by him are known; with the exception of a miniature landscape on copper in the manner of *Bril, which has been claimed as the earliest British landscape (Ashmolean Mus., Oxford), they are either portraits (mainly of members of his family) or kitchen still-lifes (*Cookmaid with Still-Life of Vegetables and Fruit*, c.1625, Tate, London). His ambitious full-length self-portrait (c.1620, Gorhambury, Hertfordshire) displays a more coherent realization of space, greater subtlety of colouring, and sharper characterization than had hitherto been achieved in English portraiture and shows he was the equal of *Mytens or Cornelius *Johnson, the leading portraitists in England before the arrival of van *Dyck.

Badile, Antonio. See VERONESE.

'Bad Painting'. See NEO-EXPRESSIONISM.

Baen, Jan de (b Haarlem, 20 Feb. 1633; bur. The Hague, 8 Mar. 1702). Dutch painter, one of his country's most successful portraitists in the later 17th century. He was a pupil of Jacob *Backer, but van *Dyck's works were the main influence on his elegant style. In 1660 he settled in The Hague and there became the leading portrait painter of the House of Orange. He also worked for Charles II of England (he probably visited England in the early 1660s) and Frederick William I, Elector of Brandenburg (who tried unsuccessfully to persuade him to move to Berlin), but for patriotic reasons he refused a commission from Louis XIV of France in 1672.

Baerze, Jacques de (active 1380s and 1390s). Netherlandish woodcarver active in Termonde (Dendermonde), near Ghent. His only known surviving works are two altarpieces commissioned by Philip the Bold, Duke of *Burgundy, for the Chartreuse de Champmol at Dijon and now in the Musée des Beaux-Arts there. The more elaborate of the two altarpieces has painted wings (1394–9) by Melchior *Broederlam. De Baerze's style was more conservative than Broederlam's and his flat compositions, dominated by the richly gilded *Gothic framework, make a strong contrast with the solidly three-dimensional style of his great contemporary Claus *Sluter. However, Sluter was part of the committee that judged the altarpieces favourably.

Baglione, Giovanni (b Rome, c.1570; d Rome, 30 Dec. 1643). Italian painter and writer. He had a fairly successful career as a painter (mainly of religious works), but his pictures are now virtually forgotten and he is remembered rather as

the author of *Le vite de' pittori, scultori, ed architetti . . .* , published in 1642. This collection of biographies is one of the fundamental sources of information for the period covered (1572–1642); it deals mainly with Italian artists but also discusses foreigners working in Rome, such as *Bril and *Rubens. In 1603 Baglione sued *Caravaggio and three other painters for circulating coarse satirical poems about him. His hatred of Caravaggio comes out in the biography devoted to him in his *Vite*, so it is ironic that his best pictures are his most Caravaggesque (*Judith and Holofernes*, 1608, Borghese Gal., Rome).

Baillairgé. Family of French-Canadian artists (mainly architects and woodcarvers) who were a dominant force in the artistic life of Quebec City in the 18th and 19th centuries. The founder of the dynasty was **Jean Baillairgé** (1726–1805), who emigrated from France in 1741; other members included his son **François** (1759–1830), the outstanding individual, François's son **Thomas** (1791–1859), and Thomas's second cousin (Jean's great-grandson) **Charles** (1826–1906). François studied in Paris, 1778–81, and his elegant style was strongly influenced by contemporary French art. His output was varied, but he is best known for his elaborately carved church interiors, of which one of the finest is that of St Joachim (1816–29) at Montmorency, Quebec province. He said that he wanted his sculpture to be 'as rich, skilful, and natural as possible'.

Baily, Edward Hodges (b Bristol, 10 Mar. 1788; d London, 22 May 1867). English sculptor. The son of a carver of ships' figureheads, he studied with *Flaxman, becoming his favourite pupil, and at the *Royal Academy. His output included a good deal of public sculpture; his two most conspicuous works are also his most inaccessible—the statues at the top of Nelson's Column in Trafalgar Square (1843) and the almost equally tall Grey's Monument in Newcastle upon Tyne (1837). He also produced numerous portrait busts, including many of fellow artists (examples are in the National Portrait Gallery, London), as well as church monuments and ideal figures, notably *Eve at the Fountain* (1822, City AG, Bristol), which was one of the most acclaimed British sculptures of the 19th century. Although he had a busy and successful career, he was extravagant and died bankrupt.

Bakhuizen, Ludolf (b Emden, 28 Dec. 1631; d Amsterdam, 6/7 Nov. 1708). Dutch painter, mainly of marine subjects. He was born in Germany and settled in Amsterdam in about

1650, working initially as a merchant's clerk. He taught calligraphy for a time and put his penmanship to use in drawings of shipping. Later he was taught painting by Allart van *Everdingen. After the van de *Veldes moved to England in 1672/3, he became the most successful marine painter in Holland, his clients including distinguished collectors from other countries, notably Peter the Great of Russia, who visited his studio. He captured the drama and movement of ships, but seldom achieved the poetic effects of either van de Velde the Younger or Jan van de *Cappelle. His grandson **Ludolf Bakhuizen the Younger** (1717–82) imitated his work.

Bakst, Léon (b Grodno, 28 Apr. [10 May] 1866; d Paris, 27 Dec. 1924). Russian painter, graphic artist, and stage designer, active for much of his career in Paris. He was a founder member of the *World of Art group in 1898. Originally he made his reputation as a portraitist, but from about 1902 he turned increasingly to stage design and is now remembered above all for his costumes and sets for *Diaghilev's Ballets Russes, his work playing a major part in the tremendous impact the company made in the West. The Diaghilev ballets for which he made designs include some of the most celebrated works in the history of dance, notably *The Firebird* (1910, music by Stravinsky), *L'Après-midi d'un faune* (1912, music by Debussy), and *Daphnis and Chloe* (1912, music by Ravel). Bakst's work revolutionized stage design. His costumes and sets are remarkable for their sheer uninhibited splendour, combining oriental fairy-tale magnificence with the gaudy colours of Russian peasant art (he believed that colour could have a significant emotional effect on spectators).

baldachin (or **baldacchino**). A canopy over an altar or other hallowed object; it may be portable for use in processions or fixed (either supported on columns or suspended from the ceiling). The most famous baldacchino is *Bernini's huge bronze structure (1624–33) in St Peter's, Rome. This type, with twisted columns and fringed canopy, became popular in *Baroque churches. See also CIBORIUM.

Baldinucci, Filippo (b Florence, 3 June 1625; d Florence, 1 Jan. 1696). Italian writer, collector, and amateur artist. His major work is *Notizie de' professori del disegno* (6 vols., 1681–1728; the last published posthumously), an encyclopedic collection of artists' biographies from *Cimabue to his own time. It constitutes a kind of updating and expansion of *Vasari's *Lives* and is particu-

larly valuable for the information it gives about 16th-century Florentine artists and Baldinucci's contemporaries. He was an innovator as an art historian in making use of every kind of document. Apart from the *Notizie*, his most important work is his biography of *Bernini (1682), the primary source for the artist's life. He wrote several other books, including a history of engraving and etching (1686), which contains one of the earliest accounts of *Rembrandt's life (his information was supplied by Bernhard *Keil, a former pupil of Rembrandt).

Baldovinetti, Alesso (b Florence, ?1425; d Florence, 29 Aug. 1499). Florentine painter, mosaicist, and worker in stained glass. Nothing is recorded of his training, but his graceful and refined style shows strong influence from *Domenico Veneziano, who may well have been his master. Baldovinetti's finest works include a damaged but still enchanting fresco of the *Nativity* (1460–2) in the forecourt of SS. Annunziata, Florence, a *Madonna and Child* (c.1460) in the Louvre, Paris, an *Annunciation* (c.1460) in the Uffizi, Florence, and *Portrait of a Lady in Yellow* (c.1465) in the National Gallery, London. They show his remarkable sensitivity to light and landscape and his engaging blend of naivety and sophistication. In his *History of Italian Renaissance Art* (1970), Frederick Hartt writes that Baldovinetti was 'the finest painter in Florence' in the 1460s, and considers him 'a very gifted master who somehow never quite seemed to fulfil his great initial promise'.

Balduccio, Giovanni di (active 1317/18–49). Italian sculptor. He is first documented in 1317/18, working at Pisa Cathedral, and he was perhaps a pupil there of Giovanni *Pisano. In the 1320s he worked in Bologna, Florence, and elsewhere, and in about 1334 he settled in Milan, where he is last documented in 1349. His most important work is the Shrine of St Peter Martyr (1335–9) in S. Eustorgio, Milan. The Shrine of St Augustine in S. Pietro in Ciel d'Oro, Pavia, is also sometimes attributed to him, although this dates from the 1350s, after his known period of activity. He was an important figure in introducing the style of Nicola and Giovanni Pisano to Lombardy and his work had considerable influence in north Italy.

Baldung (or **Baldung Grien**), **Hans** (b ?Schwäbisch Gmünd, 1484/5; d Strasbourg, Sept. 1545). German painter, printmaker, and designer. The nickname Grien (green) perhaps referred to his liking for the colour (he must have been using the name by 1507, for it is represented by the G in his monogram, which occurs from that year). He probably trained with *Dürer in Nuremberg, but his brilliant colour, expressive use of distortion, and taste for the gruesome (he was fascinated by witchcraft) bring him closer in spirit to his other great German contemporary, *Grünewald. His output was varied and extensive, including religious works, allegories and mythologies, portraits, designs for stained glass and tapestries, and a large body of graphic work, particularly book illustrations. He was active mainly in Strasbourg, but from 1512 to 1517 he lived in Freiburg im Breisgau, where he worked on his masterpiece, the high altar for Freiburg Cathedral (unusually for an artist of the time, he came from a scholarly family and his brother was a professor at Freiburg University). The centre panel of the altarpiece (which is still *in situ*) is a radiant *Coronation of the Virgin*. Baldung's most characteristic paintings, however, are in a different vein—erotic allegories such as *Death and the Maiden*, a subject he treated several times. Eroticism is also often strongly present in his prints (mainly woodcuts), the best known of which is *The Bewitched Stable Boy* (1544), which has been interpreted as an allegory of lust.

Balen, Hendrick van (*b* Antwerp, *c*.1575; *d* Antwerp, 17 July 1632). Flemish *Mannerist painter, active mainly in Antwerp (he spent virtually all his life there apart from a sojourn in Italy in the 1590s). His speciality was mythological scenes painted in the highly finished manner of Jan *Brueghel, one of the numerous artists with whom he collaborated. Van Balen was a popular teacher, his most important pupil being van *Dyck. He also had three painter sons.

Balestra, Antonio. See CIGNAROLI.

Ball, Thomas (*b* Charlestown, Mass., 3 June 1819; *d* Montclair, NJ, 11 Dec. 1911). American sculptor. He began as a painter, but turned to sculpture without formal training in about 1850 and had a successful career with portraits and monuments. Two of his monuments are particularly well known: the equestrian statue of George Washington in Boston's Public Gardens (the plaster was completed in 1861, but the Civil War delayed its casting until 1869) and *Lincoln Freeing the Slaves*, usually known as the 'Emancipation Group' (1875, Lincoln Park, Washington), which was paid for with contributions from freed slaves. 'More than any Lincoln memorial of the time it captured the imagination of the public in its mixture of naturalism and sentimen-

tality' (Milton W. Brown et al., *American Art*, 1979). For much of his career Ball lived in Florence, where he was a friend of Hiram *Powers.

Balla, Giacomo (*b* Turin, 18 July 1871; *d* Rome, 1 Mar. 1958). Italian painter and sculptor, active mainly in Rome, one of the leading *Futurist artists. He visited Paris in 1900–1 and brought back to Italy a feeling for colour and light that he passed on to *Boccioni and *Severini. His early works included landscapes and portraits, but after the turn of the century he became increasingly interested in depicting aspects of modern industrialized life. In 1910 he joined the Futurists and soon became preoccupied with their characteristic aim of portraying movement. Unlike the other Futurists, however, Balla was not interested in machines and violence and his paintings tend towards the lyrical and the witty, as in the delightful *Dynamism of a Dog on a Leash* (1912, Albright-Knox AG, Buffalo), in which the multiple impressions of the dog's legs and tail convey movement in a manner that later became a cartoon convention. In 1913–16 he went beyond the principles of the Futurist manifestos, painting pictures that approach pure abstraction, showing only the most residual resemblance to the observations in reality that inspired them (*Abstract Speed—the Car Has Passed*, 1913, Tate, London). Following the First World War, Balla stayed true to the ideals of Futurism after his colleagues had abandoned them, but in the 1930s he turned to a more conventional style. By the end of his long life he was much admired as the last survivor of a brilliant phase of modern Italian art.

Balthus (Balthazar Klossowski de Rola) (*b* Paris, 29 Feb. 1908; *d* Rossinière, Switzerland, 18 Feb. 2001). French painter (and occasional stage designer), born in Paris of cultured Polish parents, both of whom painted. He had no formal training but was encouraged by the family friends *Derain (of whom Balthus painted a memorable portrait (1936, MoMA, New York)) and *Bonnard. His work was dominated by erotic imagery, his favourite theme being the adolescent girl awakening to sexual consciousness; characteristically these girls are shown languidly sprawled or kneeling awkwardly over books in claustrophobic interiors that have a suggestion of *Surrealist oddness (*The Living Room*, 1941–3, Minneapolis Inst. of Arts). From 1961 to 1977 he was director of the French Academy in Rome, but otherwise he spent most of his life living in seclusion in France or Switzerland. He worked slowly and his output was small, but his highly distinctive images made him internationally famous, indeed something of a cult figure. His work was generally warmly received by critics as well as the public (although some have accused him of having a Lolita complex) and he is widely regarded as one of the 20th century's leading upholders of the great tradition of figure painting.

Bamboccianti. See LAER.

Bandinelli, Baccio (b Florence, 12 Nov. 1493; d Florence, 7 Feb. 1560). Florentine sculptor, painter, and draughtsman. He was a favourite of the *Medici family, but he is remembered more for his belligerent character and the antipathy of his contemporaries than for the quality of his work. His most famous and conspicuous sculpture is *Hercules and Cacus* (1527–34, Piazza della Signoria, Florence), a pendant to *Michelangelo's *David*. The commission had originally been intended for Michelangelo himself, and Bandinelli's ponderous figure, which he had boasted would surpass *David*, was ridiculed by *Cellini and others. Bandinelli had a habit of failing to fulfil his commissions and Cellini's accusations of incompetence had much justification. In return, Bandinelli attempted to sabotage Cellini's career, as he also did with another rival, *Ammanati. Bandinelli was at his best as a draughtsman. His paintings include a pompous self-portrait in the Isabella Stewart Gardner Museum, Boston, and his high opinion of himself also comes out in an account he wrote of his life and career, *Memoriale* (first published 1905).

Banks, Thomas (bapt. London, 22 Dec. 1735; d London, 2 Feb. 1805). English sculptor. He was one of the most serious-minded of British *Neoclassical artists, aiming at noble treatment of elevated subjects. Like-minded contemporaries greatly admired him (*Reynolds called him 'the first British sculptor who has produced works of classic grace' and *Flaxman ranked him alongside *Canova), but he had limited opportunities to produce works in the *antique vein, and he was less successful in worldly terms than his contemporaries John *Bacon and Joseph *Nollekens, who were more in tune with the demands of the market. Banks trained as a mason and ornamental carver, and also studied in the evenings in Peter *Scheemakers's studio. In 1772 he was awarded a *Royal Academy scholarship to Rome, where he remained until 1779. During this period he met *Fuseli, who became a lifelong friend. Back in England, he had little initial success, and in 1781–2 he visited Russia,

hoping for major commissions from Catherine the Great (see HERMITAGE). However, his stay was brief, partly because he disliked the climate. After his return to England, he at last began to prosper, but mainly with church monuments, rather than with classical subjects such as *Thetis Dipping the Infant Achilles in the River Styx* (c.1788, V&A, London); he also produced a few portrait busts. His most famous work is the monument to Penelope Boothby (1793, Ashbourne church, Derbyshire), in which the 6-year-old child is shown sleeping rather than dead; several people, including Queen Charlotte, are said to have been moved to tears when it was shown at the Royal Academy before installation. His larger monuments, however, tend to be somewhat ponderous.

Barbari, Jacopo de' (b ?Venice, active c.1497; d Netherlands, 1511/16). Venetian painter and printmaker. His early career is obscure and he is first documented in 1500 in connection with his huge (nearly 3 m (9 ft) wide) woodcut view of Venice, which had taken three years to complete. Most of his known career was spent in Germany and the Netherlands, where he worked for several royal patrons. His delicate engravings, many of mythological figures, helped to spread the Italian conception of the nude in northern Europe. As a painter he is best known for his *Dead Bird* (1504, Alte Pin., Munich), an early example of an independent still-life. He was described as old and sick in 1511 and had died by 1516.

Barberini. Italian family who achieved prominence with the election of **Maffeo** (1568–1644) as Pope Urban VIII in 1623 and ranked among the chief art patrons in 17th-century Rome. Urban's favourite artist was *Bernini, from whom he commissioned two great works in St Peter's—the statue of St Longinus and the *baldacchino over the high altar. Some of the enormous quantity of bronze required for the baldacchino was taken from ancient metal stripped from the Pantheon, giving rise to the adage *Quod non fecerunt barbari, fecerunt Barberini* (What the barbarians failed to do, the Barberini did). Urban used most of the metal to cast cannon for the Castel Sant'Angelo, saying it was more important to defend the pope than to keep rain out of the Pantheon. Apart from Urban, the most important member of the family was his nephew Cardinal **Francesco Barberini** (1597–1679), who was *Poussin's first important patron in Rome. The Barberini also employed Pietro da *Cortona, *Romanelli, Andrea *Sacchi, and others in the decoration of the family palace and of St Peter's. The Palazzo Barberini, in the design of which Bernini and two other outstanding contemporary architects—Carlo Maderno and Francesco Borromini—all played parts, now houses part of the Galleria Nazionale.

Barberini Faun (or *Sleeping Satyr*). *Hellenistic marble statue of a satyr sprawled in drunken sleep (Glyptothek, Munich). It is first recorded in the possession of Cardinal Franceso *Barberini in 1628, and during the 17th and particularly the 18th century it was generally regarded as one of the greatest works of antiquity. The figure is still admired (unlike most of the formerly celebrated antique statues) and is considered by some authorities to be an original work of around 200 BC, although others believe it to be merely a good copy. It has been several times restored, sometimes with substantial changes to its posture.

Barbizon School. An informal group of French landscape painters, active from the 1830s to about 1870, who took their name from a small village on the outskirts of the Forest of Fontainebleau, where they worked and where some of them eventually settled. The central figure of the group was Théodore *Rousseau; the other members included Charles-François *Daubigny, Narcisse *Diaz, Jules Dupré (1811–89), Charles Jacque (1813–94), and Constant *Troyon. They were united in their opposition to the conventions of the classical tradition stemming from *Claude and *Poussin and by their interest in landscape painting for its own sake, a fairly new development in French art. Their inspiration came partly from England, particularly *Constable, and partly from the 17th-century Dutch painters whom Constable so admired. They advocated painting direct from nature, but unlike the *Impressionists, they usually painted only studies in the open air; their finished pictures were almost always done in the studio. *Corot, who was one of the first artists to work in the forest, is often associated with the group, but his work has a poetic and literary quality that sets him somewhat apart. *Millet is also often linked with the School, as he settled in Barbizon in 1849 and during his last period painted pure landscapes. Most of the Barbizon painters initially struggled in their careers, but their fortunes improved during the 1850s and all the main figures eventually won official honours. The peak of their popularity came (posthumously for most of them) in the 1880s and 1890s.

Barendsz., Dirck (*b* Amsterdam, 1534; *bur.* Amsterdam, 26 May 1592). Netherlandish painter. He spent all his career in Amsterdam apart from a period in Italy, *c.*1555–*c.*1562, during which he is said to have worked in *Titian's studio. On his return to the north he became a leading representative of the fashionable Italianate style. Most of his few surviving pictures are on religious subjects; the *Adoration of the Shepherds* (*c.*1565, Stedelijk Mus., Gouda) is usually cited as his best work. He also painted portraits, including group portraits of Amsterdam's civic guards, a type of picture later particularly associated with Frans *Hals, and made designs for engravings.

Bargello (Museo Nazionale del Bargello), Florence. Museum housing an unrivalled collection of Italian *Renaissance sculpture. It is located in one of the city's best-preserved medieval buildings, the Palazzo del Podestà, begun in 1255; initially it was the residence of the chief magistrate of the city and then of the head of government (Podestà). In 1574 it was converted into a prison and assigned to the head of the police ('Bargello'), and in 1857–65 it was restored and remodelled as a museum. The collection contains works by virtually all the leading Italian Renaissance sculptors (including the celebrated bronze statues of David by *Donatello and *Verrocchio) and also has an extensive collection of applied arts, including armour, enamels, medals, and tapestries.

Barker, Thomas (*b* Pontypool, May 1769; *d* Bath, 11 Dec. 1847). British painter and lithographer, mainly of landscapes and *genre scenes. He was born in Wales but is known as Barker of Bath from his main place of work. His paintings were strongly influenced by the landscapes and *fancy pictures of *Gainsborough (the most famous artist to work in Bath), and he made his name mainly as a painter of rustic scenes. He was successful for most of his career, but his popularity declined and he died in poverty. His brother **Benjamin Barker** (1776–1838) and his son **Thomas Jones Barker** (1815–82) were also painters, mainly of landscapes and military scenes respectively.

Barlach, Ernst (*b* Wedel, nr. Hamburg, 2 Jan. 1870; *d* Rostock, 24 Oct. 1938). German sculptor, printmaker, and writer, a major figure of *Expressionism. Until he reached his thirties Barlach was as much a ceramicist as a sculptor, working in a fairly derivative *Art Nouveau style, but a turning point in his career came in 1906, when he visited Russia. The vast empty landscapes and the sturdy Russian peasants made a great impact on him; these hard-working people, with their simple faith, symbolized for him 'the human condition in its nakedness between Heaven and Earth' and helped inspire him to create a massively powerful figure style. He was influenced also by medieval German carving, with which he recognized both a spiritual and a technical affinity—he preferred to carve in heavy, close-grained woods, but even when his figures were modelled in clay and cast in bronze they retain the broad planes and sharp edges typical of woodcarving. In 1910 Barlach settled at Güstrow, a small town near Rostock, where he spent the rest of his life. By this time he had created his mature style, which changed little thereafter. His most characteristic works are massive, blocklike, heavily robed single figures or pairs of figures symbolizing some aspect of the human condition (*The Solitary One*, 1911, Kunsthalle, Hamburg). He also produced several monuments commemorating the First World War and he was a prolific maker of lithographs and woodcuts, particularly of illustrations to his own plays, of which he published seven; they are sombre works, typically showing the individual wrestling with the ties of the material world in search of God, but they sometimes have a grotesque humour not seen in his sculpture.

After the First World War (in which he served briefly in the army) Barlach was much honoured, but when the Nazis came to power in 1933 he was declared a *degenerate artist and his war memorials at Güstrow, Kiel, and Magdeburg were dismantled. In 1937 he wrote: 'A pimp or a murderer is better off. He at least gets a legal hearing and can defend himself. But we are simply repudiated, and whenever possible purged.' He died the following year. The memorial in Güstrow Cathedral was restored after the Second World War and a copy made for the Antoniterkirche in Cologne; it takes the form of a hovering bronze angel and is considered by many to be Barlach's most deeply spiritual work. His studio in Güstrow is now a museum of his work and there are also museums dedicated to him in Hamburg and Ratzeburg.

Barlow, Francis (*b* ?Lincolnshire, ?1626; *bur.* London, 11 Aug. 1704). English painter, etcher, and draughtsman, mainly of animal subjects, known as 'the father of British sporting painting'. He painted numerous large canvases for decorative schemes (examples are at Ham House in London and Clandon Park in Surrey)

and was also a prolific book illustrator, his etchings for an edition of Aesop's *Fables* published in 1666 being particularly well known. His work is vividly observed, with an almost naive charm.

Barna da Siena (active *c*.1350). Sienese painter. The source material on him is vague and confusing, and although he has been described as the leading Sienese painter of his period, some scholars think that he is a fictitious character and prefer to assign the works attributed to him to other hands. In his *Commentarii*, *Ghiberti said that Barna worked in the Collegiata at S. Gimignano, and the fresco series on the life of Christ there is the core around which attempts have been made to reconstruct his oeuvre (among the works that have been given to him is *Christ Carrying the Cross* in the Frick Collection, New York). As with Simone *Martini (traditionally Barna's master), drawing plays a dominant part in this oeuvre, but whereas Simone's line is graceful, Barna's is direct and thrusting, his figures having a more dramatic vigour than any in previous Sienese painting. According to *Vasari, Barna died in a fall from scaffolding.

Barnard, George Grey. See METROPOLITAN MUSEUM OF ART.

Barnes, Dr Albert C. (*b* Philadelphia, 2 Jan. 1872; *d* Chester County, Pa., 24 July 1951). American drug manufacturer and art collector. He made a fortune with the antiseptic Argyrol, which he created in 1901 (its success is said to have depended largely on its being adopted as the standard anti-venereal treatment of the French army), and by 1913 he was devoting his life to collecting. His greatest interest was in modern French painting, but he also bought Old Masters and primitive art. In 1922 he established the Barnes Foundation at Merion, Pennsylvania, to house his collection and to provide education in art appreciation, and in 1931 he commissioned *Matisse to paint a mural decoration for the building. When the mural turned out to be unusable because of an error in the measurements he had been given, Matisse did a new version; the abortive scheme, *The Dance I* (1931–2), is in the Musée d'Art Moderne de la Ville de Paris, and the second scheme, *The Dance II* (1932–3), is *in situ* in the Barnes Foundation.

Barnes has been described as 'perhaps the greatest single American art collector of the twentieth century' (Joseph Alsop, *The Rare Art Traditions*, 1982), but he was a highly unattractive character: John *Rewald (who was among the distinguished art historians refused admission to the Foundation) refers to his 'dreadful, crude, and unspeakably stupid manners', and Kenneth *Clark wrote that 'His stories of how he had extracted Cézannes and Renoirs from penniless widows made one's blood run cold.' (His redeeming feature was his outspoken promotion of racial equality.) The museum Barnes created was closed to the public during his lifetime, but after his death (in a car accident) legal moves were made to try to force the trustees to open it or lose its tax-exempt status. An agreement was reached in 1960 allowing restricted public entry, but it retained its reputation as a virtually inaccessible treasure house. In his will Barnes had stipulated that his pictures should remain exactly as he left them, but in 1991 a court ruled that this directive could be overruled to raise funds for the upkeep of the building, and in 1993–4 a selection of paintings went on tour to Paris, Tokyo, and several American cities.

Barocci (or Baroccio), **Federico** (b Urbino, ?1535; d Urbino, 30 Sept. 1612). Italian painter and draughtsman, generally considered the greatest and most individual artist of his time in central Italy. Apart from two visits to Rome early in his career (1556, 1560–3), he was based in Urbino all his life. During the second visit he is said to have abandoned his frescos in the Casino of Pius IV in the Vatican gardens because he thought that rivals were trying to poison him, and for the rest of his life he suffered from debilitating stomach pains (possibly the result of ulcers rather than poison). Whether the cause of his illness was physical or psychosomatic, he certainly had an acutely sensitive temperament that comes out in his work, in which he combined the influence of *Correggio and *Raphael (also a native of Urbino) in a refined and highly personal manner. His colour harmonies are sharp but subtle, and although his paintings often convey a feeling of intimate tenderness, his handling has great vigour. Apart from a few portraits, such as that of his chief patron Francesco Maria II della *Rovere, Duke of Urbino (c.1572, Uffizi, Florence), he concentrated almost exclusively on religious subjects; he was the leading painter of altarpieces in Italy in the second half of the 16th century and he also produced numerous smaller devotional pictures (Madonna and Child with St Joseph and the Infant Baptist, c.1575, NG, London).

Although he was based outside the main centres of art, Barocci's work was widely sought after, his patrons including the Emperor Rudolf II (see HABSBURG), for whom he painted his only

known classical subject (The Flight of Aeneas from Troy, 1586–9, Borghese Gal., Rome). And although his illness limited the hours he could work, he had a long and productive career; he was especially prolific as a draughtsman (more than 2,000 sheets of drawings by him survive) and he was one of the first artists to make extensive use of *pastels (he also made a handful of etchings). Certain features of his work are thoroughly in the *Mannerist tradition (his rather indefinite treatment of space, for example, and his delight in fluttering draperies), but in his directness and freshness he looked forward to the *Baroque. *Bellori, the pre-eminent biographer of the Baroque age, considered him the finest Italian painter of his period and lamented that he had 'languished in Urbino'.

Baroque. A term used in the literature of the arts with both historical and critical meanings and as both an adjective and a noun. The term has a long, complex, and controversial history. Until the late 19th century it was used mainly as a synonym for 'absurd' or 'grotesque' (it possibly derives from a Portuguese word for a misshapen pearl), but in English it is now current with three principal meanings. Primarily, it designates the dominant style of European art between *Mannerism and *Rococo. This style originated in Rome and is associated with the Catholic Counter-Reformation, its salient characteristics—overt rhetoric and dynamic movement—being well suited to expressing the self-confidence and proselytizing spirit of the reinvigorated Catholic Church. It is by no means exclusively associated with religious art, however, and aspects of the Baroque can be seen even in works that have nothing to do with emotional display—for example in the dynamic lines of certain Dutch still-life paintings. Secondly, it is used as a general label for the period when this style flourished: broadly speaking, the 17th century and in certain areas much of the 18th century. Hence such phrases as 'the age of Baroque', 'Baroque music', 'Baroque poetry', 'Baroque politics', 'Baroque science', and so on. This type of usage can be more confusing than helpful, for what literary historians call 'Baroque', for example, more often shows characteristics that the art historian would label 'Mannerist'. Thirdly, the term 'Baroque' (often written without the initial capital) is applied to art of any time or place that shows the qualities of vigorous movement and emotional intensity associated with Baroque art in its primary meaning. Much *Hellenistic sculpture could therefore be described as 'baroque'. The older meaning of the word, as a synonym for 'capricious', 'over-wrought', or 'florid', still has some currency, but not in serious criticism.

*Caravaggio and Annibale *Carracci are the two great figures who stand at the head of the Baroque tradition, bringing a new solidity and weightiness to Italian painting, which in the late 16th century had generally been artificial and often convoluted in style. In doing so they looked back to some extent to the dignified and harmonious art of the High *Renaissance, but Annibale's work has an exuberance that is completely his own, and Caravaggio created figures with an unprecedented sense of sheer physical presence. From the Mannerist style the Baroque inherited movement and fervent emotion, and from the Renaissance style solidity and grandeur, fusing the two influences into a new and dynamic whole. The supreme genius of Baroque art was Gianlorenzo *Bernini, an artist of boundless energy, total spiritual conviction, and the utmost virtuosity, whose work dominates the period sometimes called the 'High Baroque' (c.1625–75). Slightly later, Andrea *Pozzo marks the culmination in Italy of the Baroque tendency towards overwhelmingly grandiose display.

In the 17th century Rome was the artistic capital of Europe, and the Baroque style soon spread outwards from it, undergoing modification in each of the countries to which it migrated, as it encountered different tastes and outlooks and merged with local traditions. In some areas it became more extravagant (notably in the fervent religious atmosphere of Spain and Latin America) and in others it was toned down to suit more conservative tastes. In Catholic Flanders it had one of its finest flowerings in the work of *Rubens, but in neighbouring Holland, a predominantly Protestant country, the Baroque made comparatively slight inroads; nor did it ever take firm root in England. In France the Baroque found its greatest expression in the service of the monarchy rather than the Church. Louis XIV realized the importance of the arts as a propaganda medium in promoting the idea of his regal glory, and his palace at Versailles—with its grandiose combination of architecture, sculpture, painting, decoration, and (not least) the art of the gardener—represents one of the supreme examples of the Baroque fusion of the arts to create an overwhelmingly impressive whole. (The term *Gesamtkunstwerk—'total work of art'—has been applied to this ideal.) In France, as in other countries, the Baroque style merged imperceptibly with the Rococo style that followed it.

Barr, Alfred H., Jr. (b Detroit, 28 Jan. 1902; d Salisbury, Conn., 15 Aug. 1981). American art historian and museum administrator who played an enormously influential role in establishing an intellectual framework for the study and appreciation of modern art; his obituary in the *International Herald Tribune* described him as 'possibly the most innovative and influential museum man of the 20th century'. For most of his career Barr worked at the *Museum of Modern Art in New York, of which he became director when it was founded in 1929 (he resigned this post in 1943 so he could devote more time to writing, but he continued as director of research, and retired in 1967 with the title of director of museum collections). Barr was chiefly responsible for building the museum's collections and establishing its reputation. He widened the traditional concept of the art museum to embrace visual arts as a whole, including architecture, industrial design, and motion pictures, and he did much to create the modern idea of an art exhibition, through such means as special lighting, expository wall captions, and scholarly, fully illustrated catalogues (he organized more than 100 exhibitions at the museum, including such famous shows as 'Cubism and Abstract Art' and 'Fantastic Art, Dada, Surrealism', both in 1936). He wrote numerous books and catalogues himself, setting impressive standards of scholarship but presenting his findings in an accessible style; his monographs on *Picasso (1946) and *Matisse (1951) are still considered standard works. In spite of the praise he received for his work, Barr was a controversial figure. He was attacked by sectarians within the world of modern art as well as by conservatives, and some critics thought that the museum he created had too powerful an influence in shaping—rather than reflecting—the course of modern art.

Barra, Didier. See 'MONSÙ DESIDERIO'.

Barret, George (b Dublin, ?1732; d London, 29 May 1784). Irish landscape painter in oils and watercolour. In 1763 he moved to London, where he quickly made a reputation and became a foundation member of the *Royal Academy in 1768. Although he sometimes imitated the classical manner of his rival Richard *Wilson (who described Barret's foliage as 'spinach and eggs'), he was primarily a painter of topographical views. His most famous work in his day was a panorama of the Lake District painted in *distemper on the walls of a room at Norbury Park in Surrey (c.1780; in situ). Many other pictures by him are still in stately home collections. In spite of his success with aristocratic clients, Barrett had an improvident and quarrelsome nature and became bankrupt. He had three painter sons, **George Jun., James,** and **Joseph,** and his daughter **Mary** was a *miniaturist.

Barry, James (b Cork, 11 Oct. 1741; d London, 22 Feb. 1806). Irish painter, active mainly in England. In 1763, in Dublin, he met Edmund *Burke, who encouraged him to move to London and financed a lengthy Continental visit (1766–71), which he spent mainly in Rome. There Barry was overwhelmed by the work of the great masters of the *Renaissance, underlining his ambition to paint elevated subjects with moral messages. In a British art world dominated by portraiture there was little patronage for this type of picture, but Barry pursued his independent path with fervour—he was the only British artist of his time who adhered consistently to *Reynolds's precepts for *history painting in the *Grand Manner. His most famous work, a scheme of six large decorative paintings entitled *The Progress of Human Culture* (1777–83), for the Great Room of the Society of Arts, London, is the most grandiose achievement of this kind by any artist of the British School, but its weak draughtsmanship and flabby rhetoric show that his ambitions far outstripped his talent. Barry's portraits have appealed more to modern taste. They include several self-portraits, in which he suggests the truculent nature that caused friction with his fellow *Royal Academicians. He was appointed professor of painting at the Academy in 1782, but he was expelled in 1799 for making slanderous attacks on his colleagues (he had something of a persecution complex). He died in poverty, but he was sufficiently esteemed to be buried in St Paul's Cathedral and some British artists of the following generation regarded him as a kind of anti-establishment hero.

Barry, Robert. See CONCEPTUAL ART.

Bartholdi, Frédéric-Auguste (b Colmar, Alsace, 2 Apr. 1834; d Paris, 4 Oct. 1904). French sculptor. His accomplished academic style and ability to handle grandiose projects won him numerous official commissions and he is remembered mainly for two enormous public works. The first is the *Lion of Belfort* (1875–80), carved into sandstone blocks below the fort that overlooks the town to commemorate its heroic defence during the Franco-Prussian War. Even bigger and now far more famous is Bartholdi's second great work, *Liberty Enlightening the World* (the Statue of Liberty), in New York Harbour, which was presented by France to the USA to commemorate the alliance between the two countries during the American Revolution. Made of copper sheets riveted around an iron framework designed by the engineer Gustave Eiffel, the figure was constructed in 1875–84, dismantled for shipping across the Atlantic, then reassembled and dedicated in 1886.

Bartlett, Jennifer. See NEW IMAGE PAINTING.

Bartolo di Fredi (active 1353; d Siena, 26 Jan. 1410). One of the leading Sienese painters of the late 14th century. He continued the narrative style of the *Lorenzetti but gave it a flatter, more decorative character. His major surviving work is the Old Testament fresco cycle in the Collegiata, S. Gimignano (1367). In addition to being a successful painter, he held several civic offices in Siena. His son **Andrea di Bartolo** (c.1360–1428) was also a painter.

Bartolommeo, Fra (Baccio della Porta) (b Florence, 28 Mar. 1472; d Florence, 31 Oct. 1517). Florentine painter, a leading figure of the High *Renaissance. He trained under Cosimo *Rosselli and in about 1494 set up a joint workshop with Mariotto *Albertinelli, who had been his fellow pupil. Little survives of his early work, and he is said to have destroyed his profane pictures and drawings under the influence of Girolamo Savonarola's fiery preaching against worldliness. He was greatly distressed by Savonarola's execution in 1498, and in 1500 he gave up painting and became a novice at the Dominican convent at Prato. The following year he took his vows, assumed the name Fra Bartolommeo, and moved to the convent of S. Marco in Florence (famous for its Fra *Angelico paintings). In 1504 the prior of S. Marco authorized him to resume painting, and the rest of his life was devoted to religious art. After 1509 (by which time *Leonardo, *Michelangelo, and *Raphael had all left Florence), he was the leading painter in the city, although he was rivalled by Andrea del *Sarto in the second decade of the century.

Bartolommeo's style was strongly influenced by Leonardo, and his work has much in common with Raphael's. His most characteristic subjects are the Madonna and Child with saints and the Holy Family; the figures are noble, calm, and remote from the everyday world, dressed in timeless draperies and sometimes placed in non-specific settings, with a complete absence of the kind of anecdotal details beloved of the *quattrocento. In 1508 he visited Venice and his work became richer, warmer, and more atmospheric in style under the influence of Giovanni *Bellini; his *Mystic Marriage of St Catherine* (1512, Accademia, Florence) has the kind of majestic architectural setting used by Bellini in several of his major altarpieces and such Belliniesque motifs as music-making angels seated at the foot of the Virgin's throne. In 1514 he visited Rome, and some of his later work has a tendency towards empty rhetoric, as he struggled to come to terms with Michelangelo's Sistine Ceiling. A very different side to his art is seen in his drawings, which are often remarkably fresh and spontaneous, particularly his landscapes. With Leonardo, he was one of the first artists to produce drawings of pure landscape, and they seem to have been made simply for his own pleasure.

Bartolommeo Veneto (active 1502; *d* Turin, Dec. 1531). Italian painter. An obscure figure, not mentioned by *Vasari or *Ridolfi, he is usually classed as a member of the Venetian School, but he signed himself as '*mezo venizian e mezo cremonexe*' (half Venetian and half Cremonese) and seems to have worked in various parts of north Italy. He painted both religious works and portraits of fashionably dressed sitters. The religious pictures are fairly undistinguished derivations from Gentile and Giovanni *Bellini (he probably studied with Gentile), but some of the portraits are impressive and distinctive (*Ludovico Martinengo*, 1530, NG, London).

Bartolozzi, Francesco (*b* Florence, 25 Sept. 1728; *d* Lisbon, 2 Mar. 1815). Italian engraver, active mainly in England, where he settled in 1764 with the position of official engraver to George III. In 1768 he was a founder member of the *Royal Academy (admitted as a painter, as engravers were not originally eligible). He engraved the works of many of his leading contemporaries, such as *Copley, *Kauffmann, and *Reynolds, but he was also celebrated for prints after the Old Masters. Much of his work was in the *stipple engraving technique. His output was enormous and he had many assistants and pupils. In 1802 he moved to Lisbon to become director of the Academy.

Bartsch, Adam von (*b* Vienna, 17 Aug. 1757; *d* Vienna, 21 Aug. 1821). Austrian art historian. He studied engraving at the Vienna Academy and became a renowned authority on printmaking.

Most of his career was spent at the Imperial Library in Vienna and he was also adviser to Archduke Albert of Sachsen-Teschen (see ALBERTINA). From 1803 to 1821 he published in twenty volumes *Le Peintre graveur*, the pioneering work in the systematic study of Dutch, Flemish, German, and Italian painter-engravers (see PEINTRE-GRAVEUR) from the 15th to the 17th century. It is now outdated in certain respects, but still remains of fundamental importance in the study of many artists (particularly Italians) and its numbering system has been referred to by most subsequent works in its field. There have been various continuations and supplements and in 1979 a series of illustrations to the work (known as *The Illustrated Bartsch*) began publication; a similar series (*Le Peintre graveur illustré*) was begun in 1971, but only the first volume ever appeared.

Barye, Antoine-Louis (*b* Paris, 24 Sept. 1796; *d* Paris, 25 June 1875). French sculptor, painter, and printmaker. Barye was the most famous animal sculptor of the 19th century and was largely responsible for making the small animal bronze a recognized genre; artists specializing in this kind of work became known as *animaliers*. He trained as a goldsmith (his father's profession) and also studied sculpture and painting (*Gros was briefly his teacher). His knowledge of animals came partly from observing them in the Jardin des Plantes, Paris, and partly from extensive reading. In 1831 he had his first notable success at the *Salon with *Tiger Devouring a Gavial* (Louvre, Paris, and other casts) and this launched his career; only two years later he was made a member of the Legion of Honour. Much of his work is in a similar *Romantic vein, stressing the drama and savagery of nature. Barye also created large-scale sculptures, including a stone pediment relief of *Napoleon Crowned by History and the Arts* (1857) on the Sully Pavilion of the *Louvre and a bronze equestrian statue of Napoleon (1860–5) at Ajaccio, the emperor's birthplace in Corsica.

Basaldella, Afro, Dino, and **Mirko.** See AFRO.

basalt. A hard igneous rock that is very durable and takes a fine polish. It is widely distributed and has many varieties, differing in consistency and ranging in colour from black, brown, or dark green to pale blue. It is almost as difficult to work as *granite. Black basalt was much used by the ancient Egyptians for portrait sculpture and was also used in the Middle East.

In the context of *Neoclassicism the potter Josiah *Wedgwood experimented with pottery materials simulating the stones favoured for sculpture in antiquity. Basalt-ware, a hard black stoneware, was the first of these materials to be successfully produced, in 1766.

Baschenis, Evaristo (*b* Bergamo, 7 Dec. 1617; *d* Bergamo, 16 Mar. 1677). Italian painter, the outstanding member of a dynasty of artists. Although he was an ordained priest, almost all his pictures depict arrangements of musical instruments—beautifully poised and polished works that led Rudolf *Wittkower to describe him as 'probably Italy's greatest still-life painter'. His inclination for his favourite subject may have been influenced by the contemporary fame of the Amati family of violin makers of Cremona, which is near to Baschenis's native town of Bergamo. The Accademia Carrara there has the best collection of his paintings.

Baselitz, Georg (*b* Deutschbaselitz, Saxony, 23 Jan. 1938). German painter and sculptor. He is regarded as one of the leading exponents of *Neo-Expressionism and his work has often been the subject of controversy, particularly since, in 1969, he began painting the images in his pictures upside down. Since 1980 he has also made sculptures; in these the figures are the normal way up.

Basire, James. See BLAKE, WILLIAM.

Baskin, Leonard (*b* New Brunswick, NJ, 15 Aug. 1922; *d* Northampton, Mass., 3 June 2000). American sculptor, printmaker, draughtsman, and book designer. He believed that art should express moral and social concerns—a view that put him at odds with the prevailing abstraction of the early years of his career. His most characteristic sculptures are brooding full-length standing figures (in bronze, stone, or wood) portraying 'anxiety-ridden man imprisoned in his ungainly self' (*Man with a Dead Bird*, 1951–6, MoMA, New York). They have a kinship with the graphic art of *Barlach and *Kollwitz—the two modern artists Baskin admired most. Baskin himself was a prolific printmaker, especially of woodcuts, many of which were used as book illustrations. His interest in books encompassed the whole of their design, including typography and binding, and in 1952 he founded the Gehenna Press to produce limited editions. He won numerous awards for his work, including the Printmaking Prize at the 1961 São Paulo *Bienale.

Basquiat, Jean-Michel. See GRAFFITI ART.

Bassa, Ferrer (active 1324–48). Spanish painter and *miniaturist who worked for the Aragon court in Barcelona. He is considered the founder of the Catalan School, but the only certain surviving work by his hand is a series of murals (in oil rather than fresco) in the chapel of S. Miguel at the convent of Pedralbes near Barcelona, executed in 1345–6 and strongly Italianate in style.

Bassano, Jacopo (Jacopo da Ponte) (*b* Bassano [now Bassano del Grappa], *c*.1515; *d* Bassano, 13 Feb. 1592). Italian painter, the most celebrated member of a family of artists who took their name from the small town of Bassano, about 65 km (40 miles) north-west of Venice. Jacopo is regarded as a member of the Venetian School and among his contemporaries is ranked inferior only to the great triumvirate of *Titian, *Tintoretto, and *Veronese. However, apart from a period in the 1530s when he worked with *Bonifazio Veronese, he was not resident in Venice itself; he lived almost all his life in his native town, where he was easily the leading artist of the day, producing a large and varied output. Although he painted only a handful of pictures for churches or other public buildings in Venice, his work was popular with private collectors there and he also had clients in other cities of north Italy, including Treviso and Vicenza, and occasionally commissions from as far away as Florence. His father **Francesco the Elder** (*c*.1475–1539) was a village painter and Jacopo always retained a certain earthiness in his work, but in other ways his style was sophisticated and it was constantly developing: in the 1540s and 1550s, for example, he was influenced by the elongated forms of *Parmigianino's etchings, and in his late paintings he responded to the dramatic lighting effects of Tintoretto. Frederick Hartt (*A History of Italian Renaissance Art*, 1970) writes that 'Bassano's work can be dazzling in its unexpected combination of rustic naturalism with a daring freshness of invention and color.' Most of his pictures are on religious subjects, but he often treated biblical themes in the manner of rural *genre scenes, using genuine country types and portraying animals with real interest. In this way he helped to develop the taste for paintings in which the genre or still-life element assumes greater importance than the ostensible religious subject.

Bassano had four painter sons who continued his style and sometimes collaborated with him—**Francesco the Younger** (1549–92), **Gerolamo** (1566–1621), **Giovanni Battista** (1553–1613), and **Leandro** (1557–1622). Francesco and Leandro both acquired some distinction and popularity working in Venice—indeed Leandro was knighted by the doge in 1595 or 1596 (thereafter he sometimes added *Eques* to his signature). Francesco was mentally unstable and died after throwing himself from a window. Leandro's death in 1622 brought the artistic dynasty to an end. The work of the family is well represented in the Museo Civico at Bassano and there are examples in many other collections.

Bassen, Bartholomeus van (*b* ?*c*.1590; *bur.* The Hague, 28 Nov. 1652). Dutch architectural painter and architect. He is first recorded in 1613, in Delft, and in 1622 he settled in The Hague. As a painter he specialized in views of church interiors, usually imaginary, although some are based on real buildings. From 1638 until his death he was municipal architect in The Hague, and he also worked on buildings in Arnhem.

Bastien-Lepage, Jules (*b* Damvillers, Meuse, 1 Nov. 1848; *d* Paris, 10 Dec. 1884). French painter. He grew up on a farm and is best known for sentimental scenes of rural life such as *The Haymakers* (1877, Mus. d'Orsay, Paris). Émile *Zola described Bastien-Lepage's work as 'Impressionism corrected, sweetened and adapted to the taste of the crowd', and he was highly influential in spreading a taste for *plein-air* painting, not only in France, but also in Britain (*Clausen and *La Thangue were among his admirers), in other European countries, in the USA, and even—via Tom *Roberts—in Australia. He was also much admired as a portraitist. His early death was caused by cancer.

Batlle Planas, Juan (*b* Torroella de Montgri, nr. Girona, 3 Mar. 1911; *d* Buenos Aires, 8 Oct. 1966). Argentine painter, printmaker, designer, and writer, considered the father of *Surrealist art in his country. He was born in Spain and moved to Buenos Aires with his family in 1913. Although he had lessons from his painter uncle **José Planas-Casas** (1900–60), he was essentially self-taught. He was an energetic publicist for modern art and trained and influenced numerous Argentinian artists. His work included murals in public and private buildings, stage designs, and book illustrations, and he also wrote poetry and numerous articles about the psychological response to colour and form.

Batoni, Pompeo (*b* Lucca, 25 Jan. 1708; *d* Rome, 4 Feb. 1787). Italian painter and draughtsman, the son of a distinguished goldsmith. He has been described as 'Italy's last Old Master'

and he was certainly the last great Italian personality to dominate painting in Rome, where he spent virtually his whole career (he settled there in 1727). Initially he made his name with exquisite drawings of ancient statuary (which were much prized by antiquarians), then as a history painter, mainly of religious subjects. However, by the 1750s he was devoting most of his time to portraits and it is for these that he is principally famous. After *Mengs left Rome for Madrid in 1761, Batoni's pre-eminence in this field was unchallenged, and he was particularly favoured by foreign visitors making the *Grand Tour, whom he often portrayed in an *antique setting; one of his most celebrated works shows the sitter in spectacular Highland dress against a backdrop of the Colosseum (*Colonel William Gordon*, 1766, Fyvie Castle, Aberdeenshire, NT). Batoni's characterization is not profound, but it is usually vivid (he had a reputation for creating a good likeness), and he presented his sitters with dignity and élan. His polished and learned style shows his admiration for the classical tradition of *Raphael, *Reni, and *Maratta, but his work also has a *Rococo grace and delicacy of touch. Batoni earned a fortune from his work and his large house was a social, intellectual, and artistic centre, frequented by many distinguished visitors to Rome. At the time of his death he was probably the most famous artist in Europe, but his reputation went into eclipse in the 19th century and did not seriously revive until the later 20th century.

Battistello. See CARACCIOLO.

Bauchant, André (*b* Château-Renault, Indre-et-Loire, 24 Apr. 1873; *d* Montoire-sur-le-Loir, 12 Aug. 1958). French *naive painter. He was a market gardener until 1914 and did not begin painting until 1919, when he was demobilized after war service (in the army he had shown a talent for drawing and had been trained as a map-maker). In 1921 his work was shown at the *Salon d'Automne, and he soon became one of the best-known painters of his type. He was promoted by Wilhelm *Uhde, and his admirers and patrons included *Diaghilev, *Le Corbusier, *Lipchitz, and *Ozenfant. Bauchant's favourite subjects were history and mythology, for which he found inspiration in old illustrated books (*Greek Dance in a Landscape*, 1937, Tate, London). His style was meticulously detailed.

Baudelaire, Charles (*b* Paris, 9 Apr. 1821; *d* Paris, 31 Aug. 1867). French poet and critic. As well as being a major poet, Baudelaire was one of the liveliest art critics of his day, passionate and partisan in his views. He thought that there are no universal aesthetic standards, but a different type of beauty for different peoples and cultures. He also believed that the individuality of the artist is essential to the creation of beauty, and if it is suppressed or regimented, art becomes banal: 'the beautiful is always bizarre' was a favourite maxim. His favourite contemporary artist was *Delacroix, whom he extolled for his imagination, intelligence, and technical skills. However, he singled out the relatively minor Constantin *Guys as the representative *par excellence* of contemporary society, and wrote a long appreciation of his work entitled 'Le Peintre de la vie moderne', published as a series of articles in *Le Figaro* in 1863. The other artists with whom Baudelaire was involved include *Courbet (he is one of the people depicted in *The Painter's Studio* (1854–5, Mus. d'Orsay, Paris)), *Manet (he likewise appears in *Music in the Tuileries Gardens* (1863, NG, London)), and *Rops, whose career he helped to launch. His writings later had great influence on the *Symbolists.

Baugin, Lubin (*b* Pithiviers, *c*.1610; *d* Paris, 11 July 1663). French painter. He specialized in religious works and has earned the nickname 'Le Petit Guide' (Little Guido) because he was strongly influenced by Guido *Reni. This suggests that he visited Italy, but there is no documentary evidence. A small group of strikingly austere still-lifes, signed simply 'Baugin' (examples are in the Louvre), has also been attributed to him; however, there is little in common between these pictures and the religious works and some scholars think they are by an otherwise unrecorded namesake.

Bauhaus. A school of art and design founded by Walter *Gropius in Weimar in 1919 and closed by the Nazis in 1933 after moving successively to Dessau (1925) and Berlin (1932); although it had such a short life it was the most famous art school of the 20th century, playing key roles in establishing the relationship between design and industrial techniques and in breaking down the hierarchy that had previously divided 'fine' from 'applied' arts. The Bauhaus was created when Gropius was appointed head of two art schools in Weimar in 1919 and united them in one; they were the Kunstgewerbeschule (Arts and Crafts School) and the Hochschule für Bildende Kunst (Institute of Fine Arts). He gave his new school the name Staatliches Bauhaus in Weimar (Weimar State 'Building

House'), coining himself the word 'Bauhaus' (an inversion of 'Hausbau'—house construction). His prospectus formulated three main aims for the school: first, to unite the arts so that painters, sculptors, and craftsmen could in future embark on cooperative projects, combining all their skills harmoniously; secondly, to raise the status of the crafts to that enjoyed by the fine arts; and thirdly, to establish 'constant contact with the leaders of the crafts and industries of the country' (an important factor if the school were to survive in a country that was in economic chaos after the war).

All students had to take a six-month 'preliminary course' (*Vorkurs*) in which they studied the principles of form and colour, were acquainted with various materials, and were encouraged to develop their creativity. After that they moved on to workshop training in the field of their choice. Gropius brought together a remarkable collection of teachers at the Bauhaus. The first head of the preliminary course was Johannes *Itten, and when he left in 1923 he was succeeded by László *Moholy-Nagy, who replaced Itten's rather metaphysical approach with an austerely rational one. The other teachers included some illustrious painters, most notably *Kandinsky and *Klee. Several students went on to become teachers at the school, among them Josef *Albers. In 1924 right-wingers gained power in the provincial elections and cut funding to the Bauhaus, which consequently was moved to Dessau the following year; it was housed in a group of new buildings designed by Gropius. The school had been involved in architectural commissions from the beginning, but it was only in 1927 that an architectural department was established, with the Swiss architect Hannes Meyer (1889–1954) as its first professor. When Gropius resigned in 1928 to devote himself to his own practice he named Meyer as his successor. It was an unpopular choice with the staff, as Meyer was a Marxist and instituted a sociological approach that changed the whole tone of the school, with politics occupying an important place in the curriculum.

In 1930 Meyer was forced to resign and was replaced by Ludwig Mies van der Rohe (1886–1969), one of the greatest architects of the 20th century. Mies tried to rid the Bauhaus of its political associations and thereby make it a less easy target for its right-wing opponents, but in 1932 the Dessau parliament closed the school. In an attempt to keep it alive Mies rented a disused factory in Berlin and reopened the Bauhaus there as a private enterprise, but it was closed by the Nazis in April 1933, soon after Hitler assumed power. In its last few years the Bauhaus was dominated by architecture, but it produced a great range of goods, with many of them (furniture, textiles, and electric light fittings in particular) being adopted for large-scale manufacture. They were highly varied in appearance, but the style that is thought typical of the Bauhaus was severe, geometric, and undecorated.

The Bauhaus published a journal (*Bauhaus*, 1926–31) and a series of books, and its ideas were spread also by the emigration of many of its teachers before and during the Second World War. It has had an enormous influence on art education in the Western world and on visual creativity in general: 'The look of the modern environment is unthinkable without it. It left an indelible mark on activities as varied as photography and newspaper design . . . [and] achieved a language of design liberated from the historicism of the previous hundred years' (Frank Whitford, *Bauhaus*, 1984). After the Second World War Dessau became part of East Germany and the Bauhaus buildings were left derelict. In 1976 the school was faithfully restored for the 50th anniversary of its opening in Dessau, and after the reunification of Germany in 1990 it was reopened as a design institution.

Baumeister, Willi (*b* Stuttgart, 22 Jan. 1889; *d* Stuttgart, 31 Aug. 1955). German abstract painter. Unlike most significant German painters of his time, he stood apart from *Expressionism and is regarded as the most 'European' in spirit of his contemporaries. Between 1911 and 1914 he had several stays in Paris (sometimes in company with his close friend Oskar *Schlemmer) and his early work was influenced by *Cubism. After military service in the First World War, he began to develop a personal style in a series (1919–23) of *Mauerbilder* (wall paintings), so called because he added sand, putty, etc., to his pigments to give a textured effect. In the mid-1920s his work became more figurative, in a manner recalling *Léger and the *Purists (he met Léger, *Le Corbusier, and *Ozenfant when he revisited Paris in 1924), and his work received considerable acclaim in France. In 1928 he was appointed professor of typography at the Städel School in Frankfurt, but in 1933 he was dismissed by the Nazis, who declared his work *degenerate. From then until the end of the Second World War he worked in obscurity in Stuttgart. During this time his painting became freer, with suggestions of primitive imagery, creating a kind of abstract

*Surrealism. His interest in imagery from the subconscious was described in his book *Das Unbekannte in der Kunst* (The Unknown in Art), written in 1943–4 and published in 1947. After the war Baumeister became a hero to a younger generation of German abstract artists. From 1946 until his death he was a professor at the Stuttgart Academy.

Baumgarten, Alexander Gottlieb. See AESTHETICS.

Bawden, Edward (*b* Braintree, Essex, 10 Mar. 1903; *d* Saffron Walden, Essex, 21 Nov. 1989). British watercolour painter, illustrator, and designer of posters, wallpaper, tapestries, and theatre decor. He was an *Official War Artist in the Second World War (in France and the Middle East) and painted numerous murals (for example, at Queen's University, Belfast, 1965), but he is best known for his book illustrations. Most of them were done in pen and ink in an incisive economical style, but he also worked with linocut, lithography, and stencil.

Baxter, George (*b* Lewes, Sussex, 31 July 1804; *d* Sydenham, Kent [now Greater London], 11 Jan. 1867). English engraver and printer. In 1835 he patented a method of making colour prints—the first commercially viable alternative to the hand-coloured print. The basic design, usually in *aquatint, was printed from a steel plate, and the colours were superimposed from up to twenty wooden blocks. Around the middle of the century 'Baxter prints' enjoyed a great vogue, making coloured reproductions of paintings widely available. Baxter licensed other firms to employ the process and did not himself profit greatly from the invention; indeed he became bankrupt in 1865. By this time his process was being superseded by colour *lithography.

Bay Area Figuration. See DIEBENKORN.

Bayes, Gilbert (*b* London, 4 Apr. 1872; *d* London, 10 July 1953). British sculptor, the son of **Alfred Walter Bayes** (1832–1909), a painter and etcher. A leading exponent of the *New Sculpture, he concentrated on romantic themes taken from such sources as medieval chivalry and Wagner, and his work was much admired by conservative critics. One such critic, Herbert Maryon, wrote that Bayes's small bronze *Sigurd* (*c*.1910, Tate, London), judged as a 'decorative composition', was 'unsurpassed by any other equestrian group in existence' (*Modern Sculpture*, 1933). Bayes's other works include the stone relief of sporting figures (1934) outside Lord's cricket ground, London, and the design of the Great Seal of King George V.

His brother **Walter Bayes** (b London, 31 May 1869; d London, 21 Jan. 1956) was a painter and writer on art. He was art critic of the *Athenaeum* from 1906 to 1916 (succeeding Roger *Fry), a founder member of the *Camden Town Group (1911) and of the *London Group (1913), and a highly regarded teacher as principal of Westminster Art School, 1919–34, and director of painting at the Lancaster School of Arts and Crafts, 1944–9. His work as a painter consisted mainly of figure subjects, landscapes, and decorations. He wrote several books, including *The Art of Decorative Painting* (1927) and *A Painter's Baggage* (1932). **Jessie Bayes** (1878–1940), sister of Gilbert and Walter, was a painter.

Bayeu, Francisco (*bapt.* Saragossa, 9 Mar. 1734; d Madrid, 4 Aug. 1795). Spanish painter. He had an eminently successful career, becoming court painter to Charles IV and director of the Academy of S. Fernando, but he is now remembered mainly because he was the brother-in-law of *Goya, who spent some time in Bayeu's studio in the 1760s and later painted a memorable portrait of him (1795, Prado, Madrid). Bayeu painted portraits and also did much decorative work, particularly making *cartoons for the royal tapestry factory, where he succeeded *Mengs as director in 1777. His younger brothers **Manuel** (1740–1809) and **Ramón** (1746–93) were also painters.

Bayeux Tapestry. The most famous of all pieces of needlework (actually an embroidery rather than a tapestry), depicting William the Conqueror's successful invasion of England in 1066 and the events that led up to it. It was probably commissioned by William's half-brother Bishop Odo of Bayeux (who has a prominent role in the story shown), within a few years of the conquest, and it was almost certainly made in England, at this time famous for embroidery. The tapestry is worked in eight different colours of wool (used decoratively rather than naturalistically) on a plain linen ground. It is made up of eight pieces of linen joined together, with a total length of almost 70 m (230 ft); the concluding end is damaged and some scenes are lost. The average height is about 50 cm (20 in). The narrative is arranged in a continuous horizontal line of action, one scene merging into another without any vertical division. A running text in Latin provides a commentary, and a border extends above and below the main scenes; these borders contain mainly

decorative elements but also elements of sub-plot. Stylistically the tapestry has much in common with English *illumination of the period. The drawing is clear, vivid, and full of action and the composition leads on skilfully from one incident to the next. Considering its great length it is remarkably unified, suggesting close supervision by the overall designer. In addition to being a unique and highly impressive work of art, it is an immensely important historical document, containing a wealth of information on topics ranging from shipbuilding to fashionable clothes.

The tapestry is first recorded in the 15th century, when it hung in Bayeux Cathedral, and engravings of it were first published in 1739. During the French Revolution it narrowly escaped destruction. In 1842 it was placed on permanent public display, and after having various unsatisfactory homes (including the town hall and the municipal library), it is now housed in a purpose-built museum, the Musée de la Tapisserie de la Reine Mathilde. (The Queen Matilda referred to is William the Conqueror's wife, who according to an old local tradition made the Tapestry.)

Bazille, Frédéric (b Montpellier, 6 Dec. 1841; d Beaune-la-Rolande, 28 Nov. 1870). French painter, one of the early *Impressionist group. In 1862 he became a student at *Gleyre's studio in Paris and there met *Monet, *Renoir, and *Sisley, with whom he painted out of doors at Fontainebleau and in Normandy. He was primarily a figure painter rather than a landscapist, but he sometimes set his compositions in the open air, as in his best-known work, the large *Family Reunion* (1867–8, Mus. d'Orsay, Paris). Bazille died in action during the Franco-Prussian War, cutting short a promising career. He came from a wealthy family and had given generous financial support to Monet and Renoir.

Baziotes, William (b Pittsburgh, 11 June 1912; d New York, 4 June 1963). American painter, one of the minor masters of *Abstract Expressionism. From 1936 to 1941 he worked for the *Federal Art Project, and during the Second World War he became interested in *Surrealism and experimented with various types of *automatism. In the early 1950s he developed his characteristic style, which was not fully abstract but used strange *biomorphic shapes, akin to those of *Miró, suggesting animal or plant forms in an underwater setting (*Mammoth*, 1957, Tate, London). He said, 'It is the mysterious that I love in painting. It is the stillness and the silence. I want my pictures to take effect very slowly, to obsess and to haunt.'

Beale, Mary (née Cradock) (*bapt.* Barrow, Suffolk, 26 Mar. 1633; *bur.* London, 8 Oct. 1699). English portrait painter, active in London, where she moved in intellectual circles. She was the daughter of a clergyman and many of her portraits are of churchmen. They are mostly bland derivations from *Lely, but she was in considerable demand at the peak of her career, in the 1670s. Much of our knowledge of her work comes from notebooks kept by her husband recording sitters, payments, and other information; they provide a fascinating insight into contemporary artistic practice. A son, **Charles** (1660–?1714), was mainly a *miniaturist.

Beardsley, Aubrey (*b* Brighton, 21 Aug. 1872; *d* Menton, 16 Mar. 1898). English illustrator and writer. Beardsley showed a talent for drawing from an early age and he had almost no formal training in art (he attended evening classes at Westminster School of Art for a few months). However, he read voraciously and studied the art of the past and present, and his work drew on a variety of influences, including the sinuous line of *Burne-Jones (who encouraged him) and the strong patterns of Japanese prints (see UKIYO-E). In spite of these influences, his style is highly distinctive in the way he contrasts subtle use of line with bold masses of black and in his blending of grotesque humour with a sense of morbid depravity. He made a name for himself with illustrations for an edition of Malory's *Morte d'Arthur* (1893–4), and in 1894 he became notorious with the publication of his illustrations to the English version of Oscar Wilde's *Salome* and the appearance of the first issue of the *Yellow Book*, a quarterly periodical of which he was art editor. The decadent nature of his work horrified many contemporaries and the scandal of Wilde's arrest for homosexual offences in 1895 led to his dismissal from the *Yellow Book* (even though he disliked Wilde and his own personal life was blameless). In 1896 he worked for another short-lived periodical, the *Savoy*, which published extracts from his main work as a writer, the unfinished erotic novel *Under the Hill* (an unexpurgated edition, with his own pornographic illustrations, was privately published in 1907 under the title *The Story of Venus and Tannhäuser*). Although he was only 25 when he died of tuberculosis, his output was large. He became one of the best-known artists of his day (he was satirized in *Punch* as 'Aubrey Weirdsley')

and he ranks as a major figure of *Aestheticism and of *Art Nouveau.

Beaumont, Sir George (*b* Great Dunmow, Essex, 6 Nov. 1753; *d* Coleorton, Leicestershire, 7 Feb. 1827). English collector, connoisseur, and amateur painter, the friend of numerous artists and men of letters; his best-known painting, *Peele Castle in a Storm* (1806, priv. coll.), moved Wordsworth to write 'Elegaic Stanzas Suggested by a Picture of Peele Castle' (published 1807). Beaumont was a key figure in the creation of the *National Gallery; in 1823 he offered his small but choice collection of pictures to the nation on condition that a suitable building was provided for them, and this encouraged the government to buy the Angerstein collection (the nucleus of the gallery) the following year. Beaumont's favourite painting among those he presented was *Claude's *Hagar and the Angel* (1646), which he frequently took with him when he travelled and which had a great impact on his friend *Constable. Constable's famous painting *The Cenotaph* (*c.*1833, NG, London) shows the memorial to Sir Joshua *Reynolds that Beaumont erected in the grounds of his house at Coleorton, Leicestershire.

Beauneveu, André (*b* Valenciennes, *c.*1330/40; *d* ?Bourges, *c.*1403). Franco-Netherlandish artist, primarily a sculptor but also active as an *illuminator and a designer of stained glass. He is first documented in about 1360 and by 1364 he was in Paris working on a series of royal tombs commissioned by King Charles V for the abbey of Saint-Denis, near Paris. Most of the work was carried out by assistants, but the sensitively characterized effigy of Charles himself is regarded as entirely Beauneveu's work; it is the first French royal effigy to show the subject alive. For unknown reasons Beauneveu left Charles's employment in 1366. He possibly spent some years in England before moving to the Netherlands. In 1372 he was in Tournai and in 1374–7 he worked for Louis de Male, Count of Flanders, in Courtrai. From this period dates a handsome alabaster statue of St Catherine (church of Our Lady, Courtrai). In 1386 he entered the service of Jean, Duc de Berry (brother of Charles V), and evidently remained in his employment for the rest of his life, working mainly in Bourges. His only documented works as an illuminator date from this period—24 *grisaille miniatures of prophets and Apostles in Jean's Psalter (*c.*1390, Bib. Nat., Paris). Beauneveu was one of the leading artists of his day and his style, in both sculpture and painting, heralds the general northern European trend towards naturalism in the 15th century.

Beaux, Cecilia (b Philadelphia, 1 May 1855; d Gloucester, Mass., 17 Sept. 1942). American painter, active mainly in Philadelphia and New York. Her training included a period in Paris, where she studied at the *Académie Julian. She was a highly successful and much honoured society portraitist, working in a dashing and fluid style similar to that of *Sargent. Her sitters included celebrities such as Henry James and Theodore Roosevelt. She wrote an autobiography, *Background with Figures*, published in 1930.

Beaux-Arts, École des, Paris. The chief of the official art schools of France. Its origins go back to 1648, the foundation date of the Académie Royale de Peinture et de Sculpture (see ACADEMY), but it was not established as a separate institution until the Académie was dissolved in 1793, during the administrative reforms of the French Revolution. It moved to its present site, in the rue Bonaparte, in 1816. The École des Beaux-Arts controlled the path to traditional success with its awards and state commissions, notably the prestigious *Prix de Rome, and teaching remained conservative until after the Second World War. Entry was difficult—among the artists who failed were *Rodin and *Vuillard—and students often preferred the private *académies. Many progressive artists, however, obtained a sound technical grounding there— *Degas, *Manet, *Matisse, *Monet, and *Renoir all attended classes. The École, which is housed in a complex of early 19th-century buildings, has a large and varied collection of works of art. Many of them are primarily of historical interest (including a vast number of copies and portraits of teachers), but the collection of drawings is of high quality.

Beazley, Sir John. See BERLIN PAINTER.

Beccafumi, Domenico (b nr. Siena, c.1485; d Siena, Jan./May 1551). Sienese painter, sculptor, and printmaker. He is now generally considered the outstanding Sienese *Mannerist artist, although *Sodoma was more highly esteemed by his contemporaries. According to *Vasari, he visited Rome early in his career, and he was certainly aware of the work of *Michelangelo and *Raphael, as well as of contemporary Florentine art, combining the new ideas of the High *Renaissance with the bright and decorative colouring of Sienese tradition. His work is noteworthy for its sense of fantasy and striking

effects of light, as in the *Birth of the Virgin* (c.1543), one of several outstanding examples of his work in the Pinacoteca, Siena. Late in his career he turned to sculpture, producing a series of eight bronze angels (1547–51) for Siena Cathedral. He also worked as an illuminator and occasionally made engravings and woodcuts.

Becerra, Gaspar (b ?Baeza, c.1520; d ?Madrid, 22/23 Jan. 1568). Spanish *Mannerist painter and sculptor. He spent much of his early career in Italy and he was one of *Vasari's assistants in his decoration of the Cancelleria Palace, Rome (1546). In about 1557 he returned to Spain and in 1558 he began the main altarpiece of Astorga Cathedral, his most important work as a sculptor. In 1562 he was appointed court painter to Philip II (see HABSBURG), for whom his work included a ceiling fresco of *Perseus and the Golden Fleece* (1562–7) in the palace of El Pardo. His up-to-date knowledge of Italian art gave him a high contemporary reputation.

Becker, Felix. See THIEME.

Beckford, William (b London, 29 Sept. 1760; d Bath, 2 May 1844). English collector, writer, and eccentric. A pampered millionaire from boyhood (at the age of 5 he had piano lessons from the 8-year-old Mozart), he became a legendary figure in his own lifetime. One of his cousins referred to him as 'a second Lucifer' (a reference to both his youthful beauty and his depravity), and in 1784 he left England after a homosexual scandal involving a 13-year-old boy. For the next decade he travelled widely on the Continent and after his return to England he lived in eccentric seclusion at Fonthill in Wiltshire, where the architect James Wyatt built for him Fonthill Abbey (1796–1807, now mainly destroyed), a huge mansion dressed in ecclesiastical garb. He formed an excellent library and a vast collection of objects of every kind, both natural and artificial; it drew from William *Hazlitt the wry comment that 'the only proof of taste he has shown in this collection is his getting rid of it', but it included some outstanding paintings (twenty of them are now in the National Gallery, London). In 1826 when his fortunes had declined Beckford built Lansdowne Tower, Bath, a lesser but still highly impressive classical folly that now enlivens a cemetery. Beckford's most famous literary work was the fantastic oriental tale *Vathek*, written in French, but published first in English in 1786, a successor to Horace *Walpole's *The Castle of Otranto* in the vogue for the Gothic novel. The nightmarish visions of Beckford's book were inspired partly, as he himself said, by *Piranesi's engravings.

Beckmann, Max (*b* Leipzig, 12 Feb. 1884; *d* New York, 27 Dec. 1950). German painter and graphic artist, one of the most powerful and individual of *Expressionist artists. Early in his career Beckmann painted in a conservative, more or less *Impressionist style, with which he made a good living, but his experiences as a medical orderly in the First World War completely changed his outlook and his style. Although he rarely depicted scenes from the war itself, his work became full of horrifying imagery, and his forms were expressively distorted in a manner that reflected the influence of German *Gothic art. The combination of brutal realism and social criticism in his work led him to be classified for a time with the artists of the *Neue Sachlichkeit, but Beckmann differed from such artists as *Dix and *Grosz in his concern for allegory and symbolism and in his highly personal blend of the real and the visionary. His paintings were intended as depictions of lust, sadism, cruelty, etc., rather than illustrations of specific instances of those qualities at work, and he ceased to regard painting as a purely aesthetic matter, and thought of it as an ethical necessity.

In 1933 Beckmann was dismissed by the Nazis from his professorship at the Städelsches Kunstinstitut in Frankfurt; at the time he was working on *Departure* (1932–5, MoMA, New York), the first of a series of nine great *triptychs painted between then and his death in which he expressed his philosophy of life and society, and his horror at man's cruelty. He moved to the Netherlands in 1937 (the year in which his work was included in the infamous Nazi exhibition of *degenerate art), settling in Amsterdam until 1947. The last three years of his life were spent in the USA, where he taught in Washington and New York. Beckmann's philosophical outlook, which he expressed in *My Theory of Painting* (a lecture delivered in London in 1937 and published in 1941), is somewhat incoherent, but his work forms one of the most potent artistic commentaries on the disorientation of the modern world. Apart from his allegorical figure compositions, Beckmann is best known for his portraits, particularly his self-portraits, in which he charted his spiritual experiences. He was also a prolific draughtsman and printmaker (mainly of etchings and drypoints).

Beechey, Sir William (*b* Burford, Oxfordshire, 12 Dec. 1753; *d* London, 28 Jan. 1839).

English portrait painter. Beechey's careful, somewhat insipid style changed little throughout his successful career. He was appointed portrait painter to Queen Charlotte in 1793 and was knighted in 1798 in recognition of his most ambitious painting, the huge *Review of the Horse Guard with King George III and the Prince of Wales* (formerly Royal Coll.; destroyed in the fire at Windsor Castle, 1992).

Beeck, Jan van der. See TORRENTIUS.

Beer, Jan de. See ANTWERP MANNERISM.

Beerbohm, Sir Max (*b* London, 24 Aug. 1872; *d* Rapallo, 20 May 1956). British writer, caricaturist, and broadcaster, whose ironic wit was usually directed at the absurd or pretentious in fashionable society. The first of his many books, *Caricatures of Twenty-Five Gentlemen*, was published in 1896. He usually worked in pen and ink, rapidly and from memory; he was self-taught and believed that 'to sit down to write is a business requiring thought and conscience. Caricaturing, on the other hand, is pure instinct without any trouble at all.' However, in spite of the spontaneity of the drawings themselves, he often thought about them in advance, taking notes on his subjects for future use—of Oscar Wilde, for example, he wrote: 'Wax statue; huge rings; fat white hands; feather bed; pointed fingers; cat-like tread; heavy shoulders; enormous dowager.' In 1910 he married an American actress (who seldom understood his English humour) and settled at Rapallo in Italy, where he spent the rest of his life apart from the war years. Late in life he won a new audience with talks on BBC radio. His best-known literary work is his only completed novel, *Zuleika Dobson* (1911), a satire on Oxford student life.

Beerstraten, Jan (*bapt.* Amsterdam, 31 May 1622; *bur.* Amsterdam, 1 July 1666). Dutch painter, the best-known member of a family of artists. He specialized in topographical views of Dutch towns and castles, often shown in winter (*The Castle of Muiden in Winter*, 1658, NG, London), and he also painted imaginary seaports (possibly based on drawings by *Lingelbach) and a few sea battles.

Beert, Osias (*b* ?Antwerp, *c.*1580; *d* Antwerp, 1623/4). Flemish painter of still-life and flower pieces. Beert became a master in the Antwerp painters' guild in 1602 and also carried on business as a cork merchant. He is specially noted for his paintings of oysters, which show a masterly feeling for colour and texture.

Beetham, Isabella. See SILHOUETTE.

'Beggarstaff, J. & W.' (or 'Beggarstaff Brothers'). Pseudonym used by the brothers-in-law William *Nicholson and James *Pryde for their poster designs. 'They joined forces in 1894, and for the next five years they produced a series of posters which by their bold simplicity and clarity of design revolutionized certain aspects of poster art throughout Europe . . . they presented the image in its starkest form: the background is stripped bare of un-necessary detail and the fullest use is made of the silhouette . . . Despite the brilliant original-ity of their work, or perhaps because of it, they received relatively few commissions and several of their designs never reached the hoardings' (Dennis Farr, *English Art: 1870–1940*, 1978). Nicholson explained their choice of the name 'Beggarstaff' thus: 'Pryde and I came across it one day in an old stable, on a sack of fodder. It is a good, hearty, old English name, and it appealed to us, so we adopted it immediately.' They signed their work 'J. & W. Beggarstaff'; in due course some people started referring to the 'Beggarstaff Brothers', but the artists themselves did not care for this version.

Beham, Sebald (*b* Nuremberg, 1500; *d* Frank-furt, 22 Nov. 1550) and **Barthel** (*b* Nuremberg, 1502; *d* Italy, 1540). German printmakers, broth-ers. They were expelled from Nuremberg in 1525 for making anarchistic and atheistic statements supporting the Peasants' Revolt. Although they were allowed to return later that year, Barthel soon left to work for Duke William IV of Bavaria in Munich and Sebald settled in Frankfurt in about 1531. Both brothers produced a great number of prints (engravings, etchings, and woodcuts), including illustrations to the Bible, mythology, and history, strongly influenced by *Dürer. They also painted, and several impres-sive portraits by Barthel survive.

Behnes, William (*b* London, *c*.1795; *d* London, 3 Jan. 1864). English sculptor, the son of a German piano manufacturer who had settled in London. After training at the *Royal Acad-emy Schools, he quickly became successful as a maker of busts, the best of which rival those of Sir Francis *Chantrey, and he was appointed sculptor in ordinary to Queen Victoria on her accession in 1837. He also made monuments and statues (*Sir Henry Havelock*, 1861, Trafalgar Square, London). His work was uneven in qual-ity and despite the demand for his services his extravagance led him to bankruptcy and he died

in the Middlesex Hospital after being found lying 'literally in the gutter with threepence in his pocket'. His brother **Henry** (1802–37) was also a sculptor. He adopted the name Henry Bur-lowe, evidently to distance himself from the dissolute William.

Bell, Clive (*b* East Shefford, Berkshire, 16 Sept. 1881; *d* London, 17 Sept. 1964). British writer on art. In 1910 he met Roger *Fry and quickly became his chief disciple in helping to spread an appreciation of *Post-Impressionism in Britain. Bell helped with the organization of Fry's first Post-Impressionist exhibition (1910), and he chose the British section of the second one (1912), including work by his wife Vanessa *Bell, Fry himself, and Duncan *Grant among *Bloomsbury Group artists, with Spencer *Gore and Wyndham *Lewis representing the more radical wing. His aesthetic ideas, expressed most fully in his book *Art* (1914), were much concerned with the theory of 'significant form'. He invented this term to denote 'the quality that distinguishes works of art from all other classes of objects'—a quality never found in nature but common to all works of art and existing independently of representational or symbolic content. The book is not now taken seriously as philosophy, and it contains some absurd statements ('The bulk of those who flour-ished between the high Renaissance and the contemporary movement may be divided into two classes, virtuosi and dunces'); however, it is written with fervour, and his ideas were influen-tial in spreading an attitude that placed emphasis on the formal qualities of a work of art (see FORMALISM).

Quentin Bell (1910–96), son of Clive and Van-essa Bell, was a painter, sculptor, potter, and author, probably best known for his writings on art, mainly on the Victorian period and the Bloomsbury Group. Between 1962 and 1975 he was a professor successively at the universities of Leeds, Hull, and Sussex. Quentin's son, **Julian Bell** (1952–), is a painter and writer on art; his books include a monograph on *Bonnard (1994).

Bell, Graham (*b* Durban, 21 Nov. 1910; *d* Newark-on-Trent, 9 Aug. 1943). British painter and art critic, born in South Africa. He moved to England in 1931 and became a pupil of Duncan *Grant. In the early 1930s he painted abstracts, but from 1934 to 1937 he abandoned painting for journalism, writing art criticism in a socialist vein. When he returned to painting it was in the soberly naturalistic style associated with the *Euston Road School. His work included portraits, landscapes, interiors, and still-lifes. He was killed on an RAF training flight in the Second World War. In 1947 Kenneth *Clark wrote of Bell: 'his critical intelligence was extremely acute . . . I think he would have become a very good painter. There is an air of largeness and essential truth in his best work which only needs filling out and enriching in order to become great.'

Bell, Vanessa (b London, 30 May 1879; d Firle, Sussex, 7 Apr. 1961). British painter and designer. She married Clive *Bell in 1907, and like him and her sister Virginia Woolf was a central figure of the *Bloomsbury Group. Her early work, up to about 1910, and her paintings produced after the First World War are tasteful and fairly conventional, in the tradition of the *New English Art Club, but in the intervening years she was briefly in the vanguard of progressive ideas in British art. At this time, stimulated by the *Post-Impressionist exhibitions of Roger *Fry (with whom she had an affair), she worked with bright colours and bold designs and by 1914 was painting completely abstract pictures. Her designs for Fry's *Omega Workshops included a folding screen (1913–14, V&A, London) clearly showing the influence of *Matisse. From 1916—while remaining on good terms with her husband—she lived with Duncan *Grant. They spent a good deal of time in London and travelling abroad, but they lived mainly at Charleston Farmhouse, at Firle, Sussex, and did much painted decoration in the house; it has been restored as a Bloomsbury memorial and is open to the public (the couple are buried together nearby in Firle churchyard). In addition to the work at Charleston, they collaborated on other decorative schemes, including a series of murals at Berwick church, Sussex, a few miles away. Bell's independent paintings included portraits, landscapes, interiors, and figure compositions. After the Second World War, her work—like that of Grant—went out of fashion, but she continued painting vigorously into her old age, even though the death of her son, the poet Julian Bell (1908–37), in the Spanish Civil War was 'the end of all real happiness' (Richard Shone, *Bloomsbury Portraits*, 1976).

Bella, Stefano della (b Florence, 18 May 1610; d Florence, 22 July 1664). Italian etcher and draughtsman. He was one of the greatest and most prolific printmakers of his day, producing more than 1,000 etchings (as well as a huge number of drawings). Most of his career was spent in his native Florence, where his patrons included the *Medici family, but he also worked in Rome (1633–9) and in Paris (1639–50). His output was highly varied, including military scenes, landscapes, animal subjects, and designs for masques. Early in his career he was strongly influenced by *Callot, but later his style became more naturalistic, reflecting his admiration for *Rembrandt's prints (he visited the Netherlands in 1647).

Bellange, Jacques (d Nancy, 1616). French painter, etcher, draughtsman, and designer, active in Nancy, where he worked for the dukes of Lorraine from 1602. Much of his work has perished, including murals and ephemeral decorative work, and only a handful of surviving paintings are confidently attributed to him, notably the *Lamentation* (Hermitage, St Petersburg), the *Stigmatization of St Francis* (Mus. Historique, Nancy), and a pair of panels of the *Virgin* and *Angel of the Annunciation* (Kunsthalle, Karlsruhe). His reputation now rests mainly on his etchings, which are among the finest of their time and represent the final flowering of the *Mannerist tradition. They are mainly on religious subjects, with very elegant, elongated figures—highly artificial in style yet expressing an intense mystical feeling. He also produced a few prints on *genre subjects, which are more naturalistic in style, notably *The Blind Hurdy-Gurdy Player*.

Bellano, Bartolommeo. See RICCIO.

Bellany, John (b Port Seton, 18 June 1942). Scottish painter, working in a vigorous—at times rather tormented—*Expressionist style. He was born and brought up in a fishing village near Edinburgh, and the imagery of his work is often derived from the sea, although it is transformed into a kind of personal mythology. His most characteristic pictures are large allegorical compositions involving hybrid human and animal forms, painted with explosive brushwork and suggesting some vague menace. In addition to such works, Bellany has painted many portraits, including a well-known one of the cricketer Ian Botham (1985, NPG, London). In the late 1980s he became seriously ill and he had a liver transplant in 1988; after his recovery his work became more optimistic in spirit. This is expressed in the coloured etchings he began to produce in the early 1990s as well as his paintings.

Bellechose, Henri (d ?Dijon, 1440/4). Netherlandish painter who in 1415 succeeded *Malouel as court painter to John the Fearless, Duke of *Burgundy, in Dijon. Only one documented work by him survives, the *Martyrdom of St Denis* (*c*.1416, Louvre, Paris). The traditional view (based on some rather vague documentary evidence) is that this work was begun by Malouel and completed by Bellechose, but scholarly opinion now inclines to attribute it to Bellechose alone.

Bellegambe, Jean (*b* Douai, *c*. 1470/80; *d* Douai, 1535/6). Netherlandish painter and designer, active in Douai, where he was the leading artist of his day. Douai, now in northern France, was neither typically Flemish nor typically French, and the same is true of Bellegambe, who was one of the most individual Netherlandish painters of his period—notably in his sense of fantasy and his feeling for delicate colour harmonies. His output consisted mainly of altarpieces for local churches, for example a large *polyptych for the Benedictine abbey at Anchin, known as the *Credo* Altarpiece (1508–13, Mus. de la Chartreuse, Douai); this is generally considered his masterpiece. Although his elaborate architectural settings show some kinship with *Antwerp Mannerism, Bellegambe's dignified figures reveal his allegiance to the 15th-century Netherlandish tradition.

Bellini. Family of Venetian painters who played a dominant role in the art of their city for three-quarters of a century. **Jacopo** (*b* Venice, *c*.1400; *d* Venice, 1470/1) was the father of Gentile and Giovanni and the father-in-law of *Mantegna. He was a pupil of *Gentile da Fabriano, with whom he probably worked in Florence in the early 1420s (although the documentation is equivocal). From the 1430s he carried out a number of prestigious commissions in north Italy, including a fresco of the *Crucifixion* in Verona Cathedral (1436) and (after defeating *Pisanello in competition) a portrait of Lionello d'*Este in Ferrara. However, all these works have perished, and his surviving pictures are mainly fairly simple and traditional representations of the Madonna and Child, of which only one is dated (1448, Brera, Milan). Attractive though they are, they do little to suggest why he achieved such high esteem in his day, and a better indication of his quality and originality as an artist can be gained from his drawings. Two large, bound volumes of these survive (BM, London, and Louvre, Paris); together they contain almost 300 drawings, mainly finished compositions, some of them very elaborate. They show that he was keenly alert to new ideas, and many of them are remarkable for bold perspective effects conveying an exhilarating sense of space. The volumes were inherited by Jacopo's sons, who used them as quarries for ideas.

Gentile (*b* Venice, *c*.1430/5; *bur*. Venice, 23 Feb. 1507) is generally thought to have been the elder son, although the evidence for this (and for his birthdate) is inconclusive. He presumably trained with his father, and is known to have collaborated with him around 1460. By 1465 he was working independently, and for the next 40 years he was one of the leading painters in Venice. As with his father, however, most of the major works on which his reputation was based have perished. They included a good deal of decorative work in the Doges' Palace, Venice, and erotic scenes painted for the harem of Sultan Mehmet II, when Gentile worked at his court in Constantinople in 1479–81; his portrait of Mehmet, however, survives (albeit much restored) in the National Gallery, London. The most famous of his extant works are probably the *Procession of the Relic of the True Cross* (1496) and the *Miracle at Ponte di Lorenzo* (1500), two huge canvases crowded with anecdotal detail of contemporary Venetian life. Both are in the Accademia, Venice.

Giovanni (*b* ?Venice, *c*.1430/5; *d* Venice, ?29 Nov. 1516) was far and away the most important member of the family—one of the greatest and most influential artists of the *Renaissance. During his long and prolific career he transformed Venice from a city that was provincial in terms of its painting into a centre rivalling Florence and Rome in significance. He not only brought Venetian painting a prominence it had never known before, but also gave it a distinctive character, expressing himself through colour, light, and atmosphere in a way that contrasted with the traditional Florentine preoccupation with line, and he was a direct inspiration to the numerous Venetian painters of the following generation who trained in his studio. His importance in Venetian art is indeed so great that Kenneth *Clark considered that 'No other school of painting is to the same extent the creation of one man.' In spite of his fame, his career is in general poorly documented. He seems to have lived a life of uneventful devotion to his art, rarely if ever leaving the Veneto, and there are only scraps of biographical information about him. Few of his paintings bear a date or can be convincingly dated on external evidence. Therefore his development can usually be followed only in broad outline rather than precise detail, as—over a period of more than half a century—he moved from a sharp, linear manner with roots in the Middle Ages to a style of mellow breadth and classical dignity.

Giovanni was presumably trained by his father Jacopo, but the major influence on his formative years was that of his brother-in-law Mantegna. This—and Bellini's own originality—is made clear by a comparison of their celebrated pictures of the *Agony in the Garden*, both painted about 1460–5 and both now in the National Gallery, London. The compositions are closely related, both deriving from one of Jacopo's drawings, but there is great difference in treatment, particularly of the landscape: Mantegna's is sharp, precise, and analytical, Bellini's is lyrical and atmospheric. Another important influence on him was *Antonello da Messina, who was in Venice in 1475–6; Bellini admired not only his mastery of the new technique of *oil painting (of which he too became a consummate exponent), but also his lucid handling of space and form. To the end of his long life he continued to absorb new ideas; from the year before his death dates the dreamy *Woman with a Mirror* (KH Mus., Vienna), which is strongly influenced by *Giorgione, who was young enough to be his grandson. But despite his borrowings, Bellini always remained distinctly himself, for he had an extraordinary ability to assimilate ideas and blend them into a harmonious synthesis: as the Bellini specialist Jennifer Fletcher put it, 'Some artists invented more but none perfected so much.' His genius remained undiminished by advancing years, and it is easy to credit the remark made by *Dürer on his visit to Venice in 1505–7 that although Bellini was 'very old' he was still 'the best painter'. (Dürer's account of his meeting with Bellini gives a rare—and very complimentary—glimpse of his personality: whereas other Venetian artists were hostile to the German visitor and jealous of his skills, the great man treated him with courtesy and respect.)

Bellini painted excellent portraits, of which the *Doge Leonardo Loredan* (c.1501–4, NG, London) is the best-known example, and a few mythologies and allegories, notably the *Feast of the Gods* (1514, NG, Washington; altered after his death by *Titian). Like his brother Gentile, he also painted several scenes from Venetian history (destroyed) in the Doges' Palace. However, he was above all a religious painter. His most characteristic subject was the Madonna and Child, and only *Raphael has rivalled him in the beauty and variety of his treatment of the theme, ranging from the wistful melancholy of *The Madonna of the Meadow* (c.1510, NG, London), one of the loveliest examples of his ability to bring together figures and landscape in perfect harmony, to the monumentality of the

S. Zaccaria Altarpiece (1505, S. Zaccaria, Venice), perhaps the grandest of all *sacre conversazioni*. Another favourite subject was the Dead Christ, which was particularly suited to the combination of gravity and tenderness at which he excelled. He rarely attempted subjects with a strong narrative element, as he was much more interested in atmosphere than action. This concern with the evocation of mood was one of his most important legacies to his pupils. From about 1490 almost all the painters who became eminent in Venice during the next generation (including Giorgione, *Sebastiano del Piombo, and Titian) are either known to or believed to have trained in his workshop. Bellini also had some influence in Florence, via Fra *Bartolommeo, who visited Venice in 1508.

Bellmer, Hans (b Kattowitz, Germany [now Katowice, Poland], 13 Mar. 1902; d Paris, 24 Feb. 1975). Polish-French graphic artist, painter, sculptor, photographer, and writer, all of whose work is explicitly erotic. In 1933 he constructed an articulated plaster figure of a young girl, inspired partly by an infatuation with his 15-year-old cousin Ursula. He photographed his creation in various attitudes and states of dismemberment (sometimes partly clothed) and published a collection of the photographs as *Die Puppe* ('The Doll') in Karlsruhe in 1934; a French edition, *La Poupée*, was published in Paris in 1936. Bellmer sent samples of the photographs to André *Breton in Paris, and the *Surrealists were highly excited by these striking images of 'vice and enchantment'. In 1938, in danger of arrest by the Nazis, Bellmer fled from Berlin to Paris to join the Surrealists. He was interned at the beginning of the war (with Max *Ernst), then lived in the south of France, 1942–6, before returning to Paris, where he began a long series of drawings and etchings that developed the violent eroticism of his dolls. Bellmer also produced paintings and sculpture in a similar vein. His work includes some of the acknowledged masterpieces of erotic art, but it was not well known until a large retrospective in 1971–2 at the Centre National d'Art Contemporain, Paris.

Bellori, Giovanni Pietro (b Rome, 15 Jan. 1613; d Rome, 19 Feb. 1696). Italian biographer, art theorist, antiquarian, and collector. His most important work—a basic source for the history of 17th-century art—is *Le vite de' pittori, scultori et architetti moderni* (1672), in the preparation of which he was helped by his friend *Poussin. In contrast to most authors of biographical compilations, Bellori was highly selective in the artists he discussed, limiting himself to twelve subjects—*Algardi, *Barocci, *Caravaggio, Agostino and Annibale *Carracci, *Domenichino, François *Duquesnoy, van *Dyck, the architect Domenico Fontana, *Lanfranco, Poussin, and *Rubens. The preface to the work (originally delivered as a lecture at the Accademia di S. Luca, Rome, in 1664) became the classic statement of the concept of *ideal art. It had a decisive influence on French academic theory and later became the theoretical basis of the *Neoclassicism preached by *Winckelmann. Bellori planned a sequel to his *Lives*, for which he wrote biographies of *Maratta, *Reni, and *Sacchi. The life of Maratta was published in 1732 and the three biographies together, edited from his manuscript, in 1942.

Bellotto, Bernardo (*b* Venice, 30 Jan. 1721; *d* Warsaw, 17 Nov. 1780). Italian painter, draughtsman, and etcher, nephew, pupil, and assistant of *Canaletto in Venice. He became a member of the Venetian painters' guild in 1738 and in the 1740s he travelled widely in Italy, painting views of Florence, Rome, and other cities. In 1747 he left Italy for good, spending the rest of his life working successfully at various European courts, notably Dresden (1747–58 and 1761–6) and Warsaw (where he lived from 1767 until his death). He called himself Canaletto, and this caused confusion (perhaps deliberate) between his work and his uncle's, particularly in views of Venice. Bellotto's early work is indeed sometimes difficult to tell apart from his uncle's, but his mature style is more individual, distinguished by an almost Dutch interest in massed clouds, cast shadows, and rich foliage. His colouring is also generally more sombre than Canaletto's, much of his work being characterized by a steely grey. The best collections of his work are in Dresden (Gemäldegalerie) and Warsaw (Nat. Mus.). In the rebuilding of Warsaw after the Second World War his pictures were used as guides, even in the reconstruction of architectural ornament.

Bellows, George Wesley (*b* Columbus, Oh., 12 Aug. 1882; *d* New York, 8 Jan. 1925). American painter and lithographer, a leading pupil and follower of Robert *Henri. An outstanding athlete in his youth and noted for his hearty, outgoing character, Bellows is best known for his boxing scenes. The most famous of them is *A Stag at Sharkey's* (1907, Cleveland Mus. of Art), remarkable for its vivid sense of movement and energetic, sketchy brushwork (a 'stag' was a boxing match held in a private club). Such works rapidly won him a reputation, and in 1909—aged 27—he became the youngest person ever elected an associate member of the *National Academy of Design. He took a highly active part in the art life of his day and was one of the organizers of the *Armory Show in 1913. After this, his work tended to become less concerned with movement, placing more emphasis on formal balance. He was a man of strong social conscience, and his work included scenes of the urban poor—of which the most famous is the crowded tenement scene *Cliff Dwellers* (1913, Los Angeles County Mus. of Art)—and a series of paintings and lithographs about First World War atrocities. He did not take up lithography until 1916, but in the nine remaining years of his life he produced almost 200 prints, and he is accorded a high place among modern American printmakers. In the last five years of his life Bellows turned to landscapes and portraits and was considered one of the finest American portraitists of his day. His early death was caused by a ruptured appendix. See also ASHCAN SCHOOL.

Belvedere Torso. A marble fragment showing the torso and upper legs of a powerful male figure seated on a rock, now in the Vatican Museums and named after the Belvedere Court in the Vatican in which it was once displayed. It is signed by a Greek sculptor 'Apollonius, son of Nestor, Athenian', about whom nothing is known, and there is scholarly debate as to whether it is an original *Hellenistic work or a Roman copy. (It is sometimes alleged that the signature of Apollonius occurs also on the famous and stylistically similar bronze figure of a seated boxer in the Terme Museum in Rome, but most authorities now consider that this is a mirage.) The date of the discovery of the torso is uncertain, but it is first mentioned in the 1430s. It had become well known by 1500 and its majestic portrayal of heroic muscularity had a profound influence on *Michelangelo among other *Renaissance artists. From then until the 19th century it was widely regarded as one of the greatest works of art in the world, rivalled in status probably only by the *Apollo Belvedere and the *Laocoön among ancient sculptures, although its fame was generally more academic than popular. It was often referred to simply as 'the Torso'. Unusually, the figure has always been left unrestored, but various artists have attempted to reconstruct the work, notably *Flaxman, who made of it a group as *Hercules and Hebe* (1792, University College London, on loan to V&A). Although Hercules has been the most popular suggestion for the identity of the figure, there have been several others, including Ajax and Polyphemus. Between 1798 and 1815 the *Belvedere Torso* was in Paris, one of the many antique statues taken there by Napoleon.

bench end. In Christian churches, an upright panel, often richly carved, terminating either end of the benches (now usually called 'pews') on which the congregation sits. Such seating in the naves of medieval churches became general only towards the end of the 14th and during the 15th century. This was one of the symptoms of the growing importance of the laity in church life; pews were provided for their convenience, and their decoration reflects secular rather than ecclesiastical taste. Carvings on bench ends often have subjects from popular piety or fables and they generally verge on folk art, although the quality of the carving is often extremely high. In England such carvings are particularly common in East Anglia and the West Country, reflecting the prosperity of the middle classes in these regions.

Benedetto da Maiano. See MAIANO.

Benedictional of St Ethelwold. See WINCHESTER SCHOOL.

Benesch, Otto (*b* Ebenfurth, 29 June 1896; *d* Vienna, 16 Nov. 1964). Austrian art historian. He had wide interests, but he was best known as an authority on graphic art and he was director of the *Albertina in Vienna from 1947 to 1961. An industrious and painstaking scholar, he compiled the standard illustrated catalogue of *Rembrandt's drawings (6 vols., 1954–7, 2nd edn. 1973), and his other publications include *The Art of the Renaissance in Northern Europe* (1947) and monographs on *Altdorfer (1939) and *Schiele (1950); his father **Heinrich Benesch** (1862–1947), a railway executive and art collector, was one of Schiele's most important patrons.

Bénézit, Emmanuel (*b* Jersey, 1854; *d* Paris, 1920). French art historian, editor of the *Dictionnaire critique et documentaire des peintres, dessinateurs, sculpteurs et graveurs*, first published in three volumes in 1911–23. The fourth edition, in fourteen volumes, appeared in 1999. Apart from the *Lexikon* of *Thieme–Becker, it is the largest and most comprehensive dictionary of artists' biographies in current use.

Bening (or **Benig**). The name of two Netherlandish book *illuminators, father and son. **Sanders** (sometimes called Alexander) (*d* Ghent, 1519) worked in Ghent and Bruges. No documented works by him are known, but it has been suggested that he should be identified with the *Master of Mary of Burgundy, which would give him an artistic status appropriate to the contemporary reputation he enjoyed. **Simon** (*b* ?Ghent, *c*.1483; *d* Bruges, 6 Nov. 1561) worked in Bruges and was the most famous illuminator of his time, representing the final sparks of the tradition as the manuscript was supplanted by the printed book. There is a self-portrait *miniature (1558) by him in the Victoria and Albert Museum, London, and various documented manuscripts by him survive. His daughter **Levina Teerlinc** (*d* London, 23 June 1576) was also a miniaturist. She settled in London in about 1545 and worked for Henry VIII, Mary I, and Elizabeth I.

Benois, Alexandre (*b* St Petersburg, 21 Apr. [3 May] 1870; *d* Paris, 9 Feb. 1960). Russian painter, stage designer, art historian, and critic, a leader and spokesman of the *World of Art group. He was a close friend and collaborator of *Diaghilev, in Russia and later in Paris, and he is best known for his stage designs for the Ballets Russes (notably for Stravinsky's *Petrushka*, 1911), in which he harmonized the tradition of Russian folk art with French *Rococo elements. Following a difference of opinion with Diaghilev he worked at Stanislavsky's Moscow Arts Theatre, 1912–14. After the Revolution he was appointed curator of paintings at the *Hermitage in Leningrad. He held this post from 1918 to 1925, then settled permanently in Paris. His writings include several volumes of memoirs and books on art, including ones translated into English as *The Russian School of Painting* (1916), *Reminiscences of the Russian Ballet* (1941), and *Memoirs* (1960). Benois's son **Nikolai** (1901–88) was a stage designer at La Scala, Milan; his niece **Nadia Benois** (1896–1975) settled in London in 1920 and worked as a ballet designer. The actor and writer Peter Ustinov is her son.

Benoit, Rigaud. See HYPPOLITE.

Benozzo Gozzoli. See GOZZOLI.

Benson, Ambrosius (*d* Bruges, Jan. 1550). Netherlandish painter of religious works and portraits. He was born in Italy (he was originally called Ambrogio Benzone), but from 1518 he worked in Bruges, where he continued the tradition of Gerard *David, to whom he worked as assistant for a time. Many of his pictures were done for the export trade to Italy and Spain, and he evidently had a flourishing business. There is a slightly southern flavour to his compositions and for a long time many of them were thought to be by an anonymous Spanish painter known as the Master of Segovia. His comparatively rare portraits are generally more individualized than his religious works.

Benson, Frank W. See TEN.

Benton, Thomas Hart (b Neosho, Mo., 15 Apr. 1889; d Kansas City, Mo., 19 Jan. 1975). American painter, the great-nephew of a famous American statesman of the same name. In 1908–11 he lived in Paris, where he studied at the *Académie Julian and became a friend of the *Synchromist Stanton *Macdonald-Wright. After his return to the USA he settled in New York and painted in the Synchromist manner for some years, but having failed to win success working in an avant-garde style, he abandoned modernism around 1920 and gained fame as one of the leading exponents of *Regionalism. His style became richly coloured and vigorous, with restlessly energetic rhythms and rather flat, sometimes almost cartoonish figures. His work included several murals, notably scenes of American life (1930–1) at the New School for Social Research in New York. In 1935 he left New York to become director of the City Art Institute and School of Design in Kansas City, Missouri, and he lived in that city for the rest of his life. When Regionalism declined in popularity in the 1940s Benton turned more to depicting scenes from American history, and some of his later work introduced American types into representations of Greek myths or biblical stories. Benton wrote two autobiographies, *An Artist in America* (1937) and *An American in Art* (1969). A passage from the second shows how completely he turned his back on the modernism he had espoused in his youth: 'Modern art became, especially in its American derivations, a simple smearing and pouring of material, good for nothing but to release neurotic tensions. Here finally it became like a bowel movement or a vomiting spell.' In view of these words, it is ironic that Benton was influential on Jackson *Pollock, whom he taught at the *Art Students League of New York in the early 1930s.

Bentvueghels. See SCHILDERSBENT.

Berain, Jean (bapt. Saint-Mihiel, Lorraine, 4 June 1640; d Paris, 24 Jan. 1711). French designer, decorator, and engraver. He was chief designer at the court of Louis XIV and also worked for the Paris Opéra and various eminent private patrons. His large and highly varied output included designs for stage scenery, furniture, wall decorations, costumes, and festivities. Few of the objects he created survive, but many of his designs were published as engravings; they display a light and whimsical style that heralds the *Rococo. His son **Jean Berain II** (1678–1726) was also a designer.

Bérard, Christian (b Paris, 20 Aug. 1902; d Paris, 12 Feb. 1949). French designer, painter, and draughtsman. With *Berman and *Tchelitchew he was the leading representative of *Neo-Romanticism in French painting, but his career was devoted mainly to design, particularly for the theatre and also for the cinema and the fashion world. He had a particularly fruitful relationship with Jean *Cocteau, whom he met in 1926 and whose portrait he painted in 1928 (MoMA, New York). Bérard made designs for several of his plays and three of his films, most famously *Beauty and the Beast* (1946), which was perfectly suited to his gift for fantasy and 'may be considered in some respects almost as much the achievement of Bérard as of Cocteau' (*The Oxford Companion to Film*, 1976). His other work included fashion drawings in such magazines as *Harper's Bazaar* and *Vogue*.

Berchem, Nicolaes (bapt. Haarlem, 1 Oct. 1620; d Amsterdam, 18 Feb. 1683). Dutch painter, active mainly in Haarlem but also in Amsterdam. He was the son of the still-life painter Pieter *Claesz., and it is not known why he adopted a different surname. Claesz. was his first teacher, but although Berchem tried his hand at most subjects, no still-lifes by him are known. His speciality was the Italianate pastoral landscape, and among his contemporaries only Jan *Both rivalled his fame in this field. There is no documentary evidence that he visited Italy, but he was probably there at least once (the early 1650s is thought to be the likeliest time). His career was highly successful and he had numerous pupils and followers; later he exerted a strong influence on 18th-century English and French landscape painters, *Gainsborough and *Watteau being among the artists who particularly admired his work. His large output is well represented in British galleries. About 700 paintings by him survive, as well as more than 300 drawings and about 50 etchings.

Berckheyde, Gerrit (b Haarlem, 6 June 1638; d Haarlem, 10 June 1698). Dutch painter of town views and architectural scenes, active in Haarlem, Amsterdam, and The Hague. His representations of these cities have documentary accuracy, but they are never dry, achieving a poetic harmony by a subtle use of light and shade (three of his pictures of Haarlem, including a church interior, are in the National Gallery, London). The work of Gerrit's elder brother **Job** (*b* Haarlem, 27 Jan. 1630; *d* Haarlem, 23 Nov. 1693) is often very similar, although he also painted other subjects, including *genre and biblical scenes.

Berenson, Bernard (*b* Butremancz, 26 June 1865; *d* Settignano, 6 Oct. 1959). American art historian, critic, and connoisseur. He was born in Lithuania and educated in Boston and at Harvard University (his family emigrated to the USA when he was 10), but he spent most of his long life in Italy, first visiting the country in 1888 and settling there permanently in 1899. He built up a formidable reputation as an authority on Italian *Renaissance painting and was associated with several prominent dealers and collectors, notably Lord *Duveen and Isabella Stewart *Gardner, advising them on purchases. The fortune he earned in the picture trade has caused his impartiality to be questioned, and many of his attributions have been downgraded, but his lists of the work of Renaissance painters formed a basis for further work for many years. His most enduring work of scholarship is *The Drawings of the Florentine Painters* (1903, 2nd edn. 1938, 3rd edn.—in Italian—1961). He amassed a huge library of books and photographs and an impressive art collection at his villa, I Tatti, at Settignano, near Florence, which he left to Harvard University. In 1961 it opened as the Harvard University Center for Italian Renaissance Studies. Dapper and polylingual, Berenson often played host to visiting art historians and intellectuals at I Tatti and was a renowned conversationalist, diarist, and bon viveur. See also TACTILE VALUES.

Berg, Claus (*b* Lübeck, *c*.1470/80; *d* ?Lübeck, *c*.1535). German woodcarver, active mainly at Odense in Denmark, where he was invited *c.* 1504 by the country's queen, Christina of Saxony. He ran a large workshop and his masterpiece is a huge altarpiece (1517–22) made for the Franciscan church in Odense and now in St Canute's Cathedral. His dramatic and emotional late *Gothic style has affinities with that of Veit *Stoss and he is presumed to have trained in Stoss's circle in south Germany. Berg left Denmark in 1532, perhaps because of the spread of the Reformation there.

Berger, John. See KITCHEN SINK SCHOOL.

Bergh, Richard (*b* Stockholm, 28 Dec. 1858; *d* Saltsjö-Storängen, nr. Stockholm, 29 Jan. 1919). Swedish painter, writer, and art administrator, son of a landscape painter, **Edvard Berghe** (1828–80). From 1878 to 1881 he studied at the Academy in Stockholm, where his father was a professor, then spent the next three years in Paris. His work was strongly influenced by French open-air painting and *Symbolism, but he made them the basis of a distinctive Swedish national romanticism, as in his most famous work, *Nordic Summer Evening* (1899–1900, Konstmuseum, Gothenburg). It shows a man and a woman on a veranda looking out over a lake in an atmosphere heavy with psychological tension. Bergh was also a fine portraitist, notably of his artist and intellectual friends. He took a keen interest in political and social issues and was a founding member (1885) of the Artists' Union, which revolted against the conservatism of the Stockholm Academy. In 1915 he was appointed director of the Nationalmuseum in Stockholm, which he reorganized into a modern, dynamic institution. Collections of his articles on art were published in 1908 (revised 1919) and (posthumously) in 1921.

Bergognone (or Borgognone), **Ambrogio** (Ambrogio da Fossano) (*b* ?Fossano, *c*.1455; *d* Milan, 21 May 1523). Italian painter, active mainly in and around Milan. He is one of the best examples of the continuance of a native Milanese tradition into the 16th century, for unlike so many of his Lombard contemporaries he was virtually unaffected by the art of *Leonardo. On the other hand, he was open to influence from Netherlandish painting and his nickname (meaning 'Burgundian') may indicate that he spent some time in northern Europe. His style is static and undramatic, aiming at a typically late *quattrocento mood of devotional calm, which is often enhanced by pale landscape backgrounds of great delicacy. He was fairly prolific as a painter of both frescos (notably at the Certosa di Pavia) and altarpieces; there are examples of his work in several churches in Milan and in numerous public collections, including the National Gallery, London. His brother **Bernardino** (*c*.1460–*c*.1524), likewise known as Bergognone, was also a painter and sometimes worked as Ambrogio's assistant.

Berlinghieri. Family of Italian painters active in Lucca during the 13th century. **Berlinghiero Berlinghieri** (*d c*.1235) was the founder of the family and had three painter sons, **Barone**, **Bonaventura** (d. *c*.1274), and **Marco**. A painted

Crucifix (Mus. Naz. di Villa Guinigi, Lucca) signed 'Berlingeri' without Christian name is generally attributed to Berlinghiero, and several other works have been given to him on the basis of it. Bonaventura, evidently the most talented of his sons, is known chiefly for his signed and dated altarpiece of *St Francis and Scenes from his Life* (1235) in the church of S. Francesco at Pescia. It is one of the earliest pictorial representations of Franciscan ideas, produced only nine years after the saint's death. There are no other signed or documented works by Bonaventura, but several have been attributed to him on stylistic evidence.

Berlin Painter. Greek vase painter, active in Athens *c*.500–*c*.460 BC, one of the outstanding masters of the *red-figure technique. He is named after a large amphora (wine jar) (*c*.480 BC) in the Antikenmuseum, Berlin, featuring a group of Hermes, a satyr, and a faun—'a marvellous composition of three superimposed figures united in a single harmonious contour' (Martin Robertson, *A History of Greek Art*, 1975). About 300 vases are attributed to him, usually depicting one lithe, elegant figure on either side. The Berlin Painter is often compared and contrasted with his great contemporary the *Cleophrades Painter. Sir John Beazley (1885–1970), the most renowned of all authorities on Greek vase painting, characterized them respectively as 'the painter of grace and the painter of power', and wrote that the Cleophrades Painter 'may be said to play a kind of Florentine to the Berlin Painter's Sienese'.

Berman, Eugene (*b* St Petersburg, 4 [16] Nov. 1899; *d* Rome, 14 Dec. 1972). Russian-born painter and stage designer who became an American citizen in 1937. In 1918 he fled the Russian Revolution and settled in Paris. There he became friendly with *Tchelitchew (another Russian émigré) and a group of painters who became known as *'Neo-Romantics', painting dreamlike scenes with mournful, drooping figures. In 1935 he emigrated to New York, where he worked mainly as a designer for ballet and opera, in which field he was considered one of the outstanding artists of his day. In his later years he spent much of his time in Italy.

Bermejo, Bartolomé (*b* ?Córdoba, ?*c*.1440; *d* ?Barcelona, *c*.1498). Spanish painter, evidently from Córdoba, but active in northern Spain—in Aragon and then from 1486 in Barcelona. His name was originally Bartolomé de Cárdenas; his nickname 'Bermejo' (Spanish for 'red') presum-

ably indicates that he had red hair or a ruddy complexion. He was one of the first Spanish painters to work in *oils and it has been suggested that he learned the technique in the Netherlands. His most celebrated work is the powerfully emotional *Pietà in Barcelona Cathedral, signed and dated 1490. It is one of the acknowledged masterpieces of the period and Bermejo is 'generally recognised as the greatest painter active in Spain in the Middle Ages' (Eric Young, *Bartolomé Bermejo*, 1975). See also HISPANO-FLEMISH STYLE.

Bernard, Émile (*b* Lille, 28 Apr. 1868; *d* Paris, 16 Apr. 1941). French painter and writer. In 1884–6 he studied in the studio of *Cormon, where he became a friend of *Toulouse-Lautrec and also of Louis *Anquetin, with whom he developed *Cloisonnism in 1887–8. Between 1888 and 1891 he worked closely with *Gauguin at *Pont-Aven; he had a stimulating effect on his great colleague and together they created *Synthetism. Thereafter, however, Bernard's work as a painter greatly declined in importance, and he became of interest chiefly for his activities as a writer, playing a significant role as a sponsor of *Post-Impressionism. In 1890 he helped to organize the first retrospective exhibition of van *Gogh's work (soon after his death), he published much journalism and criticism on *Cézanne, *Redon, and other artists, and his correspondence with some of the leading painters of the time has been a rich quarry for art historians.

Bernini, Gianlorenzo (*b* Naples, 7 Dec. 1598; *d* Rome, 28 Nov. 1680). Italian sculptor, architect, painter, and designer, the supreme artist of the Italian *Baroque. His father **Pietro** (1562–1629) was a *Mannerist sculptor of some distinction, active in Naples and then from c.1605 in Rome, and Gianlorenzo owed to him not only his early training in the handling of marble but also his introduction to the powerful patrons, the *Borghese and the *Barberini, who fostered his early career. For Cardinal Scipione Borghese he executed a remarkable series of life-size marble sculptures: *Aeneas, Anchises, and Ascanius* (1618–19), the *Rape of Proserpine* (1621–2), *David* (1623), and *Apollo and Daphne* (1622–5), all in the Borghese Gallery in Rome. In their dramatic vigour and movement these works made a complete break with the Mannerist tradition, and they showed unprecedented virtuosity in making cold stone seem as supple as living flesh (Bernini's biographer *Baldinucci commented that 'his chisel was applied in such a way that one could believe it had been cutting wax instead of marble').

After the election of Maffeo Barberini as Pope Urban VIII (1623) Bernini became the principal artist in the papal court and in Rome. According to Baldinucci, Maffeo had 'scarcely ascended the sacred throne' when he summoned Bernini and told him: 'It is your great fortune to see Cardinal Maffeo Barberini pope, but our fortune is far greater in that Cavalier Bernini lives during our pontificate.' In 1629 he was appointed architect to St Peter's, for which his work included the great bronze *baldacchino over the high altar (1624–33), the huge marble statue of St Longinus (1629–38), which stands in a niche in one of the piers of the crossing (see also MOCHI), and Urban's tomb (1628–47), which is in bronze and white and coloured marbles. However, after Urban's death in 1644 Bernini fell under a cloud. This was partly because of one of his rare failures (a bell tower he added to the façade of St Peter's was demolished in 1646 because of structural problems), but as much because of the different artistic tastes of the new pope, Innocent X (Giambattista *Pamphili), who favoured Bernini's rival, *Algardi.

During Innocent's papacy (1644–55) Bernini worked mainly for private patrons, his masterpiece from this period being the Cornaro Chapel (1645–52) in S. Maria della Vittoria, with the celebrated marble group of the *Ecstasy of St Teresa*. Although the chapel is fairly small, it is the supreme example of Bernini's aims and achievement in the fusion of sculpture, architecture, and painting into a decorative and emotional whole. Bernini never lost his position as architect to St Peter's, however, and he did do some work for Innocent X, including the Fountain of the Four Rivers (1648–51) in the Piazza Navona. This is the most famous and spectacular of his fountains, and with these, his buildings, and his outdoor statuary he has had a greater effect on the face of Rome than any other artist.

After Innocent's death in 1655 and the accession of Alexander VII (Fabio *Chigi), Bernini was restored to full favour and was almost immediately given two major commissions at St Peter's: the decoration of the *Cathedra Petri* (Throne of St Peter), and the building of the vast colonnade round the piazza in front of the church. The *Cathedra Petri* (1657–66), a setting for the wooden chair believed to have been used by St Peter, provides an appropriately spectacular sight to conclude the vista at the east end of the church. Four immense bronze figures of doctors of the Church support the

chair, also encased in bronze, and gilt angels and cherubs float above on stucco clouds; they surround a window bearing an image of the Dove of the Holy Spirit, from which a burst of light seems to emanate. The enclosure of the piazza in front of St Peter's is his greatest achievement as an architect—a design of the utmost dignity and grandeur, expressing the overwhelming authority of the Church. Bernini himself compared the sweeping colonnades to motherly arms that reach out to 'embrace Catholics to reinforce their belief'.

In 1665–6 Bernini visited Paris with the aim of designing the east front of the *Louvre, but his plans were abandoned in favour of a French design, and the trip—which he had made unwillingly—was not a success (the 'invitation' from Louis XIV was in effect a command—one of a series of humiliations that he inflicted on Alexander VII and a sign that the balance of artistic power was beginning to shift from Italy to France). After his return to Rome Bernini continued to be extremely active into his old age (he was renowned for his phenomenal energy—an aspect of his fiery and quick-tempered personality). His late religious works were intensely spiritual, reflecting his own ardent faith (*The Blessed Lodovica Albertoni*, 1671–4, S. Francesco a Ripa, Rome). As an architect his late work included both secular and religious buildings, notably the façade (begun 1664) of the Palazzo Chigi, which had great influence on Baroque palace design throughout Europe, and S. Andrea al Quirinale (1658–70), a fairly small church but one of his most sophisticated designs in its use of rich architectural and sculptural decoration to create an appropriate setting for the mysteries of the Catholic faith.

In addition to large works of sculpture and architecture, Bernini executed many portrait busts, among the finest of which are those of Louis XIV (1665, Versailles) and Costanza Buonarelli (c.1635, Bargello, Florence), the wife of one of his assistants, with whom he had a stormy love affair before he made a happy marriage in 1639. He was also a brilliant wit, a *caricaturist, and—for his private pleasure—a painter of such high quality that his rare surviving works (which include several self-portraits) have sometimes been attributed to *Velázquez; his portrait of *Poussin (c.1627, York AG) was long considered a self-portrait by the French artist. Bernini also had a passionate interest in the theatre. There are few material remains of his activity in this field, but the diarist John Evelyn saw a remarkable demonstration of his versatility when visiting Rome in 1644: 'Bernini . . . gave a public opera wherein he painted the scenes, cut the statues, invented the engines [stage machinery], composed the music, writ the comedy, and built the theatre.'

Bernini's work was a dominant influence on sculpture in Italy (and to a certain degree in other Catholic countries) until well into the 18th century, but thereafter his reputation plummeted. To the *Neoclassical taste of the later 18th century, his approach to sculpture was anathema, to *Ruskin in the 19th century it seemed 'impossible for false taste and base feeling to sink lower', and to the devotees of the idea of *truth to materials in the 20th century he appeared, in the words of his most distinguished apologist, Rudolf *Wittkower, as 'the Antichrist personified'. It was only in the second half of the 20th century that he came to enjoy a reputation, comparable with his status in his lifetime, as the greatest sculptor since *Michelangelo and one of the giants of Baroque architecture.

Bernward of Hildesheim (*b* c.960; *d* Hildesheim, 20 Nov. 1022). German ecclesiastic and art patron. He was abbot of the Benedictine monastery at Hildesheim in Saxony from 993 until his death, and for the church of St Michael there (begun 1001) he commissioned the famous bronze doors (c.1008–15) and a great bronze column (c.1018–20), probably intended to support the paschal candle. They are important not only for being among the outstanding European works of their period, but also for marking the revival of the *cire-perdue* technique of casting, which had virtually disappeared since the time of Charlemagne. A contemporary biographer records that Bernward himself practised metalwork and manuscript *illumination, but no work can be attributed to him. He was canonized in 1192 and is a patron saint of goldsmiths.

Berruguete. Spanish artists, father and son, who are respectively associated with the beginnings of the *Renaissance and *Mannerist styles in their country. **Pedro** (*b* Paredes de Nava, nr. Valladolid, c.1450; *d* Paredes de Nava, c.1504) is said to have been court painter to Ferdinand and Isabella. He may be identifiable with the 'Pietro Spagnuolo' employed in 1477 with *Joos van Wassenhove on the decoration of the palace library at Urbino, but it is not until the 1480s that there is any firm documentation on his career. He did a good deal of work in fresco in Toledo Cathedral, but little of this survives. Most of his surviving paintings are altarpieces (several examples are in the Prado, Madrid); they are

essentially in the Netherlandish idiom that prevailed in Spain at this time, but they show Renaissance influence in their spatial clarity and use of classical architectural details. **Alonso** (*b* Paredes de Nava, c.1488; *d* Toledo, 13/26 Sept. 1561), sculptor and painter, was the son and probably pupil of Pedro. Between about 1504 and 1517, he was in Italy, where his work included the completion of Filippino *Lippi's *Coronation of the Virgin* (Louvre, Paris). By 1517 Berruguete was back in Spain (in Valladolid), and in the following year he was appointed court painter to Charles I (Emperor Charles V; see HABSBURG). However, his career flourished mainly as a sculptor, chiefly in Toledo, where he spent most of his time between 1539 and his death. Among his finest works is a set of wooden choir stalls with carvings of biblical figures in Toledo Cathedral (1539–43). The emotional intensity and expressive *contrapposto* characteristic of his style reflected the influence of *Michelangelo (who refers to Berruguete in his letters) and of the *Laocoön*, which he had studied in Rome. He is generally considered the greatest Spanish sculptor of the 16th century, his work having something of the spirit of El *Greco, who succeeded him as the outstanding artist in Toledo.

Berry, Jean, Duc de. See LIMBOURG.

Bertin, Jean-Victor. See COROT.

Bertoldo di Giovanni (*b* ?Florence, c.1430; *d* Poggio a Caiano, nr. Florence, 28 Dec. 1491). Florentine sculptor. He was a fairly minor talent, but he is remembered for three things. First, he was the pupil and assistant of *Donatello and briefly the teacher or mentor of *Michelangelo, thus forming a link between the greatest Italian sculptors of the 15th and 16th centuries. Secondly (and relatedly), he was the 'guide and chief' (*Vasari) of the informal art *academy that Lorenzo the Magnificent maintained in the *Medici garden near S. Marco (it was there that he knew Michelangelo). Thirdly, he developed a new type of sculpture—the smallscale bronze, intended, like the *cabinet picture, for the private collector. Bertoldo was responsible for the completion of two pulpits in S. Lorenzo left unfinished by Donatello at his death. His own most noteworthy work is a bronze *relief of a battle scene (c.1480, Bargello, Florence), which inspired one of Michelangelo's first works, the *Battle of the Lapiths and Centaurs* (c.1491, Casa Buonarroti, Florence). Bertoldo was also recognized as one of the leading portrait medallists of his time.

bestiary. A type of medieval book in which accounts of real and imaginary creatures (and also plants and minerals) were used to point moral lessons. The first known illustrated examples date from the early 12th century and in the late 12th and early 13th centuries the bestiary was one of the most popular types of *illuminated manuscript. It declined in popularity after the mid-13th century, but many of the exotic and fanciful creatures it had helped to make familiar, such as the unicorn, continued to be prevalent in medieval art, for example in the decoration of initials in manuscripts and later on *misericords.

Beuckelaer, Joachim. See BUECKELAER.

Beuys, Joseph (b Krefeld, 12 May 1921; d Düsseldorf, 23 Jan. 1986). German sculptor, draughtsman, teacher, and *Performance artist, regarded as one of the most influential figures in avant-garde art in Europe in the 1970s and 1980s. Like Yves *Klein, he was a leading light in shifting emphasis from what an artist makes to his personality, actions, and opinions, and he succeeded in creating a kind of personal mythology. (As a Luftwaffe pilot he was shot down in the Crimea in 1943 and according to his own account, which has been doubted, he was looked after by nomadic Tartars who kept him warm with fat and felt—materials that came to figure prominently in his work. The hat that he habitually wore hid the head injuries he received in the crash.) After the war he studied at the Düsseldorf Academy, 1946–51, and he became professor of sculpture there in 1961. He worked in various media, but is perhaps best known for his performances, of which the most famous was probably *How to Explain Pictures to a Dead Hare* (1965). In this he walked around an exhibition in the Schmela Gallery in Düsseldorf, his face covered in honey and gold leaf, carrying in his arms a dead hare, to which he gave an explanation of various pictures. He described the performance as 'A complex tableau about the problems of language, and about the problems of thought, of human consciousness and of the consciousness of animals.'

In 1962 Beuys became a member of *Fluxus, an international group of artists, opposed to tradition and professionalism in the arts, and he was also active in politics, aligning himself with the West German ecology party, the Greens. His 'presumptuous political dilettantism' eventually led to conflict with authority and in 1972 he was dismissed from his professorship. The protests that followed included a strike

by his students, and a settlement was eventually reached whereby he kept his title and studio but his teaching contract was ended. He devoted a good deal of his later career to public speaking and debate, and in 1982 he had a meeting with the Dalai Lama in Paris. By the end of his life he was an international celebrity and was regarded by his admirers as a kind of art guru. To many people, however, his work is pretentious or incomprehensible.

Bevan, Robert (b Hove, Sussex, 5 August 1865; d London, 8 July 1925). British painter and lithographer. During the 1890s he travelled a good deal and he met *Gauguin at Pont-Aven in 1894. In 1900 he settled in London, where he became a member of *Sickert's circle (he was a founding member of the *Camden Town Group in 1911 and of the *London Group in 1913). His work was much influenced by Gauguin's bold colour and flat patterning, and in his last years his style became increasingly simplified and schematic. He is best known for paintings featuring horses. His wife, the Polish-born **Stanislava de Karlowska** (1880–1952), whom he married in 1897, was also a painter. He made several visits to Poland with her.

Bewcastle Cross. See CELTIC ART.

Bewick, Thomas (b Cherryburn farm, Eltringham, Northumberland, 10 or 12 Aug. 1753; d Gateshead, 8 Nov. 1828). English engraver, active for most of his life in Newcastle upon Tyne. There he ran a thriving workshop; his account books and other records (many of which are in the Laing AG, Newcastle) show that he had clients in more than 50 towns throughout England, and he was renowned for his scrupulous honesty as a businessman. Most of the workshop's day-to-day jobs involved copper engraving, but for his own projects Bewick preferred *wood engraving, and he was the first artist to show the full potential of this technique. He had a great love of the countryside, and his finest works are natural history illustrations, particularly those to his celebrated books *A General History of Quadrupeds* (1790) and *A History of British Birds* (2 vols., 1797 and 1804), for which he wrote most of the text himself. The animals and birds are characterized with great skill, but Bewick is as much admired for his tailpieces—little (sometimes tiny) vignettes with which he concluded his account of each animal or bird. These miniature scenes give a wonderfully shrewd and sensitive picture of rural life, bringing out its bleakness and cruelty as well as its beauty and humour. Bewick himself punningly called these scenes 'Tale-pieces', for they were 'seldom without an endeavour to illustrate some truth or point some moral'. The success of his books helped to make wood engraving the dominant medium for book illustration for most of the 19th century and his work was carried on by several followers in Newcastle, notably his son **Robert** (1788–1849).

Bewick wrote an autobiography, which was posthumously published (edited by his daughter) in 1862; a more authoritative text, based on the original manuscript (BL, London), appeared in 1975. A year before his death he was visited by *Audubon, another great artist-naturalist, who left a touching account of his meeting with this 'perfect old Englishman', who was 'kind and attentive' and still—at the age of 74—'active and prompt in his labours', using 'delicate and beautiful tools . . . all made by himself'.

Beyeren, Abraham van (b The Hague, 1620/1; d Overschie, 1690). Dutch painter, little regarded in his day but now considered one of the greatest of still-life painters. He initially specialized in fish subjects, but in the 1650s he began to devote himself to sumptuous banquet tables laden with silver and gold vessels, Venetian glassware, fine fruit, and expensive table coverings of damask, satin, and velvet. Works of this kind, in which he was rivalled only by *Kalf, gave him even greater opportunity than his fish pieces to demonstrate his ability to show the play of light on varied surfaces and organize forms and colours into an opulent composition. He worked in various towns before settling in Overschie in 1678. In addition to still-lifes he painted seascapes.

Bibiena (or **Galli-Bibiena**). Family of Italian architects, *quadraturisti, and stage designers based in Bologna, members of which practised from the 1680s until the 1780s throughout Europe, from Lisbon to St Petersburg. The founder of the dynasty was **Giovanni Maria Galli** (1625–65), who adopted the name of his birthplace, Bibbiena, a small town in Tuscany. Other members of the family included **Alessandro** (1687–1769), **Antonio** (1700–74), **Carlo** (1728–87), **Ferdinando** (1657–1743), **Francesco** (1659–1739), and **Giuseppe** (1696–1757). Their work included fantastically elaborate stage settings for operas, balls, and various kinds of festivities, mainly produced in the service of the *Habsburg family in Vienna and of various German princelings. They also built several theatres in Italy and elsewhere, but most of these have been destroyed or much altered. The most illustrious and prolific member of the family was Ferdinando, who produced several books on architecture and scenography.

Bible historiale. See BONDOL.

Bible moralisée (French: 'moralized Bible'). A type of very lavish illuminated manuscript containing illustrated extracts and paraphrases from the Bible accompanied by a parallel series of pictures and commentaries supplying moral and allegorical interpretations. This type of book originated in France in the 13th century and only a small number were ever produced (the last c.1470) as they were so expensive and time-consuming to make. 'The explanatory pictures are of great variety and by no means confined to *typology, though this naturally plays a part . . . In arrangement the relationship of the text to the commentary is fairly uniform. The page is divided into columns, a narrow one with the written text followed by a broad one with the illustrations. In the thirteenth-century copies these are often placed in roundels giving the appearance of stained-glass windows' (Cambridge History of the Bible, vol. ii, 1969).

Biblia pauperum (Latin: 'poor man's bible'). A type of late medieval picture book for elementary instruction about the Bible, showing in pictures (with short explanatory texts) how the principal events from the life of Christ are prefigured in the Old Testament (see TYPOLOGY); in effect it was a Bible 'rendered in a compressed and popular manner that might supply poor preachers of no great intellectual attainment with material for their sermons and with pictures which could be shown to simple and unlettered folk' (Cambridge History of the Bible, vol. ii, 1969). The Biblia pauperum is thought to have originated in the mid-13th century in south Germany or Austria. There are about 80 manuscript examples surviving from the 14th century and about a dozen *block book editions were published in the 15th century, originally in the Netherlands. Images from the book were copied and adapted in sculpture, tapestries, stained glass, and easel paintings. Unlike the *Speculum humanae salvationis, the Biblia pauperum is strictly scriptural, with no historical or secular subjects among its types.

Bicci di Lorenzo. See LORENZO DI BICCI.

Biederman, Charles (b Cleveland, Oh., 23 Aug. 1906). American abstract artist and art theorist. From 1937 he abandoned painting and concentrated on coloured geometric reliefs, to which for some years he applied the word 'Structurist' (*Structurist Relief, Red Wing No. 20*, 1954–65, Tate, London): 'a Structurist work is neither painting nor sculpture, but a structural extension of the two.' His promotion of such works in his book *Art as the Evolution of Visual Knowledge* (1948) had an important influence on British *Constructivists, notably Kenneth and Mary *Martin and Victor *Pasmore, each of whom corresponded with Biederman. He has written other books and many articles on art theory.

Biedermeier. Term applied to an intimate, unassuming style characteristic of much German and Austrian art and interior decoration in the period from about 1815 (the end of the Napoleonic Wars) to 1848 (the Year of Revolutions). The name derives from an invented character, an unintentionally comic poet called Gottlieb Biedermaier [*sic*], who in the 1850s was a 'contributor' to the Munich journal *Fliegende Blätter* (Flying Leaves); *bieder* means plain or solid and *Maier* is a common surname, like Smith or Jones in English, so the character was meant to exemplify conventional bourgeois values. When the term was applied to the visual arts, it was originally used pejoratively, implying sentimentality and parochial dullness, but later it came to suggest more positive values, including comfort, good craftsmanship, and unostentatious charm. Biedermeier painting is concerned with the everyday world, in subjects such as portraiture and still-life, contrasting with the grand gestures of *Neoclassicism and *Romanticism. *Spitzweg and *Waldmüller are among the painters who best exemplify the style. The term is sometimes extended to cover the work of artists in other countries, for example *Købke in Denmark.

Biennale (or **Bienale**). An art exhibition held every two years, particularly a large and prestigious exhibition of international scope. The first to be founded and still the most famous is the Venice Biennale, instituted in 1895 as the 'International Exhibition of Art of the City of Venice', and claiming to represent 'the most noble activities of the modern spirit without distinction of country'. At this first Biennale, artists from sixteen different countries were represented, and the committee included such famous personalities as *Burne-Jones, *Israëls, *Liebermann, *Moreau, and *Puvis de Chavannes. The exhibition soon acquired worldwide prestige, and after it resumed in 1948 following the Second World War it became the leading showplace for the established international avant-garde. Henry *Moore, for example, set the seal on his reputation when he won the International Sculpture Prize in 1948. Other exhibitions founded on the Venice model include the São Paulo Bienale, first held in 1951, and the Paris Biennale, first held in 1959.

Bierstadt, Albert (*b* Solingen, nr. Düsseldorf, 7 Jan. 1830; *d* New York, 18 Feb. 1902). German-born American painter, active mainly in New York. He made several trips to the Far West and was the leading figure of the *Rocky Mountain School, specializing in grandiose pictures of awesome mountain scenery. His paintings—often huge in size—were immensely popular in his lifetime, but his on-the-spot sketches are now generally found much more appealing.

Bigaud, Wilson. See NAIVE ART.

Bigot, Trophime (*bapt.* Arles, 8 June 1579; *bur.* Avignon, 21 Feb. 1650). French *Caravaggesque painter, active in Rome (*c*.1620–34), then in the Aix-en-Provence area. His career is obscure (it was once surmised there were two painters of the same name, one older than the other), but he has been identified as the author of a number of paintings, mainly intimate candlelit scenes, some of which were previously grouped under the name of 'the Candlelight Master'. He sometimes painted unusual subjects (*Doctor Examining a Sample of Urine*, Ashmolean Mus., Oxford).

Biguerny, Philippe. See VIGARNY.

Bijlert, Jan van. See UTRECHT CARAVAGGISTI.

'bilingual' pottery. See BLACK-FIGURE VASE PAINTING.

Bill, Max (*b* Winterthur, 22 Dec. 1908; *d* Berlin, 9 Dec. 1994). Swiss painter, sculptor, architect, designer, teacher, and writer. From 1927 to 1929 he studied at the *Bauhaus, then returned to Switzerland, where he lived mainly in Zurich. He regarded himself primarily as an architect, but he was active in a variety of fields, his ultimate aim being to establish a unity among the individual branches of the visual arts—he once defined art as the 'sum of all functions in harmonious unity'. However, he has probably become best known for his sculptures, which characteristically employ smooth, elegant, spiralling abstract forms in stone or polished metal. He took the term *'Concrete art' from van *Doesburg to describe his work in this vein and popularized the term in Switzerland in place of 'abstract'. In

1941 he visited Argentina and Brazil, introducing the concept of Concrete art there, and he was a vigorous publicist of his ideas (he wrote several books and numerous articles, in English as well as German, and he organized exhibitions of abstract art). His sculptures have been considered precursors of *Minimal art, but in fact they represent a subtle blending of mathematics and intuition, and some Minimalists, including Donald *Judd and Robert *Morris, have denied his influence. As an architect Bill's work included his own house in Zurich (1932–3) and the much-praised Hochschule für Gestaltung (College of Design) in Ulm (1951–5), where, working on a limited budget, he created an austerely elegant complex of buildings delicately placed in a romantic setting. He was co-founder of the school and head of the departments of architecture and produce design from 1951 to 1957.

Bing, Siegfried. See ART NOUVEAU.

Bingham, George Caleb (*b* Augusta County, Va., 20 Mar. 1811; *d* Kansas City, Mo., 7 July 1879). American painter. He worked mainly in Missouri (where he held several political posts), painting the life of the frontier people. Except for a short period studying at the Pennsylvania Academy of Fine Arts, he was self-taught. His finest canvases, particularly the celebrated *Fur Traders Descending the Missouri* (1845, Met. Mus., New York), distil visual poetry from the commonplace, but after a trip to Düsseldorf (a major art centre that attracted several American painters) in 1856–8 his work lost much of its racy freshness and charm, tending to become self-conscious and sentimental.

biomorphic. A term applied to forms in abstract art that derive from or suggest organic (rather than geometric) shapes, as, for example, in the sculpture of Henry *Moore.

Bird, Francis (*b* London, 1667; *d* London, 27 Feb. 1731). English sculptor. He trained in Flanders and later visited Rome at least once. This Continental background meant that he could work in a *Baroque idiom more convincingly than most of his English contemporaries, as is seen in his best-known work, the *Conversion of St Paul* (1706) in the west pediment of St Paul's Cathedral, London. Bird did other carving at St Paul's, but most of his output consisted of tomb sculpture. His work is uneven, but he ranks as the most significant figure in English sculpture between *Gibbons (for whom he worked for a time) and *Rysbrack.

Birolli, Renato (*b* Verona, 10 Dec. 1905; *d* Milan, 3 May 1959). Italian painter whose outspoken political views and advanced and energetic artistic outlook gave him a prominent place in his country's avant-garde. His early work was *Expressionist, influenced by *Ensor and van *Gogh, and a visit to Paris in 1936 introduced him to the work of the *Fauves. In 1938 he was one of the founders of the anti-Fascist *Corrente organization; he published articles in many journals and was persecuted and imprisoned for his political activities. After the Second World War he was strongly influenced by *Picasso and gradually moved towards abstraction, his work eventually coming within the orbit of *Art Informel. In 1947 he joined the *Fronte Nuovo delle Arti. From 1948 his work was shown at the Venice *Biennale on several occasions and was much exhibited elsewhere in Italy.

Bissière, Roger (*b* Villeréal, Lot-et-Garonne, 22 Sept. 1886; *d* Boïssiérettes, Lot-et-Garonne, 2 Dec. 1964). French painter, sculptor, teacher, and writer on art. He was slow to mature as an artist and did not exhibit his work until 1920, first at the *Salon d'Automne, then at the *Salon des Indépendants. At this time he was influenced by *Cubism, which he attempted to 'humanize'. From 1925 to 1938 he taught at the *Académie Ranson, where he was a popular and influential figure among his students, who included *Manessier. His success as a teacher came partly from the fact that he regarded himself as still learning about art, so in this sense he put himself on the same plane as his students: 'I prefer those artists who make a blunder from time to time, especially those who don't always do the same thing, who try a new turn every day, unknown, dangerous, risking their neck every time, those who can't catch sight of a door without wanting to see what's behind it, even if behind it there's a booby trap.' He was one of the first French artists to recognize the importance of Paul *Klee, whose ideas he introduced to his classes. Although Bissière played an important part in shaping the careers of his students, he had still not found a distinctive artistic voice of his own and remained little known as a painter. In 1938 he retired to his home in Lot-et-Garonne and the following year he contracted an eye ailment that left him unable to paint. He started painting again in 1945 and an operation in 1948 partially restored his sight. Thereafter he worked with renewed vigour and from the early 1950s he belatedly achieved an international reputation. His mature paintings are rich and glowing tapestry-like compositions. Representational elements were gradually submerged in scintillating patterns of colour, but Bissière said that they were always based on natural appearances and refused to accept the term 'abstract' for his work. In addition to paintings, from 1957 he made designs for stained glass, notably for Metz Cathedral (1960–1). Despite his success, he continued living quietly in Lot for the rest of his life.

bistre. A transparent brown *pigment derived from the soot of burned wood. The colour varies depending on the type of wood. It is often used as a *wash for pen-and-ink drawings and watercolours. *Claude and *Rembrandt were among the artists who most memorably exploited its potentialities. See also SEPIA.

bitumen (or **asphaltum**). A resinous substance soluble in oils that can be used to produce a brown paint. At the time of use this gives a rich glowing quality, but it later becomes almost black and increasingly opaque. It never completely hardens and eventually develops a pronounced and often disfiguring *craquelure. It was most popular in the 18th century, and its damaging effects can be seen in works by *Reynolds and other British painters of the period.

Black, Dorrit. See LINOCUT.

black-figure vase painting. Technique of vase painting, originating in Corinth in the 7th century BC, in which figures were painted in black silhouette on the light red clay background. Details were added by incising through the black pigment or sometimes by overpainting in red or white. The technique had its finest flowering around the mid-6th century BC, notably in the work of *Execias; it then began to give way to *red-figure painting, although black-figure vases continued to be produced for another two centuries. Sometimes the two techniques were combined on the same piece of pottery (for an example see EPICTETUS); such pieces are described as 'bilingual'.

Black Mountain College. American art educational establishment at Black Mountain, North Carolina, founded by a group of progressive academics in 1933 and closed after longstanding financial problems in 1957. It was run by the teaching staff, with no outside control, and was kept deliberately small (with an average of about 50 students a year) to reduce administration; a variety of arts were taught and interaction between them was encouraged. Mary

Emma Harris describes the college as 'a unique combination of liberal arts school, summer camp, farm school, pioneer village, refugee centre and religious retreat' and writes that it was 'a catalyst for the emergence of the American avant-garde after the Second World War' (catalogue of the exhibition 'American Art in the 20th Century', Royal Academy, London, 1993). In the visual arts, the teacher most associated with Black Mountain College was Josef *Albers, who arrived there with his wife Anni (who taught weaving) soon after it opened and stayed until 1949. Other illustrious figures who taught at Black Mountain include Robert *Motherwell and the composer John Cage (1912–92), whose ideas on chance and indeterminacy in the arts were widely influential. In 1952 he organized there a partly programmed performance (involving paintings and readings) that was later designated the first *happening. Famous former students of the college include John *Chamberlain, Kenneth *Noland, and Robert *Rauschenberg.

Blake, Sir Peter (b Dartford, Kent, 25 June 1932). British painter, printmaker, sculptor, and designer, a leading exponent of *Pop art. His use of imagery from comics, pin-up magazines, consumer goods, and advertisements captures the flavour of the times in a manner that now evokes nostalgia for the 'swinging sixties', as was made clear during his enormously popular retrospective exhibition at the Tate Gallery, London, in 1983 (his most famous work is the cover design for the Beatles LP *Sergeant Pepper's Lonely Hearts Club Band*, 1967). The combination of sophistication and naivety typical of Blake's style is seen particularly clearly in his work as a member of the Brotherhood of Ruralists, a group of seven painters based in the West Country, of which Blake (then living near Bath) was one of the founders in 1975. The members had several group exhibitions, took working holidays together, and shared a commission to design covers for the New Arden edition of Shakespeare's work, but they had common ideals rather than a common style, taking as their inspiration 'the spirit of the countryside'. A series of winsome fairy paintings are characteristic of this facet of Blake's work, and many critics found the work of the group as a whole insufferably twee—one newspaper review of a 1981 Ruralists exhibition was headed 'Tinkerbell lives'. The Brotherhood last exhibited as a group at Blake's retrospective at the Tate in 1983. The other members were: Ann Arnold (1936–) and her husband Graham Arnold (1932–); the American-born Jann Haworth (1942–), who was married to Blake, 1963–81; David Inshaw (1943–); Annie Ovenden (1945–) and her husband Graham Ovenden (1943–).

Blake, William (*b* London, 28 Nov. 1757; *d* London, 12 Aug. 1827). English printmaker, painter, poet, and mystical philosopher, one of the most remarkable figures of the *Romantic period and one of the supreme individualists in the history of art. He was equally gifted in poetry and the visual arts, and in both fields he worked in a highly original, intensely personal idiom that expressed his unconventional views and fiercely independent personality. His unorthodoxy was bound up with his hatred of materialism and rationalism, which he thought fettered the mind and spirit and led to misery and oppression. He was deeply religious and often depicted Christian subjects in his paintings and prints, but he used private as well as traditional imagery in them, and he came to regard art, imagination, and religion as indivisible. In matters of technique he was comparably original, developing new methods of printing to publish his poetry and pictures together. He had a few loyal patrons and admirers, but for most of his life he struggled to earn a living, being ignored or dismissed as eccentric (or mad) by the world at large. It was not until long after his death that he was widely recognized as one of the great men of his age.

Blake's parents were Nonconformists in religion, and his own individuality was evident from childhood (he first claimed to see angels when he was 10). From 1772 to 1779 he was apprenticed to the engraver James Basire (1730–1802), for whom his work included making drawings in Westminster Abbey for illustrations in antiquarian books. This helped to give him an enduring love of medieval art. After his apprenticeship ended he enrolled as a student at the *Royal Academy, but he was unhappy there (he particularly disliked *Reynolds) and soon left to set up as a commercial engraver, mainly producing book illustrations from other artists' drawings. His own first book, *Poetical Sketches*, appeared in 1783, partly sponsored by *Flaxman, one of his closest friends (his other friends included *Fuseli, who, like Blake, was one of the few painters in Britain to excel at imaginative subjects at a time when the country's art was dominated by portraiture and landscape).

Poetical Sketches was conventionally produced, but all Blake's other books were done by his own

method of 'illuminated printing', in which he combined illustrations and handwritten text on the same plate, making of them a decorative unity. The technique he used was a form of *relief etching; he experimented for a while with applying colours to the plate, but settled on hand colouring the pages with ink and watercolour, with the result that each copy of his books (which were produced in very small editions) differed in varying degrees from the others. Blake claimed that he was helped to solve the technical problems of creating his books by the spirit of his beloved younger brother Robert, who died of consumption in 1787, aged 19. In the practical business of hand tinting and binding the pages he was assisted by his devoted wife Catherine. Apart from some experimental booklets, Blake's first publication using his new method was *Songs of Innocence* (1789). In 1794 he added *Songs of Experience*, never issuing this separately, but always bound with the first volume to make *Songs of Innocence and Experience*. The two parts were intended to show the 'two contrary states of the human soul': *Songs of Innocence* are meditations on childhood, whereas *Songs of Experience* (which include the celebrated 'Tyger, Tyger') deal with the corruption of innocence by adult life.

Blake used several other techniques in his work. He avoided oils, which he thought encouraged blurring of forms, as clarity of line was essential to him (he saw his visions—whether of angels or his dead brother—so intensely that they seemed part of the real world). For paintings he sometimes used tempera (confusingly he called the medium 'fresco'), which he associated with the predominantly linear style of the early *Renaissance, and in printing he produced some outstanding wood engravings. In 1795 he began a series of *monotypes that are usually referred to as the 'Large Colour Prints'. Twelve are now known; the subjects derive from the Bible, Milton, and Shakespeare, as well as from Blake's own writings, and the overall theme (if there is one) is uncertain. They have no accompanying text and in them Blake emerges for the first time as a great visual artist independent of Blake the writer (*Elohim Creating Adam*, 1795, Tate, London). None of these 'colour printed drawings' (as Blake called them) is known in more than three impressions, and the technique perhaps appealed to him more for its textural qualities than as a means of reproducing his work.

In about 1795 Blake met Thomas Butts (1757–1845), a minor civil servant who from 1799 became his main patron for many years, paying him what was virtually a regular wage. He had a less happy relationship with another patron, the poet and biographer William Hayley, who (through Flaxman's agency) employed Blake from 1800 to 1803 at his home at Felpham, on the Sussex coast—the only time he lived outside London. The work provided by Hayley (such as decorating his library) was ill suited to Blake's temperament and he described his employer as 'a corporeal friend and spiritual enemy'. After the interlude in Sussex he found it harder to pick up commercial engraving work, and in 1809–10 he mounted an exhibition of his paintings and drawings in an effort to appeal directly to the public. Few people came to see it and the only review called Blake 'an unfortunate lunatic' and described his accompanying catalogue as 'a far-rago of nonsense . . . the wild effusions of a distempered brain'. During the next few years he was sometimes close to destitution, but in 1818 he met his second great patron, John *Lin-nell, and largely thanks to him, his final decade was comparatively free of financial worries and one of the happiest and most productive periods of his life. His work for Linnell included a series of watercolour illustrations to Dante's *Divine Comedy*, begun in 1824 and left unfinished at his death. These include some of his finest work, in which he reached new heights in radiant use of colour and in the rendering of visionary experi-ence.

Linnell introduced Blake to a circle of idealis-tic young painters—the *Ancients—who ad-mired him and his work and brought to his old age a degree of protective sympathy he had never known before. One of them, George *Richmond, said that he 'died like a saint . . . singing of the things he saw in heaven'. In the next generation his memory was kept alive by a few admirers (including *Rossetti—another painter-poet with mystical leanings), but when the first substantial biography of him appeared in 1863—Alexander Gilchrist's *Life of William Blake*—it was subtitled 'Pictor Ignotus' (the un-known painter). The centenary of his death in 1927 stimulated a major revival of interest, and thereafter his reputation grew rapidly. His vast output now supports an academic industry of its own. There are major collections of his work in London (BM, Tate, V&A), Cambridge (Fitzwil-liam Mus.), and several American museums.

Blanchard, Jacques (*b* Paris, 1 Oct. 1600; *bur.* Paris, 10 Nov. 1638). French painter. From 1624 to 1628 he was in Italy and his style reflects both the polished classicism of contemporary Bolognese painting and the sensuous richness of the Venetian School. His contemporary repu-tation rested largely on decorative work, but little of this survives and he is now known chiefly as a painter of small, sensitive pictures of religious and mythological subjects (*Charity*, 1637, Courtauld Gal., London).

Blanche, Jacques-Émile (*b* Paris, 31 Jan. 1861; *d* Offranville, 30 Sept. 1942). French painter. The son of Émile Blanche, a noted pathologist, he grew up in a cultured atmosphere and became a well-known figure in artistic and soci-ety circles—he was a friend of *Degas, *Renoir, *Whistler, the writers Henry James and Marcel Proust, and many other celebrities. His best-known works are stylish portraits of people from this milieu; the finest collection is in the Musée des Beaux-Arts at Rouen, and there are several examples in London (Tate). Blanche lived mainly at Offranville, near the Channel port of Dieppe (the local church has decorative painting by him), and he was a frequent visitor to Britain, painting numerous views of London (the Tate has an example). He wrote several books of criticism and reminiscence.

Blast. See VORTICISM.

Blaue Reiter, Der (The Blue Rider). A loose association of artists formed in Munich in De-cember 1911 as a splinter group from the *Neue Künstlervereinigung; it held only two exhib-itions (poorly received by press and public) and was broken up by the First World War, but its brief life is considered to mark the high point of German *Expressionism. The name was also used as the title of an 'Almanac' (a collection of essays and illustrations) published in May 1912 by *Kandinsky (the driving force behind the group) and *Marc (another of the major figures); the cover of the Almanac featured a drawing by Kandinsky of a blue horseman (blue was the favourite colour of Marc, who regarded it as particularly spiritual, and the horse was his most cherished subject; Kandinsky, too, liked blue and often painted horses with riders, evok-ing ideas of medieval knights or warrior saints).

Unlike the members of Die *Brücke, the main artists associated with Der Blaue Reiter (including *Klee and *Macke) were not stylistic-ally unified, although their work tended towards the spiritual (contrasting with the more earthy concerns of Die Brücke) and also towards ab-straction. They had no artistic or social pro-gramme and no plans for communal activities apart from exhibitions. According to a statement in the catalogue of their first exhibition, their aim was 'simply to juxtapose the most varied manifestations of the new painting on an international basis . . . and to show, by the variety of forms represented, the manifold ways in which the artist manifests his inner desire'. The exhibition, arranged at very short notice, was held in Munich in December 1911 and featured 43 works by fourteen artists; in March 1912 it travelled to Berlin to inaugurate the *Sturm Gallery, and it was also shown (with some additions) in Cologne, Frankfurt, and Hagen. The second exhibition, held in Munich in February–April 1912, included only watercolours, drawings, and prints, but it was larger and broader in scope than the first show, featuring 315 works by 31 artists, among them *Braque, *Derain, *Goncharova, Klee, *Larionov, *Picasso, and *Vlaminck. Although *Jawlensky's work was not included in either of the two official group shows, he did exhibit alongside Kandinsky, Klee, Macke, and Marc at the Sturm Gallery in 1913 and he is generally considered part of the Blaue Reiter circle; indeed, it is to these five that the idea of a Blaue Reiter 'group' chiefly applies. *Feininger, also, showed his work with this group at the Sturm exhibition.

Blaue Vier, Die (The Blue Four). A group of four painters—*Feininger, *Jawlensky, *Kandinsky, and *Klee—formed in 1924 at the instigation of the German art dealer Galka Scheyer (1889–1945) with the aim of promoting their work abroad (where there was a better market for art than in economically depressed Germany). The four had all been associated with Der *Blaue Reiter, and Scheyer chose the name 'Blaue Vier' because 'a group of four would be significant though not arrogant . . . the colour blue was added because of the association with the early group of artists in Munich that founded the "Blue Horseman" . . . and also because blue is a spiritual colour'. In addition, Kandinsky wanted a name that did not suggest an 'ism'. Between 1925 and 1934 Scheyer organized exhibitions and lectures in the USA and Mexico (as well as Germany). The venture was a moderate financial success and an important factor in spreading the reputation of the four artists. Scheyer settled in the USA and became an American citizen. Her own collection of paintings by the Blaue Vier is now in the Norton Simon Museum, Pasadena, California.

Blechen, Karl (b Cottbus, Brandenburg, 29 July 1798; d Berlin, 23 July 1840). German painter.

His career was short, for he did not turn to art seriously until 1822, when he gave up his job as a bank clerk to study at the Berlin Academy, and in 1836 he showed the first signs of the mental illness that led to his early death. However, he gained a high reputation in his lifetime and is now considered one of the leading German landscape painters of the 19th century. Initially he worked in the *Romantic idiom of *Friedrich (whom he probably met in Dresden in 1823), but following a visit to Italy in 1828 he developed a more naturalistic style. In 1831 he was appointed professor of landscape painting at the Berlin Academy, but he resigned in 1836 because of his illness. He died insane.

Bles, Herri met de (b ?Bouvines or Dinant; active first half of 16th century). Netherlandish painter of landscapes with figures. He is an enigmatic artist, presumed to be one and the same as the Herri de Patinir who became a member of the Antwerp painters' guild in 1535. As van *Mander informs us, 'Herri met de Bles' is simply a nickname meaning 'Herri with the white forelock', and it is generally assumed that he was a relative of Joachim *Patinir, who certainly had a decisive influence on his work. No signed or documented work by Herri exists, but a small group of distinctive works has been ascribed to him, characterized by panoramic landscapes dominating the figure groups in the manner of Patinir. His work was popular with Italian collectors, who called him Civetta (little owl) because he often included an owl in his pictures.

Bleyl, Fritz. See BRÜCKE.

Bliss, Lillie P. See MUSEUM OF MODERN ART.

block book. A type of illustrated book in which the words and image on each page are printed from a single *woodcut block, as distinct from books that use movable type for the words. Block books were made in China probably as early as the 6th century AD, but in Europe the earliest known examples seem to date from around 1450, that is, at very much the same time that Gutenberg introduced printing from movable metal type. (At one time they were thought to pre-date movable type, but it is now thought more likely that they were introduced very slightly after it.) As the entire text had to be cut letter by letter on wood blocks, the process was extremely laborious and suitable only for short books in continuous demand, usually popular religious texts (see ARS MORIENDI, BIBLIA PAUPERUM, and SPECULUM HUMANAE SALVATIONIS).

Very few block books were executed after 1480 and their place in the history of printing is as sterile descendants of the woodcut rather than as ancestors of the modern illustrated book.

Bloemaert, Abraham (*b* Gorinchem, 25 Dec. 1566; *d* Utrecht, 13 Jan. 1651). Dutch historical and landscape painter and engraver, the son of a sculptor and architect, **Cornelis I Bloemaert** (*c*.1540–93). Most of his life was spent in Utrecht, where for many years he was the leading painter and an outstanding teacher. *Both, *Honthorst, *Terbrugghen, and virtually all the Utrecht painters of the period who attained any kind of distinction trained with him. Bloemaert was a good learner as well as a good teacher and rapidly assimilated the new ideas his pupils brought back from Italy. For a time he became a *Caravaggesque painter and late in his career adopted some aspects of the *classicism of the *Carracci. Although his landscape paintings are firmly in the *Mannerist tradition, his landscape drawings are naturalistic and constitute his most original works. Many of his drawings were etched and published by his son **Frederick** (*c*.1616–90) in an instructional book for the use of art students (it first appeared *c*.1650 and continued to be reprinted into the 19th century). Bloemaert had three other painter sons, who like Frederick were his pupils: **Hendrick** (*c*.1601–72), **Cornelis II** (*c*.1603–*c*.1684), and **Adriaen** (*c*.1609–66).

Blondeel, Lancelot (*b* ?Poperinghe, 1498; *bur.* Bruges, 4 Mar. 1561). Netherlandish painter, active mainly in Bruges, where he became a member of the painters' guild in 1519. He was highly versatile and also worked as a printmaker, architect, civil engineer, cartographer, and designer of sculpture, tapestries, and pageant decorations. In his day he was well known and highly regarded (he is mentioned by *Vasari) and in 1550 he and Jan van *Scorel were given the prestigious commission to restore the van *Eycks' celebrated Ghent Altarpiece. The *triptych of the *Martyrdom of Sts Cosmas and Damian* (1523, St Jacques, Bruges) is typical of his work as a painter in its profusion of Italianate ornament. By the 16th century Bruges had declined greatly in importance as a trading centre as its port silted up, and Blondeel represents one of the last sparks of its great artistic tradition.

Bloomsbury Group. A loose association of writers, artists, and intellectuals that was a distinctive force in British cultural life during the early decades of the 20th century. Leading members of the group included the writers E. M. Forster, Lytton Strachey, and Virginia Woolf, and the economist John Maynard Keynes; among the artists and critics were Clive *Bell, Vanessa *Bell, Dora Carrington (1893–1932), Roger *Fry, Duncan *Grant, and Henry *Lamb. The group takes its name from the Bloomsbury district of London, where members often met at the houses of Clive and Vanessa Bell or of Vanessa's sister Virginia Woolf, and it stemmed from student friendships formed at Cambridge University; most of the 'Bloomsberries' had been at either King's College or Trinity College and many had been 'Apostles'— members of an exclusive, semi-secret intellectual club. However, the Bloomsbury Group had no formal membership and no common social or aesthetic ideology. The members were united mainly by their belief in the importance of the arts and—in revolt against the restrictions of Victorian society—by their frankness and tolerance in sexual matters (several of them were homosexual or bisexual and their love lives were often complexly intertwined).

In the visual arts, the Bloomsbury Group made its most significant impact in the 1910s, after it had been joined by Roger Fry (he had lived in New York from 1906 to 1910). Fry was highly influential in promoting an awareness of modern art—through his writing and lecturing, through his two *Post-Impressionist exhibitions (1910 and 1912), and through his founding of the *Omega Workshops (1913). It was at this time, too, that Vanessa Bell and Duncan Grant were at their most adventurous, both of them producing pure abstracts by 1914. However, the richly coloured figurative style in which the couple worked in the period between the two world wars is considered the 'typical' Bloomsbury style. By the early 1930s the Bloomsbury Group had ceased to exist in its original form. After the Second World War, its ideas fell out of fashion and its members were attacked as dilettantish and elitist. However, from the late 1960s there has been a great revival of interest in all aspects of the group.

blot drawing. A technique devised by Alexander *Cozens, whereby an accidental mark or 'blot' on the paper is used as the starting point for an imaginative landscape composition. A comparable suggestion had been made much earlier by *Leonardo da Vinci and somewhat similar techniques were later used by the *Surrealists for stimulating subconscious imagery (see AUTOMATISM).

Blue Rider. See BLAUE REITER.

Blue Rose. Group of Russian painters active in the first decade of the 20th century, named after an exhibition held in Moscow in 1907. Their style was essentially *Symbolist, although there was also influence from *Fauvism and an interest in *primitivism. Their acknowledged inspiration was the short-lived Victor Borisov-Musatov (1870–1915), whose work has an exquisite feeling for colour and pattern. His most talented follower among the Blue Rose painters was Pavel Kuznetsov (1878–1968). The origin of the group's name is uncertain, but the colour blue was particularly significant for Symbolists, associated with the sky and spirituality, and the rose has many symbolic associations.

Blunt, Anthony (*b* Bournemouth, Hampshire, 26 Sept. 1907; *d* London, 26 Mar. 1983). British art historian and spy. He was director of the *Courtauld Institute of Art from 1947 to 1974, Surveyor of the King's (later Queen's) Pictures from 1945 to 1972, and one of the leading figures in establishing art history as an academic discipline in Britain. His career was loaded with honours, but in 1979 he suffered disgrace (including being stripped of his knighthood) when it was sensationally revealed that he had spied for the Soviet Union during his service at the War Office in the Second World War. He coped calmly with the ignominy and continued with his scholarly work until the end of his life. During the 1930s he had written a good deal of journalism on contemporary art, expressing Marxist views that he later repudiated, but after the war his publications were mainly on French and Italian art and architecture of the 16th and 17th centuries, and he was particularly renowned as the leading authority on *Poussin. His books include *Artistic Theory in Italy: 1450–1600* (1940), *Art and Architecture in France: 1500–1700* (1953 and subsequent edns.), *The Art of William *Blake* (1959), and *Guide to Baroque Rome* (1982). His brother **Wilfrid** (1901–87) was drawing master at Eton 1938–59, curator of the *Watts Gallery at Compton 1959–85, and the author of numerous books on art and other subjects, notably *The Art of Botanical Illustration* (1950) and *'England's Michelangelo'* (1975), a biography of Watts.

Boccioni, Umberto (*b* Reggio di Calabria, 19 Oct. 1882; *d* Sorte, nr. Verona, 17 Aug. 1916). Italian *Futurist painter, sculptor (the only major one in the movement), and art theorist. He signed the two Futurist manifestos of painting (both 1910), wrote the one on sculpture (1912), and became the most energetic member of the group. Calling for a complete break with the art of the past, Boccioni was centrally concerned with the two main preoccupations of the Futurists—the production of emotionally expressive works and the representation of time and movement. In his early Futurist works he often showed an interest in social themes, particularly big city life, but later (especially after a visit to Paris in 1912, when he was influenced by *Cubism) he tended to use his paintings more as vehicles for his theories than as comments on life around him. Eventually this tendency led him close to abstraction, in pictures such as *Dynamism of a Human Body* (1913, Gal. d'Arte Moderna, Milan). In common with the other Futurists, Boccioni believed that physical objects have a kind of personality and emotional life of their own, revealed by 'lines of force' with which the object reacts to its environment. This notion is perhaps best shown in his most famous piece of sculpture, *Unique Forms of Continuity in Space* (1913, casts in Tate, London, MoMA, New York, and elsewhere), which vividly expresses bodily movement. His ideas about sculpture were extremely forward-looking. He advocated the use of materials such as glass and electric lights and the introduction of electric motors to create movement. However, he died aged only 33 (following a fall from a horse whilst serving in the Italian army) before most of his ideas could be put into practice.

Böcklin, Arnold (*b* Basle, 19 Oct. 1827; *d* San Domenico, nr. Fiesole, 16 Jan. 1901). Swiss painter. With *Hodler he ranks as the most important Swiss painter of the 19th century, and in the 1880s and 1890s he was the most influential artist of the German-speaking world, even though from 1850 he had spent most of his time in Italy. He established his reputation with *Pan in the Reeds* (1857, Neue Pin., Munich), the beginning of his preoccupation with the world of nymphs and satyrs, naiads, and tritons, the results of which are sometimes slightly absurd. Later his style became more sombre and charged with mystical feeling, bringing him into the orbit of *Symbolism, as in his best-known picture, *The Island of the Dead*, of which he painted five versions between 1880 and 1886 (an example of 1880 is in the Met. Mus., New York). This haunting work, which inspired a symphonic poem by Rachmaninov (1909), shows a rocky mausoleum-island approached by a boat carrying spectral figures; such morbid imagery appealed to the *Surrealists. A curious aspect of Böcklin's career is that like *Leonardo—whom he disliked—he spent much of his time experimenting with flying machines.

Bode, Wilhelm von (*b* Calvörde, nr. Magdeburg, 10 Dec. 1845; *d* Berlin, 1 Mar. 1929). German art historian. His career was centred in Berlin; he became director of the Gemäldegalerie there in 1890 and from 1905 until his retirement in 1920 was director general of all the royal museums of Prussia. Under his administration the Gemäldegalerie became one of the world's outstanding collections. Apart from being a noted scholar, he was one of the pioneers of modern museum organization and display, combining pictures, sculptures, and frames in harmonious arrangements and achieving a balance between creating an up-to-date setting for works of art and reconstructing their historical milieu. His numerous publications were mainly on Italian *Renaissance sculpture and 17th-century Dutch painting (particularly *Rembrandt).

bodegón. Spanish term that was originally used to describe a low-class tavern and by the 1590s was applied to pictures featuring scenes of humble life in which food or drink play a part. Some *bodegones* actually depict tavern interiors, but others are set in kitchens or unspecific surroundings. *Velázquez painted several *bodegones* early in his career, and these are the most famous examples of the type. *Bodegones* usually have a prominent still-life element, and in modern Spanish the term is used as a synonym for still-life.

Body art. A type of art in which the artist uses his or her own body as the medium; it is closely related to *Conceptual art and *Performance art, and flourished mainly at the same time that these forms of expression were at their peak—the late 1960s and 1970s (there was something of a revival in the 1990s). Sometimes works of Body art are carried out in private and communicated by means of photographs or films; sometimes the execution of the 'piece' is public. The performance may be pre-choreographed or extemporaneous. Spectator participation is not usually invited. Body art is often playful in spirit, but several leading exponents have been concerned with self-inflicted pain or ritualistic acts of endurance. For example, in 'Seedbed' (1972) the American Body artist Vito Acconci (1940–) spent several hours daily masturbating under a gallery-wide ramp while the sounds of his activity were relayed via loudspeakers to visitors

overhead. Even more extreme is another American, Chris Burden (1946–): 'In 1974 his roster of activities included one in which the spectators were invited to push pins into his body, one in which he had himself crucified to the roof of a Volkswagen, and one in which he was kicked down two flights of concrete stairs. In the name of art, Burden has also had himself shot, and has had his body splashed with burning alcohol' (Edward Lucie-Smith, *Art of the Seventies*, 1980). Other artists who have put themselves through unpleasant and potentially harmful experiences include Rudolf *Schwarzkogler and the French artist Orlan (1947–), whose means of expression consists of having her face and body reshaped by plastic surgery to give her features based on Renaissance masterpieces, such as the chin from a *Botticelli Venus. The philosophy behind such works is obscure.

body colour. Paint that is opaque rather than transparent. The term usually refers to opaque *watercolour, which is also known as *gouache.

Boethus. Greek sculptor and metalworker active in the 2nd century BC. *Pliny singles out a bronze sculpture by him representing 'a child hugging a goose until he throttles it', though he adds that Boethus was more famous for his work in silver. Several Roman copies of the sculpture are known and adaptations or echoes of it appear in *Renaissance art. There seem to have been several Greek sculptors called Boethus (it was a fairly common name) and the evidence concerning them is tangled.

Bogaert, Martin van den. See DESJARDINS.

Bohemian School. Term applied to art produced in Bohemia in the second half of the 14th century during a period of cultural efflorescence associated with Charles IV (1316–78), who was King of Bohemia from 1346 and Holy Roman Emperor from 1355. His favourite residence was Prague, where he founded a university and drew to his court scholars and artists from all over Europe. Manuscripts were imported from France and Italy and inspired a local school of book *illumination, but the main achievements of the Bohemian School were in *panel painting and *fresco. The artists who created these works are mainly anonymous and of uncertain nationality. They fused many influences and contributed to the formation of the *International Gothic style. During the 1350s, in the work of the *Master of Vyšší Brod, the flavour was strongly Italian; Sienese models in particular seem to have been used. Later, with the *Master of Třeboň, who must have worked during the last two decades of the century, French elements became stronger. Under Charles's son Wenceslas, painting, and in particular illumination, still flourished, but the importance of Prague as an artistic centre declined early in the 15th century, when many works perished during the Hussite wars.

Boilly, Louis-Léopold (*b* La Bassée, nr. Lille, 5 July 1761; *d* Paris, 4 Jan. 1845). French painter and printmaker. Boilly painted portraits, domestic and *genre scenes, and also *scènes galantes* that brought him into disrepute at the time of the Revolution. Generally he worked on a small scale, with a smooth and meticulous technique. He was extremely prolific, claiming to have produced 5,000 portraits. In the 1820s he took up *lithography and used this technique to popularize his scenes from contemporary life.

Boizot, Louis-Simon (*b* Paris, 9 Oct. 1743; *d* Paris, 10 Mar. 1809). French sculptor. A pupil of René-Michel *Slodtz, he won the *Prix de Rome in 1762 and was in Italy from 1765 to 1770. He was at his best working on a small scale and had high standards of craftsmanship; appropriately he spent much of his career (1773–1800) in charge of the sculpture section of the Sèvres porcelain factory. His output also included portrait busts.

Bol, Ferdinand (*bapt.* Dordrecht, 24 June 1616; *bur.* Amsterdam, 24 July 1680). Dutch painter and etcher, active mainly in Amsterdam. He was a pupil of *Rembrandt in the mid-1630s and in his early work imitated his master's style so well as to create occasional difficulty in distinguishing between them. The portrait of Elizabeth Bas in the Rijksmuseum, Amsterdam, is the best-known instance; it was acknowledged as a Rembrandt until 1911, when it was attributed to Bol by *Bredius, and although this opinion is still widely accepted, there has been renewed support for Rembrandt as the author (as well as some for Jacob *Backer). As Bol's career prospered, both as a portraitist and a painter of historical subjects, his style moved away from that of Rembrandt, becoming blander and more elegant in the manner of van der *Helst. In 1669 he married a wealthy widow and seems to have stopped painting. *Kneller was Bol's most distinguished pupil.

Boldini, Giovanni (*b* Ferrara, 31 Dec. 1842; *d* Paris, 11 Jan. 1931). Italian painter, one of the most renowned society portraitists of his day. He was at his best with portraits of glamorous women;

*Sickert referred to his 'wriggle-and-chiffon' style. His vivacious brushwork and gift for making his sitters look graceful and poised recall the work of his even more successful contemporary John Singer *Sargent, and like Sargent he had an international career; he worked mainly in Paris, where he settled in 1871, but he travelled widely. Together with another flamboyant portraitist, Antonio Mancini (1852–1930), he was probably the best-known Italian artist at the turn of the century. Apart from portraits, his work includes some excellent street scenes of Paris. There is a Boldini museum in his native Ferrara. As with Sargent, his work went out of favour after his death, being considered merely glossy and superficial. See also MACCHIAIOLI.

bole (or **bolus**). A type of fine, soft, slightly greasy clay with several uses in art. It is found in various colours, including greyish blue, but most commonly it is red (coloured by the presence of iron oxide). Red bole is used, mixed with *size, as a base for gilding; it provides a smooth surface for the gold leaf and its colour helps to impart a warm, glowing quality to the burnished surface. It was much used in this way in early Italian panel paintings with gold backgrounds, and it was also popular as a *ground for oil paintings in the 17th and 18th centuries. Often it has caused such paintings to darken and take on a brown or red cast as the oil paint has become more transparent with age, allowing the ground to show through in thinly painted areas (this effect can be seen in paintings by *Poussin and *Piazzetta, for example). White bole (also known as kaolin and China clay) is an essential ingredient of porcelain.

Bolgi, Andrea. See MOCHI.

Bologna, Giovanni. See GIAMBOLOGNA.

Bolognese, Il. See GRIMALDI.

Bolotowsky, Ilya (*b* St Petersburg, 1 July 1907; *d* New York, 22 Nov. 1981). Russian-born painter who became an American citizen in 1929. His family fled revolutionary Russia in 1920 and in 1923 settled in New York. In the early 1930s his work was *Expressionist, but in 1933 he was deeply impressed by paintings by *Mondrian and thereafter became one of America's most committed exponents of geometrical abstraction. He wrote: 'After I went through a lot of violent upheavals in my early life, I came to prefer a search for an ideal harmony and order which is still a free order, not militaristic, not symmetrical, not goose-stepping, not academic.'

He was a founding member of *American Abstract Artists in 1936 and his mural for the Williamsburg Housing Project, New York, of that year was one of the first abstract murals to be commissioned. In spite of his reverence for Mondrian, his approach was far from cerebral and he had a love of intense, sensuous colour (*Vibrant Reds*, 1971, National Mus. of American Art, Washington). In 1971 he began to make painted geometrical constructions that represented extensions of his paintings into three dimensions, and he was also a playwright and experimental film-maker.

Boltraffio, Giovanni Antonio (*b* Milan, *c*.1467; *d* Milan, 15 June 1516). Italian painter, the pupil and assistant of *Leonardo and the most talented of his followers in Milan. He painted religious subjects and portraits (an example of each is in the National Gallery, London). His style is more prosaic than his master's, but his best work is of high quality; the beautiful female portrait known as *La Belle Ferronnière* (Louvre, Paris) is attributed to Boltraffio by some authorities and to Leonardo by others.

Bomberg, David (*b* Birmingham, 5 Dec. 1890; *d* London, 19 Aug. 1957). British painter. He gave up an apprenticeship as a lithographer to devote himself to painting, studying under *Sickert and at the *Slade School. Whilst still a student he showed an advanced understanding of avant-garde Continental painting, particularly *Cubism and *Futurism (he visited Paris in 1913), and he exhibited with the *Vorticists (although he turned down Wyndham *Lewis's invitation to become a formal member of the group). His best-known work of this time is probably *In the Hold* (1913–14, Tate, London), a dazzlingly coloured abstraction of fragmented geometric forms. Although he received critical praise for this and other pictures, Bomberg had difficulty selling his paintings and tended to work in isolation. From the 1920s he travelled widely, and at this time began moving away from abstraction to a heavily worked, somewhat *Expressionist figurative style, painting mainly portraits and landscapes. Much of his later career was devoted to teaching, and he had a strong influence on pupils such as *Auerbach and *Kossoff. At the time of his death he was little appreciated, but his reputation has since soared; a major exhibition was devoted to him at the Tate Gallery in 1988.

Bombois, Camille (*b* Vénarey-lès-Laumes, Côte d'Or, 3 Feb. 1883; *d* Paris, 11 June 1970). French *naive painter. He was the son of a boatman and spent his childhood on canal barges until he became a farmhand at the age of 12. Later he was a road labourer and a wrestler in travelling circuses. From 1907 he lived in Paris, where, after working as a porter on the Métro, a navvy, and a docker, he took a night job in a printing establishment so that he could paint during the day. In 1922 he came to the attention of Wilhelm *Uhde and other critics. With their encouragement he was able to devote all his time to painting and he became one of the best-known naive painters of his day, exhibiting his work widely. He painted various subjects but is best known for his circus pictures; they have great strength and vigour and sometimes an unconscious *Surrealist air. For example in *Carnival Athlete* (*c*.1930, Pompidou Centre, Paris) some of the bowler-hatted figures are similar to those seen in *Magritte's paintings.

Bon, Bartolommeo. See BUON.

Bondol, Jean (active *c*.1368–81). Netherlandish painter and *miniaturist active in France. His name is spelled in various ways (Boudolf, Bandolf, and so on) and he is also known as Jean de Bruges, presumably indicating his birthplace. He is first recorded in 1368 in the service of Charles V of France, an ardent bibliophile. His only known signed work is the dedicatory miniature (1371) in a *Bible historiale* (a French translation of a Latin compilation of biblical history and legend) made for Charles (Rijksmuseum Meermanno-Westreenianum, The Hague). The only other work that can be confidently attributed to him is the design of the celebrated series of tapestries on the Apocalypse (woven 1373–82, Mus. des Tapisseries, Angers), made for Louis I, Duke of Anjou, Charles V's brother. Bondol's style combined French courtly sophistication with Netherlandish realism, looking forward to the *International Gothic style.

Bone, Sir Muirhead (*b* Glasgow, 23 Mar. 1876; *d* Oxford, 21 Oct. 1953). British draughtsman, printmaker (drypoint was his favourite medium), and occasional painter, mainly of architectural subjects. He studied architecture and painting in Glasgow, then settled in London in 1901 and became a member of the *New English Art Club. In 1916 he was the first person to be appointed an *Official War Artist and he played an important part in the founding of the Imperial War Museum in 1920; he was an Official War Artist again in the Second World War. His son **Stephen** (1904–58) was a painter and art critic.

Bonheur, Rosa (*b* Bordeaux, 16 Mar. 1822; *d* Thomery, nr. Fontainebleau, 25 May 1899). French animal painter. She was trained by her father **Raymond Bonheur** (*d* 1849), and was precociously gifted, first exhibiting at the Paris *Salon in 1841, when she was 19. In 1853 she scored an enormous hit there with *The Horse Fair* (1853, Met. Mus., New York; reduced replica in NG, London), and it repeated its success when it went on tour in Britain and the USA. She became well known not only for her work but also as a colourful and formidable character, outspoken in her feminine independence (she made drawings at such places as horse auctions and obtained police permission to wear men's clothes to avoid undue attention). In 1865 she was the first woman artist to become a member of the Legion of Honour. Her home at the Château de By, Thomery, near Fontainebleau, is now a museum devoted to her.

Bonifazio Veronese (Bonifazio de' Pitati) (*b* Verona, *c.*1487; *d* Venice, 19 Oct. 1553). Italian painter, active for all his known career in Venice, where he based his style on *Giorgione, *Titian, and *Palma Vecchio. There are few signed, dated, or documented works by him, but he appears to have run a busy studio whose output was varied in kind and variable in quality. Consequently he has become one of those artists whose names tend to be used as dustbins for dumping difficult attributions. Jacopo *Bassano was his briefly his assistant, and *Schiavone and *Tintoretto were possibly his pupils.

Bonington, Richard Parkes (*b* Arnold, nr. Nottingham, 25 Oct. 1802; *d* London, 23 Sept. 1828). English painter, active mainly in France (his family settled in Calais for business reasons when he was 15). In 1818 he moved to Paris, where he studied with *Gros and became a friend of *Delacroix. Their *Romanticism is reflected in his fondness for historical 'costume' pictures, but it was as a landscapist that he established his reputation, particularly with works he exhibited at the 'English' *Salon of 1824, at which his own paintings (which won him a gold medal) and those of *Constable were the star attractions. Bonington travelled a good deal in France in search of subjects. He also spent time with Delacroix in England in 1825, and in 1826 he visited Italy, producing some of his finest work in Venice. He was overloaded with work and his delicate health suffered; he died of consumption a month before his 26th birthday. Although his career was so brief, he was highly influential, the freshness and spontaneity

of his fluid style in both oil and watercolours attracting many imitators. Delacroix wrote of him: 'Other artists were perhaps more powerful or more accurate than Bonington, but no one in the modern school, perhaps no earlier artist, possessed the lightness of execution which makes his works, in a certain sense, diamonds, by which the eye is enticed and charmed independently of the subject or of imitative appeal.' Most of his work is on a small scale and the qualities Delacroix admired are particularly evident in his *pochades* (oil sketches done rapidly on the spot as records of transitory effects in nature); with Constable and *Turner he was instrumental in establishing a fashion for such sketches. The best collection of Bonington's work is in the Wallace Collection, London, and he is also well represented in the City Museum and Art Gallery, Nottingham.

Bonnard, Pierre (*b* Fontenay-aux-Roses, nr. Paris, 3 Oct. 1867; *d* Le Cannet, nr. Cannes, 23 Jan. 1947). French painter, lithographer, and designer. His father, an official in the War Ministry, insisted that he study law, but from 1888 he also attended classes at the École des *Beaux-Arts and at the *Académie Julian, where he met several young artists (including his lifelong friend *Vuillard), who with him formed the *Nabis. After doing military service, 1889–90, he abandoned law and became a full-time artist; his first one-man exhibition was at *Durand-Ruel's gallery in 1896. At this time, as well as painting, he was producing posters and coloured lithographs, and designing for the stage; he worked on the original production of Alfred Jarry's *Ubu-Roi* (1896), considered the first work of the Theatre of the Absurd. He prospered steadily in his career and his life was quiet and uneventful (although he travelled a good deal before the First World War). Like Vuillard, he is best known for peaceful domestic scenes to which the term *Intimiste is applied. Bonnard generally painted on a larger scale than Vuillard, however, and with greater richness and splendour of colour. His favourite model was his wife, and some of his most characteristic pictures are those in which he depicted her in the bath (she had an obsession with personal cleanliness and spent much of her time in the bathroom). His other subjects included flowers and landscapes. He also did numerous self-portraits. The late ones show his desolation after the death of his wife in 1940, but in general his work radiates a sense of warmth and well-being. This quality and his lively broken brushwork make him one of the most distinguished upholders of the *Impressionist tradition.

Bonnat, Léon (b Bayonne, 20 June 1833; d Monchy-Saint-Éloi, Oise, 8 Sept. 1922). French painter and collector. Bonnat's early works were mainly religious paintings in a *tenebrist style influenced by 17th-century Spanish painting (he lived in Madrid, 1846–53), but from about 1870 he turned increasingly to portraiture. His portraits are usually as glum as his religious paintings, but their almost photographic realism won them an appreciative audience and the fortune he earned painting them enabled him to form a superb art collection, particularly of Old Master drawings. He donated it to Bayonne, his native city, where it forms the nucleus of the Musée Bonnat, one of France's finest provincial galleries. His studio and personal effects can be seen in the nearby Musée Basque. Bonnat was a renowned teacher, his many pupils including *Toulouse-Lautrec and *Braque.

Bontemps, Pierre (b ?Sens, c.1510; d ?Verneuil-sur-Oise, c.1570). French sculptor, first documented in 1536 as an assistant to *Primaticcio at *Fontainebleau. By 1550 he was in Paris, working on two important monuments for the royal burial church at Saint-Denis—the reclining effigies and bas-*reliefs for the tomb of Francis I, designed by the great architect Philibert Delorme, and the monument for the heart of Francis I. Only one other work is documented as being by him—the tomb of Charles de Maigny (1557) in the Louvre—but other works of the period are confidently attributed to him on stylistic evidence, and he seems to have been the foremost French tomb sculptor of the mid-16th century. His style was elegant and decorative.

Book of Durrow. See BOOK OF KELLS.

Book of Hours. A medieval prayer book used by laymen for private devotion, containing prayers or meditations appropriate to certain hours of the day, days of the week, months, or seasons. This type of book originated around 1300 and replaced the *psalter as the most popular prayer book for secular use; a great many examples survive (outnumbering all other types of *illuminated manuscript) and from the late 15th century there were also printed versions illustrated by *woodcuts. Most Books of Hours are small and easily portable, but more luxurious examples were made for major patrons; the most famous example is the *Très Riches Heures du duc de Berry* (Mus. Condé, Chantilly), illuminated by the *Limbourg brothers for Jean, Duc de Berry.

Book of Kells. Illuminated manuscript of the four Gospels in Latin, named after the town of Kells in County Meath, Ireland, where it was preserved in the monastery from the 11th century or earlier until the 16th century. It is one of the most famous of all illuminated manuscripts, celebrated for its extraordinary richness of ornamentation, especially in its decorative initial letters, and it is regarded as one of Ireland's greatest national treasures. However, little is known for certain about its origins. According to tradition it is from the time of St Columba (d 597), or is even a work of his own hands, but it is certainly appreciably later (it is now generally dated to about 800). It may have been produced at Kells, but the prevailing scholarly opinion is that it was made (or at least begun) on the island of Iona, off the west coast of Scotland, where Columba founded a monastery, and brought to Ireland when the monks of Iona fled from the Vikings in 806. After the Dissolution of the Monasteries in 1539 the manuscript was in private hands until the 1660s, when it was presented to Trinity College, Dublin, by Bishop Henry Jones of Meath. At the same time he presented another celebrated early manuscript, the Book of Durrow (c.650–80), named after the monastery at Durrow, County Offaly, where it had long been preserved. As with the Book of Kells, its origins are uncertain: Ireland, Iona, and *Lindisfarne have variously been suggested as its place of production (see INSULAR ART). It marks the beginning of the idea of building initial letters into whole-page designs, a concept so richly developed in the Book of Kells. See also CELTIC ART.

Borch, Gerard ter. See TERBORCH.

Bordone, Paris (bapt. Treviso, 5 July 1500; d Venice, 19 Jan. 1571). Italian painter, active mainly in Venice, where he is first recorded as a painter in 1518. *Vasari says he was a pupil of *Titian but that he soon left because he found his teaching disagreeable (Titian is then said to have stolen Bordone's first commission). Whatever the truth of these stories, Bordone's work was certainly strongly influenced by Titian and also by *Giorgione, 'for that master's style pleased him exceedingly' (Vasari). His most characteristic subjects included Holy Families in landscape settings, half-length figures of female beauties, and reclining nudes, but his most famous work, the *Presentation of the Ring of St Mark to the Doge* (c.1535, Accademia, Venice), is in a very different vein—a large, ceremonial composition that is remarkable for its spatial complexity. Bordone had a varied and successful career in Venice and is also said to have worked in France and Augsburg. However, in his later years his style, once warm and sensuous, became increasingly mechanical.

Borduas, Paul-Émile (*b* Saint-Hilaire, Quebec, 1 Nov. 1905; *d* Paris, 22 Feb. 1960). Canadian painter, active mainly in Montreal but also in Paris and New York. He trained as a church decorator under Ozias *Leduc, then studied in Paris. In the early 1940s, under *Surrealist influence, he started to experiment with *automatism and he was the driving force behind the radical abstract group Les *Automatistes. His later paintings have an *all-over surface animation recalling the work of *Pollock, although the only American influence Borduas acknowledged was that of Franz *Kline. In 1953–5 he lived in New York, then spent his final years in Paris, where he died of a heart attack. He ranks with *Riopelle as one of the outstanding Canadian abstract painters of the post-war years.

Borghese Gallery (Galleria Borghese), Rome. Italian state museum housed in the Villa Borghese. The villa was built (1613–15) for Cardinal **Scipione Borghese** (1576–1633) as a rural retreat (it was then on the outskirts of Rome) and a place to house his magnificent art collection. The nephew of Pope Paul V (**Camillo Borghese**, 1552–1621), Scipione held numerous lucrative church positions and he used his huge income to indulge his love of fine living, which included a genuine passion for art. He was *Bernini's first important patron, and the Gallery has an unrivalled representation of the sculptor's early work, including two busts of Scipione. It also boasts more *Caravaggios than any other collection (Scipione was an early admirer). Scipione was ruthless in using his power and influence to acquire coveted works, most notably with *Raphael's *Entombment*, one of the most famous pictures in the collection; with the connivance of his uncle, he had it illegally removed from the chapel in Perugia for which it had been painted and replaced it with a copy. Other members of the family added to the collection after Scipione's death, notably Prince Marcantonio Borghese IV (1730–1800), who had much of the interior of the building remodelled in a Neoclassical style appropriate to the ancient sculpture displayed there. However, because of financial difficulties, Marcantonio's son Prince Camillo Borghese (1775–1832) sold part of the collection to his brother-in-law Napoleon Bonaparte in 1807, including the *Borghese Warrior*. In

1891 paintings, sculptures, and antiquities from other Borghese properties were installed in the villa, and in 1902 the building and its contents were bought by the Italian government.

Borghese Warrior (or *Borghese Gladiator*). Marble statue (Louvre, Paris) of a nude warrior in a vigorous attitude of combat (his sword and shield are missing, but he is evidently lunging at an opponent on horseback in a type of pose that has been described as a 'heroic diagonal'). It was discovered in 1611 at Nettuno (near Anzio), had entered the *Borghese collection by 1613, and was bought by Napoleon (brother-in-law of Prince Camillo Borghese) in 1807. The statue is signed by 'Agasias, son of Dositheos, Ephesian' and is generally considered to be a copy of a *Hellenistic work influenced by *Lysippus. It became famous soon after its discovery and for two centuries it was one of the most admired and copied of antique statues, praised particularly for its anatomical mastery: *Bernini's *David* (made for the statue's then owner, Cardinal Scipione Borghese) is an early instance of a derivation from it and a more curious adaptation is found in *Copley's *Brook Watson and the Shark*, in which the figure of Watson—horizontal in the water—is based, in reverse, on the *Warrior*. It is now much less admired as a work of art, Martin Robertson (*A History of Greek Art*, 1975) describing it as 'harsh and unappealing'.

Borglum, Gutzon (*b* Bear Lake, Ida., 25 Mar. 1867; *d* Chicago, 6 Mar. 1941). American sculptor of Scandinavian descent. He specialized in extremely large works and is best known for the 'carving' (he used dynamite and pneumatic drills) of a huge cliff at Mount Rushmore in the Black Hills of South Dakota with colossal portrait busts of Presidents Washington, Jefferson, Lincoln, and Theodore Roosevelt. The project, begun in 1927, was sponsored by the US government and cost more than $1,000,000. Washington's head was completed in 1930, Jefferson's in 1936, Lincoln's in 1937, and Roosevelt's in 1939; the final details were added in 1941, after Borglum's death, by his son Lincoln. **Solon Hannibal Borglum** (1868–1922), Gutzon's brother, was also a sculptor, mainly of Wild West subjects.

Borgognone, Ambrogio. See BERGOGNONE.

Borgognone, Il. See COURTOIS.

Borgoña, Juan de (*b* ?Burgundy, ?c.1460/70; *d* ?Toledo, c.1536). Spanish painter of northern European origin (his name means 'John of

Burgundy'). He is first documented in 1495, in Toledo, where he became the leading painter of the day. His most important work is the fresco decoration (1509–11) of the chapter house of Toledo Cathedral; there are scenes from the life of the Virgin and the Passion of Christ, with a large *Last Judgement* on the entrance wall. It has been described as 'the only great fresco ensemble of the Spanish *Renaissance' (George Kubler and Martin Soria, *Art and Architecture in Spain and Portugal and their American Dominions: 1500–1800*, 1959). The calm clarity of Borgoña's style shows the influence of Italian Renaissance art; in particular he seems to have been familiar with the work of Domenico *Ghirlandaio, and he must have spent some time in Italy. He ran a large workshop and it is sometimes difficult to distinguish his work from that of his pupils and assistants, among whom were Antonio de Comontes (*d* 1565) and Pedro de Cisneros (*d* 1548).

Borisov-Musatov, Victor. See BLUE ROSE.

Borman (or **Borreman**), **Jan II** (active 1479–1520). Netherlandish sculptor, mainly in wood. He was head of the busiest workshop in Brussels, famous for its elaborate altarpieces, several of which were exported to Scandinavia. The Altar of St George (1493, Mus. Royaux, Brussels), commissioned by the guild of crossbowmen in Louvain, is his masterpiece; it features a multitude of figures in an intricate *Gothic framework. His two sons **Jan III** and **Pasquier** continued his tradition.

Borofsky, Jonathan. See NEW IMAGE PAINTING.

Borrassà, Luis (*b* Girona, active 1380; *d* Barcelona, 1424/5). Spanish painter, active mainly in Barcelona and its neighbourhood. About a dozen of his documented works survive, for example the altarpiece for the convent of S. Clara, Vich (1412–15, Vich Mus.), and about twenty more are attributed to him on stylistic evidence, making him the most prolific Catalan painter of his day. His work shows French and Sienese influences and is representative of the *International Gothic style.

Borromeo, Cardinal Federico. See AMBROSIANA and CRESPI, GIOVANNI BATTISTA.

Bosboom, Johannes (*b* The Hague, 18 Feb. 1817; *d* The Hague, 14 Sept. 1891). Dutch painter, a member of the *Hague School. He specialized in paintings of church interiors and was much inspired by the work of Emanuel de *Witte—in many of his pictures the figures even wear 17th-century costumes.

Bosch, Hieronymus (*b* ?'s Hertogenbosch, *c.*1450; *bur.* 's Hertogenbosch, 9 Aug. 1516). Netherlandish painter, active for all his known career in 's Hertogenbosch (Bois-le-Duc in French), where he is first documented in 1474. His real name was Jerome van Aken (perhaps indicating family origins in Aachen, Germany), but on the few pictures that he signed he used the name by which he has become famous: 'Hieronymus' (or 'Jheronimus' as he spelt it) is the Latin form of Jerome, and 'Bosch' is a shortened version of the name of his town. Although it was fairly remote from the major art centres of the Netherlands, it was one of the most prosperous towns in the duchy of Brabant, with a vigorous cultural and intellectual life. Bosch, who came from a long line of artists, was the leading painter of the day there, although he was married to a wealthy woman and probably had no need to paint for a living. He was a prominent member of a local religious organization, the Brotherhood of Our Lady, but because his most characteristic paintings seem so bizarre to modern eyes, his work has inspired theories that he was involved in heresy, witchcraft, or various esoteric practices. However, all the contemporary evidence indicates that he held the orthodox religious views of his time and was a respected member of his community. It was evidently not until after his death that it was first suggested he had embodied unorthodox beliefs in his work, and it was not until the 20th century that speculation (sometimes wild speculation) about his character and motivation began in earnest. There is much about his art that is obscure and perplexing, but modern research has helped to show how his work is a reflection of the cultural traditions of his time rather than the expression of eccentric private concerns.

About 40 surviving paintings are generally regarded as autograph works by Bosch, but none is dated and it has proved difficult to construct a satisfactory chronology. More than half of these pictures are on traditional Christian subjects (*Crucifixion*, *c.*1480, Mus. Royaux, Brussels), and others deal with general moral themes, often by illustrating human greed and gullibility in a folkloric way (*The Cure of Folly*, *c.*1480–90, Prado, Madrid). Almost all his pictures have some grotesque element, but only a few are dominated by the kind of weird and disturbing imagery from which his name is now inseparable—nightmare visions of monstrous creatures illuminated by the flames of hell, showing the horrible consequences of sin (*The Garden of Earthly Delights*, c.1500–10, Prado). These works have an extraordinarily vivid imaginative power and the subjects are heavily embroidered with subsidiary narratives and symbols, but the basic themes are sometimes quite simple and much of the imagery can be explained in terms of the popular culture of Bosch's age, notably proverbs and devotional literature. In purely visual terms, the monsters he painted have analogies in the strange creatures often seen in the margins of medieval manuscripts and in the gargoyles of *Gothic architecture—the cathedral at 's Hertogenbosch has some fine examples. This connection with popular culture underlines the fact that Bosch worked in a town that was somewhat distant from the mainstream of Early Netherlandish painting stemming from Jan van *Eyck. He stands apart in technique, too, for his brushwork is vigorous and varied, rather than smooth and precise in the manner typical of the time. (His individuality also comes out in his work as a draughtsman; he was one of the first artists to make drawings as independent works.)

By the time of his death, Bosch's reputation had spread far from his own town: in Spain, Queen Isabella (*d* 1504) owned three of his pictures, and in Venice, Cardinal Domenico Grimani (see BREVIARY) owned five. Through the medium of engravings his work reached a wide audience and he was influential in the Netherlands throughout the 16th century, although most of the artists who imitated him did so very superficially, turning his deeply serious diabolic imagery into 'an infernal amusement park, a Disneyland of the afterlife' (Walter S. Gibson, *Bosch*, 1973). *Patinir, in his eerie landscapes, and *Bruegel, with his vivid sense of the grotesque, were among the few who had artistic personalities strong enough to extend Bosch's vision rather than simply pastiche it, and it was in Spain rather than the Netherlands that he found his spiritual home. Philip II (see HABSBURG) was the greatest of all collectors of his work and kept a favourite example (*Tabletop of the Seven Deadly Sins*, c.1480–90, Prado) in his bedroom at the *Escorial.

Writing about the treasures of the Escorial in 1605, a Spanish monk, José de Sigüenza, dismissed the idea that Bosch's work was 'tainted with heresy'. Far from being absurd, as some people maintained, he thought that his paintings were like 'books of great wisdom and artistic value. If there are any absurdities here, they are ours, not his . . . they are a painted satire on the sins and ravings of mankind'; other artists depicted 'people as they appear outwardly', but only Bosch had the audacity 'to paint them as they are on the inside'. In Spain, 'El Bosco' continued to be respected long after he had been forgotten elsewhere. It was not until the late 19th century that a major revival of interest in him began, and his strange and often apocalyptic imagery has appealed greatly to modern taste, not least to the *Surrealists, who regarded him as a forerunner.

Boschini, Marco. See VELÁZQUEZ.

Boshier, Derek (*b* Portsmouth, 19 June 1937). British painter, sculptor, designer, and experimental artist. He was one of the *Royal College of Art students who put British *Pop art on the map at the *Young Contemporaries exhibition of 1961. His work at this time was much concerned with the manipulative forces of advertising, treating human figures as if they were mass-produced goods. However, his involvement in Pop art was short-lived, and from 1966 he worked in sculpture, photography, film, and *Conceptual art, before returning to painting in 1979. Throughout the 1980s he taught painting at the University of Texas. Although his career has been fairly low key compared with those of some of his Pop art colleagues from the early 1960s, many critics think that Boshier's work has stood the test of time at least as well as theirs.

boss (or **roof boss**). In *Gothic architecture, an ornamental knob or projection at the intersection of ribs in a vault. Bosses were often elaborately decorated with carving (figurative, foliate, or heraldic), notably in England (where vaults tend to be lower than in Continental churches and therefore easier to see).

Bosschaert, Ambrosius (*bapt.* Antwerp, 18 Nov. 1573; *d* The Hague, 1621). Flemish flower and still-life painter, active mainly in the Netherlands (he is recorded in Middelburg from 1593 to 1613 and afterwards worked mainly in Utrecht). Although he spent the major part of his life in the Netherlands, Bosschaert's style was basically Flemish—similar to that of Jan *Brueghel, with whom he ranks in quality and in historical status as one of the pioneers of flower painting as an independent genre. He specialized in formally arranged bouquets, showing a rich variety of flowers from different seasons (they were painted from separate studies made at various times of year). His *Vase of Flowers* (c.1620, Mauritshuis, The Hague), one of the most reproduced of all flower pieces, is characteristic of his polished brushwork and beauty of colour. Bosschaert may fairly be said to have initiated the Dutch tradition of flower painting and his style was continued by his three sons **Ambrosius the Younger** (1609–45), **Abraham** (c.1613–43), and **Johannes** (c.1610–after 1628), and also by his brother-in-law Balthasar van der *Ast.

Bosse, Abraham (b Tours, 1604; d Paris, Feb. 1676). French printmaker and writer on art. His large output (more than 1,500 prints in etching and engraving) provides a rich source of documentation on 17th-century French life and manners. Many of his prints are *genre scenes, and even his religious works are in modern dress, often in elaborately descriptive interiors. However, his work is impressive artistically as well as valuable historically, for it shows a classical dignity of composition, sometimes coupled with sensitive handling of light. Bosse taught perspective at the Académie Royale (see ACADEMY) from its foundation in 1648 until 1661, when he was expelled for quarrelling with his colleagues over his opposition to *Le Brun's dogmatic theories. He wrote several treatises on art, notably *Traité des manières de graver* (1645). This was the first instruction manual for printmakers and went through many editions and translations, including one into English by *Faithorne (1662).

Botero, Fernando (b Medellín, 19 Apr. 1932). Colombian painter and sculptor. His early paintings were influenced by various styles, including *Abstract Expressionism, but in the late 1950s he evolved a highly distinctive manner in which figures look like grossly inflated dolls; some of his paintings are sardonic comments on modern life, others are parodies of the Old Masters. Since the early 1970s he has lived mainly in New York and he has acquired an international reputation accompanied by huge prices for his work in the saleroom. He has made sculpture in a similar vein to his paintings, including several public monuments in bronze, notably *Broadgate Venus* (1990, Exchange Square, London).

Both, Jan (b Utrecht, c.1618; bur. Utrecht, 9 Aug. 1652). Dutch painter, draughtsman, and etcher, with Nicolaes *Berchem the most celebrated of the Italianate landscape painters. He probably studied with *Bloemaert in Utrecht before going to Italy, where he stayed for about four years, c.1637–41. Both's output was large (in spite of his short life), but few of the more than 300 paintings attributed to him can be convincingly dated to his Italian sojourn. Nevertheless, the main influence on his work was *Claude, whom he knew in Rome. His landscapes are typically peopled by peasants with animals or by travellers gazing on Roman ruins in the light of the evening sun. Such contemporary scenes were an innovation, for the earlier Dutch painters of the Italian countryside had populated it with biblical or mythological figures. They express the yearning of northerners for the light and idyllic life of the south, and proved immensely popular with collectors, not least in England, helping to shape ideas about Italy for two centuries.

Jan's brother **Andries** (c.1612–41) moved to Italy a few years before him. They lived together in Rome, 1639–41, and are said to have collaborated on certain works, but Andries is best known for paintings and drawings of lively peasant scenes that have little in common with Jan's idyllic landscapes. He drowned in an accident in Venice.

Botticelli, Sandro (Alessandro Filipepi) (b Florence, c.1445; bur. Florence, 17 May 1510). Florentine painter, neglected for centuries but now one of the best-loved artists of the *Renaissance. The name Botticelli, meaning 'little barrel', was originally given to an elder brother, presumably because he was portly, but it was adopted as the family surname. According to *Vasari, Sandro was first apprenticed to a goldsmith and then trained under Filippo *Lippi. Lippi's sweetness and grace certainly had a strong influence on him, but Botticelli was more refined, particularly in his draughtsmanship, in which he achieved an extraordinary combination of delicacy and flowing vitality: Bernard *Berenson described him as 'the greatest artist of linear design that Europe has ever had'.

Almost all Botticelli's life was spent in Florence, his only significant journey from the city being in 1481–2, when he worked on the decoration of the Sistine Chapel in the Vatican, alongside *Ghirlandaio, *Perugino, and other artists. The fact that he was called to Rome for such a prestigious commission shows that he must have had a considerable reputation by this time, and during the 1480s he seems to have been the most sought-after painter in Florence. His clients included the civic authorities, major churches, and members of distinguished families, particularly the *Medici, and in about 1485, when Ludovico *Sforza, Duke of Milan, asked his agent in Florence for information about leading artists there, Botticelli was described as 'A most excellent painter, both on panel and on wall. His works have a virile air and are done with the best judgement and perfect proportion.' He ran a busy workshop (Filippino *Lippi was his most important pupil) and some of his paintings (particularly those on the theme of the Virgin and Child) exist in several versions or copies, attesting to the vogue they enjoyed. In the 1490s, however, Botticelli's fortunes declined, and after *Leonardo's return to the city in 1500 his linear style must have looked archaic. In his final years he had financial problems and Vasari describes him as 'old and useless, unable to stand upright and moving about with the aid of crutches'. At his death he was a relic of a bygone age.

By the standards of his time, Botticelli's output was large and varied. The bulk of his work was devoted to religious subjects, but he also painted portraits and allegorical, literary, and mythological themes. In addition—and highly unusually—he made drawings as independent works. His most remarkable drawings are a series of illustrations for a de luxe manuscript edition of Dante's *Divine Comedy* (c.1490), commissioned by Lorenzo di Pierfrancesco de' Medici. The project was never finished and the 92 surviving drawings (which are in various states of completion) are now divided between the Kupferstichkabinett, Berlin, and the Vatican Library. It was perhaps for the same patron that Botticelli painted his two most celebrated pictures, *Primavera* (c.1480) and the *Birth of Venus* (c.1485), both now in the Uffizi, Florence. In Vasari's day they hung together in the Medici villa at Castello, near Florence, and they are mentioned by him in the same sentence, since when they have always been closely linked. However, they were not necessarily painted as a pair (*Primavera* is slightly bigger than the *Birth of Venus* and is painted on panel, whilst its companion is on canvas). Botticelli was the first painter since antiquity to treat such mythological themes on a large scale and with the seriousness usually reserved for religious subjects. Vasari described the subject of *Primavera* as 'Venus as a symbol of spring [primavera in Italian] being adorned with flowers by the Graces'. Various other mythological figures are present, and a huge amount of scholarly effort has gone into trying to elucidate the symbolic meaning of the picture and of the *Birth of Venus*. While the debate about iconographical interpretation continues, the pictures are universally acknowledged as two of the most beautiful works of the Renaissance, and they are now so famous that they are virtually symbols of the age.

Like other artists (Fra *Bartolommeo for example), Botticelli seems to have been disturbed by the turbulent political climate of Florence in the 1490s. Vasari says that he became a follower of the fiery preacher Savonarola, 'which led him to abandon painting'. The second part of this statement is definitely incorrect and the evidence for the first part is inconclusive, but it is certainly true that some of Botticelli's later paintings are more obviously 'serious'—solemn, intense, sometimes ecstatic—than his early works. The most telling example is the *Mystic Nativity* (1500, NG, London); it is the only work he signed or dated and it bears a cryptic inscription in Greek suggesting that he expected the second coming of Christ. It is remarkably personal in style, disregarding all the advances in naturalism that Florentine painters had made during the 15th century; he has even used the medieval device of making the Virgin and Child bigger in scale than the other figures. Botticelli's spirituality was one of the characteristics that appealed to the Victorians, who rediscovered him after a long period of obscurity. When Walter *Pater published an essay on him in 1870 he described him as 'a comparatively unknown artist', but by the end of the century he had become something of a cult figure—a major influence on *Art Nouveau and on the wan, elongated maidens of *Burne-Jones and his followers.

Botticini, Francesco (Francesco di Giovanni) (*b* Florence, *c*.1446; *d* Florence, 16 Jan. 1498). Florentine painter. His style is based almost entirely on elements drawn from his more illustrious contemporaries—Sandro *Botticelli, Domenico *Ghirlandaio, Filippino *Lippi, Andrea del *Verrocchio. He produced one remarkable work, however, the *Assumption of the Virgin* (c.1474, NG, London), which has the distinction of being the only picture from the *quattrocento known to have been painted to illustrate a heresy. The *donor, Matteo Palmieri, who held various government positions in Florence, believed that human souls are the angels who stayed neutral when Satan rebelled against God.

boucharde (or **bush hammer**). A sculptor's mallet or hammer with a chunky steel head on which the striking faces have rows of pyramidal teeth, cut or filed into the metal. It is used, mainly with very hard rocks such as granite, 'for wearing down or uniformly reducing a stone surface by progressive, broad pulverization . . . from the coarse, initial roughing-out stages almost to the very delicate or final stages of the carving. As the work progresses, the hammers should be replaced with others having increasingly finer and more numerous teeth. The pitted, granular surface resulting . . . is generally removed by using the flat chisel' (Jack C. Rich, *The Materials and Methods of Sculpture*, 1947).

Bouchardon, Edme (*b* Chaumont-en-Bassigny, Haute-Marne, 29 May 1698; *d* Paris, 27 July 1762). French sculptor whose work marks the beginning of the *Neoclassical reaction against the *Rococo style. He won the *Prix de Rome in 1722 and was in Italy from 1723 to 1732. His best-known work of this period is a marble bust of the antiquarian Philippe Stosch (1727, Skulpturgalerie, Berlin) that is very consciously in the *antique manner. Although his style later softened somewhat, notably in the famous *Cupid Making a Bow from Hercules' Club* (*c*.1750, Louvre, Paris), it remained too severe for court taste. Bouchardon had many supporters, however, and his contemporary reputation stood high—indeed he was generally regarded as the greatest French sculptor of his time (modern taste has inclined more towards artists with greater warmth, such as *Falconet and *Pigalle). His most important work was an equestrian statue of Louis XV, commissioned by the city of Paris in 1749. It was cast in 1758 but not erected until 1763, a year after Bouchardon's death. It stood in the Place Louis XV (later the Place de la Concorde) and was destroyed during the Revolution. Several small copies exist, as well as engravings, showing that it was based on the famous *Marcus Aurelius*. Bouchardon's father **Jean-Baptiste** (1667–1742) and his brother **Jacques-Philippe** (1711–53) were also sculptors.

Boucher, François (*b* Paris, 29 Sept. 1703; *d* Paris, 30 May 1770). French *Rococo painter, draughtsman, etcher, and designer, whose work best represents the frivolity and elegant superficiality of French court life at the middle of the 18th century. His father was a minor painter, who probably gave him his first training, and he briefly studied under François *Lemoyne before winning the *Prix de Rome in 1723. There were insufficient funds to pay for his scholarship and for the next few years he earned his living mainly as a printmaker, his work including etchings after drawings by *Watteau. In 1728 he went to Rome at his own expense and returned to Paris in 1731. Thereafter he was soon launched on a varied, prolific, and enormously successful career, punctuated by a stream of honours. In 1735 he received his first royal commission (for decorations at Versailles) and many others followed. At about the same time he took up tapestry design for the Beauvais factory, and he was a dominant figure in this field, becoming director of the *Gobelins factory in 1755. In 1765 he was appointed both director of the Académie Royale (see ACADEMY) and first painter to the king. He was also the favourite artist of Louis XV's most famous mistress, Mme de Pompadour, to whom he gave lessons and whose portrait he painted several times (Wallace Coll., London; NG, Edinburgh).

Boucher was immensely productive and highly versatile. He claimed that his output amounted to more than 1,000 paintings and 10,000 drawings, and his work was everywhere in fashionable society, for it ranged from colossal schemes of decoration for royal chateaux to designs for fans and slippers. It was reproduced in porcelain figures from the Sèvres and Vincennes factories and could be seen in his stage designs for the Paris Opéra. He painted many different kinds of pictures, including delightfully artificial landscapes (*Landscape with Watermill*, 1743, Bowes Mus., Barnard Castle). In his most characteristic paintings he turned the traditional mythological themes into wittily indecorous *scènes galantes*, and he painted female flesh with a delightfully healthy sensuality, notably in the celebrated *Reclining Girl* (1751, Alte Pin., Munich), which probably represents Louis XV's mistress Louisa O'Murphy. Towards the end of his career, as French taste changed in the direction of *Neoclassicism, Boucher was attacked, notably by *Diderot, for his stereotyped colouring and artificiality; he relied on his own repertory of motifs instead of painting from the life and objected to nature on the grounds that it was 'too green and badly lit'. Certainly his work often shows the effects of superficiality and overproduction, but at its best it has irresistible charm and great brilliance of execution, qualities he passed on to his most important pupil, *Fragonard.

Boucicaut Master (active early 15th century). Franco-Flemish manuscript *illuminator, active in Paris, named after a *Book of Hours (Mus. Jacquemart-André, Paris) done for Jean II le Meingre Boucicaut (1365–1421), marshal of France. This manuscript, which probably dates from about 1410, is a magnificent example of the *International Gothic style, but in its accomplished handling of space and *aerial perspective and its delightful *genre detail it heralds the achievements of the 15th-century Netherlandish School. Many other manuscripts have been attributed to the workshop of the Boucicaut Master, who has been tentatively identified with Jacques Coene, an artist with a high contemporary reputation but by whom no documented works are known.

Boudin, Eugène (b Honfleur, 12 July 1824; d Deauville, 8 Aug. 1898). French painter. The son of a sailor, he began his career working in a stationery and picture-framing business in the port of Le Havre. His clients there included several well-known artists, notably *Millet, who encouraged him to paint. Although he studied intermittently in Paris, he spent virtually all his life on the Normandy coast and his paintings are mainly small-scale beach scenes and seascapes, notable for their luminous skies. Many of them were painted out of doors, and it was he who introduced the young *Monet to this practice. He is regarded as a link between the painters of the generation of *Corot and the *Impressionists, and he exhibited in the first Impressionist exhibition of 1874. Boudin was highly prolific; there is a museum devoted to him in Honfleur and a large collection of his work in the Musée des Beaux-Arts, Le Havre.

Boudolf, Jean. See BONDOL.

Bouguereau, William (b La Rochelle, 30 Nov. 1825; d La Rochelle, 19 Aug. 1905). French painter. In 1850 he won the *Prix de Rome, and after his return to France in 1854 he became an immensely successful and influential exponent of academic art, upholding traditional values and contriving to exclude avant-garde work from the *Salon—*Cézanne once expressed regret at being excluded from the 'Salon de Monsieur Bouguereau'. He painted portraits of photographic verisimilitude, slick and sentimental religious works, and coyly erotic nudes. His reputation sank after his death and for many years his work was regarded as irredeemably empty and vulgar. However, he has recently achieved something of a rehabilitation, his work becoming the subject of serious study and fetching huge prices in the saleroom.

Boullogne. Family of French painters active in and around Paris in the 17th and early 18th centuries. The most important members were **Louis the Elder** (1609–74) and his two sons **Bon** (1649–1717) and **Louis the Younger** (1654–1733). Louis the Elder was one of the founder members of the Académie Royale (see ACADEMY) in 1748;

his work included religious pictures and a good deal of decorative painting at the Louvre, Versailles, and elsewhere. Bon and Louis the Younger similarly had successful careers as decorative painters (both worked extensively at Versailles) and are considered among the pioneers of the *Rococo style. Louis was much honoured, ending his career as director of the Académie (1722) and first painter to the king (1724). His sisters **Geneviève** (1645–1708) and **Madeleine** (1646–1710) were still-life painters.

Bourdelle, Émile-Antoine (b Montauban, 30 Oct. 1861; d Le Vésinet, nr. Paris, 1 Oct. 1929). French sculptor, the son of a cabinet-maker, from whom he received his first experience of carving. In 1876 he began to study at the École des Beaux-Arts, Toulouse, from where he won a scholarship to the École des *Beaux-Arts, Paris, in 1884. However, he shortly left the school and worked for a while with Jules *Dalou before becoming *Rodin's chief assistant from 1893 to 1908. Bourdelle's work has been somewhat overshadowed by his association with Rodin (whom he revered), but he was already an accomplished artist when he started working for him and developed an independent style. His energetic, rippling surfaces owe much to Rodin, but his flat rhythmic simplifications of form, recalling *Romanesque art, are more personal. He was particularly interested in the relationship of sculpture to architecture, and his reliefs for the Théâtre des Champs-Élysées (1912) are among his finest works. Bourdelle had many other prestigious public commissions and also achieved great distinction as a teacher. From about 1910 he was generally regarded as the outstanding sculptor in France apart from Rodin himself. He was also a talented painter and draughtsman. His house and studio in Paris have been converted into the Musée Bourdelle, opened in 1961 to mark the centenary of his birth.

Bourdichon, Jean (b ?Tours, c.1457; d Tours, 1521). French painter and manuscript illuminator, *Fouquet's successor as the leading French painter of the time. He was active in Tours, where he worked for several royal patrons, including Charles VIII, Louis XII, and Anne of Brittany, who married both these kings in turn. For Anne, Bourdichon produced his most celebrated work—the Hours of Anne of Brittany (completed 1508, Bib. Nat., Paris), one of the loveliest of all *Books of Hours. It contains numerous exquisite borders of plants and insects, together with 49 full-page miniatures (originally there were probably two more)—

mainly scenes from the New Testament and lives of the saints, but also including a portrait of Anne at prayer. Some of the religious scenes show strong Italianate influence and it is possible that Bourdichon had visited Italy. He is recorded as having painted works on a larger scale, but apart from a *triptych of the *Madonna and Child with Saints* in the Museo di Capodimonte, Naples, all his other known works are manuscript *illuminations. He effectively ends the great French tradition in this art.

Bourdon, Sébastien (*b* Montpellier, 2 Feb. 1616; *d* Paris, 8 May 1671). French painter. From about 1634 to 1637 he lived in Rome, where he worked for a picture dealer and developed a talent for imitating the work of other artists—*Claude, *Dughet, van *Laer—sometimes probably with intent to deceive. He continued in this vein when he returned to France and his oeuvre is still ill defined (contemporaries praised his work and admired his versatility but also criticized him for failing to find an individual style). From 1652 to 1654 he was court painter to Queen Christina of Sweden, of whom he did several portraits, and after his return to France he worked mainly as a portraitist. It was in this field that he produced his most distinctive works, using soft tonalities and skilful play with cascading draperies to create a languorous, romantic effect.

Bourgeois, Louise (*b* Paris, 25 Dec. 1911). French-born American sculptor. Her early life was spent in Paris, where part of her training was with *Léger, but after marrying the American art historian Robert Goldwater (1907–73) in 1938 she settled in New York and she became an American citizen in 1953. Bourgeois started as a painter and engraver and turned to sculpture only in the late 1940s. She first achieved recognition in the 1950s for her wood constructions painted uniformly black or white, which preceded the similar works of Louise *Nevelson. Subsequently she has worked in various materials, including stone, metal, and latex, and she has built up a reputation as one of the leading contemporary American sculptors. Although her work is typically abstract, it is often suggestive of the human figure, sometimes with sexual overtones. She has continued to be active into old age and in 1993 she represented the USA at the Venice *Biennale.

Bourgeois, Sir Peter Francis (*b* London, 1756; *d* London, 7 Jan. 1811). English painter and collector of Swiss parentage (his father was a

wealthy émigré watchmaker). He enjoyed some success as a painter (mainly of landscapes), but his work as an artist is now forgotten. His importance lies rather in his role in creating Dulwich College Picture Gallery, the first public art gallery in England; it opened in 1814, predating the National Gallery in London by a decade. Bourgeois was the protégé of Noel Desenfans (*b* Douai, 1745; *d* London, 8 July 1807), a French picture dealer who settled in London. There, in Anthony *Blunt's words, 'he became a friend of most of the leading artists, including *Reynolds and *Gainsborough, and exasperated his rival dealers by his successful pose as a gentleman who only sold pictures out of consideration for his friends and not for profit' (*The Nation's Pictures*, 1950). Desenfans also became consul general for Poland and in 1790 he was commissioned on behalf of King Stanislas II to put together a collection of pictures for a projected National Gallery in Warsaw. In 1795, however, Poland ceased to exist as an independent state when it was annexed by Austria, Prussia, and Russia, leaving Desenfans in possession of the pictures he had collected (for which he had not been paid). He tried to persuade the British government to buy them as the nucleus of a National Gallery, but his proposal came to nothing. Some of the paintings were sold in 1802, and those that remained with him at his death in 1807 were left jointly to his widow and Bourgeois, in the hope that they would be used to form a public collection.

At his own death in 1811 Bourgeois left the paintings and many others he had acquired himself—a total of 371 works—to Dulwich College, a distinguished boys' school in south London, which already had a small picture collection, based on that presented by its founder, the actor Edward Alleyn (1566–1626). Mrs Desenfans (who died in 1814) generously waived her lifetime interest in the paintings and helped to finance the building of a gallery designed by Sir John Soane, the most original English architect of his time and a friend of Bourgeois. The first building of its type in England, it has a series of top-lit galleries and is built of brick in a plain but eloquent classical style (the budget was tight); it incorporates a mausoleum for the three founders (Bourgeois and Mr and Mrs Desenfans). Other pictures have subsequently been added to the gallery, but the Desenfans–Bourgeois collection remains its core. Although fairly small in size, the collection is of very high quality and is particularly rich in 17th-century paintings, with choice groups of works by Aelbert *Cuyp, van

*Dyck, *Poussin, *Rembrandt, *Rubens, and *Wouwerman. The building was badly damaged by bombing in the Second World War (the pictures had been evacuated) but has been restored; an extension was opened in 2000. The gallery is administratively separate from the school and its name was changed to Dulwich Picture Gallery (dropping the word 'College') in 1979.

Boursse, Esaias (b Amsterdam, 3 Mar. 1631; d at sea, 16 Nov. 1672). Dutch painter, active mainly in his native Amsterdam. He joined the Dutch East India Company in 1661 and made two voyages to the Indies, on the second of which he died aboard ship. His few surviving paintings include some exquisite interior scenes that invite comparison with *Vermeer because of their tranquil beauty and subtle colour harmonies (*Interior with Woman Cooking*, 1656, Wallace Coll., London).

Boussot & Valadon. See GOUPIL.

Bouts, Dierec (or **Dirk**) (b ?Haarlem, ?c.1420; d Louvain, 6 May 1475). Netherlandish painter. Bouts evidently spent his early career in Haarlem, but all his documented works were produced in Louvain, where he is first recorded in 1457 and was city painter from 1468. His major commissions there were the *Last Supper* altarpiece for the church of St Peter (still *in situ*, 1464–7) and two panels (out of a projected set of four, left incomplete at Bouts's death) on the justice of Emperor Otto for the town hall (1470–5, Mus. Royaux, Brussels). Apart from these, there are no documented works, but his style is highly distinctive—characterized most obviously by stiff, solemn, exaggeratedly slender and graceful figures—and a convincing oeuvre has been built up for him. Most of his pictures are of religious subjects, but there are also a few portraits, including *Portrait of a Man* (1462, NG, London). This is his earliest dated work and perhaps the first Netherlandish portrait to include a landscape viewed through a window—an arrangement that had become common by the end of the century. Bouts often includes exquisite landscape backgrounds in his religious works, the setting helping to create the mood of the picture; there is little action, but deep poetic feeling. Sources for his work have been sought in the mysterious Albert van *Ouwater (who likewise seems to have had Haarlem connections), Rogier van der *Weyden (in spite of the great difference in emotional temperature), and Petrus *Christus, but the individuality of Bouts's

work transcends any models. His style was continued by his two sons **Dieric the Younger** (c.1448–90/1) and **Aelbrecht** (c.1455–1549), and was widely influential, in Germany as well as the Netherlands. Particularly popular were small devotional images of the *Mater Dolorosa* and Christ Crowned with Thorns (a pair of pictures showing these two subjects, catalogued as 'Workshop of Bouts', is in the National Gallery, London).

Bowes, John (b London, 19 June 1811; d Streatlam, Co. Durham, 9 Oct. 1885). English collector. The illegitimate son of the 10th Earl of Strathmore, he married Josephine Coffin-Chevallier (1825–74), a French actress and amateur painter, in 1852, and they devoted much of their wealth and energy to collecting. In 1869 they began to build an enormous museum at Barnard Castle in County Durham (near to the Strathmores' home at Streatlam) and it was opened to the public in 1892 (by which time the founders were dead). The building was designed by a French architect, Jules Pellechet, and Niklaus *Pevsner describes it as 'big, bold, and incongruous, looking exactly like the town hall of a major provincial town in France . . . gloriously inappropriate for the town to which it belongs'. The museum is particularly rich in French paintings and applied art of the 18th century (it has been called 'the *Wallace Collection of the North'), and it also has the best representation of Spanish painting in Britain outside London.

Bowler, Henry Alexander. See PRE-RAPHAELITE BROTHERHOOD.

Boyd, Arthur (b Murrumbeena, nr. Melbourne, 24 July 1920; d Melbourne, 24 Apr. 1999). Australian painter, printmaker, sculptor, designer, and ceramicist. He was the most famous member of a dynasty of artists founded by his grandfather **Arthur Merric Boyd** (1862–1940) and his wife **Emma Minnie Boyd** (1858–1936), both of whom were landscape painters. His father **William Merric Boyd** (1888–1959) was a sculptor and potter, and his mother **Doris Boyd** (c.1883–1960) was a painter and potter, but he was largely self-taught as an artist. He held his first one-man show at the age of 17, but his artistic career was then interrupted by the Second World War. In the 1950s he became well known in Australia, particularly for his large ceramic totem pole at the entrance to the Olympic Pool, Melbourne (for the 1956 Olympic Games), and for his series (twenty pictures) *Love, Marriage and Death of a Half-Caste* (1957–9) concerned with the life and death of an Aboriginal stockman and his half-caste bride. They are done in a style combining elements of *Expressionism and *Surrealism. Boyd moved to England in 1959 and soon established a reputation, which he subsequently consolidated, becoming probably the best-known Australian artist of his generation apart from Sidney *Nolan (his brother-in-law). He returned to Australia in 1971 but continued to spend a good deal of time in England and also in Italy.

Boydell, John (*b* Dorrington, Shropshire, 19 Jan. 1719; *d* London, 12 Dec. 1804). English engraver and print publisher. He made a fortune in the 1740s by publishing views of England and Wales, which he engraved from his own drawings. Later he published the work of other engravers and by developing a large foreign trade he spread the fame of English artists and engravers on the Continent. In 1790 he was lord mayor of London. His most ambitious undertaking was his celebrated Shakespeare Gallery: from 1786 he commissioned major artists (including *Fuseli, *Reynolds, and *Romney) to produce oil paintings (162 in all) illustrating Shakespeare's plays, and in 1789 he opened a purpose-built gallery in Pall Mall to exhibit them. Some of the engravings after them were published as illustrations to a nine-volume edition of Shakespeare in 1802 and others appeared separately in larger format in 1803. Boydell hoped by this venture to encourage the rise of a 'great national school of *history painting', and he intended to leave the collection to the nation, but he had heavy losses during the French wars and it was sold by lottery in 1805 shortly after his death (William *Tassie won the main prize). Few of the paintings survive. Boydell's nephew **Josiah Boydell** (1752–1817) was a painter and engraver, his uncle's partner and successor in his engraving business.

Boys, Thomas Shotter (*b* London, 2 Jan. 1803; *d* London, 10 Oct. 1874). English watercolour painter and lithographer. From 1825 to 1837 he was based mainly in France, where he was a friend of *Bonington, whose watercolours have sometimes been confused with those of Boys. He specialized in Continental urban scenes and in 1839 he published *Picturesque Architecture in Paris, Ghent, Antwerp, Rouen, etc.*, a work that marked the transition from hand-tinted *lithography to chromolithography. In 1842 he published *Original Views of London as It Is*, the plates of which constitute a fine topographical record of Regency London. In spite of the high quality of his work, Boys's career went into decline in the later 1840s (partly because of ill health) and he was often reduced to doing hackwork.

bozzetto. A small rough model, usually in wax or clay, made in preparation for a larger sculpture in more durable material. By extension, the term (a diminutive of the Italian *bozzo*, 'rough stone') is sometimes also applied to an oil sketch. In this second sense, the word is not always clearly differentiated from *modello*, but it is useful to reserve the latter word for a somewhat more elaborate type of preliminary design, especially one intended to be shown to a patron.

Brabazon, Hercules Brabazon (*b* Paris, 27 Nov. 1821; *d* Oaklands, nr. Battle, Sussex, 14 May 1906). English watercolourist, mainly of landscape subjects. He was born Hercules Brabazon Sharpe, but he adopted his mother's maiden name as a condition of inheriting the Brabazon family estates in Ireland in 1847. Later he inherited his father's estate, Oaklands in Sussex. He travelled widely in Europe and also visited Africa, the Middle East, and India, finding subjects for his large output wherever he went. He regarded himself as an amateur artist, and although he had distinguished supporters, including *Ruskin and *Sargent, his work was little known to the public until he showed it at the *New English Art Club in 1891 and then was reluctantly persuaded to hold a one-man exhibition, at the *Goupil Gallery, London, in 1892. Thereafter he quickly became a favourite with collectors, admired for his broad, fluid style. He has been described as 'A country gentleman who at seventy years old made his debut as a professional artist and straightaway became famous' (Sir Frederick Wedmore, *Hercules Brabazon Brabazon*, 1906).

Bracquemond, Félix (*b* Paris, ?28 May 1833; *d* Sèvres, 27 Oct. 1914). French printmaker, draughtsman, painter, and designer. He worked mainly as an etcher and played a leading role in the revival of the medium as a creative rather than merely a reproductive technique. He was also one of the first French artists to discover Japanese prints (see UKIYO-E). His own prints included landscapes, portraits, and subjects involving animals, particularly birds. Among the portraits are several of his artist friends, including *Degas and *Manet; he gave advice about printmaking to both Manet and Camille *Pissarro. Braquemond took part in three of the *Impressionist exhibitions (1874, 1879, 1880). His wife **Marie Bracquemond** (1840–1916) was a painter and printmaker; she too exhibited with the Impressionists (1879, 1880, 1886).

Brailes, William de (active c.1230–c.1260). English manuscript *illuminator. His signature, which appears in two manuscripts, gives his name only as 'W. de Braile', but he is almost certainly to be identified with a William de Brailes who is recorded in various civic records in Oxford; they mention no profession, but he lived in Catte Street, which was favoured by people working in the book trade. The two signed works by him (both c.1240) are a Book of Hours (BL, London) and a psalter (Fitzwilliam Mus., Cambridge). In an illustration of the Last Judgement in the Psalter, he depicts himself with a tonsure, from which it may be concluded that he was an ecclesiastic, but whether monastic or secular cannot be certain. The character of his work, however, has led to the assumption that he was secular. Several other manuscripts or illustrations have been attributed to him, and differences in quality of execution suggest that he was head of a workshop with various assistants. His style was lively and inventive, and with Matthew *Paris he ranks as one of the few distinctive personalities in English illumination of his time.

Bramante, Donato (Donato di Angelo) (b probably Monte Asdrualdo [now Fermignano], nr. Urbino, c.1444; d Rome, 11 Apr. 1514). Italian architect and painter. Bramante was the creator and greatest exponent of the High *Renaissance style in architecture, but most of his early career, which is ill documented, seems to have been devoted to painting. He probably trained in Urbino and the first record of him dates from 1477, when he is said to have worked on fresco decorations at the Palazzo del Podestà in Bergamo. In about 1480 he settled in Milan, and in 1481 he produced his earliest surviving dated work, the design of an engraving of an elaborate architectural fantasy (the British Museum, London, possesses one of only two known impressions). At about the same time he began his first building, S. Maria presso S. Satiro, Milan, in which his knowledge of *perspective was used to create an illusion of recession in the choir, which is in reality only a few inches deep. Various fresco fragments are attributed to him (mainly in the Brera, Milan), but the best evidence of his skill as a painter is the only panel painting that is generally accepted as his (on the testimony of *Lomazzo)—a sombre and poignant Christ at the

Column (c.1490, Brera), which shows some influence from his friend *Leonardo. In 1499 Bramante left Milan and settled in Rome, where in 1506 he began the rebuilding of St Peter's for Julius II (Giuliano della *Rovere). There is no evidence of any activity as a painter in Rome, but *Vasari says that Bramante designed the majestic architectural setting of *Raphael's fresco The School of Athens in the Vatican Stanze. Certainly Raphael paid tribute to Bramante by introducing his portrait into this painting as the mathematician Euclid. Bramante had an enormous influence as an architect, and his interest in perspective and *trompe-l'œil left a mark on Milanese painting, notably in the work of his follower *Bramantino.

Bramantino (Bartolomeo Suardi) (b ?Milan, c.1460; d Milan, 1530). Milanese painter and architect, a follower of *Bramante, from whom he takes his nickname (meaning 'little Bramante'). He was appointed court painter and architect to Duke Francesco II *Sforza in 1525. His style as a painter is complex and eclectic, drawing on *Piero della Francesca and *Leonardo as well as Bramante; at its best it has a certain stolid dignity. Perhaps his most individual characteristic is his use of sombre classical architectural backgrounds, as in the Adoration of the Magi (c.1500, NG, London).

Bramer, Leonaert (b Delft, 24 Dec. 1596; bur. Delft, 10 Feb. 1674). Dutch *genre and history painter. He worked mainly in Delft, but he travelled widely in Italy and France, 1614–28, and drew on a variety of influences for his most characteristic paintings—small nocturnal scenes with vivid effects of light. Works such as the Scene of Sorcery (Mus. B.-A., Bordeaux) have earned him the reputation of 'an interesting independent who cannot be pigeonholed' (Seymour Slive, Dutch Painting: 1600–1800, 1995). Bramer was also one of the few Dutch artists to paint frescos in Holland, but none of his work in the medium has survived. In 1653, when *Vermeer's future mother-in-law was trying to prevent him from marrying her daughter, Bramer came to the young man's defence. Because of this, it has been plausibly suggested that he may have been Vermeer's teacher.

Bramley, Frank. See NEWLYN SCHOOL.

Brancusi, Constantin (b Hobitza, 19 Feb. 1876; d Paris, 16 Mar. 1957). Romanian sculptor, active for almost all his career in Paris (he became a French citizen the year before his death), one of the most revered and influential of 20th-century artists. He settled in Paris in 1904 (according to his own romanticized account he had walked from Romania) and spent several years of poverty and hardship there. In 1906 he was introduced to *Rodin, whose offer to take him on as assistant Brancusi refused with the famous comment that 'No other trees can grow in the shadow of an oak.' His work of this time was in fact influenced by Rodin's surface animation, but from 1907 Brancusi began creating a distinctive style, based on his feeling that 'what is real is not the external form but the essence of things'. From this time his work (in both stone and bronze) consisted largely of variations on a small number of themes (heads, birds, a couple embracing—The Kiss) in which he simplified shapes and smoothed surfaces into immaculately pure forms that sometimes approach complete abstraction. He was particularly fond of ovoid shapes—their egglike character suggesting generation and birth and symbolizing his own creative gifts. (His woodcarvings, on the other hand, are rougher—closer to the Romanian folk-art tradition and to African sculpture.)

Brancusi's name was established abroad after five of his sculptures were shown at the *Armory Show, New York, in 1913, and during the 1920s he became newsworthy when he was involved in two celebrated art scandals. In 1920 his Princess X was removed by police from the *Salon des Indépendants because it had been denounced as indecent (there is a clear resemblance to a phallus); and in 1926 he had a dispute with the US Customs authorities. They attempted to tax his Bird in Space (one of his most abstract works) as raw metal, rather than treat it as sculpture, which was duty free. Brancusi was forced to pay up to get the work released for exhibition, but he successfully sued the Customs Office, winning the court decision in 1928. By this time he had a growing international reputation and during the 1930s he travelled widely, notably to India in 1937–8 to discuss designs for a Temple of Meditation (never built) for the Maharaja of Indore. Later in 1938 his largest work was inaugurated—a complex of sculpture (including the enormous Endless Column, nearly 30 m (100 ft) high) for the public park at Tîrgu Jiu near his birthplace. By the time of his death he was widely regarded as the greatest sculptor of the 20th century.

Brancusi's originality in reducing natural forms to their ultimate—almost abstract—simplicity had profound effects on the course of 20th-century sculpture. He introduced *Modigliani to sculpture, *Archipenko and *Epstein owed much to him, and *Gaudier-Brzeska was his professed admirer. Later, Carl *Andre claimed to have been inspired by Endless Column, converting its repeated modules into his horizontal arrangements of identical units. More generally, Henry *Moore wrote of Brancusi: 'Since the Gothic, European sculpture had become overgrown with moss, weeds—all sorts of surface excrescences which completely concealed shape. It has been Brancusi's special mission to get rid of this undergrowth and to make us once more shape-conscious.' On his death Brancusi bequeathed to the French government his studio and its contents, which included versions of most of his best works (they often exist in multiple replicas in different materials). The studio has now been reconstructed at the *Pompidou Centre in Paris. There is another outstanding Brancusi collection in the Philadelphia Museum of Art.

Brandl, Petr (b Prague, 24 Oct. 1668; d Kutná Hora, nr. Prague, 24 Sept. 1735). The outstanding Bohemian painter of his period. Most of his work consisted of altarpieces and portraits in a lively, painterly *Baroque style. Many of his best paintings are still in the churches for which they were created, but he is also well represented in the National Gallery, Prague.

Brangwyn, Sir Frank (b Bruges, 12 May 1867; d Ditchling, Sussex, 11 June 1956). British painter, printmaker, draughtsman, and designer, the son of a Welsh architect who specialized in church furnishings and who was working in Belgium at the time of the boy's birth. In 1882–4 Brangwyn served an apprenticeship with William *Morris, and like his master he was active in a variety of fields. He was an *Official War Artist in the First World War, for example, he was one of the finest draughtsmen of the day and a skilful etcher and lithographer, and he made designs for a great range of objects (furniture, textiles, ceramics, glassware, jewellery, and so on); however, he became best known for his murals. His most famous undertaking in this field was a series of eighteen panels on the theme of the British Empire, commissioned by the House of Lords. They were begun in 1926 and rejected—amid great controversy—in 1930, being considered too flamboyant for their setting. Offers for the panels came from all over the world, and in 1934 they were installed in the Guildhall in Swansea. Brangwyn's work at its most characteristic was floridly coloured, crowded with detail and incident, and rather *Rubensian, although it became somewhat flatter, lighter, and more stylized later in his career. During his lifetime he was one of the most famous of British artists (probably *the* most famous worldwide); there is a museum devoted to him in Bruges and another almost entirely given over to his work in Orange. His reputation crumbled after his death, his work tending to be dismissed as facile and sentimental, but there has recently been a modest revival of interest in him.

Braque, Georges (*b* Argenteuil, 13 May 1882; *d* Paris, 31 Aug. 1963). French painter, graphic artist, and designer. Initially he followed his father's trade of house painter, but in 1902–4 he took lessons at various art schools in Paris, including briefly the École des *Beaux-Arts. Through his friendship with his fellow students *Dufy and *Friesz, he was drawn into the circle of the *Fauves, and in 1905–7 he painted in their brightly coloured, impulsive manner. In 1907, however, two key events completely changed the direction of his work: first, he was immensely impressed by the *Cézanne memorial exhibition at the *Salon d'Automne; and secondly, he met *Picasso, in whose studio he saw *Les Demoiselles d'Avignon*. Although he was initially disconcerted by it, he soon began experimenting with the dislocation and fragmentation of form it had introduced, and the two men worked in close association until the outbreak of the First World War, jointly creating *Cubism. At times it is difficult to tell their work apart, but John *Golding (*Braque*, 1966) senses some fundamental differences of outlook: 'Picasso's approach was predominantly linear and sculptural; it was he who formulated the concept of "simultaneous vision"—that is to say, the concept of combining different viewpoints of a subject into a single, coherent image. Braque's approach was more painterly, more poetic; significantly, of all the major Cubist painters, only he retained an interest in the evocative properties of light. And he was the technician who through patient research was able to solve so many of the pictorial problems which arose in the creation of this supremely complex and sophisticated style.'

In 1914 Braque enlisted in the French army and was twice decorated for bravery before being seriously wounded in the head in 1915 and demobilized in 1916. After the war his work diverged sharply from that of Picasso. Whereas Picasso went on experimenting restlessly, Braque's painting became a series of sophisticated variations on the heritage of his pre-war years. His style became much less angular,

tending towards graceful curves. He used subtle muted colours and sometimes mixed sand with his paint to produce a textured effect. Still-life and interiors remained his favourite subject, and many critics regard his *Studio* series, begun in 1947, as the summit of his achievement. From the 1930s his reputation had become international, and in his later years he accumulated an impressive list of prizes and honours, including the main prize for painting at the 1948 Venice *Biennale. The final accolade was a state funeral—an occasion that seemed at odds with his life of unassuming dedication to his art. In addition to the type of paintings for which he is best known, Braque also did much book illustration, designed stage sets and costumes, and carried out some decorative work, notably the ceiling of the Etruscan Gallery in the Louvre, 1952–3.

brass, monumental. A funerary monument consisting of an engraved sheet of brass, a golden yellow metal, affixed to the floor or wall of a church or sometimes to a tomb chest. Brasses, which were cheaper than sculptured tombs, originated in the Low Countries in the 13th century and flourished chiefly in England, where about 8,000 are extant (the earliest date from about 1300 and the practice of making them continued into the 17th century). About half of them represent figures, and others have heraldic devices, Christian symbols, or (in later examples) religious scenes. The material used was not pure brass (copper and zinc), but an alloy called at the time 'latten', composed of approximately 60 per cent copper and 30 per cent zinc, with 10 per cent lead and tin. Latten was produced in the Low Countries and Germany and imported into England, where it was engraved; large-scale English manufacture of the material began only in the 16th century. The main centre of production seems to have been London, and the majority of medieval brasses are in the Home Counties and East Anglia; there are comparatively few in the north, although the Thornton Brass (*c.*1430) in St Nicholas's Cathedral, Newcastle upon Tyne, is said to be the largest in the country. The best examples are of outstanding artistic merit and collectively brasses are of great importance as a source of detailed information on the evolution of armour and costume in medieval England. See also BRONZE.

Bratby, John (*b* Wimbledon, Surrey [now in Greater London], 19 July 1928; *d* Hastings, Sussex, 20 July 1992). British painter and writer.

Bratby was a versatile artist: he painted portraits, still-lifes, figure compositions, landscapes, and flower pieces, and also designed film sets. He is probably best known for the scenes of drab domestic life he painted in the 1950s, when he was a member of the *Kitchen Sink School. Later his work became lighter and more exuberant. His talent for self-promotion helped to make him one of the best-known British artists of his generation. Among his publications are the novel *Breakdown* (1960) and a book on Stanley *Spencer (1970).

Braun, Matyáš Bernard (*b* Sautens, nr. Innsbruck, 24 Feb. 1684; *d* Prague, 15 Feb. 1738). Austrian-born sculptor who settled in Prague in 1710 and became with Ferdinand Maximilián *Brokof the leading sculptor of the time in Bohemia. His dynamic, emotional style and virtuosity in stone carving show the influence of *Bernini and he is presumed to have visited Italy as a young man. Much of his work is in Prague, including parts of the sculptural decoration of the Charles Bridge and two magnificent entrance portals (*c*.1713), featuring powerful *atlas figures, on the street façade of the Clam-Gallas Palace. However, the largest groups of his work are at Kuks (Kukus), north-east of Prague, where his highly cultured patron, Count Franz von Sporck, had a country estate. There von Sporck created a novel kind of religious nature park, for which Braun made figures of penitents and hermits, some of them of colossal size and carved from the living rock (*St Garinus*, 1726). Earlier Braun and his workshop made a series of figures of the Beatitudes and the Virtues and Vices (1712–20) for the garden of the hospital church at Kuks.

Bray, Jan de (*b* Haarlem, *c*.1627; *bur.* Haarlem, 4 Dec. 1697). Dutch painter, principally of portraits. He worked in his native Haarlem and his vigorously characterized work shows the lasting influence of *Hals in the city, although de Bray's handling is much smoother, in the manner of van der *Helst. Jan's father **Salomon** (1597–1664) was an architect and painter of biblical and allegorical scenes (see HUYGENS). He wrote a book, *Architectura moderna* (1631), describing the buildings of Hendrick de *Keyser.

Bredius, Abraham (*b* Amsterdam, 18 Apr. 1855; *d* Monte Carlo, 13 Mar. 1946). Dutch art historian and collector. Bredius excelled at archival research and published a large amount of new documentation relating to 17th-century Dutch artists. His best-known work is his complete illustrated catalogue of *Rembrandt's paintings, originally published in German in 1935 and then in an English edition in 1937; a second English edition, revised by Horst Gerson, Bredius' collaborator on the original edition, appeared in 1969. It is still a standard work (although the illustrations are of poor quality) and the Bredius numbering system is widely used in Rembrandt scholarship. Bredius made a choice collection of Dutch paintings; he presented or bequeathed many to the *Rijksmuseum in Amsterdam and the *Mauritshuis in The Hague (of which he was director from 1889 to 1909) and others are in the Bredius Museum in The Hague. His reputation as a connoisseur was blighted because he was taken in by the work of the *Vermeer forger Han van Meegeren (1880–1947); however, Bredius was very old at the time (1937) and almost all his contemporaries were similarly deceived.

Breenbergh, Bartholomeus (*bapt.* Deventer, 13 Nov. 1598; *bur.* Amsterdam, 5 Oct. 1657). Dutch painter, etcher, and draughtsman, with *Poelenburgh the leading pioneer of the taste for Italianate landscapes in the Netherlands. Breenbergh spent about ten years in Italy (*c*.1619–*c*.1629) and thereafter lived in Amsterdam. His work as a painter is very similar to Poelenburgh's, featuring biblical and mythological characters set in well-balanced views of the Roman Campagna, often complete with classical ruins. His drawings are fresher and bolder, and have often passed under the name of *Claude, as is the case with two examples in Christ Church, Oxford. Late in his career Breenbergh painted a few portraits.

Bregno, Andrea (*b* Osteno, nr. Lugano, 1418; *d* Rome, Sept. 1506). Italian sculptor, active mainly in Rome, where he settled in the 1460s and became the leading monumental sculptor of the second half of the 15th century. With the assistance of a large workshop he produced numerous altars and tombs, showing a command of fashionable antique motifs that no doubt accounted for much of his success. Sir John *Pope-Hennessy described him as 'a sculptor of great taste and technical proficiency, but of limited inventiveness'. His work often includes elegant architectural ornament and it has been suggested that he was involved in the design of certain buildings in Rome, including the Palazzo della Cancelleria. Bregno came from a family of sculptors, several other members of which worked in Venice; the precise familial links among them are often unclear.

Breitner, George Hendrik (*b* Rotterdam, 12 Sept. 1857; *d* Amsterdam, 5 June 1923). Dutch painter and photographer. He trained in The Hague, where he became a friend of van *Gogh, whom he encouraged. His most characteristic early works were military scenes, particularly of cavalry manoeuvres, but a six-month visit to Paris in 1884 introduced him to *Impressionism and he became the leading Dutch exponent of the style. In 1886 he settled in Amsterdam and he is best known for scenes of its busy harbour, its architecture, and its bustling street life. The unposed 'snapshot' compositions of many of these paintings reflect his interest in photography (he seems to have taken his camera with him everywhere). After 1910 he virtually gave up painting because of ill health.

Breker, Arno. See DESPIAU.

Brera (Pinacoteca di Brera), Milan. One of Italy's greatest picture galleries. It is housed in an impressive building (the Palazzo di Brera), largely 17th and 18th century in date, that was originally a Jesuit college. After the Jesuits were suppressed in 1772 it was used by various learned bodies, including the Accademia di Belle Arti. In 1796 Milan was taken over by Napoleon (he was crowned King of Italy in the cathedral in 1805) and the Brera was made the centre for paintings from north Italy that had been displaced by the closing of religious houses; in this way it came into possession of some of the finest altarpieces of the *Renaissance. It was opened as a public gallery in 1809 and became administratively separate from the Accademia in 1882. The collection is still dominated by Italian Renaissance works, but it has been continuously enlarged by purchase and bequest and includes paintings from other schools and periods, extending into the 20th century.

Breton, André (*b* Tinchebray, Orne, 19 Feb. 1896; *d* Paris, 28 Sept. 1966). French poet, essayist, critic, and editor, the founder of the *Surrealist movement and its chief theorist and promoter. In 1924 he marked the official launch of the movement by publishing his *Manifeste du surréalisme* (dedicated to the memory of his friend *Apollinaire), and in 1925 he helped organize the first Surrealist exhibition, at the Galerie Pierre, Paris. He wrote numerous other books and articles on Surrealism and was also the driving force behind two of the major periodicals of the movement—*La Révolution surrealiste* (1924–9) and *Le Surréalisme au service de la révolution* (1930–3). In 1941–6 he lived in New York, where he was one of a group of expatriate Surrealists who had an important influence on the genesis of *Abstract Expressionism. After his return to Paris he continued to be regarded as the 'Pope of Surrealism', even though the movement was now long past its prime, and his death in 1966 was regarded by many as marking its end.

Breton, Jules (*b* Courrières, Pas-de-Calais, 1 May 1827; *d* Paris, 5 July 1906). French painter, the leading successor to *Millet in the vogue for pictures of peasant life. His many admirers included van *Gogh, who at the outset of his career walked about 80 km (50 miles) from the Borinage region of Belgium to Breton's home at Courrières in northern France to meet him; however, he was dismayed by the discrepancy between the hard work portrayed in Breton's pictures and the comfortable life the painter himself led. At the time Breton was considered a *Realist, but his peasants now look very well scrubbed and almost *Raphaelesque compared with van Gogh's.

Brett, John (*b* Bletchingley, Surrey, 8 Dec. 1831; *d* London, 7 Jan. 1902). English painter, mainly of coastal scenes and landscapes. He was influenced by the *Pre-Raphaelites and by *Ruskin (whose work he read avidly), and a handful of his early paintings such as *The Stonebreaker* (1857–8, Walker AG, Liverpool) are tours de force of minute and brilliant detail. His later work, however, tended to become laboured and he died virtually forgotten.

Breu, Jörg the Elder (*b* Augsburg, *c*.1475; *d* Augsburg, May/Oct. 1537). German painter and designer of woodcuts, a pupil of Ulrich *Apt. Breu was one of the leading painters of his time in Augsburg, but his most important works there—a series of frescos in the town hall—are no longer extant. His patrons included the Emperor Maximilian I (see HABSBURG) and also Duke William IV of Bavaria, for whom he painted the *Battle of Zama* (1529, Alte Pin., Munich) in the same series as *Altdorfer's celebrated *Battle of Issus*. His style was complex, sharing something of Altdorfer's passion and love of landscape, and showing strong influence from *Dürer and from a journey he is thought to have made to Italy in about 1514. His son **Jörg the Younger** (*c*.1510–47) was his pupil and assistant. In his independent work he was a prolific illustrator of manuscripts.

Breughel. See BRUEGEL.

Breuil, Henri. See ALTAMIRA.

breviary. A liturgical book containing the hymns, lessons, prayers, etc., to be recited at appointed times by clergy in the Roman Catholic Church. Originally these various observances were distributed in different books, but from the 11th century they began to be collected in one book; *breviarum*, from which the word derives, is Latin for 'abridgement'. Usually neither the small, portable breviary nor the larger choir breviary was much illustrated; sumptuous *illumination was reserved for the breviaries destined for the use of kings, nobles, or church dignitaries. 'The splendid Breviaries must often have been chanted by the domestic chaplains rather than by the nobility in person. The aristocrats were the patrons, not the daily readers' (Christopher de Hamel, *A History of Illuminated Manuscripts*, 1986). Probably the most lavish of all is the Grimani Breviary (*c*.1510–20, Biblioteca Marciana, Venice), named after Cardinal Domenico Grimani (1461–1523), the great bibliophile and art collector who owned it when it is first documented in 1520 (although it was not made for him). It was produced in the Netherlands, and Marcantonio Michiel (see GIORGIONE) records that it was 'illuminated by many masters over a period of many years'. The wealth of illumination includes 110 large pictures, among them scenes from the New Testament, the Old Testament, and the lives of saints.

Bril, Paul (*b* Antwerp, *c*.1554; *d* Rome, 7 Oct. 1626). Flemish landscape painter, active mainly in Rome, where he is first documented in 1582. Early in his career he specialized in large decorative pictures, including frescos, but he turned increasingly to small easel paintings and it is on these that his fame now rests. He lived long enough to assimilate some of the qualities of *Elsheimer's and Annibale *Carracci's landscapes and his work forms a transition between the fantastic, highly detailed 16th-century Flemish *Mannerist style and the more idealized, atmospheric Italian landscapes of the 17th century. He also made views of Rome for the tourist trade, and marine pictures. His conception of both these types of subject had considerable influence on Agostino *Tassi, *Claude's teacher, and on Claude himself. Paul's brother **Matthew** or **Mattheus** (1550–83) also worked successfully in Rome, and their work is hard to differentiate.

Bristol board. A type of stiff cardboard with a smooth, firm surface. It is used particularly by black-and-white illustrators, for it allows a pen line and *hatching to be drawn with great clarity and sharpness, an important factor when a drawing has to be reduced in size for reproduction.

British Museum, London. Britain's national museum of archaeology and antiquities, which formerly also housed the national library of manuscripts and printed books. It was established by Act of Parliament in 1753 when the government acquired the private collection of Sir Hans Sloane (1660–1753), who was a successful physician by profession but a naturalist and antiquarian by inclination; it consisted of 'books, manuscripts, prints, drawings, pictures, medals, coins, seals, *cameos and natural curiosities'. Sloane left the collection to the nation on condition that his family was paid £20,000 (far less than he had spent in acquiring it). In 1759 the museum opened in Montagu House, a large 17th-century mansion in Bloomsbury. Initially it was not freely accessible to the public; for nearly 50 years it was necessary to make formal application for admission. With the acquisition of Sir William Hamilton's collection of classical vases and antiquities (1772), a plethora of Egyptian antiquities (including the Rosetta Stone donated by George III) at the turn of the century, the *Elgin Marbles (1816), the magnificent library of George III (1823), and many other bequests and purchases, the Museum became established as one of the world's greatest treasure houses. Montagu House was now too small for its purpose and it was demolished in the course of construction of the present huge structure (1823–47), one of the masterpieces of Greek Revival architecture. The architect was Sir Robert Smirke and the great circular Reading Room at the centre of the building, designed by Smirke's brother Sydney, was completed in 1857. There have subsequently been various other additions to the building.

Originally the Museum's collections embraced natural history, and one of its greatest attractions was a stuffed giraffe in the entrance hall, but the holdings in this area were transferred to the Natural History Museum in South Kensington, which opened in 1881. The Department of Prints and Drawings was originally part of the Library, but it led a separate existence from 1808 onwards. It began with over 2,000 drawings from the Sloane collections, which included an album of *Dürer's drawings. Among the most important acquisitions since was the Richard Payne *Knight bequest (1824) of over 1,000 drawings, including 273 by *Claude.

It is now one of the largest and most comprehensive collections in the world, containing more than two million items. The British Museum Library (as it was formerly known) was reconstituted by Act of Parliament as part of the British Library in 1973, and has been transferred to a new building, near St Pancras Station, opened in 1997.

Britton, John. See CATTERMOLE.

Briulov, Karl. See BRYULOV.

Brock, Sir Thomas (b Worcester, 1 Mar. 1847; d London, 22 Aug. 1922). British sculptor, one of the most successful specialists in monuments and public statues at the turn of the century. His most famous work is the huge Queen Victoria Memorial (unveiled 1911), in stone, marble, and gilt bronze, outside Buckingham Palace, London, and also well known is his equestrian statue of the Black Prince (1903) in Leeds.

Brockhurst, Gerald Leslie (b Birmingham, 31 Oct. 1890; d Franklin Lakes, NJ, 4 May 1978). British-born painter and etcher who became an American citizen in 1949. Precociously gifted, an excellent draughtsman, and a fine craftsman, Brockhurst won several prizes at the *Royal Academy Schools and went on to have a highly successful career as a society portraitist, first in Britain and then in the USA, where he settled in 1939, working in New York and New Jersey. He is best known for his portraits of glamorous women, painted in an eye-catching, dramatically lit, formally posed style similar to that later associated with *Annigoni. As an etcher Brockhurst is remembered particularly for *Adolescence* (1932), a powerful study of a naked girl on the verge of womanhood staring broodingly into a mirror—one of the masterpieces of 20th-century printmaking.

Broederlam, Melchior (b Ypres, c.1350; d Ypres, c.1411). Netherlandish painter. For much of his career he was court painter to Philip the Bold, Duke of *Burgundy, and he also worked for his own native city of Ypres. Documents show that he was a busy and versatile artist, but his only surviving works are the painted outer faces of the wings of a *triptych altarpiece carved by Jacques de *Baerze for the Chartreuse de Champmol, Dijon (see SLUTER): on one wing are the *Annunciation and Visitation* and on the other the *Presentation and Flight into Egypt* (1394–9, Mus. B.-A., Dijon). They are among the first and finest examples of the *International Gothic style, combining lavish decorative display with realistic touches that look forward to the later development of the Netherlandish School; the figure of St Joseph in the *Flight into Egypt*, for example, is represented as an authentic peasant. Erwin *Panofsky describes Broederlam as 'the greatest of all pre-*Eyckian panel painters insofar as their work has been preserved'.

Broeucq, Jacques Du. See DUBROEUCQ.

Brokof, Ferdinand Maximilián (b Červený Hrádek [German Rothenhaus], Bohemia, 12 Sept. 1688; d Prague, 8 Mar. 1731). Bohemian sculptor, the son and pupil of **Jan Brokof** (1652–1718), a Hungarian-born sculptor who moved to Prague in 1675. The younger Brokof ranks with *Braun as the leading Bohemian *Baroque sculptor. His work is less emotionally intense than Braun's, but it has great dignity. He is best known for various pieces on the Charles Bridge in Prague (on which his father also worked), among them the over-life-size group of *St John of Matha, St Felix of Valois, and St Ivan* (1714), which features a famous figure of a Turkish guard. Another outstanding work (designed by the architect Johann Bernard Fischer von Erlach) is the tomb of Count Vratislav Mitrovic (1714–16) in St Jacob's church, Prague. Brokof's reputation extended outside Bohemia and he had commissions from churches in Breslau (now Wrocław, Poland), Vienna, and elsewhere. His brother **Michael Jan Josef Brokof** (1686–1721) was also a sculptor.

Bronchorst (or Bronckhorst), **Jan van.** See UTRECHT CARAVAGGISTI.

bronze. An alloy consisting mainly of copper (usually about 90 per cent) and tin, often also containing small amounts of other metals such as lead or zinc. From Greek and Roman times it has been the metal most commonly used in *cast sculpture, and it has also been employed for—among much else—bells, drinking vessels, mirrors, weapons, architectural ornament, and coins ('copper' coins are usually bronze). Its popularity and versatility come from its strength, its durability, its ability to take fine detail and lustrous polish, and the fact that it is easily workable—both hot and cold—by a variety of processes. It is easier to cast than copper because it has a lower melting point, and its great tensile strength gives it an advantage over *marble sculpture, in which it is much more difficult to create unsupported parts (such as protruding limbs). However, making a large bronze figure is a complex industrial process, and *Cellini has left a classic account of the difficulties he faced in casting his *Perseus*. The colour of bronze is affected by the proportion of tin or other metals present, varying from silverish to a rich, coppery red, and its surface beauty can be enhanced when it acquires a *patina.

The word 'bronze' evidently did not enter the English language until the 18th century, and before then all copper alloys were commonly referred to as *'brass'. The words still tend to be employed fairly loosely, sometimes even in serious art-historical writing, and without scientific examination it may indeed be impossible to tell whether bronze or brass has been used in a particular work. See also CIRE-PERDUE.

Bronzino, Agnolo (Agnolo di Cosimo) (*b* Monticelli, nr. Florence, 17 Nov. 1503; *d* Florence, 23 Nov. 1572). Florentine *Mannerist painter, the pupil of *Pontormo, who virtually adopted him as a son and introduced his portrait as a child into his painting *Joseph in Egypt* (*c*.1518, NG, London). The origin of Bronzino's nickname (literally 'bronze-coloured') is uncertain, but possibly derived from his having a dark complexion. He was deeply attached to Pontormo and his style was heavily indebted to his master (in paintings of *c*.1530 it is sometimes difficult to distinguish the hand of one from the other). However, Bronzino lacked the emotional intensity that was such a characteristic of Pontormo's work, his colouring and brushwork were typically harder, and he excelled as a portraitist rather than a religious painter. In 1539 he first worked for Duke Cosimo I de' *Medici and he spent most of the rest of his career in his service, becoming the leading painter in Florence and creating an unforgettable array of images of his patron's family and courtiers—immaculately polished works that convey the splendour and formality of the sophisticated world in which they lived.

Bronzino was also a poet, and his most personal portraits are perhaps those of other literary figures (*Laura Battiferri*, *c*.1560, Palazzo Vecchio, Florence). With few exceptions he was less successful as a religious painter, tending towards empty, elegant posturing, as in the *Martyrdom of St Lawrence* (1569, S. Lorenzo, Florence), in which almost every one of the extraordinarily contorted poses can be traced back to *Michelangelo, whom Bronzino idolized, or to *Raphael. It is the type of work that got Mannerism a bad name and has been described as a 'fusion of ballet and Turkish bath'.

Late in life, Bronzino (like *Ammanati) seems to have had a crisis of conscience about the use of naked figures in religious works, thinking that they tended to inspire lewd thoughts rather than holy ones, and his skill with the nude was certainly better deployed in the celebrated *Allegory with Venus and Cupid* (*c*.1545, NG, London), which conveys a feeling of icy eroticism under the pretext of a moralizing allegory (one of the subsidiary figures has recently been interpreted as symbolizing the effects of syphilis). His other major works include the design of a series of tapestries on the story of Joseph (1545–55) for the Palazzo Vecchio. He was a much respected figure who took a prominent part in the activities of the Accademia del Disegno (see ACADEMY), of which he was a founder member in 1563. His pupils included Alessandro *Allori, who—in a curious mirroring of his own early career—was also his adopted son.

Brooking, Charles (*b* ?London, *c*.1723; *bur*. London, 25 Mar. 1759). English marine painter. Little is known of his short career, but he was the finest British marine painter of his day, equally adept at calm or rough seas. In his early years he was evidently employed in some capacity at Deptford dockyard and he had an intimate knowledge of the ships he painted.

Brotherhood of Ruralists. See BLAKE, SIR PETER.

Brouwer, Adriaen (*b* ?Oudenaarde, *c*.1605; *bur*. Antwerp, 1 Feb. 1638). Flemish painter who spent a great part of his short working life at Haarlem in Holland. He moved there in about 1625 and according to *Houbraken was a pupil of Frans *Hals. In about 1631 he left Holland for Antwerp and evidently spent the rest of his career there. He perhaps died from the plague that swept the city in 1638. Brouwer was an important link between the Dutch and Flemish schools and played a major role in popularizing low-life *genre scenes in both countries in which he worked. Early sources depict him as a colourful bohemian character (he was imprisoned in 1633, perhaps for debt) and his most typical works represent peasants brawling and drinking. Although the subject matter is humorously coarse, his technique is delicate and sparkling. The virtuosity of brushwork and economy of expression are perhaps even more evident in his landscapes, which are among the finest of his period. *Rembrandt and *Rubens were among the admirers and collectors of Brouwer's paintings (Rubens at one time owned seventeen), and Adriaen van *Ostade and David *Teniers the Younger were among his followers.

Brown, Ford Madox (*b* Calais, 16 Apr. 1821; *d* London, 6 Oct. 1893). English painter. The son of a retired ship's purser, he spent his early life on the Continent; his training included a period with *Wappers in Antwerp. In 1840–3 he lived in Paris, then settled in London in 1844; he visited Rome in 1845–6 and was impressed by the work of the *Nazarenes. In 1848 he met *Rossetti and through him became part of the *Pre-Raphaelite circle; he was never a formal member of the Brotherhood, but he shared its beliefs that art should be true to nature and morally edifying. His *Chaucer at the Court of Edward III* (1851, AG of NSW, Sydney) contains portraits of several of the Brotherhood, and his best-known picture, *The Last of England* (1852–5, City AG, Birmingham), was inspired by the departure of *Woolner, the Pre-Raphaelite sculptor, for Australia. Brown's other famous anthology piece, *Work* (1856–63, Manchester AG), shows his dedicated craftsmanship and brilliant colouring, but is somewhat swamped by its social idealism (it is a crowded street scene presenting a cross-section of contemporary society engaged in various activities, emphasizing the moral value of labour). In 1865 Brown organized a one-man exhibition in London, in which *Work* was the centrepiece; the catalogue contains his highly detailed commentary on the picture. By organizing such an exhibition he showed his independence of the *Royal Academy, which he avoided after he thought some of his pictures had been badly hung there. He had a prickly temperament and sometimes had difficulty selling his work. In 1878, however, he was given a major commission for a cycle of paintings in Manchester Town Hall on the history of the city. This occupied him until his death and he was based in Manchester from 1881 to 1887. Apart from paintings, his work included the design of stained glass and furniture for William *Morris's decorative arts company, of which he was a founder member in 1861.

Brown, Frederick. See SLADE.

Brown, Mather (*b* Boston, 7 Oct. 1761; *d* London, 25 May 1831). American painter who settled in England in 1781. He had lessons from Gilbert *Stuart as a boy and studied with Benjamin *West in London. Initially he had great success as a portraitist, especially with American visitors to England, but later he became obsessed with painting grandiose historical and religious pictures that proved unsaleable and he died in poverty.

Browne, Hablot Knight ('Phiz') (*b* Kennington, Surrey [now in London], 12 July 1815; *d* Hove, Sussex, 8 July 1882). English book illustrator (mainly in etching) and painter. He is chiefly remembered as the original illustrator of eight of Charles Dickens's novels, beginning with *Pickwick Papers* (1837), on which he replaced Robert Seymour (1798–1836), who had committed suicide, and ending with *A Tale of Two Cities* (1859). Brown made these illustrations under the pseudonym 'Phiz' (suggesting a depicter of physiognomies), which he adopted to harmonize with Dickens's nickname of 'Boz'. He illustrated the works of several other novelists, including Anthony Trollope (*Can You Forgive Her?*, 1864), and he also painted numerous watercolours and some oils. In 1867 he was partially paralysed and thereafter he worked less.

Brücke, Die (The Bridge). Group of German *Expressionist artists formed in Dresden in 1905 and disbanded in Berlin in 1913. The founders were four architecture students at the Dresden Technical School: Fritz Bleyl (1880–1966), Erich *Heckel, Ernst Ludwig *Kirchner, and Karl *Schmidt-Rottluff (Bleyl dropped out in 1906 and other artists joined from time to time, including Max *Pechstein in 1906, Emil *Nolde temporarily in 1906–7, and Otto Müller (1874–1930) in 1911). The name was chosen by Schmidt-Rottluff and indicated the members' faith in the art of the future, towards which their own work was to serve as a bridge. Their aims were vague, but in essence they were in revolt against passionless middle-class conventions and wished to create a radically new style of painting that would be in tune with modern life. Their subjects were mainly landscapes and figure compositions (a favourite theme being nudes in the open air); these were treated in an emotional style characterized by strong (and often unnaturalistic) colour and simplified, energetic, angular forms.

Although there is some kinship of spirit with *Fauvism (founded in the same year), notably in the bold colour and sense of spontaneity, the work of the Brücke artists was markedly different in feeling and technique: in place of exuberance there was restlessness and anxiety, and in place of French sophistication there was the crude vigour of artists who had had almost no professional training as painters. They were influenced not only by late medieval German art, which is often extremely intense emotionally, but also by *primitive art, of which the Museum of Ethnology in Dresden had a substantial collection. By 1911 all the members of Die Brücke had moved to Berlin, where there was a more vigorous cultural scene. They were now beginning to achieve national recognition (they promoted their work in more than twenty exhibitions), but they were also losing their group identity as their individual styles emerged more clearly. The personal rifts that had been present from the beginning became more intense and led to the dissolution of the group in 1913, but by this time it had given a powerful impetus to Expressionism in Germany.

Bruegel (or **Brueghel**), **Pieter the Elder** (*b* ?nr. Breda, *c*.1525; *d* Brussels, ?(5 Sept.) 1569). Netherlandish painter, draughtsman, and printmaker, the greatest artist of his time in northern Europe. There is little documentary evidence concerning his career, our knowledge of him depending mainly on Karel van *Mander's laudatory biography, published in 1604. This is a lively and useful source of information, but it misleadingly projects an image of him as 'Pieter the Droll', essentially a comic painter: 'there are few works by his hand which the observer can contemplate solemnly and with a straight face.' Certainly there is humour in his work, but this is part of what Kenneth *Clark calls his 'all-embracing sympathy with humanity', and his vision also includes tragedy, horror, and the implacable forces of nature. Far from being the yokel of popular tradition—'Peasant' Bruegel—he seems to have been a man of some culture; he was a townsman rather than a countryman throughout his known career (in spite of his memorable scenes of village life), he had distinguished patrons, and he was a friend of the eminent geographer Abraham Ortelius (who described him as 'the most perfect painter of his century').

His place of birth is unknown (van Mander says he came from a village near Breda and adopted the name of this village as his own, but none of the villages called Bruegel is near Breda), and there is no documentation on his life until 1550/1, when he is recorded in Malines, working on an altarpiece that is now lost. In 1551/2 he became a master in the painters' guild in Antwerp, where according to van Mander he had been the pupil of Pieter *Coecke van Aelst (who died in 1550); there is no stylistic affinity between their work, but Bruegel later married Coecke's daughter, so it is likely that he had links with her father.

Soon after becoming a master, Bruegel made a lengthy visit to Italy, travelling as far south as Sicily. In Rome he met the miniaturist Giulio *Clovio, who bought several of his paintings. By 1555 he was back in Antwerp, designing engravings for the print publisher Jerome *Cock, who was his main source of employment for the next few years. The experience of crossing the Alps affected Bruegel much more than the example of any art he had seen in Italy, as was acknowledged by van Mander, who wrote that he 'swallowed all the mountains and rocks and spat them out again, after his return, on to his canvases and panels'. His work for Cock included a series of prints now known as the Twelve Large Landscapes (*c*.1555–8), featuring wonderfully spacious mountain views. (However, most of the drawings of Alpine scenery associated with Bruegel's visit to Italy—as well as many other drawings traditionally given to him—have recently been reattributed to Jacob and Roelandt *Savery, who perhaps made them as deliberate forgeries.) Bruegel's work for Cock also included figure compositions of various subjects, including proverbs like 'Big fish eat little fish'. The engraving after Bruegel's drawing of this subject (published in 1557), bears the inscription 'Hieronymus Bos Inventor', an attempt by Cock to cash in on the continued popularity of *Bosch, whose moralistic outlook and sense of the grotesque influenced Bruegel considerably (he was indeed referred to in his lifetime as 'a second Bosch').

In 1563 Bruegel moved to Brussels and married there in that year. The move coincided with a change of direction in his career, for although he still made designs for engravings, he now worked primarily as a painter, and in the remaining six years of his short life he produced his best-known works. His patrons included Cardinal Granvelle, chief counsellor to Margaret of Parma (half-sister of Philip II (see HABSBURG) and his regent in the Netherlands), and the wealthy banker Niclaes Jonghelinck, who in 1565 commissioned the series of the Months, of which five survive today. Three of these (including the celebrated *Hunters in the Snow*) are in the remarkable collection of fourteen pictures by Bruegel in the Kunsthistorisches Museum, Vienna, which comprises nearly one-third of his surviving output as a painter; the other two are in the Metropolitan Museum, New York, and the National Gallery, Prague. His style changed during this final period; he abandoned the crowded panoramas typical of his earlier years, making his figures bigger and bolder, as is seen most notably in his novel treatment of proverbs, a genre that had previously been of minor account (*The Blind Leading the Blind*, 1568, Mus. di Capodimonte, Naples).

Bruegel enjoyed a considerable reputation in his lifetime (he is mentioned by *Vasari and slightly later by *Lomazzo), and—through his original works and the many prints after them—he had an enormous influence on later Flemish painting, particularly landscape and *genre. It was not until the 20th century, however, that he was recognized also as a profound religious painter and an artist whose human sympathy and understanding have hardly been excelled. In compositional prowess, too, he ranks with the very greatest masters, showing extraordinary skill in arranging large numbers of figures and integrating them with their surroundings.

Bruegel's two painter sons were infants when he died and so they had no training from him (they were reputedly taught by their grandmother—the widow of Pieter Coecke—Mayken Verhulst). Both sons spelled their surname 'Brueghel', retaining the letter 'h' that their father had dropped (for unknown reasons) in about 1559.

Brueghel, Jan (*b* Brussels, 1568; *d* Antwerp, 13 Jan. 1625). Flemish painter and draughtsman, the younger son of Pieter *Bruegel. From 1590 to 1596 he worked in Italy, then settled in Antwerp, where he spent the rest of his highly successful career. His specialities were still-lifes, especially flower paintings, and landscapes; he worked in an entirely different spirit from his father, depicting brilliantly coloured, lush woodland scenes, often with mythological figures, in the manner of *Coninxloo and *Bril. His exquisite flower paintings were rated the finest of the day, and his virtuoso skill at depicting delicate textures earned him the nickname Velvet Brueghel. Often he collaborated with other artists (notably his close friend *Rubens), painting backgrounds, animals, or flowers for them. He had considerable influence, notably on his pupil Daniel *Seghers, his sons **Jan II** (1601–78) and **Ambrosius** (1617–75), and his grandson Jan van *Kessel. Further descendants and imitators carried his style into the 18th century.

Brueghel, Pieter the Younger (*b* Brussels, 1564/5; *d* Antwerp 1637/8). Flemish painter, the elder son of Pieter *Bruegel. He spent his career in Antwerp, where he became a master in the painters' guild in 1584/5. He is best known for his copies and variants of his father's peasant scenes, which sold well and are often of high quality, in contrast to the work of lesser copyists such as his

son **Pieter Brueghel III** (1589–*c*.1640). His other speciality was scenes of fires, which earned him the nickname Hell Bruegel. Frans *Snyders was his most notable pupil.

Brüggemann, Hans (*b* Walsrode, Lower Saxony, *c*.1480/90; *d* Husum, Schleswig-Holstein, after 1523). German *Gothic sculptor. He is remembered primarily for one work, a huge oak altarpiece with scenes from Christ's Passion (*c*.1514–21) in Schleswig Cathedral. It is often known as the Bordesholmer Altar because it was carved for a church in Bordesholm, Schleswig-Holstein (it was moved to Schleswig in 1666). Standing over 15 m (50 ft) high and containing almost 400 figures (many of them showing influence from *Dürer's prints), it carries to the furthest extreme the virtuoso German tradition in woodcarving and has been described as the last of the great medieval carved altars. Brüggemann is said to have died in poverty, and it is possible that his career was ruined by the Reformation killing the market for altar carvings.

Brugghen, Hendrick ter. See TERBRUGGHEN.

Brülloff, Karl. See BRYULOV.

Brunelleschi, Filippo (*b* Florence, 1377; *d* Florence, 15 Apr. 1446). Florentine architect and sculptor. Brunelleschi was one of the most famous of all architects—a Florentine hero on account of the celebrated dome (1420–36) he built for the city's cathedral—and one of the group of artists, including *Alberti, *Donatello, and *Masaccio, who created the *Renaissance style. He trained as a goldsmith and was defeated by another great goldsmith/sculptor, Lorenzo *Ghiberti, in the competition (1401–2) for the new Baptistery doors for Florence Cathedral; their competition panels are in the Bargello. The disappointment of losing is said to have caused Brunelleschi to give up sculpture and turn to architecture, but he seems to have taken up architecture fairly gradually and one important sculptural work of later date is attributed to him—a painted wooden Crucifix (*c*.1412) in S. Maria Novella. Although he was not a painter, Brunelleschi was a pioneer of *perspective; in about 1413 he is said to have produced two demonstration pictures (representing buildings in Florence), in which he used a single vanishing point to represent pictorial depth in a completely consistent way.

Brunswick Monogrammist. See MASTER OF THE BRUNSWICK MONOGRAM.

Brus, Gunter. See VIENNA ACTIONISTS.

brush. A painting or drawing implement consisting of flexible fibres set in a handle. Prehistoric artists used materials such as feathers and leaves to apply paint and the Egyptians used an implement consisting simply of a reed with the end macerated to separate the fibres, but animal hairs have been used since the ancient Greeks and are still the most important materials. For watercolour painting the 'sable' brush (made from the fur of the Siberian mink) is the best type; the 'camel-hair' brush (usually made from squirrel hair) is cheaper, but lacks springiness and durability. For oil painting a stiffer type of brush is needed; the best-quality ones are made of white hog bristles. Synthetic fibres have been used since the 1960s; polyester has proved superior to nylon and has sometimes been blended with animal hairs to combine toughness with resilience. See also PENCIL.

Brussels tapestries. Tapestries woven at factories in Brussels, which during the 16th and 17th centuries was one of the most important centres in Europe for the art. Production of tapestries began in the city in the 14th century or possibly earlier, and in 1447 tapestry weavers formed their own guild, independent of other woolworkers. By this time Brussels tapestries were being exported to Italy, and an indication of the renown they enjoyed is that Leo X (Giovanni de' *Medici) had *Raphael's tapestry designs for the Sistine Chapel sent to Brussels to be woven (1516–19) in the workshop of Pieter van Aelst (*d* c.1530) (not to be confused with Pieter *Coecke van Aelst). The original set of ten tapestries is now in the Vatican Museums; several more sets were woven over the next two decades. The great fame of these tapestries not only definitively established Brussels's pre-eminence in the field, but also marked a turning point in the history of the art, for henceforth the designer of the tapestry was accorded greater status than the weavers. In the 17th century *Rubens made numerous such designs and his prestige was an important factor in the continuing international success of Brussels tapestries. After the reorganization of the *Gobelins factory in 1662 the leadership in tapestry production moved to Paris, but Brussels continued to be an important centre for the art into the 18th century.

Bruyas, Alfred. See COURBET.

Brygos Painter. Greek *red-figure vase painter, active in Athens c.500–c.475 BC, named after a potter called Brygos, several of whose signed works he decorated (it is possible that the potter and the painter are the same person). He is perhaps best known for a cup in the Louvre depicting the sack of Troy. Showing consummate mastery of composition and movement, it is regarded as one of the masterpieces of Greek painting and is sometimes referred to simply as 'the Brygos cup'. More than 200 other vases have been attributed to the artist.

Bryulov (or **Brülloff** or **Briulov**), **Karl** (*b* St Petersburg, 12 [23] Dec. 1799; *d* Marciano, nr. Rome, 12 [24] June 1852). Russian painter. He spent much of his life in Italy (1822–34 and 1849–52), where he painted the work from which his name is inseparable, *The Last Day of Pompeii* (1830–3, Russian Mus., St Petersburg), inspired by a performance of the opera of that name by Giovanni Pacini. An enormous (6 m (20 ft) wide) melodramatic composition, it was a sensational success, drawing crowds and rapturous praise when it was shown in several Italian cities and at the Paris *Salon (where it was awarded a gold medal). Sir Walter Scott is said to have seen it in Bryulov's studio in 1832 and after sitting in front of it for an hour declared it an epic, and it inspired Edward Bulwer-Lytton's novel *The Last Days of Pompeii* (1834). Bryulov was the first Russian painter to win such European fame, but he had difficulty living up to his masterpiece and the rest of his career was an anticlimax, although he produced some excellent portraits. There were several other artists in his family, notably his brother **Alexander** (1798–1877), an architect and watercolourist.

Bueckelaer, Joachim (*b* Antwerp, c.1535; *d* ?Antwerp, c.1574). Netherlandish painter of large still-lifes—market and kitchen pieces. The nephew and pupil of Pieter *Aertsen, he followed his uncle's preference for scenes in which a religious subject is relegated to the background by the still-life or *genre content (*Christ in the House of Mary and Martha*, 1565, Mus. Royaux, Brussels). He seems to have been the first painter to depict fish stalls.

Buffalmacco (Buonamico di Martino) (active first half of 14th century). Italian painter, a tantalizingly enigmatic figure. Various early sources, not only *Ghiberti and *Vasari, but also the authors Boccaccio and Sacchetti, attest to his celebrity as an artist—evidently one of the leading painters of the post-*Giotto generation—and also as a practical joker (hence his nickname, which might be translated as 'jester').

Their cumulative testimony is impressive, but no works can be securely attributed to him and there has been a tendency to regard him as a figure more of legend than of history. In the 1970s, however, he was proposed as the painter of the famous frescos of the *Triumph of Death* in the Campo Santo, Pisa (see TRAINI), an attribution that if correct would give him a stature commensurate with his literary reputation. Another school of thought has it that Buffalmacco may be identified with another obscure personality, the *Master of St Cecilia.

Buffet, Bernard (*b* Paris, 10 July 1928; *d* Tourtour, Var, 4 Oct. 1999). French painter, etcher, lithographer, designer, and occasional sculptor. Precociously gifted, he had developed a distinctive style and won considerable critical acclaim by the age of 20. His work, which includes religious scenes, landscapes, still-lifes, and portraits, is instantly recognizable, characterized by elongated, spiky forms with dark outlines, sombre colours, and an overall mood of loneliness and despair. It seemed to express the existential alienation and spiritual solitude of the post-war generation, and Buffet enjoyed enormous success in the 1950s. Later his work became more stylized and decorative, losing much of its original impact, but he continued to be highly prolific, eagerly collected, and very wealthy. His final years were marred by Parkinson's disease and he committed suicide.

Bugatti, Rembrandt (*b* Milan, 16 Oct. 1885; *d* Paris, 8 Jan. 1916). Italian sculptor and draughtsman, son of **Carlo Bugatti** (1856–1940), who is best known as a furniture designer but also worked as a painter, and brother of the famous automobile designer **Ettore Bugatti** (1881–1947). He worked mainly in Paris (where his family settled in 1904) and Antwerp (where he was based from 1907 until the outbreak of the First World War). Precociously gifted, he was stimulated by making visits to *Trubetskoy's studio when he was a boy, but he had no formal training in art. His speciality was bronze animal sculptures, in which he moved from an impressionistic style to a more abstracted idiom. He was one of the most acclaimed artists of the day in his field, but he committed suicide (gassing himself in his Paris studio) because of a combination of illness, depression (partly caused by a failed love affair), and financial problems (the war had ruined his market). After his death his reputation faded, but by the 1970s it had greatly revived. In 1979 an exhibition entitled 'The Amazing Bugattis' (featuring the work of

Carlo, Ettore, and Rembrandt) was held at the *Royal College of Art, London.

Bunny, Rupert (*b* St Kilda, nr. Melbourne, 29 Sept. 1864; *d* Melbourne, 26 May 1947). Australian painter, active for most of his career in Paris, where he settled in 1886. His work became deeply French in spirit and was well received in his adopted country; he also exhibited with success at the *Royal Academy during his frequent visits to London. Bunny's paintings included landscapes, portraits, and mythological subjects, but he is best known for leisurely scenes involving elegant, beautifully dressed women (*Returning from the Garden*, 1906, AG of NSW, Sydney). He remained in France until 1933, when he returned to Australia following the death of his French wife and settled near Melbourne. Although he continued to work, he was little appreciated in Australia until very near the end of his life. However, Bernard Smith (*Australian Painting: 1788–1990*, 1991) writes that 'Since his death his work has been held in in the highest regard . . . some critics . . . considering him the finest of all Australian painters.'

Buon (or **Bon**), **Bartolommeo** (*b* ?Venice, *c*.1400; *d* ?Venice, *c*.1467). Venetian sculptor and architect. With his father **Giovanni** (*c*.1360–*c*.1443), he ran the most successful Venetian sculpture workshop of the period. Its major works include the decoration of the Cà d'Oro (1422–34) and the Porta della Carta (1438–42) of the Doges' Palace. They epitomize the survival of the *Gothic style into the mid-*quattrocento.

Burchfield, Charles (*b* Ashtabula Harbor, Oh., 9 Apr. 1893; *d* West Seneca, NY, 10 Jan. 1967). American painter, mainly in watercolour. In 1921 he settled permanently in Buffalo, where he worked as head designer in a wallpaper factory until he was able to devote himself full-time to art in 1929. Burchfield's work divides into three clear phases. Up to about 1918 he painted scenes of nature that have an obsessive, macabre quality, often based on childhood memories and fantasies. In his second phase—during the 1920s and 1930s—he was one of the leading *American Scene Painters, portraying the bleakness of small-town life and the grandeur and power of nature. In the early 1940s, however, he became disenchanted with realism and changed his style again, reviving the subjective spirit of his youthful work but in a more monumental vein, as he turned to a highly personal interpretation of the beauty and mystery of nature (*The Sphinx and the Milky Way*, 1946, Munson-Williams-Proctor Inst.,

Utica). In the 1950s Burchfield taught at several institutions including the Buffalo Fine Arts Academy and the University of Buffalo. The Charles E. Burchfield Foundation, Buffalo, possesses his papers and a good collection of his paintings.

Burckhardt, Jacob (b Basle, 25 May 1818; d Basle, 8 Aug. 1897). Swiss historian, professor at the universities of Zurich (1855-8) and Basle (1858-93). Much of his work was devoted to the history of art and culture and he is best known for his book *Die Kultur der Renaissance in Italien* (The Civilization of the Renaissance in Italy), published in 1860. In this survey of the arts, philosophy, politics, etc., of the period he propounds the view that it was at this time that man, previously conscious of himself 'only as a member of a race, people, party, family or corporation', became aware of himself as 'a spiritual individual'. This romanticized view has been highly influential but also much attacked. Burckhardt's other books include *Cicerone* (1855), a guidebook to Italian art that was a popular handbook for German tourists for many years, and *Erinnerungen aus Rubens* (Recollections of Rubens), published posthumously in 1898. *Wölfflin, his former student, succeeded him at Basle University.

Burden, Chris. See BODY ART.

Bürger, W. See THORÉ.

Burgkmair, Hans the Elder (b Augsburg, 1473; d Augsburg, May/Aug. 1531). German painter and designer of woodcuts, the leading artist of his day in Augsburg. He was the son of a painter, **Thoman Burgkmair** (c.1445-1523), who was probably his first teacher, and in about 1498-90 he studied with *Schongauer in Colmar. After his return to Augsburg he was soon busy producing illustrations for publishers and he kept up this work throughout his career, in addition to his output as a painter. Most of his paintings are on religious subjects, but he was also a good portraitist. In 1507 he is documented in Italy, and he probably made another visit or visits before this, for his work shows strong *Renaissance influence, in the breadth and dignity of his figures, his warmth of colour, and his use of classical motifs. Indeed, he occupied a place in Augsburg comparable to that of *Dürer in Nuremberg in introducing the new style. Like Dürer, he worked a good deal for Maximilian I (see HABSBURG); his *chiaroscuro woodcut of the emperor (1508) is one of the first examples of this type of print. His other

patrons included Duke William IV of Bavaria, for whom he painted the *Battle of Cannae* (1529, Alte Pin., Munich), part of the same series as *Altdorfer's celebrated *Battle of Issus*. Burgkmair was married to the sister of Hans *Holbein the Elder. Their son, **Hans Burgkmair the Younger** (c.1500-59), was a painter and engraver, also active in Augsburg.

Burgundy, House of. French ducal dynasty that included several leading art patrons in the 14th and 15th centuries. Burgundy is a historic region in east central France, but it has given its name to several larger political formations, and at its peak in the 15th century the duchy of Burgundy was one of the most wealthy and powerful states in Europe. Its great period began in 1363, when John II of France presented the duchy to his youngest son, **Philip the Bold** (1342-1404). At this time it was fairly small, but Philip greatly enlarged it, mainly through his marriage in 1369 to Margaret of Flanders, which eventually brought him Flanders and other territories. Although he lived in various residences, his capital was at Dijon, to which he attracted many leading artists, most notably Claus *Sluter. He had one of the best libraries of his time, the illuminators who worked for him including Jean and Pol de *Limbourg. The Limbourgs also worked for his brother Jean, Duc de Berry, who was an even greater bibliophile.

Philip was succeeded by his son **John the Fearless** (1371-1419). He likewise employed Sluter, and his painters included Jean *Malouel and Henri *Bellechose. He was assassinated in 1419 on the orders of the regent of France (later King Charles VII), who saw John's power as a threat to his authority; at this time Burgundy was allied with England, which was at war with France (it was Burgundians who captured Joan of Arc in 1430 and sold her to the English to face trial and execution).

John was succeeded by his son **Philip the Good** (1396-1467), who extended the boundaries of Burgundy by conquest, marriage, and purchase, and in 1435 established peace with France, reversing his previous policy by supporting the country in its continuing war against England. There was military action in Burgundian territory for about a decade after this, but the later years of Philip's reign marked a peak of peace and prosperity for the duchy. His favourite artist was Jan van *Eyck and he also employed the other supreme Netherlandish painter of his time, Rogier van der *Weyden (Rogier painted at least two portraits of Philip; both are lost, but they are known through copies). By making Brussels (where Rogier worked) one of his courts, Philip helped bring the city into the forefront of cultural affairs.

Philip was succeeded by his son **Charles the Bold** (1433–77). He employed many artists, including Hugo van der *Goes, but he was more interested in conquest than culture. He was killed whilst besieging Nancy, the capital of the neighbouring duchy of Lorraine, in furtherance of his expansionist aims. He died without a male heir and this brought an end to Burgundy's golden age. The southern territories were annexed by France, and the northern ones became part of the Holy Roman Empire, through the marriage in 1477 of Charles's daughter Mary of Burgundy to the future Maximilian I (see HABSBURG).

burin (or **graver**). The engraver's principal tool, consisting of a short steel rod mounted in a rounded wooden handle. Usually the rod is lozenge shaped in section, cut obliquely at the end to provide a point. The handle is pushed by the palm of the hand while the fingers guide the point.

Burke, Edmund (*b* Dublin, 1 Jan. 1729; *d* Beaconsfield, Buckinghamshire, 9 July 1797). British statesman and philosopher. He was a Whig MP from 1765 until his retirement in 1794 and was renowned as one of the greatest orators of his day. His substantial literary output includes a major treatise on aesthetics, *A Philosophical Enquiry into the Origin of our Ideas of the Sublime and Beautiful* (1757), which went through seventeen editions in his lifetime and ranks as one of the most important works of its kind written in the 18th century. Its influence was felt not only in Britain, but also abroad, notably by *Kant and Gotthold Ephraim *Lessing (it was translated into French in 1765, German in 1773, Italian in 1804, and Spanish in 1807). The book marked a move away from the *classical rationalist ideas of the early 18th century in the direction of what would later be called *Romanticism. Burke argued that we are most powerfully affected in art not by what is most clearly stated but by what is suggested: 'It is our ignorance of things that causes all our admiration and chiefly excites our passions.' In particular, he thought that fear was an important ingredient in our enjoyment of the *Sublime: 'Whatever is fitted in any sort to excite the ideas of pain, and danger . . . or is conversant about terrible objects, or operates in a manner analogous to terror, is a source of the sublime; that is, it is

productive of the strongest emotion which the mind is capable of feeling.' Among the artists influenced by his ideas was James *Barry, whose visit to Italy was sponsored by Burke.

Burliuk, David (*b* Kharkiv, Ukraine, 21 July 1882; *d* Southampton, Long Island, NY, 15 Jan. 1967) and **Vladimir** (*b* Chernyanka, Ukraine, 27 Mar. 1886; *d* Salonika, Greece, 1916). Russian painters, brothers, leading members of the avant-garde in the period leading up to the First World War. Some of their early work was in a vein of exaggerated primitivism close to that of *Goncharova and *Larionov, and they were among the first exponents of *Futurism in Russia, *c.*1911. They were friendly with *Kandinsky, and through him participated in the second *Neue Künstlervereinigung exhibition in Munich in 1910 and in the *Blaue Reiter exhibition there in 1911. Vladimir, who was considered by Kandinsky to be the more talented of the two, was killed in action in the First World War. David settled in New York in 1922 and became an American citizen in 1930. He edited an art magazine, *Color Rhyme*, and ran an art gallery. There was another painter brother, **Nikolai** (1890–1920), and two painter sisters, **Lyudmila** and **Nadezhda**.

Burlowe, Henry. See BEHNES.

Burman, Thomas. See BUSHNELL.

Burne-Jones, Sir Edward (*b* Birmingham, 28 Aug. 1833; *d* London, 16/17 June 1898). English painter, illustrator, and designer, a key figure in the second phase of *Pre-Raphaelitism. In 1853 he began studying at Oxford University, intending to train for the priesthood, but his interest was turned to art first by William *Morris, his fellow student, and then by *Rossetti, who remained the decisive influence on him. He left Oxford without taking a degree in 1856 and settled in London. Rossetti gave him a few informal lessons and he attended life drawing classes for a while, but essentially he was self-taught; his taste was more classical than Rossetti's and his elongated forms owed much to the example of *Botticelli. He favoured medieval and mythical subjects and hated such modernists as the *Impressionists, describing their subjects as 'landscape and whores'. His own ideas on painting are summed up as follows: 'I mean by a picture a beautiful romantic dream, of something that never was, never will be—in a light better than any that ever shone—in a land no-one can define or remember, only desire—and the forms divinely beautiful.'

Burne-Jones had a fairly low-key career until 1877, when he became famous overnight with the showing of eight large paintings at the opening exhibition of the *Grosvenor Gallery. Thereafter he acquired huge fame and prestige, not only in Britain, but also on the Continent; he had considerable influence on the French *Symbolists and the ethereally beautiful women who people his paintings, like the more sensuous types of Rossetti, had many imitators at the end of the century. Although he was lauded for his poetic qualities by many critics, some thought his pictures 'morbid' and 'unmanly'. His paintings tend to be flat and friezelike in composition, with richly textured surfaces (*Laus Veneris*, 1873–5, Laing AG, Newcastle upon Tyne), and his feeling for pattern was put to good use in his work as a designer; he was a founder member of William Morris's decorative arts company in 1861 and designed some outstanding stained glass and tapestries for it, as well as making illustrations for *Kelmscott Press books. Burne-Jones's reputation crumbled after his death and did not seriously revive until the 1960s. The best collection of his work is in the City Art Gallery at Birmingham.

burr. A term applied in printmaking to the tiny upturned edge of the incision made in the metal plate by the cutting tool (in *line engraving or *drypoint) and also to the overall sandpaper-like roughening of the plate created by the rocker in *mezzotint. In line engraving, where maximum sharpness is required, the burr is removed, but in drypoint it is allowed to remain because the soft, velvety quality it gives to the printed line is considered one of the attractions of the medium. In mezzotint it is the foundation of the process. With both drypoints and mezzotints, only a limited number of impressions can be taken before the burr wears down.

Burra, Edward (*b* London, 29 Mar. 1905; *d* Hastings, Sussex, 22 Oct. 1976). English painter, draughtsman, and stage designer, one of the most delightfully eccentric figures in British art. From childhood he was ravaged continuously by ill health (he had arthritis and anaemia) and he lived almost all his life in the genteel Sussex seaside town of Rye (he called it an 'overblown gifte shoppe'), but he travelled indomitably and had a tremendous zest for life. His career, in fact, represents a revolt against his respectable middle-class background (his father was a barrister), for he was fascinated by low-life and seedy subjects, which he experienced at first hand in places such as the streets of Harlem in New York

and the dockside cafés of Marseilles. By his mid-twenties he had formed a distinctive style, depicting squalid subjects with a keen sense of the grotesque and a delight in colourful detail. Usually he worked in watercolour, but on a larger scale than is generally associated with this medium and using layer upon layer of pigment so that—in reproduction at any rate—his pictures appear to have the physical substance of oil paintings.

Burra's work has been compared with that of George *Grosz, whom he admired, but whereas Grosz bitterly castigated evil and ugliness, Burra concentrated on the picturesque aspects of his subjects, which he depicted with warmth and humour. Particularly well known are his Harlem scenes of 1933–4, with their flamboyant streetwise dudes and other shady characters. Burra's style changed little, but around the mid-1930s his imagery underwent a radical change and he became fascinated with the bizarre and fantastic (*Dancing Skeletons*, 1934, Tate, London). Many of his recurrent images—such as the bird-man—and his manner of juxtaposing incongruous objects have a *Surrealist air, and although he generally kept aloof from groups, he exhibited with the English Surrealists (he was also a member of *Unit One, organized by his friend Paul *Nash). The Spanish Civil War and the Second World War evoked a sense of tragedy in Burra that found expression in occasional religious pictures, and during the 1950s and 1960s his interest turned from people to landscape. By this time he had achieved critical and financial success, but he reacted with sardonic humour towards his growing fame.

Burrell, Sir William (*b* Glasgow, 9 July 1861; *d* Berwick-upon-Tweed, 29 Mar. 1958). Scottish art collector. He made an immense fortune from the family shipping business, from which he more or less retired in 1916 to devote himself to collecting, which had been his passion since boyhood (he is said to have once annoyed his father by spending his pocket money on a picture rather than a cricket bat). His interests were extremely diverse, but his collection became particularly strong in medieval art and in 19th-century French painting (some of his finest pictures were bought from the Glasgow dealer Alex Reid (1854–1928), who helped to pioneer interest in this field in Scotland). Burrell eventually amassed 8,000 objects, which he presented to the city of Glasgow in 1944, followed by the sum of £450,000 to build a new museum to house them. Because he was worried about air pollution, he stipulated that the museum should be located several miles outside the city centre, and it was not until 1967, when Pollok Country Park was presented to the city, that a suitable site became available. The museum opened there in 1983 in an impressive new building by the British architect Barry Gasson; externally it is mainly of glass and steel, but stone predominates inside and fragments of medieval buildings collected by Burrell are sensitively incorporated into the structure. In the period since Burrell's death, most of his collection had been in storage, giving it something of a legendary reputation as a hidden treasure trove, and after the museum's keenly awaited opening it soon became one of the most popular artistic attractions in Britain. Burrell also gave paintings to the Museum and Art Gallery at Berwick-upon-Tweed; in his later years he lived nearby at Hutton Castle (three rooms from the castle have been reconstructed within the Burrell Collection, complete with their furniture and fittings).

Burri, Alberto (b Città di Castello, Umbria, 12 Mar. 1915; d Nice, 13 Feb. 1995). Italian painter, *collagist, and designer. In 1943 he was captured whilst serving as a doctor with the Italian army in North Africa and he began to paint in 1944 as a prisoner of war in Hereford, Texas, using whatever materials were to hand, including sacking. After the war he settled in Rome and abandoned medicine for art. In 1948 his work became abstract, and in 1949 he began incorporating sacking in his pictures as collage elements; often he splashed red paint on the cloth in a way that suggested bloodsoaked bandages (*Sacking with Red*, 1954, Tate, London). From the late 1950s he also began to use more substantial materials in his pictures; they included objects such as pieces of charred wood or rusty metal that again reflected his experience of the carnage of war, even though the pictures are elegantly constructed. Burri was a fairly reclusive character, but he won international fame for his work; he was one of the first artists to exploit the evocative force of waste materials, looking forward to *Junk art in America and *Arte Povera in Italy. He also designed stage decor for La Scala in Milan and other theatres.

Burton, William Shakespeare. See PRE-RAPHAELITE BROTHERHOOD.

Bury, Pol (b Haine-Saint-Pierre, 26 Apr. 1922). Belgian artist, best known as one of the leading exponents of *Kinetic sculpture. Originally he was a painter; from 1947 he exhibited with the *Jeune Peinture Belge group and was also active in the *Cobra group. In 1953, however, he abandoned painting for Kinetic sculpture. His early works could be rotated at will, inviting spectator participation, but from about 1957 he began to incorporate electric motors. The movement was usually very slow and the impression made was humorous and poetic, in contrast to the violent effects of *Tinguely. Bury's work also includes films and stage designs. Since 1961 he has lived mainly in Paris.

Bury St Edmunds Bible and **Bury St Edmunds Cross.** See MASTER HUGO.

Bush, Jack Hamilton (b Toronto, 20 Mar. 1909; d Toronto, 24 Jan. 1977). One of Canada's leading abstract painters, active mainly in Toronto. Initially he worked in the tradition of the *Group of Seven, but in the early 1950s, inspired by Jock *Macdonald and by *Borduas's paintings, he began to experiment with *automatism. In 1952 he made the first of what became regular visits to New York. The influence of these brought him, by the mid-1950s, to a type of *Abstract Expressionism. Later, however, he developed a more individual style, exploring the unaffectedly emotional use of colour, as in his most famous painting, *Dazzle Red* (1965, AG of Ontario), in which the colour is placed in joyous, broadly brushed bands. Bush worked as a commercial designer for most of his career and did not devote his whole time to painting until 1968, but by the end of his life he had an international reputation. See also PAINTERS ELEVEN.

bush hammer. See BOUCHARDE.

Bushnell, John (b c.1630; d London, 15 May 1701). English sculptor. He fled to the Continent when he was an apprentice, after his master, Thomas Burman (1618–74), forced him to marry a servant he had himself made pregnant. In Italy Bushnell assimilated much of the *Baroque style (he probably saw *Bernini's work in Rome) and helped to produce a monument to Alvise Mocenigo (1663–4) in S. Lazzaro del Mendicanti, Venice. After his return to England, c.1670, he received numerous commissions and would have received more but for his difficult and unstable temperament (he died bankrupt and insane). His best-known works include statues of Charles I, Charles II, and Sir Thomas Gresham (1671) for the Royal Exchange, London (now in the Old Bailey), and the monument to Elizabeth Pepys (d 1669), wife of Samuel Pepys, in St Olave's, Hart Street, London. Bushnell's output is extremely uneven, but he is an important figure, for he showed untravelled Englishmen for the first time something of the possibilities of Baroque sculpture.

bust. A piece of sculpture representing the head and upper part of the body of a human figure, usually a portrait of a specific individual. The term entails no precise limits as to how much of the body is included; some busts show little more than the neck, and at the opposite extreme they include arms and even hands. More typically, however, they include the shoulders and the chest. Such parts of the body as are shown may serve simply as a base for the portrait head, or they may be draped to serve a decorative purpose or dressed in garments indicating the sitter's status. The form is particularly associated with the ancient Romans.

Bustelli, Franz Anton (b Locarno, 12 Apr. 1723; d Munich, 18 Apr. 1763). Swiss-born German sculptor. From 1754 until his death he was chief modeller at the Nymphenburg porcelain factory housed in the Nymphenburg Palace, outside Munich. Apart from *Kändler at Meissen, he was the most gifted of all the porcelain modellers in the German *Rococo style.

Butler, Elizabeth (Lady Butler, née Thompson) (b Lausanne, Switzerland, 3 Nov. 1846; d Gormanston Castle, Co. Meath, 2 Oct. 1933). British painter who concentrated almost exclusively on military scenes. She initially had no military connections (although she married an army officer in 1877) and took up such subjects because she thought they were comparatively neglected in Britain, offering an ambitious artist scope to 'distinguish herself from the ruck'. This idea was vindicated and during her heyday in the 1870s and early 1880s she was one of the most popular and talked-about artists in Britain. Her paintings appealed to popular patriotic sentiment, but she was also admired by critics such as *Ruskin, who in 1875 wrote that her 'Amazon's work' had forced him to admit he had been wrong in believing that 'no woman could paint'. She said, 'I never painted for the glory of war, but to portray its pathos and heroism,' and, although her pictures often have a glossy, Hollywood quality, they are sincerely felt, and she has been praised for trying to show the experience of the common soldier rather than concentrating—as was then usual—on the heroic deeds of officers. Her best-known painting is probably *Scotland for Ever!* (1881, City AG, Leeds), showing the charge of the Royal Scots Greys at the Battle of Waterloo. She pub-

lished her autobiography in 1922 and continued working almost to the end of her life; her final paintings were of First World War subjects. Her husband, Lt. Gen. Sir William Francis Butler, wrote numerous books on military history, and her sister was the writer Alice Meynell.

Butler, Reg (b Buntingford, Hertfordshire, 28 Apr. 1913; d Berkhamsted, Hertfordshire, 23 Oct. 1981). British sculptor. He trained as an architect and did not take up sculpture full-time until 1950. In 1953 he suddenly came to prominence on being awarded first prize (£4,500) in an international competition for a 'Monument to the Unknown Political Prisoner' (defeating *Calder, *Gabo, and *Hepworth among other established artists). The competition, financed by an anonymous American sponsor and organized by the *Institute of Contemporary Arts, was intended to promote interest in contemporary sculpture and 'to commemorate all those unknown men and women who in our times have been deprived of their lives or their liberty in the cause of human freedom'. Butler's design was characterized by harsh, spindly forms, suggesting in his own words 'an iron cage, a transmuted gallows or guillotine on an outcrop of rock'. The monument was never built, but the competition established Butler's name and he won a high reputation among British sculptors of his generation. He had learned iron-forging when he had worked as a blacksmith during the Second World War (he was a conscientious objector) and his early sculpture is remarkable for the way in which he used his feeling for the material to create sensuous textures. His later work, which was more traditional (and to many critics much less memorable), included some bronze figures of nude girls, realistically painted and with real hair, looking as if they had strayed from the pages of 'girlie' magazines. Butler was an articulate writer and radio broadcaster and he vigorously argued the case for modern sculpture. Five lectures he delivered to students at the *Slade School in 1961 were published in book form the following year as *Creative Development*. He was a widely read man, who numbered leading intellectuals among his friends, and his liberal sympathies were shown by his donation of works to such causes as the campaign against capital punishment.

Buys, Cornelis. See MASTER OF ALKMAAR.

Buytewech, Willem (b Rotterdam, 1591/2; d Rotterdam, 23 Sept. 1624). Dutch painter and etcher, nicknamed Geestige Willem (witty, or inventive, William). He was active in his native Rotterdam and in Haarlem, where he is said to have been friendly with Frans *Hals. Although he died young and his surviving output as a painter is tiny (about ten pictures), he is one of the most interesting artists during the first years of the great period of Dutch painting. His pictures of dandies, fashionable ladies, topers, and lusty wenches are among the most spirited Dutch *genre scenes, and instituted the category known as the 'merry company' (*Merry Company*, Boymans Mus., Rotterdam). His etchings are more numerous, and include genre scenes, fashion plates, and views of the Dutch countryside. He had an important influence on painting in Haarlem. His posthumously born son **Willem the Younger** (1625–70) was also a painter. An example of his very rare work—a landscape—is in the National Gallery, London.

Bylert, Jan van. See UTRECHT CARAVAGGISTI.

Byrne, William. See HEARNE.

Byzantine art. Art produced in or under the influence of the Eastern Roman (Byzantine) Empire; the empire was founded in AD 330 by Constantine (the first Christian emperor of Rome) and ended in 1453 when the capital Constantinople (originally named Byzantium) was captured by the Turks and under the name of Istanbul became the capital of the Ottoman Empire. The split between the Western and Eastern empires had become permanent in 395, when each adopted a separate ruler, and after the Western Empire was overrun by barbarians in the 5th century the Byzantine Empire became the great upholder of Christianity and of the cultural traditions of Greece and Rome. Byzantine territories varied greatly in extent; at one time they covered almost the entire Mediterranean basin, but from the 7th century many provinces were lost, first to the Arabs and later to the Turks. However, Byzantine art extended beyond the political or geographical boundaries of the empire, penetrating, for example, into the Slav countries, and in certain areas—where the Eastern Orthodox Church flourished—its tradition continued long after the collapse of the empire.

Byzantine art was, above all, a religious art. It was serious, otherworldly, and conservative; the Byzantine artist did not aspire to freedom of individual interpretation but was the voice of orthodox dogma. The choice of subjects and the attitudes and expressions of figures were determined according to traditional schemes charged with theological meaning. In the domes of churches, for example, Christ was usually shown as ruler of the universe (the Greek term is Pantocrater, meaning 'all-powerful'). Although Byzantine artists produced panel paintings, frescos, manuscript illuminations, ivories, enamels, textiles, jewellery, and metalwork of high quality, Byzantine art is seen at its finest and most typical in the mosaic decoration of churches. Mosaics were applied to all available surfaces of the interior, the luminous shimmering of the colours and the remote, implacably staring figures creating—in the finest works—a truly awe-inspiring effect, raising the art to unprecedented levels of grandeur and expressive power. Figures are flat and arranged frontally, occupying a spiritual dimension rather than a realistic space. Also typical of Byzantine art is the *icon, which usually represented the head of Christ, the Virgin and Child, or a particular saint, although there are also much more complex figure groups of subjects such as the Crucifixion. Icons tended to become cult images, and the view that this was idolatrous led to the various outbursts of iconoclasm (image-breaking), particularly in the 8th and 9th centuries, when many figurative works were destroyed and artists had to revert to ornamental forms or symbols such as the cross. The austere conventions of Byzantine art spread to Italy, where they were eventually challenged by the less ritualistic, more naturalistic ideals of artists such as *Giotto and *Duccio.

C

Cabanel, Alexandre (b Montpellier, 28 Sept. 1823; d Paris, 23 Jan. 1889). French painter. The winner of the *Prix de Rome in 1845, he ranked with *Bouguereau as one of the most successful and influential academic painters of the period and one of the sternest opponents of the *Impressionists. *The Birth of Venus* (1862, Mus. d'Orsay, Paris) is his best-known work and typical of the slick and titillating (but supposedly chaste) nudes at which he excelled. It was the hit of the official *Salon of 1863, the year of the *Salon des Refusés, and was bought by the emperor Napoleon III, who gave Cabanel several prestigious commissions. His reputation quickly faded after his death.

Cabel. See ARENTSZ.

cabinet painting. Term applied to fairly small *easel paintings, especially ones intended to be displayed in a domestic setting and viewed at close range. It is often used, for example, in relation to 17th-century Dutch *genre paintings, which were usually painted to fit into unpretentious bourgeois interiors.

cadavre exquis. A game in which a small group of people contribute in turn to make up a sentence or a drawing, no member of the group being aware of what the others have contributed (in the case of a drawing, the paper is usually folded in such a way that the edge of the previous participant's work—meaningless in itself—is visible, providing a starting point for the next person). This old party game, usually called 'consequences', was given a new seriousness and significance by the *Surrealists as a device for tapping the collective subconscious or exploiting the element of chance that they believed to be a path to creativity. The name (Fr: 'exquisite corpse') comes from the sentence produced by this method: 'The exquisite corpse will drink the new wine'.

Cadell, F. C. B. See SCOTTISH COLOURISTS.

Cadmus, Paul (b New York, 17 Dec. 1904; d Weston, Conn., 12 Dec. 1999). American painter and draughtsman. He painted with an extremely meticulous technique, usually in egg *tempera, and often used the poses and compositional techniques of the Old Masters. However, his subjects were taken from modern American life, on which he commented pungently and satirically. This sometimes led to scandal, as with the work that established his reputation, *The Fleet's In!* (1934, Naval Historical Center, Washington), portraying sailors on shore leave; it was described by the secretary of the navy as 'a most disgraceful, sordid, disreputable, drunken brawl, wherein apparently a number of enlisted men are consorting with a party of streetwalkers and denizens of the red-light district'. Because Cadmus worked very slowly his output as a painter was small, but he was a comparatively prolific draughtsman: 'drawings are more saleable than paintings', he wrote, 'they're less expensive.'

Cage, John. See BLACK MOUNTAIN COLLEGE.

Cagnacci, Guido (b Sant'Arcangelo di Romagna, nr. Rimini, 13 Jan. 1601; d Vienna, 1663). Italian painter. He trained in Bologna (perhaps under Guido *Reni) and Rome and worked in various places in central and north Italy, including Venice, where he lived for about a decade, c.1650–c.1660. His final years were spent in Vienna as court painter to the emperor Leopold I. By this time he had altered his name to Canlassi, presumably because of the resemblance of 'Cagnacci' to *cagnaccio*, the Italian word for 'cur'. Cagnacci essentially worked in the tradition of Reni, and he is regarded as one of the best and most distinctive of the master's followers, often showing a personal sensuous quality in his paintings. They are mainly on religious and classical subjects; he also produced a few portraits.

Cahill, Holger. See FEDERAL ART PROJECT.

Caillebotte, Gustave (b Paris, 18 Aug. 1848; d Gennevilliers, nr. Paris, 21 Feb. 1894). French painter and collector. He came from a very wealthy family (he was rich enough to build and race yachts as a hobby) and for many years after his death he was remembered primarily for the financial help he gave the *Impressionists, by purchasing their paintings and sometimes by direct gifts of money. Since the 1960s, however, his own work as a painter has been reassessed and he is now regarded as an artist of considerable, although uneven, achievement. He exhibited at five of the eight Impressionist exhibitions, concentrating on scenes from everyday life. The most striking feature of his work is his liking for unusual viewpoints and bold perspective effects, as in *Paris: A Rainy Day* (1877, Art Inst. of Chicago), which has become a much-reproduced favourite. On his death he bequeathed his collection of 67 pictures to the state. Against the opposition of various academic artists representing the taste of the École des *Beaux-Arts and the official *Salon (*Gérôme called the works offered 'filth'), 38 of the pictures were accepted after much wrangling and formed the nucleus of the Impressionist collection of the Luxembourg Museum. They are now in the Musée d'Orsay, Paris.

Calcar, Jan Joest van. See JOEST.

Caldecott, Randolph (*b* Chester, 22 Mar. 1846; *d* St Augustine, Fla., 12 Feb. 1886). English illustrator, painter, and occasional sculptor. With Walter *Crane and Kate *Greenaway he 'formed the triumvirate of great British children's illustrators of the late Victorian period . . . but his drawings were far less rigid than Crane's and far more humorous than Greenaway's' (*Oxford Companion to Children's Literature*). His output was large, in spite of his short career and the ill health that led to his early death; he worked as a bank clerk until he was 26 and he died aged only 39 on a sketching visit to America (he suffered from rheumatic fever and encountered a surprisingly cold winter in Florida). From 1938 the American Library Association has awarded the Caldecott Medal to 'the artist of the most distinguished American picture book for children published . . . during the preceding year'.

Calder, Alexander (*b* Lawnton, Pennsylvania [now part of Philadelphia], 22 July 1898; *d* New York, 11 Nov. 1976). American sculptor and painter, famous as the inventor of the *mobile and thereby as one of the pioneers of *Kinetic art. His grandfather **Alexander Milne Calder** (1846–1923) and his father **Alexander Stirling Calder** (1870–1945) were sculptors and his mother was a painter, but he began to take an interest in art only in 1922, after studying mechanical engineering. From 1923 to 1926 he studied at the *Art Students League, New York, where his teachers included *Luks and *Sloan. Calder and his fellow students made a game of rapidly sketching people on the streets and in the subway and Calder was noted for his skill in conveying a sense of movement by a single unbroken line. From this he went on to produce wire sculptures that were essentially line drawings in space; the earliest, made on a visit to Paris in 1926, were amusing, toylike figures of animals, but he also made much larger works in this manner, including the group *Romulus and Remus* (1928, Guggenheim Mus., New York), which features a wolf about 3 m (10 ft) long. His first exhibition of such works was in New York in 1928. From now on he divided his time between the USA and France and he knew many leading avant-garde artists in Paris, notably *Miró, who became his lifelong friend. In 1931 he joined the *Abstraction-Création association and in the same year produced his first non-figurative moving construction. Marcel *Duchamp baptized these constructions 'mobiles' and *Arp suggested 'stabiles' as a name for the non-moving constructions.

Calder's first mobiles were moved by hand or by motor-power, but in 1934 he began to make the unpowered mobiles for which he is most widely known. Constructed usually from pieces of shaped and painted tin suspended on thin wires or cords, these were light enough to respond to the faintest air currents. They were described by Calder as 'four-dimensional drawings', and in a letter to Duchamp written in 1932 he spoke of his desire to make 'moving Mondrians'. Calder was greatly impressed by a visit to *Mondrian in 1930, and no doubt envisaged himself as bringing movement to Mondrian-type geometrical abstracts. However, the personalities of the two men were very different: Calder's delight in the comic and fantastic, which can often be seen even in his largest works, was at the opposite pole to the messianic seriousness of Mondrian. Nevertheless, for all his humour, Calder made a major contribution to the development of abstract and kinetic art: he was 'the first sculptor, European or American, to explore so intently the implications of motion . . . the first to allow process and chance to alter the forms of his pieces. No other American had yet contributed so fundamentally to the progress of modern art' (Matthew Baigell, *A Concise History of American Painting and Sculpture*, 1984). After winning first prize for sculpture at the 1952 Venice *Biennale, Calder received numerous public commissions. Some of his late works are very large: the motorized hanging mobile *Red, Black, and Blue* (1967) at Dallas Airport, for example, is 14 m (45 ft) wide. He also worked in other fields, painting *gouaches and designing rugs and tapestries, for example.

Calderon, Philip Hermogenes. See ST JOHN'S WOOD CLIQUE.

Caliari. See VERONESE.

Callcott, Sir Augustus Wall (*b* London, 20 Feb. 1779; *d* London, 25 Nov. 1844). English painter. He studied with the portraitist John *Hoppner, but he soon changed course and went on to have a highly successful career as a landscape painter, patronized by numerous distinguished clients who preferred his work to that of his more innovative contemporaries *Constable and *Turner. His style, influenced by *Claude and 17th-century Dutch painters, was similar to that of Turner (who was a friend), but his work is rather pedestrian in comparison: *Ruskin commented that he 'painted everything tolerably, nothing excellently'. In 1827 he married the writer Maria Graham (1785–1842), author of numerous books on topography and painting, and their home in London became a leading cultural salon. He was knighted in 1837 and in 1844 was appointed Surveyor of the Queen's Pictures.

Callimachus. Greek sculptor of the late 5th century BC. His work is not known in the original or in any certain copies, but his fame in ancient writings has led to a number of works being associated with his name. He is said to have pioneered the use of the drill in sculpture and his style was graceful and fastidious—indeed overfastidious, as he was known as *catatexitechnus* (the one who spoils his art by overelaboration). According to *Vitruvius, he invented the Corinthian *capital after seeing some acanthus leaves growing around a basket on a girl's grave; as the earliest known Corinthian capital dates from about 425 BC, at the time Callimachus flourished, there may be some truth in the story.

Callot, Jacques (*b* Nancy, Mar. / Aug. 1592; *d* Nancy, 25 Mar. 1635). French etcher and draughtsman. He spent most of his life in Nancy (at this time capital of the independent duchy of Lorraine), but in his early career he worked in Italy, *c.*1611–21, initially in Rome but principally in Florence. His main patron there was Grand Duke Cosimo II de' *Medici; it was his premature death in 1621 that led Callot to return to Nancy.

Cosimo was a great lover of festivities, and Callot's work for him included scenes of fêtes and ceremonies, some of them large plates featuring scores of figures. Among his numerous other subjects were beggars and characters from the *commedia dell'arte*. He combined the sense of fantasy and the sophisticated exaggerations of late *Mannerism with witty and acute observation of real life to create a highly distinctive style. In some respects he comes close to *Bellange, also active in Nancy, but Callot was more realistic. After his return to Lorraine he concentrated on religious subjects and his output became more serious in tone. His most famous work is the series of eighteen etchings entitled *Les Misères et les malheurs de la guerre*, published in 1633, which harrowingly depict the atrocities of the Thirty Years War (in the year in which they were published Lorraine was invaded by France). They were admired by *Goya and influenced his treatment of barbarity in his *Disasters of War* prints. Callot's output was prodigious; more than 1,000 etchings and more than 1,000 drawings by him are extant. He was one of the greatest of all etchers and one of the first major creative artists to work exclusively in the *graphic arts.

calotype. See DAGUERRE.

Calraet, Abraham. See CUYP.

Calvaert, Denys (Dionisio Fiammingo) (*b* Antwerp, *c.*1540; *d* Bologna, 16 Apr. 1619). Flemish painter active in Italy. After training in Antwerp he settled permanently in Bologna in about 1560. His work is in an undistinguished *Mannerist style, but he played an important role as a teacher. In about 1575 he established an *academy, at which he taught more than 100 pupils, among them some of the most distinguished artists of the Bolognese School—*Albani, *Domenichino, and *Reni. The more celebrated academy of the *Carracci was probably inspired by Calvaert's.

calvary. A sculptural representation of the Crucifixion, which took place on the hill of Calvary, or Golgotha, outside Jerusalem. The term is sometimes applied to any wayside Crucifix or to chapels with a series of carvings of Christ's Passion, but it is more appropriate to groups of figures that represent or symbolize the whole scene, such as those found in the open air in Brittany, dating from the late 15th century to the early 17th century. Some are extremely simple, others include great numbers of figures variously arranged, usually on one or more stone bases. The remarkable concentration of calvaries in Brittany is unexplained, but it is clear that only in a remote and isolated region could the creation of such essentially medieval works have persisted so late. According to one theory the Breton calvaries are translations into stone of the medieval mystery plays in which scenes from the life of Christ were enacted in front of the churches.

Calvert, Edward (*b* Appledore, Devon, 20 Sept. 1799; *d* London, 14 July 1883). English painter and wood engraver. The son of a soldier, he spent five years in the navy, before moving to London in 1824 and studying at the *Royal Academy. He was introduced to William *Blake and became one of his group of followers known as the *Ancients. Even before this, however, he had created an outstanding work that was very much in Blake's spirit—*A Primitive City* (1822, BM, London), a tiny watercolour full of poetic ardour. Calvert continued in this vein for about a decade, but after producing his masterpiece in wood engraving, *The Chamber Idyll* (1831), he created no more work of comparable quality. From this time he became something of a recluse and painted mainly for his own pleasure (he was wealthy and had no need to sell his work). Many of his later pictures were inspired by his love of ancient Greece.

camaieu. A painting executed in several shades of a single colour; such a painting in greyish tones is known as a *grisaille.

Camaino, Tino di. See TINO DI CAMAINO.

Cambiaso, Luca (*b* Moneglia, nr. Genoa, 18 Oct. 1527; *d* Escorial, 6 Sept. 1585). Genoese painter and draughtsman. He was the outstanding Genoese painter of the 16th century, indeed the only one who was of more than local significance. Much of his large output consisted of fresco decorations in churches and palaces in and near Genoa, and he also produced numerous altarpieces and devotional pictures. Some of his finest devotional works are austere night scenes and they have been claimed as sources for Georges de *La Tour, even though it is not clear how he could have known them. Cambiaso visited Rome at least twice and *Michelangelo was a powerful influence on the massiveness of his figures, although in softness of modelling they have more in common with *Correggio. He was an almost compulsively busy draughtsman as well as a prolific painter; in some of his drawings the figures are constructed with simplified cubic shapes, giving them a remarkably modern look. In 1583 he accepted an invitation

from Philip II of Spain (see HABSBURG) to join the team of artists at the *Escorial. The work he accomplished there in the remaining two years of his life was carried out very hastily and includes an enormous and extremely dull ceiling fresco of the *Holy Trinity in Glory* in the basilica. He was succeeded at the Escorial by Federico *Zuccaro and then Pellegrino *Tibaldi.

Camden Town Group. Group of British painters formed in 1911 who took their name from the drab working-class area of London (as it was then) made popular as a subject by *Sickert, who lived in the borough for several years. In addition to being the prime inspiration of the group, Sickert suggested the name. The group lasted only two years, but its name is also used in a broader sense to characterize a distinctive strain in British painting from about 1905 to 1920, and as Wendy Baron, the group's leading historian, has written, 'If we define Camden Town painting as the objective record of aspects of urban life in a basically Impressionist-derived handling, and recognize it as a distinct movement in British art, then we must accept that the heyday of Camden Town painting was over by the time the Camden Town Group was born.' Many of Sickert's disciples showed their work at the exhibitions of the *Allied Artists' Association, founded in 1908, and several of them also did so at the *New English Art Club, but for some of them these institutions were not progressive enough, which led to the decision to form the Camden Town Group in 1911. Women were excluded and it was decided to limit the membership to sixteen, who were originally: Walter *Bayes, Robert *Bevan, Malcolm Drummond (1880–1945), Harold *Gilman, Charles *Ginner, Spencer *Gore (president), J. D. *Innes, Augustus *John, Henry *Lamb, Wyndham *Lewis, Maxwell Gordon Lightfoot (1886–1911), J. B. Manson (1879–1945), who was secretary, Lucien *Pissarro, William Ratcliffe (1870–1955), Sickert himself, and John Doman Turner (*c*.1873–1938), an amateur painter who had been a pupil of Gore. Lightfoot soon resigned (and committed suicide a few months later); he was replaced by Duncan *Grant.

These artists varied considerably in their aims and styles. Their subjects included not only street scenes in Camden Town, but also landscapes, portraits, and still-lifes. Several of them painted with a technique that can loosely be described as *Impressionist, with broad, broken touches, but particularly after Roger *Fry's *Post-Impressionist exhibitions of 1910 and

1912, the use of bold, flat areas of colour became characteristic of others, notably Bevan, Gilman, Ginner, and Gore. These four best represent a distinctive Camden Town 'style', one that was much imitated by painters of the urban scene up to the Second World War and beyond. The Camden Town Group held three exhibitions at the Carfax Gallery, London, in 1911–12. They were financial failures, and as the gallery then declined to put on more exhibitions, they merged with a number of smaller groups to form the *London Group in November 1913. The new body organized a collective exhibition in Brighton at the end of 1913, but although the exhibition was advertised under the name of the Camden Town Group, it may be regarded rather as the first exhibition of the London Group.

cameo. Small-scale sculpture in which the design stands in *relief above the surface. It is the opposite of *intaglio. Often, the term refers specifically to a portrait cut in a gemstone; this form was highly popular among the Greeks and Romans for jewellery and it was revived during the *Renaissance. Commonly a banded or multicoloured stone, such as agate, was used, in such a way as to exploit the different layers of colour—with one colour for the background and another for the carving, for example.

camera lucida (Latin: 'light chamber'). An apparatus used as an aid in drawing and copying, patented in 1807 by William Hyde Wollaston (1766–1828), a well-known man of science. It received its misleading name—for it is not a 'chamber' at all—because it performed the same function as the *camera obscura, but in full daylight. It consists essentially of a prism mounted on a metal arm above a drawing board. The draughtsman sets the prism between his eye and the paper in such a way that he can see an image of the object he wishes to draw apparently lying on the paper and can trace its outline. Various refinements were added to the basic format, including a lens to aid focusing. David *Hockney, who is fascinated by the history of artists' techniques, began experimenting with a camera lucida in 1999, using it to draw portraits.

camera obscura (Latin: 'dark chamber'). An apparatus that projects the image of an object or scene onto a sheet of paper or other surface so that the outlines can be traced. It consists of a shuttered box or space with a small hole or lens in one side through which light from a brightly lit scene enters and forms an inverted image on a screen placed opposite the opening. The optical

principle is essentially that of the photographic camera. For greater convenience a mirror is sometimes installed, reflecting the image the right way up onto a suitably placed drawing surface. The principle was known as early as Aristotle, but the first account of its use for drawing was published in 1558, in *Magia naturalis* (1558), a scientific book by Giambattista della Porta, an Italian physician. Various 17th-century painters are known or thought to have used a camera obscura in their work, and by the 18th century it had become a craze. Both amateurs and professionals—among them *Canaletto—used it for topographical painting, and there are accounts of an apparatus, somewhat like a sedan chair, inside which an artist could sit and draw, at the same time actuating bellows with his feet to improve the ventilation. More modest versions were easily portable and even pocketable. See also HOCKNEY and VERMEER.

Campagnola, Giulio (b Padua, c.1482; d Venice, c.1518). Italian artist, active mainly as an engraver. He was the son of a humanist scholar and is said to have been skilled in ancient languages and in music. After working at the *Gonzaga court in Mantua and the *Este court in Ferrara, by 1507 he had moved to Venice. It is with this city that he is chiefly associated, his engravings of idyllic landscape subjects playing a major role in spreading the style of *Giorgione and *Titian. His many copies after *Dürer likewise disseminated knowledge of this artist in Italy. Giulio's pupil and adopted son **Domenico** (b ?Venice, c.1500; d Padua, 10 Dec. 1564) was also a printmaker, but his preferred medium was woodcut rather than engraving. In addition he sold his drawings (mainly landscapes) as finished compositions, sometimes passing them off as the work of Titian. In about 1520 he settled in Padua and became one of the city's leading painters, as well as continuing his activities as printmaker and draughtsman.

Campaña, Pedro de. See KEMPENEER.

Campbell, Steven. See GLASGOW SCHOOL OF ART.

Campen, Jacob van (b Haarlem, 2 Feb. 1595; d Randenbroek [his country seat], nr. Amersfoort, 13 Sept. 1657). Dutch architect and painter. He was the greatest Dutch architect of the 17th century and occupied a role in his country similar to that of his contemporary Inigo *Jones in England by introducing a fully mature classical style; Constantijn *Huygens described him as the man 'who vanquished Gothic folly with Roman stateliness and drove old heresy forth before an older truth'. His most important building is Amsterdam Town Hall (begun 1648, later renamed the Royal Palace), a triumphant symbol of the city during its greatest period. The building was richly decorated; Artus *Quellin I led a team of sculptors, and *Rembrandt was among those who provided paintings, although his *Conspiracy of Julius Civilis* (1661–2, Nationalmuseum, Stockholm) was removed soon after installation and replaced with a picture by his pupil Juriaen Ovens (1623–78). Van Campen's other buildings include the beautiful *Mauritshuis in The Hague (begun 1633), designed as a royal palace and now a celebrated picture gallery. As a painter he concentrated on historical and decorative work and was one of the team who worked on the decoration of the Huis ten Bosch, the royal villa at The Hague.

Camphuysen, Govert (b ?Gorinchem, c.1623/4; bur. Amsterdam, 4 July 1672). Dutch painter. He spent most of his career in Amsterdam, but from about 1652 to about 1663 he lived in Stockholm, where he worked for the court. His output included portraits and still-lifes, but he is best known for bucolic landscape and *genre scenes in the manner of Aelbert *Cuyp and Paulus *Potter. Camphuysen's paintings have sometimes been attributed to these better-known masters and his *Two Peasants with Cows* (Dulwich Picture Gal., London) bears a false Potter signature. His masterpiece is generally reckoned to be *A Farm at Sunset* (Wallace Coll., London). The brothers **Raphael** (c.1598–1657) and **Jochem Camphuysen** (c.1602–59), cousins of Govert and likewise active in Amsterdam, painted moonlight and winter scenes in the style of their friend Aert van der *Neer.

Campin, Robert. See MASTER OF FLÉMALLE.

Canaday, John. See DERAIN.

Canadian Group of Painters (CGP). A group of Canadian painters formed in Toronto in 1933 and disbanded in 1969. The CGP regarded itself as a successor to the *Group of Seven, whose last exhibition had been in 1931, and it aimed 'to encourage and foster the growth of art in Canada which has a national character'. Although landscape continued to be the dominant subject among the members of the group (who included some of the leading Canadian painters of the time), it recognized 'the right of Canadian artists to find beauty and character in all things' and encouraged 'more modern ideas of technique and subject'.

Canaletto (Giovanni Antonio Canal) (b Venice, 28 Oct. 1697; d Venice, 19 Apr. 1768). Venetian painter, etcher, and draughtsman, the most famous view painter of the 18th century. He was the son of a theatrical scene painter, Bernardo Canal (c.1674–1744), and he perhaps adopted his nickname ('Little Canal') to distinguish himself from his father, whom he began his career by assisting; their work included sets for Vivaldi operas in Venice and Alessandro Scarlatti operas in Rome, which they visited in 1719–20. Whilst he was in Rome Canaletto made drawings of ancient monuments and famous modern buildings, and after his return to Venice he abandoned theatrical work for topographical painting (see VEDUTA). His early paintings of Venice include some intimate views of unremarkable pieces of townscape, treated with great freshness of observation and liveliness of touch (*The Stonemason's Yard*, c.1727, NG, London). However, he soon began to specialize in much grander views showing the public face of the city, including festivities on the canals. His colouring became stronger and brighter and his handling smoother and more precise. He worked from drawings made on the spot and also made use of a *camera obscura, but although his pictures give the feeling of being extremely accurate records, he in fact often made departures from topographical correctness in the interests of creating a better composition—changing the proportions of a building or shifting its position and so on. He also produced imaginary views (see CAPRICCIO).

Canaletto's work appealed greatly to wealthy visitors to Venice and his best customers were British aristocrats making the *Grand Tour, for whom he sometimes produced series of views in uniform size. His dealings with his British clients were mainly done through an agent, Joseph Smith (c.1674–1770), who moved to Venice in about 1700 to work as a banker and stayed for the rest of his life. In addition to being an art dealer (with an efficient organization for shipping Canaletto's pictures to England), he was a publisher, and in 1744 he was appointed British consul in Venice—he is sometimes known as Consul Smith and also as the Merchant of Venice. He had a superb art collection of his own, most of which he sold to George III in 1762, thus accounting for the fact that the *Royal Collection has the world's best representation of Canaletto's work.

Canaletto's business was badly hit by the War of the Austrian Succession (1740–8), which severely curtailed Continental travel and therefore cut him off from his main patrons. In the early 1740s he concentrated on drawings and etchings, and in 1746 he moved to England, evidently at the suggestion of Jacopo *Amigoni. He was based in England for the next decade (although during this time he made two visits to Venice). Initially he was very successful, painting views of London and of various country houses. However, some of the work he produced in England was mechanical (even though he never lost his gift for handsome composition), and rumours were put about, probably by rivals, that he was not in fact the famous Canaletto but an impostor. In about 1756 he returned permanently to Venice. He continued active for the remainder of his life, but he never recovered his former popularity, and by the time of his death he seems to have been far from prosperous. His work was much copied and was highly influential in Italy and elsewhere; his nephew Bernardo *Bellotto took his style to central Europe and his followers in England included William *Marlow and Samuel *Scott.

Candlelight Master. See BIGOT.

Cano, Alonso (*bapt.* Granada, 19 Mar. 1601; *d* Granada, 3 Sept. 1667). Spanish sculptor, painter, architect, and draughtsman, sometimes called 'the Spanish *Michelangelo' because of the diversity of his talents. He spent most of his career successively in Seville, Madrid, and Granada, but he also worked in Valencia and Málaga. Some of his movements were dictated by his eventful personal life, for more than once he left a city hastily or under a cloud after brushes with the law. In 1636 he was imprisoned for debt; in 1637 he wounded a colleague in a duel; and in 1644 he was accused of murdering his wife but was released after torture (by royal command, his right arm and hand were not harmed). In spite of his stormy temperament, his work tends to be serene and often sweet. From 1614 to 1638 Cano lived in Seville, where he studied painting with *Pacheco (his fellow student *Velázquez became a lifelong friend) and probably also spent some time in the workshop of the sculptor *Montañés (early in his career he worked more as a sculptor than a painter). In 1638 he moved to Madrid to become painter to the Count-Duke Olivares and was employed by Philip IV (see HABSBURG) to restore pictures in the royal collection. Thus he became acquainted with the work of the 16th-century Venetian masters, whose influence is evident in his later paintings; they are much softer in technique than his earlier pictures, which are strongly lit in the manner

of *Zurbarán. From 1652 he worked mainly in Granada, where he designed the façade of the cathedral (1667), one of the boldest and most original works of Spanish *Baroque architecture. He was ordained a priest in 1658, as this was necessary for him to further his career at the cathedral. It houses several of his works in painting and sculpture, including a *polychrome wooden statue of the *Immaculate Conception* (1655) that is sometimes considered his masterpiece.

Canova, Antonio (*b* Possagno, nr. Treviso, 1 Nov. 1757; *d* Venice, 13 Oct. 1822). Italian sculptor, mainly in marble. He was the most successful and the most influential sculptor of the *Neoclassical movement, outdoing even *Thorvaldsen and *Flaxman in international fame and prestige and being celebrated in prose and verse by some of the leading writers of the day. The son of a stonemason, he was apprenticed as a boy to a local sculptor, with whom he moved to Venice in about 1770. His early work is lively and naturalistic (*Daedalus and Icarus*, 1779, Mus. Correr, Venice), but after he settled in Rome in 1780 his style became graver and thoroughly imbued with *antique influence. *Theseus and the Minotaur* (1781–3, V&A, London) was his first major work in Rome, and he soon followed this with the prestigious commissions for the tombs of Pope Clement XIV in SS. Apostoli (1783–7) and Pope Clement XIII (1783–92) in St Peter's. After this Canova never looked back and he worked for a galaxy of European notables, including Napoleon, Catherine the Great, and the Emperor Francis II; these three invited him to settle in Paris, Russia, and Vienna respectively, but he said he could work only in Rome. His most celebrated works include a huge nude statue of Napoleon (original marble, 1802–6, Wellington Mus., London; bronze replica in the courtyard of the Brera, Milan); a portrait of Napoleon's sister (*Pauline Borghese as Venus*, 1805–7, Borghese Gal., Rome), a marble equivalent to *David's *Mme Récamier*; and two versions of the *Three Graces*, the first commissioned by the Empress Josephine, Napoleon's first wife (1812–16, Hermitage, St Petersburg), the second by the 6th Duke of Bedford (1814–17, owned jointly by the V&A, London, and the NG, Edinburgh).

Canova worked much for the papal court and after the Napoleonic Wars he became Pope Pius VII's representative in recovering works of art looted by the French. He visited Paris in this role in 1815 and later in the same year he went to London to see the *Elgin Marbles. On both occasions he was fêted as a celebrity. In 1816 he was created Marchese d'Ischia by the pope and soon afterwards retired to his native Possagno, where he built a church, known as the temple of Canova, in which he was buried. Nearby is the house in which he was born; a sculpture gallery was added in the 1830s and this contains a large collection of his work, including examples of the paintings he occasionally produced.

Canova was renowned for his generosity to young sculptors and was highly influential, but he went out of favour in the later 19th century, when—in the wake of *Romanticism and the rediscovery of Greek sculpture—his work seemed cold or insipid to many critics. His reputation greatly revived in the later 20th century, when his distinctive qualities, long obscured by the blanket condemnation of Neoclassicism, were rediscovered. Canova, in fact, was much more individual than many of his Neoclassical contemporaries and he placed great importance on the personal handling of his material; he employed numerous assistants, but he always took responsibility for the final carving himself, and he advised young sculptors to 'study nature, consult the works of the great masters of antiquity, and, after careful comparisons, arrive at your own original style'. In at least one respect his work was strikingly forward-looking, for his *Cupid and Psyche* (1783–93, Louvre, Paris) was designed to be rotated and displayed under coloured lighting—an anticipation of *Kinetic art.

Cantarini, Simone (*bapt*. Pesaro, 21 Aug. 1612; *d* Verona, 15 Oct. 1648). Italian painter and engraver, sometimes called Il Pesarese after his place of birth. He was one of Guido *Reni's most distinguished pupils, although he was already an accomplished artist when he entered the master's workshop at the age of about 22. Most of his work is on religious subjects, but he also painted portraits, including a poignant one of the aged Reni (*c*.1640, Pinacoteca Nazionale, Bologna).

canvas. A woven cloth used as a *support for painting. The best-quality canvas is made of linen; other materials used are cotton, hemp, and jute. It is now so familiar a material that the word 'canvas' has become almost a synonym for an *oil painting, but it was not until around 1500 that it began to rival the wooden *panel as the standard support for movable paintings. Canvas had the advantages over panel of being cheaper, easier to produce, and more portable (it can be rolled for transport), as well as providing

an attractive surface 'tooth' that encouraged the textural possibilities of oil paint. The transition to canvas took place first in Italy, with panels remaining popular in northern Europe well into the 17th century. Canvas is not suitable for painting on until it has been coated with a *ground, which isolates the fabric from the paint; otherwise it will absorb too much paint, only very rough effects will be obtainable, and parts of the fabric may be rotted by the *pigments. It must also be made taut on a *stretcher or by some other means.

canvas board. Sheet of cardboard or pasteboard covered with sized and primed cloth, usually cotton. It was first made commercially in the 1870s and is now chiefly used by amateurs as a cheap substitute for canvas. See also ACADEMY BOARD.

Čapek, Josef (*b* Hronov, 23 Mar. 1887; *d* Bergen-Belsen, Apr. 1945). Czech painter, graphic artist, stage designer, and writer. Like *Filla and *Gutfreund, he was one of the earliest artists outside France to work in a *Cubist idiom, and with them he was one of the founders of the Group of Plastic Artists, which was established in Prague in 1911 with the object of combining Cubism and German *Expressionism into a new national style. Later the Expressionist current in his work prevailed, revealing his deep concern with fundamental moral and social questions (*Bad Conscience*, 1926, Moravian Gal., Brno). His humanist outlook was shared by his more famous younger brother, the writer Karel Čapek, several of whose books he illustrated. Both of them fervently opposed the threat from Nazi Germany in the 1930s; Karel died the year before the outbreak of the Second World War, but Josef lived to see its full horrors and died in Belsen concentration camp. His work as a writer included poetry, a novel, and plays written in collaboration with Karel, most notably *The Insect Play* (1920), a comic fantasy satirizing greed and selfishness.

capital. In architecture, the crowning feature of a column, forming a transition between the shaft of the column and the member it supports. Capitals are often carved (and sometimes painted) with decorative or figurative elements (see HISTORIATED INITIAL) and in classical architecture the various types of capitals mark the most obvious distinctions between the standard 'Orders'.

Cappelle, Jan van de (*bapt*. Amsterdam, 25 Jan. 1626; *bur*. Amsterdam, 22 Dec. 1679). Dutch marine and landscape painter. He was a wealthy Amsterdam dyer who painted in his spare time, but there is nothing of the Sunday painter in his work. Typically his paintings show handsome vessels on calm rivers or seas; they have a grandeur of composition, a limpid quality of light, and an exquisite sense of tonality that place them among the finest marine paintings of any time or place. Cappelle also painted winter landscapes and beach scenes. His work is fairly rare; the best collection is in the National Gallery in London. He used his wealth to make a remarkable art collection. An inventory of it drawn up after his death lists some 200 paintings and more than 7,000 drawings, including 500 by *Rembrandt. It also mentions portraits of Cappelle by Rembrandt and *Hals; he is the only person known to have been portrayed by both these great contemporaries, but neither portrait has been identified.

capriccio. Italian term, meaning 'caprice', that can be applied to any fantasy subject, but is most commonly used of a type of townscape popular in the 18th century in which real buildings are combined with imaginary ones or are shown with their locations rearranged. *Canaletto and *Guardi often painted pictures of this type, and there is a painting by William *Marlow in Tate Britain, London, showing St Paul's Cathedral overlooking a Venetian canal. *Goya's Los caprichos are etchings of fantastic subjects of a completely different kind.

Caracciolo, Giovanni Battista (also known as Battistello) (bapt. Naples, 7 Dec. 1578; d Naples, Dec. 1635). Neapolitan painter. He was one of the greatest of *Caravaggio's followers, and his powerful work was an important factor in making Naples a stronghold of the Caravaggesque style. The decisive impact that Caravaggio made on him can be seen from his Liberation of St Peter (c.1615), painted for the same church (the Chiesa del Pio Monte della Misericordia, still in situ) as the master's Seven Acts of Mercy. It shows how Caracciolo, unlike so many of the *Caravaggisti, looked beyond the obvious trademarks of Caravaggio's work, aspiring to its depth of feeling as well as its mastery of dramatic light and shade. In 1614 he visited Rome and his late work is more classical in style, influenced perhaps by the *Carracci. Unusually for a Caravaggesque artist, he was an accomplished fresco painter, and his finest late works are decorations in the Certosa di S. Martino in Naples, finished in 1631.

Caravaggio, Michelangelo Merisi da (b Caravaggio or Milan, autumn 1571; d Port'Ercole, 18 July 1610). The most powerful, original, and influential Italian painter of the 17th century. Although his career was short (he was only 38 when he died) and his output was fairly small (there are about 60 surviving pictures by him), he had an immense impact on his contemporaries, creating a bold and naturalistic style that broke decisively with the prevailing vapid *Mannerism and inspired a host of imitators. He was perhaps born in Milan, but he grew up in Caravaggio, near Bergamo, and takes his name from the town. From 1584 to about 1588 he served an apprenticeship in Milan under the undistinguished Simone Peterzano (c.1540–c.1596) and by about 1592 he had moved to Rome, the main centre of his activity. His career there is not firmly documented until 1599 and in his early years he is said to have endured hardship, taking on whatever hackwork he could to scrape a living. He progressed to assisting reputable artists, notably Giuseppe *Cesari, then to independent work, and in the mid-1590s a dealer sold some of his pictures to Cardinal Francesco del Monte, who became his first important patron (Caravaggio was a paid retainer in his household for about three years).

Del Monte was a sophisticated and many-sided man who enjoyed various pleasures, including music and, so it is said, parties at which boys dressed up as girls. Caravaggio's earliest surviving works are mainly pictures involving fleshy, effeminate young men, and they presumably reflect his own sexual tastes (he seems to have been bisexual but predominantly homosexual) as well as those of his patron. These pictures are fairly small in size and very intimate in feeling, with a startling sense of physical presence; the strongly lit, sharply detailed figures are brought up close to the front of the picture space and typically gaze at the spectator with a look of blatant erotic invitation (Bacchus, c.1597, Uffizi, Florence). Caravaggio kept this sense of closeness and immediacy throughout his career, his figures usually standing out against a plain background with little sense of depth, but in the late 1590s he abandoned clear lighting in favour of the murky *chiaroscuro that is one of the most distinctive features of his mature paintings; *Bellori describes his early work as 'sweet, clean and without those shadows that he later used'.

It was probably through del Monte that Caravaggio gained his first public commission—two large canvases of the Calling of St Matthew and the Martyrdom of St Matthew for the side walls of the Contarelli Chapel in S. Luigi dei Francesi; they were painted in 1599–1600 and are his first documented works. An altarpiece of *St Matthew and the Angel* was added in 1602 and by this time Caravaggio had already completed a second major public commission—two paintings for the Cerasi Chapel in S. Maria del Popolo showing the *Crucifixion of St Peter* and the *Conversion of St Paul* (1600–1). All these pictures, and particularly the last two, were immensely original in their dramatic use of light and shade, their economy and force of design, and their down-to-earth realism—the familiar stories being seen in a completely new way and played out by solid, substantial, flesh-and-blood people rather than the traditional idealized figures. They established Caravaggio as the most exciting painter in Rome and changed the direction of his career; from now on he devoted himself mainly to large, deeply serious religious pictures for public settings, rather than intimate works for the rarefied taste of connoisseurs.

From the beginning of his public career, Caravaggio's work was controversial, as many contemporaries found his realism inappropriate or abhorrent in a religious context. Between 1602 and 1606 he painted five major altarpieces for Roman churches and three of them were refused on such grounds of decorum or theological incorrectness. Among the rejected pictures was the *Death of the Virgin* (1605–6, Louvre, Paris), which shows the Virgin as a thoroughly believable corpse rather than in the traditional way as a woman who appeared to be merely sleeping before being received into heaven. It was turned down by the church of S. Maria della Scala and replaced with a more conventional picture by *Saraceni. *Baglione writes that Caravaggio's picture was removed because he 'so disrespectfully made the Madonna swollen up and with bare legs', and another early account says that her figure was based on the body of a drowned prostitute that had been fished out of the River Tiber. However, the controversial painting was soon bought by Vincenzo *Gonzaga, Duke of Mantua (on the recommendation of *Rubens), and Caravaggio's other rejected pictures were likewise quickly acquired by discerning collectors.

Whilst Caravaggio was becoming the most famous painter in Rome on account of such works, he was also achieving notoriety for his violent and loutish way of life. In the years 1600–5 he built up a lengthy criminal record for various cases of assault and insulting behaviour, then in 1606 he killed a man in a fight over a

wager on a tennis match. He fled Rome, fearing he would be charged with murder, and spent the remaining four years of his life as a fugitive from justice, his travels taking him to Naples (1606–7), Malta (1607–8), Sicily (1608–9), and back to Naples again (1609–10). Wherever he went he gained important commissions and had a major influence on local artists. During these years his work became more austere and poignant, as in the *Beheading of St John the Baptist* (1608, Valletta Cathedral, Malta), his largest painting and a work of the utmost tragic power. His life continued to be fraught with danger: in 1608 he was imprisoned on Malta but escaped, and in 1609 he was badly wounded in the face in Naples. He died of fever on the way to Rome, where he thought a pardon was imminent. He had no pupils, but a legion of followers (the *Caravaggisti), and his work, together with that of the *Carracci, inaugurated a new era in Italian painting (see BAROQUE).

Caravaggio continued to be a famous name throughout the 17th century, but he was regarded by many as an 'evil genius' (in the words of Vicente *Carducho, writing in 1633), whose influence on other artists was pernicious. Baglione (1642) wrote that 'Some people consider him to have been the very ruination of painting, because many young artists, following his example, simply copy heads from life without studying the fundamentals of drawing and the profundity of art . . . and are . . . incapable of putting two figures together or of composing a story because they do not understand the high value of the noble art of painting.' In 1672 Bellori wrote that 'There is no doubt Caravaggio advanced the art of painting, because he came upon the scene when realism was not much in fashion and when figures were made according to convention and satisfied more the taste for gracefulness than for truth'; however, Bellori also thought that he had 'debased the majesty of art', and that because of him 'everyone did as he pleased, and soon the value of the beautiful was discounted. The *antique lost all authority, as did *Raphael . . . some artists began to revel in filth and deformity.'

Interest in Caravaggio declined in the 18th century (he is not mentioned in *Reynolds's *Discourses*), but revived in the mid-19th century. By this time his rejection of ideal beauty could be seen to have the advantage of truth, although there were still those, like *Ruskin, who saw in him 'perpetual seeking for and feeding upon horror and ugliness, and filthiness of sin' (*Modern Painters*, vol. ii, 1846). Serious historical research on him began in the early years of the 20th century, since when he has attracted an enormous amount of critical commentary and speculation, so much so that Ellis *Waterhouse has written that 'the innocent reader of art-historical literature could be forgiven for supposing that his place in the history of civilization lies somewhere in importance between Aristotle and Lenin.'

Caravaggio, Polidoro da. See POLIDORO DA CARAVAGGIO.

Caravaggisti. Term applied to painters who imitated the style of *Caravaggio in the early 17th century. Caravaggio's revolutionary approach to painting, particularly his dramatic use of *chiaroscuro, had extraordinary influence in Rome in the first decade of the century, not only on Italian painters, but also on artists from other countries who flocked to what was then the artistic capital of Europe. His fame was already spreading outside Italy by 1604, when Karel van *Mander, in Haarlem, wrote of 'Michelangelo da Caravaggio, who is doing extraordinary things in Rome', and in 1642 *Bellori commented: 'The painters then in Rome were greatly impressed by his novelty and the younger ones especially gathered around him and praised him as the only true imitator of nature. Looking upon his works as miracles, they outdid each other in following his method.' The most prominent of the Italian Caravaggisti included Orazio *Gentileschi, one of the few followers to have close personal contact with the master, and Bartolommeo *Manfredi, who popularized gaming and drinking scenes, subjects that Caravaggio himself had rarely painted. In Naples, where Caravaggio worked intermittently between 1606 and 1610, *Caracciolo, Artemisia *Gentileschi, and *Ribera, a Spaniard by birth, ensured that the style took firm root. In Rome, Caravaggism went out of favour in the 1620s, but it persisted elsewhere in Italy, and in other parts of Europe, particularly in Sicily (which Caravaggio visited), Utrecht, and Lorraine, lingering into the 1650s in all three places. *Baburen, *Honthorst, and *Terbrugghen were the three most important artists in making Utrecht the Dutch centre of Caravaggism (see UTRECHT CARAVAGGISTI), and in Lorraine Georges de *La Tour created perhaps the most personal and poetic interpretation of the style. Few major painters worked in a Caravaggesque style throughout their careers; some, such as Guido *Reni, had a brief flirtation with it (Caravaggio is said to have threatened to 'break his skull' for stealing his ideas), while others, such as Honthorst (who became a court portraitist), had a complete change of direction. Echoes of the Caravaggesque style can be found in the work of some of the giants of 17th-century art: *Rembrandt, *Rubens, and *Velázquez.

cardboard. A thin but stiff board usually made from paper pulp or sheets of paper, sometimes used as an inexpensive *support for paintings. Millboard is a term applied to a relatively stout type. *Etty (for his nude studies) and *Toulouse-Lautrec are among the artists who have made extensive use of these materials. See also ACADEMY BOARD.

Carducho, Bartolomé (b Florence, c.1560; d Madrid, 1608) and **Vicente** (b Florence, c.1576; d Madrid, 1638). Spanish painters, brothers, of Florentine birth (they were originally called Bartolommeo and Vincenzo Carducci). They settled permanently in Spain in 1585 when Bartolomé accompanied Federico *Zuccaro to carry out work at the *Escorial (Vicente was a child at the time). Bartolomé became a court painter in 1598 and worked on royal commissions in Madrid, Segovia, and Valladolid. He painted in fresco as well as oils, and was influential in introducing Italian ideas to Spain. Vicente was appointed a court painter in Madrid in 1609, but he is now remembered mainly for his book *Diálogos de la pintura* (1633). In this he defended the heroic Italian tradition (championing *Michelangelo in particular), and excoriated the naturalism of *Caravaggio. This has been interpreted as a veiled attack on *Velázquez, whose success overshadowed Carducho.

Cariani, Giovanni (b ?nr. Bergamo, ?c.1485; d ?Venice, after 1547). Italian painter, active mainly in Venice, where he is first recorded in 1509, but also in Bergamo. There are few documented works by him and stylistically he has been described as 'something of a chameleon', so there is great difficulty in defining his oeuvre. Some pictures have been disputed between him and artists of the calibre of *Palma Vecchio and even *Giorgione, but the works reliably associated with Cariani are much more earthbound, with heavy, angular forms. They include portraits, altarpieces, and devotional paintings.

caricature. A form of art, usually portraiture, in which characteristic features of the subject represented are distorted or exaggerated for comic effect or to make critical comment. The term is sometimes used more broadly to denote other forms of pictorial burlesque or ludicrous representation, such as the *grotesque heads of

*Leonardo. The invention of caricature in the more limited sense is usually credited to Annibale *Carracci, who possibly also coined the word 'caricatura'. He defended this type of art as a counterpart to idealization (see IDEAL): just as the serious artist penetrates to the idea behind appearances, so the caricaturist also brings out the essence of his victim, the way he should look if Nature wholly had her way. Few of Annibale's caricatures survive, but his pioneering role is well attested by early sources; *Bellori, for example, wrote that 'He was not only adroit in making witticisms and jests with words but also with the jocularities of drawings, many of them done by pen. Thus originated the delightful burlesque portraits or caricatures, as those drawings are sometimes called, of figures altered according to their natural defects, making us laugh by their ridiculous likeness.' Many other leading 17th-century artists were brilliant caricaturists (notably *Bernini), but the first artist to earn a substantial part of his living by caricature was probably Pier Leone Ghezzi (1674–1755). Political caricature as we know it today emerged in the late 18th century in Britain, notably in the work of *Gillray. It has remained a field in which British artists have excelled, but the greatest of all political caricaturists was a Frenchman, *Daumier. Many leading artists of the 19th and 20th centuries have shown a gift for caricature, but mainly as a sideline.

Carlevaris, Luca (b Udine, 20 Jan. 1663; d Venice, 12 Feb. 1730). Italian painter, active mainly in Venice. He is regarded as the father of 18th-century Venetian viewpainting (see VEDUTA), for although he was not (as is sometimes asserted) the first to specialize in the genre, he approached it with a new seriousness, his interest in mathematics being reflected in his rigorous perspective settings. His paintings and his set of 104 etched views of the city, published in 1703, are the foundation on which *Canaletto and *Guardi built. A collection of oil sketches from nature in the Victoria and Albert Museum, London, shows his lively powers of observation.

Carline, Hilda. See SPENCER.

Carmichael, Franklin. See GROUP OF SEVEN.

carnations. A term used in the 18th and early 19th centuries for the flesh colours in a painting.

Caro, Annibale. See CONDIVI.

Caro, Sir Anthony (b New Malden, Surrey [now in Greater London], 8 Mar. 1924). British sculptor, one of the most influential figures in post-war British art. After training as an engineer at Cambridge University and serving in the navy in the Second World War, he studied sculpture in London, then from 1951 to 1953 worked as part-time assistant to Henry *Moore. His early works were figures modelled in clay, but a radical change of direction came after he visited the USA and met David *Smith in 1959. In the following year he began making abstract metal sculpture, using standard industrial parts such as steel plates and lengths of aluminium tubing together with pieces of scrap, which he welded and bolted together and then generally painted a single rich colour. The colour helped to unify the various shapes and textures and often set the mood for the piece, as with the bright and optimistic red of *Early One Morning* (1962, Tate, London). This, like many of Caro's sculptures, is large in scale and open and extended in composition (he describes it as 'dancing along'); it rests directly on the ground, and Caro has been one of the leading figures in challenging the 'pedestal' tradition. He taught part-time at *St Martin's School of Art in London 1953–79, and he had a major influence on several of the young sculptors who trained under him, initiating a new school of British abstract sculpture (see NEW GENERATION). In the 1970s his work became much more massive and rougher in texture, sometimes incorporating huge chunks of metal. In the 1980s he returned to more traditional materials and techniques and began making figurative (or semi-abstract) works in bronze, including (in the early 1990s) a series inspired by the Trojan War. His reputation is high in the USA as well as Britain, but he is not without detractors; the critic Peter Fuller described the work with which he became famous as 'nothing if not of its time: it reflected the superficial, synthetic, urban, commercial American values which dominated the 1960s'.

Carolingian art. The art and architecture of the time of Charlemagne (742–814) and of his successors until about 900; he was King of the Franks 768–814 and the first Holy Roman Emperor 800–14. Charlemagne's reign was noteworthy for reforms in many fields; his guiding principle was a renewal of the values of the Roman Empire, and this was felt in the arts no less than in administrative, judicial, and religious matters. His capital was at Aachen (Aix-la-Chapelle), which became the centre of a cultural revival following a bleak period for the arts in the Franco-German lands that formed the heart of his vast empire. Charlemagne recognized the value of the arts for the education of his subjects and was himself the principal initiator of the cultural revival. The most important Carolingian building to survive largely intact is his Palatine (i. e. imperial palace) Chapel at Aachen. Little remains of Carolingian mural paintings or mosaics, but several manuscripts survive, showing a classical, naturalistic figure style, but also at times a vivid expressiveness. Among the best known are the Ebbo Gospels (Bibliothèque Municipale, Épernay), made for Ebbo, Archbishop of Reims 816–35 (see REIMS SCHOOL), and the *Utrecht Psalter. There was no large-scale sculpture, but Carolingian ivory sculpture and metalwork (on book covers, for example) often reached a high level. Carolingian art had great influence on *Ottonian and *Romanesque art.

Carolus-Duran (pseudonym of Charles-Émile-Auguste Durand) (b Lille, 4 July 1837; d Paris, 18 Feb. 1917). French painter. His early works included peasant scenes influenced by *Courbet's *Realism, but from about 1870 he concentrated on portraits (particularly of women), becoming a great fashionable success with his slick style. *Sargent was the most important of his many pupils and was influenced by his rich, fluid brushwork. In 1905–10 he was director of the French School in Rome.

Caron, Antoine (b Beauvais, 1521; d Paris, 1599). French *Mannerist painter. He is one of the few French painters of his time with a distinctive artistic personality, and his work reflects the refined but unstable atmosphere of the Valois court during the Wars of Religion (1560–98). He worked at *Fontainebleau under *Primaticcio in the 1540s and later became court painter to Catherine de *Médicis, wife of Henry II of France. His few surviving works include historical and allegorical subjects in the manner of court ceremonies, scenes of magic and prediction, and massacres, as in Massacres under the Triumvirate (1566, Louvre, Paris), his only signed and dated painting. His style is characterized most obviously by extremely elongated, precious-looking figures set in open spaces that seem too large for them. He had a penchant for gaudy colours and bizarre architectural forms. Some of the works attributed to him may be by other hands, however, for French painting of his period is such an obscure area that Caron's name is liable to be attached to anything similar to his known oeuvre.

Carpaccio, Vittore (b Venice, c.1460; d Venice, 1525/6). Venetian painter. His life is poorly documented, and it is not known with whom he trained, but it is generally agreed that the chief influence on his work was Gentile *Bellini. This is especially evident in the first of the two great cycles of paintings that are his chief claim to fame—the scenes from the life of St Ursula, executed in the 1490s for the Scuola di S. Orsola and now in the Accademia, Venice. Carpaccio's salient characteristics—his taste for anecdote, and his eye for the crowded detail of the Venetian scene—found their happiest expression in these paintings, one of which, the Miracle of the Cross, looks forward to the 18th-century compositions of *Canaletto and *Guardi. His other great cycle, mainly on the lives of St George and St Jerome, painted for the Scuola di S. Giorgio degli Schiavone, Venice, in 1502–7 (still in the Scuola), combines fantasy with wittily observed detail. After these two major commissions, however, Carpaccio's work declined in quality, although he still remained busy and continued to attract important patrons. In his later work he did an increasing number of altarpieces, a type of work for which he had little flair. On the other hand he was an excellent portraitist, as is seen particularly in his deservedly famous Two Courtesans (c.1510, Mus. Correr, Venice), probably a fragment of a larger work. It was a favourite work of *Ruskin, who contributed to the great popularity Carpaccio enjoyed in the 19th century. His fame has perhaps declined somewhat since, but he is still rated as second only to Giovanni Bellini as the outstanding Venetian painter of his generation.

Carpeaux, Jean-Baptiste (b Valenciennes, 11 May 1827; d Courbevoie, 11 Oct. 1875). The outstanding French sculptor of his period (also a painter, draughtsman, and etcher). He studied for ten years at the École des *Beaux-Arts (where *Rude was his main teacher), before eventually winning the *Prix de Rome in 1854. His major work in Rome was Count Ugolino and his Sons (1860, Mus. d'Orsay, Paris, and other versions), a tragic scene from Dante. It made his reputation (although conservatives disliked it) and after his return to Paris in 1862 he won favour at Napoleon III's court, receiving many commissions for portrait busts. He also had several larger commissions, of which the most famous is La Danse (1866–9), a high-relief group for the façade of the Paris Opéra (the original is now in the Musée d'Orsay). This uninhibitedly dynamic and sensuous work caused a sensation, was denounced as immoral, and had ink thrown over it. Partially because of such attacks on his work, Carpeaux suffered from a persecution complex in his final years before his early death from cancer. He was a pivotal figure in French sculpture, for his exuberance of feeling and vivacious modelling made a decisive break with the *Neoclassical tradition and presaged the work of *Rodin.

Carr, Emily (*b* Victoria, British Columbia, 13 Dec. 1871; *d* Victoria, 2 Mar. 1945). Canadian painter of *Expressionist landscapes. She felt the urge to paint from an early age, but her artistic development was slow and halting, interrupted by ill health and the need to undertake other work to earn a living. Her training was mainly in San Francisco, 1889–95, England, 1899–1904, and Paris, 1910–11. During her stay in France she probably studied briefly with the New Zealand painter Frances *Hodgkins, but the main influence on her at this time was the work of the *Fauves. After her return to Canada she painted the landscape of her native British Columbia with passionate feeling for the power of nature, executing much of her work out of doors. Discouraged by years of neglect, she had almost ceased to paint when in 1927 she was overwhelmed when she first saw the work of the *Group of Seven in Toronto. Thereafter she worked with renewed energy and deepened spirituality, overcoming her earlier neglect to attain the status of a national heroine. She wrote several autobiographical books.

Carrà, Carlo (*b* Quargnento, Piedmont, 11 Feb. 1881; *d* Milan, 13 Apr. 1966). Italian painter and writer on art, a prominent figure in both *Futurism and *Metaphysical Painting. He joined the Futurists in 1909, and visits to Paris in 1911 and 1912 introduced *Cubist influence into his work. In his best-known painting, *The Funeral of the Anarchist Galli* (1911, MoMA, New York), for example, he combined the dynamism typical of Futurism with a sense of Cubist structural severity. In 1915 he met Giorgio de *Chirico and turned to Metaphysical Painting, producing about twenty works with de Chirico's paraphernalia of posturing mannequins, half-open doors, mysteriously significant interiors, etc., though generally without his typically sinister feeling (there is even sometimes a touch of humour). In 1919 Carrà published a book entitled *Pittura metafisica*, but in the same year he broke with de Chirico and abandoned the style. In the 1920s and 1930s he supported the classical ideals of the *Novecento Italiano, championing the return to traditional values in the journal *Valori plastici* and also in the Milan newspaper *L'Ambrosiano*,

of which he was art critic from 1921 to 1938. From 1941 to 1952 he was professor of painting at the Brera Academy. In his work after the Second World War his style became somewhat looser, with freer brushwork.

Carracci. Family of Bolognese painters, the chief members of which were the brothers **Agostino** (*bapt*. Bologna, 16 Aug. 1557; *d* Parma, 23 Feb. 1602) and **Annibale** (*bapt*. Bologna, 3 Nov. 1560; *d* Rome, 15 July 1609) and their cousin **Ludovico** (*bapt*. Bologna, 21 Apr. 1555; *d* Bologna, 13/14 Nov. 1619). These three were major figures in the transition from *Mannerism to *Baroque and were largely responsible for establishing Bologna (previously something of an artistic backwater) as the centre of the most distinctive tradition in 17th-century Italian painting. In reaction against the artificiality of Mannerism, they revived the solidity and grandeur of the High *Renaissance, to which they added a vigour and warmth reflecting their admiration for Venetian painting. They often worked together early in their careers, and it is not easy to distinguish their individual shares in, for example, the cycle of frescos on the history of the founding of Rome in the Palazzo Magnani, Bologna (*c*.1589–90).

In the early 1580s the Carracci opened a private *academy in Ludovico's studio, and it soon became a centre for progressive art. It is uncertain how it operated in its early days, but by about 1590 it had become a teaching institution. Originally it was called the Accademia dei Desiderosi ('Desiderosi' meaning 'desirous of fame and learning'), but it later changed its name to Accademia degli Incamminati (Academy of the Progressives). In their teaching the Carracci put particular emphasis on drawing from the life, and vigorous draughtsmanship became a quality particularly associated with artists of the Bolognese School, notably *Domenichino and *Reni, two of the leading members of the following generation who trained at the academy. All three Carracci were themselves outstanding draughtsmen, and *Malvasia writes that even when eating they had 'bread in one hand and a pencil or charcoal in the other'. Their naturalistic outlook was in tune with the reforming ideals of the Counter-Reformation Church; in 1582 the Bishop of Bologna, Gabriele Paleotti, published a treatise on religious art in which he spoke out against 'obscure and ambiguous paintings' and praised the kind of artist who 'knows how to explain his ideas clearly . . . and to render them intelligible and plain to see'.

By the mid-1590s Annibale had emerged as the greatest artist of the family. His early work included landscapes, portraits, and *genre pictures, but his reputation was mainly based on a succession of large altarpieces for churches in Bologna and other cities in north Italy, in which he showed a growing mastery of composition and expression. In 1594 he was called to Rome by Cardinal Odoardo *Farnese to discuss decorations for his family palace, and after returning to Bologna to finish various commissions he had in hand, he settled in Rome in 1595 and embarked on the work in the Palazzo Farnese from which his fame is inseparable. He first decorated a small room called the Camerino (the cardinal's private study) with mythological scenes, mainly involving Hercules, then in 1597 began his masterpiece—the decoration of the Farnese Gallery. The gallery is one of the most imposing rooms in the palace and at this time was used to display choice pieces from the celebrated family collection of ancient sculpture. Annibale's paintings complemented these sculptures by evoking the world of classical antiquity, the overall theme of his frescos being the loves of the gods, or, as *Bellori described it, 'human love governed by celestial love'.

The ceiling was completed in 1600 or 1601, and the decoration of the walls, which is of much less importance, was done over the next two or three years, mainly by assistants, including Domenichino, who was part of a flow of Bolognese artists who followed Annibale to Rome and capitalized on his success. His contemporaries regarded the Farnese Ceiling as the successor to the great Vatican frescos of *Michelangelo and *Raphael, and throughout the 17th and 18th centuries it ranked almost as high in critical esteem. There are obvious similarities with Michelangelo's Sistine Ceiling, notably in the majesty of the nude figures, but Annibale's ceiling is entirely different in spirit, conveying a wonderful feeling of movement and exuberance. It was enormously influential, not only as a pattern book of heroic figure design, but also as a model of technical procedure; Annibale made hundreds of drawings for the ceiling, and until the age of *Romanticism such elaborate preparatory work became accepted as a fundamental part of composing any really large and ambitious work. In this sense, Annibale exercised a more profound influence than his great contemporary *Caravaggio, for the latter never worked in fresco, which was still regarded as the greatest test of a painter's mettle and the most suitable vehicle for painting in the *Grand Manner.

Although his work in the Farnese Palace occupied most of his time, Annibale carried out other important commissions in Rome and made momentous contributions in other branches of painting. Most tellingly, he was the inventor of *ideal landscape, in which *Claude and *Poussin were his greatest followers; the *Flight into Egypt* (c.1604, Gal. Doria Pamphili, Rome) is Annibale's masterpiece in this genre (see ALDOBRANDINI). His altarpieces and devotional pictures are amongst the finest of the time and have an important place in the tradition of history painting; Poussin was influenced by the force, economy, and precision of composition and gesture seen in paintings such as *Domine, Quo Vadis?* (c.1602, NG, London), in which Annibale was at his most severely classical, whereas other artists, for example *Rubens, responded to the muscular energy of his work.

In his final years Annibale was overcome by a debilitating illness and after 1606 he virtually abandoned painting (according to Bellori he sank into depression after being meagrely rewarded by Cardinal Farnese for his work in the Palazzo Farnese, but his sickness probably had physical as well as mental causes). When he died he was buried according to his wishes near Raphael in the Pantheon. It is a measure of his achievement that artists as important and diverse as *Bernini (who referred to Annibale's 'great big brain'), Poussin, and Rubens found so much to admire and praise in his work. They were aware mainly of the public face of his art, but it also had a less formal side that comes out in his *caricatures (he is generally credited with inventing the form) and in his early genre paintings, which are remarkable for their lively observation and free handling (*The Butcher's Shop*, c.1582, Christ Church, Oxford).

Agostino was Annibale's principal assistant in the Farnese Gallery from 1597 until 1599, when they quarrelled and Agostino moved to Parma. Although they had originally been so close artistically, the brothers were very different in character: Agostino was socially ambitious and inclined to put on airs, whereas Annibale was, in Bellori's words, 'amiable and modest'. In Parma, Agostino began his own 'Farnese Ceiling', decorating a vault in the Palazzo del Giardino with mythological scenes for Duke Ranuccio Farnese, but it was unfinished at his death. Among his paintings the most famous is probably the *Last Communion of St Jerome* (c.1592, Pinacoteca Nazionale, Bologna), which inspired Domenichino's celebrated picture of the same subject. However, his contemporary reputation was based mainly on his engravings, of which he produced more than 200. They include original compositions as well as reproductions of the paintings of other artists (notably *Tintoretto).

Ludovico left Bologna only for brief periods (although he received many invitations from distinguished patrons to work elsewhere), and after his cousins had gone to Rome, he directed the Carracci academy by himself, regarding teaching as a central part of his life. Early in his career he painted some portraits, but most of his paintings are on religious subjects. His work is uneven in quality, but at his best he was an artist of power and originality. He was less classical in style than his cousins—often emotional or even mystical in feeling. In his later years, the suave style of Guido Reni made Ludovico's work look old-fashioned, but he continued on his own path, sometimes producing pictures of an almost *Expressionist force (Christ Crucified above Figures in Limbo, 1614, S. Francesca Romana, Ferrara).

The Carracci fell from grace in the 19th century along with all the other Bolognese painters, who were one of *Ruskin's pet hates and whom he considered (1847) had 'no single virtue, no colour, no drawing, no character, no history, no thought'. They were saddled with the label *'eclectic' and thought to be ponderous and lacking in originality. Their full rehabilitation did not come until the second half of the 20th century (the great Carracci exhibition held in Bologna in 1956 was a notable landmark), but Annibale has now regained his place as one of the giants of Italian painting.

Three other members of the Carracci family became artists: **Paolo** (1568–1625), who was Ludovico's younger brother; **Francesco** (1595–1622), the nephew of Agostino and Annibale; and **Antonio** (c.1583–1618), Agostino's illegitimate son (the only offspring of the three major figures). Paolo and Francesco were undistinguished, but Antonio had a considerable reputation in his day. However, after his early death he was virtually forgotten, and it is only recently that his work has been rediscovered. He mainly painted religious works, in a graceful style influenced by Reni.

Carrara marble. See MARBLE.

Carreño de Miranda, Juan (b Avilés, nr. Oviedo, 25 Mar. 1614; d Madrid, 3 Oct. 1685). Spanish painter, active mainly in Madrid. Initially he concentrated on religious works, but after he was appointed one of the royal painters in 1669 he worked mainly as a portraitist. Except for his

friend *Velázquez, he was the outstanding court portraitist of 17th-century Spain; he was of noble birth and his paintings have an aristocratic dignity and something of Velázquez's sensitivity and taste, especially in his portrayals of the sickly Charles II (see HABSBURG). His religious paintings (which include several frescos, notably in Toledo Cathedral) are, however, more extravagantly *Baroque.

Carriera, Rosalba (b Venice, 7 Oct. 1675; d Venice, 15 Apr. 1757). Venetian *pastel portraitist, the sister-in-law of *Pellegrini. She had a European reputation and made triumphant visits to Paris (1720–1) and Vienna (1730). Her success helped to popularize pastel; Maurice Quentin de *La Tour, for example, was converted to the medium through his admiration for her. It is now hard to appreciate why there should have been so much enthusiasm for her work, which is highly accomplished but generally rather insipid. After becoming blind in 1746, she had her sight temporarily restored by an operation, but lost it permanently in 1749 and retired into a state of melancholy dejection.

Carrier-Belleuse, Albert-Ernest. See DECAMPS.

Carrière, Eugène. See ACADÉMIE.

Carrington, Dora. See BLOOMSBURY GROUP.

Carrington, Leonora. See ERNST.

Carstens, Asmus Jakob (b St Jürgen, Schleswig-Holstein [then part of Denmark; now in Germany], 10 May 1754; d Rome, 25 May 1798). Danish-German draughtsman and painter who spent the key years of his career in Rome. Apart from some initial training at the Copenhagen Academy he was largely self-taught. In 1783 he set out for Rome, but got only as far as Mantua before lack of funds obliged him to return north. After eking out a living in Germany for several years, in 1788 he became a teacher at the Berlin Academy, and in 1792 he was given a grant by the Prussian government to go to Rome, where he spent the rest of his life. He had a very high-minded concept of art, in tune with his inflated idea of his own genius, and he concentrated on heroic figure compositions (mainly drawings and tempera pictures, for he virtually abandoned oils after settling in Rome). In its austerity and insistence on the primacy of draughtsmanship, his style was essentially *Neoclassical, but it is often touched with a strong current of *Romanticism (the Romantic strain in his temperament was also expressed in his view of himself as a rebel against authority). His serious outlook was influential on northern artists of the next generation in Rome, notably *Thorvaldsen and the *Nazarenes.

cartoon (Italian: *cartone*, 'pasteboard', 'stiff paper'). A full-size drawing made for the purpose of transferring a design to a painting or tapestry or other (usually large) work. The drawing can represent the whole composition or merely a part of it, such as a single figure. Cartoons were an essential part of the process of making stained glass, and it was perhaps from this art that painters borrowed the idea; they were certainly employed in painting by the late 14th century and by the middle of the 15th century they were used extensively by, for example, *Piero della Francesca. The design was transferred either by pressing heavily along the outlines with a pointed metal implement called a stylus or by dusting powdered charcoal through a series of pinpricks—a process called *pouncing (see also SPOLVERO). Piero sometimes created mirror-image figures in a painting by pouncing through a cartoon from one side and then turning it over and repeating the process through the other side. The clearest example is in his *Madonna del Parto* (Madonna of Childbirth) fresco in the cemetery chapel at Monterchi, near Arezzo, in which the two angels flanking the Virgin are in exactly the same poses but reversed left to right relative to one another.

Cartoons were used for *easel paintings as well as frescos. A celebrated example is *Leonardo's *Virgin and Child with St Anne and the Infant St John* (NG, London), although a painting was never made from this. For tapestries, cartoons were made in full colour; famous examples are *Raphael's series on the Acts of the Apostles (Royal Coll., on loan to V&A, London), made as designs for tapestries woven for the Sistine Chapel.

In 1843 designs submitted in a competition for frescos in the Houses of Parliament in London were parodied in the magazine *Punch*. From this the word has acquired its most common meaning today—a humorous drawing or parody.

caryatid. A carved female figure, usually clad in long robes, serving as a column. Caryatids were first used in Greek architecture and the most famous examples are on the Erechtheum at Athens (c.421–406 BC). The male equivalent is the *atlas, and the term 'canephorae' is applied to caryatids supporting baskets on their heads. Caryatids are mentioned by *Vitruvius and speculative illustrations of them appear in several architectural treatises of the *Renaissance, but Jean *Goujon (in the *Louvre in 1550–1) was the only artist of the time to use them on an ambitious scale. They returned to favour during the *Neoclassical period. The well-known examples at St Pancras church, London (1819–22), designed by William Inwood and his son Henry William Inwood, are copied from those of the Erechtheum.

Casanova, Giovanni Battista. See LOUTHERBOURG.

casein. A substance with strong adhesive powers made from the curd of milk, formerly used in art as a binding material for certain types of paints (particularly for wall painting) and *grounds and as a glue for joining parts of a wooden *panel together.

Cassatt, Mary (b Allegheny [now part of Pittsburgh], 22 May, 1844; d Château de Beaufresne, Le Mesnil-Théribus, Oise, 14 June 1926). American painter and printmaker active mainly in France, where she enjoyed a highly successful career (she came from a prosperous family but she also made a good deal of money from her work). She settled in Paris in 1874 (following earlier studies there) and became friendly particularly with *Degas. He invited her to exhibit with the *Impressionists and she took part in four of their eight group shows (1879, 1880, 1881, 1886). Cassatt specialized in everyday life scenes, her favourite theme being a mother with her child or children (although she never married). In the 1880s her work was thoroughly Impressionist in style, but from about 1890 her forms became more solid and firmly outlined; comparing her with Berthe *Morisot, the other leading woman Impressionist, *Gauguin said, 'Miss Cassatt has as much charm but more strength.' She was an outstanding pastellist and printmaker, her finest prints being in colour and in a combination of techniques (aquatint, drypoint, etching). Their bold flattened forms and unconventional viewpoints were influenced by an exhibition of Japanese prints she saw in Paris in 1890. Cassatt's eyesight began to fail when she was in her fifties and she had virtually stopped working by 1914; following an unsuccessful operation for cataracts in 1921 she was almost blind. In her later years she encouraged her wealthy American friends to buy Impressionist works and in this way exercised an important influence on American taste.

cassone. Italian term for a large, decorated chest, especially one that contained a bride's dowry or was given as a wedding present. They were popular from the 14th century to the 16th century, and *cassoni* with painted fronts were particularly fashionable in 15th-century Florence. These paintings usually represented episodes from the Bible or classical history or mythology that pointed a lesson or contained a happy augury for the newly-weds. Often the *cassoni* were made as pairs, bearing the coats of arms respectively of the bride and groom, as with a pair, dated 1472, in the Courtauld Gallery, London (this pair is particularly noteworthy in retaining the original backboards—*spallieri*). *Cassone* paintings are rarely of high quality, although some major artists, including *Domenico Veneziano, *Uccello, and *Botticelli, seem to have done them once in a while. The chief documented exponent was Apollonio di Giovanni (1415–65). Often panels have been detached from *cassoni* and are now displayed as independent paintings. Any *Renaissance picture of appropriate subject, size, and proportions (roughly three or four times as long as it is high) is likely to be described as a *cassone* panel, although similar pictures were used in other furnishings (for example on beds).

cast. An object, particularly a piece of sculpture, made by pouring or pressing liquid, molten, or malleable material into a mould. Typically the sculptor produces a model in an easily workable material such as clay or wax, then constructs from this a mould, usually in plaster, into which the more durable material of the finished work, bronze for example, is poured. The most common method of casting a bronze statue is called *cire-perdue. Moulds can also be used to make copies of existing sculptures. A mould that is made up of various separate pieces—like a three-dimensional jigsaw—is called a piece mould.

Castagno, Andrea del (Andrea di Bartolo di Bargilla) (*b* Castagno, nr. Florence, *c*.1418; *bur.* Florence, 19 Aug. 1457). One of the most powerful Florentine painters in the generation after *Masaccio. Nothing is known of his training, and the first recorded episode in his career dates from 1440, when he painted frescos at the Palazzo del Podestà depicting rebels against Cosimo de' *Medici who were sentenced to be hanged by the heels, earning him the sobriquet Andreino degli Impiccati (Little Andrew of the hanged men). These have been destroyed, and Andrea's earliest known surviving works are frescos in the church of S. Zaccaria in Venice (1442), painted in collaboration with an obscure

artist called Francesco da Faenza. By 1444 he was back in Florence, designing a stained-glass window for the cathedral, and soon after he began his greatest work, a series of frescos on Christ's Passion for the monastery of S. Apollonia (now a Castagno museum), dominated by one of the most celebrated of all portrayals of the Last Supper (1447). In their emotional vigour and sinewy realism these paintings have been regarded as the pictorial equivalent of the sculpture of *Donatello, but they also have something of Masaccio's monumentality. Andrea's other noteworthy works in Florence include a frescoed equestrian portrait in the cathedral—*Niccolò da Tolentino* (1455–6), a pendant to *Uccello's earlier *Sir John Hawkwood*—and two extraordinarily intense altar frescos for SS. Annunziata (*c*.1455) showing *St Julian Receiving Absolution from Christ* and *The Trinity Appearing to Sts Jerome, Paula, and Eustochium*. *Vasari wrote that Castagno murdered his friend *Domenico Veneziano, and it was not until the 19th century that it was discovered that Castagno had died young of the plague and that Domenico had in fact outlived him. The story, however, makes it easy to believe that the intensity of his work reflected a fierce temperament.

Castelli, Leo (*b* Trieste, 4 Sept. 1907; *d* New York, 21 Aug. 1999). Italian-born American art dealer. He settled in New York in the late 1940s and originally sold modern European works, acquired mainly through contacts he had established during the 1930s, when he had been a dealer in Paris. However, finding this market dominated by more established dealers, he turned to American art, and in 1958 he first showed work by Jasper *Johns and Robert *Rauschenberg, the two artists with whom he is most closely identified. In the catalogue of the exhibition 'American Art in the 20th Century' (Royal Academy, London, 1993), Castelli is described as 'perhaps the most influential art dealer of the twentieth century . . . The reputations of most of the major artists of the 1960s were made under his guidance. He established the careers of Cy *Twombly, Frank *Stella and Roy *Lichtenstein, before enhancing the standing of Andy *Warhol . . . With his first exhibition of Claes *Oldenburg in 1974, Castelli completed his group of *Pop celebrities . . . In the early years he helped to change the American gallery system by introducing a European-type retainer (monthly wages advanced against royalties from future sales), enabling his artists to concentrate exclusively on their art.'

Castiglione, Giovanni Benedetto (Il Grechetto) (*bapt.* Genoa, 23 Mar. 1609; *d* Mantua, 5 May 1664). Italian painter, printmaker, and draughtsman, active in his native Genoa and also in Rome, Naples, and Mantua (where he ended his career working at the *Gonzaga court). He was versatile and prolific, and was unusual among Italian artists of his period in being particularly responsive to foreign influence; Rudolf *Wittkower writes that he 'ran through almost the whole gamut of stylistic possibilities in the course of his astonishing career'. In painting, his fluid manner owed something to *Rubens, van *Dyck, and Bernardo *Strozzi, all of whom worked in Genoa, whilst his etchings are indebted to *Rembrandt. His paintings are mainly on religious subjects, but they are often most notable for their superb treatment of animals and still-life details. Some of his other works have a sense of fantasy recalling Salvator *Rosa, notably the etching *The Genius of Castiglione* (1648). In addition to being one of the finest Italian etchers and draughtsmen of his period, he is credited with inventing the *monotype (see also SOFT-GROUND ETCHING). He had a high reputation in his day and his work continued to be influential in the 18th century, notably on *Fragonard and Giambattista *Tiepolo. His brother **Salvatore** (1620–76) was a minor artist and a diplomat for the Gonzaga court, and his son **Giovanni Francesco** (1641–1710) was a painter—a skilful imitator of his father's work.

Castiglione, Giuseppe (Chinese name Lang Shih-ning) (*b* Milan, 19 July 1688; *d* Peking [Beijing], 16 July 1766). Italian Jesuit missionary and painter who settled in China in 1715 and worked for three successive emperors. It is said that he studied Chinese painting by imperial command, and his landscapes and animal and *genre paintings, in which Chinese brushwork and Western naturalism were combined for the first time, enjoyed great success at the court. He was the first Western painter to be appreciated by the Chinese, and was commissioned to paint portraits, scenes of court life, and imperial military expeditions. His work is well represented in the Musée Guimet, Paris.

Catena, Vincenzo (*b* ?Venice, *c.*1470/80; *d* Venice, Sept. 1531). Venetian painter of religious subjects and portraits. Catena was a man of good birth and independent means who moved in humanist circles and may have been the link between these circles and *Giorgione. He is first mentioned in 1506 in an inscription on the back of Giorgione's portrait *Laura* (KH Mus., Vienna), according to which they had entered into some kind of partnership. Nothing else is known of this arrangement. The main influence on his style was Giovanni *Bellini. His early paintings can be awkward and stiff, but from *c.*1510 his work matured under the influence of the late Bellini, *Cima, and *Titian into a style that was derivative but handsome, with pleasing handling of diffused light and warm colours. There are several paintings by or attributed to Catena in the National Gallery, London.

Catherine II (Catherine the Great), Empress of Russia. See HERMITAGE.

Catlin, George (*b* Wilkes-Barre, Pa., 26 July 1796; *d* Jersey City, 23 Dec. 1872). American painter and writer, renowned for his portrayal of American Indian life. He practised law before becoming an artist in the early 1820s (initially as a portraitist in Philadelphia) and was completely self-taught. In 1830 he began a series of visits to various Indian tribes and from 1837 to 1845 he exhibited the resulting paintings as the 'Gallery of Indians' in the USA and Europe. He was better received in England and France than in his native country (*Baudelaire wrote about him enthusiastically), but the venture was not a commercial success and he became bankrupt in 1852. In addition to his paintings, he published various illustrated books on Indian life. Most of his work is in the Smithsonian Institution in Washington.

Cattermole, George (*b* Dickleburgh, nr. Diss, Norfolk, 10 Aug. 1800; *d* London, 24 July 1868). English watercolour painter and book illustrator. At about the age of 14 he began working as a draughtsman for the antiquarian publisher John Britton (1771–1857), whose handsomely illustrated books transformed the study of medieval architecture, and this background served Cattermole well when he turned to depicting swashbuckling historical subjects in the late 1820s. He enjoyed great success with these and also with his illustrations to *Barnaby Rudge* and *The Old Curiosity Shop* (both 1841) by his close friend Charles Dickens (who called him 'Kittenmoles'). However, in the 1850s he attempted to establish himself as a painter in oils and his works in this medium were poorly received. His brother, the Revd **Richard Cattermole** (*c.*1795–1858), also worked as a draughtsman for Britton in his early years.

Caulfield, Patrick (*b* London, 29 Jan. 1936). British painter and printmaker. He is often described as a *Pop artist, but he dislikes the label and his work has a distinct individuality. His deadpan handling, with flat colours contained by uniform black outlines, is very much in the Pop vein, but he has generally avoided imagery from popular culture, concentrating instead on more traditional subjects such as landscape, still-life, and domestic interiors. He took up *screen-printing in 1964 and the following year won a prize for graphics at the Paris *Biennale. Subsequently much of his output has consisted of prints.

Cavalcanti, Emiliano di (b Rio de Janeiro, 6 Sept. 1897; d Rio de Janeiro, 26 Oct. 1976). Brazilian painter, draughtsman, and writer, a pioneer of modern art in his country. In 1922 he helped to organize the Semana de Arte Moderna in São Paulo, which is regarded as a turning point in Brazilian culture; it included dance spectacles, poetry readings, and an art exhibition. From 1923 to 1925 he was based in Paris as a correspondent for the newspaper *Correio de manha* (he began his career as a caricaturist); during this time he got to know many leading avant-garde artists, including *Braque, *Cocteau, *Léger, *Matisse, and *Picasso, and he travelled widely in Europe. He returned to Europe in 1938–40. His work draws on a wide range of influences, including *Cubism, *Fauvism and Picasso's *Neoclassicism of the 1920s, which he blended into an extravagantly colourful style, well suited to the high-keyed Brazilian subjects he favoured: sensuous mulatto women, carnival and festival scenes, poor fishermen, and prostitutes were among his favourite themes. His cheerful, conservative brand of modernism and his preference for local subjects won him great popularity in Brazil. He published two volumes of memoirs (1955 and 1964).

Cavalcaselle, Giovanni Battista. See CROWE.

Cavaliere d'Arpino. See CESARI.

Cavallini, Pietro (active c.1270–c.1330). Italian painter and mosaic designer, active mainly in Rome, where he must have been the leading artist of his day. His two major surviving works (both dating from the 1290s) are mosaics of the Life of the Virgin (S. Maria in Trastevere, Rome) and a fragmentary fresco cycle, the most important part of which is a *Last Judgement* (S. Cecilia in Trastevere, Rome). In 1308 Cavallini was invited to Naples by the reigning king, Charles II of Anjou, and various frescos in S. Maria Donnaregina have been attributed to him. His final work (c.1325–30) was probably a mosaic on the façade of S. Paolo fuori le Mura, Rome; this was destroyed by fire in 1823, but something of its appearance (as of other lost works) is known from copies. According to his son, a scribe at the papal court, Cavallini lived to be 100, but little else is recorded about him (*Vasari's account of his life is poorly informed). Although he is an obscure figure, he occupies an important place in the history of Italian painting. He softened the rigidity of *Byzantine art, and his majestic figures have a real sense of weight and three-dimensionality. His achievements were built on by his great contemporary *Giotto, whose *Last Judgement* in the Arena Chapel at Padua features Apostles enthroned exactly as in Cavallini's fresco of the subject.

Cavallino, Bernardo (bapt. Naples, 25 Aug. 1616; d ?Naples, ?1656). Neapolitan painter. He was the most individual and sensitive Neapolitan painter of his time, but his career is somewhat obscure. About 80 paintings by him are extant, but only one is dated, St Cecilia in Ecstasy (1645, Palazzo Vecchio, Florence; a *modello is in the Mus. di Capodimonte, Naples). Most of his pictures are small-format religious works, peopled by exquisitely elegant and refined figures who evoke a feeling of tender melancholy. Their fragile sensitivity is in complete contrast to the earthy vigour of much of Neapolitan painting of his period. Cavallino trained under Massimo *Stanzione, but his style has more in common with that of van *Dyck, whose work was fairly well known in Naples. He is presumed to have died in the plague that devastated Naples in 1656.

cave painting. See ALTAMIRA and LASCAUX.

Caylus, Comte de (Anne-Claude-Philippe de Tubières) (b Paris, 31 Oct. 1692; d Paris, 5 Sept. 1765). French antiquarian, collector, patron, writer, and amateur printmaker. Caylus came from a wealthy aristocratic family and at an early age distinguished himself as a soldier in the War of the Spanish Succession, but in 1715 he abandoned his military career to indulge a lifelong passion for the arts and antiquity. He was a friend of *Watteau, of whom he wrote a biography (1748), but generally he was more interested in classical art than in the fashionable *Rococo style. Among the artists he championed were *Bouchardon and *Vien, both of whom were in the vanguard of *Neoclassicism. Caylus made a large collection of coins and ancient artefacts, which he catalogued in *Recueil d'antiquités égyptiennes, étrusques, grecques, romaines et gauloises* (7 vols., 1752–67). This is the most serious work of antiquarian research published in the 18th century and one of the most influential in spreading knowledge and enthusiasm for the works of classical antiquity. Caylus indeed is credited with being the first to conceive archaeology as a scientific discipline and in this respect *Winckelmann acknowledged indebtedness to him.

Cazes, Pierre-Jacques. See CHARDIN.

Celant, Germano. See ARTE POVERA.

Cellini, Benvenuto (*b* Florence, 3 Nov. 1500; *d* Florence, 13 Feb. 1571). Florentine sculptor, goldsmith, medallist, and writer—the author of one of the most celebrated of all autobiographies. This racy book has been famous since the 18th century (it was first published in 1728) for its vivid picture of a *Renaissance craftsman proud of his skill and independence, boastful of his feats in art, love, and war, quarrelsome, superstitious, and devoted to the great tradition embodied in *Michelangelo. It has given him a wider reputation than could have come from his artistic work alone; but to modern eyes he also appears as one of the most important *Mannerist sculptors, and his *Perseus* statue is one of the glories of Florentine art. He spent most of his life in Florence, but he worked in several other places, his movements sometimes being influenced by his violent and vain temperament; he made enemies wherever he went, was several times imprisoned, and in 1534 killed a rival goldsmith in Rome (he was pardoned by Pope Paul III (Alessandro *Farnese)).

Cellini trained as a goldsmith and in his early career (which was spent mainly in Rome) he worked predominantly in precious metals; little survives from this phase of his life apart from some medals. Between 1540 and 1545 he worked in France in the service of Francis I (see FONTAINEBLEAU), for whom he created a famous salt cellar of gold enriched with enamel (1540–3, KH Mus., Vienna), the most important piece of goldsmith's work that has survived from the Italian Renaissance and the only one that is securely documented as Cellini's. He also made for the king a bronze *relief, the *Nymph of Fontainebleau* (*c.*1543, Louvre, Paris), which was his first large-scale sculpture. The remainder of Cellini's life was spent in Florence, and it was only in this period that he took up large-scale sculpture in the round with his celebrated bronze *Perseus* (1545–54, Loggia dei Lanzi, Florence), made for Cosimo I de' *Medici. He also made two bronze portrait busts, of Cosimo I (1545–8, Bargello,

Florence) and Bindo Altoviti (*c.*1550, Gardner Mus., Boston), and several marble sculptures, including a *Crucifix* (*c.*1555–62, Escorial, near Madrid). The somewhat dry, niggly quality of these sculptures shows that the exquisite precision of handling of his goldsmith's work did not always transfer easily to a larger scale. The triumphant completion of the *Perseus* in 1554 marked the summit of Cellini's career. In 1557 he was sentenced to four years' imprisonment for sodomy, and it was whilst under house arrest that he wrote his autobiography. Apart from the *Crucifix* (which he intended for his own tomb), his only substantial works after this were treatises on goldsmithing and sculpture, which he published in 1568.

Celtic art. The art of the Celts, a group of ancient peoples identifiable by common cultural and linguistic features; in pre-Roman times they inhabited much of central and western Europe, including parts of the British Isles, France, Germany, and Spain. A distinctive type of Celtic art first emerged in the 5th century BC. It survives mainly in the form of metalwork, a field in which the Celts showed extraordinary skill. They decorated practical objects, such as weapons, armour, and drinking vessels, and also made jewellery, working chiefly in bronze and gold and using sophisticated inlay techniques. Motifs were borrowed from many sources, including Greek art, but they were transformed by the Celtic genius for abstract ornament; vigorous geometrical and spiral designs are characteristic, often combined with stylized animal forms. Human figures are rarer and are usually depicted in a similarly non-naturalistic manner.

This early Celtic art, from the time of its emergence to the coming of the Romans (*c.*450–*c.*50 BC), is often referred to as La Tène art, after an archaeological site at the east end of Lake Neuchâtel, Switzerland, where substantial remains were found in the 19th century. The spread of Roman power tended to submerge native forms in a provincial classicism, and the Celtic tradition survived most strongly in areas on the fringes of Europe, outside the Roman Empire. Metalwork skills declined, but with the Christianizing of Ireland Celtic art took on a new lease of life in illuminated manuscripts, the written text sometimes being eclipsed by intricate ornamentation. The most famous manuscript in this vein is the *Book of Kells (*c.*800).

After the Romans abandoned Britain in the 5th century AD, there was an influx of Celtic influence from Ireland, felt particularly in the north of England and most notably in the *Lindisfarne Gospels (c.700). In sculpture, Celtic art found expression in the free-standing stone cross, a type of work that is found only in Britain and Ireland at this time. Remains of thousands of these crosses survive, some of them substantially complete. The most famous example is at Ruthwell in Dumfriesshire, Scotland, vigorously carved with Bible scenes, vine leaves (a symbol of Christ), and runic inscriptions—combining Christian imagery with pagan decorative motifs. Also well known and probably of about the same date (8th century) is the example at Bewcastle, Cumberland. Such crosses served various purposes, for example as gravestones and centres of outdoor worship.

Although much modified by Scandinavian influence, the Celtic tradition continued to flourish in Ireland until the 12th century, when following the Anglo-Norman invasion of 1169–72 the country came much more into the mainstream of *Romanesque art. Vestiges of the Celtic style of ornamentation survived, however, into the 14th century.

The term **Celtic Revival** refers to a vogue for the imitation of Celtic decorative forms in the applied arts (mainly in Ireland but also elsewhere) that began in the 1840s, reached its peak around 1900, and continued well into the 20th century. It was an expression of a growing nationalistic interest in Ireland's past and was also related to the *Arts and Crafts movement. See also INSULAR ART.

Cennini, Cennino (b Colle de Val d'Elsa, nr. Florence, c.1370; d Florence, c.1440). Florentine painter and writer. No paintings survive that are certainly by him, but he is remembered as the author of Il libro dell'arte, the most important source concerning artistic practice in the late Middle Ages. Cennini states in the book that he was a pupil of Agnolo *Gaddi, who learnt from his father Taddeo Gaddi, who in turn was a pupil of *Giotto, so his detailed descriptions of *tempera and *fresco painting no doubt reflect, even if at several removes, the technical procedures of the founder of the great tradition of Florentine painting. The earliest extant manuscript of the treatise (evidently made by a copyist in the debtors' prison in Florence) is dated 1437, but most authorities put the date of composition at around 1400. Although it is mentioned by *Vasari, the book was long forgotten, until the discovery of one of the three surviving manuscript copies in the early 19th century; the first printed edition of the text was published in 1821. The standard English translation, by Daniel V. Thompson Jr., is entitled The Craftsman's Handbook (1933); it supersedes two 19th-century translations (1844 and 1899).

Cephisodotus. Athenian sculptor of the early 4th century BC, probably the father of *Praxiteles. His most famous work, the bronze Eirene [Peace] Holding the Infant Plutus [Wealth], which stood in the agora at Athens, is known through Roman copies; the heavy draperies and intimate expressions are features that were to characterize 4th-century sculpture in general and that of Praxiteles in particular. Another sculptor called Cephisodotus was the son of Praxiteles and inherited his workshop. He and his younger brother Timarchus specialized in marble statues of divinities and in portraits, mainly in bronze. Cephisodotus' son Praxiteles was also a sculptor (these two names evidently alternated in the family).

Cerano, Il. See CRESPI, GIOVANNI BATTISTA.

Cercle et Carré (Circle and Square). A discussion and exhibition society for abstract artists formed in Paris in 1929 by the critic Michel *Seuphor and the painter Joaquín *Torres-García. They published a journal of the same name, of which three numbers appeared in 1929–30. The association held only one exhibition, at Galerie 23 in April 1930, but this has the distinction of being the first group exhibition ever devoted solely to abstract art; 46 artists showed work, including *Mondrian and *Vantongerloo but also such non-geometricians as *Kandinsky and *Schwitters. In 1931 Cercle et Carré was superseded by the larger and longer-lived *Abstraction-Création association, but it had a sequel in Uruguay: in 1935 Torres-Garcia formed an Asociación de Arte Constructivo in Montevideo and edited a journal Círculo y Cuadrado, of which seven numbers appeared between 1936 and 1938.

cerography (Greek: keros, 'wax', and graphein, 'to write'). The art or act of writing or painting on or with wax; an archaic term for *encaustic.

Cerquozzi, Michelangelo (b Rome, 18 Feb. 1602; d Rome, 6 Apr. 1660). Italian painter, known as 'Michelangelo of the Battles' because of his predilection for scenes of combat. He spent all his career in Rome, where he had considerable contact with northern painters; his friendship with the Dutchman Pieter van *Laer led to his becoming the leading

Italian exponent of *bambocciate* (small pictures of low-life and peasant scenes).

César (César Baldaccini) (*b* Marseilles, 1 Jan. 1921; *d* Paris, 6 Jan. 1998). French sculptor and experimental artist. His work was highly varied, but he became best known for ingenious use of scrap material. In the mid-1950s he began to make sculptures from objects that he found in refuse dumps—scrap iron, springs, tin cans, etc.—building these up with wire into strange winged or insect-like creatures. These had closer affinities, however, with the insect-creatures of Germaine *Richier than with American *Junk art. In 1960 he began making works consisting of car bodies crushed with a hydraulic press into dense packages (he called such sculptures *Compressions*) and it is on these that his international reputation was mainly based (*The Yellow Buick*, 1961, MoMA, New York). In 1965 he started working with plastics, and in 1967, as a counterpart to his *Compressions*, he began making *Expansions*, using plastics that expand rapidly and quickly solidify; sometimes he made such works in public as a kind of *happening.

Cesare da Sesto (*b* Sesto Calende, nr. Varese, *c*.1477; *d* Milan, 27 July 1523). Italian painter. He seems to have spent most of his career in Milan, where he was one of the leading followers of *Leonardo, but he also worked in Rome, in Naples, and probably in Sicily. His suavely accomplished paintings (mainly altarpieces and other religious works) were influential in spreading elements of Leonardo's style to south Italy and elements of Raphael's style (which he encountered in Rome) to north Italy.

Cesari, Giuseppe (also known as Cavaliere d'Arpino) (*b* Arpino, ?1568; *d* Rome, 3 July 1640). Italian *Mannerist painter, active mainly in Rome. He had an enormous reputation in the first two decades of the 17th century, when he gained some of the most prestigious commissions of the day, most notably the designing of the mosaics for the dome of St Peter's (1603–12). Although some of his early work is vigorous and colourful, his output is generally repetitious and vacuous, untouched by the innovations of *Caravaggio (who was briefly his assistant) or the *Carracci. He was primarily a fresco painter, but he also did numerous *cabinet pictures of religious or mythological scenes in a finicky Flemish manner (*The Expulsion from Paradise*, versions in Louvre, Paris, Christ Church, Oxford, Wellington Mus., London, and elsewhere). Cesari's alternative name, Cavaliere

d'Arpino (Knight of Arpino), refers to the title he was awarded by Pope Clement VIII (Ippolito *Aldobrandini) and to his place of birth, between Rome and Naples (although *Baglione claimed he was born in Rome and that it was his father who came from Arpino).

Cézanne, Paul (*b* Aix-en-Provence, 19 Jan. 1839; *d* Aix-en-Provence, 22 Oct. 1906). French painter, with *Gauguin and van *Gogh the greatest of the *Post-Impressionists and a key influence on the development of 20th-century art. He was the son of a prosperous hat manufacturer who was also part-owner of a bank in Aix-en-Provence. In 1861 he abandoned the study of law, and his father reluctantly gave him permission (and a modest allowance) to train as an artist in Paris. He studied at the *Académie Suisse, where he met Camille *Pissarro, but after a few months he went back to Aix discouraged (he was a touchy character who hid his insecurities by posing as a provincial boor, once refusing to shake hands with the elegant *Manet because he claimed he had not washed for days and did not wish to dirty the great man). The following year he resumed his studies in Paris and in 1863 he exhibited at the *Salon des Refusés (his attempts to get his work accepted for the official *Salon regularly ended in failure).

At this time Cézanne's work consisted mainly of portraits and imaginative figure subjects, with occasional still-lifes. The portraits—mostly of members of his family (including self-portraits)—are sombre, using thick, slablike paint, often applied with a palette knife. The imaginative pictures are very different, their subjects typically being erotic or violent and the handling of paint impetuous (*The Murder*, *c*.1868, Walker AG, Liverpool). They show Cézanne's admiration for *Delacroix (of whose pictures he made several copies), but they have none of Delacroix's sophistication. Compared with Delacroix's work, indeed, they look brutally crude, and even with the benefit of hindsight it is hard to see the seeds of Cézanne's future greatness in them. In 1869 he met Hortense Fiquet, a model and seamstress, who became his mistress and bore him a son, Paul, in 1872. Cézanne initially managed to keep them a secret from his family in Aix—he was terrified of his domineering father—but the truth was discovered in 1878 and he eventually married Hortense in 1886, shortly before the death of his father (who had at last become reconciled to the relationship).

After the birth of his son, Cézanne could no longer afford to live in Paris, so he moved to

Pontoise, about 30 km (20 miles) away to the north-west, joining his friend Pissarro, who had recently settled there. The following year, 1873, he moved to nearby Auvers-sur-Oise, then in 1874 returned to Paris. Although this rural interlude was fairly brief, it was highly important in Cézanne's development, for under Pissarro's influence he took up landscape painting seriously, and the close study of nature this involved led him to move away from the imaginative subjects of his youth and concentrate instead on the real world around him. In line with this change of subject, he abandoned the gloomy tonality of his early work and discovered the joys of light and colour, as his style came under the influence of *Impressionism (*House of the Hanged Man*, 1873, Mus. d'Orsay, Paris). He exhibited at the first (1874) and third (1877) Impressionist group exhibitions (his work was critically savaged on both occasions), but he always stood somewhat apart from the group and never wholly adopted their aims and techniques. He was interested in structural analysis rather than in surface effects, and his objective was to combine the formal grandeur of the Old Masters with the naturalism and colour of the best contemporary painting. His aims were summed up in two celebrated remarks: that it was his ambition 'to do *Poussin again, from Nature' and that he wanted to make of Impressionism 'something solid and enduring, like the art of the museums'.

After the death of his father in 1886, Cézanne inherited the family estate (the Jas de Bouffan, which features in many of his paintings), and lived mainly in Aix (he often visited Paris, but otherwise travelled little, only once going abroad in his whole life, to Switzerland in 1890). He was now free of financial worries for the first time in his career and able to concentrate entirely on his art; in the remaining twenty years of his life he did little else but paint—pursuing his ideals with extraordinary patience and self-discipline. He devoted himself principally to certain favourite themes—portraits of his wife, still-lifes, and above all the landscape of Provence, particularly the Mont Sainte-Victoire, which came to have something of the same emotional significance for him that Mount Fuji has for Japanese artists. His painstaking analysis of nature differed fundamentally from Monet's exercises in painting repeated views of subjects such as *Haystacks* or *Poplars*. Monet's ideal was to finish a landscape painting in only one session of work so that it captured the feeling of a particular moment, whereas Cézanne returned to the same place again and again to create a deeply

pondered image that presented his accumulated vision of the subject; his pictures rarely give any obvious indication of the time of day or even the season represented. He worked slowly and intuitively, creating a sense of depth and solidity not through conventional draughtsmanship and perspective, but through extremely delicate variations of tone, and he distorted natural appearances—subtly tilting and stretching forms—to achieve the pictorial balance that was his central concern. In his final years he created works of luminous beauty and classical dignity that are a world away from the wild, impulsive pictures of his youth. The culminating paintings of his career include three large pictures of *Bathers* (female nudes in a landscape setting) that are among his most majestic creations; one of them, in the Philadelphia Museum of Art, was perhaps entirely painted in 1906, the year of his death.

Cézanne had worked in comparative obscurity until he was given a one-man show in Paris by Ambroise *Vollard in 1895. It made little impact on the public but excited many younger artists, and because Cézanne himself was rarely seen he began to acquire a legendary reputation. By the end of the century he was revered as the 'Sage' by many of the avant-garde and in 1904 the *Salon d'Automne devoted a special exhibition to him. A memorial exhibition of his work at the same venue in 1907 was a major factor in the genesis of *Cubism, and his subsequent influence has been profound, varied, and enduring, earning him the title 'the father of modern art'; the belief that the picture surface has an integrity of its own irrespective of what it represents—a characteristic of so much modern painting—stems directly from him. It is not only the quality of his work that has proved an inspiration, but also the example he set of complete devotion to art: Henri *Matisse bought a picture by Cézanne in 1899 and in 1936 wrote that 'It has sustained me spiritually in the critical moments of my career as an artist; from it I have drawn my faith and perseverance.'

Cézanne often worked on pictures over a long period—he is said to have had over 100 sittings for a portrait of Ambroise Vollard (1899, Petit Palais, Paris) before abandoning it with the comment that he was not displeased with the shirt front. In spite of this laborious slowness, he left a substantial body of work (drawings and watercolours as well as oils). There are examples in many major museums, with particularly fine collections in, for example, the Courtauld Gallery, London, the Barnes Foundation,

Merion, Pennsylvania, the Pushkin Museum, Moscow, the Metropolitan Museum, New York, the Musée d'Orsay, Paris, the Hermitage, St Petersburg, and the National Gallery, Washington. His studio in Aix is now a Cézanne museum, reconstructed as it was at the time of his death and displaying personal mementoes such as his hat and clay pipe.

Chadwick, Lynn (*b* Barnes, Surrey [now Greater London], 24 Nov. 1914; *d* Stroud, Gloucestershire, 24 Apr. 2003). British sculptor. Initially he concentrated on *mobiles, often derived from insect forms (*Dragonfly*, 1951, Tate, London), and these were followed by ponderous, bristling, rough-finished metal structures supported on thin legs. In 1956 he won the International Sculpture Prize at the Venice *Biennale, which helped him gain recognition as one of the leading British sculptors of his generation. His work is generally based on the human figure (often in couples), but is sometimes so strongly schematized that it comes close to abstraction. In the early 1960s, influenced by *Minimal art, it became more blocklike, but in the later 1960s he returned to figuration, typically contrasting highly polished faceted surfaces with rougher areas. In the 1970s his sculpture became less aggressive in feeling, and in the 1980s he began experimenting with sheet steel.

Chagall, Marc (*b* Vitebsk [now Vitsyebsk, Belarus], 7 July 1887; *d* Saint-Paul-de-Vence, 28 Mar. 1985). Russian-born painter and designer, active mainly in France. In 1910–14 he lived in Paris, where he was a member of an avant-garde circle including *Apollinaire, *Delaunay, *Léger, *Modigliani, and *Soutine. After going to Berlin in 1914 for his first one-man show (at the *Sturm Gallery) he visited Russia and had to remain because of the outbreak of war. Following the Revolution in 1917 he was appointed Fine Arts Commissar for his home province of Vitebsk, where he founded and directed an art academy. *Malevich was among the other teachers there, and after disagreements with him Chagall left in 1920 and moved to Moscow, where he made designs for the newly founded Jewish Theatre. He returned to Paris in 1923 at the invitation of Ambroise *Vollard, who commissioned much work from him, including illustrations for Gogol's *Dead Souls*, La Fontaine's *Fables*, and the Bible (these were not published until 1948, 1952, and 1956 respectively). In 1937 he became a French citizen, but he was stripped of his new nationality under the anti-Jewish laws passed after the German invasion. He escaped to Spain in 1941 and from there moved to the USA, where he lived for the next seven years. In 1948 he returned to Paris, and from 1949 he lived on the Riviera, near Nice, working to the end of his very long life—the last survivor of the generation of artists who had revolutionized painting in the years leading up to the First World War.

Chagall was prolific as a painter and also as a book illustrator and designer of stained glass (in which he did some of his most impressive late work) and of sets and costumes for the theatre and ballet. His work was dominated by two rich sources of imagery: memories of the Jewish life and folklore of his early years in Russia; and the Bible (he was born into a deeply religious family). He derived some of his spatial dislocations and prismatic colour effects from *Cubism and *Orphism, but he created a highly distinctive style, remarkable for its sense of fairy-tale fantasy. Because the scenes he depicted made no rational sense, André *Breton claimed him as one of the precursors of *Surrealism (and it was during the heyday of Surrealism—the 1930s—that his reputation became international), but Chagall himself stated in his autobiography *Ma vie* (1931) that however fantastic and imaginative his pictures appeared, he painted only direct reminiscences of his early years. Rather than exploring the unconscious mind, he was interested in great timeless themes, such as birth, love, marriage, and death, which he interpreted in his own warm and whimsical way. There is a museum devoted to Chagall's religious art in Nice. The work there does not always show him at his best, for he could be sentimental and overblown, but his finest paintings have won him an enduring reputation as one of the greatest masters of the *École de Paris.

chalk. Drawing material made from various soft stones or earths (or latterly from synthetic equivalents). There are three main types of natural chalk: black chalk (made from stones such as carbonaceous shale); red chalk, also called sanguine (made from red ochre or other red earths); and white chalk (made from various limestones). Chalk drawings are known from prehistoric times, but the medium really came into its own in the late 15th century, notably in the hands of *Leonardo, who made many drawings in red and black chalk. Some artists, notably *Watteau, used black, red, and white chalks in the same drawing. Synthetic, or 'fabricated', chalks are made from powdered pigments mixed with a binding medium, then rolled or pressed into sticks and dried. They were in use by the 17th century, but were not common until the 18th century. Fabricated chalks are not always clearly distinguished from crayons and *pastels, and there is much ambiguity in the historical literature of the subject. However, crayons, as the term is now generally understood, are sticks of colour made with an oily or waxy binding substance, and pastels are sticks of powdered pigment bound with gum, producing a softer, more powdery effect than chalk.

chalk roll. See ROULETTE.

Chamberlain, John (*b* Rochester, Ind., 16 Apr. 1927). American sculptor. His early sculpture, influenced by that of David *Smith, was made largely from metal pipes, but in 1957 he began to incorporate scrap metal parts from cars in his work and from 1959 he concentrated on sculpture made entirely from crushed automobile parts welded together. Usually he retains the original colours, and the expressive energy of his work, with its twisted planes and crumpled surfaces, has been compared to that of *Action Painting. Many of his compositions are intended for wall hanging rather than to stand on the ground. An example is *Dolores James* (1962, Guggenheim Mus., New York). Although he has continued with work of this type, which has been widely acclaimed, Chamberlain has also experimented with other types of sculpture and other media. In 1966, for example, he started using urethane foam, as in *Koko-Nor II* (1967, Tate, London). He has also done abstract paintings and made experimental films.

Chambray, Roland Fréart de. See FRÉART.

Champaigne, Philippe de (*bapt.* Brussels, 26 May 1602; *d* Paris, 12 Aug. 1674). Flemish-born painter who settled in Paris in 1621 and became a French citizen in 1629. His training was mainly under the landscape painter Jacques Fouquier or Foucquières (*c.*1591–1659), but almost all his work consists of religious pictures or portraits (his few landscapes serve as settings for religious subjects). As a religious painter he ranks high among his French contemporaries, and as a portraitist he stands head and shoulders above them. He worked for several distinguished patrons, including Louis XIII, the queen mother (Marie de *Médicis), and Cardinal Richelieu. Two of his finest portraits of Richelieu (late 1630s) are in the National Gallery, London: a commanding full-length and a triple view of the head intended to be used by a sculptor as the model for a bust. They bring the personality of the cardinal vividly to life and show how

Champaigne moderated the *Baroque idiom of *Rubens towards a classical dignity in line with French taste in the middle of the 17th century. He was a friend of *Poussin, and Anthony *Blunt has written that 'His portraits and his later religious works are as true a reflection of the rationalism of French thought as the classical compositions of Poussin in the 1640s.' His style became even more severe after he came under the influence of the Jansenists—a Catholic sect of great austerity—in the early 1640s. Some of his finest work was done for the Jansenist convent at Port-Royal, where his daughter was a nun: he commemorated her miraculous recovery from paralysis in his most celebrated work, the *Ex-Voto de 1662* (Louvre, Paris), of which Blunt writes that 'In its restraint and simplicity this painting is as typical of the Jansenist approach to a miracle as *Bernini's "St Theresa" is of the Jesuit.' His masterpiece in portraiture might well have been his self-portrait of 1668, which is lost, but survives in a copy by his nephew and pupil **Jean-Baptiste de Champaigne** (1631–81) in the Louvre and in a superb engraving (1676) by Gerard *Edelinck.

Champfleury (pseudonym of Jules Husson) (*b* Laon, 17 Sept. 1821; *d* Sèvres, 6 Dec. 1889). French writer whose huge and varied output included a good deal about art. He was a leading spokesman for the *Realism of *Courbet, declaring that art should depict the social scene as it is without moralizing or idealizing it; a collection of his essays transposing Courbet's ideas to literature was published in 1857 as *Le Réalisme*, and this is regarded as the chief manifesto of the movement. His other writings include a massive history of caricature (6 vols., 1865–88). He was also interested in ceramics and in 1872 he was appointed curator of the collections at the Sèvres porcelain factory. He is portrayed in Courbet's *The Painter's Studio* (1854–5, Mus. d'Orsay, Paris), *Manet's *Music in the Tuileries Gardens* (1862, NG, London), and *Fantin-Latour's *Homage to *Delacroix* (1864, Mus. d'Orsay).

Chantelou, Paul Fréart de. See FRÉART.

Chantrey, Sir Francis (*b* Norton, nr. Sheffield, 7 Apr. 1781; *d* London, 25 Nov. 1841). English sculptor. Initially he tried to establish himself as a portrait painter, but after about 1805 he painted only occasionally (a self-portrait, *c.*1810, is in Tate Britain, London). He made his reputation with a bust of the Revd John Horne-Took (Fitzwilliam Mus., Cambridge), exhibited at the *Royal Academy in 1811, and he succeeded *Nollekens as the most successful portrait sculptor in England. His enormous practice also included church monuments and statues; the monument to the Robinson children (1817) in Lichfield Cathedral and the bronze equestrian statue of George IV (1828) in Trafalgar Square are his best-known works in these fields. Although he had studied intermittently at the Royal Academy, Chantrey was essentially self-taught and his work often has an impressive directness, unburdened by academic theory: 'I hate allegory; it is a clumsy way of telling a story.' He became extremely wealthy, and besides being very generous during his life he left the bulk of his fortune of £150,000 to the Royal Academy, the interest to be used for the purchase of 'works of Fine Art of the highest merit executed within the shores of Great Britain'. These are now housed in Tate Britain. See also CUNNINGHAM.

Chapman, Dinos and **Jake.** See YOUNG BRITISH ARTISTS.

charcoal. Charred twigs or sticks used for drawing. Its use dates back to Roman times and possibly much earlier. An essential characteristic of charcoal is that it is easily rubbed off the drawing surface unless a *fixative is used, so it has been much favoured for preparatory work, either for sketches or *cartoons or for outlining on wall or panel a design that could be gone over with a more permanent medium. The soft-edged effect it produces has been notably exploited by 16th-century Venetian painters, *Baroque artists, and the *Impressionists. *Pencils and *chalks have now taken its place to some extent, but it remains well suited to large-scale work and broad, energetic draughtsmanship; outstanding modern exponents include *Barlach and *Kollwitz.

Chardin, Jean-Siméon (b Paris, 2 Nov. 1699; d Paris, 6 Dec. 1779). French painter of still-life and *genre, in which fields he was one of the greatest masters of all time. (His Christian names have usually been given as Jean-Baptiste-Siméon, but the 'Baptiste' seems to have been a scribe's error, and Jean-Siméon is now the accepted form.) He was the contemporary of *Boucher and he briefly taught *Fragonard, but his work is a contrast to theirs in every way, representing the naturalistic strain—influenced by 17th-century Dutch painting—that ran through 18th-century French art alongside the more fashionable *Rococo style. Almost all his pictures are modest in size and simple in subject, depicting objects and scenes from everyday

middle-class life, and they create their magic through an extraordinarily subtle mastery of composition and colour, tone and texture (he was a notoriously slow and fastidious worker).

Chardin studied under two history painters, Pierre-Jacques Cazes (1676–1754) and Noël-Nicolas *Coypel, but he gained little from them and seems to have been more or less self-taught in his specialities. In 1728 he was received into the Académie Royale as a 'painter skilled in animals and fruits'. It was customary for new members to give an example of their work to the Académie and Chardin presented two pictures— *The Rayfish* (c.1725) and *The Buffet* (1728), both now in the Louvre, Paris. *The Rayfish* is, by Chardin's standards, an unusually flamboyant work; the gutted fish has a strangely human-like 'face' twisted in a macabre grimace, and its raw flesh is depicted with virtuoso skill. For the rest of his life Chardin was a dedicated member of the Académie; he punctiliously attended its meetings and for almost twenty years he served as treasurer (1755–74), a position to which he was well suited, as he had an exemplary reputation for honesty and integrity. He reached his peak of esteem in the 1750s, when Louis XV granted him an annual allowance (1752) and gave him lodgings in the Louvre. In spite of royal favour, he led a life of uneventful dedication to his art; apart from short visits to Versailles or Fontainebleau, he is never known to have left Paris.

Chardin's career can be broadly divided into three phases, plus an epilogue. In the first phase, up to about 1733, he painted mainly still-lifes, generally featuring dead game or kitchen utensils; in such works he goes far beyond matter-of-fact realism and through his simplicity and directness of vision achieves a sense of deep seriousness, in spite of the humble objects he portrayed. For about the next fifteen years he concentrated on genre scenes; they usually contain only one or two figures, and like his still-lifes are completely without sentimentality or affectation (*The Young Governess*, c.1735, NG, London, and other versions; he often produced replicas or variants of favourite designs). In the late 1740s he returned again to still-life as his main subject, often depicting more elaborate and costly objects than he had in his early career (*The Attributes of the Arts*, 1766, versions in Hermitage, St Petersburg, and Minneapolis Inst. of Arts). Finally, in the 1770s he abandoned oils (evidently because the lead in certain colours aggravated an eye complaint) and took up pastel portraiture. Although he had rarely painted portraits before and had no previous experience of pastel, he immediately showed that he was a match for any of the great contemporary specialists in the field. He exhibited pastels at each of the *Salons from 1771 to 1779; the year of his death; they included several self-portraits and pictures of children and fellow artists.

In spite of acclaim for these unexpected products of his old age, by this time Chardin was regarded—with the growing taste for *Neoclassicism—as something of an ancient relic, and after his death he was quickly forgotten. His reputation revived in the mid-19th century, when his integrity and directness impressed the exponents of *Realism. Subsequently, the formal strength of his paintings has appealed enormously to modern taste, and he is now one of the best-loved artists of the 18th century and perhaps the most revered of all exponents of still-life.

Chares of Lindos. See COLOSSUS OF RHODES.

Charlemagne. See CAROLINGIAN ART.

Charles I, King of England, Scotland, and Ireland. See ROYAL COLLECTION.

Charles II, King of England, Scotland, and Ireland. See ROYAL COLLECTION.

Charles II, King of Spain. See HABSBURG.

Charles IV, Emperor. See BOHEMIAN SCHOOL.

Charles V, Emperor. See HABSBURG.

Charles the Bold, Duke of Burgundy. See BURGUNDY.

Charonton, Enguerrand. See QUARTON.

Chase, William Merritt (*b* Williamsburg, Ind., 1 Nov. 1849; *d* New York, 25 Oct. 1916). American painter. He was a versatile and prolific artist, but is remembered chiefly as the most important art teacher of his generation in the USA. His principal posts were in New York—at the *Art Students League, 1878–94, and at his own Chase School, 1896–1908—but he also taught in Chicago, Philadelphia, and elsewhere. From 1891 to 1902 he ran the Shinnecock Summer School on Long Island, the first important school of open-air painting in America, and he also pioneered study trips abroad (he visited Europe regularly throughout his career). A flamboyant and popular man, he was active in virtually every art organization in New York and he did a great deal to promote the art of his colleagues and countrymen. Apart from teaching, he made his living mainly through portraiture, but he was often in financial difficulties. His

other subjects included still-lifes, interiors, and landscapes. He took great joy in the process of painting, and the vigorous brushwork and fresh colour that characterizes much of the best American painting of the early 20th century owes much to his example. His students included Charles *Demuth, Marsden *Hartley, Edward *Hopper, Georgia *O'Keeffe, and Charles *Sheeler. See also TEN.

Chassériau, Théodore (*b* Sainte-Barbe de Samano, Santo Domingo [now Dominican Republic], 20 Sept. 1819; *d* Paris, 8 Oct. 1856). French painter and printmaker, born in the West Indies, where his father was a French consul. He was the most gifted pupil of *Ingres, with whom he began to study when he was 11, but in the 1840s he came under the influence of *Delacroix and attempted, with considerable success, to combine Ingres's *classical linear grace with Delacroix's *Romantic colour. His chief work was the decoration of the Cour des Comptes in the Palais d'Orsay, Paris, with allegorical scenes of Peace and War (1844–8), but these were almost completely destroyed by fire in 1871. There are other examples of his decorative work, however, in various churches in Paris. Chassériau was also an outstanding portraitist and painted nudes and North African scenes (he visited Algeria in 1846). As a printmaker he is best known for a series of fifteen etchings illustrating Shakespeare's *Othello* (1844). His friend Gustave *Moreau was among the artists influenced by his work.

Chastel, André (*b* Paris, 15 Nov. 1912; *d* Paris, 18 July 1990). The best-known French art historian of his generation. For most of his career he taught at the Sorbonne, Paris, but his activities extended into various fields outside the university. His scholarly publications were mainly on *Renaissance art, but he wrote on a wide range of subjects and reached a large popular audience through regular articles in the newspaper *Le Monde*.

Chavannes, Pierre Puvis de. See PUVIS DE CHAVANNES.

Cheere, Sir Henry (*b* London, 1703; *d* London, 15 Jan. 1781). English sculptor, possibly of French descent. In about 1729 he went into partnership with Henry *Scheemakers (they jointly signed several small monuments) and after Scheemakers left England in about 1733 Cheere extended the practice, his output including much work for Oxford University. His art is markedly *Rococo in feeling, and in his charming smaller monuments he often used coloured marbles (*Dean Wilcocks, c.*1756, Westminster Abbey, London). He was well thought of by his fellow artists and furthered the career of *Roubiliac by gaining him his first important commission in England—the statue of Handel (1738) for Vauxhall Gardens (now in the V&A, London). Cheere was also prominent in public affairs and devoted efforts to an abortive scheme to found an academy of arts a decade before the *Royal Academy came into being. He was knighted in 1760 and made a baronet in 1766. His brother **John** (1709–87) was also a sculptor—a prolific supplier of lead garden figures and other modestly priced works.

Chéret, Jules (*b* Paris, 31 May 1836; *d* Nice, 23 Sept. 1932). French lithographer, designer, and painter, the first notable specialist in poster design. Chéret was the son of a typographer and trained as a lithographer. He designed his first poster in 1858 (for Offenbach's *Orpheus in the Underworld*), but he did not become prolific in the medium until the 1870s, when improvements in printing technology enabled large colour lithographs to be produced economically on cheap paper. In all he created about 1,200 posters, for all manner of products and performances. His work is predominantly light in spirit and often features attractive women. In 1898 he retired to Nice, and the Musée des Beaux-Arts there has an outstanding collection of his work. His brother **Gustave-Joseph Chéret** (1838–94) was a sculptor and designer.

Chéron, Louis. See ST MARTIN'S LANE ACADEMY.

Chevreul, Eugène. See DIVISIONISM.

Chia, Sandro. See NEO-EXPRESSIONISM.

chiaroscuro (Italian: 'bright-dark'). Term describing the effects of light and shade in a work of art, particularly when they are strongly contrasting. *Leonardo was the great pioneer of bold chiaroscuro, but the term is associated above all with 17th-century artists, particularly the *Caravaggisti and *Rembrandt, whose handling of light and shade is unsurpassed in subtlety and expressiveness, not only in his paintings, but also in his etchings and drawings.

chiaroscuro woodcut. A type of *woodcut in which tonal effects are created by printing successively onto the same sheet from different blocks of varying tone. Two or more tones of a single colour are used, or of two closely related colours, one of which is darker than the other. It is usual to make a key block with the design in

outline, and to cut this first so that the main lines can be transferred to the other blocks to ensure correct registration. The technique was invented in the first decade of the 16th century and initially it was chiefly used for the reproduction of drawings. It developed more or less simultaneously in Germany and Italy, though there is an interesting difference of approach in the work of the two schools. In Germany great importance was given to the key block, which was to all intents and purposes a complete design in itself, the resulting print being a richly worked woodcut with the addition of background tints. In Italy the medium was handled with much greater breadth, the design being visualized in large areas of tone punctuated by dark accents.

One of the earliest dated examples of a chiaroscuro woodcut is *The Emperor Maximilian on Horseback* of 1508, designed by Hans *Burgkmair; other notable German exponents were *Cranach, *Baldung Grien, and *Altdorfer. In Italy, where the medium was used more extensively, *Ugo da Carpi (who is sometimes credited with inventing the technique) made many prints after designs by *Raphael and *Parmigianino, the latter artist being a prolific designer for the process. Although in some cases an accurate facsimile was intended, in others the cutter interpreted his original with some freedom. The technique was little used after the 17th century and its later history tends to overlap with that of colour woodcut and colour *wood engraving, but even today any *relief print cut on several blocks with the intention of rendering light and shade as opposed to colour may be claimed as a descendant of the chiaroscuro woodcut.

Chicago, Judy. See FEMINIST ART.

Chigi, Agostino (*b* Siena, 29 Nov. 1466; *d* Rome, 11 Apr. 1520). Italian banker and merchant, one of the greatest patrons of the *Renaissance. Chigi was the leading financier in Europe (his family bank had branches throughout Italy and others in places as far apart as London and Cairo) and he also had various industrial and trading interests. He was Sienese by birth (and he favoured Sienese artists such as *Peruzzi and *Sodoma), but he spent most of his life in Rome. His two most important commissions there were a villa in the suburbs of the city (now called the Villa Farnesina, as it was later owned by the *Farnese family) and a burial chapel in the church of S. Maria del Popolo. The villa was designed by *Peruzzi and begun in about 1506; it is the most sophisticated residence of its time, with painted decoration by *Raphael and *Sebastiano del Piombo, as well as Sodoma and Peruzzi himself. The lavish chapel was designed by Raphael and begun in 1512. It was unfinished when he and Chigi died within days of each other in 1520 and was not completed until the 1650s by *Bernini, working for **Fabio Chigi** (1599–1667), a descendant of Agostino who became Pope Alexander VII in 1655. In 1664 his nephew Cardinal **Flavio Chigi** (1631–93) commissioned Bernini to design the façade of the Palazzo Chigi (now Palazzo Chigi-Odescalchi).

Chinese ink. See INK.

Chinnery, George (b London, 7 Jan. 1774; d Macao, 30 May 1852). English painter, active for almost all his career in the Eastern world. After leaving London in 1802 he worked in India until 1825 and then for the rest of his life in Macao, from which he made visits to Canton and Hong Kong. He made his living principally as a portraitist, but his reputation now rests mainly on the pictures of Indian and oriental life and scenery that he painted for his own pleasure.

chinoiserie. The imitation or evocation of Chinese styles in Western art and architecture. The term is applied particularly to art of the 18th century, when pseudo-Chinese designs in a whimsical or fantastic vein were an aspect of the prevailing light-hearted *Rococo style. By the middle of the 18th century the enthusiasm for things Chinese affected virtually all the decorative arts, and there was also a vogue for Chinese-style buildings in garden architecture. The taste for chinoiserie faded during the dominance of the *Neoclassical style in the second half of the century, but there was something of a revival in the early 19th century.

Chirico, Giorgio de (b Volos, Greece, 10 July 1888; d Rome, 20 Nov. 1978). Italian painter, sculptor, designer, and writer, the originator of *Metaphysical Painting. He trained in Athens, Florence, and Munich, where he was influenced by the *Symbolist work of *Böcklin and *Klinger, with their juxtaposition of the commonplace and the fantastic. In 1909 he moved to Italy (dividing his time between Florence, Milan, and Turin) and there painted his first 'enigmatic' pictures, which convey an atmosphere of strangeness and uneasiness through their empty spaces, illogical shadows, and unexpected perspectives. From 1911 to 1915 he lived in Paris, becoming friendly with many members of the avant-garde, including *Apollinaire (who championed his work) and *Picasso. During this period he developed a more deliberate theory of 'metaphysical insight' into a reality behind ordinary things by neutralizing the things themselves of all their usual associations and setting them in new and mysterious relationships. To help empty the objects in his paintings of their natural emotional significance he depicted statues and faceless tailors' dummies in place of human beings (from 1914).

In 1915 de Chirico was conscripted into the Italian army and sent to Ferrara. There he suffered a nervous breakdown, and in 1917 met *Carrà in the military hospital and converted him to his views, launching Metaphysical Painting as a movement. It was short-lived, virtually ending when de Chirico and Carrà quarrelled in 1919, but it was highly influential on *Surrealism, and it was during the later 1920s, when Surrealism was becoming the most talked-about artistic phenomenon of the day, that de Chirico's international reputation was established. However, it was his early work that the Surrealists admired and they attacked him for adopting a more traditional style in the 1920s, when his output included some distinctive pictures featuring horses on unreal seashores with broken classical columns. In the 1920s and 1930s he spent much of his time in Paris (and in 1935–7 he lived in the USA) before settling permanently in Rome in 1944. By this time his paintings had become repetitive and obsessed with technical refinement. His other work included a number of small sculptures and set and costume designs for opera and ballet; his writings include a Surrealistic novel, *Hebdomeros* (1929), and two volumes of autobiography (1945 and 1960) translated into English as *The Memoirs of Giorgio de Chirico* (1971).

His brother **Alberto Savinio** (1891–1952), originally Andrea de Chirico, was a musician, writer, painter, and designer; he adopted his pseudonym to avoid confusion with Giorgio, with whom he worked closely for a time (they lived together in Paris, 1911–15). Savinio's work as a painter was rather heavy-handed, but his ideas helped inspire his brother's use of faceless mannequins.

Chodowiecki, Daniel Nikolaus (b Danzig [now Gdańsk, Poland], 16 Oct. 1726; d Berlin, 7 Feb. 1801). German painter, illustrator, and printmaker of Polish ancestry. He spent his career in Berlin, where he settled in 1743. Largely self-taught, he began with miniatures and progressed to oil paintings and etchings. From the late 1760s he concentrated on book illustrations and became the most prolific and famous German artist of his time in this field, with a huge and varied output. His illustrations of literary works include many attractive scenes of contemporary bourgeois life, and it is for these that he is chiefly remembered. In 1797 he became director of the Berlin Academy.

choir stalls. Term in Christian church architecture for sets of fixed, enclosed seats arranged in one or more rows on either side of the choir, for the use of clergy during services. By the 12th century a form of stalls had evolved that remained basically constant throughout the Middle Ages. The back was continuous and the long bench, with ends, was divided into separate seats by low partitions. Hinged seats, which could be raised to a vertical position when the occupant was standing, were in use by this period. In the later Middle Ages the stalls often had gabled canopies rising to great height, and these and the *misericords on the seats became vehicles for virtuoso feats of woodcarving. Among later choir stalls those carved by Grinling *Gibbons (1695–7) in St Paul's Cathedral in London are probably the most celebrated.

Christie's. The popular name for the firm of Christie, Manson & Woods, the oldest fine art auctioneers in the world (*Sotheby's was founded earlier, but originally sold only books). It was founded by James Christie (1730–1803), who gave up a commission in the navy to become an auctioneer and held his first sale on 5 December 1766 in rooms in Pall Mall, in the same premises in which the exhibitions of the *Royal Academy were held until 1779. He was a friend of *Gainsborough and *Reynolds, and Christie's developed a tradition of holding the studio sales of prominent artists. The firm acquired its present name in 1859, when James Christie's grandsons took new partners. Its headquarters are still in London and there are branches and offices in many other cities throughout the world.

Christmas, Gerard (or **Garrett**) (*bapt.* London, 15 Jan. 1576; *d* London, 1634). English sculptor and designer, active in London. There is a fair amount of documentary information about his career, but his only surviving work is the monument to Sir Robert Crane and his two wives (1626, Chilton, Suffolk). His lost works include an equestrian figure in relief of James I (*c.*1617) carved on the city gate at Aldersgate, which is known through poor engravings. Christmas worked as master carver to the navy

on the decoration of ships and was also much employed in devising pageantry for the Lord Mayor's Shows and other festivities. His sons **John** (1599–1654) and **Matthias** (1605–54) worked with him and succeeded him as master carvers to the navy. There are a number of monuments jointly signed by the brothers, the most important being the tomb of George Abbot, Archbishop of Canterbury (*c.*1634, Holy Trinity church, Guildford), which was evidently commissioned from Gerard but made by his sons after his death. Their work is competent but uninspired, giving a good idea of the average level of production of the day.

Christo (Christo Javacheff) (*b* Gabrovo, 13 June 1935). Bulgarian-born sculptor and experimental artist who settled in New York in 1964 and became an American citizen in 1973. After brief periods in Prague, Vienna (where he studied sculpture with *Wotruba), and Geneva, he moved to Paris, where he lived from 1958 to 1964. Initially he earned his living there as a portrait painter, but soon after his arrival he invented 'empaquetage' (packaging), a form of expression he has made his own and for which he has become world-famous. It consists of wrapping objects in materials such as canvas or semi-transparent plastic and dubbing the result art. He began with small objects such as paint tins from his studio (in this he had been anticipated by *Man Ray), but they increased in size through trees and motor cars to buildings and sections of landscape. He spends a great deal of time and effort negotiating permission to carry out such work and in planning the operations, which can involve teams of professional rock climbers as well as construction workers. He finances such massive enterprises through the sale of his smaller works. The buildings that he has succeeded in wrapping include the Pont Neuf in Paris (1985, after nine years of negotiations), and the Reichstag in Berlin (1995). Among the landscape projects he has carried out is *Running Fence*, something like a fabric equivalent of the Great Wall of China, undulating through 38 km (24 miles) of Sonoma and Marin Counties, California (1976). Christo says of his work: 'You can say it's about displacement. Basically even today I am a displaced person, and that is why I make art that does not last . . . Unlike steel, or stone, or wood, the fabric catches the physicality of the wind, the sun. They are refreshing. And then they are quickly gone.' Christo's wife Jeanne-Claude (née de Guillebon) (1935–) collaborates with him in his work.

Christus, Petrus (*b* ?Baerle-Duc [now Baarle-Hertog], ?*c*.1410; *d* Bruges, 1475/6). Netherlandish painter, active in Bruges. He is first documented there in 1444 and was the leading artist in the city in the generation after Jan van *Eyck, who died in 1441. Traditionally he has been regarded as Jan's pupil (and it has been suggested that he completed works the master left unfinished at his death), but it is now thought likely that he received his training elsewhere before arriving in Bruges. Nevertheless, he was strongly influenced by Jan and helped to spread his style. Christus' work is plainer and more summary, however, and his figures tend to be rather doll-like. The influence of Rogier van der *Weyden is also evident in some of Christus' work; his *Lamentation* (*c*.1450, Mus. Royaux, Brussels), for example, is clearly based on Rogier's celebrated *Descent from the Cross* (*c*.1440, Prado, Madrid), but the figures have completely lost their dramatic impact. Christus' most personal works are his portraits, notably *Edward Grimston* (1446, Earl of Verulam Coll., on loan to NG, London), in which he abandons the dark backgrounds of Jan and Rogier and places his sitter in a clearly defined interior. His interest in representing space also comes out in some of his religious works, notably the *Virgin and Child in a Chamber* (*c*.1450–60, Nelson–Atkins Mus., Kansas City, Mo.), which has a particularly complex and attractive setting.

chromolithography. The process of making coloured prints by *lithography, using a separate stone or plate for each colour. The term is usually applied to reproductive prints rather than to original works.

chryselephantine. Term describing statues incorporating gold (Greek: *khrusos*) and ivory (Greek: *elephantinos*), the gold typically being used for draperies and the ivory for flesh. The technique was used on a small scale in ancient Egypt, Mesopotamia, and Crete, and in colossal statues by the Greeks from the 6th century BC, the gold and ivory being carried on a wooden framework. Because of the cost, the technique was used only in the most important religious images, the most famous being the enormous statues of Athena and Zeus that *Phidias made respectively for the Parthenon at Athens and the temple of Zeus at Olympia.

Church, Frederic Edwin (*b* Hartford, Conn., 4 May 1826; *d* New York, 7 Apr. 1900). American landscape painter. Church was a pupil and friend of *Cole and continued the *Hudson River School's interest in depicting spectacular natural scenery; his *Niagara* (1857, Corcoran Gal., Washington) established him as the most famous painter in the USA. However, Church looked beyond his native country for subjects, travelling widely and painting, for example, the tropical forests of South America, icebergs, and exploding volcanoes, often on a huge scale. His work was immensely popular in his day, and after a period of neglect is returning to favour again. His house, Olana, on the Hudson River, is now a museum.

Churchill, Sir Winston. See AMATEUR.

Churrigueresque. Term applied to an extravagant style of architecture and ornament popular in Spain (and also Latin America) in the 18th century and sometimes used more loosely to refer to the *Rococo period as a whole in Spanish architecture. It is named after the Churriguera family of architects and sculptors, who were active mainly in Seville. The most important member of the family was José Benito de Churriguera (1665–1725), whose work is well represented by the main altarpiece (1693–1700) of the church of S. Esteban in Salamanca, an important early example of the style, full of lavishly decorated barley-sugar columns. In spite of its richness, it still retains a sense of architectural solidity, and is restrained compared with later manifestations of the style, in which surface ornament runs riot to such a degree that the underlying structure is hidden. To *Neoclassical taste the Churrigueresque style represented the last word in decadence and it died out completely in the last quarter of the 18th century.

Cibber, Caius Gabriel (*b* Flensborg, Denmark [now Flensburg, Germany], *c*.1630; *d* London, 1700). English sculptor of Danish birth. He arrived in England shortly before the Restoration in 1660, probably via Amsterdam, and worked for John Stone, son of Nicholas *Stone. When Stone died in 1667, Cibber set up on his own. His first important work was the large *relief of *Charles II Succouring the City of London* (1674) on the base of the Monument erected in memory of the Great Fire of 1666. Other works in London included the dramatic figures of *Raving* and *Melancholy Madness* (*c*.1675) for the gate of old Bedlam Hospital (now in the Bethlem Royal Hospital Mus., Beckenham). Much of his later career was taken up with decorative sculpture, notably for Sir Christopher Wren at Hampton Court and St Paul's Cathedral. With the exception of the figures of *Raving* and *Melancholy Madness*, which are powerful and original pieces, and the dignified tomb of Thomas Sackville at Withyham, Sussex (1677), Cibber's work is usually competent but uninspired; it is of interest, however, in reflecting *Baroque influence (still unusual in England at this time) from Italy (where Cibber is said to have studied early in his career) and also from the Netherlands. He was the father of Colley Cibber, the actor-manager and dramatist.

ciborium. A term applied to (i) a liturgical vessel, often chalice shaped, used for holding the consecrated Host; and (ii) an altar canopy supported on columns, popular particularly in Italy in the *Romanesque and *Gothic periods. In the second sense the word is not easily distinguished from *baldachin.

Cignani, Carlo (*b* Bologna, 15 May 1628; *d* Forlì, 6 Sept. 1719). Bolognese painter. He was a pupil of *Albani, but his style was more influenced by *Domenichino and Guido *Reni, and he became the main force in upholding the tradition of Bolognese classicism into the 18th century; his sweetness and grace also show his admiration for *Correggio. He was a slow-working perfectionist, but he employed numerous assistants in his decorative commissions. Most of his work was religious, but he also painted mythological subjects and several self-portraits. He had an international reputation and was so highly regarded by his fellow artists in Bologna that when the Accademia Clementina, the city's first municipal art academy, was founded in 1709, he was appointed director for life.

Cignaroli, Giambettino (*b* Verona, 4 July 1706; *d* Verona, 1 Dec. 1770). Italian historical, religious, and decorative painter, active mainly in and around Verona. Cignaroli was the leading artist of his period there, working in an elegantly classical style. He was also a writer; in 1749 he published a history of painting in Verona, and in 1762 a biography of his teacher Antonio Balestra (1666–1740), who had likewise upheld the classical tradition.

Cigoli, Il (Ludovico Cardi) (*b* Castello di Cigoli, nr. San Miniato, 21 Sept. 1559; *d* Rome, 8 June 1613). The outstanding Florentine painter of his generation, whose work represents the complex stylistic cross-currents in the period of transition from *Mannerism to *Baroque. He was a pupil of Alessandro *Allori, from whom he inherited the tradition of late Mannerism, but his sensuous colour and brushwork reveal the influence of *Barocci, *Correggio, and Venetian painting.

From 1604 he spent most of his time in Rome, and his dramatic handling of light shows the impact of *Caravaggio (*Ecce Homo*, 1606, Pitti, Florence). Cigoli also worked as an architect. He had scholarly inclinations and was a friend of Galileo.

Cimabue (Cenni di Peppi) (*b* c.1240; *d* Pisa, ?1302). Florentine painter. His nickname means 'Ox-head' or 'De-horner of oxen', perhaps indicating that he had an abrasive temperament. He was a contemporary of Dante, who in *The Divine Comedy* (*Purg*. xi. 94–6) describes him as an artist who was 'believed to hold the field in painting' only to be eclipsed by *Giotto's fame. This passage, meant to illustrate the brevity of earthly glory, has ironically become the basis for Cimabue's reputation; for, embroidering on this reference, later writers made him into the discoverer and teacher of Giotto and regarded him as the first in the long line of great Italian painters, the pioneer of the movement from *Byzantine stylization towards *Renaissance realism. *Vasari, for example, places Cimabue's biography at the very beginning of his *Lives* and says that he gave 'the first light to the art of painting'.

There is little solid evidence against which to test this estimate, only one surviving work being securely documented as Cimabue's, a *St John* forming part of a larger mosaic in Pisa Cathedral (1301–2). However, tradition has tended to attribute to him many works of outstanding quality from the end of the 13th century, such as the *S. Trinità Madonna* (Uffizi, Florence), a cycle of frescos in the Upper Church of S. Francesco in Assisi, and a majestic Crucifix in S. Croce, Florence (badly damaged in the Florence flood of 1966). If these highly plausible attributions are correct, Cimabue was indeed the leading master of the generation before Giotto. The movement towards greater naturalism, however, may owe more to contemporary Roman painters and mosaicists (*Cavallini, *Torriti) than to him; he is documented in Rome in 1272 and could have known their work.

Cima da Conegliano, Giovanni Battista (*b* Conegliano, ?1459/60; *bur*. Conegliano, 3 Sept. 1517 or 1518). Italian painter, named after the town of his birth and active mainly in nearby Venice, where he was one of the leading artists from about 1490 to 1510. His major works are almost all altarpieces, and he also produced numerous smaller pictures for private devotion, usually of the Virgin and Child. Nothing is known of his training, but his handsome and reflective style, which changed very little in the course of his career, was strongly influenced by Giovanni *Bellini, not least in his use of beautiful landscape settings. He has indeed been called 'the poor man's Bellini', although because of his calm and weighty figures he was also known in the 18th century (rather incongruously) as 'the Venetian *Masaccio'. In addition to his religious pictures he painted a few mythological works. Nine of his paintings are in the National Gallery, London.

cinquecento. See QUATTROCENTO.

Cione, Andrea, Nardo, and **Jacopo di.** See ORCAGNA.

Cipriani, Giovanni Battista (*b* Florence, 1727; *d* London, 14 Dec. 1785). Florentine decorative painter and designer, active mainly in England. In 1755 he was brought to London by the architect Sir William Chambers and the sculptor Joseph *Wilton, who had met him in Rome. He was employed in the decoration of many public buildings and private houses and in some cases designed such architectural details as plasterwork, woodwork, and stone carving. Good examples of his paintings are at Somerset House (where he worked for Chambers) and in the Philadelphia Museum of Art (a series originally executed for Lansdowne House, London). He was also active as a teacher at the *Royal Academy (he was a foundation member in 1768 and designed its diploma), and his numerous decorative designs (many engraved by *Bartolozzi, his friend since student days) had wide influence. Cipriani's work is accomplished rather than inspired, but he was, in the words of Ellis *Waterhouse, 'one of the great backroom figures of the *Neoclassic style in England'.

Circle. A collective manifesto of *Constructivism published in London in 1937, edited by the architect Leslie Martin (1908–2000), the painter Ben *Nicholson, and the sculptor Naum *Gabo. Subtitled 'International Survey of Constructive Art', it is nearly 300 pages long, with numerous illustrations, and was originally intended as an annual. The volume contains an editorial by Gabo entitled 'The Constructive Idea in Art', *Mondrian's essay 'Plastic Art and Pure Plastic Art', and a short statement by *Moholy-Nagy on 'Light Painting'. There are also essays or statements by, among others, *Hepworth (who took much of the responsibility for the layout and production), *Le Corbusier, *Moore, and *Read. The artists illustrated included (in addition to those already mentioned), *Malevich, *Lissitzky, Antoine *Pevsner, and many others whose work did not conform with the theoretical concept of Constructivism, including *Brancusi, *Braque, *Giacometti, and *Picasso. Dennis Farr (*English Art: 1870–1940*, 1978) writes of *Circle*: 'In the context of British art of the 1930s it not only provided the key to much that was most vital and exciting on the international front, but showed, too, there were Englishmen able to make a significant contribution to the modern movement in art and architecture.' *Circle* was reprinted in 1971.

cire-perdue (French: 'lost wax'). A method of making cast metal sculpture. In essence the technique involves producing a model of the sculpture consisting of a thin layer of wax over a heat-resistant core of clay or plaster; the wax is then covered with another heat-resistant layer, and when the wax is melted and drained off, molten metal is poured into the cavity that the 'lost wax' has created. The technique, developed independently in every continent except Australasia, was used by the Egyptians, Greeks, and Romans and is still the main means of casting used for traditional bronze sculpture. Casting sculptures of any size is an industrial process requiring great expertise, and there is a celebrated account in *Cellini's autobiography of the difficulties he encountered (and heroically overcame) with his figure of Perseus.

Cisneros, Pedro de. See BORGOÑA.

Čiurlionis, M. K. See ABSTRACT ART.

Civetta. See BLES.

Čizek, Franz. See LINOCUT.

Claesz., Pieter (*b* Burgsteinfurt, Westphalia, *c*.1597; *bur.* Haarlem, 1 Jan. 1661). Dutch still-life painter of German birth, active in Haarlem, where he had settled by 1617. He and *Heda, who also worked in Haarlem, were the most important exponents of the *ontbijt* or breakfast piece. They painted with subdued, virtually monochromatic palettes, the subtle handling of light and texture being the prime means of expression. Claesz. generally chose objects of a more homely kind than Heda, although his later work became more colourful and decorative. The two men founded a distinguished tradition of still-life painting in Haarlem, but Claesz.'s son Nicolaes *Berchem became famous as a landscape painter.

Clark, Kenneth (Lord Clark of Saltwood) (*b* London, 13 July 1903; *d* Hythe, Kent, 21 May 1983). British art historian, administrator, patron, and collector, born into a wealthy family whose fortune had been made in thread manufacturing: 'My parents belonged to a section of society known as "the idle rich", and although, in that golden age, many people were richer, there can have been few who were idler.' After working for two years as assistant to *Berenson in Florence, he was keeper of fine art at the *Ashmolean Museum in Oxford (1931–3), then director of the *National Gallery, London (1934–45), and at the same time Surveyor of the King's Pictures (1934–44). Clark also served on numerous boards and committees and was chairman of the *Arts Council (1953–60) and of the Independent Television Authority (1954–7). He published more than twenty books, his forte being appreciation and interpretation rather than exact scholarship, although his monographs on *Leonardo da Vinci (1939) and *Piero della Francesca (1951), both of which have been issued in revised editions, still remain standard works. He described his catalogue of the Leonardo drawings at Windsor Castle (1935, revised. edn. 1968–9) as 'my only claim to be considered a scholar'. His other books include The Gothic Revival (1928), Landscape into Art (1949), and The Nude (1956). He regarded The Nude as 'without question my best book, full of ideas and information, simplifying its complex subject without deformation, and in places eloquent'.

Clark was a polished television performer as well as an elegant and stimulating writer, and he did a great deal to popularize art history, most notably with his television series Civilisation (1969; also published then as a book), which was shown in over 60 countries. The part he played as a patron and collector (he inherited substantial wealth from his parents) is less well known, but was of considerable importance. He bought the work of *Moore, *Pasmore, *Piper, and *Sutherland in the 1920s and 1930s when they were little known and helped to establish their reputations (he also made a regular allowance—in strict secrecy—to several artists), and during the Second World War he had a major influence as chairman of the War Artists' Advisory Committee (see OFFICIAL WAR ART). His two volumes of autobiography—Another Part of the Wood (1974) and The Other Half (1977)—are highly entertaining, if not always accurate in detail, but some of the potboilers that appeared in his old age would have been better left unpublished.

Clark, Lygia (b Belo Horizonte, 23 Oct. 1920; d Rio de Janeiro, 26 Apr. 1988). Brazilian sculptor, painter, and experimental artist. She studied in Rio de Janeiro under Roberto Burle Marx (best known as a garden designer) and then in Paris, 1950–2, under *Léger. After her return to Brazil she became a leading figure in the country's vogue for *Concrete art. In 1959 she turned from painting to sculpture, making first reliefs and hinged pieces that could be manipulated by the spectator. She often worked with non-rigid materials such as corrugated rubber, and in 1964 she initiated 'vestiary' sculpture, designed to be worn by the spectator. In the 1970s her work became more experimental as she became concerned with *environments and 'situations'; she was a practising psychologist and particularly interested in stimulating spectator participation. Clark was one of the most internationally known of Brazilian artists; she received many awards and represented her country at the Venice *Biennale in 1960, 1962, and 1968.

Clarke, Geoffrey (b Darley Dale, Derbyshire, 28 Nov. 1924). British abstract sculptor, designer, and printmaker. His sculpture is mainly in forged, welded, and cast metal, initially iron and lead and then aluminium. Unusually for an artist working in such a modern idiom, he has devoted a good deal of his career to religious commissions, including a number of works for Coventry Cathedral (1953–62) and a pulpit (1966) in Chichester Cathedral, made of stone-faced reinforced concrete and cast aluminium. Such works have been praised for showing the potentialities of modern art in a religious setting: in Church Furnishing and Decoration in England and Wales (1980) Gerald Randall describes his high altar cross in Coventry Cathedral as 'abstract, but vividly conveying the agony and contortion of crucifixion'. Clarke's secular work includes commissions for numerous public buildings, and reliefs for the liners Canberra and Oriana. He has worked in various media other than sculpture, including enamel, mosaic, stained glass, and etching.

Clarke, Harry (b Dublin, 17 Mar. 1889; d Coire, Switzerland, 6 Jan. 1931). Irish artist, chiefly famous as one of the 20th century's greatest designers of stained glass, but also a mural painter, textile designer, and book illustrator. He had his main training at the Dublin Metropolitan School of Art, 1910–13, and scholarships then enabled him to study medieval glass in France. On his father's death in 1921 he took over his church decorating business and he had a large output in spite of his short life (he died from tuberculosis). The Harry Clarke Stained Glass Studios Ltd. continued in business until

1973. Clarke's glass was sumptuous and often rather bizarre in style—in the spirit of French *Symbolist painters. As an illustrator he had a taste for the macabre and is particularly remembered for his black-and-white drawings for an edition of Edgar Allan Poe's *Tales of Mystery and Imagination* (1923). His wife **Margaret Clarke** (née Crilley) (1888–1961), whom he married in 1914, was a painter. After Harry's death she became director of the stained-glass studios.

classicism. Term that, with the related words 'classic' and 'classical', is used in various (and often confusing) ways in the history and criticism of the arts. In its broadest sense, classicism is used as the opposite of *Romanticism, characterizing art in which adherence to recognized aesthetic ideals is accorded greater importance than individuality of expression. In this sense, *Alberti defined beauty in architecture as 'the harmony and concord of all the parts achieved by following well-founded rules and resulting in a unity such that nothing could be added or taken away or altered except for the worse'. The rules that Alberti referred to were those embodied in Greek and Roman architecture, and the word 'classicism' often implies direct inspiration from *antique art, but this is not a necessary part of the concept, and according to context the word might be intended to convey little more than the idea of clarity of expression, or alternatively of conservatism.

In the Western tradition, the term 'classical' usually does suggest a line of descent from the art of Greece and Rome, however indirect or impure, and 'classical beauty' is sometimes used to indicate a facial and bodily type reduced to mathematical symmetry about a median axis and freed from the irregularities that are normally present in living people. 'Classical architecture' is that which uses the repertoire of forms developed in Greece and Rome, as opposed to, say, the pointed arches of the *Gothic period, and the term thus covers most of European architecture from about 1500 to about 1900. In the context of Greek art, the term 'Classical' (with a capital C) has a more precise meaning, referring to the period between the *Archaic and *Hellenistic periods, when Greek culture is thought to have attained its highest peaks.

The term 'classic' is used to refer to the best or most representative example of its kind in any field or period. This is what *Wölfflin meant when he gave the title *Classic Art* to his book on the Italian High *Renaissance. Thus, in this sense, it would be legitimate, if wilfully confusing, to refer to *Delacroix as the classic Romantic artist. The three terms 'classic', 'classical', and 'classicism' are, then, often not used with discrimination or exactness, the conflation of historical term and value judgement reflecting the idea (dominant for centuries) that the art of the Greeks and Romans set a standard for all future achievement. To clear up (or perhaps add to) the confusion, the rather ungainly words 'classicistic' and 'classicizing' have also entered the lists—they convey the idea of dependence on ancient models but without any sense of qualitative judgement.

Claude (Claude Gellée) (*b* Chamagne, Lorraine, ?1604/5; *d* Rome, 23 Nov. 1682). French painter, draughtsman, and occasional etcher, active for almost all his career in Rome; he is often called Le Lorrain (in France), or Claude Lorrain(e) (in the English-speaking world), after his place of birth, but he is usually referred to simply as Claude, a familiarity reflecting his enormous fame as the most celebrated of all exponents of *ideal landscape. At an early age (probably shortly before 1620) he moved to Rome, where he is said to have initially worked as a pastry-cook (a favourite trade of Lorrainers). He then entered the household of Agostino *Tassi, progressing from domestic servant to studio assistant, and he also spent two years studying in Naples with the obscure German-born landscapist Goffredo Wals (*c*.1595–*c*.1640); he was deeply impressed by the beauty of the Gulf of Naples, memories of which recur in his paintings throughout his career.

The chronology of this early period of Claude's life is obscure, and it is not certain whether his association with Tassi began before or after his time with Wals; he is first firmly documented in Rome in 1623. In 1625 he returned to Lorraine, and collaborated with the court painter Claude *Deruet on church frescos (destroyed) in Nancy, but by 1627 he was back in Rome, where except for local journeys he remained for the rest of his life. He lived near the Piazza di Spagna, an area favoured by foreign artists in the city, and had a very settled existence, moving house only once in more than half a century's continuous residence in the city. He never married but had an illegitimate daughter (perhaps by his maid).

Claude's earliest surviving dated painting is of 1629 (*Pastoral Landscape*, Philadelphia Mus. of Art), although one or two undated pictures may precede it. In 1633 he became a member of the Accademia di S. Luca, and by this time he was already establishing himself as one of the leading landscape painters in Rome. Indeed his work soon attracted imitators, and, according to his biographer *Baldinucci, it was to guard against forgeries that he began keeping a detailed record of his paintings in what he called his *libro di verità* (book of truth); it is now known by the Latin form of the name—*Liber veritatis*. Claude began this album of drawings (which is now in the British Museum) in about 1635; it contains 195 sheets documenting virtually every picture he painted from that time until the end of his life. Each sheet has a drawn copy of the painting on the front and details about the patron on the back, and because of this, Claude's output is exceptionally well documented. By the end of the 1630s his clients included Pope Urban VIII (Maffeo *Barberini) and Philip IV of Spain (see HABSBURG) and he was unrivalled as the foremost landscape painter in Italy. He charged high prices for his work, but he was a dedicated craftsman who worked at his own pace, so he generally produced only a few pictures a year and he became moderately prosperous rather than wealthy. He lived very modestly, holding various minor offices in the Accademia di S. Luca but taking no part in public affairs; his friend *Sandrart describes him as a 'good-hearted and pious' man who 'searched for no other pleasure beside his profession'. The effects of age and illness (he suffered from gout or arthritis) caused his output to decrease (the *Liber veritatis* indicates that he completed only one picture in 1671, for example), but the quality of his work did not decline at all; indeed he produced some of his greatest paintings in the final decade of his life.

At the beginning of his career Claude belonged essentially to the northern European tradition of landscape painting, exemplified by *Bril and *Elsheimer, as well as by his teacher Wals, with its emphasis on lively, picturesque charm. Soon, however, Claude blended this with the Italian tradition of classical or ideal landscape that had been initiated by Annibale *Carracci; he retained the northern sense of richness and variety, but his compositions became much grander (although not so austere as those of Annibale or *Poussin). His early pictures are usually fairly modest in size and several of them are on copper (a material that Bril, Elsheimer, and Wals often used), but as he matured and prospered, he tended to work on a larger scale—appropriate for the palatial homes of his distinguished patrons. Similarly, the figures in his early works tend to be anonymous and dressed in contemporary costume, but from

about 1640 they are usually taken from religious or mythological stories (although unlike his friend Poussin he never tried to recreate these stories accurately). To the northern and Italian traditions Claude added something entirely his own—an extraordinary sensitivity to light that does so much to unify his pictures and create their particular moods. This sensitivity was based on loving observation of nature; Sandrart records that he would sometimes spend all day in the countryside around Rome watching the effects of light, and he made hundreds of drawings—works of great breadth and freedom—recording his impressions (many of them are in the British Museum).

During the 1640s and 1650s, when Claude's work reached a peak of classical balance, the mood of his paintings was typically one of serenity, with the cool light of morning or the warm glow of evening suggesting harmony and contentment; in his grand views of seaports—a type of picture that he made his own—he often specifically shows sunrise or sunset (*Seaport with the Embarkation of the Queen of Sheba*, 1648, NG, London). In his later years, his style became more deeply personal: his compositions are more open and less solidly constructed; forms (whether of the human figure, trees, or architecture) are strangely elongated and ethereal, colours have a magical silvery quality, and the mood is often solemn and mysterious. All these characteristics are seen in his last painting, done in the year of his death, the dreamlike *Ascanius and the Stag* (1682, Ashmolean Mus., Oxford).

Until well into the 19th century Claude's reputation as the greatest of all landscape painters was virtually unassailable. He was particularly revered in England, where the aristocracy not only collected his work avidly but even tried to make the parkland of their country estates resemble his pictures, with artfully placed clumps of trees, classical 'temples', and so on. He had a great impact on *Wilson and *Turner, and in 1836 *Constable wrote that 'He has been deemed the most perfect landscape painter the world ever saw, and he fully merits the distinction.' However, it was also in England that the first serious critical attack was made on Claude, in 1846 by *Ruskin, who considered his work artificial and lacking in invention. By 1900 his reputation had greatly declined, and it did not seriously revive until after the Second World War. See also PENDANT.

Claude glass. A small tinted mirror, with a slightly convex surface, used for reflecting landscapes in miniature so as to show their broad tonal values, without distracting detail or colour. The device is named after *Claude, who is said to have used one, and was particularly popular in the 18th century, when it was much employed by cultural travellers as well as by artists (the poet Thomas Gray is known to have had one). Its use continued into the 19th century, a notable devotee being *Corot, who regarded tonal unity in painting as supremely important.

Claudel, Camille. See RODIN.

Clausen, Sir George (b London, 18 Apr. 1852; d Cold Ash, nr. Newbury, Berkshire, 22 Nov. 1944). British painter (mainly of landscapes and scenes of rural life), the son of a decorative painter of Danish descent. His training included a few months at the *Académie Julian, Paris, in 1883 and his work was influenced by French *plein-air painting. He was particularly interested in effects of light, often showing figures set against the sun, but he always retained a sense of solidity of form. With other like-minded painters he was a founder of the *New English Art Club in 1886. From 1904 to 1906 he was professor of painting at the *Royal Academy. His lectures were published as Six Lectures on Painting (1904) and Aims and Ideals in Art (1906); a collected edition appeared as Royal Academy Lectures on Painting in 1913. In them he urged the traditional study of the Old Masters.

claw chisel (or **tooth chisel**). A chisel in which the cutting edge has sawlike serrations. It was evidently invented by the ancient Greeks and is employed mainly in marble carving as an intermediary tool between the point, used for preliminary shaping, and the flat chisel, used for the final cutting (harder stones would quickly blunt the teeth and softer stones can be worked satisfactorily with the flat chisel alone, without the need for the extra 'bite' provided by the claw). The claw is sometimes used to produce a grooved texture, and its marks can also be seen in unfinished sculptures, notably by *Michelangelo. Usually a claw chisel has four or more teeth, but examples with two and three have also been used.

clay. A sticky, fine-grained earth, composed essentially of rock dust and water, that can be moulded and cut into shape; it has been used in most civilizations for practical purposes, notably for making bricks, tiles, and pottery, and to a lesser but still significant extent in sculpture and decoration. Clay suitable for use as a modelling material is found in virtually every part of the world, in many different colours and qualities. Coloured clay is commoner than white. For sculptural purposes, lighter-coloured earths are generally preferred, as they show workmanship more clearly. Clay is worked mainly with the fingers, although many different wooden and metal implements have been employed as secondary tools. Often clay sculpture is fired in a kiln to make it more permanent; the resultant material is called *terracotta. Like *wax, clay has been used a good deal for making preparatory models but also for finished works of sculpture, usually fairly small ones, such as portrait busts (because of its comparative fragility, it has seldom been used for large pieces, although the Etruscans, for example, made impressive life-sized terracotta figures). The surface is often left in its natural state, but it can also be painted and/or glazed; Luca della *Robbia and his family made a speciality of coloured, glazed terracotta reliefs. See also BOLE.

Clement VII, Pope. See MEDICI.

Clement XIV, Pope. See VATICAN MUSEUMS.

Clemente, Francesco. See NEO-EXPRESSIONISM.

Cleophrades Painter (or **Kleophrades Painter**). Greek vase painter, active in Athens c.505–c.475 BC, one of the most distinguished masters of the *red-figure technique. He is named after a cup signed by a potter called Cleophrades (Bib. Nat., Paris). More than 100 works are attributed to him, distinguished by their expressive energy. His subjects were taken from everyday life as well as from myth. John Boardman (Athenian Red Figure Vases: The Archaic Period, 1975) writes that the Cleophrades Painter and the *Berlin Painter 'are the two greatest pot painters of the early fifth century, arguably the two greatest red figure artists whose works and careers we can judge'.

Clerck, Hendrik de (b ?Brussels, ?c.1570; bur. Brussels, 27 Aug. 1630). Flemish painter. Early in his career he visited Italy (he is documented in Rome in 1587), then settled in Brussels, where he was appointed court painter to the Archduke Ernest in 1594 and later continued in the service of his successor, the Archduke Albert. He is said to have been a pupil of the *Mannerist painter Maerten de *Vos and he carried the Mannerist tradition far into the 17th century. Much of his output consisted of altarpieces and other pictures for churches in Brussels and its neighbourhood; a characteristic example is the *Holy Kinship* (1590, Mus. Royaux, Brussels), his earliest dated work, with Italianate figures clad in restless draperies and placed in a coldly classical building. He also painted historical and mythological scenes.

Cleve, Joos and **Cornelis van.** See JOOS VAN CLEVE.

cliché-verre. See GLASS PRINT.

Clique, The. A short-lived group of young British painters, active in the late 1830s. The members, who met as students at the *Royal Academy, were Richard *Dadd, Augustus *Egg, W. P. *Frith, Henry Nelson O'Neil (1817–80), and John *Phillip. They held discussions and socialized together and were united by a dissatisfaction at the stuffy traditionalism of the Academy, but they had no particular policy. The group is not to be confused with the later *St John's Wood Clique.

Clodion (real name Claude Michel) (*b* Nancy, 20 Dec. 1738; *d* Paris, 28 Mar. 1814). French sculptor (known by the diminutive form of his first name), who created some of the most charming works of his age. The son-in-law of *Pajou and the nephew of L.-S. *Adam, he trained with the latter and briefly with *Pigalle. He produced a few large-scale works, but he excelled chiefly in small statuettes and *terracotta figures and groups. They are often of light-hearted classical subjects—nymphs and satyrs and so on—and have the wit and verve of the best *Rococo art. After the Revolution he changed his style completely to suit the sterner *Neoclassical taste; his later work included carvings on the Arc de Triomphe du Carrousel (1806–9) in Paris, which was built to commemorate Napoleon's victories.

Cloisonnism. Style of painting associated with some of the painters who worked at *Pont-Aven at Brittany in the 1880s and 1890s, characterized by dark outlines enclosing areas of bright, flat colour, in the manner of stained glass or cloisonné enamel (*cloison* is French for 'partition'). *Anquetin and *Bernard first developed the style, and *Gauguin also worked in it. The term was coined by the critic Édouard Dujardin in 1888.

Cloisters, the. See METROPOLITAN MUSEUM OF ART.

Close, Chuck (*b* Monroe, Wash., 5 July 1940). American painter. His early work was *Abstract Expressionist, but he soon turned to *Superrealism, becoming well known for huge portrait heads (mainly of friends), seen frontally like gigantic passport photographs—his self-portrait (1968) in the Walker Art Center, Minneapolis, is almost 3 m (9 ft) high. Originally he worked in black and white, but in about 1970 he turned to colour. He works from photographs, dividing them into a grid and then transferring the grid to the canvas. In some of his later work he has deliberately emphasized the grid, creating 'low-resolution' images resembling a computer scan or a face seen through frosted glass. In 1988 Close was partly paralysed following an injury to a spinal blood vessel, but he resumed painting with the aid of a brace support on his wrist.

Clouet, Jean (*d* Paris, 1540/1). French painter of Netherlandish descent. He was celebrated in his lifetime, but no documented works survive. A handful of portraits, however, including *Man Holding Petrarch's Works* (Royal Coll., Windsor), and a number of drawings (mainly in the Musée Condé, Chantilly) are attributed to him on fairly strong circumstantial evidence. The paintings belong to the tradition of Netherlandish *naturalism that dominated French portraiture at this time, but the drawings are more personal and often of very high quality. They have been compared to those of Clouet's contemporary Hans *Holbein the Younger, with which they share a keenness of observation; whereas Holbein's drawings are overwhelmingly linear, however, Clouet's are subtly modelled in light and shade with a delicate system of *hatching that recalls *Leonardo, whose work he could well have known.

Jean's son **François** (*b* ?Tours, *c*.1510; *d* Paris, 22 Sept. 1572) succeeded him as court painter in 1541. His work is somewhat better documented than his father's, but his career is still fairly obscure (they were known by the same nickname, Janet, which has caused much confusion, and one of the finest works attributed to him, the celebrated portrait of Francis I in the Louvre, showing the king in a lavish gold doublet, has also been given to Jean). François, too, was mainly a portraitist, his signed works including *Pierre Quthe* (1562, Louvre, Paris), much more Italianate than any of his father's paintings, and *Lady in her Bath* (*c*.1570, NG, Washington). This mysterious and captivating work has been traditionally identified as representing Diane de Poitiers, mistress of Henry II, but it is more probably a likeness of Marie Touchet, mistress of

Charles IX. A number of drawings, mostly in the Musée Condé, are also attributed to François.

Clovio, Giulio (*b* Grisone [Grizane], *c*.1498; *d* Rome, 3 Jan. 1578). Italian *illuminator and painter, born in Croatia, which at this time was part of Venetian territory. He moved to Italy in 1516 and spent most of his career in Rome, although he also worked in several other cities. Clovio was the outstanding Italian illuminator of the 16th century and enjoyed a very high contemporary reputation—his friend *Vasari described him as a '*Michelangelo of small works'. His illuminations do indeed make frequent use of motifs from the work of Michelangelo and *Raphael, adapting the fashionable *Mannerist style to a miniature scale. From 1540 he worked mainly for Cardinal Alessandro *Farnese, to whom he recommended the young El *Greco. El Greco painted Clovio's portrait (*c*.1570, Mus. di Capodimonte, Naples), showing him holding the Farnese Hours (*c*.1546, Pierpont Morgan Lib., New York), the manuscript that is generally regarded as his masterpiece. In addition to illuminations, he sometimes painted small independent pictures (*Pietà*, 1551, Uffizi, Florence).

clunch. A generic name for harder types of chalk or soft *limestones, varying in colour from white to greenish-grey. Clunch has occasionally been used as a building stone, but is more suitable for interior carved work and sculpture, for which purposes it was much used in England in the late Middle Ages. It is very light in weight and Alec Clifton-Taylor (*The Pattern of English Building*, 1972) writes that it 'could be worked with such facility that it offered an almost irresistible temptation to the carvers to be over-elaborate and finicky'. An example of such virtuoso carving is Bishop Alcock's Chapel (1488–1500) in Ely Cathedral.

Coade stone. An artificial stone manufactured in London in the late 18th and early 19th centuries, used for figure sculpture, monuments, architectural dressings, and decorative work. Essentially a type of clay, fired in a kiln at high temperature, it was named after Eleanor Coade (1733–1821), who set up in business in Lambeth in 1769. She claimed that it resisted frost and therefore retained sharpness of outline better than natural stone, and time has proved her right. It was mixed into a kind of paste and formed into the required shape with moulds, meaning that popular designs could be more or less mass produced. Usually it was a pale cream colour, but through the use of various additives it could be made greyer, pinker, or almost white. The business was an immediate success; Robert Adam was one of the notable architects who used the material and several good sculptors, particularly John *Bacon the Elder, worked for the firm. Monuments made of Coade stone exist in many English churches, and some garden sculpture remains. Mrs Coade's successor in the business, her distant relative William Croggon, died bankrupt in 1835 and Coade stone soon vanished from the market.

Coates, Robert. See ABSTRACT EXPRESSIONISM.

Cobra. A group of *Expressionist painters formed in Paris in 1948 by a number of Netherlandish and Scandinavian artists. The name derived from the first letters of the capital cities of the three countries of the artists involved—Copenhagen, Brussels, and Amsterdam. The Dutchman Karel *Appel, the Belgian *Corneille, and the Dane Asger *Jorn were the leading figures among the founders. Those who joined later included Pierre *Alechinsky and the Scottish painter William Gear (1915–97). The Belgian writer and painter Christian Dotrement (1922–79), who suggested the name, was the group's main spokesman. The aim of the Cobra painters was to exploit free expression of the unconscious, unimpeded and undirected by the intellect. In their emphasis on spontaneous gesture, they had affinities with the American *Action Painters, but they differed in their strange and fantastic imagery, related in some cases to Nordic mythology and folklore, in others to various magical or mystical symbols of the unconscious. Their approach was similar to the exponents of *Art Informel, but was more savage and vigorously expressive. The group arranged Cobra exhibitions at Copenhagen (1948), Amsterdam (1949), and Liège (1951), before disbanding in 1951.

Cochin, Charles-Nicolas the Younger (*b* Paris, 22 Feb. 1715; *d* Paris, 29 Apr. 1790). French engraver, trained by his father **Charles-Nicolas the Elder** (1688–1754). He was one of the outstanding French engravers of the 18th century, and his huge output forms an invaluable record of contemporary society, particularly life at the court of Louis XV, whose personal favour he enjoyed. However, he is now just as well known for his other roles in the art world. He wrote a good deal, notably the first biography of *Chardin (the account was written in 1780, the year after Chardin's death, but it was not published until 1875–6), and he played a key role in art administration as secretary of the Académie Royale (see ACADEMY) from 1755. In his writings he tried to educate the public, for example by denouncing the excesses of the *Rococo style, and his friend *Diderot often sought his advice when writing his own *Salon reviews.

Cock, Jan Wellens de (*d* Antwerp, *c.*1526). Netherlandish painter, perhaps to be identified with a 'Jan van Leyden' who became a master in the Antwerp painters' guild in 1503. He is a shadowy figure and the reconstruction of his oeuvre is controversial, but he is noteworthy as one of the earliest followers of *Bosch, his penchant seemingly being small pictures of hermits and saints in weird landscapes. He had two artist sons, **Matthys** (*c.*1509–*c.*1548) and **Hieronymus** or Jerome (*c.*1510–70), both of whom worked in Antwerp. Matthys was renowned in his day as a landscapist and is mentioned by *Vasari as well as van *Mander, but little is known for certain of his work. Jerome was an etcher and the leading print publisher of his time in northern Europe; his business was called 'Aux Quatre Vents' (At the Sign of the Four Winds). Pieter *Bruegel was much employed by Cock in the earlier part of his career, when he excelled at prints in the tradition of Bosch.

Cockerell, Sir Sydney. See FITZWILLIAM MUSEUM.

Cocteau, Jean (*b* Maisons-Laffitte, nr. Paris, 5 July 1889; *d* Milly-la-Forêt, nr. Fontainebleau, 11 Oct. 1963). French writer, film director, designer, painter, and draughtsman. One of the most dazzling figures of his time in the intellectual avant-garde, he was the friend of leading painters such as *Modigliani and *Picasso, and in his work for the theatre he collaborated with, for example, *Diaghilev and the composers Erik Satie and Igor Stravinsky. His work included poetry, novels, plays, films, and a large amount of paintings, drawings, theatrical designs, and pottery articles. He was self-taught in the visual arts. In his painting and drawing he was much influenced by Picasso, and his favourite themes included the figures of Harlequin, embodying the theatre, and Orpheus, the personification of the poet. His most lasting achievement was in the cinema, his reputation resting mainly on his beautiful adaptation of the famous story of Beauty and the Beast (*La Belle et la Bête*, 1946; with design by Christian *Bérard), and on three films dealing with the role of the artist and the

nature of his inspiration—Cocteau's recurrent preoccupation—*Le Sang d'un poète* (1930), *Orphée* (1950), and *Testament d'Orphée* (1960). There is a Cocteau museum at Menton on the Côte d'Azur; in discussing it Michael Jacobs and Paul Stirton comment that 'It is unlikely that Cocteau would have achieved any reputation at all as an artist had he not been so talented in other fields; his strongly linear works seem made to reflect all that was sentimental and slapdash in the art of his friend Picasso' (*The Mitchell Beazley Traveller's Guides to Art: France*, 1984).

Codazzi, Viviano. See LAER.

Codde, Pieter (*bapt.* Amsterdam, 11 Dec. 1599; *bur.* Amsterdam, 12 Oct. 1678). Dutch *genre and portrait painter, active in Amsterdam. His genre pictures are mainly scenes of fashionable life (with ladies and cavaliers drinking or making music) or of military life (typically soldiers in guardrooms or plundering). His best works, marked by subtle silvery-grey tonalities, are usually fairly small, but he achieved one memorable feat on a much larger scale. In 1637 he was called upon to finish the group portrait of the Amsterdam civic guards known as the *Meagre Company* (Rijksmuseum, Amsterdam) that Frans *Hals began in 1633 and refused to finish because he would not come to Amsterdam for sittings, and Codde succeeded so well in capturing Hals's spirit and the touch of his brush that experts still disagree where the work of the one ends and the other begins. Codde also wrote poetry.

Codex Egberti. See OTTONIAN ART.

Coecke van Aelst, Pieter (*b* Aelst, 14 Aug. 1502; *d* Brussels, 6 Dec. 1550). Netherlandish painter, architect, sculptor, designer of tapestries and stained glass, writer, and publisher. He was probably a pupil of Bernard van *Orley in Brussels, but he was active mainly in Antwerp, where he became a member of the painters' guild in 1527. Some time before then he had probably been to Rome and in 1533–4 he visited Constantinople. His mission to gain business there for the Brussels tapestry works was unsuccessful, but the drawings he made on his journey were later published by his widow, the painter **Mayken Verhulst** (*c.*1520–1600), as woodcut illustrations in *Les Mœurs et fachons de faire des Turcz* (The Manners and Customs of the Turks, 1553). He ran a large workshop and was regarded as one of the leading Antwerp painters of his day, but his work is fairly run-of-the-mill and he is generally more important for his publishing activities. Like his paintings, his books are saturated in Italian influence, and the translation that he and his widow issued of the architectural treatise of Sebastiano Serlio (1549–53) played a large part in spreading *Renaissance ideas in the Netherlands (it was from his edition, too, rather than from the Italian original, that the English translation of 1611 was made). Pieter *Bruegel the Elder was his son-in-law and, according to van *Mander, his pupil, but there is no trace of Coecke's influence in his work. Coecke van Aelst is not to be confused with Pieter van Aelst (see BRUSSELS TAPESTRIES).

Coello, Alonso Sánchez. See SÁNCHEZ COELLO.

Coello, Claudio (b Madrid, 2 Mar. 1642; d Madrid, 20 Apr. 1693). Spanish painter, the last important master of the Madrid School of the 17th century. He was primarily a religious painter, but he also produced portraits. His masterpiece, *Charles II Adoring the Host* (1685–90), a huge canvas in the sacristy of the *Escorial, combines a mystical religious subject with realistic portraiture and is an outstanding example of *Baroque *illusionism, mirroring the architecture of the building in which it hangs. He had other noteworthy successes, particularly in work he carried out for Toledo Cathedral, but he died a disappointed man because he was passed over in favour of the Italian Luca *Giordano for the commission to carry out a huge programme of decoration at the Escorial. Coello had travelled to Italy as a young man and also studied the work of *Titian in the royal collection, and his skill as a colourist and painterly brushwork reflect the influence of the great Venetian masters.

Coene, Jacques. See BOUCICAUT MASTER.

Cohen, Bernard and **Harold.** See SITUATION.

Colantonio, Niccolò. See ANTONELLA.

Coldstream, Sir William (b Belford, Northumberland, 28 Feb. 1908; d London, 18 Feb. 1987). British painter, mainly of portraits, but also of landscape and still-life. He studied at the *Slade School, 1926–9, and worked on documentary films for the GPO, 1934–7. In 1937 he was one of the founders of the *Euston Road School, which helped to establish a tradition of sober figurative painting of which he was one of the main representatives. In 1939 he joined the Royal Artillery and in 1943–5 he was an *Official War Artist, working in the Near East and then Italy. After the war he taught at Camberwell School of Art, 1945–9, then was professor at the Slade School, 1949–75. He exerted an important influence not only through his teaching but also through his appointment as chairman of the National Advisory Council on Art Education in 1959. The Coldstream Report of 1960 helped to change the structure of art school teaching in Britain, introducing the compulsory study of art history for art students and eventually leading to degree status being awarded to recognized art school courses. Coldstream's own work was typically austerely naturalistic: 'I find I lose interest unless I let myself be ruled by what I see.' Kenneth *Clark had been an early supporter, but he came to see Coldstream's attitude to art as one of 'dismal rectitude'.

Cole, Sir Henry. See GREAT EXHIBITION and VICTORIA AND ALBERT MUSEUM.

Cole, Thomas (b Bolton, Lancashire, 1 Feb. 1801; d Catskill, NY, 8 Feb. 1848). The outstanding American landscape painter of the first half of the 19th century, a founder of the *Hudson River School. His family emigrated to America from England in 1818 and he became passionately devoted to the natural scenery of his new country. He studied at the Pennsylvania Academy of the Fine Arts in Philadelphia, 1823–5, then moved to New York, where he was an immediate success, his work being bought by *Dunlap, *Durand, and *Trumbull. He soon began making sketching trips in the Hudson River Valley, and he settled there, in the village of Catskill, in 1836. In 1829–32 he visited Europe, and it was partly the influence of *Turner and John *Martin that encouraged him to turn from the depiction of natural scenery towards grandiose historical and allegorical themes, notably in two great series of paintings: *The Course of Empire* (1836, New-York Historical Society) and *The Voyage of Life* (1839–40, Munson-Williams-Proctor Inst., Utica). He visited Europe again in 1841–2, and after this he was increasingly attracted to religious subjects.

collage. A term applied to a type of picture (and also to the technique used in creating such pictures) in which photographs, news cuttings, and other suitable objects are pasted onto a flat surface, often in combination with painted passages (the word comes from the French *coller*, 'to gum'). Long popular as a leisure-time occupation for children and amateurs (in scrapbooks for example), it first became an acknowledged artistic technique in the early 20th century, when it drew much of its material from the proliferation of mass-produced images in newspapers, advertisements, cheap popular illustrations, etc. The

*Cubists were the first to make collage a systematic and important part of their work. Picasso began using the technique in 1912, one of the earliest examples being *Still-Life with Chair Caning* (Mus. Picasso, Paris, 1912), in which the caning is represented by a piece of oilcloth printed with a lattice pattern. Braque soon followed with his own distinctive type of collage, the *papier collé*, in which he applied strips or fragments of paper to a painting or drawing. Picasso also extended the principle of collage to three dimensions, making sculptures from scrap materials that influenced *Tatlin's creation of *Constructivism and stand at the beginning of the tradition of *assemblage. Subsequently collage has been used in many major art movements, for example *Dada, *Surrealism, and *Pop art. For some artists—notably Kurt *Schwitters—it has been the central concern of their work, and others have created personal versions of it. Examples are Max *Ernst, with his 'collage novels', and *Matisse with his late *gouaches découpées* (paper cut-outs). See also MONTAGE and PHOTOMONTAGE.

Collins, Cecil (*b* Plymouth, 23 Mar. 1908; *d* London, 4 June 1989). British painter of visionary subjects. He had a mystical outlook and was influenced by the prophetic writings of William *Blake and by the American artist Mark *Tobey, who introduced him to the Baha'i religion and to the culture of the Far East. In 1947 Collins published his book *The Vision of the Fool*, in which he explains his philosophy of art and life. He attacks the 'great spiritual betrayal' of the modern world, 'the betrayal of the love and worship of life by the dominance of the scientific technical view of life in practically all the fields of human experience'. The artist, together with the poet and the saint, 'is the vehicle of the continuity of that life, and its guardian, and his instrument is the myth, and the archetypal image'. His own archetypal image was the Fool, who represented purity and spontaneity in contrast to modern commercialism and materialism. In 1940 he began a long series of paintings and drawings, originally entitled 'The Holy Fool' but later renamed 'The Vision of the Fool' in accordance with the title of his book; *The Sleeping Fool* (1943, Tate, London) is an example. Some recent writing on Collins has come close to hagiography, but he also has detractors who find his reputation overblown.

Collins, William (*b* London, 18 Sept. 1788; *d* London, 17 Feb. 1847). English painter. He was initially taught by *Morland (of whom his father, a picture dealer, wrote a biography) and specialized in sentimental rustic landscapes and *genre scenes that won him great popularity; he also painted portraits. As with Morland, his work became very repetitive. He was a lifelong friend of *Wilkie, after whom he named his elder son, the novelist Wilkie Collins, who published a biography of his father in 1848. His second son was **Charles Allston Collins** (*b* Hampstead [now in London], 25 Jan. 1828; *d* London, 9 Apr. 1873), whose middle name was a reference to another distinguished artist friend of his father's, Washington *Allston. Charles was a contemporary of *Hunt, *Millais, and *Rossetti at the *Royal Academy Schools and was closely associated with the *Pre-Raphaelites, although he was never a formal member of the Brotherhood. His best-known picture is *Convent Thoughts* (1851, Ashmolean Mus., Oxford), which *Ruskin rated highly because of its fastidious botanical detail. Tall and handsome but dismally lacking in self-confidence and plagued by emotional problems, Collins abandoned painting in 1858 and took up writing, publishing three novels among other works. In 1860 he married Charles Dickens's younger daughter Kate; there were no children of the marriage and it was rumoured that Collins was impotent. He died of stomach cancer.

Collinson, James (*b* Mansfield, Nottinghamshire, 9 May 1825; *d* London, 24 Jan. 1881). English painter. He was one of the original members of the *Pre-Raphaelite Brotherhood in 1848, but he left it in 1850 because he felt it was incompatible with his Roman Catholic faith and in 1852 began training to be a Roman Catholic priest. Another change of heart followed, and in 1854 he returned to painting, specializing in pretty and sentimental *genre scenes, the best known of which is *The Empty Purse* of 1857 (versions in Tate, London, and Graves AG, Sheffield). He is probably the least known of the PRB and the most remarkable talent he showed at their meetings was his ability to fall asleep at any time.

Colman, Samuel (*b* 1780; *d* London, 21 Jan. 1845). English painter, active for most of his known career in Bristol, 1816–38. Local directories of the time describe him as a portrait painter and drawing master, but he is now known for a small number of grandiose apocalyptic scenes in the manner of Francis *Danby (likewise active in Bristol) or John *Martin. Until recently he was so obscure that when one of these paintings, *The Edge of Doom* (1836–8), was acquired by the

Brooklyn Museum, New York, in 1969, it was thought to be by an unrelated American namesake, **Samuel Colman** (1832–1920), a painter of the *Hudson River School.

Colnaghi's (P. & D. Colnaghi & Co. Ltd.), London. Firm of art dealers, said to be the oldest in the world. It takes its name from the Italian-born printseller **Paul Colnaghi** (1751–1833), although it traces its ancestory back to 1760. Colnaghi began his career in Paris and moved to London in 1785, becoming naturalized a few years later. In 1805 his son **Dominic Colnaghi** (1790–1879) became his partner and the firm was officially named P. & D. Colnaghi. Dominic's nephew **Martin Colnaghi** (1821–1908) also worked for the firm for a while, although he was never a partner and eventually set up on his own account. He bequeathed several pictures and a large amount of money to the National Gallery. The family firm moved to its present location in New Bond Street in 1911 (for most of the 19th century it had been based in Pall Mall) and it adopted its present name in 1937. By this time it was one of the world's most prestigious dealers in Old Master paintings and drawings, a position it still maintains.

Cologne School. Term applied to painting produced in Cologne from the late 14th century to the early 16th century. There was not, as the term might imply, a specifically local style at this time, but in the early 19th century, when roman-tically inclined collectors began to look for old German pictures, it so happened that many of their panels came from the Cologne region, and the city, with its huge unfinished *Gothic cathedral, became a symbol for the spirit of the Middle Ages. The alleged founder of the 'School', Master Wilhelm, is a semi-legendary figure and no pictures can be attributed to him with certainty. During the first quarter of the 15th century painting in Cologne had all the characteristics of the lyrical 'soft style', that is of *International Gothic. This style may have been perpetuated by guild rules and guild super-vision; in any case it was still employed by *Lochner in the middle of the 15th century. A little later, Netherlandish naturalism was influ-ential on artists in Cologne. The great Flemish centres are not far away, and one of Rogier van der *Weyden's principal works (the Columba Altarpiece, now in the Alte Pinakothek, Munich) was in Cologne from probably about 1460. Of many anonymous painters of the time, the *Master of the Life of the Virgin is perhaps the most attractive.

Colombe, Michel (*b* ?Bourges, *c.*1430; *d* Tours, ?1514). French sculptor. He had a great name in his day, but only two works that are certainly by him survive, both from late in his life. They are: the tomb of Francis II of Brittany and Marguerite de Foix (1502–7, Nantes Cathedral), done in col-laboration with Jean *Perréal and Girolamo da Fiesole, an Italian sculptor working in France; and a relief of *St George and the Dragon* (1508–9, Louvre, Paris), done for an altarpiece for the chapel of the Château de Gaillon. The altarpiece too was a work of collaboration, for the frame was carved by Jérôme Pacherot, another Italian expatriate (he was perhaps originally called Girolamo Pacchiarotti). Colombe's fame rests mainly on the *St George*, for it is a captivating work, blending the fantasy of the French *Gothic style with elements of the Italianate *Renaissance taste that was coming into vogue in southern France at this time, yet without copying particular Italian models. His brother **Jean Colombe** (*d c.*1495) was a manuscript illu-minator; his work included the completion of the *Très Riches Heures* of the *Limbourg broth-ers.

Colonna, Gerolamo Mengozzi. See QUADRATURA and TIEPOLO.

colore. See DISEGNO.

Colossus of Rhodes. A huge bronze statue of Helios the sun god, regarded as one of the Seven Wonders of the World. It stood beside (not astride as it is shown in some reconstruc-tions) the harbour at Rhodes and commemor-ated the city's successful defence against a siege in 305–304 BC; it was financed by the sale of equipment and stores left behind by the enemy. There was an enormous siege engine among the equipment, and this may have suggested the *Colossus* or been used in its construction. The sculptor was Chares of Lindos, a pupil of *Lysippus, and the statue was finished in about 280 BC after twelve years' work. In about 225 BC it collapsed in an earthquake, but the fallen figure remained until AD 653, when it was broken up by Arab raiders and sold as scrap. According to *Pliny, it had stood 70 cubits (32 m; 105 ft) high, and 'even lying on the ground it is a marvel. Few people can get their arms around its thumb, and the fingers are larger than most statues.' There are many other references to the *Colossus* in ancient sources, but no accurate visual records survive.

Colour Field Painting. A type of abstract painting in which the whole picture consists of large expanses of more or less unmodulated colour, with no strong contrasts of tone or obvious focus of attention. Some Colour Field Paintings use only one colour; others use several that are similar in tone and intensity. This type of painting developed in the USA in the late 1940s and early 1950s, leading pioneers including Barnett *Newman and Mark *Rothko. It is thus an aspect of *Abstract Expressionism and it has also been seen as a type—or precursor—of *Minimal art. From 1952 Helen *Frankenthaler developed Colour Field Painting by soaking or staining diluted paint into unprimed canvas, so that the paint is integral with the surface rather than superimposed on it. The term **Colour Stain Painting** is applied to works of this type.

Colquhoun, Robert (*b* Kilmarnock, 20 Dec. 1914; *d* London, 20 Sept. 1962). British painter, graphic artist, and designer. In 1933–8 he studied at *Glasgow School of Art, where he became the inseparable companion of his fellow student Robert MacBryde (*b* Maybole, Ayrshire, 5 Dec. 1913; *d* Dublin, 6 May 1966). They settled in London in 1941. During the war Colquhoun was an ambulance driver in the Civil Defence Corps by day and painted by night (MacBryde was exempt from military service because of tuberculosis). Within a few years the studio of the Roberts (as they were generally known) at 77 Bedford Gardens, Campden Hill, had become a centre for a group of young artists and writers, among them Keith *Vaughan. The Polish immigrant Jankel *Adler took a studio in the same building in 1942 and was an important influence on Colquhoun. Following a successful one-man show in 1943 he developed a reputation as one of the outstanding British painters of his generation; his characteristic angular figure compositions owed something to *Cubism, but had an expressive life of their own. After he and MacBryde were evicted from their studio in 1947, however, his fortunes began to decline and he died (of a heart attack) in relative obscurity. The Roberts had always been fond of the bottle, and after Colquhoun's death, MacBryde drank more than ever and led an aimless existence; he died after being knocked over by a car. Apart from painting, both Colquhoun and MacBryde produced many lithographs and worked together on stage designs. Although he has been overshadowed by his more imaginative and forceful partner, some critics maintain that MacBryde had a better sense of colour than Colquhoun.

Colt (or **Coulte**), **Maximilian** (*b* Arras; *d* ?*c*.1650). French-born sculptor who settled in London *c*.1595 (probably as a Huguenot refugee), Anglicized his surname from Poultrain, and became an English citizen in 1607. His career 'began with great promise, and then dwindled, apparently, almost to nothing' (Margaret Whinney, *Sculpture in Britain: 1530–1830*, 1964). In 1605–6 he made the tomb of Queen Elizabeth I in Westminster Abbey, a splendid example of a conventional type. Much more original is his tomb of Robert Cecil, 1st Earl of Salisbury (*c*.1612–18), at Hatfield, in which the effigy lies on a black marble bier carried on the shoulders of four solemn and beautifully cut kneeling Virtues. Before this Colt had carried out much work at Hatfield House for Cecil, including two magnificent fireplaces. In 1608 James I appointed Colt his master sculptor, an office he continued holding under Charles I. However, his art, excellent as it was by Jacobean standards, was too conservative for Charles, from whom he received only minor commissions. Very little is known about Colt's later life. He was evidently still alive in about 1645 but dead by the Restoration in 1660.

Column of Marcus Aurelius. See TRAJAN'S COLUMN.

Colville, Alexander (*b* Toronto, 24 Aug. 1920). Canadian painter. He was an *Official War Artist during the Second World War, then taught until 1963, when he was able to devote himself full-time to painting. He is regarded as a leading exponent of *Magic Realism, his work showing a remarkable ability to infuse a sense of haunting mystery into mundane situations (*Couple on a Beach*, NG, Ottawa, 1957). Less typical work by Colville has included a mural, *History of Mount Allison* (1948), for Mount Allison University, Sackville (where he studied and taught), and the designs for the special issues of Canadian coinage commemorating the centenary of Confederation (1967).

combine painting. A term coined by Robert *Rauschenberg for a type of work he invented in the early 1950s—a very radical form of *collage—in which a painted surface is 'combined' with various real objects, or sometimes photographic images, attached to it. The most famous example is *Monogram* (1955–9, Moderna Museet, Stockholm), featuring a stuffed goat with a tyre around its middle.

Comontes, Antonio de. See BORGOÑA.

Conca, Sebastiano (*b* Gaeta, 8 Jan. 1680; *d* Naples, 1 Sept. 1764). Italian painter. He was a pupil of *Solimena in Naples, then in about 1706 moved to Rome, where he became one of the leading decorative painters during the first half of the 18th century, developing an elegant *Rococo style out of the High *Baroque tradition. There are examples of his altarpieces and frescos in several churches in Rome, the *Coronation of St Cecilia* (1721–4) on the ceiling of the nave of S. Cecilia in Trastevere often being cited as his masterpiece. He also produced pictures of historical and mythological subjects for private collectors. In about 1752 Conca returned to Naples, where he remained active until almost the end of his long life.

Conceptual art. A type of art in which the idea or ideas that a work represents are considered its essential component and the finished 'product', if it exists at all, is regarded primarily as a form of documentation rather than as an artefact. Its origins go back to Marcel *Duchamp, but it was not until the later 1960s that Conceptual art became a recognizable movement and acquired its name. It flourished most vigorously in the early 1970s, becoming an international phenomenon and often overlapping with other art forms and movements that were fashionable at this time, notably *Arte Povera, *Body art, *Land art, and *Performance art. These have all been seen as aspects of the reaction against the *formalism and commercialism of *Minimal art. However, Conceptual art has proved just as susceptible to commercial exploitation as other forms of avant-garde expression, with dealers selling the documentation of Conceptual works to collectors and museums. Such documentation takes varied forms, including photographs, sound and video cassettes, texts, maps, diagrams, and sets of instructions, but some Conceptual works do not have any physicality at all, an example being *Telepathic Piece* (1969) by the American artist Robert Barry (1936–), consisting of a statement that 'during the exhibition I will try to communicate telepathically a work of art, the nature of which is a series of thoughts that are not applicable to language or image'. His other activities have included releasing small quantities of inert gases into the atmosphere and taking photographs of their dispersal (which is completely invisible). He writes that 'The world is full of objects, more or less interesting; I do not wish to add any more. I prefer, simply, to state the existence of things in terms of time and/or space.' Although some Conceptual art purports to deal with serious political issues, much of it is

concerned with deliberately abstruse analysis of language or with the kind of eccentric private concerns shown by Barry. Exponents and admirers of Conceptual art see such activities as posing questions about the nature of art and provocatively expanding its boundaries. Robert *Morris, for example, wrote in 1970 that 'The detachment of art's energy from the craft of tedious object production . . . refocuses art as an energy driving to change perception.' To the uninitiated or the sceptical, however, Conceptual art is as pointless as it is pretentious; in 1972 Keith *Vaughan wrote that 'the term is a contradiction in itself, art being the realization of concepts, not just having them'. The initial wave of enthusiasm for Conceptual art was over by the mid-1970s, but there was a substantial revival of interest in it in the mid-1980s (for example in the work of some of the exponents of *Neo-Geo). The term 'Neo-Conceptual' is sometimes applied to this revival.

Concrete art. Term applied to abstract art that is intended to be totally autonomous, repudiating all figurative references and symbolic associations. The name was coined by Theo van *Doesburg, who in Paris in 1930 issued a manifesto called *Art Concret* (it took the form of the first number of a periodical with this title, but no other numbers were issued). Although Concrete art is typically severely geometrical, it is not necessarily so; for example, the sculpture of Max *Bill (an artist particularly associated with Concrete art) often uses graceful spiral or helix shapes.

Conder, Charles (*b* London, 24 Oct. 1868; *d* Virginia Water, Surrey, 9 Feb. 1909). English painter, a direct descendant of the sculptor *Roubiliac. He lived in Australia from 1884 to 1890, then moved to Paris, where he studied at the *Académie Julian and became friendly with several leading avant-garde artists, notably *Toulouse-Lautrec, whose notoriously dissipated lifestyle he shared. In 1897 he settled in London. His work, which is often tinged with a feeling of *fin-de-siècle* decadence, was included in numerous exhibitions and he became a well-known figure in the art world, but he fell seriously ill in 1906—a result of his debauched life—and stopped painting. He is best known for landscapes, Arcadian fantasies, and designs for fans; he also painted portraits and made a few lithographs and etchings. He was influenced by *Whistler, but William *Rothenstein commented that 'Whistler never liked Conder and didn't care for his work . . . He probably thought him too involved with his ladies of Montmartre, too fond of his absinthe.'

Condivi, Ascanio (*b* Ripatransone, nr. San Benedetto, 1525; *d* nr. Ripatransone, 10 Dec. 1574). Italian painter, sculptor, and writer, a pupil and friend of *Michelangelo. He was an insignificant artist and his only claim to fame is his *Life of Michelangelo*, published in Rome in 1553. Three years earlier the first edition of Giorgio *Vasari's *Lives* had appeared, and Michelangelo seems to have taken exception to some of the statements made there. Condivi's *Life* was meant as a corrective, and he writes not only from intimate personal knowledge, but obviously at times almost at dictation from the master. Johannes *Wilde (*Michelangelo*, 1978) considers that Condivi was a 'simpleton' who could not have composed 'such an eminently readable book' unaided, and thinks that Annibale Caro (1507–66), a humanist man of letters, was probably the ghost writer. One of Condivi's few extant works is a painting of the *Holy Family* (also called 'Epifania') in the Casa Buonarroti, Florence, done from a cartoon by Michelangelo in the British Museum, London; Wilde says it 'shows an appalling degree of incompetence'.

Coninxloo, Gillis van (*b* Antwerp, 24 Jan. 1544; *bur.* Amsterdam, 4 Jan. 1607). The outstanding member of a large and prolific family of Netherlandish painters, many of whom are not clearly distinguishable personalities. He left his native Antwerp after it was captured by the Spanish in 1585, and like other Protestant refugees he fled to Holland. In 1587 he moved to Frankenthal (near Frankfurt) in Germany, where he became the most important figure among a small group of Netherlandish landscape painters, now known as the Frankenthal School. In 1595 he settled permanently in Amsterdam. Coninxloo's early landscapes are panoramic views of vast valleys and great mountain ranges populated by biblical or mythological figures, in the tradition of *Bruegel. In later works, such as the majestic *Forest* (c.1600, KH Mus., Vienna), his field of vision is narrower and he concentrates on the mood evoked by luxuriant nature. Van *Mander described Coninxloo as 'the best landscape painter of his time' and said 'his style is now frequently imitated in Holland'. He was indeed a major figure in the transition from the *Mannerist landscape tradition to the much more realistic idiom characteristic of 17th-century Dutch painters. His younger countrymen Roelandt *Savery and David *Vinckboons, who had come to Holland at about the same

time as Coninxloo, were influenced by his late works, and his pupils included Hercules *Segers and Esaias van de *Velde.

Conroy, Stephen. See GLASGOW SCHOOL OF ART.

Constable, John (*b* East Bergholt, Suffolk, 11 June 1776; *d* Hampstead [now in London], 31 Mar. 1837). English painter, ranked with his contemporary *Turner as one of the two greatest figures in the history of British landscape painting. Both of them brought a new freedom and inventiveness to their subject and they had a good deal of mutual respect. However, their temperaments and goals differed greatly and their careers were strongly contrasting. Whereas Turner was precocious and soon achieved critical and financial success, Constable was slow to mature and had difficulty in making a name in England (he was more appreciated in France).

He was the son of a prosperous corn merchant and was trained for a career in the family business. However, his passion for art was so strong that in 1799 his father reluctantly allowed him to become a student at the *Royal Academy Schools in London. He continued studying there until 1802, and during this time he also had informal tuition from his friend Sir George *Beaumont (whom he first met in 1796). However, he learnt most by copying the work of great landscape masters of the past, so essentially he was self-taught. He continued living in London, but he spent much of his time painting in his home area (now known as 'Constable country') and in 1809 he became engaged to Maria Bicknell, granddaughter of the rector of East Bergholt. Her family disapproved of the match as Constable's career had made little progress, and he did not marry Maria until 1816, when his father's death made him more financially secure. The marriage was very happy, but Maria died of tuberculosis in 1828, leaving Constable emotionally devastated and with seven young children to care for. In 1824 his most famous work, *The Hay Wain* (1821, NG, London), had won a gold medal at the Paris *Salon, but it was not until 1829, when he was over 50, that he was grudgingly made a full member of the Royal Academy, elected by a majority of only one vote. In 1833, buttressed by this new status, he began lecturing on landscape painting, showing impressive knowledge as well as great love for the subject. Although his skill as a lecturer helped to consolidate his reputation, by the time of his death he still remained only moderately successful. The biography by his friend C. R. *Leslie, published in 1843, helped to establish his posthumous fame.

Constable's early work was strongly influenced by *Gainsborough (likewise a native of Suffolk) and by 17th-century Dutch landscape painting (he revered *Ruisdael in particular). However, he developed a highly personal approach by trying to communicate the feelings he felt in front of nature, conveying a sense—in his own words—of 'light, dews, breezes, bloom'. Just as his contemporary William Wordsworth rejected what he called the 'poetic diction' of his predecessors, so Constable turned away from the pictorial conventions of 18th-century landscape painters, who, he said, were always 'running after pictures and seeking the truth at second hand'. He thought that 'No two days are alike, nor even two hours; neither were there ever two leaves of a tree alike since the creation of the world.' Unlike the much-travelled Turner, he never went abroad, and his finest works are of the places he knew and loved best, particularly Suffolk and Hampstead (at this time a village north of London), where he lived from 1821. To render the changing effects of light and weather he abandoned traditional ideals of smooth finish, using rough, vigorous brushwork to suggest the sparkle of sunlight, the movement of clouds across the sky, or the drama of storms. To many contemporaries his work looked unfinished, but Henry *Fuseli was among those who applauded the freshness of his approach: C. R. Leslie records him as saying 'I like de landscapes of Constable; he is always picturesque, of a fine colour, and de lights always in de right places; but he makes me call for my greatcoat and umbrella.'

Constable worked extensively in the open air, sketching in oils, but his finished pictures were produced in the studio. For his most ambitious works—'six-footers' as he called them—he followed the unusual technical procedure of making a full-size oil sketch, and recently there has been a tendency to praise these even more highly than the finished works because of their boldness and freedom of brushwork. (The full-size sketch for The Hay Wain is in the Victoria and Albert Museum, London, which has the finest collection of Constable's work, the bulk of it presented by his daughter.) In England Constable had no real successor and the many imitators (who included his son Lionel, 1825–87) turned rather to the formal compositions than to the more direct sketches. In France, however, he was a major influence on *Romantic painters such as *Delacroix and on the members of the *Barbizon School.

Constantine, Arch of. See TRIUMPHAL ARCH.

Constructivism. A movement or ideology in abstract art that originated in Russia in about 1914, became dominant there for a few years after the 1917 Revolution, and in the 1920s spread to the West, where it has subsequently been influential on a wide spectrum of artists. Constructivism is typically characterized by the use of industrial materials—such as glass, plastic, and standardized metal parts—arranged in clear formal relationships, but the meaning to be attached to the word varies according to context, and some writers prefer to use the terms 'Soviet Constructivism' (or 'Russian Constructivism') and 'European Constructivism' (or 'International Constructivism') to make a distinction between the original movement and its much more diffuse aftermath. Even in the context of revolutionary Russia, however, the meaning of the word is far from clear-cut.

The father of Constructivism was Vladimir *Tatlin, who visited Paris in 1914 and on his return to Russia began making abstract Relief Constructions using materials such as sheet metal, wood, and wire. He was influenced by the sculptural experiments of *Picasso, who had used a variety of ingeniously assembled odds and ends, and perhaps also by the *Futurist sculptural manifesto (1913), in which *Boccioni similarly advocated a move away from the traditional techniques of modelling and carving in favour of sculpture that was constructed from various new materials—this was the essential idea behind Constructivism. From his reliefs Tatlin went on to develop small openwork structures (sometimes hanging), and several other artists, including Alexander *Rodchenko, created similar works in the years immediately after the 1917 Revolution. The Revolution created a ferment of enthusiasm in Russia for the building of a better society, with machinery seen as a liberating force, and in this climate Tatlin's idea of investigating and exploiting industrial materials came into its own. Initially Soviet Constructivism was inseparable from politics, and the revolutionary zeal for socially useful art led many Soviet artists to conclude that traditional 'fine art' was dead. In this way, a term that had originated in Tatlin's modest reliefs expanded to embrace the whole of applied art, and 'by 1925 Constructivism had become a blanket term for any angular designs applied to furniture, fabrics, porcelain or theatre sets' (Robert Auty and Dimitry Obolensky (eds.), An Introduction to Russian Art and Architecture, 1980).

Many artists who were not prepared to abandon traditional art for industrial design left Russia at this time. Among them were the brothers Naum *Gabo and Antoine *Pevsner, who left in 1922 and 1923 respectively. Although they wanted to reflect modern technology in their work, they rejected the idea that art must serve an obvious social purpose; they thought that 'fine art' could make an important contribution to society by being spiritually uplifting and they conceived a purely abstract type of sculpture that used industrial materials such as plastic and glass. It is from their work that European or International Constructivism derives and each of them played an important part in spreading their ideals. In England Gabo was co-editor of *Circle (1937), in which he published his essay 'The Constructive Idea'. The subtitle of Circle is International Survey of Constructive Art, an indication of the 'international constructive tendency' that was recognized at this time. Among the other contributors to the volume, *Moholy-Nagy was particularly influential in the spread of Constructivism through his teaching at the *Bauhaus and elsewhere. (Meanwhile, Constructivism in the Soviet Union was dead by this time, killed—like all other modern forms of expression—by *Socialist Realism.)

Gabo's concept of Constructivism, as expressed in his essay in Circle, was vague, being equated with 'creative human genius' in art, science, or any other sphere, and since the Second World War the term has been applied to a very broad range of work. Sometimes it is used as a rough equivalent of 'geometrical abstraction'. In Britain, however, the word is often used to refer specifically to a type of work—reliefs and freestanding constructs in metal or perspex—that became popular with a group of abstract artists in the 1950s and 1960s, including Kenneth and Mary *Martin, and Victor *Pasmore.

consular diptych. See DIPTYCH.

conté crayon. A type of hard crayon, named after Nicolas-Jacques Conté (1755–1805), a French scientist who worked as a portrait painter in his youth and invented the modern graphite *pencil in the early 1790s. Conté crayons are similar to *chalk, but they have a slightly greasy quality that makes them less liable to crumble. Black and warm red are the most common colours. *Seurat made some of his best drawings in black conté crayon.

continuous representation (or **continuous narrative**). A pictorial convention whereby two or more consecutive incidents from a narrative are combined in the same image. It is most common in medieval art, but occasionally occurs later. In *Pontormo's *Joseph in Egypt* (c.1518, NG, London), for example, four episodes from Genesis are shown in the same panel and the figure of Joseph appears separately in each of them.

contrapposto. Term (Italian: 'set against') applied to poses in which one part of a figure twists or turns away from another part. It was originally applied, during the *Renaissance, to a relaxed asymmetrical pose characteristic of much Greek and Roman sculpture in which the body's weight is borne mainly on one leg, so that the hip of that leg rises relative to the other (the *Doryphorus* of *Polyclitus is a classic example). The term is now, however, used in a much broader sense and applied as much to painting as to sculpture. The acknowledged master of *contrapposto* was *Michelangelo, and his *Mannerist followers (for example *Bronzino) often devised poses of wilful complexity in order to demonstrate their skill in the field.

conversation piece. A portrait showing two or more full-length figures engaged in conversation or other polite social activity, generally in a domestic or landscape setting. Conversation pieces are usually, though not always, fairly small in size. They were especially popular in Britain during the 18th century, when Arthur *Devis, Thomas *Gainsborough, William *Hogarth, Philip *Mercier (the pioneer exponent), and Johann *Zoffany were notable practitioners, but the use of the term is not confined to British painting or to this period.

Cook, Beryl (b Reading, 10 Sept. 1926). British *naive painter. She took up painting seriously when she was about 40 and in 1975 had her first exhibition, at the Plymouth Arts Centre. It was a great success and within a few years she was well known through other exhibitions, television appearances, and the publication of the first of several collections of her work in book form (*The Works*, 1978), with the paintings accompanied by her own amusing commentaries. Her chubby, usually jovial characters have also been much used on greetings cards. Cook's subjects are drawn from everyday life and frequently involve the kind of saucy humour associated with seaside holidays (she used to run a boarding house in Plymouth) and tabloid Sunday newspapers (often she incorporates newsprint as a collage element in her work).

Cooper, Douglas (*b* London, 20 Feb. 1911; *d* London, 1 Apr. 1984). British art historian and collector. He lived in France for much of his life and was severely critical of the British for what he regarded as their failure to appreciate or patronize modern art. His main interest was *Cubism, and in 1932 he decided to devote part of his inheritance to forming a collection of its four leading exponents—*Picasso, *Braque, *Gris, and *Léger—in its greatest period, 1907–14. He later added works by other artists, but the Cubists remained the core. In the Second World War he worked in intelligence and helped to identify, protect, and repatriate works of art. Picasso was later a neighbour and visitor in southern France, but their friendship turned to hostility. Cooper, indeed, had a notoriously difficult temperament and enjoyed controversy; in the 1950s he became particularly well known for his attacks on the *Tate Gallery and its director Sir John *Rothenstein. He was a formidable scholar and published substantial books on all four major Cubists.

Cooper, Samuel (*b* ?London, ?1608; *d* London, 5 May 1672). English *miniaturist, the nephew and pupil of John *Hoskins. The greatest English miniaturist of the 17th century, Cooper enjoyed a prosperous career and a European reputation (he is said to have travelled on the Continent as a young man). He worked for both sides during the Civil War and Commonwealth, and his sitters included Oliver Cromwell and Charles II. His portraits are almost always of the bust only, but within this limitation his range is remarkable: he presents each sitter (man or woman) with an individuality of characterization that can make the life-size portraits of contemporaries such' as *Lely appear doll-like, and his vigorous *Baroque sense of design marks a complete break with the tradition of *Hilliard and Hoskins. His brother **Alexander** (*bapt.* London, 11 Dec. 1609; *d* ?Stockholm, *c*.1658) was also a miniaturist. He worked mainly on the Continent—in the Netherlands and at the court of Queen Christina in Stockholm.

Coorte, Adriaen (active 1683–1707). Dutch still-life painter, active around Middelburg. Nothing is known of his life, and his work was completely forgotten for more than two centuries after his death. Only a handful of paintings by him survive, but they show him to have been one of the most individual still-life painters of his time. They are the complete opposite of the lavish pieces by such celebrated contemporaries as Jan van *Huysum and Rachel *Ruysch, for they are small in scale and depict a few humble objects, characteristically placed on a bare ledge. The intensity of his scrutiny is such, however, that they take on something of the mystical quality of the still-lifes of *Sánchez Cotán or *Zurbarán, and the hovering butterfly that Coorte sometimes incorporates in his work may have allegorical significance. One of his favourite subjects was a bundle of asparagus (examples in Rijksmuseum, Amsterdam, Fitzwilliam Mus., Cambridge, and Ashmolean Mus., Oxford).

Copley, John Singleton (*b* ?Boston, 3 July 1738; *d* London, 9 Sept. 1815). The greatest American painter of the 18th century. He was the stepson of the engraver Peter Pelham (*c*.1695–1751), from whose large collection of prints he gained a considerable knowledge of European art, but he was virtually self-taught as a painter. While still in his teens he established his own practice in Boston and by his early twenties he was painting portraits that, in their sense of life and character, completely outstripped anything previously produced by Colonial portraitists (*Colonel Epes Sargent*, *c*.1760, NG, Washington). He had little competition, as the best Colonial portraitists of the previous generation—*Feke, *Greenwood, and *Smibert—all disappeared from the scene in the 1750s, and he became extremely successful. However, Copley was diffident and self-doubtful by nature and came to see himself as a provincial figure, cut off from the mainstream of art. He longed to know how he would measure up against his best European contemporaries, but for many years he hesitated to leave the security of Boston (where he earned 'as much as if I were a *Raphael or a *Correggio'), even after his portrait of his half-brother Henry Pelham (*The Boy with a Squirrel*, 1765, MFA, Boston) had been highly praised by both *Reynolds and *West when it was exhibited in London in 1766. He finally left America in 1774, when revolutionary activity was beginning to threaten his practice, and settled in London in 1775 after a study trip to Italy.

In England Copley's style changed markedly, as he sacrificed the forthright vigour of his Colonial work for a more fashionable and ornate manner. He continued to paint fine portraits that were more than a match for the work of most of his contemporaries, but it is generally agreed that those he painted in America have greater originality and conviction. In compensation for this decline as a portraitist, he was able to turn his hand to *history painting, in which he had long been eager to make a success but for which the opportunities in America were almost non-existent. The first major work in this field was *Brook Watson and the Shark* (1778, NG, Washington; a copy Copley made for himself is in the Museum of Fine Arts, Boston, and a smaller variant, 1782, is in the Detroit Institute of Arts). In this he followed the innovation of his countryman West in using modern dress, and went beyond him in depicting a subject not because it was of historical importance or moral significance, but merely because it was exciting. It was not until a generation later that the French *Romantics took up this revolutionary idea. His other history paintings have more conventional themes, mainly patriotic and military, such as the *Death of Major Peirson* (1783, Tate, London). In such works Copley revealed a magnificent gift for depicting heroic action in multi-figure compositions that none of his British contemporaries could approach, and these paintings won him great acclaim. They also brought on him the wrath of the *Royal Academy (of which Copley had become a full member in 1779) when they were shown privately, for this constituted a rival attraction to the Academy's own exhibitions.

Copley's success in England, however, was fairly short-lived and from the later 1780s his work began to go out of favour, a turning point being the poor reception accorded his portrait of the three daughters of George III (1785, Royal Coll.), which was considered fussy (John *Hoppner, a jealous rival, wrote a malicious review when the picture was shown at the Academy). In his final years Copley went into a sad decline. *Morse visited him in 1811 and wrote: 'His powers of mind have almost entirely left him; his late paintings are miserable; it is really a lamentable thing that a man should outlive his faculties.' He died leaving debts that had to be paid off by his son and namesake, who was ennobled as Baron Lyndhurst and was three times lord chancellor.

copper point. See METALPOINT.

Coppo di Marcovaldo (active 1260–76). Italian painter, one of the earliest about whom there is a body of documented knowledge. He served in the army of Florence and evidently settled in Siena after his capture at the Battle of Montaperti (1260). In 1261 he painted the signed and dated *Madonna and Child Enthroned* (called the *Madonna del Bordone*) for S. Maria dei Servi, Siena (still *in situ*), and between 1265 and 1276 he is documented several times working at Pistoia Cathedral, which has a Crucifix that is assumed to be one of two he was commissioned to produce (although the workmanship is thought by some critics to be largely by his son **Salerno**). On the basis of these two works, other paintings have been attributed to Coppo, notably a *Madonna and Child Enthroned* in the Cathedral Museum in Orvieto, and a Crucifix in the Pinacoteca at San Gimignano. He introduced new solidity and humanity to the *Byzantine tradition, in the way, for example, that he represents the Virgin with her head inclined towards the Child, and with *Guido da Siena he ranks as one of the founders of the Sienese School.

Coques, Gonzales (*b* Antwerp, ?1618; *d* Antwerp, 18 Apr. 1684). Flemish *genre and portrait painter, known as the 'little van *Dyck', although his style is much closer to *Terborch. He worked mainly in Antwerp, but he also travelled to Holland and England. His best works, charming and daintily executed, are small-scale fashionable group portraits such as *A Family Group* (*c.*1664, NG, London).

Corinth, Lovis (*b* Tapiau, East Prussia [now Gvardeysk, Russia], 21 July 1858; *d* Zandvoort, Netherlands, 17 July 1925). German painter and printmaker. Part of his training was with *Bouguereau in Paris (1884–7), but he was more strongly influenced by the painterly work of French artists such as *Courbet and *Manet, as well as by *Hals, *Rembrandt, and *Rubens. On his return to Germany he lived mainly in Munich before settling in Berlin in 1901. With *Liebermann and *Slevogt (both of whom also lived in Berlin) he was recognized as one of the leading German exponents of *Impressionism and in the first decade of the century he was a great fashionable success. However, in 1911 he was partially paralysed by a stroke and when he began to paint again (with great difficulty) it was in a much looser and more powerful *Expressionist manner, to which he had previously been strongly opposed (he has been described as 'an eleventh-hour convert to modernism'). He was varied and prolific as a painter and printmaker. His paintings included landscapes, portraits, and still-lifes, and he had a fondness for voluptuous allegorical and religious subjects (*Temptation of St Anthony*, 1908, Tate, London). His prints were mainly drypoints and in his later years lithographs (which he used for the numerous commissions he had for book illustrations). He also made a few etchings and woodcuts. After the Nazis came to power in 1933 his later works were declared *degenerate. *Kirchner said of

Corinth, 'In the beginning, he was only of average stature; at the end he was truly great.'

Cormon, Fernand (pseudonym of Fernand-Anne Piestre) (b Paris, 24 Dec. 1845; d Paris, 20 Mar. 1924). French painter. He had a successful career both as a painter and as a teacher (his pupils included *Matisse, *Toulouse-Lautrec, and van *Gogh), but his reputation has not lasted well. His work included decorations at the Museum of Natural History and the Petit Palais in Paris and some excellent portraits, and he also had a penchant for paintings of prehistoric history (*The Age of Stone*, 1884, Mus. du Prieuré, Saint-Germain-en-Laye).

Corneille (Cornelis van Beverloo) (b Liège, 3 July 1922). Belgian painter, active mainly in Paris. He was a founder member of *Cobra in 1948 and his paintings typically display brilliant colour and vigorous brushwork, with childlike imagery suggesting mythical beings.

Corneille de Lyon (b The Hague, c.1500/10; bur. Lyons, 8 Nov. 1575). Netherlandish-born painter who became a French citizen in 1547. He was a native of The Hague (in France he is still often known as Corneille de La Haye), but he had settled in Lyons by 1533 (the first record of him) and in 1540 he became court painter to the dauphin, later Henry II. Contemporary references to Corneille indicate that he had a considerable reputation as a portrait painter, but only one work survives that is unquestionably from his hand, a portrait of Pierre Aymeric (1534, Louvre, Paris), authenticated by an inscription in the sitter's handwriting on the back of the picture. Many other works in a similar style go under his name. They are mostly small in scale and sharply naturalistic in manner, with the sitter usually set against a plain green or blue background. The National Gallery, London, has four examples of the type, catalogued as 'attributed to' or 'style of Corneille de Lyon'.

Cornelis van Haarlem (Cornelis Cornelisz.) (b Haarlem, 1562; d Haarlem, 11 Nov. 1638). Dutch painter who ranks with Hendrick *Goltzius and Karel van *Mander as one of the leading representatives of *Mannerism in the Netherlands. He is best known for his large biblical and historical pictures packed with athletic, life-size Italianate nudes in wrenched and sharply foreshortened positions. But he also did a few forceful portraits of individuals and groups that show he was an important forerunner of Frans *Hals. Both facets of his work can best be seen in the Frans Hals Museum in Haarlem, the city where he spent most of his life.

Cornelisz. van Oostsanen, Jacob (also called Jacob van Amsterdam) (b Oostsanen, nr. Amsterdam, c.1475; d ?Amsterdam, 1533). Netherlandish painter and designer, active mainly in Amsterdam, where he was a successful painter and the leading designer of woodcuts in his period. The woodcuts include a series illustrating the Passion (1512–17) and among the paintings are a self-portrait (1533, Rijksmuseum, Amsterdam) and an *Adoration of the Shepherds* (1512, Mus. di Capodimonte, Naples), which contains pudgy angels playing toylike instruments, singing, and decorating an improbable *Renaissance manger with garlands. Although his work is somewhat provincial, he marks the beginning of the great artistic tradition of Amsterdam, and his keenness of observation was to be one of the trademarks of later Dutch art. Jan van *Scorel was possibly his pupil. Several other members of Jacob's family were artists, notably his brother Cornelis Buys, who has been identified as the *Master of Alkmaar.

Cornelius, Peter (b Düsseldorf, 23 Sept. 1783; d Berlin, 6 Mar. 1867). German painter, draughtsman, and teacher. He trained at the Düsseldorf Academy, where his father was a teacher, and from the beginning of his career his primary ambition was to produce monumental wall paintings. He moved to Rome in 1811 and the following year became a member of the *Nazarenes. In 1819 he was called to Munich by Crown Prince Ludwig of Bavaria (later Ludwig I), for whom he worked extensively, notably on a series of frescos in the Ludwigskirche (1836–9), including a *Last Judgement* that is larger than *Michelangelo's in the Sistine Chapel. In 1841 he moved to Berlin to work for Frederick William IV of Prussia. His major commission there was for a series of frescos in a mausoleum for the royal family. The project was officially cancelled after the revolution in 1848, but Cornelius continued to work on his drawings for it for the rest of his life. From 1853 to 1861 he lived in Rome again. His style is rather self-conscious in its desire to revive the heroic pictorial language of *Raphael and Michelangelo, and combine it with the didactic philosophy of German *Romanticism, but his work has an impressive epic sweep. He was director of the academies at Düsseldorf (1821–5) and Munich (from 1825) and he helped to make these institutions the most important centres in Germany for the teaching of *history painting. His work was a major influence in promoting a revival of fresco decoration in Germany and his reputation in the field was such that in 1841 he visited London to give advice on the projected mural decorations for the Houses of Parliament.

Cornell, Joseph (*b* Nyack, NY, 24 Dec. 1903; *d* New York, 29 Dec. 1972). American sculptor, one of the pioneers and most celebrated exponents of *assemblage. He had no artistic training, but in about 1931, influenced by *Surrealism, he began making collages, and from these developed the distinctive type of work that he made his own—small wooden boxes, usually glass fronted, in which he arranged collections of photographs, magazine illustrations, trinkets, and all manner of bric-a-brac. His work is sometimes compared with that of *Schwitters, but whereas Schwitters was fascinated by refuse, Cornell concentrated on fragments of once beautiful and treasured possessions, using the Surrealist technique of irrational juxtaposition to evoke a feeling of nostalgic reverie. From the late 1940s—perhaps influenced by *Mondrian, whom he much admired—his work began to become more abstract. Cornell also painted and from the late 1930s he made several Surrealist films, sometimes using discarded Hollywood movie footage. Towards the end of his life several major exhibitions were devoted to his work, notably one at the Guggenheim Museum, New York, in 1967.

Corot, Camille (*b* Paris, 17 July 1796; *d* Paris, 22 Feb. 1875). French painter, mainly of landscapes. His father was a textile merchant and his mother a fashionable dressmaker, and he was expected to follow them into the clothing business. In 1822, however, at the age of 26, he was allowed to give up his commercial career, to which he was ill suited, and devote himself to art, which was his passion; his parents gave him generous financial support, so he was able to follow his own interests without having to worry about earning a living. He studied briefly with Achille-Etna *Michallon (who died soon after their association began) and then with Jean-Victor Bertin (1767–1842). Both his teachers had been pupils of *Valenciennes, and through them Corot inherited the classical tradition of which Valenciennes had been the main upholder in the previous generation. However, he brought a personal poetry to this tradition and an unaffected naturalness reflecting the sketches from nature that formed the basis for his finished pictures; his work has a wonderful feeling of clarity and balance, but he seems to achieve

this instinctively, without any striving for effect. He was based in Paris all his life but travelled a good deal in France and abroad, visiting Switzerland several times and also Italy (1825–8, 1834, and 1843), the Low Countries (1854), and England (1862).

From 1827 Corot exhibited regularly at the *Salon; his reputation grew steadily from the 1830s and by 1850 he was established as a major figure. His public success was based mainly on a type of picture that was very different from his topographical work—more traditionally Romantic in its evocation of an Arcadian past, and painted in a misty soft-edged style that contrasts sharply with the luminous clarity usually associated with him. Throughout his career Corot also painted figure studies, as well as portraits of friends and relatives, and from the 1850s figure painting (notably of the female nude) assumed greater importance in his output; this aspect of his work has only fairly recently emerged from neglect. His directness of vision and sincerity of feeling were greatly admired by landscape painters of the later 19th century, and he took a lively interest in the work of younger artists; *Daubigny, *Pissarro, and *Sisley were among those who profited from his advice. His popularity with collectors was (and is) such that he is said to be the most forged of all painters (this in addition to an already large output). In his lifetime he was held in great esteem as a man as well as an artist, for he had a noble, generous, almost saintly nature and was completely unspoilt by his success (even the normally caustic *Degas described him as 'an angel who smokes a pipe'); he supported *Millet's widow, for example, and gave a cottage to the impoverished and almost blind *Daumier.

Correggio (Antonio Allegri) (*b* Correggio, *c*.1490; *d* Correggio, 5 Mar. 1534). Italian painter, named after the small town in Emilia where he was born and died. Although he worked mainly in provincial centres, he was one of the most sophisticated artists of his time, blending disparate sources into a potent synthesis, and although his reputation in his lifetime was modest, he had enormous posthumous fame and influence. His early career is poorly documented and his artistic education has to be conjectured on stylistic grounds. He probably received a rudimentary training from his uncle, the painter **Lorenzo Allegri** (*d* 1527), but the most obvious source of inspiration for his early development is *Mantegna, and he may well have studied in Mantua (which is fairly near his home town), possibly even with the aged Mantegna himself. His first surviving documented work is the *Virgin of St Francis* (1514–15, Gemäldegalerie, Dresden), commissioned by the church of S. Francesco in Correggio; by the time he painted this he was also influenced by Lorenzo *Costa (in the pearly colouring) and by *Leonardo (in the characteristic pointing finger of St John). Later he absorbed more of Leonardo's introspection and his soft *sfumato*, which helped to create his fluid, elegant, and alluring style. Another strong source of influence on Correggio's work comes from Rome; it is now generally assumed that he visited the city early in his career, probably around 1518, although *Vasari implies that he never went there and the impact of *Raphael and *Michelangelo could be accounted for by drawings and prints, which were known all over Italy.

Correggio's most characteristic paintings are altarpieces and small devotional works, often very tender and intimate in feeling. However, he also produced a number of major frescos in Parma, which is about 30 km (20 miles) away from his home town. He is first documented there in 1520, but the earliest of his commissions in the city was probably carried out a year or so before this—the fresco decoration of the abbess's room in the convent of S. Paolo. The theme of the paintings is Diana, goddess of chastity and the chase (an unusual subject for a convent, but the abbess was a worldly and intellectual woman); in the vaulted ceiling Correggio uses Mantegna's idea of a leafy trellis framing *putti and symbols of the hunt. This work was followed by two great dome paintings in Parma, in which Correggio developed the *illusionist conception—already used by Mantegna—of depicting a scene as though it were actually taking place in the sky above (see *sotto in sù*). The first of the domes (1520–4) is in the church of S. Giovanni Evangelista. Its subject is the *Vision of St John the Evangelist on Patmos*; the twelve Apostles sit on clouds round the base, while Christ is shown in steep foreshortening ascending to heaven. In the second dome, that of Parma Cathedral, Correggio painted the *Assumption of the Virgin* (1526–30), using the same principle, but on a larger scale and with still more daring foreshortening. These works reveal Correggio as one of the boldest and most inventive artists of the High *Renaissance. They were too audacious for some contemporaries (a priest at the cathedral described the fresco there as a 'stew of frogs legs'), but they were highly influential on the development of *Baroque dome painting (one of the most important artists in this field, *Lanfranco, was a native of Parma).

Other aspects of Correggio's work were even more forward-looking, for his extraordinarily sensuous mythologies foreshadow the paintings of *Rococo artists such as *Boucher. His most famous works in this field are four pictures representing the loves of Jupiter (*c*.1530–2), commissioned by Federico II *Gonzaga as a gift for the Emperor Charles V (see HABSBURG): *Ganymede* and *Jupiter and Io* (KH Mus., Vienna); *Leda* (Gemäldegalerie, Berlin); and *Danaë* (Borghese Gal., Rome). Correggio's renown was at its height in the 18th century, when he was ranked almost on the same level as Raphael (*Mengs was named after both of them by his artist father). Subsequently his reputation has declined somewhat, but his place as one of the greatest painters of his age is secure.

Corrente. An anti-Fascist association of young Italian artists formed by Renato *Birolli in Milan in 1938; *Guttuso was among the other founder members. The association had no fixed programme, but it was opposed to the provincialism of the official *Novecento. The members stood for the defence of 'modern' art at a time when the Nazi campaign against *degenerate art was spreading to Italy. Corrente arranged two exhibitions in Milan in 1939, and it published a fortnightly review of literature, politics, and the arts entitled *Corrente di vita giovanile* (Stream of Youthful Life), later renamed simply *Corrente*. This ceased publication in 1943 and the activities of the group were dissipated by the Second World War.

'Cor-Ten' steel. See IRON.

Cortese. See COURTOIS.

Cortona, Pietro da (Pietro Berrettini) (*b* Cortona, Tuscany, 1 Nov. 1596; *d* Rome, 16 May 1669). Italian painter, architect, decorator, and designer; he was the most influential Italian painter of his generation and ranks second only to *Bernini as the most versatile genius of the full Roman *Baroque style. Cortona is named after the town of his birth, where he probably had some training with his father, a stonemason, before settling in Rome in about 1612. His first major works there were frescos in the church of S. Bibiana (1624–6), commissioned by Urban VIII (Maffeo *Barberini), and the patronage of the Barberini family played a major part in his career. For their palace he painted his most famous work, a huge fresco, *Allegory of Divine Providence and Barberini Power*, on the ceiling of the Gran Salone. He began this in 1633, but interrupted the work in 1637 to go to Florence, where he painted two frescos commissioned by the Grand Duke Ferdinand II de' *Medici on the walls of the Sala della Stufa in the *Pitti Palace; the subjects are the *Golden Age* and the *Silver Age*. After returning to Rome he completed the Barberini ceiling in 1639. One of the key works in the development of Baroque painting, it is a triumph of *illusionism, for the centre of the ceiling appears open to the sky and the figures seen from below (*di *sotto in sù*) appear to come down into the room as well as soar out of it. It demonstrates Cortona's belief, which came out in a debate with Andrea *Sacchi in the Accademia di S. Luca in about 1636, that a history painting could be compared with an epic and was entitled to use many figures; Sacchi, intent on *classical simplicity and unity, argued for using as few figures as possible.

For most of the period from 1640 to 1647 Cortona again worked in Florence, continuing his decorations in the Pitti Palace. He first completed his Four Ages of Man decorations in the Sala della Stufa with scenes of the *Bronze Age* and the *Iron Age*, then began a series of allegorical ceiling paintings in five rooms named after the planets (the work was completed by his pupil Ciro Ferri (1634–89)). These paintings are combined with sumptuous *stucco ornamentation, and this form of decoration was widely influential, not only in Italy, but also in France. (Cortona turned down an invitation to visit Paris from Cardinal Mazarin, but his style was taken there by his best pupil, *Romanelli.) From 1647 until his death Cortona again worked in Rome, his major paintings from this period being an extensive series of frescos in S. Maria in Vallicella (the Chiesa Nuova, 1647–65), in which, as in his Pitti decorations, paint and stucco are magnificently combined. Throughout his career he painted easel pictures of religious and mythological subjects, and he also designed cartoons for a number of tapestries on the history of Constantine (1626–41) for the Palazzo Barberini (now in the Philadelphia Museum of Art), completing a series that had been begun by *Rubens.

Cortona once wrote that architecture was merely a pastime for him, but he ranks among the greatest architects of his period. His masterpiece is the church of SS. Martina e Luca in Rome (1635–50), which was the first Baroque church designed and built as a unified whole. Although his architecture has all the vigour of his painting, there is less correspondence between the two fields than might be imagined.

He never decorated any of his own churches, and indeed they were not designed with fresco decoration in mind, making their impact through grandeur of form rather than richness of ornament. His great contemporary reputation sank in the next century with that of many other Baroque artists. In a famous passage in his *Dizionario delle belle arti* (1797), Francesco Milizia wrote: 'Borromini in architecture, Bernini in sculpture, Pietro da Cortona in painting . . . represent a diseased taste—one that has infected a great number of artists.'

Cosmati work. A type of geometrical decorative inlaywork using coloured marbles and mosaic that flourished in Rome between c.1100 and c.1300. The term derives from the Cosmatus family, several members of which are documented as creating such work. At one time it was believed they were responsible for all of it, but it has now been established that many other craftsmen were active in this field, some of them belonging to families whose work extended over several generations. Cosmati work was used to adorn church furnishings such as tombs and pulpits and also for architectural enrichment and floors. Several examples are in Westminster Abbey, executed by imported Italian craftsmen.

Cossa, Francesco del (*b* Ferrara, c.1435; *d* Bologna, c.1477). Italian painter, active mainly in Ferrara, where with Cosimo *Tura and Ercole de' *Roberti he was the leading artist of the period. His style has many affinities with that of Tura and the same background of development from *Mantegna and *Piero della Francesca, but Cossa's work reveals a more genial and relaxed temperament. This found expression in the delightful frescos of the Months in the Palazzo Schifanoia at Ferrara; Cossa, Roberti, and Tura are all thought to have contributed to the scheme, but Cossa seems to have been the principal figure. In the early 1470s he moved to Bologna, where his work included an altarpiece for the Griffoni Chapel in the church of S. Petronio (1473); the central panel is in the National Gallery, London.

Cossington Smith, Grace. See SMITH, GRACE COSSINGTON.

Costa, Lorenzo (*b* Ferrara, c.1460; *d* Mantua, 5 Mar. 1535). Italian painter. He probably trained in Ferrara and his early work was much influenced by *Tura and Ercole de' *Roberti. In the early 1480s he settled in Bologna, where he entered into partnership with *Francia and worked for the ruling Bentivoglio family. In 1504–5 he painted an *Allegory* (Louvre, Paris) for Isabella d'*Este and in 1507 he succeeded *Mantegna as court painter at Mantua. He was the leading artist there until the arrival of *Giulio Romano in 1524, but little of his large-scale work survives. His mature style is often rather sweetly *Peruginesque, with a delicate feeling for landscape, and has been suggested as one of the sources of *Giorgione's work. There are good examples of Costa's work in the National Gallery, London, including *The Concert*, one of the first examples of a type of picture (a close-up of a group of musicians) that was later to have a considerable vogue. His son **Ippolito Costa** (1506–61) was a painter, as was another **Lorenzo Costa** (1537–83), who was probably Ippolito's son.

Cosway, Richard (*bapt.* Okeford, Devon, 5 Nov. 1742; *d* London, 4 July 1821). English painter, mainly of *miniatures. A friend of the Prince of Wales (later Prince Regent), Cosway was by far the most fashionable miniaturist of his day, giving his sitters an air of great elegance. The larger portraits in oils that he occasionally painted are considered less successful. In 1781 he married Maria Hadfield (1759–1838), who was a miniaturist and etcher.

Cotán, Juan Sánchez. See SÁNCHEZ COTÁN.

Cotes, Francis (*b* London, 20 May 1726; *d* London, 19 July 1770). English portrait painter, a pupil of *Knapton. He began as a specialist in *pastel and never altogether gave up the medium, but in the 1760s he turned mainly to oils and became a great fashionable success, the only serious rival to *Gainsborough and *Reynolds. Like them, he was a founder member of the *Royal Academy. His work is charming and vivacious and totally unintellectual; in the words of Ellis *Waterhouse, 'He went all out for health and youth and fine clothes, a strong likeness and no nonsense.' Cotes died from the effects of a toxic potion he took to try to cure the gallstones or kidney stones from which he was suffering. His studio in Cavendish Square in London (and something of his position in the market) was later taken over by *Romney.

Cotman, John Sell (*b* Norwich, 16 May 1782; *d* London, 24 July 1842). English landscape painter (mainly in watercolour) and etcher. He moved from Norwich to London in 1798, aged 16, and became a member of Dr *Monro's circle. As far as is known, he had no formal tuition in art, but by 1800 he was already accomplished enough to have six of his watercolours accepted

for the annual *Royal Academy exhibition. Between 1800 and 1805 he made several sketching tours to Wales and Yorkshire and these resulted in some of his finest works. They did not bring him much success, however, and in 1806 he returned to his native city, where, together with *Crome, he became the most important representative of the *Norwich School. As well as depicting local scenery, he made several trips to France, which bore fruit in *Architectural Antiquities of Normandy* (1822), one of various books he illustrated with his etchings. In 1834 he moved to London to become professor of drawing at King's College, a position he held until his death. He was delighted to be offered the post, as he often had difficulty in making a living with his work and he was in debt at the time. Throughout his life he was also subject to periods of melancholia and despondency.

Cotman's early watercolours, such as the celebrated *Greta Bridge* (c.1805, BM, London; a later version, 1810, is in the Castle Museum, Norwich), include some of the greatest examples of the classic English watercolour technique, showing remarkable boldness and sureness of hand. He used large flat *washes to build up form in clearly defined planes and shapes of almost geometrical simplicity. In his later years, however, his style became much more flamboyant; he sometimes mixed flour or rice paste with his watercolours to produce an *impasto that echoed the effects of oil paint. Throughout his career he also painted in oils, but this side of his work has been overshadowed by his achievements as a watercolourist.

Cotton, Sir Robert. See LINDISFARNE GOSPELS and UTRECHT PSALTER.

Coulte, Maximilian. See COLT.

Counihan, Noel. See ANGRY PENGUINS.

counterproof (also called **offset**). A reproduction made from a drawing or print by pressing it when damp against a blank sheet of paper; the image is therefore reversed left to right and is also fainter than the original. With drawings, both the original and the paper are slightly dampened; with prints, a fresh impression, on which the ink is still wet, is used. Counterproofs were often made for working purposes by designers of ornament who needed to have a copy of a design in reverse, or to complete one half of a symmetrical design, and they have also been used to create forgeries of Old Master drawings. The process harms the original, making it flatter and fainter, and is mainly used with drawings in red chalk rather than more delicate media. Often a counterproof forgery is touched up by hand to strengthen it. With prints, a counterproof is in reverse as regards the impression from which it is taken, but in the same direction as the image on the block or plate. For this reason counterproofs were sometimes used by printmakers to check on work in progress against the block or plate. In similar fashion, they could be used to monitor the final effect of any composition intended for an end product (such as a tapestry) that reverses the original design.

Courbet, Gustave (*b* Ornans, Franche-Comté, 10 June 1819; *d* La Tour de Peilz, Switzerland, 31 Dec. 1877). French painter, one of the most powerful personalities in 19th-century art. He was the son of a prosperous farmer at Ornans, at the foot of the Jura Mountains, near the Swiss border. His country upbringing was important to his art, for although he spent most of his career in Paris, he rarely painted urban subjects ('His palette smells of hay,' *Cézanne said of him). He was a man of independent character and obstinate self-assurance, and claimed to be self-taught. In fact he studied with various minor masters in Ornans, Besançon, and Paris, where he moved in 1839, but he learnt more from copying the work of 17th-century naturalists such as *Caravaggio and *Velázquez in the Louvre. It was largely from them that he derived his very solid and weighty style, with its strong contrasts of light and shade.

Courbet's earliest pictures (including several narcissistic self-portraits) were in the *Romantic tradition, but with three large canvases exhibited at the *Salon of 1850 he established himself as the leader of the *Realist movement: these are *A Burial at Ornans* (Mus. d'Orsay, Paris), *Peasants at Flagey* (Mus. B.-A., Besançon), and *The Stone Breakers* (formerly in Dresden, but destroyed in the Second World War). The huge burial scene in particular made an enormous impact; it was attacked by some critics for its alleged crudity and deliberate ugliness, but also hailed for its powerful naturalism (he got the idea for the picture at his grandfather's funeral). Never before had a scene from everyday life been presented in such an epic manner and Courbet was cast in the role of a revolutionary socialist. He gladly accepted this role (although it is unlikely that he painted the picture with political intention) and he became a friend and follower of the anarchist philosopher Pierre-Joseph Proudhon (1809–65), who gave him a prominent

place in his book *Du principe de l'art et de sa destination sociale* (1865). Courbet's boldness and self-confidence are as evident in his technique as in his choice of subjects. He often used a palette knife to apply paint and his work shows an unprecedented relish for the physical substance of his materials.

Courbet's unconventionality and hatred of authority were expressed most forcefully in 1855, when two of his paintings were rejected for exhibition at the Paris Exposition Universelle (World Fair) and he organized instead a one-man show in a building he titled 'The Pavilion of Realism' situated near the Exposition entrance. The painting that formed the centrepiece of the exhibition (one of the two rejected pictures) is now his most celebrated work, *The Painter's Studio* (1854–5, Mus. d'Orsay). This huge (6-m (20-ft) wide) canvas was subtitled by Courbet 'a real allegory [a seeming contradiction in terms] summing up seven years in my artistic life'. In a letter to his friend *Champfleury printed in the accompanying catalogue he wrote a long (but not very clear) account of it, describing it as 'the moral and physical history of my studio' and saying it showed 'all the people who serve my cause, sustain me in my ideal and support my activity'. These friends and mentors are shown on the right (among them are *Baudelaire, Champfleury, Proudhon, and the collector Alfred Bruyas (1821–77), Courbet's most important patron); on the left are symbolic figures of the poor and their exploiters. Between the two groups Courbet sits proudly at his easel, watched by a magnificent female nude model; in presenting himself as the artist-hero, and in taking as his subject the activity of creating art, he sounded a note that reverberated into the 20th century.

Interpretations of the picture have been many and varied; it has been seen as an esoteric representation of Freemasonry, for example, or more plausibly as containing a covert attack on Napoleon III. Many contemporaries were baffled or repelled by the mixture of allegory, portraiture, and social comment, and the exhibition drew a low attendance. Subsequently Courbet's work became less doctrinaire. His colours were less sombre and he often chose more obviously attractive subjects—landscapes from the Forest of Fontainebleau, the Jura, or the Mediterranean, seascapes, still-lifes, or comely and sensual nudes.

Following the abdication of Napoleon III, Courbet was appointed head of the arts commission of the Commune, the short-lived revolutionary government of Paris (March–May 1871). When the Commune was brutally suppressed, he was sentenced to six months' imprisonment for his role in the destruction of the Vendôme Column, a symbol of Bonapartism. He was released in 1872, but the following year he was decreed to be personally responsible for the cost of re-erecting the Column. Unable to pay and fearing arrest, he went into exile in Switzerland. He stayed there for the remaining four years of his life, painting mainly landscapes and portraits.

Courbet's resounding rejection of idealization and his concentration on the tangible reality of things had an enormous influence on 19th-century art: 'Superbly plebeian . . . Courbet acted as the bull that smashed the china shop of polite art, whether academic or preciously avant-gardist, thus enabling a new generation (including the *Impressionists) to concentrate on the problem of expressing visual experience' (Lorenz Eitner, *An Outline of 19th Century European Painting*, 1987). 'Painting', Courbet said, 'is an essentially concrete art and can only consist of the representation of real and existing objects.' When asked to include angels in a painting for a church he replied: 'I have never seen angels. Show me an angel and I will paint one.'

Courtauld, Samuel (*b* Braintree, Essex, 7 May 1876; *d* London, 1 Dec. 1947). British industrialist, collector, and philanthropist. He came from a family of prosperous silk merchants and was chairman of the textile firm Courtaulds Ltd. from 1921 to 1946. He began collecting in 1922, buying mainly *Impressionist and *Post-Impressionist works, and in 1923 he gave the Tate Gallery £50,000 for the purchase of French paintings in his own area of interest (which was poorly represented). This fund was used to buy 23 paintings over the next few years, transforming the Tate's collection (most of the pictures have subsequently been transferred to the National Gallery). His interests also extended to living artists, and in 1925 he joined his friend Maynard Keynes (see BLOOMSBURY GROUP) in founding the London Artists' Association to provide financial assistance to young painters and sculptors.

In 1931 came his most famous benefaction when he endowed the Courtauld Institute of Art, London, Britain's first specialist centre for the study of the history of art. The Institute opened in 1932 and in the same year Courtauld presented most of his collection to the University of London, together with funds for a building to house them. The co-founders of the Institute were Lord Lee of Fareham (1868–1947), a soldier and politician, who in 1921 had presented his country house—Chequers—to the nation to be the prime minister's country residence, and Sir Robert Witt (1872–1952), a lawyer who formed a library of reproductions of paintings and drawings that is now one of the cornerstones of the Institute's pre-eminence in art-historical studies. Both men left collections to the Courtauld Institute—Lee mainly of paintings, Witt of drawings and watercolours—and there have been several other important bequests, including that of the painter and critic Roger *Fry. The most recent of the major bequests, that of the Anglo-Austrian art historian Count Antoine Seilern (1901–78) in 1978, raised an already outstanding collection to new heights. Seilern's bequest is varied, reflecting his own scholarly interests, but its chief glory is its superlative group of works by *Rubens. The Institute was originally located in Courtauld's former house at 20 Portman Square (a fine 18th-century building by James Wyatt and Robert Adam), while the galleries (opened in 1958) occupied a building about a mile away, next to the *Warburg Institute in Woburn Square. In 1989–90, however, all the Institute's activities and collections were brought together under one roof at Somerset House in the Strand, fulfilling Courtauld's intention that students should work in intimate contact with original works of art.

Kenneth *Clark described Courtauld as a 'quiet modest man . . . a man of principle, if ever there was one', and Dennis Farr writes that 'He brought to his collecting that combination of flair, energy, and sense of public duty that had marked his successful career as a leading industrialist. He did not seek to acquire social status by virtue of his collecting. Indeed, he refused a peerage in the 1937 Coronation Honours List, preferring to keep his independence and integrity' (*Impressionist & Post-Impressionist Masterpieces: The Courtauld Collection*, 1987). Courtauld himself said that art was 'religion's next-of-kin'.

Courtois, Jacques (*b* Saint Hippolyte, Franche-Comté, 12 Dec. 1621; *d* Rome, 14 Nov. 1676) and **Guillaume** (*b* Saint Hippolyte, 1628; *d* Rome, 14 June 1679). French painters, brothers, active in Italy and often known by the Italian forms of the names, Giacomo and Guglielmo Cortese. They came from Burgundy and both had the nickname Il Borgognone or Le

Bourguignon. Jacques was a prolific painter of battle scenes, fairly close in style to those of Salvator *Rosa, but more colourful; his work was influential in popularizing the genre in Italy. Guillaume was a pupil of Pietro da *Cortona and mainly painted altarpieces. He was an outstanding draughtsman and also made a few etchings. Both brothers worked in Rome for much of their careers and they sometimes collaborated.

Courtois, Marie. See NATTIER.

Cousin, Jean the Elder (b ?Sens, c.1490; d ?Paris, c.1560). French painter, engraver, and designer, active in Sens and then from about 1538 in Paris. He had a successful career as a painter and a designer of stained glass and tapestries, but very little surviving work can be securely attributed to him. The only certain documented works are three tapestries from a series on the life of St Mammès, which he contracted to design in 1543 (two are in Langres Cathedral, for which they were woven, the other is in the Louvre, Paris). The painting *Eva Prima Pandora* (Louvre), however, can also be confidently given to him, as the attribution goes back almost to his lifetime, and two windows in Sens Cathedral are also traditionally attributed to him. In 1560 he published a treatise on perspective. A similar pattern emerges with his son **Jean the Younger** (b ?Sens, c.1525; d ?Paris, c.1595), a painter and engraver. He too worked in Sens and Paris and had a great contemporary reputation, but again little documented work survives. His most important painting is a *Last Judgement* (Louvre); he also produced a book of *emblem drawings entitled *Livre de fortune* (1568, Institut de France, Paris) and in 1595 published an instructional book on drawing the human figure, *Livre de pourtraicture*, which went through several editions and remained in use until the 19th century. The work of both father and son shows strong Italian influence and is remarkable for its independence from the prevailing style of the École de *Fontainebleau.

Cousin, Victor. See AESTHETICISM.

Coustou, Guillaume I (b Lyons, 25 Apr. 1677; d Paris, 22 Feb. 1746). The best-known member of a dynasty of French sculptors. He was trained by *Coysevox (his mother's brother), and like him worked a good deal for the court. His vigorous style was formed partly on the example of *Bernini, whose work he saw in Rome, where he worked c.1697–1700. His masterpieces are the celebrated pair of *Horse Tamers* (the Marly Horses, 1739–45), originally made for the royal chateau at Marly, then moved to the Place de la Concorde, Paris, and now in the Louvre. **Nicolas** (1658–1733), Guillaume's brother, was also employed in court circles, and his work can be seen at Versailles and in the Tuileries Gardens in Paris. He was probably the teacher of *Roubiliac. **Guillaume II** (1716–77), the son of Guillaume I, inherited his father's technical skill but little of his originality. Nevertheless, he enjoyed a successful career, his most important work being the monument to Louis de Bourbon (son of Louis XV) and his wife in Sens Cathedral (1766–77). **François** (d 1690), the father of Guillaume I and Nicolas and the founder of the dynasty, was a minor woodcarver working in Lyons.

Couture, Thomas (b Senlis, 21 Dec. 1815; d Villiers-le-Bel, 30 Mar. 1879). French historical and portrait painter, a pupil of *Gros and *Delaroche. He is chiefly remembered for his vast 'orgy' picture *The Romans of the Decadence* (Mus. d'Orsay, Paris), which was the sensation of the 1847 *Salon. As with other 'one-hit wonders', his reputation has sunk with that of his big work, which now is often cited as the classic example of the worst type of bombastic academic painting, impeccable in every detail and totally false in overall effect. His more informal works, however, are often much livelier in conception and technique, and as a teacher he encouraged direct study from landscape. *Manet was his best-known pupil, and among the others were *Fantin-Latour and *Puvis de Chavannes.

Cowie, James (b Cuminestown, Aberdeenshire, 16 May 1886; d nr. Cuminestown, 18 Apr. 1956). One of the most individual Scottish painters of the 20th century. Whereas the central tradition of modern Scottish painting has been one of rich colouring and lush, free brushwork (see, for example, SCOTTISH COLOURISTS), Cowie worked in a strong, hard, predominantly linear style—highly disciplined rather than intuitive (he made many preparatory drawings and often worked on a picture for several years). He took his subjects from what he saw around him, but he was also inspired by the Old Masters, often using their compositions as a starting point, without actually imitating them. Among his contemporaries he was perhaps closest in spirit to John *Nash, an artist he greatly admired. They shared an ability to infuse the ordinary with a sense of the mysterious. Cowie taught at several art schools in Scotland, his pupils including Robert

*Colquhoun, Robert MacBryde, and Joan *Eardley.

Cox, David (*b* Birmingham, 29 Apr. 1783; *d* Harborne, 7 June 1859). English landscape painter, mainly in watercolour. In his youth he worked as a scene painter in Birmingham, then in 1804 he moved to London, where he took up watercolour and had lessons from John *Varley. He lived in Hereford, 1814–27, and in London, 1827–41, before retiring to Harborne, near Birmingham (it is now a suburb of the city), from where he made annual sketching tours to the Welsh mountains. In spite of a certain anecdotal homeliness, his style was broad and vigorous, and in 1836 he began to paint on a rough Scottish wrapping paper that was particularly suited to it. A similar paper was made commercially and marketed as 'Cox Paper'. Cox devoted much of his time to teaching and wrote several instructional books on watercolour; in the last two decades of his life he also worked a good deal in oils. His son **David Cox the Younger** (1809–85) was also a landscape watercolourist.

Cox, Stephen. See PORPHYRY.

Coypel. Dynasty of French painters of which **Noël** (*b* Paris, 25 Dec. 1628; *d* Paris, 24 Dec. 1707) was the head. He worked in an academic style based on the example of *Poussin and *Le Brun, was much employed on the large decorative schemes of Louis XIV, notably at Versailles, and was director of the French Academy in Rome (1672–4) and then of the Académie Royale in Paris (1695–9). His son **Antoine** (*b* Paris, 12 Apr. 1661; *d* Paris, 7 Jan. 1722) accompanied his father to Rome as a boy (he was a child prodigy) and there is a strong Italian element in his style. This comes out particularly in his most famous work, the ceiling of the chapel at Versailles (1708), which derived from *Gaulli's ceiling in the Gesù in Rome. This and Coypel's decorations at the Palais Royal in Paris (1702–5, destroyed) rank as the two most completely *Baroque schemes found in French art of this period. The Versailles ceiling is more successful than much of Coypel's work, which often combines, in the words of Anthony *Blunt, 'the bombast of the Baroque and the pedantry of the *classical style without the virtues of either'. He became director of the Académie Royale in 1714 and chief painter to the king in 1715. His half-brother **Noël-Nicolas** (*b* Paris, 17 Nov. 1690; *d* Paris, 14 Dec. 1734) painted with much more charm, mainly mythological subjects, but he seems to have had a rather timid personality and did not

achieve the worldly success of the other members of the family. Indeed, he was the best painter of the family, but is the least famous. *Chardin was briefly his pupil. Antoine's son **Charles-Antoine** (*b* Paris, 11 July 1694; *d* Paris, 14 June 1752) was a much more forceful character than Noël-Nicolas and had a resoundingly successful career. In 1747 he became director of the Académie Royale and chief painter to the king. He also wrote verse, plays (several of which were performed at court), and art criticism. As a painter he was versatile and prolific, but the weakest member of the family; his *Supper at Emmaus* (1746) in St Merri, Paris, has been described by Sir Michael Levey as 'pathetically inept'.

Coysevox, Antoine (*b* Lyons, 29 Sept. 1640; *d* Paris, 10 Oct. 1720). French sculptor, with *Girardon the most successful of Louis XIV's reign. His style was more *Baroque than Girardon's and he overtook his rival in popularity towards the end of the 17th century as the king's taste turned away from the *classical. By 1679 Coysevox was working at Versailles, where he made numerous statues for the gardens and did much interior decoration, including a large stucco *relief of the *Triumph of Louis XIV* (c.1682) in the Salon de la Guerre. He was at his best, however, as a maker of portrait busts, showing a naturalism of conception and an animation of expression that look forward to the *Rococo. This is particularly so with his portraits of friends, but even his formal commissions can be remarkably lively. The Wallace Collection, London, has an outstanding example of both his formal and informal portraits: the bronze *Louis XIV* (c.1686) and the terracotta *Charles Le Brun* (1676).

Cozens, Alexander (*b* Russia, ?1717; *d* London, 23 Apr. 1786). English landscape draughtsman. Cozens was one of the first major British artists to work exclusively as a landscapist and he helped to bring intellectual respectability to his speciality by stressing its poetic and imaginative qualities rather than its topographical function. He grew up in St Petersburg, the son of a shipbuilder employed by Peter the Great (there is no truth in the legend that Peter was his real father), and although he was educated in England, he later returned to Russia and did not settle in Britain until he was about 30. For much of his career he worked as a fashionable teacher, and he published several treatises. The most famous of these is *A New Method of Assisting the Invention in Drawing Original*

Compositions of Landscape (1786), in which he explains his method of 'blot drawing'—using accidental marks on the drawing paper to stimulate the imagination by suggesting landscape forms that could be developed into a finished work (see AUTOMATISM). Cozens observes that 'something of the same kind had been mentioned by *Leonardo da Vinci, in his Treatise on Painting' and that reading the passage in question 'tended to confirm my own opinion'. He worked almost exclusively in monochrome, and both his 'blot drawings' and his more formal compositions use intense lights and darks with masterly effect to suggest the power and mystery of nature.

His son **John Robert Cozens** (*b* London, 1752; *d* London, *c*.14 Dec. 1797) was the outstanding landscape watercolourist of his generation. Much of his work derived from two Continental journeys, in 1776–9 and 1782–3, during which he visited Italy and Switzerland. On the first he was draughtsman to Richard Payne *Knight, and on the second he was part of the entourage of William *Beckford (a former pupil of his father). Throughout his life he was subject to fits of severe depression and in 1794 he became insane, thereafter being cared for by Dr *Monro. His work was more naturalistic than his father's, but nevertheless was more concerned with evocation of mood (typically one of poetic melancholy) than with topographical accuracy. Unlike his father, he does not seem ever to have worked wholly from imagination, but he often transposed landscape features in the interests of obtaining a more pleasing composition. His work was admired and copied by *Constable (who called him 'the greatest genius that ever touched landscape'), *Girtin, and *Turner.

Crabeth, Dirck (*d* Gouda, 1574) and **Wouter** (*d* Gouda, 1589). Netherlandish designers of stained-glass windows, brothers, the most important members of a family of artists active mainly in Gouda. They are best known for their work on the city's St Janskerck; it was virtually destroyed by fire in 1552 and the brothers were prominent among the artists who designed new windows after the church was rebuilt. Between 1555 and 1571 Dirck made nine windows and Wouter made four; some of their *cartoons are preserved in the church. Dirck is regarded as one of the outstanding stained-glass designers of his time, his figures having great vigour and dignity. Wouter's style was more influenced by *Renaissance ideas. His grandson **Wouter Crabeth II** (*c*.1594–1644) was a painter.

He spent about a decade in Rome (*c*.1615–*c*.1625) and was a founder member of the *Schildersbent. His style was influenced by *Caravaggio.

Cragg, Tony. See NEW BRITISH SCULPTURE.

Craig, Gordon (*b* Stevenage, 16 Jan. 1872; *d* Vence, 29 July 1966). British theatrical designer and graphic artist, the illegitimate son of the actress Ellen Terry and the architect and theatre critic E. W. Godwin ('Craig' was a stage name he adopted in his early days as an actor, later formalized by deed poll). Tall and handsome, with the theatre in his veins, he became a successful leading man, but in 1897 he gave up acting to concentrate on design and directing. His approach was highly unconventional, aiming for simplicity and unity in place of Victorian elaboration. From 1907 he lived on the Continent, first in Italy and then from 1931 in France. In 1913 he founded a theatre school in Florence at which he made experiments with moving lights and scenery that give him a claim to be regarded as a pioneer of *Kinetic and *Light art. After his theatre school closed in 1915 because of the First World War he concentrated more on writing, notably in his quarterly periodical the *Mask* (1908–29). He also developed his talent as a printmaker (he had learnt wood engraving from his friends William *Nicholson and James *Pryde). In this field, Craig is best known for his strikingly bold illustrations to the Cranach Press (see PRIVATE PRESS) edition of *Hamlet* (1927). By the time of his death at the age of 94 he had 'seen the best of his former revolutionary ideas pass into general theatre practice' (*DNB*).

Craig had many children, legitimate and illegitimate; one of them, **Edward Anthony Craig** (1905–98), was a painter, book illustrator, and designer for the stage and cinema. He sometimes worked under the name Edward Carrick. His son **John Craig** (1931–) and daughter **Helen Craig** (1934–) continue the family tradition as illustrators.

Cranach, Lucas the Elder (*b* Kronach, Franconia, 1472; *d* Weimar, 16 Oct. 1553). German painter and designer of woodcuts. He takes his name from the small town in south Germany where he was born. Very little is known of his life before he moved to Vienna in 1501/2 and started working for the humanist circles associated with the newly founded university. His stay in Vienna was brief (he left in 1504), but in this period he painted some of his finest and most original works. They include portraits, notably those of Johannes Cuspinian, a lecturer at the university, and his wife Anna (1502–3, Reinhart Coll., Winterthur), and several religious works in which he shows a remarkable feeling for the beauty of landscape characteristic of the *Danube School. The finest example of this manner is perhaps the *Rest on the Flight into Egypt* (Gemäldegalerie, Berlin), which shows the Holy Family resting in the glade of a German pine forest. It was painted in 1504, just before Cranach moved to Wittenberg as court painter to Frederick III (the Wise), Elector of Saxony.

Cranach remained in Wittenberg until 1550, when he followed the Elector John Frederick (the Unfortunate) into exile, to Augsburg, Innsbruck, and finally Weimar. During his time in Wittenberg he became extremely wealthy and one of the city's most respected citizens, serving as burgomaster for several years. His paintings were eagerly sought by collectors, and his busy studio often produced numerous replicas of popular designs, particularly those in which he showed his skill at depicting female beauty—more than ten versions are known of his *Reclining Nymph*. He excelled at such erotic nudes, which are influenced by Italian *Renaissance models but totally different in spirit, and he also had a penchant for pictures of coquettish women wearing large hats, sometimes shown as Judith or the goddesses in the *Judgement of Paris*. The most innovative works of his Wittenberg period, however, are probably his full-length portraits (*The Duke* and *Duchess of Saxony*, 1514, Gemäldegalerie, Dresden).

Wittenberg was at the centre of the Protestant Reformation and Cranach supported the Lutheran cause. He painted several portraits of Luther and also designed the woodcut illustrations for his translation of the New Testament (1522). However, always an astute businessman, he also worked for Catholic patrons. During his later years he was assisted by his son **Lucas the Younger** (1515–86), who carried on the tradition of the workshop and imitated his father's style so successfully that it is often difficult to distinguish between their hands.

Cranach Press. See PRIVATE PRESS.

Crane, Walter (*b* Liverpool, 15 Aug. 1845; *d* Horsham, Sussex, 14 Mar. 1915). British illustrator, designer, painter, writer, and administrator. His career was very varied, but he is best remembered today as an illustrator of children's books, a field in which he was prolific throughout his life. He took this work very seriously, believing that 'We all remember the little cuts that coloured the books of our childhood. The inef-

faceable quality of these early pictorial and literary impressions affords the strongest plea for good art in the nursery and the schoolroom.' Originally he worked in black and white, but he adapted well to the photomechanical colour processes that came in at the end of the 19th century and was one of the pioneers of the full-colour picture book for children. He was also one of the first illustrators to treat a double-page spread as a visual unity. His work for adults included designing wallpaper, and he was a leading figure in the *Arts and Crafts movement that tried to rehabilitate good design and craftsmanship. He was greatly interested in art education, serving on various examination boards; in the 1890s he taught in Manchester and Reading, and in 1898–9 he was principal of the *Royal College of Art. His writings included *Of the Decorative Illustration of Books* (1896). Crane said that he enjoyed illustrating children's books because 'in a sober and matter-of-fact age' they afforded an 'outlet for unrestrained flights of fancy'. He evidently carried the fairy-tale world he depicted into his own domestic life, for his wife once received astonished guests 'dressed as a sort of sunflower'.

craquelure. A network of small cracks that appears on the surface of a painting when in the course of time the paint or *varnish has become brittle.

Craven, Thomas. See REGIONALISM.

Crawford, Thomas (*b* New York, 22 Mar. 1813 or 1814; *d* London, 10 Oct. 1857). American sculptor. He moved to Rome in 1835, studied with *Thorvaldsen, and became the most thoroughgoing *Neoclassicist among American sculptors of his generation. Although he settled permanently in Rome (the first American sculptor to do so), he made visits to his native country and attained an extraordinary reputation there, receiving numerous prestigious public commissions. The most notable is the bronze *Armed Liberty* on top of the dome of the Capitol in Washington, which was begun in 1855 and set in place in 1863 after Crawford's early death from cancer.

crayon. See CHALK.

crayon manner. A printmaking technique, a variant of *etching, used for the reproduction of red or brown chalk drawings. The technique evolved in the 1750s in France, where such drawings were highly popular at the time (*Boucher and *Fragonard were among the artists whose work was reproduced). Jean-Charles François (1717–69), a skilled and resourceful engraver, is generally credited as the inventor. Various multi-pointed tools were used on the etching *ground, creating closely dotted lines and strokes that imitated with uncanny accuracy the grainy effect of chalk on rough paper, especially when the image was printed in red or brown ink. An offshoot of crayon manner soon developed in the form of pastel manner, in which several plates were inked with different colours to give the appearance of *pastel drawings; and in England crayon manner was developed into *stipple engraving. All three techniques were virtually rendered obsolete by *lithography early in the 19th century.

Credi, Lorenzo di (b Florence, c.1458; d Florence, 12 Jan. 1537). Florentine painter. He was a fellow pupil of *Leonardo in *Verrocchio's workshop and he seems to have stayed there until Verrocchio's death in 1488, managing the painting side of his master's varied business. He was a very fine craftsman, but his style lacked individuality. His early work is in an extremely prosaic version of Leonardo's youthful style; later he absorbed some of the ideas of the High *Renaissance. He had several pupils and seems to have had a fairly successful career with his solid, unspectacular skills. It is said that in the 1490s he was influenced by the teachings of Savonarola (see BARTOLOMMEO and BOTTICELLI) and destroyed all his pictures with profane subjects.

Creed, Martin. See TURNER PRIZE.

Crespi, Daniele (b ?Milan, c.1597; d Milan, 19 July 1630). Milanese painter. Although he died young of the plague, his output was large and his work is considered to be one of the most typical expressions of the zealous spirit of the Counter-Reformation that affected Milan during his time. His acknowledged masterpiece is St Charles Borromeo at Supper (c.1628, S. Maria della Passione, Milan); in its simple composition and emotional directness it reflects the ideals of painting advocated by the Council of Trent and marks a move from *Mannerism to *Baroque. He was probably a relative of Giovanni Battista *Crespi, whose work influenced him.

Crespi, Giovanni Battista (Il Cerano) (b ?Cerano, nr. Novara, c.1575; d Milan, 23 Oct. 1632). Italian painter, sculptor, engraver, architect, and writer, active mainly in Milan, where he was one of the leading artists of his time. He had settled there by the late 1590s, probably following a period in Rome, and became a protégé of Cardinal Federico Borromeo (1564–1631), Archbishop of Milan from 1595. Borromeo (cousin of St Charles Borromeo) was an important art patron; he appointed Crespi head of the painting section of the Accademia *Ambrosiana, which he founded in 1620, and in 1629 put him in charge of the sculptural decoration of Milan Cathedral. Crespi's paintings, often mystical in feeling, are complex stylistically; there is a strong *Mannerist current in his colouring and in the elegant posturing of his figures, but his work also shows a solidity and a feeling for realistic details that give it a place in the vanguard of the *Baroque.

Crespi, Giuseppe Maria (Lo Spagnuolo) (b Bologna, 14 Mar. 1665; d Bologna, 25 Mar. 1747). Bolognese painter. His nickname (the Spaniard) was given to him in his student days because of his manner of dress. He reacted against the academic tradition in which he was trained (*Cignani was one of his teachers) and is now best known for low-life *genre scenes. They are in the tradition of the everyday life paintings of the *Carracci, but go far beyond them in their sombre gravity and sense of unvarnished reality (The Hamlet, c.1705, Pinacoteca Nazionale, Bologna). He also painted many other subjects, and after the death of his wife in 1722 he became very pious and concentrated on religious works. From this time he became reclusive, rarely leaving his house except to go to Mass, but earlier in his career he had travelled a good deal in Italy; he had an international reputation and was particularly influential on Venetian painters, most notably *Piazzetta. Rudolf *Wittkower called him 'the only real genius of the late Bolognese school'. His son **Luigi Crespi** (1708–79) was a painter, picture dealer, and writer on art. His books include a collection of biographies of contemporary Bolognese artists (1769), a supplement to *Malvasia's Felsina pittrice.

Critius. Greek sculptor, active in Athens in the early 5th century BC. He worked in collaboration with another sculptor called Nesiotes, their chief work being the bronze Tyrannicides, erected in 477 BC, to replace the group by *Antenor that had been taken as booty after the Persian sack of Athens in 480. The group by Critius and Nesiotes is lost, but Roman copies of it survive (the most complete is in the Archaeological Museum, Naples). Other works have been attributed to Critius, including a beautiful marble *kouros known as 'The Critius Boy' in the

Acropolis Museum, Athens. This and the *Tyrannicides* group are regarded as marking the beginning of the *Severe (or early *Classical) style in Greek sculpture.

Critz, John de (*b* Antwerp, *c*.1551; *bur*. London, 14 Mar. 1642). British painter, the son of an Antwerp goldsmith who settled in London to escape religious persecution. In 1603 he was appointed serjeant-painter by James I and held the post until his death. No works certainly by him survive, but a number of portraits have been given to him on circumstantial evidence, including one of James I (1610) in the National Maritime Museum, London. Three of his sons were also painters: **John the Younger** (*c*.1591–*c*.1642), **Thomas** (1607–53), and **Emanuel** (1608–65). Little is known about any of them, but an impressive group of portraits of the Tradescant family (*c*.1640–50, Ashmolean Mus., Oxford) is probably by Thomas or Emanuel (the Tradescant and de Critz families were related). These portraits have a weighty gravity combined with a certain eccentric melancholy that puts them among the most remarkable English paintings of their period.

Crivelli, Carlo (*b* ?Venice, *c*.1430/5; *d* Ascoli Piceno, 1493/5). Italian painter. He always signed himself as a Venetian, but he is only once recorded in the city (in 1457 when he was fined and sentenced to six months' imprisonment for committing adultery) and he spent most of his career working in the Marches, particularly at Ascoli Piceno; he also lived for some time at Zara in Dalmatia (now Zadar, Croatia), which at this time was part of Venetian territory. Ascoli Piceno was for a time controlled by Naples and in 1490 Crivelli was knighted by Prince Ferdinand of Capua (later Ferdinand II of Naples), an indication of the high contemporary reputation he enjoyed. His paintings are all of religious subjects, done in an elaborate, old-fashioned style that owes much to the wiry Paduan tradition of *Squarcione and *Mantegna and yet is highly distinctive, with a rich vein of fantasy. Their dense ornamentation is often increased by the use of *gesso decoration combined with the paint. The finest collection of his works is in the National Gallery in London and includes the delightful and much reproduced *Annunciation* (1486). **Vittore Crivelli** (*d* 1501/2), Carlo's younger brother, was a faithful but pedestrian follower.

Croce, Benedetto (*b* Pescasseroli, 25 Feb. 1866; *d* Naples, 20 Nov. 1952). Italian philosopher, historian, critic, and statesman. Croce was regarded as the foremost Italian philosopher of the 20th century. His large literary output included a good deal about art, his views being set out most fully in his book *Estetica come scienza dell'espressione e linguistica generale* (1902; English translation, *Aesthetic as Science of Expression and General Linguistic*, 1909). In this work he regards all art as a form of imaging—a conjuring into being of images of particulars—and considers that good art is successful expression of emotion. But Croce uses 'expression' in a special sense, as a synonym for 'intuition', and not in the usual sense that involves some form of external manifestation. His theories have been criticized partly on the ground of inherent confusion of concepts, more generally on the ground that his identification of art with the mental process of intuition/expression does less than justice to the problems of communicating an idea or intuition in concrete form—a work of art as understood in ordinary language. Nevertheless, because of his 'attempt to understand the distinction between representation and expression', Croce has been described as 'the founder of modern aesthetics' (*Oxford History of Western Philosophy*, 2000). His other writings on aesthetics include the article on the subject in the 14th edition (1929) of the *Encyclopaedia Britannica* and many contributions to the journal *La critica*, which he founded in 1903 (in 1944 it became *Quaderni della critica*). He was briefly minister of education before Benito Mussolini came to power in 1922 and served in the government again in 1944, after Mussolini had been deposed; his staunch opposition to Fascism made him a symbol of liberty of thought and moral courage.

Crome, John (*b* Norwich, 22 Dec. 1768; *d* Norwich, 22 Apr. 1821). English landscape painter and etcher, with *Cotman the major artist of the *Norwich School. Whereas Cotman was primarily a watercolourist, Crome painted mainly in oils. He was based in Norwich all his life, earning a major part of his living as a drawing master; he made regular trips to London and visited other parts of the country, but his only journey abroad was to Paris in 1814 to see the exhibition of pictures looted by Napoleon. Of humble origin, he was first apprenticed to a coach and sign painter and taught himself principally by copying works in the collection of Thomas Harvey, a local collector and amateur painter who befriended him. The Dutch painters *Ruisdael and *Hobbema were particularly influential on him and he also admired *Gainsborough and *Wilson, but his work was based as much on direct observation of nature as on study of the Old Masters. His favourite subjects included heathland, woods, and tranquil stretches of river, and his style was fresh, clear, and unaffected. In addition to his paintings he made 34 etchings, which were posthumously published by his widow and his eldest son **John Bernay Crome** (1794–1842). The elder Crome is sometimes referred to as 'Old Crome' to distinguish him from his son, who painted in his manner but with less distinction.

Cropsey, Jasper F. See HUDSON RIVER SCHOOL.

Cross, Henri-Edmond. See NEO-IMPRESSIONISM.

Crowe, Sir Joseph Archer (b London, 20 Oct. 1825; d Gamburg an der Tauber, Germany, 6 Sept. 1896). English journalist, diplomat, and art historian, brother of the painter **Eyre Crowe** (1824–1910). He had a distinguished career as a commercial attaché in Berlin, Paris, and Vienna and was also a war correspondent in the Crimea and elsewhere, but he is best known for his writings on art history done in collaboration with the Italian draughtsman and connoisseur Giovanni Battista Cavalcaselle (b Legnano, 22 Jan. 1819; d Rome, 31 Oct. 1897). They met by chance in 1847 and became firm friends when Cavalcaselle was later a political refugee in London; for a time they lived in the same house. Every detail of their books was discussed between them, but Crowe did all the actual writing because Cavalcaselle's English was inadequate; in the words of John *Pope-Hennessy, 'Crowe was the synthesizer and historian, Cavalcaselle was the eye.' Their prodigious output included *The Early Flemish Painters* (1857), *A New History of Painting in Italy* (3 vols., 1864–8), *A History of Painting in North Italy* (2 vols., 1871), *Titian: His Life and Times* (2 vols., 1877), and *Raphael: His Life and Works* (2 vols., 1882). These works, all of which have appeared in subsequent editions, either in English or translation, set new standards of methodical research, bringing to light masses of new information, and they are still considered valuable.

Crozat, Pierre (b Toulouse, 1655; d Paris, 24 May 1740). French banker and collector. He was immensely wealthy and the greatest private collector in 18th-century France. His collection was varied but was particularly rich in drawings—he owned about 19,000, mainly by Italian artists.

These were sold after his death (catalogued by *Mariette), but the bulk of his paintings passed to his nephew **Louis-Antoine Crozat** (1699–1770), whose heirs sold them to Catherine the Great of Russia. Most of them are now in the *Hermitage, St Petersburg, including *Rembrandt's celebrated *Danaë* (1636).

Cruikshank, George (b London, 27 Sept. 1792; d London, 1 Feb. 1878). English *caricaturist, illustrator, and painter. The son of a caricaturist, **Isaac Cruikshank** (1764–1811), he was highly precocious and was successful whilst still in his teens. By the time *Gillray died in 1815, Cruikshank was already recognized as his successor as the leading political cartoonist of the day (he had completed various works Gillray had been too ill to finish and could imitate his style fluently). The dissolute private life of the Prince Regent was one of his favourite topics, but when his target became king as George IV in 1820, Cruikshank was paid £100 'in consideration of a pledge not to caricature His Majesty in any immoral situation'. From this time he began to turn from political satire to social observation and from prints to book illustrations. His output in this field was enormous and gained him a European reputation. Among his most famous illustrations are the 24 etchings he made for Dickens's *Oliver Twist* (1837). In 1847 he suddenly took up the cause of temperance, producing moral narratives in series of prints (*The Bottle*, 1847; *The Drunkard's Children*, 1848) and a vast painting, *The Worship of Bacchus* (1860–2, Tate, London). His brother **Robert Cruikshank** (1789–1856), with whom he sometimes collaborated, was a printmaker, illustrator, and painter.

Cruz-Diez, Carlos (b Caracas, 17 Aug. 1923). Venezuelan painter and *Kinetic artist, active mainly in Paris since 1960. His work (which is often made in series) has been much concerned with the role of colour in Kinetic art. In his *Physiochromie* series—low reliefs that he started making in 1959—he created shifting geometric images that emerge, intensify, change, and dematerialize as the viewer moves in front of them. He achieved this effect by using narrow strips of painted metal or plastic arranged in parallel lines or at right angles to each other (*Physiochromie 113*, 1963, reconstructed by the artist 1976, Tate, London). His work has been shown in many exhibitions and he has won several awards, including the International Painting Prize at the São Paulo *Bienale in 1967. His later work has included architectural installations, or 'chromatic environments' as he calls them, in public buildings.

Cubism. A term describing a revolutionary style of painting created jointly by *Braque and *Picasso in the period 1907–14 and subsequently applied to a broad movement, centred in Paris but international in scope, in which their ideas were adopted and adapted by many other artists. These artists were mainly painters, but Cubist ideas and motifs were also used in sculpture, and to a more limited and superficial degree in the applied arts and occasionally in architecture. Cubism was a complex phenomenon, but in essence it involved what Juan *Gris (its leading exponent apart from the two founders) called 'a new way of representing the world'. Abandoning the idea of a single fixed viewpoint that had dominated European painting for centuries, Cubist pictures used a multiplicity of viewpoints, so that many different aspects of an object could be simultaneously depicted in the same picture. Such fragmentation and rearrangement of form meant that a painting could now be regarded less as a kind of window through which an image of the world is seen, and more as a physical object on which a subjective response to the world is created. This new approach proved extraordinarily influential, and John *Golding has described Cubism as 'perhaps the most important and certainly the most complete and radical artistic revolution since the *Renaissance'.

Braque and Picasso met in October 1907. At this time, Braque had recently been overwhelmed by the memorial exhibition of *Cézanne's work at the *Salon d'Automne, and Picasso had spent much of the year working on *Les Demoiselles d'Avignon* (1906–7, MoMA, New York), in which the angular and aggressive forms owed much to the influence of African sculpture. These two sources—Cézanne and *primitive art—were of great importance in the genesis of Cubism. Cézanne's late work, with its subtle overlapping patches of colour, showed how a sense of solidity and pictorial structure could be created without traditional perspective or modelling; and primitive art offered an example of expressively distorted forms and freedom from inhibition.

The pictures to which the term 'Cubism' was first applied were a group of landscapes painted by Braque in the summer of 1908, when he was staying at L'Estaque, near Marseilles. They were shown later that year at *Kahnweiler's gallery, and in reviewing this exhibition Louis Vauxcelles (see FAUVISM) made reference to Braque's way of

reducing 'everything—sites, figures, and houses—to geometric outlines, to cubes'. The following year Vauxcelles used the expression 'bizarreries cubiques' (cubic eccentricities), and by 1911 the term 'Cubism' had entered the English language. The word is undoubtedly apposite for the blocklike forms in some of the Braque landscapes that occasioned Vauxcelles's gibes and in a few similar works by Picasso, but it is not really appropriate to their later Cubist pictures, in which the forms tend to be broken into facets rather than fashioned into cubes. However, they soon accepted the term, as did their followers.

Braque and Picasso's mature Cubist work is usually divided into two phases—Analytical Cubism (1909–11) and Synthetic Cubism (1912–14). In the 'Analytical' phase, the relatively solid massing of their earliest Cubist paintings gave way to a process of composition in which the forms of the object depicted are fragmented into a large number of small, intricately hinged planes that fuse with one another and with the surrounding space. This fascination with pictorial structure led to colour being downplayed, and the archetypal Analytical Cubist paintings are virtually monochromatic, painted in muted browns or warm greys. Examples—showing how similar the two artists were in style at this date—are Braque's *The Portuguese* (1911, Kunstmuseum, Basle) and Picasso's *The Accordionist* (1911, Guggenheim Mus., New York). At times they worked in such close harmony—'like mountaineers roped together' in Braque's memorable phrase—that even experts can have difficulty in differentiating their hands. In *The Portuguese*, Braque introduced the use of stencilled lettering, and by the following year he was experimenting with mixing materials such as sand and sawdust with his paint to create interesting textures. He refined this notion again by imitating the effect of wood graining. Later in the same year, 1912, Picasso took this a stage further when he produced his first *collages, and Braque quickly followed with his own type of collage—the *papier collé*.

These developments—marking a move away from the very cerebral near-abstraction of Analytical Cubism to a more relaxed and decorative art incorporating everyday ephemera—ushered in Synthetic Cubism. This reversed the compositional principle of Analytical Cubism, the image being built up ('synthesized') from pre-existing elements or shapes rather than being created through a process of fragmentation. One consequence of this concern with greater surface richness was that Braque and Picasso reintroduced colour to their paintings. In the Synthetic phase of Cubism, Juan Gris played as important a role as Braque or Picasso, and by this time many other artists had been won over to the movement (including Fernard *Léger, who is often considered the fourth major Cubist). Indeed, Cubism had become the dominant avant-garde idiom in Paris as early as 1911, *Delaunay, *Gleizes, *La Fresnaye, *Metzinger, and *Picabia being among the adherents by this time.

Cubism proved immensely adaptable and was the starting point or an essential component of several other movements, including *Constructivism, *Futurism, *Orphism, *Purism, and *Vorticism, as well as a spur to the imagination of countless individual artists. These included not only painters, but also sculptors, who adapted Cubist ideas in various ways, notably by the opening up of forms so that voids as well as solids form distinct shapes. Picasso himself made Cubist sculpture, and other leading artists who worked in the idiom include *Archipenko (whose international success played a great part in spreading Cubist ideas), *Duchamp-Villon, *Laurens, *Lipchitz, and *Zadkine. Another noted Cubist sculptor was the Czech Otto *Gutfreund, who was part of a remarkable flowering of Cubist art and design in Prague in the years immediately before the First World War. This was the only place where there was a significant adaptation of Cubism to architecture; several Czech architects broke up the façades of their buildings with abstract, prismatic forms in a way that clearly recalls the fragmentation of Analytical Cubism. In the applied arts, Cubism was one of the sources of *Art Deco, and more generally it has had a huge and varied impact on modern pictorial culture, becoming part of the common currency of ideas: 'Cubist painting gave to artists complete freedom to deal with reality in art in any way they chose. Cubist collage gave them in addition the equally radical freedom to *make* art out of anything they chose. These developments have been enormously fruitful—they have been and they continue to be the basis of much of the best of modern art' (Simon Wilson, *What is Cubism?*, 1983).

Cullen, Maurice (*b* St John's, Newfoundland, 6 June 1866; *d* Chambly, Quebec, 28 Mar. 1934) Canadian painter, whose work was influential in introducing *Impressionism to his country. From 1889 to 1895 he lived in Paris and elsewhere in France, with trips to Venice and North Africa;

he made two shorter trips to Europe before settling for good in Canada in 1902. His subjects included city scenes (*Old Houses, Montreal, c.*1900, Montreal Mus. of Fine Arts) and landscapes on the St Lawrence River, in the Laurentian hills, at St John's in Newfoundland, and in the Rocky Mountains. After about 1920 he lived in virtual retirement in a cabin he built at Lac Tremblant in the Laurentians. His friend J. W. *Morrice said of his work: 'he gets at the guts of things.'

Cumberland Market Group. A small group of painters formed in London in 1914, with Robert *Bevan, Harold *Gilman, and Charles *Ginner as the core members; all three had belonged to the recently defunct *Camden Town Group and were at this time members also of its successor, the *London Group. The Cumberland Market Group was named after 49 Cumberland Market in Camden, the address of Bevan's studio, where the members used to meet. They held only one exhibition, at the Goupil Gallery, London, in April 1915, by which time John *Nash had joined the group. It never officially disbanded but lapsed in about 1918.

Cunningham, Allan (*b* Keir parish, Dumfriesshire, 7 Dec. 1784; *d* London, 30 Oct. 1842). Scottish miscellaneous writer. He served an apprenticeship with his stonemason brother but turned to literature. His large output included a good deal on Scottish poetry, songs, and legends, notably an eight-volume edition (1834) of the works of Robert Burns (as a boy he had walked in Burns's funeral procession). In 1810 he moved to London and in 1814 became assistant to Sir Francis *Chantrey, a post he held until Chantrey's death in 1841. This gave him a good knowledge of the contemporary artistic scene, which he put to use in his *Lives of the Most Eminent British Painters, Sculptors, and Architects* (6 vols., 1829–33). He also edited a revised edition of Pilkington's *Dictionary of Painters* (1840; see FUSELI) and wrote a life of *Wilkie, posthumously published in 1843. See also NOLLEKENS.

Cure. Family of English sculptors and stonemasons of Netherlandish origin. The founder, **William I** (*d* 1579), moved to England in about 1540 to work on Henry VIII's Nonesuch Palace and became an English citizen in 1552. There are no surviving documented works by William, but several tombs are attributed to him. His son **Cornelius** (*d c.*1609) was master mason to Elizabeth I and James I, and his most important commission was the tomb of Mary Queen of Scots in Westminster Abbey (c.1605–12), although some of the work, perhaps including the very fine effigy, must have been done after his death by his son **William II** (d 1632). He succeeded his father as master mason and held the post until his death, but he was described as 'careless and negligent' of his duties and in 1619 was replaced as mason to Inigo *Jones's Banqueting House by Nicholas *Stone, who succeeded him as master mason in 1632. His work as a sculptor consisted mainly of tombs, but he also carved figures (1614–15) of Henry VIII, Anne of Denmark, and Prince Charles (later Charles I) on the Great Gate of Trinity College, Cambridge; they are now badly weathered.

Currie, Ken. See GLASGOW SCHOOL.

Currier & Ives prints. Popular *lithographs published in New York by Nathaniel Currier (b Roxbury, Mass., 27 Mar. 1813; d New York, 20 Nov. 1888) and James M. Ives (b New York, 5 Mar. 1824; d Rye, NY, 3 Jan. 1895). Currier began issuing prints in 1834 and the name 'Currier & Ives' was first used in 1857, when Ives (the firm's bookkeeper) became a partner. They advertised their lithographs as 'Coloured Engravings for the People', and they represented almost every aspect of contemporary America, including sporting, sentimental, patriotic, and political subjects, together with portraits, landscapes, disasters, scenes of city life, railroads, Mississippi steamboats, and so forth. A number of artists, most of whom specialized in particular subjects, were retained by the firm to draw the lithographs in black and white; afterwards the prints were coloured by hand on a production-line system (one assistant to each colour) and sold cheaply to the public by agents, printsellers, and pedlars. The business was carried on until 1907 by the sons of the founders.

Curry, John Steuart (b nr. Dunavant, Kan., 14 Nov. 1897; d Madison, Wis., 29 Aug. 1946). American painter. From 1919 to 1926 he worked as an illustrator for pulp magazines, then spent a year in Europe, before settling in New York, where he was encouraged and supported by Gertrude Vanderbilt *Whitney. He believed that art should grow out of everyday life and be motivated by affection, and his subjects were taken from the Midwest he loved (he was born on a farm in Kansas and never forgot his roots). Two of his most famous works are *Baptism in Kansas* (1928, Whitney Mus., New York) and *Hogs Killing a Rattlesnake* (1930, Art Inst. of Chi-

cago); they show his anecdotal, rather melodramatic style (he often depicted the violence of nature)—sometimes weak in draughtsmanship, but always vigorous and sincere. In the 1930s Curry was recognized—along with *Benton and *Wood—as one of the leading exponents of *Regionalism, and he was given commissions for several large murals; the best known—generally regarded as his masterpieces, even though the scheme was never completed—are in the state capitol in Topeka, Kansas (1938–40); the subjects include the activities of John Brown, the famous campaigner against slavery.

Cuyp. The name of a family of Dutch painters of Dordrecht, of which three members gained distinction. **Jacob Gerritsz. Cuyp** (b Dordrecht, Dec. 1594; d Dordrecht, 1652) was the son of a glass painter and according to *Houbraken was a pupil of Abraham *Bloemaert in Utrecht. His output was varied, but he is now best known as a portraitist—his portraits of children are particularly fine. **Benjamin Gerritsz. Cuyp** (bapt. Dordrecht, Dec. 1612; bur. Dordrecht, 28 Aug. 1652) was the half-brother of Jacob. He is known mainly for paintings of biblical and *genre scenes that use melodramatic light and shade in the manner of the young *Rembrandt.

Aelbert Cuyp (bapt. Dordrecht, Oct. 1620; bur. Dordrecht, 15 Nov. 1691) is the most famous member of the family and now one of the most celebrated of all landscape painters, although he also painted many other subjects. He was the son and probably the pupil of Jacob Gerritsz. Cuyp. His early works also show the influence of Jan van *Goyen. Although he is so closely associated with Dordrecht, Aelbert seems to have travelled along his country's great rivers to the eastern part of the Netherlands, and he also painted views of Westphalia. A prodigious number of pictures are ascribed to him, but his oeuvre poses many problems. He often signed his paintings but rarely dated them, and a satisfactory chronology has proved hard to establish. Although he had little influence outside Dordrecht, Cuyp had several imitators there, and some of the paintings formerly attributed to him are now given to Abraham Calraet (1642–1722), who signed himself 'AC' (the same initials as Cuyp). In 1658 Cuyp married a rich widow, and in the 1660s he seems to have virtually abandoned painting. He was almost forgotten for two generations after his death, then was rediscovered in the late 18th century, when he started to become particularly popular with

British collectors. He is still much better represented in British collections, public and private, than in Dutch museums (there are eleven pictures by him in the National Gallery, London, for example). His finest works—typically river scenes and landscapes with placid, dignified-looking cows—show great serenity and masterly handling of glowing light (usually Cuyp favoured the effects of the early morning or evening sun). He approaches *Claude more closely in spirit than any of his countrymen who travelled to Italy.

Cycladic. Name applied to the Bronze Age art and civilization of the Cyclades (a group of islands in the Aegean Sea between Greece and Turkey), flourishing from about 2500 BC to about 1400 BC, when the islands began to be assimilated into *Mycenaean culture. Surviving Cycladic art consists mainly of various types of decorated pottery and of white marble figurines (marble was abundant on the islands, particularly Naxos and Paros). The figurines (of uncertain purpose) are often of a distinctive type, in which the forms of body and facial features are pared down to a radically elegant simplicity that has greatly appealed to modern taste (they have been much forged). Because of the extensive maritime activities of the natives of the islands, Cycladic art was widely disseminated throughout the Mediterranean.

D

Dada. A movement in European art (with manifestations also in New York), c.1915–c.1922, characterized by a spirit of anarchic revolt against traditional values. It arose from a mood of disillusionment engendered by the First World War, to which some artists reacted with irony, cynicism, and nihilism. Originally Dada appeared in two neutral countries (Switzerland and the USA), but near the end of the war it spread to Germany and subsequently to a few other countries. The unprecedented carnage of the war led the Dadaists to question the values of the society that had created it and to find them morally bankrupt. Their response was to go to extremes of buffoonery and provocative behaviour to shock people out of corruption and complacency. One of their prime targets was the institutionalized art world, with its bourgeois ideas of taste and concern with market values. The Dadaists deliberately flouted accepted standards of beauty and they exaggerated the role of chance in artistic creation. Group activity was regarded as more important than individual works, and traditional media such as painting and sculpture were largely abandoned in favour of techniques and devices such as *collage, *photomontage, and *ready-mades, in which there was no concern for fine materials or craftsmanship; in literature the nonsense poem was a characteristic form of expression. Although the Dadaists scorned the art of the past, their methods and manifestos—particularly the techniques of outrage and provocation—owed much to *Futurism; however, Dada's nihilism was very different from Futurism's militant optimism.

European Dada was founded in Zurich in 1915 by a group of artists and writers including Hans *Arp, the German painter, sculptor, and filmmaker Hans Richter (1888–1976), and the Romanian poet Tristan Tzara (1896–1963). According to the most frequently cited of several accounts of how the name (French for 'hobby-horse') originated, it was chosen by inserting a penknife at random in the pages of a dictionary, thus symbolizing the anti-rational stance of the movement. By the end of the war the movement

was spreading to Germany, and there were significant Dada activities in three German cities: Berlin, Cologne, and Hanover. In Berlin the movement had a strong political dimension that was expressed particularly through the brilliant photomontages of Raoul Hausmann (1886–1971) and John *Heartfield and through the biting social satire of Otto *Dix and George *Grosz; eventually it gave way to *Neue Sachlichkeit. In Cologne a brief Dada movement (1919–20) was centred on two figures: Arp, who moved there from Zurich when the war ended; and Max *Ernst, who made witty and provocative use of collage and organized one of Dada's most notorious exhibitions, at which axes were provided for visitors to smash the works on show. In Hanover Kurt *Schwitters was the only important Dada exponent but one of the most dedicated of all.

Dada in New York arose independently of the European movement and virtually simultaneously. It was mainly confined to the activities of Marcel *Duchamp, *Man Ray, and Francis *Picabia; their work tends to be more whimsical and less violent than that of their counterparts in Europe, although they still liked to shock. Duchamp was the most influential of all exponents of Dada and Picabia was the most vigorous in promoting its ideas, forming a link between the European and American movements. He founded his Dada periodical *391* in Barcelona and he introduced the movement to Paris in 1919. In Paris the movement was mainly literary in its emphasis, and its tendency towards the fanciful and the absurd formed the basis for *Surrealism, which was officially launched there in 1924 but began to emerge a few years earlier. Other Dada groups appeared in Austria, Belgium, the Netherlands, and elsewhere. There was a Dada festival in Prague in 1921, in which Hausmann and Schwitters participated, and an international Dada exhibition was held in Paris in 1922. However, by this time the impetus was flagging, and at a meeting in Weimar in 1922, attended by Arp, Schwitters, and others, Tzara delivered a funeral oration on the movement.

Although it was fairly short-lived and confined to a few main centres, Dada was highly influential in its questioning and debunking of traditional concepts and methods, setting the agenda for much subsequent artistic experiment. Its techniques involving accident and chance were of great importance to the Surrealists and were also later exploited by the *Abstract Expressionists. *Conceptual art, too, has its roots in Dada. The spirit of the Dadaists, in fact, has never completely disappeared, and its tradition has been sustained in, for example, *Junk sculpture and *Pop art, which in the USA was sometimes known as *Neo-Dada.

Dadd, Richard (b Chatham, Kent, 1 Aug. 1817; d Broadmoor Hospital, Berkshire, 8 Jan. 1886). English painter who murdered his father in 1843 and spent the rest of his life in Bedlam and Broadmoor asylums. Before his mental breakdown he was considered one of the most promising artists of his generation (his friend *Frith called him 'a man of genius that would assuredly have placed him high in the first rank of painters') and after his incarceration he was encouraged to continue painting. Although most of his work before the murder had been fairly conventional, he had begun to paint fairy and fantasy subjects and in the asylums he developed these along highly imaginative lines; *The Fairy Feller's Master-Stroke* (1855–64, Tate, London) is probably the best known. Dadd was virtually forgotten for many years, but he became well known in the 1970s, when a major exhibition was devoted to him at the Tate (1974) and several books on him appeared.

Daddi, Bernardo (d ?Florence, 1348). Florentine painter, the outstanding painter in Florence in the period after the death of *Giotto (who was possibly his teacher). Daddi ran a busy workshop specializing in small devotional panels and portable altarpieces—types that he helped to popularize. His signed and dated works include a *polyptych of the *Crucifixion with Eight Saints* (1348, Courtauld Gal., London), and the works attributed to him include frescos of the martyrdoms of Sts Lawrence and Stephen in S. Croce. His style—a sweetened version of Giotto's, combining firm draughtsmanship with lightness and grace—was influential into the second half of the century.

Daguerre, Louis (b Cormeilles-en-Parisis, 18 Nov. 1787; d Bry-sur-Marne, 10 July 1851). French artist and inventor. He invented the *diorama (1822) and the daguerreotype, the first practic-able photographic process, in which the image was produced on a silvered copper plate sensitized by iodine. Each image was unique, as it was made directly onto the plate without an intervening 'negative'. Daguerre made the process public in 1839, only a few weeks before the English scientist William Henry Fox Talbot (1800–77) announced the invention of the calotype, which could produce multiple prints from a single negative. This ultimately represented the way ahead, but the daguerreotype produced a more detailed and attractive image and dominated the first twenty years of photography.

Dahl, Johan Christian (b Bergen, 24 Feb. 1788; d Dresden, 14 Oct. 1857). Norwegian landscape painter, active mainly in Dresden, where he became a professor at the Academy in 1824. In spite of his long residency in Germany, he took his subjects mainly from his native country and began its tradition of landscape painting—he is often called the discoverer of the Norwegian landscape. He was a friend of *Friedrich and he shared with him a feeling for *Romantic grandeur in nature, although Dahl's work does not have the mystical element found in Friedrich. Dahl often returned to Norway, and his strong patriotic feelings were expressed not only in his paintings, but also in his helping to found (1837) the National Gallery in Christiania (now Oslo), to which he presented his own impressive art collection.

Dahl, Michael (b Stockholm, 29 Sept. ?1659; d London, 20 Oct. 1743). Swedish portrait painter, active mainly in England. He settled permanently in London in 1689 (following an earlier stay in 1682–5) and became *Kneller's principal rival. His work is less dashing and fluent than Kneller's, but at his best he surpasses him in sincerity and humanity. There are several paintings by him or from his busy studio in the National Portrait Gallery in London.

Dalí, Salvador (b Figueras, Catalonia, 11 May 1904; d Figueras, 23 Jan. 1989). Spanish painter, sculptor, graphic artist, designer, film-maker, and writer. After working in a variety of styles, influenced by *Cubism, *Futurism, and *Metaphysical Painting, he had turned to *Surrealism by 1929. In that year he had a sell-out exhibition at the Galerie Camille Goemans in Paris; André *Breton wrote the catalogue preface, and this marked Dalí's official membership of the movement. His talent for self-publicity rapidly made him its most famous representative—its symbol in the mind of the general public. Throughout his life he cultivated eccentricity and exhibitionism, claiming that this was the source of his creative energy (one of his most outrageous stunts was delivering a lecture at the London International Surrealist Exhibition in 1936 dressed in a diving suit; he almost suffocated when the helmet got stuck). He adopted the Surrealist idea of *automatism but transformed it into a more positive method that he named 'critical paranoia'. This involved elaborating on the images of his dreams and fantasies and substituting them for—or merging them with—the world of natural appearances. It resulted particularly in the ambiguous double images that play such a large part in his work, in which a form can be read, for example, as part of a landscape or part of a human body.

During the heyday of Surrealism in the 1930s Dalí produced several of the established 'icons' of the movement, using a meticulous academic technique that was contradicted by the unreal 'dream' space he depicted and by the strangely hallucinatory character of his imagery. He described his pictures as 'hand-painted dream photographs' and had certain favourite and recurring images, such as the human figure with half-open drawers protruding from it, burning giraffes, and watches bent and flowing as if made of melting wax (*The Persistence of Memory*, 1931, MoMA, New York). Dalí himself said that the melting watches—one of the most parodied images in 20th-century art—were inspired by eating a ripe Camembert cheese, but some commentators have sought deeper meanings, seeing them, for example, as expressing a fear of impotence.

In the late 1930s Dalí made several visits to Italy and adopted a more traditional style; this together with his political views (he was a supporter of General Franco) led Breton to expel him from the Surrealist ranks in 1939. He moved to the USA in 1940 and remained there until 1948. During this time he devoted himself largely to self-publicity and making money (Breton coined the anagram 'Avida Dollars' for his name). From 1948 he lived mainly at Port Lligat in Spain, but he also spent much time in Paris and New York. Among his late paintings the best known are probably those on religious themes (*Crucifixion of St John of the Cross*, 1951, St Mungo Mus., Glasgow), although sexual subjects and pictures centring on his wife Gala were also continuing preoccupations. In old age he became one of the world's most famous recluses, generating rumours and occasional scandals to the end.

Apart from painting, Dalí's output included sculpture, book illustration, jewellery design, and work for the theatre. In collaboration with the director Luis Buñuel he also made the first Surrealist films—*Un chien andalou* (1929) and *L'Âge d'or* (1930)—and he contributed a dream sequence to Alfred Hitchcock's *Spellbound* (1945). He also wrote a novel, *Hidden Faces* (1944), and several volumes of flamboyant autobiography. Although he is undoubtedly one of the most famous artists of the 20th century, his status is controversial; many critics consider that he did little if anything of consequence after his classic Surrealist works of the 1930s. There are several museums devoted to Dalí's work, notably in Figueras, his home town in Spain, and in St Petersburg, Florida.

Dalmau, Luis (active 1428–61). Spanish painter, first recorded in 1428 in Valencia, where he worked for Alfonso V of Aragon. In 1431 Alfonso sent him to Bruges to study tapestry weaving. After his return to Spain he settled in Barcelona, and his most important work, the *Virgin of the Councillors* (1445, Barcelona Mus.), was painted for the town hall there. Dalmau's visit to Flanders is the first recorded contact of a Spanish painter with the Netherlandish School, and this painting is very strongly influenced by Jan van *Eyck. See also HISPANO-FLEMISH STYLE.

Dalou, Jules (*b* Paris, 31 Dec. 1838; *d* Paris, 15 Apr. 1902). French sculptor. Among French sculptors of his generation he ranks second only to *Rodin. His work was more conventional than Rodin's, sometimes using the heroic language and allegorical devices of *Baroque tradition, but it has a naturalistic warmth that is far removed from the chilliness of much statuary of the time. He had left-wing political views and after supporting the Commune (the short-lived revolutionary government of Paris in 1871) he spent the period 1871–9 in exile in London. On his return to Paris he began work on his best-known achievement, a huge bronze group of the *Triumph of the Republic*, eventually unveiled in 1899 (Place de la Nation, Paris). An even more ambitious work, a vast *Monument to Labour*, was left uncompleted at his death, but clay models for many of the figures are preserved in the Petit Palais, Paris. Dalou's other public statuary included the memorial to *Delacroix in the Luxembourg Gardens, Paris (1890), and he also produced smaller works, including portrait busts.

Dalwood, Hubert (*b* Bristol, 2 June 1924; *d* London, 2 Nov. 1976). British abstract sculptor. He was one of the leading figures of the generation that broke away from the raw, expressive manner in wrought and welded metal that was so prominent in British sculpture in the 1950s (his own earliest work was in this vein). His favourite medium was aluminium, which he sometimes painted. With this he created volumetric objects that contrast ribbed and edged forms with smoother and more fluid areas (*Large Object*, 1959, Tate, London). He also made sensitively modelled reliefs in aluminium. In the late 1960s, following a stay in the USA, he turned to bigger, shiny, columnar forms. In the 1970s he began making large room installations in wood.

Dalziel Brothers. Firm of English *wood engravers founded in London in 1839 by **George Dalziel** (*b* Wooler, Northumberland, 1 Dec. 1815; *d* London, 4 Aug. 1902) and **Edward Dalziel** (*b* Wooler, 5 Dec. 1817; *d* London, 25 Mar. 1905). Two other brothers, **John** (1822–69) and **Thomas** (1823–1906), worked for the firm, which was the most prolific source of book illustrations in Victorian England, producing more than 50,000 images. *Leighton, *Millais, and *Tenniel were among the artists whose work they engraved. George and Edward collaborated on the book *The Brothers Dalziel: A Record of Fifty Years' Work . . . 1840–1890* (1901).

dammar. A generic name for *resins obtained from various species of tropical trees growing mainly in South-East Asia. In art they are used for varnishes, lacquers, and as a base for painting media.

'dampfold' draperies. See MASTER HUGO.

Danby, Francis (*b* Common, nr. Wexford, Ireland, 16 Nov. 1793; *d* Exmouth, Devon, 10 Feb. 1861). Irish-born painter, active in England. He worked mainly in Bristol and London, but between 1830 and 1838, owing to financial and marital problems, he lived in Paris and Switzerland. His early work was naturalistic, but in the 1820s he turned to melodramatic apocalyptic paintings, such as *The Delivery of Israel out of Egypt* (1825, Harris Mus. and AG, Preston), which were a direct challenge to John *Martin. It is for these that he is chiefly remembered, but his best works are now usually considered to be the romantic landscapes of his later years, with their mood of melancholy and solemn serenity (*Temple of Flora*, 1840, Tate, London). In 1847 he retired to Exmouth, embittered by his failure to achieve financial success or academic honours.

Dance, Nathaniel (Sir Nathaniel Dance-Holland) (*b* London, 18 May 1735; *d* Winchester, 15 Oct. 1811). English painter, primarily of portraits. He studied under *Hayman and spent the years 1754–65 in Rome, where he was much influenced by the sophisticated portrait style of Pompeo *Batoni. In 1768 he became a foundation member of the *Royal Academy, but on inheriting a fortune in 1776 he retired from professional practice. He became an MP in 1790 and in 1800 he was created a baronet and assumed the surname Dance-Holland. One of his best-known portraits is *Captain Cook* (1766, Nat. Maritime Mus., London). He was the son and brother of architects, both called **George Dance**.

Dandridge, Bartholomew (*bapt.* London, 17 Dec. 1691; *d* after 1754). English portrait painter who had a considerable practice in London in the 1730s and 1740s (he took over *Kneller's studio in 1731). He is a minor figure, but his best work has a lively *Rococo charm and he is notable as one of the first English artists to paint *conversation pieces (*The Price Family*, *c.*1728, Met. Mus., New York).

Daniele da Volterra (Daniele Ricciarelli) (*b* Volterra, *c.*1509; *d* Rome, 4 Apr. 1566). Italian *Mannerist painter and sculptor, perhaps trained in Siena under *Sodoma. In about 1536 he moved to Rome, where he became a friend of *Michelangelo and one of his most gifted and individual followers. Michelangelo helped to gain him commissions and (as with *Sebastiano del Piombo) supplied him with drawings to work from, but Daniele's finest picture owes little to the direct influence of the master. This is his fresco of the *Deposition* (*c.*1545) in the Orsini Chapel in SS. Trinità dei Monti, a powerful and moving work, based compositionally on *Rosso Fiorentino's famous painting of the same subject in Volterra, but with an eloquent richness of its own. It was one of the most admired works of its generation in Rome and continued to be influential into the next century: *Domenichino (Hatton Gal., Newcastle upon Tyne) was among the artists who copied it, and *Rubens was clearly inspired by it in his painting of the subject in Antwerp Cathedral. Daniele was present at Michelangelo's deathbed and his most famous work of sculpture is a bronze bust of him based on the death mask (casts are in the Casa Buonarroti, Florence, the Louvre, and elsewhere). Ironically, in view of his devotion to the master, Daniele is perhaps best remembered for painting draperies (1564–5) over parts of the nude figures in Michelangelo's *Last Judgement*, a concession to Counter-Reformation prudery that earned him the nickname Il Braghettone (the breeches maker).

Danti, Vincenzo (*b* Perugia, 17 Apr. 1530; *d* Perugia, 26 May 1576). Italian sculptor, architect, and writer, active for most of his short career in Florence, where he was based from 1557 to 1573. His work reveals his admiration for *Michelangelo, whose funeral ceremonies in 1564 he helped to plan. Danti's style, however, is more elegant and much less powerful than the master's. His best-known works are (in Florence) the bronze group of the *Execution of the Baptist* over the south door of the Baptistery (finished 1571), and (in his native Perugia) the bronze figure of Pope Julius III outside the cathedral (1555). He also worked in marble, his masterpiece in this medium being *Honour Trimphant over Falsehood* (*c*.1571, Bargello, Florence). In 1573 he was appointed Perugia's city architect and he helped found the city's Accademia del Disegno. He was the author of a treatise on proportion (1567), dedicated to Duke Cosimo I de' *Medici, and he also wrote poetry.

Danube School. Term applied to a number of German and Austrian artists working in the early 16th century who were among the pioneers in depicting landscape (particularly the forests and hills of the Danube Valley) for its own sake (in drawings and prints as well as paintings). *Altdorfer, *Cranach the Elder (in his earlier work), and *Huber are the most important artists covered by the term. They worked independently of one another, so 'Danube School' (German *Donauschule*) is a term of convenience rather than an indication of any group affiliation.

Daret, Jacques (*b* Tournai, *c*.1405; *d c*.1468). Netherlandish painter. From 1428 to 1432 he was apprenticed in Tournai to Robert Campin along with Rogelet de la Pasture (assumed to be identical with Rogier van der *Weyden); the similarity of Daret's style to that of the *Master of Flémalle is one of the main reasons for thinking that Campin and this master are one and the same. Four panels survive from Daret's chief work, an altarpiece for the abbey of St Vaast in Arras (1432–5), and one of these—the *Nativity* (Thyssen Mus., Madrid)—is obviously based on the Master of Flémalle's painting of the subject in Dijon (Mus. B.-A.). Two of the other three panels from the St Vaast Altarpiece are in Berlin (Gemäldegalerie), and the fourth is in Paris (Petit Palais). Daret's other work included tapestry *cartoons and manuscript *illuminations.

Darwin, Sir Robert. See ROYAL COLLEGE OF ART.

Dashwood, Sir Francis. See DILETTANTI.

Daubigny, Charles-François (*b* Paris, 15 Feb. 1817; *d* Paris, 19 Feb. 1878). French landscape painter, one of the earliest exponents of *plein-air painting in France. He came from a family of artists and was taught initially by his father **Edmé-François** (1789–1843), likewise a landscape painter; he also learnt a good deal by copying 17th-century Dutch pictures in the Louvre. Although he is considered a member of the *Barbizon School, he never actually lived in the locality, and his favourite subjects were river—rather than forest—scenes (he often painted from a specially fitted boat). His work, which is notable for the sensitivity with which he depicted the effects of light on trees and water, was an important influence on early *Impressionism. He was influential not only stylistically but also through the support and encouragement he gave to younger painters; as a member of the *Salon jury in 1868, he helped to get the work of several of the Impressionists shown, and it was he who introduced *Monet and *Pissarro to the dealer *Durand-Ruel, when all four of them had taken refuge in England during the Franco-Prussian War of 1870–1. His son **Karl Daubigny** (1846–86) continued the family tradition in landscape painting.

Daumier, Honoré (*b* Marseilles, 26 Feb. 1808; *d* Valmondois, 10 Feb. 1879). French caricaturist, painter, and sculptor. During his lifetime he was known chiefly as a political and social satirist, but since his death he has been increasingly recognized as a painter. In 1830, after learning the still fairly new process of *lithography, he began to contribute political cartoons to the newly launched anti-monarchist weekly *La Caricature* (see PHILIPON). He was an ardent Republican and in 1832 was sentenced to six months' imprisonment for his attacks on King Louis-Philippe, whom he represented as 'Gargantua swallowing bags of gold extorted from the people'. In 1835 the government prohibited political caricature and Daumier turned to social satire, mainly in *Le Charivari*, but at the time of the 1848 Revolution, in which Louis-Philippe was deposed, he returned to political subjects. He is said to have produced more than 4,000 lithographs, wishing each time that the one he had just made could be his last.

Daumier's paintings were probably done for the most part fairly late in his career. He had examples accepted four times by the *Salon, but otherwise he never exhibited them and they remained practically unknown up to the time of an exhibition held at *Durand-Ruel's gallery in 1878, the year before his death. Most of them depict contemporary life and manners with satirical overtones, but he also did a number on literary and mythological themes (*Don Quixote and Sancho Panza*, c.1865, Courtauld Gal., London). His technique was remarkably broad and free. As a sculptor he specialized in caricature heads and figures, and these too are in a very spontaneous style. In particular he created the memorable figure of Ratapoil (meaning 'skinned rat'), who embodied the sinister agents of the government of Louis-Philippe. (A similar political type in his graphic art was Robert Macaire, who personified the unscrupulous profiteer and swindler.)

As a caricaturist Daumier stands head and shoulders above all others of the 19th century. The essence of his satire lay in his power to interpret mental states in terms of physical absurdity, but in his directness of vision and lack of sentimentality he has affinities with the *Realism of *Courbet. Although he never made a commercial success of his art, he was appreciated by the discriminating, his friends and admirers including *Baudelaire, *Degas, *Delacroix, and *Forain. In his final years he was almost blind and was saved from destitution by *Corot.

Davey, Grenville. See NEW BRITISH SCULPTURE.

David, Gerard (*b* Oudewater, nr. Gouda, ?c.1460; *d* Bruges, 13 Aug. 1523). Netherlandish painter, active for almost all his career in Bruges. He had settled there by 1484, when he became a member of the painters' guild, and after the death of *Memlinc in 1494 he became the city's leading painter. At this time the economic importance of Bruges was declining, but it still maintained its prestige as a centre of art and David played an important role in the flourishing export trade in paintings that it developed in the first quarter of the 16th century. Late in his career he probably also ran a workshop in Antwerp (he is thought to be the 'Meester Gheraert van Brugghe' who became a master in the painters' guild there in 1515). His work—extremely accomplished, but conservative and usually rather bland—was very popular and his stately compositions were copied again and again. Among his followers were *Benson and *Ysenbrandt, who carried on his tradition until the middle of the

16th century. Almost all his work was on traditional religious themes, but for Bruges Town Hall he painted a pair of pictures on an obscure secular legend, the judgement of Cambyses (1498, Groeningemuseum, Bruges), a gory subject (concerning the trial and execution of an unjust judge) to which his reflective style was not ideally suited. They were no doubt intended to rival the judgement paintings by Rogier van der *Weyden and Dirk *Bouts for the town halls of Brussels and Louvain respectively.

David, Jacques-Louis (*b* Paris, 30 Aug, 1748; *d* Brussels, 29 Dec. 1825). French history painter and portraitist. He was the greatest of *Neoclassical painters and one of the most influential European artists of his time. On the advice of the aged *Boucher, a distant relative, he was apprenticed to *Vien in 1766 and in the same year he became a student at the Académie Royale. In 1774 he won the *Prix de Rome at the fifth attempt, and the following year he went to Italy with Vien, who had been appointed director of the French Academy in Rome.

David remained in Italy until 1780 and during this period he purged his work of *Rococo mannerisms and developed a heroic style heavily influenced by his study of *antique sculpture and his admiration for *Poussin and *Raphael. After his return to Paris he quickly rose to be the leading painter of the day. His success depended not only on the grandeur and dignity of his work, but also on its moral seriousness, which was in keeping with the spirit of the time. The Rococo style was associated with the frivolity of court life, and as the royal family and the aristocracy became increasingly unpopular, David's sternly Neoclassical paintings could be seen as expressions of the desire for social as well as aesthetic change. The work that more than any other established his pre-eminence was the *Oath of the Horatii* (Louvre, Paris), painted during a return visit to Rome in 1784–5, which shows three ancient Roman brothers dedicating their lives to the state as they prepare to face three enemy champions in mortal combat. Hugh Honour (*Neo-Classicism*, 1968) describes it as 'an image of extraordinary lucidity and visual punch . . . a clarion call to civic virtue and patriotism'. Its ideals of austerity, stoical self-sacrifice, and devotion to duty were repeated in two other celebrated masterpieces, the *Death of Socrates* (1787, Met. Mus., New York) and the *Lictors Bringing Brutus the Bodies of his Sons* (1789, Louvre). These three works mark the summit of Neoclassical painting.

After the Revolution in 1789, with which he was entirely in sympathy, David became actively involved in politics (he served on various committees and voted for the execution of Louis XVI) and he used his art directly as propaganda. He made designs for revolutionary festivals, and his paintings of the time included three pictures of 'martyrs of the Revolution', in which he moved portraiture into the domain of universal tragedy. They were: the *Death of Lepeletier* (1793, destroyed, but known from an engraving), the *Death of Marat* (1793, Mus. Royaux, Brussels), and the *Death of Bara* (1794, Mus. Calvet, Avignon; unfinished). After the fall of his friend Robespierre (1794), however, David was imprisoned for having supported him, narrowly escaping the guillotine; he was released after pleas from his wife, who had previously divorced him because of his revolutionary sympathies (she was a royalist). They were remarried in 1796, and David's *Intervention of the Sabine Women* (1794–9, Louvre), begun while he was in prison, is said to have been painted to honour her, its theme being one of love prevailing over conflict. It was also interpreted at the time, however, as a plea for reconciliation in the civil strife that France suffered after the Revolution and it was the work that re-established David's fortunes. By the time it was finished, Napoleon had restored order to France. David transferred his allegiance to him ('Bonaparte is my hero', he said after first meeting him in 1798) and became one of the leading artists in depicting his life and legend. Napoleon, in turn, showered David with honours and after he was crowned emperor in 1804 gave him the title of first painter (although he eventually came to prefer the work of *Gros, David's former pupil).

David's commissions from Napoleon included various portraits and a projected series of four huge pictures of events from his life, of which only two were produced: the *Coronation of Napoleon* (1805–7, Louvre) and the *Presentation of the Eagle Standards* (1808–10, Versailles). These two pictures show a change in technique and feeling from his earlier work, severe compositions and cold colours giving way to a new feeling for pageantry and an almost *Romantic warmth and ardour (he hated the Romantic movement, but he influenced it greatly). After the final defeat of Napoleon in 1815, David (who had signed a declaration of loyalty to the emperor) left France and settled in Brussels in 1816. He was now approaching 70 and the paintings from his final decade in exile have generally been regarded as an undistinguished coda to his life, his work

weakening as the possibility of exerting a moral and social influence receded. However, the sensuous qualities of his late mythological paintings are now winning appreciation, and he continued to be an outstanding portraitist, although he never surpassed such earlier achievements as the stirring *Napoleon Crossing the Alps* (1800, KH Mus., Vienna, one of four versions) or the coolly erotic *Mme Récamier* (1800, Louvre).

David was the most important teacher of his day and he was loyally supported by his many former pupils (notably Gros, who took over the master's studio in Paris and tried to bring about his return to France, even though David was content in Brussels). His other pupils included *Gérard, *Girodet, and *Ingres, and he also had prominent followers among artists who did not actually study with him, notably *Guérin. These artists, sometimes referred to as the 'School of David', formed the most prestigious group of painters in Europe in the early 19th century; David was perhaps the last great painter to create such a following.

David, Pierre-Jean (b Angers, 12 Mar. 1788; d Paris, 6 Jan. 1856). French sculptor, known after his birthplace as David d'Angers. He won the *Prix de Rome in 1811 and from then until 1815 lived in Italy, where he met and admired *Ingres and was also influenced by *Canova and *Thorvaldsen. However, *Neoclassical influence was tempered by a strong inclination towards naturalism, and his contemporaries considered him a *Romantic. His most prestigious commission was the high-relief pedimental sculpture of the Pantheon in Paris, which shows an allegorical figure of France distributing wreaths to great Frenchmen (1830–7), but his best works are to be found among his busts and medallions of famous men. He left a large collection of them to the Musée des Beaux-Arts in his native city.

Davie, Alan (b Grangemouth, Stirlingshire, 28 Sept. 1920). British painter, graphic artist, poet, musician, silversmith, and jeweller. After service in the army and a short period as a professional jazz musician (he plays several instruments), he travelled in Europe, 1948–9. This gave him the chance to see works by Jackson *Pollock and other American painters in Peggy *Guggenheim's gallery in Venice, and he was one of the first British artists to be affected by *Abstract Expressionism. Other influences on his eclectic but extremely personal style are African sculpture and Zen Buddhism. His work is full of images suggestive of magic or mythology (some based on ancient forms, some of his own invention) and he uses these as themes around which—like a jazz musician—he spontaneously develops variations in exuberant colour and brushwork. From the 1960s he developed an international reputation.

Davies, Arthur Bowen (*b* Utica, NY, 26 Sept. 1862; *d* Florence, 24 Oct. 1928). American painter, printmaker, and tapestry designer. During his lifetime he had a high reputation as an artist, but he is now remembered mainly for his role in promoting avant-garde art (even though his own work was fairly conservative). He was a member of The *Eight and president of the Association of American Painters and Sculptors that was created to organize the *Armory Show; his enthusiasm for the project was largely responsible for the scope of the show and the force of its impact. His own work was varied and embraced remarkably diverse influences (he was a man of wide culture and unlike the other members of The Eight he did not specialize in modern urban scenes). In his early career he showed an enthusiasm for the *Pre-Raphaelites, *Whistler, and *Puvis de Chavannes, and specialized in idyllic landscapes inhabited by dreamlike, visionary figures of nude women or mythical animals (*Unicorns*, 1906, Met. Mus., New York). After the Armory Show his work displayed superficial *Cubist influence, but in the 1920s he returned to a more traditional style.

Davis, Stuart (*b* Philadelphia, 7 Dec. 1894; *d* New York, 24 June 1964). American painter. He grew up in an artistic environment, for his father was art director of the *Philadelphia Press*, a newspaper that had employed *Glackens, *Luks, *Shinn, and *Sloan—the four artists who were to form the nucleus of The *Eight—and his mother, Helen Stuart Foulke, was a sculptor. In 1910–13 he studied with Robert *Henri in New York, and in 1913 he was one of the youngest exhibitors in the *Armory Show, which made an overwhelming impact on him. After this he began experimenting with a variety of modern idioms and in the 1920s he achieved a sophisticated grasp of *Cubism, but it was only after spending a year in Paris in 1928–9 that he forged a distinctive style. Using motifs from the characteristic environment of American life, he rearranged them into flat poster-like patterns with precise outlines and sharply contrasting colours (*House and Street*, 1931, Whitney Mus., New York). In this way he became the only major artist to treat the subject matter of the *American Scene Painters—extraordinarily popular at the time—in avant-garde terms; he

was both distinctly American and distinctively modern—a rare combination that won him wide admiration. Later his work became more purely abstract, although he often introduced lettering or suggestions of advertisements etc. into his bold patterns (*Owh! in San Pao*, 1951, Whitney Mus.). The zest and dynamism of such works reflect his interest in jazz.

Davis is generally regarded as the most important American painter to come to maturity between the two world wars and the outstanding American artist to work in a Cubist idiom. He made witty and original use of it and created a distinctive American style, for however abstract his work became he always claimed that every image he used had its source in observed reality: 'I paint what I see in America, in other words I paint the American Scene.' He was an articulate defender of modern art, a major influence on many younger artists, including his friends *Gorky and *de Kooning, and a precursor of *Pop art, forming an important link between the pioneering avant-garde artists of the Armory Show generation and the triumphant New York art scene of the post-war years.

Dayes, Edward (*b* London, 6 Aug. 1763; *d* London, May 1804). English painter (mainly in watercolour), draughtsman, and printmaker. He is best known for his topographical watercolours and drawings, which are in a meticulous manner that he upheld against the 'new and more dashing style' that was coming to the fore. His traditional outlook is expressed in his treatise *Instructions for Drawing and Colouring Landscapes*, which appeared in his posthumously published *Works* in 1805; this volume also includes an attack on the 'wild effusions of the perturbed imaginations' of *Fuseli. *Girtin was a pupil of Dayes, who is said to have resented his success and contrived to have him imprisoned. There is no documentary evidence for this story, but Dayes certainly became an embittered man and he committed suicide.

Deacon, Richard. See NEW BRITISH SCULPTURE.

Dean, Graham. See SUPERREALISM.

De Andrea, John (*b* Denver, Colo., 24 Nov. 1941). American *Superrealist sculptor. As with Duane *Hanson, his figures are made of fibreglass and are realistic to the last detail, but De Andrea specializes in nude figures and his models are usually young and attractive, if rather vapid (*Model in Repose*, 1981, Scottish NG of Modern Art, Edinburgh).

decalcomania. A technique for producing pictures by transferring an image from one surface to another. It is thought to have been invented by the Spanish *Surrealist Oscar Domínguez (1906–58) in Paris in about 1935, although the term had been applied in the 19th century to a similar idea used in ceramic design (the word comes from the French *décalquer*, 'to transfer', and *manie*, 'mania', and in the 1860s there was indeed a craze for transferring pictures to glass, porcelain, etc.). In Domínguez's method, splashes of colour were laid with a broad brush on a sheet of paper. This was then covered with another sheet and rubbed gently so that the wet pigment flowed haphazardly from one surface to the other, typically producing effects resembling fantastic grottoes or jungles or underwater growths. The point of the process, which had the blessing of *Breton, was that the picture was made without any preconceived idea of its subject or form (*sans objet préconçu*). Several other Surrealists adopted it, most notably Max *Ernst, who sometimes began a picture by decalcomania and finished it by conventional means. See also AUTOMATISM.

De Camp, Joseph R. See TEN.

Decamps, Alexandre-Gabriel (*b* Paris, 3 May 1803; *d* Fontainebleau, 22 Aug. 1860). French painter and printmaker. Decamps was one of the first and most successful specialists in *Orientalism. He first exhibited an oriental picture at the *Salon in 1827 (*A Janissary*, Wallace Coll., London) and in 1828–9 he made an extensive journey through Greece, the Middle East, and North Africa, bringing back weapons, costumes, and other souvenirs, as well as sketches—a fund of reference material for his work. Typically he painted on a fairly small scale, with bright colours and richly *impasted brushwork. He accumulated a long list of honours, and a statue of him was erected in Fontainebleau (where he settled in 1857) only two years after his death; it is by Albert-Ernest Carrier-Belleuse (1824–87), one of the most prolific French sculptors of the time. Subsequently Decamps's reputation faded. His work is well represented in the Louvre, Paris, and the Wallace Collection, London.

de Chirico, Giorgio. See CHIRICO.

decorative arts. Term generally used more or less synonymously with *applied art but which can also embrace objects made purely for decoration, without any practical purpose.

de Critz, John. See CRITZ.

Defrance, Léonard (*b* Liège, 5 Nov. 1735; *d* Liège, 25 Feb. 1805). Flemish painter. He spent most of his life in Liège, but he travelled a good deal and a trip to Holland in 1773 gave him a love for 17th-century Dutch *genre painting, which influenced the lively scenes of contemporary life that are his most characteristic works (*Brigands Dividing Booty*, c.1780, Met. Mus., New York). Such paintings sold well in Paris, which Defrance visited several times. A supporter of the French Revolution and an anticlerical, he was involved in the destruction of Liège's cathedral and the removal of works of art to France after it annexed the city in 1794. He wrote treatises on drawing (1772) and colour (1782).

Degas, Edgar (*b* Paris, 19 July 1834; *d* Paris, 27 Sept. 1917). French painter, draughtsman, printmaker, and sculptor. He was the son of a wealthy art-loving banker and was initially trained for the law. In 1854, however, he began studying with Louis Lamothe (1822–69), a pupil of *Ingres, who handed on the master's insistence on the primacy of draughtsmanship (in 1855 he met the aged Ingres himself, who advised: 'Draw lines, young man, many lines, from memory or from nature'). Degas also attended classes at the École des *Beaux-Arts, but the most important part of his artistic education was gained through assiduous study of the Old Masters, both in the Louvre and in Italy, where he lived 1856–9 (he had Italian relatives and made several subsequent visits to the country). Most of his early works were portraits or history paintings on classical themes (*Young Spartans Exercising*, c.1860, NG, London), but in 1862 he met *Manet (while copying a *Velázquez in the Louvre) and this helped to bring about a decisive change of direction in his art. Manet introduced him to the circle of the young *Impressionists and during the next few years he abandoned historical pictures and turned to contemporary subjects; they included scenes of the ballet and theatre, café interiors, laundresses at work, and women bathing—no other painter of his time portrayed such a rich variety of themes from contemporary urban society.

Degas exhibited in seven out of the eight Impressionist exhibitions and he figures prominently in all accounts of the movement. However, he was Impressionist only in certain restricted aspects of his work and like Manet (who also came from an upper-middle-class background) he stood somewhat aloof from the rest of the group. He had little interest in landscape and therefore did not share the Impressionist concern for rendering the effects of changing light and atmosphere (his favourite outdoor subject was horse racing, but he painted the pictures in the studio and usually left the setting generalized). As with the other Impressionists, he depicted the world around him in a fresh and informal way, and liked to give the suggestion of spontaneous and unplanned scenes, often using unfamiliar viewpoints or figures cut off as if in a snapshot (he was very interested in photography). However, the appearance of spontaneity was an appearance only; in reality his pictures were carefully composed. 'Even when working from nature, one has to compose,' he said, and 'No art was ever less spontaneous than mine.'

Up to 1874, because of his prosperous background, Degas never had any need to sell his work, but in that year his father died leaving unexpected debts, which Degas largely paid off himself, selling his house and his picture collection to do so (going far beyond what was legally required of him). Unlike the other Impressionists, however, he never had any difficulty marketing his work (his formidable skill as a draughtsman made him more immediately acceptable to most buyers) and by 1880 he had overcome his financial crisis and was a well-established and prosperous figure in the art world. After the final Impressionist exhibition in 1886 he stopped showing his work in public, selling it selectively through a number of dealers. By this time he had turned 50 and was having serious trouble with his eyesight. Because of this he turned increasingly from oils to pastel, in which he was physically closer to the surface on which he was working; the figures in his later pictures are often shown in intimate close-up, as if he is peering at them from a very near viewpoint. His failing eyesight and his use of pastel led to a broadening and blurring of form and the use of richer colour, with the somewhat ironic result that in the 1890s—by which time the Impressionist group had broken up—his work came closer in style to mainstream Impressionism than it had ever been before. He experimented boldly with pastels, as he did with other techniques; he sometimes mixed different kinds of paints in the same picture, for example, and he sometimes steamed his pastels, so he could manipulate the colours more fluidly. Degas also made prints in various techniques, and from the late 1860s he produced wax sculptures; as his sight failed this tactile medium became of more importance to him. Most of his sculptures were small, private works, but a few were more ambitious, including the only

one he exhibited in his lifetime, the famous *Little Fourteen-Year-Old Dancer*, dressed in a real tutu, which was shown at the fifth Impressionist exhibition in 1881 (like his other sculptures, it was cast in bronze after his death; one cast is in Tate Modern, London).

After the turn of the century Degas could produce little work and in his final years he was virtually blind. Contrary to what is sometimes said, he was not a misanthrope (he had numerous friends and was good with children, and it was only in old age, when his eyesight made life difficult for him, that he became reclusive and cantankerous). However, he was a formidable personality, feared for his biting wit, and his complete devotion to his art made him seem cold and aloof to many people (as far as is known he never had any kind of romantic or sexual involvement). Among his fellow artists, though, his genius compelled universal respect (*Renoir ranked him above *Rodin as a sculptor, and in 1883 Camille *Pissarro described him as 'certainly the greatest artist of our epoch'). By the time of his death he was almost a national monument and his reputation as one of the giants of 19th-century art has endured undimmed. His influence on 20th-century art was rich and varied—on artists whom he knew personally, such as *Sickert, and on later admirers. His work has appealed greatly to other outstanding draughtsmen, such as *Hockney and *Picasso, and his mastery of pastel has been an inspiration to *Kitaj.

degenerate art. A term coined in Germany in the 1930s to discredit all contemporary art that did not correspond to the ideology of the Nazi party. Such art, which included most avant-garde work, was systematically defamed and suppressed in Germany throughout the period when the Nazis ruled the country, 1933–45. Adolf Hitler and Alfred Rosenberg (the chief theoretical spokesman of Nazism) linked art with political doctrines and racial theories, attacking modern art as 'political and cultural anarchy'. The ruthless campaign against modern ideas in art also included the closing of the *Bauhaus ('a breeding-ground of cultural Bolshevism') in 1933. Hitler made his first speech against 'degenerate art' (in German *entartete Kunst*) at Nuremberg in 1934, and a series of exhibitions designed to ridicule modern art culminated in an infamous show (also called Entartete Kunst) that opened in Munich in 1937 and then went on tour round Germany. In Munich it was shown alongside the first annual

'Great German Art Exhibition' of Nazi-approved art; this was thoroughly traditional in concept and technique, and favoured themes (often militaristic) that glorified Hitler and his ideals of Aryan supremacy.

The works on display in the Entartete Kunst exhibition were mocked by being shown together with pictures done by inmates of lunatic asylums. More than 700 works were shown out of a total of about 16,000 confiscated from museums throughout the country. The artists represented were mainly German (by birth or residence), but a few foreigners were included. Among the total of over a hundred were many distinguished figures and several of the giants of 20th-century art: *Beckmann, *Ernst, *Grosz, *Kirchner, *Klee, *Kokoschka, *Marc, *Mondrian, *Picasso (the inclusion of Marc caused some embarrassment, for he had been killed in action fighting for Germany—as a volunteer—in the First World War). As a propaganda exercise the exhibition was a huge success: more than two million people visited it in Munich alone, and huge numbers also went to see it in other major German cities. Living German artists whose work was declared 'degenerate' were forbidden to exhibit or even to work, and people who sympathized with modern art were deprived of their posts in museums and teaching posts. Some of the confiscated works were sold at auction, Nazi officials helped themselves to others, and the 'unsaleable stock' is said to have been burnt in Berlin (although it has been doubted whether this really happened).

Although degenerate art was linked so closely with political and racial doctrines, it is significant that the artist who had the 'distinction' of having the most works confiscated (more than 1,000, mainly graphics) was Emil *Nolde, who was racially 'pure' and had even been a member of the Nazi party. He protested in vain to Joseph Goebbels, the propaganda minister: 'My art is German, strong, austere and sincere.' The suppression of degenerate art was not, therefore, simply a matter of political expediency, but also a symptom of the general antipathy to new forms of artistic expression that was such a feature of the history of 20th-century art. In the normal course of events such hostility rarely goes beyond verbal abuse and occasional acts of vandalism, but in Nazi Germany aesthetic revulsion was armed with political power.

Deineka, Alexander. See SOCIALIST REALISM.

De Keyser, Nicaise. See KEYSER, NICAISE DE.

de Kooning, Willem (b Rotterdam, 24 Apr. 1904; d East Hampton, Long Island, NY, 19 Mar. 1997). Dutch-born painter (and latterly sculptor) who became an American citizen in 1961, one of the major figures of *Abstract Expressionism. He went to America as a stowaway in 1926 and the following year settled in New York. His early work was conservative, but in 1929 he met Arshile *Gorky, who became one of his closest friends and introduced him to avant-garde circles. During the 1930s and 1940s he experimented vigorously and by the time of his first one-man show in 1948 (at the Egan Gallery, New York) he was painting in an extremely energetic abstract style (often in black and white) close to that of Jackson *Pollock. The exhibition established his reputation (although prosperity was still some years away) and after it he was generally regarded as sharing with Pollock the unofficial leadership of the Abstract Expressionist group.

Unlike Pollock, de Kooning usually retained some suggestion of figuration in his work, and in 1953 he caused a sensation when his Women series (Women nos. I–VI) was exhibited at his third one-man show, at the Sidney *Janis Gallery. Woman I (1950–2, MoMA, New York), with its grotesque leer and frenzied brushwork, shocked the public and dismayed those critics who believed in a rigorously abstract art. One of these was Clement *Greenberg, but New York's other most influential critic of avant-garde art—Harold *Rosenberg—supported de Kooning. Woman I became one of the most reproduced paintings in the USA and de Kooning was enormously influential on young painters at this time. By the end of the 1950s, however, he was beginning to be regarded as an elder statesman whose best days as a creative force were past. From the 1960s he had honours heaped on him. His paintings continued to mix abstract and semi-figurative work and in 1969 he began making sculpture—figures modelled in clay and later cast in bronze. He continued working well into his eighties, until he was incapacitated by Alzheimer's disease.

In 1994 a large retrospective of de Kooning's work was shown in Washington (NG), New York (Met. Mus.), and London (Tate). The catalogue suggested that he was 'the supreme painterly painter of the second half of the century and the greatest painter of the human figure since *Picasso', but the controversial British critic Brian Sewell (1929–) wrote: 'Wandering round the Tate . . . I wonder at the awe and adulation expended on this man, most of whose paintings reveal not the slightest merit.'

His wife **Elaine de Kooning** (1919–89) was also a painter, notably of *Expressionist portraits, and a writer on art. The couple married in 1943, separated amicably in 1957, and reunited in 1975. A collection of her writings, *The Spirit of Abstract Expressionism*, was published in 1994. Sewell maintains that Willem's reputation was founded by 'her busy bedding of critics in exchange for favourable reviews'.

Delacroix, Eugène (*b* Charenton-Saint-Maurice, nr. Paris, 26 Apr. 1798; *d* Paris, 13 Aug. 1863). French painter, draughtsman, and lithographer. He was one of the towering figures of the *Romantic movement and one of the last major artists to devote a large part of his career to mural painting in the heroic tradition. Lorenz Eitner (*An Outline of 19th Century European Painting*, 1987) describes him as 'the last great European painter to use the repertory of humanistic art with conviction and originality. In his hands, antique myth and medieval history, Golgotha and the Barricade, Faust and Hamlet, Scott and Byron, tiger and Odalisque yielded images of equal power.' He was the son of a diplomat, Charles Delacroix, who at the time of his son's birth was ambassador in The Hague, but it has been suggested that his natural father was the great statesman Talleyrand, a friend of the family. His mother, Victoire Oeben, was the daughter of Jean-François Oeben, one of the most distinguished furniture makers of his day.

Delacroix had a good education and grew up with a love of literature and music as well as art. In 1815 he began studying with Pierre *Guérin, who had earlier taught *Géricault (whose work greatly influenced Delacroix), and the following year he enrolled at the École des *Beaux-Arts. His real artistic education, however, was gained by copying Old Masters in the *Louvre, where he delighted particularly in *Rubens and the 16th-century Venetian painters. Throughout his life he remained a keen and perceptive student of his predecessors, and Rubens—with his richness of imagination, warmth of colour, and enormous energy—was a constant source of inspiration. In 1822 his career was brilliantly launched when his first submission to the *Salon, the *Barque of Dante* (Louvre, Paris), a melodramatic scene from Dante's *Inferno*, was the talking point of the exhibition and was bought by the state. Two years later he had another success at the Salon with the *Massacre at Chios* (Louvre), inspired by a Turkish atrocity in the recent Greek War of Independence. It aroused much hostile criticism (*Gros, who had admired the *Barque of*

Dante, called it 'the massacre of painting'), but it was awarded a gold medal and once again was bought by the state (with Talleyrand perhaps pulling strings in the background).

The success of the *Massacre at Chios* funded a trip to England in May–August 1825 (Delacroix had earlier met *Bonington and admired *Constable's *Hay Wain*, which had been exhibited to great acclaim in the 1824 Salon). After this visit, English literature became an important source of inspiration in his work for several years; his next major Salon success, for example, the violent and erotic *Death of Sardanapalus* (1827, Louvre), was based on a play by Byron. He was also influenced by contemporary English painting; his portrait of his friend Louis-Auguste Schwiter (1826–30, NG, London) is almost like an act of homage to *Lawrence, of whom he had a high opinion personally as well as professionally. Another major source of imagery in Delacroix's work came from North Africa. In 1832 he visited Spain, Morocco, and Algeria in the entourage of the Comte de Mornay (who headed a diplomatic mission to the Sultan of Morocco), and acquired a rich fund of exotic visual imagery that he exploited for the rest of his life, lion hunting becoming one of his favourite themes (*Lion Hunt*, 1861, Art Inst. of Chicago). In spite of his love of such quintessentially Romantic subjects and his open enmity with *Ingres, who was upheld as the great champion of the classical tradition, Delacroix always regarded himself as part of this tradition, and for his large works he followed the time-honoured course of making numerous preparatory drawings. Although his work often gives the feeling of great spontaneity, he thought deeply about all aspects of his art and craft.

In 1833 Delacroix received a commission to decorate the Salon du Roi in the Palais Bourbon (now the Assemblée Nationale), Paris, and from this point much of his career was devoted to large-scale wall and ceiling painting. He finished the work in the Salon du Roi in 1837 and followed this with decorations in the library of the same building (1838–47). His other major decorative schemes (all in Paris) include those in the Library of the Luxembourg Palace (1841–6), the Galerie d'Apollon in the Louvre (1850), and the Chapelle des Anges of the church of St Sulpice (1853–61), with its celebrated scenes of *Jacob and the Angel* and *Heliodorus Expelled from the Temple*. All these works are in oils (he only once experimented with fresco). In addition to these huge public undertakings, he continued to produce a wide range of smaller paintings, and he also made lithographs, the best known of which are his illustrations to Goethe's *Faust* (1828) and Shakespeare's *Hamlet* (1843).

Delacroix was awarded many honours for his work, and his charm, intelligence, and dashing looks meant that he was in demand by fashionable society. However, he was fairly solitary by nature (he never married) and had only a few close friends, including another archetypal Romantic genius, Chopin, of whom he painted a portrait (1838, Louvre) and whom he described as 'the truest artist I have ever met' (he had a piano installed in his studio so the great man could play there). Although he carefully trained the assistants he used on his decorative commissions, he otherwise had few pupils, and none of them attained any independent distinction. Nevertheless, he had enormous influence on a wide range of artists, particularly through his vibrant and uninhibited use of colour. He was 'the supreme colourist of the first half of the nineteenth century' (Lee Johnson, *Delacroix*, 1963), and the artists who were most clearly influenced by this aspect of his work include *Monet, *Renoir, and *Seurat. Among those who copied his work and valued its liberating effect on the imagination were *Cézanne, *Degas, van *Gogh, and *Redon, and among the professed admirers depicted in *Fantin-Latour's *Homage to Delacroix* (1864, Mus. d'Orsay, Paris) are *Baudelaire, *Manet, and *Whistler.

Delacroix's output was enormous. After his death his executors found more than 9,000 separate works in his studio, including several hundred paintings and more than 6,000 drawings. He drew every day, like a musician practising scales, and he prided himself on the speed at which he worked, declaring 'If you are not skilful enough to sketch a man falling out of a window during the time it takes him to get from the fifth storey to the ground, then you will never be able to produce monumental work.' Delacroix also left behind a substantial literary legacy, for few other great painters have written so copiously or so interestingly about art. He was a voluminous letter-writer and kept a journal from 1822 to 1824 and again from 1847 until his death—a wonderfully rich source of information and opinion on his life and times. His studio in Paris is now a museum devoted to his life and work, but the Louvre has the finest collection of his paintings.

Delaroche, Paul (*b* Paris, 17 July 1797; *d* Paris, 4 Nov. 1856). French painter, one of the leading pupils of *Gros. He achieved European fame with his melodramatic, Hollywoodesque history scenes, engravings of which hung in thousands of homes. Often he chose subjects from English history, as with three of his most famous works, *Cromwell Gazing at the Body of Charles I* (1831, Mus. B.-A., Nîmes), *The Princes in the Tower* (1831, Louvre, Paris; reduced replica in Wallace Coll., London), and the *Execution of Lady Jane Grey* (1833, NG, London). They are *Romantic in flavour, but academically impeccable in their draughtsmanship and detailing. After a period when such pictures were totally out of favour, his work is once again being treated seriously. Delaroche also painted religious works and portraits, and he was a highly respected teacher, his pupils including *Couture, *Gérôme, and *Millet (see also GLEYRE). In 1835 he married the daughter of Horace *Vernet; her early death in 1845 cast a pall over his final years.

Delaunay, Robert (*b* Paris, 12 Apr. 1885; *d* Montpellier, 25 Oct. 1941). French painter. Initially he painted in an *Impressionist style, but in 1906 he began the experiments with the abstract qualities of colour that were to provide the central theme of his career. His starting point was *Neo-Impressionism, but instead of using *Seurat's pointillist technique he investigated the interaction of large areas of contrasting colours. He was particularly interested in the interconnections between colour and movement. By 1910 he was making an individual contribution to *Cubism, combining its fragmented forms with vibrant colours (rather than the muted browns and greys typical of *Braque and *Picasso at this time) and depicting the dynamism of city life rather than the standard Cubist repertoire of still-life and so on. In particular he did a memorable series of paintings of the Eiffel Tower, in which the huge monument seems to be unleashing powerful bursts of energy (*Eiffel Tower*, 1910, Guggenheim Mus., New York). By 1912 he was painting completely abstract pictures (the first French artist to do so). *Apollinaire gave the name *Orphism to Delaunay's work of this period because of its analogies with the abstract art of music. In 1913 he had a one-man show at the *Sturm Gallery in Berlin, and his work was a major influence on German *Expressionists such as *Klee, *Macke, and *Marc; it also powerfully affected the *Futurists in Italy and the American *Synchromists. Delaunay was notoriously competitive and fully aware of the importance of his work; at about this time he drew up a list of all the artists, no matter how minor, he thought he had influenced. However, the period when he was a key figure in modern art was fairly brief; he lived in Spain and Portugal during the First World War and after his return to Paris in 1920 his work lost its inspirational quality and became rather repetitive. His home became a meeting place for *Dada artists, but Delaunay's own paintings continued to be related to colour theories. His last major works were two large murals (destroyed) for pavilions in the Paris World Fair of 1937.

Delaunay-Terk, Sonia (*b* Gradizhsk, Ukraine, 14 Nov. 1885; *d* Paris, 5 Dec. 1979). Russian painter and textile designer, active in Paris, the wife of Robert *Delaunay. She settled in Paris in 1905, married Delaunay in 1910 (after a short-lived marriage of convenience to Wilhelm *Uhde), and became associated with him in the development of *Orphism. During the 1920s she worked mainly as a designer of hand-printed fabrics and tapestries; she made a strong impact on the world of international fashion, designing creations for such famous women as Nancy Cunard and Gloria Swanson. The Depression affected her business, however, and in the 1930s she returned primarily to painting and became a member of the *Abstraction-Création association. After the death of her husband in 1941 she continued to work as a painter and designer.

Delphi Charioteer. Greek bronze statue of a standing charioteer, excavated at Delphi in 1896 and now in the museum there. Fragments of the chariot, horses, and the figure of a groom also survive, and an inscription indicates that the group commemorated a victory of a Sicilian prince, Polyzalus, in the games at Delphi in 478 or 474 BC. The charioteer is one of the most celebrated pieces of Greek sculpture and is generally considered a masterpiece (in *The Story of Art*, *Gombrich describes it as 'a convincing image of a human being, of wonderful simplicity and beauty'); however, Andrew Stewart (*Greek Sculpture*, 1990) calls it a 'much over-rated work'.

Delvaux, Laurent (*b* Ghent, 17 Jan. 1696; *d* Nivelles, 24 Feb. 1778). Flemish sculptor. From 1717 to 1728 he worked in England, sometimes in collaboration with his fellow Fleming Peter *Scheemakers, with whom he made a number of church monuments. In 1728 they visited Rome together; Scheemakers returned to England in 1730, but Delvaux remained until 1733, when he moved back permanently to Flanders, settling at Nivelles, between Brussels and Charleroi, where he ran a busy workshop. His commissions came largely from churches and the court in Brussels, and occasionally from English clients. He worked in wood as well as marble and also made lively models in terracotta.

Delvaux, Paul (*b* Antheit, nr. Huy, 23 Sept. 1897; *d* Veurne, 20 July 1994). Belgian painter. After working in *Neo-Impressionist and *Expressionist manners, he discovered *Surrealism in 1934 and became an instant convert, destroying much of his earlier work. He was never formally a member of the movement, and was not in sympathy with its political aims, but he became one of the foremost upholders of its tradition. Most of his paintings show nude or semi-nude women in incongruous settings. The women are always of the same type—beautiful, statuesque, unattainable dream figures, lost in thought or reverie or even in a state of suspended animation. These dream beauties are often placed in elaborate architectural settings, reflecting both de *Chirico's strange perspectives and Delvaux's interest in the buildings of ancient Rome (he visited Italy in 1938 and 1939). Sometimes he included skeletons in his pictures (influenced by *Ensor) and trains were another recurrent motif. A large retrospective of Delvaux's work was held at the Palais des Beaux-Arts, Brussels, in 1944, and this marked the beginning of his international reputation.

De Maria, Walter (*b* Albany, Calif., 1 Oct. 1935). American sculptor and experimental artist. He was one of the earliest exponents of *Minimal art, producing examples of the type *c.*1960, before the term was current, and he was also a pioneer of *Land art. Some of his work can also be regarded as *Conceptual art, as for example *Mile Long Drawing* of 1968, two parallel chalk lines 12 ft (3.5m) apart in the Mojave Desert.

Demeter of Cnidus. A marble figure (*c.*330 BC) of the goddess Demeter found at Cnidus in Asia Minor and now in the British Museum. It represents the goddess majestically seated on a throne; originally, perhaps, a figure of her daughter Persephone stood beside her. It is considered one of the finest Greek sculptures to survive from the 4th century and has been attributed to *Leochares. See also APHRODITE OF CNIDUS.

De Morgan, Evelyn (*b* London, 30 Aug. 1855; *d* London, 2 May 1919). British painter, born Evelyn Pickering; in 1887 she married **William De Morgan** (*b* London, 16 Nov. 1839; *d* London, 15 Jan. 1917), famous as a designer of pottery, tiles, and ceramics, but also a painter himself (late in life he also became a successful novelist).

She specialized in literary subjects, done in a style owing much to the *Pre-Raphaelites and to such *Renaissance artists as *Botticelli (she and her husband spent each winter in Italy for the sake of his health). At the end of her career she painted several allegories relating to the First World War, exhibiting them to raise money for the Red Cross.

Demuth, Charles (b Lancaster, Pa., 8 Nov. 1883; d Lancaster, 23 Oct. 1935). American painter and illustrator, a pioneer of modern art in his country. He visited Europe in 1904, 1907–8, and 1912–14, staying mainly in Paris, and during the last of these visits he became seriously interested in avant-garde art, particularly *Cubism. From about 1916 its influence is evident in his paintings of architectural subjects, with which he became one of the leading exponents of *Precisionism. His most personal paintings are what he called 'poster portraits' (pictures composed of words and objects associated with the person 'represented'). The most famous example is *I Saw the Figure Five in Gold* (1928, Met. Mus., New York), a tribute to the poet William Carlos Williams and named after one of his poems. Demuth was lame from childhood and in the last decade of his life was debilitated by diabetes. Often he worked on a small scale in watercolour, rather than in more physically demanding media. The fastidious taste and concentrated energy of his work are suggested by his comment: 'John *Marin [another great American watercolourist] and I drew our inspiration from the same source, French modernism. He brought his up in buckets and spilt much along the way. I dipped mine out with a teaspoon, but I never spilled a drop.'

Denis, Maurice (b Granville, Normandy, 25 Nov. 1870; d Paris, 13 Nov. 1943). French painter, designer, lithographer, illustrator, and writer on art theory. Early in his career he was a *Symbolist and a member of the *Nabis. He was the chief theorist of the group and one of his articles, 'Definition of Neo-Traditionalism' (1890), contains a pronouncement that has become famous as an anticipation of the underlying principle of much modern—especially abstract—art: 'Remember that a picture—before being a war horse or a nude woman or an anecdote—is essentially a flat surface covered with colours assembled in a certain order.' Denis's early work, strongly influenced by *Gauguin, did indeed place great emphasis on flat patterning, but he did not intend to encourage non-representational art, for he was also very much concerned with subject matter; he was a devout Catholic and wanted to bring about a revival of religious painting. Many of his easel paintings have religious subjects, and in 1899 he carried out his first large-scale religious commission—a mural in the Chapelle de la Sainte-Croix at Vésinet. Numerous others followed, and in 1919 he founded the Ateliers d'Art Sacré with Georges Desvallières (1861–1950) to provide church decorations of various kinds, including mosaics and stained glass. Typically Denis's style in his religious work was tender and mild, with pale colours and relaxed lines. He also did a good deal of secular decoration, but his most famous work is probably *Homage to Cézanne* (1900, Mus. d'Orsay, Paris) showing Denis himself and a number of *Cézanne's other admirers, including *Bonnard, *Redon, *Sérusier, and *Vuillard, gathered round a still-life by the master. His best paintings were done early in his career; after about 1900 they became more classical in style (influenced by visits to Italy) and increasingly bland. From 1914 Denis lived in a 17th-century building in Saint-Germain-en-Laye; it has been attractively converted into the Musée du Prieuré, housing a fine collection of works by him and his associates.

Denny, Robyn. See SITUATION.

Denon, Dominique-Vivant, Baron (b Givry, nr. Chalon-sur-Saône, 4 Jan. 1747; d Paris, 28 Apr. 1825). French engraver, draughtsman, archaeologist, diplomat, museum official, and writer. He was a much-travelled and much-liked man who had a highly varied career. In 1798 he accompanied Napoleon on his expedition to Egypt, recording his travels in *Voyage dans la Basse et la Haute Égypte* (1802), illustrated from his own drawings (it was published in English in the same year as *Travels in Upper and Lower Egypt*). From 1804 to 1815 he was director of the national museums, and he played an important role in developing the collections of the *Louvre, advising Napoleon on his choice of works of art to be looted from conquered territories. After Napoleon's final defeat in 1815 Denon went into retirement and worked on a general history of art, which he left incomplete at his death; it was posthumously published in four volumes in 1829. As an artist he worked mainly as an engraver, but he was also one of the first Frenchmen to take up lithography (1809).

De Piles, Roger. See PILES.

Derain, André (b Chatou, nr. Paris, 17 June 1880; d Garches, 8 Sept. 1954). French painter, printmaker, theatrical designer, and sculptor. In the first two decades of the 20th century he was near the centre of avant-garde developments in Paris: he was one of the creators of *Fauvism, an early adherent of *Cubism, one of the first to 'discover' *primitive art, and a pioneer of *direct carving. A good example of his Fauve period is his portrait of *Matisse (1905) in Tate Modern, London, which also has Matisse's portrait of Derain, executed at the same time, when they were painting together at Collioure, near the Mediterranean border with Spain. In the 1920s he moved away from his pre-war experimentation to a much more conservative style reflecting his admiration for the Old Masters. The works he painted in this manner (including landscapes, portraits, still-lifes, and nudes) made him wealthy and famous (he exhibited widely abroad), but they dismayed many supporters of avant-garde art. He polarized opinion so much that in January 1931 the periodical *Les Chroniques du jour* published a feature entitled 'André Derain: pour ou contre'. Among those quoted in this was Jacques-Émile *Blanche, who—even though he was a fairly conservative painter himself—wrote: 'Youth has departed: what remains is a highly cerebral and rather mechanical art.'

The differences of opinion he had provoked in his life continued after Derain's death. Many critics think that his work after the First World War was essentially a long anticlimax, but some admirers have thought extraordinarily highly of him, notably *Giacometti, who wrote in 1957: 'Derain excites me more, has given me more and taught me more than any painter since *Cézanne; to me he is the most audacious of them all.' Two years later the American critic John Canaday (1907–85) summed up the situation in his book *Mainstreams of Modern Art*: 'His detractors think of him as a parasite on both the past and the present, but . . . some critics award Derain unique status as the only twentieth-century painter to achieve an individual compound of the great tradition of French culture as a whole with the spirit of his own time . . . This opinion is particularly held in France—where, of course, it is most legitimate.'

Deruet, Claude (*b* Nancy, *c.*1588; *bur.* Nancy, 20 Oct. 1660). French painter who, like *Bellange and *Callot, worked mainly for the court of the dukes of Lorraine at Nancy. He ran a busy studio and had a highly successful career (his other patrons included Louis XIII and Cardinal Richelieu), but much of his work has been destroyed and his surviving paintings are in a pedestrian *Mannerist style that was a generation out of date at the time of his death. The best known are four vast allegorical scenes representing the Elements (*c.*1640, Mus. B.-A., Orléans), painted for Richelieu. In 1625–6 the young *Claude worked as Deruet's assistant.

desco da parto (Italian: 'tray of childbirth'). A type of circular or twelve-sided painted wooden tray used in medieval and *Renaissance Italy to present small gifts, sweetmeats, and wine to a mother after childbirth. *Deschi da parto* were often decorated on both sides, typically with an appropriate narrative or symbolic scene on one side and a coat of arms or family device on the other. Many of them were produced in workshops specializing in *cassoni*, although they were occasionally commissioned from distinguished artists. One of the best surviving examples of a *desco da parto* is that marking the birth of Lorenzo de' *Medici in 1449 (Met. Mus., New York); it shows the *Triumph of Fame* and was painted by *Masaccio's brother Lo Scheggia.

Desenfans, Noel. See BOURGEOIS, SIR PETER FRANCIS.

'Desiderio, Monsù'. See 'MONSÙ DESIDERIO'.

Desiderio da Settignano (*b* Settignano, nr. Florence, *c.*1430; *bur.* Florence, 16 Jan. 1464). Florentine sculptor, born into a family of stonemasons (the village from which he takes his name was renowned for this trade). Like most of his contemporaries Desiderio formed his style on *Donatello's work of the 1430s. He learnt from him the practice of carving in very low *relief, and the lively, thick-set figures of children on the master's *Singing Gallery* for Florence Cathedral (1433–9) provided models for Desiderio's various reliefs of the Madonna and Child. Desiderio's artistic personality, however, was more delicate than Donatello's, and for refinement of handling in marble he is unsurpassed by any Italian sculptor of his period, as is seen particularly in his portrait busts of women, good examples of which are in Florence (Bargello) and Washington (NG). He died young and his only important public work was the tomb of the Florentine humanist and statesman Gregorio Marsuppini (*d* 1453) in S. Croce. This is architecturally dependent on the tomb of Leonardo Bruni by Bernardo *Rossellino (possibly Desiderio's teacher), executed for the same church about ten years earlier, but is sculpturally richer and more animated.

Desjardins, Martin (*bapt*. Breda, 11 Nov. 1637; *d* Paris, 2 May 1694). Dutch-born sculptor who spent almost all his career in France. His name was originally Martin van den Bogaert, but he adopted an approximate French equivalent (*bogaard* is Dutch for 'orchard', and *jardin* French for 'garden'). His most important work was a huge bronze statue of Louis XIV for the Place des Victoires, Paris (1686). It was destroyed during the French Revolution, but parts of the pedestal survive in the Louvre, and an earlier, smaller version of the statue in marble is at Versailles. His other work included tombs, portrait busts, and a good deal of decorative sculpture at Versailles and in various buildings in Paris.

Despiau, Charles (*b* Mont-de-Marsan, 4 Nov. 1874; *d* Paris, 28 Oct. 1946). French sculptor and illustrator. He was one of *Rodin's assistants from 1907 to 1914, after which he turned from his master's intense, vigorous style to a more static, generalized manner in the vein associated with *Maillol. His best-known works are his portrait busts, with their intimate delineation of character (*Head of Mme Derain*, 1922, Phillips Coll., Washington). He also made several monuments. In the 1920s and 1930s his reputation stood very high in France, but at the end of his life he was ostracized because of his friendship with the Nazi sculptor Arno Breker (1900–91); they had known each other since before the war and in 1942 Despiau attended an exhibition of the German's work in occupied Paris.

Desportes, Alexandre-François (*b* Champigneul, Champagne, 24 Feb. 1661; *d* Paris, 20 Apr. 1743). French painter, mainly of animal and still-life subjects. In his early career he worked much as a portraitist, notably in 1695–6 at the court of Jan Sobieski (John III) in Poland, but on his return to France he took up subjects related to the hunt, especially pictures of dogs with dead game. He became a leading specialist in his field, rivalled only by *Oudry, and his patrons included Louis XIV, Louis XV, and a host of aristocrats (he was also appreciated in England, which he visited in 1712). Although he continued the lavish Flemish tradition exemplified by *Snyders, Desportes was among the first artists of the 18th century to make landscape studies from nature for his backgrounds—a practice for which he was considered eccentric. His work is well represented in the Louvre (which has his handsome *Self-Portrait as a Huntsman*, 1699) and in the Wallace Collection, London.

De Stijl. See STIJL.

Desvallières, Georges. See DENIS.

Detroy, Jean-François. See TROY.

Deutsch, Niklaus Manuel (*b* Berne, *c*.1484; *d* Berne, 28 Apr. 1530). Swiss painter, draughtsman, designer, writer, and politician, active mainly in Berne. Deutsch was one of the outstanding Swiss artists of his period, but much of his energy was expended in other activities. He fought as a mercenary in Italy in 1516 and 1522 and he took an active part in the political and religious affairs of Berne, serving on the town council for many years; he was a passionate supporter of the Reformation, writing satirical poems against the pope, whom he equated with Antichrist. In their feeling for the grotesque, his paintings are related to those of *Baldung Grien and *Grünewald (*Temptation of St Anthony*, 1520, Kunstmuseum, Berne). Deutsch also made designs for woodcuts, stained glass, metalwork, and sculpture.

Deverell, Walter Howell (*b* Charlottesville, Va., 1 Oct. 1827; *d* London, 2 Feb. 1854). British painter, closely associated with the *Pre-Raphaelites (he was proposed for membership of the Brotherhood, to replace *Collinson, but was never actually elected). In 1849 he 'discovered' Elizabeth Siddal, the archetypal Pre-Raphaelite model and *Rossetti's future wife. Deverell was noted for his good looks and charm and Elizabeth was probably in love with him. He died aged 26 from Bright's disease, leaving only a small number of paintings.

Devis, Arthur (*b* Preston, Lancashire, 12 Feb. 1712; *d* Brighton, 25 July 1787). English painter, active mainly in London but also in his native Preston, the best-known member of a family of artists. He was one of the first specialists in the small *conversation piece and also painted single portraits of similar scale. His sitters are often somewhat artificially posed, with less animation than in *Zoffany's conversation pieces of the next generation. Devis was a minor artist in his day and virtually forgotten until the 1930s, but since then his work has attained considerable popularity because of the doll-like charm of his figures and the delicate detail of his settings. It has also become of interest to social historians, as most of his clients were from the newly prosperous middle class—merchants and country squires. There are good examples of his work in the Harris Art Gallery, Preston. His half-brother **Anthony Devis** (1729–1816) was a landscape painter, and two of Arthur's sons were also artists: **Arthur William Devis** (1763–1822) and

Thomas Anthony Devis (1757–1810). Arthur William spent the years 1785–95 in India, where he painted portraits and a series of pictures representing the arts, manufactures, and agriculture of Bengal (two examples are in the Ashmolean Museum, Oxford), which were engraved. He lived in London from 1795, working mainly as a portraitist, but also painting the *Death of Nelson* (c.1806, Nat. Maritime Mus., London). Thomas Anthony painted undistinguished portraits and *fancy pictures. Little of his work survives.

devotional painting. A fairly small religious painting suitable as a focus for private worship, as opposed to an altarpiece intended for public display. Certain prints and sculptures can also be considered devotional images.

Dewing, T. W. See TEN.

De Wint, Peter (*b* Stone, Staffordshire, 21 Jan. 1784; *d* London, 30 June 1849). English landscape painter of Dutch extraction. From 1802 to 1806 he was apprenticed to John Raphael *Smith, and he later studied at the *Royal Academy, had advice from John *Varley, and frequented the house of Dr *Monro. Although he painted in oils a good deal, he achieved little success in this field and is best known as one of the finest watercolourists of his generation. His only journey abroad was a short visit to Normandy in 1828, and almost all his work is devoted to the English countryside. He is particularly associated with views of the area around Lincoln (where his wife's parents lived), in which he often uses broad *washes of colour somewhat in the manner of *Cotman. De Wint loved painting—'Mine is a beautiful profession'—and was popular as a teacher.

Diaghilev, Sergei (*b* Grusino, Novgorod province, 19 [31] Mar. 1872; *d* Venice, 19 Aug. 1929). Russian impresario, famous above all as the founder of the Ballets Russes, through which he exerted great influence on the visual arts as well as on dancing and music. From 1890 to 1896 he studied law in St Petersburg, where he became part of a circle of musicians, painters, and writers including Léon *Bakst and Alexandre *Benois. In 1899 he founded the magazine *World of Art*, with the object of interchanging artistic ideas with western Europe. When it ceased publication in 1904 he concentrated for a while on organizing exhibitions, including one of Russian painting at the 1905 *Salon d'Automne in Paris—the most comprehensive to have been seen in the West up to that time. In 1907 he organized a series of concerts of Russian music in Paris, and in 1909 he brought a ballet company for the first time (this is usually described as the Ballets Russes, but the name was first used in 1911). The company was a sensational success, as much for the exotic designs of Bakst as for the music and choreography (the dancers included Nijinsky and Pavlova). For the next two decades, until his death in 1929, Diaghilev toured Europe and America with his ballet (he never returned to Russia after the 1917 Revolution and Paris was the main centre of his operations). He was often on the verge of bankruptcy, but he had a remarkable flair for spotting young talent and for integrating various interests and people, enabling him to bring together as his collaborators some of the foremost artistic personalities of his time; the painters who designed sets and costumes for him included *Braque, de *Chirico, *Derain, *Matisse, and *Picasso. He liked to use painters rather than artists who had trained as stage designers, as he thought specialists were likely to be too tied to old ideas.

diaper. An all-over pattern made up of small repeated geometric units (usually squares or lozenges) capable of indefinite extension in any direction. It is found carved in low relief on wall surfaces in *Romanesque and *Gothic architecture, in stained glass, and in the backgrounds of manuscript illuminations, especially of the late 13th and 14th centuries.

Diaz de la Peña, Narcisse (*b* Bordeaux, 21 Aug. 1807; *d* Menton, 18 Nov. 1876). French painter, born of Spanish parents who had settled in France as political refugees. He began his career (c.1823) as a colourist in a porcelain factory and took up painting in the late 1820s, first exhibiting at the *Salon in 1831. His early paintings included *scènes galantes*, imaginative oriental subjects, and still-lifes, usually small in size and rich in colour and texture, but after meeting Théodore *Rousseau in 1836 he became a member of the *Barbizon School of landscape painters. Stylistically, however, he stood somewhat apart from his Barbizon colleagues; his liking for melodramatic lighting contrasts with the sense of quiet communion with nature that was typical of the group and his restless brushwork remained highly distinctive. Indeed, he never lost the Romantic leanings of his youth, and carried on painting mythological pictures (typically featuring nymphs) throughout his career. He achieved success earlier than most of his friends and was generous in helping younger painters by purchasing their work.

Several of the *Impressionists were influenced by him, notably *Renoir, who said that meeting Diaz led him to lighten his palette.

Dick, Sir William Reid. See PORTLAND STONE.

Dickinson, Edwin (*b* Seneca Falls, NY, 11 Oct. 1891; *d* Cape Cod, Mass., 2 Dec. 1978). American painter and draughtsman. He often treated enigmatic or disquieting subject matter and he has been described as 'perhaps the first American artist about whom some knowledge of dream theory is essential for decoding his works' (Matthew Baigell, *A Concise History of American Painting and Sculpture*, 1984). His personal symbolism is seen at its most disturbing and provocative in his self-portraits, in which he sometimes depicted himself as dead. He is best known, however, for large compositions such as *The Fossil Hunters* (1926–8, Whitney Mus., New York). Dickinson often worked on his big pictures for a number of years and said that they were never 'really finished'. He has been called a *Surrealist and also seen as a sophisticated culmination of the 19th-century *Romantic tradition.

Dickinson, Preston (*b* New York, 9 Sept. 1891; *d* Irún, Spain, 30 Nov. 1930). American painter. He spent five years in Europe, 1910–15, and in Paris he was influenced particularly by the structural features of *Cézanne's work and the high-keyed colour of the *Fauves. In the 1920s, however, his work became less experimental as he became associated with the *Precisionists. Like others of the group, he favoured subjects (notably machinery) that were adapted to representation in terms of semi-geometrical abstract design (*Industry*, c.1924, Whitney Mus., New York).

Dicksee, Sir Frank (*b* London, 27 Nov. 1853; *d* London, 17 Oct. 1928). British painter, the best-known member of a family of artists. He specialized in romantic historical scenes (often from his own imagination rather than based on a particular event or literary source) and—in the later part of his career—portraits; he also occasionally produced scenes of modern social drama. At his best, he painted with a sumptuous technique and a feeling for bold and unusual lighting effects, but he could be rather twee. He was at the height of his esteem at the turn of the century; in 1900 he was awarded a medal at the Paris Exposition Universelle, and in the same year his pious medieval pageant scene *The Two Crowns* (Tate, London) was voted the most popular picture at the *Royal Academy summer exhibition. By the

end of his career, however, he was regarded a distinctly old-fashioned, and when he was electe president of the Royal Academy in 1924, this wa seen as a concession to his seniority rather tha as an indication of his standing in the art worlc He was strongly opposed to modern art and h speeches as president fit the stereotype of the ol attacking the new.

Other painter members of his family include his brother **Herbert** (1862–1942) and his siste **Margaret** (1858–1903).

Diderot, Denis (*b* Langres, 5 Oct. 1713; *d* Pari 31 July 1784). French philosopher and write perhaps best known as the chief editor of th *Encyclopédie* (1751–72), a work of fundamenta importance in shaping the rationalist and ht manitarian ideals of the Age of Enlightenmen He was a highly versatile author, his vast outpt including novels, plays, scientific writings, an criticism. His views on art appear in variou places, notably in articles in the *Encyclopédi* and in his reviews of the *Salons from 1759 t 1781, which appeared in the journal *Correspor dance littéraire*. They are written in a lively cor versational style and formed the model for th criticism of *Baudelaire. His aesthetic view which are sometimes inconsistent, reflect bot his common-sense approach and the 18th century taste for sentiment. He was enthusiastt about *Greuze because of what seemed ht moral seriousness, but he berated *Bouche whom he regarded as frivolous. Some of ht best writing is on *Chardin, whose close scrt tiny of the real world set him apart from th prevailing *Rococo artificiality.

Diebenkorn, Richard (*b* Portland, Ore., 2 Apr. 1922; *d* Berkeley, 30 Mar. 1993). America painter, active in California for almost all ht career, mainly in the San Francisco Bay are From 1947 to 1950 he taught at the Californi School of Fine Arts, San Francisco, where ht fellow teachers included Mark *Rothko an Clyfford *Still; under their influence he abar doned the still-lifes and interiors he had bee painting and adopted an *Abstract Expressionis manner. In the mid-1950s, however, he move away from the subjective emotionalism c this way of painting and developed a styl in which he tried to apply the vigorou brushwork of Abstract Expressionism to studie of figures in an environment. (The terms Ba Area Figuration and West Coast Figuratio have been applied to work in this vein; severa other California painters, including Davi Park (1911–60), worked in a similar idiom.

Subsequently Diebenkorn moved between abstraction and figuration, his work in both modes making use of large areas of colour that owed much to the example of *Matisse. His best-known works are a series of large pictures entitled *Ocean Park* begun in 1967 (*Ocean Park No. 96*, Guggenheim Mus., New York, 1977). They are abstract, but the light-filled colours suggest sky, sea, and sand.

Dietrich, Christian Wilhelm Ernst (*b* Weimar, 30 Oct. 1712; *d* Dresden, 24 Apr. 1774). German painter and etcher, active mainly in Dresden, although he travelled a good deal. He was prolific and versatile, his work ranging from altarpieces to porcelain decoration for the Meissen factory, and he was renowned for his ability to produce pictures in the style of various 17th-century masters. His career was highly successful: in 1741 he became court painter to the Elector Frederick Augustus II of Saxony (King Augustus III of Poland); in 1748 inspector of the Gemäldegalerie, Dresden; and in 1764 a professor at the Dresden Academy. At the peak of his career his work was in demand all over Europe, but his reputation is now much faded. There are examples of his paintings in the National Gallery and the Wallace Collection, London.

Dietterlin, Wendel (*b* Pfullendorff, nr. Ludwigshafen, *c*.1550/1; *d* Strasbourg, 1599). German painter, engraver, and designer. He worked mainly in Strasbourg, where he specialized in painting façade, ceiling, and wall decorations. None of these has survived and only one easel picture can certainly be credited to him, the signed *Raising of Lazarus* (?1582 or ?1587, Kunsthalle, Karlsruhe). His claim to fame is his book *Architectura* (2 vols., 1593–4; enlarged 2nd edn. in one vol., 1598), an extraordinary collection of engravings in which the Orders of architecture are used as the starting point for weird and extravagant decorative fantasies, full of bizarre animal and plant forms. It had an international vogue as a pattern book.

dilettante. See AMATEUR.

Dilettanti, Society of. Society of British connoisseurs founded in London in 1732; it was originally a dining club for young noblemen and gentlemen who had been on the *Grand Tour, but it came to play a prominent role in matters of taste, and particularly in the study of *antique art. The original members met on the first Sunday of the month in a tavern (drinking a toast to 'Grecian taste and Roman spirit'), so provoking the sneer of Horace *Walpole, never one of them, that 'the nominal qualification for membership is having been in Italy and the real one being drunk'. One of them at least, Sir Francis Dashwood (1708–81), was a member of the notorious Hell Fire Club. The serious interests of the group prevailed, however, and after an unsuccessful attempt to sponsor Italian opera in England, the Dilettanti turned to the study of the architectural and archaeological remains of Italy and Greece, which had stirred their interest and imagination on their travels. They financed a succession of expeditions and published the results in various magnificently illustrated books that helped lay the foundations of the serious and systematic study of classical antiquities and contributed to the growth of *Neoclassicism. Many of the finest treasures of the Department of Classical Antiquities of the *British Museum were acquired by purchase or bequest from members of the Society—among them Sir William Hamilton (1730–1803), Richard Payne *Knight, and Charles Townley (1737–1805). One serious lapse, however, was the failure of the Dilettanti, through the misjudgement of Payne Knight, to recognize the importance of the *Elgin Marbles.

From the earliest meetings the Society appointed a painter, one of whose duties was to provide a portrait of each member on election at his own expense. The first holder of the title was George *Knapton, and his successors have included Sir Joshua *Reynolds, Sir Thomas *Lawrence, Sir Martin Archer *Shee, Sir Charles *Eastlake, Frederic Lord *Leighton, Sir Edward *Poynter, John Singer *Sargent, and Sir William *Coldstream. Many portraits so commissioned are still among the treasured possessions of the Society. It has never owned its own premises, meeting at various places in the St James's area of London. Since 1976 it has been based at Brooks's Club.

Diller, Burgoyne (*b* New York, 13 Jan. 1906; *d* New York, 30 Jan. 1965). American painter and sculptor. His early work was influenced by *Impressionism and *Cubism, but by the mid-1930s he had become probably the earliest American exponent of *Mondrian's type of geometrical abstraction. He remained committed to this style for the rest of his career, in his sculpture (which is restricted to rectangular elements and primary colours) as well as his painting. He was a member of *American Abstract Artists and from 1935 to 1940 supervisor of the Mural Division of the *Federal Art Project.

diluent. A liquid used to dilute a paint and give it the fluidity the painter desires, e.g. *turpentine in *oil painting, and water in *watercolour. See also VEHICLE.

Dine, Jim (*b* Cincinnati, 16 June 1935). American painter, printmaker, experimental artist, and poet. In 1959 he was one of the pioneers of *happenings and in the early 1960s he became one of the most prominent figures in American *Pop art (he also made an impact in England, where he lived 1967–71). His Pop canvases were vigorously handled in a manner recalling *Abstract Expressionism, but he often attached real objects to them—generally everyday items such as clothes and household appliances (including a kitchen sink). Characteristically the objects were Dine's personal possessions and his work often has a strong autobiographical flavour. In addition to such *assemblages, he also made freestanding works and *environments, but since the mid-1970s he has concentrated more on traditional two-dimensional work, especially drawings (he has written and illustrated several books of poetry) and prints.

Dionysius of Fourna (*b* Fourna [Fournás], Greece, *c*.1670; *d c*.1744). Greek painter and writer on art. A monk, he worked in Constantinople, at Mount Athos, and elsewhere. Several paintings by him survive, but he is remembered chiefly as the author of an artistic treatise (*c*.1730) written in Greek and usually known in English as *The Painter's Manual*. As well as describing technical methods, it contains extensive material on *iconography, and shows the continuation of *Byzantine tradition. There are numerous manuscripts of the treatise; it first appeared in print in a Russian edition in 1909, and an English translation was published in 1974.

diorama. A form of public entertainment, popular in the 19th century, featuring a large, partially translucent scenic painting, which by means of varied illumination simulated such effects as sunrise, changing weather, etc. By extension the term was also applied to the building in which the display was housed. The audience sat in darkness and the spectacle was an ancestor of the cinema. The diorama was invented by *Daguerre, who gave his first demonstration in Paris in 1822, and the following year he opened one in London. *Constable went to see it and wrote to a friend: 'I was at the private view of the "Diorama"; it is in part a transparency; the spectator is in a dark chamber, and it is very pleasing, and has great illusion. It is

without the pale of art, because its object is deception. The art pleases by *reminding*, not *deceiving*. The place was filled with foreigners, and I seemed to be in a cage of magpies.' Other cities also had dioramas, but none has survived (although the building that housed the London example still exists, much altered internally). Today the term is more usually applied to various kinds of model, particularly a type of museum display; it consists of a miniature scene, viewed through a window or screen, in which the foreground details, modelled in the round, join imperceptibly with the more distant parts, which are painted in perspective on a vertical panel.

diorite. A hard, coarse-grained igneous rock, similar to *granite and sometimes known as 'black granite' (it is usually black or grey in colour). In ancient times it was sometimes used for sculpture in Egypt and the Near East.

dipper. A small container, usually made of metal, that clips onto the edge of the oil painter's *palette and holds *medium or *diluent. They are often made in pairs—a 'double dipper'. The American term is 'palette cup'.

diptych. A picture or other work of art consisting of two equal-sized parts facing one another like the pages of a book. Diptychs are usually fairly small in size and often the two parts are hinged together so the work could be folded when not in use and easily transported. The type seems to have originated in ivory carvings in the late Roman Empire. Initially they were used for writing tablets, the outer surfaces being carved, with wax on the hollowed inner surfaces. They were sometimes used to commemorate family events such as weddings, but they were mainly used to mark the appointment of a new consul; it became the custom for the office holder to distribute such panels as gifts to friends, relatives, and persons of rank. The earliest 'consular diptych' to survive is of 428, and the practice ceased in 541. Because they can be precisely dated by the name of the official they bear, they are important tools in scholarship of the period. Many were later reused for Christian purposes, and in the Middle Ages the diptych became a popular format for portable altarpieces; the Wilton Diptych (see INTERNATIONAL GOTHIC) is the most celebrated example. See also POLYPTYCH and TRIPTYCH.

direct carving. The practice of producing carved sculpture (particularly stone sculpture) by cutting directly into the material, as opposed to having it reproduced from a plaster model using mechanical aids and assistants. Although this might seem a purely technical matter, in the early 20th century it became associated with aesthetic and ethical issues, particularly in Britain and in France. During the 19th century it was customary for sculpture to be exhibited in plaster; it was much more expensive and time-consuming to produce marble carvings (or bronze casts), so these were usually made only when firmly commissioned. A successful sculptor could become the administrator of a large studio producing numerous, almost identical versions of popular works (*Rodin employed many assistants, including artists of the calibre of *Bourdelle, *Despiau, and *Pompon, and he rarely touched hammer and chisel himself, only occasionally adding final touches to his works in marble). This kind of procedure was attacked by John *Ruskin, who in 1872 denounced the 'modern system of modelling the work in clay, getting it into form by machinery [by this he means the *pointing machine], and by the hands of subordinates'. Ruskin argued that the sculptor of such works thinks in clay and not in marble and that 'neither he nor the public recognize the touch of the chisel as expressive of personal feeling and that nothing is looked for except mechanical polish'. However, it was not until the early years of the 20th century that his ideas on direct carving were put into practice by sculptors in Britain. Among the most important pioneers were Jacob *Epstein, Eric *Gill, and Henri *Gaudier-Brzeska, who collectively illustrate some of the range of issues involved. For Epstein, the activity of carving was linked to his interest in sculpture from outside the Graeco-Roman tradition, such as that of Assyria and Africa, and it reflected his contact in Paris with *Brancusi and *Modigliani, who had similar interests. For Gill, a return to carving was a return to a medieval practice, through which he hoped to overcome the iniquitous effect of industrialism in dividing the work of the thinker and the maker. For Gaudier-Brzeska, carving was equated with a struggle that was both manual and creative, an aspect of a 'virile' art that contrasted with the 'feminine' modelling that had dominated the previous generation of *New Sculptors.

After the First World War a number of British sculptors, including Barbara *Hepworth and Henry *Moore, practised direct carving as a dogma (see TRUTH TO MATERIAL), while others, such as Frank *Dobson and Leon *Underwood, worked as both carvers and modellers. In France, direct carving moved from being chiefly an avant-garde concern before 1914 to wider acceptance in the 1920s, and at the same time it was taken up in other countries; Fritz *Wotruba was an influential exponent in Austria, for example, as was William *Zorach in the USA. After the Second World War the carving versus modelling debate was rendered largely obsolete by the prevalence of newer techniques, although for many older sculptors the sense of personal engagement with the material through carving still remained of central importance.

Discobolus (Discus Thrower). See MYRON.

disegno. An Italian word that in art-historical contexts can sometimes be translated straightforwardly as 'drawing' or 'design' but which in the *Renaissance often carried the broader meaning of the total imaginative concept of a work of art; in this sense, the word has been translated as 'creative capacity'. In the 16th century some theorists used the phrase *disegno interno*, implying a divinely inspired idea in the artist's mind, and Federico *Zuccaro punningly derived *disegno* from *segno di Dio* ('sign of God'). Central Italian (particularly Florentine) artists and writers laid particular stress on the importance of *disegno*, in contrast with the Venetian emphasis on *colore* ('colour'). These different approaches were formalized in 17th-century France when the Académie Royale (see ACADEMY) split into opposing factions—the Poussinists, who adhered to the intellectual approach of *Poussin, and the Rubénistes, led by Roger de *Piles, who admired the colour and warmth of *Rubens. Echoes of the controversy lingered in the rivalry between *Ingres and *Delacroix in the 19th century and perhaps even in that between *Picasso and *Matisse in the 20th.

distemper. Type of paint in which the pigment is mixed with water and glue or *size. Its principal use is in stage scenery, as it is cheap but impermanent. Whitewash is a form of distemper.

divisionism. A method of painting in which colour effects are obtained by applying small areas or dots of pure, unmixed colours on the canvas in such a way that to a spectator standing at an appropriate distance they appear to interreact, producing greater luminosity and brilliance than would have resulted if the same colours had been physically mixed together. The method was employed empirically by the *Impressionists, but it was not developed systematically and scientifically until *Seurat and the *Neo-Impressionists. Camille *Pissarro, who was closely associated with Seurat in the later 1880s, said that the optimum viewing distance for a picture painted by the divisionist method was three times the diagonal measurement. Seurat (in common with other contemporaries) spoke of an 'optical mixture', but (contrary to what is usually stated) the dots do not really fuse in the viewer's eye to make different colours, for they remain visible as dots. Rather, they seem to vibrate, creating something of the shimmering effect experienced in strong sunlight. The effect is noted in *Modern Chromatics* (1879) by the American physicist Ogden Rood (1831–1902), a treatise on colour theory well known to the Neo-Impressionists through the French translation of 1881. Another treatise they found stimulating was *De la loi du contraste simultané des couleurs* (1839) by the French chemist Eugène Chevreul (1786–1889). Two separate English translations were published in the 1850s: *The Principles of Harmony and Contrast of Colours* (1854) and *The Laws of Contrast of Colour* (1857).

The terms divisionism and *pointillism are not always clearly differentiated, but whereas divisionism refers mainly to the underlying theory, pointillism describes the actual painting technique associated with Seurat and his followers. 'Divisionism' (usually with a capital 'D') was also the name of an Italian movement, a version of Neo-Impressionism, that flourished in the last decade of the 19th century and the first decade of the 20th century. It was one of the sources of *Futurism.

Dix, Otto (*b* Untermhaus, Thuringia, 2 Dec. 1891; *d* Singen, 25 July 1969). German painter and printmaker (in woodcut, etching, drypoint, and lithography). In the 1920s he was, with George *Grosz, the outstanding artist of the *Neue Sachlichkeit movement, his work conveying his disillusionment and disgust at the horrors of war and the depravities of a decadent society with complete psychological truth and devastating emotional effect. *The Match Seller* (1920, Staatsgalerie, Stuttgart), for example, is a pitiless depiction of indifference to suffering, showing passers-by ignoring a blind and limbless ex-soldier begging in the street, and Dix's 50 etchings entitled *The War* (1924) have been described by George Heard Hamilton (*Painting and Sculpture in Europe: 1880–1940*, 1967) as 'perhaps the most powerful as well as the most unpleasant anti-war statements in modern art'. Another favourite theme was prostitution and he was a brilliantly incisive

portraitist (*Sylvia von Harden*, 1926, Pompidou Centre, Paris).

In 1927 Dix was appointed a teacher at the Dresden Academy, but his anti-military stance angered the Nazis and he was dismissed from his post soon after they took power in 1933. The following year he was forbidden to exhibit, and eight of his paintings were shown in the infamous exhibition of *degenerate art in 1937. They included *The Trench* (1923), a large triptych that had been his most controversial painting on account of its horrific depiction of war; it was destroyed by the Nazis in 1939. From 1936 Dix had lived quietly in the country near Lake Constance, where he painted traditional landscapes, yet he still aroused suspicion; in 1939 he was arrested on a charge of complicity in a plot on Hitler's life, but was soon released. He was conscripted into the *Volkssturm* (Home Guard) in 1945 and was a prisoner in France 1945–6; he then returned to Lake Constance. His post-war work—which was much more loosely handled and often inspired by religious mysticism—did not compare in originality or strength with his great achievements of the 1920s, but he remained a highly respected figure, receiving major awards from both East and West Germany.

Dobell, Sir William (*b* Newcastle, NSW, 24 Sept. 1899; *d* Wangi Wangi, NSW, 13 May 1970). Australian painter. In 1929 he won a travelling scholarship that enabled him to study at the *Slade School (he also had some private tuition from *Orpen) and he did not return to Australia until 1938. By this time his style had changed from the carefully studied, solidly constructed naturalism of his early works to a much looser and more *Expressionist manner, sometimes with a satirical air. The rich colours and textures were influenced by art he saw on his travels in Europe, particularly the paintings of *Soutine. He immediately acquired a circle of admiring patrons in Sydney, and in 1944 he became a household name in Australia when he was involved in a *cause célèbre* for modernism. In January of that year he was awarded the 1943 Archibald Prize for portraiture, given annually by the Art Gallery of New South Wales, Sydney. His winning picture was *Portrait of an Artist* (damaged beyond repair by fire in 1958), representing his fellow painter Joshua Smith (1905–95). Two of the unsuccessful competitors contested the award in the Supreme Court of New South Wales, on the grounds that the winning work was not a portrait but a caricature—a 'pictorial defamation of character'. Their suit was dismissed and the case was regarded as a significant victory for the cause of modern art in Australia. Some critics think that this marks the peak of Dobell's career and that much of his later work shows a decline in confidence. However, he continued to be much in demand as a portraitist and also painted landscapes, some of them inspired by visits to the highlands of New Guinea in 1949 and 1950.

Dobson, Frank (b London, 18 Nov. 1886; d London, 22 July 1963). British sculptor. His early work consisted mainly of paintings, the few surviving examples showing how impressed he was by the *Post-Impressionist exhibitions organized by Roger *Fry. After the First World War (when he was on active service with the Artists' Rifles), he turned increasingly to sculpture, and during the 1920s and 1930s he gained an outstanding reputation: in 1925 Fry described his work as 'true sculpture and pure sculpture . . . almost the first time that such a thing has been even attempted in England'. The monumental dignity of his work and its repudiation of literary or illustrative elements relates him to *Maillol, and like him Dobson found the female nude the most satisfactory subject for three-dimensional composition, as in Cornucopia (1925–7, Univ. of Hull), described by Clive *Bell as 'the finest piece of sculpture by an Englishman since—I don't know when'. His work was more stylized than Maillol's, however, and his sophisticated simplifications of form made him one of the pioneers of modern sculpture in Britain. Dobson was also outstanding as a portrait sculptor, his best-known work in this field being the head of Sir Osbert Sitwell in polished brass (1923, Tate, London). He worked in various other materials including bronze, terracotta, and stone; his craftsmanship in all these materials was superb and he played an important role as a liberal-minded and kind-hearted teacher at the *Royal College of Art, where he was professor of sculpture from 1946 to 1953. With the rise of a younger generation led by Henry *Moore, however, Dobson's prestige waned; his work was regarded as dated, and the memorial exhibition organized by the *Arts Council in 1966 was poorly received. Since then his reputation has greatly revived and he has again been recognized as one of the outstanding figures in 20th-century British sculpture.

Dobson, William (bapt. London, 4 Mar. 1611; bur. London, 28 Oct. 1646). English portrait painter. He was described by John Aubrey in his Brief Lives (c.1690) as 'the most excellent painter that England hath yet bred' and he is indeed regarded as the most accomplished native-born painter (other than miniaturists) before *Hogarth. About 60 paintings by him are known, all the securely dated examples being from the years 1642–6, when he was painter to Charles I's wartime court at Oxford. The city surrendered to the Parliamentarians in 1646 and Dobson moved to London. Said to have been 'somewhat loose and irregular in his way of living', he was imprisoned for debt, and his early death followed shortly after his release. His style is superficially similar to van *Dyck's, but his colouring is richer and his paint texture rougher, very much in the Venetian tradition. He also had an uncompromisingly direct way of presenting character that is considered quintessentially English, as in his most celebrated work, Endymion Porter (c.1643, Tate, London). Various paintings by Dobson other than portraits are mentioned by early writers, but only two survive: the allegorical Civil Wars of France (Rousham House, Oxfordshire); and the Executioner with the Baptist's Head (Walker AG, Liverpool), which is a copy of a work by *Stom and the only known *Caravaggesque picture by an English artist.

Documenta. A large international exhibition of contemporary art held at Kassel, Germany, every four or five years since 1955. The first such exhibition was of great cultural and political significance, as it marked Germany's reacceptance of avant-garde art, which had been banned by the Nazis as *degenerate.

Doesburg, Theo van (b Utrecht, 30 Aug. 1883; d Davos, Switzerland, 7 Mar. 1931). Dutch painter, designer, architect, and writer on art. His early work was influenced variously by *Impressionism, *Fauvism, and *Expressionism, but in 1915 he met *Mondrian and rapidly underwent a transition to complete abstraction. In 1917 he was one of the founders of De *Stijl and he devoted the rest of his life to propagating the association's ideas and the austerely geometrical style it stood for, seeing himself as a crusader fighting to cleanse the world of cultural impurities. He spent much of the 1920s travelling to promote his beliefs, particularly in Germany, and from 1922 to 1924 he taught intermittently at the *Bauhaus. By the mid-1920s he had abandoned the rigid horizontal-vertical axes insisted upon by Mondrian and introduced diagonals into his paintings in a series of works entitled Counter-compositions; he called this new departure *Elementarism. In 1929 he moved to Paris and designed a house and studio for himself in the suburb of Meudon in a stark and stripped style (1929–31); he thought that an artist's studio should resemble a medical laboratory. In 1930 he published a manifesto of *Concrete art and in 1931, shortly before his death from a heart attack, a meeting of artists in his new studio led to the formation of the *Abstraction-Création association.

Van Doesburg died a disappointed man, feeling that his ideas had been rejected, but only five years later Alfred H. *Barr gave De Stijl a central place in his book *Cubism and Abstract Art* (originally published to accompany an exhibition at the Museum of Modern Art, New York) and described van Doesburg as 'painter, sculptor, architect, typographer, poet, novelist, critic, lecturer and theorist—a man as versatile as any figure of the Renaissance'. Although he has a secure place in history, he has provoked conflicting opinions: 'Some historians and critics have visualized and described van Doesburg as a scorned prophet, shouting the truth in a wilderness of conventional deceit, while others now view him as just one of the many self-proclaimed messiahs who shouted their way through the 1920s' (Theodore M. Brown in *Macmillan Encyclopedia of Architects*, 1982).

Dolci, Carlo (*b* Florence, 25 May 1616; *d* Florence, 17 Jan. 1686). Florentine painter, active in his native city for virtually his whole career. He was intensely devout and most of his paintings are of religious subjects, done in a cloyingly sweet and meticulously smooth style. They were enormously popular in his lifetime (many of his favourite compositions exist in multiple versions), but have appealed less to modern taste. His portraits, on the other hand, are now much admired for their sober objectivity. Dolci's work was highly prized by contemporary British visitors to Florence, and one of these, the physician Sir John Finch, made an impressive collection of it. Dolci painted a portrait of Finch and one of his friend Sir Thomas Baines (*c.*1665–70), both in the Fitzwilliam Museum, Cambridge. His work is best represented in the Pitti, Florence, and there are examples in many other public collections.

Domenichino (Domenico Zampieri) (*b* Bologna, ?21 Oct. 1581; *d* Naples, 6 Apr. 1641). Bolognese painter and draughtsman. He was a favourite pupil of Annibale *Carracci and one of the most important upholders of the tradition of Bolognese classicism. After studying with *Calvaert and Ludovico Carracci he moved to Rome

in 1602 and joined the group of artists working under Annibale on the decoration of the gallery in the Palazzo *Farnese. His only undisputed work there is the *Maiden with the Unicorn*, a charming, gentle fresco over the entrance of the gallery. For most of the second and third decades of the century he was Rome's leading painter; during this time he painted numerous altarpieces and had a succession of major decorative commissions, among them a series of scenes from the life of St Cecilia in S. Luigi dei Francesi (1613–14). The dignified friezelike composition of the figures reflects his study of *Raphael's tapestries, and in turn influenced *Poussin. His chief work of the 1620s is a series of frescos (1624–8) in S. Andrea della Valle, representing the four Evangelists in the pendentives of the dome and scenes from the life of St Andrew in the apse. The pendentives show a move away from classicism towards an ampler *Baroque style; but compared with his rival *Lanfranco (who at this time was overtaking him in popularity) Domenichino never abandoned the principles of clear, firm drawing for the sake of more painterly effects. In 1631 he moved to Naples, and in his frescos in the S. Gennaro chapel in the cathedral he made even greater concessions to Baroque taste. Some Neapolitan artists were jealous of his success and were hostile towards him, leading him to flee the city in 1634 (he had an anxious and timid personality). He returned the following year, but he died (it was rumoured by poisoning) before completing his work in the cathedral.

Although he was renowned mainly for his fresco decorations and altarpieces, Domenichino was also important in other fields, particularly as an exponent of *ideal landscape, in which he formed the link between Annibale Carracci and *Claude (four of his landscapes are in the Louvre). He was one of the finest draughtsmen of his generation (the Royal Library at Windsor Castle has a superb collection of his drawings) and also an excellent portraitist (*Pope Gregory XV and Cardinal Ludovico Ludovisi*, *c.*1621–3, Mus. B.-A., Béziers). In the 18th century his reputation was enormous—his *Last Communion of St Jerome* (1614, Pinacoteca, Vatican) was generally regarded as one of the greatest pictures ever painted—but he fell from grace in the 19th century under the scathing attacks of *Ruskin, along with the other Bolognese painters. In the later 20th century his reputation greatly revived.

Domenico Veneziano (*b* ?Venice; *bur.* Florence, 15 May 1461). Italian painter, an important but enigmatic figure, whose life is poorly documented. His name indicates that he came from Venice, but he is first documented in Perugia, in 1438, and was active mainly in Florence. *Vasari credits him with introducing *oil painting into Tuscany. Although this is incorrect, it seems to be true that he was responsible for bringing a new interest in colour and texture to a tradition in which draughtsmanship normally ruled supreme. His only documented fresco cycle, showing scenes from the life of the Virgin (1439–45) in S. Egidio, Florence, on which *Piero della Francesca was one of his assistants, is destroyed (except for a few fragments), and only two signed works survive. These are a *Virgin and Child Enthroned*, the largest of three much-damaged and repainted fragments from a frescoed street tabernacle (c.1440, NG, London), and the celebrated *St Lucy* altarpiece of c.1445, painted for the church of S. Lucia de' Magnoli, Florence (the central panel is in the Uffizi, Florence, and the *predella panels are dispersed in Cambridge (Fitzwilliam Mus.), Washington (NG), and Berlin (Gemäldegalerie)). This is one of the great masterpieces of 15th-century Italian painting; its pearly beauty of colouring, mastery of light, and airy lucidity of spatial construction are reflected in the work of Domenico's assistant Piero, and also, for example, in that of *Baldovinetti. See also CASTAGNO.

Domínguez, Oscar. See DECALCOMANIA.

Dominici, Bernardo de. See 'MONSÙ DESIDERIO'.

Donagh, Rita. See HAMILTON, RICHARD.

Donatello (Donato di Niccolo) (*b* Florence, c.1386; *d* Florence, 13 Dec. 1466). Florentine sculptor. He was the greatest European sculptor of the 15th century and one of a remarkable group of artists—including his friends *Alberti, *Brunelleschi, and *Masaccio—who created the *Renaissance style in Florence. His long career was hugely productive, and he was unrivalled in the variety of his output, his emotional range and depth, his formal inventiveness, and his versatility in the handling of materials, which included bronze, stone, wood, terracotta, and stucco. He worked in Padua, Pisa, Rome, and Siena as well as Florence (he also turned down invitations to work in Mantua, Modena, and Naples), and he had an enormous impact on his contemporaries and artists of the following generation—painters as well as sculptors—through his wide repertoire of pose and expression, his use of *antique motifs, and

his sophisticated handling of perspective in his *reliefs; indeed he was unquestionably the most influential Italian artist of his time in any medium. In spite of his fame and success, and the high opinion in which he was held by his eminent patrons, he is said to have lived simply, utterly devoted to his work and preferring criticism to praise, as it inspired him to greater heights.

At the outset of his career Donatello worked as an assistant to *Ghiberti (1404–7), but he developed a style that departed radically from his master's *Gothic elegance. He was unconcerned with the surface polish or linear grace so typical of Ghiberti, and excelled rather in emotional force. His individuality was first revealed in a series of powerfully realistic but deeply spiritual figures (mainly in marble) that he made for the external decoration of Florence Cathedral, the adjacent campanile, and the church of Orsanmichele. The series began with the imperious *St John the Evangelist* (1408–15) for the cathedral (now Cathedral Mus.), included the celebrated *St George* (c.1415–17) for Orsanmichele (now in the Bargello, Florence), and culminated in the uncompromisingly unidealized *Habakkuk* (completed 1436), usually known by its nickname of *Zuccone* (bald-pate), for the campanile (now Cathedral Mus.).

*Vasari conveys the brilliance of Donatello's characterization in his description of the *St George*: 'The head exhibits the beauty of youth, its spirit and valour in arms, a proud and terrifying lifelikeness, and a marvellous sense of movement within the stone.' With this acute psychological insight went a technique of daring originality that shows how concerned Donatello was with the optical effects of his works. He carefully took into consideration the position from which they would be viewed, adjusting the proportions of a figure when it would be seen from below, for example, and carving with almost brutal power and boldness when it was positioned to be seen at a distance. On the other hand, his relief of *St George and the Dragon* (1417, Bargello), done for the base of his *St George* statue, is executed with great delicacy in the technique Donatello invented called *rilievo schiacciato* (relief so low it is like 'drawing in stone'); originally situated on the north side of Orsanmichele, the relief was seen in a soft, diffused light, so the subtlety of the carving could be appreciated.

In 1430–3 Donatello worked in Rome, and the impact of the antique art he saw there can be seen most clearly in his famous *Cantoria* (Singing

Gallery) for Florence Cathedral (now Cathedral Mus., 1433–9), which makes a lavish show of freely interpreted classical motifs. His bronze statue of *David* (Bargello), which is credited with being the first free-standing nude statue since antiquity, is also sometimes seen as a response to Donatello's visit to Rome and assigned to the 1430s, but some scholars date it much later. The subject as well as the date is controversial, for it has been proposed that it represents Mercury with the head of Argus rather than David.

From 1443 to 1453 Donatello was based in Padua, where he carried out three major commissions. Two of them were for the church of S. Antonio (the Santo) and they are still there: a life-size bronze Crucifix (1443–9), originally made for the rood-screen but now placed above the high altar, and the high altar itself (begun 1446), an imposing architectural structure featuring seven free-standing bronze statues, four large reliefs of the miracles of St Anthony, and various other elements (the altar has been remodelled several times and no longer looks as Donatello intended). His third great work in Padua is the famous monument to the *condottiere* Erasmo da Narni, known as Gattamelata, in the Piazza del Santo (1447–53), which begins the modern tradition of the equestrian statue (see MARCUS AURE-LIUS). It has been imitated many times but never surpassed in grandeur and dignity.

From 1454 until his death Donatello was based mainly in Florence, although he also worked in Siena on an abortive project for a set of bronze doors for the cathedral. In his final years his style became even more emotionally intense. The most important works of this period include the bronze *Judith and Holofernes* (Palazzo Vecchio, Florence), which is an allegory of humility triumphing over pride, and a series of bronze reliefs (mainly of scenes from Christ's Passion) for a pair of pulpits in S. Lorenzo. The harrowing and emaciated *Mary Magdalene* in painted wood (Cathedral Mus.) has also traditionally been considered one of his late works, but there is evidence to suggest it belongs to an earlier period. Although the S. Lorenzo reliefs were unfinished at Donatello's death and were completed by his pupil *Bertoldo, they are essentially the master's work and show how freely he exploited the expressive possibilities of distortion, creating what has been called 'the first style of old age in the history of art'.

In addition to his major independent works, Donatello produced three important tombs in partnership with *Michelozzo di Bartolommeo, and he also made numerous smaller works.

They include bronze *plaquettes, reliefs of the Virgin and Child in marble and stucco, which became prototypes for the following generation of sculptors, and a portrait bust in painted terracotta (*Niccolò da Uzzano*, Bargello), which is thought to date from the 1430s and is probably the earliest portrait bust of the Renaissance, preceding the first dated example (by *Mino da Fiesole, 1453) by several years.

Dongen, Kees van (*b* Delfshaven, nr. Rotterdam, 26 Jan. 1877; *d* Monte Carlo, 28 May 1968). Dutch-born painter and printmaker who settled in Paris in 1897 and took French nationality in 1929. His early work was *Impressionist, but he became a member of the *Fauves in 1906 and in 1908 exhibited with the German *Expressionist group Die *Brücke. He had a reputation as a ladies' man, and his work (mainly nudes and female portraits) was often erotic in spirit; in 1913 one of his pictures was removed from the *Salon d'Automne by the police on the grounds of alleged indecency. After the First World War he became internationally famous for his paintings of fashionable life, particularly portraits of insolently glamorous women in which he created a type that has been described as 'half drawing-room prostitute, half sidewalk princess'. He kept the brilliant colouring and bold handling of his Fauve days, but his great facility led to repetition and banality and it is generally agreed that his best work was done before 1920. From 1959 he lived in Monaco.

Donkey's Tail. Title of an exhibition organized in Moscow in 1912 by *Goncharova and *Larionov after they had dissociated themselves from the *Knave of Diamonds group in 1911. They accused that group of being too much under foreign influence, and advocated a nationalist Russian art; at this time they were painting in a 'Neo-primitivist' manner based partly on icon painting and peasant art. The title of the exhibition referred to an incident in 1910 when three pictures painted with a brush tied to a donkey's tail were shown at the jury-free *Salon des Indépendants in Paris (a stunt devised by a journalist to poke fun at modern art; the pictures were hung as works of the fictitious 'Boronali', an anagram of *aliboron*, 'jackass'). At the Moscow exhibition there was an outcry because some of the paintings on view had religious subjects and it was thought to be irreverent to show religious works under such a title (the police ordered several to be removed). Goncharova and Larionov followed it up with the *Target exhibition in 1913.

Donner, Georg Raphael (*bapt*. Esslingen im Marchfeld [now in Vienna], 25 Apr. 1693; *d* Vienna, 15 Feb. 1741). The outstanding Austrian *Baroque sculptor, active mainly in Salzburg, Bratislava, and Vienna. His acknowledged masterpieces are the figures from the fountain in the Mehlmarkt, Vienna (1737–9, Österreichisches Barockmuseum, Vienna), and the group of *St Martin and the Beggar* (c. 1735, Bratislava Cathedral), in which the saint is dressed in hussar's uniform rather than the traditional armour. These works are in lead, which Donner preferred to the Austrian speciality of wood; his smooth surfaces have led some critics to see his work as presaging *Neoclassicism, although his elongated figures seem to place him closer to Italian *Mannerism. His brother **Matthäus** (1704–56) was also a sculptor.

donor. A term applied to a person who commissions and pays for a work of religious art and has his or her portrait incorporated in it as an act of devotion. By having themselves included in the picture, donors sought to associate themselves in a special way with the sacred figures portrayed there, either in thanks for favours received or in the hope of future protection and salvation. A famous example is *Giotto's portrayal of Enrico Scrovegni in the Arena Chapel, Padua (c.1305); Scrovegni, who had the chapel built and decorated in expiation of his father's sins, is shown kneeling in front of the Virgin Mary and presenting her with a model of the building. In Netherlandish art of the 15th century, a favourite format for donor paintings, popularized by Rogier van der *Weyden, was to show the Virgin and Child on one wing of a *diptych and a portrait of the donor in prayer facing them on the other. None of Rogier's diptychs of this type survives intact, the two panels in all cases having been separated, with one sometimes lost, but a well-known intact example by *Memlinc is the Nieuwenhove Diptych (1487, Memlingmuseum, Bruges).

Doort, Abraham van der. See ROYAL COLLECTION.

Doré, Gustave (*b* Strasbourg, 6 Jan. 1832; *d* Paris, 23 Jan. 1883). French illustrator, painter, and sculptor. He was the most celebrated book illustrator of the mid-19th century and was so prolific that at one time he employed more than 40 wood engravers. His best-known works are lavishly illustrated editions of literary classics, including Dante's *Inferno* (1861), *Don Quixote* (1862), and the Bible (1866)—works that helped to give European currency to the illustrated book of large format. Characteristically his style was rich and exuberant, with a strong vein of grotesque fantasy, but he worked in a more sombre and realistic manner in his illustrations for *London: A Pilgrimage* (1872). In these images he presented the grim life of the poor in a way that was admired by van *Gogh among others. Doré had an amazing appetite for work, and in addition to his huge output of illustrations he produced numerous paintings, including some very large religious compositions that became a popular attraction at the Doré Gallery in New Bond Street, London, open from 1868 to 1892 (examples are in the Petit Palais, Paris). In the 1870s he also took up sculpture, his best-known work in this medium being the monument to the dramatist and novelist Alexandre Dumas in the place Malesherbes in Paris, erected in 1883.

Doria Pamphili. See PAMPHILI.

Doryphorus (Spear Carrier). See POLYCLITUS.

Dossi, Dosso (Giovanni di Luteri) (*b* ?Ferrara, ?c.1490; *d* Ferrara, 1541/2). The outstanding painter of the Ferrarese School in the 16th century. His early life and training are obscure, but *Vasari's assertion that he was born around 1474 is now thought unlikely. He is first recorded in 1512 in Mantua (the name 'Dosso' probably comes from a place near Mantua—he is not called 'Dosso Dossi' until the 18th century). By 1514 he was in Ferrara, where he spent most of the rest of his career, collaborating with the poet Ariosto in devising entertainments, triumphs, tapestries, etc. for the *Este court. Dosso painted various kinds of pictures—mythological and religious works, portraits, and decorative frescos—and he is perhaps most important for the part played in his work by landscape, in which he continued the romantic pastoral vein of *Giorgione and *Titian (he is documented in Venice in 1516 and 1518 and may well have made an earlier visit or visits). Dosso's work, however, has a personal quality of fantasy and an opulent sense of colour and texture that give it an individual stamp (*Melissa*, c.1523, Borghese Gal., Rome). His brother **Battista Dossi** (c.1497–1548) often collaborated with him (even though Vasari said they disliked each other), but there is insufficient evidence to know whether he made an individual contribution.

Dotrement, Christian. See COBRA.

dotted manner. See MANIÈRE CRIBLÈE.

Dou, Gerrit (*b* Leiden, 7 Apr. 1613; *bur.* Leiden, 9 Feb. 1675). Dutch painter. He spent all his career in Leiden, where he became the first pupil of the young *Rembrandt in 1628. His early work was closely based on his master's, but after Rembrandt moved to Amsterdam in 1631/2, Dou developed a style of his own characterized by minute detail and a surface of almost enamelled smoothness (he had initially trained in his father's profession of glass engraving and this background must have helped instil a love of glossy surfaces). He was astonishingly fastidious about his tools and working conditions, with a particular horror of dust, and sometimes painted with the aid of a magnifying glass. In about 1640 he was visited by *Sandrart, who 'praised the great care that he had lavished on painting a broomstick hardly larger than a fingernail', only for Dou to reply that 'he would need three more days to finish it'. He painted various subjects, but is best known for domestic interiors. They usually contain only one or two figures, typically framed by a window or by the drapery of a curtain, and surrounded by books, musical instruments, or household paraphernalia, all minutely depicted. He excelled at depicting scenes lit by artificial light. With Jan *Steen, Dou was among the founders of the Guild of St Luke at Leiden in 1648. Unlike Steen he was prosperous and respected throughout his life; indeed he had an international reputation and turned down an invitation from Charles II to visit England. His pictures continued to fetch big prices (consistently higher than those paid for Rembrandt's work) until the advent of *Impressionism influenced taste against the neatness and precision of his style. Dou had a workshop with many pupils who perpetuated his style (notably *Schalken), and Leiden continued the *fijnschilder* (fine painter) tradition into the 19th century.

Doughty, Thomas (*b* Philadelphia, 19 July 1793; *d* New York, 24 July 1856). American painter, one of the first artists from his country to specialize exclusively in landscapes. Doughty was active mainly in his native Philadelphia, but he also worked in Boston and New York. He was essentially self-taught as a painter. In 1837 and again in 1845 he travelled to Europe, visiting England on both occasions. As one of the first to recognize the American landscape as a viable subject for painting, he is regarded as a forerunner of the *Hudson River School. His best-known painting is probably *In Nature's Wonderland* (1835, Detroit Inst. of Arts). Doughty

was also one of the first American artists to take up lithography.

Douglas, Aaron. See HARLEM RENAISSANCE.

Douris. Greek potter and vase painter in the *red-figure technique, active in Athens in the early 5th century BC. About 40 signed vases by him are known (he signs mainly as painter, but occasionally as potter) and many others are attributed to him. The subjects represented on them include everyday life and mythological scenes (*Eos Carrying the Dead Memnon*, Louvre, Paris). His work is noted for its fine draughtsmanship and rhythmic composition.

Dove, Arthur (*b* Canandaigua, NY, 2 Aug. 1880; *d* Huntington, Long Island, NY, 23 Nov. 1946). American painter, a pioneer of abstract art. For most of his career he earned his living as a commercial illustrator and he was often in great financial difficulty (even though he was supported by *Stieglitz and Duncan *Phillips). He visited Europe in 1907–9, coming into contact with *Fauvism and other avant-garde movements, and in 1910 he painted the first abstract pictures in American art (*Abstraction No. 1–Abstraction No. 6*, priv. coll.), which are somewhat similar to *Kandinsky's work of the same time. He never exhibited these in his lifetime, but he displayed similar work at his first one-man exhibition at Stieglitz's 291 Gallery in 1912. Typically his abstractions are based on natural forms, suggesting the rhythms of nature with their pulsating shapes (*Sand Barge*, 1930, Phillips Coll., Washington). During the 1940s he experimented with a more geometric type of abstraction (*That Red One*, 1944, William H. Lane Foundation, Leominster, Massachusetts). In his later years he took a leading part in the campaign to win artists royalty rights for the reproduction of their work.

Doves Press. See PRIVATE PRESS.

Downman, John (*b* Ruabon, nr. Wrexham, Wales, *c*.1750; *d* Wrexham, 24 Dec. 1824). British portrait painter. His best work is on a small scale and he often worked in a distinctive technique using pencil or charcoal lightly tinted with watercolour (four examples of the type are in the Wallace Collection, London). He lived mainly in London, but he travelled widely about the country, often staying in great houses whilst he painted a series of portraits of members of the family.

Doyle, Richard (*b* London, Sept. 1824; *d* London, 10 Dec. 1883). British draughtsman, printmaker, and painter, the best-known member of a family of artists. He was one of the leading humorous illustrators of his time and he also painted fairy subjects, which had a great vogue in Victorian England. From 1843 to 1850 he was on the staff of *Punch*, for which among other things he designed the cover that was used for over a century, from 1849 to 1954. He left *Punch* because of the magazine's attacks on the papacy (he was a devout Catholic) and thereafter worked mainly as a book illustrator, particularly of children's stories. Among them was *Ruskin's *The King of the Golden River* (1851), which he had written a decade earlier for the 12-year-old Effie Gray, whom he later married with unhappy consequences.

Doyle's father, the Irish-born **John Doyle** (1797–1868), was a failed portrait painter who became a successful political caricaturist. In addition to Richard, three other sons worked as artists, although with little distinction: **James** (1822–92), **Henry** (1827–92), and **Charles** (1832–93). Henry, who painted portraits and religious subjects, was director of the National Gallery of Ireland from 1869 until his death. Charles, who was a civil servant most of his life and worked as an illustrator in his spare time, was the father of Sir Arthur Conan Doyle.

drapery painter (or **draperyman**). A specialist in the painting of costume and other accessories employed by a portraitist with a large practice. Such subcontractors (to be distinguished from studio assistants) seem to have emerged in the late 17th century, perhaps in the Netherlands, and almost all the leading British portraitists of the early and mid-18th century employed one or more (the main exceptions were *Hogarth and *Gainsborough, who were too individual to subscribe to the idea). The doyen of the draperyman's profession at this time was the Flemish-born Joseph van *Aken, who worked for *Highmore, *Hudson, *Knapton, *Ramsay, and others, including provincial painters (they sent their unfinished pictures to his London studio or sometimes painted the head on a separate piece of canvas that could be pasted onto the costumed figure). Van Aken had a repertoire of poses and costumes that his clients evidently used as a kind of pattern book: the same features sometimes occur virtually identically in the work of different painters, leading *Vertue to comment that van Aken 'puts them so much on a level that it is difficult to know one hand from another'. By the end of the century such production-line methods were

falling out of favour and the separate profession of drapery painter was dying out.

drawing frame. A rectangular frame strung with wires or threads that create a network of squares through which a subject can be viewed by an artist and copied onto a correspondingly squared sheet of paper. It detaches the subject from its surroundings, helping the artist to concentrate on it. *Alberti and *Leonardo describe drawing frames and *Dürer and other artists made illustrations of the device. Following Dürer's example, van *Gogh constructed one and in a letter to his brother made a sketch of himself using it. A very small frame or viewfinder, which could be held in the hand, was used in the 18th century by topographical painters and travellers in search of the *Picturesque. Some devices of this type were adjustable, so that the ratio of upright to horizontal could correspond to that of the drawing.

Dreier, Katherine S. (*b* New York, 10 Sept. 1877; *d* Milford, Conn., 29 Mar. 1952). American painter, patron, and collector, a wealthy heiress remembered mainly for her missionary zeal in promoting modern art in the USA. Her early paintings consisted of traditional portraits and still-lifes, but in 1913 the *Armory Show converted her into an ardent supporter of avant-garde art and she devoted much of the rest of her life to championing it. She did this mainly through the *Société Anonyme, which she founded in 1920 with Marcel *Duchamp and *Man Ray. 'A domineering woman of tireless energy and Wagnerian proportions, she was the antithesis of Duchamp in every possible way, and they got along famously' (Calvin Tomkins, *The World of Marcel Duchamp*, 1966). In addition to organizing exhibitions (the main business of the Société Anonyme), she did a good deal of lecturing, and she also promoted avant-garde music and dance. Her best-known painting is her portrait of Duchamp (1918, MoMA, New York). Soon after she painted this, her work became abstract, influenced by *Kandinsky.

Droeshout, Martin. The name of two English engravers of Netherlandish extraction, father (*d* c.1642) and son (*b* 1601). The elder Martin's parents settled in London in the mid-16th century as Protestant refugees from Brussels. Both Martins were mediocre and obscure craftsman, but their name lives by the engraved portrait of Shakespeare (signed 'Martin Droeshout Sculpsit London') on the title page of the First Folio edition of the plays (1623). Traditionally the portrait has been regarded as a work of the younger Martin, but some authorities now think it is more likely to be by the father. Other members of the family were artists, but they are similarly obscure. See also JOHNSON, GERARD THE ELDER.

drollery. A comic picture or 'clownish representation', as John Evelyn put it when he saw 'Landscips and Drolleries' at the annual Rotterdam fair (*Diary*, 13 Aug. 1641). The term is now mainly applied to *grotesque or comic figures or scenes in the borders of medieval manuscripts.

Droochsloot, Joost Cornelisz. (*b* ?Utrecht, *c*.1586; *d* Utrecht, 14 May 1666). Dutch painter, active in Utrecht, where he was dean of the painters' guild in 1623 and 1641. He specialized in scenes of village life, full of incident and sometimes with a biblical or military subject (*Plunder of a Village*, 1626, Centraal Mus., Utrecht). Among his other works are interesting self-portraits in the Hermitage, St Petersburg (showing him in a landscape), and the Musée des Ursulines, Mâcon (showing him in the studio, with an apprentice grinding colours). There is strong Flemish influence in his style and he perhaps studied in Antwerp. Jakob *Duck is thought to have been among his pupils. His work was imitated by his son **Cornelis Droochsloot** (1630–73).

Drost, Willem (active mid-17th century). Dutch painter, perhaps of German origin. According to *Houbraken he was a pupil of *Rembrandt and lived in Rome for several years, but otherwise almost nothing is recorded of his life, and only a small number of paintings (and a few drawings and etchings) are attributed to him (several of them are signed). All the works that are dated are from the period 1652–63, and it would seem that at this time Drost was one of Rembrandt's closest and most talented followers. It has even been proposed that Drost is the author of several paintings that have traditionally been regarded as Rembrandt's, most notably the celebrated and enigmatic *Polish Rider* (Frick Coll., New York), which figures in many books as one of the master's most poetic creations. Among Drost's undisputed works the masterpiece is the sensuous *Bathsheba* (1654, Louvre, Paris), painted in the same year as Rembrandt's famous depiction of the subject (likewise in the Louvre) and evidently inspired by it.

Drouais, François-Hubert (*b* Paris, 14 Dec. 1727; *d* Paris, 21 Oct. 1675). French portrait painter. He trained under *Boucher (among others) and became a rival to *Nattier as a fashionable portraitist. His portraits have a gracious and artificial charm and at their best bear comparison with those of Boucher. He was particularly successful with children, but his best-known painting is probably the very grand portrait of Mme de Pompadour in the National Gallery, London (1763–4), completed after the sitter's death. His father and his son were painters. **Hubert Drouais** (1699–1767) had a successful career as a miniaturist and pastel portraitist. **Jean-Germain Drouais** (1763–88) was *David's favourite pupil and won the *Prix de Rome in 1784; David regarded him as his greatest potential rival ('He alone could trouble my sleep'), but he died of smallpox aged 24.

Drummond, Malcolm. See CAMDEN TOWN GROUP.

Drury, Alfred. See NEW SCULPTURE.

drying oils. Fatty oils of vegetable origin that harden into a solid transparent substance on exposure to air and are much used as *vehicles in paints. Those that have been in commonest use since the Middle Ages are *linseed, *walnut, and *poppy oil. Almond and olive oil are not suitable as they do not harden. Sunflower oil has been used in Russia but has never become popular.

drypoint. A printmaking method in which the design is scratched directly into a copper plate with a pointed tool. This is usually a thick steel needle, sharpened to a point or diamond tipped. It is held like a pen, though considerable force is needed to scratch the metal to any depth. A distinctive feature of the method is created by the *burr—the tiny upturned edge of the furrow made by the cutting tool. The burr retains the ink when the plate is wiped, giving to the drypoint line its characteristic rich and velvety quality, but because the edge is soon worn down by the pressure of the printing process, only a limited number of good impressions can be taken. The degree of blackness of the burred line changes with the variation in pressure of the artist's hand. Drypoint is therefore a more spontaneous and personal technique than *line engraving, but it is not as fluent as *etching, for the point is continuously up against the resistance of the metal.

Drypoint seems to have originated in the last quarter of the 15th century, the *Master of the Housebook being the main pioneer. His prints are in pure drypoint, but the technique has more often been used in combination with other processes, particularly etching. *Rembrandt, for example, often added dark accents in drypoint to his etchings. He also made a few prints purely in drypoint, notably one of his most celebrated works, *The Three Crosses*, and he sometimes used special papers to bring out the softness of the burr.

Drysdale, Sir Russell (b Bognor Regis, Sussex, 7 Feb. 1912; d Sydney, 29 June 1981). Australian painter of English birth. His family had owned land in Australia since the 1820s and he spent several years of his childhood there. The family settled in Melbourne in 1923 and in the late 1930s Drysdale gave up farming to study art. After moving to Sydney in 1940, he devoted himself full-time to painting and his work became well known throughout Australia during the 1940s. It revived the tradition of hardship, tragedy, and melancholy associated with the Australian bush that had been obscured by the much more optimistic interpretation developed during the 1890s by the city-based painters of the *Heidelberg School. However, in place of the basically *Impressionist style of the Heidelberg painters, Drysdale blended *Expressionist and *Surrealist features founded on his knowledge of contemporary European painting. In 1949 Kenneth *Clark, on a visit to Sydney, encouraged Drysdale to exhibit in London and in 1950 he had a one-man show there at the Leicester Galleries; this marked the beginning of a new interest in Australian art in Britain and in Europe—a trend that peaked in the early 1960s. *Dobell and *Nolan were two other artists whose work became well known in the northern hemisphere in this period and together with Drysdale they represented Australia at the 1954 Venice *Biennale. Of these three, Drysdale remained closest to the Australian soil. In the 1950s he travelled widely in the vast tract of northern Australia, which he described as 'magnificent in dimension, old as time, curious, strange, and compelling'. As well as the landscape, he painted the life of the Aborigines. During the early 1960s he experienced periods of depression accentuated by the death of his son and his wife. He was knighted in 1969.

Dubois, Ambroise (b Antwerp, c.1543; d Fontainebleau, 1614). Netherlandish-born painter who settled in France as a young man and became a French citizen in 1601. With *Dubreuil and *Fréminet (who married his widow) he ranks as one of the leading artists of the Second School of *Fontainebleau. Much of his decorative work still survives at Fontainebleau, showing him to have been an accomplished practitioner of an elegant, conventional *Mannerist style.

Dubreuil, Toussaint (b ?Paris, c.1561; d Paris, 22 Nov. 1602). French painter, one of the leading artists of the second School of *Fontainebleau. His most important works, such as the frescos of the story of Hercules for the Gallery of Diana at Fontainebleau, and the decorations in the Galerie d'Apollon of the *Louvre, have been destroyed; but a reasonable idea of his style can be formed from copies, works done from his designs, and his few original surviving paintings. His style was less obviously *Mannerist than that of his closest contemporaries (his figures, for example, are less elongated) and Anthony *Blunt writes that he 'forms a link between *Primaticcio and the classicism of *Poussin in the following century'.

Dubroeucq (or **Du Broeucq**), **Jacques** (b ?Mons, c.1505; d Mons, 30 Sept. 1584). Netherlandish sculptor and architect. He is believed to have been in Italy from about 1530 to about 1535, when he returned to the Netherlands to work on a major commission in St Waudru (Waltrudis), Mons, involving a huge *rood-screen and other furnishings (finished c.1550). The screen, his masterpiece, was destroyed during the French Revolution, but much of the alabaster sculpture from it survives and has been reused in other contexts in the church. It shows how assiduously Dubroeucq had studied the work of his contemporaries in *Renaissance Italy and reveals him as one of the outstanding Netherlandish sculptors of his period. In his day he also had a high reputation as an architect, but none of his buildings survive. *Giambologna was his pupil.

Dubuffet, Jean (b Le Havre, 31 July 1901; d Paris, 12 May 1985). French painter, sculptor, lithographer, and writer. He studied painting as a young man but was engaged mainly in the wine trade until 1942, when he took up art seriously again, his first exhibition coming in 1945. He preferred rough spontaneity to professional skill and was fascinated by graffiti and by what he called *Art Brut (Raw Art), the products of psychotics or wholly untrained persons. His own work is aggressively reminiscent of such 'popular' art, often featuring subjects drawn from the street life of Paris (*Man with a Hod*, 1956, Tate, London). Frequently he incorporated materials such as sand and plaster into his paintings, and he also produced sculptures made from junk materials. He was constantly experimenting with new styles and techniques and his output was enormous (he also wrote copiously expounding his ideas). His work initially provoked outrage, but then found acceptance and in some quarters reverence, and it has proved highly influential, foreshadowing many of the trends of the 1960s and beyond, and exemplifying the tendency in contemporary art to depreciate traditional materials, methods, and standards; Edward Lucie-Smith, indeed, writes that 'Dubuffet probably exercised a greater influence over both his European and his American contemporaries than any other artist of the immediately post-war epoch' (*Lives of the Great Twentieth Century Artists*, 1986).

Duca, Giacomo del (*b* Cefalù, *c*.1520; *d* Cefalù, 9 July 1604). Sicilian architect and sculptor, active mainly in Rome, where he was one of *Michelangelo's main assistants from the 1540s to the master's death in 1564. His tomb of Elena Savelli in S. Giovanni in Laterano (*c*.1570) is an impressive work showing Michelangelo's influence, but Giacomo was active more as an architect than a sculptor. In about 1590 he returned to Sicily, where he worked mainly in Messina. Earthquakes have destroyed most of his buildings there, but the dome he added to S. Maria di Loreto in Rome (*c*.1575) shows him to have been the boldest of Michelangelo's architectural disciples.

Duccio di Buoninsegna (*d* Siena, 1318/19). The most famous painter of the Sienese School. Little is known of his life: he is first recorded in 1278, records of several commissions survive, and he is known to have been fined on several occasions for various minor offences (one perhaps involving sorcery), but only one fully documented work by him survives. This is the famous *Maestà* commissioned by Siena Cathedral and completed in 1311 (it is usually said to have been begun in 1308, but *Pope-Hennessy has argued that a document of that year is an interim contract, not the initial contract, and that the elaborate double-sided altarpiece must have taken more than three years to paint). Today most of the altarpiece is in the cathedral museum in Siena, but several of the *predella panels are scattered outside Italy—in London (NG), Washington (NG), and elsewhere. It has been described by John White (*Art and Architecture in Italy: 1250–1400*, 1966) as 'probably the most important panel ever painted in Italy. It is certainly among the most beautiful. Compressed within the compass of an altarpiece is

the equivalent of an entire programme for the fresco painting of a church.' The whole of the front of the main panel is occupied by a scene of the Virgin and Child in majesty surrounded by angels and saints, and corresponding to this on the back are twenty-six scenes from Christ's Passion. Originally there were subsidiary scenes from Christ's life above and below the main panel. Although Duccio drew much on *Byzantine tradition, he introduced a new warmth of human feeling that gives him a role in Sienese painting comparable to that of *Giotto in Florentine painting. He recreates the biblical stories with great vividness, and as no one else before him he succeeds in making the setting of a scene—a room or a hillside—a dramatic constituent of the action, so that figures and surroundings are intimately bound together.

The other major work attributed to Duccio is the *Rucellai Madonna* (Uffizi, Florence), a large panel that is probably the picture documented as having been painted by him for S. Maria Novella, Florence, in 1285. Several other smaller panels can be attributed to him or his workshop with a fair degree of confidence, but there is no evidence that he ever worked in fresco. His exquisite colouring and supple draughtsmanship set enduring standards in Siena (Simone *Martini was his greatest disciple) and his influence reached as far as France, notably in the work of *Pucelle. It is possible that he visited France: a 'Duche de Siene' is documented in Paris in 1296 and 1297.

Duchamp, Marcel (*b* Blainville, Normandy, 28 July 1887; *d* Neuilly-sur-Seine, 2 Oct. 1968). French-born artist and art theorist who became an American citizen in 1955, the brother of Raymond *Duchamp-Villon and Jacques *Villon. His output was small (most of his key works are in the Philadelphia Museum of Art) and for long periods he was more or less inactive, but he is regarded as one of the most potent figures in modern art because of the originality and fertility of his ideas. His early works, influenced by *Post-Impressionism and *Fauvism, were unexceptional, but he sprang to notoriety with *Nude Descending a Staircase, No. 2* (Philadelphia), which was the most discussed work at the *Armory Show in 1913. It depicts a stylized, semi-abstract figure walking down a spiral staircase, movement being suggested by the use of overlapping images, in the manner of rapid-fire multiple-exposure photography. The attention the picture received was mainly negative, but the publicity made Duchamp suddenly much better known in the USA than he had ever been in France. This first conspicuous achievement as a painter was also Duchamp's last, for from this point he virtually abandoned conventional media.

From 1915 to 1923 he lived mainly in New York, where with *Man Ray and Francis *Picabia he formed the nucleus of the city's *Dada movement. His main contribution to this was the *ready-made, the best known of which was *Fountain* (1917), consisting of a urinal bowl signed 'R. Mutt', which was rejected by the *Society of Independent Artists. Another of his celebrated provocative gestures was adding a moustache and beard and an obscene inscription to a reproduction of the *Mona Lisa* (1919). During his years in New York Duchamp was engaged intermittently on his most complex and ambitious work—an enigmatic construction on glass entitled *The Bride Stripped Bare by her Bachelors, Even*, often known for short as 'The Large Glass' (Philadelphia; replica by Richard *Hamilton, 1965–6, in Tate Modern, London). He abandoned it as 'definitively unfinished' in 1923, but it was damaged whilst being transported in 1926 and ten years later he made repairs, incorporating cracks in the shattered glass as part of the image and declaring it completed 'by chance'. Scholars have produced voluminous interpretations of this work, but to many people it is an incomprehensible joke.

In 1923 Duchamp returned to Paris and lived there until 1942 (although he made several visits to New York), devoting much of his time in this period to his passion for chess. He was one of the best players in France and his obsessive devotion to the game ruined his first—rather frivolous—marriage in 1927, of which Man Ray wrote: 'Duchamp spent the one week they lived together studying chess problems, and his bride, in desperate retaliation, got up one night when he was asleep and glued the chess pieces to the board. They were divorced three months later.' (With his aristocratic looks and enormous charm, Duchamp was highly attractive to women, and a friend wrote that he 'could have had his choice of heiresses'; in 1954 he made a happy second marriage to Alexina Sattler, who had previously been the wife of the art dealer Pierre Matisse, son of Henri *Matisse.)

In 1942 Duchamp settled permanently in New York, although he regularly visited France. By this time he seemed to have long abandoned art, but he had in fact continued to experiment quietly, for example with rotating coloured discs that anticipate *Kinetic art. He also did a good deal to promote avant-garde art, particularly *Surrealism, in France and the USA, notably through the activities of the *Société Anonyme, but in the exciting post-war New York art world he was for many years a marginal figure. From the late 1950s, however, avant-garde artists began to rediscover his work and ideas and in his final years he was revered as a kind of patron saint of modern art. Near the end of his life he revealed that he had been working in secret for twenty years (1946–66) on a large mixed-media construction called *Étant donnés*: 1° *La Chute d'eau*, 2° *Le Gaz d'éclairage* (Given: 1. The Waterfall, 2. The Illuminating Gas). It features a naturalistic painted sculpture of a nude reclining woman holding a gas lamp, with behind her a simulated landscape, including a trickle of water representing a waterfall; this elaborate tableau is viewed through peepholes in a heavy wooden door. He presented it to the Philadelphia Museum of Art, where it joined the majority of his other works.

Duchamp's iconoclasm and experimental attitude have been enormously influential, most obviously on *Conceptual art, but also for example on *Minimal art and on *Pop art, in which the ready-made has played such a big part. His wit and irony have been sadly lacking in most of his followers, however, and it could be argued that his influence has been disastrous, encouraging people of no discernible talent to believe that anything they do, say, or think is worthy of attention as art.

Duchamp-Villon, Raymond (*b* Damville, Eure, 5 Nov. 1876; *d* Cannes, 7 Oct. 1918). French sculptor, the brother of Marcel *Duchamp and of Jacques *Villon (he adopted the name Duchamp-Villon in about 1900). After illness forced him to give up his medical studies in 1898, he took up sculpture, at which he was self-taught. For the next dozen years or so he experimented with various styles until in about 1910 he became involved with *Cubism. Several other Cubists used to meet in the studios of Duchamp-Villon and Villon and from these meetings the *Section d'Or group emerged. In 1914 Duchamp-Villon enlisted in the army as an auxiliary doctor, and he contracted typhoid fever in 1916; he spent his last two years as an invalid before he died in a military hospital. His death cut short a career of great promise, for his major work, *The Horse* (1914), has been described by George Heard Hamilton (*Painting and Sculpture in Europe: 1880–1940*, 1967) as 'the most powerful piece of sculpture produced by any strictly Cubist artist' (there are casts in Tate Modern,

London, the Museum of Modern Art, New York, and elsewhere). This 'abstract diagram of the muscular tensions developed by a leaping horse' (Hamilton) has been compared with the work of the *Futurists, particularly that of *Boccioni, who met Duchamp-Villon in 1913. In the success with which it suggests taut energy it certainly achieves at least one of the things the Futurists were aiming at in their attempts to represent 'the dynamics of movement'.

Duck, Jakob (b ?Utrecht, c.1600; bur. Utrecht, 28 Jan. 1667). Dutch painter and occasional etcher, active mainly in Utrecht (where he was perhaps a pupil of *Droochsloot) but also in Haarlem and The Hague. He is best known as a lively exponent of guardroom and 'merry company' scenes, but he also painted other subjects, including domestic interiors (Woman Ironing, Centraal Mus., Utrecht).

Dufresnoy, Charles-Alphonse (b Paris, 1611; d Villiers-le-Bel, nr. Paris, 16 Jan. 1668). French painter and writer, active in Italy (mainly Rome) for much of his career, 1634–55. His few surviving paintings are unremarkable works in the manner of *Poussin, and he is chiefly remembered for his Latin poem De arte graphica, which sets out the doctrines of French *classicism in epigrammatic form. It was published in 1668, soon after his death, and a French translation by his friend Roger de *Piles appeared later in the same year. De Piles included copious notes in which he emphasized the importance of colour that Dufresnoy had rather tentatively asserted. There were also translations into English (1695, by the poet John Dryden), German (1699), Italian (1713), and Dutch (1733), and it remained influential as an expression of academic theory throughout the 18th century; further English translations appeared in 1754 and 1783 (the latter with annotations by *Reynolds).

Dufy, Raoul (b Le Havre, 3 June 1877; d Forcalquier, 23 Mar. 1953). French painter, graphic artist, and designer. His early work was *Impressionist in style, but he became a convert to *Fauvism in 1905 after seeing *Matisse's Luxe, calme et volupté ('this miracle of creative imagination in colour and line') at the *Salon des Indépendants. He exhibited with the Fauves in 1906 and 1907, but in 1908 he worked with *Braque at L'Estaque, near Marseilles, and abandoned Fauvism for a more sober style influenced by *Cézanne. However, he soon returned to a lighter style and in the next few years developed the highly distinctive personal manner for which he has become famous. It is characterized, in both oils and watercolours, by rapid calligraphic drawing on backgrounds of bright, thinly washed colour and was well suited to the scenes of luxury and pleasure Dufy favoured. He had achieved considerable success by the mid-1920s and the accessibility and joie de vivre of his work helped to popularize modern art. In 1910 Dufy made friends with the fashion designer Paul Poiret, and he did design work for him and for Bianchini-Férier, a silk manufacturer of Lyons. His other work included stage designs, numerous book illustrations, and several murals, the largest of which was The Spirit of Electricity, commissioned for the Pavilion of Light at the 1937 Paris World Fair and now in the Musée d'Art Moderne de la Ville de Paris. In 1952 he was awarded the main painting prize at the Venice *Biennale. His popularity has continued undiminished since his death, not least in Japan, where he is a favourite with collectors.

dugento. See QUATTROCENTO.

Dughet, Gaspard (Gaspard Poussin) (b Rome, 4 June 1615; d Rome, 25 May 1675). Franco-Italian landscape painter, draughtsman, and etcher, the son of a French cook and his Italian wife. He never left Italy, spending almost all his life in or near Rome, but he is traditionally considered a member of the French School. In 1630 his sister married Nicolas *Poussin, with whom he studied c.1631–5 and whose surname he adopted. A few paintings have been disputed between the two artists, but usually Dughet's work is fairly distinct in spirit from that of his illustrious brother-in-law. He combined something of Poussin's solidity with *Claude's romanticism, but he preferred a more rugged type of scenery, and he was particularly fond of the countryside near Tivoli (where he often stayed), with its cliffs, cascades, and dense vegetation (View of Tivoli, c.1645–50, Hatton Gal., Newcastle upon Tyne). Very few of his paintings can be securely dated—the main exceptions are his frescos (c.1647–50) on the history of the Carmelite Order in S. Martino ai Monti, Rome (these too are landscapes)—and it has proved difficult to establish a chronology for him. However, in spite of the lack of detailed knowledge of his work, it is clear that he enjoyed a successful career and in the 18th century his reputation stood very high, particularly in England. His pictures were avidly sought by English collectors and he influenced painters such as Richard *Wilson and the supporters of the *Picturesque.

Dujardin, Karel (*b* Amsterdam, 1626; *d* Venice, Oct./Nov. 1678). Dutch painter and etcher of landscapes, cattle, *genre scenes, portraits, and religious subjects, active mainly in Amsterdam. He is best known for his small paintings of humble bucolic scenes set in an Italianate or a Dutch landscape and diffused with a clear, warm light. These works reveal the impact of Nicolaes *Berchem (who was probably his teacher) and his admiration for Paulus *Potter and Adriaen van de *Velde. He was also an excellent portraitist and his large religious pictures show that he was familiar with the pictorial ideas of Italian *Baroque art. It is generally assumed, on such stylistic evidence, that he visited Italy in the 1640s, but there is no documentary proof. He did, however, spend his last four years in Italy. Like so many of the 17th-century Dutch artists who made the journey to Italy, Dujardin was a Catholic.

Dulac, Edmund (*b* Toulouse, 22 Oct. 1882; *d* London, 25 May 1953). French-born illustrator, designer, painter, and sculptor who settled in London in 1905 and became a British citizen in 1912. Dulac is best known as a book illustrator, particularly of fairy-tale and legendary subjects, in which his sense of fantasy and gifts as a colourist were put to brilliant effect (he was much influenced by Middle and Far Eastern art). He was also a portrait painter, a caricaturist, a sculptor, and a highly versatile designer; his output included much work for the stage, and one of his last commissions was a stamp commemorating the coronation of Queen Elizabeth II in 1953. See also RACKHAM.

Dulwich Picture Gallery. See BOURGEOIS, SIR PETER FRANCIS.

Du Maurier, George (*b* Paris, 6 Mar. 1834; *d* London, 6 Oct. 1896). English illustrator and writer. The son of a French father and an English mother, he trained in Paris under *Gleyre, 1856–7, his fellow students including *Poynter and *Whistler. In 1857 he suddenly lost the sight in one eye, and this persuaded him to give up painting and turn to illustration. He illustrated numerous books but is better known for his work for *Punch*. After John *Leech's death in 1864 he became the magazine's leading social cartoonist and he memorably satirized artistic snobbery and pretension with characters such as Mrs Cimabue Brown, a culture-loving hostess, and her aesthetic acolytes Maudle the painter and Postlethwaite the poet. However, in the

1880s his work declined in quality (partly because of weariness with the routine and the strain it imposed on his eyesight). He had begun to write humorous verse in the 1860s, and in his final years he became a successful novelist. The best known of his three novels, all of which he illustrated himself, is *Trilby* (1894), which reflects his time as an art student in Paris; one of the principal characters is based on Fred *Walker. The actor-manager Sir Gerald Du Maurier was his son, and the writer Dame Daphne Du Maurier was his granddaughter.

Dumonstier. Family of French artists, active in various fields but mainly as portrait painters. About a dozen members of the family are recorded and several of them held court appointments. The earliest of any significance was **Geoffroy** (*c*.1510–73), and the best-known member of the dynasty was **Daniel** (1574–1645), who continued the tradition of the *Clouets into the middle of the 17th century.

Dunlap, William (*b* Perth Amboy, NJ, 19 Feb. 1766; *d* New York, 28 Sept. 1839). American painter, writer, and theatrical manager. He trained as a painter, studying with *West in London 1784–7, but he became fascinated by the theatre during this time, and it was his main profession for the next twenty years. In 1798–1805 and again in 1806–11 he managed the Park Theatre, New York, the interruption being caused by his bankruptcy (he was considered too good-natured to be a successful businessman). He wrote, adapted, or translated (from French and German) about 50 plays and has been described as 'the father of American drama'. In 1817 he returned to painting, hoping (in vain) to make a better living at that profession, and in 1825 he was one of the founders of the *National Academy of Design. His paintings, which included portraits and large religious scenes, are now virtually forgotten, and his most enduring works are two books he produced near the end of his life: *History of the American Theatre* (1832) and *History of the Rise and Progress of the Arts of Design in the United States* (2 vols., 1834). The latter is the most valuable sourcebook on the subject, rich in information and anecdote, and has earned him the nickname 'the American *Vasari'.

Dunoyer de Segonzac, André (*b* Boussy-Saint-Antoine, nr. Paris, 7 July 1884; *d* Paris, 17 Sept. 1974). French painter, printmaker, and designer. Early in his career he went through a period of *Cubist influence, but after the First

World War he became recognized as one of the leading upholders of the naturalistic tradition in a period dominated by anti-naturalistic tendencies. His oil paintings (mainly landscapes, still-lifes, and figure compositions) are often sombre in tone and usually executed in thick paint, emphasizing the weight and earthiness of the forms. His watercolours and etchings, however, are more elegant and spontaneous, with a wider range of subject matter, including dancers and boxers. He also did designs for the theatre and ballet. His reputation was at its height in the 1930s; he won first prize at the Carnegie International in Pittsburgh in 1933 and the main painting prize at the Venice *Biennale in 1934.

Dupont, Gainsborough (b Sudbury, Suffolk, 24 Dec. 1754; d London, 20 Jan. 1797). English painter and engraver, the nephew and only assistant of Thomas *Gainsborough. He made copies and *mezzotints of his uncle's pictures, completed others left unfinished at his death, and painted some original works in his manner. The best known are probably his portraits of actors, examples of which are in the Garrick Club, London, but his landscapes are sometimes regarded as his best works.

Dupré, Jules. See BARBIZON SCHOOL.

Duque Cornejo, Pedro (b Seville, 14 Aug. 1678; d Córdoba, 1757). Spanish sculptor, the grandson and pupil of Pedro *Roldán and the leading sculptor in Seville in the first half of the 18th century. He also worked elsewhere in southern Spain, including Granada and Córdoba, where he settled after being commissioned to design and carve choir stalls for the cathedral in 1747. This work occupied him for the rest of his life and the stalls are regarded as the finest to be produced in Spain in the 18th century. His style was lively and ornate.

Duquesnoy, François (bapt. Brussels, 12 Jan. 1597; d Livorno [Leghorn], 19 July 1643). Flemish sculptor, active mainly in Rome. He settled there in 1618 and with *Algardi became the outstanding sculptor in the city apart from the great *Bernini. In 1627–8 he worked for Bernini on the decoration of the *baldacchino in St Peter's, but his style—like Algardi's—was much more restrained and less *Baroque than the master's. He was indeed a leading figure in circles devoted to classical art (initially he earned his living mainly by restoring *antique sculpture and he shared a house for a time with his friend *Poussin). Duquesnoy produced only two major public works—the marble statues of

St Susanna (S. Maria di Loreto, 1629–33) and St Andrew (St Peter's, 1629–40; see MOCHI)—but his fame was spread by numerous smaller works: reliefs and statuettes of mythological and religious subjects in bronze, ivory, terracotta, and wax. He was particularly renowned for his handling of *putti, and it is curious that someone who so unaffectedly depicted the beauty and charm of children was depressive and perhaps mentally unstable; his biographer *Passeri wrote that he was 'so hesitant and careful in every particular that he wore out his life in irresolution', and the diarist John Evelyn, visiting Rome in 1644, said that he 'died mad' because his St Andrew 'was placed in a bad light' (he had died the previous year on his way to Paris to work for Louis XIII).

Duquesnoy's father and brother were sculptors; **Jerome I** (c.1570–1641/2) and **Jerome II** (1602–54). Jerome I is remembered mainly for the famous Manneken-pis fountain (1619) behind the town hall in Brussels, showing a boy urinating. Jerome II worked with François in Rome and took a somewhat diluted Baroque style back to Brussels with him. The tomb of Bishop Anton Trest in Ghent Cathedral (1651–4) is considered his finest work. He moved to Ghent to complete this, but soon after his arrival he was accused of committing sodomy in the cathedral with his pupils and was executed.

Durand, Asher B. (b Jefferson Village [now Maplewood], NJ, 21 Aug. 1796; d Jefferson Village, 17 Sept. 1886). American painter and engraver. His early work was mainly as an engraver and he established his reputation with his print after John *Trumbull's Signing of the Declaration of Independence and with portraits of eminent contemporaries. In the 1830s he turned increasingly to painting. At first he worked mainly as a portraitist, but then devoted himself to landscape, becoming a leading figure of the *Hudson River School. Thomas *Cole was a major source of inspiration, and Durand's most famous painting, Kindred Spirits (1849, New York Public Lib.), was painted as a memorial to him; it shows Cole (who had died the previous year) and the poet William Cullen Bryant admiring spectacular scenery in the Catskill Mountains, New York State.

Durand-Ruel, Paul (b Paris, 31 Oct. 1831; d Paris, 5 Feb. 1922). The best-known member of a family of French picture dealers, renowned as the first dealer to give consistent support to the *Impressionists. In 1865 he took over the family firm (established by his father in the 1820s) and became the main dealer of the *Barbizon School painters. It was one of these—*Daubigny—who introduced him to *Monet and *Pissarro when all four had taken refuge in England from the Franco-Prussian War of 1870–1. Durand-Ruel's championship of the Impressionists often brought him near to bankruptcy, but in 1886 he achieved a breakthrough with an exhibition of their work in New York, the success of which encouraged him to open a branch of his firm there. This played a major role in building up some of the great American collections of Impressionist pictures. After Durand-Ruel's death, Monet wrote to one of the dealer's sons: 'I shall never forget all that my friends and I owe to your father, in a very special way.' Under his sons and grandson the firm continued to operate until the 1980s.

Duranty, Edmond (*b* Paris, 6 June 1833; *d* Paris, 9 Apr. 1880). French writer, primarily a novelist but also an art critic. In the history of art he is most notable as an early champion of the *Impressionists, specifically as the author of a pamphlet entitled *La Nouvelle Peinture* (1876), the first publication to discuss the group as a whole (although it does not use the word 'Impressionist'). He was a particular friend of *Degas, who produced a memorable portrait of him (1879, Burrell Coll., Glasgow) and helped organize an auction of paintings to benefit his widow after his early death. Duranty also features in *Fantin-Latour's *Homage to Delacroix* (1864, Mus. d'Orsay, Paris).

Dürer, Albrecht (*b* Nuremberg, 21 May 1471; *d* Nuremberg, 6 Apr. 1528). German printmaker, painter, draughtsman, and writer, the greatest figure of *Renaissance art in northern Europe. He was the son of a goldsmith, Albrecht Dürer the Elder, who trained him in his profession. Both his grandfathers had also been goldsmiths, but from an early age Dürer had intellectual ambitions that reached far beyond the confines of the medieval craftsman's workshop. His godfather was Anton Koberger, Nuremberg's leading publisher, whose books were sent all over Europe, and his best friend from childhood was Willibald Pirckheimer, who became a poet and scholar and had the best private library in Germany. In 1486, aged 15, Dürer left his father's workshop to study with Michael *Wolgemut, the leading local painter. By this time he had already shown remarkable talent as a draughtsman, as is seen in his exquisite silverpoint self-portrait dated 1484 (Albertina, Vienna). (This is the earliest of several memorable self-portraits

by Dürer; he was the first artist to produce a series of them at various stages of his life rather than one or two isolated examples, and they show his high conception of the artist's profession as well as his pride in his appearance—in addition to drawings there are three highly finished paintings in which he presents himself as a beautifully dressed and immaculately groomed gentleman, or even as a Christlike figure, rather than as a humble craftsman.)

Wolgemut was a prolific book illustrator as well as a painter and Dürer must have learned the technique of *woodcut from him. After completing his apprenticeship he spent the years 1490–4 travelling and gaining experience of the world. In 1492 he visited Colmar, hoping to meet Martin *Schongauer, the most illustrious German painter and engraver of the day. He arrived too late, as Schongauer had recently died, but the master's brothers furnished Dürer with introductions that gained him work as a book illustrator in Basle (a major publishing centre), where he remained for over a year in 1492–3. After visiting Strasbourg, he returned to Nuremberg in 1494 and in the same year made an arranged marriage to the daughter of a local coppersmith. The union was childless and evidently unhappy (his wife had none of his intellectual interests), but it lasted until Dürer's death. A few months after the wedding he left his bride behind to make a study visit to north Italy, mainly Venice.

After his return to Nuremberg in spring 1495, Dürer quickly established himself as the city's leading artist. Although he was also active as a painter, his reputation was made mainly as a printmaker, his first great success being a series of fifteen woodcuts of the Apocalypse (1498). Most of his woodcuts were on traditional religious subjects, but they were much more ambitious than the work of his predecessors—large in size, elaborate in technique, vivid in imagery, and rich in human feeling, marking the highest development of the technique before it was virtually superseded by copper engraving. These early works tend to have crowded compositions and emphatic emotions, but Dürer became much more classical and restrained, as he learned to reconcile his native love of precise detail with Italian ideals of grandeur and harmony. In 1505–7 he made a second visit to Italy, again staying mainly in Venice. This time he was something of a celebrity, not the promising youngster of his first trip, and he painted a major altarpiece for the German church of S. Bartolommeo, Venice (*Feast of the Rose

Garlands, 1506, NG, Prague). In richness of colour it was intended to compete with Venetian artists on their own ground, or in Dürer's words 'to silence those who said that I was good as an engraver but did not know how to handle the colours in painting'. Some of the local artists were evidently jealous of Dürer (he even said that he feared being poisoned by them), but he was warmly treated by Giovanni *Bellini, for whom he had great admiration.

Back in Nuremberg Dürer consolidated his position as Germany's leading artist and by 1509 he was prosperous enough to buy a large house (now a museum dedicated to him). Apart from prints, his work included altarpieces such as the *Adoration of the Trinity* (1511, KH Mus., Vienna). In 1512 the Emperor Maximilian I (see HABSBURG) visited Nuremberg and he subsequently gave Dürer several commissions (he often failed to pay for these, but in 1515 he directed the civic authorities to give the artist a substantial annual allowance). Dürer's largest project for Maximilian was the design (finished 1515) of an enormous woodcut triumphal arch, laden with history and allegory, glorifying the emperor and his family. At the same time Dürer found creative outlets entirely of his own choosing, notably in three celebrated prints that are sometimes known as the 'Master Engravings': *The Knight, Death, and the Devil* (1513), showing a Christian soldier passing resolutely through the perils of life; *St Jerome in his Study* (1514); and *Melencolia I* (1514), a brooding, enigmatic allegory. In these prints he attained a mastery of *line engraving that has never been surpassed, achieving a richness of shading and texture that rivalled the effects of painting. The works that he produced for his own satisfaction also included much more modest pieces; like his contemporary *Leonardo da Vinci, with whom he is often compared, he found visual stimulation all around him and he made many wonderful drawings and watercolours of subjects that few other artists of the time would have noticed (*A Hare*, 1502, Albertina).

In 1519 the Emperor Maximilian died, and in 1520–1 Dürer journeyed north to meet his successor Charles V, to whom he successfully appealed for a renewal of his annual allowance. He attended Charles's coronation in Aachen and visited various places in the Netherlands, where he was fêted as the acknowledged leader of his profession. The day-to-day diary that Dürer kept on this tour, together with his drawings showing the people and places he saw, is the first record of its kind in the history of art. A good deal of other personal writing by Dürer survives, including letters and a family chronicle that he composed in 1524. These sources reveal much about his personality and beliefs, including his religious views and fears. He thought deeply about religion and became a convert to Lutheranism in about 1520, but he was moderate in his opinions, wanting toleration rather than theological conflict. After his return to Nuremberg in 1521 he dedicated much of his time to writing, producing three learned treatises—on measurement (published 1525), fortifications (1527), and proportion in the human body (published soon after his death in 1528). However, he continued his activities as a printmaker and painter, and his final works include two panels with the Four Apostles (1526, Alte Pin., Munich) that are often considered his masterpieces in painting. In these he summed up his life's work: the study of the ideal human figure—here depicted in forms of heroic dignity—and the expression of a deeply felt religious message.

At his death Dürer was acknowledged as the leading artist of his time outside Italy and as the greatest of all printmakers. He was the first artist of the very highest rank to devote the major part of his career to prints, and their portability gave them international currency—*Vasari wrote that they 'astonished the world'. Even in Dürer's lifetime his prints were extensively imitated and forged and they were reprinted and copied for generations afterwards, often as illustrations in prayer books and devotional works. A new phase of posthumous fame came in the *Romantic period, when he was acclaimed as a German national hero—the statue of him (by *Rauch) unveiled in Nuremberg in 1840 was the first such public monument ever erected to an artist. His enormous reputation has endured, and in Germany the 400th anniversary of his death (in 1928) and the 500th anniversary of his birth (in 1971) were celebrated as 'Albrecht Dürer Years'.

Durrow, Book of. See BOOK OF KELLS.

Dusart, Cornelis (*b* Haarlem, 24 Apr. 1660; *d* Haarlem, 1 Oct. 1704). Dutch painter of peasant scenes. He was the pupil and assistant of Adriaen van *Ostade and completed several works left unfinished at his master's death. There is sometimes confusion between their hands, although Dusart's work is in general coarser, with a tendency towards caricature.

Dutch mordant. A solution of dilute hydrochloric acid with potassium chlorate used for biting the plate in *etching and similar printmaking techniques. It has a milder action than nitric acid and is used particularly when very delicate effects are desired. 'Mordant' in this sense means a corrosive liquid (French: *mordre*, 'to bite').

Duveen, Joseph (Baron Duveen of Millbank) (*b* Hull, 14 Oct. 1869; *d* London, 25 May 1939). English art dealer, patron, and philanthropist. In 1886 he entered the firm of his father Sir **Joseph Duveen** (1843–1908) and with his enormous energy, larger-than-life personality, and great gift for salesmanship expanded it into the leading firm of art dealers in the world, operating on an unprecedented scale. He employed Bernard *Berenson to give his seal of authenticity to the *Renaissance paintings he sold and he was the main agent in forming the collections of such fabulously wealthy Americans as *Frick, *Kress, and Andrew *Mellon. Duveen's benefactions to the arts were also on a princely scale. In addition to giving many pictures to national collections, he paid for extensions or new galleries at the *National Gallery, the *National Portrait Gallery, the *Tate Gallery, and the *British Museum (to house the *Elgin Marbles). He also bore the cost of decorations at the *Wallace Collection and of Rex *Whistler's murals at the Tate Gallery and endowed a professorship in the history of art at London University.

Duvet, Jean (*b* ?Dijon, *c*.1485; *d* ?Langres, 1561/70). French engraver and goldsmith, sometimes called the Master of the Unicorn from his series of engravings (probably from the 1540s) on the medieval theme of the hunting of the unicorn. Little is known of his life; he lived mainly in Langres and Dijon, but the *Renaissance influence in his early work strongly suggests that he spent some time in Italy. His most famous work, a set of 24 engravings illustrating the Apocalypse, published at Lyons in 1561, is, however, completely different in style. The engravings borrow many features from *Dürer's famous series on the same subject, but they are a world apart in spirit, for Duvet treats the subject with a visionary intensity and expressive freedom that anticipate William *Blake (who may well have known Duvet's prints). His work reflects the disturbed religious conditions that prevailed in Langres and is in complete contrast to the mannered elegance of the School of *Fontainebleau, then the dominant force in French art.

Duyster, Willem (*bapt.* Amsterdam, 30 Aug. 1599; *bur.* Amsterdam, 31 Jan. 1635). Dutch painter of *genre scenes and portraits, active mainly in Amsterdam. Most of his paintings depict soldiers, sometimes fighting or looting, but more usually drinking, gaming, or wooing. His delicate skill at painting textiles, his ability to characterize individuals, and his power to express subtle psychological relationships between them, suggest that if he had not been carried off by the plague in his mid-thirties he might well have rivalled *Terborch. There are two examples of his fairly rare work in the National Gallery, London.

Dyce, William (*b* Aberdeen, 19 Sept. 1806; *d* London, 15 Feb. 1864). Scottish painter, designer, and administrator, active mainly in London. In the 1820s he twice visited Italy, where he was influenced by *Renaissance painting and by the *Nazarenes, with whom he became friendly. Dyce was highly cultured and widely talented (he was an accomplished musician and wrote learned essays on antiquities and a prizewinning paper on electromagnetism), but for some time he was successful mainly as a rather conventional portraitist in Edinburgh. In 1837 he moved to London to work for the newly founded School of Design (which developed into the *Royal College of Art) and he made a tour of state art schools in France and Germany to study their methods. His report on his findings led to his appointment as superintendent (director) of the School in 1840. He resigned in 1843, but he remained a central figure in the art world—indeed 'there was no major [artistic] undertaking in mid nineteenth-century Britain in which he did not play either an executive or advisory role' (David and Francina Irwin, *Scottish Painters at Home and Abroad*, 1975). In particular he was a key figure in the revival of fresco painting, which was stimulated mainly by the mural decoration (begun 1843) of the new Houses of Parliament. Dyce's own work there has deteriorated badly, but his *Neptune Resigning to Britannia the Empire of the Sea* (1847, Osborne House, Isle of Wight) is one of the best preserved of all Victorian frescos. This was one of several royal commissions for Dyce, who was a favourite of Prince Albert.

In addition to murals, Dyce produced a varied range of easel paintings, from high-minded religious scenes (he was a devout Christian) to the delightfully sentimental *Titian's First Essay in Colour* (1856–7, Aberdeen AG); his *Pegwell Bay, Kent* (1859–60, Tate, London) is considered one of the most remarkable of all Victorian landscapes. His strong colours, firm outlines, naturalistic detail, and thoughtful sincerity of approach formed a bridge between the Nazarenes and the *Pre-Raphaelites, and *Ruskin said that it was Dyce who gave him his 'real introduction' to the Pre-Raphaelites when, at the 1849 *Royal Academy exhibition, he 'dragged me literally up to the *Millais picture of the Carpenter's Shop, which I had passed disdainfully, and forced me to look for its merits'.

Dyck, Sir Anthony van (*b* Antwerp, 22 Mar. 1599; *d* London, 9 Dec. 1641). Apart from *Rubens, the outstanding Flemish painter of the 17th century, renowned chiefly as one of the greatest of all portraitists. In 1609 he was apprenticed to Hendrick van *Balen. He was exceptionally precocious and on his earliest dated painting (*Portrait of a Man Aged Seventy*, 1613, Mus. Royaux, Brussels) he has proudly inscribed his own age (14) as well as that of the sitter. From about 1617 to 1620 he was Rubens's chief assistant, but in this period he also painted works of his own and established an independent reputation: in 1620 the Earl of *Arundel's secretary wrote from Antwerp to tell his employer that 'Van Dyck is still with Signor Rubens, and his works are hardly less esteemed than those of his master.'

Van Dyck's early work was based very firmly on that of Rubens (there is no trace of influence from van Balen); experts still sometimes have difficulty in differentiating their hands, although van Dyck's style was typically less energetic and more nervously sensitive than that of his supremely robust mentor, reflecting differences in character and constitution (van Dyck was highly strung in temperament and comparatively slight in physique). In addition to learning so much from Rubens's paintings, van Dyck also consciously imitated his aristocratic demeanour and way of life: *Bellori wrote that 'His manners were those of a lord rather than an ordinary man, for he had been accustomed to consort with noblemen in Rubens's studio.' However, he did not have Rubens's prodigious intellectual powers or force of personality and although he was intelligent and charming, he sometimes struck people as haughty (he was certainly vain about his good looks, as his numerous self-portraits testify).

In 1620–1 van Dyck visited London, where he spent a few months in the service of James I, then in 1621 moved to Italy, where he stayed until 1627. At the beginning of this period he was primarily a painter of figure compositions (and he always nursed unfulfilled ambitions to pro-

duce grand decorative schemes in the manner of Rubens), but in Italy he turned increasingly to portraiture, a field in which *Titian was his chief inspiration. He travelled a good deal, but worked mainly in Genoa, where he painted a series of grand portraits of the nobility in which he established a distinctive aristocratic type, with slender figure and proud bearing. A superb example is the full-length *Marchesa Elena Grimaldi* (1623, NG, Washington), of which Sir David Piper wrote (*Van Dyck*, 1968): 'this is how one imagines any feminine aristocrat worthy of her rank must feel herself essentially to be, yet did not know it till van Dyck showed her—aloof and formally regal, but endowed with an elegance and grace that are infinitely seductive.'

After leaving Italy, van Dyck worked mainly in Antwerp for the next few years, 1628–32. During this period he painted some of his finest religious works, including a series of major altarpieces for local churches, beginning in 1628 with the *Martyrdom of St Augustine* (church of St Augustine, Antwerp, on loan to the city's Koninklijk Mus.). He was a devout Catholic and his religious pictures are often highly emotional in tone. In 1632 he moved to London to become court painter to Charles I, who knighted him in that year. Van Dyck was based in England for the rest of his life (he married one of the queen's ladies-in-waiting in 1640), but he never really settled there and was always on the lookout for opportunities elsewhere: between 1634 and 1641 he made three visits to the Continent (he was away for about two years in all), and during the second trip he went to Paris in the hope of winning the commission to decorate the Grande Galerie of the Louvre (which went instead to *Poussin). Nevertheless, in spite of his frustrations in England (which included dilatory payments from the king), it is probably for his portraits of Charles, his family, and his courtiers that van Dyck is best remembered; he depicted his royal and aristocratic sitters in images of such beguiling beauty and glamour that it is hard to envisage the era other than through his eyes, and these pictures have had a profound and lasting influence on British art. *Gainsborough, in particular, revered van Dyck, but he was an inspiration to many others until the early 20th century, when society portraiture ceased to be a major form of artistic expression.

The contemporary poet Edmund Waller described van Dyck's studio as a 'shop of beauty', and he is often characterized as a shameless flatterer of his sitters: when Charles I's niece Sophia of Bavaria first met Queen Henrietta Maria in

1641 she wrote, 'Van Dyck's handsome portraits had given me so fine an idea of the beauty of all English ladies that I was surprised to find that the Queen, who looked so fine in painting, was a small woman raised up on her chair, with long skinny arms and teeth like defence works projecting from her mouth.' However, not all his sitters felt that their looks had been enhanced: when the Countess of Sussex saw the portrait van Dyck painted of her in 1639–40 (now lost) she felt 'quite out of love with myself. The face is so big and fat that it pleases me not at all. It looks like one of the winds puffing—but truly I think tis like the original.'

In addition to his painted portraits, van Dyck planned a series of etchings of famous contemporaries, to be known as the *Iconography.* He etched a few plates himself and had others made from his drawings by various printmakers. The project was unfinished at his death, but 100 etchings were issued as a set in 1645. After he moved to England, he had little time or opportunity to produce paintings other than portraits, but for his own pleasure he made some remarkably fresh and informal drawings and watercolours of the English countryside. This aspect of his work—looking forward to the great English watercolour tradition—is all the more surprising considering that any landscape elements in his oil paintings are usually treated in summary or conventional fashion.

Dying Gaul. Marble statue in the Capitoline Museum, Rome, showing a fallen warrior straining to support himself on one arm as blood gushes from a wound in his side. The statue is first recorded in 1623, in the collection of Cardinal Ludovico Ludovisi (see GUERCINO) in Rome, and thereafter it quickly became one of the most celebrated of *antique works. It is a Roman copy of a Greek work in the *Pergamene style of the late 3rd century BC. Sometimes it is called the 'Dying Gladiator' (hence Lord Byron's famous line alluding to the figure as one 'butchered to make a Roman holiday'), but this title is a misnomer, as the hairstyle and accessories are scrupulously Gallic. It was among the works looted from Italy by Napoleon and was in Paris from 1798 to 1815. Unlike many once famous antique statues, the *Dying Gaul* is still a highly regarded work, admired particularly for its sense of pathos.

E

Eakins, Thomas (*b* Philadelphia, 25 July 1844; *d* Philadelphia, 25 June 1916). American painter, primarily of portraits, regarded by most critics as the outstanding American painter of the 19th century and by many as the greatest his country has yet produced. He spent almost all his career in Philadelphia, where he studied at the *Pennsylvania Academy of the Fine Arts, 1862–6. This was followed by his only substantial period away from his native city, when he spent four years in Europe, 1866–70. In Paris he continued his training under *Gérôme, 1866–9, but he learnt more from a six-month visit to Spain at the end of his stay in Europe, the unaffected naturalism and sombre dignity of *Velázquez's work making a particularly strong impact on him. In 1870 he returned to Philadelphia and in 1876 he began teaching at the Pennsylvania Academy. He caused controversy with his radical ideas, particularly his insistence on basing study on nude models rather than plaster casts, and in 1886 he was forced to resign after allowing a mixed-sex class to draw from a completely nude male model. Such desire for realism also led Eakins to study anatomy and to make use of *Muybridge's photographic researches, but the scientific bent in his work is of less importance than his honesty and depth of characterization; his portraits are often compared with Rembrandt's because of their dramatic play of sombre lighting and sense of inner truth.

Eakins's most famous work is *The Gross Clinic* (1875, Thomas Jefferson Univ., Philadelphia), which has been described as 'very possibly the greatest picture ever painted by an American artist' (John Wilmerding, *American Art*, 1976). It depicts a famous Philadelphia surgeon, Dr Samuel Gross, presiding over an operation watched by a class of students. Eakins painted it for a major exhibition in Philadelphia celebrating the centenary of the Declaration of Independence, but it was rejected by the art jury because of its gory realism and instead was displayed in the medical section of the exhibition. He later suffered a similar rejection with another picture of surgery, *The Agnew Clinic*

(1889, Univ. of Pennsylvania, Philadelphia). Because he had a small private income and modest needs, Eakins could continue on his chosen course despite public condemnation, but much of his later career was spent working in bitter isolation; in 1894 he wrote, 'My honours are misunderstanding, persecution, and neglect, enhanced because unsought.' It was only near the end of his life that he achieved recognition as a great master, and in the first two decades of the 20th century his desire to 'peer deeper into the heart of American life' was reflected in the work of the *Ashcan School and other realist painters. In 1917 a memorial exhibition of his work was held at the Metropolitan Museum, New York, and Robert *Henri—one of Eakins's greatest admirers—wrote an open letter to his students at the *Art Students League, urging them to study the work of the great man: 'His quality was honesty. "Integrity" is the word which seems best to fit him. Personally I consider him the greatest portrait painter America has produced.'

In addition to portraits, Eakins painted memorable *genre scenes of Philadelphia life; boating and rowing were favourite themes, reflecting his love of outdoor exercise (*Max Schmitt in a Single Scull*, 1871, Met. Mus., New York). He also took photographs and made a few sculptures. His wife **Susan Hannah Macdowell Eakins** (1851–1938), whom he married in 1884, was likewise a painter and photographer, as well as an accomplished pianist.

Eardley, Joan (*b* Warnham, Sussex, 18 May 1921; *d* Glasgow, 16 Aug. 1963). British painter, born in England but considered Scottish (her mother was Scottish and she lived in Scotland from 1940). One of her teachers was James *Cowie; he perhaps helped to shape her preference for subjects drawn from everyday experience, but her approach was more earthy and sensuous than his. She divided her time between Glasgow (where she painted *Kitchen Sink subjects) and the fishing village of Catterline, about 30 km (20 miles) south of Aberdeen on the north-east coast. Her favourite subjects in her later years were the village and the sea, especially in stormy weather (she is said to have set off from her Glasgow home as soon as she heard reports of gales). The freely painted, often bleak and desolate works that resulted are among the most powerful and individual landscapes in 20th-century British art. After her early death from breast cancer her ashes were scattered on the beach at Catterline. Her work is well represented in the Scottish National Gallery of Modern Art, Edinburgh.

Earl, Ralph (*b* Shrewsbury, Mass., 11 May 1751; *d* Bolton, Conn., 16 Aug. 1801). American painter, active in Connecticut, Massachusetts, New York, and Vermont, and also in England (1778–85), when his loyalty to the British put his life in danger in his homeland. He painted landscapes and battle scenes of the Revolution, but was primarily a portraitist. Although his style became softer and more sophisticated after studying with *West in London, his work generally has a sincerity and freshness of vision that makes him one of the finest American artists of the 18th century. His presentation of character is extremely forthright and his portraits convey the immense pride his New England sitters took in their possessions. Earl's personal life was a disaster. He was imprisoned for debt and died an alcoholic after deserting both of his wives in turn.

Several other members of his family were artists, notably his brother **James Earl** (1761–96), his son **Ralph E. W. Earl** (*c.*1785–1838), who is remembered mainly for his portraits of President Andrew Jackson, whose niece he had married, and his nephew (who preferred a different spelling of the surname) **Augustus Earle** (1793–1838). Earle was born and died in London, but he spent much of his career abroad, in South America, Australia, and elsewhere, and most of his work depicts the exotic places he visited. In 1832 he became artist to Charles Darwin's expedition on HMS *Beagle*, but because of ill health he was replaced the following year.

Earlom, Richard (*b* London, 1743; *d* London, 9 Oct. 1822). English reproductive printmaker. He was reckoned one of the most skilful engravers of his day and produced a wide range of work, after contemporary artists as well as the Old Masters. His most celebrated work is his set of prints (in outline etching combined with mezzotint) after *Claude's drawings in his *Liber veritatis*, published by *Boydell in two volumes in 1777. These prints inspired *Turner's *Liber studiorum*. A third volume reproducing other draw-

ings by Claude was added in 1819 when the first two were reprinted.

Early Christian art. Term generally applied to Christian art from the 3rd century AD until about 750, particularly in Italy and the western Mediterranean. The art of the Eastern Empire during this time is termed *Byzantine art, but there is no hard-and-fast demarcation between the two traditions.

Earthwork. See LAND ART.

easel. Stand on which a painting is supported while the artist works on it. The oldest representation of an easel is on an Egyptian relief of the Old Kingdom (*c.*2600–2150 BC). *Pliny mentions a *machina* in an anecdote about *Apelles and this presumably refers to an easel. *Renaissance illustrations of the artist at work show all kinds of contrivances, the commonest being the three-legged easel of a type still used today, with pegs to support the picture. Lightweight folding easels were not made until the 18th and 19th centuries, when painters took to working out of doors. The studio easel, a 19th-century invention, is a heavy piece of furniture that runs on castors or wheels, and served to impress the clients of portrait painters. Oil painters need an easel that will support the canvas almost vertically or tip it slightly forward to prevent reflection from the wet paint, whereas the watercolourist must be able to lay his paper nearly flat so that the wet paint will not run down. The term 'easel painting' is applied to any picture small enough to have been painted on a standard easel.

Eastlake, Sir Charles Lock (*b* Plymouth, 17 Nov. 1793; *d* Pisa, 24 Dec. 1865). English painter, art historian, and administrator. He studied under *Haydon and achieved early fame with his *Napoleon on Board the Bellerophon* (1815, Nat. Maritime Mus., London), made from sketches when he witnessed Napoleon on board ship (in Eastlake's native Plymouth) en route to exile on St Helena. Using the proceeds from the sale of this work he lived in Rome 1816–30, and there painted picturesque scenes of the Roman Campagna, often peopled by *banditti*, that became very popular in England. After his return to Britain, however, he turned increasingly to administration and achieved a remarkable record as a public servant. Most notably he was president of the Royal Academy from 1850 and director of the National Gallery (the first holder of this post) from 1855 until his death. His informed purchases of early Italian paintings for the National

Gallery were largely responsible for its outstanding representation in this area. Among his writings are *Materials for a History of Oil Painting* (1847), a pioneering work, and a translation of *Goethe's *Theory of Colours* (1840). His wife **Elizabeth**, *née* Rigby (1809–93), was in her own right a figure in the literary-artistic world of the day. She wrote several books on art and also translated Gustav *Waagen's *Treasures of Art in Great Britain* (1854). Eastlake's nephew **Charles Locke Eastlake** (1836–1906) was keeper of the National Gallery, 1878–98, and published several works on art and decoration, the best known of which was *Hints on Household Taste* (1868), in which he advocated quality of materials and workmanship. It was highly influential in England and even more so in America, although so-called 'Eastlake furniture' often has little to do with his ideas.

Ebbo Gospels. See CAROLINGIAN ART.

Eckersberg, Christoffer Wilhelm (*b* Blåkrog, southern Jutland, 2 Jan. 1783; *d* Copenhagen, 22 July 1853). Danish painter. He was one of the leading figures in his country's art in the first half of the 19th century, and is sometimes called 'the father of Danish painting' because of the influence he exerted on his contemporaries. After training in Copenhagen and under J.-L. *David in Paris (1811–13), he continued his studies in Rome (1813–16), where he executed a masterly portrait of his friend *Thorvaldsen (1815, Academy, Copenhagen). In 1816 he returned to Copenhagen and in 1818 he was appointed a professor at the Academy, where he revolutionized teaching by introducing painting from nature into the curriculum. His pupils included J. C. *Dahl and Christen *Købke. In addition to portraits, which were his financial mainstay, Eckersberg painted landscapes, marine subjects, scenes from Danish history, and occasional religious works. His style combines *Neoclassical clarity of form with freshness of observation.

eclectic, eclecticism. Terms in criticism for a person or style that conflates features borrowed from various sources. Such a style often arises from the overt or tacit doctrine that the excellences of great masters can be selected and combined in one work of art. After *Vasari had praised *Raphael for his skill in selecting the best from the art of his predecessors, it became commonplace to use the same formula in eulogies of other artists. Thus it was said that *Tintoretto had set himself to combine the drawing of *Michelangelo with the colour of

*Titian. In the 18th century, 'eclectics' became label for the *Carracci family and their Bo ognese followers, and gradually the term cam to be used mainly pejoratively, implying lack originality. Such usage has been abandoned serious criticism, and it is clear that the Carrac never adopted eclecticism as a fundament principle. As Denis *Mahon has said: 'Anniba Carracci, the greatest member of the family an one of the founders of 17th-century paintin, was . . . contemptuous of art theory, and (f from being a dispenser of learned recipes ar synthetic systems) was in practice one of th most insatiable experimentalists known to th history of art.'

École de Paris (School of Paris). A term th was originally applied to a number of artists non-French origin, predominantly of Jewi background, who in the years immediate after the First World War lived in Paris an painted in figurative styles that might loose be called poetic *Expressionism, forming th most distinctive strand in French painting b tween *Cubism and *Surrealism. *Chaga (Russian), *Foujita (Japanese), *Modigliani (Ital ian), *Pascin (Bulgarian), and *Soutine (Lith anian) are among the most famous artis embraced by the term. However, particular outside France, the meaning of the term wa soon broadened to include all foreign artis who had settled in Paris since the beginning the century (van *Dongen, *Gris, *Picasso, fe example), and then it expanded still further cover virtually all progressive art in the 20t century that had its focus in Paris. In th broadest sense, the term reflects the intens concentration of artistic activity, supported b critics, dealers, and connoisseurs, that mac Paris the world centre of advanced art durir the first 40 years of the 20th century. After th Second World War, however, New York replace Paris as the world capital of avant-garde art.

École des Beaux-Arts, Paris. See BEAU ARTS.

écorché (French: 'flayed'). A representation a figure with the skin removed, displaying th muscles. Drawings, prints, and statues of suc figures, both human and animal (horses wer particularly popular), were much used in a teaching from the 16th century. *Stubbs's *écorch* figures of animals are well known and *Houdc made a celebrated human *écorché* statue (176 Schlossmuseum, Gotha).

Eddy, Don. See SUPERREALISM.

Edelfelt, Albert (*b* Kiiala Estate, nr. Porvoo, 21 July 1854; *d* Haikko, nr. Porvoo, 18 Aug. 1905). Finnish painter, who with *Gallen-Kallela ranks as his country's leading artist in the 19th century. He trained in Antwerp and then in Paris, where under the influence of his friend *Bastien-Lepage he took up *plein-air* naturalism. His paintings gave a fresh interpretation of Finnish country life and he sometimes set biblical scenes in the Finnish landscape (*Christ and Mary Magdalene*, 1890, Atheneum, Helsinki). Much of his later work was on themes from Finnish history, a type of patriotic work that reflected opposition to Russia's growing oppression of his country. Edelfelt was also an outstanding book illustrator and portraitist.

Edelinck, Gerard (*bapt.* Antwerp, 20 Oct. 1640; *d* Paris, 2 Apr. 1707). Flemish-born engraver who settled in Paris in 1666 and became a French citizen in 1675. He was the son-in-law of *Nanteuil and like him was celebrated as a portrait engraver. His prints after the Old Masters are also highly distinguished, notably that of *Rubens's copy of *Leonardo's *Battle of Anghiari*.

Édouart, Augustin. See SILHOUETTE.

Edwards, Edward (*b* London, 7 Mar. 1738; *d* London, 10 Dec. 1806). English painter and writer. He was part of the first intake of students at the *Royal Academy, in January 1769 (even though he was 30 at the time), and from 1789 he taught perspective there (he was a good teacher, but he was controversially denied the title of professor as he was only an ARA, not a full Academician). He painted 'all manner of subjects' (Ellis *Waterhouse), but his pictures are now forgotten and he is remembered rather for his *Anecdotes of Painters Who Have Resided or Been Born in England*, posthumously published in 1808, which was intended as a continuation of Horace *Walpole's *Anecdotes of Painting in England*. In the introduction to a facsimile reprint published in 1970, R. W. Lightbown describes Edwards as 'a just biographer and a temperate critic', although some contemporaries thought he had been hard on James *Barry. Edwards also wrote *A Practical Treatise of Perspective* (1803).

Eeckhout, Gerbrand van den (*b* Amsterdam, 19 Aug. 1621; *d* Amsterdam, 22 Sept. 1674). Dutch painter. He was a pupil of *Rembrandt and, according to *Houbraken, his 'great friend'. His religious paintings were deeply influenced by Rembrandt; *St Peter Healing the Cripple* (1667, M. H. de Young Memorial Mus., San Francisco), for example, shows how well he understood the broad touch and warm colours of the master's mature works. Eeckhout's *genre scenes, on the other hand, are close to *Terborch in style (*The Music Lesson*, 1655, Statens Mus., Copenhagen). His other works included portraits and a few landscapes. He also made etchings and was a prolific draughtsman.

Egbert Codex. See OTTONIAN ART.

Egg, Augustus (*b* London, 2 May 1816; *d* Algiers, ?26 Mar. 1863). English painter. He painted historical, anecdotal, and literary themes (he was a friend of Dickens and a talented actor), and under the influence of the *Pre-Raphaelites (Holman *Hunt was another friend) he also turned to overtly moralizing subjects. His most famous work in this vein is *Past and Present* (1858, Tate, London), a series of three pictures melodramatically illustrating the dire consequences of adultery. At the 1858 *Royal Academy exhibition *Past and Present* attracted great attention (only *Frith's *Derby Day* conspicuously outshone it), some commentators finding it horrible but compelling. Egg suffered from asthma and in his later years he spent a good deal of time travelling abroad for the sake of his health; his much-reproduced painting *The Travelling Companions* (1862, City AG, Birmingham) shows two sisters in a train near the Riviera resort of Menton.

egg tempera. See TEMPERA.

Eidophusikon (Greek: 'image of nature'). An entertainment invented by P. J. de *Loutherbourg in which spectacular scenic effects were created on a small-scale stage set. Loutherbourg first exhibited his invention in London in 1781 with immediate popular success (more than 100 paying spectators could be seated in the room in which it was displayed). The stage area in which the spectacle was performed was roughly 2 m wide, 1 m high, and 3 m deep (6 ft × 3 ft × 9 ft), and the effects were produced by means of lights, gauzes, coloured glass, and smoke; musical accompaniment was provided by a harpsichord. Among the scenes presented were views of London and other cities, a storm at sea (ships, figures, and the like were moved by a system of rods and pulleys), and 'Satan arraying his Troops on the Banks of the Fiery Lake, with the Raising of the Palace of Pandemonium; from Milton'. *Gainsborough and *Reynolds were among the artists who were impressed by the Eidophusikon. Loutherbourg ran it for several seasons, then sold it to an assistant, who took it on a provincial tour.

Eight, The. A group of American painters who exhibited together in 1908, united by opposition to the conservative *National Academy of Design and a determination to bring painting into direct touch with modern life. The eight members were: Arthur B. *Davies, Maurice *Prendergast, Ernest *Lawson, Robert *Henri, George *Luks, William J. *Glackens, John *Sloan, and Everett *Shinn. They banded together when the Academy rejected work by Glackens, Luks, and Sloan for its 1907 exhibition. Henri, who was the dominant personality of the group and a member of the Academy's jury, withdrew his own work in protest, and Davies was then asked to organize an independent exhibition at the Macbeth Gallery, New York. This took place in February 1908; it was the only exhibition in which The Eight showed together as a group, but it was subsequently circulated to nine other venues over a period of a year and gained a good deal of publicity for their work and ideals. The members of the group were not unified stylistically (one hostile reviewer referred to the 'clashing dissonances of eight differently tuned orchestras'), but their predominant theme was contemporary urban life (several of them were part of the broader trend known as the *Ashcan School). Their exhibition is regarded as an important landmark in American art, helping to lead the way to the *Armory Show of 1913.

The Eight was also the name of a group of progressive Czech artists formed in Prague in 1907, and of a group of Hungarian painters, inspired by *Post-Impressionism, founded in Budapest in 1909. Emil *Filla and Bohumil Kubišta (1884–1918) were the best-known members of the Czech group, and Károly Kernstok (1873–1940) was the leader of the Hungarian group.

Eleanor crosses. A series of twelve carved stone crosses erected by Edward I in 1291–4 to commemorate his wife Eleanor of Castile (*c*.1242–90), 'whom living I have dearly cherished and whom dead I shall not cease to love'. Eleanor died at Harby in Nottinghamshire and the crosses marked the places where her funeral cortège halted each night on its way to her burial place in Westminster Abbey (where there is a magnificent bronze effigy of the queen by William *Torel, also commissioned by Edward). The crosses were almost certainly inspired by those erected to mark the progress of the body of Louis IX of France from Aigues Mortes to Paris in 1270. None of the French crosses (known as 'montjoies') survive, but there are substantial remains of three of the Eleanor crosses (they lac their upper parts, but otherwise they are i reasonably good condition)—at Hardingston Geddington (both Northamptonshire), and Wa tham Cross (Hertfordshire). They are similar t each other in essentials (polygonal in plan ar raised on steps) but different in their lavish an graceful ornamentation. The final cross, Charing Cross in London, survived until 164 when it was pulled down, much decayed, b order of Parliament. Hubert *Le Sueur's eque trian statue of Charles I now occupies the site (was moved there in 1676), and a replica of th cross was erected nearby, in the forecourt (Charing Cross Station, in 1863. Another Elean cross in London, at Cheapside, was demolishe in 1643 (fragments are in the Museum (London).

Elementarism. A modified form of *Ne Plasticism propounded by van *Doesburg i the mid-1920s, notably in a manifesto publishe in the journal De *Stijl in 1926. Whilst maintai ing Mondrian's restriction to the right angl Elementarism abandoned his insistence on th use of strict horizontals and verticals. By intr ducing inclined lines and forms van Doesbu sought to achieve a quality of dynamic tension i place of Mondrian's classical repose. Mondria was so offended by this rejection of his principl that he left De Stijl.

Elgin Marbles. A collection of Greek scul ture and architectural fragments from th Acropolis in Athens acquired by the British di lomat Thomas Bruce, 7th Earl of Elgin (176 1841), in 1801–3, when he was ambassador to th Sultan of Turkey, who at this time ruled Greec The collection (now in the British Museun London) consists mainly of sculptures from th Parthenon (most of what had survived), b includes other pieces, notably a *caryatid fro the Erechtheum. They were shipped to Britai over a period of several years and part of th collection was first exhibited to selected visito (including some of the most distinguished artis of the day) in 1807. Before this, original Gree sculpture of the *Classical age had been virtual unknown in Britain (people had been famili only with Roman and late *Hellenistic copie and they made an enormous impact. *Flaxma was bowled over, declaring them 'the fine works of art I have seen', and *Haydon wrot 'I consider it truly the greatest blessing that ev happened to this country their being broug here.' When asked to restore them, *Cano said 'it would be a sacrilege in him or any man to presume to touch them with a chisel'.

Many other artists, including *Chantrey, *Lawrence, *Nollekens, and *West, expressed similar opinions, but a dissenting voice came from Richard Payne *Knight, who said, 'You have lost your labour, my Lord Elgin. Your marbles are overrated: they are not Greek: they are Roman of the time of Hadrian.' The enormous expense involved in buying and transporting the marbles left Elgin in debt and in 1811 he offered to sell them to the nation for what amounted to the price they had cost him. Eventually, after the deliberations of a special committee of the House of Commons, they were bought for the British Museum in 1816 for £35,000—about half the sum Elgin had spent. The committee rightly dismissed Payne Knight's objections and the sculptures have come to be universally recognized as one of the summits of ancient art. However, they have continued to be the subject of controversy on another count—that of the morality or legality of their removal when Greece was under the dominion of a foreign power. Byron wrote of them as 'poor plunder from a bleeding land' (*Childe Harold's Pilgrimage*, Canto ii, 1812), and a campaign to have them restored to Greece is active today. See also PHIDIAS.

El Greco. See GRECO, EL.

Eliasz., Nicolaes. See PICKENOY.

Elsheimer, Adam (*bapt.* Frankfurt, 18 Mar. 1578; *bur.* Rome, 11 Dec. 1610). German painter, etcher, and draughtsman, active mainly in Italy. Although he died young and his output was small, he played a key role in the development of 17th-century landscape painting. He absorbed the *Coninxloo tradition in his native Frankfurt before moving to Italy in 1598. In Venice he worked with his countryman *Rottenhammer, then in 1600 settled in Rome. There his early *Mannerist style gave way to a more naturalistic manner in which he showed great sensitivity to effects of light; his nocturnal scenes are particularly original, bringing out the best in his lyrical temperament, and he is credited with being the first artist to represent the constellations of the night sky accurately (*Flight into Egypt*, 1609, Alte Pin., Munich). He painted a few pictures in which figures are the dominant element, but generally they are fused into a harmonious unity with their landscape settings. His paintings are invariably on a small scale and on copper (the only exception is a self-portrait in the Uffizi, Florence, of doubtful attribution); they are exquisitely executed but have a grandeur out of all proportion to their size.

Elsheimer's work was highly regarded by discerning contemporaries, but his life was unhappy and he died in poverty (he evidently spent some time imprisoned for debt); *Sandrart says he suffered from melancholia and was often unable to work. His posthumous fame spread quickly, partly through engravings of his pictures made by the Dutch artist Hendrik Goudt (1573–1648), who seems to have been his patron as well as his pupil (Elsheimer himself made a number of etchings). *Rubens was a friend of Elsheimer and after his death lamented his 'sin of sloth, by which he has deprived the world of the most beautiful things'; he also wrote: 'I have never seen his equal in the realm of small figures, of landscapes, and of so many other subjects.' Both Rubens (Staatliche Kunstsammlungen, Kassel) and *Rembrandt (NG, Dublin) made paintings of the *Flight into Egypt* inspired by Elsheimer's masterpiece, and his influence is apparent in the work of many other 17th-century artists.

emblem. A visual image carrying a symbolic meaning and often accompanied by texts to explain this meaning. In its most typical form the emblem consisted of a picture, a motto, and an explanatory verse called an epigram. For example, one of the most famous emblems depicted a dolphin and an anchor with the Latin motto *Festina lente* (Make haste slowly), to symbolize the idea that maturity is achieved by a combination of the speed and energy of the dolphin and the steadiness and gravity of the anchor. The aim of the emblem therefore was to give symbolic expression to a moral adage. Printed collections of emblems ('emblem books') enjoyed a great vogue in the 16th and 17th centuries and were often used as sources of pictorial imagery. The first and most popular of such books was *Emblematum liber* (1531) by Andrea Alciati (1492–1550), an Italian lawyer and scholar; it went through dozens of editions before the end of the century. In terms of art history, the most important emblem book is *Iconologia* (1593; first illustrated edition, 1603) by the Italian writer Cesare Ripa (*c.*1555–1622), which became the standard handbook on *iconography for artists.

Emin, Tracey. See YOUNG BRITISH ARTISTS.

emulsion. A watery liquid combined with an oily or resinous substance in such a way that they will not separate out. Oil proverbially will not mix with water, but if an emulsifying agent—such as albumen—is added, it will surround the drops of oil and prevent them from coming together. The *medium of *tempera painting is always an emulsion. The natural emulsions used most commonly in painting are egg yolk and *casein. Both have the advantage that once they have set they are not soluble in water. Modern emulsion paint, typically used for covering walls and ceilings, consists of pigments bound in a synthetic resin that forms an emulsion with water.

enamel. A smooth, glossy material made by fusing glass to a prepared surface, usually of metal, by means of intense heat. The term is also applied to any object made of, or decorated with, this material. Though easily fractured, enamel is otherwise extremely durable and gives great brilliance of colour, especially when used in translucent form against a ground of precious material. The colour can come from the use of coloured glass or from the application of colour to plain enamel. Enamel is thought to be of western Asiatic origin and was well known in the ancient Mediterranean world, the Egyptians, Greeks, and Romans making extensive use of it in jewellery. In the Middle Ages—in both Byzantium and western Europe—enamels were much used for the decoration of various types of ecclesiastical art—book covers, reliquaries, Crucifixes, and so on—and they were sometimes used on a larger scale, as for example in *Nicolas of Verdun's Klosterneuburg Altar, completed in 1181. Nicolas came from the *Mosan region (in present-day Belgium), which in his time was the centre of the highest-quality enamelwork. Later in the Middle Ages the French city of Limoges became the best-known centre of production, catering for the mass market and making secular objects (caskets, rings, and so on) as well as religious ones. The great days of enamel were over by the end of the 16th century, although it continued to be used for jewellery and decorative work.

Enamel paints, as used on *stained glass, were made from powdered glass mixed with various substances. Today the word 'enamel' is loosely used of any glossy protective covering such as durable paint or varnish applied to the surface of objects made from metal, wood, etc.

encarnado (Spanish: 'flesh-coloured'). Term applied in Spanish art to the painting of the flesh parts of wooden sculptures in more or less naturalistic colours. The term 'estofado' (literally 'quilted') is applied to the painting of

draperies. In the 16th century the paint of both flesh and draperies was given a glossy finish, but in the 17th century a matt finish was adopted for greater realism. Such work was sometimes done by distinguished painters as well as by specialist craftsmen—*encarnadores* and *estofadores*. For example, *Pacheco often painted figures by *Montañes. See also POLYCHROME.

encaustic painting. Technique of painting with *pigments mixed with molten wax. It is a laborious method, but it produces a very durable and stable surface, as wax resists moisture and does not yellow with age. The name derives from a Greek word meaning 'burnt in'—a reference to the fact that the paint was bonded to the *support by passing a heated metal rod close to it, probably immediately after the paint was applied. It was one of the principal painting techniques of the ancient world; the first great practitioner is said to have been *Pausias in the 4th century BC, and the most remarkable surviving examples are the mummy portraits from *Faiyum, dating from the early centuries AD. *Pliny (in the 1st century AD) describes two methods that were already 'ancient' in his day (one of them on ivory) and a third newer method that had been devised since it became the practice to paint ships; he records that stood up to sun, salt, and winds. Encaustic was evidently also employed for colouring statues but it was not used for painting directly on walls for which *fresco was the standard technique. The older methods described by Pliny were done with a knife or spatula; the newer technique with a brush. Signs of the brush can be seen in some of the Faiyum portraits.

Encaustic was the commonest painting technique in the early centuries of the Christian era but it fell into disuse in the Middle Ages, to be replaced by *tempera and eventually *oil. There have been various attempts to revive (e.g. by Julius *Schnorr von Carolsfeld, who painted several scenes in encaustic in the Residenz at Munich in the 1830s). Jasper *Johns has used encaustic in his Flag and Target paintings but the time-consuming technique finds few exponents today, even though electrical heating equipment makes it more manageable.

Engelbrechtsz. (or Engebrechtsz.), Cornelis (b Leiden, c.1460; d Leiden, 1527). Netherlandish painter, the leading artist of his day in Leiden. He was influenced by the fashionable Italianate style stemming from Antwerp, but his work has an emotional intensity that is *Gothic rather than *Mannerist in spirit. His compositions are crowded and lively, full of dramatic gestures and agitated movement; the figures are tall and slender, often wearing exotic costumes, and the colour is rich and resonant. He is closer in feeling to the *Master of the Virgo inter Virgines in Delft than to any Antwerp artist. The altarpieces of the *Crucifixion* and the *Lamentation* in the Lakenhal Museum, Leiden, are typical of his work. In addition to religious works he painted a few portraits. *Lucas van Leyden was his greatest pupil and tends to overshadow his achievements. The other pupils in his large studio included his three sons **Pieter, Cornelis,** and **Lucas,** as well as Lucas van Leyden's brother Aertgen.

English, Michael. See SUPERREALISM.

engraving. Term applied collectively to the various processes of cutting a design into a plate or block of metal or wood, and to the prints taken from these plates or blocks (see PRINT for a classification of these processes). In everyday usage, the term usually refers more specifically to one of the processes, known technically as *line engraving. In a different sense, the term 'engraving' is applied to the incising of designs on stone, especially in prehistoric art.

Ensor, James (*b* Ostend, 13 Apr. 1860; *d* Ostend, 19 Nov. 1949). Belgian painter and etcher (his father was English and he had British nationality until 1929). One of the most original artists of his time, Ensor had links with *Symbolism, was a major influence on *Expressionism, and was claimed by the *Surrealists as a forerunner, but his work defies classification within any school or group. Apart from a period studying at the Academy in Brussels, 1877–80, and a few brief trips abroad, he rarely left his home town of Ostend, where his parents kept a souvenir shop. His early works were mainly bourgeois interiors painted in a thick and vigorous technique. When several were rejected by the Salon in Brussels in 1883, Ensor joined the progressive group Les *Vingt. From about this time his subject matter changed and he began to introduce the fantastic and macabre elements that are chiefly associated with his name. He made much use of carnival masks, grotesque figures, and skeletons, his bizarre and monstrous imaginings recalling the work of his Netherlandish forebears *Bosch and *Bruegel. The interest in masks probably originated in his parents' shop, but he was also one of the first European artists who appreciated African art, in which they play such a great part. Through his 'suffering, scandalized, insolent,

cruel, and malicious masks', as he called them, he portrayed life as a kind of hideous carnival. Often his work had a didactic or satirical flavour involving social and religious criticism; his most famous painting, the huge *Entry of Christ into Brussels* (1888, Getty Mus., Los Angeles), shows how he imagined Christ might be greeted on a new Palm Sunday. It provoked such an outburst of criticism among his associates in Les Vingt (who refused it for exhibition) that he was almost expelled from the group.

From this time Ensor became something of a recluse and his work became even more misanthropic. Nevertheless, from about the turn of the century his reputation grew rapidly, and in 1903 he was made a knight of the Order of Leopold. The culmination of his career came in 1929, when the inaugural exhibition of the Palais des Beaux-Arts in Brussels was devoted to his work (the *Entry of Christ into Brussels* was shown in public for the first time) and he was created a baron by King Albert. His work changed little after about 1900, however, and he was content to repeat his favourite themes. From 1904 he also gave up printmaking (he was one of the greatest etchers of his time and also made lithographs). There is a museum of his work in Ostend.

entartete Kunst. See DEGENERATE ART.

Environment (or **Environmental**) **art.** An art form in which the artist creates a three-dimensional space in which the spectator can be completely enclosed and involved in a multiplicity of sensory stimulations—visual, auditory, kinetic, tactile, and sometimes olfactory. This type of art was prefigured in the Merzbau of Kurt *Schwitters and in the elaborate decor of some of the *Surrealist exhibitions of the 1930s, as well as in certain types of entertainments at funfairs, but as a movement it originated in the late 1950s and flourished chiefly in the 1960s, when it was closely connected with *happenings. The leading figures who have worked in Environment art include *Kaprow, *Kienholz and, *Oldenburg, and one of the most celebrated works in the genre was created by Niki de *Saint Phalle. The term has been loosely used, and confusingly it has sometimes been applied to *Land art or its analogues—that is, to type of art that manipulates the natural environment, rather than creating an environment to enfold and absorb the spectator.

Epictetus. Greek vase painter and potter, active in Athens *c.* 520–*c.*500 BC. He was unusual in that he was equally accomplished in *black-figure and *red-figure techniques, and he has been described as 'one of the most skilful as well as the most charming of all Greek draughtsmen' (Martin Robertson, *A History of Greek Art*, 1975). More than a hundred pieces by him are known, including plates, in which he did some of his best work. Often he depicted a single figure of an athlete or warrior, the pose adapted with consummate mastery to the shape of the pottery. A characteristic example is a cup in the British Museum, London, with a red-figure exterior and a black-figure interior showing a horseman carrying spears.

Epstein, Sir Jacob (*b* New York, 10 Nov. 1880; *d* London, 19 Aug. 1959). American-born sculptor (and occasional painter and illustrator) who settled in England in 1905 and became a British citizen in 1911. Before then, in 1902–5, he had studied in Paris and visits to the Louvre aroused an interest in ancient and *primitive sculpture that lasted all his life and powerfully affected his work. His first important commission was executed in 1907–8: eighteen over-life-size figures for the façade of the British Medical Association's headquarters in the Strand. The nude figures aroused a furore of abuse on the grounds of alleged obscenity and were mutilated in 1937 when the building was bought by the government of Southern Rhodesia. Such verbal attacks and acts of vandalism were to become a feature of Epstein's career. The next scandal came with his tomb of Oscar Wilde (1912, Père Lachaise Cemetery, Paris), a magnificently bold and original piece featuring a hovering angel inspired by Assyrian sculpture; it was banned as indecent until a bronze plaque had been placed over the angel's sexual organs, and after the plaque was removed in a night raid by a group of artists and poets, a tarpaulin was placed over the tomb and remained in place for two years. Epstein carved the tomb in London (it is in *Hopton Wood stone), but he spent a good deal of time in Paris during the initial period of controversy; he met *Brancusi, *Modigliani, and *Picasso there and was influenced by their formal simplifications. Back in England he became involved with Wyndham *Lewis and the *Vorticists (although he was never a formal member of the movement), and at this time he created his most radical work—*The Rock Drill* (1913–15, Tate, London, and other casts), a robot-like figure that was originally shown mounted on an enormous drill; he said it symbolized 'the terrible Frankenstein's monster we have made ourselves into'.

Epstein's later work was generally much less audacious than this, but his public sculptures were still attacked with monotonous regularity, their expressive use of distortion being offensive to conservative critics even when they were immune to charges of indecency. *Rima*, a stone relief memorial to the naturalist W. H. Hudson in Hyde Park, London (1922), roused perhaps the greatest storm of any of Epstein's works. It was daubed with green paint and a number of well-known figures petitioned for its removal; they included *Dicksee and *Munnings (present and future president of the Royal Academy) and Sir Arthur Conan Doyle. Muirhead *Bone came to its defence with a letter in *The Times*, signed by an equally impressive line-up, including Frank *Dobson, Eric *Kennington, and George Bernard Shaw. In the face of such controversy Epstein concentrated increasingly on bronze portrait busts, which found a more appreciative audience than his monumental works. Many notable men and women sat for him and he portrayed them with psychological intensity and great mastery of expressive surfaces, carrying on the tradition of *Rodin. It was only after the Second World War that his work began to achieve public acceptance, and in the 1950s he belatedly received a stream of honours (including a knighthood in 1954) and of major commissions, including the enormous bronze group of *St Michael and the Devil* (1958) at Coventry Cathedral. See also LEAD.

Eragny Press. See PRIVATE PRESS.

Erbslöh, Adolf. See NEUE KÜNSTLER-VEREINIGUNG MÜNCHEN.

Ercole de' Roberti. See ROBERTI.

Ernst, Max (*b* Brühl, nr. Cologne, 2 Apr. 1891; *d* Paris, 1 Apr. 1976). German-born painter, printmaker, collagist, and sculptor who became an American citizen in 1948 and a French citizen in 1958, one of the major figures of *Dada and even more so of *Surrealism. He studied philosophy and psychology at Bonn University, but he became fascinated by the art of psychotics (he visited the insane as part of his studies) and neglected academic work for painting. After serving in the First World War he became with *Arp (his lifelong friend) the leader of the Dada movement in Cologne. In 1920 he organized one of Dada's most famous exhibitions in the conservatory of a restaurant there: visitors entered through the lavatories, and axes were provided so they could smash the exhibits if they felt so inclined.

In 1922 Ernst settled in Paris, where he joined the Surrealist movement on its formation in 1924. Even before then, however, he had painted works that are regarded as Surrealist masterpieces, such as *Celebes* (1921, Tate, London), in which an elephant is transformed into a strange mechanistic monster. The irrational and whimsical imagery seen here, in part inspired by childhood memories, occurs also in his highly original collages. In them he rearranged parts of banal engravings from sources such as trade catalogues and technical journals to create strange and startling scenes, showing, for example, a child with a severed head in her lap where a doll might be expected. He also arranged series of such illustrations with accompanying captions to form 'collage novels'; the best known and most ambitious is *Une semaine de bonté* (A Week of Kindness), published in Paris in 1934. Another imaginative technique of which he was a leading exponent was *frottage, which he invented in 1925. In 1930 he appeared in the Surrealist film *L'Âge d'or*, created by Luis Buñuel and Salvador *Dalí, and in 1935 he made his first sculpture (he worked seriously but intermittently in this field, characteristically creating totemic-like figures in bronze).

In 1938 Ernst broke with the Surrealist movement, but this did not affect his work stylistically. He was interned for a short while after the German invasion of France and in 1941 moved to New York, remaining in America until 1953 (apart from a visit to France in 1949). While in the USA he collaborated with *Breton and *Duchamp in the Surrealist periodical *VVV*. He settled permanently in France in 1953 and in his late years acquired many honours, including the main painting prize at the Venice *Biennale in 1954. His painting of this time became more lyrical and abstract.

Ernst was married four times. His third (very brief) marriage was to Peggy *Guggenheim; his fourth wife (married 1946) was Dorothea Tanning (1910–), one of the outstanding American Surrealist painters. In the late 1930s he lived in Paris with the British-born (later Mexican) Surrealist painter and writer Leonora Carrington (1917–). His son **Jimmy Ernst** (1920–84) was also a painter.

Errard, Charles (*b* Nantes, *c.*1606; *d* Rome, 25 May 1689). French painter, draughtsman, architect, writer, and administrator, active in Italy for much of his career. He was the son of a painter of the same name (*c.*1570–1630), with whom he had his first training. From 1627 to 1643 he lived in Rome, where he studied the *antique, on which he based his academic style. After returning to Paris in 1643 he became one of the leading decorative painters of the day, but little of his work survives. In 1648 he was one of the founder members of the Académie Royale (see ACADEMY) and he helped to determine its intellectual and rational approach to art. His scholarly interests were also expressed in his work on the first printed edition of *Leonardo's treatise on painting (published in Paris in French and Italian in 1651; see FRÉART), for which he made illustrations. In 1666 he returned to Rome as first director of the French Academy. During this final period of his life he made designs for his only known work as an architect, the 'clumsy and pedantic' (Anthony *Blunt) church of the Assumption in the rue Saint-Honoré in Paris (1670–6; destroyed 1898).

Erté (Romain de Tirtoff) (*b* St Petersburg, 10 [22] Nov. 1892; *d* Paris, 21 Apr. 1990). Russian-born French designer, painter, and sculptor. In 1912 he moved to Paris, where he studied at the *Académie Julian (his adopted name derives from the French pronunciation of his initials, 'r' and 't'). Erté was best known for his fashion illustrations (particularly for the American magazine *Harper's Bazaar*) and for his costume and set designs for theatre, cabaret, opera, ballet, and cinema (he designed costumes for Mata Hari among other celebrities). However, he also painted, and in the 1960s he produced lithographs and made sculpture from sheet metal.

Escher, M. C. (Maurits Cornelis) (*b* Leeuwarden, 17 June 1898; *d* Hilversum, 27 Mar. 1972). Dutch printmaker, working principally in the techniques of woodcut and lithography. His early prints were mainly landscapes and townscapes in a bold but fairly naturalistic style; however, from the mid-1930s he turned increasingly to what he described as 'inner visions'. Many of these were expressed as sophisticated designs in which repeated figures of stylized animals, birds, or fish are arranged in dense, interlocking patterns. From about 1940 the bizarre element in his work became more overtly *Surrealist, particularly in the kind of print for which he is now most famous—views of strange imaginary buildings in which he made brilliant play with optical illusion to represent, for example, staircases that seem to go both up and down in the same direction (*Ascending and Descending*, 1960). Such prints have been of considerable interest to mathematicians as well as to psychologists involved with visual perception; an exhibition of them was shown at the International Mathematical Congress in Amsterdam in 1964. From the 1960s Escher's work has also found a large popular audience, especially among young people, some of whom felt that his images complemented the 'mind-expanding' experiences gained through hallucinogenic drugs.

Escorial. A small village about 50 km (30 miles) north-west of Madrid that gives its name to the monastery-palace built there by Philip II (see HABSBURG), one of the great monuments of Spanish architecture and one of the great treasure houses of Spanish art. Philip built the Escorial to honour the wishes of his father, the Emperor Charles V (d 1558), who in his will had specified the creation of a religious foundation in which he was to be buried alongside his wife, Isabella of Portugal (d 1539). In addition to this function as a royal mausoleum (almost every Spanish monarch from Charles V onwards has been buried there), the Escorial was built as a palace, a monastery, and a seminary, all centred on an imposing domed church. The huge complex was begun in 1563, with Juan Bautista de Toledo as architect; he died in 1567 and was succeeded by Juan de Herrera, under whom it was officially completed in 1584 (although construction went on for some time after this).

Externally the Escorial is built of grey granite and is overpoweringly austere, with forms of almost geometric clarity and virtually no ornament. Internally, however, it contains an extraordinary wealth of decoration (including vast areas of wall and ceiling frescos), which engaged teams of artists long after Philip's death. The plan is a large rectangle, roughly 160 m × 200 m (175 × 220 yds), and the layout has been compared to a gridiron; this is the attribute of St Lawrence (a 3rd-century martyr said to be of Spanish origin), to whom the monastery was dedicated in acknowledgement of Philip II's victory over the French at Saint Quentin on Lawrence's feast day in 1557. Many of the works of art in the Escorial feature the saint, including *Titian's great altarpiece of the *Martyrdom of St Lawrence*, commissioned by Philip in 1564.

Philip failed to persuade Titian (his favourite painter) to come to Spain, but he imported many other Italian artists to work at the Escorial, including the painters Luca *Cambiaso, Pellegrino *Tibaldi, and Federico *Zuccaro, and the sculptor Pompeo *Leoni. Such artists formed the main channel through which the *Mannerist style entered Spain. Among the Spanish artists employed by Philip on the decoration of the

Escorial were *Navarrete and *Sánchez Coello El *Greco too painted a major altarpiece for him the *Martyrdom of St Maurice and the Theban Legio (1580–2), but Philip disliked it (evidently becaus it did not sufficiently 'inspire devotion') and ha it replaced (although it remains in the Escorial)

Artists of later generations who made import ant contributions to the decoration of the buil ing include Claudio *Coello and Luc *Giordano, both of whom worked there in th late 17th century. In the 18th century Charles I used the Escorial as a hunting seat and furnishe the hitherto unoccupied state rooms of th palace; many of the tapestries with which th walls were hung were designed by *Goya. Othe outstanding works of art in the Escorial includ a marble Crucifix carved by Benvenuto *Cellin and paintings by *Dürer, *Bosch, *Ribera, an *Velázquez.

Structurally the Escorial has changed little i essentials since Philip II's time, although it wa repaired after fires in 1671, 1731, 1763, and 1825. programme of restoration began in 1953, and i 1963 a new museum was established, containin material relating to the construction of th building as well as works of art. The Escori still functions as a monastery, but it is nov administered by the Patrimonio Nacional—th organization in charge of national art treasures

Esquivel, Antonio María (b Seville, 8 Ma 1806; d Madrid, 9 Apr. 1857). Spanish painte active in Madrid from 1831. His output include religious, historical, and *genre subjects (h early works imitated the style of *Murillo), bu he is remembered as one of the leading Spanis portraitists of his time. One of his best-know works is *Zorrilla Reciting his Poems* (1846, Mu Romántico, Madrid), showing the poet an dramatist in Esquivel's studio, together wit many leading figures of the literary and artisti society of mid-19th-century Madrid.

Este. Italian family, rulers of Ferrara, Moden and Reggio from the late 13th century until 159 when Ferrara was annexed by the papacy, an thereafter of Modena and Reggio until 179 when the family was deposed by the invadin French. Various members were notable patron of the arts and letters. **Leonello** (1407–5 reigned from 1441) made Ferrara into an impor ant cultural centre; he was the friend of *Albert and a patron of Jacopo *Bellini, *Piero dell Francesca, and *Pisanello; Rogier van de *Weyden painted his illegitimate son **Francesc** (Met. Mus., New York), who spent most of hi life in the Netherlands. Leonello's brother **Bors**

(1413–71; reigned from 1450) commissioned the outstanding work of 15th-century Ferrarese painting—the series of frescos in the Hall of the Months in the Palazzo Schifanoia, attributed mainly to Francesco del *Cossa. **Isabella** (1474–1539), daughter of **Ercole I** (1431–1505), the half-brother of Leonello and Borso, was the greatest of the Este patrons and one of the most brilliant women of her time. She secured paintings from Mantegna, *Perugino, *Costa, and later *Correggio to decorate her famous *Studiolo in Mantua (she was married to Francesco *Gonzaga) and is said to have implored art dealers not to show her their wares so she would not spend herself even further into debt. A portrait drawing of her by *Leonardo is in the Louvre, Paris. Her brother **Alfonso I** (1476–1534; reigned from 1505) commissioned mythological paintings by Giovanni Bellini and *Titian for his Studiolo. Alfonso's son, Cardinal **Ippolito II** (1509–72), commissioned the Villa d'Este at Tivoli, near Rome, together with its celebrated gardens, designed by Pirro *Ligorio. Dosso and Battista *Dossi, *Garofalo, and *Scarsellino were among the other painters employed by the Este during the 16th century. In the next century they continued their activities in Modena. **Francesco I** (1610–58; reigned from 1629) commissioned portraits of himself from *Bernini and *Velázquez. Both portraits are now in the Galleria Estense in Modena, which houses many other works from the Este collections. However, in 1744 **Francesco III** (1698–1780) sold 100 of his most splendid pictures to Augustus III of Poland (as Elector of Saxony Augustus had his court in Dresden and these paintings are now among the treasures of the Gemäldegalerie there).

Estes, Richard. See SUPERREALISM.

estofado. See ENCARNADO.

etching. A printmaking method in which the design is bitten into the plate with acid; the term is also applied to the print so produced. Although there are alternative ways of carrying out some of the processes involved, the procedure is essentially as follows. A plate of polished metal—usually copper—is coated with a substance that will resist the action of acid. This 'etching *ground' is typically made of beeswax, *bitumen, and *resin; often it is darkened by coating it with soot from a smoking flame so that the lines drawn on it can be more easily seen. These lines are made with a steel etching needle, which cuts through the ground and exposes the bright metal beneath. After covering the back and edges of the plate with an acid-resisting *varnish, the etcher immerses it in a bath of dilute acid, which bites into the metal wherever the ground has been pierced by the needle. The depth to which the lines are bitten (and hence the darkness with which they will print) depends on how long the plate is immersed in the acid, and it is possible to achieve subtle variations of tone by 'stopping out' part of the design (covering it with the protective varnish) while other parts are bitten more deeply. This process of graduated biting may be repeated any number of times. Finally, when all is bitten as required, the ground is cleaned off and the plate is inked and printed. Etching is frequently combined with other processes, particularly *drypoint; by this means additional work may be done on the plate after proofing without re-laying the ground, and the drypoint lines also provide a convenient method of adding strong black accents to the design.

Etching is a much more spontaneous technique than *line engraving, as it is possible to draw on the waxy ground with virtually the same fluency as with pen or pencil. It is even possible to carry a grounded etching plate like a sketchbook to be used as the occasion demands; it seems that *Rembrandt may sometimes have worked in such a way, for the picture dealer Edmé Gersaint (*Watteau's friend) recorded that he made his famous etching 'Six's Bridge' (1645) 'against time for a wager at the country house of a friend, Jan Six, while the servant was fetching the mustard, that had been forgotten for a meal, from the neighbouring village'. Similarly, a quick portrait sketch can be made direct from the sitter, ready for biting and printing when convenient. This would be unthinkable with line engraving, where the laborious action of pushing the *burin through the metal is incompatible with drawing from life.

Close examination of the lines themselves sometimes reveals these different methods of working. Engraved lines swell and taper according to the pressure of the engraver's hand and end in a point as the needle comes to the surface. They are hard and true, whereas etched lines, especially if bitten with nitric acid, sometimes have slightly irregular edges. Such differences often make it easy to tell whether a print is an etching or a line engraving, but sometimes it is much more difficult to distinguish between the two processes, especially with examples from the early days of etching, for etching was initially used as a labour-saving method of achieving the effects of line engraving and consequently had to resemble engraving as closely as possible. Moreover, the practice arose, again in order to ease the engraver's labours, of beginning a plate with etching and finishing it by engraving. Thus etching was not at the beginning the free and spontaneous art it later became.

The first etchings belong to the early years of the 16th century (the earliest dated example, of 1513, is by Urs *Graf), though the basic principle, that of corroding a design into a metal plate, had been utilized earlier for the decoration of armour. *Dürer made a few etchings, of which the best known is *The Cannon* of 1518. He used iron plates, the biting is strong and rather coarse, and there is no stopping out to vary the tone of the lines. Other northern pioneers were *Altdorfer and *Lucas van Leyden. In Italy *Parmigianino was etching soon after 1520; his prints are attractively luminous and free in drawing, indicating the direction the technique was to take in later years. The greatest of all etchers was Rembrandt, who made a complete break from the tradition of line engraving, drawing freely on the plate with great vigour and power, and often radically transforming his designs as he went along. His early plates are in the medium of etching alone. Later he added drypoint to the etched lines, and finally he came to rely still more on drypoint in plates that are remarkable for their boldness of handling and intensity of feeling.

Several major artists of the 18th century made memorable use of etching, including *Canaletto, *Piranesi, and *Goya (who usually combined it with *aquatint), but during the first half of the 19th century the technique was employed mainly for commercial illustration. From the 1860s to the First World War, however, there was a great renewal of interest in it as a medium for original expression, especially in Britain. *Whistler and *Sickert were leading lights of this movement, which is called the Etching Revival. The technique remains popular, *Hockney being a leading contemporary exponent.

Etty, William (*b* York, 10 Mar. 1787; *d* York, 13 Nov. 1849). English painter, one of the few British artists to specialize almost exclusively in the nude. He spent most of his career in London, where he trained at the *Royal Academy Schools and then (1807–8) with *Lawrence, who had a great influence on him; this was later modified by the impact of Venetian art, which he admired on a lengthy tour of France and Italy in 1822–4. Etty's paintings are often of mythological or historical subjects, sometimes

on an ambitious scale, but he also made lit studies in the RA Schools throughout his caree and these are now probably his most admire works. He was often attacked for the allege indecency of his work, *The Times* considering 'entirely too luscious for the public eye'. How ever, by the time of his death he was wealthy an respected. He summed up his attitude to h favourite subject thus: 'Finding God's most glor ous work to be Woman, that all human beaut had been concentrated in her, I dedicated myse to painting—not the Draper's or Milliner work—but God's most glorious work, mor finely than ever had been done.' His draught manship is often criticized, but it is generall agreed that he attained a glowing voluptuou ness in the painting of flesh that few Britis artists have approached. The best collection c Etty's work is in York Art Gallery.

Euphranor. Greek painter and sculptor of th mid-4th century BC, a leading contemporary c *Praxiteles. He was one of the most celebrate artists of his day and exceptional in achievin equal fame as a painter and sculptor. Only on surviving work can be associated with him o literary evidence, a headless and armless marb statue of Apollo (*c*.330 BC, Agora Mus., Athens but other sculptures have been attributed to hir on the basis of this. His lost works include paintings in the Stoa of Zeus in Athens and bronze group of Philip of Macedon and his so Alexander the Great in their chariots. He is als said to have written treatises on proportion an colour.

Euphronios. Greek vase painter and potte active in Athens *c*.520–*c*.500 BC, one of the ou standing early exponents of the *red-figure styl He signed work as both a painter and a potte His best-known work, which well exemplifies h majestic style, is probably the *krater* (wine bow in the Louvre, Paris, showing Herakles wrestlin with Antaios. His rival was *Euthymides.

Euston Road School. A group of Britis painters centred round the 'School of Drawin and Painting' that opened in a studio at 12 Fit roy Street, London, in 1937, and soon transferre to nearby 316 Euston Road. Its founding teache were William *Coldstream, Victor *Pasmor and Claude *Rogers; Graham *Bell and Law rence *Gowing were also leading members c the circle. These artists advocated a move awa from modernist styles to a more straightforwar naturalism; by encouraging sound skills i representational painting, they hoped to en the isolation of artist from public that avant-garde movements had created. The outbreak of the Second World War in 1939 caused the School to close, but although it was so short-lived, it was influential; the term 'Euston Road' was used for a decade or so afterwards as a generic description for painting done in a style similar to that practised by the founders. Coldstream, through his position as professor at the *Slade School, was the chief upholder of the tradition.

Euthymides. Greek *red-figure vase painter and potter, active in Athens c.520–c.500 BC, the great contemporary of *Euphronios. He signed work as both a painter and a potter. As a painter he was exceptional in his mastery of movement and foreshortening. On an amphora (wine jar) showing revellers (Antikensammlungen, Munich) he inscribed next to a particularly skilfully drawn figure the (probably friendly) boast 'Euphronios never did anything like this'.

Evenepoel, Henri (b Nice, 3 Oct. 1872; d Paris, 27 Dec. 1899). Belgian painter active in France for most of his short career. He settled in Paris in 1892 and became a pupil of Gustave *Moreau, with *Matisse and *Rouault among his fellow students. His early work had been sombre, but his style became much more colourful under the influence of *Impressionism, and after a visit to Algeria in 1897–8 he adopted an even brighter palette. His work included portraits, particularly of family and friends, and scenes of Paris street life. He died of typhoid at the age of 27, at a time when he was showing promise of becoming one of the outstanding Belgian painters of his day.

Everdingen, Allart van (bapt. Alkmaar, 18 June 1621; bur. Amsterdam, 8 Nov. 1675). Dutch landscape and marine painter. He is said to have been a pupil of *Savery in Utrecht and *Molyn in Haarlem. In 1644–5 he visited Scandinavia, where he developed a taste for subjects inspired by the scenery there—above all mountain torrents—and helped to popularize such themes in the Netherlands. *Ruisdael, in his pictures of majestic waterfalls, was one of the artists influenced by him. Allart was also a fine etcher and a prolific draughtsman. His elder brother **Caesar** (b Alkmaar, ?1616/17; bur. Alkmaar, 13 Oct. 1678), who painted portraits and historical pictures, was attracted by the south rather than the north. Although he never went to Italy, he captured the spirit of Italian art better than many of his countrymen who crossed the Alps: witness his beautiful Four Muses with Pegasus (c.1650),

part of the decoration of the royal villa—the Huis ten Bosch—at The Hague (see HUYGENS).

Evergood, Philip (b New York, 26 Oct. 1901; d Bridgewater, Conn., 11 Mar. 1973). American painter. He was educated in England, at Eton and Cambridge (his mother came from a cultured British family), and much of his early life was spent travelling and studying in Europe. His early works were mainly of biblical and imaginative subjects, but after settling in New York in 1931 he became a leading figure among the *Social Realists who used their art as an instrument of social protest and propaganda during the Depression years. He was active in several organizations concerned with the civil rights of artists, and under the banner of the *Federal Art Project he produced militant paintings of social criticism, his best-known work in this genre being American Tragedy (1937, Whitney Mus., New York), which commemorates a police attack on striking steel workers in Chicago. Even his allegorical religious painting The New Lazarus (1954, Whitney Mus.) has sociological overtones, with its figures of starving children. He experimented technically (sometimes, for example, mixing marble dust with his paint to obtain a textured surface) and his work was varied stylistically; at times his inclination for the bizarre and the grotesque brought his work close to *Surrealism, as is seen particularly in his most famous painting, Lily and the Sparrows (1939, Whitney Mus.). Evergood taught at various universities and won numerous awards.

Evesham, Epiphanius (b Herefordshire, ?1570; d ?c.1634). English sculptor; his unusual Christian name suggests he was born on or about the feast of the Epiphany (6 Jan.). He was the first distinctive personality in English sculpture since the Reformation, but details of his career are scanty. From 1601 to c.1614 he worked as a sculptor and painter in Paris (he perhaps moved there for religious reasons, as he was evidently a Catholic), but though he had a studio of some size and several works in both arts are recorded, none has survived. After his return to England he made a number of tombs that stand out for their humanity, freshness of invention, and refinement of handling at a period when most English tomb sculpture was mass produced. His signed tomb of Lord Teynham (c.1622, Lynsted, Kent), for example, has, in addition to the recumbent effigy, a distinguished kneeling figure of the widow and a series of touching *reliefs of mourning children. *Vertue called him 'that most exquisite artist'.

Eworth, Hans (*b* ?*c*.1520; *d* ?London, ?1573). Netherlandish painter active in England. He is first documented in Antwerp in 1540 and had settled in England by 1545. About 30 surviving paintings are credited to him, almost all portraits (there are also a few allegories), dating from 1549 to 1570. He is known also to have painted for pageants and masques. Although he is an obscure figure and his work is uneven, he was the outstanding personality in the history of English painting in the mid-16th century, rivalled only by Gerlach *Flicke. He painted Queen Mary and Queen Elizabeth I, but his masterpiece is perhaps the striking allegorical portrait of Sir John Luttrell (1550, Courtauld Gal., London).

Execias. Greek vase painter and potter, active in Athens in the second half of the 6th century BC, the most famous exponent of the *black-figure technique. His work is distinguished by grandeur of composition, precision of draughtsmanship, and a remarkable subtlety of characterization (he was capable of conveying a sense of pathos or psychological tension in spite of the inherent limitations of the black-figure technique). John Boardman (*Athenian Black Figure Vases*, 1974) writes that 'the hallmark of his style is a near statuesque dignity which brings vase painting for the first time close to claiming a place as a major art' and that his figures make those of earlier artists look like 'at best, elegant puppets'. Many of his subjects were taken from the Trojan War, as with his best-known work, an amphora (wine jar) showing Achilles and Ajax gaming (Vatican Mus.), which he signed as both potter and painter: 'Execias made and decorated me.'

Exhibition, Great. See GREAT EXHIBITION.

Expressionism. A term employed in the history and criticism of the arts to denote the use of distortion and exaggeration for emotional effect. The term is used in several different ways and can be applied to various art forms. In the pictorial arts, it can be used in its broadest sense to describe art of any period or place that raises acute subjective feeling above objective observation, reflecting the state of mind of the artist rather than images that conform to what we see in the external world. The paintings of *Grünewald and El *Greco, which convey intense religious emotion through distorted forms, are outstanding examples of expressionism in this sense (when used in this way the word is usually spelled with a small 'e'). More commonly, the term is applied to a trend in modern European art in which strong, non-naturalistic colours and distorted or abbreviated forms were used to project inner feelings. More specifically, the term is used for one aspect of that trend—a movement that was the dominant force in German art from about 1905 until about 1930. (In the German-speaking countries Expressionism also had a powerful effect on other arts in this period, notably drama, poetry, and the cinema, which often show a common concern with the eruption of irrational forces from beneath the surface of the modern world. Some music, too, is described as Expressionist because of its emotional turbulence and lack of conventional logic, and there are also a few remarkable Expressionist buildings, although the most startling architectural designs remained on paper.)

In the second (broad European) sense described above, Expressionism traces its beginnings to the 1880s, but it did not become a distinct trend until about 1905, and as a description of a movement the term itself is thought to have been first used in print in 1911—in an article in *Der* *Sturm* (it was used more loosely long before this, in English and in German). The most important forerunner of Expressionism was van *Gogh, who consciously exaggerated natural appearances 'to express . . . man's terrible passions'. He was virtually unknown at the time of his death, but his reputation grew rapidly after that and his work made a major impact at a number of exhibitions in the early years of the 20th century. Van Gogh's friend *Gauguin was also important for the development of Expressionism. He simplified and flattened forms, and used colour in a way that gave up all semblance of realism. As a counterpart to his stylistic innovations, he sought freshness of subject matter and found it first in the peasant communities of Brittany and later in the islands of the South Pacific. In turning away from European urban civilization, Gauguin discovered folk art and *primitive art, both of which later became of absorbing interest to the Expressionists.

A third fundamental influence on Expressionism (especially in Germany, where he spent much of his career) was the Norwegian Edvard *Munch, who knew the work of van Gogh and Gauguin well. From the mid-1880s he began to use violent colour and linear distortions to express the most elemental emotions of fear, love, and hatred. In his search to give pictorial form to the innermost thoughts that haunted him he came to appreciate the abrasive expressive potential of the woodcut—its revival as an independent art form (in which Gauguin also played a prominent role) was a distinctive feature of Expressionism; many of the leading German artists of the movement did outstanding work in the medium. Another artist whose formative influence on Expressionism was spread partly through the medium of prints (in this case etchings) was the Belgian James *Ensor, who depicted the baseness of human nature by the use of grotesque and horrifying carnival masks.

The first Expressionist groups appeared almost simultaneously in 1905 in France (the *Fauves) and Germany (Die *Brücke). *Matisse, the leader of the Fauves, summed up their aims when he wrote in 1908: 'What I am after above all is expression . . . The chief aim of colour should be to serve expression as well as possible . . . The expressive aspect of colours imposes itself on me in a purely instinctive way. To paint an autumn landscape I will not try to remember what colours suit this season; I will be inspired only by the sensation that the season arouses in me.' Even at their most violent, however, the Fauves always retained harmony of design and a certain decorativeness of colour, but in Germany restraint was thrown to the winds. Forms and colours were tortured to assert a sense of revolt against the established order. Kirchner, the dominant figure of Die Brücke, wrote in 1913: 'We accept all the colours that, directly or indirectly, reproduce the pure creative impulse.'

The high point of German Expressionism came with the *Blaue Reiter group, formed in Munich in 1911 with *Kandinsky and *Marc as leaders. These two and other members tried to express spiritual feelings in art and their work was generally more mystical in outlook than that of the Brücke painters. The Blaue Reiter was dispersed by the First World War (during which Marc and another key member, August *Macke, were killed), but after the war Expressionism became widespread in Germany. Even artists such as Otto *Dix and George *Grosz, who sought a new and hard realism (see NEUE SACHLICHKEIT), kept a good deal of Expressionist distortion and exaggeration in their work. However, Expressionism was suppressed by the Nazis when they came to power in 1933, along with all other art they considered *degenerate. It revived after the Second World War, and Germany has been one of the main homes of its descendant *Neo-Expressionism.

In its broadest sense, the influence of Expressionism can be seen in the work of artists of many different persuasions—*Chagall and *Soutine for example—and in movements such as *Abstract Expressionism.

Exter, Alexandra (*b* Bielostok, Kiev region, Ukraine, 6 [18] Jan. 1882; *d* Fontenay-aux-Roses, Paris, 17 Mar. 1949). Russian painter and designer. In 1908 she went to Paris for the first time and from then until the outbreak of the First World War she made regular visits, forming a link between the Western avant-garde and that in Russia (she knew *Apollinaire, *Braque, and *Picasso, among other luminaries). Her early paintings were influenced by various modernist styles, including *Cubism and *Futurism, and by 1917 she had arrived at complete abstraction, using interpenetrating, semi-geometrical slabs of colour in a manner that is something like a cross between *Delaunay's *Orphism and *Malevich's *Suprematism. From 1917 to 1921 she taught at her own studios, first in Odessa (1917–18) and then in Kiev (1918–21). Her pupils, who included Pavel *Tchelitchew, helped her to create huge abstract designs for agit-steamers (propaganda boats) and agit-trains, which the new Soviet government used to celebrate the Russian Revolution and spread knowledge of it. Her most impressive and original work, however, was as a stage designer, particularly for Alexander Tairov's Kamerny (Chamber) Theatre in Moscow between 1916 and 1921. In powerful *Constructivist sets she explored the architectural potential of the stage, avoiding both traditional decorative illusionism and flat stylization. In 1924 she settled in Paris, and she lived in France for the rest of her life. In her later career she was mainly active as a theatre, ballet, and fashion designer. A good collection of her drawings for stage designs is in the Victoria and Albert Museum, London.

ex-voto (Latin: 'from a vow'). A painting or other work of art made as an offering to God or a saint in gratitude for a personal favour or blessing or in the hope of receiving some miraculous benefit. There is a famous example by Philippe de *Champaigne.

Eyck, Jan van (*b* ?Maaseik, *c.*1390; *d* Bruges, June 1441). The most celebrated painter of the Early Netherlandish School. Within a few years of his death he had a reputation on both sides of the Alps as a painter of great stature and importance, and although he is no longer credited with being the 'inventor' of *oil painting, as was long maintained, his fame has continued undimmed to the present day. Nothing is known for certain of his early life and he is first recorded in 1422, working in The Hague at the court of John of Bavaria, Count of Holland. In 1425 John died and later in the same year Jan entered the service of

Philip the Good, Duke of *Burgundy, in Bruges, moving soon afterwards to Lille. Jan remained in Philip's employment for the rest of his life, serving him as 'varlet de chambre' (equerry) as well as painter. Philip evidently held him in personal affection as well as high professional regard (he was godfather to one of his children), and when his accountants once questioned the high payments made to Jan they were told that they must be made 'without further argument, delay, alteration, variation, or difficulty whatever', for the duke 'would never find a man equally to his liking nor so outstanding in his art and science'. On several occasions Jan was sent on diplomatic missions, most notably to Portugal in 1428–9 as part of an embassy that arranged a marriage between Philip and a Portuguese princess. After his return from Portugal, he seems to have settled permanently in Bruges, where he bought a house in 1432.

It is only from this point that Jan's career as an artist comes into focus, for all his dated paintings belong to the period 1432–9 and only a few that are earlier in style have been plausibly attributed to him, including some controversial miniatures in the *Turin Hours (according to a 16th-century source he trained as an illuminator). The central problem of his career—and one of the most discussed in the history of art—concerns the work that has always been the basis of his resounding fame, the great altarpiece of the *Adoration of the Lamb* (completed 1432) in Ghent Cathedral. An inscription on the frame states that it was begun by 'the painter Hubert van Eyck, than whom none was greater', and completed by 'Jan, second in art'. Jan's brother **Hubert** is such an obscure figure that some scholars have questioned the authenticity of the inscription and doubted his existence. There is certainly no obvious division between the work of two hands in the altarpiece, but the prevailing opinion now is that the inscription is essentially genuine, although debate continues as to how far work had progressed at Hubert's death (a now destroyed gravestone in Ghent is said to have given his date of death as 18 September 1426). Thus, Jan's contribution to the central masterpiece of Early Netherlandish painting is uncertain.

*Dürer called the Ghent Altarpiece 'a stupendous painting' and the comment is appropriate both to the majesty and *iconographical richness of the huge *polyptych, and also to its breathtaking technical mastery. It consists of twelve panels, eight of which are painted on both sides (they are hinged so they can fold over the central section),

making twenty images in all; the central scene depicts throngs of people and adoring angels grouped around the Lamb of God, which spills its blood into a chalice, symbolizing Christ's sacrifice on the cross. The panels are overwhelming in their beauty and brilliance of colour and remarkably wide-ranging in the things they represent: vivid portraits of the *donors (Joos Vyd, a wealthy citizen of Ghent, and his wife Elisabeth), realistic full-length nudes (of Adam and Eve), landscapes, townscapes, interior views, sumptuous costumes, and manifold still-life details. Collectively the altarpiece is almost like a manifesto of everything that oil painting could achieve in naturalistic effects.

Apart from the Ghent Altarpiece, about two dozen other paintings are reasonably attributed to Jan. They are all either religious works or portraits, although he is known to have painted pictures of other subjects (including a nude woman at her bath), which are now lost. Outstanding among the surviving works are the famous double portrait *Giovanni Arnolfini and his Wife* (1434, NG, London) and two paintings of the Virgin and Child with donors—the *Madonna of Chancellor Rolin* (c.1435, Louvre, Paris) and the *Madonna of Canon van der Paele* (1436, Groeningemuseum, Bruges). The Louvre painting, with large figures in the foreground set against a distant panoramic landscape, shows Jan's all-embracing vision of the natural world and his mastery of light and space, as well as detail and texture—in Erwin *Panofsky's words, 'his eye operates as a microscope and as a telescope at the same time'. The 'Man in a Red Turban' (1433, NG, London) is generally considered to be a self-portrait. All Jan's single portraits are fairly similar in format, showing the sitter bust-length in three-quarter view against a plain background. They are more objective than those of his great contemporary Rogier van der *Weyden, with the features subjected to relentlessly close scrutiny, but they nevertheless convey a sense of inner life.

Jan stands with the *Master of Flémalle as the founder of the Early Netherlandish School and his technique became the accepted model for his successors. His closest follower and chief successor in Bruges was Petrus *Christus, but his influence was wide (it is seen, for example, in the work of Luis *Dalmau in Spain) and profound. In the Netherlands itself, however, the more emotional style of Rogier van der Weyden came to have even more influence and the very perfection of Jan's work must have made him the most daunting of models.

F

Fabre, François-Xavier (*b* Montpellier, 1 Apr. 1766; *d* Montpellier, 16 Mar. 1837). French painter and collector, active in Italy for most of his career. A pupil of J.-L. *David, he won the *Prix de Rome in 1787 and lived in Italy (mainly Florence) until 1826. He initially made his name as a history painter, then became a successful fashionable portraitist, but he is now perhaps most highly regarded for his landscapes, which are among the most impressive of the age of *Neoclassicism (*A View of Florence from the North Bank of the Arno*, 1813, NG, Edinburgh). Fabre was also a major collector, particularly of 16th- and 17th-century Italian art and of the work of his French contemporaries. On his return to France he presented his collection to his native city of Montpellier to found the Musée Fabre, opened in 1828.

Fabritius, Carel (*bapt.* Midden-Beemster, nr. Hoorn, 27 Feb. 1622; *d* Delft, 12 Oct. 1654). Dutch painter. He was *Rembrandt's most gifted pupil and a painter of outstanding originality and distinction, but he died tragically young when the Delft gunpowder magazine exploded, devastating the town, and only a tiny body of his work survives (much may have perished in the disaster). In his youth he worked as a carpenter and it was once thought that he derived his name from this profession (*faber* is Latin for 'craftsman'), but it is now known that his father, an amateur painter, had used it. Fabritius was probably in Rembrandt's studio in the early 1640s and he settled in Delft in about 1650. Although only about a dozen paintings by him are known, they show great variety. His earliest works (*Raising of Lazarus*, c.1645, Nat. Mus., Warsaw) are strongly influenced by Rembrandt, but he broke free from his master's manner and developed a personal style marked by an exquisite feeling for cool colour harmonies and (even though he often worked on a small scale) unerring handling of a loaded brush (*The Goldfinch*, 1654, Mauritshuis, The Hague). These qualities, together with an interest in perspective, occur in the work of *Vermeer, the greatest of Delft

painters, and Fabritius certainly influenced him, although it is not likely (as is sometimes maintained) that he was his master, this distinction perhaps belonging to *Bramer. Carel's brother **Barent** (*bapt.* Midden-Beemster, 16 Nov. 1624; *bur.* Amsterdam, 20 Oct. 1673) was also a painter, but of much lesser quality. He also may have studied with Rembrandt; his output consisted mainly of portraits and religious works.

Faithorne, William (*b* London, ?c.1616; *bur.* London, 13 May 1691). English engraver. He fought as a Royalist in the Civil War and later spent some time in exile in France, where he worked with *Nanteuil. In about 1650 he returned to London and he became the most distinguished of English 17th-century engravers, especially of portraits. He reproduced the work of painters (van *Dyck, *Dobson, *Lely) as well as making engravings of his own drawings from the life, many published as frontispieces to books. He also drew sensitive portrait heads as independent works (*John Aubrey*, 1666, Ashmolean Mus., Oxford). In 1662 he published a translation of *Bosse's *Traité des manières de graver* as *The Art of Graving and Etching*—the first manual on the subject in English. His son **William** (1656–1710) was also an engraver.

Faiyum (or **Faiyumic** or **Fayyumic**) **portraits.** Romano-Egyptian funerary portraits of a type that have been found in various parts of Egypt but particularly in the Faiyum (El Faiyûm) area, about 80 km (50 miles) south of Cairo. They date from about the 1st to the 4th century AD and represent the head and shoulders of the deceased. The portraits are painted life-size in *encaustic or *tempera on wood or canvas and they were enclosed in the wrapping around the corpse's face. Several hundred examples survive (in the British Museum, London, the Louvre, Paris, and other collections). The quality varies considerably, but the finest are among the most vivid and naturalistic portraits from the ancient world, suggesting that they were done while the sitter was still alive.

Falcone, Aniello (*b* Naples, 15 Nov. 1607; *d* Naples, ?July 1656). Neapolitan painter, one of the leading artists in Naples in the generation before the plague of 1656 (in which he died). He painted numerous religious subjects, including frescos for Neapolitan churches, but he is now remembered mainly as the first specialist in battle pieces, a genre that won him an international reputation and in which he inspired his pupil Salvator *Rosa. His pictures generally show war as a confused struggle between anonymous soldiers, creating a type that the Austrian-born British art historian Fritz Saxl (1890–1948) described as 'the battle scene without a hero'. Falcone was also an outstanding draughtsman.

Falconet, Étienne-Maurice (*b* Paris, 1 Dec. 1716; *d* Paris, 24 Jan. 1791). French sculptor and writer on art, a pupil of J. B. *Lemoyne. Falconet was perhaps the most quintessentially *Rococo of all French sculptors, his forte being gently erotic figures such as the celebrated marble *Bather* (1757, Louvre, Paris). Like many other of his works, this was reproduced in porcelain by the Sèvres factory, where he was director of the sculpture studios from 1757 to 1766, a position that he gained through the influence of his patron Mme de Pompadour, mistress of Louis XV. Falconet had other sides to his talent, however, and his masterpiece—the equestrian statue of Peter the Great in St Petersburg—is in a completely different vein. He moved to Russia in 1766, recommended to the Empress Catherine the Great by *Diderot, and stayed for twelve years; the statue was unveiled in 1782, four years after his return to France. The huge horse is represented with its forelegs raised and unsupported—a daring technical feat—and the heroic vigour of the statue gives it a place among the greatest examples of the type.

Falconet suffered a stroke in 1783 and thereafter produced no more sculpture, devoting himself to the revision of his writings, a six-volume edition of which had appeared in 1781. His best-known literary work is 'Réflexions sur la sculpture' (1760), originally written for Diderot's *Encyclopédie*. In this Falconet was one of the first to argue that the modern artists were superior to those of the ancient world (he was a man of humble origins and fierce independence of thought, and it is significant that unlike most of his distinguished contemporaries he never saw the need to visit Italy).

Fancelli, Domenico (*b* Settignano, *c*.1469; *d* Saragossa, 21 Apr. 1519). Florentine sculptor whose major works were made for Spain and played an important role in introducing the *Renaissance style to that country. These works—all tombs—were made in Italy, but Fancelli visited Spain to install them. They include the tomb of Cardinal Hurtado de Mendoza, Archbishop of Seville (1509, Seville Cathedral), that of Prince John, son of Ferdinand and Isabella (1512–13, convent of St Thomas, Ávila), and that of Ferdinand and Isabella (1514–17, Chapel Royal, Granada).

fancy picture. A term applied in 18th-century Britain to certain types of sentimental *genre pictures. The term is difficult to define with precision, but it refers to pictures that have a rather charmingly contrived air, showing figures—particularly children—playing out various roles. *Gainsborough's fancy pictures usually have contemporary pastoral settings, depicting idealized peasants who behave rather more as if they are in the studio than the countryside, although recently they have been interpreted as 'harrowing' portrayals of rural poverty. *Reynolds, in contrast, favoured classical or allegorical themes, with titles such as *Hope Nursing Love* and *Venus Chiding Cupid*; he often used beggar children from the streets as models for these pictures, fitting in the work in gaps between portrait sessions. His pupil *Northcote wrote that he used to 'fill his painting room' with such children and 'When any of the great people came, Sir Joshua used to flounce them into another room until he wanted them again.'

Fantastic Realism (Phantastischer Realismus). A style of painting that developed in Vienna in the late 1940s. Its exponents, of whom the best known is Ernst Fuchs (1930–), were mainly pupils of Albert Paris Gütersloh (1887–1973), who was a renowned teacher at the Vienna Academy. They shared an interest in the art of the past, notably that of Pieter *Bruegel (supremely well represented in the Kunsthistorisches Museum in Vienna), and their paintings were often literary and anecdotal in character, depicting a fairy-tale world of fantasy and imagination with minute detail.

Fantin-Latour, Henri (*b* Grenoble, 14 Jan. 1836; *d* Buré, Orne, 25 Aug. 1904). French painter and lithographer. He is best known for his luxurious flower pieces, but he produced many other kinds of work, including several group portraits that are important historical documents and show his friendship with leading avant-garde artists and writers. *Homage to Delacroix* (1864, Mus. d'Orsay, Paris) shows Fantin-Latour himself, with *Baudelaire, *Manet, *Whistler, and others grouped round a portrait of *Delacroix; and *A Studio at Batignolles* (sometimes called *Homage to Manet*) (1870, Mus. d'Orsay) shows *Monet, *Renoir, and others in Manet's studio. In spite of his associations with such progressive artists, Fantin-Latour was essentially a traditionalist, and his portraits particularly are in a precise, detailed style. Much of his later career was devoted to lithography; he greatly admired Richard Wagner and did imaginative lithographs illustrating his music and that of other Romantic composers. His wife **Victoria Fantin-Latour** (née Dubourg) (1840–1926) was also a painter, mainly of flower pieces.

Farington, Joseph (*b* Leigh, Lancashire, 21 Nov. 1747; *d* Didsbury [now in Greater Manchester], 30 Dec. 1821). English landscape painter and topographical draughtsman, best known today for his copious diary (1793–1821), which contains valuable information about the London art world of the time. Most of the original manuscript is in the Royal Library at Windsor Castle. The full text was published in sixteen volumes in 1978–84 (an index volume was added in 1998); previous editions had been heavily abridged.

Farnese. Italian family of humanists and patrons of the arts which rose to importance with the creation of **Alessandro Farnese** (1468–1549) as a cardinal in 1493. In 1534 he became Pope Paul III and in this role he was the most important patron of *Michelangelo's later years, commissioning from him the *Last Judgement* in the Sistine Chapel and the *Conversion of St Paul* and the *Crucifixion of St Peter* in his private chapel in the Vatican (the Cappella Paolina), and also appointing him architect to St Peter's. Michelangelo also had a hand in the design of the Palazzo Farnese, the finest palace built in Rome in the 16th century. Among the other artists Paul patronized was *Titian, who visited Rome at his invitation in 1545–6.

Paul's 'nephew' (actually his grandson—the Italian word 'nipote' is conveniently ambiguous), another **Alessandro** (1520–89), was made a cardinal in 1534 at the age of 14 and held many lucrative church appointments. Much of his enormous wealth was spent on artistic projects, and he ranks among the greatest patrons of the 16th century. He built up the largest collection of antiquities in Rome (now mainly in the Archaeological Museum in Naples; see FARNESE BULL and FARNESE HERCULES), encouraged *Vasari to write his *Lives*, engaged Giacoma da Vignola to complete the Palazzo Farnese at Caprarola, and

commissioned some of the most important *Mannerist frescos. He gave special support to the Jesuits and built for them the church of Il Gesù, Rome (designed by Vignola, begun 1568), one of the most influential buildings in the history of architecture. Alessandro's great-nephew Cardinal **Odoardo** (1573–1626), great-great-grandson of Paul III, commissioned Annibale *Carracci to decorate the gallery in the family palace in Rome.

By this time, however, the family was declining as a power in Rome, and the most important centre of its activities had passed to Parma, where Paul III had installed his son Pier Luigi as duke in 1545. The Farnese continued to rule there until 1731, when the line became extinct. Among the notable patrons of this branch of the family was the 4th duke, **Ranuccio I** (1569–1627; reigned from 1592). The artists he employed included Agostino Carracci, Francesco *Mochi, and Bartolomeo *Schedoni.

The family collections eventually passed to Elizabeth Farnese, who married Philip V of Spain in 1715, and then to her son Charles, who was King of Naples from 1734 to 1759 (as Charles VII) and King of Spain from 1759 until his death in 1788 (as Charles III). It was in this way that the collections moved to Naples, where they remain—in the Archaeological Museum and the Museo di Capodimonte.

Farnese Bull. Ancient marble sculpture group (probably a Roman copy of a Greek original of *c.*150 BC); it was found in the Baths of Caracalla in Rome in 1545, was acquired for the *Farnese collection soon afterwards, and is now in the Archaeological Museum in Naples. The subject, taken from Greek legend, involves the punishment of Dirce, who for her cruelty to Antiope was tied to the horns of a bull by Antiope's sons (Dirce's stepsons) and trampled to death. The figures are life-size, and the group is one of the most spectacular examples of the technical virtuosity 'and dramatic movement typical of *Hellenistic art; Federico *Zuccaro described it as a 'marvellous mountain of marble'.

Farnese Hercules. Gigantic ancient marble statue of Hercules leaning sideways on his club and resting after his labours; it is said to have been discovered in the Baths of Caracalla in Rome in 1546, is first certainly recorded in 1556, in the *Farnese collection, and is now in the Archaeological Museum in Naples. The statue is signed by an Athenian sculptor named Glycon and is a copy of a lost original of the 4th century BC, probably by *Lysippus. From virtually the time of its discovery the figure was much admired and copied; its powerful musculature and realistic surface treatment were particularly influential on *Baroque artists.

Farquharson, Joseph (*b* Edinburgh, 4 May 1846; *d* Finzean, Aberdeenshire, 15 Apr. 1935). Scottish painter who combined his artistic career with the inherited role of laird of Finzean, an estate midway between Aberdeen and Balmoral. He trained in Edinburgh and in Paris under *Carolus-Duran, from whom he gained a feeling for richly handled paint. Unlike his teacher, however, Farquharson was primarily a landscape painter, and he became famous for his snow scenes, which were favourites with the public for many years at the *Royal Academy summer exhibition and were much reproduced in prints. These snowscapes often include sheep, earning him the nickname 'frozen mutton Farquharson'. His reputation soon declined after his death. **David Farquharson** (1840–1907), another Scottish landscape painter, was no relation.

Fattori, Giovanni. See MACCHIAIOLI.

Fautrier, Jean (*b* Paris, 16 May 1898; *d* Châtenay-Malabry, Seine-et-Oise, 21 July 1964). French painter, sculptor, and printmaker. He is best known for the paintings in his *Hostages* series, inspired by his horror at the brutality and suffering of the Second World War. These strange paintings feature layer upon layer of heavy paint creating a central image that is abstract but suggests a decaying human head. The pale powdery colours evoke death, but the delicacy of the handling gives them a mysterious ambivalence. They were first exhibited at the Galerie René Drouin in Paris in 1945 and were much acclaimed. They have been seen as forerunners of *Art Informel, and with the postwar vogue for this kind of expressive abstraction Fautrier gained a reputation as one of the leading painters of the *École de Paris. In 1960 he won the Grand Prix at the Venice *Biennale. His other works included sculpture and prints (notably lithographs illustrating Dante's *Inferno*, 1928), and he developed a novel type of work called 'multiple originals', printing a basic drawing on anything up to 300 canvases and then completing each work by hand. He first exhibited such works in 1950.

Fauvism. Movement in early 20th-century painting based on the use of intensely vivid, non-naturalistic colours; centred on a group of French artists who worked together from about 1905 to 1907, it was the first of the major avant-garde movements in European art in the period of unprecedented experimentation between the turn of the century and the First World War. The dominant figure of the Fauvist group was Henri *Matisse; he used vividly contrasting colours as early as 1899 and came to realize the potential of colour freed from its traditional descriptive role when he painted with *Signac in the bright light of Saint Tropez in the summer of 1904 and with *Derain at Collioure in the summer of 1905. The Fauves first exhibited together at the *Salon d'Automne of 1905 and their name was given to them by the critic Louis Vauxcelles (1870–1943), who pointed to a Renaissance-like sculpture in the middle of the same gallery and exclaimed: '*Donatello au milieu des fauves!' (Donatello among the wild beasts). The remark was printed in the daily newspaper *Gil Blas* on 17 October and the name immediately caught on. Predictably, the Fauvist pictures came in for a good deal of mockery and abuse; the critic Camille Mauclair (1872–1945), for example, wrote that 'A pot of paint has been flung in the face of the public.' However, there were also some sympathetic reviews, and Gertrude and Leo *Stein bought Matisse's *Woman with a Hat* (priv. coll.) the picture that was attracting the worst abuse. This greatly helped to restore Matisse's battered morale and marked the beginning of a dramatic rise in his fortunes.

Among the artists who exhibited with Matisse at the 1905 Salon d'Automne were Derain, *Friesz, *Marquet, *Rouault, *Vlaminck, and the Dutch-born van *Dongen. Later they were joined by *Dufy (1906) and *Braque (1907). All of these were a few years younger than Matisse (mainly in their twenties, whereas he was 35). Lesser figures associated with the group included Jean Puy (1876–1960) and Louis Valtat (1869–1952). These artists were influenced in varying degrees by *Cézanne, van *Gogh, *Gauguin, and the *Neo-Impressionists. Their most characteristic subject was landscape and the outstanding feature of their work was extreme intensity of colour, often used arbitrarily for emotional and decorative effect. Apart from this, they had no programme in common.

As a concerted movement Fauvism reached its peak in the Salon d'Automne of 1905 and the *Salon des Indépendants of 1906, and by 1907 the members of the group were drifting apart. For most of them Fauvism was a temporary phase through which they passed in the development of widely different styles (Valtat was an exception, for he continued to explore the use of pure colour throughout his life), and their work never again displayed such similarity. Although short-lived, however, Fauvism was highly influential, for example on German *Expressionism and the work of the *Scottish Colourists.

Federal Art Project. A project run by the US government from 1935 to 1943 with the dual purpose of helping artists through the Depression years and of deploying the artistic potential of the country in the decoration of public buildings and places. There were also a Federal Writers' Project, a Federal Theater Project, and a Federal Music Project, and collectively they are known as the Federal Arts Projects. They were part of the Works Progress Administration (later called Work Projects Administration, both abbreviated to WPA), a work programme for the unemployed executed as part of President F. D. Roosevelt's New Deal. The Federal Art Project grew out of a previous scheme of a similar nature—the Public Works of Art Project; this was set up to assist artists over the winter of 1933–4 by employing them on public works for a weekly wage. As a sequel, in October 1934 the Section of Painting and Sculpture in the Treasury Department was established to commission murals and sculpture for new public buildings. This was not a relief project, artists being paid only if their designs were accepted, but the following year the Federal Art Project was set up with the primary aim of helping the unemployed. There was also a smaller Treasury Relief Art Project (TRAP), set up in 1935 to commission art for existing public buildings; this was essentially a relief project, although it also employed some established artists. These schemes are sometimes known collectively as the Federal Art Projects. Thus it is possible to distinguish between the Federal Art Project (the main scheme), the Federal Art Projects (the main scheme plus the various other ones), and the Federal Arts Projects (the WPA schemes for the visual arts, music, theatre, and writing collectively). Not surprisingly, the terms are very often confused.

The Federal Art Project was directed by Holger Cahill (1887–1960), a museum administrator and expert on American folk art. It employed people on a monthly salary and at its peak there were more than 5,000 on the payroll. They not only decorated public buildings, but also produced prints, posters, and various works of craft, and they set up community art centres and galleries in parts of the country where art was virtually unknown. The Project also involved an Index of American Design, a gigantic documentation of the decorative arts in America. Almost all the major American artists of the period were involved in the Project, either as teachers or practitioners (Barnett *Newman is one of the rare exceptions). A huge amount of work was produced, but most of it was unremarkable in quality.

Fedotov, Pavel (*b* Moscow, 22 June [4 July] 1815; *d* St Petersburg, 14 [26] Nov. 1852). Russian painter. He was an army officer until 1844, when he resigned his commission to concentrate on art, in which he was mainly self-taught (although he attended classes at the St Petersburg Academy). In his brief professional career he became one of the most popular Russian painters of the day with amusingly satirical pictures mocking the vanities and pretensions of middle-class society. His most famous painting is *The Major's Courtship* (1848, Tretyakov Gal., Moscow; later version in Russian Mus., St Petersburg), showing a middle-aged army officer, aristocratic but penniless, calling at the house of a rich merchant to seek marriage with his daughter. The main influences on Fedotov's work were 17th-century Dutch and Flemish *genre paintings and the engravings of *Hogarth (he has even been called 'the Russian Hogarth', but the English artist's work is much more biting in its moralistic purpose). Fedotov also painted portraits. In his last years his work expressed disenchantment with life, and he died in a lunatic asylum aged only 37.

Feininger, Lyonel (*b* New York, 17 July 1871; *d* New York, 13 Jan. 1956). American painter who spent most of his career in Europe. He was born into a German-American musical family; in 1887 he moved to Germany with the intention of studying music, but he turned instead to art. He had drawings published in Berlin's humorous weeklies and by the turn of the century he was Germany's leading political cartoonist. In 1906–8 he lived in Paris and under the influence of Robert *Delaunay turned seriously to painting. By 1912 he had evolved a personal style (influenced by *Cubism but highly distinctive) in which natural forms were treated in terms of a rhythmic pattern of prismatically coloured interpenetrating planes bounded by straight lines—a manner that he applied particularly to architectural and marine subjects. Although—as an American citizen—he was an alien, he remained in Germany throughout the First World War and afterwards taught at the *Bauhaus from its foundation in 1919 (one of his woodcuts appeared on the cover of its manifesto) until its closure by the Nazis in 1933; he was the only person to be on the staff from start to finish, although he did little teaching in its later years. In 1935 he visited the USA and in 1937 (the year in which the Nazis declared his work *degenerate) he returned there permanently. He settled in New York and adopted the architecture of Manhattan as one of his favourite subjects, working with vigour into his eighties. His son Andreas Feininger (1906–99) was a distinguished photographer and writer on photography. See also BLAUE VIER.

Feke, Robert (b ?Oyster Bay, Long Island, NY, c.1705; d ?Barbados, ?1752). American Colonial portrait painter. Little is known of his life until 1741, when he executed a large portrait group in Boston, *Isaac Royall and his Family* (Harvard Univ.). Later he worked in Philadelphia, and he is last securely documented in 1751. There are about a dozen signed portraits from his hand and about 50 more are reasonably attributed to him. His works are somewhat lacking in characterization, but their strength and clarity of design and delicacy of touch give them a high place among Colonial portraits.

Félibien, André (b Chartres, May 1619; d Paris, 11 May 1695). French administrator and writer on art. He is remembered chiefly for his *Entretiens sur les vies et sur les ouvrages des plus excellens peintres anciens et modernes*, first published in 1666–88, often reprinted, and translated into several languages. This massive compilation is a history of European art from antiquity to his own days. It contains the fullest contemporary biography of *Poussin (who became a friend of Félibien when he was secretary to the French ambassador in Rome, 1647–9). His other writings include a textbook on artists' techniques with a dictionary of art terms: *Des principes de l'architecture, de la sculpture, de la peinture, et des autres arts qui en dépendent, avec un dictionnaire des termes propres à chacun de ces arts* (1676).

Felixmüller, Conrad. See NEUE SACHLICHKEIT.

Feminist art. A term applied to art that deals with issues specifically relating to women's identity and experience. As a movement it originated in the late 1960s, in parallel with the militant Women's Liberation Movement. It is not associated with any particular style or medium, but rather is concerned with a range of endeavour aimed at giving women a just place in the world and specifically in the art world, which feminist artists regard as heavily biased in favour of men. Much of this endeavour has been collective—for example in the organization of exhibitions (de-

voted to reviving the reputations of women artists of the past as well as promoting the work of women artists of the present), in the setting up of courses dealing with women's art, and in the publishing of periodicals, several of which have appeared since the early 1970s. Some feminist art has been fairly traditional in presentation—for example the paintings of Sylvia Sleigh (1916–) (see ALLOWAY), in which longstanding stereotypes of the nude are reversed by presenting males as a subject for female erotic delectation. However, much feminist art uses more avant-garde types of expression; indeed, as many feminist artists feel that traditional forms are tainted by patriarchy, they tend to be interested in newer forms, such as *Performance art and *Video art.

The imagery of feminist art often focuses on sexuality, both in celebrating female eroticism and in attacking male sexual violence, and another common theme is matriarchy. Some feminist art, however, is more concerned with technique than imagery. Indeed, an important aspect of the movement has been the desire to revive interest in art forms such as quiltmaking that employ skills traditionally regarded as female and which have generally been given a low status compared with the *fine arts. This return to craft skills is emphasized in what is probably the most famous 'icon' of feminist art, *The Dinner Party* (1974–9, Through the Flower Corporation) by the American Judy Chicago (1939–); more than a hundred women (and also some men) worked on the elaborate china painting and needlework it involved. It takes the form of an open triangular banquet table, with 39 place settings, each representing a significant woman in Western civilization. *The Dinner Party* has been seen by large audiences at several venues in the USA and elsewhere (its first showing was at the San Francisco Museum of Modern Art in 1979, when it attracted 100,000 visitors in three months).

Fénéon, Félix. See NEO-IMPRESSIONISM.

Fergusson, J. D. (John Duncan) (b Leith, 9 Mar. 1874; d Glasgow, 30 Jan. 1961). Scottish painter (mainly of landscapes and figure subjects) and occasional sculptor, the best known of the *Scottish Colourists. From about 1895 he made regular visits to Paris and he lived there 1907–14. His early work was *Whistlerian and he then came under the influence of *Manet, but by 1907 he had adopted the bold palette of *Fauvism and became the most uncompromising adherent to the style among British artists (*Blue Beads*, 1910,

Tate, London). In 1914 the war brought him back to Britain; he lived in London, 1914–29, in Paris, 1929–40, and finally in Glasgow, 1940–61. Soon after his arrival in Glasgow he founded the New Art Club to provide better exhibiting facilities for the city's progressive artists, and out of it grew the New Scottish Group (1942), of which Fergusson was first president. At this time he was also editor of the periodical *Scottish Art and Letters*, and he wrote a book entitled *Modern Scottish Painting* (1943).

Fernández, Alejo (b ?Germany, c.1475; d Seville, 1545). Spanish painter, probably of German origin, as he is referred to as 'Maestro Alexos—pintor Alemán'. He married the daughter of a painter called Pedro Fernández at Córdoba and took her name, but he worked mainly in Seville, where he was the leading painter of the first third of the 16th century. His work, which is well represented in Seville Cathedral, was essentially Flemish *Mannerist in style, but it has a personal lyrical quality. One of his finest paintings is the *Virgin of the Navigators* (c.1530–40, Alcázar, Seville), a rare example of a picture reflecting the Spanish conquest of the Americas.

Fernández (or **Hernández**), **Gregorio** (b Sarria, Galicia, c.1576; d Valladolid, 22 Jan. 1636). Spanish sculptor, active for all his known career in Valladolid, where he is first recorded in 1605. He was one of the great masters of the *polychrome wooden statue, continuing the expressive tradition of *Juan de Juni but in a more realistic manner (he abandoned the earlier practice of lavish use of gold in favour of naturalistic colouring). Among the numerous altarpieces from his workshop are those of S. Miguel, Valladolid (1606), and Plasencia Cathedral (1624–34). He is well represented in the Museo Nacional de Escultura, Valladolid.

Ferrari, Gaudenzio (b Valduggia, nr. Varallo, c.1470/80; d Milan, 3 Jan. 1546). Italian painter and sculptor, active over a wide area of Lombardy and his native Piedmont. His early paintings were strongly influenced by *Leonardo and his Milanese followers, and throughout his life he remained *eclectic, absorbing into his highly charged, emotional style elements from *Pordenone and *Lotto and also, for example, from the engravings of *Dürer. He was prolific and an artist of considerable power and individuality, but his work has remained comparatively little known because much of it is in fairly remote locations. His most remarkable works are the *Stations of the Cross* (c.1520–6) in a series of chapels at the sanctuary of Sacro Monte, Varallo; here he combined highly realistic life-size sculptures in painted terracotta with a frescoed background.

Ferri, Ciro. See CORTONA.

Ferrucci, Francesco. See PORPHYRY.

fête champêtre (French: 'outdoor feast'). Type of painting in which figures are shown in an idealized outdoor setting, usually eating, dancing, flirting, or listening to music, and typically evoking a mood of reverie. Since the Gardens of Love represented in medieval manuscripts, the theme has had great popularity in European art, undergoing several transformations. It was particularly favoured in 16th-century Venetian painting and the *Concert champêtre* in the Louvre (traditionally by *Giorgione, but now usually given to *Titian) is the most celebrated of all examples of the type. The term 'fête galante' (courtship party) was invented by the Académie Royale in Paris in 1717 to describe *Watteau's variants on the theme, in which figures in ball dress or masquerade costume disport themselves amorously in a parkland setting.

Feti (or **Fetti**), **Domenico** (b ?Rome, c.1589; d Venice, 16 Apr. 1623). Italian painter. He studied in Rome under Ludovico *Cigoli, was court painter to Vincenzo *Gonzaga in Mantua from 1613 to 1622, and then moved to Venice. His most characteristic works are of religious themes turned into scenes of everyday contemporary life. Though small in scale, they are broadly painted, with characteristic 'windswept' brushstrokes. Their great popularity is shown by the fact that they often exist in numerous very similar versions (*The Parable of the Labourers in the Vineyard*, c.1622, versions in Gemäldegalerie, Dresden, NG, Dublin, and elsewhere). Feti, who was also an excellent portraitist, was one of a group of non-Venetian artists (including the German *Liss and the Genoan *Strozzi) who revivified painting in the city when there was a scarcity of native talent. Consequently, he is often classed as a member of the Venetian School, even though he spent only a few months there (from September 1622 until his death in April 1623).

Feuchtmayer, Joseph Anton (b Linz, 3 June 1696; d Mimmenhausen, 2 Jan. 1770). German *Rococo sculptor and *stuccoist, the most famous member of a family of artists from Wessobrunn in Bavaria. He and his workshop produced a large amount of decorative work for buildings in the Lake Constance area (mainly churches, although he also had secular commissions). The greatest ensemble of his work is in the pilgrimage church of Neu-Birnau (1746–53): it includes his most famous single figure, the *Honey-licking Putto*.

Feuerbach, Anselm (*b* Speyer, 12 Sept. 1829; *d* Venice, 4 Jan. 1880). German painter. He studied in Düsseldorf, Antwerp, and Paris (with *Couture), then lived in Italy from 1855 to 1873. His father was a professor of classical archaeology (he had written a book on the *Apollo Belvedere*) and Feuerbach grew up in an atmosphere saturated with the high-minded ideals of humanistic philosophy. He wished to become the founder of a new school that was to combine noble, didactic, and idealist subjects with a style derived from the most grandiose 16th-century Venetian painting. His subjects are usually taken from Greek antiquity (*Plato's Symposium*, 1869, Kunsthalle, Karlsruhe). Feuerbach's fervent desire to preach a philosophy through pictorial means was usually a source of weakness rather than strength, and his best works are now generally considered to be his portraits of his model and mistress Nanna Risi, which have a statuesque beauty lacking in his more elaborate paintings; she also posed for subject pictures such as *Iphigenia* (1862, Hessisches Landesmuseum, Darmstadt). Feuerbach moved to Vienna in 1873 to become professor of history painting at the Academy, but he returned to Italy in 1876 following criticism of his work. Throughout his life he complained that he was being misunderstood and not receiving the recognition due to a very great artist. It is this element of self-pity that makes his book *Ein Vermächtnis* (A Testament) one of the most pathetic and repellent autobiographies ever written. It was posthumously published in 1882.

Fiammingo (Italian: 'Fleming'). The name given to, or adopted by, a number of Flemish artists working in Italy, especially in the 17th century, when there was a sizeable Flemish colony in Rome. Among the important artists who were so known were Denys *Calvaert, who founded an *academy in Bologna, and the sculptor François *Duquesnoy, who frequently signed himself 'Fiammingo'.

Fielding, Copley (Anthony Vandyck Copley Fielding) (*b* Sowerby Bridge, nr. Halifax, 22 Nov. 1787; *d* Worthing, Sussex, 3 Mar. 1855). English watercolour painter, the best-known member of a family of artists. He was a pupil of *Varley, whose sister-in-law he married in 1813. Early in his career he specialized in scenes of Wales and the Lake District, but from 1817 he spent much of his time on the south coast because of his wife's health, and turned increasingly to seascapes. He was enormously prolific and much of his later work is repetitive.

Field Painting. A type of painting developed in the USA from about 1950 in which the picture is no longer regarded as a structure of interrelated elements but as a single indivisible expanse. Field Painting has affinities with *Systemic art and with the *all-over style associated with Jackson *Pollock. The term *Colour Field Painting has been used when emphasis is placed on brilliance and saturation of colour. Rather than being a specific style, it may be regarded as an aspect of a very general tendency during the 1950s and 1960s to eschew traditional composition in favour of a single 'total' theme.

Figari, Pedro (*b* Montevideo, 29 June 1861; *d* Montevideo, 24 July 1938). Uruguayan painter. He had a versatile and distinguished career as a lawyer, politician, writer, and editor, and although he had studied painting in his youth he did not devote himself full-time to art until 1921, when he moved to Buenos Aires. By this time he was already 60, but he rapidly made a name for himself as an artist and his work was widely exhibited in Uruguay, the USA, and Europe. From 1925 to 1933 he lived in Paris, then returned to Montevideo. Edward Lucie-Smith (*Latin American Art of the 20th Century*, 1993) writes: 'Figari's work shows the direct influence of the French *intimistes, that of *Vuillard perhaps even more clearly than that of *Bonnard, spiced with a certain deliberate naïveté. His thematic range, however, is wider than that of either of the French artists. It is also specifically Latin-American, since it includes not only bourgeois interiors but historical and literary scenes, and also Creole and Afro-American subjects.' His work is well represented in the National Museum at Montevideo.

figurative art. Art in which recognizable figures or objects are portrayed. The term 'representational art' is used synonymously; the opposite is non-figurative or *abstract art.

Filarete (Antonio Averlino) (*b* ?Florence, *c*.1400; *d* ?Rome, *c*.1470). Florentine sculptor, architect, and writer on art. His nickname, which he adopted late in life, derives from the Greek for 'lover of virtue' (or better '*virtù'). He probably trained with *Ghiberti and his most important work in sculpture—the bronze doors for St Peter's in Rome (c.1433–45)—are heavily indebted to Ghiberti's doors for the Baptistery in Florence, although much less accomplished (*Vasari called them 'deplorable'); they are one of the few parts of Old St Peter's to survive in the present building. In 1448 Filarete fled Rome under suspicion of stealing holy relics. After stays in Florence and Venice, in 1451 he settled in Milan. There he was active mainly as an architect, his principal work being the Ospedale Maggiore (begun 1457, completed in the 18th century), which helped to introduce the *Renaissance style to Lombardy and created new standards of comfort and sanitation in hospital design. His novel ideas came out also in his *Treatise on Architecture*, written in 1461–4 but not published until 1896. It includes a vision of an ideal city, Sforzinda (named after his patron, Francesco *Sforza), which is the first symmetrical town-planning scheme of modern times. Among his ingenious proposals for his ideal city was a Tower of Virtue and Vice, a ten-storey structure with a brothel on the ground floor and an astronomical observatory at the top. Vasari described the treatise as 'perhaps the most stupid book ever written'.

Fildes, Sir Luke (b Liverpool, 18 Oct. 1844; d London, 27 Feb. 1927). English painter and illustrator. Early in his career he worked mainly as an illustrator, notably of Dickens's last novel, *Edwin Drood* (1870), but in the 1870s he turned increasingly to painting, achieving success particularly with scenes of social concern such as *Applicants for Admission to a Casual Ward* (1874, Royal Holloway and Bedford New College, Egham; reduced replica in Tate, London). His last and most famous painting in this vein is *The Doctor* (1891, Tate, London), showing a kindly physician attending a seriously ill child in a working-class home. Its pathos made it one of the most popular pictures of the age—it was endlessly reproduced and was one of the star attractions when the Tate Gallery opened in 1897 (Sir Henry *Tate had commissioned it). Subsequently Fildes worked mainly as a fashionable portraitist. He also painted colourful Venetian genre scenes, typically featuring pretty girls—a great contrast to his sombre pictures dealing with poverty in Britain.

Filla, Emil (b Chropyně, Moravia, 4 Apr. 1882; d Prague, 6 Oct. 1953). Czech painter, sculptor, graphic artist, and writer on art. Between 1907 and 1914 he spent much of his time in France, Germany, and Italy, and during this period he

turned from his early *Expressionist manner to *Cubism, becoming the pioneer and one of the most distinguished exponents of the style in Czechoslovakia in both painting and sculpture. He spent the First World War in the Netherlands and returned to Prague in 1920. His most characteristic paintings of this time were still-lifes, but in the late 1930s he turned to themes of violence, presaging the horrors of the Second World War (during which he was imprisoned in the concentration camp at Buchenwald). His post-war work was more naturalistic in style and included some large landscapes. He wrote numerous articles on art and several books.

Filonov, Pavel (b Moscow, 20 Jan. 1883; d Leningrad, 3 Dec. 1941). Russian painter, illustrator, designer, teacher, and poet. He was one of the most individual Russian artists of his time, developing a style that has been described as proto-*Surrealist and remaining untouched by the general trend towards *Constructivism. In 1925 he founded a school named 'The Collective of Masters of Analytical Art' in Leningrad and ran it until 1932, when the state—intent on imposing *Socialist Realism—disbanded all existing art groups. His paintings (often in watercolour or gouache) are elaborately finished and highly eclectic stylistically: Alan Bird (*A History of Russian Painting*, 1987) writes that they owe 'a little to child art, a little to icon painting, mosaic, primitivism and analytical *Cubism, and much more to his own researches into Oriental and African art as well as that of the Middle Ages . . . they are deeply pessimistic about the human condition'. Filonov died in the siege of Leningrad during the Second World War.

Finch, Willy (Alfred William) (b Brussels, 28 Nov. 1854; d Helsinki, 1930). Finnish painter and ceramicist of Belgian-British extraction. He was a friend of Georges *Seurat and Paul *Signac and helped to introduce their *Neo-Impressionist style to Belgium. In 1897, having temporarily abandoned painting for ceramics, he moved to Finland to direct the Iris pottery factory at Porvoo, near Helsinki, and had a notable influence on the modernization of Finnish design. The Iris factory closed in 1902, and although Finch continued to work in ceramics he also resumed painting in 1905. He taught at the Drawing School of the Finnish Arts' Association, 1902–5, and at the Finnish Central School of Applied Art, 1905–30, and in these roles he was an important force in bringing the fine and applied arts of Finland into contact with contemporary European trends.

fine arts. Term that came into use in the 18th century to describe the 'higher' non-utilitarian arts, as opposed to *applied or *decorative arts. Usually the term is taken to cover painting, sculpture, and architecture (even though architecture is obviously a 'useful' art), but it is often extended to cover poetry and music too. See also LIBERAL ARTS.

Finiguerra, Maso (b Florence, Mar. 1426; bur. Florence, 24 Aug. 1464). Florentine goldsmith, engraver, designer, and the most famous craftsman of the day in *niello (a type of decorative metal inlay). *Vasari asserts that Finiguerra was the inventor of copper engraving and, although this claim has been discredited, the technique did develop in Italy as an extension of niello work. He is said to have often worked from designs by Antonio *Pollaiuolo.

Firenze, Andrea da. See ANDREA DA FIRENZE.

Fisher, Sandra. See KITAJ.

Fitzwilliam Museum. The museum and art gallery of the University of Cambridge. It was founded in 1816 and is one of the oldest public museums in Great Britain. Like the *Ashmolean Museum in Oxford, it has been built up almost entirely from private benefactions. The founder, the 7th Viscount Fitzwilliam (1745–1816), was a highly cultured man with a deep interest in literature and music as well as the visual arts. He never married and on his death he left his library (including 130 illuminated manuscripts) and art collection to the University of Cambridge (where he had studied as a young man) 'for the purpose of promoting the increase of learning and the other great objects of that noble Foundation'. His collection included Italian *Renaissance paintings (among them a *Titian and a *Veronese) and the best representation of *Rembrandt etchings then in England. He also left £100,000 to provide 'a good substantial convenient Museum Repository or other Building'; this was begun in 1837 by George Basevi and continued by C. R. Cockerell after Basevi's death in 1845. It opened to the public in 1848, but the grand entrance hall (by E. M. Barry), with its magnificent staircase, was not finished until 1875. Subsequently there have been several extensions to the building. The most noteworthy bequest after the founder's was that of Charles Brinsley Marlay (1831–1912), who left the museum a large sum of money as well as a varied collection that enriched all departments.

Among several distinguished directors of the Fitzwilliam, the most famous was M. R. James (1862–1936), eminent medievalist and celebrated writer of ghost stories, who was in charge from 1893 to 1908. However, the most important administrator in the museum's history was his successor, Sir Sydney Cockerell (1867–1962), who was director from 1908 to 1937. According to the *Dictionary of National Biography*, he 'transformed a dreary and ill-hung provincial gallery into one which set a new standard of excellence which was to influence museums all over the world. This he achieved by the skilful and uncrowded display of pictures against suitable backgrounds, and by the introduction of fine pieces of furniture, Persian rugs, and flowers provided and arranged by lady admirers, fired by his enthusiasm.' In Cockerell's own words, 'I found it a pig stye, I turned it into a palace.', and the Fitzwilliam has maintained the reputation he gave it as a pleasurable place to visit. Its collections are now extremely wide-ranging; the areas of greatest richness include Italian painting and Greek coins.

fixative. An adhesive liquid applied to drawings in *chalk, *charcoal, or *pastel (usually by means of spraying) to prevent the *pigments from rubbing off, by binding them together and securing them to the *ground. It is most needed for pastels, but it tends to reduce their brilliance.

Flack, Audrey. See SUPERREALISM.

Flandrin, Hippolyte (b Lyons, 23 Mar. 1809; d Rome, 21 Mar. 1864). French painter. He was one of the favourite pupils of *Ingres and won the *Prix de Rome in 1832. In Italy he was influenced by the monumental decorative tradition and after his return to Paris in 1838 he became the leading muralist of his day, painting vast compositions in such churches as St Vincent-de-Paul (1849–53) and St Germain-des-Prés (1856–61) in Paris. He was a zealous but rather frigid upholder of Ingres's theories. Flandrin was an excellent portraitist and also painted historical and mythological pictures. He came from a family of artists. His brothers **Auguste** (1804–43) and **Paul** (1811–1902) were likewise pupils of Ingres, and concentrated mainly on portraiture and landscape respectively; his son **Paul-Hippolyte** (1856–1921) painted religious, historical, and *genre scenes.

Flavin, Dan (b New York, 1 Apr. 1933; d Riverhead, Long Island, NY, 29 Nov. 1996). American sculptor and experimental artist. Apart from some lessons at the Hans *Hofmann School in 1956 he had no formal training in art and did not take it up seriously until 1959. In 1961 he began to make 'icons', in which plainly painted, square-fronted constructions were combined with lights, and in 1963 he began using coloured fluorescent tubes; it is for this type of work that he became best known. In general he eschewed complicated effects of pulsating or flashing lights, preferring a bare and simple presentation that brought him within the orbit of *Minimal art. By 1968 his work had developed into room *environments. He had many commissions, including the lighting of several tracks at New York's Grand Central Station in 1976.

Flaxman, John (*b* York, 6 July 1755; *d* London, 9 Dec. 1826). English sculptor, draughtsman, and designer, an outstanding figure of the *Neoclassical movement. He was the son of a moulder of plaster figures, and after studying at the *Royal Academy Schools (where he met his lifelong friend *Blake) he worked for the potter Josiah Wedgwood from 1775 to 1787. The designs he produced for Wedgwood not only strengthened his interest in *antique art but also developed the innate sensitivity to line that was his greatest gift. In the same period he gradually built up a practice as a sculptor. From 1787 to 1794 he lived in Rome. While there he drew illustrations, much influenced by Greek vase painting, to the *Iliad* and the *Odyssey*, engraved and published in Rome in 1793, followed by illustrations to Aeschylus (1795) and Dante (1802). These engravings, which are of exceptional purity of outline, were republished in several editions, and won him international fame. His later illustrations to Hesiod (1817) were engraved by Blake.

Flaxman returned to England in 1794 with a well-established reputation and quickly became one of the busiest sculptors in the country. His monument to the poet William Collins (1795, Chichester Cathedral) and the more important one to Lord Mansfield (1795–1801, Westminster Abbey) were commissioned while he was in Rome. His enormous practice as a maker of monuments included large groups with free-standing figures (*Lord Nelson*, 1809, St Paul's Cathedral), but his most characteristic work appears in simpler and smaller monuments, sometimes cut in low *relief. In these his great gift for linear design was given full play. Flaxman was appointed the first professor of sculpture at the Royal Academy in 1810 and his reputation among Neoclassical sculptors was exceeded only by those of *Canova and possibly *Thorvaldsen. He was one of the first English artists to be famous outside his own country, although his

reputation and influence were based principally on engravings after his drawings rather than his sculpture. University College London has a large collection of Flaxman's drawings and models, and examples of his monuments can be seen in churches throughout England.

Flegel, Georg (*b* Olmütz, Moravia [now Olomouc, Czech Republic], 1566; *d* Frankfurt, 1638). German painter, one of the first artists to specialize in still-life. His life is poorly documented, but he seems to have started his career as a landscape painter, working as an assistant to Lucas I van *Valckenborch in Vienna, and to have followed Valckenborch to Frankfurt, which was a leading centre for the art trade. Flegel's paintings characteristically depict foodstuffs on a table; in his precise handling of detail his approach is naturalistic, but he arranges objects into compositions of charming—almost naive—simplicity.

Flicke, Gerlach (*b* ?Osnabrück; *d* London, Jan./Feb. 1558). German portrait painter who worked in England from about 1545 until his death. With *Eworth he was the outstanding painter working in England in the generation after *Holbein, but few of his works survive. The most important are the signed and dated (1547) portrait of an unknown man (sometimes identified with the 13th Lord Grey of Wilton) in the National Gallery of Scotland, Edinburgh, and the signed portrait of Archbishop Cranmer (probably 1546) in the National Portrait Gallery, London. Both of these are strong, vigorous works, showing Flicke as a painter of considerable distinction.

Flight, Claude. See LINOCUT.

Flinck, Govert (*b* Cleve, Germany, 25 Jan. 1615; *d* Amsterdam, 2 Feb. 1660). Dutch painter, active mainly in Amsterdam. He studied with *Rembrandt from about 1633 to 1636, and his early work, including portraits, religious subjects, and landscapes, was overwhelmingly influenced by his master (several of his paintings have indeed at some time been assigned to Rembrandt). From the mid-1640s, however, Flinck adopted the elegant style of van der *Helst, with which he had great success. In 1659 he was awarded the most prestigious commission given to any Dutch painter of his time: he was asked to paint twelve pictures for van *Campen's new town hall in Amsterdam, eight of which (each about 5 m (16 ft) high) were to represent the story of the revolt of the Batavians. However, Flinck died suddenly three months after signing the contract and the commission was divided among Rembrandt, *Lievens, and *Jordaens.

Flint, Sir William Russell (b Edinburgh, 4 Apr. 1880; d London, 27 Dec. 1969). British painter and graphic artist. He trained as a lithographer and was a prolific book illustrator, but is now best remembered for his watercolours (particularly his mildly erotic nudes), painted in a distinctive and rather flashy style. 'He was a modest and unassuming man, a fine and versatile craftsman, entirely detached from everything that was controversial or experimental in the art of his time' (DNB). His son **Francis Russell Flint** (1915–77) was also a painter.

flock prints. Prints imitating patterned velvet. They were evidently made by coating a *woodcut block with glue or paste instead of ink, impressing it on paper, and then sprinkling the paper with cloth shavings which adhered to the paste. Very few such prints exist, all made probably in south Germany in the third quarter of the 15th century; an example is *Christ on the Cross with the Virgin and St John* in the Ashmolean Museum, Oxford. A similar process was used in the 17th and 18th centuries for wallpapers.

Tinsel prints are similar to flock prints but use tinsel (small fragments of sparkling metal) in place of cloth. The rare surviving examples are thought to date from c.1430–60.

Floris (or **Floris de Vriendt**). Netherlandish family of artists active in Antwerp. The most important members were the brothers **Cornelis** (b Antwerp, c.1514; d Antwerp, 20 Oct. 1575) and **Frans** (b Antwerp, 1519/20; d Antwerp, 1 Oct. 1570). Both of them spent some time in Rome and returned to Antwerp with a desire to emulate the Italian *Renaissance manner. Cornelis was an architect and sculptor and also published engravings of Italianate motifs, which were used by many northern artists. He is famous principally as the architect of Antwerp Town Hall (1561–5), the finest and most influential building of the 16th century in Flanders. Frans was a painter and studied with Lambert *Lombard before going to Italy, where he was overwhelmed by *Michelangelo's *Last Judgement* (he was in Rome at about the time it was unveiled in 1541). The impression it made on him is reflected in his most characteristic works—large religious and mythological pictures crowded with athletic *Mannerist nudes (*Fall of the Rebel Angels*, 1554, Koninklijk Mus., Antwerp). In his portraits, however, he combined powerful brushwork with forthright

characterization in a way that anticipates Frans *Hals (*Old Lady*, 1558, Mus. B.-A., Caen). According to van *Mander, every Flemish youth with artistic leanings studied with him, but in spite of his success he died in debt because of his extravagant lifestyle.

Flötner, Peter (b Thurgau canton, Switzerland, c.1490; d Nuremberg, 23 Nov. 1546). German sculptor, medallist, designer, and printmaker, active mainly in Nuremberg. He visited Italy early in his career and he was one of the first German sculptors to be strongly influenced by *Renaissance ideas. His best-known work is the Apollo Fountain (1532, Stadtmuseum Fembohaus, Nuremberg), which is classical in inspiration but with a flowing elegance that is Flötner's own.

Fluxus. A loosely organized international group of avant-garde artists set up in Germany in 1962 and flourishing until the early 1970s. There was no common stylistic identity among the members, but they revived the spirit of *Dada and were opposed to artistic tradition and everything that savoured of professionalism in the arts. Their activities were mainly concerned with *happenings (usually called 'Aktions' in Germany), street art, and so on. Fluxus festivals were held in various European cities (including Amsterdam, Copenhagen, Düsseldorf, London, and Paris), and also in New York, which became the centre of the movement's activities. The most famous artist involved with Fluxus was Joseph *Beuys; among the others were Wolf *Vostell and the Japanese-born American Yoko Ono (1933–). The group's chief coordinator and editor of its many publications was the Lithuanian-born American George Maciunas (1931–78), who coined its name—Latin for 'flowing', suggesting a state of continuous change.

Focillon, Henri (b Dijon, 7 Sept. 1881; d New Haven, 3 Mar. 1943). French art historian. He was a celebrated teacher and held various university appointments, notably at the Sorbonne in Paris, where in 1924 he succeeded Émile *Mâle as professor of medieval archaeology. He also taught in the USA. Focillon's work ranged from studies of medieval sculpture to 20th-century painting; he also wrote much on prints (his father was an engraver), notably a book on *Piranesi (1918). His best-known work is *Art d'Occident* (The Art of the West, 1938), a study of *Romanesque and *Gothic art in which he placed great emphasis on the technical aspects of artistic creation, stressing how the artist responds to his raw materials, their potentialities, and limitations. This outlook also finds expression in Focillon's *Vie des formes* (1934), translated as *The Life of Forms in Art* (1942).

Fontainebleau, School of. Term applied to art produced for the French court at Fontainebleau c.1530–c.1610, and more broadly used to refer to any French art of the period influenced by the distinctive style created there; in this broader sense it was the dominant strain in French art in the 16th century. The driving force behind the School of Fontainebleau was Francis I (1494–1547; reigned from 1515), whose favourite residence was at Fontainebleau, about 65 km (40 miles) south-east of Paris. In 1528 he began enlarging the building (at the time no more than a hunting lodge) into a palace, making it the most important expression of his desire to glorify the French crown by emulating the lavish patronage of the great humanist princes of Italy. As France lacked an indigenous tradition of mural painting adequate to his ambitions, he brought in first-rate Italian artists, most notably *Rosso Fiorentino, who moved to France in 1531, and *Primaticcio, who followed in 1532. The Italian masters succeeded in adapting their own styles to the courtly ideals of the French taste and were assisted by French and Flemish artists. From the association was born a distinctive *Mannerist style—elegant, sophisticated, and often voluptuous, expressed most characteristically in mural painting combined with stucco ornament. Much of the stuccowork was in high *relief, but Rosso also developed a distinctive motif known as *strapwork, in which the stucco is formed into shapes resembling leather or parchment that has been rolled and cut into decorative patterns; this became a particularly popular form of ornament in England and the Low Countries (Fontainebleau motifs were widely spread through engravings). Primaticcio's distinctive figure style—characterized by long limbs, small heads, and sharp, elegant profiles—became virtually canonical in French art until the end of the 16th century.

Other Italian artists who worked at Fontainebleau included Niccolò dell' *Abate and *Cellini, but much of the work associated with the school is by unknown hands, although often of high quality, as with the celebrated painting *Diana the Huntress* (c.1550, Louvre, Paris). The mythological subject matter, elongated elegance, idyllic landscape setting, and air of sophis-ticated artificiality in this work are wholly typical of the School, the influence of which left few French artists of the time untouched. After the hiatus caused by the Wars of Religion (1562–98) the decorative painting of royal palaces was revived under the patronage of Henry IV (reigned 1589–1610). The name **Second School of Fontainebleau** is usually given to the artists who carried out this work for Henry, notably Ambroise *Dubois, Toussaint *Dubreuil, and Martin *Fréminet. Their work was accomplished, but without the inventive brilliance of the best work of the First School.

Fontana, Lucio (b Rosario, Santa Fé, Argentina, 19 Feb. 1899; d Comabbio, nr. Varese, 7 Sept. 1968). Italian painter, sculptor, and ceramicist. He worked mainly in Milan, where in 1930 he had his first one-man show at the Galleria del Milione; this was the first exhibition in which abstract sculpture was seen in Italy and Fontana became a leading figure in promoting abstract art in his country. In 1935 he moved to Paris, where he became a member of the *Abstraction-Création association, then in 1940 to Argentina (his mother was Argentinian), where in 1946 he issued his *White Manifesto*. This introduced a new concept of art called *Spatialism (Spazialismo), which aimed for cooperation with scientists in synthesizing new ideas and materials. In 1947 he returned to Milan, and in the same year officially launched the Spatialist movement and issued the *Technical Manifesto of Spatialism* (four more Spatialist manifestos followed, the last in 1952). His most characteristic works, which he began producing in 1958, are paintings in which completely plain surfaces are penetrated by gashes in the canvas, but he also made *environments (for example using neon lights in blackened rooms) and carried out various decorative projects.

Fontana, Prospero (b Bologna, c.1512; d Bologna, 1597). Italian painter. He worked in various Italian cities, notably Florence, Genoa, and Rome, assisting *Vasari and other artists on decorative projects, and was also employed at *Fontainebleau (c.1560) under *Primaticcio. Most of his career, however, was spent in Bologna, where he was the leading painter during the 1570s. He was a favourite artist of Gabriele Paleotti, Bishop of Bologna, one of the churchmen who, in line with the ideals of the Counter-Reformation, called for greater clarity in painting as an aid to devotion, but Fontana's work—elegant but rather spineless—is generally seen as exemplifying everything that the *Carracci opposed in their move towards naturalism. Most of Fontana's work is still in and around Bologna. His daughter and pupil **Lavinia Fontana** (1552–1614) was much esteemed in her day as a portraitist.

Foppa, Vincenzo (b Bagnolo, nr. Brescia, 1427/30; d Brescia, 1515/16). Italian painter, the leading figure in Lombard painting until the arrival of *Leonardo da Vinci in Milan in 1481/2. He worked a good deal in Brescia, but his main places of activity at the height of his career were Pavia and Milan. According to *Vasari he trained in Padua, and his robust style owed much to *Mantegna, not least in his interest in perspective. His major works include frescos in S. Eustorgio, Milan, and S. Maria del Carmine, Brescia.

Forain, Jean-Louis (b Reims, 23 Oct. 1852; d Paris, 11 July 1931). French painter, lithographer, and caricaturist. In the first half of his career he worked mainly on satirical illustrations for various Paris journals, combining something of the realistic outlook of *Manet and the mordant satire of *Daumier. However, he exhibited at four of the *Impressionist exhibitions between 1879 and 1886, and after the turn of the century he concentrated more on painting. His most distinctive work included some court scenes, two examples of which are in Tate Modern, London: *The Court of Justice* (c.1902) and *Counsel and Accused* (1908). Forain was much influenced by his friend *Degas, who said, 'he paints with his hand in my pocket'.

Forbes, Stanhope. See NEWLYN SCHOOL.

Ford, Edward Onslow. See NEW SCULPTURE.

formalism. A term used in the discussion of the arts to describe an approach (on behalf of creator or critic) in which the formal qualities of a work—such as line, shape, and colour—are regarded as self-sufficient for its appreciation, and all other considerations—such as representational, ethical, or social aspects—are treated as secondary or redundant. The idea that formal qualities can have meaning or resonance independently of representative function was essential to the development of *abstract art, and several notable writers on art in the 20th century were basically formalist in outlook, including Clive *Bell, Roger *Fry, and Clement *Greenberg. Many other writers have been strongly opposed to their ideas, believing that form and 'content' are to a large extent interdependent.

Formalism has been particularly opposed in Communist countries, especially Stalinist Russia, where art was supposed to serve a moral purpose in the education and inspiration of the masses (see SOCIALIST REALISM), and anything that suggested cultural elitism was condemned. The Soviet authorities regarded formalism as a sign of Western decadence—so much so that the word was used virtually as an all-purpose term of abuse for Western art or its influence. Artists guilty or suspected of formalism were persecuted and encouraged to make public recantations for their offences. This applied to writers and composers as well as painters and sculptors. In 1936, for example, Dmitri Shostakovich was attacked in *Pravda* for producing 'leftist confusion instead of music for the people' in his opera *Lady Macbeth of the Mtsensk District*, which 'tickles the perverted tastes of bourgeois audiences abroad'. In literature, 'The charge of formalism will commonly mean that a novelist has devoted too much attention to plot, characterization and description, and that his work lacks the requisite inspirational quality' (C. Hunt, *Guide to Communist Jargon*, 1957).

Forment, Damián (b ?Valencia, c.1475; d Santo Domingo de la Calzada, 22 Dec. 1540). Spanish sculptor, active mainly in Saragossa, where he settled in 1509. On stylistic grounds it has been proposed that he trained in Florence; certainly he was the leading sculptor of his generation in introducing *Renaissance elements to eastern Spain. Early works, such as the altarpiece at the church of the Pilar, Saragossa (1509–12), incorporate Renaissance-style figure sculpture within *Gothic architectural frameworks, but by the time of his altarpiece for the monastery church at Poblet, Tarragona (1527–9), he had abandoned Gothic. He worked mainly in alabaster, but in 1537–40 he made a large wooden altarpiece (gilded and *polychromed after his death) for the church at Santo Domingo de la Calzada; the twisted poses of the figures foreshadow *Mannerism.

Fortuny y Carbo (or **Fortuny y Marsal**), **Mariano** (b Reus, 11 June 1838; d Rome, 21 Nov. 1874). Spanish painter, son-in-law of Federico de *Madrazo. He worked mainly in Rome and enjoyed international success with anecdotal costume pieces, often set in the 18th century. They have something in common with the work of *Meissonier but they are much livelier in colour and particularly brushwork. He made a fortune from his work but died aged only 36; the cause of death is uncertain, but it was possibly malaria. His son **Mariano Fortuny y Madrazo** (1871–1949) was a painter, sculptor, designer, photographer, and inventor.

Forum Exhibition (in full, Forum Exhibition of Modern American Painters). An exhibition arranged in New York in 1916 by the critic Willard Huntington Wright with the support of the magazine *The Forum*, to which he was a regular contributor. The purpose of the exhibition was to pinpoint the best of progressive American painting in order to convince the public that it could stand up to the work of the European avant-garde, which had made a great impact at the *Armory Show three years earlier. Robert *Henri and Alfred *Stieglitz were on the selection committee. The exhibition consisted of about 200 pictures by seventeen artists, including *Benton (ironically, later a vociferous enemy of modernism), *Dove, *Macdonald-Wright (Wright's brother), *Marin, *Sheeler, and *Zorach. Anticipating that some of the work on show might be too advanced for public taste, Wright wrote in the catalogue, 'Not one man represented in this exhibition is either a charlatan or a maniac,' and he vigorously defended abstraction: 'It is neither the subject-matter nor the painter's approximation to nature which makes his work great: it is the inherent aesthetic qualities of order, rhythm, composition and form.'

Foster, Myles Birket (*b* Tynemouth, Northumberland [now Tyne and Wear], 4 Feb. 1825; *d* Weybridge, Surrey, 27 Mar. 1899). English painter and illustrator. He was trained as a wood engraver and early in his career designed many book illustrations. After *c*.1858, however, he devoted himself primarily to watercolour painting of rustic subjects in a sweetly sentimental style that has made him a favourite artist for manufacturers of greetings cards.

Foucquières, Jacques. See CHAMPAIGNE.

Foujita, Tsuguharu (or Léonard) (*b* Edogawa [now a district of Tokyo], 27 Nov. 1886; *d* Zurich, 29 Jan. 1968). Japanese-French painter and graphic artist. He moved to Paris in 1913 and spent most of the rest of his life in the city, with the exception of a long interlude, 1933–50, when he returned to Japan. In the 1920s he developed a distinctive style of delicately mannered *Expressionism, combining Western and Japanese traits, and he became recognized as a leading figure of the group of émigrés who made up the *École de Paris—the only Japanese artist of his time to earn a considerable reputa-

tion in Europe. Characteristic works in his large and varied output include landscapes, portraits, nudes, pictures of cats (once very popular in reproduction), and compositions in which still-life and figures are combined. In 1959 he converted to Roman Catholicism and adopted the forename Léonard in recognition of his admiration for Leonardo da Vinci. From this time he began painting religious subjects, and in his later career he tended to lapse into sentimentality.

Fouquet (or Foucquet), **Jean** (*b* Tours, *c*.1420; *d* Tours, *c*.1481). The outstanding French painter of the 15th century, active mainly in his native Tours. Between 1446 and 1448 he was in Rome, where he painted a portrait, now lost, of Pope Eugenius IV. Much has been made of this Italian journey, the influence of which can be detected in the perspective effects and classical architecture of his subsequent paintings, but in certain respects—notably his close, unidealized scrutiny of the human face—his work remained deeply rooted in northern tradition and did not succumb to Italian influence. On his return from Italy, Fouquet worked much for the French court. His first patron was Étienne Chevalier, the royal secretary and lord treasurer, for whom he produced a *Book of Hours (1450–60), now dismembered but mainly in the Musée Condé at Chantilly, and who appears in the Melun Diptych (*c*.1452), now divided between Antwerp (Koninklijk Mus.) and Berlin (Gemäldegalerie). The figure of the Virgin in the panel in Antwerp is said to be a portrait of Agnes Sorel, Charles VII's mistress, whom Chevalier had also loved.

It was not until 1475 that Fouquet became royal painter (to Louis XI), but in the previous year he was asked to prepare designs for the king's tomb, and he must have been the leading court artist for many years. In both his manuscript illuminations and his panel paintings, his art had the same clarity and dignity, his figures being modelled in broad planes defined by lines of magnificent purity. His sculptural sense of form went with a cool and detached temperament, and in his finest works the combination creates a deeply impressive gravity.

Fouquier, Jacques. See CHAMPAIGNE.

Fox-Strangways, William. See ASHMOLEAN MUSEUM.

Fragonard, Jean-Honoré (*b* Grasse, 5 Apr. 1732; *d* Paris, 22 Aug. 1806). French painter whose scenes of frivolity and gallantry are among the most complete embodiments of the *Rococo spirit; he has been described as the 'fragrant essence' of the 18th century. After a brief period studying with *Chardin, to whom he was temperamentally unsuited, Fragonard became *Boucher's most brilliant pupil and in 1752 won the *Prix de Rome, even though he was not officially qualified to enter the competition as he was not a student at the Académie Royale (Boucher said, 'It does not matter; you are *my* pupil'). From 1756 to 1761 he lived in Rome, where he eschewed the work of the approved masters of the High *Renaissance and instead found inspiration in a freer and more colourful tradition, represented above all by *Tiepolo. His best friend in Rome was Hubert *Robert, with whom he spent several weeks at the Villa d'Este, Tivoli, in the summer of 1760; he made some beautiful drawings of the villa's gardens, memories of which occur in paintings throughout his career (he saw the villa again on a second visit to Italy in 1773–4).

In 1765 Fragonard became a member of the Académie with *Coroesus Sacrificing himself to Save Callirhoe* (Louvre, Paris), a mythological scene in the *Grand Manner. Although the picture won lavish praise, he soon abandoned this idiom for the erotic canvases by which he is chiefly known. His delicate colouring, witty characterization, and spontaneous brushwork ensured that even his most intimate or voyeuristic subjects are never vulgar, and his finest works have an irresistible verve and joyfulness (*The Swing*, 1767, Wallace Coll., London). After his marriage in 1769 he also painted children and pictures of domestic life and his large output included various other subjects, including landscapes, portraits, and occasional religious scenes.

Fragonard stopped exhibiting at the *Salon in 1767 and almost all his work was done for private patrons. Among them was Mme du Barry, Louis XV's most beautiful mistress, for whom he painted the works that are often regarded as his masterpieces—the four canvases representing the progress of love (c.1770–3, Frick Coll., New York; he later added other pictures to the series). Mme du Barry, however, returned the pictures and had them replaced with works by *Vien—an early indication that taste in court circles was beginning to turn against Fragonard's light-hearted style. He adapted to some extent to the new *Neoclassical vogue, notably by using more polished brushwork, but after the French Revolution his scenes of frivolous aristocratic pleasure were completely outmoded and he seems to have abandoned painting in about 1792. Jacques-Louis *David, who as a young

unknown had been helped by Fragonard, returned the kindness by finding him an administrative job at the *Louvre, which had opened as a national museum in 1793. Fragonard worked there until 1800, then lived the rest of his life in obscurity.

There were several other painters in Fragonard's family, including his son **Alexandre-Évariste Fragonard** (1780–1850), who specialized in historical subjects, and his sister-in-law Marguerite Gérard (1761–1837), who was regarded as one of the finest women artists in France (her work consisted mainly of portraits and *genre scenes). Gérard had a close professional relationship with Fragonard as his pupil, protégée, and colleague (they sometimes collaborated on pictures, an example being *The Reader* in the Fitzwilliam Museum, Cambridge). According to popular legend they were also lovers, in spite of the almost 30-year age gap between them, but there is no contemporary evidence to support this idea. Berthe *Morisot was Fragonard's great-granddaughter.

Frampton, Sir George (*b* London, 16 June 1860; *d* London, 21 May 1928). British sculptor. Early in his career he was one of the leading exponents of the *New Sculpture, experimenting with unusual materials and polychrome and working in a style imbued with elements of *Art Nouveau and *Symbolism (*Mysteriarch*, 1892, Walker AG, Liverpool). Later his work became more traditional and he had a successful career with accomplished but uninspired monuments, including two well-known sights of London—the bronze Peter Pan statue (1911) in Kensington Gardens and the Edith Cavell Memorial (1920) in St Martin's Place; the figure of the First World War heroine is in marble and the rest of the structure in granite. Frampton's wife, née **Christabel Annie Cockerell** (1863–1951), was a painter of landscapes and children.

Their son **Meredith Frampton** (*b* London, 17 Mar. 1894; *d* Mere, Wiltshire, 16 Sept. 1984) was a painter, primarily of portraits. Like his father, he studied at the *Royal Academy, and he exhibited there from 1920, his work winning increasing critical recognition. However, he gave up painting in 1945 because his sight was deteriorating and he was almost entirely forgotten until an exhibition of his work was held at the Tate Gallery, London, in 1982, revealing him as an artist of great distinction. His work is beautifully finished, with a sense of hypnotic clarity (the images seem almost palpable yet at the same time strangely remote), and he excelled at conveying the intellectual qualities of his sitters. He was a slow worker and his output was small. He wrote of his own work: 'I think my principal aim has always been to paint the sort of picture that I would like to own and live with had it been painted by someone else.'

Francavilla, Pietro (Pierre de Francheville or Francqueville) (b Cambrai, c.1548; d Paris, 25 Aug. 1615). Franco-Netherlandish sculptor active mainly in Italy and usually known by the Italian form of his name. He settled in Florence in about 1570 and worked extensively with *Giambologna (as his partner, rather than merely as an assistant). In 1604 he moved to Paris to execute the four bronze figures of slaves for Giambologna's equestrian statue of Henry IV for the Pont Neuf; the statue itself is destroyed, but Francavilla's figures (not cast until 1618, after his death) are in the Louvre. In both bronze and marble he was a highly accomplished exponent of Giambologna's style.

Francesco da Faenza. See CASTAGNO.

Francesco del Cossa. See COSSA.

Francesco di Giorgio (bapt. Siena, 23 Sept. 1439; bur. Siena, 29 Nov. 1501). Sienese painter, sculptor, architect, military engineer, and writer, a pupil of the equally versatile *Vecchietta. He painted mainly during the early part of his career and few pictures certainly by him survive; the most important are a signed Nativity (c.1475) and a documented Coronation of the Virgin (1472–4), both in the Pinacoteca at Siena. As a sculptor, his major works are two bronze angels (1489–97) on the high altar of Siena Cathedral. Francesco was widely travelled, and the latter part of his career was spent mainly as an architect and military engineer (he was an expert in fortifications and is said to have exploded the first mine). As a technological innovator he was second only to his friend *Leonardo, whom he certainly influenced. Among his patrons was Federico da *Montefeltro, and Francesco may have had a hand in the designing of his celebrated palace in Urbino. He also designed churches, notably S. Maria del Calcinaio, near Cortona, begun in 1484. Francesco wrote a treatise on architecture in the last years of his life; it was not published until 1841.

Francheville, Pierre de. See FRANCAVILLA.

Francia, Francesco (Francesco Raibolini) (b Bologna, c.1450; d Bologna, 1517/18). The outstanding Bolognese painter of his period. He originally trained as a goldsmith and had several other skills, being recorded as a sculptor, miniaturist, and engraver of *nielli. However, from about 1485 he worked mainly as a painter, principally of altarpieces for churches in Bologna and neighbouring towns and of small devotional works; he was also an accomplished portraitist. His softly rounded style was strongly influenced by *Perugino. According to *Vasari, Francia died of 'grief' after seeing *Raphael's St Cecilia (c.1515, Pinacoteca Nazionale, Bologna), which made his own paintings look hopelessly old-fashioned. There are several examples of his work in the National Gallery, London.

Franciabigio (Francisco di Cristofano) (b Florence, 30 Jan. 1484; d Florence, 14 Jan. 1525). Florentine painter, a minor master of the High *Renaissance style. He was a pupil of Mariotto *Albertinelli and later shared a workshop with Andrea del *Sarto, who was the dominant influence on his style. His best works are generally considered to be his portraits, particularly those of young men (A Knight of Rhodes, c.1514, NG, London).

Francis I, King of France. See FONTAINEBLEAU.

Francis, Sam (b San Mateo, Calif., 25 June 1923; d Santa Monica, Calif., 4 Nov. 1994). American painter, one of the leading second-generation *Abstract Expressionists. While serving in the US Army Air Corps he injured his spine in a plane crash and he took up painting in 1944 when he was recovering in hospital. In 1950 he settled in Paris, where he studied under *Léger and was friendly with *Riopelle and other *Art Informel painters; his style was influenced by these artists as well as by Americans such as Jackson *Pollock. He visited Japan several times, and the thin texture of his paint, his drip and splash technique, and his asymmetrical balance of colour against powerful voids (he often left areas of canvas blank) have led critics to speak of influences from Japanese traditions of contemplative art. In 1961 Francis returned to his native California, settling first at Santa Barbara and then in Santa Monica. From the mid-1960s the feeling of oriental simplicity in his painting increased, bringing his work into closer affinity with *Minimal art. Francis carried out several mural commissions, but he often worked on a small scale in watercolour. He also made lithographs (from 1960) and sculpture (from 1965).

Francken. Family of Flemish painters active in the 16th and 17th centuries, mainly in Antwerp. The individual contributions of the many artists in the family are often difficult to distinguish, but the two most important members were **Frans I** (*b* Herentals, 1542; *d* Antwerp, 2 Oct. 1616) and particularly his son **Frans II** (*bapt*. Antwerp, 6 May 1581; *d* Antwerp, 6 May 1642). The father mainly painted religious and historical compositions. His early works were often large in scale; the late ones were small, usually done on copper, and crowded with exotic figures and accessories. Frans II frequently adopted his father's subjects and style, but his range was wider. He painted landscapes and *genre scenes as well as historical pictures, and was also one of the first artists to use the interior of a picture gallery as a subject, giving faithful miniature reproductions of the works in the collection. His paintings were even smaller and more crowded than his father's; they were also more colourful. Frans II was frequently employed by his fellow artists in Antwerp to paint the figures in their landscapes and interiors.

François, Guy (*b* Le Puy [Le Puy-en-Velay], Haute-Loire, *c*.1578; *d* Le Puy, Oct./Dec. 1650). French painter. In 1608 he is documented in Rome and by 1613 he was back in Le Puy, where he was based for the rest of his career, painting numerous pictures for local churches, many of them still *in situ*. He has been described as 'the first painter to introduce post-*Mannerist Italian fashions into France' (Benedict Nicolson, *Caravaggism in Europe*, 1989), and his *Caravaggesque style is sometimes particularly close to *Saraceni, with whom he presumably had contact in Rome (a few paintings have even been disputed between them). François was virtually unknown until an exhibition was devoted to him in Le Puy in 1974.

François, Jean-Charles. See CRAYON MANNER.

Francqueville, Pierre de. See FRANCAVILLA.

Frankenthaler, Helen (*b* New York, 12 Dec. 1928). American painter, an important figure in the transition from *Abstract Expressionism to *Colour Field Painting. In her early work she was influenced by Jackson *Pollock and she developed his drip technique by pouring and running very thin paint—like washes of watercolour—onto canvases laid on the floor. She first used this method in *Mountains and Sea* (1952, artist's collection, on loan to NG, Washington), which is regarded as one of the seminal works of post-war American painting. It particularly impressed Morris *Louis and Kenneth *Noland when they saw it in her studio in 1953. In 1962

Frankenthaler switched from oils to acrylic paint, which allowed her to achieve more richly saturated colour. Her limpid veils of colour float on the surface of the canvas, but they often evoke suggestions of landscape. Since 1960 Frankenthaler has also made aquatints, lithographs, and woodcuts; in 1964 she began to work in ceramics; and in 1972 she made her first sculpture. From 1958 to 1971 she was married to Robert *Motherwell.

Frankenthal School. See CONINXLOO.

Fréart, Roland, Sieur [Master] de Chambray (*b* Le Mans, 13 July 1606; *d* Le Mans, 11 Dec. 1676). French civil servant and writer. He wrote, translated, or edited several works relating to art, architecture, and mathematics. These include the first printed edition of *Leonardo da Vinci's treatise on painting, published in Paris in 1651 in French and Italian. In his own treatise, *Idée de la perfection de la peinture* (1662), he expresses his intellectual conception of painting; he greatly admired *Poussin, whom he had met in Rome, and he condemned *Caravaggio and *Rubens, among other painters, for their disregard of classical principles. His brother **Paul Fréart**, Sieur de Chantelou (*b* Le Mans, 25 Mar. 1609; *d* ?1694), likewise a civil servant, was Poussin's main patron in France. They corresponded a good deal from 1639 until Poussin's death in 1665; Chantelou's letters to Poussin are lost, but Poussin's to Chantelou survive and they are an important source of information. Mainly they deal with practical matters, but they also set forth some of Poussin's views on art. When *Bernini visited Paris in 1665–6 Chantelou was appointed his guide and companion, and he kept a diary documenting the visit; it was published in 1885 and an English translation appeared in 1985.

Frederick, Prince of Wales. See ROYAL COLLECTION.

Frederick-Augustus II, Elector of Saxony. See GEMÄLDEGALERIE.

freestone. Any good-quality, fine-grained *limestone or sandstone that can be 'freely' cut in any direction, making it suitable for carving or masonry.

Fréminet, Martin (*b* Paris, 23 Sept. 1567; *d* Paris, 18 June 1619). French painter, one of the leading artists of the Second School of *Fontainebleau. In about 1587 he moved to Italy and worked there until 1603, when he was recalled to Paris by Henry IV following the death of *Dubreuil. The ceiling for the chapel of the

Trinity at Fontainebleau (begun 1606) is the most important of Fréminet's few surviving works. Italian *Mannerist influence, particularly that of Giuseppe *Cesari (whom he had known in Rome), is evident in the rather strained poses of the figures, which nevertheless are effectively integrated with the *stucco decoration. In 1617 Fréminet married the widow of Ambroise *Dubois. Their son **Louis Fréminet** (d c.1651) was a painter but no works certainly by him are known.

French, Daniel Chester (b Exeter, NH, 20 Apr. 1850; d Stockbridge, Mass., 7 Oct. 1931). American sculptor. He made his name with the famous bronze statue of the *Minute Man* (1875) in Concord, Massachusetts, a monument to commemorate the rising of the citizens of the town during the early years of the Revolution (the figure was ready to fight for his country in a minute). After this success, French went on to become the most illustrious sculptor of public monuments of his day, his best-known work being the huge seated marble figure of Abraham Lincoln (dedicated in 1922) on the Lincoln Memorial in Washington.

fresco. A method of wall painting in which powdered *pigments mixed only in water are applied to wet plaster freshly laid on the wall (the word 'fresco' is Italian for 'fresh'). As the wall dries an irreversible chemical reaction occurs that binds the pigment with the plaster, making the picture an integral part of the wall (the lime (calcium hydroxide) of the plaster combines with carbon dioxide in the atmosphere to form a crust of calcium carbonate). This technique is also called *buon fresco* or *fresco buono* (true fresco) to distinguish it from painting on dry plaster, which is called by analogy *fresco secco* or simply *secco*. *Buon fresco* is exceptionally permanent in dry climates, but if damp penetrates the wall, the plaster is liable to crumble and the paint with it. Consequently the art has been practised chiefly in dry countries, particularly in Italy (though less often in watery Venice), and seldom in northern Europe. The technique is of great antiquity. *Minoan and Greek wall paintings were probably in fresco; those at Pompeii certainly are and the Roman writer *Vitruvius describes a method much like that in use during the *Renaissance. Fresco painting is also found outside Europe, for example in China and India.

The Italian practice was described in detail by *Cennini in the early 15th century. The wall was first given a coating of plaster, prepared from lime and sand in water. When this rough surface (the *arricciato) had dried, any horizontal, vertical, or diagonal guidelines needed were produced by 'snapping' a stained cord or string between appropriate points on the wall, and the basic design was drawn in charcoal. Over the charcoal the design was indicated in more detail in a red chalk called sinopia. A layer of finer plaster, called the *intonaco, was now applied over one section of the rougher arricciato. This was the actual painting ground and was made very smooth. Because the sinopia was covered by it, the essential lines of the buried drawing had to be quickly indicated again on the intonaco. At any one time, only as much plaster was applied as could be painted in one day, before it had time to dry. This might be a fairly large area if little detail were involved, for example in the sky, but a much smaller area might be given a day to itself if it required special care, for example the head of an important figure. On close examination joins can be discerned between areas of plaster that correspond to each day's work (*giornato* in Italian), so it is possible to calculate reasonably accurately the number of days' work that have gone into a fresco. In *Giotto's Arena Chapel, for example, 852 *giornate* have been counted, so even allowing for the fact that assistants would almost certainly have painted repetitive areas such as decorative borders, the work probably took a minimum of two years. Cennini's account of fresco technique was written before the use of *cartoons, which generally supplanted sinopie around the middle of the 15th century. Cartoons had the advantage not only of transferring the design accurately but also of transferring it directly onto the final painting surface (intonaco) rather than onto the arricciato.

The fresco painter had to work rapidly, before the plaster could dry; corrections were almost impossible to make without chipping away the plaster and applying a fresh surface, so the technique demanded a sure hand and purpose. The colours available were limited (they had to be chemically compatible with the process), and as they were apt to become lighter in drying, depth of tone was hard to attain. Blending, too, was difficult, so much use was made of *hatching to produce tonal effects. Finishing touches were sometimes added after the plaster was dry (*al secco*), but this had to be done with egg tempera or *size paint instead of pure pigment and water. *Vasari called it a 'vile practice' and the parts done *al secco* were liable to flake off, but many of the greatest exponents of the art resorted to it. The difficulties and limitations of the technique encouraged the artist to design the subject broadly and treat it boldly, and did much to foster the purity, strength, and monumentality of Italian Renaissance painting.

Giotto stands at the head of the glorious Italian tradition of fresco painting, and from his time many of the leading Italian masters produced their most famous works in the medium: *Masaccio, in the Brancacci Chapel, Florence; *Piero della Francesca in S. Francesco, Arezzo; *Michelangelo in the Sistine Chapel; *Raphael in the Stanze at the Vatican; *Correggio in his church domes at Parma; Annibale *Carracci in the Farnese Gallery. It became less common in the 18th century and Giambattista *Tiepolo was the last in the line of great Italian painters who used it. The medium was revived in the 19th century, notably by German painters such as the *Nazarenes and *Cornelius, but some notable decorators of the time, such as *Delacroix and *Puvis de Chavannes, preferred to use the method of *marouflage. In the 20th century the greatest exponents of fresco were the Mexican muralists *Orozco, *Rivera, and *Siqueiros.

Fresnoy, Charles-Alphonse du. See DUFRESNOY.

Freud, Lucian (b Berlin, 8 Dec. 1922). German-born British painter, draughtsman, and etcher, a grandson of Sigmund Freud. In 1932 he settled in England with his parents, and he acquired British nationality in 1939. His earliest love was drawing and he began to work full-time as an artist after being invalided out of the merchant navy in 1942. He first exhibited his work in 1944 and first made a major public impression in 1951 when his *Interior at Paddington* (Walker AG, Liverpool) won a prize at the Festival of Britain; it shows the sharply focused detail, pallid colouring, and obsessive, slightly bizarre atmosphere characteristic of his work at this time. Because of the meticulous finish of such paintings, Freud has sometimes been described as a 'Realist' (or rather absurdly as a *Superrealist), but the subjectivity and intensity of his work has always set him apart from the sober tradition characteristic of most British figurative art since the Second World War. From the late 1950s he painted with much broader handling and richer colouring, without losing any of his intensity of vision. His work includes still-lifs, interiors, and urban scenes, but his specialities are portraits and nudes, often observed in arresting close-up, with the flesh painting given an extraordinary quality of palpability (*The Painter's Mother* 1982, Tate, London). He prefers to paint people he knows well: 'If you don't know them, it can only be like a travel book.'

Freud's work has been shown in numerous one-man and group shows and he has steadily built up a formidable reputation as one of the most powerful contemporary figure painters. In 1993 Peter *Blake wrote that since the death of Francis *Bacon the previous year, Freud was 'certainly the best living British painter', and by this time he was also well known abroad (a major retrospective exhibition of his work in 1987–8 was seen in Paris and Washington as well as London). His fame has been won in spite of an aversion to self-publicity.

Freundlich, Otto (b Stolp, Pomerania [now Słupsk, Poland], 10 July 1878; d Maidanek concentration camp, nr. Lublin, 9 Mar. 1943). German painter, sculptor, and designer (of mosaics, tapestries, and stained glass), active mainly in France. From 1909 to 1914 he spent much of his time in Paris, where he was a member of *Picasso's circle and flirted briefly with *Cubism. In 1918 he was a member of the *Novembergruppe in Berlin and soon afterwards he began producing purely abstract paintings, composing with interlocking swathes of colour. From 1924 to 1939 he lived in Paris, where he was a member of *Cercle et Carré and *Abstraction-Création. In his own country his work was condemned as *degenerate (his sculpture *The New Man* (1912) was reproduced on the cover of the catalogue of the infamous 'Degenerate Art' exhibition held in Munich in 1937 and was later destroyed by the Nazis). He did not seriously devote himself to sculpture until 1928, but his few surviving works in this field are generally considered his finest achievements, notable for their feeling of sombre mystery. After fleeing Paris he was arrested in the Pyrenees and died in a concentration camp.

Frick, Henry Clay (b West Overton, Pa., 19 Dec. 1849; d New York, 2 Dec. 1919). American industrialist, art collector, and philanthropist. He made an enormous fortune in coke and steel operations and devoted much of his wealth to his passion for art and to philanthropy (he endowed several hospitals for example). Although he sometimes took expert advice (notably from Roger *Fry), Frick essentially relied on his own taste and eye for quality. In addition to paintings, his purchases included drawings, prints, enamels, bronzes, and porcelain. On his death he left his New York mansion and a large fund to form the Frick Collection, which was opened to the public in 1935. It is generally regarded as one of the finest small museums in the world, with a choice collection of works from the Middle Ages to the late 19th century. Giovanni *Bellini's *St Francis*, *Fragonard's 'Progress of Love' series, *Holbein's *Thomas More*, and *Rembrandt's *Polish Rider* are among the celebrated masterpieces in the collection. Frick's will stipulated that further acquisitions could be made and a few pictures have subsequently been added to the collection, maintaining the superb standards he set. Attached to the Frick Collection is the Frick Art Reference Library, which has major collections of books and photographs. It was founded in 1920 by Frick's daughter **Helen Clay Frick**. In 1970 she established the Frick Art Museum in Pittsburgh, the city where her father had made his fortune.

Friedlaender, Walter (b Berlin, 10 Mar. 1873; d New York, 6 Sept. 1966). German-American art historian. He was originally a Sanskrit scholar and took up art history seriously when he was 30. In 1914 he became a professor at the university of Freiburg im Breisgau, where he numbered Erwin *Panofsky among his pupils. He was dismissed by the Nazis in 1933 and two years later he emigrated to the USA to become a professor at the Institute of Fine Arts, New York University, where he exercised a great influence on American art historians. His major publications include *Von David bis Delacroix* (1930; translated as *From David to Delacroix*, 1952), *Caravaggio Studies* (1955), *Mannerism and Anti-Mannerism in Italian Painting* (1957), monographs on *Poussin in German (1914) and English (1966), and (with Anthony *Blunt) a complete catalogue of Poussin's drawings (5 vols., 1939–74).

Friedländer, Max J. (b Berlin, 5 June 1867; d Amsterdam, 11 Oct. 1958). German art historian. The successor to Wilhelm von *Bode as director of the Gemäldegalerie in Berlin, he enriched the collection particularly in his own field of Early Netherlandish painting. In 1934 he retired to the Netherlands. His magnum opus is *Die altniederländische Malerei* (14 vols., 1924–37). In a prefatory note to the English edition (*Early Netherlandish Painting*, 16 vols., 1967–76) Erwin *Panofsky described it as 'one of the few uncontested masterpieces produced by our discipline'. Friedländer covered the same ground in a much briefer format in *Die frühen niederländischen Maler von Van Eyck bis Bruegel* (1916), translated as *From Van Eyck to Bruegel* (1956). His other books include *On Art and Connoisseurship* (1942) and *Landscape, Portrait, Still Life* (1949).

Friedrich, Caspar David (b Greifswald, 5 Sept. 1774; d Dresden, 7 May 1840). The greatest German *Romantic painter and one of the most original geniuses in the history of landscape painting. His home town is near the Baltic coast, and the sea and shipping often feature in his work—although he depicted them imaginatively rather than topographically. He studied at the Copenhagen Academy under *Juel and *Abildgaard from 1794 to 1798 before settling permanently in Dresden. There he led a quiet life, interrupted only by occasional excursions to the mountains or to his homeland coast, single-mindedly pursuing his personal insight into the spiritual significance of landscape. He was intensely introspective and often melancholic (although his marriage at the age of 44 brought him much happiness), and he relied on deep contemplation to summon up mentally the images he was to put on canvas. 'Close your bodily eye, so that you may see your picture first with your spiritual eye', he wrote, 'then bring to the light of day that which you have seen in the darkness that it may react on others from the outside inwards.'

Friedrich began his career with topographical drawings in pencil and *sepia wash and did not take up oil painting until 1807. One of his first works in the new medium, *The Cross in the Mountains* (1808, Staatliche Kunstsammlungen, Dresden), caused great controversy because it was painted as an altarpiece, and to use a landscape in this unprecedented way was considered sacrilege by some critics. His choice of subjects often broke new ground and he discovered aspects of nature so far unseen: an infinite stretch of sea or mountains, snow-covered or fog-bound plains in the strange light of sunrise, dusk, or moonlight. Even when he does not use any overt religious symbolism, his landscapes convey a sense of haunting spirituality. Friedrich had a severe stroke in 1835 and returned to his small sepias. Although he enjoyed considerable success and renown earlier in his career, by the time of his death he was virtually forgotten and his immediate influence was confined to members of his circle in Dresden, notably G. F. *Kersting, who sometimes painted the figures in Friedrich's work. It was only at the end of the 19th century, with the rise of *Symbolism, that his greatness began to be recognized. Most of his work is still in Germany; *Winter Landscape* (c.1811), acquired by the National Gallery, London, in 1988, is the first Friedrich oil to enter a British public collection.

Friesz, Othon (*b* Le Havre, 6 Feb. 1879; *d* Paris, 10 Jan. 1949). French painter (of landscapes, portraits, figure compositions, and still-lifes), graphic artist, and designer. His early work was *Impressionist in style, then from 1905 to 1907 he was one of the *Fauves—his best work dates from this brief period. In 1907 he abandoned Fauvism and reverted to a more traditional and solidly constructed style, under the influence of *Cézanne, and from 1911 he adopted looser, freer handling. As well as paintings, he made book illustrations and tapestry designs. By the end of his life he was a much honoured figure, but his later career is generally seen as marking a steep decline from his Fauve days.

Frink, Dame Elisabeth (*b* Thurlow, Suffolk, 14 Nov. 1930; *d* Blandford Forum, Dorset, 18 Apr. 1993). British sculptor and graphic artist. Some of her early work—influenced by *Giacometti—was angular and menacing. During the 1960s her figures—typically horses and riders or male nudes—became smoother, but she retained a feeling of the bizarre in the polished goggles that feature particularly in her over-life-size heads. 'I think my sculptures are about what a human being or an animal feels like, not necessarily what they look like. I use anatomy to create the essence of human and animal forms.' She became one of the best-known British sculptors of her generation and her work included numerous public commissions, beginning with the concrete *Wild Boar* (1957) for Harlow New Town; a characteristic work is the bronze *Horse and Rider* (1975) in Piccadilly, London (at the corner of Dover Street), commissioned by Trafalgar House Investments Ltd. Later in her career she also did numerous portrait busts of distinguished sitters. In addition to sculpture she also made prints and drawings. She was created a dame in 1982.

Frith, William Powell (*b* Aldfield, nr. Ripon, Yorkshire, 9 Jan. 1819; *d* London, 2 Nov. 1909). English painter. He began his career as a portraitist and painter of literary subjects (from Shakespeare, Scott, and other authors), but in the 1850s he turned to contemporary scenes, with which he had enormous commercial success. Three of his pictures are particularly renowned—crowded, anecdote-packed scenes that rank among the most familiar images of Victorian life: *Life at the Seaside* (or *Ramsgate Sands*) (1854, Royal Coll.), *Derby Day* (1858, Tate, London), and *The Railway Station* (1862, Royal Holloway and Bedford New College, Egham). *Derby Day* was so popular when shown at the *Royal Academy that it had to be railed off from the throng of admirers—a distinction previously accorded only to *Wilkie's *Chelsea Pensioners* in 1822. Frith's *My Autobiography and Reminiscences* (1887) and *Further Reminiscences* (1888) give lively accounts of the art world of his time. He continued exhibiting until 1902 and by the end of his long life he was regarded as a 'specimen of Victorian philistinism' (Jeremy Maas, *Victorian Painters*, 1969). His reputation greatly revived as part of the general re-evaluation of Victorian art after the Second World War.

Froment, Nicolas (*d* ?Avignon, 1483/4). French painter. He perhaps came from northern France, but his known career was spent in the south; he is first recorded in 1465 at Uzès in Languedoc and he worked mainly in Avignon. Two documented works by him survive, both *triptychs: the *Raising of Lazarus* (1461, Uffizi, Florence) and *The Burning Bush* (1476, Aix-en-Provence Cathedral). They show that with *Quarton he introduced Netherlandish naturalism to French art. His figures have strong if sometimes clumsy expressions and gestures, and his draperies have an angularity reminiscent of some of the works of the Spanish and German followers of Rogier van der *Weyden.

Fromentin, Eugène (*b* La Rochelle, 24 Oct. 1820; *d* Saint-Maurice, nr. La Rochelle, 27 Aug. 1876). French painter and writer. As a painter he was a specialist in *Orientalism (he visited North Africa in 1846, 1847–8, and 1853). His pictures in this vein were much admired in his day but are now little known; his reputation rests instead on his book *Les Maîtres d'autrefois* (The Masters of Past Time, 1876), a study of Dutch and Flemish painting, particularly of the 17th century. He also wrote a lyrical novel, *Dominique* (1862).

Fronte Nuovo delle Arti (New Art Front). An association of Italian artists founded in 1946 with the aim of combating the pessimism of the post-war world and revitalizing Italian art, which had not been a leading force in Europe since the heyday of *Futurism. *Birolli and *Guttuso were the best-known figures in the group, which embraced artists of very different styles and ideologies. Incompatibilities between abstractionists and realists led to the dissolution of the association in 1948.

Frost, Sir Terry (*b* Leamington Spa, Warwickshire, 13 Oct. 1915; *d* nr. Newlyn, Cornwall, 1 Sept. 2003). British painter, one of the leading

*St Ives painters. He started painting in 1943 when he was a prisoner of war, encouraged by his fellow prisoner Adrian *Heath, then studied at St Ives and under *Coldstream and *Pasmore at the Camberwell School of Art, 1947–50. He began painting in the sober, naturalistic tradition of the *Euston Road School, but he soon turned to abstraction. His work remained based on observations of nature, however, often the harbour at St Ives. Characteristically he used patterns of interlinked shapes—strongly outlined but avoiding geometrical regularity. He taught at various art schools, notably at Reading University, 1965–81. His son **Anthony Frost** (1951–) is also an abstract painter of the St Ives School.

frottage (French: 'rubbing'). A technique of creating an image by placing a piece of paper over some rough surface such as grained wood or sacking and rubbing the paper with a crayon or pencil until it acquires an impression of the surface quality of the substance beneath. The resulting image is usually taken as a stimulus to the imagination, forming the point of departure for a picture expressing unconscious imagery. The technique was invented in 1925 by Max *Ernst, who described how he was inspired by some floorboards, 'the grain of which had been accentuated by a thousand scrubbings'; many other *Surrealists adopted it. See also AUTOMATISM.

Fry, Roger (b London, 14 Dec. 1866; d London, 9 Sept. 1934). British critic, painter, and designer. He took a first-class degree in natural sciences at Cambridge in 1888, but by this time he was already more interested in art, and in the 1890s he built up a reputation as a writer and lecturer (and a much more modest one as a painter). His success as a public speaker depended partly on his mellifluous voice; George Bernard Shaw said it was one of only two he knew that were worth listening to for their own sake—the other was that of the actor Sir Johnston Forbes-Robertson. In 1901 he became the regular art critic of the *Athenaeum*, a prestigious literary review, and from 1906 to 1910 he was curator of paintings at the Metropolitan Museum, New York. He had won his scholarly reputation writing on Italian Old Masters (his first book was on Giovanni *Bellini, 1899), but in the year he took up his New York appointment he began to be strongly drawn to *Cézanne and he developed into his period's most eloquent champion of modern French painting. After returning to London in 1910 he organized two exhibitions of *Post-Impressionist painting at the Grafton Galleries

(1910 and 1912) that are regarded as milestones in the history of British taste. They attracted an enormous amount of publicity, most of it unfavourable, and many people thought that Fry was a charlatan or possibly even insane (his wife unfortunately was insane, which prompted the unkind idea that her condition had somehow infected him). Certain young artists were immensely impressed by the exhibitions, however, and Fry became an influential figure among them. They included Vanessa *Bell and Duncan *Grant, both of whom worked for the *Omega Workshops, which Fry founded in 1913.

For the rest of his life Fry kept up a steady output of writing and lecturing and also continued to work seriously as a painter (he always regarded this activity as an important aspect of his career); at the time of his death he was Slade professor at Cambridge University. His books include monographs on Cézanne (1927) and *Matisse (1930), an edition of *Reynolds's *Discourses* (1905), and several collections of lectures and essays. In spite of the initial opposition to his ideas, he probably did more than anyone else to awaken public interest and understanding of modern art in England. Kenneth *Clark called him 'incomparably the greatest influence on taste since *Ruskin' and said: 'In so far as taste can be changed by one man, it was changed by Roger Fry.' As a painter Fry was experimental (his work includes a few abstracts), but his best pictures are fairly straightforward naturalistic portraits; his sitters included several of his *Bloomsbury Group friends (examples, including a self-portrait, are in the NPG, London).

Fuchs, Ernst. See FANTASTIC REALISM.

Führich, Joseph (b Kratzau, Bohemia, 9 Feb. 1800; d Vienna, 13 Mar. 1876). Austrian painter, draughtsman, and printmaker. Initially he was strongly influenced by *Dürer, but his style and outlook were most fundamentally shaped by his contact with the *Nazarenes in Rome (1827–9); he assisted with their frescos in the Villa Massimo and adopted their clear draughtsmanship and pious sentiment. After he returned to Austria he became the main upholder of Nazarene ideas there, as both a painter and a teacher (he became professor of historical composition at the Vienna Academy in 1840). His work included large fresco cycles in churches in Vienna, but he is probably better known for his various series of prints (etchings and wood engravings) on biblical subjects; these were highly popular in his day and earned him the nickname of 'der Theologe mit dem Stifte' (the theologian with the pencil).

Fuller, Isaac (*b* ?c.1606; *d* London, 17 July 1672). English decorative and portrait painter. He is said to have studied in France with *Perrier, then worked in Oxford and London. Fuller painted altarpieces for Oxford colleges (his *Resurrection* in All Souls was described by the diarist John Evelyn in 1644 as 'too full of nakeds for a chapel') and did decorative painting for taverns in London, including mythological scenes for the Mitre Tavern, Fenchurch Street, but these works have disappeared. His largest surviving pictures are five canvases, each about 3 m (10 ft) wide, showing Charles II's escape after the Battle of Worcester in 1651 (NPG, London). Otherwise, Fuller is remembered for his highly idiosyncratic portraits. He was a notorious drunkard and his self-portraits are painted with a bravura worthy of a larger-than-life character; there are three of these, all of similar type (c.1670, NPG; Bodleian Lib., Oxford; Queen's College, Oxford), and a related drawing (BM, London).

Funk art. Term applied to a type of art that originated in California (specifically the San Francisco area) around 1960 in which tatty or sick subjects—often pornographic or scatological—are treated in a deliberately distasteful way (the word 'funky' has various meanings, including 'smelly'; when applied to music it can mean 'earthy' or 'authentic'). Such art has been seen as a subversive reaction against the seriousness of *Abstract Expressionism and the New York art scene in general. Although the first Funk works were paintings, its most characteristic products are three-dimensional, either sculpture or *assemblages. Edward *Kienholz was the best-known practitioner of the genre.

Furini, Francesco (*b* Florence, 10 Apr. 1603; *d* Florence, 19 Aug. 1646). One of the leading Florentine painters of his period. He specialized in morbidly sensual pictures involving female nudes. In their idealization of the figure they show the influence of *Reni, but they have a distinctive dark, brooding atmosphere. Rudolf *Wittkower writes that Furini's 'highly sophisticated, over-refined' work has 'a sweetish, sickly flavour, but nobody can deny that he had a special gift for rendering the melodious calligraphy of the female body'. In 1633 Furini became a priest, the result of a crisis of conscience that led him to paint nothing but religious themes for a while. Even in his religious works, however, he showed his love of female beauty (*Lot and his Daughters*, c.1634, Prado, Madrid). Furini's pictures are usually fairly small and aimed at the private collector. In a very different vein, however, he painted two imposing allegorical frescos on *Medici history (1636–7) in the *Pitti Palace.

Fuseli, Henry (Johann Heinrich Füssli) (*b* Zurich, 6 Feb. 1741; *d* Putney [now in London], 16 Apr. 1825). Swiss-born painter, draughtsman, and writer on art, active mainly in England, where he was one of the outstanding figures of the *Romantic movement. He was the son of a portrait painter, **Johann Caspar Füssli** (1706–82), but he originally trained as a Zwinglian minister; he took holy orders in 1761, but soon abandoned the priesthood. In 1764 he moved to London at the suggestion of the British ambassador in Berlin, who had been impressed by his drawings. *Reynolds encouraged him to take up painting, and he spent the years 1770–8 in Italy, engrossed in the study of *Michelangelo, whose elevated style he sought to emulate for the rest of his life. After his return to England in 1779 he exhibited highly imaginative works such as *The Nightmare* (1781, Detroit Inst. of Arts), the picture that secured his reputation when it was shown at the *Royal Academy in 1782 (there is another version in the Goethe-museum, Frankfurt). An unforgettable image of a woman in the throes of a violently erotic dream, this painting shows how far ahead of his time Fuseli was in exploring the murky areas of the psyche where sex and fear meet. His fascination with the horrifying and fantastic also comes out in many of his literary subjects, which formed a major part of his output; he painted several works for *Boydell's Shakespeare Gallery, and in 1799 he followed this example by opening a Milton Gallery in Pall Mall with an exhibition of 47 of his own paintings.

From 1799 to 1805 Fuseli was professor of painting at the *Royal Academy and he was re-elected to the post in 1810. He was a popular teacher and a much respected figure (he was buried in St Paul's Cathedral next to Reynolds), but his work was generally neglected for about a century after his death until the *Expressionists and *Surrealists saw in him a kindred spirit. His work can be clumsy and overblown, but at its best it has something of the imaginative intensity of his friend *Blake, who described Fuseli as 'The only man that e'er I knew | who did not make me almost spew'. Fuseli's extensive writings on art include *Lectures on Painting* (1801) and a translation of *Winckelmann's *Reflections on the Painting and Sculpture of the Greeks* (1765). He also produced a revised edition (1805) of Matthew Pilkington's *Dictionary of Painters* (originally published in 1770), the first book of its kind in English.

Futurism. Italian avant-garde art movement, launched in 1909, that exalted the dynamism of the modern world; it was literary in origin, but most of its major exponents were painters, and it also embraced sculpture, architecture, music, the cinema, and photography. The First World War brought the movement to an end as a vital force, but it lingered in Italy until the 1930s, and it had a strong influence in other countries, particularly Russia.

The founder of Futurism was the writer Filippo Tommaso *Marinetti, who launched the movement with a manifesto published in French in the Parisian newspaper Le Figaro on 20 February 1909. In bombastic, inflammatory language, he attacked established values ('set fire to the library shelves . . . flood the museums') and called for the cultural rejuvenation of Italy by means of a new art that would celebrate technology, speed, and all things modern. Although he repeatedly used the word 'we' in the manifesto, there was no Futurist group when it was published (the movement was unusual not only in choosing its own name but also in that it started with an idea and only gradually found a way of expressing it in artistic form). However, he soon attracted adherents among other Italians, notably a group of painters based in Milan, whom he helped to produce the Manifesto of Futurist Painters, published in February 1910. It was drawn up by *Boccioni, *Carrà, and *Russolo, and also signed by *Balla (who lived in Rome) and *Severini (who was in Paris at this time). The same five (the main painters of the movement) signed the Technical Manifesto of Futurist Painting, published in April 1910. Whereas the first painters' manifesto is little more than a repetition of Marinetti's bombast, the Technical Manifesto does suggest—although in vague terms—the course that Futurist painting would take, with the emphasis on conveying movement (or the experience of movement). In trying to work out a visual idiom to express such concerns, the Futurist painters at first were strongly influenced by *Divisionism, in which forms are broken down into small patches of colour—suitable for suggesting sparkling effects of light or the blurring caused by high-speed movement. From 1911, however, some of them—influenced by *Cubism—began using fragmented forms and multiple viewpoints, often accentuating the sense of movement by vigorous diagonals. Their subjects were typically drawn from urban life, and they were often political in intent, but at times their work came close to abstraction.

Boccioni (the only major sculptor in the group) showed a similar concern with movement in his Manifesto of Futurist Sculpture, published in April 1912. There was also a Manifesto of Futurist Architecture (1914)—by Antonio Sant'Elia (1888–1916), whose powerful and audacious designs remained on paper—as well as musical manifestos (see RUSSOLO), and several on other topics, including a Manifesto of Futurist Lust (1913). Marinetti had a prodigious talent for publicity (backed by substantial inherited wealth) and Futurism was promoted not only through such manifestos, but also by exhibitions, lectures, press conferences, and various attention-seeking stunts, some of which foreshadowed *Performance art.

In keeping with this talent for self-promotion, the Futurists had widespread influence in the period immediately before and during the First World War. Stylistically, the influence is clear in the work of the *Vorticists and *Nevinson in England, for example, and that of Marcel *Duchamp in France and Joseph *Stella in the USA, whilst the use of provocative manifestos and other shock tactics was most eagerly adopted by the *Dadaists. Outside Italy, however, it was in Russia that Futurism made the greatest impact, although there were significant differences between the movements in the two countries: Russian Futurism was expressed as much in literature and the theatre as in the visual arts, and it combined modern ideas with an interest in *primitivism. In terms of Russian painting, Futurism was particularly influential on *Rayonism.

Russian Futurism flourished into the 1920s, but Italian Futurism—as an organized movement—was virtually ended by the First World War (during which Boccioni, its outstanding artist, and also Sant'Elia died; ironically, Marinetti had welcomed the war as a means of cleansing the world). Of the leading painters of the pre-war phase, only Balla remained true to Futurism, and its centre of activity moved from Milan to Rome, where he lived. After the war, Marinetti continued with his literary and political activities, supporting Fascism (he was a friend of Mussolini). Fascism and Futurism shared an aggressive nationalism and the names are often linked; Futurism has even been described as 'the official art of Fascism'. This, however, is untrue. Although Fascism was ideologically close to Nazism, it was much more tolerant and open in artistic matters; there was no official art of the regime, but in the 1930s the pompous style favoured by some *Novecento artists came much closer to this than Futurism ever did.

Fyt, Jan (*bapt.* Antwerp, 15 June 1611; *d* Antwerp, 11 Sept. 1661). Flemish painter and etcher, primarily of still-life and hunting pieces. He worked mainly in Antwerp, where he was a pupil of *Snyders, but he also visited Paris, Italy, and possibly the Netherlands. He had a successful and prolific career and often collaborated with other artists. His most characteristic paintings are in the Snyders tradition, depicting trophies of the hunt, dead stags, hares, and birds, all treated with a vigorous feeling for texture. His rare flower paintings are exceptionally fine and perhaps more attuned to modern taste.

G

Gabo, Naum (Naum Neemia Pevsner) (*b* ?Klimovichi, Belarus, 5 Aug. 1890; *d* Waterbury, Conn., 23 Aug. 1977). Russian-born sculptor who became an American citizen in 1952, the most influential exponent of *Constructivism. He was the younger brother of Antoine *Pevsner, and adopted another family name, Gabo, in 1915 to avoid confusion between the two. After studying medicine, natural sciences, and engineering in Munich, he was introduced to avant-garde art when he visited his brother in Paris in 1913–14, and in 1915 he began to make geometrical constructions in Oslo, where they had taken refuge during the First World War. In 1917 the brothers returned to Russia and in 1920 they published their *Realistic Manifesto*, which set forth the basic principles of Constructivism. They advocated a pure abstract sculpture, but official policy in the new Soviet Russia increasingly insisted on art being channelled into industrial design and other socially useful work (as exemplified by *Tatlin). Gabo therefore left Russia in 1922 and spent the next ten years in Berlin, where he knew many of the leading artists of the day, particularly those connected with the *Bauhaus. In 1932 he moved to Paris, where he was a prominent member of the *Abstraction-Création group, and in 1935 he settled in England, living first in London (where in 1937 he was co-editor of the Constructivist review *Circle*) and then from 1939 in Cornwall (see ST IVES SCHOOL).

In 1946 Gabo moved to the USA, settling at Middlebury, Connecticut, in 1953. In the last three decades of his life he received many prestigious awards and carried out numerous public commissions in Europe and America. He often worked on themes over a long period; his Torsion Fountain outside St Thomas's Hospital in London, for example, was erected in 1975, but is a development from models he was making in the 1920s. (Small models are a feature of his work; there are numerous examples in Tate Modern, which has an outstanding collection of Gabo material.)

Gabo never trained as an artist, but came to art by way of his studies of engineering and physical science, and was one of the first artists to embody in his work modern concepts of the nature of space. He was one of the earliest to experiment with *Kinetic sculpture and to make extensive use of semi-transparent materials for a type of abstract sculpture that incorporates space as a positive element rather than displacing or enclosing it. He was throughout his life an advocate of the Constructivist idea not merely as an artistic movement but as the ideology of a way of life.

Gabriël, Paul Joseph Constantin (*b* Amsterdam, 5 July 1828; *d* Scheveningen, 23 Aug. 1903). Dutch painter, primarily of landscapes (but also of flower pieces). Best known for views of meadows, canals, and windmills, he is regarded as a member of the *Hague School, even though he spent much of his life in Brussels (1860–84) and was more appreciated in Belgium and France than in his own country. His liking for cheerful colours also distinguishes him from other members of the Hague School, who favoured grey, atmospheric effects; in 1901 he wrote, 'Although I may sometimes seem rather grumpy, I really love it when the sun shines on the water; and, quite apart from that, I think my country is colourful.' *Mondrian admired the almost geometrical quality of Gabriël's compositions and in 1895 he made a copy of his *In the Month of July* (Rijksmuseum, Amsterdam).

Gaddi, Taddeo (*d* Florence, 1366). Florentine painter, the son of a painter and mosaicist, **Gaddo Gaddi** (*d* c.1330). According to Cennino *Cennini, Taddeo was *Giotto's godson and worked with him for 24 years. He was one of the leading Florentine artists of his day, as is indicated by the fact that in about 1347 he headed a list of 'the best masters of painting who are in Florence' drawn up by the authorities of the church of S. Giovanni Fuorcivitas in Pistoia; the altarpiece he painted for the church (a *polyptych of the *Virgin and Child Enthroned with Saints*, completed 1353) is still *in situ*. Taddeo's best-known works were painted for S. Croce, Florence, notably the frescos devoted to the life of the Virgin in the Baroncelli Chapel (*c*.1330), and the panels illustrating the life of Christ (*c*.1330), originally meant for the doors of a sacristy cupboard and now divided among museums in Florence (Accademia), Munich (Alte Pin.), and Berlin (Gemäldegalerie). Many other panels are attributed to him and he must have had a flourishing workshop. Although he was heir to the tradition of Giotto, his style is less heroic and more anecdotal.

Taddeo had three painter sons, of whom the most important was **Agnolo** (*bur*. Florence, 16 Oct. 1396), who continued the Giotto manner but modified it still further in the direction of decorative elegance. He is particularly notable for his cool, pale colours, which influenced the refined late *Gothic art of artists of the next generation such as *Lorenzo Monaco. Agnolo's works include frescos on the story of the Cross in the chancel of S. Croce (*c*.1390) and on the story of the Virgin and her girdle in the chapel of the Holy Girdle in Prato Cathedral (1392–5). Many panel paintings also are attributed to him.

Gainsborough, Thomas (*bapt*. Sudbury, Suffolk, 14 May 1727; *d* London, 2 Aug. 1788). English painter of portraits, landscapes, and *fancy pictures, one of the most individual geniuses in British art. He showed artistic talent from an early age and around 1740 (aged about 13) he moved from his home in Sudbury to London, where he studied with *Gravelot and perhaps also with *Hayman. In 1748 he returned to Sudbury and in 1752 he set up as a portrait painter in Ipswich, the largest town in the county. His work at this time consisted mainly of heads and half-lengths, but he also produced some small portrait groups in landscape settings, including the celebrated *Mr and Mrs Andrews* (*c*.1748–9, NG, London), remarkable for its 'dewy freshness' (Ellis *Waterhouse). In addition he painted pure landscapes (*Cornard Wood*, 1748, NG, London). His patrons in Ipswich were mainly the merchants of the town and local squires, but in 1759 he moved to Bath, where he worked for much more fashionable clients, many of them wealthy visitors to the spa town. From now on all his portraits were life-size and many of them were full-lengths, in which he cultivated a distinctively free and elegant manner (*Mary, Countess Howe*, *c*.1764, Kenwood House, London). In 1768 he was elected a foundation member of the *Royal Academy (the only portraitist from outside London to be so honoured), and in 1774 he settled permanently in the capital. Here he further developed the personal style he

had evolved at Bath, working with light and rapid brushstrokes and delicate and evanescent colours. He became a favourite painter of the royal family, even though his rival *Reynolds was appointed principal painter to the king.

Gainsborough said that while portraiture was his profession, landscape painting was his pleasure, and he continued to paint landscapes long after he had left a country neighbourhood, sometimes basing them on materials such as twigs and pebbles, which he arranged in the studio as a stimulus to his imagination; Reynolds recorded that he used 'broken stones, dried herbs, and pieces of looking glass, which he magnified and improved into rocks, trees, and water'. Gainsborough also produced many landscape drawings, some in pencil, some in charcoal and chalk (he liked to experiment technically and sometimes used mixed media, for example combining chalk with oils). In his later years he extended his range to include fancy pictures of pastoral subjects (*Peasant Girl Gathering Sticks*, 1782, City AG, Manchester). He is only once known to have left England, making a brief visit to the Netherlands in 1783.

Gainsborough's style had diverse sources. His early works show the influence of French engraving and of Dutch landscape painting; at Bath his change of portrait style owed much to a close study of van *Dyck, whose work he saw in nearby country houses (his admiration is most clear in *The Blue Boy*, 1770, Huntington Art Coll., San Marino); and in his later landscapes he was sometimes influenced by *Rubens (*The Watering Place*, 1777, NG, London). But he was an independent and highly original artist, able to assimilate to his own ends what he learnt from others, and he always relied mainly on his own resources. With the exception of his nephew Gainsborough *Dupont, he had no assistants and unlike most of his contemporaries he never employed a *drapery painter. He was in many ways the antithesis of Reynolds. Whereas Reynolds was sober-minded and the complete professional, Gainsborough (even though his output was prodigious) was much more easygoing and often overdue with his commissions, writing that 'painting and punctuality mix like oil and vinegar'. Although he was an entertaining letter-writer, Gainsborough, unlike Reynolds, had no interest in literary or historical themes, his great passion outside painting being music (his friend William Jackson the composer wrote that he 'avoided the company of literary men, who were his aversion . . . he detested reading').

Gainsborough and Reynolds had great mutual respect, however; Gainsborough asked for Reynolds to visit him on his deathbed, and Reynolds paid posthumous tribute to his rival in his Fourteenth *Discourse*. Recognizing the fluid brilliance of his brushwork, Reynolds praised 'his manner of forming all the parts of a picture together', and wrote of 'all those odd scratches and marks' that 'by a kind of magic, at a certain distance . . . seem to drop into their proper places'. Examples of Gainsborough's work are in many collections in Britain and the USA, including the museum devoted to him in Sudbury, located in the attractive house in which he was born.

Gallego, Fernando (*b* Salamanca, ?*c*.1440; *d* Salamanca, ?*c*.1550). Spanish painter, first documented in 1468. He worked mainly in Salamanca, where *Palomino says he was born, and was the major Castilian painter of his period. Gallego's sober, impassive style has affinities with that of Dirk *Bouts, and it has been suggested that he visited the Netherlands early in his career. His works include a *triptych of *The Virgin, St Andrew and St Christopher* (*c*.1470) in the new cathedral of Salamanca (one of his few signed paintings), an altarpiece of *St Idelfonso* (*c*.1475–80) in the cathedral of Zamora, and ceiling frescos on astrological subjects (*c*.1480, much repainted) in the Old Library in the university of Salamanca. Gallego had considerable influence in Castile. He is last documented in 1507, but Palomino says he died 'at an advanced age' around 1550. One of his followers, **Francisco Gallego**, was presumably a relative.

Gallen-Kallela, Akseli (*b* Pori, 26 Apr. 1865; *d* Stockholm, 7 Mar. 1931). Finnish painter, graphic artist, designer, and architect. A major figure in the *Art Nouveau and *Symbolist movements, Gallen-Kallela travelled widely and was well known outside Finland, particularly in Germany (he had a joint exhibition with *Munch in Berlin in 1895 and exhibited with Die *Brücke in Dresden in 1910). He was deeply patriotic (he volunteered to fight in the War of Independence against Russia in 1918, even though he was in his fifties) and he was inspired mainly by the landscape and folklore of his country, above all by the Finnish national epic *Kalevala* ('Land of Heroes'). His early work was in the 19th-century naturalistic tradition, but in the 1890s he developed a flatter, more stylized manner, well suited to the depiction of heroic myth, with bold simplifications of form, strong outlines, and vivid—sometimes rather garish—

colours. Apart from easel paintings, Gallen-Kallela did a number of murals for public buildings (including the Finnish National Museum, Helsinki, 1928). His work also included book illustrations (notably for an edition of *Kalevala*, 1922) and designs for stained glass, fabrics, and jewellery. He is regarded not only as his country's greatest painter, but also as the chief figure in the creation of a distinctive Finnish art, and he was given a funeral befitting a national hero. His former home (which he designed himself) at Tarvaspää near Helsinki is now a museum dedicated to him.

Galli-Bibiena. See BIBIENA.

Gambart, Ernest (*b* Courtrai [Kortrijk], 12 Oct. 1814; *d* Nice, 12 Apr. 1902). Belgian-born picture dealer and print publisher who settled in London in 1840 and became a dominant figure in these fields; he adopted British nationality in 1846. In the three decades between his arrival in England and his retirement to the Continent in 1871, 'Gambart, more than any other individual, transformed the London art world. He founded a system for the promotion and sale of pictures on an international scale; contributed increasingly to the status of the artist in society; and brought the London, if not the European, art trade from infancy to maturity . . . [He] became a print publisher of international repute, who exploited the possibilities of the print so as to raise it to the level of pure popular art' (Jeremy Maas, *Gambart: Prince of the Victorian Art World*, 1975).

Games, Abram. See AIRBRUSH.

Garbo, Raffaellino del. See SARTO.

Gardner, Isabella Stewart (*b* New York, 14 Apr. 1840; *d* Boston, 17 July 1924). American socialite and art collector. She married into a prominent Boston family and spent most of her life in that city, where she patronized numerous artistic causes (including the Boston Symphony Orchestra) and dazzled and occasionally mildly scandalized polite society (for example by attending boxing matches). Her interest in art was guided by Bernard *Berenson, one of her protégés, who helped her to assemble a superb collection of Italian Renaissance paintings, including *Titian's *Rape of Europa*, which has often been claimed as the greatest painting in America. Other highlights of her collection include some outstanding 17th-century Dutch paintings and her full-length portrait (1888) by *Sargent (to whom she had been introduced in

London by Henry James). The portrait shows off her celebrated figure (she wears her pearls round her waist rather than her neck) and was considered rather shocking—in the spirit of Sargent's earlier *Madame X* (some contemporaries assumed that he and Mrs Gardner were lovers, but this seems highly unlikely). Her husband, the financier Jack Gardner, died in 1898, and the following year she began building Fenway Court in Boston as both a home and a museum. The building, which was formally opened in 1903, is modelled on a Venetian Renaissance palace and incorporates various architectural fragments that she bought on her numerous trips to Europe. She supervised the construction with immense care, acting virtually as site foreman. In her will she left the Isabella Stewart Gardner Museum to Boston as a public institution, with the proviso that the collection should be maintained exactly as she had arranged it. The British art historian Sir Philip Hendy, who published a catalogue of the Gardner Museum in 1931, described it as 'probably the finest collection of its compact size in the world'. In addition to paintings, sculpture, drawings, and prints, it contains objects of many other types, including furniture, textiles, ceramics, glassware, manuscripts, and books.

Gargallo, Pablo. See IRON.

gargoyle. A spout in the form of a grotesque figure—animal, human, or monstrous—projecting from a cornice or parapet and allowing the water from the roof gutters to escape clear of the walls. There are many examples on *Gothic cathedrals and churches throughout Europe, bearing witness to the lively imagination of medieval craftsmen. In the 14th and 15th centuries, sculptures similar to gargoyles but not serving their function were used to decorate walls, and the term gargoyle is sometimes loosely applied to these. With the introduction of lead drainpipes in the 16th century gargoyles were no longer needed, but examples were occasionally made in lead.

Garofalo (Benvenuto Tisi) (*b* Ferrara, ?1481; *d* Ferrara, 6 Sept. 1559). Italian painter, active mainly in Ferrara. His nickname is said to come from his liking for including a gillyflower (Italian: *garofano*) in a corner of his paintings. According to *Vasari he twice visited Rome, and his work—derivative but beautifully crafted—was heavily influenced by *Raphael. He was the first to paint in such a manner in Ferrara and was influential in spreading the High *Renaissance style.

His output was large and varied (frescos, altarpieces, small devotional works, also a few mythologies); there are many examples in Ferrarese churches and, for example, in the National Gallery, London. In about 1550 he went blind.

Garwood, Tirzah. See RAVILIOUS.

Gaudí, Antoni. See ART NOUVEAU.

Gaudier-Brzeska, Henri (Henri Gaudier) (*b* Saint-Jean-de-Braye, nr. Orléans, 4 Oct. 1891; *d* Neuville-Saint-Vaast, 5 June 1915). French sculptor and draughtsman, active in England for most of his short career and usually considered part of the history of British rather than French art. In 1910 he took up sculpture in Paris without formal training, and in the same year he met Sophie Brzeska, a Polish woman twenty years his senior, with whom he lived from that time, both of them adopting the hyphenated name. In 1911 they moved to London, which Gaudier had visited briefly in 1906 and 1908, and lived for a while in extreme poverty. He became a friend of Wyndham *Lewis and other leading literary and artistic figures, and his work was shown in avant-garde exhibitions, such as the *Vorticist exhibition of 1915. In 1914 he enlisted in the French army and was killed in action the following year, aged 23.

Gaudier developed with astonishing rapidity from a modelling style based on *Rodin towards a highly personal manner of carving in which shapes are radically simplified in a manner recalling *Brancusi (*Red Stone Dancer, c.*1913, Tate, London). In England, only *Epstein was producing sculpture as stylistically advanced as Gaudier at this time. In his lifetime his work was appreciated by only a small circle, but since his death he has become widely recognized as one of the outstanding sculptors of his generation and has acquired something of a legendary status as an unfulfilled genius. In addition to his sculptures he left behind some splendid animal drawings.

Gauguin, Paul (*b* Paris, 7 June 1848; *d* Atuona, Marquesas Islands, 8 May 1903). French painter, printmaker, sculptor, and ceramicist, with *Cézanne and van *Gogh the greatest of the *Post-Impressionists and like them a seminal figure in the development of modern art. His father was a radical journalist and his mother, who was half French and half Peruvian Creole, also had strong political convictions. They were opponents of the regime of Louis Napoleon (later Napoleon III), and in 1851 the family left France for exile in Peru. Gauguin spent part of his childhood in

Lima before returning to France with his mother in 1855 (his father had died on the outward journey). He joined the merchant marine in 1865, in 1868 transferred to the French navy, and from 1871 worked successfully as a stockbroker. In the early 1870s he became a keen amateur painter and in 1874 he saw the first *Impressionist exhibition. At about the same time he met *Pissarro, who encouraged him, and began to make a collection of Impressionist pictures. He had a landscape accepted by the *Salon in 1876 and his work was shown in the fifth to eighth (and last) Impressionist exhibitions (1880–6). In 1883 he gave up his employment to become a full-time artist, but had little success and sold his collection to support himself and his family.

After the last Impressionist exhibition Gauguin moved to Brittany (where he spent much of his time until 1890), having abandoned his family in Copenhagen (his wife was Danish). He was inspired not only by the rugged Breton landscape but also by the humble faith of the peasants in this region, which was still almost medieval in some of its ways. His main place of work in Brittany was *Pont-Aven, where he became the centre of a group of artists who were attracted by his powerful personality and stimulating ideas about art. The pivotal work he produced there was *The Vision after the Sermon*, also known as *Jacob Wrestling with the Angel* (1888, NG, Edinburgh), in which he broke away completely from the Impressionist style, using areas of pure, flat colour for expressive and symbolic purposes. In 1887–8 he visited Panama and Martinique, and in 1888 he spent a short time at Arles with van *Gogh, a visit that ended in a disastrous quarrel as van Gogh suffered one of his first attacks of madness.

Gauguin had had a taste for colourful, exotic places since his childhood in Peru and in 1891 he left France for Tahiti. In the account he wrote of his life there, *Noa Noa* (first published in 1897), he said: 'I have escaped everything that is artificial and conventional. Here I enter into Truth, become one with nature. After the disease of civilization, life in this new world is a return to health.' Earlier he had found something of the same untainted quality—a 'great rustic and superstitious simplicity'—among the peasants of Brittany, and his theory and practice of art reflected his desire to deal with earthy human feelings rather than the concerns of polite society. He was one of the first to find visual inspiration in the arts of ancient or *primitive peoples, and he reacted vigorously against the naturalism

of the Impressionists and the scientific preoccupations of the *Neo-Impressionists. As well as using colour unnaturalistically for its decorative or emotional effect, he employed emphatic outlines forming rhythmic patterns suggestive of stained glass or Japanese colour prints (see UKIYO-E). Gauguin also produced woodcuts in which the black and white areas formed almost abstract patterns and the tool marks were incorporated as parts of the design. Along with those of Edvard *Munch, these prints played an important part in stimulating the major revival of the art of woodcut in the 20th century. His other work included woodcarving and pottery.

In Tahiti Gauguin endeavoured to 'go native' and despite the constant pressure of poverty he painted his finest pictures there. His colours became more resonant, his drawing more grandly simplified, and his expression of the mysteries of life more profound. In 1893 poverty and ill health forced him to return to France, but he had a financial windfall when an uncle died and he was back in Tahiti in 1895. At the end of 1897 he painted his largest picture, the celebrated allegory of life *Where Do We Come From? Who Are We? Where Are We Going?* (MFA, Boston), before attempting suicide (although he had deserted his family he had been devastated that year by the news of the death of his favourite daughter). In September 1901 he settled at Dominica in the Marquesas Islands, where he died two years later. Until his death he worked continuously in the face of poverty, illness (he had syphilis), and lack of recognition. He was often unable to obtain proper materials and was forced to spread his colours thinly on coarse sacking, but from these limitations he forged a style of rough vigour wholly appropriate to the boldness of his vision.

Gauguin was by no means forgotten in France during his years in the South Seas, but at the time of his death few would have agreed with his self-assessment: 'I am a great artist and I know it. It is because I am that I have endured such suffering.' His reputation was firmly established, however, when 227 of his works were shown at the *Salon d'Automne in Paris in 1906, and his influence has been enormous. The *Nabis were formed under his inspiration, and he was a leading figure of the *Symbolist movement and one of the sources for *Fauvism. Later, he was one of the major influences on the general non-naturalistic trend of 20th-century art. Because of the romantic appeal of his life and personality, particularly his willingness to sacrifice everything for his art, Gauguin (like his friend van Gogh) has also been an inspiration for popular and fictional biography, including the novel *The Moon and Sixpence* (1919) by Somerset Maugham, and the opera (1957) of the same title by John L. Gardner.

Gaulli, Giovanni Battista (Il Baciccio) (*b* Genoa, 8 May 1639; *d* Rome, 2 Apr. 1709). Italian painter; the name Baciccio, by which he is often known, is a dialect contraction of his forenames. He worked mainly in Rome, where he settled in 1657 and was a friend and protégé of *Bernini (his portrait of Bernini (*c.*1675, NG, Edinburgh) became a kind of official likeness of the Grand Old Man, serving as the basis for the frontispiece engraving of *Baldinucci's biography of 1682). Gaulli achieved success as a painter of altarpieces and portraits (he painted each of the seven popes from Alexander VII to Clement XI as well as many cardinals), but he is remembered mainly for his decorative work and above all for his *Adoration of the Name of Jesus* (1674–9) on the ceiling of the nave of the Gesù. This is one of the supreme masterpieces of *illusionistic decoration, ranking alongside *Pozzo's slightly later ceiling in S. Ignazio, and it appears in countless books as an archetypal example of Counter-Reformation art. The *stucco figures that are so brilliantly combined with the painted decoration (from the ground it is not always possible to tell which is which) are the work of Bernini's pupil Antonio Raggi (1624–86).

Gavarni, Paul (pseudonym of Sulpice-Guillaume Chevalier) (*b* Paris, 13 Jan. 1804; *d* Paris, 24 Nov. 1866). French lithographic caricaturist, a leading satirist of French bourgeois life (he is often seen as the equivalent in social satire of *Daumier in political satire, although he was an artist of lesser stature). Gavarni was described as 'the best-dressed man in France' and his style was appropriately elegant and witty. His work, which appeared in various journals, including *La Caricature* (see PHILIPON), was popular in England as well as France, and he visited England in 1847 and 1851. While there he studied the life of the poor in London and in *Gavarni in London* (1849) he contrasted it with the life of the rich, the benign irony of his earlier works giving way to a more trenchant satire. As he aged he became reclusive and his work expressed disenchantment with life.

Gear, William. See COBRA.

Geertgen tot Sint Jans (*b* ?Leiden, ?*c.*1460; *d* ?Haarlem, ?*c.*1490). Netherlandish painter, active in Haarlem, where he was the outstanding artist

of his day. Almost nothing is known of his career, but van *Mander says that he was a pupil of *Ouwater and that he died when he was about 28. His name means 'Little Gerard of the Brethren of St John', after the Order in Haarlem of which he was a lay brother. For the monastery church of the Brethren he painted his only documented work, a *triptych of the *Crucifixion*, of which two large panels (originally two sides of a wing) survive (KH Mus., Vienna): the *Lamentation of Christ* and the *Burning of the Bones of St John the Baptist*. Certain features of these paintings—particularly the slender, doll-like figures with smooth, rather egglike heads—are highly distinctive, and a small oeuvre of about fifteen paintings has been attributed to Geertgen on stylistic grounds. Unlike the Vienna panels, most of the other pictures given to him are fairly small. They include such remarkably beautiful works as the *Nativity* (NG, London), a radiant nocturnal scene, and *St John the Baptist in the Wilderness* (Gemäldegalerie, Berlin), which shows an exquisite feeling for nature. The vein of tender melancholy that pervades Geertgen's work, the beguilingly innocent charm of his figures, and his sensitivity to light are perhaps the salient qualities that make him one of the most irresistibly attractive artists of the Early Netherlandish School.

Gelder, Aert de (*b* Dordrecht, 26 Oct. 1645; *d* Dordrecht, 27 Aug. 1727). Dutch painter, active mainly in Dordrecht. After studying with *Hoogstraten, he became one of *Rembrandt's last pupils in Amsterdam. He was not only one of the most talented of Rembrandt's pupils, but also one of his most devoted followers, for he was the only Dutch artist to continue working in his style into the 18th century, remaining completely resistant to new trends. His religious paintings, in particular, with their imaginative boldness and preference for oriental types, are very much in the master's spirit, although de Gelder often used colours—such as lilac and lemon yellow—that were untypical of Rembrandt, and his palette was in general lighter. One of his best-known works, *Jacob's Dream* (Dulwich Picture Gal., London), was long attributed to Rembrandt.

Gemäldegalerie. German word meaning 'picture gallery'; it is the name in particular of two of the world's greatest collections of Old Masters, in Berlin and Dresden.

The Dresden Gemäldegalerie had its origins in the collections of the ruling house of Saxony. In 1722 the finest pictures from various churches and palaces were brought together in a group of buildings in Dresden (known incongruously as the Stables), and the collection was greatly augmented by Frederick-Augustus II, Elector of Saxony (1696-1763; reigned from 1733, also as King Augustus III of Poland). *Winckelmann said that he 'brought the arts to Saxony' and he did indeed devote much of his money and energy to collecting; his most famous purchase was *Raphael's *Sistine Madonna*. In 1831 the gallery became state property, and in 1855 (by which time the collection had about 2,200 paintings) it was transferred to the present building, designed by Gottfried Semper (one of the architects of the *Kunsthistorisches Museum, Vienna).

The Berlin Gemäldegalerie was created as part of a policy to demonstrate that Prussia (the most powerful German state, of which Berlin was the capital) was fit to lead Germany culturally as well as politically (Dresden and Munich already had world-renowned collections). It was founded in 1823 (the nucleus of pictures coming from various royal residences in Prussia) and opened in 1830 in a magnificently severe *Neoclassical building designed by *Schinkel. This building is now known as the Altes Museum (Old Museum). In 1904 the Gemäldegalerie transferred to the newly built Kaiser Friedrich Museum (now renamed the Bode Museum, after Wilhelm von *Bode). After the Second World War, Berlin was divided into East and West and the Gemäldegalerie's paintings were similarly divided between the Bode Museum (East) and the Dahlem Museum (West). Following the unification of Germany in 1990, however, Berlin's museums were reorganized and in 1999 the Gemäldegalerie moved into a new building in the Tiergarten complex (also known as the Kulturforum), alongside numerous other cultural institutions.

Generalić, Ivan (*b* Hlebine, 21 Dec 1914; *d* Koprivnica, 27 Nov. 1992). Yugoslav (Croatian) *naive painter, the best-known member of the school of peasant painters centred on his native village of Hlebine; the other members included his friends Franjo Mraz (1910–81) and Mirko Virius (1889–1943). Unlike most naive painters, Generalić had a wide repertory. Many of his pictures depict scenes from village life—weddings, funerals, farm work, fairs, and so on—but he also painted landscapes, portraits, still-lifes, and imaginative subjects. Some of his pictures are idyllic in mood, but in others there is an element of grotesque fantasy or of *Surrealist strangeness. Usually he painted on glass and his pictures often have a kind of inner glow. After the Second World War he became internationally recognized as one of the finest of all naive artists, his work featuring in numerous group and solo exhibitions and winning him various awards. In spite of his success, he continued to live the life of a peasant and to paint only in his spare time.

genre. Term for paintings or other works depicting scenes from daily life. It may be applied to appropriate art of any place or period, but most commonly suggests the type of domestic subject matter favoured by Dutch 17th-century artists. In a broader sense, the term is used to mean a particular branch or category of art; landscape and portraiture, for example, are genres of painting, and the essay and the short story are genres of literature.

Gentile da Fabriano (*b* Fabriano, ?*c*.1385; *d* Rome, 1427). Italian painter, named after his birthplace in the Marches. His birthdate has been traditionally estimated as *c*.1370, but expert opinion now inclines to put it about fifteen years later. Gentile carried out important commissions in several major Italian art centres and was recognized as one of the foremost artists of his day, but most of the work on which his great contemporary reputation was based has been destroyed. It included frescos in the Doges' Palace in Venice (1408) and for St John Lateran in Rome (1427). In between he worked in Florence, Siena, and Orvieto. His major surviving work is the celebrated altarpiece of the *Adoration of the Magi* (1423, Uffizi, Florence), painted for the church of S. Trinità in Florence, which places him alongside *Ghiberti as one of the greatest exponents of the *International Gothic style in Italy. It is remarkable not only for its exquisite decorative beauty but also for the naturalistic treatment of light in the *predella, where there is a night scene with three different light sources. Gentile had widespread influence (much more so initially than his great contemporary *Masaccio), notably on Jacopo *Bellini, who probably worked with him in Florence, *Pisanello, who completed work in Rome he left unfinished at his death, and Fra *Angelico, who was his greatest heir.

Gentileschi, Orazio (*bapt.* Pisa, 9 July 1563; *d* London, 7 Feb. 1639). Italian painter, active mainly in Rome, where he settled in about 1576. Initially he worked in a *Mannerist style, but he became one of the closest and most gifted of *Caravaggio's followers. He was one of the few

*Caravaggisti who were friends of the master, and in 1603 he and Caravaggio and two other artists were sued for libel by Giovanni *Baglione. Gentileschi's work does not have the power and uncompromising naturalism of Caravaggio, however, tending rather towards the lyrical and refined. His figures are graceful, stately, and clearly disposed, and have sharp-edged drapery—qualities recalling his Tuscan heritage. In 1621 he moved to Genoa, where he stayed until 1623; while there he painted an *Annunciation* (Gal. Sabauda, Turin) that is often considered his masterpiece. After working for Marie de *Médicis in Paris, he settled in England in 1626 and became court painter to Charles I. He was held in great esteem in England and remained until his death. His travels were a factor in spreading the Caravaggesque manner, but by the end of his career he had long abandoned heavy *chiaroscuro in favour of light colours. His major works in England were a series of ceiling paintings (1635–8) commissioned by Charles I for the Queen's House at Greenwich, now in Marlborough House, London.

His daughter **Artemisia Gentileschi** (*b* Rome, 8 July 1593; *d* Naples, 1652/3) was one of the greatest of Caravaggesque painters and a formidable personality. She showed remarkable talent whilst still in her teens, built up a European reputation, and lived a life of independence rare for a woman of the time. Up to about 1630 she worked mainly in her native Rome, apart from the years 1612–20, when she lived in Florence (in 1616, aged only 23, she became the first ever female member of the city's Accademia del Disegno). In about 1630 she settled in Naples, but in 1638–41 she visited England, presumably initially to see her ailing father. Although she had doubtless been trained by Orazio, her powerful and dramatic style was very different from his. It is seen at its most characteristic in paintings of *Judith and Holofernes*, a subject she made her own (one of the finest examples is in the Uffizi, Florence). Her predilection for the bloodthirsty theme has been related to events in her own life. At the age of 17 she was allegedly raped by Agostino *Tassi and was tortured during his ensuing trial; thus the fierce intensity with which she depicted a woman decapitating a man has been seen as pictorial 'revenge' for her sufferings.

Geometric art. Term applied to Greek art in the 9th and 8th centuries BC, named after the decoration associated with the pottery of the period. Vases are characteristically divided into painted horizontal bands filled with various forms of geometric ornament, developing into stylized human and animal forms.

George III, King of Great Britain and Ireland. See ROYAL COLLECTION.

George IV, King of Great Britain and Ireland. See ROYAL COLLECTION.

Gérard, François (*b* Rome, 4 May 1770; *d* Paris, 11 Jan. 1837). French painter, born in Rome, where his father worked for the French ambassador to the Vatican (his mother was Italian). His family returned to Paris in 1782 and in 1786 Gérard began studying with J.-L. *David, becoming one of his favourite pupils. In the *Salon of 1796 he won acclaim with his portrait *Jean-Baptiste Isabey and his Daughter* (Louvre, Paris) and by the turn of the century he was established as France's leading society portraitist. He also produced historical and mythological pictures, notably *Psyche Receiving Cupid's First Kiss* (1798, Louvre). He successfully negotiated the various political changes of the day and received a series of honours, culminating in 1819 when he was made a baron. His style derived from David but was much less taut and heroic, tending at times towards a rather mannered gracefulness.

Gérard, Marguerite. See FRAGONARD.

Gerasimov, Alexander (*b* Kozlov [now Michurinsk], 12 Aug. 1881; *d* Moscow, 23 July 1963). Russian painter, stage designer, architect, and administrator, a dominant figure in Soviet art. He painted various types of picture, and his most admired works are now perhaps those in which he recalled his peasant upbringing, notably *The Slaughter* (1929, Gerasimov Mus., Michurinsk), a powerful scene of a bull being killed. However, he is best known for his hagiographical pictures of Stalin (*Stalin and Voroshilov in the Kremlin Grounds*, Tretyakov Gal., Moscow, 1938), indeed as the archetypal artist of the repressive Stalinist era (see SOCIALIST REALISM): 'Gerasimov was president of the Academy of Arts of the USSR from 1947 to 1957; and also dominated the USSR Union of Artists, showing an implacable hostility towards the slightest signs of advanced art and meriting the epithets of "sinister" and "evil" which were showered upon him by Western critics and the more courageous of his countrymen' (Alan Bird, *A History of Russian Painting*, 1987). After Stalin had been denounced by his successor Khrushchev in 1956, Gerasimov was out of official favour. He had a heart attack the same year and never recovered his health.

Gerhaert, Nicolaus (*b* ?Leiden; *d* Wiener Neustadt, Austria, ?1473). Sculptor, perhaps of Netherlandish origin, active in Germany and Austria, an artist of great power and originality. He is first recorded in 1462 in Trier and he is known to have worked also in Strasbourg and Vienna; several signed or documented works survive, in sandstone and marble (woodcarvings have also been attributed to him), but the details of his life are mostly obscure. His work is extraordinarily vivid and unconventional, capturing an intense feeling of inner life, as in the celebrated sandstone *Bust of a Man* (Mus. de l'Œuvre Notre-Dame, Strasbourg), which is usually considered to be a self-portrait. In signatures and documents he is sometimes called Nicolaus 'of Leyden', which implies that he came from Leiden, but the voluminous style of his draperies and his boldness of approach suggest that he was trained in a Burgundian workshop where Claus *Sluter's style was still predominant. His work had considerable influence in central Europe.

Géricault, Théodore (*b* Rouen, 26 Sept. 1791; *d* Paris, 26 Jan. 1824). French painter and lithographer, one of the prime movers and most original figures of *Romanticism. He studied in Paris with Carle *Vernet and Pierre *Guérin, but was influenced more by making copies of the Old Masters in the *Louvre, developing in particular a passion for *Rubens. In 1816–17 he visited Italy and there became an enthusiastic admirer of *Michelangelo and the *Baroque. After his return to Paris he began work on the picture for which he is most famous, *The Raft of the Medusa* (Louvre, Paris), which caused a sensation at the 1819 *Salon; although it was awarded a medal, it created a furore both on account of its realistic treatment of a horrific event and because of its political implications (it depicts the ordeal of the survivors of the shipwreck of the *Medusa* in 1816, a disaster ascribed by some to government incompetence). The huge picture, which was remarkably original in treating a contemporary event with epic grandeur, also attracted great attention in England, where Géricault spent the years 1820–2 (more than 50,000 visitors paid to see it when it was exhibited in London). During his stay in England he painted jockeys and horse races (*Derby at Epsom*, 1821, Louvre) and was one of the first to bring English painting to the attention of French artists (he was particularly enthusiastic about *Bonington and *Constable).

Géricault was a passionate horseman and his death at the age of 32 was hastened by a riding accident. In his temperament and lifestyle as well as in his work he ranks as an archetypal Romantic artist. His tempestuous career lasted little more than a decade and in that time he displayed a meteoric and many-sided genius (his teacher Guérin said that he had 'the stuff of several painters' in him). His love of stirring action, his sense of swirling movement, his energetic handling of paint, and his taste for the macabre were all to become features of Romanticism. He was, at the same time, forward-looking in his realism: he made studies from corpses and severed limbs for the *Raft of the Medusa* and painted an extraordinary series of portraits of mental patients in the clinic of his friend Dr Georget, one of the pioneers of humane treatment for the insane (*A Kleptomaniac*, c.1822–3, Mus. B.-A., Ghent). His work had enormous influence, most notably on *Delacroix.

Germ. See PRE-RAPHAELITE BROTHERHOOD.

Gero Crucifix. See OTTONIAN ART.

Gérôme, Jean-Léon (*b* Vesoul, nr. Besançon, 11 May 1824; *d* Paris, 10 Jan. 1904). French painter and (in his later career) sculptor. He was a pupil of Paul *Delaroche and inherited his highly finished academic style, with which he had a career of great public success. Lorenz Eitner writes that 'In the variety and sensationalism of his subjects . . . Gérôme . . . surpassed all his rivals at the *Salon—murder in the Roman Senate and carnage in the gladiatorial arena; luscious nudity at the slave auction or the harem bath; Bonaparte contemplating the Sphinx, and Molière breakfasting with Louis XIV—all served equally well for his carefully plotted picture-plays, graced with sex, spiced with gore, and polished into waxwork lifelikeness by a technique that his admirers took for realism' (*An Outline of 19th Century European Painting*, 1987). Gérôme had considerable influence as an upholder of academic tradition and enemy of progressive trends in art; he opposed, for example, the acceptance by the state of the *Caillebotte bequest of *Impressionist pictures.

Gersaint, Edmé. See ETCHING and WATTEAU.

Gerstl, Richard (*b* Vienna, 14 Sept. 1883; *d* Vienna, 4 Nov. 1908). Austrian painter. His early painting was in the style of the Vienna *Sezession, but by 1905 he had developed a highly personal type of *Expressionism. His finest works are portraits, notably two groups of the family of the composer Arnold Schoenberg (Österreichische Gal., Vienna), remarkable for their psychological intensity. He was a tormented character, and after running off with Schoenberg's wife he committed suicide. His work, which anticipates that of such painterly Expressionists as *Kokoschka, remained little known until the 1930s, when he was hailed as an 'Austrian van *Gogh'.

Gertler, Mark (b London, 9 Dec. 1891; d London, 23 June 1939). British painter. He was born to poor Polish-Jewish immigrant parents and he spoke only Yiddish up to the age of 8. In 1908–12 he studied at the *Slade School, where he won several prizes. After the First World War he spent a good deal of time in the south of France for the sake of his delicate health (he had tuberculosis). Gertler was influenced by *Post-Impressionism, but his style was highly individual, with strong elements of eastern European folk art. His favourite subjects included female portraits, still-lifes, and nudes, such as the earthy and voluptuous *Queen of Sheba* (1922, Tate, London), painted in his characteristic feverishly hot colours. His best-known work is perhaps *Merry-Go-Round* (1916, Tate, London), a powerful image—probably a satire on militarism—in which figures spin on fairground horses in a mad, futile whirl. Gertler had many admirers, including distinguished figures in the literary world; D. H. Lawrence made him the model for the sculptor Loerke in *Women in Love* (1920). The word 'genius' was frequently applied to him, and he was seen by many as the acceptable face of modernism. However, he began to lose popularity in the early 1930s, when he adopted a more avant-garde style characterized by a flatter sense of space and a greater emphasis on surface pattern. He had always been subject to fits of depression, and after the failure of an exhibition at the Lefevre Gallery, London, in 1939, he committed suicide.

Gesamtkunstwerk (German: 'total work of art'). A term used to describe the cooperation of several arts in a single expressive aim. The term was coined by the composer Richard Wagner in his book *Das Kunstwerk der Zukunft* (The Artwork of the Future, 1849), although the idea of uniting music, poetry, the visual arts, and dance is as old as opera. Subsequently the term has been applied (often retrospectively) to various ensembles embracing painting, sculpture, and architecture or other combinations of arts (see BAROQUE, for example).

Gessner, Salomon (b Zurich, 1 Apr. 1730; d Zurich. 2 Mar. 1788). Swiss painter, etcher, and writer. As both a writer (of poetry and lyrical prose) and visual artist he concentrated on pastoral subjects treated in a sweet, idealized style that brought him great popularity. He was the son of a bookseller and publisher, whose business he inherited in 1775, and he made numerous charming illustrations for books (including his own) issued by the family firm. His best-known literary works (both of which appeared in numerous editions and translations) are *Idyllen* (Idylls, 1756) and the prose epic *Der Tod Abel* (The Death of Abel, 1758). As a painter he was self-taught, and he describes his process of learning in *Brief Über die Landschaftsmalerei* (Letters on Landscape Painting), first published in a five-volume edition of his writings (1770–2). He advocates love of nature and imitation of the great masters, in particular *Claude, as the best training for the landscape painter who wishes to express true feeling, and he asserts that poetry and painting should support one another. His son **Konrad Gessner** (1764–1826) was a painter and etcher.

gesso. Brilliant white preparation of powdered chalk mixed with glue, used during the Middle Ages and the *Renaissance as a *ground to prepare a panel or canvas for painting or gilding. The gesso was applied in several layers, with the proportion of chalk to glue progressively increasing. When applied to frames and furniture it could be painted and gilded in the same way, and was often modelled (*gesso rilievo*). In the 20th century the term 'gesso' came to be used loosely for any white substance that can be mixed with water to make a ground; in reference to sculpture it often means *plaster of Paris.

Gestel, Leo (b Woerden, 22 Nov. 1881; d Hilversum, 26 Nov. 1941). Dutch painter. Although he was a painter of modest talent, he was significant as one of the first Dutch artists to experiment with *Expressionism and *Cubism, and he helped to introduce these trends to his country. His knowledge of avant-garde art came partly from two visits to Paris—in 1904 (with Jan *Sluyters) and 1910–11. His work included landscapes, nudes, and still-lifes. He also made lithographs.

gestural painting. A term describing the application of paint with expansive gestures so that the sweep of the artist's arm is deliberately emphasized. The term carries an implication that the artist's actions express his or her emotions and personality, just as in other walks of life gestures express a person's feelings. It has been applied particularly to *Abstract Expressionism and is sometimes used more or less as a synonym for *Action Painting. However, it can also apply to figurative painting, notably *Neo-Expressionism.

Getty, J. Paul (*b* Minneapolis, 15 Dec. 1892; *d* Sutton Place, nr. Guildford, Surrey, 6 June 1976). American oil magnate and art collector. Reputedly the richest man in the world, he amassed a large collection of works of art, his main areas of interest being, as he wrote in his book *The Joys of Collecting* (1966), 'Greek and Roman marbles and bronzes; Renaissance paintings; sixteenth-century Persian carpets; Savonnerie carpets and eighteenth-century French furniture and tapestries'. The J. Paul Getty Museum was opened in 1954 in a wing of his home in Malibu, Los Angeles, and in 1974 a new museum, housed in a re-creation of a Roman villa, was opened nearby. One of the archetypes of the eccentric, parsimonious millionaire, Getty lived in England from the 1950s and never saw his creation. On his death it became the most richly endowed museum in the world, and has become famous for its spectacular purchases (see LYSIPPUS), which have aroused fears that it would monopolize the world market for masterpieces. In 1997 a second Getty Museum opened at Brentwood, Los Angeles; this now houses all the collections other than antiquities, which remain at Malibu. The new museum is part of the enormous Getty Center, which includes various facilities for art research and education. **Sir Paul Getty** (1932–2003), one of Getty's five sons by his five wives, spent much of his life in England (he adopted British nationality in 1988) and was a princely benefactor to British art institutions; most notably he gave £50,000,000 to the National Gallery, London, in 1985.

Ghe, Nikolai. See WANDERERS.

Gheeraerts, Marcus the Younger (*b* Bruges, 1562; *d* London, 19 Jan. 1636). Flemish-born portrait painter, active in England. He settled there in 1568 with his father **Marcus the Elder** (*c.*1530–*c.*1590), an engraver and painter who had fled from Bruges because of religious persecution. Marcus the Younger was probably the leading society portraitist in London at the peak of his career (his popularity declined after about 1615). About 30 paintings can be confidently assigned to him on the basis of signatures or inscriptions, the best known among them

being the splendid full-length portrait of Elizabeth I known as the 'Ditchley' portrait (*c.*1592, NPG, London), in which the queen is shown standing on a map of England. Many other portraits have been attributed to him, but it is not easy to disentangle his work from that of some of his contemporaries.

Gheyn, Jacob de, II (*b* Antwerp, 1565; *d* The Hague, 29 Mar. 1629). Dutch draughtsman, engraver, and painter. He was probably a pupil of his father **Jacob de Gheyn I** (1537/8–?1581), a glass painter and engraver. From *c.*1585 to 1590 he studied with Hendrick *Goltzius in Haarlem. He worked in various other Dutch towns, notably for the court at The Hague, where he designed the grotto (the earliest in the Netherlands) and other ornamentation of Buitenhof, the garden of Prince Maurice. His drawings and engravings are of greater importance than his paintings, for in their liveliness and informality they are outstanding documents of the period of transition from *Mannerism to *naturalism in Dutch art. His son **Jacob de Gheyn III** (*c.*1596–1641) was also an engraver, specializing in mythological subjects.

Ghezzi, Pier Leone. See CARICATURE.

Ghiberti, Lorenzo (*b* Florence, *c.*1380; *d* Florence, 1 Dec. 1455). Florentine sculptor, goldsmith, and designer, one of the most important artists of his period. He came to prominence in 1401 when he competed successfully (defeating *Brunelleschi, Jacopo della *Quercia, and four other artists) for a commission, offered by the merchant guild, to make a pair of gilded bronze doors for the Baptistery of Florence. His competition *relief of the *Sacrifice of Isaac* is in the Bargello, Florence. Work on the doors lasted until 1424 and in 1425 he was asked to make a second pair for the same building, which occupied him until 1452. Both sets of doors are divided into panels showing biblical scenes or figures in high relief. The two commissions had immense prestige, and Ghiberti's workshop became a kind of academy for a whole generation of artists, attracting some of the best talent of the day: *Donatello, *Masolino, and *Uccello were among those who had at least part of their training there. Although the two sets of doors dominated his career, Ghiberti was involved in numerous other projects; indeed, he boasted that 'Few works of importance were made in our city that were not designed or devised by my hand.' He served on the committee in charge of the architectural works of Florence Cathedral, designed stained-glass windows, goldsmith's work, and reliquaries (none of his work in precious metals survives), and made three over-life-size bronze statues for the church of Orsanmichele: *St John the Baptist* (1413–17), *St Matthew* (1419–22), and *St Stephen* (c.1425–9). The *St John* was the first bronze statue of such size to be produced since antiquity. In addition to his own works, Ghiberti said he gave help to 'many painters, sculptors, and stonecarvers', for whom he made 'models in wax and clay'.

Ghiberti was also a writer, leaving a lengthy incomplete manuscript entitled *Commentaries*. It contains a survey of ancient art based on *Pliny and observations on the science of optics, as well as valuable records of Italian painters and sculptors of the 14th century, and also Ghiberti's autobiography, the first by an artist that has survived. The same interest in the new humanist ideals that is reflected in Ghiberti's writings also prompted him to collect *classical sculptures. However, in spite of the prominent place that he occupies in the classical revival, his style was deeply rooted in the tradition of *Gothic craftsmanship. His first pair of Baptistery doors was modelled on the pattern of Andrea *Pisano's earlier doors for the same building, and the 28 panels (twenty showing episodes from the Life of Christ and eight depicting saints) have much of the spirit of *International Gothic about them, with their emphasis on graceful lines, lyrical sentiment, and close attention to landscape detail. These traits survive in Ghiberti's second pair of doors, but they are here subordinated to the new principles of the *Renaissance. The doors are divided into ten large panels in which episodes from the Old Testament are represented on carefully constructed perspective stages. As the reliefs were designed by 1437, they must rank among the most 'advanced' works of Florentine art of their time, particularly in the mastery of composition within a spatial framework. The fame of these doors has always stood high. *Michelangelo's dictum, recorded by *Vasari, that they were worthy to form the Gates of Paradise secured their prestige even in times less sympathetic to *quattrocento art.

Ghika, Nikolas (*b* Athens, 26 Feb. 1906; *d* Athens, 3 Sept. 1994). Greek painter and graphic artist. He studied under *Bissière at the *Académie Ranson, Paris, and his early work was strongly influenced by *Braque and *Picasso. However, after his return to Athens in 1934 he became interested also in Mediterranean landscape and Greek popular art. From the late 1930s he was recognized at home and abroad as Greece's leading painter, admired for his success in achieving a synthesis between his country's ancient traditions and contemporary artistic movements. In 1942 he was appointed a professor at the university of Athens and he continued to teach there until his retirement in 1960. Besides painting, Ghika made numerous book illustrations, notably for a collected edition of the work of Constantine Cavafy, Greece's most famous modern poet (1966).

Ghirlandaio, Domenico (*b* Florence, c.1449; *d* Florence, 11 Jan. 1494). Florentine painter. According to *Vasari he trained with *Baldovinetti and it has been suggested that he also spent some time in *Verrocchio's workshop. His style was solid, prosaic, and rather old-fashioned (especially when compared with that of his great contemporary *Botticelli), but he was an excellent craftsman and good businessman and had one of the most prosperous workshops in Florence. In this he was assisted by his younger brother **Davide** (1452–1525); another brother, **Benedetto** (c.1458–97), seems to have spent much of his career in France. Domenico's largest undertaking was the fresco cycle in the choir of S. Maria Novella, Florence, illustrating scenes from the lives of the Virgin and St John the Baptist (1485–90). This was commissioned by Giovanni Tornabuoni, a partner in the *Medici bank, and Ghirlandaio depicts the sacred story as if it had taken place in the home of a wealthy Florentine burgher. It is this talent for portraying the life and manners of his time (he often included portraits in his religious works) that has made Ghirlandaio popular with many visitors to Florence. But he also had considerable skill in the management of complex compositions and a certain grandeur of conception that sometimes hints at the High *Renaissance.

Ghirlandaio worked on frescos in Pisa, San Gimignano, and Rome (in the Sistine Chapel) as well as in Florence, and his studio produced numerous altarpieces. He also painted portraits, the finest of which is *Old Man and a Boy* (c.1485, Louvre, Paris); this depicts the man's diseased features with ruthless realism, but has a remarkable air of tenderness. Ghirlandaio's son **Ridolfo** (1483–1561) was a friend of *Raphael and a portrait painter of some distinction. He probably had his initial training from his father, but Domenico's most famous pupil was *Michelangelo.

Ghislandi, Giuseppe (Fra Galgario) (*b* Borgo di San Leonardo, nr. Bergamo; *bapt.* Bergamo, 4 Mar. 1655; *d* Bergamo, Dec. 1743). The outstanding Italian portrait painter of his time. He spent most of his early career in Venice, where he became a lay brother at the monastery of S. Francesco di Paola. In 1702 he returned permanently to Bergamo, where he lived at the Convento di Galgario, from which he takes the name Brother Galgario by which he is often known. Although he led an isolated life at the convent, he had a large practice and built up a reputation that extended far beyond his locality. His portraits are renowned for their strength and directness of characterization, recalling those of *Moroni, his great predecessor in Bergamo. The best collection of them is in the Accademia Carrara, Bergamo.

Giacometti, Alberto (*b* Borgonovo, nr. Stampa, 10 Oct. 1901; *d* Chur, 11 Jan. 1966). Swiss sculptor and painter, active mainly in Paris. He was the son of **Giovanni Giacometti** (1868–1933), a painter influenced by *Impressionism and *Post-Impressionism. After short periods at the École des Arts et Métiers, Geneva, and in Italy, he moved to Paris, where he worked under *Bourdelle from 1922 to 1925. In the latter year he abandoned naturalistic sculpture and began a period of restless experimentation. From 1930 to 1935 he participated in the *Surrealist movement, developing a highly individual attenuated manner exemplified in the cagelike construction of *The Palace at 4 a.m.* (1933, MoMA, New York). In 1935, however, he abandoned Surrealism and began to work again from the model. From 1941 to 1944 he lived in Geneva to escape the German occupation of France, but he then returned permanently to Paris, and in 1947 he began evolving the style for which he became famous, characterized by the use of human figures of extremely elongated proportions and emaciated, nervous character (*Man Pointing*, 1947, Tate, London). These fragile, isolated figures often have a suggestion of existentialist tragedy, and Giacometti was indeed a friend of the existentialist philosopher Jean-Paul Sartre, who wrote on his work, notably the introduction to the catalogue of his exhibition at the Pierre *Matisse Gallery, New York, in 1948. It was this exhibition that established Giacometti's post-war reputation, and his work soon had widespread influence, which can be seen, for example, in many of the entries for the *Unknown Political Prisoner* competition of 1953 (see BUTLER, REG). He impressed many people not only through the quality of his work, but also by his force of personality, integrity, and devotion to his work. Simone de Beauvoir, Sartre's companion,

wrote: 'Success, fame, money—Giacometti was indifferent to them all.' He is generally considered one of the outstandingly original sculptors of the 20th century, and from the late 1950s his reputation as a painter began to increase. Most of his paintings and drawings are portraits of his family and friends; his brother **Diego** (1902–85), who was a skilled technician and a lifelong assistant, was a favourite model and the subject of dozens of sculptures, paintings, and drawings (in his own right he is notable as the designer of furniture and light fittings for the Musée Picasso in Paris, 1984–5). Their cousin **Augusto Giacometti** (1877–1947) was a painter, one of the first to produce pure abstracts.

Giacomo del Duca. See DUCA.

Giambologna (Giovanni Bologna, originally Jean Boulogne) (*b* Douai [now in France], 1529; *d* Florence, 13 Aug. 1608). Netherlandish-born Italian sculptor. He was the greatest sculptor of the age of *Mannerism and for about two centuries after his death his reputation was almost equal to that of *Michelangelo. Virtually all his career was spent in Florence, but he was admired throughout Europe and patrons and collectors of his work included several popes, the Holy Roman Emperors Maximilian II and Rudolf II (see HABSBURG), and kings of France (Henry IV) and Spain (Philip III).

Giambologna trained in Flanders under Jacques *Dubroeucq. In 1550 he went to Italy to further his studies and spent two years in Rome, where he met the elderly Michelangelo. He intended returning to Flanders, but on the way he visited Florence and settled there for life. The work that made his name, however, was for Bologna—the Fountain of Neptune (1563–6), with its impressive nude figure of Neptune, which he had designed for a similar fountain in Florence (*Ammanati defeated him in the competition). Even before working on the fountain in Bologna, though, Giambologna had begun in Florence the first of a series of celebrated marble groups demonstrating his formidable mastery of complex twisting poses: *Samson Slaying a Philistine* (c.1561–2, V&A, London); *Florence Triumphant over Pisa* (completed 1575, Bargello, Florence); *The Rape of a Sabine* (1581–2, Loggia dei Lanzi, Florence); *Hercules and the Centaur* (1594–1600, Loggia dei Lanzi). These were made for members of the *Medici family, his greatest patrons (he was court sculptor to three successive Medici grand dukes of Tuscany: Cosimo I, Francesco I, and Ferdinando I). His monument to Cosimo I (1587–95) was the first equestrian statue made in Florence and an immensely influential design, becoming the pattern for similar statues all over Europe, including two from his own workshop: that to Henry IV in Paris (destroyed), which was completed after Giambologna's death by his colleague Pietro *Francavilla; and that to Philip III in Madrid, which was installed after the master's death by his most important pupil, Pietro *Tacca.

It was for the Medici also that Giambologna made his largest work—the colossal (about 10 m (33 ft) high) figure of the mountain god *Appennino* (1577–81) in the gardens of the family's villa at Pratolino. Constructed of brick and stone, the god crouches above a pool and seems to have emerged from the earth, blending harmoniously with the landscape. Giambologna, however, was as happy working on a small scale as in a monumental vein. His bronze statuettes were enormously popular (they continued to be reproduced almost continuously until the 20th century) and being portable helped to give his style European currency. The most famous of them is *Mercury* (originally made c.1565), of which several versions and many copies exist. It is such a potent image of speed and grace that it has been adapted in several ways in the modern world, for example as the symbol of Interflora. Many of Giambologna's preliminary models also survive (uniquely for an Italian sculptor of his period), giving insight into his creative processes. The best collection is in the Victoria and Albert Museum.

Giaquinto, Corrado (*b* Molfetta, nr. Bari, 8 Feb. 1703; *d* Naples, 18 Apr. 1766). Italian painter. Giaquinto was the most distinguished pupil of *Solimena in Naples and is generally considered a member of the Neapolitan School, but he spent most of his highly successful career in Rome (he was based there 1727–53) and subsequently in Spain (1753–62), where he worked for Ferdinand VI. He was mainly a fresco decorator, and apart from Giambattista *Tiepolo he was probably the most renowned European artist of his day in this field; he also painted altarpieces. His style was light, colourful, and elegant. He returned to Naples in 1762, evidently not because Tiepolo and *Mengs had replaced him in royal favour in Spain (as is often assumed) but because of ill health. Most of his major works remain *in situ* in the churches and palaces for which he painted them, but examples of the lively oil sketches he made in preparation for them are in many collections, including the National Gallery, London.

Gibbings, Robert (*b* Cork, 23 Mar. 1889; *d* Oxford, 19 Jan. 1958). British wood engraver, book designer, and travel writer. He founded the Society of Wood Engravers in 1919 and ran the Golden Cockerel Press (see PRIVATE PRESS) from 1924 to 1933, illustrating many of its books himself and also employing engravers such as Eric *Gill and Eric *Ravilious. He went through a nudist phase at about this time and sometimes typeset in the nude. Gibbings's books typically combine topographical impressions, personal anecdote, and observations of nature, illustrated with his own engravings; they include two on the River Thames—*Sweet Thames Run Softly* (1940) and *Till I End my Song* (1957).

Gibbons, Grinling (*b* Rotterdam, 4 Apr. 1648; *d* London, 3 Aug. 1721). Anglo-Dutch woodcarver and sculptor, the son of English parents who had business interests in the Netherlands (his father was a draper). He settled in England c.1667 and was 'discovered' by John Evelyn (see *Diary*, 18 Jan. 1671). Evelyn introduced him to King Charles II and to Sir Christopher Wren, who employed him on decorations at Hampton Court and St Paul's Cathedral. In 1693 he was appointed royal master carver. Gibbons was chiefly celebrated for naturalistic decorative carving of fruits, flowers, and shells, strung together in garlands and festoons, with small animals, cherubs' heads, etc. Horace *Walpole said of him: 'There is no instance of a man before Gibbons who gave to wood the loose and airy lightness of flowers, and chained together the various productions of the elements with the free disorder natural to each species.' Because of his fame an enormous amount of work has been attributed to him, but he lived in a great age of English craftsmanship and much of the carving that is connected with his name was done by artists influenced by his style. Apart from his work for Wren, his documented commissions include outstanding ensembles at Burghley House, Lincolnshire, and Petworth House, Sussex. His virtuosity in wood (especially *limewood) was not equalled in marble or bronze, and George *Vertue said of him: 'He was a most excellent carver in wood, he was neither well skill'd or practized in Marble or Brass for which works he employd the best artists he coud procure.' In about 1684 he took as partner Artus *Quellin III, who is thought to have been mainly responsible for some of the figure sculpture for which Gibbons was officially credited, notably the impressive bronze statue of James II (1686) outside the National Gallery in London.

Gibson, Charles Dana (*b* Roxbury, Mass., 14 Sept. 1867; *d* New York, 23 Dec. 1944). American illustrator and painter. He studied at the *Art Students League of New York, 1884–5, and in the 1890s became a great success with pen-and-ink drawings contributed to such magazines as *Collier's Weekly, Harpers*, and *Life*. He specialized in scenes of fashionable social life and achieved immortality with his creation of the 'Gibson Girl', a type (modelled on his wife) representing an ideal of American womanhood—feminine and gracefully attired, but a lover of sports and the outdoor life. His work was immensely popular until about 1914, influencing fashions in women's clothes and hairstyles, and he earned a fortune. He also tried to gain recognition as a portrait painter, but he was much less successful in this field.

Gibson, John (*b* Gyffin, nr. Conway, Wales; *bapt.* Conway, 19 June 1790; *d* Rome, 27 Jan. 1866). British *Neoclassical sculptor. His early years were spent as a monumental mason in Liverpool, where he became a protégé of William Roscoe (1753–1831), a lawyer, collector, and historian (he wrote books on Lorenzo de' *Medici (1796) and his son Leo X (1806)). In 1817 Gibson moved to London, where he met *Flaxman, on whose encouragement he went to Rome that year with an introduction to *Canova, whose pupil he became. Later he was also taught by *Thorvaldsen. He spent nearly all the rest of his life in Rome apart from occasional visits to England, the longest being from 1844 to 1847. Gibson won recognition internationally as one of the outstanding Neoclassical sculptors, and in his enthusiasm for Greek art he experimented with the ancient practice of colouring statues (see POLYCHROMY), arousing much controversy. His best-known work of this type is the *Tinted Venus* (1851–6, Walker AG, Liverpool). He left most of the fortune he made from his work to the *Royal Academy.

Giersing, Harald (*b* Copenhagen, 24 Apr. 1881; *d* Valdal, 15 Jan. 1927). Danish painter and critic, the most energetic advocate of modern art in Denmark at the beginning of the 20th century. In 1906–7 he visited Paris, where he was influenced by *Bonnard, *Cézanne, *Matisse, and *Vuillard. From these artists he took a feeling for vigorous simplified shapes, which he combined with deep, saturated colours. From about 1917 he was influenced by *Cubism. His work included landscapes, still-lifes, and figure compositions. He exercised an important influence on young Danish artists, not only through his work, but also through his teaching (he ran his own art school for ten years) and writing (he was one of his country's leading art critics).

Gierymski, Alexander (*b* Warsaw, 30 Jan. 1850; *d* Rome, 6/8 Mar. 1901). Polish painter. He had an unstable temperament, led a wandering life, often in poverty, and at the time of his death (in an asylum) was virtually unknown to the art world. However, he is now considered one of the greatest of Polish painters. His work, which includes landscapes, *genre scenes, and urban views, is remarkable for its subtle handling of light, particularly in his nocturnes (*The Louvre at Night*, 1892, Nat. Mus., Poznań). His brother **Maximilian Gierymski** (1846–74), a painter and illustrator, died young of lung disease.

Gilabertus. See GISLEBERTUS.

Gilbert, Sir Alfred (*b* London, 12 Aug. 1854; *d* London, 4 Nov. 1934). British sculptor and metalworker. He originally intended becoming a surgeon, but after failing the entrance examination at the Middlesex Hospital in 1872 he turned to art, training at the *Royal Academy, and then from 1875 to 1878 at the École des *Beaux-Arts in Paris. After spending six years in Italy, he returned to England in 1884 and worked on several major projects, the best known of which is his Shaftesbury Memorial Fountain in Piccadilly Circus (1887–93). The celebrated figure of Eros that surmounts the fountain is cast in aluminium, one of the earliest examples of the use of this metal in sculpture. Its light weight allowed Gilbert to achieve a more delicately poised pose than if he had been restricted to the traditional medium of bronze. Although Gilbert was hard-working, respected, and sought-after, he was unworldly and a hopeless businessman; his refusal to delegate work or compromise his standards meant that he took on more work than he could handle and he sometimes lost money on commissions. In 1901 he became bankrupt, and in 1909 he moved into self-imposed exile in Bruges, where he did little work. In 1926, however, he returned to London, and in 1926–8 he completed his masterpiece, the tomb of the Duke of Clarence in St George's Chapel, Windsor Castle, which he had begun in 1892. The sinuous and labyrinthine detailing, crafted with consummate skill, reveals Gilbert as one of the major practitioners of *Art Nouveau, although he was disparaging about the style. Characteristically for Gilbert, the tomb employs a variety of materials: marble, bronze, aluminium, brass, and ivory. His final major work was the bronze memorial to Queen Alexandra at Marlborough Gate, London (1926–32); on its completion he was knighted. His reputation sank after his death because he was so clearly outside the mainstream of 20th-century art (stylistically the Alexandra Memorial looks more like a work of the 1890s than the 1930s), but he is now regarded as the greatest British sculptor of his generation. See also NEW SCULPTURE.

Gilbert & George (Gilbert Proesch, b Dolomites, 17 Sept. 1943; and George Passmore, b Plymouth, 8 Jan. 1942). British artists (Gilbert is Italian born) who met whilst studying at *St Martin's School of Art in London in 1967 and since 1968 have lived and worked together as self-styled 'living sculptures': 'Being living sculptures is our life blood, our destiny, our romance, our disaster, our light and life.' They initially attracted attention as *Performance artists, their most famous work in this vein being *Underneath the Arches* (1969), in which—dressed in their characteristic neat suits and with their hands and faces painted gold—they mimed mechanically to the 1930s music-hall song of the title. Although they gave up such 'living sculpture performances' in 1977, they still see themselves as living sculptures, considering their whole lifestyle a work of art. Since the early 1970s their work has consisted mainly of photo-pieces—large and garish arrangements of photographs, usually in black and white and fiery red, and often violent or homoerotic in content, with scatological titles. The images are often drawn from the street life of the East End of London in which they live. Gilbert & George have become the most famous British avant-garde artists of their generation. Their work has been shown worldwide and has attracted an enormous amount of commentary. In 1986 they won the *Turner Prize. Critical opinion on them is sharply divided, however: to some they are geniuses, to others tedious poseurs.

Gill, Eric (b Brighton, 22 Feb. 1882; d Harefield, Middlesex [now in Greater London], 17 Nov. 1940). British sculptor, engraver, typographer, and writer. He began to earn his living as a letter cutter in 1903 and carved his first figure piece in 1910. In 1913 he became a convert to Roman Catholicism and was commissioned to make fourteen relief carvings of the Stations of the Cross for Westminster Cathedral (1914–18). These and the *Prospero and Ariel* group on Broadcasting House, London (1929–31), are his best-known sculptures. Gill was one of the chief protagonists in the movement for the revival of *direct carving, and his work usually has an impressive simplicity of conception; he wrote that his 'inability to draw naturalistically was, instead of a drawback, no less than my salvation. It compelled me . . . to concentrate upon something other than the superficial delights of fleshly appearance . . . to consider the significance of things.' In life, as in his work and writing, he was an advocate of a romanticized medievalism, and he tried to revive a religious attitude towards art and craftsmanship. His unconventionality was well known in his own time (he disliked trousers, for example, preferring to wear smocks), but the most bizarre and unpleasant aspects of his life were not revealed until the publication of Fiona MacCarthy's biography in 1989: he had incestuous relationships with two of his sisters and two of his daughters and sexual congress with a dog (apart from religion, sex is the main subject of his work). Gill was an important figure in book design and typography as well as sculpture. He illustrated many books, and his 'Perpetua' and 'Gill Sans-Serif' typefaces are among the classics of 20th-century typography. His books include *Christianity and Art* (1927), *Art* (1934), and *Autobiography* (1940).

Gillot, Claude (b Langres, 27 Apr. 1673; d Paris, 4 May 1722). French painter, draughtsman, and etcher. Few of his paintings survive, but his interest in scenes from the popular theatre (*Quarrel of the Cabmen*, Louvre, Paris) was inherited by his pupil *Watteau. His work is known mainly in the form of drawings and etchings, and he excelled at designs in the elegant *Rococo manner of *Audran.

Gillray, James (b London, 13 Aug. 1756; d London, 1 June 1815). English caricaturist. He was one of the greatest of all caricaturists and probably the first significant artist to devote himself almost exclusively to this field. Initially he trained as a commercial engraver and although he later studied at the *Royal Academy Schools, he seems to have been largely self-taught. By the mid-1780s his vividness and fecundity of imagination had gained him recognition as the leading caricaturist in Britain and he made a small fortune for the printseller Hannah Humphrey, above whose London shop he lived and for whom he worked almost exclusively from about 1790 (they were rumoured to be lovers). Although he produced a good deal of social satire, his most characteristic works are his political cartoons, in which his targets included

George III and other members of the royal family. Another frequent subject was Napoleon, whom he depicted as a belligerent midget. Gillray drank heavily and from about 1810 had fits of madness; by the time of his death he was hopelessly insane. His successor was George *Cruikshank.

Gilman, Harold (*b* Rode, Somerset, 11 Feb. 1876; *d* London, 12 Feb. 1919). British painter of interiors, portraits, and landscapes. He became interested in art during a long convalescence after an accident and he had his main training at the *Slade School, 1897–1901; his fellow student Spencer *Gore became a close friend. In 1907 he met *Sickert and became one of the leading figures in his circle; he was a founder member of the *Camden Town Group in 1911 and of the *London Group (of which he was first president) in 1913. His early work was rather sombre, but under the influence of Sickert he adopted a higher colour register and a technique of using a mosaic of opaque touches. From Sickert also he derived his taste for working-class subjects. After Roger *Fry's first *Post-Impressionist exhibition (1910) and a visit to Paris (1911) he used very thick paint and bright (sometimes garish) colour. He was one of the most gifted English painters of his generation and one of the most distinctive in his reaction to Post-Impressionism, but his career was cut short by the influenza epidemic of 1919.

Gilpin, Sawrey (*b* Carlisle, 30 Oct. 1733; *d* London, 8 Mar. 1807). English animal painter. He began his career as an apprentice to Samuel *Scott, the marine painter, but turned to the painting of horses, making a name with 'portraits' of celebrated racers. In occasional works he also contrived his own blend of horse and history painting (*The Election of Darius*, c.1772, York AG). His son **William Sawrey Gilpin** (1762–1843) began his career as a watercolourist but turned to landscape gardening, a field in which he had great success, in spite of his lack of professional training.

The Revd **William Gilpin** (*b* Scaleby, Cumberland, 4 June 1724; *d* Boldre, Hampshire, 5 Apr. 1804), brother of Sawrey, was a writer, draughtsman, and printmaker. He spent much of his life as a schoolmaster and country parson and wrote a good deal on religious topics, but he is chiefly remembered as one of the most important advocates of the *Picturesque. From 1768 to 1776 he made summer tours in various parts of Britain and he later published accounts of his travels illustrated by his own aquatints, beginning with

Observations on the River Wye . . . (1782). These books, which stress pleasure rather than instruction, helped to promote a boom in domestic tourism, and they were parodied in the adventures of Dr Syntax, memorably illustrated by *Rowlandson. Gilpin's other publications include *An Essay on Prints* (1768), which was translated into French, German, and Dutch and achieved lasting success as a standard work on print collecting.

Ginner, Charles (*b* Cannes, 4 Mar. 1878; *d* London, 6 Jan. 1952). British painter. He grew up in France (his father, a doctor, practised there) and settled in London in 1910. He was already a friend of *Gilman and *Gore and through them he was drawn into *Sickert's circle, becoming a founder member of the *Camden Town Group in 1911 and the *London Group in 1913. His Continental background made him a respected figure among his associates, who were united by an admiration for French painting. Ginner was primarily a townscape and landscape painter and he is known above all for his views of London (often drab areas, although he also depicted the hustle and bustle of places such as Leicester Square and Victoria Station). He painted with thick, regular brushstrokes and firm outlines, creating a heavily textured surface and a feeling of great solidity. Once he had established his distinctive style (by about 1911) it changed little and he became one of the main upholders of the Camden Town tradition after the First World War (ironically, unlike other members of the group, he never actually lived in Camden Town). He worked for the Canadian War Records Commission in the First World War and was an *Official War Artist in the Second.

Giordano, Luca (*b* Naples, 18 Oct. 1634; *d* Naples, 3 Jan. 1705). Neapolitan painter, the most important Italian decorative artist of the second half of the 17th century. He was nicknamed Luca Fa Presto (Luke work quickly) because of his prodigious speed of execution and huge output. His early works were in the *tenebrist manner of *Ribera, but his style became much more colourful under the influence of such great decorative painters as *Veronese, whose works he saw on his extensive travels. Indeed, he absorbed a host of influences and was said to be able to imitate other artists' styles with ease. His work was varied also in subject matter, although he was primarily a religious and mythological painter. In addition to the frescos for which he is principally famed, he produced a large number of easel paintings and was a prolific draughtsman. He worked mainly in Naples, but also extensively in Florence and Venice, and he was widely influential in Italy. In 1692 he was called to Spain by Charles II (see HABSBURG) and stayed there for ten years, painting in Madrid, Toledo, and the *Escorial. His last works, after his return to Naples, included the decoration of the dome of the Treasury Chapel of the Certosa di S. Martino (1704). He died a very wealthy man and one of the most famous artists in Europe. In his personal self-confidence and courtliness, and in the open, airy compositions and light luminous colours of his work, Giordano presages such great 18th-century painters as *Tiepolo.

Giorgione (Giorgio da Castelfranco) (b Castelfranco [now Castelfranco Veneto], c.1477; d Venice, Oct. 1510). Venetian painter. Almost nothing is known of his life and only a handful of paintings can be confidently attributed to him, but he holds a momentous place in the history of art. He had achieved legendary status soon after his early death (evidently from plague) and through succeeding centuries he has continued to excite the imagination in a way that few other painters can match. The extraordinary discrepancy between his enormous fame and the tiny size of his oeuvre is explained by the fact that he initiated a new conception of painting. He was one of the earliest artists to specialize in *cabinet pictures for private collectors rather than works for public or ecclesiastical patrons, and he was the first painter who subordinated subject matter to the evocation of mood—it is clear that his contemporaries sometimes did not know what was represented in his pictures. *Vasari, who says that Giorgione earned his nickname—meaning 'big George'— 'because of his physical appearance and his moral and intellectual stature', ranked him alongside *Leonardo as one of the founders of 'modern' painting.

Giorgione's home town is about 40 km (25 miles) north-west of Venice, where as far as is known he spent all his career. According to Vasari he trained with Giovanni *Bellini (although it has also been suggested that *Carpaccio may have been his teacher). He had two important public commissions in Venice: in 1507-8 he worked on a canvas (now lost without trace) for the audience chamber of the Doges' Palace; and in 1508 (together with *Titian) he painted frescos on the exterior of the Fondaco dei Tedeschi (the German warehouse), now known only through engravings and ruinous

fragments. Apart from this, the only certain contemporary documentation on any of his surviving paintings is an inscription on the back of a female portrait known as *Laura* (KH Mus., Vienna), which says it was painted by 'Master Zorzi da Castelfranco' in 1506; it also records that Giorgione was a colleague of Vincenzo *Catena, a partnership about which nothing else is known. (An inscription on *Portrait of a Man* in the San Diego Museum of Art is more doubtful.)

The main document for reconstructing Giorgione's oeuvre is a series of notes by the Venetian collector and connoisseur Marcantonio Michiel (c.1484-1552), written intermittently between 1521 and 1543. Michiel, who is a scrupulous and reliable source, mentions a number of paintings by Giorgione, four or five of which can be plausibly identified with extant works: *The Tempest* (Accademia, Venice), *The Three Philosophers* (KH Mus.), *Sleeping Venus* (Gemäldegalerie, Dresden), *Boy with an Arrow* (a copy?, KH Mus.), and (an oblique and less explicit reference than the others) *Christ Carrying the Cross* (S. Rocco, Venice). He says that *The Three Philosophers* was finished by *Sebastiano del Piombo and that the *Sleeping Venus* (the work that founded the tradition of the reclining female nude) was finished by Titian. The problem of attribution was, then, complicated from the start by the fact that some of Giorgione's paintings were completed after his death by other hands, and confusion soon arose; in the first edition of his *Lives* (1550) Vasari attributed the S. Rocco painting to Giorgione, but in the second edition (1568) he gave it in one place to Giorgione and in another to Titian, even though 'many people believed it was by Giorgione'. Distinguishing between the work of Giorgione and the young Titian continues to be one of the knottiest problems in connoisseurship, the celebrated *Concert champêtre* in the Louvre being the picture most hotly disputed between them.

Among the other paintings given to Giorgione are the *Castelfranco Madonna*, in the cathedral of his home town (first mentioned by *Ridolfi in 1648 and accepted by almost all critics), and several male portraits, including a self-portrait in the Herzog-Anton-Ulrich Museum in Brunswick (perhaps a copy). Giorgione is said to have been handsome and amorous, and he initiated a type of dreamily romantic portrait that became immensely popular in Venice. The powerful influence that his work exerted in the generation after his death (even the venerable Bellini succumbed to it) is one of the main factors in making the

construction of a catalogue of his work so difficult, for there are scores of paintings of the
period, particularly pastoral landscapes, that
can be described as Giorgionesque, and many
are of high quality.

The problems of *iconography that Giorgione's paintings present are sometimes every
bit as difficult as those of attribution. The most
famous instance is *The Tempest*, one of his most
enigmatic and poetic creations. Michiel saw it in
1530 and described it as a 'little landscape with the
tempest with the gipsy and soldier', so he evidently did not know what subject, if any, was
represented. X-rays have shown that Giorgione
radically altered the figures in a way that suggests
he was here indulging his imagination rather
than illustrating a particular theme, although
many ingenious attempts have been made to
unravel a subject. This creation of the 'landscape
of mood', in which he used colour and atmosphere with great subtlety, was, indeed, his most
momentous contribution to the history of art—
an innovation of great originality and influence.
Apart from the artists already mentioned,
*Palma Vecchio and Dosso *Dossi were among
the contemporaries who fell under Giorgione's
spell, and among later artists *Watteau was his
most sensitive heir. See also PARAGONE.

Giottesques. A term applied to the 14th-
century followers of *Giotto. The best-known
artists embraced by the term are the Florentines
Bernardo *Daddi, Taddeo *Gaddi, *Maso di
Banco, and to a lesser extent the *Master of
St Cecilia. Giotto's most loyal follower was
Maso, who concentrated on the essential and
maintained the master's high seriousness.

Giottino. See MASO DI BANCO.

Giotto di Bondone (*b* ?Colle di Vespignano,
nr. Florence, *c.*1270; *d* Florence, 8 Jan. 1337). Florentine painter and architect. Giotto is regarded
as the founder of the central tradition of Western painting because his work broke away decisively from the stylizations of *Byzantine art,
introducing new ideals of naturalism and creating a convincing sense of pictorial space. His
momentous achievement was recognized by
his contemporaries (Dante praised him in a
famous passage of *The Divine Comedy*, saying he
had surpassed his master *Cimabue), and to
succeeding generations it was clear that a new
artistic era began with him; in about 1400 Cennino *Cennini wrote that 'Giotto translated the
art of painting from Greek into Latin and made
it modern.' He was the first artist since antiquity

to achieve widespread fame, the demand for his
services coming from all over Italy: early sources
suggest that he worked in Assisi, Bologna,
Ferrara, Lucca, Milan, Naples, Padua, Ravenna,
Rimini, Rome, Urbino, and Verona, as well as
Florence, and according to *Vasari he also
visited Avignon in France, where he is said to
have carried out commissions for Pope Clement
V (reigned 1305–14). However, these early references tend to be frustratingly vague, many of the
works they refer to are unidentifiable or have
been destroyed, and no surviving painting can
be given to Giotto on the basis of unimpeachable
contemporary documentation. His work, indeed, poses some formidable problems of attribution, but it is universally agreed that the fresco
cycle in the Arena Chapel at Padua is by him (he
is credited with it in two separate literary references dating from *c.*1313), and it forms the starting
point for any consideration of his work.

The Arena Chapel (so called because it occupies the site of a Roman arena) was built by
Enrico Scrovegni (see DONOR), one of Padua's
leading citizens, in expiation for the sins of his
father, a notorious usurer mentioned by Dante.
It was begun in 1303 and Giotto's frescos are
usually dated *c.*1303–6. They run right round
the interior of the chapel, which is virtually
devoid of architectural ornament and clearly
was conceived with painted decoration in mind
(Giotto himself may well have been involved in
the design of the building); the west wall is
covered with a *Last Judgement*, there is an *Annunciation* over the chancel arch, and the main wall
areas have three tiers of paintings representing
scenes from the life of the Virgin and her
parents, St Anne and St Joachim, and events
from the ministry and Passion of Christ. Below
these scenes are figures personifying Virtues and
Vices, painted to simulate stone *reliefs—the
first *grisailles. The figures in the main narrative
scenes are about half life-size, but from reproductions it is easy to imagine they are much
bigger, because Giotto's conception is so grand
and powerful. His figures have a completely new
sense of three-dimensionality and physical presence, and in portraying the sacred events he
creates a feeling of moral weight rather than
divine splendour. He seems to base the scenes
on personal experience, and no artist has surpassed his ability to go straight to the heart of a
story and express its essence with gestures and
expressions of unerring conviction.

The other major fresco cycle associated with
Giotto's name is that on the life of St Francis in
the Upper Church of S. Francesco at Assisi. This

was first specifically given to him by Vasari and the attribution was not doubted until the 19th century; subsequently the question of its authorship has become one of the most controversial issues in the history of art. The St Francis frescos are clearly the work of an artist of great stature (their intimate and humane portrayals have done much to determine posterity's mental image of the saint), but they are more anecdotal and less powerful than the Arena Chapel frescos—stylistic differences that to many critics seem so pronounced that they cannot accept a common authorship. Other authorities, however, argue that the differences can be explained by Giotto maturing as his career progressed (the Assisi frescos are probably earlier than the Arena Chapel frescos, but their dating too is contentious). Attempts to attribute other frescos at Assisi to Giotto have met with similar controversy (see also MASTER OF THE LEGEND OF ST FRANCIS and MASTER OF ST CECILIA). There is a fair measure of agreement, however, about the frescos associated with Giotto in S. Croce in Florence. He probably painted in four chapels there, and work survives in the Bardi and Peruzzi chapels, generally dated to the 1320s. The frescos are in very uneven condition (they were whitewashed in the 18th century), but some of those in the Bardi Chapel on the life of St Francis remain deeply impressive.

Among Giotto's other major works was an external mosaic for Old St Peter's, Rome, showing *Christ Walking on the Waters* and popularly known as the *Navicella* ('little boat'—a reference to the vessel carrying the Apostles, which symbolizes the Church, in which the faithful find refuge). The mosaic was saved when Old St Peter's was demolished and part of it is displayed in the portico of the present church, but it has been so heavily restored that it can no longer be regarded as Giotto's work. It is not known when he visited Rome, but during his stay he would have seen the work of Pietro *Cavallini, which was as important an influence on him as that of Cimabue, who is traditionally (and highly plausibly) said to have been his teacher. The best documented period of Giotto's career is the time (1328–33) he spent at the court of Robert of Anjou, King of Naples. He had an honoured place in the royal household, but only small fragments survive of the paintings he carried out for Robert (Vasari says they included 'portraits of many famous men', including a self-portrait—rare examples of secular works by Giotto). In 1334, following his return from Naples, he was appointed city architect in

Florence and in this role began the celebrated campanile (bell tower) of the cathedral (the design was altered after his death, but his essential concept was followed and the building is sometimes called 'Giotto's Tower').

The panel paintings associated with Giotto are not as controversial as the frescos, but they nevertheless present numerous problems. Several panels bear his signature, but it is generally agreed that the signature is a trademark showing that the works came from his shop rather than an indication of his personal workmanship. Similarly, the Stefaneschi Altarpiece (Vatican Mus.) is connected with Giotto in a credible early source, but it is now regarded as having only tenuous links with him. On the other hand, the *Ognissanti Madonna* (c.1305–10, Uffizi, Florence) is neither signed nor firmly documented (it is first recorded in 1418), but it is a work of such grandeur and humanity that Giotto's authorship has never been seriously questioned. Among the other panels attributed to him, the finest is the Crucifix in S. Maria Novella, Florence (returned to the church in 2001 after a lengthy process of restoration, which confirmed its outstanding quality).

In the generation after his death Giotto had an overwhelming influence on Florentine painting; this declined with the growth of *International Gothic, but his work was later an inspiration to *Masaccio, and even to *Michelangelo. These two giants were his true spiritual heirs. By the time Michelangelo's friend Vasari wrote his *Lives of the Artists*, however, Giotto was regarded more as the herald of the Renaissance than as a towering figure in his own right. This view persisted for centuries, compounded by the fact that Giotto's greatest works were virtually inaccessible until 1880, when the Arena Chapel, until then in private hands, was bought by the city of Padua. Its opening to the public was a major landmark in the revival of his reputation.

Giovanni Bologna. See GIAMBOLOGNA.

Giovanni da Maiano. See MAIANO.

Giovanni da Udine. See UDINE.

Giovanni di Balduccio. See BALDUCCIO.

Giovanni di Paolo (*b* Siena, *c.*1400; *d* Siena, 1482). One of the most attractive and idiosyncratic painters of the Sienese School, sometimes called Giovanni dal Poggio, from the district of the city where he lived. Little is known of his life, but there are a considerable number of surviving works by him—all small-format religious panels (the earliest known dates from 1426). He may have been taught by *Taddeo di Bartolo and was influenced notably by *Gentile da Fabriano and *Sassetta, but his style is highly personal and engaging, with rather whimsical figures inhabiting strange landscapes. After centuries of neglect his reputation was revived by *Berenson, who called him 'the El *Greco of the *quattrocento'.

Girardon, François (b Troyes, 10 Mar. 1628; d Paris, 1 Sept. 1715). French sculptor. He ranked with *Coysevox as the outstanding sculptor of Louis XIV's reign, but his style was more restrained and *classical, embodying the ideas of the Académie Royale (see ACADEMY). Much of his work was done for Versailles, where he collaborated with *Le Brun; it includes a marble group of *Apollo Tended by the Nymphs* (1666–75) that is regarded as one of the most purely classical works of French 17th-century sculpture. (The group was originally in a grotto room, but is now in the palace gardens.) His other work includes the marble monument to Cardinal Richelieu (1675–94) in the church of the Sorbonne, Paris. He also made a bronze equestrian statue of Louis XIV (1683–92) for the Place Vendôme in Paris, but this was destroyed during the French Revolution. Girardon died on the same day as Louis XIV.

Girodet, Anne-Louis (b Montargis, Loiret, 29 Jan. 1767; d Paris, 9 Dec. 1824). French painter and illustrator, usually known as Girodet-Trioson, a name he took in honour of a surgeon, Dr Trioson, who adopted him after he was orphaned at an early age and who was probably his natural father. He studied with J.-L. *David, won the *Prix de Rome in 1789, and spent the years 1790–5 in Italy. In style and technique he followed David, but in his choice of themes and his emotional treatment of them he was *Romantic in spirit. He was particularly interested in unusual colour effects and melodramatic lighting, as in the *Sleep of Endymion* (1791) and the *Entombment of Atala* (1808), both in the Louvre. In addition to works on literary subjects such as these, Girodet painted pictures glorifying Napoleon (*The Revolt of Cairo*, 1810, Versailles Mus.) and he was a fine portraitist. One of his best-known portraits, *Mlle Lange as Danaë* (1799, Minneapolis Inst. of Arts), caused a scandal because of its scurrilous sexual allusions (the woman portrayed was a well-known actress with whom Girodet had quarrelled). His book illustrations included work for editions of Racine and Virgil. In 1815 he inherited a fortune when Dr Trioson died and thereafter devoted himself mainly to writing unreadably boring poems and treatises on aesthetics.

Girolamo da Carpi (b Ferrara, c.1501; d Ferrara, ?(c.1 Aug.) 1556). Italian painter, architect, and stage designer, active mainly in Ferrara (where he was much employed by the *Este court), but also in Bologna early in his career and later in Rome (where he did some architectural work at the Vatican for Pope Julius III). Girolamo's eclectic style was influenced by his teacher *Garofalo and by several of the leading painters of the early 16th century, including *Correggio, *Raphael, and *Giulio Romano, and his oeuvre is not well defined (much of the work that *Vasari mentions has perished). At his best, however, he was an artist of distinction (*Mystic Marriage of St Catherine*, c.1534, S. Salvatore, Bologna). In addition to religious works he painted portraits and a few mythological subjects.

Girolamo da Fiesole. See COLOMBE.

Giroust, Marie-Suzanne. See ROSLIN.

Girtin, Thomas (b London, 18 Feb. 1775; d London, 9 Nov. 1802). English painter and printmaker, one of the supreme masters of the watercolour landscape. His earlier works were tinted drawings in the 18th-century topographical tradition, but by the end of his short life he had developed a technique that revolutionized watercolour painting. He used strong colour in broad *washes, influenced to some extent by J. R. *Cozens but going beyond him in the boldness of his compositions, the grandeur with which he created effects of space, and the power with which he suggested mood. His work stands at the beginning of the classic English tradition of watercolour painting, freed from its dependence on line drawing, and *Turner acknowledged his friend's greatness with the words 'If Tom Girtin had lived, I should have starved.' Girtin made tours in various parts of Britain, and spent six months in Paris in 1801–2, making a series of etchings of the city that were posthumously published in 1803. In 1802 he exhibited an enormous panorama of London, painted in oils or distemper—the *Eidometropolis*; this is no longer extant, but sketches for it survive. He died of tuberculosis.

gisant. French term used from the 15th century onwards for a recumbent effigy on a funerary monument. In *Renaissance monuments *gisants* often formed part of a lower register, where the deceased person was represented as a corpse (sometimes in decomposition), while on the upper part he or she was represented *orant* (praying), as if alive.

Gislebertus (active first half of 12th century). French *Romanesque sculptor. He was one of the great geniuses of medieval art, but his name has survived only because he carved his signature—*Gislebertus hoc fecit* (Gilbert made this)—beneath the feet of the central figure of Christ in the tympanum of the west doorway of Autun Cathedral in Burgundy. The unusually prominent position of his signature suggests that his greatness was appreciated in his own time. The tympanum represents the Last Judgement; it is a huge work (over 6 m (20 ft) wide at the base) and a masterpiece of expressionistic carving, conveying with visionary intensity both the horror of the damned and the serenity of the elect. Most of the rest of the sculptural decoration of the cathedral can be confidently attributed to Gislebertus. It includes the decoration of 60 or so capitals and a large-scale reclining nude figure of Eve that is without parallel in medieval art (this piece, a fragment of the north doorway, is now in the Musée Rolin, Autun). These carvings display Gislebertus's great fecundity of imagination and range of feeling. It has been surmised that he was trained in the workshop responsible for the decoration of the abbey of Cluny, the most influential of all Romanesque monasteries, and that he worked at the cathedral at Vézelay before going to Autun (all three places are in Burgundy). He was already a mature artist when he started at Autun, where he worked *c.*1125–35, and his style changed little while he was there. His influence was felt in the sculpture of various Burgundian churches, and many of his ideas had a long-term effect on the development of French *Gothic sculpture.

He is not to be confused with **Gilabertus,** a sculptor of the same period who signed two figures at the cathedral of St Étienne, Toulouse (they are now in the Musée des Augustins, Toulouse).

Giuliano da Maiano. See MAIANO.

Giulio Romano (Giulio Pippi) (*b* Rome, ?1499; *d* Mantua, 1 Nov. 1546). Italian painter, architect, and designer. He was the only major *Renaissance artist who was a native of Rome, but he was active mainly in Mantua. In his youth he was *Raphael's chief pupil and assistant (although exactly what part he played in his workshop is uncertain) and later one of the outstanding figures of *Mannerist art and architecture. It is not

known when Giulio began working for Raphael, but it was probably in about 1515, when he was still very young; after the master's death in 1520 he became his main artistic executor, completing a number of his unfinished works, including the decorations of the Villa Madama. His independent works of this time include the *Holy Family* (*c.*1522) in S. Maria dell'Anima, Rome, and the design of some pornographic prints that caused such a scandal that their engraver Marcantonio *Raimondi was imprisoned (their notoriety was sustained by the sonnets that the poet Pietro Aretino wrote inspired by them soon after their publication). Giulio had moved to Mantua in 1524 and escaped Raimondi's fate. He remained there for the rest of his life and dominated the artistic affairs of the *Gonzaga court.

The great monument to Giulio's genius is the Palazzo del Tè, begun in 1526 for Federico Gonzaga. This was one of the first Mannerist buildings, deliberately flouting the canons of classical architecture as exemplified by *Bramante in order to shock or surprise the spectator. The same tendency is shown in Giulio's fresco decoration in the palace, especially in the Sala dei Giganti, where the whole room is painted from floor to ceiling to give an overall illusionistic effect, and the spectator feels overwhelmed by the rocks and thunderbolts hurled down on the rebellious Titans who attempted to storm Olympus. Giulio painted several other frescos in the Palazzo del Tè and in the Sala di Troia of the Ducal Palace at Mantua that testify to his classical learning and exuberant invention. His muscular style owed much to *Michelangelo as well as to Raphael, but was less daunting than that of either and proved widely influential. Indeed, he became one of the most famous painters of his day and has the distinction of being the only modern artist mentioned by Shakespeare; he called him 'that rare Italian master Julio Romano', but mistakenly imagined him a sculptor (*The Winter's Tale*, v. ii). Among Giulio's other architectural works, the most important is his own house in Mantua (1544–6).

Giusti, Giovanni (*b* nr. Florence, 1485; *d* Tours, 1549). Italian-born sculptor who settled at Tours in France in about 1504 and became known by a French form of his name, Jean Juste. He was a leading figure in the introduction of the *Renaissance style to France. His masterpiece is the tomb of Louis XII and Anne of Brittany (1517–31) in the abbey of Saint-Denis, near Paris. He was probably assisted in the work by his brother **Antonio** (1479–1519), who settled with him in France and became known as Antoine Juste. It features seated figures of the twelve Apostles in purely Italian style, allegorical figures of the Virtues, and *reliefs depicting the king's Italian victories. Antoine's son **Juste de Juste** (1505–59) and Jean's son **Jean II** (1510–79) were also sculptors.

Giustiniani. Prominent Italian family, branches of which were established in many parts of Italy, especially Genoa and Venice, where they played important roles in politics, literature, and religion. For the arts the most interesting member of the family was the enormously wealthy Marchese **Vincenzo Giustiniani** (1564–1637). He owned the finest collection of *antique sculpture in Rome—published in the *Galleria Giustiniana* (1631), the first ever illustrated catalogue of an art collection—and was an enthusiastic and discriminating patron of painters, especially *Caravaggio (he owned no fewer than fifteen pictures by him) and his northern followers.

Glackens, William James (*b* Philadelphia, 13 Mar. 1870; *d* Westport, Conn., 22 May 1938). American painter and draughtsman. His early career was spent mainly as a newspaper illustrator in Philadelphia, but he was encouraged to take up painting by Robert *Henri, whom he met in 1891. In 1896 he settled in New York and in 1908 he was one of the group of painters who exhibited together as The *Eight. He is considered one of the central figures of the *Ashcan School, but he was less concerned with *Social Realism than with representing the life of the people as a colourful spectacle, and he was heavily influenced by the *Impressionists. By the time of the *Armory Show (1913), which he helped to organize, Glackens was painting in a style reminiscent of the early *Renoir. From 1912 he was employed as art consultant by Dr Albert C. *Barnes (an old school friend) and toured Europe buying paintings that formed the nucleus of the celebrated Barnes Foundation at Merion, Pennsylvania. In 1917 he was elected first president of the *Society of Independent Artists.

glair. A term for white of egg when used as the *medium in *illuminating manuscripts, in *tempera painting, and in gilding with gold dust. It is also used as an adhesive substance to fix gold leaf.

Glasgow School. A term that has been applied to several groups of artists whose activities have centred on Glasgow. The first and largest of these groups was a loose association of artists active from about 1880 to the turn of the century; there was no formal membership or programme, but the artists involved (who preferred to be known as the Glasgow Boys) were linked by a desire to move away from the conservative and parochial values they thought were represented by the Royal Scottish Academy in Edinburgh. Sir James Guthrie (1859–1930) and Sir John *Lavery were probably the best-known members of the group. Several of them had worked in France and were proponents of open-air painting. The heyday of the group was over by 1900 and it did not survive the First World War, but it provided a powerful stimulus for Scottish art in the 20th century, breaking ground where the *Scottish Colourists were soon to follow. A slightly later group, active from about 1890 to 1910, created a distinctive version of *Art Nouveau. Its most important member was the architect and designer Charles Rennie *Mackintosh. More recently, the term 'Glasgow School' (or facetiously 'Glasgow pups') has been applied to a group of figurative painters working in the city from the 1980s. They include Ken Currie (1960–), Peter Howson (1958–), and Adrian Wiszniewski (1958–), all of whom were students at *Glasgow School of Art at much the same time.

Glasgow School of Art. Art school founded in 1840 as the School of Design in Ingram Street, Glasgow. In 1869 it moved to its present site in Sauchiehall Street, and in 1896 Charles Rennie *Mackintosh won a competition to design a new building. This was erected in 1897–9, with a library block and other extensions added in 1907–9. Together they form one of the most original and dramatic works of architecture of the period anywhere in Europe. At this time the School was enjoying its golden age, under the directorship (1885–1918) of the painter Francis (Fra) Newbery (1855–1946), who had admirable skill as an administrator and a flair for recognizing and encouraging talent. He had good connections abroad and helped the School to win an international reputation. It continues to enjoy high status and produced a particularly outstanding crop of graduates in the 1980s, including the painters Steven Campbell (1953–), Stephen Conroy (1964–), and Alison Watt (1965–). Their work marks a return to an interest in figurative art after the 'anything goes' 1970s.

glass print (or **cliché-verre**). An image made by exposing sensitized photographic paper to the sun beneath a glass plate on which the design has been drawn. Such images resemble *etchings and are sometimes classified as a type of *print. The medium was popular in France from about 1850 to 1870; during this period it was used by several distinguished artists, above all *Corot, and it has occasionally been used subsequently.

glaze. A transparent or semi-transparent layer of paint applied over another layer so as to modify its colour; the light passing through is reflected back by the under surface and altered by the glaze. The effect produced by glazing differs from any obtainable by directly mixing colours together, for the technique imparts a special depth and luminosity. From the 15th to the 19th century most oil paintings were built up as an elaborate structure of superimposed layers, glazes, and *scumbles over an *underpainting, but since *alla prima painting became the norm such a highly deliberate, craftsmanly approach has fallen into disfavour.

Gleizes, Albert (b Paris, 8 Dec. 1881; d Avignon, 23 June 1953). French painter, printmaker, and writer. His early work was *Impressionist in style, but in 1909 he took up *Cubism. In 1912 he was among the founders of the *Section d'Or group and in 1912, with *Metzinger, he wrote the book Du Cubisme (an English translation, Cubism, appeared in 1913). This was the first book on the movement and it remains Gleizes's main claim to fame. Much of his later career was devoted to trying to achieve a synthesis of medieval and modern art, expressing Christian ideas through pseudo-Cubist forms. In this he is generally reckoned to have been conspicuously unsuccessful and his modest reputation as a painter rests on his pre-war work. He expounded his views in several books and pamphlets.

Gleyre, Charles (b Chevilly, nr. Lausanne, 2 May 1806; d Paris, 5 May 1874). Swiss painter, active mainly in Paris, where he settled in 1838 after four years travelling in the Near East (see ORIENTALISM). His successful career was based mainly on figure compositions, sometimes in an *antique setting, and portraits. He had a highly polished technique and was a renowned teacher; when *Delaroche retired from teaching in 1843, the majority of his students transferred to Gleyre. He taught *Whistler and several of the *Impressionists—*Bazille, *Monet, *Renoir, and *Sisley—and although his own paintings were academic in spirit, he encouraged open-air painting (see PLEIN AIR). Renoir, however, said that his main strength as

a teacher was that he left his pupils 'pretty much to their own devices'. Gleyre closed his studio in 1864 because of an eye ailment.

Gobelins. French tapestry manufactory, named after a family of dyers and cloth makers who set up business on the outskirts of Paris in the 15th century. Their premises became a tapestry factory in the early 17th century, and in 1662 it was taken over by Louis XIV, who appointed *Le Brun its director. For Louis it made not only tapestries but also every kind of product (except carpets, which were woven at the Savonnerie factory) required for the furnishing of the royal palaces—its official title was Manufacture Royale des Meubles de la Couronne. The celebrated tapestry designed by Le Brun showing Louis XIV Visiting the Gobelins (c.1667, Gobelins Mus., Paris) gives a good idea of the range of its activities. In 1694 the factory was closed because of the king's financial difficulties, and although it reopened in 1699, thereafter it made only tapestries. For much of the 18th century it retained its position as the foremost tapestry manufactory in Europe. *Oudry and *Boucher successively held the post of director (1733-70). The Gobelins continues in production today and also houses a tapestry museum.

Godefroid de Clair (Godefroid de Huy). *Mosan goldsmith and enamellist, active in the mid-12th century. He may have trained in the workshop of *Rainer of Huy. Early sources praise his great skill and suggest he was a prolific artist, but his career is obscure and most of the numerous attributions to him of reliquaries and *enamels are highly speculative. Peter Lasko (Ars Sacra: 800-1200, 1972) considers that 'On the whole, the introduction of the personality of Godefroid has hindered rather than helped our understanding of the development of the Mosan style.' His name continues to be one to conjure with, however. In 1978 two small enamels attributed to him were bought at *Sotheby's (at the sale of the collection of Robert von Hirsch) for more than £1,000,000 each. They are now in the Germanisches Nationalmuseum, Nuremberg, and the Kunstgewerbemuseum, Berlin.

Godward, J. W. See ALMA-TADEMA.

Goes, Hugo van der (b ?Ghent, ?c. 1440; d Rode Klooster, nr. Brussels, 1482). Netherlandish painter, one of the greatest and most individual of his period. Nothing is known of his life before 1467, when he became a master in the painters' guild at Ghent. He had numerous commissions from the town of Ghent for work of a temporary nature such as processional banners, and in 1475 he became dean of the painters' guild. At about the same time he became a lay brother at a monastery near Brussels (the Rode Klooster: 'Red Cloister'), but he continued to paint and also to travel. In 1481 he suffered a mental breakdown (he had a tendency to acute depression) and, although he recovered, died the following year. An account survives of his illness written by Gaspar Ofhuys, a monk at the monastery; Ofhuys was evidently jealous of Hugo and his description has been called by Erwin *Panofsky 'a masterpiece of clinical accuracy and sanctimonious malice'.

No paintings by Hugo are signed and the only work attributed to him on solid early evidence is his masterpiece, a large *triptych of the Nativity known as the Portinari Altarpiece (c.1475–6, Uffizi, Florence). This was commissioned by Tommaso Portinari, the representative of the *Medici bank in Bruges, for the church of the Hospital of S. Maria Nuova in Florence, and its masterful handling of the oil technique made a powerful impact on Italian painters. There is a great variety of surface ornament and detail, but this is combined with lucid organization of the figure groups and a convincing sense of spatial depth. As remarkable as Hugo's skill in reconciling grandeur of conception with keen observation is his psychological penetration in the depiction of individual figures, notably the awestruck shepherds.

Other works have been convincingly attributed to Hugo on the basis of similarity of style with the Portinari Altarpiece. They include two large panels painted c. 1478 for the church of Holy Trinity in Edinburgh, showing the Holy Trinity Adored by Sir Edward Bonkil (the provost of the church) and the Royal Family of Scotland (both Royal Coll., on loan to NG of Scotland). His last work is perhaps the Death of the Virgin (Groeningemuseum, Bruges), a painting of remarkable tension and poignancy that seems a fitting swansong for such a tormented personality.

Goethe, Johann Wolfgang von (b Frankfurt, 28 Aug. 1749; d Weimar, 22 Mar. 1832). German writer, scientist, patron, and amateur artist, one of the giants of European culture. Throughout his career he devoted much time to studying art and was a prolific draughtsman. His talent in this field was modest, but his writings were influential on the visual arts, particularly in the growth of *Romanticism. Initially he stressed the role of passion in art, but after visiting Italy in 1786–8 he had a greater appreciation of the *classical tradition. His writings on art included a book on colour theory (Zur Farbenlehre, 1810; translated into English by *Eastlake, 1840), in which he purported to refute the Optics of Newton, and a German translation of *Cellini's Autobiography (1798). Many other pieces were published in the periodical Die Propyläen (1798–1800), which he founded as a mouthpiece for his views, and in a series of occasional volumes he edited entitled Über Kunst und Altertum (Art and Antiquity, 6 vols., 1816–32). He was a friend and patron of numerous artists, including *Friedrich and *Tischbein, and his imaginative works were an inspiration to many others; *Delacroix, for example, produced a set of lithographs (1828) illustrating his Faust. See also MINIMAL ART.

Gogh, Vincent van (b Zundert, North Brabant, 30 Mar. 1853; d Auvers-sur-Oise, 29 July 1890). Dutch painter and draughtsman, active for much of his brief career in France, with *Cézanne and *Gauguin the greatest of *Post-Impressionist artists. His uncle was a partner in *Goupil, the international firm of art dealers, and in 1869 van Gogh got a job as a clerk in the branch at The Hague. Between 1873 and 1876 he worked in the London and Paris branches; initially he did well, but early in 1876 he was obliged to resign because of his erratic behaviour. During his time in London he fell unsuccessfully in love with his landlady's daughter (or perhaps with the widowed landlady herself; the evidence is vague)—the first of several disastrous attempts to find happiness with a woman. Throughout most of 1876 he was again in England, working as a teacher in Ramsgate, Kent, and Isleworth, Middlesex, and as an assistant to a Methodist minister, his experience of urban squalor having awakened a religious zeal and a longing to serve his fellow men. His father was a Protestant pastor, and after returning to the Netherlands van Gogh began to train for the ministry; however, he abandoned his studies in 1878 and went to work as a lay preacher among the impoverished miners of the grim Borinage district in Belgium. In his zeal he gave away his own worldly goods to the poor and was dismissed for his literal interpretation of Christ's teaching. He remained in the Borinage, suffering acute poverty and a spiritual crisis, until 1880, when he found that art was his vocation and the means by which he could bring consolation to humanity. From this time he worked at his new 'mission' with single-minded intensity, and although he often suffered from extreme poverty and undernourishment, his output in the ten remaining years of his life was prodigious: about 1,000 paintings and a similar number of drawings. The spontaneous, irrational side of his character has often been stressed, but he was a cultivated and well-read man, who in spite of his speed of work thought deeply about his paintings and planned them carefully.

From 1881 to 1885 van Gogh lived in the Netherlands, sometimes with his parents, sometimes in lodgings, supported by his devoted brother **Theo** (1857–91), a picture dealer in Paris who regularly sent him money from his own small salary as well as art materials and prints. Their correspondence is an extraordinarily rich source of information on van Gogh's life and art. Initially he confined himself to drawings, and they dominate the first half of his career. He experimented with various media, including waxy black lithographic chalk, which encouraged the bold, strongly outlined style he favoured in his early works; later he preferred pen and ink, which he used with much greater spontaneity in rapid dots and flicks that pulsate with the same kind of life as the swirling brushstrokes that came to characterize his paintings. He took up oils in 1882 and in keeping with his humanitarian outlook he painted peasants and workers, the most famous picture from this early period being *The Potato Eaters* (1885, Van Gogh Mus., Amsterdam). Of this he wrote to Theo: 'I have tried to emphasize that those people, eating their potatoes in the lamp-light, have dug the earth with those very hands they put in the dish, and so it speaks of manual labour, and how they have honestly earned their food.'

In 1885 van Gogh moved to Antwerp on the advice of Anton *Mauve (a cousin by marriage), and studied for some months at the Academy there. Academic instruction had little to offer such an individualist, however (essentially he was self-taught), and in February 1886 he moved to Paris, where he met *Degas, Gauguin, *Pissarro, *Seurat, and *Toulouse-Lautrec. At this time his painting changed abruptly in style under the combined influence of *Impressionism and Japanese prints (see UKIYO-E), losing its moralistic flavour and revelling in the beauty of colour. Unlike the Impressionists, however, he did not use colour for the reproduction of visual appearances, atmosphere, and light. 'Instead of trying to reproduce exactly what I have before my eyes,' he wrote, 'I use colour more arbitrarily so as to express myself more forcibly.' Of his *Night Café* (1888, Yale Univ. AG), he said:

'I have tried to express with red and green the terrible passions of human nature.' For a time he was influenced by Seurat's delicate *pointillist manner, but he abandoned this for broad, vigorous brushstrokes.

After two years in Paris van Gogh felt tired of city life and longed 'to look at nature under a brighter sky', so in February 1888 he settled at Arles in the south of France, where he painted more than 200 canvases in fifteen months (most of the celebrated masterpieces on which his huge reputation rests were produced in the last two or three years of his life—an unparalleled creative outpouring). Throughout 1888 he lived in poverty and suffered recurrent nervous crises with hallucinations and depression. However, he became enthusiastic for the idea of founding an artists' cooperative at Arles and in October he was joined by Gauguin. As a result of a quarrel between them van Gogh suffered a crisis in which (24 December 1888) he cut off his left ear (or part of it; contemporary sources disagree on this point), an event commemorated in his *Self-Portrait with Bandaged Ear* (1889, Courtauld Gal., London); epilepsy and schizophrenia are among the causes that have been suggested to account for his mental disturbances. In May 1889 he went at his own request into an asylum at Saint Rémy, near Arles, but during the year he spent there he continued a fervent output of pictures such as *Starry Night* (1889, MoMA, New York). He produced 150 paintings (as well as drawings) in the course of this year. In 1889 Theo married and in May 1890 van Gogh moved to Auvers-sur-Oise, to the north of Paris, to be near him, lodging with the patron and connoisseur Dr Paul Gachet. There followed another tremendous burst of activity and during the last 70 days of his life he painted 70 canvases. But his spiritual anguish and depression became more acute and on 27 July 1890 he shot himself in the chest and died two days later; Theo, who died six months afterwards, is buried alongside him in Auvers.

Van Gogh sold almost nothing during his lifetime and was little known to the art world at the time of his death, but thereafter his reputation grew rapidly (initially his fame was mainly in France and the Netherlands, but in the period between the turn of the century and the First World War it became international). His influence on *Expressionism, *Fauvism, and early abstraction was enormous, and it can be seen in many other aspects of 20th-century art. His passionate life and unswerving devotion to his ideals have made him one of the great cultural heroes of modern times, providing the most auspicious material for the 20th-century vogue in romanticized psychological biography, notably Irving Stone's novel *Lust for Life* (1934) and the Hollywood film of the same name (1956).

Golden Cockerel Press. See PRIVATE PRESS.

Golden Section. A proportion in which a straight line or rectangle is divided into two unequal parts in such a way that the ratio of the smaller to the greater part is the same as that of the greater to the whole. Like the mathematical value pi, it cannot be expressed as a finite number, but an approximation is 8:13 or 0.618:1. The proportion has been known since antiquity (it is discussed by Euclid and *Vitruvius) and has been said to possess inherent aesthetic value because of an alleged correspondence with the laws of nature or the universe. It was much studied during the *Renaissance, and Luca Pacioli (*c*.1445–*c*.1514), the most famous mathematician of his day and a friend of *Leonardo and of *Piero della Francesca, wrote a book on it called *Divina proportione* (1509); some of its illustrations are by Leonardo. In accordance with the tendencies of the time, Pacioli credits this 'divine proportion' with various mystical properties and exceptional beauties both in science and in art. Like many other learned men of the Middle Ages and Renaissance, he was anxious to harmonize the knowledge of pagan antiquity with the Christian faith, and in the chapter in which he justifies his choice of title he explains that this ratio cannot be expressed by a number and, being beyond definition, is in this respect like God, 'occult and secret'; further, this three-in-one proportion is symbolic of the Holy Trinity.

Goldie, C. F. (Charles Frederick) (*b* Auckland, 20 Oct. 1870; *d* Auckland, 11 July 1947). New Zealand painter, trained in Paris at the *Académie Julian. He was brought up at a time when the Maori people were commonly (but erroneously) regarded as a 'dying race' and he devoted most of his career to producing a pictorial record of them for posterity, paying close attention to such details as facial tattoos. His work is best represented in the City Art Gallery, Auckland.

Golding, John (*b* Hastings, Sussex, 10 Sept. 1929). British painter and art historian. He is probably best known as an eminent scholar of 20th-century art, particularly for his standard book *Cubism: A History and an Analysis, 1907–1914* (1959, revised edns. 1968 and 1988), but he has also made a reputation as an abstract painter. He taught history of art at the *Courtauld Institute 1962–81 and in 1976–7 he was *Slade professor at Cambridge University. He began painting seriously in the late 1950s (his first one-man exhibition was in 1962) and gradually devoted more of his time to it. In 1971 he started to teach at the *Royal College of Art and in 1981–6 (having given up his post at the Courtauld Institute) was senior tutor there. His abstracts are typically large in format, with broad expanses of glowing colour; he sees them as 'basically reflective or contemplative'.

Goldsworthy, Andy (*b* Sale Moor, Cheshire, 25 July 1956). British sculptor and *Land artist. He works mainly with found natural materials such as leaves, pebbles, twigs, and even snow and ice, typically using no tools other than objects that come easily to hand. Many of his sculptures are inherently short-lived and are recorded by him in colour photographs (examples are in many public collections). He says that 'each work grows, stays, decays—integral parts of a cycle which the photograph shows at its height, marking the moment when it is most alive. There is an intensity about a work at its peak which I hope is expressed in the image. Process and decay are implicit.' In addition to his transient sculptures, Goldsworthy has produced more permanent pieces, including two large earthworks in County Durham, and he has published several books documenting his output. He was born in Cheshire, grew up in Yorkshire, and has spent much of his life in Scotland, but he works internationally, his projects taking him to Japan and the Canadian Arctic for example.

Goldwater, Robert. See BOURGEOIS, LOUISE.

Goltzius, Hendrick (*b* Mühlbracht [now Bracht-am-Niederrhein], Jan./Feb. 1558; *bur.* Haarlem, 1 Jan. 1617). Dutch printmaker, draughtsman, and painter of German descent, one of the most influential figures of his time in northern European art. He was the best-known line engraver of his day (he also made a few etchings) and the leader of a group of *Mannerist artists who worked in Haarlem, where he founded some kind of 'academy' (perhaps a life class) with *Cornelis van Haarlem and Karel van *Mander. In 1590–1 he visited Rome and after this his style became more *classical. Goltzius' right hand was crippled, but in spite of this handicap he was renowned for his technical virtuosity and for his skill in imitating the work of other great engravers such as *Dürer and *Lucas van

Leyden. In his early career much of his work was reproductive, but he also produced many original compositions, including a splendid series on Roman heroes (1586). His portrait drawings are also outstanding, and the landscape drawings he made after 1600 mark him as a forerunner of the great 17th-century landscape artists. His paintings are generally less interesting than his drawings and much less advanced stylistically.

Gombrich, Sir Ernst (b Vienna, 30 Mar. 1909; d London, 3 Nov. 2001). Austrian-born British art historian. He settled in England in 1936 and began a long association with the *Warburg Institute in the University of London, where he was director and professor of the history of the classical tradition from 1959 to 1976. He was also *Slade professor at both Oxford and Cambridge. His scholarly work, which shows a remarkable ability to combine great breadth of learning with lucidity and wit, was devoted largely to the theory of art, the psychology of pictorial representation, and Renaissance symbolism, and won him a position of the highest esteem in his profession. His writings bore witness to his interest in scientific method and helped to promote interchange between art history and other disciplines. Gombrich's best-known book, however, is a popular work, *The Story of Art*, which was first published in 1950 and has ever since held its place as the most congenial introduction to the history of art. It reached its 16th English edition in 1995 and has been translated into twenty languages.

Among Gombrich's other books the best known is probably *Art and Illusion* (1960 and subsequent editions). This highly influential work deals with conventions of representation and examines how styles change and develop, challenging many orthodox views and received opinions about visual perception. The notion of the 'innocent eye'—the idea of the artist simply representing what he sees—is shown to be untenable and the evolution of style ('why different ages and different nations have represented the visible world in . . . different ways') is explained in terms of the modification of schematic images to match the objective reality of the subject. Using the findings of experimental psychology, Gombrich examines the way the viewer looks at works of art and shows that we tend to see what we expect to see. In *Thinkers of the Twentieth Century* (ed. Elizabeth Devine et al., 1983) J. M. Massing wrote: 'For his scholarly method, his theoretical approach and his defence of cultural values, Gombrich will be remembered as one of the leading art historians of this century. Through his study of the psychology of perception, he is also one of the very few to have widened our understanding of the visible world.'

Gonçalves, Nuno (active 1450–71). Portuguese painter, first recorded in 1450, when he was appointed court painter by Alfonso V. No works certainly by his hand survive, but there is strong circumstantial evidence that he was responsible for the *St Vincent* *polyptych (c.1460–70, Mus. Nacional de Arte Antiga, Lisbon), the outstanding Portuguese painting of the 15th century. The style is rather dry, but powerfully realistic, and the polyptych contains a superb gallery of highly individualized portraits of members of the court, including a presumed self-portrait. There are affinities with contemporary Burgundian and Flemish art, especially the work of *Bouts.

Goncharova, Natalia (b Lodyzhino or Negayevo, Tula province, 4 [16] June or 21 June [3 July] 1881; d Paris, 17 Oct. 1962). Russian-French painter, designer, printmaker, and illustrator, born into a distinguished family (she was related to the poet Pushkin). In Moscow in 1900 she met her fellow student Mikhail *Larionov, who became her lifelong companion. In the years leading up to the First World War they were among the most prominent figures in Russian avant-garde art, taking part in and often helping to organize a series of major exhibitions in Moscow. Her early paintings were *Impressionist, but from 1906 she began to develop a *primitivist style combining her interest in peasant art and icon painting with influences from modern French art, particularly *Fauvism and *Cubism, to which was later added *Futurism. By the time of the *Target exhibition of 1913 she was painting in a near-abstract *Rayonist style (*Cats*, 1913, Guggenheim Mus., New York). In 1915 she left Russia with Larionov and after settling in Paris in 1919 she devoted herself mainly to designing settings and costumes for the theatre, particularly *Diaghilev's Ballets Russes. Goncharova and Larionov became French citizens in 1938 and were married in 1955. By this time they had been virtually forgotten, but there was a great revival of interest in them in the early 1960s.

Goncourt, Edmond de (b Nancy, 26 May 1822; d Champrosay, 16 July 1896) and **Jules de** (b Paris, 17 Dec. 1830; d Paris, 20 June 1870). French writers, brothers, who worked in close collaboration. They wrote on various artistic topics, their most important work of criticism being a book made up of a collection of articles, *L'Art du dix-huitième siècle* (1875), which helped to revive the reputation of 18th-century French artists such as *Watteau. The brothers inherited a substantial fortune when their aristocrat mother died in 1848, and their lives were divided between writing and self-indulgence; the *Journal* that they began in 1851, and which Edmond continued after Jules died until his own death, provides a richly detailed record of Paris in the second half of the 19th century. Edmond's books on Utamaro (1891) and Hokusai (1896) helped to popularize Japanese art (see UKIYO-E). The brothers also wrote novels and painted. The Académie Goncourt, founded under Edmond's will, is a body of ten men or women of letters that awards an annual prize (the Prix Goncourt) for imaginative prose.

Gonzaga. Italian family, rulers of Mantua from 1328 to 1707, who at various times attracted to their court some of the greatest Italian and other European artists. Under **Ludovico** (1412–78; reigned from 1444) *Mantegna was appointed court painter and *Alberti began the church of S. Andrea. The presence of Isabella d'*Este, who married **Francesco II** in 1490, helped to make Mantua one of the greatest centres of art collecting and patronage. Under **Federico II** (1500–40; reigned from 1519) *Giulio Romano built and decorated the Gonzaga pleasure house, the Palazzo del Tè, and turned Mantua into one of the main centres of *Mannerist art. The other artists who worked for Federico included *Correggio, who painted a celebrated series of mythological pictures for him. **Vincenzo I** (1562–1612; reigned from 1587) was one of the greatest collectors of his day and *Rubens's chief patron during his years in Italy. **Ferdinando** (1587–1626; reigned from 1612) employed van *Dyck, Domenico *Feti, *Albani, and other artists. In 1627 most of the family collections were sold by **Vincenzo II** (1594–1627; reigned from 1626), principally to Charles I of England (see ROYAL COLLECTION), and important Gonzaga patronage came to an end after Mantua was sacked by Austrian troops in 1630.

González, Julio (*b* Barcelona, 21 Sept. 1876; *d* Arcueil, nr. Paris, 27 Mar. 1942). Spanish sculptor, draughtsman, metalworker, and painter, active mainly in France, the leading pioneer in the use of *iron as a sculptural medium. He learnt to work metals under his father, a goldsmith and sculptor, but his early career was spent mainly as a painter. In about 1900 he moved to Paris and formed a lifelong friendship with *Picasso, whom he had earlier met in his native Barcelona. He initially supported himself mainly by making metalwork and jewellery, and it was not until the late 1920s, when he was already 50, that he devoted himself wholeheartedly to sculpture and turned to welded metal as a material. His best-known work, *Montserrat* (1937, Stedelijk Mus., Amsterdam), is a fairly naturalistic piece, showing a woman with a child in her arms, and commemorates the suffering of the people of Spain in the Civil War (Montserrat is Spain's holy mountain). More usually, however, his sculptures are semi-abstract, as in his series of *Cactus People*, formidable pieces with some of Picasso's savage humour. González's work had great influence, notably on Picasso, to whom he taught the techniques of iron sculpture, and on a generation of British and American artists exemplified by Reg *Butler and David *Smith. His brother **Joan González** (1868–1908) was a draughtsman and painter.

Gordon, Douglas. See TURNER PRIZE.

Gore, Spencer (*b* Epsom, Surrey, 26 May 1878; *d* Richmond, Surrey [now in Greater London], 27 Mar. 1914). British painter of landscapes, music-hall scenes, interiors, and occasional still-lifes. He was the son of Spencer Walter Gore, who won the first Wimbledon tennis championship in 1877, and nephew of Charles Gore, Bishop of Oxford. In 1896–9 he studied at the *Slade School, where he was a particular friend of Harold *Gilman. In 1904 he visited *Sickert in Dieppe; this marked the beginning of his close acquaintance with recent French painting (he returned to France in 1905 and 1906), and his enthusiasm helped to decide Sickert to return to Britain in 1905. For the rest of his short career Gore was part of Sickert's circle, becoming a founder member successively of the *Allied Artists' Association in 1908, the *Camden Town Group (of which he was first president) in 1911, and the *London Group in 1913. His early work was *Impressionist in style, but he was strongly influenced by Roger *Fry's *Post-Impressionist exhibitions (Gore's own work was included in the second in 1912) and his later pictures show vivid use of flat, bright colour and boldly simplified forms. He died of pneumonia aged 35 and was much lamented by his many friends in the art world. Sickert said Gore was 'probably the man I love and admire most of any I have known', and his obituary in the *Morning Post* remarked that 'his personal character was so exceptional as to give him a unique influence in the artistic affairs of London in the last dozen years'. His son **Frederick Gore** (1913–) is also a painter.

Gorky, Arshile (Vosdanig Manoog Adoian) (*b* Dzov, 15 Apr. 1904; *d* Sherman, Conn., 21 July 1948). American painter, born in Turkish Armenia, who formed a link between European *Surrealism and American *Abstract Expressionism. He emigrated to the USA in 1920 and adopted the pseudonym Arshile Gorky, the first part of the name being derived from the Greek hero Achilles, the second part (Russian for 'the bitter one') from the Russian writer Maxim Gorky, to whom the painter sometimes claimed he was related (evidently not realizing that the writer's name, too, was a pseudonym). In 1925 he settled in New York, where he first studied and then taught at the Grand Central School of Art. Gorky took a romantic view of his vocation and is said to have hired a Hungarian violinist to play during his classes to encourage his students to put emotion into their work. His early paintings were strongly influenced by *Cézanne (whom he considered 'the greatest artist that has lived') and he also fell under the spell of *Picasso, as can be seen both in the haunting *The Artist and his Mother* (*c*.1926–9, Whitney Mus., New York) and in his experimentation with *Cubism at this period. Much of his work of the 1930s represents an attempt to synthesize the flatness of Cubist structure (in which he was influenced also by Stuart *Davis) with the improvisatory fluidity and energy of *Surrealist *automatism.

In the early 1940s Gorky came into contact with the European Surrealists who had emigrated to New York to escape the Second World War and under their influence (particularly that of *Matta and *Miró) he created the distinctive style of his last phase, featuring delicately drawn shapes, suggestive of living organisms, floating in brilliant colour. However, just as Gorky began to emerge as a powerful original voice in American art, he suffered a tragic series of misfortunes. In 1946 a fire in his Connecticut studio destroyed a large proportion of his recent work, and in the same year he was operated on for cancer. In 1948 he broke his neck in an automobile accident, and when his wife left him soon afterwards he hanged himself. Gorky has been called both the last of the great Surrealists and the first of the Abstract Expressionists, and his work in the 1940s was a potent factor underlying the emergence of a specifically American school of abstract art. He was particularly influential on his friend *de Kooning.

Gormley, Antony (*b* London, 30 Aug. 1950). British sculptor. His work has been mainly concerned with the human figure and is often based on moulds from his own body. He won the *Turner Prize in 1994 and achieved much wider fame in 1998 when his enormous *Angel of the North* was erected near Gateshead, overlooking the A1 trunk road, and thereafter quickly became one of Britain's most instantly recognizable sights. Made of steel, it stands 20 m (65 ft) high and has a wingspan of 54 m (177 ft). It was commissioned by Gateshead Metropolitan Borough Council in 1994, and its creation and erection was a complex industrial undertaking. Gormley has also made prints (see SOFT-GROUND ETCHING).

Gospels of Henry the Lion. An illuminated manuscript of the Four Gospels made *c*.1175–80 for Henry the Lion (*c*.1129–95), Duke of Brunswick and Saxony. The ruler of vast territories in Germany, Austria, Italy, and Scandinavia, 'He was by far the most important man of his time and was recognised as such not only in Germany but throughout the civilised world' (A. L. Poole, *Henry the Lion*, 1912). The manuscript was made at Helmarshausen Abbey, which was a famous centre of artistic production (see THEOPHILUS), for presentation to Brunswick Cathedral. It is an extraordinarily lavish book, with abundant use of gold, and was intended to symbolize Henry's wealth and power and to set forth his claim (which remained unfulfilled) to the title of Holy Roman Emperor; the dedication page justifies this claim on the basis of his descent from Charlemagne. The provenance of the manuscript is obscure in some places, but it was for centuries in Prague Cathedral until sold to the King of Hanover in 1861. In 1983 it came on the open market for the first time and was sold at *Sotheby's, London, which justifiably described it as 'the finest illuminated manuscript remaining in private hands'. It was bought by the West German government for £8,140,000—at the time the highest price paid for any work of art, and more than ten times the price ever realized by an illuminated manuscript. It is held jointly by the Bayerische Staatsbibliothek, Munich, and the Herzog August Bibliothek, Wolfenbüttel, alternating between the two locations.

Gossaert, Jan (also called Mabuse) (*b* ?Maubeuge, *c*.1478; *d* ?Antwerp, 1 Oct. 1532). Netherlandish painter, probably from Maubeuge (now in France), from which his name Mabuse derives. In 1503 he became a master in the Antwerp painters' guild, but a few years afterwards he entered the service of Philip of Burgundy (illegitimate son of Duke Philip the Good and later Bishop of Utrecht). In 1508–9 he was part of Philip's retinue when he visited Rome as ambassador to the Vatican. After his return to the Netherlands, Gossaert seems to have settled in Zeeland, although it is not known in which town he made his home. His work before his Italian journey is in the tradition of Hugo van der *Goes and Gerard *David, whose influence can still be seen in the *Adoration of the Magi* (NG, London), probably painted soon after his return. His later work, however, was transformed by the experience of Italy, although the motifs he learned there were never thoroughly digested and coexisted with Flemish forms and details. *Vasari acclaimed him for being the first 'to bring the true method of representing nude figures and mythologies from Italy to the Netherlands', but in, for example, *Neptune and Amphitrite* (1516, Gemäldegalerie, Berlin), the life-size muscle-bound figures are in fact closer to *Dürer than to any Italian contemporary, and the curious classical temple in which they stand has bizarrely hybrid architectural elements.

Gossaert was highly thought of by his contemporaries. His commissions took him to various towns in the Netherlands, his patrons included Margaret of Austria (see HABSBURG) and Christian II of Denmark, and his work was widely influential. However, to modern eyes there seems justice in Dürer's assessment of him as better in execution than in invention ('nit so gut im Haupstreichen als im Gemäl'). Jan van *Scorel was Gossaert's pupil for a short time.

Gosse, Sir Edmund. See NEW SCULPTURE.

Gotch, Thomas Cooper. See NEWLYN SCHOOL.

Gothic. Style of architecture and art that succeeded *Romanesque and prevailed in Europe (particularly northern Europe) from the mid-12th century to the 16th century. Like many other stylistic labels, the word was originally a term of abuse; it was coined by Italian artists of the *Renaissance to denote the type of medieval architecture they condemned as barbaric (implying, quite wrongly, that this architecture was created by the Gothic tribes who had destroyed the classical art of the Roman Empire). The Gothic style is still characterized chiefly in terms of architecture—in particular by the use of pointed arches, rib vaults, and flying buttresses. None of these features was first used in the Gothic period (they are all found in late Romanesque architecture), but when employed together they created a new type of skeletal structure and a sense of graceful resilience that was very different in spirit from the massive solidity of Romanesque buildings.

By extension, the term 'Gothic' has also been applied to the ornament, sculpture, and painting of the period in which Gothic architecture was built; it has less precise meaning in these contexts, although a swaying elegance is often considered typical of Gothic figures, which are generally much more naturalistic and less remote than those of the Romanesque period. There were great sculptural ensembles (particularly around portals) at several Gothic cathedrals, but the most characteristic sculptural product of the age is perhaps the standing figure of the Virgin and Child, notably in *ivory. In late Gothic Germany carving in *limewood reached great heights of beauty and elaboration. Gothic pictorial art is seen at its best in manuscript illumination and in stained glass. Panel painting came more into its own with the development of the late branch of the style known as *International Gothic, which flourished at the turn of the 14th and 15th centuries. Among the other arts that flourished in the period were embroidery (see OPUS ANGLICANUM) and tapestry.

The **Gothic Revival** is the name given to a fashion involving the reintroduction of Gothic forms in architecture and associated arts. It began in the mid-18th century, in a fairly lighthearted way, medieval forms being used for their picturesque qualities, in a *Rococo spirit, with no regard for archaeological accuracy. However, the movement became much more serious in tone and developed into a major strand in 19th-century art.

Gottlieb, Adolph (b New York, 14 Mar. 1903; d East Hampton, Long Island, NY, 4 Mar. 1974). American painter, one of the leading *Abstract Expressionists. His early work was *Expressionist and in 1935 he was one of the founding members of the Expressionist group The *Ten. In 1936 he worked for the *Federal Art Project. Some of his landscapes of the late 1930s were influenced by *Surrealism, and from the early 1940s this tendency was enhanced by contact with expatriate European Surrealists and by an interest in Freudian psychology. His personal style began to emerge in 1941 and from then until the end of his life he worked on three main series: *Pictographs* (1941–51), *Imaginary Landscapes* (1951–7, and again in the mid-1960s), and *Bursts* (1957–74). The *Pictographs* use a loose grid- or compartment-like arrangement with schematic shapes or symbols suggesting some mythic face; the *Imaginary Landscapes* feature a zone of astral shapes against a foreground of heavy *gestural strokes; and the *Bursts*, becoming still freer, suggest solar orbs and astral bodies hovering above violently coloured terrestrial explosions (*Blast I*, 1957, MoMA, New York). Gottlieb also designed stained glass and other works for churches and synagogues, suggesting a religious mood without any specific representation.

gouache. Opaque *watercolour, sometimes also known as *body colour. It differs from transparent watercolour in that the *pigments are bound with glue and the lighter tones are obtained by the admixture of white pigment. Its degree of opacity varies with the amount of white that is added, but in general it is sufficient to prevent the reflection of the *ground through the paint and it therefore lacks the luminosity of transparent watercolour painting. It is, however, easier to use, as trials and errors can be painted over. The colours sold as poster paints by commercial colourmen are usually a form of gouache.

Goudt, Hendrik. See ELSHEIMER.

Goujon, Jean (*b* c.1510; *d* ?Bologna, ?1568). French sculptor. He ranks second only to Germain *Pilon as the greatest French sculptor of the 16th century and he created a distinctive *Mannerist style as sophisticated as the finest works of painting and decoration of the contemporary School of *Fontainebleau. Nothing is known of his early life and he is first recorded in 1540 as the carver of the impressive columns supporting the organ loft in the church of St Maclou at Rouen. The pure *classicism of these columns has caused some critics to assume that he had earlier visited Italy. He had moved to Paris by 1544, when he was working on the screen in the church of St Germain-l'Auxerrois, in collaboration with the architect Pierre Lescot. Low-*relief panels (now in the Louvre) from this screen show that Goujon had evolved a style of extreme grace and delicacy, owing something to the influence of Benvenuto *Cellini. The style is seen at its most mature in his decorations (now in the Louvre) for the Fontaine des Innocents, Paris (1547–9). The six relief panels of nymphs from the fountain, with their exquisitely carved rippling draperies, are generally considered his masterpieces. Goujon's most extensive undertaking

was on the sculptural decoration of the *Louvre; he worked there from 1549 to 1562 in collaboration with Lescot, mainly on decorative panels forming part of the architectural scheme. Unfortunately all Goujon's work there has been heavily restored, including the famous *caryatids (1550–1) in the Salle des Caryatides. Using caryatids on a monumental scale was a novelty, perhaps inspired by his reading of *Vitruvius (he made illustrations for the first French translation of his treatise in 1547). There is no indication of any work executed after 1562 and it is possible that Goujon left France because of religious persecution and died in Bologna (there is some doubt concerning the documentation).

Goupil. Firm of printsellers and art dealers founded in Paris in 1827 by **Adolphe Goupil** (1806–93). Initially it specialized in selling reproductions, but it expanded to become a leading picture dealer, marketing works by a wide range of contemporary artists. In 1841 a branch was opened in London and in 1846 one in New York (this later became *Knoedler's). Later there were branches in Berlin, Brussels, The Hague, and Vienna. Van *Gogh's uncle was a partner in the branch in The Hague and at the outset of his career van Gogh himself worked for the firm for several years; it also employed his brother Theo. After Goupil's retirement in 1875 the firm was run by his partner Léon Boussot and Boussot's son-in-law René Valadon, although it continued to be known familiarly as Goupil's for some time after this. Boussot & Valadon continued in business until 1919. It dealt in work by several of the *Impressionists, among other artists, and the Glasgow dealer Alex Reid (see BURRELL), who helped introduce modern French painting to Scotland, worked for the firm in 1887–9.

Gower, George (*b* ?c.1540; *bur.* London, 30 Aug. 1596). English portrait painter. He was appointed serjeant-painter to Queen Elizabeth in 1581 and seems to have been the leading English portraitist of his day. His *Sir Thomas Kytson* and *Lady Kytson* (1573, Tate, London) show his clear and individual, if unsubtle, style. Gower was a gentleman by birth and his *Self-Portrait* (1579, priv. coll.) depicts his coat of arms outweighed in a balance by a pair of dividers, a symbol of the painter's craft.

Gowing, Sir Lawrence (*b* London, 21 Apr. 1918; *d* London, 5 Feb. 1991). British painter and writer on art. He had a distinguished academic career, during which he was deputy director of the Tate Gallery (1965–7) and a professor at several universities (notably at the *Slade School, 1975–85), and he wrote books and exhibition catalogues, valued for their critical insights, on numerous artists, among them *Cézanne, *Matisse, and *Vermeer. As a painter he began as a pupil of *Coldstream working in the *Euston Road tradition, and much of his subsequent work was in this sombre vein. His work also included abstracts, however, and in 1976 he began producing large pictures in which he traced the outline of his own naked body stretched on the canvas, the paint being applied by an assistant.

Goya, Francisco de (*b* Fuendetodos, Aragon, 30 Mar. 1746; *d* Bordeaux, 16 Apr. 1828). Spanish painter, printmaker, and draughtsman. He was the most powerful and original European artist of his time, but his genius was slow in maturing and he was well into his thirties before he began producing work that set him apart from his contemporaries. The son of a gilder, he trained initially with a local painter in Saragossa, then in 1763 moved to Madrid, where he continued his studies under Francisco *Bayeu (he twice failed in attempts to enrol at the Academy of S. Fernando). After a visit to Italy (*c.*1768–71), he worked in Saragossa, then after marrying Bayeu's sister in 1773 he settled in Madrid in 1774. Bayeu secured him employment making designs for the royal tapestry factory, and this took up most of his working time from 1775 to 1780 (he continued the work more sporadically until 1792). Goya made 63 tapestry designs in all (most of them are in the Prado, Madrid). Although they are usually referred to as '*cartoons', they are in fact finished oil paintings, many of them of impressive size (the largest are more than 6 m (20 ft) wide). The subjects range from idyllic scenes to realistic depictions of incidents of everyday life; they are conceived in a lively and romantic spirit and executed with *Rococo decorative charm, but they are sometimes spiced with a sardonic humour that looks forward to Goya's later work.

During the 1780s Goya progressed steadily in his career, becoming a sought-after portraitist, achieving success as a religious painter, and winning a series of official distinctions. He was elected to the Academy of S. Fernando in 1780 and became deputy director of painting there in 1785; in 1786 he was appointed one of the painters to the king and in 1789 he was promoted to the more prestigious post of painter to the royal household (he marked his elevation by

adding the aristocratic 'de' to his name). A more important turning point in his career than any of these appointments, however, was the mysterious, traumatic, and near-fatal illness he experienced in the winter of 1792–3 (syphilis and lead poisoning from paint are among the causes that have been suggested). The illness paralysed him and partially blinded him for a while and left him stone deaf for the rest of his life. Whilst convalescing in 1793 he painted a series of small pictures as a kind of therapy, 'to occupy my imagination, vexed by consideration of my sufferings, and . . . to make observations that normally are given no place in commissioned works, where caprice and invention cannot be developed'. This marks the beginning of his preoccupation with the morbid, bizarre, and menacing that was to be such a feature of his mature work. It was given vivid expression in the first of his great series of prints, *Los caprichos* (Caprices), issued in 1799. The set consists of 80 plates dealing with the ills and disorders of society.

In 1795 Goya succeeded Bayeu as director of painting at the Academy of S. Fernando and in 1799 he was appointed principal painter to the royal household, producing his most famous portrait group, the *Family of Charles IV* (Prado), in the following year. The weaknesses of the royal family are revealed with unsparing realism, though evidently without the deliberate satirical intent that has sometimes been claimed for the picture. Goya's early portraits had followed the manner of *Mengs, but stimulated by the study of *Velázquez's paintings in the royal collection he developed a much more natural, lively, and personal style, showing increasing mastery of pose and expression, heightened by dramatic contrasts of light and shade. From about the same date as the royal group portrait are the celebrated pair of paintings the *Clothed Maja* and *Naked Maja* (Prado), whose erotic nature led Goya to be summoned before the Inquisition. Popular legend has it that they represent the Duchess of Alba, the beautiful widow whose relationship with Goya caused scandal in Madrid.

During the French occupation of Spain (1808–13) Goya retained his appointment of royal painter under Joseph Bonaparte (installed as king by his brother Napoleon), but his activity as a painter of court and society decreased, and—like many others—he may have been torn between welcoming the regime (which potentially brought freedom from royal tyranny) and feeling patriotic abhorrence against foreign military rule. He never openly expressed his political opinions and to a certain extent he was prepared to bend with the prevailing wind for the sake of his career (during the occupation he painted the Duke of Wellington, Napoleon's eventual conqueror, as well as supporters of the French). After the restoration of Ferdinand VII in 1814 Goya was exonerated from the charge of having 'accepted employment from the usurper' by claiming he had not worn the medal awarded him by the French, and he painted for the king two powerful and harrowing pictures of Spain's 'glorious insurrection', the bloody uprising of the citizens of Madrid against the occupying forces—the *Second of May, 1808* and the *Third of May, 1808* (both 1814, Prado). Even more savage are the 65 etchings *Los desastres de la guerra* (The Disasters of War, 1810–14), which depict atrocities committed by both French and Spanish.

Goya virtually retired from public life after 1815, subsequently working for himself and friends. He kept the title of court painter but was superseded in royal favour by Vicente *López. Towards the end of 1819 he fell seriously ill for the second time (a remarkable self-portrait in the Minneapolis Institute of Arts shows him with the doctor who nursed him). Earlier that year he had bought a country house on the outskirts of Madrid, the Quinta del Sordo (House of the Deaf Man), and it was here, after his recovery, that he executed fourteen large murals (now in the Prado) known as the *Black Paintings* (1820–3) on account of their nightmarish subjects as well as their dark tonality. Painted almost entirely in blacks, greys, and browns, they feature religious and mythological scenes as well as ones entirely from Goya's imagination; they are executed with an almost ferocious intensity and freedom of handling and have been seen as reflections on death. By the time he completed these extraordinary works, many Spanish liberals were leaving the country because of the oppressive regime of Ferdinand VII, and in 1824 Goya obtained permission to visit France, ostensibly for reasons of health, and settled at Bordeaux. He made two brief visits to Spain, on the first of which (1826) he officially resigned as court painter and was granted a pension. In these last years he took up the new medium of *lithography (in four bullfighting scenes known collectively as the *Bulls of Bordeaux*, 1824–5), while his final paintings illustrate his progress towards a style anticipating *Impressionism in its freedom and lightness of touch.

Goya's output was enormous; there are about 700 surviving paintings by him, some 300 prints, and nearly 1,000 drawings. He was exceptionally versatile and his work expresses a very wide range of emotion. His technical freedom and originality likewise are remarkable—he sometimes manipulated paint with knives or fingers (and with more unconventional tools, including sponges and a wooden spoon, if Théophile Gautier's account in *Voyage en Espagne*, 1845, is to be believed), and in his prints he often used more than one technique on the same plate, especially combining *etching with *aquatint. In his own day he was chiefly celebrated for his portraits (which account for more than half of his painted output), but his enormous reputation now rests equally on work that was virtually unknown to his contemporaries: the *Disasters of War* etchings were not published until 1863 and the *Black Paintings* were not publicly exhibited until the 1870s.

Goyen, Jan van (*b* Leiden, 13 Jan. 1596; *d* The Hague, 27 Apr. 1656). Dutch painter, one of the foremost pioneers of realistic landscape painting in the Netherlands. His earliest works are heavily indebted to his master Esaias van de *Velde, but he then created a distinctive type of monochrome landscape in browns and greys with touches of vivid blue or red to catch the eye. He was one of the first painters to capture the quality of the light and air in a scene and to suggest the movement of clouds. Most of his paintings seem to be based on drawings made as he travelled about the countryside, and he evidently used the same drawings again and again because the same themes and motifs recur repeatedly in his works: gnarled oaks, wide plains, usually seen from a height, low horizons, and clouded skies are typical of his repertoire. His finest work has a sense of poetic calm as well as great freshness and luminosity of atmosphere. Van Goyen worked in Leiden, Haarlem, and The Hague. He was hugely prolific and had many pupils and imitators. With Salomon van *Ruysdael, whose paintings are often virtually indistinguishable from his, he was the outstanding master of the 'tonal' phase of Dutch landscape painting, when the depiction of atmosphere was the artist's prime concern.

Gozzoli, Benozzo (Benozzo di Lese) (*b* Florence, *c*.1421; *d* Pistoia, 4 Oct. 1497). Florentine painter. He probably trained under Fra *Angelico and he later worked as his assistant in Rome (1447) and Orvieto (1448). His reputation rests on only one work—but one of the most enchanting in all Italian *Renaissance art: the decoration of the chapel of the Palazzo

*Medici in Florence with frescos of the *Journey of the Magi* (1459–61). This is the most glittering fresco cycle of the century, recalling, and perhaps consciously rivalling, *Gentile da Fabriano's *Adoration of the Magi* of 1423. Its secular outlook is far removed in spirit from the work of his master Fra Angelico. The rest of Benozzo's career was busy but fairly unremarkable. His biggest undertaking was a fresco cycle of Old Testament scenes in the Campo Santo in Pisa; he began work on it in 1467 and spent most of the rest of his life in Pisa. The frescos were badly damaged by bombing in the Second World War. Benozzo also painted altarpieces, one of which (*Madonna and Child with Saints*, 1461–2) is in the National Gallery, London.

Grabar, Igor (*b* Budapest, 13 Mar. 1871; *d* Moscow, 16 May 1960). Hungarian-born Russian painter, art historian, and administrator. Early in his career as an artist he worked mainly as a landscapist, and Alan Bird (*A History of Russian Painting*, 1987) comments that he 'was one of the first Russian painters to take over the manner and the palette of *Impressionism, producing some extremely sensitive scenes of the landscape under snow' (*September Snow*, 1903, Tretyakov Gal., Moscow). Grabar continued to paint throughout his life, his work including portraits of some of his distinguished contemporaries, but after the Revolution he became better known as a scholar and administrator (even before this, in 1913, he had been appointed director of the *Tretyakov Gallery, a position that he held until 1925). He was a professor of art history at Moscow University until 1946 and also held important posts in the state establishments for art restoration and scientific research in art history. In these varied roles he did much to preserve his country's artistic heritage. His writings included numerous books and articles on Russian art, including a two-volume monograph on *Repin (1937, 2nd edn. 1963–4), for which he was awarded a Stalin Prize in 1941, and he was editor of the standard work *Istoriya russkogo iskusstva* (History of Russian Art, 6 vols., 1906–16) and co-editor of the revised and expanded version (13 vols., 1953–68). His autobiography appeared in 1937.

gradual. See MISSAL.

Graf, Urs (*b* Solothurn, *c*.1485; *d* ?Basle, 1529/30). Swiss draughtsman, printmaker, designer, goldsmith, and painter, active mainly in Basle. He is best known for his drawings, which survive in considerable number, often signed and dated.

They are done in a bold and energetic style, with virtuoso curling strokes of the pen; favourite subjects are soldiers (Graf himself spent some time as a mercenary in Italy), peasants, and flamboyantly dressed ladies of easy virtue. Graf also designed stained glass, made woodcuts, and executed the earliest extant dated etching, *Girl Washing her Feet* (1513).

Graff, Anton (*b* Winterthur, 18 Nov. 1736; *d* Dresden, 22 June 1813). Swiss-born German painter, mainly of portraits (but occasionally of landscapes). He spent most of his life in Dresden, where he settled in 1766, but he made numerous visits to Berlin and Leipzig, where his work was much in demand, as well as to Switzerland. His large output (more than 2,000 paintings) gives a vivid picture of German aristocratic and middle-class society of his time. He was at his best in portraits of intellectual, literary, and artistic sitters. In these he sometimes recalls *Reynolds in his direct and penetrating characterization, while his more elegant society pieces are reminiscent of *Gainsborough. There are numerous examples of his work in the Gemäldegalerie in Dresden, including one of the most memorable of his many self-portraits (1795).

Graffiti art. A style of painting based on the type of spray-can vandalism familiar in cities all over the world and specifically in the New York subway system; the term can apply to any work in this vein, but refers particularly to a vogue in New York in the 1980s (several commercial galleries specialized in it at this time and a Museum of American Graffiti opened there in 1989). The best-known figures of Graffiti art are Jean-Michel Basquiat (1960–88) and Keith Haring (1958–90), both of whom enjoyed huge reputations (and prices) during their brief careers, which were ended for Basquiat by a drugs overdose and for Haring by AIDS. Basquiat was a genuine street artist who 'crossed over' into the gallery world; Haring had an art school training but adopted a primitivistic style based on graffiti. Robert *Hughes satirized them as 'Keith Boring and Jean-Michel Basketcase'.

graffito (or **sgraffito**) (Italian: 'scratched'). Term now most commonly applied (usually in the plural—'graffiti') to an illicit design or inscription (often obscene) drawn, painted, or scratched on a wall; in a broader sense it is applied to any technique of producing a design by scratching through a layer of paint or other material to reveal a *ground beneath it. In a medieval panel painting, for instance, decorative areas would be covered with gold leaf, burnished, and painted, and a design would then be scratched through the paint.

Graham, Maria. See CALLCOTT.

Gran, Daniel (*bapt.* Vienna, 22 May 1694; *d.* St Pölten, 16 Apr. 1757). One of the leading Austrian fresco painters of his period. In 1719–23 he visited Italy, where he studied with *Solimena amongst others, and his work has something of Solimena's classical dignity and firmness of construction, eschewing the more extravagant effects typical of *Baroque decorative painting. His masterpiece is the decoration of the dome (1726–30) of the grand hall of the Hofbibliothek (now Österreichische Nationalbibliothek (Austrian National Library)), Vienna; the frescos glorify the Emperor Charles VI, the founder of the library.

Granacci, Francesco (*b* Villamagna, nr. Florence, *c.*1469; *d* Florence, 30 Nov. 1543). Florentine painter, a minor master of the High *Renaissance. He trained under Domenico *Ghirlandaio at the same time as *Michelangelo, who became his friend. In 1508 Michelangelo called Granacci and other Florentine painters to Rome to assist him on the Sistine Ceiling, but he soon dismissed them and carried out the work with little more than menial help. According to *Vasari, Granacci was an easygoing character, and this is suggested in his work, which is suave and unadventurous, drawing heavily on other artists, particularly Fra *Bartolommeo. It is well represented in the Accademia, Florence.

Grand Manner. Term applied to the lofty and rhetorical manner of *history painting that in academic theory was considered appropriate to the most serious and elevated subjects. The classic exposition of its doctrines is found in *Reynolds's Third and Fourth *Discourses* (1770 and 1771), where he asserts that 'the *gusto grande* of the Italians, the *beau idéal* of the French, and the *great style, genius,* and *taste* among the English, are but different appellations of the same thing'. Cecil Gould (*An Introduction to Italian Renaissance Painting,* 1957) rightly points out that 'the Grand Manner is an attitude rather than a style' and goes on to give a lucid exposition of some of its characteristics. 'The general aim is to transcend Nature . . . The Subject itself must be on an elevated and elevating plane . . . Similarly, the individual figures in such a scene must be shown purged of the grosser elements of ordinary existence . . . Landscape backgrounds

or ornamental detail must be reduced to a minimum and individual peculiarities of human physiognomy absolutely eliminated. Draperies should be simple, but ample and noble, and fashionable contemporary costume absolutely shunned. Alternatively, the figures should be nude.' The idea of the Grand Manner took shape in 17th-century Italy, notably in the writings of *Bellori. His friend *Poussin and the great Bolognese painters of the 17th century were regarded as outstanding exponents of the Grand Manner, but the greatest of all was held to be *Raphael.

Grand Tour. An extensive Continental journey, chiefly through France, the Netherlands, and above all Italy, sometimes in the company of a tutor, to complete the education of an aristocrat or gentleman. The origins of the Grand Tour go back to the 16th century, but its heyday was the 18th century, when it was an almost obligatory part of the tutelage of the sons (or at least eldest sons) of noble families in Britain (similar tours were also undertaken by young men from other countries, but they are associated above all with British travellers). The traveller was usually aged about 17–22 and the tour typically lasted a year or longer. Such tours laid the basis for many art collections among the landed gentry, helping to spread the fashion for *Neoclassicism and an enthusiasm for Italian painting. Among the native artists who catered for this demand were *Batoni, *Canaletto, *Panini, and *Piranesi, and British artists (such as Gavin *Hamilton, William *Kent, and Joseph *Nollekens) were sometimes able to support themselves while in Italy by working for the dealers and restorers who supplied the tourist clientele, particularly in Rome. There was also a flourishing market in guidebooks (see RICHARDSON). Between 1792 and 1815 the French Revolutionary and Napoleonic Wars virtually ended foreign travel, and although the Grand Tour resumed after this, its golden age was over. By the middle of the 19th century, railways were beginning to open up Europe to middle-class travellers and the Grand Tour was defunct.

Grandville (pseudonym of Jean-Ignace-Isidore Gérard) (*b* Nancy, 15 Sept. 1803; *d* Vanves, nr. Paris, 17 Mar. 1847). French caricaturist and illustrator. In 1825 he settled in Paris, where he became one of the leading political cartoonists until censorship outlawed such work in 1835. Subsequently he turned mainly to book illustration, notably of classic texts such as *Don Quixote,* *Gulliver's Travels,* and especially La Fontaine's

Fables (1838). He often satirized people by depicting them as animals, and in some of his work he created bizarre hybrid forms of animate and inanimate objects. In 1844 he published a collection of nonsense drawings entitled *Un autre monde*, loosely linked by a text. The book has been postulated as a source for *Tenniel's illustrations to *Alice in Wonderland* (1865) and even for parts of Lewis Carroll's text. Later the book appealed to the *Surrealists. Grandville died in a lunatic asylum.

Granet, François-Marius (*b* Aix-en-Provence, 7 Dec. 1775; *d* Malvalat, nr. Aix, 21 Nov. 1849). French painter and museum official. Granet was a pupil of J.-L. *David and subsequently spent the years 1802–19 in Rome (he returned to Italy several times thereafter). He made a speciality of sombre tonal effects and changing light in dimly lit interiors, his pictures recalling 17th-century Dutch interiors rather than expressing the *Neoclassical tradition in which he was trained. His *Choir of the Capuchin Church in Rome* (Met. Mus., New York) was exhibited at the 1819 *Salon with such success that he made more than a dozen replicas of it. Granet also painted Italian landscapes, constructed with firm, cubic volumes, in which some critics have seen a foreshadowing of *Cézanne. In 1826 he became a curator at the *Louvre and in 1833 he was appointed curator of the newly established museum at Versailles. During the Revolution of 1848 he retired to Aix-en-Provence, where he founded the museum that bears his name. It contains a celebrated portrait of him by *Ingres.

granite. A general term for a class of very hard igneous rock consisting essentially of quartz, feldspar, and mica. Granite is one of the commonest of all rocks, found throughout the world, and it has many varieties, differing in texture and coarseness. It occurs in a wide range of colours—grey, green, rose, yellow—and the small scales of mica give it a lively sparkle. It takes a brilliant polish on a mirror-smooth surface and is extremely durable and resistant to weather, but it is one of the most difficult stones to carve. Consequently it has been used a good deal for building and paving but much less for sculpture—mainly for large outdoor works, most notably in ancient Egypt. Among modern sculptors, Masayuki *Nagare has made memorable use of it.

Grant, Duncan (*b* Rothiemurchus, Inverness-shire, 21 Jan. 1885; *d* Aldermaston, Berkshire, 9 May 1978). British painter and designer. Through

the writer Lytton Strachey (his cousin) he became a member of the *Bloomsbury Group, and he was also familiar with avant-garde circles in Paris (he met *Matisse in 1909 and *Picasso soon afterwards). Up to about 1910 his work—which included landscapes, portraits, and still-lifes—was fairly sober in form and restrained in colour, but he then underwent a rapid development to become one of the most advanced of British artists in his response to modern French painting (he exhibited at Roger *Fry's second *Post-Impressionist exhibition in 1912). From about 1913 he was also influenced by African sculpture, and he was one of the first British artists to produce completely abstract pictures. However, this extreme avant-garde phase was fairly short-lived and he soon reverted to a figurative style. In 1913 he began working for the *Omega Workshops, and having discovered a taste and talent for interior decoration, he sought similar commissions when the Workshops closed in 1919. In this field he worked much in collaboration with Vanessa *Bell, with whom he lived from 1916. He was at the height of his popularity and esteem in the 1920s and 1930s, but after the Second World War his work went out of fashion. However, he lived long enough to see a great revival of interest in the Bloomsbury Group, which brought a renewed appreciation of his own work. Apart from paintings, his work included designs for textiles, pottery, stage scenery, and costumes.

Grant, Sir Francis (*b* Edinburgh, 18 Jan. 1803; *d* Melton Mowbray, Leicestershire, 5 Oct. 1878). Scottish painter, one of the most fashionable portrait painters of his day. His best works are generally considered to be his sporting *conversation pieces. In 1866 he succeeded *Eastlake as president of the *Royal Academy.

graphic art. Term current with several different meanings in the literature of the visual arts. In the context of the *fine arts, it most usually refers to those arts that rely essentially on line or tone rather than colour—i.e. drawing and the various forms of engraving. Some writers, however, exclude drawing from this definition, so that the term 'graphic art' is used to cover the various processes by which prints are created. In another sense, the term—sometimes shortened to 'graphics'—is used to cover the entire field of commercial printing, including text as well as illustrations.

graphite. Mineral—a form of carbon—used as the 'lead' in *pencils, among other purposes. It is mined in various parts of the world and can also be made synthetically.

Grasser, Erasmus (*b* Schmidmuhlen, nr. Regensburg, *c*.1450; *d* Munich, Apr./May 1518). German sculptor, active mainly in Munich. He worked in an animated and expressive late *Gothic style and was the leading sculptor of his day in south Bavaria, with a flourishing workshop and numerous pupils. His best-known works are ten (originally sixteen) limewood figures of morris dancers for the ballroom of the old town hall in Munich (1480, Stadtmuseum, Munich). Grasser was also an architect and hydraulic engineer.

Gravelot (pseudonym of Hubert-François Bourguignon) (*b* Paris, 26 Mar. 1699; *d* Paris, 19 Apr. 1773). French draughtsman, engraver, and painter, active for several years (1732–45) in London, where he became the leading book illustrator of the day. He worked on more than 50 English books, including John Gay's *Fables* (1738) and Samuel Richardson's *Pamela* (1742), one of the first novels to be illustrated. On *Pamela* he collaborated with his friend *Hayman. His other friends included *Hogarth and he taught at the *St Martin's Lane Academy, where *Gainsborough was among his pupils. Although not an artist of outstanding talent, he played an important role in introducing the French *Rococo style to England.

graver. See BURIN.

Graves, Nancy. See SERRA.

Great Exhibition. The first international industrial exhibition ever held, open to the public from 1 May to 11 October 1851 in Hyde Park, London; its full title was 'The Great Exhibition of the Works of Industry of all Nations, 1851'. Prince Albert was chairman of the committee that planned it and the chief organizer was Sir Henry Cole, later the first director of the *Victoria and Albert Museum. A competition to design a suitable building for the exhibition attracted more than 200 entries; none was considered entirely suitable and the committee produced a composite design for a domed brick building. However, Joseph Paxton, uninvited, then submitted a revolutionary design for a vast structure of iron and glass (originally a gardener, he was experienced in building large greenhouses) and—using ingenious prefabrication methods—this was erected in only six months (it was completed just in time for the opening). Paxton was knighted for creating his masterpiece, which ranks as one of the most important structures of the 19th century (it was the first really conspicuous prefabricated building and it established iron and glass as worthy materials for architecture). It was popularly known as the 'Crystal Palace', a term first applied to it by *Punch* in its issue of 2 November 1850, before it had been built.

The exhibition was an extraordinary success, attracting more than six million visitors (among them Queen Victoria, who went on several occasions). There were nearly 14,000 exhibitors (7,381 British and 6,556 foreign), with over 100,000 exhibits. In 1852 the building was dismantled and re-erected in a modified form at Sydenham, Kent (now south London), where it remained a major attraction until it was destroyed by fire in 1936. The profits from the exhibition were used to promote science and art, mainly by purchasing a large area of land in South Kensington as a site for the group of museums and colleges including the Victoria and Albert Museum, the Science Museum, the Natural History Museum, the Imperial College of Science and Technology, the *Royal College of Art, and the Royal College of Music. The success of the exhibition encouraged similar enormous international shows (world fairs) aimed at promoting trade and reflecting cultural progress; the first of these was the Exposition Universelle in Paris in 1855 (see COURBET).

Greaves, Derrick. See KITCHEN SINK SCHOOL.

Greaves, Walter. See WHISTLER, JAMES McNEILL.

Greco, El (*b* Candia [now Iraklion], Crete, *c*.1541; *d* Toledo, 7 Apr. 1614). Cretan-born painter, sculptor, and architect who settled in Spain and is regarded as the first great genius of the Spanish School. His real name was Domenikos Theotocopoulos and it was thus that he signed his paintings throughout his life, always in Greek characters, and sometimes followed by *Kres* (Cretan). To avoid the tongue-twisting name, he was known in Spain as Domenico Griego or simply El Griego (the Greek). Evidently it was not until after his lifetime that the curious form 'El Greco' was adopted (curious because 'El' is Spanish and 'Greco' is Italian). Little is known of his early years, and only a few works survive by him in the *Byzantine tradition of *icon painting, notably the signed *Dormition of the Virgin* discovered in 1983 (church of the Dormition, Syros). Between 1566 and 1568 he moved to Venice (Crete was then a Venetian possession), and late in 1570 he is described as 'recently arrived' in Rome. The miniaturist Giulio *Clovio, who became a friend of El Greco there, referred to him as a 'disciple' of *Titian, but of all Venetian painters *Tintoretto influenced him most, with his sense of movement and dramatic lighting (El Greco's turbulent skies are often particularly reminiscent of Tintoretto).

It is generally presumed that El Greco remained in Rome until 1577 (when he is first recorded in Spain), but he is only once securely documented in the city after 1570 (in 1572, when he became a member of the Accademia di S. Luca), and it has been suggested that he returned to Venice for a while. Clovio was an influential friend, and through him El Greco evidently gained accommodation in the Palazzo *Farnese; however, he received no public commissions in Italy and worked on a fairly small scale. Among his surviving pictures of the period are two paintings of the *Purification of the Temple* (Minneapolis Inst. of Arts, and NG, Washington), a favourite theme with him, and a portrait of Clovio (Mus. di Capodimonte, Naples).

Accomplished though these works are, they give little hint of the explosion of genius that occurred after El Greco settled in Spain. His decision to move to Toledo (where he lived for the rest of his life) was presumably influenced by the young Spanish priest Luis de Castilla, part of his circle in Rome, whose father was dean of Toledo Cathedral and a man of considerable influence. El Greco quickly gained major commissions in his new home, beginning with the main altarpiece of the church of S. Domingo el Antiguo (1577). The central part of the altarpiece, a 4-m (13-ft) high canvas of the *Assumption of the Virgin* (Art Inst. of Chicago), was easily his biggest work to date, but he carried off the dynamic composition triumphantly. A succession of great altarpieces followed throughout his career, the two most famous being *El Espolio* (Christ Stripped of his Garments) (1577–9, Toledo Cathedral) and the *Burial of Count Orgaz* (1586–8, S. Tomé, Toledo). These two mighty works convey the awesomeness of great spiritual events with a sense of mystic rapture, and in his late work El Greco went even further in freeing his figures from earth-bound restrictions; the *Adoration of the Shepherds* (1612–14, Prado, Madrid), painted for his own tomb, is a prime example. His style has something in common with Italian *Mannerism in its use of elongated figures and non-rational space, but his flamelike forms, electric colours, and ecstatic emotion are intensely personal. Toledo at this time was the spiritual capital of Spain, with more than 100 religious establishments, so El Greco had little need to look beyond it for commissions; he attempted to win royal favour but failed, as Philip II (see HABSBURG) rejected an altarpiece he painted for the *Escorial.

Although he was primarily a religious painter, El Greco excelled also as a portraitist. His sitters were mainly ecclesiastics (*Felix Paravicino*, 1609, MFA, Boston) or gentlemen, although one of his most beautiful works is a portrait of a lady (c.1577–80, Pollok House, Glasgow), traditionally identified as a likeness of Jerónima de las Cuevas, his common-law wife. He also painted two views of Toledo (Met. Mus., New York, and Mus. del Greco, Toledo), both late works, and a mythological painting, *Laocoön* (c.1610, NG, Washington), that is unique in his oeuvre. The unusual choice of subject is perhaps explained by the local tradition that Toledo had been founded by descendants of the Trojans. El Greco also designed complete altar compositions, working as architect and sculptor as well as painter, for instance at the Hospital de la Caridad, Illescas (1603). *Pacheco, who visited El Greco in 1611, refers to him as a writer on painting, sculpture, and architecture, and an inventory of his books drawn up after his death indicates he had wide intellectual interests. He had a strong sense of professional pride and expected to be well rewarded for his work; on several occasions he engaged in legal disputes over payments, and the failure of one such lawsuit seems to have caused him financial difficulties near the end of his life. His workshop produced a great many replicas of his paintings, but his style was so personal that his influence was slight, his only followers of note being his son **Jorge Manuel Theotocopoulos** (c.1578–1631) and Luis *Tristán.

At the time of his death El Greco was famous and respected, but his reputation soon declined and in 1724 *Palomino described his work as 'contemptible and ridiculous, as much for his disjointed drawing as for the unpleasant colour'. By the time the *Prado opened in 1819 he was so little regarded that it did not display a single example of his work. Interest in his art revived at the end of the 19th century and his great popular fame has come in the wake of modern art, particularly *Expressionism, of which he has been seen as a forerunner. The strangeness of his art has inspired unlikely theories to account for it, for example that he was mad or suffered from defective eyesight, but his rapturous paintings make complete sense as an expression of the religious fervour of his adopted country.

Greek Revival and **Greek Taste.** See NEO-CLASSICISM.

Green, Anthony (b London, 30 Sept. 1939). British painter. He specializes in scenes from his own middle-class domestic life portrayed with loving attention to detail and an engaging sense of whimsy. Often he uses oddly *shaped canvases that accentuate his strange perspective effects, and his subjects are frequently erotic as well as humorous. His work, which is sometimes on a large scale, is instantly recognizable and is generally highly popular with the public at the *Royal Academy summer exhibition, for he vividly communicates the loving feeling he puts into his paintings.

Green, Valentine (b Salford, nr. Chipping Norton, Oxfordshire, 3 Oct. 1739; d London, 29 June 1813). English printmaker, chiefly in *mezzotint. In 1765 he settled in London, where he became one of the leading engravers of the day. Initially he made his reputation with prints after history paintings by *West, but he is now probably best remembered for his prints of female portraits by *Reynolds. In 1779 he began a series of these issued under the title 'Beauties of the Present Age'; there were originally six in the series, but they proved so popular that three more were added. However, in 1783 he quarrelled with Reynolds and this ended their association. In 1789 Green obtained a patent from the Elector of Bavaria to engrave and publish pictures in the Düsseldorf gallery, but this ambitious venture fell foul of warfare on the Continent, and Green, who had invested a good deal of money in it, had financial difficulties in his later years. In addition to his large output of engravings, he wrote a good deal on antiquarian and artistic topics, notably *A Review of the Polite Arts in France . . . Compared with their Present State in England* (1792).

Green, William. See ACTION PAINTING.

Greenaway, Kate (b London, 17 Mar. 1846; d London, 6 Nov. 1901). English painter, illustrator, and writer, famous for her children's books. Her delicate skill and fragile sentimentality won her many distinguished admirers, including *Ruskin and (perhaps for her feeling for flat pattern) *Gauguin. She often illustrated her own texts, for example in *Kate Greenaway's Almanack*, of which she issued a series (1888–97), and her work became so popular that the quaint clothes that are such a feature of her illustrations influenced children's costume. In 1955 the Library Association of Great Britain established the Kate Greenaway Medal to be awarded annually for the most distinguished work in the illustration of a children's book during the previous year.

Greenberg, Clement (b New York, 16 Jan. 1909; d New York, 7 May 1994). American art critic. With Harold *Rosenberg he was his country's most influential writer on contemporary art in the post-war years when American painting and sculpture first achieved a dominant position in world art. His approach to criticism is sometimes described as *formalist, and the artists to whose works he gave the most powerful advocacy were chiefly uncompromising abstractionists—most famously Jackson *Pollock and David *Smith, and later the *Post-Painterly Abstractionists (Greenberg coined this term) and the British sculptor Anthony *Caro. In painting he laid particular stress on the flatness of the picture surface and the rejection of any kind of illusionistic modelling, and he opposed the mere 'novelty' art of painters such as *Rauschenberg. Although he regarded aesthetic judgements as autonomous, he also believed that history possessed order and purpose (the result of early contacts with Marxism) and this allowed him to endow his 'disinterested aesthetic' verdicts on art with a claim for historical certainty. His influence was at its height in the 1950s and 1960s, but thereafter it waned in the face of such developments as *Conceptual art and *New Figuration. His best-known book is probably *Art and Culture* (1961), an anthology of his writings; his other books include monographs on *Miró (1948), *Matisse (1953), and *Hofmann (1961).

Greene, Balcomb. See AMERICAN ABSTRACT ARTISTS.

Greenhill, John (b Orchardleigh, nr. Frome, Somerset, 14 July 1642; d London, 19 May 1676). English portrait painter. He was *Lely's outstanding pupil and 'one of the few British-born painters of this age who showed real promise' (Ellis *Waterhouse), but he led a dissipated life and died young. There are several examples of his work, including a self-portrait, in Dulwich Picture Gallery, London.

Greenough, Horatio (b Boston, 6 Sept. 1805; d Somerville, Mass., 18 Dec. 1852). American *Neoclassical sculptor who spent the greater part of his working life in Italy (1825–6, 1828–51). He is sometimes described as the first professional American sculptor and his major work, the colossal marble figure of George Washington (1833–41), was the first important state commission given to an American sculptor. It was originally placed in the rotunda of the Capitol in Washington, but is now in the National Museum of American History. The seated figure is based on *Phidias' celebrated statue of Zeus at Olympia, but the head follows *Houdon's portrait of Washington—an uneasy mixture of idealism and naturalism. Greenough's work is in general rather uninspiring, and the essays he wrote on art in the final decade of his life are considered more interesting; his views on architecture have been claimed as precursors of modern functionalism. His brother **Richard Saltonstall Greenough** (1819–1904) was also a sculptor, best known for his statue of Benjamin Franklin (1855) outside Boston City Hall.

Greenwood, John (b Boston, 7 Dec. 1727; d Margate, Kent, 16 Sept. 1792). American-born painter, printmaker, and art dealer who spent most of his career in England. Although his work is rather wooden, for a brief period he probably ranked as the best portraitist in Boston; however, he left the city permanently in 1752, a few years before the rise of *Copley, who would soon have eclipsed him. Greenwood moved first to Surinam in the Dutch East Indies, where he painted his most famous work, *Sea Captains Carousing in Surinam* (c.1758, St Louis Art Mus.), which has something of the spirit of *Hogarth and was perhaps influenced by prints of his work. In 1758 he moved to Amsterdam, where he became involved in the picture trade, and in about 1763 he settled in London, where he became a leading auctioneer.

Gregory XV, Pope. See GUERCINO.

Greuze, Jean-Baptiste (b Tournus, 21 Aug. 1725; d Paris, 21 Mar. 1805). French painter. He had a great success at the 1755 *Salon with a group of paintings including *Father Reading the Bible to his Children* (Louvre, Paris) and he went on to win enormous popularity with similar sentimental and melodramatic *genre scenes. His work was praised by *Diderot as 'morality in paint' and as representing the highest ideal of painting in his day. He also wished to succeed as a *history painter, but when he presented his *Septimius Severus Reproaching Caracalla* (1769, Louvre) to the Académie Royale as his reception piece he was accepted only as a genre painter, causing him acute embarrassment. Much of Greuze's later work consisted of titillating pictures of young girls, which contain thinly veiled sexual allusions under their surface appearance

of mawkish innocence; *The Broken Pitcher* (Louvre), for example, alludes to loss of virginity. With the swing of taste towards *Neoclassicism his work went out of fashion and after the Revolution in 1789 he sank into obscurity. At the very end of his career he received a commission to paint a portrait of Napoleon (1804–5, Versailles), but he died in poverty. His huge output is particularly well represented in the Louvre, the Wallace Collection in London, the Musée Fabre in Montpellier, and the museum dedicated to him in Tournus, his native town.

Grien, Hans Baldung. See BALDUNG.

Grimaldi, Giovanni Francesco (b Bologna, 1606; d Rome, 28 Nov. 1680). Italian landscape painter, sometimes called Il Bolognese after his place of birth. He developed an attractive landscape style in the manner of the mature Annibale *Carracci, and his work, which was popular with collectors and much engraved, helped to spread the tradition of *ideal landscape in Europe. Grimaldi worked mainly in Rome, painting frescos as well as easel paintings, notably at the Villa Doria Pamphili, where he was also employed as an architect. In 1649–51 he worked in Paris.

Grimani, Cardinal Domenico. See BOSCH and BREVIARY.

Grimm, Samuel Hieronymus (bapt. Burgdorf, 18 Jan. 1733; d London, 14 Apr. 1794). Swiss-born painter (mainly in watercolour) and draughtsman, who settled in England in 1768. He was a prolific topographical draughtsman, much of his work being done on commission for antiquarian patrons. Most notably he made drawings for *The Natural History and Antiquities of Selborne* (1789) by Gilbert White. Grimm also made caricatures and drawings of Shakespearian subjects, and himself wrote poetry. His work is well represented in the British Museum and the Victoria and Albert Museum.

Grimmer. Two Netherlandish painters, **Jacob** (c.1526–90) and his son **Abel** (c.1570–c.1619), whose styles are so similar that it is often difficult to distinguish between their hands. They worked in Antwerp, mainly painting landscape and *genre subjects in an attractive style, full of lively anecdote, that places them among the best followers of *Bruegel. Jacob's work was praised by van *Mander and others.

Grimshaw, Atkinson (b Leeds, 6 Sept. 1836; d Leeds, 31 Oct. 1893). English painter. He specialized in a distinctive type of nocturnal townscape, usually featuring gas lights and wet streets, and *Whistler said of him: 'I considered myself the inventor of Nocturnes until I saw Grimmy's moonlit pictures.' Grimshaw's paintings, however, unlike Whistler's, are sharp in focus and rather acidic in colouring, although often remarkably atmospheric. They were very popular (in spite of the fact that he rarely exhibited at the *Royal Academy) and he was much imitated, not least by two of his sons, **Arthur** (1864–1913) and **Louis** (1870–?1944). Their father worked in his native Leeds and in other northern towns, as well as in London.

Gris, Juan (b Madrid, 23 Mar. 1887; d Boulogne-sur-Seine, nr. Paris, 11 May 1927). Spanish painter, sculptor, illustrator, and designer, active mainly in Paris, where he settled in 1906. In his early years there he earned his living mainly with humorous drawings for various periodicals and he did not begin painting in earnest until 1910. By this time he was strongly influenced by his fellow Spaniard *Picasso and his serious painting was almost entirely in the *Cubist manner. He made such rapid strides that by 1912 he was becoming recognized as the leading Cubist painter apart from the founders of the movement, Picasso and *Braque. His work stood out at the *Section d'Or exhibition in that year, attracting the attention of collectors and dealers (Gertrude *Stein was among those who bought his paintings and *Kahnweiler gave him a contract). In 1913–14 he developed a personal version of Synthetic Cubism, in which *papier collé played an important part. He said that he conceived of his paintings as 'flat, coloured architecture' and his methods of visual analysis were more systematic than those of Picasso and Braque. His subjects were almost all taken from his immediate surroundings (mainly still-lifes, with occasional landscapes and portraits), but he began with the image he had in mind rather than with an object in the external world: 'I try to make concrete that which is abstract . . . *Cézanne turns a bottle into a cylinder, but I make a bottle—a particular bottle—out of a cylinder.'

In 1919 Gris had his first major one-man exhibition (at the Galerie l'Effort Moderne in Paris), but in the following year he suffered a serious attack of pleurisy and from then on his health was poor; for this reason he spent much of his time in the south of France. In this last period of his life his style became more painterly (*Violin and Fruit Dish*, 1924, Tate, London). Apart from paintings, his work included polychrome sculp-

ture, book illustrations, and set and costume designs for *Diaghilev. He wrote a few essays on his aesthetic ideas and a collection of his letters, edited and translated by Douglas *Cooper, was published in 1956. Although Gris was of a logical turn of mind, Cooper writes that he 'always tempered his science with the workings of his personal sensibility, and the many *pentimenti* and freely invented passages in his paintings are evidence of his constant concern that the reality of natural forms should not be subjected to "monstrous" distortions dictated by some pre-determined design'.

grisaille. A painting done entirely in shades of grey or another neutral greyish colour. The idea was evidently first used in stained glass. The earliest known examples in painting are in *Giotto's frescos in the Arena Chapel, Padua (c.1305), where they imitate the appearance of stone sculpture. Grisaille was sometimes also used for underpainting or for oil sketches (notably in the work of *Rubens). See also CAMAIEU.

Gromaire, Marcel. See LURÇAT.

Gropius, Walter (b Berlin, 18 May 1883; d Boston, 5 July 1969). German-born architect, designer, and teacher who became an American citizen in 1944. In 1919 he founded the *Bauhaus, of which he was principal until 1928, when he resumed his architectural practice in Berlin. In 1934, after the Nazis had come to power, he left Germany for England, where he practised in partnership with the British architect Maxwell Fry. In 1937 he settled in the USA, where he taught at Harvard until 1951. He remained active until the end of his life and had an exceptional list of notable buildings to his credit. Although Gropius's practical work was in the field of architecture, his influence upon modernist trends in all the visual arts has probably not been exceeded by that of any other man. Nowhere else have so many major artists of outstanding originality been brought into collaboration as those whom Gropius gathered at the Bauhaus.

Gropper, William (b New York, 3 Dec. 1897; d Manhasset, Long Island, NY, 6 Jan. 1977). American graphic artist and painter. In 1920 he joined the staff of the *New York Herald Tribune* as a cartoonist, but he was soon dismissed because of his left-wing political sympathies and then worked as a freelance cartoonist, contributing to fashionable periodicals such as *Vanity Fair* as well as radical publications such as *The New Masses*. His Communist sympathies led him to make a visit to the USSR in 1927, during which he worked for the Party newspaper *Pravda* in Moscow; the following year he published a book entitled *Fifty-Six Drawings of the USSR*. His paintings were closely related to his caricatures in subject and style; he was concerned with exposing social injustice, sympathizing with the downtrodden, and attacking businessmen and politicians in a formally simplified, satirical manner bordering on *Expressionism (he has been called 'the Expressionist *Daumier'). His best-known painting is probably *The Senate* (1935, MoMA, New York). In his later years he moved from satire to themes of broader social concern, his work taking on a more spiritual feeling.

Gros, Antoine-Jean (*b* Paris, 16 Mar. 1771; *d* Meudon, nr Paris, 25 June 1835). French painter. He trained with his parents, both of whom were miniaturists, and then with J.-L. *David. Although he revered David and became one of his favourite pupils, Gros had a passionate nature and he was drawn more to the colour and vibrancy of *Rubens and the great Venetian painters than to the *Neoclassical severity of his master. From 1793 to 1800 he worked in Italy, where he met Napoleon and was commissioned to paint portraits documenting his campaigns. After his return to Paris he continued this vein in huge paintings such as the *Battle of Eylau* (1808, Louvre, Paris) that are among the most stirring images of the Napoleonic era. Compared with the contemporary war scenes of *Goya, they are glamorous lies, but they are painted with such dramatic skill and panache that they cannot but be admired on their own terms. When David went into exile in 1816 after the fall of Napoleon, he entrusted his studio to Gros, who subsequently tried to work in a more consciously Neoclassical style. He never again approached the quality of his Napoleonic pictures, however (although he continued to paint excellent portraits), and haunted by a sense of failure, unhappily married, and in poor health, he drowned himself in the Seine. In spite of the sad end to his career, Gros is regarded as the most gifted of David's immediate followers and an important figure in the development of *Romanticism; the colour and drama of his work influenced *Géricault, *Delacroix, and his pupil *Bonington amongst others. See also ORIENTALISM.

Grosvenor Gallery, London. A commercial gallery founded in 1877 by the wealthy dilettante painter Sir Coutts Lindsay (1824–1913) and Charles E. Hallé, son of the famous musician Sir Charles Hallé. *Whistler showed eight paint-

ings at the opening exhibition, and *Ruskin's notorious outburst against one of them led to the libel trial that caused the painter's financial ruin. The other artists who showed at the gallery included such distinguished academics as *Leighton and *Poynter, but it became particularly associated with the Aesthetic Movement (see AESTHETICISM) and was memorably satirized in Gilbert and Sullivan's *Patience* (1881): 'A greenery-yallery, Grosvenor Gallery, | Foot-in-the-grave young man' (an allusion to the deathly pallor possessed by many of the figures in works by painters such as *Burne-Jones). In 1888 the Grosvenor Gallery was taken over by the New Gallery; by this time it 'had become little more than an overflow from the *Royal Academy' (Dennis Farr, *English Art: 1870–1940*, 1978).

Grosz, George (*b* Berlin, 26 July 1893; *d* West Berlin, 6 July 1959). German-born painter and draughtsman who became an American citizen in 1938. He began as a caricaturist and through his drawings he expressed his disgust at the depravity of the Prussian military caste. During the First World War he twice served in the German army and each time was discharged as being unfit for service. In 1917, with *Heartfield, he Anglicized his name (adding an 'e' to 'Georg') as a protest against the hatred being whipped up against the enemy. The most famous of the satirical anti-war illustrations he made at this time is the drawing *Fit for Active Service* (1918, MoMA, New York), in which a fat, complacent doctor pronounces a skeleton fit for duty. From 1917 to 1920 Grosz was a prominent figure in the *Dada movement in Berlin, and in the 1920s, with *Dix, he became the leading exponent of the *Neue Sachlichkeit. In 1917 he published the first of several collections of drawings, through which he established an international reputation. The most famous are *The Face of the Ruling Class* (1921) and *Ecce Homo* (1927). In these and in his paintings he ruthlessly denounced a decaying society in which gluttony and depravity are placed beside poverty and disease; prostitutes and profiteers were frequently among his cast of characters. Grosz often used watercolour, and in spite of the nastiness of the subject matter and the bluntness of his satire, his works in this medium are remarkable for the sheer beauty and delicacy of their technique. His more conventional works of this time include a number of incisive portraits. He was prosecuted several times for obscenity and blasphemy, and in 1933, despairing at the political situation in Germany, he moved to America to take up the offer of a teaching post at the *Art Students League of New York.

In America Grosz largely abandoned his satirical manner for more romantic landscapes and still-lifes, with from time to time apocalyptic visions of a nightmare future. Although he won several honours in his later years, he regarded himself as a failure because he was unable to win recognition as a serious painter rather than a brilliant satirist, and he painted several self-portraits showing how isolated and depressed he was in his adopted country (*The Wanderer*, 1943, Memorial AG, Univ. of Rochester, New York). His autobiography, *A Little Yes and a Big No*, was published in New York in 1946. He returned to Berlin in 1959, saying 'my American dream turned out to be a soap bubble', and died there shortly after his arrival following a fall down a flight of stairs.

grotesque. A term originally used in the visual arts to describe a type of fanciful wall decoration (painted, carved, or moulded in *stucco) characterized by the use of interlinked floral motifs, animal and human figures, masks, etc., often arranged in an vertical, column-like format. Such decoration was inspired by the ornament found in the excavated rooms (popularly called *grotte*, 'grottoes') of certain ancient Roman buildings, notably the Golden House of Nero in Rome, which began to be uncovered at the end of the 15th century. During the 16th century this kind of decoration spread from Italy to most of the countries of Europe. In France the word 'grotesque' was applied as an adjective to literature and even to people fairly early in the 17th century, and later in the same century this meaning spread to England, and the word began to assume its current sense in everyday parlance, suggesting the ridiculous, absurd, monstrous, or abnormal.

ground. The surface or *support on which a painting or drawing is executed, typically paper for watercolours, for example, and canvas for oils; or, more specifically, a preparatory coating applied to such a surface before the picture is begun. The purpose of the ground in the second, more technical, sense is to isolate the paint from the support so as to prevent chemical interaction, to render the support less absorbent, to provide a satisfactory surface for painting or drawing on, and to heighten the brilliance of the colours. *Gesso is the ground that occurs most often in the literature of art history. In *etching the ground is the acid-resisting

mixture that is spread over the plate before work is begun.

Groupe de Recherche d'Art Visuel (GRAV). A group of *Kinetic artists formed in Paris in 1960. The members, who included Julio *Le Parc and *Vasarely's son Yvaral, adopted a scientific approach and investigated the use of modern industrial materials for artistic purposes. As well as creating individual works, they often worked together on anonymous collective projects, and it was one of their aims to produce art that called for involvement from the spectator. The group had its base at the Galerie Denise René, but on various occasions it attempted to bring art into the life of the streets. It disbanded in 1968.

Groupe des Vingt. See VINGT.

Group of Plastic Artists. See ČAPEK.

Group of Seven. Group of 20th-century Canadian painters, based in Toronto, who found their main inspiration in the landscape of northern Ontario and created the first major national movement in Canadian art. The group was officially established in 1920, when it held its first exhibition in the Art Gallery of Toronto, the seven painters involved being Franklin Carmichael (1890–1945), Lawren *Harris, A. Y. *Jackson, Frank Johnston (1888–1949), Arthur Lismer (1885–1969), J. E. H. MacDonald (1873–1932), and Frederick Varley (1881–1969). Some members of the group had, however, been working together since 1913, and Tom *Thomson, who was one of the early leaders, had died in 1917. Other artists joined after the 1920 exhibition. The members made group sketching expeditions and worked in an *Expressionist style characterized by brilliant colour and bold brushwork. After initial critical abuse, they won public favour and Emily *Carr was inspired by their example. The last group exhibition was held in 1931 and two years later the name was changed to the *Canadian Group of Painters; thereafter the members worked more as individuals and developed separately.

Group X. See LEWIS, WYNDHAM.

Gruber, Francis (*b* Nancy, 15 Mar. 1912; *d* Paris, 1 Dec. 1948). French painter. His early work was often of visionary subjects, but from about 1933 he began to paint mainly from the model in the studio; he also did still-lifes, views through windows, and from 1937 landscapes painted out of doors. Gruber's mature style was grave and melancholy, featuring long, drooping figures, and he is regarded as the founder of the 'Misérabiliste' strain in French painting, later particularly associated chiefly with *Buffet. A typical work is *Job* (1944, Tate, London), painted for the *Salon d'Automne of 1944, which was known as the Salon of the Liberation because it was held soon after Paris was freed from the German occupation; the picture symbolizes oppressed peoples who like Job in the Bible had endured a great deal of suffering. In spite of the tuberculosis that caused his early death, Gruber worked with great energy and had a substantial output.

Grünewald, Mathis (*b* ?Würzburg, *c*.1475/80; *d* Halle, 30/31 Aug. 1528). German painter, the greatest of *Dürer's contemporaries. His real name was Mathis Gothardt or Neithardt, but this was not discovered until the 1930s. The origin of the nickname Grünewald ('green-wood') is unknown, but it was evidently not used before the 17th century, notably by *Sandrart, who published the first biography of the artist in his *Teutsche Akademie* (1675). This haziness about his identity reflects the isolation and individuality of his work and the obscurity into which he fell after his death; he had no known pupils and (unlike most of his German contemporaries) he did not make woodcuts or engravings, which would have spread his name. He was successful for most of his career, working as court painter to two successive archbishops of Mainz, but his reputation did not long survive, and in 1597, when the Emperor Rudolf II (see HABSBURG) tried to buy his masterpiece, the Isenheim Altarpiece, the name of the painter had already been forgotten.

The surviving documentation on Grünewald is meagre and sometimes confusing, for it appears that some references that have previously been assumed to allude to him are in fact concerned with other artists called 'Master Mathis' (the name was fairly common at the time). He spent much of his career in Aschaffenburg, a town near Frankfurt, and it is there that he is first firmly documented in 1504/5. By 1510 he was working for the Archbishop of Mainz, Uriel von Gemmingen, whose official residence was in Aschaffenburg. Von Gemmingen died in 1514 and Grünewald was also employed by his successor Albrecht von Brandenburg (who was also Archbishop of Magdeburg). In addition to being a painter, he is known to have worked as a hydraulic engineer and supervisor of architectural works. The little that is recorded of his personal life comes from Sandrart, who says he

was melancholy and withdrawn and made an unhappy marriage late in life. There is no documentary confirmation of his marriage, but he is known to have had an adopted son called Andreas Neithardt, whose surname the painter sometimes used for himself in documents relating to the boy, thus creating one of the sources of confusion about the painter's identity.

Grünewald's work forms a complete contrast to that of Dürer. Whereas Dürer—an intellectual imbued with *Renaissance ideas—had limitless curiosity about the visual world, Grünewald concentrated exclusively on religious themes, and in particular the Crucifixion, a subject he was to make his own. His most famous treatment of it is the central panel of his masterpiece, the altarpiece for the hospital church of the Anthonite abbey at Isenheim in Alsace, completed in about 1515 and now in the Musée d'Unterlinden, Colmar. The hospital at Isenheim cared particularly for plague victims, and the concentration on Christ's appalling physical agonies, his body gruesomely mangled and torn, must have bolstered the faith of the sick by reminding them that he too had suffered horribly before triumphing over death. In the *Resurrection*, Christ displays his nail and lance wounds, but the lacerations that cover his body in the *Crucifixion* have disappeared, affirming that the patients at the hospital could be cleansed of their diseases and sins. The altarpiece is marked by extreme emotional intensity, brought about by expressive distortion and by colouring of an extraordinary incandescent beauty. Grünewald was familiar with Renaissance ideas of *perspective, but spiritually he belongs to the late medieval world. His other work includes Crucifixions in Basle (Öffentliche Kunstsammlung), Karlsruhe (Staatliche Kunsthalle), and Washington (NG), and several drawings survive.

The end of Grünewald's career was marked by a decline in his fortunes. He had Protestant sympathies, and following the Peasants' War, in which Archbishop Albrecht's palace was besieged, he left his service and moved to Frankfurt. There he made a meagre living at a variety of jobs, including selling artists' colours and a curative balm, the latter presumably something he had learnt about at Isenheim. In 1527 he became convinced his life was in danger and fled to Halle, where he died of plague the following year. His effects included 'much Lutheran trash'. Although his influence can be seen in the paintings of contemporaries such as *Baldung Grien and *Ratgeb, it was not until the advent of *Expressionism in the early 20th century that his work started to arouse widespread interest and he began his rise to his present pinnacle of esteem as one of the most awe-inspiring artists of his, or any other, time.

Guardi, Francesco (*b* Venice, 5 Oct. 1712; *d* Venice, 1 Jan. 1793). Venetian painter, the best-known member of a family of artists. He is now famous for his views of Venice, indeed next to *Canaletto he is the most celebrated view painter (see *VEDUTA*) of the 18th century, but he produced work on a great variety of subjects and seems to have concentrated on views only after the death of his brother **Gianantonio** (*bapt.* Vienna, 27 May 1699; *d* Venice, 22 Jan. 1760). Until then Francesco's personality was largely submerged in the family studio, of which Gianantonio was head and which handled commissions of every kind. Francesco's career was unsuccessful in worldly terms; he was still working for other artists when he was over 40, he never attracted the attention of foreign visitors in the way Canaletto did, and he died in poverty. Recognition of his genius came in the wake of *Impressionism, when his vibrant and rapidly painted views were seen as having qualities of spontaneity, bravura, and atmosphere lacking in Canaletto's more sharply defined works.

Francesco was enormously prolific and his work is in many public collections in Italy, Britain, and elsewhere. Few paintings from the Guardi studio are signed, dated, or reliably documented, and there has been a good deal of scholarly controversy about certain works. The major problem concerns the authorship of paintings representing the Story of Tobit that decorate the organ loft of S. Raffaele in Venice. Critical opinion is divided as to whether these brilliant works, painted with brushwork of breathtaking freedom, are by Francesco or Gianantonio (there is dispute also over the dating), but if they are indeed by the latter, he too must rank as a major figure. Giambattista *Tiepolo was married to the sister of the Guardi brothers, and it was possibly through his influence that Gianantonio became a founder member of the Venetian Academy in 1756. Francesco was not elected until 1784, during the presidency of his nephew Giandomenico Tiepolo. After Francesco's death, the studio was inherited by his son **Giacomo Guardi** (1764–1835), who produced a large number of Venetian views, mainly drawings.

Guercino (Giovanni Francesco Barbieri) (*bapt.* Cento, nr. Bologna, 8 Feb. 1591; *d* Bologna, 22 Dec. 1666). One of the outstanding Italian painters and draughtsmen of the 17th century; his nickname Guercino (Squinter) was given to him because of an eye defect that is said to have been caused by a childhood accident. He seems to have been mainly self-taught, and his early work drew on a variety of north Italian sources, notably Ludovico *Carracci and Venetian painting, to create a highly individual style characterized by dramatic and capricious lighting, strong colour, and broad, vigorous brushwork. In 1621 one of his patrons, Cardinal Alessandro Ludovisi (1554–1623), became Pope Gregory XV and summoned him to Rome. Among other commissions there he painted the celebrated ceiling fresco of *Aurora* (1621) in the Casino of the Villa Ludovisi for Gregory's nephew, Cardinal Ludovico Ludovisi (1595–1632). This exuberant work, with its illusionistic architectural framework designed by Agostino *Tassi, is much more *Baroque in style than Guido *Reni's treatment of the subject of a decade earlier.

On the death of the pope in 1623 Guercino returned to Cento, but his short stay in Rome introduced a more classical feeling to his work. This trend became more pronounced after he moved to Bologna in 1642 to take over the mantle of Reni, who died in that year. For the next quarter of a century, until his own death, he was Bologna's leading painter, and his late works can be remarkably similar to Reni's, calm and light in colouring, with little of the lively movement of his early style (*St Luke Displaying a Painting of the Virgin*, 1652, Nelson–Atkins Mus., Kansas City, Mo). His career is especially well documented because of *Malvasia's scrupulous biography, which lists his main commissions, coupled with the survival of a studio account book covering the period from 1629 until his death.

As well as being a major painter, Guercino was one of the most brilliant draughtsmen of his age. In addition to preparatory studies for his paintings, he made many informal drawings for his own pleasure (including landscapes, *genre scenes, and caricatures) and these—usually executed in pen and brown ink—often show remarkable freedom and vitality. The finest collection of his drawings is in the Royal Library at Windsor Castle. Guercino's reputation remained high until the mid-19th century, when it crumbled, along with those of the other great Bolognese painters, under the attacks of *Ruskin. His rehabilitation in the mid-20th century owed much to the championship of Denis *Mahon.

Guérin, Pierre-Narcisse (*b* Paris, 13 Mar. 1774; *d* Rome, 16 July 1833). French painter. He was one of the most successful French artists of his time, but his reputation did not long survive his death. In 1797 he won the *Prix de Rome, and his later distinctions included becoming director of the French *Academy in Rome in 1822 and being created a baron in 1829. His style was derived mainly from J.-L. *David (who said, 'I think he has been eavesdropping at the door of my studio'), but his scenes from classical history and mythology are less severe and more stagy. Apart from David he was the most sought-after teacher of his period, his pupils including *Géricault and *Delacroix, and he was an important figure in the transition from *Neoclassicism to *Romanticism. As a teacher he laid particular emphasis on the painted sketch and was instrumental in establishing a sketch competition as a preliminary to the Prix de Rome.

Guggenheim, Solomon R. (*b* Philadelphia, 2 Feb. 1861; *d* Sands Point, Long Island, NY, 3 Nov. 1949). American industrialist, collector, and philanthropist, a member of a famous family of financiers whose fortunes were based on the mining and smelting of metals. Like other members of his family, he devoted much of his vast wealth to philanthropy and in 1937 he founded the Solomon R. Guggenheim Foundation 'for the promotion and encouragement of art and education in art'. In 1943 he commissioned Frank Lloyd Wright to design a museum in New York to house his collection, and the Solomon R. Guggenheim Museum was opened in 1959, a decade after his death. It is renowned not only for the outstanding collection of late 19th-century and 20th-century art it contains, but also for the radical nature of the architecture, which marks a complete departure from traditional museum design; the exhibition space is a continuous spiral ramp, six 'storeys' high, encircling an open central space. It is architecturally exhilarating, but its suitability for displaying paintings and sculptures has been much questioned.

Guggenheim's niece **Peggy Guggenheim** (*b* New York, 26 Aug. 1898; *d* Venice, 23 Dec. 1979) was a noted patron, collector, and dealer, who played an important role in promoting avant-garde art, in particular by helping to introduce *Surrealism to the USA and by furthering the career of many leading *Abstract Expressionists. She spent much of her life in Europe, but during its brief existence (1942–6) her Art of This Century gallery in New York was the main showcase for Abstract Expressionism in its formative period. Notorious for her loose living, she had affairs with several artists and in 1941 married and divorced Max *Ernst. Her own superb collection is open to the public in Venice under the administration of the Solomon R. Guggenheim Foundation.

In 1997 a new Guggenheim Museum opened in Bilbao, Spain. Designed by the American architect Frank Gehry, it is one of the most spectacular buildings of the age—huge, eccentrically shaped, and clad largely in titanium. It is intended particularly for the display of works that are too large to be shown in the Guggenheim Museum in New York.

Guglielmo della Porta (*d* Rome, 6 Jan. 1577). Italian sculptor. He is first documented in Genoa, in 1534, but he spent most of his career in Rome. *Vasari says he moved there in 1537, but he is not documented in the city until 1546. The following year he succeeded *Sebastiano del Piombo as keeper of the papal seals. Guglielmo had a prolific and varied career, his work including several papal busts and a number of tombs in Roman churches, the most important being that of Paul III (Alessandro *Farnese) in St Peter's (1549–75). He also produced numerous small devotional and pagan statuettes and worked as a restorer and copier of *antique works. The major influence on his style was *Michelangelo and he had a penchant for reclining figures in the manner of the master's *Day* and *Night, Dawn* and *Evening* in the Medici Chapel, Florence.

Guido da Siena. Sienese painter active during the 13th century. Nothing is known of his life, and his only certain work is a *Madonna and Child* in the Palazzo Pubblico, Siena. The picture bears an inscription with the date 1221, but this has been the subject of much controversy, as stylistically the painting seems to belong about half a century later. It has been suggested that the inscription may have some commemorative purpose, the significance of which is now lost, rather than being a record of the date of execution. Although the painting is majestic in effect and follows *Byzantine conventions of *iconography, the figures to some extent relax the stiff linear patterns that had been conventional in central Italian painting up to that time. On the basis of this picture a number of other panels, most of which are in the Siena Pinacoteca, have been assigned to Guido or his school. Despite his great obscurity, he is regarded as sharing with *Coppo di Marcovaldo the honour of founding the Sienese School.

Guillaumin, Armand (*b* Paris, 16 Feb. 1841; *d* Paris, 26 June 1927). French landscape painter, one of the lesser-known figures of the *Impressionist group. Lack of success made him take a post with the department of bridges and causeways until he won a prize in a lottery in 1891 and was able to devote all his time to painting. Often his paintings include industrial elements, but he also painted seascapes. In his later work he sometimes used an almost *Fauve-like boldness of colour. He was the last survivor of those who exhibited in the first *Impressionist exhibition in 1874, dying the year after *Monet.

Gulbenkian, Calouste (*b* Constantinople [now Istanbul], 23 Mar. 1869; *d* Lisbon, 20 July 1955). Turkish-born oil magnate and collector who became a British citizen in 1902 and adopted Persian nationality in 1926. He made an enormous fortune in the oil industry in the Middle East and used his wealth to form one of the finest private collections of the 20th century. It included European paintings and sculpture, Islamic and Indian art, coins and medals, illuminated manuscripts, furniture, and much else. He was one of the collectors who benefited when the Soviet government sold works from the *Hermitage: 'Gulbenkian had an inside track with the Soviets because he had helped them importantly with sales of Baku oil, and he was given first choice' (Joseph Alsop, *The Rare Art Traditions: The History of Collecting and its Linked Phenomena*, 1982). In 1942 Gulbenkian settled in Lisbon. He left part of his collection to Portugal's Museu Nacional de Arte Antiga and the rest was used to form the Museu Calouste Gulbenkian, inaugurated in Lisbon in 1969; it is the foremost international collection of art in the country.

Gully, John (*bapt.* Bath, 21 Mar. 1819; *d* Nelson, 1 Nov. 1888). British-born painter who settled in New Zealand in 1852 and became one of the country's most successful painters. He specialized in grandiose scenes of natural beauty, including lake and mountain views, and earned the flattering nickname of the 'New Zealand *Turner'.

gum. A sticky liquid exuded by certain trees and shrubs, various types of which have been used in making paints from ancient times. The most commonly used is gum arabic, obtained from a species of acacia, which is the normal binding agent for watercolours.

Gunn, Sir James (*b* Glasgow, 30 June 1893; *d* London, 30 Dec. 1964). British portrait painter.

Gunn enjoyed a successful career with portraits of eminent soldiers, academics, judges, and so on, painted in a solid, forthright, traditional style. He was a more interesting painter in less conventional work, notably his portrait of the blind composer Delius (City AG, Bradford), which was the public's choice as 'picture of the year' at the *Royal Academy in 1933. Also well known is Gunn's *Conversation Piece at the Royal Lodge, Windsor*, 1950 (NPG, London), showing George VI, Queen Elizabeth (later the Queen Mother), and Princesses Elizabeth (later Elizabeth II) and Margaret.

Günther, Ignaz (*b* Altmannstein, Bavaria, 22 Nov. 1725; *d* Munich, 26 June 1775). German sculptor. After a varied training culminating in several months at the Vienna Academy, he settled in Munich in 1754. He was one of the great woodcarvers of his age (occasionally he worked in other materials), combining an elegant *Rococo style with highly emotional religious feeling. In 1759–62 he produced his chief work, the almost entire furnishing of the church at Rott-am-Inn.

Guston, Philip (*b* Montreal, 27 June 1913; *d* Woodstock, NY, 7 June 1980). American painter. After travelling in Mexico in 1934, studying the work of *Orozco and *Rivera in particular, he settled in New York and from 1934 to 1941 worked as a muralist on the *Federal Art Project. In 1941 he moved to Iowa City to teach at the State University there, and from 1945 to 1947 he was artist-in-residence at Washington University, St Louis. After leaving New York he switched from mural to easel painting, and during the 1940s his work changed in another fundamental way, moving from social and political subjects to abstraction; by 1950 (when, after travels in Europe, he settled in New York again) he had eliminated all figurative elements from his work. His most characteristic paintings feature luminous patches of overlapping colours delicately brushed in the central area of a canvas of light background (*Dial*, 1956, Whitney Mus., New York). This manner of his has been described as *'Abstract Impressionism' and he was associated with the more lyrical wing of *Abstract Expressionism—he was the only member of the group who had already had a successful career as a figurative painter. During the 1960s shades of grey encroached on the earlier brilliant colours and vague naturalistic associations crept in, until in the 1970s he returned to figurative painting in a satirical, garishly coloured, cartoonlike style that has been seen as the source of

*New Image Painting. His subjects in this manner included scenes of fantastic social comment, involving, for example, the Ku Klux Klan.

Gutai Group. A group of Japanese artists founded at Osaka in 1954, led by Jiro *Yoshihara. The group was best known for *Performance art. In 1960, for example, it produced a Sky Festival: 'Large balloons bearing banners by the artists, and some invited foreigners . . . were released from the roof of a department store in Osaka, recalling a similar piece by Yves *Klein done in 1957' (Adrian Henri, *Environments and Happenings*, 1974). The Gutai artists also produced abstract paintings, mainly in an *Abstract Expressionist vein. The group held numerous exhibitions and published fourteen numbers of its magazine before breaking up following Yoshihara's death in 1972.

Gütersloh, Albert Paris. See FANTASTIC REALISM.

Gutfreund, Otto (*b* Dvůr Králové, 3 Aug. 1889; *d* Prague, 2 June 1927). Czech sculptor. After training in Prague, he spent several months in Paris, 1909–10. He studied under *Bourdelle but he was inspired more by paintings he saw by *Braque and *Picasso and he became one of the first artists to try to apply the principles of *Cubism to sculpture. On his return to Prague in 1911 he joined the Group of Plastic Artists (see ČAPEK), whose members attempted to fuse Cubism with *Expressionism. An example of his work from this time is *Cubist Bust* (1912–13, Tate, London). After the First World War he developed a more naturalistic style based on folk art. He committed suicide by drowning.

Guthrie, Sir James. See GLASGOW SCHOOL.

Guttuso, Renato (*b* Bagheria, nr. Palermo, 2 Jan. 1912; *d* Rome, 18 Jan. 1987). Italian painter. He was a forceful personality and Italy's leading 20th-century exponent of *Social Realism; he never subordinated artistic quality to political propaganda, but his art was often the direct expression of his hatred of injustice and of the abuse of power. In 1931 he abandoned legal studies for painting, in which he was mainly self-taught. He settled in Rome in 1937 and in the following year became a founder member of the anti-Fascist association *Corrente. Fascism was not his only target, however, for he also pilloried the Mafia and in 1943 published a series of drawings protesting against the massacres that took place under the German occupation of Italy. After the war (in which he worked with the Resistance) he became a member of the *Fronte Nuovo delle Arti in 1946. His post-war works were often inspired by the struggles of the Sicilian peasantry, and his other subjects included the 1968 student riots in Paris, a city he often visited. Many of his paintings were large, with allegorical overtones, typically painted in a vigorous *Expressionist style.

Guys, Constantin (*b* Flushing [Vlissingen], 3 Dec. 1802; *d* Paris, 13 Mar. 1892). French illustrator. Early in his career he travelled widely and adventurously, fighting in the Greek War of Independence in the 1820s, for example, and in 1855 he covered the Crimean War as a correspondent for the *Illustrated London News*. After he settled in Paris in the late 1850s, however, he became famous for his vigorous drawings of fashionable life, which were published in various journals. He seems to have been self-taught as an artist. In 1863 *Baudelaire immortalized him as 'The Painter of Modern Life' in his celebrated essay of that name. Many of the leading avant-garde painters of the day admired his work, including *Degas and *Manet, and because of his realistic approach to contemporary subjects and his liveliness of touch he has been seen as a precursor of *Impressionism. In spite of his renown, he had difficulty earning a living with his work and died in poverty at the age of 89.

H

Haarlem, Cornelis van. See CORNELIS VAN HAARLEM.

Habsburg (or **Hapsburg**). One of the major ruling dynasties of European history, the members of which have included several important art patrons and collectors. The family can be traced back to the 10th century and it established a hereditary monarchy in Austria in the 13th century. From 1452 it held the title of Holy Roman Emperor almost continuously until the empire was dissolved by Napoleon in 1806. The family's territories reached their greatest extent in the early 16th century under Charles V, who—as a result of diplomacy, marriage, and conquest—ruled one of the largest empires ever created; in addition to its heartland in central Europe, it included Spain, the kingdom of Naples and other parts of Italy, and most of the Netherlands, as well as vast colonial possessions in the Americas. When Charles abdicated in 1556 the empire was divided between his son Philip, who inherited Spain, the New World colonies, the Italian possessions, and the Netherlands, and his brother Ferdinand, who inherited the rest (the 'Austrian' territories), as well as the title of emperor. The Habsburgs ruled in Spain until 1700 and in Austria until 1918, when the upheavals of the First World War brought the dynasty to an end.

Maximilian I (1459–1519), who became emperor in 1493 and reigned until his death, was one of the most cultured rulers of his time (he was himself an accomplished writer) and the first of the great Habsburg patrons. He is sometimes known as the 'Last Knight', because in certain respects he represents a final flowering of the ways of the medieval world (he was, for example, his period's leading patron of armourers, and the graceful style of German armour characteristic of the time is known as Maximilian after him). In other ways, however, he was forward-looking, notably in his appreciation of the power of the printing press and the propaganda value of art. The most remarkable example of his use of visual propaganda was a huge woodcut triumphal arch, made up of more than a hundred blocks, celebrating his family's achievements; 700 copies were produced for distribution throughout the empire. *Dürer, the designer-in-chief, finished his work in 1515, but the cutting of the blocks took two more years, and the printing was not finished until 1518. Among the other artists who worked for Maximilian were Hans *Burgkmair the Elder and Bernhard *Strigel. They often had to wait a long time for payment, for the emperor was constantly in financial trouble. His tomb (or more strictly monument, as he is buried elsewhere) in the Hofkirche, Innsbruck, was begun in 1508 as a vast dynastic memorial, but the design was much truncated by the time it was completed more than half a century later. Various artists worked on it, including Peter *Vischer the Elder.

Maximilian was succeeded by his grandson **Charles** (1500–58), who ruled the empire as Charles V, 1519–56, and was also King of Spain as Charles I, 1516–56; he relinquished both titles two years before his death and retired to a life of religious devotion. By this time his unwieldy empire was becoming ungovernable, in the face of numerous problems, not least the spread of Protestantism. Charles had wide-ranging interests, and he collected maps, globes, and scientific instruments, as well as pictures, tapestries, books, arms and armour, coins, jewellery, and even featherwork from the Americas. His favourite painter was *Titian, who twice visited the imperial court at Augsburg, and the other artists he patronized included the sculptor Leone *Leoni and the architect Pedro *Machuca.

Charles's aunt **Margaret of Austria** (1480–1530), and his sister **Mary of Hungary** (1505–58), were successively regent of the Netherlands (1507–30 and 1530–56 respectively). Both of them were art lovers and each of them in turn owned Jan van *Eyck's *'Arnolfini Marriage'* (1434, NG, London) for a time; Mary also owned another celebrated masterpiece of Early Netherlandish painting—Rogier van der *Weyden's *Descent* *from the Cross* (c.1440, Prado, Madrid). Bernard van *Orley served as court painter to both of them. Charles's nephew **Maximilian II** (1527–76), who became emperor in 1564, was a devotee of the arts and learning and one of the main patrons of Giuseppe *Arcimboldo.

Arcimboldo also worked for Maximilian's son **Rudolf II** (1552–1612), who became emperor in 1576. He was the most remarkable of all Habsburg patrons and collectors, indeed one of the most impassioned art lovers in history. Politically his career was a disaster; he was subject to fits of morbid depression and spent long periods in semi-seclusion, making him incapable of governing effectively (in 1611 he was forced to abdicate as King of Bohemia in favour of his brother Mathias). However, his fervour for art and science turned his capital Prague into one of the leading cultural centres of Europe. His patronage attracted a roster of distinguished artists, scientists, and scholars to the city (including the astronomers Tycho Brahe and Johann Kepler) and his collection of pictures was one of the greatest ever assembled. The artists who worked for him in Prague included Hans von *Aachen, Roelandt *Savery, Bartholomeus *Spranger, and Adriaen de *Vries. He also commissioned work from some of the leading Italian masters of the day, including *Barocci, *Tintoretto, and *Veronese. Among earlier artists he particularly loved the work of *Bruegel and Dürer. In addition to paintings and sculptures, he collected applied art and curiosities of all kinds.

Rudolf's collections were dispersed after his death, but several of the paintings he owned are in the *Kunsthistorisches Museum, Vienna, which is the greatest monument to the artistic interests of the Habsburgs. The real father of its picture collection was Archduke **Leopold William** (1614–62). He was governor of the Spanish Netherlands from 1646 to 1656 and during this period at the hub of the international art market he bought pictures on a grand scale, taking advantage of the political upheavals of the time (including the dispersal of the collection of Charles I of England after his execution in 1649; see ROYAL COLLECTION). His court painter, David *Teniers the Younger, produced several pictures showing his remarkable collection. It was particularly rich in Italian (especially Venetian) pictures of the 16th century and in Flemish pictures of the 15th to the 17th century.

Among the later Habsburg patrons were **Maria-Theresa** (1717–80; Holy Roman Empress 1740–65), who bought numerous pictures, particularly by *Rubens, and patronized *Bellotto,

and her son **Joseph II** (1741–90; reigned from 1765), who opened the imperial collections to the public in 1781. Joseph was succeeded by his brother **Leopold II** (1747–92). He reigned for only two years before his death, but earlier, as Grand Duke Pietro Leopoldo, he had played an important role in the artistic life of Florence (see UFFIZI).

The Habsburg monarchs of Spain included two patrons and collectors who rank among the greatest in history, **Philip II** (1527–98; reigned from 1556) and his grandson **Philip IV** (1605–65; reigned from 1621). Philip II, the son of Charles V, lived an austere life in many ways—he was intensely religious and obsessively devoted to bureaucratic paperwork—but he also had a genuine passion for art. The greatest artistic memorial of his reign is the *Escorial, the huge monastery-palace near Madrid, begun in 1563. Philip imported many Italian artists to work on its decoration, and he also collected pictures on a scale that had not previously been seen in Spain. By the end of his life he owned about 1,500 and they were the basis of the Spanish royal collection that now forms the heart of the *Prado. His favourite living artist was Titian and he was the most important patron of his later career. Among earlier painters, he particularly admired *Bosch. In addition to paintings he also collected books and manuscripts, as well as sculpture, tapestries, arms and armour, antiquities, and other objects. At the beginning of his reign, Spain was at the height of its power and wealth, but he suffered various setbacks in his later years, including the defeat of the Spanish Armada in 1588, and by the end of his life the country was in decline.

Under Philip IV this political decline accelerated, but his reign witnessed a glorious flowering of Spanish art. His favourite artist was *Velázquez, who produced numerous portraits of him and his family, and he employed many other eminent artists of this golden age, particularly on the decoration of royal buildings. In addition to the Escorial, these included the Buen Retiro Palace, built in Madrid in the 1630s, and the Torre de la Parada, a hunting lodge near Madrid that Philip enlarged in 1635–7. Rubens and his assistants painted more than 100 mythological scenes for the Torre de la Parada, and so much art was required to furnish the Buen Retiro that large numbers of pictures were commissioned from the Netherlands and Italy (*Claude was among the artists involved) as well as from Spanish painters, including *Mayno (who had taught Philip drawing when he was a child), *Pereda, and *Zurbarán. Philip also bought pictures by earlier artists, including works by some of the greatest Renaissance masters, notably *Raphael and Titian.

Philip was succeeded by his sickly son **Charles II** (1661–1700; reigned from 1665), whose mental and physical infirmities reflected generations of Habsburg inbreeding. He inherited some of the family love of art, and his court painters included *Carreño de Miranda, *Coello, and *Palomino. In 1692 he brought Luca *Giordano to Spain to work at the Escorial. By the time Charles died childless in 1700, Spain's power had declined so much that Louis XIV of France was able to install his grandson (Charles's great-nephew) as Philip V, bringing the Spanish Habsburg line to an end and provoking the War of the Spanish Succession.

Hackaert, Jan (*bapt.* Amsterdam, Feb. 1628; *d* Amsterdam, *c.*1685). Dutch landscape painter, active mainly in Amsterdam. Most of his work consists of Italianate landscapes and woodland scenes. He travelled in Switzerland in the 1650s, but there is no documentary evidence that he visited Italy; however, he captured the golden Italian sunlight so successfully that his *Lake of Zurich* (*c.*1673, Rijksmuseum, Amsterdam) was long thought to be a view of Lake Trasimene in Umbria. The figures in his paintings are often the work of other artists, notably *Berchem and Adriaen van de *Velde.

Hackert, Jakob Philipp (*b* Prenzlau, 15 Sept. 1737; *d* San Pietro di Carreggio, nr. Florence, 24 Apr. 1807). German landscape painter, active in Italy from 1768. In 1786 he became court painter to Ferdinand IV of Naples. He was a sensitive upholder of the *ideal landscape tradition of *Claude, which he seasoned with touches of *Romanticism. Much of his output was devoted to views of famous sites, which were eagerly sought by foreign visitors to Italy. *Goethe met Hackert in 1787 and edited his memoirs (published 1811). His work is exceptionally well represented at Attingham Park in Shropshire. Hackert came from a family of artists and often collaborated with his brother **Johann Gottlieb Hackert** (1744–73). Three other brothers were artists.

Hadfield, Maria. See COSWAY.

Haecht, Willem van. See VERHAECHT.

Haecken. See AKEN.

Hagenauer (or Hagnower), **Niclas** (active 1490s–1520s). German woodcarver, documented in Strasbourg from 1493 to 1526. A good deal of

sculpture has been associated with his name, but often on insecure grounds. The most famous work attributed to him is the carving of the Isenheim Altarpiece (Mus. d'Unterlinden, Colmar), celebrated for its paintings by *Grünewald. The sculptural element of the altarpiece has been much praised, and even described as worthy of the paintings, but Michael Baxandall (*The Limewood Sculptors of Renaissance Germany*, 1980) says 'it suffers from heavy-handed drapery as well as coarse characterization'. **Friedrich Hagenauer** (*c.*1500–after 1546), a sculptor and one of the outstanding medallists of his time, was probably the son of Niclas.

Haggadah (plural: Haggadot) (Hebrew: 'story, parable'). A set of Jewish texts, including the Exodus narrative, to be ritually recited as part of the celebrations of Passover; the term also refers to a book containing these texts, the only Hebrew book with a long and consistent tradition of illustration. Most of the illustrated manuscript Haggadot date from the 14th and 15th centuries, a famous example being the Sarajevo Haggadah (National Mus. Sarajevo), produced in Spain in the 14th century. Illustrated printed texts of the Haggadah were produced from 1516; editions published in Prague (1526), Mantua (1560, 1568), Venice (1609), and Amsterdam (1695) are among the most artistically noteworthy. Ben *Shahn is among the artists who have illustrated more modern editions.

Hague School. Informal group of Dutch artists who worked mainly in The Hague between about 1860 and 1900. The group is particularly associated with landscapes and beach scenes, but the members also painted street scenes, views of everyday life, and church interiors. In some ways this was a *Romantic revival of the 17th-century tradition, and this nostalgic strain—particularly in pictures made during the first years the group worked together—is one of the things that distinguishes them from their French counterparts, the painters of the *Barbizon School and the *Impressionists. They shared with the great Dutch landscapists of the 17th century a special interest in recording light and atmospheric effects. Leading members of the Hague School included *Bosboom, *Israëls, the *Maris brothers, *Mauve, *Mesdag, and *Weissenbruch. The group was the leading force in Dutch painting in the late 19th century and van *Gogh was strongly influenced by Mauve and Israëls.

Halicka, Alicia. See MARCOUSSIS.

Hall, Fred. See NEWLYN SCHOOL.

Hall, Peter Adolf (*b* Borås, 23 Feb. 1739; *d* Liège, 15 May 1793). Swedish portrait painter, active mainly in Paris, where he moved in 1766. He was most renowned as a miniaturist, but he also made life-size portraits in oils and pastels (his miniatures are very lively in technique, with broader brushwork than is usually found in the medium). Hall quickly became a fashionable success in Paris, but his market was ruined by the Revolution, and he left France destitute in 1791, moving to Brussels and then Liège. His work is well represented in the Nationalmuseum, Stockholm, and there are examples in the Wallace Collection, London.

Hals, Frans (*b* Antwerp, 1582/3; *d* Haarlem, 29 Aug. 1666). Dutch painter. He was Flemish by birth; his parents left Antwerp after the city was captured by the Spaniards in 1585 and moved to Holland. They had settled in Haarlem by 1591 and Hals spent the rest of his long life there. He was twice married, had at least ten children, and was constantly in financial trouble. *Houbraken says he was 'filled to the gills every evening', but there is no real foundation for the popular image of him as a drunken wife-beater. His second wife, however, was more than once in trouble for brawling. During his last years he was destitute and the municipal authorities of Haarlem awarded him a small annual stipend four years before his death.

Hals was the first great artist of the 17th-century Dutch School and is regarded as one of the most brilliant of all portraitists. Almost all his works are portraits and even those that are not (some *genre scenes and an occasional religious picture) are portrait-like in character. He is said to have been taught in Haarlem by Karel van *Mander, but there is no discernible influence from him in Hals's early works, which are not numerous or well documented. The earliest dated picture associated with him is a portrait of Jacobus Zaffius (1611, Hals Mus., Haarlem; perhaps a copy), and on stylistic evidence a few other paintings can be dated around the same time. Nothing he did before 1616 anticipated the way he shattered well-established traditions that year with his life-size group portrait of the *Banquet of the Officers of the St George Militia Company* (Hals Mus.). There is no real precedent in either his own work or that of his predecessors for the vigorous composition and characterization of this picture, which has become a symbol of the strength and healthy optimism of the men who established the new Dutch Republic.

It demonstrates to the full his remarkable ability—his greatest gift as a portraitist—to capture a sense of fleeting movement and expression and thereby convey a compelling feeling of life.

From 1616 onwards there are numerous dated or documented works by Hals and his artistic development is clear. He was at the height of his popularity in the 1620s and 1630s. During these decades he made five large group portraits of civic guards; one (finished by Pieter *Codde) is in the Rijksmuseum and the others are in the museum named after Hals in Haarlem, the only place where one can get a comprehensive view of his range and power. In the 1630s his compositions became simpler and monochromatic effects took the place of the bright colours of the earlier paintings (*Lucas de Clercq* and *Feyntje van Steenkiste*, 1635, Rijksmuseum, Amsterdam). The group portrait of the *Regents of the St Elizabeth Hospital* (1641, Hals Mus.) sets the key for the sober restraint of the late period, when his pictures became darker and his brushstrokes more economical. His career culminated in his group portraits of the *Regents* and the *Regentesses of the Old Men's Alms House* (*c*.1664, Hals Mus.), which rank among the most moving portraits ever painted. By this time Hals was using in his commissioned portraits the bold brushwork and the *alla prima technique that early in his career he reserved for genre pictures. No drawings by him are known and he presumably worked straight onto the canvas.

Hals had two painter brothers and five painter sons, but the only artist of substance among them was his brother **Dirk** (*bapt.* Haarlem, 19 Mar. 1591; *bur.* Haarlem, 17 May 1656), who painted charming small interior scenes. Apart from his sons, Hals taught numerous pupils, including (with varying degrees of certainty) Judith *Leyster, Jan Miense *Molenaer, Adriaen van *Ostade, Adriaen *Brouwer, and Philips *Wouwerman. His reputation did not long outlive him, however, and it was only in the second half of the 19th century that there was a renewed appreciation of his genius. The spontaneity of his work appealed to the generation of the *Impressionists, and from about 1870 to about 1920 he was one of the most popular of the Old Masters, becoming a model for society portraitists. Lord Hertford's purchase of his most famous work, *The Laughing Cavalier* (1624, Wallace Coll., London), in 1865 for the then enormous sum of 51,000 francs (more than six times the auction estimate), was a milestone in the revival of his fortunes, and the buoyant confidence of his paintings later made him a particular favourite with the new generation of fabulously rich American collectors—self-made men—who were beginning to dominate the picture market. This explains why so many works by him are in American collections.

Hamel, Théophile (b Sainte-Foy, nr. Quebec, 8 Nov. 1817; d Quebec, 23 Dec 1870). Canadian painter of portraits and religious subjects, active mainly in Quebec. He was the most distinguished pupil of *Plamondon and his early portraits combine his master's classicism with the simplicity of folk art (1842, *Léocadie Bilodeau*, Université Laval, Quebec). Later, following a visit to Europe (1843–6), he was influenced by *Romanticism. He was regarded as the best Canadian painter of his time and his sitters included many leading contemporaries.

Hamilton, Gavin (b Murdieston House, Lanarkshire, 1723; d Rome, 4 Jan. 1798). Scottish painter, archaeologist, and picture dealer. From 1748 he lived mainly in Rome, where he was a leading member of the *Neoclassical circle of *Mengs and *Winckelmann. As an artist he concentrated on *history paintings, and he is one of the few British artists (with *Barry and the Anglo-Americans *Copley and *West) to make a significant contribution in this field. He was particularly interested in Homeric subjects, in his treatment of which he was influenced by *Poussin as well as by the *antique (*Achilles Lamenting the Death of Patroclus*, 1763, NG, Edinburgh). His pictures in this vein were never very numerous and today are generally regarded as ponderous, but they became well known through engravings, and greatly influenced the development of the Neoclassical style amongst both his contemporaries and the younger generation, including *David. His occasional portraits generally appeal more to modern taste (*The 8th Duke of Hamilton with Dr John Moore and Ensign John Moore*, 1775–7, NPG, Edinburgh). Hamilton met and encouraged virtually all the British artists who visited Rome in the second half of the 18th century, but he remained better known on the Continent than in Britain, where his name was more familiar for his lucrative activities in selling Old Masters and classical antiquities. From about 1769 he directed archaeological excavations himself, notably at Hadrian's Villa at Tivoli.

Gavin Hamilton is not to be confused with **Gawen Hamilton** (c.1697–1737), a minor portrait painter remembered for his *Conversation of Virtuosis . . . at the Kings Armes* (1735, NPG, London), which shows himself and several other artists of the day.

Hamilton, Hugh Douglas (b Dublin, 1736; d Dublin, 10 Feb. 1808). Irish painter, mainly of portraits, active for much of his career in England and Italy. He worked in London 1764–79, then in Italy 1779–91 (mainly Rome and Florence), before returning in 1792 to Dublin, where he became the leading portraitist of the day. Early in his career he worked mainly in pastel and it was in this medium that he produced his masterpiece, *Antonio *Canova in his Studio* (c.1789, V&A, London), which shows the celebrated sculptor with Henry Tresham (?1751–1814), an Irish painter, art dealer, and writer; in front of them is a full-size plaster model for Canova's *Cupid and Psyche*. The picture is unusually large and ambitious for a pastel (it is a metre (3 ft) wide), and it is the work with which Hamilton relaunched his career in Britain, at the *Royal Academy exhibition in 1791, after his long residence in Italy. Dignified in composition and masterly in its richness of technique, it is regarded as the greatest pastel ever produced by an artist from the British Isles.

Hamilton, Richard (b London, 24 Feb. 1922). British painter, printmaker, teacher, exhibition organizer, and writer, one of the leading pioneers of *Pop art. As a young man he worked in advertising and commercial art and he is best known for his montages featuring scenes from the fields of advertisement and contemporary life, notably *Just what is it that makes today's homes so different, so appealing?* (1956, Kunsthalle, Tübingen), which is sometimes considered to be the first Pop art work. Hamilton has had a distinguished career as a teacher, notably at King's College, Newcastle upon Tyne (which later became Newcastle University), 1953–66, and has organized several exhibitions, including 'The Almost Complete Works of Marcel *Duchamp' at the Tate Gallery, London, in 1966. An anthology of his writings, *Collected Works*, appeared in 1982. His second wife (whom he married in 1991) is the painter **Rita Donagh** (1939–). See also INDEPENDENT GROUP.

Hamilton, Sir William. See DILETTANTI.

Hammershøi, Vilhelm (b Copenhagen, 15 May 1864; d Copenhagen, 13 Feb. 1916). Danish painter. He painted portraits, architectural subjects (including two murals for Copenhagen Town Hall), and landscapes, but is best known for his quiet interior scenes. They are painted in muted colours, and have a certain affinity with

*Vermeer, often featuring a single standing or seated figure. Most of Hammershøi's paintings are in Denmark, but two of his interiors are in Tate Modern, London.

Hanneman, Adriaen (*b* The Hague, *c.*1604; *bur.* The Hague, 11 July 1671). Dutch portrait painter. He studied under Anthonie van *Ravesteyn, then from about 1626 to 1638 he lived in England, where he perhaps worked as an assistant to van *Dyck for a time. On his return to the Netherlands he became one of the leading portraitists in The Hague, his sitters including many English Royalists who had gone into exile after the Civil War as well as officials of the Dutch government. His style—elegant and dignified, although sometimes a little stiff—was strongly influenced by van Dyck. In spite of his success Hanneman had financial problems late in his career (for unknown reasons).

Hanson, Duane (*b* Alexandria, Minn., 17 Jan. 1925; *d* Boca Raton, Fla., 6 Jan. 1996). American sculptor. Hanson was probably the best-known exponent of *Superrealism in sculpture, producing minutely detailed fibreglass resin figures dressed in real clothes and accompanied by real props. He commented pungently on the depressing or tasteless aspects of everyday American life, his subjects including down-and-outs, exhausted shoppers, or, in one of his most famous works, a pair of fat, ageing, and garishly dressed sightseers (*Tourists*, 1970, Scottish NG of Modern Art, Edinburgh).

happening. A form of entertainment, often carefully planned but usually including some degree of spontaneity, in which an artist performs or directs an event combining elements of theatre and the visual arts. The term was coined in 1959 by Allan *Kaprow, to whom the concept of the happening was bound up with his rejection of traditional principles of craftsmanship and permanence in the arts. Happenings had close affinities with *Performance art (the two terms have sometimes been used more or less synonymously) and they were not restricted like environments to the confines of a gallery or some other specific site. The composer and artist John Cage (1912–92), one of Kaprow's teachers, organized a performance at *Black Mountain College in 1952 that has sometimes been described as the first happening. Kaprow's own first happening, *Intermission Piece*, staged at the Reuben Gallery, New York, in 1959; in October of the same year he performed *18 Happenings in 6 Parts* at the same venue, and this was the first event to be actually

titled a happening. Apart from Cage and Kaprow, the artists chiefly responsible for the development of the form in the USA include Jim *Dine, Roy *Lichtenstein, Claes *Oldenburg, and Robert *Rauschenberg. Outside America, the happening was widely exploited during the 1960s and 1970s—in Japan, for example, and by many artists in Europe. The term has often been used to cover staged demonstrations for political or social propaganda, as for example in the work of the *Fluxus group (whose happenings in Germany were usually called 'Aktions').

Hapsburg. See HABSBURG.

Hard-Edge Painting. A type of abstract painting in which forms, although not necessarily geometrical, have sharp contours and are executed in flat colours. It was one of the types of painting that developed as a reaction against the spontaneity and painterly handling of *Abstract Expressionism (see POST-PAINTERLY ABSTRACTION). Major exponents have included Ellsworth *Kelly and Kenneth *Noland. The term was coined by the American critic Jules Langsner in 1958.

Hare, David (*b* New York, 10 Mar. 1917; *d* Jackson Hole, Wyo., 21 Dec. 1992). American sculptor, painter, and photographer. He initially studied chemistry and had no formal training in art, which he approached as a form of experimentation. In the late 1930s he worked as a commercial photographer and in about 1940 he began to experiment with the technique of 'heatage' (gently heating the emulsion of a photographic plate so that it melted and the image flowed). His interest in this technique brought him into contact with the European *Surrealists who had moved to New York during the Second World War, and Hare founded and edited the Surrealist magazine *VVV*, which ran from June 1942 to February 1944 In 1942 he began to make sculpture, using various materials and showing a typically Surrealist interest in visual puns. He was friendly with several leading *Abstract Expressionist painters and his sculptures have been seen as three-dimensional analogues of their work. From 1948 to 1953 he lived in France. By the time he returned to New York he was working mainly in metal—welded or cast. In the 1960s he took up painting, but he returned to sculpture as his main medium in the 1970s.

Haring, Keith. See GRAFFITI ART.

Harlem Renaissance. A term describing a flowering of activity among black American artists in the 1920s, centred on the Harlem district of New York. It was primarily a literary movement, but there were also visual artists involved, notably Aaron Douglas (1899–1979), who is regarded as the first black American painter consciously to incorporate African imagery in his pictures. An exhibition entitled 'Rhapsodies in Black: Art of the Harlem Renaissance' was held at the Hayward Gallery, London, in 1997.

Harnett, William Michael (b Clonakilty, Co. Cork, 10 Aug. 1848; d New York, 29 Oct. 1892). American still-life painter. He was born in Ireland and brought to America as a child, living first in Philadelphia and then from 1869 in New York (with the exception of a stay in Europe, 1880–6). He specialized in elaborate *trompel'œil compositions, often involving firearms or musical instruments (After the Hunt, 1885, California Palace of the Legion of Honor, San Francisco). Although his works were long popular with the public, they were generally dismissed by critics as mere sleight of hand until about 1940, when they began to win favour for their strength of composition.

Harpignies, Henri (b Valenciennes, 24 July 1819; d Saint-Privé, Yonne, 28 Aug. 1916). French landscape painter (and occasional printmaker). He did not take up painting seriously until 1846, but he was then very prolific and won considerable success and fame. He is sometimes classed with the *Barbizon School, but his work shows more specifically the influence of *Corot.

Harris, Lawren Stewart (b Brantford, Ontario, 23 Oct. 1885; d Vancouver, 29 Jan. 1970). Canadian painter, active mainly in Toronto and (from 1940) in Vancouver. From 1904 to 1908 he studied in Berlin, where his work was influenced by *Expressionism. Early in his career his favourite subjects were cityscapes and views of houses, but in about 1911 he also took up landscape and from 1920 (when he was one of the founder members of the *Group of Seven) this became his main interest. Harris was a follower of Theosophy and he used spectacular scenery as a way of expressing spiritual values. To this end he sought out the most overpowering landscapes he could find—in the Rockies and even the Arctic. The transcendental quality in his work was maintained when he turned to abstraction in the 1930s. In the later part of his career he became a patriarchal figure in Canadian painting.

Harris, Max. See ANGRY PENGUINS.

Hartley, Marsden (b Lewiston, Me., 4 Jan. 1877; d Ellsworth, Me., 2 Sept. 1943). American painter, whose work represents a diverse yet also highly personal response to European modernism. In 1909 he was given a one-man exhibition by *Stieglitz, and in 1912 help from Stieglitz and Arthur B. *Davies enabled him to travel to Europe—the beginning of the almost compulsive travels that lasted throughout his life (he was a lonely, reclusive, rather haunted character who never achieved much worldly success). Apart from a visit to New York in 1913, he lived in Europe until 1916. During these years he created a distinctive semi-abstract manner seen most famously in Painting No. 5 (1914–15, Whitney Mus., New York); this work represents a remarkably personal synthesis of modernist trends, being more closely structured and objective than German *Expressionism and more freely patterned and highly coloured than French *Cubism. In 1916 Hartley returned to America, and in 1918 said that he had grown weary of 'emotional excitement in art'. He turned to landscape as his principal subject, working in a more representational but still highly formalized style. In 1921 he returned to Europe, stayed there for a decade, then continued his wandering life in the early 1930s, visiting Mexico in 1932, for example, when he painted a series of pictures of the volcano Popacatepetl. In 1934 he settled in his native Maine. The work of his final years (usually rugged mountain and coastal scenes) was characterized by blunt blocklike forms, showing a powerful feeling for the beauty and grandeur of nature.

Hartung, Hans (b Leipzig, 21 Sept. 1904; d Antibes, 7 Dec. 1989). German-born abstract painter and printmaker who settled in Paris in 1935 and became a French citizen in 1946. During the Second World War he fought in the French Foreign Legion; he was badly wounded in 1944 and had a leg amputated without anaesthetic. Hartung was an individualist who pursued his own path, unconcerned with fashion and sustained by what he called 'stubborn staying power'. He had begun painting abstracts in 1922, when he was only 17, and he developed a sensuous, freely improvised style that anticipated post-war developments. It was only after the war that he made a reputation and was hailed as one of the pioneers of *Art Informel. His fame was at its peak around 1960, in which year he was joint winner of the main painting prize at the Venice *Biennale. In some of his paintings the vibrant thick black lines and blotches have a kinship with the work of Franz *Kline, but Kline is more brusquely energetic and less subtle.

Hassam, Childe (*b* Dorchester, Mass., 17 Oct. 1859; *d* East Hampton, Long Island, NY, 27 Aug. 1935). American painter and printmaker. He was one of his country's earliest and most accomplished exponents of *Impressionism, which he discovered on his second visit to Europe in 1886–9. On his return to America he settled in New York, and the life of the city became one of his main sources of subject matter; scenes of rainy streets were something of a speciality. Another favourite theme was a woman in an interior. His early paintings are fresh and clear but sometimes rather slick and saccharine. After the turn of the century, his style tended towards greater simplification and flatness in composition and his colour became lusher—somewhat in the manner of *Bonnard. Hassam was immensely prolific in oils, watercolour, pastel, and a variety of drawing media; in his fifties he also took up printmaking seriously, producing a large number of etchings and lithographs (notably harbour scenes in a style reminiscent of *Whistler). He received many honours and died a wealthy man, although by this time he was seen in artistic circles as a very conservative figure. See also TEN.

hatching. The use of closely spaced parallel lines to suggest shading. The technique is found mainly in drawing and engraving, but is also used, for example, in *tempera painting. When intersecting sets of lines are used, the term cross-hatching is applicable.

Hausmann, Raoul. See DADA and PHOTOMONTAGE.

Haworth, Jann. See BLAKE, SIR PETER.

Haydon, Benjamin Robert (*b* Plymouth, 25 Jan. 1786; *d* London, 22 June 1846). English painter and writer, a mediocre artist but a fascinating personality. Inspired by *Reynolds's *Discourses*, he aimed to bring a new seriousness to British art by producing historical and religious works in the *Grand Manner and through them to educate and improve public taste. His life, which was punctuated by bankruptcy, imprisonment, and disputes with patrons, was a story of bombastic frustration and stubborn opposition to the establishment (particularly the *Royal Academy), as he fought continuously for personal recognition and argued for the social purpose of art. However, his talents fell far short of his lofty ambitions, his multi-figure compositions degenerating into turgid melodrama. His great monument, rather, is the massive collection of autobiographical writings he left behind him (various editions have been published), which gives fascinating insights into the contemporary artistic scene and paints a vividly detailed picture of his disturbed mind and tragicomical life. He was closely linked with the *Romantic movement in literature, particularly with William Wordsworth, who wrote a sonnet to him, and with John Keats, painting portraits of both of them (NPG, London), and but for his lack of talent he would exemplify all the traits traditionally ascribed to the Romantic concept of genius. In true Romantic fashion his death came by suicide.

Hayez, Francesco (*b* Venice, 11 Feb. 1791; *d* Milan, 12 Dec. 1882). Italian painter, active mainly in Milan. Hayez was the most important figure in the transition from *Neoclassicism to *Romanticism in Italian painting, but his Romantic leanings come out mainly in subject matter rather than in technique, the clear outlines he favoured revealing his training in Rome in the circle of *Canova and *Ingres. He painted religious, historical, and mythological works in a vein owing something to *Delacroix and *Delaroche, and portraits that are sometimes thought worthy of comparison with those of Ingres. Some of the most eminent Italians of the day sat for him. For many years he taught at the Brera in Milan (he became director in 1860) and he exercised great influence on his pupils. The Brera has an outstanding collection of his work.

Hayman, Francis (*b* ?Exeter, *c*.1708; *d* London, 3 Feb. 1776). English painter and book illustrator. He was the most versatile British painter of his period, his work including subjects from literature and the theatre (notably Shakespeare), scenes of rural folklore, and portraits (his *conversation pieces anticipated those of *Gainsborough, who early in his career probably worked with him). Hayman also had the reputation of being 'unquestionably the best historical painter in the kingdom before the arrival of *Cipriani' (Edward *Edwards, *Anecdotes of Painters . . .* , 1808), but little of his work in this vein survives. In addition he was a prolific designer of book illustrations, sometimes collaborating with *Gravelot. His biggest undertaking (*c*.1741) was the painting of about 50 large pictures to decorate the supper boxes and pavilions at Vauxhall Gardens, the fashionable

London pleasure resort. Few of these survive intact (two are in the Victoria and Albert Museum, London), but several are known through drawings and engravings; the subjects included children's games, popular festivities, and scenes from plays. Amiable and popular with his fellow artists, Hayman was president of the *Society of Artists, 1766–8, and became a foundation member of the *Royal Academy in 1768; he was appointed librarian in 1771. His best work has a certain *Rococo charm, but there is some justification in Horace *Walpole's comment that his paintings are 'easily distinguishable by the large noses and shambling legs of his figures'.

Hayter, Sir George (*b* London, 17 Dec. 1792; *d* London, 18 Jan. 1871). English historical and portrait painter. The son of a miniaturist, **Charles Hayter** (1761–1835), he studied at the *Royal Academy Schools and in Rome. In 1837 he was appointed portrait and history painter to Queen Victoria, and on the death of *Wilkie in 1841 he was made 'principal painter in ordinary to the queen'. He is known chiefly for his royal portraits and his huge groups (*House of Commons, 1833*, 1833–43, NPG, London), unexciting in their handling, but composed with dexterity and accomplished grandiloquence. In spite of his royal favour he was never a member of the Royal Academy, seemingly because, after an unfortunate early marriage, he lived with a woman who was not his wife.

Hayter, S. W. (Stanley William) (*b* London, 27 Dec. 1901; *d* Paris, 4 May 1988). British printmaker and painter, a descendant of Sir George *Hayter. He spent most of his life in Paris, where in 1927 he founded an experimental workshop for the graphic arts—Atelier 17—that played a central role in the 20th-century revival of the print as an independent art form. (The name was adopted in 1933 when Hayter moved his establishment from its original home to 17 rue Campagne-Première.) In 1940–50 he lived in New York, taking Atelier 17 with him. Hayter was a chemist by training and had an unrivalled knowledge of the technicalities of printmaking, on which he wrote two major books, *New Ways of Gravure* (1949) and *About Prints* (1962). Although his historical importance has long been acknowledged (probably no modern British artist has been so influential internationally), it is only recently that his own work has won him belated recognition as one of the outstanding graphic artists of his time. His prints are varied in technique and style, but most characteristically are influenced by the abstract vein of *Surrealism and are notable for their experiments with texture and colour.

Hazlitt, William (*b* Maidstone, Kent, 10 Apr. 1778; *d* London, 18 Sept. 1830). English critic. He is known mainly for his literary criticism, but he also wrote much on the fine arts and he ranks as the most important British writer on the subject between *Reynolds and *Ruskin. Early in his career he worked briefly as a portrait painter (*Charles Lamb*, 1804, NPG, London), but he lived mainly by journalism, writing for numerous newspapers and journals. He was a *Romantic in outlook, placing more importance on the role of genius in artistic creation than on rules or theories. Thus he admired Reynolds's paintings, but attacked his ideas. A notable feature of Hazlitt's writing is that (unlike most previous art criticism) it was produced for the general reader rather than for the connoisseur or practising artist.

Heade, Martin Johnson. See LUMINISM.

Heaphy, Charles (*b* London, c.1820; *d* Brisbane, 3 Aug. 1881). English painter and colonial official, active mainly in New Zealand. He studied at the *Royal Academy Schools, and in 1839 was appointed draughtsman to the New Zealand Company. For the next three years he travelled through the country, which was largely an unexplored wilderness, and the paintings and sketches he made of it (Alexander Turnbull Lib., Wellington) form a unique visual record. In 1842 he returned to England and in the same year published *Narrative of a Residence in Various Parts of New Zealand*, which was intended to encourage settlers. Soon afterwards he went back to settle there himself. Since a raw colony had no need for professional painters, he abandoned art for a distinguished career as an administrator and politician and for a time as a soldier (in 1867 he was awarded the Victoria Cross for his bravery in the third Maori War, during which he was severely wounded). His father **Thomas Heaphy Sen.** (1775–1835) and his brother **Thomas Jun.** (1813–73) were watercolour painters, and two sisters, **Mary Ann** (Mrs Musgrave) and **Elizabeth** (Mrs Murphy), were miniaturists.

Hearne, Thomas (*b* Marshfield, nr. Bath, 22 Sept. 1744; *d* London, 13 Apr. 1817). English topographical draughtsman and watercolourist, originally trained as an engraver. From 1771 to 1775 he worked in the Leeward Islands as draughtsman to the governor Sir Ralph Payne (later Lord Lavington). After his return to England he concentrated on British scenery and architecture, travelling very widely in connection with *The Antiquities of Great Britain*, for which his drawings were engraved by William Byrne (1743–1805). The engravings were issued from 1778 and bound as a book in 1786, the 52 plates setting a new standard in antiquarian illustration; a second volume, with 32 plates, appeared in 1807. Hearne was a friend of Dr *Monro, who owned many of his drawings; these were copied by Monro's protégés, including the young *Girtin and *Turner.

Heartfield, John (Helmut Herzfelde) (*b* Berlin, 19 June 1891; *d* Berlin, 26 Apr. 1968). German designer, painter, and journalist, a leading light of *Dada in Berlin, best known as one of the pioneers and perhaps the greatest of all exponents of *photomontage. With *Grosz he Anglicized his name during the First World War as a protest against German nationalistic fervour and his finest works are brilliantly satirical attacks—often in the form of book covers and posters—against militarism and Nazism. Harassed by the Nazis he left Germany in 1938 and moved to London, where his work included designs for Penguin Books. He returned to Germany in 1950.

Heath, Adrian (*b* Burma, 23 June 1920; *d* Montmirail, France, 15 Sept. 1992). British abstract painter. In 1949 and 1951 he visited St Ives, where he met Ben *Nicholson, and he formed a link between the *St Ives School and London-based *Constructivists such as Victor *Pasmore and Kenneth and Mary *Martin, with whom he was also associated. During the early 1950s he was an important figure in promoting abstract art—by organizing collective exhibitions at his London studio (at 22 Fitzroy Street) in 1951, 1952, and 1953, and by writing a short popular book on the subject, *Abstract Painting: Its Origin and Meaning* (1953), which begins with the sentence: 'There seems to be little understanding of the values of abstract painting and consequently no general appreciation of its qualities.' Heath's paintings of this time featured large, blocklike slabs of colour, heavily brushed. He also made a few constructions. Later his paintings became freer and more dynamic.

Heckel, Erich (*b* Döbeln, nr. Dresden, 31 July 1883; *d* Radolfzell am Bodensee, 27 Jan. 1970). German painter and graphic artist, one of the founders of Die *Brücke. His work was somewhat more lyrical than that of the other members of the group and he showed a particular concern for depicting sickness and inner anguish. His landscapes, too, sometimes have a decorative quality foreign to most German *Expressionism. During the First World War, when he worked as a medical orderly in Flanders, his work became more melancholic and tragic. After the war, however, his painting lost much of its intensity, with pastel tones replacing the bold, sometimes harsh colours he had earlier used. In 1937 his work was declared *degenerate by the Nazis and in 1944 his Berlin studio was destroyed in an air raid. Heckel then moved to Hemmenhofen on Lake Constance. From 1949 until his retirement in 1955 he taught at the Karlsruhe Academy. Apart from *Kirchner, Heckel was the most prolific printmaker among the Brücke artists, producing more than 400 woodcuts, about 400 lithographs, and nearly 200 etchings, mainly in the period 1903–23.

Heda, Willem Claesz. (*b* Haarlem, *c.*1594; *d* Haarlem, 1680). Dutch still-life painter, active in Haarlem. He and Pieter *Claesz. are the most important representatives of *ontbijt* (breakfast piece) painting in the Netherlands. His overall grey-green or brownish tonalities are very similar to those of Claesz., but Heda's work was usually more highly finished and his taste was more aristocratic. He showed a preference for ham, mincemeat pie, and oysters, and after 1629 never included a herring in his pictures. His son **Gerrit** (*d* before 1702) was his pupil and a close imitator of his style.

Heem, Jan Davidsz. de (*b* Utrecht, Apr. 1606; *d* Antwerp, 1683/4). One of the greatest Dutch still-life painters. He worked mainly in Antwerp, where he settled in about 1635. His early pictures are in the style of Balthasar van der *Ast and he also studied the restrained and simple works of the Haarlem still-life artists *Claesz. and *Heda. In Antwerp, however, he turned to a different idiom, producing splendid flower pieces and large compositions of exquisitely laid tables in the opulent spirit of Flemish *Baroque art. His work formed a link between the Dutch and Flemish still-life traditions and he is claimed by both schools. He came from a large family of painters and his many followers in Flanders and Holland included his sons **Cornelis de Heem** (1631–95) and **Jan Jansz. de Heem** (1650–after 1695).

Heemskerck, Maerten van (*b* Heemskerck, 1498; *d* Haarlem, 1 Oct. 1574). Netherlandish painter and draughtsman, named after his native town and active mainly in nearby Haarlem, where he was the leading artist of the day. The most important part of his training was with Jan van *Scorel in Utrecht, *c.*1527–9. Although Heemskerck was only three years younger than Scorel and was a mature man when he entered his studio (he had already studied with two other teachers), the experience left a distinctive mark on him. In some pictures, particularly portraits, experts still have difficulty differentiating their hands. As a rule, however, Heemskerck's paintings are more crowded and nervous than Scorel's balanced and harmonious compositions. Equally significant for Heemskerck's development was a visit to Italy (1532–6), where he was overwhelmed by *Michelangelo and deeply impressed by the remains of ancient buildings and sculpture, of which he made sensitive drawings (some of them in a sketchbook that is now in the Kupferstichkabinett, Berlin); he later included a view of the Colosseum in the background of his arresting Self-Portrait (1553, Fitzwilliam Mus., Cambridge). After his return to the Netherlands, the impact of Michelangelo (and of the *Laocoön) is clearly seen in such forceful, emotive works as the Crucifixion (1540, Linköping Cathedral). Later his style became more restrained, but sometimes no less eloquent, as in the Lamentation (1566, Prinsenhof Mus., Delft), a work of great pathos. In addition to his paintings, Heemskerck made designs for hundreds of prints, and through these he played a major role in disseminating *Mannerism in northern Europe. See also MAULSTICK.

Heidelberg School. Group of Australian painters who worked together at Heidelberg, Victoria (at the time a village, now a suburb of Melbourne), from 1886 to about 1900. Tom *Roberts (the dominant figure) and Arthur *Streeton were among the members. The work of the group, based on the *Impressionist ideal of painting in the open air, featured local subject matter and was associated with the emergence of a distinctive Australian literature. By 1900 the group had broken up, many of the leading members having gone to Europe, but its vision of Australian life and landscape came to dominate the country's painting in the early 20th century and inspired many other artists in later decades.

Heizer, Michael. See LAND ART.

Held, Al (*b* New York, 12 Oct. 1928). American painter. His early work was in the prevailing *Abstract Expressionist idiom, being particu-

larly influenced by Jackson *Pollock. From about 1960, however, he began to develop a more individual style characterized by clean-edged, bold, brightly coloured geometrical forms. It had affinities with *Hard-Edge Painting, but Held's work was distinguished by his use of very heavily textured paint. He often worked on a huge scale, giving his paintings an extremely forceful physical impact. In 1967 he began making black-and-white paintings, using white linear structures on a black ground or black lines on a white ground to create overlapping and interlocking boxlike forms that demonstrate his interest in Renaissance perspective. In the 1980s he reintroduced colour with a vengeance, as in his 17-m (55-ft) long mural Mantegna's Edge (1983, Southland Center, Dallas), a work of tremendous high-keyed vigour.

Helladic. A term conventionally applied to the culture of the Greek mainland during the Bronze Age, from about 3000 BC to about 1000 BC. Late Helladic is alternatively called *Mycenaean.

Hellenic. An adjective meaning 'Greek' that in non-technical usage is applied to ancient Greek culture in general, but which in archaeological terminology is more specifically applied to the cultures of Greek-speaking societies from the beginning of the Iron Age (late 11th century BC) to about 323 BC (the death of Alexander the Great). It embraces the *Geometric, *Archaic, and *Classical periods. Earlier periods in Greece are 'Prehellenic', or *Helladic, to which *Minoan and *Mycenaean art belong; the subsequent period is called *Hellenistic.

Hellenistic. A term applied to Greek culture in the late 4th to late 1st century BC, conventionally from 323 BC, when Alexander the Great died, to 27 BC, when Augustus became the first Roman emperor. During this period Greece itself had lost its political importance as Rome rose to power, but Greek culture was adopted by diverse peoples in the Mediterranean world and beyond. Hellenistic art is more varied in inspiration than that of the *Classical age which preceded it, and the sculpture of the period is often remarkable for its technical bravura and overt display of emotion, as in the celebrated *Laocoön, the most famous of Hellenistic works of art. After original Greek works of the Classical period became widely known in the course of the 19th century much Hellenistic art was generally dismissed as decadent, but it is now recognized as a rich field of study. J. J. Pollitt writes (*Art in the*

Hellenistic Age, 1986), 'Hellenistic art was not tied to a single country or ethnic group: rather, like Hellenistic culture as a whole, it was adopted and produced by diverse peoples in widely separated geographical areas. Further, it throve in a world where many of the familiar figures of the modern "art world"—private patrons, collectors, and even dealers—made their first appearance. The Hellenistic age also seems to have been the first epoch in western art in which an intense sense of "art history" influenced art itself. Systematic histories of art were first written during the period; artists revived the style of earlier centuries; sculptors' workshops began to specialize in the reproduction of "old masters"; different styles came into simultaneous use. The result of these historical conditions was an art which, like much modern art, was heterogeneous, often cosmopolitan, increasingly individualistic, and frequently elitist in its appeal.'

Helst, Bartholomeus van der (*b* Haarlem, *c.*1613; *bur.* Amsterdam, 16 Dec. 1670). Dutch portrait painter, active in Amsterdam. In the 1640s he took over from *Rembrandt as the most popular portraitist in the city, his detailed, tasteful, and slightly flattering likenesses appealing more to the fashionable burghers than the master's work, which was becoming more individual and introspective. Van der Helst was highly influential during his lifetime. For example, Rembrandt's talented pupils *Bol and *Flinck abandoned the style of their master in order to follow his more popular manner. His reputation endured into the next century and as late as 1781 *Reynolds described his *Banquet of the Amsterdam Civic Guard in Celebration of the Peace of Münster* (1648, Rijksmuseum, Amsterdam) as 'perhaps, the first picture of portraits in the world', adding that it as far exceeded his expectations as Rembrandt's *Night Watch* fell below them.

Hemessen, Jan Sanders van (*b* Hemessen, nr. Antwerp; active 1519–56). Netherlandish painter, active mainly in Antwerp, where he was the outstanding painter between the death of *Massys in 1530 and the emergence of *Bruegel in the 1550s. After visiting Italy early in his career, he was established in Antwerp by 1524 Like his contemporary *Marinus van Reymerswaele he specialized in scenes exposing human vanities and follies, such as greed and loose living (*The Prodigal Son*, 1536, Mus. Royaux, Brussels). The figures in these compositions are muscular and strongly three-dimensional, placed close to the *picture plane. Although the sub-jects are often religious, the pictures typically have a strong feeling of everyday life and they helped to found the Flemish tradition of *genre painting. Hemessen also painted portraits, as did his daughter and pupil **Catharina van Hemessen** (1528–after 1587). See also MAULSTICK.

Hendriks, Wybrand (*b* Amsterdam, 24 June 1744; *d* Haarlem, 28 Jan. 1831). Dutch painter and administrator. His work included landscapes, topographical views, still-lifes, portraits, and *genre scenes, often done in a manner recalling 17th-century Dutch masters. From 1785 to 1819 he was the first curator of the art collections of the Teylers Foundation (now the Teylers Museum) in Haarlem, named after the financier, collector, and philanthropist Pieter Teyler (1702–78); this was the first public museum in the Netherlands (opened 1784). During his time in charge Hendriks made some important additions to the collections; his own work is represented in the city's Frans Hals Museum.

Henri, Robert (*b* Cincinnati, 24 June 1865; *d* New York, 12 July 1929). American painter, teacher, and writer, a major figure in combating conservative attitudes in American art in the early 20th century. From 1886 to 1888 he trained at the Pennsylvania Academy of the Fine Arts, Philadelphia, under Thomas Anshutz (1851–1912), who passed on the tradition of Thomas *Eakins, an artist Henri came to admire deeply. In 1888–91 he lived in Paris, studying mainly at the *Académie Julian. After returning to Philadelphia he became the leader of a circle of young artists—*Glackens, *Luks, *Shinn, *Sloan—that later became the nucleus of The *Eight and the *Ashcan School. In 1895–7 and 1898–1900 he again lived in Paris, then in 1900 settled in New York. There he became an outstanding teacher, first at the New York School of Art, 1902–9, then at his own school, 1909–12, at the Modern School of the Ferrer Center (a radical educational establishment), 1911–18, and finally at the *Art Students League, 1915–28. The essence of his teaching was that art should grow from life, not from theories. He said that he wanted his own paintings to be 'as clear and as simple and sincere as is humanly possible', and he was a powerful force in turning young American painters away from academism to look at the rich subject matter provided by modern urban life; indeed he was 'regarded by many of his contemporaries as the most influential single force affecting the development of American art in the generation preceding the *Armory Show of 1913' (William Innes Homer, *Robert Henri and his Circle*, 1969).

Henri was open-minded about the new developments seen at the Armory Show but he was not interested in experiment for experiment's sake and his own painting was little affected by it. His early work had been *Impressionist, but in the 1890s he adopted a darker palette, with rapid slashing brushwork geared to creating a sense of vitality and immediacy. From 1909 his work became more colourful again. Apart from scenes of urban life, he painted many portraits, and also landscapes and seascapes (which have been rather neglected). He made frequent visits to Europe and found inspiration there for figure studies of picturesque characters—Irish peasants, gypsies, and so on. His paintings are dashing but rather superficial and they are generally regarded as much less important than his teaching and crusading. Henri wrote numerous articles on art and in 1923 published *The Art Spirit*, a collection of his letters, lectures, and aphorisms, in which art is seen as an expression of love for life.

Henry VIII, King of England. See ROYAL COLLECTION.

Henry the Lion. See GOSPELS OF HENRY THE LION.

Hepworth, Dame Barbara (*b* Wakefield, Yorkshire, 10 Jan. 1903; *d* St Ives, Cornwall, 20 May 1975). British sculptor, one of the most important figures in the development of abstract art in Britain. She trained at Leeds School of Art, where she became a friend of Henry *Moore, and at the *Royal College of Art. Her early sculptures were quasi-naturalistic and had much in common with Moore's work (*Doves*, 1927, Manchester AG), but she already showed a tendency to submerge detail in simple forms, and by the early 1930s her work was entirely abstract. At this time she worked in both stone and wood, and she described an important aspect of her early career as being 'the excitement of discovering the nature of carving'. In this preference for *direct carving she was again united with Moore, but whereas his abstractions always remained based on natural forms, hers were often entirely unrepresentational in origin. Yet she consistently professed a *Romantic attitude of emotional affinity with nature, speaking of carving both as a 'biological necessity' and as an 'extension of the telluric forces which mould the landscape'.

From 1925 to 1931 Hepworth was married to the sculptor John Skeaping (1901–80). In 1931 she met Ben *Nicholson, who became her second husband in 1938, and through him she became aware of contemporary European developments. They joined *Abstraction-Création in 1933 and were among the founders of *Unit One in the same year. During the 1930s Hepworth, Nicholson, and Moore worked in close harmony and became recognized as the nucleus of the abstract movement in England. In 1939 Hepworth moved with Nicholson to St Ives in Cornwall and lived there for the rest of her life (see ST IVES SCHOOL). During the late 1930s and 1940s she began to concentrate on the counterplay between mass and space in sculpture. In 1931 in *Pierced Form* (destroyed during the Second World War) she first introduced into England the use of the 'hole', and she now developed this with great subtlety, making play with the relationship between the outside and inside of a figure, the two surfaces sometimes being linked with threaded string, as in *Pelagos* (1956, Tate, London). *Pelagos* also shows her sensitive use of painted surface to contrast with the natural grain of the wood. In all her work she displayed a deep understanding of her materials and superb standards of craftsmanship.

By the 1950s Hepworth had an international reputation and from this time she received many honours and prestigious public commissions, among them the memorial to Dag Hammarskjöld—*Single Form*—at the United Nations in New York (1963). She now worked more in bronze, especially for large pieces, but she always retained a special feeling for direct carving. Occasionally she diversified into other areas, notably with her sets and costumes for the first production of Michael Tippett's opera *The Midsummer Marriage* in 1955.

Hepworth died tragically in a fire at her studio in St Ives, which is now a museum dedicated to her work. Her obituary in the *Guardian* described her as 'probably the most significant woman artist in the history of art to this day'. She was 'small and intense in appearance, deeply reserved in character, and totally dedicated to her art. It was always a measure of surprise that such a frail woman could undertake such demanding physical work, but she had great toughness and integrity' (*DNB*).

Hering, Loy (*b* Kaufbeuren, Bavaria, *c*.1485; *d* Eichstätt, Bavaria, *c*.1555). The most prolific German sculptor of the first half of the 16th century. He trained and spent his early career in Augsburg, then in about 1512 settled in Eichstätt, where he lived for the rest of his life and held several high civic offices. His best-known work is the monument to St Willibald, the first bishop of Eichstätt, in the city's cathedral (c.1512–15). He also produced tomb sculpture, but in his later career he concentrated on small figures and reliefs, sometimes of secular subjects. These are typically in Solnhofen stone, an exceptionally fine limestone that was quarried near Eichstätt. Hering's style shows traces of a late *Gothic heritage and at the same time influence from the Italian *Renaissance (he perhaps visited Italy early in his career); he also often borrowed motifs from *Dürer's prints.

Herkomer, Sir Hubert von (b Waal, Bavaria, 26 May 1849; d Budleigh Salterton, Devon, 31 Mar. 1914). German-born painter, printmaker, designer, teacher, and writer who settled in England in 1857 with his father (a woodcarver) and became a British citizen. He established his reputation with The Last Muster—Sunday at the Royal Hospital, Chelsea (1875, Lady Lever AG, Port Sunlight), a work appealing to the public taste for patriotic sentiment, and then became a successful and prolific portrait painter. His best-known works today, however, are his scenes of social concern, which were then still something of a novelty in English art (On Strike, 1891, Royal Academy, London). Herkomer was a versatile artist and a man of many parts. He composed operas, which were performed at his private theatre at Bushey, Hertfordshire, and as well as performing in them and designing the sets, he experimented with new forms of stage lighting; he also designed sets for the cinema. From 1883 to 1904 he ran his own art school at Bushey (William *Nicholson was one of his pupils) and he lectured widely. His books include the autobiographical My School and my Gospel (1908).

herm. A type of sculpture consisting of an armless *bust or head of a man surmounting a quadrangular shaft that tapers slightly towards the bottom. Herms appear in Greek art from the 6th century BC and in early examples the shaft was usually carved with an erect phallus protruding from it (the name derives from Hermes, who was a fertility deity and the god of roads and boundaries, as well as the messenger of the gods). They were used mainly out of doors, as milestones, signposts, boundary markers, memorials, and so on. Similar sculptures were also made by the Romans; some of them were adorned with representations of Terminus, the god of boundaries, from which the word 'term' derives. Herms and terms are not always precisely distinguished, but the figurative sculpture

on a term can feature the torso and arms, whereas that on a herm is confined to the head or little more. Since the *Renaissance both types have become part of the general vocabulary of decorative art (see SAMBIN).

Hermitage, St Petersburg. Russia's pre-eminent collection of art and antiquities, one of the world's greatest museums. It takes its name from a pleasure pavilion (now known as the Little Hermitage) created in the late 1760s for the Empress Catherine II (Catherine the Great) (1729–96; ruled from 1762) as an extension to the recently built Winter Palace, providing a place to entertain friends and display some of her art treasures ('hermitage' meaning 'place of retreat'). In 1787 Catherine completed another similar extension (now known as the Old Hermitage). Apart from a devotion to antique gems she had little personal enthusiasm for art, but she bought voraciously for the sake of prestige and at her death the imperial collections contained about 4,000 pictures (including works from the *Crozat and *Walpole collections), as well as many other treasures. In 1837 the Winter Palace was ravaged by fire, but the Little and Old Hermitages were saved. The palace was extensively reconstructed in sumptuous style and Nicholas I added a custom-built museum, designed by the German architect Leo von Klenze. This building, known as the New Hermitage, was opened to the public in 1852. After the 1917 Revolution the imperial collections were nationalized and the whole vast palace complex was gradually turned into a museum, known as the State Hermitage.

In the 1930s the Soviet government sold numerous works from the museum, including celebrated masterpieces, to raise foreign currency; Calouste *Gulbenkian and Andrew *Mellon were among the major purchasers. In spite of these losses, the Hermitage's collection of Western painting is rich in virtually every period and school, perhaps most notably in 17th-century Dutch and Flemish painting and in French painting of the late 19th and early 20th centuries (almost all the great figures of *Impressionism and *Post-Impressionism are well represented). Many of the French paintings come from the collections of two Moscow businessmen who were among the outstanding collectors and patrons of their time: Ivan Morozov (1871–1921) and Sergei Shchukin (1851–1936). They commissioned new works as well as buying through dealers. *Matisse was a particular favourite of both men, and Shchukin's interest also extended to *Cubism. After the Revolution their collections were nationalized and later distributed between the Hermitage and the Pushkin Museum in Moscow. Although primarily famous for its paintings, the Hermitage includes much else, notably extensive collections of central Asian and oriental art.

Hernández, Gregorio. See FERNÁNDEZ.

Heron, Patrick (b Leeds, 30 Jan. 1920; d St Ives, 20 Mar. 1999). British painter, writer, and designer. His early paintings were influenced by *Braque and *Matisse, but in 1956 he turned to abstraction; in the same year he settled in Cornwall, becoming a member of the *St Ives School. His abstracts were varied, including stripe paintings—vertical and horizontal—as well as looser types with soft-edged shapes, but all his work is notable for its vibrancy of colour. He wrote several books, including *The Changing Forms of Art* (1955), *The Shape of Colour* (1973), and studies of *Vlaminck (1947), *Hitchens (1955), and Braque (1958).

Herrera, Francisco the Elder (b Seville, c.1590; d Madrid, 29 Sept. 1654). Spanish painter and engraver, a representative of the transition from *Mannerism to *Baroque. He spent most of his career in his native Seville and with his older contemporary *Roelas, under whose influence he developed, he helped to prepare the way for the naturalistic style characteristic of the following generation of painters in the city. *St Basil Dictating his Rule* (c.1639, Louvre, Paris), which is generally considered his masterpiece, shows his work at its most bold and vigorous. In about 1650 Herrera moved to Madrid. According to *Palomino, he was a 'harsh and ill-tempered man' whose pupils never stayed with him very long. *Velázquez is said to have been one of these short-lived pupils, as was his son **Francisco Herrera the Younger** (bapt. Seville, 28 June 1627; bur. Madrid, 25 Aug. 1685), a painter and architect. After fleeing from home, he evidently spent several years in Italy, although there is no documentary evidence for his visit. He worked for several years in Seville but mainly in Madrid, where he was appointed a royal painter to Charles II (see HABSBURG) in 1672 and royal architect in 1677. His greatest achievement was the design (subsequently modified) of the church of El Pilar at Saragossa, begun in 1681. His work as a painter, airy and colourful, owed much to the example of Murillo.

Herring, John Frederick Sen. (b Surrey, 1795; d Meopham, Kent, 23 Sept. 1865). British painter, the best-known member of a family of sporting and animal artists. He had great success as a painter of racehorses, regularly doing portraits of the winners of the Derby and St Leger, and his work enjoyed wide popularity in engravings. His three painter sons included **John Frederick Jun.** (d 1907), and he also had a painter brother, **Benjamin Herring Sen.** (1806–30). It is often not easy to distinguish between the work of the various members of the family.

Hesse, Eva (b Hamburg, 11 Jan. 1936; d New York, 29 May 1970). German-born American sculptor. Her family fled the Nazis, settling in New York in 1939, and she became a US citizen in 1945. She studied at various art schools in New York, then at Yale University under Josef *Albers, graduating in 1959. She did not take up sculpture until 1964, so her career lasted only six years, before her early death from a brain tumour. However, in that time she gained a high reputation as an exponent of 'Eccentric Abstraction' (the title of an exhibition in which her work was included at the Fischbach Gallery, New York, in 1966, organized by her friend the art critic Lucy Lippard (1937–), who is particularly known for her writings on *Conceptual art and *Feminist art). Hesse is sometimes described as a *Minimalist, but her work was too restlessly experimental to fit neatly into any category. It often shared with Minimal art the use of repeated units and severely limited colour, but she made inventive use of materials (including fibreglass, wood, wire, various fabrics, and rubber tubing), and her work is far from the emotional reserve associated with Minimalism; her forms are often organic and sexually suggestive.

Heyden, Jan van der (b Gorinchem, 5 Mar. 1637; d Amsterdam, 28 Mar. 1712). Dutch painter, draughtsman, printmaker, and inventor, active in Amsterdam. He painted some landscapes and still-lifes, but is renowned mainly as one of the greatest of all townscape painters. His views of Amsterdam and other towns are done with loving attention to detail, with precise rendering of foliage, bricks, and architectural detail. However, this treatment never appears dull or dry, for the detail is underpinned by dignified composition and his handling of colour and light is highly attractive. In spite of the seemingly objective nature of his work, van der Heyden often took liberties with topographical accuracy and he also painted *capricci. Painting was only a part of his activity, for he was also involved in civic administration in Amsterdam. In 1669 it became the first European city to enjoy street lighting when it adopted the oil lamps he proposed. The fire hose is also said to have been his invention and features in his *Brandspuiten-boek* ('Fire Engine Book', 1690), which is illustrated with plates from his own drawings, some of which he etched and engraved himself. His varied activities made him a wealthy man.

Heysen, Sir Hans (*b* Hamburg, 8 Oct. 1877; *d* Hahndorf, nr. Adelaide, 2 July 1968). German-born Australian landscape painter in oils and watercolour. His family emigrated to Australia when he was 6 and he worked mainly in or near Adelaide. Robert *Hughes (*The Art of Australia*, 1970) writes: 'Heysen's large body of work was immensely popular; it has most of the textbook virtues and, for many years, no Australian business firm was considered quite solid unless it had a Heysen in its boardroom . . . The only deficiency of his art is that it has no imagination . . . He was, in fact, the Alfred *Munnings of the gum-tree.' His work is represented in all Australian state galleries and many provincial galleries.

Hiberno-Saxon art. See INSULAR ART.

Hicks, Edward (*b* Attleboro [now Langhorne], Bucks County, Pa., 4 Apr. 1780; *d* Newtown, Bucks County, 23 Aug. 1849). The best-known American *naive painter of the 19th century, active in Bucks County, Pennsylvania. He was a coach and sign painter early in life, but for many years he devoted himself to preaching—the pleasure he derived from painting conflicted with his austere Quaker outlook and caused him much conscience searching. Some of his pictures are farm scenes or landscapes, but he is best known for his many versions (he reputedly made more than 100) of *The Peaceable Kingdom*. Exemplifying the pacifism of the Quaker society in which he lived, they depict with a vivid and charming literalness the prophecy in the eleventh chapter of Isaiah that all men and beasts will live in peace. His cousin **Thomas Hicks** (1823–90) was also a painter, mainly of portraits.

Highmore, Joseph (*b* London, 13 June 1692; *d* Canterbury, 3 Mar. 1780). English painter (mainly of portraits) and writer. He studied at *Kneller's Academy and had a considerable practice as a portraitist by the 1720s. His early work is in the manner of Jonathan *Richardson, but from the 1730s his portraits became more elegant as he responded to the *Rococo influences that began to pervade English painting at this time. Some of his more informal works, however, have a dir-

ectness and freshness that recall *Hogarth (*Mr Oldham and Friends*, c.1750, Tate, London). Highmore was a friend of the novelist Samuel Richardson and in 1743–4 painted a series of twelve illustrations to his *Pamela* (Tate; Fitzwilliam Mus., Cambridge; NG of Victoria, Melbourne) which link him with *Hayman and Hogarth as one of the initiators of a British school of narrative painting. He also painted several portraits of Richardson (two are in the NPG, London). In 1762 he gave up painting and retired to Canterbury to devote himself to writing, including much on artistic topics.

Hildebrand, Adolf von (*b* Marburg, 6 Oct. 1847; *d* Munich, 18 Jan. 1921). German sculptor and writer on art. He spent much of his career in Italy and is regarded as one of the main upholders in his period of the classical tradition in sculpture. His most characteristic works were nude figures—timeless and rather austere, in the high-minded tradition of Greek art—although he also made several large monuments, including a statue of Johannes Brahms in Meiningen (1898). He is now, however, better known for his treatise *Das Problem der Form in der bildenden Kunst* (1893) than for his highly accomplished but rather bland sculpture. The book went through many editions (an English translation, *The Problem of Form in Painting and Sculpture*, was published in 1907) and it was influential in promoting a move against surface naturalism in sculpture.

Hill, Carl Fredrik (*b* Lund, 31 May 1849; *d* Lund, 22 Feb. 1911). Swedish painter and draughtsman. In 1873 he moved to France, where he was strongly influenced by *Corot and other contemporary French landscape painters (for a time he lived at *Barbizon). His work showed great promise (indeed he is regarded as the finest Swedish landscape painter of his time), but in 1878 his public career was ended by mental illness. After a period of hospitalization in Paris, he returned to Sweden and was cared for in his parents' home. There he produced thousands of drawings of imaginary subjects, including apocalyptic visions. Many of these drawings are in the Malmö Museum and the Nationalmuseum, Stockholm.

Hilliard, Nicholas (*b* Exeter, c.1547; *bur.* London, 7 Jan. 1619). English *miniaturist, the most celebrated of all practitioners of his art and a central figure in establishing the portrait miniature as a distinctive genre in Britain. He was the son of an Exeter goldsmith and himself trained in this craft, completing a seven-year apprenticeship in London in 1569. It is not known how he learnt miniature painting, but his first surviving examples were done when he was only 13. By 1572 he was working for Elizabeth I (his earliest portrait of her, dating from that year, is in the NPG, London). Later he also worked for James I, but after the turn of the century his position as the leading miniaturist in the country was challenged by his former pupil Isaac *Oliver; these two were head and shoulders above their contemporaries. Although he won great prestige through his work, Hilliard sometimes experienced financial problems (in 1617 he was briefly imprisoned for debt); his perfectionist approach limited his output and he is known to have lost money in a venture to find gold in Scotland.

In about 1600 Hilliard wrote a treatise entitled *The Arte of *Limning* (not published until 1912), which gives fascinating insights into his technical and aesthetic approach (see LIBERAL ARTS). He stressed the importance of a calm and clean working environment, for example, even cautioning the artist to ensure that no dandruff fell on his tiny picture. Stylistically he declared himself a follower of the tradition of *Holbein. In particular he avoided the use of shadow for modelling and he records that this was in agreement with Queen Elizabeth's taste—'for the lyne without shadows showeth all to good jugment, but the shadowe without lyne showeth nothing'. But whereas for Holbein a miniature was always a painting reduced to a small scale, Hilliard developed in the miniature an intimacy and subtlety peculiar to the art. He combined his unerring use of line with a jeweller's exquisiteness in detail, an engraver's elegance in calligraphy, and a unique realization of the individuality of each sitter. His portraits are often freighted with enigmatic inscription and allegory (e.g. a hand reaching from a cloud), but this usually heightens the vividness with which the sitter's face is impressed. Apart from the queen herself, many other great Elizabethans sat for him, including Sir Francis Drake, Sir Walter Raleigh, and Sir Philip Sidney. The best collection of his miniatures is in the Victoria and Albert Museum, including the celebrated *Young Man Leaning on a Tree among Roses* (c.1587). Hilliard is known also to have worked on a large scale and among the paintings attributed to him are portraits of Elizabeth I in the National Portrait Gallery, London, and the Walker Art Gallery, Liverpool. His son **Laurence** (c.1582–1647/8) was also a miniaturist.

Hillier, Tristram (b Peking [Beijing], 11 Apr. 1905; d Bristol, 18 Jan. 1983). British painter of landscape, still-life, and occasional religious subjects. During the 1930s he lived mainly in the south of France, with visits to Spain, which he 'came to love above all other countries' (he also kept contacts with the London art world, however, and in 1933 was a member of *Unit One). In the Second World War he served in the Royal Naval Volunteer Reserve, 1940–4, and then settled in Somerset, where he often painted agricultural subjects. He continued to travel regularly, spending much time in Spain and Portugal. Early in his career Hillier was influenced by a variety of modern idioms, and his work (which included abstracts) showed little individuality. In the mid-1930s, however, he evolved a distinctive style to which he remained faithful for most of his life; he painted with great sharpness of definition and smoothness of finish, creating scenes of stillness and calm that evoke an air of *Surrealist strangeness and otherworldliness through the juxtaposition of incongruous objects and the use of unreal perspectives. He came to regard himself as 'the slave of my own style', but in some of his later work he used freer brushwork or applied paint with a palette knife. In 1954 he published an autobiography, *Leda and the Goose*.

Hilton, Roger (b Northwood, Middlesex [now in Greater London], 23 Mar. 1911; d Botallack, Cornwall, 23 Feb. 1975). British painter of German extraction (Aby *Warburg was his father's cousin). He trained at the *Slade School, and in the 1930s also studied in Paris under *Bissière. In 1950 he began painting abstracts; initially he was influenced by developments in Paris (to which he regularly returned), but on a visit to the Netherlands in 1953 he was inspired more by *Mondrian. From 1955 he reintroduced a sense of a shallow pictorial space, and from 1956, when he began making visits to St Ives (see ST IVES SCHOOL), there are suggestions of beaches, boats, rocks, and water in his work. In 1961 he returned to overt figuration with a series of exuberant, jokey female nudes. These dismayed some of his admirers, who regarded him as a standard-bearer for abstraction, but they were now among his most popular works (*Oi yoi yoi*, 1963, Tate, London). For the last few years of his life he was bedridden with a muscular disease, but his ill health was belied in the series of colourful, good-humoured gouaches he did in this period. He won numerous awards, including the Unesco prize at the 1964 Venice *Biennale.

Hiltunen, Eila (*b* Sortavala, Karelia [now in Russia], 1922). Finnish sculptor. She began her career working in a naturalistic style and made her name as a sculptor of war memorials, of which the one at Simpele is considered the best. In the 1940s and 1950s she also did portrait busts of distinguished Finns. She worked in bronze, marble, and granite, but in the late 1950s she discovered the technique of welding and concentrated on this after meeting *Archipenko during a visit to the USA in 1958. Initially her welded pieces were figurative, but she then turned to abstraction, as in her most famous work, the Sibelius Monument (1967) in Sibelius Park, Helsinki. This consists of a nest of polished steel tubes that have been likened both to organ pipes and to the pine trunks of the Finnish forests.

Hippolite, Hector. See HYPPOLITE.

Hiroshige, Ando. See UKIYO-E.

Hirschvogel, Augustin (*b* Nuremberg, *c*.1503; *d* Vienna, 1553). German glass painter, etcher, cartographer, and mathematician, the best-known member of a family of artists. He began his career in the family stained-glass workshop, the most important in Nuremberg. However, the Reformation (which was accepted in Nuremberg in 1525) badly affected the market for church art and Hirschvogel branched out into other fields. From 1536 to 1543 he worked in Ljubljana and during this period he emerged as a leading cartographer, notably with a large map of Austria (1542) for the *Habsburg Emperor Ferdinand I. In 1544 he settled in Vienna, where he was employed by the civic authorities to make accurate views and plans of the city and to help design new fortifications (following the Turkish siege of 1543). In this work he used surveying methods of his own devising. During this last period of his life Hirschvogel also made numerous etchings, notably of landscapes—works that give him a place among the minor masters of the *Danube School.

Hirshfield, Morris. See JANIS.

Hirst, Damien (*b* Bristol, 7 June 1965). British sculptor, painter, designer, and entrepreneur, whose flair for self-publicity has helped him become the most famous and controversial British artist of his generation. Whilst still a student at Goldsmiths College, London, he made a name for himself by organizing an exhibition of student work ('Freeze', 1988) and persuading leading dealers and critics to come and see it. From his youth he had a fascination with death,

and his most famous work is *The Physical Impossibility of Death in the Mind of Someone Living* (1991, Saatchi Gal., London), consisting of a dead tiger-shark balanced and weighted so that it floats in preserving fluid in a large tank made of glass and steel. In 1995 he was awarded the *Turner Prize. The work he showed at the exhibition of shortlisted candidates' work at the Tate Gallery was *Mother and Child Divided*, consisting of four tanks each containing half of a cow or calf bisected lengthways. According to the accompanying catalogue, 'Hirst strips the closest of bonds between living creatures to its starkest reality', but many people hated the work, and a letter to *The Times* suggested that the Tate authorities must be suffering from mad cow disease. Hirst himself said, 'It's amazing what you can do with an E in A Level art, a twisted imagination and a chainsaw.' His other works include paintings consisting of rows of coloured spots and circular pictures made by dripping paint on a spinning canvas. See also YOUNG BRITISH ARTISTS.

Hispano-Flemish style. A term applied to the main trend in Spanish (especially Castilian) painting of the second half of the 15th century and the early 16th century, in which influence from Flanders (with which Spain had strong trading links), particularly a new naturalism of detail made possible by the adoption of oil paint, was combined with the intense religious sentiment typical of Spanish art. At the beginning of the Hispano-Flemish tradition stands the *Virgin of the Councillors* (1445, Barcelona Mus.) by Luis *Dalmau, who visited Flanders in 1431. The most celebrated exponent of the style is Bartolomé *Bermejo; the standard book on him (by Eric Young, 1975) is subtitled *The Great Hispano-Flemish Master*.

historiated initial. In an illuminated manuscript, an enlarged initial letter incorporating a narrative scene illustrating the text. *Capitals containing narrative scenes are sometimes also described as historiated. See also INHABITED INITIAL.

history painting. A term applied to pictures showing figures involved in momentous or morally edifying scenes, treated in a suitably grand and noble way. The term derives from the Italian *istoria* ('story') and is applied not only to pictures representing actual historical events but also to appropriate subjects from legend and literature. Thus scenes from the Bible, Greek mythology, Dante, or Shakespeare would usually come under the heading 'history painting', whereas scenes drawn from a domestic novel might be considered as *genre pictures, even if set in a period before the painter's own. In conventional academic theory, history painting was considered the highest branch of art, to which the *Grand Manner was appropriate. Its status derived not only from its elevated aims, but also from the fact that it was considered the most difficult branch of painting to master, involving the skilful arrangement of figures with convincing gestures and expressions. The American painters *West and *Copley were pioneers in painting history pictures in modern dress.

Hitchens, Ivon (b London, 3 Mar. 1893; d Lavington Common, nr. Petworth, Sussex, 29 Aug. 1979). British painter, mainly of landscapes. He created a highly distinctive style on the borderline between abstraction and figuration in which broad, fluid areas of vibrant colour, typically on a canvas of wide format, evoke but do not represent the forms of the English countryside that were his main inspiration. From 1940, after his London studio was destroyed by bombing, he lived in Sussex. By this time his characteristic manner was fully developed and subsequently his work altered little, apart from the fact that his palette changed from naturalistic browns and greens to much more vivid colours such as bright yellows and purples. Contrary to what often happens when an artist remains constant in one style over a period of decades, Hitchens's work did not become stereotyped or banal. In addition to landscapes, he painted flowers and figure subjects (usually nudes) and he did several large murals, for example at Nuffield College, Oxford (1959), and the University of Sussex (1963). His work is represented in many public collections. His son **John Hitchens** (1940–) is also a painter, mainly of landscapes and flower pieces.

Hlebine School. See GENERALIĆ.

Hoare, William (b Eye, Suffolk, c.1707; d Bath, 12 Dec. 1792). English portrait painter. He spent the formative years of his career in Italy (1728–37), but his style is a continuation of *Richardson's. By 1738 he had settled in Bath, and until the arrival of *Gainsborough in 1759 he was the leading portrait painter there. Sir Ellis *Waterhouse has described his style as 'serious, but a little blank'. He worked much in *pastel, and in this was followed by his daughter **Mary** (c.1753–1820), also a portraitist.

Hobbema, Meindert (bapt. Amsterdam, 31 Oct. 1638; d Amsterdam, 7 Dec. 1709). Dutch landscape painter, active in Amsterdam, where he was the friend and only documented pupil of Jacob van *Ruisdael. Some of his pictures are very like Ruisdael's, but Hobbema was brighter in temperament and narrower in range, painting favourite subjects—particularly watermills and trees around a pool—over and over again. In 1668 he began working for Amsterdam customs and excise, supervising the weighing and measuring of imported wine, and thereafter seems to have painted only in his spare time. However, his most famous work, *The Avenue at Middelharnis* (NG, London), dates from 1689; it is considered the swansong of the great age of Dutch landscape. Hobbema has long been a popular artist in England (his influence is clear in *Gainsborough's early landscapes) and he is outstandingly well represented in English collections.

Höch, Hannah. See PHOTOMONTAGE.

Hockney, David (b Bradford, 9 July 1937). British painter, draughtsman, printmaker, photographer, designer, and writer, active mainly in the USA. After a brilliant prize-winning career as a student at the *Royal College of Art, Hockney had achieved considerable success by the time he was in his mid-twenties, and he has since consolidated his position as by far the best-known and most critically acclaimed British artist of his generation. His phenomenal success has been based not only on the flair and versatility of his work, but also on his colourful personality, which has made him a recognizable figure even to people not particularly interested in art. In 1961 he emerged as one of the leaders of British *Pop art at the *Young Contemporaries exhibition. Hockney himself disliked the label 'Pop', but his work of this time makes many references to popular culture (notably in the use of graffiti-like lettering) and is often jokey in mood. His first retrospective exhibition came as early as 1970, at the Whitechapel Art Gallery, London (it subsequently toured to Hanover, Rotterdam, and Belgrade). By this time he was painting in a weightier, more traditionally representational manner, in which he did a series of large double portraits of friends, including the well-known *Mr and Mrs Clark and Percy* (1970–1, Tate, London). These portraits are notable for their airy feeling of space and light and the subtle flattening and simplification of forms, as well as for the sense of stylish living they capture. Hockney often paints the people and places he knows best (his art is frequently autobiographical) and has memorably celebrated his romance with Los Angeles (he first visited the city in 1963 and settled there in 1976), particularly in his many paintings featuring swimming pools (*A Bigger Splash*, 1967, Tate, London). In these works he skilfully exploited the qualities of the new *acrylic paint.

Hockney has also been outstanding as a graphic artist; his work in this field includes etched illustrations to Cavafy's *Poems* (1967) and *Six Fairy Tales of the Brothers Grimm* (1969), as well as many individual prints, often on homo-erotic themes. From the 1970s he has also worked a good deal as a stage designer, his first notable successes being his set and costume designs for Stravinsky's *The Rake's Progress* and Mozart's *The Magic Flute*, produced by Glynde-bourne Festival Opera in 1975 and 1978 respectively. The broader style demanded by stage design has been reflected in his subsequent easel paintings. In the 1980s he experimented a good deal with photography, producing, for example, photographic collages and—since 1986—prints created on a photocopier. Hockney is a perceptive commentator on art and has published several books on his own life and work, as well as *Secret Knowledge: Rediscovering the Lost Techniques of the Old Masters* (2001), in which he argues that the use of optical aids such as the *camera lucida and *camera obscura has been much more common in European art than previously thought.

Hodges, William (b London, 28 Oct. 1744; d Brixham, Devon, 6 Mar. 1797). English painter, mainly of landscapes. He was the pupil and assistant of Richard *Wilson 1758–65 and became a skilful imitator of his style. His work took on a more personal character when he travelled as draughtsman with Captain James Cook on his second voyage to the South Pacific in 1772–5, and his finest paintings are those based on drawings he made of such exotic places as Tahiti and Easter Island (examples are in the National Maritime Museum, London). In 1779–84 he worked in India (where he earned a good deal of money) and in 1790 he visited the Continent, going as far as Russia. He did pictures for *Boydell's Shakespeare Gallery and also some allegorical subjects, but in 1795 he abandoned painting and opened a bank in Dartmouth. It failed shortly before he died.

Hodgkin, Sir Howard (b London, 6 Aug. 1932). British painter and printmaker, regarded as one of the outstanding colourists in contemporary art. His paintings, which are usually fairly small, sometimes look completely abstract, but in fact he bases his work on specific events,

usually an encounter between people. He has travelled widely, making several visits to India, and his preference for flat colours and decorative borders reflects his admiration for Indian miniatures. A well-known figure in the art world, he has been a trustee of the Tate Gallery and the National Gallery, and in 1985 he was awarded the *Turner Prize. He was knighted in 1992.

Hodgkins, Frances (b Dunedin, 28 Apr. 1869; d Herrison House psychiatric hospital, nr. Dorchester, 13 May 1947). New Zealand painter, active mainly in England, where she settled in 1914 after some time alternating between the two hemispheres. She was the daughter of **William Matthew Hodgkins** (1833–98), a barrister and amateur painter who had emigrated from England in 1859 and became a leading figure in the artistic life of Dunedin. Her father taught her watercolour painting, but she did not begin to paint in oils until 1915. Until that time her work had been conventional, but she gradually developed a more individual style, echoing *Matisse and *Dufy in its use of vibrant colour (she spent a good deal of time in France). She mainly painted landscapes and still-lifes. Her later paintings approach abstraction in a manner akin to *Hitchens's work.

Hodler, Ferdinand (b Berne, 14 Mar. 1853; d Geneva, 19 May 1918). Swiss painter, active mainly in Geneva. He ranks alongside *Böcklin as the outstanding Swiss artist of his time, but his early work was rather unimaginatively naturalistic, his landscapes amounting to ambitious colour postcards for tourists. However, in 1890, with his brooding *Night* (Kunstmuseum, Berne), Hodler began a sudden change of style. This picture, depicting a black-shrouded, phantom-like presence amid a number of semi-naked sleeping figures, set the pattern for his most characteristic works—allegories featuring stately groups of flat, stylized figures composed into a rhythmic and repetitive pattern of lines, forms, and colours. Often the same basic figure is repeated throughout the picture with only slight variations. Hodler called his method 'Parallelism'; he used the same principles in scenes from Swiss history and landscapes. By the turn of the century he had become immensely popular throughout the German-speaking world and in 1904 a group of 31 of his paintings was the main attraction at the Vienna *Sezession's international exhibition. In the last decade of his life he returned more to landscape painting. As well as being a major figure of Symbolism and *Art

Nouveau, Hodler has been seen as one of the harbingers of *Expressionism.

Hofer, Karl (*b* Karlsruhe, 11 Oct. 1878; *d* Berlin, 3 Apr. 1955). German painter. Early in his career he lived in Rome (1903–8) and Paris (1908–13) and also visited India. Thereafter he lived mainly in Berlin, where he taught at the Hochschule für Bildende Künste. He achieved considerable success and his reputation spread outside Germany, but in 1933 his work was declared *degenerate by the Nazis and he was removed from his teaching post. His studio and much of his work were destroyed by bombing in 1943. At the end of the Second World War he was reinstated at the Hochschule and appointed its director. He wrote several theoretical works on art and also an autobiography, *Aus Leben und Kunst* (Life and Art), published in 1952. In this book he said that 'One must have the courage to be unmodern', and although his subjects were taken from modern life, he rejected the *Expressionism that was the dominant force in German art of his time. Except for a brief experiment with abstract painting in 1930–1, he concentrated on a small range of obsessively recurrent images, through which he expressed a dark and disillusioned vision of the world. His most typical works portray brooding figures, singly or in couples, but he also did portraits, landscapes, and large figure compositions. The simplicity and strength of design of his compositions reflect his lasting admiration for *Cézanne, but their cool, chalky colours are distinctive.

Hofmann, Hans (*b* Weissenberg, Bavaria, 21 Mar. 1880; *d* New York, 17 Feb. 1966). German-born painter and teacher who became an American citizen in 1941. From 1904 to 1914 he lived in Paris, where he knew many of the leading figures of *Fauvism, *Cubism, and *Orphism. In 1915 he founded his own art school in Munich and taught there successfully until 1932, when he emigrated to the USA (following visits in 1930 and 1931, during which he taught at the university of California, Berkeley). He founded the Hans Hofmann School of Fine Arts in New York in 1934 (followed the next year by a summer school at Provincetown, Massachusetts) and became a teacher of great influence on the minority group of American artists who practised abstract painting during the 1930s. Hofmann continued teaching until 1958, when he closed his schools so that he could concentrate on his own painting. This was to counter opinions that he was merely an academic figure and a symbol of the avant-garde rather than a significant creative artist himself. In the course of his career he experimented with many styles, and was a pioneer of the technique of dribbling and pouring paint that was later particularly associated with Jackson *Pollock. His later works, in contrast, feature rectangular blocks of fairly solid colour against a more broken background. As a painter and teacher he was an important influence on the development of *Abstract Expressionism. The essence of his approach was that the picture surface had an intense life of its own.

Hofstede de Groot, Cornelis (*b* Dwingeloo, 9 Nov. 1863; *d* The Hague, 14 Apr. 1930). Dutch art historian, author of the monumental catalogue *Beschreibendes und kritisches Verzeichnis der Werke der hervorragendsten holländischen Maler des XVII Jahrhunderts* (10 vols., 1907–28). An English edition of volumes i–viii appeared in 1908–27, entitled *A Catalogue Raisonné of the Works of the Most Eminent Dutch Painters of the Seventeenth Century*. Covering the work of 40 of the leading painters of the period, the catalogue has been superseded in some areas, but is still regarded as a major source of information and its numbering system is frequently referred to. Hofstede de Groot also published the first complete catalogue of *Rembrandt's drawings (1906) and he wrote numerous articles for *Thieme–Becker. With *Bode and *Bredius he ranks as one of the founders of the modern study of 17th-century Dutch art.

Hogarth, William (*b* London, 10 Nov. 1697; *d* London, 25/26 Oct. 1764). English painter and engraver, the outstanding British artist of his period. During his childhood, his father, a schoolteacher, was imprisoned for debt, and this early experience of the seamy side of life left a deep mark on Hogarth (much of his output is concerned with the contrast between success and failure, and he depicted prisons in several works). He trained as an engraver of silver plate and by 1720 had set up his own business in London, doing various kinds of commercial work. In his spare time he studied painting, first at the *St Martin's Lane Academy and later under Sir James *Thornhill, whose daughter he married in 1729.

By the early 1730s Hogarth had achieved some success as a painter of *conversation pieces and at about the same time he invented the idea of using a sequence of anecdotal pictures 'similar to representations on the stage' to point a moral and satirize social abuses. *A Harlot's Progress* (six scenes, *c*.1731; destroyed by fire) was followed by *A Rake's Progress* (eight scenes, *c*.1735, Soane

Mus., London), and *Marriage à la Mode* (six scenes, c.1743, NG, London), each of them unfolding a cautionary tale of vanity, corruption, and betrayal leading to decline and death. Hogarth produced all three series with a view to engraving them, and the prints had a wide sale and were popular with all classes. They were indeed so successful that unauthorized copies were marketed and Hogarth's campaigning against the profiteers led to the Engravers' Copyright Act of 1735, which made such copies illegal. In addition to engravings based on his paintings, he produced many independent prints, among them *Industry and Idleness* (twelve scenes, 1747), *Beer Street* and *Gin Lane* (1751), and *The Four Stages of Cruelty* (four scenes, 1751). There is a good deal of witty observation in his work, but he could also be brutally direct when he was moved by undeserved suffering: *The Four Stages of Cruelty* 'were done in the hopes of preventing that cruel treatment of poor animals which makes the streets of London more disagreeable to the human mind than anything whatever'.

Hogarth wrote of his 'modern moral subjects' that 'I have endeavoured to treat my subjects as a dramatic writer: my picture is my stage, and men and women my players.' However, he was much more than a preacher in paint. His satire was directed at pedantry and affectation as well as at immorality, and he saw himself to some extent as a defender of native common sense against a fashion for French and Italian mannerisms. In spite of his xenophobia, he made some attempts to show he could paint in the Italian *Grand Manner, including a huge altarpiece for St Mary Redcliffe, Bristol (1755–6, now City AG, Bristol). These, however, are generally considered his weakest works, and apart from his morality subjects he excelled mainly in portraiture. *Captain Thomas Coram* (1740, Foundling Mus., London), which he regarded as his highest achievement in this field, shows that he could paint a portrait in the *Baroque manner with complete confidence and vivid characterization. However, wealthy clients generally preferred bland flattery to Hogarth's robust directness, so he was not financially successful as a portraitist. His other ventures included establishing an academy in St Martin's Lane in 1735 (a successor to the one at which he had studied), and this became an important forerunner of the *Royal Academy. In 1753 he published *The Analysis of Beauty*, a treatise on aesthetic theory written with the conviction that the views of a practising artist should carry greater weight than the theories of the connoisseur or dilettante. It

reveals him as an original if somewhat muddled thinker.

Hogarth was far and away the most important British artist of his generation. He was equally outstanding as a painter and engraver, and by the force of his pugnacious personality as well as by the quality and originality of his work he freed British art from its domination by foreign artists. Moreover, he gave a focus to this newly emerging national spirit in art by persuading his fellow artists—including Francis *Hayman, Thomas *Hudson, Allan *Ramsay, Samuel *Scott, and Richard *Wilson—to present examples of their work to London's famous Foundling Hospital (established in 1739 by his friend Thomas Coram), where they could be seen by the public; in effect, if not in name, it was Britain's first public art gallery. Because so much of his own work has a 'literary' element, Hogarth's qualities as a painter have often been overlooked, but his more informal pictures in particular show that his brushwork could live up to his inventive genius. The vigour and spontaneity of *The Shrimp Girl* (c.1740, NG, London), for example, have made it deservedly one of the most popular British paintings of the 18th century.

Hokusai, Katsushika. See UKIYO-E.

Holanda (or **Hollanda**), **Francisco de** (*b* Lisbon, 1517; *d* Lisbon, 19 June 1584). Portuguese draughtsman, miniaturist, painter, architect, and writer on art, the son of a Netherlandish miniaturist, **Antonio de Holanda** (*d* 1557), who spent part of his career in Lisbon. In 1538–40 Francisco visited Italy, where he produced a volume of drawings (now in the Escorial, near Madrid) documenting various sights he saw there, including fortifications and antiquities. Although he became court painter in Lisbon, his influence in propagating the Italianate style in Portugal was exercised mainly through his writings. In 1548 he completed a manuscript entitled *Da pintura antigua* (Of Ancient Painting); this was the first treatise on painting written in the Iberian peninsula, but it was not published until 1890–6. It contains four dialogues (English translation 1928) in which Holanda purportedly discusses theories of art with *Michelangelo, the miniaturist Giulio *Clovio, and others. As an appendage Holanda completed in 1549 ten dialogues entitled *Do tirar polo natural* (On Drawing from Nature).

Holbein, Hans (*b* Augsburg, ?1497; *d* London, Oct./Nov. 1543). German painter and designer, chiefly celebrated as one of the greatest of all portraitists. He trained in his native Augsburg with his father **Hans Holbein the Elder** (c.1465–1534), one of the leading artists of the day there; another son, **Ambrosius** (c.1494–?c.1519), was also a painter but evidently died young. By 1515 the brothers had moved to Basle. There Hans quickly found employment as a designer for printers, and in 1516 he painted portraits of Jacob Meyer, mayor of the city, and his wife (Kunstmuseum, Basle). From 1517 to 1519 he worked in Lucerne, assisting his father on the decoration of a house for the city's chief magistrate (only a fragment of the work survives, in the Lucerne museum). It is possible that during this time Holbein crossed the Alps to Lombardy, for on his return to Basle, where he was to remain until 1526, his work had more dignity and authority and his modelling had become softer. The harrowing *Christ in the Tomb* (1521 or 1522, Kunstmuseum, Basle), for example, has a power of expression combined with a mastery of *chiaroscuro that almost rivals *Leonardo.

Holbein was now the leading artist in Basle, producing a highly varied output, including portraits, altarpieces, murals, and designs for stained glass. He also continued to work for printers, producing between about 1523 and 1526 his best-known work in this field, the *Dance of Death* series. This was not published until 1538 but then enjoyed enormous popularity, running into many editions. His most notable portraits in these years are three of Desiderius Erasmus, all dating from c.1523 (Louvre, Paris; Earl of Radnor Coll., Longford Castle, Wiltshire; and Kunstmuseum, Basle). In them, perhaps by the sitter's wish, he used the formula of the scholar in his study, first devised by Quentin *Massys, also for a portrait of Erasmus. A visit to France in 1524 gave Holbein further knowledge of *Renaissance painting, especially through the works of *Raphael in the royal collection, and the effect may be seen in the *Meyer Madonna* (1526, Schlossmuseum, Darmstadt). Mother and Child alike have an ideal beauty that is quite un-German, though the *donor portraits have a splendid naturalism.

The disturbances of the Reformation meant a decline of patronage in Basle, and in 1526, armed with an introduction from Erasmus to Sir Thomas More, Holbein sought work in England. His great group portrait of the More family (lost, but later copies in NPG, London, and Nostell Priory, Yorkshire) is a landmark in European art, for no previous artist had produced a group portrait of full-length figures

in their own home. A number of single portraits of eminent sitters also date from this visit and Holbein seems to have prospered financially. However, in 1528 he returned to Basle, probably because there was a risk of losing his citizen's rights if he was absent too long. He bought a house in the city soon after his return and again was in demand for a variety of work. His biggest commission in Basle was the decoration of the council chamber of the town hall with murals (of which only fragments remain) on the theme of justice; they were begun in 1521 and completed after his return from England. While he had been away the religious strife in Basle had intensified, and in 1532 he returned to England, leaving behind his wife and two children. He saw them only once more, on a brief visit to Basle in 1538, and was based in London for the rest of his life.

England too had changed since his first visit. More had resigned as lord chancellor and gone into retirement and members of his circle who had patronized Holbein were similarly out of favour. He found new patrons among the prosperous German merchant community in London, and in about 1533 he painted a portrait of Thomas Cromwell (Frick Coll., New York), soon to be Henry VIII's secretary. Cromwell may have obtained for Holbein the commission for his celebrated double portrait *The Ambassadors* (1533, NG, London; see ANAMORPHOSIS), and almost certainly helped him to gain royal patronage. By 1536 he was working for the king, and in the next year he produced the work that his contemporaries regarded as the masterpiece of his English years, the wall painting in Whitehall Palace of Henry VIII with his father and mother and his third wife, Jane Seymour. Though the picture perished in a fire in 1698, part of the *cartoon survives (NPG, London) and the massively assertive full-length figure of the king is well known through copies. Visitors to Whitehall Palace are said to have been 'abashed' and 'annihilated' by this overpowering image of royal authority. The only portrait of the king indisputably from Holbein's hand is a bust-length picture in the Museo Thyssen-Bornemisza, Madrid, a type of which numerous replicas exist. The king also twice sent Holbein abroad to produce portraits of prospective brides—*Christina, Duchess of Milan* (1538, NG, London) and *Anne of Cleves* (1539, Louvre). Henry married Anne in 1540, but divorced her in the same year without consummating the marriage. According to popular tradition, he had been misled by Holbein's portrait, but in fact it was

Anne's dullness rather than her looks that disappointed him, and he blamed his ambassadors' reports, not his painter's likeness. Numerous other members of Henry's court were portrayed by Holbein—in paintings and in drawings, a superb collection of which is in the Royal Library at Windsor Castle.

Holbein also made many designs for the royal household, ranging from substantial architectural elements to buttons, but there are no surviving objects based on his drawings. At about the time he entered royal service he also took up *miniature painting, to which his exquisitely detailed craftsmanship was eminently suited. Holbein's portraits were much copied, but none of his followers in England approached the penetration of his characterization or the virtuosity of his technique. Only in miniature painting did he have a worthy successor in *Hilliard.

Holguín, Melchor Pérez (b Cochabamba, c.1660; d Potosí, c.1725). Bolivian painter, active mainly in Potosí, which in his time was the biggest and wealthiest city in the Americas because of its exploitation of the local silver. He is regarded as the leading painter of his period in the Spanish colonies, but his work is undistinguished by European standards. It mixed various European influences, from *Mannerism to *Rococo, with certain native Indian features.

Hollanda, Francisco de. See HOLANDA.

Hollar, Wenceslaus (or Wenzel) (b Prague, 23 July 1607; d London, 25 Mar. 1677). Bohemian etcher and watercolourist, active mainly in England. He had part of his training in the workshop of *Merian in Frankfurt. In 1636, while working in Cologne, he met the Earl of *Arundel, whom he accompanied on a diplomatic mission through central Europe, returning with him to England. Hollar remained in England for most of the rest of his life (he lived in Antwerp 1644–52 and went on an expedition to Tangier 1668–9); during the Civil War he fought on the Royalist side. He was one of the outstanding draughtsmen and etchers of the 17th century and his views of London form an invaluable record of its appearance before the Great Fire of 1666. His large output also included many other subjects.

Home, Henry (Lord Kames) (b Kames, nr. Greenlaw, Berwickshire [now Scottish Borders], 1696; d Edinburgh, 27 Dec. 1782). Scottish judge and writer. His literary output was large and varied, including publications on agriculture, antiquities, and law. However, his writing was devoted mainly to philosophy, his major book

being *Elements of Criticism* (1762), the most elaborate treatise on aesthetics written in English up to that time. It went through many editions and was used as a textbook until superseded by Germanic philosophy in the 19th century.

Homer, Winslow (b Boston, 24 Feb. 1836; d Prout's Neck, Me., 29 Sept. 1910). American landscape, marine, and *genre painter. Next to *Eakins and the expatriate *Whistler, he is probably regarded as the greatest American painter of his period. He came to painting from illustration (chiefly for *Harper's Weekly*) and *Prisoners from the Front* (1866, Met. Mus., New York), one of his first important oils, has a quality of vivid, unromanticized reportage: 'When I have selected the thing carefully, I paint it exactly as it appears.' In 1867 he visited Paris; he was impressed by *Manet's work, but he explored the rendering of light and colour in a different way from the *Impressionists—instead of dissolving forms into light and atmosphere, he sought luminosity within a firm construction of clear outline and broad planes of light and dark (*Long Branch, New Jersey*, 1869, MFA, Boston). The sea was Homer's favourite subject, and after staying at Cullercoats (home of a flourishing artists' colony) on the rugged coast of northeast England in 1881–2 he settled at Prout's Neck on the Maine coast, where he lived in isolation. His pictures of the Maine coast, which represent the power and solitude of the sea and the contest of man with the forces of nature, are his best-known works. He was an artist of considerable originality and power who created an imaginative vision of nature that has come to be accepted as a reflection of the American pioneering spirit. He used watercolour with the force and authority of oil (*Inside the Bar, Tynemouth*, 1883, Met. Mus.).

Hondecoeter, Melchior d' (b Utrecht, 1636; d Amsterdam, 3 Apr. 1695). Dutch painter, the best-known member of a family of artists. He was the Netherlands' most renowned painter of birds, winning an international reputation with his lively and brightly coloured canvases. They show both domestic and exotic birds, often in vigorous movement and sometimes pointing a moral. Hondecoeter also painted still-lifes. He was a prolific artist and is represented in many museums. His father **Gysbert** (1604–53) was also a bird painter, and his grandfather **Gillis** (d. 1638) was a landscapist. Melchior trained with his father and with his uncle Jan Baptist *Weenix; he worked in Utrecht, The Hague, and Amsterdam.

Hondius, Abraham (b Rotterdam, c.1625/30; bur. London, 17 Sept. 1691). Dutch painter and etcher. He produced various kinds of picture, including religious and mythological works, landscapes, and still-lifes, but most of his output consists of scenes of hunting and animal combat. These are typified by vigorous movement and show the influence of Flemish artists such as *Fyt and *Snyders. Hondius worked in his native Rotterdam until 1659, then in Amsterdam until about 1666, when he settled in London. There are two examples of his work in the Fitzwilliam Museum, Cambridge, including the unusual Arctic Adventure (c.1675).

Hone, Nathaniel (b Dublin, 24 Apr. 1718; d London, 14 Aug. 1784). Irish portrait painter (he began his career as a miniaturist), who settled permanently in London after studying in Italy, 1750–2, and became a foundation member of the *Royal Academy in 1768. He is now remembered mainly for one painting, The Conjurer (1775, NG, Dublin), in which he satirized *Reynolds's practice of borrowing poses from the Old Masters. The picture was accepted at the RA, but was withdrawn after Angelica *Kauffmann (whose name had been linked romantically with Reynolds's) objected that a nude figure in the background was meant to represent her. (Hone painted out the nude figures, but they can be seen in his sketch for the picture (Tate, London).) In protest at the removal of his painting Hone exhibited it in a one-man show in St Martin's Lane, the first of its kind recorded in Britain. Hone's sons **Horace** (c.1755–1825) and **Camillus** (1759–1836) were also painters, as was a brother, **Samuel** (1726–?). Camillus was the subject of some of his father's best portraits.

Evie Hone (b Dublin, 22 Apr. 1894; d Rathfarnham, Co. Dublin, 13 Mar. 1955), a direct descendant of a brother of Nathaniel, was one of the greatest stained-glass designers of the 20th century. Her masterpiece is the huge east window of Eton College Chapel, commissioned in 1949 to replace glass destroyed in the Second World War and completed in 1952. The subjects are The Crucifixion and The Last Supper. Sir Nikolaus *Pevsner (The Buildings of England: Buckinghamshire, 1960) describes the window as 'a triumph for the authorities of Eton, which refused to be satisfied with the anaemic glass put into so many churches of England before and after the Second World War. Here is bold, vigorous design and strong, glowing colour.'

Honthorst, Gerrit van (b Utrecht, 4 Nov. 1592; d Utrecht, 27 Apr. 1656). Dutch painter of biblical, mythological, and *genre scenes, and of portraits. He was a pupil of *Bloemaert in his native Utrecht, but his style was formed by a long stay in Italy, where he probably spent most of the second decade of the century. On his return to Utrecht in 1620 he became, along with *Baburen and *Terbrugghen, one of the leading followers of *Caravaggio in the Netherlands (see UTRECHT CARAVAGGISTI). The candlelight effects he used in some of his Roman pictures (Christ before the High Priest, c.1617, NG, London) earned him the nickname Gherardo delle Notti (Gerard of the night scenes). In the late 1620s, however, he abandoned his Caravaggesque style for a lighter manner in which he achieved international success (rare for a Dutch artist) as a court portraitist. His distinguished patrons included Christian IV of Denmark and Charles I of England (see ROYAL COLLECTION); he spent most of 1628 in England, where he painted several portraits, including one of Charles (NPG, London). From 1637 to 1652 he was court painter in The Hague, where he worked on the decoration of the Huis ten Bosch (see HUYGENS).

Hooch, Pieter de (bapt. Rotterdam, 20 Dec. 1629; bur. Amsterdam, 24 Mar. 1684). Dutch *genre painter. He was born in Rotterdam, is said to have studied in Haarlem (as a pupil of *Berchem), and spent the last two decades of his life in Amsterdam, but he is particularly associated with Delft. His period of residence there was fairly brief (c.1655–c.1661), but during this time he painted the pictures on which his reputation rests—a small number of tranquil masterpieces that perfectly evoke the well-being of his peaceful and prosperous country. Typical subjects include a sunny yard (Courtyard of a House in Delft, 1658, NG, London) or light streaming into the interior of a corner of a burgher's house (The Pantry, c.1658, Rijksmuseum, Amsterdam). There is a kinship of spirit with his great Delft contemporary *Vermeer, and de Hooch sometimes approaches him in delicate observation of light and lucidity of composition, although not in beauty of brushwork. After de Hooch moved to Amsterdam in the early 1660s, however, the quality of his work declined. Instead of the simple brick and plaster settings of his earlier groups he chose sumptuous marble interiors, and towards the end these backgrounds acquired something of the harsh quality of a stage backdrop. He died in a madhouse.

Hoogstraten, Samuel van (b Dordrecht, 2 Aug. 1627; d Dordrecht, 19 Oct. 1678). Dutch painter, printmaker, and writer on art. He painted *genre scenes in the style of de *Hooch and *Metsu, and portraits, but he is best known as a specialist in perspective effects, notably in his *peep-show boxes, which show a painted toy world viewed through a small opening. Only in his early works can it be detected that he was a pupil of *Rembrandt. Hoogstraten visited London, Rome, and Vienna, worked in Amsterdam and The Hague as well as his native Dordrecht, and was a man of many parts. He was an etcher, poet, director of the mint at Dordrecht, and art theorist. His *Inleyding tot de hooge schoole der schilderkonst* (Introduction to the Art of Painting, 1678) contains one of the rare contemporary appraisals of Rembrandt's work.

Hope, Thomas (*b* Amsterdam, 30 Aug. 1769; *d* London, 2 Feb. 1831). British collector, patron, and writer. He was born in the Netherlands into a wealthy banking family, and travelled extensively before and after settling in England in 1795. In 1801 he was described as being reputedly 'the richest, but undoubtedly far from the most agreeable man in Europe', and he used his great wealth to spend lavishly on art for his London mansion in Duchess Street (to which the public could buy admission tickets) and his country seat at Deepdene, Surrey. He was a devotee of *Neoclassicism, and the artists he patronized included *Canova, *Flaxman, and *Thorvaldsen. Hope also had notable collections of paintings and antique statuary. He trained craftsmen to make furniture from his own Greek and Egyptian designs, and his publications included *Household Furniture and Interior Decoration* (1807).

Hopper, Edward (*b* Nyack, NY, 22 July 1882; *d* New York, 15 May 1967). American painter and etcher. He spent almost all his career in New York, but he travelled extensively in the USA, making long journeys by car. His main training was at the New York School of Art, where Robert *Henri was one of his teachers. Between 1906 and 1910 he made three trips to Europe (mainly Paris), but these had little influence on his style. In 1913 he exhibited (and sold) a picture at the *Armory Show, but for the next ten years he earned his living entirely by commercial illustration such as magazine covers. After a successful one-man show in 1924, however, he was able to devote himself full-time to painting and thereafter enjoyed a fairly rapid rise to recognition as the outstanding exponent of *American Scene Painting (he was given a retrospective exhibition by the *Museum of Modern Art in 1933 and this set the seal on his reputation).

Hopper's distinctive style was formed by the mid-1920s and thereafter changed little. The central theme of his work is the loneliness of city life, generally expressed through one or two figures in a spare setting—his best-known work, *Nighthawks* (1942, Art Inst. of Chicago), has an unusually large 'cast' with four. Typical settings are motel rooms, filling stations, cafeterias, and almost deserted offices at night. He was the first artist to seize on this specifically American visual world and make it definitively his own. However, although his work is rooted in a particular period and place, it also has a peculiarly timeless feel and deals in unchanging realities about the human condition. He never makes feelings explicit or tries to tell a story; rather he suggests weariness, frustration, and troubled isolation with a poignancy that rises above the specific. Hopper himself enjoyed solitude (although he was happily married to another ex-student of Henri) and he disliked talking about his work. When he did, he discussed it mainly in terms of technical problems; one of his best-known pronouncements is that he wanted only to 'paint sunlight on the side of a house'. Of *Nighthawks* he said: 'I didn't see it as particularly lonely . . . Unconsciously, probably, I was painting the loneliness of a big city.' Deliberately so or not, in his still, reserved, and blandly handled paintings he exerts a powerful psychological impact that makes him one of the great painters of modern life.

Hopper worked in watercolour as well as oil and also made etchings, beginning in 1915—in fact his individual vision emerged in this medium before it did in painting. His best-known print is *Evening Wind* (1921), establishing a theme that would later often recur in his paintings—the female nude in a city interior. He virtually abandoned printmaking in 1923, but in spite of his short career in the medium he has been described as 'undoubtedly the greatest American etcher of this century' (Frances Carey and Antony Griffiths, *American Prints: 1879–1979*, 1980).

Hoppner, John (*b* London, 4 Apr. 1758; *d* London, 23 Jan. 1810). British portrait painter. He trained as a chorister in the Chapel Royal, St James's Palace, and later received an allowance from George III to study at the *Royal Academy Schools. This royal favour led to rumours that he was the king's illegitimate son. In 1789 he was appointed portrait painter to the Prince of Wales (later George IV) and after the death of *Reynolds, he and *Lawrence were the leading portraitists in the country. Hoppner rarely achieved striking individuality (his portraits often recall Reynolds and *Romney and later Lawrence and *Raeburn), but his best work, particularly when depicting women and children, has great charm.

Hopton Wood stone. A very hard limestone quarried at Middleton, Derbyshire (Hopton is nearby), varying in colour from light grey to light tan and speckled with dark-grey crystals. It can be cut to a smooth face and sharp ridge and takes a good polish. Jacob *Epstein (notably for his tomb of Oscar Wilde), Henry *Moore, and Barbara *Hepworth are among the sculptors who have used it.

Hornebolte, Lukas. See MINIATURE.

Hornton stone. Limestone named after quarries at Hornton in north-west Oxfordshire. It is usually a rich tawny brown in colour, but green and greyish-blue tints also occur. It was a favourite stone of Henry *Moore, the *Madonna and Child* (1943–4) in St Matthew's, Northampton, being one of his best-known works in this material. The quarries at Hornton are now closed, but similar stone is obtained at nearby Edge Hill in Warwickshire.

Hoskins, John (*b* *c*.1590/5; *bur.* London, 22 Feb. 1665). The leading English portrait miniaturist between *c*.1620 and *c*.1640 (from the death of *Hilliard to the emergence of Samuel *Cooper, Hoskins's nephew and pupil). His early work is a development of Hilliard's style. Later he became a specialist in miniature versions of van *Dyck's large-scale portraits, but his work often has a charm and originality of its own. His son **John Hoskins the Younger** (*c*.1620–after 1692) was also a miniaturist.

Houbraken, Arnold (*b* Dordrecht, 28 Mar. 1660; *d* Amsterdam, 14 Oct. 1719). Dutch painter and writer on art. His paintings are now forgotten, but he is important for his biographical compilation *De groote schouburgh der Nederlantsche konstschilders en schilderessen* (The Great Theatre of Netherlandish Men and Women Painters, 3 vols., 1718–21). This was intended as a sequel to van *Mander's *Schilder-boeck* of 1604 and is the main source of information on many 17th-century Dutch and Flemish painters. Arnold's son **Jacobus** (1698–1780) was a leading portrait engraver. His work includes engraved plates after his father's designs for the *Groote schouburgh*.

Houckgeest, Gerrit (*b* The Hague, *c*.1600; *d* Bergen-op-Zoom, Aug. 1661). Dutch painter of architectural views. He began his career in The Hague, ended it in Bergen-op-Zoom, where he settled in 1653, and in between worked in Delft (he perhaps also visited England in the 1630s). Initially he painted imaginary architectural views, but in about 1650 he changed to depicting real church interiors. His works in this vein—luminous and precisely delineated—are among the most sensitive architectural paintings of the time (*Interior of the New Church at Delft*, 1651, Mauritshuis, The Hague).

Houdon, Jean-Antoine (*b* Versailles, 25 Mar. 1741; *d* Paris, 15 July 1828). French sculptor. A pupil of Michel-Ange *Slodtz, Jean-Baptiste *Lemoyne, and Jean-Baptiste *Pigalle, he won the *Prix de Rome in 1761. During his stay in Rome, 1764–8, he produced two works that made his reputation: a life-size male *écorché* figure (1767, Schlossmuseum, Gotha), casts of which were widely used in art academies, and the dignified, contemplative *St Bruno* (1767, S. Maria degli Angeli), a kind of classical riposte to Slodtz's more animated and *Baroque statue of the saint in St Peter's. After returning to Paris in 1768, he was successful in the popular mythological idiom, becoming a member of the Academy in 1777 with his *Morpheus* (Louvre, Paris). His greatest strength, however, was with portraits, in which he showed a brilliant gift for catching lively gesture and expression. By the mid-1780s he was acknowledged as the leading portrait sculptor of Europe and in 1785 he visited America in connection with his statue of George Washington (marble original, 1788, in Virginia State Capitol, Richmond; bronze copy outside the NG, London). His other well-known works include several portraits of Voltaire (e.g. in the Comédie-Française, Paris, and V&A, London). During the French Revolution he narrowly escaped imprisonment and although he found favour again under Napoleon (a terracotta bust of him, 1806, is in the Musée des Beaux-Arts, Dijon), he produced little of importance after the turn of the century. He last exhibited in 1814 and in his final years his mind was impaired following a stroke.

Hours of Turin. See TURIN HOURS.

Howson, Peter. See GLASGOW SCHOOL and OFFICIAL WAR ART.

Hoyland, John. See SITUATION.

Hsü Pei-hung. See XU BEIHONG.

Huber, Wolfgang (or **Wolf**) (*b* ?Feldkirch, *c*.1480/90; *d* Passau, 3 June 1553). Austrian painter, printmaker, and architect, active mainly in

Passau in Germany, where he was court painter and architect to the prince-bishop. He was first and foremost a poetic interpreter of landscape and is usually counted among the masters of the *Danube School. His landscape drawings are particularly delicate and his religious paintings and portraits sometimes have landscape backgrounds.

Hudson, Thomas (b Devon, 1701; d Twickenham, Middlesex [now Greater London], 26 Jan. 1779). English portrait painter, a pupil of Jonathan *Richardson, whose daughter he married. From the mid-1740s to the mid-1750s he was the leading fashionable portraitist in London, rivalled only by *Ramsay. His studio produced a great deal of work, with much help from specialist assistants (see DRAPERY PAINTER), and Hudson has been described by Ellis *Waterhouse as 'the last of the conscienceless artists, of whom *Lely was the first in England, who turned out portraits to standard patterns and executed comparatively little of the work themselves'. Hudson went into semi-retirement in the late 1750s, when his former pupil *Reynolds was rapidly rising in success. His other pupils included John Hamilton *Mortimer and Joseph *Wright. He made an impressive collection of paintings and drawings, dispersed after his death.

Hudson River School. Term applied retrospectively to a number of American landscape painters, active c.1825–c.1875, who were inspired by pride in the beauty of their homeland. This patriotic spirit won them great popularity in the middle years of the century. The early leaders and the three most important figures in the group were Thomas *Cole, Thomas *Doughty, and Asher B. *Durand, who painted the Hudson River Valley, the Catskill Mountains, and other remote and untouched areas of natural beauty. These three artists and many of those who followed, including Jasper F. Cropsey (1823–1900) and John Frederick Kensett (1862–72), had studied in Europe and part of their inspiration came from painters of the grandiose and spectacular such as *Turner and John *Martin. Painters of a similar outlook who found their inspiration in the far West are known collectively as the *Rocky Mountain School.

hue. The name of a colour or the attribute by virtue of which it is discerned as red, green, blue, etc. The spectrum is conventionally divided into six basic hues—red, yellow, and blue (the primary colours) and green, orange, and violet (the secondary colours, made by mixing the primary colours). In normal parlance the word 'hue' tends to be used so loosely that it is no more than a synonym for colour.

Huet, Christophe (b Pontoise, 22 June 1700; d Paris, 2 May 1759). French *Rococo painter, engraver, and designer, a member of a family of artists. He belongs to the decorative tradition stemming from *Berain and *Audran and is best known for paintings and engravings involving animals dressed up and acting like humans (see SINGERIE). Good examples of his work are in the Musée Condé at Chantilly. Among other members of his family the best known is his nephew **Jean-Baptiste Huet I** (b Paris, 15 Oct. 1745; d Paris, 27 Jan. 1811), a painter and engraver specializing in more realistic animal subjects (Dog Attacking Geese, 1769, Louvre, Paris). Jean-Baptiste had three artist sons.

Hughes, Arthur (b London, 27 Jan. 1832; d Kew, Surrey [now in Greater London], 22 Dec. 1915). English painter and illustrator. In the 1850s he was one of the most distinguished of the *Pre-Raphaelite sympathizers, remarkable for his lyrical delicacy of colour and drawing. Two paintings are particularly well known—April Love (1856, Tate, London), which *Ruskin called 'exquisite in every way', and The Long Engagement (1859, City AG, Birmingham). After about 1870, however, his work declined in quality, although he did some good book illustrations. He was shy and withdrawn and in later life he lived in suburban obscurity.

Hughes, Robert (b Sydney, 28 July 1938). Australian art critic, active mainly in the USA. In 1964 he moved to Europe (first to Italy, then England) and in 1970 settled in New York as art critic of Time magazine. He writes mainly on 20th-century art and has a richly deserved reputation as a witty and penetrating observer of the contemporary art scene. His books include The Art of Australia (1966, revised 1970), Heaven and Hell in Western Art (1969), and Nothing If Not Critical: Selected Essays on Art and Artists (1990). He has also made films for television, notably two much-praised series: The Shock of the New (1980) and American Visions (1996), both with accompanying books of the same title. In his work for television he has received the kind of praise previously enjoyed by Kenneth *Clark, but Hughes's approach is very different—forceful rather than suave.

Hugo, Master. See MASTER HUGO.

Hugo, Victor (*b* Besançon, 26 Feb. 1802; *d* Paris, 22 May 1885). French poet, novelist, playwright, and draughtsman. As well as being one of the giants of French literature, he was an accomplished and highly prolific draughtsman. His early drawings were fairly conventional, but from the 1840s his style became much more imaginative, free, and emotional, revealing some of the same *Romantic spirit as his literary works. Sometimes he used inkblots in a way recalling *Cozens and anticipating the *automatism of the *Surrealists. There are many examples of his drawings in the Maison de Victor Hugo, Paris.

Huguet, Jaime (*b* Valls, ?*c*.1415; *d* Barcelona, 1492). Spanish painter, the most prominent figure in the Catalan School during the second part of the 15th century. For most of his career he worked in Barcelona, where he had settled by 1448. He continued the Catalan tradition of Bernardo *Martorell, but was highly individual in his characterization. His studio produced many sumptuous composite altarpieces of the type that became typical in Spanish art and his work exercised a wide influence on the painting of Catalonia and Aragon.

Hulten, Pontus (*b* Stockholm, 1924). Swedish art historian and administrator, whose international career has been largely concerned with the founding of major collections of modern art. In 1958 he was appointed director of the Moderna Museet, Stockholm, and in 1973 he became director of the Musée National d'Art Moderne, Paris, in which role he supervised the inauguration of the *Pompidou Centre. From 1980 to 1982 he was first director of the Museum of Contemporary Art, Los Angeles, and from 1981 to 1993 he was first director of the Palazzo Grassi, Venice, a centre for temporary exhibitions, largely sponsored by the car firm Fiat. Hulten has organized numerous major exhibitions in these and other posts, including 'Paris–New York' (1977), the first of a series of blockbusters at the Pompidou Centre in which Paris was linked with other great art centres, and 'Futurism and Futurisms' (1986), the inaugural show of the Palazzo Grassi and the largest *Futurist exhibition ever held.

Hume, David. See ADDISON.

Hume, Gary. See YOUNG BRITISH ARTISTS.

Humphry, Ozias (*b* Honiton, Devon, 8 Sept. 1742; *d* London, 9 Mar. 1810). English portrait painter. He worked for a time as a miniaturist in Bath, but settled in London in 1764 on the encouragement of *Reynolds. In 1772 a riding accident that affected his eyes made him abandon miniatures and after a visit to Italy in 1773–7 (he made the outward journey with *Romney), he practised in oils. From 1785 to 1788 he was in India, where he resumed miniature painting, but again he found the work too great a strain. He then took up pastel and in this medium was highly successful (being given the title of portrait painter in crayons to his majesty in 1792) until he went blind in 1797.

Hundertwasser, Fritz (Friedrich Stowasser) (*b* Vienna, 15 Dec. 1928; *d* at sea, on board the *Queen Elizabeth II*, 19 Feb. 2000). Austrian painter and graphic artist. He took the name Hundertwasser in 1949, translating the syllable 'sto' (which means 'hundred' in Czech) by the German 'hundert'. From about 1969 he signed his work 'Friedensreich Hundertwasser', symbolizing by the word 'Friedensreich' (Kingdom of Peace) his boast that by his painting he would introduce the observer into a new life of peace and happiness. He often added 'Regenstag' (Rainy Day) to the name—making it in full 'Friedensreich Hundertwasser Regenstag'—on the ground that he felt happy on rainy days because colours then began to sparkle and glow. This exaggerated concern with the name is a symptom of the braggadocio, conceit, and talent for self-advertisement that are apparent in his work as well as his life. Standing outside most contemporary artistic movements, though borrowing from many, he worked mainly on a small scale, often in watercolour. His work has sometimes been compared with that of *Klee, but although it is in the same tradition of figurative fantasy it lacks his elegance and wit. In his concern with the dehumanizing aspects of 20th-century society, he was an outspoken critic of modern architecture and his work included the design of an idiosyncratic, multi-coloured, fairy-tale-like housing unit in Vienna (completed 1986).

Hunt, William Henry (*b* London, 28 Mar. 1790; *d* London, 10 Feb. 1864). English painter, mainly in watercolour. Hunt had deformed legs and suffered a good deal of ill health, but he worked indefatigably and became one of the most renowned watercolourists of his time, numbering *Ruskin among his many admirers. Initially he specialized in landscapes, but later he was famous chiefly for his highly detailed still-lifes of fruits, flowers, and birds' nests, which earned him the nicknames 'Hedgerow Hunt' and 'Bird's Nest Hunt'.

Hunt, William Holman (*b* London, 2 Apr. 1827; *d* London, 7 Sept. 1910). English painter, co-founder of the *Pre-Raphaelite Brotherhood in 1848. He was the only member of the Brotherhood who throughout his entire career remained faithful to Pre-Raphaelite aims, which he summarized as finding serious and genuine ideas to express, direct study from nature in disregard of all arbitrary rules, and envisaging events as they must have happened rather than in accordance with artistic conventions. Hunt's work was remarkable for its minute precision of handling, its accumulation of incident, and its didactic emphasis on moral or social symbolism, and he made three visits to the Middle East so he could paint biblical scenes with accurate local detail. One of the most famous paintings that resulted from his fanatical devotion to authenticity is *The Scapegoat* (1854–5, Lady Lever AG, Port Sunlight), showing the outcast animal on the shore of the Dead Sea. His colour tends to be painfully harsh and his sentiment mawkish, but he created some of the most enduring images of the Victorian age, among them *The Hireling Shepherd* (1851, Manchester AG), *The Awakening Conscience* (1853, Tate, London), and *The Light of the World* (1851–3, Keble College, Oxford; a smaller version, 1853–7, is in Manchester AG, and a larger replica, 1900–4, is in St Paul's Cathedral, London). Like the other Pre-Raphaelites, Hunt suffered critical attacks early in his career, but the moral earnestness of his work later made it immensely popular with the Victorian public and he earned a fortune from the sale of engravings of his paintings. In old age he became a patriarchal figure in the art world and he was awarded the Order of Merit in 1905. In the same year he published his autobiographical *Pre-Raphaelitism and the Pre-Raphaelite Brotherhood*, which is a basic sourcebook on the subject, though somewhat biased.

Hunter, Leslie. See SCOTTISH COLOURISTS.

Huntington, Henry E. (*b* Oneonta, NY, 27 Feb. 1850; *d* Philadelphia, 23 May 1927). American businessman, collector, and philanthropist. He made an enormous fortune mainly in the railway industry, but by about 1910 he had retired from most of his business interests to devote himself to collecting art and books. In the remaining years of his life he built up a huge library of early books that ranks in importance with those of the great national collections. With art he was more selective, concentrating on British paintings of the late 18th and early 19th centuries. In 1919 he signed a deed creating what is now the Huntington Library, Art Collections, and Botanical Gardens at his home at San Marino, California, his aim being 'to promote and advance learning, the arts and sciences, and to promote the public welfare by founding, endowing and having maintained a library, art gallery, museum and park'. The chief glory of the art collection is the array of full-length British portraits in the main gallery—probably the finest group of such works to be seen anywhere in the world, including *Gainsborough's *Blue Boy* (1770) and *Reynolds's *Mrs Siddons as the Tragic Muse* (1784). Since Huntington's death the collection has expanded and now also has a good representation of American and French paintings. Huntington's cousin (later also his stepson) **Archer M. Huntington** (1870–1955), a poet, Spanish scholar, and philanthropist, founded the Hispanic Society of America, New York, in 1908 and commissioned *Sorolla to paint mural panels for the interior. Archer's wife **Anna Hyatt Huntington** (1876–1973) was a sculptor of animal subjects in a traditional style. Her work includes an equestrian statue of El Cid outside the Hispanic Society of America (another cast is in Seville). She continued working almost up to her death at the age of 97.

Hutcheson, Francis (*b* Drumalig, Co. Down, 1694; *d* Dublin, 1746). British philosopher, professor of moral philosophy at Glasgow University from 1730 until his death. His major work is *An Inquiry into the Original of our Ideas of Beauty and Virtue* (1725). In this he argues that aesthetic (and moral) judgement is founded on a special kind of perception. Just as our sense of sight enables us to see colours directly, so we possess an analogous 'inner' sense enabling us to perceive aesthetic or ethical values. To stimulate this inner sense aesthetically, an object must possess the right kind of ratio between 'uniformity and variety'. Beauty, although a property of the object, also depends for its existence on our subjective engagement. This attempt to harmonize objective and subjective elements of aesthetic experience set a pattern for later British thought in the field.

Huygens, Constantijn (*b* The Hague, 4 Sept. 1596; *d* The Hague, 28 Mar. 1687). Dutch diplomat, writer, patron, and collector. Huygens was 'a well-travelled, cultivated man who combined a full life of service to his country with a mastery of the polite accomplishments' (Seymour Slive, *Dutch Painting: 1600–1800*, 1995); he spoke six languages, played several musical instruments, and his writings included a translation into

Dutch of some of the poems of John Donne. Early in his career he worked in the Dutch embassies in Venice and London, and in 1625 he was appointed secretary to the stadholder (head of the Dutch state), Prince Frederick Henry of Orange. He held similar posts under Frederick Henry's successors until his own death at the age of 90. His duties included being court art adviser, and in this role he devised the iconographical scheme for the decoration of the Oranjezaal (Orange Hall) of the Huis ten Bosch, a newly built royal villa (designed by Pieter *Post) just outside The Hague. After the death of Prince Frederick Henry in 1647 it was decided to decorate the central hall of the building with murals honouring him. These were painted in 1648–52; the team of Dutch and Flemish artists involved, overseen by Jacob van *Campen, included Salomon de *Bray, Caesar van *Everdingen, Gerrit van *Honthorst, Jacob *Jordaens, and Jan *Lievens. Some of the individual contributions are impressive, but overall the scheme has not generally been judged a success; when *Reynolds saw it in 1781 he commented: 'The different hands that have been employed here make variety it is true; but it is variety of wretchedness.' In 1629–31 Huygens wrote a journal-cum-autobiography in Latin and this contains interesting comments about contemporary artists, notably Lievens and *Rembrandt. Lievens was one of several artists who painted Huygens's portrait; another was Thomas de *Keyser (1627, NG, London).

His son **Constantijn Huygens the Younger** (1628–97) was a diplomat and draughtsman (his drawings are mainly landscapes, many of them made on his official travels). Another son, Christiaan Huygens (1629–95), was a music theorist, physicist, and astronomer—'after Newton, the most influential physical scientist of the late 17th century' (*Cambridge Dictionary of Scientists*, 1996).

Huysum, Jan van (*b* Amsterdam, 15 Apr. 1682; *d* Amsterdam, 7/8 Feb. 1749). Dutch painter, with Rachel *Ruysch the most distinguished flower painter of his day. He had a European reputation and was much imitated, his light colours and intricate, flamboyant compositions becoming characteristic of 18th-century Dutch flower painting. Occasionally he painted subjects other than flowers—mainly landscapes, although there is also a self-portrait in the Ashmolean Museum, Oxford. He was a pupil of his father, **Justus van Huysum the Elder** (1659–1716), and he had three painter brothers: **Justus the Younger** (*c*.1684–1707); **Michiel** (*d* 1759); and

Jacob (*c*.1687–1740). Father and sons were all flower painters, apart from Justus the Younger, who specialized in battle scenes.

Hyperrealism. See SUPERREALISM.

Hypnerotomachia Poliphili. A printed book, a kind of philosophical prose romance, published in Venice in 1499, celebrated as one of the supreme masterpieces of the printer's art; it has 'never been bettered for balance of type and illustration' (David Bland, *A History of Book Illustration*, 1958). The *Hypnerotomachia* was published by the great scholar-printer Aldus Manutius (1449–1515), whose Aldine Press, founded in 1494, was one of the most influential book producers of the *Renaissance. His most characteristic books were 'pocket editions' (a format he created) of Greek and Roman classics and they were normally unillustrated, but the *Hypnerotomachia* is a substantial folio with abundant woodcuts. No author is named in the book, but there is convincing evidence for attributing the text to Francesco Colonna, a Venetian Dominican friar. The pseudo-Greek title can be translated as 'the dream of a battle for love fought by Poliphilo', and the abstruse text, which describes a lover searching for his mistress Polia (Poliphilo means 'lover of Polia'), is an exotic mixture of Italian, Latin, and Greek. It has been seen as both 'a jumble of mystical nonsense' and 'an allegory of remarkable subtlety in which Poliphilo's pursuit of his lost love in a dream symbolizes man's striving after unattainable spiritual ideals' (Alan G. Thomas, *Great Books and Book Collectors*, 1975). The illustrations, of exquisite linear purity, are so intimately integrated with the text that the artist who created them must have worked in close consultation with the author and publisher, but the identity of this artist remains unknown.

Anthony *Blunt (*Artistic Theory in Italy: 1450–1600*, 1940) writes of the *Hypnerotomachia*: 'The wanderings of the unhappy lover Poliphilus in search of his Polia are accompanied by all the adventures and allegories traditional in the romances of the Middle Ages. But the author has used this medieval form to express above all his overwhelming passion for antiquity . . . the buildings described are in the ancient manner; the monuments are covered in Latin or Greek inscriptions, or with hieroglyphs which the author painstakingly transcribes and explains . . . Many of the buildings he describes are in a state of ruin, and in talking of them he betrays a romantic feeling . . . indulging in that sentimental and melancholy delight in ruins as symbols of the impermanence of things which became so popular at a later date, particularly in the eighteenth century . . . The *Hypnerotomachia* was not of great use to architects who wished to learn about the methods and structure of ancient building, but to the painters, sculptors, engravers and maiolica painters it was an endless source of themes.' An Italian translation, *La hypnerotomachia di Poliphilo*, appeared in 1545, a French translation, *Le Songe de Poliphile* (almost as beautiful as the original), in 1546, and a partial English translation (a meagre reflection of the original) in 1592 under the title *The Strife of Love in a Dreame*.

Hyppolite (or Hippolite), **Hector** (*b* Saint-Marc, 15 Sept. 1894; *d* Port-au-Prince, 9 June 1948). Haitian painter. He is the most famous of his country's remarkable crop of *naive painters, but he did not achieve recognition until the final years of his life, after André *Breton encountered his work on a visit to the island in 1945 and arranged exhibitions of his paintings in Europe. Before this, Hyppolite spent most of his life in poverty and obscurity. He earned part of his living as a house painter, and his artistic work began with the decoration of doors and walls. It was only towards the end of his career that he began painting easel pictures, and he is said to have regretted that they distracted him from his duties as a Voodoo priest. Many of his paintings were inspired by his religious beliefs, featuring Voodoo scenes and symbols. He used bold, flat forms and vivid colours, and had no interest in technical refinement, his paint sometimes being applied with chicken feathers or his fingers. His success helped to inspire other Haitian naive painters, notably Rigaud Benoit (1911–86), who married Hyppolite's daughter, and Wilson Bigaud (1931–), who as a boy was a neighbour of Hyppolite in Port-au-Prince.

I

Ibbetson, Julius Caesar (*b* Farnley Moor, nr. Leeds, 29 Dec. 1759; *d* Masham, Yorkshire, 13 Oct. 1817). English painter. His unusual Christian names were given to him because of his Caesarean birth. He specialized in fairly small landscapes with figures and animals, and his style has been characterized by Ellis *Waterhouse as 'more natural than de *Loutherbourg's, and more civilized than *Morland's'; Benjamin *West called him 'the *Berchem of England'. Ibbetson worked mainly in his native Yorkshire, but also at times in London, Scotland, and the Lake District, and in 1787–8 he was draughtsman on a British mission to China, during which he visited Java. He worked in watercolour as well as oil and also made etchings. In 1803 he published a manual on painting. Like his friend Morland, Ibbetson is said to have been given to dissipation, but his work did not obviously suffer because of this as Morland's did.

ICA. See INSTITUTE OF CONTEMPORARY ARTS.

icon. An image of a saint or other holy personage, particularly when the image is regarded by the devotee as sacred in itself and capable of facilitating contact between him or her and the personage portrayed. The term, which derives from the Greek word *eikōn*, meaning 'likeness', has been applied particularly to sacred images of the *Byzantine Church and the Orthodox Churches of Russia and Greece.

iconography. The aspect of art history dealing with the identification, description, classification, and interpretation of the subject matter of the figurative arts. In his book *Studies in Iconology* (1939) Erwin *Panofsky proposed that the term 'iconology' should be used to distinguish a broader approach towards subject matter in which the scholar attempts to understand the total meaning of the work of art in its historical context. However, in practice an exact distinction between the two terms is rarely made, and 'iconography' is much the more commonly used of the two. The term 'iconography' can also be applied to collections (or the classification) of portraits. Van *Dyck, for example, made a series of etchings of famous contemporaries entitled *Iconography*, and the detailed catalogues of the National Portrait Gallery in London have a section called 'iconography' in the entry for each sitter, in which other portraits of the person represented are listed and discussed. Thus it is possible to speak of 'the iconography of Shakespeare' or 'the iconography of Queen Victoria'.

iconology. See ICONOGRAPHY.

iconostasis. In *Byzantine and Russian churches, an *icon-covered screen separating the sanctuary from the main body of the building, comparable to the *rood-screen in a Western church.

ideal. A conception of something that is perfect, referring in the visual arts to works that attempt to reproduce the best of nature, but also to improve on it, eliminating the inevitable flaws of particular examples. The notion derives ultimately from Plato, according to whom all perceptible objects are imperfect copies approximating to unchanging and imperceptible Ideas or Forms. This idea reappeared with the revival of Platonism in the Italian *Renaissance, and throughout much of subsequent European art the model of ideal beauty was supplied by classical statuary (see ANTIQUE). Its most influential formation was in a lecture by *Bellori delivered before the Accademia di S. Luca (see ACADEMY) in Rome in 1664, and published as a preface to his *Lives* in 1672. To Bellori, the contemporary artist who best exemplified the doctrine was *Poussin, whose example greatly influenced the French Académie Royale (see ACADEMY) in the 17th century. The doctrine provided the philosophical justification for the *Grand Manner, and was the basis of criticism of anti-idealistic artists such as *Caravaggio and *Rembrandt, who were thought to have broken the 'rules' of good art. Although the doctrine has been responsible for much arid art, it has also been an inspiration to such great artists as *Raphael, who said, 'To paint a beautiful woman I must see several, and I have also recourse to a certain ideal in my mind', and Guido *Reni, who said, 'The beautiful and pure *idea* must be in the mind, and then it is no matter what the model is.'

ideal landscape. A type of landscape painting, invented by Annibale *Carracci in the first decade of the 17th century, in which natural elements are composed into a grand and highly formalized arrangement suitable as a setting for small figures from serious religious or mythological subjects. It was an extraordinarily influential invention, developed most memorably by *Claude and *Poussin.

illuminated manuscripts. Books written by hand, decorated with pictures and ornaments of different kinds. The word 'illuminated' comes from a usage of the Latin word *illuminare* in connection with oratory or prose style, where it means 'adorn'. The decorations are of three main types: (*a*) *miniatures* or small pictures incorporated into the text or occupying the whole page or part of the border; (*b*) *initial letters* either containing scenes (*historiated initials) or with elaborate decoration; (*c*) *borders*, which may consist of miniatures but more often are composed of decorative motifs. They may enclose the whole of the text space or occupy only a small part of the margin of the page.

Manuscripts are for the most part written on *parchment or vellum. From the 14th century paper was used for less sumptuous copies. The pigments were usually mixed with *glair (white of egg) and water, sometimes with the addition of egg yolk or gum. Although a number of books have miniatures and ornaments executed in outline drawing only, the majority are fully coloured. After the introduction of printing in the mid-15th century the illuminated book became outmoded, although fine examples were produced well into the 16th century. During the 15th and 16th centuries illuminations were often added to printed books.

illusionism. Term applied in its broadest sense to the basic principle of *naturalistic art whereby verisimilitude in representation causes the spectator in various degrees to seem actually to be seeing the object represented, or the space in which it is represented, even though with part of his mind he knows that he is looking at a pictorial representation. In a somewhat narrower sense 'illusionism' refers to the use of pictorial techniques such as *perspective and foreshortening to deceive the eye (if not the

mind) into taking that which is painted for that which is real, or in architecture and stage scenery to make the constructed forms seem visually more extensive than they are. Two specific forms of illusionism in painting are *quadratura, in which painted architecture appears to extend the real space of a room, and *trompe-l'œil, in which the spectator is genuinely, if momentarily, tricked into thinking that a painted object is a real one.

impasto. Thickly applied opaque paint (usually oil paint) showing the marks of the brush or other instrument of application.

Imperial War Museum. London. See OFFICIAL WAR ART.

Impressionism. A movement in painting that originated in France in the 1860s and had an enormous impact on Western art over the following half-century. As an organized movement, Impressionism was purely a French phenomenon, but many of its ideas and practices were adopted in other countries, and by the turn of the century it was a dominant influence on avant-garde art in Europe (and also in the USA and Australia). In essence, its effect was to undermine the authority of large, formal, highly finished paintings in favour of works that more immediately expressed the artist's personality and response to the world.

The Impressionists were not a formal group with clearly defined principles and aims; rather they were a loose association of artists linked by some community of outlook who banded together for the purpose of exhibiting, most of them having had difficulty in getting their work accepted for the official *Salon (they held eight group shows, all in Paris, in 1874, 1876, 1877, 1879, 1880, 1881, 1882, and 1886). The main figures involved were (in alphabetical order) *Cézanne, *Degas, *Manet, *Monet, Camille *Pissarro, *Renoir, and *Sisley; Berthe *Morisot, too, played a central role in the movement. Frédéric *Bazille was part of the original nucleus but died tragically early in 1870; the minor figures included Armand *Guillaumin, who was the last survivor of those who showed in the 1874 exhibition, dying in 1927. Monet, Renoir, and Sisley met as students, and the others came into contact with them through the artistic café society of Paris. There were friendly ties of varied degrees of intimacy linking each of them to most of the others, but Degas and even more Manet were set somewhat apart because they came from a higher stratum of society than the others, and the artists' commitment to Impressionism varied considerably (Manet was much respected as a senior figure, but he never exhibited with the group). They were united, however, in rebelling against academic conventions to try to depict their surroundings with spontaneity and freshness, capturing an 'impression' of what the eye sees at a particular moment, rather than a detailed record of appearances. Their archetypal subject was landscape (and painting out of doors, directly from nature, was one of the key characteristics of the movement), but they treated many other subjects, notably ones involving everyday city life. Degas, for example, made subjects such as horse races, dancers, and laundresses his own, and Renoir is famous for his pictures of pretty women and children.

In trying to capture the effects of light on varied surfaces, particularly in open-air settings, the Impressionists transformed painting, using bright colours and sketchy brushwork that seemed bewildering or shocking to traditionalists. The name 'Impressionism', in fact, was coined derisively, when the painter and critic Louis Leroy (1812–85) latched onto a picture by Monet, *Impression: Sunrise* (1872, Mus. Marmottan, Paris), at the group's first exhibition, heading his abusive review 'Exposition des Impressionistes' (*Le Charivari*, 25 Apr. 1874); he dismissed the group as a whole as 'hostile to good manners, to devotion to form, and to respect for the masters'. Although the critical response to the Impressionists was not as one-sided as is sometimes suggested, Leroy's attitude prevailed in conservative circles for many years; for example, when Gustave *Caillebotte left his superb Impressionist collection to the French nation in 1894, Jean-Léon *Gérôme wrote that 'For the Government to accept such filth, there would have to be a great moral slackening.' However, by the time of the final exhibition in 1886 the Impressionists as a whole were starting to achieve critical praise and financial success (helped by the dedicated promotion of *Durand-Ruel), and during the 1890s their influence began to be widely felt (by this time the group had broken up and only Monet continued to pursue Impressionist ideals rigorously).

Few artists outside France adopted Impressionism wholesale, but many lightened their palettes and loosened their brushwork as they synthesized its ideas with their local traditions. It was perhaps in the USA that it was most eagerly adopted, both by painters such as Childe *Hassam and the other members of The *Ten and by collectors (Mary *Cassatt helped to de-

velop the taste among her wealthy picture-buying friends). It also made a significant impact in Australia, with Tom *Roberts playing the leading role in its introduction. In Britain, *Sickert and *Steer are generally regarded as the main channels through which Impressionism influenced the country's art, but the differences between their work shows how broadly and imprecisely the term has been used (at the time, D. S. *MacColl commented that it was applied to 'any new painting that surprised or annoyed the critics or public'). For a few years around 1890, Steer painted in a sparklingly fresh Impressionist manner, but his style later became more sober; Sickert adopted the broken brushwork of Impressionism (as did his followers in the *Camden Town Group), but he used much more subdued colour, and he had a taste for quirky, distinctively English subject matter. In contrast, the painters of the *Newlyn School often painted out of doors in conscious imitation of the French and used comparatively high-keyed colour, but they generally did not adopt Impressionist brushwork. Accordingly, many authorities think that among British artists, only Steer—and he only briefly—can be considered a 'pure' Impressionist.

In addition to prompting imitation and adaptation, Impressionism also inspired various counter-reactions—indeed its influence was so great that much of the history of late 19th-century and early 20th-century painting is the story of its aftermath. The *Neo-Impressionists, for example, tried to give the optical principles of Impressionism a scientific basis, and the *Post-Impressionists began a long series of movements that attempted to free colour and line from purely representational functions. Similarly, the *Symbolists wanted to restore the emotional values that they thought the Impressionists had sacrificed through concentrating so strongly on the fleeting and the casual.

imprimatura. A thin layer of transparent colour applied to a white *ground to reduce its absorbency and tone down its brightness.

Inchbold, J. W. (John William) (*b* Leeds, 29 Aug. 1830; *d* Leeds, 23 Jan. 1888). English painter. In the 1850s he was friendly with the *Pre-Raphaelites and with *Ruskin (with whom he visited Switzerland in 1858) and at this time he painted some outstanding Pre-Raphaelite landscapes, with meticulous detail (*In Early Spring*, 1855, Ashmolean Mus., Oxford). Later his style became broader. Inchbold had a difficult temperament and never enjoyed much success.

He travelled a good deal and lived in Switzerland for most of the final decade of his life.

Independent Group. A small and informal discussion group that met intermittently between 1952 and 1955 at the *Institute of Contemporary Arts, London. Its members included Lawrence *Alloway, Richard *Hamilton, and Eduardo *Paolozzi. The issues they discussed included advertising and mass culture, and the first phase of British *Pop art grew out of the group.

Indiana, Robert (b New Castle, Ind., 13 Sept. 1928). American painter, sculptor, and graphic artist. His original name was Robert Clark, but he adopted the name of his native state as his own. He is regarded as one of the leading American *Pop artists, and although he has done some figurative paintings he is best known for pictures involving geometric shapes emblazoned with lettering and signs. His vivid colours often create effects of visual ambiguity reminiscent of those of *Op art.

Indian ink. See INK.

Informalism. See ART INFORMEL.

infra-red reflectography. See UNDER-DRAWING.

Ingres, Jean-Auguste-Dominique (b Montauban, 29 Aug. 1780; d Paris, 14 Jan. 1867). French painter, the son of a minor painter and sculptor, **Jean-Marie-Joseph Ingres** (1755–1814). After an early academic training in the Toulouse Academy he moved to Paris in 1797 to study in *David's studio. He won the *Prix de Rome in 1801, but because of the unsettled political situation in France his departure for Italy was postponed until 1806. In the interval he produced his first portraits. These fall into two categories: portraits of himself and his friends, often *Romantic in spirit (Self-Portrait, 1804, Mus. Condé, Chantilly), and portraits of well-to-do clients characterized by purity of line and enamel-like colouring (Mlle Rivière, 1805, Louvre, Paris). Their expressive contours have a sensuous beauty of their own beyond their function to contain and delineate form, and this was characteristic of Ingres's painting throughout his life.

During his first years in Rome Ingres continued to execute portraits and began to paint bathers, a theme that was to become one of his favourites (Valpinçon Bather, 1808, Louvre). When his four-year scholarship ended, he decided to stay in Rome, where he earned his living mainly with pencil portraits of members of the French colony. However, he also received more substantial commissions, including two decorative paintings for Napoleon's palace in Rome (Triumph of Romulus over Acron, 1812, École des Beaux-Arts, Paris; and Ossian's Dream, 1813, Mus. Ingres, Montauban). In 1820 he moved from Rome to Florence, where he remained for four years, working mainly on his *Raphaelesque Vow of Louis XIII, commissioned for the cathedral of Montauban. Ingres's work had often been severely criticized in Paris because of its 'Gothic' distortions, and when he accompanied this painting to the *Salon of 1824 he was surprised to find it acclaimed and himself set up as the leader of the academic opposition to the Romanticism exemplified by Delacroix (whose Massacre at Chios was shown at the same Salon).

Ingres stayed in Paris for the next decade and received the official success and honours he had always craved. During this period he devoted much of his time to executing two large works: the Apotheosis of Homer, for a ceiling in the *Louvre (installed 1827), and the Martyrdom of St Symphorian (shown at the 1834 Salon) for the cathedral of Autun. When the latter painting was badly received, however, he accepted the directorship of the French Academy in Rome, a post he retained until 1840. He was a model administrator and teacher, greatly improving the academy's facilities, but he produced few major works in this period. In 1841 he returned to France, once again acclaimed as the champion of traditional values. He was heartbroken when his wife died in 1849, but he made a happy second marriage in 1852, and he continued working with great energy into his eighties. In this final period he produced some of his best portraits (Mme Moitessier, 1856, NG, London), and one of his acknowledged masterpieces dates from the last years of his life, the extraordinarily sensuous Turkish Bath (1863, Louvre). At his death he left a huge bequest of his work (several paintings and more than 4,000 drawings) to his home town of Montauban and they are now in the museum bearing his name there.

Ingres is a puzzling artist and his career is full of contradictions. By the end of his life he was perceived as the great upholder of the French classical tradition, yet he had spent much of his early career obstinately persisting with work that was unappreciated in Paris. In his way of life he was bourgeois, but as *Baudelaire remarked, his finest works 'are the product of a deeply sensuous nature'. The central contradiction of his career is that although he was held up as the guardian of classical rules and precepts, it is his personal obsessions and mannerisms that make him such a great artist. His technique as a painter was academically unimpeachable—he said paint should be as smooth 'as the skin of an onion'—but he was often attacked for the expressive distortions of his draughtsmanship; critics said, for example, that the abnormally long back of *La Grande Odalisque* (1814, Louvre) had three extra vertebrae. Unfortunately his influence was mainly seen in those shortcomings and weaknesses that have come to be regarded as the hallmark of inferior academic work; he had scores of admiring pupils, but *Chassériau was the only one to attain distinction. In terms of calligraphic draughtsmanship, his true successors were *Degas and *Picasso. See also TROUBADOUR STYLE.

inhabited initial. In an illuminated manuscript, an enlarged initial letter decorated with a figure or figures. The figures may be purely decorative or only loosely related to the text, whereas *historiated initials contain scenes directly illustrating it.

ink. Coloured fluid used for writing, drawing, or printing. Inks usually have staining power without body, but printers' inks—pigments mixed with oil and varnish—are opaque. The use of inks goes back in China and Egypt to at least 2500 BC. The earliest known type was produced from lampblack (a pigment made from soot) ground into a solution of glue or gums. These materials could be moulded into dry sticks or blocks, which were then mixed with water for use. Ink brought from China or Japan in such dry form came to be known in the West as 'Chinese ink' or 'Indian ink'. The names are also given to a similar preparation used today. Other materials that have been used to make ink include plant dyes, soot (see BISTRE), and fluids from marine creatures (see SEPIA). Most modern inks use soluble synthetic dyes as the colouring agent.

Innes, J. D. (James Dickson) (*b* Llanelli, 27 Feb. 1887; *d* Swanley, Kent, 22 Aug. 1914). British painter, mainly of landscapes (particularly mountain scenes) but also occasionally of figure subjects. He often painted with his friend Augustus *John, particularly in their native Wales in 1911 and 1912. His early work was in an *Impressionist manner influenced by *Steer, but he developed a more expressive *Post-Impressionist style combining hot colour and decorative pattern. He usually painted on a fairly small scale and worked a good deal in watercolour.

Inness, George (*b* nr. Newburgh, NY, 1 May 1825; *d* Bridge of Allan, Scotland, 3 Aug. 1894). American landscape painter. He was largely self-taught, learning a good deal during several lengthy visits to Europe (the *Barbizon School in particular had a powerful impact on him). His early work was influenced by the detailed handling and *Romantic approach of the *Hudson River School, but his style became much freer and more atmospheric, and he turned away from grandiose scenes to intimate subjects lacking in conventional picturesque appeal. He was a deeply spiritual man and some of his later work has a mystical, *Symbolist flavour. At the beginning of his career he worked in New York, but in 1859 he moved to the village of Medfield, near Boston, where he found the isolation more conducive to his work; later he settled in New Jersey. Inness is considered by many to be the greatest American landscape painter of the 19th century. His son **George Inness Jr.** (1854–1926) was also a painter and published an account of his father's career (1917).

Inshaw, David. See BLAKE, SIR PETER.

installation. A term that can be applied very generally to the disposition of objects in an exhibition (the hanging of paintings, the arrangement of sculptures, and so on), but which also has the more specific meaning of a one-off work (often a large-scale *assemblage) conceived for and usually more or less filling a specific interior (generally that of a gallery). This type of work has various precedents, including the room-filling Merz constructions of Kurt *Schwitters, but it was not until the 1970s that the term came into common use and not until the 1980s that certain artists started to specialize in this kind of work, creating a genre of 'Installation art'. In the 1970s installations were often impermanent and could be seen as part of the movement against the collectable art 'object' that was so fashionable at the time. However, many installations are now intended for permanent display, and even some of the most unlikely works have proved collectable. A well-known example is *20:50* (1987) by the British sculptor Richard Wilson (1953–), which consists of a room filled with used sump oil; this was created for the Matt's Gallery, London, but it was subsequently resited at the Royal Scottish Academy, Edinburgh, and it is now in the Saatchi Gallery, London.

Institute of Contemporary Arts (ICA), London. Cultural centre founded by Roland

*Penrose and Herbert *Read in 1947 to encourage new developments in the arts and cater for some of the functions fulfilled by the *Museum of Modern Art in New York—organizing exhibitions, lectures, films, and so on. Its original home was in Dover Street, but it moved to Nash House, the Mall, in 1968. Many leading artists have been members of the ICA and it has played an important role in certain developments; for example, in the 1950s it was the cradle of British *Pop art (see INDEPENDENT GROUP), and in 1969 it was the venue for the first exhibition of *Conceptual art in Britain, 'When Attitudes Become Form'.

Institut Néerlandais, Paris. See LUGT.

Insular art. A term applied to art produced in the British Isles (more specifically northern England, Ireland, and Scotland) from about AD 500 to 900. It is used mainly in the field of illuminated manuscripts, where its neutrality circumvents the controversies (sometimes fuelled by national loyalties) about the place of origin of certain works, such as the *Book of Kells, as well as underlining the close cultural links between Ireland and the north of Britain during this period (see CELTIC ART). The term Hiberno-Saxon art is used in a similar way.

intaglio. Carving or engraving on a small scale, as for example on a gemstone or seal, in which the design is hollowed into the surface—the opposite of *cameo, in which the design projects above the surface. In the graphic arts, 'intaglio printing' refers to any process of printmaking in which the parts of the plate or block that will take the ink are recessed into it rather than raised above it ('relief printing'). *Etching is thus a form of intaglio printing (see PRINT).

intarsia. Method of creating a picture or design on a wooden surface (typically wall panelling or a piece of furniture) by attaching small pieces of variously coloured woods to it. Intarsia was popular in *Renaissance Italy; the most famous examples of the technique decorate the Studiolo of Federico II da *Montefeltro in the Palazzo Ducale, Urbino.

International Gothic. Style in painting, sculpture, and the decorative arts that spread widely over western Europe between c.1375 and c.1425. The style was characterized by aristocratic elegance and delicate naturalistic detail and was formed by a blending of elements from Italy and northern Europe, a situation encouraged by the cultural rivalry of major courts and the growing frequency with which leading artists travelled between them. Lombardy, Franco-Flemish Burgundy, and Bohemia were among the most important centres of the style, major exponents of which included *Gentile da Fabriano, *Pisanello, and the *Limbourg brothers. Elements of the style are present in the work of many of the leading artists of the early *Renaissance, such as Fra *Angelico, *Ghiberti, and *Uccello. In the context of English art, the finest work in the style is the celebrated Wilton Diptych (NG, London), named after Wilton House, Wiltshire, where it was in the collection of the earls of Pembroke for more than two centuries. This painting testifies to how genuinely international the International Gothic style was, for although it is a work of extraordinary beauty and must be from the hand of an artist of the highest rank, authorities disagree as to his likely nationality (English, French, Italian, and Bohemian have been proposed). It shows Richard II (reigned 1377–99) being presented to the Virgin and Child by John the Baptist, Edward the Confessor, and Edmund the Martyr (his patron saints), but its purpose and significance are uncertain. It probably dates from late in Richard's reign (heraldic evidence suggests it cannot be earlier than c.1395) and was presumably commissioned by him.

Intimisme. A type of painting featuring intimate domestic scenes, more or less *Impressionist in technique, particularly associated with *Bonnard and *Vuillard, who practised it from the 1890s (this is when the term was first used). Whereas the Impressionists usually aimed at accurately reflecting the colours of the natural world, Bonnard and Vuillard often exaggerated and distorted colour to express mood, conveying the warmth and comfort of an untroubled domestic life.

intonaco. In *fresco painting, the final layer of plaster on the wall; the paint is applied to it while the plaster is still wet.

iron. A widely available metal (it makes up about 5 per cent of the earth's crust) that has been used for practical and to a lesser extent decorative purposes since prehistoric times. In its pure state it is soft and silvery white, but it is rarely found in this form, almost always containing impurities, particularly carbon, that affect its properties; the more carbon present, the more brittle the metal generally is. As used in manufacturing and art, iron divides into two main types—cast iron and wrought iron. Cast iron has a high carbon content and is consequently brittle, but it is cheap to produce and resists corrosion well. Wrought iron has a lower carbon content, making it more pliable; it can be hammered into elaborate shapes and has been much used in decorative work, for example in ornamental gateways. Steel is iron that has been purified and alloyed with small quantities of other elements, producing an extremely strong material that is a basic element in modern industry. 'Cor-Ten' steel is a proprietary name for a type of 'self-weathering' steel popular with some contemporary sculptors. It contains a small amount of copper and acquires a *patina that resists corrosion.

Some cast iron sculpture was made in the 19th century, but it was not until the 20th century that iron and steel became important additions to the sculptor's materials. The Spanish sculptor Pablo Gargallo (1881–1934) was one of the first modern artists to use iron, making hammered masks in the material from about 1907. His work helped inspire *Picasso to create what has been described as the first steel sculpture, *Guitar* (1912, MoMA, New York), made of sheet metal and wire. (Iron and steel are not always clearly differentiated; up to about the Second World War, the material used in sculpture was generally referred to as iron, but much of it could probably be more accurately described as steel.) Picasso's sculptural experimentation was an inspiration to *Tatlin, the founder of *Constructivism, in which steel (along with other modern materials) played a large part, its association with engineering making it appropriate to the creation of forms expressing the machine age. Picasso also played an important part in the development of welded sculpture, collaborating from 1928 to 1931 with Julio *González, the main pioneer of the technique. González (who came from a family of metalworkers) taught Picasso welding, in which pieces of metal are joined by melting them together with a blowtorch (first made commercially available in 1901). Welding produces a very strong joint, making it possible to connect pieces of metal in free-flowing, openwork constructions, such as Picasso's *Woman in a Garden* (1929–30, Mus. Picasso, Paris).

Among the many sculptors influenced by such 'drawing in space' was David *Smith. Like González, he was highly influential on sculpture after the Second World War, and more than anyone else he established steel as a material with its own expressive qualities, notably by grinding and polishing the surface of his work. Smith also helped encourage the use of scrap metal and prefabricated industrial parts in sculpture. Scrap has been much used in *Junk art, for example, and industrial parts in the work of Anthony *Caro, who inspired a generation of British abstract sculptors. *Minimal artists, too, have made much use of steel, valuing its impersonal qualities.

Isakson, Karl (*b* Stockholm, 16 Jan. 1878; *d* Copenhagen, 19 Feb. 1922). Swedish painter, active mainly in Denmark. He worked in Paris 1905–7 and 1911–14 and was one of the first Scandinavians to show the influence of *Cézanne and the *Cubists. His work had considerable influence on other Scandinavian artists, although it was virtually unknown in Sweden until 1922, when an exhibition was held in Stockholm soon after his death. He painted still-lifes, nudes, and landscapes, and towards the end of his life visionary religious subjects, which he treated with the same regard for structure.

Isenbrandt, Adriaen. See YSENBRANDT.

Israëls, Jozef (*b* Groningen, 27 Jan. 1824; *d* Scheveningen, 12 Aug. 1911). Dutch painter. He studied in Amsterdam and Paris and began his career as a portrait and historical painter, but in the 1850s he turned to the kind of work for which he is principally known—scenes of fishermen and peasants and the milieu in which they lived. In 1870 he moved from Amsterdam to The Hague and thereafter became one of the leading members of the *Hague School. He has been called 'the Dutch *Millet' and he won great popularity because of his piously sentimental approach; indeed, in his time he was the most famous living Dutch artist, with an international reputation. His son **Isaac** (1865–1934) also worked mainly in The Hague, but in a style almost completely independent of his father's. His pictures of the social life of his time are influenced by *Breitner and characterized by the vivid colours and vigorous brushwork of the *Impressionists.

Itinerants. See WANDERERS.

Itten, Johannes (*b* Südern-Linden, 11 Nov. 1888; *d* Zurich, 25 May 1967). Swiss painter, designer, writer on art, teacher, and administrator. In 1916 he opened his own school of art in Vienna, then from 1919 to 1923 he taught at the *Bauhaus, where he was in charge of the 'preliminary course', obligatory for all students. In 1923 he left the Bauhaus and opened another school of his own in Berlin, then from 1932 to 1938 he taught at the Krefeld School of Textile

Design. In 1938 he settled in Zurich, where he held four posts concurrently—as director of the School of Arts and Crafts, the Museum of Arts and Crafts, the Rietberg Museum, and the School of Textile Design. He held the first three posts until 1953 and retired from the fourth in 1961. Itten wrote several books on art theory and his work as a painter consisted mainly of geometrical abstractions exemplifying his researches into colour. However, he is best remembered as a teacher, especially for his preliminary course at the Bauhaus, which had a great influence on instruction in other art schools. He emphasized the importance of knowledge of materials, but also encouraged his pupils to develop their imaginations through, for example, automatic writing (see AUTOMATISM). His mystical ideas were opposed to the technological outlook of *Gropius (their quarrels caused Itten's departure from the Bauhaus) and he had a reputation as a crank (he followed an obscure faith called Mazdaznan, shaved his head, and wore a long robe), but he influenced many of his students. Frank Whitford (*Bauhaus*, 1984) describes him as 'a perplexing mixture of saint and charlatan'.

Ivanov, Alexander (*b* St Petersburg, 28 July 1806; *d* St Petersburg, 15 July 1858). Russian painter. He studied at the St Petersburg Academy under his father, the painter **Andrei Ivanov** (*c.*1772–1848). Most of his career was spent in Rome, where he settled in 1831. Initially he was preoccupied with subjects from the classical world, but partly under the influence of the *Nazarenes (he was a friend of *Overbeck) he turned to religious painting, and his fame is inseparable from his main work, which occupied him for twenty years, *Christ's First Appearance to the People* (1837–57, Tretyakov Gal., Moscow). This enormous painting achieved European celebrity long before its completion, but it had a disappointing reception when it was finally exhibited in St Petersburg in 1858, its *Raphaelesque composition being at odds with the naturalistic setting and details, the result of hundreds of preparatory studies. Ivanov accompanied the painting to St Petersburg and died there of cholera a few months afterwards. He had no immediate followers, but the moral sincerity of his work was influential on many Russian painters, notably *Kramskoi and *Repin; when Repin first saw *Christ's First Appearance to the People* in 1867 he pronounced it 'the greatest work in the whole world, by a genius, born in Russia'.

ivory. A hard, smooth, creamy white substance obtained from the tusks or teeth of certain animals, widely used as a carving material from prehistoric times onwards. Elephant tusks have been the commonest source of ivory, but mammoth tusks (from deposits in Siberia), hippopotamus teeth, and walrus tusks have been much used (the famous Bury St Edmunds Cross (see MASTER HUGO) is in walrus ivory); carvings made from narwhal and rhinoceros horn, stag horn, and even bone have also been embraced by the term. True ivory is an excellent material for high-quality, small-scale sculpture, for although it is difficult to carve it can be easily worked with saws, drills, files, and rasps, and it can take a fine polish and detailed surface treatment. In the ancient world it was classed with gold and precious stones as a luxury material, and the Greeks used it for colossal *chryselephantine (gold and ivory) cult statues. Unless separate pieces are joined together (as in such statues), the size and shape of a carving are limited by the dimensions of the tusk, the curvature of which has sometimes been exploited to give a graceful swing to the figure, notably in *Gothic statuettes of the Virgin. Though ivory was often painted in the Middle Ages, its natural lustre, translucence, and satin smoothness have always been valued, making it an ideal material for small objects that must be handled to be fully appreciated, such as chessmen and Japanese netsuke. After the 14th century ivory carving declined steadily in Europe, but the art revived in the 17th century, Georg *Petel being a noted exponent in this period.

J

Jabach, Everard (*b* Cologne, 10 July 1618; *d* Paris, 6 Mar. 1695). German-born French financier and collector. He inherited a vast fortune, as well as numerous works of art, from his banker father, who died in 1636. In about 1638 he settled in Paris, where he became a leading financier and built up a princely collection. He was one of the chief buyers of works from the *Royal Collection sold after the execution of Charles I in 1649, for example, and he also acquired part of Lord *Arundel's collection. His portrait was painted by van *Dyck, *Le Brun, and *Rigaud, and he owned many celebrated pictures, including *Caravaggio's *Death of the Virgin* and the *Concert champêtre* attributed at the time to *Giorgione but now usually given to *Titian (both pictures are now in the Louvre, Paris); however, his collection was renowned above all for its drawings. In 1662 he sold some works to Louis XIV and in 1671, after suffering financial reverses, he was obliged to sell most of the rest of the collection to the king on very unfavourable terms. Subsequently he prospered again and made another collection—less remarkable than the first but still of high quality. After his death this was gradually dispersed by his children; many of the drawings were bought by *Crozat.

Jack of Diamonds. See KNAVE OF DIAMONDS.

Jackson, A. Y. (Alexander Young) (*b* Montreal, 3 Oct. 1882; *d* Kleinburg, Ontario, 5 Apr. 1974). Canadian landscape painter, active mainly in Toronto, where he settled in 1913 after extensive travels in Europe. He was one of the leading artists in the *Group of Seven and in the later years of his long career became a venerated senior figure in Canadian painting. Jackson visited virtually every region of Canada, including the Arctic, and responded particularly to the hilly region of rural Quebec along the St Lawrence River. From 1921 he returned there almost every spring, and the canvases he prepared from sketches made there are probably his finest work. Their easy, rolling rhythms, and rich and full colouring had a major impact on Canadian landscape painting.

Jacomart, Master. See BAÇO.

Jacopo della Quercia. See QUERCIA.

Jacque, Charles. See BARBIZON SCHOOL.

James, M. R. See FITZWILLIAM MUSEUM.

Jameson, Anna Brownell (née Murphy) (*b* Dublin, 17 May 1794; *d* London, 17 Mar. 1860). British writer, daughter of an Irish miniaturist, Denis Brownell Murphy (*d* 1842), who moved to England in 1798. She married a barrister, Robert Jameson, in 1825, but they soon separated. By this time she was already a successful author and for the rest of her life she kept up a prodigious and varied literary output. Her most famous book is probably *Characteristics of Women* (1832), later retitled *Shakespeare's Heroines*; it is illustrated with her own etchings and dedicated to the actress Fanny Kemble, one of her many famous and influential friends. In the last two decades of her life her writings were mainly on art and she has been described as the first professional English art historian. Her first major book in the field was *A Handbook to the Public Galleries of Art in and near London* (1842). She modestly said it 'ought to have fallen into the hands of Dr *Waagen, or some such bigwig, instead of poor little me', but in fact it is an impressively detailed and accurate work. Her other books include several on Christian iconography, among them *Sacred and Legendary Art* (2 vols., 1848) and *Legends of the Madonna* (1852). Although antiquated in certain respects, they are clearly written, full of information, and still useful.

Jamesone, George (*b* Aberdeen, 1589/90; *d* Aberdeen, late 1644). Scottish portrait painter, active in Aberdeen and Edinburgh. His name has been indiscriminately attached to a great number of Scottish portraits of the period, as he is virtually the only 17th-century Scottish painter about whom anything is known. A now discounted tradition has it that he trained with *Rubens and he has been flatteringly called 'the Scottish van *Dyck', but his style was closer to Cornelius *Johnson's. It is difficult to assess, however, as many of the works that are certainly by him are in a bad state of preservation. John Michael *Wright was his pupil.

Janet. See CLOUET.

Janis, Sidney (*b* Buffalo, NY, 8 July 1896; *d* New York, 23 Nov. 1989). American art dealer and writer on art. Between the departure of Peggy *Guggenheim from the USA in 1947 and the rise of Leo *Castelli in the 1960s he was the most important figure in promoting the work of avant-garde American artists, particularly the *Abstract Expressionists. He was also interested in *naive art and in 1939 'discovered' one of the outstanding American naive painters, Morris Hirshfield (1872–1946). Janis wrote *They Taught Themselves: American Primitive Painters of the 20th Century* (1942), *Abstract and Surrealist Art in America* (1944), and (with his wife Harriet) *Picasso: The Recent Years, 1939–1946* (1946).

Janssen (or **Janssens**), **Abraham** (*b* c.1575; *bur.* Antwerp, 25 Jan. 1632). Flemish figure and portrait painter, active mainly in Antwerp. In 1598 and 1601 he is documented in Rome and by 1602 he was back in Antwerp. A second visit to Italy has been postulated, for although in 1601 he was painting in a *Mannerist style (*Diana and Callisto*, MFA, Budapest), by 1610 (*Scaldis and Antwerpia*, Koninklijk Mus., Antwerp) his work had become much more solid, sober, and classical, suggesting close knowledge of *Caravaggio in particular. For the next decade Janssen was one of the most powerful and individual painters in Flanders, but during the 1620s his work became less remarkable as he fell under the all-pervasive influence of *Rubens. His pupils included Gerard *Seghers and Theodoor *Rombouts.

Japanese prints. See UKIYO-E.

Jawlensky, Alexei von (*b* Torzhok, 13 [25] Mar. 1864; *d* Wiesbaden, 15 Mar. 1941). Russian *Expressionist painter, active mainly in Germany. Originally he was an army officer, but in 1906 he resigned his commission and moved to Munich in order to devote himself to art. Munich was to be his home until the outbreak of the First World War, but he travelled a good deal in this period, notably making several visits to France (he was the first of his Munich associates to have direct contact with advanced French art). In 1905 he met *Matisse in Paris and was influenced by the strong colours and bold outlines of the *Fauves. He combined them with influences from the Russian traditions of icon painting and peasant art to form a highly personal style that expressed his passionate temperament and mystical conception of art. A mood of melancholy introspection—far removed from the ebullience of Fauvism—is characteristic of much of his work and it has been said that he 'saw Matisse through Russian eyes'. In 1909 he was one of the founders of the *Neue Künstlervereinigung, and apart from *Kandinsky he was the outstanding artist of the group. His most characteristic works of this period are a series of powerful portrait heads, begun in 1910 (*Alexander Sacharoff*, 1913, Städtisches Mus., Wiesbaden). On the outbreak of war in 1914 Jawlensky took refuge in Switzerland, where he remained until 1921. His work there included a series of 'variations' on the view from a window—small, semi-abstract landscapes with a meditative, religious aura. Like Kandinsky and others, Jawlensky believed in a correspondence between colours and musical sounds and he named these pictures *Songs without Words*. In 1918 he began a series of nearly abstract heads, in which he reduced the features to a few curves and lines. Unlike Kandinsky, however, he always based his forms on nature. From 1921 he lived in Wiesbaden, and in 1924 he joined with Kandinsky, *Klee, and *Feininger to form the *Blaue Vier. From 1929 he suffered from arthritis and by 1938 this had forced him to abandon painting completely.

Jean de Bruges. See BONDOL.

Jean de Paris. See PERRÉAL.

Jeanneret, Charles-Édouard. See LE CORBUSIER.

Jegher, Christoffel. See WOODCUT.

Jervas, Charles (*b* Dublin, c.1675; *d* London, 2 Nov. 1739). Irish painter, active mainly in London. His surname was pronounced, and often spelled, Jarvis. After studying with *Kneller he spent ten years in Italy, mainly Rome, before settling in London in 1709. Jervas had a great reputation and succeeded Kneller as principal painter to George II in 1723, but his fame depended on his friendship with various literary figures, who trumpeted his praises, rather than on the quality of his work, which does not rise above the level of that of any other of Kneller's pupils or followers. He has perhaps more claim to literary distinction, for he made a well-regarded translation of Cervantes' *Don Quixote*, posthumously published in 1742. His conceit was enormous: once, having copied a painting by

363

*Titian, he looked from one to the other and said complacently, 'Poor Little Tit! How he would stare!'

Jeune Peinture Belge. An avant-garde artists' association founded in Brussels in 1945 with the aim of holding exhibitions of contemporary Belgian art throughout Europe. The members of the group (who included Pierre *Alechinsky and Pol *Bury) were strongly individualistic and had no common programme, but they were basically abstract in their outlook and were influenced particularly by the expressive abstraction of the post-war *École de Paris. The group dissolved in 1948.

Joest, Jan (b ?Wesel, c.1450/60; d Haarlem, 1519). German-Netherlandish painter, often known as Joest van Calcar (or Kalkar), after one of his main places of work, Kalkar in the Rhine valley. It was there that he produced his masterpieces—twenty scenes on the life of Christ (1505–8) decorating the shutters of the high altar in the church of St Nicholas (in situ). These show the influence of *Geertgen, particularly in their delicate handling of landscape, but they have a dignity that is personal. Joest was probably the 'Juan de Holanda' who painted an altarpiece of the Seven Sorrows of the Virgin for Palencia Cathedral in Spain (in situ), commissioned by the Bishop of Palencia when he visited the Netherlands in 1505. From 1509 Joest lived in Haarlem. He was a significant figure in transmitting Netherlandish influence to Germany.

John, Augustus (b Tenby, Pembrokeshire, 4 Jan. 1878; d Fordingbridge, Hampshire, 31 Oct. 1961). British painter and draughtsman. He studied at the *Slade School, 1894–8. In his early days there 'he appeared a neat, timid, unremarkable personality' (DNB), but after injuring his head diving into the sea while on holiday in Pembrokeshire in 1897 he became a dramatically changed figure, described by Wyndham *Lewis as 'a great man of action into whose hands the fairies had placed a paintbrush instead of a sword'. He grew a beard and became the very image of the unpredictable bohemian artist. His work, too, changed startlingly; previously it had been described by *Tonks as 'methodical', but it became vigorous and spontaneous, especially in his brilliant drawings—his draughtsmanship was already legendary by the time he left the Slade. In the first quarter of the 20th century John was identified with all that was most independent and rebellious in British art and he became one of the most talked-about figures of the day. In

1911–14 he led a nomadic life, sometimes living in a caravan and camping with gypsies. As well as romanticized pictures of gypsy life he painted deliciously colourful small-scale landscapes, sometimes working alongside his friend J. D. *Innes. During the same period he also painted ambitious figure compositions, with stylized forms that bring him close to French *Symbolist painters (The Way Down to the Sea, 1909–11, Lamont AG, Exeter, New Hampshire). In the First World War he was an *Official War Artist. It is as a portraitist, however, that John is best remembered. He was taken up by society and painted a host of aristocratic beauties as well as many of the leading literary figures of the day. Increasingly, however, the painterly brilliance of his early work degenerated into flashiness and bombast, and the second half of his long career added little to his achievement, although he remained a colourful, newsworthy figure until the end of his life. He was one of the few British artists who have become familiar to the general public, and his image changed from that of rebel to Grand Old Man (he was awarded the Order of Merit in 1942). He wrote two volumes of autobiography, Chiaroscuro (1952) and Finishing Touches (posthumously published in 1964). A new edition entitled The Autobiography of Augustus John appeared in 1975. His reputation was in decline by the time of his death, but there has subsequently been a revival of interest in him, especially in his early work.

John, Gwen (b Haverfordwest, Pembrokeshire, 22 June 1876; d Dieppe, 18 Sept. 1939). British painter. She was the sister of Augustus *John, but his complete opposite artistically, as she was in personality, living a reclusive life and favouring introspective subjects. After studying at the *Slade School, 1895–8, she took lessons in Paris from *Whistler, and adopted from him the delicate greyish tonality that characterizes much of her work (once when Augustus John mentioned to Whistler that Gwen had a fine sense of character, he replied: 'Character? What's that? It's the tone that matters. Your sister has a fine sense of tone'). In 1899 she returned to London, but in 1904 she settled permanently in France, living first in Paris (earning her living modelling for other artists—including *Rodin, who became her lover), then from 1911 in Meudon, on the outskirts of the city. In 1913 she became a Catholic, and she said: 'My religion and my art, these are my life.' Most of her paintings depict single figures (typically girls or nuns) in interiors, painted with great sensitivity and an unobtrusive originality (*Self-Portrait*, c.1900, NPG, London). She had only one exhibition devoted to her work during her lifetime (at the New Chenil Galleries, London, in 1936) and at the time of her death was little known. However, her brother's prophecy that one day she would be considered a better artist than him has been fulfilled, for as his star has fallen hers has risen, and since the 1960s she has been the subject of numerous books and exhibitions. 'Few on meeting this retiring person in black', said Augustus, 'with her tiny hands and feet, soft, almost inaudible voice, and delicate Pembrokeshire accent would have guessed that here was the greatest woman artist of her age, or, as I think, of any other . . . Fifty years from now [he was speaking in 1946] I shall be known as the brother of Gwen John.'

Johns, Jasper (*b* Augusta, Ga., 15 May 1930). American painter, sculptor, and printmaker. His career has been closely associated with that of Robert *Rauschenberg, and they are considered the leading figures in the move away from *Abstract Expressionism to the types of *Pop art and *Minimal art that succeeded it. They met in 1954 and were close friends until 1962, when they broke up with some bitterness (for a time they were lovers, sharing a triangular relationship with a woman). Soon after meeting they formed a partnership to design window displays for up-market stores, the money they earned allowing them to pursue their artistic experiments. Johns had his first one-man show at Leo *Castelli's gallery in New York in 1958. This was an enormous success, and since then he has become one of the most famous (and wealthy) living artists. Much of his work has been done in the form of series of paintings presenting commonplace two-dimensional objects—for example *Flags*, *Targets*, and *Numbers*—and his sculptures have most characteristically been of equally banal subjects such as beer cans or brushes in a coffee tin. Such works—at one and the same time laboriously realistic and patently artificial—are seen by his admirers as brilliant explorations of the relationship between art and reality; to others, they are as uninteresting as the objects depicted. Much of his later work has been in the form of prints.

Johnson, Cornelius (Cornelis Jonson van Ceulen) (*bapt.* London, 14 Oct. 1593; *d* Utrecht, 5 Aug. 1661). Anglo-Dutch portrait painter. He was born in England of Flemish parents and perhaps trained in Holland. By about 1618 he was active in London and he worked there until 1643, when he left England because of the Civil War and settled in Holland. There are several hundred portraits by him, mainly of people from the upper (but not the highest) levels of society. He was a conservative artist but a sensitive one, with a delicate feeling for colour and characterization. Most of his portraits are in head-and-shoulders format, but he occasionally painted full-lengths.

Johnson, Eastman (*b* Lovell, Me., 29 July 1824; *d* New York, 5 Apr. 1906). American painter and printmaker. He spent his early career in Boston (where he trained as a lithographer) and Washington, then from 1848 to 1855 studied in Europe—in Düsseldorf, The Hague, and Paris. After his return to the USA he worked in various places before settling in New York in 1859. He spent a good deal of time in rural areas, and his best pictures are generally thought to be his outdoor *genre scenes, which are vigorous and fresh in observation (*Cranberry Harvest*, 1880, Timken AG, San Diego). In his later career he devoted himself mainly to fashionable portraiture, with which he earned a handsome living.

Johnson, Gerard the Elder (originally Garat Janssen) (*bur.* London, 30 July 1611). Netherlandish-born sculptor and mason who moved to London, probably as a Protestant refugee, and became an English citizen in 1568. He built up a large practice chiefly as a tomb maker, though chimney-pieces and basins for fountains were also made in his Southwark workshop. A good example of his accomplished but uninspired work is the tomb of the 2nd Earl of Southampton at Titchfield, Hampshire (1592). Two of his sons became sculptors, **Nicholas** (*d* 1624) and **Gerard the Younger**. The latter's name lives on because he made the monument to Shakespeare (*d* 1616) in Holy Trinity church, Stratford-upon-Avon. As a work of art this is feeble, but it is one of only two portraits of Shakespeare generally accepted as an authentic likeness (the other is the *Droeshout engraving). The most distinguished artist in the family seems to have been another son of Gerard the Elder, **Bernard**, as he is said to have been the principal mason for Northumberland House in the Strand and Audley End, Essex, which, although partially demolished, is still, in Sir John Summerson's words, 'the most powerful and impressive of Jacobean houses'.

Johnston, Frank. See GROUP OF SEVEN.

John the Fearless, Duke of Burgundy. See BURGUNDY.

Jones, Allen (*b* Southampton, 1 Sept. 1937). British painter, printmaker, sculptor, and designer, one of the most committed exponents of *Pop art. Although he has worked primarily as a painter, printmaker, and designer, he is best known to the public for a distinctive type of sculpture in which figures of women—more or less life-size, dressed in fetishistic clothing, and with what Jones calls 'high definition female parts'—double as pieces of furniture; for example, a woman on all fours supporting a sheet of glass on her back becomes a coffee table, and a standing figure with outstretched hands becomes a hatstand. He began making such sculptures in the late 1960s and continues to do so, although in a manner that he calls 'less aggressive' and 'easier to take' (they have come in for a good deal of criticism for alleged demeaning of women as sex objects; an article in the feminist journal *Spare Rib* in 1973 suggested that they expressed a castration complex). His work as a designer includes sets and costumes for the erotic review *Oh! Calcutta!* (1969).

Jones, David (*b* Brockley, Kent, 1 Nov. 1895; *d* Harrow, Greater London, 28 Oct. 1974). British painter, draughtsman, printmaker, and writer. A convert to Roman Catholicism in 1921, he met Eric *Gill in 1922 and under his influence achieved a sense of purpose (his studies at the Camberwell School of Art, 1909–15, had left him, as he said, 'completely muddle-headed as to the function of art in general'). Gill not only introduced him to wood engraving, but also guided him in rejecting the current concern with formal properties in favour of an art that aspired to reveal universal and symbolic truths behind the appearance of things. Jones worked mainly in pencil and watercolour, his subjects including landscape, portraits, still-life, animals, and imaginative themes; Arthurian legend was one of his main inspirations. As a writer he is best known for *In Parenthesis* (1937), a long work of mixed poetry and prose on the subject of the First World War (in which he had fought). T. S. Eliot declared this to be a work of genius and it was awarded the Hawthornden Prize. After the Second World War Jones retired to Harrow and concentrated on calligraphic inscriptions in the Welsh language (he was of Welsh extraction).

Jones, Inigo (*bapt.* London, 19 July 1573; *d* London, 21 June 1652). English architect, stage designer, draughtsman, and painter. Jones was one of the greatest of English architects and certainly the most influential, introducing a pure classical style based on the work of the Italian architect Andrea Palladio to a country where *Renaissance influence had previously been fairly superficial. It was not until he was in his forties, however, that he showed his genius as an architect, and the first known mention of him as an artist is as a 'picture maker' in 1603. No paintings certainly by him are known, but his drawings survive in large numbers (the finest collection is at Chatsworth). They are mainly costume and scenery designs for the court masques, on which he worked from 1605 to 1640, and in which he introduced movable scenery and the proscenium arch into England. Inigo's lively and fluent style as a draughtsman reflects two lengthy visits to Italy (*c.*1600 and 1613–14), the second of them accompanying the great collector the Earl of *Arundel. He advised Arundel on the purchase of Italian antiques while developing his own knowledge of Italian and *antique architecture, and his learning as well as his skills gave him immense prestige in England at the courts of James I and Charles I. His principal collaborator in the masques was the formidable Ben Jonson, with whom he had a running feud about the rival claims of words and spectacle. Few of Jones's buildings survive in anything like their original state. The two most important are in London: the Queen's House at Greenwich (1616–35), for which Orazio *Gentileschi provided decorations, and the Banqueting House in Whitehall (1619–22), with its painted ceiling by *Rubens.

Jones, Thomas (*b* Trevonnen, Radnorshire [now Powys], 26 Sept. 1742; *d* Pencerrig, Radnorshire, 29 Apr. 1803). Welsh landscape painter, a pupil of Richard *Wilson. He painted some ambitious classical landscapes in Wilson's manner, but he is now best known for his remarkably fresh and unaffected oil sketches done in and around Naples and Rome during a period in Italy, 1776–83 (examples are in the National Museum and Gallery, Cardiff). They are among the earliest British examples of this kind of open-air sketch and have a directness that looks forward to *Corot. In 1789 Jones inherited the family estate and thereafter painted comparatively little.

Jongkind, Johan Barthold (*b* Lattrop, 3 June 1819; *d* La-Côte-Saint-André, 9 Feb. 1891). Dutch landscape painter and etcher, active mainly in France, where he was a precursor of *Impressionism. Although he was better appreciated during his lifetime than van *Gogh, in some ways his career is similar to that of his more famous countryman. Both artists made a greater impression abroad than in their own country; both failed to adjust to the society of their time; both endured much poverty and were troubled by serious psychological problems; and sensational aspects of their lives—in Jongkind's case it was alcoholism—have interfered with a balanced appraisal of their achievement. Jongkind studied in The Hague under *Schelfhout. From 1846 he spent much of his time in France and from 1860 he made his home there permanently. He worked and exhibited with members of the *Barbizon School, and during the 1860s he played an important part in the development of Impressionism; his friend *Monet acknowledged him, together with *Boudin, as the most significant formative influence on his work. Jongkind's output was varied, but he is perhaps best known for his atmospheric coastal and river scenes.

Jonson van Ceulen, Cornelis. See JOHNSON, CORNELIUS.

Joos van Cleve (b ?Cleves, c.1490; d Antwerp, 1540/1). Netherlandish painter, presumably from Cleves in the lower Rhine region and active mainly in Antwerp, where he became a member of the painters' guild in 1511. He seems to have been one of the city's leading painters, but his eclectic style and the lack of documented works mean that his career is ill defined. Some of the pictures attributed to him were formerly grouped under the name of the Master of the Death of the Virgin, called after two similar triptychs of this subject in Cologne (1515, Wallraf-Richartz-Mus.) and Munich (Alte Pin.). There is sometimes a flavour of *Leonardo in his paintings, and he may have visited Italy. Almost certainly he worked in France in the early 1530s, and he possibly visited England at about the same time, as a portrait of Henry VIII (c.1536) in the Royal Collection is attributed to him. According to van *Mander he collaborated with Joachim *Patinir: a Rest on the Flight into Egypt (Mus. Royaux, Brussels) is possibly a joint work. The large output from his studio consisted mainly of religious works, particularly pictures of the Virgin and Child and the Holy Family. Joos's son **Cornelis van Cleve** (1520–67) was also a painter. He was known as Sotte Cleve (mad Cleve) after becoming insane in 1556—evidently a result of failing to win the patronage of Philip II of Spain (see HABSBURG).

Joos van Wassenhove (active c.1460–80). Netherlandish painter, part of whose career was spent in Italy, where he was known as Giusto da Guanto (Justus of Ghent). He became a member of the Antwerp painters' guild in 1460, but by 1464 he had moved to Ghent, where he was a friend of Hugo van der *Goes. At some time after 1469 he moved to Rome, and by 1473 he had settled in Urbino, where he worked for Duke Federico da *Montefeltro. Joos's only documented work is the Communion of the Apostles (also known as the Institution of the Eucharist, 1473–4), which is still at Urbino, in the Galleria Nazionale. Like Hugo's Portinari Altarpiece, it was an important work in spreading knowledge of the Netherlandish oil technique in Italy. Of the other works attributed to Joos, the most important are a series of 28 famous men (Gal. Naz., Urbino, and Louvre, Paris), commissioned for the Ducal Palace. Their authorship is controversial, and they may have been a work of collaboration between Joos and the Spanish painter Pedro *Berruguete.

Jordaens, Jacob (b Antwerp, 19 May 1593; d Antwerp, 18 Oct. 1678). Flemish painter, the pupil and son-in-law of Adam van *Noort. Early in his career he often assisted *Rubens, but he had a flourishing studio of his own by the 1620s, and after Rubens's death in 1640 he was the leading figure painter in Flanders. His style was heavily indebted to Rubens, but was much more earthbound, using thick *impasto, strong contrasts of light and shade, and colouring that is often rather lurid. His physical types, too, are coarser than Rubens's and his name is particularly associated with large canvases of hearty rollicking peasants. Two of his favourite subjects, which he depicted several times, are The Satyr and the Peasant, based on one of Aesop's fables, and The King Drinks, which depicts a boisterous group enjoying an abundant Twelfth Night feast. Jordaens's prodigious output, however, included many other subjects, including religious works and portraits, and he also etched and made designs for tapestries. He rarely left his native Antwerp, but he received commissions from several courts in northern Europe, the most important being The Triumph of Frederick Henry (1651–2), an enormous composition painted for the Huis ten Bosch, the royal villa near The Hague (see HUYGENS). In about 1655 Jordaens became a convert to Protestantism; he continued to paint pictures for Catholic churches, but the work of the last two decades of his life is more subdued.

Jorn, Asger (Asger Oluf Jørgensen) (b Vejrum, Jutland, 3 Mar. 1914; d Århus, 1 May 1973). Danish painter, sculptor, printmaker, ceramicist, designer, collector, and writer, active in Paris for much of his career. He was one of the founders of the *Cobra group in 1948, and his most characteristic works are highly coloured abstracts executed with violently expressive brushwork. In 1951 he became ill with tuberculosis and returned to Silkeborg in Denmark, where he had grown up, and spent ten months in a sanatorium. After his recovery he travelled widely, but he divided his time mainly between Paris and Albisola Marina in northern Italy. Late in life he took up sculpture. His other works include numerous book illustrations and he also wrote several books himself. Although he lived mainly elsewhere, he retained a great affection for his homeland, and he carried out several major works for sites there, notably a ceramic wall (installed 1959) and a tapestry (1960) for Århus State High School. He presented many works by himself and by his contemporaries to the Silkeborg Museum.

Joseph II, Emperor. See HABSBURG.

Josephson, Ernst (b Stockholm, 16 Apr. 1851; d Stockholm, 22 Nov. 1906). Swedish painter and draughtsman. He travelled widely in Europe early in his career and in 1882–8 he lived in Paris, where he was the leader of a group of anti-academic Swedish artists. At this time he moved from a naturalistic style to a much more fantastic idiom, often inspired by Nordic myth, and his work is particularly remarkable for its intensity and vitality of colouring. In 1887 he began suffering from mental instability and never fully recovered. None the less, he continued to work intensively, and the bizarre paintings he produced—although little known in his lifetime—were influential on *Expressionism in Sweden. Josephson's work is particularly well represented in the Konstmuseum in Göteborg and the Nationalmuseum in Stockholm.

Jouvenet, Jean (b Rouen, 1 May 1644; d Paris, 5 Apr. 1717). French painter, the outstanding member of a family of artists from Rouen. He moved to Paris in 1661 and became one of *Le Brun's assistants. His early works, including decorations for the Salon de Mars at Versailles (1671–4), were usually imitative of his master's style, although he was also influenced by Eustache *Le Sueur (St Bruno in Prayer, Nationalmuseum, Stockholm). He worked on numerous major decorative schemes throughout his career, but he is now best remembered as the leading French religious painter of his generation, creating many altarpieces (some of huge size) for churches in Paris and elsewhere. His later work

was marked both by *Baroque emotionalism and by a realistic treatment of details foreign to the principles encouraged by the Académie Royale. It is recorded, for example, that before painting his Miraculous Draught of Fishes (c.1706, Louvre, Paris) he studied fishing scenes on the spot at Dieppe. Throughout his career he also painted portraits. In 1713 his right hand was paralysed, but he learnt to paint with his left.

Juan de Flandes (d ?Palencia, c.1519). Netherlandish painter active in Spain, where he is first documented in 1496. He was one of a number of northern European artists employed by Queen Isabella of Castile. A portable altarpiece he painted for her in a delicate miniaturistic style was once much renowned, but it is now dismembered and the surviving 27 panels (out of the original 47) are widely scattered (one is in the NG, London). After Isabella's death in 1504 he worked for churches in Salamanca and Palencia.

Juan de Juanes. See MAÇIP.

Juan de Juni (b ?Joigny, c.1507; d Valladolid, Apr. 1577). French sculptor, active in Spain from c.1533. He worked in León and Salamanca before settling in Valladolid in 1540. A prolific sculptor of religious subjects, he excelled in the dramatic expression of emotion, and is generally ranked next to Alonso *Berruguete as the outstanding Spanish sculptor of his period. Berruguete himself called him 'the best foreign carver in Castile'. Juni's most famous works are probably the Entombment groups in Valladolid Museum (1545) and Segovia Cathedral (1571). On stylistic grounds he is believed to have visited Italy early in his career and he has been proposed as the author of the famous St Roch (SS. Annunziata, Florence), usually attributed to *Stoss.

Juarez (or **Xuarez**). Dynasty of Mexican painters active in the 17th and 18th centuries. The founder was **Luis Juarez** (c. 1585–c. 1638) and the most distinguished member was his son **José Juarez** (1619–62), who was the leading Mexican painter of his time. He specialized in large altarpieces, some of which show the influence of Zurbarán (Adoration of the Kings, 1655, Pinacoteca Verreinal, Mexico City).

Judd, Donald (b Excelsior Springs, Mo., 3 June 1928; d New York, 12 Feb. 1994). American sculptor, designer, and writer on art, one of the leading exponents of *Minimal art. From 1959 to 1965 he earned his living as an art critic, working mainly for Arts Magazine. He began his career as a practising artist as a painter, but in the early 1960s he took up sculpture with heavily textured monochrome reliefs. In 1963 he began making the type of work for which he is best known—arrangements of identical rectangular boxlike shapes cantilevered ladder-like from a wall. Initially he worked mainly in wood, but after a successful exhibition at the Green Gallery, New York, in 1963-4 he began having them industrially manufactured in various metals (or sometimes coloured perspex). In 1970 he started making works for the specific space in which they were to be exhibited, and in 1972 he began producing outdoor works. In spite of great financial success, Judd (who was notoriously touchy) disliked the New York 'art crowd' and in 1973 moved to Marfa, Texas, where he converted the buildings of an old army base into studios and installation spaces. In the 1980s he began designing furniture in a similar style to his sculptures. His *Complete Writings, 1959–75* was published in 1976, and *Complete Writings, 1975–86* in 1987.

Juel, Jens (*b* Balslev, Funen [now Fyn], 12 May 1745; *d* Copenhagen, 27 Dec. 1802). Danish painter. He had a distinguished career both in Denmark and on his wide travels; he studied in Hamburg and between 1772 and 1779 he worked successively in Dresden, Rome, Paris, and Geneva. After settling in Copenhagen he became court painter (1780) and a professor at the Academy (1784), although he had little interest in teaching. Juel painted landscapes, *genre scenes, and still-lifes (particularly flowers), but he is most renowned for his sensitive portraits.

Jugendstil. See ART NOUVEAU.

Julian, Rodolphe. See ACADÉMIE.

Julius II, Pope. See ROVERE.

Junius Bassus, sarcophagus of. See SARCOPHAGUS.

Junk art. Art constructed from the waste products of urban life. In so far as Junk art represented a revolt against traditional materials and a desire to show that works of art can be constructed from the humblest and most worthless things, it may be plausibly traced back to *Cubist collages, *Duchamp's *ready-mades, and the work of Kurt *Schwitters. However, it is not until the 1950s that it is possible to speak of a Junk movement, particularly with the work of Robert *Rauschenberg, who used rags and tatters of cloth, torn reproductions, and other waste materials in his *combine paintings. Lawrence *Alloway, in 1961, was the first to apply the name 'Junk art' to such works, and the term was then extended to sculpture made from scrap metal, used timber, and so on. Californian *Funk art sometimes made use of similar materials. The Junk art of the USA had analogies in the work of *Tàpies and others in Spain, *Burri and *Arte Povera in Italy, and similar movements in most European countries and in Japan, where debris from the Second World War was sometimes converted to artistic use.

Juste. See GIUSTI.

Justus of Ghent. See JOOS VAN WASSENHOVE.

K

Kahlo, Frida (*b* Mexico City, 6 July 1907; *d* Mexico City, 13 July 1954). Mexican painter. In 1925, when she was still at school, she suffered appalling injuries in a traffic accident, leaving her a permanent semi-invalid, often in severe pain. During her convalescence she began painting portraits of herself and others. She remained her own favourite model and her art was usually directly autobiographical: 'I paint myself because I am so often alone and because I am the subject I know best.' In 1928 she married Mexico's most famous artist, Diego *Rivera, who was twice her age and twice her size. Their relationship was often strained, but it lasted to her death, through various separations, divorce and remarriage (1939–40), and infidelities on both sides (one of her lovers was Leon Trotsky, who was assassinated while living in Mexico City in 1940). Kahlo was mainly self-taught as a painter. She was influenced by Rivera, but more by Mexican folk art, and her work has a colourful, almost *naive vigour, tinged with *Surrealist fantasy. Her paintings of her own physical and psychic pain are narcissistic and nightmarish, but also—like her personality—fiery and flamboyant. They were widely shown in Mexico and she had successful exhibitions in Paris and New York in 1938 and 1939 respectively, but during her lifetime she was overshadowed by her husband. Since her death, however, her fame has grown and she has become something of a feminist heroine, admired for her refusal to let great physical suffering crush her spirit or interfere with her art and her left-wing political activities. Her house in the suburb of Coyoacán, Mexico City, was opened as a museum dedicated to her in 1958.

Kahnweiler, Daniel-Henri (*b* Mannheim, 25 June 1884; *d* Paris, 11 Jan. 1979). German-born art dealer, publisher, and writer, who became a French citizen in 1937. In 1907 he opened a gallery in Paris. His first purchases were of *Fauvist works, but he is best known as the friend and promoter of the *Cubists. In 1912 *Braque and *Picasso signed contracts giving Kahnweiler exclusive rights to buy their entire outputs. He was also a friend and supporter of Juan *Gris, of whom he wrote a standard biography (1947). As a publisher he brought out numerous books illustrated by his artist friends. In 1961 he published an autobiography, *Mes galeries et mes peintres*; in the introduction to the English translation, *My Galleries and Painters* (1971), John Russell wrote: 'Where the old-style dealers did their artists a favour by inviting them to luncheon, Kahnweiler lived with Picasso, Braque, Gris, Derain, and Vlaminck on a day-to-day, hour-to-hour basis. The important thing was not so much that they should sell as that they should be free to get on with their work; and Kahnweiler, by making this possible, helped to bring into being what now seems to us that last great flowering of French art.'

Kalf, Willem (*b* Rotterdam, 1619; *d* Amsterdam, 31 July 1693). Dutch painter, one of the most celebrated of all still-life painters. From about 1640 to 1646 he worked in Paris; on his return to the Netherlands he lived in Hoorn and then in 1653 settled in Amsterdam. His early works were modest kitchen and courtyard scenes, but he soon became the outstanding exponent of a type of still-life in which fruit and precious objects—porcelain, oriental rugs, Venetian glass—are arranged in grand *Baroque displays. He was an art dealer as well as a painter, so some of the objects he used as models may have been objects he had in stock. His pictures have been compared with those of *Vermeer because of his masterly handling of texture and his ability to manipulate warm and cool colours (he frequently contrasts the reddish browns in a carpet with the yellow of a peeled lemon and the blue and white of porcelain).

Kallimachos. See CALLIMACHUS.

Kandinsky, Wassily (*b* Moscow, 22 Nov. [4 Dec.] 1866; *d* Neuilly-sur-Seine, 13 Dec. 1944). Russian-born painter, printmaker, designer, teacher, and art theorist, who became a German citizen in 1927 and a French citizen in 1939, one of the most important figures in the development of *abstract art. He abandoned a promising university career teaching law, partly under the impact of an exhibition in Moscow of French *Impressionists, at which one of *Monet's *Haystack* pictures made a powerful impression on him, and in 1896 he moved to Munich to study painting. Munich was to be the centre of his activities until 1914, but he travelled widely in this period and spent a year in Paris, 1906–7. His pictures at the turn of the century combined features of *Art Nouveau with reminiscences of Russian folk art, to which he added a *Fauve-like intensity of colour.

In 1909 (the year in which he was one of the founders of the *Neue Künstlervereinigung) Kandinsky began a series of *Improvisations*, in 1910 of *Compositions*, and in 1911 of *Impressions*; in these he eliminated all representational content to arrive—in about 1910—at pure abstraction. The choice of names, deriving from musical terminology, was significant, for like the *Symbolists he was interested in analogies between colours and sounds (a great lover of music, he played the cello and piano and was a friend of Arnold Schoenberg, whose revolutionary atonality he equated with his own experiments). Kandinsky himself described how he came to recognize that colour and line in themselves could be sufficient vehicles for the expression of emotions; he returned to his studio one evening and failed to recognize one of his own paintings that was lying on its side, seeing in it a picture 'of extraordinary beauty glowing with an inner radiance . . . Now I knew for certain that the subject-matter was detrimental for my paintings.' He discussed the issue of abstraction in his book *Über das Geistige in der Kunst* (Concerning the Spiritual in Art), which was published late in 1911 (it bears the date 1912) and is the best known of his writings. His views about the nature of art were influenced by mysticism and Theosophy; he did not completely repudiate representation, but he held that the 'pure' artist seeks to express only 'inner and essential' feelings and ignores the superficial and fortuitous.

In 1911 Kandinsky was one of the founders of the *Blaue Reiter, and the brief lifetime of this group (broken up by the First World War) marked a period of intense achievement and growing fame for him. A major work from this period is *Composition VI* (1913, Hermitage, St Petersburg), a huge, gloriously coloured apocalyptic vision. On the outbreak of the war in 1914 Kandinsky returned to Russia, where he was highly active as a teacher and administrator in various cultural organizations instituted by the new Soviet regime. However, he was out of sympathy with the growing tide of ideas that subordinated fine art to industrial design in the service of the proletariat (even though he made designs for cups and saucers himself), and in 1922 he accepted an offer to take up a teaching post at the *Bauhaus, where he remained until it was closed by the Nazis in 1933. His painting of this period became more geometrical, but in addition to circles and triangles he used arrow-like forms and wavy lines in a manner that ran counter to the typical Bauhaus concern with geometrical purity (*Swinging*, 1925, Tate, London).

In 1926, to mark his 60th birthday, an exhibition of Kandinsky's work toured Germany, and by this time he was an internationally renowned figure (his reputation was spread in the USA by the *Blaue Vier). He left Germany for France in 1933 and settled at Neuilly-sur-Seine, a suburb of Paris. The paintings of his last period represent something of a synthesis between the organic style of his Munich period and the more geometrical manner of his Bauhaus period, but there was also a new element of fantasy in the use of amoeba-like forms that show the influence of *Surrealism (*Sky Blue*, 1940, Pompidou Centre, Paris). Examples of his paintings are in many of the world's leading collections, with particularly rich representations in, for example, the Lenbachhaus, Munich (see LENBACH), the Guggenheim Museum, New York, and the Pompidou Centre, Paris (many presented by his widow).

Kändler, Johann Joachim (*b* Fischbach, 15 June 1706; *d* Meissen, 18 May 1775). German sculptor and porcelain modeller. From 1733 until his death he was chief modeller at the Meissen factory near Dresden, which during this time was the arbiter of European taste in porcelain. Kändler's brilliance and inventiveness was a major factor in its success. He is widely regarded as the greatest of all porcelain modellers, and his work has great vivacity as well as a *Rococo delicacy and charm. Examples of his large output are in many museums, notably the Porzellansammlung, Dresden.

Kane, John (*b* West Calder, 19 Aug. 1860; *d* Pittsburgh, 10 Aug. 1934). American *naive painter, born in Scotland. He emigrated to the USA in 1879 and moved around a good deal, working at various labouring jobs. However, he considered Pittsburgh his home. In 1891 he lost a leg when he was struck by a train, but he became so agile with his artificial limb that few realized he was disabled. He took to drink after his son died soon after birth in 1904 and his wife consequently left him, taking their two daughters with her. Kane then led a wandering life, scraping a living by house painting and carpentry. His first oil paintings were done *c*.1910; he produced portraits—an intense self-portrait (1929, MoMA, New York) is his best-known work—landscapes, interiors, and cityscapes of industrial Pittsburgh, combining meticulous observation with naive stylization and imaginative reconstruction. In 1927 he achieved sudden fame, at the age of 67, when one of his paintings was accepted for the Carnegie International Exhibition in Pittsburgh. Kane was the first American naive painter to achieve such recognition; some people thought his picture was a hoax, but in the remaining seven years of his life he achieved considerable acclaim and became something of a celebrity (in consequence of which he was reunited with his wife). His autobiography *Sky Hooks* (named after the supports of a house painter's scaffold) was posthumously published in 1938.

Kane, Paul (*b* Mallow, Co. Cork, 3 Sept. 1810; *d* Toronto, 20 Feb. 1871). Irish-born Canadian painter of landscape and Indian subjects. He was active mainly in Toronto, but he journeyed as far as the Pacific coast, publishing an account of his travels and adventures in *Wanderings of an Artist* (1859). About half his paintings are portraits of Indians and he took great care over accurate recording of details of costume and ornament, giving his work much historical value. He also had considerable skill, however, in composing figure groups in a way akin to the European *Grand Manner. His work is well represented in the National Gallery, Ottawa, and the Royal Ontario Museum, Toronto.

Kanoldt, Alexander. See NEUE KÜNSTLER-VEREINIGUNG MÜNCHEN.

Kant, Immanuel (*b* Königsberg, East Prussia [now Kaliningrad, Russia], 22 Apr. 1724; *d* Königsberg, 12 Feb. 1804). German philosopher. Kant spent all his life in provincial Königsberg, where he was appointed professor of logic and metaphysics at the university in 1770. He is widely regarded as 'the greatest philosopher of the last three hundred years' (*Oxford Dictionary of Philosophy*) and his broad-ranging writings were enormously influential; in the words of Roger Scruton (*The Aesthetics of Architecture*, 1979), his 'division of the mental faculties, into theoretical,

practical and aesthetic (or, as he put it, understanding, practical reason and judgement), provided the starting point for all later investigations, and gave to aesthetics the central position in philosophy which it occupied through much of the nineteenth century'. Kant's writings on aesthetics are principally in his *Kritik der Urteilskraft* (Critique of Judgement, 1790), the third of his three great systematic treatises.

Kapoor, Anish (*b* Bombay [Mumbai], 12 Mar. 1954). British abstract sculptor, born in India, the son of a Hindu father and Jewish-Iraqi mother. He settled in London in 1973. Although his sculpture is not obviously indebted to his Asian background, he feels an affinity with the spirituality of Indian art: 'I don't want to make sculpture about form . . . I wish to make sculpture about belief, or about passion, about experience that is outside of material concern.' His early work was predominantly in fairly lightweight materials, including wood and mixed media, and was often brightly coloured, but in the late 1980s he changed direction. Having acquired a large ground-floor studio where he could handle heavy materials, he turned to working in stone. Typically his sculptures from this time have consisted of large, rough-hewn blocks; he has also made smooth, organic pieces in cast metal. Kapoor was Britain's representative at the Venice *Biennale in 1990 and in 1991 he was awarded the *Turner Prize.

Kaprow, Allan (*b* Atlantic City, NJ, 23 Aug. 1927). American artist and art theorist, best known as the main creator of *happenings. His studies included a period with the musician John Cage (see BLACK MOUNTAIN COLLEGE), from whom he took over the idea of chance and indeterminacy in aesthetic organization. In the mid-1950s he gave up painting for *assemblages and then *environments, and in 1958 he published an article in *Art News* in which he argued for the abandonment of craftsmanship and permanence in the fine arts and advocated the incorporation of perishable materials. His first happenings took place at the Reuben Gallery, New York, in 1959. Kaprow has been an evangelic promoter of his ideas through his teaching at various universities and his voluminous output of writings, as well as through his own performances.

Karlowska, Stanislava de. See BEVAN.

Kauffer, E. McKnight (*b* Great Falls, Mont., 14 Dec. 1890; *d* New York, 22 Oct. 1954). American-born painter and designer, active mainly in England, where he settled in 1914. He was a member of Wyndham *Lewis's Group X and of the *Cumberland Market Group, but he abandoned painting in 1921 and is best known for his brilliant and witty poster designs, notably for the London Transport Board and the Great Western Railway. In 1940 he returned to the USA and settled in New York. His work in America included posters (for government agencies during the Second World War and afterwards for American Airlines) and also book-jackets and illustrations.

Kauffmann, Angelica (b Chur, 30 Oct. 1741; d Rome, 5 Nov. 1807). Swiss painter, active mainly in Italy and England. From an early age she travelled with her father, the painter **Joseph Johann Kauffmann** (1707–82), in Switzerland and Italy, and she formed her style in Rome. She impressed several British visitors to Italy and in 1776 she moved to London, where her work and her person were vastly admired. A foundation member of the *Royal Academy in 1768, she was a close friend of the president, Sir Joshua *Reynolds, their relationship giving rise to gossip and to a satirical picture by Nathaniel *Hone. (*Canova, *Fuseli, *Goethe, and *Winckelmann were among the other distinguished men who were charmed by her.) Kauffmann began in England as a fashionable portraitist, but then devoted herself more to historical scenes and also did decorative work for Robert Adam and other architects. Although her work owes much to the *Neoclassical tradition, it has a prettiness that can be described as *Rococo. At its best it has great charm, but it can be rather insipid, and she was much more successful with ladylike decorative vignettes than with scenes from Homer or Shakespeare. In 1767 she married an unscrupulous adventurer from whom she was quickly estranged. Following his death in 1780 she married the decorative painter Antonio Zucchi (1726–95) and in 1781 moved with him to Italy, where she continued her successful career, mainly in Rome.

Kaulbach, Wilhelm von (b Arolsen, nr. Kassel, 15 Oct. 1805; d Munich, 7 Apr. 1874). German painter and illustrator, active mainly in Munich, the best-known member of a family of artists. He was a favourite of King Ludwig I of Bavaria and in his day one of the most celebrated of German painters, but the kind of bombastic and didactic historical scenes in which he specialized have dated badly. Much more to modern taste are his drawings from nature and his charming illustrations to *Goethe's *Reinecke*

Fuchs, which admirably catch the spirit of this animal satire; Kaulbach made the drawings (Lenbachhaus, Munich) in 1846–7 and they appeared in numerous editions.

Keating, Tom. See PALMER, SAMUEL.

Keene, Charles (b London, 10 Aug. 1823; d London, 4 Jan. 1891). English caricaturist and illustrator. He illustrated many books, but he is best known for his association with *Punch*, which lasted from 1852 until his death. His work mainly deals with contemporary social life.

Keil, Bernhard (Eberhard Keilhau) (b Helsingør [Elsinore], 1624; d Rome, 3 Feb. 1687). Danish painter, active mainly in Italy, where he was known as 'Monsù Bernardo'; he was the first painter from his country to enjoy more than a local reputation. Keil studied in Copenhagen and then with *Rembrandt in Amsterdam, c.1642–4. In 1651 he moved to Italy, where he lived for the rest of his life, settling in Rome in 1656. 'Life-size genre pictures of a few figures were his speciality. His themes are often related to simple allegorical subjects such as the Five Senses, the Seasons, and the Four Elements, and as protagonists he favoured dignified old people or children dressed in old clothes and rags' (Seymour Slive, *Dutch Painting: 1600–1800*, 1995). Keil provided Filippo *Baldinucci with information about Rembrandt that he used in his book on engraving and etching (1686).

Keim's process. See WATER-GLASS PAINTING.

Kells, Book of. See BOOK OF KELLS.

Kelly, Ellsworth (b Newburgh, NY, 31 May 1923). American painter, sculptor, and printmaker. In the mid-1950s he became recognized as one of the leading exponents of the *Hard-Edge style that was one of the reactions against *Abstract Expressionism. His paintings are characteristically very clear and simple in conception, sometimes consisting of a number of individual panels placed together, identical in size but each painted a different uniform colour (he started using this formula in 1952). He was also one of the first artists to develop the idea of the *shaped canvas. Kelly has also worked in various printmaking techniques and in sculpture (using painted cut-out metal forms—often industrially manufactured—related to those in his paintings).

Kelly, Sir Gerald (b London, 9 Apr. 1879; d London, 5 Jan. 1972). British painter. One of the leading society portraitists of his day, he had many distinguished friends, among them Somerset Maugham, whose portrait by Graham *Sutherland he wittily attacked. From 1949 to 1954 he was president of the *Royal Academy; in this position he devoted much of his time to organizing loan exhibitions, and became well known for his appearances in related television programmes. His popularity helped to revitalize the Academy's image after the damage done by his predecessor, the arch-conservative *Munnings. Apart from portraits, Kelly painted landscapes and also pictures of Asian dancing girls (he had spent some time in Burma) that were once very popular in reproduction.

Kelmscott Press. A private printing press founded in 1890 by William *Morris at Hammersmith, London, and named after the village near Oxford where he had lived since 1871. Between 1891 and 1898, two years after Morris's death, the press issued more than 50 titles, including editions of several of Morris's own works. Deeply influenced by his study of early printing, Morris himself designed most of the type, borders, ornaments, and title pages. The press's greatest book, and by common consent one of the world's masterpieces of book production, is the 1896 edition of Geoffrey Chaucer's works, with illustrations by *Burne-Jones. Although short-lived, the Kelmscott Press had enormous influence on the *private presses that followed in its wake.

Kempeneer, Pieter de (b Brussels, c.1503; d Brussels, c.1580). Netherlandish painter and tapestry designer, active for much of his career in Spain, where he was known as Pedro de Campaña. He is documented in Seville from 1537 to 1561 and in the later part of this period he was the leading painter in the city (several examples of his work are in the cathedral). Before arriving in Spain he is said to have spent several years in Italy. This has been doubted, as the fairly superficial Italian influence in his *Mannerist style could have been gained from prints. By 1563 he was back in Brussels, designing tapestry cartoons. He is also said to have worked as an architect and sculptor.

Kemp-Welch, Lucy. See OFFICIAL WAR ART.

Kennington, Eric (b London, 12 Mar. 1888; d Reading, 13 Apr. 1960). British painter, sculptor, and draughtsman. He was an *Official War Artist in the First and Second World Wars and is best known for his paintings and drawings of the daily life of ordinary soldiers and airmen. Between the wars he worked mainly as a

portraitist but also did book illustrations, including those for T. E. Lawrence's *Seven Pillars of Wisdom* (1926). His sculptures include the monument to the 24th Division in Battersea Park, London (1926) (the writer Robert Graves was the model for one of the three soldiers); figures (in carved brick) for the Shakespeare Memorial Theatre in Stratford-upon-Avon (1930); and the recumbent effigy of T. E. Lawrence on his tomb in St Martin's church, Wareham, Dorset (1940).

Kensett, John Frederick. See HUDSON RIVER SCHOOL.

Kent, Rockwell (b Tarrytown, NY, 21 June 1882; d Ausable Forks, NY, 13 Mar. 1971). American painter, graphic artist, and writer. His preference was for scenes of the great outdoors, painted in a vivid, dramatic style with strong contrasts of light and shade. They reflected his own lifestyle, for he loved exploring remote areas (including Alaska, Greenland, and Tierra del Fuego) and early in his career he supported himself by working at such jobs as lobsterman and ship's carpenter. His pictures appealed to the American pioneer spirit and by the 1920s he was one of the country's most popular artists. However, he had outspoken left-wing political sympathies and at the time of the anti-Communist witch hunts in the 1940s and 1950s he was dogged by various investigating committees. He was chairman of the National Council for American-Soviet Friendship and in 1967 was awarded the International Lenin Peace Prize by the Soviet government; he gave the money part of the award to the people of North Vietnam. Kent illustrated numerous books, including his own accounts of his travels, such as *Wilderness* (1920). His other writings include an autobiography, *It's Me, O Lord* (1955).

Kent, William (bapt. Bridlington, 1 Jan. 1686; d London, 12 Apr. 1748). English architect, designer, landscape gardener, and painter, the most versatile British artist of his time. He began his career as a painter and spent a decade (1709–19) in Italy, mainly Rome, where in 1717 he painted a ceiling in the church of S. Giuliano dei Fiamminghi (offering to work without payment for the chance to establish his reputation). As a guide and art dealer for Englishmen on the *Grand Tour he met the architect and patron Lord Burlington, with whom he returned to London in 1719. From then until Kent's death in 1748 the two were inseparable partners. Initially Kent was employed mainly as a decorative painter (notably at Burlington House and

Kensington Palace, both in London), but his talent in this field was described by Horace *Walpole as 'below mediocrity' and he turned increasingly to architecture and design. His biggest architectural commission was Holkham Hall, Norfolk, begun in 1734 for the 1st Earl of Leicester, whom he had initially met in Rome. Externally it is in a severe Palladian style, but the opulent interior has been described by Nikolaus *Pevsner as 'more consistently palatial than that of almost any other house in England'. Kent was the first British artist to envision an interior and its furnishings as a unified scheme and he designed some impressively grand furniture, including the magnificent state bed (1732) at Houghton Hall, Norfolk. His other work as a designer was highly varied; it included book illustrations, sculpture (notably the Isaac Newton Monument (1731), carved by *Rysbrack, and the Shakespeare Monument (1740), carved by *Scheemakers, both in Westminster Abbey), and a state barge (1731–2, Nat. Maritime Mus., London) for Frederick, Prince of Wales (see ROYAL COLLECTION). In his later years he worked mainly as a garden designer, in which field he was a key figure in the development of the informal style later particularly associated with Capability Brown. Although he was a painter of little talent, Kent has the distinction of painting the earliest medieval history subjects in British art—a series of three pictures for Queen Caroline depicting scenes from the life of Henry V (c.1730, Royal Coll.). There is no attempt to re-create the scenes accurately, and in fact there is some doubt whether one of the pictures is intended to represent the Battle of Agincourt (1415) or the Battle of Crécy (1346).

Kephisodotos. See CEPHISODOTUS.

Kernstok, Károly. See EIGHT.

Kersting, Georg Friedrich (b Güstrow, 22 Oct. 1785; d Meissen, 1 July 1847). German painter. After studying at the Copenhagen Academy 1805–8, he settled in Dresden, where he specialized in small portraits set in delicately rendered interiors. They include three similar pictures showing his friend *Friedrich in his studio (1811, Kunsthalle, Hamburg; 1812, Staatliche Museen, Berlin; 1819, Kunsthalle, Mannheim).

Kessel, Jan van (bapt. Antwerp, 5 Apr. 1626; d Antwerp, 18 Oct. 1679). Flemish still-life and flower painter active in Antwerp, where he became a member of the painters' guild in 1645. He continued the tradition of his grandfather, Jan 'Velvet' *Brueghel, and was also influenced by Daniel *Seghers. Van Kessel painted garlands and bouquets of flowers, but is best known for small, jewel-like pictures, often on copper, of insects or shells against a light background, depicted with vivid colour and great exactitude of detail. Good examples of his large output are in Oxford (Ashmolean Mus.), Cambridge (Fitzwilliam Mus.), and Madrid (Prado).

Ketel, Cornelis (b Gouda, 18 Mar. 1548; d Amsterdam, 8 Aug. 1616). Dutch portrait and history painter. He worked mainly in Gouda and Amsterdam, but also in France and in England (1573–81). Van *Mander, who was well informed about him, mentions that he painted a portrait of Queen Elizabeth I in 1578, and this has been identified with a picture in the Siena Pinacoteca. Ketel's finest works are his group portraits (examples in the Rijksmuseum, Amsterdam), which prefigure those of *Hals.

Kettle, Tilly (b London, 31 Jan. 1735; d Aleppo, Turkey [now Halab, Syria], ?July 1786). English portrait painter. After working in the Midlands and London, he became one of the first British painters to risk a long visit to India, where he lived 1769–76, making a fortune painting nabobs and princes. He died on his way out a second time, having found it much harder to achieve success in England. His style was derivative (of *Reynolds, *Cotes, and *Romney), but he 'ranks fairly high among the lesser portraitists of his time' (Ellis *Waterhouse).

Key, Willem (b Breda, c.1515; d Antwerp, ?5 June 1568). Netherlandish painter, mainly of portraits. He was probably a pupil of Lambert *Lombard c.1540 in Liège. In 1542 he became a master in the painters' guild in Antwerp, where he spent the rest of his working life. **Adriaen Thomasz. Key** (b ?Antwerp, c.1544; d ?Antwerp, after 1589), was probably his pupil and perhaps a distant relative (although not his nephew, as previously believed). He became a master in the Antwerp guild in 1568. Both artists were highly regarded in their day and did assured and solid portraits of famous people. Their religious works are less well known, and many of Willem's are known to have perished at the hands of iconoclasts.

Keyser, Hendrick de (b Utrecht, 15 May 1565; d Amsterdam, 15 May 1621). The outstanding Dutch sculptor and one of the leading Dutch architects of his period. Most of his career was spent in Amsterdam, where he was appointed municipal sculptor and architect in 1594. His most important buildings are the Zuiderkerk

(South Church, 1606–14), Holland's first large Protestant church, and the Westerkerk (West Church, 1620–38), which broke with the *Mannerist tradition, looking forward to the *classicism of Jacob van *Campen. The splendid towers of these two churches are still among Amsterdam's chief landmarks. As a sculptor, de Keyser excelled particularly as a portraitist in a soberly realistic style (*Unknown Man*, 1608, Rijksmuseum, Amsterdam), but his best-known work is the tomb of William the Silent (1614–21) in the Niewe Kerk at Delft.

Thomas de Keyser (*b* ?Amsterdam, *c*.1597; *bur.* Amsterdam, 7 June 1667), Hendrick's son and pupil, was Amsterdam's municipal architect from 1662 until his death (he added the cupola to van Campen's town hall), but he is better known as a portrait painter. He was, indeed, Amsterdam's leading portraitist before being overtaken in popularity by *Rembrandt in the 1630s. His life-size portraits look stiff compared with Rembrandt's and he is more attractive and original on a small scale. *Constantijn *Huygens and his Clerk* (1627, NG, London) is an excellent example of his small portraits of full-length figures in an interior, forerunners of the *conversation piece. His small equestrian portraits were also a new type (*Pieter Schout*, 1660, Rijksmuseum).

Two other sons of Hendrick, **Pieter** (1595–1676) and **Willem** (1603—after 1678), were sculptors. Willem worked for some years in England, probably with Nicholas *Stone, Hendrick's son-in-law and former pupil.

Keyser, Nicaise de (*b* Zandvliet, nr. Antwerp, 26 Aug. 1813; *d* Antwerp, 16 July 1887). Belgian painter. He made his name with the huge *Battle of the Golden Spurs* (1836, destroyed in the Second World War) and went on to have a highly successful career with similar historical scenes in *Romantic vein, often taken from his country's past. He was also in demand as a portraitist, not just in Belgium, but also at several foreign courts (he travelled widely). From 1855 to 1879 he was director of the Academy in Antwerp (where *Alma-Tadema was one of his pupils) and he won numerous honours. However, his reputation faded after his death.

Khnopff, Fernand (*b* Grembergen, nr. Antwerp, 12 Sept. 1858; *d* Brussels, 12 Nov. 1921). Belgian painter, active mainly in Brussels, a leading exponent of *Symbolism. He came from a wealthy family and gave up law to study art. His work was influenced by diverse sources, including *Burne-Jones and Gustave *Moreau,

both of whom he discovered in 1878, at the Exposition Universelle in Paris (Khnopff was fluent in English and later became friendly with Burne-Jones, making several visits to England). In 1883 he was a founder member of Les *Vingt in Brussels, but he showed his work mainly in Paris, notably at the *Salon de la Rose + Croix. By the 1890s he had an international reputation. His output included many portraits, but he is best known for exotic, sometimes sinister reveries involving beautiful, decadent women (*I Lock my Door upon Myself*, 1891, Neue Pin., Munich). In addition to paintings, he produced book illustrations and sculpture, and he wrote a good deal on art, including several articles in English for *The Studio* magazine.

Kiefer, Anselm (*b* Donaueschingen, 8 Mar. 1945). German painter. Early in his career he was a *Conceptual artist, but he turned to painting and has become one of the leading exponents of *Neo-Expressionism, with an international reputation. He produces large, heavily worked canvases, often with objects or vegetable matter (such as plants or straw) attached to them (he has also mixed blood with his paint). Sometimes the surface is further 'distressed' by such means as scorching it with a blowtorch. Many of his pictures refer to German history or Nordic mythology and show an attempt to come to terms with his country's Nazi past. Another subject that has interested him is the Chinese Communist leader Mao Zedong (*Let a Thousand Flowers Bloom*, 2000, Tate, London).

Kienholz, Edward (*b* Fairfield, Wash., 23 Oct. 1927; *d* Hope, Ida., 10 June 1994). American sculptor specializing in life-size tableaux. Typically he created situations of a bizarre and gruesome character in which death and decay are common themes (his work is sometimes categorized as *Funk art). A much reproduced example is *The State Hospital* (1964–6, Moderna Museet, Stockholm), showing a mentally ill patient strapped to his bed with his own self-image (in a thought bubble) strapped to the bed above. Both figures are modelled with revolting realism but have glass bowls for heads. H. H. Arnason (*A History of Modern Art*, 1969) describes the work as 'one of the most horrifying concepts created by any modern artist'.

Kiki of Montparnasse. See MAN RAY.

Kinetic art. Term applied to art that moves or appears to move (from the Greek *kinesis*, 'movement'). In its broadest sense the term can encompass a great deal of phenomena, including cinematic motion pictures, *happenings, and the animated clockwork figures found on clock towers in many cities of Europe. More usually, however, it is applied to sculptures such as *Calder's mobiles that are moved either by air currents or by some artificial means—usually electronic or magnetic. In addition to works employing actual movement, there is another type of Kinetic art that produces an illusion of movement when the spectator moves relative to it (and *Op art paintings are sometimes included within the field of Kinetic art because they appear to flicker).

The idea of moving sculpture had been proposed by the *Futurists as early as 1909, and the term 'kinetic' was first used in connection with the visual arts by *Gabo and *Pevsner in their *Realistic Manifesto* in 1920. Gabo produced an electrically driven oscillating wire construction in this year, and at the same time Marcel *Duchamp was experimenting with *Rotative Plaques* that incorporated movement. Various other works over the next three decades made experiments in the same vein, for example *Moholy-Nagy's *Light-Space-Modulator* (1922–30, Busch-Reisinger Mus., Harvard Univ.), one of a series of constructions he made using reflecting metals, transparent plastics, and sometimes mechanical devices to produce real movement. However, for many years Calder was the only leading figure who was associated specifically with moving sculpture (and many people regarded him as eccentric), and it was not until the 1950s that the phrase 'Kinetic art' became a recognized part of critical vocabulary; the exhibition 'Le Mouvement' at the Denise René Gallery, Paris, in 1955 was a key event in establishing it as a distinct genre. The artists represented included *Agam, *Bury, Calder, Duchamp, *Tinguely, and *Vasarely. See also CANOVA.

King, Sir Phillip (*b* Kheredine, Tunisia, 1 May 1934). British sculptor. He is probably the most renowned of the generation of avant-garde British sculptors (mainly, like himself, pupils of *Caro) who came to prominence at the *New Generation exhibition in 1965. His work at this time was characteristically in smooth, manmade materials such as plastic or fibreglass, often brightly coloured, with the cone shape being a favourite motif (*And the Birds Began to Sing*, 1964, Tate, London). At the end of the decade he began using more rugged materials, including steel and wood. With Bridget *Riley he represented Britain at the Venice *Biennale of 1968 and his work has been included in many

other international exhibitions. He has taught at various art schools in Britain and elsewhere and from 1980 to 1990 he was professor of sculpture at the *Royal College of Art. In 1999 he became president of the *Royal Academy.

Kip, Johannes (*b* Amsterdam, 1653; *d* London, Apr. 1722). Dutch topographical engraver who settled in England in about 1690. He is best known for his engravings of country houses in the sumptuous *Britannia illustrata* (1708 and subsequent volumes). They are of modest artistic merit but have great historical interest.

Kiprensky, Orest (*b* Oranienbaum district, Petersburg province, 24 Mar. 1782; *d* Rome, 24 Oct. 1836). Russian painter, active for much of his career in Italy. He was the leading Russian portraitist of the *Romantic era, combining the then fashionable attitude of 'Byronic' melancholy with an elegance that earned him the nickname 'the Russian van *Dyck'.

Kirchner, Ernst Ludwig (*b* Aschaffenburg, 6 May 1880; *d* Frauenkirch, Switzerland, 15 June 1938). German *Expressionist painter, printmaker, and sculptor, the dominant figure in the *Brücke group. Like the other members of the group, he was influenced by *Post-Impressionism, particularly *Gauguin and van *Gogh, by *Fauvism, and by *Munch. He also claimed that he was the first of the group to appreciate Polynesian and other *primitive art (which he saw in the Zwinger Museum in Dresden), but this had little obvious effect on his work. His paintings are usually of the human figure, including portraits and nudes (he often spent the summer months in seclusion in the country or on the coast, where he could draw and paint nude models in natural movement). There is often an explicit erotic quality in his work and sometimes a feeling of malevolence. His forms are typically harsh and jagged, and his colours dissonant. From 1910 he began to spend much of his time in Berlin and he settled there in 1911. During the next few years his work developed more independently of the other members of Die Brücke, and his criticisms of his associates were an important factor in the break-up of the group in 1913. His most celebrated paintings of this period are a series of street scenes of Berlin that are regarded as marking one of the highpoints of Expressionism. In a style that had become more spiky and aggressive he depicted the pace, the glare, and the tension of big city life (*Street, Berlin*, 1913, MoMA, New York).

Kirchner was drafted into the German army in 1915, but he was soon discharged after a mental and physical collapse. In 1916 he was hit by a car in Berlin and during his long period of recuperation he settled in Frauenkirch, near Davos, in Switzerland, which became his home for the rest of his life. By 1921 he had recovered from heavy dependence on drugs, but he never fully regained mental equilibrium. When he started painting again he concentrated on mountain landscapes and peasant scenes, his work gaining in serenity what it lost in vigour. From the late 1920s his style began to move towards abstraction, as he painted less directly from nature. Many exhibitions of his work were held in the 1930s, in Germany and elsewhere, but in the middle of the decade he was overcome again by mental anxiety and physical deterioration. The inclusion of his work in the Nazi exhibition of *degenerate art in 1937 caused him acute distress and the following year he shot himself. Throughout his career, printmaking (in woodcut, etching, and lithography) was as important to him as painting and he ranks as one of the 20th century's greatest masters in this field. He also made wooden sculpture, rough-hewn and harshly coloured.

Kisling, Moïse (*b* Cracow, 22 Jan. 1891; *d* Sanary-sur-Mer, nr. Toulon, 29 Apr. 1953). Polish-born painter who became a French citizen in 1915. He moved to Paris in 1910 and became friendly with numerous members of the avant-garde, particularly his fellow expatriates *Chagall, *Modigliani, and *Soutine (his work has a similar melancholy character to theirs); he also knew *Derain, *Gris, and *Picasso, and *Cubism was one of the influences on his eclectic early work. After the First World War (in which he fought in the Foreign Legion) he consolidated the various influences on his work into a personal style marked by elegant draughtsmanship and delicately modulated colours. He had considerable success as a portraitist and also painted nudes and landscapes.

Kitaj, Ron B. (*b* Cleveland, Oh., 29 Oct. 1932). American painter, printmaker, and draughtsman, active mainly in England, where he has been one of the most prominent figures of the *Pop art movement. Before studying at the *Royal College of Art in 1959–61 Kitaj had travelled widely (he was a merchant seaman, then served in the US army) and his wide cultural horizons gave him an influential position among his contemporaries (he studied with *Hockney and Allen *Jones), particularly in holding up his preference for figuration in opposition to the prevailing abstraction. After a visit to Paris in 1975 he was inspired by *Degas to take up pastel, which he has used for much of his subsequent work. Late 19th-century French art has been a major source of inspiration, as has a preoccupation with his Jewish identity, and he has said: 'I took it into my cosmopolitan head that I should attempt to do *Cézanne and Degas and Kafka over again, after Auschwitz.' Unlike the majority of Pop artists, Kitaj has had relatively little interest in the culture of the mass media and has evolved a multi-evocative pictorial language, deriving from a wide range of visual and literary sources—indeed he has declared that he is not a Pop artist. Typically he uses broad areas of flat colour within a strong linear framework, creating an effect somewhat akin to comic strips. In 1994 a retrospective exhibition of his work at the Tate Gallery, London, received strongly negative reviews; his wife, the American artist Sandra Fisher (1947–94), died of a brain haemorrhage only months later, and Kitaj caused much controversy by blaming this on his critics: 'They tried to kill me and they got her instead.'

kit-cat. A canvas measuring 36 × 28 in (91 × 71 cm). The name derives from *Kneller's portraits of the Kit-Cat Club (c.1702–21, NPG, London), all but one of which (there are 42) are of this size. Members of the club, founded in the last years of the 17th century, met originally at a tavern near Temple Bar kept by Christopher Cat (or Kat) that was famous for its mutton pies known as 'Kit-cats'. One of the members, the architect Sir John Vanbrugh, described it as 'the best club that ever met'; it included many of the leading Whigs of the day. Kneller's portraits were commissioned by the publisher Jacob Tomson, the club's secretary and moving spirit, for a room in which its meetings were held in his house at Barn Elms near Putney. In 1735 Tomson published a folio volume of *mezzotint engravings of the portraits; the paintings remained in the possession of his descendants until 1945. The kit-cat size canvas is particularly suited to life-size portraits showing the sitter's head and shoulders and one or both hands, and Kneller's portraits popularized the format. Previously canvases of 30 × 25 in (76 × 64 cm, bust length) and 50 × 40 in (127 × 102 cm, three-quarter length) had been more or less standard.

Kitchen Sink School. A group of British *Social Realist painters active in the 1950s who specialized in drab working-class subjects, notably interior scenes and still-lifes of domestic clutter and debris; the term was coined by the critic David Sylvester (1924–2001) in an article in the December 1954 issue of the journal *Encounter*. The main artists covered by the term were John *Bratby, Derrick Greaves (1927–), Edward Middleditch (1923–87), and Jack Smith (1928–), who were supported by the Beaux Arts Gallery in London (they became known as the Beaux Arts Quartet) and by the left-wing critic John Berger (1926–); in 1956 they exhibited together at the Venice *Biennale. By their choice of dour and sordid themes and their harsh aggressive style they expressed the same kind of dissatisfaction with the social and moral values of post-war British society as the 'Angry Young Men' in literature (writers such as John Osborne, whose *Look Back in Anger* was first produced in 1956, were sometimes referred to as 'kitchen sink dramatists'). The mood did not last and from the late 1950s the painters of the Kitchen Sink School developed in different ways, Bratby, for example, emphasizing his *Expressionist handling and Smith eventually turning to abstraction. Berger denounced his former protégés.

Kitson, Linda. See OFFICIAL WAR ART.

Klee, Paul (*b* Munchenbuchsee, nr. Berne, 18 Dec. 1879; *d* Muralto, nr. Lucarno, 29 June 1940). German-Swiss painter, printmaker, teacher, and writer on art, one of the most individual and best-loved figures in 20th-century art. He is often referred to as Swiss (his mother's nationality), but he held German citizenship (through his father) all his life. From 1898 to 1901 he studied in Munich, principally at the Academy under Franz von *Stuck. After travelling in Italy, 1901–2, he lived in Berne for the next four years, then in 1906 moved to Munich after marrying the German pianist Lily Stumpf (both Klee's parents were musicians and he was himself a violinist of professional standard). In 1911 he became friendly with *Jawlensky, *Kandinsky (whom he had first met as a student ten years earlier), *Macke, and *Marc, and in the following year he took part in the second *Blaue Reiter exhibition. Also in 1912 he visited Paris for the second time (he had earlier been there with Louis *Moilliet in 1905); he met *Delaunay on this occasion and saw *Cubist pictures. At this point he was principally an etcher, his most notable prints including a series of eleven *Inventions* (1903–5)—bizarre and satirical works with freakishly distorted figures. However, in 1914 he visited Tunisia with Macke and Moilliet and was dramatically awakened to the beauty of colour. Two weeks after arriving he wrote: 'Colour

possesses me. I no longer need to pursue it: it possesses me forever, I know. Colour and I are one—I am a painter.'

During the war Klee served in the German army, engaged for part of the time on painting aeroplane wings. After the war he returned to Munich, and a large exhibition of his work there in 1919 secured his reputation and led *Gropius to invite him to teach at the *Bauhaus, where he worked from 1921 to 1931. He proved an inspired, undogmatic teacher, both in his specialist work in the stained-glass, bookbinding, and weaving workshops and in the more general classes of the introductory course devoted to the understanding of basic principles of design (his popularity with his students was so great that to mark his 50th birthday in 1929, one of them, Anni *Albers, hired an aeroplane to drop bouquets of flowers on his house). However, he found the internal disputes at the school increasingly tiresome and in 1931 he moved to the Düsseldorf Academy. He was dismissed from this post by the Nazis in 1933 and left Germany for Berne; four years later works by him were included in the notorious exhibition of *degenerate art.

Although Klee was not politically inclined, his mood during his last years was one of profound disappointment. In 1935 he suffered the first symptoms of the illness that killed him—a rare debilitating skin disease called scleroderma—and although he remained highly productive to the end, his earlier playfulness gave way to a preoccupation with malign and malevolent forces. His exquisitely sensitive line grew deliberately rough and crude and his sense of humour became macabre; his imagery was haunted by premonitions of death, as in *Death and Fire* (1940, Paul Klee Foundation, Kunstmuseum, Berne), one of his starkest and most powerful works. It depicts a ghastly, ashen face, the features of which are made up of letters forming the word 'Tod'—German for 'death'.

Klee was one of the most inventive and prolific of modern masters, his complete output being estimated at some 9,000 works. He usually worked on a small scale; initially he painted only in watercolour, but he took up oils in 1919 and sometimes used both media in one painting. It is impossible to categorize his work stylistically, for he moved freely between figuration and abstraction, absorbing countless influences and transforming them through his unrivalled imaginative gifts as he explored human fantasies and fears. In spite of this variety, his work—in whatever style or medium—is almost instantly recognizable as his, revealing a joyous spirit

Klein, Yves

that is hard to parallel in 20th-century art. Various collections of his writings (including his notebooks and diaries) have been published. The best-known individual work is *Pädagogisches Skizzenbuch*, published in 1925 and translated into English as *Pedagogical Sketchbook* (1953).

Klein, Yves (*b* Nice, 28 Apr. 1928; *d* Paris, 6 June 1962). French painter and experimental artist, one of the most influential figures in European avant-garde art in the post-war period. Both his parents were painters, but he had no formal artistic training, and for much of his short life he earned his living as a judo instructor (in 1952–3 he lived in Japan, where he obtained the high rank of black belt, fourth dan). In the mid-1950s he began exhibiting 'monochromes', pictures in which a canvas was uniformly painted a single colour, usually a distinctive blue that he called 'International Klein Blue'. He used this also for other works including sculptured figures, and reliefs of sponges on canvas. In a lecture given at the Sorbonne in 1959, he explained his theory of monochrome painting as an attempt to depersonalize colour by ridding it of subjective emotion and thus giving it a metaphysical quality. Klein also made pictures by a variety of unorthodox methods, including the action of rain on prepared paper (these he called *Cosmogonies*), the use of a flame-thrower (*Peintures de feu*), or imprints of the human body (*Anthropométries*). In 1958 he created a sensation (and almost a riot) at the Galerie Iris Clert in Paris by an 'exhibition of emptiness'—an empty gallery painted white. It was called *Le Vide* (The Void). In 1960 he gave his first public exhibition of the *Anthropométries*: naked women smeared with blue pigment dragged each other over canvas laid on the floor to the accompaniment of his *Symphonie monotone*—a single note sustained for ten minutes and alternating with ten minutes' silence.

Critical reception to Klein's work was very mixed. He became a celebrity in Europe, but an exhibition at the Leo *Castelli gallery in New York in 1961 was a dismal failure. Although he died aged only 34 (of a heart attack), he produced a large amount of work and had wide influence, particularly on the development of *Minimal art. A great showman, he exemplifies the tendency in 20th-century art for the personality of the artist to assume greater importance than the things he makes—a tendency continued most notably by Joseph *Beuys.

Kleinmeister. See LITTLE MASTERS.

Kleophrades Painter. See CLEOPHRADES PAINTER.

Klimt, Gustav (*b* Baumgarten, nr. Vienna, 14 July 1862; *d* Vienna, 6 Feb. 1918). Austrian painter, draughtsman, and designer, one of the leading figures in one of the most exciting epochs of Vienna's cultural history. Early in his career he was highly successful as a painter of sumptuous decorative schemes in the grandiose tradition of *Makart, whose staircase decoration in the Kunsthistorisches Museum in Vienna he completed after Makart's death in 1884. In this and other schemes, he worked in collaboration with his brother **Ernst** (1864–92) and Franz von Matsch (1861–1942), who had been fellow students at the Kunstgewerbeschule (School of Applied Art) in Vienna. In spite of his official academic successes, Klimt was drawn to avant-garde art, and his work was influenced by *Impressionism, *Symbolism, and *Art Nouveau. Discontent with the conservative attitudes of the Viennese Artists' Association led him and a group of friends to resign in 1897 and set up their own organization, the *Sezession, of which he was elected president.

In a short time Klimt thus went from being a pillar of the establishment to a hero of the avant-garde, and this new role was confirmed when his enormous allegorical mural paintings for Vienna University were denounced as nonsensical and pornographic. (Klimt was given the commission in 1894 and abandoned it in 1905; the paintings—on the themes of Jurisprudence, Medicine, and Philosophy—were destroyed by fire in 1945.) Although official commissions dried up after this, he continued to be much in demand from private patrons, as a portraitist as well as a painter of mythological and allegorical themes. He was highly responsive to female beauty (he was a great womanizer) and in both his portraits and his subject pictures he stresses the allure and mystery of womanhood. Notable examples are the magnificent full-length portrait of his sister-in-law and close friend Emilie Flöge (1902, Historisches Mus. der Stadt, Vienna) and *Judith I* (1901, Österreichische Gal., Vienna), one of the archetypal images of the *femme fatale*.

Characteristically, the figures in Klimt's paintings are treated more or less naturalistically but embellished—in the background or their clothing—with richly decorative patterns recalling butterfly or peacock wings, creating a highly distinctive style of extraordinarily lush sensuality. The erotic aspect of his work is even more pronounced in his drawings, most of which were done as independent works rather than as preparatory studies for paintings; typically they show naked or semi-naked women in a state of sexual arousal. In addition to paintings and drawings, he did a good deal of design work for the *Wiener Werkstätte. Most of this was fairly modest, but the great exception was the major commission of his later years—the mosaics (executed 1909–11) for the dining room of the Palais Stoclet in Brussels, a luxury home built at huge expense for the young Belgian industrialist Adolphe Stoclet, who had just inherited the family fortune. Klimt had a great reputation in his day and was influential on some of his Viennese contemporaries, notably *Kokoschka and *Schiele, but his work was too personal to find much of a following.

Kline, Franz (b Wilkes-Barre, Pa., 23 May 1910; d New York, 13 May 1962). American painter, generally considered one of the most individual of the *Abstract Expressionists. He began as a representational painter, notably of urban landscapes, but turned to abstraction at the end of the 1940s. This change of direction reflected the influence of *de Kooning and was also stimulated by his seeing some of his own drawings enlarged by a projector, an experience that made him realize their potential as abstract compositions. Once he had embarked on this new path he very quickly developed a highly individual style, converting the brushstrokes of these drawings into large-scale abstract paintings, using bold black patterns on a white ground reminiscent of oriental calligraphy, but with a distinctive rough vigour (he used commercial paints and house painter's brushes, sometimes up to 20 cm (8 in) wide). Towards the end of his life he sometimes incorporated vivid colours but for the most part remained loyal to his characteristic black-and-white style. He died of heart disease.

Klinger, Max (b Leipzig, 18 Feb. 1857; d Grossjena, nr. Naumburg, 5 July 1920). German painter, sculptor, and printmaker. He studied in Karlsruhe and Berlin, then, after brief periods in Brussels, Berlin, and Munich, he spent the years 1883–6 in Paris, 1886–8 in Berlin, and 1888–93 in Rome. After his return to Germany in 1893 he settled in his native Leipzig, where his home became one of the centres of the city's cultural life. His work reveals a powerful imagination and an often morbid interest in themes of love and death. As a painter he is best known for his enormous *Judgement of Paris* (1885–7, KH Mus., Vienna), in which the frame is part of the decorative scheme. As a sculptor he experimented

with *polychromy in the manner of Greek *chryselephantine statues; the culmination was his statue of Beethoven (1899–1902, Mus. der Bildenden Künste, Leipzig) in white and coloured marbles, bronze, alabaster, and ivory. It is as a printmaker, however, that Klinger is now best known and most clearly showed his originality, especially in *Adventures of a Glove* (three series, begun 1881), a grotesque exploration of fetishism that antedated the publication of Freud's theories. These etchings concern a hapless young man and his involvement with an elusive lost glove that has clearly sexual connotations. Together with other works of Klinger, they have been claimed as forerunners of *Surrealism, and his influence can be seen in the work of de *Chirico (one of his greatest admirers), *Dalí, and *Ernst, amongst others.

Knapton, George (b London, 1698; d London, Dec. 1778). English portrait painter, a pupil of *Richardson. He was in Italy 1725–32 and in 1736 he became a foundation member of and official painter to the Society of *Dilettanti. His 23 portraits of his fellow members (1741–9, several still in the possession of the Society) are considered his finest works. Most of them show the members in fancy dress. These portraits are in oil, but otherwise Knapton worked mainly in pastel. He had a great reputation as a connoisseur and from 1765 until his death he was Surveyor of the King's Pictures. By the time of this appointment he seems to have given up painting. *Cotes was his most important pupil.

Knave of Diamonds (or Jack of Diamonds). An artists' association, formed in Moscow in 1910, that was for a time the most important of the avant-garde groups in Russia. There are various explanations of how the name came about, one being that it refers to the diamond markings on the uniforms of civil prisoners; the artists involved thus wanted to indicate that they were revolutionaries. In 1911 *Goncharova and *Larionov broke away from the group, accusing it of being too dominated by the 'cheap orientalism of the Paris School' and the 'Munich decadence', and founded their own association, the *Donkey's Tail, to promote an art based on native inspiration. The Knave of Diamonds held regular exhibitions up to 1917, then broke up.

Kneller, Sir Godfrey (originally Gottfried Kniller) (b Lübeck, ?8 Aug, 1646; d London, 19 Oct. 1723). German-born painter who settled in England and became the leading portraitist there in the late 17th century and early 18th century. He studied in Amsterdam under *Bol, a pupil of *Rembrandt, and later in Italy, before moving to England, probably in the mid-1670s. The opportune death of serious rivals (notably *Lely in 1680) and his own arrogant self-assurance enabled him to establish himself as the dominant court and society painter by the beginning of the reign of James II (1685). On the accession of William III and Mary II in 1689 he was appointed their principal painter jointly with *Riley (becoming sole bearer of the title when Riley died in 1691), in 1692 he was knighted, and in 1715 he was created a baronet by George I, an unprecedented honour for a painter.

Kneller's output was vast and he made extensive use of assistants. Sitters were required to pose only for a drawing of the face, and efficient formulas were worked out for the accessories. He is said sometimes to have accommodated as many as fourteen sitters in a day, but the idea of his running a kind of picture factory has been exaggerated. The average portrait turned out from his studio was slick and mechanical (and the heavy wigs then fashionable make for great monotony in male portraits), but Kneller was capable of work of much higher quality when he had a sitter to whom he especially responded; outstanding examples are *The Chinese Convert* (1687, Kensington Palace, London) and *Matthew Prior* (1700, Trinity College, Cambridge). Many other examples of his work, including the portraits of the *Kit-Cat Club, are in the National Portrait Gallery, London. Ellis *Waterhouse writes that 'he had a wonderfully sharp eye for character, could draw and paint a face with admirable economy, and maintains, even in his inferior work, a certain virility and down-to-earth quality which is refreshing after the languishments of the age of Lely'. Nevertheless, the influence of his mass-produced work was stultifying; he was the last foreign-born artist to dominate English painting, but it needed a *Hogarth and a *Reynolds to break through the conventions he had popularized.

Knight, Dame Laura (née Johnson) (*b* Long Eaton, Derbyshire, 4 Aug. 1877; *d* London, 7 July 1970). British painter and printmaker. In the first half of the 20th century she was one of the most highly regarded of British artists and in 1936 she became the first woman to be elected a *Royal Academician since the two original women members, Angelica *Kauffmann and Mary *Moser. At the height of her considerable fame (she was regarded as a 'character'—the nearest equivalent to a female Augustus *John) she won great popularity for her colourful scenes of circus life and the ballet, but these now often seem rather corny. On the other hand, her early *Newlyn School landscapes and beach scenes, which at their best have a sparkling sense of *joie de vivre*, have recently come back into favour (she lived in Newlyn 1907–18). Some of the work she did as an *Official War Artist during the Second World War is also now highly regarded. In 1946 she went to Nuremberg to make a pictorial record of the War Criminals' Trial; she made scores of sketches from which she produced a large painting (*The Dock, Nuremberg*, 1946, Imperial War Mus., London). Her husband **Harold Knight** (1874–1961), whom she married in 1903, was also a painter, mainly of portraits.

Knight, Richard Payne (*b* Wormsley Grange, Herefordshire, 11 Feb. 1751; *d* London, 23 Apr. 1824). English collector, connoisseur, and writer, a leading member of the Society of *Dilettanti. His collections were highly varied, but particularly outstanding were his drawings and antique coins and bronzes, which he bequeathed to the *British Museum. He was a leading advocate of the *Picturesque, and his country house, Downton Castle, Herefordshire (1774–8), which he helped to design himself, was novel in being in a pseudo-medieval 'castellated' style and deliberately irregular in plan and outline. His writings include *An Account of the Remains of the Worship of Priapus* (1786), which some contemporaries condemned as obscene, and *An Analytical Inquiry into the Principles of Taste* (1805). See also ELGIN MARBLES.

Knoedler's (M. Knoedler & Co.), New York. Firm of art dealers that traces its origin to 1846 when Michel (or Michael as he was later known) Knoedler (*d* 1878) moved from Paris to New York to manage a branch of the French firm *Goupil. In 1857 he bought the business and prospered selling American paintings. His son Roland opened branches in London and Paris, and by the turn of the century the firm was one of the world's leading dealers in Old Masters, a position it has maintained through various changes of ownership and location. It also deals in modern art, especially by American artists.

Knüpfer, Nicolaus. See STEEN.

Købke, Christen (*b* Copenhagen, 26 May 1810; *d* Copenhagen, 7 Feb. 1848). Danish painter, a pupil of *Eckersberg. Although he visited Italy in 1838–40, this had little influence on his work, which was rooted in his native land. He concentrated on everyday scenes in and around Copenhagen and on portraits of family and friends, displaying great sensitivity in his treatment of colour and light and a warm intimacy of characterization. Købke was little appreciated in his lifetime, but he began to win recognition at the end of the 19th century and is now considered the outstanding Danish painter of his period.

Koch, Joseph Anton (b Obergibeln, Tyrol, 27 July 1768; d Rome, 12 Jan. 1839). Austrian painter, active mainly in Rome, where he settled in 1795. He was influenced by *Carstens and worked with the *Nazarenes on the decorations of the Casino Massimo (1825–9) in Rome, choosing Dante's *Inferno* for his subject, but he is now best known for his landscapes. They were directly descended from the heroic and *ideal landscape of *Poussin, but have a distinctive *Romantic flavour, particularly in his paintings of mountains.

Koekkoek, Barend Cornelis (b Middelburg, 11 Oct. 1803; d Cleve, 5 Apr. 1862). The best-known member of a family of Dutch painters. He spent much of his career in Germany, where he found inspiration for his *Romantic views of forests and mountains; they are painted in a precise and detailed style, often with rosy light effects recalling the work of Jan *Both. His work was highly popular in his lifetime, leading to many imitations and forgeries. Other members of his large and prolific family specialized mainly in seascapes.

Kokoschka, Oskar (b Pöchlarn, 1 Mar. 1886; d Montreux, Switzerland, 22 Feb. 1980). Austrian *Expressionist painter, printmaker, and writer (he became a Czech citizen in 1937 and a British citizen in 1947, but he reverted to Austrian nationality in 1975). His formative years were spent in Vienna, where in 1909 he began to make an impact with his 'psychological portraits', in which the soul of the sitter was thought to be laid bare. A good example is his portrait of the architect Adolf Loos (1909, Staatliche Museen, Berlin), showing the sensitive, quivering line through which Kokoschka captured what he called the 'closed personalities, so full of tension' of his sitters. Later his brushwork became much broader and more broken, with high-keyed flickering colours.

In 1915 Kokoschka was badly wounded whilst serving in the Austrian army, and in 1917—still recuperating—he settled in Dresden, where he taught at the Academy from 1919 to 1924. After

this he embarked on a period of wide travel that lasted for seven years, and during this time his attention turned more from portraits to landscapes, including a distinctive type of townscape seen from a high viewpoint (*Jerusalem*, 1929–30, Detroit Inst. of Arts). In 1931 he returned to Vienna, but he was outspokenly opposed to the Nazis (who later declared his work *degenerate) and he moved to Prague in 1934 and then to London in 1938. By this time he had an international reputation, but his work was as yet little known in England and he was poor throughout the war years. After the war his fortunes soon improved and he came to be generally regarded as one of the giants of modern art. From 1953 he lived mainly at Villeneuve in Switzerland, and from 1953 to 1963 he ran a summer school at Salzburg. In his later years Kokoschka continued to paint landscapes and portraits, but his most important works of this time are allegorical and mythological pictures, including the *Prometheus* ceiling (1950) for the house of Count Seilern (see COURTAULD) at Princes Gate in London, and the *Thermopylae* triptych (1954) for Hamburg University.

Kokoschka remained steadfastly unaffected by modern movements and throughout his long and energetic life he pursued his highly personal and imaginative version of pre-1914 Expressionism. Unlike many other Expressionists, however, he was essentially optimistic in outlook. His writings include an autobiography (1971), and several plays, the most important of which is *Mörder Hoffnung der Frauen* (Murderer Hope of Women), an early example of Expressionist theatre that caused outrage when it was first perfomed in 1908 because of its violence.

Kollwitz, Käthe (née Schmidt) (b Königsberg, East Prussia [now Kaliningrad, Russia], 8 July 1867; d Moritzburg, nr. Dresden, 22 Apr. 1945). German graphic artist and sculptor. She came from a family of strong moral and social convictions, and after marrying a doctor of similar outlook, Karl Kollwitz, in 1891, she moved to one of the poorer quarters of Berlin, where she gained first-hand knowledge of the wretched conditions in which the urban poor lived. The two series of etchings that established her reputation were inspired by a spirit of protest against working conditions of the day, although their subjects are set in the past—*Weavers' Revolt* (1893–7) and *Peasants' War* (1902–8). After about 1910 lithography replaced etching as her preferred medium (she also made woodcuts), and after the First World War she turned from illustrating particular subjects to depicting abstract concepts and great timeless themes such as the Mother and Child. Her work is uncompromisingly serious and often deeply pessimistic in spirit, and many of her later drawings and prints are pacifist in intention (her son was killed in the First World War and her grandson in the Second World War). Appropriately, her best-known sculpture is a war memorial—that at Dixmuiden, Flanders, completed in 1932.

In line with her left-wing views Kollwitz visited the Soviet Union in 1927, but she subsequently became disillusioned with Soviet Communism. In 1919 she had been made the first ever woman member of the Berlin Academy, but when Hitler came to power in 1933 she was forced to resign. She suffered harassment, but she was never declared a *degenerate artist (in fact the Nazis sometimes used her images—without her name or authorization—in their propaganda), and she continued to produce outstanding work. Her masterpiece is arguably the series of eight lithographs on *Death* (1934–5), memorably showing the powerful breadth of her style, in which all accidentals and inessentials are eliminated. In its poignant concern for suffering humanity, her work represents one of the highpoints of German *Expressionism and of 20th-century graphic art. 'I should like', she wrote in 1922, 'to exert influences in these times when human beings are so perplexed and in need of help.'

Komar and Melamid. See SOTS ART.

Koninck (or de Koninck), **Philips** (b Amsterdam, 5 Nov. 1619; bur. Amsterdam, 6 Oct. 1688). Dutch painter, the best-known member of a family of artists. He studied with his brother **Jacob** (b Amsterdam, c.1615; d Amsterdam, after 1690) in Rotterdam, and *Houbraken says he was also a pupil of *Rembrandt in Amsterdam, where he settled in 1641. Although he painted various subjects (the poet Vondel praised his portraits and history pictures), his fame now rests on his landscapes. He specialized in extensive views—powerful and majestic works that rival the similar scenes of *Ruisdael; the National Gallery in London has four outstanding examples. Like many Dutch painters he had a second occupation; he ran a prosperous shipping firm and evidently painted little in the last decade of his life. His wealth enabled him to collect drawings. He was a prolific draughtsman himself and his sketchy penmanship can be deceptively close to Rembrandt's. **Salomon Koninck** (b Amsterdam, 1609; bur, Amsterdam,

8 Aug. 1656), a relative (perhaps a cousin) of Philips and Jacob, was also a painter and likewise active in Amsterdam. He was a follower of Rembrandt, imitating him in pictures of hermits, old men, and philosophers in their studies, as well as in religious scenes, and exaggerating the master's early predilection for rich exotic costumes, emphatic gestures, and dramatic contrasts of light and shadow. His work is fairly rare; there are examples in the Rijksmuseum, Amsterdam, and the Mauritshuis, The Hague.

Kooning, Willem de. See DE KOONING.

Koons, Jeff. See NEO-GEO.

kore. Greek word for 'maiden', applied to the draped standing female statues characteristic of the *Archaic period. The plural is korai. See also KOUROS.

Kossoff, Leon (b London, 7 Dec. 1926). British painter, born of Russian-Jewish immigrant parents in the East End of London, an area that has provided the chief subject matter of his paintings. His training included evening classes under David *Bomberg, 1950–2, and his work has close affinities with that of another Bomberg student, Frank *Auerbach—in choice of subject, emotional treatment of it, and use of extremely heavy *impasto. Kossoff generally retains a firmer sense of structure than Auerbach, however, often using thick black outlines, and unlike him does not approach abstraction. His reputation was slow to grow, but there was a major retrospective exhibition of his work at the Tate Gallery, London, in 1996. See also SCHOOL OF LONDON.

Kosuth, Joseph (b Toledo, Oh., 31 Jan. 1945). American experimental artist, a well-known exponent of *Conceptual art. He has been much concerned with linguistic analysis of concepts of art, his best-known work being *One and Three Chairs* (1965, MoMA, New York), which presents an actual chair alongside a full-scale photograph of a chair and an enlarged photograph of a dictionary definition of a chair. 'Actual works of art', he said, 'are little more than historical curiosities.'

kouros. Greek word for 'young man', applied to the nude standing male statues typical of the *Archaic period. The plural is kouroi. See also KORE.

Kraft, Adam (d Schwabach, nr. Nuremberg, Jan. 1509). German sculptor, active in Nuremberg, where he is first recorded in 1490. He was a virtuoso stone carver and his most celebrated work, the tabernacle in St Lawrence, Nuremberg (1493–6), is a gigantic stone imitation (c.18 m (60 ft) high) of a subtle piece of goldsmith's work. The richly decorated structure houses a multitude of human figures, animals, amphibians, etc. One of the supporting figures at the base is said to be a self-portrait of Kraft.

Kramskoi, Ivan (b Novaya Sotnya, nr. Ostrogozhsk, 8 June 1837; d St Petersburg, 6 Apr. 1887). Russian painter. In 1863 he led a revolt of fourteen students at the St Petersburg Academy; they left together in protest because they thought its approach was out of touch with modern life, and in 1870 they formed the nucleus of the *Wanderers, of which Kramskoi was a leading light. A sensitive and highly principled man, he believed that 'only a sense of social purpose can give an artist strength and multiply his powers . . . only confidence that the artist's work is needed and appreciated by society can help those exotic plants called pictures to ripen.' He was one of the outstanding Russian portraitists of his time and also painted deeply serious religious works. The most famous is *Christ in the Wilderness* (1872, Tretyakov Gal., Moscow), of which Tolstoy said: 'This is the best Christ I know.' His style was clear and sharply focused, perhaps reflecting the fact that he had been a photographic retoucher in his youth. Kramskoi was a hero and intellectual father to a generation of Russian painters, including *Repin, who called him a 'mighty man'.

Krasner, Lee. See POLLOCK.

Kress, Samuel H. (b Cherryville, Pa., 23 July 1863; d New York, 22 Sept. 1955). American businessman, art collector, and philanthropist. He became immensely wealthy from his chain of stores and in 1929 he established the Samuel H. Kress Foundation 'to promote the moral, physical and mental welfare of the human race'. His philanthropic work included contributions to medical research and restoring historic buildings in Europe after the Second World War, but he is best known for donations of works of art to American museums. Above all, his donation of 375 paintings and eighteen sculptures to the newly formed National Gallery of Art in Washington in 1939 (together with subsequent gifts) formed one of the cornerstones of the collection. Kress was a friend of Bernard *Berenson and his main field of interest was Italian *Renaissance painting.

Krieghoff, Cornelius (b Amsterdam, 19 June 1815; d Chicago, 8 Mar. 1872). Dutch-born Canadian painter. He studied in Düsseldorf, moved to New York c.1835, and from 1840 spent most of his career in Canada (mainly in Montreal and Quebec), although he also had periods in Europe and the USA. His pictures of the Indians, French-Canadian life, and the landscape, done in a colourful, detailed, and often anecdotal style, proved highly popular, and he has been much imitated and forged.

Kris, Ernst. See MESSERSCHMIDT.

Kritios. See CRITIUS.

Krohg, Christian (b Aker, nr. Christiania [now Oslo], 13 Aug. 1852; d Oslo, 16 Oct. 1925). Norwegian painter, active mainly in Christiania/Oslo, although he had a lengthy stay in Paris from 1902 to 1909. He took his subjects mainly from ordinary life—often from its sombre or unsavoury aspects. In particular, he is well known for his paintings of prostitutes, and he wrote a controversial novel on the same subject (*Albertine*, 1886). His work was often attacked by conservative critics, but his vigorous and forthright tackling of modern issues made him a hero to many Norwegian artists of a younger generation, most notably *Munch. His son **Per Krohg** (b Asgardstrand, 18 June 1889; d Oslo, 3 Mar. 1965) was also a painter. In his early work he specialized in scenes of city life, using bright *Fauvist colours (he studied under *Matisse in Paris) and exaggerated gestures that sometimes border on caricature (*Kiki of Montparnasse*, 1928, NG, Oslo). From about 1930, however, his style became more naturalistic and he worked mainly as a muralist, decorating many public buildings, particularly in Oslo. Father and son both held the post of director of the Academy of Fine Arts in Oslo, Christian from 1909 until his death, Per from 1955 to 1958.

Kröller-Müller, Hélène. See VELDE, HENRY VAN DE.

Krøyer, P. S. (Peder Severin) (b Stavanger, 23 July 1851; d Skagen, 21 Nov. 1909). The most famous Danish painter of his period. After studying at the Copenhagen Academy he travelled extensively in Europe 1875–81. During this period he spent two years in Paris, 1877–9, and he was influenced by French *plein-air painting, showing a particular interest in capturing complex effects of light—the fusion of daylight and lamplight, for example. From 1882 he spent much of his time at the village of Skagen on the Jutland coast, where he was a prominent figure in a colony of artists (see ANCHER); his work is well represented in the museum there. The pictures he painted at Skagen include poetic views of figures on the beach in the blue light of summer evenings. He was also a succesful portraitist. From 1900 his career was marred by mental illness.

Kruseman, Cornelis (*b* Amsterdam, 25 Sept. 1797; *d* Lisse, 14 Nov. 1857). Dutch painter, active for much of his career in Italy (1821–5 and 1841–8). In his day he was renowned for his scenes of life in Italian villages and his idealized and historical scenes, but they now seem sugary and his straightforward portraits (as well as the sketches for his more ambitious works) are considered his best works. He had two painter nephews, the cousins **Jan Adam Kruseman** (1804–62), who specialized in portraits and historical scenes, and **Frederik Marinus Kruseman** (1817–*c*.1860), a landscapist.

Krylov, Porfirii. See KUKRYNIKSY.

Kubin, Alfred (*b* Leitmeritz [now Litomerice], Bohemia, 10 Apr. 1877; *d* Schloss Zwickledt, nr. Wernstein, 20 Aug. 1959). Austrian draughtsman, illustrator, painter, and writer. From 1906 he lived mainly at Zwickledt in Upper Austria, although he travelled a good deal. He was a friend of *Kandinsky and showed his work in the second *Blaue Reiter exhibition in 1912, but his preoccupations were very different from those usually associated with the group. His work shows a taste for the morbid and fantastic, which he combined with pessimistic social satire and allegory. Often he depicted weird creatures in the kind of murky nightmare world associated with Odilon *Redon, whom he met in 1905. Kubin's imagery reflects his disturbed and traumatic life (he had an unhappy childhood, attempted suicide on his mother's grave in 1896, and in 1903 underwent a mental breakdown after the death of his fiancée). He was obsessed with the theme of death (he is said to have liked to watch corpses being recovered from the river) and with the idea of female sexuality as a symbol of death. In 1909 he wrote a fantastical novel *Die andere Seite* (The Other Side) and he illustrated many books, often ones whose subject matter matched his own macabre interests, such as the stories of Edgar Allan Poe. From the 1920s his reputation was widespread and he was influential on the *Surrealists. His spidery style changed little throughout his career.

Kubišta, Bohumil. See EIGHT.

Kuhn, Walt (*b* New York, 27 Oct. 1877; *d* White Plains, NY, 13 July 1949). American painter, illustrator, and designer, best known for the major role he played in planning and organizing the *Armory Show of 1913; he and Arthur B. *Davies were its chief architects. In spite of his involvement with this milestone in modern art, his own work was fairly conservative, although influenced superficially by, for example, the bright colours of the *Fauves. His best-known paintings are of clowns and circus life. From the 1920s he worked much as a designer for musical revues and also of industrial products. After suffering a nervous breakdown he died in a mental hospital.

Kukryniksy. A collective pseudonym of three Soviet artists who always worked together: Mikhail *Kupriianov* (1903–91), Porfirii *Krylov* (1902–90), and Nikolai *Sokolov* (1903–2000). The collective produced oil paintings but was famous primarily for political and social caricatures in newspapers and periodicals, particularly *Pravda*. The members started working as a group in 1925, began making joint contributions to exhibitions in 1929, and joined the permanent staff of *Pravda* in 1933. In the late 1930s and during the Second World War they did many biting caricatures of Hitler and Mussolini. After the war they continued as political caricaturists and also excelled as book illustrators for classics of Russian literature. In 1965 they were awarded the Lenin Prize.

Kulmbach, Hans Süss von (*b* ?Kulmbach, Upper Franconia, *c*.1480; *d* Nuremberg, Nov./ Dec. 1522). German painter and designer of woodcuts and stained glass. He worked mainly in Nuremberg, where he probably had part of his training with *Dürer; his clear, Italianate style was also influenced by Jacopo de' *Barbari, who visited the city in 1500–3. In the second decade of the 16th century Kulmbach was second only to Dürer as Nuremberg's leading painter. His work included altarpieces, among them several for churches in Cracow in Poland, which he probably visited, and also portraits. In addition he was an important designer of stained glass; several of his windows are in the church of St Sebald, Nuremberg, and his drawings for such work constitute the largest body of such work surviving from the early 16th century (an imposing example is a cartoon of St Peter in the British Museum, London).

Kunsthistorisches Museum, Vienna. Museum of painting, sculpture, and decorative arts (the title means 'Art History Museum') based on the accumulation of treasures by members of the imperial *Habsburg dynasty from the 16th century onwards. The imperial collections were first opened to the public in 1781 in the Belvedere Palace, which became informally known as the Belvedere Gallery. The present museum, a huge structure in neo-Renaissance style, was built in 1872–82. It is one of a series of very grand buildings erected around the Ringstrasse, the great circular boulevard created on the line of the city's ancient ramparts, which were demolished in 1858–64. The architects of the museum were Gottfried Semper (who also designed the *Gemäldegalerie, Dresden) and Karl von Hasenaur, and the extremely lavish decoration includes murals by *Makart and *Klimt on the main staircase. The collection of Old Master paintings in the Kunsthistorisches Museum is one of the most celebrated in the world, particularly rich in works by the great 16th-century Venetians (*Giorgione, *Titian, *Tintoretto, *Veronese), and by *Bruegel, *Dürer, van *Dyck, *Rubens, and *Velázquez. There are also major holdings in other areas, including antiquities, sculpture, and coins.

Kunstkammer. German term (literally 'art chamber') used to describe a type of collection of pictures and curios popular with princely connoisseurs in the 16th and 17th centuries. The pieces in such collections (which were by no means confined to Germany) might include anything from a watch to a fossil. In 16th- and 17th-century inventories the term *Kunstkammerstück* means an object of art, a jewel, or a devotional article of particularly remarkable character or quality ordered specially for display in the *Kunstkammer*.

Kupecký, Jan (b ?Prague, 1667; d Nuremberg, 16 July 1740). Bohemian portrait painter, active outside his native country for almost his whole career. His family were Protestants (members of the Moravian Brethren) and had to emigrate from Bohemia to Slovakia when Kupecký was a boy. He trained in Vienna, then in about 1687 moved to Italy, where he remained for more than twenty years, mainly in Rome. In about 1709 he returned to Vienna to work for Prince Adam von Liechtenstein. He remained based in Vienna until 1723 (during this time he made brief visits to Bohemia), then moved to Nuremberg (perhaps because of renewed religious persecution), where he spent the rest of his life. In this final period he became a friend of Johann Caspar

Füssli (see FUSELI), who wrote a biography of him, published in 1758. Kupecký's portraits are notable for their vigorous characterization and strong *chiaroscuro. He was a great admirer of *Rembrandt and like him painted numerous self-portraits.

Kupka, František (or Frank, François) (b Opočno, Bohemia, 22 Sept. 1871; d Puteaux, Paris, 24 June 1957). Czech painter and graphic artist, active mainly in France, a pioneer of *abstract art. He studied in Prague and Vienna, and settled in Paris in 1895 or 1896, working first mainly as a satirical draughtsman and book illustrator; his paintings of the time were influenced by *Symbolism and then *Fauvism. From an early age he had been interested in the supernatural (later in Theosophy), and from this grew a concern with the spiritual symbolism of colour. It became his ambition to create paintings whose colours and rhythms would produce effects similar to those of music, and in his letters he sometimes signed himself 'colour symphonist'. From 1909 (inspired by high-speed photography) he experimented—in a manner similar to that of the *Futurists—with ways of showing motion, and by 1912 this had led him to complete abstraction in *Amorpha: Fugue in Two Colours* (NG, Prague). This created something of a sensation when exhibited at the *Salon d'Automne in 1912. As with *Delaunay and the *Orphists, to whom his work is closely related, Kupka excelled at this stage in his career in the creation of lyrical colour effects.

At the outbreak of the First World War Kupka volunteered for military service; he fought on the Somme and he also did a good deal of propaganda work such as designing posters. After the war the Prague Academy appointed him a professor in Paris with the brief of introducing Czech students there to French culture. In 1931 he was one of the founder members of the *Abstraction-Création group. His later work was in a more geometrical abstract style. Although Kupka gradually established a considerable reputation, his pioneering role in abstraction was not generally realized in his lifetime. The re-evaluation of his career began with an exhibition of his work at the Musée National d'Art Moderne, Paris, in 1958, a year after his death.

Kupriianov, Mikhail. See KUKRYNIKSY.

Kuznetsov, Pavel. See BLUE ROSE.

L

Lachaise, Gaston (b Paris, 19 Mar. 1882; d New York, 18 Oct. 1935). French-born sculptor who emigrated to the USA in 1906 and became an American citizen in 1916, one of the pioneers of modern sculpture in his adopted country. He settled first in Boston, then in 1912 moved to New York, where he became assistant to Paul *Manship. Lachaise was a consummate craftsman in stone, metal, and wood (his father was a cabinetmaker), but his most characteristic works are in bronze. He did a number of portrait busts remarkable for their psychological insight and he earned a good deal of his living from decorative animal sculptures, but he is best known for his female nudes—monumental and anatomically simplified figures, with voluptuous forms and a sense of fluid rhythmical movement (*Standing Woman*, 1912–27, Whitney Mus., New York). Their smooth modelling links them with the work of *Nadelman, who was also at this time helping to lead American sculpture away from the 19th-century academic tradition, but Lachaise's figures are more powerful than those of Nadelman and have an overt sexuality that has caused them to be compared with the nudes of *Renoir. The inspiration for the figures—Lachaise's embodiment of female beauty—was Isabel Dutaud Nagle, a married American woman with whom he fell in love when he was about 20; she was the reason for his move to America and he was eventually able to marry her in 1917.

Laer, Pieter van (bapt. Haarlem, 14 Dec. 1599; d ?c.1642). Dutch painter, active for much of his career (c.1625–38) in Rome. There he was nicknamed Il Bamboccio (which may be translated as 'little clumsy one' or 'rag doll') because he was crippled or deformed in some way. His self-portrait in the Pallavicini Gallery in Rome (c.1625–30) suggests that he bore his handicap with good humour, and he was one of the leaders of the *Schildersbent, a fraternal organization set up by the Netherlandish artists in Rome to protect their interests. Van Laer was the first artist to specialize in scenes of street life in Rome. His work proved popular with collectors and he inspired numerous followers who were known as the 'Bamboccianti'. They were mainly other northerners working in Rome, such as the Flemings Jan Miel (1599–1663) and Michiel *Sweerts, but also included Italians such as Michelangelo *Cerquozzi and Viviano Codazzi (1611–72). Their pictures are called *bambocciate* (the singular is *bambocciata*—Italian for childishness) or in French *bambochades*; an English equivalent—bambocciade—exists, but it is rarely used. In about 1638 van Laer returned to his native Haarlem. He is said to have set off for Rome again in 1642, and nothing is heard of him thereafter.

La Fosse, Charles de (b Paris, 15 June 1636; d Paris, 13 Dec. 1716). French painter, one of the pre-eminent decorative artists of Louis XIV's reign. He was a pupil of *Le Brun and his assistant at Versailles, but his style was more strongly affected by his stay in Italy (1658–63), where he absorbed the *Baroque manner of Pietro da *Cortona and was influenced by the colour and warmth of such north Italian artists as *Correggio and *Veronese. In the 1680s he turned more to *Rubens as a source of inspiration. From 1689 to 1692 La Fosse worked in London for the 1st Duke of Montagu on the decoration of Montagu House (destroyed; the site is now occupied by the British Museum), then returned to Paris to decorate the church of the Invalides. Originally he was commissioned to paint the entire building, but eventually he did only the dome and pendentives (1702–4), in a style that heralds something of the lightness and elegance of the ensuing *Rococo. La Fosse's work was much more free and colourful than that of most of his contemporaries, and Anthony *Blunt described him as 'almost the only 17th-century French artist whom *Watteau may have studied with profit'.

La Fresnaye, Roger de (b Le Mans, 11 July 1885; d Grasse, 27 Nov. 1925). French painter. In 1912–14 he was a member of the *Section d'Or group, and his work shows an individual response to *Cubism; his paintings were more naturalistic than those of *Braque and *Picasso, but he adopted something of their method of analysing forms into planes. The effect in La Fresnaye's work, however, is more decorative than structural, and his prismatic colours reflect the influence of *Delaunay, as in his most famous and personal work, *The Conquest of the Air* (1913, MoMA, New York), in which he portrays himself and his brother in an exhilaratingly airy setting with a balloon ascending in the background. La Fresnaye's health was ruined during his service in the army during the First World War and he never again had the energy for sustained work. In his later paintings he abandoned Cubist spatial analysis for a more linear style.

Laguerre, Louis (*b* Versailles, 1663; *d* London, 20 Apr. 1721). French decorative painter, active for almost all his career in England. He was the son of the keeper of the royal menagerie at Versailles and Louis XIV was his godfather. After working for a short time under Charles *Le Brun in Paris he moved to England in 1683/4, initially collaborating with *Verrio but soon branching out on his own, working mainly in country houses, notably Burghley House, Chatsworth, and Blenheim Palace. He was a better painter than Verrio (although still unexceptional judged by European standards) and was also a more attractive personality, but he never achieved the extravagant worldly success of the Italian. From about 1710 *Thornhill began to succeed him in popularity. Late in his career Laguerre turned increasingly to portraits and history paintings.

La Hyre, Laurent de (*b* Paris, 26 Feb 1606; *d* Paris, 29 Dec. 1656). French painter. He painted religious and mythological scenes, portraits, and landscapes and also made engravings. His earlier work owed much to *Primaticcio and the *Fontainebleau schools, but from about 1638 his style became more classical, under the influence of Nicolas *Poussin and then of Philippe de *Champaigne. The *Birth of Bacchus* (1638, Hermitage, St Petersburg) is a good example of his work—obviously indebted to Poussin, but showing a certain individuality in the soft and romantic treatment of the landscape.

Lairesse, Gérard de (*b* Liège, 11 Sept. 1640; *bur.* Amsterdam, 28 July 1711). Flemish-born Dutch painter, etcher, and writer on art. He settled in Amsterdam in about 1665 and became the leading decorative painter in Holland in the second half of the 17th century, working in an academic classical style that inspired his over-enthusiastic contemporaries to call him 'the Dutch *Raphael' and 'the Dutch *Poussin'. In about 1690, however, he suddenly went blind and thereafter devoted himself to art theory. His lectures were collected in two books—*Grondlegginge der teekenkonst* (Principles of Drawing, 1701) and *Het groot schilderboek* (The Great Painting Book, 1707)—which went through many editions and translations during the 18th century. Lairesse's writings reveal the same academic approach as his paintings and he somewhat naively confessed that he had a special preference for *Rembrandt until he learned 'the infallible rules of art'. Rembrandt had painted a portrait of the young Lairesse in 1665 (Met. Mus., New York), sympathetically showing his disease-ravaged face (he was disfigured by congenital syphilis, which probably caused his blindness).

Lam, Wifredo (*b* Sagua la Grande, 8 Dec. 1902; *d* Paris, 11 Sept. 1982). Cuban painter. His father was Chinese and his mother of mixed African, Indian, and European origin, and Lam's career was appropriately cosmopolitan. After studying in Havana, he settled in Madrid in 1924, then in 1938 moved to Paris, where he became a friend of *Picasso. He also met André *Breton (whose book *Fata Morgana* he illustrated in 1940) and in 1939 joined the *Surrealist movement. In 1941 Lam sailed from Marseilles for Martinique on the same ship as *Masson, Breton, and many other intellectuals who were fleeing the Germans. After his return to Cuba in 1942 he came increasingly under the spell of African and Oceanic sculpture, and following visits to Haiti in 1945 and 1946 he also began incorporating images of Voodoo gods and rites in his work. In 1952 he returned to Paris and from the 1960s also spent much of his time at Albisola Mare, near Genoa. In the 1970s he began making bronze sculpture. Lam's work successfully reconciles the artistic vigour of Latin America with the European avant-garde and with the powerful mystique of African and Oceanic tradition, fusing human, animal, and vegetable elements in menacing semi-abstract images. He won numerous prestigious prizes and his work is included in many leading collections of modern art.

Lamb, Henry (*b* Adelaide, 21 June 1883; *d* Salisbury, 8 Oct. 1960). British painter, mainly of portraits. He was born in Australia, where his father, Sir Horace Lamb, was professor of mathematics at Adelaide University, and was brought up in Manchester, where his father became professor in 1885. Under parental pressure he studied medicine, but abandoned it for art in 1904. (On the outbreak of the First World War, however, Lamb returned to medicine, qualifying at Guy's Hospital, London, in 1916 and then serving as a medical officer in France, Macedonia, and Palestine; he was gassed and won the Military Cross. He also worked as an *Official War Artist, as he did again in the Second World War.) Lamb was associated with the *Bloomsbury Group and is best known for his sensitive portraits of fellow members, painted in the restrained *Post-Impressionist style that characterized his work throughout his career. Above all he is remembered for his portrait of Lytton Strachey (1914, Tate, London), in which he 'has relished emphasizing Strachey's gaunt, ungainly figure, and the air of resigned intellectual superiority with which he surveys the world from that incredible slab-like head' (*DNB*); Sir John *Rothenstein described it as 'one of the best portraits painted in England in this century'. Apart from portraits, Lamb also painted landscapes and (especially in later life when his health was failing) still-lifes.

Lambert, George (*b* ?Kent, ?1700; *d* London, 30/31 Jan. 1765). The leading English landscape painter of his day. He began his career working in the style of John *Wootton and also learned something of the principles of *ideal landscape composition from studying the work of Gaspard *Dughet. As well as painting handsome works essentially in Dughet's manner, Lambert also did more realistic topographical views. Ellis *Waterhouse has written of him: 'Lambert was the first native painter to apply the rules of art to the English rural scene, and, in this sense, *Wilson followed him.' The figures in Lambert's paintings were done by other artists—sometimes, according to plausible tradition, by *Hogarth. He also collaborated with Samuel *Scott (who painted the shipping) in views of the East India Company's settlements (1732, India Office Library, London).

Lami, Eugène (*b* Paris, 12 Jan. 1800; *d* Paris, 19 Dec. 1890). French painter and lithographer. A pupil of Horace *Vernet and *Gros, he made his name with military subjects, including battle scenes in oils, but he became best known for watercolours and lithographs of fashionable society and court life, in which he took particular delight in recording details of costume. In 1832 he was appointed official painter to King Louis-Philippe. He visited England in 1826–7, and again

in 1848–52, when he followed Louis-Philippe into exile. There are large collections of his work in the Royal Library at Windsor Castle and in the Victoria and Albert Museum, London.

Lamothe, Louis. See DEGAS.

Lancret, Nicolas (*b* Paris, 22 Jan. 1690; *d* Paris, 14 Sept. 1743). French painter. He studied under Claude *Gillot, who slightly earlier had taught *Watteau, and he became a great admirer of Watteau's work, imitating the style and themes he had made popular. In 1719 he was received into the Académie Royale in Paris as a painter of *fêtes galantes*—a category that had been created especially for Watteau only two years earlier. Although his work is prosaic compared with Watteau's, it has great charm and he had a successful career. He is well represented in the Wallace Collection, London.

Land art (or **Earth art** or **Earthworks**). Terms applied to a type of art that uses earth, rocks, soil, and so on as its raw materials. The terms are not usually clearly differentiated, although 'Earthworks' generally refers to very large constructions. Land art emerged as a movement in the late 1960s and has links with several other movements that flourished at that time: *Minimal art in that the shapes created are often extremely simple; *Arte Povera in the use of 'worthless' materials; *happenings and *Performance art because the work created was often impermanent; and *Conceptual art because the more ambitious earthwork schemes frequently exist only as projects. There are affinities also with the passion at this time for the study of prehistoric mounds and ley lines—part of the hippie back-to-nature ethos that expressed a disenchantment with the sophisticated technology of urban culture. The desire to get away from the traditional elitist and money-orientated gallery world was also very much typical of the time, although large earthworks have in fact necessitated very hefty expenditure, and far from being populist and accessible, such works are usually in remote areas; some are intelligible only from the air and therefore can rarely be appreciated other than by people rich enough to own or hire aeroplanes. Moreover, in spite of the desire to sidestep the gallery system, dealers have proved capable of exploiting this kind of art, just like any other, and some land artists at least have made handsome livings from it.

The artist associated more than any other with large-scale earthworks *in situ* was Robert *Smithson, whose *Spiral Jetty* (1970) in the Great

Salt Lake, Utah, is easily the most reproduced work of this kind. The most ambitious of all such enterprises is probably the Roden Crater Project by James Turrell (1941–), involving the reshaping of an extinct volcano in Arizona (begun in the mid-1970s). Most of the other leading exponents are—like Smithson and Turrell—Americans. They include Alice Aycock (1946–), whose work has included underground mazes, and Michael Heizer (1944–), whose best-known work is *Double Negative* (1969–70) in the Nevada desert—two massive cuts 30 ft (9 m) wide and 50 ft (15 m) deep in an area where he said he found 'that kind of unraped, peaceful religious space artists have always tried to put in their work'. Some critics, however, consider that earthworks can themselves constitute a type of rape or violation.

*Christo is sometimes grouped with Land artists, although his work really defies classification. The leading British exponents are Andy *Goldsworthy and Richard *Long.

Landseer, Sir Edwin (*b* London, 7 Mar. 1802 or 1803; *d* London, 1 Oct. 1873). English painter, sculptor, and engraver, mainly of animal subjects. He was the son of an engraver and writer, **John Landseer** (1769–1852), and was an infant prodigy. His career was a story of remarkable social as well as professional success; he was the favourite painter of Queen Victoria (who considered him 'very good looking although rather short') and his friends included Dickens and Thackeray. The qualities in his work that delighted the Victorian public, however, subsequently caused his reputation to plummet, for although he had great skill in depicting animal anatomy, he tended to humanize his subjects to tell a sentimental story or point a moral. His most familiar works in this vein include *The Old Shepherd's Chief Mourner* (1837, V&A, London), *Dignity and Impudence* (1839, Tate, London), and *The Monarch of the Glen* (1850, Guinness plc, Edinburgh). Other paintings by Landseer have been attacked for their cruelty (he made many visits to the Scottish Highlands and frequently painted scenes of deer hunting). Apart from animal subjects, he also painted portraits and historical scenes. Although he had no previous experience as a sculptor, in 1858 he was commissioned to make four huge bronze lions for the base of Nelson's Column in Trafalgar Square, London; they were cast by *Marochetti and unveiled in 1867. By this time Landseer's health had broken down (it was for this reason that he declined the presidency of the *Royal Academy

in 1865), and in his last years he suffered from bouts of madness, aggravated by alcohol.

His brother **Thomas** (1798–1880) was an engraver, whose prints played a great part in popularizing Edwin's work. Another brother, **Charles** (1800–79), bequeathed £10,000 to the Royal Academy to found Landseer scholarships.

Lane, Fitz Hugh. See LUMINISM.

Lane, Sir Hugh (*b* Ballybrack House, Co. Cork, 9 Nov. 1875; *d* at sea, 7 May 1915). Irish dealer, patron, collector, and administrator. He made his fortune as a picture dealer in London and had no particular interest in Ireland until about 1900, when through the influence of Sarah *Purser and the playwright Lady Gregory (his aunt) he became caught up in the rising tide of nationalism in the arts. He commissioned John Butler *Yeats to paint a series of eminent contemporary Irishmen (it was completed by *Orpen, a distant cousin and close friend of Lane's) and he helped to found Dublin's Municipal Gallery of Modern Art, opened in temporary premises in 1906. In addition to giving and lending numerous works to the gallery, he offered to bequeath his finest late 19th- and early 20th-century French paintings to Dublin, if a suitable gallery were built to house them. This caused arguments with Dublin's city authorities, however, and he moved the pictures to the National Gallery in London. Lane was killed when the *Lusitania* (on which he was returning from business in the USA) was torpedoed by a German submarine. A codicil to his will expressed his intention of returning the pictures to Dublin, but it was unwitnessed, creating a long-term legal dispute about their ownership. In 1959 an agreement was eventually reached whereby the paintings were divided into groups to be shown alternately in Dublin and London. This arrangement has subsequently been somewhat modified. The Municipal Gallery of Modern Art was given a permanent home in Dublin in 1933, and in 1979 it was renamed the Hugh Lane Municipal Gallery of Modern Art.

Lanfranco, Giovanni (*bapt.* Parma, 26 Jan. 1582; *d* Rome, 29 Nov. 1647). Italian painter, who with *Guercino and Pietro da *Cortona ranks as one of the founders of the High *Baroque style of painting. He trained in Parma under Agostino *Carracci before going to Rome in 1602 to assist Annibale Carracci in the Palazzo Farnese. After Annibale's death in 1609, he returned for a while to Emilia, but by about 1612 was back in Rome, where he gradually superseded his arch-rival *Domenichino as the leading fresco decorator in the city. Their work can be compared in the church of S. Andrea della Valle; Domenichino painted the apse and the pendentives of the dome, but Lanfranco was awarded the commission for the *Assumption of the Virgin* (1625–7) in the dome itself. This fresco is one of the key works of Baroque art and it ended the dominance of Bolognese classicism in Rome. The heroic figure style derives from the Carracci, but the dynamic foreshortening is based on *Correggio's dome paintings in Lanfranco's native Parma, here carried to new extremes. *Bellori compared the way in which Lanfranco handles the multitude of figures to the harmonious blending of voices in a choir, and the energetic design became a pattern for decorative painters throughout Europe.

Between 1634 and 1646 Lanfranco was based in Naples, where he produced numerous frescos in the cathedral and other major churches. His work was an inspiration to such Neapolitan masters as Mattia *Preti, Luca *Giordano, and *Solimena. He returned to Rome in 1646, the year before his death; his final (unfinished) work, a fresco of *S. Carlo Borromeo in Glory* in the apse of S. Carlo ai Catinari, exemplifies the airy luminosity of his final style.

Lanfranco is much less renowned as an easel painter, but he created some outstanding works in this field also. Particularly remarkable are his *Ecstasy of the Blessed Margaret of Cortona* (1622, Pitti, Florence), which possibly influenced *Bernini's *St Teresa*, and *St Mary Magdalene Transported to Heaven* (c.1605, Mus. di Capodimonte, Naples), a bizarre and highly original work in which the rapturous saint is carried by angels above a poetically evoked view of the Roman Campagna.

Langley, Walter. See NEWLYN SCHOOL.

Lanyon, Peter. See ST IVES SCHOOL.

Lanzi, Luigi (b Monte dell'Olmo, nr. Macerata, 13 June 1732; d Florence, 31 Mar. 1810). Italian art historian, archaeologist, and philologist. He was appointed curator of the antiquarian collections of the *Uffizi, Florence, in 1775, and he ranks second only to *Winckelmann as a pioneer in the systematic study of ancient art. However, he is best known for his history of Italian painting from the 13th century until his own time, *Storia pittorica della Italia . . .* (1792, 2nd edn. 1795–6, 3rd edn. 1809). Lanzi classified his material by regional schools and based his work on a thorough knowledge of previous writings on the subject and of the paintings themselves (he visited churches and collections throughout central and northern Italy in the course of his work). His methodical arrangement and his synthesis of solid research with sensitive analysis of style make his work a landmark in art-historical writing, and Rudolf *Wittkower has described it as 'still unequalled for knowledge of the material and breadth of approach'. There have been numerous editions since Lanzi's death, including an English translation in 1828. His other writings included a scholarly but controversial work on the Etruscan language (1789) and a book on ancient vases (1806) in which he correctly perceived that vases traditionally called Etruscan were in fact Greek in origin.

Laocoön. An antique marble group (Vatican Mus.) representing the Trojan priest Laocoön and his two sons being crushed to death by serpents as a penalty for warning the Trojans against the wooden horse of the Greeks, an incident related by Virgil in the *Aeneid* ii. 199–231. It is usually dated to the 2nd or 1st century BC or the 1st century AD, although whether it is an original *Hellenistic piece or a Roman copy has long been a matter of dispute. *Pliny states that in his time it stood in the palace of the Emperor Titus in Rome, records that it was made by the sculptors Hagesander, Polydorus, and Athenodorus of Rhodes, and describes it as 'a work to be preferred to all that the arts of painting and sculpture have produced'. This praise echoed long after the sculpture had disappeared, and its dramatic rediscovery in a vineyard in Rome in 1506 made an overwhelming impression, notably on *Michelangelo, who went to see it immediately. Its liberating influence for the expression of the emotions continued to be important for *Baroque sculpture and until the 19th century it was ranked (with the *Apollo Belvedere and the *Belvedere Torso) as one of the greatest works of antiquity. (As early as about 1530 *Titian satirized the adulation it received in a woodcut showing the figures changed to monkeys.) It was given a new aesthetic significance by *Winckelmann, who saw it as a supreme symbol of the moral dignity of the tragic hero and the most complete exemplification of the 'noble simplicity and quiet majesty' that he regarded as the essence of Greek idealistic art and the key to true beauty. In 1766 *Lessing chose *Laokoon* as the title of the book in which he attacked Winckelmann's ideas.

The *Laocoön* was one of the greatest prizes taken from Italy by Napoleon and was in Paris

1798–1815. It has been restored several times since its discovery, and a complete renovation was made in the 1950s, when Laocoön's original right arm was returned to the figure and replaced in its correct position behind his head. Although no longer considered one of the world's supreme masterpieces, it has slipped in esteem much less than some once-revered antique marbles; it continues to be a work with a powerful hold over the imagination and still finds a place in almost all general histories of art.

Study of the *Laocoön* was revolutionized in 1957 by one of the most spectacular archaeological discoveries of the 20th century, when several groups of marble figures representing events in Homer's *Odyssey* were found at Sperlonga (ancient Spelunca) near Naples; the names Hagesander, Polydoros, and Athenodoros are inscribed on one of the groups (now in the museum at Sperlonga), which are close in style to the *Laocoön*. The cave in which these sculptures were found was evidently used as a banqueting hall by the Emperor Tiberius (reigned AD 14–37), and there is other evidence linking them with the 1st century AD, so this date is now finding favour among classical archaeologists for the *Laocoön* also.

Largillière (or Largillierre), **Nicolas de** (*b* Paris, 10 Oct. 1656; *d* Paris, 20 Mar. 1746). French painter, mainly of portraits. He spent his youth in Antwerp and from 1675 to 1679 he worked in England, assisting *Lely and *Verrio. After settling in Paris in 1679 he soon established his position as a leading portraitist, rivalled only by *Rigaud, his almost exact contemporary. The two men were friends and seldom in direct competition, for Largillière specialized in portraits of the rich middle classes and Rigaud painted the aristocracy. Largillière's successful career continued into old age: he was director of the Académie Royale (see ACADEMY) in his eighties (1734–5 and 1738–42). His output of portraits was prodigious (contemporary sources indicate he painted about 1,500), and he also did religious works (once highly regarded), still-lifes, and landscapes. At his best, his paintings are vigorous, forthright, and colourful; at his worst, they are pompous and vacuous.

Larionov, Mikhail (*b* Tiraspol [now in Moldova], 22 May [3 June] 1881; *d* Fontenay-aux-Roses, nr. Paris, 10 May 1964). Russian-French painter and designer, one of the leading figures in the development of modernism in Russia in the period before the First World War. His early work was influenced by *Impressionism, but from 1908, together with Natalia *Goncharova (his lifelong companion and collaborator), he developed a style known as Neo-Primitivism, in which he blended *Fauvist colour with elements drawn from Russian folk art. Together they were involved in a series of avant-garde groups and exhibitions, notably the *Knave of Diamonds group, founded in 1910, the *Donkey's Tail exhibition in 1912, and the *Target exhibition in 1913, at which Larionov launched *Rayonism, a near abstract movement that was a counterpart to Italian *Futurism. In May 1914 Larionov and Goncharova accompanied *Diaghilev's Ballets Russes to Paris. They returned to Russia in July on the outbreak of the First World War, and Larionov served in the army and was wounded. After being invalided out, he and Goncharova left Russia permanently in 1915, moving first to Switzerland and then settling in Paris in 1919 (they became French citizens in 1938). In Paris he practically abandoned easel painting and concentrated on theatrical designing for the Ballets Russes. After Diaghilev's death in 1929 Larionov took up painting again, but he gradually sank into obscurity and his final years were marred by illness and poverty. His reputation was revived shortly before his death with retrospective exhibitions (jointly with Goncharova) in London (Arts Council, 1961) and Paris (Mus. d'Art Moderne de la Ville de Paris, 1963).

Larkin, William (*d* London, Apr./May 1619). English portrait painter. He emerged from total obscurity in 1952 with the publication of his only documented works—a pair of small oval portraits (1609–10) at Charlecote Park, Warwickshire (the sitters are Lord Herbert of Cherbury, who mentions the portrait in his celebrated autobiography, and his friend Sir Thomas Lucy). Subsequently, on circumstantial evidence, several other portraits have been attributed to Larkin; they are in a very different vein from the Charlecote pictures—full-lengths featuring elaborate Turkey carpets, dazzling metallic curtains, and poses of a starched magnificence, notably a breathtaking group at Ranger's House, London. If they are indeed all by Larkin he was the genius of Jacobean painting; Ellis *Waterhouse considered the Ranger's House portraits to be the work of 'at least three different hands' (one of them perhaps Isaac *Oliver's), but technical examination in the 1980s indicated they are all from the same studio.

Laroon, Marcellus (*b* Chiswick, Middlesex [now Greater London], 2 Apr. 1679; *d* Oxford, 1 June 1772). English painter, the son of a

Franco-Dutch painter of the same name (d 1701/2) who moved to England as a young man and was one of *Kneller's assistants. The younger Laroon was a colourful character who in his long and strenuous life was a musician, singer, soldier, and man of pleasure; he drew and painted 'for diversitions', to use the words of *Vertue, and did not concentrate on art until he retired from the army in 1732. He painted portraits, *conversation pieces, and *genre scenes, usually fanciful in character. His nearly monochromatic, feathery style added a touch of French daintiness to the stolid English tradition and he anticipated *Gainsborough by his lightness of touch. After a long period of neglect, he was rediscovered in the 20th century.

Larsson, Carl (b Stockholm, 28 May 1853; d Falun, 22 Jan. 1919). Swedish painter, illustrator, printmaker, and writer. His work included numerous portraits and book illustrations, as well as several large murals (the best known are those on Sweden's artistic history in the Nationalmuseum, Stockholm, 1896), but he is now remembered mainly for the house he created in the village of Sundborn in Dalarna (Dalecarlia) and for his watercolours of the idyllic life he enjoyed there with his wife **Karin** (1853–1928), a textile designer. The house—called Lilla Hyttnäs—was opened as a museum in 1942. To Swedes it epitomizes a healthy, happy society, and it has exercised a lasting influence on Scandinavian interior design.

Lascaux. Site of a cave near Montignac in the Dordogne region of France containing some of the finest examples of prehistoric paintings ever discovered. The cave was found in 1940 by some boys searching for a lost dog and rapidly attracted great interest; it opened to the public in 1948. Although the paintings (probably dating from about 15,000 BC) were remarkably well preserved, they deteriorated so rapidly because of the effect of the large number of tourists on the cave's environment that it had to be closed in 1963; a facsimile was opened nearby in 1983. Various animals are portrayed, some over-life-size, and it is generally believed that the cave served as a centre for magical hunting rites rather than as a dwelling. As well as the paintings there are some engravings cut in the rock. See also ALTAMIRA.

Lassaw, Ibram. See ABSTRACT EXPRESSIONISM.

Lastman, Pieter (b ?Amsterdam, c.1583; bur. Amsterdam, 4 Apr. 1633). Dutch painter, highly esteemed in his day but now remembered mainly as the most significant of *Rembrandt's teachers. Most of his career was spent in Amsterdam, but in about 1603–7 he was in Italy, where *Caravaggio and *Elsheimer made a strong impact on his style. He specialized in small-scale religious, historical, and mythological scenes and often chose unusual subjects that showed off his learning (*The Roman Women and Children Beseeching Coriolanus not to Attack Rome*, 1625, Trinity College, Dublin). The glossy colours, the animated gestures and facial expressions, and the dramatic lighting of Rembrandt's early works all owe much to Lastman, and his *Balaam and the Ass* (1626, Mus. Cognacq-Jay, Paris), for example, is clearly based on a prototype by his master (1622, priv. coll.). Lastman also taught Rembrandt's friend Jan *Lievens.

László, Philip de (b Budapest, 30 Apr. 1869; d London, 22 Nov. 1937). Hungarian-born portrait painter (and occasional sculptor) who settled in London in 1907 and became a British citizen in 1914 (although he was interned during the First World War). He trained in Budapest, Munich, and Paris (at the *Académie Julian) and already had an international reputation as a society portraitist when he moved to England. There his career continued in its successful course, his sitters including Edward VII and numerous members of the aristocracy (examples are in the NPG, London). According to the *Dictionary of National Biography*, he had 'a pleasing, courteous, and exuberant manner, and was very popular in society'. He was a fast and fluent worker and his style was elegant and dashing.

La Tène art. See CELTIC ART.

La Thangue, H. H. (Herbert Henry) (b Croydon, Surrey [now Greater London], 19 Jan. 1859; d London, 21 Dec. 1929). British painter. He studied mainly at the *Royal Academy in London and the École des *Beaux-Arts in Paris. In 1887 he described the Academy as 'the diseased root from which other evils grow', and he was one of the leading figures in founding the *New English Art Club in opposition to it and in introducing French *plein-air painting to Britain. He lived in the countryside (first in Norfolk, then in Sussex), and *Clausen wrote: 'Sunlight was the thing that attracted him: this and some simple motive of rural occupation, enhanced by a picturesque surround.' From about 1898 he turned to peasant scenes set in Provence or Italy, places he often visited. As the countryside changed, his work became increasingly nostalgic, as he hankered after what *Munnings called a 'quiet old world village where he could live and find real country models'.

La Tour, Georges de (*bapt.* Vic-sur-Seille, Lorraine [now Moselle], 14 Mar. 1593; *d* Lunéville, Lorraine [now Meurthe-et-Moselle], 30 Jan. 1652). French painter, active mainly at Lunéville in the duchy of Lorraine; it was his wife's home town and he settled there in 1620, three years after his marriage. He was highly regarded in his day (his paintings were owned by Louis XIII, Cardinal Richelieu, and the Duke of Lorraine), but his name sank into oblivion after his death and it was not until the 20th century that he was rediscovered (see voss) and hailed as the most inspired of *Caravaggesque painters. Little is recorded of his life (although he is known to have been arrogant and unpopular with his neighbours) and it is a matter of dispute whether he gained his knowledge of Caravaggio's style by visiting Italy, via painters of the Utrecht School such as *Honthorst, or through a local intermediary such as Jean Le Clerc, who had worked with *Saraceni in Rome and returned to Lorraine in 1622 (after the record of his baptism, La Tour is not certainly documented until 1616, when he was 23, and it has been proposed that he travelled abroad in this early period; nothing at all is known of his training). Like Honthorst he is particularly associated with nocturnal scenes and with the use of a candle as the light source in a painting. La Tour's handling of light is more subtle and sensitive, however, and he is grander in conception and more sombre in mood. In his mature work he smoothed the forms of his figures until they approached geometric simplicity and achieved a feeling of monumental stillness that is considered to represent the spirit of 17th-century French *classicism no less than the paintings of *Poussin and Philippe de *Champaigne in their different fields.

Several of La Tour's paintings are signed, but only three of them bear a date—the *Payment of Taxes* (date barely legible—various readings have been proposed; Picture Gal., Lviv, Ukraine); the *Penitent St Peter* (1645, Cleveland Mus. of Art); and the *Denial of St Peter* (1650, Mus. B.-A., Nantes)—and there is much scholarly debate about his chronology. The works associated with the beginning of his career are daylit scenes of such subjects as peasants and card-sharpers; they are very different in spirit from the calm and majestic religious images of his maturity and have become controversial as regards attribution as well as dating. It has been argued (and hotly disputed) that the *Fortune-Teller* (Met. Mus., New York) is a modern fake, and although the status of most of the other early works as authentic (and high-quality) 17th-century French paintings is not denied, their attribution to La Tour (which rests almost entirely on stylistic evidence) has been questioned. Another problem in La Tour studies is that many of his undeniably authentic compositions exist in more than one version, and the studio replicas (as they appear to be) are sometimes of extremely high quality; the versions of *St Sebastian Tended by St Irene* in the Louvre, Paris, and the Gemäldegalerie, Berlin, for example, are each extraordinarily beautiful. La Tour's son **Étienne** (1621–92) worked in his father's studio and may have been responsible for some of the replicas. No independent works certainly by him are known, but the *Education of the Virgin* (Frick Coll., New York), signed 'de la Tour', has been attributed to him.

La Tour, Maurice-Quentin de (*b* Saint-Quentin, 5 Sept. 1704; *d* Saint-Quentin, 17 Feb. 1788). With *Perronneau the most celebrated and the most successful French *pastel portraitist of the 18th century. His portraits are remarkable for their beauty of colour, their mastery of texture, and above all their brilliant handling of expression, which gives them a feeling of great vivacity. La Tour himself said, 'I penetrate into the depths of my subjects without their knowing it, and capture them whole.' He portrayed many of the most famous men and women of his day and in 1750 he became portraitist to Louis XV. He made a fortune from his work and late in life he used much of it for philanthropic purposes, in both Paris and his native Saint-Quentin. The museum there has a good collection of his work.

Laurana, Francesco (*b* Vrana, nr. Zara, Dalmatia [now Zadar, Croatia], *c*.1430; *d* Marseilles, ?1502). Italian sculptor, born in Dalmatia, at that time subject to Venice. He is first recorded in 1453 in Naples, where he was one of several sculptors who worked on the decorations to the triumphal arch of Alfonso I that forms the entrance to Castelnuovo. By 1461 he was working in Provence and thenceforward he divided his time between France and Italy, mainly the south of Italy, including Sicily, although he is thought to have visited Urbino, and was possibly related to Luciano Laurana, the chief architect of the celebrated Ducal Palace there. In France his most important work was the chapel of St Lazare (1475–81) in the Old Cathedral at Marseilles, described by Anthony *Blunt as 'probably the earliest purely Italian work on French soil'. He is best known, however, for his female portrait busts of royal and aristocratic sitters. In these remarkably sensitive works the forms of the face are subtly generalized in a search for basic geometric shapes, and their simple naturalism was sometimes enhanced by heightening the marble with colour, as with the bust of Isabella of Aragon (c.1470, KH Mus., Vienna).

Laurencin, Marie (b Paris, 31 Oct. 1883; d Paris, 8 June 1956). French painter, illustrator, and stage designer. In 1907 she was introduced to *Apollinaire, *Picasso, and their circle, and in 1908 she painted a group portrait of several of her famous friends (The Guests, Baltimore Mus. of Art). For several years she lived with Apollinaire, and she exhibited with the *Cubists. Her work, however, was entirely peripheral to the Cubist movement. She specialized in portraits of oval-faced, almond-eyed young girls painted in pastel colours, and although she borrowed a few tricks of stylization from her Cubist friends, her style remained essentially unaffected by them. Her work was lyrically charming and rather repetitive. From 1914 to 1920 she lived in Spain and Germany, then returned to Paris. Apart from paintings, her work included book illustrations and set and costume designs for the ballet and theatre.

Laurens, Henri (b Paris, 18 Feb. 1885; d Paris, 5 May 1954). French sculptor, printmaker, designer, and illustrator. He trained as an ornamental stonemason. His early work shows the influence of *Rodin, but in 1911 he became a friend of *Braque (he later met *Gris, *Léger, and *Picasso) and he was one of the first artists to adapt the *Cubist style to sculpture. He made collages, reliefs, and constructions of wood and metal, mainly still-lifes using the familiar Cubist repertory of bottles, glasses, and fruit. Much of his work was coloured, but he retained a genuine sculptor's feeling for mass, and his distrust of intellectual speculation preserved his independence from Cubist theorizing. In the mid-1920s he moved away from his geometrical style to one that featured curved lines and voluptuous forms, notably in female nudes. Many of his fellow artists regarded him as one of the greatest sculptors of his time, but financial success and official recognition were slow in coming. When he failed to win the first prize for sculpture at the 1948 Venice *Biennale, *Matisse was so disgusted that he offered to share his own painting prize with him. In 1953, however, Laurens won the Grand Prix at the São Paulo Bienale. Apart

from sculpture, his work included stage design for *Diaghilev and numerous book illustrations.

Lavery, Sir John (b Belfast, 20 Mar. 1856; d Kilmaganny, Co. Kilkenny, 10 Jan. 1941). British painter, mainly of portraits. He studied in Glasgow, in London, and then in the early 1880s in Paris (at the *Académie Julian and elsewhere). Between 1885 and 1896 he lived mainly in Glasgow (see GLASGOW SCHOOL), then settled in London, although he travelled a good deal and often wintered in Morocco, where he bought a house in about 1903. Lavery had an immensely successful career as a fashionable portraitist (particularly of women), painting in a dashing and fluid, if rather facile, style; in his autobiography, The Life of a Painter (1940), he wrote, 'I have felt ashamed of having spent my life trying to please sitters and make friends instead of telling the truth and making enemies.' He also painted interiors, landscapes, and outdoor scenes such as tennis and bathing parties, and he was an *Official War Artist, 1917–18. His reputation did not long survive his death, but there has recently been a revival of interest in his work.

Law, Bob. See SITUATION.

Lawrence, Sir Thomas (b Bristol, 13 Apr. 1769; d London, 7 Jan. 1830). The outstanding English portrait painter of his generation. Lawrence was a child prodigy and was almost entirely self-taught. He was also handsome and charming, and after a resounding early triumph with his portrait of Queen Charlotte (1789–90, NG, London) he never looked back in terms of professional and social success. On the death of *Reynolds in 1792 he succeeded him as official painter to George III, and in 1794, aged 25, he became the youngest person ever to be elected a Royal Academician (although Mary *Moser was a founder member when even younger). On the death of *Hoppner in 1810 he was recognized as the leading portrait painter of the time, and also to some extent as head of the profession of painting in Britain. The high point of his career came in 1818, when he was sent to Europe as the envoy of the Prince Regent (later George IV) to paint the heads of state and military leaders who were involved with the allied victory over Napoleon. As a preliminary gesture he was knighted, and on his return in 1820 he succeeded Benjamin *West as president of the *Royal Academy. The portraits painted on this tour are now in the Waterloo Chamber, Windsor Castle.

Lawrence was devoted to the memory and example of Reynolds and in some respects he was the last of the great portrait painters in the 18th-century tradition. In others he was a *Romantic, responding to the glamour of the historic years through which he lived. His fluid and lush brushwork won the admiration of French painters when his work was exhibited at the Paris *Salon of 1824 and after *Delacroix visited London in the following year he paid Lawrence the compliment of painting a portrait in his style (*Louis-Auguste Schwiter*, 1826–30, NG, London). Lawrence's reputation declined after his death, however, and has never revived to its former heights. He was constantly in debt in spite of his success and took on too many commissions, so his work is uneven and sometimes careless (and like Reynolds he was a failure as a history painter), but at his best he has a feeling for paint that few British artists can rival.

Lawrence was a man of great taste and made one of the finest collections of Old Master drawings ever assembled, particularly rich in works by *Michelangelo and *Raphael (these are now among the greatest treasures of the Ashmolean Museum in Oxford). He played a part in founding the *National Gallery and in securing the *Elgin Marbles for the nation, and was noted for the unselfish help he gave to young artists; Delacroix described him as the 'flower of politeness'.

Lawson, Ernest (*b* Halifax, Nova Scotia, 22 Mar. 1873; *d* Miami, Fla., 18 Dec. 1939). American painter, the least distinguished and most orthodox member of The *Eight. Unlike the other members of the group, he was primarily a landscapist (although he did also paint urban scenes), and his style was essentially *Impressionist.

lay figure. A doll-like model of the human figure, jointed so that it can be given all kinds of poses. It may be anything from a few inches in height to life-size (an example about half life-size that belonged to the sculptor *Roubiliac is in the Museum of London). Articulated dolls and marionettes were known in antiquity, but the first description of an artist's lay figure is given by *Filarete in his *Treatise on Architecture* (1461–4). Although *Vasari mentions a life-size wooden model made by Fra *Bartolommeo, early lay figures were mostly small and were called manikins. Some 18th-century portrait painters used a life-size figure, completely jointed and covered with fabric. They could arrange the costumes on it and work on that part of the picture in the absence of the sitter. When *Millais painted *The Black Brunswicker* (1859–60, Lady Lever AG, Port Sunlight), the models for the two lovers—with Victorian decorum—posed separately, embracing a life-size lay figure.

Lazzarini, Gregorio. See TIEPOLO.

lead. A heavy, soft, silvery-coloured metal that tarnishes to bluish grey. Since ancient times it has been used for numerous practical and decorative purposes, notably in plumbing and roofing, as it is durable and easily worked. It can be hammered, carved, or filed when cold, and because of its low melting point it can be cast with much simpler facilities than those required for *bronze, although it does not take such fine detail. It was used by the Greeks for statuettes, by the Romans for garden ornaments, in the *Romanesque period for fonts (especially in England), and in the *Renaissance for *medals and *plaquettes. However, it was not generally used for large sculptures until the late 17th century, when it was much employed for garden statuary at Versailles. This began a fashion for lead garden sculpture that lasted throughout most of the 18th century, John *Nost being the leading exponent of this kind of work in England. It is 'singularly appropriate for use in garden sculpture because of its delicate texture and soft appearance, which blends beautifully with foliage' (Jack C. Rich, *The Materials and Methods of Sculpture*, 1947). In the 18th century it was also sometimes used for more ambitious works, for example by Georg Raphael *Donner. During the 19th century it was used less often, but there is, for example, some outstanding lead ornamental work on the Albert Memorial (1863–76) in Kensington Gardens, London. In the 20th century it has been employed fairly infrequently by sculptors, partly because of a growing awareness of its toxic qualities, but it was used by *Epstein in his large *Madonna and Child* (1953) in Cavendish Square, London, as a considerable amount of lead from war-damaged roofing was available at the convent it adorned. More recently, Richard *Serra has used splashed molten lead in his sculpture.

Leader, Benjamin Williams (*b* Worcester, 12 Mar. 1831; *d* Shere, nr. Guildford, Surrey, 22 Mar. 1923). English landscape painter, chiefly remembered for one work. He was originally called Benjamin Leader Williams (he was the brother of the engineer Sir Edward Leader Williams), but he transposed his names because there were several other contemporary landscape painters called Williams from whom he wanted to distinguish himself. His career was only modestly successful until he caught the public imagination with *February Fill Dyke* (City AG, Birmingham), exhibited at the *Royal Academy in 1881 (it represents a November—not a February—evening after rain; the title comes from an old country rhyme). It was acclaimed for its vividness of atmosphere, and 'By the end of the century . . . had achieved the kind of popular immortality that in British landscape art had previously only been granted to *Constable' (catalogue of the exhibition 'Great Victorian Paintings', RA, London, 1978). Leader continued exhibiting with success until the end of his long life, but many 20th-century critics were dismissive about his work (in *Landscape into Art* (1949), Kenneth *Clark held up *February Fill Dyke* as an example of 'false naturalism'). However, with the general growth of interest in Victorian art, Leader's reputation has revived.

lead point. See METALPOINT.

Lear, Edward (*b* London, 12 May 1812; *d* San Remo, 29 Jan. 1888). English painter, draughtsman, writer, and traveller. Although he is now remembered principally for his nonsense poems and as the popularizer of the limerick, he earned his living mainly through drawing and painting. He began his career as a draughtsman for the Zoological Society, but when the exacting work began to affect his eyesight he turned to topographical painting in the 1830s, initially in watercolour and later in oils. His style is very clear and brightly lit. He travelled widely and published several illustrated accounts of his journeys. In 1871 he settled in San Remo, Italy.

Le Brun, Charles (*bapt.* Paris, 24 Feb. 1619; *d* Paris, 12 Feb. 1690). French painter, designer, and art theorist, the dominant artist of Louis XIV's reign. He trained under *Vouet and quickly made a name for himself, winning a commission from Cardinal Richelieu when he was barely out of his teens; the only surviving picture from this commission (for the Palais Cardinal in Paris) is *Hercules and the Horses of Diomedes* (*c*.1640, Castle Mus., Nottingham). In 1640 Le Brun went to Rome in company with *Poussin, who was returning from his visit to Paris, and remained there until 1646. After his return to Paris he was soon busy with varied commissions and during the 1650s he established himself as the leading decorative painter in France. In 1662 he was raised to the nobility and named first painter to the king, and in 1663 he was made director of the *Gobelins factory and of the Académie Royale. For the next two decades, until the death of his patron Jean-Baptiste Colbert (Louis XIV's chief

minister) in 1683, Le Brun was virtually the dictator of the visual arts in France. He not only supervised all the great royal commissions, but also turned the Académie into a channel for imposing a codified system of artistic orthodoxy (see ACADEMY). His lectures, formulated on the classicism of Poussin, provided the official standards of artistic correctness and gave authority to the view that every aspect of artistic creation can be reduced to teachable rule and precept. In 1698 his illustrated treatise *Méthode pour apprendre à dessiner les passions* . . . was posthumously published; in this, again following theories of Poussin, he purported to codify the visual expression of the emotions in painting. The treatise went through numerous editions in French and other languages and remained a standard textbook for art students until well into the 19th century.

Despite the classicism of his theories, Le Brun's own talents lay rather in the direction of flamboyant and grandiose effects. Among the most outstanding of his works for the king were the decoration of the Galerie d'Apollon at the *Louvre (1663), and of the famous Galerie des Glaces (1679–84) and the Great Staircase (1671–8, destroyed in 1752) at Versailles. Because his artistic domination became so closely identified with the political despotism of Louis XIV, Le Brun's posthumous reputation suffered, but it rose again in the second half of the 20th century, a major exhibition of his work at Versailles in 1963 being a landmark in demonstrating the range and quality of his work. In addition to his achievements as a decorative painter, he was a fine portraitist and an extremely prolific draughtsman.

Leck, Bart van der (*b* Utrecht, 26 Nov. 1876; *d* Blaricum, 13 Nov. 1958). Dutch painter and designer. After working for eight years in stained-glass studios, he studied painting in Amsterdam, 1900–4. His early work was influenced by *Art Nouveau and *Impressionism, but from about 1910 he developed a more personal style characterized by simplified and stylized forms; his work remained representational, but he eliminated perspective and reduced his figures (which included labourers, soldiers, and women going to market) to sharply delineated geometrical forms in primary colours. In 1916 he met *Mondrian and in 1917 was one of the founders of De *Stijl. At this time his work was purely abstract, featuring geometrically disposed bars and rectangles in a style close to those of Mondrian and van *Doesburg. However, he found the dogmatism of the movement uncongenial and left it in 1918, reverting to geometrically simplified figural subjects. In the 1920s he became interested in textile design and during the 1930s and 1940s he extended his interests to ceramics and interior decoration, experimenting with the effects of colour on the sense of space. His work can best be seen at the Rijksmuseum Kröller-Müller, Otterlo.

Le Clerc, Jean. See SARACENI.

Le Corbusier (Charles-Édouard Jeanneret) (*b* La Chaux-de-Fonds, 6 Oct. 1887; *d* Roquebrune-Cap-Martin, 27 Aug. 1965). Swiss-born architect, painter, designer, and writer who became a French citizen in 1930. Although chiefly celebrated as one of the greatest and most influential architects of the 20th century, Le Corbusier also has a niche in the history of modern painting as one of the founders of *Purism. Up to 1929 he painted only still-life, but from that time he occasionally introduced the human figure into his compositions. He adopted the pseudonym Le Corbusier in 1920, but continued to sign his paintings 'Jeanneret'. The pseudonym derives from the name of one of his grandparents and is also a pun on his facial resemblance to a raven (French: 'corbeau'). Apart from paintings and architecture, his enormous output included drawings, book illustrations, tapestry designs, furniture, and numerous books, pamphlets, and articles.

lectionary. See SIFERWAS.

Leduc, Ozias (*b* Saint-Hilaire, Quebec, 8 Oct. 1864; *d* Saint-Hyacinthe, Quebec, 16 June 1955). Canadian painter, active mainly in his native Saint-Hilaire. His career was devoted principally to church decoration, but he also painted portraits, *genre scenes, and still-life—mostly for his own pleasure or for friends. In 1897 he visited Paris, and his later work was affected by *Symbolist ideas. He lived modestly and unambitiously away from the main centres of art, but he was an inspiration to many of those who knew him, notably Paul *Borduas.

Lee, Arthur Hamilton (Viscount Lee of Fareham). See COURTAULD.

Leech, John (*b* London, 29 Aug. 1817; *d* London, 30 Oct. 1864). English caricaturist and illustrator, one of the leading artists working for *Punch* from its foundation in 1841 until his death. He made over 3,000 pictures for *Punch* alone (including political cartoons and scenes of everyday life) and he was also particularly associated with the sporting novels of R. S. Surtees. The

other books he illustrated included R. H. Barham's *The Ingoldsby Legends* (1840) and Charles Dickens's *Christmas Books* (1843). Dickens said of his pictures that they were 'always the drawings of a gentleman', and he more than any other set the gentlemanly tone for *Punch*.

Le Fauconnier, Henri (*b* Hesdin, Pas-de-Calais, July 1881; *d* Paris, Jan. 1946). French painter, mainly of figure subjects, including nudes and allegories. From about 1910 he was influenced by *Cubism, but in about 1914 he moved to a more *Expressionist style, although he still retained structural features derived from Cubism. He spent the First World War in the Netherlands, where he laid the basis of a European reputation and exercised considerable influence on the development of northern Expressionism (his work is better represented in Dutch collections than it is in French). After his return to Paris in 1920 he gradually abandoned his Expressionist manner for a more restrained and austere style. He is not now generally highly regarded as a painter, but he played an important role in spreading the mannerisms of Cubism.

Lega, Silvestro. See MACCHIAIOLI.

Léger, Fernand (*b* Argentan, Normandy, 4 Feb. 1881; *d* Gif-sur-Yvette, Seine-et-Oise, 17 Aug. 1955). French painter and designer. After passing through various early influences he turned to *Cubism in 1909. Although he is regarded as one of the major figures of the movement, he always stood somewhat apart from its central course; he disjointed forms but did not fragment them in the manner of *Braque and *Picasso, preferring bold tubular shapes (he was for a time known as a 'tubist'). During the First World War he served as a sapper in the front line, then as a stretcher-bearer, and his experiences were 'a complete revelation to me as a man and a painter'. They enlarged his outlook by bringing him into contact with people from different social classes and walks of life and also by underlining his feeling for the beauty of machinery. Henceforward he made it his ambition to create an art that would be accessible to all ranks of modern society. After being gassed, he spent more than a year in hospital and was discharged in 1917. During the next few years, his work showed a fascination with machine-like forms, and even his human figures were depicted as almost robot-like beings (*The City*, 1919, Philadelphia Mus. of Art). In 1920 he met *Le Corbusier and *Ozenfant, who shared his interest in a machine aesthetic, and in the mid-1920s his work became flatter and more stylized, in line with their *Purist style. He used bold, poster-like contrasts of form and colour, with strong black outlines and extensive areas of flat, uniform colour. In the inter-war years he expanded his range beyond easel painting with murals (sometimes completely abstract) and designs for the theatre and cinema. He was also busy as a teacher and travelled widely, making three visits to the USA in the 1930s. The contacts that he made during these visits stood him in good stead when he lived in America during the Second World War.

Léger's work of the war years included pictures of acrobats, cyclists, and musicians, and after his return to France in 1945 he concentrated on the human figure rather than the machine. He joined the French Communist Party soon after his return and favoured proletarian subjects. Some of his pictures in this vein were very big, especially *The Great Parade* (1954, Guggenheim Mus., New York), and in his later career he also worked a good deal on large decorative commissions, notably stained-glass windows and tapestries for the church at Audincourt (1951) and a glass mosaic for the university of Caracas (1954). Many honours came to him late in life, including the Grand Prix at the 1955 São Paulo *Bienale. Shortly before his death he bought a large house at Biot, a village between Cannes and Nice, and his widow built a museum of his work there, opened in 1960.

In the catalogue of the exhibition 'Léger and Purist Paris' (1970, Tate, London), John *Golding wrote of Léger: 'No other major twentieth-century artist was to react to, and to reflect, such a wide range of artistic currents and movements. *Fauvism, Cubism, *Futurism, Purism, *Neo-Plasticism, *Surrealism, *Neo-Classicism, *Social Realism, his art experienced them all. And yet he was to remain supremely independent as an artistic personality.' However, despite Léger's centrality in modern art, Edward Lucie-Smith thinks that he 'still ranks as an under-appreciated artist, one who is on the whole more respected than loved. His work has a deliberate harshness which repels many spectators' (*Lives of the Great Twentieth Century Artists*, 1986). Certainly he never achieved the popularity with ordinary working-class people that he aimed for.

Legros, Alphonse (b Dijon, 8 May 1837; d Watford, 8 Dec. 1911). French-born painter, printmaker, and designer who settled in England in 1863 (encouraged by *Whistler) and became a British citizen in 1881, although he never acquired fluency in English. His chief importance was as an influential teacher (particularly of etching) at the *Slade School, where he was professor 1876–92 in succession to *Poynter. He encouraged a respect for the tradition of the Old Masters. See also MEDAL.

Legros, Pierre I (*bapt.* Chartres, 27 May 1629; d Paris, 10 May 1714). French sculptor. He was a pupil of Jacques *Sarrazin and worked extensively at Versailles, notably on the sculptural decoration of the gardens. His son **Pierre II** (b Paris, 12 Apr. 1666; d Rome, 3 May 1719) was a more illustrious figure. He trained with his father in Paris but spent almost all his career in Rome, where he became one of the leading sculptors of his time. Much of his work was produced for the Jesuits, including the memorial to St Stanislas Kostka (1703) in S. Andrea al Quirinale, showing the saint on his deathbed; the memorial is in the very room where the saint died in 1568 and is described by Anthony *Blunt as 'one of the most remarkable examples of *Baroque illusionism in coloured marbles'. **Jean Legros** (b Paris, 3 Oct. 1671; d Saint-Germain-en-Laye, 27 Jan. 1741), half-brother of Pierre II, was a portrait painter, a pupil of *Rigaud.

Lehmbruck, Wilhelm (b Meiderich, nr. Duisburg, 4 Jan. 1881; d Berlin, 25 Mar. 1919). German sculptor. His early work was in a fairly conservative academic manner, but when he was living in Paris from 1910 to 1914 he developed a much more personal style, influenced by the formal simplifications of *Archipenko, *Brancusi, and *Modigliani, although still essentially in the tradition of *Rodin and *Maillol. It is exemplified in the extremely attenuated forms, angular pose, and melancholic expression of his *Kneeling Woman* (1911, MoMA, New York). On the outbreak of the First World War he returned to Germany and worked in a hospital, the suffering he witnessed being reflected in the poignancy of his last works. The war brought him to a state of acute depression and he committed suicide in 1919. Lehmbruck often used marble, but he was by temperament a modeller rather than a carver, working in clay over a spindly armature, and several of his works were cast in artificial stone to preserve the texture of the clay. With *Barlach he ranks as the outstanding German *Expressionist sculptor. Lehmbruck also made etchings and lithographs, painted, and wrote poetry. There is a museum dedicated to him in Duisburg.

Leibl, Wilhelm (*b* Cologne, 23 Oct. 1844; *d* Würzburg, 4 Dec. 1900). German painter, one of the leading exponents of *Realism in his country. He studied at the Academy in Munich and in 1869 he met *Courbet, who was visiting the city for an international exhibition. Later that year he moved to Paris to work with Courbet, but the outbreak of the Franco-Prussian War in 1870 forced him to return to Germany. However, he continued to exhibit his work in Paris and during his lifetime he had a higher reputation in France than in his own country. Disgusted with the intrigues of the Munich art world, from 1873 he withdrew to the Bavarian countryside, where he found his favourite models in simple country folk, as in his best-known work *Three Women in Church* (1878–82, Kunsthalle, Hamburg). This is in the hard, objective manner of his so-called '*Holbein period'; later his technique became more fluid. Leibl also painted a number of portraits. His work is well represented in the Wallraf-Richartz-Museum in Cologne.

Leighton, Frederic (Baron Leighton of Stretton) (*b* Scarborough, 3 Dec. 1830; *d* London, 25 Jan. 1896). English painter and sculptor, one of the dominant figures of late Victorian art. The son of a doctor who gave up his practice and travelled widely on the Continent, Leighton gained his artistic education successively in Frankfurt, Rome, and Paris. It was not until 1859 that he settled in England, but he had earlier made his name with *Cimabue's Celebrated Madonna is Carried in Procession through the Streets of Florence*, which he painted in Rome; it was exhibited at the 1855 *Royal Academy exhibition and bought by Queen Victoria (it is now on loan from the Royal Collection to the National Gallery, London). In spite of this success, Leighton was for several years regarded as an alien presence in the British art world, but from the mid-1860s he enjoyed a degree of worldly success that was matched perhaps only by *Millais, his almost exact contemporary; he became president of the Royal Academy in 1878, was made a baronet in 1886, and a few days before he died was raised to the peerage, the first English artist to be so honoured. Intelligent, cultured, and of distinguished appearance (although rather austere), he was one of the chief adornments of London society. His varied output included portraits and book illustrations, but he is best known for his paintings of classical Greek subjects, the finest of which are distinguished by magnificently opulent colouring as well as splen-did draughtsmanship (*Garden of the Hesperides*, 1892, Lady Lever AG, Port Sunlight). As a sculptor he is best known for the bronze *Athlete Struggling with a Python* (1874–7), which can be seen in Leighton House (on loan from Tate Britain), the sumptuously decorated house and studio he built in Holland Park Road, Kensington, now a Leighton museum.

Leinberger, Hans (documented 1510–30). German sculptor, active mainly in Landshut, Bavaria. His life is obscure, but he was one of the greatest German sculptors of his period—majestic in style and versatile in technique (he worked mainly in wood but also in stone and bronze, and he produced reliefs as well as figures in the round). Most of his work is in churches in Bavaria, for example the *Virgin and Child* (*c*.1515–20) in St Martin's, Landshut, but there are also examples in the Bayerisches Nationalmuseum, Munich.

Lely, Sir Peter (*b* Soest, Westphalia, 14 Sept. 1618; *d* London, 30 Nov. 1680). Painter of Dutch origin who spent almost all his career in England and was naturalized in 1662. His family name was originally van der Faes, and the name Lely is said to have come from a lily carved on the house in The Hague where his father was born. Lely was born in Germany (where his father, a captain of infantry, was stationed) and trained in Haarlem. He moved to England in the early 1640s (early biographers say 1641 or 1643), and although he first painted figure compositions in landscapes (*Sleeping Nymphs*, *c*.1650, Dulwich Picture Gal.), he soon turned to the more profitable field of portraiture. Fortune shone on him, for within a few years of his arrival the best portraitists in England disappeared from the scene; van *Dyck and William *Dobson died in 1641 and 1646 respectively, and Cornelius *Johnson returned to Holland in 1643. In 1654 he was described as 'the best artist in England'.

Lely portrayed Charles I and his children, Oliver Cromwell and his son Richard, and other leading figures of the Interregnum, but he is associated chiefly with the Restoration court of Charles II. He was made principal painter to the king in 1661 and enjoyed a lavish lifestyle, described in the *Diary* of Samuel Pepys, who called him 'a mighty proud man, and full of state'. With the aid of a team of assistants he maintained an enormous output, and his fleshy, sleepy beauties clad in exquisite silks and his bewigged courtiers have created the popular image of Restoration England. Van Dyck was the strongest influence on his style, but Lely was more earthy and less refined. Much of his work is repetitive (it is sometimes hard to tell sitters apart), but he was a fluent and lively colourist and had a gift for impressive composition. He completely dominated English painting in his time, and his tradition of society portraiture, developed by *Kneller, *Jervas, and *Richardson, endured well into the 18th century until it was challenged by *Hogarth. He was a notable connoisseur and amassed one of the finest collections of Old Master drawings ever assembled; it was sold after his death.

Lemoyne. Family of French sculptors. **Jean-Louis Lemoyne** (1665–1755) was a pupil of *Coysevox and is remembered mainly for portrait busts in his master's manner. His brother **Jean-Baptiste the Elder** (1679–1731) was a figure and portrait sculptor of no great distinction. Jean-Louis's son **Jean-Baptiste the Younger** (b Paris, 19 Feb. 1704; d Paris, 25 May 1778) was the outstanding member of the family and worked a good deal for Louis XV. He did much large-scale work at Versailles and elsewhere, but is renowned particularly for the vivacity of his portraits. Among his pupils were *Falconet, *Houdon, *Pajou, and *Pigalle.

Lemoyne (or Lemoine), **François** (b Paris, 1688; d Paris, 4 June 1737). French painter. He was one of the leading decorative artists of the day, continuing the grand tradition of *Le Brun but adapting it to the lighter taste of the court of Louis XV, to whom he became official painter in 1736. Much of his work can be seen at Versailles, notably in the Salon d'Hercule. He was a man of wide pictorial culture, learning from *Rubens in his use of colour and from 17th-century Bolognese painters in his clarity and grace of drawing. The polished fluency of his style belies his disturbed personality; he committed suicide a few hours after completing *Time Revealing Truth* (1737, Wallace Coll., London). *Boucher was his most important pupil.

Lempicka, Tamara de (née Tamara Gorska) (b ?Moscow, ?c.1895; d Cuernevaca, Mexico, 18 Mar. 1980). Painter of Polish-Russian birth active mainly in Paris and the USA. According to her own account she was born in Warsaw on 16 May 1898, but there is evidence to indicate that the place of her birth (and upbringing) was Moscow and that she deducted a few years from her age. In 1916 she married Tadeusz Lempicki, a Russian lawyer and socialite, and in 1918 they fled the Russian Revolution to Paris, where she studied with Maurice *Denis and André *Lhote. She quickly established a reputation as a painter of portraits, mainly of people in the smart social circles in which she moved—writers, entertainers, the dispossessed nobility of eastern Europe. Her style owes something to the 'tubism' of *Léger, but is very distinctive in its hard, streamlined elegance and sense of chic decadence—better than anyone else she represents the *Art Deco style in painting. Apart from portraits, her main subjects were hefty erotic nudes and still-lifes of calla lilies. She received considerable critical acclaim and also became a social celebrity, famed for her aloof Garboesque beauty, her parties, and her voracious sexual appetite (with women as well as men). In 1939 she moved to the USA with her second husband, Baron Raoul Huffner, repeating her artistic and social success in Hollywood and New York. By the 1950s, however, her work was going out of fashion. She tried painting pictures in a different, much looser style, but these were coolly received. Interest in her earlier work began to revive in the 1970s and by the 1990s she had again become something of a stylish icon, with her paintings fetching huge prices in the saleroom and featuring in television advertisements as symbols of the high life.

Le Nain, Antoine (b ?Laon, c.1600; d Paris, 25 May 1648), **Louis** (b ?Laon, c.1600; d Paris, 23 May 1648), and **Mathieu** (b ?Laon, c.1607; d?: Paris, 20 Apr. 1677). French painters, brothers, who came from Laon but had all moved to Paris by 1630. The traditional birthdates for Antoine and Louis are 1588 and 1593 respectively, but it is now thought likely that they were born around 1600, so that all three brothers were of much the same generation. Mathieu was made painter to the city of Paris in 1633, and all three were foundation members of the Académie Royale (see ACADEMY) in 1648 (both Antoine and Louis died two months after its first meeting, presumably of some contagious illness). Apart from this, little is known of their careers and the attribution of works to one or the other of them is fraught with difficulty and controversy, for such paintings as are signed bear only their surname, and of those that are dated none is later than 1648, when all were still alive.

The finest and most original works associated with the brothers—powerful and dignified *genre scenes of peasants—are conventionally given to Louis; Antoine has been credited with a group of richly coloured family scenes, mainly on copper; and in a third group, traditionally attributed to Mathieu, are paintings of a more *eclectic style, chiefly portraits and group portraits in a manner suggesting influence from Holland. All these pictures are fairly small, but there are also some slightly larger paintings, mainly of religious subjects, associated with the brothers. Examples of all these types are in the Louvre, Paris. Early accounts of the brothers, as well as technical examination of the pictures, indicate that they sometimes collaborated, making the issue of assigning works to individual hands even more difficult. In 1978–9 a major exhibition in Paris brought together most of the pictures associated with the brothers, but it raised as many problems as it solved. It also, however, confirmed the stature of 'Louis', whose sympathetic and unaffected peasant scenes are the main reason why the Le Nains have attracted so much attention.

Lenbach, Franz von (*b* Schrobenhausen, Bavaria, 13 Dec. 1836; *d* Munich, 6 May 1904). German painter, active mainly in Munich but also in Italy, Vienna, and elsewhere. He painted various subjects, but is remembered chiefly as the most successful German portraitist of his day. His rich Venetian technique combined with his solid, respectful characterization appealed greatly to the prosperous ruling classes of Germany. He painted about 100 portraits of Bismarck, whom he first met in 1878 and with whom he had a reserved friendship. Lenbach was a dominant figure in Munich's artistic life in the late 19th century; his splendid house there, which he designed himself, is now a museum.

Lens, A. C. (Andries Cornelis) (*b* Antwerp, 31 Mar. 1739; *d* Brussels, 30 Mar. 1822). Flemish painter and writer on art, active mainly in Antwerp until 1781 and then for the rest of his career in Brussels. In 1764–8 he lived in Rome, where he was strongly influenced by *Winckelmann's ideas, and on his return to Flanders he became his country's leading exponent and promoter of *Neoclassicism. His work included religious, mythological, and allegorical scenes in a graceful but vapid style, as well as occasional portraits. He also wrote two treatises—on ancient costume (1776) and on beauty and taste in painting (1811).

Leo X, Pope. See MEDICI.

Leochares. Greek (probably Athenian) sculptor active in the mid-4th century BC. He is recorded in several ancient sources but is an elusive figure. In about 350 BC he is thought to have worked with *Scopas and two other sculptors on the friezes of the celebrated Mausoleum of Halicarnassus, but it is not possible confidently to assign any of the surviving portions (BM, London) to him. He is also said to have worked for Philip of Macedon and his son Alexander the Great. On rather tenuous evidence, the original of the *Apollo Belvedere* is sometimes attributed to Leochares, and the *Demeter of Cnidus* has been proposed as a work from his own hand.

Leonard, Michael. See SUPERREALISM.

Leonardo da Vinci (*b* Anchiano or Vinci, 15 Apr. 1452; *d* chateau of Cloux, nr. Amboise, 2 May 1519). Florentine artist, scientist, and thinker, the most versatile genius of the Italian *Renaissance and one of the most revered and influential of all painters. Leonardo was born in or near the small town of Vinci, a day's journey from Florence. His father was a notary, and Leonardo was his illegitimate son by a peasant girl. *Vasari's biography and other early sources testify that he was blessed with remarkable beauty and charm as well as an extraordinary mind. In 1472 he was enrolled as a painter in the fraternity of St Luke in Florence, after serving an apprenticeship with *Verrocchio. Vasari attributed to Leonardo one of the angels in Verrocchio's *Baptism of Christ* (*c*.1470, Uffizi, Florence), and the head of the angel on the left of the picture does indeed far surpass its companion in spirituality and beauty of technique, giving the first demonstration of the combined languor and intensity that is so characteristic of Leonardo's work. Verrocchio is said to have been so impressed that he gave up painting to concentrate on sculpture, and it is possible that he was content to entrust the painting side of his business to Leonardo, who was still living in his master's house in 1476.

Leonardo remained in Florence until 1481 or 1482, when he settled in Milan. Several pictures are reasonably attributed to the period before this move, among them an exquisite *Annunciation* (*c*.1473, Uffizi), generally regarded as his earliest surviving independent painting, and a portrait of Ginevra de' Benci (NG, Washington), probably painted *c*.1476 for the Venetian ambassador Bernardo Bembo. The most important work of the period is an altarpiece of the *Adoration of the Magi* (Uffizi), commissioned in 1481 by the monks of S. Donato a Scopeto near Florence and left unfinished when Leonardo moved to Milan. This painting and the numerous preparatory drawings for it show the astonishing fecundity of his mind. The range of gesture and expression was unprecedented, and such features as the contrasting figures of wise old sage and beautiful youth who stand at either side of the painting, and the rearing horses in the background, became permanent obsessions in his work.

Leonardo lived in Milan until 1499 (when the city was captured by French invaders), working mainly at the court of Duke Ludovico *Sforza (Il Moro). He is said to have been initially recommended as a musician (he was a virtuoso performer on the *lira da braccio*, an instrument somewhat like a large viola), and in a letter to the duke listing his accomplishments he gives some idea of his versatility, writing of himself first and foremost as a designer of instruments of war and adding his attainments as an artist almost as an afterthought. This many-sidedness comes out in his notebooks, which are filled with technological schemes and investigations of all kinds into the natural world; Kenneth *Clark called him 'the most relentlessly curious man in history'. The price he paid for his versatility was a tendency to leave tasks uncompleted, as his restless mind wandered to some new venture. His dilatoriness dismayed his patrons and he left a high proportion of his pictures unfinished; as Vasari wrote, he 'could have profited more if he had not been so changeable and unstable, for he was able to study many things, but as soon as he had started, he abandoned them'. Although he surpassed all of his contemporaries in the sheer beauty of his technique as a painter, this 'mechanical' aspect of his work was less appealing to him than solving problems of composition and characterization in his drawings, of which there is a wonderful collection at Windsor Castle (he was the greatest and most prolific draughtsman of his time, using chalk, ink, and metalpoint with equal skill). This stress on the intellectual aspects of painting was one of the most momentous features of Leonardo's career, for he was largely responsible for establishing the idea of the artist as a creative thinker, not simply a skilled craftsman (see LIBERAL ARTS).

Leonardo's two main artistic undertakings in Milan were a project for a huge equestrian statue (about three times life-size) to Ludovico Sforza's father, which got as far as a full-size model of the horse but is now known only in preliminary drawings, and the wall painting of the *Last Supper* (c.1495–7) in the refectory of the monastery of S. Maria delle Grazie. The *fresco method of mural painting was not flexible or subtle enough for the slow-working Leonardo, so he adopted an experimental technique that quickly caused

the picture to deteriorate disastrously. In spite of its sad condition, however, it has for five centuries been perhaps the most revered painting in the world. There have been many attempts to restore it, the most recent (which has proved highly controversial) being unveiled in 1999. Leonardo's other works in Milan included portraits, notably the superb picture of Duke Ludovico's mistress Cecilia Gallerani known as the *Lady with an Ermine* (c.1490, Czartoryski Gal., Cracow) and an altarpiece of the *Virgin of the Rocks*, which exists in two problematically related versions, the earlier (Louvre, Paris) possibly painted when Leonardo was still in Florence, the later (NG, London) still being worked on in 1508. There may have been some studio assistance in the London version (see PREDIS), but the finest passages, notably the heads of the Virgin and the angel, with their exquisitely curled hair and heavy-lidded eyes, can be by no one but Leonardo himself. The larger, bolder forms of the London picture show Leonardo's move towards the more monumental style of the High Renaissance, of which he was the main creator; incidental detail is reduced to create a greater unity of form and atmosphere.

Between 1499, when he abandoned Milan, and 1516/17, when he left Italy for France, Leonardo moved about a good deal. In 1500 he visited Venice and briefly Mantua (where he drew a profile portrait of Isabella d'*Este, now in the Louvre; see PASTEL), in 1502–3 he worked as a military engineer for Cesare Borgia, in 1508–13 he was based again in Milan, and in 1513 he moved to Rome, but the artistic activity of his later years was chiefly centred in Florence in the years 1500–8. From this time dates his most celebrated work, the *Mona Lisa* (begun c.1503, Louvre), in which he showed a subtlety and naturalness of pose and expression that make most earlier portraits look rigid, and the wall painting of the *Battle of Anghiari* (1503–6) in the Palazzo Vecchio, Florence, where he worked in rivalry with *Michelangelo. The battle piece was abandoned unfinished and the remains were painted over by Vasari in 1557, but something of its appearance is known from copies; fittingly, the most famous is a drawing by *Rubens (Louvre) (a copy of a copy), for Leonardo's painting anticipated the dynamism of the *Baroque and influenced battle painters up to the 19th century. During this intermittent period in Florence Leonardo also worked out variations on a theme that fascinated him and presented a great challenge to his skill in composing closely knit groups of figures—the Virgin and Child with St Anne. In addition to various sketches, there survive a painting of the subject in the Louvre and the incomparably beautiful *cartoon (which includes also the infant John the Baptist) in the National Gallery, London; the exact dates of these two famous works are controversial.

During his subsequent period based in Milan (1508–13) Leonardo's main artistic project was for another equestrian statue, ironically to Gian Giacomo Trivulzio, the Italian general who had led the French army that drove Ludovico Sforza from the city. This got no further than drawings, and Leonardo received no important commissions after moving to Rome, where Pope Leo X (Giovanni de *Medici) was wary of him because of his reputation for failing to complete work. In 1516 or 1517 he accepted an invitation from Francis I (a great lover of Italian culture) to move to France, and he died at Cloux in 1519. Officially he was 'first painter, architect, and mechanic to the king', but Francis treated him as an honoured guest rather than an employee, allowing him to spend his time as he pleased. Although he made designs for court festivities, there is no certain evidence that he continued painting in France. The last paintings from his hand are probably two pictures of St John the Baptist (one later converted into a *Bacchus*), both in the Louvre (c.1510–15). They show the enigmatic smile, the dense shadow, the pointing finger, and the thick curling hair that rapidly became clichés in the work of his followers.

As a painter Leonardo triumphantly reconciled grandeur of form with exquisite precision of detail, and he introduced an unprecedented subtlety in handling gesture and expression. His work marked the greatest advance in naturalism since *Masaccio, and he had enormous influence (as is indicated by the large number of contemporary copies and adaptations of his pictures). His heroic figures and beautifully balanced compositions (particularly his use of pyramidal grouping) were the basis of the High Renaissance style, influencing particularly his two greatest contemporaries, Michelangelo and *Raphael, and his delicate modelling through light and shade (see SFUMATO) showed the potentialities of the *oil medium, which he was one of the first Italians to exploit. *Correggio and *Giorgione were among those most deeply affected by this aspect of his work, and they also responded to his sense of fantasy and mystery.

Leonardo's writings on painting were influential too; they were first published from his scattered notes as the *Treatise on Painting* (in Italian and French) in 1651, but they were well known

before then. In sculpture and architecture no work that is indisputably by him survives, but his expertise and ideas were important in both fields. His friend *Bramante, the greatest architect of the High Renaissance, was influenced by his designs for 'ideal' churches, for example, and when the sculptor Giovanni Francesco Rustici (1474–1554) was making his bronze group of *St John the Baptist between a Pharisee and a Levite* (1506–11) for the Baptistery in Florence, he would, as Vasari tells us, 'allow no one near save Leonardo, who never left him while he was moulding and casting until the work was finished'. He is one of the very few artists whose reputation has from his own time onward always remained at the highest level, even though his output of completed works was small—a reflection of his remarkable personal magnetism, his extraordinary force of intellect, and his virtually single-handed creation of the idea of the artist as genius.

Leoni, Leone (*b* ?Menaggio, nr. Lake Como, *c*.1509; *d* Milan, 22 July 1590). Italian *Mannerist sculptor who worked in many parts of Italy and in the service of the Emperor Charles V (see HABSBURG) in Germany and the Netherlands. He was trained in goldsmithery, but none of his works in that medium survives. From 1538 to 1540 he worked as a coin engraver in the papal mint in Rome, but he was then condemned to the galleys for attacking and maiming the papal jeweller. He was released in 1541 and for most of the rest of his life was master of the imperial mint in Milan. In 1549 and 1556 he visited the imperial court in Brussels and in 1551 the imperial court in Augsburg. He also worked for Charles's son Philip II of Spain. His own son **Pompeo Leoni** (*b* ?Venice, *c*.1533; *d* Madrid, 13 Oct. 1608) settled in Spain in 1556 and gave the finishing touches to works his father sent there. The most important commission was a group of fifteen bronze statues (installed 1591) for the high altar of the *Escorial, to which Pompeo later added several others. Pompeo also executed several tombs in Spain on his own account, and was, like his father, a goldsmith and medallist. Again like his father, he had a dangerous brush with authority, being briefly imprisoned by the Inquisition for unorthodox views.

Leopold II, Emperor. See HABSBURG.

Leopold William, Archduke. See HABSBURG.

Le Parc, Julio (*b* Mendoza, 23 Sept. 1928). Argentinian painter, sculptor, and experimental artist, regarded as one of the leading exponents

Lépicié, Nicolas-Bernard

of *Kinetic art. In 1958 he settled in Paris and in 1959 became a founder member of the *Groupe de Recherche d'Art Visuel. Le Parc professes to adopt a rational attitude to his work, working according to scientific principles. He often uses the idea of spectator participation, but tries to eliminate subjective response on the part of the spectator, looking for an objective and predictable perceptual response to a planned stimulus. Much of his work consists of devices for disorientating the spectator (distorting glasses and so on), but he has also made some outstanding *mobiles, using perspex or metallic elements to scatter or reflect light.

Lépicié, Nicolas-Bernard (*b* Paris, 16 June 1735; *d* Paris, 14 Sept. 1784). French painter. His output included portraits and historical subjects, but he is best known for his domestic *genre scenes, which have something of the tranquil beauty of *Chardin and something of the sentimentality of *Greuze (*The Reading Lesson*, *c.*1774, Wallace Coll., London). His father **François-Bernard** (*b* Paris, 6 Oct. 1698; *d* Paris, 17 Jan. 1755) was an engraver and writer on art. In 1737 he was appointed secretary and official historian of the Académie Royale (see ACADEMY) and he played an important role in its administration.

Le Prince, Jean-Baptiste. See AQUATINT.

Leroy, Louis. See IMPRESSIONISM.

Leslie, C. R. (Charles Robert) (*b* London, 19 Oct. 1794; *d* London, 5 May 1859). British painter and writer on art of American parentage. In his day he was well known for his paintings of literary themes, but he is now remembered mainly as a writer, above all for his *Memoirs of the Life of John Constable* (1843), which is regarded as one of the classics of artistic biography (*Constable was a close friend). Leslie's other books include *A Handbook for Young Painters* (1855), based on lectures he gave as professor of painting at the *Royal Academy, 1847–52, and the posthumously published *Autobiographical Recollections* (1860). His sons **Robert Charles Leslie** (1826–1901) and **George Dunlop Leslie** (1835–1921) were painters.

Lessing, Gotthold Ephraim (*b* Kamenz, 22 Jan. 1729; *d* Brunswick, 15 Feb. 1781). German writer. He was a man of formidable intellect and great versatility who played a leading role in the development of German theatre, but he is known mainly for his treatise on aesthetics, *Laokoon* (1766). This takes as its starting point a passage in *Winckelmann's writings in which

he discussed the celebrated antique statue *Laocoön. Winckelmann contrasted what he considered the stoical beauty of Laocoön in the sculpture with the loud cries that Virgil causes him to utter in the *Aeneid*, interpreting the alleged difference (to most people he appears to be howling with pain in the sculpture too) as a superior serenity in Greek art. Lessing dissented, and argued that each art achieves its effects by the means appropriate to its medium and that the artist must exploit the potentialities of his medium to the full, whilst respecting its limitations. Poetry, he held, is most adapted to the representation of action in time but lacks visual vividness. Painting and sculpture are best adapted to the representation of idealized human beauty in repose. Owing to the non-temporal character of the medium they cannot well represent the body in action. Only by selecting the 'critical' or 'fruitful' moment, which simultaneously preserves physical beauty and concentrates within itself the suggestion of past and future action, can the plastic artist even indirectly represent a sequence of events in action. He thought that the *Laocoön* group was a masterly example of this, a work whose beauty and significance made it at once a delight to the eye and a stimulus to the imagination. The impact of Lessing's book stemmed from its emphasis on the aesthetic functions of art in contrast with the traditional view of art as the handmaid of religion and philosophy, with a duty primarily to instruct. See also THEOPHILUS.

Lessing, Karl Friedrich (*b* Breslau [now Wrocław, Poland], 15 Feb. 1808; *d* Karlsruhe, 5 June 1880). German painter, the great-nephew of Gotthold Ephraim *Lessing. In 1826 he settled in Düsseldorf and he became one of the leading figures in the tradition of history painting associated with the city. He combined earnestly melodramatic poses with studiously correct historical detail, so that many of his pictures look like scenes from plays or pageants. His best-known works have subjects taken from the Hussite Rebellion of the 15th century (*Hussite Sermon*, 1836, Kunstmuseum, Düsseldorf) and were identified with the spirit of rebellion against the political and religious repression of the day. Lessing also painted landscapes. In 1858 he became director of the gallery at Karlsruhe, and settled there permanently.

Lessore, Thérèse. See SICKERT.

Le Sueur, Eustache (*b* Paris, 19 Nov. 1616; *d* Paris, 30 Apr. 1655). French painter. He was a pupil of *Vouet, whose influence is strong on his early works (*Presentation of the Virgin*, c.1640, Hermitage, St Petersburg). In the 1640s he was profoundly affected by the paintings of *Poussin (who visited Paris 1640–2) and his work became more classical. He lacked Poussin's heroic grandeur, and he added a tenderness of his own to the master's manner, as in his most important works, a series of paintings (begun 1645) illustrating the life of St Bruno, done for the Charterhouse of Paris and now in the Louvre. In the last years of his life his chief model became *Raphael, particularly through engravings of his tapestry designs. Le Sueur was a founder member of the Académie Royale (see ACADEMY) in 1648. In his own day he was almost as well thought of as Poussin, and in the 18th century he was known as 'the French Raphael', but his reputation declined in the 19th century and he now has the status of an attractive minor master.

Le Sueur, Hubert (b Paris, c.1580; d Paris, after 1658). French sculptor, active for much of his career in England, where he is first recorded in 1626. He was employed a good deal by Charles I, and his most famous work is the equestrian statue of the king (1633) at Charing Cross in London (commissioned by Baron Weston, the lord high chancellor). This shows the skill as a bronze caster for which he was renowned, but also his smooth, lifeless surfaces, which give his works, in the words of Margaret Whinney (*Sculpture in Britain: 1530–1830*, 1964), 'a curious, inflated appearance, as if they were not modelled, but blown up from within'. He was remarkably conceited, on occasions signing himself '*Praxiteles Le Sueur', but Charles recognized him as a second-rate artist and sometimes reduced the prices he asked for his work. By 1643 Le Sueur was back in Paris. His main influence in England was in popularizing the portrait bust.

Leu, Hans the Younger (b Zurich, c.1490; d Gubel, nr. Zurich, 24 Oct. 1531). Swiss painter, draughtsman, and occasional printmaker, the son of a painter of the same name. He probably worked with *Dürer in Nuremberg and possibly with *Baldung Grien in Freiburg, before returning to settle in Zurich, where he became the leading painter of the day. His work is remarkable mainly for the prominence given to landscape, relating him to the masters of the *Danube School (*Orpheus*, 1519, Kunstmuseum, Basle). Few of his paintings survive, but there are numerous landscape drawings by him. His career was ruined by the religious conflict of the Reformation and he became a soldier, dying at the Battle of Gubel.

Leutze, Emanuel Gottlieb (b Schwäbisch Gmünd, 24 May 1816; d Washington, DC, 18 July 1868). German painter who lived in America from 1825 to 1841 and again from 1859 until his death and is usually considered a member of the American School. He is remembered mainly for his *Washington Crossing the Delaware* (1851, Met. Mus., New York), painted in Düsseldorf, where he spent most of his career, and for another work that similarly appeals more for its patriotic sentiments than for its aesthetic merits—his large mural *Westward the Course of Empire Takes its Way* (1861–2) in the Capitol at Washington. His portraits and rare landscapes are more distinguished, but remain little known.

Levasseur. Family of Canadian woodcarvers of French origin active in Quebec in the 17th and 18th centuries. Their work included a good deal of interior decoration of churches and other buildings. The most distinguished member of the family was **Noël** (1680–1740), who worked in stone as well as wood and made statues as well as decorative features.

Levitan, Isaak. See WANDERERS.

Lewis, John Frederick (b London, 14 July 1805; d Walton-on-Thames, Surrey, 15 Aug. 1876). English painter, mainly in watercolour, son of the engraver and landscape painter **Frederick Christian Lewis** (1779–1856). He travelled extensively and spent the years 1841–51 in Cairo. His colourful and highly detailed scenes of life in the harem and bazaar were a huge success in London, and after his return there in 1851 he concentrated on them exclusively, playing a major part in creating the vogue for *Orientalism. Several other members of the family were painters, including his brother **Frederick Christian Lewis Jun.** (1813–75). He worked in India for many years and is sometimes known as Indian Lewis to distinguish him from his brother.

Lewis, Wyndham (b on his parents' yacht, off Amherst, Nova Scotia, 18 Nov. 1882; d London, 7 Mar. 1957). British painter, novelist, and critic, the son of a British mother and a wealthy American father. He came to England as a child, studied at the *Slade School, 1898–1901, then lived on the Continent for seven years, mostly in Paris. In 1909 he returned to England and in the years leading up to the First World War emerged as one of the leading figures in British avant-garde art. From 1911 he developed an angular, machine-like, semi-abstract style that had affinities with both *Cubism and *Futurism. He worked for a short time with Roger *Fry at the *Omega Workshops, but after quarrelling with him in 1914 he formed his own organization, the Rebel Art Centre, intended as a place in which artists and craftsmen could meet, work, and hold discussions. This lasted only a few months, but out of it grew *Vorticism, a movement of which Lewis was the central figure and whose journal *Blast* he edited. He served with the Royal Artillery, 1915–17, and as an *Official War Artist, 1917–18, carrying his Vorticist style into works such as *A Battery Shelled* (1918, Imperial War Mus., London). In 1919 he founded Group X as an attempt to revive Vorticism, but this failed, and from the late 1920s he devoted himself mainly to writing, in which he often made savage attacks on his contemporaries (particularly the *Bloomsbury Group). His association with the British Fascist Party and his praise of Hitler alienated him from the literary world. The best-known paintings of his later years are his incisive portraits, more naturalistic than his earlier works but still with a bold, hard simplification of form; the rejection of that of T. S. Eliot (Durban AG) caused Augustus *John to resign in disgust from the *Royal Academy in 1938.

Lewis was the most original and idiosyncratic of the major British artists working in the first decades of the 20th century, and he was among the first artists in Europe to produce completely abstract paintings and drawings. He built his personal style on features taken from Cubism and Futurism but did not accept either. He accused Cubism of failure to 'synthesize the quality of LIFE with the significance or spiritual weight that is the mark of all the greatest art' and of being mere visual acrobatics. The Futurists, he wrote, had the vivacity that the Cubists lacked, but they themselves lacked the grandness and the 'great plastic qualities' that Cubism achieved. His own work, he declared, was 'electric with a mastered and vivid vitality'. He wrote several books, including novels, notably *Tarr* (1918), and collections of essays and criticism. *Blasting and Bombardiering* (1937), *Wyndham Lewis the Artist* (1939), and *Rude Assignment* (1950) are autobiographical.

LeWitt, Sol (*b* Hartford, Conn., 9 Sept. 1928). American sculptor, printmaker, writer, and *Conceptual artist. His career did not take off until the early 1960s, when he turned to sculpture and became one of the leading exponents of *Minimal art. His 'structures', as he prefers to call them, characteristically involve permutations of simple basic elements, sometimes arranged in box- or table-like constructions. He is also an exponent of Conceptual art; in 1968, for example, he fabricated a metal cube and buried it in the ground at Visser House at Bergeyk in the Netherlands, documenting photographically the object's disappearance (this has also been considered an example of *Land art). LeWitt has also written numerous articles on Conceptual art. His other work includes prints in various techniques.

Leyden, Lucas van. See LUCAS VAN LEYDEN.

Leys, Henri (*b* Antwerp, 18 Feb. 1815; *d* Antwerp, 26 Aug. 1869). Belgian painter. He specialized in painting events from his country's history in a sober detailed style and in historical *genre scenes that recall those of his 17th-century Flemish forebears and also reflect his admiration for 16th-century German painting. His work was immensely popular in his day and he won a succession of honours; most notably he was created a baron in 1862. There are two characteristic examples of his work in the Wallace Collection, London: *Soldiers Playing Cards* (1849) and *Frans *Floris Going to a St Luke's Day Feast, 1540* (1853). *Alma-Tadema was for a time his assistant.

Leyster, Judith (*bapt.* Haarlem, 28 July 1609; *bur.* Heemstede, 10 Feb. 1660). Dutch painter of *genre scenes, portraits, and still-life. She was probably a pupil of Frans *Hals in Haarlem, where she spent her early career. After her marriage to Jan Miense *Molenaer in 1636 she moved to Amsterdam, where she shared a studio with her husband, using the same models and props. In 1648 they bought a house in Heemstede and thereafter lived mainly there and in Haarlem. Leyster was one of Hals's best followers and her work has sometimes passed as his, an example being the *Lute Player* in the Rijksmuseum, Amsterdam. Her monogram includes a star, a play on 'Ley/ster' (lode star).

Lhermitte, Léon (*b* Mont-Saint-Père, Aisne, 31 July 1844; *d* Paris, 27 July 1925). French painter, printmaker, and draughtsman. He is best known for his pictures of peasant subjects—van *Gogh, a great admirer of his work, called him a second *Millet—but he also enjoyed success with large decorative paintings, for example *Les Halles* (1894), commissioned for the Hôtel de Ville, Paris, and now in the Petit Palais.

Lhote, André (*b* Bordeaux, 5 July 1885; *d* Paris, 24 Jan. 1962). French painter, sculptor, teacher, and writer on art. He worked initially as a commercial woodcarver and was largely self-taught as a painter. His early work was *Fauvist in spirit, but from 1911 he adopted *Cubist mannerisms in his varied range of subjects, including landscapes, still-lifes, interiors, mythological scenes, and portraits. Lhote, however, was more important as a teacher and critic than as a practising artist. In 1922 he opened his own school in Paris, the Académie Montparnasse, and through this had an extensive influence on younger artists, French and foreign; he founded a South American branch on a visit to Rio de Janeiro in 1952. His writings included treatises on landscape painting (1939) and figure painting (1950).

liberal arts. In the context of *Renaissance art, a term applied to pursuits that were considered primarily as exercises of the mind rather than of practical skill and craftsmanship. The concept of a distinction between 'liberal' (worthy of a free man: Latin *homo liber*) and 'vulgar' arts goes back to classical antiquity, and survived in one form or another up to the Renaissance, forming the basis of secular learning in the Middle Ages. The name *quadrivium* was given to the subjects concerned with physical reality (arithmetic, astronomy, geometry, and music—that is the mathematical theory of music) and *trivium* to the arts of grammar, rhetoric, and logic. Collectively these were known as the seven liberal arts, and were subservient to philosophy, the supreme art. In these, as in all classifications that preceded the concept of the *fine arts, the word 'art' carries a very different signification from that which it bears in normal language today—closer to the meaning that survives in academic terminology such as 'arts degree'.

In the early Renaissance the lowly position accorded to the visual arts was increasingly contested, providing a theoretical basis for the social struggle that took place to raise them from the status of manual skill to the dignity of a liberal exercise of the spirit. The most formidable champion of the visual arts was *Leonardo, who more than anyone else was responsible for creating the idea of the painter as a creative thinker. His revolutionary approach is illustrated in the following anecdote told by *Vasari. When Leonardo was painting his *Last Supper* the prior of the monastery was puzzled by the way in which 'he sometimes spent half a day at a time

contemplating what he had done so far; if he had had his way, Leonardo would have toiled like one of the labourers hoeing in the garden and never put down his brush for a moment'. When the prior complained to the Duke of Milan, Leonardo explained 'that men of genius sometimes accomplish most when they work the least, for they are thinking out inventions and forming in their minds the perfect ideas that they subsequently express and reproduce with their hands'. By about 1500 painting and sculpture were generally accepted as liberal arts by Italian humanists (significantly so in Baldassare Castiglione's influential *Book of the Courtier* of 1528, which was translated into English in 1561). However, as Anthony *Blunt points out (*Artistic Theory in Italy: 1450–1600*, 1940), 'As soon as the visual arts became generally accepted as liberal, the protagonists began to quarrel among themselves about which of them was the noblest and most liberal' (see PARAGONE). The acceptance came later in other parts of Europe than in Italy. *Hilliard was one of the first English artists to make a claim for the nobility of his profession. In his treatise *The Arte of Limning* (written *c*.1600) he suggests that miniature painting is especially suited to gentlemen as it is such a private art; the miniaturist can work in secret and his portraits are intended for intimate enjoyment.

The original seven liberal arts (sometimes paired with the seven principal virtues—faith, hope, charity, etc.) are often represented in painting and sculpture, personified as women holding various *attributes and being followed by famous masters of the arts concerned (e.g. Cicero with Rhetoric). The system was formulated by the 5th-century scholar Martianus Capella in his elaborate allegorical treatise *The Marriage of Philologia and Mercury*, which was much studied in the Middle Ages (more than 200 manuscripts of it survive). For the *Baroque age the types of the liberal arts were codified by Cesare Ripa (see EMBLEM) in his handbook of *iconography.

Liber studiorum. See TURNER, J. M. W.

Liber veritatis. See CLAUDE.

Libre Esthétique, La. See VINGT.

Lichtenstein, Roy (*b* New York, 27 Oct. 1923; *d* New York, 29 Sept. 1997). American painter, sculptor, and printmaker. In the late 1950s his style was *Abstract Expressionist, but in the early 1960s he changed to *Pop art and his first one-man exhibition in this style, at the Leo *Castelli gallery, New York, in 1962, was a sensational success. In common with other Pop artists, Lichtenstein adopted the images of commercial art, but he did so in a highly distinctive manner. He took his inspiration from comic strips but blew up the images to a large scale, reproducing the primary colours and dots of the cheap printing processes (*Whaam!*, 1963, Tate, London). The initial stimulus is said to have come from one of his young children, who pointed to a comic book and challenged, 'I bet you can't paint as good as that.' Despite their use of such kitsch material, his paintings show an impressive feeling for composition and colour and Lichtenstein enjoyed continued critical success as well as popular appeal. In the mid-1960s he began making Pop versions of paintings by modern masters such as *Cézanne and *Mondrian, and also started making screenprints. In the 1970s he expanded his range to include sculpture, mostly in polished brass and imitating the *Art Deco forms of the 1930s. His later work included several large commissions for public places.

Liebermann, Max (*b* Berlin, 20 July 1847; *d* Berlin, 8 Feb. 1935). German painter (of portraits, figure subjects, and landscapes), etcher, and lithographer, active principally in Berlin. From 1873 to 1878 he lived mainly in Paris, and together with *Corinth and *Slevogt he came to be considered one of the leading German representatives of *Impressionism. In 1899 he became first president of the Berlin *Sezession, but he did not keep abreast of developments and a decade later he was regarded as a pillar of the traditionalism against which the German *Expressionists were in revolt. He was one of the dominant figures in the German art world and in the later part of his career he accumulated many honours. When the Nazis came to power, however, he was forced—as a Jew—to resign as president of the Prussian Academy and from his other prestigious positions. His widow committed suicide in 1943 rather than suffer at the hands of the Gestapo.

Liédet, Loyset (*b* ?Hesdin, *c*.1420; *d* Bruges, 1479). Netherlandish manuscript illuminator, active first in Hesdin and then in Bruges, where he became a guild member in 1469. His patrons included Philip the Good and Charles the Bold, dukes of *Burgundy, and he was perhaps the most prolific illuminator of his time. He sometimes worked in *grisaille but more usually in colour; his figures are long-limbed and gawky.

Lievens, Jan (*b* Leiden, 24 Oct. 1607; *d* Amsterdam, 4 June 1674). Dutch painter and print-

maker. He was extremely precocious, and after training in Amsterdam with *Lastman he is said to have begun practising independently in his native Leiden when he was barely into his teens. From *c*.1625 to 1631/2 he worked in close collaboration and friendly rivalry with *Rembrandt. They shared the same models (and probably a studio) and contemporaries sometimes had difficulty distinguishing between their hands (a few works are still disputed between them). Constantijn *Huygens visited them in 1629 and thought they showed equal promise of greatness. He wrote that Rembrandt surpassed Lievens in vivacity of expression, but that Lievens was superior in 'a certain grandeur of invention and boldness of subjects and forms'. That this was not excessive praise is borne out by Lievens's marvellously melodramatic *Raising of Lazarus* (1631, Brighton Mus. and AG), in which the only parts of Lazarus shown are his arms emerging from the tomb. After the paths of the two young artists separated in 1631/2, however, Lievens did not sustain his early brilliance, although in his later years he was more successful than Rembrandt in worldly terms. In 1632–5 he visited England, then from 1635 to 1644 he lived in Antwerp, where he adopted a more elegant and facile style, influenced by van *Dyck, that brought him a good deal of work as a fashionable portraitist. In 1644 he returned to the Netherlands and was based in Amsterdam for the rest of his life, although he made visits to other Dutch cities and to Germany. It is not known whether he had any contact with his old friend Rembrandt when both were living in Amsterdam. In addition to his work as a painter, Lievens was a talented etcher and also made some woodcuts.

lift-ground etching. See AQUATINT.

Light art. A general term for works that use artificial light (usually electric) as an artistic medium of its own or as an important constituent of a piece. The idea can be traced back to the 18th century, when the French scientist Louis-Bertrand Castel became interested in the relationship between sound and colour (both of which, he argued, were products of vibration) and constructed various 'ocular harpsichords', some of which incorporated coloured glass. However, his experiments do not seem to have been followed up until the 20th century. Various artists in the first half of the century made works incorporating artificial light, for example *Moholy-Nagy, but it was not until the 1960s that it is possible to think of Light art constituting a movement. During this decade there were several large exhibitions devoted to Light art in Europe and the USA, and it often overlapped with other genres, particularly *Kinetic art, but also for example *Minimal art, notably in the work of Dan *Flavin, who typically used arrangements of fluorescent tubes. In the 1960s, also, lasers and holography (which was made possible by lasers) became available to the artist. Lasers have been used most characteristically to create spectacular nocturnal displays. Many artists, including Salvador *Dalí, have experimented with holograms, and they have been sold by leading dealers such as Leo *Castelli, but in the art world holography is generally regarded as a curiosity rather than a serious means of expression.

The term *Luminism is sometimes used as an alternative to 'Light art'. However, this usage is potentially confusing, as the word already has other meanings in art-historical writing.

Lightfoot, Maxwell Gordon. See CAMDEN TOWN GROUP.

Ligorio, Pirro (*b* Naples, *c*.1513; *d* Ferrara, 26 Oct. 1583). Italian architect, antiquarian, draughtsman, designer, and painter, active mainly in Rome, where he settled in about 1534. He began his career as a fresco painter, but very little remains of his activity in this field, and he is more important for his excavations and antiquarian research, which bore fruit in his *Antichità di Roma* (1553). In addition to this book he left a large body of manuscript writings on antiquities, now divided among several libraries in Italy and elsewhere. His best work as an architect is the richly ornamented Casino (summer house) built for Pius IV in the Vatican gardens (begun 1559), which has been described by Jacob *Burckhardt as 'the most beautiful afternoon retreat that modern architecture has created'. Ligorio also designed the Villa d'Este at Tivoli (begun *c*.1560) for Cardinal Ippolito II d'*Este and was the mastermind behind the villa's spectacular gardens, which are among the most famous in Europe. In 1564 he was appointed *Michelangelo's successor as architect to St Peter's, but in the following year he was imprisoned on suspicion of defrauding the papacy both in his architectural work and in regard to the purchase of antiquities. He was soon released, but in 1569 he left Rome and settled in Ferrara, where he again worked for the Este family, notably as court antiquarian to Duke Alfonso II and as a designer of festivities.

Limbourg. Netherlandish manuscript illuminators, the brothers **Herman**, **Jean** (Jannequin), and **Pol** (Paul) **de Limbourg**, all three of whom died in 1416, presumably victims of the plague or other epidemic. Pol was probably the head of the workshop, but it is not possible to distinguish his hand from those of his brothers. The Limbourgs came from Nijmegen and were nephews of Jean *Malouel. In 1402 Jean and Pol were working for Philip the Bold, Duke of *Burgundy, and after Philip's death in 1404 all three Limbourgs worked for his brother Jean, Duc de Berry (1340–1416), remaining in his service until their deaths and holding privileged positions at his court, which moved with him around France from one magnificent residence to the next. He was one of the most extravagant patrons and collectors in the history of art, and the Limbourgs illuminated two manuscripts for his celebrated library: the *Belles Heures* (*c*.1408, Met. Mus., New York) and the *Très Riches Heures* (Mus. Condé, Chantilly), which was begun *c*.1413 and left unfinished at their deaths (it was completed by the French illuminator Jean *Colombe about 70 years later). The *Très Riches Heures* (see BOOK OF HOURS) is by common consent one of the supreme masterpieces of manuscript illumination and the archetype of the *International Gothic style. Its most original and beautiful feature is the series of twelve full-page illustrations of the Months (the first time a calendar was so lavishly treated), full of exquisite ornamentation and beautifully observed naturalistic detail. The *miniatures are remarkable, too, for their mastery in rendering space, strongly suggesting that one or more of the brothers had visited Italy, and they occupy an important place in the development of the northern traditions of landscape and *genre painting.

limestone. A general term for sedimentary rocks composed mainly of calcium carbonate. Limestones vary considerably in colour and hardness. Certain types that will take a polish are often referred to as marbles; *Purbeck marble, the best-known example, was a favourite material for tomb sculpture in England in the Middle Ages, but generally limestone has been used much more for building than for carving.

limewood. Wood of the lime tree, which together with oak and walnut has been the material most commonly used in Europe for large wooden sculpture. The tree is often called by its alternative name of linden, which helpfully distinguishes it from the tropical citrus tree also called lime. There are several species of linden, but they have similar qualities. The wood is pale in colour and very uniform in character. It is lighter and easier to carve than walnut or especially oak, but it is less durable and more vulnerable to damp. Although it has been used in various times and places, it is particularly associated with the great tradition of woodcarving in southern Germany in the late 15th and early 16th centuries; it was the standard material for the spectacular altarpieces that were one of the most characteristic art forms of the region in this period. Often the wood was *polychromed and gilded. The ease with which it could be carved encouraged virtuoso naturalistic effects that were impossible in other woods—hence *Vasari's amazement (the material being relatively unfamiliar in Italy) at Veit *Stoss's statue of St Roch (c.1510–20, SS. Annunziata, Florence). Another celebrated virtuoso in the medium was Grinling *Gibbons, one of whose most famous creations is a lace cravat carved in limewood (V&A, London); it was once owned by Horace *Walpole, who wore it at a reception.

limner. A word for a painter that has been used in various ways in different contexts. In the Middle Ages it was applied to manuscript *illuminators, and from the 16th century it was used of painters of *miniature portraits (Nicholas *Hilliard's treatise is called *The Arte of Limning*). In terms of American art, it denotes the anonymous and often itinerant painters, particularly portraitists, of the 17th and 18th centuries. Limners in this last sense are sometimes given invented names in the same manner in which the term 'Master of' is used in European painting—the Schuyler Limner, named after one of the families he portrayed, is an example.

linden. See LIMEWOOD.

Lindisfarne Gospels (British Library). Illuminated manuscript of the four Gospels in Latin, named after the island of Lindisfarne (also known as Holy Island), off the coast of Northumberland, where it was produced in the monastery, c.700. Regarded as 'one of the first and greatest masterpieces of medieval European book painting' (Janet Backhouse, *The Illuminated Manuscript*, 1979), it includes full-page portraits of the four Evangelists but is celebrated mainly for its vigorous ornament, some purely abstract and some including animal and bird life; there are pages devoted solely to ornament ('carpet pages') as well as elaborately decorated enlarged initial letters. For a work of its period it is excep-

tionally well documented, thanks to a colophon (end note) added in the 10th century explaining its origins. According to this note the book was written by Eadfrith (Bishop of Lindisfarne 698–721) in honour of God and St Cuthbert (also named are the binder and the decorator of the binding). Cuthbert (d 687), northern England's most popular saint, was Bishop of Lindisfarne and was buried on the island. In 698 his body was moved to a new shrine and the manuscript may well have been made to mark this event (the body was found to be incorrupted and from this time became the object of special veneration). In 875 Lindisfarne was sacked by the Danes; the monks fled with the saint's shrine, which had no permanent resting place for more than a century until a safe home was found for it in Durham in 995 (Cuthbert's remains are now in the cathedral). The Lindisfarne Gospels shared the wanderings of the shrine, and the colophon was written by a priest called Aldred, who became provost of Chester-le-Street in County Durham. He also added an interlinear Anglo-Saxon translation of the text, the first surviving version of the Gospels in any form of the English language. In 1539, following the Dissolution of the Monasteries, the book was separated from the shrine and in the early 17th century it was acquired by the antiquarian Sir Robert Cotton (1571–1631), who had a collection of manuscripts of European fame. The collection was bequeathed to the nation by his grandson in 1700 and became part of the British Museum on its foundation in 1753. See also CELTIC ART and INSULAR ART.

Lindner, Richard (*b* Hamburg, 11 Nov. 1901; *d* New York, 16 Apr. 1978). German-born painter who became an American citizen in 1948. He fled from the Nazi regime in 1933 and settled in Paris, then moved to the USA in 1941. At first he worked as a magazine and book illustrator (in Germany he had been art director of a publishing firm), and he did not begin to paint seriously until the early 1950s. His most characteristic works take their imagery from New York life, often with overtly erotic symbolism, and are painted with hard outlines and harsh colours. The effects he created owed something to *Expressionist exaggeration, *Surrealist fantasy, and *Cubist manipulations of form, but his style is vivid and distinctive and anticipates aspects of *Pop art.

Lindsay. Family of Australian artists. The members included five of the children of Dr R. C. Lindsay of Creswick, Victoria: **Percy**

Lindsay (1870–1952), painter and graphic artist; **Sir Lionel Lindsay** (1874–1961), art critic, water-colour painter, and graphic artist in pen, etching, and woodcut, who helped to create an interest in the collection of original prints in Australia; **Norman Lindsay** (*b* Creswick, 23 Feb. 1879; *d* Sydney, 21 Nov. 1969), painter, graphic artist, critic, and novelist; **Ruby Lindsay** (1887–1919), graphic artist; and **Sir Daryl Lindsay** (1889–1976), painter and director of the National Gallery of Victoria from 1942 to 1956. Norman's son **Raymond** (1904–60) and Daryl's wife **Joan** (1896–1984) were also painters. For over half a century this family, through one or other of its members, played a leading role in Australian art. The most interesting character among them was Norman Lindsay, who according to Robert *Hughes (*The Art of Australia*, 1970) 'has some claim to be the most forceful personality the arts in Australia have ever seen'. He believed that the main impulse of art and life was sex, and his work was often denounced as pornographic. However, when he saw some of Lindsay's works at an exhibition of Australian art in London in 1923, Sir William *Orpen commented that they were 'certainly vulgar, but not in the least indecent. They are extremely badly drawn, and show no sense of design and a total lack of imagination.' Norman's son **Jack Lindsay** (1900–90) was a writer who settled in England in 1926. His books include biographies of several major artists, notably *Courbet (1973) and *Turner (1966).

Lindsay, Sir Coutts. See GROSVENOR GALLERY.

line engraving. Term applied to a method of making prints (and the print so made) in which the design is cut directly into the surface of a metal (usually copper) plate. In normal parlance the word *'engraving' usually refers to line engraving, but the word is also used as a generic term, covering a variety of printmaking processes (see PRINT). The line engraver uses a tool called a *burin, holding it in his right hand (presuming he is right-handed) and pushing it through the surface of the copper, cutting a clean V-shaped furrow. Both hands are in action, for the engraver steadies the plate with his left hand against the pressure exerted by the burin; when cutting curves, he holds the burin still with the right hand while the left rotates the plate onto the point of the tool. The shreds of metal excavated by the tool and the slight *burr thrown up at the sides of the lines are cut off by a scraper. The essential character of the medium is linear, though shading and tone may be suggested by parallel strokes, cross-*hatching, or textures compounded of various dots and flicks. Typically, line engravings have a quality of metallic hardness and austere precision, compared with the easy spontaneity of *etching or *lithography, in which the artist draws the design freely. Often, however, engraving has been combined with etching (or with other *intaglio techniques such as *mezzotint) on the same plate.

Line engraving seems to have originated somewhat before the middle of the 15th century in the workshops of goldsmiths, arising independently in Germany and Italy (see NIELLO), though slightly earlier in Germany (the first known impressions date from the 1430s). The early German engravers are mostly anonymous and are identified by a system of initials and *noms de plume*, as with the *Master of the Playing Cards and the *Master E. S., who were certainly goldsmiths as well as engravers. Martin *Schongauer, who died in 1491, was the first major artist to work mainly as an engraver, and the medium had its finest flowering in the early 16th century, in the work of Albrecht *Dürer (trained initially as a goldsmith) and *Lucas van Leyden. Active at the same time in Italy was Marcantonio *Raimondi, who was the great pioneer in the use of engraving as a means of reproducing the works of other artists. This soon became the primary function of the medium, and 'the entire history of Western art would have been quite different if engravings had not rapidly disseminated every stylistic innovation all around Europe' (Antony Griffiths, *Prints and Printmaking*, 1980). *Rubens, for example, realized the value of having his works broadcast in the form of prints, and several excellent engravers worked for him, his favourite being Paul Pontius (1603–58). A little later there arose in France a celebrated school of portrait engraving, in which the greatest names were those of Claude *Mellan, Robert *Nanteuil, and the Flemish-born Gerard *Edelinck.

During the 18th century line engraving began to decline in importance even as a reproductive process, especially in England, where tonal processes such as mezzotint and *stipple were popular. In the 19th century *wood engraving came to dominate the mass market for illustrations, but copper engraving continued to be used where fine detail was required, as for example in high-quality reproductions of paintings (several eminent artists of the time, particularly in Britain, earned more from the reproduction rights of their pictures than they did from the pictures themselves). From about 1820 steel plates came into common use when a large print run was required, as they lasted longer than copper plates before showing signs of wear. They had the disadvantage of being very difficult to work, but this problem was got round by steel plating—a process patented in 1857—whereby an extremely thin coating of steel is deposited on a copper plate by means of electrolysis.

The development of photomechanical processes towards the end of the 19th century made line engraving virtually obsolete as a reproductive technique. In the 20th century, however, there was a modest revival of interest in it as a means of original expression, the greatest impetus coming from S. W. *Hayter's experimental workshop for the graphic arts—'Atelier 17'—established in Paris in 1927.

Lingelbach, Johannes (*bapt.* Frankfurt, 10 Oct. 1622; *d* Amsterdam, ?Nov. 1674). Dutch painter of German birth. He settled in Amsterdam as a child and lived there for the rest of his life apart from a period abroad in his twenties, when he visited France and Italy (he is documented in Rome from 1647 to 1649). Lingelbach painted various types of warmly illuminated Italianate scenes, including views of harbours, and also pictures involving horses (hunting scenes and so on) in the manner of *Wouwerman. At the end of his career he produced a few pictures of sea battles, probably inspired by the anniversary of the Battle of Lepanto (1571). In addition he painted the figures in the work of many other artists. He was a fine craftsman and his work was popular with 18th- and 19th-century collectors. There are examples in many major galleries.

Linnell, John (*b* London, 16 June 1792; *d* Redhill, Surrey, 20 Jan. 1882). English painter. He made his reputation and his fortune as a fashionable portraitist, but was devoted to landscape painting. His wealth enabled him to patronize William *Blake, and his early landscapes occasionally have something of the visionary quality of the master and of Samuel *Palmer, who married Linnell's daughter in 1837. In the 1840s Linnell gave up portraiture and after settling at Redhill in 1851 most of his large output was devoted to idyllic scenes in Surrey, done in a lush and more conventional pastoral idiom than his early work. Such works were highly popular and Linnell became even wealthier. In spite of his success he was denied membership of the *Royal Academy, this being a reflection of his unpopularity with his fellow artists (his admiration for Blake was the saving grace in an otherwise unsavoury character).

linocut. A term applied to the technique of making a print from a thick piece of linoleum and to the print so made. Linoleum was invented in the 1860s, but it was not used for printing (in the manufacture of wallpaper) until the 1890s. The technique is essentially a development of *woodcut, the earliest of printmaking methods, but linocuts are much simpler to make because the material is soft and grainless and therefore easier to work. For this reason (and because the material is cheap) linocuts have been much used in the art education of children, the pioneer in this field being the Austrian painter and teacher Franz Čizek (1865–1946), who toured Europe and North America with examples of his pupils' work and had a great influence on art teaching. Because of the close association with children's art, the medium has been somewhat lightly regarded, but it has also been used by numerous eminent artists. The members of Die *Brücke were among the earliest to adopt it (*Heckel, who was making linocuts by 1903, before the group was founded, was probably the first major figure to take up the technique). *Kandinsky was making colour linocuts by about 1907.

In Britain, the most important popularizer of the medium was Claude Flight (1881–1955). He was probably the first artist to specialize in the technique and he wrote two books on the subject: *Lino-Cuts: A Handbook of Linoleum-Cut Colour Printing* (1927, revised edn. 1948) and *The Art and Craft of Lino Cutting and Printing* (1934). Flight taught at the Grosvenor School of Modern Art in London, where his pupils included the Australian painter and printmaker Dorrit Black (1881–1951). After returning to Australia in 1929 she tried to promote the linocut as a form of original art that was cheap enough to be bought by the ordinary person.

The two most famous artists to use linocut are *Matisse and *Picasso. Matisse took up the medium in 1938 and made about 70 linocuts between then and 1952. Picasso made his first black-and-white linocut in 1939 and began making linocut posters in the early 1950s. In 1958–9 he made a series of 45 colour linocuts and in 1962–3 a series of 55 more. The medium is particularly suitable for colour prints, as several large blocks may be used without undue expense (Picasso, however, used a method of printing in several colours from one block).

linseed oil. The *medium most often used in *oil painting, obtained from the seeds of the flax plant (the plant from which linen—the material for the best canvas—is also made). 'The best quality linseed oil is superior to all other *drying oils in resistance to embrittlement . . . [and] resistance to yellowing' (Ralph Mayer, *A Dictionary of Art Terms and Techniques*, 1969).

Liotard, Jean-Étienne (*b* Geneva, 22 Dec. 1702; *d* Geneva, 12 June 1789). Swiss painter (mainly in pastels) and printmaker. He travelled widely in Europe and also spent four years in Constantinople (1738–42), after which he adopted 'Turkish' dress and beard (actually more Moldavian); his eccentric appearance, which was a useful form of self-publicity, is familiar from his numerous self-portraits (after his marriage he reluctantly shaved off the beard to please his wife). His delicate and polished style brought him fashionable success as a portraitist in London (which he visited in 1754–5), Paris, Vienna, and the Netherlands. The best collection of his work is in the Musée d'Art et d'Histoire in Geneva, his native city.

Lipchitz, Jacques (*b* Druskieniki [now Druskininkai], 10 [22] Aug. 1891; *d* Capri, 26 May 1973). Lithuanian-born sculptor who became a French citizen in 1925 and an American citizen in 1958. After studying engineering in Lithuania he moved to Paris in 1909; by about 1912 he was part of a circle of avant-garde artists including *Matisse, *Modigliani, and *Picasso, and from 1914 he became one of the first sculptors to apply the principles of *Cubism in three dimensions (*Man with Guitar*, 1916, MoMA, New York). During the 1920s his style changed, as he became preoccupied with open forms and the interpenetration of solids and voids, and from about 1930 he began to use allegorical subject matter drawn from the Bible or classical mythology. In 1941 he moved to the USA, where he returned to greater solidity of form, but with a desire for greater spirituality. At times the tortured, bloated forms of his late work look rather like inflated shrubbery, as in *Prometheus Strangling the Vulture* (1944–53, Walker Art Center, Minneapolis). His output included several large public commissions, for example *Peace on Earth* (1967–9, Los Angeles Music Center). This, like most of his work, is in bronze, but he also made stonecarvings. In 1972 he published an autobiography, *My Life in Sculpture*, coinciding with a major exhibition of his work at the Metropolitan Museum, New York, entitled 'Jacques Lipchitz: His Life in Sculpture'. He died on holiday in Capri (he usually spent several months each year in Italy) and was buried in Jerusalem (he first visited Israel in 1963 and regarded it as his spiritual home).

Lippard, Lucy. See HESSE.

Lippi, Filippino (*b* Prato, c.1457; *d* Florence, 18 Apr. 1504). Florentine painter, the son and pupil of Filippo *Lippi, who died when the boy was about 12. Filippino ('little Filippo') later studied with *Botticelli and learned much from his expressive use of line, but Filippino's style, although sensitive and poetic, is more earthy than his master's. His first major commission (c.1485) was the completion of *Masaccio's fresco cycle in the Brancacci Chapel of S. Maria del Carmine, a task he carried out with such skill and tact that it is sometimes difficult to tell where his work begins and that of more than half a century earlier ends. Among his other frescos, the most important are cycles on the life of St Thomas Aquinas (1488–93) in the Caraffa Chapel, S. Maria sopra Minerva, Rome, and the lives of St Philip and St John (c.1495–1502) in the Strozzi Chapel, S. Maria Novella, Florence. In these he created picturesque, dramatic, and even bizarre effects that reveal him as one of the most inventive of late *quattrocento painters. Filippino also painted many altarpieces, the most famous of which is the *Vision of St Bernard* (c.1485, Badia, Florence), an exquisitely tender work, full of beautiful detail. Although he is now somewhat overshadowed by Botticelli, Filippino enjoyed a great reputation in his lifetime, being described by Lorenzo de' *Medici as 'superior to *Apelles'.

Lippi, Fra Filippo (*b* Florence, c.1406; *d* Spoleto, 10 Oct. 1469). Florentine painter. He was brought up as an unwanted child in the Carmelite friary of S. Maria del Carmine, where he took his vows in 1421. Unlike the Dominican Fra *Angelico, however, Lippi was a reluctant friar and had a scandalous love affair with a nun, Lucrezia Buti, who bore him his son Filippino and a daughter Alessandra. The couple were released from their vows and allowed to marry, but Lippi continued to sign himself 'Frater Philippus'. His biography (romantically embroidered to include capture by Moorish pirates) is one of the most colourful in *Vasari's *Lives* and has given rise to the picture of a worldly *Renaissance artist, rebelling against the discipline of the Church—an image reflected in Robert Browning's poem about Lippi ('Fra Lippo Lippi' in *Men and Women*, 1855). He must undoubtedly have had a more eventful life than most, but there is little documentary evidence of his character and personality.

Vasari writes that Lippi was inspired to become a painter by watching *Masaccio at work in the Carmine church, and his early work, notably the *Tarquinia Madonna* (1437, Gal. Naz., Rome) is certainly overwhelmingly influenced by him. From about 1440, however, his style changed direction, becoming more linear and preoccupied with decorative motifs—thin, fluttering draperies, brocades, etc. Lippi is associated particularly with paintings of the Virgin and Child, which are sometimes in the form of *tondi, a format he was among the first to use— a beautiful example (c.1453), showing the wistful delicacy and exquisite pale lighting that characterizes his best work, is in the Pitti, Florence. Another formal innovation with which Lippi is closely linked is the *sacra conversazione*—his Barbadori Altarpiece (begun 1437, Louvre, Paris) is sometimes claimed as the earliest example of the type. As a fresco painter Lippi's finest achievement is his cycle on the lives of St Stephen and St John the Baptist (1452–66) in Prato Cathedral.

Lippi was highly regarded in his day (he was patronized by the *Medici, who came to his aid when he was imprisoned and tortured for alleged fraud) and his influence is seen in the work of numerous artists, most notably *Botticelli, who was probably his pupil. Four centuries later he was one of the major sources for the second wave of *Pre-Raphaelitism.

Lipton, Seymour. See ABSTRACT EXPRESSIONISM.

Lisboa, António Francisco (*b* Vila Rica [now Ouro Prêto], c.1738; *d* Vila Rica, 18 Nov. 1814). Brazilian mulatto sculptor and architect, the illegitimate son of a Portuguese-born architect and stonemason, **Manuel Francisco Lisboa** (*d* c.1767), and an African slave. He was known as O Aleijadinho (little cripple) because he suffered from a disease (possibly leprosy or syphilis) that from his late thirties progressively deformed his limbs and caused him to lose some of his fingers and toes (he died in pain and poverty). He is said to have worked with chisel and mallet tied to half paralysed hands, but in spite of his handicap, he is considered the greatest sculptor as well as the greatest architect of colonial Brazil. Much of his work is in Ouro Prêto, a town that grew extremely wealthy as a gold-mining centre, but his masterpiece is the group of twelve life-size prophets (1800–5), carved in *soapstone, adorning the great staircase leading to the pilgrimage church of Nosso Senhor Bom Jesus de Matozinhos at Congonhas do Campo. These figures have been described as 'the most dynamic ensemble of open-air statuary in the Lusitanian world' (George Kubler and Martin

Soria, *Art and Architecture in Spain and Portugal and their American Dominions: 1500–1800*, 1959).

Lismer, Arthur. See GROUP OF SEVEN.

Liss (or Lys), **Johann** (*b* Oldenburg, c.1597; *d* Verona, 5 Dec. 1631). German painter, active mainly in Italy. Apart from *Elsheimer, he was perhaps the most gifted German painter of the 17th century. He trained in the Netherlands (probably in Amsterdam, possibly with *Goltzius) and visited Paris before moving to Italy c.1620. Venice seems to have been the main centre of his activity, but he also worked in Rome, and *Caravaggesque influence is clearly seen in such vivid and strongly lit works as *Judith and Holofernes* (c.1622, NG, London). His work enjoyed considerable popularity in Venice (where there was a dearth of talented native painters at this time) and his *Vision of St Jerome* in the church of S. Nicolo da Tolentino (c.1628) was much copied. It shows the remarkably free brushwork and brilliant use of high-keyed colour that were the salient features of his style and which were influential on Venetian painting when its glory revived in the 18th century. It was formerly assumed that Liss perished in the Venetian plague of 1629–30, but it is now known that he died in Verona in 1631.

Lissitzky, El (Eliezer Markowich) (*b* Pochinok, nr. Smolensk, 10 [22] Nov. 1890; *d* Moscow, 30 Dec. 1941). Russian painter, designer, graphic artist, and architect. He studied engineering in Darmstadt and architecture in Moscow. In 1919 he became professor of architecture and graphic art at the art school in Vitebsk run by *Chagall. One of his other colleagues there was *Malevich, whose advocacy of the use of pure geometric form greatly influenced Lissitzky, notably in his series of abstract paintings to which he gave the collective name 'Proun' and which he referred to as 'the interchange station between painting and architecture'. They do indeed look like plans for three-dimensional constructions, and at the same time Lissitzky made ambitious architectonic designs that were never realized. In 1921 he was sent to Berlin to arrange and design a major exhibition of abstract art at the Van Diemen Gallery—the show that first comprehensively presented the modern movement in Russia to the West (it was later shown in Amsterdam). While in Berlin he made contact with van *Doesburg and members of De *Stijl and with *Moholy-Nagy, who spread Lissitzky's ideas through his teaching at the *Bauhaus. In 1923 he went with *Gabo to a Bauhaus exhibition at Weimar and there met *Gropius. From 1923 to 1925 he lived in Switzerland, and (after a short visit to Russia) from 1925 to 1928 in Hanover. He returned to Russia in 1928 and settled in Moscow. By this time he had abandoned painting and devoted himself mainly to typography and industrial design. His work included several propaganda and trade exhibitions, notably the Soviet Pavilion of the 1939 World's Fair in New York, and his dynamic techniques of *photomontage, printing, and lighting had wide influence. For a considerable time Lissitzky was the best known of the Russian abstract artists in the West. In his mature work he achieved a fusion between the *Suprematism of Malevich (often using his diagonal axis), the *Constructivism of *Tatlin and *Rodchenko, and features of the *Neo-Plasticism of *Mondrian.

lithography (Greek: *lithos*, 'stone', and *graphein*, 'to write'). A method of printing from a design drawn directly onto a slab of stone or other suitable material. The design is neither raised in relief as in *woodcut nor incised as in *line engraving, but simply drawn on the flat printing surface; initially this surface was provided by a slab of special limestone, but metal sheets are now usually preferred, as they are less cumbersome. The process is based on the antipathy of grease and water. The artist draws his design with a greasy ink or crayon on the stone, which is then treated with certain chemical solutions so that the drawing is fixed. Water is then applied. The moisture is repelled by the greasy design but is readily accepted by the remainder of the porous surface of the stone. The stone is now rolled with greasy ink, which adheres only to the drawing, the rest of the surface, being damp, repelling it. A sheet of paper is placed on the stone, they are passed through a press, and an exact replica of the drawing is transferred, in reverse as with all prints, to the paper.

The most recent of the principal printmaking techniques, lithography was invented in 1798 by Aloys *Senefelder, a Bavarian playwright who was experimenting with methods of duplicating his plays; he records that the idea came to him when he made a laundry list with a greasy pencil on a piece of stone. Senefelder appears to have realized at once the significance of his invention and how it could be used. He called it 'Chemical Printing', insisting that the chemical principles involved were of more importance than the stone on which the designs were made, and in this he was right, for metal plates produce virtually identical results; zinc was first used in about

1830 and aluminium in about 1890. Senefelder also introduced the use of transfer paper, whereby the design is drawn on paper and transferred subsequently to the stone for printing—a method much used by artists ever since.

As its inventor foresaw, lithography has proved to be a highly flexible medium, capable of producing the most varied effects of transparency and texture. Instead of being drawn with pen or crayon, the design may be painted on the stone with a brush; the *washes may be opaque or dilute, they may be scratched or scraped to produce white lines on a background of black, or they may be textured in any way the artist's ingenuity can suggest (*Toulouse-Lautrec, one of the greatest masters of the technique, sometimes created tonal effects by spattering ink on the stone with a toothbrush). Colour lithographs, first made in the 1830s, are produced in much the same way as in any other graphic method, that is by preparing a separate stone for each of the colours in the design.

The lithographic principle has also been widely used in the commercial printing industry. Offset lithography, in which the ink is printed from the stone or metal onto a rubber-coated cylinder before being transferred to the paper, allows the design to be made the right way round instead of in reverse and also enables a very thin film of ink to be used, thus permitting the reproduction of the finest lines. Photo litho offset involves the photographic printing of an image, usually by means of a half-tone screen, onto a sensitized metal plate, which is then, after certain chemical treatments, printed on an offset lithographic machine. By contrast with these complex commercial procedures, the simplicity and directness of lithography in its basic form has attracted many artists of the 19th and 20th centuries to use it as a means of original expression (the artist need do nothing more than draw on the stone, plate, or transfer paper—the printer can handle all the technicalities).

*Goya, in his old age, was one of the first major artists to take up the new medium. Those who followed him included *Géricault, *Delacroix, *Daumier (the first great artist to execute the bulk of his life's work in lithography), *Manet, *Degas, *Whistler, *Redon, *Bonnard, and *Vuillard. Meanwhile, in the USA, the firm of *Currier & Ives was producing a series of lithographs that had little in common with the sophisticated European prints of the period but show us a cross-section of the life of the American nation in terms of a genuinely popular art. Among more recent artists,

*Picasso has been one of the most notable exponents of lithography, producing a large and varied oeuvre in the medium.

Little Masters. A once popular but now little-used term (a translation of the German *Kleinmeister*) applied to a group of 16th-century German printmakers who produced small, delicately worked images (mainly engravings), some of them no bigger than a postage stamp. The artists most frequently referred to by the term are the brothers Sebald and Barthel *Beham and Georg *Pencz, all three of whom worked in Nuremberg and were strongly influenced by *Dürer. Albrecht *Altdorfer and Heinrich *Aldegrever are sometimes included within the grouping.

Liu Haisu. See XU BEIHONG.

livre d'artiste (artist's book). A type of luxury illustrated book in which each illustration is printed directly from the surface on which the artist has worked (etching plate, lithographic stone, etc.). The genre was originated by the dealer Ambroise *Vollard, a great promoter of printmaking, and the first example is regarded as *Parallèlement* (1900), a book of poetry by Paul Verlaine illustrated with lithographs by Pierre *Bonnard. Vollard commissioned about 50 such books, the artists involved including *Braque, *Maillol, *Picasso, *Rodin, and *Rouault, and he was soon followed by other publishers, among them *Kahnweiler, who in 1909 issued *Apollinaire's *L'Enchanteur pourrissant* with wood engravings by *Derain. The livre d'artiste has continued to flourish particularly in France, but notable examples have also been produced elsewhere, for example David *Hockney's edition of Cavafy's *Poems* (1967).

Usually livres d'artiste are published in unsewn sheets, rather than bound (this means that they can be specially bound to the owner's requirement or dismantled for individual display of particular illustrations). The number of copies in an edition typically ranges from about twenty to 300. Printing is done by specialist establishments, using carefully selected paper, inks, and typefaces, and the artists and publishers often go to great lengths to secure the exact results they require.

Llanos, Fernando. See YAÑEZ.

local colour. The 'true' colour of an object or area seen under normal daylight, without regard for the modifying effect of such factors as distance or reflections from other objects. Thus, the local colour of a typical grass field is green, although at a certain distance it may appear blue because of *atmospheric perspective.

Lochner, Stefan (*b* ?Meersburg, ?*c*.1415; *d* Cologne, ?1451). German painter. The works associated with him have long been regarded as the finest paintings produced in Cologne in the mid-15th century, but there has recently been some doubt about the artist's identity. A painter called Stefan Lochner is first documented in Cologne in 1442 and died there in 1451, but there are no signed or documented works by him. In 1520 *Dürer visited the city and saw 'with wonder and astonishment' an unspecified altarpiece by 'Master Stefan'. The altarpiece that Dürer saw is usually identified as a large triptych of the *Adoration of the Magi*, painted for Cologne's town hall but now in the city's cathedral, and the 'Master Stefan' has been assumed to be Lochner. However, certain works attributed to the same hand as the altarpiece are now thought to date from after 1451, Lochner's known date of death. In spite of the difficulties, Lochner's name is still usually retained for convenience. The work associated with him is characterized by exquisite colouring and delicate sentiment.

Loggan, David (*bapt.* Danzig [now Gdańsk], 27 Aug. 1634; *bur.* London, 1 Aug. 1692). British engraver and draughtsman. He was born in Poland, of Anglo-Scottish descent, and moved to London in the late 1650s. He is best known for his topographical books on the universities, *Oxonia illustrata* (1675) and *Cantabrigia illustrata* (1690), but he also made sensitive portrait drawings.

Lohse, Richard (*b* Zurich, 13 Sept. 1902; *d* Zurich, 16 Sept. 1988). Swiss painter and printmaker. In his early works he experimented with various subjects and styles, but in the 1940s he became one of the leading representatives of *Concrete art. His paintings are mathematically based, often featuring chequerboard or gridlike patterns, but they are not cold or analytical in effect; indeed his work is particularly noted for its beauty and refinement of colour, and has a certain resemblance to *Op art of the kind associated with Bridget *Riley. From about 1950 he gained an international reputation.

Lomazzo, Giovanni Paolo (*b* Milan, 26 Apr. 1538; *d* Milan, 13 Feb. 1600). Milanese painter and writer. At the age of 33 he went blind and thereafter devoted himself to writing, publishing two treatises on art: *Trattato dell'arte de la pittura, scoltura, et architettura* (1584) and *Idea del tempio* *della pittura* (1590). The *Trattato* was the largest and most comprehensive treatise on art published in the 16th century and has been described as 'the Bible of *Mannerism'. It is divided into seven books, whose themes are Proportion, Motion, Colour, Light, Perspective, Practice, and History, the last containing a guide to Christian and classical *iconography. Throughout the book runs the assumption that the arts can be taught by detailed precepts. It was widely influential and an English translation by the Oxford physician Richard Haydocke was published in 1598, entitled *A Tracte Containing the Artes of Curious Paintinge, Carvinge & Buildinge*. The translation adds details of English artists such as *Hilliard, not mentioned in Lomazzo's original. Lomazzo's second treatise is a shorter and more abstract work; he also wrote poetry and treatises on other subjects. An example of his rare surviving paintings is a self-portrait (1568) in the Brera, Milan.

Lombard, Lambert (*b* Liège, 1505/6; *d* Liège, Aug. 1566). Netherlandish painter, draughtsman, engraver, architect, and antiquarian, active mainly in Liège. He trained in Antwerp and was influenced by *Gossaert and Jan van *Scorel. A man of scholarly inclinations, Lombard visited Rome in 1537–8 and made drawings of the *antique, some of which were engraved in the workshop of Jerome *Cock. He corresponded with *Vasari, providing him with information about Netherlandish artists, and Vasari said of him: 'Of all the Flemish artists I have named none is superior to Lambert Lombard of Liège, a man well versed in letters, a painter of judgement, a learned architect and—by no means his least title to merit—the master of Frans *Floris and Willem *Key.' This opinion was echoed by van *Mander, who wrote in 1604: 'One can confidently rank him among the best Netherlandish painters, past and present.' Few paintings survive to bear witness to his high contemporary reputation, but his work is known from drawings (almost 500 by him are preserved), copies, and engravings. A formidable *Portrait of the Artist* in the Musée de l'Art Wallon, Liège (another version is in the Staatliche Kunstsammlungen, Kassel) is among the best paintings given to him, but some critics think it is by his pupil Frans Floris. The portraits associated with Lombard—lively and strongly characterized—generally appeal more to modern taste than his somewhat academic religious paintings.

Lombardo. Family of Italian artists, the leading Venetian sculptors of their period: **Pietro** (*b* Carona, Lombardy, *c*.1435; *d* Venice, June 1515) and his sons **Tullio** (*b c*.1455; *d* Venice, 17 Nov. 1532) and **Antonio** (*b c*.1458; *d* Ferrara, ?1516). Pietro settled in Venice in about 1467. He was an architect as well as a sculptor, and his church of S. Maria dei Miracoli (1481–9) is one of the gems of Venetian *Renaissance architecture; his sons assisted him on its sculptural decoration. Of his numerous tombs in Venetian churches, the best known is that of Doge Pietro Mocenigo (*c*.1476–81, SS. Giovanni e Paolo). His style is distinguished by polished mastery of marble cutting and an interest in the *antique. These features recur in the sculpture of Tullio, whose most imposing work is the Vendramin Monument (*c*.1488–94) in SS. Giovanni e Paolo; the figure of *Adam* from this—a sensuously beautiful free-standing nude—is in the Metropolitan Museum, New York. Antonio has less substance as an independent artist. His work included a series of mythological reliefs in marble for Alfonso d'*Este (mainly in the Hermitage, St Petersburg).

London, School of. See SCHOOL OF LONDON.

London Artists' Association. See COURTAULD.

London Group. An exhibiting society of British artists formed in 1913 by an amalgamation of the *Camden Town Group with several smaller groups and various individuals. The first president was Harold *Gilman. Initially it was dominated by *Futurists and those who would soon be called *Vorticists, among them *Bomberg, *Epstein (who suggested the name), *Nevinson, and *Wadsworth. It soon became less aggressively avant-garde, although it still represented advanced taste. Several artists associated with the *Bloomsbury Group joined in the early years, including Roger *Fry (1918), who wrote that the London Group had 'done for *Post-Impressionism in England what the *New English Art Club did in a previous generation for *Impressionism'. By the time of the Second World War the group had lost its place as a significant force in British art, but it still exists.

London Institute. See ST MARTIN'S SCHOOL OF ART.

Long, Edwin. See ALMA-TADEMA.

Long, Richard (*b* Bristol, 2 June 1945). British avant-garde artist whose work brings together sculpture, *Conceptual art, and *Land art. Since 1967 his artistic activity has been based on long solitary walks that he makes through landscapes, initially in Britain, and from 1969 also abroad, often in remote or inhospitable terrain. Sometimes he collects objects such as stones and twigs on these walks and brings them into a gallery, where he arranges them into designs, usually circles or other fairly simple geometrical shapes (*Circle of Sticks*, 1973, *Slate Circle*, 1979, both Tate, London). He also creates such works in their original settings, and documents his walks with photographs, texts, and maps. Long has an international reputation (as early as 1976 he represented Britain at the Venice *Biennale) and has attracted a great deal of commentary, much of it laudatory, although the critic Peter Fuller described his work as 'the barren arrangement of gathered stones'. In 1989 Long won the *Turner Prize.

Longhi, Pietro (*b* Venice, 15 Nov. 1701; *d* Venice, 8 May 1785). Venetian painter. Although he carried out some fresco commissions he is known principally as a painter of small *genre scenes of contemporary patrician and low life. These charming and often gently satirical scenes were very popular, although surprisingly he does not seem to have been patronized by English visitors to Venice. He was prolific and occasionally painted more than one version of his own compositions; these again were often duplicated by pupils and followers. His son **Alessandro Longhi** (*b* Venice, 1733; *d* Venice, ?8 Nov. 1813) was a successful portraitist. He was the official portrait painter to the Venetian Academy, so he was in a good position for compiling his book *Compendio delle vite de' pittori veneziani istorici* (1762), a collection of biographies of Venetian artists; each subject is illustrated by a portrait that Longhi etched himself.

Longhi, Roberto (*b* Alba, 28 Dec. 1890; *d* Florence, 3 June 1970). Italian art historian. Longhi was a scholar of great industry, and published much new material, particularly in the area with which he is most associated—*Caravaggio and Caravaggism (he catalogued the great exhibition of the work of Caravaggio and the *Caravaggisti held in Milan in 1951, which is regarded as a landmark in this field). He was involved with various periodicals, and in 1950 founded a new journal, *Paragone*, in Florence, where he was a professor at the university. His villa in Florence is now an art-historical foundation, housing his picture collection and his library of books.

Loo, Carle van (Carle Vanloo) (*b* Nice, 15 Feb. 1705; *d* Paris, 15 July 1765). French painter of Flemish descent, the most illustrious member of a family of artists. He won the *Prix de Rome in 1724 (he was in Italy 1727–34) and enjoyed a career of unbroken success, ending his life as first painter to the king (1762) and director of the Académie Royale (1763). Industrious and versatile, he was primarily a history painter but also produced works in several other genres, including portraits, landscapes, and hunting scenes. His eclectic style was fluent but rather bland. Some of his contemporaries considered him the greatest painter in Europe, but after his death his work soon went out of favour, seeming flimsy and superficial to *Neoclassical taste, and his reputation did not seriously revive until the later 20th century.

Lopes, Gregório (*b* Lisbon, *c*.1490; *d* Lisbon, *c*.1550). Portuguese painter, court painter successively to Manuel I and John III. Among Portuguese painters of his period he was the most directly inspired by *Renaissance influence. Most of his surviving works (mainly altarpieces) are in the Museu Nacional de Arte Antiga, Lisbon.

López y Portaña, Vicente (*b* Valencia, 19 Sept. 1772; *d* Madrid, 22 Apr. 1850). Spanish painter. He painted many different subjects but was primarily a portraitist, continuing the tradition of *Mengs into the 19th century; his sitters included some of the leading Spanish personalities of his period. In 1814 he was appointed principal court painter to Ferdinand VII (jointly with the elderly *Goya), in 1817 director of the Academy of S. Fernando, and in 1823 curator of the *Prado.

Lorenzetti, Pietro (active 1320–45) and **Ambrogio** (active 1319–48). Sienese painters, brothers. They were among the outstanding Italian artists of their time, but their lives are poorly documented; it is possible that both died in the Black Death of 1348. Pietro is usually said to have been the elder brother, but the evidence is not conclusive. His first dated work is of 1320—a *polyptych of the *Virgin and Child with Saints* in the Pieve di S. Maria at Arezzo; Ambrogio's earliest reliably attributed work is of a year earlier—a *Virgin and Child* for a church at Vico l'Abate (Mus. Diocesano, Florence). Apart from collaborating in a cycle on the life of Mary, which they painted in fresco on the façade of Siena's public hospital in 1335 (now lost), the brothers worked independently. They shared a certain affinity of style, however, the weightiness of their figures showing the influence of *Giotto and clearly setting them apart from the elegance of their greatest Sienese contemporary, Simone *Martini. Ambrogio was the more innovative of the brothers, and his greatest work, the fresco series representing Good and Bad Government in the Palazzo Pubblico in Siena (1338–9), is one of the most remarkable achievements in 14th-century Italian art. In it he broke new ground in the naturalistic painting of landscape and townscape, and the talkative crowds of figures show he was an acute observer of his fellow men. Ambrogio's other dated work includes altarpieces of the *Presentation in the Temple* (1337–42, Uffizi, Florence) and the *Annunciation* (1344, Pinacoteca, Siena). Pietro's work is noted for its emotional expressiveness, his fresco of the *Descent from the Cross* in the Lower Church of S. Francesco at Assisi having remarkable pathos and dramatic power. The extent and the date of Pietro's contribution at Assisi are matters of controversy, but his other work includes dated altarpieces of the *Virgin and Child Enthroned* (1340, Uffizi) and the *Birth of the Virgin* (1342, Cathedral Mus., Siena).

Lorenzo di Bicci (*b* Florence, *c*.1350; *d* Florence, ?*c*.1410/20). Florentine painter. His life is poorly documented and only a few works are securely attributed to him, but he is regarded as one of the best Florentine painters of his period. His style is clear and lively (*Crucifixion*, 1399, Mus. della Collegiata di Sant'Andrea, Empoli). The workshop he established was taken over by his son and pupil **Bicci di Lorenzo** (*b* Florence, 1373; *d* Florence, 6 May 1452). Bicci's style was conservative (he was untouched by the innovations of *Masaccio), but his work is elegant and beautifully crafted, and he had a constant flow of commissions for altarpieces and frescos. There are examples of his work in numerous churches and museums in Florence. The family tradition was continued by his son **Neri di Bicci** (*b* Florence, 1418; *d* Florence, 4 Jan. 1492). He too was unadventurous in style, but his work is colourful and decorative (*Annunciation*, 1464, Accademia, Florence) and was much in demand. An exceptional amount is known about his activities because of the survival of a workshop diary he kept from 1453 to 1475 (now in the Uffizi, Florence); it is the most extensive piece of documentation on any 15th-century painter.

Lorenzo Monaco (*b* *c*.1370; *d* ?Florence, *c*.1425). Italian painter. He perhaps came from Siena, but all his known professional activity was in Florence. In 1391 he took his vows as a monk of the Camaldolese monastery of S. Maria degli Angeli. He rose to the rank of deacon, but in 1402 he was enrolled in the painters' guild under his lay name, Piero di Giovanni (Lorenzo Monaco means 'Laurence the Monk'), and was living outside the monastery. The monastery was renowned for its manuscript *illuminations and several *miniatures in books in the Laurentian Library in Florence have been attributed to him, but he was primarily a painter of altarpieces, good examples of which are in the National Gallery in London and the Uffizi in Florence. His only known works in fresco are the scenes of the life of the Virgin in the Bartolini Chapel of S. Trinità, Florence. His style is distinguished by luminous beauty of colouring and a graceful, rhythmic flow of line. He stands in complete contrast to his great contemporary *Masaccio and represents the highest achievement of the last flowering of *Gothic art in Florence.

Lorrain, Claude. See CLAUDE.

Lorsch Gospels. See ADA GROUP.

lost wax. See CIRE-PERDUE.

Loth, Johann Carl. See ROTTMAYR.

Lotto, Lorenzo (*b* Venice, *c*.1480; *d* Loreto, 1556/7). Venetian painter. According to his own testimony he was born in Venice, and *Vasari suggests that he was trained there, but he worked in many other places, had an idiosyncratic style, and stands somewhat apart from the central Venetian tradition. He is first recorded in 1503 in Treviso, where he was based until 1506. He then had a period in central Italy, during which he worked for Julius II (Giuliano della *Rovere) in the Vatican (nothing survives by him there). From 1513 to 1525 he worked mainly in Bergamo, then returned to Venice. He remained there until 1532, then was peripatetic for the remainder of his career, working mainly in various towns in the Marches. In 1554, when he was partially blind, he became a lay brother at the monastery at Loreto, where he died. (These movements are unusually well documented because his account book for the period 1538–54 survives, together with numerous letters from the earlier part of his career.)

Lotto's rootless existence reflects his anxious, difficult temperament, and his work is extremely uneven. It draws on a wide variety of sources, from northern Europe as well as Italy, but at the same time shows acute freshness of observation. He is now perhaps best known for his portraits, in which he often conveys a mood of psychological unrest (*Young Man in his Study*, c.1527, Academy, Vienna), but he worked mainly as a religious painter. An outstanding example of how original and poetic his altarpieces could be is the *Annunciation* (c.1527, Pinacoteca Civica, Recanati), a bizarre and captivating work full of brilliant colours and lighting effects, odd expressions and poses, and unusual and beautifully painted details, including a startled cat.

Louis, Morris (Morris Louis Bernstein) (*b* Baltimore, 28 Nov. 1912; *d* Washington, DC, 7 Sept. 1962). American painter, a major pioneer of the movement from *Abstract Expressionism to Colour Stain Painting (see COLOUR FIELD PAINTING). His career was spent first in Baltimore and then from 1947 in nearby Washington. He isolated himself from the New York art world, concentrating on his own experiments and supporting himself by teaching. However, it was a visit to New York in 1953 with Kenneth *Noland that led to the breakthrough in his art. He and Noland went to Helen *Frankenthaler's studio, where they were immensely impressed by her painting *Mountains and Sea*, and Louis immediately began experimenting with her technique of applying liquid paint on to unprimed canvas, allowing it to flow over and soak into the canvas so that it acted as a stain and not as an overlaid surface. He was secretive about his methods and it is uncertain how he achieved his control over the flow of colour (his technique allowed him no possibility for alteration or modification), but towards the end of his life he suffered from severe back problems caused by his constant bending and stooping over the canvas. Whatever his methods, the effect was to create suave and radiant flushes of colour, with no sense of brush gesture or hint of figuration.

Louis painted various series of pictures in his new technique, the first of which was *Veils* (1954; he did another series in 1957–60). The other major series were *Florals* (1959–60), *Unfurleds* (1960–1), and *Stripes* (1961–2). The *Veils* consist of subtly billowing and overlapping shapes filling almost the entire canvas, but his development after that was towards rivulets of colour arranged in rainbow-like bands, often on a predominantly bare canvas. It was not until 1959 that his career began to take off and he had little time to enjoy his success before dying of lung cancer. However, his reputation now stands very high and he has had enormous influence on the development of Colour Stain Painting. In the introduction to the catalogue of the 1974 Arts Council exhibition of his work, John Elderfield

wrote: 'Morris Louis is one of the very few artists whose work has really changed the course of painting . . . With Louis, fully autonomous abstract painting came into its own for really the first time, and did so in paintings of a quality that matches the level of their innovation.'

Loutherbourg, Philippe Jacques de (*b* Strasbourg, 31 Oct. 1740; *d* Chiswick [now in London], 11 Mar. 1812). French painter, stage designer, and illustrator, active mainly in England. He was the son of an engraver and miniaturist. In 1755 he moved to Paris, where he trained under Carle van *Loo and Giovanni Battista Casanova (1728–95) (brother of the famous amorist), a painter of battle, hunting, and equestrian scenes. During the 1760s he enjoyed considerable success at the *Salon, mainly with landscapes. In 1771 he settled in London, armed with an introduction to David Garrick, for whom he became a highly inventive designer of spectacular stage sets at Drury Lane Theatre. After Garrick's retirement in 1776, Loutherbourg continued under his successor Richard Brinsley Sheridan, but in 1781 he left Drury Lane and launched his own theatrical entertainment, the *Eidophusikon. This was a popular success, and in the 1780s Loutherbourg also made an impact as a landscape painter at the *Royal Academy exhibitions (he became an RA in 1781). He travelled widely in England and Wales, and although his landscapes can be rather stagy, they are also lively, and their feeling for *Picturesque and *Sublime qualities provided an influential alternative to the dominant Italianate tradition. In 1786 he became involved with the occultist Count Cagliostro and in 1788–9 he abandoned painting for faith healing; however, he was forced to give this up because of public opposition and thereafter returned successfully to art. In his later work he turned more to history painting, including battle scenes and biblical subjects. He made numerous book illustrations and also published two collections of engravings of his work: *The Picturesque Scenery of Great Britain* (1801) and *The Romantic and Picturesque Scenery of England and Wales* (1805).

Louvre (Musée du Louvre), Paris. The national museum and art gallery of France. The first building on the site, begun c.1190 by Philip II as a fortress and arsenal, held the royal treasures of jewels, armour, illuminated manuscripts, etc. It was enlarged and beautified by Charles V (reigned 1364–80), and his successor Charles VI used it as a residence for visiting royalty. Francis I began to demolish it in the 1520s and in 1546 he commissioned the architect Pierre Lescot to build a new palace of four wings around a square court, roughly of the same size as the old castle and on the same site. Only the west and half of the south wings were completed by Lescot, but his work forms the heart of the present vast structure, and his elegant and sophisticated classical style set the tone for the additions to the Louvre that were made by virtually every French monarch up to Napoleon III in the mid-19th century (although for much of the early 18th century it was neglected, after Louis XIV had moved the court to Versailles).

In 1699 one of the infrequent exhibitions of the Académie Royale (see ACADEMY) was held in the Louvre, and from 1737 the palace's Salon Carré became the venue for more regular exhibitions—hence the term *Salon. In 1784 Louis XVI began converting the Grande Galerie into a museum to display the royal collection (Hubert *Robert was in charge), and as a result of the democratic fervour of the Revolution the Louvre was opened as the first national public gallery in 1793 (though as a public museum it was preceded by others, including the *Ashmolean Museum in Oxford and the *Vatican Museums). It was originally called the Muséum Central des Arts, but in 1803 Napoleon renamed it the Musée Napoléon and exhibited there the works of art he had looted from conquered territories. Most were returned after his fall from power. In 1851 his nephew Napoleon III opened new rooms, housing *Rubens's Marie de *Médicis cycle (transferred from the Luxembourg Palace) and other works. Subsequently there have been various other additions, including a spectacular glass pyramid (1985–9) in the main courtyard serving as a new entrance to the museum; it was designed by the American architect I. M. Pei.

In addition to one of the world's greatest collections of paintings, the Louvre houses many other treasures, including large holdings of Greek and Roman antiquities. Among the famous ancient statues are the *Borghese Warrior, the *Venus de Milo, and the *Victory of Samothrace. To relieve congestion after the Second World War a special museum for Impressionist art was formed at the Jeu de Paume in the gardens of the Tuileries. The paintings from the Jeu de Paume, together with certain other works from the Louvre, have now been moved to the *Musée d'Orsay.

Low, Sir David (b Dunedin, 7 Apr. 1891; d London, 19 Sept. 1963). New Zealand cartoonist, active in Britain from 1919. He worked for numerous papers but is best known for his association with the London *Evening Standard*, 1927–50. His socialist views conflicted with the Conservative policy of this paper, but its proprietor Lord Beaverbrook thought so highly of him that he offered him 'complete freedom in the selection and treatment of subject matter'. In 1932 Winston Churchill described him as 'the greatest of our modern cartoonists—the greatest because of the vividness of his political conceptions, and because he possesses what few cartoonists have—a grand technique of draughtsmanship'. As well as satirizing well-known figures, Low invented imaginary characters to symbolize policies and attitudes of mind, the most famous of whom was 'Colonel Blimp', whose name has passed into the language to describe a type of muddle-headed complacent reactionary. Many collections of his cartoons appeared in book form, and he wrote *Ye Madde Designer* (1935), about the technique of cartooning, and *British Cartoonists, Caricaturists and Comic Artists* (1942) in the 'Britain in Pictures' series.

Lowry, L. S. (Laurence Stephen) (b Stretford, Lancashire [now Greater Manchester], 1 Nov. 1887; d Glossop, Derbyshire, 23 Feb. 1976). British painter. He lived all his life in or near Manchester (mainly in Salford) and worked as a rent collector and clerk for a property company until he retired in 1952. His painting was done mainly at night after his day's work, but he was not a *naive painter, having studied intermittently at art schools from 1905 to 1925. The most important of his teachers—at Manchester School of Art—was Adolphe Valette (1876–1942), a French painter who settled in Manchester in 1905 and whose work includes some memorably atmospheric views of the city. Lowry, too, concentrated on urban subjects, but his style was very different from Valette's and much more in the tradition of certain painters of the *Camden Town Group. His most characteristic pictures feature firmly drawn backgrounds of industrial buildings, often bathed in a white haze, against which groups or crowds of figures, painted in his distinctive sticklike manner, move about their affairs. Many of them record his immediate surroundings, but others are semi-imaginary views. There is sometimes an element of humour, but the prevailing feeling is generally what Sir John *Rothenstein calls 'a kind of gloomy lyricism' (Lowry was a solitary character and said, 'Had I not been lonely I should not have seen what I did'). His first one-man exhibition, at the Reid and Lefevre Gallery, London, in 1939, established his name outside his home area for the first time, and his reputation steadily increased thereafter, although he continued to lead a spartan life. In 1976, a few months after his death, a comprehensive retrospective exhibition of his work at the Royal Academy brought considerable divergence of opinion among critics. Some thought of him as a great artist with an important original vision. Others represented him as a very minor talent, although interesting as a social commentator. The best collection of his work is in the Lowry, a large arts centre that opened in Salford in 2000.

Luca della Robbia. See ROBBIA.

Lucas, Sarah. See YOUNG BRITISH ARTISTS.

Lucas van Leyden (*b* Leiden, ?1494; *d* Leiden, May / Aug. 1533). Netherlandish engraver and painter. The only evidence for the birthdate of 1494 is van *Mander's biography, and some scholars think it is likely Lucas was born a few years earlier than this, around 1490. He was the pupil of his father, from whose hand no works are known, and of Cornelis *Engelbrechtsz., but both these were painters whereas Lucas himself was principally an engraver. How he learnt engraving is unknown, but he showed precocious skill in the art; the earliest dated print by him (*Mohammed and the Murdered Monk*, 1508) was made when he was probably still in his teens, yet it reveals no trace of immaturity in inspiration or technique. In 1514 he became a member of the Leiden painters' guild. He seems to have travelled a certain amount, and on a visit to Antwerp in 1521 he met Albrecht *Dürer, who drew his portrait (Mus. B.-A., Lille).

An unbroken series of dated engravings makes it possible to follow Lucas's career as a printmaker and to date many of his paintings, but no clear pattern of stylistic development emerges. Dürer was the single greatest influence on him, but Lucas was less intellectual in his approach, tending to concentrate on the anecdotal features of the subject and to take delight in caricatures and incidents from everyday life. Van Mander characterizes him as a pleasure-loving dilettante, who sometimes worked in bed, but he left a large oeuvre, in spite of his fairly short life, and must have been a prodigious worker.

Lucas had a great reputation in his day (*Vasari even rated him above Dürer in certain respects) and he is universally regarded as one of the greatest figures in the history of *graphic art

(he made etchings and woodcuts as well as engravings and was a superb draughtsman). His status as a painter is less elevated, but nevertheless he occupies a significant place in this field too. He was a pioneer of the Netherlandish *genre tradition, as witness his *Chess Players* (*c*.1508, Gemäldegalerie, Berlin)—which actually represents a variant game called 'courier'—and his *Card-Players* (*c*.1517, Wilton House, Wiltshire), while his celebrated *Last Judgement* *triptych (1526–7, Lakenhal Mus., Leiden) shows the heights to which he could rise as a religious painter. It eloquently displays his vivid imaginative powers, his superb skill as a colourist, and his deft and fluid brushwork. Lucas left no pupils or direct followers, but his work was a stimulus to an even greater Leiden-born artist, *Rembrandt.

His brother **Aertgen van Leyden** (?1498–1564) was a painter, draughtsman, and designer of stained glass; few works can be securely associated with him.

Luchism. See RAYONISM.

Lucian of Samosata (2nd century AD). Greek writer. His surviving literary output is large and varied. In the history of art he is notable for his *Eikones* (Images or Portraits), often known by its Latin title *Imagines*, which contains descriptions of works (now lost) by some of the leading Greek artists, including *Phidias and *Praxiteles. Lucian's writings were well known in the *Renaissance (the first printed collected edition of his works was published in Florence in 1496) and his description of *Calumny* by *Apelles, for example, was the source for the painting of this subject by *Botticelli (Uffizi, Florence).

Ludovisi, Alessandro (Pope Gregory XV). See GUERCINO.

Ludovisi, Cardinal Ludovico. See DYING GAUL and GUERCINO.

Ludwig I, King of Bavaria. See PINACOTHECA.

Ludwig, Peter (*b* Koblenz, 9 July 1925; *d* Aachen, 22 July 1996). German businessman and art collector. He studied art history at Mainz University (writing a doctoral thesis on *Picasso in 1950), then went into business and became chairman of various firms. His collecting interests were initially very broad, but he came to concentrate on contemporary art, in which he built up one of the world's largest collections, particularly rich in American *Pop art. He made many donations to public collections, and several cultural bodies in Germany and Austria now bear his name, notably the Ludwig Museums in Aachen (1977) and Cologne (1986).

Lugt, Frits (*b* Amsterdam, 4 May 1884; *d* Paris, 15 July 1970). Dutch collector and art historian, one of the most renowned of all connoisseurs of Old Master drawings and prints. He was self-taught and pursued an independent career, working a good deal as an agent and adviser for other collectors. His main field of interest was Dutch and Flemish art of the 16th and 17th centuries, *Rembrandt being his favourite artist. He was an extremely industrious scholar, his most notable publications being *Les Marques de collections de dessins et d'estampes* (1921, supplement 1956), a fundamental reference work on collectors and the marks they used to identify their drawings and prints, and *Répertoire des catalogues de ventes publiques* (3 vols., 1938–64; a 4th volume appeared posthumously in 1987), which lists tens of thousands of art sale catalogues from *c*.1600 to 1925. During the Second World War he lived in the USA and he spent his final years in Paris, where in 1953 he established a cultural foundation, the Institut Néerlandais, to house his own superb collection; it opened in 1957.

Luini, Bernardino (*b* ?Luino, Lake Maggiore, ?*c*.1480; *d* ?Lugano, 1532). Milanese painter, one of the most prominent of *Leonardo's followers in Lombardy. Little is known of his life (estimates of his birthdate have ranged from 1460 to 1490), but his large output indicates that he must have enjoyed a successful career (he was unusual among Leonardo's followers in that he painted numerous frescos as well as easel pictures). His work is well represented in the Brera in Milan and many of his frescos and altarpieces are in Lombard churches. He also painted mythological subjects (*Cephalus and Procris*, *c*.1522, NG, Washington). Luini adapted Leonardo's style to conservative taste; he also sentimentalized it, and this helps account for his great popularity with the Victorians. His best work is of high quality, but he ran a busy workshop and some of his followers and copyists vulgarized his style into almost a parody of Leonardo, with sickly smirks and exaggerated *chiaroscuro.

Lukasbrüder. See NAZARENES.

Luks, George (*b* Williamsport, Pa., 13 Aug. 1867; *d* New York, 29 Oct. 1933). American painter and graphic artist. In 1894, after a decade's travel in Europe, he became an illustrator on the *Philadelphia Press* and made friends with other newspaper artists—*Glackens, *Shinn, and *Sloan—who introduced him to Robert *Henri. In 1896 Luks moved to New York, where he turned more to painting and became a member of The *Eight and the *Ashcan School. A flamboyant character who identified himself with the poorer classes and made a pose of bohemianism, he was much given to tall tales and sometimes posed as 'Lusty Luks', an ex-boxer. His work was uneven and unpredictable. It had vigour and spontaneity but often lapsed into superficial vitality. One of his best-known works is *The Wrestlers* (1905, MFA, Boston), which shows his preference for earthy themes and admiration for the bravura painterly technique of artists such as *Manet. Luks taught for several years at the *Art Students League and also ran his own school.

Luminism. Term coined *c*.1950 by John Baur, director of the Whitney Museum in New York, to describe a trend in mid-19th-century American landscape painting in which the rendering of light and atmosphere was paramount. He defined Luminism as 'a polished and meticulous realism in which there is no sign of brushwork and no trace of impressionism, the atmospheric effects being achieved by infinitely careful gradations of tone, by the most exact study of the relative clarity of near and far objects, and by a precise rendering of the variations in texture and color produced by direct or reflected rays' ('American Luminism', *Perspectives USA*, autumn 1954). At their most characteristic, Luminist paintings are concerned chiefly with the depiction of water and sky. Leading Luminists included *Bingham, *Durand, Martin Johnson Heade (1819–1904), also known for pictures of birds and flowers, and the marine painter Fitz Hugh Lane (1804–65), and aspects of the trend can be seen in the work of the *Hudson River School. By about 1880 Luminism was becoming outmoded by French influences.

In the field of 20th-century art the term 'luminism' has also been used in completely different senses: as a name for *Neo-Impressionism in Belgium and as a term applied to works of art incorporating electric light (see LIGHT ART).

lunette (French: 'little moon'). A semicircular or crescent-shaped window or space, typically one framed by an arch or vault; the term is also applied to a painting filling such a shape. For examples see ALDOBRANDINI.

Lurçat, Jean (*b* Bruyères, Vosges, 1 July 1892; *d* Saint-Paul-de-Vence, 6 Jan. 1966). French painter and designer. For a time he was influenced by *Cubism, but more important and lasting influences on his painting came from his extensive travels during the 1920s in the Mediterranean countries, North Africa, and the Middle East. His pictures were dominated by impressions of desert landscapes, reminiscences of Spanish and Greek architecture, and a love of fantasy that led him to join the *Surrealist movement for a short period in the 1930s. Lurçat is chiefly remembered, however, for his work in the revival of the art of tapestry. His designs combined exalted themes from human history with fantastic representations of the vegetable and insect worlds, and he succeeded in reconciling the stylizations of medieval tapestry with modern modes of abstraction. In 1939 he was appointed designer to the tapestry factory at Aubusson and together with Marcel Gromaire (1892–1971) he brought about a renaissance in its work. He made more than 1,000 designs, the most famous probably being the huge *Apocalypse* for the church of Notre-Dame-de-Toute-Grâce at Assy (1948). From 1930 onwards he also produced coloured lithographs, stage designs, and book illustrations, and in the 1960s he renewed his painting activities. Lurçat also wrote poetry and books on tapestry.

Luttrell Psalter. See PSALTER.

lyrical abstraction. A rather vague term, used differently by different writers, applied to a type of expressive but non-violent abstract painting flourishing particularly in the 1950s and 1960s; the term was evidently coined by the French painter Georges *Mathieu, who in 1947 spoke of 'abstraction lyrique'. European critics often use it more or less as a synonym for *Art Informel or *Tachisme; Americans sometimes see it as an emasculated version of *Abstract Expressionism. To some writers it implies particularly a lush and sumptuous use of colour.

Lysippus. Greek sculptor from Sicyon, near Corinth, active in the middle and later 4th century BC. He was one of the most famous of Greek sculptors, with a long and prolific career (he worked from perhaps as early as c.360 BC to as late as c.305 BC and *Pliny said he made 1,500 works—all in bronze). Nothing is known to survive from his own hand, but some idea of his style can be gained from Roman copies of his work, the best and most reliable being the *Apoxyomenus* (a young athlete scraping himself with a strigil) in the Vatican Museums. The figure is tall and slender, bearing out the tradition current in antiquity that Lysippus introduced a new scheme of proportions for the human body to supersede that of *Polyclitus, and the pose—with one arm outstretched—is novel. Lysippus was famous also for his portraits of Alexander the Great, who is said to have let no other sculptor portray him; several copies survive, including examples in the British Museum, London, and the Louvre, Paris. Among his other works was a colossal statue of Hercules at Sicyon, which was probably the original of the celebrated *Farnese Hercules* in the Archaeological Museum in Naples. It shows the realism that was said to be another hallmark of his work. Of the works associated with him on stylistic grounds, the best known is a bronze statue of a victorious athlete found in the Adriatic Sea in 1964; this was bought by the *Getty Museum, Los Angeles, in 1977 for $3,900,000, then the highest price ever paid for a piece of sculpture, and it is now sometimes known as 'the Getty Victor'. Even from the second-hand evidence that survives, it is clear that Lysippus was an outstandingly original sculptor whose stylistic innovations, like those of his great contemporary *Praxiteles, became common currency in the Greek world; J. J. Pollitt (*Art in the Hellenistic Age*, 1986) describes him as 'probably the single most creative and influential artist of the entire *Hellenistic period'. His pupils included Chares of Lindos, creator of the *Colossus of Rhodes*.

Lysistratus. Greek sculptor of the later 4th century BC, brother of *Lysippus. No works by him are known to survive in originals or copies, but *Pliny's account indicates that he pursued even further the naturalism that was such a feature of his brother's work. Pliny says that he tried to make portraits lifelike rather than beautiful, and that he was the first to make life masks and to take casts from statues (presumably to make copies).

M

Mabuse. See GOSSAERT.

MacBryde, Robert. See COLQUHOUN.

McCahon, Colin (*b* Timaru, 1 Aug. 1919; *d* Auckland, 27 May 1987). New Zealand painter. With Rita *Angus and Toss *Woollaston, he formed 'the trinity of native-born painters who pioneered the modern movement in New Zealand art' (Gil Docking, *Two Hundred Years of New Zealand Painting*, 1971) and he is generally considered his country's foremost 20th-century artist. His paintings—intense and visionary in style—are mainly landscapes and religious subjects, and he often combined the two, as in his *Stations of the Cross* series, in which Christ's Passion is placed in the North Otago hills. In 1953 McCahon was appointed keeper of the Auckland City Art Gallery and in 1964 he became lecturer in painting at the University of Auckland.

Macchiaioli. Group of Italian painters, active mainly in Florence *c*.1855–65, who were in revolt against academic conventions and emphasized painterly freshness through the use of spots or patches (*macchie*) of colour. The name Macchiaioli (spot makers) was applied facetiously to them in 1862 and the painters themselves adopted it. They were influenced by the *Barbizon School, but they painted *genre scenes, historical subjects, and portraits as well as landscapes. Leading members included Giovanni Fattori (1825–1908), Silvestro Lega (1826–95), and Telemaco Signorini (1835–1901). *Boldini and de *Nittis were among the artists who sympathized with their ideas. Their main supporter was the critic and collector Diego Martelli (1839–96), who was also interested in contemporary French painting—he was a friend of *Degas, who painted his portrait (1879, NG, Edinburgh). In spite of Martelli's championship, the Macchiaioli had little commercial success, but they are now considered the most important phenomenon in 19th-century Italian painting. Sometimes they are even claimed as proto-*Impressionists, but the differences between the two groups are as striking as the similarities;

there is often a strong literary element in the work of the Macchiaioli, for example, and however bright their lighting effects, they never lost a sense of solidity of form.

MacColl, D. S. (Dugald Sutherland) (*b* Glasgow, 10 Mar. 1859; *d* London, 21 Dec. 1948). British painter, critic, lecturer, and administrator. From 1890 to 1895 he was art critic of the *Spectator* and from 1896 to 1906 of the *Saturday Review* (and again from 1921 until 1930, when he moved to the newly founded *Week-End Review*). In these positions he helped to influence public taste in favour of *Impressionism, and his book *Nineteenth Century Art* (1902) contains one of the earliest balanced assessments of the movement. He did not care for the *Post-Impressionists, however, and thought that *Cézanne must have suffered from an eye defect. MacColl was keeper of the Tate Gallery, 1906–11, and of the Wallace Collection, 1911–24, one of the founders of the *National Art Collections Fund in 1903, and a vigorous controversialist; in the *Dictionary of National Biography* he is described as 'highly versatile, volcanically energetic, utterly honest and self-confident'. As a painter he concentrated on landscape watercolours, although he also did portraits in oils, including one of Augustus *John (1907, Manchester AG). His books include *Confessions of a Keeper* (1931) and *Philip Wilson *Steer* (1945).

McCubbin, Frederick (*b* Melbourne, 25 Feb. 1855; *d* Melbourne, 20 Dec. 1917). Australian painter. In the 1890s he was a member of the *Heidelberg School, and he is best known for the scenes of pioneer life he painted at this time (*Bush Burial*, 1890, Geelong AG). After a visit to Europe late in life in 1906, his work was more directly influenced by *Impressionism. From 1886 until his death he taught drawing at the Melbourne National Gallery School. His son **Louis** (1890–1952) was also a painter. His major work is a huge mural of battle scenes for the Australian National War Museum in Canberra (1920–9). From 1936 to 1950 he was director of the National Gallery of South Australia.

MacDonald, J. E. H. See GROUP OF SEVEN.

Macdonald, Jock (*b* Thurso, 31 May 1897; *d* Toronto, 3 Dec. 1960). Canadian painter, born in Scotland. He emigrated to Canada in 1926 to teach at the new Vancouver School of Decorative and Applied Arts. His early work was in the *Group of Seven tradition, but in 1934 he painted his first abstract work, *Formative Colour Activity* (NG, Ottawa). In the late 1930s he became a friend of Emily *Carr, and in 1940 of Lawren *Harris, who encouraged him in his abstract experiments. These included *automatic paintings in a *Surrealist vein. During the last five years of his life Macdonald's output was prodigious, as he threw himself into experimenting with various techniques and media. He taught at several art colleges over the course of his career and played a leading role in advancing the cause of modern art in Canada.

Macdonald, Margaret. See MACKINTOSH.

Macdonald-Wright, Stanton (*b* Charlottesville, Va., 8 July 1890; *d* Pacific Palisades, Calif., 22 Aug. 1973). American painter, designer, and experimental artist, remembered chiefly as a pioneer of abstract art. In 1907 he moved to Paris, where he met Morgan *Russell in 1911; together they evolved *Synchromism—a style of painting based on the abstract use of colour. They first exhibited their works in this style in 1913 and claimed that they, rather than *Delaunay and *Kupka (whose work of the time was very similar), were the originators of a new type of abstract art. In 1914–16 Macdonald-Wright lived in London, then returned to the USA. In 1919 he moved to California, where he abandoned Synchromism and became involved with experiments with colour film and various other projects. He was deeply interested in oriental art and from 1958 he spent part of every year in a Zen monastery in Japan. His brother Willard Huntington Wright (1888–1939) began his career as an art and literary critic (see FORUM EXHIBITION), but turned to crime fiction in the 1920s; under the pen name S. S. Van Dine, he made a fortune as the author of a series of books featuring the super-sleuth Philo Vance, whose scholarship and urbanity were modelled on his own.

McEvoy, Ambrose (*b* Crudwell, Wiltshire, 12 Aug. 1878; *d* London, 4 Jan. 1927). English painter. He began as a painter of restful interiors, but from about 1915 he gained great success as a portraitist. His most characteristic pictures are of beautiful society women, often painted in watercolour in a rapid, sketchy style. They can be merely flashy or cloyingly sweet (during the First World War one critic joked that at a time of suger shortage McEvoy was 'a positive asset to the nation'), but the finest have something of the romantic air of refinement of *Gainsborough, an artist he greatly admired. His wife **Mary McEvoy** (1870–1941), whom he married in 1902, was a painter of interiors with figures, flowers, and portraits.

Mach, David. See NEW BRITISH SCULPTURE.

Machuca, Pedro (*b* Toledo, ?*c*.1490; *d* Granada, 4 Aug. 1550). Spanish architect and painter, active mainly in Granada. He worked in Italy in his early career (which is ill documented) and was one of the first Spanish artists to break entirely with medieval tradition and become steeped in *Renaissance ideas. His earliest dated work, the *Virgin with the Souls of Purgatory* (1517, Prado, Madrid), was painted in Italy and is thoroughly *Raphaelesque in style. Machuca was back in Spain by 1520; he continued painting, but after Charles V (see HABSBURG) appointed him architect of his new palace in Granada (begun 1527), he devoted himself mainly to this great building. It is strongly Italianate in style; indeed the majestic circular courtyard expresses the ideals of the High Renaissance more completely than any surviving building of the same date in Italy.

McIntire, Samuel (*bapt*. Salem, Mass., 16 Jan. 1757; *d* Salem, 6 Feb. 1811). American architect and woodcarver. He worked all his life in Salem, Massachusetts, and his gracious and refined work helped make the town the handsomest in New England during the early years of the American Republic. His ideas were borrowed from English pattern books, but he did not copy complete designs, and his decorative carving shows superb craftsmanship. The Gardner House (1804–5) is regarded as his masterpiece.

Maçip (or Masip), **Vicente** (*b* ?Andilla, *c*.1475; *d* Valencia, 1550). Spanish painter, one of a dynasty of artists working in Valencia. Little is known of his life, but his major work, the main altarpiece of Segorbe Cathedral (1528–30), shows him to have been a leading representative of the Italianate style. During his later years he collaborated with the outstanding member of the family, his son and follower **Juan** (known as Juan de Juanes, *b* Valencia, *c*.1510; *d* Bocairente, Valencia province, 21 Dec. 1579). Juan's work combines figures in the Italian *Mannerist style with a polished Netherlandish technique. He was the leading painter of his time in Valencia and had many followers.

Maciunas, George. See FLUXUS.

Macke, August (b Meschede, Westphalia, 3 Jan. 1887; d nr. Perthes-les-Hurlus, Champagne, 26 Sept. 1914). German *Expressionist painter. His training included a period studying with *Corinth in Berlin. Between 1907 and 1912 he visited Paris several times and he came closer in spirit to French art than any other German painter of his time, evolving a personal synthesis of *Impressionism, *Fauvism, and *Orphism (he met Robert *Delaunay in 1912). His subjects were generally light-hearted, without any of the angst associated with other Expressionists, and although his colour was bright it was never strident; often he showed people enjoying themselves. In 1909–10 he met *Kandinsky and Franz *Marc in Munich and in 1911 he joined them in forming the *Blaue Reiter, but apart from a few experiments his work moved less towards abstraction than that of other members of the group. Early in 1914 he made a trip with Paul *Klee and Louis *Moilliet to Tunisia, and the watercolours he did there are considered his finest achievements. He volunteered for the army soon after the outbreak of the First World War and was killed in action a few weeks later. Max *Ernst (a great admirer, even though their work was very different stylistically) described him as 'a subtle poet, the very image of just and intelligent enthusiasm, generosity, judgement and exuberance'.

Mackennal, Sir Bertram. See NEW SCULPTURE.

Mackintosh, Charles Rennie (b Glasgow, 7 June 1868; d London, 10 Dec. 1928). Scottish architect, designer (chiefly of furniture), and watercolourist, active mainly in Glasgow. He was one of the most original and influential artists of his time and a major figure of *Art Nouveau. His most famous building is *Glasgow School of Art (1897–9), to which he later added a library block and other extensions (1907–9). They are strikingly original in style—clear, bold, and rational, yet with an element of fantasy. In his interior decoration and furniture design, often done in association with his wife **Margaret Macdonald** (1865–1933), he worked in a sophisticated calligraphic style but avoided the exaggerated floral ornament often associated with Art Nouveau. He had an enormous reputation among the avant-garde on the Continent, especially in Germany and Austria, where the

advanced style of the early 20th century was sometimes known as 'Mackintoshismus', but admiration was more restrained in his own country, where he antagonized fellow architects by criticizing traditional values. The First World War brought a decline in his career, for there was little call for work as sophisticated as his. In 1914 he moved to London and thereafter virtually gave up architecture. He did, however, do some fine work as a designer, particularly of fabrics. From 1923 to 1927 he lived at Port Vendres in the south of France, where he devoted himself to watercolour painting, mainly landscapes. By the time of his death his reputation had declined, but it now stands very high in all the fields of his activity.

Maclise, Daniel (bapt. Cork, 2 Feb. [b ?25 Jan.] 1806; d London, 25 Apr. 1870). Irish painter and caricaturist, active in London from 1827. An outstanding draughtsman, Maclise became the leading British history painter of his period, his most prestigious commissions being two enormous murals in the House of Lords on the *Meeting of Wellington and Blücher at Waterloo* (completed 1861) and the *Death of Nelson at Trafalgar* (completed 1865). They were done in the *water-glass technique and are poorly preserved (a sketch for the *Nelson* in the Walker Art Gallery in Liverpool gives an idea of the original colouring), but they are powerful works—fully coherent in spite of the huge numbers of figures involved—and they remain the most stirring examples of his heroic powers of design. Maclise was handsome, charming, and popular with fellow artists, and *Frith wrote that he was spoken of in academic circles as 'out and away the greatest artist that ever lived'. Grandiose history painting was only one side to his talent, however, for he also excelled as a caricaturist, and is particularly noted for a series of character portraits of literary men and women he contributed to *Fraser's Magazine* in the 1830s. There are examples of his conventional portraits in the National Portrait Gallery, London, including one of his friend Charles Dickens (1839).

MacMonnies, Frederick (b New York, 28 Sept. 1863; d New York, 22 Mar. 1937). American sculptor, a pupil of *Saint-Gaudens. From 1884 to the outbreak of the First World War he worked mainly in Paris, but he sent work back to the USA and became one of the leading American sculptors of public monuments in his generation. His most notable works include a statue of Shakespeare (1895) and a set of bronze doors representing the Art of Printing (c.1898) for the Library of Congress in Washington, and the fountain figures *Truth* and *Inspiration* (1913) for the New York Public Library. He worked in a traditional style but sometimes caused controversy because of the alleged indecency of his nudes. After he returned to the USA in 1915 he took up portrait painting. By the end of his career the 'bright young sculptor of the 1890s' had become 'the quintessential academic, and the modern movements of the early 20th century took place without his notice' (Matthew Baigell, *Dictionary of American Art*, 1979).

McQueen, Steve. See TURNER PRIZE.

McTaggart, William (*b* Aros croft, Laggan of Kintyre, Argyllshire, 25 Oct. 1835; *d* Broomieknowe, nr. Edinburgh, 2 Apr. 1910). The leading Scottish landscape painter of his period. He has been called 'the Scottish *Impressionist', but although he was much concerned with light and atmosphere, the sense of the drama of nature in his work brings him closer in spirit to *Constable. His brushwork was free and fervent and he often depicted rough seas and scudding clouds. He was an influential figure, his followers including his grandson **Sir William MacTaggart** (1903–81).

Maddox, Conroy. See SURREALISM.

Maderno, Stefano (*b* ?Rome, *c*.1576; *d* Rome, 17 Sept. 1636). Italian sculptor. He was one of the leading sculptors in Rome during the papacy of Paul V (1605–21) before *Bernini came into the ascendancy, working on statues and reliefs in numerous churches, notably the chapel that the pope had built (the Cappella Paolina, begun 1605) in S. Maria Maggiore. One of his sculptures has attained lasting fame: the recumbent figure of St Cecilia (1600) in S. Cecilia in Trastevere, a lyrical and poignant work that is said to show the body of the Early Christian martyr in the exact position in which it was discovered in the church in 1599.

Madrazo, José (*b* Santander, 22 Apr. 1781; *d* Madrid, 8 May 1859). Spanish painter, the best-known member of a dynasty of artists. He studied with J.-L. *David in Paris and also worked in Rome, and he became the leading *Neoclassical painter in Spain. His history paintings are generally rather cold, but he was a spirited portraitist. He was director of the *Prado from 1838 to 1851. His son **Federico** (1815–94) was the foremost Spanish portraitist of the time and a leading figure in the art establishment, holding various prestigious posts, including the directorship of

the Prado. Three other sons were involved with the arts: **Pedro** (1816–98) was an art historian and critic, **Luis** (1825–97) a painter, and **Juan** (*c*.1829–80) an architect. Other members of the family continued the tradition into the 20th century.

Maes, Nicolaes (*b* Dordrecht, Jan. 1634; *bur.* Amsterdam, 24 Dec. 1693). Dutch painter. In about 1648 he became a pupil of *Rembrandt in Amsterdam, staying there until 1653, when he returned to his native Dordrecht. In his early years he concentrated on *genre pictures, rather sentimental in approach, but distinguished by deep glowing colours he had learnt from his master. Old women sleeping, praying, or reading the Bible were favourite subjects. In the later 1650s, however, Maes began to turn more to portraiture, and from about 1660 he worked exclusively in this field. His style changed too, becoming closer to van *Dyck than to Rembrandt. He abandoned the reddish tone of his earlier manner for a wider, lighter, and cooler range (greys and blacks in the shadows instead of brownish tones). In 1673 he settled in Amsterdam and had great success with this kind of picture. He was a fairly prolific artist and is well represented in, for example, the National Gallery, London, and the museum at Dordrecht.

Maestà. Term (Italian: 'majesty') used to describe a representation of the Virgin and Child in which the Virgin is enthroned as Queen of Heaven, often surrounded by a court of saints and angels. The most famous example is by *Duccio.

Mafai, Mario. See SCIPIONE.

Maffei, Francesco (*b* Vicenza, *c*.1605; *d* Padua, 2 July 1660). Italian painter, active for much of his career in Venice. He had a refreshingly individualistic style, carrying on the great painterly tradition of *Tintoretto and *Bassano, reinforced by the example of *Liss, *Feti, and *Strozzi, to which he added his own note of mysterious and sometimes bizarre fantasy. He painted religious and mythological scenes and also allegorical portraits of local officials.

Magic(al) Realism. Term coined by the German critic Franz Roh in 1925 to describe the aspect of *Neue Sachlichkeit characterized by sharp-focus detail. In the book in which he originated the term—*Nach-Expressionismus, Magischer Realismus, Probleme der neuesten Europäischen Malerie* (1925)—Roh also included a rather mixed bag of non-German painters as 'Magic Realists', among them *Miró and

*Picasso. Subsequently critics have used the term to cover various types of painting in which objects are depicted with photographic naturalism but which because of paradoxical elements or strange juxtapositions convey a feeling of unreality, infusing the ordinary with a sense of mystery. The paintings of *Magritte are a prime example. In the English-speaking world the term gained currency with an exhibition entitled 'American Realists and Magic Realists' at the Museum of Modern Art, New York, in 1943. The director of the museum, Alfred H. *Barr, wrote that the term was 'sometimes applied to the work of painters who by means of an exact realistic technique try to make plausible and convincing their improbable, dreamlike or fantastic visions'.

The term has been adopted in the field of literary criticism to describe 'a kind of modern fiction in which fabulous and fantastical events are included in a narrative that otherwise maintains the "reliable" tone of objective realistic report' (*Concise Oxford Dictionary of Literary Terms*, 1990).

Magnasco, Alessandro (b Genoa, 4 Feb. 1667; d Genoa, 12 Mar. 1749). Italian painter, known as Lissandrino (little Alessandro) on account of his small stature. Although he was born and died in Genoa, he spent most of his working life in Milan. At the beginning of his career he was a portraitist, but virtually nothing is known of this aspect of his career. Later he turned to the type of work for which he is now known—highly individual melodramatic scenes set in storm-tossed landscapes, ruins, convents, and gloomy monasteries, peopled with small, elongated figures of monks, nuns, gypsies, mercenaries, witches, beggars, and inquisitors. His brushwork is nervous and flickering and his lighting effects macabre. He was prolific and his work is rarely dated or datable. Marco *Ricci and Francesco *Guardi were among the artists influenced by him.

Magnelli, Alberto (b Florence, 1 July 1888; d Meudon, nr. Paris, 20 Apr. 1971). Italian painter, active mainly in Paris, where he settled in 1931. In his early work he moved from a naturalistic style to one influenced by *Futurism and then *Cubism. After the First World War his style became more representational under the influence of *Metaphysical Painting. In the late 1930s he turned to pure abstraction, his work characteristically making use of a dynamic interplay of hard-edged shapes. An exhibition at the Galerie René Drouin, Paris, in 1947 established his repu-

tation and from the 1950s he was much honoured and recognized as one of Italy's leading abstract artists.

Magritte, René (b Lessines, 21 Nov. 1898; d Brussels, 15 Aug. 1967). Belgian painter, one of the leading exponents of *Surrealism. After initially working in a *Cubist-Futurist style, he turned to Surrealism in 1925 under the influence of de *Chirico and by the following year had already emerged as a highly individual artist with *The Menaced Assassin* (MoMA, New York), a picture that displays the startling and disturbing juxtapositions of the ordinary, the strange, and the erotic that were to characterize his work for the rest of his life. In 1927–30 he lived near Paris, participating in Surrealist affairs, but like many others in the movement he fell out with André *Breton, and he spent almost all of the rest of his life working in Brussels, where he lived a life of bourgeois regularity (the bowler-hatted figure who often features in his work is to some extent a self-portrait).

Apart from a period in the 1940s when he experimented first with pseudo-*Impressionist brushwork and then with a *Fauve technique, Magritte worked in a precise, scrupulously banal manner (a reminder of the early days when he made his living working in a wallpaper factory) and he always remained true to Surrealism. He had a repertory of obsessive images that appeared again and again in ordinary but incongruous surroundings. Enormous rocks that float in the air and fishes with human legs are typical leitmotivs. He repeatedly exploited ambiguities concerning real objects and images of them (many of his works feature paintings within paintings), inside and out of doors, day and night. In a number of paintings, for example, he depicted a night scene, or a city street lit only by artificial light, below a clear sunlit sky. He also made Surrealist analogues of a number of famous paintings—for example *David's *Mme Récamier* and *Manet's *The Balcony*, in which he replaced the figures with coffins. Late in life he also made wax sculptures based on such paintings, and some of them were cast in bronze after his death (*Mme Récamier*, Pompidou Centre, Paris). He also made prints and a few short comic films, using his friends as actors.

Magritte's work was included in many Surrealist exhibitions, but it was not until he was in his fifties that he began to achieve international success and honours. By the time of his death his work had had a powerful influence on

*Pop art, and it has subsequently been widely imitated in advertising. In the fertility of his imagery, the unforced spontaneity of his effects, and not least his rare gift of humour, he was one of the very few natural and inspired Surrealist painters. J. T. Soby (*René Magritte*, 1965) summed this up felicitously when he wrote: 'In viewing Magritte's paintings . . . everything seems proper. And then abruptly the rape of commonsense occurs, usually in broad daylight.'

mahlstick. See MAULSTICK.

Mahon, Sir Denis (*b* London, 8 Nov. 1910). British art historian and collector. A private scholar with private means, he has devoted himself to the study of 17th-century Italian (particularly Bolognese) painting, and has not only built up a choice collection in this field, but also played a greater part than anyone else in the rehabilitation of such once-scorned artists as the *Carracci, *Guercino, and *Reni. He is also a leading *Poussin scholar. His publications include *Studies in Seicento Art and Theory* (1947), a brilliant pioneering work, and catalogues of Carracci drawings (1956) and Guercino paintings (1968) and drawings (1969) for major exhibitions of their work in Bologna.

Maiano, Benedetto da (*b* Maiano, *c*.1442; *d* Florence, 24 May 1497). One of the leading Florentine sculptors of his generation, a member of a family of artists from Maiano, near Florence, a village renowned for its quarries. He often worked with his brothers **Giuliano** (*c*.1432–90), who was primarily an architect, and **Giovanni I** (*c*.1439–78), and he also sometimes collaborated with the painter Domenico *Ghirlandaio, whose essentially conservative outlook and high standards of craftsmanship were similar to his own. Nothing is documented of Benedetto's training. He is first recorded as a woodcarver, in 1467, and he continued working in wood throughout his career, but his most important works are in marble and he perhaps learnt his skills with this material from Antonio *Rossellino. His masterpiece is the pulpit in S. Croce, Florence (*c*.1475–80), which features five relief panels on the life of St Francis (terracotta models for three of the panels are in the V&A, London). The pulpit was commissioned by the Florentine merchant Pietro Mellini, of whom Benedetto carved a portrait bust (1474, Bargello, Florence). He also produced a bust of the banker Filippo Strozzi (1475, Louvre, Paris); the terracotta model for this is in the Skulpturengalerie, Berlin, and this is the only instance of a 15th-century portrait bust in which both model and finished marble survive.

Benedetto's son **Giovanni II** (*c*.1487–*c*.1542) was also a sculptor. From about 1520 to about 1536 he worked in England (possibly recruited by *Torrigiano) and he helped to introduce *Renaissance influence to the country. His most important documented works in this respect are eight terracotta roundels of Roman emperors (1521) made for Cardinal Wolsey for the external decoration of his palace at Hampton Court (*in situ*). The superb wooden screen (*c*.1533–6) at King's College Chapel, Cambridge, has been attributed to him.

Maillol, Aristide (*b* Banyuls-sur-Mer, 8 Dec. 1861; *d* Banyuls-sur-Mer, 24 Sept. 1944). French sculptor, painter, illustrator, and tapestry designer. His early career was spent mainly as a tapestry designer, but he also painted, exhibiting with the *Nabis. Although he first made sculpture in 1895, it was only in 1900 that he decided to devote himself to it after serious eyestrain made him give up tapestry. In 1902 he had his first one-man exhibition, which drew praise from *Rodin; in 1905 came his first conspicuous public success at the *Salon d'Automne; and after about 1910 he was internationally famous and received a constant flow of commissions. With only a few exceptions, he restricted himself to the female nude, expressing his whole philosophy of form through this medium. Commissioned in 1905 to make a monument to the 19th-century revolutionary Louis-Auguste Blanqui, and asked by the committee what form he proposed to give it, he replied: 'Eh! une femme nue.' More than any other artist before him he brought to conscious realization the concept of sculpture in the round as an independent art form stripped of literary associations and architectural context, and in this sense he forms a transition between Rodin and the following generation of modernist sculptors. However, he rejected Rodin's emotionalism and animated surfaces; instead, Maillol's weighty figures, often shown in repose, are solemn and broadly modelled, with simple poses and gestures. His work consciously continued the classical tradition of Greek and Roman sculpture (Maillol visited Greece in 1908), but at the same time has a quality of healthy sensuousness (his peasant wife sometimes modelled for him). Maillol took up painting again in 1939 when he returned to his birthplace, Banyuls, but apart from his sculpture the most important works of his maturity are his book illustrations. His finest achievements in this field are the woodcut illustrations (which he cut himself) for an edition of Virgil's *Eclogues* (begun 1912 but not published until 1926), which show superb economy of line. A museum dedicated to Maillol opened in Paris in 1995 and his work can also be seen in many important collections of modern art.

Mainardi, Sebastiano (*b* San Gimignano, 23 Sept. 1466; *d* ?Florence, Sept. 1513). Florentine painter, a pupil or assistant of Domenico *Ghirlandaio, whose half-sister he married in 1494, a few months after Domenico's death. His name has often been indiscriminately attached to school pieces from the Ghirlandaio workshop (with which he continued his association after Domenico's death), but little is known for certain of his work.

Maitani, Lorenzo (*b* Siena, *c*.1270; *d* Orvieto, June 1330). Sienese architect, perhaps also active as a sculptor. From 1310 until his death he was master of the works at Orvieto Cathedral and is presumed to be the designer of the west façade—one of the most impressive examples of Italian *Gothic architecture. The rich sculptural decoration of the façade has also been attributed to Maitani, but the extent of his involvement is conjectural (there is no conclusive evidence that he worked as a sculptor).

Makart, Hans (*b* Salzburg, 28 May 1840; *d* Vienna, 3 Oct. 1884). Austrian painter. He studied under *Piloty in Munich and from 1869 worked in Vienna, where he was enormously successful and became a leading society figure. His pictures, often vast in size, were characteristically of mythological, historical, and allegorical subjects, treated in the manner of grand opera or Hollywood epics in an exuberant, somewhat *Rubensian style. They were produced in a huge studio that was one of the sights of Vienna (Makart liked to paint in front of visitors). His work had great influence in Austria and Germany, notably on the early work of *Klimt, but his reputation soon declined after his death.

Malatesta, Sigismondo (*b* Rimini, 1417; *d* Rimini, 9 Oct. 1468). Italian nobleman, ruler of Rimini from 1432 until his death. A brilliant and totally unscrupulous *condottiere*, he is the archetype of the megalomaniac, paganizing tyrant once thought to be characteristic of the Italian *Renaissance. His contemporaries accused him of incest, murder, and rape, amongst other crimes, and he was publicly consigned to hell while still alive—the only man ever to suffer this fate—by Pope Pius II. However, he was also a noted patron of art and scholarship. In particular, his name is indissolubly linked to one of the most remarkable artistic projects of the 15th century—the conversion (begun 1447) of the church of S. Francesco in Rimini into a memorial to himself and his mistress (later wife) Isotta degli Atti. *Alberti was responsible for the exterior cladding of the building in a noble classical style and *Agostino di Duccio and *Piero della Francesca were among the artists who worked on the decoration of the interior. The scheme was never completed, but under Sigismondo's direct inspiration it became the most self-conscious return to the *antique yet seen, and even in its unfinished state it is one of the gems of Renaissance art. Much of the sculpted ornament makes allusion to classical literature and philosophy, prompting Pius II's remark that the church was 'so full of pagan images that it seems like a temple for the worshippers of demons and not for Christians'. However, it was not until the 18th century that the building was dubbed the Tempio Malatestiano—the name by which it is still known.

Mâle, Émile (*b* Commentry, 2 Jun. 1862; *d* Chaalis, Oise, 6 Oct. 1954). French art historian. A pioneer in the study of French medieval art, he became professor of the history of art at the Sorbonne in 1912. His best-known book is probably *L'Art religieux du XIIIe siècle en France* (1902), translated into English as *The Gothic Image* (1913). His work is distinguished not only by great learning but also by literary merit, his style being praised by Marcel Proust amongst others.

Malevich, Kasimir (*b* nr. Kiev, 11 [23] Feb. 1878; *d* Leningrad, 15 May 1935). Russian painter, designer, and writer, with *Mondrian the most important pioneer of geometric *abstract art. He began working in an unexceptional *Post-Impressionist manner, but by 1912 he was painting peasant subjects in a massive 'tubular' style similar to that of *Léger, as well as pictures combining the fragmentation of form of *Cubism with the multiplication of the image of *Futurism (*The Knife Grinder*, 1912, Yale Univ. AG). Malevich, however, was dissatisfied with representational art or—as he put it—fired with the desire 'to free art from the burden of the object'. He was a devout Christian, with mystical leanings, and he thought that by abandoning the need to depict the external world he could break through to a deeper level of meaning and 'swim in the white free abyss' (he often used the analogy of flight and space when discussing his paintings). His first abstract work was a backdrop for the Futurist opera *Victory over the Sun*, produced in the Luna Park Theatre, St Petersburg, in December 1913; his original drawing (now in the Theatrical Museum, St Petersburg) shows a rectangle divided almost diagonally into a black upper segment and a white lower one. He claimed that he made a picture 'consisting of nothing more than a black square on a white field' as early as 1913, but Suprematist paintings were first made public in Moscow in 1915 (there is often difficulty in dating his work and also in knowing which way up his paintings should be hung, photographs of early exhibitions sometimes providing conflicting evidence).

Over the next few years Malevich moved away from absolute austerity, tilting rectangles from the vertical, adding more colours, and introducing a suggestion of the third dimension by overlapping forms (*Suprematist Composition*, *c*.1915, Stedelijk Mus., Amsterdam); there is sometimes even a degree of painterly handling (*Yellow Parallelogram on White*, *c*.1917, Stedelijk Museum). However, around 1918 he returned to his purest ideals with a series of *White on White* paintings, in which a tilted white square is placed on a background of the same colour, the difference between them being visible only through variations in the brushwork (*Suprematist Composition: White on White*, *c*.1918, MoMA, New York). After this he seems to have realized he could go no further along this road and virtually gave up abstract painting, turning more to teaching, writing, and making three-dimensional models that were important in the growth of *Constructivism. In 1919, at the invitation of *Chagall, he started teaching at the art school at Vitebsk, where he exerted a profound influence on *Lissitzky, and in 1922 he moved to Petrograd (Leningrad), where he lived for the rest of his life. He went to Warsaw and Berlin in 1927, accompanying an exhibition of his works, and during this trip he visited the *Bauhaus. In the late 1920s he returned to figurative painting, but he was out of favour with a political system that now demanded *Socialist Realism from its artists and he ran into trouble with the authorities. However, he remained a revered figure among artists and after his death he lay in state at the Leningrad Artists' Union in a coffin—which he had designed himself—bearing Suprematist designs.

Malevich wrote various theoretical tracts (several collections of his writings have been published) and his influence was spread through these as well as his paintings. In *Cubism and Abstract Art* (1936) Alfred H. *Barr gave the following assessment of his significance: 'In the history of abstract art Malevich is a figure of fundamental importance. As a pioneer, a theorist and an artist he influenced not only a large following in Russia but also, through Lissitzky and *Moholy-Nagy, the course of abstract art in Central Europe. He stands at the heart of the movement which swept westward from Russia after the war and, mingling with the Dutch De *Stijl group, transformed the architecture, furniture, typography and commercial art of Germany and much of the rest of Europe.'

Malouel, Jean (*b* ?Nijmegen, ?*c*.1360; *d* Dijon, 12 Mar. 1415). Netherlandish painter, the uncle of the *Limbourg brothers. From 1397 he was court painter to Philip the Bold, Duke of *Burgundy, and his successor John the Fearless. No documented works by him survive, but he has been proposed as the author of several paintings, including a *tondo of the *Trinity* in the Louvre, Paris. It has all the refinement of French court art combined with a strength of modelling and a realistic naturalism derived from Flanders. See also BELLECHOSE.

Malraux, André (*b* Paris, 3 Nov. 1901; *d* Créteil, nr. Paris, 23 Nov. 1976). French writer and statesman. From 1959 until his retirement in 1969 he served as France's minister of culture (in this role he initiated a programme of cleaning the great buildings and monuments of Paris and commissioned ceiling decorations for the Paris Opéra from Marc *Chagall, 1963–4). Before the Second World War he had written several novels, but his post-war books were devoted mainly to art, in a philosophical—at times metaphysical—vein. His writings reflect the broadening of aesthetic outlooks in the 20th century, when for the first time it was possible to have some familiarity with the art of the whole world throughout the entire course of human history. He thought that art should be appraised entirely by aesthetic standards, expressing this notion in his now famous concept of the 'museum without walls', in which all works of art—whatever their origin—are available to be appreciated for their formal qualities, independently of whatever they originally signified (the phrase comes from the title of one of his books, *Le Musée imaginaire* (1946), translated as *Museum without Walls* (1949)).

Malton, Thomas. See TURNER, J. M. W.

Malvasia, Count Carlo (*b* Bologna, 18 Dec. 1616; *d* Bologna, 9 Mar. 1693). Italian writer and antiquarian. His major work, *Felsina pittrice: vite* *dei pittori bolognesi* (1678), is the most important source for knowledge of the great period of the Bolognese School that began with the *Carracci (Felsina was the Etruscan name for Bologna). It contains a particularly revealing biography of his friend *Reni. Malvasia also wrote a guide to the paintings of Bologna (*Le pitture di Bologna*, 1686), one of the first books of its kind.

Mancini, Antonio. See BOLDINI.

Mander, Karel van (*b* Meulebeke, nr. Courtrai, 1548; *d* Amsterdam, 11 Sept. 1606). Netherlandish painter and writer on art, active mainly in Haarlem. He is sometimes known as the 'Dutch *Vasari', for his fame rests primarily on his work as a biographer of artists, published in *Het schilder-boeck* (The Book of Painters) in 1604. The most important part of the book is made up of about 175 biographies of Netherlandish and German artists from the van *Eycks to van Mander's own younger contemporaries. This is the first systematic account of the lives of northern European artists, and our only source of information about some of them. The book also contains the lives of Italian artists from *Cimabue up to his own time. Most of this material is a condensed translation into Dutch of Vasari, but it also has valuable information collected by van Mander himself when he was in Italy in 1573–7 or from friends and correspondents; he is sufficiently up to date to mention *Caravaggio, 'who is doing extraordinary things in Rome'. Another part of the book is a long poem that gives practical advice to artists and sums up much of the theory and practice of 16th-century Netherlandish art. About 30 of van Mander's own pictures survive; they are mainly of religious and allegorical subjects, characterized by elongated *Mannerist forms. With *Cornelis van Haarlem and Hendrick *Goltzius, he is said to have founded an academy in Haarlem. Frans *Hals was probably his pupil.

mandorla (Italian: 'almond') (also called **aureole** or **vesica piscis** (Latin: 'fish's bladder')). An oval or almond-shaped aura (sometimes consisting of a series of radiating lines) enclosing or emanating from the body of a figure to indicate divinity or holiness. The device often appears in medieval and early *Renaissance art, but then fell into disuse as more naturalistic ideals prevailed. It is most commonly found in portrayals of Christ, particularly in post-Resurrection scenes (but also notably in representations of the Transfiguration) when he is seen in his heavenly glory. The Virgin Mary, too, is often shown with a mandorla and she and Christ sometimes share one.

Mánes, Josef (*b* Prague, 12 Apr. 1820; *d* Prague, 9 Dec. 1871). Czech painter, illustrator, and designer, the most illustrious member of a family of artists. An ardent patriot at a time when his country, part of the Austro-Hungarian Empire, was struggling for autonomy, he is regarded as the founder of Czech national painting. Much of his work reflects his study of his country's landscape, costumes, and peasant life, notably his series of twelve paintings of the Months (1865–6) for the clock of Prague's Old Town Hall (replaced by copies; the originals are now in the City Museum). He was also a prolific portraitist. His work was an inspiration to many of his countrymen, notably Mikuláš Aleš (1852–1913), the most prolific Czech decorative painter of his time, and his name was honoured in the Mánes Union of Artists, founded in Prague in 1887. An association somewhat analogous to the *Salon d'Automne in Paris, it was largely responsible for introducing progressive trends to Czech art in the early years of the 20th century.

Manessier, Alfred (*b* Saint-Ouen, 5 Dec. 1911; *d* Orléans, 1 Aug. 1993). French painter, lithographer, and designer of tapestries and stained glass, a pupil of *Bissière. During the 1930s his work was influenced by *Cubism and *Surrealism, but after staying at a Trappist monastery in 1943 he became deeply committed to religion and turned to expressing spiritual meaning through abstract art. Characteristically his paintings feature rich colours within a loose linear grid, creating an effect reminiscent of stained glass (a medium in which he did some of his best work). After the Second World War he came to be regarded as one of the leading exponents of expressive abstraction in the *École de Paris and won numerous awards, notably the main painting prize at the 1962 Venice *Biennale. He died as a result of a car crash.

Manet, Édouard (*b* Paris, 23 Jan. 1832; *d* Paris, 30 Apr. 1883). French painter and printmaker, one of the giants of 19th-century art. He was the son of a senior civil servant in the Ministry of Justice and inherited considerable wealth when his father (who disapproved of his choice of career) died in 1862. His upper middle-class background was important, for although he was seen as an artistic rebel, he always sought traditional honours and success and he cut an impeccable figure as a man about town. He trained under *Couture, 1850–6, but his own style was based mainly on a study of the Old Masters at the *Louvre, and particularly Spanish painters such as *Velázquez (his greatest artistic hero) and *Ribera. During the 1850s he visited museums in the Netherlands, Germany, Austria, and Italy and it is one of the ironies of Manet's career that a painter with such reverence for the art of the past should be so much attacked for his modernity. His initial taste of official disfavour came when his first submission to the *Salon—*The Absinthe Drinker* (1859, Ny Carlsberg Glyptothek, Copenhagen)—was rejected. He had two paintings accepted in 1861, but then in 1863 his *Déjeuner sur l'herbe* (Mus. d'Orsay, Paris) caused a scandal. It was turned down by the Salon and was shown instead at the *Salon des Refusés, set up specially for such rejected paintings. Its hostile reception was based on moral as well as aesthetic grounds, for nudity was considered acceptable only if it was sufficiently remote in time or place and this showed a naked woman having a picnic with two contemporary, clothed men.

Manet caused even greater outrage two years later when his *Olympia* (Mus. d'Orsay, 1863) was exhibited at the Salon. The reclining nude figure was based on *Titian's *Venus of Urbino* (which Manet had copied in Florence ten years earlier), but her blatant sexuality was thought an affront to accepted standards of decorum, and one critic wrote, 'Art sunk so low does not even deserve reproach.' Manet was denounced also for his bold technique, in which he eliminated the fine tonal gradations of academic practice and created vivid contrasts of light and shade: 'The shadows are indicated by more or less large smears of blacking', wrote another critic, 'The least beautiful woman has bones, muscles, skin, and some sort of colour. Here there is nothing, we are sorry to say, but the desire to attract attention at any price.' From this time, Manet reluctantly found himself acquiring a reputation as a leader of the avant-garde, and in particular was respected and admired by the *Impressionists. However, he always stood somewhat aloof from them (although he enjoyed going to the races with *Degas, who was also from the upper middle class) and did not participate in their exhibitions. He did, however, adopt the Impressionist technique of painting out of doors (encouraged by Berthe *Morisot, who became his sister-in-law in 1874), and his work became freer and lighter in the 1870s under their influence.

In the late 1870s Manet became ill with a disease diagnosed as locomotor ataxia (associated with the late stages of syphilis), which caused him bouts of great pain and extreme tiredness. Increasingly he preferred to work in pastels, which were less physically demanding than oils, but his last great painting, *A Bar at the Folies-Bergère* (1882, Courtauld Gal., London), is unsurpassed in 19th-century art for sheer beauty of technique. He died in appalling pain a week after having a gangrenous leg amputated. The official honours he had craved—in the form of a second-class medal at the Salon and membership of the Legion of Honour—came too late (1881) to be enjoyed.

Manet was a complex and many-sided artist. He painted a great variety of subjects (he was also a skilled etcher and lithographer) and rarely repeated himself. His approach was completely undogmatic and he was reluctant to theorize; his friend Émile *Zola wrote of him: 'In beginning a picture, he could never say how it would come out.' His work often has a feeling of complete freshness and spontaneity, yet he would often repaint and rework pictures or even cut them into fragments. His greatest strength was with modern-life subjects (he sketched constantly in the boulevards and cafés of Paris), but although he is accused by some critics of having no imagination, of being able to paint something only if he had it in front of him, his pictures are far from being straight transcriptions of nature. They are, indeed, sometimes enigmatic and elusive, as with *A Bar at the Folies-Bergère*, and seem to be more concerned with the act of painting than with the ostensible subject. It is partly in this freedom from the traditional literary, anecdotal, or moralistic associations of painting that he is seen as one of the founders of 'modern' art, and it is significant that the official title of the first *Post-Impressionist Exhibition, organized by Roger *Fry in 1910–11, was 'Manet and the Post-Impressionists'.

Manfredi, Bartolommeo (*bapt.* Ostiano, nr. Mantua, 25 Aug. 1582; *d* Rome, 12 Dec. 1622). Italian painter, active mainly in Rome, where he was one of *Caravaggio's leading followers. It is not known when he settled in Rome (his life is poorly documented), but it was probably not later than about 1605 and he could well have been personally acquainted with the master (who left the city in 1606). Most of Manfredi's work was on religious subjects, but he is particularly important for his low-life scenes of drinkers, card-players, fortune-tellers, etc., for it was he rather than Caravaggio himself who was mainly responsible for popularizing this kind of work, especially among painters from France and the

Netherlands who visited or settled in Italy (*Tournier and *Valentin, for example). None of Manfredi's paintings are signed, dated, or documented, and several of the 40 or so works that are now given to him were formerly attributed to Caravaggio, for example *Mars Punishing Cupid* (c.1607, Art Inst. of Chicago).

manière criblée (French: 'sieved manner') (or **dotted manner**). A technique used in some *metal cuts, in which dots were stamped with a punch over selected parts of the plate to create a textured effect in those areas, the dots showing as white against the inked background. The technique was uncommon after the end of the 15th century, but there was something of a revival in the late 18th century.

Mannerism. Term used in the study of the visual arts (and by transference in the study of literature and music) with a confusing variety of critical and historical meanings. Even more than with most stylistic labels, there is little agreement amongst scholars as to its delimitations, and John Shearman begins his book on the subject (*Mannerism*, 1967) with the frank admission: 'This book will have at least one feature in common with all those already published on Mannerism; it will appear to describe something quite different from what all the rest describe.'

The word derives from the Italian *maniera*, meaning 'style' or 'stylishness', and it was popularized mainly by the writings of *Vasari, who used it as a term of praise, signifying qualities of grace, poise, facility, and sophistication—characteristics that are indeed apparent in much of the art that he admired from his own time—the mid-16th century. From the 17th century, however, most critics thought that Italian art of Vasari's period marked a decline from the peaks of grandeur and harmony reached during the High *Renaissance. Faced with such unsurpassable models as *Leonardo, *Michelangelo, and *Raphael, their unfortunate successors were deemed to have been reduced to artistic inbreeding, feebly plagiarizing and distorting the work of the masters. From being a stylistic label the term expanded its meaning to become a period designation, so that 'Mannerism' came to indicate the era in Italian art between the High Renaissance and the *Baroque—that is, from about 1520 to about 1600. The term is still applied mainly to Italian art and architecture, but it is also used of art in other countries.

It was not until the 20th century—and particularly the period between the two world wars—that a more sympathetic attitude towards Mannerist art emerged, and the word began to be used neutrally, without the implication of decadence that it had long carried. At this time, after the revolutionary achievements of early 20th-century art, Mannerist art was looked at with new eyes, and the work of artists who had long been ignored or disparaged began to seem exciting and original to modern taste. The qualities associated with Mannerist art include tension, emotionalism, elongation of the human figure, strained poses, unusual or bizarre effects of scale, lighting, or perspective, and vivid—sometimes harsh or lurid—colours. Often the subject is approached in an unconventional way, with the artist drawing attention to his own learning or virtuosity. In the hands of the greatest Mannerist artists (for example *Pontormo or *Parmigianino) such preoccupations led to works that are not only highly sophisticated, but also powerful, disturbing, and moving. The work of less accomplished Mannerists (for example Vasari as a painter) often degenerated, however, into insipid or frenzied gesturing and grimacing.

With Mannerism no longer receiving blanket condemnation, more subtle issues occupied the minds of historians, for example to what extent the term could be applied to art outside Italy (e.g. El *Greco in Spain, the École de *Fontainebleau in France, and *Hilliard in England) or to architecture (where what might be taken in one context as playful or capricious disregard for the rules of classical architecture might in another be regarded as provincial clumsiness). While some critics wish to expand the use of the term, others wish to contract it, and still others seek to distinguish what they regard as the central elements of the style within the general period label by using the term '*maniera*'. The following sentence from S. J. Freedberg's book *Painting in Italy: 1500–1600* (1971) in the Pelican History of Art series shows how potentially bewildering the terminology can be: 'The first generation of Mannerism, its inventors, thus could achieve *maniera*, but this requires to be distinguished not only chronologically but in degree and in some respects of kind from the "high Maniera" or Maniera proper.' Thus while the term 'Mannerism' can generally be taken to imply an elegant, refined, artificial, self-conscious, and courtly style, the shade of meaning to be attached to it varies very much according to the context and the outlook of the writer using it.

Man Ray (*b* Philadelphia, 27 Aug. 1890; *d* Paris, 18 Nov. 1976). American painter, photographer, draughtsman, sculptor, and film-maker, active for much of his career in France. He was born Emmanuel Radinsky, but he was known only as Man Ray from about the age of 15 because other youngsters jeered at his foreign-sounding name. After seeing the *Armory Show in 1913 he began painting in a *Cubist style. In 1915 he began a lifelong friendship with Marcel *Duchamp, and these two together with *Picabia were the mainstays of the New York *Dada movement. He also collaborated with Duchamp and Katherine *Dreier in forming the *Société Anonyme in 1920. In 1921 he settled in Paris, where he continued his Dada activities and then became a member of the *Surrealist movement. For several years he earned his living mainly as a fashion and portrait photographer, but he painted regularly again from the mid-1930s. In 1940 he went back to America to escape the Nazi occupation of Paris and settled in Hollywood, then in 1951 returned permanently to Paris.

From the 1940s photography took a secondary place in Man Ray's activities, but it is as a photographer that his reputation is now most secure. In the 1920s and 1930s he was one of the most imaginative artists in this field, particularly for his exploitation of the 'Rayograph' (also known as photogram), a photograph produced without a camera by placing objects directly on sensitized paper and exposing them to light, and for his development of the technique of 'solarization' (the complete or partial reversal of the tones of a photographic image). The glamorous women who appear in his photographs include Meret *Oppenheim, the model Kiki of Montparnasse (Marie Prin, 1901–53), with whom he lived for several years, and his assistant Lee Miller, who herself became a distinguished photographer and later married Roland *Penrose. In addition to his celebrity as a photographer, he gained an international reputation as one of the most prominent figures of Dada and Surrealism. Several of his *objects have become icons of the movements, notably *Gift* (1921), consisting of a flat iron with a row of nails sticking out of its smooth face (the original is no longer extant; a reconstruction is in the Museum of Modern Art, New York).

Manship, Paul (*b* St Paul, Minn., 25 Dec. 1885; *d* New York, 31 Jan. 1966). American sculptor, active mainly in New York. He worked in an elegant, streamlined style, his beautifully crafted figures characterized by clarity of outline and suave generalized forms, and he achieved great success as a sculptor of public monuments. One of his best-known works is the gilded bronze *Prometheus* (1933) in Rockefeller Center Plaza, New York. Manship was also an excellent portraitist. Because of the stylization of his work, derived partly from his interest in archaic sculpture, he had for a time a reputation as a pioneer of modern sculpture in America, but his modernism was fairly superficial and by about 1940 he was being labelled an academic artist.

Manson, J. B. See CAMDEN TOWN GROUP.

Mantegna, Andrea (*b* ?Isola di Carturo, Piazzola, nr. Padua, *c.*1431; *d* Mantua, 13 Sept. 1506). Italian painter and printmaker, one of the most renowned and influential artists of the 15th century. He was the pupil and adopted son of *Squarcione in Padua (which is near his probable birthplace), growing up in a humanist atmosphere that was to colour his whole approach to art. Squarcione exploited his pupils for his own ends and in 1448, when he was only about 17, Mantegna gave an early indication of his formidable strength of character by taking him to court and forcing him to recognize his independence. He was remarkably precocious, and the distinctive style he created at the beginning of his career changed little in essentials over the next half century. It was a style characterized by sharp clarity of drawing, colouring, and lighting, a passion for archaeology that fed on the abundance of *classical remains in northern Italy, and a mastery of *perspective and foreshortening unequalled in his time. These qualities were evident in his first major commission (1448), the decoration of the Ovetari Chapel of the Eremitani church in Padua with frescos on the lives of St Christopher and St James (almost completely destroyed by bombing in the Second World War), and they can also be seen in the celebrated *Agony in the Garden* (*c.*1460–5, NG, London). For all his learning, however, Mantegna was never dry. His work, indeed, often shows wit and fancifulness, and he was a delightful painter of animals—witness the rabbits in the *Agony in the Garden.*

In 1460 Mantegna was appointed court painter to Ludovico *Gonzaga in Mantua, and apart from a visit to Rome in 1488–90 he remained there for the rest of his life. He was held in the highest esteem by Ludovico, by his son and successor Federico, and by Isabella d'*Este, who married Federico's successor Francesco. At this time Mantua was becoming one of the leading centres of humanist culture in Europe, and Mantegna glorified the Gonzaga family and court in his most famous work—the fresco decoration (1465–74) of the Camera degli Sposi (Bridal Chamber) in the Ducal Palace. Group portraits of the Gonzaga family, arranged in various courtly scenes, line the walls and above them are bust medallions of the Caesars, indicating that the reigning house was worthy to continue the traditions of the Roman Empire. The most remarkable feature of the room, however, is the *illusionistic painting of the architecture (particularly of the ceiling), which appears to extend the real space of the room. This was the first time since antiquity that such a scheme had been carried out and Mantegna's work became the foundation for much subsequent decorative painting (see QUADRATURA).

Mantegna's other great undertaking for the Gonzaga was his series of nine paintings on the Triumphs of Caesar (c.1480–1500, Royal Coll., Hampton Court, London); it is often said that they were done for Francesco, but in fact it is not known which member of the family commissioned them. These large and fragile canvases have suffered dreadfully at the hands of 're-storers' in former centuries, but they were successfully cleaned in the 1960s and 1970s, and although they are battered and faded they still give a superb picture of Mantegna's magnificent powers of invention and design and rank alongside *Raphael's tapestry *cartoons as one of the greatest ensembles of *Renaissance art outside Italy.

Besides these large commissions for the Gonzaga, Mantegna painted many other types of work, including altarpieces, devotional pictures, portraits, and allegories. He also produced engravings of outstanding quality (they are the finest of their time in Italy) and was one of the first artists to use such prints to disseminate his compositions (initially he probably cut the plates himself but later relied on specialist assistants). In addition he designed his own house in Mantua, and it is generally thought that he modelled the bronze bust of himself in his memorial chapel in the church of S. Andrea (a cast of the bust is in the National Gallery, London). By the time of his death he was a widely venerated figure and his reputation has remained high. His influence was profound, not only on Italian artists such as his brother-in-law Giovanni *Bellini, but also, for example, on *Dürer, one of the many northern artists who found his version of the *antique particularly easy to assimilate.

Manuel Deutsch, Niklaus. See DEUTSCH.

Manutius, Aldus. See HYPNEROTOMACHIA POLIPHILI.

Manzoni, Piero (b Soncino, nr. Milan, 13 July 1933; d Milan, 6 Feb. 1963). Italian experimental artist. He was born into an aristocratic family and was mainly self-taught as an artist, although he studied briefly at the Brera, Milan. Until 1956 he painted in a traditional style (mainly landscapes), but he then turned to avant-garde work. In 1957 he began to produce Achromes, textured white paintings influenced by *Burri and *Klein (whom he met in 1957), and from 1959 he devised a series of provocative works and gestures that included signing people's bodies and designating them works of art, a block on which is inscribed upside down 'The base of the world' (1961, Herning Park, Denmark), and cans of his own excrement. He is regarded as one of the forerunners of *Arte Povera and *Conceptual art. His early death was caused by cirrhosis.

Manzù, Giacomo (b Bergamo, 22 Dec. 1908; d Rome, 17 Jan. 1991). Italian sculptor. From the age of 11, he worked successively for a wood-carver, a gilder, and a stuccoworker, but he was virtually self-taught as an artist. His early work was influenced by Egyptian and Etruscan art, but he then turned to a more *Impressionistic style owing much to the example of *Rodin and Medardo *Rosso. In the 1940s he simplified his style, so that although the surface of his work is often animated, the feeling it produces is one of classic calm. His sculpture included nudes, portraits, and scenes from everyday life, but he was best known for religious subjects. In 1938 he produced his first figure of a cardinal, a type of work that became particularly associated with him. These figures have been variously interpreted as expressions of an anticlerical attitude or as glorifications of ecclesiastical dignity, but Manzù himself always said that he regarded them as still-lifes with no deeper significance than a plate of apples, representing 'not the majesty of the church but the majesty of form'. His most famous work is the set of bronze doors he made for St Peter's in Rome after winning an international competition in 1950 (they were not completed until 1964). In 1958 he also completed a set of doors for Salzburg Cathedral and in 1968 one for the church of St Lawrence in Rotterdam. These works have been much praised and show the possibility of producing sculpture that fits within a traditional religious context and yet is in a modern and personal idiom. Manzù also worked as an etcher, lithographer, and painter.

maquette. A small preliminary model, typically in clay or wax, for a work of sculpture. The word implies something in the nature of a rough sketch, not so fully worked out as a *bozzetto.

Maratta (or Maratti), **Carlo** (b Camerano, 15 May 1625; d Rome, 15 Dec. 1713). Italian painter, the leading painter in Rome in the latter part of the 17th century. A pupil of Andrea *Sacchi, he continued the classical tradition of *Raphael, and he gained an international reputation particularly for his paintings of the Madonna and Child, which are reworkings of types established during the High *Renaissance. However, the rhetorical splendour of his work is thoroughly in the *Baroque idiom, and the numerous altarpieces he painted for Roman churches (many still in situ) give whole-hearted expression to the dogmas of the Counter-Reformation. Maratta was also an accomplished fresco painter and the finest portraitist of the day in Rome. He had a large studio and his posthumous reputation suffered when the inferior works of his many pupils and imitators were confused with his own paintings.

marble (Greek: marmaros, 'shining or sparkling stone'). A word sometimes loosely applied to any stone that is sufficiently close in texture to take a good polish; more strictly, it refers to *limestones whose structure has been recrystallized by heat or pressure, rendering the stone particularly hard and dense. Marbles are widely distributed and occur in a great variety of colours and patterns, but certain types have been particularly prized by sculptors. In the ancient world the most famous of Greek marbles was the close-grained, golden-toned Pentelic, which was quarried at Mount Pentelicon in Attica. The *Elgin Marbles are carved in Pentelic. Also widely used were the somewhat coarser-grained translucent white marbles from the Aegean islands of Paros and Naxos. Parian marble was used for the celebrated Mausoleum at Halicarnassus. The pure white Carrara marble, quarried at Carrara, Massa, and Pietra Santa in Tuscany from the 3rd century BC, is the most famous of all sculptors' stones. It was used for the *Apollo Belvedere, and was much favoured in the *Renaissance, particularly by *Michelangelo, who often visited the quarries to select material for his work. *Neoclassical sculptors also favoured Carrara marble because of its ability to take a sleek surface, but it can look rather 'dead' compared with some of the finest Greek marbles.

Marc, Franz (b Munich, 8 Feb. 1880; d nr. Verdun, 4 Mar. 1916). German painter, active mainly in Munich. His early work was in an academic style, but visits to Paris in 1903 and 1907 introduced him to *Impressionism and *Post-Impressionism. He was particularly impressed by the work of van *Gogh, under whose influence his style moved towards *Expressionism. In 1910 he met August *Macke, who became his closest friend, and also *Kandinsky; with them he was a leading member of the *Blaue Reiter group, founded in 1911. Marc was of a deeply religious disposition (in 1906 he visited Mount Athos in Greece with its famous monasteries) and was troubled by a profound spiritual malaise; through painting he sought to uncover mystical inner forces that animate nature. His ideas were expressed most intensely in paintings of animals, for he believed that they were both more beautiful and more spiritual than man. Using non-naturalistic symbolic colour and simplified, rhythmic shapes, he tried to paint animals not as we see them, but as they feel their own existence (Blue Horses, 1911, Minneapolis Inst. of Arts). In a letter to Macke in December 1910 he explained the emotional value he assigned to colours: 'Blue is the main principle, astringent and spiritual. Yellow is the female principle, gentle, gay and spiritual. Red is matter, brutal and heavy and always the colour to be opposed and overcome by the other two.'

In 1912 Marc saw an exhibition of *Futurist paintings in Berlin and also met *Delaunay in Paris. These events helped to move his work towards abstraction, as in Animal Destinies (1913, Kunstmuseum, Basle), one of his most celebrated paintings, which uses panic-stricken animals to symbolize a world on the edge of destruction; on the back of the picture he wrote: 'Und alles Sein ist flammend Leid' (And all being is flaming suffering). By 1914, his paintings had become still more abstract, losing almost entirely any representational content, as in Fighting Forms (1914, Neue Pin., Munich), an image of convulsive fury in which there are the merest suggestions of beak- and clawlike forms. These last paintings are considered among the culminating works of German Expressionism. Marc was killed in action in the First World War.

Marcantonio Raimondi. See RAIMONDI.

Marcoussis, Louis (b Warsaw, 10 Nov. 1878; d Cusset, nr. Vichy, 22 Oct. 1941). Polish-born French painter and etcher, originally called Louis Markus (his adopted name, suggested by *Apollinaire, came from the village of Marcoussis near Paris). He moved to Paris in 1903 and was granted French nationality on the basis of his distinguished army service in the First World War. His early paintings were *Impressionist in style, but in 1910 he met Apollinaire, *Braque, and *Picasso and joined the *Cubist group. He remained faithful to Cubism for the rest of his career and is regarded as one of the most appealing minor masters of the movement, combining clarity and simplicity of structure with delicacy of handling. Marcoussis's wife, whom he married in 1913, was the Czech painter **Alicia Halicka** (1895–1975).

Marcus Aurelius. Over-life-size bronze statue (Capitoline Mus., Rome) of the Emperor Marcus Aurelius mounted on horseback, probably made during his reign (AD 161–80). It is the only bronze equestrian statue to survive from antiquity, although another one, the *Regisole* (Sun King), survived in Pavia until 1797, and two marble equestrian statues were excavated at Herculaneum in the 1740s (they are now in the Archaeological Museum in Naples). The *Marcus Aurelius* is also one of the few famous *antique statues that always remained unburied and visible after the fall of the Roman Empire. During the Middle Ages it was commonly thought to represent Constantine, the first Christian emperor, and this perhaps saved it from destruction. The history of the statue can be traced back to about the 10th century, although early references to it are vague. For centuries it stood outside the Lateran Palace in Rome, but in 1538 Pope Paul III (Alessandro *Farnese) had it transferred to the Capitoline Hill, where *Michelangelo made it the focal point of the piazza he created there; he also designed a new base for the statue. It remained in the open air until 1981, when—because it was being damaged by atmospheric pollution—it was transferred to the Capitoline Museum. A full-size copy was erected in the piazza in 1997, as part of the celebrations to mark the 2,750th anniversary of the traditional date of the foundation of Rome. The original statue was too fragile for a cast to be taken from it, so the copy was made with the aid of moulds created from computerized photographs. From the 15th century the *Marcus Aurelius* was one of the most copied and reproduced of ancient works—in statuettes, engravings, and other forms. It influenced the two greatest equestrian monuments of the *Renaissance—*Donatello's *Gattamelata* and *Verrocchio's *Colleoni*—and many others subsequently. Such influence has usually been general rather than precise, but is fairly specific in Sir Richard *Westmacott's two equestrian statues of George III (1818–22,

Monument Place, Liverpool, and 1824–30, Windsor Great Park, Berkshire). For the Column of Marcus Aurelius, see TRAJAN'S COLUMN.

Marées, Hans von (*b* Elberfeld, 24 Dec. 1837; *d* Rome, 5 June 1887). German painter, active mainly in Italy (he lived there 1864–9 and settled permanently in 1873). Like his friends *Böcklin, *Feuerbach, and *Hildebrand, he was one of the Germanic artists working in Italy who turned to the tradition of *ideal art at a time when naturalism was becoming dominant in their own countries. He devoted himself mainly to the theme of the human figure in a landscape setting (*Three Youths under Orange Trees*, 1875–80, Neue Pin., Munich). In 1873 he carried out a major commission to paint a series of large frescos in the Zoological Institute in Naples, but he lacked self-confidence, and died disappointed and practically unknown. It was only at the beginning of the 20th century that the statuesque dignity of his work became appreciated and was hailed as a symbol of a new spirit of modernity in German art.

Margaret of Austria. See HABSBURG.

Margarito (or **Margaritone**) **of Arezzo** (active *c*.1262). Italian painter, active in Arezzo. He is one of the very few 13th-century Italian painters and the only early Aretine by whom we have signed works (examples are in the National Gallery, London, and the National Gallery, Washington). His paintings are clumsy, but they have something of the vividness and lucid brevity of a comic strip. *Vasari, who also came from Arezzo, included a biography of Margarito in his *Lives* (saying he was an architect as well as a painter), and this is virtually the only source of knowledge on him, although a document of 1262 probably refers to him.

Maria-Theresa, Empress. See HABSBURG.

Marieschi, Michele (*b* Venice, 1 Dec. 1710; *d* Venice, 18 Jan. 1743). Venetian painter and etcher. He painted fanciful landscapes, somewhat in the spirit of Marco *Ricci, and also views of Venice, influenced by the work of *Canaletto but less grand and more animated. In 1741 he published a set of 21 etchings of Venice accompanied by a self-portrait. If he had not died so young (according to tradition through overwork) he might have developed into a serious rival to Canaletto. His work probably influenced Francesco *Guardi.

Mariette, Pierre-Jean (*b* Paris, 7 May 1694; *d* Paris, 11 Sept. 1774). French print dealer, publisher, collector, and writer. He was descended from a line of engravers and print publishers. Early in his career he worked in Vienna and travelled in Italy before settling in Paris in about 1720. He corresponded with connoisseurs throughout Europe and was renowned for his art-historical knowledge, in particular his expertise in prints and drawings (he catalogued the sale of *Crozat's celebrated collection in 1741, and here he pioneered the use of *provenances to support attributions). In 1750 he sold his print business to concentrate on his own collection and his scholarly activities. He owned about 10,000 drawings, a large number of prints (among them more than 400 *Rembrandt etchings), and a few paintings and sculptures, including terracotta models by his friend *Bouchardon. His collections were sold by auction after his death and about 1,000 of his drawings are now in the Louvre. Mariette worked for many years on two major books—a dictionary of artists and a history of engraving. These were never completed, but selections from his extensive notes were published in six volumes in 1851–62.

Marin, John (*b* Rutherford, NJ, 23 Dec. 1870; *d* Cape Split, Me., 1 Oct. 1953). American painter and printmaker. From 1905 to 1910 he lived in Europe, mainly Paris, where he was influenced by *Whistler's watercolours and etchings, but he first came into contact with avant-garde movements after his return to America, when he became a member of *Stieglitz's circle. The *Armory Show also made a great impact on him. Responding especially to German *Expressionism and the late work of *Cézanne, he developed a distinctive semi-abstract style that he used most characteristically in powerful watercolours of city life and the Maine coast (where he often painted in the summer). His oil paintings (which became more important in his work from the 1930s) are often similar in effect to watercolours, leaving parts of the canvas bare. Marin also made etchings, especially early in his career. From the 1920s he enjoyed a high reputation. He was an individualist, belonging to no movement, and one of the finest watercolourists of the 20th century. See also DEMUTH.

Marinetti, Filippo Tommaso (*b* Alexandria, 22 Dec. 1876; *d* Bellagio, 2 Dec. 1944). Italian writer and artistic entrepreneur, the founder of *Futurism and the movement's chief theorist and promoter. He was the son of a wealthy lawyer, and family money later allowed him the freedom to pursue his artistic interests. He spent much of his early life in Paris (up to 1912 his poetry was written in French) and it was there that he launched Futurism in 1909 with a famous manifesto published on the front page of *Le Figaro*. Over the next few years, up to the beginning of the First World War, he was extremely vigorous in promoting Futurist ideas, travelling widely around Europe, organizing exhibitions, giving lectures, holding press conferences, and so on. Wherever he went, he attracted attention because of his outspoken and provocative behaviour. The First World War had a disastrous effect on the Futurist movement, but Marinetti continued promoting it afterwards and throughout his life he kept up a stream of writing, often in an experimental vein; he also occasionally tried his hand in the visual arts, making collages, for example. Although he is not regarded as a major writer or artist himself, he had an enormous influence as a provocateur—so much so that he is described by Robert *Hughes as 'one of the key figures of twentieth-century culture. He was the prototype of avant-garde promoters. For how do you create interest in something as utterly marginal to the public as new art? By turning it into fresh copy. The Futurists . . . realized that the newspapers wanted to run sensational stories about weirdos, not virtuously tolerant reviews of the avant-garde. Marinetti brilliantly used this appetite by trumpeting an art movement as a broad "revolution" in living that aims to change life itself, embracing everything from architecture to athletics, politics and sex.'

Marini, Marino (*b* Pistoia, 27 Feb. 1901; *d* Viareggio, 6 Aug. 1980). One of the outstanding Italian sculptors of the 20th century, also a painter, lithographer, and etcher. His travels (particularly his visits to Paris) brought him into contact with many distinguished modern artists (*Braque, *Giacometti, *González, *Maillol, *Picasso—to name only a few), but he did not ally himself with any avant-garde movements, remaining essentially isolated in his artistic aims. Although he experimented with various materials, he worked mainly in bronze and concentrated on a few favourite themes, most notably the horse and rider, a subject in which he seemed to express an obscure but poignant tragic symbolism (*Horseman*, 1947, Tate, London). His other subjects include female nudes and he also made numerous portrait busts, remarkable for their psychological penetration and sensuous exploitation of the surface qualities of the material. Often he polychromed his bronzes, sometimes working with corrosive dyes. In 1952 he won the main sculpture prize at the Venice *Biennale, setting the seal on his international reputation. There are Marini museums in Florence, Milan, and Pistoia and his work is represented in many major collections of modern art.

Marinus van Reymerswaele (b ?Roymerswaele, c.1490; d ?Middelburg, ?1567). Netherlandish painter, presumably from Roymerswaele (once in Zeeland but now under the sea). He specialized in two types of picture, both with more or less life-size half-length figures: representations of St Jerome in his study (influenced by *Dürer) and *genre scenes of bankers, usurers, misers, and tax collectors. The genre scenes show the sin of avarice and the vanity of earthly possessions; according to a Flemish proverb a banker, a usurer, a tax collector, and a miller were the four evangelists of the devil. These paintings must have been very popular, for they exist in numerous versions and copies, but it is not known what kind of clientele bought pictures of such unpleasant characters, grotesquely presented in a manner deriving (via *Massys) from *Leonardo's 'caricatures'. A 'Marinus . . . of Romerswael' is mentioned in Middelburg in 1567, when he was condemned to walk in a penitential procession for taking part in the looting of a church, but he may not be identical with the painter, who is described as deceased in another document of that year.

Maris. Family of three brothers who played a leading part in Dutch painting during the second half of the 19th century. **Jacob** (Jacobus Hendricus) (b The Hague, 25 Aug. 1837; d Karlsbad, 7 Aug. 1899) was one of the leaders of the *Hague School, specializing in views of the Dutch countryside and scenes in Dutch towns. **Matthias** (Matthijs, Thijs) (b The Hague, 17 Aug. 1839; d London, 22 Aug. 1917) began in similar fashion, but came to specialize in figure compositions of visionary subjects. In 1869 he moved to Paris and then in 1877 to London, where he lived for the rest of his life and was influenced by the *Pre-Raphaelites in his choice of poetic subjects, although not in style. **Willem** (b The Hague, 18 Feb. 1844; d The Hague, 10 Oct. 1910) was a pupil of his two brothers and was influenced by *Mauve. His subjects are almost entirely confined to meadows and cattle. In his later years he became a leader of Dutch *Impressionism, urging his pupils—among them *Breitner—to paint in the open air and to use vivid colours.

Marlow, William (b London, 1740; d Twickenham, Middlesex [now Greater London], ?14 Jan. 1813). English landscape and marine painter, a pupil of Samuel *Scott and possibly also of Richard *Wilson. His early landscapes were topographical views, including pictures of country houses, but after a visit to the Continent (1765–6) he painted largely from his memories of France and Italy. In the 1780s he went into semi-retirement, devoting himself to making scientific instruments. See also CAPRICCIO.

Marmion, Simon (b ?Amiens, ?c.1425; d Valenciennes, 25 Dec. 1489). Franco-Flemish manuscript *illuminator and painter. In 1449–54 he lived in Amiens, and he joined the Tournai painters' guild in 1468, but most of his working life was spent in Valenciennes, where he is first documented in 1458. He had a great reputation in his day, but no works certainly from his hand survive. The main paintings attributed to him are two wings of an altarpiece (1455–9) from the abbey of St Bertin, Saint-Omer (Gemäldegalerie, Berlin; fragments from the altarpiece are in the National Gallery, London). Several manuscripts also are attributed to him. His style was very tender, with delicate, almost pastel colouring, and does not belong to the mainstream of either French or Netherlandish art.

Marochetti, Carlo (b Turin, 14 Jan. 1805; d Paris, 29 Dec. 1867). Italian sculptor. He had an internationally successful career, being made a baron in his native country, awarded the Legion of Honour in France, and patronized by Queen Victoria and Prince Albert in England, where he settled in 1848. His dramatic style, exemplified in his equestrian statue of Richard the Lionheart (1851–60) outside the Houses of Parliament, was, however, considered rather flashy by some English critics. See also LANDSEER.

marouflage (French: maroufler, 'to stick down'). Term for gluing a *canvas permanently to a wall, whether before painting it or afterwards. The adhesive used is traditionally white lead in oil. The term is also applied to the sticking down onto canvas of oil sketches done on paper.

Marquet, Albert (b Bordeaux, 26 Mar. 1875; d Paris, 14 June 1947). French painter and draughtsman. He was one of the *Fauves, and for a time his boldness of colour almost matched that of *Matisse (his lifelong friend). However, he soon abandoned Fauvism and turned to a comparatively naturalistic style. He painted some fine portraits and did a number of powerful female nudes (1910–14), but he was primarily a landscapist. His favourite—eventually almost exclusive—themes were ports and the bridges and quays of Paris, subjects he depicted with unaffected simplicity and great sensitivity to tone. Marquet was an outstanding draughtsman and from 1925 worked mainly in watercolour. He travelled widely and built up an international reputation, but he lived very quietly (he was timid in personality) and refused all honours.

Marsh, Reginald (*b* Paris, 14 Mar. 1898; *d* Dorset, Vt., 30 July 1954). American painter. Until 1930 he worked mainly as a newspaper illustrator, but he took up painting seriously after a study trip to Paris in 1925–6, and in the 1930s he became well known for his paintings depicting shabby and tawdry aspects of life in New York. His favourite subjects included Coney Island, the amusement arcades of Times Square, and the cheap and grubby street life of the Bowery district (*Tattoo and Haircut*, 1932, Art Inst. of Chicago). He was also capable of bitter satire against the smug complacency of the wealthy, but in general his work shows a love of depicting teeming life through ugly yet colourful subjects rather than a desire for social protest. His aim was to represent contemporary subjects in the manner of the Old Masters and he worked mainly in *tempera, also experimenting with other venerable techniques. He came from a wealthy family and to some extent his work expressed a rejection of the affluent and genteel circumstances in which he grew up.

Marshall, Benjamin (*b* Seagrave, Leicestershire, 8 Nov. 1768; *d* London, 24 July 1835). English sporting painter, one of the best followers of *Stubbs. He was briefly a pupil of the portrait painter L. F. *Abbott, but from *c*.1792 he turned to animal painting. In 1812 he settled at Newmarket, famous for its racecourse, but he returned to London in 1825.

Marshall, Edward (*b c*.1598; *d* London, 10 Dec. 1675). English mason and sculptor. He was one of the leading English tomb sculptors of his time, although 'his work was uneven and his scope limited' (Margaret Whinney, *Sculpture in Britain: 1530–1830*, 1964); the dignified monument to Elizabeth, Lady Culpeper, at Hollingbourne, Kent (1638), shows him at his best. At the Restoration in 1660 he was appointed master mason to Charles II, a post in which he was succeeded by his son **Joshua** (*bapt.* London, 24 June 1629; *d* London, 6 Apr. 1678), the only one of his fourteen children who survived him. Joshua was

much employed on the rebuilding of the city of London after the Great Fire of 1666. He also carved the pedestal for Hubert *Le Sueur's equestrian statue of Charles I at Charing Cross. His monuments are less accomplished than those of his father.

Martelli, Diego. See MACCHIAIOLI.

Martin, Elias (*bapt.* Stockholm, 8 Mar. 1739; *d* Stockholm, 25 Jan. 1818). The leading Swedish landscape painter of his period. He lived for several years in England (1768–80 and 1788–91) and his style was influenced by *Gainsborough and *Wilson as well as by *Claude. He painted in both oils and watercolour and also worked in various printmaking techniques. His brother **Johan Fredric Martin** (1755–1816) was an engraver and etcher.

Martin, John (*b* Haydon Bridge, Northumberland, 19 July 1789; *d* Douglas, Isle of Man, 17 Feb. 1854). English *Romantic painter and *mezzotint engraver, celebrated for his melodramatic scenes of cataclysmic events crowded with tiny figures placed in vast architectural or landscape settings. He caught the public imagination with spectacular paintings such as *Joshua Commanding the Sun to Stand Still* (1816, United Grand Lodge of Great Britain, London), the work that made his reputation, and in 1821 *Lawrence referred to him as 'the most popular painter of the day'. His work was indeed truly popular, for he made his living mainly through the sale of prints of his pictures rather than the paintings themselves. He became famous in France as well as Britain, he was knighted by Leopold I of Belgium (1833), and his influence was felt by American artists such as *Cole. However, while he pleased a large public and was regarded by some admirers as one of the greatest geniuses who ever lived, Martin was reviled by *Ruskin and other critics, who considered his work vulgar sensationalism. Few artists, indeed, have been subject to such extremes of critical fortune, and he later sank so much in esteem that very large and once famous paintings by him were sold in the 1930s for as little as £2. By the 1970s his reputation had greatly revived.

Martin made mezzotints not only as a means of reproducing his paintings but also as original compositions. Most of them are of biblical subjects, and he also made celebrated illustrations to John Milton's *Paradise Lost* (1825–7). These show that although he had great weaknesses as an artist, especially in his drawing of the human figure, he also had a vividness and grandiloquence of imagination not unworthy of such an elevated subject; indeed, C. H. Collins Baker writes that 'he leaves *Blake and all the other illustrators far behind in suggesting the scale of Milton's conceptions, and in creating a world, supernatural and Paradisean, conforming with Milton's' (*Some Illustrators of Milton's Paradise Lost*, 1948).

He is sometimes called Mad Martin, but the sobriquet is undeserved and applies more to his brother Jonathan, who set fire to York Minster in 1829, badly damaging the building, and was confined to an asylum for the rest of his life (another brother, William, was an eccentric writer and inventor). John Martin was eminently sane and in the 1830s almost bankrupted himself with extremely ambitious but entirely practical plans for improving the water supply and sewage system of London. His schemes did not come to fruition, but they reveal a heroic desire to put the architectural visions of his paintings into a concrete form. His work is best represented in Tate Britain, London, and in the Laing Art Gallery in Newcastle upon Tyne, near his native Haydon Bridge.

Martin, Kenneth (b Sheffield, 13 Apr. 1905; d London, 18 Nov. 1984). British painter and sculptor. In 1930 he married Mary Balmford (a fellow student at the *Royal College of Art), whose artistic development as **Mary Martin** (b Folkestone, 16 Jan. 1907; d London, 9 Oct. 1969) was closely linked with his own. In the 1930s he painted in a naturalistic style, but during the 1940s his work became less representational until in 1948–9 he produced his first abstract pictures. His wife soon followed suit and in the early 1950s they began making abstract constructions. With Victor *Pasmore and others they became recognized as leaders of the *Constructivist movement that burgeoned in England in the 1950s. Kenneth Martin's contribution came not only through his work, but also by writing and organizing exhibitions. Mary Martin had numerous major commissions, among them a screen for Musgrave Park Hospital, Belfast (1957).

Martin, Sir Leslie. See CIRCLE.

Martini, Simone (b ?Siena, ?1284; d Avignon, July/Aug. 1344). Next to *Duccio, the most distinguished painter of the Sienese School. Nothing certain is known of him before 1315. *Vasari says that he was a pupil of *Giotto, but the prevailing opinion is that he probably trained in Duccio's circle; certainly he learnt much from the decorative use of outline, colour, and patterning characteristic of Duccio's work. The main features of his style are present in his earliest surviving work, the large fresco of the *Maestà (1315; reworked 1321) in Siena Town Hall: the sumptuous materials and the aloofness of the Madonna derive from the *Byzantine style of the older generation; the decorative line, gesture, and expression are informed by the gracious *Gothic fashion that was now current in Siena; and the use of foreshortening to create depth shows the awakening desire for more lifelike effects. Two years later he painted an altarpiece (1317, Mus. di Capodimonte, Naples) for Robert of Anjou (King of Naples, 1309–43) showing his elder brother St Louis of Toulouse, newly canonized, resigning his crown to him. The *predella scenes contain the boldest compositions in perspective that had been produced up to that date. Perhaps at about the same time (although the evidence for the dating is inconclusive) he carried out the fresco decoration of the chapel of S. Martino in the Lower Church of S. Francesco, Assisi.

The next major work associated with Simone is a fresco, bearing the date 1328, on the wall opposite his *Maestà* in Siena Town Hall, commemorating the *condottiere* Guidoriccio da Fogliano, who in that year had won a great victory for the Sienese and liberated the town of Montemassi, depicted in the background. This highly original work, which shows the general riding in stately but solitary triumph, is generally regarded as one of the first equestrian portraits since antiquity; however, it has recently been the subject of great controversy, some scholars considering that it is not by Simone and appreciably later than assumed (this opinion is based on technical evidence allegedly showing that part of the fresco lies on top of another fresco known to date from 1363). The work that is generally regarded as the epitome of Simone's style is the *Annunciation* (Uffizi, Florence, 1333), although this is jointly signed with his brother-in-law Lippo *Memmi. It is a ravishing blend of fragile grace and sweet sentiment and for sheer beauty of craftsmanship is unsurpassed in its age.

Simone's work is more fully Gothic in spirit than that of any other major Italian painter; it is therefore not surprising that he was appreciated in France, and from about 1335 until his death he worked at the papal court in *Avignon. During this period he painted the unusual subject *Christ Reproved by his Parents* (1342, Walker AG, Liverpool) and the frontispiece to a Virgil manuscript belonging to the poet Petrarch (Ambrosiana

445

Lib., Milan). He also did a portrait of Petrarch's beloved Laura; it is lost, but mentioned in one of the poet's sonnets. Simone's style and compositions were taken over by illuminators from France and Flanders and generations of Italian panel and fresco painters copied him too. He was one of the main sources of the *International Gothic style.

Martorell, Bernardo (d Barcelona, Dec. 1452). Spanish painter and manuscript illuminator. He worked in Barcelona (where he is first documented in 1427) and was the outstanding painter in Catalonia in the second quarter of the 15th century, the successor to *Borrassá, who perhaps taught him. Only one surviving work is securely documented—the altarpiece of St Peter of Púbol (1437–42, Gerona Mus.)—but on stylistic grounds a group of paintings formerly given to 'the Master of St George' has been attributed to him. The group includes (and formerly took its identity from) an altarpiece of St George; the central panel is in the Art Institute of Chicago and the four wings are in the Louvre, Paris. Martorell's work, influenced by Franco-Flemish painting and *illumination, was essentially *International Gothic in style, but reveals a highly distinctive personality, particularly in its vigorous sense of drama and delicate handling of light. Among the painters of the next generation, *Huguet was most obviously indebted to him.

Mary of Burgundy. See MASTER OF MARY OF BURGUNDY.

Mary of Hungary. See HABSBURG.

Marzal de Sax, Andrés (active 1393–1410). Painter of German origin (Sax indicating Saxony) who worked in Valencia, Spain. Only one fragment survives of his documented works—the Incredulity of St Thomas in Valencia Cathedral, part of an altarpiece he completed for the cathedral in 1400. Among the works given to him on stylistic grounds the most important is the huge and sumptuous St George altarpiece (V&A, London), featuring the varied tortures of the saint in grisly detail. The somewhat rough vigour of Marzal de Sax's style had considerable influence in Valencia; he is last mentioned in 1410, impoverished and ill, receiving free lodging from the city in recognition of the quality of his work and his generosity in training local painters.

Masaccio (Tommaso di Ser Giovanni di Mone Cassai) (b Castel San Giovanni [now San Giovanni Valdarno], nr. Florence, 21 Dec. 1401; d Rome, ?June 1428 [or perhaps 1429]). Florentine painter. Although he died aged only 26 or 27, he brought about a revolution in painting and he ranks alongside his friends *Alberti, *Brunelleschi, and *Donatello as one of the founding fathers of the *Renaissance. His affectionate nickname, which may be translated as 'hulking Tom' or 'sloppy Tom', was given to him, so *Vasari says, because he was so completely absorbed in art that 'he refused to give any time to worldly matters, even to the way he dressed'.

Masaccio became a member of the painters' guild in Florence in 1422, but nothing is known of his training, the tradition that he was taught by *Masolino, later his collaborator, now being discounted. The earliest work attributed to him is the S. Giovenale *Triptych (1422, S. Pietro, Cascia di Reggello), which is somewhat uncouth but reveals a totally individual spirit in its rejection of all *Gothic elegance and concentration on the weight and bulk of the figures. Instead of learning from contemporary painters, Masaccio looked back to *Giotto for inspiration, recapturing the gravity of feeling and grandeur of form that characterized his work. But whereas Giotto set his figures in space intuitively, Masaccio grappled with and solved the problem of creating a completely coherent and consistent sense of three dimensions on a two-dimensional surface, his work thus becoming part of 'the bedrock of European art' (in Kenneth *Clark's phrase). His enormous achievement was based on his mastery of the new science of *perspective and his use of a single consistent light source to define the structure of the body and its draperies. Among contemporary artists he was closest in spirit to Donatello. Both artists were less concerned with surface appearances and isolated detail than with the underlying construction of objects and both excelled at the depiction of emotion with great force and directness.

Masaccio has left three great works to posterity in which he enunciated his new principles: a *polyptych (1426) for the Carmelite church in Pisa (the central panel is in the National Gallery in London, and the other ten surviving panels—probably representing about half the original total—are in the Gemäldegalerie, Berlin, the Getty Museum, Los Angeles, the Museo di Capodimonte, Naples, and the Museo Nazionale, Pisa); a fresco cycle, done in collaboration with Masolino, on the life of St Peter (with additional scenes of the Temptation of Adam and Eve and the Expulsion from Paradise) in the Brancacci Chapel of S. Maria del Carmine, Florence (c.1425–8); and a fresco of the *Trinity* in S. Maria Novella, Florence (*c*.1428). Masaccio moved to Rome in 1428, leaving the frescos in the Brancacci Chapel unfinished, and died so suddenly that Vasari said 'there were some who even suspected he had been poisoned'. Vasari adds that 'during his lifetime he had made only a modest name for himself', and certainly many of his Florentine contemporaries and successors were unmoved by his innovations. He was a great inspiration to the progressive masters of the next generation, however (Fra *Angelico, Filippo *Lippi, *Piero della Francesca), and Vasari records a whole roster of major artists, including *Leonardo, *Michelangelo, and *Raphael, who studied his work with profit.

Masaccio's younger brother, Giovanni di Ser Giovanni (1406–86), was also a painter, known by the nickname Lo Scheggia (the splinter); this presumably indicates he was slight in stature or marks his connections with woodworking (his grandfather made wooden boxes and much of his own work consisted of decorating objects such as *cassoni and *deschi da parto).

Masereel, Frans (*b* Blankenberge, 30 July 1889; *d* Avignon, 3 Jan. 1972). Belgian graphic artist and painter, active mainly in France. He was a prolific illustrator of books and periodicals. Much of his work was motivated by social concern, one of his chief themes being the suffering caused by war. He often used the formula of *romans in beelden* (novels in pictures), which are series of woodcuts telling a story without a text. His style was mildly *Expressionist.

Masip, Vicente. See MAÇIP.

Maso di Banco (active second quarter of the 14th century). Florentine painter. Almost nothing is known of his career (*Vasari does not mention him by name and attributes some of his work to an obscure—possibly fictitious—artist called Giottino). However, he is regarded as the greatest of *Giotto's followers on the strength of *Ghiberti's testimony that he was the painter of the frescos illustrating the legend of St Sylvester in the Bardi Chapel of S. Croce, Florence. The stately figures here are sometimes even more massive than Giotto's and the lucid and beautifully coloured compositions are of almost geometric clarity (although it has been argued that some of the effect of monumental simplicity may be due to restoration). On stylistic grounds other works have been attributed to Maso, including panels in Budapest (MFA),

Chantilly (Mus. Condé), and New York (Brooklyn Mus. and Met. Mus.).

Masolino da Panicale (Tommaso di Cristofano) (*b* ?Panicale, ?*c*.1383; *d* ?*c*.1435/40). Italian painter, an enigmatic and intriguing figure. He presumably came from Panicale in Umbria, and he worked in various places in Italy (and also in Hungary), but he is regarded as a member of the Florentine School. According to *Vasari he trained as a sculptor and goldsmith under *Ghiberti, but his early life is obscure. For a short period his career was closely linked to that of *Masaccio, but the exact nature of their association remains ill defined (the nickname Masolino, meaning 'little Tom', almost suggests that he and Masaccio—'big' or 'hulking Tom'—were thought of as a kind of double act). The tradition that he was Masaccio's master is now dismissed, for he became a member of the painters' guild in Florence only in 1423 (a year after Masaccio) and although he was evidently almost two decades older, it was he who was influenced by Masaccio rather than the other way round. On stylistic grounds they are thought to have collaborated on the *Madonna and Child with St Anne* (*c*.1425, Uffizi, Florence), and Vasari records that they worked together on the decoration of the Brancacci Chapel of S. Maria del Carmine in Florence (*c*.1425–8). Masolino's style was softer and more graceful than Masaccio's and there is a fair measure of agreement about the division of hands in the chapel. The contrast in style is seen most clearly in the frescos of the *Temptation of Adam and Eve* and the *Expulsion from Paradise*; Masolino's nude figures in the *Temptation* have an almost doll-like daintiness, whereas Masaccio's in the *Expulsion* are massively powerful and convey a feeling of tragic intensity. After Masaccio's early death in 1428 Masolino's style became more decorative. At his best he was a painter of great distinction; his masterpiece is perhaps the fresco of the *Baptism of Christ* (*c*.1435) in the Baptistery at Castiglione d'Olona, near Como, a graceful and lyrical work that is a world away from Masaccio's sombre *Baptism of the Neophytes* in the Brancacci Chapel.

Masson, André (*b* Balagny, 4 Jan. 1896; *d* Paris, 28 Oct. 1987). French painter, printmaker, sculptor, stage designer, and writer, one of the major figures of *Surrealism. During the First World War he was seriously wounded and deeply scarred emotionally. His pessimism was accompanied by a profound and troubled curiosity about the nature and destiny of man and an obscure belief in the mysterious unity of the universe; he devoted the whole of his artistic activity to penetrating and expressing this belief. In the early 1920s he was influenced by *Cubism, but in 1924 he joined the Surrealist movement and remained a member until 1929, when he left in protest against *Breton's authoritarian leadership. His work belonged to the spontaneous, expressive, semi-abstract variety of Surrealism, and included experiments with automatic drawings (see AUTOMATISM), chance effects, and unusual materials (he sometimes incorporated sand in his paintings). Themes of metamorphosis, violence, psychic pain, and eroticism dominated his work. In 1934–6 he lived in Spain until the Civil War drove him back to France and in 1941–5 he took refuge from the Second World War in the USA. There his work formed a link between Surrealism and *Abstract Expressionism. In 1945 he returned to France and two years later settled at Aix-en-Provence, where he concentrated on landscape painting, achieving something of the spiritual rapport with nature seen in some Chinese paintings.

Massys (or **Matsys** or **Metsys**), **Quentin** (b Louvain, c.1466; d Antwerp Apr./Sept. 1530). Netherlandish painter, the leading artist of his day in Antwerp. He became a master in the painters' guild there in 1491, but his early career is obscure and his training is a matter of conjecture (van *Mander says he was self-taught, and according to another early account he originally followed his father's trade as a blacksmith but took up art to woo his sweetheart away from a painter she admired). His first dated works are the altarpieces of St Anne (1507–9, Mus. Royaux, Brussels) and the Lamentation (1508–11, Koninklijk Mus., Antwerp). Massys continued the tradition of the great masters of 15th-century Netherlandish art, but he was also clearly aware of Italian art (particularly the work of *Leonardo) and may well have crossed the Alps at some point in his career. In his exquisite Madonna and Child with Angels (c.1505, Courtauld Gal., London), for example, the *iconographic type of the standing Virgin goes back to Jan van *Eyck, but the *putti holding a garland reveal *Renaissance influence. The landscape backgrounds of some of his religious works were probably done by his friend *Patinir. Massys also painted portraits and *genre scenes. The satirical quality in his pictures of bankers, tax collectors, and avaricious merchants has been linked with the writings of the great humanist Erasmus. Certainly the two met, for in 1517 Massys painted a pair of portraits of Erasmus

and his friend Petrus Aegidius (respectively Royal Coll. and Earl of Radnor Coll., Longford Castle, Wiltshire) as a gift for Sir Thomas More. They instituted a new type—the scholar in his study—that influenced *Holbein among others. Massys had two painter sons, **Jan** and **Cornelis**.

Master Bertram (b ?Minden, Westphalia, active 1367; d Hamburg, 1414/15). German painter, active mainly in Hamburg, where he was the leading master of his day. His main work is a huge *polyptych for the church of St Peter in Hamburg, now known as the Grabow Altarpiece (completed 1383, Kunsthalle, Hamburg). The softly modelled figures show how the influence of the *Bohemian School, notably *Master Theodoric, extended as far as Hamburg.

Master E. S. (sometimes called the Master of 1466 from the date on one of his engravings). German engraver working in the mid-15th century, named after the monogram on several of his surviving prints. He was the most prolific and influential of the early German engravers, working on profane and fantastic subjects as well as religious images and producing more than 300 known prints (about a third of them survive in unique copies). Earlier engravers had been content with pure outline, but E. S. created rich tonal effects by the ingenious use of *hatching and cross-hatching.

Master Francke. German painter, active in Hamburg in the early 15th century. His major surviving work is an altarpiece (now fragmentary) for the guild of merchants trading with England (1424, Kunsthalle, Hamburg), showing Passion scenes and incidents from the life of St Thomas Becket. Francke was a leading exponent of *International Gothic in northern Germany and he had wide influence there and along the shores of the Baltic.

Master Hugo (active second quarter of the 12th century). English illuminator, metalworker, and sculptor. He was a lay artist, but he worked for Bury St Edmunds Abbey, Suffolk. A late 13th-century chronicle of the abbey names him as the illuminator of a 'large Bible', which is almost certainly to be identified with a book that survives in part in Corpus Christi College, Cambridge. Known as the Bury Bible or the Bury St Edmunds Bible and datable to c.1135, it is one of the masterpieces of *Romanesque illumination, distinguished by its rich colouring, powerful draughtsmanship, and vivid characterization. There is strong *Byzantine influence, notably in the use of 'dampfold' draperies that seem to cling to the body like wet cloth. Master Hugo's curvilinear variety of dampfold was highly influential and 'can be found in nearly all the major English paintings between about 1140 and 1170' (catalogue of the exhibition 'English Romanesque Art', Hayward Gallery, London, 1984). No other documented works by Master Hugo survive, but he is mentioned in early sources as a sculptor and metalworker, and on stylistic grounds an *ivory altar cross, known as the Bury St Edmunds Cross (Met. Mus., New York), has been attributed to him, although some scholars date it a generation after his time, and 'the association with Bury rests upon stylistic resemblances that cannot be held entirely conclusive' (T. S. R. Boase, *English Art: 1100–1216*, corrected impression, 1968). The cross is notable not only for its superb quality, but also for its mysterious history (it came to light only in 1955) and its unusual anti-Semitic inscriptions.

Master Jacomart. See BAÇO.

Master of . . . Term used in art history to label the author of anonymous works or groups of works for convenience in discussing them. This use of invented names is more common in the study of painting and printmaking than of sculpture, and historians of architecture hardly ever resort to it. It began in Germany in the early 19th century with the description of Early Netherlandish painting. Initially the choice of names was often more lyrical than descriptive, as with the 'Master of the Pearl of Brabant', named after a small gemlike altarpiece (Alte Pin., Munich), now usually attributed to Dieric *Bouts. Nowadays invented names tend to be more prosaic and more directly appropriate. Often the anonymous master is named after a particular picture and/or the collection to which it belongs, e.g. 'Master of the Louvre Annunciation'. Alternatively, the name can refer to some aspect of the artist's style, as in the 'Master of the Anaemic Figures' (a 15th-century Spanish painter), who shows that the designation 'master' is used neutrally and is not a term of approbation. The practice of creating artistic personalities in this way has been overdone, but is often useful.

Master of 1466. See MASTER E.S.

Master of Alkmaar (active early 16th century). Netherlandish painter named after the altarpiece of the *Seven Works of Mercy* painted for the church of St Lawrence in Alkmaar in 1504

and now in the Rijksmuseum, Amsterdam. The painter has been plausibly identified with Cornelis Buys (active 1490–1524), who was the brother of Jacob *Cornelisz. van Oostsanen. The figure style is reminiscent of *Geertgen tot Sint Jans and the altarpiece is important as an early instance of the characteristically Dutch delight in the representation of everyday life.

Master of Flémalle. Netherlandish painter, named after three paintings in the Städelsches Kunstinstitut in Frankfurt that in the 19th century were wrongly said to have come from an 'abbey of Flémalle, near Liège' (no such abbey ever existed). Scholarly opinion now generally identifies him with Robert Campin (*c.*1375–44), who settled in Tournai in about 1405 and became the city's leading painter, earning a handsome living. There are various contemporary references to him, including records of his being charged with leading a dissolute life (he was married but living with another woman); in 1432 he was sentenced to a year's banishment for this, but the punishment was commuted to a fine. However, none of Campin's documented pictures survives, and the identification of him with the Master of Flémalle depends on the similarity between the paintings given to the Master and those of Jacques *Daret and Rogier van der *Weyden, for Daret was Campin's pupil and Rogier almost certainly was. The once popular hypothesis that the Master of Flémalle's paintings are early works by Rogier now has few adherents.

While there may still be doubt about the Master of Flémalle's identity and the limits of his oeuvre, there is no argument about his achievement, for he made a radical break with the elegant *International Gothic style and ranks with Jan van *Eyck as one of the founders of the Early Netherlandish School of painting. None of the paintings given to him is dated—with the exception of the wings of the Werl Altarpiece of 1438 in the Prado, a doubtful attribution—but it seems likely that his earliest works antedate any surviving picture by van Eyck. The earliest of all is generally thought to be the *Entombment* (Courtauld Gal., London) of about 1410/20. This still has the decorative gold background of medieval tradition, but the influence of Claus *Sluter is clear in the sculptural solidity and dramatic force of the figures. The most famous work generally associated with the Master of Flémalle is the Mérode Altarpiece (Met. Mus., New York), and he is indeed sometimes referred to as the Master of Mérode.

However, the attribution of this painting has also been questioned. Among the other works associated with him are the *Marriage of the Virgin* (Prado, Madrid), the *Nativity* (Mus. B.-A., Dijon), and the *Virgin and Child before a Firescreen* (NG, London; now catalogued as 'follower of Campin'), which shows the homely detail and down-to-earth naturalism characteristic of the artist (the firescreen behind the Virgin's head doubles as a halo). The National Gallery also has three portraits attributed to the Master of Flémalle. In spite of the many problems associated with him, he ranks as a very powerful and important artistic personality.

Master of Frankfurt (active *c*.1500). Netherlandish painter. He almost certainly worked in Antwerp, but he is named after two works painted for clients in Frankfurt and now in the Städelsches Kunstinstitut there: a *Holy Kinship* altarpiece and a *Crucifixion* triptych. About 40 pictures are attributed to him, including *Portrait of the Artist with his Wife* (Koninklijk Mus., Antwerp). This is dated 1496 and gives his age as 36, so he was presumably born in 1459 or 1460. He has been tentatively identified with Hendrik van Wueluwe, who was active in Antwerp from 1483 and died there in 1533. With his contemporary Quentin *Massys, the Master of Frankfurt stands at the beginning of Antwerp's great tradition in painting.

Master of Hohenfurth. See MASTER OF VYŠŠÍ BROD.

Master of Liesborn (active *c*.1470). German painter, named after an altarpiece painted for the Benedictine abbey of Liesborn in Westphalia; various panels and fragments of it survive (notably in the National Gallery, London). His attractive gentle style was influenced by the *Cologne School.

Master of Mary of Burgundy. Netherlandish manuscript illuminator, active in the last quarter of the 15th century. He is named after a *Book of Hours painted for Mary of Burgundy, who married the Emperor Maximilian I (see HABSBURG) in 1477 and died in 1482 (Österreichische Nationalbibliothek, Vienna). This is among the finest illuminated books of the period, with many charming everyday life and still-life details, and other high-quality works in a similar style have been attributed to him, including a Book of Hours in the Bodleian Library, Oxford. It has been suggested that he is to be identified with Alexander *Bening.

Master of Moulins (active *c*.1480–*c*.1500). French or Netherlandish painter, named after a *triptych of the *Madonna and Child with Saints and Donors* (*c*.1498) in Moulins Cathedral. The style of this work is highly distinctive, and has enabled a considerable oeuvre to be built up around it. The Master of Moulins's sculptural precision of form (recalling *Fouquet), the poise of his figures, his brilliant palette, the harmony of his compositions, and his taste for splendid and meticulous details make him one of the outstanding painters of his period in northern Europe. Various suggestions have been made for identifying him with named artists; these include Jean *Perréal, who had the biggest contemporary reputation of any French artist of this period, but the most plausible candidate is now thought to be Jean Hey, a Netherlandish painter who is known to have worked in France around 1500.

Master of Naumburg. Name given to the head of the workshop which produced a group of works in Naumburg Cathedral around 1240 that are generally regarded as the finest works of *Gothic sculpture in Germany. They include twelve sensitively characterized statues in the west chancel representing the benefactors of the original cathedral (notably the famous figures of Ekkehard and Uta) and the decoration of the screen at the entrance of the chancel with a *Crucifixion* group and a series of Passion reliefs. The Master of Naumburg was probably trained in northern France, but there is little doubt that he was a German by birth; his Germanic temperament emerges in the pathos and vehement gestures of his figures. However, he loses nothing of the monumental dignity and idealism of his predecessors, and in his art the two worlds of feeling seem to meet and enrich one another as in the work of perhaps no other medieval artist.

Master of St Cecilia (active *c*.1300). Italian painter named after the St Cecilia Altarpiece (Uffizi, Florence), which came from the church of S. Cecilia, Florence, destroyed by fire in 1304. Presumably he was a Florentine, but nothing is known about him. Other works have been attributed to him because of their resemblance to the Uffizi picture, the most important being the first scene and the three concluding scenes of the great fresco cycle of the life of St Francis in the Upper Church of S. Francesco at Assisi (see MASTER OF THE LEGEND OF ST FRANCIS). The painter of these scenes resembles *Giotto in lucidity of presentation and the solid drawing of his figures, but he is more genial in feeling. His figures are more vivacious, his colour warmer and sweeter. Some critics have attempted to identify him with the famous but elusive *Buffalmacco.

Master of St George. See MARTORELL.

Master of St Giles (active c.1480–c.1500). French or Netherlandish painter named after two panels representing scenes from the life of St Giles (NG, London). Other paintings in the same style have been grouped round them. Their attention to detail and their meticulous finish have prompted the view that the artist was trained in the Netherlands, but the inclusion of views of Paris in some of his works indicates that he worked there, whatever his origin. His work is of high quality and he must have been one of the best painters of the day in northern France.

Master of Segovia. See BENSON.

Master of the Amsterdam Cabinet. See MASTER OF THE HOUSEBOOK.

Master of the Brunswick Monogram (active c.1520–40). Netherlandish painter, named after a picture in the Herzog-Anton-Ulrich Museum in Brunswick of the *Parable of the Great Supper* (Luke 14). There is no agreement as to how the interlinked letters of the monogram should be read. A dozen or so small pictures have been attributed to the same hand; about half depict religious subjects in the open air, and most of the others are brothel scenes. The quality of the pictures is uniformly high. The artist's observation of nature, his fine drawing, and his ability to integrate figures into a landscape make him an important forerunner of Pieter *Bruegel the Elder. Suggestions have been made for identifying him with various named painters, including Jan Sanders van *Hemessen.

Master of the Death of the Virgin. See JOOS VAN CLEVE.

Master of the Housebook (active late 15th century). German (or according to some authorities Netherlandish) printmaker and draughtsman, so called from a number of drawings contained in a kind of commonplace book in Castle Wolfegg in Germany. He has also been called the Master of the Amsterdam Cabinet, since the largest collection of his prints (all drypoints) is in the print room of the Rijksmuseum. They often represent very worldly subjects and are done in a lively sketchy manner. *Dürer must have known them, as their influence can be traced in several of his early drawings. A few

paintings have also been attributed to this master. Various suggestions have been made for identifying him with named artists, but none has met with general acceptance.

Master of the Legend of St Barbara (active c.1470–c.1500). Netherlandish painter, one of the ablest followers of Rogier van der *Weyden. He probably worked in Bruges and/or Brussels. He is named after the subject of a *triptych (c.1475), the centre panel of which is now in the Musées Royaux, Brussels, the left wing in the Confrérie du S. Sang, Bruges, and the right one lost.

Master of the Legend of St Francis. A name for the main painter of the famous cycle of frescos on the nave walls of the Upper Church of S. Francesco in Assisi, depicting the life of St Francis and probably dating from about 1300, although some critics put them as late as the 1330s. This cycle was praised by *Vasari as one of the principal works of *Giotto and figures as such in much art-historical literature, but many scholars now challenge the attribution, feeling that Giotto's undoubted works in the Arena Chapel at Padua differ so thoroughly from those of Assisi in both sentiment and formal organization that it is hard to imagine that he should have painted both. There are 28 scenes in the cycle; the first one and the last three differ in style from the rest and have been attributed to the *Master of St Cecilia.

Master of the Life of the Virgin (or **Master of the Life of Mary**) (active c.1460–90). German painter, named after a series of eight panels (from a dismembered alterpiece) illustrating the life of the Virgin, of which the *Presentation in the Temple* is in the National Gallery, London, and the remainder in the Alte Pinakothek, Munich. He was one of the outstanding Cologne painters of his time, and his affinities with Dieric *Bouts and Rogier van der *Weyden suggest that he trained in the Netherlands. None of the pictures attributed to him is dated; a *Crucifixion* *triptych in the hospital church at Bernkastel-Kues on the Moselle, is generally regarded as his earliest work (c.1460–5).

Master of the Playing Cards (active mid-15th century). German engraver, named after a set of playing cards depicting human figures, animals, flowers, etc., now mainly divided between the Kupferstichkabinett in Dresden and the Bibliothèque Nationale in Paris. They have been dated as early as the 1430s and he was one of the first distinct artistic personalities in the history of engraving. More than 100 prints have been attributed to him, his style being characterized by closely observed naturalistic detail and the use of short, densely packed parallel strokes to create shading.

Master of the Unicorn. See DUVET.

Master of the View of St Gudule (active c.1470–c.1500). Netherlandish painter, named after a picture that has in the background a view of the façade of the church (now cathedral) of St Gudule in Brussels (*The Pastoral Sermon*, also known as *St Géry Preaching*, Louvre, Paris). Other Brussels buildings figure in pictures attributed to this artist. In the background of his *Portrait of a Man Holding a Heart-Shaped Book* (NG, London), for example, there is a view of Notre-Dame-du-Sablon. His style was influenced by Rogier van der *Weyden.

Master of the Virgo Inter Virgines (active c.1480–c.1500). Netherlandish painter, named after a picture representing the Virgin Mary with the virgin saints Barbara, Catherine, Cecilia, and Ursula (Rijksmuseum, Amsterdam). He is thought to have worked in Delft, for his style is reflected in the woodcut illustrations (which he presumably designed) to several books published there between 1482 and 1498. About twenty paintings have been attributed to him, revealing a very distinctive and distinguished artist, who obtained his highly emotional effects through intense colours, desolate landscapes, and gaunt figures. His work is sometimes awkward but always sincere and involving. Two of his finest paintings are the *Crucifixion* (Bowes Mus., Barnard Castle) and the *Entombment* (Walker AG, Liverpool).

Master of Třeboň (or of **Wittingau**) (active late 14th century). Bohemian painter, named after his main work, three panels (c.1380–90) from an altarpiece originally in the monastery at Třeboň (Wittingau in German) in the Czech Republic and now in the National Gallery, Prague. He was the outstanding Bohemian painter of his time and because of his combination of elegant forms and naturalistic details he is sometimes claimed as a pioneer of the *International Gothic style.

Master of Vyšší Brod (or of **Hohenfurth**). Bohemian painter, so called after his main work, a large altarpiece with scenes from the life of Christ (c.1350, NG, Prague) painted for the monastery of Vyšší Brod (Hohenfurth in German) in the Czech Republic. He combined knowledge of Italian painting with Bohemian traditions to create the courtly style characteristic of Prague in the third quarter of the 15th century.

Master of Wittingau. See MASTER OF TŘEBOŇ.

masterpiece. A term now loosely applied to the finest work by a particular artist or to any work of art of acknowledged greatness or of pre-eminence in some particular respect or field. Originally it meant the piece of work by which a craftsman, having finished his training, gained the rank of 'master' in his guild.

Master Theodoric (active mid-14th century). Bohemian painter. He is first certainly documented in 1359, when he is described as court painter to the Emperor Charles IV in Prague. However, he may well be identical with a Theodoric who in 1348 became first head of the newly founded painters' guild in Prague. In 1367 he was rewarded for his only documented work—the extraordinarily rich decoration of the chapel of the Holy Cross in Karlstein Castle near Prague. The decoration features more than 100 panels of saints, prophets, and angels, most of them still *in situ*, together with frescos and coloured stone inlays. His figures are rather heavy in form but softly modelled, and he is regarded as one of the originators of the 'Soft Style' that was characteristic of much central European painting in the late 14th and early 15th centuries.

Master Wilhelm. See COLOGNE SCHOOL.

mastic. A soft *resin from the mastic tree (*Pistacia lentiscus*), native of the shores of the Mediterranean. It has been used in art as a painting medium (see MEGILP) and in varnishes. Because it yellows with age, however, it has been superseded as a varnish by *dammar and synthetic resins.

Matejko, Jan (*b* Cracow, 24 June 1838; *d* Cracow, 1 Nov. 1893). The most famous Polish painter of his time. Apart from periods of study in Munich and Vienna, he was based in Cracow all his career, and in 1873 he was appointed director of the city's School of Fine Arts (his pupils there included *Wyspiański). Matejko specialized in huge colourful canvases depicting notable events from Poland's history (*Battle of Grunwald*, 1875–8, Nat. Mus., Warsaw). He also painted portraits.

Mateo de Compostela (active late 12th century). Spanish *Romanesque architect and possibly sculptor. An inscription dated 1188 on the Portico de la Gloria at the cathedral of Santiago de Compostela names Mateo as the director of works. It has usually been assumed that he was the sculptor as well as the architect of the portico (which features the greatest ensemble of Spanish sculpture of this period), but this is by no means certain.

Mathieu, Georges (b Boulogne-sur-Mer, 27 Jan. 1921). French painter. In the 1950s he gained an international reputation as one of the leading exponents of expressive abstraction. This was partly because of a flair for publicity that has led to him being described as 'the Salvador *Dalí of *Art Informel'. He works rapidly, often on a large scale, with sweeping, impulsive gestures, sometimes squeezing paint straight from the tube onto the canvas. He regards himself as a traditional history painter working with abstract means, and he has painted dressed in armour in front of an audience.

Matisse, Henri (b Le Cateau-Cambrésis, nr. Cambrai, 31 Dec. 1869; d Nice, 3 Nov. 1954). French painter, sculptor, draughtsman, print-maker, and designer, one of the most illustrious artists of the 20th century. From the 1920s he enjoyed an international reputation alongside *Picasso as the foremost painter of his time. Unlike Picasso, he was a late starter in art, and he was not quite so prolific or versatile, but for sensitivity of line and beauty of colouring he stands unrivalled among his contemporaries.

Matisse began studying art in 1891 after abandoning a legal career. His early pictures—mainly still-lifes and landscapes—were sober in colour, but in the summer of 1896, painting in Brittany, he began to adopt the lighter palette of the *Impressionists. In 1899 he started to experiment with the *Neo-Impressionist technique, which he still used five years later in one of his first major works—the celebrated *Luxe, calme et volupté* (1904–5, Mus. d'Orsay, Paris), exhibited at the *Salon des Indépendants in 1905 and bought by *Signac. During this period he had been painting with *Marquet, and had met *Derain and through him *Vlaminck; in 1905, together with these and other friends from student days, he took part in the exhibition at the *Salon d'Automne that launched *Fauvism. In the same year (Matisse's *annus mirabilis*) he acquired his first important patrons—the expatriate Americans Gertrude, Leo, and Michael *Stein—and they were soon followed by others. Previously he had struggled to earn a living, but he was now free from financial worries and could afford to travel (before the First World War he visited Germany, where his work was

becoming influential among the *Expressionists, Morocco, Russia, and Spain). His growing reputation also attracted many pupils to the art school he ran in Paris from 1907 to 1911.

Matisse had met Picasso as early as 1906, and during the second decade of the century he was influenced by *Cubism (or rather responded to its challenge) and painted some of his most austere and formal pictures (*Bathers by a River*, 1916–17, Art Inst. of Chicago). In the 1920s, however, he returned to the luminous serenity that characterized his work for the rest of his long career. From 1916 he spent most of his winters on the Riviera, mainly at Nice and also at Vence. The luxuriously sensual works he painted there—odalisques, still-lifes of tropical fruits and flowers, and glowing interiors—are irradiated with the strong sun and rich colours of the south. During the 1930s he travelled widely again, but in 1940 he moved to the south of France to escape the German occupation of Paris and settled there permanently. Following two major operations for duodenal cancer in 1941, he was confined to bed or a wheelchair, but he worked until the end of his life and one of his greatest and most original works was created in 1949–51, when he was in his eighties. This is the chapel of the Rosary at Vence, a gift of thanksgiving for a woman who had nursed him after his operations then become a nun at this Dominican convent. Matisse designed every detail, including the priests' vestments. The stained-glass windows show his familiar love of colour, but the walls feature murals of pure white ceramic tiles decorated with black line drawings of inspired simplicity. Matisse was not a believer, but he created here one of the most moving religious buildings of the 20th century and expressed what he called 'the nearly religious feeling I have for life'.

In his bedridden final years Matisse also embarked on another kind of highly original work, using brightly coloured cut-out paper shapes (*gouaches découpées*) arranged into purely abstract patterns (*L'Escargot*, 1953, Tate, London). 'The paper cut-out', he said, 'allows me to draw in the colour. It is a simplification for me. Instead of drawing the outline and putting the colour inside it—the one modifying the other—I draw straight into the colour.' The colours he used in his cut-outs were often so strong that his doctor advised him to wear dark glasses. They must rank among the most joyous works ever created by an artist in old age. Unlike many of his great contemporaries, Matisse did not attempt to express in his work the troubled times through which he lived. 'What I dream of', he wrote, 'is an art of balance, of purity and serenity devoid of troubling or disturbing subject-matter . . . like a comforting influence, a mental balm—something like a good armchair in which one rests from physical fatigue.'

Matisse made sculptures at intervals throughout his career, the best known probably being the four bronzes called *The Back I–IV* (1909–c.1929, casts in Tate Modern, London, and elsewhere), in which he progressively removed all detail, paring the figure down to massively simple forms. He also designed sets and costumes for *Diaghilev and was a brilliant book illustrator. His work is represented in most important collections of modern art, the finest holdings being at the *Barnes Foundation in Merion, Pennsylvania, the Hermitage, St Petersburg, and the Pushkin Museum, Moscow. There are also Matisse museums in Le Cateau (his birthplace) and Nice.

His son **Pierre Matisse** (1900–89), an art dealer, settled in the USA in 1925 and became an American citizen in 1942. His gallery in New York (opened 1932) dealt particularly in the work of leading *Surrealists, but he also represented artists as varied as *Balthus, *Chagall, and *Giacometti.

Matsch, Franz von. See KLIMT.

Matsys, Quentin. See MASSYS.

Matta (Roberto Matta Echaurren) (b Santiago, Chile, 11 Nov. 1911; d Civitavecchia, Italy, 23 Nov. 2002). Chilean painter and sculptor, active mainly in Paris, but also in Italy and the USA. He trained as an architect but turned to painting in 1937 and in the same year joined the *Surrealist movement. In 1939 he fled from Europe to New York, where with other émigrés including *Breton, *Ernst, *Masson, and *Tanguy he formed a strong and influential Surrealist presence. He played a particularly significant role in encouraging *Gorky, *Pollock, and other *Abstract Expressionists to experiment with *automatism; he, 'more than any other of the Surrealists, made himself available to young New Yorkers.' A keen intellectual and scintillating conversationalist, he was able to focus attention on issues, to crystallize and dramatize them verbally' (Irving Sandler, *Abstract Expressionism*, 1970). From about 1944 he began to create his most characteristic works—large canvases bordering on abstraction that evoke fantastic subjective landscapes and take as their theme the precariousness of human existence in a world dominated by machines and hidden forces; he was described in his obituary in *The Times* as 'a master visionary of the 20th century'. In 1948 he broke with the Surrealists and returned to Europe, but his work continued in a similar vein. He lived in Rome in the early 1950s, then mainly in Paris, although he travelled widely. In 1957 he began making sculpture.

Matteo di Giovanni (b Borgo San Sepolcro [now Sansepolcro], c.1430; d Siena, 1495). Italian painter. He came from the same town as *Piero della Francesca, and he painted the wings and *predella (Pinacoteca, Sansepolcro) of the altarpiece of which Piero's *Baptism of Christ* (NG, London) was the centre panel. However, he spent most of his career in Siena, where he seems to have been one of the most popular and prolific painters of the second half of the 15th century. His style was elegant, linear, and decorative.

matting wheel. See ROULETTE.

Mauclair, Camille. See FAUVISM.

Maulbertsch (or **Maulpertsch**), **Franz Anton** (b Langenargen, Lake Constance, 7 June 1724; d Vienna, 7 Aug. 1796). The greatest Austrian decorative painter of the 18th century. For most of his career he was based in Vienna, where he studied at the Academy and was early influenced by Paul *Troger, but he was active (and extremely productive) over a wide area of central Europe; he is recorded working in almost 60 different places and most of his paintings (altarpieces as well as frescos) are still in the churches and secular buildings in Austria, the Czech Republic, Hungary, and Slovakia for which they were produced. His vivacious, colourful, and emotional style was almost completely resistant to *Neoclassical influences, representing the last glorious flowering of the *Baroque and *Rococo tradition, although his final paintings understandably reveal signs of tiredness. Examples of his work that show him at the exhilarating height of his powers are the altar and ceiling frescos (1757–8) in the church at Sümeg, Hungary. His painterly dash is even more apparent in his oil sketches, which are well represented in the Barockmuseum, Vienna, and he was also an outstanding etcher.

maulstick (or **mahlstick** or **rest-stick**) (Dutch: *malen*, 'to paint', and *stok*, 'stick'). A wooden rod about a metre (3 ft) long with a padded knob at one end, used by painters to support and steady the brush hand, particularly when working on detailed passages. Maulsticks are first recorded in the 16th century, their introduction coinciding roughly with the adoption of oil on canvas as the standard technique for producing easel pictures (as oils are slower drying than *tempera there was more risk of smudging wet paint). They are sometimes shown in pictures of St Luke painting the Virgin, for example by a follower of Quentin *Massys (c.1520, NG, London) and by Maerten van *Heemskerck (1532, Hals Mus., Haarlem). From the mid-16th century they are seen occasionally in artists' self-portraits, and from the 17th century they often appear; one of the first dated examples (1548) is by Catharina van *Hemessen (Kunstmuseum, Basle).

Mauritshuis. The royal picture gallery in The Hague, opened to the public in 1820. The building, designed by Jacob van *Campen in 1633 as a palace for Count Johan Maurits of Nassau-Siegen (Maurice of Nassau), is one of the masterpieces of Dutch architecture. It houses one of the world's choicest collections of 17th-century Dutch painting (with pictures also from the 15th, 16th, and 18th centuries), including such celebrated works as *Rembrandt's *Anatomy Lesson of Dr Tulp* and *Vermeer's *View of Delft*.

Mauve, Anton (b Zaandam, 18 Sept. 1838; d Arnhem, 5 Feb. 1888). Dutch painter, one of the leading artists of the *Hague School. He concentrated on small pictures of unpretentious subjects—dunes, meadows, and beaches—painted in light, silvery tones. His sincere and modest spirit made a deep impression on van *Gogh, who was a cousin of Mauve's wife and spent some time working with him in 1881–2. Mauve was a prolific and popular artist and is represented in many museums in the Netherlands and elsewhere.

Maximilian I, Emperor. See HABSBURG.

Maximilian II, Emperor. See HABSBURG.

May, Phil (b Leeds, 22 Apr. 1864; d London, 5 Aug. 1903). English illustrator and caricaturist. He began his career as a theatrical scene painter (he also did some acting) and was self-taught as an illustrator. In 1885–8 he lived in Australia for the sake of his health, working for the *Sydney Bulletin*, and after his return to England he became one of the most popular and prolific illustrators of the day, contributing to *Punch*, the *Illustrated London News*, and various other periodicals, and also publishing numerous collections of his drawings. He worked at a time when most British magazines were switching to photomechanical methods of reproduction, and the new techniques suited his vigorous and economical style of pen-and-ink drawing. His subjects were taken mainly from London street life—in contrast to those of Aubrey *Beardsley, the other great but short-lived black-and-white illustrator of the 1890s. May was bohemian in his habits ('draw firm and live jolly' was his motto), squandering a good deal of money, and he died of cirrhosis and tuberculosis at the age of 39.

Mayer, Constance. See PRUD'HON.

Mayno (or Maino), **Juan Bautista** (b Pastrana, Jan. 1578; d Madrid, 1 Apr. 1641). Spanish painter. According to *Palomino he was a pupil of El *Greco in Toledo, but there is no suggestion of this in Mayno's clear and firm style, which was formed in Italy (his stay is not precisely documented, but he seems to have spent most of the first decade of the 17th century there). Paintings such as the *Adoration of the Shepherds* (1611, Prado, Madrid) show echoes of *Caravaggio (no other Spanish artist was so directly influenced by him) and of Guido *Reni, who is said to have been a friend of Mayno. In 1613 he took holy orders and subsequently did little painting, but after moving from Toledo to Madrid in about 1620 he was drawing master to the future Philip IV (see HABSBURG). The most important painting of his later career is the *Recovery of Bahía* (1634–5, Prado), part of a series of battle pictures for the Buen Retiro Palace that also included the *Surrender of Breda* by his friend *Velázquez.

Mazo, Juan Bautista Martínez del (b Cuenca province (probably Beteta), c.1612/15; d Madrid, 10 Feb. 1667). Spanish painter. He was a pupil of *Velázquez, married his daughter in 1633, and succeeded him as court painter in 1661. His life is fairly well documented, but his work is not. Among his very few signed paintings is a portrait of Queen Mariana (1666, NG, London), and many of the works attributed to him were formerly given to Velázquez, whose mature style he imitated with great assurance. In addition to portraits he painted some excellent landscapes.

Mazzoni, Sebastiano (b Florence, c.1611; d Venice, 22 Apr. 1678). Italian painter, poet, and architect, active mainly in Venice, where he settled in 1646/8. He was one of the most individualistic of Italian *Baroque painters, often choosing unusual subjects and expressing a vivid sense of movement with his brilliantly free brushwork. His work looks forward to 18th-century Venetian painting and he may have been Sebastiano *Ricci's first teacher.

Meadows, Bernard (b Norwich, 19 Feb. 1915). British sculptor, mainly in bronze, studio assistant to Henry *Moore, 1936–9. In the Second World War he served in the RAF and spent some time on the Cocos Islands in the Indian Ocean, from which he derived the crab motif that he used in many of his works (*Black Crab*, Tate, London, 1952). Characteristically his sculpture is abstract but suggests animal and plant forms—during the 1960s he sometimes used real fruits in his casting. From 1960 to 1980 he was professor of sculpture at the *Royal College of Art.

Meckenem, Israhel van, the Younger (b Meckenheim, c.1440/50; d Bocholt, 10 Nov. 1503). German engraver, the son of an engraver of the same name, active c.1450–65. He is thought to have trained with his father and probably with *Master E.S., whose work he copied. His oeuvre is bigger than that of any other 15th-century engraver; about 600 plates are attributed to him, and in some instances over 100 prints have been preserved from each plate. Like many early engravers, he also worked as a goldsmith. Although he was a minor figure as a creative artist (much of his work consisted of copies), he is important in showing the growing popularity of engraving. He was the first artist to engrave his own features (in a double portrait together with his wife, c.1490) and looks a very shrewd individual.

medal. A small, flat piece of metal bearing a design commemorating a person or event and produced in multiple copies; usually it resembles an outsize coin, with a portrait on one side and a complementary image on the other. Although there are precedents of a sort in Roman art, medals as we know them originated in the 15th century, inspired by the *Renaissance interest in antique coins (with their vivid portraits of emperors). *Pisanello is regarded as the father of the art form. The first of his twenty-odd medals honoured the Byzantine emperor John VIII who visited Italy in 1438. On one side is a profile portrait of the emperor, and on the other is an image of him praying at a shrine. Pisanello subsequently made medals for the ruling families of several Italian states, including the *Este of Ferrara and the *Gonzaga of Mantua. His innovation was soon imitated and during the second half of the 15th century the production of medals

was established in virtually every notable art centre in Italy. In the early 16th century the fashion spread outside Italy, particularly to Germany, where a specialist profession of medallist soon developed.

Although there is considerable variation in detail, most Renaissance medals follow the same basic format. Occasionally they are ovals or other shapes, but the vast majority are circular and usually between about 5 and 10 cm (2–4 in) in diameter (that is, appreciably larger than coins, although a few are coin sized). Some of them commemorate significant events (for example battles), but most were made in honour of a particular individual. One side (the obverse) almost always has a profile portrait, and the other (the reverse) generally has a symbol or image alluding to the subject's character or achievements. Both sides usually have an inscription in Latin (or occasionally Greek); typically these identify the subject and sometimes they name the artist. Most early medals were made of bronze (lead and silver were also occasionally used), and they were produced by casting, like miniature works of sculpture. In the early 16th century, however, machinery was introduced by means of which the design could be stamped on to a blank piece of metal. This mechanization meant that more impressions of a medal could be made, and consequently they could be more widely circulated.

Improvements in technology led to mass production of medals, with a consequent general drop in artistic standards. However, there have been periodic revivals of interest in producing cast medals in the original Renaissance fashion. Alphonse *Legros, for example, began producing cast medals in the 1880s and—as an influential teacher at the *Slade School—he inspired several other artists in Britain to follow his example.

Medici. Italian family of bankers and merchants that ruled Florence and later Tuscany for most of the period from 1434 to 1737 and was famous for its patronage of learning and the arts throughout the *Renaissance. Unlike most of the great Italian ruling dynasties, the Medici were not primarily military men, gaining their power through wealth and political astuteness rather than force. Their influence extended beyond the city and the region, for the family produced three popes and two queens of France.

The Medici name appears in Florentine records as early as the 12th century, but the real founder of the family fortune was **Giovanni di**

Bicci de' Medici (1360–1429), who became one of the leading bankers in Italy and in 1421 was appointed gonfalonier (head of Florence's governing council). He also began the family tradition of art patronage, notably by commissioning *Brunelleschi to build the Old Sacristy of the church of S. Lorenzo in 1419. His son **Cosimo** (1389–1464) was effectively ruler of Florence from 1434, although in theory he was an ordinary citizen of the republic. His major artistic undertaking was the building of the family palace (now known as the Palazzo Medici-Riccardi), designed by *Michelozzo and begun in 1445. The other artists he employed included *Donatello and *Uccello, and he was an important collector of manuscripts, founding what is now the Laurentian Library in Florence. His son **Piero** (1416–69), known as Piero the Gouty, is best remembered in artistic terms for commissioning Benozzo *Gozzoli's celebrated frescos in the family palace.

Piero's son and successor **Lorenzo the Magnificent** (1449–92) was the most famous member of the family. A poet and scholar, he had a great interest in the classical world and made a fine collection of antiquities, including sculpture, gems, and cameos. He also patronized some of the best contemporary artists, including the young *Michelangelo, who was treated almost like an adopted son (he lived in the Medici Palace for a time and had access to Lorenzo's sculpture garden, which served as a kind of informal art *academy). Lorenzo's most important architectural commission was the Villa Medici at Poggio a Caiano, near Florence, designed by Giuliano da Sangallo and built in the 1480s. For another villa, near Volterra, he commissioned paintings from *Botticelli and other artists. This building has been destroyed, but Botticelli produced other work for the Medici; his *Primavera* and *Birth of Venus* were certainly owned by the family and were perhaps painted for Lorenzo's second cousin **Lorenzo di Pierfrancesco** (1463–1503). Lorenzo the Magnificent was succeeded by his son **Piero** (1471–1503), who was exiled from Florence in 1494 after being forced to make humiliating concessions to Charles VIII of France, who had invaded Italy.

The Medici were absent from Florence until 1512, when Piero's brother **Giuliano** (1479–1516) returned and assumed power. From 1527 to 1532 the family was again expelled, then **Alessandro** (1511–37), an illegitimate descendant of Lorenzo the Magnificent, regained control and assumed the title of Duke of Florence. A despotic ruler, he was assassinated in 1537 and succeeded by a distant cousin **Cosimo** (1519–74), who restored stability to the city. In 1557 Cosimo gained control of Siena and most of its dependent territories, giving him dominion over much of the region, and in 1569 Pope Pius V awarded him the hereditary title of Grand Duke of Tuscany. Unlike some other Medici rulers, Cosimo was not a connoisseur, but he appreciated the propaganda value of art and he spent lavishly on glorifying himself and his family and on embellishing Florence. *Bronzino was his favourite artist, and the others he employed included *Ammanati, *Cellini, *Giambologna, *Pontormo, and *Vasari, who designed the *Uffizi, originally used as offices but soon adapted to include gallery space for the family art collections. Its great collection of artists' self-portraits was founded by Cardinal **Leopoldo de' Medici** (1617–75), who in this way made perhaps the most distinctive contribution to the arts of any of the later members of the family. Cosimo's descendants ruled until 1737, when the last Medici grand duke, **Gian Gastone**, died without a male heir and was succeeded by a distant relative, Francis Stephen, Duke of Lorraine. At this point Gian Gastone's sister **Anna Maria Luisa** (1667–1743) presented the family collections to the city of Florence.

The three Medici popes were Leo X (reigned 1513–21), Clement VII (1523–34), and Leo XI (reigned for a month in 1605); the first two were notable art patrons. Leo X (born **Giovanni de' Medici** in 1475) was the second son of Lorenzo the Magnificent. As pope he continued his predecessor Julius II's projects in the rebuilding of St Peter's and the decoration of the Vatican Stanze (see RAPHAEL). His extravagant spending (on war and personal pleasures as well as art) left the papal treasury in heavy debt. Clement VII (born **Giulio de' Medici** in 1478) was a nephew of Lorenzo the Magnificent. The artists he patronized included Cellini, Michelangelo, and *Sebastiano del Piombo. (Giovanni Angelo Medici (1499–1565), who became Pius IV in 1559, came from a Milanese family that was not related to the Florentine Medici.)

The two Medici queens of France were **Catherine de' Medici** (1519–89), known in France as Catherine de Médicis, and **Maria de' Medici** (1573–1642), known in France as Marie de Médicis. Catherine was the wife of Henry II and after his death in 1559 she was regent or adviser to three of their sons who became king in turn: Francis II, Charles IX, and Henry III. The artists she patronized included Niccolò dell' *Abate, Germain *Pilon, and Francesco *Primaticcio.

Maria was the second wife of Henry IV and after his death in 1610 she became regent for their son Louis XIII. *Rubens painted a great cycle of paintings glorifying her life (1622–5, Louvre, Paris). The image it presents of her is far from the truth, for she was politically inept and ended her life in exile.

Medici Venus. Marble statue of naked Venus (Uffizi, Florence), first recorded for certain in 1638 in the Villa Medici in Rome. It is signed by 'Cleomenes son of Apollodorus', but in the 18th century its fame as a model of female beauty was so great that the signature's authenticity was doubted and the statue was attributed to such illustrious names as *Phidias and *Praxiteles (to whose *Aphrodite of Cnidus it bears some resemblance in pose). Several other statues of similar type exist, but in spite of the *Medici Venus'* quite severe restorations, it far outdid its rivals in fame, and it was one of the greatest prizes that Napoleon brought to France when Italy was under his dominion (it was in Paris 1803–15). As late as 1840 it was described by *Ruskin as 'one of the purest and most elevated incarnations of woman conceivable', but its reputation has since crumbled, Martin Robertson (*A History of Greek Art*, 1975) describing it as being 'among the most charmless remnants of antiquity'. It is now considered to be a copy of *c*.100 BC deriving from an original of the time of Praxiteles.

Medina, Sir John (John Baptiste de Medina) (*b* Brussels, *c*.1659; *d* Edinburgh, 5 Oct. 1710). Painter of Spanish extraction active principally in Scotland. He moved from Flanders to London in 1686 and in about 1693 settled in Edinburgh, where he became the leading portraitist of his time—'*Kneller's equivalent in Scotland' (Ellis *Waterhouse). His pupil William Aikman (1682–1731) succeeded to his position—'the equivalent in Scotland of both *Richardson for his men's portraits and *Jervas for his women's portraits' (Waterhouse). In about 1723 Aikman settled in London.

medium. Term used to refer to the material or form of expression employed by an artist; thus painting, sculpture, and drawing are three different media, and bronze, marble, and wood are three of the media of sculpture. In a more restricted sense, the term refers to the substance with which *pigment is mixed to make paint; for example, gum arabic in *watercolour, egg yolk in *tempera, *linseed oil (most usually) in *oil painting. See also VEHICLE.

Meegeren, Han van. See BREDIUS.

Meer, Jan van der. See VERMEER VAN HAARLEM.

Megillah (plural: Megillat; Hebrew: 'scroll'). A scroll containing any of five biblical texts appointed to be read on certain notable Jewish days; when the text is not specified, the term commonly refers to the scroll of the Old Testament Book of Esther, read during the feast of Purim, commemorating the deliverance of the Jews from Babylon. Esther scrolls read in synagogues are unornamented, but those for domestic use in prosperous families were often richly decorated—it is one of the few Jewish works with a consistent tradition of illumination. The earliest known illustrated Megillat are from 16th-century Italy, where the tradition flourished until the 18th century. They were also particularly popular in the Low Countries.

megilp. A gel-like painting *medium consisting of *mastic varnish mixed with *linseed oil. It makes oil paint glossy and easy to manipulate, for which reason it was popular in the 18th and 19th centuries; however, it is a dangerous aid, in time rendering the paint yellow and brittle.

Meissonier, Ernest (*b* Lyons, 21 Feb. 1815; *d* Paris, 31 Jan. 1891). French painter, illustrator, and sculptor. He was immensely successful with his small-format, nigglingly detailed historical paintings and historical *genre pieces (particularly scenes in *Three Musketeers* vein or from the Napoleonic campaigns) and from the 1840s he received the highest official honours, including the Grand Cross of the Legion of Honour in 1889—he was the first painter to win this award. Astonishingly conceited as well as mean-spirited, he cultivated a huge white beard and liked to be photographed or painted in attitudes of fiercely profound thought, as in his self-portrait of 1889 in the Musée d'Orsay, Paris. He did his best work when he was at his least pretentious. His landscapes are attractive descriptive exercises and his *Rue de la Mortellerie* (1848, Mus. d'Orsay), which shows a corpse-strewn Paris street during the revolutionary events of 1848, has genuine pathos and impressed *Delacroix. There are large collections of Meissonier's work in the Musée d'Orsay and in the Wallace Collection, London.

Meissonnier, Juste-Aurèle (*b* Turin, 1695; *d* Paris, 31 July 1750). French goldsmith, designer, and architect. In 1726 he succeeded Jean *Berain II as chief designer to Louis XV. His charming and fanciful designs were widely known in engravings and were an important factor in spreading the *Rococo style.

Meit, Conrad (b Worms, c.1475; d Antwerp, 1550/1). German sculptor. From about 1506 to 1510 he worked in Wittenberg at the court of Frederick the Wise, Elector of Saxony, collaborating with *Cranach. Soon afterwards he moved to the Netherlands, where he was court sculptor to the *Habsburg rulers for most of his career. His work included a number of large monuments, but his most characteristic sculptures are small figures and portraits, most notably sensuous free-standing nudes such as the well-known alabaster *Judith with the Head of Holofernes* (c.1510–15, Bayerisches Nationalmuseum, Munich). In these he created a distinctive type of German *Renaissance sculpture, combining Italian idealism with northern particularity of detail.

Meldrum, Max (b Edinburgh, 3 Dec. 1875; d Melbourne, 6 June 1955). Scottish-born Australian painter and teacher, active mainly in Melbourne. In 1917 he established a school there at which he disseminated his highly opinionated ideas on art. They were based on study of the Old Masters, particularly *Velázquez, whom he revered above all other painters. He regarded painting as a wholly objective exercise in defining and translating optical impressions by analysing tone in a rationally ordered way, and he thought that modern art, with its emphasis on colour and individual expression, spelt social decadence. Meldrum's paintings faithfully reflect his doctrines, being competently handled but singularly lacking in inspiration. In spite of his obvious limitations as an artist, his views gained many adherents in Melbourne and Sydney in the interwar period. He was a powerful personality (Norman *Lindsay called him 'the mad Mullah') and inspired great devotion in his students, none of whom achieved much distinction.

Meléndez, Luis (b Naples, 1716; d Madrid, 11 July 1780). Spanish painter, active in Madrid. He painted various subjects, but from the 1760s he specialized in still-life and is regarded as the finest Spanish painter in this field in the 18th century (he is sometimes called 'the Spanish *Chardin'). However, he spent much of his life in poverty. His work is rare outside Spain, but there are examples of his still-lifes in the National Gallery, London, and York Art Gallery, and there is a striking self-portrait of 1746 in the Louvre, Paris. Several other members of his family were painters, including two sisters.

Mellan, Claude (bapt. Abbeville, 23 May 1598; d Paris, 9 Sept. 1688). French engraver. One of the most renowned engravers of his period, he was best known for his portraits, but he also made prints after *Poussin and *Vouet, for example. He was a technical virtuoso and instead of using cross-*hatching he obtained his effects of light and shade by varying the thickness of his lines. The most famous example of his prowess is his *Sudarium of St Veronica* (1642), a portrait of Christ made up of a single continuous spiral line that goes round from the centre to the edge like the groove on a gramophone record. Mellan also painted, but few of his pictures survive.

Mellon, Andrew W. (b Pittsburgh, 24 Mar. 1855; d Southampton, NY, 26 Aug. 1937). American businessman, public official, art collector, and philanthropist. A banker and steel, coke, and oil magnate, he became secretary to the US Treasury (1921–32), ambassador to England (1932–3), and one of the richest men in the world. In 1937, shortly before his death, he donated his collection (particularly rich in Dutch and British painting) to the nation, together with funds to build a gallery to house them, thus creating the National Gallery of Art in Washington, which opened in 1941. Some of the finest works he owned, including *Raphael's *Alba Madonna*, had been sold from the *Hermitage by the Soviet government. His son **Paul Mellon** (b Pittsburgh, 11 June 1907; d Upperville, Va., 1 Feb. 1999) was also one of the greatest collectors of his generation, his main field of interest being British art. In 1966 he founded the Yale Center for British Art at New Haven. Opened in 1977, the Center is not only a major gallery, but also a research institution, with important collections of books and photographs. Its sister institution, the Paul Mellon Centre for Studies in British Art, was established in London in 1970. It is an educational charity whose purpose is to advance the study of British art and architecture, mainly by sponsorship of publications and support of research.

Melozzo da Forlì (b Forlì, 8 June 1438; d Forlì, 8 Nov. 1494). Italian painter, active mainly in Loreto, Rome, and Urbino. He was an attractive and idiosyncratic painter who achieved a high reputation in his time, but little of his work survives intact and he has been a neglected figure until fairly recently. His style was indebted to *Piero della Francesca and he was renowned for his skill in perspective and illusionism; he was, indeed, credited with being the inventor of the extreme form of foreshortening known as *sotto in sù*, of which *Mantegna was another great exponent. Melozzo's skill in this field is seen in his fresco of the *Ascension* (1478–80) for the dome of SS. Apostoli in Rome, fragments of which are in the Quirinal Palace and the Vatican.

Memlinc (or **Memling**), **Hans** (*b* Seligenstadt, nr. Frankfurt, *c*.1430/40; *d* Bruges, 11 Aug. 1494). Netherlandish painter, active in Bruges from 1465. He was German by birth, but there is no indication of this in his paintings, which show close connections with Rogier van der *Weyden, by whom—according to plausible tradition—he was taught. His softened and sweetened version of Rogier's style (there is some influence also from *Bouts) made him the most popular Netherlandish painter of his day. Whereas Rogier excelled in the depiction of intense emotion, Memlinc's impeccably crafted paintings are quiet, restrained, pious, and beautifully balanced. Tax records indicate that he was one of Bruges's wealthiest citizens and his large output shows he must have had a busy workshop. His style changed very little and it is difficult to place undated paintings in a chronological scheme. He painted numerous portraits and showed rather more originality in this field than in religious painting. Among his patrons were Italians then living in Bruges (*Tommaso Portinari* and his wife *Maria Portinari*, *c*.1468, Met. Mus., New York), and his portraits seem to have influenced artists such as Giovanni *Bellini in northern Italy. Gerard *David was among the local artists who continued his tradition. Memlinc's work is in many major collections, but it can be best seen in the museum devoted to him in Bruges.

Memmi, Lippo (active 1317–47). Sienese painter, Simone *Martini's brother-in-law and most able follower. They jointly signed the celebrated *Annunciation* (1333, Uffizi, Florence) and their respective shares in it are uncertain. Several other works are signed by Memmi, including Madonnas in the Gemäldegalerie, Berlin, and S. Maria dei Servi, Siena, showing his refined draughtsmanship, delicate palette, and extremely sensitive modelling. He was not an innovator, but an indication of the high quality of his work is that several paintings are disputed between him and Simone.

Mena, Pedro de (*bapt.* Grenada, 20 Aug. 1628; *d* Málaga, 13 Oct. 1688). Spanish sculptor, son of the sculptor **Alonso de Mena** (1587–1646), who ran the busiest workshop in Granada. Pedro worked in the city until 1658 (sometimes collaborating with Alonso *Cano), then moved to Málaga to carry out a commission for the cathedral—40 *relief panels for the choir stalls (1658–62). He was based in Málaga for the rest of his life, but he visited Madrid in 1662 and his reputation became widespread. His most characteristic works are *polychromed wooden figures of saints—pious, dignified, and graceful, if sometimes rather vapid.

Meneses Osorio, Francisco. See MURILLO.

Mengs, Anton Raphael (*b* Aussig, Bohemia [now Ústí nad Labem, Czech Republic], 12 Mar. 1728; *d* Rome, 29 June 1779). German painter, the son of a court painter in Dresden, **Ismael Mengs** (1688–1764). His father brought him up with harsh severity to be a great painter, on the models particularly of *Correggio and *Raphael (from whom he gained his Christian names). In 1740 he was taken to Rome and there established a reputation as a youthful prodigy. He returned to Germany in 1744 and in the next few years achieved success as a portraitist in Dresden. In 1748–9 he made another visit to Rome, during which he married an Italian girl, and in 1752 he settled in the city, becoming a close friend of *Winckelmann, who provided much of the theoretical inspiration for his work. It was for Winckelmann's patron, Cardinal *Albani, that Mengs painted his most famous work, the ceiling fresco *Parnassus* (1761) in the Villa Albani (now the Villa Torlonia), Rome. The fresco now seems flimsy and simpering, but it was the basis of Mengs's enormous contemporary reputation (he was widely regarded not only as a leader of the *Neoclassical movement, but also as the greatest living painter). It breaks completely with *Baroque *illusionism, treating the scene exactly as if it were to be seen at normal eye level (see QUADRO RIPORTATO), and is full of allusions to the *antique and the High *Renaissance. In 1761–9 and 1774–7 he worked as court painter in Spain, carrying out a large amount of decoration in the Royal Palace, Madrid. His frescos there are dull and sterile, but it is a sign of the move in taste towards Neoclassicism that certain of his works were preferred to those of Giambattista *Tiepolo, now regarded as an incomparably greater artist. Mengs was influential through his writings on art (which appeared in or soon after his lifetime in English, French, German, Italian, and Spanish) as well as his paintings. Today his portraits are considered more successful than his history paintings, and he was *Batoni's main rival as the leading portraitist in Rome.

Menpes, Mortimer. See WHISTLER, JAMES MCNEILL.

Menzel, Adolph (*b* Breslau, Silesia [now Wrocław, Poland], 8 Dec. 1815; *d* Berlin, 9 Feb. 1905). German painter and printmaker, active mainly in Berlin, where in 1832 he took over his dead father's lithographic business. He was extremely industrious and achieved fame with 400 illustrations (wood engravings from his lively drawings) for Franz Kugler's *History of Frederick the Great* (1840–2). In painting he worked on similar themes and with comparable success, creating the popular image of the founder of the Prussian state. From the 1860s he turned to subjects from modern life and was one of the first German painters to depict the picturesque qualities of industry (*The Steel Mill*, 1872–5, Alte NG, Berlin). Today, however, Menzel is most highly regarded not for the works that brought him contemporary acclaim (in his later years he was one of the most admired artists in Germany), but for a series of informal landscapes and interiors dating from the 1840s that remained virtually unknown in his lifetime. They are remarkably free and fresh in technique, unorthodox in composition, and both bold and refined in their treatment of light, presaging the developments of *Impressionism (*The Artist's Sister with a Candle*, 1847, Neue Pin., Munich). His attitude towards these paintings was strange; he kept them hidden and referred to Impressionism as 'the art of laziness', and when he visited Paris in 1855, 1867, and 1868 the artist he most admired was the tiresomely meticulous *Meissonier.

Mercier, Philip (*b* Berlin, 1689/91; *d* London, 18 July 1760). German-born painter and etcher of French extraction who spent all his known career in England, where he settled in about 1716. He was 'no genius' (Ellis *Waterhouse), but his work has considerable charm and he has the distinction of introducing the *conversation piece to England—*Party on a Terrace: The Schutz Family* (1725, Tate, London) is the first dated example; he also pioneered the *fancy picture. Many engravings were made of his work, helping to spread the *Rococo style in England. His patrons included several Hanoverian courtiers and in 1729 he was appointed principal painter to Frederick, Prince of Wales (see ROYAL COLLECTION), who had moved to England from Hanover the previous year. From 1739 to 1751 he lived in York (in this period he visited Ireland and Scotland), then returned to London. His daughter **Charlotte** (1738–62) was a pastel portraitist. She died in a workhouse, which

suggests that her father's career may have declined in his final years.

Merian, Matthäus (*bapt.* Basle, 25 Sept. 1593; *d* Bad Schwalbach, 19 June 1650). German printmaker and publisher of Swiss origin, active mainly in Frankfurt, where he ran an enormously prolific business. It published thousands of prints, many of them views of European towns for various topographical books. Much of this output came from the hands of assistants, among them Wenceslaus *Hollar. Merian's daughter **Maria Sibylla Merian** (*b* Frankfurt, 2 Apr. 1647; *d* Amsterdam, 13 Jan. 1717) trained as a flower painter. From 1685 she lived mainly in Amsterdam and in 1699–1701 she visited Surinam in South America, returning with numerous drawings and specimens of insects, including butterflies. In 1705 she published a book on these, illustrated with hand-coloured engravings that are remarkable for their scientific accuracy as well as their delicate beauty. Her brother **Matthäus Merian the Younger** (*bapt.* Basle, 25 Mar. 1621; *bur.* Frankfurt, 15 Feb. 1687) ran the family business in Frankfurt after his father's death.

Mérida, Carlos (*b* Guatemala City, 2 Dec. 1891; *d* Mexico City, 21 Dec. 1985). Guatemalan painter, active mainly in Mexico. In 1910–14 he studied in Paris under van *Dongen, meeting *Modigliani, *Picasso, and other members of the avant-garde. He returned to Guatemala in 1914 and in 1919 moved to Mexico, where he worked as *Rivera's chief assistant for several years. In 1927–9 he was again in Europe, where he became friends with *Klee and *Miró, then returned to Mexico. His early work was in a politically conscious figurative style, but in the 1930s he was influenced by *Surrealism and he eventually developed a completely abstract manner. From the 1950s much of his work was done for architectural settings, and he often worked in mosaic (for example at the Municipal Palace, Guatemala City, 1956) as well as in fresco.

Meryon, Charles (*b* Paris, 23 Nov. 1821; *d* Charenton, nr. Paris, 14 Feb. 1868). French etcher, the illegitimate son of an English doctor and a French dancer. After serving in the navy for several years, he took up painting in 1848, but he soon discovered he was colour blind and turned instead to etching. In the early 1850s he produced a series of views of Paris that are his most famous works. They feature a good deal of precise architectural detail, but they are remarkable more for their intense, sometimes sinister atmosphere than for their topographical qualities. Meryon had an extremely unhappy life, suffering from melancholia and a persecution complex, and in 1858–9 he was confined to an asylum at Charenton. After his release his work became looser and more subjective, culminating in *The Ministry of the Marine* (1865), which features flying *Bosch-like demons. In 1866 he was readmitted to the Charenton asylum and died there insane. During his lifetime he had some distinguished admirers, notably *Baudelaire, but in general his work was little appreciated. Now, however, he is recognized as a central figure in the revival of etching as a creative art form.

Merz. See SCHWITTERS.

Mesdag, Hendrik Willem (*b* Groningen, 23 Feb. 1831; *d* The Hague, 10 July 1915). Dutch painter and collector. He abandoned the family profession of banking in 1866 and became one of the leading artists of the *Hague School, particularly noted for his beach and sea scenes. His best-known work is the vast panorama (1881) of the fishing village of Scheveningen—about 120 m (400 ft) in circumference—housed in a specially designed building in The Hague. The Mesdag Museum, in the same city, contains his excellent collection of paintings, rich in works by members of the *Barbizon and Hague Schools, which he presented to the nation in 1903.

Mesens, E. L. T. (*b* Brussels, 27 Nov. 1903; *d* Brussels, 13 May 1971). Belgian musician, poet, collagist, exhibition organizer, and dealer. His interest in the visual arts developed under the influence of *Duchamp and *Picabia, whom he met in Paris in 1921, and he was influenced towards *Surrealism by the paintings of de *Chirico. He became a friend and champion of *Magritte and a highly active figure in the Surrealist movement, although more as an organizer than an artist. In 1938 he settled in London and became director of the London Gallery in Cork Street, the headquarters of Surrealism in England, organizing exhibitions of the work of many European artists there (including *Ernst, *Schwitters, and *Tanguy); he also edited the gallery's publication, the *London Bulletin*, an important documentary source for the period (it ran for twenty issues, 1938–40). He returned to Belgium in the 1950s. In his own work as an artist, Mesens was best known for his collages, which he created from an assortment of materials—tickets, ribbons, pieces of paper and print, etc. He made extensive use of printed words to create disconcerting or amusing ambiguities and

suggested meanings, some of which might almost be regarded as anticipations of *Conceptual art.

Messerschmidt, Franz Xaver (*b* Wiesensteig, nr. Ulm, 6 Feb. 1736; *d* Pressburg [now Bratislava, Slovakia], ?19 Aug. 1783). Austrian sculptor. He was trained initially by his uncles Johann Baptist Straub (1704–84) and Philipp Jakob Straub (1706–74) (two of five German sculptor brothers) in Munich and Graz respectively, then in 1755 moved to Vienna, where he continued his studies at the Academy. He remained based in Vienna until 1774, although he spent several months in Rome in 1765 (he visited London in the same year). In 1769 he began teaching at the Academy and in 1770 he bought a substantial house, an indication of the success he was enjoying as a portrait sculptor. However, he began to suffer from mental disturbances, because of which he was turned down for a professorship at the Academy in 1774. Deeply offended, he left Vienna, moving first to his native Wiesensteig, then to Munich, and finally to Pressburg, where he settled in 1777. In this final period he continued to work as a portraitist, but he lived as a famous recluse and devoted himself mainly to a series of 'character heads' (*Charakterköpfe*), in which he depicted in exaggerated, grimacing fashion the expressions associated with various states of mind. At his death, 69 of these heads (mainly in lead) were found in his studio, of which 49 survive (mainly in the Österreichisches Barockmuseum, Vienna). They were first exhibited in 1793 and have subsequently attracted a good deal of attention and varied interpretations. All of them depict the same bald, middle-aged man, essentially a self-portrait, and they have been seen as therapy for his mental illness. The Austrian-born American scholar Ernst Kris (1900–57), who was a psychoanalyst as well as an art historian, published two papers on Messerschmidt in 1932–3 in which he concluded that 'we are indeed dealing with a psychosis with predominant paranoid trends, which fits the general picture of schizophrenia'.

Meštrović, Ivan (*b* Vrpolje, 15 Aug. 1883; *d* South Bend, Ind., 16 Jan. 1962). Yugoslavian (Croatian)-born sculptor who became an American citizen in 1954. He studied at the Academy in Vienna, 1900–4, and in 1908–9 lived in Paris, where he met *Rodin. After returning to Yugoslavia he worked in a style that was basically classical but furbished with a superficial air of modernity. He spent the First World War in Rome, Geneva, Paris, and London, and in 1919 returned to Yugoslavia, where he received many public commissions, including an enormous mausoleum outside Belgrade in commemoration of the Unknown Soldier (1934), one of the many works in which he expressed his ardent patriotism. From 1943 to 1946 he lived in Switzerland, then settled in the USA, where he was professor of sculpture at Syracuse University, New York, 1947–55, and at the University of South Bend, Indiana, from 1955 until his death. His work in the USA included a number of monuments. The great reputation he enjoyed in his lifetime has declined since his death, the rhetoric of his large-scale works now seeming rather ponderous; his smaller, more lyrical pieces have dated less. There are Meštrović museums in Split (his former house, which he designed himself) and Zagreb.

metal cut. A print made from a metal plate in which the parts of the design that take the ink are raised in *relief (as in a *woodcut) rather than incised into the plate as in a *line engraving. Prints done in the *manière criblée are examples of the type and William *Blake used a personal version of the technique in his illuminated books.

metalpoint. Method of drawing using a small metal-tipped rod on paper or other material that has been coated with a special *ground. This coating is slightly granular, causing a trace of the metal to rub off on it. The metal may be copper, gold, lead, or (most commonly) silver, which gives an attractive fine grey line that oxidizes to a light brown. Often the ground is tinted with pigment, increasing the opportunity for delicate colouristic effects. The strength of tone can hardly be varied at all, so the technique depends on the quality of the drawn line and is best suited to work on a small scale. It demands great certainty of purpose and hand, for the line cannot be removed except by disturbing the ground. Silverpoint first appeared in medieval Italy and was particularly popular in the 15th century; *Dürer and *Leonardo were perhaps the greatest exponents of the medium. It went out of fashion in the 17th century, probably because the graphite *pencil was coming in, but was revived in the 18th century by miniaturists, especially in France.

Metaphysical Painting. A style of painting invented by de *Chirico in about 1913 and practised by him, *Carrà (from 1917), *Morandi (from 1918), and a few other Italian artists until about 1920. The term (Pittura Metafisica) was coined by de Chirico and Carrà in 1917, when both were patients at a military hospital in Ferrara, although *Apollinaire had earlier applied the word 'metaphysical' to de Chirico's pictures. The meaning attached to the word, which occurs in the titles of several pictures by de Chirico particularly, was never precisely formulated, but the style is characterized by images conveying a sense of mystery and hallucination (one definition of 'metaphysical' is 'transcending physical matter'). This enigmatic feeling was achieved partly by unreal perspectives and lighting, partly by the adoption of a strange iconography involving, for example, the use of tailor's dummies and statues in place of human figures, and partly by an incongruous juxtaposition of realistically depicted objects in a manner later taken over by some of the *Surrealists. However, the dreamlike quality conveyed by Metaphysical Painters differed from that of the Surrealists because of their concern with pictorial structure; their works often have an architectural sense of repose deriving from Italian *Renaissance art.

Metcalf, Willard L. See TEN.

Meteyard, Sidney Harold. See PRE-RAPHAELITE BROTHERHOOD.

metope. In *Classical architecture the square space or block that alternates with the ornamental features called triglyphs in the frieze of the Doric Order. Metopes may be left plain (they were originally left open), but in Greek art are often carved with *relief sculptures. The most famous examples are the metopes from the Parthenon in Athens (see PHIDIAS).

Metropolitan Museum of Art, New York. The largest and most comprehensive collection of art in the USA and one of the greatest in the world. It was founded in 1870 by a group of art collectors, civic leaders, and philanthropists, and after two temporary locations for the museum, it opened at its present site in Central Park in 1880. The building was designed by Calvert Vaux (one of the designers of Central Park) in Gothic style, and the grandiose classical façade overlooking Fifth Avenue was added in the early 20th century. There have been numerous other extensions over the years, and the original building now forms only a small part of the vast structure. The museum is owned by the city, but is supported mainly by private endowment, and the history of its foundation and growth illustrates the rapid rise of New York at the end of the 19th century as the financial and cultural

463

capital of North America, as well as the growing economic supremacy of America over Europe. In the first half-century or so of its existence, at a time when the major public collections in Europe were engaged in consolidation, relying largely on their purchase grants and other state aid, the Metropolitan Museum was being built up out of the private fortunes of great businessmen, who collected for prestige rather than out of connoisseurship, but collected only first-class works of art. It has also benefited from a number of endowed purchase grants, many of them unconditional, and its collections are now rich in virtually every field of the *fine and *applied arts from all parts of the world. Notable scholars who have been employed at the museum include Roger *Fry, John *Pope-Hennessy, and William *Valentiner.

Much of the collection of medieval art is housed in a separate building called the Cloisters in Fort Tryon Park, overlooking the Hudson River. Opened in 1938, the Cloisters is a medieval-style structure, largely made up of parts of *Romanesque and *Gothic buildings transported from Europe. Many of the works it houses were collected by the American sculptor George Grey Barnard (1863–1938), who lived in France for much of his career.

Metsu, Gabriel (b Leiden, Jan. 1629; bur. Amsterdam, 24 Oct. 1667). Dutch painter, active in Leiden, then in Amsterdam, where he had settled by 1657. *Houbraken says he was a pupil of *Dou, but Metsu's early works are very different from his—typically historical and mythological scenes, broadly rather than minutely painted. Metsu also painted portraits and still-lifes, but his most characteristic works are *genre scenes, some of which rank among the finest of their period. He concentrated on scenes of genteel middle-class life, fairly close to de *Hooch and *Terborch in style, but with a personal stamp. One of his best-known pictures, *The Sick Child* (c.1660–5, Rijksmuseum, Amsterdam), is often compared with *Vermeer's work because of its strength of design. His masterpiece, however, is perhaps *Woman Reading a Letter* (c.1660–5, NG, Dublin), in which the secondary figure of a maid examines a picture on the wall—a telling indication of the wide social appeal of art in 17th-century Holland. Metsu's paintings are rarely dated, so his development and relationships with other artists are difficult to trace.

Metsys, Quentin. See MASSYS.

Metzger, Gustav. See AUTO-DESTRUCTIVE ART.

Metzinger, Jean (b Nantes, 24 June 1883; d Paris, 3 Nov. 1956). French painter and writer on art. After passing through *Neo-Impressionist and *Fauvist phases he became one of the earliest devotees of *Cubism and a central figure of the *Section d'Or group. However, he is remembered less for his paintings than as the co-author with *Gleizes of *Du Cubisme* (1912), the first book to be published on the movement.

Meulen, Adam Frans van der (bapt. Brussels, 11 Jan. 1632; d Paris, 15 Oct. 1690). Flemish painter and tapestry designer, active mainly in France. He moved to Paris in 1664, became an assistant to *Le Brun, and was made one of Louis XIV's court painters, specializing in military scenes. He accompanied the king on his campaigns, and his paintings and designs for *Gobelins tapestries are accurate historical documents of the battles they represent. His work of this type is well represented at Versailles. He also made much less grandiose pictures of such subjects as hunting parties and landscapes.

Meunier, Constantin (b Brussels, 12 Apr. 1831; d Brussels, 4 Apr. 1905). Belgian sculptor and painter, well known for his sincere but rather heavy-handed glorification of the nobility of labour in his treatment of such subjects as miners, factory workers, and stevedores. In the early 20th century he had considerable influence on younger sculptors interested in *Social Realist subjects. There is a museum of his work in Brussels and his most ambitious work, the Monument of Labour (erected after his death), is in the Place de Trooz there.

Meyer, Hannes. See BAUHAUS.

mezzotint (Italian: *mezzotinto*, 'half tint'). A printmaking method that produces subtly graduated tones rather than lines; the term also applies to a print made by this method, which is essentially as follows. A metal (usually copper) plate is laboriously roughened with a serrated chisel-like steel tool called a rocker, creating a texture somewhat like that of fine sandpaper over the whole surface. If inked and printed from in this condition, the plate would produce solid black. The design is formed by scraping away the textured *burr to varying degrees. When the plate has been inked and then wiped, the ink is retained where the plate is rough and will print an intense black, but where it has been smoothed, less ink is held and a lighter tone results (for the highlights the burr is completely removed and the metal polished smooth). Unlike other types of print, a mezzotint is thus evolved from dark to light. *Engraved or *etched lines are sometimes introduced if greater definition is required; this procedure is known as mixed mezzotint. Like *drypoint, mezzotint yields only a small number of good impressions before the burr wears down.

Mezzotint was invented in the Netherlands in the early 1640s by Ludwig von *Siegen. Another notable pioneer, formerly thought to be the inventor, was Prince *Rupert, who was perhaps responsible for introducing the rocker, which was an improvement over the *roulette used by von Siegen. The Netherlands remained the chief centre for the technique in the 17th century, but in the 18th century it became recognized as a British speciality and was an extremely popular method for reproducing portraits. This was the heyday of mezzotint, when specialists such as Richard *Earlom and Valentine *Green flourished, but memorable use was also made of it in the following century by John *Martin, one of the few eminent artists to make original creative use of the medium rather than reproducing someone else's designs. The technique virtually died out in the later 19th century with the development of photographic methods of reproduction, but it is still used by some original printmakers who value its rich tonal qualities.

Michallon, Achille-Etna (b Paris, 22 Oct. 1796; d Paris, 24 Sept. 1822). French landscape painter, the first artist to win the *Prix de Rome in the historical landscape category that was established in 1817. He was a pupil of *David and *Valenciennes and in his turn taught *Corot, who was influenced by his severe compositions and cool colour harmonies. His early death was caused by pneumonia.

Michel, Georges (b Paris, 12 Jan. 1763; d Paris, 7/8 June 1843). French landscape painter. He achieved little recognition in his lifetime, but he is now regarded as an important forerunner of the *Barbizon School. His paintings were influenced by 17th-century Dutch artists (he worked as a copyist and restorer of their work), but they have a modest directness reflecting the many studies he made in the open air (see PLEIN AIR). He lived in Paris all his life and most of his work depicts scenes within a few miles of the city.

Michelangelo (Michelangelo Buonarroti) (b Caprese [now Caprese Michelangelo], nr.

Arezzo, 6 Mar. 1475; d Rome, 18 Feb. 1564). Florentine sculptor, painter, architect, draughtsman, and poet, one of the giants of the *Renaissance and, in his later years, one of the forces that shaped *Mannerism. Michelangelo's career lasted more than 70 years and for most of that time he was the dominant figure in Italian art. His contemporaries regarded him with awe, and the word *terribilità*, which may be translated as 'frightening power', was often applied to his work. He was the subject of two detailed biographies in his lifetime, both of them by people who knew him well (*Vasari and *Condivi), and because of these and other sources (including his own letters, about 500 of which survive), more is known about him—his personal qualities as well as the details of his career—than about any previous artist. He was utterly devoted to art and religion, living frugally in spite of his fame. However, although he was scornful of the conventional trappings of success, he was sure of his own worth and was concerned about his place in society. He tended to be suspicious and withdrawn, and had a sharp temper and a sarcastic tongue, but he was affectionate and generous to his family and friends (see PRESENTATION DRAWING).

His father, a member of the gentry, claimed noble lineage and throughout his life Michelangelo was touchy on the subject; pride of birth had much to do with the family opposition to his choice of an artistic career as well as with Michelangelo's own insistence on the status of painting and sculpture among the *liberal arts. In 1488 he was apprenticed to the painter Domenico *Ghirlandaio, but the following year he transferred to a kind of informal *academy sponsored by Lorenzo de' *Medici and overseen by the sculptor *Bertoldo di Giovanni. Michelangelo later claimed to be largely self-taught and this is probably true as far as marble carving is concerned (Bertoldo was a specialist in bronze), but Ghirlandaio was an excellent craftsman and in his workshop Michelangelo probably at least laid the foundations of his technical skill in fresco painting. Stylistically, however, he learned much more from the austere grandeur of *Giotto and *Masaccio (his earliest surviving drawings, done c.1490, include copies of figures from their frescos).

After the death of Lorenzo de' Medici in 1492 the political situation in Florence became unstable, and in October 1494 Michelangelo left for Bologna, where he carved three small figures for the Shrine of St Dominic (see NICCOLÒ DELL'ARCA). He returned briefly to Florence in

1495 but in June 1496 moved to Rome, where he remained for the next five years; during this time he carved the two statues that established his fame when he was still in his early twenties—*Bacchus* (*c.*1496–7, Bargello, Florence) and the **Pietà* (1498–9, St Peter's, Rome). The latter is the masterpiece of his early years—a tragically expressive and yet beautiful and harmonious solution to the problem of representing a full-grown man lying dead in the lap of a woman. There are no marks of suffering—as were common in northern representations of the period—and the carving has a flawless beauty and polish demonstrating his absolute technical mastery. For unclear reasons, Michelangelo returned to Florence in 1501, leaving unfinished an altarpiece of the *Entombment* (NG, London) commissioned by the church of S. Agostino, Rome, one of only two or three surviving panel paintings by him (see also TONDO).

He remained in Florence until the spring of 1505, the major completed work of the period being the marble *David* (1501–4, Accademia, Florence), which has become a symbol of Florence and Florentine art (it was originally intended for the cathedral but was instead set up outside the Palazzo Vecchio, the seat of government, David being regarded as a virtuous fighter for freedom, as the citizens of the Florentine republic liked to see themselves). Soon after the *David* was completed, Michelangelo received another great commission from the Florentine government—a huge mural of the *Battle of Cascina* for the new Council Chamber in the Palazzo Vecchio; here he worked in rivalry with **Leonardo*, who was engaged on the *Battle of Anghiari* for the same room. Neither painting came to fruition, but Michelangelo completed the full-size **cartoon* or part of it, and during its brief life this was highly influential (Vasari says that it was 'torn apart and divided into many pieces' because it was 'placed too freely in the hands of artists'). It is now known through a copy of the central section, as well as from some magnificent preliminary drawings (for example in the British Museum, London).

Michelangelo left the battle piece unfinished when Pope Julius II (Giuliano della **Rovere*) summoned him to Rome in 1505 to make his tomb. However, the following year Julius began the rebuilding of St Peter's, which deflected his attention from the tomb, and at his death in 1513 little had been accomplished on it. Afterwards the project dragged on for decades, causing Michelangelo to lament, 'I have wasted all my youth chained to this tomb.' It was originally conceived on the most grandiose scale, but was whittled down in successive contracts with Julius's heirs, and of the monument finally erected in S. Pietro in Vincoli, Rome, in 1545 only three figures, including the celebrated *Moses* (*c.*1515), are from Michelangelo's own hand. (Two figures of *Slaves*, *c.*1513, carved by Michelangelo for the tomb are now in the Louvre, Paris.)

The other great work commissioned from Michelangelo by Julius—the frescoing of the ceiling of the Sistine Chapel (1508–12)—was equally daunting, but was brought to sublime fruition. Michelangelo, who always regarded himself as a sculptor first and foremost, was reluctant to undertake the work, but he made of it his most heroic achievement, not only for its quality as a work of art, but also in terms of the endurance and stamina he showed in completing so quickly and virtually unaided such a huge and physically uncomfortable task. There is still much debate about the exact interpretation of the scores of figures that adorn the ceiling, but the main images represent scenes from Genesis—from the Creation to the Drunkenness of Noah—forming the background to the frescos on the life of Moses and of Christ on the walls below by a number of 15th-century artists (see PERUGINO). Prophets and sibyls who foretold Christ's birth are at the sides of the ceiling, and at each corner of the central scenes are figures of beautiful nude youths (usually called the *Ignudi*). Their exact significance is uncertain, but as Kenneth **Clark* wrote, 'Their physical beauty is an image of divine perfection; their alert and vigorous movements an expression of divine energy.' From the moment of its completion the ceiling has always been regarded as one of the supreme masterpieces of pictorial art (the cleaning in the 1980s revealed anew the beauty of the colouring), and Michelangelo, at the age of 37, was recognized as the greatest artist of his day, a position he retained unchallenged until his death half a century later.

In 1516 Michelangelo was commissioned by Julius II's successor, Leo X (Giovanni de' Medici), to design a façade for the Medici parish church in Florence, S. Lorenzo, which had been left unfinished by **Brunelleschi*. The project came to nothing and wasted a good deal of Michelangelo's time, but it led to two other works for S. Lorenzo—the Medici Chapel, or New Sacristy, planned as a counterpart to Brunelleschi's Old Sacristy, and the Biblioteca Laurenziana, which houses the Medici collection of books and manuscripts. Neither project was completed in accordance with Michelangelo's plans, but they nevertheless rank among his finest creations. He began work on the Medici Chapel in 1519, broke off when the Medici were expelled from Florence in 1527, restarted in 1530, and left the work incomplete in 1534 when he settled permanently in Rome. The powerful architectural forms of the building are conceived as the setting for the wall tombs of Giuliano and Lorenzo de' Medici, who are characterized in their marble figures as representatives of the Active and Contemplative Life; below them are allegorical reclining figures symbolizing *Day* and *Night* (for *Vita activa*) and *Dawn* and *Evening* (for *Vita contemplativa*). Anthony *Blunt has written of the Medici Chapel sculptures: 'there is still that superhuman quality visible in the Sistine frescoes . . . but in addition there is a feeling of brooding, of sombre disquiet, which becomes from this time a hall-mark of Michelangelo's work. They are no longer only symbols of eternal beauty; they also reflect the tragedy of human destiny.'

In the 30 years that remained to him in Rome, Michelangelo worked mainly for the papacy. He was at once commissioned to paint the *Last Judgement* in the Sistine Chapel and began the actual painting in 1536. It was unveiled on 31 October 1541, 29 years to the day after the unveiling of the Sistine Ceiling but a whole world away from it in feeling and meaning, with its massive and menacing figures and mood of wrathful desolation. In the interval the world of Michelangelo's youth had collapsed in the horror of the Sack of Rome (1527), and its confident humanism had been found insufficient in the face of the rise of Protestantism and the new, militant spirit of the Counter-Reformation. For Paul III (Alessandro *Farnese), who commissioned the *Last Judgement*, Michelangelo also executed his final works in painting, the *Conversion of St Paul* and the *Crucifixion of St Peter* (1542–50), frescos in the Cappella Paolina (Paul's private chapel) in the Vatican. The figures here are even more blunt, heavy, and unconcerned with physical allure, totally repudiating his own early ideals. Something of the same deep and troubled spirituality is seen in Michelangelo's late drawings of the Crucifixion and in two sculptures known as Pietàs (although they might more accurately be described as representing the Deposition). One (now in Florence Cathedral) was intended for his own tomb and contains a self-portrait as Nicodemus; it was begun c.1546 and mutilated and abandoned by Michelangelo in 1555. The other (Castello Sforza, Milan) was his last work, left unfinished at his death.

For the last twenty years of his life, however, Michelangelo devoted most of his attentions to architecture, and in this field his stature is just as great as in sculpture and painting (no other artist has approached this domination in the three major visual arts). His most important commission—indeed the most important in Christendom—was the completion of St Peter's, which had been begun under Julius II in 1506. When Michelangelo became architect in 1546, the building had advanced little since *Bramante's death in 1514. As with the Sistine Ceiling, he was initially unwilling to undertake the task, but he then proceeded with formidable energy, and by the time of his death work had advanced so far that the drum of the dome was nearly complete. Michelangelo also designed the dome itself, but as executed after his death it is probably a good deal steeper in outline than he intended. The addition of a long nave in the early 17th century altered Michelangelo's plan for a centralized church, but nevertheless the exterior of the building owes more to him than to any other architect and forms a fitting conclusion to his titanic career.

In architecture, Michelangelo's decorative vocabulary soon attained widespread currency, but it was not until the 17th century that his massive and dynamic style was fully appreciated and emulated; it is fitting that *Bernini, the great sculptor-architect of the age, should complete St Peter's with his glorious piazza. In painting and sculpture, Michelangelo's means of expression was limited almost entirely to the heroic male figure, usually nude, but in this domain he reigned supreme as no artist has done before or since, and for centuries afterwards it was virtually impossible for any artist to work in the field without referring, consciously or unconsciously, to his example.

Michelozzo di Bartolommeo (sometimes incorrectly called Michelozzo Michelozzi) (*b* Florence, 1396; *bur.* Florence 7 Oct. 1472). Florentine architect and sculptor. As a sculptor he worked for *Ghiberti (on both his sets of doors for the Baptistery in Florence) and in partnership with *Donatello (1425–c.1433). With Donatello he produced three major tombs—those of antipope John XXIII (1424–8, Baptistery, Florence), Cardinal Rinaldo Brancacci (1426–8, S. Angelo a Nilo, Naples), and Bartolommeo Aragazzi (1427–38, Montepulciano Cathedral, but now disassembled; two angels are in the Victoria and Albert Museum, London). His style was vigorous and forthright. In his later career Michelozzo worked mainly as an architect, and he ranks as one of the leading figures of the generation after *Brunelleschi, whom he succeeded as *capomaestro* at Florence Cathedral (1446). His most famous building is the Palazzo Medici-Riccardi in Florence (begun 1445), often described as the first *Renaissance palace. Michelozzo was influential in spreading the Renaissance style; he worked in Milan, Yugoslavia, and the island of Chios.

Michiel, Marcantonio. See GIORGIONE.

Middleditch, Edward. See KITCHEN SINK SCHOOL.

Miel, Jan. See LAER.

Miereveld (or Mierevelt), **Michiel van** (*b* Delft, 1 May 1567; *d* Delft, 27 June 1641). Dutch portrait painter, active mainly in Delft and The Hague. He was court painter to the House of Orange, highly successful, and very prolific: *Sandrart reports that Mierevelt himself estimated that he made about 10,000 portraits. Even though this figure must be a considerable exaggeration, his portraits certainly tend to be dull and formulaic; however, they are meticulously crafted and of great value as historical records.

Mieris, Frans van (*b* Leiden, 16 Apr. 1635; *d* Leiden, 12 Mar. 1681). Dutch painter, the most distinguished member of a family of artists active in Leiden. He was one of the best pupils of Gerrit *Dou and followed his master in choice of subjects (mainly domestic *genre scenes) and in his highly polished technique. The tradition was continued by his sons **Jan** (1660–90) and **Willem** (1662–1747) and by Willem's son **Frans II** (1689–1763).

Miers, John. See SILHOUETTE.

Mies van der Rohe, Ludwig. See BAUHAUS.

Mignard, Pierre (*b* Troyes, 17 May 1612; *d* Paris, 30 May 1695). French painter, one of the most successful of *Vouet's pupils. His career culminated in 1690, when, on the death of *Le Brun, he became director of the Académie Royale and first painter to the king. He was one of the principal supporters of de *Piles and the 'Rubénistes' in their battle against the *classicism of the 'Poussinistes' (see POUSSIN). His own historical and religious paintings, however, did not exemplify his theories, being more in the classical tradition of *Domenichino and Poussin (he spent much of his career in Italy, 1635–57). His best works are his portraits; he painted many of

the members of Louis XIV's court, sometimes fitting out his sitters with allegorical trappings. Pierre's brother **Nicolas** (1606–68) also trained with Vouet and had a successful career painting portraits and religious subjects.

Millais, Sir John Everett (*b* Southampton, 8 June 1829; *d* London, 13 Aug. 1896). English painter and book illustrator. A child prodigy who was hard-working as well as naturally gifted, he became the youngest ever student at the *Royal Academy Schools when he was 11, and although he suffered some temporary setbacks in his twenties, his career was essentially one of the great Victorian success stories. In 1848, with *Rossetti and *Hunt, he founded the *Pre-Raphaelite Brotherhood, and he had his share of the abuse heaped on the members until *Ruskin stepped in as their champion. (In 1854 Millais married Effie Gray, formerly Ruskin's wife, after this first marriage had been annulled.) In the 1850s his style changed, as he moved away from the brilliantly coloured, minutely detailed Pre-Raphaelite manner to a broader and more fluent way of painting—with a family to support he said he could not afford to spend a whole day working on an area 'no larger than a five shilling piece'. His subjects changed also, from highly serious, morally uplifting themes to scenes that met the public demand for sentiment and a good story. Many of them featured children, whom he painted with great affection, often modelling them on his own family; *The Boyhood of Raleigh* (1870, Tate, London), for example, shows his two eldest sons. He became enormously popular, not only with subject pictures such as this (colour reproductions of his best-loved works sold in hundreds of thousands), but also as a portraitist and book illustrator; his drawings for the novels of Anthony Trollope were such a success that Trollope said they influenced the way he developed the characters in sequels.

Millais lived in some splendour on his huge income and was loaded with honours; most notably, in 1885 he was awarded a baronetcy, and in the year of his death was elected president of the Royal Academy. To some contemporaries it seemed that he wasted his talents pandering to public taste, and many 20th-century critics presented him as a young genius who sacrificed his artistic conscience for money. Millais, an easygoing and much-liked man, certainly enjoyed his success, but he was far from being a cynic. He was always proud of his skills (near the end of his career he wrote 'I may honestly say that I have never consciously placed an idle touch upon canvas'), and few of his contemporaries could match his late works for sheer beauty of handling (*Bubbles*, 1886, A. & F. Pears Ltd.). See also LAY FIGURE.

millboard. See CARDBOARD.

Miller, Lee. See MAN RAY and PENROSE.

Milles, Carl (*b* Lagga, nr. Uppsala, 23 June 1875; *b* Lidingö, 19 Sept. 1955). Sweden's greatest sculptor. From 1897 to 1904 he lived in Paris, where he worked for a time as assistant to *Rodin, then moved to Munich (1904–6), where he was influenced by *Hildebrand. In the following two years he lived in Rome, Stockholm, and Austria, then settled at Lidingö, near Stockholm, in 1908. His travels had given him a wide knowledge of ancient, medieval, and Renaissance art, as well as of recent developments, and he forged from these varied influences an eclectic but vigorous style. He is best known for his numerous large-scale fountains, distinguished by rhythmic vitality and inventive figure types (he liked to fuse classical and Nordic types such as tritons and goblins), and sometimes by a grotesque humour. From 1931 to 1945 he was professor of sculpture at the Cranbrook Academy at Bloomfield Hills, Michigan; his work in the USA includes fountains in Chicago, Kansas City, New York, and St Louis. He became an American citizen in 1945 but returned to Sweden in 1951 and died at Lidingö, where his home is now an open-air museum of his work, known as Millesgården.

Millet, Francisque (Jean-François) (*bapt.* Antwerp, 27 Apr. 1642; *bur.* Paris, 3 June 1679). French landscape painter of Flemish birth. He worked mainly in Paris, but he is said to have visited England and Holland. No signed or documented paintings are known, but several are authenticated by early engravings. His work was influenced by *Poussin and *Dughet, sometimes enlivened by romantic touches in the manner of Salvator *Rosa, as in *Mountain Landscape with Lightning* (NG, London), one of the most original works of an artist usually content to be an able follower. His son **Jean** (*c.*1666–1723) was a landscape painter, and he too had a painter son, **Joseph** (*c.*1688–1777).

Millet, Jean-François (*b* Gruchy, nr. Cherbourg, 4 Oct. 1814; *d* Barbizon, 20 Jan. 1875). French painter, draughtsman, and printmaker, born in Normandy into a prosperous and cultured farming family. After studying with local painters, he moved to Paris in 1837 and for two years continued his training under *Delaroche at the École des *Beaux-Arts. His early work consisted of portraits and then small mythological and pastoral scenes, but with *The Winnower* (NG, London), exhibited at the *Salon in 1848, he turned to the pictures of rustic life from which his name is now inseparable. *The Winnower* perfectly caught the spirit of the time, for earlier in the year in which it was shown, King Louis-Philippe had been deposed, helping to create a taste for pictures of ordinary people such as this (it was indeed bought by a minister in the new republican government). Critics of the time tended to interpret Millet's work in terms of their own social views, so whereas republicans thought he was showing the dignity of working people in a progressive spirit, conservatives regarded his paintings as coarse and subversive, the peasantry being to them a potential source of civil unrest. Millet himself, however, saw his work in aesthetic and personal rather than political terms, and the feeling of sad solemnity that so often characterizes it is an expression of his own melancholic temperament. In 1854 he commented: 'I must confess, at the risk of being taken for a socialist, that it is the treatment of the human condition which touches me most in art . . . I never see the joyous side; I do not know where to find it, for I have never seen it. The happiest thing I know is the calm and the silence one so deliciously experiences in the forest or in the fields.' This 'calm and silence' he expressed through figures of great strength and dignity, reflecting his admiration for Old Masters such as *Poussin.

In 1849 Millet settled at *Barbizon, where he remained for the rest of his life apart from the period of the Franco-Prussian War (1870–1), when he took refuge in Cherbourg. Late in his career he turned increasingly to pure landscape, influenced by Théodore *Rousseau, one of his closest friends. Rousseau sometimes helped Millet financially, for he spent much of his career in poverty, but in the 1860s—his work now being much less controversial—he began to build an international reputation (he became especially popular with American collectors). By the time of his death he was a celebrated figure (although still not financially secure—the ever-generous *Corot supported his widow), and he had considerable influence on late 19th-century art. *Seurat, for example, greatly admired the grand simplicity of his draughtsmanship, and van *Gogh copied reproductions of his work when he was teaching himself to draw. As well as achieving great respect among fellow artists, Millet also pleased a large popular audience, above all with *The Angelus* (1859, Mus. d'Orsay, Paris), which became perhaps the most widely reproduced painting of the 19th century. This had a harmful effect on his subsequent critical fortunes, for largely on the strength of it he was pigeon-holed for much of the 20th century as a purveyor of pious sentimentality (it shows a farmer and his wife pausing in their work to pray as a church bell tolls the evening Angelus). A major exhibition of his work in Paris and London in 1975–6 was a landmark in his critical rehabilitation.

Mills, Clark (*b* Onondaga County, NY, 13 Dec. 1810; *d* Washington, DC, 12 Jan. 1883). American sculptor, a jack-of-all-trades, who was self-taught as an artist. In 1848 he won a competition for the monument to President Andrew Jackson in Lafayette Square, Washington, and worked for five years on this, the first equestrian statue in the USA. He built his own foundry to cast the statue, which daringly has the rearing horse supported only by its hind legs, and eventually succeeded at the seventh attempt. The ecstatic response when the statue was unveiled in 1853 brought him great financial rewards and the commission for an equestrian statue to George Washington in Washington Circle (1860). He spent his final years under a cloud, however, suspected of dishonesty in handling the metal assigned to him.

Milne, David B. (*b* nr. Paisley, Ontario, 8 Jan. 1882; *d* Bancroft, Ontario, 26 Dec. 1953). Canadian painter, mainly of landscape. In 1904 he gave up his job as a schoolteacher to study at the *Art Students League, New York, and he remained based in the USA until 1928 (although in 1918–19 he served with the Canadian army and became an *Official War Artist in Britain, France, and Belgium). After returning to Canada he lived in seclusion in various parts of Ontario, although he was a regular visitor to Toronto. His love of solitude limited the impact he made in his lifetime, but he is now regarded as one of the finest Canadian painters of his time. He greatly admired the work of Tom *Thomson, but he was not interested in the aggressive nationalism of Thomson's followers in the *Group of Seven. Rather, he was concerned with 'pure' painting. His style was vigorous and spontaneous, with a calligraphic quality in the handling. From 1937 he worked mainly in watercolour, a medium he used in an oriental-like way as a sensitive means of expressing his emotional response to nature (*Rites of Autumn*, 1943, NG, Ottawa). Late in life he also painted fantasy subjects, some of a whimsically religious nature.

miniature. A term applied to two different kinds of pictures: first, representational images (as distinct from decorative motifs) in *illuminated manuscripts; and secondly, very small independent paintings, particularly portraits that can be held in the hand or worn as a piece of jewellery. The word derives from the Latin *minium*, the red lead used to emphasize initial letters in manuscripts, decorated by the *miniator*. However, on account of a mistaken etymology, the term has become connected with 'minute' (small). In the Middle Ages a manuscript 'miniature' was called *historia*, and the portraits painted by *Hilliard and others were named 'limnings' or 'pictures in little' by the Elizabethans. They were usually painted in watercolour on vellum (see PARCHMENT), or occasionally on ivory or card, and in the 17th and 18th centuries there was a vogue for miniatures done in an *enamelling technique.

Portrait miniatures developed from a fusion of the traditions of medieval illumination and the *Renaissance *medal and they perhaps originated in France in the 1520s; in 1526—in the first known reference to such works—Marguerite d'Alençon, sister of Francis I of France, sent Henry VIII of England two lockets that opened up to reveal portraits. These do not survive, but at much the same time the Flemish-born Lukas Hornebolte (*c*.1490–1544) began producing miniatures at Henry's court, including one of Henry himself (Fitzwilliam Mus., Cambridge). Hornebolte was a fairly mediocre artist, but he began the renowned English tradition in miniature painting, and according to van *Mander he gave lessons in the technique to *Holbein, the first great exponent of the art. Holbein's work was in turn an inspiration to Hilliard, who begins the golden age of miniature painting in the late 16th and early 17th centuries. The art continued to flourish in England (and to varying degrees in other countries) until the mid-19th century, when photography virtually killed it as a serious form of expression.

Minimal art. A type of abstract art, particularly sculpture, characterized by extreme simplicity of form and a deliberate lack of expressive content; it emerged as a trend in the 1950s and flourished particularly in the 1960s and 1970s. There are numerous precedents for the stark simplicity of Minimal art. In 1777, for example, *Goethe designed an Altar of Good Fortune for his garden in Weimar consisting of two utterly pure geometrical stone shapes—a sphere sur-mounting a cube; and in 1883 the journalist Alphonse Allais (1855–1905) created a burlesque version of minimalism when he exhibited in Paris a plain sheet of white paper with the title *First Communion of Anaemic Young Girls in the Snow*. Such byways aside, the roots of Minimal art can be traced to the stark geometric abstractions of *Malevich and the *ready-mades of *Duchamp in the second decade of the century, and after this the idea of extreme reductivism occurred in various aspects of avant-garde art—certain sculptures of *Brancusi, for example, the *Spatialism of Lucio *Fontana, and the mono-chromatic canvases of Yves *Klein. As a move-ment, however, Minimal art developed in the USA and its impersonality is seen as a reaction against the emotiveness of *Abstract Expres-sionism. Leading sculptors of the movement include Carl *Andre, Don *Judd, and Tony *Smith; leading painters (for whom the imme-diate precursors were *Albers and *Reinhardt) include Frank *Stella (in his early work), and *Hard-Edge abstractionists such as Ellsworth *Kelly and Kenneth *Noland.

According to *The Tate Gallery: An Illustrated Companion* (1979), 'The theory of minimalism is that without the diverting presence of "compos-ition", and by the use of plain, often industrial, materials arranged in geometrical or highly sim-plified configurations we may experience all the more strongly the pure qualities of colour, form, space and materials.' Minimal art has close links with *Conceptual art (Minimalist sculpture often has a strong element of theoretical dem-onstration about it, with the artist leaving the fabrication of his designs to industrial special-ists), and sometimes there are affinities with other contemporaneous movements, such as *Land art. There is even a kinship with *Pop art in a shared preference for slick, impersonal surfaces (some Minimal artists, however, have used 'natural' materials such as logs rather than machine finished products). Like Pop art, Minimal art proved a commercial success for many of its leading practitioners, and it gener-ated a huge amount of critical commentary; sometimes it seemed that the less there was to see in a work, the more verbiage it attracted. See also PRIMARY STRUCTURES.

Minne, Georg. See SYMBOLISM.

Minoan art. A term applied to the art of an-cient Crete, particularly that produced from c.3000 BC to c.1100 BC. The term was first used in 1894 by the British archaeologist Sir Arthur Evans, who, from 1898 to 1935, conducted exten-sive excavations at Crete, principally at Knossos, where the royal palace he uncovered was named the Palace of Minos (hence Minoan) after the legendary king of Crete. Minoan civilization is in many ways mysterious (Minoan scripts have not been deciphered), but it must have been settled and sophisticated, for the palace at Knossos is immense and entirely without fortification. Apart from architecture, Minoan art survives in sculpture, pottery, and wall painting, often fea-turing highly spirited depictions of animals, par-ticularly the bull, which had ritual significance (the best collection is in the Archaeological Museum at Heraklion in Crete). Minoan civil-ization is believed to have been destroyed partly by earthquake and partly by invasion, and by about 1100 BC Minoan art had been absorbed into the tradition of the mainland.

Mino da Fiesole (*b* Papiano, nr. Poppi, Tuscany, 1429; *d* Florence, 1484). Florentine sculptor. According to *Vasari he was a pupil of *Desiderio da Settignano, but this seems un-likely, as Mino was about the same age as him—possibly even a year or so older (he presumably spent some time training in Fiesole, overlooking Florence, a town famous for its stoneworkers). Mino is remembered mainly for his portrait busts. Whereas Desiderio's are all of women, Mino's are almost all of men; the earliest—that of Piero de' *Medici (1453, Bargello, Florence) is the first dated portrait bust of the *Renaissance (although an undated example by *Donatello probably precedes it). Mino also worked as a tomb sculptor, but much of his work in this field has been altered or destroyed or is of uncer-tain attribution because he collaborated with other sculptors. The one that most clearly shows his own workmanship is that of Count Hugo of Tuscany (completed 1481, Badia, Flor-ence), which Vasari describes as 'the most beau-tiful work that he ever produced'. Mino had three documented stays in Rome (1454, 1463, and 1474–80) and also worked briefly in Naples (1455). His reputation was at its height in the 19th century, when his delicate carving of marble was much admired.

Minton, John (*b* Great Shelford, Cambridge-shire, 25 Dec. 1917; *d* London, 20 Jan. 1957). British painter, illustrator, and designer. In 1938–9 he spent a year in Paris, where he shared a studio with Michael *Ayrton. Among the artists whose work he saw in Paris, he was par-ticularly influenced by the brooding sadness of *Berman and *Tchelitchew. From 1943 to 1946 he had a studio in London at 77 Bedford Gardens (the house in which *Colquhoun and MacBryde lived) and from 1946 to 1952 he lived with Keith *Vaughan. Minton was a leading exponent of *Neo-Romanticism and an influential teacher at Camberwell School of Art (1943–7), the Central School of Arts and Crafts (1947–8), and the *Royal College of Art (1948–56). He was extremely energetic, travelling widely and producing a large body of work as a painter (of portraits, landscapes, and figure compositions), book illustrator, and designer. After about 1950, however, his work went increasingly out of fashion. He made an effort to keep up with the times with subjects such as the *Death of James Dean* (1957, Tate, London), but stylistically he changed little. Minton was renowned for his charm and generosity, but he was also melancholic and troubled by self-doubt. He committed suicide with an overdose of drugs.

Mir Iskusstva. See WORLD OF ART.

Mirko. See AFRO.

Miró, Joan (*b* Barcelona, 20 Apr. 1893; *d* Palma de Mallorca, 25 Dec. 1983). Spanish painter, sculptor, printmaker, and designer. He first visited Paris in 1919 and from then until 1936 (when the Spanish Civil War began) his regular pattern was to spend the winter in Paris and the summer at his family's farm near Barcelona. His early work shows the influence of various modern movements—*Fauvism, *Cubism (he was a friend of *Picasso), and *Dadaism—but he is particularly associated with the *Surrealists, whose first manifesto he signed in 1924. Throughout his life, whether his work was purely abstract or whether it retained figurative suggestions, Miró remained true to the basic Surrealist principle of releasing the creative forces of the unconscious mind from the control of logic and reason. However, even though André *Breton wrote that he was 'probably the most Surrealistic of us all', Miró was never a formal member of the movement and always stood somewhat apart because of the variety, geniality, and lack of attitudinizing in his work, which shows none of the superficial devices beloved of other Surrealists. One of the works in which he first displayed an unmistakable personal vision is *Harlequin's Carnival* (1924–5, Albright-Knox Art Gallery, Buffalo), featuring a bizarre assembly of insect-like creatures dancing and making music—a scene inspired by 'my hallucinations brought on by hunger'. Much of his work has the delightful quality of playfulness

seen in this picture, but he was inspired to much more sombre and even savage imagery by the Spanish Civil War, during which he designed propaganda posters for the Republicans fighting against Franco.

Miró settled in Paris in 1936 because of the Civil War, but in 1940 he returned to Spain to escape the German occupation of France and thereafter lived mainly on the island of Majorca. It was from about this time that he began to achieve international recognition. For the rest of his long life he worked with great energy in a wide variety of fields. In 1944 he began making ceramics and slightly later he took up sculpture, initially small terracottas but eventually large-scale pieces for casting in bronze. He visited the USA for the first time in 1947 and did a large mural for the Terrace Hilton Hotel in Cincinnati. This fulfilled his desire to communicate with a large public, and several of his major works of the 1950s were in a similar vein: a mural for Harvard University in 1950 (now replaced by a ceramic copy; the original is in MoMA, New York) and two vast ceramic wall decorations, *Wall of the Sun* and *Wall of the Moon* (installed 1958), for the Unesco building in Paris. Another aspect of his desire to make his art widely accessible is his productivity as a printmaker (etchings and lithographs). He continued to explore new techniques into his old age, taking up stained-glass design when he was in his eighties. In spite of the worldwide fame he acquired he was a modest, retiring character, utterly devoted to his work, and in one of his rare public statements he criticized Picasso for what seemed to him a mania for publicity. The Foundation Joan Miró was opened in 1975 on the heights of Montjuic overlooking Barcelona. It is designed both as a memorial museum housing a collection of Miró's works and as a centre of artistic activity.

misericord. In Christian church architecture, a bracket or ledge projecting from the underside of a hinged tip-up seat in the choir, against which an elderly or infirm clergyman could lean and rest during long services whilst still appearing to stand. The term, which derives from the Latin *misericordia* ('compassion'), is first recorded in Germany in the 11th century, but the earliest surviving examples date from the early 13th century. Misericords are often richly carved, and England has a particularly impressive tradition in them. The subject matter of the carving is predominantly secular and frequently humorous, illustrating fables and proverbs for example, but there is often a moral attached. Misericords were at their peak of development in the 14th and 15th centuries in England, but they continued to be produced into the 17th century.

missal. A liturgical book containing prayers, readings, and so on used in the celebration of the Mass throughout the year. It evolved from the 10th century, combining the functions of other books such as the sacramentary (which gave the appropriate rites and prayers for each sacrament) and the gradual (containing various sung parts of the service) and, to a large extent, eventually replacing them. Early manuscript missals often contain an elaborate *miniature of the Crucifixion, but otherwise usually have comparatively little decoration. During the later Middle Ages, however, they were sometimes sumptuously illustrated, the Sherborne Missal by John *Siferwas being a notable example. In the late 15th century printed editions appeared, illustrated with woodcuts.

mixed media. A term used to describe works of art composed of a variety of different materials. Such works have been made since ancient times, but the term is applied particularly to modern pieces in which a range of unconventional materials is used, thereby making a succinct statement of medium (such as 'oil on canvas') impossible. Mixed media in this sense was popularized by the *Dadaists and *Surrealists, to whom the use of unconventional materials was an aspect of artistic anarchy and freedom. The term 'composite media' is sometimes used synonymously with 'mixed media', but some critics prefer to apply it to works in which different forms of art (rather than different materials) are combined, for example *installation with *Performance art or *Video art.

mobile. Term coined by Marcel *Duchamp in 1932 to describe the motor- or hand-powered *Kinetic sculptures of Alexander *Calder and soon extended to others he produced in which the movement is caused by a combination of air currents and their own structural tension. Typically Calder's mobiles consisted of flat metal parts suspended on wires. Many other sculptors (notably Lynn *Chadwick) have experimented with the genre, and mobiles have also been adopted as articles of interior decoration and (on a miniature scale) as playthings for babies.

Mochi, Francesco (*b* Montevarchi, nr. Arezzo, 29 July 1580; *d* Rome, 6 Feb., 1654). Italian sculptor. He was the outstanding Italian sculptor of his generation, but after brilliant early achievements he was eclipsed by *Bernini and his career petered out. His first notable work is the dynamic *Annunciation* (1603–8, Orvieto Cathedral), made up of separate marble figures of Mary and Gabriel, originally placed on either side of the high altar; it has been described as the first *Baroque sculpture or, in Rudolf *Wittkower's words, 'a fanfare raising sculpture from its slumber'. Even more impressive are two bronze equestrian statues Mochi executed in Piacenza for Ranuccio *Farnese, Duke of Parma and Piacenza. The first of the pair (1612–20), representing Ranuccio himself, is still in the tradition of *Giambologna, but the second (1620–5), commemorating Ranuccio's father Alessandro, has a magnificent Baroque sweep: 'Never before . . . had the figure of the rider held its own so emphatically against the bulk of the horse's body' (Wittkower). Mochi's last major work was the huge marble *St Veronica* (1629–39) adorning one of the crossing piers of St Peter's, Rome, which suffers from comparison with Bernini's powerful *St Longinus*. (The two other companion statues are *St Andrew* by François *Duquesnoy and *St Helena* by Andrea Bolgi (1605–56), whom Wittkower describes as 'the driest among Bernini's protégés'.)

modello. A preparatory drawing or painting for a larger work, particularly one made to be shown to a patron. Since the object was to impress the patron and give him a clear idea of the picture that the artist had in mind, a *modello* was more elaborate and fully worked out than a sketch or *bozzetto. *Rubens's work is particularly rich in *modelli*.

Modernista. See ART NOUVEAU.

Modern Style. See ART NOUVEAU.

Modersohn-Becker, Paula (née Becker) (*b* Dresden, 8 Feb. 1876; *d* Worpswede, 20 Nov. 1907). German painter. In 1898 she joined the artists' colony at *Worpswede and in 1901 she married **Otto Modersohn** (1865–1943), another member of the group. Her early work—mainly landscapes and scenes of peasant life—was in the lyrical, rather sentimental manner associated with Worpswede at this time, but she developed a massively powerful style through which she expressed a highly personal vision of the world. Her artistic evolution was influenced by four visits she made to Paris between 1900 and her early death in 1907. The work of *Gauguin and van *Gogh in particular helped her to find the 'great simplicity of form' for which she had been searching, and in her mature work she concentrated on single figures, including self-portraits and portraits of peasants. In her self-portraits she typically shows herself with wide, staring eyes and often in the nude. Although she had a weak physical constitution, she worked with great discipline and perseverance, and in a career that lasted only a decade she produced a substantial output of paintings and drawings as well as a few etchings. She died of a heart attack three weeks after giving birth to her first child. She was little known at the time of her death (she had sold only a handful of pictures), but is now regarded as one of the outstanding German artists of her time. Her symbolic use of colour and pattern, her subjective outlook (she wrote that 'the principal thing is my personal feeling'), and the almost primitive force of some of her work give her a place among the most important precursors of *Expressionism.

Modigliani, Amedeo (b Livorno [Leghorn], 12 July 1884; d Paris, 24 Jan. 1920). Italian painter, sculptor, and draughtsman, active mainly in Paris. Although virtually his whole career was spent in France, he laid the foundations of his style in Italy with his study of the masters of the *Renaissance. In particular he is often seen as a spiritual heir of *Botticelli because of the linear grace of his work, and his reclining nudes continue a tradition begun by *Giorgione and *Titian. He moved to Paris in 1906; apart from visits to his family in Italy and a year spent at Nice and Cagnes, 1918–19, this was his home for the rest of his life, and he became a familiar figure in the café and night life of Montmartre. Initially he was strongly influenced by *Cézanne, from whom he learnt much about simple dignity of composition and subtle handling of colour harmonies. However, in 1909 he met *Brancusi and under his influence devoted himself mainly to stone carving until 1914, when the war made it impossible for him to get materials. He then returned to painting and his finest pictures were produced in the last five years of his short life.

Both as a sculptor and as a painter Modigliani's range was limited. Almost all his two dozen or so surviving sculptures are heads and the great majority of his paintings are portraits or female nudes. Common to virtually all his work are extremely elongated, simplified forms and a superb sense of rhythmic vitality, but there is a great difference in mood between, for example, his sculptures (Head, c.1911–12, Tate, London), which have the primitive power of the African masks that inspired them, and his gloriously sensual nudes (Reclining Nude, c.1919, MoMA,

New York), which were censured for their open eroticism (the only one-man exhibition he held in his lifetime, at the Galerie Berthe Weill, Paris, in 1917, was closed by the police because of the 'filth' on display). Modigliani's early death from tuberculosis was hastened by his notoriously dissolute lifestyle, and his mistress Jeanne Hébuterne, pregnant with their second child, committed suicide the day after he died. At this time he was beginning to make a name among enthusiasts of modern art but was virtually unknown to the world at large; his posthumous fame was established by an exhibition at the Galerie Bernheim-Jeune, Paris, in 1922 and a colourful biography by the poet and critic André Salmon (1881–1969) published in 1926—Modigliani, sa vie et son œuvre. His reputation as one of the outstandingly original artists of his time is now secure, but his fame rests even more on his reputation as the bohemian par excellence: in the popular imagination he is the archetypal romantic genius, starving in a garret, the victim of drugs and alcohol, an inveterate womanizer, but painting and carving obsessively.

Moholy-Nagy, László (b Bácsborsod, 20 July 1895; d Chicago, 24 Nov. 1946). Hungarian-born painter, sculptor, experimental artist, and writer who became an American citizen in 1944. After qualifying in law at Budapest University and serving in the First World War, he moved to Vienna in 1919 and then in 1921 to Berlin, where he painted abstract pictures influenced by *Lissitzky (himself newly arrived from Russia). He also experimented with *collage and *photomontage and in 1922 had his first one-man exhibition, at the *Sturm Gallery. From 1923 to 1928 he taught at the *Bauhaus, taking over from *Itten the running of the preliminary course. The difference in approach between these two highly distinctive characters is summed up by Frank Whitford (Bauhaus, 1984): 'Even Moholy's appearance proclaimed his artistic sympathies. Itten had worn something like a monk's habit and had kept his head immaculately shaved with the intention of creating an aura of spirituality and communion with the transcendental. Moholy sported the kind of overall worn by workers in modern industry. His nickel-rimmed spectacles contributed further to an image of sobriety and calculation belonging to a man mistrustful of the emotions, more at home among machines than human beings.'

Although Moholy was regarded as a brilliant teacher, his assertiveness and his rejection of a spiritual dimension in art made him unpopular with some of his colleagues. He resigned when Hannes Meyer replaced Gropius as director in 1928, then worked for some years in Berlin, chiefly on stage design and experimental film. In 1934 he left Germany because of the Nazis, moving to Amsterdam and then in 1935 to London, where he made designs for the science fiction film *Things to Come* (1936), produced by his fellow Hungarian Alexander Korda, and contributed to the *Constructivist review *Circle* (1937). In 1937 he emigrated to Chicago, where he became director of the short-lived New Bauhaus (1937–8), then founded his own School of Design (1939; it changed its name to the Institute of Design in 1944), directing it until his death. He was one of the most influential teachers of the 20th century and one of the most inventive and versatile of Constructivist artists, pioneering especially in his use of light, movement (see KINETIC ART), photography, film, and plastic materials. His views, emphasizing the Constructivist doctrine that so-called *fine art must be integrated with the total environment, were most fully expressed in his posthumously published book *Vision in Motion* (1947).

Moilliet, Louis (*b* Berne, 6 Oct. 1880; *d* Vevey, 24 Aug. 1962). Swiss painter and designer of stained glass. In 1911 he introduced *Klee (a friend since schooldays) to the *Blaue Reiter circle, and in 1914 he visited Tunisia with Klee and *Macke. After the First World War he travelled extensively, especially in the Mediterranean. As a painter he worked mainly in watercolour in a style influenced by *Orphism. The same feeling for colour comes out in the stained-glass windows he designed for Swiss churches, notably the Lucaskirche at Lucerne (1934–6) and the Zwinglikirche at Winterthur (1943–4).

Mola, Pier Francesco (*bapt.* Coldrerio, nr. Lugano, 9 Feb. 1612; *d* Rome, 13 May 1666). Italian *Baroque painter. Although he spent most of his life in Rome, his style, characterized by warm colouring and soft modelling, was formed mainly on the example of *Guercino and Venetian art (his early career is not well documented, but he probably spent much of the period 1633–47 in north Italy). He painted frescos in Roman churches and palaces, and his best-known picture is the striking *Barbary Pirate* (1650, Louvre, Paris), but his most characteristic works are fairly small canvases with religious or mythological figures set in landscapes (two examples are in the National Gallery, London).

They are somewhat reminiscent of *Albani, but much freer, and closer in spirit to Salvator *Rosa; with the latter, Mola was one of the chief representatives of a distinctively romantic strain in Roman painting in the mid-17th century.

Molenaer, Jan Miense (*b* Haarlem, *c.*1610; *bur.* Haarlem, 19 Sept. 1668). Dutch painter, active in his native Haarlem and in Amsterdam, where he moved in 1636 after marrying Judith *Leyster; both belonged in their youth to the circle of Frans *Hals. He and his wife probably collaborated and sometimes it is difficult to differentiate their work. Molenaer, however, was more prolific and more versatile. His *genre scenes range from pictures of the indecorous activities of peasants to exquisitely finished interiors showing well-to-do families. He also painted portraits and religious scenes. His early works (which are considered his best) have a grey-blond tonality and touches of bright colour; his later ones are darker, in the manner of *Brouwer or *Ostade. He had two painter brothers, **Bartholomaeus** (*d* 1650) and **Claes** (*d* 1676), both active in Haarlem.

Molyn (or Molijn), **Pieter de** (*bapt.* London, 6 Apr. 1595; *bur.* Haarlem, 23 Mar. 1661). Dutch landscape painter, born in England (it is not known why his parents had moved there) and active mainly in Haarlem. With Jan van *Goyen, and Salomon van *Ruysdael, also active in Haarlem, he ranks as one of the pioneers of naturalistic landscape painting in Holland. It is not known if these three painters worked together, if they arrived at similar solutions independently, or if one of them began experiments with monochromatic pictures of dunes and cottages and the others followed his lead. However, Molyn's *Sand Dune* (1626, Herzog-Anton-Ulrich Mus., Brunswick) is earlier than any comparable dated picture by van Goyen or Ruysdael. Molyn's later career was less distinguished, and he seems then to have worked more as a draughtsman than a painter. He also produced a few etchings.

Momper, Joos (or Jodocus) **II de** (*b* Antwerp, 1564; *d* Antwerp, 5 Feb. 1635). Flemish landscape painter, the outstanding member of a family of artists. He worked in his native Antwerp, where he became a master in the painters' guild in 1581, but mountains are so much a prevailing theme in his work that it seems likely he crossed the Alps to Italy at some time in his career (frescos in the church of S. Vitale in Rome have recently been attributed to him). His chief inspiration was *Bruegel and his work stands halfway between the constructed landscapes of the 16th century and the naturalistic landscapes of the 17th century. Judging by the great number of extant pictures in his manner, his work must have enjoyed great popularity. They vary greatly in quality, but the best works that are indisputably from his own hand, for example the majestic *Winter Landscape with the Flight into Egypt* (Ashmolean Mus., Oxford), show that he was one of the greatest landscape painters of his period and worthy to be mentioned in the same breath as Bruegel. His style seems to have changed little and his work is difficult to date. Figures in his paintings are often the work of other artists, notably Jan *Brueghel I.

Monaco, Lorenzo. See LORENZO MONACO.

Monamy, Peter (*b* London, 12 Jan. 1681; *d* London, 1 Feb. 1749). English marine painter, perhaps of French extraction. He was one of the first English imitators of the van de *Veldes. His work, which is meticulous and has little variety, is well represented in the National Maritime Museum, London.

Mondrian, Piet (*b* Amersfoort, 7 Mar. 1872; *d* New York, 1 Feb. 1944). Dutch painter, one of the most important figures in the development of *abstract art. His early paintings were naturalistic and direct, often delicate in colour, but between 1907 and 1910 his work took on a *Symbolist character, partly under the influence of *Toorop and perhaps partly owing to his conversion to Theosophy. Between 1912 and the outbreak of the First World War in 1914 he divided his time between Paris and the Netherlands, and in this period he was strongly influenced by *Cubism, painting a series of pictures on the theme of a tree in which the image became progressively more fragmented and abstract (*Flowering Apple Tree*, 1912, Gemeentemuseum, The Hague). By 1914 he had virtually eliminated curved lines from his work, using a structure that was predominantly horizontal and vertical, with the merest suggestion of natural forms underlying the patterning. In 1915 he met Theo van *Doesburg, and two years later he joined him in founding the association De *Stijl; it promoted a new kind of rigorously geometrical abstract painting of which Mondrian became the main exponent. In this style, which he named *Neo-Plasticism, he limited himself to straight lines and basic colours to create an art of great clarity and discipline that

he thought reflected the laws of the universe, revealing immutable realities behind the ever-changing appearances of the world. Typically he used a bold grid of black lines (all completely straight and either strictly horizontal or strictly vertical) to form an asymmetrical network of rectangles of various sizes that were painted with a narrow range of colours (the three primaries—blue, red, and yellow—plus black, white, and initially grey, although this was later dropped).

From 1919 to 1938 Mondrian lived in Paris, where in 1931 he joined the *Abstraction-Création group. For many years he had struggled to earn a living, but in the 1920s he gradually became known to an international circle of admirers, including the American Katherine *Dreier (from 1926). In 1938 he left Paris because of the threat of war, and for the next two years he lived in London, near Naum *Gabo and Ben *Nicholson. After the house next door to his studio was hit by a bomb, he moved to New York in 1940 and spent his remaining years there, adapting well to his new home even though he was now almost 70. In America he developed a more colourful style, with syncopated rhythms that reflect his interest in jazz and dancing (*Broadway Boogie-Woogie*, 1942–3, MoMA); he was noted for his immaculate tidiness and rather fussy lifestyle, but he had a passion for social dancing and took lessons in fashionable steps. John Milner (*Mondrian*, 1992) writes: 'Even in middle age, when he was already enjoying some celebrity, his studio was stark and denuded of all but the most necessary comforts. His only indulgence was a gramophone. Some of his furniture was constructed from wooden boxes . . . He had no wife, no children, to enrich and complicate the simplicity of his daily life . . . He rarely smiled for photographs, appearing reserved, austere, preoccupied and a little awkward in company . . . [but] he was welcoming and helpful to visitors.'

Mondrian's enormous influence was not limited to artists whose style and aesthetic outlook were similar to his own. He also had a powerful impact on much industrial, decorative, and advertisement art from the 1930s onwards; indeed Ian Dunlop writes that 'it is no exaggeration to say that his effect on the look and style of contemporary life has been greater than that of any modern artist, even of such supreme masters as *Matisse and *Picasso' (*Piet Mondrian*, 1967). This influence was spread by his writings (including numerous articles in the periodical *De Stijl*) as well as his paintings.

Mone, Jean (*b* ?Metz, *c*.1480/90; *d* ?Malines [Mechelen], ?1549). Franco-Netherlandish sculptor, active mainly in Malines. He is presumed to have visited Italy early in his career, and he also worked in Spain (as assistant to Bartolomé *Ordóñez in Barcelona) before settling in the Low Countries in about 1520. In 1522 he became sculptor to the Emperor Charles V (see HABSBURG). Mone was the first sculptor working in the Netherlands to break completely with the *Gothic tradition, using a repertoire of *Renaissance forms (pilasters, friezes, and so on), as in the high altar (1533) of the pilgrimage church of Notre-Dame-de-Hal, near Brussels, perhaps his best-known work.

Monet, Claude (*b* Paris, 14 Nov. 1840; *d* Giverny, 5 Dec. 1926). French *Impressionist painter. He is regarded as the archetypal Impressionist in that his devotion to the ideals of the movement was unwavering throughout his long career, and it is fitting that one of his pictures—*Impression: Sunrise* (1872, Mus. Marmottan, Paris)—gave the group its name. His youth was spent in Le Havre, where he first excelled as a caricaturist but was then converted to landscape painting by his early mentor *Boudin, from whom he derived his enthusiasm for painting out of doors. In 1859 he studied in Paris at the *Académie Suisse and formed a friendship with *Pissarro. After two years' military service in Algiers, he returned to Le Havre and met *Jongkind, to whom he said he owed 'the definitive education of my eye'. Then, in 1862, he entered the studio of *Gleyre in Paris and there met *Renoir, *Sisley, and *Bazille, with whom he was to form the nucleus of the Impressionist group. Monet's devotion to painting out of doors is illustrated by the famous story concerning one of his most ambitious early works, *Women in the Garden* (1866–7, Mus. d'Orsay, Paris). The picture is about 2.5 m (8 ft) high and to enable him to paint all of it outside he had a trench dug in the garden so the canvas could be raised or lowered by pulleys to the height he required. *Courbet visited him when he was working on it and said Monet would not paint even the leaves in the background unless the lighting conditions were exactly right. However, although he always liked to maintain this image as an outdoor painter, he later came to rely more and more on studio work.

During the Franco-Prussian War (1870–1) Monet took refuge in England with Pissarro: he painted the Thames and London parks, and met the dealer *Durand-Ruel, who was to become one of the great champions of the Impressionists. From 1871 to 1876 he lived at Argenteuil, a village on the Seine near Paris, and here were painted some of the most joyous and famous works of the Impressionist movement, not only by Monet, but by his visitors *Manet, Renoir, and Sisley. In 1878 he moved to Vétheuil and in 1883 he settled at Giverny, also on the Seine, but about 65 km (40 miles) from Paris. Early in his career he had experienced extreme poverty, but in the 1880s he began to prosper. By 1890 he was successful enough to buy the house at Giverny he had previously rented and in 1892 he married his mistress, with whom he had begun an affair in 1876, three years before the death of his first wife.

From 1890 Monet concentrated on series of pictures in which he painted the same subject at different times of the day in different lights—*Haystacks* or *Grainstacks* (1890–1) and *Rouen Cathedral* (1891–5) are the best known. He continued to travel widely, visiting London and Venice several times (and in 1895 Norway, where he painted with his beard 'covered in icicles'), but increasingly his attention was focused on the celebrated water-garden he created at Giverny, which served as the theme for the series of paintings on *Waterlilies* (*Nymphéas*) that began in 1899 and grew to dominate his work completely (in 1914, by now wealthy and famous, he had a special studio built in the grounds of his house so he could work on the huge canvases). From 1908 he was troubled by failing eyesight (he had a cataract operation in 1923), but he painted until the end, completing a great decorative scheme of waterlily paintings that he donated to the nation in 1926, the year of his death. They were installed in the Orangerie, Paris, in 1927. In these late works his style had become so loose and free that the forms almost disappear in a blur of vibrant brushstrokes. It has even been suggested that they anticipate *Abstract Expressionism, but the subject matter always remained important to Monet.

Monnoyer, Jean-Baptiste (*bapt*. Lille, 12 Jan. 1636; *d* London, 16 Feb. 1699). Franco-Flemish painter. He was the most renowned flower painter of his time, specializing in large and opulent canvases for the decoration of grand interiors. After initial training in Antwerp, he moved to Paris in about 1650 and collaborated with *Le Brun on the decoration of royal palaces. He also made designs for the Beauvais and *Gobelins tapestry factories. He spent most of the final decade of his life in England, working for the 1st Duke of Montagu, a great lover of French culture, and other patrons; a good collection of his work is at Boughton House, Northamptonshire. Monnoyer's work was much imitated, and pictures in his style, sometimes designated by his nickname 'Baptiste', often appear in the saleroom. His son **Antoine** (1672–1747) was also a flower painter.

monotype. A method of making an image (on the borderline between painting and printmaking) in which a design is painted (usually in oil colours) on a flat sheet of metal or glass and is then transferred directly to a sheet of paper; the term is also applied to the print so made. With glass plates, pressure has to be applied to the back of the paper by hand; in other cases monotypes may be printed in a press. Strictly speaking, only one print may be taken by this process (hence the term 'monotype'); in practice the colour on the slab may be reinforced after printing and another one or two impressions taken, although they will often differ considerably from the first. Various modifications of the principle are known. G. B. *Castiglione is generally credited with the invention of the monotype in the 1640s. William *Blake and Edgar *Degas are among the artists who have made memorable use of the technique.

Monro, Dr Thomas (*b* London, 29 June 1759; *d* Bushey, Hertfordshire, 14 Feb. 1833). English collector, patron, and amateur painter, a physician by profession. He played an important role in encouraging some of the outstanding watercolour painters of his period, his protégés including *Cotman, *De Wint, *Girtin, *Turner, and many others. They used his houses in London and Bushey, Hertfordshire, as places to meet and work, and were given the run of his superb collection. Late in life Turner recalled how he and Girtin had often made 'drawings for good Dr Monro at half a crown apiece and a supper'.

'Monsù Bernardo'. See KEIL.

'Monsù Desiderio'. A name under which two obscure French painters working in Naples in the early 17th century were for many years conflated. The two painters, who probably sometimes collaborated, are Didier Barra (*c.*1590–after 1647) and François de Nomé (*c.*1593–after 1644), both of whom came from Metz, and the name 'Monsù Desiderio' is a corruption of 'Monsieur Didier'. The main—but often unreliable—source of information on Neapolitan art of this period, *Vite de' pittori, scultori ed architetti napoletani* (1742–5) by the local painter and writer

Bernardo de Dominici (1683–1759), describes Monsù Desiderio as a 'highly praised painter of perspectives and city scenes', and it was not until the 1950s that the separate identities of Barra and de Nomé were clearly established. De Nomé is now regarded as the artist principally responsible for producing the pictures previously given to 'Monsù Desiderio'—strange architectural fantasies, with crumbling cities under stormy skies, sometimes with a religious scene played out by tiny figures in the foreground (*Fantastic Ruins with St Augustine and the Child*, 1623, NG, London). One of the few works reliably associated with Barra is the signed and dated *Panoramic View of Naples* (1647, Mus. di S. Martino, Naples).

montage (French: 'mounting'). A pictorial technique in which a number of cut-out illustrations, or fragments of them, are arranged together and mounted on a suitable background; the term also refers to the picture so created. Ready-made images alone are used and they are generally chosen for their subject and message; in both these respects montage can be distinguished from *collage, in which materials of varied kinds can be used, often primarily with an interest in their decorative qualities. Montage is now associated particularly with advertising, but it has also been used by artists. *Photomontage is montage using photographic images only. In cinematic usage, the term 'montage' refers to the assembling of separate pieces of film into a sequence or superimposed image.

Montagna, Bartolomeo (*b* ?Orzinuovi, nr. Brescia, *c.*1450; *d* Vicenza, 11 Oct. 1523). Italian painter. He probably trained in Venice, but he worked mainly in Vicenza, where he was the leading painter of his day, producing many altarpieces for local churches. His style has been well characterized by S. J. Freedberg (*Painting in Italy: 1500–1600*, 1971) as 'gloomily impressive'. There are examples of his work in the National Gallery, London.

Montañés, Juan Martínez (*bapt.* Alcalá la Real, nr. Granada, 16 Mar. 1568; *d* Seville, 18 June 1649). The greatest Spanish sculptor of the 17th century, known as 'el dios de la madera' (the god of wood) because of his mastery as a carver. He was active mainly in Seville, his most famous work being the *Christ of Clemency* (1603–6) in the cathedral there, which shows the new naturalism he brought to the *polychromed wooden statue (*Pacheco often painted his figures). In this he occupied a role comparable to Gregorio

*Fernández in Valladolid, but Montañés was more aristocratic in style, tempering *Baroque emotionalism with a classical sense of dignity. In 1635-6 he visited Madrid to undertake his only recorded secular work, a portrait head (now lost) of Philip IV (see HABSBURG) to serve as model for the equestrian statue of the king executed by Pietro *Tacca in Florence, and it was at this time that *Velázquéz painted his well-known portrait of Montañés (Prado, Madrid). His work influenced painters such as *Zurbarán as well as sculptors such as *Cano (whom he probably taught), and his style was spread by his flourishing workshop.

Montefeltro. Italian noble family that ruled Urbino from 1234 with short intervals until 1508, when the line became extinct. For most of this period Urbino was of only local importance, but under **Federico II da Montefeltro** (1422-82; ruled from 1444) the city had a brief golden age as one of the most important centres of *Renaissance culture. Federico fulfilled the ideal of the Renaissance prince, for he was a brave soldier and a humane ruler as well as an enlightened patron of literature and the arts. His library was the finest in Italy and his palace is one of the most beautiful buildings of the Renaissance. For us he chiefly survives—broken nose, warts, and all—in the famous portrait (Uffizi, Florence) by *Piero della Francesca, who was one of the leading lights of his court. Federico's ideals lived on in his son **Guidobaldo** (1472-1508), whose court is commemorated in Castiglione's famous book *The Courtier* (1528). Guidobaldo was deposed by Cesare Borgia in 1502, but recovered Urbino the following year. When he died childless in 1508, the dukedom passed to his nephew Francesco Maria I della *Rovere.

Monticelli, Adolphe (b Marseilles, 14 Oct. 1824; d Marseilles, 29 June 1886). French painter, active in his native Marseilles and in Paris. He was a pupil of Paul *Delaroche, but he learned more from his studies of Old Masters in the Louvre; he was also influenced by his friends *Delacroix and *Diaz de la Peña. His subjects included landscapes, portraits, still-lifes, *fêtes galantes* in the spirit of *Watteau, and scenes from the circus, painted in brilliant colours and thick impasto that influenced van *Gogh. He enjoyed great success in Paris in the 1860s, but after the outbreak of the Franco-Prussian War in 1870 he returned to Marseilles and led a retiring life. His work is represented in many French museums, and he has been much forged.

Moore, Albert (b York, 4 Sept. 1841; d London, 25 Sept. 1893). English painter, son of a portrait painter, **William Moore** (1790-1851). His early works were in a *Pre-Raphaelite vein, but in the mid-1860s, under the influence particularly of the *Elgin Marbles, he turned to classical subjects. He specialized in elaborately, and sometimes diaphanously, draped female figures, singly or in groups—'subjectless' pictures akin to those of his friend *Whistler. The two men met in 1865 and influenced each other. Like Whistler, Moore was a colourist of great sensitivity, although his colours tend to be much higher keyed, and he ranks with him as one of the leading figures of *Aestheticism. Four of Moore's brothers were artists, most notably **Henry** (1831-95), a successful marine painter.

Moore, George. See ACADEMY.

Moore, Henry (b Castleford, Yorkshire, 30 July 1898; d Much Hadham, Hertfordshire, 31 Aug. 1986). British sculptor, draughtsman, and printmaker. He is regarded as one of the greatest sculptors of the 20th century and from the late 1940s until his death he was unchallenged as the most celebrated British artist of his time. After service in the British army in the First World War, he trained at Leeds School of Art and from there obtained a scholarship to the *Royal College of Art in 1921; he completed his training in 1924, then taught there until 1931. From 1932 to 1939 he was the first head of sculpture in a new department at Chelsea School of Art. During the 1930s he lived in Hampstead in the same area as Ben *Nicholson, Barbara *Hepworth, the critic Herbert *Read, and other leading figures of the avant-garde. In 1940, after the bombing of his studio, he moved to Much Hadham in Hertfordshire, where he lived for the rest of his life.

Most of Moore's early work was carved, rejecting the academic tradition of modelling in favour of the doctrine of *truth to material, according to which the nature of the stone or wood—its shape, texture, and so on—was part of the conception of the work. He also rejected the *classical and *Renaissance conception of beauty and put in its place an ideal of vital force and formal vigour that he found exemplified in much ancient sculpture (Mexican, Sumerian, etc.), which he studied in the British Museum, and also in the frescos of *Giotto and *Masaccio, which he saw in Italy in 1925 in the course of a travelling scholarship. During the 1930s his work was more directly influenced by European avant-garde art, particularly the *Surrealism of *Arp. Although he produced some purely abstract pieces, his work was almost always based on forms in the natural world—often the human figure, but also, for example, bones, pebbles, and shells. The reclining female figure and the mother and child were among his perennial themes.

By the late 1930s Moore was well known in informed circles as the leading avant-garde sculptor in England (Kenneth *Clark and Jacob *Epstein were among his early supporters), and his wider fame was established by the poignant drawings he did as an *Official War Artist (1940–2) of people sheltering from air raids in underground stations. Subsequently his reputation grew rapidly (particularly after he won the International Sculpture Prize at the 1948 Venice *Biennale), and from the 1950s he carried out many public commissions in Britain and elsewhere. During this time there were major changes in his way of working. Bronze took over from stone as his preferred medium and he often worked on a very large scale. There was a tendency also for his works to be composed of several elements grouped together rather than made up of a single object. Some critics discerned a falling away of his powers in his later work, marked in particular by a tendency towards inflated rhetoric, but for others he remained a commanding figure to the end.

A man of great integrity and unaffected charm, Moore was held in almost universally high esteem. He held broad socialist principles, was pleased to find that his work could be appreciated by a wide audience and not just an elite, and gave his time generously to serve on public bodies. The tributes paid after his death made it clear that he was widely regarded not only as one of the greatest artists of the century, but also as one of the greatest Englishmen in any field. He was a lucid and perceptive commentator on his own and other people's art, and his writings have been collected as *Henry Moore on Sculpture* (1966). His output was huge, and it has been reasonably claimed that by the time of his death 'his work had been distributed more widely throughout the Western world than that of any other sculptor, living or dead' (catalogue of the exhibition 'Henry Moore', Royal Academy, London, 1988). From the late 1960s he also worked a good deal as an printmaker, producing several series of etchings such as *Elephant Skull* (1969). There are particularly fine holdings of his work in Leeds (City Art Gallery), London (Tate), Toronto (Art Gallery of Ontario), and Washington (Hirshhorn Museum and Sculpture Garden).

Moorman, Charlotte. See VIDEO ART.

Mor, Anthonis (*b* Utrecht, *c*.1517/20; *d* Antwerp, 1576/7). Netherlandish portrait painter, one of the outstanding pupils of Jan van *Scorel. He was the most successful court portraitist of his day, leading an international career that took him to England, Germany, Italy, Portugal, and Spain. In England he painted a portrait of Mary Tudor (1554, Prado, Madrid, and other versions), for which he is said to have been knighted—he is sometimes known as Sir Anthony More (it is thus that he appears in the *Dictionary of National Biography*) and the Spanish version of his name, Antonio Moro, is also commonly used. His work shows little variation throughout his career; sitters are shown life-size or a little larger, half-, three-quarter-, or full-length, turned slightly to the side, with an air of unruffled dignity. His composition is simple and strong and his grasp of character firm but undemonstrative. He owed much to *Titian, but his surfaces are more detailed and polished, in the northern manner. Mor had great influence on the development of royal and aristocratic portraiture, particularly in Spain, where his ceremonious but austere style ideally suited the rigorous etiquette of the court. *Sánchez Coello was his pupil. From 1567 he worked mainly in Antwerp.

Morales, Luis de (*b* ?Badajoz, ?*c*.1520; *d* Badajoz, *c*.1586). Spanish painter. He worked for most of his life in Badajoz, a town on the Portuguese border, and his style—formed away from the influence of the court or great religious and artistic centres such as Seville—is highly distinctive. His pictures are usually fairly small and he concentrated on devotional images such as the *Mater Dolorosa* or *Ecce Homo*, painted with intense spirituality. The piety of his work has earned him the nickname El Divino. His style owes something to Netherlandish art, but his misty modelling seems to derive more from *Leonardo da Vinci. He is last documented in 1584 and *Palomino says he died in about 1586, aged 67.

Moran, Thomas. See ROCKY MOUNTAIN SCHOOL.

Morandi, Giorgio (*b* Bologna, 20 July 1890; *d* Bologna, 18 June 1964). Italian painter and etcher. He lived in Bologna all his life, and apart from brief associations with *Futurism and *Metaphysical Painting, he stood aloof from modern aesthetic experiments. Early in his career (and again in the 1940s) he painted landscapes, but he came to specialize almost exclusively in still-life, eschewing literary and symbolic content, and using subtle combinations of colour within a narrow range of tones. His style has something in common with *Purism, but is more subtle and intimate; the greatest influence on his work was *Cézanne, whom he revered. After the Second World War Morandi won an international reputation, and his work won great respect among younger Italian artists for its poetic quality and devotion to purely aesthetic values.

morbidezza (Italian: 'delicacy' or 'softness'). The rendering of the flesh tints in painting with softness and delicacy. It was a popular term in criticism of the 18th century, when it was applied in particular to *Correggio, but it is now antiquated.

Moreau, Gustave (b Paris, 6 Apr. 1826; d Paris, 18 Apr. 1898). French painter, one of the leading *Symbolist artists. He was a close friend of *Chassériau and was influenced by his exotic *Romanticism, but Moreau went far beyond him in his feeling for the bizarre and developed a style that is highly distinctive in subject and technique. His pictures are typically mystically intense images treated with an extraordinary sensuousness, his paint encrusted and jewel-like. Often the subjects are religious or mythological (Orpheus was a favourite theme), but sometimes they more vaguely evoke long-dead civilizations. Although he had some success at the *Salon, Moreau was highly sensitive to criticism and for long periods did not exhibit his work. He had no need to sell his paintings, as he had private means, and much of his life was spent in seclusion. Nevertheless, his paintings became well known, partly because they appealed strongly to some of the leading writers of the day; most notably, there is a lengthy description of his work in J. K. Huysmans's novel *A rebours* (1884), one of the key texts of the Symbolist movement. In 1892, Moreau became a professor at the École des *Beaux-Arts and proved an inspired teacher, bringing out his pupils' individual talents rather than trying to impose his own ideas on them. His pupils included *Marquet and *Matisse, but his favourite was *Rouault, who became the first curator of the Moreau Museum in Paris (the artist's house), which Moreau left to the nation on his death. The bulk of his work is preserved there. Much of it consists of small pictures and watercolours, as he executed comparatively few major oils.

Moreau, Louis-Gabriel (b Paris, Jan./Apr. 1740; d Paris, 12 Oct. 1805). French landscape painter and etcher. He was not particularly successful in his time, but he is now recognized as one of the outstanding French landscape painters of the 18th century, the freshness, directness, and sincerity of his work looking forward to the naturalism of *Corot. He is often called Moreau the Elder, to distinguish him from his brother **Jean-Michel** (b Paris, 26 Mar. 1741; d Paris, 30 Nov. 1814), Moreau the Younger, a draughtsman, printmaker, and painter. His output was varied, but he is best known for his drawings and engravings of fashionable manners and morals. Carle *Vernet was his son-in-law and Horace Vernet his grandson.

Moreelse, Paulus (b Utrecht, 1571; d Utrecht, 5 Mar. 1638). Dutch painter and architect, active in his native Utrecht, where he was the first dean of the painters' guild, founded in 1611. He painted various types of picture, including portraits (similar to those of his teacher *Miereveld, but less severe) and religious works. More interesting than these are his Arcadian scenes with shepherds and shepherdesses; he was one of the first Dutch artists to paint such pictures. As an architect he designed the Catherine Gate (destroyed) and possibly the façade of the Meat Market in Utrecht. He served on the town council and was involved in founding Utrecht's university in 1636.

Morelli, Giovanni (b Verona, 25 Feb. 1816; d Bergamo, 28 Feb. 1891). Italian critic. He trained as a physician and spent most of his career as a politician, but from 1873 he began to write articles on Italian art. These were written in German (he was educated in Switzerland and Germany), and at first he published them as supposed translations from the Russian of Ivan Lermolieff (an anagram of his surname with a Russian termination). His work appeared in English as *Italian Masters in German Galleries* (1883) and *Italian Painters: Critical Studies of their Works* (2 vols., 1892–3). Morelli concentrated mainly on the problems of attribution and claimed to have reduced the matter to scientific principles. He maintained that an artist's method of dealing with subordinate details, such as the treatment of fingernails or ears (here his anatomical training was useful), is tantamount to a signature and that by systematic study of such details attribution can be put beyond doubt. This method, still sometimes referred to as 'Morellian criticism', was influential on connoisseurs such as *Berenson, but it has proved much less productive of scientific certainty than Morelli hoped; it is now felt that we recognize the work of individual artists more by general effect than by details, and that the details rather than the general effect are what an imitator will be able to reproduce most convincingly. Morelli himself made some brilliant attributions, but also some noteworthy blunders. A devoted patriot, he declined the directorship of the *Uffizi because he did not want to be distracted from his political duties, and he helped to secure legislation restricting the export of works from Italy. His own collection of pictures was left to the Pinacoteca of his adopted city of Bergamo.

Moretto da Brescia (Alessandro Bonvicino) (*b* Brescia, *c*.1498; *d* Brescia, Nov./Dec. 1554). Italian painter, active mainly in his native Brescia and the neighbourhood. His nickname Moretto means 'blackamoor'. *Ridolfi says he was a pupil of *Titian, and certainly his influence is apparent in Moretto's work. He was the leading Brescian painter of his day, mainly producing altarpieces and other religious works, the best of which display an impressive gravity and a poetic feeling for nature (*St Giustina with a Donor*, *c*.1530, KH Mus., Vienna). However, his portraits, although much less numerous, are considered to be generally of higher quality and of greater importance historically. It seems likely that he introduced the independent full-length portrait to Italy, for although *Vasari credits Titian with this distinction, Moretto's *Portrait of a Gentleman* of 1526 in the National Gallery, London, antedates any known example by Titian by several years. The National Gallery has an outstanding collection of works by Moretto, including two other portraits, which show the thoughtful qualities he passed on to his pupil *Moroni.

Morgan, Evelyn De. See DE MORGAN.

Morgan, J. Pierpont (*b* Hartford, Conn., 17 Apr. 1837; *d* Rome, 31 Mar. 1913). American financier, industrialist, and art collector. The son of a financier and head of one of the most powerful banking houses in the world, Morgan used his personal fortune to spend lavishly on works of art. His main collecting interests were manuscripts and rare books and after his death his son, also **J. Pierpont Morgan** (1867–1943), endowed the Pierpont Morgan Library in New York as a research institute and museum in memory of his father. It has superb collections of illuminated manuscripts and Old Master drawings and also contains stained glass, sculpture, and metalwork. The Metropolitan Museum in New York also received an important bequest from the elder Morgan, who was chairman of its governing board for many years.

Morghen, Raphael (*b* Naples, 19 June 1758; *d* Florence, 8 Apr. 1833). Italian engraver, the best-known member of a family of printmakers. He was one of the leading reproductive engravers of his day, and his print of *Leonardo's *Last Supper* (1800) brought him European fame. After his death, however, his reputation declined and his name came to stand for a style of engraving that was extremely precise and technically accomplished but somewhat mechanical and lacking in spirit.

Morisot, Berthe (*b* Bourges, 14 Jan. 1841; *d* Paris, 2 Mar. 1895). French painter and printmaker, a central figure of the *Impressionist group. The daughter of a high-ranking civil servant and the great-granddaughter of *Fragonard, she was brought up in a cultured atmosphere; her training included some informal tuition from *Corot. In 1864, at her first attempt, she had two pictures accepted by the *Salon, and she showed several more there over the next few years, receiving encouraging reviews. However, she was attracted to progressive ideas in art, particularly after she met *Manet in 1868 (she married his brother in 1874), and she made her last submission to the Salon in 1873. Instead she became one of the mainstays of the Impressionist exhibitions, taking an active part in their organization; she participated in seven out of the eight (missing the fourth in 1879 because she was ill following the birth of her only child). In addition her home was a social meeting place for the Impressionists, as well as for writers (she was renowned for her beauty and charm and often posed for Manet). Morisot produced various types of picture, including marine views, but she is best known for gentle domestic scenes, painted in a delicate but lively technique, showing the influence of Manet (in turn she is said to have persuaded Manet to experiment with Impressionist methods, particularly painting out of doors). Her watercolours are as accomplished as her oils, and she also produced pastels, drypoints, and lithographs. Although she has been overshadowed by her celebrated male colleagues, her reputation stands high.

Morland, George (*b* London, 26 June 1763 [or, according to his own account, 26 May 1762]; *d* London, 29 Oct. 1804). English painter, mainly of scenes from rural life, the son and pupil of **Henry Morland** (?1716–97), a painter of portraits and *fancy pictures who was also a dealer, forger, and restorer. George was precocious and a fluent worker and produced a huge amount of work, in spite of leading a dissolute life and often being drunk, in hiding from his creditors, or in prison. His name is particularly associated with small scenes of middle- and lower-class rural life, usually drawn more from the tavern and the stable than the cottage. The quality of his work is uneven, but at his best he showed a spirited technique and a sure sense of tone. His paintings became extremely popular and he was much imitated and forged; numerous prints were made after his work, some of them by his brother-in-law William *Ward. With *Wheatley and *Ibbetson he established the village scene in the English painter's repertory.

Morley, Malcolm (b London, 7 June 1931). British painter, active mainly in the USA. In the 1960s he turned from abstract to figurative work and became one of the pioneers of *Superrealism. From about 1970, however, his paintings became increasingly loose in handling, often depicting animals in lush landscapes (the critic Peter Fuller described these works as 'incoherent and overblown canvases based on his masturbatory fantasies'). In 1984 he was the first winner of the *Turner Prize, awarded for 'the greatest contribution to art in Britain in the previous twelve months', a decision that occasioned much controversy as Morley had been living in New York since 1958.

Moro, Antonio. See MOR.

Morone, Domenico (b Verona, c.1440; d Verona, c.1518). The leading Veronese painter of his time. He was strongly influenced by *Mantegna, but the most important of his few surviving works, the *Expulsion of the Bonacolsi* (1494), in the Palazzo Ducale in Mantua, is an extensive, multi-figure townscape recalling Gentile *Bellini and *Carpaccio. It commemorates the beginning of *Gonzaga rule in Mantua, when the rival Bonacolsi family were defeated in battle in 1328. Domenico's son and pupil **Francesco** (?1471–1529) succeeded him as the leading painter in Verona, working in a calm, dignified style showing the impact of High *Renaissance ideals. There are examples of the work of father and son in the National Gallery, London.

Moroni, Giovanni Battista (b Albino, c.1520/4; d Albino, ?(5 Feb.) 1578). Italian painter. He trained under *Moretto in Brescia and worked mainly in his home town of Albino and in nearby Bergamo. His style was based closely on that of his master, but whereas his religious paintings are unexceptional, his portraits are worthy successors to Moretto's, being among the finest of their time (several of them indeed have formerly been attributed to *Titian). They are remarkable for their psychological penetration, dignified air, and exquisite silvery tonality. The National Gallery, London, has the best collection of his work, including the celebrated portrait known as '*The Tailor*' (c.1570).

Morozov, Ivan. See HERMITAGE.

Morrice, James Wilson (b Montreal, 10 Aug. 1865; d Tunis, 23 Jan. 1924). Canadian landscape and figure painter, active mainly in Paris, where he settled in 1890. He was friendly with many leading artists, notably *Whistler, who was an influence on his early work; later his style became mildly *Fauvist. He was widely travelled and made several return visits to Canada, playing an important role in introducing modern trends to his country.

Morris, Robert (b Kansas City, Mo., 9 Feb. 1931). American artist and writer. He is regarded as one of the most prominent exponents and theorists of *Minimal art, and has also worked in other fields, including *Conceptual art, *Land art, and *Performance art. His most characteristic sculptures consist of large-scale, hard-edged geometric forms, but he has also produced 'anti-form' pieces in soft, hanging materials.

Morris, William (b Walthamstow, Essex [now Greater London], 24 Mar. 1834; d London, 3 Oct. 1896). English designer, craftsman, writer, painter, and social reformer. As a student at Oxford University he formed a lifelong friendship with *Burne-Jones and began to write poetry and to study medieval architecture. In 1856 he was apprenticed to the architect G. E. Street, but soon left to paint under *Rossetti's guidance—his only completed oil painting, *Queen Guenevere* (1858, Tate, London), is strongly *Pre-Raphaelite. In 1859 Morris married Jane Burden, who appears in numerous paintings by Rossetti as an archetypal *femme fatale*; Morris's architect friend Philip Webb built for the couple the famous Red House, Bexley Heath, Kent (now Greater London). With Webb, Rossetti, Burne-Jones, Ford Madox *Brown, P. P. Marshall (a surveyor), and Charles Faulkner (an accountant), Morris founded the manufacturing and decorating firm of Morris, Marshall, Faulkner & Co. in 1861 (reorganized in 1875 as Morris & Co.).

After a shaky start, the firm prospered, producing furniture, tapestry, stained glass, furnishing fabrics, carpets, and much more. Morris's wallpaper designs are particularly well known (they are still produced commercially today) and Burne-Jones did some superb work for the firm, particularly in stained glass and tapestry.

Morris repudiated the concept of *fine art and his company was based on the ideal of a medieval guild, in which the craftsman both designed and executed the work. As a socialist he wished to produce art for the masses, but there was an inherent flaw in his ambition, for only the rich could afford his expensive handmade products. His ideal of universal craftsmanship and his glorification of manual skill thus proved unrealistic in failing to come to terms with modern machine production. However, his work bore lasting fruit, in England (see ARTS AND CRAFTS MOVEMENT) and abroad, in the emphasis it laid on the social importance of good design and fine workmanship in every walk of life. He also played an important part in the history of book production through the founding of the *Kelmscott Press, which initiated the *private press movement. Morris's homes at Walthamstow in London and Kelmscott Manor in Oxfordshire contain good examples of work designed by him and his associates.

Morse, Samuel F. B. (b Charleston, Mass., 27 Apr. 1791; d New York, 2 Apr. 1872). American painter and inventor. He had ambitions as a history painter and studied with *West during a period in London, 1811–15, but for financial reasons he had to work mainly as a portraitist. After his return to the USA he lived in Boston and then in New York, where he was a founder member of the *National Academy of Design and its first president from 1826 to 1845. Disenchanted by his failure to achieve major commissions as a history painter, however, he turned to invention, and in the 1830s conceived the idea of the telegraph and developed the Morse Code, which eventually made him a fortune. His first telegraph line was established between Washington and Baltimore in 1844, by which time Morse had abandoned painting as a profession.

Mortimer, John Hamilton (b Eastbourne, Sussex, 17 Sept. 1740; d London, 4 Feb. 1779). English painter. He studied under *Hudson and became a lifelong friend of his fellow pupil Joseph *Wright. Like Wright, he painted portraits as well as subject pieces of a pioneering *Romantic nature. His *conversation pieces bear comparison with those of *Zoffany, but he found his true

bent in the 1770s with pictures representing the exploits of soldiers and banditti in the 'savage' style of Salvator *Rosa (Bandit Taking up his Post, c.1775, Detroit Inst. of Arts). Many of his paintings have disappeared and are now known only through engravings. Mortimer led an eccentric and disorderly life, but he became more settled after marrying in 1775 and his early death cut short the career of one of the most individual British painters of his generation.

Mortlake Tapestry Factory. See ROYAL COLLECTION and TAPESTRY.

mosaic. The art of making patterns and pictures by arranging small (usually multicoloured) pieces of glass, marble, and other suitable materials and fixing them into a bed of cement or plaster. It was first developed extensively by the Romans in pavements. But it is also well suited to the adornment of walls and vaults, and great use was made of wall mosaic by the Christian churches of Italy and the *Byzantine Empire throughout the Middle Ages. As an exterior decoration it has sometimes appeared on the façades of medieval churches and in modern architecture (see O'GORMAN). More rarely it has been made into portable pictures, or inlaid in furniture and small objects, as in the Aztec art of Mexico.

Mosan School. Tradition of manuscript illumination, metalwork, and enamelwork flourishing from the late 11th to the early 13th century in the valley of the Meuse (or Maas). The river rises in France and empties into the Rhine estuary in the Netherlands, but in the context of medieval art the term Mosan refers to the stretch of river and its tributaries in present-day Belgium, particularly the area around Liège and the Benedictine monastery of Stavelot. The most important artists of the school are *Godefroid de Claire, *Nicolas of Verdun, and *Rainer of Huy. The Mosan style is part of *Romanesque art, but is distinctive because of its more naturalistic, if idealized, attitude towards the human figure. In Rainer of Huy's font at Liège, for example, the figures are three-dimensional and well proportioned and their draperies are notably *antique-like. Mosan art is also noteworthy for its sheer sumptuousness, and Mosan metalworkers in particular were famed throughout Europe; Abbot *Suger employed a number at Saint-Denis.

Moser, Lukas (active 1432). German painter, known only from one work, the Magdalene altarpiece in the church at Tiefenbronn (signed and dated 1432—not 1431, as had previously been read). The altarpiece is remarkably advanced stylistically, showing a detailed naturalism in the treatment of figures and landscape and an interest in light that have much in common with the paintings of *Witz, who worked in nearby Switzerland. Also remarkable is an enigmatic inscription on the frame (perhaps no more than the lament of an underpaid artist): 'schri kunst schri und klag dich ser din begert iecz niemen mer' (Cry out, art, cry out and wail! No one wants you now).

Moser, Mary (b London, 27 Oct. 1744; d London, 2 May 1819). English flower painter, the daughter of **George Moser** (1706–83), a Swiss goldsmith, enameller, and medallist who settled in England and became the first keeper of the *Royal Academy. Like her father she was a foundation member of the Academy in 1768 (Angelica *Kauffmann was the only other woman so honoured). Aged 24 at the time, Moser was the youngest ever Academician, and in 1805 she was proposed as a candidate for the presidency. Her small flower pieces in the Dutch manner were highly popular in her day.

Moses, Grandma (born Anna Mary Robertson) (b Greenwich, Washington County, NY, 7 Sept. 1860; d Hoosick Falls, NY, 13 Dec. 1961). The most famous of American *naive painters. She took up painting in her seventies (initially copying postcards and *Currier & Ives prints) after arthritis made her unable to continue with embroidery, with which she had regularly won prizes at country fairs. Her first exhibition was held in a drugstore at Hoosick Falls, NY, in 1938. She was then 'discovered' by a collector, Louis J. Caldor, and had a one-woman show in New York in 1940 at the age of 80. Thereafter she rapidly became famous and something of a national institution, her work being widely reproduced, notably on Christmas cards (her winter scenes were ideal for this; she sometimes dusted 'glitter' over the snow to make it look more realistic to her eye). In 1949 she was received at the White House by President Harry Truman and in 1960 Governor Nelson Rockefeller proclaimed her 100th birthday, 7 September, 'Grandma Moses Day' in New York State. She produced more than 1,000 pictures (working on a sort of production line system, three or four at a time, painting first the skies and last the figures), her favourite subjects being scenes of what she called the 'old-timey' farm life she had known in her

younger days. Examples are in many American collections, notably the Bennington Museum, Vermont.

Mostaert, Jan (b ?Haarlem, c.1475; d Haarlem, 1555/6). Netherlandish painter. He worked mainly in Haarlem and the influence of *Geertgen tot Sint Jans can clearly be seen in his rather stiff and gangling figures. Most of his paintings are religious works or portraits (for a period of unknown duration, probably c.1516–26, he was court portraitist to Margaret of Austria, regent of the Netherlands; see HABSBURG). However, his most remarkable painting is a 'West Indies Landscape' (c.1545, Hals Mus., Haarlem), which is now thought to represent New Mexico. He presumably based it on written accounts.

Motherwell, Robert (b Aberdeen, Wash., 24 Jan. 1915; d Provincetown, Mass., 16 July 1991). American painter, collagist, writer, editor, and teacher, one of the pioneers and principal exponents of *Abstract Expressionism. He took up painting seriously in 1941 after studying philosophy at Stanford and Harvard universities and the erudite approach of his writings played a large part in setting the intellectual tone of the Abstract Expressionist movement. Motherwell was unusual among Abstract Expressionists in that his painting was essentially abstract from the beginning of his career. However, his work was deeply influenced by *Surrealism (particularly in the use of *automatism) and there is often a suggestion of figuration in the large amorphous shapes of his paintings. Moreover, the intellectual sensibilities he brought to his work are reflected in the inspiration from literature, history, or his personal life. For example, he painted a series of works (more than 100 pictures) entitled *Elegy to the Spanish Republic*. By the late 1960s his style had moved towards *Colour Field Painting. He was an extremely prolific artist and also displayed great energy as a writer, teacher, and lecturer. From 1958 to 1971 he was married to Helen *Frankenthaler.

mould. See CAST.

Mount, William Sidney (b Setauket, Long Island, NY, 26 Nov. 1807; d Setauket, 19 Nov. 1868). American painter, his country's first notable specialist in *genre scenes. Although he worked intermittently in New York City, he spent most of his life on rural Long Island, which supplied him with many of the subjects for his work. He came from a farming family and began his career as a sign painter, but in 1826–7 he took drawing lessons at the recently founded

*National Academy of Design. Initially he painted portraits and historical scenes, but in 1830 he had a great success with his first genre picture, *Rustic Dance after a Sleigh Ride* (MFA, Boston), when it was exhibited at the National Academy of Design, and he continued to work in this lively, affectionate, anecdotal vein. He had, 'like his countryman Mark Twain, a sure instinct for the kind of subject that Americans would respond to as somehow distinctly their own' (Matthew Baigell, *Dictionary of American Art*, 1979), and his work was widely distributed in engravings. In spite of this popular appeal, he was a sophisticated artist with a polished technique (he took a great deal of interest in the painter's craft and made various experiments with pigments, brushes, and so on). Far and away the largest collection of his work is at the Stony Brook Museum, Long Island, near his birthplace.

Moynihan, Rodrigo (*b* Santa Cruz, Tenerife, 17 Oct. 1910; *d* London, 6 Nov. 1990). British painter, born in the Canary Islands to an Irish father (a fruit broker) and a Spanish mother. He moved to England at the age of 8 and studied at the *Slade School, 1928–31. His work was varied and fluctuated between figuration and abstraction. In the early 1930s he was one of the most radical of British abstract painters, but he then turned to figurative art and taught at the *Euston Road School. However, unlike his fellow teacher *Coldstream, who advocated a socially relevant art, Moynihan approached his subjects in a more impersonal way. After being invalided out of the army, he became an *Official War Artist in 1943, concentrating on the everyday life of the troops. From 1948 to 1957 he was professor of painting at the *Royal College of Art, and one of his best-known works is the large *Portrait Group* (1951, Tate, London), showing the nine members of the teaching staff of the painting school there (himself included). In 1956 he reverted to abstract art, in a style influenced by *Abstract Expressionism, but in the 1970s he took up figurative art again (mainly portraits and still-lifes), characteristically painting in pale, muted colours. From 1957 he lived mainly in France.

Mraz, Franjo. See GENERALIĆ.

Mucha, Alphonse (*b* Ivančice, Moravia, 24 July 1860; *d* Prague, 14 July 1939). Czech painter and designer, active for much of his career in Paris. He settled there in 1888, and it was his centre of activity until about 1905, when he began to spend an increasing amount of time in his homeland. His output was highly varied, but he is best known for his luxuriously flowing poster designs, which rank among the most distinctive products of the *Art Nouveau style. They often feature beautiful women, but have nothing of the morbid sexuality typical of the period. Some of the best known were made in the 1890s for the celebrated actress Sarah Bernhardt. Mucha also designed sets, costumes, and jewellery for her. He was successful in the USA as well as Europe, making four journeys there between 1903 and 1922; a Chicago industrialist and Slavophile, Charles Richard Crane, sponsored a series of twenty huge paintings entitled *Slav Epic* (1909–28, Moravsky Krumlov Castle). Although he is so strongly associated with Paris, Mucha was an ardent patriot, and after Czechoslovakia became independent in 1918 he did a good deal of work for the new nation (giving his services free), including designing its first banknotes and stamps. When the Germans occupied Prague in 1939 (a few months before his death) he was one of the first to be arrested and questioned by the Gestapo. After the war his work was long out of fashion, but interest in him has revived so strongly that in the popular imagination he is now one of the symbols of the turn-of-the-century era.

Mueck, Ron. See SUPERREALISM.

Muehl, Otto. See VIENNA ACTIONISTS.

Müller, Otto. See BRÜCKE.

Mulready, William (*b* Ennis, Co. Clare, 1 Apr. 1786; *d* London, 7 July 1863). Irish-born painter, active in England, the pupil and brother-in-law of John *Varley. After undistinguished beginnings with historical *genre and landscape he turned with great success to scenes of contemporary life in the vein made popular by *Wilkie. *The Fight Interrupted* (1816, V&A, London), which shows a vicar intervening between two boys who have come to blows, made his reputation and set the course for his career. At first his meticulous brushwork showed the influence of 17th-century Dutch painting, but in the 1820s he began to develop a more distinctive technique, using light colours over a white ground. This, together with his clear draughtsmanship and the poetic quality of some of his later paintings (*The Sonnet*, 1839, V&A), has led him to be seen as a precursor of the *Pre-Raphaelites, although they themselves regarded his work as trivial. Mulready made numerous book illustrations and also designed the first penny postage envelope (issued 1840).

multiples. A term designating works of art other than prints or cast sculpture that are designed to be produced in a large—potentially limitless—number of copies. Whereas prints and casts of sculptures are copies of an original work hand-made by the artist, multiples are different, for the artist often produces only a blueprint or set of specifications for an industrial process of manufacture in materials such as plastic. Multiples were first made in the 1960s, *Le Parc and *Oldenburg being early exponents. In theory, they represented a democratization of art—works were no longer to be regarded as rare items for collectors and connoisseurs but as consumer goods for the masses like any other industrial product. In practice, however, they are too expensive for a mass market and have been sold through galleries rather than high street shops or supermarkets (although Richard *Hamilton designed a plastic relief showing the exterior of the Guggenheim Museum, New York, that was sold in the museum shop). In 1971 substantial exhibitions of multiples were held at the Philadelphia Museum of Art ('Multiples: The First Decade') and the Whitechapel Art Gallery, London ('New Multiple Art'). By about 1980 the idea seemed to be dying out, but there was a revival of interest in the 1990s.

Multscher, Hans (*b* Reichenhofen, Bavaria. *c.*1400; *d* Ulm, *c.*1467). German sculptor, active in Ulm, where he is first documented in 1427. The solid naturalism of his style, reminiscent of *Sluter, suggests that he trained in the Netherlands or northern France. He ran a large workshop, which was influential in spreading this manner in southern Germany. Paintings were often integral to his altarpieces, but it is a matter for debate whether he practised painting himself. Among his most important works was the high altar (1456–8) for the church at Sterzing in the Tyrol (now in Italy and known as Vipiteno), parts of which are in the Multscher museum there.

Munch, Edvard (*b* Løten, 12 Dec. 1863; *d* Oslo, 23 Jan. 1944). Norwegian painter and printmaker, his country's greatest artist. He began painting in a conventional naturalistic manner, but by 1884 he was part of the world of bohemian artists in Christiania (now Oslo) who had advanced ideas on ethics and sexual morality, Christian *Krohg being his early mentor. In 1885 he made the first of several visits to Paris, where over the next few years he was influenced by the *Impressionists and *Symbolists and, above all, by *Gauguin's use of simplified forms and non-naturalistic colours. Soon after his return from the initial visit he painted the first work in which he showed a distinctly personal vision, *The Sick Child* (1885–6, NG, Oslo). Munch himself described this hauntingly sad scene (of which he painted five later versions) as 'the breakthrough in my art. Most of what I have done since had its birth in this picture.' The choice of subject was highly significant, for it reflected his own tragic childhood (his mother and eldest sister died of consumption when he was young, and as a result his grief-stricken father became almost dementedly pious). 'Illness, madness and death were the black angels that kept watch over my cradle', he wrote, and in his paintings he gave expression to the neuroses that haunted him. Certain themes—jealousy, sickness, the awakening of sexual desire—occur again and again, and he painted extreme psychological states with an unprecedented conviction and an intensity that sometimes bordered on the frenzied.

In 1892 Munch was invited to exhibit at the Verein Berliner Künstler (Association of Berlin Artists) and the anguished intensity of his work caused such an uproar in the press that the exhibition was closed. The scandal made him famous overnight in Germany, so he decided to base himself there and from 1892 to 1908 he lived mainly in Berlin (although he moved around restlessly, staying in boarding houses, and made frequent visits to Norway as well as journeys to France and Italy). During this period—the heart of his creative life—he devoted much of his time to an ambitious open-ended series of pictures that he called the 'Frieze of Life'—'a poem of life, love and death'. The most famous of the paintings from the series, *The Scream* (1893, NG, Oslo), and several others were translated by Munch into etching, lithography, or woodcut. He was one of the greatest of all printmakers, and his woodcuts (often in colour) are particularly remarkable, exploiting the grain of the wood to contribute to their effect of rough vigour. Together with the woodcuts of Gauguin (who likewise took up the medium in the 1890s) they were the major stimulus for the great revival of the technique in the 20th century, especially among the German *Expressionists. By a process of artistic feedback, Munch's prints also influenced his own paintings, for after refining his ideas as he turned a composition from painting to print, he often translated the image back into a painting in a simpler and more powerful form.

In 1908 Munch suffered what he called 'a complete mental collapse', the legacy of heavy drinking, overwork, and a wretched love affair, and after recuperating he made his home permanently in Norway, where he was by now an honoured figure. He realized that his mental instability was part of his genius ('I would not cast off my illness, for there is much in my art that I owe to it'), but he made a conscious decision to devote himself to recovery and abandoned his familiar imagery. The tormented quality of his art disappeared and his work became much more extroverted. He announced this change of direction in a series of murals decorating the Assembly Hall of Oslo University (1910–16); they are concerned with what Munch called 'great eternal forces' (*History* and *The Sun* are two of the subjects) and they are strong and fresh in colour and optimistic in spirit. In 1916 he bought a large house called Ekely, at Skøyen on the outskirts of Oslo, and he spent most of the rest of his life there, leading an increasingly isolated existence, although he continued to travel a good deal. His subjects in his later years, during which he kept up a prodigious output, included landscapes, portraits (he made much of his living through commissions), and workmen, often seen trudging through snow. However, he sometimes returned to the themes that haunted his youth, and occasionally he rekindled the passion and profundity of his early years, as in the last of his numerous self-portraits, *Between the Clock and the Bed* (1940–2, Munch Mus., Oslo), in which he shows himself old and frail, hovering on the edge of eternity. At his death he left the huge body of his work still in his possession to the City of Oslo to found the Munch Museum (opened in 1963 to mark the centenary of his birth).

Munch ranks as one of the most powerful and influential of modern artists. His impact was particularly strong in Scandinavia and Germany, where he and van *Gogh are regarded as the two main sources of Expressionist art. The intensity with which he communicated mental anguish opened up new paths for art. 'Just as *Leonardo da Vinci studied human anatomy and dissected corpses', he said, 'so I try to dissect souls.'

Munkácsy, Mihály (*b* Munkács [now Mukacheve, Ukraine], 20 Feb. 1844; *d* Endenich, near Bonn, 1 May 1900). Hungarian painter. After training in Budapest, Munich, and Düsseldorf, he lived mainly in Paris. He had a resounding early success when he won a gold medal at the 1870 *Salon with the *Last Day of a Condemned Man* (NG, Budapest) and won an international reputation with his *Milton and his Daughters* (1877–8, New York Public Lib.). These theatrical costume pieces were enormously popular with rich collectors and Munkácsy became one of the wealthiest artists of his day. His best works are now, however, considered to be his landscapes, in which, although he did not paint out of doors, he continued the tradition of the *Barbizon School. He despised the *Impressionists, but his work is often very free in handling. Munkácsy is generally regarded as Hungary's greatest painter; appropriately the best collection of his work is in the National Gallery in Budapest.

Munnings, Sir Alfred (*b* Mendham, Suffolk, 8 Oct. 1878; *d* Dedham, Essex, 17 July 1959). English painter, a specialist in scenes involving horses, which he loved passionately. He was at the height of his popularity in the inter-war years, when he cut a figure in fashionable society and was often invited to the grandest country houses to paint the owners with their horses (he was also besieged with commissions when he visited the USA in 1924). From 1944 to 1949 he was president of the *Royal Academy (he beat Augustus *John in the election by 24 votes to 11). He had no interest in administration or the Academy's finances and his presidency was remarkable mainly for a splenetic speech attacking modern art that he delivered at the RA annual dinner in 1949. It was broadcast live on radio and was a national talking point the next day. His successor as PRA, Sir Gerald *Kelly, did much to restore the damage done to the Academy's prestige. Munnings was an artist of considerable natural ability, but he became rather slick and repetitive and his continued popularity is more with lovers of horses and the countryside than with lovers of painting. His work can best be seen at Castle House, Dedham, Essex, his home from 1919, which his widow converted into a Munnings Museum.

Münter, Gabriele. See NEUE KÜNSTLERVEREINIGUNG MÜNCHEN.

mural. A painting, usually large, painted on a wall or for mounting on a wall as a permanent part of the decoration of a building. In European art the classic technique for mural painting is *fresco, but other methods have been used, especially in northern Europe, where the generally damper climate makes fresco unsuitable (see WATER-GLASS PAINTING). For interior murals the most successful alternative has simply been to paint in oils on canvas and glue the canvas to the wall either before or after painting (see MAROUFLAGE).

Murillo, Bartolomé Esteban (*bapt.* Seville, 1 Jan. 1618; *d* Seville, 3 Apr. 1682). Spanish painter, active for almost all his life in Seville. His early career is not well documented, but he started working in a naturalistic *tenebrist style, showing the influence of *Zurbarán. After making his reputation with a series of eleven paintings on the lives of Franciscan saints for the Franciscan monastery in Seville (1645–6, the pictures are now dispersed in Spain and elsewhere), he displaced Zurbarán as the city's leading painter and was unrivalled in this position for the rest of his life. His pre-eminence was acknowledged in 1660 when an academy of painting was founded in Seville (the first in Spain) and Murillo, together with Francisco *Herrera the Younger, was appointed joint president. Most of his paintings are of religious subjects, appealing strongly to popular piety and illustrating the doctrines of the Counter-Reformation Church, above all the Immaculate Conception, which was his favourite theme. His mature style was very different from that seen in his early works; it is characterized by idealized figures, soft, melting forms, delicate colouring, and sweetness of expression and mood. The term *estilo vaporoso* ('vaporous style') is often used of it. Murillo also painted *genre scenes of beggar children that have a similar sentimental appeal, but his fairly rare portraits are strikingly different in feeling—much more sombre and intellectual (an outstanding self-portrait, *c.*1670, is in the NG, London). He died from the effects of injuries he sustained when he fell from scaffolding whilst painting a huge altarpiece of the *Mystic Marriage of St Catherine* for the Capuchin church in Cadiz; the picture, completed by his pupil Francisco Meneses Osorio (*c.*1640–1721), is now in the city's Museo de Bellas Artes.

Murillo had many assistants and followers, and his style continued to influence Sevillian painting into the 19th century. His fame in the 18th century and early 19th century was enormous. With *Ribera he was the only Spanish painter whose work was widely known outside his own country and he was ranked by many critics amongst the greatest artists of all time. Later his reputation plummeted, and he was dismissed as facile and sugary, but now that his own work is being distinguished from that of his numerous imitators his star is rising again.

Murillo, Gerardo. See ATL.

Musée d'Orsay, Paris. The French national museum of *fine and *applied arts from *c.*1848 to *c.*1914, opened in 1986. It is housed in a large building that was originally a railway station, the Gare d'Orsay (1897–1900). The main train service to it closed in 1939 and the building was subsequently put to various uses (for example as a theatre) before it was decided to transform it into a museum. Structural work began in 1979, and in 1980 the Italian architect Gae Aulenti began the conversion of the interior; her design has proved controversial, as some critics feel that it clashes with and obscures the handsome original fabric of the building and provides an unsympathetic setting for many of the works on show. The collections cover the period between those assigned to the *Louvre and the *Pompidou Centre. Not surprisingly, the museum is particularly strong in French art, and at its heart is the superb collection of *Impressionist and *Post-Impressionist paintings formerly housed in the Jeu de Paume. It also includes pictures transferred from the Louvre and decorative art from other state collections.

Musée du Luxembourg, Paris. See POMPIDOU CENTRE.

Musée National d'Art Moderne, Paris. See POMPIDOU CENTRE.

Museum of Modern Art (MoMA), New York. The world's pre-eminent collection of art from the late 19th century to the present day, privately founded in 1929 by a group of collectors. Among them were Lillie P. Bliss (1864–1931) and Abby Aldrich Rockefeller (1874–1948), who became two of the museum's greatest benefactors. It operated first in rented premises, holding loan shows, but the nucleus of a permanent collection was established with the bequest of Miss Bliss at her death in 1931. The present building, in 53rd Street, was opened in 1939 and was inaugurated with a large exhibition entitled 'Art in our Time', celebrating the museum's tenth anniversary. The catalogue of the exhibition recorded that in its first decade the museum had held 112 exhibitions attended by about 1.5 million people. By this time the balance of its collections and activities had moved strongly from 19th-century to 20th-century art: in the words of the 'Art in our Time' catalogue, 'our aim has been to present to the public the living art of our own time and its sources'. Subsequently the museum has expanded greatly in size in various stages (in 1966 it took over the adjacent premises when the *Whitney Museum moved from them to its new home). Apart from its unrivalled holdings of painting, sculpture, and the graphic arts, it has collections of photographs, films, and architectural documentation, and a large library. Through its permanent collections, exhibitions, and many other activities it exercises a strong influence both on taste and on artistic production. The numerous publications it has produced include some of the standard texts on modern art, several of them written by Alfred H. *Barr Jr., the first director of the museum.

'museum without walls'. See MALRAUX.

Muybridge, Eadweard (*b* Kingston upon Thames, Surrey [now Greater London], 9 Apr. 1830; *d* Kingston upon Thames, 8 May 1904). British-born photographer and pioneer of motion photography who emigrated to the USA in about 1852. He became director of photographic surveys to the US government, and while surveying the Pacific coast in 1872, he was asked by the railroad magnate Leland Stanford, then governor of California, to photograph a horse in motion, evidently to settle a bet as to whether a horse ever had all four legs off the ground simultaneously. Muybridge experimented with a battery of cameras with high-speed shutters operated by the horse itself passing across trip threads (he worked at Stanford's stud farm, and at his expense), and succeeded in proving that all four legs of a horse are indeed at times in the air simultaneously. He published his photographs in *The Horse in Motion* (1878), and then went on to study the movement of other animals, including humans, publishing his results in volumes such as *Animal Locomotion* (1887). In 1880 he invented the zoopraxiscope to project the pictures and recreate the movements he had photographed, and this he showed to scientific bodies all over Europe and America. This predecessor of the modern cinema caused a sensation. Muybridge's photographs were much used as a source by artists, among them *Eakins and the *Futurists.

Mycenaean art. A term applied to the art of Greece in the Late Bronze Age (Late Helladic Period), that is, from about 1500 to about 1100 BC. Usually the term embraces the art not only of the mainland, but also of the Greek Islands with the exception of Crete (see MINOAN ART). Mycenaean art is named after the fortress-city of Mycenae, the site of the most important remains, which was excavated by the German archaeologist Heinrich Schliemann in the 1870s.

Myron. Greek sculptor active in Athens in the mid-5th century BC. He was one of the leading Greek sculptors of the period and is celebrated for his bronze *Discobolus* (Discus Thrower), which survives in Roman marble copies; the best of them is in the Terme Museum in Rome. As an example of compositional equilibrium it achieved a fame comparable to the *Doryphorus* of *Polyclitus. Copies also exist of Myron's group of *Athena and Marsyas*, but no visual record survives of the work for which he was most renowned in his own time—the bronze *Cow* in the market place at Athens, which was said to display remarkable naturalism. See also SEVERE STYLE.

Myslbek, Josef Václav (*b* Prague, 20 June 1848; *d* Prague, 2 June 1922). The leading Czech sculptor of the late 19th and early 20th centuries. He created numerous statues of national heroes in Prague, most notably the famous St Wenceslas Monument in Wenceslas Square, which was conceived in 1887 but not completed until 1923, the year after Myslbek's death. His work is in the *Renaissance tradition but has a suitably Romantic Slavonic ardour. He had an international reputation, winning awards in Chicago, Paris, and elsewhere.

Mytens, Daniel (*b* Delft, *c*.1590; *d* The Hague, *c*.1647). Anglo-Dutch portrait painter. He trained in The Hague (probably under *Miereveld), but almost all of his known career was spent in England, where he is first recorded in 1618 working for the Earl of *Arundel. By 1620 he was employed by James I and in 1625 he was appointed 'one of our picture drawers' by Charles I. Mytens introduced a new elegance and grandeur into English portraiture, especially in his full-lengths, and he was the dominant painter at court until the arrival of van *Dyck in 1632. Van Dyck completely outclassed him, however, and he returned to The Hague in about 1634. Few paintings are known from his final years, but he continued to work as Arundel's agent. His finest picture is acknowledged to be *The First Duke of Hamilton* (1629, NPG, Edinburgh), distinguished by its imposing composition and lovely silvery-grey colouring; Ellis *Waterhouse described it as 'the great masterpiece of pre-Vandyckian portraiture in England'. Mytens belonged to a dynasty of painters active into the 18th century. Among the other members was his great-nephew **Daniel Mytens the Younger** (1644–88), also a portraitist.

N

Nabis. A group of painters, mainly French, active in Paris in the 1890s; their outlook was essentially *Symbolist and they were particularly influenced by *Gauguin's expressive use of colour and rhythmic pattern. The name Nabis (Hebrew: 'prophets') was coined in reference to the missionary zeal with which they promoted Gauguin's teachings. *Sérusier, who met Gauguin at Pont-Aven in 1888, was the driving force behind the group and with *Denis was its main theorist. Other members included *Bonnard, *Maillol (before he turned to sculpture), Ranson (see ACADÉMIE), the Hungarian Josef Rippl-Rónai (1861–1927), *Vallotton, *Vuillard, and Vuillard's brother-in-law Ker-Xavier Roussel (1867–1944). They were active in design (of posters, stained glass, and theatrical decor) and book illustration as well as painting. Group exhibitions were held between 1892 and 1899, after which the members gradually drifted apart. Several of them, however, continued Nabis ideas into the 20th century, notably Denis and Sérusier, whose work remained esoteric in spirit and bound up with their religious beliefs.

Nadelman, Elie (*b* Warsaw, 20 Feb. 1882; *d* New York, 28 Dec. 1946). Polish-born sculptor who became an American citizen in 1927. After brief studies in his native Warsaw and in Munich, he settled in Paris in 1903 or 1904 and lived there until 1914. With the outbreak of the First World War, Nadelman moved to London and then New York. He had a successful one-man show at *Stieglitz's gallery in 1915 and was befriended by Paul *Manship and Gertrude Vanderbilt *Whitney among others. His patrons included Helena Rubinstein (he had known her in Paris), who commissioned him to make sleek marble heads for her beauty salons. He married a wealthy widow in 1919 and his work has a witty sophistication appropriate to the high-society world he moved in, as with the delightful bowler-hatted bronze *Man in the Open Air* (1915, MoMA, New York). With his humour went a bold simplification and distortion of forms that

places him alongside *Lachaise as one of the pioneers of modern sculpture in America. The Depression had a disastrous effect on his market and his career virtually ended when much of his work was accidentally destroyed in 1935.

Nagare, Masayuki (*b* Nagasaki, 14 Feb. 1923). Japanese sculptor. He had a samurai upbringing and his interest in martial arts led him to study with a swordsmith, laying the foundations of the understanding of materials and superb craftsmanship that he later displayed in his sculpture. His work is abstract but often evokes the human figure or other forms, such as the sharp edges and subtle curves of samurai sword blades. Most characteristically he works in *granite, polished to mirror smoothness; often he contrasts sleek shapes with raw, rough surfaces, and he has also used other materials, including bronze and steel, with a similar feeling for their own special qualities. In the 1960s and 1970s he spent much of his time in the USA, where his work included *Cloud Fortress* (1969–75) in the plaza outside the World Trade Center, New York, consisting of two gigantic triangular clusters in black granite (it was destroyed as a result of the terrorist attack on 11 September 2001).

Nagler, Georg Kaspar (*b* Oberfiesbach, Oberbayern, 6 Jan. 1801; *d* Munich, 20 Jan. 1866). German art historian and bookseller. He was the author of two massive works of reference, *Neues allgemeines Künstler-Lexikon* (New General Dictionary of Artists, 22 vols., 1835–52), the largest dictionary of artists before *Thieme–Becker, and *Die Monogrammisten* (5 vols., 1858–79), a dictionary of artists' monograms that was completed by associates after his death. His other writings included a monograph on *Raphael (1836).

naive art. Term applied to painting (and to a much lesser degree sculpture) produced in more or less sophisticated societies but lacking conventional expertise in representational skills. Colours are characteristically bright and non-naturalistic, perspective non-scientific, and the vision childlike or literal-minded. The term *'primitive' is sometimes used more or less synonymously with naive, but this can be confusing, as 'primitive' is also applied loosely to paintings of the pre-Renaissance era as well as to art of 'uncivilized' societies. Other terms that are sometimes used in a similar way are 'folk', 'popular', or 'Sunday painters', but these too have their pitfalls, not least 'Sunday painter', for many amateurs do not paint in a naive style, and naive artists (at least the successful ones) often paint as a full-time job. Sophisticated artists may also deliberately affect a naive style, but this 'false naivety' (*faux naïf*) is no more to be confused with the spontaneous quality of the true naive than the deliberately childlike work of say *Klee or *Picasso is to be confused with genuine children's drawing. Naive art has a quality of its own that is easy to recognize but hard to define. Scottie *Wilson summed it up when he said, 'It's a feeling you cannot explain. You're born with it and it just comes out.'

Naive art, as the term is now generally understood, developed in the 19th century (before then, pictures that have a naive quality might more reasonably be classified as folk art or simply as amateurish works) and the first notable exponent was perhaps the American Edward *Hicks. It was not until the early years of the 20th century, however, that there was a vogue for naive art. Henri *Rousseau was the first naive painter to win serious critical recognition and he remains the only one who is regarded as a great master, but many others have won an honourable place in modern art. The critic Wilhelm *Uhde was mainly responsible for putting naive painters on the map in the years after the First World War. At first their freshness and directness of vision appealed mainly to fellow artists, but a number of major group exhibitions in the 1920s and 1930s helped to develop public taste for them, notably 'Masters of Popular Painting: Modern Primitives of Europe and America' at the Museum of Modern Art, New York, in 1938.

Most of the early naive painters to make reputations were French (mainly because Uhde was active in discovering and promoting them in France); they included *Bauchant, *Bombois, *Séraphine, and *Vivin. In Britain the best-known figures include Beryl *Cook and Henry *Wallis (two painters who show the huge difference of approach and style that can exist between artists given the same label). L. S. *Lowry is also often claimed as a naive painter, but some critics regard him as outside this classification because

of his many years of study at art school. In the USA the leading figures include John *Kane and Grandma *Moses. The richest crop of naive painters, however, has been in Croatia, where Ivan *Generalić has been the most famous figure. Haiti is also particularly noteworthy in that naive painting has been the country's central tradition in modern art, stemming from the success of Hector *Hyppolite.

Nanni di Banco (*b* Florence, ?*c*.1380; *d* Florence, 12 Feb. 1421). Florentine sculptor, one of the major figures of the transition from *Gothic to *Renaissance. Much of his work was designed for one or other of two architectural settings in Florence, the cathedral and the church of Orsanmichele, which together formed the chief source of demand for sculpture in the city during the first quarter of the 15th century, and he often worked alongside *Donatello. His work has a Gothic elegance, but also shows the influence of the *antique; his masterpiece, the group of the *Quattro santi coronati* (Four Crowned Saints) at Orsanmichele, for example, features grave and dignified figures modelled on Roman senator statues. Because this and other major works are of controversial dating, however, it is uncertain whether he was in advance of Donatello in his use of *classical exemplars.

Nanteuil, Robert (*b* Reims, 1623; *d* Paris, 9 Dec. 1678). French engraver, draughtsman, and pastellist, almost exclusively of portraits. He is considered the greatest European portrait engraver of the 17th century, and in France stands as the counterpart of Philippe de *Champaigne among painters. He often engraved the work of Champaigne and other painters, but also made original compositions, in which he showed both great technical mastery and penetrating characterization. Louis XIV appointed him royal draughtsman in 1658 and he made many pastel portraits as well as engravings of the king and royal family.

Nash, Paul (*b* London, 11 May 1889; *d* Boscombe, Hampshire, 11 July 1946). English painter, book illustrator, writer, photographer, and designer. Nash was one of the most individual British artists of his period, taking a distinguished place in the English tradition of deep attachment to the countryside whilst at the same time responding imaginatively to European modernism. He saw himself as a successor of *Blake and *Turner. After training at the *Slade School he served in the First World War, was wounded, and worked as an *Official War

Artist, creating memorable images of the devastation the war wrought on the countryside. During the 1920s and particularly the 1930s he was influenced by *Surrealism (above all by de *Chirico, an exhibition of whose work he saw in London in 1928) and often concentrated on mysterious aspects of the landscape (*Monster Field*, 1939, Durban AG). For much of this time he lived in rural areas (Kent, Sussex, Dorset), basing his work on scenes he knew well but imaginatively transforming them. He continued to be involved in the London art world, however, and in 1933 he was the prime mover in the formation of *Unit One; he also helped to organize and exhibited in the International Surrealist Exhibition in London in 1936. In the Second World War he was again an Official War Artist. He was already very sick with the asthmatic condition that killed him, but he produced one of the best-known works to be inspired by the conflict, *Totes Meer (Dead Sea)* (1940–1, Tate, London), which portrays shot-down aircraft with their wings looking like undulating waves. Nash was regarded as one of the finest book illustrators of his time; he also designed scenery, fabrics, and posters, and was a photographer and writer, his books including a guide to Dorset. His brother **John** (1893–1977) was also a painter and illustrator, excelling in meticulous flower drawings for botanical publications. Like Paul he was an Official War Artist in both world wars.

Nasmyth, Alexander (*b* Edinburgh, 9 Sept. 1758; *d* Edinburgh, 10 Apr. 1840). Scottish painter. He worked mainly in Edinburgh, but he was a pupil and assistant of *Ramsay in London 1774–8, and in 1782–4 he visited Italy. There he became interested in landscape painting, which eventually took over from portraiture as his main concern. In his landscapes he blended classical elements stemming from *Claude with naturalistic observation and became the founder of the Scottish landscape tradition, influencing many younger painters. He was a man of wide culture, interested in science as well as art, and he worked as a stage designer and architectural consultant. One of his friends was the poet Robert Burns, whose portrait he painted against a romantic landscape background (1787, NPG, Edinburgh). Nasmyth had several artist sons and daughters, of whom the most important was his eldest child **Patrick** (*b* Edinburgh, 7 Jan. 1787; *d* London, 17 Aug. 1831). He worked mainly in London and won great popularity with his landscapes in the manner of the 17th-century Dutch masters, earning him the nickname 'the English *Hobbema'.

National Academy of Design, New York. A professional association of artists founded in New York in 1825 in opposition to the conservative American Academy of the Fine Arts (which ran from 1802 to 1841; see TRUMBULL). The National Academy was originally called the Society for the Improvement of Drawing; it adopted its present name in 1828. For most of the 19th century it was the leading art institution in America, its annual exhibitions helping to make New York the country's major art centre. *Morse was first president, and most ambitious artists of the time sought membership. However, its views became unprogressive, prompting certain artists to break away (notably to found The *Eight in 1908). Today it exists mainly as a historical institution.

National Art Collections Fund. The UK's largest art charity, established in 1903 to assist public collections to acquire works of art they would not otherwise be able to afford. The founders, who included Roger *Fry and D. S. *MacColl, shared a concern about the amount of art leaving the country, and the Fund's first conspicuous achievement came in 1906 when, by means of a public appeal, it bought *Velázquez's *Rokeby Venus*, which was in danger of being sold abroad, and presented it to the *National Gallery, London (the painting cost £45,000 and at this time the Gallery's annual purchase grant was £5,000). Many similar successes have followed, most memorably that with *Leonardo da Vinci's *cartoon of the *Virgin and Child with St Anne and St John the Baptist*: in 1962 financial problems forced the *Royal Academy to sell the cartoon, its greatest treasure, and the Fund's campaign to secure it for the National Gallery caught the public imagination to such an extent that an estimated 300,000 people made contributions to the purchase price of £800,000 (see also WHEELER). Most of the Fund's work deals with more modest art, however, and by the time of its centenary in 2003 it had helped more than 600 museums, galleries, and historic houses throughout the UK to make more than 400,000 acquisitions, ranging from prehistoric artefacts to contemporary experimental pieces. More broadly, the Fund aims to increase public enjoyment and understanding of art and has, for example, played a leading role in the campaign to abolish admission charges to national museums—an object that was achieved in 2001. The Fund is an independent charity, without government aid, and is supported mainly by members' subscriptions, bequests, and donations.

In 1910 the Contemporary Art Society was founded as a specialist counterpart in the field of modern art, acquiring works by living artists for gift or loan to public collections in Britain (and later in the Commonwealth and occasionally elsewhere). In 1991 it published a book celebrating its 80th anniversary and by this time had presented more than 4,000 works, mainly by British artists.

National Gallery, London. The British national collection of European paintings from c.1300 to c.1900 (it also includes a few earlier pictures and has recently started to acquire works from the early 20th century). It was founded in 1824 when the government purchased 38 paintings from the collection of John Julius Angerstein (1735–1823), a Russian-born merchant. They were mainly Italian works of the 16th and 17th centuries, but there were also examples by British, Dutch, Flemish, and French masters. Initially they were displayed in Angerstein's former house at 100 Pall Mall, but further acquisitions (including the bequest of Sir George *Beaumont) soon necessitated larger premises, and the present building in Trafalgar Square, designed by William Wilkins, was opened in 1838 (architecturally it is undistinguished: Sir John Summerson has memorably described the rather feeble central dome and side turrets as being 'like the clock and vases on a mantelpiece, only less useful'). In its early days the Gallery was run in rather haphazard fashion, but Charles *Eastlake, director 1855–65, brought professionalism, flair, and drive to its administration (other notable directors have included Edward *Poynter and Kenneth *Clark). The Gallery shared the premises with the *Royal Academy until 1869, by which time it had grown into one of the great collections of the world. Since then there have been various enlargements of the building and in 1991 a major extension was opened—the Sainsbury Wing, the gift of Sir John, Simon, and Timothy Sainsbury. This wing now houses the Gallery's early paintings, up to about 1510.

The collection as a whole now has about 2,200 pictures. This is a fairly small number compared with the holdings of some of the great Continental galleries based on former royal collections, but the National Gallery's paintings surpass those of any other collection in giving a balanced view of the mainstream of European painting from *Giotto to *Cézanne. Best represented of all are the early Italian and Dutch Schools. The

representation of the British School is selective because of the existence of *Tate Britain as a separate national gallery of British art.

Other well-known national galleries, with their dates of foundation, are: the National Gallery of Scotland in Edinburgh (1850); the National Gallery of Ireland in Dublin (1854); the National Gallery of Victoria in Melbourne (1859); the National Gallery of Canada in Ottawa (1880); the National Museum and Gallery in Cardiff (1907; originally called the National Museum of Wales); the National Gallery of Art in Washington (1937; see KRESS and MELLON); and the Australian National Gallery in Canberra (1976).

National Portrait Gallery, London. The national collection of portraits of eminent British men and women. It was founded in 1856 at the urging of the historian and politician Philip Henry Stanhope, 5th Earl Stanhope, who was the first chairman of the trustees. The collection was originally housed at 29 Great George Street, Westminster, and the present premises, adjoining the National Gallery, were opened in 1896. The criterion for inclusion in the Gallery is the celebrity of the sitter rather than the quality of the portrait, so the pictures in the collection vary enormously in artistic merit, from an acknowledged masterpiece such as *Holbein's cartoon of Henry VIII to the wholly amateurish representation of the three Brontë sisters by their brother Branwell. Nevertheless, because portraiture has played such a great part in the history of British art, many illustrious artists are well represented. Recently the Gallery has begun to commission portraits of living sitters, and since 1980 it has organized a series of annual portrait awards for artists under 40 years old. From the 1970s it has collaborated with several historic houses outside London, in which works from the Gallery are displayed in appropriate period settings: the main ones are Montacute House in Somerset, Beningbrough Hall in Yorkshire, and Bodelwyddan Castle in Wales. The Scottish National Portrait Gallery was established in Edinburgh in 1882, and the National Portrait Gallery in Washington in 1962.

Nattier, Jean-Marc (b Paris, 17 Mar. 1685; d Paris, 7 Nov. 1766). French painter. His father Marc (c.1642–1705) was a painter and his mother Marie (née Courtois) (c.1655–1703) was a miniaturist. Nattier had early ambitions to be a history painter, but he came to specialize in portraits, and from the 1730s he was one of the most successful artists at the court of Louis XV, excelling in the vogue for painting women in mythological or allegorical fancy dress—or undress—transforming his matrons into goddesses (*The Duchesse d'Orléans as Hebe*, 1744, Nationalmuseum, Stockholm). The pastel-like delicacy of his handling led to the accusation that he 'painted with make-up'. His portraits are little concerned with individual characterization, but they show fluency, vivacity, and a relaxed charm. Towards the end of his career taste began to turn against him and some of his later work shows signs of fatigue. His brother **Jean-Baptiste** (1678–1726) was also a painter; he committed suicide after being expelled by the Académie Royale. *Tocqué was Nattier's pupil and son-in-law.

naturalism. Term denoting an approach to art in which the artist endeavours to represent objects as they are empirically observed, rather than in a stylized or conceptual manner. *Bellori (1672) was the first to apply the term to a particular type of painting in discussing the followers of *Caravaggio, with reference to their doctrine of copying nature faithfully whether it seems to us ugly or beautiful. Naturalism, however, is not incompatible with the *idealization of nature, for Greek sculpture may be naturalistic in its command of anatomy, but idealistic in that it sets up a standard of physical beauty remote from the everyday world. Nor need the term imply minute attention to detail, although this is often part of a naturalistic approach. The shade of meaning to be attached to the word can thus vary greatly according to context; when used in its broadest sense it may suggest little more than that a work is representational rather than *abstract. The terms 'naturalistic' and 'realistic' are often used more or less synonymously, but *Realism with a capital 'r' has a specific meaning in the history of art and should not be used loosely.

Navarrete, Juan Fernández de (b Logroño, c.1538; d Toledo, 28 Mar. 1579). Spanish painter from the Navarre region, called El Mudo (the mute) because he was deaf and dumb. He spent several years in Italy (where according to *Palomino he was a pupil of *Titian) and returned to Spain in about 1565. In 1568 he was appointed a court painter to Philip II (see HABSBURG) and he spent most of the rest of his life painting altarpieces for the *Escorial. His work was significant in spreading Italian influence in Spain.

Nazarenes. A group of young, idealistic German painters of the early 19th century who believed that art should serve a religious or moral purpose and desired to return to the spirit of the Middle Ages. The nucleus of the group was established in 1809 when six students at the Vienna Academy formed an association called the Brotherhood of St Luke (*Lukasbrüder*), named after the patron saint of painting. The name Nazarenes (first used c.1817) was given to them facetiously because of their devout way of life and adoption of flowing biblical hairstyles. They wished to revive the working environment as well as the spiritual sincerity of the Middle Ages, and lived and worked together in a quasi-monastic fashion. In 1810 *Overbeck, *Pforr, and two other members moved to Rome, where they occupied the disused monastery of S. Isidoro. Here they were joined by Peter *Cornelius and others. One of their aims was the revival of monumental *fresco painting and they obtained two important commissions that made their work internationally known (Casa Bartholdy, 1816–17, the paintings are now in the Alte Nationalgalerie, Berlin; and Casino Massimo, 1817–29, *in situ*). Stylistically they were much indebted to *Perugino, and their work is clear and prettily coloured, but often insipid. In general, modern taste has been more sympathetic towards the Nazarenes' simple and sensitive landscape and portrait drawings than to their ambitious and didactic figure paintings. They broke up as a formal group in the 1820s, but their ideas continued to be influential and the name was applied to younger followers until about 1850. In 1819 Cornelius had moved to Munich, where he attracted a large number of pupils and assistants who in turn carried his style to other German centres. The studio of Overbeck (the only Nazarene to remain permanently in Rome) was a meeting place for artists from many countries (the Russian *Ivanov was his friend, for example); *Ingres admired him and Ford Madox *Brown visited him. William *Dyce introduced some of the Nazarene ideals into English art and there is a kinship of spirit with the *Pre-Raphaelites.

NEAC. See NEW ENGLISH ART CLUB.

Neeffs (or Neefs), **Pieter the Elder** (b Antwerp, c.1578; d Antwerp, 1656/61). Flemish painter, active in Antwerp. Most of his pictures are interiors of *Gothic churches, some of them night scenes illuminated by artificial light. They are generally small, painted on copper, and executed in a precise, neat way—similar in style to those of the *Steenwycks, but more mechanical. His son **Pieter Neeffs the Younger** (b Antwerp,

23 May 1620; d Antwerp, after 1675) painted the same subjects, and it is very difficult to distinguish between their hands. Another son, **Lodewijk** (b Antwerp, 22 Jan. 1617; d Antwerp, ?1649), was also a painter, but little is known of his work.

Neer, Aert (or Aernout) **van der** (b Amsterdam, ?1604; d Amsterdam, 9 Nov. 1677). Dutch landscape painter, active in Amsterdam. He had two specialities: moonlit scenes, of which he is the acknowledged master among Dutch painters; and winter landscapes with skaters, as an exponent of which he is in the first rank. In both types he displayed his mastery of light effects and subtle modulations of colour. He was a prolific painter and his work was much copied and imitated, but he had difficulty earning a living as an artist. In 1658 he opened a wine shop in Amsterdam, but this venture was a failure and in 1662 he became bankrupt. Two of his sons were artists. **Eglon** (b Amsterdam, c.1634; d Düsseldorf, 3 May 1703) is best known for *genre pieces done in the style of *Terborch and *Metsu. He was conspicuously more successful than his father and from 1690 worked as court painter in Düsseldorf. The few works that can be attributed to **Jan** (c.1638–65) show that he was an imitator of his father.

Neizvestny, Ernst. See UNOFFICIAL ART.

Neoclassicism. The dominant movement in European art and architecture in the late 18th and early 19th centuries, characterized by a desire to re-create the spirit and forms of the art of ancient Greece and Rome. A new and more scientific interest in *classical antiquity, greatly stimulated by the discoveries at Pompeii (where excavations began in 1748) and Herculaneum, was one of the features of the movement, and it is also seen as a reaction against the light-hearted and frivolous *Rococo style. The order, clarity, and reason of Greek and Roman art appealed greatly in the Age of Enlightenment, and the Neoclassical style could have moral as well as aesthetic implications, particularly in France, where it is associated with the Revolution and a desire to restore ancient Roman values into civil life. It is, indeed, in the paintings of *David, with their antique grandeur and simplicity of form, and their heroic severity of tone, that Neoclassicism finds its purest expression, but the style was born and had its focal point in Rome. *Mengs and *Winckelmann were in the vanguard of the movement there, and other leading figures from all over Europe—including *Canova, *Flaxman, Gavin *Hamilton, and *Thorvaldsen—spent the main or important parts of their careers in the city. Many American artists worked there too—notably the sculptor Horatio *Greenough, who was a pupil of Thorvaldsen—and took the Neoclassical style back to their country.

Because Neoclassicism placed respect for approved models above personal expression it was a style that particularly lent itself to this kind of international currency. The 18th century saw a great growth in the publication of lavishly illustrated volumes on classical art, architecture, and antiquities, and this helped to spread the ideals of the movement. There was, however, considerable stylistic variation within Neoclassicism; Angelica *Kauffmann, for example, painted in a delicate and pretty manner that is far removed from David's severity. Moreover, there is no firm dividing line between Neoclassicism and *Romanticism, even though in some ways they appear to be at opposite spiritual poles. In the revival of interest in antique art, archaeological zeal could easily give way to a nostalgic yearning for a lost golden age, and the term 'Romantic Classicism' is sometimes used to characterize an aspect of Neoclassicism in which an interest in antiquity is tinged with Romantic feeling. In fact the antipathy between Classics and Romantics (exemplified by *Ingres and *Delacroix, for example) was unknown before the 19th century, and it was only in the mid-19th century, at a time when the antique revival style was out of fashion, that the word 'Neoclassicism' was coined—originally a pejorative term with suggestions of lifelessness and impersonality. These negative connotations have clung tenaciously to the term, and the ardent aspirations of the founders of Neoclassicism have been obscured by the fact that the more decorative aspects of the movement—*Wedgwood pottery, for example—have become more closely associated with the word in the public consciousness than have the great masterpieces of David and Canova.

Neoclassicism is related to but can be distinguished from Greek Taste, which was a fairly superficial fashion for Greek-inspired decoration, and from the Greek Revival, which in architecture was a movement expressing a new interest in the simplicity and gravity of ancient Greek buildings. It began seriously in the 1790s and culminated in the 1820s and 1830s. Greek architecture became widely known in the West only around 1750–60 and in the early days of Neoclassicism it was regarded as primitive and few architects cared to imitate it.

In the context of modern art, the term Neo-classicism has been applied to a revival of the spirit of classicism among avant-garde artists in the second and third decades of the 20th century, marking a return to restraint after a period of unprecedented experimentation. Other terms for this phenomenon include 'the New Classicism', 'the classical revival', 'the return to order', and 'the call to order' (this last being the title of a book by Jean *Cocteau, published in 1926—*Le Rappel à l'ordre*).

Neo-Dada. A term that has been applied to various styles, trends, or works that are perceived as reviving the methods or spirit of *Dada. It has been used as a synonym for *Pop art, for example, and has been applied to the work of Jasper *Johns.

Neo-Expressionism. Movement in painting (and to a lesser extent sculpture) emerging in the late 1970s, characterized by intense subjectivity of feeling and aggressively raw handling of materials. Neo-Expressionist paintings are typically large and rapidly executed, sometimes with materials such as straw or broken crockery embedded in their surfaces. They are usually figurative, often with violent or doom-laden subjects, but the image is sometimes almost lost in the welter of surface activity. To some extent Neo-Expressionism marked a return to more traditional forms after the 'anything goes' experimentation of the 1970s. Perhaps partly for this reason it was welcomed by art dealers and collectors, but critical reaction to it has been very mixed. Several exponents, above all the American Julian *Schnabel, have become rich and famous, but to many critics their work seems deliberately bad, ignoring all conventional ideas of skill; indeed the term 'Bad Painting' (from the title of an exhibition at the New Museum, New York, in 1978) has been applied to certain works in the vein (Punk Art and Stupid Painting are alternative terms). Distinguishing between good 'Bad Painting' (i.e. that which deliberately cultivates crudeness for its emotional value) and bad 'Bad Painting' (something that is just a mess) is an unenviable critical task. Neo-Expressionism has flourished mainly in Germany (where its exponents are sometimes called Neue Wilden—'New Wild Ones'), Italy, and the USA. Leading exponents include: in Germany, Georg *Baselitz and Anselm *Kiefer; in Italy, Sandro Chia (1946–) and Francesco Clemente (1952–); in the USA, David Salle (1952–) and Julian Schnabel. See also NEW IMAGE PAINTING.

Neo-Geo. Term (short for Neo-Geometric Conceptualism) applied to the work of a group of American artists active in New York in the mid-1980s who employed a variety of styles and media but were linked by the fact that their paintings, sculpture, or other products were predominantly cool and impersonal, in reaction from the emotionalism of *Neo-Expressionism. Jeff Koons (1955–), who exhibited consumer products such as vacuum cleaners in a reworking of *Dada *ready-mades, is the best-known figure of the group. Many critics have seen their work as cynical and empty ('dead on arrival' is one memorable description), but Neo-Geo has been a hit with certain collectors, most notably Charles *Saatchi, who has bought it in bulk.

Neo-Impressionism. A movement in French painting—both a development from *Impressionism and a reaction against it—in which the Impressionist approach to depicting light and colour was made more rational and scientific. Georges *Seurat was the founder of the movement and far and away its outstanding artist. His friend Paul *Signac was its main theoretician, and Camille *Pissarro was briefly a leading adherent. All three showed Neo-Impressionist pictures at the final Impressionist exhibition in 1886 (the term Neo-Impressionism was coined by the critic Félix Fénéon (1861–1944) in a review of this exhibition). The theoretical basis of Neo-Impressionism was *divisionism, with its associated technique of *pointillism—the use of dots of pure colour applied in such a way that when seen from an appropriate distance they achieve a maximum of luminosity. In each painting the dots were of a uniform size, chosen to harmonize with the scale of the work. In Seurat's paintings, this approach combined solidity and clarity of form with a vibrating intensity of light; in the hands of lesser artists, it often produced works that look rigid and contrived. As an organized movement Neo-Impressionism was short-lived, but it had a significant influence on several major artists of the late 19th and early 20th centuries, notably *Gauguin, van *Gogh, and also *Matisse, who worked with Signac and another Neo-Impressionist, Henri-Edmond Cross (1856–1910), at Saint Tropez in 1906.

Neo-Plasticism. Term coined by Piet *Mondrian for his style of austerely geometrical abstract painting and more broadly for the philosophical ideas about art that his work embodied. He claimed that art should be 'denaturalized', by which he meant that it must be purely abstract, with no representational relation to the natural world. To this end he limited the elements of pictorial design to the straight line and the rectangle (the right angles in a strictly horizontal–vertical relation to the frame) and to the primary colours—blue, red, and yellow—together with black, white, and grey. In this way he thought that one might escape the particular and achieve expression of an ideal of universal harmony. Mondrian took the term 'nieuwe beelding' (which might be translated as 'new image creation') from the writings of Dr Matthieu Schoenmaekers, a Dutch author of popular books on philosophy and religion, whom he admired for a time but later considered to be a charlatan. The Dutch term was rendered in French by Mondrian himself as 'néo-plasticisme', and this in turn was translated into English as Neo-Plasticism.

Neo-Primitivism. See LARIONOV.

Neo-Romanticism. A movement in British painting and other arts c.1935–55, in which a number of loosely affiliated artists looked back to certain aspects of 19th-century *Romanticism, particularly the 'visionary' landscape tradition of William *Blake and Samuel *Palmer, and reinterpreted them in a more modern idiom. The term was coined by the critic Raymond Mortimer in 1942. Painters and graphic artists representative of the movement include John *Minton, John *Piper, and Graham *Sutherland, who all worked in a landscape tradition that was regarded as distinctly national, and projected a Romantic image of the countryside at a time when it was under threat from Nazi Germany. Other artists whose work has been dubbed Neo-Romantic include the poet Dylan Thomas, the film director Michael Powell, and photographers such as Bill Brandt and Edwin Smith. The term Neo-Romanticism has also been applied to certain painters working in France in the 1930s, notably *Berman and *Tchelitchew, who typically painted dreamlike imaginary landscapes with rather mournful figures. Their work influenced the British Neo-Romantics.

In the 1980s 'Neo-Romanticism' was one of the many terms used as a synonym for *Neo-Expressionism, but it did not catch on in this sense.

Neri di Bicci. See LORENZO DI BICCI.

Neroccio de' Landi (b Siena, 1447; d Siena, 1500). Sienese painter and sculptor. He was probably a pupil of *Vecchietta and in the early 1470s he worked in partnership with *Francesco di Giorgio. Most of his paintings are devotional images of the Virgin and Child with saints, but he produced various other kinds of picture, one of his finest works being *Portrait of a Lady* (c.1490, NG, Washington). He continued the elegant and refined Sienese tradition that stretched back to *Duccio and his work is particularly noted for its delicate colouring. His work as a sculptor includes a marble statue of St Catherine of Alexandria (1487) in Siena Cathedral.

Netscher, Caspar (b ?Prague, ?1635/9; d The Hague, 15 Jan. 1684). Dutch painter. *Houbraken, who says Netscher was born in 1639, makes inconsistent statements about his birthplace, mentioning both Heidelberg and Prague; according to Roger de *Piles, he was born in Prague and died aged 48, which would place his birth in 1635 or 1636. Most of his career was spent in The Hague, where he settled in 1661/2, but he trained in Deventer with *Terborch. From his master he took his predilection for depicting costly materials—particularly white satin. He painted *genre scenes and some religious and mythological subjects, but from about 1670 he devoted himself almost exclusively to portraits, often for court circles in The Hague. His reputation was such that Charles II invited him to England (*Vertue says that he came, de Piles and Houbraken that he declined). His work, elegant, Frenchified, small in scale, and exquisitely finished, influenced Dutch portraiture into the 18th century; his followers included his sons **Constantijn** (1688–1723) and **Theodoor** (1661–1732).

Neue Künstlervereinigung München (NKV) (New Artists' Association of Munich). An association of artists founded in Munich in 1909 to provide a more liberal alternative to existing exhibiting venues, particularly the *Sezession. *Kandinsky was elected president; Alexander Kanoldt (1881–1939) was secretary and Adolf Erbslöh (1881–1947) was chairman of the exhibition committee. Other members included *Jawlensky, *Kubin, Kandinsky's lover Gabriele Münter (1877–1962), and Jawlensky's lover Marianne von Werefkin (1870–1938). They were strongly influenced by *Fauvism and the three exhibitions that they held (1909, 1910, and 1911) were far too advanced for the critics and public and were met with torrents of abuse (the first two exhibitions were held in the gallery of the Munich dealer Heinrich Thannhauser, who said he had to clean spit off the paintings each evening). The second exhibition was European in character, including works by the Russians

David and Vladimir *Burliuk, by *Le Fauconnier, *Picasso, and *Rouault, and by members of the Fauves (*Braque, *Derain, van *Dongen, *Vlaminck), some of whom had already moved on to *Cubism. Franz *Marc came to the NKV's defence after this exhibition and it was in this way that he met Kandinsky. When Erbslöh rejected an abstract painting submitted by Kandinsky for the third exhibition, Kandinsky resigned and with Marc founded the *Blaue Reiter. They moved so quickly that the Blaue Reiter's first exhibition opened on the same day as the NKV's last and stole its thunder.

Neue Sachlichkeit (New Objectivity). Movement in German painting in the 1920s and early 1930s reflecting the resignation and cynicism of the post-war period. The name was coined in 1923 by Gustav Hartlaub, director of the Kunsthalle, Mannheim, and used as the title of an exhibition he staged there in 1925, featuring 'artists who have retained or regained their fidelity to positive tangible reality'. The movement was not characterized by a unified style or by any kind of group affiliation, but its major trend involved the use of meticulous detail and violent satire to portray the face of evil. This marked a continuation of the interest in social criticism that had characterized much of *Expressionism, but Neue Sachlichkeit rejected the abstract tendencies of the *Blaue Reiter, in which Expressionism had reached its high point just before the First World War. *Dix and *Grosz were the greatest figures of the movement, which was dissipated in the 1930s with the rise of the Nazis. Other artists associated with Neue Sachlichkeit include Conrad Felixmüller (1897–1977), Christian Schad (1894–1982), and Rudolf Schlichter (1890–1955).

Nevelson, Louise (b Kiev, 23 Sept. 1899; d New York, 17 Apr. 1988). Russian-born American sculptor, painter, and printmaker. Her family emigrated to the USA in 1905 and she settled in New York in 1920. Her serious study of art began at the *Art Students League in 1929–30 and she then studied under Hans *Hofmann in Munich. In 1932–3 she worked with Ben *Shahn as assistant to Diego *Rivera on his frescos in New York. She started to make sculpture in 1932 and in 1944 began experimenting with abstract wooden assemblages. It was towards the end of the 1950s that she began the 'sculptured walls' for which she became internationally famous. These are wall-like *reliefs made up of many boxes and compartments into which abstract shapes are assembled together with commonplace objects such as chair legs, bits of balustrades, and other 'found objects' (An American Tribute to the British People, 1960–4, Tate, London). These constructions, painted a uniform black, or later in her career white or gold, won her a reputation as a leader in both *assemblage and *environment sculpture. They have great formal elegance, but also a strange ritualistic power. In the late 1960s she started working in a greater variety of materials and also began to receive commissions for large open-air and environmental sculptures, which she executed in aluminium or steel.

Nevinson, C. R. W. (Christopher Richard Wynne) (b London, 13 Aug. 1889; d London, 7 Oct. 1946). British painter and printmaker. As a student at the *Académie Julian, Paris, in 1912–13 Nevinson met several of the *Futurists and he became the outstanding British exponent of their style. His work included landscapes, urban scenes, figure compositions, and flowers, but he found his ideal subjects during the First World War. He served in France with the Red Cross and the Royal Army Medical Corps, 1914–16, before being invalided out, and his harsh, steely images of life and death in the trenches received great acclaim when he held a one-man exhibition at the Leicester Galleries, London, in 1916. Stylistically they drew on certain *Cubist as well as Futurist ideas, but they are closer to the work of the *Vorticists (with whom he had exhibited in 1915). In 1917 Nevinson returned to France as an *Official War Artist, and he was the first to make drawings from the air. Some of his work was considered too unpleasant for public viewing and was censored, but a second one-man exhibition at the Leicester Galleries in 1918 was another triumph. At the end of the war Nevinson renounced Futurism and his later, more conventional paintings are generally regarded as an anticlimax; an example is Twentieth Century (1932–5, Laing AG, Newcastle upon Tyne), an ambitious but rather turgid attempt to portray a world on the brink of catastrophe.

Newbery, Francis. See GLASGOW SCHOOL OF ART.

New British Sculpture. A term sometimes applied to the work of a loosely connected group of British sculptors who emerged in a series of exhibitions at the beginning of the 1980s, notably 'Objects and Sculpture' shown at the *Institute of Contemporary Arts and the Arnolfini Gallery, Bristol, in 1981. There is no single common factor linking these sculptors, but predominantly their work is abstract (although sometimes with human associations), using industrial or junk material, and most of them are represented by the same dealer—the Lisson Gallery, London. Among the leading figures are: Tony Cragg (1949–), Grenville Davey (1961–), Richard Deacon (1949–), Anish *Kapoor (each of these four has won the *Turner Prize), David Mach (1956–), Julian Opie (1958–), Richard Wentworth (1947–), Alison Wilding (1948–), and Bill Woodrow (1948–). Most of these are well represented in the *Saatchi Gallery.

New Contemporaries. See YOUNG CONTEMPORARIES.

New English Art Club (NEAC). An artists' society founded in London in 1886 in reaction against the conservative and complacent attitudes of the *Royal Academy. The founders—largely artists who had worked in France and had been influenced by *plein-air painting—included *Clausen, *La Thangue, *Sargent, *Steer, and *Tuke. There were about 50 members when the inaugural exhibition was held in April 1886 at the Marlborough Gallery. In 1889 the NEAC came under the control of a minority group led by *Sickert, who had joined in 1888; he and his associates were interested in the *Impressionists, and in 1889 they held an independent exhibition under the name 'The London Impressionists'. Sickert resigned in 1897 (he returned in 1906) and from then up to about the First World War the NEAC was effectively controlled by Frederick Brown (see SLADE), Henry *Tonks, and Steer. In this period it contained most of the best painters in England. From about 1908, however, it began to lose initiative to progressive groups such as the *Allied Artists' Association and the *Camden Town Group. After the war the NEAC occupied a position midway between the Academy and the avant-garde groups. With the gradual liberalization of the Academy exhibitions its importance diminished, but it still exists.

New Figuration. A very broad term for a general revival of figurative painting in the 1960s following a period when abstraction (particularly *Abstract Expressionism) had been the dominant mode of avant-garde art in Europe and the USA. The term is said to have been first used by the French critic Michel Ragon, who in 1961 called the trend 'Nouvelle Figuration'.

New Generation. The title of four exhibitions, sponsored by the Peter Stuyvesant [tobacco company] Foundation, held at the Whitechapel Art Gallery, London, in 1964, 1965, 1966, and 1968, with the aim of introducing young British painters and sculptors to the public. *Op and *Pop art were well represented, but the series is best remembered for the 1965 exhibition, which featured a group of sculptors who were seen as creating a new school of British abstract sculpture, largely under the influence of Anthony *Caro (most of them had been his pupils at St Martin's School of Art). Subsequently their work has been referred to as 'New Generation Sculpture'. The leading figures were Phillip *King, Tim Scott (1937–), and William *Tucker. William *Turnbull is generally grouped with them, even though he did not train at St Martin's or show at the New Generation exhibition. Their work had in common a liking for simple shapes and strong colours—sometimes close to *Minimal art, sometimes with a Pop flavour.

New Image Painting (or **New Image art**). A vague term applied since the late 1970s to the work of certain painters who work in a strident figurative style, often with cartoon-like imagery and abrasive handling owing something to *Neo-Expressionism. The term was given currency by an exhibition entitled 'New Image Painting' at the Whitney Museum, New York, in 1978. The accompanying catalogue unhelpfully informs us that the New Image painters 'felt free to manipulate the image on canvas so that it can be experienced as a physical object, an abstract configuration, a psychological associative, a receptacle for applied paint, an analytically systemized exercise, an ambiguous quasi-narrative, a specifically non-specific experience, a vehicle for formalist explorations or combinations of any'. Philip *Guston, who in the 1970s abandoned *Abstract Expressionism for a comic-strip style of figuration, is regarded as the progenitor of New Image Painting. Other American artists who have been labelled New Image Painters include Jennifer Bartlett (1941–), Jonathan Borofsky (1942–), and Susan Rothenberg (1945–). In Britain the term 'New Image' has been applied particularly to painters of the 1980s *Glasgow School.

Newlyn School. A name applied to the painters who worked in the Cornish fishing port of Newlyn (now a suburb of Penzance) from the 1880s, particularly those directly linked with Stanhope Forbes (1857–1947), who was the founder and leader of the school. One of the attractions of Newlyn was the mild climate, which made it particularly suitable for outdoor work, and Forbes and his associates were among the pioneers of *plein-air painting in Britain. Apart from Forbes and his wife Elizabeth Armstrong (1859–1912), the artists most closely associated with Newlyn in its heyday include: Frank Bramley (1857–1915); Thomas Cooper Gotch (1854–1931), better known for his later work, particularly his allegorical pictures of children; Fred Hall (1860–1948), Walter Langley (1852–1922), and Henry Scott *Tuke. Many of the Newlyn artists were members of the *New English Art Club, but they also showed their work at the *Royal Academy. The golden period of Newlyn was over by the turn of the century; thereafter it was vulgarized by an influx of inferior talent, and *St Ives came to have a greater attraction for 20th-century artists. However, distinguished painters continued to be associated with Newlyn: Harold and Laura *Knight lived there, 1907–18, for example, and Dod Procter (1892–1972) and her husband Ernest Procter (1886–1935) studied with Forbes and settled in the village after their marriage in 1912.

Newman, Barnett (b New York, 29 Jan. 1905; d New York, 4 July 1970). American painter, one of the leading figures of *Abstract Expressionism and one of the initiators of *Colour Field Painting. During the 1930s he had a hard time financially; the Depression almost ruined his father's clothing business, and unlike most American painters of the time Newman did not work for the *Federal Art Project, being unwilling to accept state handouts. Part of his living came from teaching art in high schools. He destroyed most of his early work and stopped painting in the early 1940s, but he began again in 1944, and in the second half of the 1940s evolved a distinctive style of mystical abstraction—he considered 'the sublime' to be his ultimate subject matter. The work with which he announced this style was Onement I (1948, MoMA, New York), a monochromatic canvas of dark red with a single stripe of lighter red running down the middle. Such stripes (or 'zips' as Newman preferred to call them) became a characteristic feature of his work. By the time he painted Onement I Newman already had a reputation as a controversialist and a spokesman for avant-garde art (in catalogue essays and in articles in journals). In 1949 he painted his first wall-size pictures (he was one of the pioneers of the very large format) and in 1950 he had his first one-man exhibition, at the Betty *Parsons Gallery. This was coolly received by critics and fellow artists, and by the mid-1950s his very spare style had separated him from the predominantly *gestural idiom of his colleagues. For a time he became a somewhat marginalized figure and he stopped painting in 1956. He had a heart attack in 1957, but in the following year a resurgence began with a series of paintings in black and white, and in the last decade of his life his output and his reputation soared. From 1965 he made steel sculptures (vertical strips recalling his paintings) and in his late years he also experimented with *shaped canvases, painting several triangular pictures.

New Realism. A vague term, of dubious value, that has been used in at least three distinct senses in connection with art of the 1960s and later. First, it has been used in a way similar to the term *New Figuration to describe a revival of figurative art after a dominant period of abstraction; whereas 'New Figuration' has been used very broadly, however, 'New Realism' has often been applied more specifically to works that are objective in spirit, particularly *Superrealist pictures or those of Philip *Pearlstein. In a second sense, 'New Realism' has been used as a straight translation of the French term 'Nouveau Réalisme' and applied to works incorporating three-dimensional objects, typically mass-produced consumer goods, in *assemblages or attached to the surface of a painting. Thirdly—and perplexingly—it has been used as a synonym for *Pop art.

New Sculpture, the. A trend in British sculpture between about 1880 and 1910 characterized chiefly by an emphasis on naturalistic surface detail and a taste for the spiritual or *Symbolist in subject matter, in reaction against the blandness of much Victorian sculpture. The name was coined by the critic Edmund Gosse (1849–1928) in a series of four articles, 'The New Sculpture, 1879–1894', published in the Art Journal in 1894. Leading representatives of the trend include Gilbert Bayes (1872–1953), Alfred Drury (1856–1944), Edward Onslow Ford (1852–1901), Sir George *Frampton, Sir Alfred *Gilbert, the Australian-born Sir Bertram Mackennal (1863–1931), Sir William Reynolds-Stephens (1862–1943), Sir Hamo *Thornycroft, Albert Toft (1862–1949), and Derwent Wood (1871–1926). Their archetypal product was the 'ideal' free-standing figure, often with imagery drawn from mythology or poetry. Most typically these ideal figures were in bronze, but polychromy—using such materials as ivory and coloured stones—was also a feature of the New Sculpture. Although the New Sculpture did not survive the First World War as a major force, some of the practitioners went on working in the idiom long after this.

Newton, Algernon (*b* London, 23 Feb. 1880; *d* London, 21 May 1968). British painter, grandson of one of the founders of Winsor & Newton, the firm of artists' colourmen. He specialized in urban views painted in a sombre, naturalistic style; his penchant for scenes involving waterways earned him the nickname 'the Canaletto of the canals' (*The Surrey Canal, Camberwell*, 1935, Tate, London). He also painted landscapes in Cornwall and Yorkshire and was in demand for 'portraits' of country houses.

Newton, Eric (*b* Marple Bridge, Cheshire, 28 Apr. 1893; *d* London, 10 Mar. 1965). British mosaicist and writer on art. From 1913 to 1933 (interrupted by army service in the First World War) he worked as a mosaic designer and craftsman with the firm of L. Oppenheimer, Manchester, but he is much better known as a writer. He was art critic of the *Manchester Guardian* and the *Sunday Times*, and wrote many books, including *European Painting and Sculpture* (1941 and several times revised and reprinted), *The Meaning of Beauty* (1950), and *The Romantic Rebellion* (1962). He was a clear and polished writer and also an articulate lecturer and radio broadcaster. In 1959–60 he was *Slade professor at Oxford University. His second wife, **Stella Mary Newton** (née Pearce) (1901–2001), was a leading authority on the history of dress. She played a central role in establishing her subject as a serious academic discipline, partly through founding a specialist postgraduate course at the *Courtauld Institute.

New York Realists. Informal name given during the early years of the 20th century to Robert *Henri and his disciples, whose work included scenes of unidealized contemporary urban life.

New York School. Name applied to the innovatory painters, particularly the *Abstract Expressionists, who worked in New York during the 1940s and 1950s and whose critical and financial success helped the city to replace Paris as the world's leading centre of avant-garde art.

Niccolò dell'Arca (*d* Bologna, 2 Mar. 1494). Italian sculptor. He was probably of south Italian origin, but his known career was spent in Bologna, where he is first documented in 1462. His name comes from his work on the Arca di S. Domenico (Shrine of St Dominic) in S. Domenico Maggiore, Bologna, for which he carved a marble canopy and small free-standing

figures (1469 onwards). The work was unfinished at his death and *Michelangelo carved three missing figures. Niccolò's greatest work is a highly emotional group of the *Lamentation over the Body of Christ* in S. Maria della Vita, Bologna, executed in *terracotta and originally painted. It is of uncertain date. According to tradition the figure of Nicodemus is a self-portrait.

Nicholson, Ben (*b* Denham, Buckinghamshire, 10 Apr. 1894; *d* London, 6 Feb. 1982). British painter and maker of *reliefs, one of his country's most distinguished pioneers of abstract art. From his father Sir William *Nicholson he inherited a feeling for simple and fastidious still-lifes, which with landscapes made up the bulk of his early work. In 1921 he first saw *Cubist paintings on a visit to Paris and in the following years his still-lifes showed a personal response to the standard Cubist repertoire of jugs and glasses, which he arranged as flat shapes on the picture plane. Nicholson was also influenced by the *naive painter Alfred *Wallis, whose work he discovered in 1928 and whose roughly textured surfaces he emulated. From the early 1930s he turned to abstraction, partly because of the influence of Barbara *Hepworth (they shared a studio from 1932 and married in 1938) and partly because of the impact of several visits he made to Paris at this time. He joined the *Abstraction-Création association in 1933 and became friendly with several leading avant-garde artists, *Mondrian's work in particular coming as a revelation to him. In 1933 he made his first abstract relief and in 1934 his first strictly geometrical 'white relief' in painted wood, using only straight lines and circles. Such works were the most uncompromising examples of abstract art made by a British artist up to that date (*White Relief*, 1935, Tate, London). He also did paintings in a similar intellectual vein but with a poetic refinement of colour that offsets their severity of composition (*Painting*, 1937, Tate). By this time Nicholson was recognized as being at the forefront of the modern movement in England. He was a member of *Unit One (1933), and one of the editors of *Circle* (1937). In 1939 he and Hepworth moved to Cornwall, where they became the nucleus of the *St Ives School. They divorced in 1951 and in 1958 Nicholson settled in Switzerland with his third wife, the Swiss photographer Felicitas Vogler. After the Second World War he won an international reputation, accompanied by many awards. He returned to England in 1971. His late work moved freely between abstraction and figuration and included large, free-standing reliefs, notably one in marble in the garden of Sutton Place, Surrey (1982).

Nicholson's first wife **Winifred Nicholson** (1893–1981), also known by her maiden name of Roberts and her mother's surname Dacre, was a painter of distinction. She is best known for her flower paintings, but she also did other subjects and abstracts, all her work showing her joy in colour and light. Even after they separated in 1931 (they divorced in 1938) she and Ben Nicholson took a keen interest in each other's work; he said, 'I learnt a great deal about colour from Winifred Nicholson and a great deal about form from Barbara Hepworth.'

Nicholson, Sir William (*b* Newark-on-Trent, Nottinghamshire, 5 Feb. 1872; *d* Blewbury, Berkshire [now Oxfordshire], 16 May 1949). British painter and graphic artist. He is perhaps best remembered for his brilliant early work as a poster designer, done in collaboration with his brother-in-law James *Pryde under the name J. & W. *Beggarstaff. As a painter he was successful mainly as a portraitist, but he is now particularly admired for his still-lifes, typically small, unpretentious, and sensitively handled.

Nicias. Greek painter, active in Athens during the latter part of the 4th century BC, a younger contemporary of the sculptor *Praxiteles, some of whose statues he coloured. None of his work survives, but it is described in some detail by *Pliny and he is 'the first Greek painter of whose work some echo can probably be identified in Roman painting' (Martin Robertson, *A History of Greek Art*, 1975). He was famous for his skill in *chiaroscuro and in painting female figures, and he held that a great artist should concentrate on noble and heroic themes.

Nicolas of Verdun (active late 12th century–early 13th century). *Mosan goldsmith, enameller, and metalworker. He is considered the greatest goldsmith and enameller of his day and a major figure in the transition from *Romanesque to *Gothic. Two signed works by him survive: an *enamelled pulpit frontal made for the abbey church at Klosterneuburg, near Vienna (completed in 1181, damaged in 1320, and then remodelled into its present *triptychaltar form); and the Shrine of St Mary for Tournai Cathedral (1205). Among the works attributed to him the most important is the Shrine of the Three Kings, made for Cologne Cathedral in about 1190, which is the largest and most sumptuous reliquary of the period. All three works still belong to the churches for which they were commissioned. The Klosterneuburg Altar is his masterpiece, featuring 45 enamel plaques in an elaborate *typological programme, events from the New Testament being paralleled by ones in the Old Testament. His figure style is expressive and dynamic, with individualized faces and richly articulated drapery suggesting influence from the *antique.

niello (from Latin: *nigellus*, diminutive of *niger*, 'black', dark'). A black substance (typically sulphur, silver, lead, and copper) used as a decorative inlay on metal surfaces; the term can also be used to refer to the process of making such an inlay, and to a surface or object so decorated. The craft flourished particularly in *Renaissance Italy, most notably in Florence and to a lesser extent Bologna. Niello prints are impressions taken from surfaces decorated in niello and are invariably Italian work of the second half of the 15th century. They were probably initially taken as proofs by niellists who wanted to see their work clearly, but it appears that these craftsmen then took to engraving plates with the express purpose of taking impressions from them, and many early examples of Italian *line engraving show the influence of the niello craft. Maso *Finiguerra, whom *Vasari credits with the invention of line engraving, was both niellist and line engraver. In the 18th and 19th centuries there was a revival of interest in niello in Russia, where it was known as Tula-work, from the name of one of the towns notable for producing it. Typically the Russian craftsmen decorated small luxury items such as silver snuff boxes.

Nitsch, Hermann. See VIENNA ACTIONISTS.

Nittis, Giuseppe de (*b* Barletta, 25 Feb. 1846; *d* Saint-Germain-en-Laye, nr. Paris, 21 Aug. 1884). Italian painter, mainly of landscapes and scenes of city life. Early in his career he was associated with the *Macchiaioli. He settled in Paris in 1868, became a friend of *Degas and *Manet, and took part in the first *Impressionist exhibition in 1874 (because de Nittis had already enjoyed some success at the *Salon, Degas thought that the presence of his work among the Impressionists would mean that critics 'won't be able to say that ours is an exhibition of rejected artists'). The best collection of his work is in the Pinacoteca Communale of his native Barletta.

NKV. See NEUE KÜNSTLERVEREINIGUNG MÜNCHEN.

Noguchi, Isamu (*b* Los Angeles, 17 Nov. 1904; *d* New York, 30 Dec. 1988). American sculptor and designer, the son of a Japanese father and an American mother, both of whom were writers. He was brought up in Japan, 1906–18, and after returning to the USA he was briefly apprenticed in 1922 to Gutzon *Borglum, who told him he would never make a sculptor. For the next two years he studied medicine in New York until in 1924 he decided definitively to be an artist. In 1927 he won a Guggenheim Fellowship that enabled him to spend two years in Paris, where he worked as *Brancusi's assistant and under his influence turned from figuration to abstraction. He returned to New York in 1929. Although he used various materials, including wood, bronze, and iron, Noguchi was essentially a stone carver, and his work has a kinship with Brancusi's in its craftsmanship and respect for materials as well as its expressive use of organic shapes. For several years he supported himself mainly by making academic portrait busts, but in 1938 he scored his first major success, winning a competition to make a huge stainless-steel piece for the façade of the Associated Press building in Rockefeller Center, New York. Before this he had already begun what was to be a highly distinguished career as a stage designer, working most notably for the choreographer Martha Graham. After the Second World War he became recognized internationally as one of the leading sculptors of the day and from the 1960s he had many major commissions for public spaces that allowed him to fulfil his long-held ambition to combine Western modernism with Eastern traditions of contemplative art. A notable example is Hart Plaza, Detroit (1975), with its huge Dodge Memorial Fountain in stainless steel and granite. Throughout his career he often returned to Japan and his work is regarded as a successful marriage of East and West. He published an autobiography, A Sculptor's World, in 1968.

Nolan, Sir Sidney (b Melbourne, 22 Apr. 1917; d London, 28 Nov. 1992). The most internationally famous of Australian painters. He turned from odd jobs to art after attending night classes in Melbourne, and became a full-time painter when he was 21. His early work was abstract, but while serving in the Australian army (1941–5) he painted a series of landscapes of the Wimmera district of Victoria that gave the first unmistakable signs of the originality of his vision, capturing the heat and emptiness of the bush. In 1946 he began a series of paintings on the notorious bushranger Ned Kelly, who had become a legendary figure in Australian folk history, and it was with these works that he made his name. He

returned to the Kelly theme throughout his career and he also drew on other events from Australian history. In such works Nolan created a distinctive idiom to express this novel Australian subject matter and memorably portrayed the hard, dry beauty of the desert landscape. Technically, his work is remarkable for the lush fluidity of his brushwork and sometimes he painted on glass or other smooth materials. Nolan first visited Europe in 1950 and from 1955 he lived mainly in England. (One of his staunchest British supporters was Kenneth *Clark, who first saw Nolan's work in 1949 during a visit to Australia and was 'confident that I had stumbled on a genius . . . an entirely original artist'.) Nolan also worked in Paris (where he studied printmaking with *Hayter in 1957) and in the USA, and he travelled extremely widely (the Australian airline Qantas commissioned him to fly around the world gathering material for a series of paintings to decorate their offices). Among the places he visited, Antarctica and New Guinea in particular inspired him, and he also painted pictures on literary themes such as the legend of Leda and the Swan.

Noland, Kenneth (b Asheville, NC, 10 Apr. 1924). American abstract painter and sculptor. In 1949 he settled in Washington, where he became a close friend of Morris *Louis. On a visit to New York in 1953 they were greatly impressed by Helen *Frankenthaler's Mountains and Sea and they began experimenting with the kind of pouring and staining techniques she pioneered. They became the leading figures of a group of *Colour Field Painters known as the Washington Color Painters, but from the late 1950s Noland tended to use more precisely articulated geometrical forms, and in the 1960s he became one of the chief exponents of *Hard-Edge Painting. Initially he used concentric circles on a square canvas. This was followed by a chevron motif, sometimes on a diamond- or lozenge-shaped canvas, and this again was gradually lengthened into horizontal stripes running across a canvas of a very long rectangular format. In 1966 he began to make sculpture, influenced by his friend Anthony *Caro.

Nolde, Emil (b Nolde, Schleswig-Holstein, 7 Aug. 1867; d Seebüll, 13 Apr. 1956). German painter and printmaker, one of the most powerful representatives of *Expressionism. Born of a peasant family, he was originally called Emil Hansen, but he adopted the name of his village as a surname when he married in 1902. He trained as a woodcarver and came late to artistic maturity. His studies took him from his native north Germany to Munich and Paris, and from 1906 to 1907 he was a member of the *Brücke in Dresden, but he was essentially an isolated figure, standing apart from his great German contemporaries. He moved around a good deal in Germany and was well travelled elsewhere (in 1913–14 he visited Russia, the Far East, and the South Sea islands as part of an ethnographic expedition), but at times he lived almost like a hermit. His travel broadened his knowledge of the kind of *primitive art that was then beginning to excite avant-garde artists, but Nolde had already established the essential features of his style before his contact with such art, and when the term 'primitive' is applied to his work it refers to its brutal force, not to any exotic trappings. He was a deeply religious man and is now famous for his paintings of Old and New Testament subjects, in which he expresses intense emotion through violent colour, radically simplified drawing, and grotesque distortion. The majority of his pictures, however, were landscapes, and he was also one of the outstanding 20th-century exponents of flower painting, working with gloriously vivid colour, often in watercolour. He was also a prolific etcher and lithographer. Although he was a member of the Nazi Party, he was declared a *degenerate artist by the Nazis and in 1941 forbidden to paint. He did, however, execute small watercolours in secret (these are called the 'unpainted pictures') and from these made larger oils after the war. From 1926 he lived at Seebüll, where there is now a Nolde Foundation that has an outstanding collection of his work.

Nollekens, Joseph (b London, 11 Aug. 1737; d London, 23 Apr. 1823). English sculptor, mainly in marble but also in terracotta. He was the son of a Flemish painter, **Joseph Francis Nollekens** (Old Nollekens) (1702–48), who settled in London in 1733. After training under *Scheemakers, the younger Nollekens worked in Rome from 1762 to 1770, making a handsome living by copying, restoring, faking, and dealing in *antique sculpture. He also produced a few portrait busts, including that of Laurence Sterne (1766, NPG, London), a splendid character study in the antique manner, and on his return to England it was chiefly as a portraitist that he built up his great reputation and fortune. His best portraits are among the finest of their age, but there are many inferior studio copies of his more popular works. He also made statues in a slightly erotic antique manner, and produced numerous funerary monuments. In addition to being very hardworking, he was an excellent businessman and something of a skinflint, with the result that at his death he left the huge sum of £200,000. A former pupil, J. T. *Smith, who was one of his executors, received a legacy of £100, much less than he had been hoping for, and had his revenge by writing the venomous *Nollekens and his Times* (1828); this gives such a cruelly exaggerated picture of the miserliness and coarseness of Nollekens and his wife that it has been described as probably 'the most candid, pitiless and uncomplimentary biography in the English language' (Rupert Gunnis, *Dictionary of British Sculptors: 1660–1851*, 1953). Allan *Cunningham's account of Nollekens (1830) is more charitable.

Nomé, François de. See 'MONSÙ DESIDERIO'.

Non-Objective art. General term for abstract art that is intended to be completely non-representational, rather than derived (however remotely or obliquely) from appearances in the world around us; most commonly it is applied to severely geometrical works. The term was coined by *Rodchenko, who used it in the title of some of his paintings (*Non-Objective Painting: Black on Black*, 1918, MoMA, New York), and it is also particularly associated with *Malevich.

Noort, Adam van (b Antwerp, 1562; d Antwerp, ?Sept. 1641). Flemish history and portrait painter, remembered chiefly as one of the teachers of *Rubens. Too little is known of the style of either man at the time to estimate what influence he may have had. Another famous pupil was *Jordaens, who became van Noort's son-in-law in 1616.

Northcote, James (b Plymouth, Devon, 22 Oct. 1746; d London, 13 July 1831). English painter and writer. He was largely self-taught until he moved to London in 1771 and became the pupil and assistant of *Reynolds, a fellow Devonian. From 1770 to 1780 he was in Italy, where he gained ambitions to be a history painter; however, his exercises in this field, notably for *Boydell's Shakespeare Gallery, are ponderous and awkward. As a portraitist he was an uninspired follower of Reynolds, and it is as a writer that he has the main claim to distinction; he was something of a character and a lively commentator on the artistic scene. *Memoirs of Sir Joshua Reynolds* (1813, supplement 1815) is his major publication.

Norwich School. A group of English landscape painters associated with the Norwich Society of Artists, which was founded in 1803. It held annual exhibitions 1805–25 and again in 1828–33 after it had been reformed as the Norfolk and Suffolk Institution for the Promotion of the Fine Arts—the first instance of a provincial institution holding regular exhibitions. John *Crome was a founder member and became president in 1808; when he died in 1821, *Cotman took over the role. The Norwich artists, who included amateurs as well as professionals, consisted almost entirely of landscape painters in oil and watercolour; they concentrated on local scenery and often sketched out of doors, but they also found inspiration in 17th-century Dutch painting. Although the heyday of the Norwich School ended with the demise of the annual exhibitions in 1833, the term is often extended to cover artists of the area working in a similar spirit up to the 1880s. James Stark (1794–1859) is probably the best-known representative of the later generation.

Nost (originally **van Ost**), **John** (d London, 1711/13). Flemish-born sculptor who settled in England in about 1678. By 1686 he was foreman to Artus III *Quellin, whose widow he later married. He is chiefly notable as a maker of lead garden statues, some based on Italian or *antique models but others of his own creation. Examples remain at Melbourne Hall, Derbyshire, Hampton Court, and elsewhere. His tombs are less interesting. His son—not, as long thought, his nephew—of the same name (d 1780) settled in Dublin in about 1750 and became the leading sculptor of the day there.

Notke, Bernt (b ?Lassan, Pomerania, c.1440; d Lübeck, c.1509). German sculptor, the leading woodcarver in the Baltic area during his period. He worked mainly in Lübeck, where he is first recorded (as a painter) in 1467, but his masterpiece was executed in Sweden, where he was summoned c.1483 to make a monument commemorating a victory by the regent, Sten Sture, over the Danes. The victory was attributed to the assistance of St George, and Notke's stirring group of St George and the Dragon (completed 1489) in the Storkyrka (Stockholm's main church) is one of the greatest of all votive images. Its spiky forms represent the most expressionistic strain in late *Gothic art and the vividly naturalistic details include the use of real elk antlers for the dragon's horns.

novecento. See QUATTROCENTO.

Novecento Italiano (Italian 20th Century). Association of Italian artists, founded in 1922; it aimed to reject European avant-garde movements and revive a naturalistic type of art based on classical Italian tradition. The Novecento had no clear artistic programme (although it wished to revive large-scale figurative compositions) and numbered within its ranks artists of very different styles and temperaments, among them *Carrà and *Marini. Increasingly it came to be associated with Fascist propaganda and during the 1930s it was the main bastion of reactionary attitudes. It disbanded in 1943.

November Group. An association of Finnish *Expressionist artists founded in Helsinki in November 1917. This was only a month after the declaration of independence from Russia and the members of the November Group were sometimes aggressively nationalistic in outlook, creating a distinctively Finnish form of Expressionism. Tyko *Sallinen was the leading figure of the group, which held annual exhibitions until 1924.

Novembergruppe. A group of radical left-wing German artists formed in Berlin in December 1918; it took its name from the revolution that had broken out in Germany the previous month, at the end of the First World War, and the professed aim of the Novembergruppe was to bring about national renewal by means of a closer relation between progressive artists and the public. Max *Pechstein was among the prime movers. In 1919 the founders of the association created the Arbeitsrat für Kunst (Workers' Council for Art) in an attempt to bring about a dialogue between art and the masses, but this collapsed in 1921 and interest and support came mainly from the middle classes. Artistically the group covered a wide spectrum of ideas and styles. Through its numerous exhibitions it did a good deal to foster an artistic revival, and many of its aims were more fully realized at the *Bauhaus. The group disbanded in 1929.

O

oak. See LIMEWOOD.

obelisk. A tall, generally monolithic, stone shaft, square or rectangular in section, slightly tapering towards the top, and with a pyramidal apex. Obelisks originated in Egypt in the 3rd millennium BC as solar symbols, and many were removed to Rome as trophies after the conquest of Egypt in 30 BC. Their rediscovery during the *Renaissance led to the adaptation of the obelisk form for monuments and in architectural ornament. During the 19th century others were transferred to Paris, London, and New York and few now remain standing in Egypt. The so-called Cleopatra's Needle in London (it dates from about 1500 BC, long before Cleopatra) originally stood at Alexandria; it was presented to Britain in 1819 by the Turkish viceroy of Egypt, but because of the difficulty of transporting the huge granite object it was not moved to London until 1877 and was erected there in 1878.

object. A term applied to a type of three-dimensional work (generally fairly small) made up of any materials that take the artist's fancy and usually put together with some symbolic or ironic meaning. Works in this vein were produced by the *Dadaists, but it was the *Surrealists who really cultivated the object. It is impossible to define the term with any great precision, and in addition to the *objet trouvé and the *ready-made, both of which have a fairly clearly understood meaning, the Surrealists listed (or invented) various categories, many of which seem intended to mystify rather than clarify. The most famous of all Surrealist objects is probably Meret *Oppenheim's *Cup, Saucer and Spoon in Fur* (MoMA, New York, 1936), also known simply as *Object*.

object of virtu (or **objet de vertu**). See VIRTU.

objet trouvé (French: 'found object'). An object found by an artist and displayed with no, or minimal, alteration as (or as an element in) a work of art. It may be a natural object, such as a pebble, a shell, or a curiously contorted branch, or a man-made object such as a piece of pottery or old piece of ironwork or machinery. The essence of the matter is that the finder-artist recognizes such a chance find as an 'aesthetic object' and displays it for appreciation by others as he would a work of art. The practice began with the *Dadaists (especially Marcel *Duchamp) and was particularly cultivated by the *Surrealists. George Heard Hamilton (*Painting and Sculpture in Europe: 1880–1940*, 1967) writes that the devotees of the *objet trouvé* believed that such pieces 'by their unexpected isolation from their customary purpose and environment could open magic casements on interior psychic seas . . . But the technique was easily abused, especially by interior decorators, until no bit of driftwood or broken bone was free from Surrealist implications.' Subsequently, found material has been much used in *assemblage. See also READY-MADE.

Ochtervelt, Jacob (*bapt*. Rotterdam, ?1 Feb. 1634; *bur* Amsterdam, 1 May 1682). Dutch *genre painter. He was mainly active in Rotterdam, but he is said to have been a pupil of *Berchem in Haarlem, and from 1674 he lived in Amsterdam. Apart from a few portraits and some early hunting party and 'merry company' scenes, his paintings are almost all elegant upper-class interiors, in which he showed off a skill in painting silks and satins to rival that of *Terborch. His figures are extremely refined, but there is often a sexual element in his paintings—a couple eating oysters (believed to be an aphrodisiac) was a favourite subject.

O'Conor, Roderic (*b* Milton, Co. Roscommon, 17 Oct. 1860; *d* Nueil-sur-Layon, nr. Saumur, 18 Mar. 1940). Irish painter and etcher, active for most of his life in France (mainly Paris), where he settled in 1883 after studying in London and Antwerp. He was strongly influenced by *Gauguin and van *Gogh, and by the early 1890s he was painting in a full-blooded *Post-Impressionist style with bold colour—often used non-naturalistically—and thick brushwork. He lived a fairly reclusive life (although he was friendly with many British visitors to France, including Clive *Bell and Roger *Fry) and he was virtually unknown in the British and Irish art worlds. It was only after his death that he was recognized as the outstanding pioneer of Post-Impressionism among English-speaking artists. He did, however, notably influence Matthew *Smith, whom he met in 1919. O'Conor was mainly a landscapist, but he also painted still-lifes, portraits, interiors, and figure subjects.

Official War Art. Art sponsored by the British government during the First and Second World Wars to make a visual record of all aspects of the war effort for information and propaganda purposes. By extension the term is also applied to art produced under official auspices for other Allied countries. Australia commissioned work for the Australian War Memorial in Canberra (originally intended to commemorate the First World War, but extended to encompass all wars in which the country was involved); Canada had a Canadian War Records Office that commissioned paintings and drawings; and the USA had a War Portraits Commission.

In the First World War, official art was directed by the Ministry of Information, which was advised by a committee drawn from distinguished figures in the art world and public life, among them Campbell Dodgson, keeper of prints and drawings at the British Museum, and Eric MacLagan, later director of the Victoria and Albert Museum. In 1916 the Ministry launched the Official War Artists scheme, under which artists were recruited, with appropriate military ranks, to serve as chroniclers (Germany already had a similar scheme in operation). The first artist to be commissioned was Honorary 2nd Lieutenant Muirhead *Bone, who left for France on 16 August 1916 and toured the front in a chauffeur-driven car. Many others soon followed, among them some of the most illustrious British artists of the time. They included men who had already been serving in the armed forces, such as Paul *Nash, C. R. W. *Nevinson, and Stanley *Spencer, and others who were too old for active duty. The works produced varied enormously in style and quality (the committee was admirably broad in its choice of artists) and included imaginative evocations of the war as well as sober factual records. There were many portraits of participants, but two of the most notable portraitists who worked as Official War Artists—*Orpen and *Sargent—showed a different and unexpected side to their talents, powerfully depicting the horrors they saw.

In the autumn of 1939, soon after the outbreak of the Second World War, the Ministry of Information appointed Kenneth *Clark chairman of a small group that became known as the War Artists' Advisory Committee (Muirhead Bone was one of the members). It met weekly at the National Gallery, of which Clark was director, and its functions were principally 'to draw up a list of artists qualified to record the War at home and abroad . . . [and] . . . to advise on the selection of artists from this list for war purposes and on the arrangement for their employment'. Clark regarded his work on the committee as 'my only worthwhile activity' during the war: 'We employed every artist whom we thought had any merit, not because we supposed that we would get records of the war more truthful or striking than those supplied by photography, but because it seemed a good way of preventing artists being killed' (*Ravilious was one of the rare fatalities). Several painters who had been Official War Artists in the First World War were employed in the same capacity in the Second, among them Nash and Spencer, but the committee mainly employed men of a younger generation. The terms in which they were employed varied: some were given salaried posts for a specific period, while others were given one-off commissions. The committee also encouraged artists, whether serving or civilian, to submit pictures for consideration. Generally the commissions in the Second World War were on a smaller scale than those in the First, with many works being executed in watercolour (Spencer's huge canvases of shipbuilding on the Clyde are a conspicuous exception). Henry *Moore's drawings of Londoners sheltering from air raids in underground stations are perhaps the best known of all the works produced under the auspices of Clark's committee.

In both wars women were employed as Official War Artists on the home front, notably the animal painter Lucy Kemp-Welch (1869–1958) in the First and Laura *Knight in the Second. A huge number of works was produced. The largest collection (about 10,000 items) is in the Imperial War Museum, London, which was opened in 1920 and moved to its present home (the former Royal Bethlehem Hospital) in 1936. The Tate has another major collection, and many provincial museums have good examples.

Since the Second World War the tradition of Official War Art has been maintained on a lesser scale by the Artistic Records Committee of the

Imperial War Museum. Linda Kitson (1945–) went on its behalf to the Falkland Islands during the war there against Argentina in 1982, for example, and Peter Howson (1958–) went to Bosnia in 1993. His exhibition 'War in Bosnia' at the Imperial War Museum the following year attracted considerable attention because of its unsparing depiction of atrocities: 'Now that I've actually seen dead bodies, and guts and brains, and starving children, it has made the work authentic.'

offset. An alternative term for *counterproof; it is also used as an abbreviation for 'offset *lithography'.

Ofili, Chris. See TURNER PRIZE and YOUNG BRITISH ARTISTS.

O'Gorman, Juan (b Mexico City, 6 July 1905; d Mexico City, c.18 Jan. 1982). Mexican architect and painter. Early in his career he designed a series of houses in Mexico City (notably those for himself and for Diego *Rivera) that were among the first in the Americas to show the functionalist ideas of *Le Corbusier. In the 1930s, however, he abandoned architecture for painting. His work was strongly nationalistic and his anti-fascist, anti-Church frescos at Mexico City airport (1937–8) were destroyed in 1939 during a political swing to the right. In the 1950s he returned to architecture, now advocating a more 'organic' approach inspired in part by Frank Lloyd Wright. His most celebrated work in this vein is the Library of the National University in Mexico City (1951–3), in which a modern structural design is completely covered externally in mosaics of his own design that symbolically represent the history of Mexican culture. In 1953–6 O'Gorman built a second home for himself outside Mexico City. This too was lavishly decorated in mosaics externally and internally and it was designed to harmonize with the lava formation of the landscape. He committed suicide.

oil paint. Paint in which *drying oils (usually *linseed oil) are used as the *medium. It was long believed—on the authority of *Vasari—that oil painting was invented by Jan van *Eyck in the early 15th century, but it is now known that its origins are older and obscurer (the treatise of *Theophilus, for example, written probably in the 12th century, describes 'grinding colours with oil'). There is no doubt, however, that van Eyck revolutionized the technique and brought it to a sudden peak of perfection. He showed the medium's flexibility, its rich and dense colour, its wide range from light to dark, and its ability to achieve both minute detail and subtle blending of tones. Other painters soon took up his innovations—first in northern Europe, then in Italy—and over the next century oil progressively superseded *tempera as the standard medium for serious painting (other than for murals, in which *fresco continued to be the norm).

During the period of transition, oil was often combined with tempera. Giovanni *Bellini, for example, began his long career using tempera exclusively and ended it using oil exclusively, but in most of his work he seems to have combined the two methods, typically beginning a picture in the older technique and completing it in the newer. His portrait of Doge Leonardo Loredan (c.1501–4, NG, London) is one of the earliest examples of the use of deliberately rough oil paint to convey texture; in the doge's ornate costume he suggests light catching the gold thread in a way that would be impossible in tempera. This kind of handling was taken much further by Bellini's pupil *Titian, who was the first artist to fully exploit the rich textural qualities of oil paint, giving the surface of his pictures an expressive life of their own. The revolution he wrought in technique was bound up with his increasing preference for *canvas in place of wooden *panels; in his later work he often used fairly coarse types, in which the rough grain shows through the brushwork and is part of the surface texture of the picture.

This ability to show an artist's personal 'handwriting' has been a major factor in the long dominance of oil paint; it can attain any variety of surface from porcelain smoothness to violent *impasto. Its versatility was increased still further in the 19th century with the invention of the collapsible metal *tube (devised in 1841), which made it convenient to work out of doors. In the 20th century, however, *acrylic became a serious rival to oil paint.

O'Keeffe, Georgia (b Sun Prairie, Wis., 15 Nov. 1887; d Santa Fe, N. Mex., 6 Mar. 1986). American painter. One of the pioneers of modernism in America, she was a member of the circle of *Stieglitz, whom she met in 1916 and married in 1924. She is best known for her near-abstract paintings based on enlargements of flower and plant forms, works of great elegance and rhythmic vitality, whose sensuous forms are often sexually suggestive (*Black Iris*, 1926, Met. Mus., New York). In the 1920s she also painted townscapes of New York in a manner close to that of the *Precisionists and landscapes done in broad, simple forms. From the 1930s she spent each winter in New Mexico and she settled there after Stieglitz's death in 1946, the desert landscape appearing frequently in her paintings (bleached animal bones were a favourite subject). She began to travel widely in the 1950s and many of her later paintings were inspired by views of the earth, sky, and clouds seen from an aeroplane. She became partially blind in 1971 and did little work thereafter. A museum dedicated to her opened in Santa Fe in 1997.

Oldenburg, Claes (*b* Stockholm, 28 Jan. 1929). Swedish-born sculptor and graphic artist who became an American citizen in 1953. He was educated at Yale University and studied at the Art Institute of Chicago (earning his living with part-time jobs as a reporter and illustrator), then in 1956 settled in New York. There he came into contact with a group of young artists, including *Dine, *Kaprow, and *Segal, who were in revolt against *Abstract Expressionism and from about 1958 he became interested in *happenings, *environments, 'situations', etc. His inspiration was drawn largely from New York's street life—shop windows, graffiti, advertisements, and so on—and in 1961 he opened 'The Store', at which he sold painted plaster replicas of foods and other domestic objects. This led to the work with which his name is most closely associated—giant-size sculptures of foodstuffs and 'soft sculptures' of normally hard objects (*Dual Hamburger*, 1962, MoMA, New York). With these he was hailed as one of the leaders of American *Pop art. Oldenburg is also well known for his projects for colossal monuments—for example, *Lipsticks in Piccadilly Circus, London* (1966, Tate, London), consisting of a magazine cutting of an array of lipsticks pasted onto a picture postcard. The first of these projects to be realized was a giant lipstick erected at Yale University in 1969. Since 1976 he has concentrated almost exclusively on such large-scale projects, for example the 20 m (70 ft) high *Match Cover* erected in Barcelona in 1992.

Old Master. An imprecise but useful term employed as a blanket phrase to cover European artists (particularly painters) from the *Renaissance up to about 1800; the term is applied also to their works, so an Old Master can be a picture as well as a person. Often the term carries an implication of high quality, but this is not necessarily so. In major auction houses, for example, the term is used chronologically rather than aesthetically, as 19th-century and later paintings

are usually sold separately from earlier works. Thus an 'Old Master sale' may contain entirely undistinguished pictures or even feeble copies as well as masterpieces.

oleograph. A coloured *lithograph impressed with a canvas grain and varnished to make it look like an oil painting. Oleographs were popular—but often considered rather vulgar—in the second half of the 19th century.

Olitski, Jules (*b* Snovsk [now Shchors, Ukraine], 27 Mar. 1922). Russian-born American painter and sculptor, one of the leading figures of *Post-Painterly Abstraction, specifically of *Colour Field Painting. His early paintings were influenced by *Fauvism and they were followed by heavily textured abstracts, but in 1960 the direction of his work changed radically when he began experimenting with stain techniques in the manner of *Frankenthaler and *Louis. In 1964 he began using a spray gun and in the second half of the 1960s he developed the type of painting for which he is best known—vast canvases covered with luscious mists of atmospheric colour; he said that ideally he would like 'nothing but some colours sprayed into the air and staying there'. Sometimes there are some heavier touches at the edges of the canvas in a sort of ironic reference to *Abstract Expressionism, and in the 1970s Olitski returned to a more textural handling of paint, often reducing his colour to delicate modulations of greys and brown. He took up sculpture seriously in 1968 and has worked mainly with painted metal.

Oliver, Isaac (*b* ?Rouen, *c*.1565; *bur.* London, 2 Oct. 1617). English *miniaturist of French origin, the son of a refugee Huguenot goldsmith who settled in England in about 1568. Although he was naturalized in 1606, he always considered himself French and his command of written English was shaky. He trained under *Hilliard (whose main rival he later became) and by 1590 was established in his own practice. Hilliard continued to receive royal favour under James I, but Oliver was made *limner to the queen, Anne of Denmark, in 1604, and he was also patronized by Henry, Prince of Wales, and his circle. His style was more naturalistic than Hilliard's, using light and shade to obtain modelling and generally dispensing with the emblematic trappings so beloved of the Elizabethan age. In 1596 he is documented in Venice, and unlike Hilliard he produced copies of Renaissance pictures in miniature. Contemporary sources indicate that he probably also painted life-size portraits, and he has been proposed as the author of some of the pictures more usually attributed to William *Larkin. His son **Peter Oliver** (?1594–1647) was also a miniaturist; he began as a portraitist but from the 1620s specialized in miniature copies after the Old Masters.

Olsen, John (*b* Newcastle, NSW, 21 Jan. 1928). One of Australia's leading abstract painters, active mainly in Sydney. In 1957–60 he travelled in Europe, where his work was strongly influenced by the *Expressionism of the *Cobra group and the totemic imagery of Alan *Davie, whom he met in London. Back in Australia, he applied the lessons he had learned to an imaginative exploration of the bush landscape, notably in his series *Journey into You Beaut Country* (1961), in which lively calligraphic brushwork evokes a feeling of vegetation and insect life. In 1972 Olsen painted a mural for the newly completed Sydney Opera House, and in 1978 he made an extensive painting tour of Africa.

Omega Workshops. Decorative arts company founded by Roger *Fry in London in 1913 with the twin aims of improving the standard of design in Britain and providing work for the young avant-garde artists in his circle. (Omega is the last letter of the Greek alphabet and it has been suggested that Fry chose the name to indicate its products were 'the last word' in design, but in fact he seems to have picked it because it was anonymous but easy to remember and in addition to being a word was a sign that could be used as a trademark.) Fry disliked the smooth finish of machine products, and Omega works characteristically have the irregularities of hand craftsmanship, although the furniture it sold was originally bought ready-made and then painted on the premises, and its linens were expertly printed in France. Its other products included ceramics and carpets. The favourite Omega motifs included flowers, nudes, and abstract patterns, and colour was often very bright; *Cubism and *Fauvism were strong influences.

Apart from Fry himself, the designers most closely associated with Omega were Vanessa *Bell and Duncan *Grant, and several other distinguished artists worked for the enterprise, including Paul *Nash and William *Roberts. However, all the work was sold anonymously. Artists were paid a regular wage, the financing coming from Fry himself and from subscribers, including George Bernard Shaw. The Workshops made a promising start, but the First World War had a disastrous effect on sales (Fry in any case had little business aptitude) and in

June 1919 Omega's remaining stock was sold off; the company was officially liquidated in 1920. The best idea of Omega furnishings in a contemporary setting can be gained at Charleston, the country home of Bell and Grant at Firle in Sussex. There are also good examples in London at the Courtauld Gallery and the Victoria and Albert Museum.

O'Neil, Henry Nelson. See CLIQUE.

Ono, Yoko. See FLUXUS.

Oostsanen, Cornelisz. van. See CORNELISZ. VAN OOSTSANEN.

Op art (abbreviation of Optical art, on the analogy of Pop art). A type of abstract art that exploits certain optical phenomena to cause a work to seem to vibrate, pulsate, or flicker. It flourished mainly in the 1960s; the term was first used in print in the American magazine *Time* in October 1964 and had become a household phrase by the following year, partly through the attention given to the exhibition 'The Responsive Eye' held at the Museum of Modern Art, New York, in 1965. This was the first international exhibition with a predominance of Op paintings. The development of Op art as a recognizable movement had begun a few years earlier than this, in about 1960, the works and theories of Josef *Albers being among the main sources. The devices employed by Op artists (after-images, effects of dazzle and vibration, and so on) are often elaborations on the well-known visual illusions to be found in standard textbooks of perceptual psychology, and maximum precision is sought in the control of surfaces and edges in order to evoke an exactly prescribed retinal response. Many Op paintings employ repeated small-scale patterns arranged so as to suggest underlying secondary shapes or warping or swelling surfaces. This kind of work can retain much of its effect in reproduction, but Op art also embraces constructions that depend for their effects on light and/or movement, so Op and *Kinetic art sometimes overlap.

The two most famous exponents of Op art are Bridget *Riley and Victor *Vasarely. Their work illustrates the considerable impact that Op made on fashion and design in the 1960s—its instant popular success (accompanied by a fairly cool critical reception) is hard to parallel in modern art. Op art became something of a craze in women's fashion and in 1965 Riley unsuccessfully tried to sue an American clothing company that used one of her paintings as a fabric design. One of Vasarely's designs was used on the plastic carrier bags of France's chain of COOP stores. Among other exponents of Op art the best known is probably the American Richard Anuszkiewicz (1930–), a former pupil of Albers; his work is typically concerned with radiating expanses of lines and colours.

Opie, John (*b* St Agnes, Cornwall, May 1761; *d* London, 9 Apr. 1807). English painter. He was something of a child prodigy and was discovered by the political satirist John Wolcot (better known by his pen name Peter Pindar), who in 1781 successfully launched him in London as an untaught genius (the Cornish Wonder). At this time Opie was painting strongly modelled portraits and rustic *fancy pictures with rich *Rembrandtesque lighting. He soon lost the rugged freshness of his early work and his later paintings were undistinguished and repetitive. His career continued to flourish, however, and he became professor of painting at the *Royal Academy in 1805, his lectures being posthumously published in 1809 (prefaced with a memoir by his wife, the novelist and poet Amelia Opie). Apart from portraits and *genre scenes, he also painted history pictures, notably for *Boydell's Shakespeare Gallery.

Opie, Julian. See NEW BRITISH SCULPTURE.

Oppenheim, Meret (*b* Berlin, 6 Oct. 1913; *d* Basle, 15 Nov. 1985). German-Swiss painter, sculptor, and maker of objects. In 1932 she moved to Paris, where she was introduced to the *Surrealist group by *Giacometti and became for a while the model and disciple of *Man Ray. He described her as 'one of the most uninhibited women I have ever known' and she became celebrated among the Surrealists as the 'fairy woman' whom all men desire. She had a long career, but she is remembered mainly for one early work: *Object* (1936, MoMA, New York), a fur-lined tea cup and saucer. This became famous as a symbol of artistic anarchy after being shown at major Surrealist exhibitions in London and New York in 1936. See also OBJECT.

opus anglicanum (Latin: 'English work'). Term used on the Continent in the late 13th and 14th centuries to describe the sumptuous English embroidery of that period and all other embroidery in similar style. English embroiderers were recognized as the best in Europe at this time and their church vestments were widely exported (a Vatican inventory of 1295 contains more than 100 references to such work). Surviving examples mainly date from *c.*1250 to *c.*1350 (the reasons for the decline in the art after this date are unclear). Typically they feature small figures or religious scenes, comparable in style with East Anglian manuscript illumination of the time (the vestments were presumably sometimes designed by painters), framed by foliaged scrolls or in geometrical or architectural compartments; these designs are worked in coloured silks, generally on backgrounds of gold thread. Fine examples remain in the treasuries of several major Continental churches, and *opus anglicanum* is also well represented in the Victoria and Albert Museum, London, notably with the celebrated Syon Cope (*c.*1300–20).

opus sectile (Latin: 'cut work'). An inlaid design made of pieces of marble that are individually shaped to fit the pattern or picture, as distinct from *mosaic, where the design is built up from countless small pieces (tesserae) of stone or glass. It is a rarer and more luxurious art than mosaic, since the plates of marble are larger, more fragile, and more precious than tesserae; and it was in Egypt and Asia Minor, lands rich in coloured marble, that it had its origin. The Book of Esther (1: 6) describes 'a pavement of red and blue and white and black marble' in the palace of Ahasuerus (probably to be identified with the Persian king Xerxes I). However, little survives from before the time of the Romans, who used *opus sectile* extensively for wall and floor decoration. It was later used in Early Christian and Byzantine churches, and evolved into more specialized crafts such as *Cosmati work. Geometrical *opus sectile* continued to be popular in Italy for decorating church floors throughout the Middle Ages and *Renaissance.

orant. See GISANT.

Orcagna, Andrea (Andrea di Cione) (*b* Florence, ?*c.*1320; *d* Florence, ?1368). The leading Florentine artist of the third quarter of the 14th century, a painter, sculptor, architect, and administrator. His nickname 'Orcagna' was evidently local slang for 'Archangel' (*Arcangelo*). In 1343/4 he was admitted to the painters' guild in Florence and in 1352 to that of the masons. His only certain work as a painter is the altarpiece of *The Redeemer with the Madonna and Saints* (1354–7) in the Strozzi Chapel of S. Maria Novella. This is the most powerful Florentine painting of its period, and in spite of the massiveness of the figures it represents a reversion from *Giotto's naturalism to the hieratic ideals of *Byzantine art. Colours are resplendent, with lavish use of gold, and the figures are remote and immobile.

Among paintings attributed to Orcagna, the most important is a fragmentary fresco trilogy of the *Triumph of Death, Last Judgement*, and *Hell* in S. Croce. As a sculptor and architect he is known through one work, the tabernacle in Orsanmichele (finished 1359), a highly elaborate ornamental structure housing a painting of the *Virgin Enthroned* by Bernardo *Daddi. Orcagna was *capomaestro* of Orvieto Cathedral from 1358 to 1362, supervising the mosaic decoration of the façade. He was also an adviser on the construction of Florence Cathedral. During 1368 he fell mortally ill while painting the *St Matthew* altarpiece (Uffizi, Florence) and this work was finished by his brother **Jacopo di Cione** (*d* 1398/1400), who worked in his style and continued it to the end of the century. Another brother, **Nardo di Cione** (*d* 1365/6), was also a painter. *Ghiberti attributes to him the series of frescos of the *Last Judgement, Hell*, and *Paradise* in the same chapel in S. Maria Novella that houses Andrea's great altarpiece. A fourth brother, **Matteo di Cione** (*d* c.1390), was a sculptor, but almost nothing is known of his work.

Orchardson, Sir William Quiller (*b* Edinburgh, 27 Mar. 1832; *d* London, 13 Apr. 1910). Scottish painter of *genre subjects and portraits, active in London from 1862. He made his name with historical costume pieces, but later did his most memorable work in modern-day scenes of upper-class married life. In these he used large empty spaces to create feelings of psychological tension or despair. The best-known are *The First Cloud* (1887, Tate, London) and a pair representing *A Marriage of Convenience* (1883, Glasgow AG, and 1886, Aberdeen AG).

Ordóñez, Bartolomé (*b* Burgos, c.1485; *d* Carrara, 5/10 Dec. 1520). Spanish sculptor, active mainly in Barcelona. On stylistic grounds, he is presumed to have trained in Florence, perhaps with Andrea *Sansovino, and he was certainly in Italy in 1517–18 and 1520. His main work there is the marble altarpiece of the Caracciolo Chapel in the church of S. Giovanni a Carbonara, Naples, where he perhaps worked in collaboration with Diego de *Siloé (there is evidence that the altarpiece was made c.1515, but some authorities connect it with Ordóñez's visit to Italy in 1517–18). By 1519 he was working on the decoration of the choir stalls in Barcelona Cathedral, and in the same year he began work on two tombs—that of Philip I and Joanna of Castile (Chapel Royal, Granada) and that of Cardinal Francisco Jiménez de Cisneros (S. Ildefonso, Alcalá de Henares). He died at Carrara

(see MARBLE) in Italy before these were finished, but his will indicates that he had completed major parts, including the effigies of Philip and Joanna. Although he died young, his elegant and imaginative work played an important role in introducing the High *Renaissance style to Spain.

Orientalism. A term that in its broadest sense can allude to any aspect of Eastern culture adopted, imitated, or portrayed in the West but which in the history of art usually refers specifically to a fashion in 19th-century painting and other arts, particularly in France, for imagery drawn from the Near and Middle East and North Africa (rather than the Far East of China and Japan). The fashion came in the wake of Napoleon's invasion of Egypt in 1798 and was facilitated by improving means of travel in the 19th century, which enabled many European artists to visit regions that would previously have been closed to them.

Although he never visited the Near East himself, Antoine-Jean *Gros was one of the first artists to create pictures that can be described as orientalist, in his scenes of the Army of the Orient's campaigns in Egypt and Syria (*Napoleon Visiting the Pesthouse at Jaffa*, 1804, Louvre, Paris). Alexandre-Gabriel *Decamps was among the pioneers in actually visiting exotic lands (in 1828–9) and in making them his speciality. Those who followed him included *Delacroix, *Fromentin, *Gleyre, and *Gérôme. Among sculptors, the most notable specialist in Orientalism was Charles Cordier (1827–1905), best known for busts of North African people, in which he used *polychromy and semi-precious stones to suggest the opulence of the East. Outside France, the artists who made a career out of the fashion included J. F. *Lewis and David *Roberts.

There were many different types of orientalist picture, including biblical scenes re-created in authentic settings (Holman *Hunt was a noted exponent), erotic images of the harem or slave market (although he never travelled outside Europe, *Ingres painted some memorable pictures of odalisques), and gory scenes of torture and execution such as Decamps's *The Punishment of the Hooks* (1837, Wallace Coll., London). By the end of the 19th century the genre was more or less exhausted, but various 20th-century artists continued to explore orientalist themes, most notably *Matisse.

Orientalizing period. A term sometimes applied to Greek art of the 7th century BC, between the *Geometric and *Archaic periods. The term reflects the influence of eastern peoples such as the Assyrians and Phoenicians, particularly in vase painting, where the rectilinear patterns of the Geometric period gave way to motifs involving plant and animal life, including fabulous beasts.

Orlan. See BODY ART.

Orley, Bernard (or **Barend**) **van** (b Brussels, c.1490; d Brussels, 6 Jan. 1542). Netherlandish painter of religious subjects and portraits and designer of tapestries and stained glass. He was the leading artist of his day in Brussels, becoming court painter to Margaret of Austria (see HABSBURG), regent of the Netherlands, in 1518 and to her successor Mary of Hungary in 1532. His work is full of Italianate motifs, often rather ill digested. There is no evidence that he visited Italy, and his knowledge presumably came from engravings and from *Raphael's tapestry *cartoons, which were in Brussels c.1516–19; he has (very flatteringly) been called 'the Raphael of the Netherlands'. His best-known work is the turbulent *Job* altarpiece (1521, Mus. Royaux, Brussels). As a portraitist his style was quieter and more thoughtful (*Georg Zelle*, 1519, Mus. Royaux, Brussels). None of van Orley's paintings bears a date later than 1530; after that time he was chiefly occupied with designing tapestries and stained-glass windows.

Orozco, José Clemente (b Zapotlán el Grande [now Ciudad Guzmán], 23 Nov. 1883; d Mexico City, 7 Sept. 1949). Mexican painter, with his contemporaries *Rivera and *Siqueiros one of the trio of politically and socially committed muralists who dominated modern Mexican art. Following the first outburst of revolutionary activity in Mexico in 1910 (which was to last on and off until 1920), Orozco took up work as a political cartoonist. In 1912 he began a series of watercolours called 'House of Tears' dealing with prostitutes (a favourite symbol of human degradation for Orozco). The angry reaction of critics and moralists to these works was one of his reasons for leaving for the USA, where he spent three unhappy and unproductive years, 1917–20. His career as a muralist began after he returned to Mexico in 1920. The country was now relatively stable under the government of Alvaro Obregón, who encouraged nationalistic subjects as a way of creating a positive identity for the country after years of turmoil.

Orozco's first frescos were in the Escuela Nacional Preparatoria (National Training School),

1923–4. They were controversial because of their caricatural style, and all except *Maternity* and *The Rich Banquet while the Workers Quarrel* were subsequently destroyed or altered. In the period 1927 to 1934 (broken by a brief trip to Europe in 1932) he again worked in the USA. This time he was much more successful, carrying out a number of important mural commissions, most notably a cycle for Dartmouth College, New Hampshire, on the coming and the return of Quetzalcoatl (1932–4). This huge scheme showed his outlook crystallizing into a contrast between a pagan paradise and a capitalist hell. Unlike Rivera and Siqueiros, Orozco did not align himself with a political movement, but his work had an intense humanitarian mission. He returned to Mexico in 1934 with a big reputation after his success in the USA, and he spent most of the rest of his life engaged on mural projects in Mexico City and Guadalajara, the country's second city. In his last years his work became ever more violent in expression, moved by a passionate concern for the suffering and miseries of mankind. His studio in Guadalajara is now a museum dedicated to him.

Orpen, Sir William (b Blackrock, Co. Dublin, 27 Nov. 1878; d London, 29 Sept. 1931). British painter, chiefly famous as one of the leading fashionable portraitists of his day. Orpen was a child prodigy and had a brilliant student career at the *Slade School. He worked mainly in London but he kept up links with his native Ireland, teaching part-time at the Metropolitan School in Dublin, 1902–14. His style had much in common with that of his friend Augustus *John, being vigorous and painterly but sometimes rather flashy. He was at his best when he was away from his standard boardroom and drawing-room fare, and his numerous self-portraits are often particularly engaging, as he pokes fun at himself in character roles. Up to the First World War he had a steady rise in worldly success and after the war he earned an average of about £35,000 a year, rising to over £50,000 a year in 1929—a colossal sum then. In 1920 a story appeared in London newspapers that he had refused an offer of £1,000,000 to work for a dealer in the USA, and he was one of the few British artists of his time capable of attracting public attention in such a way. Apart from portraits, Orpen also painted *genre subjects, landscapes, interiors, nudes, and allegories, and he did memorable work as an *Official War Artist in France (he also attended the 1919 Peace Conference in Paris and painted a large group portrait showing the *Signing of the Peace in the Hall of Mirrors, Versailles, 28 June, 1919* (Imperial War Mus., London)). His reputation faded badly after his death but revived greatly in the 1970s.

Orphism (or **Orphic Cubism**). Terms coined by *Apollinaire to describe a type of painting—a development from *Cubism—practised by Robert *Delaunay and some of his associates between 1911 and the outbreak of the First World War in 1914. The reference to Orpheus, the singer and poet of Greek mythology, reflected the desire of the artists involved to bring a new element of lyricism and colour into the austere intellectual Cubism of *Picasso, *Braque, and *Gris. Apart from Delaunay, the artists whom Apollinaire mentioned as practitioners of Orphism were Marcel *Duchamp, Fernand *Léger, and Francis *Picabia (all members of the *Section d'Or), but František *Kupka, another member of their circle, was in fact closer in style to Delaunay than these three. By 1912 both Delaunay and Kupka were painting completely non-representational pictures characterized by intensely vibrant, fragmented colours. Despite its short life, Orphism was highly influential, notably on several major German painters, particularly *Klee (who visited Delaunay in 1912), *Macke, and *Marc. It was also closely related to *Synchromism.

Orsi, Lelio (*b* Novellara, *c*.1511; *d* Novellara, 3 May 1587). Italian *Mannerist painter, active mainly in his birthplace, near Parma, and in nearby Reggio Emilia. His large-scale work in fresco has almost all perished and he is now known mainly by *cabinet pictures of religious subjects (*The Walk to Emmaus*, *c*.1570, NG, London). He was influenced by various sources (*Correggio, *Giulio Romano, *Michelangelo, *Parmigianino, and perhaps also German woodcuts), but his style has a leaning towards the bizarre, with dramatic stage-lighting effects, that gives it a distinctly personal touch. Orsi was an outstanding draughtsman and also worked as an architect.

Os, van. Dutch family of painters active during the late 18th and 19th centuries, mainly in The Hague. **Jan** (1744–1808) was the founder. He and his daughter **Maria Margaretha** (1780–1862) and his son **Georgius** (1782–1861) specialized in painting flowers and fruits in the lavish detailed manner of Jan van *Huysum. Another of Jan's sons, **Pieter Gerardus** (1776–1839), specialized in landscapes with cattle. His son and pupil **Pieter Frederik** (1802–92) taught *Mauve.

Osona, Rodrigo de (*d* Valencia, 1518). Spanish painter. He was one of the leading painters of his day in Valencia, introducing both Netherlandish and Italian *Renaissance influence to the area. His most important work is a *Crucifixion* (1476) in the church of S. Nicolás, Valencia. On the basis of an altarpiece of the *Adoration of the Magi* (V&A, London) signed 'the son of Master Rodrigo', several works have been attributed to **Rodrigo de Osona the Younger** (*d* Valencia, *c*.1514). His style is similar to his father's, but weaker and more Italianate.

Ostade, Adriaen van (*bapt*. Haarlem, 10 Dec. 1610; *d* Haarlem, 27 Apr. 1685). Dutch painter, draughtsman, and etcher, active in Haarlem. Although he turned his hand to many subjects, he was principally a *genre painter. According to *Houbraken, he and Adriaen *Brouwer (whose work is similar) were fellow pupils of Frans *Hals. Ostade's early pictures depict lively scenes of peasants carousing or brawling in crowded taverns or hovels. In his later works (after *c*.1650) his peasants learn better manners and the rooms they live in are tidier. These later pictures are lighter in key and more colourful; thus they follow the general trend of Dutch painting around this time. Ostade was successful, prolific, and much imitated. He is said to have taught Jan *Steen and his other pupils included his brother **Isaak van Ostade** (*bapt*. Haarlem, 2 June 1621; *bur*. Haarlem, 16 Oct. 1649), who likewise worked in Haarlem. As well as painting genre scenes in the manner of Adriaen, Isaak was an outstanding exponent of the winter landscape, and his early death cut short a career of great promise. Good examples of the work of both brothers are in the National Gallery, London.

Osthaus, Karl Ernst. See SONDERBUND.

ottocento. See QUATTROCENTO.

Ottonian art. Term applied to art of the Holy Roman Empire in the 10th century and most of the 11th century. The period is named after Otto the Great, who was crowned King of the Germans in 936 and was Holy Roman Emperor from 963 until his death in 973. He re-established a strong royal authority after the fall of the Carolingian Empire. The Ottonian period saw the revival of large-scale bronze casting (see BERNWARD OF HILDESHEIM) and of life-size sculpture (in the celebrated Gero Crucifix in Cologne Cathedral, the gift of Archbishop Gero (reigned 969–76)), but the most typical sculptural products of the time were in ivory and metalwork, notably for book covers and altar reliefs. Though wall paintings still survive, the character of Ottonian art is better seen in a rich store of illuminated manuscripts. One of the most celebrated is the Codex Egberti (Egbert Codex) (Stadtbibliothek, Trier), made for Egbert, who was Archbishop of Trier 977–93 and a great patron of the arts. In spite of differences in local schools, all Ottonian illumination has certain things in common, notably the pre-eminence given to the human figure, which is often imbued with strong expression and marked by exaggerated gestures. Ottonian art was one of the sources out of which *Romanesque grew.

Oudry, Jean-Baptiste (b Paris, 17 Mar. 1686; d Beauvais, 30 Apr. 1755). French painter, tapestry designer, and illustrator. He was a pupil of *Largillière and painted some portraits, but he is renowned chiefly as one of the outstanding animal painters of the 18th century. With *Desportes he was his period's foremost exponent of hunting scenes and still-lifes with dead game. Some of his best work was done as a tapestry designer, and he was head of the Beauvais and *Gobelins factories from 1734 and 1748 respectively. He also did book illustrations, notably for an edition of La Fontaine's *Fables* (1755–9).

Outsider art. See ART BRUT.

Ouwater, Albert van (active mid-15th century). Netherlandish painter. There is no known contemporary information on him (an alleged reference to him in 1467 is now thought to be a misreading of the document), and knowledge of his life depends on the account in van *Mander's *Schilder-boeck* (1604). According to this, Ouwater was the founder of the Haarlem School and the teacher of *Geertgen tot Sint Jans. Van Mander also praised Ouwater's skill as a landscapist, so it is ironic that the only painting that can be identified as his from the descriptions of his work in the *Schilder-boeck* is an interior scene—the *Raising of Lazarus* (c.1440–50, Gemäldegalerie, Berlin). The thoughtful, unemotional style of this picture has some affinities with the work of Dieric *Bouts, who was probably a native of Haarlem.

Ovenden, Annie and **Graham.** See BLAKE, SIR PETER.

Ovens, Juriaen. See CAMPEN.

Overbeck, Friedrich (b Lübeck, 3 July 1789; d Rome, 12 Nov. 1869). German painter, the leading member of the *Nazarenes. He moved to Rome in 1810 and was based there for the rest of his life, although he made several visits to Germany. In 1813 he was converted to Roman Catholicism and apart from a few portraits (there is a self-portrait in the Uffizi, Florence) his work was almost exclusively on religious themes. He painted in a consciously archaic style—clear and sincere but rather pallid—based on the work of *Perugino and the young *Raphael. His best-known painting is perhaps the *Rose Miracle of St Francis* (Porziuncola Chapel, S. Maria degli Angeli, Assisi, 1829). The high-minded and didactic tone of his work won it a more sympathetic acceptance (particularly in England) than its artistic quality alone merited. William *Dyce and Ford Madox *Brown were among his supporters and there were affinities between his aspirations and those of the *Pre-Raphaelite Brotherhood.

Ozenfant, Amédée (b Saint-Quentin, 15 Apr. 1886; d Cannes, 4 May 1966). French painter, writer, and teacher. In 1918 he met *Le Corbusier, with whom he founded *Purism, but he is more important as a writer and teacher than as a painter. He lived in London, 1935–9, then in New York, 1939–55, founding art schools in both cities. After returning to France he settled in Cannes, where he directed a studio for foreign art students. His most important book is *Art* (1927), translated as *Foundations of Modern Art* (1931, enlarged edn. 1952). This is a study of the interrelationship of all forms of human creativity, including science and religion, and is one of the most widely read books by any modern artist. However, the great reputation Ozenfant enjoyed in the interwar period declined sharply afterwards. Indeed in 1973 John *Golding wrote that 'Perhaps no other artistic reputation of comparable stature within the contemporary field has undergone, during the past decades, such an almost total eclipse.'

P

Pacheco, Francisco (*bapt.* Sanlúcar de Barrameda, nr. Cadiz, 3 Nov. 1564; *d* Seville, 1644). Spanish painter and writer, active in Seville. He was a highly cultured man, a poet and scholar as well as a painter, and his house was the focus of Seville's artistic life (*Palomino describes it as a meeting place for 'the greatest minds' in the city). As a painter he was undistinguished, working in a stiff academic style (though his portraits are fresher than his religious works). He was an outstanding teacher, however, for (in spite of his own limitations) he was sympathetic to the more naturalistic style that was then developing. Moreover, he was generous enough in spirit to acknowledge openly that his greatest pupil, *Velázquez (who became his son-in-law in 1618), was a much better painter than himself: 'I consider it no disgrace for the pupil to surpass the master.' Alonso *Cano was his other outstanding pupil, and Pacheco often collaborated with the great sculptor *Montañés, painting his wooden figures. In 1649 his book *Arte de la pintura* (Art of Painting) was posthumously published; part theoretical, part biographical, this is a major source of information for the period (it includes accounts of his meeting with El *Greco in Toledo in 1611 and of Velázquez's early career). Pacheco was an official overseer of religious images for the Inquisition and the highly detailed *iconographical prescriptions in his book were often strictly adhered to by contemporary artists; he believed that the main aim of painting was to inspire people 'to adore and love God and to cultivate piety'.

Pacher, Michael (*b* ?*c*.1435; *d* Salzburg, July/Aug. 1498). Austrian painter and sculptor, active mainly at Bruneck in the Tyrol, where he is first documented in 1467 (although there are records of lost works dating back to 1462). He worked mainly for local churches, carrying out the carving as well as the painting of his altarpieces, and much of his work is still *in situ*. His most celebrated work is the *St Wolfgang* altarpiece (1471–81) in the church of St Wolfgang on the Abersee, a huge *polyptych with some astonishingly intricate woodcarving and painted wings. Although Pacher's sculpture is thoroughly late *Gothic in spirit, his painting is strongly influenced by Italian art. He is particularly close to *Mantegna, especially in the way dramatic effects are obtained by using a low viewpoint and setting the figures close to the picture plane. There is no documentary evidence that Pacher visited Italy, but because of its proximity to the Tyrol it seems overwhelmingly likely that he did. Pacher's work had wide influence and before *Dürer he was the most important interpreter of *Renaissance ideas for painting in the German-speaking world. His son **Hans Pacher** was a painter, and Michael sometimes collaborated with a **Friedrich Pacher**, who was perhaps also a relative (although the surname is not uncommon).

Pacherot, Jérôme. See COLOMBE.

Pacioli, Luca. See GOLDEN SECTION.

Paeonius. Greek sculptor from Mende in Thrace, active in the second half of the 5th century BC. The only surviving work certainly by him is a marble statue of winged Nike (Victory) (*c*.420 BC) found at Olympia in 1875 and now in the museum there. An inscription on the pedestal names him as the sculptor and also says he won a competition to make the *acroteria of the temple of Zeus at Olympia. This perhaps misled *Pausanias into saying that he made the sculpture of the east pediment of the temple, for this is appreciably earlier in date and clearly different in style (Pausanias also seems to have erred in his attribution of the west pediment; see ALCAMENES). The Nike—a virtuoso piece of carving in its depiction of clinging, wet drapery and the first representation of a partially nude divinity in *Classical Greek art—is a key work in the sculpture of its period, announcing a new flamboyant or 'rich' style, just as the *Tyrannicides* group (see CRITIUS) marks the beginning of the *Severe style.

Paik, Nam June. See VIDEO ART.

Painters Eleven. A group of Toronto abstract painters active from 1953 to 1960. The most important member was William *Ronald. Apart from being abstract rather than figurative artists, the painters had little in common and for this reason the non-committal name of the group was deliberately chosen. They were united mainly by the desire to promote their work in an environment unfavourable to abstract art and in this achieved considerable success, especially after they were guest exhibitors with *American Abstract Artists in New York in 1956. A group of their works is in the Robert McLaughlin Gallery, Oshawa, Ontario.

Pajou, Augustin (b Paris, 18 Sept. 1730; d Paris, 8 May 1809). French sculptor, a pupil of J.-B. *Lemoyne the Younger. He won the *Prix de Rome in 1748 and was in Italy from 1752 to 1756. After his return to Paris he had a successful and varied career, aided by his industrious and amiable character; Louis XV and his mistress Mme du Barry were among his patrons, but in spite of his royal connections he successfully negotiated the French Revolution. His output included portrait busts, among them several of fellow artists (*Hubert Robert*, 1789, École des Beaux-Arts, Paris), mythological works, notably the seductive *Psyche Abandoned* (completed 1790, Louvre, Paris), and the elegant sculptural decoration of the opera house at Versailles (1768–70), which Sir Michael Levey describes as 'the most attractive monument to his basically thin talents' (*Painting and Sculpture in France: 1700–1789*, 1993). The sculptor *Clodion was his son-in-law.

pala. An Italian term for an altarpiece consisting of a single large painting, as distinct from a *polyptych with many panels.

Palacios, Francisco de. See PEREDA.

Palamedesz., Anthonie (b Delft, c.1601; d Amsterdam, 27 Nov. 1673). Dutch portrait and *genre painter, active mainly in his native Delft. He was a pupil of *Miereveld and Dirk *Hals and his paintings resemble those of his masters—his portraits rather wooden, his 'merry company' groups of soldiers, cavaliers, and their ladies livelier and pleasantly coloured. His younger brother **Palamedes I Palamedesz.** (1607–38) and his son **Palamedes II Palamedesz.** (1633–1705) were both painters.

palette. A flat board, usually rectangular, ovoid, or kidney shaped, on which artists arrange their paints ready for use; early examples sometimes had a handle, rather like a table-tennis bat, but a thumb-hole is now standard. Palettes first appeared c.1400; before then individual containers (sometimes shells) were used for mixing colours. For oil painting, mahogany is traditionally considered the best material for palettes, although other close-grained hardwoods have been used. Materials such as porcelain or ivory have been used by watercolour or *miniature painters and also sometimes by oil painters—*Millais, for example, used a porcelain palette early in his career, when he painted with fastidious detail and wished to avoid muddying his colours.

For many artists, choice of their pigments and the order in which they are arranged on the palette is a very important and personal matter; instructional manuals of the 18th and 19th centuries published much advice on how to 'set' a palette, and *Baudelaire describes *Delacroix placing the pigments on his palette with the fastidious care of a woman arranging a bouquet of flowers. By extension, the term 'palette' thus refers to the range of colours characteristic of an artist; *Caravaggio has a dark or restricted palette, *Monet a bright or rich palette.

palette knife. A thin, flexible, dull-edged blade, set in a handle, used for mixing paint, scraping it off the *palette or canvas, and also as a painting instrument (although more delicate tools—'painting knives', shaped like miniature trowels—are often preferred for this purpose). Palette knives became popular in the 18th century, ordinary knives being used for the purpose before this. Today the blades are invariably made of steel, but other materials, including ivory, have been used in the past. *Courbet is sometimes credited with inventing the specialized painting knife, but *Constable had earlier used a similar implement.

Palma Giovane (Giacomo or Jacopo Palma) (b Venice, c.1548; d Venice, 1628). Venetian painter, great-nephew of *Palma Vecchio. He is said to have been a pupil of *Titian, but this tradition has been doubted (it is probably based on the fact that he completed the *Pietà* that Titian left unfinished at his death). In the late 1560s and early 1570s he worked in central Italy, mainly Rome, but thereafter he spent the rest of his life in Venice, and after the death of *Tintoretto in 1594 he was the leading painter in the city. His style was influenced by several of his great Venetian predecessors—*Veronese as well as Titian and Tintoretto—and by central Italian *Mannerism. He was extremely prolific, fulfilling many commissions from abroad as well as for Venetian churches, and his later work is often mechanical. As well as religious pictures, he painted historical and mythological works, and he also made etchings.

Palma Vecchio (Giacomo or Jacopo Palma) (*b* Serina, nr. Bergamo, *c*.1480; *d* Venice, 30 July 1528). Italian painter, active for all his known career in Venice, where he is first documented in 1510. His original surname was Negreti, but he was using the name Palma by 1513. He is called Palma Vecchio (Old Palma) to distinguish him from *Palma Giovane (Young Palma), his great-nephew. Nothing is known of his training, and there is indeed very little secure knowledge about his life and works, none of his pictures being dated or reliably signed and very few of them being certainly identifiable from early sources. His style is distinctive, however, and in practice the definition of his oeuvre is much less problematic than with many of his contemporaries. He painted a few altarpieces for Venetian churches, but most of his work was done for private clients, his speciality being half-length portrayals of beautiful and voluptuous blonde-haired women, sometimes in religious or mythological guise. In opulence of colour and beauty of handling they show the influence of the early work of *Titian, and the finest, such as the celebrated *La Bella* (*c*.1525, Thyssen Mus., Madrid), are worthy of his name. Palma also painted some *Giorgionesque reclining nudes and some male portraits. His work was influential on painters of the next generation in Venice, notably *Bonifazio Veronese.

Palmer, Erastus Dow (*b* Pompey, nr. Syracuse, NY, 2 Apr. 1817; *d* Albany, NY, 4 Mar. 1904). American sculptor. Self-taught, he rarely left Albany in his native New York State, and he was the most successful American sculptor of his period to work in the USA rather than in Europe. He began with *cameo portraits and had a flourishing business with portrait busts and bas-*reliefs on religious subjects, but his most celebrated work, now as in his own day, is the *White Captive* (1858, Met. Mus., New York). Inspired by *Powers's *Greek Slave*, it shows a naked young girl who has been captured by Red Indians and is sustained by her Christianity—this accompanying storyline undoubtedly contributed to its popularity. The statue is fresher in observation than Powers's *Greek Slave*, for although the marble surfaces are impeccably smooth, the chubby proportions of the figure are unidealized and the strikingly characterized head is a portrait of Palmer's daughter.

From the 1860s he worked increasingly in bronze.

Palmer, Samuel (*b* London, 27 Jan. 1805; *d* Redhill, Surrey, 24 May 1881). English landscape painter and etcher. He was precocious, exhibiting landscape drawings at the *Royal Academy when he was only 14. In 1822 he met John *Linnell, who introduced him to William *Blake in 1824. Palmer had had visionary experiences from childhood and the effect of Blake upon him was to intensify his inherent mystical leanings. In 1826 he moved to Shoreham, near Sevenoaks, Kent, where he was the central figure of the group of artists known as the *Ancients and produced what are now his most famous works—landscapes charged with a sense of pantheistic fecundity and otherworldly beauty. In about 1832 what he called his 'primitive and infantine feeling' for landscape began to fade, and after returning to London in 1835, marrying Linnell's daughter in 1837, and spending a two-year honeymoon in Italy, the break with his visionary manner was complete. His later paintings were in a much more conventional topographical or pastoral mode, highly wrought and often sentimental in feeling. In his etchings, however, something of his early genius remained; at his death he was working on an edition of Virgil's *Eclogues*, translated and illustrated by himself. His early work was virtually forgotten until the 1920s, but it subsequently influenced modern romantic landscape artists such as Paul *Nash and Graham *Sutherland. Palmer was also the favourite subject for the notorious forger Tom Keating (1917–84), whose work was exposed amid great publicity in 1976.

Palomino, Antonio (*bapt.* Bujalance, nr. Córdoba, 1 Dec. 1655; *d* Madrid, 12 Aug. 1726). Spanish painter and writer on art, active mainly in Madrid, where in 1688 Charles II (see HABSBURG) appointed him one of his court painters. He was famous in his day for frescos in churches in Madrid and elsewhere, but he is now best known for his book *El museo pictórico y escala óptica* (The Pictorial Museum and Optical Scale, vol. i, 1715; vols. ii and iii, 1724). The first two volumes are devoted respectively to the theory and the practice of art, and the third volume is a collection of biographies, the most important source for the history of Spanish art from the 16th to the early 18th century. It earned Palomino the nickname 'the Spanish *Vasari'.

Pamphili (or **Pamphilj**). Italian noble family that assumed an important role in art patronage in Rome when **Giambattista Pamphili** (1574–1655) became Pope Innocent X in 1644. Conservative in taste, he tended to reject artists who had been favoured by his predecessor Urban VIII (Maffeo *Barberini); most notably, *Algardi replaced *Bernini as the leading sculptor at the papal court, although Bernini did do some work for Innocent, including the celebrated Four Rivers Fountain in the Piazza Navona. Innocent concentrated much of his patronage on this piazza, in which the family palace stood (it is now the Brazilian embassy). In 1651–5 Pietro da *Cortona decorated the ceiling of the gallery of the palace with scenes from the *Aeneid* (the Pamphili family claimed to be descended from Aeneas); this was Pietro's last major commission as a decorative painter. Innocent's most famous connection with the arts, however, is as the subject of a superlative portrait by *Velázquez. His nephew **Prince Camillo Pamphili** (1622–66) was a significant patron and collector. In 1647 he renounced his cardinalship to marry Olimpia *Aldobrandini, heir to Cardinal Pietro Aldobrandini, and in this way the Aldobrandini palace and art collection passed to the Pamphili family. Camillo's own collecting interests lay mainly in contemporary landscape painting (he owned several choice *Claudes) and in the work of Dutch and Flemish painters active in Rome. In 1760 the male Pamphili line became extinct and the family's possessions passed to Prince Giovanni Andrea Doria, who was descended from a daughter of Camillo. His family palace in Via del Coiso is now called the Palazzo Doria Pamphili. It still houses the family's paintings—the best privately owned collection of Old Masters in Italy. See also PENDANT.

panel. Term in painting for a *support of wood or other rigid material, as distinct from *canvas or other flexible material such as silk. Until the introduction of canvas in the 15th century, nearly all movable paintings in Europe were executed on wood, and it was probably not until the early 17th century that canvas overtook wood in popularity and could be regarded as the standard support for oil painting. When the word 'panel' is used without qualification in art-historical contexts, it therefore almost invariably implies wood, but many other rigid materials have been used as supports. Painters who worked on a small scale often used copper plates, like those of engravers or etchers (*Elsheimer is a leading example), and in the colonial art of South America copper and tin and even lead and zinc were employed. Various stones have also been used as

supports, including marble (see STELLA, JACQUES) and, on a larger scale, slate, notably by *Sebastiano del Piombo in several works and by *Rubens in his altarpiece for S. Maria in Vallicella (the Chiesa Nuova) in Rome; the picture he originally painted, on canvas (*Virgin and Child Adored by St Gregory and Other Saints*, 1607, Mus. B.-A., Grenoble), was said to reflect the light unpleasantly and slate was used for the replacement to produce a more matt finish (1608, *in situ*). In a more experimental vein, *Stubbs painted numerous pictures on earthenware panels, using *enamel paints, hoping that works produced in this way would retain their freshness and resist cracking better than oil paintings. Technically his results were impressive, but the smooth, glossy finish was not to everyone's taste, and the process was too demanding and expensive to attract imitators.

The choice of wood for panels depended mainly on local availability. In Italy, poplar was most commonly used, and oak was preferred in northern Europe. Many other types were used, however; analysis of the contents of art galleries has yielded a long list, including beech, cedar, chestnut, fir, larch, linden, mahogany, olive, and walnut. Today cedar, teak, and dark walnut are favourites. The panel must be well seasoned to remove resin and gum as otherwise it may warp and split. *Cennini advised that small panels should be boiled to prevent splitting, presumably because this removes some of the resin, and modern experts recommend steaming for the same reason. For a large picture several pieces had to be accurately jointed together and glued with *casein, a difficult operation that is described in medieval treatises. Modern painters have also used plywood, fibre-board, and other synthetic materials as supports (see also ACADEMY BOARD).

Painting directly on wood is not satisfactory because the wood absorbs too much of the paint and does not reflect enough light, besides reacting chemically with some of the *pigments. Moreover, some woods darken in course of time. Normally, therefore, after any filling up of holes that was necessary, the panel was *sized and coated with several layers of *gesso, or of chalk, so that it presented a smooth, even *ground. The backs of panels also require protection against woodworm and against damp, which can cause warping and rot.

Panini (or **Pannini**), **Giovanni Paolo** (or **Gianpaolo**) (*b* Piacenza, 17 June 1691; *d* Rome, 21 Oct. 1765). Italian painter. He trained as a *quadraturista and stage designer in Piacenza, then in 1711 settled in Rome, where he became the pre-eminent painter of real and imaginary views of the city. He was the first painter to make a special feature of ruins—an aspect of his work that links him with Hubert *Robert and *Piranesi—and he also did paintings of public festivities and events of historical importance. Panini taught perspective at the French Academy in Rome and his influence was strong with French as well as Italian artists. He was a prolific painter and many galleries have examples of his work.

Panofsky, Erwin (*b* Hanover, 30 Mar. 1892; *d* Princeton, 14 Mar. 1968). German-American art historian, a professor at Hamburg University 1926–33, until dismissed by the Nazis. In 1934 he settled in the USA, where he had been a visiting professor at New York since 1931, and was then visiting professor at Princeton University, 1934–5, and from 1935 professor at the Institute for Advanced Study, Princeton. Kenneth *Clark described him as 'unquestionably the greatest art historian of his time', and he is renowned particularly for his immensely learned contributions to the study of *iconography. His books include *Studies in Iconology* (1939), *Albrecht Dürer* (1943), *Early Netherlandish Painting* (1953), and *Tomb Sculpture* (1964). *Meaning in the Visual Arts* (1955) is a collection of his most important essays and articles representing a cross-section of his work. Panofsky enjoyed teaching and was influential through his work in the classroom and lecture hall as well as through his writings. Many scholars have tried to emulate his way of analysing works of art as part of a broad philosophical, intellectual, and cultural pattern, but few have rivalled his learning or finesse, and some of his followers have been accused of 'over-interpreting' pictures in their desire to uncover 'hidden symbolism'. Panofsky himself warned of this possibility, writing: 'there is admittedly some danger that iconology will behave, not like ethnology as opposed to ethnography, but like astrology as opposed to astrography.'

panorama. 'A picture of a landscape or other scene, either arranged on the inside of a cylindrical surface round the spectator as a centre (a *cyclorama*), or unrolled or unfolded and made to pass before him, so as to show the various parts in succession' (*OED*). In 1787 a patent for such a 360-degree painting was granted to Robert Barker (1739–1806), an Irish-born painter working in Edinburgh, and the type soon became a popular form of entertainment: 'Pan-

orama painting seems all the rage', *Constable wrote in 1803. Panoramas were indeed a kind of forerunner of the popular cinema and tended to be remarkable for sheer spectacle rather than artistic merit. Distinguished artists were sometimes associated with them, however, notably *Girtin, who made a panorama of London, now lost, and *Mesdag, whose panorama of Scheveningen can still be seen in The Hague. More typical is the panorama of the Battle of Gettysburg (1883) at Gettysburg National Military Park by the French painter Paul Philippoteaux (1846–?). In more general parlance, the term 'panorama' is used of any wide, uninterrupted view over a scene, particularly a landscape.

Pan Painter. Greek *red-figure vase painter, active in Athens *c*.480–*c*.450 BC, named after a *krater* with an amusing scene of Pan amorously pursuing a shepherd boy (MFA, Boston). He was one of the best painters of his time, fluent and vigorous in style, and also the most versatile, decorating various types of vase with images that encompass tragedy as well as comedy: 'His range of subjects is unrivalled—all types of genre, myth scenes and figures restated or invented' (John Boardman, *Athenian Red Figure Vases: The Archaic Period*, 1975).

pantograph. An instrument, known since the 17th century, for copying a drawing or design, either same size or on a larger or smaller scale. By a simple system of levers, the outline of the original work traced with a point attached to one arm can be repeated on to another surface by a drawing instrument that is attached to another arm.

Pantoja de la Cruz, Juan (*b* Valladolid, *c*.1553; *d* Madrid, Oct./Nov. 1608). Spanish painter. He was a pupil of *Sánchez Coello and succeeded him as the leading portraitist at the court of Philip II (see HABSBURG) and later Philip III. His style was stiff and stately, well expressing the formality of court life. He also painted religious pictures and still-lifes, although none of the still-lifes are known to survive. His work is well represented in the Prado, Madrid.

Paolozzi, Sir Eduardo (*b* Leith, Edinburgh, 7 Mar. 1924). British sculptor, printmaker, and designer of Italian parentage. He had his first one-man exhibition as a sculptor in 1947 and in the same year he began making *collages using cuttings from American magazines, advertising prospectuses, technological journals, etc. (*I was a Rich Man's Plaything*, 1947, Tate, London).

paper

Paolozzi regarded these collages as 'ready-made metaphors' representing the popular dreams of the masses, and they have been seen as forerunners of *Pop art (he eventually amassed a large collection of pulp literature, art, and artefacts, which he presented to the University of St Andrews). From the 1950s he has worked primarily as an abstract sculptor, often on a large scale. His work of the 1950s was characteristically heavy and bulky, often incorporating industrial components, showing his interest in technology as well as in popular culture. In the 1960s his work became more colourful, including large totem-like figures made up from casts of pieces of machinery and often brightly painted. In the 1970s he made solemn machine-like forms and also boxlike low reliefs, both small and large, in wood or bronze, sometimes made to hang on the wall, compartmented and filled with small carved items. His more recent work has included several large public commissions, for example mosaic decorations for Tottenham Court Road underground station in London (installed 1983–5). Paolozzi has taught at various art schools and universities in Britain, Europe, and the USA. He was knighted in 1989 and has been awarded many other honours. See also INDEPENDENT GROUP.

paper. A material made from the pulp of wood or other fibrous substances, manufactured in thin sheets as a surface for writing, drawing, or printing. Paper was invented in China about 2,000 years ago and was first made in Europe in the 11th century, in Spain. Other European countries followed, and by the end of the 14th century France, southern Germany, Italy, and Switzerland had well-developed paper industries. The first record of a papermill in England dates from 1494. The growing availability of paper (in place of the much more expensive *parchment) was a great stimulus to the development of drawing during the *Renaissance. Until 1800 European paper was made entirely of rags pulped in water, and drawing paper of the best quality is still made by hand in the traditional way. Writing papers, less expensive drawing papers, and some book papers are machine made of a mixture of cotton, hemp, esparto, and wood, with a good deal of china clay added to make them smooth and opaque, *size to make them non-absorbent, and starch to make them stiff. Cheaper papers are machine made wholly of wood. Oriental papers made of bamboo, rice straw, and mulberry bark are imported for artists' use.

papier collé (French: 'pasted paper'). A type of *collage in which pieces of decorative or printed paper are incorporated into a picture or—when stuck on a ground such as canvas—themselves constitute the picture. The technique was invented by *Braque in September 1912 in his *Fruit-Dish and Glass* (priv. coll.) and was almost immediately adopted by *Picasso. *Gris too made extensive use of *papier collé*, and *Matisse's use of cut-out paper shapes in his late work is a development of the technique.

papyrus. A writing material made from the stem of the marsh plant of the same name, growing in antiquity principally in Egypt and now in the Sudan. Its use in Egypt goes back to at least the third millennium BC and it was the standard writing material in ancient Greece and throughout the Roman Empire. From the 4th century AD it was increasingly replaced by *parchment.

paragone (Italian: 'comparison'). A term referring to a long-running debate on the relative merits of painting and sculpture that was a distinctive feature of aesthetic theory in the Italian *Renaissance. The foremost champion of the superiority of painting was *Leonardo, who regarded it as a more intellectual art than sculpture. He wrote that 'the sculptor's work entails greater physical effort and the painter's greater mental effort', and he contrasted the way in which a painter could work in fine clothes whilst listening to music with the sweaty, noisy labour involved in sculpture. Partisans of sculpture praised its grandeur, its permanence, and the fact that it could show a figure in three dimensions, whereas a painting offered only two. According to *Vasari, *Giorgione countered the last argument by painting a picture of a naked man in which he showed 'the front, the back, and the profile on either side'; this he did by depicting a 'limpid pool of water' at his feet, a mirror on one side, and a burnished breastplate on the other, thereby achieving 'more at one single view of a living figure than does sculpture'. (The painting does not survive. Another early source describes a similar Giorgione picture of St George in armour; both accounts perhaps refer in muddled fashion to the same work.)

In 1547 the Florentine scholar Benedetto Varchi (1503–65) delivered a lecture in Florence contributing to the debate, and he asked several leading artists for their thoughts on the matter, among them *Bronzino, *Cellini, *Michelangelo (whose funeral oration Varchi later delivered),

*Pontormo, and Vasari. Their replies were published in Varchi's *Due lezzioni* (Two Lectures) in 1549. Varchi concluded that all the arts are one, since they have the same aim, and in the second edition of his *Lives* (1568) Vasari resolved the question in a similar way, seeing *disegno* as the common foundation of architecture, painting, and sculpture. Thereafter interest in the debate waned, although echoes of it occur long afterwards, for example in *Lessing's *Laokoon* (1766).

parchment. Writing material made from the skins of sheep or calf, less frequently pig, goat, and other animals; it has also been used for painting, and occasionally for printing and bookbinding. *Pliny says that it was invented in the second century BC in Pergamum; hence the name 'parchment' from the Latin *pergamena*, 'of Pergamum'. Skin had been used as a writing material before this, but the refined methods of cleaning and stretching involved in making parchment enabled both sides of a leaf to be used, leading eventually to the supplanting of the manuscript roll by the bound book. Vellum is a fine kind of parchment made from the delicate skins of young (sometimes stillborn) animals. *Paper began to replace parchment from about the 14th century in Europe, but parchment is still used for certain kinds of documents, and the name is often applied to high-quality writing paper.

Pareja, Juan de. See VELÁZQUEZ.

Paris, Matthew (*b* ?c.1200; *d* ?St Albans, ?1259). English chronicler and manuscript illuminator. He became a monk at the monastery of St Albans in 1217 and was appointed monastery chronicler in 1236. In 1248 he was sent to Norway to reform the monastery of St Benet-Holme, but this is his only recorded visit abroad (the surname Paris is found elsewhere in England in the 13th century and does not necessarily imply that he had any French associations). Matthew carried on the abbey's *Chronica majora* from 1235 until 1259, which was presumably the year of his death (it is now divided between Corpus Christi College, Cambridge, and the British Library, London) and also wrote a summary of the chief events between 1200 and 1250 that is known as the *Historia minor* or *Historia Anglorum* (BL). His historical manuscripts are almost unique in being illustrated with numerous marginal scenes and symbols from his own hand. He also composed several lives of the saints (the *Life of St Alban*, Trinity College, Dublin, is autograph) in which the illustrations occupy the upper half of the page and are of equal importance with the text. The frontispiece to his *Historia Anglorum* is his only signed work—a self-portrait showing him on his knees dedicating the manuscript to the Virgin. It is a tinted outline drawing, and because of his fame there has been a mistaken tendency to assign all mid-13th-century English work of this character to St Albans in general and, if at all plausible, to his hand.

Paris, School of. See ÉCOLE DE PARIS.

Park, David. See DIEBENKORN.

Parler, Peter (*b* ?Schwäbisch Gmünd, c.1330; *d* Prague, 13 July 1399). German architect and sculptor, the most famous member of a dynasty of masons active in the 14th century and early 15th century. In the 1350s he settled in Prague, where he was architect to the cathedral (much of the present structure was designed by him). He also built the celebrated Charles Bridge over the River Vltava. As a sculptor he is best known for a series of portrait busts in the triforium of the cathedral, including a portrait of himself and one of the Emperor Charles IV.

Parmigianino (Girolamo Francesco Maria Mazzola) (*b* Parma, 11 Jan. 1503; *d* Casalmaggiore, nr. Parma, 24 Aug. 1540). Italian *Mannerist painter, draughtsman, and printmaker; his nickname (the little Parmesan) comes from his native city, which was also his main place of work. He was precociously gifted, and as early as 1522–3 he painted highly accomplished frescos in two chapels in S. Giovanni Evangelista, Parma; they show his admiration for *Correggio, who was working in the same church at this time. The originality and sophistication he displayed from the beginning, particularly his love of unusual spatial effects, is most memorably seen in his celebrated *Self-Portrait in a Convex Mirror* (1524, KH Mus., Vienna), in which *Vasari said he looks 'so beautiful that he seemed an angel rather than a man'.

In 1524 Parmigianino moved to Rome, possibly via Florence, and his work became both grander and more graceful under the influence of *Raphael and *Michelangelo. The *Vision of St Jerome* (1526–7, NG, London) is his most important work of this time, showing the disturbing emotional intensity he created with his elongated forms, disjointed sense of space, chill lighting, and lascivious atmosphere. Parmigianino left Rome after it was sacked by German troops in 1527 and moved to Bologna. In 1530 he returned to Parma and contracted to paint frescos in S. Maria della Steccata. He failed to complete the work, however, and in 1539 was imprisoned for breach of contract. Vasari says he neglected the work because he was infatuated with alchemy—'he allowed his beard to grow long and disordered . . . he neglected himself and grew melancholy and eccentric'. His later paintings show no falling off in his powers, however, and his work reaches its apotheosis in his celebrated *Madonna of the Long Neck* (c.1535, Uffizi, Florence). The forms of the figures are extraordinarily elongated and tapering and the painting has a refinement and grace that place it among the archetypal works of Mannerism.

Parmigianino's range extended beyond religious works. He painted a highly erotic *Cupid Carving his Bow* (1535, KH Mus., Vienna), and was one of the subtlest portraitists of his age (two superb examples are in the Museo di Capodimonte, Naples). The landscape backgrounds to his religious works have a mysterious and visionary quality that influenced Niccolò dell' *Abate and through him French art (see FONTAINE-BLEAU). Parmigianino, whose draughtsmanship was exquisite, also made designs for engravings and *chiaroscuro woodcuts and seems to have been the first Italian artist to produce original etchings from his own designs.

Parrhasius. Greek painter from Ephesus, active in the later 5th century BC. He is said to have been particularly skilful in the use of contour and in depicting character through facial expression, and his mastery of illusionism is recorded in one of *Pliny's most famous anecdotes. It concerns a contest Parrhasius had with *Zeuxis, who painted some grapes so naturalistically that birds came to peck at them. Victory seeming to be his, he called on Parrhasius to draw back the curtain concealing his picture, but this turned out to be a painted curtain. Zeuxis conceded the contest; he had deceived the birds, but Parrhasius had deceived him.

Parrish, Maxfield (b Philadelphia, 25 July 1870; d Plainfield, NH, 30 Mar. 1966). American painter and illustrator. He studied at the Pennsylvania Academy of the Fine Arts with the author-illustrator Howard Pyle (1853–1911), celebrated for his children's books. In 1895 Parrish designed a cover for *Harper's Weekly* and thereafter rapidly made a name for himself with illustrations, posters, and advertisements. His greatest fame and popularity came with colour prints designed for the mass market. Sentimental scenes such as the *Garden of Allah* (copyrighted 1919) and *Dawn* (1920) sold by the million. They are in a lush and romantic style, set in an escapist world combining elements of the Arabian Nights, Hollywood, and classical antiquity, with languorous maidens and idyllic landscape backgrounds. His draughtsmanship and detailing are immaculate and his colouring distinctively high keyed and luminous. Many of his advertisements were in a similar vein. In the 1930s his style went out of fashion and he retired to paint landscapes, working up to his death at the age of 95. Shortly before this there was a revival of interest in his work, which had long been dismissed as kitsch; in 1964, for example, the Metropolitan Museum, New York, bought his painting *Errant Pan* (c.1915).

Parsons, Betty (b New York, 31 Jan. 1900; d New York, 23 Aug. 1982). American art dealer, collector, painter, and sculptor. After Peggy *Guggenheim closed her New York gallery in 1946, Parsons became for a few years the leading dealer of the *Abstract Expressionists, until several of the major figures left her for Sidney *Janis in the early 1950s. She continued to support avant-garde art, and by the time her New York gallery closed in 1977 she had represented many of the most famous names in American art over the previous three decades, especially *Colour Field and *Minimal painters. Her own work as an artist was predominantly abstract.

Parthenon sculptures. See ELGIN MARBLES and PHIDIAS.

Pascin, Jules (Julius Pincas) (b Vidin, 31 Mar. 1885; d Paris, 2 June 1930). Bulgarian-born painter and draughtsman (his father was Spanish and his mother Italian). He led a wandering life, and although he acquired American citizenship when he moved to New York during the First World War, he is chiefly associated with Paris, where he belonged to the circle of émigré artists who gravitated around *Chagall, *Modigliani, and *Soutine. His work includes portraits of his friends, café scenes, and flower pieces, as well as a few large paintings with biblical themes, but the bulk of his output consists of erotically charged studies of nude (or very flimsily dressed) teenage girls. They have been compared to the work of *Degas and *Toulouse-Lautrec, but Pascin's paintings are less penetrating and more obviously posed. He can be rather repetitive, but his best work has great delicacy of colour and handling and a poignant sense of lost innocence. Pascin's work brought him financial success, but he led a dissolute life and was emotionally unstable; on the day on which a major exhibition of his work was due to open at the Galerie Georges Petit in Paris he committed suicide in his studio (slashing his wrists and then hanging himself).

Pasiteles. Greek sculptor and writer, active in Rome in the 1st century BC (he became a Roman citizen in about 89 BC). He was one of the most famous artists of his time, working in various materials, and he exemplifies the shift in Greek art towards production for Roman tastes. Apart from a signed statue base (Mus. Romano, Verona), none of his work survives, but a marble figure of an athlete signed by Stephanus, his best pupil, is in the Villa Torlonia (formerly Villa Albani), Rome. *Pliny, one of the few sources of information on Pasiteles, says that he wrote a five-volume treatise entitled *Noble* [or *Marvellous*] *Works of Art throughout the World*.

Pasmore, Victor (*b* Chelsham, Surrey, 3 Dec. 1908; *d* Malta, 23 Jan. 1998). British painter and maker of constructions who is unusual in having achieved eminence as both a figurative and an abstract artist. After early experiments with abstraction he reverted to naturalistic painting, and in 1937 he joined with William *Coldstream and Claude *Rogers in forming the *Euston Road School. Characteristic of his work at this time and in the early 1940s are some splendid female nudes and lyrically sensitive Thames-side landscapes that have been likened to those of *Whistler (*Chiswick Reach*, 1943, NG, Ottawa). In the late 1940s he underwent a dramatic conversion to pure abstract art, and by the early 1950s he had developed a personal style of geometrical abstraction. As well as paintings he made abstract *reliefs, partly under the influence of Ben *Nicholson and partly under that of Charles *Biederman's book *Art as the Evolution of Visual Knowledge*, lent to him in 1951 by Ceri *Richards. Pasmore's earlier reliefs had a handmade quality but later, through the introduction of transparent perspex, he gave them the impersonal precision and finish of machine products. Through work in this vein he came to be regarded as one of the leaders of *Constructivism in Britain. Later paintings are less austere and more organic.

Pasmore was an influential teacher, notably at King's College, Newcastle upon Tyne (now Newcastle University), where he was head of the painting department, 1954–61. The 'basic design' course he taught there (based on *Bauhaus ideas) spread to many British art schools. He was also much concerned with bringing abstract art to the general public. In 1955, for example, he was appointed consulting

director of architectural design for Peterlee New Town, County Durham, and designed an urban centre in the form of a Pavilion that integrated architectural design with abstract relief painting. In his later career Pasmore was also a prolific printmaker. He won many honours and Kenneth *Clark described him as 'one of the two or three most talented English painters of this century'.

Passarotti, Bartolommeo (*bapt.* Bologna, 28 June 1529; *d* Bologna, 3 June 1592). Italian painter. After spending much of his early career in Rome (*c*.1551–*c*.1565) he settled in his native Bologna, where he had a large studio that became the focal point of the city's artistic life. The religious paintings that were the basis of his success are fairly conventional, and he is now remembered mainly for his pioneering *genre scenes of butchers' shops (one of the few surviving examples is in the Galleria Nazionale, Rome). They reflect the influence of northern painters such as *Aertsen and in their lively observation marked a break with the prevailing *Mannerism. Annibale *Carracci (whose brother Agostino studied with Passarotti) was influenced by these genre scenes in his early career, although Annibale's approach was more serious. In addition to his religious and genre works, Passarotti painted excellent portraits throughout his career. His son **Tiburzio** (d. *c*.1612) imitated his style, and he in turn had two artist sons, **Gaspare** and **Archangelo**.

Passe, van de. Family of Dutch artists, mainly engravers, whose members worked in various parts of northern Europe. The founder was **Crispijn** (1564–1637), who began his career in Antwerp, then worked in Cologne and Utrecht. He was prolific and his work is wide-ranging in subject. Two of his children, **Simon** (?1595–1647) and **Willem** (*c*.1598–*c*.1636), worked in England, mainly as portrait engravers. Another son, **Crispijn the Younger** (*c*.1597–1670), and a daughter, **Magdalena** (?1596–1638), were also engravers.

Passeri, Giovanni Battista (*b* Rome, *c*.1610/15; *d* Rome, 22 Apr. 1679). Italian painter and writer on art. He is of no significance as a painter, but he is important for his collection of biographies of contemporary artists, *Vite de' pittori, scultori ed architetti che anno lavorato in Roma morti dal 1641 fino al 1673*, not published until 1772, almost a century after his death. Passeri's accounts are detailed and on the whole accurate, forming one of the most important sources for the study of Roman *Baroque art. His nephew **Giuseppe Passeri** (1654–1714) was a painter and draughtsman, a favourite pupil of *Maratta.

pastel. A drawing or painting material consisting essentially of a stick of colour made from powdered *pigments mixed with just enough *resin or *gum to bind them (in addition there is usually a mineral filler to give support to the stick); the term is also applied to a work produced with this medium. Pastel is applied directly to paper, with no diluent, and a significant difference between this and other methods of painting is that the colour as applied represents the final result—no allowance has to be made for changes during drying. It can produce very rich and subtle effects, but it has the disadvantage of being extremely fragile and easily dislodged from the paper. This can be counteracted by using a *fixative, but fixing is apt to reduce the brilliance of the colour. As they are so delicate, pastels are generally used on a small scale, and they have always been especially popular for portraits.

Pastels originated at the end of the 15th century as a development from the use of *chalk for drawing: *Leonardo's famous profile drawing of Isabella d'*Este (1500, Louvre, Paris) is in black and red chalk with touches of pastel (see also PERRÉAL). At first colours were generally limited to black, white, and red or flesh-colour, but a full range of colours had been developed by the early 18th century. The first notable artist to devote herself almost exclusively to the medium was the Venetian Rosalba *Carriera, who was internationally successful and helped inspire the great vogue for pastel portraiture in 18th-century France (*Chardin, Maurice-Quentin de *La Tour, and *Perronneau being famous exponents). During the first half of the 19th century the medium declined in popularity, but there was a great revival of interest in the second half of the century, especially among the French *Impressionists, who found it well suited to their characteristic freshness of observation and speed of work. *Cassatt, *Manet, *Redon, *Renoir, *Toulouse-Lautrec, and *Whistler were all notable exponents, but the supreme master of pastel at this time was undoubtedly *Degas, who used the medium with a power, freedom, and inventiveness that none of his contemporaries matched. He described himself as a 'colourist with line', underlining the fact that pastel lies on the borderline between drawing and painting.

pastel manner. See CRAYON MANNER.

Pasternak, Leonid (b Odessa, 23 Mar. [4 Apr.] 1862; d Oxford, 31 May 1945). Russian painter and draughtsman. He was a friend of many literary, musical, and political personalities, notably Leo Tolstoy, whose works he illustrated (War and Peace; Resurrection), and whom he portrayed on many occasions. In 1921 he left the Soviet Union and settled in Berlin, where he worked mainly as a portraitist (his sitters included Max *Liebermann and Albert Einstein). He left Germany because of the rise of Nazism and settled in England in 1938, spending his last years in Oxford. The celebrated writer Boris Pasternak was his son.

pastiche (or **pasticcio**). A work of art that imitates the style of another work, artist, or period; more specifically, in the visual arts, a picture or other work that (often with fraudulent intent) imitates the style of a particular artist by borrowing and rearranging motifs from his authentic works.

Patch, Thomas (bapt. Exeter, 31 Mar. 1725; d Florence, 30 Apr. 1782). English painter and engraver who lived in Italy from 1747. In Rome he first made a reputation as a view painter, especially among English tourists, but after settling in Florence in 1755 he was best known for good-humoured caricature *conversation pieces and it is for these that he is chiefly remembered today. Patch knew *Reynolds, who included a portrait of him in his own caricature of *Raphael's School of Athens (1751, NG, Dublin), and it is uncertain who influenced whom in the genre.

Patel, Pierre (b ?Picardy, ?c.1605; d Paris, 5 Aug. 1676). French landscape painter, active in Paris. He was a pupil of *Vouet but worked in the manner of *Claude, with whose paintings his own have sometimes been confused (although Patel's style is harder). Much of his work was done in the form of panels set into the decoration of rooms; two examples (c.1647) from the Cabinet de l'Amour of the Hôtel Lambert, Paris, are in the Louvre. His son **Pierre-Antoine** (b Paris, 22 Nov. 1648; d Paris, 15 Mar. 1707) painted in the same vein as his father. Both men often featured classical ruins in their paintings, looking forward to the *Picturesque.

Patenier, Joachim. See PATINIR.

Pater, Jean-Baptiste (b Valenciennes, 29 Dec. 1695; d Paris, 25 July 1736). French painter, the only pupil of *Watteau (a fellow native of Valenciennes), with whom he had a somewhat touchy relationship. An unlikely legend has it that Watteau dismissed him from his studio (c.1713) because he thought he was a threat to his own pre-eminence; whatever the reason for their differences, they were reconciled soon before Watteau's death. Like Watteau's other chief imitator, *Lancret, Pater repeated the master's type of *fêtes galantes* (see FÊTE CHAMPÊTRE) in a fairly stereotyped fashion. He showed more originality in scenes of military life and groups of bathers (in which he gave freer rein to the suggestiveness often seen in his *fêtes galantes*). Examples of all types of his work are in the Wallace Collection, London.

Pater, Walter (b London, 4 Aug. 1839; d Oxford, 30 July 1894). English critic and essayist. A bachelor don at Brasenose College, Oxford, he lived uneventfully with his two spinster sisters and was the unlikely standard-bearer for *Aestheticism, which set a supreme value upon the enjoyment of beauty. His best-known book is *Studies in the History of the Renaissance* (1873), which includes essays on *Winckelmann, the then neglected *Botticelli, and *Leonardo, with his celebrated evocation of the *Mona Lisa*: 'She is older than the rocks among which she sits . . . ' This volume (which concludes 'To burn always with this hard gem-like flame, to maintain this ecstasy, is success in life'), though attacked by some as unscholarly and morbid, had a profound influence on the undergraduates of the day and was acclaimed by Oscar Wilde as 'the holy writ of beauty'.

patina. Incrustation, usually green, on the surface of a metal (typically bronze) object, caused by corrosion. Such discoloration occurs naturally with age through exposure to the atmosphere and can be accelerated or modified when an object is buried in the sea or soil, where various substances present will cause chemical reactions. Patination can produce an attractive, mellowing effect, and since the *Renaissance bronze statues have often been artificially patinated, usually by treatment with acid. By extension, the term 'patina' can be applied to any form of surface discoloration or mellowing, for example dirty varnish on a painting.

Patinir, Herri de. See BLES.

Patinir (or Patenier or Patinier), **Joachim** (b ?Dinant or Bouvignes, c.1480; d Antwerp, 1524). Netherlandish painter, a pioneer of landscape as an independent genre. Although his paintings nominally represent religious or mythological subjects, the figures are often dwarfed by the natural world and he has been described as the first landscape specialist in European art, or, in Kenneth *Clark's words, 'the first painter to make his landscapes more important than his figures'. Nothing is known of his early life, but he probably came from Dinant or its neighbourhood, in the craggy gorge of the River Meuse; his native scenery—so different from the flat countryside of most of the Netherlands—no doubt helped to inspire the rocky backgrounds that feature in his paintings. In 1515 he was enrolled in the painters' guild in Antwerp, and when *Dürer visited the city in 1521 he became friendly with Patinir and described him as a 'good landscape painter' (perhaps the first occurrence of this term). There are only a very few signed paintings, for example the *Baptism of Christ* (KH Mus., Vienna), but many others have been attributed to him or his busy workshop. He also painted landscape backgrounds for other artists, including his friend Quentin *Massys (who after Patinir's death became guardian of his children); the most securely authenticated instance of such collaboration is the *Temptation of St Anthony* (Prado, Madrid), which in a 1574 inventory of the *Escorial is described as having 'the figures by Master Quentin and the landscape by Master Joachim'. Patinir's work combines naturalistic observation of detail with a wonderful sense of fantasy, forming a link between *Bosch and *Bruegel.

Paton, Sir Joseph Noel (b Dunfermline, 13 Dec. 1821; d Edinburgh, 26 Dec. 1901). Scottish painter. A friend of *Millais (a fellow student at the *Royal Academy), he had a kinship with the *Pre-Raphaelites early in his career. He painted mythological and historical scenes and later gained great success with his rather portentous and sentimental religious pictures, which went on tour and were much reproduced. His brother **Waller Hugh Paton** (1828–95) was also a painter, mainly of landscapes in watercolour.

Paul III, Pope. See FARNESE.

Paul V, Pope. See BORGHESE GALLERY.

Pausanias (2nd century AD). Greek traveller and geographer, the author of a *Description of Greece* in ten books that is the single most important literary source for the history of Greek art (painting and sculpture as well as architecture). It is a guidebook written for tourists—simple, unpretentious, detailed, and in the main reliable, as is frequently attested by the remains of the monuments he describes. Occasionally he has lapses; he saw several statues said to be the work of the legendary Daedalus and accepted that he really existed. Sir James Frazer, who produced one of the several English translations of the work (6 vols., 1898), said of Pausanias: 'without him the ruins of Greece would for the most part be a labyrinth without a clue, a riddle without an answer.'

Pausias of Sicyon. Greek painter of the mid-4th century BC. He was renowned for his small pictures of boys and of flowers, and he was said to be the first painter who fully mastered the *encaustic technique. According to *Pliny he was also the first to paint ceiling coffers, but this is considered unlikely.

Peake, Mervyn (b Kuling, 9 July 1911; d Burcot, Oxfordshire, 17 Nov. 1968). British writer and illustrator, born in China, the son of medical missionaries. He is now best known as a novelist, but he studied at the *Royal Academy Schools and spent much of his career teaching drawing in London art schools. His reputation rests mainly on his trilogy of novels *Titus Groan* (1946), *Gormenghast* (1950), and *Titus Alone* (1959), a work of grotesque Gothic fantasy to which his vividly imaginative drawing style was well matched (originally, however, the books were published without his accompanying illustrations). Peake illustrated numerous other books, including Stevenson's *Treasure Island* (1949) and several by himself (among them an instructional manual, *The Craft of the Lead Pencil*, 1946). In 1946 he was commissioned by the Ministry of Information to make drawings of people liberated from Belsen concentration camp—an experience that left him emotionally scarred. In the last decade of his life he was gradually incapacitated by Parkinsons' disease. Peake is described in the *Dictionary of National Biography* as 'Tall, thin, dark, and haggard . . . gentle, gracious, unworldly, and unpractical. He lived in many ways outside convention, wearing strange clothes and behaving in a gently whimsical fashion which puzzled the ordinary.'

Peale, Charles Willson (b Queen Annes County, Md., 15 Apr. 1741; d Philadelphia, 22 Feb. 1827). American painter, inventor, naturalist, and patriot, the founder and most distinguished member of a family of artists. Peale was a highly versatile craftsman, and early in his career he worked as a saddler, watchmaker, silversmith, and upholsterer, as well as a sign painter. He received advice and encouragement from *Copley and spent two years in London (1767–9), where he studied under *West. In 1776

he settled in Philadelphia, where he became the most fashionable portraitist in the Colonies, Copley having left for England in 1774. He fought as a colonel of the militia in the War of Independence and became a Democratic member of the Pennsylvania Assembly. In 1782 he built an exhibition gallery next to his studio, the first art gallery in the United States, and there displayed his own portraits of leading personalities of the Revolutionary War (he painted George Washington several times). This expanded into a natural history museum, which attained a vast size and included as its star exhibit the first mastodon skeleton to be exhumed in America. Two of his most famous paintings celebrate his scientific interests—*The Exhumation of the Mastodon* (1806) in the Peale Museum, Baltimore, and *The Artist in his Museum* (1822) in the *Pennsylvania Academy of the Fine Arts, an institution he helped to found in 1805. His inventions included new types of spectacles and false teeth. As a painter, Peale generally worked in a solid, dignified style, but his most celebrated work is a witty piece of *trompe-l'œil. This is *The Staircase Group* (1795, Philadelphia Mus. of Art), a life-size portrait of two of his sons mounting a staircase, with a real step at the bottom and a real door jamb as a frame; George Washington is said to have been deceived into doffing his hat to the boys' images.

Peale married three times and had seventeen children, of whom several became artists. They included **Raphaelle** (1774–1825), one of America's most distinguished still-life painters, **Rembrandt** (1778–1860), a gifted though uneven portraitist, and **Titian Ramsay II** (1799–1885), who continued his father's tradition as an artist-naturalist. Apart from his portraits, Rembrandt won fame with *The Court of Death* (1821, Detroit Inst. of Arts), a huge, melodramatic allegory that toured the country with success for over half a century. Charles Willson's brother **James** (1749–1831) was also a painter and his son and four daughters carried on the family tradition. The Peales were largely responsible for establishing Philadelphia as one of the country's leading cultural centres.

Pearce, Edward. See PIERCE.

Pearlstein, Philip (b Pittsburgh, 24 May 1924). American painter, a leading proponent of the return to naturalism and interest in the human figure that was one aspect of the move away from the dominance of *Abstract Expressionism. His early works (mainly landscapes) were painted with vigorous *gestural handling, but in the 1960s he developed a cooler, more even type of brushwork. He specializes in starkly unidealized portrayals of the nude figure (singly or in pairs), usually set in domestic surroundings. Because of the clarity of his compositions and the relentlessness of his scrutiny, he is sometimes described as a *Superrealist, but his work has an individuality that puts him outside this classification. He uses harsh lighting, oblique angles, and cropping of the image (heads are often excluded and the body is seen in voyeuristic close-up) in a way that suggests candid photography, but his pictures do not try to counterfeit the effect of photographs; the handling of paint is smooth—but vigorous rather than finicky.

Pechstein, Max (b Eckersbach, nr. Zwickau, 31 Dec. 1881; d West Berlin, 19 June 1955). German *Expressionist painter and printmaker. He studied in Dresden and in 1906 became a member of the *Brücke. In 1908 he settled in Berlin; his energy and charm quickly made him a leading figure in the city's artistic life and in 1910 he was elected president of the Neue *Sezession. In 1913–14, showing an interest in the exotic shared with other Expressionists, Pechstein visited the Palau Islands in the Pacific and he painted bright and lively anecdotal pictures depicting the paradisal life of the island fishermen in a near-*Fauvist manner. His other subjects included nudes, landscapes, portraits, and opulent flower pieces. He was the most French in spirit of the German Expressionists (he was particularly influenced by *Matisse) and probably because his work was decorative rather than emotionally intense, he was the first of the Brücke to achieve success and general recognition; the 1920s marked the height of the fashion for his work. Since then his reputation has faded whilst those of his former colleagues have grown. In 1918 he was one of the founders of the *Novembergruppe and he taught in the Berlin Academy from 1923, being dismissed in 1933 by the Nazis and reinstated in 1945. His later work became repetitive and the high quality of his work during his Brücke period is sometimes forgotten.

peep-show box. An enclosed cabinet with scenes painted on the interior surfaces in such a way that when viewed through a small opening or eyepiece they give a strong illusion of three-dimensional reality. *Alberti may have been the inventor of the peep-show box, for some such device is ascribed to him in a contemporary, anonymous biography, but they had their greatest popularity in 17th-century Holland. Six examples survive from this time, three of them by Samuel van *Hoogstraten (the best, c.1655–60, is in the National Gallery, London).

Peeters, Bonaventura, the Elder (bapt. Antwerp, 23 July 1614; d Hoboken, 25 July 1652). Flemish marine painter. He was virtually the only noteworthy practitioner in the genre in his country, seascapes being much more a Dutch than a Flemish speciality. He is best known for his depictions of storms and shipwrecks, but he also produced various other types of marine pictures, including imaginary Mediterranean port scenes. Several other members of the family were artists, including his sister **Catharina** (1615–76), a seascape and still-life painter, but **Clara Peeters** (?1594–?1657), an outstanding (albeit obscure) Antwerp still-life painter, was evidently no relation.

peintre-graveur. A French term for an artist who makes original prints from his own designs, as opposed to reproductive prints of another artist's work.

Péladan, Joséphin. See SALON DE LA ROSE + CROIX.

Pelham, Peter. See COPLEY.

Pellegrini, Giovanni Antonio (b Venice, 29 Apr. 1675; d Venice, 5 Nov. 1741). Venetian painter, the brother-in-law of Rosalba *Carriera. Pellegrini played a major part in the spread of the Venetian manner of large-scale decorative painting in northern Europe, working in Austria, England, France, Germany, and the Netherlands. He was in England from 1708 to 1713 (and briefly in 1719). He and Marco *Ricci were the first Venetian artists known to work there; they arrived together, accompanying Charles Montagu (later the 1st Duke of Manchester), the British ambassador to Venice. Pellegrini's work in England included murals at Montagu's country seat, Kimbolton Castle, Cambridgeshire, and the dome paintings (destroyed by fire in 1940) at Castle Howard, Yorkshire. His airy, *illusionistic compositions, with their bright flickering colour and purely decorative intention, set a new standard of *Rococo elegance for English decoration, but by European standards most of his output is routine. *Thornhill defeated him in competition for the commission to decorate the dome of St Paul's Cathedral, London.

pen. Writing and drawing instrument used with ink or a similar coloured fluid. From Early Christian times until the 19th century the standard form of pen in Europe was the quill, made from bird feathers, and most of the pen drawings of the Old Masters were done with such instruments. Goose, swan, and turkey quills have commonly been used for writing and crow quills provide a very fine point for drawing. The reed pen, made from stems of bamboo-like grasses, was already in use in classical antiquity and is probably older than the quill. The point is much coarser, producing a bold, thick line, sometimes slightly blurred at the edges. For drawing it has been used much less than the quill, though *Rembrandt, for example, was a master of the broad energetic technique appropriate to it. The metal pen dates back at least to Roman times, but steel nibs of the modern type were not made until late in the 18th century and began to replace the quill only after machine methods of producing them were developed in the 1820s. More recent developments include the fountain pen (the first efficient model was patented by the American inventor L. E. Waterman in 1884), the ballpoint (the first satisfactory model was developed in the 1930s by Laszló Biró, a Hungarian inventor living in Argentina), and the fibre-tip pen (first produced in Japan in the 1970s).

No other drawing tool can produce such a variety of texture as the pen or reveal so intimately the personal 'handwriting' of an artist. It is the ideal medium for rapidly noting down the first idea and has been used in this way by draughtsmen as different as *Pisanello, *Michelangelo, *Dürer, and Rembrandt. However, it has also been used with great effect in a careful, calligraphic manner, as in *Botticelli's illustrations to Dante's *Divine Comedy*. Often pen drawing is combined with *washes of ink.

pencil. Writing or drawing instrument consisting of a slender rod of *graphite or similar substance encased in a cylinder of wood (or less usually metal or plastic). Although the material is graphite, the term 'lead' pencil came into use because it superseded the lead point (see METALPOINT). The first known reference to a wooden pencil dates from the 1560s, but instruments of predetermined hardness or softness were not produced until the 1790s, when Nicolas-Jacques *Conté undertook to solve the problem of making pencils when France—at war with England—was cut off from the English supply of graphite (the mines in Borrowdale, Cumbria, which had opened in 1664, being the main source). Conté found that the graphite could be eked out with clay and fired in a kiln,

and that more clay meant a harder pencil. He obtained a patent for his process in 1795. It was only then that the pencil became the universal drawing instrument that it is today. *Ingres, who often used pencil with great delicacy in his portrait drawings, was one of the first to show its potential. Although the *Oxford English Dictionary* records the usage of the phrase 'a pencil of black lead' as early as 1612, until the end of the 18th century the word 'pencil' more commonly meant a brush (particularly a small brush). 'Pencilling' could mean 'colouring' or 'brushwork' as well as 'drawing'. According to a handbook published in 1859 (*Painting Popularly Explained* by Thomas J. Gullick and John Timbs) 'The smaller kinds of brushes are still sometimes termed "pencils"; but the use of the word "pencil" instead of "brush" as distinctive of and peculiar to water-colour is now obsolete.'

Pencz, Georg (Jörg Bencz) (*b* c.1500; *d* Leipzig, 10/15 Oct. 1550). German painter and engraver of religious and mythological subjects and portraits. He is first documented in 1523 in Nuremberg, where he is presumed to have studied with *Dürer, who strongly influenced him. In 1525 he was expelled from Nuremberg with the *Beham brothers, two other 'godless artists', for their radical Protestant views, but the sentence was soon revoked and he returned to the city. On stylistic evidence he is thought to have visited Italy in the late 1520s and again c.1540. The sharp outlines and glossy textures of his portraits show, in particular, a kinship with *Bronzino (*Man Holding a Mirror*, 1544, Hessisches Landesmuseum, Darmstadt). In 1550 he was appointed painter to Duke Albrecht of Prussia, but he died on the way to take up the post.

pendant. A painting created by an artist to be displayed as one of a pair. Pendants are usually exactly the same size as each other and closely related in theme; portraits of husband and wife were often produced as pendants, for example. Several of *Claude's landscapes were painted as pairs, sometimes related by composition or mood rather than by subject. Examples are *Landscape with the Marriage of Isaac and Rebecca* ('*The Mill*') and *Seaport with the Embarkation of the Queen of Sheba* (both 1648, NG, London). They were commissioned by Cardinal Camillo *Pamphili, Claude's leading patron of the mid-1640s. However, before the pictures were finished, Pamphili relinquished his cardinalship so he could marry, causing Pope Innocent X (his uncle) to exile him temporarily from Rome. This evidently led the commission to fall through and the paintings were bought instead by the Duc de Bouillon, a French general serving in the papal army. Pamphili then seems to have commissioned a second version of 'The Mill', together with a new companion, a *View of Delphi*, both now in the Doria Pamphili Gallery in Rome. Unlike these Claudes, many pendants have become separated over the course of time and now hang in different locations.

pendentive. One of the curved, slightly concave, triangular surfaces (usually four in number) that form the transition between the base or drum of a circular or elliptical dome and its supporting walls, piers, or columns; by this means, a circular or elliptical dome can rise over a square or polygonal space. Pendentives are often used as a field for painted (and sometimes sculpted) decoration, especially in *Baroque churches (see DOMENICHINO, for example).

Penni, Giovanni Francesco (*b* Florence, *c*.1496; *d* Naples, ?*c*.1536). Italian painter, active mainly in Rome, where he and *Giulio Romano were *Raphael's main assistants (he was nicknamed Il Fattore, which might be translated as 'right-hand man'). Various parts of works by the master have been attributed to him (*Vasari says he was employed on the tapestry *cartoons for the Sistine Chapel), but he is a shadowy figure. After Raphael's death he collaborated with Giulio. A rare signed work by Penni is the *Portrait of a Young Man* (NG, Dublin). His brother **Luca Penni** (*c*.1500–1557) was a painter and designer. He settled in France in about 1530 and worked at Fontainebleau.

Pennsylvania Academy of the Fine Arts, Philadelphia. The oldest surviving art institution in the USA, founded in 1805 to encourage local interest in art. Charles Willson *Peale was among the founders, but initially it was run by businessmen rather than artists. Teaching was for many years very sporadic, but when the present building opened in 1876 it was fully equipped with classrooms. Designed by the Philadelphia architect Frank Furness, it is in a powerful and very personal *Gothic style. Thomas *Eakins, who began work there in the year the building opened, is the most distinguished artist who has taught at the Academy. It owns an impressive collection of work by American artists.

Penny, Edward. See WEST.

Penrose, Sir Roland (*b* London, 14 Oct. 1900; *d* Chiddingly, Sussex, 23 Apr. 1984). British writer, exhibition organizer, and artist. As an artist he holds a distinguished place among British *Surrealists (he produced collages and 'objects' as well as paintings), but he is remembered mainly for the missionary zeal with which he promoted Surrealism and contemporary art in general in England. He was one of the organizers of the 1936 International Surrealist Exhibition in London, and he was closely involved with many leading artists, including *Ernst, *Miró, and above all *Picasso, who became a lifelong friend. During the Second World War he was a camouflage instructor. In 1947 he was co-founder (with Herbert *Read) of the *Institute of Contemporary Arts, of which he was first chairman. His books include *Picasso: His Life and Work* (1958, 3rd edn. 1981), regarded as a standard work on the artist. Penrose's second wife, whom he married in 1947, was the American photographer Lee Miller (1907–77), who had formerly been the pupil, lover, and favourite model of *Man Ray.

pentimento. Term (Italian: 'repentance') describing a part of a picture that has been overpainted by the artist but which has become visible again (often as a ghostly outline) because the superimposed layer of pigment has become semi-transparent with age. The presence of pentimenti is often used as an argument in matters of attribution, as it is felt that such evidence of an artist's second thoughts is much more likely to occur in an original painting than in a copy.

Peploe, S. J. See SCOTTISH COLOURISTS.

Perceval, John. See ANGRY PENGUINS.

Pereda, Antonio de (*bapt*. Valladolid, 20 Mar. 1611; *d* Madrid, 30 Jan. 1678). Spanish painter, active mainly in Madrid. He began as a history painter—his *Relief of Genoa* (1634–5, Prado, Madrid) was painted for Philip IV's (see HABSBURG) Buen Retiro Palace in Madrid as part of the same series as *Velázquez's *Surrender of Breda*— but he is now best known for his still-lifes. The most famous painting associated with him is *The Knight's Dream* (also called *The Dream of Life* or *Life is a Dream*, *c*.1650, Academy, Madrid), a splendidly sensuous composition, full of brilliantly painted still-life details, in which worldly pleasures and treasures are seen to be as insubstantial as a dream. It was a key work in the development of the moralizing still-life in Spain, influencing *Valdés Leal in particular. However, the attribution to Pereda has recently been questioned, and Francisco de Palacios (1622/5–52) has been suggested as the author.

Peredvizhniki. See WANDERERS.

Pereira, Manuel (*b* Oporto, 1588; *d* Madrid, 29 Jan. 1683). Portuguese sculptor, active chiefly in Spain; he is first recorded there in 1624 and spent the rest of his life working in and around Madrid. Pereira was one of the outstanding masters of the *polychrome statue in the generation after Gregorio *Fernández and Juan Martínez *Montañés. He worked not only in wood, but also in stone, as in the statue of St Bruno (*c*.1635–40, Academy, Madrid). The grand austerity and spiritual conviction he shows here brings to mind the paintings of *Zurbarán. Pereira 'became very wealthy, was favoured by fortune, and was esteemed by all' (*Palomino).

Pérelle, Gabriel (*bapt.* Vernon-sur-Seine, 7 Mar. 1604; *d* Paris, 6 Mar. 1677). French draughtsman and engraver, mainly of topographical views and landscapes. His engravings of buildings are of great use to the architectural historian. He was assisted by his sons **Adam** (1640–95) and **Nicholas** (1631–*c*.1695).

Performance art. An art form combining elements of theatre, music, and the visual arts. It is related to the *happening (the two terms are sometimes used synonymously), but Performance art is usually more carefully programmed and generally does not involve audience participation. The tradition of Performance art can be traced back to the *Futurists, *Dadaists, and *Surrealists, who often staged humorous or provocative events to promote their work or ideas, then through such activities as Georges *Mathieu painting in front of an audience in the 1950s and Yves *Klein directing nude models smeared with paint in the early 1960s. However, it was only in the later 1960s and particularly in the 1970s that Performance art became recognized as a category of art in itself. 'At that time', RoseLee Goldberg writes, 'Conceptual art was in its heyday and performance was often a demonstration, or an execution, of [its] ideas . . . Art spaces devoted to performance sprang up in the major international art centres, museums sponsored festivals, art colleges introduced performance courses, and specialist magazines appeared' (*Performance Art: From Futurism to the Present*, 1988).

The form and tone of Performances have varied enormously. Some practitioners have cultivated sado-masochism and scatology, for example the *Vienna Actionists (the abuse of the performer's body is something that often occurs also in *Body art, with which Performance art sometimes overlaps). In Britain, however, the field has more often been characterized by whimsicality (in the 1970s there was a fad for Performance groups with quaint names and for wacky newsworthy stunts). Performance art has also been used as an adjunct to rock music (the American Laurie Anderson (1947–) is the most noted exponent) and as a vehicle for political dissent, as well as for the exploration of private fantasies. Among the artists in whose work it has played a large role are Joseph *Beuys and *Gilbert & George.

Pergamene School. A trend in *Hellenistic sculpture, associated with the city of Pergamum in Asia Minor, whose great period coincided with the Attalid dynasty (241–133 BC). Works of the Pergamene School are characterized by an exaggeration of the general tendency of Hellenistic sculpture towards emotional display and virtuoso naturalistic detail. They include a series of *Dying Gauls* (the most famous is in the Capitoline Museum, Rome) that have been identified as copies of statues dedicated by Attalus I to celebrate a victory over the Gauls, and the Great Altar of Zeus (*c*.180–150 BC, Pergamum Museum, Berlin), which features relief carvings of the fight between gods and giants depicted with an extraordinary sense of movement and dramatic tension. It is perhaps the 'Satan's seat' of Revelation 2: 13. Other Hellenistic works from places other than Pergamum (above all the celebrated *Laocoön*) are clearly similar in their restless energy, and some scholars deny that there is adequate reason for recognizing a separate Pergamene School. However, T. B. L. Webster in his *Hellenistic Poetry and Art* (1964) maintains that although the artists employed by the Attalid kings came from various places, they 'achieved a unity of style which justifies the name Pergamene'.

Perino del Vaga (Piero Buonaccorsi) (*b* Florence, ?1501; *d* Rome, 19/20 Oct. 1547). Florentine painter. He took his name (del Vaga) from a minor painter with whom he worked after studying with Ridolfo *Ghirlandaio. In about 1517 he moved to Rome, where he became one of *Raphael's assistants, working mainly on the Vatican Loggie. After the Sack of Rome in 1527 he moved to Genoa, where he was based until the late 1530s and where his *Mannerist style had great influence. His major work there was a series of mythological frescos in the Palazzo Doria. During this period he also worked in Pisa. By 1538 he was back in Rome, where he became the principal decorative artist employed by Pope Paul III (Alessandro *Farnese), his work for him including frescos on the history of Alexander the Great (1545–7) in the Sala Paolina of the Castel Sant'Angelo. Perino's style derives from Raphael and *Giulio Romano, but is ornamental rather than monumental. He was one of the leading decorative artists of his generation, and his work has been aptly described by S. J. Freedberg (*Painting in Italy: 1500–1600*, 1971) as 'intelligent but facile'. He also did a number of devotional pictures in a Raphaelesque vein, notably the unfinished *Holy Family* (Courtauld Gal., London).

Permeke, Constant (*b* Antwerp, 31 July 1886; *d* Ostend, 4 Jan. 1952). Belgian painter and sculptor, one of the leading exponents of *Expressionism in Belgium in the period between the two world wars. In 1914 he was badly wounded serving in the Belgian army and was evacuated to England. He returned to Belgium in 1919 and lived in Antwerp and Ostend before building his own house and studio at Jabbeke, near Bruges, now a Permeke museum (he called his home De Vier Windstreken, 'The Four Corners of the Earth'). His subjects were taken mainly from the life of the coastal towns of Belgium and he is best known for his strong and solemn portrayals of sailors and fishermen with their women (*The Fiancés*, 1923, Mus. Royaux, Brussels). In addition to figure paintings, he painted numerous seascapes. From 1935 he also made sculpture, carving in artificial stone.

Permoser, Balthasar (*b* Kammer, Upper Bavaria, 13 Aug. 1651; *d* Dresden, 20 Feb. 1732). German sculptor. He worked in Italy 1675–89 and his lively *Baroque style was much influenced by *Bernini. In 1689 he became court sculptor in Dresden and spent most of the rest of his life there. His most important work was the sculptural decoration of the Zwinger—Augustus the Strong's pleasure palace in Dresden, designed by the architect M. D. Pöppelmann (begun 1711, badly damaged in the Second World War). Permoser carved in wood and ivory as well as stone and also made ingenious use of coloured marble (*Damned Soul*, c.1715, Mus. der Bildenden Künste, Leipzig). *Roubiliac is said to have studied with him.

Perov, Vasily. See WANDERERS.

Perréal, Jean (or Jean de Paris) (*b* ?c.1450/60; *d* Paris, 1530). French painter, architect, sculptor, and designer. He was the most renowned French artist of his time, painter to three successive kings (Charles VIII, Louis XII, and Francis I),

but few works survive that can be confidently associated with him. They are mainly manuscript illuminations, but a portrait of Louis XII (c.1514) in the British Royal Collection is attributed to him by some authorities (others consider it a copy). These works show Perréal as a master of scrupulous naturalism, and it has been suggested that he is to be identified with the *Master of Moulins. Perréal travelled to Italy several times; on one of these visits he met *Leonardo, who mentions him in his notebooks and says he was introduced by him to 'the manner of dry colouring'—what we now call *pastel.

Perrier, François (*b* ?Burgundy, ?c.1590; *d* Paris, Nov. 1649). French history painter and engraver. He had two stays in Rome (c.1625–8 and 1635–45) and his style was formed on the example of *Lanfranco (in whose studio he worked during his first visit), Pietro da *Cortona, and the *Carracci. His decorative work helped to introduce the grand *Baroque style to France, but almost all of it has been destroyed or altered. However, his influence can be seen in the work of Charles *Le Brun, who was briefly his pupil.

Perronneau, Jean-Baptiste (*b* Paris, ?1715; *d* Amsterdam, 19 Nov. 1783). French painter and engraver. He worked principally as a portraitist and mainly in *pastel. In this medium he was overshadowed in his lifetime by Maurice-Quentin de *La Tour, whose style was more vivacious; however, posterity has judged the more sober but more penetrating Perronneau to be at least his equal. From about 1755 he led a wandering life, visiting England, the Netherlands several times, Italy, Poland, and Russia. He was a prolific artist and is represented in many galleries in France and elsewhere.

perspective. Method of giving a sense of depth on a flat or shallow surface, utilizing such optical phenomena as the apparent convergence of parallel lines and diminution in size of objects as they recede from the spectator. Perspective is by no means common to the art of all epochs and all peoples. For example, the pictorial art of the ancient Egyptians, although a richly developed tradition, did not take account of the optical effects of recession. Systematic, mathematically founded perspective, based initially on a fixed central viewpoint, was developed in Italy in the early 15th century, when it was invented by *Brunelleschi, described by *Alberti in his treatise *De pictura*, and put into majestic practice by *Masaccio. Various names are given to this type of perspective—geometric, linear, mathematical, optical, *Renaissance, or scientific perspective—which remained one of the foundations of European painting until the late 19th century. In pre-Renaissance Europe and in the East, more intuitive systems of representing spatial recession were used. In medieval paintings, for example, lines that would in strict perspective converge are often shown diverging (this 'inverted perspective' can look much more convincing in practice than it sounds in theory); and in Chinese art 'parallel perspective' was a common convention in the depiction of buildings. See also AERIAL PERSPECTIVE.

Perugino, Pietro (Pietro Vannucci) (b Città della Pieve, Umbria, c.1450; d Fontignano, nr. Perugia, Feb./Mar. 1523). Italian painter, active mainly in Perugia, from which his nickname derives. His early career is obscure, but he seems to have formed his style chiefly in Florence, where *Vasari says he studied with *Verrocchio—this would have been at about the same time that *Leonardo da Vinci was training with him (he is also said to have been a pupil of *Piero della Francesca; this could have preceded his training in Florence). In 1472 he was enrolled as a painter in the fraternity of St Luke in Florence (the same year as Leonardo) and in 1475 he was back in Perugia. By 1481 he was sufficiently well known to be commissioned to paint frescos on the walls of the newly built Sistine Chapel, Rome, for Pope Sixtus IV (Francesco della *Rovere), along with *Botticelli, Domenico *Ghirlandaio, and Cosimo *Rosselli (*Signorelli later completed the work). Vasari says that Botticelli was head of the team, but some modern scholars think that Perugino was more likely to have been leader, partly because of the prominence of his contributions. His main work there is *Christ Delivering the Keys to St Peter*; he also did the frescoed altarpiece, but this was destroyed to make way for *Michelangelo's *Last Judgement*.

His reputation firmly established, Perugino received commissions from various places in central Italy, and in the 1490s he maintained a workshop in Florence as well as in Perugia. In 1500 he was described as the best painter in Italy (by Agostino *Chigi), and he was indeed at his peak at about this time. He was a fine portraitist as well as a fresco painter, but today he is best known for his altarpieces, which are usually gentle, pious, and rather sentimental in manner. His style does not seem to have been a reflection of his personality, for Vasari says he 'was not a religious man' and that he 'would have gone to any lengths for money'. In about 1505 he left the competitive atmosphere of Florence, where his work now seemed old-fashioned, and settled permanently in Perugia, although he returned to Rome in about 1508 to paint a ceiling for Pope Julius II (Giuliano della *Rovere) in the Stanza dell'Incendio in the Vatican. His later work is often routine and repetitive, but at his best, as in the Vatican fresco, he has the authority of a great master. The harmony and spatial clarity of his compositions and his idealized physical types strongly influenced the young *Raphael, who worked with him early in his career, so Perugino can be seen as one of the harbingers of the High *Renaissance. A second wave of his influence came in the 19th century, when he was glorified by the *Pre-Raphaelites.

Peruzzi, Baldassare (b Ancaiano, nr. Siena, 15 Jan. 1481; d Rome, 6 Jan. 1536). Sienese architect, painter, and stage designer, active mainly in Rome, where he settled in 1503. He worked under *Bramante on St Peter's, and eventually became architect to the building after *Raphael's death in 1520. Amongst High *Renaissance architects he ranks almost alongside these two celebrated contemporaries, but his style was very different: sophisticated and delicate rather than monumental and grave. His greatest work—indeed the greatest secular building of the High Renaissance—is the Villa Farnesina (begun c.1506) in Rome, built for the banker Agostino *Chigi. The Farnesina contains decorations by Raphael, *Sebastiano del Piombo, and *Sodoma, as well as Peruzzi's own masterpiece in painting—the Sala delle Prospettive (c.1517), a brilliant piece of feigned architectural painting that confirms early accounts of his skill in perspective and stage design. In spite of his genius and his open, friendly nature he had little material success, and *Vasari lamented that 'The great abilities and labours of this noble artist benefited him but little, but assisted others, for though he was employed by popes, cardinals and other great wealthy men, not one of them ever rewarded him richly, though this was due more to his own retiring nature than to any want of liberality in his patrons.'

Pesellino (Francesco di Stefano) (b Florence, c.1422; d Florence, 29 July 1457). Florentine painter. He perhaps had his initial training with his maternal grandfather, a painter called Pesello (c.1367–1446), from whom the nickname Pesellino (little Pesello) derives. On stylistic grounds it is thought likely that he also studied with Filippo *Lippi. His only surviving documented work is an altarpiece of the *Trinity with Saints*, begun in 1455, left incomplete at his early death, and finished in Lippi's workshop. It was afterwards cut into several pieces, which entered the National Gallery, London, at different dates and have since been reassembled (one section is on loan from the Royal Collection). Numerous other pictures, including several *cassone* panels, are reasonably attributed to Pesellino (in spite of his short life); they are characterized by a jewel-like beauty of craftsmanship that makes him one of the most attractive Italian painters of his time.

Petel, Georg (*b* Weilheim, Bavaria, ?1601/2; *d* Augsburg, ?1634). German sculptor, active mainly in Augsburg. Although he died young of the plague, Petel was the most renowned German sculptor of his time, with a reputation extending far outside his own country; he travelled widely, visiting France, Italy, and (several times) the Low Countries, and he was a friend of van *Dyck, who painted his portrait (*c*. 1628, Alte Pin., Munich), and of *Rubens, who influenced his style. His work included large pieces in bronze and wood, but he is chiefly famed for his skill as an ivory carver (*Venus and Cupid*, 1624, Ashmolean Mus., Oxford).

Peters, Matthew William (*b* Freshwater, Isle of Wight, 1741/2; *d* Brasted Place, Kent, 20 Mar. 1814). English painter of portraits, *genre and historical scenes, and *fancy pictures. He studied with *Hudson in the late 1750s and between *c*.1762 and 1784 he made several visits to Italy and Paris. Foreign influence is clearly seen in his rich technique (admirers called him 'the English *Titian') and in the pin-up type of picture of pretty women—reminiscent of *Greuze—with which he caused mild scandal and attained great popularity in engravings. He was ordained a priest in 1782 and retired from professional practice in 1788, but he continued to paint for his own pleasure. His later works include some mawkish religious paintings and some dull pictures for *Boydell's Shakespeare Gallery.

Peterzano, Simone. See CARAVAGGIO.

Peto, John Frederick (*b* Philadelphia, 21 May 1854; *d* Island Heights, NJ, 23 Nov. 1907). American still-life painter. With his friend *Harnett he is now considered the outstanding American still-life painter of his period, but he was little known during his lifetime and after his death was completely forgotten until redis-covered in the 1940s by the critic Alfred Franken-stein. His style was strongly influenced by Harnett (whose signature has sometimes been fraudulently added to paintings by Peto), but his work was softer and more anecdotal, often depicting discarded objects. Peto worked in his native Philadelphia, then from 1889 in seclusion at Island Heights, New Jersey.

Petrarch Master. See WEIDITZ.

Pettie, John (*b* Edinburgh, 17 Mar. 1839; *d* Hastings, 21 Feb. 1893). Scottish painter, active in London from 1862. He had a successful career with dramatic and anecdotal historical subjects, particularly dashing military episodes evoking the novels of Sir Walter Scott (*A Sword and Dagger Fight*, also known as *To the Death*, 1877, Mappin AG, Sheffield). These pictures were influenced by *Meissonier, whose work was popular in Britain at this time, but Pettie used broader handling, showing his admiration for *Rembrandt. Pettie also painted portraits and contemporary *genre scenes.

Pettoruti, Emilio (*b* La Plata, 1 Oct. 1892; *d* Paris, 16 Oct. 1971). Argentine painter. From 1913 to 1923 he studied and worked in Europe, taking part in the *Futurist movement in Italy, and experimenting with the *Cubism of Juan *Gris, whom he met in Paris. After his return to Argentina in 1924 he had a great influence on the younger generation of painters there through his advocacy of European modernism. An exhibition of his paintings at the Galeria Witcomb in Buenos Aires in 1924 provoked a scandal, even though the pictures were mild and decorative by European standards, and in 1930 he caused further controversy, when as director of the Museum of Fine Arts in La Plata he exhibited current European art (he had two terms as director of the museum, both short-lived because of official disapproval of his activities). By the late 1940s his own work had become abstract. In 1952 he returned to Europe and settled in Paris. He published a book of memoirs, *Un peintre devant son miroir*, in 1962.

Pevsner, Antoine (*b* ?Orel, 18 Jan. 1886; *d* Paris, 12 Apr. 1962). Russian-born sculptor and painter who became a French citizen in 1930. He was the elder brother of Naum *Gabo and like him one of the pioneers and chief exponents of *Constructivism. Between 1911 and 1914 he made lengthy visits to Paris, where *Archipenko and *Modigliani were among his friends. After two years in Norway with Gabo he returned to Russia in 1917. In 1920 he was co-signatory of

Gabo's *Realistic Manifesto*, which set forth the ideals of Constructivism, and in 1922 he helped to organize a major exhibition of Soviet art in Berlin. He left Russia in 1923 because the authorities were turning against the 'pure' art in which he was interested in favour of utilitarian work, and later that year he settled permanently in Paris. Up to this time he had been a painter, but he now turned to sculpture, at first working mainly in plastic, then in welded metal. Initially his sculptures retained vestiges of representation, as in his witty *Portrait of Marcel Duchamp* (1926, Yale Univ. AG), but by 1927 he had arrived at pure abstraction. His later work was characterized by bold spiralling forms (*Dynamic Projection in the 30th Degree*, 1950–1, Baltimore Mus. of Art). Pevsner was a founder member of *Abstraction-Création and was influential in transmitting Constructivist ideas to other artists in the group. His style was similar to that of Gabo, but his outlook was different in important ways, for he had a religious rather than a scientific cast of mind; he thought that 'the power of the constructive work must be like that of painting, which represents the divine song and music; it must have an active life of great power and eternal salvation.' By the end of his career he was a much-honoured figure.

Pevsner, Sir Nikolaus (*b* Leipzig, 30 Jan. 1902; *d* London, 18 Aug. 1983). German-born British art historian. He worked at the Gemäldegalerie in Dresden and taught at Göttingen University (1929–33) before moving to England because of the rise of Nazism. As well as teaching at Birkbeck College in the University of London, he was *Slade professor at both Cambridge (1949–55) and Oxford (1968–9). He is best known for his writings on architecture, above all for the celebrated series of county-by-county guides *The Buildings of England* (46 vols., 1951–74), which he conceived, edited, and largely wrote himself. The series is one of the great achievements of 20th-century scholarship, for the books are, in the words of Gerald Randall (*Church Furnishing and Decoration in England and Wales*, 1980), 'such indispensable guides to the traveller and works of reference to the student that it is amazing how people coped without them'. Companion series on the buildings of Ireland (from 1979), Scotland (1978), and Wales (1979) are in course of publication. The four series are now known collectively as the Pevsner Architectural Guides. Pevsner's many other books included important studies on painting, sculpture, and design as well as architecture.

They include *Academies of Art, Past and Present* (1940), *An Outline of European Architecture* (1942 and numerous other editions), and *The Englishness of English Art* (1956). He also conceived and edited the Pelican History of Art (which began publication in 1953), the largest, most comprehensive, and most scholarly history of art ever published in English, many of the individual volumes of which have become classics. Anthony *Blunt, Ellis *Waterhouse, and Rudolf *Wittkower are among the scholars who have written volumes in the series.

Pforr, Franz (*b* Frankfurt, 5 Apr. 1788; *d* Albano, nr. Rome, 16 June 1812). German painter. He was one of the founders of the *Nazarenes and moved to Rome with other members of the group in 1810. Two years later he died of tuberculosis. His work evokes a fairy-tale type of medievalism, with bright colours and picturesque details. It is best represented in the Städelsches Kunstinstitut, Frankfurt.

Phalanx. An association of artists organized in Munich in 1901 in opposition to the conservative views of the Academy and the *Sezession. *Kandinsky was one of the founders of the association and its leading figure, becoming president in 1902. For the first group exhibition, in August 1901, he designed a magnificent poster in *Art Nouveau style showing Greek warriors advancing across a battlefield in phalanx formation. The militaristic name of the association was chosen to suggest its aggressive, progressive spirit. Eleven more exhibitions followed before Kandinsky dissolved Phalanx in 1904 because of lack of public support. In addition to work by members, the exhibitions featured 'guest' artists, notably French *Post-Impressionists and *Neo-Impressionists at the tenth exhibition in 1904. This was the most important of the exhibitions, confirming Kandinsky's internationalism and having a marked effect on several young artists, notably *Kirchner. In 1902–3 Phalanx ran an art school; one of the first students was Gabriele Münter, who became Kandinsky's mistress.

Phidias (*d* c.430 BC). Greek sculptor, active mainly in Athens, the most famous artist of the ancient world. No work survives that is certainly from his own hand, but through copies, descriptions, and above all the surviving sculpture of the Parthenon at Athens, which Phidias supervised, a fair idea can be gained of his style. In antiquity he was most celebrated for two enormous *chryselephantine cult statues—of Athena, inside the Parthenon, and of Zeus in the temple dedicated to the god at Olympia. The statue of Zeus, a seated figure about 12 m (40 ft) high and one of the Seven Wonders of the World, is known through reproductions on Roman coins. The statue of Athena (dedicated 438 BC), a standing figure about 9 m (30 ft) high, is known through several (much smaller) copies. Phidias also made two bronze statues of Athena for the Acropolis in Athens: the huge *Athena Promachos* (champion), in which the goddess was shown holding a spear; and the *Lemnian Athena* (so called because it was dedicated by Athenian colonists going to Lemnos between 451 and 448 BC). The *Athena Promachos* is represented on coins and the *Lemnian Athena* can be partially reconstructed from what are thought to be two fragmentary copies: a remarkably sensitive head in Bologna (Mus. Civico Archeologico) and a substantially complete figure in Dresden (Albertinum). Other copies have been credibly associated with works of Phidias mentioned in ancient sources, and recently the two bronze statues of warriors found in the sea near Riace in 1972 ('The Riace Bronzes') have been linked with his name because of their superlative quality; they are now in the archaeological museum at Reggio di Calabria.

The greatest testimony to his genius, however, is the sculpture of the Parthenon (447–432 BC), the most ambitious sculptural undertaking of the age, consisting originally of a low-*relief frieze about 160 m (525 ft) long, 92 *metopes in high relief, and groups of free-standing figures on both pediments. Much of the sculpture still survives, mainly in the British Museum, London (see ELGIN MARBLES). The quality is variable, as a team of sculptors was involved, and Phidias could not have carved more than a tiny fraction of the work himself, but the finest parts exemplify the harmony and serene majesty that earned the raptures of ancient commentators and stand as the greatest surviving examples of the *Classical period in Greek art.

In spite of his fame and the prominent works on which he was employed, there is much that is enigmatic about Phidias' career, not least about the end of his life. When the great statesman Pericles, his friend and patron, fell out of favour, Phidias was accused of misappropriating gold supplied to him for the statue of Athena. Then, according to Plutarch, having cleared himself of this charge, he was thrown into prison for impiety on the ground that he had introduced portraits of Pericles and himself on the shield of the goddess (a copy of the shield—the 'Strangford Shield'—is in the British Museum). Plutarch says that Phidias

died in prison, but according to another ancient source he escaped and went to Olympia to work on his statue of Zeus, the date of which is uncertain. In 1954–8 Phidias' workshop at Olympia was excavated. Moulds, scraps of ivory, and other fragments were discovered, and, remarkably, a cup bearing the inscription 'I belong to Phidias'—the great man's tea-mug, as it were. This poignant relic is in the Olympia Museum.

Philip II, King of Spain. See HABSBURG.

Philip IV, King of Spain. See HABSBURG.

Philipon, Charles (*b* Lyons, Sept. 1802; *d* Paris, 25 Jan. 1862). French caricaturist, journalist, and publisher. He was a major figure in the history of political caricature, establishing several humorous publications in Paris that helped make topical cartoons a regular feature of journalism, notably *La Caricature* (founded 1830) and *Le Charivari* (founded 1832). *La Caricature*, a weekly political journal, was forced to close in 1834 after a barrage of legal actions (Philipon was imprisoned several times for his outspokenness); *Le Charivari* was more social than political in its satire and inspired the English comic journal *Punch, or the London Charivari*, which began publication in 1841. Philipon ran *La Caricature* until 1838 and it continued to appear into the 20th century. Some of the best caricaturists of the time worked for his journals, including *Daumier, *Gavarni, and *Grandville. As an artist, Philipon himself was less distinguished, but in 1831 he created a famous and much-imitated comic image when he caricatured the unpopular, heavy-jowled King Louis-Philippe as a pear (*poire* has the slang meaning of blockhead or simpleton).

Philippoteaux, Paul. See PANORAMA.

Philip the Bold, Duke of Burgundy. See BURGUNDY.

Philip the Good, Duke of Burgundy. See BURGUNDY.

Phillip, John (*b* Aberdeen, 19 Apr. 1817; *d* London, 27 Feb. 1867). Scottish painter, active mainly in London. He began as a specialist in paintings of Scottish life and character in the manner of *Wilkie, but following visits to Spain in 1851, 1856, and 1860 he became celebrated for picturesque Spanish *genre scenes and was known as Spanish Phillip or Phillip of Spain. His style was fluent and colourful, often with a picture postcard flavour. He also painted portraits.

Phillipps, Sir Thomas (*b* Manchester, 2 July 1792; *d* Cheltenham, 6 Feb. 1872). English antiquary and collector. He had a passion for books from childhood and after inheriting his father's title and Worcestershire estates in 1818 he became the greatest of all collectors of manuscripts, amassing material 'of all ages, countries, languages, and subjects' (*DNB*); he described himself as 'a perfect vello-maniac'. In 1822 he established a private printing press at his house, Middle Hill, Broadway, Worcestershire, which published catalogues of his collection and other antiquarian material, and in 1862 he moved the collection and the press to larger premises, Thirlestane House, Cheltenham. He allowed scholars and other collectors access to his manuscripts, but he was an irascible character and his plans to leave his collection to the British Museum or another library as a monument to his passion floundered because he imposed impossible conditions (such as banning Catholics—whom he hated—from seeing the material). The collection instead passed to one of his daughters, who in 1886 began the decades-long process of dispersing it by auction at Sotheby's.

Phillips, Duncan (*b* Pittsburgh, 26 June 1886; *d* Washington, DC, 9 May 1966). American collector and writer on art. His family had made a fortune in steel and glass and he devoted much of his substantial inheritance to collecting. Mainly he bought the work of late 19th- and 20th-century artists, and when he opened his Washington home to the public (three afternoons a week) in 1921 it represented the first permanent museum of modern art in the USA (the *Société Anonyme was founded a year earlier but initially concentrated on temporary exhibitions). It proved so popular that Phillips made the house over completely as a gallery and moved to another home. The Phillips Collection retains its intimate, domestic air, and is widely regarded as one of the world's finest small museums. Its star exhibit is *Renoir's celebrated *Luncheon of the Boating Party* (1880–1). As a writer on art Phillips is best known for his book *The Leadership of Giorgione* (1937). He also edited a short-lived periodical, *Art and Understanding* (1929).

Phillips, Peter (*b* Birmingham, 21 May 1939). British painter. He studied at the *Royal College of Art, 1959–62, and with his fellow students Derek *Boshier, David *Hockney, Allen *Jones, and R. B. *Kitaj he emerged as one of the leading exponents of British *Pop art at the *Young Contemporaries exhibition in 1961. Typically his imagery is drawn from modern American culture—juke boxes, pinball machines, automobiles, film star pin-ups, and so on—painted in the tight, glossy manner of commercial art. However, the images are usually set into bold heraldic frameworks or fragmented into sections and reorganized, so that illusionism and abstraction are combined.

Phillips, Thomas (*b* Dudley, Warwickshire, 18 Oct. 1770; *d* London, 20 Apr. 1845). English painter. He began his career with ambitions as a history painter but he turned to portraiture and is best known for depicting some of the outstanding literary figures of his day, including William *Blake (1807, NPG, London), Lord Byron in Albanian costume (1813, NPG), and Samuel Taylor Coleridge (1821, Dove Cottage and Wordsworth Mus., Grasmere). T. S. R. Boase (*English Art: 1800–1870*, 1959) writes that 'he caught as no other the noble gloom of the romantic pose and the inspired intensity of the creative imagination'. Phillips was professor of painting at the *Royal Academy, 1825–32. His son and pupil **Henry Wyndham Phillips** (1820–68) was also a portrait painter.

Phillips, Tom (*b* London, 24 May 1937). British painter, graphic artist, musician, and writer. Phillips's work resists classification and has been much concerned with the fusion of words and images. Simon Wilson (*British Art from Holbein to the Present Day*, 1979) writes that his 'primary source material is the modern, photographically based, coloured picture postcard of which he is an obsessional collector . . . Phillips typically develops some specific human or social theme and then submits the source image to an elaborate painting process so devised that the theme is embodied in a visual scheme of maximum richness and subtlety.' In 1966 he began using texts from a Victorian novel (*A Human Document* by W. H. Mallock, 1892) and has produced various suites of prints and other works based on it under the collective title *A Humument*. A by-product of this work is his opera *Irma* (first produced 1973, recorded 1980). Another ambitious project is his set of illustrations to Dante's *Inferno* (1979–83), consisting of etchings, lithographs, and screenprints accompanying his own translation. His writings include the book *Music in Art* (1997).

Philostratus. The name of three or four members of a family of Greek writers active in the 3rd and 4th centuries AD, two of whom ('Philostratus the Lemnian' and his grandson

'Philostratus the Younger') wrote series of descriptions of real or imaginary paintings under the title *Eikones* (or in Latin *Imagines*, 'Images'). They are primarily literary exercises, but they contain some useful information concerning *Hellenistic painting. *Goethe published an essay on them in 1818.

Philoxenos of Eretria. See ALEXANDER MOSAIC.

'Phiz'. See BROWNE, HABLOT KNIGHT.

Photographic Realism. See SUPERREALISM.

photomontage. Term applied to a technique of making a pictorial composition from parts of different photographs and to the composition so made. The technique has antecedents in the 19th century, particularly in the work of O. G. Rejlander (1813–75), a Swedish photographer and painter active in England. He tried to expand the expressive range of photography by experimenting with double exposures and printing from several negatives onto a single sheet, as in his elaborate allegory *The Two Ways of Life* (1857), printed from 30 negatives onto two sheets joined together. However, as the term is now understood, photomontage involves cutting out, arranging, and pasting down pre-existing photographic images rather than the manipulation of negatives taken for a particular purpose. Photomontage in this sense was largely the creation of the *Dadaists (specifically the Berlin Dadaists), who used the technique for political propaganda, social criticism, and generally to assist the shock tactics in which they indulged. Raoul Hausmann (1886–1971) claimed to have invented photomontage in 1918; this is a dubious claim, but certainly he ranks with *Heartfield and Hannah Höch (1889–1978) as one of the main pioneers and most brilliant exponents of the technique. Photomontage has also been memorably used by, for example, Max *Ernst and other *Surrealists and by *Pop artists such as Richard *Hamilton, but it is now mainly associated with advertising.

photo-work. A term used since the 1970s to describe various types of works of art based on photographic images that have been manipulated by the artist in some way. It is a difficult term to define with any precision, as artists have routinely made use of photographic imagery since the days of *Pop art. However, it generally carries with it the suggestion that a photograph is physically the essential component of the work, rather than merely a part of a mixed media work or the starting point for a work in some other medium. Many *Conceptual artists in particular work with photographs, and Gilbert & George create spectacular wall-sized panels in which black-and-white photographs arranged into regular grids are overlaid with garish tints; the artists themselves call these images 'photopieces', rather than 'photo-works'. They first exhibited such pieces in 1971; earlier they had made 'postcard sculptures'. David *Hockney, also, has created elaborate images using photographs—in his case 'photocollages' made up of as many as 600 overlapping prints. At the other extreme are the pictures of the American Cindy Sherman (1954–), in which the 'manipulation' occurs before the photograph is taken, rather than after it, and the photographic print itself is presented perfectly 'straight'. Sherman photographs herself acting out roles from imaginary movies, sometimes dressed in elaborate costume, as a way of examining female stereotyping. It is questionable to what extent such images should be called 'photo-works' rather than simply 'photographs', but they routinely feature in books on art as well as on photography. Some critics prefer to use such terms as 'fabricated photography', 'set-up photography', or 'staged photography' to describe them.

Piazzetta, Giovanni Battista (*b* Venice, 13 Feb. 1683; *d* Venice, 29 Apr. 1754). Venetian painter and draughtsman. After preliminary training in Venice he spent about two years in Bologna, where he was strongly influenced by G. M. *Crespi. By 1705 he had returned to Venice and he spent the rest of his life there. He was one of the most individual Venetian painters of his period, his dramatic style, with its powerful *chiaroscuro, looking back to work done a century earlier by *Feti, *Liss, and *Strozzi. Unlike several of his leading contemporaries, he preferred to paint in oils rather than fresco; he was a notoriously slow worker, but his pictures seem fresh and spontaneous rather than laboured. He had a large family and although he was not without wealthy patrons (*Algarotti among them) he relied much on drawings and book illustrations to earn money. As a painter he did religious and historical works and portraits, as well as some hauntingly enigmatic *genre scenes that reflect his admiration for Crespi. In 1750 Piazzetta became the first director of the Venice Academy of Fine Arts, but in his last years he was eclipsed by the new generation. The young *Tiepolo was greatly influenced by him, but later the influence was reversed, as

Piazzetta's style became softer and lighter—more *Rococo—in feeling.

Picabia, Francis (b Paris, 22 Jan. 1879; d Paris, 30 Nov. 1953). French painter, designer, writer, and editor. His talent as an artist was modest, but his restless and energetic personality gave him a significant role successively in the *Cubist, *Dadaist, and *Surrealist movements, and through his publications he helped to disseminate avant-garde ideas. A private income enabled him to carry on his activities without having to worry about earning a living, as well as to indulge his love of fast cars, fast women, and wild living in general. Early in his career he was a successful painter of *Impressionist landscapes. In 1908–9 he experimented with *Neo-Impressionism, and then with *Fauvism and Cubism. In 1911 he met Marcel *Duchamp, who was to be the most important influence on his career, and with him became an exponent of *Orphism. He painted his first purely abstract works in 1912. In 1913 he visited New York as spokesman for the Cubist pictures in the *Armory Show, and he returned to the USA in 1915–16, when he, Duchamp, and *Man Ray were involved in the first stirrings of Dada. After moving to Barcelona (where he lived 1916–17), he launched a magazine entitled 391 (1917–24). In 1917 he spent six months in New York, then lived in Zurich (1918–19) before returning to Paris, where he helped to launch the Dada movement. However, in 1921 he denounced Dada for being no longer 'new', and became involved with André *Breton and the nascent Surrealist movement. In 1924 he attacked this, too, but some of his later works are in a Surrealist idiom. From 1925 to 1945 he lived mainly on the Côte d'Azur, experimenting with various styles. In 1945 he settled permanently in Paris and in his final years returned to abstract painting.

Apart from his contributions to avant-garde magazines, Picabia published various pamphlets and wrote poetry. He also conceived the fantasy ballet Relâche (1924), with music by Erik Satie, together with the film Entr'acte (directed by René Clair), which was used to fill the intermission between the ballet's two acts. Among Picabia's paintings, the most highly regarded today are those in his 'machinist' style, in which mechanistic and *biomorphic forms are combined in dynamic compositions. The most famous is I See Again in Memory my Dear Udnie (1914, MoMA, New York).

Picasso, Pablo (b Málaga, 25 Oct. 1881; d Mougins, nr. Cannes, 8 Apr. 1973). Spanish painter, sculptor, printmaker, draughtsman, ceramicist, and designer, the most famous, versatile, prolific, and influential artist of the 20th century. Although it is conventional to divide his work into certain phases, all such divisions are to some extent arbitrary, as his energy and imagination were such that he often worked simultaneously on a wealth of themes and in a variety of styles. He himself said: 'The several manners I have used in my art must not be considered as an evolution, or as steps toward an unknown ideal of painting. When I have found something to express, I have done it without thinking of the past or future. I do not believe I have used radically different elements in the different manners I have used in painting. If the subjects I have wanted to express have suggested different ways of expression, I haven't hesitated to adopt them.'

Picasso was the son of a painter and drawing master and was absorbed in art from childhood (his first word is said to have been piz, baby talk for lapiz, 'pencil'). In 1900 he made his first visit to Paris and by this time had already absorbed a wide range of influences. Between 1900 and 1904 he alternated between Paris and Barcelona, and these years coincide with his Blue Period, when he took his subjects from social outcasts and the poor, and the predominant mood of his paintings was one of slightly sentimentalized melancholy expressed through cold and ethereal blue tones (La Vie, 1903, Cleveland Mus. of Art). He also made a number of powerful etchings in a similar vein (The Frugal Repast, 1904). In 1904 he settled in Paris and quickly became part of a circle of avant-garde artists and writers. A brief phase in 1904–5 is known as his Rose Period. The predominant blue tones of his earlier work gave way to pinks and greys and the mood became less austere. His favourite subjects were acrobats and dancers, particularly the figure of the harlequin. In 1906 he met *Matisse, but although he seems to have admired the work being done by the *Fauves, he did not share their interest in the decorative and expressive use of colour (indeed his work often shows little concern with colour, and it is significant that—unlike most painters—he liked to work at night by artificial light). The period around 1906–7 is sometimes called Picasso's Negro Period, because of the impact that African sculpture made on his work, but *Cézanne was an equally powerful influence at this time, when he was engrossed in the analysis of form. His explorations climaxed in Les

Demoiselles d'Avignon (1906–7, MoMA, New York), which in its distortions of form and disregard of any conventional idea of beauty was as violent a revolt against tradition as the paintings of the Fauves in the realm of colour. At the time, the picture was incomprehensible even to other avant-garde artists, including Matisse and *Derain, and it was not publicly exhibited until 1916 or reproduced until 1925. It is now seen not only as a pivotal work in Picasso's personal development but also as the most important single landmark in the development of 20th-century painting. It was the herald of *Cubism, which he developed in close association with *Braque and then *Gris from 1907 up to the First World War.

During the war Picasso continued working in Paris, but in 1917 he went to Rome with his friend Jean *Cocteau to design costumes and scenery for the ballet *Parade*, which was being produced by *Diaghilev. Picasso fell in love with one of the dancers, Olga Koklova, and married her in 1918; they moved into a grand apartment in a fashionable part of Paris, as the bohemian days of his youth were left behind. The visit to Italy was an important factor in introducing the strain of monumental classicism that was one of the features of his work in the early 1920s (*Mother and Child*, 1921, Art Inst. of Chicago), but at this time he was also involved with *Surrealism—indeed André *Breton hailed him as one of the initiators of the movement. However, his predominant interest in the analysis and synthesis of form was at bottom opposed to the irrational elements of Surrealism, its exaltation of chance, or its fascination with material drawn from dreams or the unconscious.

Following his serene classical paintings, Picasso entered on a period when his work was characterized by violent emotions and expressionist distortion, the elements of the human face often being rearranged to convey intensity of feeling. This phase began with *The Three Dancers* (1925, Tate, London), a savage parody of classical ballet, painted at a time when his marriage was becoming a source of increasing unhappiness and frustration (he could not obtain a divorce, so he remained officially married to Olga until her death in 1955; he remarried in 1961). The period culminated in his most famous work, *Guernica* (1937, Centro Cultural Reina Sofía, Madrid), produced for the Spanish Pavilion at the Paris Exposition Universelle of 1937 to express horror and revulsion at the destruction by bombing of the Basque capital Guernica during the Civil War. It was followed by a number of other paintings attacking the cruelty and destructiveness of war, including *The Charnel House* (1945, MoMA, New York): 'Painting is not done to decorate apartments', he said: 'it is an instrument of war against brutality and darkness.'

Picasso remained in Paris during the German occupation, but from 1946 he lived mainly in the south of France, where he added pottery to his many other activities. His later output as a painter does not compare in momentousness with his pre-war work (indeed some critics think there was a sad decline in his powers), but it remained prodigious in terms of sheer quantity. It included a number of variations on paintings by other artists, including 44 on *Las meninas* of *Velázquez (the theme of the artist and his almost magical powers is one that exercised him greatly throughout his long career). In his old age he was haunted by the idea of death, and images of physical decay and the contrast between youth and age occur frequently in his work, as if he hoped to ward off his own end through the potency of his art. Some of his late paintings are aggressively sexual in subject and almost frenzied in brushwork (*Reclining Nude with Necklace*, 1968, Tate); they have been seen as sources for *Neo-Expressionism.

Picasso's status as a painter has perhaps overshadowed his work as a sculptor, but in this field too (although his interest was sporadic) he ranks as one of the outstanding figures in 20th-century art. He was one of the first artists to make sculpture that was assembled from varied materials rather than modelled or carved (in this way he helped to inspire *Constructivism), and made brilliantly witty use of found objects (see OBJET TROUVÉ). The most celebrated example is *Head of a Bull, Metamorphosis* (1943, Mus. Picasso, Paris), made of the saddle and handlebars of a bicycle. Alan Bowness has written (*Modern Sculpture*, 1965): 'Picasso's sculpture sparkles with bright ideas—enough to have kept many a lesser man occupied for the whole of a working lifetime . . . it is not inconceivable that the time will come when his activities as a sculptor in the second part of his life are regarded as of more consequence than his later paintings.'

As a graphic artist (draughtsman, etcher, lithographer, linocutter), too, Picasso ranks with the greatest of the century, showing a remarkable power to concentrate the impress of his genius in even the smallest and slightest of his works. His emotional range is as wide as his varied technical mastery; by turns tragic and playful, his work is suffused with a passionate love of life, and no artist has more devastatingly exposed the cruelty and folly of his fellow men or more rapturously celebrated the physical pleasures of love. There are several museums devoted to him in France and Spain, the largest being in Barcelona and Paris, and other examples of his huge output are in collections throughout the world. Just as this extraordinary oeuvre has been more discussed than the work of any other modern artist, so Picasso's personal life has inspired a flood of writing, particularly regarding his relationships with women. He once characterized them as either 'goddesses or doormats' and he has been criticized for allegedly demeaning them in his work (especially his later erotic paintings) as well as mistreating them in person.

Pickenoy, Nicolaes Eliasz. (*bapt.* Amsterdam, 10 Jan. 1588; *d* Amsterdam, 1650/6). Dutch painter who, with Thomas de *Keyser, was the leading portraitist in Amsterdam until the arrival of *Rembrandt in 1631/2. In the 1640s, however, his career seems to have gone into decline. His work is well represented in the Rijksmuseum, Amsterdam, and in the Louvre, Paris. He is sometimes referred to in art-historical literature as 'Nicolaes Eliasz., called Pickenoy', but Pickenoy was his family name.

picture plane. In the imaginary space of a picture, the plane corresponding to the physical surface of the work. *Perspective appears to recede from the picture plane, and objects painted in *trompe-l'œil may appear to project from it.

Picturesque. Term covering a set of aesthetic ideas about landscape and its depiction in art that flourished in Britain in the late 18th and early 19th centuries. It indicated an approach that found pleasure in roughness and irregularity, and one of its main devotees, Sir Uvedale *Price (in his *Essay on the Picturesque*, 1794), proposed that it should be regarded as a new critical category between the 'Beautiful' and the '*Sublime', as formulated by Edmund *Burke in his treatise of 1757. Picturesque scenes were thus neither serene (like the Beautiful) nor awe-inspiring (like the Sublime), but full of variety, curious details, and interesting textures—medieval ruins were quintessentially Picturesque. Natural scenery tended to be judged in terms of how closely it approximated to the paintings of favoured artists such as Gaspard *Dughet, and in 1801 George Mason's *Supplement* to Samuel Johnson's *Dictionary* defined 'Picturesque' as: 'what pleases the eye; remarkable for

singularity; striking the imagination with the force of painting; to be expressed in painting; affording a good subject for a landscape; proper to take a landscape from.' The Picturesque Tour in search of suitable subjects was a feature of English landscape painting of the period, exemplified, for example, in the work of *Girtin and (early in his career) of *Turner, and the Picturesque generated a large literary output; much of it was pedantic and obsessive and it became a popular subject for satire (see GILPIN). *Romanticism has some of its roots in the Picturesque.

piece mould. See CAST.

Pieneman, Jan Willem (*b* Abcoude, nr. Amsterdam, 4 Nov. 1779; *d* Amsterdam, 8 Apr. 1853). Dutch painter and museum official. His contemporary reputation was based mainly on the enormous *Battle of Waterloo* (1824, Rijksmuseum, Amsterdam). It established him as his country's foremost history painter, but it is now regarded as having greater historical interest than artistic merit (it features portraits of many of the leading British commanders at the battle, based on oil sketches from the life; these are now in the Wellington Museum, London). Pieneman was a well-regarded teacher, Jozef *Israëls being among his pupils, and he was director of the Rijksmuseum, Amsterdam, from 1844 to 1847. His son **Nicolaas** (1809–60) was a painter and lithographer. Like his father, he specialized in historical scenes and portraits.

Pierce (or **Pearce**), **Edward** (*b* c.1635; *d* London, ?Apr. 1695). English sculptor and mason, son of a painter (*d* 1658) of the same name, some of whose decorative work survives at Wilton House, Wiltshire. Little is known of his early career, but from 1671 he was much employed by Christopher Wren on the rebuilding of the City of London churches, both as a mason and as a stonecarver. He was a woodcarver too, and his work in this field is of such quality that it has sometimes been credited to Grinling *Gibbons. There are also a few portrait busts by Pierce, the most notable being the life-size marble of Wren (c.1673, Ashmolean Mus., Oxford), brilliantly characterized and more convincingly *Baroque than anything else of the date in English art. It is generally considered the best piece of English sculpture of the 17th century, but it has been suggested that the workmanship does not live up to the boldness of the conception and that Pierce is here perhaps copying a lost bust by *Coysevox. Pierce also worked as an architect, the Bishop's Palace, Lichfield

(1686–7), being his chief documented building. There are several drawings by him in the British Museum, London.

Piero della Francesca (*b* Borgo San Sepolcro [now Sansepolcro], Umbria, *c*.1415; *d*. Borgo San Sepolcro, 12 Oct. 1492). Italian painter, virtually forgotten for centuries after his death, but now regarded as one of the supreme artists of the *Renaissance. He spent much of his life in his native town and evidently had great affection for it, as he took an active part in its civic affairs (he twice served as a town councillor) and the surrounding countryside often features in the backgrounds of his paintings. At various times he also worked in Arezzo, Ferrara, Florence, Rimini, Rome, and Urbino, but his career is scantily documented and it is not possible to follow his movements in detail. (Arezzo and Urbino are close to Sansepolcro and Piero probably spent a good deal of time in both places, but he is only once actually documented in either, in Urbino in 1469).

He is first heard of in 1431, when he received payment for painting some candle poles used in processions, and between 1432 and 1438 he is several times recorded working with an obscure local painter, Antonio d'Anghiari, who was perhaps his teacher. In 1439 he is documented outside Sansepolcro for the first time, assisting *Domenico Veneziano on frescos (now lost) in S. Egidio, Florence. This is the only time he is recorded in Florence, but he must have been well acquainted with the city, for his paintings show that he had carefully studied the work of his great Florentine predecessors and contemporaries. He is perhaps closest in spirit to *Masaccio, with whom he shared a sense of massive dignity and deep spiritual authority, but he had more interest in colour than Masaccio, and in this respect is closer to Fra *Angelico and *Masolino, as well as Domenico Veneziano. His fascination with perspective was something he shared with *Uccello. Piero refined and unified the discoveries these artists had made in the previous twenty years and created a style in which monumental, meditative grandeur and almost mathematical lucidity are combined with limpid beauty of colour and light.

Piero's first surviving documented work is the *polyptych of the *Madonna della Misericordia* (Pinacoteca, Sansepolcro), commissioned in 1445 but not completed until about 1460. Such a lengthy period of gestation was typical of Piero, who was a habitually slow worker. This meant that the traditional method of *fresco painting, demanding swiftness and sureness of hand, was not ideally suited to him, and he experimented with ways of modifying the technique. He sometimes applied wet cloths to the plaster at night so that—contrary to normal fresco practice—he could work for more than one day on the same section, and he also tried using some kind of oil medium. His major work in fresco is the great series on the legend of the True Cross in the choir of S. Francesco at Arezzo (*c*.1450–*c*.1465). The subject derived from a complex medley of medieval stories, but Piero made from its fanciful details some of the most solemn and serene images in Western art—even the two battle scenes have a feeling of grim deliberation rather than violent movement.

These frescos were painted for a wealthy local family and several of Piero's other paintings were done for religious institutions in his home town. However, he also worked for illustrious patrons further afield. They included Leonello d'*Este in Ferrara, Sigismondo *Malatesta in Rimini, and Pope Pius II in Rome. Nothing survives of his work in Ferrara or Rome, but his fresco of *Sigismondo Malatesta Venerating St Sigismund* (1451, Tempio Malatestiano, Rimini) provides one of the rare firm dates in his career. The most important of his patrons was Federico da *Montefeltro and Piero probably spent much of his later career working at his court in Urbino. There he painted the portraits of Federico and his wife (*c*.1465–75, Uffizi, Florence) and the celebrated *Flagellation* (*c*.1450–60), which is still at Urbino, in the Galleria Nazionale (housed in the Ducal Palace). The *Flagellation* is Piero's most enigmatic work, and it has called forth varied interpretations; *Gombrich suggested that the subject is rather *The Repentance of Judas* and *Pope-Hennessy that it is *The Dream of St Jerome*.

Piero is last mentioned as a painter in 1478 (in connection with a lost work) and his two final works are probably the *Madonna and Child with Federico da Montefeltro* (*c*.1475, Brera, Milan) and the unfinished *Nativity* (NG, London). Thereafter he seems to have devoted himself to mathematics and perspective (three treatises by him survive on these subjects). *Vasari said Piero was blind when he died, and failing eyesight may have been his reason for giving up painting, but in a legal document of 1487 he writes in his own clear hand that he is 'sound in mind, in intellect and in body'. His paintings had considerable influence, notably on *Signorelli (in the weighty solemnity of his figures) and *Perugino (in the spatial clarity of his compositions). Both are said to have been Piero's pupils. However, after his death, Piero was remembered mainly as a mathematician rather than as a painter, and even Vasari, who as a native of Arezzo must have known the frescos in S. Francesco well, is lukewarm in his enthusiasm for his work. Most of his major paintings were in locations that were off the beaten track and they were more or less neglected for centuries (although for an instance of his work influencing a 17th-century painter see TOURNIER). The process of rediscovery did not seriously begin until the later 19th century and it was not until the 20th century that he was widely acclaimed.

Piero di Cosimo (*b* ?Florence, ?1461; *d* Florence, ?1521). Florentine painter, a pupil of Cosimo *Rosselli, whose Christian name he adopted as a patronym. There are no signed, documented, or dated works by him, and reconstruction of his oeuvre depends on the account given in *Vasari's Lives*. It is one of Vasari's most entertaining biographies, for he portrays Piero as a highly eccentric character who lived on hard-boiled eggs, 'which he cooked while he was boiling his glue, to save the firing'. The paintings for which he is best known are appropriately idiosyncratic—fanciful mythological inventions, inhabited by fauns, centaurs, and primitive men. There is sometimes a spirit of low comedy about these delightful works, but in the so-called *Death of Procris* (NG, London) he created a poignant scene of the utmost pathos and tenderness. He was a wonderful painter of animals and the dog in this picture, depicted with a mournful dignity, is one of his most memorable creations. Piero also painted portraits, the finest of which is that of Simonetta Vespucci (Musée Condé, Chantilly), in which she is depicted as Cleopatra with the asp around her neck. His religious works are somewhat more conventional, although still distinctive, and Frederick Hartt (*A History of Italian Renaissance Art*, 1970) has written that 'His whimsical Madonnas, Holy Families, and Adorations provide a welcome relief from the wholesale imitation of *Raphael in early Cinquecento Florence.' One of his outstanding religious works is the *Immaculate Conception* (Uffizi, Florence), which seems to have been the compositional model for the *Madonna of the Harpies* by his pupil Andrea del *Sarto.

Pietà. Term (Italian: 'pity') applied to a painting or sculpture showing the Virgin Mary supporting the body of the dead Christ on her lap. Other figures, such as St John the Evangelist

or Mary Magdalene, may also be included. The theme originated in Germany in the 13th century and was more popular in northern Europe than in Italy. However, the most celebrated of all Pietàs is that by *Michelangelo in St Peter's, Rome; and one of the most sublime is by *Titian (Accademia, Venice), said to have been painted for his own tomb. The subject is not always clearly distinguished from the scene known as the Lamentation. However, whereas the Lamentation represents a specific moment from Christ's Passion, between the Descent from the Cross and the Entombment, the Pietà is a timeless image, divorced from narrative content.

pietra dura (plural: pietre dure; Italian: 'hard stone'). A term applied to various hardstones, including agate, chalcedony, jasper, and *porphyry, that are used either singly or in combination with one another to make decorative objects. In particular the term is applied to panels in which these stones are used to imitate as far as possible the effect of painting (the stones vary widely in colour, so a great range of tones and effects can be created). Hardstones were used by the ancient Greeks and Romans and their techniques were revived during the *Renaissance (special tools are needed to work such materials, similar to those used in diamond cutting). The main centre of the art was Florence, where in 1588 the Grand Duke Ferdinando I de' *Medici established the Opificio delle Pietre Dure (Workshop of Hard Stones). This became famous throughout Europe for its pictorial panels, typically decorated with birds and flowers or landscapes, which were used mainly as table-tops and in other pieces of furniture. Sometimes whole rooms were embellished in pietre dure, most notably the Cappella dei Principi (Chapel of the Princes), the Medici funeral chapel (begun 1604) in S. Lorenzo, Florence.

Pietro da Cortona. See CORTONA.

Pietro Spagnuolo. See BERRUGUETE.

Pigalle, Jean-Baptiste (*b* Paris, 26 Jan. 1714; *d* Paris, 21 Aug. 1785). French sculptor. He studied under J.-B. *Lemoyne and then in Rome (1736–40). In his early career he endured poverty and sickness (his studies in Rome were made at his own expense and he walked there from Paris), but after he was received into the Académie Royale in 1744 with his rapturously acclaimed *Mercury* (Louvre, Paris; terracotta model in the Met. Mus., New York), he rapidly went on to become one of the leading French sculptors of his period (in terms of worldly success he probably outdid all his contemporaries). He was a superb craftsman and highly versatile and inventive, equally adept at small *genre pieces and the most grandiloquent tomb sculpture. As a portraitist he was noted for his warmth and vivacity. His most famous works are the startling nude figure of Voltaire (1770–6, Louvre) and the spectacular and majestic tomb of Maurice of Saxony (designed 1753) in St Thomas, Strasbourg.

pigment. Any substance used as a colouring agent, particularly the finely ground particles that when held in suspension in a *medium constitute a paint. Most pigments are now manufactured synthetically, but in the past they have been made from a great variety of mineral, plant, and animal sources: the brown colour *sepia, for example, comes from the inky secretions of the cuttlefish, and ultramarine blue was originally made from the semi-precious stone lapis lazuli. The history of pigments is a highly specialized field with little practical importance today for artists who use commercial paints, but it is often vitally important to the expert in relation to authentication and attribution.

Pijnacker, Adam. See PYNACKER.

Piles, Roger de (b Clamecy, 7 Oct. 1635; d Paris, 5 Apr. 1709). French writer on art, amateur painter, and diplomat. De Piles was employed by Louis XIV on various confidential missions (he was imprisoned as a spy in Holland, 1692–7) and his travels enabled him to study the arts at first hand in various European countries. His best-known book is *Cours de peinture par principes avec une balance des peintres* (1708), which has become notorious for the section (the 'balance des peintres') in which he awarded marks to great artists of the past for their skill at composition, drawing, colour, and expression, then added up the scores to form a sort of league table of genius (his criticism, however, is usually much less crude than this). *Raphael and *Rubens come out with the joint highest marks in his scheme, and his admiration for the latter was shown in the famous controversy of the 'Rubénistes' against the 'Poussinistes' (see POUSSIN) that split the French Académie Royale (see ACADEMY) in the second half of the 17th century. De Piles took the side of the Rubénistes, who believed that colour is of prime importance in painting, in opposition to those who upheld the academic emphasis on drawing. He also recognized the value of genius, imagination, and 'enthusiasm', as opposed to skills that can be learnt.

Pillement, Jean-Baptiste (b Lyons, 24 May 1728; d Lyons, 26 Apr. 1808). French painter and designer. As a painter he is best known for his charming landscapes, which are strongly indebted to *Boucher but more atmospheric. His importance, however, lies more in the engravings made after his drawings, which were popular throughout Europe and influential in spreading the *Rococo style, particularly the taste for *chinoiserie. Pillement himself was well travelled, visiting Austria, England, Poland, Portugal, and Spain.

Pilo, Carl Gustaf (b Göksäter, nr. Nyköping, ?5 Mar. 1711; d Stockholm, 2 Feb. 1793). Swedish portrait painter. In about 1740 he settled in Copenhagen, where he became court painter and director of the Academy, but he left for Stockholm in 1772 because of strained relations between Denmark and Sweden. He continued his success in his home country, working for the royal family and becoming director of the Academy. His best-known work is the huge *Coronation of Gustavus III* (begun 1782, Nationalmuseum, Stockholm); although it was left unfinished at his death it is considered one of the masterpieces of Swedish painting. Pilo's style was characterized by nervously sensitive drawing and refined colouring in a personal *Rococo vein.

Pilon, Germain (b Paris, c.1525; d Paris, 3 Feb. 1590). The most powerful and original French sculptor of the 16th century. He was born in Paris, the son of a sculptor, **André Pilon,** and spent most of his career there. His first known work is the group of *Three Graces* on the monument for the heart of Henry II (1561–2, Louvre, Paris), which shows that his early manner was based on the elegant decorative style of the School of *Fontainebleau, in particular on *Primaticcio's *stuccowork. Although Pilon's style never lost its tendency towards graceful *Mannerist elongation, it developed in the direction of greater naturalism and emotional intensity. These qualities are seen most memorably in his marble *gisants on the tomb of Henry II and Catherine de *Médicis at Saint-Denis Abbey (1563–70), poignant works in which the seminude figures are shown relaxed in death. The kneeling effigies of Henry and Catherine on the upper tier of the tomb are in bronze and Pilon excelled in this medium as well as marble, both as a portrait sculptor (*Charles IX,* c.1574, Wallace Coll., London) and a medallist—he was appointed controller general of the Paris mint in 1572. Pilon's early work was influential on his successors, but the deeply felt emotion of his later style proved too personal to inspire imitation. Several examples of his sublime late work are in the Louvre, notably the tomb of Valentine Balbiani (c.1580).

Piloty, Karl von (b Munich, 1 Oct. 1826; d Ambach, nr. Munich, 21 July 1886). German painter, active in Munich, where in 1856 he became a professor at the Academy and in 1874 its director. He was highly successful with large, opulent history paintings in which the settings, furnishings, and costumes were reconstructed with great accuracy. They gave the public the same kind of feast for the eye as Hollywood epics and now have a distinctly hollow ring. His pupils included *Makart.

pinacotheca (Greek: 'picture repository'). A name originally applied to a picture gallery in the Propylaea (gateway) of the Acropolis at Athens; it was open to the public by the 2nd century AD. The word was adopted by the Romans for galleries of private collectors, and in modern times it has been applied to numerous public galleries in Italy (for example the *Vatican Pinacoteca) and a few in other countries, notably the Alte Pinakothek (Old Picture Gallery) in Munich. This was built by the art-loving King Ludwig I of Bavaria (1786–1868; reigned 1825–48) and was opened in 1836; the architect was Leo von Klenze and the design is a kind of free interpretation of a very large *Renaissance *palazzo*. Originally it was called simply the Pinakothek, but it was renamed Alte Pinakothek when a gallery for more recent pictures—the Neue Pinakothek—opened in 1853. The Alte Pinakothek has one of the world's greatest collections of Old Masters, particularly rich in German Renaissance works.

Pintoricchio (or **Pinturicchio**) (Bernardino di Betto) (b Perugia, c.1454; d Siena, 11 Dec. 1513). Italian painter. His nickname has been variously explained as being a reference to 'his small stature and unprepossessing appearance', as meaning 'rich painter' (alluding to his liking for gold leaf and expensive colours), and as meaning 'dauber'. He worked in various places but always kept contact with his native Perugia. In 1481–2 he assisted the city's leading painter, *Perugino, with his frescos in the Sistine Chapel, Rome. His style was strongly influenced by Perugino, especially in his sweet, elegant figure types, but Pintoricchio lacked Perugino's lucidity of design and was more interested in decorative effects. His chief works are frescos in the Borgia rooms

in the Vatican (1492–5) and the colourful scenes from the life of Aeneas Sylvius Piccolomini (i.e. Pope Pius II) in the Piccolomini Library of Siena Cathedral (1503). In these he showed the brilliant colours, ornamental detail, and fanciful charm that make him at his best, in the words of Frederick Hartt (*A History of Italian Renaissance Art*, 1970), 'one of the most endearing masters of the *Quattrocento . . . a kind of Perugian Benozzo *Gozzoli'. Pintoricchio was a prolific painter of panels as well as frescos—there are several examples of his work in the National Gallery, London.

Piper, John (b Epsom, Surrey, 13 Dec. 1903; d Henley-on-Thames, Oxfordshire, 28 June 1992). English painter, printmaker, draughtsman, designer, and writer. He reluctantly became an articled clerk in his father's legal firm, but took up the study of art after his father's death in 1926, first at the Richmond School of Art and then at the *Royal College of Art. From 1928 to 1933 he wrote as an art critic for the *Listener* and the *Nation* and was among the first to recognize such contemporaries as William *Coldstream, Ivon *Hitchens, Victor *Pasmore, and Ceri *Richards. By the mid-1930s he was one of the leading British abstract artists, but by the end of the decade he had become disillusioned with non-representational art and reverted to naturalism. He concentrated on landscape and architectural views in a subjective, emotionally charged style that continued the English *Romantic tradition. Some of his most memorable works were done as an *Official War Artist when he made pictures of bomb-damaged buildings. A similar stormy atmosphere pervades his famous views of country houses of the same period. Piper's work diversified in the 1950s and he became recognized as one of the most versatile British artists of his generation. He was a prolific printmaker and did much work as a designer of stained glass (notably at Coventry Cathedral) and of stage decor (notably for Benjamin Britten's operas; Piper's wife Myfanwy Evans wrote the librettos for three of these). In addition he made book illustrations and designed pottery and textiles. As a writer he is probably best known for his book *British Romantic Artists* (1942). He also compiled architectural guidebooks to several English counties, usually in collaboration with the poet Sir John Betjeman.

Piranesi, Giovanni Battista (b Mogliano, nr. Venice, 4 Oct. 1720; d Rome, 9 Nov. 1778). Italian etcher, designer, archaeologist, and architect, active for almost all his career in Rome, where he settled in 1740. Earlier, in Venice, he had studied perspective and stage design and in Rome he achieved great popularity with his spectacular etchings of the ancient and modern city—the *Vedute*—published from 1745 onwards. He often altered the scale of buildings to make them look even grander than they are in actuality (Horace *Walpole said he 'conceived visions of Rome beyond what it boasted even in the meridian of its splendour') and his work played a major role in shaping the popular mental image of the city. Even more dramatic and original are his images of *Carceri d'invenzione*, fantastic imaginary prisons, begun c.1745 and reworked in 1761. These striking and obsessive works were later claimed by the *Surrealists as an anticipation of their ideas and their influence can be seen in 20th-century horror movies. Only one building was erected to Piranesi's designs (S. Maria del Priorato, Rome, 1764–6), but he was important as an architectural polemicist, most notably in his *Della magnificenza ed architettura de' Romani* (1761), in which he championed the superiority of Roman architecture over Greek. He influenced not only architects, but also stage designers and painters of *capricci such as his friend Hubert *Robert, and he had a powerful impact on the literary imagination. William *Beckford, for example, said that in writing his Gothic novel *Vathek* (1786) 'I drew chasms, and subterranean hollows, the domain of fear and torture, with chains, racks, wheels and dreadful engines in the style of Piranesi.' His etchings continued to be published for many years after his death and his work was continued by his son **Francesco** (1758–1810).

Pisanello (Antonio Pisano) (b ?Pisa, c.1394; d ?Rome, ?1455). Italian painter, draughtsman, and medallist. He presumably came from Pisa (hence his nickname—the little Pisan), but he spent his early years in Verona, a city with which he kept up an association for most of his life. His successful career also took him to Rome, Naples, and several courts of north Italy, particularly those of the *Este (Ferrara) and *Gonzaga (Mantua). With *Gentile da Fabriano, he is regarded as the foremost exponent of the *International Gothic style in Italian painting, but most of his major works have perished, including frescos in the Doges' Palace, Venice (in which he collaborated with Gentile), and in St John Lateran, Rome (in which he completed work left unfinished by Gentile at his death). His surviving documented frescos are the *Annunciation* (c.1426, S. Fermo, Verona) and *St George and the Princess of Trebizond* (c.1433–8, S. Anastasia, Verona), and confidently attributed to him are fragmentary murals showing scenes of war and chivalry in the Palazzo Ducale, Mantua, uncovered in 1968 and one of the most spectacular art discoveries of recent years. A handful of panel paintings is also given to him, including two in the National Gallery, London. On the other hand, a good many of his drawings survive, those of animals being particularly memorable. They show his keen eye for detail and his ability to convey an animal's personality. Pisanello was also the inventor of the portrait *medal and arguably the greatest of all exponents of this art form, his work having an extraordinary dignity and strength considering the small size of the objects. His first medal commemorated a visit to Italy by the Byzantine emperor John VIII in 1438, and he subsequently made more than twenty others, mainly for the ruling families of the courts at which he worked.

Pisano, Andrea (b ?Pontedera, nr. Pisa, c.1290; d ?Orvieto, 1348/9). Italian sculptor and architect, not related to Nicola and Giovanni *Pisano. He probably came from Pontedera near Pisa (he is sometimes called Andrea da Pontedera), but he is first documented in Florence in 1330, when he began work on a pair of bronze doors for the Baptistery. The doors, finished in 1336, are the first of the three great sets for the Baptistery (the other two are by *Ghiberti), and represent twenty scenes from the life of St John the Baptist and eight Virtues—melodious in line and with a jeweller's refinement of handling. By 1340 Andrea was architect to Florence Cathedral (succeeding *Giotto) and the only other works certainly by him or from his workshop are *reliefs and statues for the cathedral's campanile. In their clear-cut designs the reliefs show the influence of Giotto's painting. In 1347 Andrea was appointed master of works at Orvieto Cathedral, where he was succeeded by his son **Nino** (d 1368) in 1349. Nino is known from documents to have been active as a goldsmith and architect, but all his surviving works are sculptures in marble. He was much less distinguished as an artist than his father, but noteworthy in being one of the first sculptors to specialize in freestanding life-size statues.

Pisano, Nicola (b Apulia, c.1220; d ?Pisa, 1278/84) and **Giovanni** (b Pisa, c.1245/50; d Siena, 1314/19). Italian sculptors and architects, father and son. They were the greatest sculptors of their period and stand at the head of the tradition of Italian sculpture in the same way that *Giotto stands at the head of the tradition of Italian painting. They often worked together, but their styles are distinctive. Nicola came from Apulia, where the Emperor Frederick II (d 1250) had encouraged a revival of interest in ancient art, and his first known work, the pulpit in the Baptistery at Pisa (dated 1260 Pisan style, i.e. 1259), shows his brilliant adaptation of *antique forms to a new context. He transformed a Dionysus into Simeon at the Presentation of Christ, a nude Hercules into a personification of Christian Fortitude, and a Phaedra into the Virgin Mary. Instead of following the *Romanesque convention of separating episodes into compartments arranged in bands, he created unified high-*relief images on each of the five decorated faces of the hexagonal pulpit, carving with great power and dramatic effect. Several of the figures were directly inspired by ancient sarcophagi that Nicola saw in the Campo Santo in Pisa, but they are much more than simple borrowings, for he made them the vehicle for expressing richly varied human feeling.

Nicola followed the Pisa pulpit with a similar but more complex work for Siena Cathedral (1265–8). The carving is deeper, the contrasts between light and shadow sharpened, the reliefs more densely packed and full of movement. By then Nicola had a large workshop, his assistants including his son Giovanni and *Arnolfo di Cambio. His last great project was the large fountain in the public square of Perugia, which he and Giovanni finished in 1278. The dozens of reliefs are a typical medieval mixture—biblical scenes, heraldic beasts, personifications of seasons and places, and local dignitaries—but the vigour and spontaneity of the carving express a new freedom and naturalness.

By 1284 Nicola was dead. Between the Perugia fountain and this date, Giovanni, alone or in collaboration with his father, had carved the sculpture for the outside of the Pisa Baptistery (now in the Museo Nazionale). Here for the first time in Tuscany a scheme of monumental statuary was incorporated into an architectural setting. Giovanni developed this much further in Siena, where from 1284 onwards he designed the façade of the cathedral and carried out much of the sculptural decoration (some of the figures have been transferred to the cathedral museum and a magnificent fragment—the upper part of the figure of the prophet Haggai—is in the Victoria and Albert Museum, London). It is the most richly decorated of all the great Italian *Gothic cathedral façades, and the statuary has tremendous energy and inner life.

Giovanni's last two great works were pulpits for S. Andrea, Pistoia (1300–1), and Pisa Cathedral (1302–10). They are based on those of his father, but more elegant in style (showing French Gothic influence) and also more emotionally charged. The Pisa pulpit was damaged in a fire in 1599, then dismantled and reassembled, some parts being dispersed; several museums, including the Metropolitan Museum, New York, have fragments that are said to come from it. Giovanni also made a number of free-standing statues, the best known of which is the *Madonna and Child* on the altar of the Arena Chapel in Padua (c.1305). Its grandeur and humanity suggest a close kinship with Giotto, amid whose celebrated frescos it stands.

Pissarro, Camille (b Charlotte Amalie, St Thomas, Virgin Islands, 10 July 1830; d Paris, 13 Nov. 1903). French painter, printmaker, and draughtsman, born in the West Indies, where his parents (a French Jewish father and a Creole mother) ran a prosperous general store. He was educated at boarding school in Paris, but he then returned to the Caribbean and did not settle in France until 1855. Before this he had been mainly self-taught, but he now studied at the École des *Beaux-Arts and the *Académie Suisse, as well as copying in the Louvre. In 1859 he met *Monet, and with him became a central figure of *Impressionism. Pissarro in fact was the only artist who exhibited at all eight Impressionist exhibitions and he was a much-respected father figure to his colleagues (he was about a decade older than most of the other members of the group). His talents as a teacher made him influential even among artists of greater stature than himself—*Cézanne and *Gauguin, for example, spoke glowingly of him—and his roles as a guide and mediator have perhaps tended to obscure his own high quality as a painter.

During the Franco-Prussian War of 1870–1, when his home at Louveciennes was overrun by the German invaders and many of his paintings were destroyed, Pissarro joined Monet in England. In 1872 he settled at Pontoise, where he introduced Cézanne to painting out of doors. From 1884 he lived at Eragny in Normandy, although he travelled a good deal. In 1885 he met *Seurat and for several years afterwards he experimented with *Neo-Impressionism; in about 1890, however, he reverted to his Impressionist style, though with freer brushwork than in his early work. By this time, following early hardships, he was beginning to prosper, and by the end of his career his work was selling well in

Germany and the USA as well as France. From about 1895 deterioration of his eyesight caused him to give up painting out of doors and many of his late works are urban scenes painted from windows (usually of hotels) in Paris and elsewhere. Although he is best known for his landscapes and city views, he painted various other subjects, including portraits, still-lifes, and *genre scenes. In addition to a large output of paintings and drawings, he was the most prolific printmaker among the Impressionists, working in a variety of techniques and sometimes mixing them. The best representation of his paintings is in the Musée d'Orsay, Paris. There is another good collection of his work (including numerous drawings) in the Ashmolean Museum, Oxford.

Pissarro had five painter sons, of whom the most important was the eldest, **Lucien** (*b* Paris, 20 Feb. 1863; *d* Hewood, Somerset, 10 July 1944). He took part in the final Impressionist exhibition (1886) and with Seurat in the second *Salon des Indépendants, adopting the *pointillist technique for a time. In 1890 he settled in England, and he became a British citizen in 1916. From 1905 he was part of *Sickert's circle and he was a member of the *Camden Town Group and afterwards of the *London Group. He was a distinguished book illustrator and from 1894 to 1914 ran the Eragny Press, one of the best of the *private presses that flourished at this period. A modest and unassuming character, he has been overshadowed by his more famous father, but he was an important figure in helping to introduce Impressionism and Neo-Impressionism to England. His daughter **Orovida Pissarro** (1893–1968) often known simply as 'Orovida', was a painter and etcher, mainly of animal subjects.

Pitti Palace (Palazzo Pitti), Florence. Art gallery, originally built as a palace for Luca Pitti, a wealthy rival of the *Medici. Construction work began in about 1457, so the traditional attribution of its design to *Brunelleschi (who died in 1446) is unlikely; it has also been attributed to *Alberti. The Pitti family had taken up residence by 1469, but their fortunes later declined and the building remained unfinished. In 1550 it was bought by Eleonora of Toledo, the wife of Cosimo de' Medici (later the first Grand Duke of Tuscany). It now became the main Medici residence and from 1560 it was enlarged by *Ammanati. At about the same time the land around the building was developed into the Boboli Gardens. Most of the present vast structure dates from the 16th and 17th centuries, although additions continued to be made into the 19th century. The interior includes opulent decoration by Pietro da *Cortona. After the Medici dynasty came to an end in the 18th century, the family collections became state property and the Pitti was opened as a public gallery in 1833. Among its treasures are about 500 paintings from the Medici collections, mainly from the 16th and 17th centuries; in quality they rival the masterpieces in its sister institution, the *Uffizi. The Pitti also contains a good representation of Italian pictures of the 18th, 19th, and 20th centuries, and collections of costume and of precious objects such as jewels, cameos, and ivories.

Pittoni, Giambattista (*b* Venice, 20 June 1687; *d* Venice, 17 Nov. 1767). Venetian painter of religious, historical, and mythological pictures. He had a highly successful career and ranks as one of the best contemporaries of *Tiepolo, whom he succeeded as president of the Venetian Academy in 1758. As far as is known, Pittoni never left Italy, but he nevertheless received important foreign commissions, being particularly highly regarded in Germany. He also painted altarpieces for churches in numerous Italian towns and he had a reputation for being diligent and dependable. His early work was much indebted to *Piazzetta and Sebastiano *Ricci.

Pius VI, Pope. See VATICAN MUSEUMS.

Place, Francis (*b* Dinsdale, Co. Durham, 1647; *d* York, 21 Sept. 1728). English gentleman draughtsman and printmaker, active mainly in York. In 1665 he met *Hollar in London (where he had initially intended to study law) and this seems to have been the decisive factor in his taking up art seriously. His early topographical and architectural drawings are near to Hollar's in style, but his later drawings rely on a fuller use of *wash, anticipating the technique characteristic of 18th-century watercolour painting. Place also made portraits and was a pioneer of the *mezzotint technique. His work is best represented in York Art Gallery.

Plamondon, Antoine (*b* L'Ancienne-Lorette, nr. Quebec City, 29 Feb. 1804; *d* Neuville, Quebec City, 4 Sept. 1895). Canadian painter of portraits, religious subjects, and figure compositions, active mainly in Quebec. He was the first Canadian to study in France after Quebec was ceded to Britain in 1763, training in Paris, 1826–30. His portraits, which are his best works, are painted in an austerely classical style. He also executed numerous church commissions in Quebec.

Planas-Casas, José. See BATLLE PLANAS.

plaquette. A type of small decorative *relief in metal (usually bronze or lead, sometimes silver) made in multiple copies. Plaquettes originated in Italy in the 1440s, flourished there for about a century, and were popular in France, Germany, and the Netherlands into the 17th century. They were almost always cast by the *cire-perdue process and new editions could be made from a wax image of an existing plaquette; if this wax were altered a new 'state' would result. A very few were struck like coins. After casting, the best plaquettes were usually chiselled and chased, and finished with a *patina or gilding. They were used to decorate such objects as sword-hilts, inkwells, or caskets; small ones served as buttons. Because they were easily transportable they helped to disseminate *Renaissance taste—like the engravings of which they are the three-dimensional counterpart. *Flötner's plaquettes, for example, helped to make his designs common property among German artists. *Donatello is the greatest name connected with the art (there are several plaquettes by or attributed to him), but most examples are of unknown authorship.

plaster of Paris. A fine white or pinkish powder, made from gypsum (see ALABASTER), that when mixed with water forms a quick-setting paste that dries to form a uniform, solid, and inert mass. It is used in sculpture for making moulds and casts.

Plastov, Arkady. See SOCIALIST REALISM.

plein air (French: 'open air'). Term used to characterize paintings (usually landscapes) done outdoors rather than in the studio, or more generally to describe pictures that give a strong feeling of the open air. Although there are earlier instances, painting outdoors did not become common until the 19th century, when the development of portable equipment made it much easier in practical terms. It became a central feature of *Impressionism and is especially associated with *Monet.

Pleydenwurff, Hans (b ?Bamberg, c.1425; d Nuremberg, 9 Jan. 1472). German painter and designer of stained glass, the leading painter of his day in Nuremberg, where he was active from about 1450. His work shows a move away from the *International Gothic style to a more naturalistic idiom influenced by Netherlandish painting. A large Crucifixion (c.1470, Alte Pin., Munich) is characteristic of his refined style.

Michael *Wolgemut married his widow and later took over his workshop. Pleydenwurff's son **Wilhelm** (d 1494) was a painter and designer of woodcuts, also active in Nuremberg.

Pliny the Elder (Gaius Plinius Secundus) (b Comum [now Como], AD 23/24; d Stabiae [now Castellammare di Stabia], 24 Aug. 79). Roman writer. As a sideline to his career in public office, Pliny produced (among many other things) the Historia naturalis (Natural History), a massive compilation in 37 books intended to embrace not only the whole of the natural sciences but also their application to the arts and crafts of civilized life. His only extant work, it has been condemned as uncritical, unreliable, and superficial, but it contains a great deal that is interesting and entertaining. Much of its information would have been completely lost but for Pliny's labours, and the material on painting and sculpture is especially interesting because earlier treatises on classical art have not survived. It is typical of Pliny's thirst for knowledge that he perished through asphyxiation when making observations of the eruption of Vesuvius that destroyed Pompeii and Herculaneum.

plumbago. An antiquated term for *graphite, as used in *pencils.

pochade. See BONINGTON.

Poelenburgh, Cornelis van (b ?Utrecht, 1594/5; d Utrecht, 12 Aug. 1667). Dutch painter, mainly of landscapes. He studied in Utrecht with *Bloemaert and from about 1617 to 1626 was in Rome, becoming one of the leading members of the first generation of Dutch painters of Italianate landscapes. His pictures are typically small scale (he often worked on copper), with biblical or mythological figures set in Arcadian landscapes, sometimes scattered with antique remains. They are strongly influenced by *Elsheimer, but cooler in colour than the German artist's work and without his sense of mystery. After returning to Utrecht Poelenburgh enjoyed a career of great success. He was *Rubens's guide when he visited the city in 1627, was popular in aristocratic and even royal circles (he visited England in 1637 at the invitation of Charles I), and was imitated until the early 18th century. There are examples of Poelenburgh's work (and of the work of imitators) in the Fitzwilliam Museum, Cambridge, including his portrait of Jan *Both, in whose landscapes he sometimes painted the figures (an example of their collaboration is in the NG, London).

pointillism. Technique of using regular small touches of pure colour in such a way that when a picture is viewed from a suitable distance they seem to react together optically, creating more vibrant colour effects than if the same colours were physically mixed together. The term ('peinture au point') was coined in 1886 by the French critic Félix Fénéon in reference to *Seurat's *La Grande Jatte*, but Seurat, and also *Signac, preferred the broader term *divisionism. See also NEO-IMPRESSIONISM.

pointing. A method of creating an exact copy of a statue or of enlarging a model into a full-size sculpture by taking a series of measured points on the original and transferring them by means of mechanical aids to the copy or enlargement. The ancient Greeks devised elementary methods of pointing using callipers, and some kind of mechanical device was in use by the 1st century BC, when the copying of Greek statues for Roman patrons had become an industry. Various techniques of transfer, using for example a frame and plumb-line, have been used since the *Renaissance, but it was not until the late 18th and early 19th century that sophisticated pointing machines became established in the sculptor's workshop (see BACON, JOHN). Such devices typically consisted of an upright stand carrying movable arms, each arm having attached to it an adjustable measuring rod that showed the depth to which each point must be drilled. Sometimes hundreds and even thousands of points would be taken. In the late 19th and early 20th centuries most stone sculpture was produced by this mechanical method, but thereafter sculptors increasingly rejected it in favour of *direct carving.

Polack, Jan (*b* ?Poland, ?*c*.1450; *d* Munich 1519). Painter, presumably of Polish origin, active in Munich, where he is documented from 1482 and was city painter from 1488. A substantial number of paintings by him survive, including portraits as well as religious works, and he must have run a busy workshop. His style was vigorous but rather clumsy, with characteristic grimacing expressions. There are several examples of his work in the Alte Pinakothek, Munich.

Poliakoff, Serge (*b* Moscow, 8 Jan. 1906; *d* Paris, 12 Oct. 1969). Russian-born painter, printmaker, and designer who settled in Paris in 1923 and became a French citizen in 1962. For many years he earned his living as a guitarist, but he began to study painting in 1930, attending various art schools, including the *Slade School during a two-year stay in London, 1935–7. His early work was figurative, but after his return to Paris in 1937 he met *Kandinsky and Robert and Sonia *Delaunay, and under their influence he turned to abstraction. During the 1950s he gained recognition as one of the leading abstract painters in the *École de Paris; his pictures characteristically feature bold irregular slabs of matt, roughly textured colour (*Abstract Composition*, 1954, Tate, London). He adopted an almost religious attitude towards painting, saying: 'You've got to have the feeling of God in the picture if you want to get the big music in.'

Polidoro da Caravaggio (Polidoro Caldara) (*b* Caravaggio, nr. Bergamo, *c*.1499; *d* Messina, ?1543). Italian painter, named after his birthplace in Lombardy. At an early age he moved to Rome, where he assisted *Raphael in the decoration of the Vatican Loggie and then achieved great success painting palace façades with monochrome scenes imitating classical sculpture. Almost all these works have perished (only the heavily restored decoration of the Palazzo Ricci remains *in situ*), but they were highly regarded in the 16th and 17th centuries and became widely known through engravings and drawings (*Rubens was among the artists who copied them), making Polidoro, together with *Giulio Romano, the most influential of Raphael's followers. Polidoro's other claim to fame is his decoration of the chapel of Fra Marino Fetti in S. Silvestro al Quirinale (*c*.1525) with two murals of scenes from the lives of St Mary Magdalene and St Catherine of Siena; here he gave an entirely new prominence to the landscape, which dominates the figures. In this he was influenced by ancient Roman painting and foreshadowed the classical landscapes of *Claude and *Poussin. Polidoro fled Rome after the sack of the city in 1527, moving to Naples and then Messina; *Vasari says that he was murdered there by an assistant for the sake of his money.

Pollaiuolo, Antonio (*b* Florence, *c*.1432; *d* Rome, ?4 Feb. 1498) and **Piero** (*b* Florence, *c*.1441; *d* Rome, *c*.1496). Florentine artists, brothers, who jointly ran a flourishing workshop, first in their native city and then from about 1484 in Rome. Both of them are recorded as being painters and sculptors and there are considerable problems in attempting to disentangle their individual contributions to their output. However, Antonio was evidently the dominant figure and primarily a goldsmith and worker in bronze, whilst Piero was mainly a painter. Several documented paintings by Piero are known, all of fairly mediocre quality, but none by Antonio, and as certain pictures from the studio of the two brothers are so much better than Piero's independent works, it is generally assumed that Antonio had a major involvement in them. The most important of these pictures is the *Martyrdom of St Sebastian* in the National Gallery, London, probably painted in 1475. The figures of the archers in the foreground reveal a mastery of anatomy paralleled in certain bronzes generally accepted as Antonio's (e.g. the *Hercules and Antaeus*, c.1475–80, in the Bargello, Florence), in his only surviving engraving (*Battle of the Nude Men*, c.1460), and in his numerous pen drawings in which his typically wiry figures are seen in vigorous and expressive movement. His main contribution to Florentine painting lay in his searching analysis of the human figure in movement or under conditions of strain, but he is also important for his pioneering interest in landscape, seen in the National Gallery *St Sebastian* and other works. He is said to have anticipated *Leonardo in dissecting corpses in order to study the anatomy of the body.

Antonio's two principal public works were the bronze tombs of Pope Sixtus IV (Francesco della *Rovere) (signed and dated 1493) and Pope Innocent VIII (c.1492–8), both in St Peter's, Rome. The latter contains the first sepulchral effigy that simulated the living man.

Pollock, Jackson (*b* Cody, Wyo., 28 Jan. 1912; *d* East Hampton, Long Island, NY, 11 Aug. 1956). American painter, the commanding figure of the *Abstract Expressionist movement. In 1929–31 he studied at the *Art Students League under Thomas Hart *Benton and was influenced not only by Benton's restlessly energetic style, but also by his image as a virile, hard-drinking macho man (Pollock began treatment for alcoholism in 1937 and in 1939 he started therapy with Jungian psychoanalysts, using his drawings in sessions with them). During the 1930s he painted in Benton's *Regionalist vein, and he was influenced also by the work of the Mexican muralists (he attended an experimental workshop run by *Siqueiros in New York in 1936) and by certain aspects of *Surrealism, particularly the use of mythical or totemic figures as archetypes of the unconscious. From 1935 to 1942 he worked for the *Federal Art Project, and in 1943 he was given a contract by Peggy *Guggenheim; his first one-man show was held at her Art of This Century gallery in that year. A characteristic work of this time is *The She-Wolf* (1943, MoMA, New York), a semi-abstract picture with vehe-

mently handled paint and ominous imagery recalling the monstrous creatures of *Picasso's *Guernica* period.

By the mid-1940s Pollock's work had become completely abstract, and the 'drip and splash' style of *Action Painting for which he is best known emerged with some suddenness in 1947. Instead of using the traditional easel, he laid his canvas on the floor and poured and dripped his paint from a can (using commercial enamels and metallic paint because their texture was better suited to the technique); instead of using brushes, he manipulated the paint with 'sticks, trowels or knives' (to use his own words), sometimes obtaining textured effects by the admixture of 'sand, broken glass or other foreign matter'. As he worked, Pollock moved around (and sometimes through) his paintings, creating a novel *all-over style that avoided any points of emphasis and abandoned traditional ideas of composition; the design of the painting had no relation to the size or shape of the canvas—indeed in the finished work the canvas was sometimes docked or trimmed to suit the image.

The drip paintings were first publicly shown at Betty *Parsons's New York gallery in 1948. Initially they shocked most observers, but Irving Sandler (*Abstract Expressionism*, 1970) writes that 'a small number of artists and critics were stunned by the originality and dynamism of his painting . . . he opened the way to a kind of painting that was more direct, improvisational, abstract, and larger in size than that of the Abstract Surrealists of the time or of such earlier pioneers of improvisation as *Kandinsky. Pollock revitalized American abstraction, giving other artists the confidence to risk basing their own painting on the spontaneous gesture, knowing that it could yield a unified picture full of energy, drama, and passion . . . it was Pollock who unleashed the creative energies of the Abstract Expressionists.' Willem *de Kooning summed up the impact of the 1948 exhibition when he commented, 'Jackson's broken the ice.'

Pollock's drip period lasted only from 1947 to 1952 (afterwards he went back to quasi-figurative work), but it is on the paintings of these five years that his enormous reputation rests. Among the most celebrated are *Autumn Rhythm* (1950, Met. Mus., New York) and *Lavender Mist* (1950, NG, Washington), which Robert *Hughes describes as 'his most ravishingly atmospheric painting'. Pollock's novel methods gave rise to a good deal of mockery (he was nicknamed Jack the Dripper), but he was supported by advanced critics, particularly Clement *Greenberg and

Harold *Rosenberg, and as early as 1949 the French painter Georges *Mathieu said that he considered him the 'greatest living American painter'. By 1960 he was generally recognized as the most important figure in the most important movement in the history of American painting, but a movement from which artists were already in reaction. His unhappy personal life and his premature death in a car crash contributed to his status as one of the legends of modern art; he was the first American painter to become a 'star'.

In 1945 Pollock married **Lee Krasner** (1908–84), who was an Abstract Expressionist painter of some distinction, although it was only after her husband's death that she received serious critical recognition. She was also an important source of encouragement and support to Pollock, whose attitude to his work fluctuated from supreme confidence to dismal uncertainty.

polychrome. Term meaning 'many coloured' applied in art-historical writing particularly to sculpture painted in this fashion. Until the *Renaissance the practice was extremely common, whether the colours were conventionalized, as in much ancient art, or more or less naturalistic, as became more common during the Middle Ages, but because of fading of the pigments the colouring is rarely obvious today. Spain has a particularly rich tradition of polychrome sculpture (see ENCARNADO).

Polyclitus (active c.450–c.420 BC). One of the most celebrated of Greek sculptors. He was probably a native of Argos, although *Pliny says he came from Sicyon. No original works by him survive, but several are known through Roman copies. He is now most famous for his *Doryphorus* (Spear Carrier), the best copy of which is in the Archaeological Museum in Naples. In this figure he is said to have embodied the system of mathematical proportions on which he wrote a book, and the statue—long regarded as a standard for ideal male beauty—is sometimes referred to as 'The Canon'. Copies also exist of a *Diadumenus* (a youth wreathing a band round his head) by Polyclitus and of an Amazon with which, according to Pliny, he defeated *Phidias in a competition. In antiquity his greatest work was held to be the colossal *chryselephantine statue of Hera in her temple—the Heraeum—near Argos. It is now known only through descriptions and representations on coins, but ancient writers compared it favourably with Phidias' statue of Zeus at Olympia; Strabo, for example, said the Zeus was more

magnificent but the Hera more beautiful in workmanship.

Polygnotus of Thasos. Greek painter, active chiefly in Athens in the mid-5th century BC. None of his works survive, but ancient sources credit him with being the first great figure in Greek painting. He painted large compositions (mainly mythological) with many figures and some indication of landscape. His style was said to be serious and dignified, and his lively and expressive faces marked an advance on earlier art.

polyptych. A picture or other work of art made up of four or more linked parts (usually wooden panels). It was a popular form for altarpieces from the 14th century to the early 16th century. Italian polyptychs of this time typically include a *predella beneath the main panel or tier, the whole enclosed in an elaborate frame. In northern Europe, polyptychs often had panels hinged together and painted on both sides, so that they could be folded to create different pictorial compositions (sometimes ones that were appropriate for particular liturgical seasons or events). Jan van *Eyck's Ghent Altarpiece and *Grünewald's Isenheim Altarpiece are among the famous examples of this type. See also DIPTYCH and TRIPTYCH.

Pomarancio, Il. See RONCALLI.

Pompidou Centre (in full, Centre National d'Art et de Culture Georges-Pompidou). Cultural centre in Paris named after Georges Pompidou (1911–74), the President of France from 1967 to 1974. In 1969 he expressed a 'passionate wish' for 'a place where the plastic arts, music, cinema, literature, audio-visual research, etc. would find a common ground'. The site chosen for the Centre was the Plateau Beaubourg (hence its colloquial name 'Beaubourg Centre'), a once thriving area near the centre of Paris that had become derelict between the world wars. An international competition for the building produced almost 700 submissions, including bizarre ideas such as a giant egg and an enormous hand extended towards the sky, each finger being intended to house a separate department. The winning design was submitted by the Italian-British team of Renzo Piano and Richard Rogers (later Lord Rogers). Their huge building was constructed in 1971–7 and soon became one of the most famous sights of the city. A leading example of 'high-tech' architecture, it has been described as looking like a 'crazy oil refinery' and has attracted extremes of praise and censure. The large plaza in front of the building is conceived as part of the Centre and is the main forum for the city's street performers. Also outside the building is the ebullient Beaubourg Fountain (1980) by Jean *Tinguely and Niki de *Saint Phalle. The Centre is divided into various departments, including a library, an industrial design centre, and an institute for the development and promotion of avant-garde music. The largest of the departments and the main reason for the Centre's popularity is the national collection of modern art—the Musée National d'Art Moderne—which was formerly housed in the Palais de Tokyo. It was opened there in 1947, but its origins are much older, for it is the heir to the Musée du Luxembourg, opened in 1818 as a showcase for the work of living artists. Its collection of modern art is exceeded in scope and quality probably only by that of the *Museum of Modern Art in New York.

pompier, l'art. A term applied pejoratively to French academic art (more particularly pretentious *history painting) of the late 19th century. It is said to derive from the habit of posing nude models wearing firemen's helmets to substitute for ancient military headgear (*pompier* is French for 'fireman').

Pompon, François (*b* Saulieu, nr. Dijon, 9 May 1855; *d* Paris, 6 May 1933). French sculptor. Much of his career was spent working as an assistant to other sculptors (including *Rodin) and recognition came to him late in life after his *Polar Bear* (Pompidou Centre, Paris) was a great success at the 1922 *Salon d'Automne. The work became enormously popular, reproduced in a variety of forms, and Pompon was hailed as the greatest animal sculptor since *Barye.

Pont-Aven, School of. Term applied to a group of painters associated with *Gauguin during his periods of work at the town of Pont-Aven in Brittany (1886, 1888–9, 1894), and inspired by his anti-naturalistic style. Émile *Bernard was among them, and he and Gauguin together developed *Synthetism.

Pontius, Paul. See LINE ENGRAVING.

Pontormo (Jacopo Carucci) (*b* Pontormo, nr. Empoli, 26 May 1494; *d* Florence 31 Dec. 1556). Italian painter, active in and around Florence, where he was one of the outstanding artists of his generation. According to *Vasari, he studied successively with *Leonardo da Vinci, *Albertinelli, *Piero di Cosimo, and Andrea del *Sarto, whose workshop he is said to have

entered in 1512; Andrea was certainly a major influence on his early work. Pontormo was precocious (he was praised by *Michelangelo whilst still a youth) and by the time he painted his *Joseph in Egypt* (NG, London) in about 1518 he had already created a distinctive style—full of restless movement and disconcertingly irrational effects of scale and space—that put him in the vanguard of *Mannerism. The emotional tension evident in this work reaches its climax in Pontormo's masterpiece, the altarpiece of the *Entombment* (*c*.1526–8) in the Capponi Chapel of S. Felicità, Florence, which is regarded as one of the summits of Mannerist art. It is sometimes described as the *Deposition* or the *Lamentation*, rather than the *Entombment*, and the uncertainty over the subject reflects its sublime otherworldliness; there is almost no conventional setting, the colours have an unearthly intensity, and the figures—lost in a trance of grief—seem to occupy a spiritual rather than a physical dimension.

Pontormo was primarily a religious painter, but he was also an outstanding portraitist (he was a major influence on his pupil and adopted son *Bronzino) and in 1520–1 for the *Medici villa at Poggio a Caiano he painted a memorable mythological work (*Vertumnus and Pomona* according to Vasari, but the identification is disputed) in which an apparently idyllic scene reveals a strong undercurrent of neurosis. In his later work his style was enriched by the study of Michelangelo and *Dürer's prints, but this stage of his career is known mainly through his superb drawings (best represented in the Uffizi, Florence), as the great fresco scheme in S. Lorenzo, Florence, that occupied him from 1546 until his death was destroyed in the 18th century. In the last two years of his life Pontormo kept a diary—a remarkable document that not only gives a day-to-day account of his progress in S. Lorenzo but also reveals his obsession with his failing health, as he notes every ache and pain and records every morsel he ate. It is a poignant testimony of a melancholy and introspective man; Vasari described him as 'temperate and polite', but also 'solitary beyond belief'.

Pop art. A movement based on the imagery of consumerism and popular culture, flourishing from the late 1950s to the early 1970s, chiefly in the USA and Britain. The term was coined *c*.1955 by Lawrence *Alloway. Comic books, advertisements, packaging, and images from television and the cinema were all part of the iconography of the movement, and it was a feature of Pop art in both the USA and Britain that it rejected any distinction between good and bad taste.

In the USA Pop art was initially regarded as a reaction from *Abstract Expressionism because its exponents brought back figural imagery and made use of *Hard-Edge techniques. It was seen as a descendant of *Dada (in fact Pop art is sometimes called *Neo-Dada) because it debunked the seriousness of the art world and embraced the use or reproduction of common-place subjects (comic strips, soup tins, highway signs) in a manner that had affinities with *Duchamp's *ready-mades. The most immediate inspiration, however, was the work of Jasper *Johns and Robert *Rauschenberg, both of whom began to make an impact on the New York art scene in the mid-1950s. They opened a wide new range of subject matter with Johns's paintings of flags, targets, and numbers and his sculptures of objects such as beer cans and Rauschenberg's *collages and *combine paintings featuring Coca-Cola bottles, stuffed birds, and photographs from magazines and newspapers. While often using similar subject matter, Pop artists generally favoured commercial techniques in preference to the painterly manner of Johns and Rauschenberg. Examples are Andy *Warhol's screenprints of soup tins and so on, Roy *Lichtenstein's paintings in the manner of comic strips, and Mel *Ramos's brash pin-ups. Claes *Oldenburg, whose subjects include ice-cream cones and hamburgers, has been the major Pop art sculptor. John Wilmerding (American Art, 1976) writes that Pop art 'cannot be separated from the culmination of affluence and prosperity during the post-World-War-II era. America had become a ravenously consuming society, packaging art as well as other products, indulging in commercial manipulation, and celebrating exhibitionism, self-promotion, and instant success . . . Pop's mass-media orientation may further be related to the acceleration of uniformity in most aspects of national life, whether restaurants or regional dialects. Shared by all Americans were the principal preoccupations of Pop art—sex, the automobile, and food.'

In Britain, too, Pop art revelled in a new glossy prosperity following years of post-war austerity. British Pop was nurtured by the *Independent Group and the work that is often cited as the first fully-fledged Pop art image was produced under its auspices—Richard *Hamilton's collage Just what is it that makes today's homes so different, so appealing? (1956, Kunsthalle, Tübingen). However, British Pop art first made a major impact at the *Young Contemporaries

exhibition in 1961 (at about the same time that American Pop art became a force). The artists in this exhibition included Derek *Boshier, David *Hockney, Allen *Jones, R. B. *Kitaj, and Peter *Phillips, who had all been students at the *Royal College of Art. In the same year the BBC screened Ken Russell's Monitor film 'Pop goes the Easel', in which Peter *Blake was one of the featured artists. Although there are exceptions (notably the erotic sculptures of Allen Jones), British Pop art was generally less brash than American, expressing a more romantic view of the subject matter in a way that can now strike a note of nostalgia. Much of the imagery, however, came directly from the American world of pin-ups and pin ball machines.

Richard Hamilton defined Pop art as 'popular, transient, expendable, low-cost, mass-produced, young, witty, sexy, gimmicky, glamorous, and Big Business', and it was certainly a success on a material level, getting through to the public in a way that few modern movements do and attracting big-money collectors. However, it was scorned by many critics. Harold *Rosenberg, for example, described Pop as being 'Like a joke without humour, told over and over again until it begins to sound like a threat . . . Advertising art which advertises itself as art that hates advertising.'

Pope-Hennessy, Sir John (b London, 13 Dec. 1913; d Florence, 31 Oct. 1994). British art historian. He was director of the *Victoria and Albert Museum, 1967–73, director of the *British Museum, 1974–6, and from 1977 to 1987 consultative chairman, department of European paintings, *Metropolitan Museum, New York, and professor of fine arts at New York University. His many publications made him perhaps the doyen in the field of Italian Renaissance art among English writers. They include the magisterial An Introduction to Italian Sculpture in three parts (all of which have subsequently appeared in revised editions), Italian Gothic Sculpture (1955), Italian Renaissance Sculpture (1958), and Italian High Renaissance and Baroque Sculpture (1963), an edition of *Cellini's Autobiography (1949), and monographs on *Giovanni di Paolo (1937), *Sassetta (1939), *Uccello (1950, revised 1972), Fra *Angelico (1952, revised 1974), *Raphael (1970), Luca della *Robbia (1980), and Cellini (1985). His autobiography, Learning to Look, was published in 1991.

Popova, Lyubov (b nr. Ivanovskoye, Moscow province, 24 Apr. 1889; d Moscow, 25 May 1924).

Russian painter and designer. She was one of the leading figures of Russian avant-garde art in its most exciting period, but she died tragically young of scarlet fever. After studying painting in Moscow, 1907–8, she travelled extensively (she came from a wealthy bourgeois family) and in 1912–13 worked in Paris, frequenting the studios of two *Cubist artists, *Le Fauconnier and *Metzinger. When the First World War broke out she returned from Italy to Moscow, where she worked with *Tatlin and contributed to major avant-garde exhibitions. From Cubism she developed to complete abstraction in a series of pictures she called *Painterly Architectonics* (1916– 20). They owe something to both Tatlin and *Malevich, but have a distinctive voice, especially in her rich colouring. Popova also worked as a designer of costumes and sets for the stage and of textiles.

poppy oil. Oil extracted from poppy seeds, one of the most popular of the *drying oils used as a *medium for *oil painting. It is less viscous than *linseed and *walnut oil and does not easily turn rancid. It is, however, slow drying. This turned out to be an advantage rather than a disadvantage when *alla prima* painting came into vogue about the middle of the 19th century and for a time during the second half of that century poppy oil was much used by commercial colourmen.

Porcellis, Jan (b Ghent, c.1584; d Zouterwoude, 1632). Dutch painter, etcher, and draughtsman of marine subjects. Porcellis was Flemish by birth, but he spent most of his career in Holland, working in various towns before settling at Zouterwoude, near Leiden. He was regarded as the greatest marine painter of his day and his work marks the transition from the busy and brightly coloured seascapes of the early 17th century, with their emphasis on the representation of ships, to monochromatic paintings that are essentially studies of sea, sky, and atmospheric effects. His favourite theme was a modest fishing boat making its way through a choppy sea near the shore. *Rembrandt and Jan van de *Cappelle collected his works. His son **Julius** (c.1609–45) was also a marine painter.

Pordenone (Giovanni Antonio de Sacchis) (b Pordenone, ?c.1483; d Ferrara, ?13 Jan. 1539). Italian painter, named after the town of his birth, near Venice, and active in various parts of northern Italy. After working in a provincial style at the very start of his career (his master is unknown and *Vasari says he was self-taught), by the beginning of the second decade of the 16th century he had come close to the contemporary Venetian (specifically *Giorgionesque) manner of painting. In the second half of the decade, however, he was in central Italy, and his style changed under the impact particularly of *Michelangelo, acquiring great weight and solidity. Pordenone was influenced also by *Mantegna's illusionism and by German prints, and the style he forged from these diverse influences was highly distinctive and original. He always retained something of provincial uncouthness—at times vulgarity—but he was, in Vasari's words, 'very rich in invention . . . bold and resolute', and he excelled at dramatic spatial effects. These qualities are seen at their most forceful in his fresco of the *Crucifixion* (1520–1) in Cremona Cathedral; the densely packed, bizarrely expressive figures are seen as if on a stage through a painted proscenium arch and they lunge violently out into the spectator's space. From 1527 Pordenone lived mainly in Venice and in the 1530s he was the most serious rival there to *Titian. His major works in Venice have been destroyed, however. In the year before his death he moved to Ferrara to design tapestries for Ercole II d'*Este.

porphyry. A hard volcanic stone, difficult to carve and polish, varying in colour from red to green. The porphyry used by ancient sculptors was a very hard, durable stone of a deep purplish red. It was greatly prized by the Romans and became particularly associated with the sacred aura of the emperor, purple being the imperial colour. Large numbers of Roman works in porphyry have been preserved—gems, vases, urns, sarcophagi, busts, and statues (in figural work sometimes only the clothing is in porphyry, with the flesh parts in another stone). The Eastern emperors in Byzantium also used porphyry, often despoiling Roman monuments to get it. During the Italian *Renaissance this costly stone of the ancients (*pórfido rosso antico*) again came into favour, especially with the *Medici. The sculptor Francesco Ferrucci (1497–1585) was the leading figure in rediscovering the virtually lost art of cutting it. He produced various works in the medium, including a portrait relief of Cosimo de' Medici (c.1570, V&A, London). Porphyry has sometimes been used by modern sculptors, for example by Stephen Cox (b 1946) in an abstract piece (1996–7) alluding to the Eucharist (the purple colour suggesting Christ's blood) in St Nicholas' Cathedral, Newcastle upon Tyne.

Portinari, Cândido (*b* Brodósqui, São Paulo state, 30 Dec. 1903; *d* Rio de Janeiro, 6 Feb. 1962). Brazilian painter of Italian descent. He is best known for his portrayals of Brazilian workers and peasants, but he dissociated himself from the revolutionary fervour of his Mexican contemporaries, and painted in a style that shows affinities with *Picasso's *'Neoclassical' works of the 1920s (which he saw during a three-year period he spent in Europe, 1928–31). In the 1940s his work took on greater pathos and he also turned to biblical subjects. He gained an international reputation and his major commissions included murals for the Hispanic section of the Library of Congress in Washington (1942) and for the United Nations Building in New York (two panels representing *War* and *Peace*, 1953–5).

Portland stone. *Limestone from Portland in Dorset. It has been quarried there since the Middle Ages, but it was not used extensively until the 17th century, when it was much employed in the rebuilding of London after the Great Fire of 1666 (St Paul's Cathedral is mainly in Portland stone). Subsequently (in spite of its relative scarcity and the expense of transporting it) the best-quality Portland stone became a favourite material for dignified public buildings throughout England, because of its attractive colour and texture (it bleaches white on exposure to the elements, and its close grain means that it can be precisely cut and carved). It has also been used for outdoor monuments, for example the statue of George V (1947) in Old Palace Yard, London, by Sir William Reid Dick (1878–1961).

Posada, José Guadalupe (*b* Aguascalientes, 2 Feb. 1851; *d* Mexico City, 20 Jan. 1913). Mexican printmaker and draughtsman. His enormous output was largely devoted to political and social issues, revealing, for example, the dreadful conditions in which the poor lived. From 1890 his studio in Mexico City functioned as an open shop fronting the street, where he turned out sensational broadsheets and cheap cartoons aimed at a largely illiterate public. His work had the vigour and spontaneous strength of genuinely popular art, with the inborn Mexican taste for the more gruesome aspects of death— one of his recurring motifs is the *calavera* or animated skeleton. He made a major impression on *Orozco and *Rivera during their student days.

Post, Frans (*b* Haarlem, *c.*1612; *bur.* Haarlem, 17 Feb. 1680). Dutch landscape painter, active mainly in his native Haarlem. In 1637–44 he was a member of the Dutch West India Company's voyage of colonization to Brazil, where he produced 'the first firmly documented landscapes painted in the New World by a trained European artist' (Seymour Slive, *Dutch Painting: 1600–1800*, 1995). He observed the unfamiliar flora and fauna with an appropriate freshness, creating scenes of remarkable vividness and charm, and he continued to paint Brazilian landscapes after his return to the Netherlands (indeed he is not known to have painted any other type of picture). Because of his *'naive' style, he has been called the Douanier *Rousseau of the 17th century, and he was virtually forgotten or regarded as a curiosity until the 20th century. Examples of his fairly rare work are in the Louvre, Paris, the National Gallery of Ireland, Dublin, and Ham House, London. His brother **Pieter** (1608–69) was one of the outstanding Dutch architects of the 17th century (the Huis ten Bosch near The Hague is his most famous work) and also occasionally painted.

Post-Impressionism. Term applied to various trends in painting, particularly in France, that developed from *Impressionism or in reaction against it in the period *c.*1880–*c.*1905. Roger *Fry coined the term as the title of an exhibition, 'Manet and the Post-Impressionists', which he organized at the Grafton Galleries, London, in 1910. The exhibition was dominated by the work of *Cézanne, *Gauguin, and van *Gogh, who are considered the central figures of Post-Impressionism. These three artists varied greatly in their response to Impressionism: Cézanne, who wished 'to make of Impressionism something solid and enduring, like the art of the museums', was preoccupied with pictorial structure; Gauguin renounced 'the abominable error of naturalism' to explore the symbolic use of colour and line; and van Gogh's uninhibited emotional intensity was the fountainhead of *Expressionism. Georges *Seurat, a figure of almost equal importance, concentrated on a more scientific analysis of colour (see NEO-IMPRESSIONISM. The general drift of Post-Impressionism was to lead away from the naturalism of Impressionism towards the series of avant-garde movements (such as *Fauvism and *Cubism) that revolutionized European art in the decade leading up to the First World War. (Some writers extend the notion of Post-Impressionism to cover these developments, making the term embrace the period *c.*1880–*c.*1914, but this makes an already broad concept less rather than more useful.)

Fry organized his first Post-Impressionist exhibition at short notice and in an almost casual atmosphere, but he brought together a highly impressive (if far from balanced) collection of pictures, mainly loaned by leading French dealers. The exhibition created what the *Daily Mail* called 'an altogether unprecedented artistic sensation' or what *Sickert more succinctly described as a 'rumpus'. The reviews were mainly unpleasant, sometimes viciously so. Some visitors were angry (Duncan *Grant recalled people shaking their umbrellas at the pictures) and others mocked. The prevailing opinion was that the pictures on show were childish, crude, and the product of moral degeneracy or mental derangement. Duncan Grant, however, said that he and Vanessa *Bell were 'wildly enthusiastic' about the exhibition, and it powerfully affected the work of several of the painters in Sickert's circle (see CAMDEN TOWN GROUP), in general encouraging the use of strong, flat colours.

In 1912 Fry organized a second Post-Impressionist exhibition at the Grafton Galleries. This was more wide-ranging, coherent, and up to date than the first (it included several *Cubist works), with a British section chosen by Clive Bell and a Russian section organized by Boris *Anrep. It too caused a great deal of controversy, but did not have quite the same impact as the first.

Post-Painterly Abstraction. A term coined by the critic Clement *Greenberg to characterize a broad trend in American painting, beginning in the 1950s, in which abstract painters reacted in various ways against the *gestural 'painterly' qualities of *Abstract Expressionism. Greenberg used the term as the title of an exhibition he organized at the Los Angeles County Museum of Art in 1964. He took the word 'painterly' (in German *malerisch*) from Heinrich *Wölfflin, who had discussed it in his book *Principles of Art History*. By it he understood 'the blurred, broken, loose definition of colour and contour'; Post-Painterly Abstractionists, in contrast, moved towards 'physical openness of design, or toward linear clarity, or toward both'. The characterization was never a very exact one, but essentially it described a rejection of expressive brushwork in favour of broad areas of unmodulated colour. The term thus embraces more precisely defined types of abstract art including *Colour Field Painting and *Hard-Edge Painting. Among the leading figures of the trend are Helen *Frankenthaler, Al *Held, Ellsworth *Kelly, Morris *Louis, Kenneth *Noland, Jules *Olitski, and Frank *Stella.

Pot, Hendrik (*b* ?Haarlem, *c.*1585; *d* Amsterdam, 1657). Dutch painter. Most of his paintings are small portraits and guardroom scenes, although he also produced a few large allegorical pictures. In 1632 he visited England, where he painted a portrait of Charles I (Louvre, Paris) and a group portrait of Charles with Queen Henrietta Maria and the Prince of Wales (Royal Coll.).

Potter, Paulus (*bapt.* Enkhuizen, 20 Nov. 1625; *bur.* Amsterdam, 17 Jan. 1654). Dutch painter and etcher of animals in landscapes, active in Delft, The Hague, and Amsterdam. His best-known work, the life-size *Young Bull* (1647, Mauritshuis, The Hague), was in the 19th century one of the most famous of all Dutch paintings. Subsequent taste has found its detailed and precise manner rather dry and laboured and preferred his more characteristic works, which are much smaller. His speciality was scenes of cattle and sheep in sunlit meadows. His father **Pieter Potter** (*c.*1600–1663) was a versatile minor painter, working in all the main genres of the day.

pouncing. A method of transferring a drawing or design to another surface (typically a *cartoon to a wall for *fresco painting) by making a series of pinpricks along the outlines of the drawing, then dabbing pounce (a fine powder of charcoal or similar substance) through them, thus creating a dotted replica of the outlines on the surface below. See also SPOLVERO.

Pound, Ezra. See VORTICISM.

Pourbus. Family of Netherlandish painters, distinguished mainly as portraitists. **Pieter** (*b* Gouda, *c.*1523; *d* Bruges, 30 Jan. 1584) spent most of his life in Bruges, where he became a member of the painters' guild in 1543 and at about the same time married the daughter of Lancelot *Blondeel. He was a civil engineer, surveyor, and cartographer as well as a painter. Van *Mander wrote: 'I have never seen a better equipped studio than his.' As well as portraits he painted religious and allegorical scenes, one of the most splendid of which is the *Allegory of True Love* (*c.*1547, Wallace Coll., London). Pieter's son **Frans the Elder** (*b* Bruges, 1545; *d* Antwerp, 19 Sept. 1581) was active in Antwerp, where he was a pupil and follower of Frans *Floris (he married a daughter of Cornelis Floris). The most famous member of the family is his son **Frans the Younger** (*b* Antwerp, 1569; *bur.* Paris, 19 Feb. 1622), who was one of the principal court portraitists of Europe. After spending a year working for the Archduke Albert and the Infanta

Isabella in Brussels, he was employed in Mantua from 1600 to 1609 (at the same time as *Rubens) by Vincenzo I *Gonzaga. In 1609 he was called to Paris by Marie de *Médicis and worked as her court painter until his death. His style—more concerned with the meticulous reproduction of rich costumes and jewellery than with interpretation of character—was typical of international court portraiture of the day.

Poussin, Gaspard. See DUGHET.

Poussin, Nicolas (b Les Andelys, Normandy, June 1594; d Rome, 19 Nov. 1665). French painter and draughtsman, active mainly in Rome. Although he spent almost all his career in Italy, he is regarded not only as the greatest French painter of the 17th century, but also as the mainspring of the *classical tradition in French painting. His early interest in art was given direction when Quentin Varin (c.1570–1634), a mediocre late *Mannerist painter, visited his home town, Les Andelys, in 1611–12 to carry out a church commission. Soon afterwards Poussin moved to Paris, where he probably spent most of his time until his departure for Rome in 1623, although these years are poorly documented and he may have travelled around France a good deal. The only surviving works from this period that are certainly by him are a series of mythological drawings (1622–3, Royal Lib., Windsor Castle) commissioned by the Italian poet Giovanni Battista Marino, who at this time lived in Paris. Encouraged by Marino, Poussin set out for Rome (he had already made two unsuccessful attempts to get there) and arrived in March 1624. Apart from an interlude in Paris in 1640–2, he lived in Rome for the rest of his life and his art was largely shaped by the cultural traditions of his adopted city.

Poussin initially endured hardship in Rome, but Marino's influence gained him an introduction to Cardinal Francesco *Barberini, for whom he painted the Death of Germanicus (1626–8, Minneapolis Inst. of Arts), generally regarded as his first masterpiece. The cardinal's secretary, Cassiano dal Pozzo (1588–1657), became Poussin's most important patron in Rome. He was not particularly wealthy, but he had a huge collection of prints and drawings relating to his passion for antiquity, and Poussin absorbed a great deal from this 'paper museum', as Pozzo called it. In the ancient world he found guiding moral principles as well as stylistic models—*Reynolds described him as having 'a mind thrown back two thousand years and, as it were, naturalized in antiquity'. In such an intellectual climate, his

style began to shed an earlier tendency towards Mannerist elongation, becoming more classical, but for a time he was also influenced by the dynamic *Baroque style that was emerging in these years. This is seen most clearly in the only picture he painted for a public setting in Rome, the altarpiece of the Martyrdom of St Erasmus, commissioned by Cardinal Barberini for St Peter's (1628–9, Pinacoteca, Vatican). His most personal work during this period is the Inspiration of the Poet (c.1628, Louvre, Paris), classical in design but Venetian in its rich colouring.

In about 1629 Poussin became seriously ill (*Passeri says he was stricken by venereal disease) and was nursed back to health by the family of Jacques Dughet, a French cook working in Rome, whose daughter he married in 1630. The illness coincided with a change of direction in his work. His altarpiece for St Peter's had been coolly received and in 1630 he had tried unsuccessfully to win a commission for a fresco in S. Luigi dei Francesi, the French church in Rome; these failures seem to have convinced him that his talent was not for large public works, and henceforth he concentrated on pictures of fairly modest size for private collectors whose interests were similar to his own (several of them were indeed his friends). In the early 1630s he specialized in literary subjects from Ovid and Tasso, treated with a lyrical warmth (Rinaldo and Armida, c.1630, Dulwich Picture Gal., London), and he also painted some full-blooded bacchanalian scenes. From the mid-1630s, however, he put more stress on clarity of design, and *Raphael replaced Titian as his chief inspiration among *Renaissance painters. In addition to his pagan subjects, he painted religious themes, and he seems to have been able to reconcile Christian beliefs with certain philosophical ideas of the ancient world, particularly the Stoical ideal that virtuous equanimity sustains a wise person in any misfortune. He lived a quiet, simple life, in spite of his growing success, and although he had been something of a hothead in his youth, he came to believe that 'peace and tranquillity of mind are possessions without equal'.

By the later 1630s Poussin had a high reputation in France as well as Italy, and in 1640 he reluctantly succumbed to official pressure and returned to Paris to work for Louis XIII. He was commissioned to superintend the decoration of the Grande Galerie of the *Louvre (work wholly alien to his temperament), to paint altarpieces, and to design frontispieces for the royal press. His visit was ruined by jealousy and intrigue, and in September 1642 he returned to Rome—ostensibly to collect his wife, but in reality with no intention of ever going back to Paris. Fortunately for Poussin, both the king and his chief minister, Cardinal Richelieu, died within months of his departure and no attempt was made to coerce him back to France to complete the projects he had left unfinished. Although the visit was such an unhappy one, it had the positive effect of introducing him to cultivated admirers of his work in Paris, and from this point he worked more for French than Italian patrons. The most important among them was Paul *Fréart de Chantelou, a civil servant. Poussin not only painted some of his finest works for Chantelou, but also corresponded with him at length, revealing much about his deeply thoughtful approach to his art. Clarity and rationality were the qualities he sought above all; in 1642 he told Chantelou, 'My nature constrains me to seek and to love well-ordered things, and to flee confusion, which is as much my antithesis and my enemy as light is to dark.' His working procedure was appropriately methodical, for he not only made numerous drawings, but also used wax models on a kind of miniature stage set (like *Tintoretto before him) so he could study the composition and lighting with great deliberateness. He preferred to work in solitude and—unlike most artists of the time—never employed assistants.

During the 1640s Poussin's work reached a peak of classical grandeur, lucidity, and harmony. At this time his interest in landscape increased, and many of his finest late paintings have magnificent open-air settings in which the natural elements are treated with the same sense of order that he brought to his figures—trees and mountains being turned into forms of almost geometrical clarity. These characteristics are wonderfully exemplified in two great works of 1648 illustrating the death of Phocion, a Stoical story from Greek history (Earl of Plymouth Coll., on loan to National Museum and Gallery, Cardiff; and Walker AG, Liverpool). Together with the work of his friend *Claude and his brother-in-law *Dughet, Poussin's paintings in this vein were the basis for *ideal landscape for the next two centuries. In the 1650s Poussin's style changed again, becoming imbued with an almost mystical feeling. His figures sometimes attain a superhuman grandeur and marmoreal detachment (*Holy Family*, c.1655, Hermitage, St Petersburg), his landscapes take on a new wildness and splendour, suggesting awe at the fecundity and power of nature, and his colouring

has a silvery, otherworldly quality. The last works he completed were a set of four pictures representing the Seasons (1660–4, Louvre). By this time he had become almost a hermit, but nevertheless he was revered as one of the greatest artists of the age.

After his death Poussin's high-minded and rational approach made him the perfect embodiment of the ideals of the Académie Royale (see ACADEMY), founded in 1648, but in the 1670s his authority was challenged in an ongoing debate in the Académie between those who believed in the primacy of design (see DISEGNO) in painting (Poussinistes) and those who—inspired by *Rubens—emphasized the importance of colour (Rubénistes). Although the Rubénistes won the day, Poussin continued to be a major inspiration to classically minded artists into the early 19th century—indeed Anthony *Blunt describes him as 'the key to the whole later evolution of French art'. During the *Romantic era, with its stress on self-expression, his influence declined, but his spirit was revived again by *Cézanne, who declared that he wanted 'to do Poussin again, from Nature'.

Powers, Hiram (*b* Woodstock, Vt., 29 July 1805; *d* Florence, 27 June 1873). American sculptor, active in Italy from 1837. He first achieved success with portrait busts, but his great international fame came with his marble statue *The Greek Slave* (1841–3), which caused a sensation at the *Great Exhibition in London in 1851 and was for a time one of the most talked about and reproduced works of art of the age (there are several versions of it, for example in the Corcoran Gallery, Washington). The naked girl (a captive of the infidel Turks in the Greek War of Independence, 1821–32) is bound in chains and the astonishing popularity of the statue (which now seems rather insipid) no doubt depended on the way in which its sentimentality licensed its eroticism.

Poynter, Sir Edward (*b* Paris, 20 Mar. 1836; *d* London, 26 July 1919). English painter and administrator, son of the architect Ambrose Poynter, and great-grandson of the sculptor Thomas *Banks. He formed his academic style in Italy (1853–4), where he met Frederic *Leighton and admired *Michelangelo above all other artists, and in Paris (1856–9), where he studied with *Gleyre. His reputation was made with the huge *Israel in Egypt* (1867, Guildhall AG, London) and he became one of the most popular painters of the day with similar elaborate historical tableaux in which he displayed his great prowess as a draughtsman (*The Catapult*, 1868, Laing AG, Newcastle upon Tyne). In the latter part of his career, however, he confined himself to much smaller works, similar to *Alma-Tadema's classical *genre scenes, as he devoted himself much more to administration; he was first *Slade professor at University College London, 1871–5; director for art at the South Kensington Museum (now Victoria and Albert Museum) and principal of the National Art Training School (now the *Royal College of Art), 1875–81; director of the National Gallery, 1894–1904; and president of the *Royal Academy, 1896–1918. At the Slade he established an emphasis on draughtsmanship that became characteristic of the school and at South Kensington he revived a stagnant curriculum (by virtue of this office he was also supervisor of the chief provincial art schools, and in these too he raised standards). However, he was hostile towards recent developments in art, castigating the 'clique of self-styled *"Impressionists" and their apologists in the Press' for 'their incompetency in drawing and slovenliness in execution' (preface to the fourth edition of his *Lectures on Art*, 1897).

Pozzo, Andrea (*b* Trento, 30 Nov. 1642; *d* Vienna, 31 Aug. 1709). Italian painter and architect, one of the greatest exponents of the *Baroque style of *illusionist ceiling decoration. He became a lay brother in the Jesuit order in 1665 (he is sometimes give the courtesy title Padre Pozzo) and worked much for Jesuit churches, both as a painter and architect. His masterpiece is the huge ceiling fresco *Allegory of the Missionary Work of the Jesuits* (1688–94) in S. Ignazio, Rome, perhaps the most stupendous feat of *quadratura ever painted. Pozzo worked in several other Italian cities apart from Rome, and from 1703 until his death he lived in Vienna, where he decorated the Jesuit church, the University church, and the Liechtenstein Garden Palace. His influence was spread not only by his paintings, but also by his treatise *Perspectiva pictorum et architectorum* (2 vols., 1693 and 1700), which was soon translated into several European languages and also (by Jesuit missionaries) into Chinese. As an architect, he designed several churches and numerous altars, but his work in this field was unexciting compared with his paintings and the engravings in his treatise.

Pozzo, Cassiano dal. See POUSSIN.

Prado (Museo Nacional del Prado), Madrid. Spain's national museum of art, opened to the public in 1819. 'Prado' is Spanish for 'meadow' and the museum takes its name from a nearby tree-lined walk called the Paseo del Prado. The building, one of the finest examples of Spanish *Neoclassical architecture, was designed by Juan de Villanueva and begun in 1787. It was originally intended to house an academy of sciences and a museum of natural history, but before it opened it was pillaged by the invading French army in 1808. After the restoration of the Spanish monarchy, Ferdinand VII had the building repaired and decided to use it as an art gallery rather than for scientific purposes. It became national property after Queen Isabella II was deposed in 1868. The major part of the collection derives from the royal collections made in the course of three centuries by the *Habsburg and Bourbon monarchs of Spain, who included some of the most discriminating and lavish patrons in Europe, most notably Philip II and Philip IV. It is not comprehensive in its coverage but is supremely rich in certain areas. Above all, it contains what is far and away the world's greatest collection of Spanish painting, with about 50 pictures by *Velázquez (roughly half his surviving output) and more than 100 by *Goya. It has more pictures by *Bosch, *Rubens, and *Titian than any other collection in the world, and among the other artists who are particularly well represented are van *Dyck, *Tintoretto, and *Veronese.

Praxiteles. Greek sculptor from Athens, active in the mid-4th century BC. His fame among Greek sculptors, today as in his own time, is second only to that of *Phidias. Various works of his described by ancient authors are known through Roman copies, and a marble statue of *Hermes and the Infant Dionysus*, found at Olympia in 1877 in the location where it was described by *Pausanias (now in the Olympia Museum), is considered by some authorities to be from his own hand. If this is so, it can be claimed as the only surviving original statue by an identified Greek sculptor of the first rank. Certainly it has a delicacy in the modelling of forms and a subtlety of finish far removed from the workmanship seen in most Roman copies, and it shows the sensuous charm and gentle grace for which he was renowned. In antiquity his most famous work was the *Aphrodite of Cnidus*, known through several copies. This much-imitated work was the first free-standing life-size female nude in Greek art and *Pliny described it as 'the finest statue not only by Praxiteles but in the whole world'. Praxiteles' influence was profound. The tenderness and intimacy of his work marked a move away from the remote idealization of the *Classical period, to an art more concerned with human emotion, and his graceful, sinuous poses, with the figure often shown leaning on a support, became part of the general currency of *Hellenistic sculptors. His preference for working in marble made the material popular again after it had long been eclipsed by bronze.

Precisionism. A movement in American painting, originating c.1915 and flourishing in the inter-war period, particularly the 1920s, in which urban and especially industrial subjects were depicted with a very smooth, and precise technique, creating clear, sharply defined, sometimes quasi-*Cubist forms. The terms 'Cubist-Realists', 'Immaculates', and 'Sterilists' have also been applied to Precisionist painters. They were not a formal group, but they often exhibited together. *Demuth, *O'Keeffe, and *Sheeler were among the leading figures. In Precisionist painting the light is typically brilliantly clear (although George Ault (1891–1948) was best known for his night scenes) and forms are often chosen for their geometric interest. Human presence is excluded and there is no social comment. Rather, the American industrial and technological scene is endowed with an air of epic grandeur. The degree of Cubist influence varied greatly. Some of Sheeler's paintings are in an almost photographically realistic style, whereas other works are semi-abstract. Precisionism was influential in both imagery and technique on American *Magic Realism and *Pop art.

predella (Italian: 'platform', 'altar step'). A small painting or series of paintings beneath the main part of an *altarpiece. Predellas are often found in Italian *polyptychs of the 14th and 15th centuries; they are less common in other countries. By extension, the term is sometimes applied to any subsidiary picture forming an appendage to a larger one.

Predis (or Preda), **Ambrogio de** (b Milan, c.1455; d after 1508). Milanese painter. He was court painter to Ludovico *Sforza and worked mainly as a portraitist, but he is chiefly remembered for his association, together with his elder half-brother **Evangelista de Predis** (d after 1490), with *Leonardo da Vinci in the 1483 contract for the Virgin of the Rocks in the National Gallery, London. The wings of this altarpiece, depicting angels with musical instruments, are of much lower quality than the centre panel and are

presumed to be by Ambrogio and/or Evangelista. The National Gallery also has a portrait by Ambrogio (Profile Portrait of a Lady, c.1500), showing his rather wooden imitation of Leonardo's style.

Preece, Patricia. See SPENCER.

Prendergast, Maurice (b St John's, Newfoundland, 10 Oct. 1859; d New York, 1 Feb. 1924). Canadian-born American painter and printmaker. He was a member of The *Eight, but stood somewhat apart from the rest of the group. Boston was his home for most of his life and he spent much of his career travelling and painting abroad; it was only in 1914 that he moved to New York, the centre of The Eight's activities. The main thing he had in common with other members was a desire to revive American art from academic stagnation, and his work is remarkable for its brilliant decorative colour. His paintings were often of people enjoying themselves in innocent pleasures (Central Park in 1903, 1903, Met. Mus., New York). He was one of the first American artists to be influenced by *Post-Impressionism, notably in the way in which he emphasized flat pattern rather than illusionistic space. In 1913 he showed seven works in the *Armory Show and at this time he stood out as one of the most stylistically advanced American artists. Most of his paintings were in watercolour, but in later years he turned increasingly to oils. He also made about 200 *monotypes (mainly between 1891 and 1902), an unusually large oeuvre for this medium.

Pre-Raphaelite Brotherhood (PRB). The name adopted in 1848 by a group of young English artists who shared a dismay at what they considered the moribund state of British painting and hoped to recapture the sincerity and simplicity of early Italian art (i.e. before the time of *Raphael, whom they saw as the fountainhead of academism). The nucleus of the group was formed by three fellow students at the *Royal Academy—William Holman *Hunt, John Everett *Millais, and Dante Gabriel *Rossetti (to whom, son of an Italian ex-revolutionary, the sealing of the group into a secret Brotherhood was due). The other four original brethren were the painter James *Collinson, the sculptor Thomas *Woolner, and the art critics W. M. Rossetti (1829–1919) and F. G. Stephens (1828–1907). Ford Madox *Brown was closely allied with them, though not at any time a member of the Brotherhood. The movement had a strong literary flavour from the start, and the members published a short-lived journal called the *Germ* (4 issues, 1850); Rossetti was distinguished as a poet as well as a painter. His brother defined the aims of the Brotherhood as follows: '(1) To have genuine ideas to express; (2) to study Nature attentively, so as to know how to express them; (3) to sympathise with what is direct and serious and heartfelt in previous art, to the exclusion of what is conventional and self-parading and learned by rote; and (4) and most indispensable of all, to produce thoroughly good pictures and statues.' Their desire for fidelity to nature was expressed through detailed, rather literal-minded observation of flora, etc., and the use of a clear, bright, sharp-focus technique; and their moral seriousness is seen in their choice of religious or other uplifting themes. The kind of pictures they hated were academic 'machines' and trivial *genre scenes.

The initials PRB were first used on Rossetti's picture *The Girlhood of Mary Virgin* (Tate, London), exhibited in 1849, and were adopted by the other members of the Brotherhood. When their meaning became known in 1850 the group was subjected to furious criticism and abuse. Charles Dickens led the attack in his periodical *Household Words*, calling Millais's *Christ in the House of His Parents* (1849–50, Tate) 'mean, odious, revolting and repulsive' (later he became a friend of Millais). Dickens was outraged by the implied rejection of Raphael (still unquestioningly thought of by many critics as the greatest painter who ever lived), and he regarded the claim to go behind Raphael as an anti-progressive reversion to primitivism and ugliness. The fortunes of the Pre-Raphaelites improved greatly after they were publicly defended by *Ruskin in 1851, and they attracted numerous followers. These included John *Brett, Charles Allston *Collins, Walter Howell *Deverell, Augustus *Egg, Arthur *Hughes, Henry *Wallis, and two artists who are each remembered for only a single Pre-Raphaelite masterpiece—Henry Alexander Bowler (1824–1903), painter of *The Doubt: 'Can These Dry Bones Live?'* (1855, Tate), and William Shakespeare Burton (1824–1916), painter of *The Wounded Cavalier* (1856, Guildhall AG, London).

By 1853, however, the Brotherhood itself had virtually dissolved. Apart from their youthful revolutionary spirit (they were very young in 1848) and their romantic if uninformed medievalism, the prime movers had little in common as artists and they went their separate ways. Of the original members only Hunt remained true to PRB doctrines. Millais adopted a much looser

style and went on to become the most popular and successful painter of the day. Curiously, however, it was Rossetti, the least committed to PRB ideals (he never cultivated painstaking detail), who continued the name. Although his later work, made up principally of languorous depictions of *femmes fatales*, is entirely different from his early Pre-Raphaelite pictures, the name stuck to him and to his followers. Thus in the popular imagination the term 'Pre-Raphaelite' conjures up pictures of medieval romance, and ironically a movement that began as a rebellion against artificiality and sentimentality is now itself identified with a kind of escapism. This second wave of pseudo-medieval Pre-Raphaelitism had its roots in the decoration of the newly built Oxford Union Society debating hall (now the Old Library) with scenes from Arthurian legend (1857), a scheme in which Rossetti was joined by *Burne-Jones, William *Morris, Val Prinsep (1838–1904), and other artists (the paintings, in *distemper, were technically unsound and have faded badly). Rossetti's influence endured after his death and the smouldering temptresses he painted, together with the more pallid and ethereal beauties of Burne-Jones, were much imitated at the turn of the century, when they were part of the taste for *Symbolism.

The Pre-Raphaelite tradition was continued well into the 20th century in the work of artists such as Evelyn *De Morgan, Sidney Harold Meteyard (1868–1947), John Byam Shaw (1872–1919), and John Melhuish Strudwick (1849–1937). After the First World War, however, work in this style was increasingly considered old-fashioned, and the reputations of the original Pre-Raphaelites slumped. In 1948 the centenary of the founding of the PRB was marked by several exhibitions and the publication of a substantial book (*Pre-Raphaelite Painters* by Robin Ironside and John Gere), but it was not until the 1960s that there was a general revival of interest in the subject.

presentation drawing. A highly finished drawing intended as an independent work of art rather than as a stage in the preparation of some other work; the term is applied particularly to such drawings made in the Italian *Renaissance. The earliest known drawings of the type, probably dating from the 1420s, are by *Lorenzo Monaco (*Visitation* and *Journey of the Magi*, both Kupferstichkabinett, Berlin), and the first artist known to have produced a drawing specifically for presentation to a patron is *Leonardo da Vinci; *Vasari records that he made such a drawing, of Neptune (c.1503), for 'his good friend Antonio Segni', a collector with antiquarian tastes, but it does not survive. *Michelangelo is the artist who above all others is associated with presentation drawings and the term was coined (by Johannes *Wilde) with reference to his work. In the 1530s he made a series of such drawings, some of which he gave to Tommaso Cavalieri, a young nobleman of great physical beauty whom he met in 1532 and to whom he had a passionate emotional attachment. The drawings, in delicately stippled chalk, were of mythological subjects or fanciful heads (Vasari calls them 'divine heads'), the earliest surviving one being the *Punishment of Tityus* (1532, Royal Lib., Windsor). Later Michelangelo made presentation drawings on religious subjects for Vittoria Colonna, a pious widow who became a close friend from about 1538 (*Crucifixion*, c.1539, BM, London).

Preston, Margaret (née Macpherson) (*b* Port Adelaide, 29 Apr. 1875; *d* Sydney, 28 May 1963). Australian painter, printmaker, writer, and lecturer, active mainly in Sydney. In 1904–7 and 1910–20 she lived in Europe. During the second period, spent mainly in Paris and London, she moved from an academic style to a more modern idiom influenced by *Fauvism. She was 'a woman of great independence of mind, volatile in temperament, ardently patriotic and consumed by a passion for experimentation in painting media and all kinds of graphic techniques' (Bernard Smith, *Australian Painting: 1788–1990*, 1991). In 1927 the journal *Art in Australia* devoted a special issue to her and by this time she was recognized as one of the leading painters in the country. Her characteristic subjects included bush landscapes and flower paintings of native flora, and she was passionately devoted to the idea of creating a distinctive national art, promoting this through writing and lecturing as well as painting. She was one of the first to appreciate Aboriginal art, and much of her own work from the 1940s onwards shows its influence, particularly in her adoption of earthy colours.

Preti, Mattia (Il Cavaliere Calabrese) (*b* Taverna, 24 Feb. 1613; *d* Valletta, Malta, 3 Jan. 1699). Italian *Baroque painter. He came from the Calabria region of southern Italy (hence his nickname) and his busy career took him to many different parts of the country; he is also said to have visited Flanders and Spain, but these journeys are not documented. His early work includes groups of musicians and card-players,

strongly *Caravaggesque in style, but later he excelled mainly in frescos on religious subjects. In this field his main model was *Lanfranco, whom he succeeded in the decoration of S. Andrea della Valle in Rome (1650–1). After the plague of 1656 carried off virtually a whole generation of artists in Naples, Preti worked with great success there, gaining many important commissions. They included a series of seven frescos commemorating the plague for the city gates; they no longer survive, but two *modelli* for them are in the Museo di Capodimonte in Naples and give some idea of how powerful the huge frescos must have been. In 1661 Preti moved to Malta, where he lived for the rest of his life. Several churches on the island, including the cathedral of Valletta, have decorations by him.

Price, Sir Uvedale (*b* ?Foxley Hall, Herefordshire, 1747; *d* Foxley Hall, 14 Sept. 1829). English landed gentleman and writer, a leading proponent of the *Picturesque. He laid out his Herefordshire estate, Foxley, on Picturesque principles, aiming for variety and irregularity, and his *Essay on the Picturesque* (1794) is one of the main literary works of the movement. His other writings include a translation of selections from *Pausanias (1780).

primary colours. In painting, those colours—blue, red, and yellow—that cannot be made from mixtures of other colours. When two of the primaries are mixed together, the result is known as a secondary colour, red and yellow making orange, red and blue making purple, and yellow and blue making green.

Primary Structures. A type of abstract sculpture that became fashionable in the mid-1960s, characterized by a preference for extremely simple geometrical shapes and frequently a use of industrially fabricated elements. The term was popularized by an exhibition entitled 'Primary Structures' at the Jewish Museum, New York, in 1966. Among the artists who worked in this vein were Carl *Andre, Donald *Judd, Sol *LeWitt, Robert *Morris, and Tony *Smith. Primary Structures comes within the scope of *Minimal art and the two terms have sometimes been used synonymously.

Primaticcio, Francesco (*b* Bologna, 1504/5; *d* Paris, Mar./Sept. 1570). Italian painter, architect, and decorator, mainly active in France. He was born in Bologna and developed his all-round skills as *Giulio Romano's assistant in Mantua. In 1532 he was called to France by Francis I and worked with *Rosso at Fontainebleau. Together they were mainly responsible for establishing the distinctive French type of *Mannerism associated with the School of *Fontainebleau. Their respective shares in the creation of the new manner—particularly the highly influential combination of paintings with *stucco ornament—are uncertain. Rosso is often accorded primacy, but *Vasari said 'the first works in stucco that were done in France, and the first labours in fresco of any account, had their origin, it is said, in Primaticcio.' His elongated figure style also had wide influence in France. Primaticcio took over the direction of the work at Fontainebleau on Rosso's death in 1540 and in the 1540s he twice visited Rome to buy antiquities or have casts made for Francis. In his later years he turned more to architecture, but little survives of his work in this field. On the other hand, examples of his drawings are in several major collections; there are also a few easel paintings by him.

priming. A coating applied to a canvas, panel, or other *support to prepare the surface for painting; more specifically, the final thin layer of this coating. In the broader sense, the term is synonymous with *ground.

primitive. Term used with various meanings in the history and criticism of the arts. In its widest sense it is applied to art of societies outside the great Western, Near Eastern, and oriental civilizations, even though much of it was produced by highly sophisticated peoples. Pre-Columbian art, North American Indian art, African art south of the Sahara, and Oceanic art are the main areas embraced by the term. Originally the term was derogatory or patronizing, as such art generally seemed uncouth or savage to Western eyes, but it is now used as a label of convenience, without any implied value judgement. By extension it has been applied to other fields of art that appear unsophisticated relative to some particular standard. It was once widely used, for example, of pre-Renaissance European painting, particularly of the Italian and Netherlandish schools (as in the expression 'the Flemish primitives'); the Renaissance had established the idea of painting as the imitation of nature that dominated Western art for centuries, so paintings from earlier periods were long found wanting in the representational skills that had become accepted as the norm. This usage of the word 'primitive' is now much less common and no longer has derogatory implications.

In the context of modern art, the term 'primitivism' has been employed to refer to the use by Western artists of forms or imagery derived from the art of so-called primitive peoples, or more broadly to describe an approach in which the artist seeks to express or celebrate elemental forces by using unconventional procedures or techniques that bypass the methods normally associated with the trained painter or sculptor. In the broader sense, the term 'primitivism' has been used to embrace such diverse phenomena as child art, *naive art (which is sometimes known as primitive art), the art of the mentally ill (see ART BRUT), and *Graffiti art. These varied forms of art are linked to each other and to the art of 'primitive' peoples by a belief that such 'innocent' expression can have a freshness and emotional honesty often lacking in mainstream Western art.

For centuries, the art of 'primitive' peoples was known in the West mainly as colonial booty, and it attracted interest either for its curiosity value or (if made of precious materials) for its monetary worth (in 1520 *Dürer enthused about Aztec treasures sent to the Emperor Charles V (see HABSBURG) from 'the new land of gold'). Although the idea of the 'noble savage' untainted by European civilization had a vogue in the 18th century, it was not until the 1890s that primitivism made a significant impact on Western art—in the work of *Gauguin, who tried to escape 'the disease of civilization' among the natives of Tahiti. From about 1905 many other avant-garde artists followed his example in cultivating primitive art as a source of inspiration, finding in it a vitality and sincerity that they thought had been polished out of Western art. Usually they followed Gauguin in spirit rather than body, although *Nolde and *Pechstein, for example, visited Oceania. Many artists in Paris collected African masks (which could be bought very cheaply in curio shops), among them *Derain, *Matisse, *Picasso, and *Vlaminck, and their influence is particularly clear in Picasso's Les Demoiselles d'Avignon, the painting that stands as the fountainhead of *Cubism. Other artists studied primitive art in museums—Henry *Moore, for example, was impressed by the powerful blocklike forms of Mayan sculpture he saw in the British Museum.

Such visual 'appropriation' of the culture of 'primitive' peoples has sometimes been interpreted as a kind of exploitation, akin to the exploitation of native labour or resources by colonial powers. However, certain modern artists seem to have approached primitive art in a spirit that was far from cynical or opportunist. For example, in 1931 the Paris *Surrealists used tribal art in their exhibition 'The Truth about the Colonies', which was a protest against a recently opened official exhibition celebrating French colonialism.

Prinsep, Val. See PRE-RAPHAELITE BROTHERHOOD and ST JOHN'S WOOD CLIQUE.

print. A picture or design made (usually on paper) from an inked impression of an engraved metal plate, wooden block, etc. Prints are made by a great variety of processes, but they fall into three main groups, depending on whether the ink is carried on raised parts of the printing surface (relief methods), in grooves made in the surface (intaglio methods), or on the surface itself (planographic or surface methods). It is fairly common for different processes from the same group to be combined in one print, and in *Baxter prints, for example, intaglio and relief methods are used together.

(a) *Relief Methods*. In these, the parts of the wood block or metal plate that are to print black are left in relief and the remainder is cut away. The principal methods are *woodcut, *wood engraving, and *linocut. To these may be added certain techniques such as *metal cut, *manière criblée, and *relief etching, in which metal plates are engraved and printed like woodcuts.

(b) *Intaglio Methods*. In intaglio printing the principle is the reverse of that in the relief methods; the surface of the plate does not print, the ink being held only in the engraved furrows. The main techniques are: *line engraving, in which the design is engraved on the metal plate with a *burin; *drypoint, where the lines are drawn by scratching the plate with a strong steel needle; *etching, *soft-ground etching, and *aquatint, where the designs are bitten into the plate by means of acid. In addition there are the mainly reproductive (and largely defunct) processes of *mezzotint, *stipple engraving, and *crayon manner. The various intaglio processes have often been used in combination with one another on the same plate. *Rembrandt, for example, frequently combined etching and drypoint.

(c) *Planographic Methods*. In these the design is neither raised in relief nor incised. The main method is *lithography, in which the design is printed from a perfectly flat slab of limestone or a prepared metal plate. The process utilizes the antipathy of grease and water to separate those areas that receive and those areas that reject the printing ink. *Stencilling and *screenprinting are sometimes considered

planographic methods, although they really form a separate category because the image is created through a barrier rather than printed from a surface.

The *monotype and the *glass print are traditionally grouped with prints, although the former is really a type of painting and the latter a type of photograph. The term 'print' is also more loosely applied to reproductions of works of art made by photomechanical methods.

private press. A printing establishment operated on a small scale by a private individual or group, producing limited numbers of books with the emphasis on high quality of typography, illustration, binding, and other physical characteristics. In a general sense private presses are almost as old as printing itself, but the 'private press movement' was initiated by William *Morris, whose *Kelmscott Press (1890–8) provided both the impetus and the model for a revival of interest in typography and book production around 1900 (the movement was mainly associated with Britain, but there were similar establishments in other countries, such as the Cranach Press in Weimar, Germany, founded in 1913). Although aims and accomplishment varied considerably among the private presses Morris inspired, some emphasizing typography and layout to the exclusion of illustration, the movement as a whole was characterized by (1) an interest in type design, often shown in the use by individual presses of types produced specially for them; (2) an interest in illustration; (3) the appeal to bibliophiles implicit in the production of limited editions of carefully designed and produced books. Among the private presses that followed Morris's lead were the Eragny Press (1894–1914, run by Lucien *Pissarro), the Vale Press (1896–1904; see RICKETTS), the Doves Press (1900–16), whose books were noted for the austere beauty of their typography and had no illustrations, and the Golden Cockerel Press (founded 1920; see GIBBINGS). Such presses played an important part in stimulating a revival of *wood engraving for illustration; Eric *Gill and Eric *Ravilious were among the artists employed by the Golden Cockerel Press, for example. The movement was in decline by the 1930s and was virtually ended by the Second World War, but there have subsequently been revivals of its ideals.

Prix de Rome. A scholarship, founded concurrently with the French *Academy in Rome (1666), that enabled prizewinning students at the Académie Royale de Peinture et de Sculpture in Paris to spend a period (usually 3–5 years) in Rome at the state's expense, engaged in study and creative work. The award soon acquired great prestige and was regarded as a stepping stone to the highest honours. Competition rules were complex and they varied over the years, but as many as six painters and four sculptors might be staying as prizewinners in Rome at any one time (prizes for architects were added in the 18th century and for engravers and musicians in the 19th century). In some years, the Grand Prix was not awarded, as none of the entrants was thought good enough, but lesser prizewinners could still qualify to stay in Rome. The rules were sometimes bent; in 1752 *Fragonard won the Grand Prix even though he was not a student at the Académie.

In painting, as many as 100 students might enter for the Prix de Rome each year, but this number was reduced by preliminary tests to a maximum of ten finalists for the competition proper. The finalists had to make an oil sketch on an allotted subject (always something from the Bible or ancient history) and then were given ten weeks to produce a full-scale picture from this (a standard-sized canvas was used, measuring roughly 1 × 1.5 m (3 × 5 ft)). They had to work in individual supervised rooms, to prevent them from receiving outside help and to keep their work secret from their rivals. The winner was decided by a vote of all the members of the Académie Royale. Unsuccessful competitors could try again; J.-L.*David won at the fifth attempt (his fourth as a finalist) in 1774.

After a hiatus during the French Revolution, the Prix de Rome continued under the auspices of the École des *Beaux-Arts, which effectively replaced the Académie, and it maintained its prestige well into the 19th century. However, in the 20th century it came to be regarded as a relic from another age and it was abolished in 1968. Similar scholarships have been awarded by other academies, including the *Royal Academy in London.

Procaccini, Giulio Cesare (b Bologna, 30 May 1574; d Milan, 14 Nov. 1625). Italian painter and sculptor, the most distinguished member of a family of artists. He worked mainly in Milan, where the family settled when he was a child, and also in Modena and Genoa. Early in his career he was primarily a sculptor, but after about 1600 he concentrated on painting and became one of the leading painters in Milan. His style was eclectic but often very powerful, combining something of the emotional tension of *Mannerism with the dynamism and sense of physical presence of the *Baroque. His colours tend to be acidic, his handling of light and shade dramatic. Many of his paintings are still in Milan, but two large scenes from Christ's Passion (perhaps part of a series) are in Edinburgh (NG) and Sheffield (Graves AG). His father, **Ercole** (1520–95), and his brothers, **Camillo** (c.1555–1629) and **Carlo Antonio** (1571–?1630), were also painters.

Procter, Dod and **Ernest.** See NEWLYN SCHOOL.

Proto-Renaissance. Term that can be applied to any revival of the style or spirit of classical antiquity before the *Renaissance proper. In particular it is used of the 'proto-Renaissance of the twelfth century', often simply called 'the twelfth-century Renaissance', which Erwin *Panofsky described as a classicizing movement that began in the latter part of the 11th century, reached its climax in the 12th century, and continued into the 13th century; it was a 'Mediterranean phenomenon, arising in southern France, Italy and Spain'.

Proudon, Pierre-Joseph. See COURBET.

Prout, Samuel (b Plymouth, 17 Sept. 1783; d London, 10 Feb. 1852). English painter, best known for his watercolour views of *Picturesque buildings and streets in Normandy. Many of them appeared as engravings in illustrated books and they helped to build up the British *Romantic image of the Continent. His work was greatly admired by *Ruskin.

provenance. The record of the ownership of a movable work of art. An unbroken provenance accounts for the whereabouts of a work from the time of its creation to the present day, and the nearer a work's pedigree approaches this ideal, the more secure its *attribution is likely to be.

Provost, Jan (b Mons, c.1465; d Bruges, Jan. 1529). Netherlandish painter, active mainly in Bruges, where he settled in 1494. He was perhaps a pupil of *Marmion, whose widow he married soon after the master's death in 1489. His style was fairly close to Gerard *David, then the leading painter in Bruges, but Provost, although clumsier, was more inventive. *Dürer was his guest when he visited Bruges in 1521.

Prud'hon, Pierre-Paul (b Cluny, 4 Apr. 1758; d Paris, 16 Feb. 1823). French portrait and historical painter. His main training was at the Dijon Academy, from which he won a scholarship to

Rome in 1784. He became a friend of *Canova there and formed his style on the example of the *sfumato and sensuous charm of *Leonardo and *Correggio. In 1788 he returned to Paris and after working in obscurity for some time he flourished under Napoleon, becoming a favourite of both his empresses, Josephine and Marie-Louise. In addition to painting portraits of the imperial court (*Josephine at Malmaison*, 1805, Louvre, Paris), he designed decorations for important ceremonies, including Napoleon's marriage to Marie-Louise in 1810. He remained in official favour after the fall of Napoleon in 1815, but he painted little in his final years. He had a neurotic personality and the shock of the suicide of his mistress—his pupil Constance Mayer (1775–1821)—hastened his own death.

Prud'hon was the most independent-minded of the leading French painters of his generation—the only one who did not fall under the dominant influence of *David. He belongs to both the 18th and the 19th centuries. In his elegance, his grace, and his exquisite fancy he recalls the epoch of Louis XVI (David referred to him slightingly as 'the *Boucher of his time'), but his deep personal feeling aligns him with the *Romantics. *Gros said of him: 'He will bestride the two centuries with his seven league boots.' Among his best-known pictures are *Justice and Divine Vengeance Pursuing Crime* (1808, Louvre) and *Venus and Adonis* (1810–12, Wallace Coll., London). He was one of the finest draughtsmen of his time (especially in his nude studies), typically working with black and white chalk on blue or grey paper. However, many of his paintings are in poor condition because of his use of *bitumen.

Pryde, James (*b* Edinburgh, 30 Mar. 1866; *d* London, 24 Feb. 1941). British painter and designer. In the 1890s he designed posters with his brother-in-law William *Nicholson under the name J. & W. *Beggarstaff and these are probably his most famous works. Pryde sometimes supplemented his income at this time by taking small parts on the stage (he was a friend of Gordon *Craig, who began his career as an actor). As a painter he is best known for dramatic and sinister architectural views, with figures dwarfed by their gloomy surroundings. They have something of the spirit of *Piranesi's prison etchings, but they are broadly brushed. Pryde—'tall and handsome', but 'dilatory, extravagant, and unproductive for long periods' (*DNB*)—produced little after 1925. However, in 1930 he designed the sets for Paul Robeson's memorable *Othello* at the Savoy Theatre, London.

psalter. A manuscript (particularly one for liturgical use) or a printed book containing the text of the 150 Psalms of the Old Testament. In its worship the Christian Church makes more use of the Psalms than of any other part of the Old Testament, and the psalter was the most popular type of *illuminated book from the 11th to the 14th century. Thereafter the *Book of Hours became the most important channel for illuminations. The Psalms are hymns of praise to God, and it is very difficult to illustrate them literally (although this was done with great imagination in the *Utrecht Psalter). Often, therefore, psalters are adorned with images that have little direct relevance to the text. A famous example is the Luttrell Psalter (*c*.1340, BL, London), made for Sir Geoffrey Luttrell of Irnham, Lincolnshire, which is renowned for its scenes of contemporary life. These are sometimes rather crudely drawn and painted, but they are so lively and cover such a wide range of activities, including sports and games, that they have been reproduced again and again as illustrations in books on medieval life.

Public Works of Art Project. See FEDERAL ART PROJECT.

Pucelle, Jean (*d* ?Paris, ?1334). French manuscript *illuminator. Little is known of his career, but his large workshop dominated Parisian painting in the first half of the 14th century. His work commanded high prices and—unusually for the time—his reputation endured after his death. Among the manuscripts attributed to him is the *Book of Hours of Queen Jeanne d'Évreux (1325–8, Met. Mus., New York). Certain features of his work—particularly his mastery of space—indicate that he probably travelled in Italy early in his career, and he was also familiar with Netherlandish developments.

Puget, Pierre (*b* Marseilles, 16 Oct. 1620; *d* Marseilles, 2 Dec. 1694). The greatest French sculptor of the 17th century. He worked mainly in his native Marseilles and in Toulon, for although he sought success at court, his work was much too impassioned to fit into the scheme of *Le Brun's artistic dictatorship. Moreover, he was arrogant and headstrong in temperament and he fell victim to the intrigues of fellow artists. His *Baroque style was formed in Italy, where he worked from about 1638 to 1643; for part of this time he is said to have been an assistant to Pietro da *Cortona in Florence and Rome, presumably as a stuccoist. Subsequently he made several visits to Genoa, where he established a consider-

able reputation. His first major work was a pair of
*atlas figures for the entrance to Toulon Town
Hall (1656) and in these (now in the Musée Naval)
he showed the physical vigour and emotional
intensity that were the hallmarks of his style.
These characteristics occur most memorably in
his celebrated *Milo of Crotona* (1671–82, Louvre,
Paris), which was one of his few works accepted
for the palace at Versailles. Puget spent his final
years embittered by his failures. He worked as a
painter, architect, and decorator of ships as well
as a sculptor, and was an outstanding draughtsman. His son **François** (1651–1707) was a painter,
working mainly in Toulon and Marseilles. He did
a few religious works but was mainly a portraitist; his sitters included his father (Louvre).

Purbeck marble. A hard, shelly *limestone
from quarries in the Isle of Purbeck (a peninsula
rather than an island), Dorset. It is the nearest
approximation to a true *marble quarried in
England and can be cut to moderately fine
detail. When quarried it is light grey in colour,
often tinged with brown or green, but it polishes
to a darker hue (sometimes almost black). It
began to be used in English art and architecture
in the 12th century and was widely employed in
the 13th century—for architectural elements
(particularly column shafts), fonts (superseding
the black marble fonts imported from Tournai),
and tombs, including the first royal tomb in
England, that of King John (c.1230) in Worcester
Cathedral. It went out of fashion in the early 14th
century, replaced by cheaper and more easily
worked *freestone.

Purism. A movement in French painting advocating an art of clarity and objectivity in tune
with the machine age; its founders and sole
exponents were Amédée *Ozenfant and *Le
Corbusier, who met in Paris in 1918, and it flourished from then until 1925. Feeling that
*Cubism—'the troubled art of a troubled
time'—was degenerating into an art of decoration, they regarded their association as 'a campaign for the reconstitution of a healthy art',
aiming to 'inoculate artists with the spirit of
the age'. They set great store by 'the lessons
inherent in the precision of machinery' and
held that emotion and expressiveness should be
strictly excluded from art, apart from the beauty
of functional efficiency—the 'mathematical lyricism' that is the proper response to a well-
composed picture. Their characteristic paintings
are still-lifes—cool, clear, almost diagrammatic-
ally flat, and impersonally finished.

Despite the anti-emotionalism of this functionalist outlook, Ozenfant and Le Corbusier
advocated Purism with missionary fervour and
dogmatic certainty in their book *Après le Cubisme*
(1918) and other writings. However, they seemed
to realize that it represented something of a dead
end pictorially and moved on to much looser
styles. The movement's main sequel is to be
found in Le Corbusier's architectural work and
theories and more generally in the field of
design, where there is some kinship with the
contemporary ideals of the *Bauhaus. As
George Heard Hamilton writes (*Painting and
Sculpture in Europe: 1880–1940*, 1967), 'Purism
did encourage a serious look at the products
and the methods of producing objects in
modern times . . . Whenever we admire the
simple contour or refined shape of an article of
daily use, we share in the Purist aesthetic.'

Purser, Sarah (*b* Dún Laoghaire, nr. Dublin,
22 Mar. 1848; *d* Dublin, 7 Aug. 1943). Irish painter,
designer, patron, collector, and administrator.
She was a successful society portraitist, who in
her own words 'went through the British aristocracy like the measles', but she is more important for her other roles in Irish art. She knew
everyone who mattered (from 1911 she held
regular social gatherings for Dublin's intelligentsia at her home, Mespil House) and in 1924 she
founded the Friends of the National Collections
of Ireland. One of its aims was to campaign for
the return of Sir Hugh *Lane's pictures from
London to Dublin and she helped to secure
Charlemont House as the home for what
became the Hugh Lane Municipal Gallery of
Modern Art. Perhaps most importantly, she
was the founder of the stained-glass workshop
An Túr Gloine (The Tower of Glass), which
operated in Dublin from 1903 to 1944; the work
it produced, which can be seen in so many Irish
churches, is her finest memorial. With the exception of Harry *Clarke, most of the leading
Irish stained-glass designers of the day worked
there at one time or another, among them Evie
*Hone.

putto (Italian: 'little boy'). Term applied to a
representation of a chubby, naked child, sometimes winged, appearing—usually as a subsidiary figure—in a work of art. Putti have been a
frequent motif of decorative art since classical
antiquity and may have a pagan, human, or
divine status. They derived from a type of figure
used in ancient art to represent Eros, the Greek
god of love, and from the *Renaissance onwards
a putto has often been used to represent his

Roman counterpart, Cupid. More commonly, however, putti are anonymous figures, pictured attending classical gods, or, for example, the Virgin Mary. In this sense they are sometimes known as *amoretti* (singular *amoretto*).

Puvis de Chavannes, Pierre (*b* Lyons, 14 Dec. 1824; *d* Paris, 24 Oct. 1898). The foremost French mural painter of the second half of the 19th century. He decorated many public buildings in France (for example, the Panthéon, the Sorbonne, and the Hôtel de Ville, all in Paris) and also Boston Public Library (*Abbey and *Sargent did murals here too). His paintings were done on canvas and then affixed to the walls (see MAROUFLAGE), but their pale colours imitated the effect of *fresco. He had only modest success early in his career (when a private income enabled him to work for little payment), but he went on to achieve an enormous reputation, and he was respected even by artists of very different aims and outlook from his own. *Gauguin, *Seurat, and *Toulouse-Lautrec were among his professed admirers. His reputation has since declined, his idealized depictions of antiquity or allegorical representations of abstract themes now often seeming rather anaemic. He remains important, however, because of his extensive influence on younger artists. His simplified forms, respect for the flatness of the picture surface, rhythmic line, and use of non-naturalistic colour to evoke the mood of the painting appealed to both the *Post-Impressionists and the *Symbolists. In addition to murals he produced easel paintings and pastels, and he was a prolific draughtsman. According to some accounts he was the father of *Utrillo.

Puy, Jean. See FAUVISM.

Pyle, Howard. See PARRISH.

Pynacker (or **Pijnacker**), **Adam** (*b* Schiedam, nr. Rotterdam, *c.*1620; *bur.* Amsterdam, 28 Mar. 1673). Dutch landscape painter, active in Schie-dam and possibly in Delft before settling in Amsterdam in about 1661. According to *Houbraken he spent three years in Italy (perhaps *c.*1645–8) and he was one of the outstanding Dutch exponents of Italianate landscapes. His style resembles that of Jan *Both and Jan *Asselyn, but his mature work often has a distinctive and attractive silvery tonality. A splendid example of his work, showing his ability to compose boldly on a large scale, is *Landscape with Sportsmen and Game* (*c.*1665, Dulwich Picture Gal., London), which features some unnaturally (but attractively) blue leaves, caused by yellow pigment fading in the greens.

Pynas, Jan (*b* Alkmaar, *c.*1582; *bur.* Amsterdam, 27 Dec. 1631) and **Jacob** (*b* Amsterdam, *c.*1592; *d* ?Delft, ?1650). Dutch painters, brothers. Jan visited Italy *c.*1605–7 (he was there at the same time as *Lastman) and again about ten years later. On stylistic grounds it is likely that Jacob too went there at some time. Both brothers produced small-format history paintings in the manner of *Elsheimer, and both of them usually signed their works 'J. Pynas', causing difficulties in differentiating their hands. *Rembrandt is said to have studied briefly with Jacob.

Pythagoras. Greek sculptor in bronze, active in the early 5th century BC. He evidently emigrated from Samos to Rhegium (now Reggio di Calabria) in Italy. Ancient writers rank him among the greatest Greek sculptors, but no work survives—either original or copy—that can be securely attributed to him. *Pliny describes him as 'the first to represent sinews and veins and to bestow attention on the treatment of hair' and the Greek biographer Diogenes Laertius writes that he is 'thought to have been the first to aim at rhythm and proportion'. Though doubtless exaggerations, these comments indicate that his work must have seemed remarkably naturalistic and harmonious. He made several statues of athletes and in this field he is said to have excelled *Myron.

Q

quadratura. A type of *illusionistic decoration in which architectural elements are painted on walls and/or ceilings in such a way that they appear to be an extension of the real architecture of the room into an imaginary space. It was common in ancient Roman art, was revived by *Mantegna in the 15th century, and reached its peaks of elaboration in *Baroque Italy. The greatest of all exponents of quadratura was probably Andrea *Pozzo, in whose celebrated ceiling in S. Ignazio, Rome, architecture and figures surge towards the heavens with breathtaking bravura. Especially when applied to ceilings, quadratura demands formidable skill with perspective, for the painted architecture can all too easily look as if it is collapsing, and the illusion may be convincing only when the spectator stands at a particular point. Ellis *Waterhouse writes of Pozzo's S. Ignazio ceiling: 'From most points of view—and especially from the sides of the church—the effect is wholly unnerving. Columns fall inwards or sideways and the spectator feels as Samson must have felt after he had started work on the Temple at Gaza. But there is one point in the centre of the nave (marked by an indicator on the floor) from which all this nonsense appears in correct perspective—and the effect is extremely impressive.' Unlike Pozzo, many artists relied on specialists—called quadraturisti—for this part of their work. Agostino *Tassi, for example, painted the architectural setting for *Guercino's celebrated *Aurora*, and Giambattista *Tiepolo worked much in collaboration with the brilliant quadraturista Gerolamo Mengozzi Colonna (c.1688–1766).

quadro riportato (Italian: 'carried—or transferred—picture'). Term applied to a ceiling picture that is intended to look as if it is a framed easel picture placed overhead; there is no *illusionistic foreshortening, figures appearing as if they were to be viewed at normal eye level. *Mengs' *Parnassus* (1761) in the Villa Albani (now Villa Torlonia), Rome, is a famous example—a kind of *Neoclassical manifesto

against *Baroque illusionism. Often, however, quadro riportati were combined with illusionistic elements, as in Annibale *Carracci's Farnese Ceiling (1597–1600) in Rome.

Quarton (or **Charonton**), **Enguerrand** (active 1444; d ?1466). French painter, active in Provence. His career is unusually well documented for a provincial artist of his date; he worked in Aix, Arles, and Avignon, and there are various records of him dating from 1444 to 1466, in which year he perhaps died in an outbreak of the plague in Provence. However, there are only two extant works that are certainly by him: the *Virgin of Mercy* (1452) in the Musée Condé at Chantilly, painted in collaboration with an obscure artist called Pierre Villatte, and the *Coronation of the Virgin* (1454) in the Musée Municipal at Villeneuve-lès-Avignon. They are highly impressive works, uniting Flemish and Italian influence whilst having something of the monumental character of the sculpture of Quarton's region. Indeed, they show Quarton to have been a painter of such commanding stature that there is an increasing tendency to attribute to him the celebrated *Avignon Pietà* (c.1460, Louvre, Paris), the greatest French painting of the period (see AVIGNON). Several *illuminated manuscripts have also been attributed to Quarton.

Quast, Pieter (b ?Amsterdam, c.1606; bur. Amsterdam, 29 May 1647). Dutch painter and draughtsman, active in Amsterdam and The Hague. He is best known for peasant *genre scenes in the manner of *Brouwer and Adriaen van *Ostade, but he also painted more refined types in 'merry companies', as well as theatrical subjects (which are fairly rare in Dutch art). Sometimes he combined elegant and peasant types in the same picture (*A Man and Woman in a Stableyard*, NG, London). In addition to paintings he made finished drawings, presumably for sale—to be used as amusing and cheap decorations for taverns and homes (similar sheets hang in many of the interiors painted by 17th-century Dutch artists). His work has a personal feeling of caricature or exaggeration. It is often of high quality, but he died in poverty.

Quatremère de Quincy, Antoine (b Paris, 28 Oct. 1755; d Paris, 28 Dec. 1849). French writer. He initially studied law, then trained as a sculptor, but he turned to writing and became one of the chief spokesmen of *Neoclassicism. In his writings he vigorously promoted a severe, grand style, and he also expressed strong views on administrative and political matters. He argued, for example, that the Académie Royale (see ACADEMY) should concern itself solely with teaching and that its members should cease to have a monopoly on state commissions, and he opposed the removal of Italian art treasures to France in the wake of Napoleon's conquests. He was imprisoned during the French Revolution and lived in exile in Germany in 1797–1800. Later he returned to public life in France, but by this time his ideas were becoming regarded as outmoded. His many books include a biography of *Canova (1823), whom he met in Rome as a young man and corresponded with thereafter.

quattrocento. Term (Italian: 'four hundred') applied to the 15th century (the 1400s) in Italian art. It can be used as a noun ('painting of the quattrocento') or as an adjective ('quattrocento sculpture'). Terms used in the same way for other centuries are: dugento (or duecento) for the 13th century; trecento for the 14th century; cinquecento for the 16th century; seicento for the 17th century; settecento for the 18th century; ottocento for the 19th century; and novecento for the 20th century.

Queen's Gallery. See ROYAL COLLECTION.

Quellin (or **Quellinus**), **Artus I** (or **Arnoldus**) (bapt. Antwerp, 30 Aug. 1609; d Antwerp, 23 Aug. 1668). Flemish sculptor, the most distinguished member of a family of artists. He trained with his father **Erasmus I** (c.1584–1640). In 1634 he moved to Rome, where he worked in the studio of François *Duquesnoy. He was back in Antwerp in 1639, and by 1648 he had moved to Amsterdam, where from c.1650 to 1664 he directed the sumptuous sculptural decoration of the new town hall (now Royal Palace). His dignified style was singularly appropriate for van *Campen's great building, and the decoration forms the most impressive sculptural ensemble of the time in northern Europe. Quellin also produced tomb sculpture and portrait busts. His collaborators at Amsterdam Town Hall included his cousin **Artus II Quellin** (1625–1700), whose independent work was more *Baroque in style. The commanding figure of God the Father (1682) adorning the rood-screen in Bruges Cathedral is perhaps his finest work.

Artus III Quellin (1653–86), usually called Arnold, son of Artus II, settled in England in about 1680. By 1684 he was working with Grinling *Gibbons, and the drop in quality of Gibbons's large-scale figure work (not his forte) after Quellin's death indicates that the latter was probably the dominant personality in producing such fine statues as the bronze James II (1686) outside the National Gallery, London. Quellin's outstanding independent work is the tomb of Thomas Thynne (1682, Westminster Abbey), which features a *relief of Thynne's murder in his coach in Pall Mall.

Other members of the Quellin family included Artus I's two brothers **Erasmus II** (1607–78), a painter who often collaborated with *Rubens, and **Hubert** (?1619–1687), an engraver who produced numerous prints after works by his relatives.

Quercia, Jacopo della (b Siena, c.1374; d Siena, 20 Oct. 1438). The greatest sculptor of the Sienese School, the son of an undistinguished goldsmith and woodcarver, **Piero di Angelo** (Quercia, from which Jacopo takes his name, is a district of Siena). Like his father, he carved in wood and also worked in bronze, but marble was his preferred material. He was one of the outstanding figures of his generation in Italian sculpture, the only non-Florentine who can be mentioned in the same breath as *Donatello and *Ghiberti, but his career is difficult to follow, as he worked in numerous places and sometimes left one commission unfinished while he took up another elsewhere. Contrary to *Vasari's assertions that he led a 'well-ordered life', he seems to have been inveterately dilatory. He is first firmly documented in 1401, unsuccessfully competing for the commission (won by Ghiberti) for the Baptistery doors in Florence. His first surviving works are generally agreed to be a marble statue of the Virgin and Child, commissioned in 1403 for Ferrara Cathedral (now Cathedral Mus.), and the tomb of Ilaria del Carretto, wife of the ruler of Lucca, Paolo Guinigi (c.1406, Lucca Cathedral), which was eulogized by *Ruskin. There are Renaissance *putti and swags round the base of the tomb, but the serene and graceful effigy is in the northern manner and suggests that Jacopo had knowledge of work done in the circle of Claus *Sluter in Burgundy.

Jacopo's major work for his native city was a fountain called the Fonte Gaia (commissioned in

1408, executed in 1414–19), which is now—much damaged—in the loggia of the Palazzo Pubblico (a copy stands in the Piazza del Campo, where the original was first located). Its *relief carvings include some beautifully draped female figures and a terribly battered but still awesomely powerful panel of the *Expulsion from Paradise*. Between 1417 and 1430 Jacopo worked on reliefs for the font in the Baptistery at Siena (Donatello and Ghiberti were also involved in this commission), and in 1425 he began his last great work (left unfinished at his death), the sculptural decoration of the main doorway of S. Petronio, Bologna. The principal feature of the doorway is a series of relief panels with subjects taken from Genesis and the Nativity of Christ. The figures—usually only two or three to a relief, in contrast to the crowded panels of Ghiberti—have a directness and strength that won the admiration of *Michelangelo, who visited Bologna in 1494. Several of the motifs are to be found, reinterpreted, on the Sistine Ceiling.

Quesnel, François (*b* Edinburgh, *c*.1545; *d* Paris, 1619). The best-known member of a dynasty of French painters active in the 16th and 17th centuries. His father **Pierre** (*d c*.1574) worked at the Scottish court, but François spent his career in France. He was active in various fields, but mainly as a portraitist, carrying on the *Clouet tradition into the 17th century. His work is known mainly through his polished drawings. Numerous paintings are attributed to him, but only one is securely identified as his by his monogram—*Mary Ann Waltham* (1572, Earl Spencer Coll., Althorp, Northamptonshire).

Quinn, Marc. See YOUNG BRITISH ARTISTS.

R

Rackham, Arthur (*b* London, 19 Sept. 1867; *d* Limpsfield, Surrey, 6 Sept. 1939). British illustrator, celebrated for his work in children's books. He established his reputation with *Fairy Tales of the Brothers Grimm*, published in 1900, and from then until the First World War he had his golden period, when Edmund *Dulac was the only serious rival in his field. The two artists were very different in style. Dulac was much more painterly, using strong expressive colour, whereas Rackham relied on wiry line and subtle, muted colour. He said he believed in 'the greatest stimulating and educative power of imaginative, fantastic and playful pictures and writings for children in their most impressionable years', and he worked in a striking vein of Nordic fantasy, creating a bizarre world populated by goblins, fairies, and weird creatures (he looked rather like a gnome himself). After the First World War the market for expensive children's books declined, but he continued to prosper from gallery sales of his work.

Raeburn, Sir Henry (*b* Stockbridge [now a district of Edinburgh], 4 Mar. 1756; *d* Edinburgh, 8 July 1823). The leading Scottish portrait painter of his period, active mainly in Edinburgh. On leaving school he was apprenticed to a goldsmith and he appears to have been largely self-taught as a painter. In 1784–6 he visited Italy (going via London, where he is said to have met *Reynolds), but his distinctive style was already formed by this time—one of his finest works, the *Revd Robert Walker Skating* (NG, Edinburgh), is traditionally said to date from 1784. He painted directly on to the canvas without preliminary drawings, and his vigorous, bold handling—sometimes called his 'square touch'—could be extraordinarily effective in conveying the character of rugged Highland chiefs or bluff legal worthies. He also had a penchant for vivid and original lighting effects (*William Glendonwyn*, *c*.1795, Fitzwilliam Mus., Cambridge) and could be remarkably sensitive when painting women (*Isabella McLeod, Mrs James Gregory*, *c*.1798, Fyvie Castle, Aberdeenshire, NT). At times, however,

his technical facility degenerated into empty virtuosity. In 1822, on the occasion of George IV's visit to Edinburgh, he was knighted and appointed His Majesty's *Limner for Scotland. Since he had all the sitters he needed in Scotland, there was no need for him to compete with *Lawrence and *Hoppner in London (although he did consider moving there after Hoppner's death in 1810), and in the history of British portraiture he is an isolated and perhaps underrated figure.

Raffaellino del Garbo. see SARTO.

Raggi, Antonio. See GAULLI.

Raimondi, Marcantonio (*b* ?Argini, nr. Bologna, *c*.1480; *d* ?Bologna, 1527/34). Italian *line engraver, a pioneer in the use of prints to reproduce the work of other artists. He studied in Bologna with *Francia, and from about 1506 to 1508 lived in Venice, where he learned much from *Dürer's engravings (Dürer, indeed, brought legal proceedings against him for plagiarism). In about 1510 he settled in Rome, and thereafter worked mainly for *Raphael, his engravings helping to spread the master's style throughout Europe. Apart from his association with Raphael, Raimondi is best known for a series of erotic engravings (after designs by *Giulio Romano) that led to his imprisonment in 1524. He left Rome after the Sack of 1527 and died in obscurity.

Rainer (or Renier) **of Huy.** *Mosan metalworker active in the early 12th century. Nothing is known of his life, but in a 14th-century chronicle he is credited with one of the great masterpieces of his period—a bronze font (1107–18) originally made for Notre-Dame-des-Fonts, Liège, and now in St Bartholomew, Liège. It is a large bowl supported on ten (originally twelve) oxen (a reference to the 'sea of cast metal . . . mounted on twelve oxen' made for King Solomon (1 Kings 7: 23–5)) and adorned with scenes appropriate to the sacrament of baptism. The figures are much more naturalistic and classical than in most *Romanesque art. Very little other work can be attributed to Rainer or his workshop, but his masterpiece had great influence on Mosan art. It has recently been suggested, however, that he is more or less a mythical figure and that the font was made in the imperial foundry in Constantinople.

Ramos, Mel (*b* Sacramento, Calif., 24 July 1935). American painter. Ramos is usually described as a *Pop artist, but his smooth, impersonal handling (in oils and watercolour) brings him also within the orbit of *Superrealism. He specializes in paintings of nude women of the calendar pin-up or 'playmate' type. Sometimes they are posed with oversized products such as pieces of cheese and sometimes they allude to the work of leading painters of the past (more rarely the present). The jokey quality of his work is reflected in his titles; two typical series are 'You Get More Spaghetti with Giacometti' and 'You Get More Salami with Modigliani'.

Ramsay, Allan (*b* Edinburgh, 2 Oct. 1713; *d* Dover, 10 Aug. 1784). Scottish painter, active mainly in London, where he was the outstanding portraitist from about 1740 until the rise of *Reynolds in the mid-1750s. He studied in Edinburgh and London, and then from 1736 to 1738 in Italy (including a period with *Solimena in Naples), and when he returned to London he brought a cosmopolitan air to British portraiture. His pictures of women have a decidedly French grace (*The Artist's Wife*, *c*.1755, NG, Edinburgh) and in this field he continued to be a serious rival to Reynolds. He was preferred to Reynolds by the royal family and in 1767 was appointed principal painter to George III. However, after injuring his right arm in an accident in 1773 he gave up painting (although his studio continued to produce replicas of royal portraits) and devoted himself to his other interests. He was the son of the poet Allan Ramsay, and he inherited his father's literary inclinations. Political pamphleteering, classical archaeology (he revisited Rome in 1754–7 and 1775–7), and conversation took up much of his later years. He was a prominent figure in literary circles and Samuel Johnson said of him: 'You will not find a man in whose conversation there is more instruction, more information, and more elegance.'

Rand, John G. See TUBE.

Ranson, Paul. See ACADÉMIE.

Raphael (Raffaello Sanzio) (*b* Urbino, 6 Apr. [or less likely 28 Mar.] 1483; *d* Rome, 6 Apr. 1520).

Italian painter, draughtsman, architect, and designer, the artist who most completely expresses the ideals of the High *Renaissance. He was the son of the painter and writer Giovanni *Santi, through whom he must have gained early familiarity with the humanist court of Federico da *Montefeltro. This cultured background stood him in good stead throughout his career, for unlike many artists he was renowned for his social poise. *Vasari says that 'Raphael came to be of great help to his father in the numerous works that Giovanni executed in the state of Urbino', but Santi died in 1494, when Raphael was only 11, and nothing is documented about his training. Presumably he did receive his first lessons in art from his father, and it has been suggested that he was subsequently a pupil of Timoteo Viti (1469–1523), a local painter, but the overwhelming influence on his early work was *Perugino. Raphael took from him not only general qualities such as sweetness of expression and elegance of drawing, but also such characteristic details as daintily crooked little fingers and wispy background trees. According to Vasari, Raphael was Perugino's pupil, but this is perhaps not strictly true. He was highly precocious and is documented as an independent artist (described as 'magister'—master) in 1500, when he was only 17; his close contact with Perugino seems to have come a little later (*c*.1502–3), when he was probably his colleague rather than assistant. By the time he was 21 he had already outstripped Perugino, as is clearly seen by comparing Raphael's *Marriage of the Virgin* (1504, Brera, Milan) with Perugino's slightly earlier painting of the same subject (Mus. B.-A., Caen). The two compositions are closely similar in many ways, but Raphael far surpasses Perugino in lucidity and grace.

In his early career Raphael had commissions from various places in Umbria. From 1504 to 1508 he spent much of his time in Florence, and these years are usually referred to as his Florentine period, although he never took up permanent residence in the city. The experience of Florence greatly affected his art; he moved away from Perugino's manner and his work became grander and more sophisticated under the inspiration of *Leonardo, *Michelangelo, and also Fra *Bartolommeo (whose 'pleasing manner of colouring' is cited by Vasari as an influence). To this period belong some of Raphael's most celebrated depictions of the Virgin and Child (*Madonna of the Meadow*, 1505, KH Mus., Vienna). In these and his paintings of the Holy Family he showed his developing mastery of composition and expression (from Leonardo he particularly learned how to group figures fluently and compactly). He paints the sacred figures as splendid, healthy human beings, but with a serenity, a sense of some deep inner integrity, that removes any doubt as to the holiness of the subject. This sense of well-being distinguishes the art of Raphael from the more disturbingly intellectual work of Leonardo or the overwhelmingly powerful creations of Michelangelo, and evidently reflects his own balanced nature. Unlike his two great contemporaries, he was not a solitary genius but a sociable and approachable figure, whom Vasari describes as 'so gentle and so charitable that even animals loved him'. He must, however, have had considerable toughness to produce the large amount of work he did in a short lifetime.

In 1508 Raphael moved to Rome, where Pope Julius II (Giuliano della *Rovere) entrusted him with the fresco decoration of the Stanza della Segnatura, one of a suite of rooms he was having remodelled in the Vatican. It is not known how Raphael (still only 25) came to the attention of the pope, but he was perhaps recommended by *Bramante, who was a distant relative. Raphael had never before worked on a project of such size and prestige and he had little experience in fresco, but he fulfilled the commission triumphantly and he spent most of the rest of his career in the service of Julius and his successor Leo X (Giovanni de' *Medici). The Stanza della Segnatura was probably used by Julius as his private library and its decoration is based on a complex theological programme concerning the relationship between classical learning and Christian thought. On one main wall, in the celebrated painting known as *The School of Athens*, are shown the great thinkers of the ancient world, led by Plato and Aristotle, arranged in a majestic architectural setting, a masterpiece of perspective drawing. Opposite, in the painting called the *Disputà* (the Disputation over the Sacrament), the Doctors of the Church adore the Sacrament, while above them the Trinity is surrounded by the saints and martyrs.

After the completion of the Stanza della Segnatura in 1511 or 1512 Raphael was entrusted with decorating three adjacent rooms in the Vatican, but by the time he had completed the first of these—the Stanza d'Eliodoro—in 1514, his services were so much in demand that he had to leave the execution of his work increasingly to assistants (of whom *Giulio Romano was the most distinguished). The *cartoons for his tapestries for the Sistine Chapel (1515–16, Royal Coll., on loan to V&A, London), for example,

rank among his noblest designs, but probably little of the actual brushwork is from his own hand (for the tapestries woven from them see BRUSSELS TAPESTRIES and ROYAL COLLECTION). In the Stanze and the cartoons Raphael showed a prodigious ability to arrange groups of varied figures into grandly harmonious compositions and—like Michelangelo's Sistine Ceiling—these works have had a profound and enduring influence on the whole European tradition of *history painting.

Apart from Julius II and Leo X, Raphael's most important patron in Rome was the enormously wealthy Agostino *Chigi. Raphael's work for him included fresco decoration at his villa (now known as the Villa Farnesina), just outside the city walls of Rome, and the design of his burial chapel in the church of S. Maria del Popolo. Most of the work at the Farnesina was carried out by assistants, but the celebrated *Galatea* (c.1512) was painted by Raphael himself. For the Chigi Chapel (begun c.1512) he designed the entire scheme, comprising architecture, sculpture, painting, mosaic, stuccowork, and marble inlay. The richness of effect was an important source for similar works in the *Baroque era, and it is fitting that the chapel (left unfinished when Chigi and Raphael died within a week of each other in 1520) was completed by *Bernini.

In addition to his great decorative schemes, Raphael painted many portraits and it is in these that the quality of his own workmanship in his later years is best seen. They rival Leonardo in subtlety of characterization and *Titian in richness of colouring, show great inventiveness in creating psychological situations, and provide a remarkable record of the intellectual circles in which he moved (*Baldassare Castiglione*, c.1515, Louvre, Paris). His portrait of Julius II (1511, NG, London) established a type for papal portraits that endured for about two centuries. Other important works from his Roman period that are largely from his own hand are the *Sistine Madonna* (c.1512–14, Gemäldegalerie, Dresden), his most famous painting of the Virgin and Child, and the great altarpiece of the *Transfiguration* (Pinacoteca, Vatican), on which he was working at his death, and which—in its agitated movement and emotion—is regarded as one of the wellsprings of the *Mannerist style. From about 1512 he began to work as an architect, and after the death of Bramant in 1514 he was placed in charge of the rebuilding of St Peter's. Raphael ranks second only to him among High Renaissance architects, but it is difficult to appreciate his status, as little of his work survives as he designed it. His huge workload increased further in 1517 when Leo X appointed him Rome's superintendent of antiquities, in which capacity he planned a detailed survey of the city's ancient monuments.

Vasari says that Raphael's early death from fever (evidently on his 37th birthday) 'plunged the entire papal court into grief'. He was rich, famous, and honoured, and his influence was widely spread even in his lifetime through the prints of Marcantonio *Raimondi. His posthumous reputation was even greater, for until well into the 19th century he was regarded by almost all critics as the greatest painter who had ever lived—the artist who expressed the basic doctrines of the Christian Church through figures that have a physical beauty worthy of the *antique. He became the ideal of all *academies and *Reynolds said of him: 'It is from his having taken so many models that he became himself a model for all succeeding painters: always imitating and always original.' In the later 19th century and particularly the 20th century there was a reaction against such adulation. The modern world likes its artistic heroes to show human frailties and preferably to be eccentrics or rebels, and Raphael—with his obliging personality, efficient management skills, and career of unbroken success—is completely lacking in this kind of appeal. Nevertheless, although his reputation is slightly less exalted than it once was, he remains one of the brightest beacons of European art.

Raspe, Rudolph Eric. See TASSIE.

Ratcliffe, William. See CAMDEN TOWN GROUP.

Ratgeb, Jörg (b ?Schwäbisch Gmünd, c.1480; d Pforzheim, 1526). German painter, active in Swabia. His few surviving paintings show him to have been closer in spirit to *Grünewald than practically any of his contemporaries. The most important is the Herrenberg Altarpiece (1519, Staatsgalerie, Stuttgart), which has some harrowing Passion scenes. Ratgeb himself met a gruesome end—executed for his part in the Peasants' Revolt.

Rauch, Christian Daniel (b Arolsen, nr. Kassel, 2 Jan. 1777; d Dresden, 3 Dec. 1857). The leading German sculptor of the first half of the 19th century, active mainly in Berlin. His training included lessons from Johann Gottfried *Schadow. From 1804 to 1818 he lived mainly in Italy, where he was influenced by *Canova and *Thorvaldsen, but he modified their *Neoclassical idealism with a close study of nature, particularly noticeable in his portraits. He worked for the court in Berlin, the royal houses of Bavaria and Hanover, and numerous aristocratic patrons in Germany and elsewhere. His most famous work is the elaborate equestrian monument of Frederick the Great (c.1835–51) in Unter den Linden, Berlin, and also well known is his monument to Albrecht *Dürer in Nuremberg (1828–40). These are in bronze, but he worked mainly in marble, notably in his portraits; his sitters included many eminent contemporaries.

Rauschenberg, Robert (b Port Arthur, Tex., 22 Oct, 1925). American painter, printmaker, designer, and experimental artist. With his friend Jasper *Johns, whom he met in 1954, he is regarded as one of the most influential figures in the move away from the *Abstract Expressionism that had dominated American art in the late 1940s and early 1950s. He studied at various art schools, most notably *Black Mountain College. In the mid-1950s he began to incorporate three-dimensional objects into what he called '*combine paintings'. The best-known example is probably Monogram (1955–9, Moderna Museet, Stockholm), which features a stuffed goat with a rubber tyre around its middle, splashed with paint in a manner recalling *Action Painting. Other objects he used included Coca-Cola bottles, fragments of clothing, electric fans, and radios, and because of his preoccupation with such consumer products he has been hailed as one of the pioneers of *Pop art. In 1958 he had a one-man show at Leo *Castelli's gallery and from this time his career began to take off. By the early 1960s he was building up an international reputation, and in 1964 he was awarded the Grand Prize at the Venice *Biennale. This caused great controversy, the Vatican newspaper L'osservatore romano describing the award as 'the total and general defeat of culture'. In the 1960s Rauschenberg returned to working on a flat surface and was particularly active in the medium of *screenprinting. He has been interested in combining art with new technological developments and in 1966 he helped to form EAT (Experiments in Art and Technology), an organization to help artists and engineers work together. In 1985 he launched Rauschenberg Overseas Cultural Interchange (ROCI), an exhibition dedicated to world peace that toured the world and included works created specifically for each place visited.

Raverat, Gwen (b Cambridge, 26 Aug. 1885; d Cambridge, 11 Feb. 1957). British printmaker, theatre designer, painter, and writer, the

577

daughter of Sir George Darwin, professor of astronomy at Cambridge University, and granddaughter of Charles Darwin. She studied at the *Slade School, but was mainly self-taught in wood engraving, which was her primary activity. Her best-known works are her book illustrations, notably of collections of poems by her cousin Frances Cornford. Her style was bold and vigorous and she was uninterested in technical virtuosity. Although she was art critic for *Time and Tide* from 1928 to 1939, she did not consider herself a writer and was surprised at the success of *Period Piece* (1952), an account of her childhood with her own illustrations, which became a best-seller on both sides of the Atlantic.

Ravesteyn, Jan van (*b* The Hague, *c*.1572; *bur*. The Hague, 21 June 1657). Dutch portrait painter. Like the more famous *Miereveld (with whose work his own is sometimes confused) he was a fine craftsman but limited in imagination, his large output being of more historical than artistic interest. His sitters included many members of the court in The Hague. There were several other artists in Ravesteyn's family, notably his brother **Anthonie** (*c*.1580–1669), likewise a portrait painter.

Ravilious, Eric (*b* London, 22 July 1903; *d* off Iceland, 2 Sept. 1942). British watercolour painter, printmaker, and designer. In addition to painting, his highly varied output included book illustrations and book-jackets, and designs for furniture, glass, textiles, and the Wedgwood pottery factory (notably a mug commemorating Edward VIII's coronation; this was withdrawn following Edward's abdication, but the design was used in revised form for the coronations of George VI and Elizabeth II). He was one of the outstanding wood engravers of his time, his book illustrations in this medium making striking use of bold tonal contrasts and complex patterning (some of his work was done for Robert *Gibbings's Golden Cockerel Press). In 1940–2 he was an *Official War Artist, and he produced some memorable watercolours of naval scenes off Norway (*Norway, 1940*, Laing AG, Newcastle upon Tyne). His plane disappeared on a flying patrol near Iceland in 1942, and he was officially presumed dead the following year.

His wife **Tirzah Ravilious** (née Garwood) (1908–51) was a painter and illustrator. She gave up her career for motherhood (they had three children), but she started work again after Eric's

death, even though she was already suffering from the cancer that caused her own early death.

Ray, Man. See MAN RAY.

Rayonism (Russian: Luchism). A type of abstract or semi-abstract painting practised by the Russian artists *Goncharova and *Larionov and a few followers from about 1912 to 1914 and representing their own adaptation of *Futurism. Rayonism was launched at the *Target exhibition in Moscow in 1913. In the same year Larionov published a manifesto on the subject, stating that 'Rayonism is a synthesis of *Cubism, Futurism and *Orphism', and Rayonist pictures do indeed combine something of the fragmentation or splintering of form of Cubism, the dynamic movement of Futurism, and the colour of Orphism. The style was bound up with a very unclear theory of invisible rays, in some ways analogous to the 'lines of force' that were postulated by the Futurists. In early Rayonist paintings an underlying subject is broken up into bundles of slanting lines, but in later ones the lines take over the picture completely so that there is no discernible naturalistic starting point and the work becomes completely abstract, as in Larionov's *Rayonist Composition: Domination of Red* (dated on painting 1911, but thought to have been executed *c*.1913–14, MoMA, New York). Rayonism was short-lived as both Goncharova and Larionov virtually abandoned easel painting after they left Russia in 1915 and they had no significant followers.

Read, Sir Herbert (*b* Kirkbymoorside, Yorkshire, 4 Dec. 1893; *d* Stonegrave, Yorkshire, 12 June 1968). British poet and critic, who throughout the middle third of the 20th century was virtually unchallenged as his country's foremost advocate and interpreter of modern art. After serving with distinction in the army in the First World War he worked at the Treasury, then in the ceramics department of the Victoria and Albert Museum, 1922–31, before becoming professor of fine arts at Edinburgh University, 1931–3. By this time he had published several collections of his verse as well as various art-historical studies (including *English Stained Glass*, 1926, still a standard work), critical works on English literature, and the first of his philosophical works on art, *The Meaning of Art* (1931). In 1933 he returned to London as editor (1933–9) of the *Burlington Magazine*, Britain's foremost scholarly art journal, and his attention turned increasingly to contemporary art; in 1933 he published *Art Now*, the first comprehensive defence in English of modern European art, and in 1934 he edited the modernist manifesto *Unit One*. At this time he lived near Henry *Moore, Barbara *Hepworth, and Ben *Nicholson, and he acted as the public mouthpiece of the group of artists of which they were the centre. He was interested in *Surrealism as well as abstraction and was one of the organizers of the 1936 International Surrealist Exhibition in London. In 1947 he was co-founder (with Roland *Penrose) of the *Institute of Contemporary Arts in London. Among his many books the most influential was probably *Education through Art* (1943), which used the insights of psychoanalysis to promote the idea of teaching art as an aid to the development of the personality. His other books include *A Concise History of Modern Painting* (1959) and *A Concise History of Modern Sculpture* (1964), both of which have been frequently reprinted. By the time he wrote them he was becoming disenchanted with contemporary artistic developments, but he was known as 'The Pope of Modern Art' and was regarded as 'an international authority and indeed something of a sage. It was not a role to which he ever pretended, for he was a man of conspicuous modesty' (*DNB*).

Read, Nicholas. See ROUBILIAC.

ready-made. A name given by Marcel *Duchamp to a type of work he invented consisting of a mass-produced article isolated from its functional context and displayed as a work of art. His first ready-made (1913) was a bicycle wheel, which he mounted on a kitchen stool. Strictly speaking, this was a 'ready-made assisted', but other 'pure' ready-mades soon followed, notably *Bottle Rack* (1914), *In Advance of the Broken Arm* (a snow shovel, 1915), and the celebrated *Fountain* (1917), consisting of a urinal which he signed 'R. Mutt' (the name of a firm manufacturing sanitary ware); most of the originals have disappeared, but several replicas exist. The ready-made can be considered a type of *objet trouvé* (found object), although Duchamp himself made a clear distinction between them, pointing out that whereas the *objet trouvé* is discovered and chosen because of its interesting aesthetic qualities, its beauty and uniqueness, the ready-made is one—any one—of a large number of indistinguishable mass-produced objects. Therefore the *objet trouvé* implies the exercise of taste in its selection, but the ready-made does not. In creating such works he demonstrated his belief in the absurdity of life and aesthetic values. The ready-made was one of *Dada's most enduring legacies to modern art. It was much used in

*Pop art, for example, and Robert *Rauschenberg called *Bicycle Wheel* 'one of the most beautiful pieces of sculpture I've ever seen'.

realism. Term used with various meanings in the history and criticism of the arts. In its broadest sense the word is used as vaguely as *naturalism, implying a desire to depict things accurately and objectively. Often, however, the term carries with it the suggestion of the rejection of conventionally beautiful subjects, or of idealization, in favour of a more down-to-earth approach, often with a stress on low life or the activities of the common man. In a more specific sense, the term (usually spelled with a capital R) is applied to a movement in 19th-century (particularly French) art characterized by a rebellion against the traditional historical, mythological, and religious subjects in favour of unidealized scenes of modern life. The leader of the Realist movement was *Courbet, who said: 'painting is essentially a concrete art and must be applied to real and existing things.'

The term *Social Realism has been applied to 19th- and 20th-century works that are realistic in this second sense and make overt social or political comment. It is to be distinguished from *Socialist Realism, the name given to the type of art that was officially promoted in the Soviet Union and some other Communist countries; far from implying a critical approach to social questions, it involved toeing the Party line in an academic style.

*Magic Realism and *Superrealism are names given to two 20th-century styles in which extreme realism—in the sense of acute attention to detail—produces a markedly unrealistic overall effect. Since the 1950s the term 'realism' has also been used in a completely different way, describing certain types of art that eschew conventional illusionism. This usage is found mainly in the terms *New Realism and Nouveau Réalisme, which have been applied to works made of materials or objects that are presented for exactly what they are and are known to be. See also VERISM.

Rebel Art Centre. See LEWIS, WYNDHAM.

Recco, Giuseppe (*b* Naples, 12 June 1634; *d* Alicante, 29 May 1695). Neapolitan still-life painter, the outstanding member of a family of artists. He is best known for pictures of fish, painted in an impressively grand style, but more austere than those of *Ruoppolo, with whom he ranks as the most distinguished Italian still-life painter of his period.

red-figure vase painting. One of the two major divisions of Greek vase painting, the other being *black-figure. In the red-figure technique, the background was painted black, leaving the figures in the unpainted red colour of the pottery. Details of the figure could thus be added with a brush rather than incised through the black paint, allowing much greater flexibility and subtlety of treatment. Because of this advantage the red-figure technique, which developed in Athens from about 530 BC, superseded the black-figure technique.

Redgrave, Richard (*b* London, 30 Apr. 1804; *d* London, 14 Dec. 1888). English painter, writer, and art administrator. He began as a painter of anecdotal literary subjects, often in 18th-century costume, but in the 1840s he became a pioneer of scenes of contemporary social concern (*The Poor Teacher*, 1845, Shipley AG, Gateshead). 'It is one of my most gratifying feelings', he wrote, 'that many of my best efforts in art have aimed at calling attention to the trials and struggles of the poor and the oppressed.' In his later career his output as an artist was limited mainly to landscapes painted when he was on holiday, as most of his time was taken up with administration: he was Surveyor of the Queen's Pictures (see ROYAL COLLECTION) from 1857 to 1880, and also held various posts at the School of Design (which became the *Royal College of Art) and the South Kensington (later Victoria and Albert) Museum. His brother **Samuel Redgrave** (*b* London, 3 Oct. 1802; *d* London, 20 Mar. 1876) was a writer on art, the author of a still-useful *Dictionary of Artists of the English School* (1874). The brothers collaborated on *A Century of Painters of the English School* (1866; later retitled *A Century of British Painters*), a valuable source of information on 18th- and 19th-century artists, many of whom they knew personally.

Redon, Odilon (*b* Bordeaux, 20 Apr. 1840; *d* Paris, 6 July 1916). French painter, draughtsman, and printmaker, one of the outstanding figures of *Symbolism. He led a retiring life, first in Bordeaux, then from 1870 in Paris, and until he was in his fifties he worked almost exclusively in black and white—in charcoal drawings and lithographs. In these he developed a highly distinctive repertoire of weird subjects—strange amoeboid creatures, insects, and plants with human heads and so on, influenced by the writings of Edgar Allan Poe. He remained virtually unknown to the public until the publication of J. K. Huysmans's celebrated novel *A rebours* in 1884; the book's hero, a disenchanted aristocrat who lives in a private world of perverse delights, collects Redon's drawings, and with his mention in this classic expression of decadence, Redon too became a figurehead of the movement. During the 1890s he turned to painting and revealed remarkable powers as a colourist that had previously lain dormant. Much of his early life had been unhappy, but after undergoing a religious crisis in the early 1890s and a serious illness in 1894–5, he was transformed into a much more buoyant and cheerful personality, expressing himself in radiant colours in visionary subjects, flower paintings, and mythological scenes (the chariot of Apollo was one of his favourite themes). He showed equal facility in oils and pastel and after 1900 he carried out a number of large decorative schemes. His flower pieces, in particular, were much admired by *Matisse, and the *Surrealists regarded him as one of their precursors. By the end of his life he was a distinguished figure, although still a very private person.

Redouté, Pierre-Joseph (*b* Saint-Hubert, Luxembourg [now in Belgium], 10 July 1759; *d* Paris, 20 June 1840). French botanical illustrator of Flemish birth, the best-known member of a family of artists. He settled in Paris in 1782 and throughout his career he successfully negotiated France's varied political upheavals, becoming official flower painter in turn to Queen Marie Antoinette, both Napoleon's empresses (Josephine and Marie-Louise), and Queen Marie-Amélie (wife of King Louis-Philippe). His large output included black-and-white illustrations for serious scientific treatises, but he is best known for lavish colour plates in deluxe books, notably *Les Roses* (1817–24). He was highly extravagant and died in debt in spite of his successful career.

Regionalism. A movement in American painting, flourishing chiefly in the 1930s, concerned with the depiction of scenes and types from the American Midwest. The term is often used more or less interchangeably with *American Scene Painting, but Regionalism can be more precisely thought of as the Midwestern branch of this broader category. Like all American Scene Painters, the Regionalists were motivated by a patriotic desire to establish a genuinely American art by using local themes and repudiating avant-garde styles from Europe. Specifically they were moved by a nostalgic desire to glorify, or at least to record, rural and small-town America, and it was on this that their widespread popularity depended. The period when they flourished coincided with the Great Depression, and at this time of profound national doubt, they reasserted America's faith in itself, giving the public pictures with which they could readily identify. Their work was often produced under the auspices of the *Federal Art Project and it was supported by the fanatically patriotic critic Thomas Craven (1889–1969).

The three major Regionalists were Thomas Hart *Benton, John Steuart *Curry, and Grant *Wood, who were all Midwesterners but differed greatly in temperament and style. They scarcely knew one another personally, but the idea of a group identity was skilfully promoted by Maynard Walker, a Kansas art dealer. Walker got a Benton self-portrait onto the cover of the Christmas 1934 issue of *Time* magazine and this largely created the image of Regionalism in the public eye; thus, as Robert *Hughes writes, 'it became the only art movement ever launched by a mass-circulation magazine', or as Benton put it, 'A play was written and a stage erected for us. Grant Wood became the typical Iowa small towner, John Curry the typical Kansas farmer, and I just an Ozark hillbilly. We accepted our roles.' On the fringes of the Regionalist movement were Charles *Burchfield and Ben *Shahn. Burchfield's work has a streak of fantasy absent from that of the others, and Shahn was driven by a spirit of social protest. Specifically local styles did not develop anywhere and Regionalism died out in the 1940s in the more international spirit that prevailed during and after the Second World War.

Regnault, Henri (b Paris, 30 Oct. 1843; d Buzenval, 19 Jan. 1871). French history painter, son of a notable scientist and photographer, Victor Regnault. He won the *Prix de Rome in 1866 and spent two years in Italy before moving to Spain, where he was allowed to continue working under the terms of his scholarship, and then in 1870 to Morocco. The pictures that he sent back for exhibition at the *Salon were acclaimed for their ardour, colour, and vigorous handling (*Automedon Taming the Horses of Achilles*, 1868, MFA, Boston) and he was spoken of as the heir of *Delacroix. However, after volunteering for service in the Franco-Prussian War he was killed in action at the age of 27. His patriotic death, coupled with his talent and his attractive personality, made him a national hero. There were several memorial books and exhibitions over the next few years and a monument to him was placed in the courtyard of the École des *Beaux-Arts.

Rego, Paula (b Lisbon, 26 Jan. 1935). Portuguese-born British painter of figure, animal, and fantasy subjects. She studied at the *Slade School, where she met her husband, the painter Victor Willing (1928–88). In the 1980s Rego became well known for her enigmatic figurative paintings, which often have a feeling of caricature as well as of fantasy. In 1990 she was appointed the first associate artist of the National Gallery, London. She painted murals in the restaurant of the gallery's new Sainsbury Wing in 1991, and in 1992 she became the first living artist to be given an exhibition in the gallery.

Reichenau School. Term used to cover *illuminated manuscripts of the *Ottonian period that have been associated with the abbey of Reichenau situated on an island in Lake Constance. It was once commonly believed that Reichenau was the pre-eminent centre of illumination in this period, but this view was strongly challenged in the 1960s, notably by C. R. Dodwell, who in his Pelican History of Art volume, *Painting in Europe: 800–1200* (1971), writes, 'my own view is that Reichenau was a small artistic outpost rather than a central headquarters'. He considers Lorsch and Trier to be more important centres.

Reid, Alex. See BURRELL.

Reid, Robert. See TEN.

Reid Dick, Sir William. See PORTLAND STONE.

Reims School. A term describing a tradition of manuscript illumination in the diocese of Reims in the early 9th century. From 816 to 835 the Bishop of Reims was Ebbo, a notable patron who had formerly been Charlemagne's librarian, and at this time his diocese was Europe's foremost centre for book production. The most famous manuscripts of the school are the Ebbo Gospels (Bibliothèque Municipale, Épernay) and the *Utrecht Psalter (University Lib., Utrecht). See also CAROLINGIAN ART.

Reinhardt, Ad (b Buffalo, NY, 24 Dec. 1913; d New York, 30 Aug. 1967). American painter. From the beginning of his career his painting was abstract, but it changed radically in style over the years. During the 1930s he worked in a crisp, boldly contoured geometrical style that owed something both to *Cubism and to the *Neo-Plasticism of *Mondrian. In the 1940s he passed through a phase of *all-over painting which has been likened to that of Mark *Tobey, and in the late 1940s he was close to certain of the *Abstract Expressionists, particularly *Motherwell, with whom he jointly edited *Modern Artists in America* (1950), a book based on conversations with contemporary artists. During the 1950s he turned to monochromatic paintings. At first they were usually red or blue, but from the late 1950s he devoted himself to all-black paintings with geometrical designs of squares or oblongs barely perceptibly differentiated in value from the background colour—works that were influential on the development of *Minimal art. His reduction of his work to 'pure aesthetic essences' reflects his belief in the complete separation between art and life—'Art is Art. Everything else is everything else.' Reinhardt's views were extremely uncompromising and he was a noted critic of trends in modern art of which he did not approve, as a polemical writer, as a lecturer, and as a satirical cartoonist.

Rejlander, O. G. See PHOTOMONTAGE.

relief (or **relievo**). Term (Italian: *rilevare*, 'to raise') applied to sculpture that projects from a background surface rather than standing freely. Since ancient times such sculpture has been particularly used for architectural decoration, but many sculptors have also made reliefs as independent works. According to the degree of projection, reliefs are usually classified as high (*alto rilievo*), medium (*mezzo rilievo*), or low (*basso rilievo* or bas-relief). The name *rilievo schiacciato* is given to a form of very low relief invented by *Donatello and memorably used also by *Desiderio da Settignano. Another distinctive type of low relief was used by the ancient Egyptians, figures being carved within deeply incised outlines rather than projecting beyond the surface. It is sometimes called *cavo relievo* or sunken, incised, or coelanaglyphic relief (Greek: *koilos*, 'hollow', and *anagluphe*, 'work in relief').

*Intaglio is the reverse of relief, the design being incised and sunk below the surface of the block.

relief etching. A method of *etching in which the parts of the design that take the ink are raised above the surface of the plate rather than incised into the plate (as in conventional etching). The design is drawn on the plate in an acid-resisting *varnish. The plate is then immersed in acid, which eats away the unprotected parts so that the design stands out in relief and prints can be taken in the same way as from a *woodcut block. The method dates from the 18th century, but was little used except by

William *Blake, who called it 'woodcut on copper'. In the 20th century the process was revived by S. W. *Hayter and Joan *Miró.

Rembrandt (Rembrandt Harmensz. van Rijn) (*b* Leiden, 15 July 1606; *d* Amsterdam, 4 Oct. 1669). Dutch painter, etcher, and draughtsman, his country's greatest artist. The son of a prosperous miller, he attended Leiden's Latin school and in 1620 he registered at the city's university, although he probably never actually studied there. At about this time he was apprenticed to the mediocre local painter Jacob van *Swanenburgh, with whom he is said to have studied for about three years. However, much more important for Rembrandt's development were six months spent in Amsterdam with Pieter *Lastman, *c*.1624. From Lastman he took not only his predilection for mythological and religious subjects, but also his manner of treating them, with exaggerated gestures and expressions, vivid lighting effects, and a meticulous, glossy finish, as in his earliest dated work—the *Stoning of St Stephen* (1625, Mus. B.-A., Lyons).

*Houbraken says that Rembrandt also studied with Jacob *Pynas and perhaps with Joris van Schooten (1587–1651), but any such associations must have been brief, for by 1625 he was working as an independent master in Leiden. There he had a close association with his friend Jan *Lievens, but they parted company when Rembrandt moved to Amsterdam (his home for the rest of his life) in 1631/2. His paintings of his Leiden period are mainly figure subjects, often involving old men depicted as philosophers or biblical characters. He also did portraits of himself and of members of his family, but it is not until 1631 that he painted his earliest known formal commissioned portraits, notably that of Nicolaes Ruts, a prosperous Amsterdam merchant (Frick Coll., New York). Rembrandt no doubt realized that here he had a recipe for success, as this type of work dominated his output in his early years in Amsterdam. It was the busiest period of his life, as he quickly established himself as the leading portraitist in the city. The work that most clearly demonstrated his superiority to rivals such as Thomas de *Keyser is the *Anatomy Lesson of Dr Tulp* (1632, Mauritshuis, The Hague), which brought a wholly new vitality to the group portrait. Rembrandt's great energy in his early years in Amsterdam comes out also in his religious works. The most important commission he received during the 1630s was from the stadholder (head of state) Prince Frederick Henry of Orange for five pictures depicting scenes of the Passion (Alte Pin., Munich), and the *Baroque tendencies of his work at this time are even more emphatically expressed in his sensational, life-size *Blinding of Samson* (1636, Städelsches Kunstinstitut, Frankfurt). Rembrandt presented this picture to Constantijn *Huygens, who had probably secured the commission for the Passion series from the stadholder.

Rembrandt's success in the 1630s was personal as well as professional. In 1634 he married Saskia van Uylenburgh, cousin of a picture-dealer associate, and from the evidence of his wonderfully tender portraits of her it must have been a blissful union. In 1639 he bought an imposing house (now a Rembrandt museum), and he spent lavishly on works of art and anything else that took his fancy or looked as if it might be useful as a prop—armour, old costumes, etc. His domestic happiness was, however, marred by a succession of infant deaths; of the four children Saskia bore him, only his son Titus (1641–68), who became one of his favourite models, lived longer than two months.

Saskia died in 1642, and in the same year Rembrandt finished his most famous picture, *The Night Watch* (Rijksmuseum, Amsterdam), which Jacob Rosenberg, in his standard monograph on the artist (1948), calls 'a thunderbolt of genius'. The erroneous title dates from the late 18th century when the painting was so discoloured with dirty varnish that it looked like a night scene. Its correct title is *The Militia Company of Captain Frans Banning Cocq and Lieutenant Willem van Ruytenburch*, and it is the culminating work of the Dutch tradition of civic guard portraits (a genre particularly associated with Frans *Hals). It is also the most ambitious picture of any kind painted by a Dutch artist up to this date, and Rembrandt showed remarkable originality in making a pictorial drama out of an insignificant event. To do this he subordinated the individual portraits to the demands of the composition, and according to popular legend the sitters who had paid for the picture were appalled at this and demanded that Rembrandt make radical changes, paint a new picture, or refund their money. Rembrandt's refusal is supposed to have been his downfall and to have led him into penniless obscurity. There is, however, no basis in fact for the story, which seems to be a 19th-century invention; indeed all the available evidence suggests that the picture was well received by contemporaries. Samuel van *Hoogstraten, for example, wrote: 'It is so painter-like in thought, so dashing in movement, and so powerful' that the pictures beside which it hung were made to seem 'like playing cards'.

Nevertheless, in the 1640s Rembrandt's worldly success did decline as the direction of his art changed. Formal portraiture took up much less of his time and he concentrated more on religious painting, while his style grew less flamboyant and more introspective. The change has been explained as a response to the death of Saskia (and of his mother in 1640), and religion may well have been a solace to him in this difficult period. At the same time, some of his market in portraiture must have gone to pupils such as *Bol and *Flinck, who imitated his style so well. It seems just as likely, however, that Rembrandt was tired of routine portraiture and wanted to return to his first love—painting subjects from the Bible. In the 1640s he also developed an interest in landscape and it has been suggested that he spent more time in the countryside during this period to escape from the domestic problems he encountered after Saskia's death. A widow called Geertge Dircx was employed as Titus's nurse, and she sued Rembrandt for breach of promise after his affections turned to Hendrickje Stoffels, a servant some twenty years his junior who entered the household in about 1645. After some unpleasant legal action Rembrandt succeeded in having Geertge shut up in a reformatory and the litigation did not end until her death in 1656. Hendrickje remained with Rembrandt for the rest of her life and bore him two children, including a daughter, Cornelia, born in 1654, who was the only one of his children to outlive him. Rembrandt's portrayals of Hendrickje are just as loving as those of Saskia, but he was unable to marry her because of a restrictive clause in Saskia's will.

After he turned his back on fashionable portraiture, Rembrandt's extravagance led him into financial difficulties, which became acute by the early 1650s. In 1656 he was declared insolvent (by convincing the authorities that he had acted honestly and in good faith he avoided the worse fate of bankruptcy, which carried the possibility of imprisonment); his collections were sold and by 1660 he had to leave his house and move to lodgings in a poorer district of the city. Houbraken says that 'in the autumn of his life he kept company mainly with common people and such as practised art', but the romantic image of him as a pauper and a recluse is grossly exaggerated. He continued to be a respected figure who received important commissions, some of them from abroad (his patrons included the Sicilian nobleman and collector Don Antonio Ruffo (1610–78)), and Hendrickje and Titus established an art firm with Rembrandt technically their employee, a device that protected him from his creditors. Indeed, with some weight thus lifted from his shoulders, Rembrandt may well have felt renewed energy, and there are more dated paintings from 1661 than from any year since the early 1630s. In 1661–2 he painted two of his greatest works—*The Sampling Officers of the Cloth-Makers' Guild* (sometimes called *The Syndics*, Rijksmuseum) and *The Conspiracy of Claudius Civilis*, painted for Amsterdam Town Hall, but for unknown reasons removed in 1663 and cut down (evidently by Rembrandt himself)—the magnificent fragment is now in the Nationalmuseum, Stockholm.

Rembrandt's final years were clouded by the deaths of Hendrickje in 1663 and Titus in 1668, but his art was in no way impaired. On the contrary, his work seemed to grow in human understanding and compassion to the very end, and his last self-portraits, the culmination of an incomparable series that began 40 years earlier, show him facing his hardships with the utmost dignity—someone who has no illusions about life, but equally no bitterness. Two self-portraits date from the last year of his life (NG, London, and Mauritshuis), but the painting that best stands as his spiritual testimony is perhaps the *Return of the Prodigal Son* (c.1669, Hermitage, St Petersburg), a work of the utmost tenderness and poignancy, described by Kenneth *Clark as 'a picture which those who have seen the original . . . may be forgiven for claiming as the greatest picture ever painted'. The emotional depth and range of Rembrandt's work was matched by the expressive mastery of his technique. Even as a young man, when surface polish and attention to detail were a necessary part of his skill as a fashionable portraitist, he had experimented boldly in his more private works, sometimes, for example, using the butt end of the brush to scrape through the paint. When he began to paint more to please himself in the 1640s, his handling grew much broader, and Houbraken wrote that 'in the last years of his life, he worked so fast that his pictures, when examined from close by, looked as if they had been daubed with a bricklayer's trowel.'

It is not only the quality of Rembrandt's work that sets him apart from all his Dutch contemporaries, but also its range. Although portraits and religious works bulk largest in his output, he made highly original contributions to other genres, including still-life (*The Slaughtered Ox*,

1655, Louvre, Paris), and he painted some pictures, such as *The Polish Rider* (c.1655, Frick Coll., New York), that virtually defy classification (see also DROST). Rembrandt was prodigious, too, as an etcher and draughtsman. He is universally regarded as the greatest of all exponents of etching (and *drypoint), capable of expressing the airy breadth of the Dutch countryside with a few quick strokes, but also prepared radically to rework a complex religious scene such as *The Three Crosses* perhaps a decade after he had begun it in 1653 to create one of the most awesome of all images of Christ's Passion. His drawings were done mainly as independent works rather than as studies for paintings and often with the thick bold strokes of the reed pen, of which he was an unsurpassed master.

Rembrandt was a great teacher; Gerrit *Dou became his first pupil in 1628 and Aert de *Gelder, who was with him in the 1660s, continued his master's style into the 18th century. Between these two, Rembrandt taught such illustrious figures as Carel *Fabritius (his greatest pupil), Phillips *Koninck, and Nicolaes *Maes. He continued to have many admirers after his death, and his work often fetched high prices in the 18th century. He was generally regarded as incomparable in his mastery of light and shade, but most critics considered his chief failing was his 'vulgarity' and lack of decorum. It was during the age of *Romanticism, when it was felt that artists should give expression to their innermost feelings and flout conventions, that his reputation began to rise towards its present supremely exalted heights. In 1851 *Delacroix suggested that one day Rembrandt would be rated higher than *Raphael—'a piece of blasphemy that will make every good academician's hair stand on end'; his prophecy came true within 50 years.

Remington, Frederic (b Canton, NY, 4 Oct. 1861; d Ridgefield, Conn., 26 Dec. 1909). American painter, sculptor, illustrator, and writer, the most famous portrayer of the 'Wild West'. He was a burly, athletic man and after studying art at Yale University he travelled widely in the West, prospecting and cow-punching as he worked to establish himself with his illustrations. Reproductions in *Harper's Weekly* and other popular journals made him a household name, and with his success he was able to turn more to painting and sculpture. In 1885 he settled in New York, but he continued to make visits to the West. His love of horses was so great that he had barn doors built in his studio so he could bring them inside. Remington travelled to Europe and North Africa as well as in America, and he wrote a good deal. He covered the Indian Wars of 1890–1 and the Spanish-American War (in Cuba) of 1898 as a newspaper correspondent and he published eight books, including *The Way of an Indian* (1906). There is a collection of his work at the Remington Art Memorial, Ogdensburg, New York State.

Renaissance. Term meaning 'rebirth' applied to an intellectual and artistic movement that began in Italy in the 14th century, culminated there in the 16th century, and influenced other parts of Europe in a great variety of ways. The notion of a rebirth refers to a revival of the values of the classical world, and the concept was used as early as the 15th century, by Italians who thought they were living at a time when the qualities of ancient art and literature were blossoming anew after centuries of barbarism. In the following century *Vasari gave the idea of such a revival a systematically developed form; he thought that art had declined in the Middle Ages, had been set once again on its true path by *Giotto, and had risen to its greatest heights in the work of his friend and hero *Michelangelo.

The extension of the meaning of the term from a cultural movement to a period of history began in the 18th century and this usage became firmly established in the mid-19th century. John *Ruskin used the expression 'The Renaissance period' in *The Stones of Venice* in 1851, for example, Jules Michelet called a volume of his history of France *La Renaissance* (1855), and in 1860 Jacob *Burckhardt published his highly influential book *Die Kultur der Renaissance in Italien* (The Civilization of the Renaissance in Italy). Michelet saw the Renaissance as the antithesis of the Middle Ages, and although Burckhardt did not share this view, he too had a rather romantic conception of the movement, seeing it as representing a great blossoming of the human spirit—'the discovery of the world and of man'. In *Gombrich's words, 'The nineteenth century regarded the Renaissance as a movement of liberation from the monkish dogmatism of the Middle Ages expressing its new-found enjoyment of sensuous pleasure in the artistic celebration of physical beauty.'

To modern historians these ideas seem too simple, and the Renaissance is seen more as a period of gradual change than as a sudden break with the past (art did become more secular in many ways, for example, but traditional religious subjects still provided the staple for most painters and sculptors of the time). Nevertheless, the intellectuals of the Renaissance were the first people to conceive a period identity for themselves, and this in itself gives the label a certain coherence. Scholars may debate endlessly over the exact interpretation of many aspects of the period, but in the general historical scheme of things, the Renaissance has come to represent the time when 'Medieval' turns into 'Modern'.

In the visual arts, the revival of the antique can be seen most clearly in architecture, for classical architecture uses a 'vocabulary' of forms that distinguishes it unambiguously from the Gothic style, and there can be no doubt that *Brunelleschi is entitled to rank as the first Renaissance architect. He was interested in Roman buildings probably more for what he could learn about engineering problems than for stylistic reasons, and he was undogmatic and unarchaeological in his use of antique detail, but he had an instinctual understanding of classical design, and his buildings—based on simple mathematical ratios—have a lucidity and harmony worthy of comparison with the finest ancient models. In sculpture, the beginnings of the Renaissance are sometimes traced as far back as Nicola *Pisano in the late 13th century because he is known to have been directly influenced by Roman sarcophagi. However, it is not until *Donatello, in the early 15th century, that we find a sculptor who had thoroughly assimilated the spirit of ancient sculpture, rather than simply borrowing motifs from it. In painting, it is harder to define the Renaissance in terms of antique influence, as very little ancient painting survived compared with the fairly abundant remains of Roman architecture and sculpture to be found in Italy. From the writings of ancient authors, however, classical painters were known to have excelled in fidelity to nature, so this quality was seen as a keynote of Renaissance painting. Because Giotto made such great advances in naturalism he is sometimes put at the head of the Renaissance tradition in painting, but it is more consistent to give this position to *Masaccio, who brought a new scientific rigour to the problems of representation.

Masaccio, like his friends Brunelleschi and Donatello, was a Florentine, and it is thus reasonable to see Florence as the cradle of the Renaissance, and the period around 1425, when they were producing some of their most innovative works, as a major turning point in European art. Florence continued to be of pre-eminent importance throughout the

15th century, but in the 16th century Rome and Venice were equally significant centres for the arts. The culmination of the Renaissance came in the period from about 1500 to 1520—a time that is now known as the High Renaissance. During this time the three most famous artists of the age—*Leonardo, Michelangelo, and *Raphael—produced works that have for centuries been regarded as touchstones of perfection and the fulfilment of all the ideals that artists had pursued since Giotto. In architecture, *Bramante represents a similar peak, and his noble and grave designs were regarded in his own time as having recaptured the majesty of Roman buildings.

The ideals and imagery of the Italian Renaissance did not generally begin to spread to the rest of Europe until about 1500. Albrecht *Dürer was the outstanding artist of the 'Northern Renaissance', making it his mission to transplant the new Italian ideas onto German soil. His work was of enormous importance in spreading Italian ideas, and during the 16th century it became a normal part of the career of ambitious young artists from northern Europe to follow in his footsteps across the Alps. By this time, however, Italian art had entered the phase called *Mannerism, and much Italian-inspired art of this period in Germany, France, and the Netherlands can be classified as Mannerist rather than Renaissance. Most northern artists imitated only the superficial characteristics of Italian art, and only a few—such as Jan van *Scorel—absorbed something of the order, poise, and dignity associated with the High Renaissance. Although Italian artists worked in England (notably Pietro *Torrigiano and Giovanni II da *Maiano), Renaissance influence there was fairly limited during the 16th century, being confined mainly to decorative motifs (and many of these were used in debased or misunderstood forms). It was not until the 17th century that there emerged an English artist—Inigo *Jones—who thoroughly understood Renaissance ideals, and by this time Italian art had progressed through Mannerism to the *Baroque. See also PROTO-RENAISSANCE.

Reni, Guido (*b* Bologna, 4 Nov. 1575; *d* Bologna, 18 Aug. 1642). Bolognese painter, draughtsman, and occasional etcher. From about 1584 to 1593 he was a pupil of *Calvaert, then transferred to the academy run by the *Carracci, where he absorbed their tradition of clear, firm draughtsmanship. By 1601 he had moved to Rome and he was based there until 1614, although he made frequent visits to Bologna. He flirted briefly with the *Caravaggesque manner (*Crucifixion of St Peter*, 1603, Pinacoteca, Vatican), but *Raphael and the *antique were the main inspiration for his graceful classical style, as is seen in his most celebrated work, *Aurora* (1614, Casino dell'Aurora, Palazzo Rospiglioso-Pallavacini, Rome), a captivatingly beautiful ceiling fresco painted for Cardinal Scipione *Borghese. Reni was also a favourite artist of Borghese's uncle, Pope Paul V, but in spite of his success in Rome he settled in Bologna in 1614 and seldom left the city again. After Ludovico Carracci's death in 1619, he was unrivalled as Bologna's most important artist; indeed by this time he was probably the most sought-after painter in Italy. The products of his large studio (mainly religious works) were sent all over Europe and *Rubens was the only contemporary painter who had a more glittering international clientele.

Reni cut an impressive, aristocratic figure, always fashionably and expensively dressed and usually attended by servants. He earned a huge amount of money from his work, but he was often in debt because of his addiction to gambling. This was one aspect of his complex and decidedly odd character, which is described in detail by his friend and biographer *Malvasia. Because of this remarkable account, more is known about Reni's inner life than that of any previous artist. In spite of his love of gambling, he was deeply religious and also rather prim, hating to hear anyone swearing or even making double entendres. He was devoted to his mother, but otherwise was fearful and suspicious of women: 'It was generally thought that he was a virgin . . . When observing the many lovely young girls who served as his models, he was like marble' (it has been suggested that he was a repressed homosexual). He was renowned for his generosity to friends, colleagues, pupils, and good causes (to which he often gave money anonymously), but he was notoriously touchy, falling out with several of his fellow artists, including *Albani, *Domenichino, and two of his teachers—Calvaert and Ludovico Carracci. Other quirks were a fear of witchcraft and a dread of being poisoned.

The great reputation Reni enjoyed in his lifetime was maintained in the 18th and early 19th centuries, many critics ranking him second only to Raphael. He was known as 'the Divine Guido' and was lauded for the celestial grace of his work. However, he fell from favour under the scornful attacks of *Ruskin (who detested the Bolognese painters in general), and was long dismissed as vulgar and sentimental. Until well into the 20th century a just appreciation of his stature was impeded by the failure to distinguish between his own works and those by his countless (often extremely insipid) imitators. A major exhibition devoted to him in Bologna in 1954 was a turning point in his critical fortunes, and his status as one of the greatest Italian painters of the 17th century is now firmly re-established. His late works in particular show a beauty of colouring that sets him apart from any of his contemporaries. In his early career he had typically used strong, rich colours, but he came to favour cooler harmonies, with prominent use of ice blue, apple green, pink, and pearly grey, and in the 1630s his tonality lightened even further, his pictures taking on a soft (sometimes almost ethereal), silvery glow. At the same time his brushwork became looser and the mood of his pictures more languid. These changes, particularly the less detailed handling, may have been partly a consequence of the speed at which he worked to pay off his gambling debts (he was once so desperate for money that he hired himself out by the hour), but the best of his late works have an exquisite delicacy and refinement. The largest and finest collection of his paintings is in the Pinacoteca Nazionale in Bologna.

Renier of Huy. See RAINER OF HUY.

Renoir, Pierre-Auguste (*b* Limoges, 25 Feb. 1841; *d* Cagnes-sur-Mer, 3 Dec. 1919). French *Impressionist painter. He was born into a poor family and in 1854, aged 13, he began work as a painter in a porcelain factory in Paris, gaining experience with the light, fresh colours that were to distinguish his Impressionist work and also learning the importance of good craftsmanship. His predilection for light-hearted themes was also influenced by the great *Rococo masters, whose work he studied in the Louvre. In 1862, having saved enough money to pay for tuition, he became a pupil in *Gleyre's studio and there formed lasting friendships with *Monet, *Sisley, and *Bazille, with whom he formed the early nucleus of the Impressionist group. His relationship with Monet was particularly close at this time, and their paintings of the beauty spot called La Grenouillère done in 1869 (an example by Renoir is in the Nationalmuseum, Stockholm) are regarded as the classic early statements of the Impressionist style.

Like Monet, Renoir endured much hardship early in his career, but in the late 1870s he began to achieve success as a portraitist (he was well suited to this work temperamentally, as his shy but friendly personality put sitters at their ease). In 1881 the dealer Paul *Durand-Ruel began buying his work regularly and henceforth he was free of major financial worries. By this time Renoir had 'travelled as far as Impressionism could take me', and a visit to Italy in 1881–2 inspired him to seek a greater sense of solidity in his work. The change in attitude is seen in *The Umbrellas* (NG, London), which was begun before the visit to Italy and finished afterwards; the two little girls on the right are painted with the feathery brushstrokes characteristic of his Impressionist manner, but the figures on the left are done in a crisper and drier style, with duller colouring. In the mid-1880s Renoir experimented for a while with this 'manière aigre' (harsh or sour manner) as he called it, but he then developed a softer and more supple kind of handling combined with warmer colour. At the same time he began to turn from contemporary themes to more timeless subjects, particularly nudes, but also pictures of young girls in unspecific settings. As his style became grander and simpler he also took up mythological subjects (*The Judgement of Paris*, c.1913–14, Hiroshima Museum of Art), and the female type he preferred became more mature and ample.

In the 1890s Renoir began to suffer from rheumatism, and from 1903 (by which time he was world-famous) he lived in the warmth of the south of France. The rheumatism eventually crippled him (by 1912 he was confined to a wheelchair), but he continued to paint until the end of his life, and in his last years he also took up sculpture, directing assistants (usually Richard Guino, a pupil of *Maillol) to act as his hands (*Venus Victorious*, 1914, Tate, London). The house at Cagnes-sur-Mer in which he spent his final years is now a museum devoted to him.

Renoir is perhaps the best loved of all the Impressionists, for his subjects—pretty children, flowers, beautiful scenes, above all lovely women—have instant appeal, and he communicated the joy he took in them with great directness. 'Why shouldn't art be pretty?', he said, 'There are enough unpleasant things in the world.' He was one of the great worshippers of the female form, and he said: 'I never think I have finished a nude until I think I could pinch it.' His output was enormous (about 6,000 paintings) and examples are in collections all over the world.

One of his sons was the celebrated film director Jean Renoir (1894–1979), who wrote a lively and touching biography published in both French and English (*Renoir, my Father*) in 1962.

Repin, Ilya (*b* Chuguyev, Ukraine, 24 July [5 Aug.] 1844; *d* Kuokkala, Finland [now Repino, St Petersburg region], 29 Sept. 1930). The most celebrated Russian painter of his day and a central figure in his country's cultural life. Although *Bryulov and *Ivanov had earlier won great renown in the West with a classical and a biblical picture respectively, and *Aivazovsky had gained international success with his seascapes, Repin was the first Russian painter to achieve European fame with specifically Russian themes. In addition to portraits of a host of celebrities, he painted colourful scenes of Russian history, pictures of peasant life, and contemporary subjects in which he attacked political abuses and social ills; his friend Tolstoy said that he 'depicts our national way of life much better than any other artist'. His main training was at the St Petersburg Academy, where he won a scholarship that enabled him to travel in Europe, 1873–6. He spent most of this time in Paris and returned there several times, becoming a highly respected figure in France (he was made a member of the Legion of Honour in 1901). Repin had mixed feelings about the *Impressionists, who became a great artistic talking point during his scholarship period in Paris (their first group exhibition was in 1874). He admired their lively use of light and colour but thought their work was lacking in serious moral purpose. The importance he attached to such moral values was clearly evident in his first great success, *Barge Haulers on the Volga* (1870–3, Russian Mus., St Petersburg), which won a medal at an international exhibition in Vienna in 1873. He showed his social conscience in revealing the appalling working conditions of the barge haulers, but the picture also celebrates their dignity and fortitude.

In 1878–83 Repin lived in Moscow, then settled in St Petersburg, but he spent a good deal of time travelling in remote areas of Russia to gather material for his paintings. He was at his peak in the 1880s, when he produced most of his finest works, including *The Zaporozhian Cossacks Writing a Mocking Letter to the Turkish Sultan* (1880–91, Russian Mus.), a characteristically full-blooded evocation of Russian history; *They Did Not Expect Him* (1884, Tretyakov Gal., Moscow), showing the unexpected return of a political exile from Siberia; and *Modest Mussorgsky* (1881, Tretyakov Gal.), which is often considered his greatest achievement as a portraitist. Although he sometimes worked painstakingly for years on his big historical paintings, the portrait of Mussorgsky was a brilliant impromptu performance, produced in a few hours during a temporary improvement in the health of the dying composer; Mussorgsky himself referred to the 'fearsome sweeps' of Repin's brush.

In 1894 Repin began teaching at the St Petersburg Academy and became a revered figure among his pupils. Following the 1905 Revolution he resigned his post as he did not want to be associated with a government he considered 'behind the times, stupid and ready for a complete downfall'. He returned in 1906 after pleas from his pupils but resigned for good in 1907. In 1899 he had bought a country estate at Kuokkola, which is near St Petersburg but at this time was part of Finland. After Finland declared independence from Russia in 1917 and closed the border, Repin found himself cut off from his native country and never returned. He remained highly respected there, however, and after Stalin's imposition of *Socialist Realism in the 1930s he was extolled as an 'artist-democrat' and held up as a model for Soviet painters. Kuokkola is now part of Russia again and has been renamed Repino in his honour; his home there is now a museum dedicated to him.

repoussoir (French: *repousser*, 'to push back, set off'). A figure or object in the foreground of a picture (and usually at the side) used to 'push back' the principal scene or episode, thereby increasing the sense of depth.

reredos. See ALTARPIECE.

resin. A sticky substance, insoluble in water, used in art particularly as a constituent of *varnish. Resins are secreted by many trees and plants; those used by painters in the past are not always easy to identify, but they include both soft resins from living trees (such as mastic, dammar, sandarac, Canada balsam, and *turpentine), and hard fossil resins (such as copal and amber). Resins can now also be made synthetically.

rest-stick. See MAULSTICK.

retable. See ALTARPIECE.

Rethel, Alfred (*b* Diepenbend, nr. Aachen, 15 May 1816; *d* Düsseldorf, 1 Dec. 1859). German painter and printmaker. His biggest work, a cycle of frescos from the life of Charlemagne (town hall, Aachen), was once much admired as a great achievement of heroic *history painting, but today seems hollow and theatrical. The cycle was begun in 1847 but left unfinished because of the madness that ended Rethel's career in 1853. He is now mainly remembered for his series of wood engravings *Another Dance* *of Death* (1849), much in the spirit of *Holbein's famous depictions of the subject, but satirizing the revolutionary events of 1848, with Death seen as the embodiment of anarchy. In 1851 he returned to the theme of death, but in a personal rather than political vein, with a pair of prints that were once extremely popular—*Death as an Avenger* and *Death as a Friend*.

retroussage (French: 'dragging up'). In *intaglio methods of printmaking, a technique of gently passing a fine cloth over an inked plate, thereby drawing out a little of the ink and spreading it over the edges of the lines. It produces a soft effect in printing.

Révoil, Pierre. See TROUBADOUR STYLE.

Rewald, John (*b* Berlin, 12 May 1912; *d* New York, 2 Feb. 1994). German-born American art historian, a professor at the university of Chicago 1963–71 and thereafter at the City University, New York. He was the doyen of the field of *Impressionist and *Post-Impressionist scholarship, and is famous for two magisterial works, *The History of Impressionism* (1946, 4th edn. 1973) and *Post-Impressionism: From Van Gogh to Gauguin* (1956, 3rd edn. 1978). These show his total command of the voluminous material and his remarkable powers of organization and exposition in forming it into a highly readable narrative, and are, by common consent, among the greatest works of art history ever written (even though some critics have accused him of being strong on facts but weak on interpretation); *The History of Impressionism* used to enjoy the 'distinction' of being the book most frequently stolen from the *Courtauld Institute library. Rewald's other writings include studies of many leading 19th-century French artists, particularly *Cézanne (he received a gold medal from Cézanne's home town, Aix-en-Provence, in 1984), and two collections of his articles have appeared: *Studies in Impressionism* (1985) and *Studies in Post-Impressionism* (1986).

Rexach, Juan and **Pere.** See BAÇO.

Reymerswaele, Marinus van. See MARINUS VAN REYMERSWAELE.

Reynolds, Sir Joshua (*b* Plympton, Devon, 16 July 1723; *d* London, 23 Feb. 1792). English painter and writer on art. Reynolds was the leading portraitist of his day, the first president of the *Royal Academy, a major art theorist, and perhaps the most important figure in the history of British painting, for through his social and intellectual eminence he raised his profession to a new level of dignity. He was the son of a scholarly clergyman and was brought up in an atmosphere of learning (he said he owed his 'first fondness' for art to Jonathan *Richardson's *Essay on the Theory of Painting*, which he read in his father's library). From 1740 to 1743 he studied painting in London under *Hudson (likewise a Devon man), then set up independently as a portraitist a year before his apprenticeship was due to end (the parting was amicable—he and Hudson remained on good terms).

In 1750–2 Reynolds spent 2½ years in Italy (mainly Rome), where he made an intensive study of the *antique and the great masters of the 16th and 17th centuries (whilst copying *Raphael in the wintry chill of the Vatican he caught a cold that left him hard of hearing for the rest of his life). He not only absorbed the formal language of his models, but also developed a deliberate cult of learning and classical allusion that coloured his whole approach to art. In tune with established art theory, he thought that *history painting was the highest branch of art, but he believed that portraiture could rise above its traditional status as mere 'face-painting' by making reference to the great art of the past. Thus, in the work that established his reputation after he settled in London in 1753—*Commodore Keppel* (1753–4, Nat. Maritime Mus., London)—the sitter's heroic attitude is based directly (albeit in reverse) on that of the *Apollo Belvedere*, then regarded as the matchless ideal of male beauty. However, his approach involved far more than simply borrowing poses from approved models, for he tried to create an image that was in keeping with the character and status of each particular sitter. In the Keppel portrait, for example, he not only alludes to an ancient statue, but also depicts a contemporary man of action with great verve.

Reynolds quickly achieved a leading position in his profession. He had 150 sitters a year by 1758, and by 1764 was earning the enormous annual sum of £6,000. His success was achieved through hard work and careful business management as well as talent; on the day he was knighted (21 April 1769) his visit to St James's Palace was fitted in between two sittings with clients. Moreover, although he always retained traces of his provincial origins (notably his Devon accent), he was completely at home with his eminent sitters. His pupil James *Northcote said that 'His general manner, deportment and behaviour were amiable and prepossessing; his disposition was naturally courtly. He . . . contrived to move in a higher sphere of society than any other English artist had done before. Thus he procured for the Professors of the Arts a consequence, dignity and reception which they never possessed in this country.'

Reynolds's elevation of the status of the artist depended, then, not only on the intellectual quality of his work, but also on his social acceptability, and it is significant that his friends were mainly men of letters—notably Samuel Johnson and Oliver Goldsmith—rather than other painters (James Boswell dedicated his celebrated *Life of Johnson* to Reynolds). On the foundation of the Royal Academy in 1768, he was the obvious choice for president, and he arranged for Johnson and Goldsmith to be appointed to the honorary positions of professors of ancient history and literature. Between 1769 and 1790 he delivered a series of lectures to the Academy's students, and these fifteen *Discourses* are one of the most impressive bodies of writing ever made by a practising artist, forming the classic expression of the academic doctrine of the *Grand Manner (each *Discourse* was published separately and the first collected edition appeared in 1797). In 1789 failing eyesight forced Reynolds to give up painting and by the time of his death he was almost completely blind. He bore his final illness with what his friend Edmund *Burke called a 'mild and cheerful fortitude' and was buried in St Paul's Cathedral with ceremonial never before accorded a British painter; his ten pallbearers were made up of three dukes, three earls, two marquesses, a viscount, and a baron.

As a portraitist Reynolds is remarkable above all for his versatility—his inexhaustible range of response to the individuality of each sitter, man, woman, or child. The celebrated remark of his rival *Gainsborough, 'Damn him! How various he is!', is echoed in the praise of *Ruskin: 'Considered as a painter of individuality in the human form and mind, I think him the prince of portrait painters. *Titian paints nobler pictures and van *Dyck had nobler subjects, but neither of them entered so subtly as Sir Joshua did into the minor varieties of human heart and temper.' His huge output necessitated the employment of assistants and *drapery painters, and his experimentation with *bitumen has resulted in some of his pictures being in poor condition, but there is nevertheless much beauty of handling in his work, and his finest pictures rank among the great masterpieces of British portraiture. On the other hand, his history paintings, dating mainly from the end of his career, are generally considered ponderous failures (Hester Thrale—a friend of Dr Johnson—said he had 'a rage for

sublimity ill-understood'). Reynolds's work is in numerous public collections, great and small, in Britain and elsewhere, and many of his best pictures are still in the possession of the families for which they were painted. His output was so varied that no single collection can be regarded as fully representative.

Frances Reynolds (1729–1807), Joshua's sister and for many years his housekeeper, was an amateur painter, but evidently not a very good one, for he said of her copies of his work: 'They make other people laugh and me cry.'

Reynolds-Stephens, Sir William. See NEW SCULPTURE.

Reyntiens, Patrick. See STAINED GLASS.

Riace Bronzes. See PHIDIAS.

Ribalta, Francisco (*bapt.* Solsona, Catalonia, 2 June 1565; *d* Valencia, 13 Jan. 1628). Spanish painter, an important figure in the transition from *Mannerism to a more naturalistic style. He spent most of his early career in Madrid, but by 1599 he had settled in Valencia. Up to about 1620 his work was *eclectic, but he then developed a more personal and powerful style, with dramatic lighting that echoes *Caravaggio (*Christ Embracing St Bernard*, 1625–7, Prado, Madrid). *Zurbarán was among the artists who were influenced by him. His son **Juan** (1596/7–1628) was an able painter in his father's style, but he died young.

Ribera, José (or **Jusepe**) **de** (*bapt.* Játiva, nr. Valencia, 17 Feb. 1591; *d* Naples, 3 Sept. 1652). Spanish painter, etcher, and draughtsman, active for all his known career in Italy, where he was called Lo Spagnoletto (the little Spaniard). He is recorded in Parma in 1611 and Rome in 1613, but little is known of his life before he settled in Naples (at the time a Spanish possession) in 1616. Naples was one of the main centres of the Caravaggesque style, and Ribera is often described as a follower of *Caravaggio. However, although his early work is markedly *tenebrist, it is much more individual than that of most Caravaggesque artists, particularly in his vigorous and scratchy handling of paint, and his later works are far removed from Caravaggio in style—rich in colour and soft in modelling. Similarly, his penchant for the typically Caravaggesque theme of bloody martyrdom has been overplayed, enshrined as it is in Byron's lines: 'Spagnoletto tainted/His brush with all the blood of all the sainted' (*Don Juan*, xiii. 71). He did paint some powerful scenes in this vein, notably the celebrated *Martyrdom of St Philip* (1639, Prado, Madrid; formerly identified as the *Martyrdom of St Bartholomew*), but his treatment is invariably dignified rather than merely gory. Moreover he was capable of great tenderness, as in the *Adoration of the Shepherds* (1650, Louvre, Paris), and his work is remarkable for his feeling for individual humanity. This feature is evident in his secular pictures as well as his religious works, for example in *The Clubfooted Boy* (1642, Louvre). His range of secular subjects was fairly wide, for he was the first Spanish painter to show much interest in mythological themes (*Apollo and Marsyas*, 1637, Mus. Royaux, Brussels) and he also created a novel type of picture in which he depicted philosophers as beggars or vagabonds (*Archimedes*, 1630, Prado). He was the leading painter in Naples in his period (*Velázquez visited him during his second visit to Italy and probably during his first) and his work was influential in Spain (where much of it was exported) as well as in Italy. *Giordano was among his pupils. His reputation remained high after his death, and until the Napoleonic Wars he and *Murillo were virtually the only Spanish painters whose work was widely known outside their native country.

Ricci, Juan and **Francisco.** See RIZI.

Ricci, Sebastiano (*bapt.* Belluno, 1 Aug. 1659; *d* Venice, 15 May 1734). Italian decorative painter. He was born in the Veneto and is considered a member of the Venetian School, but before he settled permanently in Venice in 1717 he led a peripatetic life, working in numerous Italian cities and also in England, Flanders, France, and Germany. His unsettled existence is a reflection not only of the demand for his talents but also of his penchant for illicit love affairs, which often led to his having to move in haste, and once almost resulted in his execution. In view of this it is not surprising that his work is uneven and sometimes shows signs of carelessness, but he had a gift for vivid, fresh colouring, and his itinerant career was important in spreading knowledge of Italian decorative painting. He was in England in 1711/12–16. Little of the decorative work he did there survives except the *Resurrection* in the apse of the chapel at Chelsea Hospital and some large but damaged canvases on the staircase at Burlington House (now the Royal Academy). He is, however, extremely well represented in the Royal Collection.

Marco Ricci (*b* Belluno, 5 June 1676; *d* Venice, 21 Jan. 1730), Sebastiano's nephew, came from the same town and similarly travelled extensively.

He made two visits to England (1708 and 1711/12–16), and during the second worked in partnership with his uncle; the collaboration continued after they returned to Venice. Examples of their joint works are in the Royal Collection. Marco was primarily a landscape painter, working in a freely handled style that owed something to *Magnasco.

Riccio, Il (Andrea Briosco) (*b* Trento, Apr. 1470; *d* Padua, 8 July 1532). Italian sculptor, active in and around Padua; his nickname means 'curly head'. He was trained as a goldsmith by his father, but he turned to sculpture and studied with Bartolommeo Bellano (*c.*1440–96/7), who is said to have been one of *Donatello's assistants. Although he worked in terracotta, Riccio was primarily a virtuoso in bronze and his masterpiece is the huge (nearly 4 m (13 ft) high) Easter candlestick (1507–16) in the Santo (S. Antonio) at Padua, which with its relief scenes of classically draped figures, its satyrs, sphinxes, and decorative conceits, is an endlessly inventive work. He is best known, however, for small bronze pieces, including statuettes and items such as inkstands and oil lamps. They are done in an *antique manner and greatly appealed to humanist circles in Padua and Venice (he was on friendly terms with leading scholars). Riccio was much imitated, but works from his own hand are distinguished by a vivacity and delicacy of surface that none of his rivals could match.

Richards, Ceri (*b* Dunvant, nr. Swansea, 6 June 1903; *d* London, 9 Nov. 1971). British painter, printmaker, designer, and maker of reliefs, born into a Welsh-speaking family. From 1924 he spent most of his life in London, but he remained close to his Welsh roots. His output was many-sided, and Sir John *Rothenstein writes that 'Richards's work is widely admired but there is little consensus of opinion about its essential character.' In 1936 he took part in the International *Surrealist Exhibition in London and he said that Surrealism 'helped me to be aware of the mystery, even the "unreality", of ordinary things'. At this time he was also strongly influenced by *Picasso, notably in a series of semi-abstract relief constructions begun in 1933. After the Second World War his painting drew inspiration from the large exhibition of Picasso and *Matisse at the Victoria and Albert Museum in 1945. His best-known works include the *Cathédrale engloutie* series, based on a Debussy prelude (which Richards used to play on the piano), and '*Do not go gentle into that good night*' (1956, Tate, London), based on a poem by

Dylan Thomas (whom he once met). Richards's work also included book illustrations, theatre designs, mural decorations for ships of the Orient line, and designs for stained glass and furnishings for the Blessed Sacrament Chapel in Liverpool Roman Catholic Cathedral (1965).

Richardson, Jonathan the Elder (*b* London, ?1665; *d* London, 28 May 1745). English portrait painter, writer, and collector. John *Riley's most important pupil, he was one of the leading portraitists in the generation after *Kneller's death. This period, however, has been described by Ellis *Waterhouse as 'the most drab in the history of British painting', and Richardson is now remembered more for his writings than his pictures. His most important book is *An Essay on the Theory of Painting* (1715), which was the first significant work of art theory written in English; it was an immediate success and its claims for the intellectual seriousness of painting inspired the young *Reynolds. *An Account of Some of the Statues, Bas-Reliefs, Drawings, and Pictures in Italy* (1722), which he wrote in collaboration with his son **Jonathan the Younger** (*b* London, 1694; *d* London, 10 June 1771), also a portraitist, was much used as a guidebook by young Englishmen making the *Grand Tour. Richardson the Elder was an excellent draughtsman (a self-portrait in black and red chalk, *c*.1735, is in the NPG, London) and he made a superb collection of Old Master drawings.

Richier, Germaine (*b* Grans, nr. Arles, 16 Sept. 1902; *d* Montpellier, 31 July 1959). French sculptor. She had a traditional training as a carver, working under *Bourdelle from 1925 to 1929, but from about 1940 she began to create a distinctive type of bronze sculpture. Her figures became long and thin, combining human with animal or insect (and sometimes vegetal) forms. The surfaces of these powerful and disquieting works have a tattered and lacerated effect, creating a macabre feeling of decomposition, and she was one of the pioneers of an open form of sculpture in which enclosed space becomes as important as the solid material. Such figures were often extremely difficult to cast and she showed great technical resourcefulness in bringing them to completion. The public sometimes found her work shocking, especially her *Crucified Christ* (1950, church of Nôtre-Dame-de-Toute-Grâce, Assy), which caused a storm of controversy. Nevertheless, her international prestige grew steadily in the years after the

Second World War. Late in her career she also produced engravings and paintings.

Richier, Ligier (*b* Saint-Mihiel, Lorraine, *c*.1500; *d* Geneva, 1567). French sculptor, the head of a dynasty of artists. Ligier's work is powerful and emotional and although there is some *Renaissance influence in his style, he has been described as the 'last of the great masters of French *Gothic sculpture'. His largest work is the life-size stone *Entombment* group (1554–64) in the church of St Étienne, Saint-Mihiel, and his best-known work is perhaps the tomb of René de Châlons (*d* 1544) in St Pierre, Bar-le-Duc. It is surmounted by a gruesome standing skeleton with shreds of skin attached to its bones; in its outstretched hand it lifts up its own heart to heaven. Late in life Richier became a convert to Protestantism and he died a religious refugee in Switzerland. His son **Gérard Richier** (1534–*c*.1603) was a sculptor, and he in turn had three sculptor sons, who continued the family tradition into the 17th century, **Jacob** (*d c*.1640), **Jean** (*d* 1625), and **Joseph** (1581–1624).

Richmond, George (*b* London, 28 Mar. 1809; *d* London, 19 Mar. 1896). The best-known member of a family of English painters. He was a pupil of his father, the miniaturist **Thomas Richmond Sen.** (1771–1837), and also studied at the *Royal Academy, where he became a friend of Samuel *Palmer. With Palmer and others he was one of the group of William *Blake's followers known as the *Ancients. However, his imitation of Blake's mannerisms was heavy-handed (*The Eve of Separation*, 1830, Ashmolean Mus., Oxford). From about 1830 he turned from poetic and religious themes to portraiture and became a great fashionable success. He was highly prolific, his account books listing about 2,500 portrait paintings and drawings. His brother **Thomas Richmond Jun.** (1802–74) and his son **Sir William Blake Richmond** (*b* London, 29 Nov. 1842; *d* London, 11 Feb. 1921) were also painters. Thomas specialized in portraits, but Sir William had a more varied output and was also a sculptor and a designer (notably of numerous mosaics in St Paul's Cathedral, London).

Richter, Hans. See DADA.

Richter, Ludwig (*b* Dresden, 28 Sept. 1803; *d* Dresden, 19 June 1884). German painter, printmaker, and illustrator. Richter is usually regarded as one of the leading figures of late *Romanticism in Germany, alongside Moritz von *Schwind, but his work has a modest, intimate quality that also relates it to

*Biedermeier. He spent most of his career in Dresden (where he was a professor at the Academy), but in 1823–6 he lived in Rome, where he was in close touch with the *Nazarenes and studied with the landscape painter Joseph Anton *Koch. In his paintings as well as his illustrations—often for children's books—his favourite subjects included the pleasures of the countryside, fairy tales, and the more idyllic incidents of sacred and legendary art. His autobiography, *Lebenserinnerungen eines deutschen Malers* (Memoirs of a German Painter, 1885), is not only a charming piece of writing but also an important source for the artistic ideas of his time.

Ricketts, Charles (b Geneva, 2 Oct. 1866; d London, 7 Oct. 1931). British painter, designer, sculptor, collector, and writer on art. In 1882, whilst studying wood engraving at Lambeth School of Art, he met fellow student Charles *Shannon, who became his lifelong companion. Ricketts initially made his mark in book production, first as an illustrator, then as the driving force behind the Vale Press (1896–1904), one of the finest *private presses of the day, for which he designed founts, initials, borders, and illustrations. After the closure of the Press (following a disastrous fire), Ricketts turned to painting and occasional sculpture, and in 1906 he began to make designs for the theatre. His paintings—typically rather melodramatic, heavy-handed figure subjects—have not worn well, but his colourful stage designs are still much admired. He had a great reputation as a connoisseur and in 1915 turned down the offer of the directorship of the National Gallery. Later he regretted this decision, but he served on various committees and put much energy into trying to combat modernism in art. Most of the highly varied collection he made with Shannon was bequeathed to the Fitzwilliam Museum in Cambridge, although the gem of the collection—*Piero di Cosimo's *Fight between Lapiths and Centaurs*—went to the National Gallery. Ricketts's main books were *The Prado and its Masterpieces* (1903), *Titian* (1910), and *Pages on Art* (1913); *Self-Portrait* (taken from his letters and journals) was posthumously published in 1939.

Ridolfi, Carlo (b Lonigo, nr. Vicenza, 1 Apr. 1594; d Venice, 5 Sept. 1658). Italian painter and writer. He is insignificant as an artist, but he is remembered as the biographer of *Tintoretto (1642) and author of *Le miraviglie dell' arte* (The Marvels of Art), published in two volumes in 1648. This is a source of great importance for the history of Venetian art, which was somewhat scantily treated by *Vasari. Ridolfi was also a notable collector of drawings; many of those he owned are now at Christ Church, Oxford.

Riegl, Alois (b Linz, 14 Jan. 1858; d Vienna, 17 Jan. 1905). Austrian art historian, professor of the history of art at Vienna University from 1897 until his death. He is remembered mainly as the originator of the concept of *Kunstwollen* ('will for art' or, as it is more usually translated, 'will to form'). He wished to understand why style changed through the ages, and thought it was inadequate to explain the changes in terms of materials and techniques. Instead he proposed the idea of a dynamic aesthetic impulse, reflecting an innate desire for change, each generation seeing differently from its predecessor. His main publications are *Stilfragen* (Style Questions, 1893), which deals with ornament, *Die spätrömische Kunstindustrie* (The Late Roman Art Industry, 1901), which *Gombrich calls 'the most ambitious attempt ever made to interpret the whole course of art history in terms of changing modes of perception', *Die holländische Gruppenporträt* (The Dutch Group Portrait, 1902), and *Die Enstehung der Barockkunst in Rom* (The Genesis of *Baroque Art in Rome, published posthumously in 1907). His *Kunstwollen* concept had considerable influence; it can be seen, for example, in Kenneth *Clark's *The Nude*.

Riemenschneider, Tilman (b Heiligenstadt, c.1460; d Würzburg, 7 July 1531). German sculptor, active in Würzburg, where he settled in 1483. With *Stoss, he was the outstanding German late *Gothic sculptor, and his workshop was large and productive (his activities are exceptionally well documented for the time). He worked a good deal in stone, but he was primarily a woodcarver, and he was evidently the first German sculptor to leave his wooden figures un-*polychromed (although they were not entirely uncoloured, as he used pigmented varnish and picked out details such as eyes and lips in colour). His style was intricate, but also balanced and harmonious, with none of the extreme emotionalism often seen in German art of the period. He held various offices in city government, and in 1525 he was briefly imprisoned and perhaps tortured because he was one of the councilmen who refused to support the use of force against the rebels in the Peasants' War.

Much of Riemenschneider's surviving work is still in the churches for which it was created, a celebrated example being the magnificent *Holy Blood* altarpiece (1501–5) in St Jacobskirche,

Rothenburg ober der Tauber. It formed a kind of giant reliquary for a drop of Christ's blood, and this dictated the iconography, the main scene showing the institution of the Eucharist. Riemenschneider is also well represented in the Bayerisches Nationalmuseum, Munich, and the Mainfränkisches Museum, Würzburg. Two of his sons, **Jörg** and **Hans**, were sculptors, and two others, **Bartholomäus** (a pupil of *Dürer) and **Tilman**, were painters.

Rietveld, Gerald. See STIJL.

Rigaud, Hyacinthe (*b* Perpignan, 18 July 1659; *d* Paris, 29 Dec. 1743). French portrait painter, the friend and rival of *Largillière. He began his career in Montpellier and worked in Lyons before settling in Paris in 1681. His reputation was established in 1688 with a portrait (now lost) of Monsieur, Louis XIV's brother, and he became the outstanding court painter of the latter part of Louis's reign, retaining his popularity after the king's death. He was less interested in showing individual character than in depicting the rank and condition of the sitter by nobility of attitude and expressiveness of gesture. These qualities are seen most memorably in his celebrated state portrait of Louis XIV (1701, Louvre, Paris), one of the classic images of royal majesty. Louis so admired this portrait that although he had intended it as a present for Philip V of Spain, he kept it himself. Rigaud's unofficial portraits, such as *The Artist's Mother* (1695, Louvre), are much more informal and show a debt to *Rembrandt, several of whose works he owned. The output from Rigaud's studio was vast and examples are in many collections.

Rijksmuseum, Amsterdam. The Dutch national art collection. Its origins go back to a National Art Gallery opened in 1800 in the Huis ten Bosch, a 17th-century palace on the outskirts of The Hague. At this time Holland was under French rule and the creation of such a museum was typical of the centralizing reforms beloved of Napoleon. In 1808 the gallery was relocated to Amsterdam and renamed the Royal Museum—the 'royal' referring to Louis Bonaparte (Napoleon's brother), who had been created King of Holland in 1806. It was housed in the town hall (renamed by Louis the Royal Palace). After Louis abdicated in 1810 it was renamed the Great Dutch Museum, and after the French were expelled in 1813 it was renamed the National Museum. In 1815 it was given its present title of State Museum (Rijksmuseum), and in 1817 it opened in a new home, a 17th-

century building called the Trippenhuis (Trip House), named after its original owners. The idea of the museum was to assemble Netherlandish paintings of national importance and also to stimulate contemporary art. The Trippenhuis proved too small for the growing collection, but it was not until 1877 that a new purpose-built museum was begun. This building, the present Rijksmuseum, opened in 1885. Designed by P. J. H. Cuypers, the outstanding Dutch architect of the 19th century, it is in an eclectic style mixing Gothic and Renaissance features and is of immense size—at the time it opened it was the largest building in the country. In 1895 it transferred its pictures by living artists to Amsterdam's newly opened Stedelijk Museum (Municipal Museum) and from this point it virtually gave up collecting modern works.

The most important official in the history of the museum has been Frederick Schmidt-Degener (1881–1941), who was director from 1922 until his death. He modernized its displays and began the acquisition of foreign works of art. Since the Second World War the Rijksmuseum has also greatly expanded its coverage of sculpture and applied art, but it remains chiefly famous for its collection of 17th-century Dutch paintings—the largest and most comprehensive in the world. Associated with the Rijksmuseum is the Rijksprentenkabinet, which has an outstanding collection of prints and drawings.

Riley, Bridget (*b* London, 24 Apr. 1931). British painter and designer, rivalled only by *Vasarely as the most celebrated exponent of *Op art. Her interest in optical effects came partly through her study of *Seurat's technique of *pointillism, but when she took up Op art in the early 1960s she worked initially in black and white. She turned to colour in 1966. By this time she had attracted international attention (one of her paintings was used for the cover to the catalogue of the exhibition 'The Responsive Eye' at the Museum of Modern Art, New York, in 1965, the exhibition that gave currency to the term 'Op art'), and the seal was set on her reputation when she won the International Painting Prize at the Venice *Biennale in 1968. Her work shows a complete mastery of the effects characteristic of Op art, particularly subtle variations in size, shape, or placement of serialized units in an all-over pattern. It is often on a large scale and she frequently makes use of assistants for the actual execution. Although her paintings often create effects of vibration and dazzle, her decorative scheme for the interior of the Royal Liverpool Hospital (1983) uses soothing bands of blue, yellow, pink, and white and is reported to have caused a drop in vandalism and graffiti. She has also worked in theatre design, making sets for a ballet called *Colour Moves* (first performed at the Edinburgh Festival in 1983). Unusually, the sets preceded the composition of the music and the choreography. Riley has travelled widely, and a visit to Egypt in 1981 was particularly influential on her work, as she was inspired by the colours of ancient Egyptian art.

Riley, John (b London, 1646; d London, 27 Mar. 1691). English portrait painter. His early career is obscure, but he emerged as the most distinguished figure in English portraiture in the brief interval between the death of *Lely in 1680 and the dominance of *Kneller. Although he was appointed principal painter to William III and Mary II jointly with Kneller in 1688, his finest works are not court portraits but depictions of sitters from humble callings; the two best known are *The Scullion* (Christ Church, Oxford) and *Bridget Holmes* (1686, Royal Coll.), a full-length portrayal of a nonagenarian royal housemaid who brandishes her broom at a mischievous page-boy. Riley was generally more successful painting men than women (he was no rival to Lely in depicting fine clothes and soft complexions) and his unassuming sincerity of presentation exemplifies a typically English approach to portraiture that he passed on to his pupil *Richardson.

Rimmer, William (b Liverpool, 20 Feb. 1816; d South Milford, Mass., 20 Aug. 1879). English-born American sculptor, painter, teacher, and writer. His family emigrated when he was a small child and eventually settled in Boston, which with New York was his main place of work. Rimmer was an offbeat character and had an eccentric career. He believed he was the rightful heir to the French throne and taught himself medicine (he was licensed as a physician in 1855). As an artist too he was self-taught, and although he showed brilliantly precocious talent with his gypsum figure of *Despair* (c.1830, MFA, Boston), he struggled for recognition, and for years earned his living mainly as a sign and scenery painter and as a cobbler. In his later years, however, he became famous as a teacher, notably for his instructional books, *Elements of Design* (1864) and *Art Anatomy* (1877). Rimmer's output as an artist was very small, but he was the most powerful and original American sculptor of his time; his work excels in dramatic force and

vividly displays his anatomical mastery (*Falling Gladiator*, 1861; original plaster, Nat. Mus. of American Art, Washington; bronze, MFA, Boston). As a painter, his best-known work is the nightmarish *Flight and Pursuit* (1872, MFA, Boston), which, like his sculptures, shows the freshness and unconventionality of his approach and the richness of his imagination.

Rinehart, William Henry (b nr. Union Bridge, Md., 13 Sept. 1825; d Rome, 28 Oct. 1874). American sculptor. After spending his early career as a stonecutter in Baltimore, he settled in Rome in 1855, and became one of the leading American expatriate *Neoclassical sculptors of his generation. His work included mythological and allegorical subjects and (in a more naturalistic style) portraits, but he is perhaps best known for the rather maudlin *Sleeping Children* (1859–60); this was originally made for Greenmount Cemetery, Baltimore, but it was so popular that Rinehardt produced more than twenty replicas of it. He left the bulk of his estate to promote the appreciation of sculpture and enable American sculptors to study abroad.

Ring, Ludger tom the Elder (b Münster, 1496; d Münster, 1547). German painter and designer of woodcuts, the head of a dynasty of artists active mainly in and around Münster. Most of his surviving pictures are portraits, influenced by Netherlandish art, although he also worked on an astronomical clock for Münster Cathedral (1540, *in situ*) and produced a set of fifteen pictures of sibyls and ancient sages for the cathedral, six of which survive (Westfälisches Landesmuseum, Münster). His sons **Hermann tom Ring** (b Münster, 2 Jan. 1521; d Münster, 1597) and **Ludger tom Ring the Younger** (b Münster, 19 Nov. 1522; d Brunswick, 1584) painted portraits and religious works, and Ludger was also an early exponent of still-life (unlike his father and brother he was a Protestant, which explains his move to Brunswick, an early supporter of the new faith). Hermann's *Portrait of a Musician* (1547, Westfälisches Landesmuseum) is regarded as one of the outstanding German portraits of the period. His sons **Nikolaus tom Ring** (1564–1622) and **Johann tom Ring** (1571–1604) were unexceptional religious painters.

Riopelle, Jean-Paul (b Montreal, 7 Oct 1923; d Île-aux-Grues, Quebec, 12 Mar. 2002). Canadian painter, sculptor, and printmaker. Riopelle was considered the leading Canadian abstract painter of his generation, even though he spent most of his career in Paris. His early works were landscapes, but he turned to abstraction under the influence of *Borduas and became a member of his group Les *Automatistes in 1946 before settling in Paris in 1947. His paintings of the late 1940s were in a lyrical manner, but in the 1950s his work became tauter, denser, and more powerful, the paint often applied with a palette knife, creating a rich mosaic-like effect (*Pavane*, 1954, NG, Ottawa). Later his handling became more calligraphic. Riopelle was a prolific artist and at home in various media. In spite of his long residence in France, he kept up a close association with his native country and from 1970 he spent a good deal of time in his native Montreal.

Ripa, Cesare. See EMBLEM.

Rippl-Rónai, Josef. See NABIS.

Rivalz. Dynasty of French painters that was the main force in painting in Toulouse over three generations, from the mid-17th century to the late 18th century. **Jean-Pierre Rivalz the Elder** (1625–1706), an architect as well as a painter, worked in Rome for several years, in the circle of *Poussin, before settling in Toulouse in 1657. His son **Antoine Rivalz** (1667–1735), an engraver as well as a painter, was the most distinguished member of the family. He too worked in Rome, 1687–1702, and his work—mainly history paintings—shows strong Italian influence. In 1726 he founded an *academy in Toulouse, one of the few such institutions in provincial France at this time, although initially its operations were modest. His pupils included *Subleyras and his son **Jean-Pierre Rivalz the Younger** (1720–85), who was curator of the municipal art collection as well as a painter. Like his father and grandfather he worked in Rome early in his career and he was awarded a knighthood for a portrait of Pope Benedict XIV (he is sometimes known as Chevalier Rivalz). The work of the family is best represented in the Musée des Augustins, Toulouse.

Rivera, Diego (*b* Guanajuato, 13 Dec. 1886; *d* Mexico City, 24 Nov. 1957). Mexican painter, the most celebrated figure in the revival of monumental fresco painting that is his country's most distinctive contribution to modern art. He visited Paris in 1909 and after a brief return to Mexico he settled there from 1911 to 1920. During this time he became one of the lions of café society and was friendly with many leading artists. He was familiar with modern movements, but although he made some early experiments with avant-garde idioms, notably *Cubism, his mature art was firmly rooted in Mexican tradition. At about the

time of the Russian Revolution he had become interested in politics and in the role art could play in society. In 1920–1 he visited Italy to study Renaissance frescos (already thinking in terms of a monumental public art), then returned to his homeland, eager to be of service to the Mexican Revolution.

In 1920 Alvaro Obregón, an art lover as well as a reformist, had been elected President of Mexico, and Rivera, who was an extremely forceful personality, swiftly emerged as the leading artist in the programme of murals he initiated glorifying the history and people of the country in a spirit of revolutionary fervour. Many examples of his work are in public buildings in Mexico City, and they are often on a huge scale, a tribute to his enormous energy. His most ambitious scheme, in the National Palace, covering the history of Mexico, was begun in 1929; it was still unfinished at his death, but it contains some of his most magnificent work. Rivera's murals were frankly didactic, intended to inspire a sense of nationalist and socialist identity in a still largely illiterate population; their glorification of creative labour or their excoriation of capitalism can be crude, but his best work has astonishing vigour. He showed formidable skill in choreographing his incident- and figure-packed compositions, in combining traditional and modern subject matter, and in blending stylized and realistic images.

In 1927 Rivera visited the Soviet Union and in 1930–4 he worked in the USA, painting several frescos that were influential on the muralists of the *Federal Art Project. His main work in America was a series on Detroit industry (1932–3) in the Detroit Institute of Arts (commissioned by William *Valentiner); another major mural, *Man at the Crossroads* (1933), in the Rockefeller Center, New York, was destroyed before completion because he included a portrait of Lenin. It was replaced with a mural by *Brangwyn. Throughout his career he also painted a wide range of easel pictures, in some of which he experimented with the *encaustic (wax) technique. Rivera was an enormous man, and although he was notoriously ugly he was irresistibly attractive to women. He had numerous love affairs and was married three times, his second wife (and his third, for they divorced and remarried) being the painter Frida *Kahlo; her parents said it was like a marriage between an elephant and a dove.

Rivers, Larry (*b* New York, 17 Aug. 1923). American painter, sculptor, printmaker, and designer, a leading figure in the revival of figurative art that was one aspect of the reaction against the dominance of *Abstract Expressionism. He was a professional jazz saxophonist in the early 1940s and began painting in 1945, studying at the Hans *Hofmann School, 1947–8, and then at New York University under *Baziotes in 1948. His work of the early and mid-1950s continued the vigorous painterly handling associated with Abstract Expressionism, but was very different in character. Some of his paintings were fairly straightforwardly naturalistic, but others looked forward to *Pop art in their quotations from well-known advertising or artistic sources, their use of lettering, and their deadpan humour. An example is *Washington Crossing the Delaware* (1953, MoMA, New York), based on the picture by *Leutze. In the late 1950s and 1960s his work came more clearly within the orbit of Pop, sometimes incorporating cut-out cardboard or wooden forms, electric lights, and so on, but his sensuous handling of paint set him apart from other Pop artists. Rivers has also made sculpture, collages, and prints, designed for the stage, acted, and written poetry.

Rizi (or **Ricci**), **Juan** (*b* Madrid, 1600; *d* Monte Cassino, 29 Nov. 1681) and **Francisco** (*b* Madrid, 19 Apr. 1614; *d* Madrid, 2 Aug. 1685). Spanish painters, brothers, sons of **Antonio Ricci** (*d* 1631), a mediocre Italian painter who moved to Spain in 1585 when he accompanied Federico *Zuccaro to work on the *Escorial. Juan became a Benedictine monk in 1627 and worked mainly for monasteries of his order in Castile in an austere, deeply felt *tenebrist style that at times shows an affinity of spirit with *Zurbarán (*Last Mass of St Benedict*, *c.*1650–60, Academy of S. Fernando, Madrid)—indeed he has been called 'the Castilian Zurbarán'. Juan was also a fine portraitist, with a strong grasp of character. He wrote treatises on painting and architecture (both published 1930), as well as on theological topics. In 1662 he moved to Rome and eventually settled at the abbey of Monte Cassino (the mother house of the Benedictine Order). There are no known paintings from his two decades in Italy, although *Palomino says he 'did many pictures that were celebrated in Rome' (any that were at Monte Cassino would presumably have perished when the abbey was destroyed during the Second World War).

Francisco was an artist of very different character. He worked mainly at the court of Philip IV (see HABSBURG) and his religious works are much more colourful than his brother's, at times

almost *Rubensian. In 1656 he was appointed one of the royal painters and he was also chief designer for the royal theatre at the Buen Retiro Palace, Madrid. He also had commissions from outside Madrid, notably from Toledo Cathedral, for which he painted several works, including the *Blessing of the Cathedral by Archbishop Jiménez de Rada* (1653, *in situ*).

Robbia, Luca della (*b* ?Florence, *c.*1399 / 1400; *d* Florence, 20 Feb. 1482). Florentine sculptor, the most famous member of a family of artists. Nothing is known of his early career, and he was a mature artist by the time of his first documented work—a *Cantoria* (Singing Gallery, 1431–8) for Florence Cathedral, now in the Cathedral Museum. It is a work of considerable originality as well as enormous charm, antedating by a year or two the companion gallery by *Donatello (now also in the Cathedral Museum). Its marble *reliefs of angels and children singing, dancing, and making music reflect *antique prototypes, but are conceived in a more cheerful, less heroic spirit than Donatello's figures. In his own time Luca had the reputation of being one of the leaders of the modern (i.e. *Renaissance) style, comparable to Donatello and *Ghiberti in sculpture and *Masaccio in painting, but he is now remembered mainly for his development of coloured, glazed *terracotta as a sculptural medium—in particular for his highly popular invention of the type of the half-length Madonna and Child in white on a blue ground. The family workshop seems to have kept the technical formula a secret and it became the basis of a flourishing business; among the major works by Luca in the medium are the roundels of Apostles (*c.*1450) in *Brunelleschi's Pazzi Chapel in S. Croce.

Luca's business was carried on by his nephew **Andrea** (1435–1525), and later by Andrea's five sons, of whom **Giovanni** (1469–after 1529) was the most important. The famous roundels of infants on the façade of the Foundling Hospital in Florence (1463–6) were probably made by Andrea. His successors tended to sentimentalize Luca's warm humanity, and in course of time the artists' studio became a potters' workshop-industry.

Robert, Hubert (*b* Paris, 22 May 1733; *d* Paris, 15 Apr. 1808). French landscape painter. From 1754 to 1765 he lived in Italy (mainly Rome), where he became a friend of *Fragonard and made a large number of drawings that were a source for his pictures after his return to Paris. Like Fragonard, he had a lively touch and in their drawings they are sometimes so close in style that it is difficult to distinguish their hands. However, whereas Fragonard was primarily a figure painter, Robert became the chief pioneer and leading exponent of scenes involving ruined buildings (he was nicknamed Robert des Ruines). Some of his paintings are fairly accurate depictions of real architecture, but he also produced various types of imaginary ruinscapes, including pictures in which he showed contemporary buildings as they might look after falling into decay. His work was much in demand—part of the vogue for rather artificial, idealized landscape that was one aspect of *Rococo taste. As well as delicacy and charm, however, his paintings have grandeur and he could work convincingly on a large scale; many of his pictures were intended for a specific decorative context in grandiose interiors. In 1784 Louis XVI appointed him keeper of his pictures and gave him responsibility for creating a museum at the *Louvre. However, he fell foul of intrigue during the Revolution and was imprisoned in 1793–4, narrowly escaping execution (he owed his life to a mistake whereby another person of the same name was guillotined in his stead). After his release he returned to his successful career and is said to have died 'brush in hand'.

Roberti, Ercole de' (b Ferrara, c.1450; d Ferrara, May/June 1496). Italian painter, active mainly in Ferrara. He succeeded *Tura as court painter to the *Este in 1486, but little is known of his life. Earlier he appears to have assisted *Cossa for some years, and with Cossa and Tura he ranks as the leading artist of the 15th-century Ferrarese School. His only surviving documented painting is the altarpiece with a *Madonna Enthroned with Saints* (1480) painted for S. Maria in Poroto at Ravenna and now in the Brera, Milan. Other works, however, can be confidently given to him because of his distinctive style. He inherited the tradition of Tura and Cossa, with their precise line and metallic colours against elaborately fanciful ornamentation, but he developed this manner with great originality, modifying it with a subtlety of handling that seems to derive from Giovanni *Bellini. His work is often remarkable for its almost mystical intensity of feeling, as in his *Pietà* in the Walker Art Gallery, Liverpool.

Roberts, David (b Stockbridge [now a district of Edinburgh], 24 Oct. 1796; d London, 25 Nov. 1864). Scottish painter. He was apprenticed to a house painter, then worked as a scene painter for theatres in Edinburgh and Glasgow. In 1822 he settled in London and worked at the Drury Lane Theatre with his friend Clarkson *Stanfield. From 1833 he travelled widely in Europe and the Mediterranean basin and made a fortune with his topographical views in oil and watercolour. Several collections of these were published in lavishly illustrated books, among them the six-volume *Views in the Holy Land, Syria, Idumea, Arabia, Egypt and Nubia* (1842–9). Near the end of his career he also painted some views of London (*The Houses of Parliament from Millbank*, 1861, Mus. of London). His work can be monotonous when seen en masse, but at his best Roberts combines bold design with precise observation.

Roberts, Tom (b Dorchester, 9 Mar. 1856; d Kallista, Victoria, 14 Sept. 1931). British-born Australian painter, active mainly in and around Melbourne. He was the most important figure in introducing *Impressionism to Australia and he is regarded as the father of the country's indigenous tradition of landscape painting. Much of his career was spent in Europe and he first acquired some knowledge of Impressionism in 1883 in Spain, where he met artists who had studied in Paris. After returning to Melbourne in 1885 he was soon the leading figure of the *Heidelberg School, whose work was based on open-air painting. In addition to landscapes (and portraits—with which he earned a major part of his living), Roberts painted scenes of rural *genre and history (including outlaw life). He continued to make journeys to Europe, where he exhibited with modest success at the *Royal Academy, the Paris *Salon, and elsewhere. By the time of his death, however, 'he had been overshadowed by the more prolific, and by then shallower, talents of his old friend, Arthur *Streeton' (Robert *Hughes, *The Art of Australia*, 1970).

Roberts, William (b London, 5 June 1895; d London, 20 Jan. 1980). British painter, chiefly of figure compositions and portraits. After travelling in France and Italy, he worked briefly for the *Omega Workshops, then in 1914 joined the *Vorticist movement. His style at this time showed his precocious response to French modernism and was close to that of *Bomberg in the way he depicted stiff, stylized figures through geometrically simplified forms. After the First World War (in which he served in the Royal Artillery and as an *Official War Artist) his forms became rounder and fuller in a manner reminiscent of the 'tubism' of *Léger. Often his paintings showed groups of figures in everyday settings, his most famous work being *The*

Vorticists at the Restaurant de la Tour Eiffel: Spring 1915, 1961–2, Tate, London), an imaginative reconstruction of his former colleagues celebrating at a favourite rendezvous to mark the publication of the first issue of *Blast*. In response to the exhibition 'Wyndham *Lewis and the Vorticists' at the Tate Gallery in 1956, Roberts wrote a series of pamphlets (1956–8) disputing Lewis's claim (in the catalogue introduction) that 'Vorticism, in fact, was what I, personally, did, and said, at a certain period.' However, in 1974 Roberts issued another pamphlet in which he strangely contradicted his earlier statements, declaring that the term Vorticism 'should only be used in reference to his [Lewis's] own work; and that the term Cubist should be employed to describe the abstract painting of his contemporaries of the 1914 period'.

rocaille. Term applied from the mid-16th century onwards to fancy rock-work and shell-work for fountains and grottoes, and later to ornament based on such forms. The word *Rococo derives from it and the two terms have sometimes been used synonymously by French art historians.

Rockefeller, Abby Aldrich. See MUSEUM OF MODERN ART.

rocker. The serrated metal tool used to prepare the plate in *mezzotint.

Rockwell, Norman (*b* New York, 3 Feb. 1894; *d* Stockbridge, Mass., 8 Nov. 1978). American illustrator and painter. He studied at various art schools in New York and by the time he was 18 was a full-time professional illustrator. In 1916 he had a cover accepted by the *Saturday Evening Post*, the biggest-selling weekly publication in the USA (its circulation was then about 3,000,000), and hundreds of others followed for this magazine until it ceased publication in 1969. He also worked for many other publications. Rockwell's subjects were drawn from everyday American life and his style was anecdotal, sentimental, and lovingly detailed; he described his pictorial territory as 'this best-possible-world, Santa down-the-chimney, lovely-kids-adoring-their-kindly-grandpa sort of thing'. Such work brought him immense popularity, making him something of a national institution. For most of his career critics dismissed his work as corny, but he began to receive serious attention as a painter late in his career. In his later years, too, he sometimes turned to more serious subjects, producing, for example, a series on racism for *Look* magazine. From 1953 until his death he lived at Stockbridge, Massachusetts, where there is a museum devoted to him.

Rocky Mountain School. Term applied retrospectively to 19th-century American artists who painted large pictures of the Rocky Mountains in a reverential spirit similar to that adopted by the *Hudson River School. The German-born Albert *Bierstadt and the English-born Thomas Moran (1837–1926) are the best-known artists embraced by the term.

Rococo. Style of art and architecture, characterized by lightness, grace, playfulness, and intimacy, that emerged in France *c*.1700 and spread throughout Europe in the 18th century. The word is said to have been coined in 1796–7 by one of J.-L. *David's students, wittily combining *rocaille* and *barocco* (*Baroque), to refer disparagingly to the taste fashionable in the mid-18th century. Thus, like so many stylistic labels, it began life as a term of abuse, and it long retained its original connotations, implying an art that was, in the words of one of the definitions given to it in the *Oxford English Dictionary*, 'excessively or tastelessly florid or ornate'. However, the word is now used without any pejorative connotations.

The Rococo was both a development from and a reaction against the weightier Baroque style, and initially it was expressed mainly in interior decoration. It shared with the Baroque a love of complexity of form, but instead of a concern for solidity and mass, there was a delicate play on the surface, with sombre colours and heavy gilding giving way to lighter tones and delicate ornament, and much use of asymmetrical curves and pretty decorative motifs. The style was in general less suited to exteriors, but something of the Rococo spirit—of its refinement and charm—can be seen even in such a regular and relatively unadorned building as Ange-Jacques Gabriel's Petit Trianon (1763–9) at Versailles. In painting, the first great master of the Rococo style was *Watteau, and the painters who most completely represent the light-hearted (often gently erotic) spirit of the mature Rococo style are *Boucher and *Fragonard. *Falconet is perhaps the best representative of the style in French sculpture, but generally the Rococo spirit is seen more clearly in small porcelain figures than in large-scale statues (Falconet himself was director of the sculpture studios at the famous porcelain factory at Sèvres).

From Paris the Rococo was disseminated by French artists working abroad and by engraved publications of French designs (see BERAIN, for example). It spread to Germany, Austria, Russia, Spain, and northern Italy (*Tiepolo, *Longhi, *Guardi). In England it had somewhat less of a vogue, although a substantial exhibition of English Rococo art was held at the Victoria and Albert Museum in 1984 and there are clear reflections of the style even in the work of so xenophobic an artist as *Hogarth. *Gainsborough's delicacy of characterization and sensitivity of touch (although completely personal) are also thoroughly in the Rococo spirit. In each country the style took on a national character and in addition many local variants may be distinguished. Outside France, it had its finest flowering in Germany and Austria, where it merged with a still vigorous Baroque tradition. In churches such as Vierzehnheiligen (1743–72) by Balthasar Neumann, the Baroque qualities of spatial variety and of architecture, sculpture, and painting working together are taken up in a breathtakingly light and exuberant manner. The Rococo flourished in central Europe until the end of the century (as in the work of *Maulbertsch), but in France and elsewhere the tide of taste had begun to turn from frivolity towards the sternness of *Neoclassicism by the 1760s.

Rodchenko, Alexander (*b* St Petersburg, 23 Nov. [5 Dec.] 1891; *d* Moscow, 3 Dec. 1956). Russian painter, sculptor, industrial designer, and photographer, one of the leading *Constructivists. His artistic evolution was rapid, as he moved from *Impressionistic pictures in 1913 to pure abstracts, made with a ruler and compass, in 1916. He was influenced by *Malevich's *Suprematism, his *Black on Black* (1918, MoMA, New York) being a response to Malevich's *White on White* paintings. Rodchenko, however, was without Malevich's mystical leanings, and he coined the term *'Non-Objective' to describe his own more scientific outlook. In 1917 he began making three-dimensional constructions under the influence of *Tatlin, and some of these developed into graceful hanging sculptures. Like Tatlin and other Constructivists, however, Rodchenko came to reject pure art as a parasitic activity, and after 1922 he devoted his energies to industrial design, typography, film and stage design, propaganda posters, and photography. It was perhaps in photography that he made his most original and enduring contribution to art. Although his photographs were geared towards reportage and creating a pictorial record of the new Russia, many of them are outstanding for their 'abstract' qualities, partly created by his novel exploitation of unusual angles and viewpoints; his dramatic use of light and shadow influenced, for example, the great Soviet film director Sergei Eisenstein. In the mid-1930s, after Stalin's imposition of *Socialist Realism, Rodchenko returned to easel painting. Initially he produced circus scenes, but in 1943 he began to paint abstract 'drip' pictures that—amazingly—prefigure those of Jackson *Pollock. Rodchenko's wife **Varvara Stepanova** (1894–1958) was a painter and designer.

Rodin, Auguste (*b* Paris, 12 Nov. 1840; *d* Meudon, nr. Paris, 17 Nov. 1917). French sculptor and draughtsman, one of the greatest and most influential European artists of his period. He was the first sculptor since the heyday of *Neoclassicism to occupy a central position in public attention and he opened up new possibilities for his art in a manner comparable to that of his great contemporaries in painting—*Cézanne, *Gauguin, and van *Gogh. His beginnings, however, were not auspicious. He came from a poor background, was rejected three times by the École des *Beaux-Arts, and for many years worked mainly as an ornamental mason. In the winter of 1875–6 he visited Italy, where (as he later wrote to *Bourdelle) '*Michelangelo freed me from academism.' Michelangelo was the inspiration for his first major work, a male nude, *The Age of Bronze*, which was exhibited at the 1877 *Salon. (Like many of Rodin's statues, this exists in several casts or versions; the Rodin Museum in Paris has examples of virtually all his work. There is also a Rodin museum in Philadelphia.) It caused a sensation because the naturalistic treatment of the naked figure was so different from the idealizing conventions then current—he was even accused of having cast it from a live model.

Three years later, in 1880, his reputation now established, Rodin was commissioned by the state to make a bronze door for a proposed Musée des Arts Décoratifs. He never definitively finished the huge work—*The Gates of Hell*— (he worked on it intermittently until 1900 and the museum never came into being in its proposed form), but he poured some of his finest creative energy into it, and many of the nearly 200 figures that are part of it formed the basis of famous independent sculptures, most notably *The Kiss* and *The Thinker*. The several casts of the complete structure that exist were made after Rodin's death. Rodin's overall design is a kind of *Romantic reworking of *Ghiberti's *Gates of Paradise* for the Florence Baptistery, the twisted and anguished figures, irregularly arranged, reminiscent of Michelangelo's *Last Judgement* and Gustave *Doré's illustrations for the *Divine Comedy*. The modelling is often rough and 'unfinished' and anatomical forms are exaggerated or simplified in the cause of intensity of expression.

These traits were taken further in some of Rodin's monuments, beginning with the famous group of *The Burghers of Calais* (1884–9), commissioned by the city of Calais for a site in front of the town hall (there are several other casts, including one in Victoria Tower Gardens, London). In the figures of the six hostages who face the threat of death, Rodin showed a variety of responses—including anguish as well as courage—to an extreme emotional crisis. The civic authorities had wanted something in a more traditional heroic-patriotic vein, and the monument was unveiled in 1895 only after years of wrangling. Even worse hostility was aroused a few years later by his statue of Balzac. This was commissioned by the Société des Gens de Lettres in 1891, but Rodin's design was so radical—an expression of the elemental power of genius rather than a portrait of an individual—that it was rejected, and the monument was not finally cast and set up until 1939—at the intersection of the boulevards Raspail and Montparnasse in Paris. It ranks as the most original piece of public statuary created in the 19th century, and *Brancusi wrote that it was 'indisputably the starting point of modern sculpture'. Rodin himself described it as 'the sum of my whole life'.

In spite of the controversy his work caused, by 1900 Rodin was widely regarded as the greatest living sculptor, and in that year a pavilion was devoted to his work at the Paris World Fair. From this point he created no more major monuments, his sculpture consisting mainly of portrait busts, including many of eminent personalities. In his later years he was also a prolific draughtsman, mainly of the female nude, some of the drawings being highly erotic. (He was famed for his voracious sexual appetite, but this was excused as an aspect of his Olympian stature; his lovers included Gwen *John and his pupil Camille Claudel (1864–1943).) He left his collection of his own work to the state to found the Musée Rodin in Paris, opened in 1919. His villa at Meudon (now a suburb of Paris) is an outstation of the museum. Rodin is buried in the garden at Meudon, with a cast of *The Thinker* overlooking his grave.

Although the literary and symbolic significance he attached to his work has been out of keeping with the conception of 'pure' sculpture that predominated in the 20th century, Rodin's influence on the development of modern art has been immense, for single-handedly he revived sculpture from a period of relative stagnation when it had lagged behind the momentous achievements of contemporary painters and made it once again a vehicle for intense personal expression. His sense of movement and energy and his use of the partial figure (particularly the torso) as a legitimate subject were among his most potent legacies, inspiring Bourdelle (his long-time assistant) for example. Just as important as his direct influence was the fervent reaction against his dominance among the avant-garde. As George Heard Hamilton writes (*Painting and Sculpture in Europe: 1880–1940*, 1967), 'Perhaps the proof of his greatness is to be seen in the work of such men as *Maillol, Brancusi, *Lipchitz, and others, who had to reject his method and his programme in order to assert their independence. Through the loyal opposition, so to speak, Rodin's inexhaustible energies reach to the present.'

Roelas, Juan de (*b* ?Valladolid, *c.*1560; *d* Olivares, nr. Seville, 25 May 1625). Spanish painter. Roelas was a priest and virtually all his work was done for churches and religious houses in and around Seville, where he was the leading painter of his period. He has been called 'the Spanish *Tintoretto' and 'the Spanish *Veronese', and the painterly richness of his large multi-figure compositions suggests he had studied in Italy. His work, however, has a religious fervour that is typically Spanish rather than Italian, and his blending of mysticism with naturalism was deeply influential in Seville. Most of his work remains there; his masterpiece is perhaps the huge *Martyrdom of St Andrew* (1609, Mus. B.-A., Seville).

Roerich, Nikolai (*b* St Petersburg, 27 Sept. [9 Oct.] 1874; *d* Nagar, nr. Kulu, Himachal Pradesh, India, 13 Dec. 1947). Russian painter, designer, archaeologist, anthropologist, and mystical philosopher. He was a prolific painter of landscapes and of imaginary historical scenes that evoke a colourful pagan image of Russia's past. They reveal the same feeling for exotic splendour and bold, sumptuous colour that he displayed in his set and costume designs for *Diaghilev's Ballets Russes, notably for Stravinsky's *Rite of Spring* (1913), for which Roerich created the scenario with the composer. A man of immense energy, Roerich combined his career as an artist with one as an archaeologist and anthropologist. In 1925–8 he led a 16,000-mile

(26,000-km) expedition in central Asia, and his investigations still form 'the bedrock of anthropological studies' in the region (*The Times Atlas of World Exploration*, 1991). From 1928 until his death he directed a Himalayan research station in the Kulu valley in India, and many of his later paintings feature mountain landscapes. He had a deep interest in esoteric religions and the mysteries of nature, and he developed a philosophy in which art should unite humanity. There are Roerich museums in Moscow and New York (he lived in the USA, 1920–3), but the best collection of his work is in the Russian Museum, St Petersburg.

Roger of Helmarshausen. See THEOPHILUS.

Rogers, Claude (*b.* London, 24 Jan. 1907; *d.* London, 18 Feb. 1979). British painter of portraits, landscapes, and *genre scenes. With William *Coldstream and Victor *Pasmore he founded the *Euston Road School in 1937 and he became one of the leading upholders of its sober figurative tradition, although in his later work the underlying abstract quality of the composition became of more importance. Much of his career was devoted to teaching, notably at the Slade School, 1949–63, and Reading University, where he was professor of fine art, 1963–72.

Rogers, John (*b* Salem, Mass., 30 Oct. 1829; *d* New Canaan, Conn., 26 July 1904). American sculptor. Trained as a machinist and self-taught as an artist, he became highly successful with a novel type of sculpture he made his own. His 'Rogers Groups', as they came to be called, were mass-produced plaster pieces, mainly showing sentimental scenes of rural or small-town life—characteristic titles are *The Checker Players* (1859; his first major group) and *Weighing the Baby* (1876). His subjects also covered topical events, including the Civil War, so his parlour ornaments were a kind of three-dimensional equivalent of *Currier & Ives prints. They were produced in a studio-cum-factory that he established in New York in 1859 and could be bought in general stores or by mail order. He made about 80 groups in all (he always designed and modelled them himself), and produced an average of about 1,000 copies of each. Several imitators marketed similar products, but none of them matched his success. Rogers also did a few portrait busts and more ambitious pieces, notably the equestrian statue of Major-General Reynolds (1883) in front of the city hall in Philadelphia.

Rogers, William (active *c.*1589–1605). The first English engraver of note, best known for his portraits of Queen Elizabeth I, the first of which he produced in 1589 to celebrate the defeat of the Spanish Armada the previous year. He also engraved title pages, for example for John Gerard's *Herball* (1597).

Rohlfs, Christian (*b* Niendorf, Holstein, 22 Dec. 1849; *d* Hagen, 8 Jan. 1938). German painter and printmaker. Until he was over 50 he worked in a fairly traditional naturalistic manner, but he then discovered the work of the *Post-Impressionists, in particular van *Gogh, whose brilliant colour and intense feeling were a revelation to him, and he became one of the pioneers of *Expressionism in Germany. His favourite themes were visionary views of old German towns, colourful landscapes, and flower pieces. He received considerable acclaim for work in his new style, but in 1937 he was declared a *degenerate artist by the Nazis and forbidden to paint.

Roldán, Pedro (*b* Seville, 14 Jan. 1624; *d* Seville, Aug. 1699). Spanish *Baroque sculptor. He trained in Granada but worked mainly in Seville, where he became the leading sculptor of his period. His work was often *polychromed by *Valdés Leal, as for example with his group of the *Entombment* (1670–2), which forms the centrepiece of the high altar of the church of the Hospital de la Caridad, Seville. Roldán's daughter and pupil **Luisa** (1650–*c.*1704) was also a sculptor, principally active in Cadiz and Madrid. She was the only woman to hold the position of royal sculptor, to Charles II (see HABSBURG). Roldán's grandson Pedro *Duque Cornejo succeeded him as Seville's foremost sculptor.

Rolfsen, Alf (*b* Christiania [now Oslo], 28 Jan. 1895; *d* Oslo, 10 Nov. 1979). Norwegian painter, printmaker, draughtsman, and writer on art, best known as one of his country's leading muralists. He made several visits to Paris and he was influenced by modern French painting, particularly *Cubism and the work of *Derain. His first fresco commission, for the Telegraph Building in Oslo, was carried out in 1922. Many others followed, the last one being for the Hansa Brewery in Bergen (1967). Rolfsen also produced easel paintings (including landscapes, portraits, and figure compositions), as well as lithographs and book illustrations, and he wrote and lectured on art.

Romanelli, Giovanni Francesco (*b* Viterbo, *c.*1610; *d* Viterbo, 8 Nov. 1662). Italian painter and tapestry designer. He was Pietro da *Cortona's outstanding pupil, and like his master a protégé of the *Barberini family. Romanelli's graceful style was less energetic than Cortona's (he owed much to his first teacher *Domenichino) and his restrained type of Baroque proved particularly popular and influential in France, where he worked 1646–7 and 1655–7. He introduced to Paris Cortona's characteristic manner of decoration, consisting of paintings combined with richly gilded *stuccowork, and this was one of the sources for the great schemes of *Le Brun at Versailles and elsewhere. Examples of Romanelli's decorative work survive in the Bibliothèque Nationale (painted for Cardinal Mazarin, 1646–7) and (much altered) in the Salle des Saisons of the Louvre (painted for Anne of Austria, mother of Louis XIV, 1655–7).

Romanesque. Style of art and architecture prevailing throughout most of Europe in the 11th and 12th centuries, the first style to achieve such international currency. The dominant art of the Middle Ages was architecture, and 'Romanesque', like '*Gothic', is primarily an architectural term that has been extended to the other arts of the period. As the name suggests, it indicates a derivation from Roman art, and sometimes 'Romanesque' is used to cover all the developments from Roman architecture in the period from the collapse of the Roman Empire until the flowering of the Gothic—roughly AD 500–1200. More usually, however, it is applied to a distinctive style that emerged, almost simultaneously, in several countries—France, Germany, Italy, Spain—in the 11th century. It is characterized most obviously by a new massiveness of scale, reflecting the greater political and economic stability that followed a period when Christian civilization seemed in danger of extinction.

Painting and sculpture, as well as architecture, flourished during the Romanesque period, although comparatively little large-scale painting has survived (originally the churches of the period would have been alive with colour). Many illuminated manuscripts remain, however, and the art of stained glass was perfected in the period. There are also some fine Romanesque mosaics, particularly in Italy, and the most famous work of pictorial art of the period is the *Bayeux Tapestry, which gives a wonderfully vivid account of the Norman invasion of England. Sculpture revived greatly during the period, becoming larger in scale and more ambitious, often conceived as an integral part of a building. Few names of Romanesque artists survive, but *Gislebertus carved his signature at

Autun Cathedral in France, where he created one of the great sculptural ensembles of the Middle Ages. Although Romanesque painting and sculpture show considerable variety, they are in general strongly stylized, with little of the *naturalism and humanistic warmth of *classical or later Gothic art. The forms of nature are freely translated into linear and sculptural designs that at times are majestically calm and severe and at others are agitated by a visionary, almost delirious excitement. Because of this expressionistic distortion, Romanesque art, as with other great non-naturalistic styles of the past, has had to wait for the revolution in sensibility brought about by modern art in order to be widely appreciated.

The so-called minor arts (or 'luxury arts')—work in gold, silver, ivory, bronze, precious stones, and so on—were as highly (or more highly) regarded during the Romanesque period as painting or sculpture. Often they had additional prestige because they were used in church ritual or as containers for holy relics. Many such objects have perished because they have been plundered for their valuable raw materials, but enough survive to show the superb quality of Romanesque craftsmanship.

Romano, Giulio. See GIULIO ROMANO.

Romantic Classicism. See NEOCLASSICISM and ROMANTICISM.

Romanticism. Movement in the arts flourishing in the late 18th and early 19th centuries. Romanticism is so varied in its manifestations that a single definition is impossible, but its keynote was a belief in the value of individual experience. In this it marked a reaction from the rationalism of the Enlightenment and the orderliness of the *Neoclassical style. Neoclassical artists typically stressed such ideas as duty and stoicism, whereas Romantic artists often chose subjects that were wild, exotic, or mysterious. They explored the values of intuition and instinct, exchanging the public discourse of Neoclassicism, the forms of which had a common currency, for a more private kind of expression.

Romanticism is commonly seen as the antithesis of *classicism, and the two concepts are sometimes used in a very general sense to designate polarities in attitude that may be seen in the art of any age—thus *Raphael might be described as a 'classical' artist, whereas his contemporary *Giorgione is a 'romantic' one. However, the exponents of both Romanticism and classicism share a concern with the *ideal rather than the real, and there is sometimes no firm dividing line between the two approaches, as is shown by the use of the term 'Romantic Classicism' to describe certain works that show a Romantic response to antiquity. Both Romanticism and classicism embrace concepts of nobility, grandeur, virtue, and superiority. But where the classical seems a possible ideal that will adapt man to his society and mould that society into an orderly setting for him, the Romantic envisages the unattainable, beyond the limits of society and human adaptability. The classical hero accepts the fate over which he has no control and triumphs nobly in this acquiescence, otherwise he would not be a hero. The Romantic hero pits himself against a hostile environment and at no time comes to terms with it even if he reaches his goal, otherwise he would not be Romantic.

Romanticism represents an attitude of mind rather than a set of particular stylistic traits and involves the expression of an idea that tends to have a verbal rather than a visual origin. It lends itself more easily to expression through music and literature than through the visual arts, as a sense of the infinite and the transcendental, of forces exceeding the boundaries of reason, must necessarily be vague—suggestive rather than concrete, as it must be in painting and even more so in sculpture. On the other hand, although there is no specific Romantic school in architecture, the *Gothic Revival, especially in its early, non-scholarly phase, is an aspect of Romanticism.

Almost by definition, the leading Romantic artists differ widely from one another—*Blake and *Turner in Britain, *Delacroix and *Géricault in France, *Friedrich and *Runge in Germany. The movement of which they were a part died out in the mid-19th century, but in a broader sense the Romantic spirit has lived on, representing a revolt against conservatism, moderation, and insincerity and an insistence on the primacy of the imagination in artistic expression.

Rombouts, Theodoor (b Antwerp, 2 July 1597; d Antwerp, 14 Sept. 1637). Flemish painter, mainly of religious and *genre scenes. He was a pupil of *Janssen in Antwerp, then from about 1616 to about 1625 he was in Italy. There his work became strongly *Caravaggesque and he established himself as one of the leading Flemish exponents of the style. Later, he fell under the all-pervasive influence of *Rubens and his work became much lighter in tonality.

Romney, George (b Dalton-in-Furness, Lancashire, 15 Dec. 1734; d Kendal, Cumberland, 15 Nov. 1802). English painter, mainly of portraits. He worked in the north of England until 1762, when he settled in London. There he became the most successful portraitist of the day apart from *Reynolds and *Gainsborough. His posthumous reputation was once almost the equal of theirs, but later faded considerably. Much of his work is now considered facile and repetitive compared with that of his two great contemporaries, and he was probably at his best with portraits of young people, when his delicate colour sense and graceful line were used to good effect. As with many successful portraitists, his heart lay elsewhere and he had aspirations to be a history painter. In 1773–5 he visited Italy and this had a lasting effect on him, but his plans for grandiose literary and historical works rarely advanced beyond his sepia drawings (a large collection is in the Fitzwilliam Museum, Cambridge), although he painted for *Boydell's Shakespeare Gallery. Introspective and nervous by temperament, Romney was attracted to literary circles and associated little with his fellow artists, never exhibiting at the *Royal Academy. His friends among artists tended to be others of literary inclination, such as *Flaxman. In 1781 Romney met Emma Hart, later Lady Hamilton, Nelson's mistress, and became infatuated with her, painting her many times in various guises. His final years were marred by ill health and depression and in 1799 he retired to Kendal in Cumberland. There he was cared for by his wife, whom he had rarely seen since settling in London. Romney's output was huge, and his paintings are in many collections in Britain and the USA (in the early 20th century he was a particular favourite of American collectors and his work often fetched huge sums at this time).

Ronald, William (William Ronald Smith) (b Stratford, Ontario, 13 Aug. 1926). Canadian-American painter and radio and television presenter, a leading figure in the development and acceptance of abstract art in Canada. In 1955 he moved from Toronto to New York, where he enjoyed considerable success among the second generation of *Abstract Expressionists. He lived in the USA until 1965, becoming an American citizen in 1963, but he retained a large following in Toronto and exerted a strong influence on painters there. With the decline of Abstract Expressionism his popularity waned, but after his return to Canada he achieved success as a radio and television personality, presenting chat shows and programmes on art and current affairs. He also developed a kind of road-show performance in which he painted on stage before an audience to the accompaniment of rock music.

Roncalli, Cristoforo (*b* Pomarance, nr. Volterra, *c*.1552; *bur.* Rome, 14 May 1626). Italian painter, sometimes known as Il Pomarancio, after his birthplace. With *Cesari he was one of the leading fresco decorators of his time in Rome. Although he adapted somewhat to the innovations of the *Carracci, he remained essentially in the *Mannerist tradition and his work is generally undistinguished. His unbiased, common-sense views on art, however, commended him to Vincenzo *Giustiniani, one of the most enlightened patrons of his time; Roncalli became his artistic adviser and made a tour of northern Europe with him in 1606.

Rood, Ogden. See DIVISIONISM.

rood-screen. Term in Christian church architecture for a screen separating the chancel (reserved to the clergy) from the nave (assigned to the laity). It is named after the Crucifixion figure or group, known as the rood (Old English for 'cross' or 'crucifix'), that usually surmounted it, although there is in fact no necessary connection between the rood (which originally stood on a beam) and the screen. A great many screens survive from the Middle Ages, not least in England, where there are some superb examples, particularly of the 15th century. They represent one of the great flowerings of the art of the medieval carver and in East Anglia they often incorporate painted panels (notably at Ranworth in Norfolk). The screen was often surmounted by a loft that housed the choir and sometimes a small organ. Many medieval rood figures survive in Continental churches, but during the Reformation in England they were so thoroughly 'extincted and destroyed' (in the words of an Act of 1548) that of the thousands of Crucifixes that must once have existed only a few poignant fragments remain, notably a wonderful head of Christ (*c*.1130, BM, London) from All Hallows, South Cerney, Gloucestershire. When the *Renaissance style came to dominate church architecture, an unbroken view from the nave into the chancel became the norm, and the rood-screen became virtually obsolete during the 18th century.

Rooker, Michael 'Angelo' (*b* London, ?(25 Mar.) ?1746; *d* London, 3 Mar. 1801). English painter (mainly in watercolour) and engraver. He studied engraving with his father **Edward** (?1724–74), a specialist in architectural subjects, and painting with Paul *Sandby (who is said to

have dubbed him 'Angelo'). From about 1788 he made regular sketching tours in the southern and Midland counties and he was one of the most industrious topographical artists of his time. From 1779 to 1800 he was scene painter at the Haymarket Theatre in London.

Roos. Dynasty of German painters, members of which were active from the 17th to the 19th century, in Austria, Italy, and the Netherlands as well as Germany. The founder of the family tradition was **Johann Heinrich Roos** (*b* Reipoltskirchen, 29 Sept. 1631; *d* Frankfurt, 3 Oct. 1685). He trained in Amsterdam and specialized in idyllic pastoral scenes with herdsmen and livestock in the tradition of such Italianate Dutch painters as *Berchem and *Dujardin. His works in this vein were copied and imitated into the 19th century. Roos also painted other subjects, notably portraits, as well as making etchings, and he was a prolific draughtsman. He had four painter sons, of whom the most notable was **Philipp Peter Roos** (*b* St Goar, 30 Aug. 1657; *d* Rome, 17 Jan. 1706). He settled in Italy in 1677 and in the late 1680s lived near Tivoli, from which he derives his nickname Rosa da Tivoli. Subsequently he lived mainly in Rome. Like his father he specialized in landscapes with animals. Examples of his large output are in many collections. He had two painter sons, **Jakob Roos** (1682–?), known as Rosa da Napoli, and **Cajetan Roos** (1690–1770), known as Gaetano Rosa. **Cajetan's** son **Joseph** (1726–1805) was the last significant member of the family. He worked in Vienna and continued the pastoral tradition of his ancestors in a *Rococo idiom.

Rops, Félicien (*b* Namur, 7 July 1833; *d* Essonnes [Corbeil-Essonnes], 23 Aug. 1898). Belgian printmaker (and occasional painter), active mainly in Paris (he settled at Essonnes, a few miles south of the city, in 1874). Rops was a friend of *Baudelaire, who helped to launch him in the Paris art world, and in his work he similarly showed a fascination with evil and vice, and particularly with the idea of woman as a corrupter of man. He was greatly admired by *Symbolist writers and much of his output was done as illustrations to esoteric and erotic literature. Some of his work is frankly pornographic or blasphemous (for example, he showed Mary Magdalene masturbating at the foot of the cross), but in spite of his disdain for conventional morals, he became famous and successful. Technically he was one of the most resourceful printmakers of his period, mixing different techniques (such as *aquatint with *mezzotint) and experimenting with various types of acids and varnishes. In 1886 he became a member of the avant-garde Brussels group Les *Vingt and his work was notably influential on *Ensor.

Rosa, Salvator (*b* Arenella, nr. Naples, 21 July [or less likely 20 June] 1615; *d* Rome, 15 Mar. 1673). Italian painter and etcher, a fiery and flamboyant character who was a poet and actor as well as an artist. After training in Naples, he spent most of his career in Rome, except for the 1640s, when he lived mainly in Florence; his decision to move there was probably connected with the scandal he caused by publicly satirizing the great *Bernini. Rosa was a prolific artist and painted various subjects (including spirited battle pieces in which he surpassed his teacher *Falcone), but he is best known for the creation of a new type of wild and savage landscape (*River Landscape with Apollo and the Cumaean Sibyl*, *c*.1650–60, Wallace Coll., London). His craggy cliffs, jagged, moss-laden trees, and rough bravura handling create a dank and desolate air that contrasts sharply with the serenity of *Claude or the classical grandeur of *Poussin (a situation summed up in the famous lines from James Thomson's *The Castle of Indolence* (1748): 'Whate'er Lorraine light-touched with softening hue,/Or savage Rosa dashed, or learned Poussin drew'). He is also well known for his macabre subjects (notably of witches), but he himself set store by his large historical and religious compositions, which are now considered his least attractive works. His most ambitious etchings, dating mainly from the 1660s, were done to publicize these paintings. Rosa's colourful personality and unswerving belief in his own genius made him a prototype of the *Romantic artist and his fame was greatest in the 18th and 19th centuries (the story that he was a bandit seems to be a 19th-century invention). He was highly influential on the development of the *Picturesque and the *Sublime, and he had a great vogue in England, where *Mortimer was particularly taken with his pictures of bandits. *Ruskin, however, was largely responsible for the fall of his reputation, condemning his landscapes as artificial.

Rosa da Tivoli. See ROOS.

Roscoe, William. See GIBSON, JOHN.

Rosenberg, Harold (*b* New York, 2 Feb. 1906; *d* Springs, Long Island, NY, 11 July 1978). American writer, one of the most influential critics in the field of contemporary art from the 1950s until his death. Early in his career he wrote poetry and essays on literary and general cultural issues, and his first important work devoted to the visual arts was an article in *Art News* in 1952 in which he coined the term *Action Painting. He was one of the major champions of *Abstract Expressionism, writing monographs on *Gorky (1962), *de Kooning (1974), and *Newman (1978). Unlike his rival Clement *Greenberg, who was concerned only with formal values, Rosenberg had an ethical and political conception of art, believing that the critic should less 'judge it' than 'locate it', subordinating visual analysis to intellectual understanding. He thought that authentic modern art should be perpetually disruptive and he attacked the manipulative fashions created by both the market place and the museum.

Rosenberg, Isaac (*b* Bristol, 25 Nov. 1890; *d* nr. Arras, 1 Apr. 1918). British painter and poet, born into a family of Jewish immigrants from Lithuania. He trained as an engraver and also studied at the *Slade School. In 1915 he enlisted in the army and was killed in action on the Somme. He made little impact in his lifetime, and it was not until many years after his death that he began to be mentioned in the same breath as other notable war poets such as Rupert Brooke and Wilfred Owen (who were inherently more conspicuous because they were officers). In the 1970s, however, there was an upsurge of interest in Rosenberg, who was the subject of several books and exhibitions. As a painter he did some landscapes and allegorical scenes, but the bulk of his work consists of portraits (before the war he had hoped to earn his living from them). There are several self-portraits (the National Portrait Gallery and the Tate, London, each has an example) and these convey particularly well the nervous sensitivity of his style and seriousness of attitude: 'Art is not a plaything', he wrote, 'it is blood and tears.'

Roslin, Alexander (*b* Malmö, 15 July 1718; *d* Paris, 5 July 1793). Swedish portrait painter, active mainly in France. He left his country in 1745, worked at the courts of Bayreuth (1745–7) and Parma (1751–2), and in 1752 settled in Paris. There he rapidly became one of the leading portraitists of the day, esteemed particularly for his skilful rendering of expensive fabrics and delicate complexions ('Satin, skin? Go to Roslin'). In the 1770s he visited Moscow, St Petersburg, Vienna, and Warsaw (as well as Stockholm), but in spite of his international travels his elegant work was entirely French in style. His wife **Marie-Suzanne Giroust** (1734–72) was a pastellist and miniaturist. One of Roslin's finest works is an enchanting portrait of her entitled *The Lady with a Fan* (1768, Nationalmuseum, Stockholm).

Rosselli, Cosimo (*b* Florence, 1439; *d* Florence, ?7 Jan. 1507). Florentine painter. His successful career (the high point of which was painting frescos in the Sistine Chapel, 1481–2, together with *Botticelli, *Ghirlandaio, and *Perugino) was based on his facility and high standards of craftsmanship rather than on any great distinction or originality as an artist. His pupils included Fra *Bartolommeo and *Piero di Cosimo.

Rossellino, Bernardo (*b* Settignano, *c*.1409; *d* Florence, 23 Sept. 1464) and **Antonio** (*b* Settignano, *c*.1427; *d* Florence, 1479). Florentine sculptors, brothers. The family name was Gambarelli, but Antonio's nickname (Rossellino means 'little redhead') is now applied to both of them. They had three other brothers who also worked as sculptors, and all five of them seem to have worked together under Bernardo's management. He was an architect as well as a sculptor and he combined both arts in his chief work—the tomb of the great humanist Leonardo Bruni, chancellor of the Florentine Republic, in S. Croce, Florence (*c*.1444–7). It is based on the monument of the antipope John XXIII (Baldassare Cossa) by *Donatello and *Michelozzo in the Baptistery in Florence, and although less powerful is more graceful and harmonious; the pilasters framing the serene reclining effigy have a dignity and elegance almost worthy of *Brunelleschi. It became the model for the niche tomb for the rest of the century.

Antonio was trained by his brother, and his most ambitious work—the tomb of the Cardinal Prince of Portugal in S. Miniato al Monte, Florence (1461–6)—is based on Bernardo's Bruni tomb. It is more elaborate and concerned with movement than Bernardo's masterpiece, but also a less coherent design, and Antonio was a more distinguished artist when working on a smaller scale. He was a fine portraitist (*Giovanni Chellini*, 1456, V&A, London) and also made charming reliefs and statuettes of the Madonna and Child, in which he continued the tradition of Luca della *Robbia in stressing the naturalness and humanity of the Virgin (perhaps the finest of his reliefs is that in the Metropolitan Museum, New York, known as the *Altman Madonna*).

Rossetti, Dante Gabriel (*b* London, 12 May 1828; *d* Birchington, nr. Margate, Kent, 9 Apr. 1882). English painter and poet. He came from a remarkable and talented family: his father was an exiled Italian patriot and Dante scholar, his sister the poet Christina Rossetti, and his brother the critic William Michael Rossetti. Growing up in modest circumstances but a strongly literary environment, he at first found it hard to decide whether he should devote himself to poetry or painting. Although painting became his profession (following the advice given to him by the poet and critic Leigh Hunt: 'If you paint as well as you write, you may be a rich man'), he continued to write poetry and make translations from the Italian, and he has a secure place in literary history. In 1848 he founded the *Pre-Raphaelite Brotherhood with *Hunt, *Millais, and others. His *Girlhood of Mary Virgin* (1849, Tate, London), the first picture to be exhibited bearing the Brotherhood's initials, was warmly praised and sold well, but the subsequent abuse that the Pre-Raphaelites received hurt him so much that he rarely again exhibited in public. In the 1850s he virtually gave up oils and concentrated on watercolours of medieval subjects. These found ready buyers (often contacts of *Ruskin, whom Rossetti met in 1854), and Rossetti, who was a hard and skilful businessman, proved Leigh Hunt's prediction true—by the 1860s he was earning the very substantial sum of £3,000 a year.

In 1860, after a long and sometimes vexed liaison, Rossetti married the beautiful but sickly Elizabeth Siddal (1829–62), the archetypal Pre-Raphaelite 'stunner', who under his guidance also became a minor Pre-Raphaelite painter. Her melancholy face haunted his imagination, and he portrayed 'Guggums' (as he called her) again and again—'It is like a monomania with him', wrote Ford Madox *Brown in 1855. Rossetti immortalized her mainly in drawings, for in spite of the hatred for academic discipline that made him so disdainful of the official art world, he was an outstanding draughtsman. Elizabeth died from an overdose of laudanum, possibly deliberate, in 1862, and Rossetti was devastated; as a gesture of his grief he had the only complete manuscript of his poems placed in her coffin, but he was persuaded to have them exhumed in 1869 and they were published the following year. Rossetti also painted the intensely spiritual *Beata Beatrix* (Tate) as a memorial to Elizabeth, expressing his love for her as a parallel to Dante's for Beatrice (the picture is dated 1864, but was worked on over a period of several years).

By the time of Elizabeth's death Rossetti had returned to oil painting, and in the last two decades of his life his subject matter was confined almost exclusively to beautiful women, portrayed in a richly sensuous manner and often evoking literary or mythological references. Elizabeth was replaced as his favourite model by William *Morris's wife Janey, who became in Rossetti's pictures one of the archetypal *femmes fatales*—all cascading curls, pouting lips, and smouldering eyes. Rossetti had met Morris and *Burne-Jones in 1856 and entered into partnership with them in 1861 (in the decorative arts firm later known as Morris & Co.), but both business and personal relationships became strained; Rossetti was in love with Janey and he and Morris parted acrimoniously in 1875. In his later years Rossetti became an eccentric recluse (he had a menagerie of unusual animals, including a wombat, the death of which occasioned a poem); he fought a losing battle against drugs and alcohol and he died paralysed and prematurely aged. He was nevertheless a commanding personality and his work was highly influential; his romantic medievalism inspired the second wave of Pre-Raphaelitism associated with Burne-Jones and other followers, and his *femmes fatales* appealed to the *Symbolists and had a legion of descendants during the turn-of-the-century taste for 'decadence'.

Rosso, Medardo (*b* Turin, 21 June 1858; *d* Milan, 31 Mar. 1928). Italian sculptor. He was virtually self-taught, for he was dismissed from the Brera Academy in Milan in 1883 after only a few months' training when he appealed for drawing to be taught from the nude model rather than casts of statues. In 1884 he first visited Paris, and he lived there from 1889 to 1897, the period of his most intense creative activity. It is indeed with French rather than Italian art that his work has affinity, for he created a sculptural equivalent of *Impressionism, depicting everyday subjects and capturing a feeling of movement, atmosphere, and transitory effects of light. His favourite medium was wax, which he used with great subtlety to express his view that matter was malleable by atmosphere: 'We are mere consequences of the objects which surround us.' His subjects included portraits and single figures and groups in contemporary settings (*The Bookmaker*, 1894, MoMA, New York; *Conversation in a Garden*, 1893, Gal. Naz. d'Arte Contemporanea, Rome). In his early days in Paris Rosso struggled to earn a living (he made funerary monuments for his basic income), but his career blossomed in the

1890s, partly because of the patronage of Henri Rouart (a wealthy industrialist and friend of *Degas), who helped Rosso find clients as well as purchasing works himself. *Rodin, too, tried to help him, but Rosso was suspicious of him and thought he was trying to steal his ideas (it has been suggested that the 'Impressionistic' handling of Rodin's celebrated Balzac monument is indebted to Rosso).

In 1897 Rosso returned to Italy and thereafter made almost no new sculpture, devoting his time instead to organizing exhibitions of his work throughout Europe. Through these his work became extremely well known, and after Rodin's death in 1917, *Apollinaire spoke for many when he described him as 'beyond doubt the greatest living sculptor'. His reputation remains high and he is considered one of the most original artists of his time (not even Rodin challenged so decisively the traditional preoccupations of sculpture). He was particularly influential on the *Futurists, who took over and developed many of his ideas. Rosso's output was fairly small; replicas of several of his works and a collection of his drawings are in the Museo Medardo Rosso at Barzio in Italy.

Rosso Fiorentino (Giovanni Battista di Jacopo) (*b* Florence, 8 Mar. 1494; *d* Fontainebleau or Paris, 14 Nov. 1540). Florentine painter and decorative artist; the name by which he is known means 'the red-headed Florentine'. *Vasari says that he 'would not bind himself to any master' (a story that fits in with his individuality of temperament), but in his youth he learned most from Andrea del *Sarto, and together with Andrea's pupil *Pontormo (Rosso's friend and close contemporary) he was one of the leading figures in the early development of *Mannerism. His work was highly sophisticated and varied in mood, ranging from the refined elegance of the *Marriage of the Virgin* (1523, S. Lorenzo, Florence) to the violent energy of *Moses Defending the Daughters of Jethro* (c.1523, Uffizi, Florence) and to the disquieting intensity of the *Deposition* (1521, Pinacoteca Communale, Volterra). In 1523 Rosso left Florence for Rome, where he stayed until the Sack of 1527, and he then worked briefly in several Italian towns until 1530, when he was invited to France by Francis I. With *Primaticcio he was the most important artist to work on the decoration of the Royal Palace at Fontainebleau and one of the creators of the distinctive style of French Mannerism associated with the School of *Fontainebleau. Rosso's principal work there is the Gallery of

Francis I. Many engravings were made from his designs and his influence on French art was great. Vasari, whose biography of Rosso includes an entertaining story about his pet baboon, says that he killed himself in remorse after falsely accusing a friend of stealing money from him; there is no supporting evidence for this story, but nothing to contradict it either.

Roszak, Theodore. See ABSTRACT EXPRESSIONISM.

Rothenberg, Susan, See NEW IMAGE PAINTING.

Rothenstein, Sir William (*b* Bradford, 29 Jan. 1872; *d* Far Oakridge, nr. Stroud, Gloucestershire, 14 Feb. 1945). British painter, printmaker, draughtsman, writer, and teacher. He studied for a year at the *Slade School (1888–9) under Alphonse *Legros and afterwards at the *Académie Julian in Paris. There he was encouraged by *Degas and *Pissarro. He also knew and was influenced by *Whistler; his best works are generally considered to be his early Whistlerian paintings such as *The Doll's House* (1899, Tate, London), which shows Augustus *John and Rothenstein's wife as characters in a tense scene from Ibsen's play *A Doll's House*. From about 1898, however, he specialized in portraits of the celebrated and those who later became celebrated. In his later career he was much more renowned as a teacher than a painter. His outlook was conservative (he regarded pure abstraction as 'a cardinal heresy') and as principal of the *Royal College of Art, 1920–35, he exercised an influence second only to that of *Tonks at the Slade School in earlier decades. His books included three volumes of memoirs (1931–9). His brother **Albert** (1881–1953) was a painter, designer, and prolific book illustrator. In 1914 he changed his surname to Rutherston because of anti-German feeling. William's son **Sir John Rothenstein** (1901–92) had a distinguished career as an art historian (he was director of the Tate Gallery, 1938–64, and wrote numerous books); another son, **Michael Rothenstein** (1908–93), was a painter, printmaker, and writer on art.

Rothko, Mark (*b* Dvinsk [now Daugavpils, Latvia], 25 Sept. 1903; *d* New York, 25 Feb. 1970). Russian-born American painter, one of the outstanding figures of *Abstract Expressionism and one of the creators of *Colour Field Painting. He emigrated to the USA as a child in 1913. After dropping out of Yale University in 1923 he moved to New York and studied at the *Art Students League under Max *Weber, but he regarded himself as essentially self-taught as a painter. In the 1930s and 1940s he went through phases influenced by *Expressionism and *Surrealism, but from about 1947 he began to develop his distinctive mature style. Typically his paintings feature large rectangular expanses of colour arranged parallel to each other, usually in a vertical format. The edges of these shapes are softly uneven, giving them a hazy, pulsating quality, and they seem to gently hover or float over the canvas. The paintings are often very large and the effect they produce is characteristically one of calmness and contemplation, but in spite of their tranquillity, they cost Rothko enormous emotional effort: 'I'm not an abstract artist . . . I'm not interested in the relationship of colour or form or anything else. I'm interested only in expressing basic human emotions—tragedy, ecstasy, doom and so on. And the fact that a lot of people break down and cry when confronted with my pictures shows that I can communicate these basic human emotions . . . The people who weep before my pictures are having the same religious experience as I had when I painted them.'

Rothko was poor for much of his career (from 1929 to 1959 he earned at least part of his living by teaching art), but his reputation grew in the 1950s and in 1961 he was given a major retrospective exhibition at the Museum of Modern Art, New York, that sealed his success. In spite of his soaring fame (and the money it brought), Rothko was plagued by depression. He had a prickly temperament, drank heavily, took barbiturates to excess, was fearful and suspicious of younger artists, had two unhappy marriages, and felt he was misunderstood (he disliked having his paintings discussed in *formalist terms). His early works had often been bright and vivid in colour, but from the 1950s they became increasingly sombre, typically employing blacks, browns, and maroon. He regarded his fourteen paintings for a non-denominational chapel in Houston, Texas (now known as the Rothko Chapel), 1967–9, as his masterpieces. His last paintings were a series of stark black on grey canvases that evoke his painful state of mind leading up to his suicide (he slashed his veins in his studio). His reputation stands high, but he has not been without detractors. After visiting an exhibition of his work in 1972, Keith *Vaughan wrote: 'Feeble stuff. Large decor. Boring to paint and look at. Not surprising he killed himself if that was all there was to do.'

Rothschild. The most famous of European banking dynasties, several members of which have been art collectors and patrons. The business was established in Frankfurt by Mayer Amschel Rothschild (1744–1812), who set up branches in London, Naples, Paris, and Vienna, each one run by one of his sons. Of these the most significant collector was **Baron James Meyer de Rothschild** (1792–1868). He bought objects from the Middle Ages onwards, including Old Master paintings, and commissioned *Ingres to paint family portraits. Many of the works that he and other members of the dynasty collected are still in family ownership, but the family has also given generously to public collections and the best idea of Rothschild wealth and taste can be obtained at Waddesdon Manor, Buckinghamshire, which was presented to the National Trust in 1957. It was built in 1874–89 in ornate French *Renaissance style for **Baron Ferdinand de Rothschild** (1839–98) to house his collection, particularly rich in 18th-century French paintings, porcelain, furniture, and carpets. For patronage of living artists, the most enterprising member of the family has perhaps been **Baron Philippe de Rothschild** (1902–88), who commissioned many leading artists to design labels for the famous Château Mouton-Rothschild wine, among them *Braque, *Cocteau, *Dalí, *Kandinsky, and *Warhol.

Rottenhammer, Hans (or **Johann**) (*b* Munich, 1564; *d* Augsburg, 14 Aug. 1625). German painter, active for much of his career in Italy. He moved there in about 1589, worked in Rome in the early 1590s, then settled in Venice, where he lived 1596–1606. He specialized in mythological scenes in landscape settings, working on a small scale and often on copper, and his paintings form a link between the styles of Paul *Bril, whom he knew in Rome, and Adam *Elsheimer, who was his assistant in Venice (Rottenhammer's workshop became something of a magnet for German artists visiting the city). After his return to Germany he settled in Augsburg. He became one of the leading artists there, but he died in poverty, mainly because of over-indulgence in alcohol.

Rottmann, Carl (*b* Handschuhsheim, nr. Heidelberg, 11 Jan. 1797; *d* Munich, 7 July 1850). German painter. He travelled extensively in Italy, and is best known for a series of Italian landscapes commissioned by King Ludwig I of Bavaria (see PINACOTHECA) and painted in fresco on the walls of the *Hofgarten* cloisters in Munich in 1830–4 (now in the Residenz, Munich). They

are influenced by the heroic style of *Koch. Ludwig's son Otto became King of Greece in 1832, and Rottmann spent most of the rest of his life working on a companion series of Greek landscapes (Neue Pin., Munich).

Rottmayr, Johann Michael (*bapt.* Laufen, nr. Salzburg, 11 Dec. 1654; *d* Vienna, 25 Oct. 1730). Austrian painter who stands at the beginning of the great tradition of *Baroque and *Rococo fresco decoration in the Austro-Hungarian Empire. From 1675 to 1687 he was in Venice as the pupil and assistant of Johann Carl Loth (1632–98), a painter from Munich whose studio attracted many German and Austrian artists who visited Italy. After he returned to Austria, Rottmayr lived first in Salzburg, then in about 1696 settled in Vienna. This was his home for the rest of his life, but he undertook commissions in various other places, including Breslau (now Wrocław, Poland), where he decorated the ceiling of the Jesuit church (now St Matthew) in 1704–6, and Melk, where he carried out extensive work at the great abbey church, built in 1702–14. Although primarily famous for his frescos, Rottmayr also painted easel pictures. His vigorous, colourful style was strongly influenced by *Rubens, and he followed Rubens's practice of making oil sketches in preparation for his major works.

Rouault, Georges (*b* Paris, 27 May 1871; *d* Paris, 13 Feb. 1958). French painter, draughtsman, printmaker, and designer who created a personal kind of *Expressionism that gives him a highly distinctive place in modern art. From 1885 to 1890 he was apprenticed to a stained-glass maker, his work including the restoration of medieval glass; the vivid colours and strong outlines characteristic of the medium left a firm imprint on his work. In 1892 he became a fellow pupil of *Matisse and *Marquet under Gustave *Moreau at the École des *Beaux-Arts. He was Moreau's favourite pupil and in 1898 became the first curator of the Musée Moreau in Paris. At about the same time he underwent a psychological crisis and, although he continued to associate with the group of artists around Matisse who were later known as *Fauves, he did not adopt their brilliant colour or characteristic subjects; instead he painted characters such as clowns, prostitutes, and outcasts in sombre but glowing tones. These subjects expressed his hatred of cruelty, hypocrisy, and vice, depicting the ugliness and degradation of humanity with passionate conviction. His familiar cast of characters also included judges (*The Three Judges*, *c*.1936, Tate, London), on the subject of which he said: 'If I have made them such lamentable figures, it is doubtless because I betrayed the anguish which I feel at the sight of a human being who has to pass judgement on other men.' Initially such work disturbed the public, but Rouault achieved financial security after *Vollard became his agent in 1917 and during the 1930s he gained international popularity. From about 1940 he devoted himself almost exclusively to religious art. In addition to his large output of paintings, drawings, and prints (in various techniques, often done as book illustrations), his work also included ceramics and designs for tapestry, for stained glass, and for *Diaghilev's ballet *The Prodigal Son* (1929), for which the music was written by Prokofiev. By the time of his death he was a much-honoured figure and he was given a state funeral.

Roubiliac, Louis-François (*bapt.* Lyons, 31 Aug. 1702; *d* London, 11 Jan. 1762). French-born sculptor, active in England for virtually his entire career. Little is known of his life before he settled in London in the early 1730s, although he is said to have trained under Balthasar *Permoser in Dresden and Nicolas *Coustou in Paris. He made his reputation with a full-length seated marble statue of the composer Handel (1738, V&A, London), remarkable for its lively informality, and quickly became recognized as the most brilliant portrait sculptor of the day. His busts have great vivacity, stressing small forms and rippling movement in a manner very different from the broader treatment of his contemporary Michael *Rysbrack. He was especially successful with portraits of old and ugly men, and in his series of busts at Trinity College, Cambridge, and the celebrated statue of Newton (1754–5) there, he showed an unusual gift for producing lively portraits of men long dead. Roubiliac was also outstanding as a tomb sculptor, several notable examples being in Westminster Abbey, including the wonderfully dramatic tomb of Lady Elizabeth Nightingale (1758–61), who is shown being attacked with a spear by Death (a hideous skeleton emerging from a vault), while her husband vainly tries to keep him at bay (the skeleton was carved by Roubiliac's assistant Nicholas Read (*c*.1733–87)). The Nightingale monument clearly shows the influence of *Bernini, whose work profoundly impressed Roubiliac when he visited Rome in 1752; he said that compared with Bernini's his own sculptures looked 'meagre and starved, as if made of nothing but tobacco pipes'.

Roubiliac is generally regarded as one of the greatest sculptors ever to work in England, certainly the greatest of his period. He had a vivid imagination, he was a superb craftsman, and, as Gerald Randall observes (*Church Furnishing and Decoration in England and Wales*, 1980), 'Unlike even the best of his rivals, Roubiliac seems to have been incapable of indifferent work, and even his most modest commissions are designed and executed with a master's touch.' See also LAY FIGURE.

roulette. A tool used in certain printmaking techniques, consisting essentially of a spiked wheel on the end of a handle. It was used mainly in the 18th century for making dotted lines in the plate in *crayon manner and other tonal processes that were popular at the time. However, the first known use of a roulette was by Ludwig von *Siegen, the inventor of *mezzotint; examination of his prints (the first of which dates from 1642) shows that he roughened the plate with a roulette rather than the rocker that later became standard. Two variant tools are the chalk roll and the matting wheel. They have thicker wheels or cylinders than the roulette.

Rousseau, Henri (known as Le Douanier Rousseau) (*b* Laval, 21 May 1844; *d* Paris, 2 Sept. 1910). French painter, the most celebrated of *naive artists. His nickname refers to the job he held with the Paris municipal toll-collecting service (1871–93), although he never actually rose to the rank of 'Douanier' (customs officer). Before this he had served in the army, and he later claimed to have seen service in Mexico, but this story seems to be a product of his imagination (indeed as far as is known he never set foot outside France in the whole of his life). He began to paint as a hobby, self-taught, when he was about 40, and from 1886 he exhibited regularly at the *Salon des Indépendants. In 1893 he took early retirement so he could devote himself to art. His character was extraordinarily ingenuous and he suffered much ridicule (although he sometimes interpreted sarcastic remarks literally and took them as praise) as well as enduring great poverty. However, his faith in his own abilities never wavered. He tried to paint in the academic manner of such traditionalist artists as *Bouguereau and *Gérôme, but it was the innocence and charm of his work that won him the admiration of the avant-garde. He was 'discovered' by *Vollard and members of his circle in about 1906–7, and in 1908 *Picasso gave a banquet, half serious half burlesque, in his honour.

Rousseau is now best known for his jungle scenes, the first of which was *Tiger in a Tropical Storm (Surprised!)* (1891, NG, London) and the last *The Dream* (1910, MoMA, New York). These two paintings are works of great imaginative power, in which he showed his extraordinary ability to retain the utter freshness of his vision even when working on a large scale and with loving attention to detail. He claimed such scenes were inspired by his experiences in Mexico, but in fact his sources were illustrated books and visits to the zoo and botanical gardens in Paris. His other work ranges from the jaunty humour of *The Football Players* (1908, Philadelphia Mus. of Art) to the mesmeric, eerie beauty of *The Sleeping Gypsy* (1897, MoMA). Rousseau was buried in a pauper's grave, but his greatness began to be widely acknowledged soon after his death.

Rousseau, Théodore (*b* Paris, 15 Apr. 1812; *d* Barbizon, 22 Dec. 1867). French landscape painter, the central figure of the *Barbizon School. He was one of the pioneers of landscape painting in the open air (see PLEIN AIR), and because of the non-academic outlook of his work it was for several years consistently rejected by the *Salon, earning him the nickname 'le grand refusé' (the period during which his paintings were turned down, 1836–41, was, however, shorter than is sometimes imagined and he had earlier had several pictures accepted and even won a medal, in 1834). He first made a lengthy stay in the Forest of Fontainebleau in 1834 and he settled in Barbizon in 1848. Acclaim began to come in the 1850s, but he did not achieve financial security until near the end of his life. During the later 19th century his reputation stood very high (he was widely regarded as one of the greatest of all landscape painters), but it has subsequently declined.

Roussel, Ker-Xavier. See NABIS.

Rovere. Italian family that included two popes and three dukes of Urbino, all of them art patrons. The family achieved prominence when **Francesco della Rovere** (1414–84) became pope in 1471 as Sixtus IV. He was a scholar and was strict in his personal life, but he was ruthless in pursuing his aims and unscrupulous in advancing his relatives (he made six of his nephews cardinals). As a patron, he played a key role in the transformation of Rome from a medieval to a Renaissance city, laying out new streets and widening old ones, building the Ponte Sisto over the Tiber, and restoring old buildings and

founding new ones, notably the churches of S. Maria del Popolo and S. Maria della Pace. His most famous foundation is the chapel named after him in the Vatican, the Sistine Chapel. It was built in 1477–80 and the celebrated fresco decorations by *Botticelli, *Perugino, and other artists were begun in 1481. His huge expenditure, on war as well as art, left the papal treasury depleted.

Sixtus's tomb, by Antonio *Pollaiuolo, was commissioned after his death by his nephew **Giuliano della Rovere** (1453–1513), who in 1503 became pope as Julius II. He was one of the most formidable personalities among all the popes ('hated by many and feared by all') and the greatest patron of his time, employing *Bramante, *Michelangelo, and *Raphael to create some of the central works of European art: the new St Peter's (begun 1506), the ceiling of the Sistine Chapel (1508–12), and the decoration of the Vatican Stanze (begun 1508). Howard Hibbard (*Michelangelo*, 1975) writes that 'If, as many believe, this was the greatest assembly of talent ever to work for one man at the same time, we must hail Julius as the most perspicacious as well as the most fortunate patron the world has ever known.' His political policies were aimed at making the papal state the most important power in Italy and he personally led campaigns that greatly expanded its territories (his choice of papal name reflected his admiration for the military prowess of Julius Caesar). In spite of his costly wars and his huge outlay on rebuilding St Peter's, because of his skilful administration he left the papacy more prosperous than he found it. Julius' interest in art extended to collecting *antique sculpture, and he placed several of his finest pieces (including the *Apollo Belvedere and the *Laocoön) in the Belvedere Courtyard of the Vatican, where artists and scholars were allowed to see them; this was the origin of the *Vatican Museums.

Julius's nephew **Francesco Maria I della Rovere** (1490–1538) became Duke of Urbino in 1508, when he succeeded his childless uncle Guidobaldo da *Montefeltro, who had adopted him as his heir. His favourite painter was *Titian, who painted portraits of him and his wife Eleonora *Gonzaga (*c*.1536–8, both Uffizi, Florence). Francesco Maria's son **Guidobaldo della Rovere** (1514–74) was also a great admirer of Titian and owned his celebrated *Venus of Urbino* (1538, Uffizi); the title is misleading, as the picture hung in the ducal palace in Pesaro, which was part of Guidobaldo's territories. His son

Francesco Maria II della Rovere (1549–1631) employed numerous artists and was in particular the main patron of Federico *Barocci.

Rowlandson, Thomas (*b* London, 14 July 1756 or 1757; *d* London, 21 Apr. 1827). English caricaturist. Rowlandson ranks with James *Gillray as one of the founders and supreme figures of the English caricature tradition. However, whilst Gillray was a political satirist, Rowlandson excelled in comic subjects and his work is essentially jolly rather than abrasive. He trained at the *Royal Academy, 1772–7, and began his career as a painter, mainly of portraits, but he turned to caricature to supplement his income (he was a notorious gambler), and finding his sideline highly successful he gave his career over to it completely. His talent for exuberant and flowing line had affinities with the French *Rococo (Rowlandson had a French aunt and visited Paris during his student years), but his rollicking humour and delicate tonal effects were distinctively English; the marvel of his art is that there is no inconsistency between the bawdiness or boisterousness of the subject matter and the beauty of his technique. Usually he made his caricatures in ink tinted with watercolour, and engravings were produced from them by specialist printmakers. He created an instantly recognizable gallery of social types, such as the old maid, the hack writer, and the crabbed antiquarian, and his buxom wenches have their descendants in the fat ladies of today's saucy seaside postcards. From 1797 much of his work was produced for Rudolph Ackermann (1764–1834), a major publisher of prints. He issued several collections of Rowlandson's work in book form, including *The Comforts of Bath* (1798) and three featuring Dr Syntax (1812–22), a grotesque and pedantic old schoolmaster, whose adventures are used to satirize the craze for the *Picturesque (specifically the writings of William *Gilpin). Rowlandson's output was huge, but it was only towards the end of his career that the quality of his work suffered because of overproduction.

Royal Academy of Arts (RA), London. The national art *academy of England, founded in 1768 with George III (see ROYAL COLLECTION) as its 'patron, protector and supporter'. Its main—interlinked—aims were to raise the status of British artists, to provide a venue for regular exhibitions (which have indeed been held every year since 1769), and to establish a sound system of training for students. The *Society of Artists was a forerunner in these aims, but it was soon eclipsed by the RA. *Reynolds was the first president and other foundation members included the architect Sir William Chambers (who was treasurer), *Gainsborough, *West, *Wilson, and the sculptor Joseph *Wilton. Engravers were initially admitted only as Associates of the Royal Academy (ARAs), but from 1853 they were eligible for full membership (the category of ARA was abolished in 1992).

The RA was initially based in Pall Mall, but in 1771 its art school transferred to Old Somerset House in the Strand, and in 1780 the whole institution was given rooms in the new Somerset House, a huge government office block designed by Chambers. In 1837 the RA moved to Trafalgar Square, where it shared premises with the *National Gallery in a building newly erected for this dual purpose. However, it eventually proved too small to accommodate both institutions, and in 1869 the RA moved to its present home in Burlington House, Piccadilly.

Throughout this first century of its existence, the RA had had no real rival as an art school and in general enjoyed great prestige. However, in the late 19th century it was increasingly seen as a bastion of conservatism; the *Slade School (founded 1871) and the *Royal College of Art (given its present name in 1896) became more important as teaching institutions, and organizations such as the *New English Art Club (1886), and later the *London Group (1913), were preferred as exhibiting venues by progressive artists. Adventurous work was rarely shown at the RA's exhibitions (where traditionalism ruled to such an extent that top hats and tail coats were required dress on Private View Days until 1940), and in the 1930s there were several notable instances of leading artists (*Sickert, Stanley *Spencer, Augustus *John) resigning their membership because of outmoded views and taste.

After the presidency (1944–9) of *Munnings, who was notorious for his opposition to modern art, the RA's policy became more liberal, and the gap between official and progressive art narrowed. As an art school it has also won back much of its former prestige. But something of the reputation for stuffiness continued up to the 1970s, and the RA's aim at its inception to provide exhibitions of the best contemporary work from year to year has been challenged by commercial galleries and by bodies such as the *Arts Council. The annual summer exhibition still remains a popular social event, however, and the RA regularly organizes major loan exhibitions (the first was in 1870).

Royal Collection. The collection of works of art, particularly paintings and drawings, accumulated by the British royal family over a period of five centuries—from Tudor times to the present day. It is the only great European royal or princely collection to retain its identity, the others having been mainly absorbed into state museums. Sir Oliver Millar, Surveyor of the Queen's Pictures 1972–88, writes that the collection was 'made by a succession of English Kings, Queens, Consorts and Princes; and it reflects their discernment and prejudice, their bad taste as well as their good, their friendships, diversions, loves, hates, idiosyncrasies and obsessions—and of course a network of dynastic associations—in a uniquely illuminating manner . . . The commonplace that the worst and most extravagant Kings have the best taste is well borne out by the story of the collection' (*The Queen's Pictures*, 1977). In the foreword to *The Royal Collection* (1992) by Christopher Lloyd (Millar's successor as Surveyor), Prince Charles explains that 'Although the paintings were purchased over the ages as a means of decorating the homes and official residences of sovereigns, they are not, strictly speaking, the private property of the sovereign. They are, to all intents and purposes, national heirlooms which are an integral part of the institution of monarchy and of which each successive sovereign is the guardian.'

The earliest English monarch of whose collection we have substantial records is **Henry VIII** (1491–1547; reigned from 1509), but most of the works he owned cannot be certainly identified (the inventories are imprecise) or have been lost or dispersed; they included *Raphael's exquisite *St George and the Dragon* (c.1505, NG, Washington), which is believed to have been a diplomatic gift to his father Henry VII from Guidobaldo da *Montefeltro, Duke of Urbino. Henry VIII spent lavishly on art and understood its propaganda value, but little is known of his personal taste; rather than being a connoisseur, he probably appreciated paintings, like other luxury goods, for their value as status symbols. He employed outstanding foreign artists, above all *Holbein, but the Holbeins now in the Royal Collection were acquired after Henry's reign.

Every British monarch since Henry's time has acquired paintings, but only a few of these rulers stand out for their genuine interest in art, above all **Charles I** (1600–49; reigned from 1625), who assembled one of the choicest picture collections ever created and gave England a new prominence in European cultural affairs. Charles's passion for art began early and he inherited the

nucleus of his collection from his elder brother Henry Prince of Wales, who died in 1612 aged only 18. Other works of art came to Charles as diplomatic gifts, but most of his collection was purchased, and the huge amounts he spent on it were one of the sources of the financial difficulties that helped bring about his downfall. His greatest enthusiasm was for Italian Renaissance painting, particularly of the 16th-century Venetian School (he had a superb representation of *Titian's work). In 1623 he bought Raphael's magnificent set of *cartoons of the *Acts of the Apostles* for use at the recently founded Mortlake Tapestry Factory (see TAPESTRY), and in 1627 came his greatest coup when he outmanoeuvred rivals to acquire the bulk of the celebrated *Gonzaga collection, including *Mantegna's series of canvases of the *Triumphs of Caesar*. Charles also patronized living artists, most notably *Rubens and van *Dyck, whom he knighted in 1630 and 1632 respectively.

After Charles's execution in 1649 his goods were declared state property and most of his collection was sold, the money raised to be employed for 'public uses of this Commonwealth'. More than 1,500 pictures and almost 400 pieces of classical sculpture were dispersed over a period of several years, but a few works were retained, including the Raphael tapestry cartoons and the Mantegna *Triumphs of Caesar* (these are still in the Royal Collection: the Mantegnas at Hampton Court Palace and the Raphaels on loan at the Victoria and Albert Museum). When the monarchy was restored in 1660, **Charles II** (1630–85) set about recovering as much as he could of his father's collection. He had substantial success with works that had remained in England, but most of the key paintings had gone to foreign buyers including Everard *Jabach, Philip IV of Spain, and Archduke Leopold William (for both see HABSBURG), and masterpieces that were once in Charles I's collection can now be found in some of the greatest museums of Europe; many of his beloved Titians, for example, are in the Louvre, Paris, the Prado, Madrid, and the Kunsthistorisches Museum, Vienna. In spite of these losses, Charles II—in Anthony *Blunt's words—'had a collection of which no king need have been ashamed'. Although he was much less interested in art than his father, Charles was intelligent and cultivated and he added several notable works to the Royal Collection on his own account. It was probably he who acquired the celebrated collection of *Leonardo drawings now at Windsor Castle (perhaps advised by his court painter

*Lely, a great connoisseur of drawings), although they are not recorded in the Royal Collection until 1690, five years after Charles's death.

The next major royal collector was **Frederick, Prince of Wales** (1707–51), son of George II. The antiquarian *Vertue said of Frederick that 'no prince since King Charles the First took so much pleasure nor observations on works of art or artists' and he added numerous works to the Royal Collection, notably by 17th-century painters—French, Flemish, and Italian. He also patronized contemporary artists, including *Kent, *Mercier, and *Wootton. Frederick's son **George III** (1738–1820; reigned from 1760) was a less passionate but highly purposeful collector. His most famous acquisition (in 1762) was the collection of Joseph Smith, the British consul in Venice, with its incomparable group of *Canalettos. Smith's collection was rich in drawings as well as paintings, and in the same year that he acquired it George also bought another great collection of drawings—from Cardinal Alessandro *Albani. These two acquisitions form a substantial part of the magnificent collection of Old Master drawings (one of the greatest in the world) in the Royal Library at Windsor Castle. The contemporary artists George III particularly admired included *Gainsborough, *Ramsay, *West, and *Zoffany, and he played a significant role in the creation of the *Royal Academy, funding it from its foundation in 1768 until it became self-supporting in 1780.

George's son **George IV** (1762–1830; regent from 1811 because of his father's illness, reigned from 1820) ranks second only to Charles I among British royal collectors—for reckless extravagance as well as for refined taste. Oliver Millar writes that 'Perhaps more than any other English royal connoisseur, he had a feeling for the look of a room as a whole and for the part a picture could play in its design.' He constantly altered the arrangement of the paintings and other works of art in his homes, and he had Buckingham Palace and Windsor Castle remodelled with special provision for displaying pictures. In 1826 and 1827 he lent more than 100 paintings for exhibition at the British Institution in London. His main field of interest as a collector was 17th-century Dutch and Flemish painting, and his purchases included two masterpieces particularly associated with Charles I: Rubens's *Landscape with St George and the Dragon* (in which St George and the princess are idealized portraits of Charles and his wife, Henrietta Maria) and van Dyck's triple portrait of Charles I (which had been sent to Rome in 1636 to serve

as the model for a marble bust by *Bernini). Among contemporary artists, George especially favoured *Lawrence.

George's niece **Victoria** (1819–1901; reigned from 1837) and her husband Prince **Albert** (1819–61) were the last of the major figures in shaping the character of the Royal Collection. Most of the hundreds of pictures they bought were by contemporary artists (*Landseer and *Winterhalter were among their favourites, and *Frith commented that 'they knew quite as much about art as most painters' and that 'their treatment of artists displayed a generous kindness delightful to experience'). In a very different field, Albert was a pioneer in the appreciation of early Italian painting; most of the Royal Collection's Italian pictures dating from before 1500 were acquired in the period between his marriage to Victoria in 1840 and his early death in 1861.

Under Victoria and Albert the administration of the Royal Collection was greatly improved and it was made more accessible to the public (Hampton Court was open to visitors 'free and without restriction' on certain days). Charles I had been the first monarch to appoint an administrator specifically to look after his pictures—Abraham van der Doort (c.1580–1640), a Dutch-born wax modeller and drawing master. His successors in the post of Surveyor of the King's (or Queen's) Pictures included several well-known painters, among them George *Knapton, Benjamin West, and Richard *Redgrave, who was appointed by Victoria and Albert in 1857 and who 'deserves without question to be enshrined in the annals of the collection as its greatest and most admirable servant' (Oliver Millar). In addition to achieving a great deal in cleaning and restoration, Redgrave made a manuscript inventory of the entire royal picture collection that was much more detailed and accurate than anything that had gone before (each description was accompanied by a photograph of the picture—a pioneering use of the medium in art history).

Redgrave resigned in 1880 because of declining eyesight. His successors have mainly been distinguished art historians, among them Kenneth *Clark and Anthony Blunt. It was during Blunt's surveyorship, in 1962, that the Queen's Gallery was opened at Buckingham Palace to hold exhibitions of works from the Royal Collection (the gallery has subsequently been much enlarged, reopening in its new form in 2002). Buckingham Palace itself was first opened to the public in 1993, and works from the Royal

Collection can also regularly be seen in other royal residences, including Hampton Court and Kensington Palace in London, Windsor Castle, and Holyroodhouse, Edinburgh. A second Queen's Gallery opened in Edinburgh in 2002.

Royal College of Art (RCA), London. Britain's pre-eminent training school for artists and designers. Since 1967 it has been a postgraduate university institution, but it has had many changes of status, name, and location since it was founded in 1837 at Somerset House as the School of Design (William *Dyce was a key figure in its early days). Originally it taught industrial design, the fine arts being the province of the *Royal Academy. In 1852 it moved to Marlborough House and was renamed the Central School of Practical Art. It became part of the Government Department of Science and Art in 1853 and in 1857, renamed the National Art Training School, it moved to South Kensington with the Museum of Ornamental Art (later the *Victoria and Albert Museum). In 1863 it moved to new buildings in Exhibition Road, and in 1896 it was renamed the Royal College of Art by Queen Victoria and allowed to grant diplomas. Walter *Crane was principal in 1898–9.

By the turn of the century the RCA had turned much more to fine art, away from industrial design, and by the 1920s it rivalled the *Slade School as the most important art school in the country; William *Rothenstein was principal at this time and the students included Barbara *Hepworth and Henry *Moore. By the end of the Second World War the RCA had become rather stagnant, but it was given new life by Sir Robert (Robin) Darwin (1910–74), who was head from 1948 to 1971 (in 1967 his title changed from principal to rector). Darwin introduced new departments, including fashion design and photography, aligned the RCA more closely with industry (he aimed to 'provide courses of a thoroughly practical nature in all primary industrial fields'), and revitalized the teaching staff (he said that when he joined 'two of the five professors were alleged not to have exchanged a word for fifteen years'). His overall concern was to make the RCA a 'magnet for talent'. It was during Darwin's long period in charge—generally reckoned the RCA's golden age—that it moved to its present home, a new eight-storey building in Kensington Gore (1961). Its absolute peak of esteem perhaps came in the late 1950s and early 1960s with the generation of students who were largely responsible for launching British *Pop art, including *Hockney and Allen *Jones.

Rozanova, Olga (b Malenki, Vladimir province, 22 June [4 July] 1886; d Moscow, 8 Nov. 1918). Russian painter, designer, writer, and administrator. She was an energetic figure in the avant-garde in the most momentous period of 20th-century Russian art, but her career was cut short when she died suddenly of diphtheria at the age of 32. In an essay published in 1913 she was among the first Russians to advocate abstract art. Her painting at this time was *Futurist in style and she illustrated many Futurist books, often in collaboration with her husband Alexei Kruchenykh, a poet and critic who was one the leading theorists of the movement. By the time she illustrated his book *Universal War* (1916) her style had become purely abstract in a manner close to *Suprematism (she also experimented with other abstract styles). After the 1917 Revolution, Rozanova (who was an ardent public speaker) devoted much of her energy to the reorganization of industrial art, travelling widely throughout the country, which was in a state of chaos. Her idea of reconciling art and industry was realized in the *Constructivist movement.

Rubens, Sir Peter Paul (b Siegen, Westphalia, 28 June 1577; d Antwerp, 30 May 1640). Flemish painter, draughtsman, designer, and diplomat, the greatest and most influential figure in *Baroque art in northern Europe. He was born in Germany, the son of a scholarly lawyer from Antwerp who had left the city to escape religious persecution (he had Protestant sympathies). In 1587, soon after his father's death, the boy Rubens returned to Antwerp with his mother; he had been baptized a Calvinist in Germany, but he became a devout Catholic. From about 1590 he studied successively with three fairly undistinguished masters: Tobias *Verhaecht (a distant relative), Adam van *Noort, and Otto van *Veen. The first two could teach him no more than the local tradition, but van Veen was a man of some culture, who had spent several years in Rome, and he no doubt inspired his pupil with a desire to visit Italy. Rubens became a master in the Antwerp painters' guild in 1598, and after working with van Veen for two more years he set out for Italy in 1600.

Very little of Rubens's work survives from before this date, and his style was largely formed in Italy, where he was based until 1608. Soon after his arrival he began working for Vincenzo *Gonzaga, Duke of Mantua, visiting most of the principal art centres of Italy to make copies for the ducal collection (he also went to Spain,

1603–4, when he accompanied gifts from Vincenzo to Philip III). The most significant parts of his stay in Italy were spent in Genoa and above all Rome. In Genoa he painted some stately aristocratic portraits (*Marchesa Brigida Spinola-Doria*, 1606, NG, Washington) that inspired van *Dyck when he worked in the city, and in Rome he absorbed the lessons of the *antique, the great masters of the *Renaissance, and Annibale *Carracci, basing his dignified and powerful style on these sources, but adding a distinctive energy and warmth of his own.

On learning that his mother was seriously ill, Rubens returned to Antwerp in 1608, but she died before he arrived. Italy had become his spiritual home (he usually signed himself 'Pietro Pauolo') and he considered returning for good, but his success in Antwerp was so immediate and great that he remained there, and in spite of his extensive travels later in his career he never saw Italy again. In 1609 he was appointed court painter to the Archduke Albert and his wife the Infanta Isabella, the Spanish governors of the Netherlands (Isabella was the daughter of Philip II of Spain—see HABSBURG); although the court was in Brussels, he was allowed to remain in Antwerp. In the same year he married the 17-year-old Isabella Brant, the daughter of an eminent Antwerp lawyer. The portrait of himself and his wife that he painted to mark the union (Alte Pin., Munich) gives a wonderful picture of Rubens on the threshold of his prodigious career—handsome, vigorous, and dashingly self-confident. In the next few years he established his reputation as the pre-eminent painter in northern Europe, his first two resounding successes being the huge *triptychs of the *Raising of the Cross* and the *Descent from the Cross* (1610–11 and 1611–14, Antwerp Cathedral), which showed his mastery of *history painting in the *Grand Manner and the immense vitality of his style.

The demand for Rubens's work was extraordinary, and he was able to meet it only because he ran an extremely efficient studio. It is not known how many pupils or assistants he had, because as court painter he was exempt from registering them with the guild. The idea of his running a sort of picture factory has been exaggerated, but even a man of his seemingly inexhaustible intellectual and physical stamina (he habitually rose at 4 a.m.) could not carry out all the work involved in his massive output with his own hands. He both collaborated with established artists (Jan *Brueghel, *Jordaens, Daniel *Seghers, *Snyders, and others) and retouched pictures by pupils, the degree of his intervention

being reflected in the price. Generally his assistants (of whom van Dyck was the most illustrious) did much of the work between the initial oil sketch and the master's finishing touches. Modern taste has tended to admire these sketches and his drawings (in which his personal touch is evident in every stroke of brush, chalk, or pen) more than the large-scale works, but Rubens himself would surely have found this attitude hard to comprehend, for the sheer size and grandeur of the finished paintings gives them an extra, symphonic dimension. His capacity for collaboration and delegation was an expression of his warm and well-balanced personality as well as of his management skills; he was generous towards his fellow artists and in spite of his immense worldly success he aroused little professional jealousy.

Rubens not only painted virtually every type of subject then known, but also designed tapestries, book illustrations, and decorations for festivals, as well as giving visual directives for sculptors, metalworkers, and architects. 'My talents are such', he wrote in 1621, 'that I have never lacked courage to undertake any design, however vast in size or diversified in subject.' So huge was his output, indeed, that it is difficult to put a figure on it; the *Corpus Rubenianum*, the first comprehensive catalogue of his work using all the resources of modern scholarship, began publication in 1968 and is still incomplete (34 volumes are scheduled). His biggest commission in Flanders was for the decoration of the Jesuit church in Antwerp (a building he may also have had a hand in designing), but almost all his work there was destroyed by fire in 1718. From outside Flanders, those who sought his services included the royal families of France, England, and Spain. For Marie de *Médicis (mother of Louis XIII of France) he did a series of 25 enormous paintings on her life (1622–5, Louvre, Paris); for Charles I of England (see ROYAL COLLECTION) he painted a series of canvases representing the reign of his father James I (completed 1635) for the ceiling of the Banqueting House in London (the only one of his major decorative schemes still *in situ*); and for Philip IV of Spain he embarked in 1636 on a series of more than 100 mythological pictures for his hunting lodge, the Torre de la Parada, near Madrid (the series was incomplete when Rubens died and most of the finished paintings—executed by assistants from his *modelli*—were destroyed in 1710 when the building was sacked during the War of the Spanish Succession).

After the death of the Archduke Albert in 1621, Rubens became a trusted adviser to the Infanta

Isabella. In that year a twelve-year truce between the Spanish Netherlands (Flanders) and its northern neighbour the Dutch Republic (Holland) came to an end and Rubens was entrusted with diplomatic missions aimed at securing a lasting peace between the countries. In this he was unsuccessful, but he did play an important role in the preliminary stage of ending hostilities between Spain (Flanders's overlord) and England (Holland's ally). He visited Spain in 1628–9 (when he met *Velázquez) and England in 1629–30, and he was knighted by the kings of both countries (Charles I in 1630, Philip IV in 1631) for his part in the peace negotiations. In his diplomatic role his courtly manners and linguistic skills were put to good advantage—apart from Flemish and Italian, he knew French, German, Latin, and Spanish.

Rubens found the political work a solace following the death of his beloved wife in 1626, but after he remarried in 1630 he had a desire to 'remain home all my life', and although he stayed reluctantly involved in diplomacy until the Infanta Isabella's death in 1633, he never went abroad again. His new wife, 16 when he married her, was Hélène Fourment, daughter of a rich silk merchant and the niece of his first wife. The second marriage was as happy as the first, and Rubens's love of his family shines through many of his late paintings (*Hélène Fourment with Two of her Children*, c.1636, Louvre). In 1635 he bought a country house, the Château de Steen, between Brussels and Malines, and in his final years he developed a new passion for painting landscapes—wonderfully ripe works that led *Constable to extol 'the joyous and animated character' he impressed on 'the level, monotonous scenery of Flanders', and to declare that 'In no branch of the art is Rubens greater than in landscape.' Superb examples are in the National Gallery and the Wallace Collection, London.

In his lifetime Rubens was described as 'prince of painters and painter of princes' and at his death he was mourned not just as a supreme artist but also as one of the great men of the age. His influence in 17th-century Flanders was overwhelming, and it was spread elsewhere in Europe by his journeys abroad and by pictures exported from his workshop, and also through the numerous prints he commissioned of his work; Christoffel Jegher (see WOODCUT) and Paul Pontius (see LINE ENGRAVING) were among the outstanding printmakers he employed. In later centuries, his influence has also been immense, perhaps most noticeably in France,

where his greatest admirers included *Watteau, *Delacroix (who called him 'that Homer of painting, that father of warmth and enthusiasm'), and *Renoir. Because of the unrivalled variety of his work, artists as different in temperament as these three could respond to it with equal passion.

Rublev, Andrei (*b* ?c.1360; *d* Moscow, 1430). The most famous of Russian *icon painters. The 600th anniversary of his birth was celebrated by Soviet Russia in 1960, but the date is not firmly documented and there is little secure knowledge of his life or works. In 1405 he worked as assistant to *Theophanes in the cathedral of the Annunciation in the Kremlin at Moscow, but it has not been possible to distinguish his share there or in the cathedral of the Dormition at Vladimir, where he is also said to have painted murals. The work that stands at the centre of his oeuvre is the celebrated icon of the *Old Testament Trinity* (that is, the three angels who appeared to Abraham) in the Tretyakov Gallery, Moscow (c.1411). In its gentle, lyrical beauty this marks a move away from the hieratic *Byzantine tradition, and other icons in a similar style have been attributed to Rublev.

rubrication (Latin: *rubricare*, 'to make red'). In calligraphy and typography (particularly *illuminated manuscripts and early printed books) the use of a different colour, usually red, to emphasize initial letters, section headings, etc.

Rude, François (*b* Dijon, 4 Jan. 1784; *d* Paris, 3 Nov. 1855). French *Romantic sculptor. He was a fervent admirer of Napoleon Bonaparte, and his emotionally charged work expresses the martial spirit of the Napoleonic era more fully than that of any other sculptor. In 1812 he won the *Prix de Rome, but he was unable to take it up because of the Napoleonic Wars, and after Napoleon's final defeat in 1815 he joined *David in exile in Brussels. On his return to Paris in 1827 he became highly successful with public monuments, most notably his celebrated high *relief on the Arc de Triomphe, *Departure of the Volunteers in 1792*, popularly known as *La Marseillaise* (1833–6). None of Rude's other works matches the fire, dynamism, and heroic bravura of this glorification of the French Revolution, but he created another strikingly original work in his monument *Napoleon Awakening to Immortality* (1845–7) in the Parc Noisot at Fixin, near his native Dijon, which shows the emperor casting off his shroud. In spite of the dramatic movement of his work, it always has a solidity that reveals his classical training and his lifelong admiration for the *antique.

Rudolf II, Emperor. See HABSBURG.

Ruffo, Don Antonio. See REMBRANDT.

Ruisdael, Jacob van (*b* Haarlem, ?1628/9; *d* ?Amsterdam; *bur.* Haarlem, 14 Mar. 1682). The greatest and most versatile of all Dutch landscape painters. In the absence of any evidence about his training, it is generally assumed that he was taught by his father **Isaac**, who was a painter as well as a frame maker and picture dealer (no works by him are known to survive), or by his uncle Salomon van *Ruysdael (this distinction in spelling occurs consistently in their own signatures). Whatever form his artistic education took, Ruisdael was extremely precocious; his earliest known paintings date from 1646 and already reveal a mature and distinctive artistic personality. He was also versatile and prolific (about 700 paintings are reasonably attributed to him, together with 100 or so drawings and a dozen etchings); he painted forests, grain fields, beaches and seascapes, watermills and windmills, winter landscapes and Scandinavian torrents influenced by Allart van *Everdingen (he did not visit Scandinavia himself); he could conjure poetry from a virtually featureless patch of duneland as well as from a magnificent panoramic view. Even more than his range, however, it is the emotional force of his work that distinguishes him from his contemporaries. He moved away decisively from the 'tonal' phase of Dutch landscape represented by his uncle; in place of subtle atmospheric effects he favoured strong forms and dense colours and his brushwork is vigorous and *impasted. His emotional, subjective approach is most memorably expressed in *The Jewish Cemetery* (*c*.1660, versions in Detroit Inst. of Arts and Gemäldegalerie, Dresden), where tombstones and elegiac ruins, symbols of man's transitory and ephemeral existence, are contrasted with nature's power of renewal.

Early in his career Ruisdael seems to have travelled a fair amount in search of subjects, but he never ventured far from home. His most ambitious journey was probably made in 1650 with his friend Nicolaes *Berchem and took him just over the German border, resulting in several pictures of Bentheim Castle in Westphalia. In the most famous of these views (1653, NG, Dublin), the castle heroically crowns the top of a steep, rugged hill, transformed by Ruisdael's imagination from the mild slope it is in actuality.

In about 1656 he moved to Amsterdam, where he lived for the rest of his life (although he was buried in St Bavo's Cathedral in Haarlem).

He evidently had a fairly prosperous career, but little is known about his life and it was long thought he had died insane in the workhouse at Haarlem, a fate that is now known to have befallen his cousin and near-namesake Jacob van *Ruysdael. There is still uncertainty, however, concerning the story, reported by *Houbraken and supported by other tantalizing evidence, that Ruisdael practised as a surgeon. It seems unlikely that he could have found the time for this (he is said to have taken a medical degree at Caen in Normandy in 1676, when he was in his late forties), but other prolific Dutch painters, for example *Steen (who ran a tavern), managed to pursue two careers. Ruisdael's only documented pupil was *Hobbema, but his influence was resounding, both on his Dutch contemporaries and on artists in other countries in the following two centuries—*Gainsborough, *Constable, and the *Barbizon School for example. Examples of his work are in many public collections, the finest representation being in the National Gallery, London.

Runciman, Alexander (*b* Edinburgh, 21 Apr. 1736; *d* Edinburgh, 21 Oct. 1785) and **John** (*b* Edinburgh, 1744; *d* Naples, winter 1768/9). Scottish painters, brothers, who specialized in religious, literary, and historical subjects in a proto-*Romantic manner. John, the more gifted, died young in Italy, where both brothers had gone in 1767 (his death has been variously attributed to consumption, nervous depression, and suicide). His masterpiece, *King Lear in the Storm* (1767, NG, Edinburgh), has freshness and originality, with nothing of the staginess of most 18th-century Shakespearian pictures. Alexander's major work, the decoration (1772) of Penicuik House near Edinburgh with subjects from Ossian and Scottish history, ranked with *Barry's paintings in the Society of Arts as the most ambitious British decorative scheme of the time, but it was destroyed by fire in 1899. Some of its compositions survive in his drawings and etchings. He also painted landscapes and portraits.

Runge, Philipp Otto (*b* Wolgast, Pomerania, 23 July 1777; *d* Hamburg, 2 Dec. 1810). German painter and draughtsman. Although he made a late start to his career and died young (of consumption), he ranks second only to *Friedrich among German *Romantic artists. He studied at the Copenhagen Academy (1799–1801), then moved to Dresden, where he knew Friedrich. In

1803 he moved to Hamburg, where he spent most of the rest of his life. Runge was of a mystical, pantheistic turn of mind and in his work he tried to express notions of the harmony of the universe through symbolism of colour, form, and numbers. To this end he planned a series of four paintings called *The Times of the Day*, designed to be seen in a special building and viewed to the accompaniment of music and poetry. He painted two versions of *Morning* (1808 and 1809, Kunsthalle, Hamburg), but the others did not advance beyond drawings. Runge was also one of the best German portraitists of his period; several examples are in Hamburg. His style was rigid, sharp, and intense, at times almost *naive. In 1810 he published *Farben-Kugel* (Colour Sphere) after doing several years of research on colour, during which he corresponded with *Goethe.

Ruoppolo, Giovanni Battista (*b* Naples, 1629; *d* Naples, 1693). Neapolitan still-life painter. He specialized in pictures of flowers and food (especially fruit and seafood), depicted in an exuberant and succulent style. With *Recco he was the finest Italian still-life painter of his period. His nephew **Giuseppe Ruoppolo** (*d* 1710) painted in his style but was much less accomplished.

Rupert, Prince (*b* Prague, 17 Dec. 1619; *d* London, 29 Nov. 1682). Bohemian-born soldier and amateur artist active mainly in England. Famous as a dashing cavalry commander for his uncle Charles I in the English Civil War, he also took a serious interest in science and the arts. Most notably, he introduced *mezzotint engraving to England, having perhaps learnt the technique from its inventor Ludwig von *Siegen (Rupert was himself long credited as the inventor). He demonstrated the technique to the diarist John Evelyn, who publicized it in his book *Sculptura* (1662), and he also gave instruction to professional printmakers, notably Wallerant *Vaillant. Most of Rupert's own mezzotints are experimental in character, but the largest of them, the *Great Executioner* (1658), after *Ribera, is acknowledged as a masterpiece of printmaking.

Ruralists, Brotherhood of. See BLAKE, SIR PETER.

Rusconi, Camillo (*b* Milan, 14 July 1658; *d* Rome, 9 Dec. 1728). Italian sculptor. He settled in Rome in 1686 and became the city's outstanding sculptor, a figure comparable to his friend *Maratta in painting. The vigour and boldness of his style derive from *Bernini, but Rusconi was more restrained and classical. His most important works are four over-life-size marble statues of Apostles in S. Giovanni in Laterano (1708–18) and the tomb of Pope Gregory XIII (1715–23) in St Peter's.

Rush, William (*b* Philadelphia, 4 July 1756; *d* Philadelphia, 17 Jan. 1833). American sculptor, active in his native Philadelphia. His father was a ship's carpenter and Rush worked mainly in wood, progressing from ships' figureheads to free-standing figures, such as those of *Comedy* and *Tragedy* (1808) for the new Chestnut Street Theater, Philadelphia (now the Forrest Home for Aged Actors). His work is vigorous and naturalistic and he marks the transition from the unselfconscious folk carver to the professional artist. He was one of the prime movers in the foundation of the *Pennsylvania Academy of the Fine Arts (1805), which has many examples of his work. Thomas *Eakins, another native of Philadelphia, greatly admired Rush's work.

Rusiñol, Santiago (*b* Barcelona, 26 Feb. 1861; *d* Aranjuez, 13 June 1931). Spanish painter and writer. He worked mainly in Barcelona, but he visited Paris early in his career and was one of the main channels through which the influence of modern French painting—particularly *Symbolism—was introduced to Spain. The young *Picasso was part of his circle in Barcelona.

Ruskin, John (*b* London, 8 Feb. 1819; *d* Brantwood, nr. Coniston, Cumberland, 20 Jan. 1900). English writer, artist, social reformer, and philanthropist. He was the most important English art critic of the 19th century, with a remarkable hold over public opinion, and also a talented and prolific draughtsman and watercolourist, mainly of landscape and architectural subjects. His father was a wealthy wine merchant who liked paintings and encouraged his son (his only child) in his intellectual interests; his mother too was devoted to him, but in a repressive, puritanical way. He was educated at home and travelled a good deal in Britain and on the Continent with his parents, developing an ardent love of nature (he was deeply interested in botany and geology) as well as a feeling for art. From 1837 to 1842 he studied at Oxford University, where he won the Newdigate prize for poetry in 1839 (the following year his studies were interrupted when he had a breakdown, evidently partly caused by a frustrated passion for the daughter of one of his father's business associates). His father gave him a generous allowance, so after graduating he was able to devote himself to writing and lecturing and also could afford to buy paintings, notably works by *Turner, who was his greatest artistic hero (Ruskin first met him in 1840 and became a friend and eventually executor of his will).

Most of Ruskin's art criticism was written early in his career; after about 1855 he devoted himself more to economic and political questions. It is, however, difficult to separate his thought into different strands, as he was so concerned with the relationship between art, morality, and social justice; his lectures as the first *Slade professor of fine art at Oxford (1870–7, 1883–4), for example, were as much about sociology as art. Although he later modified his views, the key ideas in his most influential works of art criticism were sincerity and truth to nature. He thought that good art is essentially moral and that bad art is insincere and immoral. When he defended the *Pre-Raphaelites against vicious attacks in 1851, it was mainly their 'labour and fidelity' he praised, and when he dismissed the 17th-century Bolognese painters such as the *Carracci and *Domenichino as 'art-weeds' it was largely because of what he perceived as their lack of genuine feeling: 'There is no entirely sincere or great art in the 17th century.' In architecture he loved the *Gothic style and believed that the key to the beauty of medieval buildings was the delight that craftsmen took in their creation. These views were particularly influential on William *Morris and the *Arts and Crafts movement. In line with his opinions on the dignity and value of manual labour, he regarded factories as degrading places and he tried to improve the conditions in which the working class lived. Many of his social ideas, such as his advocacy of old age pensions, later became commonly accepted. By the end of his life he had disposed of all his large inheritance in philanthropic work and maintained himself on the proceeds of his writings.

Ruskin's personal life was deeply unhappy. His marriage of six years was annulled in 1854 on the grounds of non-consummation (his ex-wife married *Millais in the following year) and in middle and old age he made many young girls the objects of his unhealthy affection. He proposed to one of them, the 18-year-old Rose La Touche, in 1866, but was refused; she died mad in 1875. In 1878 he lost a famous libel case against *Whistler, whom he had accused of 'flinging a pot of paint in the public face', and just before it came to court he showed the first signs of the mental illness that made his final years wretched.

After 1889, living in isolation in the Lake District, where he was cared for by his cousin Joan Severn, Ruskin wrote nothing and rarely spoke. His house, Brantwood, overlooking Lake Coniston, is now a memorial to him.

Ruskin's literary output was enormous; the standard edition of his complete works occupies 39 volumes (1903–12). His most important books dealing specifically with art are: *Modern Painters* (5 vols., 1843–60, epilogue 1888), which began as a defence of Turner and expanded into a general survey of art; *The Seven Lamps of Architecture* (1849); and *The Stones of Venice* (3 vols., 1851–3). He is accorded a distinguished place amongst English prose writers of the 19th century, and his finest flights of rhetoric, such as his descriptions of the *Tintorettos in the Scuola di S. Rocco in Venice, are classics of their kind.

Russell, Morgan (b New York, 25 Jan. 1886; d Broomall, Pa., 29 May 1953). American painter, active mainly in Paris, a pioneer of abstract art. He was born in New York, where he studied sculpture at the *Art Students League and painting under Robert *Henri. In 1908 he settled in Paris, where he briefly attended *Matisse's art school. By 1910 he was devoting himself increasingly to painting, and in 1911 he met Stanton *Macdonald-Wright, with whom he developed theories about the analogies between colours and musical patterns. In 1913 they launched *Synchromism, one of the earliest abstract movements, and Russell's *Synchromy in Orange: To Form* (1913–14, Albright-Knox Art Gallery, Buffalo) won him considerable renown in Paris. His later work, in which he reintroduced figurative elements, was much less memorable. He lived in Paris until 1946, then returned to the USA.

Russolo, Luigi (b Portogruaro, nr. Venice, 7 May 1885; d Cerro di Laveno, Lake Maggiore, 4 Feb. 1947). Italian painter and musician. He signed both the *Futurist painters' manifestos in 1910, but he is remembered mainly as 'the most spectacular innovator among the Futurist musicians' (*New Grove Dictionary of Music and Musicians*, 1980). In 1913 he published a manifesto, of *L'arte dei rumari* (*The Art of Noises*, expanded in book form in 1916), and later in the same year he demonstrated the first of a series of *intonarumori* ('noise-makers'), which produced a startling range of sounds. In 1913–14, he gave noise concerts in Milan (causing a riot), Genoa, and London. Others followed after the First World War. Several leading composers, notably Ravel and Stravinsky, thought they opened up interesting possibilities, and Russolo has been regarded as a pioneer of today's electronic music. Unfortunately his compositions and machines have been destroyed. As a painter Russolo made rather crude use of the Futurist device of 'lines of force' in his early work; after the war his style became more naturalistic.

Rustici, Giovanni Francesco. See LEONARDO DA VINCI.

Ruthwell Cross. See CELTIC ART.

Rutter, Frank. See ALLIED ARTISTS' ASSOCIATION.

Ruysch, Rachel (*b* Amsterdam, 1664; *d* Amsterdam, 12 Aug. 1750). Dutch still-life painter, with van *Huysum the most celebrated flower painter of the first half of the 18th century. The daughter of a botanist and the pupil of Willem van *Aelst, she worked mainly in Amsterdam, but also in The Hague (1701–8) and Düsseldorf, where from 1708 to 1716 she was court painter to the elector palatine. Her richly devised bouquets are painted in delicate colours with meticulous detail, and are worthy of the finest tradition of Dutch flower painting. She continued to use the dark backgrounds characteristic of van Aelst and the older generation long after van Huysum and other contemporaries had gone over to light backgrounds.

Ruysdael, Salomon van (*b* Naarden, nr. Amsterdam, ?1600/3; *bur.* Haarlem, 3 Nov. 1670). Dutch landscape painter, active in Haarlem, where he became a member of the painters' guild in 1623. His earliest pictures show the influence of Esaias van de *Velde and in the 1630s he was so close in style to Jan van *Goyen that it is sometimes difficult to differentiate their hands. Both of them excelled in atmospheric, virtually monochromatic river scenes and they are the leading masters of this type of picture. In the 1640s Ruysdael's landscapes became somewhat more solid and colourful, perhaps reflecting influence from his nephew Jacob van *Ruisdael. Late in his career he occasionally painted still-lifes. He was prolific and many galleries have examples of his work. His son **Jacob van Ruysdael** (*c.*1630–81) was also a landscape painter. An example of his rare work is *A Waterfall by a Cottage* (NG, London), which shows he worked in a style similar to that of his illustrious cousin and near-namesake, with whom he has sometimes been confused in documentary references.

Ryder, Albert Pinkham (*b* New Bedford, Mass., 19 Mar. 1847; *d* Elmhurst, NY, 28 Mar. 1917). American painter of imaginative subjects.

He lived and worked most of his life as a solitary and dreamer in New York, and his methods and approach were largely self-taught. His pictures reflect a rich inner life, with a haunting love of the sea (his birthplace, New Bedford, is a fishing port) and a constant search to express the ineffable: 'Have you ever seen an inch worm crawl up a leaf or twig, and then clinging to the very end, revolve in the air, feeling for something to reach something? That's like me. I am trying to find something out there beyond the place on which I have a footing.' This imaginative quality and eloquent expression of the mysteriousness of things is expressed typically through boldly simplified forms and eerie lighting (*The Race Track* or *Death on a Pale Horse*, Cleveland Mus. of Art). In spite of his self-imposed isolation Ryder's works became well known in his lifetime and he has been much imitated and faked. His own paintings have often deteriorated because of unorthodox technical procedures. He was greatly admired by Jackson *Pollock, and the critical and popular favour Ryder enjoyed in the 1950s and 1960s was linked to the success of *Abstract Expressionism.

Ryland, William. See STIPPLE ENGRAVING.

Rysbrack, Michael (*bapt.* Antwerp, 27 June 1694; *d* London, 8 Jan. 1770). Flemish-born sculptor (a member of an Antwerp family of artists), who settled in England about 1720. He soon achieved success and for most of the 1720s and 1730s he was the leading sculptor in the country. His best-known work is perhaps the monument to Sir Isaac Newton (designed by William *Kent) in Westminster Abbey (1731), with its eloquent reclining figure of the great scientist, and his most prestigious commission (won in preference to *Scheemakers) is the monument to William III in Queen Square, Bristol (1733–5), regarded as the finest equestrian statue made in Britain (and perhaps in western Europe) in the 18th century. However, from about 1740 (the year of Scheemakers's acclaimed Shakespeare Monument in Westminster Abbey), Rysbrack began to lose ground to Scheemakers and also to *Roubiliac, although he remained busy and prosperous. He was a versatile and prolific artist, hard-working and widely admired. His output included tombs, statues, architectural elements such as chimney-pieces, and portraits; he was largely responsible for establishing two distinct types of portrait busts in Britain—the classical presentation of the sitter *all'antica* (in the manner of a Roman general or senator) and the informal depiction of the sitter *en négligé* (in contemporary indoor costume). His style was vigorous and dignified, less sombre than that of Scheemakers. He did not quite match the brilliant vivacity that characterizes Roubiliac's work, but he rivalled him in beauty of craftsmanship, in terracotta as well as marble.

Among the other members of his family, the best known is his brother **Pieter Andreas Rysbrack** (c.1684–1748), who settled with him in England. He was a painter, his subjects including still-lifes and views of country houses.

Rysselberghe, Théo van (b Ghent, 23 Nov. 1862; d Saint-Clair, Normandy, 13 Dec. 1926). Belgian painter, designer, and sculptor. In 1883 he became a founder member of the avant-garde group Les *Vingt; it encouraged an interest in innovative art largely through contact with France, and van Rysselberghe, who met *Seurat in Paris, became the leading Belgian exponent of *Neo-Impressionism. He moved to Paris in 1898 and became friendly with the *Symbolist circle of writers and artists; his painting A Reading (1903, Mus. voor Schone Kunsten, Ghent) shows several leading literary figures including André Gide and Maurice Maeterlinck. In 1910 he settled in Provence, where he abandoned Neo-Impressionism for a broader style of painting. His work is well represented in the Rijksmuseum Kröller-Müller at Otterlo. Apart from paintings, his output included a variety of design work, including furniture, jewellery, and stained glass, much of it for Siegfried Bing's Paris gallery L'Art Nouveau, the establishment that gave the *Art Nouveau style its name. Late in his career he also took up portrait sculpture. His brother **Octave van Rysselberghe** (1855–1929) was one of Belgium's leading Art Nouveau architects.

S

Saatchi, Charles (*b* Baghdad, 9 June 1943). Iraqi-born British businessman and art collector. In 1970 he was co-founder with his brother Maurice of Saatchi & Saatchi, which became the world's largest advertising agency. He has devoted much of his enormous wealth to buying contemporary art on a huge (almost industrial) scale, and in 1985 his collection was opened to the public in a new gallery (converted from a warehouse) in St John's Wood, north London. In 2003 it transferred to a more central location in County Hall, overlooking the Thames. Saatchi's patronage has been welcomed by many (not least the artists who have benefited from it), but others have been critical of the way in which his bulk buying has given him such power in the art market. He helped to create the boom in *Neo-Expressionism and *Neo-Geo, for example, and he has been the chief patron of the *Young British Artists.

Sacchi, Andrea (*b* ?Nettuno or Rome, *c.*30 Nov. (St Andrew's day) 1599 or 1600; *d* Rome, 21 June 1661). Italian painter, one of the leading artists of his day in Rome. He was a pupil of *Albani, but he was inspired chiefly by *Raphael, and with the sculptors *Algardi and *Duquesnoy he became the chief exponent of the style sometimes called 'High *Baroque Classicism'. In the mid-1630s, defending the *classical principles of order and moderation, Sacchi engaged in a debate in the Accademia di S. Luca with Pietro da *Cortona on the question of whether history paintings should have few figures (as Sacchi maintained) or many (Cortona). Sacchi's ideas were more immediately influential, but his ponderous ceiling fresco of *Divine Wisdom* (1629–33) in the Palazzo Barberini in Rome is completely outshone by Cortona's exhilarating ceiling of the Gran Salone in the same building. Sacchi, indeed, was at his best on a much smaller scale—in altarpieces such as the grave, introspective *Vision of St Romuald* (1631, Pinacoteca, Vatican), in portraits, and not least in his drawings. His most important pupil was *Maratta. Sacchi also worked as an architect, designing the chapel of St Catherine of Siena (1637–9) in the sacristy of S. Maria sopra Minerva, a work of refined classical purity.

sacra conversazione (Italian: 'holy conversation'). A representation of the Virgin and Child with saints in which all the sacred personages are disposed in a single pictorial space rather than in the separate compartments of a *polyptych; usually the figures commune silently, rather than actually conversing. The type originated in Italy in the first half of the 15th century: Filippo *Lippi's Barbadori Altarpiece (begun 1437, Louvre, Paris) is perhaps the first dated example.

sacramentary. See MISSAL.

Saenredam, Pieter (*b* Assendelft, nr. Haarlem, 9 June 1597; *bur.* Haarlem, 31 May 1665). Dutch painter of architectural subjects, particularly church interiors, active mainly in Haarlem. He was the son of an engraver and map-maker, **Jan Saenredam** (*c.*1565–1607), and a friend of the great architect Jacob van *Campen, who made a drawing of Saenredam (1628, BM, London), which shows that he was dwarflike and evidently hunchbacked. Saenredam was the first painter to concentrate on accurate depictions of real buildings rather than the fanciful inventions of the *Mannerist tradition. His pictures were based on painstaking drawings, but they never seem pedantic or niggling and are remarkable for their delicacy of colour and airy grace. The cathedral of St Bavo (where he is buried) and the Grote Kerk in Haarlem were favourite subjects, but he also travelled to other Dutch towns to make drawings, and Utrecht is represented in several of his paintings. He also made a few views of Rome based on drawings in a sketchbook by Maerten van *Heemskerck (now in the Kupferstichkabinett, Berlin) that he (or someone in his circle) owned. His work had great influence on Dutch painting.

Saftleven, Cornelis (*b* Gorinchem, *c.*1607; *d* Rotterdam, 1 June 1681) and **Herman II** (*b* Rotterdam, 1609; *d* Utrecht, 5 Jan. 1685).

Dutch painters, brothers, the best-known members of a family of artists. Cornelis, who was active mainly in Rotterdam, was highly versatile, his output including landscapes, portraits, religious and mythological subjects, peasant scenes in the tradition of *Brouwer and *Teniers, images of hell, and allegorical and satirical pictures, sometimes with animals dressed as humans. Herman, who was active mainly in Utrecht, painted religious subjects but is best known for his imaginary river views, done in a distinctive misty blue tonality (*View on the Rhine*, 1656, Dulwich Picture Gal., London).

Sage, Kay (*b* Albany, NY, 25 June 1898; *d* Woodbury, Conn., 25 Jan. 1963). American *Surrealist painter, mainly self-taught as an artist. The daughter of wealthy parents, she spent much of her life in Italy (she was married to an Italian prince, 1925–35), and Giorgio de *Chirico was an early influence on her work. In 1937 she moved to Paris, where she met Yves *Tanguy in 1939. He followed her to the USA in 1940 and they married later that year. From the time of her return to America, architectural motifs became prominent in her work—strange steel structures depicted in sharp detail against vistas of unreal space—and her pictures also included draperies from which faces and figures sometimes mistily emerged (*Tomorrow is Never*, 1955, Met. Mus., New York). Sage also made mixed-media constructions and wrote poetry. Tanguy's sudden death in 1955 cast a shadow over her last years and she committed suicide.

Saint-Aubin, Gabriel-Jacques de (*b* Paris, 14 Apr. 1724; *d* Paris, 14 Feb. 1780). French draughtsman, etcher, and painter, the best-known member of a family of artists. He drew incessantly (*Greuze spoke of his 'priapism of draughtsmanship') and his work forms a lively record of various aspects of the Paris of his time. Throughout his career he regularly went to art sales (as well as the *Salon) and he embellished his copies of the catalogues with small drawings of the works of art and of the passing scene. A number of these catalogues survive (mainly in the Bibliothèque Nationale, Paris) and they form a valuable resource for the art historian. Saint-Aubin's relatively rare paintings are as spirited as his drawings (*A Street Show in Paris*, 1760, NG, London). Among the other members of the family was his brother **Augustin** (1736–1807); he was a draughtsman of considerable charm but is best known for his large output of engravings after *Boucher, *Fragonard, and others.

Saint-Gaudens, Augustus (*b* Dublin, 1 Mar. 1848; *d* Cornish, NH, 3 Aug. 1907). The leading American sculptor of his period. His parents (a French father and an Irish mother) settled in America when he was a baby. He began his career as a *cameo cutter in New York, then studied for three years in Paris (1867–70) and three in Rome (1870–3), returning to America in 1874. His first important commission was the Admiral Farragut Monument (1878–81) in Madison Square Park, New York, and following its successful reception he quickly achieved a leading reputation among American sculptors and retained this throughout his life. Saint-Gaudens had great energy and he produced a large amount of work in spite of the high standards of craftsmanship he set himself. His preferred material was bronze and he excelled particularly at memorials. Although his style is generally warmly naturalistic, his most celebrated work, the Adams Memorial (1886–91) in Rock Creek Cemetery, Washington, is a powerful allegorical figure. It is a monument to a wife of a friend of Saint-Gaudens who had committed suicide, and the mysterious female figure, swathed in magnificent voluminous draperies, has been interpreted as 'Grief', although the sculptor himself saw the elegiac work as embodying 'the Peace of God'. Saint-Gaudens was a highly important figure in the development of American sculpture; he turned the tide against *Neoclassicism and made Paris, rather than Rome, the artistic mecca of his countrymen. From 1885 he spent his summers at Cornish, New Hampshire, and settled there in 1900; his studio was declared a national historic site in 1964. Casts of most of his works can be seen there.

St Ives School. A loosely structured group of artists, flourishing particularly from the late 1940s to the early 1960s, who concentrated their activities in the Cornish fishing port of St Ives. Like *Newlyn, St Ives had been popular with artists long before this (for example, *Sickert and *Whistler painted there together in the winter of 1883–4), but it did not become of more than local importance in painting and sculpture until Barbara *Hepworth and Ben *Nicholson moved there in 1939, two weeks before the outbreak of the Second World War. They were anxious that their children should be safely outside London, and their friend Adrian *Stokes, who lived at Carbis Bay (virtually a suburb of St Ives), invited the family to stay with him. Hepworth lived in St Ives for the rest of her life (her studio is now a museum of her work) and Nicholson (who had discovered Alfred *Wallis on a day-trip to St Ives in 1928) lived there until 1958. They formed the nucleus of a group of avant-garde artists who made the town an internationally recognized centre of abstract art, and it is to these artists that the term 'St Ives School' is usually applied, even though many of them had little in common stylistically, apart from an interest in portraying the local landscape in abstract terms. The one with the greatest international prestige was Naum *Gabo, who lived in St Ives from 1939 to 1946. After the war a number of abstract painters settled in or near the town or made regular visits. The residents included Terry *Frost and Patrick *Heron; the visitors included Roger *Hilton (who eventually settled in Cornwall in 1965), Adrian *Heath, and Victor *Pasmore. Peter Lanyon (1918–64) was the only notable abstract artist to be born in St Ives. The heyday of the St Ives School was over by the mid-1960s, but the town continued to be an artistic centre. In 1993 the *Tate Gallery opened a branch museum there, housing changing displays of the work of 20th-century artists associated with the town. The building includes a stained-glass window commissioned from Patrick Heron.

St John's Wood Clique. A loose association of British painters, active in the 1860s and 1870s. Most of the members lived in the St John's Wood area of north London, which was then a fashionable place of residence for artists. They included Philip Hermogenes Calderon (1833–98), Val Prinsep (see PRE-RAPHAELITE BROTHERHOOD), George Adolphus Storey (1834–1919), Fred *Walker, and W. F. *Yeames; Storey's autobiography, *Sketches from Memory* (1899), is the principal source of information on the group. Although several of the members worked in a similar vein, painting sentimental genre scenes in historical settings, they were united mainly by social rather than artistic aims, and they were noted for their high spirits and love of practical jokes. The St John's Wood Clique is to be distinguished from an earlier group of British painters known as The *Clique.

St Martin's Lane Academy. The name of two successive organizations in St Martin's Lane, London, that were important training grounds for English artists in the half-century before the *Royal Academy was established in 1768. They were founded in 1720 and 1735 respectively and each was a drawing and painting class rather than a professional institution. The first St Martin's Lane Academy grew out of another

academy (London's first) established in 1711 in Great Queen Street, of which *Kneller was the head. *Thornhill replaced Kneller in 1716, and in 1720, when Thornhill himself was deposed by the French-born Louis Chéron (1660–1725) and John *Vanderbank, the academy moved to St Martin's Lane. It became defunct after a few years, but *Hogarth reconstituted it in 1735 and it remained active until his death in 1764. He described the room in which it met as 'big enough for a naked figure to be drawn after by thirty or forty people'.

St Martin's School of Art, London. Art college founded in 1854 in Shelton Street, London, near the church of St-Martin-in-the-Fields, which initially provided sponsorship. It became independent of the church in 1859. In 1913 it moved to Charing Cross Road, which is still the site of one of its principal buildings (it also occupies premises nearby in Southampton Row, Long Acre, and elsewhere). St Martin's developed into one of the largest art schools in the country, and in the 1960s it became famous for its sculpture department, where Anthony *Caro was a highly influential teacher, encouraging a generation of artists to work with welded metal. In 1989 St Martin's amalgamated with the Central School of Art and Design (founded in 1896 as the Central School of Arts and Crafts) to form the Central St Martin's College of Art and Design. This is one of five colleges that make up the London Institute, the others being Camberwell College of Arts (formerly Camberwell School of Art and Crafts), Chelsea College of Art and Design (formerly Chelsea School of Art), the London College of Fashion, and the London College of Printing and Distributive Trades (formerly London College of Printing and Graphic Art). Together, the five colleges offer Europe's largest provision for art and design education.

Saint Phalle, Niki de (b Neuilly-sur-Seine, 29 Oct. 1930; d La Jolla, Calif., 21 May 2002). French sculptor, graphic artist, and film-maker, one of the great entertainers of modern art. In 1952 she started painting without formal artistic training and she first came to public prominence in 1960 with 'rifle-shot' paintings that incorporated containers of paint intended to be burst and spattered when shot with a pistol. After she separated from her husband in 1960 she lived with Jean *Tinguely, with whom she collaborated on numerous projects, notably the enormous sculpture *Hon* (Swedish for 'she') erected at the Moderna Museet, Stockholm, in 1963 (destroyed). It was in the form of a reclining woman (more than 25 m (80 ft) long) whose interior was a giant *'environment' reminiscent of a funfair: visitors entered through the vagina. The attractions inside included a milk bar in the breasts and a cinema showing Greta Garbo movies. Externally the figure was gaudily painted in a manner similar to that of her series of *Nanas*—grotesque fat ladies. Her other works included *happenings, films, and a huge sculpture garden at Garavicchio in Italy (begun 1979). Other projects from her later years included a touching book on AIDS addressed to her son (*AIDS: You Can't Catch it Holding Hands*, 1987) and a giant figure of the Loch Ness Monster, made for an exhibition of her work in Glasgow in 1992.

Salle, David. See NEO-EXPRESSIONISM.

Sallinen, Tyko (*b* Nurmes, 14 Mar. 1879; *d* Helsinki, 18 Sept. 1955). The outstanding Finnish *Expressionist painter. He was the son of a tailor who belonged to a strict fundamentalist religious sect (the Hihhulit), and the unhappy background of his early years later formed the basis for some of his paintings. After spending several years as an itinerant jobbing tailor in Sweden, he studied art in Helsinki and in 1909 and 1914 visited Paris, where he was influenced by avant-garde French painting, particularly *Fauvism. Its influence can be seen in what is probably his most famous picture, *Washerwomen* (1911, Ateneum, Helsinki), a work that caused an outcry because of its bold colours and very rough handling. Sallinen's favourite subjects were scenes of Finnish peasant life such as this and also views of the harsh Karelian landscape. He was the leading figure of the *November Group and became regarded as the nationalist Finnish painter *par excellence*.

Salmon, André. See MODIGLIANI.

Salon. France's official art exhibition, first held in 1667 and originally limited to members of the Académie Royale de Peinture et de Sculpture (see ACADEMY). The name derives from the fact that from 1737 the exhibitions were held in the Salon Carré in the *Louvre (various other venues had previously been used). For many years their frequency was irregular (though with stretches when they were held annually or biennially); from 1831 they were mainly annual. The jury system of selection was introduced in 1748. As these were the only public exhibitions in Paris, conservative academic art gained a stranglehold on publicity; dissatisfaction with this situation led to the *Salon des Refusés in

1863. In 1881 the École des *Beaux-Arts relinquished control of the Salon and a group of artists organized the Société des Artistes Français to take responsibility for the show with a jury elected from each previous year's exhibitors. It still remained hostile to avant-garde art, and from this time a number of competing exhibitions were established, undermining what prestige the Salon still retained. The *Salon des Indépendants, for example, appeared in 1884, and the *Salon d'Automne in 1903.

Salon d'Automne. Annual exhibition founded in Paris in 1903 as a more progressive alternative to the official *Salon and other current exhibiting venues, including the *Salon des Indépendants; it was held in the autumn (October or November), so as not to clash with these other shows, which took place mainly in spring and summer. The early Salons d'Automne played an important role in establishing the reputations of *Cézanne and *Gauguin. There was a small Gauguin exhibition in 1903 (the inaugural show) and a major retrospective in 1906; Cézanne was strongly represented in 1905 and was given a memorial exhibition in 1907. However, the Salon d'Automne is famous above all for the sensational launch of *Fauvism at the 1905 exhibition.

Salon de la Rose + Croix. Art exhibition held annually in Paris from 1892 to 1897. It was organized by the Rosicrucians, an esoteric brotherhood (allegedly founded in the 15th century by one Christian Rosenkreuz) that in the late 19th century had close connections with the *Symbolist movement. The order's symbol, reflecting the name, was a rose and cross combined. Joséphin Péladan (1859–1918), a man of letters who called himself Sâr (i.e. High Priest) Péladan, founded a lodge of the brotherhood in France and this organized the exhibitions. They became a focal point of Symbolism, and the catalogue to the first exhibition said its objects were 'to destroy *Realism and to bring art closer to Catholic ideas, to mysticism, to legend, myth, allegory, and dreams'.

Salon des Indépendants. Annual exhibition held in Paris by the Société des Artistes Indépendants, an association formed in 1884 by *Seurat and other artists in opposition to the official *Salon. There was no selection committee and anyone could exhibit on payment of a fee. This meant that many interesting avant-garde works were shown, but also that they ran the risk of being swamped by a sea of mediocrity. It became the main showcase for the *Post-Impressionists (Henri *Rousseau was also a regular exhibitor) and was a major art event in Paris up to the First World War. By then, however, it had been challenged by the smaller but more discriminating *Salon d'Automne.

Salon des Refusés. Exhibition held in Paris in 1863 to show work that had been refused by the selection committee of the official *Salon. In that year there were especially strong protests from artists whose work had been rejected, so the Emperor Napoleon III, 'wishing to let the public judge the legitimacy of these complaints', ordered this special exhibition. It drew huge crowds, who came mainly to mock, and *Manet's *Déjeuner sur l'herbe* was subjected to particular ridicule. Other major artists represented included *Cézanne, Camille *Pissarro, and *Whistler. In spite of the unfavourable reaction to the works shown there, the Salon des Refusés was of great significance in undermining the prestige of the official Salon. After this, artists began to organize their own exhibitions (notably the *Impressionists in 1874) and art dealers became of increasing importance. The Salon des Refusés is thus regarded as a turning point in the history of art and 1863 has been described as 'the most convenient date from which to begin any history of modern painting' (Alan Bowness, *Modern European Art*, 1972).

Salviati, Francesco (Francesco de' Rossi) (*b* Florence, 1510; *d* Rome, 11 Nov. 1563). Florentine *Mannerist painter, a pupil of Andrea del *Sarto. In about 1530 he moved to Rome and he adopted the name by which he is now known from his main patron there, Cardinal Giovanni Salviati; he lodged in the cardinal's palace and it was for him that he painted the work that established his reputation—the fresco of the *Visitation* (1538) in S. Giovanni Decollato. In 1539 he moved to Venice, but he had left the city by 1541; the rest of his career was mainly divided between Rome and Florence, but he also worked in France in 1556-7. Salviati was one of the leading fresco decorators of his day, specializing in learned and elaborate multi-figure compositions, typically Mannerist in their artificiality and abstruseness, and similar in style to those of his friend *Vasari. He was an artist of higher calibre than Vasari, but he had a difficult temperament and many of his projects were disrupted when he alienated patrons or fellow artists. His finest works are perhaps the frescos on the story of the Roman general Furius Camillus (1543-5) in the Sala dell'Udienza of the Palazzo Vecchio, Florence, intended as an allegory of Cosimo de' *Medici's reign. Salviati's work also included portraits (Florentine in their direct characterization but north Italian in their richness of colour), altarpieces, and designs for tapestry. **Giuseppe Salviati** (*c.*1520-*c.*1575) was his pupil. He was born Giuseppe Porta, but borrowed his master's borrowed name. He worked mainly in Venice, painting numerous altarpieces and also decorations for civic buildings.

Samaras, Lucas (*b* Kastoria, 14 Sept. 1936). Greek-born sculptor and experimental artist who settled in the USA in 1948 and became an American citizen in 1955. His work has been extremely varied in scale, medium, and approach. In 1959 he took part in Kaprow's first *happening and his own work of this time included figures made from rags dipped in plaster and pastels combining *Surrealist fantasy with *Pop art imagery. During the 1960s he worked a good deal with *assemblages, creating bizarre and sometimes sinister objects studded with nails and pins. He also experimented with light and reflection, notably in his *Mirrored Room* (1966), an *environment with mirrors in which the spectator was reflected endlessly. Perhaps his best-known works are his 'Autopolaroids'— photographs of the most intimate parts of his own body that he began making in 1970 and which brought him considerable notoriety.

Sambin, Hugues (*b* Gray, nr. Dijon, *c.*1520; *d* Dijon, 1601/2). French architect, woodcarver, and designer, active mainly in Dijon. He was one of the leading French provincial artists of his time, working in a lively *Mannerist style, seen in his buildings and elaborately carved furniture. His vivid imagination comes out also in his book of engravings, *Œuvre de la diversité des termes, dont on use en architecture* (1572), which contains 36 engraved plates of terms (see HERM)—exuberantly rich designs involving all manner of motifs, including flowers, fruit, *putti, and satyrs. The book seems to have been a popular source for local carvers.

Sánchez Coello, Alonso (*b* Benifaió, nr. Valencia, ?1531/2; *d* Madrid, 8 Aug. 1588). Spanish painter of Portuguese parentage, principally a portraitist. He studied under Anthonis *Mor in Flanders in the early 1550s and from 1559 worked at the court of Philip II of Spain (see HABSBURG), becoming a personal favourite of the king, who was godfather to his two daughters. His dignified and sober style was strongly influenced by

Mor, but was more sensuous, showing his admiration for *Titian, and he is regarded as the founder of the great tradition of Spanish formal portraiture. He also painted religious works, but these are much less distinguished.

Sánchez Cotán, Juan (*bapt.* Orgaz, 25 June 1560; *d* Granada, 8 Sept. 1627). Spanish painter. He was a still-life painter in Toledo until 1603, when he retired from secular life to become a lay brother at the Carthusian monastery in Granada. The religious works he painted after this date are unexceptional, but as a still-life artist he ranks with the great names of European painting. Characteristically he depicts a few simple fruits or vegetables, arranged on a ledge or shelf with an almost geometric clarity and standing out against a dark background (*Quince, Cabbage, Melon, Cucumber, c.*1600, San Diego Mus. of Art). Each form is scrutinized with such intensity that the pictures take on a mystical quality, conveying a feeling of wonder and humility in front of the humblest items in God's creation. Sánchez Cotán's austere style had considerable influence on Spanish painting, notably on *Zurbarán.

sandarac. A soft *resin used in the preparation of *varnishes. It becomes darker and redder with age, so other resins have largely replaced it.

Sandby, Paul (*bapt.* Nottingham, 12 Jan. 1731; *d* London, 7 Nov. 1809). English topographical watercolourist and printmaker. Like his brother **Thomas** (*bapt.* Nottingham, 8 Dec. 1721; *d* Windsor, 25 June 1798) before him, he trained as a military draughtsman at the Tower of London. Both brothers saw service in Scotland, Thomas during the 1745–6 Jacobite rebellion, and Paul after it, when he worked on a survey of the Highlands as part of the government campaign to subdue the area. In about 1752 Paul returned to London, where he lived for a time with his brother. He also spent time with him at Windsor Great Park, where Thomas had held the position of deputy ranger since 1746 (they produced many views of Windsor and its environs, and the Royal Library at Windsor Castle has an outstanding Sandby collection). Thomas also worked as an architect and landscape gardener, his most important project at Windsor being the creation of Virginia Water, the largest artificial lake in the country (he earned the unfortunate nickname 'Tommy Sandbag' after a dam he constructed burst in a storm in 1768). The brothers have much in common as watercolourists, but Paul was the better artist and also more versatile, his output including lively figure compositions as well as an extensive range of landscape subjects. In his later work he often used *body-colour (he also sometimes painted in oils) and he was the first professional artist in England to publish *aquatints (1775). *Gainsborough singled him out as the only contemporary English landscape artist who painted 'real views from nature' instead of artificial *Picturesque compositions and he helped to win prestige for the medium of watercolour. Both brothers were founder members of the *Royal Academy in 1768 and Thomas was its first professor of architecture.

Sandrart, Joachim von (*b* Frankfurt, 12 May 1606; *d* Nuremberg, 14 Oct. 1688). German painter and writer on art. He travelled widely and was the most highly regarded German artist of his day but he is now remembered almost exclusively for his treatise *Teutsche Academie der Edlen Bau-, Bild- und Mahlerey-Künste* (German Academy of the Noble Arts of Architecture, Sculpture and Painting), published in Nuremberg in 1675–9 (a Latin edition followed in 1683). This treatise, organized into three main parts, is a sourcebook of major importance. The first part is an introduction to the arts of architecture, painting, and sculpture put together largely from material taken from earlier sources such as *Vasari and van *Mander. The second part, consisting of biographies of artists, likewise contains much material borrowed from previous writers but also much that is original, in particular about German artists and on contemporary artists whom the author knew personally (including *Claude and *Poussin). The third part contains information about art collections and a study of *iconography; remarkably Sandrart also included in his book a chapter on Far Eastern art. Sandrart was the first director (1662) of the Academy at Nuremberg (the earliest such in Germany). The immense prestige he enjoyed is reflected in his grand self-portrait (Historisches Museum, Frankfurt).

sanguine. A dark red colour; the word is often particularly applied to *chalk of this colour.

Sano di Pietro (Ansano di Pietro di Mencio) (*bapt.* Siena, 2 Dec. 1405; *d* Siena, 1481). Sienese painter. He ran a very busy workshop, producing altarpieces and devotional pictures, a large number of which survive. The best are of high quality, but he made extensive use of assistants and his output is repetitive and uneven. His style was strongly influenced by *Sassetta, who probably taught him.

Sansovino, Andrea (b Monte San Savino, nr. Arezzo, c.1467/70; d Monte San Savino, Mar./Apr. 1529). Italian sculptor and architect, named after his birthplace. He called himself a Florentine, but although much of his sculpture is in Florence, his fame rests on what he did elsewhere, notably in Rome. His major works there include the companion tombs of Cardinal Ascanio Sforza and Cardinal Girolamo Basso della Rovere (1505–9, S. Maria del Popolo) and the group of the *Virgin and Child with St Anne* (1512, S. Agostino), which displays classical dignity and grace combined with human tenderness. Sansovino spent much of the period 1513–27 in Loreto in charge of the sculpture (and for part of the time the architecture also) of the Shrine of the Holy House, originally designed by *Bramante. In the 1490s he twice visited Portugal, but no work that is certainly by him survives there. Jacopo *Sansovino was his main pupil.

Sansovino, Jacopo (Jacopo Tatti) (*bapt.* Florence, 2 July 1486; d Venice, 27 Nov. 1570). Florentine sculptor and architect, active mainly in Venice. He trained under Andrea *Sansovino, whose name he adopted as a sign of his admiration. In 1505/6 he followed Andrea to Rome, where he moved in the circle of *Bramante and *Raphael and worked on the restoration of ancient sculpture. From c.1510 to 1518 he was again in Florence, where he shared a studio with Andrea del *Sarto, and he then returned to Rome until the Sack of 1527, when he moved to Venice. There he was appointed state architect (1529), formed a close friendship with *Titian, and became a dominant figure in the art establishment. Sansovino played a major role in introducing the High *Renaissance style to Venice in both architecture and sculpture, and his sculptures are often important decorative elements of his buildings. His most celebrated work, one of Venice's most familiar sights, is the glorious Library of S. Marco (begun 1537). As a sculptor he is best known for the colossal marble figures of Mars and Neptune (1554–66) in the courtyard of the Doges' Palace, although the carving was done by assistants. Sansovino's sculptural style was firmly rooted in his study of antiquity, but it was in no way academic and possessed great vitality. He studied assiduously from the life as well as from the *antique, and legend has it that the model for his marble *Bacchus* (1511–12, Bargello, Florence) went mad through being made to pose for hours on end with his arm

raised and one day was found in this position standing naked on top of a chimney.

Sansovino's son **Francesco** (1521–83) was a scholar of diversified interests. His *Venetia città nobilissima* (Venice, Most Noble City), published in 1581, is an important sourcebook—the first attempt to give a systematic account of a city's artistic heritage.

Santayana, George (b Madrid, 16 Dec. 1863; d Rome, 26 Sept. 1952). Spanish-American philosopher and man of letters. He spent most of his life in Europe and always kept his Spanish nationality, but he was educated in the USA, wrote in English, and is generally considered American by adoption. His literary output included a novel, an autobiography, poetry, and literary criticism, as well as philosophical works. In these he avoided technical terms and he was admired for his unpedantic style. His ideas on art were part of an overall theory of values embracing morals and rational living, although as he became more withdrawn from the world (he spent his final years in a convent), his views became more morally detached. His best-known book is *The Theory of Beauty* (1896), in which he defined beauty as 'pleasure objectified' and argued that the justification of art is that it adds to human happiness. Some of the analogies between the visual arts and music that he expressed here looked forward to *abstract art.

Sant'Elia, Antonio. See FUTURISM.

Santerre, Jean-Baptiste (b Magny-en-Vexin, nr. Paris, 23 Mar. 1658; d Paris, 21 Nov. 1717). French painter. He was mainly a portrait painter, especially of women, but he is now known chiefly for his *Susanna at the Bath* (1704, Louvre, Paris), a graceful nude that foreshadows the work of *Boucher and *Fragonard. He caused mild scandal with another religious work, the *Ecstasy of St Teresa* (1710), which was commissioned for the chapel of the chateau of Versailles (*in situ*) and was considered by some observers to be too erotic for the context. Late in life he is said to have destroyed certain nude drawings that he considered indecent.

Santi, Giovanni (b ?Colbordola, nr. Urbino, ?c.1440; d Urbino, 1 Aug. 1494). Italian painter and writer, the father of *Raphael, active mainly in Urbino, where he worked for the court. He was 'a mediocre painter but an intelligent man' (*Vasari) and no doubt gave his illustrious son his introduction to humanist culture. Santi is now remembered less for his paintings than for a long rhymed chronicle about Federico da

*Montefeltro, Duke of Urbino, which he wrote in 1484–7 and presented to the young Guido-baldo da Montefeltro in about 1492. This work is undistinguished as literature, but it contains a good deal of useful information about court life, Federico's military campaigns, and artistic matters. Santi's house in Urbino is now a museum—the Casa di Raffaello. It contains a small fresco of the *Virgin and Child* that some authorities consider to be Santi's portrayal of Raphael and his mother, and others claim as a very early work by Raphael himself.

Santvoort, Dirck (*b* Amsterdam, *c*.1611; *bur.* Amsterdam, 9 Mar. 1680). Dutch portrait painter, great-grandson of Pieter *Aertsen. He worked in an old-fashioned style, but his rather naive-looking figures often have great charm, particularly his portraits of children (a good example is in the National Gallery, London), and his career was highly successful. By the 1640s he was a wealthy man and seems to have retired from practice, although he remained active in the Amsterdam painters' guild, of which he was head in 1658. He had two painter brothers, **Abraham** (*c*.1624–69) and **Peter** (*c*.1603–35).

Saraceni, Carlo (*b* Venice, 1579; *d* Venice, 16 June 1620). Italian painter. Although he was born and died in Venice, he spent almost all his career in Rome. There he formed his style under the influence of *Caravaggio and *Elsheimer, painting small, luminous pictures of figures in landscapes as well as much larger altarpieces, including the replacement for Caravaggio's *Death of the Virgin*, which the church of S. Maria della Scala had rejected in 1606. Caravaggio's picture is now in the Louvre, Paris, and Sarace-ni's is still in the church. He painted several other smaller variants or versions of it, so the design was evidently popular. His style was sensitive and poetic, showing a delicate feeling for colour and tone. His liking for turbans, tasselled fringes, and stringy drapery folds may have influenced Dutch artists in Rome such as *Lastman and *Pynas, and through them *Rembrandt. He also possibly had some influence in Lorraine, through his pupil, the French Caravaggesque painter Jean Le Clerc (*c*.1587–1633). Le Clerc was also an engraver; his prints include one of his master's *Death of the Virgin* (after a small version on copper, now in the Alte Pinakothek, Munich, rather than the large altarpiece in Rome).

Sarazin, Jacques. See SARRAZIN.

sarcophagus. A stone (or more rarely terra-cotta) coffin. The term is particularly applied to large and richly decorated examples from the ancient world. According to *Pliny the name (Greek: 'flesh-devouring') was derived from the custom of making or lining coffins with a slate stone found in Asia Minor that had the property of destroying the flesh of the corpse. In the 3rd and 4th centuries AD sarcophagi were the most common form of sculpture produced in the Roman Empire. Many surviving examples—more or less mass-produced—are mediocre, but some are of high quality and great historical interest, notably the sarcophagus of Junius Bassus (Vatican Grottoes, Rome). As an inscription informs us, Junius Bassus was prefect of Rome and was baptized a Christian on his deathbed in 359; the sarcophagus is richly adorned with relief carvings of subjects from the Old and New Testaments, and rather than being a memorial to an individual, it can be seen as a declaration of church teaching, marking the growing dominance of Christianity (it was not officially tolerated until 313, but by the end of the century it was the virtually compulsory religion for Roman citizens). On earlier sarcophagi the carvings are usually of pagan subjects and such sculptures were highly influential on *Renaissance artists. In the *Neoclassical era the sarcophagus form was revived.

Sargent, John Singer (*b* Florence, 12 Jan. 1856; *d* London, 15 Apr. 1925). American painter, chiefly famous as the outstanding society por-traitist of his age: *Rodin called him 'the van *Dyck of our times'. He was born in Florence, the son of prosperous and cultured parents who had settled in Europe, and he had an inter-national upbringing and career—indeed, he has been described as 'an American born in Italy, educated in France, who looks like a German, speaks like an Englishman, and paints like a Spaniard' (William Starkweather, 'The Art of John S. Sargent', *Mentor*, October 1924). His 'Spanishness' refers to his deep admiration for *Velázquez, for although he was encouraged to paint directly by his teacher *Carolus-Duran, with whom he studied in Paris, 1874–6, the vir-tuoso handling of paint that characterized his style derived more particularly from Old Masters such as Velázquez and *Hals (he visited Madrid in 1879 and Haarlem in 1880 to study their work). In 1884 he became famous when his portrait of Mme Virginie Gautreau (Met. Mus., New York) caused a sensation at the Paris *Salon because of what was felt to be its provocatively erotic character. It was shown as *Madame X*, but the sitter, a society beauty of strikingly unconventional looks, was unmistakable, and her mother wrote to Sargent imploring him to withdraw the picture, which she said had made her daughter a laughing-stock (he refused to do so). The scandal persuaded Sargent to move to London, and he remained based there for the rest of his life; he continued to travel extensively, however, and often visited America. The lavish elegance of his work brought him unrivalled success, and his portraits of the wealthy and privileged convey with brilliant bravura the glamour and opulence of high-society life. Even in his lifetime he was deprecated by some critics for superficiality of characterization, but although psychological penetration was certainly not his strength, he was admirably varied in his response to each sitter's individuality.

As with many successful portraitists, Sargent's heart lay elsewhere; indeed he came to hate portraiture, calling it 'a pimp's profession'. In 1907—at the height of his career—he announced that he would paint 'no more mugs', and although he was occasionally persuaded to relent, essentially he kept his word and in the remaining eighteen years of his life he produced only about two dozen commissioned portraits. Despite his sophistication and charm and the entrée to high society that his success gave him, he was a very private person, who never married and led a quiet life. With portraiture behind him, he was free to produce work for his own satisfaction. He loved painting landscape watercolours, showing a technique as dashing in this medium as in his oil paintings, and from the 1890s he devoted much of his energies to ambitious allegorical murals in the Public Library and Museum of Fine Arts in Boston: 'Landscape I like, but, most of all, decoration, where the really aesthetic side of art counts for so much more.' For the Library his subject was the history of religion (his friend E. A. *Abbey painted a series on the quest for the Holy Grail for the same building at the same period). Sargent began work in 1890 and the paintings (in oil on canvas) were installed in stages between 1895 and 1916. They led to the commission from the Museum, for which he painted subjects from classical mythology between 1916 and 1925, completing the work shortly before his death. (As models for the *Danaides* he used dancing girls from the chorus-line of the Ziegfeld Follies.) His murals are in a high-flown, sometimes rather dreary *Symbolist manner and have evoked mixed reactions. A very different side to his talents is revealed in the enormous *Gassed* (1918–19, Imperial War Mus., London), which he painted as an *Official War Artist. It has remarkable tragic power and is one of the greatest pictures inspired by the First World War. Sargent's reputation plummeted after his death (in 1929 Roger *Fry called him 'undistinguished as an illustrator and non-existent as an artist'), but has soared again since the 1970s.

Sarrazin (or Sarazin), **Jacques** (*bapt.* Noyon, 8 June 1592; *d* Paris, 3 Dec. 1660). The leading French sculptor of the mid-17th century. He was in Rome from about 1610 to 1628, during which time he formed his style on the example of the *antique and classicizing artists such as *Domenichino and *Duquesnoy. On his return to Paris he established himself as head of his profession, and his workshop became the main training ground for sculptors of the following generation. Much of his best work was done as architectural decoration, the finest example being his *caryatids on the Pavillon de l'Horloge at the *Louvre (1639–42). He also supervised the decoration (1652–60) of the Château de Maisons, the masterpiece of François Mansart, the greatest French architect of the 17th century. Although it does not rank on the same elevated level, Sarrazin's dignified work forms a kind of sculptural parallel to the architecture of Mansart or the paintings of *Poussin.

Sarto, Andrea del (*b* Florence, ?16 July 1486; *d* Florence, 28/29 Sept. 1530). Florentine painter. The epithet 'del sarto' (of the tailor) is derived from his father's profession; his real name was Andrea d'Agnolo di Francesco Lanfranchi. According to *Vasari, he was first apprenticed as a goldsmith and then taught by *Piero di Cosimo; another early source says he studied under Raffaellino del Garbo (*d* c.1527). However, his poised and graceful style was more obviously influenced by Fra *Bartolommeo and *Raphael, and following the departures of *Leonardo, Raphael, and *Michelangelo (all of whom had left Florence by 1509) he became established with Bartolommeo as the leading painter of the city. Apart from a visit to Fontainebleau in 1518–19 to work for Francis I, he was based in Florence all his life, although he probably visited Rome soon after his return from France, and made short visits elsewhere. He excelled as a fresco decorator (there are outstanding examples in Florence in SS. Annunziata and the Chiostro dello Scalzo), and he also painted superb altarpieces (*Madonna of the Harpies*, 1517, Uffizi, Florence) and portraits (*A Young Man*, c.1517, NG, London).

Andrea's posthumous image was largely made and marred by *Vasari, who described his works as 'faultless' but represented him as a weakling completely under the thumb of his wicked wife. In Robert Browning's poem on the painter (1855) and in a psychoanalytic essay by Freud's disciple Ernest Jones (1913) attempts are made to link a supposed lack of vigour in his mellifluous art with these traits of character. This approach, however, is hardly just and a good deal of Vasari's account of Andrea's private life has been shown to be factually inaccurate (the scandalmongering is mainly in the 1550 edition of his book and was suppressed in the 1568 edition). Andrea has suffered from being judged against such giants as Michelangelo and Raphael, but he nevertheless ranks as one of the greatest masters of his time. In grandeur and gracefulness he approaches Raphael, and he had a feeling for colour and atmosphere that was unrivalled among Florentine painters of his period. He also numbers among the finest draughtsmen of the Renaissance (the best collection of his drawings is in the Uffizi). Certain features of his art foreshadow the *Mannerist experiments of his great pupils *Pontormo and *Rosso Fiorentino. The many other artists who trained in his busy workshop included *Salviati and Vasari.

Sassetta (Stefano di Giovanni) (*b* ?Siena or Cortona, *c*.1400; *d* Siena, 1 Apr. 1450). Sienese painter; the name Sassetta was evidently first used in the 18th century and is of unknown origin, but it is now the accepted designation. His work continues Sienese tradition in its beautiful colouring and elegant line, but he was also influenced by the *International Gothic style and by contemporary Florentine developments, combining them into a highly personal manner expressive of his mystical imagination. With *Giovanni di Paolo he ranks as the outstanding Sienese painter of the 15th century. His most important work was the *St Francis* altarpiece (1437–44) painted for the church of S. Francesco at Borgo San Sepolcro and now dispersed. The central panel, *St Francis in Ecstasy* (Berenson Coll., Florence), has a monumental dignity that must have impressed *Piero della Francesca (a native of San Sepolcro), and some of the other panels (seven are in the National Gallery, London) show him at his most lyrical. Sassetta's reputation did not long survive his death and he was not rediscovered until the early 20th century.

Sassoferrato (Giovanni Battista Salvi) (*b* Sassoferrato, 29 Aug. 1609; *d* Florence or Rome, 8 Aug. 1685). Italian painter, known by the name of his town of birth and active in nearby Urbino and other cities of central Italy, notably Rome (where he is said to have been a pupil of *Domenichino) and Perugia. He produced some portraits, but he specialized in religious works painted in an extremely sweet, almost *Peruginesque style. They are very clearly drawn and pure in colouring and totally un-*Baroque in feeling—indeed, they have a deliberately archaic quality that brings to mind the paintings of the *Nazarenes. Little is known of his life (in the 18th century it was evidently generally believed he was a contemporary of *Raphael) and few of his pictures are dated or datable; they seem to have been in great demand, however, as his compositions often exist in numerous very similar versions. Most of them were presumably done for private collectors, as few are in churches (the most notable exception is the *Mystic Marriage of St Catherine*, 1643, in S. Sabina, Rome). Examples of his work are in many galleries (including the National Gallery and Wallace Collection, London), and a fine collection of his drawings (virtually his entire surviving output as a draughtsman) is in the Royal Library at Windsor Castle.

Saura, Antonio (*b* Huesca, 22 Sept. 1930; *d* Cuenca, 22 July 1998). Spanish painter, draughtsman, and printmaker, active mainly in Madrid. He was self-taught and began painting during a long illness in 1947. His early work was *Surrealist and while he was living in Paris from 1953 to 1955 he met the founder of the movement, André *Breton. Back in Spain, however, he quickly abandoned Surrealism for a violently expressive semi-abstract style that has been seen as one of the most forceful protests against the Franco regime (his sudden change of direction was partly inspired by the brutal suppression of student demonstrations soon after his return to Madrid). The stormy atmosphere and thickly textured figures in his work create a feeling of tortured humanity (*Great Crucifixion*, 1963, Boymans Mus., Rotterdam).

Savery, Roelandt (*b* Courtrai [Kortrijk], ?1576; *d* Utrecht, 25 Feb. 1639). Flemish-born Dutch painter, draughtsman, and etcher of landscapes, animal subjects, and still-life, the most distinguished member of a family of artists. He grew up in Amsterdam and in 1619 settled in Utrecht, but he is best known for his association with Prague, where he worked for the Emperor Rudolf II (see HABSBURG) from 1603 to 1613. Rudolf's famous menagerie allowed him to study in detail the exotic animals that became the trademark of his work. He painted and drew creatures such as pelicans, ostriches, camels, and the now extinct dodo, and was one of the first artists in the Netherlands to produce pictures of animals alone. His favourite subjects, however, were Orpheus and the Garden of Eden, which allowed him to include any number of colourful beasts. Savery's bright and highly finished style is similar to that of Jan 'Velvet' *Brueghel, but is somewhat more archaic. His rare flower paintings are sometimes of outstanding quality, and with *Bosschaert (likewise Flemish born) he was an influential early exponent of this genre in Holland. *Houbraken says that Savery died insane. His brother **Jacob Savery** (b Courtrai, c.1565; d Amsterdam, 1603) was a painter, draughtsman, and etcher. He was influenced by Pieter *Bruegel and numerous drawings formerly attributed to Bruegel are now considered to be deliberate forgeries by Jacob; other 'Bruegel' drawings are thought to be by Roelandt.

Saville, Jenny. See YOUNG BRITISH ARTISTS.

Savinio, Alberto. See CHIRICO.

Savoldo, Giovanni Girolamo (active 1506–48). Italian painter, perhaps born in Brescia, first documented in Parma, in 1506, and active mainly in Venice. His output was small, his career was fairly undistinguished, and he was virtually forgotten after his death, but he is now regarded as a highly attractive minor master whose work stands somewhat apart from the main Venetian tradition. His forte was night scenes, in which he gave his lyrical sensibility and liking for unusual light effects full play. One of the best-known examples is *Mary Magdalene Approaching the Sepulchre*, of which several versions exist, one in the National Gallery, London. The writer Pietro Aretino described Savoldo as 'decrepit' in 1548 and he is not heard of thereafter.

Saxl, Fritz. See FALCONE.

Scarfe, Gerald (b London, 1 June 1936). British caricaturist, designer, sculptor, printmaker, painter, film-maker, and writer. He suffered from severe asthma throughout most of his childhood and took up drawing during long periods of confinement in bed. After a brief period working for an advertising agency he became a freelance caricaturist, working for *Punch* from 1960, *Private Eye* from 1961, the *Daily Mail* from 1966, and the *Sunday Times* and *Time* magazine from 1967. The first of many

collections of his drawings, *Gerald Scarfe's People*, was published in 1966. His work is varied in subject, style, and technique, but he is best known for line drawings in which he grotesquely distorts his subjects' features: 'I like to see how far I can stretch a face and still make it recognizable.' He has also worked in other media in a similar vein and has been widely exhibited (a large, highly entertaining exhibition of his sculpture was held in the Festival Hall, London, in 1983, for example). He has done a good deal of stage and film design and he has also worked on animated films, including the Disney movie *Hercules* (1997). His autobiography, *Scarfe by Scarfe*, was published in 1986.

Scarsellino, Lo (Ippolito Scarsella) (b Ferrara, c.1551; d Ferrara, 1620). The leading Ferrarese painter of his period. He produced a good deal of large-scale work, including frescos, but he is now remembered mainly for his small mythological or religious scenes set in landscapes, several of which are in the Borghese Gallery, Rome. Their romantic feeling and spirited technique recall Venetian painting (he is said to have studied with *Veronese) and they were particularly influential on the young *Guercino.

scauper. See SCORPER.

Schad, Christian. See NEUE SACHLICHKEIT.

Schadow, Johann Gottfried (b Berlin, 20 May 1764; d Berlin, 27 Jan. 1850). German sculptor, draughtsman, printmaker, and writer on art. In 1785–7 he lived in Rome, then settled in his native Berlin. His style was essentially *Neoclassical (he became a friend of *Canova in Rome), but it retained a degree of *Baroque liveliness. He was active mainly as a portraitist and tomb sculptor, but his best-known work is the *quadriga* (four-horse chariot) (completed 1791) surmounting the Brandenburg Gate in Berlin, which was badly damaged in the Second World War and has been replaced by a copy. His finest achievement is perhaps the charming and sensitive group of the Princesses Luise and Frederika of Prussia (1795–7, Alte NG, Berlin). From 1815 until his death he was director of the Berlin Academy and his later years were mainly devoted to teaching, administration, and writing on art theory. He had three artist sons: **Felix** (1819–61), a painter, **Rudolf** (or Ridolfo) (1786–1822), a sculptor, and, most importantly, **Wilhelm von Schadow** (b Berlin, 6 Sept. 1788; d Düsseldorf, 19 Mar. 1862), who was a painter and writer on art. In 1810–19 he lived in Rome, where he became a member of the *Nazarenes. From 1826 to 1859 he was director of the Düsseldorf Academy, which he helped to make into a leading centre of history painting. In 1845 he was ennobled and added the aristocratic 'von' to his name.

Schalken, Godfried (b Made, nr. Dordrecht, 1643; d The Hague, 13 or 16 Nov. 1706). Dutch painter of biblical, allegorical, and anecdotal subjects and of portraits, active mainly in Dordrecht. He was taught there by *Hoogstraten and in Leiden by *Dou, and he was one of Dou's most distinguished successors in the *fijnschilder* (fine painter) tradition. His surfaces are as smooth, glossy, and delicately finished as Dou's, and Schalken too excelled in night scenes (he had a strong preference for the red glow of candlelight). However, he differed from his master in his penchant for scenes involving coquettish women. From 1692 to 1697 Schalken lived in London, where he painted a portrait of *William III by Candlelight* (Rijksmuseum, Amsterdam). As with Dou, Schalken's great reputation lasted throughout the 18th century.

Schapiro, Meyer. See ABSTRACT EXPRESSIONISM.

Schäufelein, Hans (b ?Swabia, ?c.1480; d Nördlingen, 1538/40). German painter and designer of woodcuts and stained glass. His work was strongly influenced by Dürer, in whose studio in Nuremberg he worked from about 1503 to 1507. He developed the master's ideas with 'a kind of fumbling audacity . . . A born, extraordinarily fertile story-teller, he was more warm-hearted, intelligible and melodious than Dürer' (Gert van der Osten and Horst Vey, *Painting and Sculpture in Germany and the Netherlands: 1500–1600*, 1969). After leaving Nuremberg he spent several years in Augsburg, where he probably worked with Hans *Holbein the Elder, and in 1515 he settled in Nördlingen, where he was the leading artist of the day. Most of his output was devoted to religious works, but he was also a fine portraitist and in 1536 he designed a large nine-sheet woodcut of the *Triumphal Procession of the Emperor Charles V* (see HABSBURG). Schäufelein's monogram includes a little shovel (German: *kleine Schaufel*), a pun on his name. His son **Hans Schäufelein the Younger** (c.1515–c.1582) was also a painter, but little is known about his work.

Schedoni, Bartolomeo (b Formigine, nr. Modena, 1578; d Parma, 23 Dec. 1615). Italian painter and draughtsman, active mainly in Modena, at the *Este court, and then from 1607 in Parma, where he was a favourite artist

of Duke Ranuccio I *Farnese. His work drew on various influences, notably *Correggio and the *Carracci, but by the end of his short life he had developed a distinctive style characterized by bold lighting, poetic feeling, and a striking use of areas of bright, almost metallic colour (*The Three Marys at the Tomb*, Gal. Naz., Parma). Although his art is often very tender in sentiment, he had a violent, unstable temperament, and he is said to have died in a 'fit of passion' (which perhaps indicates suicide) after a night of heavy gambling losses.

Scheemakers, Peter (bapt. Antwerp, 10 Jan. 1691; d Antwerp, 12 Sept. 1781). Flemish sculptor, active mainly in England, where he settled around 1720 after spending four years in Copenhagen. Apart from a visit to Rome (1728–1730) he was based in London until 1771, when he retired to Antwerp. In the 1730s he became the main rival to *Rysbrack, whose prices he undercut. Rysbrack defeated him in competition for the equestrian statue of William III in Bristol, but Scheemakers gained a great success in 1740 with his Shakespeare Monument (designed by William *Kent) in Westminster Abbey and for a few years thereafter, until overtaken by *Roubiliac, he ranked as the country's most renowned sculptor. He ran a large studio, with many assistants, and was the most prolific sculptor of his time in England, particularly as a maker of monuments, ranging from small tablets to large multi-figure compositions. He also made portrait busts, and these, like his monuments, are often severely classical, reflecting his love of the *antique.

Scheemakers' brother **Henry** (d 1748) and his son **Thomas** (1740–1808) were also sculptors; both of them worked in England, but Henry settled in France in 1733.

Scheffer, Ary (b Dordrecht, 10 Feb. 1795; d Argenteuil, 15 June 1858). Dutch-born painter and lithographer who spent virtually all his career in Paris and became a French citizen in 1850. His work was immensely popular in his lifetime, but is now generally considered sentimental. Early in his career he favoured literary themes (*Francesca da Rimini*, 1835, Wallace Coll., London, and other versions), but later he turned to mawkishly treated religious subjects (*St Augustine and St Monica*, 1854, NG, London, and other versions). He also painted many portraits. His work is well represented in the museum at Dordrecht.

Scheggia, Lo. See MASACCIO.

Schelfhout, Andreas (*b* The Hague, 16 Feb. 1787; *d* The Hague, 19 Apr. 1870). Dutch landscape painter in oils and watercolour, a forerunner of the *Hague School. He is best known for carefully depicted winter scenes reminiscent of those made by 17th-century Dutch artists, but he also painted seascapes and other subjects. His work was influential particularly on *Jongkind, his most famous pupil.

Scheyer, Galka. See BLAUE VIER.

Schiavone, Andrea (Andrea Meldolla) (*b* Zara, Dalmatia [now Zadar, Croatia], *c*.1510/15; *d* Venice, 1 Dec. 1563). Italian painter and etcher. His nickname Schiavone means 'Slav', reflecting the fact that he was born in Dalmatia (then under Venetian jurisdiction), although his family was originally from Meldola, near Rimini. He worked mainly in Venice, where he was on friendly terms with *Titian (who along with *Parmigianino was one of the main influences on his style). His most characteristic works were fairly small religious or mythological pictures for private patrons, done in a vigorous, painterly style that had considerable influence on the next generation.

Schiele, Egon (*b* Tulln, nr. Vienna, 12 June 1890; *d* Vienna, 31 Oct. 1918). Austrian painter and draughtsman. Schiele had a disturbed adolescence which had certain affinities with that of *Munch and which similarly seems to have disposed him towards angst-ridden and sexually charged imagery: when he was 15 his father died mad, he disliked his mother, and he had a strange, possibly incestuous, relationship with his younger sister. He studied at the Vienna Academy and in 1907 met *Klimt, who encouraged him and was a strong influence on his early *Art Nouveau style. By 1909, however, he had begun to develop his own highly distinctive style, which is characterized by an aggressive linear energy expressing acute nervous intensity. He painted portraits, landscapes, and semi-allegorical works, but he is best known for his drawings of nudes (including self-portraits), which have a disturbing and explicit erotic power—in 1912 he was briefly imprisoned on indecency charges (for exhibiting lewd material where it was accessible to children), and several of his drawings were burnt. The figures he portrays are typically lonely or anguished, their bodies emaciated and twisted, expressing an aching intensity of feeling. His work was much exhibited, and he was beginning to receive international acclaim when he died (three days after

his wife) in the influenza epidemic of 1918. He has since come to be recognized as one of the greatest masters of *Expressionism, and only Klimt and *Kokoschka are better known among modern Austrian artists.

Schildersbent (Dutch: 'band of painters'). A fraternal organization dedicated to social fellowship and mutual assistance, founded in about 1620 by a number of Dutch and Flemish artists living in Rome. Its members called themselves *Bentvueghels* or 'birds of a flock' and they had individual *Bentnames* that presumably related to their character or appearance. For example, Pieter van *Laer, one of the early leaders, was called Bamboccio ('little clumsy one' or 'rag doll'), *Breenbergh was dubbed Het Fret ('the ferret'), and *Swanevelt was known as Eremiet ('hermit'). In 1720 Pope Clement XI banned the Schildersbent's drunken initiation rituals, which parodied the ceremony of baptism, and the organization was disbanded.

Schinkel, Karl Friedrich (*b* Neuruppin, 13 Mar. 1781; *d* Berlin, 9 Oct. 1841). German architect, painter, and designer, active mainly in Berlin. Schinkel was the greatest German architect of the 19th century, but until 1815, when he gained a senior appointment in the Public Works Department of Prussia, he worked mainly as a painter and stage designer. His paintings are highly *Romantic landscapes somewhat in the spirit of *Friedrich, although more anecdotal in detail (*Gothic Cathedral by a River*, 1813–14, Alte NG, Berlin). He continued working as a stage designer until the 1830s, and in this field ranks among the greatest artists of his period. His most famous designs were for Mozart's *Magic Flute* (1815, Schinkelmuseum, Berlin), in which he combined the clarity and logic of his architectural style with a feeling of mystery and fantasy.

Schjerfbeck, Helene (*b* Helsinki, 10 July 1862; *d* Saltsjöbaden, nr. Stockholm, 23 Jan. 1946). Finnish painter. In the 1880s she travelled widely, working mainly in France but also in *St Ives and St Petersburg, making a name with open-air scenes notable for their fresh colouring. From about 1900 her health (always delicate) began to fail badly (although she lived into her eighties) and she adopted a solitary life at Hyvinkaa, almost forgotten, developing a much more simplified style. Her subtle colour harmonies recall those of *Whistler, and after her work was exhibited in 1937 she was recognized as one of the pioneers of modernism in Finland.

Her work included landscapes, still-lifes, figure compositions, and portraits, notably a long series of self-portraits that are regarded as being among her finest achievements.

Schlemmer, Oskar (*b* Stuttgart, 4 Sept. 1888; *d* Baden-Baden, 13 Apr. 1943). German painter, sculptor, stage designer, and writer on art. From 1920 to 1929 he taught at the *Bauhaus, in the metalwork, sculpture, and stage-design workshops. During this time he did much work for the theatre, notably designs for the *Constructivist *Triadic Ballet*, to music by Paul Hindemith, which was performed at the Bauhaus in 1923. After leaving the Bauhaus he taught in Breslau and Berlin, but in 1933 he was dismissed by the Nazis, who declared his work *degenerate. He lived in Switzerland from 1933 to 1937 and from 1940 spent most of his time in Wuppertal. Schlemmer had a mystical temperament and his ideas on art were complex. He rejected what he considered the soullessness of pure abstraction, but he wished to submit his intuition to rational control. Some of his early work was influenced by *Cubism and he showed a deep concern for pictorial structure. Characteristically his paintings represent rather mechanistic human figures, seen in strictly frontal, rear, or profile attitudes set in a mysterious space (*Group of Fourteen Figures in Imaginary Architecture*, 1930, Wallraf-Richartz-Museum, Cologne). His cool, streamlined forms are seen also in his sculpture.

Schlichter, Rudolf. See NEUE SACHLICHKEIT.

Schlüter, Andreas (*b* ?Danzig [now Gdańsk, Poland], *c*.1660; *d* St Petersburg, ?June 1714). German sculptor and architect, active mainly in Berlin. The greatest *Baroque sculptor in northern Germany and also an outstanding architect, he played a leading role in establishing Berlin as an important art centre, but his career was dogged by ill fortune, and few of his major works survive. The most important is the splendid equestrian monument to Frederick William, the Great Elector (1696–1703, Charlottenburg Castle, Berlin). After a series of structural problems with his buildings (probably mainly caused by marshy ground), Schlüter lost his appointment as royal architect in 1707 and had a nervous breakdown. In 1713 he accepted an invitation from Peter the Great to work in the recently founded St Petersburg, but he died soon after arriving.

Schmidt-Degener, Frederick. See RIJKS-MUSEUM.

Schmidt-Rottluff, Karl (*b* Rottluff, nr. Chemnitz, 1 Dec. 1884; *d* West Berlin, 10 Aug. 1976). German *Expressionist painter, printmaker, and sculptor, born Karl Schmidt; he added 'Rottluff' to his name, from his place of birth, in 1906. In 1905 he was one of the founders of Die *Brücke. He was the most independent member of the group, taking a limited part in its activities, and his style was harsher than that of the other members. It was particularly forceful in his woodcuts, which are amongst the finest representatives of Expressionist graphic art. In 1906 he stayed with *Nolde on the island of Alsten, Norway, and in 1907 he painted with *Heckel at Dangast on the coast north-west of Bremen. Apart from landscapes such as the ones he painted in these places, his work included portraits, figure compositions, and still-lifes. In 1911, with the other members of Die Brücke, Schmidt-Rottluff moved to Berlin, where he lived for most of the rest of his life. In the 1910s and 1920s he was influenced by the stylized forms of African sculpture (*Dr Rosa Schapire*, 1919, Tate, London). Later his style became somewhat more naturalistic. His work was declared *degenerate by the Nazis and in 1941 he was forbidden to paint. In 1947 he became a professor at the Berlin Hochschule für Bildende Künste. The Brücke-Museum in Berlin was founded on his initiative in 1967 and he gave 60 of his own works to the collection. There are good collections of his graphic work in the Victoria and Albert Museum, London, and the Leicestershire Museum and Art Gallery, Leicester.

Schnabel, Julian (*b* New York, 26 Oct. 1951). American painter (and latterly sculptor and film director). His paintings are characteristically large and in a *Neo-Expressionist vein; often they are on unusual materials such as carpet or velvet, and some of them are encrusted with broken crockery (*Humanity Asleep*, 1982, Tate, London) or incorporate other three-dimensional objects (sometimes the supports themselves are three-dimensional, with central projections like a chimney breast). In the 1980s he enjoyed a meteoric rise as the most touted figure in the international art world, treated more like a pop star than a painter, and many critics feel that the huge prices his works have fetched depend more on media hype and the investment value of contemporary art than on any intrinsic merit. Robert *Hughes, for example, writes that 'Schnabel's work is to painting what Sylvester Stallone's is to acting—

a lurching display of oily pectorals—except that Schnabel makes bigger public claims for himself.' In 1983 he began producing sculpture, and in 1996 he made his debut as a movie director with *Basquiat*, about the *Graffiti artist Jean-Michel Basquiat.

Schnorr von Carolsfeld, Julius (*b* Leipzig, 26 Mar. 1794; *d* Dresden, 24 May 1872). German painter and draughtsman, the most distinguished member of a family of artists. After studying at the Vienna Academy, he moved to Rome in 1818 and joined the *Nazarenes, taking part in their fresco decoration of the Casino Massimo. In 1827 he moved to Munich, where he was employed by Ludwig I on vast mural schemes in his palace, the Residenz, illustrating scenes from the legend of the Nibelung and from German history (the work was not completed until 1867). In 1846 Schnorr became a professor at the Academy in Dresden and the following year director of the Gemäldegalerie there. Because of his administrative duties and trouble with his eyesight he did comparatively little creative work in his later years. His last major project, on which he worked for many years and which brought him international recognition, was a series of illustrations to the Bible, published in the form of wood engravings as *Die Bibel in Bildern* (1852–60) and in an English edition as *Schnorr's Bible Pictures* (1855–60).

Schönfeld, Johann Heinrich (*b* Biberach an der Riss, 1609; *d* Augsburg, 1682/3). German painter and etcher. From about 1633 to 1651 he lived in Italy (mainly Rome and Naples). His career there is rather obscure and it is only after he settled in Augsburg in 1652 that his development can be traced through a succession of dated works. He was versatile and prolific, painting historical and genre subjects as well as many altarpieces for churches in southern Germany. His style was lively and *eclectic, drawing on various Italian influences, and in his delicate colouring and lightness of touch he anticipates elements of German *Rococo art.

Schongauer, Martin (*b* Colmar, Alsace, ?c.1440; *d* Breisach am Rhein, nr. Colmar, 2 Feb. 1491). German engraver and painter, active in Colmar, the best-known member of a family of artists (his father and two of his brothers were goldsmiths; two other brothers were painters and engravers). His early years are obscure and estimates of his birthdate range from c.1435 to c.1450; the first known documentary reference to him is of 1465, when he was a student at Leipzig

University. In his day Martin was probably the most famous artist in Germany; the young *Dürer hoped to study in his workshop, but when he arrived in Colmar in 1492 the master had recently died. Although he was renowned as a painter, few surviving pictures can be confidently attributed to him; the most important, and the only dated example, is the *Madonna in the Rose Garden* (1473, Dominican church, Colmar). However, about 115 of his engravings are known (all bearing his initials) and these show that he was the greatest master of the technique before Dürer. His work was strongly influenced by Netherlandish art, above all by Rogier van der *Weyden, but Schongauer had a powerful imagination of his own. Most of his prints are on religious themes, but there are also various secular subjects. In them he brought a new richness and maturity to engraving, expanding the range of tones and textures, so that an art that had previously been the domain of the goldsmith took on a more painterly quality. The gracefulness of his work became legendary, giving rise to the nicknames Hübsch (charming) Martin and Schön (beautiful) Martin.

School of London. An expression coined by R. B. *Kitaj in 1976 and given wide currency when it was used as the title of a British Council exhibition that toured Europe in 1987—'A School of London: Six Figurative Painters' (the six were Michael *Andrews, Frank *Auerbach, Francis *Bacon, Lucian *Freud, Kitaj himself, and Leon *Kossoff). In 1989 the term was used as the title of a book by Alistair Hicks—*The School of London: The Resurgence of Contemporary Painting*. The book covers other artists apart from the original six, including Howard *Hodgkin. It is not clear what the label is meant to mean and some critics have denied that any such thing as a School of London exists.

School of Paris. See ÉCOLE DE PARIS.

Schooten, Floris van (*b* c.1585; *d* Haarlem, c.1655). Dutch still-life painter active in Haarlem, a specialist in pictures of food laid on a table. His style was originally rather rigid and austere, but became more naturalistic under the influence of *Claesz and *Heda. He also painted other types of picture, including market scenes.

Schooten, Joris van. See REMBRANDT.

Schouman, Aert (*b* Dordrecht, 4 Mar. 1710; *d* The Hague, 7 May 1792). Dutch painter, printmaker, glass engraver, art dealer, and collector. He was extremely versatile, his work embracing all manner of subjects and techniques. His most appealing works are his delicate watercolours of birds and animals, which are reckoned among the best of the 18th century. He worked mainly in Dordrecht and The Hague, but he made several visits abroad, including two to England (1766 and 1775).

Schwarzkogler, Rudolf (*b* Vienna, 13 Nov. 1940; *d* Vienna, 20 June 1969). Austrian *Performance artist. Like the *Vienna Actionists, with whom he occasionally worked, Schwarzkogler was often concerned with violence and pain (he sometimes used medical instruments, recalling his father, a doctor who committed suicide in 1943 after losing both legs in the Second World War). He achieved a place in the pantheon of great artistic oddballs by reputedly cutting off his own penis as part of a performance; Robert *Hughes referred to him as 'the Vincent van *Gogh of *Body Art', who 'proceeded, inch by inch, to amputate his own penis, while a photographer recorded the act as an art event'. However, the story depends on a misreading of the photographic documentation of the work (the object that is shown being cut with a razor blade is in fact a dead fish). Schwarzkogler, though, did undoubtedly abuse his body, and he committed suicide by falling from a window.

Schwind, Moritz von (*b* Vienna, 21 Jan. 1804; *d* Niederpöcking, nr. Munich, 8 Feb. 1871). Austrian painter and illustrator, active mainly in south Germany. He trained at the Vienna Academy and then under *Cornelius at the Munich Academy (where Schwind himself became a professor in 1846). His work represents the tail-end of Germanic *Romanticism, characteristically depicting an idealized fairy-tale Middle Ages, with knights in armour, damsels in distress, enchanted woods and castles, and much loving depiction of costume, architecture, etc. He painted several murals, but he was at his best working on a small scale, as in his numerous book illustrations and his woodcuts for *Fliegende Blätter*, a humorous Munich periodical. In his young days Schwind, who was an accomplished violinist, had been friendly with Franz Schubert and late in life he depicted Schubert's Vienna circle in a number of drawings.

Schwitters, Kurt (*b* Hanover, 20 June 1887; *d* Kendal, Westmorland, 8 Jan. 1948). German painter, sculptor, maker of constructions, writer, and typographer, a leading figure of the *Dada movement who is best known for his invention of 'Merz'. Schwitters first applied this word to collages made from refuse, but he came to use it of all his activities, including poetry. He used the word as a verb as well as a noun: a fellow artist was once nonplussed when Schwitters asked him to *merz* with him. In his early work he was influenced by *Expressionism and *Cubism, but after the First World War (in which he served for a time as a draughtsman) he became the chief (indeed, virtually only) representative of Dada in Hanover. In 1918 he began making collages from refuse such as bus tickets, cigarette wrappers, and string, and in 1919 he invented Merz. The name was reached by chance: whilst he was fitting the word 'Commerzbank' (from a business letterhead) into a collage, Schwitters cut off some letters and used what was left. He called the collages Merzbilden (Merz pictures) and in about 1923 began to make a sculptural or architectural variant—the Merzbau (Merz building)—in his house in Hanover (it was destroyed by bombing in 1943). From 1923 to 1932 he published a magazine called *Merz* and in this period he was much occupied with typography. In 1937 his work was declared *degenerate by the Nazis and in the same year he fled to Norway, where at Lysaker he began a second Merzbau (destroyed by fire in 1951). When the Germans invaded Norway in 1940, he moved to England, where he lived for the rest of his life—in London (after release from an internment camp) from 1941 to 1945, and then at Ambleside in the Lake District. Here, in an old barn, he began work on his third and final Merzbau, with financial aid from the Museum of Modern Art, New York. It was unfinished at his death and is now in the Hatton Gallery, Newcastle upon Tyne. The day before he died Schwitters received British citizenship.

Scipione (Gino Bonichi) (*b* Macerata, 15 Feb. 1904; *d* Arco, 9 Nov. 1933). Italian painter. He was the son of a soldier and adopted his pseudonym (in 1927) in homage to Scipio Africanus, the Roman general who defeated Hannibal. He studied briefly (1924–5) at the Academy in Rome before being expelled with his friend Mario Mafai (1902–65), with whom he introduced a romantic *Expressionist vein into Italian painting in opposition to the pomposity of much of the art that was favoured under Mussolini's Fascist government. His subjects were mainly scenes of modern Rome, painted with violent brushwork and a feeling of visionary intensity. His career was very short, virtually ending in 1931 because of the tuberculosis that killed him, but he was highly influential, becoming a symbol of heroic individuality to Italian artists after the Second World War.

Scopas of Paros. One of the most celebrated Greek sculptors, active in the mid-4th century BC. He is recorded as working on the Mausoleum of Halicarnassus, the temple of Artemis at Ephesus, and the temple of Athena Alea at Tegea, of which *Pausanias says he was the architect. Sculptural remains from all three buildings have survived, and although none of them can be certainly associated with Scopas, it is likely that he or his workshop were responsible for certain pieces that show a distinctive style and are of a quality consonant with his elevated reputation. Among them are three slabs from the Mausoleum (BM, London) showing the Battle of Greeks and Amazons, which display the intensity of expression and the characteristically deep-set eyes that are considered typical of his work. Several other pieces have been associated with him on stylistic grounds. In spite of the lack of solid evidence, Scopas is presumed to have ranked with *Praxiteles and *Lysippus as the leading Greek sculptor of the mid- to late 4th century BC, his work heralding the emotionalism of *Hellenistic sculpture.

Scorel, Jan van (b Schoorl, nr. Alkmaar, 1 Aug. 1495; d Utrecht, 6 Dec. 1562). Netherlandish painter, the first artist to bring the ideals of the Italian *Renaissance to the area we today call Holland. His training is said to have included a period in Utrecht with *Gossaert, who probably encouraged him to visit Italy. Scorel set out in about 1518 and according to van *Mander's account he visited various German cities on his way south, including Nuremberg, where he met *Dürer. When he reached Venice, he joined a group of pilgrims going to the Holy Land and visited Crete and Cyprus as well as Bethlehem and Jerusalem. After returning to Venice he made his way to Rome, where Pope Adrian VI, a native of Utrecht, appointed him curator of the papal collection of antiquities. Adrian died in 1523, however, and the following year Scorel returned to Utrecht, where he spent most of the rest of his life. He was the illegitimate son of a priest and took holy orders himself (this did not stop him fathering six children).

Scorel soon became the dominant artist in the northern Netherlands and his reputation spread to other countries (Francis I is said to have tried to engage him to work in France). Most of his work was religious (many of his major altarpieces have been destroyed), but he was also an outstanding portraitist. His paintings show how

closely he had studied *antique sculpture and the works of *Raphael and *Michelangelo while he lived in Rome. He was also influenced by the sensuous beauty of Venetian painting, as is seen particularly clearly in his *Death of Cleopatra* (c.1523, Rijksmuseum, Amsterdam), a reclining nude in the *Giorgione tradition. Unlike the works of many other Netherlandish masters, however, Scorel's pictures are no mere jumble of Renaissance motifs. His *Presentation in the Temple* (c.1535, KH Mus., Vienna), for example, is set in a convincingly *Bramantesque building and the dignified figures are well integrated in their spatial setting. On the other hand, his interest in atmospheric effects is part of his northern heritage. Scorel was highly influential in the Netherlands, and his pupils included some of the leading artists of the next generation, notably *Heemskerck and *Mor.

scorper (or **scauper**). A metal tool used in *wood engraving for scooping out large areas of the block or for engraving broad lines. Its cutting section is usually rounded, occasionally square.

Scott, Kathleen (née Bruce) (b Carlton in Lindrick, Nottinghamshire, 27 Mar. 1878; d London, 25 July 1947). British portrait sculptor. She studied at the *Slade School and in Paris under *Rodin. In 1908 she married Captain Robert Falcon Scott (Scott of the Antarctic), who died on his return from the South Pole in 1912. Her most famous work is the statue commemorating him (unveiled 1915) in Waterloo Place, London. She did portrait busts of many other distinguished contemporaries. After her husband's death she was granted the rank of a widow of a Knight Commander of the Order of the Bath and was known as Lady Scott. In 1922 she married Lieutenant-Commander Edward Hilton-Young, who in 1935 became Baron Kennet; some reference books list her as Lady Kennet. Her son **Sir Peter Scott** (b London, 14 Sept. 1909; d Bristol, 29 Aug. 1989) was a distinguished ornithologist and conservationist (a familiar figure through radio and television broadcasts) and also a noted painter and illustrator of wildfowl.

Scott, Samuel (b London, ?1702; d Bath, 12 Oct. 1772). English marine and topographical painter. He began as a marine painter in the tradition of the van de *Veldes, but in the 1740s he turned to topographical views (usually of the London riverside) in the manner of *Canaletto, who was then enjoying great success in England.

He was not simply a mechanical imitator, however, and had a feeling for the English atmosphere that is lacking in Canaletto, who brought the Venetian light with him to England. Scott also could achieve a distinctive grandeur of design, as in *An Arch of Westminster Bridge* (*c*.1750, Tate, London), which is often considered his masterpiece. He left London in 1765 and settled in Bath for reasons of health (he suffered from gout), evidently painting little in his later years.

Scott, Tim. See NEW GENERATION.

Scott, William (*b* Greenock, nr. Glasgow, 15 Feb. 1913; *d* Coleford, Somerset, 28 Dec. 1989). British painter of still-life (usually involving kitchen objects) and abstracts. In 1937–9 he lived in France, and he said: 'I picked up from the tradition of painting in France that I felt most kinship with—the still-life tradition of *Chardin and *Braque, leading to a certain kind of abstraction which comes directly from that tradition.' His work continued to be based on still-life, but for a time in the 1950s he painted pure abstracts. They featured forms such as circles and squares, but they were not geometrically exact and were bounded by sensitive painterly lines. In the late 1960s and 1970s his style became more austere. Although his work was restricted in range and undemonstrative in character, Scott came to be regarded as one of the leading British artists of his generation.

Scott, William Bell (*b* Edinburgh, 12 Sept. 1811; *d* Penkill Castle, Ayrshire, 22 Nov. 1890). Scottish painter and poet. He was head of the Government School of Design in Newcastle upon Tyne, 1843–64, and his best-known works are near Newcastle, at Wallington Hall, Northumberland: a series (1857–61) representing Northumbrian history and including the well-known *Iron and Coal*, one of the earliest representations in art of heavy industry. The paintings are arranged around a central hall that had been converted from an open courtyard, and the decorative scheme also includes flower paintings by Lady Pauline Trevelyan, the mistress of the house, and by her friend *Ruskin. Bell was a close friend of *Rossetti, and his work has affinities with *Pre-Raphaelitism in its Romanticism and love of historical detail. His literary output included much poetry and several books on art, among them a memoir (1850) of his brother **David Scott** (1806–49), a history painter and book illustrator. Their father **Robert Scott** (1777–1841) was an engraver.

Scottish Colourists. A term applied to four Scottish painters who in the period *c*.1900–14 each spent some time in France and were strongly influenced by the rich colours and bold handling of recent French painting, notably *Fauvism: they are F. C. B. Cadell (1883–1937), J. D. *Fergusson, Leslie Hunter (1879–1931), and S. J. Peploe (1869–1933). The term was popularized by a book by T. J. Honeyman dealing with Cadell, Hunter, and Peploe (*Three Scottish Colourists*, 1950), but it is now usual to add Fergusson to their number, even though he stands apart from the rest in that he returned to live in France after the First World War, whereas the other three remained in Scotland. All four painters knew each other, and they exhibited together as 'Les Peintres de L'Écosse Moderne', at the Galerie Barbazanges, Paris, in 1924, but they did not function as a group. They have been described as the first 'modern' Scottish artists; certainly they were the main channel through which *Post-Impressionism reached their country. None of them was represented in Roger *Fry's Post-Impressionist exhibitions of 1910 and 1912, but this reflects insular English attitudes towards Scottish art rather than the quality of their work.

scraper. A tool, normally in the form of a three-sided blade, used in *line engraving and other metal-plate techniques for removing the *burr from engraved lines or for making corrections by smoothing or scraping the surface of the plate.

screenprinting. A printing technique based on *stencilling, originally used for commercial work but now popular with artists for creative printmaking. The essence of the technique is that a fine mesh screen, stretched tightly over a wooden frame, is placed above a sheet of paper and colour is forced through the mesh with a rubber blade called a squeegee. Usually the screen is made of silk—hence the terms silkscreen printing, which is preferred in the USA, and serigraphy (from *sericum*, Latin for silk); however, the screen can also be made of cotton, nylon, or metal, so the more inclusive term is useful. There are various ways of applying the design to the screen. The earliest and most basic was to attach a cut-out stencil to it. A refinement of this method is to paint the design directly on the screen with a glue- or varnish-like substance that blocks the holes in the mesh. The blocked-out areas form the negative part of the design, the colour being squeezed through the untouched parts of the screen. However, more sophisticated methods enable the artist to create a positive design directly on the screen with a waxy or waterproof medium that is eventually dissolved to allow the ink through only in the parts that have been so treated. Photographic images can be used in the design by shining a light through a transparency onto a chemically treated mesh. Screenprints are almost invariably coloured, a different screen generally being used successively for each colour. The origins of the technique are murky, but it seems to have come to Europe from Japan in the late 19th century. It was not until the early 1960s, however, that it made an important impact in the art world. It was especially favoured by *Pop artists, whose bold images were well served by its capacity for strong, flat colour and its relative crudeness of detail (subtle handling is discouraged because of the texture of the mesh). The artist who more than any other put it on the map was Andy *Warhol.

Scrotes, Guillim (William Stretes) (active 1537–53). Netherlandish portrait painter, active mainly in England. He is first heard of in 1537, when he became court painter to Mary of Hungary (see HABSBURG), regent of the Netherlands, and by 1545 he was working in England for Henry VIII, who paid him a very high salary (about twice what his predecessor *Holbein had earned). His appointment continued under Edward VI. Only a handful of paintings, all done in England, can be confidently attributed to him, among them a full-length portrait of Edward VI in the Royal Collection (several other versions exist). They show Scrotes to have been a highly accomplished practitioner in the international *Mannerist court style and he was an important figure in introducing the full-length portrait to England. He is last heard of in 1553 and may have left England after Edward's death in that year.

scumble. A layer of opaque colour brushed lightly over a previous layer of another colour in such a way that the lower layer is only partly covered and shows through irregularly. Together with *glazing, scumbling allows a range of textural and colouristic effects that ensured *oil painting's dominance over other media. Similar effects can now be obtained with *acrylic.

Sebastiano del Piombo (Sebastiano Luciani) (b ?Venice, c.1485; d Rome, 21 June 1547). Venetian painter, active mainly in Rome. According to *Vasari, he trained with Giovanni *Bellini, but his early work was most strongly influenced by *Giorgione, whose Three Philosophers (KH Mus., Vienna) Sebastiano is said to

have completed after the master's death in 1510. Their styles, indeed, can be so close as to cause paintings to be disputed between them, most notably the unfinished Judgement of Solomon (Kingston Lacy, Dorset, NT). This large and impressive work was attributed to Giorgione by *Ridolfi, but scholarly opinion now increasingly gives it to Sebastiano. The half-length Salome (or Judith?) (1510, NG, London) shows the magnificent painterly skills of an undoubted work of Sebastiano at this date; it has a sensuous beauty reminiscent of Giorgione, but also a statuesque grandeur that is Sebastiano's own.

In 1511 Sebastiano moved to Rome at the invitation of the banker Agostino *Chigi, and he remained there for the rest of his life apart from a visit to Venice in 1528–9 after the Sack of Rome. For Chigi he painted mythological frescos at the Villa Farnesina, where *Raphael also worked. It was with *Michelangelo rather than Raphael, however, that Sebastiano formed a friendship and a professional relationship. Michelangelo not only recommended him to people of influence, but also made drawings for him to work from, as with the Raising of Lazarus (1517–19, NG, London). This was commissioned by Cardinal Giulio de' *Medici (later Pope Clement VII) for the cathedral in Narbonne (of which he was archbishop); it was painted in rivalry with Raphael's Transfiguration (Pinacoteca, Vatican), intended for the same church, and Vasari suggests that Michelangelo helped Sebastiano in order to discredit the Raphael faction, who had denigrated his powers as a colourist. Under Michelangelo's guidance Sebastiano's work became grander in form whilst losing much of its beauty of handling, the lack of sensuous appeal being accentuated when he began experimenting with painting on slate (see PANEL).

Some of the finest works of Sebastiano's Roman years are his portraits, and after Raphael's death (1520) he had no rival in the city in this field, his work attaining a distinctive sombre grandeur. Clement VII, the subject of one of Sebastiano's finest portraits (1526, Mus. di Capodimonte, Naples), appointed him to the lucrative post of keeper of the papal seals in 1531 and after this he was less active as a painter. The seals were made of lead, 'piombo' in Italian, hence Sebastiano's nickname.

Secession. See SEZESSION.

secco (Italian: 'dry'). Term applied to any technique of mural painting in which the colours are applied to dry plaster, rather than wet plaster as in *fresco. The term embraces a variety of methods, but typically the paints used were some form of *casein or *tempera, or *pigments ground in water mixed with lime; if lime-water was used, the plaster had to be damped before painting, a method described by *Theophilus and popular in northern Europe and in Spain. In Italian *Renaissance art the finishing touches to a true fresco would often be painted *a secco*, as it is easier to add details in this way; because the secco technique is much less permanent, such passages have a tendency to flake off with time. Thus in *Giotto's *Betrayal* in the Arena Chapel, Padua, the details of many of the soldiers' weapons are now missing.

secondary colours. See PRIMARY COLOURS.

Section d'Or. Group of French painters who worked in loose association between 1912 and 1914, when the First World War brought an end to their activities. The name, which was also the title of a short-lived magazine published by the group, was suggested by Jacques *Villon in reference to the mathematical ratio known as the *Golden Section, reflecting the interest of the artists involved in questions of proportion and pictorial discipline. Other members of the group (who held one exhibition, in 1912) included *Delaunay, *Duchamp, *Duchamp-Villon, *Gleizes, *Gris, *Léger, *Metzinger, and *Picabia. The common stylistic feature of their work was a debt to *Cubism and several of them worked in the *Orphist style.

Segal, George (*b* New York, 26 Nov. 1924; *d* South Brunswick, NJ, 10 June 2000). American sculptor. His career was slow to mature. He studied at various art colleges and took a degree in art education at New York University in 1950, but until 1958 he worked mainly as a chicken farmer, painting *Expressionist nudes in his spare time. In 1958 he made his first sculpture and in 1960 he began producing the kind of work for which he became famous—life-size unpainted plaster figures, usually combined with real objects to create strange ghostly tableaux (*The Gas Station*, 1963, NG, Ottawa). The figures were made from casts taken from the human body; he used his family and friends as models. In the 1970s he began to incorporate sound and lighting effects in his work. Segal has been classified with *Pop art and *Environment art, but his work is highly distinctive and original, his figures and groups dwelling in a lonely limbo in a way that captures a disquieting sense of spiritual isolation.

Segall, Lasar (*b* Vilna [now Vilnius], 7 July 1891; *d* São Paulo, 2 Aug. 1957). Lithuanian-born painter and graphic artist who settled in Brazil in 1923 (following a visit in 1912) and became a Brazilian citizen. Before and after the first journey to Brazil he lived in Germany (mainly Berlin and Dresden), where he developed an *Expressionist style. He was the first to exhibit Expressionist pictures in Brazil and had a great influence on younger painters there. His work often expresses his compassion for the persecuted and downtrodden, particularly the Jews who suffered under Nazism. After his death his home and studio in São Paulo were converted into a museum of his work, opened in 1970.

Segantini, Giovanni (*b* Arco, nr. Trento, 15 Jan. 1858; *d* Schafberg, Switzerland, 28 Sept. 1899). Italian painter, mainly of figure compositions in landscape settings, active for most of his career in the Swiss Alps. His early work was naturalistic, but from the later 1880s he developed a *Divisionist technique and a liking for *Symbolist subjects (*The Punishment of Luxury*, 1891, Walker AG, Liverpool). He exhibited widely and was one of the few Italian artists of his time with an international reputation. There is a Segantini museum at St Moritz.

Segers, Hercules (*b* Haarlem, 1589/90; *d* ?The Hague, 1633/8). Dutch painter and etcher of landscapes, one of the most original and most enigmatic figures in the history of Dutch art. His name is now often spelled 'Seghers', but 'Segers' was the form used by himself and his contemporaries. Few details of his life are known. He studied with Gillis van *Coninxloo in Amsterdam, and worked also in Utrecht and The Hague, where he is last mentioned in 1633. The woman who was evidently his second wife is described as a widow in 1638. Hardly more than a dozen surviving paintings can be securely attributed to him, although contemporary documents show he certainly painted more. None of the paintings is dated and his chronology is difficult to reconstruct. He specialized in mountainous scenes, fantastic or visionary in conception but advanced in the naturalistic treatment of light and atmosphere. They are usually fairly small, but they suggest vast distances, and with their jagged rocks, shattered tree trunks, and menacing skies convey a sense of almost tragic desolation. Only *Rembrandt and *Ruisdael among Dutch artists attained a similar degree of emotional intensity in landscape painting, and Segers certainly influenced Rembrandt, who owned no less than eight of his paintings.

One of these, *Mountain Landscape* (c.1630, Uffizi, Florence), now Segers's most famous picture, was attributed to Rembrandt until 1871 and he may have touched it up when it was in his collection.

Segers's etchings are also rare (the latest catalogue lists 54, with 183 known impressions) and are perhaps even more original than his paintings. He experimented with coloured inks and dyed papers, so that extraordinarily different impressions could be made from the same plate, a dark paper printed with pale ink transforming a daylight scene into a haunting nocturnal view. Sometimes he printed on linen, which emphasized the vigorous and grainy quality of his work. Every print was an individual work rather than an item in a standardized commercial edition: *Hoogstraten said that he 'printed paintings'. These works are unique in European art of the time, and it is often pointed out that some of them have a strange spiritual kinship with Chinese art. The best collection is in the print room of the Rijksmuseum, Amsterdam.

In 1678 Hoogstraten published a highly coloured account of Segers's unhappy career, his desperate experiments with etchings, and his eventual poverty and drunkenness (he says that he was killed by falling downstairs when intoxicated). Although the account may be exaggerated, Segers certainly had financial problems (he was forced to sell his house in Amsterdam in 1631), and it seems likely that he was little appreciated in his day.

Seghers, Daniel (*b* Antwerp, 3 Dec 1590; *d* Antwerp, 2 Nov 1661). The leading Flemish flower painter of his generation. He was a pupil of Jan *Brueghel and was enrolled in the Antwerp painters' guild in 1611. In 1614 he became a Jesuit lay brother and in 1625 was ordained a priest. After spending two years at Jesuit headquarters in Rome he returned to Antwerp in 1627 and lived there for the rest of his life, working at his monastery; the words 'Society of Jesus' usually follow his signature on his paintings. He enjoyed considerable fame and his distinguished visitors included the future Charles II of England. Most of his works were not sold, but were presented by the Jesuits to dignitaries as tokens of esteem or honour; the recipients in return sent treasures including holy relics and a gold palette and brushes. Seghers's work consists mainly of garlands of flowers painted around a religious image (typically a Madonna and Child or a *Pietà) by another artist. He collaborated with his friend *Rubens in this way. Much rarer are his bouquets of flowers in a glass vase, where brilliant colours stand out against a dark background (*A Vase with Flowers*, 1643, Gemäldegalerie, Dresden). Their comparative simplicity makes it easier to appreciate his lovely creamy touch (his brushwork was broader than Brueghel's but unerringly sure) and they rank among the most beautiful flower pieces ever painted.

Seghers, Gerard (*bapt*. Antwerp, 17 Mar. 1591; *d* Antwerp, 18 Mar. 1651). Flemish painter of religious subjects, active mainly in Antwerp, where he is said to have been taught by *Janssen. He probably spent most of the second decade of the 17th century in Italy (he evidently also visited Spain during this time) and he became one of the very few noteworthy Flemish *Caravaggesque artists. By the late 1620s, however, he had fallen under the all-pervasive influence of *Rubens (*Assumption of the Virgin*, 1629, Mus. de Peinture et de Sculpture, Grenoble). Seghers enjoyed a successful career supplying altarpieces for churches in Antwerp and other Flemish cities, and he was also an international art dealer.

Seghers, Hercules. See SEGERS.

seicento. See QUATTROCENTO.

Seilern, Count Antoine. See COURTAULD.

Seisenegger, Jakob (*b* 1504/5; *d* Linz, 1567). Austrian painter, chiefly a portraitist. In 1531 he became court painter to the Emperor Ferdinand I at Augsburg and he also worked for other members of the *Habsburg family. He was a painter of modest talent, but has some importance in the development of the full-length portrait; his best-known work is the full-length of Charles V (1532, KH Mus., Vienna), which served as a model for the more famous one by *Titian (Prado, Madrid). Seisenegger travelled widely, working in Italy, the Netherlands, and Spain, as well as in various cities in central Europe—Innsbruck, Prague, Vienna.

Seligmann, Kurt (*b* Basle, 20 July 1900; *d* Sugar Loaf, NY, 2 Jan. 1962). Swiss-born painter, printmaker, designer, and writer who became an American citizen. From 1929 to 1938 he lived in Paris, where he became involved with the *Surrealist movement. His paintings of this time had a magical and apocalyptic character, with hazy shapes and swirling draperies fading into a landscape. In 1939 he emigrated to the USA and settled in New York. His work in his new country included sets for ballet and modern dance and a series of pictures called 'Cyclonic Forms' in which he purported to express his reactions to the American landscape. He made a serious study of the occult and wrote a book called *The Mirror of Magic* (1948); a British edition appeared in 1971 entitled *Magic, Supernaturalism and Religion*.

Senefelder, Aloys (*b* Prague, 6 Nov. 1771; *d* Munich, 26 Feb. 1834). German writer who in 1798 invented *lithography as a cheap means of reproducing his plays. He soon realized the artistic possibilities of his invention, which he publicized in two books (1809 and 1818). The second was translated into English as *A Complete Course of Lithography* (1819).

'Sensation'. See YOUNG BRITISH ARTISTS.

sepia. A brown pigment made from the ink of cuttlefish and other marine creatures. It is mentioned by Roman writers and was perhaps used in the ancient world for writing, but it was evidently not until the late 18th century that it was much used in art—for ink drawings and, because of its semi-transparent quality, in *washes. When first applied to paper, sepia is a warm black, but it gradually turns reddish brown. It is more opaque than *bistre, which it tended to replace in the 19th century, but it can be difficult to tell them apart (and to distinguish them from other brown pigments, especially as different types of ink were sometimes mixed). The terms tend to be used fairly loosely.

Sequeira, Domingos António de (*b* Belém, nr. Lisbon, 10 Mar. 1768; *d* Rome, 7 Mar. 1836). The leading Portuguese painter of his period, the only one with an international reputation. He studied in Rome 1788–95, and in 1802 he was appointed first court painter in Lisbon. In 1810 he was imprisoned for collaborating with the French invaders during the Peninsular War, but he successfully protested his innocence and after his release in 1811 he designed the celebrated silver table service (1813–16) presented by Portugal to the Duke of Wellington for his part in defeating the French (it is now in the Wellington Museum, London). He continued working in Lisbon until 1823, when he went into exile because of an illiberal new regime and he spent the rest of his life in Paris and (from 1826) Rome. Sequeira was a prolific and versatile painter, mainly of religious subjects and portraits. His early work was *Neoclassical in style, but some of his later work is tinged with *Romantic feel-

ing and is sketchy in handling. Although a much lesser artist, he is a kind of Portuguese equivalent of *Goya.

Séraphine (or **Séraphine de Senlis**) (Séraphine Louis) (*b* Arsy, Oise, 2 Sept. 1864; *d* Clermont, Oise, 11 Dec. 1942). French *naive painter. After being orphaned very young, she spent her youth as a farmhand and later entered domestic service in Senlis. She began painting when she was about 40 and was 'discovered' by Wilhelm *Uhde in 1912. Her pictures are mainly fantastic, minutely detailed compositions of fruit, leaves, and flowers. She was intensely devout and painted in a trancelike state of religious ecstasy, regarding her works as offerings to the Virgin Mary. In the late 1920s her reason began to fail and she became obsessed with visions of the end of the world. She died in a home for the aged.

Sergel, Johan Tobias (*b* Stockholm, 28 Aug. 1740; *d* Stockholm, 26 Feb. 1814). Swedish sculptor and draughtsman of German parentage, active mainly in Stockholm. His early works are in a French *Rococo style, but he abandoned this during an eleven-year stay in Rome (1767–78) and became the leading Swedish exponent of *Neoclassicism. He was a much livelier artist than many Neoclassical sculptors, however, and although his mature work has impressive clarity of form, it also possesses warmth and vitality. In Rome he was best known for his spirited clay sketches, but after his return to Sweden he was mainly a portraitist. He was court sculptor to Gustavus III and his most important work is a bronze statue of the king (1790–1808) in front of the Royal Palace in Stockholm. Sergel was a prolific draughtsman, many of his drawings being *Romantic in spirit, in a style similar to those of *Fuseli, who was a friend during his period in Rome. He became a professor at the Stockholm Academy in 1780 and was appointed director in 1810.

Serial art. A term that from the 1960s, especially in the USA, has been applied to two types of avant-garde art (although the two types may overlap and have in common the fact that they are usually produced by mathematically minded artists). First, it has been used to describe a kind of *Minimal art in which simple, uniform, interchangeable elements (often commercially available objects such as bricks) are assembled in a regular, easily apprehended arrangement. Carl *Andre is a noted exponent of this kind of work. Secondly, more broadly, the term has been applied to works of art that are conceived in series or as part of a larger group; often the individual work is regarded as incomplete in itself, needing to be seen within the context of the whole.

serigraphy. See SCREENPRINTING.

Serov, Valentin (*b* St Petersburg, 19 Jan. 1865; *d* Moscow, 5 Dec. 1911). Russian painter and graphic artist, son of the composer Alexander Serov. He studied privately under *Repin from an early age and then in 1880–5 at the Academy in St Petersburg, where he became a friend of *Vrubel. His work includes landscapes, genre pictures, and historical scenes, as well as book illustrations, but he is best known as a portraitist. In this field he was the greatest Russian painter of his time and a match for any artist in the world. Like *Sargent, he was a cosmopolitan figure, used to moving in high society, and he brought to his work something of the same quality of aristocratic authority and poise associated with the American's portraits. Like Sargent, too, he painted with superb technical freedom and finesse, and he was just as good with informal portraits as with grand showpieces. His two most famous paintings (both in the Tretyakov Gallery, Moscow) are intimate early works, the breathtakingly beautiful *Girl with Peaches* (1887) and the almost equally lovely *Girl in the Sunshine* (1888); later, as his fame grew, he painted many of the leading Russian celebrities of his time, particularly artists, musicians, and writers. Serov was a member of the *World of Art group and some of his later work shows a tendency towards flat *Art Nouveau stylization. The most remarkable example is a nude, almost monochromatic portrait of the dancer Ida Rubinstein (Russian Mus., St Petersburg), painted in Paris in 1910. Serov had a difficult personality (he could be gloomy and rude), but he was greatly admired for the integrity and sincerity of his work. See also ABRAMTSEVO COLONY.

Serpotta, Giacomo (*b* Palermo, 10 Mar. 1656; *d* Palermo, 27 Feb. 1732). Sicilian sculptor in *stucco. He was the greatest of all virtuosi in his medium and with the exception of *Antonello da Messina the most distinguished artist to come from Sicily. Unlike Antonello, he spent almost all his life on the island and his work is mainly found in the churches of his native Palermo. Serpotta's icing-sugar-white figures—elegant, delicate, charming, and joyous in spirit—are amongst the finest expressions of the *Rococo in Italian art. He is particularly well known for his playful *putti, but his finest single figure is generally acknowledged to be the en-

chantingly coquettish *Fortitude* (1714–17) in the Oratoria del Rosario di S. Domenico, Palermo. His father **Gaspare** (1634–70), his brother **Giuseppe** (1653–1719), and his son **Procopio** (1679–1755) were also sculptors, mainly in stucco.

Serra. The name of four Spanish painters, brothers, who seem to have been the dominant figures in painting in Barcelona in the second half of the 14th century. Little is known about them as individuals and they probably collaborated on some works. Their style was influenced by Sienese painting, probably via the papal court at Avignon. **Jaime** and **Pedro** are the most distinct personalities (documented works survive by both of them); **Francisco** and **Juan** are very obscure.

Serra, Richard (*b* San Francisco, 2 Nov. 1939). American sculptor. His early work was varied; the materials he used included wooden logs, molten lead splashed along the base of a wall, and vulcanized rubber sheets (arranged so that the weight of the material was allowed to determine the shape of the piece). In about 1970 the direction of his art changed as he began to use industrial materials, often on a gigantic scale in works intended for specific sites. His sculptures have often aroused controversy, most notably *Tilted Arc* (1981), a huge slab of curved, tilted steel commissioned by the General Services Administration for Federal Plaza, New York. It was hated by many people who worked in the area not only on aesthetic grounds (it was described as a 'hideous hulk of rusty scrap metal') but also because it interfered with the social activities of the plaza. After highly publicized legal proceedings it was destroyed in 1989. Serra refused to have it relocated, as it was intended for this particular site: 'Every site has an ideology . . . what I try to do is expose that ideology.' He claims that 'it's not the business of art to deal with human needs'. His first wife was the sculptor **Nancy Graves** (1940–95).

Sérusier, Paul (*b* Paris, 9 Nov. 1864; *d* Morlaix, Finistère, 6 Oct. 1927). French painter and art theorist. In 1888 he met *Bernard and *Gauguin at Pont-Aven. He was converted to their *Symbolist views and soon afterwards was one of the founders of the *Nabis, a group inspired by Gauguin's expressive use of colour and rhythmic pattern. After visiting the school of religious painting at the Benedictine monastery at Beuron in Germany in 1897 and 1903 his ideas became permeated with concepts of religious symbolism. His early paintings had generally featured

Breton peasants, but from about 1900 he concentrated on religious subjects. However, his paintings are generally considered of less interest than his ideas on art, notably his views about geometrical principles governing beauty, which he set out in his book *ABC de la peinture* (1921). From 1908 he taught at the *Académie Ranson.

Servaes, Albert (*b* Ghent, 4 Apr. 1883; *d* Lucerne, 19 Apr. 1966). Belgian painter. In 1905 he joined the artists' community at the village of Laethem-Saint-Martin, near Ghent. He found the mystical fervour of the community congenial and he changed from brash *Impressionist pictures to scenes from the Bible and rustic life, featuring heavy figures painted in sombre earth colours—works that have won him a reputation as one of the founders of Belgian *Expressionism. The tragic bitterness of his religious paintings aroused the hostility of the Roman Catholic authorities, which regarded him as an extremist, and several of his works were removed from churches. In 1945 he settled in Switzerland; his work after this time seldom reached the intensity of his earlier paintings.

settecento. See QUATTROCENTO.

Settignano, Desiderio da. See DESIDERIO DA SETTIGNANO.

Seuphor, Michel (*b* Antwerp, 10 Mar. 1901; *d* Paris, 12 Feb. 1999). Belgian-born painter, printmaker, writer, and editor who became a French citizen in 1954. In 1925 he settled in Paris, where he was one of the founders of the *Cercle et Carré association of abstract artists in 1929 and editor of its journal. His own paintings were in a geometrical abstract style (he also made prints in a variety of techniques), but he is better known for his writings. They include a standard book on abstract art, *L'Art abstrait: ses origines, ses premiers maîtres* (1949), and dictionaries of abstract painting (1957) and modern sculpture (1959), all of which have been translated into English. Seuphor also wrote poetry.

Seurat, Georges (*b* Paris, 2 Dec. 1859; *d* Paris, 29 Mar. 1891). French painter and draughtsman, the founder and greatest exponent of *Neo-Impressionism. Seurat was the son of comfortably-off parents and his career took an unusual course; he never had to worry about earning a living and pursued his artistic researches with single-minded dedication. In 1878 he entered the École des *Beaux-Arts in Paris, but his studies were interrupted by military service in 1879. He returned to Paris in 1880 and for the next two years devoted himself to drawing (he was one of the subtlest and most original draughtsmen of the 19th century, typically working with very broad, velvety areas of tone, using a *conté crayon on textured paper). In spite of this mastery of black and white, as a painter he turned for inspiration to artists in the colourist tradition— notably *Delacroix and the *Impressionists. In addition to studying the work of such painters, Seurat read aesthetic and scientific treatises, and he made it his aim to establish a rational system for achieving the kind of vibrant colour effects that the Impressionists in particular had arrived at instinctively. The method he evolved was to place small touches of unmixed colour side by side on the canvas, producing an effect of greater luminosity by this 'optical mixture' than if the colours had been physically mixed together on the palette.

In his first major painting, *Bathers at Asnières* (1883–4, reworked, 1887, NG, London), Seurat was still experimenting with his technique, but his next large work, *Sunday Afternoon on the Island of La Grande Jatte* (1884–6, Art Inst. of Chicago), is a completely mature statement of his ideals. *La Grande Jatte* was shown at the final Impressionist exhibition in 1886 and led to the recognition of Seurat as a leader of the avant-garde. The critic Félix Fénéon coined the term *pointillism in reference to this painting to describe the technique of using myriad dots of colour, but Seurat preferred the term *divisionism.

From 1887 Seurat began to turn his attention to the significance of line in painting, believing that certain directions of lines could express specific emotions; horizontal lines represented calmness, for example, while upward- and downward-sloping lines represented happiness and sadness respectively. He embodied his beliefs in paintings such as *Le Chahut* (1890, Rijksmuseum Kröller-Müller, Otterlo), in which the raised legs of the dancers performing 'Le Chahut' (a sort of can-can) express 'happiness'. Seurat died very suddenly at the age of 31, evidently from meningitis, although his friend *Signac said that he 'killed himself by overwork'. He was so dedicated to his work and kept himself to himself to such an extent that until his death few people knew he had a mistress and son. His mistress, Madeleine Knobloch, is represented in *Woman Powdering Herself* (1890, Courtauld Gal., London).

Seurat's work was highly influential, but his disciples rarely approached his skill, and even less his level of inspiration, in applying his theories; their paintings often look mechanical and lack his gently satirical humour. In power of composition he stands above not only his follow-ers, but also virtually all other painters of his period. He planned his pictures with extraordin-ary care, and they have nothing of the sense of the passing moment associated with Impression-ism. Rather, they have a highly formalized qual-ity and a conscious grandeur that has caused Seurat to be compared with such revered masters as *Piero della Francesca and *Poussin.

Severe style. A term applied to the style characteristic of much Greek sculpture in the period c.480 BC–c.450 BC, transitional between the *Archaic and *Classical periods. Winckel-mann had applied the word 'severe' to works of the time before *Phidias, but the term 'Severe style' did not acquire a specific meaning until the 20th century, particularly with the publication of the book *Der strenge Stil* (1937) by the Danish scholar Vagn Poulsen. Typical features of the Severe style include simplicity and severity of form, grandeur and elevation of spirit, and an increase in characterization compared with the Archaic period. *Myron is the best-known sculp-tor of the period, but his work is sometimes described as early Classical rather than Severe.

Severini, Gino (b Cortona, 7 Apr. 1883; d Paris, 26 Feb. 1966). Italian painter, designer, and writer on art, active mainly in Paris. He first settled there in 1906, and he played an important role in transmitting the ideas of French avant-garde art to the *Futurists, both of whose manifestos of painting he signed in 1910. His work was strongly influenced by *Cubism (he knew *Braque and *Picasso) and he concerned himself with the problem of conveying a sense of movement and action by breaking up his picture space into contrasting and interacting rhythms (*Suburban Train Arriving in Paris*, 1915, Tate, London). He was influenced by theories of mathematical proportion and in 1921 published a book on the subject, *Du Cubisme au classicisme*. In the 1920s his style became more traditional and he carried out several decorative commis-sions, including murals for churches in Switzer-land. He also worked as a theatrical designer. Severini returned to Italy in 1935, but in 1946 he settled permanently in Paris. In the later 1940s his style once again became semi-abstract.

Severus, Septimius, Arch of. See TRIUMPHAL ARCH.

Seymour, Robert. See BROWNE.

Sezession (or **Secession**). Name adopted by several groups of painters in Germany and Aus-tria who in the 1890s broke away ('seceded') from the official academies, which they regarded as too conservative, and organized their own, more avant-garde exhibitions. The first of these groups was formed in Munich in 1892, its leading members being Franz von *Stuck and Wilhelm Trübner (1851–1917), and there were Sezessionen also in Vienna (1897), with Gustav *Klimt as first president, and Berlin (1899), with Max *Lieber-mann as first president. When in 1910 a number of young painters were rejected by the Berlin Sezession—among them members of Die *Brücke—they started the Neue Sezession, with Max *Pechstein a prominent figure.

Sezessionstil. See ART NOUVEAU.

Sforza. Italian family who ruled Milan for most of the period from 1450 to 1535 (there were inter-ruptions in 1499–1512 and 1515–21). The most famous member of the family was **Ludovico** (1452–1508), who was effectively ruler of the city from 1480 to 1499, when he was driven out by the invading French; he was known as Il Moro (the Moor) because of his dark complexion. His court was one of the most splendid in Europe and the greatest artists to work for him were *Bramante and *Leonardo da Vinci.

sfumato (Italian: 'faded away', from *fumo* 'smoke'). Term used to describe the blending of tones or colours so subtly that they melt into one another without perceptible transi-tions—in *Leonardo's words, 'without lines or borders, in the manner of smoke'. Leonardo was a supreme exponent of *sfumato* and *Vasari regarded his ability to mellow the precise out-lines characteristic of the earlier *quattrocento as one of the distinguishing marks of 'modern' painting.

sgraffito. See GRAFFITO.

Shahn, Ben (b Kovno [now Kaunas], Lithu-ania, 12 Sept. 1898; d New York, 14 Mar. 1969). American painter, illustrator, photographer, de-signer, teacher, and writer, born in Lithuania, then part of Russia. His family emigrated to the USA in 1906 and settled in New York. Shahn's background (his father had been sent to Siberia for revolutionary activities) and early life (he grew up in a Brooklyn slum) gave him a hatred of cruelty and social injustice, which he ex-pressed powerfully in his work. He first made a name with a series of pictures (1931–2) on the Sacco and Vanzetti case (these two Italian immi-grants had been executed for murder in 1927 on very dubious evidence, and many liberals believed that they had really been condemned for their anarchist political views). Shahn's paintings on them are in a deliberately awkward, caricature-like style that vividly expresses his anger and compassion. In 1933 he was assistant to Diego *Rivera on the latter's murals for the Rockefeller Center, New York, and subsequently he painted a number of murals himself, notably for the Bronx Post Office, New York (1938–9), and the Social Security building, Washington (1940–1). From 1935 to 1938 he worked as an artist and photographer for the Farm Security Administration, a government agency that documented rural poverty. During the Second World War his work included designing posters for the Office of War Information. After the war he returned to easel painting and was also active as a book and magazine illustrator and as a designer of mosaics and stained glass. His later work tended to be more fanciful and reflective and less concerned with social issues. From the 1950s he gave more time to teaching and lecturing and in 1956–7 he was Charles Eliot Norton professor of poetry at Harvard University. His lectures there were published as *The Shape of Content* (1957), in which he summarized his humanistic, anti-abstract artistic philosophy.

Shannon, Charles (*b* Quarrington, Lincolnshire, 26 Apr. 1863; *d* Kew, Surrey [now in Greater London], 18 Mar. 1937). British painter, printmaker, and collector. In 1881–5 he studied wood engraving at Lambeth School of Art, where in 1882 he met Charles *Ricketts, who became his lifelong companion. They lived together for almost 50 years until Ricketts's death in 1931. Ricketts had the more dominant personality and Kenneth *Clark writes that he 'did most of the talking. Shannon was quiet and recessive, but his rare interpolations showed good sense and considerable learning. One could see that Ricketts turned to him as to a reasonable wife.' Shannon's output as a painter consisted mainly of portraits and imaginative subjects treated in a lush style based on 16th-century Venetian art. They were highly regarded in their day but have dated badly. He made lithographs in a similar vein. In 1929 he fell from a ladder while hanging a picture and injured his brain; although he lived for eight more years, he never fully recovered and often did not recognize Ricketts.

shaped canvas. A term that began to be used in the 1960s for paintings on *supports that departed from the traditional rectangular format. Non-rectangular pictures were of course not new at this time; *Gothic and *Renaissance altarpieces often had pointed or rounded tops, the oval was particularly popular in the *Baroque and *Rococo periods, and so on. The phrase 'shaped canvas', however, usually alludes particularly to a type of abstract painting that emphasizes the 'objecthood' of the work, proclaiming it as something that exists entirely in its own right and not as a reference to, or reproduction of, something else. Various artists have been claimed as the 'inventor' of the shaped canvas in this sense, but its most prominent exponent has undoubtedly been Frank *Stella, who has used such shapes as Vs, lozenges, and fragments of circles. The leading British exponent has been Richard Smith (1931–), who has sometimes used a kite-shaped format in which the canvas is stretched on rods that are part of the visual structure of the picture. He was one of the artists represented in an exhibition entitled 'The Shaped Canvas', organized by Lawrence *Alloway at the Guggenheim Museum, New York, in 1974. The shaped canvas has also occasionally been used by modern figurative painters, notably Anthony *Green.

Shaw, John Byam. See PRE-RAPHAELITE BROTHERHOOD.

Shchukin, Sergei. See HERMITAGE.

Shee, Sir Martin Archer (*b* Dublin, 20 Dec. 1769; *d* Brighton, 19 Aug. 1850). Irish portrait painter and writer on art, active from 1788 in London. There he became second only to *Lawrence as the leading society portraitist, and in 1830 he succeeded him as president of the *Royal Academy, which he guided through a difficult period when it was under attack from *Haydon and other disaffected artists. Examples of his work—which lies in style between the bravura of Lawrence and the precision of *West—are in the National Portrait Gallery, London. He wrote *Rhymes on Art* (1805), in which he urged national patronage of artists, and *Elements of Art* (1809), a poem in six cantos.

Sheeler, Charles (*b* Philadelphia, 16 July 1883; *d* Dobbs Ferry, NY, 7 May 1965). American painter and photographer, the best-known exponent of *Precisionism. Between 1904 and 1909 he made several trips to Europe, and he gradually abandoned the bravura handling of *Chase (his teacher at the Pennsylvania Academy of the Fine Arts) for a manner influenced by European modernism—the paintings he exhibited at the *Armory Show of 1913, for example, were much indebted to *Cézanne. In 1912 Sheeler took up commercial photography for a living while continuing to paint. He worked for a while in fashion photography, but his shy personality was not suited to this world, and he concentrated more on very mundane subjects such as plumbing fixtures. The clarity needed in such work helped to transform his style of painting to a meticulous, smooth-surfaced manner that was the antithesis of his early approach. He began to paint urban subjects in about 1920 and over the next decade shifted from simplified compositions influenced by *Cubism (on 'the borderline of abstraction' in his own words) to highly detailed photographic-like images. In 1927 he was commissioned to take a series of photographs of the Ford Motor Company's plant at River Rouge, Michigan. His powerful images, presenting a pristine view of American industry, were widely reproduced and brought him international acclaim. Increasingly, also, he was recognized as the finest painter in the Precisionist style, his work standing out as much for its formal strength as for its technical polish. Sheeler's paintings continued in this realistic vein in the 1930s, but in the mid-1940s his style changed dramatically; he began using multiple viewpoints and bold unnaturalistic colours, although his brushwork remained immaculately smooth. In 1959 he suffered a stroke and had to abandon painting and photography.

Sherborne Missal. See SIFERWAS.

Sherman, Cindy. See PHOTO-WORK.

Shinn, Everett (*b* Woodstown, NJ, 6 Nov. 1876; *d* New York, 1 May 1953). American painter and graphic artist. He began his career as a reporter-illustrator on the *Philadelphia Press*. His colleagues on the newspaper included *Glackens, *Luks, and *Sloan, who like Shinn became members of The *Eight and the *Ashcan School in New York (where he moved in 1896). Shinn differed from his associates in his choice of subject, preferring scenes from the theatre and music hall to low-life imagery. However, in 1911 he painted murals on local industrial subjects for Trenton City Hall, New Jersey, and these have been described as the earliest instance of *Social Realist themes in public mural decoration. He also did decorations for the interior of the Belasco Theatre, New York. In addition Shinn painted fashionable portraits, illustrated numerous books, wrote plays, and worked as an art director for motion pictures.

Shishkin, Ivan. See WANDERERS.

Shubin, Fedot (*b* Techkovskaya, Archangel province, 1740; *d* St Petersburg, 24 May 1805). The leading Russian sculptor of the 18th century. He trained at the Academy in St Petersburg and in 1767 won a scholarship to Paris, where he studied with *Pigalle. Before returning to Russia in 1773 he travelled in Italy (Turin, Bologna, Rome) and worked for a short while in London under *Nollekens. His output consists mainly of marble portrait busts, but his best-known work is a statue of Catherine the Great (1789–90, Russian Mus., St Petersburg). An earlier bust of Catherine (1771) is in the Victoria and Albert Museum, London.

Siberechts, Jan (*bapt.* Antwerp, 29 Jan. 1627; *d* London, *c.*1703). Flemish landscape painter who settled in England in the early 1670s. Initially he painted handsome Italianate landscapes in the manner of Dutch artists such as *Asselyn and *Both, as well as rural Flemish scenes with large-scale figures of peasants. After his move to England, however, he became best known as the first professional painter of 'portraits' of country houses; two views of Longleat, Wiltshire (1675 and 1676), are still preserved in the house. He also painted topographical views that stand at the beginning of the English landscape tradition (*Henley from the Wargrave Road*, 1698, River and Rowing Mus., Henley-on-Thames).

siccative. A substance mixed with paint (particularly oil paint) to make it dry more quickly. Siccatives (typically consisting of metallic salts) are dangerous aids, as they may cause cracking or darken a picture.

Sickert, Walter Richard (*b* Munich, 31 May 1860; *d* Bathampton, Somerset, 22 Jan. 1942). British painter, printmaker, teacher, and critic, one of the most important figures of his time in British art. He was born in Germany of a Danish-German father and an Anglo-Irish mother and his outlook was appropriately cosmopolitan. The family settled in London in 1868. Both his father and his grandfather were painters, but Sickert—after a good classical education—initially trained for a career on the stage, 1877–81. He toured with Sir Henry Irving's company but never progressed beyond small parts and in 1881 he abandoned acting and became a student at the *Slade School. In the following year he became a pupil of *Whistler, and in 1883 he worked in Paris with *Degas. Between 1885 and 1905 he spent much of his time in Dieppe, living there 1899–1905, and also visited Venice several times. From 1905, when he returned to England, he became the main channel for influence from avant-garde French painting in British art—inspiring a host of younger artists with the force of his personality as well as the quality of his work. The *Allied Artists' Association (1908), the *Camden Town Group (1911), and the *London Group (1913) were all formed largely by artists in his circle. In 1918–22 he again lived in or near Dieppe, then settled permanently in England, living in London and Brighton before moving to Broadstairs, Kent (1934), and finally to Bathampton, near Bath (1938).

Sickert took the elements of his style from various sources but moulded them into a highly distinctive manner. From Whistler he derived his subtle modulations of tone, although his harmonies were more sombre and his touch rougher, using thick, crusty paint. To Degas he was indebted particularly for his method of painting from photographs and for the informality of composition this encouraged. His favourite subjects were urban scenes and figure compositions, particularly pictures of the theatre and music-hall and drab domestic interiors. Sickert himself wrote in 1910 that 'The more our art is serious, the more will it tend to avoid the drawing-room and stick to the kitchen.' This attitude permeates his most famous painting, *Ennui*, a compelling image of a stagnant marriage, of which he painted several versions, that in the Tate, London (c.1914), being the largest and most highly finished. From the 1920s Sickert received many honours. His later works—often based on press photographs or Victorian illustrations—are very broadly handled, with the canvas often showing through the paint in places. The colour is generally much higher keyed than in his earlier work and sometimes almost *Expressionist in its boldness. The prevailing critical opinion for many years was that these late works marked a significant decline, but major claims have recently been made for them, particularly following the 1981 *Arts Council exhibition 'Late Sickert: Painting 1927 to 1942'.

As well as painting, Sickert was an outstanding etcher (he learnt the technique from Whistler) and a great teacher (he opened seven private art schools, each of brief duration, and also taught part-time at Westminster School of Art, 1908–12 and 1915–18). He was celebrated for his wit and charm and was a stimulating talker and an articulate writer on art; Osbert Sitwell edited a posthumous collection of his writings entitled *A Free House!* (1947). Sickert was married three times; his third wife (from 1926) was the painter **Thérèse Lessore** (1884–1945). His brother **Bernard Sickert** (1862/3–1932) was a landscape painter and etcher. He was a member of the *New English Art Club.

Since the 1970s there have been several misguided attempts (in books and television programmes) to implicate Sickert in the Jack the Ripper murders of 1888; apart from other considerations, he was probably in France at the time of the crimes.

Siddal, Elizabeth. See ROSSETTI.

Siegen, Ludwig von (*bapt.* Cologne, 2 May 1609; *d* Wolfenbüttel, c.1680). German soldier and amateur artist who invented the technique of *mezzotint. The earliest of his few surviving prints, a portrait of the Landgravine Amelia Elizabeth of Bohemia, dated 1642, was sent by Siegen to the Landgrave with a letter stating that the invention was his. Prince *Rupert, whom he probably met in Brussels in 1654, perhaps learnt the technique from him.

Siferwas, John (*b* c.1360; *d* c.1430). English illuminator, a Dominican friar. Siferwas is the first English illuminator whose career can be followed to some extent through documentary references and signed works. He was ordained a priest in London in 1382 and he probably trained as an artist there, but all his known work was done for religious houses in the south-west of England. His most important manuscript is the Sherborne *Missal (c.1405, BL, London), a very large and sumptuous book made for Sherborne Abbey, Dorset. It is a masterpiece of the *International Gothic style, the decoration including much flora and fauna, including some particularly sensitive depictions of birds. His other main work is the Lovell Lectionary (c.1400, BL, London), commissioned by John, 5th Lord Lovell of Titchmarsh, as a gift for Salisbury Cathedral (a lectionary is a book of extracts from the Bible appointed to be read at religious services). It includes a miniature of the artist (in Dominican habit) presenting the book to Lovell—one of the most remarkable self-portraits in medieval art. Siferwas included smaller self-portraits in the Sherborne Missal.

Signac, Paul (*b* Paris, 11 Nov. 1863; *d* Paris, 15 Aug. 1935). French painter, printmaker, and writer. He began in the *Impressionist manner, but met *Seurat in 1884 and became an ardent disciple of his views and technical method. After Seurat's death in 1891 he was the acknowledged leader of the *Neo-Impressionist group, and in

1899 he published *D'Eugène Delacroix au néo-impressionnisme*, which was long regarded as the authoritative work on the subject. The book was, however, more in the nature of a manifesto in defence of the movement than an objective history. It reflected Signac's use of more brilliant colour from about 1890, as he moved away from the scientific precision advocated by Seurat to a freer and more spontaneous manner. His work had a great influence on *Matisse, who visited him at Saint-Tropez in 1904 (a keen yachtsman, Signac spent a good deal of time on the Mediterranean and French Atlantic coasts; harbour scenes were his favourite subjects).

significant form. See BELL, CLIVE.

Signorelli, Luca (*b* Cortona, *c*.1440/50; *d* Cortona, 23/24 Oct. 1523). Italian painter, active in various cities of central Italy, including Arezzo, Florence, Orvieto, Perugia, and Rome, as well as his native Cortona. According to *Vasari (who was related to him and 'as a child of eight' met 'this good old man'), Signorelli was a pupil of *Piero della Francesca and this seems highly probable on stylistic grounds, for his solid figures and sensitive handling of light echo the work of the master. Signorelli differed from Piero, however, in his interest in the representation of action, which put him in line with contemporary Florentine artists such as the *Pollaiuolo brothers. He must have had a considerable reputation by about 1483, when he was engaged to complete the cycle of frescos on the walls of the Sistine Chapel in Rome, left unfinished by *Botticelli, *Ghirlandaio, *Perugino, and *Rosselli. (It is not known why these four artists abandoned the work in 1482, but it has been suggested that they simply downed tools because of slow payment.) Signorelli completed the scheme with distinction, but his finest works are in Orvieto Cathedral, where he painted a magnificent series of frescos illustrating the end of the world and the Last Judgement (1499–1504). In these grand and dramatic scenes he displayed a mastery of the nude in a wide variety of poses surpassed at that time only by *Michelangelo. Vasari says that 'Luca's works were always highly praised by Michelangelo' and several instances of close similarity between the work of the two men can be cited; perhaps most interesting is the enigmatic seated nude youth in Signorelli's *Last Acts and Death of Moses* in the Sistine Chapel, which is remarkably close to some of the *Ignudi* painted by Michelangelo on the ceiling of the chapel a quarter of a century later. By the end of his career, however, Luca had

become a conservative artist, working in provincial Cortona, where his large workshop produced numerous altarpieces. Several examples of his work are in the National Gallery, London.

Signorini, Telemaco. See MACCHIAIOLI.

silhouette. An outline image in one, solid, flat colour usually against a plain background, giving the appearance of a shadow cast by a solid figure. The principle goes back at least as far as Greek *black-figure vases, but the term is applied particularly to profile portraits in black against white (or vice versa), either painted or cut from paper, which were extremely popular in the period *c*.1750–*c*.1850. Silhouettes represented the quickest and cheapest method of portraiture (they have been called 'the poor man's *miniature'), and their characteristic purity and simplicity were particularly appealing in the age of *Neoclassicism. They harked back to the legend (recorded by *Pliny) that portraiture was invented when the daughter of a potter from Corinth 'drew in outline on the wall the shadow of her lover's face thrown by a lamp'; pictures representing this story and entitled either 'The Origin of Painting' or 'The Corinthian Maid' were popular in the 18th century (an example by David *Allan, 1775, is in the National Gallery of Scotland, Edinburgh). Additional intellectual prestige came from J. C. Lavater's *Essays on Physiognomy* (1775–8, English translation 1789–98), which were illustrated by silhouettes. Lavater's work was held in great respect throughout Europe, notably by *Goethe, who was himself an amateur devotee of silhouette making. The usual format was a head profile, but *conversation pieces were also fairly common, and some exponents even produced *genre scenes, history pictures, and landscapes. After about 1800 the essential purity of the silhouette was vitiated by the introduction of colour, gilding, fancy backgrounds, and other embellishments. Its death-blow, like that of the miniature, was dealt by the popularization of photography, although interesting experiments have later been made, such as the animated silhouette films of the German film-maker Lotte Reiniger (1899–1981).

During the century or so when silhouettes were at the height of their popularity there were hundreds of professional exponents of the art in Britain alone (some set up in fashionable places, while others toured the country), as well as countless amateurs. Many artists worked freehand, but some used mechanical aids, notably the 'silhouette chair' designed by Lavater. This entailed the sitter posing in front of a translucent screen, onto which a profile shadow was cast by a candle or other light. The artist, on the other side of the screen, traced the outline of the head and reduced it to the desired size by means of a *pantograph. Among the leading specialists in Britain were John Miers (1765–1821), regarded by many critics as the greatest of all silhouette painters, Isabella Beetham (née Robinson) (1753–1825), who worked mainly on glass, and the French-born Augustin Édouart (1789–1861), acknowledged as the finest of all silhouette cutters. He worked in England from 1814 to 1829, then emigrated to the USA. Édouart is said to have cut more than 200,000 silhouettes, and another indication of how quickly such works could be made comes from Miers's trade label; it says a sitting took only three minutes and that 'Mr Miers preserves all the original sketches from which he can at any time supply copies without the trouble of sitting again'.

The word 'silhouette' derives from Étienne de Silhouette (1709–67), French finance minister under Louis XV, who was notorious for his parsimony and—according to some accounts—cut shadow portraits as a hobby; hence the phrase 'à la silhouette' came to mean 'on the cheap'. In Britain silhouette portraits were generally called 'shades' or 'profiles' up to the end of the 18th century. The first recorded use of the word 'silhouette' in the *Oxford English Dictionary* dates from 1798, by which time the term had lost its original pejorative associations.

silkscreen printing. See SCREENPRINTING.

Siloé, Diego de (*b* Burgos, *c.*1495; *d* Granada, 22 Oct. 1563). Spanish architect and sculptor, one of the leading figures in the transition from *Gothic to *Renaissance in Spanish art. He was the son of **Gil de Siloé** (*d c.*1501), who is of uncertain origin (contemporary references suggest both Orléans and Antwerp as his native city) but who settled in Burgos and is regarded as the outstanding Spanish sculptor of the 15th century and the country's last great representative of the Gothic tradition. Gil's extant work includes two royal tombs (1489–93), both in alabaster, in the monastery of Miraflores, Burgos: the first is of John II of Castile and his wife Isabella of Portugal, the second of their son Prince Alfonso. Diego formed his style in Italy, where he collaborated with Bartolomé *Ordóñez. By 1519 he had returned to Burgos, where he carried out several important commissions in the cathedral. They include the impressive alabaster tomb of Bishop Luis de Acuña (1519–20), but his greatest work there is the *Escalera Dorada* (Golden Stairway) of 1519–23, and it was as an architect rather than as a sculptor that he emerged as one of the great figures of Spanish art. His masterpiece is Granada Cathedral, where he took over as architect in 1528.

silverpoint. See METALPOINT.

Silvestre, Israël (*b* Nancy, 3 Aug. 1621; *d* Paris, 11 Oct. 1691). French etcher, the best-known member of a family of artists. He worked a good deal for Louis XIII and was drawing master to the young Louis XIV. His output was large and varied, forming an invaluable source of historical information.

Simmons, Edward E. See TEN.

singerie. A depiction of monkeys (French: *singes*) engaged in playful activities, often dressed in human clothes and acting out human roles. The conceit of monkeys involved in human occupations goes back to medieval manuscripts, but the term *singerie* is most commonly applied to a type of decorative painting associated with the French *Rococo. Claude *Audran and his one-time assistant *Watteau were noted exponents.

sinopia. Term applied to a reddish-brown chalk used for the underdrawing of a *fresco and also to the drawing itself. Sinopie have sometimes been uncovered during restoration work when a fresco is detached from the wall, revealing the lower layer of plaster (see, for example, TRAINI).

Siqueiros, David Alfaro (*b* Chihuahua, 29 Dec. 1896; *d* Cuernavaca, 6 Jan. 1974). Mexican painter, one of the trio of muralists (with *Orozco and *Rivera) who dominated 20th-century Mexican art. He was a political activist from his youth and in 1914 abandoned his studies at the Academy of S. Carlos in Mexico City to join the revolutionary army fighting against President Huerta. His services were appreciated by the victorious General Carranza, who in 1919 sponsored him to continue his studies in Europe, where he was friendly with Rivera (later they became rivals). On returning to Mexico in 1922 he took a leading part in the artistic revival fostered by President Alvaro Obregón. Siqueiros was active in organizing the Syndicate of Technical Workers, Painters, and Sculptors and was partly responsible for drafting its manifesto, which set forth the idealistic aims of the revolutionary artists: 'our own aesthetic aim is to socialize artistic expression, to destroy bourgeois individualism . . . We proclaim that this being the moment of social transition from a decrepit to a new order, the makers of beauty must invest their greatest efforts in the aim of materializing an art valuable to the people, and our supreme object in art, which today is an expression for individual pleasure, is to create beauty for all, beauty that enlightens and stirs to struggle.'

Siqueiros's political activities led to his imprisonment or self-imposed exile several times; from 1925 to 1930 he completely abandoned painting for political activity and he later fought in the Spanish Civil War. It was not until 1939 that he eventually completed a mural in Mexico—*Portrait of the Bourgeoisie* for the headquarters of the Union of Electricians in Mexico City (his slow start had prompted Rivera to retort in answer to criticism from him: 'Siqueiros talks: Rivera paints!'). Thereafter, however, Siqueiros's output was prodigious. He painted many easel pictures as well as murals, and though he insisted they were subordinate to his wall paintings, they were important in helping to establish his international reputation. His murals are generally more spectacular even than those of Orozco and Rivera—bold in composition, striking in colour, freely mixing realism with fantasy, and expressing a raw emotional power. In contrast with the sense of disillusionment and foreboding sometimes seen in Orozco's work, Siqueiros always expressed the dynamic urge to struggle; his work can be vulgar and bombastic, but its sheer energy is astonishing. He often experimented technically—working on curved surfaces and using airbrushes and synthetic pigments—and his last major work, the Polyforum Siqueiros in Mexico City (completed 1971), is a huge auditorium integrating architecture, sculpture, and painting. In his late years Siqueiros was showered with honours from his own country and elsewhere; he received the Lenin Peace Prize in 1967, for example, and in the following year became the first president of the newly founded Mexican Academy of Arts.

Sisley, Alfred (*b* Paris, 30 Oct 1839; *d* Moret-sur-Loing, nr. Fontainebleau, 29 Jan. 1899). Anglo-French *Impressionist painter; although he is generally regarded as French, his parents were English and he was a British citizen throughout his life (he twice unsuccessfully tried to become a naturalized Frenchman). His father was a businessman who spent much of his life in Paris, and Sisley was destined for a commercial career before he turned to painting. In

1862 he entered the studio of *Gleyre and there met *Renoir, *Monet, and *Bazille; these four student friends formed the original nucleus of the Impressionist group. Like Monet, Sisley devoted himself almost exclusively to landscape, but his work was much less varied. He made several visits to England, but otherwise rarely travelled, and most of his pictures are of scenes in and around Paris. The best are among the most lyrical and gently harmonious works of Impressionism, delicate in touch and with a beautiful feeling for tone (*Flood at Port-Marly*, 1876, Mus. d'Orsay, Paris). Sisley was given a generous allowance by his wealthy father and his early life was happy: Renoir described him as 'a delightful human being' and said he 'could never resist a petticoat'. However, after the family business failed in 1871 because of the Franco-Prussian War, his father was unable to support him and thereafter he spent much of his life in poverty, never winning the success or renown of his former colleagues. He still remains something of a Cinderella among the Impressionists, claimed as their own by neither the French nor the English.

Situation (in full, 'Situation: An Exhibition of British Abstract Painting'). An exhibition staged in September 1960 at the Galleries of the Royal Society of British Artists, London, by a group of predominantly young British painters who were united by their admiration for American *Abstract Expressionism. The catalogue listed twenty artists, but only eighteen in fact showed their work. Paintings included had to be totally abstract and at least 30 square feet (*c*.3 sq. m) in size; the name of the exhibition came from the participants' idea that an abstract painting that occupied the whole field of vision would involve the spectator in an 'event' or 'situation'. Robyn Denny (1930–) was the organizing secretary and other artists represented included Gillian Ayres (1930–), the brothers Bernard (1933–) and Harold Cohen (1928–), John Hoyland (1934–), Bob Law (1934–), Richard Smith (see SHAPED CANVAS), and William *Turnbull. These artists felt frustrated by the lack of exposure given to large-scale abstract works by commercial galleries, and in organizing the exhibition themselves they aimed to bypass the dealer system. The following year, however, the London dealers Marlborough Fine Art staged an exhibition featuring sixteen of the eighteen who had participated in the original show, with the addition of the sculptor Anthony *Caro; this was entitled 'New London Situation: An Exhibition of

Abstract Art'. In 1962–3 the *Arts Council organized a touring exhibition of the work of the group entitled 'Situation: An Exhibition of Recent British Abstract Art'. The three exhibitions marked a move towards a more international context for British painting.

Sixtus IV, Pope. See ROVERE.

size. Glue made from animal products (such as skin or bone), or, more loosely, any fairly weak glue. It is used in art mainly for filling the porous surface of wooden *panels or *canvases to provide a suitable foundation for the *priming (see GROUND). Size is also used as a *medium—paint mixed with it is called *distemper.

Skagen artists' colony. See ANCHER.

Skeaping, John. See HEPWORTH.

sketch. 'A rough drawing or delineation of something, giving the outlines or prominent features without the detail, especially one intended to serve as the basis of a more finished picture, or to be used in its composition' (OED). This was the original meaning of the word, and it was not until the latter.part of the 18th century that it acquired the additional sense of 'a drawing or painting of a slight or unpretentious nature'. A sketch should be distinguished from a 'study', which is a representation of a detail to be used in a large composition and may be highly finished. See also BOZZETTO and MODELLO.

Škréta, Karel (b Prague, c.1610; bur. Prague, 1 Aug. 1674). The outstanding Bohemian painter of the 17th century. From about 1630 to about 1635 he was in Italy, and he subsequently worked for a time in Germany before settling in Prague in about 1638. He produced a good deal of religious work, but he is best known for his dignified and humane portraits. There are several examples in the convent of St George (part of the National Gallery), Prague, including *Dionysius Miseroni and his Family* (c.1653), which is generally regarded as his masterpiece. It shows a gem cutter with his wife and children, with a view into his workshop behind them.

Slade, Felix (b London, Aug. 1790; d London, 29 Mar. 1868). English art collector and philanthropist. He left a great part of his collection, notable particularly for glass, to the *British Museum and in his will he endowed chairs of fine art at the universities of London (University College), Oxford, and Cambridge. The professorships at Oxford and Cambridge involve only the giving of lectures, intended for a general audience, but in London the Slade School of Fine Art, opened in 1871, is an institution giving practical instruction. The first professor was Sir Edward *Poynter, who founded the Slade tradition of emphasis on drawing from the nude. Rapidly overtaking the *Royal Academy (where the teaching methods were considered arid and academic) as the most important art school in the country, the Slade had its heyday in the period from about 1895 to the First World War. Its students then included some of the most illustrious names in 20th-century British art—*Augustus and Gwen *John, Wyndham *Lewis, Paul *Nash, Ben *Nicholson, Stanley *Spencer, and so on. Poynter's successors in London have included *Legros, Frederick Brown (1851–1941), who was professor from 1892 to 1917, presiding over the School's golden age, *Tonks, *Coldstream, and *Gowing. The first Slade professors at Oxford and Cambridge respectively were *Ruskin and the architect Matthew Digby Wyatt. Their successors have included many eminent art historians.

Sleigh, Sylvia. See ALLOWAY and FEMINIST ART.

Slevogt, Max (b Landshut, Bavaria, 8 Oct. 1868; d Neukastel, Pfalz, 20 Sept., 1932). German painter and illustrator, with *Corinth and *Liebermann one of his country's leading exponents of *Impressionism. He studied in Munich, then at the *Académie Julian, Paris, 1889–90. In 1901 he settled in Berlin, where he taught at the Academy from 1917. Slevogt's early work was sombre, but from about 1900 his style became lighter, looser, and more colourful. His subjects included landscapes, portraits, and scenes from contemporary life; he loved the theatre and his best-known works include a number of portrayals of the Portuguese baritone Francesco d'Andrade in his most celebrated role as Mozart's Don Giovanni. Although his vigorous brushwork, bold effects of light, and energetic sense of movement give his work great dash, he never adopted the fragmentation of colours typical of the Impressionists and always retained something of the Bavarian *Baroque tradition. He also differed from the Impressionists in that he devoted a good deal of his time to large decorative schemes; these include a fresco of *Golgotha* in the Friedenskirche at Ludwigshafen (1932), often considered his masterpiece. He was a prolific illustrator for books and journals.

Sloan, John (b Lock Haven, Pa., 2 Aug. 1871; d Hanover, NH, 7 Sept. 1951). American painter and graphic artist. During the 1890s he worked as a newspaper illustrator in Philadelphia, and he started painting seriously in 1896, influenced by Robert *Henri. In 1904 he settled permanently in New York, where he and Henri were among the members of The *Eight. Sloan was the most political member of the group and, as well as taking his most characteristic subjects from everyday lower-class New York life, he did illustrations for socialist periodicals, including *The Masses*, of which he was art editor from 1912 to 1916. However, he was not interested in using his art for what he called 'socialist propaganda' and he resigned from the magazine after a dispute over policy. His paintings of the pre-First World War period are generally solid, broadly brushed, and low keyed in colour, typically featuring street scenes or domestic interiors; however, he could also be sharply satirical and occasionally he expressed himself in a totally different vein, as in *Wake of the Ferry* (1907, Phillips Coll., Washington), a hauntingly melancholic marine picture. After the *Armory Show he broadened the scope of his work to include landscapes and nudes and his style became harder and brighter. He also made etchings throughout his career. Sloan was a popular teacher at the *Art Students League and other schools. In 1939 he published an autobiographical-critical book, *Gist of Art*.

Slodtz. Family of French artists. The head of the family was **Sébastien** (1655–1726), a sculptor and designer, who was Flemish by birth. He had three sculptor sons: **Sébastien-Antoine** (1695–1754), **Paul-Ambroise** (1702–58), and **René-Michel** called Michel-Ange (b Paris, 27 Sept. 1705; d Paris, 26 Oct. 1764). All four of them worked for the Menus Plaisirs (the office that designed costumes, festivities, etc. for the court), as did another son of Sébastien, the painter **Dominique Slodtz** (1711–64); a fifth brother, **Jean-Baptiste** (1699–1759), was also a painter. Michel-Ange was the only member of the family to attain great distinction. From 1728 to 1747 he lived in Rome, where his admiration for *Michelangelo won him his nickname. His best-known work is the marble *St Bruno* (1744, St Peter's, Rome), which shows the nervous sensitivity of his style. In France he made several major tombs, notably that of Languet de Gergy (completed 1753, St Sulpice, Paris), which shows the influence of *Bernini in its *Baroque rhetoric and use of different coloured marbles. *Houdon was Slodtz's most important pupil.

Sluijters, Jan. See SLUYTERS.

Sluter, Claus (b Haarlem, c.1350; d Dijon, 1405/6). Netherlandish stone sculptor, active mainly in Dijon. He was the greatest sculptor of his time in northern Europe and a figure of enormous importance in the transition from *International Gothic to a more weighty and naturalistic style. Sluter is first mentioned in Brussels (c.1379) in a document that says he came from Haarlem. In 1385 he entered the service of Philip the Bold, Duke of *Burgundy, in his capital Dijon. All of Sluter's surviving work was done for Philip, and almost all of it remains in Dijon. For the Chartreuse de Champmol, a monastery founded by Philip, he carved figures for the portal of the chapel in the early 1390s, and made a fountain group, the only part of which to survive intact is the base, known as the *Well of Moses* (1395–1403). The monastery was destroyed during the French Revolution, and the portal and the *Well of Moses* are now part of the psychiatric hospital that occupies its site. The Well features six full-length figures of prophets of monumental dignity; they convey an intense sense of physical presence, and as character studies rival the prophets of *Donatello, which they preceded by about twenty years. Originally Sluter's figures were painted (by *Malouel) and the figure of Jeremiah is known to have worn copper spectacles, the record of payment for which still survives. Of the *Calvary* group that surmounted the Well (symbolizing the 'Fountain of Life') only fragments survive in the Archaeological Museum in Dijon; they include the head and torso of the figure of Christ—one of Sluter's noblest works, in which the expression of suffering stoically endured is deeply moving.

Sluter's last work was the tomb of Philip the Bold, begun in 1404 and unfinished at the sculptor's death (Mus. B.-A., Dijon). Most of the work on it was carried out by Sluter's nephew and assistant Claus de Werve (d 1439), but the figures of *pleurants* (weepers or mourners) that form a frieze around the sarcophagus are from the master's own hand, and although they are only about 40 cm (15 in) high they possess massive solemnity. They show Sluter's extraordinary ability to use the heavy folds of drapery for expressive effect; indeed some of the mourners are so completely enveloped in their voluminous cowls that they are in effect nothing else but drapery. Erwin *Panofsky has written (*Early Netherlandish Painting*, 1953) that it is 'the concentrated emanation of Claus Sluter's style which we mean when we speak of a "Burgundian school of sculpture of the fifteenth century"', and his work had great influence also on painters. The emphatic plasticity of the *Master of Flémalle's figures, for example, has Sluter as its source, and in his *Entombment* (Courtauld Gal., London, c.1410–20), which stands at the head of the Early Netherlandish tradition of painting, the angel who wipes away a tear with the back of his hand is a quotation from the *Well of Moses*.

Sluyters (or **Sluijters**), **Jan** (b 's Hertogenbosch, 17 Dec. 1881; d Amsterdam, 8 May 1957). Dutch painter, active mainly in Amsterdam. He was one of the best-known artists in the Netherlands in the inter-war period and the one in whom French modernism is most variously reflected. His early works show the influence of his countrymen van *Gogh and *Breitner, and of *Fauvism. He also experimented with *Cubism before finally developing a lively personal style of colourful *Expressionism that is best seen in his nudes—he had a predilection for painting nude children.

Smart, John (b c.1742; d London, 1 May 1811). One of the leading British miniaturists of his period. His style was meticulous, bright, and pretty. He worked mainly in London but was in India 1785–95.

Smet, Gustave de (b Ghent, 21 Jan. 1877; d Deurle, nr. Ghent, 8 Oct. 1943). One of the leading Belgian *Expressionist painters. His early work was *Impressionist in style, but he was influenced towards Expressionism by Jan *Sluyters and Henri *Le Fauconnier, whom he met in Holland when he took refuge there during the First World War. Typically de Smet painted scenes of rural and village life in which forms are treated in a schematic way owing something to *Cubism; there is often an air of unreality reminiscent of that in *Chagall's work (*Village Fair*, c.1930, Mus. voor Schone Kunsten, Ghent). His brother **Léon de Smet** (1881–1966) was also a painter.

Smibert, John (b Edinburgh, 24 Mar. 1688; d Boston, 2 Apr. 1751). Scottish-born portrait painter who emigrated to America in 1728 and settled in Boston in 1730. Previously he had travelled in Italy and practised successfully in London in an uninspired style derived from *Kneller. After he settled in America his work became somewhat more vigorous. He brought with him a small collection of copies, casts, and prints, and he opened a shop in Boston where he sold artists' materials and engravings of the works of well-known artists. His collection was displayed above the shop, forming in effect America's first art gallery, and together with his own paintings it became the cornerstone of the New England Colonial portrait style. *Copley and *Trumbull were among the artists familiar with the collection.

Smith, David (b Decatur, Ind., 9 Mar. 1906; d nr. Bennington, Vt., 23 May 1965). The most original and influential American sculptor of his generation. He began to study art at Ohio University in 1924 but soon dropped out of the course, and in the summer of 1925 he worked at the Studebaker motor plant at South Bend, Indiana, where he acquired the skills in metalwork that stood him in good stead later in his career. From 1926 to 1930 he studied painting at the *Art Students League, New York, while supporting himself by a variety of jobs. Among his friends at this time were Arshile *Gorky and Willem *de Kooning. He turned to sculpture in the early 1930s, making his first welded iron pieces (probably the first by an American artist) in 1933. These were inspired by Julio *González, to whom Smith said he owed his 'technical liberation', but he always maintained that there was no essential difference between painting and sculpture and that his aesthetic outlook was more influenced by *Kandinsky, *Mondrian, and *Cubism. By the time of his first one-man exhibition in 1938 he was producing sculpture of considerable originality, constructing compositions from steel and 'found' scrap, parts of agricultural machinery, etc. He had a love of technology, and wrote: 'The equipment I use, my supply of material, comes from factory study, and duplicates as nearly as possible the production equipment used in making a locomotive . . . What associations the metal possesses are those of this century: power, structure, movement, progress, suspension, destruction, brutality.'

Smith settled at Bolton Landing in upstate New York in 1940. In the same year he exhibited a set of fifteen bronze *relief plaques entitled *Medals for Dishonor* stigmatizing violence and greed. He was employed as a welder on defence work 1942–4, then returned to sculpture, and from this time began to build an international reputation. During the 1940s and 1950s his sculpture was predominantly open and linear, like three-dimensional metal calligraphy (*Hudson River Landscape*, 1951, Whitney Mus., New York). From the end of the 1950s, however, his style became more monumental and geometrical, with boxes and cylinders of polished metal joined at odd angles. Although the forms are often massive, the effect they create is not one of heaviness but of unstable dynamism, the exhilarating sense of freedom being enhanced by the reflection of sunlight from the bright surfaces (they are generally intended for outdoor settings). These works were often created in series, such as *Zig*, *Cubi*, and *Voltri*. They initiated a new era in American sculpture, and gave Smith a place as the peer of the great *Abstract Expressionist painters who were his contemporaries. Like the most famous of the Abstract Expressionists, Jackson *Pollock, Smith died in an automobile accident. See also IRON

Smith, Grace Cossington (*b* Sydney, 22 Apr. 1892; *d* Sydney, 20 Dec. 1984). Australian painter. In 1912–14 she visited England and Germany. After her return to Sydney she began studying at the Royal Art Society of New South Wales School, where she became interested in *Post-Impressionism. Her painting *The Sock Knitter* (1915, AG of NSW, Sydney), exhibited at the Royal Art Society show in 1915, is—in its flattened space and *Fauve-like colours—arguably the first 'modern' picture painted and exhibited in Australia. In the early 1920s Smith was briefly influenced by Max *Meldrum's all-pervasive tonal theory of painting, but she reverted to richer colour and to the application of paint in crisp strokes. In the 1930s she turned increasingly to light-filled interiors of her own home. Although her work was influenced by artists such as *Matisse and later *Cézanne, she never regarded herself as a particularly radical or innovatory artist. Her interest in modernism was inspired not by its intellectual prescriptions, but because for her it constituted a livelier approach to painting.

Smith, Jack. See KITCHEN SINK SCHOOL.

Smith, John. See VERMEER.

Smith, John Raphael (*b* Derby, 1752; *d* Doncaster, 2 Mar. 1812). English printmaker, publisher, painter, and draughtsman, son of a landscape painter, **Thomas Smith** of Derby (*d* 1767). He was one of the leading printmakers of the day, producing (most notably) numerous plates after portraits by *Gainsborough, *Reynolds, and *Romney, and also some after his own designs. Usually he worked in *mezzotint, but also in *aquatint and *stipple. In addition to his work as an artist, he was a highly successful publisher and seller of prints, exporting large numbers to France (a bon viveur, he took part of his payment in champagne and claret). The Napoleonic Wars ruined this market, however,

and in the last decade of his life Smith worked as a pastel portraitist.

Smith, John Thomas ('Antiquity Smith') (*b* London, 23 June 1766; *d* London, 8 Mar. 1833). English draughtsman, engraver, painter, antiquary, and administrator. He was the son of a sculptor, **Nathaniel Smith** (*c*.1741–after 1800), who was *Nollekens's chief assistant, and he himself spent three years training with Nollekens before he abandoned sculpture for engraving in 1781. For much of his career he worked as a topographical draughtsman, and from 1816 until his death he was keeper of prints and drawings at the British Museum. He wrote various books; they are mainly on London topography and other antiquarian matters, but he is now remembered above all for *Nollekens and his Times* (1828). In addition to the notoriously unkind account of Nollekens, it contains short biographies of other artists—a valuable source of information for the art historian.

Smith, John 'Warwick' (*b* Irthington, Cumberland, 26 July 1749; *d* London, 22 Mar. 1831). English landscape watercolourist, nicknamed Warwick Smith because he was patronized by George Greville, 2nd Earl of Warwick, and also lived in Warwick for a time. Lord Warwick paid for Smith to visit Italy in 1776–81, and he later made many sketching tours in Wales and the Lake and Peak Districts. He experimented with directly applied colour without underdrawing and his best work has strength and freshness. He was very prolific, however, and much of his later work is routine. He is represented in most major collections of watercolours.

Smith, Joseph. See CANALETTO.

Smith, Joshua. See DOBELL.

Smith, Sir Matthew (*b* Halifax, Yorkshire, 22 Oct. 1879; *d* London, 29 Sept. 1959). British painter. He studied at the *Slade School, 1905–7, and for a short time in Paris (1911) under *Matisse. Thereafter he identified strongly with French art and during the interwar years he spent much of his time in France, mainly in Paris and Aix-en-Provence. He was delicate in health and of a nervous disposition, but this is hardly apparent from his work, which uses colour in a bold, unnaturalistic manner echoing the *Fauves. His lush brushwork, too, has great vigour, and he was one of the few British painters to excel in painting the nude, his dark saturated colours and opulent fluency of line creating images of great sensuousness.

He also painted landscapes (most notably a series done in Cornwall in 1920) and still-lifes. His early progress had been halting, but after a successful one-man exhibition at the Mayor Gallery, London, in 1926 his reputation quickly grew—in 1928 Augustus *John described him as 'one of the most brilliant and individual figures in modern English painting'. Frank *Auerbach and Francis *Bacon are among the other artists who have admired Smith's painterliness; Bacon said he was 'one of the very few English painters since *Constable and *Turner to be concerned with painting—that is, with attempting to make idea and technique inseparable'. His work is in many public galleries, the best collection being in the Guildhall Art Gallery, London.

Smith, Richard. See SHAPED CANVAS and SITUATION.

Smith, Tony (*b* South Orange, NJ, 23 Sept. 1912; *d* New York, 26 Dec. 1980). American sculptor, painter, and architect. He served an apprenticeship in architecture as clerk of works to Frank Lloyd Wright and practised as an architect from 1940 to 1960, during which time he also painted. He began to take an interest in sculpture around 1940, but although he taught at various colleges in the 1940s and 1950s (in addition to his architectural career) and was closely associated with leading avant-garde figures such as *Newman, *Pollock, *Rothko, and *Still, he did not exhibit sculpture publicly until 1964. From that time he quickly emerged as one of the leading exponents of *Minimal art. His work was sometimes very large in scale, composed of bold geometrical shapes (often repeated modular units) that he had industrially manufactured in steel. Many of his works were placed outdoors, helping to bring to American sculpture a new interest in the environment. A well-known example is *Grace-hoper* (1972, Detroit Inst. of Arts), which one can walk through. His daughter **Kiki Smith** (1954–) is a sculptor and *Body artist.

Smithson, Robert (*b* Passaic, NJ, 2 Jan. 1938; *d* Amarillo, Tex., 20 July 1973). American sculptor and experimental artist. In the 1960s his work belonged mainly to the category of *Minimal art; he was interested in mathematical impersonality and as well as making blocklike steel sculptures he experimented with reflections and mirror images. From the late 1960s he turned to *Conceptual art; he expressed his ideas mainly through *Land art and became the best-known artist working in this field. In 1968 he began a

series of 'Sites' and 'Non-Sites'. The latter consisted of photographs and plans of locations he had visited (particularly derelict urban or industrial sites) displayed with specimens of rock or geological refuse he had gathered there, arranged into random heaps or in metal or wood bins: 'Instead of putting a work of art on some land, some land is put into the work of art.' Smithson then moved on to large-scale earthworks, the best known of which is the enormous *Spiral Jetty* (1970), a spiral road running out into Great Salt Lake, Utah (it has periodically become submerged and then reappeared with changing water levels). He was killed in a plane crash when he was surveying a work in progress, *Amarillo Ramp*, in Texas. Smithson wrote many articles expounding his views on art: *The Writings of Robert Smithson*, edited by Nancy Holt (his widow), was published in 1979.

Smithsonian Institution. A research institution and educational centre founded by the bequest of the English scientist James Smithson (1765–1829) 'for the increase and diffusion of knowledge' and established by congressional act in Washington, DC, in 1846. Smithson was an illegitimate son of Hugh Smithson Percy, Duke of Northumberland, and it is thought to have been resentment over the circumstances of his birth that caused him to make the bequest to the USA rather than his native country: 'My name shall live . . . when the titles of the Northumberlands . . . are extinct and forgotten.' The Smithsonian administers many prestigious cultural organizations in Washington, including the National Gallery of Art, the National Portrait Gallery, and the Joseph H. Hirshhorn Museum and Sculpture Garden.

Snyders, Frans (*bapt.* Antwerp, 11 Nov. 1579; *d* Antwerp, 19 Aug. 1657). Flemish painter of animals, hunting scenes, and still-life. He was a pupil of Pieter *Brueghel the Younger and perhaps of Hendrick van *Balen. In 1602 he became a master in the Antwerp guild, and in 1608–9 he visited Italy (mainly Rome and Milan). Back in Antwerp, he became a close friend of *Rubens, also recently returned from Italy (he was eventually executor of Rubens's will). Snyders often collaborated with Rubens; he painted animals, fruits, and flowers in Rubens's pictures, and Rubens painted figures in his. He later had the same kind of reciprocal arrangement with *Jordaens, and also collaborated with van *Dyck, *Janssen, and Cornelis de *Vos (his brother-in-law). Snyders's independent works confirm him as the finest animal painter of his time; the best are his scenes of hunts and fighting wild animals, which have a tremendous sense of *Baroque vitality. Some of his pictures are very large; his *Boar Hunt* (MFA, Boston), for example, is more than 5 m (16 ft) wide.

soapstone (also called **steatite**). A very soft smooth stone (composed of magnesium silicate), superficially like *marble or jade in appearance but with a greasy, soapy feel. It is a compact form of talc, the softest standard mineral on the Mohs scale of hardness. Usually it is a dull greenish or bluish grey or sometimes brown. It will take a smooth polish, and is so easily worked that it may even be carved with a knife. Because of this quality it has been used in many parts of the world, from ancient times onwards, mainly for fairly small objects and utensils, but also for large sculpture, for example by António Francisco *Lisboa in colonial Brazil.

Socialist Realism. The name of the officially approved type of art in Soviet Russia and other Communist countries, involving in theory a faithful and objective reflection of real life to educate and inspire the masses, and in practice the compulsory and uncritical glorification of the state. Socialist Realism was an aspect of the dictatorship of Stalin, who was leader of the Soviet Union from the death of Lenin in 1924 until his own death in 1953. Alan Bird (*A History of Russian Painting*, 1987) writes that 'He saw all aspects of avant-garde culture, including painting, as subversive infiltrations of the purity of Soviet life' and that his minister Andrei Zhdanov 'made himself responsible for imposing an iron control on artistic expression'.

The principles of Socialist Realism began to take shape in the late 1920s and were proclaimed in the 1932 decree 'On the Reconstruction of Literary and Art Organizations' (before this, the term 'Heroic Realism' had often been used, but 'Socialist Realism' now became the official label). It was never defined specifically in terms of style and in its early days it saw expression in some outstanding works, notably the paintings of Alexander Deineka (1899–1969), which are remarkable for their formal vigour as well as their humanity (*The Defence of Petrograd*, 1927, Tretyakov Gal., Moscow). However, Socialist Realism became increasingly associated with stereotyped images painted in a conventional academic manner. In the 1930s these paintings were of four main types: domestic scenes, portraits, industrial and urban landscapes, and scenes on collective farms. During the Second World War, patriotic scenes from Russian history were added to the list. After the death of Stalin there was some relaxation of strictures, but the system still remained stifling to creativity, and any form of experiment remained extremely difficult. In the West, Socialist Realism remained synonymous with repression, and its products were generally regarded as morally tragic and aesthetically comic, although the merits of painters such as Arkady Plastov (1893–1972), a specialist in farm scenes, are now being recognized.

Socialist Realism had an equally powerful grip on Russian literature and even music. In 1934 the constitution of the Union of Writers stated that Socialist Realism 'demands from the artist a true and historically concrete depiction of reality in its revolutionary development . . . combined with the task of educating workers in the spirit of Communism', and in 1948 several leading Soviet composers (including the two greatest, Prokofiev and Shostakovich) were censured for *formalism and had to make a grovelling public apology. They wrote a joint letter to 'Dear Comrade Stalin' in which they said: 'We are tremendously grateful . . . for the severe but profoundly just criticism of the present state of Soviet music . . . We shall bend every effort to apply our knowledge and our artistic mastery to produce vivid realistic music reflecting the life and struggles of the Soviet people.' For Socialist Realism in China, see XU BEIHONG.

Social Realism. A very broad term for painting (or literature or other art) that comments on contemporary social, political, or economic conditions, usually from a left-wing viewpoint, in a realistic manner. Often the term carries with it the suggestion of protest or propaganda in the interest of social reform. However, it does not imply any particular style; Ben *Shahn's caricature-like scenes on injustice and social hypocrisy in the USA, the dour working-class interiors of the *Kitchen Sink School in Britain, and the declamatory political statements of *Guttoso in Italy are all embraced by the term. See also REALISM.

Société Anonyme, Inc. (or **A Museum of Modern Art**). An association founded in 1920 by Katherine *Dreier, Marcel *Duchamp, and *Man Ray for the promotion of contemporary art in America by lectures, publications, travelling exhibitions, and the formation of a permanent collection. In French the term 'société anonyme' means 'limited company', so the name—suggested by Man Ray—was intended as a tautological *Dada jest; as Miss Dreier loved to explain, it meant 'incorporated corporation'. However, the work of the society was serious and trailblazing. Its museum, which opened at 19 East 47th Street, New York, in 1920, was the first in the USA, and one of the earliest anywhere, to be devoted entirely to modern art (although as it was concerned mainly with temporary exhibitions, the *Phillips Collection in Washington has the distinction of being the first *permanent* American museum in the field). Between 1920 and 1940 the Société organized 84 exhibitions, through which such artists as *Klee, *Malevich, *Miró, and *Schwitters were first exhibited in America. To some extent, therefore, the Société carried on the tradition that had been started by the 291 Gallery of *Stieglitz in the years before the *Armory Show, and to some extent also it prepared the way for the *Museum of Modern Art, which was founded in 1929. The Museum of Modern Art soon eclipsed the Société Anonyme and Miss Dreier's finances were in any case badly hit by the Depression, but she continued to serve as president (as Duchamp did as secretary) until the Société officially closed in 1950. Nine years earlier, in 1941, they had presented the superb permanent collection that the Société had built up (over 600 works) to Yale University Art Gallery.

Society of Artists. An association of artists founded in London in 1760 and incorporated by Royal Charter in 1765 (after which it was known as the Incorporated Society of Artists). It held annual exhibitions and was the main forerunner of the *Royal Academy. *Hayman and *Lambert were leading figures of the society in its early years; it was soon overshadowed by the Academy, but it remained active until 1791.

Society of Independent Artists. An organization formed in New York in December 1916 as a successor to the Association of American Painters and Sculptors, which had been dissolved—its task accomplished—after mounting the *Armory Show in 1913. The Society's aim was to give progressive artists an opportunity to show their work by holding annual exhibitions in rivalry with the conservative *National Academy of Design. These shows were organized on the model of the French *Salon des Indépendants, without jury or prizes, giving anyone the right to exhibit on payment of a modest fee. The first show, in April 1917, featured about 2,500 works by about 1,200 artists and was probably the largest art exhibition ever held in the USA. However, it is remembered mainly because of a work that was not shown, for Marcel *Duchamp (one of the Society's officials) resigned after his *ready-made in the form of a urinal was rejected. Although much recondite aesthetic theory has been read into this gesture, it is likely that the main purpose was to demonstrate the incongruity of a society with the professed purpose of allowing anyone to exhibit anything. The first president of the Society was William *Glackens; he was followed by John *Sloan, who held the post from 1918 until his death in 1951. Annual exhibitions continued to be held until 1944, but they soon declined in terms of quantity and quality.

Sodoma, Il (Giovanni Antonio Bazzi) (*b* Vercelli, 1477; *d* Siena, 15 Feb. 1549). Italian painter, active chiefly in and around Siena, where he settled in about 1500, but also in Rome. *Vasari, who disliked him, explains the origin of his nickname (the sodomite) in this fashion: 'His manner of life was licentious and dishonourable, and as he always had boys and beardless youths about him of whom he was inordinately fond, this earned him the nickname of Sodoma; but instead of feeling shame, he gloried in it, writing stanzas and verses on it, and singing them to the accompaniment of the lute.' Sodoma (who was married and had children) himself used the name in his signature, and Vasari's account has been questioned. Vasari also tells us that Sodoma kept a menagerie of strange animals 'so that his home resembled a veritable Noah's ark'. He was a prolific painter of frescos and easel pictures, and he drew on a variety of sources that were not always fully digested; consequently his work often has incongruous juxtapositions and a general air of uncoordination, but it also possesses charm and a flair for decoration. His fresco of the *Marriage of Alexander and Roxane* (c.1516), painted for the banker Agostino *Chigi in his villa (now the Villa Farnesina) in Rome, is often cited as his finest work. In his time Sodoma was considered the leading artist in Siena, but later critics have come to rank *Beccafumi above him.

Soest, Gerard (*b* ?Soest, Westphalia, ?c.1600; *d* London, 11 Feb. 1681). Painter of Dutch (or perhaps German) origin who spent all his known career in England (where he probably settled in the late 1640s). He was much less successful than his contemporary *Lely (he never worked at court), but he is often a more interesting painter, as he had a strong grasp of character and eschewed flattery and superficial elegance. There are examples of his work in the National

Portrait Gallery and Tate Britain, London, but his masterpiece is the full-length *Cecil, Second Lord Baltimore, with a Child and a Negro Page* (Enoch Pratt Library, Baltimore), which shows his considerable powers as a colourist; Ellis *Waterhouse describes it as 'one of the most fascinating portraits painted in England in the seventeenth century'.

Soffici, Ardengo (*b* Rignano sull'Arno, nr. Florence, 7 Apr. 1879; *d* Forte dei Marmi, nr. Viareggio, 18 Aug. 1964). Italian critic and painter. From 1900 to 1907 he spent his formative years in Paris, where he wrote for avant-garde periodicals and knew such figures as *Apollinaire, *Braque, *Modigliani, and *Picasso. In 1907 he settled in Florence and in the period before the First World War he was prominent in introducing the discussion of modern art—particularly *Cubism—to Italy. He championed the work of Medardo *Rosso, but initially he was hostile to *Futurism; however, under the influence of *Boccioni and *Carrà, he became converted to the movement in 1913. After the war his views became increasingly conservative and he joined Carrà and de *Chirico in the attacks they made on Cubism and Futurism in the journal *Valori plastici*. Soffici's own work as a painter reflects his changing critical outlook, but it is not considered to have much independent merit.

Soft art. Term applied to sculpture using non-rigid materials, a vogue of the 1960s and 1970s. The materials employed have been very diverse: rope, cloth, rubber, leather, paper, canvas, vinyl—anything in fact that offers a certain persistence of form but lacks permanent shape or rigidity. The earliest example of Soft art was perhaps the typewriter cover that Marcel *Duchamp mounted on a stand and exhibited in 1916. However, this belongs rather to the category of *ready-mades, and Soft art as a movement is generally traced to Claes *Oldenburg's giant replicas of foodstuffs (ice-cream sundaes, hamburgers, pieces of cake, etc.) made from stuffed vinyl and canvas. Other artists who have experimented with soft materials have been many and diverse, representing a variety of movements, including *Arte Povera, *Pop art, and *Surrealism.

soft-ground etching. A method of *etching that produces prints characterized by softness of line or a grainy texture. The waxy *ground used to coat the etching plate is softer and stickier than in normal etching (various recipes exist), so that it adheres to anything pressed into it. Over this ground is laid a sheet of paper on which the artist draws with a pencil. Under the pressure of the pencil strokes the ground sticks to the back of the paper, so that when it is peeled off the wax immediately underneath the lines comes away with it, while the rest remains in place. The plate is then immersed in acid, and printed in the normal way. Depending on the texture of the paper used for the drawing, the printed lines are granular, coarse, or fine: thus if the paper is smooth, the lines resemble pencil, but if rough, they are more like chalk. Soft-ground etchings bear a strong likeness to prints in the *crayon manner, but are generally a little softer and less regular.

The technique is believed to have been invented by G. B. *Castiglione in the 1640s, but only a single print by him survives (in the Royal Library, Windsor). Evidently the idea died with him, and the technique was reinvented in the mid-18th century; it flourished until about 1830, when it was generally superseded by *lithography. Although it was chiefly used for reproductive prints, a number of excellent original soft-ground etchings were produced by *Gainsborough, *Cotman, and *Girtin. Gainsborough in particular, in his landscape prints, combined the soft-ground line with *aquatint in a manner resembling spontaneous drawing in pencil and *wash. Interest in the technique has revived among some modern artists, for example Antony *Gormley, who in a print in his *Body and Soul* series (1990) pressed his mouth into the etching ground.

Soft Style. See MASTER THEODORIC.

Sokolov, Nikolai. See KUKRYNIKSY.

Solari (or **Solario**). Family of Italian artists, mainly architects and sculptors, active in Lombardy in the 15th and 16th centuries. The best-known members are **Andrea** (*c*.1465–1524), the only painter in the family, and his brother **Cristoforo** (*c*.1470–1524), known as Il Gobbo (the hunchback), a sculptor and architect. Andrea worked mainly in Milan and was strongly influenced by *Leonardo. However, his paintings also have suggestions of Flemish and Venetian art, and they are much more individual in character than those of many of the master's followers. The *Madonna with the Green Cushion* (*c*.1510, Louvre, Paris) is his best-known work. In 1507–9 Andrea painted fresco decorations (destroyed) in the Château de Gaillon in Normandy for Cardinal Georges d'Amboise, and his work played a part in introducing the

*Renaissance style to France. Like Andrea, Cristoforo spent much of his career in Milan, but he also worked in Rome, Venice, and elsewhere. His best-known work is the pair of marble effigies of Ludovico *Sforza and his consort Beatrice d'*Este (1497–9) in the Certosa di Pavia; he abandoned work on the tomb of which they were to be a part after Ludovico was deposed in 1499. **Pietro Antonio Solari** (c.1450–93), cousin of Andrea and Cristforo, an architect and sculptor, spent his final three years in Moscow, working for Ivan III, Grand Duke of Muscovy, notably on the reconstruction of the Kremlin walls.

Solario, Antonio (active 1502–18). Italian painter, known as Lo Zingaro (the gypsy), a name perhaps referring to his itinerant career. His life is fairly obscure, but in signatures he called himself a Venetian and his reflective style was certainly strongly influenced by Giovanni *Bellini. It seems that he worked in the Marches and Naples and it is possible that he visited England, for his best-known work, the Withypool Triptych (1514), features an English donor, Paul Withypool, a merchant-tailor from Bristol who worked mainly in London. The central panel (Bristol Mus. and AG) shows the Virgin and Child with Withypool, and the wings (NG, London, on deposit at Bristol Mus. and AG) feature St Catherine of Alexandria and St Ursula.

Solimena, Francesco (b Canale de Serino, nr. Naples, 4 Oct. 1657; d Barra, nr. Naples, 3 Apr. 1747). The leading Neapolitan painter of the first half of the 18th century. In a long and extremely productive career he dominated the artistic life of Naples; he painted frescos in many of the city's greatest churches, including the vast Expulsion of Heliodorus from the Temple (1725, Gesù Nuovo), and he also produced a large number of easel pictures. His vigorous style, often marked by dramatic lighting, owed much to the example of such *Baroque artists as *Giordano (his outstanding predecessor in Naples), *Lanfranco, and *Preti, but it also has a firmness of structure and a clarity of draughtsmanship that show his allegiance to the classical tradition of *Raphael and Annibale *Carracci. Although chiefly a religious painter, he was also a good portraitist (a proud self-portrait is in the Uffizi, Florence). He never travelled further than Rome, but his paintings were in demand all over Europe and he became one of the wealthiest and most famous artists of the time. His international influence was spread also by his celebrity as a teacher. *Ramsay was among his pupils

and *Fragonard copied his work when he visited Naples in 1761.

Solis, Virgil (b c.1514; d Nuremberg, 1562). German engraver and designer, active in Nuremberg. He was one of the most prolific engravers of his time, producing a huge output of book illustrations and ornamental designs.

Solomon, Simeon (b London, 9 Oct. 1840; d London, 14 Aug. 1905). British painter and illustrator, a member of a well-known family of artists. He was part of *Rossetti's circle and a friend of *Burne-Jones, and his work shows strong *Pre-Raphaelite influence. In the 1860s he built up a reputation as an illustrator as well as a painter, but then sank into a life of idleness and dissipation (in 1873 he was convicted of homosexual offences and although he was let off lightly his career was ruined by the incident). His later years were spent in a pathetically bohemian existence, and he died of alcoholism. His sister **Rebecca** (b London, 26 Sept. 1832; d London, 20 Nov. 1886), who painted portraits and anecdotal historical scenes, also died an alcoholic. Their brother **Abraham** (b London, 14 May 1823; d Biarritz, 19 Dec. 1862) painted scenes from literature and contemporary life, some of which attained great popularity and were much reproduced as prints.

Somer, Paul van (b Antwerp, c.1576; bur. London, 5 Jan. 1622). Flemish portrait painter who settled in England in 1616 and became—together with Cornelius *Johnson and Daniel *Mytens—the leading portraitist working at the court of James I. His finest work is Queen Anne of Denmark (1617, Royal Coll.), an imposing full-length, but more archaic in style than similar portraits by Mytens.

Sonderbund. An organization founded in Düsseldorf in 1909 to mount exhibitions of contemporary art; the full name was Sonderbund Westdeutscher Kunstfreunder und Künstler (Special League—or Federation—of Art-Lovers and Artists in Western Germany). The 'art-lovers' included collectors, dealers, museum officials, and writers, the first president of the Sonderbund being Karl Ernst Osthaus (1874–1921), a banker, collector, and critic. He was one of the first Germans to support the *Post-Impressionists (he had personally travelled to Aix-en-Provence to buy directly from *Cézanne) and he founded the Folkwang Museum in Hagen (opened 1902 in a building remodelled by Henry van de *Velde), one of the earliest public museums of contemporary art in

663

Germany. (After Osthaus's death, the contents of the museum were transferred to Essen, and the building in Hagen, much altered, is now the Karl Ernst Osthaus Museum.) Four Sonderbund exhibitions were held—the first three in Düsseldorf (1909, 1910, 1911) and the final one in Cologne (1912). The Cologne exhibition—held at the Kunsthalle from May to December—was by far the most important. Its aim was to provide 'a conspectus of the movement that has been termed *Expressionism'. Van *Gogh was the core of the exhibition, and Cézanne, *Gauguin, and *Munch were also very well represented. In an anteroom were paintings by El *Greco, a great forerunner of Expressionism. German painters (especially those of Der *Blaue Reiter and Die *Brücke) were naturally to the fore, but the exhibition was international in scope, with artists from eight other countries on show. It was influential on the planning of the *Armory Show, which took place the following year.

Sørensen, Henrik (b Fryksände, Sweden, 12 Feb. 1882; d Oslo, 24 Feb. 1962). Norwegian painter and book illustrator of Swedish birth. His training included a period studying with *Matisse in Paris, 1909–10, and his lively and colourful work combined certain *Expressionist features with traditional Norwegian themes. His subjects included portraits, landscapes, and religious compositions, and he did numerous murals for public buildings. The largest was for the new Town Hall in Oslo (1938–50); others were for Linköping Cathedral in Sweden (1934) and the League of Nations in Geneva (1939).

Sorolla y Bastida, Joaquín (b Valencia, 27 Feb. 1863; d Cercedilla, nr. Madrid, 10 Aug. 1923). Spanish painter and illustrator, active mainly in his native Valencia and in Madrid. He was a prolific and popular artist, working on a wide variety of subjects—genre, portraits, landscapes, historical scenes—and producing many book illustrations. His pleasant and undemanding style was marked by brilliant high-keyed colour and vigorous brushwork, representing a kind of conservative version of *Impressionism. He was well known outside Spain, and in 1910–20 he painted a series of fourteen mural panels for the Hispanic Society of America in New York (see HUNTINGTON), representing scenes typical of the various provinces of Spain. His former home in Madrid is now a museum dedicated to his work.

Sotheby's. The oldest and largest firm of auctioneers in the world. It was founded by the London bookseller Samuel Baker, whose first recorded auction was in 1744. On his death in 1778, his estate was divided between his partner George Leigh and his nephew John Sotheby. The last of the Sotheby family to be involved in the firm died in 1861. Although Sotheby's extended its range to take in prints, coins, medals, and antiquities of various kinds, books long remained the primary concern of the company, and it was not until after the First World War that paintings and other works of art became a major part of its business (before this time most important picture sales were held by *Christie's). In 1964 Sotheby's bought Parke-Bernet, America's largest fine art auctioneers, and it now has major salerooms in London, New York, Geneva, and Monaco, with numerous branches throughout the world.

Sots art (or **Sotz art**). A type of *Unofficial art practised in the Soviet Union in the 1970s and 1980s in which the officially sanctioned style of *Socialist Realism was undermined by treating its conventions in an ironic or mocking way (the term derives from the Russian for Socialist Realism—Sotsialisticheskiy realism). The best-known exponents of this kind of work are probably Vitaly Komar (1943–) and Alexander Melamid (1945–), who work together as Komar and Melamid. After being expelled from the Moscow Union of Artists for 'distortion of Soviet reality and deviation from the principles of Socialist Realism', they left the Soviet Union in 1977 and settled in the USA, becoming American citizens in 1988.

sotto in sù, di (Italian: 'from below upwards'). Term applied to an extreme form of *illusionistic foreshortening in which figures or objects painted on a ceiling appear to be floating or suspended in space above the viewer. *Mantegna's Camera degli Sposi in the Palazzo Ducale in Mantua is the first major example, but the device is associated particularly with *Baroque decoration.

Soulages, Pierre (b Rodez, 24 Dec. 1919). French abstract painter, printmaker, sculptor, and designer. He was mainly self-taught and did not take up painting in earnest until 1946, when he settled in Paris. However, he quickly gained a reputation as one of the leading exponents of *Tachisme. His paintings characteristically feature broad, powerful, sombre strokes; originally he worked entirely in black and white, to which he subsequently added subdued blues, browns, and greys. His preference for such a solemn palette exemplifies his view that 'the more limited the means, the stronger the expression'. The primitive force of his work reflects his love of the prehistoric and Romanesque art of the Massif Central region in which he was born, but the forms of his paintings sometimes also resemble blown-up hieroglyphs or Chinese characters (in 1957 he won the grand prize at the Tokyo *Biennial and in 1958 he visited the Far East, where he admired oriental calligraphy). In the 1980s he began making completely black paintings, sometimes consisting of several panels. Apart from paintings, his work has included bronze sculptures, etchings, lithographs, and designs for the stage. He has won numerous awards and his work is included in many major collections of modern art.

Soutine, Chaïm (*b* Smilovitchi, nr. Minsk, 1893; *d* Paris, 9 Aug. 1943). Lithuanian-born painter who settled in France in 1913 and became one of the leading *Expressionists of the *École de Paris. His friends in the circle of expatriate artists there included *Chagall and *Modigliani, who painted a memorable portrait of him (1917, NG, Washington). Soutine suffered from depression and lack of confidence in his own work (he was reluctant to exhibit and sometimes destroyed his own pictures), and he endured years of desperate poverty until the American collector Dr Albert C. *Barnes bought a number of his paintings in 1923. Thereafter he was free from need, although he continued to suffer from ill health and a disposition towards self-torment. Soutine's work included landscapes, portraits, and figure studies of characters such as choirboys and page-boys. His style is characterized by thick, convulsive brushwork, through which he could express tenderness as well as turbulent psychological states. There is something of an affinity with van *Gogh, although Soutine professed to dislike his work and felt more kinship with the Old Masters whose work he studied in the Louvre; his pictures of animal carcasses, for example, are inspired by *Rembrandt's *Flayed Ox*. However, the gruesome intensity of works such as *Side of Beef* (1925, Albright-Knox AG, Buffalo) was not gained simply through study of similar pictures, for Soutine visited abattoirs and even brought a carcass into the studio. His neighbours complained of the smell of the rotting meat and called the police, whom Soutine harangued on the subject of how much more important art was than sanitation. The filthy state in which he lived during his years of poverty was notorious: the poet André Salmon

recalled that Soutine once consulted a specialist about earache and that 'In the canal of the painter's ear the doctor discovered, not an abscess, but a nest of bed bugs.'

Soyer, Moses (*b* Borisoglebsk, 25 Dec. 1899; *d* New York, 2 Sept. 1974) and **Raphael** (*d* New York, 4 Nov. 1987). Russian-born painters, twins, who emigrated to America in 1912 and became US citizens in 1925. They are best known for their *Social Realist subjects, particularly those of the Depression years of the 1930s, in which they depicted the lives of working people with sympathy and at times a touching air of melancholy, as in Raphael's well-known *Office Girls* (1936, Whitney Mus., New York). Both brothers also did many self-portraits and wrote on art. Moses wrote articles defending Social Realism and attacking *Regionalism; Raphael published several autobiographical volumes and a book on Thomas *Eakins (1966). Another brother, **Isaac** (1907–81), who moved to America in 1914, was also a painter.

Spagnoletto, Lo. See RIBERA.

Spagnuolo, Lo. See CRESPI, GIUSEPPE MARIA.

spalliera. An Italian term originally used to describe a painting set into the wall panelling of a room in the *Renaissance period and now by extension applied to any similar painted piece of furniture of the time, such as the headboard or footboard of a bed or the backboard of a *cassone*. No *spalliere* survive *in situ* as wall panelling, but detached examples are in numerous museums; they are usually difficult to distinguish from detached cassone panels, as they tend to be similar in size and shape.

spandrel. Architectural term for the approximately triangular space between the outer curve of an arch and the rectangular frame enclosing the arch, or for the wall surface between two adjacent arches; more loosely the term is applied to any triangular area with curved sides, as in the series of vaulting compartments above the windows in the Sistine Chapel, painted by *Michelangelo with images of the ancestors of Christ. Spandrels are often treated ornamentally, with painting or sculpture, although the shape does not readily lend itself to decorative exploitation. Winged figures, however, have often found favour in this position—victories on triumphal arches and angels in medieval churches.

Spare, Austin. See AUTOMATISM.

Spatialism (or **Spazialismo**). A movement founded by Lucio *Fontana in Milan in 1947 in which he grandiosely intended to synthesize colour, sound, space, movement, and time into a new type of art. The main ideas of the movement were anticipated in his *Manifesto blanco* (White Manifesto) published in Buenos Aires in 1946. In it he spoke of a new 'spatial' art in keeping with the spirit of the post-war age. On the negative side it repudiated the illusory or 'virtual' space of traditional easel painting; on the positive side it was to unite art and science to project colour and form into real space by the use of up-to-date techniques such as neon lighting and television. Five more manifestos followed; they were more specific in their negative than their positive aspects, and carried the concept of Spatialism little further than the statement that its essence consisted in 'plastic emotions and emotions of colour projected upon space'. In 1947 Fontana created a 'Black Spatial Environment', a room painted black, which was considered to have foreshadowed *Environment art. His holed and slashed canvases (beginning in 1949 and 1959 respectively) are also considered to embody Spatialism. An example of the slashed type (the slash made with a razor blade) is *Spatial Concept Waiting* (1960, Tate, London). Although Fontana's ideas were vague, his outlook was influential, for he was one of the first to promote the idea of art as gesture or performance, rather than as the creation of an enduring physical work.

Speculum humanae salvationis (The Mirror of Human Salvation). A medieval textbook of Christian *typology showing how the Incarnation and Passion of Christ (antitype) had been prefigured in the Old Testament, Jewish legend, and secular history (type). The original text, in Latin verse, was probably written *c.*1320 by Ludolph of Saxony, a German monk, and versions later appeared in English, French, German, Dutch, and Czech (there was comparatively little interest in it in Italy). Many manuscripts survive, some of them illustrated. The illustrated *Speculum* is normally arranged so that on opening the book there are four pictures at the head of the pages—the antitype on the left and the types on the right. In about 1465 the *Speculum* was issued as a *block book, which enjoyed great popularity, and it was also used in painting, sculpture, stained glass, and tapestry throughout western Europe.

Spencelayh, Charles (*b* Rochester, Kent, 27 Oct. 1865; *d* Northampton, 25 June 1958). British painter. Completely resistant to any modern developments in art, Spencelayh continued the tradition of Victorian genre painting into the second half of the 20th century. He specialized in anecdotal domestic scenes, most typically showing old codgers pottering around in junk shops or other cluttered interiors. From 1892 until the year of his death he exhibited fairly regularly at the *Royal Academy, a record for longevity that has rarely been exceeded. Critics generally regarded his work as trivial and outmoded, but the public liked it, voting his *Why War?* (Harris Mus. and AG, Preston) 'picture of the year' at the RA exhibition in 1939 (in wartime he often pandered to national sentiment by depicting patriotic themes or including patriotic details). He knew his market well and part of his income came from reproduction of his works on calendars, greetings cards, and so on. His son **Vernon** (1891–1980) painted in a similar style.

Spencer, Sir Stanley (*b* Cookham, Berkshire, 30 June 1891; *d* Cliveden, nr. Cookham, 14 Dec. 1959). English painter, one of the most original figures in 20th-century British art. He lived for most of his life in his native village of Cookham, which played a large part in the imagery of his paintings. His education was fairly elementary, but he grew up in a family in which literature, music, and religion were dominant concerns and his imaginative life was extremely rich. He said he wanted 'to take the inmost of one's wishes, the most varied religious feelings . . . and to make it an ordinary fact of the street', and he is best known for his pictures in which he set biblical events in his own village; his visionary attitude has been compared to that of William *Blake.

Spencer was a prizewinning student at the *Slade School (1908–12) and served in the army from 1915 to 1918, first at the Beaufort War Hospital in Bristol, then in Macedonia. He was appointed an *Official War Artist in 1918, but his experiences during the war found their most memorable expression a decade later when he painted a series of murals for the Sandham Memorial Chapel at Burghclere in Hampshire (1927–32), built to commemorate a soldier who had died from an illness contracted in Macedonia. The arrangement of the murals consciously recalls *Giotto's Arena Chapel in Padua, but Spencer painted in oil, not fresco, and he concentrated not on great events, but on the life of the common soldier, which he depicted with deep human feeling. There is no violence, and Spencer said that the idea for one of the scenes—*The Dug-*

Out—occurred to him 'in thinking how marvellous it would be if one morning, when we came out of our dug-outs, we found that somehow everything was peace and the war was no more'.

By this time Spencer was a celebrated figure, his greatest public success having been *The Resurrection: Cookham* (1924–6, Tate, London), which when exhibited in 1927 was hailed by the critic of *The Times* as 'the most important picture painted by any English artist in the present century'. He continued: 'What makes it so astonishing is the combination in it of careful detail with modern freedom of form. It is as if a *Pre-Raphaelite had shaken hands with a *Cubist.'

Spencer was again an Official War Artist during the Second World War, when he painted a series of large canvases showing shipbuilding on the Clyde (Imperial War Mus., London) that memorably capture the heroic teamwork that went into the war effort. His career culminated in a knighthood in the year of his death, but his life was not a smooth success story, and in the 1930s he somewhat alienated his public with the expressive distortions and erotic content of his work. In 1935 he resigned as an Associate of the *Royal Academy when two of his pictures, considered caricature-like and poorly drawn, were rejected for the annual summer exhibition, but he rejoined the Academy in 1950.

In 1937 Spencer divorced his first wife, the painter **Hilda Carline** (1889–1950), and married **Patricia Preece** (1900–71), also a painter, but the second marriage was a disaster and Hilda continued to play a large part in his life; he painted pictures in memory of her and even wrote letters to her after her death. Some of his nude paintings of Patricia vividly express not only the sexual tensions of his life, but also his belief in the sanctity of human love; the best known is the double nude portrait of himself and Patricia known as *The Leg of Mutton Nude* (1936, Tate). In his later years Spencer acquired a reputation as a landscapist as well as a figure painter. He also occasionally did portraits. There is a gallery devoted to him at Cookham, containing not only paintings, but also memorabilia such as the pram that this eccentric figure used for pushing his painting equipment around the village.

His younger brother **Gilbert Spencer** (b Cookham, 4 Aug. 1892; d Walsham le Willows, Suffolk, 14 Jan. 1979) was also a painter of imaginative subjects and landscapes, working in a style close to that of Stanley.

Spinario (Latin: *spina*, 'a thorn'). Ancient bronze statue of a seated boy extracting a thorn from his left foot (Capitoline Mus., Rome). It is recorded in Rome as early as the 12th century and during the *Renaissance it was one of the most influential and copied of ancient sculptures. Its fame endured and it was one of the ancient works taken by Napoleon to Paris, where it remained from 1798 to 1815. Various stories grew up from the Renaissance onwards to explain the subject, the most popular being that the statue commemorates a shepherd boy called Gnaeus Martius who delivered an important message to the Roman Senate and only when his task was accomplished stopped to remove a thorn from his foot. It is now generally thought that the *Spinario* is a Roman *pastiche of about the 1st century BC, combining a *Hellenistic body with a head of earlier date (the way in which the hair falls suggests that the head was meant to be in an upright position rather than looking down as it is now).

Spinelli, Parri. See SPINELLO ARETINO.

Spinello Aretino (b Arezzo, *c*.1350; d Arezzo, 1410/11). Italian painter, the most distinguished member of a family of artists (mainly goldsmiths) from Arezzo (hence the name Aretino). Spinello probably trained in Florence, perhaps under Agnolo *Gaddi. He painted numerous altarpieces and was the most prolific muralist of his time, undertaking large fresco cycles all over Tuscany. The last of these was devoted to the Sienese pope Alexander III in Siena Town Hall (1408–10); Spinello was the first non-Sienese painter to work in the building. He borrowed ideas freely from other painters, notably *Giotto, but his style was sturdy and vigorous. Several fresco fragments by him are in the National Gallery, London. His son **Parri Spinelli** (1387–1453) was also a painter.

Spitzweg, Carl (b Munich, 5 Feb. 1808; d Munich, 23 Sept. 1885). German painter and illustrator, active in Munich. He began his career as a pharmacist, but he gave this up for art in 1833 when a legacy made him financially independent; he had been interested in art from childhood but had no professional training. Although he travelled widely (England, France, Italy, and elsewhere), he was provincial in his choice of subjects and is an outstanding representative of the *Biedermeier style. His pictures are generally small, humorous in content, and full of lovingly depicted anecdotal detail (*The Poor Poet*, 1839, Neue Pin., Munich, and other versions). He also painted excellent landscapes that show a debt to the *Barbizon School.

spolvero (Italian: *polvere*, 'dust'). A copy of a *cartoon made specifically to be pricked for *pouncing with charcoal dust, enabling the original cartoon to be preserved in good condition.

Spranger, Bartholomeus (*b* Antwerp, 21 Mar 1546; *d* Prague, 1611). Netherlandish painter and designer who had an international career and played an important part in the spread of *Mannerism in northern Europe. He trained in Antwerp, where he came under the influence of Frans *Floris, then travelled via France to Italy, where he spent a decade (1565–75), mainly in Rome. After five years in Vienna, he finally settled in Prague, where he was appointed court painter by the Emperor Rudolf II (see HABSBURG) in 1581. His paintings are often of mythological or allegorical subjects and are highly polished and sophisticated—close in style to those of his fellow court painter Hans von *Aachen. Spranger had met van *Mander in Rome and through drawings that he gave him his style was carried to Haarlem. *Goltzius and other engravers made many prints of his designs (Spranger also made a few etchings himself) and his work was widely influential in the years around 1600.

Squarcione, Francesco (*b* Padua, *c*.1395; *d* Padua, *c*.1468). Italian painter, active in Padua. He is an enigmatic figure, who is important in terms of the pupils he trained, rather than for his own work. In a history of Padua published in 1560 he is patriotically described as a famous and benevolent master, with many pupils and a large collection of *antique sculpture gathered on youthful journeys through Greece and Italy. Modern research, however, shows that for many years he was discreditably involved in a series of lawsuits with pupils who, resentful of his exploitation of their talents, had broken their apprenticeships with him (*Mantegna was the most famous litigant). No traces of his collection remain, but it is likely that something of the antiquarian erudition of the university town of Padua rubbed off on the young men who spent time in his workshop. It is impossible to assess any stylistic debt to Squarcione himself, however, as so little is known about his work, and his traditional role as the founder of a distinctive 'Paduan style' is highly questionable. Only two paintings are firmly associated with his shop—a *polyptych in the museum in Padua and a half-length *Virgin and Child* in the Gemäldegalerie, Berlin—both very dry in style.

Staël, Nicolas de (*b* St Petersburg, 5 Jan. 1914; *d* Antibes, 16 Mar. 1955). Russian-French painter, son of an aristocrat, Baron Vladimir Ivanovich de Staël-Holstein. In 1919 his family was forced to leave Russia (he would later become incensed if anyone suggested they had 'fled') and moved to Poland. Both parents had died by 1922 and Nicolas and his two sisters were adopted by a family of rich Russian expatriates in Brussels, where he studied at the École des Beaux-Arts, 1932–6. In the next two years he travelled widely (France, Italy, Spain, North Africa), then in 1938 settled in Paris, where he studied briefly with *Léger. On the outbreak of war in 1939 he joined the Foreign Legion and was sent to Tunisia. He was demobilized in 1941 and moved to Nice, where he turned from figurative to abstract art, although the forms he used were usually suggested by real objects. In 1943 he returned to Paris and after the war he quickly gained a reputation as one of the leading abstract painters of the *École de Paris, his work showing a sensuous delight in handling paint that was unrivalled at the time. Typically his works feature luscious blocks or patches of thick paint (often applied with a knife), subtly varied in colour and texture. In 1951 he began to reintroduce figurative elements into his work, his subjects including landscapes and still-life. From 1952 he spent much of his time working in the bright light of the south of France, and his late works are often very intense in colour. In spite of critical and financial success, de Staël felt that he had failed to reach a satisfactory compromise between abstraction and figuration, and he committed suicide.

staffage. Term applied to small figures and animals in a painting that are not essential to the subject but are used to animate the composition. Landscape painters, notably in 17th-century Flanders and Holland, often employed other artists to paint the staffage in their work (see, for example, POELENBURGH).

stained glass. Glass that has been given translucent colour in any of various ways, used particularly in church windows. Although the term 'stained glass' is now hallowed by long usage, much window glass could more strictly be described as 'coloured' (when it is dyed in its substance) or 'painted' (when pigments are applied to its surface). The art began in the service of the Christian Church and in its most characteristic development and its highest achievements it is essentially an art of Western Christendom, practised most splendidly in the west and north of Europe as an adjunct to *Gothic architecture. Its early history is obscure, as there are few survivals before the *Romanesque period (the church of St Paul at Jarrow, near Newcastle upon Tyne, has some fragments—placed in a window in 1980—that are probably more or less contemporary with the foundation of the monastery there in the late 7th century). The earliest known complete windows still *in situ*—in Augsburg Cathedral—are variously dated between 1050 and 1150, and show an art already nearly perfect, with a technique that has endured in principle to the present day, developed or modified only in inessential details.

Medieval windows are generally made up of hundreds of small pieces of glass of varied colours and shapes held together by strips of lead—somewhat like a jigsaw puzzle with dark outlines around the pieces. Windows of any size were made up of several panels so treated, and these were set in a framework of iron ('armature') that served not only as a support against wind pressure, but also to accentuate the main lines of the design of the window. The period from roughly 1150 to 1250 was the greatest age of stained glass: colours were strong and simple; designs were bold and fresh; and the feelings conveyed were lofty and awe-inspiring. The glass was coloured by adding various metallic oxides at the molten stage (copper for red, for example, and cobalt for blue). Such glass that is dyed one colour throughout its thickness is known as pot glass or pot metal. Details—such as facial features—were added to it by black pigment, which was fixed to the surface by means of a light firing. True 'staining' was introduced in the 14th century and was achieved by applying silver salts to white glass and firing it in a kiln; this produced a yellow colour, and orange could be obtained by repeating the process.

From the 15th century, stained glass generally became more pictorial, imitating the effects of oil painting, and this tendency was accentuated in the 16th century with the introduction of a range of *enamel colours, with which the artist could paint on the glass more or less as he would on canvas (aided by the fact that improving technology enabled glass to be made in larger and flatter sheets than previously). This trend reached its height in the 18th century with such works as the west window of the chapel of New College, Oxford, designed by *Reynolds and executed in 1778–85; it includes a Nativity scene inspired by *Correggio, whose fluid, soft forms are a world away from the firm black outlines of

medieval glass. Windows of this kind can have a charm of their own, but they are anathema to many students of the subject: E. Liddell Armitage, in his book *Stained Glass* (1959), describes the use of enamel as 'an artistic poison . . . which killed practically every aesthetic faculty the craftsman of the period might inherently have possessed'. With the *Gothic Revival in the 19th century there came a return to medieval principles, and William *Morris and his associates (notably *Burne-Jones) were among the foremost designers in this spirit. In the 20th century many noteworthy artists have designed stained-glass windows, in both figurative and abstract veins—among them *Chagall, *Matisse, *Piper, and Patrick Reyntiens (1925–), a leading specialist in the field who as well as creating his own glass has manufactured that designed by Piper.

The distinctive beauty of stained glass has been well described by Gerald Randall in *Church Furnishing and Decoration in England and Wales* (1980): 'However intrinsically interesting wall and ceiling paintings may be, there is no doubt that the contribution of glass to our churches is more important. Glass has the advantage of transmuting light instead of merely reflecting it, and at its best has a sparkle and vitality that no opaque surface can match. Its effect changes with the light, from one day to another and from one hour to the next, and there are moments when the whole interior of a church seems to take fire from it.'

Stanfield, Clarkson (*b* Sunderland, 3 Dec. 1793; *d* London, 18 May 1867). English painter, best known for his marine subjects. From 1808 to 1816 he was a sailor, mainly in the merchant service, although he was in the Royal Navy for a time after being press-ganged. He began his artistic career as a theatrical scene painter and creator of *dioramas, sometimes working in collaboration with his friend David *Roberts, but from the 1830s he concentrated on easel paintings. With these he gained the reputation of being 'England's van de *Velde', and apart from *Turner he was indeed the best British marine painter of his period. His work is represented in numerous British collections, including the National Maritime Museum, London, and the art gallery of his native Sunderland.

Stantons of Holborn. A family of English mason-sculptors with a large workshop at Holborn in London managed successively by **Thomas Stanton** (1610–74), his nephew **William** (1639–1705), and the latter's son **Edward**

(1681–1734). They were much patronized by the lesser aristocracy and the professional classes, and their monuments are found in many parts of England. Their designs are usually conservative, but William was one of the best English sculptors of his generation.

Stanzione, Massimo (*b* ?Orta di Atella, nr. Caserta, ?1585; *d* ?Naples, ?1656). Neapolitan painter. Like so many artists in his city at this time, he was strongly influenced by *Caravaggism, but his style has a distinctive refinement and grace that has earned him the nickname 'the Neapolitan Guido *Reni'. He was head of the busiest studio in Naples, and many of his works are still in the churches of the city, his masterpiece being the eloquent *Lamentation* (1638) in the Certosa di S. Martino. His most important pupil was *Cavallino. Stanzione probably died in the terrible plague that struck Naples in 1656.

Stark, James. See NORWICH SCHOOL.

state. Term applied to any of the identifiable stages through which a *print has passed as an artist creates or alters the design. The first state is represented by the initial proof taken from the plate. If no alterations are made, this will also be the 'only state'. Often, however, particularly in *etching, the artist will alter the design several times before reaching the final state; several impressions may be taken from the printing surface each time it is altered, but sometimes only a unique impression may exist. Differences in states may be so subtle that experts can disagree as to whether they are in fact intentional or are simply the result of chance or wearing of the plate. Some of *Rembrandt's etchings, however, exist in radically different states involving a major rethinking of the design.

Statue of Liberty. See BARTHOLDI.

steatite. See SOAPSTONE.

Stedelijk Museum, Amsterdam. See RIJKS-MUSEUM.

steel. See IRON.

steel engraving and **steel facing.** See LINE ENGRAVING.

Steen, Jan (*b* Leiden, 1625/6; *bur.* Leiden. 3 Feb. 1679). Dutch painter. He is best known for his humorous *genre scenes, warm-hearted and animated works in which he treats life as a vast comedy of manners. In Holland he ranks next to *Rembrandt, *Vermeer, and *Hals in popularity and the expression a 'Jan Steen household' has become part of the Dutch language to describe the kind of lively, untidy home depicted in so many of his paintings. According to *Houbraken, Steen's 'paintings are like his way of life and his way of life like his paintings', and in his biography of the artist he concentrates on the 'buffoonery' of his work. This, however, gives a misleadingly one-sided view of Steen, for he has many other facets. He painted portraits, historical, mythological, and religious subjects (he was a Catholic), and the animals, birds, and still-lifes in his pictures rival those by any of his specialist contemporaries. As a painter of children he was unsurpassed. Moreover, even his most comic paintings often have a serious underlying theme, as he points out human folly or frailty—his favourite topics include various forms of immoderation, such as excessive drinking, squandering money, or giving way to lust or anger (in many of his pictures he includes inscriptions that explain or underline the meaning).

Although he was born and died in Leiden, Steen moved around a good deal and spent much of his career in The Hague and Haarlem. He is said to have studied successively with the history painter Nicolaus Knüpfer (1603–55) in Utrecht, with Adriaen van *Ostade in Haarlem, and with Jan van *Goyen (whose daughter he married) in The Hague. About 800 paintings are attributed to him, but in spite of his productivity he often had difficulty earning a living and at his death his widow (his second wife) was left with a large family and heavy debts. His financial problems were caused partly by a series of wars against England (and later France), 1652–78, which had a ruinous effect on the Dutch economy in general and the art market in particular. In 1654 his father, a brewer, set him up in a brewery in Delft, but the venture was unsuccessful, and in 1672 he opened a tavern in Leiden, although he continued to paint.

Because of these beery connections, Steen is seen in the popular imagination as a drunken profligate, but there is nothing in the known facts of his life to justify this reputation; many of his pictures are indeed set in taverns, but he also painted scenes of impeccable genteelness, and he must have been a dedicated worker to produce his large output in a fairly short career. His work is uneven, but at its best is remarkable for sheer beauty of technique, as well as for richness of characterization and inventiveness in composition. *Reynolds praised his 'strong and manly' brushwork, and his deftness of touch is sometimes reminiscent of Hals, although his handling is more detailed. As a colourist he was one of the subtlest artists of his time, his use of salmon-red, rose, pale yellow, dove grey, and blue-green being highly distinctive. He had no recorded pupils, but his work was much imitated.

Steenwyck, Hendrick van the Elder (*b* Steenwijk, ?*c*.1550, *d* Frankfurt, 1 June 1603) and **Hendrick van the Younger** (*b* ?Antwerp, *c*.1580; *d* ?Leiden, 1649). Flemish painters, father and son, specialists in architectural views. Little is known of the career of either man, but the father, who was probably a pupil of *Vredeman de Vries, is regarded as the creator of the church interior as a special branch of painting. Both father and son painted small pictures of real and imaginary *Gothic churches, sometimes as eerie nocturnal scenes. There are several examples of the work of Hendrick the Younger in the National Gallery, London; in two of them the figures are credited to Jan *Brueghel the Elder.

Steer, Philip Wilson (*b* Birkenhead, 28 Dec. 1860; *d* London, 21 Mar. 1942). English painter (of landscapes and occasional portraits and figure compositions), son of an undistinguished portrait painter, **Philip Steer** (1810–71). With *Sickert (his friend and exact contemporary), Steer was the leader among the progressive British artists of his generation who looked to France for inspiration. He had his main training in Paris, 1882–4, first at the *Académie Julian and then the École des *Beaux-Arts, and he revisited France on several occasions. With other admirers of French painting, he was one of the founders of the *New English Art Club in 1886 and he regularly exhibited there. In 1892 the Anglo-Irish novelist George Moore wrote, 'it is admitted that Mr Steer takes a foremost place in what is known as the modern movement', and around this time Steer was indeed at his peak, producing the beach scenes and seascapes that are regarded not only as his finest works but also as the best *Impressionist pictures painted by an Englishman. They are remarkable for their great freshness and their subtle handling of light, and unlike Sickert's paintings they are devoid of any social or literary content. Among them are several depicting the seaside resort of Walberswick in Suffolk, where Steer had friends and often stayed at this period.

After about 1895 Steer's work became more conventional and more closely linked to the English tradition of *Gainsborough (especially in his portraits), *Turner, and *Constable. In the 1920s he turned increasingly to watercolour.

He taught at the *Slade School from 1893 to 1930 and in 1931 was awarded the Order of Merit. His sight began to fail in 1935 and he had stopped painting by 1940. In character he was benign, modest, and dryly amusing, inspiring affectionate regard in almost everyone who knew him. He was a confirmed bachelor and a hypochondriac who carried his worries about his health to comic lengths: in his own home 'he donned a hat to go downstairs, because of the changes of temperature between one room and another' (Bruce Laughton, *Philip Wilson Steer*, 1971).

Stefano da Zevio (or **Stefano di Giovanni da Verona**) (*b* *c*.1375; *d* ?*c*.1438). Italian painter of French extraction, active mainly in Verona. He was the son of Jean d'Arbois (Giovanni d'Arbosio), a painter who had worked for Philip the Bold, Duke of *Burgundy, but by whom no works are known. Stefano's life is obscure, and the information about him is confusing, but he is regarded as one of the leading Italian exponents of the *International Gothic style. His work is very much in the northern manner, with rather insubstantial figures and an abundance of pretty details, and has almost no local character (*Adoration of the Magi*, ?1435, Brera, Milan).

Stefano della Bella. See BELLA.

Stein, Gertrude (*b* Allegheny [now part of Pittsburgh], 3 Feb. 1874; *d* Neuilly-sur-Seine, 27 July 1946). American writer, collector, hostess, eccentric, and self-styled genius. She settled in Paris in 1903 and her home at 27 rue de Fleurus became famous as a literary and artistic salon; many distinguished American visitors to Paris found it their introduction to modern French painting. With her brother, the art critic **Leo Stein** (*b* Allegheny, 11 May 1872; *d* Settignano, nr. Florence, 29 July 1947), who lived with her from 1903 to 1912, she was one of the first collectors of the work of *Braque, *Matisse, and *Picasso (who painted a well-known portrait of Gertrude, 1905–6, Met. Mus., New York); another brother, **Michael** (1865–1938), and his wife **Sarah** (1870–1953), were also collectors. Gertrude's writings, which she claimed to be a literary counterpart to *Cubism, are often opaque in style, concerned with the rhythm and sound of words rather than their meaning. The best-known and most approachable of her many books is *The Autobiography of Alice B. Toklas* (1933), which in fact is her own autobiography, composed as though by Miss Toklas (1877–1967), her secretary and companion from 1907. Alfred

H. *Barr writes that Leo Stein was 'the critic who first felt that Matisse *and* Picasso were the two important artists of his time', but Stein later turned his back on their work, describing Cubism as 'godalmighty rubbish'. Clive *Bell maintained that 'Neither Gertrude or Leo had a genuine feeling for visual art . . . Pictures were pegs on which to hang hypotheses.'

stela or **stele** (plural: stelae or steles) (Greek: 'standing block'). An upright slab, usually of stone, that serves as a grave marker or other monument. The term is chiefly applied to the ancient Mediterranean world (particularly classical Greece), but similar objects are found in many other times and places. Greek grave stelae were sometimes plain, but by the 6th century BC they were often carved or painted.

Stella, Frank (*b* Malden, Mass., 12 May 1936). American painter, a leading figure of *Post-Painterly Abstraction. In his early work he was influenced by *Abstract Expressionism, but after settling in New York in 1958 he was impressed by the flag and target paintings of Jasper *Johns and the direction of his art changed completely. He began to emphasize the idea that a painting is a physical object rather than a metaphor for something else, saying that he wanted to 'eliminate illusionistic space' and that a picture was 'a flat surface with paint on it—nothing more'. These aims were first given expression in a series of black 'pinstripe' paintings in which regular black stripes were separated by very thin lines. They made a big impact when four of them were shown at the Museum of Modern Art's '16 Americans' exhibition in 1959, inspiring a mixture of praise and revulsion. Soon after this he began using flat bands of bright colour (*Hyena Stomp*, 1962, Tate, London), then—to identify the patterning more completely with the shape of the picture as a whole—he started working with notched and *shaped canvases. In the 1970s he began to experiment with paintings that included cut-out shapes in relief and he abandoned his impersonal handling for a spontaneous, almost graffiti-like manner (*Guadalupe Island, Caracara*, 1979, Tate). He has been an influential figure, not only in painting but also on the development of *Minimal sculpture (his friends have included Carl *Andre and Donald *Judd).

Stella, Jacques (*b* Lyons, 19 Sept. 1596; *d* Paris, 29 Apr. 1657). French painter, engraver, and draughtsman. From about 1619 to 1634 he lived in Italy, first in Florence, where he worked

for Cosimo II de' *Medici, making engravings of his festivities, and then from 1623 in Rome, where he became a friend of *Poussin and one of his closest followers. He had a high reputation in his day, in both Italy and France, but it is now much faded. Most of his surviving paintings are fairly close to Poussin in style and spirit, although without the master's power of design and intellectual complexity (*Adoration of the Child*, 1639, Bowes Mus., Barnard Castle). However, he also painted a different type of work—small pictures on marble or other expensive stone, in which the veining is allowed to show through the paint in places and form part of the composition. These luxury items were popular in Florence at the time but were unusual for a French artist.

Stella, Joseph (*b* Muro Lucano, nr. Potenza, 13 June 1877; *d* New York, 5 Nov. 1946). Italian-born American painter. He emigrated to the USA in 1896, but from 1909 to 1912 he lived in Italy and France, where he had his first significant contacts with modern art. He was particularly influenced by *Futurism and he became the leading American exponent of the style. His first and most famous Futurist painting was *Battle of Lights, Coney Island, Mardi Gras* (1913–14, Yale Univ. AG), a densely fragmented portrayal of a crowded amusement park at night. In works such as this Stella gave a romanticized image of the industrialized townscape of New York. In particular he was obsessed with Brooklyn Bridge, which he described as 'a shrine containing all the efforts of the new civilization of America' (*Brooklyn Bridge*, 1917–18, Yale Univ. AG). He soon abandoned the Futurist idiom, but industrial and urban themes continued to inspire him. Stella was active in the administration of two leading avant-garde associations—the *Society of Independent Artists and the *Société Anonyme—and in the early 1920s he experimented with various styles, including *Precisionism. In the 1920s and 1930s he spent much of his time in Italy and France (he lived in Paris 1930–4). From the mid-1920s his work grew more conservative and included mystical and sacred subjects.

stencil. A thin sheet of metal, paper, or other suitable material perforated with a design (or often lettering) that is reproduced on paper, fabric, or other surface when the sheet is laid on them and colour is brushed, rubbed, or sprayed through the openings. A 'negative stencil' is one in which an object is placed on a surface and colour is deposited around it. Stencilling was probably the earliest method to be devised of duplicating a design and it has a long history in fabric printing, for example. Prints made entirely by stencilling are uncommon, but the method was often used to add colour to cheap popular *woodcuts. In France, where it is called *pochoir*, stencilling has been much employed in book illustration. The more sophisticated technique of *screenprinting is based on stencilling.

Stepanova, Varvara. See RODCHENKO.

Stephanus. See PASITELES.

Stephens, F. G. See PRE-RAPHAELITE BROTHERHOOD.

stereochromy. The Victorian name for *water-glass painting.

Stern, Irma (*b* Schweizer-Renecke, Transvaal, 2 Oct. 1894; *d* Cape Town, 23 Aug. 1966). South African painter. From 1913 to 1920 she studied in Germany, mainly Berlin. She was influenced particularly by *Expressionism and was the most important figure in introducing European modernism to South Africa, where her work (mainly figure subjects) initially caused outrage. Her home in Cape Town is now a museum dedicated to her.

Stevens, Alfred (*b* Blandford Forum, Dorset, 31 Dec. 1817; *d* London, 1 May 1875). English sculptor, painter, and designer, the son of a house painter. With the assistance of the local clergyman, who recognized his talent, Stevens was sent to study in Italy in 1833, at the age of 15, and remained there until 1842. He worked with *Thorvaldsen in Rome, and laid the foundations of his style in the study of the *Renaissance masters, above all *Raphael. After his return to England he taught at the Government School of Design (later the *Royal College of Art), 1845–7, and in 1850–7 he was chief designer to a Sheffield firm of bronze- and metalworkers. In 1856 he entered the competition for the Wellington Monument to be erected in St Paul's Cathedral, and although his design was placed sixth, he was eventually awarded the commission. It occupied him for the rest of his life and was plagued with bureaucratic problems. It was not finally completed until 1912, when the equestrian group at the top was cast from Stevens's model. Nevertheless, it is not only Stevens's masterpiece (indeed, the only one of his large schemes to come to fruition and survive), but also arguably the greatest piece of sculpture produced in England in the 19th century. The architectural elements form a splendid, bold composition, and the two bronze groups *Valour and Cowardice* and *Truth and Falsehood* have an almost *Michelangelesque grandeur and vigour.

Apart from the Wellington Monument, Stevens's finest work was the decoration for the dining room at Dorchester House, London (*c*.1856), a sumptuous residence built for the millionaire R. S. Holford. It was demolished in 1929 (the Dorchester Hotel now occupies the site), but a fireplace is in the Victoria and Albert Museum, London, and many of the fittings are in the Walker Art Gallery, Liverpool, which has an outstanding Stevens collection. He was a masterful craftsman in numerous media— marble, bronze, silver, porcelain—and was also a painter, although he destroyed much of his work because it did not satisfy him. His unexecuted designs included schemes for the decoration of the interior of the dome of St Paul's Cathedral and the Reading Room at the British Museum, recorded in his superb drawings, which are particularly well represented in Cambridge (Fitzwilliam Mus.), Liverpool (Walker AG), London (Tate Britain), Oxford (Ashmolean Mus.), and Sheffield (Mappin AG). These drawings are very much in the High Renaissance tradition, and it is to this era that Stevens belonged in spirit.

Stevens, Alfred-Émile (*b* Brussels, 11 May 1823; *d* Paris, 24 Aug. 1906). Belgian painter, active mainly in Paris, where he settled in 1852. From about 1860 he achieved immense success with his pictures of young ladies in elegant interiors dressed in the height of fashion. His skill in rendering fine materials earned him the title 'the *Terborch of France'. He was a friend and supporter of *Manet and influenced *Whistler, with whom he was one of the first enthusiasts for Japanese art. Stevens also painted coastal and marine scenes in a rather freer, more *Impressionistic style, similar to that of *Boudin or *Jongkind. His brother **Joseph** (*b* Brussels, 26 Sept. 1816 [or 1819 according to some accounts]; *d* Brussels, 2 Aug. 1892) was also a painter, mainly of animals, and in his day was almost as famous and successful as Alfred (both brothers were made members of the Legion of Honour). Another brother, **Arthur** (1825–99), was an art critic and dealer, and Alfred's son **Léopold** (1866–1935) was a painter.

Stieglitz, Alfred (*b* Hoboken, NJ, 1 Jan. 1864; *d* New York, 13 July 1946). American photographer, editor, and art dealer who, during the first two decades of the 20th century, did more than anyone else to bring European avant-garde art before the American public. The son of a German immigrant, he spent most of the 1880s in Berlin and returned to the USA in 1890 with an international reputation as a photographer. His 291 Gallery (at 291 Fifth Avenue, New York), which he opened in 1905, presented the first American exhibitions of *Matisse (1908), *Toulouse-Lautrec (1909), the Douanier *Rousseau (1910), *Picabia (1913), and *Severini (1917), and the first one-man exhibition of *Brancusi anywhere (1914). It also gave the first exhibition of children's art and the first major exhibition of African art in America. Stieglitz also championed American artists, among them Georgia *O'Keeffe, whom he married in 1924. From 1903 to 1917 he edited the journal *Camera Work*, which he published from the 291 Gallery. At first devoted to photography, it was later extended to cover all the visual arts and opened its pages to avant-garde American writers. The 291 Gallery was closed in 1917 when the building was pulled down, but Stieglitz continued his work with the Intimate Gallery (1925–9) and An American Place (1929–46). In his own medium of photography, he was a brilliant innovative artist. Learning from the avant-garde paintings that he exhibited, he experimented with various modes of abstraction and his work went a long way to revolutionize the concept of the photographic image and to establish photography as an independent art form. He formed an impressive collection of art, much of which was donated to the Art Institute of Chicago.

Stifter, Adalbert (*b* Horní Planá [German: Iglau], Bohemia, 23 Oct. 1805; *d* Linz, 28 Jan. 1868). Austrian writer and painter. Up to about 1840 painting took priority in his artistic output, but thereafter he dedicated himself more to writing. He is now regarded as one of the outstanding Austrian novelists of the 19th century, but he enjoyed little success in his lifetime, and full recognition of his stature came only after the First World War. For much of his career he worked as a tutor, then an educational administrator. His later years were clouded by the suicide of an adopted daughter in 1859 and he took his own life, cutting his throat with his razor, whilst suffering agonizing pain from what was thought to be cancer. As a painter he was self-taught, and as in his writing eschewed heroic events in favour of simple, everyday happenings. His sensitive perception of nature comes out in his remarkably fresh landscapes. There is a museum devoted to his work in Vienna.

Stijl, De (Dutch: 'the style'). The name of a group of mainly Dutch artists founded in Leiden in 1917 and of the journal they published to set forth their ideas. It was a very loose association, held together mainly by Theo van *Doesburg. The other members were, like him, mainly painters (*Mondrian was the most important), but they also included the sculptor Georges *Vantongerloo and the architect and designer Gerald Rietveld (1888–1964). Their common aim was to find laws of equilibrium and harmony that would be applicable to life and society as well as art, and their style was one of austere abstract clarity (see NEO-PLASTICISM). The journal was founded by van Doesburg and Mondrian in 1917 and van Doesburg continued to edit it until 1928 (it appeared roughly monthly, but irregularly; the place of publication—befitting van Doesburg's peripatetic career—also varied). A final issue (number 90) was published in 1932 by Mme van Doesburg in memory of her husband, after whose death in 1931 the group disbanded. At first the journal was devoted exclusively to Neo-Plasticism, but a *Dadaist element crept in. Mondrian ceased to contribute to *De Stijl* after 1924 and in 1926 van Doesburg published the manifesto of a splinter movement that he called *Elementarism. Despite this lack of cohesion, *De Stijl* was probably the most influential of the many avant-garde publications in Europe between the two wars. It was, however, in architecture and the applied arts (including furniture design and typography), rather than painting and sculpture, that it had its greatest influence—notably at the *Bauhaus and in the clean-lined architectural style known as 'International Modern', of which Rietveld's Schröder House in Utrecht (1924) is an early and famous example.

Stile Liberty. See ART NOUVEAU.

Still, Clyfford (*b* Grandin, N. Dak., 30 Nov. 1904; *d* Baltimore, 23 June 1980). American painter, one of the major figures of *Abstract Expressionism but the one least associated with the New York art scene. In the 1930s he taught at Washington State College, Pullman, and after working in war industries in California, 1941–3, he taught for two years at the Richmond Professional Institute, Richmond, Virginia. He then lived briefly in New York (1945–6), where he had a one-man exhibition at Peggy *Guggenheim's Art of This Century gallery in 1946. Although he stood somewhat apart from the other Abstract Expressionists, he was friendly with Mark *Rothko (they had met in 1943), the two men sharing a sense of almost mystical fervour about their work. In 1946–50 he taught at the California School of Fine Arts in San Francisco, then lived in New York, 1950–61. By the time he returned to New York, Still had created his mature style and had a rapidly growing reputation. He was one of the pioneers of the very large, virtually monochromatic painting. But unlike *Newman and Rothko, who used fairly flat, unmodulated pigment, Still used heavily loaded, expressively modulated impasto in jagged forms. His work can have a raw aggressive power, but in the 1960s it became more lyrical.

In 1961 Still moved to Maryland to work in tranquillity away from the art world. Scorning galleries, dealers, and critics, and rarely exhibiting, he considered himself something of a visionary who needed solitude to give expression to his high spiritual purpose, and he gained a reputation for cantankerousness and pretentiousness—his comment on his painting *1953* (1953, Tate, London) is typical of his high-flown prose: 'there was a conscious intention to emphasize the quiescent depths of the blue by the broken red at its lower edge while expanding its inherent dynamic beyond the geometries of the constricting frame . . . In addition, the yellow wedge at the top is a re-assertion of the human context—a gesture of rejection of any authoritarian rationale or system of politico-dialectical dogma.' Still presented large groups of his paintings to the Albright-Knox Art Gallery, Buffalo, the Metropolitan Museum, New York, and the San Francisco Museum of Art, and his work is represented in many other major collections.

Stimmer, Tobias (b Schaffhausen, 17 Apr. 1539; d Strasbourg, 14 Jan. 1584). Swiss painter, draughtsman, and designer of woodcuts, active mainly in Schaffhausen and Strasbourg. He was a versatile artist, whose work included façade decorations (notably that of the Haus zum Ritter, 1568–70, now in the Museum zu Allerheiligen, Schaffhausen), portraits in a *Holbeinesque style, and a large output of prints. He also decorated the astronomical clock in Strasbourg Cathedral (1571–4). His reputation in his lifetime stood very high. Several other members of his family were artists, notably his brother **Abel** (1542–1606), a painter and etcher.

stipple engraving. A printmaking technique, a mixture of *etching and *engraving, in which the design is made up of countless small dots or flecks, producing softly graded tones. It derived from *crayon manner, but instead of creating lines to reproduce the appearance of a drawing, the whole plate was covered with dots or flecks to build up varied tonal areas (as in crayon manner, however, stipple prints were often made in shades of red or brown). The basic design was created in etching, a needle being used to dot through the waxy *ground; after the plate was bitten in acid, the ground was cleaned off it and the design was strengthed or modified with a *burin.

Stipple engraving was evidently first used in 1774 by the English engraver William Ryland (1732–83), who had learnt crayon manner in Paris, and it remained almost entirely confined to England. Francesco *Bartolozzi was the most famous exponent of the technique, and John Raphael *Smith also used it a good deal. Sometimes it was combined with *mezzotint, the other main tonal process of the time. The softness of effect it creates is somewhat similar to that of mezzotint, though with less depth of tone. Stipple yielded more impressions than mezzotint, as the plate did not wear down so quickly. It remained popular into the early years of the 19th century, but was then more or less superseded by *lithography.

William Ryland, stipple's inventor, was engraver to George III and made a good deal of money from his work, but he lived extravagantly and he was executed for forging bills of exchange. The young William *Blake is said to have foreseen this, turning down an apprenticeship with Ryland because he was repelled by him and remarking that he 'looks as if he will live to be hanged'.

Stokes, Adrian (b London, 27 Oct. 1902; d London, 15 Dec. 1972). British writer and painter. In the 1920s he visited Italy several times, leading to his first important book *The Quattro Cento* (1932), in which he articulated his 'love of stone'. This preoccupation led him to friendship with a number of artists—particularly Barbara *Hepworth and Henry *Moore—to whom *direct carving was important. In 1936 Stokes took up painting and in 1937 he studied at the *Euston Road School; his work included landscapes and still-lifes. From 1939 to 1946 he lived at Carbis Bay, Cornwall, and by encouraging Hepworth and Ben *Nicholson to settle near him at the outbreak of the Second World War he helped to bring about the heyday of the *St Ives School. His books sold badly, but he had a loyal following, and some of his admirers today consider him the most eloquent and poetic British art critic since *Ruskin. Others find his prose hard going. An intensely subjective writer, with an interest in psychoanalysis, Stokes responded passionately, even ecstatically, to art, believing its task was to show the 'utmost drama of the soul as laid-out things'. His books include *The Stones of Rimini* (1934), *Colour and Form* (1937), and *Painting and the Inner World* (1963); *The Critical Writings of Adrian Stokes*, edited by Lawrence *Gowing, appeared in three volumes in 1978.

He is not to be confused with another **Adrian Stokes** (1854–1935), a landscape painter and author of *Landscape Painting* (1925).

Stom, Matthias (*b* Amersfoort, nr. Utrecht, *c*.1600; *d* ?Sicily, *c*.1650). Dutch painter, active mainly in Italy. In art-historical literature he is often called Matthias Stomer, but 'Stom' is the form that occurs in contemporary documents and on his only signed and dated picture, *St Isidore Agricola* (1641, Chiesa degli Agostiniani, Caccamo, Sicily). The details of his life are obscure, but he was one of the most prolific and committed of *Caravaggesque artists, working in the master's idiom long after it had gone out of fashion in most places. He is first documented in 1630, in Rome; a few years later he moved to Naples, and from about 1640 he lived in Sicily. There are about 200 surviving pictures by him, mainly religious works but also including mythological and *genre scenes. They are remarkable for their psychological intensity and their distinctive claylike treatment of flesh.

Stone, Frank (*b* Manchester, 22 Aug. 1800; *d* London, 18 Nov. 1859). English painter and illustrator. He began his working life as a cotton spinner and was evidently self-taught as an artist. Initially he concentrated on watercolours but later took up oils. His work included portraits and sentimental genre scenes. He was a friend of Charles Dickens, whom he helped with his theatrical productions, and knew several other writers, including William Makepeace Thackeray, whose portrait he painted (*c*.1839, NPG, London). His son **Marcus Stone** (*b* London, 4 July 1840; *d* London, 24 Mar. 1921) was also a painter and illustrator and likewise a friend of Dickens. He made something of a speciality of sentimental scenes of romance in 18th- or early 19th-century costume (*In Love*, 1888, Castle Mus., Nottingham). They were enormously popular in engravings and made him a fortune.

Stone, Nicholas (*b* nr. Exeter, *c*.1587; *d* London, 24 Aug. 1647). English sculptor, mason, and architect. The son of a Devon quarryman, he trained in London, where he met Hendrick de *Keyser, who visited the city in 1606–7. Stone went to Amsterdam with de Keyser and worked for him until 1613, when he married his daughter and returned to England. He quickly established himself as the outstanding tomb sculptor in the country, surpassing his contemporaries in technical skill as a marble cutter and outdoing them in introducing new ideas: the monument to Francis Holles (*d* 1622; Westminster Abbey), for example, has the first English example of a figure in Roman armour.

In 1619 Stone became master mason for Inigo *Jones's Banqueting House in Whitehall, and in 1632 master mason to the Crown. His contact with the court gave him a knowledge of the *antique sculpture in Charles I's collection and his work after *c*.1630 shows a change in style, marked by an attempt to imitate antique drapery, as in the monument to John and Thomas Lyttelton (1634, Magdalen College, Oxford). His large workshop produced monuments of many types, and we are unusually well informed about its activities, as an office notebook covering the period 1614–41 and an account book for the period 1631–42 still survive (Soane Mus., London). Much less of his work as an architect is extant (and it is sometimes not clear whether he was the designer as well as the mason of the buildings on which he worked), but he is recognized as the creator of 'a vernacular classical architecture of considerable charm and accomplishment' (Howard Colvin, *A Biographical Dictionary of British Architects 1600–1840*, 1978). The outbreak of civil war in 1642 seems to have brought his career to an end. Stone may have been the author of *Enchiridion of Fortification, or a Handfull of Knowledge in Martiall Affairs*, published anonymously in London in 1645, but the book has also been attributed to the youngest of his three sons, **John Stone** (1620–67), who ran the family practice after his father's death (even though he does not appear to have been a sculptor himself).

Stone, Reynolds (*b* Eton College, Windsor, 13 Mar. 1909; *d* Dorchester, Dorset, 23 June 1979). British engraver, letter cutter, designer, and painter. After working for the Cambridge University Press and a commercial printer, he set up on his own as a wood engraver in 1934 and from 1939 also practised (self-taught) as a letter cutter in stone. His highly varied output included book illustrations (his speciality was quiet rural scenes), memorial tablets (including that to Sir Winston Churchill in Westminster Abbey, 1965), and the design of £5 and £10 notes for the Bank of England (1963–4).

stopping-out varnish. An acid-resisting varnish used in *etching and similar printmaking processes.

Storey, George Adolphus. See ST JOHN'S WOOD CLIQUE.

Stoskopff, Sébastien (*bapt.* Strasbourg, 31 July 1597; *d* Idstein, nr. Frankfurt, 11 Feb. 1657). French still-life painter, active in Paris, where he lived 1621–40 (in this period he also made a visit to Venice, in 1629), and thereafter mainly in Strasbourg. He painted in a spare, stiff, almost archaic style that has appealed greatly to modern taste—most of his paintings have come to light since the 1930s. The best collection is in the Musée de l'Œuvre de Notre Dame, Strasbourg.

Stoss, Veit (*b* ?Horb am Neckar, Swabia, *c.*1450; *d* Nuremberg, Sept. 1533). German sculptor, with *Riemenschneider the greatest woodcarver of his age (he also worked in stone). He is first recorded in 1477, when he moved from Nuremberg to Cracow in Poland. There he carved his largest work, the huge altarpiece for St Mary's church (1477–89), and also made the red marble tomb of King Casimir IV in the cathedral (1492). In 1496 he returned to Nuremberg, where he continued to prosper. However, in 1503 his career was blighted when he forged a document in an attempt to recoup some money he regarded as having been misappropriated in an investment—an offence for which he was tried, convicted, and branded through both cheeks. He was also confined to the city limits of Nuremberg (he fled but returned), and although he was to some extent rehabilitated, he never regained his former position. He died a wealthy man, but his old age was embittered by disputes with the city authorities.

A good many documented and signed works by Stoss survive and his style is distinctive—bold and powerfully characterized, with exaggerated gestures and expressions and draperies rendered in an ornate, almost calligraphic manner. Indeed, Stoss's work is so individual that the famous figure of St Roch (*c.*1510–20) in SS. Annuziata, Florence, is almost universally accepted as his (see VOSS), even though it is undocumented and was attributed by *Vasari to 'Janni Francese' (Janni the Frenchman; see JUAN DE JUNI). Vasari wrote eloquently of the virtuosity of the carving, describing the draperies as 'cut almost to the thinness of paper, and with a beautiful flow in

the arrangement of the folds, so that nothing more wonderful is to be seen'. Stoss sometimes, as here, left his figures unpainted, but otherwise his work is entirely in the late *Gothic spirit. He is recorded as being a painter and engraver as well as a sculptor and he also declared himself competent as a civil engineer. See also LIME-WOOD.

Stothard, Thomas (*b* London, 17 Aug. 1755; *d* London 27 Apr. 1834). English painter, book illustrator, and designer. He was a prolific and versatile artist, admired for his work in various fields. His paintings were mainly small-scale historical pieces in a charmingly sentimental manner, but he also did occasional more ambitious works, for example the decoration of the staircase at Burghley House, near Peterborough (1799–1803), and of the dome of the Advocates' Library, Edinburgh (1822). His book illustrations were mainly for English novels and poetry. As a designer he ranged from monuments to jewellery. His son **Charles Alfred Stothard** (1786–1821) was a draughtsman and antiquarian.

Stradano (or **Stradanus**), **Giovanni.** See STRAET.

Straet, Jan van der (*b* Bruges, 1523; *d* Florence, 3 Nov. 1605). Netherlandish painter and designer, active for almost all his career in Italy, where he was known as Giovanni Stradano (or Stradanus or della Strada). He had his main training in Antwerp with *Aertsen, and moved to Italy in about 1545. A protégé of *Vasari, he worked in various Italian cities, but mainly in Florence, where he was much employed by the *Medici family. He assisted Vasari with frescos in the Palazzo Vecchio, for example, but his main work for the Medici was as a tapestry designer. His *Mannerist style was influenced by Vasari, but it always retained a Netherlandish accent and he was admired for his skill in *genre painting, a northern speciality. Several of his designs were published in engravings.

strapwork. A type of ornament consisting of decorative forms resembling strips of leather or parchment that have been elaborately cut, pierced, and twisted. Although the origins of strapwork have been traced back earlier in the 16th century, it was first given prominence by *Rosso Fiorentino in his stucco decoration of the Gallery of Francis I (*c.*1533–40) at *Fontainebleau. It spread rapidly to Flanders and from there, by means of engraved pattern books and refugee craftsmen, to England, where it was profusely used in Elizabethan and Jacobean decoration in wood, metal, stucco, stone, and printer's ornament.

Straub, Johann Baptist and **Philipp Jakob.** See MESSERSCHMIDT.

Streeter, Robert (*bapt.* London, 16 Dec. 1621; *bur.* London, 23 Apr. 1679). English painter, appointed serjeant-painter to Charles II in 1660. In the words of Ellis *Waterhouse, 'he left no branch of painting untried and would have been a universal genius had he been endowed with the requisite talent.' The most important of his few surviving works is the allegorical ceiling painting of *Truth Inspiring the Arts and Sciences* (1668–9) in the Sheldonian Theatre, Oxford. This is a heavy-handed work, but noteworthy as the most ambitious attempt at a piece of *Baroque decoration by any Englishman before *Thornhill (Streeter had travelled in Italy during the Commonwealth). His reputation was evidently high in his day, for Samuel Pepys in his celebrated *Diary* calls him a 'famous history-painter' who 'lives very handsomely', and Robert Whitehall, whose ability as a poet happily matched that of Streeter as a painter, eulogized the Sheldonian ceiling in the immortal lines ' . . . future ages must confess they owe | To Streeter more than Michael Angelo' (*Urania, or a Description of the Painting of the Top of the Theatre at Oxford*, 1669). Streeter's son **Robert** (*d* 1711) succeeded him as serjeant-painter.

Streeton, Sir Arthur (*b* Mount Duneed, Victoria, 8 Apr. 1867; *d* Olinda, Victoria, 2 Sept. 1943). Australian painter, active mainly in Melbourne. He was a prolific landscape painter, working in an *Impressionist style similar to that of his friend Tom *Roberts. Between 1898 and 1924 he spent most of his time abroad (in 1918 he was an *Official War Artist with the Australian forces in France). His work became stereotyped, but he was enormously popular in his own country, regarded as the foremost portrayer of the remote and awesome Australian landscape. By the end of his life he had long enjoyed the status of a national institution.

stretcher. The wooden framework on which a *canvas is stretched and fixed. Wedges in the inner corners enable the canvas to be tightened if it slackens.

Stretes, William. See SCROTES.

Strigel, Bernhard (*b* Memmingen, Swabia, Nov./Dec. 1460; *d* Memmingen, Apr./May 1528). German painter, mainly active in Memmingen, near Ulm, where he was a leading figure in the period of transition from late *Gothic to *Renaissance. Most of his paintings are on religious subjects, but in his later years he turned more to portraiture, notably in the service of the Emperor Maximilian I (see HABSBURG). In 1515 he was summoned to Vienna by the emperor and there painted the *Family of Maximilian I* (KH Mus., Vienna), one of the earliest group portraits in German art.

Strong, Sir Roy. See VICTORIA AND ALBERT MUSEUM.

Strozzi, Bernardo (*b* Genoa, 1581; *d* Venice, 2 Aug. 1644). The leading Genoese painter of his period. He became a Capuchin monk in 1598, hence his nicknames, Il Prete Genovese (the Genoese priest) and Il Cappuccino (the Capuchin). In 1610 he was allowed to leave his monastery to support his sick and widowed mother and his unmarried sister. By 1630 his mother was dead and his sister had married, and Strozzi is said to have been pressurized to return to the monastery, this accounting for his move in 1630/1 to Venice (where he spent the rest of his life). Strozzi was successful and prolific in both Genoa and Venice, painting portraits and allegorical and genre scenes (often of musicians) as well as religious works. The sensuous richness of his style was influenced by *Rubens (who worked in Genoa), but his paintings are highly distinctive, with an air of refinement and tenderness that recalls van *Dyck (who also worked in Genoa). During Strozzi's time in Venice there was a dearth of native talent in the city, and with two other 'foreigners', *Feti and *Liss, he kept alive the painterly tradition of the 16th century.

Strudwick, John Melhuish. See PRE-RAPHAELITE BROTHERHOOD.

Stuart, Gilbert (*b* North Kingstown, RI, 3 Dec. 1755; *d* Boston, 9 July 1828). American portrait painter. With *Copley he was the outstanding American portraitist of his period and he is regarded as the creator of a distinctively American style of portraiture. Much of his early career was spent in Scotland (*c.*1771–2), England (1775–87), and Ireland (1787–92). After he settled permanently in America in 1793, he worked briefly in New York City, then moved to Philadelphia (1794/5), Washington (1803), and finally Boston, where he settled in 1805. He quickly established himself as the outstanding portraitist in the country and painted many of the notables of the new republic. His portraits of George Washington are his most famous works—he created three types, all of which were endlessly copied: the 'Vaughan' type (1795, NG, Washington), the 'Lansdowne' type (1796, Pennsylvania Academy of the Fine Arts, Philadelphia), and the 'Athenaeum' type (1796, MFA, Boston), which is one of the most famous images in American art, being used on the country's $1 bill. Stuart's style is notable for its strength of characterization (Benjamin *West said he '*nails* the face to the canvas') and its fluent brushwork. His work had great influence on the next generation of American painters.

Stubbs, George (*b* Liverpool, 25 Aug. 1724; *d* London, 10 July 1806). English animal painter and engraver, celebrated as the greatest of all horse painters. He was the son of a leather-worker, and he followed his father's trade until he was about 16. As an artist he was virtually self-taught, although he worked briefly with Hamlet Winstanley (1694–1756), a portrait painter and engraver. His life up to his mid-thirties (which is poorly documented) was spent mainly in the north of England. Early in his career he seems to have earned his living mainly as a portraitist, and he also made the illustrations (based on his own dissections) for Dr John Burton's treatise on midwifery (1751); Stubbs had studied anatomy at the County Hospital in York, where Burton was a doctor. In 1754 he visited Rome, then spent eighteen months working in isolation in Lincolnshire, dissecting and drawing horses in preparation for a book on equine anatomy. He moved to London in about 1758 and, unable to find an engraver to do the work, he made the plates himself, and in 1766 published his famous book *The Anatomy of the Horse*. It was a great success, prized for its beauty as well as its scientific accuracy, and Stubbs was soon in demand as a painter, not only for his 'portraits' of horses with their owners or grooms, but also for *conversation pieces in which the sitters were grouped in and around a carriage.

His command of anatomy was matched by his ability to depict the beauty and grace of his equine subjects without sentimentalizing them and his range of feeling was wide, extending from the lyrical calm of *Mares and Foals in a River Landscape* (*c*.1763–8, Tate, London) to the full-blooded *Romanticism of his series of pictures on the theme of a horse attacked by a lion (the largest—*c*.1762—is in the Yale Center for British Art, New Haven). He is said to have derived his fascination for the subject from having witnessed a lion attacking a horse in

Morocco on his way back from Italy, but he may also have been familiar with a much copied *antique statue on the theme.

Stubbs painted many other animals apart from horses—among them numerous dogs and several exotic beasts that were exhibited in England (including a moose, a rhinoceros, and a zebra). At his death he was working on *A Comparative Anatomical Exposition of the Structure of the Human Body with that of a Tiger and a Common Fowl*, the drawings for which are in the Yale Center for British Art. His scientific curiosity extended to the materials he used and he experimented with painting in *enamel, first on copper and then on larger earthenware *panels specially manufactured for him by Josiah *Wedgwood. Such projects took up much time but did not make him money and in his final years he was in financial difficulties. He kept his great powers until the end, however, and one of his finest works, painted when he was 75, is the enormous *Hambletonian, Rubbing Down* (1799, Mount Stewart House, County Down, NT), showing the champion horse looking strained and exhausted after winning a race in which it was 'much cut with the whip' and 'shockingly goaded' with the spur. It is a magnificent, heroic, almost tragic image. Stubbs was for long classified merely as a superior sporting painter, but his reputation now stands very high; indeed he is placed alongside *Gainsborough and *Reynolds in the front rank of English painters of his age.

His son **George Townly Stubbs** (?1756–1815) was a printmaker, mainly in *mezzotint and *stipple. Most of his work consisted of reproductions of his father's paintings.

stucco. A light, malleable plaster-like substance made from dehydrated lime (calcium carbonate) mixed with powdered *marble and glue and sometimes reinforced with hair. It is used for sculpture and architectural decoration, both external and internal. In a looser sense, the term is applied to a plaster coating applied to the exterior of buildings, and the words plaster and stucco are often used more or less interchangeably; in strict usage of the terms, however, plaster can be differentiated by the fact that it is made from calcium sulphate. Stucco has been known to virtually every civilization. In Europe it was exploited most fully from the 16th century to the 18th century, notable exponents being the artists of the School of *Fontainebleau and Giacomo *Serpotta. By adding large quantities of glue and colour to the stucco mixture *stuccatori* were able to produce a material that could take a high polish and assume the appearance of marble. Indeed, sometimes it is difficult to distinguish from real marble without touching it (marble feels colder).

Stuck, Franz von (*b* Tettenweis, Bavaria, 23 Feb. 1863; *d* Munich, 30 Aug. 1928). German painter, sculptor, and graphic artist, active mainly in Munich, where he was a founding member of the *Sezession in 1893. In 1895 he became a professor at the Munich Academy, where *Kandinsky and *Klee were among his pupils. His favourite subjects were mythological and allegorical scenes, often treated in a morbidly erotic *Symbolist style: he did at least eighteen pictures of a naked woman entwined with an enormous snake under such titles as *Sensuality*, *Sin*, and *Vice*. He had an extraordinarily high reputation in his day (now badly faded) and enjoyed a princely lifestyle. The house in which he lived in Munich is now a museum dedicated to him. He designed and decorated it, attempting to create the ideal of the *Gesamtkunstwerk* ('total work of art').

studiolo (Italian: 'little study'). A term applied in *Renaissance Italy to an intimate domestic chamber used by rulers and other distinguished people as a place of retreat. Such rooms became a badge of culture and they were often specially designed or hung with pictures commissioned specifically for them. The most famous surviving example is that of Federico da *Montefeltro in his palace in Urbino. Isabella d'*Este obtained paintings from some of the leading painters of the day for her studiolo in Mantua.

stump. A short tapered stick, usually of tightly rolled leather or paper and about the length and thickness of a finger, used to soften the edges of a drawing or spread the chalk, crayon, or pencil in shading, thereby providing very delicate tonal transitions. It was much used in the 18th and 19th centuries but went out of favour in the 20th century. A tortillon is a similar implement, but smaller and with a more acute point.

Sturm, Der (The Storm). Name of a magazine and an art gallery in Berlin, both of which were founded and owned by Herwarth Walden (1878–?1941), a writer and composer whose aim was to promote avant-garde art in Germany. The magazine ran from 1910 to 1932 and the gallery from 1912 to 1932. They became the focus of modern art in Berlin, introducing the work of the *Cubists and *Futurists to Germany, for example, and publicizing the *Expressionism of the *Blaue Reiter group. Walden left Germany in 1932 be-

cause of the economic depression and the rise of Nazism and moved to the Soviet Union, where he is said to have died as a political prisoner in 1941.

stylus (or **style**). A small pointed implement, typically of metal, used to make indented marks on a surface. Originally used in the ancient world for writing on clay or wax tablets, it later served many other purposes, for example to incise the ornament on gold grounds, rule the lines for a manuscript, or trace the outlines of a composition from the *cartoon on to the plaster in *fresco painting.

Subleyras, Pierre (*b* Saint-Gilles-du-Gard, 25 Nov. 1699; *d* Rome, 28 May 1749). French painter who settled permanently in Rome in 1728 after winning the *Prix de Rome the previous year. He painted a variety of subjects, including portraits and still-lifes, but he is most highly regarded for his religious pictures, which are much more serious in spirit than most French works of the *Rococo period. His most famous work is the *Mass of St Basil*, painted for St Peter's, but now in S. Maria degli Angeli. This huge picture was highly acclaimed when it was unveiled in 1748, but Subleyras died before he could follow up his success. He has subsequently been something of an underrated figure, but a major exhibition of his work in Paris and Rome in 1987 did much to establish his reputation as one of the outstanding French painters of his period.

Sublime. An aesthetic concept that originated in ancient Greece and played a particularly important part in 18th-century writings about art. It denoted a category of aesthetic experience, associated with ideas of awe and vastness, that was held to be distinct from (although often discussed in conjunction with) the 'Beautiful' and the *Picturesque. It was first used as a term in rhetoric and poetry and gained wide currency after the French translation (1674) of a Greek treatise entitled *On the Sublime*, attributed to Longinus (*c*.1st century AD), although the word itself had occurred earlier in English—quite frequently in Milton for example. Longinus described the immensity of objects in the natural world—stars, mountains, the ocean—in terms of the Sublime, and from the literary sphere the term was extended to a wider range of aesthetic reactions, in particular the new sensibility for the wild, awe-inspiring, and stupendous aspects of natural scenery.

The outstanding work on the concept of the Sublime in English was Edmund *Burke's *A*

Philosophical Enquiry into the Origin of our Ideas of the Sublime and Beautiful (1757). This book was one of the first to realize the power of suggestion to stimulate the imagination (in contrast with the emphasis on clarity and precision during the Age of Enlightenment). Speaking of painting, Burke says that 'a judicious obscurity in some things contributes to the effect of the picture', because in art as in nature 'dark, confused, uncertain images have a greater power on the fancy to form the grander passions than those which are more clear and determinate.' The cult of the Sublime had varied expressions in the visual arts, notably the taste for the 'savage' landscapes of Salvator *Rosa and the popularity among painters of subjects from Homer, Milton, and Ossian (the legendary Gaelic warrior and bard, whose verses—actually fabrications—were published in the 1760s to great acclaim). In literature, the 'Gothic novel', in which mystery and horror were the essential ingredients, appealed to the same sentiments. The first Gothic novel was Horace *Walpole's *The Castle of Otranto* (1764), and when crossing the Alps in 1739 Walpole expressed the essence of the imaginative appeal of the Sublime in his memorable exclamation: 'Precipices, mountains, torrents, wolves, rumblings—Salvator Rosa.' The vogue for the Sublime, with that for the Picturesque, helped shape the attitudes that led to *Romanticism.

sudarium. See VERNICLE.

sugar(-lift) aquatint. See AQUATINT.

Suger, Abbot (*b* c.1081; *d* Saint-Denis, 13 Jan. 1151). French churchman, statesman, and patron. He was adviser to Louis VI and Louis VII, acting as regent in 1147–9 during the latter's absence on the Second Crusade, but he is remembered mainly for the rebuilding of the abbey of Saint-Denis, near Paris, of which he was abbot from 1122 until his death. Suger's reconstruction and redecoration of the abbey was the most important landmark in the emergence of the *Gothic style in architecture and sculpture. In the 1140s he wrote an autobiographical account of the work—a unique document of the time. It was edited and translated (1946) by Erwin *Panofsky, who wrote that Suger was 'frankly in love with splendour and beauty in every conceivable form: it might be said that his reponse to ecclesiastical ceremonial was largely aesthetic'. Suger commissioned several items of furnishing and sacred vessels for the abbey, some of which survive, notably an antique porphyry vase he had converted into the shape of an eagle (Louvre, Paris).

Suisse, Académie. See ACADÉMIE.

Sully, Thomas (*b* Horncastle, Lincolnshire, 19 June 1783; *d* Philadelphia, 5 Nov. 1872). The preeminent American portrait painter of his period, active mainly in Philadelphia. He was born in England, but moved to America as a child. Subsequently he made two visits to England—in 1809–10, when he received advice from *West, and in 1837–8, when he painted Queen Victoria for the Society of the Sons of St George of Philadelphia (another version is in the Wallace Coll., London). His style, distinguished by fluid, glossy brushwork and romantic warmth and dash, reveals his great admiration for *Lawrence. In his later work, however, he tended towards a genteel sentimentality. Sully was highly successful and extremely productive. He is said to have painted some 2,000 portraits (he also made miniatures), but his best-known work is probably one of his (also very numerous) history paintings—*Washington Crossing the Delaware* (1819, MFA, Boston).

Superrealism. Style of painting (and to a lesser extent sculpture) popular from the late 1960s, particularly in the USA and Britain, in which subjects are depicted with a minute and impersonal exactitude of detail. Hyperrealism and Photographic Realism (or Photorealism) are alternative names, and some artists who practise the style do indeed work from photographs (sometimes using colour slides projected on the canvas); sharpness of detail is evenly distributed over the whole picture (except where out-of-focus effects in the photograph are faithfully recorded), but the scale is sometimes greatly enlarged. (Some critics prefer to use the terms 'Photographic Realism' or 'Photorealism' only when a picture has been painted direct from a photograph, but most are not so restrictive.) The immediate progenitor of Superrealism was *Pop art; banal subject matter from the consumer society was common to both, and certain artists, such as Malcolm *Morley and Mel *Ramos, overlap both fields. The kind of humour found in Pop is very rare in Superrealism, however, which tends to be cool and impersonal, with subjects often chosen because they are technically challenging (involving multiple reflections, for example). Like Pop, Superrealism was a hit commercially, but it was less well received critically. Some critics, indeed, regard it as involving a great deal of painstaking work but very little else; others think that its exponents can achieve a strange kind of intensity, the effect of the indiscriminate attention to detail being—somewhat paradoxically—to create a strong feeling of unreality.

The leading American Superrealist painters include: Chuck *Close, whose speciality is giant portrait heads; Don Eddy (1944–), notable for scenes involving reflections in shop windows; Richard Estes (1936–), most of whose work is devoted to the urban landscape; and Audrey Flack (1931–), who is unusual in that she aims for emotional effect in her still-lifes of religious symbols and images of vanity and death. Philip *Pearlstein is sometimes labelled a Superrealist but stands somewhat apart. British Superrealist painters include Graham Dean (1951–), Michael English (1943–), and Michael Leonard (1933–), whose work includes highly detailed portrait drawings in a style mimicking the Old Masters. The best-known Superrealist sculptors have been the Americans John *De Andrea and Duane *Hanson, and more recently the Australian-born, British resident Ron Mueck (1958–).

In the 1930s the term 'Superrealism' was fairly commonly used as an alternative to *Surrealism, but this usage has died out.

support. The material—*canvas, wooden *panel, *paper, or other substance—on which a painting or other two-dimensional work is executed; in mural painting the support is the wall. Usually a support is prepared with a *ground before paint is applied, but in watercolour the paint is used directly on the paper, so support and ground are one and the same.

Suprematism. Russian abstract art movement, created by and chiefly associated with *Malevich. He claimed that he began producing Suprematist pictures in 1913, but he coined the name and officially launched the movement in 1915. His Suprematist paintings were the most radically pure abstract works created up to that date, for he limited himself to basic geometric shapes—the square, rectangle, circle, cross, and triangle—and a narrow range of colours, reaching the ultimate distillation of his ideas in a series of paintings of a white square on a white ground (c.1918), after which he announced the end of Suprematism. The spiritual ideas that he attempted to embody in Suprematism are difficult to summarize, for his writing is often vague and mystical; he thought that 'The Suprematists have deliberately given up the objective representation of their surroundings in order to reach the summit of the "unmasked" art and from this vantage point to view life through the prism of pure artistic feeling.' In spite of his wish to create

a pure abstract art, some artists applied Suprematist designs to functional objects such as pottery and textiles, and Malevich's work was influential for a time even on scientifically minded artists such as *Rodchenko. Suprematism, indeed, made a powerful impact on the avant-garde in Russia until the Soviet regime demanded work that was socially useful (see CONSTRUCTIVISM) and it later had great influence on the development of art and design in the West.

Surikov, Vasily. See WANDERERS.

Surrealism. Movement in art and literature flourishing in the 1920s and 1930s, characterized by a fascination with the bizarre, the incongruous, and the irrational. It was closely related to *Dada, its principal source; several artists figured successively in both movements, each of which was conceived as a revolutionary mode of thought and action—a way of life rather than a set of stylistic attitudes. Both were strongly anti-rationalist and much concerned with creating effects that were disturbing or shocking, but whereas Dada was essentially nihilist, Surrealism was positive in spirit.

The movement originated in France. Its founder and chief spokesman was the writer André *Breton, who believed that the world had been corrupted by excessive materialism and rationalism and wanted to assert the importance of emotional and imaginative values. He officially launched the movement with his first *Manifeste du surréalisme*, published in 1924; however, it had been taking shape for a few years before this and the term 'surréalisme' had been coined by *Apollinaire in 1917. The central idea of the movement was to release the creative powers of the unconscious mind, or as Breton put it, 'to resolve the previously contradictory conditions of dream and reality into an absolute reality, a super-reality'. Essentially it aimed at breaching the dominance of reason and conscious control by releasing primitive urges and imagery, and Breton and other members of the movement drew liberally on Freud's theories concerning the unconscious and its relation to dreams. The way in which they set about exploration of submerged impulses and imagery varied greatly (in spite of Breton's demands there was little doctrinal unity, and defections, expulsions, and personal attacks are a feature of the history of the movement). Some artists, for example *Ernst and *Masson, cultivated various spontaneous techniques such as *frottage in an effort to eliminate conscious control. At the other extreme, *Dalí, *Magritte, and others painted in a scrupulously detailed manner to give a hallucinatory sense of reality to scenes that make no rational sense.

Paris remained the centre of Surrealism until the Second World War, when the emigration of many European artists to the USA made New York the new hub of its activity. It made an impact in many other places and indeed became the most widely disseminated and controversial aesthetic movement of the 1920s and 1930s, spread partly by a series of major international exhibitions. Two of the most important took place in 1936: the International Surrealist Exhibition at the New Burlington Galleries in London, and 'Fantastic Art, Dada, Surrealism' at the Museum of Modern Art, New York. Surrealism did not take root in Germany (Ernst, the major German Surrealist, lived mostly in France and the USA), but it flourished vigorously in Belgium—in the work particularly of Magritte, the most inspired of all Surrealist painters, and *Delvaux, the most long-lived upholder of the tradition. Many artists who were not in sympathy with the political aims of Surrealism (for a time it was associated with the French Communist Party), and who were never formal members of the movement, nevertheless found its ideas stimulating and were influenced by its imagery. In Britain, Henry *Moore and Paul *Nash were among the major artists who went through a Surrealist phase. The English Surrealist Group was founded in 1936, but it was social rather than revolutionary in its aims.

Although it broke up as an organized movement during the war and by this time had spent its main force, the spirit of Surrealism lived on. With its stress on the marvellous and the poetic, it offered an alternative approach to the formalism of *Cubism and various types of abstract art, and its methods and techniques continued to influence artists in many countries. It was, for example, a fundamental source for *Abstract Expressionism. Among the artists who have most unwaveringly kept the Surrealist spirit alive is the British painter Conroy Maddox (1912–), who in 1978 said, 'No other movement has had more to say about the human condition, or has so determinedly put liberty, both poetic and political, above all else.'

Susini, Clemente. See WAX.

Sutherland, Graham (*b* London, 24 Aug. 1903; *d* London, 17 Feb. 1980). British painter, printmaker, and designer. He abandoned an apprenticeship as a railway engineer to study engraving and etching, 1921–6, and up to 1930 worked exclusively as a printmaker. His etchings of this period are in the *Romantic and visionary tradition of Samuel *Palmer. In the early 1930s he began experimenting with oils (following a decline in the market for prints), and by 1935 he had turned mainly to painting. His paintings of the 1930s show a highly subjective response to nature, inspired mainly by visits to Pembrokeshire. He had a vivid gift of visual metaphor and his landscapes are not topographical, but semi-abstract patterns of haunting and monstrous shapes rendered in his distinctively acidic colouring (*Entrance to a Lane*, 1939, Tate, London). From 1940 to 1945 he was employed as an *Official War Artist, mainly recording the effects of bombing; his poignant pictures of shattered buildings are among the most famous images of the home front.

Soon after the war Sutherland took up religious painting, with a *Crucifixion* (1946) for St Matthew's, Northampton (he received the commission at the dedication of Henry *Moore's *Madonna and Child* in this church), and also portraiture, with *Somerset Maugham* (1949, Tate). It was in these two fields that he chiefly made his mark in his later career. The portrait of Maugham has an almost caricature quality (Maugham's friend Sir Gerald *Kelly said it made him look 'like an old Chinese madam in a brothel in Shanghai'), and his most famous portrait, that of Winston Churchill (1954), was so hated by the sitter (who thought it made him look 'half-witted') that Lady Churchill destroyed it. Sutherland's most celebrated work, however, has become widely popular—it is the immense tapestry of *Christ in Glory* (1952–62) in Coventry Cathedral.

In addition to such figure subjects, Sutherland continued to paint landscapes—many of them inspired by the French Riviera, where he lived for part of every year from 1947—and late in his career he returned to printmaking, producing coloured lithographs. Apart from paintings and prints, his work included ceramics and designing posters and stage costumes and decor. He was one of the most famous British artists of the 20th century and received many honours, notably the Order of Merit in 1960. His reputation was high abroad; indeed in his later career he was probably more admired by foreign than by British critics, who tended to find his work old-fashioned.

Swanenburgh, Jacob van (*b* Leiden, 21 Apr. 1571; *d* Utrecht, 16 Oct. 1638). Dutch painter, a member of a family of artists active in Leiden. He was a minor figure, now remembered exclusively because he has the distinction of being the first recorded teacher of *Rembrandt. His work had no discernible influence on his great pupil, for although Rembrandt's work was wideranging, he never—so far as is known—tried his hand at either of Swanenburgh's specialities: subjects set in Italy (where he spent most of his career, c.1591–1618) and scenes of hell.

Swanevelt, Herman van (b ?Woerden, nr. Utrecht, c.1600; d Paris, 1655). Dutch landscape painter, printmaker, and draughtsman, active mainly in France and Italy. He is recorded in Paris in 1623 and from 1629 to 1641 he lived in Rome. There is no documentary evidence in support of the tradition that he once shared a house with *Claude, but he was certainly close to him in style and both artists were among those who painted landscapes for Philip IV's (see HABSBURG) Buen Retiro Palace in Madrid— 'the largest, most spectacular landscape commission awarded in Europe during the seventeenth century' (Seymour Slive, Dutch Painting: 1600–1800, 1995). Swanevelt often included *antique remains in his paintings, and according to *Sandrart he was nicknamed Eremiet ('hermit'; see SCHILDERSBENT) because of his fondness for painting amid ruins and solitary places in and around Rome. He continued producing views of Roman ruins after he left Italy and moved to Paris (The Arch of Constantine, Rome, 1645, Dulwich Picture Gal., London). For the rest of his career he was based in Paris, but he made several visits to Woerden. His work helped to spread the tradition of *ideal landscape in northern Europe. In addition to paintings he produced etchings and drawings.

Swart van Groningen, Jan (b Groningen, c.1500; d ?Antwerp, c.1560). Netherlandish painter, book illustrator, and designer of stained glass. He worked mainly in Antwerp and Gouda, and also travelled to Italy early in his career. His pictures show that he was familiar with the work of *Dürer, *Holbein, *Scorel, and other northern artists who were impressed by Italian *Renaissance art, but in spite of this his style has a certain archaic charm. He had a predilection for showing people wearing high hats, turbans, and other odd headgear.

Sweerts, Michiel (bapt. Brussels, 29 Sept. 1618; d Goa, India, 1664). Flemish painter, an enigmatic and exceedingly attractive artist. Nothing is known of his training or early career.

From about 1646 to about 1656 he lived in Rome, where he came into contact with the 'Bamboccianti' (see LAER). He painted *genre scenes in their manner, but his work is in a class apart because of the quiet, melancholy dignity of his figures and his exquisite tonality. His other pictures in Rome included views of artists' studios (an example dated 1652 is in the Detroit Institute of Arts). By 1656 Sweerts had returned to his native Brussels; he set up a life drawing class in that year and in 1659 became a member of the painters' guild. By 1661 he was in Amsterdam, where he joined a missionary group (he was almost fanatically devout and zealous—giving his possessions to the poor, sleeping on a hard floor, and so on). In 1662 he sailed from Marseilles to the Orient, but his fellow missionaries found him quarrelsome and unstable, and he was dismissed at Isfahan in Persia; he made his own way to Goa in India, where he died in a Portuguese mission station. Towards the end of his career, Sweerts seemed to have worked mainly as a portraitist. Like his genre scenes, his portraits are distinguished by delicate and subdued colour harmonies and great sensitivity of expression and handling. They have often been compared with the work of *Vermeer, to whom Sweerts's Portrait of a Girl (Leicestershire Mus. and AG, Leicester) was once attributed.

Sylvester, David. See KITCHEN SINK SCHOOL.

Symbolism. A loosely organized movement in literature and the visual arts, flourishing c.1885–c.1910, characterized by a rejection of direct, literal representation in favour of evocation and suggestion. It was part of a broad anti-materialist and anti-rationalist trend in ideas and art towards the end of the 19th century and specifically marked a reaction against the naturalistic aims of *Impressionism. Symbolist painters tried to give visual expression to emotional experiences, or as the poet Jean Moréas put it in a Symbolist Manifesto published in Le Figaro on 18 September 1886, 'to clothe the idea in sensuous form'. Just as Symbolist poets thought there was a close correspondence between the sound and rhythm of words and their meaning, so Symbolist painters thought that colour and line in themselves could express ideas or feelings. Symbolist critics were much given to drawing parallels between the arts, and *Redon's paintings, for example, were compared with the poetry of Baudelaire and Edgar Allan Poe and with the music of Claude Debussy. Many painters were inspired by the same kind of imagery as Symbolist writers (the femme fatale is a common theme), but *Gauguin and his followers (see SYNTHETISM) chose much less flamboyant subjects, often peasant scenes. Religious feeling of an intense, mystical kind was a feature of the movement, but so was an interest in the erotic and the perverse—death, disease, and sin were favourite subjects. Stylistically, Symbolist artists varied greatly, from a love of exotic detail to an almost primitive simplicity in the conception of the subject, and from firm outlines to misty softness in the delineation of form. A general tendency, however, was towards flattened forms and broad areas of colour—in tune with *Post-Impressionism in general. By freeing painting from what Gauguin called 'the shackles of probability' the movement helped to create the aesthetic premises of much 20th-century art. Although chiefly associated with France, Symbolism had international currency, and such diverse artists as *Burne-Jones, *Hodler, and *Munch are regarded as part of the movement in its broadest sense. Symbolist sculptors include the Norwegian Gustav *Vigeland and the Belgian Georg Minne (1866–1941).

Synchromism. An abstract or semi-abstract movement in painting founded in 1912 by Stanton *Macdonald-Wright and Morgan *Russell, two American artists living in Paris (they met there in 1911). The term, meaning literally 'colours together', was coined by Russell on the analogy of 'symphony'. As it suggests, he and his colleague were primarily interested in the abstract use of colour (in 1912 Russell said that he wished to do 'a piece of expression solely by means of colour and the way it is put down, in showers and broad patches, distinctly separated from each other, or blended . . . but with force and clearness and large geometric patterns'). In the period 1911–14 the Synchromists were working in a similar direction to the *Orphists but more or less independently and the two Americans were appalled when they were dismissed by some critics as followers of their European counterparts. Although Synchromism petered out with the First World War (during which Macdonald-Wright and Russell were separated), it influenced several American artists over the next few years (notably *Benton), and its founders hold distinguished places in the vanguard of abstract art.

Synthetic Cubism. See CUBISM.

Synthetism. Term applied to a manner of painting associated with *Bernard, *Gauguin, and their associates at Pont-Aven in Brittany. It involved the simplification of forms into large-scale patterns and the expressive purification of colours. Bernard believed that form and colour must be simplified for the sake of more forceful expression, and Gauguin spoke much of 'synthesis', by which he meant a blending of abstract ideas of rhythm and colour with visual impressions of nature. He advised his disciples to 'paint by heart' because in memory coloured by emotion natural forms become more integrated and meaningful. Bernard and Gauguin each claimed credit for developing Synthetism and they probably acted as mutual catalysts. Synthetism was at its most vital between about 1888 and 1894, but some artists working at Pont-Aven continued the style well into the 20th century. It was influential on the *Nabis and has affinities with the more literary *Symbolism. See also CLOISONNISM.

Systemic art. Term coined by Lawrence *Alloway in 1966 to describe a type of abstract art characterized by the use of very simple standardized forms, usually geometric in character, either in a single concentrated image or repeated in a system arranged according to a clearly visible principle of organization. The chevron paintings of *Noland are examples of Systemic art. It has been described as a branch of *Minimal art, but Alloway extended the term to cover *Colour Field Painting.

T

Tacca, Pietro (*bapt.* Carrara, 6 Sept. 1577; *d* nr. Florence, 26 Oct. 1640). Florentine sculptor, mainly in bronze, the chief pupil and follower of *Giambologna. After his master's death in 1608 Tacca completed a number of his works and succeeded him as sculptor to the *Medici grand dukes of Tuscany. His work for them included his masterpieces, the four *Slaves* (*c.*1615–24) at the foot of *Bandinelli's statue of Ferdinand I de' Medici in Livorno (Leghorn). His last major project was an equestrian statue (1634–40) of Philip IV of Spain (see HABSBURG) for the garden of the Buen Retiro Palace in Madrid (it is now in the Plaza de Oriente). The king—by his own wish—is shown on a rearing horse, an unprecented technical feat of bronze casting on this scale (Tacca had scientific advice from Galileo). The *Baroque pose had already been used in pictures of Philip by *Rubens and *Velázquez (a copy of a painting by one or the other of these artists was sent to Florence to act as a model), but the smooth, generalized treatment of the work shows that Tacca remained essentially a *Mannerist sculptor. In addition to his large works, he produced numerous graceful bronze statuettes, continuing the tradition of Giambologna. His son **Ferdinando Tacca** (1619–86) was a sculptor and stage designer.

Tachisme. A type of abstract painting popular in the late 1940s and 1950s characterized by the use of irregular dabs or splotches of colour (*tache* is French for spot or blotch). The term was first used in this sense in about 1951 and was given wide currency by the French critic Michel Tapié in his book *Un art autre* (1952). In its intuitive, spontaneous approach, Tachisme had affinities with *Abstract Expressionism (although it initially developed independently of it), and the term is often used as a generic label for any European painting of the time that parallels the American movement. However, Tachisme was primarily a French phenomenon (Jean *Fautrier, Georges *Mathieu, and the German-born but Paris-based *Wols were among the leading exponents), and Tachiste paintings are characteristically more suave, sensual, and concerned with beautiful handling (*belle facture*) than the work of the Abstract Expressionists, which can be aggressively raw in comparison. The terms 'abstraction lyrique' (*lyrical abstraction) *'Art Autre' (other art), and *'Art Informel' (art without form) are sometimes used synonymously with Tachisme, although certain critics use them to convey different nuances, sometimes corresponding with niceties of theory rather than with observable differences in practice. It seems reasonable, however, to regard Tachisme as one aspect of the broader notion of Art Informel. To add to the confusion of terminology, the word 'tachisme' was used differently in the 19th century, being applied pejoratively to the *Impressionists and the *Macchiaioli.

tactile values. Term coined by Bernard *Berenson in his *Florentine Painters of the Renaissance* (1896) to describe those qualities in a painting that he regarded as stimulating the sense of touch. He thought that *Giotto was the first master since classical antiquity whose painting demonstrated these qualities, which he considered to be a distinctive feature of Florentine painting and held to be 'life enhancing'. His theories were not very cogent, and the term is now little used.

Taddeo di Bartolo (*b* Siena, *c.*1362; *d* Siena, *c.*1422). Sienese painter. He was the leading painter in Siena in the first two decades of the 15th century and also worked in and for other cities. His style was conservative, but his frescos of Roman heroes (1413–14) in the Palazzo Pubblico in Siena are forward-looking in subject—early examples of the type of famous men cycle that became popular in the *Renaissance.

Taeuber-Arp, Sophie (*née* Taeuber) (*b* Davos, 19 Jan. 1889; *d* Zurich, 13 Jan. 1943). Swiss artist, the wife and frequent collaborator of Jean *Arp. She met Arp in Zurich in 1915 and married him in 1922. Her large output included *collages, embroideries, paintings, puppets, sculpture, and stage designs, much of her work being in an abstract style distinguished by its rhythmic vitality. She died from an accident with a leaking gas stove.

Taft, Lorado (*b* Elmwood, Ill., 29 Apr. 1860; *d* Chicago, 30 Oct. 1936). American sculptor, writer, and teacher. He studied at the École des *Beaux-Arts in Paris, 1880–6, and taught sculpture at the Art Institute of Chicago, 1886–1929. In his day Taft was well known for portraits and allegorical public sculpture, particularly fountains such as The Fountain of Time (1922, Washington Park, Chicago), but he is now remembered mainly for his books *The History of American Sculpture* (1903), the first comprehensive work on the subject, and *Modern Tendencies in Sculpture* (1921), in which he defended the academic tradition and attacked abstraction. In addition to writing and teaching, Taft spread his ideas as a public lecturer, touring clubs and schools in Illinois. His studio in Chicago has been preserved as a national monument.

Taine, Hippolyte (*b* Vouziers, Ardennes, 21 Apr. 1828; *d* Paris, 5 Mar. 1893). French philosopher, historian, and critic. He was a leading exponent of positivism, and in particular the chief figure in applying its ideas of scientific method to aesthetics and cultural history. In 1864 he was appointed professor of aesthetics and art history at the École des *Beaux-Arts, Paris, and his lecture courses there formed the basis of several books, beginning with *Philosophie de l'art* (1865; it was translated into English the same year). In this he declared that 'My sole duty is to offer you facts and show how these facts are produced', and he described art history as a sort of applied botany: 'Just as there is a physical temperature which by its variations determines the appearance of this or that species of plants, so there is a moral temperature which by its variations determines the appearance of this or that kind of art.' Although he did not rule out the ideas of self-expression and genius, he thought they were less important than environmental, social, and economic factors. Taine antagonized many people, but his ideas had wide influence.

Takis (Panayotis Vassilakis) (*b* Athens, 29 Oct. 1925). Greek experimental artist, active mainly in Paris, best known for his highly original work in *Kinetic sculpture. His creations often employ magnetic fields in which various metal objects produce changing patterns—the magnet's 'live force and vibration gives life to what has seemed to be dead material'. In 1960 he suspended the

poet Sinclair Beiles on a metal frame between two powerful magnets at the Galerie Iris Clert in Paris. Sometimes he combines light effects and music with movement.

Talbot, William Henry Fox. See DAGUERRE.

Tamayo, Rufino (*b* Oaxaca, 29 Aug. 1899; *d* Mexico City, 24 June 1991). Mexican painter, printmaker, sculptor, and collector, the son of Zapotec Indians. Apart from the trio of great muralists—*Orozco, *Rivera, and *Siqueiros—he was probably the most celebrated Mexican artist of the 20th century, but his work was very different from theirs, for he was concerned with pictorial values rather than with the political messages they held so dear. From 1921 to 1926 he worked at the National Archaeological Museum in Mexico City, and native folk art traditions helped to shape his eclectic but distinctive style; *Surrealism was another strong influence. From 1936 to 1950 he lived in New York, although he returned regularly to Mexico, and from 1957 to 1964 he lived in Paris, then settled permanently in Mexico. By this time he was internationally famous, with a list of major exhibitions and distinctions to his credit, including the Grand Prize for Painting at the 1953 São Paulo *Bienale. His work was varied in subject, including still-lifes, portraits (notably many of his pianist wife Olga), nudes, animals, and scenes of the culture and myths of the Mexican Indians. He did several murals in Mexico, but usually worked on canvas affixed to the wall rather than in fresco. His work also included a large number of prints in various techniques and sculpture in bronze and iron. Some of his late sculptures were very large (*Conquest of Space*, 1983, San Francisco International Airport). Throughout his life Tamayo was an ardent collector. He donated his collections to the city of Oaxaca to form museums of Pre-Columbian art (1974) and contemporary art (1981).

Tanagra figurines (or statuettes). A type of painted *terracotta figurine, mostly of the 3rd century BC, named after Tanagra in Boeotia, Greece, where many of them were found in the late 19th century. The favourite subjects were elegantly draped women. They became enormously popular and have been much forged.

Tanguy, Yves (*b* Paris, 5 Jan. 1900; *d* Woodbury, Conn., 15 Jan. 1955). French-born painter who became an American citizen in 1948. Whilst working at various odd jobs in Paris he began sketching café scenes that were praised by

*Vlaminck, and in 1923 he decided to take up art seriously after being greatly impressed by the work of de *Chirico; he had no formal artistic training. In 1925 he met André *Breton and joined the *Surrealist group. His work developed quickly and by the time of his first one-man exhibition, at the Galerie Surréaliste in 1927, he had already created a distinctive style. Characteristically he painted in a scrupulous technique reminiscent of that of *Dalí, but his imagery is highly individual, featuring marine- or lunar-like landscapes whose ghostly plains are scattered with structures that suggest giant weathered bones arranged into fantastic pylons. In 1939 he met the American Surrealist painter Kay *Sage in Paris; he followed her to the USA and they married in 1940. After the Second World War he built up an international reputation.

Tanning, Dorothea. See ERNST.

tapestry. A term that is often loosely applied to any heavy ornamental fabric used as a wall hanging but which more correctly signifies a textile woven on a loom with two directions of thread, running respectively top to bottom (warps) and side to side (wefts). The warps are plain backing threads, and the design is created by weaving the wefts alternately over and under them according to the requirements of colour; the image is thus an integral part of the material rather than something superimposed on it, as in embroidery. Although tapestries are most often used for wall hangings, they have also been employed in other ways, notably as upholstery fabrics. The usual materials for the warps are wool, linen, or hemp, and wool is also the most common material for the wefts, although silks and even silver and gold threads have been used in particularly luxurious examples. The technical fineness of a tapestry is expressed by the number of wefts to the centimetre; an average of ten per centimetre is fairly coarse, while thirty is considered refined (although much denser concentrations are sometimes found). Usually the weaver works from a full-sized coloured *cartoon (*Raphael, *Rubens, and *Goya are among the celebrated artists who have produced such designs).

Tapestry was known in the ancient world, but the early history of the subject is obscure. It is not until the 14th century that a continuous tradition can be traced, but from then tapestries were an essential part of medieval interior decoration, particularly in northern Europe (where in addition to their aesthetic purpose they performed the practical function of keeping out draughts). Among the most famous tapestries of the Middle Ages are a vast series on the Apocalypse (designed by Jean *Bondol) made in 1373–82 for Louis I, Duke of Anjou (brother of Charles V of France), and now displayed in a special gallery in the castle at Angers, and an enchanting series on the Lady and the Unicorn (c.1490–1500, Mus. du Moyen Age, Paris). France has the richest tradition in the art, with particularly important factories at *Arras, *Aubusson, Beauvais, and Paris (see GOBELINS), but in the 15th and 16th centuries Flanders led the way for a time, with Tournai and then *Brussels being major centres of production. Most other European countries have also produced tapestries, the most famous English manufactory being the Mortlake Tapestry Factory (1619–1703), at Mortlake in Surrey, in which Charles I (see ROYAL COLLECTION) took a close interest; the factory wove several sets of tapestries from Raphael's cartoons of the Acts of the Apostles, which Charles bought in 1623.

Tapestries continued to be popular until well into the 18th century, but they then began to give way to cheaper coverings such as wallpaper. However, there was a revival of interest in the late 19th century, for example in the work of William *Morris, and this continued in the 20th century. At the *Bauhaus, for example, tapestry design was part of the curriculum, and numerous modern artists have done impressive work in the medium, including *Braque, *Matisse, *Picasso, and Graham *Sutherland, whose huge Christ in Glory (1952–62) in Coventry Cathedral, woven at Aubusson, is probably the most famous tapestry of the 20th century.

Tàpies, Antoni (b Barcelona, 13 Dec. 1923). The leading Spanish painter to emerge in the period since the Second World War, active mainly in Barcelona. He studied law at Barcelona University from 1943 to 1946 and was largely self-taught as an artist. His early works were in a *Surrealist vein influenced by *Klee and *Miró, but in about 1953, after turning to abstraction, he began working in mixed media, in which he has made his most original contribution to art. He incorporated clay and marble dust in his paint and used discarded materials such as paper, string, and rags, and then (from about 1970) more substantial objects such as parts of furniture. He explained his belief in the validity of commonplace materials in his essay Nothing is Mean (1970). Tàpies has travelled extensively and his ideas have had worldwide influence. Apart from paintings he has also made etchings and lithographs.

Tarbell, Edmund C. See TEN.

Target exhibition. Exhibition organized in Moscow by *Larionov, *Goncharova, and *Malevich in March 1913, at which *Rayonism was launched. Malevich also showed works in his 'Cubo-Futurist' style.

Tassi, Agostino (Agostino Buonamici) (b Ponzano Romano, c.1580; d Rome, 1644). Italian painter, active mainly in Rome. He was one of the outstanding *quadratura specialists of the period, his most famous work being the illusionistic architectural setting for *Guercino's celebrated *Aurora* fresco (1621–3) in the Casino of the Villa Ludovisi, Rome. Tassi also painted small landscapes in the manner of *Bril and *Elsheimer, and for centuries he was remembered mainly because he taught *Claude, his significance as a decorative painter being forgotten. His other claim to fame is that in 1612 he stood trial for allegedly raping Artemisia *Gentileschi. The verdict of the court is unknown; Tassi is said to have spent some time in prison, but he was at liberty by 1613. However, it is certain that he was an unsavoury character (he was even suspected of murdering his wife).

Tassie, James (b Pollokshaws [now a suburb of Glasgow], 15 July 1735; d London, 1 June 1799). Scottish maker of medallion portraits and reproductions of antique gems and cameos. He began his career as a stonemason, and in 1763—intending to set up as a sculptor—he moved to Dublin. There he met Dr Henry Quin, a physician who made casts from antique gems as a hobby, and together they developed a 'white enamel composition' suitable for reproducing gems (and for creating miniature portrait heads) in imitation of marble. Tassie successfully kept the secret of his vitreous paste and learned to use it so skilfully that (as well as varying the colour) he could make his reproductions opaque or transparent and imitate the varied layers of a cameo. In 1766 he settled in London, where he attained a considerable reputation; from 1769 to 1791 he exhibited regularly at the *Royal Academy and he made casts for *Wedgwood. The German-born antiquary Rudolph Eric Raspe (1737–94), who is perhaps best remembered as the creator of the humorous character 'Baron Munchausen', issued a two-volume catalogue of Tassie's 'ancient and modern engraved gems' in 1791. In all, Tassie reproduced more than 15,000 gems, cameos, and medallions, and he made more than 500 medallion busts (his work is best represented in the Scottish National Portrait Gallery in Edinburgh).

Tassie's nephew **William Tassie** (b London, 1777; d London, 26 Oct. 1860) succeeded to his business. He was equally industrious, but less skilful. Like his uncle, he was a kindly, popular man, and his studio in Leicester Square was much frequented by artists and literary men. In 1805 he won the main prize in the lottery when *Boydell's Shakespeare Gallery pictures were disposed of. Tassie sold the pictures in the same year.

Tate, Sir Henry (b Chorley, Lancashire, 11 Mar. 1819; d London, 5 Dec. 1899). British sugar tycoon (the inventor of the sugar cube) and art collector. In 1890 he offered the nation his collection, consisting mainly of the work of Victorian contemporaries, on condition that the government found a suitable site for a gallery. Following great controversy over where it should be located, the Tate Gallery opened at Millbank, overlooking the Thames, in 1897, on a site previously occupied by part of Millbank Prison. The building is an undistinguished classical structure designed by Sidney R. J. Smith, an architect who is otherwise virtually unknown.

At the time of its opening, the Tate was not the independent gallery that had been envisaged by its founder. It was subordinate to the *National Gallery and was intended only for recent British art (its official title was the National Gallery of British Art, although it was referred to as the Tate Gallery from the beginning and this name was formalized in 1932). It began to be established as a historical collection of British art in 1910 when a collection of works by Alfred *Stevens was added and a wing was opened to accommodate most of the paintings left in *Turner's studio at his death, which had previously been housed (but in the main unexhibited) at the National Gallery. In 1916 the Tate was given the additional responsibility of forming the national collection of modern art. It was not until 1954, however, that it became completely independent of the National Gallery (although transfers are still made between the two institutions). There have been several extensions to the building (some of them paid for by Sir Joseph and Lord *Duveen), and in 1987 a new gallery—the Clore Gallery (named after Sir Charles Clore (1904–79), a businessman and philanthropist who was one of the Tate's greatest benefactors)—was opened to house works by Turner, including not only the oil paintings already at the Tate, but also watercolours and drawings previously in the *British Museum.

In 1988 a new branch of the Tate Gallery was opened in Liverpool and in 1993 another one in *St Ives. The creation of these two outstations reflected not only a desire to share the Tate's collections with regional audiences, but also the fact that the gallery had outgrown its site in London. In 1994 the Tate Trustees announced a decision to create a new museum to house the gallery's modern collections in the decommissioned Bankside Power Station, a huge, starkly magnificent building occupying a prime site on the Thames opposite St Paul's Cathedral. It was designed by Sir Giles Gilbert Scott and built in 1947–63; the remodelling into a gallery was carried out by the Swiss architects Jacques Herzog and Pierre de Meuron. This new gallery opened to the public in 2000 under the name Tate Modern and quickly became an enormously popular attraction. The original Tate Gallery at Millbank is now known as Tate Britain and has reverted to its original function as the 'National Gallery of British Art'. It has the world's most comprehensive collection of British painting from the mid-16th century onwards, but sculptural coverage does not begin until the 19th century, as the *Victoria and Albert Museum holds the national collection of earlier sculpture. Modern British works are found in both Tate Britain and Tate Modern, and they are sometimes transferred between the two institutions.

Tatlin, Vladimir (b Kharkov [now Kharkiv], Ukraine, 12 Dec. 1885; d Moscow, 31 May 1953). Russian painter, designer, and maker of abstract constructions, the founder of *Constructivism. He ran away to sea at the age of 18 and until 1914 combined painting with the life of a merchant seaman: many of his earlier pictures are of maritime subjects, notably *The Sailor* (1911–12, Russian Mus., St Petersburg), a self-portrait. From 1910 he showed work at several avant-garde exhibitions in Russia and worked in close association with *Goncharova and *Larionov, who had known him as a boy. In 1914 Tatlin visited Berlin and Paris. He haunted *Picasso's studio and on his return to Russia began making a series of abstract *Painted Reliefs, Relief Constructions*, and *Corner Reliefs* inspired by Picasso's sculptural experiments. Very few of these revolutionary works survive, most being known only from photographs; it appears that they were made of a variety of materials—tin, glass, wood, plaster, etc.

After the October Revolution of 1917, Tatlin's constructions made from 'real materials in real space' were felt to be in accordance with the new 'culture of materials' and he threw himself wholeheartedly into the demand for socially orientated art, declaring: 'The events of 1917 in the social field were already brought about in our art in 1914, when material, volume and construction were laid as its basis.' In 1919 he was commissioned to design the monument to the Third International (the organization set up by the Bolsheviks to coordinate the activities of Communist movements throughout the world). The huge monument—in the form of a leaning, openwork, spiral tower in iron and glass—was intended for a position in the centre of Moscow. It was to be both functional and symbolic, housing various offices of the revolutionary government and including such features as an immense projector for throwing propaganda images onto clouds. Tatlin described it as 'A union of purely plastic forms (painting, sculpture and architecture) for a utilitarian purpose'. A model was exhibited in December 1920 at the exhibition of the VIIIth Congress of the Soviets. *Gabo condemned the design as impracticable and it was never executed (it was intended to be much bigger than the Eiffel Tower), but it is recognized as the outstanding symbol of Soviet Constructivism. (The original model has been destroyed, but there is a reconstruction in the Moderna Museet, Stockholm.)

The monument was the culmination of Tatlin's artistic career, and the rest of it is something of an anticlimax. He was active in teaching and administration, and his own work was mainly in the field of *applied art, designing furniture, workers' clothes, etc. In the late 1920s and early 1930s he devoted his energies to designing a glider, which he called *Letatlin* (a compound of his name and the Russian word for 'to fly'). From the 1930s his main activity was theatre design, and his later years were spent in lonely obscurity. In 1948 the Soviet government, demanding *Socialist Realism in the arts, declared him an 'enemy of the people'.

Tchelitchew, Pavel (b Kaluga, 21 Sept. 1898; d Grottaferrata, nr. Rome, 31 July 1957). Russian-born American painter and stage designer. In 1918 he fled Moscow because of the Revolution and in 1923 settled in Paris, where he made a reputation as a stage designer and also became one of the leading exponents of *Neo-Romanticism in painting. His subjects included landscapes, portraits, and figure compositions (among them circus scenes recalling *Picasso's work in his Blue Period). Some of his paintings were fairly naturalistic, but others used multiple images and violent distortions of perspective. He moved to the USA in 1934 and became an American citizen in 1952. In America he was again in demand as a stage designer, but he grew tired of this kind of work and gave it up in 1942 to concentrate on painting. The best-known picture of his American period is probably *Hide and Seek* (1942, MoMA, New York), a *Surrealist-like work in which strangely coloured children's heads weirdly metamorphose into vegetable forms (such subjects reflect something of his belief in the occult—he thought he possessed magical powers). From 1949 he lived mainly in Italy.

Teerlinc, Levina. See BENING.

tempera. A term originally applied to any paint in which the pigment is dissolved in water and mixed (tempered) with an organic gum or glue, but now generally confined to the most common form of the medium—egg tempera. Egg has probably been used in paint since antiquity and it remains the principal *medium for *icons produced in the service of the Greek and Russian Orthodox churches. However, tempera is mainly associated with European art from the beginning of the 13th century until the end of the 15th century; it was the standard technique for panel painting in this period, until it began to be overtaken by *oil. A detailed description of the technique as practised by Italian painters of the time is given in Cennino *Cennini's treatise, written c.1400. According to Cennini (and later *Vasari), only the yolk of the egg was used, but scientific examination of pictures suggests that the white by itself or both yolk and white together may occasionally have been used. The yellowness of the egg had little effect on the colours, though Cennini says that town hens produce the palest and best yolks, and adds that darker yolks will do for the flesh colour of 'old people, or such, who are darker in colouring'. Pale yolks are still preferred today.

Painting with tempera is a demanding craft. Unlike in oil painting, each colour or tone required has to be pre-mixed, for they cannot be blended on the picture surface. The variety and subtlety obtained by skilful painters depended on a slow building-up process, in which each stage—*ground, *underpainting, and various layers of semi-transparent paint—would have a calculated effect upon the next. Tempera has more luminosity and depth than *fresco, but its range of colour and tone is limited and it cannot achieve the close imitation of natural effects attainable in oil painting. In the late 15th and early 16th centuries it was very common for pictures to be painted in a mixture of the two techniques, with tempera typically providing a quick-drying underpaint to which oil *glazes were applied. Subsequently tempera was virtually forgotten for centuries, until there was a revival of interest in the 19th century, stimulated by the rediscovery and publication of Cennini's treatise. Restorers, forgers, and also a few artists began to experiment with the technique, and certain 20th-century artists have favoured it, notably the Americans *Cadmus, *Tooker, and *Wyeth.

Tempesta, Antonio (*b* Florence, 1555; *d* Rome, 5 Aug. 1630). Italian painter, engraver, and draughtsman. He trained in Florence under Jan van der *Straet (which accounts for the Flemish feel in his work) and spent most of his career in Rome. Although he produced a good deal of work as a fresco decorator, he is remembered chiefly as a highly prolific engraver (he produced more than 1,000 prints) of biblical, historical, and mythological scenes—often involving battles, his forte. These engravings were widely distributed throughout Europe and were often used as sources by other artists.

Ten, The (more formally, **Ten American Painters**). A group of well-established American painters from Boston and New York who exhibited together from 1898 to 1919 after resigning from the Society of American Artists, whose exhibitions they considered too conservative and too large. Most of the members of the group had studied in Paris in the 1880s and the common factor in their work was an interest in *Impressionism. They were Frank W. Benson (1862–1951); Joseph R. De Camp (1858–1923); Thomas W. Dewing (1851–1938); Childe *Hassam; Willard L. Metcalf (1858–1925); Robert Reid (1862–1929); Edward E. Simmons (1852–1931); Edmund C. Tarbell (1862–1938); John H. Twachtman (1853–1902); Julian Alden Weir (1852–1919). On the death of Twachtman his place was taken by W. M. *Chase. The Ten held twenty annual exhibitions in New York (at various galleries) and these were sometimes shown in other cities; a final exhibition was shown in Washington in 1919. Although these shows were not particularly radical, they helped to establish a tradition of setting up exhibiting organizations independent of official bodies, foreshadowing such ventures as The *Eight and the *Armory Show.

The Ten was also the name of a group of American *Expressionist painters who exhibited together from 1935 to 1940. *Gottlieb and *Rothko were among the members.

tenebrism. Term describing predominantly dark tonality in a painting. It derives from the Italian *tenebroso* (obscure) and is applied mainly to the 17th-century followers of *Caravaggio in Italy and elsewhere.

Teniers, David the Younger (*b* Antwerp, 15 Dec. 1610; *d* Brussels, 25 Apr. 1690). Flemish painter, the most important member of a family of Antwerp artists. His output was huge and varied (about 2,000 pictures have been attributed to him), but he is best known for his peasant scenes—similar to those of *Brouwer, although less hearty. In 1651 he was appointed court painter in Brussels to Archduke Leopold William of Austria (SEE HABSBURG), governor of the Spanish Netherlands, and he was also made custodian of the archduke's art collection. He compiled a catalogue of part of it, published in 1660 as *Theatrum pictorium*, and made small copies of some of the pictures to assist the engravers who produced the illustrations (his copies are now widely dispersed; examples are in the Courtauld Gallery and Wallace Collection, London). Teniers also painted several larger pictures showing the archduke with his paintings in a fictionalized gallery setting (an example, dated 1651, is in Petworth House, Sussex, NT). His other distinguished patrons included Queen Christina of Sweden, Philip IV of Spain, and various nobles, and his success brought him considerable wealth.

His father **David the Elder** (1582–1649) was primarily a painter of religious scenes. Few pictures are known that are certainly by him, and many formerly attributed to him are now given to his son, with whom he may have collaborated. David the Younger's son **David III** (1638–85) was one of the many artists who imitated his father's work. Several other members of the family were painters.

Tenniel, Sir John (*b* London, 28 Feb. 1820; *d* London, 25 Feb. 1914). English illustrator. He is remembered chiefly for his brilliant illustrations to Lewis Carroll's *Alice's Adventures in Wonderland* (1865) and its sequel *Through the Looking-Glass* (1872), which now seem inseparable from the text, and for his long association with *Punch*. He worked for the magazine from

1850 to 1901, succeeding *Leech as chief cartoonist in 1864.

Terborch (or **Ter Borch**), **Gerard the Younger** (*b* Zwolle, Dec. 1617; *d* Deventer, 8 Dec. 1681). Dutch painter and draughtsman of interiors and small portraits. A highly precocious artist—his earliest dated drawing (in the Rijksmuseum, Amsterdam) is from 1625—Terborch studied with his father **Gerard the Elder** (1584–1662) in his native Zwolle, and with Pieter de *Molyn in Haarlem. Unlike most of the Dutch artists of his time, he travelled extensively. In 1635 he visited London, and according to *Houbraken he travelled in France, Italy, and Spain. From about 1645 to 1648 he was in Germany, where he painted the *Swearing of the Oath of Ratification of the Treaty of Münster* (1648, NG, London), a group portrait of the signatories to the treaty that gave the Dutch independence from Spain. In 1654 he finally settled in Deventer, where he won both professional and social success. He began his career with guardroom scenes, but turned to pictures of elegant society, to which his gifts for delicate characterization and exquisite depiction of fine materials were ideally suited. His best-known work, the subject of a charming passage by *Goethe, is the so-called *Parental Admonition* (c.1655, versions in the Rijksmuseum, Amsterdam, and the Gemäldegalerie, Berlin). It is symptomatic of Terborch's unvaryingly tasteful decorum that the true theme of this picture is a man making a proposition to a courtesan (the coin that he proffers to his 'daughter' has been partially erased in the Berlin version and it is omitted in the engraving Goethe knew). Terborch's most important pupil was Caspar *Netscher.

Terbrugghen (or **ter Brugghen**), **Hendrick** (*b* ?The Hague, ?1588; *d* Utrecht, 1 Nov. 1629). Dutch painter, one of the earliest and finest exponents of *Caravaggism in northern Europe. Born into a Catholic family, he grew up in Utrecht (the main Dutch centre of Catholicism), studied there with *Bloemaert, then spent several years in Italy (c.1605–14), mainly in Rome, although he also visited other cities. There are no known works by him from this period, his earliest dated painting being the *Supper at Emmaus* (1616, Toledo Mus. of Art, Toledo, Ohio). On his return to the Netherlands he became with *Baburen and *Honthorst the leader of the Caravaggism associated with Utrecht (see UTRECHT CARAVAGGISTI). A second journey to Italy, c.1620, has been postulated, as his later works are generally more thoroughly

Caravaggesque than his earlier ones; however his increased interest in Caravaggio's typical subjects and effects could have been stimulated by Baburen (who returned from Italy in about 1620 and is thought to have shared a studio with Terbrugghen for a time). Terbrugghen was chiefly a religious painter, but he also produced some remarkable *genre works, notably a pair of paintings of *Flute Players* (1621, Staatliche Kunstsammlungen, Kassel), which in their subtle tonality—with dark figures placed against a light background—anticipated by a generation the achievement of painters of the Delft School such as *Fabritius and *Vermeer. Although he was praised by *Rubens, who visited Utrecht in 1627, Terbrugghen was neglected by 18th- and 19th-century collectors and historians. The rediscovery of his sensitive and poetic paintings was part of the reappraisal of Caravaggesque art during the 20th century.

term. See HERM.

terracotta (Italian: 'baked earth'). *Clay that has been baked to make it hard. Since very early times it has been used to make figures and architectural ornaments (see, for example, TANAGRA FIGURINES), and it is to these, rather than pottery vessels, that the word 'terracotta' usually refers. The presence of certain chemicals, such as iron oxide, affects the colour of the baked product, so terracotta works are not necessarily of the reddish-brown colour that is normally associated with the word. Firing may produce a wide range of colour from light buff to deep red or black. The hardness and strength of the baked clay vary according to the temperature at which it has been fired. During the firing the clay shrinks by about one-tenth of its volume, sometimes more, sometimes less, according to its quality and the amount of moisture.

Tessin, Count Carl Gustav. See TIEPOLO.

Testa, Pietro (*b* Lucca, ?1612; *d* Rome, 1 Mar. 1650). Italian draughtsman, printmaker, and painter, born in Lucca (hence his nickname Il Lucchesino) and active mainly in Rome. He trained with *Domenichino and was employed by Nicolas *Poussin's patron Cassiano dal Pozzo to make antiquarian drawings, but his bizarre imagination brings him closer in spirit to his contemporaries of romantic temperament such as *Castiglione and *Rosa. Although he had little success as a painter and spent much of his career in poverty, he was recognized as an outstanding draughtsman and etcher. He died by

drowning, and it was rumoured that he had killed himself.

Teylers Museum, Haarlem. See HENDRIKS.

Theed, William (*b* Trentham, Staffordshire, 1804; *d* London, 9 Sept. 1891). English sculptor. He was the son of a painter and sculptor of the same name (1764–1817), best known for his pediment group *Hercules Taming the Thracian Horses* (Royal Mews, London, *c.*1816), one of the earliest works to show the influence of the *Elgin Marbles. Theed the Younger trained with his father, under E. H. *Baily, and at the *Royal Academy Schools. In 1826 he moved to Rome and worked under *Thorvaldsen and *Gibson. He returned to London in 1848 and became one of the most distinguished and prolific of Victorian sculptors. His work includes numerous busts and statues and the colossal group of *Africa* (1864–9) for the Albert Memorial in Kensington Gardens.

Theophanes the Greek (in Russian Feofan Grek) (*b c.*1330/40; *d c.*1410). Painter of *Byzantine origin, active mainly in Russia. Several fresco cycles by him are recorded in early sources, but only part of one survives, in the church of the Transfiguration at Novgorod (1378). Although fragmentary, this is one of the outstanding monuments of Russian medieval art, showing the highly personal version of the Byzantine style that Theophanes brought to Russia; his figures are vigorous and strongly characterized, and his brushwork has an almost impressionistic freedom and dash. The other main works associated with him are a series of nine large *icons (*c.*1405) in the cathedral of the Annunciation, Moscow. According to a contemporary source, Theophanes was also famous as a manuscript *illuminator. No signed or documented work in this field is known by him, but several examples have been attributed to him on stylistic grounds. He made a great impression on painting in Novgorod and Moscow in the 15th century, notably on *Rublev.

Theophilus. The pseudonym adopted by the author of a medieval treatise on arts and crafts entitled *De diversis artibus* (The Various Arts). Estimates of the date of composition range from the 9th to the 13th century. C. R. Dodwell, who produced the standard edition of the Latin text, with English translation (1961), assigns it to the period 1110–40. It is the most important source of information on medieval artistic techniques and is unusual for its time in its references to the artist's attitude to his work. Various early manuscripts are extant, but the treatise did not become generally known until the late 18th century. Gotthold Ephraim *Lessing produced the first printed edition, posthumously published in 1781, and in the same year Rudolph Eric Raspe (see TASSIE) published an edition in England from another manuscript. Raspe was mainly interested in the remarks on oil painting and the title page tells us that the treatise proves 'that the art of painting in oil was known before the pretended discovery of John and Hubert van *Eyck'.

Little or nothing is known with certainty about the writer, who adopted a pseudonym because he wanted to dedicate his skills to God rather than win fame for himself. However, internal evidence suggests that he was a German Benedictine monk and also a practising craftsman whose primary interest lay in metalwork. He has been plausibly identified with Roger of Helmarshausen, a goldsmith and monk at the abbey of Helmarshausen, near Kassel, who is documented as the maker of a portable altar (1100, Paderborn Cathedral Treasury) for Bishop Henry of Werl. Other works have been attributed to him.

Thieme, Ulrich (b Leipzig, 31 Jan. 1865; d Leipzig, 25 Mar. 1922), and **Becker, Felix** (b Sondershausen, 27 Sept. 1864; d Leipzig, 28 Oct. 1928). German art historians, editors of the *Allgemeines Lexikon der bildenden Künstler von der Antike bis zur Gegenwart* (General Dictionary of Artists from Antiquity to the Present, 37 vols., 1907–50), the largest and most comprehensive dictionary of artists' biographies ever published, familiarly known as Thieme–Becker. The high scholarly standard and profuse detail of the entries (many of them written by leading authorities) have made the dictionary a cornerstone of art-historical studies. Architects and decorative artists are covered, as well as painters, sculptors, and engravers. Work began in 1898; Becker retired because of ill health in 1910 and after Thieme's death Hans Vollmer (1878–1969) became editor and saw the immense project to completion. Vollmer also edited the supplement, *Allgemeines Lexikon der bildenden Künstler des XX. Jahrhunderts* (6 vols., 1953–62), which like the main work was published in Leipzig. The first volume of what is in effect a new edition of the complete dictionary appeared in 1983; it is entitled *Allgemeines Künstler-Lexikon*.

Thoma, Hans (b Bernau im Schwarzwald, 2 Oct. 1839; d Karlsruhe, 7 Nov. 1924). German painter. Early in his career he specialized in landscapes—mainly scenes from his native Black Forest—and these are now considered his best works. Later he turned to figurative subjects, including Wagnerian themes; these won him an immense reputation in his day, but are now considered rather ponderous. The largest collection of his works is in the Kunsthalle in Karlsruhe, of which he was director from 1899.

Thomson, Tom (b Claremont, Ontario, 4 Aug. 1877; d Canoe Lake, Algonquin Park, Ontario, 8 July 1917). Canadian landscape painter, one of the main creators of an indigenous Canadian school of painting. Most of his career was spent as a commercial artist in Toronto, and it was only in 1914 that he was able to take up painting full-time. Much of his painting was done out of doors, notably a series of fluently spontaneous oil sketches he produced in Algonquin Park, a huge nature reserve north-west of Toronto. Among his more formal paintings, the most famous is the bold and brilliantly coloured *Jack Pine* (1917, NG, Ottawa), which has become virtually a national symbol of Canada. Thomson's career ended tragically when he was mysteriously drowned in Algonquin Park, but his ideals were continued by the artists who formed the *Group of Seven, to whom he was an inspiration. His death was probably an accident, but the uncertainty surrounding it helped to establish him as a legendary figure in Canadian art.

Thoré, Théophile (b La Flèche, 23 June 1807; d Paris, 30 Apr. 1869). French writer on art. He ranks alongside *Baudelaire as the most perceptive French art critic of his time (he was among the first to acclaim *Courbet, *Daumier, *Manet, *Monet, and *Renoir and to see the weakness of *Meissonier), and he also made memorable contributions to the study of earlier art. Above all, he is remembered for virtually rediscovering *Vermeer, a brilliant feat of connoisseurship and historical detective work. He was originally a political journalist and he published much of his work under the pseudonym W. Bürger when he was living in exile.

Thornhill, Sir James (b Woolland or Weymouth, Dorset, 25 July 1675 or 1676; d Thornhill House, nr. Stalbridge, Dorset, 13 May 1734). English decorative painter. He was the only native painter to challenge the foreign decorative artists who worked in England during the period in the late 17th and early 18th centuries when there was a vogue for wall and ceiling paintings in the *Baroque manner. His two finest works are the ceiling of the Painted Hall

(1707–14) at Greenwich Hospital (now Royal Naval College), London, the main scene of which shows *William and Mary Enthroned*, and the *grisaille paintings on the life of St Paul (1716–19) in the dome of St Paul's Cathedral, London (he beat *Pellegrini and Sebastiano *Ricci in the competition for the commission). Thornhill was highly regarded by his contemporaries and won numerous distinctions. He was appointed history painter to George I in 1718 and serjeant-painter in 1720; in the same year he was knighted (the first English-born painter to be so honoured), and in 1722 he became Member of Parliament for a seat in his home county of Dorset. In addition to his decorative paintings, he also produced portraits, book illustrations, and architectural designs. *Hogarth was his pupil and son-in-law.

Thorn-Prikker, Johan (*b* The Hague, 6 June 1868; *d* Cologne, 5 Mar. 1932). Dutch painter and designer. Early in his career he passed through phases of *Impressionism and *Post-Impressionism, then changed to an elaborate linear style with which he became a leading exponent of *Symbolism and *Art Nouveau, as in his most famous painting—the mystical, erotic *The Bride* (1893, Kröller-Müller Museum, Otterlo). From 1893 he concentrated on the design of mosaics, murals, and stained glass, mainly for churches, continuing in this vein after he settled in Germany in 1904. He taught at several art schools in Germany and was a major figure in the development of modern religious art. His masterpiece is perhaps the cycle of windows in the Romanesque church of St George in Cologne, completed in 1930.

Thornycroft, Sir Hamo (*b* London, 9 Mar. 1850; *d* Oxford, 18 Dec. 1925). British sculptor, one of the leading exponents of the *New Sculpture. Early in his career he concentrated on idealized figures in which he expressed a 'poetic mood' praised by the critic Edmund Gosse; the best-known example is probably *The Mower* (1884, Walker AG, Liverpool; there are also several smaller versions). From the 1890s, however, he was increasingly preoccupied with portrait sculpture and above all public monuments, becoming perhaps the most distinguished British practitioner in this field in the early 20th century. His statues, dignified and thoughtful in tone, include those of Oliver Cromwell outside the Houses of Parliament, London (unveiled 1899), Alfred the Great in Winchester (1901), Gladstone in the Strand, London (1905), Lord Armstrong in Newcastle upon Tyne (1906), Lord Curzon in

Calcutta (1912), and Edward VII in Karachi (1915). These are all in bronze, but he also worked in stone.

Both his father **Thomas Thornycroft** (1815–85) and his mother **Mary Thornycroft** (1814–95) were sculptors. They were primarily portraitists, but Thomas is now chiefly remembered for his dramatic Boadicea Monument at Westminster Bridge, London, showing the fearsome warrior queen in her chariot. He began work on the group in 1856 and was encouraged by Prince Albert, who lent him horses as models. The plaster model was complete at Thornycroft's death, but it was not cast in bronze until 1897, after his son had presented it to the nation, and it was finally erected in 1902.

Thorvaldsen (or **Thorwaldsen**), **Bertel** (*b* Copenhagen, 13 Nov. 1768 or 19 Nov. 1770; *d* Copenhagen, 24 Mar. 1844). Danish sculptor, active mainly in Rome, next to *Canova the most celebrated sculptor of the *Neoclassical movement. The first date given above is the one on which Thorvaldsen himself believed he was born, and is generally accepted, but there is some evidence to support the second one. He studied at the Copenhagen Academy, where he won a scholarship to Italy. In 1797 he reached Rome and henceforth regarded the day of his arrival (8 March) as his 'Roman birthday'. He made his name with the statue *Jason* (1802–3, Thorvaldsens Mus., Copenhagen), which was based on the *Doryphorus* of *Polyclitus, and his growing reputation resulted in so many commissions that by 1820 he had 40 assistants in his Roman workshop. In that year, on a visit to Copenhagen, he began planning the sculptural decoration of the newly built church of Our Lady, including marble statues of Christ and the twelve Apostles, and this project occupied him intermittently until 1842. His other major works include the tomb of Pius VII in St Peter's, Rome (1824–31), and a monument to Lord Byron (1829–35, Trinity College, Cambridge). He also produced numerous portrait busts. In 1838 he returned finally to Denmark, a celebrity whose authority in the arts was sovereign. A museum was built in his honour in Copenhagen (1839–48), itself a remarkable piece of neo-antique architecture; his tomb is in the courtyard. In addition to his own sculptures, the museum contains works he collected, including pictures by contemporary painters (notably the *Nazarenes) as well as antiquities.

Thorvaldsen aimed at reviving the sublimity of Greek sculpture, but he never went to Greece and (in common with other artists of his time) based his knowledge mainly on late *Hellenistic or Roman copies. He did, however, gain close familiarity with Greek sculpture from the restorations he made to the recently excavated sculptures from the temple of Aphaia in Aegina, which in 1816 passed through Rome on their way to Munich (they are now in the Glyptothek there). Compared with Canova he is cool and calculating; his sculptures are more logically worked out and have great precision and clarity, but they lack Canova's sensitive surfaces. According to the taste of the time, his work has been praised for its nobility and classical calm or dismissed as frigid and empty.

Thulden, Theodoor van (*bapt.* 's Hertogenbosch, 9 Aug. 1606; *bur.* 's Hertogenbosch, 12 July 1669). Flemish painter and engraver, the son-in-law of Hendrick van *Balen. He spent much of his career in Antwerp, and like most contemporary painters of historical and religious subjects, he was strongly influenced by *Rubens (with whom he collaborated in the 1630s). However, his work has a distinctive and appealingly sweet charm. He had numerous commissions both inside and outside Flanders, and he also worked in The Hague and Paris.

Thyssen-Bornemisza. Dynasty of central European businessmen and collectors. **August Thyssen** (1842–1926) was an immensely wealthy German industrialist whose iron and steel business expanded into France. He was a friend of *Rodin, by whom he owned several sculptures, but otherwise he was little interested in collecting. His son **Heinrich** (1875–1947), however, was passionately devoted to art and founded one of the greatest private collections formed in the 20th century. In 1905 he married Baroness Margit Bornemisza, daughter of a Hungarian aristocrat; he became a Hungarian citizen and took the title Baron Thyssen-Bornemisza. In 1919 he moved to the Netherlands, where he flourished as a financier and over the next twenty years built up a superb collection of Old Masters. Initially he concentrated on German pictures, his prize acquisitions including *Dürer's *Christ among the Doctors* (1506) and *Holbein's *Henry VIII* (*c.*1535). He then expanded his interests to Early Netherlandish and Italian *Renaissance painting. In 1932 he bought a 17th-century house, the Villa Favorita, at Castagnola on Lake Lugano, Switzerland, and in 1937 he added a picture gallery to it.

At his death the collection was divided among his four children, but one of them, Baron **Hans**

Heinrich Thyssen-Bornemisza (1921–2002), a Swiss industrialist, determined to reunite it and gradually bought back pictures from his siblings (Fra *Angelico's *Virgin of Humility* (*c.*1440) was reaquired as late as 1986). In 1954 he began adding new works to the collection and from the 1960s he greatly expanded its range, in particular buying numerous pictures from the 19th and 20th centuries—fields in which he maintained the high standards of quality set by his father. He had always been generous in sharing the collection with the public and in the 1980s, feeling that the Villa Favorita was now too small to house it satisfactorily, he decided to find a new location for it. Various countries submitted proposals, and in 1992 the Thyssen-Bornemisza Museum opened in Madrid, housed opposite the *Prado in the Palacio de Villahermosa, originally an early 19th-century building (the *Neoclassical façade survives). About 70 pictures and a few sculptures from the collection are displayed in the monastery of Pedralbes, Barcelona.

Tibaldi, Pellegrino (*b* Puria di Valsolda, nr. Lugano, *c.*1527; *d* Milan, 27 May 1596). Italian *Mannerist painter and architect. He was brought up in Bologna, and from about 1547 to 1553 he worked in Rome; his style in painting, distinguished by grand, if sometimes rather ponderous figures, was based mainly on the work of *Michelangelo, for whom he had a lifelong admiration. His finest paintings are frescos illustrating the story of Ulysses (*c.*1555) in the Palazzo Poggi (now University), Bologna. From the mid-1560s Tibaldi worked a good deal as an architect, chiefly in and around Milan, where he was much employed by the archbishop, Charles Borromeo; he was appointed chief architect to the cathedral in 1567. In 1587 he moved to Spain to work on the decoration of the *Escorial, for which he produced a large amount of decorative painting. His work there was influential in the development of Spanish Mannerism. He returned to Milan, ennobled by Philip II (see HABSBURG), in the year of his death.

Tidemand, Adolph (*b* Mandal, 14 Aug. 1814; *d* Christiania [now Oslo], 25 Aug. 1876). Norwegian painter. He spent most of his career in Düsseldorf, but he often returned to his home country and he achieved international success with idyllic and often rather sentimental peasant scenes in romantic Norwegian settings.

Tiepolo, Giambattista (*b* Venice, 5 Mar. 1696; *d* Madrid, 27 Mar. 1770). Venetian painter, draughtsman, and etcher. He was the greatest

Italian (and arguably the greatest European) painter of the 18th century, his work bringing to a glorious conclusion the Italian tradition of fresco decoration begun by *Giotto 400 years earlier. His output was prodigious (his career is essentially a story of ceaseless work) and his services were sought from Sweden to Spain. He trained with the history painter Gregorio Lazzarini (1655–1730), but according to Lazzarini's biographer, Vincenzo da Canal (1732), Tiepolo soon departed from his master's 'diligent manner, and, being all fire and spirit, adopted one that was rapid and free'. Initially he was influenced by the sombre and dramatic style of *Piazzetta and worked mainly in oils. However, from the mid-1720s he turned increasingly to fresco and his palette lightened, with *Veronese becoming an important influence on his style. He was described by his contemporaries as 'Veronese reborn' and he shared with his great predecessor a love of pageantry and sparkling colour (and he often used 16th-century costume in his paintings). However, whereas Veronese's work always has a *Renaissance solidity, Tiepolo created exhilarating effects of airy space, particularly in his ceiling frescos, in which the central area often depicts open sky. For all its lightness, however, Tiepolo's work was always underpinned by superb draughtsmanship; it was this that allowed him to depict figures soaring overhead so fluently and convincingly.

In 1726–8 Tiepolo carried out his first major work outside Venice, the fresco decoration of the Archbishop's Palace in Udine, and this led to a string of commissions for various places in north Italy. By 1736 his fame was such that he was invited to Stockholm to decorate the Royal Palace—an invitation he declined because the fee offered was too small. Count Carl Gustav Tessin (1695–1770), the Swedish diplomat and art collector who tried to secure his services, was impressed by his 'spirited and obliging' character as well as by his 'amazing speed. He paints a picture in less time than it takes another to grind his colours.'

Up to this time, Tiepolo's work had been predominantly secular, but from the late 1730s to the late 1740s he also produced a series of major religious paintings for Venetian churches, including a series of three huge canvases depicting scenes from Christ's Passion (c.1740) for S. Alvise (still *in situ*). These three pictures make 'a tremendous emotional assault on the spectator' (Michael Levey, *Tiepolo*, 1986) and are much closer in style to *Tintoretto than to Veronese. After this period, secular decorative

commissions once again dominated Tiepolo's output, although he continued to produce altarpieces throughout his career; he also occasionally ventured into other areas, as with the ravishing *Young Woman with a Parrot* (c.1760, Ashmolean Mus., Oxford). His most important secular work of the 1740s and perhaps the greatest of all his works in Venice was the decoration of the Palazzo Labia (c.1745), which includes celebrated frescos of the *Meeting of Antony and Cleopatra* and the *Banquet of Antony and Cleopatra* (their story was one to which he returned several times). Here, as in other commissions, he was assisted by his expert in *quadratura, Gerolamo Mengozzi Colonna.

In 1750 Tiepolo left Italy for the first time, to carry out a very lucrative and prestigious commission to decorate the Rezidenz (palace) of the prince-bishop of Würzburg in Germany. The building was designed by Balthasar Neumann, the greatest architect of the age in central Europe, and it forms a worthy setting for Tiepolo's most glorious works. Like *Rubens, he could make even the most ponderous allegory come alive, and here the unpromising task of paying tribute to the lacklustre prince-bishop brought forth resplendent visions full of light and colour. Tiepolo first decorated the Kaisersaal (used as a state dining room) and then the ceiling of the grandiose Treppenhaus (stairwell), completing the work in 1753, when he returned to Venice. In 1757 another peak of his career came with the decoration of a series of rooms in the Villa Valmarana, near Vicenza, with scenes from Homer, Virgil, Ariosto, and Tasso. Here the scale is more intimate and the mood more tender, most of the subjects being concerned with the theme of love.

Tiepolo's last large-scale work in Italy was the enormous ceiling of the ballroom in the Villa Pisani at Strà, near Padua, which he began in 1760. Whilst working on it he was summoned to Madrid by Charles III—'I am bound to respond to His Majesty's urging'—and spent the remaining eight years of his life there. He was 66 when he arrived in Madrid in 1762 but he still had formidable energy and by 1766 he had completed three ceilings in the royal palace, including that of the huge throne room, on which he depicted the *Apotheosis of Spain*. His last major completed commission was a series of seven altarpieces for the church of S. Pascual in Aranjuez, near Madrid, works with a solemnity and inwardness that were new to his art.

They were finished in 1769 and installed in 1770, soon after Tiepolo's death. Within a few years, however, they had been replaced with pictures by *Mengs and other artists; this post-humous blow—a sign of the growing taste for *Neoclassicism—has been taken as an indication that Tiepolo's reputation was declining in his final years, but in fact he remained in royal favour until the end, earning a very high salary. (Moreover, there is no contemporary evidence to support the popular idea of personal animosity between Tiepolo and Mengs, and the later story that Mengs was so jealous of Tiepolo that he hired thugs to beat him up is highly implausible; he is said to have hidden in a tree to watch the attack but fell and injured himself, whereupon his rival—with characteristic nobility—did what he could to help him.) Tiepolo's Aranjuez altarpieces are now dispersed and partly lost; the five surviving *modelli for them are in the Courtauld Gallery, London, and show that he kept his masterly fluency with the brush until the end of his life. He was as prolific a draughtsman as he was a painter (an outstanding collection of his drawings is in the Victoria and Albert Museum, London) and was also one of the finest etchers of his period, although his output in this field was small; *Goya was especially indebted to his graphic work.

Tiepolo was married to Cecilia Guardi, the sister of the *Guardi brothers, and he had two painter sons, **Giandomenico** (b Venice, 30 Aug. 1727; d Venice, 3 Mar. 1804), usually known as Domenico, and **Lorenzo** (b Venice, 8 Aug. 1736; d Húmera, nr. Madrid, 2 Aug. 1776). They were their father's chief assistants on several of his major projects; both of them accompanied him to Spain and Lorenzo remained there for the rest of his life. He produced some attractive etchings and pastel portraits, but has much less independent substance as an artist than Domenico, who was a painter and etcher of some distinction. Although he imitated his father's manner closely when he assisted him, in his own work he has a distinct style—much more down-to-earth, with lively observation of everyday life. The contrast with his father can best be seen at the Villa Valmarana, where Domenico decorated the guesthouse at the same time that Giambattista was engaged on the main building; the subjects include scenes of peasant life. As an etcher he is best known for his set of 24 prints on the theme of the Flight into Egypt (1749).

Tiffany, Louis Comfort (b New York, 18 Feb. 1848; d New York, 17 Jan. 1933). American designer, interior decorator, and architect, his country's most famous exponent of the *Art Nouveau style. The son of a prosperous jeweller, he initially trained as a painter, but in the 1870s he turned more to the decorative arts and founded an interior decorating business in 1879. Tiffany became famous above all for his highly distinctive glass vases and lamps, but until about 1900 his firm was better known for stained glass and mosaic work (it did interiors for many socially prominent New Yorkers as well as for clubs). Most of his architectural work has perished, including his own mansion on Long Island, Laurelton Hall (1903–5), which was regarded as his masterpiece; however, its main entrance survived the fire that destroyed the building in 1957 and is now in the Metropolitan Museum, New York. Tiffany was also an art patron and established a foundation that provided study and travel grants for students.

Tillmans, Wolfgang. See TURNER PRIZE.

Tinguely, Jean (b Fribourg, 22 May 1925; d Berne, 30 Aug. 1991). Swiss sculptor and experimental artist. He had an international career, working in Paris, New York, and elsewhere. His work was concerned mainly with movement and the machine, satirizing technological civilization. His boisterous humour was most fully demonstrated in his auto-destructive works, which turned *Kinetic art into *Performance art. The most famous is Homage to New York, presented at the Museum of Modern Art, New York, on 17 March 1960. The object on which the work was based was constructed from an old piano and other junk; it failed to destroy itself as programmed and caused a fire. Tinguely was also an innovator in promoting the idea of spectator participation, as in his Rotozazas, in which the spectator plays ball with a machine. His most famous work is somewhat more traditional—the exuberant Beaubourg Fountain (1980) outside the *Pompidou Centre, Paris, done in collaboration with Niki de *Saint Phalle; it features fantastic mechanical birds and beasts that spout water in all directions.

Tino di Camaino (b Siena, c.1280/5; d Naples, 1337). Sienese sculptor, chiefly of tombs, active in Pisa, Florence, and Naples, as well as his native city. He was the most important follower of Giovanni *Pisano, whom he probably assisted for a time, but Tino's style was more calm and reserved, with an imposing blocklike massiveness. His early career was spent mainly in Siena and Pisa, but his chief works are in Florence (where he worked intermittently from 1318 to 1323) and Naples (where he lived from about 1324 until his death). In Florence he produced, most notably, the tomb of Bishop Antonio d'Orso (1321) in the cathedral, which features possibly the earliest example of a seated effigy. In Naples his work included tabernacled tombs for the Angevin court, notably that of Queen Mary of Hungary (c.1325) in S. Maria Donnaregina. They show a move away from the sober grandeur of his earlier work to a more elegant, ostentatious, *Gothic style. Tino also worked as an architect.

tinsel prints. See FLOCK PRINTS.

Tintoretto (Jacopo Robusti) (*b* Venice, ?1518; *d* Venice, 31 May 1594). Venetian painter. His nickname derives from his father's profession of cloth dyer (*tintore*). He ranks second only to *Titian among the Venetian painters of his time and had a prolific and successful career. Whereas most of Titian's later paintings were done for foreign patrons, Tintoretto worked mainly for Venetian clients and in particular was the dominant figure in supplying religious pictures for the city's churches and charitable institutions; he is only once recorded outside Venice (when he visited Mantua in 1580 in connection with a commission from the *Gonzaga family) and the bulk of his work remains in the buildings for which it was painted.

Little is known about Tintoretto's character or personal life, and his career up to the time he was about 30 is poorly documented. His biographer *Ridolfi says that he began an apprenticeship with Titian but was quickly dismissed because the master was jealous of his draughtsmanship. On stylistic evidence, it has been suggested that he may also have studied with *Bonifazio Veronese, Paris *Bordone, or *Schiavone. He is first documented in 1539, by which time he was working independently, but the first work in which he announced a distinctive voice is *St Mark Rescuing the Slave* (1548, Accademia, Venice), in which many of the qualities of his maturity, particularly his love of foreshortening, begin to appear. To help him with the complex poses he favoured, he made 'little models of wax and clay' (Ridolfi), which he arranged in 'little houses' (presumably something like a miniature stage set), enabling him to use artificial illumination to experiment with lighting (*Poussin later used a similar method). He sometimes suspended the models from strings, which must have helped with poses of aerial figures. This method of composing explains the frequent repetition in Tintoretto's works of the same figures seen from different angles. He was a formidable draughtsman and

Ridolfi says that he had inscribed on his studio wall the motto 'The drawing of *Michelangelo and the colour of Titian'. However, although he clearly admired these two great elder contemporaries, he was very different in spirit from either of them—more emotive, using violent movement and vivid exaggerations of light. His drawings, unlike Michelangelo's detailed life studies, are brilliant, rapid notations, bristling with energy, and his colour is generally more sombre and mystical than Titian's. It is in freedom of brushwork that he most resembles Titian, although his touch is rougher, and the qualities he shares with Michelangelo are an epic imagination and almost superhuman vigour.

St Mark Rescuing the Slave was at first rejected by the Scuola di S. Marco, which had commissioned it (presumably expecting something more traditional), and the resulting publicity helped establish Tintoretto as the most exciting young painter in Venice. From this point his career was essentially the story of a succession of major religious commissions (including further ones from the Scuola di S. Marco after it had overcome its resistance to the controversial picture). His greatest works are the vast series of paintings he produced between 1564 and 1587 for the Scuola di S. Rocco, the wealthiest of the Venetian *scuole* (literally schools)—charitable institutions that performed such functions as caring for orphans and the sick.

Tintoretto began his long association with S. Rocco with the most famous episode in his career, when in 1564 he won the competition for the initial commission—a ceiling painting of *St Roch in Glory*—by somehow managing to install a full-sized picture whilst his rivals merely produced the specified sketches (he was renowned for the speed at which he worked). This clever ruse was regarded by some as underhand tactics and Tintoretto was evidently willing to undercut competitors' prices and even to work without pay if it helped to gain him the commissions he wanted. Unlike Titian, he seems to have been unconcerned with money as an end in itself, and his religious paintings are the expression of a deeply devout nature. In S. Rocco he created one of the greatest of all interpretations of the Christian story. The work was carried out in three phases: first he decorated the *albergo* (committee room) with scenes of Christ's Passion (1565–7); this was followed by the great hall (1575–81), which has Old Testament scenes on the ceiling and New Testament scenes on the wall; and finally came the lower hall (1583–7), which has scenes of the life of the Virgin

Mary and the Nativity of Christ. There is an extraordinary range and depth of feeling in these paintings, from the cosmic drama of the *Crucifixion* (1565) to the tender intimacy of the Nativity scenes. Henry James wrote that 'We shall scarcely find four walls elsewhere that enclose within a like area an equal quantity of genius', and said of the stupendous *Crucifixion*: 'Surely no single picture in the world contains more of human life; there is everything in it, including the most exquisite beauty.'

In addition to his religious works, Tintoretto painted portraits and occasional mythological scenes (*Origin of the Milky Way*, c.1575–80, NG, London). Although portraiture was never central to his activity, he was the best Venetian portraitist of his time apart from Titian and was particularly good at depicting old men, showing the dignity and weariness of age (a self-portrait of c.1590 is in the Louvre). In his later work particularly he must have used a good deal of studio help; his son **Domenico** (c.1560–1635) became his foreman, and another son, **Marco** (1561–1637), and a daughter, **Marietta** (c.1554–90), were among his other assistants. However, he showed no diminution of powers in old age, and his career ended with one of his greatest masterpieces, the *Last Supper* (1592–4, S. Giorgio Maggiore, Venice), a scene of incandescent spirituality.

Tintoretto had considerable influence, most notably on El *Greco, who absorbed the visionary energy and intensity of his work. He continued to be a respected figure in Venice throughout the 17th century, but his reputation was lower elsewhere, and in the rational climate of the 18th century his work tended to be dismissed for an alleged lack of intellectual control (even in his lifetime *Vasari had admired his powerful imagination but lamented his 'haphazard' design and indifference to traditional ideals of finish). In the age of *Romanticism, however, his intense individuality brought him back into favour. No one played a more important role in his rehabilitation than *Ruskin, whose first encounter with the Scuola di S. Rocco in 1843 left him 'perfectly prostrated'. See also VERONESE.

tint tool. A type of *burin used in *wood engraving for cutting fine lines of even thickness. These lines, set very close together and parallel to one another, form the grey tones of 'tints' so characteristic of 19th-century reproductive wood engraving.

Tischbein. Dynasty of German painters. The best known of them, **Johann Heinrich Wilhelm Tischbein** (1751–1829), was a friend of *Goethe and is now remembered almost solely for his famous portrait *Goethe in the Roman Campagna* (1786–7, Städelsches Kunstinstitut, Frankfurt). He is often called Goethe Tischbein, and the two other leading members of the family, his uncle and cousin, were nicknamed after their main place of work: **Johann Heinrich the Elder**, Kassel Tischbein (1722–89), and **Johann Friedrich**, Leipzig Tischbein (1750–1812). They were principally portraitists. Other members of the family were active until the late 19th century.

Tissot, James (*b* Nantes, 15 Oct. 1836; *d* Château de Buillon, nr. Besançon, 8 Aug. 1902). French painter, illustrator, and printmaker. Originally he was called Jean-Jacques, but he adopted the name James as an expression of his Anglophilia. Early in his career he painted historical costume pieces, but in about 1864 he turned with great success to scenes of contemporary life, usually involving fashionable women. He is said to have supported the Commune, the short-lived revolutionary government of Paris, and its brutal suppression in 1871 may have helped prompt him to move to London, where he lived from 1871 to 1882. He was just as successful there as he had been in Paris and lived in some style in the fashionable suburb of St John's Wood; in 1874 Edmond de *Goncourt wrote sarcastically that he had 'a studio with a waiting room where, at all times, there is iced champagne at the disposal of visitors, and around the studio, a garden where, all day long, one can see a footman in silk stockings brushing and shining the shrubbery leaves'. His pictures are distinguished most obviously by his love of painting women's costumes (both his parents were involved in the clothes business and he was a dandy himself): indeed, his work—which has a fashion-plate elegance and a chocolate-box charm—has probably been more often reproduced in works on the history of costume than on the history of painting. However, he also had a gift for wittily observing nuances of social behaviour, not least in matters of sexual attraction and flirtation. In 1882, following the death of his mistress Kathleen Newton (the archetypal Tissot model—beautiful but rather vacant), he returned to France, and in 1885 he underwent a religious conversion when he went into a church to 'catch the atmosphere for a picture'. Thereafter he devoted himself to religious subjects; he visited the Holy Land in 1886–7 and 1889, and his illustrations to the Bible were enormously popular, both in book form and when the original drawings were exhibited. Tissot's reputation sank after his death and for many years he was generally dismissed as vulgar and superficial, but since the 1970s there has been an upsurge of interest in him, expressed in saleroom prices for his work as well as in numerous books and exhibitions devoted to him.

Titian (Tiziano Vecellio) (b Pieve di Cadore, c.1485; d Venice, 27 Aug. 1576). The greatest painter of the Venetian School and one of the supreme figures of world art. In the course of a very long and highly prolific career he dominated Venice's art during its golden age and also worked for many illustrious patrons outside the city; his paintings have had a profound and enduring influence on European art. Most of his career is well documented, but his early years are somewhat obscure and his date of birth has long been a subject of scholarly debate, for the evidence concerning it is contradictory; certainly he was very old when he died, although probably not quite as old as some accounts suggest (traditionally he lived to be 99).

He was probably a pupil of Giovanni *Bellini, and in his early work he came under the spell of *Giorgione, with whom he had a close relationship. In 1508 (the first secure point in his career) they collaborated on the external fresco decoration (destroyed) of the Fondaco dei Tedeschi (German warehouse) in Venice, and after Giorgione's early death in 1510 Titian is said to have completed a number of paintings that his friend left unfinished. The authorship of certain works (some of them famous) is still disputed between them. Titian's first surviving works that can be precisely dated are three frescos on the life of St Antony of Padua in the Scuola del Santo, Padua (1511), noble and dignified paintings with an almost central Italian firmness and monumentality. Although they show impressive skill in handling fresco, he hardly ever used the medium again, working almost exclusively in oils. In the same year that these murals were painted, *Sebastiano del Piombo left Venice for Rome, and with him gone and Giorgione dead, only the aged Bellini stood between Titian and supremacy. After Bellini died in 1516, he was virtually unchallenged as the leading painter in Venice until his own death 60 years later, although in his final decades he worked mainly for foreign patrons, allowing younger artists such as *Tintoretto and *Veronese to flourish in the domestic arena.

In the second decade of the century Titian moved away from Giorgione's dreamily romantic style and developed a much more robust manner of his own. There is still a good deal of Giorgione's enigmatic poetry in the allegorical *Sacred and Profane Love* (c.1514, Borghese Gal., Rome), but it is tempered by worldliness, and Titian's style soon became much more dynamic. This is seen particularly clearly in the work that more than any other stamped his authority in Venice—the huge altarpiece of the *Assumption of the Virgin* (1516–18, S. Maria dei Frari, Venice). It is one of the largest pictures he ever painted and one of the greatest, matching the achievements of his most illustrious contemporaries in Rome in grandeur of form and surpassing them in splendour of colour. The soaring movement of the Virgin, rising from the closely packed group of Apostles towards the hovering figure of God the Father, looks forward to the *Baroque.

Similar qualities are seen in Titian's two most famous altarpieces of the 1520s: the *Virgin and Child with Saints and Members of the Pesaro Family* (the Pesaro Altarpiece) (1519–26, S. Maria dei Frari), a bold diagonal composition of great magnificence, and the *Death of St Peter Martyr* (completed 1530), which he painted for the church of SS. Giovanni e Paolo, Venice, having defeated *Palma Vecchio and *Pordenone in competition for the commission. The painting was destroyed by fire in 1867, but it is known through copies and engravings; trees and figures together form a violent centrifugal composition appropriate to the action, and *Vasari described it as 'the most celebrated, the greatest work . . . that Titian has ever done'. The young Titian had important secular as well as ecclesiastical commissions, notably a set of three mythological pictures (1518–23) for Alfonso d'*Este, his first princely patron—the *Worship of Venus*, the *Bacchanal* (both in the Prado, Madrid), and *Bacchus and Ariadne* (NG, London). He was also busy as a portraitist. Many of his early portraits are of unknown sitters, as with the exquisite *Man with a Glove* (c.1520, Louvre, Paris), but later he painted some of the most famous personalities of the day.

Titian's success brought him a substantial income and from 1531 he lived in a palatial house in Venice, with gardens overlooking the lagoon. In 1533 the Emperor Charles V (see HABSBURG) appointed him court painter and elevated him to the rank of count palatine and knight of the Golden Spur. This was an unprecedented honour for a painter, and *Ridolfi tells a revealing anecdote concerning the respect Titian was accorded even by the emperor himself: Titian dropped a brush and when Charles picked it up for him he protested, 'Sire, I am not worthy of such a servant', to which the emperor replied, 'Titian is worthy to be served by Caesar.' Although he had probably had a fairly basic education (he knew no Latin), he does indeed seem to have been at ease in the elevated society of his patrons; contemporary accounts say he was well mannered and a good conversationalist, and his best friend was the celebrated poet Pietro Aretino.

Titian had first met the emperor in 1530, when he was crowned in Bologna. Although he made several short visits such as this to towns in northern Italy, he was reluctant to journey far from Venice and he turned down Charles's invitation to go to Spain to paint portraits of the royal family. In the 1540s, however, he overcame his resistance to travelling long distances, visiting Rome in 1545–6 at the invitation of Pope Paul III (Alessandro *Farnese) and then Augsburg in Germany in 1548 to work at Charles's court. He returned to Augsburg in 1550–1. His work in Rome included a celebrated portrait of the pope with his grandsons, Cardinal Alessandro and Ottavio Farnese (Mus. di Capodimonte, Naples), and he brought with him a painting of *Danaë* (c.1544–5, Mus. di Capodimonte), previously commissioned by the cardinal. It is one of his most gloriously sensuous treatments of the female nude, and a papal legate writing to the cardinal in 1544 stressed its overtly erotic character by comparing it with Titian's own slightly earlier *Venus of Urbino* (1538, Uffizi, Florence): 'the nude that Your Reverence saw . . . in the apartment of the Duke of Urbino [Guidobaldo della *Rovere] looks like a nun compared with this one.' According to Vasari, *Michelangelo praised the colouring of *Danaë* but found fault with the drawing. Titian's work in Augsburg included *Charles V on Horseback* (1548, Prado, Madrid), the largest and grandest of all his portraits.

The greatest patron of Titian's later career was Charles's son Philip II of Spain, whom he first met in 1549 in Milan. Initially Philip was unimpressed with Titian's work, finding his brushwork too broad, but he came to admire him above all other painters, and eventually—rather than commissioning specific works from him—he was content to accept whatever the master cared to send him. Like his father, Philip was intensely devout, and Titian's work for him included religious pictures as well as portraits. However, the most famous works he painted for him were a series of seven erotic mythological subjects (c.1550–c.1562) based (sometimes loosely) on Ovid's *Metamorphoses*: *Danaë* (a variant of the earlier picture for Cardinal Farnese) and *Venus and Adonis* (Prado), *Perseus and Andromeda* (Wallace Coll., London), the *Rape of Europa* (Gardner Mus., Boston), *Diana and Actaeon* and *Diana and Calisto* (Ellesmere Coll., on loan to NG of Scotland), and the *Death of Actaeon* (NG, London).

Titian referred to these pictures as *poesie* (poems), and they are indeed highly poetic visions of distant worlds, quite different from the sensual realities of his earlier mythological paintings. By this time his style had changed greatly from that of his youth, with an emphasis on inner feeling rather than external drama, his colours mellow and glowing rather than rich and resonant, and his brushwork loose and almost impressionistic. It has been argued that the extreme freedom of handling in some of his final works is a result of their being unfinished and perhaps partly a consequence of failing eyesight. The situation is complicated by the fact that in his later career Titian is known to have made extensive use of assistants, among them his brother **Francesco Vecellio** (c.1490–1559/60) and his son **Orazio Vecellio** (1525–76). Nevertheless, there can be no doubt that Titian's final works include some of his most sublime creations, and his career ends with the awe-inspiring *Pietà* (c.1575–6, Accademia, Venice), which is said to have been intended for his own tomb and was evidently finished after his death by *Palma Giovane.

Titian was recognized as a towering genius in his own time (*Lomazzo described him as 'the sun amidst small stars not only among the Italians but all the painters of the world') and his reputation as one of the giants of art has never been seriously questioned (it has been commonplace for centuries to describe him as the greatest of all colourists). He was supreme in every major branch of painting practised in his time and his achievements were so varied—ranging from the joyous evocation of pagan antiquity in his early mythologies to the depths of tragedy in his late religious paintings—that he has been an inspiration to artists of very different character. Van *Dyck, *Poussin, *Rubens, and *Velázquez are among the painters who have particularly revered him. In many subjects he set patterns that were followed by generations of artists, particularly in portraiture; more than anyone else he was responsible for widening the scope of portraiture beyond the head-and-shoulders type that prevailed in the 15th century, not only by popularizing the half-length and the full-length, but also by varying his poses and introducing accessories such as a dog, a book, or a classical column. In technique he was just as influential, for he was the first to show the limitless expressive potential of oil paint, creating a vibrant pictorial surface in which the artist's personal 'handwriting' is evident in every touch of the brush. According to Palma Giovane, 'in the final stages he worked more with his fingers than with his brush', and Vasari wrote that his late works 'are executed with bold, sweeping strokes, and in patches of colour, with the result that they cannot be viewed from near by, but appear perfect at a distance . . . The method he used is judicious, beautiful, and astonishing, for it makes pictures appear alive and painted with great art, but it conceals the labour that has gone into them.'

Titian's greatness as an artist, it appears, was not matched by his character, for he was notoriously avaricious. In spite of his wealth and status, he claimed he was impoverished, and Erwin *Panofsky comments that 'his tax declaration of 1566 . . . would land him in jail today'. However, he was lavish in his hospitality towards his friends, notably Pietro Aretino and the sculptor and architect Jacopo *Sansovino. These three were so close that they were known in Venice as the triumvirate, and they used their influence with their respective patrons to further each other's careers.

Titus, Arch of. See TRIUMPHAL ARCH.

Tobey, Mark (*b* Centerville, Wis., 11 Dec. 1890; *d* Basle, 24 Apr. 1976). American painter. In 1918 he became a convert to the Baha'i faith and much of his subsequent work was inspired by an interest in oriental art and thought. He lived mainly in Seattle, but travelled widely and from 1931 to 1938 was artist-in-residence at Dartington Hall, a progressive school in Devon, England. Following a visit to the Far East in 1934–5, he developed a distinctive style of painting that he called 'white writing', characterized by calligraphic white patterns overlying dimly discerned suggestions of colour beneath. Although he painted representational pictures in this style, he turned increasingly to abstractions. Their *all-over manner anticipated and perhaps influenced Jackson *Pollock, but unlike *Action Painters, Tobey believed that 'painting should come through the avenues of meditation rather than the canals of action.' Unusually for an American painter, he was more highly esteemed abroad than in his own country, and he was

influential on French *Tachisme in the 1950s. In 1960 he settled in Switzerland.

Tocqué, Louis (*b* Paris, 19 Nov. 1696; *d* Paris, 10 Feb. 1772). French portrait painter, a pupil of *Nattier, whose daughter he married in 1747. He was influenced by Nattier, but his style was more forthright and penetrating in characterization; indeed David Wakefield (*French Eighteenth-Century Painting*, 1984) writes that his portraits 'have a direct simplicity and honesty which strikes an entirely new note in this period'. His sitters were more varied than Nattier's, including artists and intellectuals as well as aristocrats. In addition to having a successful career in Paris, he worked in St Petersburg, 1756–8, painting the Empress Elizabeth I and members of her court. On the way back to France he spent several months in Copenhagen, where he was honoured with membership of the recently founded Academy. Nattier, too, was later made a member of the Copenhagen Academy, and he and Tocqué sent portraits of each other (1762) as their diploma works. Both portraits remain in the collection of the Academy and they make for instructive comparison: Nattier is shown convincingly at work, whereas Tocqué, although also holding palette and brushes, is posing with a graceful air.

Toft, Albert. See NEW SCULPTURE.

Tolsá, Manuel (*b* Enguera, nr. Valencia, 1757; *d* Mexico City, 24 Dec. 1816). Spanish sculptor, architect, and teacher, active from 1791 in Mexico City. He went there as director of sculpture at the Academy of S. Carlos (founded 1783) and became the central figure in the *Neoclassical reaction against the extravagances of Mexican *Churrigueresque. His best-known works are both in Mexico City: the bronze equestrian statue of Charles IV of Spain (1796–1803) and the School of Mining (1797–1813), one of the most impressive buildings of the colonial Americas.

Tolstoy, Count Leo (*b* Yasnaya Polyana, Tula province, 28 Aug. [9 Sept.] 1828; *d* Astapovo, Tambov province, 7 [20] Nov. 1910). Russian writer. He is celebrated as one of the greatest of all novelists, but much of his later career was devoted to writing on a broad range of moral issues, expressing the radical ethical views that caused him to repudiate his own earlier works and way of life and try to live like a self-sufficient peasant. His writings in this vein include *What is Art?* (1898), in which he argues that art is justifiable only if it communicates high moral and religious values in a simple and direct way.

His enormous prestige ensured a wide readership for his book (it was immediately translated into English, French, and German), but his extraordinary value judgements—dismissing as worthless *Michelangelo's *Last Judgement* and Shakespeare's *King Lear*, for example—meant that his ideas were generally considered eccentric.

Tomaso da Modena (*b* Modena, *c*.1325; *d* *c*.1379). Italian painter, one of the leading artists of his day in northern Italy. His earthy, humane, and naturalistic style is well seen in his series of frescos of famous Dominicans (signed and dated 1352) in the chapter house of S. Niccolò in Treviso. The saintly figures are shown meditating, writing, and reading (the first dated example of spectacles being worn appears here) and Tomaso shows a remarkable ability to depict intellectual activity. His reputation was such that work was commissioned from him by the Emperor Charles IV in Bohemia (see BOHEMIAN SCHOOL), and two panels by Tomaso are still in Karlstein Castle, near Prague. It is unlikely that he visited Bohemia, but there is some kinship between his work and that of his leading Bohemian contemporary, *Master Theoderic.

Tomé, Narciso (*b* *c*.1690; *d* Toledo, 13 Dec. 1742). Spanish architect, sculptor, and painter, a leading representative of the *Churrigueresque style. He is first recorded in 1715 working with other members of his family on the façade of Valladolid University. In 1721 he was appointed architect to Toledo Cathedral, where he executed his only surviving work—the Transparente (completed 1732), an extraordinary altarpiece-cum-chapel that uses dramatic natural lighting as well as the arts of architecture, sculpture, and painting to achieve its spectacular effect. John Rupert Martin (*Baroque*, 1977) writes: 'As we pass through the shadowy ambulatory of the cathedral, we suddenly come across an ornate and towering altarpiece, the face of which is brilliantly illuminated by the light from an unseen window high above the vaulting. The architectural forms of this astonishing invention are foreshortened in such a way as to give the illusion of a deep apse-like recess.' When it was completed the Transparente was hailed as the 'eighth wonder of the world', but to *Neoclassical taste it represented the ultimate in artistic decadence.

Tomlin, Bradley Walker (*b* Syracuse, NY, 19 Aug. 1899; *d* New York, 11 May 1953). American painter. In his early work he experimented with

a variety of styles, but he systematically destroyed a good deal in the 1930s when he began to question himself as an artist. In the late 1930s he began to find a more individual path with semi-abstract still-lifes that blend elements of *Cubism and *Surrealism. By 1947 his work had become completely abstract and in the last years of his life he developed into one of the minor masters of *Abstract Expressionism. His paintings of this time characteristically feature a rich but coolly coloured *all-over pattern of cryptic dashes, dots, and crosses (*Number 9: In Praise of Gertrude Stein*, MoMA, New York, 1951).

Tommaso da Modena. See TOMASO DA MODENA.

tondo. A painting or *relief sculpture of circular shape: the word is Italian for 'round'. The format became popular in Florence in the 15th century, perhaps as a development of the *desco da parto*, and was often used in depictions of the Virgin and Child, the 'perfect' geometrical form of the circle perhaps being intended to reflect the moral perfection of Christ and his mother. There are famous tondi by *Michelangelo in both painting and sculpture: the *Holy Family* (Uffizi, Florence), known as the Doni Tondo, his only completed panel painting to survive; and two early sculptures of the Virgin and Child, the Taddei Tondo (RA, London) and the Pitti Tondo (Bargello, Florence). All three date from around 1505 and all three are named after the families that commissioned them. Most portrait miniatures are circular, but the word 'tondo' is not applied to such small works.

Tonks, Henry (*b* Solihull, Warwickshire, 9 Apr. 1862; *d* London, 8 Jan. 1937). British painter, draughtsman, and teacher. He was interested in art from childhood, and in 1893 he abandoned his successful medical career to become a teacher at the *Slade School. (However, he worked in plastic surgery during the First World War.) Tonks remained at the Slade until 1930 (as professor from 1918), and became the most renowned and formidable teacher of his generation—'in appearance tall, gaunt, and severe' (*DNB*). Under him the Slade maintained its position as the dominant art school in Britain (although it was now challenged by the *Royal College of Art), and he was a major influence as an upholder of traditional values and an opponent of modern ideas: 'I don't believe I really like any modern development.' He set high standards for his pupils, particularly in draughtsmanship (his own forte), and he got on well with them, in spite of being notorious for his sarcasm and abruptness. Because of his refusal to move with the times he was increasingly looked on as a back number by more progressive artists and students, but he remained a dominant presence in the art world. Tonks's own paintings are mainly figure subjects, often consciously (or self-consciously) poetic in spirit: Sir John *Rothenstein refers to 'the sheer prettiness of much of his art', but his pictures often look rather laborious, partly because of his technique of 'Tonking', which involved using an absorbent material to soak excess oil from the canvas after each day's work and so produce a dry surface for the next session. His best-known work is probably *Saturday Night in The Vale* (1928–9, Tate, London), which shows the novelist and critic George Moore reading aloud to a gathering at Tonks's studio in The Vale, Chelsea. Moore complained that he had been made to look like a 'flabby old cook', whereas Tonks had depicted himself as a young and elegant 'demi-god'.

Tooker, George (*b* New York, 5 Aug. 1920). American painter. He studied at the *Art Students League, 1943–4. His teachers there included Reginald *Marsh, and it was from him and Paul *Cadmus (with whom he studied privately) that he acquired his preference for painting in egg *tempera. His technique is scrupulously detailed in the manner of the Old Masters, but his subjects express the spiritual desolation and debilitating uniformity of modern life. The figures in his paintings all look more or less like one another and go through life as if on a conveyer belt, tense and drained of energy. They are physically close to one another, but emotionally distant. *Subway* (1950, Whitney Mus., New York) is perhaps his most famous work—a terrifying vision of Kafkaesque isolation.

Toorop, Jan (*b* Purworedjo, Java, 20 Dec. 1858; *d* The Hague, 3 Mar. 1928). Dutch painter, graphic artist, and designer. He was born in Java (at this time a Dutch colony) and moved to the Netherlands with his family when he was 13. Toorop's work reflected many of the main stylistic currents of his time and he was a leading figure in the *Symbolist and *Art Nouveau movements. His most characteristic paintings are literary subjects depicted with flowing lines, as in his masterpiece, *The Three Brides* (1893, Rijksmuseum Kröller-Müller, Otterlo), a ghostly scene with an exotic feeling that recalls his oriental origins. In 1905 he was converted to Catholicism and thereafter concentrated mainly

on religious works. In addition to paintings his output included book illustrations, designs for stained glass, and posters. His daughter **Charley Toorop** (*b* Katwijk, 24 Mar. 1891; *d* Bergen, 6 Nov. 1955) trained as a musician but began to paint in about 1914. Her early work was influenced by her father's Symbolism, but later her style became more solid and naturalistic.

Topolski, Feliks (*b* Warsaw, 14 Aug. 1907; *d* London, 24 Aug. 1989). Polish-born painter and draughtsman who settled in England in 1935 and became a British subject in 1947. A versatile and prolific artist, he is perhaps best known for his large murals, notably the *Coronation of Elizabeth II* (1.2 × 30 m (4 × 100 ft)) in Buckingham Palace. He was an *Official War Artist 1940–5, and his other work includes portraits and book illustrations. His style is characterized by the use of vigorous swirling line.

Torel, William (active 1291–1303). English goldsmith and sculptor. In 1291 Edward I commissioned him to make three life-size gilt-bronze effigies: one of Edward's father Henry III and two of Edward's wife Eleanor of Castile (see ELEANOR CROSSES). One of the effigies of Eleanor was for Lincoln Cathedral (where her entrails were buried); it has been destroyed, but the other two works survive *in situ* in Westminster Abbey. Although they were among the first large-scale figures to be cast in England, Torel produced works of superb quality.

Torrentius, Johannes (*b* Amsterdam, 1589; *d* Amsterdam, 1644). Dutch painter whose name before he translated it into Latin was Jan van der Beeck. He specialized in still-lifes and obscene *genre scenes and was a very different character from the usual workmanlike Dutch painter of the 17th century. In 1627 he was tried in Haarlem for immorality and heresy (the authorities charged him with being the leader of the outlawed Rosicrucian sect). He was tortured and then sentenced to be burned alive, but the sentence was commuted to twenty years' imprisonment. Thanks to the intervention of Charles I (who admired his work), he was released in 1630 and permitted to go to England. He stayed there for about a decade before returning to Holland, where he again fell foul of the law and died after being tortured. In view of his extraordinary life, it is ironic that the only known painting certainly by him is an allegorical still-life on the theme of temperance (1614, Rijksmuseum, Amsterdam); it was once owned by Charles I.

Torres-García, Joaquín (*b* Montevideo, 28 July 1874; *d* Montevideo, 8 Aug. 1949). Uruguayan painter and art theorist, active mainly in Europe. In 1891 his family moved to Spain and he grew up in Barcelona, where he was part of an avant-garde circle that included the young *Picasso. After a visit to New York (1920–2), he settled in France (1924–32), where he developed a severely geometrical, two-dimensional *Constructivist style, and in 1929 founded the review *Cercle et Carré* with Michel *Seuphor. In 1934 he returned to Uruguay, where he opened an art school. He wrote various works on art theory and by his example and teaching did much to promote Constructivist and *Kinetic art in South America. There is a museum of his work in Montevideo.

Torrigiano (or **Torrigiani**), **Pietro** (*b* Florence, 22 Nov. 1472; *d* Seville, July/Aug. 1528). Florentine sculptor, active outside Italy for most of his career, particularly in England. He trained under *Bertoldo in the *Medici 'academy' and in a quarrel he broke the nose of his fellow student *Michelangelo, permanently disfiguring him. This assault on his favourite is said to have so angered Lorenzo de' Medici that Torrigiano fled Florence and in the 1490s he seems to have worked mainly in Rome; he is also said to have spent some time as a mercenary soldier (*Cellini says that he had 'a most arrogant spirit, with the air of a great warrior rather than a sculptor'). In 1504 he is documented in Avignon, and in 1509–10 he worked in the Netherlands for Margaret of Austria (see HABSBURG). By 1511 he had moved to England (probably following an earlier visit, *c.*1507–8), and it was there that he created his most important works, chief among them the tomb of Henry VII and his wife Elizabeth of York (1512–18, Westminster Abbey), which has been described by *Pope-Hennessy as 'the finest *Renaissance tomb north of the Alps'. The two sensitive bronze effigies have a *Gothic elegance, but the figures of child angels at the corners of the tomb and the exquisite decorative work introduced a pure Renaissance style into England. It had little immediate influence, however, in a country where the medieval tradition in art was still so vigorous.

In 1519 Torrigiano was commissioned to make a companion tomb for Henry VIII and his then wife Catherine of Aragon, and he visited Florence to recruit help; Cellini (who turned down the invitation when he learned that Torrigiano had broken his hero's nose) says that he continually boasted of his 'gallant feats among those beasts of Englishmen'. Torrigiano brought several Italian artists to England (including perhaps Giovanni II da *Maiano), but the tomb was abandoned when he moved to Spain in about 1522. According to *Vasari, his notoriously violent temper led to his death; infuriated by low payment for a statue of the Virgin and Child, he smashed the work, was imprisoned for this sacrilege, and starved himself to death (possibly to avoid the shame of execution).

Torriti, Jacopo (active 1290s). Italian mosaicist and painter. Nothing is known of his life, but he signed mosaics commissioned by Pope Nicholas IV for the apses of two churches in Rome, S. Giovanni in Laterano (*c.*1291), and S. Maria Maggiore (*c.*1295), and he must have been one of the leading contemporaries of *Cavallini. The mosaic in S. Giovanni in Laterano appears to have been a reworking of an earlier design and was reconstructed in the 19th century, so Torriti's style can best be assessed from the less restored mosaic in S. Maria Maggiore. Here, in the main scene of the *Coronation of the Virgin* and subsidiary scenes from the life of the Virgin, Torriti recaptures something of the vitality of late *antique mosaics; he was clearly influenced in his choice of colour by the pale delicate harmonies and silvery lights of the 5th-century mosaic on the triumphal arch of the same church. A number of frescos in the Upper Church of S. Francesco, Assisi, have been attributed to Torriti because of their stylistic similarity to the S. Maria Maggiore mosaic.

tortillon. See STUMP.

Toulouse-Lautrec, Henri de (*b* Albi, 24 Nov. 1864; *d* Château de Malromé, nr. Toulouse, 9 Sept. 1901). French painter, printmaker, and draughtsman, one of the most colourful figures in 19th-century art. The son of an outrageously eccentric nobleman, he grew up with a love of horses and sport, but as a result of inherited illness and two falls when he was in his early teens the bones in his legs atrophied and he became permanently stunted. (Accounts of his height vary, but he was certainly not the midget of popular imagination. He was about 5 ft tall—above the minimum height for military service—but his head looked disproportionately large and he walked with difficulty. Lautrec was stoical about his condition, never mentioning it except in jest; it did not prevent him from attracting women as beautiful as Suzanne *Valadon, and his courage in coming to terms with it helped to give him a hatred of any kind of pretence—a quality that emerges in the frankness of his art.)

Lautrec showed an early talent for drawing (his father and uncle were amateur artists) and in 1882 he began to study with *Bonnat. The following year he became a pupil of *Cormon, and in January 1884, aged 19, he was given an allowance and set up in a studio of his own in the Montmartre district of Paris, an area notorious for bohemianism and seedily glamorous nightlife. Almost all his work is taken from this world and his scenes of cafés, brothels, and nightclubs (notably the Moulin Rouge) have helped to create the popular image of *fin de siècle* Paris. He led a notoriously dissipated life, but he was always a dedicated professional artist, and it was a matter of pride that he kept his earnings in a separate bank account from his parental allowance (his work sold well, but he was constantly short of money because he was so extravagant). Even after a hard night's drinking he would arrive early at the printing workshop to supervise the production of his lithographs, and his output was very large considering his brief life.

Lautrec received a solid, traditional training with Bonnat and Cormon (two of the most renowned teachers of the day), and although his work often gives a wonderful feeling of spontaneity, it was in fact based on constant application as a draughtsman. In this he resembles *Degas, who was the *Impressionist he admired most. It was partly from him and partly from Japanese prints (see UKIYO-E) that Lautrec derived his striking use of oblique compositions, in which a scene is vividly observed as if in a sideways glance. Again like Degas, Lautrec was unconventional technically; he often painted on cardboard with very thin oil paint and he sometimes mixed normally separate media such as oil and pastel. However, whereas Degas had a reputation for aloofness, Lautrec was warm-hearted and his work is full of human sympathy. There is sometimes humour, but more often there are feelings of melancholy, disillusionment, or despair, especially in his brothel scenes. Prostitutes proved to be ideal models for him as they were so unselfconscious in moving around naked or semi-naked, and he represented their lives with no attempt to glamorize, moralize, or sentimentalize.

Lautrec sometimes lodged in brothels for weeks at a time and the prostitutes came to regard him as a friend. He concentrated on the tedious routine of their profession—waiting for clients, undergoing compulsory medical examinations, and so on—and he was particularly sensitive in depicting the lesbian relationships that often developed between them. A more extrovert side to his talents is seen in his celebrated poster designs, with which he achieved his greatest public success. Although he produced only about 30 posters (the first in 1891), he created such masterfully bold and arresting designs that he is almost universally regarded as the greatest of all artists in this field.

Suffering from alcoholism and syphilis, Lautrec became seriously ill in 1899 and he died two years later, aged 36. In 1922 his mother presented a large collection of his work to the museum in his native city of Albi, which was renamed the Musée Toulouse-Lautrec. The museum houses memorabilia as well as works of art, including Lautrec's walking stick, which ingeniously opens up to reveal a tiny glass and flask of brandy.

Tournier, Nicolas (*bapt.* Montbéliard, Franche-Comté, 12 July 1590; *d* Toulouse, Dec. 1638/Feb. 1639). French painter. Very little is known of his life and most of the attributions to him are speculative, but he seems to have been—with the exception of Georges de *La Tour—the most individual and sensitive of French *Caravaggesque painters. He was in Rome *c*.1619–26, then is recorded in Carcassonne in 1627 and in Toulouse from 1632. The works attributed to him in his Roman period are *genre scenes of music making, dice playing, etc. (*A Musical Party*, City Art Mus., St Louis), but after he returned to France he concentrated on religious pictures. There are examples in the Louvre, Paris, and in the Musée des Augustins, Toulouse, including a huge, badly damaged *Battle of Constantine* influenced by *Piero della Francesca's treatment of the subject at Arezzo—this at a time when Piero was virtually forgotten. More typical of Tournier's paintings in the museum at Toulouse are the *Lamentation* and the *Entombment*, which show the grace and refinement of his style.

Town, Harold (*b* Toronto, 13 June 1924; *d* Peterborough, Ontario, 27 Dec. 1990). Canadian abstract painter, printmaker, and sculptor, active mainly in Toronto, where he was a leading member of the group *Painters Eleven (1953–60). This was a channel for the influence of *Abstract Expressionism in Canada, but he subsequently worked in a variety of abstract styles, often developing themes in long series over a number of years. His work included murals for several public buildings, for example Toronto International Airport (1962). In 1956 and 1964 he represented Canada at the Venice *Biennale.

Towne, Francis (*b* ?Exeter, 1739/40; *d* London, 7 July 1816). English landscape painter, primarily in watercolour. He spent most of his life in Exeter, where he earned a good living as a teacher; in his time his work was little known outside his locality, but he is now regarded as one of the most individual watercolourists of his period. His method of painting in flat *washes over a brown pen-and-ink outline was employed with a severe economy of means and he had an eye for geometrical structure that gives his pictures an affinity with those of certain 20th-century artists such as John *Nash. His best works include some done when he passed through Switzerland in 1781 returning from a visit to Italy. Towne also visited Wales and the Lake District. In his later years he lived mainly in London.

Townley, Charles. See DILETTANTI.

Traini, Francesco (documented 1321–?63). Pisan painter. Only one work is certainly known to be by him—the signed *polyptych of *St Dominic and Scenes from his Life* (1345, Mus. Naz., Pisa). The most important works attributed to him are frescos in the Campo Santo in Pisa—the celebrated *Triumph of Death*, with accompanying scenes of the *Last Judgement, Hell*, and *Legends of the Hermits*. These, among the outstanding Italian paintings of the 14th century, were badly damaged by bombs in the Second World War, but this brought to light, by way of partial compensation, the beautiful *sinopie, which are now shown in the Museo delle Sinopie. The frescos include many telling details of death's victims and have been seen as a reflection of the horrors of the Black Death of 1348, but some authorities consider them earlier and perhaps the work of the mysterious *Buffalmacco.

Trajan's Column. A huge marble column erected in Rome by the Emperor Trajan (reigned AD 98–117) as a monument to himself; it survives largely intact and is one of the best preserved of all major Roman works of art. The monument was dedicated in 113, four years before Trajan's death, but according to a recent theory the sculptural decoration was produced under his successor Hadrian. The column itself is almost 30 m (100 ft) tall and stands on a base that is about 6 m (20 ft) high; a chamber in the base contained Trajan's funeral urn and that of his wife Pompeia Plotina. Originally a colossal bronze statue of Trajan stood on top of the monument, but it does not survive; a statue of St Peter has stood in its place since 1588. The shaft of the column is decorated with a spiral of relief sculpture, winding 23 times round it. These reliefs depict Trajan's triumphant campaigns in Dacia (now part of Romania) in 101–2 and 105–6 and are arranged as a continuous narrative strip (there are no breaks between scenes). The sculpture is of good quality and provides much detailed information about military matters (there are more than 2,000 figures; Trajan himself appears several times). The reliefs were originally painted and although this would have made them clearer, they can never have been easy to 'read', even from the upper storeys of nearby buildings; they can be more comfortably viewed in the full-size cast of the column in the Victoria and Albert Museum, London.

Columns had earlier been used in Roman art as pedestals for statuary, but Trajan's Column was novel in its great size and in its use of a spiral frieze. A similar column was erected c.180 in honour of the Emperor *Marcus Aurelius. It is in less good condition than Trajan's Column and the sculpture is less skilfully carved, but because the figures are more boldly conceived and in higher relief, the spiral design is much more legible from the ground.

Transitional style. Term applied to certain aspects of European art in the late 12th and early 13th centuries during a period of transition from *Romanesque to *Gothic. In architectural writing it is applied to buildings that manifest distinct features of both styles—in its crudest terms, those that use both round and pointed arches. In the study of the figurative arts, the meaning of the term is less clear, but it is often applied to certain works that are distinguished from both Romanesque and Gothic by their strongly *antique flavour and fluent forms: *Nicolas of Verdun's Klosterneuberg Altar is a prime example.

travertine. A *limestone of almost pure calcium carbonate found at Tivoli (Latin *Tibur*, hence *lapis Tiburtinus*—Tiburtine stone) and elsewhere in Italy. Varying in colour from pale buff to orange pink, it is sometimes porous. It has been much used in the buildings of Rome (notably the Colosseum and the colonnade of St Peter's) and has also been employed for outdoor sculpture that does not require a smooth finish, as for example by *Bernini in his Triton Fountain in Rome (1642–3).

Treasury Relief Art Project (TRAP). See FEDERAL ART PROJECT.

trecento. See QUATTROCENTO.

Tresham, Henry. See HAMILTON, HUGH DOUGLAS.

Très Riches Heures du duc de Berry. See LIMBOURG.

Tretchikoff, Vladimir (*b* Petropavlovsk, Kazakhstan, 13 Dec. 1913). Russian-born painter who settled in South Africa in 1946 and became a citizen of the country, one of the most financially successful but also one of the most critically reviled artists of the 20th century. Typically his pictures depict oriental beauties (notably *The Chinese Girl*, 1952), African tribesmen and tribeswomen portrayed as the noble savage, or flowers—often he shows a single bloom, accompanied by tearlike drops of water and with titles such as *The Weeping Rose*. His enormous popular success has depended not only on his choice and treatment of subject, but also on his skilful marketing. As well as showing extensively in South Africa, he organized several tours of his work in Britain, Canada, and the USA between 1953 and 1973 (the peak period of his fame), exhibiting in major department stores rather than galleries. The paintings themselves were generally not for sale, but reproductions of them sold in vast quantities. Tretchikoff has been the subject of several books and documentary films, including one for the BBC. To most critics, however, his work is excruciatingly vulgar, and he has been dubbed the 'King of Kitsch'.

Tretyakov, Pavel (*b* Moscow, 27 Dec. 1832; *d* Moscow, 16 Dec. 1898). Russian businessman and art collector. He made a fortune in the textile industry and devoted much of it to his passion for art. Initially he bought Western works, but he soon came to specialize in Russian art and by 1860 he had conceived the idea of a national museum; in that year he wrote, 'Being a true and ardent lover of painting, I could not think of anything better than to set up a repository of works of art that would benefit many, please everyone, and be accessible to all.' He wanted the collection to be representative, so he bought all kinds of pictures, not merely ones that appealed to him personally; he also commissioned many contemporary artists to produce work (he gave much encouragement and assistance to the *Wanderers). In 1874 his collection was opened to the public in a specially built gallery next to his Moscow mansion. After the death of his younger brother **Sergei** (1834–92), also an art lover, Tretyakov decided to present their combined collections to the city of Moscow; the reformed gallery opened in 1893 as the Pavel and Sergei Tretyakov Moscow City Art Gallery. After Tretyakov's own death, his mansion was incorporated into the gallery, the structures being unified by a new façade (1902) designed by Viktor *Vasnetsov in a picturesque 'old Russian' style. Following the 1917 Revolution, the gallery was declared national property and renamed the State Tretyakov Gallery in 1918. Up to this time there had been a few foreign works in the collection, but these were now dispersed and it became devoted exclusively to Russian art. With the addition of works confiscated after the Revolution, the collection grew to enormous size. A new wing was added in the 1930s, and in 1985–95 a huge new museum was built, incorporating the much-loved Vasnetsov façade into the structure. Modern works (from the time of the 1917 Revolution) have been transferred to the New Tretyakov Gallery, specially built for this purpose in Gorky Park. Between them, the two galleries contain more than 100,000 works, mainly paintings and graphic art, although there is also, for example, a good collection of jewellery.

Trevisani, Francesco (*b* Capodistria, nr. Trieste [now Cape of Istra, Slovenia], 9 Apr. 1656; *d* Rome, 30 July 1746). Italian painter, trained in Venice and active in Rome from about 1678. After the death of *Maratta in 1713, he succeeded him as 'the most famous, prosperous and prolific painter in Rome, with connections all over Europe' (Ellis *Waterhouse). His output included frescos, altarpieces, devotional works, mythological scenes, and portraits, including several of British visitors. His style was similar to Maratta's, but sweeter and more colourful.

triptych. A picture or carving consisting of three parts, usually a central panel flanked by wings (or folding shutters). As with the *diptych, the folding triptych lent itself to the making of portable altarpieces; the delicate inner surfaces were protected by the outer leaves, although these might be painted or carved on their outer as well as their inner surfaces. Some triptychs, however, are very large, for example the two by *Rubens in Antwerp Cathedral. See also POLYPTYCH.

Tristán, Luis (*b* nr. Toledo, *c*.1585; *d* Toledo, 7 Dec. 1624). Spanish painter, active mainly in Toledo, where he was a pupil of El *Greco *c*.1603–6. After spending some time in Italy he was back in Toledo by 1613, and the death of El Greco the following year left him the leading painter in the city. His style (notably his characteristically elongated proportions) owes much to the master, but Tristán is more sober, marking the transition from *Mannerism to a more naturalistic approach (*Adoration of the Shepherds*, 1620, Fitzwilliam Mus., Cambridge).

triumphal arch. A large, free-standing, decorative gateway erected to honour an important person or event. This type of structure originated in ancient Rome and initially the term alluded to a celebratory parade called a triumph that was awarded to a general who had won a particularly great victory; such generals led their troops into Rome through a special triumphal gate. At first triumphal arches were temporary structures, but from the 1st century BC some were built of permanent materials; they were also erected for purposes other than honouring generals, such as commemorating a new emperor. Examples were built throughout the Roman Empire, but most are in Italy, and three famous examples survive in Rome itself, each one decorated with notable sculpture.

The **Arch of Titus** (*c*. AD 81) has two large, dignified (although rather damaged) reliefs in the passageway depicting Titus' victory procession for the capture of Jerusalem in 70; it was erected by his brother Domitian, who succeeded him as emperor in 81. The **Arch of Septimius Severus** (203), erected to celebrate this emperor's victories against the Parthians and to establish the legitimacy of his new dynasty, is larger and more ornate, with extremely lavish sculptural decoration; indeed, 'As a vehicle for imperial propaganda the arch of Septimius Severus was the biggest "billboard" yet erected' (Donald Strong, *Roman Art*, 1976). The **Arch of Constantine** (dedicated in 315 to mark his victory over Maxentius and to celebrate the first decade of his reign) is the largest of all Roman triumphal arches and perhaps the most dignified. It has even more sculptural ornament than the Arch of Septimius Severus, some of it made specially for the purpose but much of it cannibalized from monuments of the previous two centuries. The contemporary sculpture is very different in style from the earlier pieces, the figures being dumpy in proportions and un-*classical in feeling. To many critics this stylistic gulf has been taken as an indication of a profound decline in Roman art, marking the virtual end of the classical world as Christianity rose to power. Bernard *Berenson, for example, wrote a book entitled *The Arch of Constantine, or, The Decline of Form* (1954). However, serious students

of the subject now consider this kind of condemnation outmoded: 'Nothing could be less classical than the style and technique of the sculpture; but there is something very effective about it as a means of conveying the character of the occasion in each case' (Strong).

Troger, Paul (*bapt.* Zell unter Welsberg, South Tyrol [now Monguelfo, Italy], 30 Oct. 1698; *d* Vienna, 20 July 1762). Austrian painter, printmaker, and draughtsman, a leading figure of central European art in the period of transition from *Baroque to the lighter *Rococo style. At the beginning of his career he spent about a decade in Italy, working successively in Venice, Rome, Naples, and Bologna, and when he returned to Austria in 1726 he probably had a more comprehensive knowledge of recent Italian painting than any other northern artist of his time. From 1728 he was based in Vienna, but he was in wide demand and travelled extensively to carry out commissions. He was primarily a fresco decorator, but he also painted altarpieces and produced etchings, engravings, and a large number of drawings. His ceiling frescos in the church (1733–4) and library (1742–3) of Altenburg Abbey are generally regarded as his masterpieces. They are characterized by light colours and vigorous movement, but also by a firmness of drawing that shows he had learnt well from *Solimena and the Bolognese tradition. From 1745 he taught at the Vienna Academy and he had a strong influence on the artists of the next generation, notably *Maulbertsch.

trompe-l'œil. Term (French: 'deceives the eye') applied to a painting (or a detail of one) that is intended to deceive the spectator (if only briefly) into thinking that it is a real object rather than a two-dimensional representation of it. Such virtuoso displays of skill often have a humorous intent, and anecdotes of almost miraculous feats of trompe-l'œil are typical of periods in which *naturalism has been cultivated, such as the *Classical age in Greece (see PARRHASIUS) and the Italian *Renaissance. *Vasari, for example, records that the young *Giotto tricked his master *Cimabue by painting on the nose of a figure on which he was engaged 'a fly so lifelike that when Cimabue returned to carry on with his work he tried several times to brush it off with his hand, under the impression that it was real, before he realized his mistake'. Petrus *Christus' *Portrait of a Carthusian* (*c*.1446, Met. Mus., New York) is an example of a painting with such a trompe-l'œil fly, here on a painted ledge at the bottom of the picture, rather than on the sitter's nose. Sometimes the term trompe-l'œil is used loosely to refer to any type of pictorial illusionism (for example *quadratura), but such usage deprives a useful term of its precision.

Troost, Cornelis (*b* Amsterdam, 8 Oct. 1696; *d* Amsterdam, 7 Mar. 1750). Dutch painter, printmaker, and draughtsman, active mainly in his native Amsterdam, the outstanding Dutch artist of the 18th century. He made his name with a lively group portrait of the *Amsterdam Inspectors of the Collegium Medicum* (1724, Rijksmuseum, Amsterdam) and continued to enjoy success as a formal portraitist and painter of *conversation pieces. However, he painted numerous other types of picture, including theatrical subjects (he had close connections with the theatre and acted professionally in his youth). His most famous work—made in his favourite technique of pastel and watercolour—is a series of five pictures entitled *NELRI* (1740, Mauritshuis, The Hague); the name is derived from the first letters of the Latin inscriptions that accompany the five views of the activities of a group of men during the night of a reunion. Troost has been described as 'the Dutch *Hogarth', but unlike his great English contemporary, he is a humorist without an ulterior motive; he never attempted to teach or preach.

Troostwijck, Wouter Johannes van (*b* Amsterdam, 28 May 1782; *d* Amsterdam, 20 Sept. 1810). Dutch painter, mainly of landscapes. He is regarded as the best Dutch landscapist of his period, but he died young before he could fulfil his promise. His freshness of vision is well exemplified in *The Rampoortje* (Rijksmuseum, Amsterdam, 1809), a view of an Amsterdam gate in winter.

trophy. A carved, painted, or engraved representation of a group of arms and armour (and usually banners), a common decorative motif on, for example, tomb sculpture and buildings. Trophies derive from the ancient practice of displaying the actual weapons of defeated enemies as spoils of war and symbols of conquest.

Troubadour style. Term applied to a vein of historical painting popular in the early 19th century, particularly in France, featuring scenes from the Middle Ages or the Renaissance treated in a way later associated with Hollywood costume dramas, with colourful apparel, amorous adventures, chivalric deeds, and sentimental anecdote to the fore. It can be seen as an aspect of *Romanticism—a kind of pictorial parallel to the poems and novels of Sir Walter Scott—and has been described as a 'style within a style'. Troubadour pictures are typically fairly small, with much detailed attention to accessories. Several major artists painted pictures of this type, notably *Ingres, as with *Leonardo da Vinci Dying in the Arms of Francis I* (1818, Petit Palais, Paris). However, the most committed exponents were fairly minor figures, for example Pierre Révoil (1776–1842), whose painting *The Tournament* (1812, Mus. B.-A., Lyons) is an archetypal example of the Troubadour style; it shows knights jousting amid the full panoply of medieval pageantry.

Troy, Jean-François de (or Jean-François Detroy) (*bapt.* Paris, 27 Jan. 1679; *d* Rome, 26 Jan. 1752). French painter and tapestry designer. His successful career was based initially on large historical and allegorical compositions (*Time Unveiling Truth*, 1733, NG, London), but he is now most highly regarded for his smaller and more spirited scenes of elegant social life. They are among the best of those that rode on the wave of *Watteau's success—indeed *The Alarm* (1723, V&A, London) was attributed to Watteau in the 19th century. In 1738 de Troy was appointed director of the French Academy in Rome, and he spent the rest of his life there. He was one of a family of painters, his father and teacher, **François de Troy** (1645–1730), being a successful painter of fashionable portraits and director of the Académie Royale from 1708 to 1711.

Troyon, Constant (*b* Sèvres, 28 Aug. 1810; *d* Paris, 20 Mar. 1865). French painter. He began his career as a porcelain decorator (the family trade) at the famous factory in his home town, Sèvres. In the 1830s, however, he took up landscape painting, and became one of the leading figures of the *Barbizon School. He visited Holland in 1847, and the influence of *Cuyp and *Potter is seen in his fondness for including cows in his pictures. Late in his career he turned to seascapes, the freshness and freedom of his work influencing *Boudin and *Monet in this genre. Troyon was a prolific and internationally successful painter, and his work is in many public collections in France and elsewhere.

Trubetskoy, Prince Pavel (or Paulo) (*b* Intra [now part of Verbania], nr. Lake Como, 15 Feb. 1866; *d* Suna, nr. Intra, 12 Feb. 1938). Russian-Italian sculptor. Trubetskoy grew up in Italy, then lived in Russia from 1897 to 1907 and afterwards in Paris, the USA (his mother was

American), and Italy. He was mainly self-taught and formed his style under the influence of *Rodin. His most important commission was the equestrian statue of Alexander III in St Petersburg (1899–1909). This is over-life-size in bronze on a granite base, but he usually worked on a much smaller scale and was known principally for statuettes of animals and Impressionistic portraits. Such works won him a great reputation at the Paris International Exhibition of 1900, and after a period of total neglect they are once again becoming fashionable. Examples are in the Tretyakov Gallery, Moscow, and the Russian Museum, St Petersburg.

Trübner, Wilhelm. See SEZESSION.

Trumbull, John (b Lebanon, Conn., 6 June 1756; d New York, 10 Nov. 1843). American painter. Trumbull fought in the American War of Independence (for a time he was aide-de-camp to George Washington) and his career was devoted mainly to depicting the outstanding events and personalities of the Revolution. He was strongly influenced by Benjamin *West, with whom he studied in London (he made several visits there, and during the first of them, 1780–3, was imprisoned in reprisal for the hanging of a British agent in America). In 1817 he became president of the American Academy of Fine Arts in New York, but his tyrannical attitude, especially towards young painters, led to many members leaving to set up the *National Academy of Design in 1825. His pictures did not sell well, so in 1831 he gave those in his studio to Yale University Art Gallery in exchange for an annuity. The most famous of his works there, and one of the most reproduced images in American art, is The Declaration of Independence (1786–97), in which most of the portraits were painted from life. His larger works are usually fairly stodgy, but his smaller pictures and sketches can be much livelier. Trumbull, who died an embittered old man, published an autobiography in 1841.

truth to material(s). A belief that the form of a work of art should be inseparably related to the material in which it is made. The phrase was much used in aesthetic discussions in the 1930s and is particularly associated with Henry *Moore, who in *Unit One (1934) wrote that 'Each material has its own individual qualities . . . Stone, for example, is hard and concentrated and should not be falsified to look like soft flesh . . . It should keep its hard tense stoniness.' Although in theory the idea could be

applied to any material, in effect it was used by Moore as an argument for *direct carving, as practised by himself and contemporaries such as Barbara *Hepworth. Moore later admitted that the idea of truth to materials had become a fetish and in 1951 he conceded that it should not be made into a criterion of value, 'otherwise a snowman made by a child would have to be praised at the expense of a *Rodin or a *Bernini'. (Bernini's virtuosity in creating lifelike effects in marble exemplified the kind of 'falsification' Moore had criticized in Unit One: according to a contemporary report, Bernini said of the elaborate curls in the wig of his bust of Louis XIV that it was 'no easy thing to attain that lightness in the hair to which he aspired, for he had to struggle against the contrary nature of the material'.)

tube. Collapsible container for paints. It was devised in 1841 by John G. Rand (1801–73), an American portrait painter working in London, and was commercially manufactured very soon afterwards. Before this time, artists either mixed their own paints or bought them in rather cumbersome bladders or in metal cylinders that were emptied by means of a piston and could be refilled at the colourman's shop. With the success of the tube, the preparation of paints now passed from the studio to the factory and the painter lost part of his character as craftsman. Moreover, a less fluid consistency had to be given to *oil paints to make them suitable for packing in tubes, and other ingredients had to be added during manufacture in order to ensure that the *pigments would stay suspended in the oil. Consequently manufactured paints do not flow from the brush as those of the Old Masters used to do and a stiffer, shorter brush is needed for handling them or a *diluent must be used. The tube, therefore, brought about a quiet revolution in painting technique. Furthermore the availability of ready-made paints in tubes made the practice of painting out of doors in oils much easier (see PLEIN AIR) and also encouraged artists to experiment with a much wider range of colours instead of mixing the smaller number with which they were familiar.

Tuby, Jean-Baptiste (b Rome, 1635; d Paris, 9 Aug. 1700). Italian-born sculptor who became a French citizen in 1666 (his father was French). He worked chiefly at Versailles, often in collaboration with *Girardon (whose niece he married). Much of his work there was garden sculpture, including a copy (1684–96) of the

Laocoön group. Tuby also made a good deal of funerary sculpture, sometimes in collaboration with *Coysevox.

Tucker, Albert. See ANGRY PENGUINS.

Tucker, William (*b* Cairo, 28 Feb. 1935). British-born abstract sculptor, writer on art, and teacher who settled in the USA in 1976 and later became an American citizen. In 1965 he was among the artists included in the *New Generation exhibition at the Whitechapel Art Gallery, London, which marked the emergence of a new British sculptural avant-garde inspired by his teacher Anthony *Caro. His work is in various materials and often makes striking use of colour. In 1974 he published *The Language of Sculpture* and in 1975 he organized a major Arts Council exhibition at the Hayward Gallery, London, entitled 'The Condition of Sculpture'.

tufa. Soft porous rock formed from the deposits of springs rich in lime. It is easily sawn and worked, but durable, hardening on exposure to air, and has been used since ancient times for buildings and sometimes for sculpture (in particular, the Romans used it for carved *sarcophagi).

Tuke, Henry Scott (*b* York, 12 June 1858; *d* Swanpool, nr. Falmouth, 13 Mar. 1929). British painter. He studied at the *Slade School, 1875–80, then in Italy and Paris, where he was strongly influenced by contemporary French *plein-air* painting. Tuke had known and loved Cornwall since childhood and after he returned to England in 1883 he settled there, living first at *Newlyn and then from 1885 in a cottage near Falmouth. His favourite subject—which he made his own—was nude boys in a sunlit atmosphere against a background of sea or shore. At first the freshness of these works—so different from the frigid studio nudes to which the public was accustomed—caused prudish objections (Tuke was a founder member of the *New English Art Club in 1886 and the sight of one of his paintings caused the dealer Martin *Colnaghi to withdraw his financial backing for the group's first exhibition). However, they soon became favourites with the public and are now regarded as being among the finest and most individual works of English *Impressionism. Tuke also painted portraits throughout his life.

Tura, Cosimo (or Cosmè) (*b* Ferrara, *c*.1430; *d* Ferrara, Apr. 1495). Italian painter, the first major artist of the Ferrarese School. Almost all his career was spent in Ferrara, where he worked

for the *Este family from 1452 and was appointed court painter in 1458. His sculptural figure style was influenced by *Mantegna and also by *Piero della Francesca (who worked in Ferrara in the 1440s), but its feverish, metallic quality is highly distinctive. Most of his surviving work is religious, including two huge shutters of the *Annunciation* and *St George and the Princess* (1469) for the organ of Ferrara Cathedral, now in the Cathedral Museum. Good examples of his work on a smaller scale are in the National Gallery, London. Tura was an important influence on the other two major painters of the 15th-century Ferrarese School—*Cossa and *Roberti. The latter replaced him as court painter in 1486 and Tura died poor.

Turin Hours. Manuscript *Book of Hours produced over an extended period with illustrations by several Franco-Netherlandish artists, one of whom was possibly Jan van *Eyck. The history of the manuscript is complex. It was begun in 1389 for Jean, Duc de Berry (the great-uncle of van Eyck's patron Philip the Good, Duke of *Burgundy), but it was not finished until about 1447, after passing through the hands of several owners, including John of Bavaria (for whom van Eyck worked in 1422–5) and possibly Philip the Good himself. Part of the manuscript was destroyed by a fire in Turin in 1904, but the illustrations that perished are known in photographs; the remaining parts are divided between Turin (Mus. Civico) and Paris (Bib. Nat. and Louvre). Three of the surviving illustrations are so close to Jan van Eyck in style and of such high quality that many scholars attribute them to him (or to his brother Hubert): *The Birth of St John the Baptist, The Mass of the Dead*, and *The Finding of the True Cross* (all three are in Turin). One of the striking features of the illustrations is their subtle observation of nature, and Kenneth *Clark thought that they included 'the first modern landscapes'. If they are by Jan, they must be his earliest surviving works, probably made before John of Bavaria's death in 1425. However, James Snyder (*Northern Renaissance Art*, 1985) thinks it more likely that they are 'the works of a talented imitator of Van Eyck's style, executed about 1435 or later'.

Turnbull, William (*b* Dundee, 11 Jan. 1922). British sculptor and painter. After serving as an RAF pilot in the Second World War he studied at the *Slade School, 1946–8, then in 1948–50 lived in Paris, where he saw a good deal of his fellow Scot and Slade student *Paolozzi and met such illustrious figures as *Brancusi and *Giacometti.

As a sculptor Turnbull moved from *Surrealistic and primitivist works to painted steel geometrical constructions in the manner of *Caro. As a painter he was one of the first British artists to work in a style similar to that of the American *Colour Field Painters. See also SITUATION.

Turner, J. M. W. (Joseph Mallord William) (*b* London, 23 Apr. 1775; *d* London, 19 Dec. 1851). English painter, one of the greatest figures in the history of landscape painting. His family called him Bill or William, but he is now invariably known as J. M. W. Turner (which is how he usually signed his pictures). He showed a talent for drawing from an early age and as a boy earned money by colouring prints. In 1789 he began working as a draughtsman for the architect Thomas Hardwick, and later in the same year he enrolled at the *Royal Academy Schools, where he studied regularly until 1793 and intermittently until 1799. Early in his student days he also had lessons from Thomas Malton (1748–1804), a topographical watercolourist who specialized in neat and detailed town views and whom Turner later described as 'my real master'. Turner first exhibited a watercolour at the Academy in 1790, when he was only 15, and from 1791 he began making regular sketching tours in various parts of Britain, producing many drawings of *Picturesque views and architectural subjects that he later used as the basis of watercolours or sold to engravers. At this time his work was more polished but less poetic than that of his friend *Girtin. Initially he painted only in watercolour, but in 1796 he first exhibited an oil at the Academy, *Fishermen at Sea* (Tate, London). Only three years later, in 1799, he was elected an Associate of the Royal Academy and in 1802, two months before his 27th birthday, he became the second youngest person ever elected a full Academician (only Thomas *Lawrence had achieved the distinction at a younger age). By this time he was also highly successful in financial terms, for he was hard-working, a good businessman, and frugal by nature (he lived rather squalidly, but he was not miserly or ungenerous, as is sometimes maintained).

From early in his career Turner was aware of his place in the tradition of landscape painting and he often produced works in homage to (or rivalry with) his great predecessors such as *Claude (whom he particularly revered) and Willem van de *Velde the Younger. However, he soon began to paint more original pictures in which he depicted the violence of nature in powerful *Romantic fashion. *The Shipwreck*

(Tate, 1805) was one of his first works in this vein, and one of the most celebrated is *Snow Storm: Hannibal and his Army Crossing the Alps* (Tate, 1812), of which a contemporary newspaper (the *Examiner*) wrote: 'This is a performance that classes Mr Turner in the highest rank of landscape painters . . . the moral and physical elements are here in powerful unison blended by a most masterly hand, awakening emotions of awe and grandeur.' During these years, however, he continued exhibiting more conventional pictures and still earned a good deal of his large income through work for engravers. His most ambitious engraving project was his *Liber studiorum* (Book of Studies), conceived in emulation of Claude's *Liber veritatis* and intended to show the range of his own work; between 1807 and 1819 he issued 71 of a projected 100 plates.

Turner made his first journey to the Continent in 1802, during a temporary peace in the war with France, visiting Paris like so many other artists to see pictures looted by Napoleon, which were then on exhibition. From Paris he travelled on to Switzerland. The resumption of war made Continental travel impossible for more than a decade, and Turner did not go abroad again until 1817, when he visited Belgium, Holland, and the Rhine. He first visited Italy two years later, and from then until 1845 made fairly regular journeys abroad (including three more to Italy, the last in 1840). Unlike his contemporary *Constable, who concentrated on painting the places he knew best, Turner was inspired to a great extent by what he saw on his travels (he lived in London all his life, but the city appears fairly infrequently in his paintings). The mountains and lakes of Switzerland and the haunting beauty of Venice, in particular, provided him with an enduring fund of subjects. He was inspired by history (especially ancient history) and literature as well as nature. Many of the paintings he exhibited at the Royal Academy were accompanied by verses printed in the catalogue, and from 1800 he added lines of poetry he had composed himself.

From the 1830s Turner's painting became increasingly personal and free, with detail subordinated to general effects of colour and light. To many critics it was incomprehensible, and one of his most celebrated pictures—*Snow Storm: Steam-Boat off a Harbour's Mouth* (Tate, 1842)—is said to have been dismissed as 'soapsuds and whitewash'. Turner's wealth and status allowed him to remain indifferent to such attacks, and he continued to have many admirers, including some who regarded him as the outstanding genius of the day. His most important patron was George Wyndham, 3rd Earl of Egremont (1751–1837), who was unusual among collectors of the time in buying contemporary British art (sculpture as well as painting) on a large scale. Turner had a studio at Petworth, Egremont's country house in Sussex, and several of his paintings are still to be seen there (although their ownership was transferred to the Tate Gallery in 1984).

Turner's other great champion was the young *Ruskin, who first met him in 1840 and wrote eloquently of him in the first volume of *Modern Painters*, published in 1843. By this time some of Turner's compositions were almost abstract, the forms dissolved in a haze of light and colour, the paint so delicate it appears almost to have been floated onto the canvas: 'He seems to paint with tinted steam, so evanescent and so airy', wrote Constable. Turner's originality lay not only in such handling of colour and light, but also in his use of the power, beauty, and mystery of nature to express deep human concerns. For example, *The Fighting Temeraire* (1839, NG, London), showing a ship that had fought at Trafalgar being towed to the breaker's yard, is not just a beautiful marine scene, but also a poignant elegy for a passing era.

For many years Turner was a prominent figure at the Royal Academy (he was professor of perspective 1807–38 and in 1845–6 he took over the president's duties when Sir Martin Archer *Shee was ill). However, he always carefully guarded his private life and in his later years he became more and more of a recluse, sometimes calling himself Mr Booth (assuming the name of his mistress Sophia Booth; he never married but had two long-term relationships, both with widows, and is rumoured to have fathered several children). After his death, Ruskin (his executor) destroyed many erotic drawings that he found among his works, thinking that they tainted his hero's memory.

In his will Turner left plans for disposing of his fortune (he wanted to found an almshouse for 'poor and decayed male artists') and for the creation of a special gallery at the National Gallery to display certain of his paintings (he had a huge stock of his work, including not only pictures that had never been sold, but also favourite paintings that he had bought back at auction). However, the will was contested by long-forgotten cousins (one of whom had a lawyer son with the splendidly Dickensian name of Jabez Tepper), and they won Turner's money

in 1856; at the same time the Court of Chancery awarded all the works remaining in his possession at his death to the National Gallery—about 300 oils and 19,000 drawings and watercolours. Most of these are now in the Clore Gallery at Tate Britain, but a few of Turner's most famous oils remain in the National Gallery.

Turner, John Doman. See CAMDEN TOWN GROUP.

Turner, William (*b* Black Bourton, nr. Witney, Oxfordshire, 12 Nov. 1789; *d* Oxford, 7 Aug. 1862). English painter, mainly in watercolour, and occasional printmaker. He studied in London under John *Varley but he worked chiefly in Oxford, and from as early as 1810 he was referred to as 'Turner of Oxford' to distinguish him from his great contemporary J. M. W. *Turner. Most of his work consists of views in Oxfordshire and neighbouring counties, although he made sketching tours in several other parts of England, Scotland, and Wales. At the outset of his career he was regarded as an artist of exceptional promise, but he settled into comfortable routine. Much of his life was devoted to teaching.

Turner Prize. An annual prize of £20,000 for British achievement in the visual arts, named after J. M. W. *Turner. It was established in 1984 by the Patrons of New Art, a body founded two years earlier (as part of the Friends of the *Tate Gallery) to encourage the collection of contemporary art. The regulations have changed somewhat since the prize was inaugurated. Originally it was awarded for 'the greatest contribution to art in Britain in the previous twelve months' and was open to critics and administrators (who were shortlisted but never won) as well as artists; since 1991 those eligible are British artists under the age of 50 who have had 'an outstanding exhibition or other presentation of their work' in the previous twelve months. The original sponsors, Drexel Burnham Lambert, suffered a financial collapse in 1990 and the prize was suspended that year; since then it has been sponsored by Channel 4 Television, which broadcasts the award ceremony live from Tate Britain. The director of the Tate is on the jury that makes the award. Like the Booker Prize in literature, the Turner Prize attracts a great deal of publicity, but much of this attention has been expressed as damning criticism, as it is regarded by many as showcasing all that is most pretentious and self-regarding in contemporary art.

The winners of the prize have been: 1984, Malcolm *Morley; 1985, Howard *Hodgkin; 1986, *Gilbert & George; 1987, Richard Deacon (1949–); 1988, Tony Cragg (1949–); 1989, Richard *Long; 1990, prize suspended; 1991, Anish *Kapoor; 1992, Grenville Davey (1961–); 1993, Rachel *Whiteread; 1994, Antony *Gormley; 1995, Damien *Hirst; 1996, Douglas Gordon (1967–); 1997, Gillian Wearing (1963–); 1998, Chris Ofili (1968–); 1999, Steve McQueen (1969–); 2000, Wolfgang Tillmans (1968–); 2001, Martin Creed (1968–); 2002, Keith Tyson (1969–).

turpentine. A *resinous liquid obtained from various species of pine tree, which in its distilled form ('spirits of turpentine') has been used since the 15th century as a *diluent, or thinner, for *oil paint.

Turrell, James. See LAND ART.

Tussaud, Marie. See WAX.

Twachtman, John H. See TEN.

Twelfth-century Renaissance. See PROTO-RENAISSANCE.

Twombly, Cy (*b* Lexington, Va., 25 Apr. 1929). American abstract painter and draughtsman. His distinctive style is characterized by apparently random scrawls and scribbles on white or black grounds. In his rejection of traditional ideas of composition he shows an affinity with the *all-over style initiated by Jackson *Pollock, though Twombly's work is looser than that of Pollock. In 1957 he settled in Rome.

291 Gallery. See STIEGLITZ.

tympanum (Greek: 'drum'; plural: tympana). Architectural term for the space enclosed between the lintel of a doorway and an arch over it; the term is also applied to similar spaces, such as the triangle enclosed by a classical pediment. The tympanum has no structural function and is often richly carved; some of the chief glories of *Romanesque sculpture are tympanum decorations (see, for example, GISLEBERTUS).

typology. In Christian *iconography a system whereby figures and scenes from the Old Testament were thought of as prefiguring those of the New Testament. It became the custom in biblical illustration for Old Testament 'types' to be juxtaposed with or subordinated to New Testament 'antitypes', to demonstrate visually that the promise of the Old Testament was fulfilled in the New. Thus Abraham's willingness to sacrifice his son Isaac was seen as foreshadowing God's sacrifice of Christ, and David was seen as a 'type' of Christ, his fight with Goliath prefiguring Christ's struggle with Satan. Occasionally classical myths or other secular sources were also accepted as types. Typological illustration is found in virtually every field of visual art throughout the Middle Ages (the earliest examples date from the 3rd century), and occasionally occurs afterwards. It reached a wide popular audience in *block books.

Tyson, Keith. See TURNER PRIZE.

Tytgat, Edgard (*b* Brussels, 28 Apr. 1879; *d* Brussels, 10 Jan. 1957). Belgian painter and printmaker. He began his career painting portraits, landscapes, and interiors in an *Impressionist style, and during the First World War he worked as a book illustrator in London, where he printed a memorial volume to his friend Rik *Wouters. After the war he returned to Belgium and turned to painting subjects such as circus and carnival themes in a mildly *Expressionistic, consciously *naive way. His work often drew on popular prints and folk art and it has a quality of humour that sets it apart from that of the other Belgian Expressionists. He wrote a good deal, including reminiscences of his childhood, but only part of his output has been published.

Tzara, Tristan. See DADA.

U

Uccello, Paolo (Paolo di Dono) (*b* Florence, *c*.1397; *d* Florence, 10 Dec. 1475). Florentine painter, one of the most distinctive artists of the early *Renaissance. *Vasari says he was called Uccello (which means 'bird') because he loved animals, and birds in particular, and he seems to have been regarded as something of an eccentric. He is first documented *c*.1412 as one of *Ghiberti's apprentices, but he is not known to have worked as a sculptor. From 1425 to 1427 he is recorded in Venice, where he worked as a mosaicist at St Mark's, but nothing survives there that can be certainly associated with him. By 1431 he was back in Florence, where he spent most of the rest of his life (he worked in Padua, 1444–5, and in Urbino, 1465–8).

In 1436 he painted his first dated surviving work—a huge fresco in Florence Cathedral depicting an equestrian statue, a monument to the English *condottiere* Sir John Hawkwood (*d* 1394). It demonstrated the fascination with perspective that was central to his style. His two other surviving large-scale works are a series of poorly preserved frescos on Old Testament themes (probably 1430s and 1440s) in the 'Green Cloister' of S. Maria Novella, Florence, and a series of three large panels (*c*.1455) depicting the Battle of San Romano, a minor Florentine victory against the Sienese in 1432. The panels formed part of a decorative scheme in the Palazzo *Medici but they are now separated, with one each in the National Gallery, London, the Louvre, Paris, and the Uffizi, Florence. Uccello's other works include the decoration of the clock-face and designs for stained-glass windows in Florence Cathedral, and two enchanting paintings that are generally considered to date from late in his career— *St George and the Dragon* (NG, London), one of the earliest known Italian paintings on canvas, and *The Hunt in the Forest* (Ashmolean Mus., Oxford). In spite of his major commissions in Florence Cathedral, his career was not particularly successful in worldly terms; Vasari says that 'he came to live a hermit's life', and in his tax return of 1469 Uccello described himself as 'old without means of livelihood . . . and unable to work'.

Uccello was long regarded more as a curiosity than a serious artist (in 1896 *Berenson dismissed him as a mathematician rather than a painter and said that artistically he 'accomplished nothing'); however, he is now one of the best-loved painters of his time, admired for the power and vigour of his forms, the beauty of his colouring, and his lively and witty imagination. His work presents a striking—and often captivating—combination of two seemingly opposing stylistic currents: the decorative tradition of *International Gothic and the scientific involvement with perspective of the early Renaissance. Vasari maintained that Uccello wasted his time 'on the finer points of perspective' and presents him as an amiable fanatic who worked into the night and when told to come to bed by his wife would reply: 'What a sweet mistress is this perspective!' He undoubtedly took his enthusiasm to extraordinary lengths (in the *Battle of San Romano* the broken weapons and even the corpses recede neatly in accordance with the perspective scheme), but his effects were appropriate to his subjects and to the decorative charm of his pictures rather than mere technical exercises. In *The Hunt in the Forest*, for example, he creates not only an atmosphere of fairy-tale romance, but also, through the way in which the horses and dogs move swiftly back into space, an exhilarating sense of darting energy. Uccello's name became so identified with the subject of perspective that he was often said to have invented it. *Ruskin, for example, wrote in a letter to Kate *Greenaway: 'I believe the perfection of perspective is only recent. It was first applied in Italian art by Paul Uccello. He went off his head with love of perspective.'

Uden, Lucas van (*b* Antwerp, 18 Oct. 1595; *d* Antwerp, 4 Nov. 1672). Flemish landscape painter and engraver, active mainly in his native Antwerp. The long-standing tradition that he worked in *Rubens's studio and painted landscape backgrounds for him is now discredited, but he was certainly strongly influenced by the master. His pictures are often large and have something of Rubens's sweep and richness. The figures were often added by other artists.

Udine, Giovanni da (b Udine, 27 Oct. 1487; d Rome, 1561/4). Italian painter, stuccoist, and architect. He was one of *Raphael's leading assistants in Rome and is chiefly important for his role in reviving antique techniques of *stucco and the ancient taste for *grotesques, inspired by archaeological discoveries. His light and graceful style, seen best in the Vatican Loggie (1517–19), was imitated all over Europe, particularly by *Neoclassical designers. In 1522 he returned to Udine; he spent most of the rest of his life there, but he had further sojourns in Rome (where he died) and also worked in Florence and Venice.

Uffizi (Galleria degli Uffizi), Florence. The chief public gallery of Florence. The nucleus of the collection derives from the art treasures of the *Medici family, and the Uffizi Palace was begun by *Vasari in 1560 for Cosimo I de' Medici, Grand Duke of Tuscany. It originally housed government offices (Italian *uffizi*), hence the building's name. In 1565 Vasari built a corridor over the Ponte Vecchio connecting the Uffizi with the *Pitti Palace. The Uffizi was completed in about 1580 and soon afterwards Francesco I de' Medici (Cosimo's son) had part of it remodelled as gallery space in which to display the family collections. Subsequently the building has been much altered, enlarged, and restored (it was damaged in the Second World War, by flooding in 1966, and by a terrorist bomb in 1993), but it remains the best testimony to Vasari's skill as an architect.

The last of the Medici line, Anna Maria Luisa, presented the collections to the city of Florence in 1737, and the transformation of the Uffizi into a public gallery was largely the work of Grand Duke Pietro Leopoldo (later the Emperor Leopold II; see HABSBURG), who reigned 1765–90. He reorganized the collections to make them more coherent, appointed scholarly staff (including *Lanzi) to care for them, and allowed public visiting free of charge. In the 19th century the Uffizi was again radically reorganized. Much archaeological material was placed in the Museo Archeologico, while the medieval and *Renaissance sculpture and the rich collection of *applied art were transferred to the *Bargello. The Uffizi picture collection on the other hand was enriched by early Italian works gained from

suppressions of churches and monasteries and confiscations of religious property. Although it is primarily famous for its incomparable representation of Florentine Renaissance painting, the Uffizi also has outstanding works from other Italian and non-Italian schools (for example, Hugo van der *Goes's Portinari Altarpiece) and important examples of *antique sculpture. The collection of prints and drawings in the Gabinetto dei Disegni e Stampe is one of the finest in the world, and the gallery of artists' self-portraits, begun by Cardinal Leopoldo de' Medici in the 17th century, is unrivalled.

Uglow, Euan (b London, 10 Mar. 1932; d London, 31 Aug. 2000). British painter. His work included landscapes, portraits, and still-lifes, but he is best known for his carefully composed nudes, in which the naturalistic tradition stemming from the *Euston Road School is combined with geometrical precision of composition. Sir John *Rothenstein wrote of him: 'He is probably the slowest of professional painters; it sometimes takes him three-quarters of an hour even to pose the model in the precise position he requires . . . His output is therefore exceptionally small, sometimes amounting to no more than three or four canvases a year.' In spite of this and his aversion to publicity, he built up a strong reputation among contemporary figurative painters, especially among his fellow artists.

Ugo da Carpi (b Carpi, Emilia, c.1480; d ?Rome, 1532). Italian printmaker, a pioneer of the *chiaroscuro woodcut. He worked in Venice, Rome, and elsewhere. In 1516 he requested from the Venetian Senate a patent for his method 'of making from woodcuts prints that seem as though painted', and although there are German examples earlier than any known by Ugo, he may have discovered the technique independently. Certainly his prints achieve their pictorial effect better than those of the Germans. They are often based on designs by *Raphael and *Parmigianino.

Ugolino di Nerio (active 1317–27). Sienese painter, a close follower of *Duccio. His only certain work is a large *polyptych painted for the high altar of S. Croce, Florence; it formerly bore the signature 'Ugolino da Siena', but this has disappeared. The altarpiece was dismantled in the 16th century and is now widely dispersed; several panels are in the National Gallery, London. *Vasari says Ugolino painted 'many pictures and chapels in all parts of Italy' and several paintings are attributed to him on stylistic grounds. His style was charming, but must have been something of an anachronism in the Florence of *Giotto's day. In the first edition of his *Lives* Vasari says he died in 1339; in the second edition he gives the date as 1349.

Uhde, Fritz von (b Wolkenburg, Saxony, 22 May 1848; d Munich, 25 Feb. 1911). German painter, active mainly in Munich, where he was a founder member of the *Sezession in 1892. He did not settle on art as a career until 1877, after spending ten years as an army officer. His work included landscapes, portraits, and *genre scenes, but he is best known for his novel treatment of biblical subjects in modern settings. The first of these was *Suffer the Little Children to Come unto Me* (1884, Mus. der Bildenden Künste, Leipzig), showing Jesus as an itinerant preacher at a village school. Such paintings aroused great controversy, as they were regarded by conservative critics as sacrilegious, but their sincerity and sentiment also won them many admirers. Often Uhde used outdoor settings, in line with his interest in *plein-air* painting, in which he was encouraged by *Liebermann.

Uhde, Wilhelm (b Friedeberg in der Neumark [now Strzelce Krajeńskie, Poland], 28 Oct. 1874; d Paris, 17 Aug. 1947). German collector, dealer, and writer on art, active mainly in France. After studying in Munich and Florence, he settled in Paris in 1904 and by the following year he was buying pictures by *Picasso and *Braque at a time when these artists were practically unknown. Uhde was also one of the first to discover the Douanier *Rousseau; he published the first monograph on him in 1911 and in 1912 organized a retrospective exhibition of his work. Subsequently he was best known for discovering and encouraging other *naive artists. In 1947 he published his best-known book, *Fünf primitive Meister*, dealing with *Bauchant, *Bombois, Rousseau, *Séraphine, and *Vivin (French and English editions appeared in 1949).

Ukiyo-e. Japanese term, meaning 'pictures of the floating world', applied to the dominant movement in Japanese art of the 17th to the 19th century. It refers to the subjects from everyday life, with its ever-shifting fashions, favoured by printmakers in this period, including such celebrated artists as Ando Hiroshige (1797–1858), Katsushika Hokusai (1760–1849), and Kitagawa Utamaro (1753–1806). Favourite subjects were theatre scenes, actors in well-known roles, and prostitutes and bath-house girls. Japanese prints began arriving in European ports in

the 1850s (*Monet bought one in Le Havre in 1856) and greatly influenced avant-garde French artists, to whom their flat decorative colour and expressive pattern came as a revelation.

underdrawing. Preliminary drawing made on the prepared canvas, panel, or other *support before the application of paint. Underdrawings are obviously not meant to be seen after the picture is completed, but they are sometimes visible to the naked eye in thinly painted passages, as well as in unfinished works. They can also be revealed through infra-red photography or through the related technique of infra-red reflectography (which can achieve greater penetration of the paint layers), developed in the 1960s by the Dutch physicist J. R. J. van Asperen de Boer. Many paintings have been examined by these methods, particularly 15th- and 16th-century works, revealing underdrawings that range from summary sketches to highly finished compositions. They can be useful tools in matters of attribution.

underpainting. The preliminary blocking out of a composition on the painting surface in which the main shapes and tones of the picture are established before being built up by layers of *glazes, *scumbles, or solid paint. Until the late 19th century, when *alla prima* painting became general, most paintings were built up in a series of such layers. Usually underpainting was monochromatic (see GRISAILLE). In *tempera, it was traditionally done in *terre verte* (green earth colour), and a greenish caste can often be seen in 14th-century paintings, especially in the shadows of the flesh. In *oil painting, various neutral colours were used for the monochrome underpainting, which might be painted over a coloured *imprimatura. In the 15th and 16th centuries it was common to use tempera for the underpainting of works in oil. By the 19th century the main design of the painting was usually put in a colour scheme similar to that planned for the finished work, though each colour might be more subdued and extreme darks and lights were avoided.

Underwood, Leon (b London, 25 Dec. 1890; d London, 9 Oct. 1975). British sculptor, painter, printmaker, teacher, and writer. A versatile and original figure, Underwood was out of sympathy with the main trends of modernism, describing abstraction as 'artfully making emptiness less conspicuous'. Nevertheless, from the 1960s critics began to speak of him as the 'father of modern sculpture in Britain', in view of the streamlined stylized forms of his stone carvings and bronzes in the 1920s and 1930s and the influence of his teaching. He taught at the *Royal College of Art (where Henry *Moore was among his pupils) from 1920 to 1923, resigning after an argument with William *Rothenstein, and at his own Brook Green School in Hammersmith, which he opened in 1921 and ran intermittently until 1938. Underwood travelled widely and wrote several books, notably on African art. He illustrated his books (and a few by other authors) with etchings and woodcuts. His painting, which was sometimes influenced by primitive art, was generally less interesting than his sculpture.

Unit One. A group of avant-garde British artists formed in 1933, its members including Barbara *Hepworth, Henry *Moore, Paul *Nash, and Ben *Nicholson. The group held one exhibition, in London in 1933 (it toured to six provincial venues in 1934–5), and published a book, *Unit One: The Modern Movement in English Architecture, Painting and Sculpture*, edited by Herbert *Read, in 1934. In the introduction to this volume (which was originally intended as the first of a series), Read explained that the name was chosen because 'though as persons, each artist is a *unit*, in the social structure they must, to the extent of their common interests be *one*'. The group had no common doctrine or programme and was breaking up by 1935. Despite its short life, however, it made a considerable impact on British art of the 1930s, helping to promote abstraction and *Surrealism.

Unofficial art. A term for art produced in the Soviet Union that did not conform to the ideals of *Socialist Realism, which became officially sanctioned by the state in 1932. Any form of artistic independence was virtually impossible under the tyrannical rule of Stalin (1924–53), but there was a slight thaw under his successor Nikita Khrushchev, who in 1956 denounced Stalin's abuse of power. Unofficial art began to appear in public a few years after this, in about 1960, and in 1962 one of its leading figures, the sculptor Ernst Neizvestny (1926–), had a public confrontation with Khrushchev about the validity of modern art. The authorities could still be highly repressive, however, and in 1974 an open-air exhibition of Unofficial art in a field near Moscow was broken up with water-cannon and bulldozers, causing it to be dubbed the 'Bulldozer Show'. Unofficial art was stylistically varied and individualistic, often reflecting avant-garde Western movements, but from about 1970 a distinctive strand emerged within it—*Sots art, in which the conventions of Socialist Realism were mocked. During the 1970s such art began to be seen in the West (for example at an exhibition at the *Institute of Contemporary Arts, London, in 1977); several Unofficial artists were allowed to leave the Soviet Union and a few achieved success in Europe and the USA, notably Neizvestny and Komar and Melamid (see SOTS ART). During the late 1980s the much more liberal policies of Mikhail Gorbachev (Soviet leader 1985–91) brought great changes, and by the time the Soviet Union broke up in 1991 there was even a company called Sovart that placed Soviet artists with Western galleries.

Urban VIII, Pope. See BARBERINI.

Ushakov, Simon (*b* Moscow, 1626; *d* Moscow, 1686). Russian *icon painter, active in Moscow. His talent was modest, but he is noteworthy as the first Russian artist to show the influence of Western painting. In about 1667 he wrote a treatise, *Words to the Lovers of Icon Painting*, in which he called for greater naturalism in the art, and although his own move in that direction was fairly superficial, he was decried by traditionalists in his own time for introducing a foreign 'heresy' and subsequently blamed by 19th-century scholars for starting the 'decline' of icon painting. Ushakov also painted portraits (although these do not survive) and made engravings for book illustration—another field in which he was a pioneer of Western influence. There are examples of his work in the Tretyakov Gallery, Moscow.

Utamaro, Kitagawa. See UKIYO-E.

Utrecht Caravaggisti. A term applied to a number of Dutch painters active in Utrecht who were strongly influenced by *Caravaggio's work and who in the 1620s made their city the chief centre of his style in northern Europe. The three main artists covered by the term are *Baburen, *Honthorst, and *Terbrugghen, each of whom had lengthy stays in Rome. Terbrugghen was the first to return to the Netherlands, in about 1614, and Baburen and Honthorst followed in about 1620. The minor figures associated with them include Jan van Bijlert or Bylert (*c*.1598–1671) and Jan van Bronchorst or Bronckhorst (*c*.1600–61), both of whom visited Rome in the early 1620s. Utrecht was the main Dutch centre of Catholicism at this time, and all these artists painted religious subjects; their other staple was *genre scenes, typically featuring gamblers or musicians. Terbrugghen's death in 1629 marked the end of the heyday of Utrecht Caravaggism (Baburen had died in 1624 and Honthorst had already moved away from the style). However, these artists exerted a lasting influence, for they 'introduced one of the main currents of *Baroque art into the Netherlands. Even the greatest masters of seventeenth-century Dutch painting, who were never in Italy—*Hals, *Rembrandt, and *Vermeer—received decisive impulses from the Caravaggesque style' (Seymour Slive, *Dutch Painting: 1600–1800*, 1995).

Utrecht Psalter (University Lib., Utrecht). The most famous of *Carolingian illuminated manuscripts and one of the most influential works of art of the early Middle Ages. It was probably made in the abbey of Hautvillers in the diocese of Reims (see REIMS SCHOOL) during the time of Archbishop Ebbo (816–35). Each Psalm is illustrated with a drawing in brown ink that translates the poetical texts into concrete images. 'The small figures are drawn with great rapidity and with only a few strokes, and they are set in hilly landscapes indicated with a line or two. Everything is movement, gesture, and expression. The crowds swarm like ants, agitated, tense, in constant motion, their robes swirling as if blown by the wind. The dynamic, expressive style obviously depends on late antique models but, at the same time, it is very personal and the work of a great artist. No wonder this style caught the imagination of many later artists' (George Zarnecki, *Art of the Medieval World*, 1975). By about 1000 the book had found its way to Canterbury, and there are three surviving free copies of it made there over the next two centuries (BL, London; Trinity College, Cambridge; Bib. Nat., Paris). After the Dissolution of the Monasteries it passed into private ownership (it was for a time in the library of Sir Robert Cotton; see LINDISFARNE GOSPELS), and it was acquired by the University of Utrecht in 1716. See also PSALTER.

Utrillo, Maurice (*b* Paris, 26 Dec. 1883; *d* Dax, 5 Nov. 1955). French painter. The illegitimate son of Suzanne *Valadon, he took his surname from the Spanish painter Miguel Utrillo (1862–1934), who legally recognized him as his son in order to help him (his real father—according to some sources—was *Puvis de Chavannes, who was 40 years older than Valadon). He began to paint in 1902 at the urging of his mother, who hoped that it would remedy the alcoholism to which he had been a victim since his boyhood. Valadon gave him his first lessons, but he was largely self-taught. He first showed his work publicly at the *Salon d'Automne in 1909. In 1923 he had a successful joint exhibition with his mother, and subsequently he became prosperous and critically acclaimed. However, he continued to be an alcoholic (in 1934 the Tate Gallery wrongly stated in a catalogue that he had died of drink that year, thus bringing on the trustees' heads a libel suit, settled out of court). In his later years he devoted as much time to religious devotions as to painting.

Utrillo was highly prolific, painting mainly street scenes in Montmartre, although he also did numerous views of churches and cathedrals (*Church at St Hilaire*, c.1911, Tate, London). The period from about 1910 to 1916 is known as his 'white period' because of the predominance of milky or chalky tones in his pictures (he sometimes mixed plaster with his paint to enhance the sense of texture), and it is generally agreed that he did his best paintings during this time. They subtly convey solitude and emotional emptiness and have a delicate feeling for tone and atmosphere, even though he often worked from postcards. His later work is livelier but less touching. His work is in many museums and (no doubt because of the deceptive simplicity of his paintings) he is among the most forged of modern artists.

Uytewael, Joachim. See WTEWAEL.

V

Vaenius, Octavius. See VEEN.

Vaillant, Wallerant (*bapt*. Lille, 30 May 1623; *d* Amsterdam, 28 Aug. 1677). Dutch printmaker, draughtsman, and painter of Flemish birth. He spent most of his career in Amsterdam, but he worked in various other places, including Paris, where he lived from 1659 to 1665, and *Vertue says he visited England. Most of his paintings are portraits, but he also produced still-lifes and *genre scenes (*A Boy Seated Drawing*, Louvre, Paris, and other versions). However, he was active mainly as a printmaker and draughtsman, and he is remembered particularly as the first professional exponent of *mezzotint. He learnt the new technique from Prince *Rupert, whom he met in Frankfurt in 1658, and produced about 200 prints in the method. Vaillant had several painter brothers and half-brothers: **Jacques** (*c*.1625–91), **Jean** (1627–?after 1688), **Bernard** (1632–98), and **Andries** (1655–93). They were active mainly as portraitists.

Valadon, Suzanne (*b* Bessines-sur-Gartempe, nr. Limoges, 23 Sept. 1865; *d* Paris, 7 Apr. 1938). French painter. As a girl she worked as a circus acrobat, but had to abandon this after a fall and then became an artists' model and the reigning beauty of Montmartre. The artists she posed for included *Renoir, *Puvis de Chavannes, and *Toulouse-Lautrec (each of whom numbered among her lovers). Lautrec brought her drawings to the attention of *Degas, who encouraged her to develop her artistic talent, and she became a full-time painter in 1896. Valadon owed little to formal training or to the influence of the artists with whom she associated and her painting has a fresh and personal vision. Her subjects included portraits and still-lifes, but she was at her best in figure paintings, which often have a splendid earthy vigour and a striking use of bold contour and flat colour. After the First World War she achieved critical and financial success, but in her final years her health was undermined by the excesses of her life. Maurice *Utrillo was her son.

Valckenborch. Family of Netherlandish landscape and *genre painters, the most important members of which were **Lucas I** (*c*.1535–97) and his brother **Marten I** (1534–1612). Both of them began their careers in Malines and ended them in Frankfurt, where they ran a flourishing workshop together (in between their paths diverged as their lives were disrupted by war and religious persecution). They worked in the tradition of Pieter *Bruegel, characteristic subjects including winter landscapes and the Tower of Babel.

Valdés Leal, Juan de (*bapt*. Seville, 4 May 1622; *bur*. Seville, 15 Oct. 1690). Spanish painter and etcher, active mainly in Seville. He settled there permanently in 1656 after spending part of his early career in Córdoba, and following *Murillo's death in 1682 he was the leading artist in the city. Like Murillo, he was primarily a religious painter, but he was very different in style and approach. He had a penchant for macabre or grotesque subject matter, and his style is characterized by feverish excitability, with a vivid sense of movement, brilliant colouring, and dramatic lighting. His most celebrated works are two powerful allegories of Death (1670–2) in the Hospital de la Caridad, Seville: *In ictu oculi* (In the Twinkling of an Eye), showing a skeleton snuffing out the flame of life and trampling on the attributes of earthly achievement; and *Finis gloriae mundi* (The End of Worldly Glory), depicting rotting corpses in a crypt. He also *polychromed *Roldán's sculpture on the high altar in the Caridad. Several other members of his family were artists.

Valenciennes, Pierre-Henri de (*b* Toulouse, 6 Dec. 1750; *d* Paris, 16 Feb. 1819). French landscape painter. Between 1769 and 1785 he spent several years in Italy, and his style was influenced most notably by Nicolas *Poussin. He became a leading upholder of the classical tradition in landscape painting and he argued that landscape should be considered equal in status to *history painting. However, although his finished pictures were in a grand, highly composed style, he was also a leading exponent of the oil sketch; he thought that direct study from nature was a prerequisite for his formal works. His ideas were promoted not only through his paintings, but also through his book *Élémens de perspective pratique* (1800) and through his teaching at the École des *Beaux-Arts in Paris, where he became a professor in 1812.

Valentin de Boulogne (also called Le Valentin and Moïse Valentin) (*bapt.* Coulommiers, ?3 Jan. 1591; *d* Rome, 18/19 Aug. 1632). French *Caravaggesque painter, active in Rome for all his known career (he is first securely documented there in 1620 but probably arrived appreciably earlier). His life is fairly obscure and his first name is unknown; the word 'Moïse' (the French form of Moses), which was sometimes used to refer to him, is not a personal name but a corruption of the Italian form of 'monsieur'. He did, however, paint one major public work—the *Martyrdom of St Processus and St Martinian* (1629–30, Pinacoteca, Vatican), commissioned by Cardinal Francesco *Barberini for St Peter's as a pendant to *Poussin's *Martyrdom of St Erasmus*. About 80 pictures are attributed to Valentin. They vary in subject—religious, mythological, and *genre scenes and portraits—but the same models often seem to reappear in them. Characteristically his work is marked by an impressively solemn, at times melancholic, dignity, but he could also create a vivid sense of menace in his portrayals of sinister drinking dives and gambling dens (*The Card-Sharps*, Gemäldegalerie, Dresden). He was one of the best of Caravaggio's followers and one of the most dedicated, still painting in his style when it had gone out of fashion in Rome. *Baglione says that he died after taking a cold bath in a fountain following a drinking bout; his death was much lamented in the city's artistic community.

Valentiner, William (*b* Karlsruhe, 2 May 1880; *d* New York, 6 Sept. 1958). German-American art historian, one of the foremost connoisseurs of Dutch painting, on which he published numerous books. From 1906 to 1908 he worked at the Kaiser-Friedrich Museum, Berlin, under *Bode, then moved to the *Metropolitan Museum in New York, where one of his innovations was to ban the attendants from smoking cigars while they were on duty. He stayed there until 1914, then served in the German army in the First World War. At this time he knew various German *Expressionist artists, notably *Schmidt-Rottluff, and helped to promote their work in the USA. In 1921 he

began working at the Detroit Institute of Arts, of which he was director from 1924 to 1945 and where he commissioned murals from Diego *Rivera. He was then director of the County Museum of Art in Los Angeles (1946–54) and the first director of the North Carolina Museum at Raleigh (1955–8). He also founded the *Art Quarterly* (1938), a leading scholarly journal.

Valette, Adolphe. See LOWRY.

Vallotton, Félix (*b* Lausanne, 28 Dec. 1865; *d* Paris, 28 Dec. 1925). Swiss-born painter, printmaker, illustrator, sculptor, and writer who settled in Paris in 1882 and became a French citizen in 1900. In the 1890s he worked a good deal in woodcut, and apart from *Gauguin he was the most important French pioneer of the revival of this medium. During the same period he exhibited with the *Nabis (he was a friend of *Bonnard and *Vuillard). After the turn of the century he concentrated on painting; in his canvases he took over something of the simplifications of form and sharp contrasts between blocks of light and shadow that characterize his woodcuts. His subjects included landscapes, portraits, nudes, and interiors. In 1930 his novel *La Vie meurtrière* was posthumously published; it is autobiographical and illustrated by himself.

Valtat, Louis. See FAUVISM.

Vanderbank, John (*b* London, 9 Sept. 1694; *d* London, 23 Dec. 1739). English painter and book illustrator of Dutch extraction. He had a considerable practice as a portraitist in the years immediately succeeding the death of *Kneller, and *Vertue says he started the fashion for depicting ladies in *Rubens costume. His best work is vigorous, but often marred by sloppy handling. He was one of the founders of the *St Martin's Lane Academy in 1720.

Vanderlyn, John (*b* Kingston, NY, 15 Oct. 1775; *d* Kingston, 24 Sept. 1852). American painter, active mainly in and around New York. Between 1796 and 1815 he lived in Europe (apart from brief visits to America) and his style was closer to mainstream *Neoclassicism and *Romanticism than that of almost any other American painter of his generation. He was the first American painter to study in Paris and also worked in Rome. His best-known painting is *Ariadne Asleep on Naxos* (1812–14, Pennsylvania Academy of the Fine Arts, Philadelphia), a reclining figure in the tradition of the Venuses of *Giorgione and *Titian that is regarded as the finest American nude before *Eakins. Although such works won him considerable renown in France, he was much less successful in America, where he worked mainly as a portraitist, and he died poor and embittered.

Van de Velde, Henry. See VELDE, HENRY VAN DE.

vanitas (Latin: 'vanity' or 'emptiness'). A type of still-life picture depicting an object or collection of objects symbolizing the brevity of life and the transience of all earthly pleasures and achievements. Typical motifs are a skull, an hourglass, a watch, a smoking candle, and a flower losing its petals. Such paintings were especially popular in Dutch and Spanish art of the 17th century. At this time vanitas elements were often found in portraits and figure paintings as well as in pure still-lifes.

Vanloo, Carle. See LOO.

Van Rysselberghe, Théo. See RYSSELBERGHE.

Vantongerloo, Georges (*b* Antwerp, 24 Nov. 1886; *d* Paris, 5 Oct. 1965). Belgian sculptor, painter, architect, and writer on art, active mainly in France, one of the pioneers of a mathematical approach to abstract art. In 1917 he joined the De *Stijl group and turned from the conventionally naturalistic style he had previously practised to abstract sculptures in which he applied the principles of *Neo-Plasticism to three dimensions (*Interrelation of Volumes*, 1919, Tate, London). From 1919 to 1927 he lived in the French Riviera resort of Menton and then for the rest of his life in Paris, where he was a member of *Cercle et Carré and one of the founders of *Abstraction-Création. From 1928 he began to design ambitious (and unrealized) architectural projects, including a 'Skyscraper City' (1930), whose cubiform structure resembles that of his sculptures. In the 1940s his sculpture became more varied as he began using wire and perspex, exploring effects of reflection and refraction. His paintings were based on horizontal and vertical lines until 1937, when he introduced rhythmic curving lines, rejecting his friend *Mondrian's idea that only constructions based on the right angle reflect the harmony of the universe.

Vanvitelli, Gaspare. See WITTEL.

Varchi, Benedetto. See PARAGONE.

Vargas, Alberto. See AIRBRUSH.

Varin, Quentin. See POUSSIN.

Varley, Frederick. See GROUP OF SEVEN.

Varley, John (*b* London, 17 Aug. 1778; *d* London, 17 Nov. 1842). English landscape painter in watercolour, a protégé of Dr *Monro. Varley represents the transition between tinted topographical drawing and the bolder, more fully developed manner of watercolour painting characteristic of the 19th century. As well as being a leading painter, he was the most popular and enthusiastic teacher of his day; his pupils included *Cox, *De Wint, *Linnell, *Mulready (his brother-in-law), and *Palmer, and he published various instructional works. He also wrote a treatise on astrology (1828), a subject in which he had an obsessive interest. His eccentricities helped endear him to William *Blake, who was a close friend. In spite of his success, Varley constantly had money problems (he had a large family and an improvident wife) and he was imprisoned for debt on several occasions. His brothers **Cornelius** (1781–1873) and **William** (1785–1856) and his sister **Elizabeth** (1783–1864), Mulready's wife, were also watercolourists, and several descendants carried on the family tradition.

varnish. Solution of natural or synthetic *resin dissolved in liquid, used as a protective coating on the surface of a painting or sometimes as a paint *medium. Ideally varnish should be colourless and transparent, but most have darkened with age. Natural resin varnishes are usually either oil based or spirit based. Oil varnishes, which have been used since the Middle Ages, are made by dissolving resins (such as *mastic or *sandarac) in hot oil (usually *linseed). These were the main types of picture varnishes until well into the 20th century, when they were largely replaced by synthetic equivalents. Spirit-based varnishes are made by dissolving resin in a rapidly evaporating liquid such as *turpentine. Other organic varnishes have used gum arabic (notably for manuscript illuminations) and egg white (particularly for temporary varnishes, removed a year or so later and replaced with a permanent varnish).

Vasarely, Victor (*b* Pécs, 9 Apr. 1908; *d* Paris, 15 Mar. 1997). Hungarian-born painter who became a French citizen in 1959, the main originator and one of the leading practitioners of *Op art. He settled in Paris in 1930, and for the next decade worked chiefly as a commercial artist, particularly on the designing of posters, showing a keen interest in visual tricks such as *trompe-l'œil effects. From 1943 he turned to painting and about four years later he adopted the method of geometrical abstraction for which he was best known. Typically he created a hallucinatory impression of movement through visual ambiguity, using alternating positive–negative shapes interrupted in such a way as to suggest underlying secondary shapes. His fascination with the idea of movement led him to experiment with *Kinetic art and he also collaborated with architects in such works as his relief in aluminium for Caracas University (1954) and the French Pavilion at 'Expo '67' in Montreal, hoping to create a kind of urban folk art. From the mid-1950s he wrote a number of manifestos, which, together with his paintings, were a major influence on younger artists working in the same fields. Among them is his son **Jean-Pierre** (1934–), who works under the name Yvaral.

Vasari, Giorgio (*b* Arezzo, 30 July 1511; *d* Florence, 27 June 1574). Italian painter, architect, and writer, active mainly in Florence and Rome. In his day he was a leading painter, architect, and artistic impresario, but his activities in these fields have been completely overshadowed by his role as the most important of all artistic biographers. His great book, generally referred to as *Lives of the Artists*, has earned him the title of the father of art history; it is not only the fundamental source of information on Italian *Renaissance art, but also a key document in shaping attitudes about the period for centuries afterwards. (The book was first published in Florence in 1550 as *Le vite de' più eccellenti architetti, pittori, et scultori italiani*—The Lives of the Most Eminent Italian Architects, Painters, and Sculptors; in 1568 there was a second, much enlarged edition, in which the title is slightly changed, the painters being mentioned first. In addition to biographies, the book contains a lengthy introduction dealing with artists' materials and techniques.)

Vasari wrote from a particular aesthetic viewpoint, and his book is not only a collection of biographical information but also a critical history of style. He believed that art is in the first instance imitation of nature and that progress in painting consists in the perfecting of the means of representation. He thought that such representational skills had been taken to high levels in *classical antiquity, that art had then passed through a long period of decline in the Middle Ages, and that it had begun to revive in the 14th century in Tuscany (he was heavily biased in favour of his own region). The main theme of the *Lives* was to set forth this revival—its initiation by *Cimabue and *Giotto, its steady advance at the hands of such artists as *Brunelleschi, *Donatello, and *Masaccio, and its culmination with *Leonardo, *Raphael, and above all *Michelangelo, whom Vasari idolized and whose biography was the only one of a living artist to appear in the first edition of his book (the second edition adds accounts of several artists then living, including Vasari's autobiography). The idea of artistic 'progress' that he promoted subsequently coloured most writing on the period.

Given the wide scope and vast size of the book (the second edition has roughly the same wordage as the Bible), it is not surprising that it contains many errors and contentious points (see, for example, Andrea del *Castagno and Andrea del *Sarto). However, by the standards of the time Vasari was a diligent researcher and he gathered together an enormous amount of invaluable information, which he presented in a lively style, full of memorable anecdotes. Moreover, his qualitative judgements have generally stood the test of time well: the artists and works he most admired are by and large still the ones we most admire today. His book became the model for artistic biographers in other countries, such as van *Mander in the Netherlands, *Sandrart in Germany, and *Palomino in Spain.

As a painter, Vasari was one of the most prolific decorators of his period, but he is not now highly regarded, his work representing the most in-bred and affected kind of *Mannerism. His best-known achievement in this field is probably the decoration (1546) of the grand salon in the Palazzo della Cancelleria, Rome, with scenes celebrating the life of Pope Paul III, commissioned by his grandson Cardinal Alessandro *Farnese. Pressed for quick results by the cardinal, Vasari enlisted a team of assistants and finished the work within 100 days, earning the room its nickname of the Sala dei Cento Giorni. When Michelangelo was told of the remarkable speed with which the work had been accomplished, he is said to have made the withering response 'E si vede' (So it appears). As an architect Vasari has a higher reputation; his most important building is the *Uffizi in Florence, and he designed and decorated his own house in Arezzo, now a museum dedicated to him. Vasari was the first important collector of drawings, using them partly as research material for his biographies, for the insight they gave into the creative process, and he also played the leading role in establishing Florence's Accademia del Disegno (see ACADEMY).

725

Vasnetsov, Viktor (b Lopyal, nr. Vyatka [now Kirov], 15 May 1848; d Moscow, 23 July 1926). Russian painter, illustrator, designer, and architect, active mainly in Moscow. His early paintings were chiefly of contemporary subjects, sometimes involving the urban poor, but from about 1880 he specialized in scenes from Russian history and legend, combining carefully researched details with a feeling for the romance of myth. He is probably best known for the huge, stirring *Bogatyrs* (1881–98, Tretyakov Gal., Moscow), showing three mighty folk heroes keeping watch on the Russian frontier, but his range extended to lyrical scenes from fairy tales (*Alenushka*, 1881, Tretyakov Gal.). Vasnetsov also worked as a portraitist, book illustrator, stage designer, and occasional architect. He designed his own house in Moscow (1894), now a museum dedicated to him, and most memorably the façade of the *Tretyakov Gallery (1902). See also ABRAMTSEVO COLONY and WANDERERS.

Vatican Museums (Musei Vaticani, Rome). Institutions housing the enormous collections of antiquities and works of art accumulated by the papacy since the beginning of the 15th century. As the leaders of the Christian Church the popes have always commanded the services of the best artists of the day, and they have also been continually showered with gifts. The Vatican collections are consequently among the largest and most important in the world, housed in a complex of buildings in the papal palace and elsewhere in the Vatican. There are several separate museums and the visitor to them is also admitted to the exhibition rooms of the Vatican Library and to various suites of *Renaissance painting, of which the most important are the Sistine Chapel, decorated by *Michelangelo and others, and the Stanze, decorated by *Raphael and others.

The museums had their origin with Julius II (Giuliano della *Rovere, ruled 1503–13), who placed some of the most famous works of *antique sculpture in the Cortile del Belvedere (Belvedere Court), accessible to artists, connoisseurs, and scholars. However, it was not until the 18th century that further development took place. Small museums of sacred and pagan art were created in 1756 and 1767 respectively, but the decisive impetus was provided by Popes Clement XIV (1769–74) and Pius VI (1775–99). They built an extension to the Vatican Palace to house classical statuary, and this—named after them as the Museo Pio-Clementino—still forms the heart of the Vatican Museums. It is in a handsome *Neoclassical style that was highly influential on museum architecture elsewhere. The Vatican Museums are still primarily famous for their classical statues, including the *Apollo Belvedere, the *Belvedere Torso, and the *Laocoön, but they also contain great riches in, for example, Egyptian art, jewellery, and vestments. The Pinacoteca (picture gallery) was founded in 1909 and the present building was opened in 1932. It has an impressive if somewhat haphazard collection, devoted mainly to Italian painting of the 13th century to the 17th century. There is also a collection of modern religious art (opened 1973), much of it merely of curiosity value.

Vaughan, Keith (b Selsey, Sussex, 23 Aug. 1912; d London, 4 Nov. 1977). British painter, draughtsman, designer, and writer. In the 1940s, with his friend John *Minton, he was one of the leading exponents of *Neo-Romanticism, characteristic works of this time being coloured drawings of moonlit houses. His later work, in which he concentrated on his favourite theme of the male nude in a landscape setting, became grander and more simplified, moving towards abstraction (*Leaping Figure*, 1951, Tate, London). Vaughan also designed textiles and book-jackets, and he taught part-time at several art schools in London, notably the *Slade. His varied activities brought him critical and financial success, but he felt deep insecurity about his work and his role in life, as is revealed in his book *Journal and Drawings* (1966), extracts from a diary he had begun in 1939 (a new edition appeared in 1989). As well as containing many perceptive comments about art, it gives a remarkably frank (and often amusing) account of his homosexual and masturbatory activities and of the struggle with cancer that led to his suicide. He made 'sex trousers' with a constricting silk codpiece and contrived an electronic masturbating device (his beloved 'black box'), and wrote that although he listed his recreations in the *International Who's Who* as 'Eating and drinking with friends, bathing in the Ionian Sea', what he should say was 'Drinking alone, sexual self-pleasuring with autoerotic devices'.

Vauxcelles, Louis. See FAUVISM.

Vecchietta (Lorenzo di Pietro) (*bapt.* Siena, 11 Aug. 1410; d Siena, 6 June 1480). One of the outstanding Sienese artists of the 15th century, a painter, sculptor, goldsmith, architect, and military engineer. His nickname, meaning 'little old one', first appears in 1442 and repeatedly thereafter in documents relating to him, but its origin is unknown. On stylistic grounds he is assumed to have been a pupil of *Sassetta, but he also came under the influence of Florentine art and his large-scale paintings have a monumentality rare in Siena in the *quattrocento. As a sculptor he worked in wood and marble and late in his career in bronze, this change in medium probably reflecting the influence of *Donatello, who was in Siena 1457–9. *The Risen Christ* (1476, S. Maria della Scala, Siena) has something of Donatello's sinewy expressiveness. Donatello's influence may also account for the strength and plasticity of Vecchietta's later paintings, such as the fresco of *St Catherine* (1461) in the Palazzo Pubblico, Siena (1461), and the triptych of the *Assumption of the Virgin* (c.1462) in Pienza Cathedral. Several of the leading Sienese artists of the next generation were taught by him, including probably *Francesco di Giorgio and *Neroccio de' Landi.

Vecellio, Francesco and **Orazio**. See TITIAN.

veduta. Term (Italian: 'view') applied to a representation of a town or landscape that is essentially topographical, specifically one that is faithful enough to allow the location to be identified (an imaginary but realistic-looking view can be called a *veduta ideata*). Painters of *vedute* (e.g. *Canaletto and *Guardi) are called *vedutisti*.

Veen, Otto van (*b* Leiden, *c*.1556; *d* Brussels, 6 May 1629). Flemish painter. From *c*.1575 to *c*.1580 he was in Italy, where he is said to have been a pupil of Federico *Zuccaro, and after working in various places in Germany and Flanders he settled in Antwerp in about 1592. He was an uninspired *Mannerist painter, but he became busy and successful, his work including portraits, illustrations for *emblem books, and altarpieces inspired by Italian masters such as *Correggio and *Parmigianino (*Mystic Marriage of St Catherine*, 1589, Mus. Royaux, Brussels). His love of Italian art and his scholarly inclinations (he sometimes Latinized his name to Octavius Vaenius) must have been appreciated by *Rubens, who completed his training in van Veen's studio. After Rubens returned from Italy in 1608, van Veen's work looked old-fashioned and his career petered out.

vehicle. The liquid in which *pigment is suspended to form paint—the 'carrier'. The word can be applied to either the *medium or the *diluent, or to a mixture of both; thus the vehicle of *oil painting might be either *linseed oil, or *turpentine, or both together.

Velázquez (or Velasquez), **Diego** (*bapt*. Seville, 6 June 1599; *d* Madrid, 6 Aug. 1660). The greatest painter of the Spanish School, chiefly celebrated as one of the supreme portraitists in world art. He spent most of his career at the court in Madrid, but he grew up in Seville, where in 1610/11 he was apprenticed to *Pacheco (possibly following a brief period of study with *Herrera the Elder). He qualified as a master painter in 1617 and the following year he married Pacheco's daughter.

Velázquez was exceptionally precocious and while he was still in his teens he painted pictures that display commanding presence and complete technical mastery. Pacheco's style in religious paintings was 'dry and insipid' (*Palomino); Velázquez revitalized it by following his master's advice to 'go to nature for everything', and in works such as the *Immaculate Conception* (c.1618, NG, London) and the *Adoration of the Magi* (1619, Prado, Madrid) he developed a more lifelike approach to religious art, in which the figures are treated like portraits rather than *ideal types (his young wife may be the model for the Virgin in both these pictures). The light, too, is realistically observed, even though it has a mysterious, spiritual quality. In their strong *chiaroscuro as well as their naturalism such pictures show an affinity with the work of *Caravaggio and his followers, but the supple, clotted brushwork is already entirely Velázquez's own. In addition to religious pictures, his early work included several *bodegones, a type of *genre scene to which he brought a new seriousness and dignity; the best known among them is *The Waterseller of Seville* (c.1620, Wellington Mus., London), in which the water dripping down the jug shows his remarkable ability to create a sense of almost palpable reality.

In 1622 Velázquez paid a short visit to Madrid, during which he painted a portrait of the poet Luis de Góngora (MFA, Boston). In the following year he was recalled to the capital by Philip IV's (see HABSBURG) chief minister, the Count-Duke Olivares, and painted a portrait of the king (now lost) which pleased Philip so much that he appointed Velázquez one of his court painters and declared that now only he should paint his portrait. Thus, at the age of 24, he suddenly became the country's most prestigious painter, and he kept his position as the king's favourite for the rest of his life.

With his appointment as court painter, the direction of Velázquez's work changed. He entirely abandoned *bodegones*, and although he painted historical, mythological, and religious pictures intermittently throughout his career, he was from now on primarily a portraitist. Technically, too, his work changed as a result of his move to Madrid, his palette lightening and his brushwork becoming broader and more fluid under the influence particularly of the *Titians in the royal collection. Although his portraits of the king and his courtiers are grand and dignified, he humanized the formal tradition of Spanish court portraiture derived from *Mor and *Sánchez Coello, setting his models in more natural poses and giving them greater life and character. The king (who was six years younger than Velázquez) had an extremely high opinion of the artist's personal qualities as well as his artistic skills, and the warmth with which he treated him was considered astonishing, given the stiff etiquette for which the Spanish court was renowned. In 1627 Philip made Velázquez 'Usher of the Chamber', the first of a series of appointments that brought him great prestige but took up much of his time in trivial bureaucratic matters, thus partly accounting for his fairly small output as a painter. He was conscientious in his duties, however, and evidently well suited to them temperamentally: the Italian painter Marco Boschini (1605–81) described him as 'a courtly gentleman of such great dignity as distinguishes any person of authority'.

In 1628–9 *Rubens visited Spain on a diplomatic mission and he and Velázquez became friends. Palomino records that the contact with Rubens 'revived the desire Velázquez had always had to go to Italy', and the king duly gave him permission to travel there. He was in Italy from 1629 to 1631, visiting Genoa, Venice, and Naples, but spending most of his time in Rome. Two major paintings date from this period—*Joseph's Coat* (Escorial) and *The Forge of Vulcan* (Prado), works that show how his brushwork loosened still further under the influence of the great Venetian masters and how his mastery of figure composition matured.

The 1630s and 1640s (before he again left for Italy) were the most productive period of Velázquez's career. His series of royal and court portraits continued and he expanded his range in a series of glorious equestrian portraits (Prado). In these he showed an unprecedented ability to attain complete atmospheric unity between foreground and background in the landscape. Their rhetorical poses are in the *Baroque tradition, but they are without bombast or allegorical embellishments and as portraits are characteristically direct. The same ability to look

beyond external trappings to the human mystery beneath is seen in his incomparable series of portraits of the pitiful court fools (Prado)—dwarfs and idiots whom Philip, like other monarchs, kept for his amusement. Velázquez presents them without any suggestion of caricature, but with pathos and human understanding, as if they too are worthy of his respect.

The most celebrated single work of this middle period of Velázquez's career is not a portrait, however, but a great masterpiece of contemporary history painting, the *Surrender of Breda* (1634–5, Prado), one of a series of twelve pictures by various court artists glorifying the military triumphs of Philip's reign that were executed for the new Buen Retiro Palace in Madrid. The composition is highly organized, but Velázquez creates a remarkable sense of actuality and no earlier picture of a contemporary historical event had seemed so convincing. Characteristically, he concentrates on the human drama of the situation, as Ambrogio Spínola, the chivalrous Spanish commander, receives the key of the town from Justin of Nassau, his vanquished Dutch counterpart, with a superb gesture of magnanimity.

Between 1648 and 1651 Velázquez paid another visit to Italy to purchase paintings and antiquities for the royal collection (he may have been there briefly in 1636 but the evidence is inconclusive). Again, he spent most of the time in Rome, where he painted several portraits, including two of his most celebrated works— *Juan de Pareja* (1650, Met. Mus., New York) and *Pope Innocent X* (1650, Gal. Doria Pamphili, Rome). Juan de Pareja (c.1610–c.1670), who was himself a painter, was Velázquez's mulatto slave (his master granted him his freedom while they were in Rome), and Velázquez painted this portrait because he felt he needed some practice before tackling that of the pope. The *Innocent X* is by common consent one of the world's supreme masterpieces of portraiture, unsurpassed in its breathtaking handling of paint and so incisive in characterization that the pope himself said the picture was 'troppo vero' (too truthful). While in Rome Velázquez fathered an illegitimate son, Antonio, by a widow named Martha, but nothing is known of what became of mother or child. They may have been on Velázquez's mind when he applied for (and was refused) permission to return to Italy in 1657, but his life and work continued to unfold with the same sober dignity and the skeleton in his cupboard remained hidden until 1983, when the documentation revealing his paternity was first published.

In his final years in Madrid, Velázquez continued to acquire new honours (the greatest was being made a knight of the Order of Santiago in 1659) and to reach new heights as a painter. His last portraits are mainly of the new young queen, Mariana of Austria (Philip's second wife, whom he married in 1649), and of the royal children. In these works his brushwork has become increasingly sparkling and free, and the gorgeous clothes the sitters wore (such a change from the sombre costumes of the king and male courtiers) allowed him to show his prowess as a colourist (several examples are in the Kunsthistorisches Museum, Vienna). Velázquez never ceased to base his work on scrutiny of nature, but his means grew increasingly subtle, so that detail is entirely subordinated to overall effect. Thus in his late works space and atmosphere are depicted with unprecedented vividness, but when the pictures are looked at closely the forms dissolve into what Kenneth *Clark called 'a fricassee of beautiful brushstrokes'. As Palomino put it, 'one cannot understand it if standing too close, but from a distance it is a miracle.'

The culmination of Velázquez's career is Las meninas (The Maids of Honour) (c.1656, Prado). It shows him at his easel, with various members of the royal family and their attendants in his studio, but it is not clear whether he has shown himself at work on a portrait of the king and queen (who are reflected in a mirror) when interrupted by the Infanta Margarita and her maids of honour or vice versa. Velázquez's prominence in the picture seems to assert his own importance and his pride in his art, but in the background he has included two pictures (copies of works by Rubens) showing the downfall of mortals who challenge the gods in the arts. Apparently spontaneous but in the highest degree worked out, it is both Velázquez's most complex essay in portraiture and an expression of the high claims he made for the dignity of his art. Luca *Giordano called it 'the Theology of Painting' because 'just as theology is superior to all other branches of knowledge, so is this the greatest example of painting'. Posterity has endorsed his verdict, for in a poll of artists and critics in the Illustrated London News in August 1985, Las meninas was voted—by some margin—'the world's greatest painting'.

The number of good contemporary copies of Velázquez's work indicates that he ran a busy studio, but of his pupils only his son-in-law *Mazo achieved any kind of distinction. As with most Spanish painters, Velázquez remained little known outside his own country until the

Napoleonic Wars brought Spain into the mainstream of European affairs. The opening of the *Prado in 1819, with 44 of his paintings on display, made his work much more accessible than it had ever been before, and from the mid-19th century his technical freedom was an inspiration to many progressive artists, above all *Manet, who regarded him as the greatest of all painters. The bulk of Velázquez's work is still in Spain, and his genius can be fully appreciated only in the Prado, which has most of his key masterpieces. Outside Spain, he is best represented in London—in the National Gallery, which has his only surviving female nude, the Rokeby Venus (c.1648), in the Wellington Museum, and in the Wallace Collection.

Velde, Esaias van de (bapt. Amsterdam, 17 May 1587; bur. The Hague, 18 Nov. 1630). Dutch painter, one of the most important figures in the development of his country's tradition of naturalistic landscape. He was perhaps a pupil of Gillis van *Coninxloo in Amsterdam, and he worked in Haarlem (c.1610–18) and The Hague (1618 onwards). His earliest works are in the *Mannerist tradition, but by 1615 he had already moved away from the panoramic effect and high viewpoint of his predecessors. His fresh brushwork and directness of vision herald the subsequent accomplishment of his pupil Jan van *Goyen and of Salomon van *Ruysdael. In addition to pure landscapes, Esaias painted various figure subjects in landscape settings; he was also a prolific etcher and draughtsman. There were other artists in his family, notably his cousin **Jan van de Velde II** (c.1593–1641), but he was not related to Willem van de *Velde.

Velde, Henry van de (b Antwerp, 3 Apr. 1863; d Zurich, 25 Oct. 1957). Belgian architect, designer, painter, writer, and teacher, one of the chief creators and exponents of the *Art Nouveau style and a key figure in the development of art teaching in the 20th century. He began his career as a painter and in 1888 adopted *Neo-Impressionism. However, he gave up painting soon afterwards—the result of acute self-questioning that followed a nervous collapse in 1889 brought on by the death of his mother—and thereafter devoted himself to architecture and applied art. In 1896 he carried out decorations for Siegfried Bing's Paris shop Maison de l'Art Nouveau, from which the name of the new style derived. From 1902 to 1917 he lived in Weimar, where he was appointed head of the new Kunstgewerbeschule (School of Arts and Crafts). The teaching here was novel in that pupils—instead of studying the art of the past—were encouraged to think in terms of the needs of the modern world. Van de Velde's successor in Weimar was Walter *Gropius, who developed these ideas at the *Bauhaus. In 1917 he moved to Switzerland, then in 1920 the Netherlands, where he began to work for the collector and patron Hélène Kröller-Müller (1869–1939), for whom he later designed the celebrated museum of modern art named after her at Otterlo (1937–54). This shows the much severer style of his later years. In 1926 he returned to Belgium, and taught in Brussels for twenty years before retiring to Switzerland in 1947. He wrote several books on his ideas and also an autobiography, *Geschichte meines Lebens*, posthumously published in 1962.

Velde, Willem van de the Elder (b Leiden, 1611; bur. London, 16 Dec. 1693). Dutch marine painter. He came from a naval family and devoted himself to the drawing and painting of ships. His pictures, which are frequently *grisailles, contain faithful and detailed portraits of vessels (of much value to naval historians) and for a time he was an official artist for the Dutch fleet. In the winter of 1672–3, when the Netherlands were at war with England, he moved to London and entered the service of Charles II; why he left his country at a critical moment in its fortunes remains unclear.

Willem the Younger (bapt. Leiden, 18 Dec. 1633; d London, 6 Apr. 1707), his son, is one of the most illustrious of all marine painters. He was the pupil of his father and of Simon de *Vlieger. Like his father, he gave very accurate portrayals of ships, but he is distinguished from him by his feeling for atmosphere and his majestic sense of composition. He left Amsterdam for England with his father in 1672–3 and in 1674 Charles II gave them a yearly retaining fee of £100 each; the father received his 'for taking and making draughts of sea fights' and the son 'for putting the said draughts into colours for our particular use'. They did not switch their allegiance to England completely; both subsequently painted pictures of naval battles for the Dutch as well as the English market. Willem the Younger's influence, however, was particularly great in England, where the whole tradition of marine painting stemmed from him.

Adriaen (bapt. Amsterdam, 30 Nov. 1636; bur. Amsterdam, 21 Jan. 1672), Willem II's younger brother, was a versatile and prolific artist in spite of his short life. He is said to have been a pupil of his father and of Jan *Wijnants. His output

included various types of landscapes (most notably some fresh and atmospheric beach scenes) and also religious and mythological works, portraits, and animal pictures. He also made etchings and often painted the figures into the landscapes of other artists, notably *Hobbema and *Ruisdael.

Vellert, Dirk (b ?Amsterdam, c.1480/90; d Antwerp, c.1549). Netherlandish artist, best known as a designer of stained glass. He was active in Antwerp, where he became a master of the Guild of St Luke in 1511. Much of his work, richly ornamented with garlands, masks, vases, and other classical motifs, was exported, and some of the windows in King's College Chapel, Cambridge, were made from his designs (it is not known whether he visited England). Vellert was also an engraver, his prints owing a good deal to *Dürer and *Lucas van Leyden; most of them are precisely dated, with the day and the month as well as the year. Several paintings have also been attributed to him, on the basis of their similarity to his prints and his documented windows.

vellum. See PARCHMENT.

Veneto, Bartolommeo. See BARTOLOMMEO VENETO.

Veneziano, Domenico. See DOMENICO VENEZIANO.

Venne, Adriaen van de (b Delft, 1589; d The Hague, 12 Nov. 1662). Dutch painter and draughtsman, active first in Middelburg and then in The Hague, where he settled in 1625. His parents were from Flanders (they had fled north to escape religious strife) and his early works show Flemish influence, being somewhat in the tradition of Jan *Brueghel's, with numerous small figures inhabiting wide landscapes with high horizons. One of the most interesting of these paintings is *Fishing for Souls* (1614, Rijksmuseum, Amsterdam), an allegory of the conflict between Catholics and Protestants. After his move to The Hague he painted various subjects, his most original works being moralizing pictures in *grisaille of poor people such as beggars, vagabonds, and peasants. Van de Venne made drawings in a similar vein for book illustrations (his brother was a publisher and he wrote poetry himself).

Venturi, Adolfo (b Modena, 4 Sept. 1856; d Santa Margherita Ligure, nr. Genoa, 10 June 1941). The most distinguished Italian art historian of his generation. He taught at the university of

Rome from 1890 to 1931, and in 1901 he was appointed professor there—the first holder of a chair in art history at an Italian university. His main work is the monumental *Storia dell'arte italiana* (11 vols. in 25 parts, 1901–40; a separate index volume was published in 1975). This covers Italian art from Early Christian times up to the end of the 16th century in great detail, with a vast number of illustrations, and it is still much used by scholars. Venturi wrote several other books and he founded *L'arte* (1898), one of the major Italian art-historical periodicals. His son **Lionello Venturi** (*b* Modena, 25 Apr. 1885; *d* Rome, 14 Aug. 1961) was professor of the history of art at the university of Turin from 1915 to 1931, but resigned because of his opposition to Fascism and moved to Paris and then the USA. After returning to Italy in 1945, he taught at the university of Rome. Like his father, he was a prolific writer, his books including *History of Art Criticism* (1936) and studies of *Caravaggio (1911 and 1952), *Cézanne (2 vols., 1936: the standard catalogue of his works for many years), and *Giorgione (1913).

Venus de Milo. A marble statue of Aphrodite (Venus), the best known of all ancient statues, found on the small Greek island of Melos (or Milos) in 1820 and now in the Louvre, Paris. A plinth (now lost) that was found with the statue was signed ' . . . andros [Alexandros or Agasandros] of Antioch on the Maeander', but nothing is known of the sculptor. Originally the statue was thought to date from the *Classical age of Greek sculpture, but it is now put appreciably later—*c.*100 BC— and is thought to be a sophisticated combination of older styles: the goddess's head derives from the later 5th century BC, her nudity from the 4th century, and her spiral, omnifacial posture from the *Hellenistic age.

The *Venus de Milo* arrived in the Louvre (1821) soon after the *Medici Venus* had been returned to Italy (1815), and its enormous fame stemmed from French determination to persuade the world that they had gained a greater treasure than they had lost; Martin Robertson (*A History of Greek Art*, 1975) writes that its 'extraordinary reputation, which started by propaganda, has become perpetuated by habit'. Many 19th-century critics went into raptures about the figure, which was thought to represent the apogee of female beauty, perfectly combining grandeur with gracefulness, but *Renoir described it as a 'big gendarme'. The statue's arms are missing and many conjectures have been made as to what the goddess might have been holding: it has been suggested for

example that she is intended as Venus Victrix, and so would have been shown with the golden apple presented to her by Paris when he adjudged her more beautiful than her rivals Juno and Minerva.

'Venus of Willendorf' (Naturhistorisches Mus., Vienna). A prehistoric limestone figurine of a naked, faceless, obese woman, discovered at Willendorf, Austria, in 1908. It is 11 cm (4¼ in) high (small enough to hold in the hand) and is generally dated to about 30,000 BC. There are traces of red colouring on the stone. More than 100 such prehistoric 'Venus' figures have been discovered, in places ranging from Italy to Siberia, but this is far and away the most famous of them, for whereas the others tend to be very heavily stylized, here there is an extraordinary sense of earthy vitality: 'she does not impress us as an abstraction, an idea or ideal of the female and the fecund; rather one feels, in spite of facelessness and gross exaggeration, that this is actual woman' (N. K. Sandars, *Prehistoric Art in Europe*, 1968). Such figures are presumed to have been made as symbols of fertility or fecundity, intended to endow or ensure fruitfulness in some form.

Verhaecht (or **van Haecht**), **Tobias** (*b* Antwerp, 1561; *d* Antwerp, 1631). Flemish painter, now remembered almost solely because he was *Rubens's first teacher. Apart from a sojourn in Italy as a young man, Verhaecht spent his career in Antwerp. He was a landscape specialist, working in a style similar to Paul *Bril's, and he had no detectable influence on his great pupil. His son **Willem van Haecht** (1593–1637) was a painter, best known for pictures of art collections (*The Picture Gallery of Cornelis van der Geest*, 1628, Rubenshuis, Antwerp).

Verhaegen, Pieter Jozef (Pierre-Joseph Verhagen) (*b* Aarschot, 1728; *d* Louvain, 1811). Flemish painter. He specialized in religious paintings and was his country's most vigorous upholder of the tradition of the *Baroque altarpiece in the 18th century. His robust, down-to-earth style owed more to *Jordaens than to *Rubens or van *Dyck.

Verhulst, Mayken. See BRUEGEL and COECKE VAN AELST.

Verhulst, Rombout (*b* Mechelen [Malines], 15 Jan. 1624; *bur.* The Hague, 27 Nov. 1698). Flemish sculptor active mainly in Holland. In the 1650s he was the most important assistant to Artus *Quellin in the sculptural decoration of the town hall in Amsterdam. By 1663 he had settled in The Hague, where he became a leading sculptor of busts and tombs. The noble and sensitively cut monument to Admiral Michiel de Ruyter (1681) in the Niewe Kerk in Amsterdam is perhaps his masterpiece.

verism. An extreme form of *realism, in which the artist makes it his aim to reproduce with rigid truthfulness the exact appearance of his subject, repudiating all imaginative interpretation. The term has been applied, for example, to certain Roman portrait sculptures. In a different sense, the term 'Veristic *Surrealism' is sometimes applied to pictures that claim to reproduce hallucination in exact and unselective detail; *Dalí is the best-known exponent of works of this type.

Vermeer, Jan (*bapt.* Delft, 31 Oct. 1632; *bur.* Delft, 16 Dec. 1675). Dutch painter. Among the great Dutch artists of the 17th century, he is now second in renown only to *Rembrandt, but he made little mark during his lifetime and then long languished in obscurity. Almost all the contemporary references to him are in colourless official documents and his career is in many ways enigmatic. As far as is known, he lived all his life in his native Delft and rarely made even local journeys outside it. He became a member of the painters' guild there in 1653 and was twice elected 'hooftman' (headman), but it is not known who taught him. His name is often linked with that of Carel *Fabritius, but it is doubtful if he can have been Vermeer's teacher in the formal sense. This distinction may belong to Leonaert *Bramer, although there is no similarity between their work; Balthasar van der *Ast, too, has been suggested as a candidate.

Only about 35 to 40 paintings by Vermeer are known, and although some early works may have been destroyed in the disastrous Delft gunpowder explosion of 1654, it is unlikely that the figure was ever much larger; this is because most of the Vermeers mentioned in early sources can be identified with surviving pictures, whilst only a few pictures now attributed to him are not mentioned in these sources—thus there are few loose ends. This small output may be at least partially explained by the fact that he almost certainly earned most of his living by means other than painting. His father kept an inn and was a picture dealer and Vermeer very likely inherited both businesses. In spite of this he had grave financial troubles (he had a large family to support—his wife bore him fifteen children, eleven of whom survived him). His

money problems increased after the French invasion of 1672, which devastated the Dutch economy, and his widow was declared insolvent the year after his death.

Only three of Vermeer's paintings are dated—*The Procuress* (1656, Gemäldegalerie, Dresden), *The Astronomer* (1668, Louvre, Paris), and its companion *The Geographer* (1669, Städelsches Kunstinstitut, Frankfurt). (Another signed and dated work, *St Praxedis Mopping up the Blood of the Martyrs* of 1655, appeared in the 1960s, but its authenticity has been questioned. It is in a private collection.) It is difficult to fit his other paintings into a convincing chronology, but his work nevertheless divides into three fairly clear phases. The first is represented by only two works—*Christ in the House of Mary and Martha* (NG, Edinburgh) and *Diana and her Companions* (Mauritshuis, The Hague)—both probably dating from a year or two before *The Procuress*. They are so different from Vermeer's other works—in their comparatively large scale, their subject matter, and their handling—that *Diana and her Companions* was for a time attributed to the obscure Jan *Vermeer of Utrecht. *The Procuress* marks the transition to the middle phase of Vermeer's career, for although it is fairly large and warm in tonality—like the two history paintings—it is a contemporary life scene, as were virtually all Vermeer's pictures from now on.

In the central part of his career (into which most of his work falls) Vermeer painted those serene and harmonious images of domestic life that for their beauty of composition, brushwork, and treatment of light raise him into a different class from any other Dutch *genre painter. The majority show one or two figures in a room lit from the onlooker's left, engaged in domestic or recreational tasks. The predominant colours are yellow, blue, and grey, arranged in flawlessly cool harmonies, and the compositions have a purity and dignity that confer on them an impact out of relation to their small size. In reproduction his pictures can look quite smooth and detailed, but Vermeer often applies the paint broadly, with variations in texture suggesting the play of light with exquisite vibrancy—Jan *Veth aptly described his paint surface as looking like 'crushed pearls melted together'. From this period of Vermeer's greatest achievement also date his only landscape—the incomparable *View of Delft* (Mauritshuis), in which he surpassed even the greatest of his specialist contemporaries in lucidity and truth of atmosphere—and his much-loved *Little Street*

(Rijksmuseum, Amsterdam). Another painting of this period is somewhat larger in size and unusual in subject for him—*The Artist's Studio* (KH Mus., Vienna), in which Vermeer shows a back view of a painter, perhaps a suitably enigmatic self-portrait.

In the third and final phase of his career Vermeer's work lost some of its magic as it became somewhat harder. There are still wonderful passages of paint in all his late works, but the utter naturalness of his finest works is gone. The only one of his paintings that might be considered a failure, the *Allegory of Faith* (Met. Mus., New York), belongs to this period. His wife was a Catholic and he may well have been converted to her religion, but this rather lumbering figure shows he was not at ease with the trappings of *Baroque allegory. There are symbolic references in other paintings by him, but they all—except for this one—make sense on a straightforward naturalistic level.

No drawings by Vermeer are known and knowledge of his working methods has largely to be deduced from close examination of his paintings. It is virtually certain, however, that he sometimes made use of a *camera obscura; the exaggerated perspective in some of his pictures (in which foreground figures or objects loom unexpectedly large) and the way in which sparkling highlights appear slightly out of focus are effects duplicated by unsophisticated lenses. The scientist Antony van Leeuwenhoek (1632–1723), celebrated for his work with microscopes, became the executor of Vermeer's estate and it may well have been an interest in optics that brought them together.

Vermeer's paintings were admired in his lifetime, but after his death his name quickly passed into obscurity. During the 18th century his pictures were sometimes attributed to other artists who were better known at the time, such as Frans van *Mieris, and in 1833 the British picture dealer John Smith (1781–1855), a pioneer in the scholarly study of Dutch art, wrote of Vermeer: 'This painter is so little known, by reason of the scarcity of his works, that it is quite inexplicable how he attained the excellence many of them exhibit.' The key figure in rediscovering Vermeer was Théophile *Thoré, who published a lengthy series of articles on him in the *Gazette des beaux-arts* in 1866 and memorably dubbed him 'the Sphinx of Delft'.

Vermeer (or **van der Meer**) **van Haarlem.** Family of Dutch painters. Four members of the family, from successive generations, were called Jan Vermeer van Haarlem. The titles of Elder and Younger have become attached to the second and third, very little being known about the other two.

Jan the Elder (1628–91) made panoramic landscapes of the dunes and woods around Haarlem. During the 19th century he was confused with the great Jan *Vermeer of Delft, but the name is the only thing they have in common. Jacob van *Ruisdael and Philips *Koninck have more affinity with his work, but he was a much less powerful artist than either of these.

His son **Jan the Younger** (1656–1705) was a pupil of his father and of Nicolaes *Berchem and was likewise a landscape painter. He spent some time in Italy and most of his pictures are idyllic views of the south.

There was also a **Jan Vermeer** of Utrecht (c.1630–after 1692), a *genre and portrait painter. The works of all three artists are fairly rare.

Vermeyen, Jan Cornelisz. (*b* Berverwijk, nr. Haarlem, c.1500; *d* Brussels, c.1559). Netherlandish painter, engraver, and tapestry designer. He spent much of his career working for members of the *Habsburg family—for Margaret of Austria and Mary of Hungary, successively regent of the Netherlands, and then the Emperor Charles V. In their service he travelled extensively, visiting Germany, Italy, Spain, and also Tunis, where he accompanied Charles on his successful campaign to capture the port in 1535. Later (c.1546–54) Vermeyen designed a set of twelve huge tapestries of the campaign; the *cartoons are in the Kunsthistorisches Museum, Vienna, and the original set of tapestries is in the Royal Palace, Madrid. His work also included portraits (similar in style to those of Jan van *Scorel), religious paintings, and engravings.

Vernet. Family of French painters, three members of which attained distinction. **Joseph Vernet** (*b* Avignon, 14 Aug. 1714; *d* Paris, 3 Dec. 1789) was one of the leading French landscape painters of his period. From 1734 to 1753 he worked in Rome, where he was influenced by the light and atmosphere of *Claude and also by the more wild and dramatic art of Salvator *Rosa. With Hubert *Robert, he became a leading exponent of a type of idealized and somewhat sentimental landscape that had a great vogue at this time. Vernet was particularly celebrated for his paintings of the seashore and ports, and on returning to Paris in 1753 he was commissioned by Louis XV to paint a series of the seaports of France. He produced fifteen (more were planned but not executed), now divided between the Louvre and the Musée Maritime, Paris. His son Antoine-Charles-Horace, known as **Carle Vernet** (*b* Bordeaux, 14 Aug. 1758; *d* Paris, 27 Nov. 1836), painted large battle pictures for Napoleon, notably the *Battle of Marengo* (1806, Versailles), and after the restoration of the monarchy he became official painter to Louis XVIII, for whom he did racing and hunting scenes. He married the daughter of Jean-Michel *Moreau. Their son **Horace Vernet** (*b* Paris, 30 June 1789; *d* Paris, 17 Jan. 1863) was one of the most prolific of French military painters, specializing in scenes of the Napoleonic era. A portrait of Napoleon and four battle pieces by him are in the National Gallery, London. He also produced animal and oriental subjects. From 1828 to 1834 he was director of the French Academy in Rome.

vernicle (or **sudarium**). 'The cloth or kerchief, alleged to have belonged to St Veronica, with which, according to legend, she wiped the face of Christ on his way to Calvary, and upon which his features were miraculously impressed' (*OED*), or, by extension, any picture of Christ's face shown on a cloth or veil in allusion to the story. A relic that purports to be the original vernicle has been in St Peter's, Rome, since the late 8th century; other places have also claimed possession of the original. The name Veronica was said in the Middle Ages to derive from *vera icon* ('true image'), and it is likely that the saint is purely fictitious and was invented to explain the relic. The alternative name, sudarium, is Latin for handkerchief or towel. In art, the vernicle was a popular subject from the 15th to the 17th century. Usually it is shown as being carried by St Veronica, although *Zurbarán, for example, painted several pictures showing the cloth by itself; Claude *Mellan likewise depicted the cloth alone in his celebrated engraving of the subject (1642).

Veronese, Bonifazio. See BONIFAZIO VERONESE.

Veronese, Paolo (Paolo Caliari) (*b* Verona, ?1528; *d* Venice, 19 Apr. 1588). Italian painter. His nickname derives from his native city of Verona. He trained there with the undistinguished Antonio Badile (*c.*1518–60), whose daughter he later married, but from about 1553 he was based in Venice and he is considered a member of the Venetian School. With *Tintoretto he became the dominant figure in Venetian painting in the generation after *Titian and he had many major commissions. Although he was sometimes in direct competition with Tintoretto, generally they worked for rather different markets and they seem to have been on good terms personally. Both of them were at their best on a large scale, but whereas Tintoretto concentrated on religious pictures, Veronese also did numerous secular commissions. Some of his finest work was produced outside Venice and in fresco, whereas Tintoretto worked almost exclusively in the city itself and in oils. Stylistically they had little in common: Tintoretto's most characteristic paintings are intensely emotional, with the drama played out in a dark, brooding atmosphere; Veronese preferred the clear light of day and subjects that made their impact through pomp rather than passion.

Veronese established a distinctive style early in his career and thereafter developed relatively little. Few of his paintings are dated or can be reliably dated, so his chronology is difficult to construct. Similarly, because he had such a highly organized studio and his output was so large, there can be problems in distinguishing the work of his own hand. Nevertheless, his status and achievement are clear. He was one of the greatest of all decorative artists, delighting in painting enormous pageant-like scenes that bear witness to the material splendour of Venice in its Golden Age. Marble columns and costumes of velvet and satin abound in his work, and he used a sumptuous but delicate palette in which pale blue, orange, silvery white, and lemon yellow predominate. In his religious works his penchant was for feast scenes from the Bible.

Veronese's love of richness and ornament got him into trouble with the Inquisition in a famous incident in 1573 when he was interrogated about a painting of the *Last Supper* that he had crowded with such irrelevant and irreverent figures as 'a buffoon with a parrot on his wrist . . . a servant whose nose was bleeding . . . dwarfs and similar vulgarities'. Veronese staunchly defended his right to artistic licence: 'I received the commission to decorate the picture as I saw fit. It is large and, it seemed to me, it could hold many figures.' He was instructed to make changes, but the matter was resolved by simply changing the title of the picture so that it represented a less solemn meal from the Bible, the *Feast in the House of Levi*. It was painted for the refectory of the monastery of SS. Giovanni e Paolo, Venice, and is now in the Accademia.

Veronese's secular works include the delightfully light-hearted frescos (including *illusionistic architecture and enchanting landscapes) decorating the Villa Barbaro at Maser, near Treviso (*c*.1561), a series of four canvases, *Allegory of Love* (*c*.1575, NG, London), probably painted for the Emperor Rudolf II (see HABSBURG), and the resplendent *Triumph of Venice* (*c*.1585) on the ceiling of the Hall of the Great Council in the Doges' Palace, Venice. He also painted portraits. His studio was carried on after his death by his brother **Benedetto Caliari** (1538–98) and his sons **Carlo** (*c*.1567–92/6) and **Gabriele** (1568–1631). He had no significant pupils, but his influence on Venetian painting was important, particularly in the 18th century, when he was an inspiration to the masters of the second great flowering of decorative painting in the city, above all *Tiepolo.

Verrio, Antonio (*b* Lecce, *c*.1639; *d* Hampton Court, Middlesex [now Greater London], 15 June 1707). Italian decorative painter who settled in England in 1671/2. He is said to have trained in Venice, and he worked in Naples and France before moving to England; there he enjoyed an enormously successful and well-remunerated career as the first of the foreign artists who dominated the fairly brief period when *Baroque wall and ceiling painting was in vogue in the country. He was much employed at royal buildings—Whitehall Palace, Windsor Castle, and Hampton Court—and also worked at great aristocratic houses such as Burghley and Chatsworth. In 1684 Charles II appointed him 'our chief and first painter' in succession to *Lely. His wealth and prestige were based on his self-assertiveness and the lack of native talent in his field rather than on his skills as an artist, for his work is at best mediocre (and sometimes dismal) judged by European standards; Sir Oliver Millar writes that his 'figure-drawing is often almost ludicrously clumsy'. *Laguerre, his one-time assistant, was a better painter but had less worldly success. The two artists are indissolubly linked because of Alexander Pope's famous lines: 'On painted ceilings you devoutly stare, | Where sprawl the saints of Verrio or Laguerre' (*Epistle to the Earl of Burlington*, 1731).

Verrocchio, Andrea del (Andrea di Cioni) (*b* Florence, *c*.1435; *d* Venice, June/July 1488). Florentine sculptor, painter, and metalworker, one of the outstanding Italian artists of his period. His nickname—Verrocchio means 'true eye'—was given to him not because of his sharpness of vision, but evidently because early in his career he worked for a family of that name. He is said to have studied in *Donatello's workshop, but his main training was as a goldsmith, and delicacy of craftsmanship is one of the salient features of his work. Only one work in precious metal by him survives, however—a silver *relief of the *Beheading of John the Baptist* (1477–80), done for the Baptistery in Florence and now in the Cathedral Museum. His major activity was as a sculptor, principally in bronze, but also in marble and terracotta, and his two most famous works rank with the statues of Donatello that inspired them among the great masterpieces of Italian sculpture, whilst also showing the great differences in approach between the two artists. Verrocchio's *David* (*c*.1475, Bargello, Florence) is more refined, but less broodingly intense than Donatello's *David* in the same museum, and Verrocchio's masterpiece, the equestrian statue of the *condottiere* Bartolommeo Colleoni in Venice (begun 1481, cast after Verrocchio's death, and unveiled in 1496), has a magnificent sense of movement and swagger, but less of the heroic dignity of Donatello's *Gattamelata* statue in Padua.

It is much harder to assess Verrocchio's stature as a painter, as very few works exist that can be convincingly assigned to his own hand. Nevertheless numerous paintings came from his workshop, which was the largest in Florence at this time, and he trained distinguished painters, most notably *Leonardo da Vinci, who assisted his master with the *Baptism of Christ* (*c*.1470, Uffizi, Florence), one of the few paintings indisputably by Verrocchio. Leonardo took his superb craftsmanship from Verrocchio and also shared his fascination with two contrasting types—the tough old warrior (as in the Colleoni Monument) and the epicene youth (as in the *David*). Leonardo's enormous fame has tended to cast a shadow over Verrocchio, but nevertheless he is generally regarded as the greatest Italian sculptor between Donatello and *Michelangelo.

Vertue, George (*b* London, 17 Nov. 1684; *d* London, 24 July 1756). English engraver and antiquarian. He was a prolific engraver of portraits and antiquarian subjects (he was appointed official engraver to the Society of Antiquaries in 1717), but he is important chiefly for the voluminous notes he collected relating to the history of art in England (now in the British Library, London). After his death they were bought by Horace *Walpole, who used them as a basis for his *Anecdotes of Painting in England* (1762–71), and the notebooks themselves—an invaluable storehouse of information—were published in six volumes, plus an index, in 1930–50.

vesica piscis. See MANDORLA.

Veth, Jan (*b* Dordrecht, 18 May 1864; *d* Amsterdam, 1 July 1925). Dutch painter, draughtsman, printmaker, poet, and writer on art, a leading figure in the Dutch art world of his time. His best-known book is his monograph on *Rembrandt, originally published to mark the 300th anniversary of the painter's birth in 1606. As an artist he worked mainly as a portraitist (in drawing and lithography as well as painting). His sitters included many distinguished Dutch contemporaries, but he also portrayed people from humble walks of life.

Victoria, Queen. See ROYAL COLLECTION.

Victoria and Albert Museum (V&A), London. Museum housing the world's greatest collection of *applied art as well as a large and varied collection of *fine art. It was the brainchild of Prince Albert and grew out of the *Great Exhibition (1851), the profits from which were used to buy a site in South Kensington for a cultural centre of museums and colleges. Whilst the site was being developed, the nucleus of the collection, consisting of objects of applied art bought from the Great Exhibition, was temporarily displayed at Marlborough House and named the Museum of Manufactures. This opened in 1852 and the following year it was renamed the Museum of Ornamental Art. At this time the Central School of Practical Art (which became the *Royal College of Art) was also based in Marlborough House. In 1857 both institutions moved to South Kensington, where the museum collections soon expanded greatly in range and size. A new building on the same site was begun in 1899, designed by Sir Aston Webb, and at the ceremony of laying the foundation stone by Queen Victoria, the name of the museum was changed to The Victoria and Albert Museum. The building was opened by King Edward VII in 1909; at this time the scientific collections were moved to the nearby Science Museum.

Prince Albert's ideal when he conceived the museum was to improve the standard of design in Britain by making the finest models available for study, and the first director, Sir Henry Cole (1808–82), echoed this when he declared his policy was 'to assemble a splendid collection of objects representing the application of fine arts to manufacture'. However, the collections have—through a flood of acquisitions—become extraordinarily diverse, and a later director, Sir Roy Strong (1935–), has written that 'Any visitor to the Victoria and Albert Museum today is likely to be bemused as to what exactly is the central thread that animates these discrepant if marvellous collections. The answer is that there is none. For over a century the Museum has proved an extremely capacious handbag.' It incorporates, for example, the national collections of post-*classical sculpture (excluding modern, the province of the *Tate), of British *miniatures, of *watercolours, and English silversmiths' work. The National Art Library is also part of the museum. There are great collections of ceramics, furniture, and musical instruments, and oriental art is strongly represented. The celebrated highlights include *Raphael's tapestry *cartoons (on loan from the Royal Collection), which form the most important ensemble of High *Renaissance art outside Italy, and the collection of *Constable's work—the largest anywhere (the bulk of it was presented by his daughter).

Victory of Samothrace. Celebrated larger-than-life Greek marble statue (Louvre, Paris) representing winged Victory (Nike) alighting on the bows of a galley. The figure, discovered on the Greek island of Samothrace in 1863, is lithely outstretched and draped with magnificent swirls. It was erected around 200 BC above a rocky pool, presumably to celebrate a victory in a sea battle; it showed its best view obliquely and from below, and now is appropriately and dramatically placed at the top of the main staircase in the Louvre.

Video art. A broad term applied to works created by visual artists in which video and television equipment and technology are used in any of various ways. Wolf *Vostell incorporated working television sets in *assemblages in 1959, but the creator of Video art as a genre is usually regarded as Nam June Paik (1932–), a Korean musician, *Performance artist, and sculptor, who settled in New York in 1964 and acquired a portable Sony video recorder in 1965 as soon as this new equipment was available there. He is said to have made his first recording on the day he bought the recorder and to have shown the tape the same evening at an artists' club, the Café-a-Go-Go. Paik had trained as a pianist, and after he turned to video he often collaborated with the cellist Charlotte Moorman (1940–94), notably in *Bra for Living Sculpture* (1969), in which she played her instrument whilst wearing a bra incorporating two miniature television screens (predictably dubbed 'boob tubes'). (Moorman was arrested for indecent exposure whilst performing in another Paik work.)

Whereas Paik sees himself as an entertainer (he has often appeared on television chat shows), another well-known specialist in Video art, the American Bill Viola (1951–), is more serious—his detractors might say portentous—in tone. A representative work is *To Pray without Ceasing* (1992), which Viola describes as 'a contemporary "book of hours" and image vigil to the infinite day, functioning as an unfolding sequence of prayers for the city'. It consists of a twelve-hour cycle of images accompanied by a recording of a voice reciting poetry by Walt Whitman. 'The images are projected continuously, 24 hours a day, seven days a week,' comments Viola. 'During the day, sunlight washes out the image and only the voice is present. The video playback is synchronized to the time of day by computer.' Rapid advances in computer and video technology have encouraged many artists to work in the field, which became highly fashionable in the 1990s; the *Turner Prize was won by Video artists in 1996, 1997, and 1999.

Vien, Joseph-Marie (*b* Montpellier, 18 June 1716; *d* Paris, 27 Mar. 1809). French painter. He won the *Prix de Rome in 1743 and was in Rome from 1744 to 1750. At this time, excavations at Herculaneum and Pompeii were causing great excitement in the art world, and Vien's interest in the ancient Roman paintings that were unearthed helped him to gain a reputation (partly self-promoted) as a pioneer of the *Neoclassical style. He was enthusiastic for the ideas of *Winckelmann, but his classicism was of a very superficial kind; his most characteristic works are sentimental *genre or allegorical pictures with pseudo-antique trappings (*The Cupid Seller*, 1763, Château de Fontainebleau). Nevertheless, he gauged the taste of the time well and had a career of exemplary success, becoming director of the French Academy in Rome (1775–81) and first painter to the king (1789). In spite of this royal appointment, he survived the Revolution and was ennobled by Napoleon in 1808. He had many pupils, of whom the most important was J.-L. *David. His son **Joseph-Marie Vien the Younger** (1762–1848) was also a painter, mainly of portraits.

Vienna Actionists (or **Viennese Actionism**) (Wiener Aktionismus). Names applied to a group of Austrian *Performance artists who worked together in the 1960s and who represent the most unsavoury, sadomasochistic trends in the genre. The three main members of the group were Gunter Brus (1938–), Otto Muehl

(1925–), and Hermann Nitsch (1938–), who first collaborated in 1961 and in 1966 began calling themselves the Institut für Direkte Kunst (Institute for Immediate Art). Other people associated with them included Rudolf *Schwarzkogler. The early work of the group had included crude *assemblages and *Action paintings, from which they progressed to deliberately extreme and provocative performances, typically involving substances such as blood and excrement and often involving nude performers. The titles of some of Muehl's 'actions' give a flavour of their content: 'Penis Action' (1963); 'Christmas Action: A Pig is Slaughtered in Bed' (1969); 'Action with Goose' (1971). He often submitted himself to degradation and humiliation, as in 'Libi' (1969), in which a broken egg was dripped into his mouth from the vagina of a menstruating woman. This kind of performance led to the arrest of the participants on several occasions. Nitsch was the chief spokesman of the group. He maintained that such work could bring liberation from violence through catharsis.

Vienna Genesis (Österreichische Nationalbibliothek, Vienna). A fragmentary *Byzantine illuminated manuscript of the Book of Genesis, usually dated to the 6th century. It was once generally thought to be the oldest surviving illustrated biblical manuscript, and although various fragments are now considered earlier, it remains one of the most precious survivals of its time. It has been intensively studied, but there is no agreement about its origins; David Talbot Rice (*Byzantine Art*, 1968) writes that 'it has been assigned . . . to practically every region in the Christian world except Greece'. The material is purple parchment and each page is essentially divided in half—the text, in silver ink, occupying the upper part, and an illustration or group of illustrations the lower.

Vigarny, Felipe (Philippe Biguerny) (*b* Langres, ?*c*.1470/5; *d* Toledo, 10 Nov. 1542). Burgundian-born sculptor who spent all his known career in Spain. He is first documented in 1498, in Burgos, when he contracted to carve three large stone reliefs of Christ's Passion for the retrochoir of the cathedral. They show Italian influence and are regarded as heralding the *Renaissance in Spain. Vigarny worked in various other places in Castile, sometimes in partnership with Alonso *Berruguete or Diego de *Siloé. His work is uneven, and 'in contrast to Berruguete, [he] was a good craftsman rather than a great artist' (George Kubler and Martin

Soria, *Art and Architecture in Spain and Portugal and their American Dominions: 1500–1800*, 1959).

Vigée-Lebrun, Élisabeth (*b* Paris, 16 Apr. 1755; *d* Paris, 30 Mar. 1842). French portrait painter, daughter of the pastellist **Louis Vigée** (1715–67), from whom she received her first lessons. Renowned for her beauty, wit, and charm as well as for her talent, she had a highly successful career, with many eminent sitters, notably Queen Marie-Antoinette; she portrayed the queen numerous times (initially in 1778, KH Mus., Vienna) and they became friends. On the outbreak of the Revolution in 1789 her royal connections became dangerous and she left France with her daughter, leaving behind her husband, the picture dealer Jean-Baptiste Lebrun, to whom she was unhappily married (he stole her earnings to fuel his gambling). She worked in Italy (1789–93), Vienna (1793–4), and St Petersburg (1795–1801), and her graceful, charming, pleasingly sentimental, and delicately executed portraits won her distinguished patronage wherever she went; she was also admitted to several *academies. In 1802 she returned to Paris, but she disliked the Napoleonic regime and worked in England in 1803–5. She then settled permanently in France, subsequently making only short visits abroad and painting only sporadically. Her memoirs (3 vols., 1835–7) give a lively picture of the Europe of her day as well as an account of her own works, and vividly demonstrate what a redoubtable woman she was: 'on the day that my daughter was born I never left my studio and I went on working . . . in the intervals between labour pains.'

Vigeland, Gustav (*b* Mandal, 11 Apr. 1869; *d* Oslo, 12 Mar. 1943). The most famous of Norwegian sculptors. He studied in Oslo and Copenhagen and then (1892–5) in Paris and Italy, spending a few months with *Rodin. At this time he worked in a painstakingly naturalistic style, but in 1900 he began studying medieval sculpture in preparation for restoration work on Trondheim Cathedral and this led to his work becoming expressively stylized. In the same year he made his first sketches for the massive project that occupied much of his energies for the rest of his life (it was completed the year after his death)—a series of allegorical groups at Frogner Park, Oslo. Originally only a fountain was planned, but with the help of assistants he went on to create numerous other groups, including a 17-m (55-ft) high column composed of intertwining bodies. The symbolism of the scheme is not clear, but essentially it represents 'a statement of the doubt, disillusion, and physical decline that beset humanity in its passage through this world' (George Heard Hamilton, *Painting and Sculpture in Europe: 1880–1940*, 1967). Reactions to the whole megalomaniac conception, involving scores of bronze and granite figures, have been mixed, some critics finding it stupendous, others tasteless and monotonous.

vignette. Term now most commonly applied to an illustration or design (especially a photograph) that fades into the space around it without a definite border. It is also applied to any small illustration placed at the beginning or end of a chapter or book, to fill up a space, and to foliage ornament (French: *vigne*, 'vine') in a manuscript, book, or decorative carving. Vignettes at the beginning of a chapter are sometimes called headpieces and those at the end tailpieces (a type particularly associated with *Bewick).

Vignon, Claude (*b* Tours, 19 May 1593; *d* Paris, 10 May 1670). French painter, active mainly in Paris. His highly eclectic style was largely formed in Italy, where he worked *c*.1616–*c*.1622, and his openness to very diverse influences was later fuelled by his activities as a picture dealer. Paradoxically, in view of his varied sources of inspiration, his style is the most distinctive of any French painter of his generation—highly coloured and often bizarrely expressive. *Elsheimer and the *Caravaggisti were strong influences on his handling of light, and his richly encrusted brushwork has striking affinities with *Rembrandt, whose work Vignon is known to have sold. There are examples of his paintings in the Louvre; he also produced etchings and book illustrations. Vignon is said to have fathered 34 children by his two wives; his sons **Claude the Younger** (1633–1703) and **Philippe** (1638–1701) and his daughter **Charlotte** (1639–?) were also painters.

Villatte, Pierre. See QUARTON.

Villon, Jacques (*b* Damville, Normandy, 31 July 1875; *d* Puteaux, nr. Paris, 9 June 1963). French painter and graphic artist, the elder brother of Marcel *Duchamp and Raymond *Duchamp-Villon. His original name was Gaston Duchamp, but he changed it in 1895 because of his admiration for the 15th-century poet François Villon. In 1894 he began studying law in Paris, but he soon abandoned it for art, initially earning his living mainly as a newspaper illustrator. In 1911 he began experimenting with

*Cubism, and the following year he was one of the founders of the *Section d'Or group. After the First World War (during which he served in the army) he began painting geometrical abstracts (*Colour Perspective*, 1921, Guggenheim Mus., New York), but in the 1920s he earned his living mainly as a printmaker (he was an expert etcher). In 1921 he had a one-man exhibition at the *Société Anonyme, New York, and for most of the inter-war period he was probably better known in the USA than in Europe. During this time he alternated between abstraction and a highly schematized type of figuration (*Portrait of the Artist's Father*, 1924, Guggenheim Mus.). After the Second World War he enjoyed substantially greater recognition than in the earlier part of his career, winning the Grand Prize for Painting at the Venice *Biennale in 1958, when he was in his eighties.

Vinci, Leonardo da. See LEONARDO DA VINCI.

Vinckboons, David (*b* Mechelen [Malines], 13 Aug. 1576; *d* Amsterdam, 1630/3). Dutch painter and printmaker of Flemish birth, the best-known member of a family of artists. His father, the painter **Philip Vinckboons** (1545–1601), left Antwerp because of religious intolerance (he was a Protestant) and David spent most of his life in Amsterdam. He specialized in *genre scenes in landscape settings and is a transitional figure between the decorative *Mannerist tradition and the more naturalistic style associated with 17th-century Dutch painting. His scenes depicting village festivals show the influence of Pieter *Bruegel, and Vinckboons is credited with introducing some of his motifs into Holland. It is sometimes claimed that his works can always be identified by the presence of a finch (*vinck*) in a tree (*boom*), but the painstaking student usually finds that the bird has flown. His son **Philips Vingboons** (1607/8–78) was a leading architect in Amsterdam.

Vingt, Les (or **Les XX**). Society of progressive Belgian painters and sculptors (originally twenty in number, hence the name), founded in 1883 in Brussels, where it held annual exhibitions from 1884 to 1893. The members included James *Ensor, Fernand *Khnopff, and Jan *Toorop. They showed not only their own work, but also paintings by non-Belgian artists such as *Cézanne, van *Gogh, and *Seurat. The society was influential in spreading the ideas of *Neo-Impressionism and *Post-Impressionism and became the main Belgian forum for *Symbolism and *Art Nouveau. After it dissolved in 1893, the society's work was carried on by an association called La Libre Esthétique, which ran from 1894 to 1914. Most of the leading Belgian avant-garde artists of the period were members.

Viola, Bill. See VIDEO ART.

Virius, Mirko. See GENERALIĆ.

virtu (or **vertu**). 'A love of or taste for works of art or curios; a knowledge of or interest in the fine arts; the fine arts as a subject of study or interest' (*OED*). The word, deriving from the Latin *virtus* ('excellence') via the Italian *virtù*, became common in England in the 18th century (Horace *Walpole in a letter of 1746 refers to 'my books, my virtu and my other follies and amusements'). It now hardly survives apart from the term 'object of virtu' (or 'object de vertu'), meaning a curio, which is still current in saleroom language.

The related term 'virtuoso' was originally used of someone who was learned in the arts or sciences, and according to Henry Peacham in *The Compleat Gentleman* (1634) it was applied particularly to those skilled in distinguishing copies of antiquities from the originals. It came to be applied to professional artists, and the 'Society of Virtuosi', founded in 1689, was composed of 'gentleman painters, sculptors and architects'. In modern usage it denotes a person who shows consummate mastery of technique and is applied primarily in music ('a virtuoso violinist') rather than in the visual arts.

Vischer. Family of German sculptors active in Nuremberg. **Hermann the Elder** (*d* 1488) established the family bronze foundry, and the business was inherited by his son **Peter the Elder** (*c*.1460–1529), the best known of the Vischers. He was assisted by five sons: **Hermann the Younger** (*c*.1486–1517), **Peter the Younger** (1487–1528), **Hans** (*c*.1489–1550), **Jacob**, and **Paulus**.

The masterpiece of the Vischer workshop is the spectacular bronze shrine over the sarcophagus of St Sebald in the church dedicated to him in Nuremberg. The first design—a drawing (by Peter the Elder?) in the Academy, Vienna—dates from 1488, but work began only in 1508 and continued until 1519. Through journeys of the younger generation the workshop had by that time gained a good deal of knowledge of Italian bronzes and in particular the work of north Italian sculptors. Thus the Sebald tomb became a fascinating mixture of *Gothic and *Renaissance styles. The canopy remained Gothic, as also the main figures of the Apostles standing before the supports; but both the base and the *baldacchino were inhabited by biblical, mythological, and decorative figures conceived in a genuine Renaissance spirit. Peter the Elder included a celebrated self-portrait (complete with tools and leather apron) among these figures. He also made two splendid free-standing figures (1512–13) of Theodoric and King Arthur for the tomb of the Emperor Maximilian I (see HABSBURG) in the Hofkirche, Innsbruck.

Georg (c.1522–92), a son of Hans, was the last artist member of the family; he seems to have specialized in small decorative bronzes such as inkwells.

Viti, Timoteo. See RAPHAEL.

Vitruvius Pollio (active second half of 1st century BC). Roman architect, the author of a treatise, *De architectura*, which is the only work of its kind to have survived from antiquity. It was well known in manuscript throughout the Middle Ages and the first printed edition appeared in Rome in 1486. Since then it has been much edited and translated and for centuries was regarded as the authoritative voice on *classical architecture. It is still a major source for the history of ancient art, for it contains much incidental information about Greek and Roman painting and sculpture as well as about architecture.

Vittoria, Alessandro (b Trento, ?1525; d Venice, 27 May 1608). Italian sculptor, active mainly in Venice, where he settled in 1543. He trained under Jacopo *Sansovino and succeeded him as the leading sculptor in the city, dominating the art in a way somewhat comparable to his contemporary *Giambologna in Florence. His output was large and varied, including tombs, altars, statues, portraits, and architectural ornament, notably the vault over the ceremonial entrance to the Doges' Palace, the Scala d'Oro (1557–9). This is in gilded *stucco, and he also worked in bronze, marble, and terracotta. Temperamentally he was a modeller rather than a carver, and his marbles tend to be lacking in warmth compared with his work in other media. His formidably characterized portrait busts are now perhaps his most admired works; his sitters included some of the leading Venetian personalities of the time.

Vivarini. Family of Venetian painters. **Antonio** (c.1420–76/84) seldom worked independently. He collaborated first with his brother-in-law, the German-born Giovanni d'Alemagna (active 1441–50), and then from the 1450s with his own younger brother **Bartolomeo** (c.1432–c.1499).

The pictures produced by these partnerships usually took the form of large *polyptychs with stiff, archaic-looking figures and very elaborate carved and gilded frames in the *Gothic tradition. Bartolomeo's independent works date from the 1460s onwards. He continued to paint polyptychs, but he modernized his style to a certain extent by imitating *Mantegna. **Alvise** (c.1445–1503/5), son of Antonio, is the best-known member of the family. He presumably trained in the family workshop, but his work was more modern in style than that of his father or uncle, influenced particularly by Giovanni *Bellini. None of the Vivarini had much originality. There are examples of the work of all three in the National Gallery, London.

Vivin, Louis (b Hadol, nr. Épinal, 27 July 1861; d Paris, 28 May 1936). French *naive painter. He had a passion for painting from childhood, but could not devote himself to it regularly until he retired from the Post Office in 1922. In 1925 he was 'discovered' by Wilhelm *Uhde and subsequently won wide recognition. His work included *genre pictures, flower pieces, hunting scenes, and views of Paris, notable for their charmingly wobbly perspective effects.

Vlaminck, Maurice de (b Paris, 4 Apr. 1876; d Rueil-la-Gadelière, Eure-et-Loir, 10 Oct. 1958). French painter, printmaker, and writer. A colourful and many-sided character, as a young man he earned his living mainly as a racing cyclist and orchestral violinist, painting in his spare time virtually without instruction. Indeed, he delighted to inveigh against all forms of academic training and boasted that he had never set foot inside the *Louvre: 'I try to paint with my heart and my loins, not bothering with style.' In 1901 an exhibition of van *Gogh's work in Paris overwhelmed him, intensifying his love of pure colour, and with *Matisse and *Derain he became a leading exponent of *Fauvism, often using paint straight from the tube in exuberant compositions—mainly landscapes. From 1908, however, his palette darkened and his work became more solidly constructed, under the influence of *Cézanne. In 1910–14 he was also mildly influenced by *Cubist stylization, although he came to dislike *Picasso and regard him as a charlatan.

After the First World War Vlaminck moved from Paris and in 1925 he settled in a farmhouse in Eure-et-Loir. Thereafter his subjects were taken mainly from the surrounding countryside. His work became rather slick and mannered, but his reputation grew steadily in France and abroad during the inter-war years. After the German invasion of France in 1940, he—like several other well-known artists—was courted by the Nazis for propaganda purposes, and in 1941 he visited Germany as part of a group that included Derain, *Despiau, van *Dongen, *Dunoyer de Segonzac, and *Friesz. In 1944, immediately after the Liberation, he was arrested and interrogated, and although no action was taken against him, the suspicions of collaboration damaged his career. By the end of his life, however, he had been more or less rehabilitated. In addition to painting he wrote novels and several volumes of memoirs.

Vlieger, Simon de (*b* Rotterdam, *c*.1601; *d* Weesp, Mar. 1653). Dutch painter, mainly of marine subjects, active in Rotterdam, Delft, and Amsterdam. One of the outstanding marine painters of his period, he moved from stormy subjects in the manner of *Porcellis to serene and majestic images that influenced van de *Cappelle (who owned a large collection of his work) and Willem van de *Velde the Younger (whom he taught). De Vlieger also painted landscapes; he was a prolific draughtsman, made etchings, and designed stained-glass windows for the Niewe Kerk in Amsterdam.

Vollard, Ambroise (*b* Saint-Denis, Réunion, Indian Ocean, 3 July 1866; *d* Paris, 22 July 1939). French dealer, connoisseur, publisher, and writer, one of the most important champions of avant-garde art in the early 20th century. In 1893 he opened a gallery in Paris and in 1895 he gave the first important exhibition of *Cézanne's work. Other landmark events included the first one-man exhibitions of *Picasso (1901) and *Matisse (1904). His clientele included some of the leading collectors of the day, among them Albert C. *Barnes and Gertrude and Leo *Stein. As well as buying and selling paintings, Vollard played an important role as a publisher by encouraging his artists to work as printmakers. He commissioned them to illustrate books (literary classics as well as contemporary works) and also issued independent portfolios of prints, notably Picasso's *Vollard Suite*, consisting of 100 etchings on various themes made between 1930 and 1937. His portrait was painted many times, among others by *Bonnard, Cézanne, Picasso, *Renoir, and *Rouault. Vollard's writings included books on Cézanne and *Degas and the autobiographical *Recollections of a Picture Dealer* (1936); a slightly expanded French version, *Souvenirs d'un marchand de tableaux*, appeared in 1937.

Vollmer, Hans. See THIEME.

Volterra, Daniele da. See DANIELE DA VOLTERRA.

Volto Santo (Italian: 'Sacred Face'). A large wooden Crucifix in Lucca Cathedral, on which Christ is shown fully robed. According to an early medieval tradition this Crucifix was an actual portrait of Christ made by Nicodemus, who had helped to bury him. It is said to have been in Lucca from the 8th century, but the present *Volto Santo* is perhaps a 13th-century copy of an 8th-century original. The commercial importance of Lucca in the Middle Ages helps to explain the appearance of a number of 12th–15th-century copies of the *Volto Santo* throughout Europe.

Vorticism. An avant-garde British art movement launched in 1914; it was related to *Cubism and *Futurism and was mainly concerned with the visual arts, but it also embraced literature (its name was suggested by the American poet and critic Ezra Pound (1885–1972), to whom the vortex represented 'the point of maximum energy', an expression of the dynamism of modern life). Vorticism was highly aggressive in tone, celebrating movement and the machine, and attacking what was considered the complacency and sentimentality of contemporary British culture. It was short-lived, its vigour being dissipated by the First World War, but it had a powerful, revitalizing impact on British art. The central figure of the movement, as a theorist as well as an artist, was Wyndham *Lewis, who edited its journal *Blast* (only two numbers appeared, in 1914 and 1915). He later claimed that 'Vorticism . . . was what I, personally, did, and said, at a certain period', but there was clearly a close similarity of style between his harsh, angular, mechanistic paintings and the work of several of his associates, including Henri *Gaudier-Brzeska, William *Roberts, and Edward *Wadsworth, each of whom signed the Vorticist manifesto that appeared in the first number of *Blast*.

The Vorticists held only one exhibition, at the Doré Gallery, London, in June 1915. Apart from the formal members of the movement, the artists taking part included David *Bomberg and Christopher *Nevinson. Jacob *Epstein was not included, but his work was reproduced in *Blast* and he is generally considered part of the movement. Several of the artists represented in the exhibition were now producing pure abstracts, and the show was far too advanced for the critics, who treated it as an incomprehensible joke. By this time the war was scattering the Vorticists (Gaudier-Breszka had already been killed in action), and Lewis failed in his attempts to revive the movement after the war.

Vos, Cornelis de (b Hulst, ?1584; d Antwerp, 9 May 1651). Flemish painter, active in Antwerp. He painted historical, allegorical, mythological, and religious works, but excelled chiefly as a portraitist. His finest paintings are his portraits of children, which have great sensitivity and charm without lapsing into sentimentality. A splendid self-portrait of *The Artist with his Family* (1621, Mus. Royaux, Brussels) shows him looking happy and proud with his own children. In style he was close to *Rubens and van *Dyck but more down to earth (his sitters were typically solid members of the bourgeoisie rather than aristocrats or intellectuals). His brother **Paul de Vos** (b Hulst, ?1595; d Antwerp, 30 June 1678) painted hunting scenes and still-lifes in the style of Frans *Snyders, who was the brother-in-law of the de Vos brothers. In 1637 all three helped Rubens execute pictures for the Torre de la Parada, Philip IV of Spain's (see HABSBURG) hunting lodge near Madrid.

Vos, Maerten de (b Antwerp, 1532; d Antwerp, 4 Dec. 1603). Netherlandish painter, active mainly in Antwerp. In about 1552 he went to Italy (perhaps in company with *Bruegel) and worked in *Tintoretto's studio in Venice; he also visited Rome and probably Florence. By 1558 he was back in Antwerp, and after the death of Frans *Floris in 1570 he became one of the leading artists in the city. The altarpieces that make up the bulk of his output show the influence of Italian *Mannerism in their slender elegance, but his warmth of colour looks forward to *Rubens and the Flemish *Baroque. His rare portraits are notably direct and in the Netherlandish rather than the Italian tradition (*Antoine Anselme and his Family*, 1577, Mus. Royaux, Brussels). He was a prolific draughtsman and many prints were made of his compositions.

Voss, Hermann (b Lüneburg, 30 July 1884; d Munich, 28 Apr. 1969). German art historian. He spent much of his career working in German museums (notably the Kaiser Friedrich Museum in Berlin and Gemäldegalerie in Dresden, of which he was director, 1942–54) and he also taught in England and the USA. His publications were mainly on 16th- and 17th-century art, and he played an important role in the revival of interest in Italian *Baroque painting, particularly with his book *Die Malerei des Barock in Rom* (Baroque Painting in Rome, 1924), which has been described by Rudolf *Wittkower as 'the basic study without which no work in the field can be undertaken'. He was a sensitive connoisseur, as he showed with articles on Veit *Stoss (1908), in which he was the first to attribute to him the celebrated *St Roch* in Florence, and Georges de *La Tour (1915), in which he began the rediscovery of this artist.

Vostell, Wolf (b Leverkusen, 14 Oct. 1932; d Berlin, 3 Apr. 1998). German artist, best known as one of Europe's leading organizers of *happenings. He first organized such events in Paris in 1958 and thereafter in numerous other cities, including Berlin and New York. In 1962 he joined the *Fluxus movement. Much of his work was politically motivated, with the accent on violence and destruction, and he described the student riots in Paris in 1968 as 'the greatest happening of all'.

Vouet, Simon (b Paris, 8 Jan. 1590; d Paris, 30 June 1649). The leading French painter in the first half of the 17th century. His early years are obscure, but according to *Félibien he was precocious and worked as a portraitist in England when he was only 14. He certainly visited Constantinople in 1611–12 before moving to Italy, where he lived from 1613 to 1627, mainly in Rome. During this period Vouet achieved a considerable reputation and became president of the Accademia di S. Luca (see ACADEMY) in 1624. His early work in Italy was much influenced by *Caravaggio (*The Fortune-Teller*, c.1618–20, NG, Ottawa), but he later developed an *eclectic style in which *Baroque tendencies were tempered by the *classicism of Guido *Reni and *Domenichino.

In 1627 Louis XIII recalled Vouet to Paris and made him his court painter, launching him on an extremely busy and prosperous career. His compromise style proved exactly to the taste of his French clients; he offered them something more lively and modern than the prevailing tired *Mannerism but less extreme than the dramatic naturalism of the Caravaggesque or the full emotionalism of the Baroque. Only when *Poussin returned from Rome to Paris in 1640–2 was Vouet's dominance threatened. He painted religious and allegorical works and portraits and was employed on several major decorative schemes, sometimes in conjunction with Jacques *Sarrazin. Little of his best decorative work survives, however. Vouet was a versatile and hard-working artist rather than a great one and his success and influence depended on his having hit upon a style that suited the taste of the day at a time when French painting was at a low ebb. He introduced new life and a tradition of solid competence and most of the leading members of the next generation of painters passed through his studio, including *Le Brun, *Le Sueur, and *Mignard. Examples of his work are in many French museums.

Vrancx, Sebastian (*bapt.* Antwerp, 22 Jan. 1573; *d* Antwerp, 19 May 1647). Flemish painter. Apart from a period in Italy as a young man, *c.*1596–1601, he spent all his career in Antwerp. He painted various types of picture, including landscapes, religious scenes, and allegories, but he is remembered chiefly for his lively scenes of battle and of soldiers plundering. His work, which was much copied and also disseminated through engravings, was largely responsible for establishing battle painting as a distinct genre in the Low Countries.

Vredeman de Vries, Hans (*b* Leeuwarden, *c.*1527; *d* ?Antwerp, *c.*1606). Netherlandish painter, architect, engineer, and designer, active in Germany and Prague, as well as in Amsterdam, Antwerp, and The Hague. He was famous in his lifetime for his skill in *illusionistic architectural decoration, but much of his work was of a temporary nature (triumphal arches for festivities and so on) and although his paintings were much admired and imitated by his contemporaries, few survive that are certainly from his own hand. An example is *Palace Scene with Strolling Figures* (1596, KH Mus., Vienna), which has a typically elaborate *Mannerist architectural setting, with rows of columns in emphatic perspective. It is signed by Hans and his son **Paul** (1567–*c.*1630), one of several painters with whom he worked (Hans doing the architecture, his collaborator the figures). He is now remembered primarily for his many books and prints containing perspective studies of fanciful palaces, courts, gardens, furniture, and decorative work. They had wide circulation in northern Europe and had great influence on architecture and decoration.

Vrel, Jacobus (active 1654–62). Dutch painter, an enigmatic figure who has only recently gained recognition as one of the most charmingly idiosyncratic masters of his time. Nothing at all is recorded of his life, his name surviving solely through the signatures on some of his paintings. About 40 pictures by him are known—either sparse interiors or quiet street scenes. They show a remarkably fresh, almost *naive vision and have a sense of tranquil poetry that has led them to be compared with the work of *Vermeer. Several of his paintings have, indeed, formerly gone under Vermeer's name, for example *Street Scene* in the Getty Museum, Los Angeles. Because of the similarity of spirit, it has been surmised that Vrel, too, worked in Delft, but some authorities consider it likely that he lived in a provincial town rather than a major art centre.

Vries, Adriaen de (*b* The Hague, *c.*1545; *bur.* Prague, 15 Dec. 1626). Netherlandish sculptor active mainly in central Europe, notably for the Emperor Rudolf II (see HABSBURG) in Prague. He spent most of the 1580s in Italy, where he assisted *Giambologna in Florence and Pompeo *Leoni in Milan. His first independent documented work is *Mercury and Psyche* (1593, Louvre, Paris), made for Rudolf II. This, like most of his sculpture, is in bronze, a material in which he imitated Giambologna's sleek and elegant *Mannerist style with great accomplishment; he played a leading role in spreading this style to northern Europe. His major works included two fountains in Augsburg (1599, 1602) and another made for Fredericksberg Castle, Copenhagen (1615–17). The figures from the Copenhagen fountain were taken by the Swedes as war booty in 1659 and are now in the Palace of Drottningholm near Stockholm. None of de Vries's commissions came from the Low Countries.

Vroom, Hendrick (*b* Haarlem, *c.*1563; *bur.* Haarlem, 2 Feb. 1640). Dutch painter and tapestry designer, regarded as the founder of the European tradition of marine painting (there had been marine pictures before him, but he was the first artist to specialize in the field). Early in his career he travelled extensively in Spain and Italy, then settled in Haarlem in about 1590. By this time he already had a reputation as a painter of ships and the sea, and he was soon commissioned to design a series of ten huge tapestries commemorating the defeat of the Spanish Armada in 1588. These were woven in Delft in 1592–5 and they hung in the House of Lords, London, until they were destroyed by fire in 1834. Their appearance is recorded in engravings, however, and some similar tapestries designed by Vroom to celebrate Dutch naval victories (woven 1595–1603) are in the Zeeuws Museum, Middelburg. Vroom's paintings are typically in the same vein as his tapestries—large works depicting historical maritime events, with great attention paid to the detail of the ships (*Arrival of Frederick V, Elector Palatine, at Flushing* [Vlissingen], *May 1613*, 1623, Hals Mus., Haarlem). In addition to these major official commissions, he also painted smaller 'portraits' of individual ships. Generally he used a high viewpoint, so he could present the information in the scene clearly; his drawings, however, are more naturalistic.

Vroom was greatly esteemed in his day, his work fetching high prices, and he ran a large studio. Among his pupils was his son **Cornelis Vroom** (*b* Haarlem, *c*.1591; *bur*. Haarlem, 16 Sept. 1661). He began his career as a marine painter but turned to landscape and became one of the pioneers of woodland views (*Landscape with a River by a Wood*, 1626, NG, London), a type of work later particularly associated with the supreme Haarlem landscapist, Jacob van *Ruisdael. Several other members of the Vroom family were artists.

Vrubel, Mikhail (*b* Omsk, 5 Mar. 1856; *d* St Petersburg, 1 Apr. 1910). Russian painter and designer, the outstanding exponent of *Symbolism in his country. His first important work was the restoration of murals in the 12th-century church of St Cyril, Kiev, and in his subsequent career he showed an affinity with the spirituality of medieval religious art. In 1889 he moved from Kiev to Moscow and there was taken up by the wealthy art patron Savva Mamontov (see ABRAMTSEVO COLONY); a portrait (1897) of him by Vrubel is in the Tretyakov Gallery, Moscow. In 1890 he began to produce interpretations of Mikhail Lermontov's poem *The Demon* and the theme became central to his work. In treating it he passed from fairly naturalistic depictions to highly idiosyncratic anguish-ridden images rendered in brilliant fragmented brushwork

that recalls the effects of medieval mosaics. The obsessive treatment of the theme reflected his own emotional instability; in 1902 the first symptoms of approaching insanity became apparent, in 1906 he went blind, and he died in a lunatic asylum. Although he was little appreciated for most of his career, he had become well known by the time of his death and had great influence on Russian painting in the early 20th century.

Vuillard, Édouard (*b* Cuiseaux, 11 Nov. 1868; *d* La Baule, nr. Saint-Nazaire, 21 June 1940). French painter, draughtsman, designer, and lithographer. In the 1890s he was a member of the *Nabis and at this time painted intimate interiors and scenes from Montmartre, his sensitive patterning of flattish colours owing something to *Gauguin and something to *Puvis de Chavannes, but creating a distinctive manner of his own. He also designed posters and theatrical sets. From about 1900 he turned to a more naturalistic style and with *Bonnard became the main practitioner of *Intimisme, making use of the camera to capture fleeting, informal groupings of his friends and relatives in their homes and gardens. He had several close female friends and preferred painting women and children to men. His work also included landscapes and portraits. Although he was financially successful, he lived modestly, sharing an apartment with his widowed mother until her death in 1928; she often features in his paintings. He was reserved and quiet in personality, although affectionate and much liked. For many years he kept a detailed journal (there are 48 volumes of it in the Institut de France, Paris), in which he revealed his thoughtful attitude towards art and life.

W

Waagen, Gustav Friedrich (*b* Hamburg, 11 Feb. 1794; *d* Copenhagen, 15 July 1868). German art historian. He made his name with a book on the van *Eycks, published in 1822, and in 1832 he was appointed director of the newly founded *Gemäldegalerie in Berlin. In 1844 he became the first holder of a university chair in art history when he was made professor at Berlin University. Waagen had a great reputation as a connoisseur, and on his travels he wrote compendious notes on works of art he saw in public and private collections. These formed the basis for various publications that are a mine of information, including *Works of Art and Artists in England* (3 vols., 1838) and, most notably, *Treasures of Art in Great Britain* (3 vols., 1854), which was translated by Lady *Eastlake; a supplementary volume entitled *Galleries and Cabinets of Art in Great Britain* was published in 1857. See also JAMESON.

Wadsworth, Edward (*b* Cleckheaton, Yorkshire, 29 Oct. 1889; *d* London, 21 June 1949). British painter, printmaker, draughtsman, and designer. A friend of Wyndham *Lewis, he was a member of the *Vorticist group (1914–15); his work of this time included completely abstract pictures such as the stridently geometrical *Abstract Composition* (1915, Tate, London). In the First World War he worked on designing dazzle camouflage for ships, turning his harsh Vorticist style to practical use. This experience provided the subject for one of his best-known paintings, the huge *Dazzle-Ships in Drydock at Liverpool* (1919, NG, Ottawa). The lucidity and precision seen here were enhanced when Wadsworth switched from oil painting to tempera in about 1922. At the same time his style changed, as he abandoned *Cubist leanings for a more naturalistic idiom. He had a passion for the sea and often painted maritime subjects, developing a distinctive type of highly composed marine still-life, typically with a *Surrealistic flavour brought about by oddities of scale, strange juxtapositions, and the hypnotic clarity of the lighting (*Satellitium*, 1932, Castle Mus., Nottingham). In the 1920s and 1930s he was among the most European in spirit of British artists. He travelled widely on the Continent and in 1933 contributed to the Paris journal *Abstraction-Création. In the same year he was a founder member of *Unit One. Around this time he again painted abstracts (influenced by *Arp), but he reverted to his more naturalistic style in 1934. During the 1930s he had several commissions for murals, notably two panels for the liner *Queen Mary* in 1938. As a graphic artist he is best known for his vigorous, angular woodcuts of ships and machinery, which played a part in the revival of the technique after the First World War. For an artist, Wadsworth was 'unusually businesslike, answering letters by return of post and punctiliously fulfilling his commissions' (*DNB*), but he has been aptly described by Sir John *Rothenstein as 'a true poet of the age of machines'.

Waldmüller, Ferdinand Georg (*b* Vienna, 15 Jan. 1793; *d* Helmstreitmühle, nr. Baden, 23 Aug. 1865). One of the leading Austrian painters of the *Biedermeier period. He painted portraits, *genre subjects, and still-life, but is perhaps best known for his landscapes, which in their loving attention to detail illustrate his belief that the close study of nature should be the basis of painting. In 1829 he became professor of painting at the Vienna Academy, but he had a stormy relationship with it because his views were at odds with its traditional teaching methods; he wrote several treatises urging academic reform.

Walker, Dame Ethel (*b* Edinburgh, 9 June 1861; *d* London, 2 Mar. 1951). British painter and occasional sculptor. In 1900 she became the first woman member of the *New English Art Club and it was there that she mainly exhibited, building a reputation as one of the outstanding British women artists of her period. She painted portraits, flower pieces, interiors, and seascapes in an attractive *Impressionist style, but her most individual works are large decorative compositions inspired by her vision of a golden age. They show the influence of French *Symbolist painting as well as of her interest in philosophy and religion (*The Zone of Hate*, 1914–15, and *The Zone of Love*, c.1930–2; both Tate, London).

Walker, Fred (*b* London, 26 May 1840; *d* St Fillans, Perthshire, 4 June 1875). English painter and illustrator. He was one of the most successful illustrators of the early 1860s, working for several leading periodicals, including *Punch* and the *Cornhill Magazine*, as well as on books. By the mid-1860s, he was turning from illustration to painting, and he became well known for scenes of rural life, treated with grace and pathos (*The Vagrants*, 1868, Tate, London). He also designed an acclaimed poster for a stage adaptation (1871) of Wilkie Collins's *The Woman in White*. His death from tuberculosis at the age of 35 was much lamented by his many friends in the art world; one of these, George *Du Maurier, later used him as the model for the character Little Billee in his novel *Trilby* (1894). See also ST JOHN'S WOOD CLIQUE.

Walker, Robert (*b* c.1600/10; *d* c.1658). English portrait painter. He has a certain niche in history as he was the portraitist most favoured by Oliver Cromwell and the Parliamentarians during the Interregnum (1649–60), but his work is generally dull and derivative (mainly of van *Dyck). His last dated pictures are of 1656 and he is said to have died 'a little before the Restoration'.

Wallace Collection, London. National museum consisting of the collection built up in the 18th and 19th centuries by the Seymour-Conway family, earls and later marquesses of Hertford; it was bequeathed to the nation in 1897 by Lady Wallace, widow of Sir Richard Wallace, the illegitimate son of the 4th marquess of Hertford, and opened to the public in 1900. It is located in Hertford House, the former London residence of the family. The collection, the largest of its date to be preserved intact, reflects the tastes of various members of the family, but particularly of the 4th marquess (Richard Seymour-Conway, 1800–70) and his son Sir Richard Wallace (1819–90), who spent much of their lives in Paris. The marquess bought most of the superb representation of 18th-century French art (furniture as well as paintings) that is the collection's chief glory; Sir Richard added much *Renaissance decorative art and the magnificent collection of armour, rivalled in Britain only by that in the Royal Armouries. Other areas in which the Wallace Collection is particularly rich are 17th-century Dutch and Flemish painting (its most famous

exhibit is Frans *Hals's *The Laughing Cavalier*); 18th-century English portraits; and the works of *Bonington (the best representation anywhere). In 2000, marking the Wallace Collection's centenary, an extension to the building was opened, created partly by glazing over what had been the central courtyard.

Wallis, Alfred (*b* Devonport, 8 Aug. 1855; *d* Madron, nr. Penzance, Cornwall, 29 Aug. 1942). British *naive painter of sailing ships and landscapes. He went to sea as a cabin boy and cook at the age of 9, and from about 1880 worked as a fisherman in Cornwall. In 1890 he opened a rag and bone store in St Ives and after retiring from this did odd jobs, including selling ice cream. He began to paint in 1925 to ease the loneliness he felt after his wife's death and was discovered by Ben *Nicholson and Christopher *Wood in 1928; the unselfconscious vigour of his paintings made a powerful impression on them and they introduced his work to friends in the art world. Wallis painted from memory and imagination, usually working with ship's paint on scraps of cardboard or wood. Although he rapidly became the best known of British naive artists, he died in a workhouse.

Wallis, Henry (*b* London, 21 Feb. 1830; *d* Croydon, Surrey [now Greater London], 20 Dec. 1916). English painter, mainly of literary and *genre subjects. Early in his career he was strongly influenced by the *Pre-Raphaelites, and he is chiefly remembered for the lovingly detailed *Death of Chatterton* (1856, Tate, London), showing the young poet after taking poison in a miserable garret. This won enormous praise at the time (*Ruskin called it 'faultless and wonderful') and has endured as an archetypal image of Romantic ardour and suffering. Wallis painted a few other impressive works in Pre-Raphaelite vein, but his later career was less distinguished, and he made more impact as an authority on ceramics. He wrote extensively on the subject and made a large collection, which he left to the Victoria and Albert Museum.

walnut. See LIMEWOOD.

walnut oil. *Drying oil obtained from the common walnut. It was one of the earliest oils used in painting, and perhaps the commonest *medium in the early days of *oil painting, but it is little used today. It dries more slowly than *linseed oil but has less tendency to turn yellow.

Walpole, Horace, 4th Earl of Orford (*b* London, 24 Sept. 1717; *d* London, 2 Mar. 1797).

English collector, connoisseur, man of letters, and amateur architect. He was the son of **Sir Robert Walpole** (1676–1745), who was Britain's first prime minister and also a notable collector of paintings. In 1739–41 Horace made the *Grand Tour, travelling in France and Italy with the poet Thomas Gray. His literary fame rests on his voluminous correspondence and on *The Castle of Otranto* (1764), the first 'Gothic novel'. In the history of taste he is primarily important for his house at Twickenham, Strawberry Hill, which he bought in 1747 and extended into a showpiece of the *Gothic Revival, employing professional architects to work from his sketches. He filled the building with his collections (dispersed after his death) and it became such a tourist attraction that he took to issuing admission tickets. In 1757 Walpole established his own printing press at Strawberry Hill, from which he published his *Anecdotes of Painting in England* (4 vols., 1762–71), a highly important source for the history of British art from the Middle Ages to his own time, based on *Vertue's notebooks but augmented by his own research. His other publications include *A Description of the Villa of Mr Horace Walpole at Strawberry Hill* (1774) and *Aedes Walpolianae* (1747), a catalogue of his father's paintings at Houghton Hall, Norfolk. These were bought en bloc by Catherine the Great of Russia in 1779 and are now in the *Hermitage, St Petersburg; among them are several works by van *Dyck, including his portrait of Inigo *Jones (*c.*1632–5), and *Rembrandt's *Sacrifice of Isaac* (1635).

Wals, Goffredo. See CLAUDE.

Walton, Henry (*b* Dickleburgh, nr. Diss, Norfolk; *bapt*. Tivetshall St Mary, nr. Dickleburgh, 5 Jan. 1746; *d* London, 19 May 1813). English painter, a pupil of *Zoffany. He was a gentleman painter and his work is rare. His portraits are unexceptional, but he painted a small number of *genre scenes that are amongst the finest of their time in English art, notable for their unaffected charm and sureness of tone (*Girl Plucking a Turkey*, 1776, Tate, London). They have something of the quiet dignity of *Chardin, with whose work he may have been familiar (he is said to have visited France).

Wanderers (or **Itinerants**) (Russian: Peredvizhniki). Association of Russian painters active from 1870 to 1923. The formal name of the organization was 'Association of Travelling [or Wandering] Art Exhibitions', the word 'travelling' referring to the fact that its exhibitions were shown successively in various Russian towns (including Astrakhan, Kharkov, Kiev, Kursk, Odessa, and Saratov), not just in the country's two elite art centres, Moscow and St Petersburg. This desire to reach a wide public was inspired by democratic social ideals; like other members of the Russian intelligentsia at this time, the Wanderers wanted to bring culture to the common people, to help educate and inspire them.

The nucleus of the association was formed by a number of art students—led by *Kramskoi—who had left the St Petersburg Academy in 1863 because of its rigid traditionalism. They had refused to accept 'The Feast of the Gods in Valhalla' as a competition subject because it was so irrelevant to contemporary social needs. In contrast to such rarefied subjects, the Wanderers not only wanted to depict ordinary people, but also to show such people a vision of moral worth and hope in the future. Consequently their paintings were realistic and easily intelligible. Sometimes they were overtly political, dealing with issues such as rural poverty or corruption in the Church, but many pictures shown in the exhibitions were unpolemical; there were, for example, numerous landscapes and portraits.

The first Wanderers' exhibition was held in 1871; it was highly successful and 47 more followed, held virtually every year until 1923. Many of the outstanding Russian painters of the late 19th century were members. Among them were Nikolai Ghe (1831–94), whose work included some starkly powerful scenes of Christ's Passion; Isaak Levitan (1860–1900), one of the leading landscapists of the time; Vasily Perov (1834–82), whose scenes of rural and urban poverty perhaps best illustrate the social conscience of the Wanderers in their early days; Ilya *Repin; Ivan Shishkin (1832–98), a landscapist particularly renowned for forest scenes; Vasily Surikov (1848–1916), best known for depicting events from his country's history; and Viktor *Vasnetsov. By the turn of the century the association had passed its peak as a major force in the country's cultural life and in its later years it was regarded as upholding conservative rather than radical values. In 1923 it merged with the Association of Artists of Revolutionary Russia, which had been founded the previous year. After the imposition of *Socialist Realism in the 1930s, the Wanderers were extolled as its precursors.

Wappers, Gustaf (*b* Antwerp, 23 Aug. 1803; *d* Paris, 6 Dec. 1874). Belgian painter, active mainly in Antwerp, where he became a professor at the Academy in 1833. He had enormous success with his elaborate historical costume pieces, catching the public imagination with patriotic themes that appealed to the Belgian people, who had just won their independence (*Episode from the Belgian Revolution of 1830*, 1834, Mus. Royaux, Brussels). However, such works have dated badly. In 1845 he was created a baron, and in 1853 he settled in Paris.

War Artists' Advisory Committee. See OFFICIAL WAR ART.

Warburg, Aby (*b* Hamburg, 13 June 1866; *d* Hamburg, 26 Oct. 1929). German art historian. He came from a prosperous banking family and his wealth enabled him to pursue his own inclinations as a private scholar. His main field of study was the art of the Florentine *quattrocento. Whereas his contemporaries, such as *Berenson and *Wölfflin, interpreted *Renaissance art largely in formal terms, Warburg tried to understand it as part of the intellectual history of the time. In particular he was impressed by the hold that religious loyalties and astrological superstition retained on the minds of patrons, indicating that the subject matter of the works of art they commissioned could be fully explained only by reference to forgotten esoteric lore.

Warburg published little, but his ideas had great influence. The superb library that he built up in his home in Hamburg developed into a research institute, which was transferred to London in 1933 to escape the Nazi regime and in 1944 was incorporated in the University of London as the Warburg Institute. Its field of study is now officially defined as 'the history of the *classical tradition' (das Nachleben der Antike), but a better idea of the intellectual range of its activities can be gauged from a comment by *Panofsky: 'It stands to reason that an institute like the Warburg . . . which was founded for the explicit purpose of eliminating the borderlines between the history of art, the history of religion and superstition, the history of science, the history of cultic practices (including pageantry) and the history of literature, could not help being important for the practitioners of all these disciplines.' Ernst *Gombrich, who wrote a biography of Warburg (1970, revised edn. 1986), is one of the many distinguished scholars associated with the Institute.

Ward, James (*b* London, 23 Oct. 1769; *d* Cheshunt, Hertfordshire, 17 Nov. 1859). English painter and printmaker. He was trained as a

mezzotint engraver by his brother **William** (1766–1826) and by John Raphael *Smith; he began painting around 1790. Until about the end of the century he mainly produced anecdotal *genre scenes in the manner of his brother-in-law George *Morland, but he then turned to the paintings of animals in landscape settings for which he is chiefly remembered. They are often dramatic and *Romantic in character and their rich colouring was influenced by *Rubens (*Bulls Fighting*, 1803, V&A, London). His taste for natural grandeur and the *Sublime is most memorably expressed in the enormous *Gordale Scar* (1812–14, Tate, London). Ward had many admirers, including *Delacroix and *Géricault, but he became disillusioned with the art world and lived in retirement in Hertfordshire from 1830. He continued to exhibit, but he became something of a religious obsessive and died in poverty aged 90.

Ward, John Quincy Adams (*b* nr. Urbana, Oh., 29 June 1830; *d* New York, 1 May 1910). American sculptor, active mainly in New York. He was the most prolific sculptor of public monuments of his period, working until the end of his long life. His portrait statues, equestrian figures, allegorical groups, war memorials, and architectural decorations have solid dignity but none of the genius of his contemporary *Saint-Gaudens. The statue of Henry Ward Beecher (1891) in Cadman Plaza, Brooklyn, New York, is often cited as his finest work.

Warhol, Andy (*b* Pittsburgh, 6 Aug. 1928; *d* New York, 22 Feb. 1987). American painter, printmaker, sculptor, draughtsman, film-maker, and writer, one of the most famous and controversial artists of the 20th century. During the 1950s he was enormously successful as a commercial artist in New York (specializing in shoe advertisements). In 1960 he began making pictures based on mass-produced images such as newspaper advertisements and comic strips, then in 1962 of Campbell's soup cans. The soup can pictures were exhibited in that year with sensational success and Warhol soon became the best-known figure in American *Pop art. In the same vein he did pictures of Coca-Cola bottles and made equally banal sculptures of Brillo soap pad boxes and similar cartons. He also embarked on a lengthy series of pictures of Marilyn Monroe, Elvis Presley, Elizabeth Taylor, and other celebrities. Similar in method but different in effect were his pictures of disasters such as car crashes and views of the electric chair. Whatever the subject in his pictures, he often made use of rows of repeated images. The *screenprinting process that he favoured allowed limitless replication, and he was opposed to the idea of a work of art as a piece of craftsmanship, hand-made and expressing the personality of the artist: 'I want everybody to think alike. I think everybody should be a machine.'

In keeping with this outlook Warhol used clippings of 'dehumanized' illustrations from the mass media as his sources, turned out his works like a manufacturer, and called his studio 'The Factory'. There he was surrounded by a crowd of helpers and hangers-on, described by Robert *Hughes as 'cultural space-debris, drifting fragments from a variety of sixties sub-cultures'. Warhol liked to give the idea that he took a paternal interest in his followers, but Eric Shanes (Warhol, 1991) writes: 'Just how cynical he could be in his dealings with his entourage is demonstrated by an incident that occurred in October 1964 when one of his hangers-on, Freddie Herko, committed suicide by jumping from a fifth-floor window in Greenwich Village while high on LSD: Warhol was heard to complain repeatedly that Herko should have forewarned him so that he could have filmed his death.'

In 1965 Warhol announced his retirement as an artist to devote himself to films and to managing the rock group the Velvet Underground, but in fact he never gave up painting. As a film-maker, he became perhaps the only 'underground' director to be well known to the general public. His first films were silent and virtually completely static: Sleep (1963)—a man sleeping for six hours—and Empire (1964)—the Empire State Building seen from one viewpoint for eight hours—'I like boring things.' Later films, such as the two-screen Chelsea Girls (1966), gained widespread attention because of their voyeuristic concentration on sex.

In 1968 Warhol was shot and severely wounded by a bit-part player in one of his films, a member of SCUM (The Society for Cutting Up Men). The incident caused him to turn away from the unconventional types who had made up his entourage and instead become associated with high society (in the 1970s he made an enormous amount of money churning out commissioned portraits of wealthy patrons). In his later years he was more famous for his celebrity-courting lifestyle and deliberately bland persona than for his art; indeed, it could be argued that his advertising skills were nowhere more brilliantly deployed than in promoting himself. In purely financial terms his success

in doing this was prodigious. At his death (following a routine gall bladder operation) he left a fortune estimated at $100,000,000, most of which went to create an arts charity, the Andy Warhol Foundation. His status as an artist, however, is controversial. Even his most fervent admirers tend to admit that he added little to his achievement as a painter after the mid-1960s, but large claims are sometimes made for his earlier works. Warhol published a celebrity magazine called Interview, and several books appeared under his name, some genuinely written by him, others put together from tapes. The Diaries of Andy Warhol appeared posthumously in 1989. In 1994 a museum dedicated to his work opened in his home town of Pittsburgh.

wash. A thin, transparent layer of *watercolour or diluted *ink spread evenly over a fairly broad area of paper and showing no brush marks.

Washington Color Painters. See NOLAND.

watercolour. Term that can, in its broadest sense, be applied to any paint bound with a *medium (generally *gum arabic) soluble in water. Its use has been widespread and varied over a long period, embracing ancient Egyptian papyruses, Chinese paintings on silk, the decorations of *illuminated manuscripts of the Middle Ages, and Elizabethan portrait *miniatures. In normal parlance, however, the term 'watercolour' usually refers specifically to a type of painting in which the lighter tones are obtained not by mixing white pigment with the colours (see GOUACHE) but by diluting them with water so that the paper or other support shows more strongly through the thinner layers of paint.

Watercolour in this more restricted sense was sometimes used in the 16th and 17th centuries (memorably by *Dürer and van *Dyck, for example), but it was not until the 18th century, in England, that it became a major medium, particularly for landscape painting, in which it lent itself to rendering subtle atmospheric effects. By the 1780s watercolours were being manufactured in small cakes of the type still used today, making them very easily portable for outdoor work. At first the medium was used mainly for topographical scenes, and the technique consisted essentially of tinting an underlying drawing. Around 1800 a transition was made to a bolder approach in which the colour was used freely and directly. *Girtin and *Turner (both born in 1775) brought watercolour to its greatest heights, Girtin being the consummate master of the classic broad technique and Turner achieving unequalled variety of effect and intensity of expression. In the wake of *Impressionism, the capacity of watercolour to achieve spontaneous expression was more widely appreciated and it ceased to be so much of an English speciality. Among the modern artists who have been great exponents of the technique (in their very different ways) are *Cézanne, *Dufy, *Grosz, *Klee, *Nolde, and *Sargent.

water-glass painting (also called **mineral painting** and **stereochromy**). A method of mural painting, intended to prove resistant to the effects of damp and pollution, invented c.1825. It is essentially a variation of *fresco; after the paint has been applied to the plaster, it is carefully sprayed with a solution of water-glass (potassium silicate or sodium silicate), which provides a protective film when it dries. As water-glass is strongly alkaline it can be used only with certain pigments. In the 1860s *Maclise and other artists used the technique in murals in the Houses of Parliament, because it was thought that they would be proof against the damp and dirty atmosphere of London, but they deteriorated within ten years. Later the method was improved as Keim's process (developed by professor Adolf Keim of Munich in the 1880s), but because of its complexity and limitations it never became popular.

Waterhouse, Sir Ellis (b Epsom, Surrey, 16 Feb. 1905; d Oxford, 7 Sept. 1985). British art historian. In a highly distinguished career he was director of the National Galleries of Scotland (1949–52), director of the Barber Institute of Fine Arts, Birmingham (1952–70), and the holder of many other prestigious posts in Britain and the USA. His publications were centred on two main areas, British painting of the 18th century and Italian *Baroque painting, his chief books being Baroque Painting in Rome (1937, revised edn. 1976), Painting in Britain: 1530–1790 (1953 and several revised edns.), Italian Baroque Painting (1962), a monograph on *Gainsborough (1958), and two on *Reynolds (1941 and 1973), The Dictionary of British 18th-Century Painters (1981), and The Dictionary of British 16th- and 17th-Century Painters (published posthumously 1988). He wore his great erudition lightly and few other art historians wrote so entertainingly.

Waterhouse, J. W. (John William) (b Rome, 6 Apr. 1849; d London, 10 Feb. 1917). English painter. Early in his career he concentrated on scenes from the Greek and Roman world in a manner similar to that of *Alma-Tadema, but in the 1880s he turned to literary themes, painted in a distinctive, dreamily romantic style. In approach he was influenced by the *Pre-Raphaelites, but his handling of paint is quite different from theirs—rich and sensuous. His work includes such classic Victorian anthology pieces as The Lady of Shalott (1888, Tate, London) and Hylas and the Nymphs (1896, City AG, Manchester). He enjoyed a great reputation in his lifetime; it declined after his death but revived as part of the general reappraisal of Victorian art in the later 20th century.

Watson, Homer (b Doon, nr. Kitchener, Ontario, 14 Jan. 1855; d Doon, 30 May 1936). Canadian landscape painter, active for most of his life in his home town of Doon. He was mainly self-taught. His early works were rather dry and descriptive, but after a visit to England in 1887–90 his style became much freer and more *Impressionistic (although it was before this visit, in 1882, that Oscar Wilde, seeing Watson's work in Toronto, dubbed him 'the Canadian Constable'). Around the turn of the century Watson was internationally famous, but after his wife's death in 1918 he devoted much of his time to spiritualism, and by the time of his own death he was bankrupt and forgotten.

Watt, Alison. See GLASGOW SCHOOL OF ART.

Watteau, Jean-Antoine (bapt. Valenciennes, 10 Oct. 1684; d Nogent-sur-Marne, nr. Paris, 18 July 1721). The greatest French painter of his period and one of the key figures of *Rococo art. His home town of Valenciennes had passed to France from the Spanish Netherlands only six years before his birth, and he was regarded by contemporaries as a Flemish painter. There are indeed strong links with Flanders in his art, but it also has a sophistication that is quintessentially French.

Watteau moved to Paris in about 1702 and c.1704–8 he was a pupil and assistant of *Gillot, who stimulated his interest in scenes from the theatre and daily life. After leaving Gillot he worked for a year or two for Claude *Audran, who as well as being a leading decorative painter was curator of the Luxembourg Palace; Watteau thus had access to *Rubens's Marie de Médicis paintings, which were an enormous influence on him, even though Rubens's robustness was far removed from the exquisite sensitivity that characterized his own art. Rubens was one of the prime inspirations for the type of picture with which Watteau is most associated—the *fête galante* (see FÊTE CHAMPÊTRE), in which beautifully dressed young people idle away their time in a dreamy, romantic, pastoral setting. The tradition of lovers in a parkland setting goes back via *Giorgione to the medieval type known as the Garden of Love, but Watteau was the first painter to make the theme his own, and his individuality in this respect was recognized by his contemporaries. In 1717 he submitted a characteristic work, *The Pilgrimage to the Island of Cythera* (Louvre, Paris; a slightly later variant is in Schloss Charlottenburg, Berlin), as his reception piece to the Academy, and owing to the difficulty of fitting him into recognized categories he was received as a 'peintre de fêtes galantes', a title created expressly for him. He was, indeed, a highly independent artist, who did not readily submit to the will of patrons or officialdom, and the novelty and freshness of his work liberated French painting from the yoke of Italian influence, creating a truly 'Parisian' outlook that endured until the *Neoclassicism of J.-L. *David.

Watteau's world is a highly artificial one (apart from scenes of love he took his themes mainly from the theatre), but underlying the frivolity is a feeling of melancholy, reflecting the certain knowledge that all the pleasures of the flesh are transient. This poetic gravity distinguishes him from his imitators, and parallels are often drawn between Watteau's own life and character and the content of his paintings. He was notorious for his irritable and restless temperament and died early of tuberculosis, and it has been suggested that the pervasive melancholic mood of his pictures was related to the constant reminders of his own mortality that his illness entailed. In 1719–20 he visited London to consult the celebrated physician Dr Richard Mead (who was also an art collector), but the hard English winter worsened his condition. His early death came when he may have been making a new departure in his art, for his last important work combines something of the straightforward naturalism of his early pictures in the Flemish tradition with the elegant sophistication of his *fêtes galantes*: it is a shop sign painted for the picture dealer Edmé Gersaint (1694–1750) and known as *L'Enseigne de Gersaint* (1721, Gemäldegalerie, Berlin).

Watteau was slipshod in matters of material technique (another aspect of his listless temperament) and many of his paintings are in consequence in a poor state of preservation. A complete picture of his genius depends all the more, then, on his numerous superb drawings, many of them scintillating studies from the life. He collected his drawings into large bound volumes and used these books as a reference source for his paintings (the same figure often appears in more than one picture). In spite of his difficult character, he had many loyal friends and supporters who recognized his genius, and although his reputation suffered with the Revolution and the growth of Neoclassicism, he always had distinguished admirers. It is perhaps as a colourist that he has had the most profound influence. His method of juxtaposing flecks of colour on the canvas was carried further by *Delacroix and later reduced to a science by *Seurat and the *Neo-Impressionists. Among his immediate followers, the principal figures were *Lancret and *Pater. He also had a nephew and a great-nephew (father and son) who worked more or less in his manner. They are both known as Watteau de Lille after their main place of work—**Louis Watteau** (1731–98) and **François Watteau** (1758–1823).

Watts, G. F. (George Frederic) (*b* London, 23 Feb. 1817; *d* London, 1 July 1904). English painter and sculptor. In 1843 he won a prize in the competition for the decoration of the Houses of Parliament; no commission resulted from this, but he used the prize money to visit Italy, where the great *Renaissance masters helped shape his high-minded attitudes towards art. After returning to England in 1847, he established a solid reputation in intellectual circles, but popular fame did not come until the early 1880s, following exhibitions of his work in Manchester (1880) and London (1881). In old age he was the most revered figure in British art, and in 1902 he was the only artist among the twelve original holders of the newly instituted Order of Merit (he had earlier refused many other honours, including a baronetcy, offered at the same time as *Millais's).

Watts's style was early influenced by *Etty, but the *Elgin Marbles, *Michelangelo, and the great Venetian painters (notably *Titian) were his avowed exemplars in his desire 'to affect the mind seriously by nobility of line and colour'. He aimed to invest his work with moral purpose and his most characteristic paintings are abstruse allegories that were once enormously popular but now seem vague and ponderous (*Hope*, 1886, Tate, London, and other versions). His portraits of great contemporaries (*Gladstone, Tennyson, J. S. Mill*, etc., NPG, London) have generally worn much better. As a sculptor, he is remembered chiefly for his equestrian piece *Physical Energy* (1904). A cast of it forms the central feature of the Cecil Rhodes Memorial, Cape Town, and another is in Kensington Gardens, London. Watts was twice married, his first wife being the celebrated actress Ellen Terry, of whom he painted several portraits, notably 'Choosing' (c.1864, NPG, London). Only 16 at the time of the wedding in 1864, she was 30 years his junior and they separated the following year (later she was the mother of Gordon *Craig). Watts's former house at Compton, near Guildford, Surrey, is now the Watts Gallery, devoted to his work. Wilfrid *Blunt was curator 1959–85.

wax. A malleable substance obtained from various animal, vegetable, and mineral sources, most commonly the matter secreted by bees as the material of honeycomb; when bleached and purified it can be used as a medium for sculpture. Since the 1830s, synthetic waxes, based on petroleum, have also been available. Wax has a long and varied history in sculpture, for it is widely available, extremely versatile, and has many advantageous qualities. It can be modelled, carved, or cast; it is easy and fairly clean to handle; it can readily be mixed with colouring matter (making it an excellent medium for naturalistic portraiture); 'it is not subject to serious chemical or physical change, only shrinking and becoming slightly more brittle with age, it is not prone to fungal and insect attacks . . . it is easy to vary its consistency by the addition of hardeners, plasticizers, and solvents . . . It is a very tractable material permitting corrections, changes, or additions to the design at any stage. This makes it the ideal material for the production of sketch models for works finished in other materials' (E. J. Pyke, *A Biographical Dictionary of Wax Modellers*, 1973). However, it also has disadvantages. Compared with clay (see TERRACOTTA), the other material most often used for models, it is fairly expensive; it tends to become dirty, and it is easily broken or damaged by heat.

In addition to being employed by countless major sculptors to make preliminary models (several by *Michelangelo survive, for example) and also as an essential part of bronze-casting by the 'lost wax' process (see CIRE-PERDUE), wax has been used since ancient times to produce finished works, particularly portraits and death masks. In the 18th century, exhibitions of waxworks (life-size, highly realistic figures of famous people, complete with real clothes and hair)

became popular entertainments. Easily the most famous exponent of this kind of work was Marie Tussaud, née Grosholtz (b Strasbourg, 1 Dec. 1761; d London, 16 Apr. 1850), who, as well as producing casts from live people, made death masks of guillotined victims of the French Revolution. In 1802 she moved to England and toured for many years with an exhibition of her work until finding a permanent home for 'Madame Tussaud's Waxworks' in London in 1835. Initially it was located in Baker Street, and in 1884 (under her grandson's management) it moved to its present site in nearby Marylebone Road; some of her work can still be seen there. Other notable waxworks can be seen in London in the collection of royal funerary effigies at Westminster Abbey. Small portraits in wax were made in the *Renaissance and became popular in the 18th and 19th centuries; they were mainly done as profile reliefs, paralleling the vogue for *silhouettes.

Among serious sculptors who have used wax as their preferred medium, Medardo *Rosso stands out. The most famous artist to use the material exclusively was probably Gaetano Giulio Zumbo (b Syracuse, 1656; d Paris, 22 Dec. 1701), who worked in various Italian cities, particularly Florence. He specialized in macabre tableaux on themes of death, with grimly realistic depictions of decomposing bodies. He also pioneered the use of wax models as tools in anatomical demonstration. This aspect of his work was developed with extreme sophistication in Florence in the 18th century, most notably in the work of Clemente Susini (1754–1814), who worked for the natural history museum 'La Specola', opened in 1775; examples of his extraordinarily detailed life-size figures (and of Zumbo's work) can still be seen there.

wax painting. See ENCAUSTIC PAINTING.

Wearing, Gillian. See TURNER PRIZE.

Weber, Max (b Belostok [now Białystok, Poland], 18 Apr. 1881; d Great Neck, NY, 4 Oct. 1961). Russian-born American painter, sculptor, printmaker, and writer, whose work more than that of any other American artist synthesized the latest European developments at the beginning of the 20th century. He emigrated to New York with his parents when he was 10. From 1905 to 1908 he travelled in Europe, studying in Paris at the *Académie Julian and with *Matisse, admiring early *Cubism and becoming a friend of Henri *Rousseau. After his return to New York in 1909 he rapidly became a controversial figure—no other American avant-garde artist of the time exhibited more widely or was more harshly attacked. His work was influenced by *Fauvism and *primitive art (he was one of the first American artists to show interest in it), but most importantly by Cubism (in sculpture as well as painting). After about 1917, however, Weber's work became more naturalistic. During the 1930s his subjects often expressed his social concern and in the 1940s his work included scenes with rabbis and Jewish scholars—mystical recollections of his Russian childhood. He published several books, including *Cubist Poems* and the autobiographical *Max Weber* (1945).

Wedgwood, Josiah (*bapt*. Burslem, Staffordshire, 12 July 1730; *d* Burslem, 3 Jan. 1795). The most famous of English pottery manufacturers. Wedgwood combined organizing ability and flair for business with scientific knowledge and artistic taste, and he was largely responsible for the great expansion of the Staffordshire pottery industry in his period. He founded his own pottery in 1759, and in 1768 he opened a new factory at Etruria, a village (now part of Stoke-on-Trent) he had built for his workmen (it was named after the ancient state of Etruria in Italy, where much ancient pottery had been found). His products established the taste for *Neoclassical designs in English ceramics and were influential as far afield as the USA and Russia. He employed excellent designers, the most distinguished of whom was *Flaxman, and also collaborated with *Stubbs, manufacturing earthenware panels that he used in place of canvas.

Weenix, Jan Baptist (*b* Amsterdam, ?1621; *d* Huis ter Mey, nr. Utrecht, ?1660/1). Dutch painter. From 1642/3 to 1646/7 he was in Italy, and on his return to his native Amsterdam he painted Italianate landscapes close in style to those of *Berchem, who is said to have been his cousin. Later he turned mainly to pictures of still-life with dead game; he also painted portraits. His son **Jan Weenix** (*b* Amsterdam, ?1642; *bur*. Amsterdam, 19 Sept. 1719) specialized in hunting trophy subjects similar to those of his father; indeed, it is often difficult to tell their work apart. Most of his career was spent in Amsterdam, but from 1702 to 1712 he worked at Düsseldorf for the elector palatine. Both artists were prolific (Jan told *Houbraken that his father could paint three life-size half-length portraits in a day) and are represented in many public collections.

Weiditz, Hans (*b* ?c.1500; *d* ?Strasbourg, ?c.1536). German designer of woodcuts, active in Augsburg (1518–22) and subsequently in Strasbourg. He seems to have had a high contemporary reputation, but his life is obscure. Very few of his works are signed, but a large number of book illustrations have been attributed to him. Much of this oeuvre was previously given to an artist called 'the Petrarch Master', named after the illustrations in an edition of Petrarch's *De remediis utriusque fortunae* published in Augsburg in 1532. The identification of Weiditz with the Petrarch Master is generally but not universally accepted. The illustrations associated with the Petrarch Master are remarkable for their acute observation, and at a time when *Dürer's influence was all-pervasive he maintained his own personal style. A few paintings have also been attributed to Weiditz. Several other members of his family were artists.

Weight, Carel (*b* London, 10 Sept. 1908; *d* London, 13 Aug. 1997). British painter. In the Second World War he served with the Royal Engineers and Army Education Corps and was appointed an *Official War Artist in 1945, working in Austria, Greece, and Italy. He began teaching at the *Royal College of Art in 1947 and was professor of painting there from 1967 until his retirement in 1973. Weight was something of a maverick figure ('I don't like the art world very much. I don't like the dealers and I don't like the critics') and his work is highly individual. His best-known paintings are imaginative figure compositions, set in suburban surroundings. They are superficially realistic, but feature idiosyncratic perspective effects and strange human dramas, producing a feeling that is sometimes humorous and sometimes menacing: 'My art is concerned with such things as anger, love, fear, hate and loneliness, emphasized by the ordinary landscape in which the dramatic scene is set.' Weight also painted portraits and landscapes.

Weir, J. Alden. See TEN.

Weissenbruch, Jan Hendrik (*b* The Hague, 19 June 1824; *d* The Hague, 24 Mar. 1903). Dutch landscape and marine painter, one of the outstanding artists of the *Hague School. His work is distinguished by its subtle handling of tone and feeling for atmosphere. His cousin **Johannes** (Jan) **Weissenbruch** (*b* The Hague, 18 Mar. 1822; *d* The Hague, 15 Feb. 1880), a painter and lithographer, specialized in town views in the detailed manner of 17th-century artists such as Jan van der *Heyden.

welding. See IRON.

Wentworth, Richard. See NEW BRITISH SCULPTURE.

Werefkin, Marianne von. See NEUE KÜNSTLERVEREINIGUNG.

Werenskiold, Erik (*b* Vingen, 11 Feb. 1855; *d* Oslo, 23 Nov. 1938). Norwegian painter, printmaker, and illustrator. He was one of the leading personalities in Norwegian art, the friend of numerous writers and intellectuals and a symbol of national culture. His work included landscapes, in which he showed an affectionate yet unsentimental approach to his native land, portraits of many of the leading Norwegians of his day (*Henrik Ibsen*, 1895, NG, Oslo), lithographs, etchings, and book illustrations. After the turn of the century he was influenced by *Cézanne.

Werff, Adriaen van der (*b* Kralingen, nr. Rotterdam, 21 Jan. 1659; *d* Rotterdam, 12 Nov. 1722). Dutch painter of religious and mythological scenes and portraits, active mainly in Rotterdam. He combined the precise finish of the Leiden tradition (learned from his master Eglon van der *Neer) with the classical standards of the French Académie Royale (see ACADEMY) and became the most famous Dutch painter of his day, winning international success and earning an enormous fortune. *Houbraken, writing in 1721, considered him the greatest of all Dutch painters and this was the prevailing critical opinion throughout the 18th century. His reputation crumbled in the 19th century, when he was thought to have betrayed the Dutch naturalistic tradition, and he is now considered an extremely accomplished but rather sentimental and repetitive minor master. Van der Werff also worked as an architect in Rotterdam, designing elegant house façades. His brother **Pieter van der Werff** (1661–1722) was his principal pupil and assistant, imitating his style closely and making many copies of his work.

Werve, Claus de. See SLUTER.

Wesselmann, Tom (*b* Cincinnati, Oh., 23 Feb. 1931). American painter, one of the best-known exponents of *Pop art. He often incorporates elements of *collage or *assemblage in his work, using household objects such as television sets and sometimes including sound effects. Typically his subjects are aggressively sexual and he is best known for his continuing series *Great American Nude* (began 1961), in which the nude becomes a depersonalized sex symbol set in a realistically depicted everyday environment. He emphasizes the woman's nipples, mouth, and genitals, with the rest of the body depicted in flat, unmodulated colour. In other works he isolates parts of the body still further, as in his *Smoker* series, in which the mouth—often depicted on a huge scale—becomes a provocatively erotic symbol. In the 1980s he began making massive 'drawings' cut from sheets of aluminium or steel. He has also made prints in a variety of techniques.

West, Benjamin (*b* Springfield [now Swarthmore], nr. Philadelphia, 10 Oct. 1738; *d* London, 11 Mar. 1820). American history and portrait painter who spent almost all his career in England. After early success as a portraitist in New York, he studied for three years in Italy (1760–3), chiefly in Rome, then settled in London. There he soon repeated the professional and social success he had enjoyed in Italy, in part because of the novelty value of being an American. Initially West had set up as a portraitist in London, but it was as a *history painter that he made his mark. In Rome he had been in contact with the circle of Gavin *Hamilton and *Mengs, and his early work is in a determined but rather flimsy *Neoclassical style (*Agrippina Landing at Brundisium with the Ashes of Germanicus*, 1768, Yale Univ. AG). With his famous *Death of Wolfe* (1770, NG, Ottawa), however, he broke new ground. This was not, as is sometimes asserted, the first history painting to feature contemporary costume (Edward Penny (1714–91), for example, had painted the same subject in modern dress in 1764 (Ashmolean Mus., Oxford)); however, it was the first picture in such vein to become a popular and critical success in Britain. It was exhibited in 1771 at the *Royal Academy (of which West had been a foundation member in 1768) and was so admired that West had to make several replicas; he also made a fortune from the sale of engravings. George III admitted he had been wrong to think it 'very ridiculous to exhibit heroes in coats, breeches, and cocked hats' and in 1772 he appointed West his official history painter. His innovation was soon adopted by other artists, most notably his countryman *Copley, and it marks an important turning point in taste.

In 1792 West succeeded *Reynolds as president of the Royal Academy; he resigned in 1805 following internal squabbles, but he resumed the post the following year and held it until his death. In his later works, his style grew away from Neoclassicism; he was in the vanguard of the *Romantic movement with paintings such as the melodramatic *Saul and the Witch of Endor* (1777, Wadsworth Atheneum, Hartford), and his *Death on a Pale Horse* (1817, Philadelphia Mus. of Art) has been hailed as a forerunner of *Delacroix. His historical importance far outweighs the quality of his work, which (in spite of its modernity in ideas) is often pedestrian. He was the first American painter to achieve an international reputation and was an inspiration to many of his countrymen. Many young Americans who followed him to London benefited from his unstinting generosity in advice and practical help, including Washington *Allston, Samuel *Morse, Charles Willson *Peale, and Gilbert *Stuart (his assistant for several years), so he well deserves his title of 'the father of American painting'.

Westall, Richard (*b* Hertford, 1765; *d* London, 4 Dec. 1836). English painter and illustrator. He painted a few pictures for *Boydell's Shakespeare Gallery, but he made his name chiefly in book illustration, in which field he was one of the most prolific artists of the day. As a watercolourist he was noted for his unusually rich colour effects.

West Coast Figuration. See DIEBENKORN.

Westhoff, Clara. See WORPSWEDE.

Westmacott, Sir Richard (*b* London, 15 July 1775; *d* London, 2 Sept. 1856). English *Neoclassical sculptor. The son of a sculptor also called **Richard** (1747–1808), he trained first under his father and then from 1793 to 1796 in Rome, where he worked in *Canova's studio. After his return to London, he soon had a very large practice, second only to *Chantrey. His best-known work is the huge *Achilles* statue (unveiled 1822) in Hyde Park; it honours the Duke of Wellington and is made of bronze from captured French cannon. At the time the figure's conspicuous nudity was considered shocking or amusing, especially considering it had been paid for by a group of lady subscribers. Westmacott's last major undertaking was the group of the *Progress of Civilization* on the pediment of the British Museum (installed 1851). His work is dignified but often rather pedestrian in handling. He was professor of sculpture at the *Royal Academy from 1827 to 1854. Two of his brothers, **George** (active 1799–1827) and **Henry** (1784–1861), were sculptors, as was his son, another

Richard Westmacott (1799–1872). See also MARCUS AURELIUS.

Weyden, Rogier van der (*b* Tournai, ?1399; *d* Brussels, 18 June 1464). The outstanding Netherlandish painter of the mid-15th century. He was one of the greatest and most influential European artists of his time, but there is little secure knowledge about his career. None of the surviving paintings associated with him is signed, dated, or verified by indisputable contemporary documentation, but several can be identified from early sources, and the style these show is so distinctive that a coherent oeuvre has been built up around them.

His early career, however, is still a particularly problematic area, as the sparse evidence relating to it is teasingly equivocal. In 1427 a certain 'Rogelet [little Roger] de la Pasture' began an apprenticeship with Robert Campin in Tournai, and in 1432 he became a master in the city's painters' guild. It is generally accepted that these two documentary records refer to Rogier van der Weyden (the French and Flemish forms of the name both meaning 'Rogier of the Meadow'), although it is uncertain why he should have started his apprenticeship so late. There are no documented pictures surviving from Campin's hand, but he is generally agreed to be identical with the *Master of Flémalle, so the whole question of Rogier's relationship with his master is based on stylistic analysis. Some scholars have argued that the Master of Flémalle should be identified with the young Rogier rather than with Campin, but the prevailing opinion is now that Rogier's work shows a development from the powerfully naturalistic and expressive style of his master towards greater refinement and spirituality. Rogier's celebrated *Descent from the Cross* (c.1440, Prado, Madrid), for example, is close to the Master of Flémalle's *Crucified Thief* fragment (Städelsches Kunstinstitut, Frankfurt) in its dramatic force and use of a plain gold background, but it has a new poignancy and exaltedness.

By 1435 Rogier had moved to Brussels and in 1436 he was appointed official painter to the city. There is evidence that he made a pilgrimage to Rome in 1450, but otherwise nothing to indicate that he ever left Brussels again. His work there included four large panels on the theme of justice for the courtroom of the town hall (these were his most famous pictures until they were destroyed during the French bombardment of the city in 1695), but all his surviving paintings are either religious pictures or portraits. The portraits are all of fairly similar type, showing the sitter, whether male or female, bust-length and in three-quarter view, with aristocratic bearing and a pious expression (*Portrait of a Young Lady*, c.1460, NG, Washington). They are among the finest of their time, but Rogier's reputation rests mainly on his religious works, which are remarkable for their magisterial power of design and their emotional intensity and sensitivity. The largest and most magnificent among them is the *Last Judgement* altarpiece (c.1445–50, Hôtel-Dieu, Beaune), which in size and ambition invites comparison with the Ghent Altarpiece of Jan van *Eyck. The contrast with the cool objectivity of this great precursor was well summed up by Erwin *Panofsky: 'Roger's world is at once physically barer and spiritually richer than Jan van Eyck's. Where Jan observed things that no painter had ever observed, Roger felt and expressed emotions and sensations—mostly of a bitter or bittersweet nature—that no painter had ever recaptured.'

Unlike Jan, Rogier seems to have had numerous assistants and pupils, for the number of good contemporary copies and versions of his paintings indicates that he ran a busy workshop. His pictures were exported to France, Germany, Spain, and Italy (where he was one of the few northern artists of the time to be highly regarded), and many of the types and motifs he invented or popularized became part of the common currency of artistic ideas until well into the 16th century (see DONOR, for example). However, although his work was revered, knowledge of the man himself quickly faded, so much so that in van *Mander's biographies he is inadvertently split into two artists—Rogier van der Weyden and Rogier of Bruges. After the destruction of his most conspicuous works in Brussels in 1695, he was virtually forgotten. Interest in him revived in the mid-19th century, but it was not until the 20th century that he took his place among the greatest European painters.

Wheatley, Francis (*b* London, 1747; *d* London, 28 June 1801). English painter. His early works were mainly small full-length portraits and *conversation pieces in the manner of *Zoffany. In 1779 he moved to Dublin to escape creditors, and after his return to London in 1783 his work broadened in scope. It included landscapes, history paintings, and life-size portraits, but he is best known for works produced to be engraved for the print market. He is particularly remembered for his enormously popular *Cries of London* (fourteen paintings, 1792–5; prints published 1793–7), showing street vendors, milkmaids, and so on. The paintings are now dispersed; examples are at Upton House, Warwickshire (NT).

Wheeler, Sir Charles (*b* Codsall, Staffordshire, 14 Mar. 1892; *d* Mayfield, Sussex, 22 Aug. 1974). British sculptor (and occasional painter). He produced many portrait busts, but the major part of his output was devoted to public sculpture; his biggest commission was for the Bank of England, for which he did various works between 1930 and 1937, including three bronze doors and a series of giant stone figures on the exterior. From 1956 to 1966 he was president of the *Royal Academy. The most notable event of his presidency was the controversial sale (1962) of the Academy's greatest treasure, *Leonardo da Vinci's cartoon of the *Virgin and Child with St Anne and St John the Baptist* (now in the National Gallery); fear that the masterpiece would leave Britain 'provoked extensive press and public obloquy', but the sale 'did secure the [Academy's] finances for almost the next 20 years' (*DNB*). The matter is discussed at length in Wheeler's autobiography, *High Relief*, published in 1968. See also NATIONAL ART COLLECTIONS FUND.

Whistler, James McNeill (*b* Lowell, Mass., 11 July 1834; *d* London, 17 July 1903). American-born painter, printmaker, and designer, active mainly in England. Originally he was called James Abbot Whistler, but after his mother's death in 1881 he added her maiden name to become James Abbot McNeill Whistler for a time, and eventually he dropped the 'Abbot'. He spent part of his childhood in Russia (where his father had gone to work as a civil engineer) and was an inveterate traveller. His training as an artist began indirectly when, after his discharge from West Point Military Academy for 'deficiency in chemistry', he learnt etching as a US navy cartographer. In 1855 he moved to Paris, where he studied intermittently under *Gleyre, made copies in the Louvre, acquired a lasting admiration for *Velázquez, and became a devotee of the cult of the Japanese print (see UKIYO-E) and oriental art and decoration in general. The circles in which he moved can be gauged from his friend *Fantin-Latour's *Homage to *Delacroix*, in which Whistler is portrayed alongside *Baudelaire, *Manet, and others. He settled in London in 1859, but often returned to France. His first major oil painting, *At the Piano* (1858–9, Taft Mus., Cincinnati), was well received at the *Royal Academy exhibition in 1860 and he soon made a name for himself, not just because of his talent, but also on account of his flamboyant personality. He was famous for his wit and dandyism, and loved controversy. His lifestyle was lavish and he was often in debt. Dante Gabriel *Rossetti and Oscar Wilde were among his famous friends.

Whistler's art is in many respects the opposite to his ostentatious personality, being discreet and subtle, but the creed that lay behind it was radical. He believed that painting should exist for its own sake, not to convey literary or moral ideas, and he often gave his pictures musical titles to suggest an analogy with the abstract art of music: 'Art should be independent of all claptrap—should stand alone, and appeal to the artistic sense of eye or ear, without confounding this with emotions entirely foreign to it, as devotion, pity, love, patriotism, and the like. All these have no kind of concern with it, and that is why I insist on calling my works "arrangements" and "harmonies".' He was a laborious and self-critical worker, but this is belied by the flawless harmonies of tone and colour he created in his paintings, which are mainly portraits and landscapes, particularly scenes of the Thames. No less original was his work as a decorative artist, notably in the Peacock Room (1876–7) for the London home of the Liverpool shipping magnate Frederick Leyland (now reconstructed in the Freer Gallery, Washington), where the graceful, stylized patterning anticipated much in the *Art Nouveau style of the 1890s (Aubrey *Beardsley saw the room in about 1891 and was greatly impressed by it).

In 1877 Whistler showed his *Nocturne in Black and Gold: The Falling Rocket* (1875, Detroit Inst. of Arts) at the opening exhibition of the *Grosvenor Gallery. *Ruskin attacked it in print, accusing him of 'wilful imposture' and 'flinging a pot of paint in the public's face', and Whistler sued him for libel. He won the action, but the awarding of only a farthing's damages with no costs was in effect a justification for Ruskin, and the expense of the trial led to Whistler's bankruptcy in 1879—a tribulation he endured with dignity. His house was sold and he spent a year in Venice (1879–80), concentrating on the etchings that helped to restore his fortunes when he returned to London. He was one of the greatest of all etchers (some critics rank him second only to *Rembrandt) and also made lithographs. In his fifties he began to achieve honours and substantial success (he also made a happy marriage, in 1888, to Beatrix Godwin, widow of the architect E. W. Godwin, with whom he had collaborated, but she died only

eight years later). In 1891 his portrait of Thomas Carlyle (1872–3) was bought by Glasgow Art Gallery and Museum, becoming the first of his oils to enter a public collection in Britain, and in the same year his most famous work, *Arrangement in Grey and Black: Portrait of the Painter's Mother* (1871), was bought by the French state (it is now in the Musée d'Orsay, Paris).

Whistler's paintings are related to *Impressionism (although he was more interested in evoking a mood than in accurately depicting the effects of light), to *Symbolism, and to *Aestheticism, and he played a major role in introducing modern ideas to British art, his magnetic personality attracting numerous followers. Those who were most immediately influenced by him included his pupils Walter Greaves (1849–1930), Gwen *John, the Australian-born Mortimer Menpes (1860–1938), and Walter *Sickert. His aesthetic creed was explained in his *Ten O'Clock Lecture* (1885) and this, and much else on art and society, was republished in *The Gentle Art of Making Enemies* (1890).

Whistler, Rex (*b* Eltham, Kent [now Greater London], 24 June 1905; *d* nr. Le Mesnil, Normandy, 18 July 1944). British painter, graphic artist, and stage designer. He is best known for his decorations in a light and fanciful style evocative of the 18th century, notably the series of murals *In Pursuit of Rare Meats* (1926–7) in the restaurant of the Tate Gallery (now Tate Britain). He also did numerous book illustrations and much work for the stage, including ballet and opera. He was killed in action in the Second World War. His brother **Sir Laurence Whistler** (1912–2000), a writer and glass engraver, published several books on him.

Whiteley, Brett (*b* Sydney, 7 Apr. 1939; *d* Thirroul, nr. Wollongong, NSW, 15 June 1992). Australian painter. His work was based on the human figure, often with erotic or violent imagery, but he sometimes came close to abstraction. He achieved success early (he won the international prize at the Paris *Biennale for Young Artists in 1961), but his later life was marred by personal problems, including divorce and a battle with addiction to alcohol and drugs; he was found dead in a motel room and the coroner's verdict was 'death by self-administered substances'. Christopher Allen (*Art in Australia*, 1997) writes that Whiteley was the artist who most 'truly speaks for middlebrow Australian culture in the seventies and eighties . . . the media loved him and his every sketch met with adulation . . . With his brilliant facility, bright colours, images of sun, sea and sexual passion, he became the acceptable face of modernism and his pictures, though growing steadily worse and more vacuous, continued to fetch higher and higher prices.'

Whiteread, Rachel (*b* London, 20 Apr. 1963). British sculptor. In 1988 she began making a novel type of sculpture consisting of casts of domestic features or the spaces around them (such as the space under a bed). These pieces, carrying 'the residue of years and years of use' culminated in *Untitled (House)* (1993), a concrete cast of an entire house in Grove Road in the East End of London. The house itself was demolished once the cast was made, leaving Whiteread's ghostly replica on the site. It helped her to win the *Turner Prize in 1993 and generated so much publicity that it made her probably the most famous artist in Britain apart from Damien *Hirst (although, unlike Hirst, she does not court attention). The Turner jury praised the work for 'its combination of austere monumentality and immediacy of reference to the everyday world', its 'haunting qualities' and its 'poetic strangeness'. Many people, however, regarded it as an ugly lump of concrete, and in spite of a vigorous campaign to save it, the work was demolished in 1994. Following her success as the first woman to win the Turner Prize, in 1997 Whiteread became the first woman to represent Britain with a solo show at the Venice *Biennale (Barbara *Hepworth in 1950 and Bridget *Riley in 1968 had shared the British Pavilion). In 2000 her memorial to Austrian Jews killed by the Nazis was installed in the Judenplatz, Vienna. It is a chamber-like structure encircled by rows of concrete books, like a library turned to stone—an image evoking the idea of the Nazis' attempt to destroy a culture.

Whitney, Gertrude Vanderbilt (*b* New York, 9 Jan. 1875; *d* New York, 18 Apr. 1942). American sculptor, patron, and collector, the founder of the Whitney Museum of American Art, New York. The daughter of Cornelius II Vanderbilt, an immensely wealthy railroad magnate, she turned seriously to art after her marriage in 1896 to Harry Payne Whitney, a financier and world-class polo player. Her training as a sculptor included periods at the *Art Students League and in Paris, where she knew *Rodin. She won several major commissions, notably for monuments commemorating the First World War, including the Washington Heights War Memorial, New York (1921). Her style was traditional, but she was sympathetic towards pro-

gressive art and is much more important as a patron than as an artist. In 1907 she opened her New York studio as an exhibition space for young artists, and in 1914 she put her patronage on a more formal basis when she bought the house adjoining her studio, converted it into galleries, and opened it as the Whitney Studio; later she founded a series of organizations in New York with the same aim of helping young artists—the Friends of Young Artists (1915), the Whitney Studio Club (1918), and the Whitney Studio Galleries (1928). In 1929 she offered to donate her own collection of about 500 American paintings, sculptures, and drawings to the *Metropolitan Museum, New York, but the gift was turned down. Consequently in 1930 she announced the founding of the Whitney Museum of American Art and it opened the following year at 10 West 8th Street in a group of converted brownstone buildings. In 1954 the museum moved to a new building at 22 West 54th Street on land provided by the *Museum of Modern Art, and in 1966 to its present home—a spectacular building designed for it by Marcel Breuer at 945 Madison Avenue. The museum now has the largest and finest collection of 20th-century American art in the world, as well as a good representation from earlier periods. Every other year it holds the Whitney Biennial, a major showcase for work by living artists. Mrs Whitney donated funds to many other good causes, artistic and otherwise, but she was 'a woman of modest disposition who carried out her public activities quietly' (*Dictionary of American Biography*).

Wicar, Jean-Baptiste (*b* Lille, 22 Jan. 1762; *d* Rome, 27 Feb. 1834). French painter, draughtsman, and collector, active in Italy for most of his career. A pupil of J.-L. *David, he was a fairly successful painter of portraits and history paintings in his master's style, but he is now best remembered as a leading collector of Old Master drawings. He sold some of the best of these to Sir Thomas *Lawrence, through the dealer Samuel Woodburn (1780–1853), but he bequeathed about 1,300 (together with paintings and engravings) to his native city of Lille, where they now form part of the Musée des Beaux-Arts.

Wiener Werkstätte (German: Viennese Workshop). Arts and crafts cooperative studio established in Vienna in 1903 by members of the *Sezession. The workshop produced everything from jewellery to complete room decorations, including mosaics (see KLIMT). Its designers and craftsmen aimed, like William *Morris, to combine usefulness with aesthetic quality. Again like Morris, they found that their necessarily high prices prevented them from reaching the wide public they hoped for. Ultimately the venture was an economic failure and it closed in 1932.

Wiertz, Antoine (b Dinant, 22 Feb. 1806; d Brussels, 18 June 1865). Belgian painter, one of the great eccentrics in the history of art. In 1832 he won the Belgian *Prix de Rome and when he visited Italy in 1834 he was overwhelmed by *Michelangelo. His other great artistic hero was *Rubens and he tried to follow in their footsteps with enormous and high-flown religious, historical, and allegorical canvases. The results now seem almost dementedly bombastic and melodramatic, but he had many admirers among his countrymen. The Belgian government was keen to promote a national school of painting and in 1850–1 built him a special studio in Brussels (now the Musée Wiertz). He worked there in isolation for the rest of his life, seeing himself as an artist-philosopher and totally convinced of his own genius. Some of his work is erotic or macabre in character and anticipates Belgian *Symbolism (*Thoughts and Visions of a Severed Head*, 1853, Mus. Wiertz).

Wijnants (or Wynants), **Jan** (b ?Haarlem, c.1632; bur. Amsterdam, 23 Jan. 1684). Dutch landscape painter, active first in Haarlem, then from about 1660 in Amsterdam, where he also ran an inn. He specialized in landscapes with dunes and sandy roads, inspired by the countryside around Haarlem—unpretentious, naturalistic views that were favourites with collectors in the 18th century. The figures in his paintings were evidently always painted by other artists, including *Wouwerman. He, too, was an excellent painter of dunescapes and it is uncertain if one influenced the other. Wijnants was prolific and his work is in many public collections. Adriaen van de *Velde is said (by *Houbraken) to have been his pupil and *Gainsborough was among the artists he influenced.

Wilde, Johannes (b Budapest, 2 June 1891; d London, 15 Sept. 1970). Hungarian-born art historian who became an Austrian citizen in 1928 and a British citizen in 1947. From 1923 to 1938 he was on the staff of the *Kunsthistorisches Museum in Vienna and he gained an international reputation with his work on the Italian (particularly the Venetian) paintings there. He made many contributions to the attribution and dating of pictures, and one of his most important

achievements was the systematic use of X-rays, not only as a tool for discovering the physical condition of a painting but also as a guide to the artist's creative process. Following the annexation of Austria by Nazi Germany in 1938, Wilde resigned from the Kunsthistorisches Museum and moved to England. From 1948 to 1958 he taught at the *Courtauld Institute, where he was an inspirational figure—Kenneth *Clark described him as 'the most beloved and influential teacher of art history of his time'. Wilde published comparatively little, and as Anthony *Blunt wrote 'his wisdom was mainly dispensed in lectures, supervisions and private conversation'. During his lifetime only two of his major contributions appeared in book form in English, both on *Michelangelo's drawings—in the catalogue of the 15th- and 16th-century drawings at Windsor Castle (1949, with A. E. Popham) and in his catalogue of Michelangelo's drawings in the *British Museum (1953). In these two works, which demonstrate his keen sensibility as well as his great learning, Wilde effectively reversed the 'revisionist' tendency whereby many genuine drawings by Michelangelo had been rejected. After his death, two collections of lectures were published: *Venetian Art from Bellini to Titian* (1974) and *Michelangelo* (1978).

Wildens, Jan (b Antwerp, c.1586; d Antwerp, 16 Oct. 1653). Flemish landscape painter, active in Antwerp, where he became a master in the painters' guild in 1604. He is best known for painting landscape backgrounds for other artists, particularly his friend *Rubens, but his finest independent work, *Winter Landscape with Hunter* (1624, Gemäldegalerie, Dresden), shows he was an accomplished master in his own right.

Wildenstein. Dynasty of French art dealers and writers. The family firm was founded in Paris in 1875 by **Nathan Wildenstein** (1851–1934), and under him became one of the world's leading dealers, specializing mainly in Old Masters. In 1902 he opened a branch of the firm in New York. His son **Georges Wildenstein** (1892–1963) began working for the firm in 1910 and took over on his father's death. He opened a London branch, in New Bond Street, in 1936. His many books include monographs on *Chardin (1933 and 1963), *Fragonard (1960), *Gauguin (1964), and *Ingres (1954). His son **Daniel Wildenstein** (1917–2001) took over the firm on his father's death. He too was a notable art historian, his major work being a huge catalogue raisonné of *Monet's paintings and letters

(5 vols., 1974–91). Many of the firm's exhibition catalogues have also been contributions to scholarship and they have often benefited good causes.

Wilding, Alison. See NEW BRITISH SCULPTURE.

Wilenski, R. H. (Reginald Howard) (*b* London, 1887; *d* 19 Apr. 1975). British writer on art (and occasional painter). Much of his writing was devoted to modern art, and in the 1920s and early 1930s (until overtaken by Herbert *Read) he ranked as the leading spokesman for Britain's artistic avant-garde, particularly in sculpture. He was a vigorous champion of *Epstein at a time when he received routine abuse from most critics, and he was an early supporter of *Hepworth and *Moore. His many books are usually smoothly written popular works, although *Flemish Painters* (2 vols., 1960) is a massively dense and rather eccentric compilation of information, many years in the making. His best-known publication is probably *Modern French Painters* (1940, 2nd edn. 1945), which John *Rewald calls 'an interesting but completely unreliable book'.

Wiligelmo (active *c*.1100). Italian sculptor. His name is known only from an inscription on the façade of Modena Cathedral—'Among sculptors, your work shines forth, Wiligelmo. How greatly you are worthy of honours.' He must have been the main sculptor of the *reliefs on the façade (scenes from Genesis together with figures of prophets), which date from soon after 1099, when the cathedral was begun. In these works he created a distinctive style (his figures are squat and full of earthy vigour) that was the fountain-head of *Romanesque sculpture in northern Italy.

Wilkie, Sir David (*b* Cults, nr. Cupar, Fife, 18 Nov. 1785; *d* at sea, off Malta, 1 June 1841). Scottish painter. He trained in Edinburgh and then in 1805 moved to London, where he studied briefly at the *Royal Academy Schools. His *Village Politicians* (priv. coll.) was the hit of the RA exhibition of 1806 and he established himself as the most popular *genre painter of the day. He was strongly influenced in technique and subject matter by 17th-century Netherlandish artists such as *Ostade and *Teniers, and the public loved the wealth of lively and often humorous incident in his paintings. His *Chelsea Pensioners Reading the Gazette of the Battle of Waterloo* (1822, Wellington Mus., London), commissioned by the Duke of Wellington, was so popular when shown at the Royal Academy that a rail had to be erected in front of it to protect it from the crowds (a precaution not repeated until 1858, with *Frith's *Derby Day*). In 1825–8 Wilkie travelled abroad for reasons of health and his style changed radically under the influence particularly of Spanish painting, becoming grander in subject matter and broader in touch. The change was regretted by many of his contemporaries. In 1840 he went to the Holy Land to research material for his biblical paintings and on the return journey died at sea; his friend *Turner commemorated him in *Peace: Burial at Sea* (1842, Tate, London).

Wilkie's success did much to establish the popularity of anecdotal painting in Britain and many Victorian artists were influenced by him. The esteem in which he was held was possible only in an age that looked first to the 'story' of a painting and the moral lesson it contained. In his *Last Judgement* (1853, Tate) John *Martin portrayed Wilkie alongside some of the world's greatest artists—*Leonardo, *Michelangelo, *Raphael, and so on—and many contemporaries would have agreed that he belonged in such company.

'Willendorff, Venus of'. See 'VENUS OF WILLENDORFF'.

Williams, Fred (*b* Melbourne, 23 Jan. 1927; *d* Melbourne, 22 Apr. 1982). Australian painter and printmaker, regarded as the most original portrayer of his country's landscape. He studied in Melbourne, 1944–9, then in London, 1951–6. His earliest etchings, often with music-hall subjects, were produced at about this time. He returned to Australia in 1957, and from the late 1950s began to paint landscapes revealing a distinctly personal vision of the country's landscape, such as *Charcoal Burner* (1959, NG of Victoria, Melbourne). Unlike other modern Australian artists who had memorably portrayed aspects of their country's landscape (notably Arthur *Boyd, Russell *Drysdale, and Sidney *Nolan), Williams rarely featured the human figure in his paintings and his work conveys a sense of primeval mystery and remoteness. In the 1970s he broadened his range to include marine subjects and murals.

Willing, Victor. See REGO.

Willmann, Michael (*bapt.* Königsberg, Prussia [now Kaliningrad, Russia], 27 Sept. 1630; *d* Leubus, Silesia [now Lubiąż, Poland], 26 Aug. 1706). German painter. He studied in Amsterdam (under Jacob *Backer according to *Sandrart) and after working in various places, including Prague and Berlin, in 1660 he settled permanently in Leubus (Lubiąż), the site of one of the largest *Baroque abbeys in central Europe, for which he did a good deal of work. He also worked for churches elsewhere and was a fine portraitist. His style was highly emotional, with bold brushwork and flickering light effects. Together with *Schönfeld, he was the outstanding German painter of the late 17th century.

Willumsen, Jens Ferdinand (b Copenhagen, 7 Sept. 1863; d Cannes, 4 Apr. 1958). Danish painter, sculptor, architect, engraver, potter, and collector. In 1888–9 he visited Paris, and he was again in France between 1890 and 1894, abandoning his early naturalistic style under the impact of *Gauguin (whom he met in Brittany) and *Symbolism. His work became highly individual, notable for its obscure and disturbing subject matter and glaringly bright colours (*After the Tempest*, 1905, NG, Oslo). His sculpture is often *polychromatic, using mixed media, showing the influence of *Klinger. Willumsen was also influenced by El *Greco, on whom he wrote a long book (2 vols., 1927). He was one of the leading personalities of his time in Danish art, idolized as a genius by his admirers, but decried by others.

Wilson, Richard (b Penegoes, Montgomeryshire [now Powys], ?(1 Aug.) 1713 or 1714; d nr. Llanberis, Denbyshire [now Clwyd], 11 May 1782). British painter, born in rural north Wales, the son of a well-connected clergyman who encouraged his interest in art as well as giving him a good classical education. Wilson became the leading British landscape painter of his generation, but initially he seems to have worked mainly as a portraitist. He began his training in London in 1729 and was working independently by 1735, but the decisive change in his career did not come until his visit to Italy in 1750–7, when he decided to devote himself exclusively to landscape. He is said to have done this at the urging of Francesco *Zuccarelli, whom he met in Venice and whose portrait (1751, Tate, London) he painted, but he was more obviously influenced by *Claude and by the natural surroundings of Rome where Claude had worked.

Back in London Wilson became successful with his Italian landscapes and applied the same classical compositional principles to English and Welsh views, as in his celebrated *Snowdon from Llyn Nantlle* (c.1765, versions in Walker AG, Liverpool, and Castle Mus., Nottingham). He also painted large historical landscapes more or less in the manner of *Dughet or Salvator

*Rosa (*Destruction of the Children of Niobe*, 1760, Yale Center for British Art, New Haven, and other versions), and these too sold well (he often repeated successful pictures, referring to a money-making composition as a 'good-breeder'). Wilson, however, had a prickly nature and a problem with drink, and in the early 1770s his career went into a sharp decline. The *Royal Academy (of which he had been a founder member in 1768) helped him out by appointing him librarian, but in 1781 his family took him (now a pitiable figure) back to Wales. His work is of great importance in the history of British art, for he transformed landscape from an art that was essentially topographical to one that could be a vehicle for ideas and emotions; *Ruskin wrote that 'with Richard Wilson the history of sincere landscape art founded on a meditative love of nature begins in England'. He had several pupils, notably Thomas *Jones, as well as numerous imitators (making connoisseurship of his work difficult), and he was admired by such later artists as *Cotman, *Crome, *Constable, and *Turner.

Wilson, Richard (1953–). See INSTALLATION.

Wilson, Scottie (b Glasgow, 28 Feb. 1891; d London, 26 Mar. 1972). British self-taught painter of imaginative subjects, born in Glasgow of working-class parents. A colourful character, he ran away from home at the age of 16, did military service in India and South Africa, and lived in Canada from about 1930 to 1945. He started to draw in the 1930s. After the Second World War he settled in London and became something of a character in the art world (he was barely literate and fond of the bottle), although he became reclusive in old age. He made a good living selling his work to dealers but lived in very modest circumstances. Unlike the work of most *naive artists (with whom he is sometimes grouped), his pictures (often in coloured inks) were not 'realistic' renderings of scenes from the daily life with which he was familiar, but decorative fantasies incorporating stylized birds, fishes, butterflies, swans, flowers, self-portraits, and totem-pole heads. The last of these, no doubt reminiscences of Canada, were rather fancifully thought by some commentators to represent the powers of evil in contrast to the powers of good symbolized in the images taken from nature. All his work, however, was decorative rather than symbolic.

Wilton, Joseph (b London, 16 July 1722; d London, 25 Nov. 1803). English sculptor. He trained in Flanders and with *Pigalle in Paris, then was in Italy from 1747 until 1755. On his return to London he rapidly became successful, his patrons including George III, for whom he did carving on a new state coach (1762, Royal Coll.), still in use today. He was a close friend of the architect Sir William Chambers, with whom he often collaborated (notably on the decorative carving of Chambers's masterpiece, Somerset House), and he was one of the original members of the *Royal Academy. His portraits are generally regarded as his best works, his monuments showing him hesitating between various styles. Much of his work was executed by assistants. His talents were considerable, but he was more interested in social life than his work; in 1768 he inherited a fortune from his father (a manufacturer of ornamental plaster) but dissipated it and became bankrupt in 1793. Considering the quality of his training and his friendship with key figures in the art world, his career is a story of wasted opportunity.

Wilton Diptych. See INTERNATIONAL GOTHIC.

Winchester School (or **Winchester Style**). Term applied to a number of Anglo-Saxon illuminated manuscripts produced in the century before the Norman Conquest in 1066. At this time Winchester was the artistic capital of England and it was once assumed that all the manuscripts embraced by the term were produced there; however, it is now known that some were made in other centres. The most distinctive feature of the Winchester School is the use of bold, leafy borders around miniatures; other characteristics include lively draughtsmanship and rich colours. The most famous example is the Benedictional of St Ethelwold (BL, London). A benedictional is a book of blessings to be said by a bishop during Mass, and this one was made for St Ethelwold, who was Bishop of Winchester from 963 until his death in 984.

Winckelmann, Johann Joachim (b Stendal, 9 Dec. 1717; d Trieste, 8 June 1768). German art historian and archaeologist, a key figure in the *Neoclassical movement and in the development of art history as an intellectual discipline. He was the son of a poor cobbler, but through hard work he gained a good education, studying at the universities of Halle and Jena. For several years he was a schoolteacher, before obtaining the post of librarian to Count Heinrich von Bünau at Nothnitz, near Dresden, in 1748. This gave him the opportunity to absorb himself in the study of classical antiquity, and in 1755 he

managed to reach his goal of Rome. The previous year he had converted to Catholicism to enhance his chances of obtaining a scholarly appointment in Rome, and this did indeed help him to become librarian to Cardinal Alberigo Archinto, whom he had met in Germany. On Archinto's death in 1758 he became librarian to Cardinal Alessandro *Albani, a leading collector of antiquities, and this allowed him to lead a life of scholarly research through which he established a European reputation as a writer. In 1768, on the way back to Rome from a visit to Germany and Austria, he was murdered in Trieste; ostensibly he was killed for the sake of some gold and silver medallions he was carrying (gifts from the Empress Maria-Theresa; see HABSBURG), but it has been suggested that he had formed a homosexual relationship with his murderer (who was executed).

Winckelmann's two most important books are *Gedanken über die Nachahmung der griechischen Werke in der Malerei und Bildhauerkunst*, published in 1755, shortly before he left for Rome (*Fuseli published an English translation in 1765 under the title *Reflections on the Painting and Sculpture of the Greeks*), and *Geschichte der Kunst des Altertums* (History of Ancient Art), published in 1764 (this is the first occurrence of the phrase 'history of art' in the title of a book). In these immensely influential works he proclaimed the superiority of Greek art and culture, combining rapturous descriptions of individual works (above all the *Apollo Belvedere*) with historical analysis. He never went to Greece and unwittingly based most of his observations on Roman copies, but his account of the stylistic development of Greek sculpture was a milestone in archaeological writing, and he is regarded as having laid the foundations of modern methods of art history. His analysis of ancient Greek culture as a unity, and his interpretation of art as an index of the spirit of the time, were novel (he thought that when social conditions in general were good, then art was good, and when one declined the other did also); these ideas were subsequently developed into an entire philosophy of culture by 19th-century German writers. He refined the notions of how a work may be dated or its place of origin located and explained the character of works of art by reference to such factors as climate, religious customs, and social conditions. His interpretation of classical antiquity influenced many contemporary artists—above all *Mengs—and it helped to determine aspects of German education into the 20th century.

Winstanley, Hamlet. See STUBBS.

Winterhalter, Franz Xaver (*b* Menzenschwand, Black Forest, 20 Apr. 1805; *d* Frankfurt, 8 July 1873). German painter. Early in his career he worked mainly as a lithographer, but he became famous as the leading court portrait painter of his time. From 1834 he was based mainly in Paris, but he travelled widely and painted royals from several European countries. He was a particular favourite of Queen Victoria, who called him 'excellent, delightful Winterhalter' (the Royal Collection has more than 100 of his paintings), and he was also much employed by Napoleon III of France and his wife the Empress Eugénie. His style was romantic, glossy, and superficial and his portraits have until recently generally been valued more as historical records than as works of art. However, a major exhibition devoted to him at the National Portrait Gallery, London, and the Petit Palais, Paris, in 1987 brought renewed appreciation of his work. His brother **Hermann** (1808–91) was his assistant. A watercolour by him, *A Girl of Frascati* (signed but until recently given to his brother), is in the Wallace Collection, London.

Wissing, Willem (*b* Amsterdam, 1655; *d* Stamford, Lincolnshire, 10 Sept. 1687). Dutch portrait painter who moved to London in 1676, became an assistant of *Lely, and after his master's death in 1680 took over much of his fashionable practice. He was particularly favoured by James II and he also painted William III and Mary II, but he died young, opening the way for *Kneller's dominance. Wissing's style was similar to Lely's, but more Frenchified.

Wiszniewski, Adrian. See GLASGOW SCHOOL.

Wit, Jacob de (*bapt.* Amsterdam, 19 Dec. 1695; *d* Amsterdam, 12 Nov. 1754). The outstanding Dutch decorative painter of the 18th century, active mainly in his native Amsterdam. He had his principal training in Antwerp and learned much from *Rubens's ceiling paintings in the Jesuit church there (his drawings became valuable records after the paintings were destroyed by fire in 1718). De Wit's style, however, was much lighter than Rubens's, with a *Rococo delicacy and charm. He was a Catholic and was the first Dutch artist since the 16th century to carry out a good deal of decorative work for Catholic churches, but he was at his best in domestic ceiling decorations (*Bacchus and Ceres in the Clouds*, 1751, Huis Boschbeek, Heemstede). His name has entered the Dutch language to describe a kind of *trompe-l'œil imitation of marble *reliefs for which he was renowned; such pictures, usually set over a chimney-piece or door, are called 'witjes' (*wit* is Dutch for 'white'). De Wit was also an etcher and a noted collector of Old Master drawings.

Witt, Sir Robert. See COURTAULD.

Witte, Emanuel de (*b* Alkmaar, *c.*1616; *d* Amsterdam, winter 1691/2). Dutch painter, born at Alkmaar and active there, then in Rotterdam (by 1639), Delft (by 1641), and Amsterdam (by 1652). His range was wide, including history paintings, *genre scenes (notably of markets), and portraits, but after he settled in Amsterdam he concentrated on architectural paintings (primarily church interiors—both real and imaginary). *Houbraken wrote that 'in the painting of churches, no one was his equal with regard to orderly architecture, innovative use of light and well-formed figures', and this verdict has been endorsed by posterity, for his paintings are very different in spirit from the sober views of most Dutch architectural specialists, making powerful use of the dramatic play of light and shadow in the lofty interiors. His life was unhappy (he was constantly in debt) and when his body was found in an Amsterdam canal it was suspected that he had committed suicide.

Wittel, Gaspar van (*b* Amersfoort, *c.*1653; *d* Rome, 13 Sept. 1736). Dutch painter and draughtsman who spent virtually his whole career in Italy, where he was known as Gaspare Vanvitelli. He lived mainly in Rome, where he is first recorded in 1675, but he also visited northern Italy and Naples. He was one of the leading view painters of his time, specializing in scenes of modern Rome and showing comparatively little interest in the ancient ruins that attracted so many other artists. His son **Luigi Vanvitelli** (1700–73) began his career as a painter but changed course to become one of the greatest Italian architects of the 18th century, celebrated particularly for his huge royal palace (begun 1751) at Caserta, near Naples.

Wittkower, Rudolf (*b* Berlin, 22 June 1901; *d* New York, 11 Oct. 1971). Anglo-German art historian. He was born and brought up in Germany, but held British citizenship through his father, who had been born in England. After studying at the universities of Munich and Berlin, he worked at the Biblioteca Hertziana in Rome from 1923 to 1933. From 1934 to 1956 he was on the staff of the *Warburg Institute in London and from 1949 to 1956 was also professor of history of art at University College London. In

1956 he moved to Columbia University, New York, as head of the Department of Fine Arts and Archaeology, which under his direction became one of the leading centres of art-historical scholarship in the USA. After he retired in 1969 he was *Kress professor at the National Gallery in Washington and *Slade professor at Cambridge. Wittkower's many books and articles were devoted mainly to Italian art and architecture of the 16th and 17th centuries, and his writings form one of the cornerstones in the study of the Italian *Baroque. His major books, several of which have appeared in revised editions, include: *Architectural Principles in the Age of Humanism* (1949), *Gian Lorenzo Bernini* (1955), *Art and Architecture in Italy: 1600–1750* (1958), *Sculpture* (1977), and (with his wife **Margot Wittkower**) *Born under Saturn: The Character and Conduct of Artists* (1963).

Witz, Konrad (*b* Rottweil, Swabia, *c*.1400; *d* Basle or Geneva, 1444/6). German-born painter active in Switzerland and generally considered a member of the Swiss School. He became a member of the painters' guild in Basle in 1434 and evidently spent the rest of his career there and in Geneva. Little else is known of him and few paintings by him survive. These few, however, show that he was remarkably advanced in his naturalism, suggesting a knowledge of the work of his contemporaries Jan van *Eyck and the *Master of Flémalle. In place of the soft lines and lyrical qualities of *International Gothic, Witz's paintings are characterized by heavy, almost stumpy, figures, whose ample draperies emphasize their solidity. His most famous works are the four surviving panels (forming two wings) from the altarpiece of *St Peter* that he painted for the cathedral in Geneva. These are now in the Musée d'Art et d'Histoire there; the central panel is lost. One of the panels, the *Miraculous Draught of Fishes*, is Witz's masterpiece and his only signed and dated work (1444). The landscape setting depicts part of Lake Geneva (one of the earliest recognizable landscapes in art) and Witz's naturalism is even more remarkable in his observation of reflection and refraction in the water.

Wölfflin, Heinrich (*b* Winterthur, 24 June 1864; *d* Zurich, 19 July 1945). Swiss art historian, professor at the universities of Basle (1893–1901), Berlin (1901–12), Munich (1912–24), and Zurich (1924–34). He was one of the most influential art historians of his period, and several of his books are still widely read. They include *Die klassische Kunst* (Classic Art, 1899), on the art of the High *Renaissance, *Kunstgeschichtliche Grundbegriffe* (Principles of Art History, 1915), and a monograph on *Dürer (1905). His work concentrated on stylistic analysis, and he attempted to show that style—in painting, sculpture, and architecture—follows evolutionary principles. *Principles of Art History* presents his ideas in the most highly developed form, discussing the transformation from Renaissance to *Baroque in terms of contrasting visual schemes—for example the development from linear to painterly ('malerisch'). Wölfflin's view that style was a force in its own right rather than an intellectual abstraction and his lack of interest in *iconography are out of tune with much modern thinking on art history, and his approach is often over-rigid; however, he was a figure of great importance in establishing his subject as an intellectually demanding discipline. Herbert *Read wrote: 'it could be said of him that he found art criticism a subjective chaos and left it a science.'

Wolgemut, Michael (*b* Nuremberg, *c*.1435; *d* Nuremberg, 30 Nov. 1519). German painter and woodcut designer, active in Nuremberg. In 1472 he married the widow of Hans *Pleydenwurff and he later purchased his workshop, which he made the most prosperous in the city. The numerous large altarpieces it produced show little sign of a distinctive individual personality, and Wolgemut is more important for his role in the history of book illustration. Most notably he and his workshop, in partnership with his stepson Wilhelm Pleydenwurff, made the pictures for Hartmann Schedel's *Weltchronik* (World Chronicle, 1493), which initiated a major shift in book production, popularizing the extensive use of *woodcut illustrations. Hitherto illustrations in printed books had been sparing and often embellished by *illumination to make the book resemble a manuscript, but in the *Weltchronik* the woodcuts are abundant—there are more than 600 of them—and determine the character of the book; in Erwin *Panofsky's words they 'opened up a new vision of the representational and expressive possibilities of the medium'. Wolgemut is also remembered as *Dürer's teacher. Dürer evidently had great affection for his master, for he painted a touching portrait of Wolgemut in old age (1516, Germanisches Nationalmuseum, Nuremberg) and added an inscription recording his death.

Wols (Wolfgang Schulze) (*b* Berlin, 27 May 1913; *d* Champigny-sur-Marne, nr. Paris, 1 Sept. 1951). German-born painter active mainly in

France; he adopted the pseudonym Wols in 1937 from fragments of his name on a torn telegram. In 1932 he studied briefly at the *Bauhaus, then moved to Paris, where he worked as a photographer. He lived in Spain 1933–5, but after being imprisoned for political activities he returned to Paris. As a German citizen he was interned at the outbreak of war, but he was liberated in 1940 and lived in poverty in the south of France. At the end of the war he returned to Paris and was befriended by the writers Jean-Paul Sartre and Simone de Beauvoir, for whose books he did illustrations. In the late 1940s he began to make a name for himself as a painter, but his irregular life, poverty, and excessive drinking undermined his health and he died aged only 38. His posthumous fame far outstripped his reputation during his lifetime and he came to be regarded as the 'primitive' of *Art Informel and one of the most original masters of expressive abstraction.

Wood, Christopher (b Knowsley, nr. Liverpool, 7 Apr. 1901; d Salisbury, 21 Aug. 1930). British painter, mainly of landscapes, harbour scenes, and figure compositions. In 1921 he studied at the *Académie Julian in Paris and subsequently travelled widely on the Continent. To influences from modern French art (*Picasso and *Diaghilev were among his friends), he added an entirely personal lyrical freshness and intensity of vision, touched with what Gwen *Raverat felicitously described as 'fashionable clumsiness'. In a remarkably short time he achieved a position of high regard in the art worlds of London and Paris, but he was emotionally unstable and his early death was probably suicide (he was killed by a train). After this he became something of a legend as a youthful genius cut off before his prime. Much of Wood's best work was done in Cornwall, where he and his friend Ben *Nicholson discovered the *naive painter Alfred *Wallis in 1928.

Wood, Derwent. See NEW SCULPTURE.

Wood, Grant (b nr. Anamosa, Ia., 13 Feb. 1892; d Iowa City, 12 Feb. 1942). American painter, active mainly in Iowa. Early in his career he was an artistic jack-of-all-trades. The turning point in his life came when he obtained a commission to make stained-glass windows for the Cedar Rapids Veteran Memorial Building in 1927 and went to Munich to supervise their manufacture the following year. Influenced by the Early Netherlandish paintings he saw there in the Alte Pinakothek, he abandoned his earlier *Impressionist style and began to paint in the meticu-

lous, sharply detailed manner that characterized his mature work (he has been called 'the *Memling of the Midwest'). His subjects were taken mainly from the ordinary people and everyday life of Iowa and he became recognized as one of the leading exponents of *Regionalism. He first came to national attention in 1930 with *American Gothic*, which depicts a farming couple (his sister and dentist were in fact the models) in front of a farmhouse with a pointed Gothic-style window; he had seen such a building in southern Iowa and said that 'I imagined American Gothic people with their faces stretched out long to go with this American Gothic house'. The painting won a bronze medal at an exhibition at the Art Institute of Chicago (which now owns the work), but it aroused violent controversy because many people regarded it as an insulting caricature of plain country folk. However, it later won great popularity and is now one of the most familiar and best-loved images in American art.

Wood never again achieved quite the same bite and freshness of his masterpiece, but his other work included some highly distinctive and original pictures. Among them are *The Midnight Ride of Paul Revere* (1931, Met. Mus., New York), which has a captivating air of fantasy, and *Daughters of the Revolution* (1932, Cincinnati Art Mus.), which Wood described as 'the only satire I have ever painted'. Depicting 'three sour-visaged, squint-eyed and repulsive-looking females', it was his pictorial revenge on members of the Daughters of the American Revolution, who had opposed the dedication of his stained-glass windows in Cedar Rapids because they had been made in Germany—America's recent enemy. His other work includes some vigorous stylized landscapes, and during the 1930s he supervised several Iowa projects of the *Federal Art Project. In 1934 he became assistant professor of fine arts at the university of Iowa.

Woodburn, Samuel. See WICAR.

woodcut. Term applied to the technique of making a print from a block of wood sawn along the grain and also to the print so made. Although the term is often loosely used for any type of print made from wood, it refers specifically to those made from blocks in which the grain runs lengthways across the surface (as in a plank of wood). It can thus be distinguished from *wood engraving, in which the print is made from wood sawn across the grain, which produces a surface that is harder to cut but capable of taking finer detail.

Woodcut is the oldest technique for making prints and its basic principles are simple. The design is drawn on a smooth block of wood (almost any wood of medium softness can be used—beech, pear, sycamore for example) and the parts that are to be white in the print are cut away with knives and gouges, leaving the parts that will print black standing up in relief. The block is then inked and the design printed on a sheet of paper (usually in a press, although it is possible to make a print using only hand pressure). Cutting blocks of any complexity is a highly skilled business and this part of the work has often been done by specialist craftsmen rather than the artist responsible for the design. Coloured woodcuts, generally made by using a separate block for each colour, have been particularly popular in Japan (see UKIYO-E).

The origins of woodcut are obscure (the principle was employed in fabric printing in China at least as early as the 3rd century AD). There is evidence that woodcut prints as we know them were being produced in Europe in the 14th century, but the earliest surviving reliably dated example is perhaps the *St Christopher* (1423) by an unknown artist in the John Rylands Library, Manchester. Many of the earliest woodcuts were crude popular religious images designed to be sold at fairs and pilgrim shrines (see also BLOCK BOOK), but in skilled hands the technique could produce much more sophisticated results. It was at its peak in the first 30 years of the 16th century, in both individual prints and book illustrations, with *Dürer being the supreme master.

The connection between woodcut and the art of the book was very close at this time, as both used essentially the same method of printing and therefore could be readily combined. In block books, the text and image were cut on the same piece of wood, but in books printed from movable metal type, the woodcut blocks and the type were locked together in the press, so that text and illustration were inked and printed together. This procedure was much cheaper and simpler than illustrating with copperplate engravings, which had to be printed separately (a heavier press was required), and bound into the book afterwards. The earliest printed books had been produced to look like manuscripts, so woodcut illustrations were usually eschewed, but they became highly popular in the 1490s, the first great landmark being Hartman Schedel's *Weltchronik* (World Chronicle), published in Nuremberg in 1493, with illustrations by Michael *Wolgemut. Although there was a vogue for the *chiaroscuro woodcut in Italy, in general woodcut was used less there than in northern Europe. Nevertheless, there were some outstanding Italian achievements in the art, notably in Venice, for example the illustrations to the *Hypnerotomachia Poliphili*, published in 1499, and Jacopo de' *Barbari's huge view of the city, published in 1500.

In spite of the versatility and relative cheapness of woodcut, during the 16th century it steadily lost ground to *line engraving, which could produce finer detail and subtler effects. By about 1600 it was little used apart from jobbing work and ephemera—broadsheets, chapbooks, playbills, and so forth—although the Flemish printmaker Christoffel Jegher (1596–1652/3) produced some vigorous woodcut reproductions of *Rubens's work. In the 18th century the technique was only sporadically employed by serious artists; *Hogarth, for example, originally had his *Four Stages of Cruelty* (1751) produced as woodcuts, seeking a popular style and market, but he changed his plans and redid the designs on copper.

In the late 19th and early 20th centuries there was a major revival of interest in the woodcut as a medium of original artistic expression. Now that photomechanical methods had taken over the reproductive functions of printmaking, all kinds of hand engraving could make a fresh start. The simplicity and directness characteristic of 15th-century prints was revived, with the difference that modern exponents of woodcut learned the craft themselves and cut their own designs on the block. *Gauguin and *Munch were the great pioneers in the 1890s, using the grain of the wood to create bold and vigorous textural effects, and they were followed by the German *Expressionists (notably the members of Die *Brücke), some of whom virtually hacked the design into the block.

wood engraving. Term applied to the technique of making a print from a block of hardwood (usually boxwood) sawn across the grain and to the print so made. The technique derives from the *woodcut, but because of the harder and smoother surface and the use of the *burin and other tools associated with the copperplate engraver, the effect is generally finer and more detailed (although there is a middle ground where the two techniques produce very similar results). As boxwood has only a small diameter, large designs necessitated joining several blocks together.

Wood engraving developed in the 18th century and its first great exponent was Thomas *Bewick (his contemporary William *Blake also made some superb wood engravings, but these were little known at the time). Bewick ushered in the technique's heyday, which coincided with a great expansion in journalism and book publishing from about 1830. From then until about 1890, when it was superseded by photomechanical processes, it was the most popular medium for illustration. The *Dalziel brothers and Gustave *Doré were among the most prolific exponents during this period. By this time the design was often photographically transferred to the block from the artist's drawing. Although it was no longer commercially viable for everyday printing, wood engraving continued to be used in the 20th century for original prints and the illustration of expensive books. It was a favourite technique of Eric *Ravilious, for example.

Woodrow, Bill. See NEW BRITISH SCULPTURE.

Woollaston, Sir Mountford Tosswill ('Toss') (b Taranaki, 11 Apr. 1910; d Upper Moutere, 30 Aug. 1998). New Zealand painter, who with Rita *Angus and Colin *McCahon pioneered a move away from conventional figuration in his country's art. His work combines influences from *Cézanne and *Expressionism and is mainly devoted to landscapes and portraits of family and friends. He spoke of his painting as 'a very quiet song hummed or murmured to myself', and the poet Charles Brasch called him 'one of the first to see and paint New Zealand as a New Zealander'. Woollaston set out some of his ideas on art in a lecture delivered at the City Art Gallery, Auckland, in 1960; two years later it was published as a pamphlet entitled The Far-Away Hills: A Meditation on New Zealand Landscape. In 1979 he became the first New Zealand painter to be knighted. His autobiography, Sage Tea, was published in 1981.

Woollett, William (b Maidstone, 15 Aug. 1735; d London, 23 May 1785). English printmaker. He was one of the outstanding reproductive printmakers of his time, his work being admired on the Continent as well as in Britain. He established his reputation in 1761 with his print after Richard *Wilson's Destruction of the Children of Niobe, and his greatest success came in 1766 with the Death of Wolfe after Benjamin *West. In the same year he was appointed engraver to George III. Usually he began his plates in etching and finished them in engraving.

Woolner, Thomas (b Hadleigh, Suffolk, 17 Dec. 1825; d London, 7 Oct. 1892). English sculptor. He was a founder of the *Pre-Raphaelite Brotherhood in 1848, the only sculptor among the members. His early career was unsuccessful, so he decided to try his hand at gold prospecting in Australia; his departure in 1852 inspired Ford Madox *Brown's picture The Last of England (1852–5, City AG, Birmingham). Woolner found little gold in Australia, but he began to prosper as a portrait sculptor, and after returning to England in 1854 he made a name for himself with his marble bust of his friend Alfred Tennyson (1857, Trinity College, Cambridge, and several replicas). His work was praised for its lifelikeness and he made portraits of many other distinguished sitters. Woolner also produced a few figure subjects and occasional paintings, and he wrote poetry.

Wootton, John (b Snitterfield, Warwickshire, c.1682; d London, 13 Nov. 1764). English landscape and sporting painter. He is best known for pictures involving horses, with which he made a handsome living, but his main contribution to British painting was the introduction of the *ideal landscape—Horace *Walpole said his works in this vein 'approached towards Gaspar Poussin [i.e. *Dughet], and sometimes imitated happily the glow of *Claude Lorrain'. His landscape manner was continued by George *Lambert. There are examples of Wootton's work in Tate Britain and other public collections, but many of his finest paintings are still in private hands—notably at Althorp, Northamptonshire, and Longleat, Wiltshire.

Works Progress Administration. See FEDERAL ART PROJECT.

World of Art (Mir Iskusstva). The name of an informal association of Russian artists formed in St Petersburg in 1898 and of the journal they published from 1899 to 1904; the association lasted, with interruptions, until 1924, but its heyday was over long before this. *Diaghilev was the journal's editor, and his contributors and collaborators included Léon *Bakst and Alexandre *Benois. The group encouraged interchange with Western art (many articles published in the journal had previously appeared in European magazines) and became the focus for avant-garde developments in Russia. In particular it promoted the *Art Nouveau style. Some of the artists involved in the group (notably Nikolai *Roerich) were also interested in evoking the spirit of ancient Russia, and this synthesis of old and new was best expressed in their decor for Diaghilev's ballet company, which revolutionized European stage design when he brought it to Paris in 1909.

Worpswede. A north German village near Bremen that in the last decade of the 19th century became the centre of a colony of artists, following the example of the *Barbizon School in France. The most famous artist to work there was Paula *Modersohn-Becker, and the 'Worpswede School' is sometimes regarded as one of the roots from which German *Expressionism sprang. Another woman artist in the group was the sculptor Clara Westhoff (1878–1954); in 1901 she married the poet Rainer Maria Rilke, who published a book on Worpswede in 1903.

Worringer, Wilhelm (b Aachen, 13 Jan. 1881; d Munich, 29 Mar. 1965). German art historian and aesthetician, professor at the universities of Bonn (1920–8), Königsberg (1928–46), and Halle (1946–50). His writings, which tend to be somewhat metaphysical in tone, encouraged a more sympathetic response to non-realist styles and *Expressionist distortion in art. His best-known books are *Abstraktion und Einfühlung* (1908) (translated as *Abstraction and Empathy*, 1953) and *Formprobleme der Gotik* (1912), which has been translated in an American edition as *Form Problems of the Gothic* (1919) and in an English edition, with an introduction by Herbert *Read, as *Form in Gothic* (1927). Charles Harrison and Paul Wood write that *Abstraktion und Einfühlung* was 'continuously reprinted for over forty years. It was influential in countering what Worringer called the "European-classical prejudice of our customary historical conception and valuation of art". It also furnished theoretical support for that widespread modern tendency in which enthusiasm for so-called *primitive art was conjoined with interest in modern forms of abstraction' (*Art in Theory: 1900–1990*, 1992).

Wotruba, Fritz (b Vienna, 23 Apr. 1907; d Vienna, 28 Aug. 1975). The leading Austrian sculptor of the 20th century. His masterly craftsmanship won him acclaim from early in his career, as when his work was shown in an exhibition of Austrian art in Paris in 1929; Aristide *Maillol is said to have refused to believe that such sculpture could have been done by a 22-year-old. In his most characteristic works he carved directly in stone, preferring a hard stone with a coarse texture. His early pieces were in a naturalistic style reminiscent of Maillol, but he moved towards abstraction by reducing his

figures to bare essentials. His approach was similar to *Brancusi's, but in contrast to Brancusi's smooth, subtle abstractions, Wotruba's figures are solid, blocklike structures. They were left in a rough state, creating a feeling of primitive power (*Feminine Rock*, 1947–8, Middelheim Open-Air Mus. of Sculpture, Antwerp). He also worked in bronze (*Standing Man*, 1949–50, Tate, London). Wotruba had many public commissions for sculptural works, and from 1959 he also made stage designs, for example costumes for a performance of Wagner's *Ring* in Berlin in 1967. Near the end of his life he branched out into architecture, designing the church of the Holy Trinity on the outskirts of Vienna (constructed 1974–6). After the Second World War he taught at the Vienna Academy and his work was admired and imitated by many younger Austrian artists, bringing about a revival of sculpture in his country.

Wouters, Rik (b Mechelen [Malines], 21 Aug. 1882; d Amsterdam, 11 July 1916). Belgian painter, sculptor, and printmaker. He is regarded as his country's leading exponent of *Fauvism, but his career was cut tragically short when he died following operations for cancer of the eye. His work is less violent in colour than that of the French Fauvists and often has a quality of serene intimacy, notably in portraits of his wife Nel, who was his favourite model (*The Artist's Wife*, 1912, Pompidou Centre, Paris).

Wouwerman (or **Wouwermans**), **Philips** (bapt. Haarlem, 24 May 1619; d Haarlem, 19 May 1668). The most celebrated member of a family of Dutch painters from Haarlem, where he worked virtually all his life. He became a member of the painters' guild in 1640 and is said by a contemporary source to have been a pupil of Frans *Hals. The only thing he has in common with Hals, however, is his nimble brushwork, for he specialized in landscapes of hilly country with horses—cavalry skirmishes, camps, hunts, travellers halting outside an inn, and so on. In this genre he was immensely prolific and also immensely successful—*Houbraken says he left his daughter a dowry of 20,000 guilders. He had many imitators, including his brother **Peter** (1623–82), and his great popularity continued throughout the 18th century, when he was a favourite with princely collectors, and engravings after his work had wide circulation. Subsequently he has perhaps been underrated, for although he was usually content to follow a successful formula, he maintained high standards; his draughtsmanship is elegant, his composition sure, his colouring delicate, and his touch lively. Examples of his work are in many galleries; the biggest collections are in Dresden (Gemäldegalerie) and St Petersburg (Hermitage), but he is also very well represented in London (Dulwich Picture Gal., NG, Wallace Coll., Wellington Mus.).

WPA. See FEDERAL ART PROJECT.

Wright, John Michael (*bapt.* London, 25 May 1617; *bur.* London, 1 Aug. 1694). English portrait painter. He was apprenticed to George *Jamesone in Edinburgh, 1636–41, then spent a long period abroad, chiefly in Rome, where in 1648 he became a member of the Accademia di S. Luca (see ACADEMY), the only British painter of the 17th century to have this distinction. On his return to England in 1656 he won many patrons among his fellow Catholics and became *Lely's chief rival, although he never had great worldly success and died in modest circumstances. His style was less glossy than Lely's but more penetrating and individual in characterization, his sitters tending to look thoughtful rather than merely glamorous (*Magdalen Aston*, Castle Mus., Nottingham). Wright's most unusual work is an allegorical ceiling painting (Castle Mus.) done for Charles II's bedroom at Whitehall Palace; it cannot be considered a success, but it is interesting as an attempt at *Baroque decoration by someone who was familiar with the works of Pietro da *Cortona (whom he described as 'the greatest master of his time'). Wright was a collector, antiquarian, and scholar, a man of considerable culture; in 1685–7 he accompanied an embassy from James II to Pope Innocent XI and wrote an account of it in Italian, published in 1687 (English translation, 1688).

Wright, Joseph (*b* Derby, 3 Sept. 1734; *d* Derby, 29 Aug. 1797). English painter, active mainly in his native city and generally known as Wright of Derby. He was one of the most original, versatile, and accomplished British artists of the 18th century and the first major English painter whose career was based outside London. In 1751–3 and again in 1756–7 he trained under *Hudson in London, and after returning to Derby he made a name as a portraitist in the Midlands, his works displaying fluent composition and a firm grasp of character. In the 1760s he began to paint candlelit scenes of various types, showing the fascination with unusual lighting effects that was to run throughout his career. He was influenced in some of these by Dutch painting, but in his depictions of the contemporary scientific world he broke new ground—he has been called 'the first professional painter to express the spirit of the industrial revolution' (Francis Klingender, *Art and the Industrial Revolution*, 1947) and his most famous work, *An Experiment on a Bird in the Air Pump* (1768, NG, London), has been described by Ellis *Waterhouse as 'one of the wholly original masterpieces of British art'. Such works won him a considerable reputation, and in 1772 James *Northcote called him 'the most famous painter now living for candle-lights'.

In 1768–71 Wright worked in Liverpool, and in 1773–5 visited Italy, where he assiduously studied the *antique but was even more impressed by the eruption of Vesuvius he witnessed and by a kind of man-made equivalent—the great fireworks display held annually at the Castel Sant'Angelo in Rome (he painted several pictures of both subjects and they have been seen as prophetic of *Romanticism). On his return to England in 1775 he moved to Bath, hoping to fill the gap left by *Gainsborough's departure for London, but his more forthright style did not please sophisticated society there and in 1777 he returned to Derby. He remained there for the rest of his life apart from short journeys when he made tours of the Lake District in 1793 and 1794 (landscape became increasingly important towards the end of his career). Appropriately, Derby Art Gallery has far and away the finest collection of his work.

Wright, Willard Huntington. See MACDONALD-WRIGHT.

Wtewael (or Uytewael), **Joachim** (*b* Utrecht, 1566; *d* Utrecht, 13 Aug. 1638). Dutch painter, mainly of religious and mythological subjects. After travelling in Italy and France *c.*1588–92, he returned to Utrecht, where he became one of the leading Dutch exponents of *Mannerism. His highly distinctive, charmingly artificial style, which remained untouched by the naturalistic developments happening around him, was characterized by acidic colours and elegant figures in wilfully distorted poses. The best collection of his work, including a self-portrait (1601), is in the Centraal Museum, Utrecht.

Wueluwe, Hendrik van. See MASTER OF FRANKFURT.

Wyeth, Andrew (*b* Chadds Ford, Pa., 12 July 1917). American painter, son and pupil of a well-known muralist and illustrator of children's books, **Newell Convers Wyeth** (1882–1945). Wyeth's work consists almost entirely of depictions of the people and places of the two areas he knows best—the Brandywine Valley around his native Chadds Ford, Pennsylvania, and the area near Cushing, Maine, where he has his summer home. He usually paints in watercolour or *tempera with a precise and detailed technique, and often he conveys a sense of loneliness or nostalgia (trappings of the modern world, such as motor cars, rarely appear in his work). He became famous with *Christina's World* (1948), which was bought by the Museum of Modern Art, New York, in 1949 and has become one of the best-known images in American art. It depicts a friend of the artist, Christina Olson, who had been so badly crippled by polio that she moved by dragging herself with her arms. She is shown in a field on her farm in Maine, 'pulling herself slowly back towards the house'. The unusual viewpoint and the heavily charged atmosphere are typical of Wyeth's work. Because Christina is seen from the back, some viewers assumed that she was an attractive young girl frolicking in the grass, and were shocked when they saw Wyeth's portraits of the gaunt, middle-aged figure. Many other viewers, however, saw in it a deeper significance as a symbol of the human condition.

Building on the picture's fame, Wyeth has gone on to have an enormously successful career. However, critical opinion on him is widely divided: J. Carter Brown, director of the National Gallery in Washington, called him 'a great master', whereas Professor Sam Hunter, one of the leading authorities on 20th-century American art, has written: 'What most appeals to the public, one must conclude, apart from Wyeth's conspicuous virtuosity, is the artist's banality of imagination and lack of pictorial ambition. He comfortably fits the commonsense ethos and non-heroic mood of today's popular culture, despite his occasional lapses into gloomy introspection.' Wyeth himself explained his popularity by saying, 'It's because I happen to paint things that reflect the basic truths of life: sky, earth, friends, the intimate things.'

Wynants, Jan. See WIJNANTS.

Wyspiański, Stanisław (*b* Cracow, 15 Jan. 1869; *d* Cracow, 28 Nov. 1907). Polish painter, designer, illustrator, and writer. He is now perhaps best known for his work in the theatre (as playwright, producer, and stage designer), which has given him a reputation as the father of modern Polish drama; revolting against naturalistic conventions, he made many innovations in stagecraft and based his plays on national themes interwoven with classical symbolism. His literary and theatrical work, however, was mainly confined to the last decade of his short life, and he was active chiefly in the visual arts, in which he was a figure of similar vigour and versatility. After training under Jan *Matejko he spent most of the period 1891–4 in Paris, where he was influenced by *Gauguin and *Symbolism. His work included church murals, stained glass, portraits, landscapes, book illustrations, and furniture design. He had an allergy to oil paint and his favourite medium was pastel. There are many examples of his work in the National Museums in Cracow and Warsaw.

X

Xenakis, Iannis (*b* Brăila, Romania, 29 May 1922; *d* Paris, 4 Feb. 2001). French composer, architect, and experimental artist, born in Romania to Greek parents. After the German invasion of Greece in 1941 he fought in the Resistance, losing the sight of an eye when he was badly wounded in 1945. In 1947 he settled in Paris, where he assisted *Le Corbusier in his architectural practice from 1948 to 1960. He became a French citizen in 1965. Xenakis was best known as a composer; his works 'are examples of a new and individual kind of musical thinking, based on models drawn from architecture, physics, and mathematics' (*The New Oxford Companion to Music*, 1983). In the visual arts he is notable for being among the most prominent creators of 'total environments' involving both spectacle and sound, in particular for pioneering the use of multiple lasers in light environments. For the French Pavilion at 'Expo '67' in Montreal he created a vast 'Polytope' made up of large concave and convex mirrors suspended on electrified cables producing 'visual melodies' by the action of light sources. In 1972 he created a still more strange and elaborate form of total spectacle at the Roman Baths off the boulevard Saint-Michel in Paris.

Xuarez. See JUAREZ.

Xu Beihong (Hsü Pei-hung) (*b* Yixing, Jiangsu province, 19 July 1895; *d* Peking [Beijing], 26 Sept. 1953). Chinese painter, teacher, and administrator, the most important figure in introducing Western ideas about art to his country. From 1919 to 1927 he lived in Europe (with one brief trip home), travelling widely and studying in Paris (at the École des *Beaux-Arts) and Berlin. After his return to China he held a variety of teaching and administrative posts in Shanghai, Peking, and Nanjing, and when the country became the People's Republic of China in 1949 he was appointed director of the newly founded Central Academy of Fine Arts and chairman of the National Artists' Association. Xu's most characteristic works were large historical compositions. They were decidedly old-fashioned by European standards or even by the standards of his only rival in importance in introducing Western art to China—Liu Haisu (1896–1994), who was influenced by *Impressionism and *Post-Impressionism and who caused a scandal by introducing drawing from live models in his teaching at the Shanghai Academy. However, Xu's style was novel to most Chinese eyes and it was highly influential, proving completely compatible with the Soviet-inspired *Socialist Realism that became the official style in Communist China in the 1950s.

Xul Solar (Oscar Agustín Alejandro Schulz Solari) (*b* San Fernando, nr. Buenos Aires, 14 Dec. 1887; *d* Buenos Aires, 10 May 1963). Argentinian painter. He was the son of German-Italian immigrants, hence his rather jumbled name, which he compressed to Xul Solar. From 1912 to 1924 he travelled widely in Europe. Although he had absorbed features from European movements such as *Cubism and *Dada, he was self-taught as an artist and his work has a highly personal sense of fantasy and humour befitting his visionary and mystic outlook. He worked on a small scale, chiefly in tempera and watercolour, rarely exhibited, and sought no honours. His friend the writer Jorge Luis Borges referred to his paintings as 'documents for the ultraterrestrial world, of the metaphysical world in which the gods take on the imaginative forms of dreams'. Xul Solar was given a major retrospective exhibition at the Museo Nacional de Belles Artes in Buenos Aires in 1964 and has had a powerful influence on younger Argentinian artists.

xylography (Greek: *xulon*, 'wood', and *graphein*, 'to write'). A term (now little used) for any kind of printing from a wooden block, thus encompassing both *woodcut and *wood engraving.

Y

Yale Center for British Art, New Haven. See MELLON.

Yáñez, Fernando (active 1506–31). Spanish painter. He is first certainly documented in 1506 in Valencia, where he collaborated with Fernando Llanos (active 1506–16) in painting twelve large panels of the life of the Virgin for the main altarpiece of the cathedral (1507–10). From the style of these paintings it is overwhelmingly likely that the 'Ferrando Spagnuolo' who in 1505 is recorded assisting *Leonardo da Vinci in Florence on the *Battle of Anghiari* was either Yáñez or Llanos. They were 'the first non-Italian painters to assimilate the style of the High *Renaissance and practice it in a foreign land' (Jonathan Brown, *Painting in Spain: 1500–1700*, 1998). Their respective shares in the altarpiece are a matter of debate, although there is a tendency now to see Yáñez as the more gifted. Various other paintings are attributed to each of them working independently, but their careers are ill defined.

YBAs. See YOUNG BRITISH ARTISTS.

Yeames, William Frederick (*b* Taganrog, Russia, 18 Dec. 1835; *d* Teignmouth, Devon, 3 May 1918). British painter. He was born in Russia, where his father was a British consul, had part of his education in Dresden, and moved to London in 1848. He specialized in scenes from British history, particularly of the Tudor and Stuart periods, treated in an anecdotal and often melodramatic way that looks forward to Hollywood 'costume' movies. Most of his work has been forgotten, but one of his pictures has achieved enduring fame as an archetypal image of Victorian sentimentality, the Cromwellian tear-jerker *'And When Did You Last See Your Father?'* (1878, Walker AG, Liverpool). See also ST JOHN'S WOOD CLIQUE.

Yeats, Jack Butler (*b* London, 29 Aug. 1871; *d* Dublin, 28 Mar. 1957). The best-known Irish painter of the 20th century, son of **John Butler Yeats** (1839–1922), a barrister who became a successful portrait painter, and brother of the poet William Butler Yeats. Initially he worked mainly as an illustrator and did not regularly paint in oils until about 1905. His subjects included Celtic myth and everyday Irish life, through which he contributed to the upsurge of nationalist feeling in the arts that accompanied the movement for Irish independence. His early paintings were influenced by French *Impressionism, but he then developed a more personal *Expressionistic style characterized by vivid colour and extremely loose brushwork (there is some similarity to the work of *Kokoschka, who became a great friend in the last decade of Yeats's life). Although he has many admirers, some critics think that his late paintings often degenerate into a muddy mess. Yeats was a writer as well as a painter—the author of several plays, novels, and volumes of poetry, as well as *Life in the West of Ireland* (1912) and *Sligo* (1930).

Yoshihara, Jiro (*b* Osaka, 1 Jan. 1905; *d* Ashiya, 10 Feb. 1972). Japanese painter. He was a wealthy industrialist and was mainly self-taught as an artist. During the 1930s he was a pioneer of abstract art in Japan, but he is best known as the central figure of the *Gutai Group, which he founded in 1954 and sustained with his wealth for the rest of his life. In 1957 he was awarded first prize at the Tokyo *Biennial. His paintings of this time are 'a sophisticated mixture of Eastern and Western modes. They mingle Zen . . . with things learned from American *Abstract Expressionism' (Edward Lucie-Smith, *Visual Arts in the Twentieth Century*, 1996).

Young British Artists (YBAs). An imprecise term applied to a number of highly publicized British avant-garde artists active from the 1980s, several of whom are well known for their grubbily glamorous lifestyles as well as for what they create; they do not form an organized group and their work is diverse, but there are ties of friendship linking many of them and they have been supported chiefly by Charles *Saatchi. Their work has been showcased in several exhibitions, most notably 'Sensation' at the Royal Academy,

London, in 1997, which generated a great deal of controversy, including various forms of protest against it. The two best-known artists who featured in 'Sensation' are Damien *Hirst and Rachel *Whiteread. Among the others are the brothers Dinos (1962–) and Jake (1966–) Chapman, whose work includes figures modelled on bland shop-window dummies but with horrible mutilations or freakish mutations; Tracey Emin (1963–), whose work is largely autobiographical and includes *My Bed* (1999, Saatchi Gal., London), featuring her own unmade bed accompanied by assorted debris from her life; Gary Hume (1962–), who paints large figurative pictures characterized by flat, reductive forms; Sarah Lucas (1962–), whose work often has sexual themes, for example *Two Fried Eggs and a Kebab* (1992, Saatchi Gal.), in which the foods, arranged on a table, mimic breasts and female genitals; Chris Ofili (1968–), whose trademark is incorporating elephant dung in his paintings (he hit on the idea whilst in Zimbabwe on a travelling scholarship in 1992); Marc Quinn (1964–), best known for *Self* (1991, Saatchi Gal.), a three-dimensional self-portrait head made of his own frozen blood (it is displayed in a refrigerated cabinet); and Jenny Saville (1970–), who paints huge pictures of mountainously obese nude women.

Young Contemporaries. Exhibition of works by British art students held in London since 1949 on a roughly annual basis (lack of funds or organization—they are generally arranged by the students themselves—has some-times prevented the shows taking place). The first Young Contemporaries exhibition was held at the Royal Society of British Artists (RBA Galleries). Other venues have included the *Institute of Contemporary Arts, and some of the exhibitions have toured the provinces. The most famous Young Contemporaries show was that of 1961, when British *Pop art first appeared in force in the work of Derek *Boshier, David *Hockney, Allen *Jones, R. B. *Kitaj, and Peter *Phillips, all of them students or former students at the *Royal College of Art. In 1974 the name was changed to 'New Contemporaries'.

Ysenbrandt (or Isenbrandt), **Adriaen** (d Bruges, c.1551). Netherlandish painter. He became a master in the Bruges painters' guild in 1510 and is said by an early source to have been a pupil of Gerard *David. Otherwise, virtually nothing is recorded of him and there are no signed or documented works. However, in 1902 the Belgian art historian Georges Hulin de Loo proposed Ysenbrandt as the author of a large group of paintings deriving from David, and the identification has generally been accepted. Previously the paintings had been attributed to Jan *Mostaert and the anonymous Master of the Seven Sorrows of the Virgin, named after a *diptych of the subject divided between the church of Notre-Dame in Bruges and the Musées Royaux in Brussels. Because of the uncertainty, some authorities prefer to use the name Ysenbrandt in inverted commas.

Yvaral. See VASARELY.

Z

Zadkine, Ossip (*b* Vitebsk [now Vitsyebsk], 14 July 1890; *d* Paris, 25 Nov. 1967). Russian-born sculptor who worked mainly in Paris and became a French citizen in 1921. He moved to Paris in 1909 after spending four years in Britain (sent there by his father—a professor of classics—to learn 'English and good manners'). By 1912 he was friendly with many leading figures in avant-garde art, among them *Apollinaire, *Archipenko, *Brancusi, *Lipchitz, and *Picasso. He deeply admired *Rodin, but *Cubism had a greater impact on his work. His experiments with Cubism, however, had none of the quality of intellectual rigour and restraint associated with Picasso and *Braque, for Zadkine's primary concern was with dramatically expressive forms. The distinctive style he evolved made great use of hollows and concave inflections, his figures often having openings pierced through them. In 1915 he joined the French army but was invalided out after being gassed. He worked in Paris through the 1920s and 1930s, and spent the Second World War in New York (where he taught at the *Art Students League), returning to Paris in 1944. Often Zadkine's work can seem merely melodramatic, but for his greatest commission—the huge bronze *To a Destroyed City* (completed 1953) standing at the entry to the port of Rotterdam—he created an extremely powerful figure that is widely regarded as one of the masterpieces of 20th-century sculpture. With its jagged, torn shapes forming an impassioned gesture mixing defence and supplication, it vividly proclaims anger and frustration at the city's destruction and the courage that made possible its rebuilding. This work gave Zadkine an international reputation and many other major commissions followed it. The house in which he lived in Paris is now a museum dedicated to his work.

Zeitblom, Bartholomäus (*b* Nördlingen, *c*.1460; *d* Nördlingen, *c*.1520). German painter of religious works. He was the leading painter of the day in Ulm (where he became a citizen in 1482), and his prosperous workshop supplied large altarpieces for a number of Swabian towns. His calm, dispassionate, lyrical style appealed strongly to certain 19th-century German critics and he was called a 'German *Perugino' or even more incongruously a 'German *Leonardo'. A few portraits have been given to him, but their attribution is disputed.

Zeuxis (active later 5th century BC). Greek painter from Heraclea (probably meaning the town of that name in southern Italy, rather than the one on the Black Sea). None of his works survive, but ancient writers describe him as one of the greatest of Greek painters and he was famed for his powers of verisimilitude, as is indicated by a famous anecdote concerning a competition with a rival (see PARRHASIUS). Another story tells how when called upon to paint a picture of Helen of Troy for a temple at Croton he assembled the five most beautiful maidens of the city and combined the best features of each into one figure of *ideal beauty—an early example of an idea that later became commonplace in aesthetic theory. He is said to have specialized in panels rather than murals. According to legend, he died laughing while painting a picture of a funny-looking old woman, and the story has occasionally formed the basis for later artists' self-portraits. Aert de *Gelder, for example, painted himself as Zeuxis (1685, Städelsches Kunstinstitut, Frankfurt) and *Rembrandt's 'Laughing' self-portrait (*c*.1665, Wallraf-Richartz-Museum, Cologne) has also been interpreted in this way.

Zick. Dynasty of German painters active over five generations in the 18th and 19th centuries. The two leading members were **Johann Zick** (1702–62) and his son and pupil **Januarius Zick** (1730–97). Both of them were primarily church decorators in the *Rococo style, although the comparative solidity and sobriety of Januarius's later work shows the influence of *Neoclassicism, as in his ceiling frescos (1786) in the Klosterkirche in Triefenstein. In addition to his frescos he painted numerous easel pictures.

Ziem, Félix (*b* Beaune, nr. Dijon, ?26 Feb. 1821; *d* Paris, ?10 Nov. 1911). French landscape painter. He travelled widely and was highly prolific, painting various types of picture, but he is best known for his views of Venice, which were enormously popular with collectors and earned him a fortune. They are usually high keyed in colour and reminiscent of *Turner's pictures of the city. Ziem had studios in Martigues (where there is now a museum devoted to him), Paris, and Venice. He also worked a good deal at *Barbizon.

Zijl, Gerard van. See ZYL.

Zimmermann, Johann Baptist (*bapt.* Wessobrunn, 3 Jan. 1680; *bur.* Munich, 2 Mar. 1758). German painter and stuccoist. Although he worked a good deal for the court in Munich, he was above all a church decorator; indeed 'the typically Bavarian-Swabian church interior, resplendent with light colours, is largely Zimmermann's creation' (Eberhard Hempel, *Baroque Art and Architecture in Central Europe*, 1965). He often worked in collaboration with his brother **Dominikus Zimmermann** (*bapt.* Wessobrunn, 1 July 1685; *d* Wies, Bavaria, 16 Nov. 1766), who began his career as a stuccoist but became one of the greatest German architects of his time. Their two most celebrated collaborations are the pilgrimage churches of Steinhausen (1727–33), which has been described as 'the first wholly *Rococo church in Bavaria', and Die Wies (1746–54), which marks one of the high points of the style; the simple white exterior gives no hint of the airy vision in pastel colours and gilt within. Both churches have ceiling paintings by Johann Baptist. His finest work as a stuccoist is the decoration of the Amalienburg hunting lodge at Schloss Nymphenburg near Munich (1734–9). Several other members of the Zimmermann family were painters and/or stuccoists.

Zoffany, Johann (*b* nr. Frankfurt, 13 Mar. 1733; *d* Chiswick, Middlesex [now Greater London], 11 Nov. 1810). German-born painter who settled in England in 1760 after working in Rome. He was patronized by the famous actor David Garrick and made his name with paintings representing scenes from plays, usually showing Garrick in one of his favourite parts. They show how quickly he adapted to English taste, and he also painted *conversation pieces of much the same small scale and in the same relaxed vein. No doubt because of his German background, he was taken up by George III and Queen Charlotte and he painted numerous works for the royal family. The two most important (still in the Royal Collection) are *The Academicians of the Royal Academy* (1772) and *The Tribuna of the Uffizi* (1772–8). For the latter he made a long visit to Florence (1772–9) and when he returned to England he found that the vogue for conversation pieces had passed its peak. Because of the slump in his market he moved to India in 1783 and made a fortune painting Indian princes and expatriate Britons before returning to England in 1789. As a wealthy man he now had no need to earn a living from his work and he seems to have stopped painting in about 1800. At the time of his death he was regarded as a curiosity from another age and for many years his paintings were valued chiefly as historical records (they are sharp and clear in detail and contain a wealth of information about costume, etc.); however, he is now also appreciated for his charm and recognized as an artist who brought new life to the conversation piece.

Zola, Émile (*b* Paris, 2 Apr. 1840; *d* Paris, 29 Sept. 1902). French writer. One of the greatest novelists of the 19th century, he also wrote outspokenly on social and political issues and was a significant art critic. Just as his novels deal vividly with contemporary life, so he rejected academic conventions in art and was one of the first supporters of the group of artists who would become known as the *Impressionists, writing about them in articles in the radical newspaper *L'Événement* from 1866. In particular he championed *Manet, publishing a pamphlet on him in 1867; Manet returned the compliment by painting a superb portrait of Zola (1868, Mus. d'Orsay, Paris). Zola had grown up in Aix-en-Provence, where as a boy he became a close friend of *Cézanne. However, their friendship ended in 1886, when Zola published his novel *L'Œuvre*, for Cézanne believed that the central character—a tormented artist who kills himself in front of his unfinished masterpiece—was based on him. They evidently never saw one another again, but when Zola died tragically in 1902—killed by fumes from a defective stove—Cézanne is said to have shut himself in his studio and wept all day.

Zoppo, Marco (*b* Cento, nr. Bologna, *c.*1432; *d* Venice ?1478). Italian painter of religious subjects. He is first documented in 1455, when he was living in Padua as the adopted son of his teacher *Squarcione. However, like *Mantegna a few years earlier, Zoppo realized he was being exploited by Squarcione, and later in 1455 he moved to Venice. He spent most of his brief career there and in Bologna (he signed himself Bononensis—'Bolognese'). His work includes altarpieces and small devotional pictures, painted in a wiry style reflecting the influence of Mantegna, softened by that of Giovanni *Bellini. Two of his paintings are in the National Gallery, London. A substantial number of his drawings survive.

Zorach, William (b Eurburg [now Yurbarkas], 1889; d Bath, Me., 15 Nov. 1966). Lithuanian-born American sculptor. Initially Zorach worked as a painter in a vivid *Fauvist style, but he took up sculpture in 1917 and abandoned painting (apart from watercolours) about five years later. His sculpture is figurative and its salient characteristics are firm contours, blocklike bulk, and suppression of details: 'I owe most', he said, 'to the great periods of primitive carving in the past—not to the modern or the classical Greeks, but to the Africans, the Persians, the Mesopotamians, the archaic Greeks and of course to the Egyptians.' He was a pioneer in America of the revival of *direct carving in stone and wood and in this as well as in his formal austerity he exercised a powerful influence on modern American sculpture. He had numerous major commissions, including relief carvings for the Municipal Court Building, New York (1958). His most famous work is not a carving, however, but the aluminium *Spirit of the Dance* (1932) for Radio City Music Hall, New York—a heroic female figure that was banished for a time because of its nudity but reinstated by public pressure. Zorach taught at the *Art Students League from 1929 to 1966. His wife **Marguerite Thompson Zorach** (1887–1968) was one of America's leading modernist painters in the years immediately before and immediately after the *Armory Show (1913), in which both she and her husband exhibited. At this time she painted in a style influenced by Fauvism and *Expressionism. In her later career, however, much of her time was spent selflessly helping her husband with his sculptural commissions, producing many of the preliminary drawings for his work.

Zorn, Anders (b Mora, 18 Feb. 1860; d Mora, 22 Aug. 1920). Swedish painter and etcher. After leaving the Stockholm Academy in 1881 because of its restrictive and outdated ideas, he travelled widely, becoming the most cosmopolitan Scandinavian artist of his time and an international success. He was based in London (1882–5), then Paris (1888–96), and visited Spain, Italy, the Balkans, North Africa, and (on several occasions) the USA, where he painted three presidents.

Originally he worked almost exclusively in watercolour, but in 1887–90 he abandoned the medium for oils. In 1896 he settled at his home town of Mora (although he continued to travel), building his own house, which is now a museum dedicated to him. He painted three main types of pictures: portraits, *genre scenes (often depicting the life and customs of the area in which he lived), and female nudes. It is for his nudes—unashamedly healthy and voluptuous works—that he is now best known. He often painted them in landscape settings and delighted in vibrant effects of light on the human body, depicted through lush brushwork that recalls the handling of his friend Max *Liebermann. Zorn also gained a great reputation for his etchings and he occasionally made sculpture, including one large work—the statue of Gustavus Vasa in Mora (1903).

Zuccarelli, Francesco (b Pitigliano, Tuscany, 15 Aug. 1702; d Florence, 30 Dec. 1788). Italian painter of landscapes, often featuring mythological subjects. He was born near Florence and studied in Rome, but he is associated chiefly with Venice, where he settled in about 1730 and worked in the vein of pastoral landscape popularized by Marco *Ricci. Like *Canaletto, Zuccarelli was patronized by the English entrepreneur Joseph Smith and his work found a ready market in England. When Richard *Wilson (still primarily a portraitist) visited Venice in 1751 he painted Zuccarelli's portrait (Tate, London) and it is said to have been Zuccarelli's encouragement that induced him to concentrate on landscape. In 1752–62 and again in 1765–71 Zuccarelli worked in England, where his delicate *Rococo style gained him great success (he was one of the founder members of the *Royal Academy in 1768). In 1772 he was elected president of the Venetian Academy, but soon afterwards he retired to Florence. There are numerous examples of his work in Britain, most notably in the Royal Collection (George III bought many of his paintings from Joseph Smith and also commissioned work from him).

Zuccaro, Taddeo (b Sant'Angelo in Vado, nr. Urbino, 1 Sept. 1529; d Rome, 2 Sept. 1566) and **Federico** (b Sant'Angelo in Vado, 18 Apr. ?1540; d Ancona, ?(20 July) 1609). Italian *Mannerist painters, brothers. Taddeo worked mainly in Rome and although he was only 37 when he died he had made a great name for himself as a fresco decorator, working most notably for the *Farnese family in their palace at Caprarola, near Viterbo. His style was based on *Michelangelo and *Raphael and tended to be rather dry and wooden.

Federico took over his brother's flourishing studio, continuing the work at Caprarola and also the decoration of the Sala Regia in the Vatican (begun by Taddeo in 1561). His talent was no more exceptional than Taddeo's, but he became even more successful and won a European reputation—indeed for a time he was probably the most famous living painter. In 1574 he travelled via Lorraine and the Netherlands to England, where he is said to have painted many court portraits, although the only works dating from this visit that can be safely attributed to him are two drawings in the British Museum portraying Elizabeth I and Robert Dudley, Earl of Leicester. (Many anonymous portraits of the period are improbably attributed to him.) After working in Florence, Rome, and Venice, he spent three years in Spain (1585–8), painting altarpieces and frescos for the *Escorial. However, his visit was not a success, partly because his arrogance offended his Spanish colleagues. Back in Rome he was elected the first president of the new Accademia di S. Luca, founded in 1593 (see ACADEMY). Like many of his contemporaries he believed that correct theory would produce good works of art and he wrote several treatises, of which the most important is *L'idea de' pittori, scultori, et architetti* (1607). Zuccaro also worked as an architect, designing a doorway in the form of a grotesque face (one enters through the open mouth) for his house in Rome, the Palazzo Zuccaro, which he bequeathed to the Accademia to use as its headquarters (it is now the Biblioteca Hertziana). The two flanking windows are treated in similar bizarre fashion.

Zucchi, Antonio. See KAUFFMANN.

Zuloaga, Ignacio (b Eibar, nr. Bilbao, 26 July 1870; d Madrid, 31 Oct. 1945). Spanish painter. He came from a long line of craftsmen (his father was a metalworker) and was mainly self-taught as an artist. Much of his career was spent in Paris, where he was on friendly terms with *Rodin, *Gauguin, and *Degas, but his art is strongly national in style and subject matter. Bullfighters, gypsies, and brigands were among his subjects, and he also painted religious scenes and society portraits (these were one of the main sources of the considerable fortune he earned). His inspiration came from the great Spanish masters of the past, notably *Velázquez and *Goya, and he is credited with being one of the first to 'rediscover' El *Greco. He had a great reputation in his lifetime (unusually for a Spanish artist, his standing was higher abroad than at home), but his work now often looks rather stagy. There are museums devoted to him in Segovia and the Basque fishing port of Zumaya, two of his principal places of work.

Zumbo, Gaetano Giulio. See WAX.

Zurbarán, Francisco de (bapt. Fuente de Cantos, Extremadura, 7 Nov. 1598; d Madrid, 27 Aug. 1664). Spanish painter, active mainly in Seville, which lies about 100 km (60 miles) to the south of the village where he was born. He trained in Seville, 1614–17, then spent the next decade working at Llerana, near his birthplace. In 1627 he made his name with a powerful *Christ on the Cross* (Art Inst. of Chicago), painted for the Dominican monastery of S. Pablo in Seville, and its success led him to settle in the city in 1629. In 1634–5 he visited Madrid, where he worked for Philip IV (see HABSBURG), painting for the Buen Retiro Palace a series of ten pictures on the Labours of Hercules and a large historical scene, *The Defence of Cadiz* (all now in the Prado, Madrid); apart from these pictures, a few portraits, and some masterly still-lifes, he devoted himself almost entirely to religious images. His most characteristic works are single figures of monks and saints in meditation or prayer (for example, two paintings of *St Francis* in the National Gallery, London, one of them dated 1639). The figures are usually depicted against a plain background, standing out with massive physical presence. In such compositionally simple and emotionally direct altarpieces, Zurbarán showed himself to be an ideal interpreter of Counter-Reformation ideals, combining austere *naturalism with mystical intensity. Many of his pictures were painted in series, notably a set of eight pictures of Hieronymite saints for the Order's monastery at Guadalupe (1639–40); these remain *in situ* and 'constitute the best surviving example of a series of monastic history painted in the seventeenth century' (Jonathan Brown, *Painting in Spain: 1500–1700*, 1998).

The 1630s marked the peak of Zurbarán's career, and after 1640 his stream of major commissions dried up. Subsequently he produced most of his work for the South American market, much of it being done by assistants. In the later 1640s *Murillo began to overtake him as the most popular painter in Seville, and Zurbarán's work lost something of its power and simplicity as he tried to come to terms with the softer, sweeter, lighter style of his rival. By the later 1650s he was experiencing financial problems, partly caused by the loss in warfare of ships bringing payments from his South American clients. In 1658 he moved to Madrid, where he spent his final years, but he failed to revive his career there.

His son **Juan** (1620–49), who died young of the plague, is known from a few impressive still-life paintings.

Zwobada, Jacques (b Neuilly-sur-Seine, 6 Aug. 1900; d Fontenay-aux-Roses, nr. Paris, 1967). French sculptor. His early inspiration was *Rodin, as can be seen in his monument to Simon Bolivar (1933) in Quito, Ecuador. In about 1935 he abandoned sculpture and taught drawing in Paris for several years, but in about 1950 he returned to sculpture, working in a semi-abstract style characterized by a rhythmic interplay of masses and voids. In 1956 his wife died

suddenly and he devoted most of the rest of his career to creating a funerary monument to her at Mentana, near Rome, where he had bought property shortly before her death. The monument consists of several figures and groups arranged in a semi-circle, with various subsidiary groups. The last group he added, shortly before his own death, was the symbolically apt *Orpheus and Eurydice*.

Zyl (or **Zijl**), **Gerard van** (b ?Haarlem, c.1607; bur. Amsterdam, 19 Dec. 1665). Dutch painter of portraits and *genre scenes, the best-known member of a dynasty of painters active in the 16th and 17th centuries. He was a pupil of Jan *Pynas in Amsterdam and from 1639 to 1641 worked in London, where he was a friend of van *Dyck.

CHRONOLOGY

This chronology (a revision of that compiled by Caroline Juler for the second edition) shows how certain key examples of Western art fit into a wider historical context. In the left-hand column it lists famous works, almost all of which are discussed in the appropriate entry in the text. The right-hand column gives a selective list of events of cultural and general historical importance.

	Key works	Other events
c. 530 BC		Invention of red-figure vase-painting
490 BC		Persian emperor Darius invades Greece and is defeated at Marathon
c. 470 BC	*Delphi Charioteer*	Temple of Zeus at Olympia begun; it houses Phidias' statue of the god, one of the Seven Wonders of the World
c. 460–429 BC		Pericles presides over a golden age in Athenian culture
c. 450 BC	Myron: *Discus Thrower*	
447 BC		Parthenon, Athens, begun
432 BC	Parthenon sculptures completed	
431–404 BC		Peloponnesian War, in which Sparta defeats Athens
399 BC		Socrates d.
c. 350 BC		Mausoleum, Halicarnassus (now Bodrum, Turkey), with sculptural decoration by Scopas and others
c. 330 BC	*Demeter of Cnidus* Praxiteles: *Hermes*	
323 BC		Alexander the Great d.
c. 300 BC	*Alexander Sarcophagus*	Euclid's *Elements* represent a breakthrough in mathematics
c. 280 BC	*Colossus of Rhodes* completed	
c. 200 BC	*Barberini Faun* *Victory of Samothrace*	
c. 180–150 BC	Pergamum altar	
146 BC		3rd Punic War ends with the destruction of Carthage, leaving Rome dominant in the western Mediterranean
c. 100 BC	*Alexander Mosaic* *Venus de Milo*	
70 BC		Virgil b.
44 BC		Julius Caesar assassinated
13–9 BC	Ara Pacis Augustae, Rome	
AD 17		Ovid d.
c. AD 30	*Laocoön*	Jesus Christ crucified
AD 43		Romans occupy Britain

Chronology

	Key works	Other events
79		Pompeii and Herculaneum destroyed by eruption of Vesuvius
c. 81	Arch of Titus, Rome	
98–117		Reign of Trajan, when Roman Empire reaches its height of power and prosperity
113	Trajan's Column, Rome, dedicated	
c. 118–c. 128		Pantheon, Rome
c. 161–80	*Marcus Aurelius* equestrian statue, Rome	
c. 200	Wall paintings, catacomb of Priscilla, Rome (one of the earliest examples of Christian art)	
203	Arch of Septimius Severus, Rome	
c. 240	Wall paintings, Dura Europos synagogue, Syria (the earliest continuous cycle of biblical images)	
306–37		Constantine rules Roman Empire
c. 312–15	Arch of Constantine, Rome	
330		Constantine establishes Byzantium as his capital and renames it Constantinople
c. 360	Sarcophagus of Junius Bassus	
402		Ravenna becomes capital of western Roman Empire
410		Visigoths sack Rome
c. 425	*Good Shepherd* mosaic, Mausoleum of Galla Placidia, Ravenna	
432		Traditional date for the beginning of St Patrick's mission in Ireland
476		Western Roman Empire falls
c. 500–600	Vienna Genesis	
532–7		Church of Hagia Sophia, Constantinople
c. 540		St Benedict of Nursia writes his 'rule', which establishes principles of Western monasticism
c. 540–7	Mosaics, S. Vitale, Ravenna (consecrated 547), one of the greatest ensembles of Byzantine art	
590–604		Pontificate of Gregory the Great, whose reforms lay foundation of medieval papacy
597		St Augustine leads Christian mission to England
632		Death of Muhammad, founder of Islamic religion
c. 650–80	Book of Durrow	
c. 700	Lindisfarne Gospels	
711		Muslim invaders begin conquest of Spain
732		Frankish leader Charles Martel wins decisive victory at Battle of Poitiers (also called Battle of Tours), halting Muslim advance in Europe
c. 750	Ruthwell Cross, Scotland	*Beowulf*, Anglo-Saxon epic poem

	Key works	Other events
800		Charlemagne crowned Holy Roman Emperor
c. **800**	Book of Kells	
c. **816–35**	Utrecht Psalter	
962–73		Otto the Great rules as Holy Roman Emperor
c. **970**	Gero Crucifix	
c. **1008–15**	Bronze doors for St Michael, Hildesheim, commissioned by Bernward of Hildesheim	
c. **1063**		St Mark's, Venice, begun
1066		Norman Conquest of England
c. **1080**	Bayeux Tapestry	
1093		Durham Cathedral begun
1096–9		First Crusade
1098		Cistercian order founded in France
c. **1107–18**	Rainer of Huy: bronze font, Liège	
c. **1120**		Cathedral of Santiago de Compostela begun
c. **1130**	Gislebertus: *Last Judgement* tympanum, Autun Cathedral	
1140–4		Rebuilding of the abbey church of Saint-Denis, near Paris, for Abbot Suger, marking the birth of the Gothic style
1163		Notre-Dame Cathedral, Paris, begun
1181	Nicolas of Verdun: Klosterneuburg Altar completed	
1216		Foundation of Dominican order
1226		St Francis of Assisi d.
1259	Nicola Pisano: Pisa pulpit	
1261	Coppo di Marcovaldo: *Madonna del Bordone*	
1265		Dante b.
c. **1280**	Cimabue: *S. Trinità Madonna*	
c. **1303–6**	Giotto: Arena Chapel frescos, Padua	
1311	Duccio: *Maestà* completed	
1333	Simone Martini and Lippo Memmi: *Annunciation*	
1337–1453		Hundred Years War between England and France
1338–9	Ambrogio Lorenzetti: *Good and Bad Government*	
1347–50		Black Death devastates Europe
1354–7	Orcagna: *The Redeemer with the Madonna and Saints*	
c. **1395–9**	Wilton Diptych	
1395–1403	Sluter: *Well of Moses*	
1401		Ghiberti wins competition for bronze doors of Florence Baptistery

Chronology

	Key works	Other events
c. 1413–16	Limbourg brothers: *Très Riches Heures du duc de Berry*	
1415		Battle of Agincourt
c. 1415–17	Donatello: *St George*	
1420–36		Dome of Florence Cathedral built (designed by Brunelleschi)
1423	Gentile da Fabriano: *Adoration of the Magi*	
c. 1428	Masaccio: *Holy Trinity*	
1431		Joan of Arc burnt at stake
1432	Jan van Eyck: Ghent Altarpiece completed	
1435		Alberti writes *De pictura*
1436	Uccello: *Sir John Hawkwood*	
c. 1438–45	Fra Angelico: S. Marco frescos	
1447–53	Donatello: *Gattamelata* equestrian statue	
1448		King's College Chapel, Cambridge, begun
c. 1450	Jean Fouquet: Diptych of Melun	
c. 1450–65	Piero della Francesca: *Legend of the True Cross*	
1452	Quarton: *Virgin of Mercy*	Leonardo b.
1453	Mino da Fiesole: *Piero de' Medici*	Turks capture Constantinople, ending Byzantine Empire
1465–74	Mantegna: Bridal Chamber, Ducal Palace, Mantua	
1469–92		Lorenzo de' Medici is head of the family and virtual ruler of Florence
1470–5	Dieric Bouts: *Justice of Emperor Otto*	
1475		Michelangelo b.
c. 1475	Pollaiuolo: *Martyrdom of St Sebastian*	
1475–6	Antonello da Messina: S. Cassiano Altarpiece	
c. 1478	Botticelli: *Birth of Venus*	
1481–2		Botticelli, Ghirlandaio, Perugino, and Rosselli paint frescos in Sistine Chapel
1481–96	Verrocchio: *Colleoni* equestrian statue	
1483		Raphael b.
1489	Notke: *St George and the Dragon* completed	
1492		Columbus lands in W. Indies Moors driven from Granada, completing the Christian reconquest of Spain
c. 1495–7	Leonardo: *Last Supper*	
1498		Portuguese navigator Vasco da Gama becomes first European to travel to India by sea
1498–9	Michelangelo: *Pietà*	
1503–13		Papacy of Julius II

	Key works	Other events
c. 1503–6	Leonardo: *Mona Lisa*	
1504	Barbari: *Dead Bird* Cranach: *Rest on the Flight into Egypt*	
1505	Giovanni Bellini: S. Zaccaria Altarpiece	
1506		Bramante begins rebuilding of St Peter's, Rome
1508	Raphael begins decoration of Vatican Stanze	
1508–12	Michelangelo: Sistine Ceiling	
1510		Giorgione d.
1512–18	Torrigiano: tomb of Henry VII and Elizabeth of York	
1513	Dürer: *The Knight, Death, and the Devil*	
c. 1515	Grünewald: Isenheim Altarpiece completed	
1516		Bosch d.
1516–18	Titian: *Assumption of the Virgin*	
1517	Andrea del Sarto: *Madonna of the Harpies*	
1519		Leonardo d. Charles V becomes Holy Roman Emperor
1520		Raphael d. Luther excommunicated
1522		First circumnavigation of the globe completed by Spanish navigator Juan Sebastián del Cano (the original leader of the expedition, Ferdinand Magellan, having died the previous year)
1526	Sebastiano del Piombo: *Clement VII*	
1527		Sack of Rome
1528		Castiglione: *The Book of the Courtier*
c. 1530	Correggio: *The Loves of Jupiter*	
1533	Holbein: *The Ambassadors*	Ivan the Terrible becomes Grand Duke of Moscow (in 1547 he is the first ruler to assume the title of Tsar of Russia)
c. 1535	Parmigianino: *Madonna of the Long Neck*	
1536–40		Dissolution of the monasteries in England and Wales
1536–41	Michelangelo: *Last Judgement*	
1543		Copernicus's *De revolutionibus orbium coelestium* lays the foundations of modern astronomy
1545		Council of Trent begins
c. 1545	Bronzino: *Allegory with Venus and Cupid*	
1546		Francis I begins rebuilding Louvre, Paris
1548	Titian: *Charles V on Horseback*	
1550		Vasari's *Lives of the Artists* published
1554	Cellini: *Perseus* unveiled	
1558–1603		Reign of Elizabeth I of England

Chronology

	Key works	Other events
1563		Accademia del Disegno founded in Florence
1564		Shakespeare b.
		Michelangelo d.
1565	Pieter Bruegel starts *The Months* series	
1565–87	Tintoretto: Scuola di S. Rocco	
***c.* 1566**		Palladio's Villa Rotunda begun
1573	Veronese: *Feast in the House of Levi*	
1577		Rubens b.
1577–9	El Greco: *El Espolio*	
1581–2	Giambologna: *Rape of a Sabine*	
1584		William the Silent, chief architect of Dutch independence, assassinated in Delft
1586–8	El Greco: *Burial of Count Orgaz*	
***c.* 1587**	Hilliard: *Young Man Leaning on a Tree among Roses*	
1588		England defeats Spanish Armada
1597–1600	Annibale Carracci: Farnese Ceiling	
1598		Edict of Nantes defines rights of Protestants at end of Wars of Religion in France
1600–1	Caravaggio: *Crucifixion of St Peter* and *Conversion of St Paul*	
1603–6	Montañés: *Christ of Clemency*	
1606		Rembrandt b.
1609	Elsheimer: *Flight into Egypt*	Dutch Republic effectively wins freedom from Spain
1610–11	Rubens: *Raising of the Cross*	
1611		Authorized Version of the Bible
1613–14	Reni: *Aurora*	
1616		Cervantes d.
		Shakespeare d.
1618–48		Thirty Years War
1619–22		Inigo Jones, Banqueting House, London
1622–5	Bernini: *Apollo and Daphne*	
1624	Hals: *The Laughing Cavalier*	
1625–7	Lanfranco: *Assumption of the Virgin*	
1632		van Dyck becomes court painter to Charles I of England
1633–9	Pietro da Cortona: Barberini Ceiling	
1634–5	Velázquez: *Surrender of Breda*	
1637		Descartes, *Discourse on Method*
1639	Ribera: *Martyrdom of St Philip*	
1642	Rembrandt: *The Night Watch*	English Civil War begins
1643–1715		Reign of Louis XIV of France
1647–52	Bernini: *Ecstasy of St Teresa*	
1648	Poussin: *The Ashes of Phocion*	Académie Royale de Peinture et de Sculpture founded in Paris
	Terborch: *The Swearing of the Oath of Ratification of the Treaty of Münster*	

	Key works	Other events
1649		Charles I executed; England becomes a republic under Oliver Cromwell
1650	Georges de La Tour: *The Denial of St Peter* Mola: *Barbary Pirate*	
1653	Ruisdael: *Bentheim Castle*	
1656	Vermeer: *The Procuress*	
***c.* 1656**	Velázquez: *Las meninas*	
1660		Restoration of the English monarchy
1661		Louis XIV begins enlarging chateau of Versailles
1662	Philippe de Champaigne: *Ex-Voto*	
1666		Fire of London
***c.* 1669**	Rembrandt: *The Return of the Prodigal Son*	
1672		Bellori, *Lives of the Modern Painters*
1674–9	Gaulli: *Adoration of the Name of Jesus*	
1675–1710		St Paul's Cathedral, London
1682	Claude: *Ascanius and the Stag*	
1683		Ashmolean Museum, Oxford, opens; the first public museum in Britain
1685		Johann Sebastian Bach b. Handel b. Louis XIV revokes Edict of Nantes
1685–90	Coello: *Charles II Adoring the Host*	
1687		Newton, *Principia mathematica*
1689	Hobbema: *The Avenue*	
1691–4	Pozzo: ceiling of S. Ignazio, Rome	
1701	Rigaud: *Louis XIV*	
1703		Peter the Great founds St Petersburg
1707		Act of Union unites England and Scotland
1717	Watteau: *The Pilgrimage to the Isle of Cythera*	
1721–32	Tomé: Transparente, Toledo Cathedral	
1728	Chardin: *The Rayfish*	
***c.* 1730**	Canaletto: *The Stonemason's Yard*	
1731	Rysbrack: Isaac Newton monument	
***c.* 1735**	Hogarth: *A Rake's Progress*	
1740	Scheemakers: Shakespeare monument	Frederick II (the Great) becomes ruler of Prussia
***c.* 1745**	Piranesi: *Carceri*	
1749		Goethe b.
1750		Bach d.
1750–3	Tiepolo: decorations for the prince-bishop's palace, Würzburg	
1751	Boucher: *Reclining Girl*	
1753		British Museum established

Chronology

	Key works	Other events
1753–4	Reynolds: *Commodore Keppel*	
1756		Mozart b.
1757	Tiepolo: decorations for the Villa Valmarana, Vicenza	
1761	Mengs: *Parnassus* Roubiliac: Nightingale monument	
1764		Winckelmann, *History of Ancient Art*
1766	Fragonard: *The Swing*	
1768	Wright: *An Experiment on a Bird in the Air Pump*	Foundation of Royal Academy, London
1770	Gainsborough: *The Blue Boy* West: *Death of Wolfe*	Beethoven b.
1776		American Declaration of Independence
1778	Copley: *Brook Watson and the Shark*	
1781	Fuseli: *The Nightmare*	
1784–5	David: *Oath of the Horatii*	
1786–7	Tischbein: *Goethe in the Roman Campagna*	
1787		Mozart, *Don Giovanni*
1789	Blake: *Songs of Innocence*	French Revolution begins
1790	Bewick: *A General History of Quadrupeds*	
1791		Mozart d.
1793	David: *Death of Marat*	Louvre, Paris, opens as first national public gallery
1797		Schubert b.
1798	Rowlandson: *The Comforts of Bath*	lithography invented
1799	Goya: *Los Caprichos* Stubbs: *Hambletonian: Rubbing Down*	
1802–3	Thorvaldsen: *Jason*	
1804		Napoleon becomes Emperor of France Beethoven, *Eroica* symphony
1805		Battle of Trafalgar Pennsylvania Academy of the Fine Arts founded
1805–7	Canova: *Pauline Borghese as Venus*	
1808	Friedrich: *The Cross in the Mountains* Gros: *Battle of Eylau* Ingres: *Valpinçon Bather*	
1809		Nazarenes formed
1812		Napoleon retreats from Moscow
1814		George Stephenson constructs the first successful steam locomotive
1815	Schinkel: designs for Mozart's *Magic Flute*	Battle of Waterloo
1819	Géricault: *Raft of the Medusa*	First Atlantic steamship crossing Prado, Madrid, opens
1820–3	Goya: *Black Paintings*	
1821	Constable: *The Hay Wain*	
1822	Wilkie: *Chelsea Pensioners*	

	Key works	Other events
1824	Delacroix: *Massacre at Chios*	National Gallery, London, founded
1825–7	Martin: illustrations to Milton's *Paradise Lost*	
1827		Beethoven d.
1827–38	Audubon: *The Birds of America*	
1828		Tolstoy b. Schubert d.
1830		July Revolution in France
1830–3	Bryulov: *The Last Day of Pompeii*	
1832		Daumier imprisoned for political satire
1833		Brahms b.
1833–6	Rude: *La Marseillaise*	
1836–9	Cornelius: *Last Judgement*	
1837		Queen Victoria accedes to throne in England
1839	Turner: *The Fighting Temeraire*	Daguerre publicizes 'daguerreotype'
1840	Cole: *The Voyage of Life*	Monet b. Rodin b.
1841		Eakins b.
1843	Powers: *The Greek Slave*	Ruskin, first volume of *Modern Painters*
1845	Bingham: *Fur Traders Descending the Missouri*	
1847	Couture: *The Romans of the Decadence*	
1848		Gauguin b. The Year of Revolutions Marx and Engels, *Communist Manifesto* Pre-Raphaelite Brotherhood formed
1849	Rossetti: *Girlhood of Mary Virgin*	
1850	Courbet exhibits *A Burial at Ornans*, *Peasants at Flagey*, and *The Stone Breakers*	
1851		The Great Exhibition, London
1853	Holman Hunt: *The Awakening Conscience*	Van Gogh b.
1853–6		Crimean War
1855	Madox Brown: *The Last of England*	
1858	Frith: *Derby Day* Ivanov exhibits *Christ's First Appearance to the People* (1837–57)	
1859	Millet: *The Angelus*	Darwin, *The Origin of Species*
1861–5		American Civil War
1863	Ingres: *The Turkish Bath* Manet: *Le Déjeuner sur l'herbe*	Salon des Réfuses
1864	Fantin-Latour: *Homage to Delacroix*	
1870	Millais: *Boyhood of Raleigh*	Metropolitan Museum, New York, founded Wanderers founded
1870–1		Franco-Prussian War
1870–3	Repin: *Barge Haulers on the Volga*	

Chronology

	Key works	Other events
1871	Whistler: *Arrangement in Grey and Black: Portrait of the Painter's Mother*	
1872	Monet: *Impression: Sunrise*	
1874		First Impressionist exhibition, Paris
1875	Eakins: *The Gross Clinic*	
1876		Bell patents telephone Battle of Little Bighorn
1878		Ruskin–Whistler libel trial Edison invents phonograph
1880	Böcklin: *The Island of the Dead* Rodin begins *Gates of Hell*	Apollinaire b. Epstein b. Kirchner b. Flaubert d. Dostoevsky, *The Brothers Karamazov*
1881	Degas: *Little Fourteen-year-old Dancer* Saint-Gaudens: Admiral Farragut monument unveiled	Bartók b. Léger b. Picasso b. Dostoevsky d. Samuel Palmer d. Ibsen, *Ghosts* Tsar Alexander II assassinated
***c.* 1881–6**	Renoir: *Umbrellas*	
1882	Manet: *A Bar at the Folies-Bergère*	Braque b. Charles Darwin d. Rossetti d.
1883		Orozco b. Manet d. Marx d. Wagner d. Nietzsche, *Also sprach Zarathustra*
1884	Sargent: *Madame X*	Beckmann b. Modigliani b. First exhibition of Salon des Indépendants, Paris Huysmans, *A rebours*
1884–6	Seurat: *Sunday Afternoon on the Island of La Grande Jatte*	
1884–93		Les Vingt group exhibitions
1885	van Gogh: *The Potato Eaters*	Victor Hugo d. General Gordon killed as Khartoum is captured by the Mahdi Zola, *Germinal*
1886	Bartholdi: Statue of Liberty dedicated Millais: *Bubbles*	Mies van der Rohe b. Rivera b. Liszt d. New English Art Club founded in London
1886–94		Gauguin intermittently active at Pont-Aven
1887	Serov: *Girl with Peaches*	Archipenko b. Chagall b. Duchamp b. Le Corbusier b. Verdi, *Otello*

	Key works	**Other events**
1888	Ensor: *Entry of Christ into Brussels* Gauguin: *The Vision after the Sermon* van Gogh: *The Night Café*	Albers b. de Chirico b. T. S. Eliot b. van Gogh settles at Arles Strindberg, *Miss Julie* Wilhelm II becomes emperor of Germany
1889		Crown Prince Rudolf of Austria and his mistress commit suicide at Mayerling, near Vienna Eiffel Tower built
1890	Edelfelt: *Christ and Mary Magdalene*	Gabo b. van Gogh d. William Morris founds Kelmscott Press
1891	Fildes: *The Doctor*	Dix b. Max Ernst b. Gaudier-Brzeska b. Prokofiev b. Stanley Spencer b. Seurat d. Gauguin sails to Tahiti
1891–5	Monet: *Rouen Cathedral* series	Trans-Siberian railway started
1892	Leighton: *The Garden of the Hesperides*	Grant Wood b. The Nabis' first exhibition
1893	Munch: *The Scream* Toorop: *The Three Brides*	Grosz b. Miró b.
1894	Beardsley: illustrations to Oscar Wilde's *Salome*	President Carnot of France assassinated
1894–1906		The Dreyfus affair
1895		First Venice Biennale Lumière brothers present the cinématographe, the first apparatus to project motion pictures on a screen Marconi invents wireless telegraph Röntgen discovers X-rays
1896		André Breton b. Millais d. William Morris d. Puccini, *La Bohème* Alfred Jarry, *Ubu Roi* First modern Olympic Games held in Athens
1897	Gauguin: *Where Do We Come From? Who Are We? Where Are We Going To?*	Tate Gallery, London, opens Brahms d.
1898		Aalto b. Calder b. Magritte b. Henry Moore b. Beardsley d. Boudin d. Burne-Jones d.
1899	Dalou: *Triumph of the Republic* unveiled	Spanish-American War
1899–1902	Klinger: Beethoven monument	Boer War

Chronology

	Key works	Other events
1900	Denis: *Homage to Cézanne*	Ruskin d. Oscar Wilde d. Freud, *The Interpretation of Dreams* Max Planck propounds quantum theory Boxer Rising in China
1901	Klimt: *Judith I*	Alberto Giacometti b. Böcklin d. Toulouse-Lautrec d. Queen Victoria d. President McKinley assassinated
1902		Zola d.
1903	Rysselberghe: *A Reading*	Hepworth b. Gauguin d. Camille Pissarro d. Whistler d. Salon d'Automne founded in Paris Wright brothers make first powered flight National Art Collections Fund founded, London
1904	Picasso: *The Frugal Repast*	Dalí b. de Kooning b. Dvořák d.
1904–5	Matisse: *Luxe, calme et volupté*	Russo-Japanese War
1905		Burra b. Bouguereau d. Fauvism launched at Salon d'Automne Die Brücke formed in Dresden Einstein publishes his special theory of relativity
1906		Cézanne d.
1906–7	Picasso: *Les Demoiselles d'Avignon*	
1907	Bellows: *A Stag at Sharkey's*	Salon d'Automne holds Cézanne memorial exhibition Kahnweiler opens gallery in Paris
1907–8	Epstein: figures for façade of British Medical Association, London	
1907–14		Braque and Picasso evolve Cubism
1908		Henry Ford designs the Model T, the first mass-production automobile
1909	Kokoschka: *Adolf Loos*	Bacon b. Marinetti launches Futurism Diaghilev brings his Russian ballet company to Paris
1910	Rousseau: *The Dream*	Tolstoy d. Roger Fry's first Post-Impressionist exhibition, London
***c.* 1910**		Birth of abstract art
1911	Braque: *The Portuguese* Brock: Queen Victoria monument unveiled Carrà: *The Funeral of the Anarchist Galli* Le Fauconnier: *Abundance* Lehmbruck: *Kneeling Woman*	Der Blaue Reiter's first show Camden Town Group formed

	Key works	**Other events**
1912	Archipenko: *Walking Woman* Balla: *Dynamism of a Dog on a Leash* Robert Delaunay: *Circular Forms* Kupka: *Amorpha: Fugue in Two Colours*	Jackson Pollock b. Gleizes and Metzinger, *Du Cubisme* 'Donkey's Tail' exhibition, Moscow
1913	Boccioni: *Unique forms of Continuity in Space* Duchamp: *Bicycle Wheel* (first ready-made) Kandinsky: *Composition VI* Kirchner: *Street, Berlin*	Reg Butler b. Camus b. Armory Show, New York Proust, *Swann's Way* 'Target' exhibition, Moscow Fry founds Omega Workshops
1913–14	Bomberg: *In the Hold*	Stravinsky, *Rite of Spring*
1914	Lamb: *Lytton Strachey* Marc: *Fighting Forms*	Birth of Vorticism
***c*. 1914**	Sickert: *Ennui*	
1914–18	Gill: *Stations of the Cross*	First World War
1915	Duchamp begins constructing *The Bride Stripped Bare by her Bachelors, Even*	Dada founded D. W. Griffiths: *The Birth of a Nation*
1916	Gertler: *Merry-Go-Round*	Eakins d.
1917	Thomson: *Jack Pine*	Rodin d. Russian Revolution De Stijl founded Carrà and de Chirico meet
1918	Grosz: *Fit for Active Service*	Apollinaire d. Poland and Czechoslovakia become republics
***c*. 1918**	Malevich: *White on White*	
1918–19	Sargent: *Gassed*	
1919		Alcock and Brown make first transatlantic flight The Bauhaus opens in Weimar
1919–20	Tatlin: model for Monument to the Third International	
1920	Dix: *The Match Seller*	Modigliani d. Group of Seven founded
1921	Ernst: *Celebes*	
1922		Mussolini's Fascists march on Rome James Joyce, *Ulysses*
1923	Frank Dobson: *Osbert Sitwell*	
1924		Lenin d. First Surrealist manifesto
1924–6	Spencer: *The Resurrection: Cookham*	
1925	Miró: *The Harlequin's Carnival*	Eisenstein, *Battleship Potemkin* Kafka, *The Trial*
1926	Magritte: *The Menaced Assassin*	Monet d. First demonstration of television
1927	Hepworth: *Doves*	*The Jazz Singer* (first film with synchronous sound)
1928	Curry: *Baptism in Kansas*	Fleming discovers penicillin
1929		Wall Street Crash Museum of Modern Art, New York, founded

Chronology

	Key works	Other events
1930	Grant Wood: *American Gothic*	Buñuel: *L'Age d'or*
1930–1		Empire State Building, New York
1931	Dalí: *The Persistence of Memory*	Abstraction-Création group founded in Paris Courtauld Institute of Art, London, founded
1932	Brockhurst: *Adolescence*	
1932–3	Rivera: *Detroit Industry*	
1932–5	Beckmann: *Departure*	
1933	Gunn: *Delius* Manship: *Prometheus*	Hitler becomes Chancellor of Germany
1934	Burra: *Dancing Skeletons*	
1935	Ben Nicholson: *White Relief*	Italy invades Ethiopia
1936	Oppenheim: *Object* Spencer: *The Leg of Mutton Nude*	International Surrealist Exhibition, London
1936–9		Spanish Civil War
1937	Brancusi: *Endless Column* González: *Montserrat* Picasso: *Guernica*	Germans bomb Guernica, Spain National Gallery of Art, Washington, founded Nazi exhibition of 'Degenerate Art', Munich
1938	Lewis: *T. S. Eliot*	Kirchner d. Germany annexes Austria
1939	Nash: *Monster Field*	Franco becomes Spanish dictator Germany invades Poland
1939–45		Second World War
1940	Klee: *Death and Fire*	
1940–2	Moore: Air-raid shelter drawings	
1941		Japanese attack Pearl Harbor Orson Welles, *Citizen Kane*
1942	Hopper: *Nighthawks*	Grant Wood d.
1943	Dobell: *Joshua Smith* Mondrian: *Broadway Boogie-Woogie*	
1944	Bacon: *Three Studies for Figures at the Base of a Crucifixion* Gruber: *Job*	Allies liberate Paris
1945		Bartók d. US drops atomic bombs on Hiroshima and Nagasaki Orwell, *Animal Farm*
1946	Burchfield: *The Sphinx and the Milky Way* Nolan's first *Ned Kelly* paintings	Moholy-Nagy d.
1947	Paolozzi: *I Was a Rich Man's Plaything*	India gains independence from UK Institute of Contemporary Arts, London, founded
1948	Newman: *Onement I* Wyeth: *Christina's World*	South Africa adopts apartheid Communists gain control in Czechoslovakia, making the country a satellite of the Soviet Union
1949	Sutherland: *Somerset Maugham*	Orozco d. Carol Reed, *The Third Man*
1950	Pollock: *Lavender Mist* Tooker: *Subway*	Beckmann d. Gombrich, *The Story of Art*

	Key works	**Other events**
1951	Armitage: *People in the Wind* Dalí: *Crucifixion of St John of the Cross* Davis: *Owh! in San Pao* Freud: *Interior at Paddington*	J. D. Salinger, *The Catcher in the Rye* Festival of Britain Harold Rosenberg coins term 'Action Painting'
1952	de Kooning: *Woman I* Frankenthaler: *Mountains and Sea* Tretchikoff: *Chinese Girl*	Samuel Beckett, *Waiting for Godot*
1953	Matisse: *L'Escargot* Zadkine: *To a Destroyed City* completed	Stalin d. Reg Butler wins international competition for monument to The Unknown Political Prisoner
1954	Burri: *Sacking with Red*	Matisse d.
1954–5	Annigoni: *Queen Elizabeth II*	
1955	John's first *Flag* paintings	Léger d.
1955–9	Rauschenberg: *Monogram*	
1956	Hamilton: *Just what is it that makes today's homes so different, so appealing?* Richards: *'Do not go gentle into that good night'*	Pollock d. Hungarian uprising crushed by USSR Suez crisis
1957		Rivera d. USSR sends world's first satellite into space Ingmar Bergman, *The Seventh Seal*
1958	Klein: *Le Vide*	
1959	Kaprow's first happenings	Epstein d. Grosz d. Spencer d. Cuban revolution: Fidel Castro becomes prime minister Guggenheim Museum, New York, opens
1960	Escher: *Ascending and Descending* Tinguely: *Homage to New York*	*Lady Chatterley's Lover* obscenity trial Sharpeville massacre, South Africa
1961		Greenberg, *Art and Culture* Joseph Heller, *Catch 22* British Pop art is put on the map at Young Contemporaries exhibition Berlin Wall erected
1962	Caro: *Early One Morning* Oldenburg: *Dual Hamburger* Warhol's first *Soup can* paintings	Birth of Fluxus, Germany Cuban missile crisis Edward Albee, *Who's Afraid of Virginia Woolf?*
1963	Hilton: *Oi yoi yoi* Lichtenstein: *Whaam!*	Braque d. President Kennedy assassinated
1964	Gottlieb: *Orb* King: *And the Birds Began to Sing*	Archipenko d.
1964–6	Kienholz: *The State Hospital*	
1965	Beuys: *How to Explain Pictures to a Dead Hare* Kosuth: *One and Three Chairs*	Le Corbusier d.
1966	Andre: *Equivalent VIII*	Breton d. Giacometti d. Floods destroy Florentine art treasures England wins football World Cup
1967	Hockney: *A Bigger Splash*	Magritte d. The Beatles, *Sergeant Pepper's Lonely Hearts Club Band* (LP cover design by Peter Blake)

Chronology

	Key works	Other events
1967–9	Rothko: paintings for the Rothko Chapel	
1968	Close: *Self-Portrait*	Duchamp d. Students and workers riot in Paris USSR invades Czechoslovakia
1969	Gilbert & George: *Underneath the Arches*	Dix d. Mies van der Rohe d. Baselitz paints his first upside-down image Kenneth Clark, *Civilisation* (television series) First lunar landing
1969–75	Nagare: *Cloud Fortress* (destroyed in 2001 as a result of World Trade Center terrorist attack)	
1970	Hanson: *Tourists* Smithson: *Spiral Jetty*	
1971		Intel develops microchip, USA Pompidou Centre, Paris, opens
1972	Tony Smith: *Gracehoper*	Palestinian terrorists murder Israeli athletes at Munich Olympic Games
1973	Long: *Circle of Sticks*	Picasso d.
1974		President Nixon resigns following Watergate scandal
1974–9	Chicago: *The Dinner Party*	
1975	Frink: *Horse and Rider*	Hepworth d.
1976	Christo: *Running Fence*	Aalto d. Albers d. Burra d. Calder d. Ernst d.
1977		Gabo d.
1978	Hockney: stage designs for Mozart's *Magic Flute*	de Chirico d.
1979		Iranian Revolution deposes Shah Margaret Thatcher becomes Britain's first woman Prime Minister Soviet Union invades Afghanistan Anthony Blunt exposed as former spy
1980		Solidarity union formed, Poland
1980–8		Iran–Iraq war
1981	De Andrea: *Model in Repose*	First known AIDS case in USA Butler d.
1982	Schnabel: *Humanity Asleep*	Argentinian–British war in Falkland Islands compact discs launched in Japan
1983		Miró d. US occupies Grenada
1984		Malcolm Morley is first winner of Turner Prize

	Key works	Other events
1985	Christo: *The Pont Neuf Wrapped*	Chagall d. Mikhail Gorbachev becomes USSR leader, and introduces liberal policies Saatchi Collection, London, opens
1986		Henry Moore d. Chernobyl disaster Musée d'Orsay, Paris, opens
1988		Tate Gallery Liverpool opens
1989		Berlin Wall torn down Communist regimes deposed in Czechoslovakia, East Germany, and elsewhere Tiananmen Square massacre, China
1990		East and West Germany reunited Nelson Mandela released from prison Iraq invades Kuwait Hubble space telescope launched
1991	Hirst: *The Physical Impossibility of Death in the Mind of Someone Living*	Gulf War Civil war breaks out in former Yugoslavia Soviet Union breaks up
1992	Saint Phalle: *Loch Ness Monster*	Bacon d. Bill Clinton elected US President
1993	Whiteread: *Untitled (House)*	Frink d. Tate Gallery St Ives opens
1994		Max Bill d. Mandela becomes South African president; apartheid abolished
1995	Christo: *Wrapped Reichstag*	Burri d.
1996		Taliban forces occupy Kabul
1997		Diana, Princess of Wales, killed in car crash Guggenheim Museum, Bilbao, opens 'Sensation' exhibition, Royal Academy
1998	Gormley: *Angel of the North* installed	Pasmore d. James Cameron, *Titanic* (wins 11 Oscars)
1999	Emin: *My Bed*	Buffet d.
2000	Kiefer: *Let a Thousand Flowers Bloom*	Lowry arts centre opens in Salford Tate Britain and Tate Modern open in London
2001		Balthus d. World Trade Center, New York, destroyed in terrorist attack
2002		Armitage d. Riopelle d. Saint Phalle d.
2003		Chadwick d. Frost d. Saatchi Gallery opens in London US-led coalition deposes Saddam Hussein in Iraq

INDEX OF GALLERIES AND MUSEUMS

This list gives basic information about 150 of the world's leading collections of Western art. It includes all the museums and galleries that have entries devoted to them in the main text, plus a selection of other notable institutions from 25 countries.

AUSTRALIA

Canberra
National Gallery of Australia
King Edward Terrace
Parkes Place
Canberra ACT 2001
Tel +61 2 62406411
Fax +61 2 62406529
www.nga.gov.au

The gallery has a small but high-quality collection of European paintings, some outstanding modern American works, a good representation of Australian art, and a sculpture garden.

Melbourne
National Gallery of Victoria
285–321 Russell Street
Melbourne VIC 8004
Tel +61 3 92080222
Fax +61 3 92080245
www.ngv.vic.gov.au

A wide-ranging and well-balanced collection of European paintings (the best in the southern hemisphere) together with an impressive array of Australian art. There is also some sculpture, including two works by Bernini.

AUSTRIA

Vienna
Graphische Sammlung Albertina
Albertinaplatz
1010 Wien
Tel +43 1 534830
Fax +43 1 5337697
www.albertina.at

A wonderful collection of Old Master drawings and prints, although only a few are on show at a time. See p. 14.

Kunsthistorisches Museum
Maria Theresien-Platz
1010 Wien

Tel +43 1 525240
Fax +43 1 52524503
www.khm.at

Austria's pre-eminent art museum, housing in particular one of the world's most celebrated collections of Old Master paintings. See p. 386.

Österreichische Galerie Belvedere
Prinz Eugenstrasse
1037 Wien
Tel +43 1 795570
Fax +43 1 7984337
www.belvedere.at

The Belvedere Palace (actually two distinct buildings, the Upper and Lower Belvedere) houses three museums that together make up the Österreichische Galerie and collectively form a national gallery of Austrian art. They are devoted respectively to medieval art up to the 16th century, to 17th- and 18th-century art (the Barockmuseum), and to 19th- and 20th-century art. Most of the leading Austrian painters and sculptors are well represented in these collections.

BELGIUM

Antwerp
Koninklijk Museum voor Schone Kunsten
(Musée Royal des Beaux-Arts)
Leopold de Waelplaats
2000 Antwerpen
Tel +32 3 2387809
Fax +32 3 2480810
www.antwerpen.be/cultuur/kmska

Next to the Musées Royaux in Brussels, this is Belgium's most important museum, and it is likewise primarily a collection of Old Master paintings (although it also has modern works). It is particularly strong in Netherlandish, Flemish, Dutch, and Belgian art (a group of Rubens altarpieces is one of the highlights), but it also has good examples from other schools, notably the French, German, and Italian.

Bruges

Groeningemuseum
Dijver 12
8000 Brugge
Tel +32 50 448711
Fax +32 50 448778
www.brugge.be/musea/nl/mgroen.htm

A fairly small but highly impressive collection of paintings, almost all from the Low Countries, from the 15th century to the 20th century. Among them are two of the most famous master-pieces of the Early Netherlandish School: Jan van Eyck's *Madonna of Canon van der Paele* and Hugo van der Goes's *Death of the Virgin*.

Brussels

Musées Royaux des Beaux-Arts (Musée d'Art Ancien)
3 Rue de la Régence
1000 Bruxelles
Tel +32 2 5083211
Fax +32 2 5083232
www.fine-arts-museum.be

Belgium's leading art museum—mainly devoted to Old Master paintings, although it also has significant holdings of sculpture. It covers painting in the Low Countries in great breadth and depth (although a few major masters, such as Jan van Eyck, are missing) and also has good representa-tions of other schools, notably the French. Nine-teenth- and 20th-century art is shown at the Musée d'Art Moderne in the Place Royale (same telephone number and website).

BRAZIL

São Paulo

Museu de Arte de São Paulo
Avenida Paulista 1578
01310–200 São Paulo
Tel +55 11 2515644
Fax +55 11 2840574
www.masp.art.br

South America's leading collection of European paintings, with work from the 15th century to the 20th century. It is richest in 19th-century French art. There are also works by South American artists.

CANADA

Montreal

Montreal Museum of Fine Arts
(Musée des Beaux-Arts de Montréal)

1379–1380 Sherbrooke Street West
Montreal
Qué H3G 2T9
Tel +1 514 2851600
Fax +1 514 8446042
www.mmfa.qc.ca

One of the country's leading collections of Can-adian and European painting. The excellent re-presentation of French art reflects Montreal's position as Canada's major French-speaking city.

Ottawa

National Gallery of Canada
380 Sussex Drive
Ottawa
Ont K1N 9N4
Tel +1 613 9901985
Fax +1 613 9934385
www.national.gallery.ca

The gallery houses the best collection of Euro-pean art in Canada (all the major national schools are represented) and also the country's leading collection of Canadian painting and sculpture.

Toronto

Art Gallery of Ontario
317 Dundas Street West
Toronto
Ont M5T 1G4
Tel +1 416 9770414
Fax +1 416 2042713
www.ago.net

Next to the National Gallery in Ottawa, the best collection of European painting in Canada. The gallery is also rich in Canadian and American art, and its Henry Moore Sculpture Center has one of the world's best collections of this artist's work.

CZECH REPUBLIC

Prague

Národni Galerie v Praze (National Gallery in Prague)
Hradčanské náměští 15
Praha 1-Hradčany
Tel +420 2 57320536
Fax +420 2 539162
www.ngprague.cz

The collections of the National Gallery are dis-persed among four locations in the city. Here, in the 18th-century Sternberg Palace, is assembled most of the non-Czech European art. The collec-tion is rich in Netherlandish, Dutch, and Flemish painting, and also has outstanding works from other schools, including Dürer's *Feast of the Rose Garlands*.

DENMARK

Copenhagen

Ny Carlsberg Glyptotek
Dantes Plads 7
1556 København V
Tel +45 33418141
Fax +45 33912058
www.glyptoteket.dk

This is primarily a museum of sculpture, including works from the ancient world, by followers of Thorvaldsen, and by 19th-century French sculptors (the best representation outside Paris). The paintings are mainly by 19th-century French artists, particularly Gauguin (whose wife was Danish).

Statens Museum for Kunst
Sølvgade 48–50
1307 København K
Tel +45 33748404
Fax +45 33748494
www.smk.dk

Denmark's pre-eminent picture collection. Apart from the incomparable representation of Danish art (with Eckersberg, Juel, and Købke to the fore), it is notable chiefly for its large collection of 17th-century Dutch painting, but it also has fine works from other schools: Cranach and Matisse, for example, are well represented. The museum also has a major collection of prints.

Thorvaldsens Museum
Posthusgade 2
1213 København K
Tel +45 33321532
Fax +45 33321771

The museum has a comprehensive collection of Thorvaldsen's sculpture and also houses works he collected, including antiquities and paintings by his contemporaries. See p. 695.

Humlebaek

Louisiana Museum for Moderne Kunst
Gl. Strandvej 13
3050 Humlebaek
Tel +45 49190719
Fax +45 49193505
www.louisiana.dk

An outstanding collection of international modern art, most of it dating from after the Second World War. The museum has a beautiful setting and much of the sculpture is displayed out of doors.

FINLAND

Helsinki

Ateneumin Taidemuseo (Atheneum Art Museum)
Kaivokatu 2
00100 Helsinki
Tel +358 9 17336401
www.fng.fi

This museum is one of three that make up the Finnish National Gallery. It is devoted to Finnish art up to about 1950, with major works by Gallen-Kallela, Sallinen, and other leading figures. The other two museums are devoted respectively to foreign art and contemporary art.

FRANCE

Aix-en-Provence

Musée Granet
Place St Jean de Malte
13100 Aix-en-Provence
Tel +33 4 42381470
Fax +33 4 42268455

The museum's collections embrace various schools and periods, but it is strongest in 19th-century French paintings, including many by its founder, François-Marius Granet. One of the highlights is a portrait of Granet by his friend Ingres.

Albi

Musée Toulouse-Lautrec et Galerie d'Art Moderne
Palais de la Berbie
81000 Albi
Tel +33 5 63494870
Fax +33 5 63494888

The museum has the world's largest collection of works by Toulouse-Lautrec, as well as paintings by some of his leading contemporaries and a few Old Masters. See p. 706.

Chantilly

Musée Condé
Château de Chantilly
60500 Chantilly
Tel +33 3 44626262
Fax +33 3 44626261
www.chateaudechantilly.com

The museum is perhaps best known as the home of one of the greatest of all illuminated manuscripts, the *Très Riches Heures du duc de Berry* by the Limbourg brothers. However, it also has many other treasures, including impressive collections of Old Master paintings and drawings. The French and Italian paintings are particularly noteworthy, Ingres, Poussin, Raphael, Rosa, and Watteau being among the artists best represented.

Dijon

Musée des Beaux-Arts
Palais des États
1 Rue Rameau
21000 Dijon
Tel +33 3 80745270
Fax +33 3 80745344
www.ville-dijon.fr

One of France's leading provincial collections. Its treasures include two celebrated works from the golden age of art in Burgundy, when Dijon was the capital of Duke Philip the Bold: Claus Sluter's tomb of Philip, and an altarpiece carved by Jacques de Baerze and painted by Melchior Broederlam.

Grenoble

Musée de Grenoble
5 Place de Lavalette
38000 Grenoble
Tel +33 4 76634444
Fax +33 4 46634410
www.museedegrenoble.fr

One of France's best collections of painting and sculpture outside Paris. Its pre-20th-century holdings are strongest in French art, although the Dutch, Flemish, and Italian schools are also well represented. The modern collection is international in scope, with some good examples of American art.

Lille

Musée des Beaux-Arts
Place de la République
59000 Lille
Tel +33 4 20067800
Fax +33 4 20067815

Outside Paris, the museum has the largest and most comprehensive collection of Old Master paintings in France. Lille is very near the border with Belgium and for a time was part of the Netherlands, so it is not surprising that it is particularly strong in Dutch and Flemish, as well as French, art. The museum also has an important collection of drawings, many of them bequeathed by the painter Jean-Baptiste Wicar, a native of Lille.

Marseilles

Musée des Beaux-Arts
Palais Longchamp
13004 Marseille
Tel +33 4 91145930
Fax +33 4 91145931

A large collection devoted mainly to French art of the 17th to the 19th century. The artists who are best represented include three who were natives of the city: Pierre Puget (a good representation of his paintings and drawings as well as the sculptures for which he is primarily known), Honoré Daumier, and Adolphe Monticelli.

Montpellier

Musée Fabre
39 Boulevard Bonne Nouvelle
34000 Montpellier
Tel +33 4 67148300
Fax +33 4 67660920
www.ville-montpellier.fr

The museum has a choice collection of Old Master and 19th-century paintings, particularly of the French, Dutch, and Italian schools, as well as some modern works. Many of the finest pictures were presented by the museum's founder, François-Xavier Fabre, and another important group came from Alfred Bruyas, Courbet's most important patron.

Paris

Centre Georges-Pompidou (incorporating the Musée National d'Art Moderne)
Place Georges Pompidou
75191 Paris
Tel +33 1 44781233
Fax +33 1 44781300
www.cnac-gp.fr

One of the world's major collections of modern art, housed in one of the most famous buildings of the 1970s. See p. 553.

Musée d'Art Moderne de la Ville de Paris
11 Avenue du Président Wilson
75116 Paris
Tel +33 1 53674000
Fax +33 1 47233598

Paris's municipal collection of 20th-century art, not to be confused with the Musée National d'Art Moderne at the Pompidou Centre. Although much less famous than the Pompidou Centre, the museum has a rich and varied collection, reflecting artistic developments in Paris from Fauvism onwards.

The palace retains much of its original decorative painting by Charles Le Brun and his followers and has also accumulated a vast number of portraits and numerous history paintings, especially ones celebrating French military triumphs. Many of these pictures are more of historical than artistic interest, but among them are impressive works by Delacroix, Gros, and other illustrious figures.

GERMANY

Berlin
Gemäldegalerie
Kulturforum
10785 Berlin
Tel +49 30 2662101
Fax +49 30 2662103
www.smb.spk-berlin.de/gg

One of the world's most celebrated collections of Old Master paintings. The representation of the Early Netherlandish School is incomparable, and there are also great riches in Dutch, Flemish, German, and Italian painting. See p. 278.

Schloss Charlottenburg
Spandauer Damm 20
10585 Charlottenburg
Tel +49 30 320911
Fax +49 30 32091200

The collection is renowned for its superb examples of 18th-century French painting, with Watteau to the fore. Nineteenth-century German painting is also well represented.

Brunswick
Herzog-Anton-Ulrich Museum
Museumstrasse 1
38100 Braunschweig
Tel +49 531 12250
Fax +49 531 12252408
www.museum-braunschweig.de

A major collection of Old Masters, particularly rich in 17th- and 18th-century paintings of the Dutch, Flemish, German, and Italian schools. The museum also houses prints and drawings, antiquities, and applied art.

Cologne
Museum Ludwig
Bischofsgartenstrasse 1
50667 Köln
Tel +49 221 26165
Fax +49 221 24114
www.museenkoeln.de

One of Europe's most important collections of international modern art, with most of the leading movements and artists represented. See p. 424.

Wallraf-Richartz-Museum
Martinstrasse 39
50667 Köln
Tel +49 221 21119
Fax +49 221 22629
www.museenkoeln.de

The museum is essentially a distinguished collection of Old Master paintings, but it also includes later paintings, as well as sculpture, drawings, and prints.

Dresden
Gemäldegalerie Alter Meister
Zwinger
Sophienstrasse
01067 Dresden
Tel +49 351 4914620
Fax +49 351 4914694
www.staatl-kunstsammlungen-dresden.de

A world-famous collection of Old Master paintings, particularly renowned for its Italian Renaissance masterpieces, among them Giorgione's *Sleeping Venus* and Raphael's *Sistine Madonna*. See p. 278.

Düsseldorf
Kunstsammlung Nordrhein-Westfalen
Grabbeplatz 5
40213 Düsseldorf
Tel +49 211 8381130
Fax +49 211 8381201
www.kunstsammlung.de

A high-quality collection of international modern art from Fauvism onwards. Paul Klee is particularly well represented.

Frankfurt
Städelsches Kunstinstitut und Städtische Galerie
Dürerstrasse 2
60596 Frankfurt am Main
Tel +49 69 6050980
Fax +49 69 610163
www.staedelmuseum.de

The museum houses one of the most important collections of paintings in Germany, with outstanding works of all periods from the Renaissance to the 20th century and from most of the major European schools. The collection of 17th-century Dutch art is especially renowned,

Rembrandt's *Blinding of Samson* being one of the highlights. There are also substantial holdings of drawings, prints, and sculpture.

Hamburg

Kunsthalle
Glockengiesserwall
20095 Hamburg
Tel +49 40 428542612
Fax +49 40 428542482
www.hamburger-kunsthalle.de

The museum has one of the largest and most comprehensive collections of paintings in Germany, from the Renaissance to the 20th century (it even has a good representation of British painting, which is unusual in Continental galleries). Drawings, prints, sculpture, coins, and medals are also represented.

Karlsruhe

Staatliche Kunsthalle
Hans-Thomastrasse 2–6
76133 Karlsruhe
Tel +49 721 9263355
Fax +49 721 9266788
www.kunsthalle-karlsruhe.de

The museum houses a large and varied collection of paintings that includes a superb representation of German art, from the Renaissance onwards. It is also strong in Dutch and French painting and has substantial holdings of prints and drawings.

Kassel

Staatliche Kunstsammlungen
Schloss Wilhelmshöhe
34131 Kassel
Tel +49 561 93777
Fax +49 561 9377666
www.museum-kassel.de

A major collection of Old Masters, particularly rich in Dutch and Flemish paintings of the 17th century. Prints, drawings, and applied art are also represented.

Munich

Alte Pinakothek
Barerstrasse 29
80799 München
Tel +49 89 23805216
Fax +49 89 23805221
www.pinakothek.de

One of the world's greatest collections of Old Masters. It has an unrivalled representation of German Renaissance painting (not least Dürer) and great strengths in Italian Renaissance art and Dutch and Flemish painting of the 17th century (above all Rubens). See p. 546.

Bayerisches Nationalmuseum
Prinzregentenstrasse 3
80538 München
Tel +49 89 2112401
Fax +49 89 21124201
www.bayerisches-nationalmuseum.de

A large collection of fine and applied art, principally from Bavaria and southern Germany. It includes an outstanding representation of Gothic and Renaissance sculpture.

Städtische Galerie im Lenbachhaus
Luisenstrasse 33
80333 München
Tel +49 89 23332000
Fax +49 89 23332003

The house of the 19th-century painter Franz von Lenbach contains many examples of his work and works he collected, but it is remarkable chiefly for a magnificent group of pictures by Jawlensky, Kandinsky, Klee, Macke, and Marc, presented in 1957 by Gabriele Münter, Kandinsky's lover. See p. 403.

Nuremberg

Germanisches Nationalmuseum
Kartäusergasse 1
90402 Nürnberg
Tel +49 911 1331200
Fax +49 911 1331200
www.gnm.de

The museum has a vast collection of art and artefacts from the Stone Age onwards. It is chiefly remarkable for its outstanding collection of German Renaissance painting and sculpture, including several works by Dürer, who spent most of his life in the city.

GREECE

Athens

National Archaeological Museum
Tossitsa 1
10682 Athens
Tel +30 210 8217724
Fax +30 210 8217724
www.culture.gr

Greece's pre-eminent museum, with one of the world's greatest collections of classical antiquities, including masterpieces of sculpture and vase painting.

HUNGARY

Budapest

Szépművészeti Múzeum
(Museum of Fine Arts)
Dózsa György út. 41
1146 Budapest
Tel +36 1 3439759
Fax +36 1 3438298

The museum's collections include antiquities, sculpture, drawings, and prints, but it is best known for its extensive and wide-ranging holdings of Old Master paintings, with particular strengths in the Dutch, Italian, and Spanish schools. Hungarian paintings are shown mainly in the Hungarian National Gallery (Magyar Nemzeti Galéria; 3757533; www.mng.hu).

IRELAND

Dublin

Hugh Lane Municipal Gallery of Modern Art
Charlemont House
Parnell Square
Dublin 1
Tel +353 1 8741903
Fax +353 1 8722182
www.hughlane.ie

A collection of late 19th-century and 20th-century art, strong in Irish painting and with a good representation of French works. Francis Bacon's London studio has been reconstructed in the gallery. See p. 39.

National Gallery of Ireland
Merrion Square West
Dublin 2
Tel +353 1 6615133
Fax +353 1 615372
www.nationalgallery.ie

Outside London, the gallery has the largest collection of Old Master and 19th-century paintings in the British Isles. Italian painting of the 16th and 17th centuries is one of the areas of greatest strength, and Irish artists are outstandingly well represented.

ITALY

Bologna

Pinacoteca Nazionale
Via delle Belle Arti 56
40126 Bologna
Tel +39 051 243222
Fax +39 051 251368
www.pinacotecabologna.it

The collection concentrates on the great 17th-century painters who made Bologna such an important art centre (the Carracci, Guercino, Reni, for example), but it also has works from other schools and periods, including Raphael's celebrated *St Cecilia*, which was painted for the church of S. Giovanni in Monte, Bologna (for an anecdote concerning this picture, see the entry on Francesco Francia, p. 263).

Florence

Galleria dell'Accademia
Via Ricasoli 60
50122 Firenze
Tel +39 055 2388609
Fax +39 055 2388609
www.sbas.firenze.it

An excellent collection of Florentine paintings is understandably overshadowed by a group of sculptures by Michelangelo, including his celebrated *David* and four unfinished *Slaves* for the tomb of Julius II.

Galleria degli Uffizi
Piazzale degli Uffizi
50122 Firenze
Tel +39 055 2388651
Fax +39 055 2388699
www.uffizi.firenze.it

One of the most famous galleries in the world, chiefly renowned for its unrivalled representation of Florentine Renaissance painting. It also has paintings from other Italian and non-Italian schools, antique sculpture, major holdings of prints and drawings, and a remarkable collection of artists' self-portraits. See p. 718.

Museo di San Marco o dell'Angelico
Piazza San Marco 3
50121 Firenze
Tel +39 055 2388608
Fax +39 0550 2388704
www.sbas.firenze.it/sanmarco

In addition to the frescos by Fra Angelico for which the convent of S. Marco is famous, the museum has a superb collection of his panel paintings, including major altarpieces. There are also works by other Florentine painters, notably Fra Bartolommeo, who like Fra Angelico was a Dominican friar and spent part of his career at S. Marco.

Museo Nazionale del Bargello
Palazzo del Bargello
Via del Proconsolo 4
50122 Firenze

Tel +39 055 2388606
Fax +39 055 2388756
www.sbas.firenze.it

The world's best collection of Italian (particularly Florentine) Renaissance sculpture. Ghiberti, Donatello, Verrocchio, Michelangelo, Cellini, and other major figures are represented by important pieces. Among later works, Bernini's bust of his mistress Costanza Buonarelli is one of the highlights. The museum also has examples of applied art and a few Italian and Netherlandish paintings. See p. 50.

Palazzo Pitti (Galleria Palatina)
Piazza Pitti
50125 Firenze
Tel +39 055 2388611
Fax +39 055 2388613

Formerly the chief residence of the Medici family, the Pitti still retains the feeling of a great princely collection. Italian artists of the 16th and 17th centuries are best represented, but there are also good examples from other schools, notably by Rubens and van Dyck. See p. 549.

Milan

Pinacoteca Ambrosiana
Piazza Pio XI 2
20123 Milano
Tel +39 02 806921
Fax +39 02 80692210
www.ambrosiana.it

A small but high-quality collection of paintings and drawings. The paintings are mainly by Italian artists, but there is an outstanding representation of Jan Brueghel's work. See p. 20.

Pinacoteca di Brera
Via Brera 28
20121 Milano
Tel +39 02 722631
Fax +39 02 72001140

One of the major Italian picture collections, renowned particularly for its superb representation of Renaissance altarpieces, including Piero della Francesca's *Madonna and Child with Federico da Montefeltro* and Raphael's *Marriage of the Virgin*. See p. 104.

Naples

Museo Archeologico Nazionale
Piazza Museo 19
80135 Napoli
Tel +39 081 440166
Fax +39 081 440013

One of the world's outstanding collections of classical antiquities. There is a vast amount of material from excavations at nearby Pompeii and Herculaneum (including an unrivalled representation of Roman painting), as well as statuary from the Farnese collection, notably the *Farnese Bull* and the *Farnese Hercules*.

Museo e Galleria Nazionale di Capodimonte
Parco di Capodimonte
80136 Napoli
Tel +39 081 7499111
Fax +39 081 7499198

A major museum, famous particularly for porcelain and for one of the most magnificent picture collections in Italy. At its heart are works acquired in the 16th century by members of the Farnese family, including a wonderful group of Titians. There are also many pictures from the golden age of Neapolitan painting in the 17th century, when it was one the main centres of the Caravaggesque style.

Rome

Galleria Borghese
Villa Borghese
Via Pinciana
00197 Roma
Tel +39 06 8548577
www.galleriaborghese.it

The museum is based on the collection made by Cardinal Scipione Borghese in the early 17th century and is especially rich in works by Bernini and Caravaggio. See p. 90.

Galleria Doria Pamphili
Palazzo Doria Pamphili
Piazza del Collegio Romano
00186 Roma
Tel +39 06 6797323
Fax +39 06 6780939
www.doriapamphilj.it

A splendid aristocratic collection (still in private hands), predominantly of 17th-century paintings, set among antique sculptures, tapestries, and 18th-century furniture. The most famous work in the collection is Velázquez's incomparable portrait of Pope Innocent X (Giambattista Pamphili). See p. 519.

Galleria Nazionale d'Arte Moderna – Arte Contemporanea
Viale delle Belle Arti 131
00196 Roma
Tel +39 06 322981
Fax +39 06 3221579

Italy's leading collection of 19th- and 20th-century art. It is devoted mainly to Italian painting and sculpture, with good representations of the work of the Macchiaioli and Futurists, for example, but artists of other nationalities are also included, among them Cézanne, Kandinsky, Klimt, and Pollock.

Galleria Nazionale Palazzo Barberini
Via Quattro Fontane 13
00184 Roma
Tel +39 06 4824184

The 17th-century Palazzo Barberini, with its celebrated ceiling painting by Pietro da Cortona, houses most of the national collection of Old Master paintings; the remainder is in the 18th-century Palazzo Corsini (Via della Lungara 10). Between them the galleries have a large collection of Italian paintings from the Renaissance to the 18th century (17th-century works are mainly in the Corsini Gallery) and examples from most of the other main European schools.

Musei Capitolini
Piazza del Campidoglio
00186 Roma
Tel +39 06 67102071
Fax +39 06 67103118

The Capitoline Museums are made up of three museums occupying two buildings (designed by Michelangelo) that face each other across the Piazza del Campidoglio. The Museo Capitolino and the Museo dei Conservatori house antiquities, including some of the most famous works of classical statuary, most notably the *Marcus Aurelius* equestrian statue, which formerly stood in the piazza. The third museum, the Pinacoteca Capitolina, is somewhat overshadowed by its neighbours, but it contains a good collection of pictures, mainly Italian works of the 16th and 17th centuries.

Musei Vaticani e Cappella Sistina
00120 Città Vaticana
Tel +39 06 69883333
Fax +39 06 69885061

A series of museums and decorated rooms in the Vatican that include some of the most celebrated works in the whole of European art, particularly Michelangelo's frescos in the Sistine Chapel. See p. 726.

Museo Nazionale Romano (Museo delle Terme)
Piazza del Cinquecento 69
00185 Roma
Tel +39 06 483617
Fax +39 06 4814125

A major collection of classical antiquities, consisting largely of material that has been excavated in and around Rome (including statues, sarcophagi, portrait busts, mosaics, and frescos). The museum appropriately occupies part of the ruins of the Baths (Terme) of Diocletian, built around AD 300.

Siena
Pinacoteca Nazionale
Palazzo Buonsignori
Via San Pietro 29
53100 Siena
Tel +39 0577 286143
Fax +39 0577 270508

The gallery is devoted mainly to Sienese painting and in this field is unrivalled, with key works by virtually every important local painter from the 13th century to the 17th century.

Turin
Galleria Sabauda
Via Accademia delle Scienze 6
10123 Torino
Tel +39 011 547440
Fax +39 011 549547

The gallery includes sculpture and applied art, but it is essentially a collection of Old Master paintings, one of the most varied in Italy, including examples from most of the major schools. Numerically the Italian School predominates, but there are also fine representations of the Early Netherlandish, Dutch, and Flemish schools.

Urbino
Galleria Nazionale delle Marche
Palazzo Ducale
61029 Urbino
Tel +39 0722 2760
Fax +39 0722 4427

A fairly small but memorable collection in the wonderful setting of Federico da Montefeltro's ducal palace, one of the loveliest of Renaissance buildings. The most famous picture in the collection is Piero della Francesca's *Flagellation*; other artists represented include Raphael, Titian, Uccello, and Joos van Wassenhove. In addition to paintings, there are superb examples of intarsia in Duke Federico's studiolo.

Venice
Gallerie dell'Accademia
Campo della Carità
30100 Venezia

Tel +39 041 5212709
Fax +39 041 5200410

The city's main picture gallery. It is devoted largely to Venetian art, but there are a few works from other Italian and non-Italian schools. See p. 7.

Raccolta Peggy Guggenheim
Palazzo Venier dei Leoni
Dorsoduro 701
30123 Venezia
Tel +39 041 2405411
Fax +39 041 5206885
www.guggenheim-venice.it

Choice collection of modern art assembled by the dealer Peggy Guggenheim, housed in her palace overlooking the Grand Canal. Max Ernst (to whom Guggenheim was briefly married) and Jackson Pollock are among the artists best represented. See p. 319.

JAPAN

Tokyo

National Museum of Western Art
7–7 Ueno-koen
Taito-ku
Tokyo 110–0007
Tel +81 3 38285131
Fax +81 3 38285135
www.nmwa.go.jp

Housed in a Le Corbusier building opened in 1959, the museum has at its core a collection consisting largely of 19th-century French painting and sculpture made by the shipping magnate Kojiro Matsukata. French art of the 19th and 20th centuries continues to be its main strength, but it has also built up an interesting collection of Old Masters, with works by Claude, Rubens, Tintoretto, and other eminent figures.

NETHERLANDS

Amsterdam

Rijksmuseum
Stadhouderskade 42
1071 ZD Amsterdam
Tel +31 20 6747047
Fax +31 20 6747001
www.rijksmuseum.nl

The Dutch national art museum. In addition to a huge collection of Dutch paintings, in which virtually all the country's leading artists are well represented, it has works from other schools, notably Italian, as well as prints and drawings, sculpture, and applied art. See p. 594.

Rijksmuseum Vincent van Gogh
Paulus Potterstraat 7
1070 AJ Amsterdam
Tel +31 20 5705200
Fax +31 20 6735053
www.vangoghmuseum.nl

As well as housing the world's largest collection of van Gogh's work, the museum has examples by some of his leading contemporaries, including Gauguin.

Stedelijk Museum
Paulus Potterstraat 13
1071 CX Amsterdam
Tel +31 20 5732911
Fax +31 20 6752716
www.stedelijk.nl

A major collection of international art from about 1850 onwards. Dutch artists (notably Mondrian) are well represented, and there are other areas of great strength, including the world's largest collection of Malevich's paintings.

Haarlem

Frans Halsmuseum
Groot Heiligland 62
2001 DJ Haarlem
Tel +31 23 5115775
Fax +31 23 5115776
www.franshalsmuseum.com

The museum is dominated by a series of great group portraits by Frans Hals, but it also has fine works by other Dutch painters (especially ones who—like Hals—lived in Haarlem) and there are a few works by artists of other nationalities.

The Hague

Haags Gemeentemuseum
Stadhouderslaan 41
2501 CB Den Haag
Tel +31 70 338111
Fax +31 70 3381112
www.hhgm.denhaag.nl

A major collection of 19th- and 20th-century art, particularly rich in work by Dutch artists; it includes the world's largest representation of Mondrian's paintings.

Mauritshuis
Korte Vijverberg 8
2513 CM Den Haag
Tel +31 70 3023456

Fax +31 70 3653819
www.mauritshuis.nl

A collection (mainly of paintings) that is fairly small in size but very high in quality. It concentrates on 17th-century Dutch artists, but there are also examples from other periods and countries. See p. 455.

Otterlo
Rijksmuseum Kröller-Müller
Houtkampweg 6
6730 AA Otterlo
Tel +31 31 8591241
Fax +31 31 8591515
www.kmm.nl

A major collection devoted mainly to international modern art from about 1870 onwards. The representation of van Gogh's work is second only to that in the museum dedicated to him in Amsterdam, and other artists who are present in strength include Gris, Mondrian, and Seurat. The sculpture park includes work by Hepworth, Moore, Rodin, and other eminent figures.

Rotterdam
Museum Boymans–van Beuningen
Museumpark 18–20
3015 CX Rotterdam
Tel +31 10 4419400
Fax +31 10 4360500
www.boijmans.nl

This museum can claim to have the most comprehensive collection of paintings in the Netherlands, for although the Rijksmuseum in Amsterdam is bigger and has more major works, its coverage does not generally extend beyond the 19th century, whereas modern art is well represented here, alongside Old Master paintings. The area of greatest strength is 17th-century Dutch art, but the French and Italian schools are also well covered. In addition to paintings, the museum has collections of drawings, prints, and sculpture.

NORWAY

Oslo
Nasjonalgalleriet (National Gallery)
Universitetsgaten 13
0164 Oslo
Tel +47 22200404
Fax +47 22361132

An impressive collection consisting mainly of Old Master and modern paintings. Apart from Scandinavian art, the greatest strength is in Dutch and

Flemish painting of the 17th century. The most famous painting in the gallery is Munch's *The Scream*. This is part of a large representation of his work, but he is even more abundantly represented in the city's Munch Museum (see p. 487).

Munch-Museet
Toyengt 53
0578 Oslo
Tel +47 23241400
Fax +47 23241401
www.munch.museum.no

POLAND

Warsaw
Muzeum Narodowe (National Museum)
Al. Jerozolimskie 3
00–495 Warsawa
Tel +48 22 6211031
Fax +48 22 6228559

A large and varied collection of Old Masters, with a few more recent paintings. It is richest in 17th-century Dutch painting, but French, German, and Italian art are also well represented (there is a superb group of works by Bellotto, who spent much of his career in Warsaw), and there are also some interesting 19th-century Russian paintings.

PORTUGAL

Lisbon
Museu Calouste Gulbenkian
Av Berna 45
1067 Lisboa
Tel +351 217935131
Fax +351 217955249
www.gulbenkian.pt

A fairly small, high-quality collection of fine and applied art reflecting the taste of its founder, the oil magnate Calouste Gulbenkian. Numerically French art dominates (in sculpture as well as painting), but there are also choice works by, for example, Cranach, Francesco Guardi, and Rembrandt. See p. 320.

Museu Nacional de Arte Antiga
Rua das Janelas Verdes
1249 Lisboa
Tel +351 213912800
Fax +351 213973703
www.ipmuseus.pt

The museum has a varied collection of fine and applied art, including the most extensive collection of Old Master paintings in Portugal. There are good examples from most of the major European schools, but the star exhibit is the *St Vincent* polyptych by Nuño Gonçalves, Portugal's great 15th-century painter.

RUSSIA

Moscow

Pushkin State Museum of Fine Arts
12 Ulitsa Volkhonka
121019 Moscow
Tel +7 095 2037998
Fax +7 095 2028481
www.museum.ru/gmii

Next to the Hermitage, this has Russia's outstanding collection of European art. It is particularly strong in French painting from the 17th century to the early 20th century.

State Tretyakov Gallery
Lavrushinsky Perculok 10
117049 Moscow
Tel +7 095 2307788
Fax +7 095 9531051
www.tretyakov.ru

Superb collection of Russian art up to the 1917 Revolution. Post-1917 works are housed in the New Tretyakov Gallery in Gorky Park. See p. 709.

St Petersburg

State Hermitage Museum
34 Dvortsovaya Naberezhaya
St Petersburg 19000
Tel +7 812 1109625
www.hermitagemuseum.org

One of the greatest museums in the world, with collections that are breathtaking in terms of quality and quantity. See p. 335.

State Russian Museum
Inzhenernaya 2
St Petersburg
Tel +7 812 5954248
Fax +7 812 3144153
www.rusmuseum.ru

Huge and magnificent collection of Russian art. This museum and the Tretyakov Gallery in Moscow between them house most of the famous masterpieces of Russian painting.

SPAIN

Barcelona

Fundació Joan Miró
Avenida de Miramar 71–75
Parc de Montjuïc
08038 Barcelona
Tel +34 93 3291908
Fax +34 93 3298609
www.bcn.fjmiro.es

A striking modern building housing a huge collection of Miró's work in various media (mostly donated by the artist himself to this, his native city), as well as examples by artists associated with him, notably his friend Alexander Calder. See p. 472.

Museu Nacional d'Art de Catalunya
Palau Nacional
Parc de Montjuïc
08038 Barcelona
Tel +34 93 6220360
Fax +34 93 6220374
www.mnac.es

The museum is memorable chiefly for medieval painting and sculpture, above all for a superb collection of Romanesque frescos removed from churches in the region; no other museum in the world shows Romanesque wall painting to such good effect. Among later works there are examples by some of the most renowned figures in Spanish painting, including Goya, El Greco, and Zurbarán, as well as by foreign artists, mainly of the Italian School.

Bilbao

Museo Guggenheim Bilbao
Abandoibarra 2
48001 Bilbao
Tel +34 94 4359080
Fax +34 94 4359010
www.guggenheim-bilbao.es

Spectacular modern building displaying contemporary art. See p. 319.

Escorial

Monasterio de San Lorenzo de El Escorial
28200 San Lorenzo de El Escorial
Tel +34 91 8905902

A vast monastery-palace begun in 1563 for Philip II of Spain. It contains a wealth of art treasures, although many major paintings have been transferred to the Prado, Madrid. See p. 240.

Madrid

Museo Nacional Centro de Arte Reina Sofía
Calle Santa Isabel 52
28012 Madrid
Tel +34 91 4675062
Fax +34 91 4673163

A collection of 20th-century art housed in an 18th-century building. The highlight is Picasso's *Guernica*.

Museo Nacional del Prado
Paseo del Prado
28014 Madrid
Tel +34 91 3302800
Fax +34 91 3302856
www.museoprado.mcu.es

Spain's national museum, famous for one of the world's greatest collections of Old Master paintings, including an unrivalled representation of the Spanish School. The museum also houses sculpture, drawings, prints, and applied art. See p. 561.

Museo Thyssen-Bornemisza
Paseo del Prado 8
28014 Madrid
Tel +34 91 4203944
Fax +34 91 4202780
www.museothyssen.org

An outstanding collection of European and American paintings from the 14th to the 20th century. Most major schools are represented, the areas of greatest strength including Italian painting and modern German and American art. See p. 696.

Seville
Museo de Bellas Artes
Convento de la Merced
Plaza del Museo 9
41001 Sevilla
Tel +34 95 4221829
Fax +34 95 4224324

Next to the Prado in Madrid, this museum has Spain's best collection of Spanish painting of the 17th century, the golden age for the country's art. It is particularly rich in works by painters active in Seville, notably Murillo, although there is nothing by Velázquez, a native of the city. The collection also features sculpture, including works by Torrigiano, who died in Seville.

Valladolid
Museo Nacional de Escultura
Cadenas de San Gregorio 1
47011 Valladolid
Tel +34 983 250375
Fax +34 983 259300

Superb collection of sculpture, rich in the painted wooden statues of religious figures that were such a distinctive feature of Spanish art in the 16th and 17th centuries.

SWEDEN
Stockholm
Moderna Museet
Skeppsholmen
10327 Stockholm
Tel +46 8 51955200
Fax +46 8 51955210
www.modernamuseet.se

One of the world's leading collections of international modern art.

Nationalmuseum
Södra Blasieholmen
10324 Stockholm
Tel +46 8 51954300
Fax +46 8 51954450
www.nationalmuseum.se

A wide-ranging collection of European art from the Middle Ages to the 20th century. In addition to an incomparable representation of Swedish painting, it has one of the best collections of 18th-century French art outside France. Dutch and Flemish painting of the 17th century are also particularly well represented.

SWITZERLAND
Basle
Öffentliche Kunstsammlung (Public Art Collection)
(also known as the Kunstmuseum)
St Albangraben 16
4010 Basel
Tel +41 61 2066262
Fax +41 61 2066252
www.kunstmuseumbasel.ch

The oldest, largest, and most distinguished collection in Switzerland (it has its origins in the first public art gallery in Europe, which opened in Basle in 1672). Its greatest strengths lie in Swiss and German painting (with an unrivalled representation of Hans Holbein the Younger) and in modern art, particularly Cubism. The sculpture collection, too, concentrates on the 20th century, although there are some Greek and Roman pieces.

Berne
Kunstmuseum
Hodlerstrasse 8–12
3000 Berne 7
Tel +41 31 3280944
Fax +41 31 3280905
www.kunstmuseumbern.ch

The museum is primarily a collection of paintings, but it also houses sculpture, prints, and drawings. Its main strengths are in Swiss painting and in 20th-century art. The artists who are best represented include Hodler (a native of Berne) and Klee (who grew up in the city).

Geneva

Musée d'Art et d'Histoire
2 rue Charles Galland
1211 Geneva 3
Tel +41 22 4182600
Fax +41 22 4182601
www.mah.ville-ge.ch

The museum's collections range from prehistoric artefacts to contemporary art. The painting collection has examples from most of the major schools, and is particularly strong in work by Swiss and Swiss-based artists, including Hodler (who spent much of his career in Geneva), Liotard (a native of the city), and Witz, whose *Miraculous Draught of Fishes* (1444) depicts part of Lake Geneva and is one of the earliest known representations of a recognizable landscape.

Zurich

Kunsthaus
Heimplatz 1
8001 Zürich
Tel +41 61 2538484
Fax +41 61 2538433
www.kunsthaus.ch

The museum has some ancient and medieval works, but its collections consist mainly of paintings, drawings, and prints from the Renaissance onwards. Its main strengths are in Swiss art (Böcklin, Fuseli, Giacometti, and Hodler are among those well represented), in 19th-century French painting, and in 20th-century art in general.

UK

Barnard Castle

Bowes Museum
Barnard Castle
County Durham
DL12 8NP
Tel +44 1833 690606
Fax +44 1833 637163
www.bowesmuseum.org.uk

One of the most remarkable provincial collections in Britain, renowned—amongst much else—for its representation of 18th-century French art. See p. 98.

Belfast

Ulster Museum
Botanic Gardens
Belfast BT9 5AB
Tel +44 28 90383000
Fax +44 28 90383003
www.ulstermuseum.org.uk

Northern Ireland's major museum, with highly varied collections embracing history, archaeology, and natural history, as well as fine and applied art. The painting collection is strongest in British and Irish art from the 18th century onwards (Sir John Lavery, born in Belfast, is among the artists who are particularly well represented), but there are also some good Continental Old Masters, particularly of the Dutch and Flemish schools, and some impressive modern American works.

Birmingham

Barber Institute of Fine Arts
University of Birmingham
Edgbaston Park Road
Birmingham B15 2TS
Tel +44 121 4147333
Fax +44 121 4143370
www.barber.org.uk

A fairly small but choice collection, primarily of paintings but also including sculpture, drawings, and prints. The paintings are mainly Old Masters, and the 17th century is particularly well represented, with fine examples by Claude, van Dyck, Hals, Murillo, Poussin, and Rubens, amongst others.

Birmingham Museums and Art Gallery
Chamberlain Square
Birmingham B3 3DH
Tel +44 121 3032834
Fax +44 121 3031394
www.bmag.org.uk

One of the largest provincial museums in Britain, with diverse collections embracing antiquities and natural history as well as fine and applied art. British painting is particularly well represented, especially the Pre-Raphaelites (and above all Burne-Jones, who was a native of Birmingham). There are also examples from all the other major schools, as well as sculptures (notably by Epstein) and large holdings of drawings, prints, and water-colours (with many examples by David Cox, another native of Birmingham).

Cambridge

Fitzwilliam Museum
Trumpington Street

Cambridge CB2 1RB
Tel +44 1223 332900
Fax +44 1223 332923
www.fitzmuseum.cam.ac.uk

A major collection of fine and applied art. The areas that are best represented include Dutch, Flemish, and Italian painting. See p. 256.

Cardiff

National Museum and Gallery Cardiff
Cathays Park
Cardiff CF10 3NP
Tel +44 29 20397951
Fax +44 29 20573321
www.nmgw.ac.uk

Although it was founded (in 1907, as the National Museum of Wales) with the aim of telling 'the world about Wales and the Welsh about their fatherland', its scope has broadened to the extent that in addition to its unrivalled Welsh material it now has a distinguished collection of foreign art; the 19th-century French paintings are particularly renowned.

Edinburgh

National Gallery of Scotland
The Mound
Edinburgh EH2 2EL
Tel +44 131 6246200
Fax +44 131 2200917
www.nationalgalleries.org

The gallery is fairly modest in size compared with some other national picture collections, but it is wide in scope and has outstanding works by some of the most illustrious figures in European art (in addition to a superb representation of Scottish painting). There are also sculptures and an important collection of drawings.

Scottish National Gallery of Modern Art
75 Belford Road
Edinburgh EH4 3DR
Tel +44 131 6246200
Fax +44 131 6237126
www.nationalgalleries.org

Next to Tate Modern, this is Britain's outstanding collection of modern art. Most of the major movements (and many of the major artists) of the 20th century are represented, and it is particularly strong as a centre for the study of Dada and Surrealism (it owns the library and archive and part of the collection of Sir Roland Penrose, one of the leading British Surrealists).

Glasgow

Burrell Collection
Pollok Country Park
2060 Pollokshaws Road
Glasgow G43 1AT
Tel +44 141 2872550
Fax +44 141 2872597
www.glasgow.gov.uk/cls

A large and diverse collection, almost all of which was accumulated by the Scottish shipping magnate Sir William Burrell; it is particularly rich in medieval art (including stained glass) and in 19th-century French painting. See p. 115.

Kelvingrove Art Gallery and Museum
Kelvingrove
Glasgow G3 8AG
Tel +44 141 2872699
Fax +44 141 2872690
www.glasgow.gov.uk/cls

A large museum with varied collections, including major holdings of armour and ceramics, for example. The picture collection ranks with that of the National Gallery in Edinburgh as the most important in Scotland. It is particularly rich in Dutch and French, as well as Scottish, painting. Closed for refurbishment until February 2006.

Liverpool

The Walker (formerly Walker Art Gallery)
William Brown Street
Liverpool L3 8EL
Tel +44 151 4784199
Fax +44 151 2981816
www.nmgm.org.uk

One of England's most distinguished provincial art collections. It has an outstanding representation of British art, particularly of Victorian painting (the most famous work in the gallery is probably Yeames's *'And When Did You Last See Your Father?'*), as well as examples from all the major European schools, including masterpieces by Simone Martini (*Christ Reproved by His Parents*), Ercole de' Roberti (*Pietà*), and Poussin (*The Ashes of Phocion Collected by His Widow*).

London

British Museum
Great Russell Street
London WC1B 3DG
Tel +44 20 73238000
Fax +44 20 73238480
www.thebritishmuseum.ac.uk

An enormously rich and varied collection, with magnificent holdings in classical antiquities, medieval art, prints and drawings, and numerous other fields. See p. 105.

Courtauld Gallery
Somerset House
Strand
London WC2R 0RN
Tel +44 20 78482526
Fax +44 20 78482589
www.courtauld.ac.uk

The collection is principally famous for its superb representation of the French Impressionists and Post-Impressionists, but it has many other treasures, including a magnificent group of works by Rubens and two paintings by Pieter Bruegel the Elder. In addition to paintings the collection includes sculpture, prints, drawings, and applied art. See p. 176.

Dulwich Picture Gallery
Gallery Road
London SE21 7AD
Tel +44 20 86935254
Fax +44 20 82998700
www.dulwichpicturegallery.org.uk

A small but choice collection, mainly of British, Dutch, Flemish, French, and Italian paintings. See p. 97.

National Gallery
Trafalgar Square
London WC2N 5DN
Tel +44 20 77472885
Fax +44 20 77472423
www.nationalgallery.org.uk

One of the world's greatest collections of paintings. It contains superb examples from all the major European schools, offering a more balanced view of the mainstream of Western painting from *c*.1300 to *c*.1900 than can be obtained in any other gallery. See p. 494.

National Maritime Museum
Romney Road
Greenwich
London SE10 9NF
Tel +44 20 88584422
Fax +44 20 83126632
www.nmm.ac.uk

The museum is concerned with all aspects of maritime history and has the world's most extensive collection of marine paintings; they are mainly by British and Dutch artists, including Willem van de Velde the Elder and Younger,

who are outstandingly well represented. There are also numerous portraits of distinguished maritime figures, among them Reynolds's celebrated *Commodore Keppel*.

National Portrait Gallery
St Martin's Place
London WC2 0HE
Tel +44 20 73060055
Fax +44 20 73060056
www.npg.org.uk

Unrivalled collection of portraits (in painting and other media) of noteworthy men and women in British life from Tudor times onwards. Most of the leading British portraitists are represented, as well as numerous distinguished foreign artists. See p. 494.

Saatchi Gallery
County Hall
Southbank
London SE1 7PB
Tel +44 20 78232363
www.saatchi-gallery.co.uk

Large collection of contemporary art formed by a leading patron. See p. 624.

Tate Britain
Millbank
London SW1P 4RG
Tel +44 20 78878000
Fax +44 20 78878007
www.tate.org.uk

The 'National Gallery of British Art'. It has an unrivalled collection of British painting from the mid-16th century onwards and also covers sculpture from the 19th century onwards. See p. 689.

Tate Modern
Bankside
London SE1 9TG
Tel +44 20 78878008
Fax +44 20 78878007
www.tate.org.uk

Britain's leading collection of international modern art. See p. 689.

Victoria and Albert Museum
Cromwell Road
London SW7 2RL
Tel +44 20 79422000
Fax +44 20 79422266
www.vam.ac.uk

Although it was originally conceived as a museum of applied and decorative art, this vast treasure house has also acquired an extraordinary wealth of fine art—paintings, sculpture, drawings, and prints. See p. 736.

Wallace Collection
Hertford House
Manchester Square
London W1U 3BN
Tel +44 20 75639500
Fax +44 20 72242155
www.the-wallace-collection.org.uk

A superb collection of fine and applied art, particularly rich in French paintings and furniture of the 18th century. See p. 746.

Manchester

Manchester Art Gallery
Mosley Street
Manchester M2 3JL
Tel +44 161 2365244
Fax +44 161 2367369
www.manchestergalleries.org

A major provincial collection, with holdings ranging from Egyptian and Greek antiquities to contemporary art. It is chiefly renowned for its impressive representation of 19th-century British paintings, including some of the most famous works of the Pre-Raphaelites, such as Ford Madox Brown's *Work* and Millais's *Autumn Leaves*. However, it has riches in many other areas, including paintings from all the major European schools. Sculpture is less well represented, but there are pieces by artists of the calibre of Algardi, Bourdelle, Dalou, and Thorvaldsen.

Oxford

Ashmolean Museum of Art and Archaeology
Beaumont Street
Oxford OX1 2PH
Tel +44 1865 278000
Fax +44 1865 278018
www.ashmol.ox.ac.uk

One of Britain's greatest museums, especially rich in classical antiquities, Italian Renaissance paintings, and Old Master drawings. It also has a good collection of British paintings, notably by the Pre-Raphaelites and members of the Camden Town Group. See p. 38.

USA

Baltimore

Walters Art Museum
600 North Charles Street
Baltimore MD 21201
Tel +1 410 5479000

Fax +1 410 7837969
www.thewalters.org

The museum is chiefly renowned for its outstanding collection of Italian Renaissance painting, and it is also strong in 19th-century French art, including sculptures by Barye.

Boston

Isabella Stewart Gardner Museum
The Fenway
Boston MA 02115
Tel +1 617 5661401
Fax +1 617 2328039
www.boston.com/gardner

A fairly small but high-quality collection of paintings and other works, reflecting the taste of its founder. See p. 275.

Museum of Fine Arts
465 Huntington Avenue
Boston MA 02115
Tel +1 617 2679300
Fax +1 617 2670280
www.mfa.org

Next to the Metropolitan Museum in New York, this is the most comprehensive collection of world art in the USA. It is rich in many fields, including 19th-century French painting: the collection of Millet's work is the largest in the world and the Impressionists are magnificently represented.

Cambridge

Fogg Art Museum
Harvard University
32 Quincy Street
Cambridge MA 02138
Tel +1 617 4959400
Fax +1 617 4959936
www.artmuseums.harvard.edu

A large and diverse collection, with major holdings of paintings, sculptures, drawings, and prints. The collection of Italian painting is one of the largest and most varied in the USA, and the American and French schools are also particularly well represented. Harvard University administers two other museums: the Busch-Reisinger Museum, which is devoted mainly to art of the German-speaking countries, especially of the 20th century; and the Arthur M. Sackler Museum, which covers ancient and non-European art.

Chicago

Art Institute of Chicago
111 South Michigan Avenue

Chicago IL 60603
Tel +1 312 4433600
Fax +1 312 4430849
www.artic.edu

The collections are extensive and varied, including a good deal of oriental art and applied art. However, the Art Institute is principally famous for Western paintings—outside New York and Washington, it has arguably the finest collection in the USA. There are superb examples from every major school and its celebrated masterpieces include Seurat's *Sunday Afternoon on the Island of La Grande Jatte*, Grant Wood's *American Gothic*, and Hopper's *Nighthawks*.

Cleveland
Cleveland Museum of Art
11150 East Boulevard
Cleveland OH 44106
Tel +1 216 4217350
www.clevelandart.org

An important collection of Western and oriental art. All the major European schools of painting are represented and the museum is also rich in American art.

Detroit
Detroit Institute of Arts
5200 Woodward Avenue
Detroit MI 48202
Tel +1 313 8337900
Fax +1 313 2233140
www.dia.org

A large and wide-ranging collection that includes one of the most comprehensive and well-balanced representations of Western painting in the USA. Its most famous exhibits include one of the two versions of Ruisdael's *Jewish Cemetery* (the other is in the Gemäldegalerie, Dresden) and Whistler's *Nocturne in Black and Gold: The Falling Rocket*, the picture that sparked off his libel trial with Ruskin. There are also murals by Diego Rivera, specially painted for the building.

Hartford
Wadsworth Atheneum
600 Main Street
Hartford CT 06103
Tel +1 860 2782670
Fax +1 860 5270803
www.wadsworthatheneum.org

The oldest continuously functioning public art museum in the USA (opened in 1844), it has wide-ranging collections, including classical antiquities, furniture, and porcelain. The extensive and varied painting collection is rich in 17th-century works of the Dutch, Flemish, French, Italian, and Spanish schools.

Los Angeles
Getty Center
1200 Getty Center Drive
Los Angeles CA 90049
Tel +1 310 4407300
Fax +1 310 4407718
www.getty.edu

A large complex housing various facilities for art research and education, including a museum with important collections of paintings, sculptures, drawings, photographs, and other objects. See p. 283.

Merion
Barnes Foundation
300 North Latch's Lane
Merion PA 19066
Tel +1 610 6670290
Fax +1 610 6644026
www.barnesfoundation.org

A famous collection, devoted mainly to late 19th-century and early 20th-century painting, in which certain artists are particularly well represented, notably Cézanne, Matisse, and Renoir. See p. 51.

New Haven
Yale Center for British Art
1080 Chapel Street
New Haven CT 06520–8280
Tel +1 203 4322800
Fax +1 203 4329628
www.yale.edu/ycba

Next to Tate Britain in London, this has the world's most comprehensive collection of British painting, and is particularly rich in the work of the leading masters of the 18th and early 19th centuries. See p. 459.

Yale University Art Gallery
1111 Chapel Street
New Haven CT 06520
Tel +1 203 4320600
Fax +1 203 4328150
www.yale.edu/artgallery

A large and diverse collection of fine and applied art. Its areas of greatest strength include American painting, Italian painting, and early 20th-century art (including the collection of the Société Anonyme (see p. 660), presented in 1941).

New York

Frick Collection
1 East 70th Street at Fifth Avenue
New York NY 10021
Tel +1 212 2880700
Fax +1 212 6284417
www.frick.org

A fairly small collection of extraordinarily high quality that retains the feel of a private home—albeit the home of a multi-millionaire with exquisite taste. See p. 266.

Metropolitan Museum of Art
Fifth Avenue at 82nd Street
New York NY 10028
Tel +1 212 8795500
Fax +1 212 5703879
www.metmuseum.org

One of the world's greatest museums, rich in virtually every field of fine and applied art, not least in Western painting, of which it has the most comprehensive collection in the USA. See p. 463.

Morgan Library
29 East 36th Street
New York NY 10016
Tel +1 212 6850610
Fax +1 212 4813484
www.morganlibrary.org

A celebrated collection primarily of books, illuminated manuscripts, and Old Master drawings. The library also has a few paintings, and its other material includes the archives of the Pierre Matisse Gallery. See p. 482.

Museum of Modern Art
11 West 53rd Street
New York NY 10019
Tel +1 212 7089400
Fax +1 212 7089889
www.moma.org

The world's largest and most comprehensive collection of international modern art from the late 19th century onwards. See p. 489.

Solomon R. Guggenheim Museum
1071 Fifth Avenue
New York NY 10128
Tel +1 212 4233500
Fax +1 212 4233650
www.guggenheim.org

A major collection of late 19th-century and 20th-century art housed in a remarkable building by Frank Lloyd Wright. Its holdings include the world's largest collection of Kandinsky's work. See p. 319.

Whitney Museum of American Art
945 Madison Avenue
New York NY 10021
Tel +1 212 5703676
Fax +1 212 5701807
www.whitney.org

The museum has the world's largest collection of 20th-century American art and a good representation of earlier periods. See p. 758.

Philadelphia

Philadelphia Museum of Art
Benjamin Franklin Parkway at 26th Street
Philadelphia PA 19130
Tel +1 215 7638100
Fax +1 215 2364465
www.philamuseum.org

Although the museum has a large collection of Old Masters, it is perhaps best known for its 20th-century holdings; they include an unrivalled representation of Marcel Duchamp's work and a major collection of Brancusi's sculpture.

San Marino

Huntington Library, Art Collections and Botanical Gardens
1151 Oxford Road
San Marino CA 91108
Tel +1 626 4052100
Fax +1 626 4495720
www.huntington.org

A remarkable institution, combining a research library, art gallery, and botanical garden—each of eminence in its own field. The art collection is mainly renowned for a wonderful group of full-length 18th-century British portraits, including Gainsborough's *Blue Boy*. See p. 35.

Washington

Hirshhorn Museum and Sculpture Garden
Independence Avenue at Seventh Street
Washington DC 20560
Tel +1 202 6334674
Fax +1 202 7862682
www.si.edu.hirshhorn

A major collection of modern art from *c*.1880 onwards, founded by the Latvian-born industrialist Joseph H. Hirshhorn. It is particularly strong in sculpture (notably the work of Henry Moore), in American painting (de Kooning is especially well represented), and in European painting since the Second World War.

National Gallery of Art
Constitution Avenue
Washington DC 20565
Tel +1 202 7374215
Fax +1 202 8426176
www.nga.gov

Together with the Metropolitan Museum in New York, this ranks as the pre-eminent collection of Western painting in the USA. Its areas of greatest strength are perhaps French and Italian painting (one of the highlights is Leonardo da Vinci's portrait of Ginevra de' Benci, the only undisputed Leonardo painting in the USA), but it has superb examples from every major school.

Phillips Collection
1600–1612 21st Street West
Washington DC 20009
Tel +1 202 3872151
Fax +1 202 3872436

A delightful collection, mainly of late 19th- and early 20th-century painting, in an intimate domestic setting. Among the artists who are best represented are Bonnard, Braque, and the pioneering American abstractionist Arthur Dove, a protégé of Duncan Phillips, the founder of the collection. See p. 538.